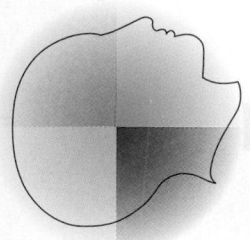

sixth edition

Biopsychology

John P. J. Pinel
University of British Columbia

PEARSON

Boston   New York   San Francisco
Mexico City   Montreal   Toronto   London   Madrid   Munich   Paris
Hong Kong   Singapore   Tokyo   Cape Town   Sydney

6/19/12

WB

Executive Editor: Karon Bowers
Series Editorial Assistant: Deborah Hanlon
Executive Marketing Manager: Pamela Laskey
Development Editor: Erin K. Liedel
Production Editor: Michael Granger
Editorial Production Service: Jane Hoover/Lifland et al., Bookmakers
Composition Buyer: Linda Cox
Manufacturing Buyer: Megan Cochran
Electronic Composition: Omegatype Typography, Inc.
Interior Design: Glenna Collett
Photo Researcher: ImageQuest—Sarah Evertson
Cover Administrator: Linda Knowles
Cover Designer: Susan Paradise
Illustration Design and Art Direction: Maggie Edwards, Gnosis Consulting Corporation

For related titles and support materials, visit our online catalog at www.ablongman.com

Between the time Website information is gathered and then published, it is not unusual for some sites to have closed. Also, the transcription of URLs can result in typographical errors. The publisher would appreciate notification where these errors appear.

Library of Congress Cataloging-in-Publication Data

Pinel, John P. J.
    Biopsychology / John P. J. Pinel.—6th ed.
        p.   cm.
    Includes bibliographical references and index.
    ISBN 0-205-42651-4
    1. Psychobiology.   I. Title.

QP360.P463   2007
612.8—dc22

2005043198

Printed in the United States of America

10 9 8 7 6 5 4 3 2   VHP   09 08 07 06

To my German daughter,
Anja Egerer

Brief Contents

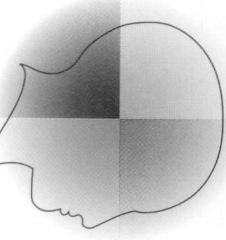

part one

What Is Biopsychology?

1 Biopsychology as a Neuroscience   1
What Is Biopsychology, Anyway?

part two

Foundations of Biopsychology

2 Evolution, Genetics, and Experience   19
Thinking about the Biology of Behavior

3 The Anatomy of the Nervous System   50
The Systems, Structures, and Cells That
Make Up Your Nervous System

**4 Neural Conduction and Synaptic
Transmission**   76
How Neurons Send and Receive Signals

**5 The Research Methods
of Biopsychology**   100
Understanding What Biopsychologists Do

part three

Sensory and Motor Systems

6 The Visual System   128
From Your Eyes to Your Cortex

**7 Mechanisms of Perception, Conscious
Awareness, and Attention**   155
How You Know the World

8 The Sensorimotor System   185
How You Do What You Do

part four

Brain Plasticity

9 Development of the Nervous System   211
From Fertilized Egg to You

10 Brain Damage and Neuroplasticity   231
Can the Brain Recover from Damage?

11 Learning, Memory, and Amnesia   260
How Your Brain Stores Information

part five

Biopsychology of Motivation

12 Hunger, Eating, and Health   288
Why Do Many People Eat Too Much?

13 Hormones and Sex   314
What's Wrong with the Mamawawa?

**14 Sleep, Dreaming, and Circadian
Rhythms**   341
How Much Do You Need to Sleep?

**15 Drug Addiction and the Brain's
Reward Circuits**   369
Chemicals That Harm with Pleasure

part six

Disorders of Cognition and Emotion

**16 Lateralization, Language, and the
Split Brain**   395
The Left Brain and the Right Brain
of Language

**17 Biopsychology of Emotion, Stress,
and Health**   425
Fear, the Dark Side of Emotion

**18 Biopsychology of Psychiatric
Disorders**   448
The Brain Unhinged

Contents

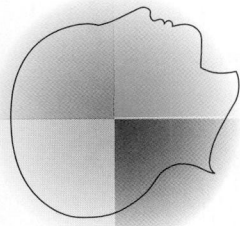

Preface   xvi
To the Student   xxiii
About the Author   xxiv

part one   What Is Biopsychology?

chapter 1

Biopsychology as a Neuroscience   1
What Is Biopsychology, Anyway?

The Case of Jimmie G., the Man Frozen in Time   2
Four Major Themes of This Book   3

1.1 What Is Biopsychology?   4
1.2 What Is the Relation between Biopsychology and the Other Disciplines of Neuroscience?   4
1.3 What Types of Research Characterize the Biopsychological Approach?   5
Human and Nonhuman Subjects   5
Experiments and Nonexperiments   5
Pure and Applied Research   7
1.4 What Are the Divisions of Biopsychology?   8
Physiological Psychology   8
Psychopharmacology   9
Neuropsychology   9
The Case of Mr. R., the Brain-Damaged Student Who Switched to Architecture   9
Psychophysiology   9
Cognitive Neuroscience   10
Comparative Psychology   11
1.5 Converging Operations: How Do Biopsychologists Work Together?   12
1.6 Scientific Inference: How Do Biopsychologists Study the Unobservable Workings of the Brain?   13

1.7 Critical Thinking about Biopsychological Claims   15
Case 1: José and the Bull   15
Case 2: Becky, Moniz, and Prefrontal Lobotomy   16
Themes Revisited   17
Think about It   18
Key Terms   18

part two   Foundations of Biopsychology

chapter 2

Evolution, Genetics, and Experience   19
Thinking about the Biology of Behavior

2.1 Thinking about the Biology of Behavior: From Dichotomies to Relations and Interactions   20
Is It Physiological, or Is It Psychological?   20
Is It Inherited, or Is It Learned?   20
Problems with Thinking about the Biology of Behavior in Terms of Traditional Dichotomies   21
The Case of the Man Who Fell Out of Bed   21
The Case of the Chimps and the Mirrors   22
The Case of the Thinking Student   23
2.2 Human Evolution   24
Evolution and Behavior   25
Course of Human Evolution   27
Thinking about Human Evolution   29
Evolution of the Human Brain   31
Evolutionary Psychology: Understanding Mate Bonding   31
2.3 Fundamental Genetics   34
Mendelian Genetics   34
Chromosomes, Reproduction, and Linkage   34
Sex Chromosomes and Sex-Linked Traits   37
Chromosome Structure and Replication   37

The Genetic Code and Gene Expression 38
Mitochondrial DNA 39
Human Genome Project: What's Next? 39

2.4 Behavioral Development: The Interaction of Genetic Factors and Experience 42
Selective Breeding of "Maze-Bright" and "Maze-Dull" Rats 42
Phenylketonuria: A Single-Gene Metabolic Disorder 44
Development of Birdsong 44

2.5 The Genetics of Human Psychological Differences 46
Development of Individuals versus Development of Differences among Individuals 46
Minnesota Study of Twins Reared Apart 46

Themes Revisited 48
Think about It 49
Key Terms 49

chapter 3

The Anatomy of the Nervous System
The Systems, Structures, and Cells That Make Up Your Nervous System 50

3.1 General Layout of the Nervous System 51
Divisions of the Nervous System 51
Meninges, Ventricles, and Cerebrospinal Fluid 53
Blood–Brain Barrier 53

3.2 Cells of the Nervous System 54
Anatomy of Neurons 54
Glial Cells: The Forgotten Majority 58

3.3 Neuroanatomical Techniques and Directions 59
Neuroanatomical Techniques 59
Directions in the Vertebrate Nervous System 61

3.4 The Spinal Cord 62

3.5 The Five Major Divisions of the Brain 64

3.6 Major Structures of the Brain 65
Myelencephalon 65
Metencephalon 65
Mesencephalon 65
Diencephalon 66
Telencephalon 67

Themes Revisited 74
Think about It 75
Key Terms 75

chapter 4

Neural Conduction and Synaptic Transmission
How Neurons Send and Receive Signals 76

The Lizard, a Case of Parkinson's Disease 77

4.1 The Neuron's Resting Membrane Potential 77
Recording the Membrane Potential 77
The Resting Membrane Potential 77
The Ionic Basis of the Resting Potential 78

4.2 Generation and Conduction of Postsynaptic Potentials 80

4.3 Integration of Postsynaptic Potentials and Generation of Action Potentials 81

4.4 Conduction of Action Potentials 83
The Ionic Basis of Action Potentials 83
Refractory Periods 84
Axonal Conduction of Action Potentials 84
Conduction in Myelinated Axons 85
The Velocity of Axonal Conduction 85
Conduction in Neurons without Axons 85
The Hodgkin-Huxley Model and the Changing View of Dendritic Function 85

4.5 Synaptic Transmission: Chemical Transmission of Signals from One Neuron to Another 86
Structure of Synapses 86
Synthesis, Packaging, and Transport of Neurotransmitter Molecules 86
Release of Neurotransmitter Molecules 87
Activation of Receptors by Neurotransmitter Molecules 88
Reuptake, Enzymatic Degradation, and Recycling 90
Glial Function and Synaptic Transmission 91

4.6 The Neurotransmitters 92
Amino Acid Neurotransmitters 92
Monoamine Neurotransmitters 92
Soluble-Gas Neurotransmitters 93
Acetylcholine 94
Neuropeptides 94

4.7 Pharmacology of Synaptic Transmission 95
How Drugs Influence Synaptic Transmission 95
Psychoactive Drugs: Five Examples 95

Themes Revisited 98
Think about It 98
Key Terms 99

chapter 5

The Research Methods of Biopsychology 100
Understanding What Biopsychologists Do

The Ironic Case of Professor P. 101

PART ONE   Methods of Studying the Nervous System 102

5.1   Methods of Visualizing and Stimulating the Living Human Brain 102
Contrast X-Rays 102
X-Ray Computed Tomography 102
Magnetic Resonance Imaging 102
Positron Emission Tomography 104
Functional MRI 105
Magnetoencephalography 106
Brain-Image Archives 106
Transcranial Magnetic Stimulation 106

5.2   Recording Human Psychophysiological Activity 106
Scalp Electroencephalography 106
Muscle Tension 108
Eye Movement 109
Skin Conductance 109
Cardiovascular Activity 109

5.3   Invasive Physiological Research Methods 110
Stereotaxic Surgery 110
Lesion Methods 110
Electrical Stimulation 113
Invasive Electrophysiological Recording Methods 113

5.4   Pharmacological Research Methods 114
Routes of Drug Administration 114
Selective Chemical Lesions 114
Measuring Chemical Activity of the Brain 114
Locating Neurotransmitters and Receptors in the Brain 115

5.5   Genetic Engineering 117
Gene Knockout Techniques 117
Gene Replacement Techniques 117

PART TWO   Behavioral Research Methods of Biopsychology 117

5.6   Neuropsychological Testing 118
Modern Approach to Neuropsychological Testing 118
Tests of the Common Neuropsychological Test Battery 119
Tests of Specific Neuropsychological Function 120
Frontal-Lobe Function 121

5.7   Behavioral Methods of Cognitive Neuroscience 121

5.8   Biopsychological Paradigms of Animal Behavior 123
Paradigms for Assessment of Species-Common Behaviors 123
Traditional Conditioning Paradigms 123
Seminatural Animal Learning Paradigms 124

Themes Revisited 126

Think about It 126

Key Terms 126

part three

Sensory and Motor Systems

chapter 6

The Visual System 128
From Your Eyes to Your Cortex

The Case of Mrs. Richards: Fortification Illusions and the Astronomer 129

6.1   Light Enters the Eye and Reaches the Retina 130

6.2   The Retina and Translation of Light into Neural Signals 132
Cone and Rod Vision 134
Eye Movement 136
Visual Transduction: The Conversion of Light to Neural Signals 138

6.3   From Retina to Primary Visual Cortex 139
Retinotopic Organization 140
The M and P Channels 140

6.4   Seeing Edges 140
Lateral Inhibition and Contrast Enhancement 142
Receptive Fields of Visual Neurons 143
Receptive Fields: Neurons of the Retina-Geniculate-Striate Pathway 143
Receptive Fields: Simple Cortical Cells 144
Receptive Fields: Complex Cortical Cells 145
Columnar Organization of Primary Visual Cortex 146
Spatial-Frequency Theory 147
The Case of Mrs. Richards, Revisited 149

6.5   Seeing Color 149
Component and Opponent Processing 150

Color Constancy and the
Retinex Theory   151

Themes Revisited   153

Think about It   154

Key Terms   154

chapter 7

**Mechanisms of Perception, Conscious
Awareness, and Attention**   155

How You Know the World

*The Case of the Man Who Could See Only
One Thing at a Time*   156

**7.1 Principles of Sensory System
Organization**   156

Hierarchical Organization   156

*The Case of the Man Who Mistook
His Wife for a Hat*   157

Functional Segregation   157

Parallel Processing   158

The Current Model of Sensory System
Organization   158

7.2 Cortical Mechanisms of Vision   159

Scotomas: Completion   159

*The Case of the Physiological
Psychologist Who Made
Faces Disappear*   160

Scotomas: Blindsight   160

*The Case of D.B., the Man Confused
by His Own Blindsight*   160

Visual Awareness and Neural Activity   161

Functional Areas of Secondary
and Association Visual Cortex   161

Dorsal and Ventral Streams   161

*The Case of D.F., the Woman Who
Could Grasp Objects She Did Not
Consciously See*   164

*The Case of A.T., the Woman Who
Could Not Accurately Grasp
Unfamiliar Objects That She Saw*   164

Prosopagnosia   164

R.P., a Typical Case of Prosopagnoisa   165

Areas of the Ventral Stream
Specialized for Recognizing
Specific Classes of Objects   165

Interim Conclusion   166

7.3 Audition   166

The Ear   166

From the Ear to the Primary
Auditory Cortex   168

Primary Auditory Cortex   169

Sound Localization   169

Effects of Auditory Cortex Damage   170

7.4 Somatosensation: Touch and Pain   170

Cutaneous Receptors   170

Dermatomes   171

The Two Major Ascending
Somatosensory Pathways   171

Cortical Areas of Somatosensation   172

Effects of Damage to the Primary
Somatosensory Cortex   173

Somatosensory Agnosias   174

*The Case of Aunt Betsy, Who Lost Half
of Her Body*   174

The Paradoxes of Pain   175

*The Case of Miss C., the Woman Who
Felt No Pain*   175

7.5 The Chemical Senses: Smell and Taste   177

The Olfactory System   178

The Gustatory System   179

Brain Damage and the Chemical Senses   180

7.6 Selective Attention   181

Themes Revisited   183

Think about It   184

Key Terms   184

chapter 8

The Sensorimotor System   185

How You Do What You Do

*The Case of Rhonda, the
Dexterous Cashier*   186

**8.1 Three Principles of Sensorimotor
Function**   186

The Sensorimotor System Is
Hierarchically Organized   186

Motor Output Is Guided by
Sensory Input   187

*The Case of G.O., the Man with
Too Little Feedback*   187

Learning Changes the Nature and Locus
of Sensorimotor Control   187

A General Model of Sensorimotor System
Function   188

8.2 Sensorimotor Association Cortex   188

Posterior Parietal Association Cortex   188

*The Case of Mrs. S., the Woman Who
Turned in Circles*   189

Dorsolateral Prefrontal Association
Cortex   191

8.3 Secondary Motor Cortex   192

8.4 Primary Motor Cortex **193**
    Belle: The Monkey That Controlled a Robot with Her Mind *194*
8.5 Cerebellum and Basal Ganglia **195**
    Cerebellum 195
    Basal Ganglia 195
8.6 Descending Motor Pathways **196**
    Dorsolateral Corticospinal Tract and Dorsolateral Corticorubrospinal Tract 196
    Ventromedial Corticospinal Tract and Ventromedial Cortico-brainstem-spinal Tract 198
    Comparison of the Two Dorsolateral Motor Pathways and the Two Ventromedial Motor Pathways 198
8.7 Sensorimotor Spinal Circuits **200**
    Muscles 200
    Receptor Organs of Tendons and Muscles 200
    Stretch Reflex 202
    Withdrawal Reflex 204
    Reciprocal Innervation 204
    Recurrent Collateral Inhibition 204
    Walking: A Complex Sensorimotor Reflex 205
8.8 Central Sensorimotor Programs **206**
    Central Sensorimotor Programs Are Capable of Motor Equivalence 206
    Sensory Information That Controls Central Sensorimotor Programs Is Not Necessarily Conscious 206
    Central Sensorimotor Programs Can Develop without Practice 207
    Practice Can Create Central Sensorimotor Programs 207
    Functional Brain Imaging of Sensorimotor Learning 208
    The Case of Rhonda, Revisited 209
    Themes Revisited **209**
    Think about It **210**
    Key Terms **210**

part four
Brain Plasticity 211

chapter 9
Development of the Nervous System 211
    From Fertilized Egg to You 212
    The Case of Genie 212
9.1 Phases of Neurodevelopment **212**
    Induction of the Neural Plate 213
    Neural Proliferation 214
    Migration and Aggregation 214
    Axon Growth and Synapse Formation 215
    Neuron Death and Synapse Rearrangement 219
9.2 Postnatal Cerebral Development in Human Infants **220**
    Postnatal Growth of the Human Brain 220
    Development of the Prefrontal Cortex 221
9.3 Effects of Experience on the Early Development, Maintenance, and Reorganization of Neural Circuits **221**
    Early Studies of Experience and Neurodevelopment 222
    Competitive Nature of Experience and Neurodevelopment 222
    Effects of Experience on Topographic Sensory Cortex Maps 222
    Mechanisms by Which Experience Might Influence Neurodevelopment 223
9.4 Neuroplasticity in Adults **223**
    Neurogenesis in Adult Mammals 223
    Effects of Experience on the Reorganization of the Adult Cortex 225
9.5 Disorders of Neurodevelopment: Autism and Williams Syndrome **225**
    Autism 225
    Some Cases of Amazing Savants 226
    Williams Syndrome 227
    Themes Revisited **229**
    Think about It **229**
    Key Terms **230**

chapter 10
Brain Damage and Neuroplasticity 231
    Can the Brain Recover from Damage? 232
    The Ironic Case of Professor P. 232
10.1 Causes of Brain Damage **233**
    Brain Tumors 233
    Cerebrovascular Disorders 233
    Closed-Head Injuries 236
    The Case of Jerry Quarry, Ex-Boxer 236
    Infections of the Brain 237
    Neurotoxins 237
    Genetic Factors 237
    Programmed Cell Death 238
10.2 Neuropsychological Diseases **239**
    Epilepsy 239

*The Subtlety of Complex Partial Seizures:
Four Cases*   240

10.3 Neuropsychological Diseases   **245**
Parkinson's Disease   241
Huntington's Disease   242
Multiple Sclerosis   242
Alzheimer's Disease   242

**10.4 Animal Models of Human
Neuropsychological Diseases**   **245**
Kindling Model of Epilepsy   246
Transgenic Mouse Model of
Alzheimer's Disease   246
MPTP Model of Parkinson's Disease   247
The Case of the Frozen Addicts   247

**10.5 Neuroplastic Responses to Nervous
System Damage: Degeneration,
Regeneration, Reorganization,
and Recovery**   **248**
Neural Degeneration   248
Neural Regeneration   248
Neural Reorganization   250
Recovery of Function after Brain Damage   252

**Neuroplasticity and the Treatment of
Nervous System Damage**   **254**
Reducing Brain Damage by Blocking
Neurodegeneration   254
Promoting Recovery from CNS Damage
by Promoting Regeneration   254
Promoting Recovery from CNS Damage
by Neurotransplantation   255
*The Case of Roberto Garcia d'Orta:
The Lizard Gets an Autotransplant*   255
Promoting Recovery from CNS Damage
by Rehabilitative Training   256
*The Cases of Tom and Philip: Phantom
Limbs and Ramachandran*   257

Themes Revisited   **258**
Think about It   258
Key Terms   **259**

chapter 11

Learning, Memory, and Amnesia   260
How Your Brain Stores Information

**11.1 Amnesic Effects of Bilateral Medial
Temporal Lobectomy**   **261**
*The Case of H.M., the Man Who
Changed the Study of Memory*   261
Formal Assessment of H.M.'s
Anterograde Amnesia   262
Scientific Contributions of
H.M.'s Case   263

*The Subtlety of Complex Partial Seizures:
Four Cases*

Medial Temporal Lobe Amnesia   264
Effects of Cerebral Ischemia on the
Hippocampus and Memory   264
*The Case of R.B., the Product of
a Bungled Operation*   265

11.2 Amnesia of Korsakoff's Syndrome   **266**
The Up-Your-Nose Case of N.A.   267

11.3 Amnesia of Alzheimer's Disease   **267**

**11.4 Amnesia after Concussion: Evidence
for Consolidation**   **268**
Posttraumatic Amnesia   268
Gradients of Retrograde Amnesia
and Memory Consolidation   268
Reconsolidation   270
The Hippocampus and Consolidation   270

**11.5 Neuroanatomy of Object-Recognition
Memory**   **271**
Monkey Model of Object-Recognition
Amnesia: The Delayed
Nonmatching-to-Sample Test   272
The Delayed Nonmatching-to-Sample
Test for Rats   273
Neuroanatomical Basis of the
Object-Recognition Deficits Resulting
from Medial Temporal Lobectomy   274

**11.6 The Hippocampus and Memory
for Spatial Location**   **277**
Hippocampal Lesions Disrupt
Spatial Memory   277
Hippocampal Place Cells   277
Comparative Studies of the Hippocampus
and Spatial Memory   278
Theories of Hippocampal Function   278

11.7 Where Are Memories Stored?   **279**
Inferotemporal Cortex   279
Amygdala   279
Prefrontal Cortex   279
*The Case of the Cook Who Couldn't
Remember H.M.*   280
Cerebellum and Striatum   280

**11.8 Synaptic Mechanisms of Learning
and Memory**   **280**
Long-Term Potentiation   281
Induction of LTP: Learning   283
Maintenance and Expression of LTP:
Storage and Recall   284
Variability of LTP   285

**11.9 Conclusion: Infantile Amnesia
and the Biopsychologist Who
Remembered H.M.**   **285**
*The Case of R.M., the Biopsychologist
Who Remembered H.M.*   286

Themes Revisited   286
Think about It   287
Key Terms   287

part five
Biopsychology of Motivation

chapter **12**
Hunger, Eating, and Health   288
Why Do Many People Eat Too Much?

The Case of the Man Who Forgot Not to Eat   289

12.1 **Digestion and Energy Flow**   289

12.2 **Theories of Hunger and Eating: Set Points versus Positive Incentives**   292
Set-Point Assumption   292
Glucostatic and Lipostatic Set-Point Theories of Hunger and Eating   293
Problems with Set-Point Theories of Hunger and Eating   293
Positive-Incentive Perspective   294

12.3 **Factors That Determine What, When, and How Much We Eat**   295
Factors That Determine What We Eat   295
Factors That Influence When We Eat   295
Factors That Influence How Much We Eat   296

12.4 **Physiological Research on Hunger and Satiety**   298
Role of Blood Glucose Levels in Hunger and Satiety   298
Myth of Hypothalamic Hunger and Satiety Centers   299
Role of the Gastrointestinal Tract in Satiety   301
Hunger and Satiety Peptides   302
Serotonin and Satiety   303

12.5 **Body Weight Regulation: Set Points versus Settling Points**   303
Set-Point Assumptions about Body Weight and Eating   303
Set Points and Settling Points in Weight Control   305

12.6 **Human Obesity**   308
Why Is There an Epidemic of Obesity?   308
Why Do Some People Become Obese While Others Do Not?   308
Why Are Weight-Loss Programs Typically Ineffective?   308
Mutant Obese Mice and Leptin   309
The Case of the Child with No Leptin   310
Insulin: Another Negative Feedback Fat Signal   310
Serotonergic Drugs and the Treatment of Obesity   310

12.7 **Anorexia Nervosa**   311
Anorexia and Dieting   311
Anorexia and Positive Incentives   311
The Puzzle of Anorexia   311
The Case of the Anorexic Student   312

Themes Revisited   313
Think about It   313
Key Terms   313

chapter **13**
Hormones and Sex   314
What's Wrong with the Mamawawa?
The Developmental and Activational Effects of Sex Hormones   315
The Men-Are-Men-and-Women-Are-Women Assumption   315

13.1 **The Neuroendocrine System**   315
Glands   315
Hormones   315
Gonads   316
Sex Steroids   316
Hormones of the Pituitary   317
Female Gonadal Hormone Levels Are Cyclic; Male Gonadal Hormone Levels Are Steady   317
Neural Control of the Pituitary   318
Control of the Anterior and Posterior Pituitary by the Hypothalamus   318
Discovery of Hypothalamic Releasing Hormones   319
Regulation of Hormone Levels   320
Pulsatile Hormone Release   320
A Summary Model of Gonadal Endocrine Regulation   320

13.2 **Hormones and Sexual Development**   321
Fetal Hormones and the Development of Reproductive Organs   322
Sex Differences in the Brain   323
Perinatal Hormones and Behavioral Development   325

Puberty: Hormones and the Development
of Secondary Sex Characteristics 326

**13.3 Three Cases of Exceptional Human
Sexual Development 327**

*The Case of Anne S., the Woman
Who Wasn't* 327

*The Case of the Little Girl Who Grew
into a Boy* 328

The Case of the Twin Who Lost His Penis 329

Do the Exceptional Cases Prove the Rule? 330

**13.4 Effects of Gonadal Hormones
in Adults 330**

Male Reproduction–Related Behavior
and Testosterone 330

*The Case of the Man Who Lost
and Regained His Manhood* 331

Female Reproduction–Related Behavior
and Gonadal Hormones 332

Anabolic Steroid Abuse 332

The Neuroprotective Effects of Estradiol 333

**13.5 Neural Mechanisms of Sexual
Behavior 334**

Structural Differences between the
Male Hypothalamus and the Female
Hypothalamus 334

The Hypothalamus and Male
Sexual Behavior 335

The Hypothalamus and Female
Sexual Behavior 336

**13.6 Sexual Orientation, Hormones,
and the Brain 337**

Sexual Orientation and Genes 337

Sexual Orientation and Early Hormones 337

What Triggers the Development of
Sexual Attraction? 337

Is There a Difference in the Brains of
Homosexuals and Heterosexuals? 337

Transsexualism 338

The Independence of Sexual Orientation
and Sexual Identity 338

Themes Revisited 339

Think about It 339

Key Terms 339

chapter **14**

Sleep, Dreaming, and Circadian Rhythms 341
How Much Do You Need to Sleep? 342

*The Case of the Woman Who
Wouldn't Sleep* 342

**14.1 The Physiological and Behavioral
Events of Sleep 343**

The Three Standard Psychophysiological
Measures of Sleep 343

Four Stages of Sleep EEG 343

14.2 REM Sleep and Dreaming 345

Testing Common Beliefs
about Dreaming 345

The Interpretation of Dreams 346

Lucid Dreams 346

**14.3 Why Do We Sleep, and Why Do
We Sleep When We Do? 347**

14.4 Comparative Analysis of Sleep 347

14.5 Circadian Sleep Cycles 348

Free-Running Circadian
Sleep–Wake Cycles 349

Jet Lag and Shift Work 350

14.6 Effects of Sleep Deprivation 350

Personal Experience of Sleep Deprivation:
A Cautionary Note 350

*Two Classic Sleep-Deprivation
Case Studies* 351

*The Case of the Sleep-Deprived
Students* 352

Experimental Studies of Sleep
Deprivation in Humans 352

The Case of Randy Gardner 352

Sleep-Deprivation Studies with
Laboratory Animals 353

REM-Sleep Deprivation 353

Sleep Deprivation Increases the Efficiency
of Sleep 355

**14.7 Four Areas of the Brain Involved
in Sleep 356**

Two Areas of the Hypothalamus Involved
in Sleep 356

*The Case of Constantin von Economo,
the Insightful Neurologist* 356

Reticular Activating System and Sleep 356

Reticular REM-Sleep Nuclei 358

**14.8 The Circadian Clock: Neural
and Molecular Mechanisms 359**

Location of the Circadian Clock in the
Suprachiasmatic Nuclei 359

Mechanisms of Entrainment 359

Genetics of Circadian Rhythms 360

14.9 Drugs That Affect Sleep 361

Hypnotic Drugs 361

Antihypnotic Drugs 361

Melatonin 361

The Drug Dilemmas: Striking the
Right Balance   384

**15.4 Biopsychological Theories
of Addiction**   **386**
Physical-Dependence and
Positive-Incentive Perspectives
of Addiction   386
Causes of Relapse   386

**15.5 Intracranial Self-Stimulation and the
Pleasure Centers of the Brain**   **387**
Fundamental Characteristics of
Intracranial Self-Stimulation   387
Mesotelencephalic Dopamine System
and Intracranial Self-Stimulation   388

**15.6 Neural Mechanisms of Motivation
and Addiction**   **389**
Two Key Methods for Measuring
Drug-Produced Reinforcement   389
Early Evidence of the Involvement of
Dopamine in Drug Addiction   390
The Nucleus Accumbens and
Drug Addition   390
Support for the Involvement of
Dopamine in Addiction: Evidence
from the Imaging of Human Brains   391
Dopamine, Nucleus Accumbens, and
Addiction: Current View   391

15.7 A Noteworthy Case of Addiction   **392**
The Case of Sigmund Freud   392

Themes Revisited   **393**

Think about It   **393**

Key Terms   **394**

part six
Disorders of Cognition and Emotion

chapter 16
**Lateralization, Language, and the
Split Brain**   **395**
The Left Brain and the Right Brain of Language   395

**16.1 Cerebral Lateralization of Function:
Introduction**   **396**
Aphasia, Apraxia, and
Left-Hemisphere Damage   397
Tests of Cerebral Lateralization   397
Speech Laterality and Handedness   398
Sex Differences in Brain Lateralization   398

Sleep Disorders   **362**
Insomnia   363
Mr. B., the Case of Iatrogenic Insomnia   363
Hypersomnia   363
REM-Sleep–Related Disorders   364
The Case of the Sleeper Who Ran
Over Tackle   364

**14.11 The Effects of Long-Term
Sleep Reduction**   **365**
Long-Term Reduction of Nightly Sleep   365
Long-Term Sleep Reduction by Napping   365
Long-Term Sleep Reduction:
A Personal Case Study   366
The Case of the Author Who Reduced
His Sleep   366

Themes Revisited   **368**

Think about It   **368**

Key Terms   **368**

chapter 15
**Drug Addiction and the Brain's
Reward Circuits**   369
Chemicals That Harm with Pleasure

15.1 Basic Principles of Drug Action   **370**
Drug Administration and Absorption   370
Drug Penetration of the Central
Nervous System   371
Mechanisms of Drug Action   371
Drug Metabolism and Elimination   371
Drug Tolerance   371
Drug Withdrawal Effects and Physical
Dependence   372
Addiction: What Is It?   372

**15.2 Role of Learning in Drug Tolerance
and Drug Withdrawal**   **373**
Contingent Drug Tolerance   373
Conditioned Drug Tolerance   373
Conditioned Withdrawal Effects   375
Thinking about Drug Conditioning   375

15.3 Five Commonly Abused Drugs   **376**
Tobacco   376
Alcohol   377
Marijuana   377
Cocaine and Other Stimulants   380
The Opiates: Heroin and Morphine   381
Comparison of the Hazards of Tobacco,
Alcohol, Marijuana, Cocaine,
and Heroin   383

14.10

16.2 The Split Brain   **399**
Groundbreaking Experiment of Myers and Sperry   399
Commissurotomy in Human Epileptics   401
Evidence That the Hemispheres of Split-Brain Patients Function Independently   402
Cross-Cuing   402
Learning Two Things at Once   403
The Z Lens   403
Dual Mental Functioning and Conflict in Split-Brain Patients   404
The Case of Peter, the Split-Brain Patient Tormented by Conflict   404

16.3 Differences between the Left and Right Hemispheres   **404**
Slight Biases versus All-or-None Hemispheric Differences   405
Some Examples of Lateralization of Function   405
What Is Lateralized—Broad Clusters of Abilities or Individual Cognitive Processes?   407
Anatomical Asymmetries of the Brain   407
Theories of Cerebral Asymmetry   408
The Case of W.L., the Man Who Experienced Aphasia for Sign Language   409
Evolution of Cerebral Lateralization of Function   410

16.4 Cortical Localization of Language: The Wernicke-Geschwind Model   **411**
Historical Antecedents of the Wernicke-Geschwind Model   411
The Wernicke-Geschwind Model   413

16.5 Evaluation of the Wernicke-Geschwind Model   **413**
Effects of Damage to Various Areas of Cortex on Language-Related Abilities   414
Electrical Stimulation of the Cortex and Localization of Language   416
Current Status of the Wernicke-Geschwind Model   418

16.6 The Cognitive Neuroscience Approach to Language   **418**
Functional Brain Imaging and Language   419

16.7 The Cognitive Neuroscience Approach and Dyslexia   **421**
Developmental Dyslexia: Cultural Diversity and Biological Unity   421
Cognitive Neuroscience Analysis of Reading Aloud: Deep and Surface Dyslexia   422
The Case of N.I., the Woman Who Read with Her Right Hemisphere   422

Themes Revisited   **423**
Think about It   **423**
Key Terms   **424**

chapter **17**
Biopsychology of Emotion, Stress, and Health
Fear, the Dark Side of Emotion   425

17.1 Biopsychology of Emotion: Introduction   **426**
Early Landmarks in the Biopsychological Investigation of Emotion   426
The Mind-Blowing Case of Phineas Gage   426
A Human Case of Kluver-Bucy Syndrome   428
Emotions and the Autonomic Nervous System   429
Emotions and Facial Expression   431

17.2 Fear, Defense, and Aggression   **433**
Types of Aggressive and Defensive Behaviors   433
Aggression and Testosterone   434

17.3 Stress and Health   **435**
The Stress Response   435
Stress and Gastric Ulcers   436
Psychoneuroimmunology: Stress, the Immune System, and the Brain   437
Early Experience of Stress   440
Stress and the Hippocampus   440

17.4 Fear Conditioning   **441**
Amygdala and Fear Conditioning   442
Anatomy of the Amygdala: A General Comment   442
Contextual Fear Conditioning and the Hippocampus   443

17.5 Brain Mechanisms of Human Emotion   **443**
Specific Brain Structures Play Specific Roles in Emotion   443
The Case of S.P., the Woman Who Couldn't Perceive Fear   444
The Right Hemisphere Is More Involved Than the Left in Human Emotion   444

Individual Differences in the Neural
Mechanisms of Emotion   445
*The Case of Charles Whitman,
the Texas Tower Sniper*   446
Themes Revisited   447
Think about It   447
Key Terms   447

chapter **18**

Biopsychology of Psychiatric Disorders   448
The Brain Unhinged

18.1 Schizophrenia   449
*The Case of Lena, the Catatonic
Schizophrenic*   449
What Is Schizophrenia?   450
Causal Factors in Schizophrenia   450
Discovery of the First Antischizophrenic
Drugs   450
Dopamine Theory of Schizophrenia   451
Current Research on the Neural Basis
of Schizophrenia   453

**18.2 Affective Disorders: Depression
and Mania**   454
The Case of P.S., the Weeping Widow   454
Major Categories of Affective Disorders   455
Causal Factors in Affective Disorders   455
Discovery of Antidepressant Drugs   456
Theories of Depression   457
Antidepressant Effect of
Sleep Deprivation   458
Brain Pathology and Affective Disorders   458

18.3 Anxiety Disorders   458
*The Case of M.R., the Woman Who
Was Afraid to Go Out*   458

Five Classes of Anxiety Disorders   459
Etiology of Anxiety Disorders   459
Pharmacological Treatment of Anxiety
Disorders   459
Animal Models of Anxiety   460
Neural Bases of Anxiety Disorders   460

18.4 Tourette Syndrome   461
The Case of R.G.—Barking Mad   461
What Is Tourette Syndrome?   461
Impediments to the Study of the
Neuropathology of Tourette Syndrome   462
Brain Mechanisms of Tourette Syndrome   462
Treatment of Tourette Syndrome   462
*The Case of P.H., the Neuroscientist
with Tourette Syndrome*   462

**18.5 Clinical Trials: Development of New
Psychotherapeutic Drugs**   463
Clinical Trials: The Three Phases   463
Controversial Aspects of Clinical Trials   464
Effectiveness of Clinical Trials   465
*The Case of S.B., the Biopsychology
Student Who Took Control*   465

Themes Revisited   466
Think about It   466
Key Terms   467

Epilogue   468
Appendixes   469
Glossary   476
References   495
Credits   531
Indexes   533

Preface

Welcome to the sixth and newest edition of *Biopsychology*. I have been through five previous editions of this text, but never have I been as excited as I am about this one. This edition builds on the strengths of its predecessors, but it also takes important new steps: In addition to introducing cutting-edge research topics, it sharpens the focus on the human element of biopsychology and promotes interactive learning.

I wrote the first edition of *Biopsychology* as a clear, engaging introduction to current biopsychological theory and research—and the sixth edition continues to fill this role. It is intended for use as a primary text in one- or two-semester courses in biopsychology—variously titled Biopsychology, Physiological Psychology, Brain and Behavior, Psychobiology, Behavioral Neuroscience, or Behavioral Neurobiology.

The defining feature of *Biopsychology* is its unique combination of biopsychological science and personal, reader-oriented discourse. It is a textbook that is "untextbooklike." Rather than introducing biopsychology in the usual textbook fashion, it interweaves the fundamentals of the field with clinical case studies, social issues, personal implications, and humorous anecdotes. It tries to be a friendly mentor that speaks directly to the reader, enthusiastically relating recent advances in biopsychological science.

The friendly persona of *Biopsychology* is more than just window dressing. I think you will find that this text's engaging pedagogical approach facilitates the acquisition and retention of information, delivering more biopsychology for less effort and with more enjoyment.

Features of the Sixth Edition

The following are major features of the previous editions of *Biopsychology* that have been maintained and strengthened in this edition.

An Emphasis on Behavior In some biopsychological textbooks, the coverage of neurophysiology, neurochemistry, and neuroanatomy subverts the coverage of behavior. *Biopsychology* gives top billing to behavior: It stresses that neuroscience is a team effort and that the unique contribution made by biopsychologists to this effort is their behavioral expertise.

A Broad Definition of Biopsychology Biopsychology is the study of the biology of behavior. *Biopsychology* focuses on the neural mechanisms of behavior but also emphasizes the evolution, genetics, and adaptiveness of behavioral processes.

A Focus on the Scientific Method *Biopsychology* emphasizes important—but frequently misunderstood—points about the scientific method, including these three: (1) The scientific method is a means of answering questions that is as applicable in daily life as it is in the laboratory. (2) The scientific method is fun—it is basically the same as the method used by detectives to solve unwitnessed crimes. (3) Widely accepted scientific theories are current best estimates—not statements of absolute fact.

An Integrative Approach *Biopsychology* has not taken the modular approach, dispensing biopsychological information as a series of brief, independent subject modules. *Biopsychology*'s approach is integrative. It creates a strong fabric of research and ideas by weaving together related subject areas and research findings into chapters of intermediate length.

An Emphasis on Personal and Social Relevance Several chapters of *Biopsychology*—particularly those on eating, sleeping, sex, and drug addiction—carry strong personal and social messages. In these chapters, students are encouraged to consider the relevance of biopsychological research to their lives outside the classroom.

Wit and Enthusiasm Most biopsychology laboratories are places of enthusiasm, dedication, and good humor. *Biopsychology* communicates these important aspects of the "biopsychological life."

Remarkable Illustrations The illustrations in *Biopsychology* are special. This is because each one was conceptualized and meticulously designed by a scientist—

artist team uniquely qualified to clarify and reinforce the text: Pinel and his artist wife, Maggie Edwards.

Emphasis on the Human and Clinical Elements of Biopsychology

Biopsychology features many case studies, which are highlighted in the text. These provocative true stories stimulate interest and allow students to learn how biopsychological principles apply to the real world. Also, chapter-opening photos emphasize the personal and social relevance of biopsychological principles.

Emphasis on Broad Themes

The emphasis of *Biopsychology* is on broad themes rather than details. Four especially important themes are highlighted by distinctive tabs:

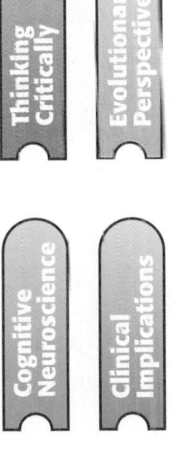

In order to emphasize "the big picture," these four themes have been selected for special prominence. A *Themes Revisited* section at the end of each chapter briefly summarizes how they were developed therein. The four themes provide excellent topics for essay assignments and exam questions.

New Features of the Sixth Edition

Three new and updated features appear in this edition of *Biopsychology*. All are designed to make the text more accessible to students.

Expanded *Beyond the Brain & Behavior* CD-ROM

The CD-ROM that accompanies *Biopsychology* differs from the CDs that come with most texts in one important respect: Most of the material in *Beyond the Brain & Behavior* has been specifically designed to support, expand, and complement *Biopsychology*. The CD accompanying this edition has been significantly expanded: It includes several new animations, videos of research laboratories, and discussions with experts on particular biopsychological topics.

ON THE CD

Visit the *Change Blindness* module. Change blindness needs to be experienced to be appreciated. This is one you'll want to share with your friends.

New Chapter-Opening Photographs Stunning new photographs introduce most chapters. Each was carefully selected by the author to generate student in-

---

terest and to emphasize the human and behavioral orientation of the text.

New Interior Design There have been major changes in the design and layout of the pages. Some are cosmetic, but one has important pedagogical consequences. Many figures have been tightened up, and text has been wrapped around them. Both of these changes are intended to reduce the space taken up by the figures and to make it easier to position figures closer to where they are discussed. This improvement will make it much easier to read and study *Biopsychology*.

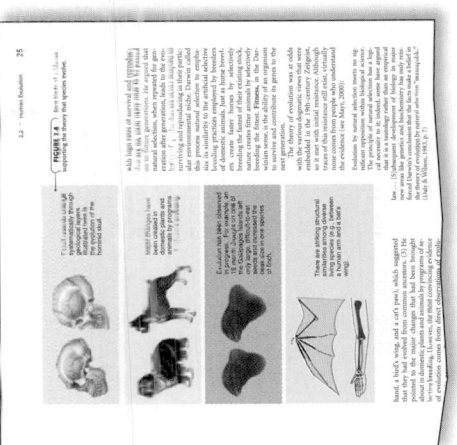

New Coverage in the Sixth Edition

Biopsychology remains one of the most rapidly progressing scientific fields. Like previous editions, this edition of *Biopsychology* has kept abreast of recent developments; it contains 653 references to articles that were not cited in the last edition. These additions have dictated changes to many parts of this text. The following is a list of some of the major content changes to this edition, organized by chapter.

Chapter 2: Evolution, Genetics, and Experience

- Description of the discovery of "number neurons" in the parietal lobes of humans, monkeys, and cats, illustrating the comparative approach
- New subsection entitled "Human Genome Project: What's Next?"

Chapter 3: The Anatomy of the Nervous System

- New subsection entitled "Glial Cells: The Forgotten Majority"

Chapter 4: Neural Conduction and Synaptic Transmission

- Recent discovery that action potentials are not generated on the axon hillock but on the adjacent part of the axon
- Recent discovery that there are few Na^+ channels on axons between the nodes of Ranvier
- Recent finding that postsynaptic potentials elicited near the ends of dendrites tend to be of larger amplitude than those elicited on the cell body
- Discussion of new findings on the recycling of vesicles
- Possible functions of the retrograde conduction of action potentials
- Recent research on gap junctions
- Explanation of the mechanisms of Botox

Chapter 5: The Research Methods of Biopsychology

- Description of the brain-image archives
- A systematic discussion of the weaknesses of fMRI
- Discussion of transcranial magnetic stimulation
- Antisense method of producing genetic knockouts

Chapter 7: Mechanism of Perception, Conscious Awareness, and Attention

- Functional brain-imaging studies of facial recognition in humans and the fusiform facial area
- New findings on the layout of human auditory cortex
- Recent report that Penfield incorrectly inverted the face of the somatosensory homunculus
- Discovery of another secondary area of somatosensory cortex

- The new one-olfactory-receptor-one-neuron rule
- Description of the topographic organization of the olfactory receptors
- Discussion of the adult neurogenesis of olfactory receptors

Chapter 8: The Sensorimotor System

- Clarification of the difference between egocentric and object-based contralateral neglect
- Emphasis on the role of the posterior parietal lobes in initiating movement
- Recent discoveries about the areas of secondary motor cortex
- Discussion of contralateral neglect and unconscious perception
- New case study on the mind control of a robot by a monkey
- Role of the cerebellum in timing

Chapter 9: Development of the Nervous System

- Discussion of radial and tangential neural migration
- Comparison of somal translocation and glia-mediated migration of neurons

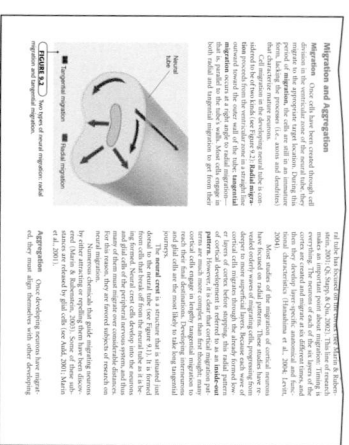

- Updated discussion of the theories of accurate axonal growth
- Systematic discussion of guidance molecules
- Improved description of the topographic gradient hypothesis
- New findings about the role of glial cells in synaptogenesis
- The issue of "promiscuity" in synaptogenesis
- Systematic discussion of neurotrophins
- Discussion of the heterogeneity of autism

Chapter 10: Brain Damage and Neuroplasticity

- Depression as a symptom of Parkinson's disease
- The sex difference in multiple sclerosis

- New material on attempts to develop treatments for Alzheimer's disease
- The possible contributions of adult neurogenesis to recovery of function after brain damage
- The results of the first double-blind placebo-control study of the treatment of Parkinson's disease with tissue transplants
- New research on stem cells and the treatment of spinal damage

Chapter 11: Learning, Memory, and Amnesia

- Discussion of the concept of reconsolidation
- New coverage of the mechanisms of the maintenance and expression of LTP
- A new section on the variability of LTP

Chapter 12: Hunger, Eating, and Health

- More systematic coverage of hunger and satiety peptides
- Recent findings that meals served to famine victims cause anorexia

Chapter 13: Hormones and Sex

- More systematic coverage of sex differences in brain structure
- Recent evidence that sex chromosomes have effects on brain development that are not mediated by sex hormones
- Discovery that sex differences in brain size result from more apoptotic cell loss in females
- The recent suicide of "John," the famous product of infantile sex reassignment
- Discussion of the neuroprotective effects of estradiol
- Evidence that ventromedial nucleus lesions disrupt the motivation to engage in male sexual behavior
- Emphasis that the direction of a person's sexual attraction (male or female) is not a matter of choice
- Discussion of transsexualism and sexual reassignment
- Independence of sexual orientation and sexual identity

Chapter 14: Sleep, Dreaming, and Circadian Rhythms

- Default theory of REM sleep
- Reorganized coverage of the neural mechanisms of sleep
- Classic observations of von Economo and the neural mechanisms of sleep
- Newly discovered circadian photoreceptors in the retinal ganglion cell layer

- Recent discovery that all cells of the body contain circadian timing mechanisms
- Role of orexin in narcolepsy and sleep
- The important recent finding that people who slept 8 hours or more per night tended to die sooner than those who slept between 5 and 7 hours per night

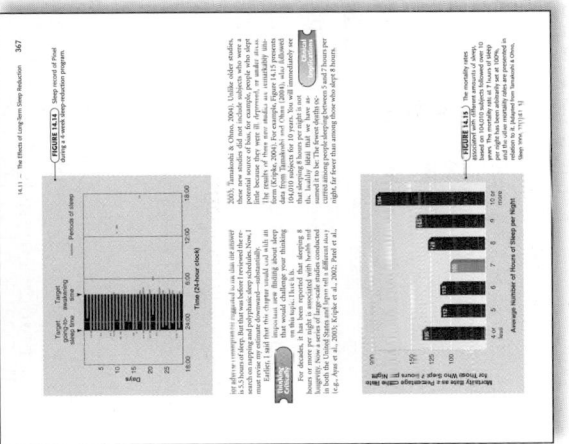

Chapter 15: Drug Addiction and the Brain's Reward Circuits

- Increased coverage of fetal alcohol syndrome
- Discussion of recent reports that marijuana causes memory problems
- Recent correlational studies linking MDMA and brain damage
- Discussion of methadone and buprenorphine treatments for opiate addiction
- New section on the causes of relapse in cases of addiction
- Support from human brain-imaging studies for the involvement of dopamine in addiction

Chapter 16: Lateralization, Language, and the Split Brain

- Description of the current, more-sophisticated view of the involvement of dopamine in addiction
- Hand preference and the asymmetry of the hand area of the motor homunculus
- Right handedness of apes
- The paradox involving right-hemisphere activity during language use and the failure of right-hemisphere lesions to disrupt language use
- Sensory and motor problems of dyslexics

Chapter 17: Biopsychology of Emotion, Stress, and Health

- How stress affects immune function—the surprising results of a recent meta-analysis

- Why decreases in immune function do not necessarily translate into increases in disease

- Systematic coverage of the effects of early stress

- Systematic coverage of the effects of stress on the hippocampus

- Fear conditioning in humans during functional brain imaging

Chapter 18: Biopsychology of Psychiatric Disorders

- The current view that the role of D_2 receptors in schizophrenia is not the entire story

- Systematic coverage of schizophrenia and brain damage

- Systematic discussion of atypical neuroleptics

- Comparison of the effectiveness of drugs in the treatment of affective disorders

- Brain pathology and affective disorders

- Posttraumatic stress disorder

- Concept of orphan drugs

Learning Aids

Biopsychology has several features that are expressly designed to help students learn and remember the material:

- Boldfaced **key terms**—additional terms of lesser importance appear in italics

- **Scan Your Brain**, study exercises that occur in the chapters at key transition points, where students can benefit most from pausing to consolidate preceding material before continuing

- **Themes Revisited**, sections that act as the conclusion to each chapter, summarizing the ways the book's four major themes have impacted that particular topic

- **Think about It**, discussion questions that challenge students to think critically about chapter information

- **Appendices**, which serve as convenient sources of important information that is too detailed for some students of biopsychology

Ancillary Materials Available with Biopsychology

The *Beyond the Brain & Behavior* CD-ROM Packaged free with every new textbook, the CD-ROM titled

Beyond the Brain & Behavior contains many activities and demonstrations designed to increase students' interest and encourage them to relate to biopsychology in an active way. Marginal annotations in *Biopsychology* direct students to CD components at the appropriate points in each chapter. Some of the key elements featured on *Beyond the Brain & Behavior* include:

- **Animations and other demonstrations.** Media demonstrations specially designed for this CD allow students to experience important textual concepts for themselves. New animations focus on the receptive fields of visual neurons, Sperry's classic eye rotation experiments, and the anatomy of neurons.

- **Neural modules.** Ten animated neural modules from the acclaimed A.D.A.M. Interactive Physiology CD-ROM (Benjamin/Cummings) help students understand fundamental physiological principles. Through audio explanations and visual demonstrations, each module brings a complex aspect of biopsychology to life on students' own computer monitors.

- **Video clips.** In some video clips, Pinel speaks personally to students and communicates his enthusiasm for biopsychology—most of these were filmed in his own home. In other video clips, students see research laboratories in action and hear from the well-known biopsychologists who run them.

- **Practice Tests.** On the CD, students will find 15 multiple-choice questions per chapter, written by Pinel himself. These self-scoring tests will help students prepare for exams.

- **Electronic flash cards.** Students can review key terms and their definitions for each chapter using convenient electronic flash cards.

Test Bank The test bank for this edition of *Biopsychology* comprises more than 2,000 multiple-choice questions. The difficulty of each item is rated—easy (1), moderate (2), or difficult (3)—to assist instructors with their test construction. Each item is also labeled with a topic and a page reference so that instructors can easily select questions to customize their tests. Textbook authors rarely prepare their own test banks; the fact that Pinel insists on preparing his own attests to its quality—and his commitment to helping students learn.

Computerized Test Bank This computerized version of the test bank is available with Tamarack's easy-to-use TestGen software, which lets instructors prepare tests for printing as well for network and online testing. The computerized test bank has full editing capability for Windows and Macintosh.

Instructor's Manual Skillfully prepared by Michael Mana of Western Washington University, the instruc-

dents quickly master the fundamentals, review a subject for understanding, or prepare for an exam.

A Colorful Introduction to the Anatomy of the Human Brain
This book provides an easy and enjoyable means of learning or reviewing the fundamentals of human neuroanatomy through the acclaimed directed-coloring method.

VideoWorkshop for Physiological Psychology CD-ROM
This CD-ROM for students and instructors contains over 50 minutes of content relevant to the Physiological Psychology course.

VideoWorkshop for Physiological Psychology Instructor Teaching Guide with CD-ROM
The Instructor Teaching Guide offers a multitude of ideas for integrating VideoWorkshop into your course, including summaries for each video clip, classroom activities, writing activities, discussion starters, correlation grids, learning objectives, and an answer key for the Student Learning Guide. The content of the CD-ROM and Student Learning Guide is also printed at the end of the Teaching Guide, giving you the complete program in one easy reference!

VideoWorkshop for Physiological Psychology Student Learning Guide with CD-ROM
The Student Learning Guide contains many in-depth learning questions, organized into the categories "Observation," "Multiple-Choice," "The Next Step," and "Connecting to the Web," to help students connect what they see to what they've learned in class.

Digital Media Archive
Allyn & Bacon's Digital Media Archive for Physiological Psychology, 2006 edition, is available to adopters of the book. This instructor's resource, available on CD-ROM from your Allyn & Bacon sales representative, provides more than 400 full-color images—including PowerPoint presentations and figures—from the text and from other sources. A booklet listing the images by chapter accompanies the CD-ROM, for easy reference.

Biopsychology Video
Instructors who adopt *Biopsychology* can obtain a 60-minute biopsychology videotape. Based on the *Films for the Humanities* series, this video provides students with glimpses of important biopsychological phenomena such as sleep recording, axon growth, memory testing in monkeys, the formation of synapses, gender differences in brain structure, human amnesic patients, rewarding brain stimulation, and brain scans.

tor's manual contains helpful teaching tools, including at-a-glance grids, activities and demonstrations for the classroom, handouts, lecture notes, chapter outlines, and other valuable course organization material for new and experienced instructors.

PowerPoint Presentation
Michelle Pilati of Rio Hondo College has created a PowerPoint package with detailed outlines of key points for each chapter, supported by charts, graphs, diagrams, and other visuals from the textbook. Go to www.ablongman.com/catalog to download this instructor supplement right from its product page!

The Allyn & Bacon Physiological Psychology Transparency Set, 2005 edition
This set of 145 full-color acetate transparencies is available upon adoption of the text from your local Allyn & Bacon sales representative. The transparency package includes images from Allyn and Bacon's major Physiological Psychology texts.

Grade Aid
This robust study guide, written by Michael Mana of Western Washington University, has been revised and expanded for the sixth edition. Grade Aid offers students a rich and highly structured learning tool. Each chapter of the study guide includes the following sections:

- "Before You Read," containing a brief chapter summary and learning objectives
- "As You Read," offering a collection of demonstrations, bidirectional study questions, activities, and exercises
- "After You Read," consisting of three short practice quizzes and one comprehensive practice test
- "When You Have Finished," presenting Web links for further information and a crossword puzzle using key terms from the text

Companion Website
Connecting the textbook to the Internet, this Website contains flash cards, learning objectives, Log-On weblinks, and online practice tests for each chapter to help students review and retain key concepts from the text. Visit this site at www.ablongman.com/pinel6e.

Study Card for Physiological Psychology, © 2005
Colorful, affordable, and packed with useful information, Allyn & Bacon/Longman's study cards make studying easier, more efficient, and more enjoyable. Course information is distilled down to the basics, helping stu-

Acknowledgments

I wrote *Biopsychology*, but Maggie Edwards took the responsibility for all other aspects of the manuscript and CD preparation—Maggie is a talented artist and technical writer, and my partner in life. I am grateful for her encouragement and support and for her many contributions to this book. I also thank her on behalf of the many students who will benefit from her efforts.

Allyn & Bacon did a remarkable job of producing this book. They shared my dream of a textbook that meets the highest standards of pedagogy but is also personal, attractive, and enjoyable. Thank you to Bill Barke, Karon Bowers, and other executives at Allyn and Bacon for having faith in *Biopsychology* and providing the financial and personal support necessary for it to stay at the forefront of its field. A special thank you goes to Erin Liedel for her development assistance, her moral support, and her willingness to put up with our eccentricities. Another special thank you goes to Michael Granger and Jane Hoover for coordinating the production—an excruciatingly difficult and often thankless job. Jane was also the copyeditor, making many improvements in the text and art, which were greatly appreciated. And thank you to Cristina Vasuta for her assistance in compiling the references and test bank.

I thank the following instructors for providing me with reviews of various editions of *Biopsychology*. Their comments have contributed substantially to the evolution of this edition and its CD-ROM.

L. Joseph Acher, Baylor University

Michael Babcock, Montana State University–Bozeman

Carol Batt, Sacred Heart University

Noel Jay Bean, Vassar College

Thomas Bennett, Colorado State University

Linda Brannon, McNeese State University

Peter Brunjes, University of Virginia

Michelle Butler, United States Air Force Academy

Donald Peter Cain, University of Western Ontario

Deborah A. Carroll, Southern Connecticut State University

John Conklin, Camosun College

Gregory Ervin, Brigham Young University

Robert B. Fischer, Ball State University

Allison Fox, University of Wollongong

Thomas Goettsche, SAS Institute, Inc.

Arnold M. Golub, California State University–Sacramento

Mary Gotch, Solano College

Kenneth Guttman, Citrus College

Melody Smith Harrington, St. Gregory's University

Theresa D. Hernandez, University of Colorado

Cindy Ellen Herzog, Frostburg State University

Peter Hickmott, University of California–Riverside

Tony Jelsma, Atlantic Baptist University

Roger Johnson, Ramapo College

John Jonides, University of Michigan

Maria J. Lavooy, University of Central Florida

Jon Kahane, Springfield College

Craig Kinsley, University of Richmond

Ora Kofman, Ben Gurion University of the Negev

Louis Koppel, Utah State University

Victoria Littlefield, Augsburg College

Linda Lockwood, Metropolitan State College of Denver

Charles Malsbury, Memorial University

Michael R. Markham, Florida International University

Michael P. Matthews, Drury College

Lin Meyers, California State University–Stanislaus

Russ Morgan, Western Illinois University

Henry Morlock, SUNY–Plattsburgh

Lauretta Park, Clemson University

Ted Parsons, University of Wisconsin–Platteville

Jim H. Patton, Baylor University

Edison Perdorno, Minnesota State University

Michael Peters, University of Guelph

Michelle Pilati, Rio Hondo College

David Robbins, Ohio Wesleyan University

Jeanne P. Ryan, SUNY–Plattsburgh

David Soderquist, University of North Carolina at Greensboro

Michael Stoloff, James Madison University

Dallas Treit, University of Alberta

Stuart Tousman, Rockford College

Dennis Vincenzi, University of Central Florida

Linda Walsh, University of Northern Iowa

Jon Williams, Kenyon College

David Yager, University of Maryland

H. P. Ziegler, Hunter College

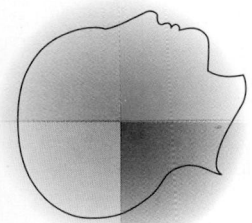

To the Student

In the 1960s, I was, in the parlance of the times, "turned on" by an undergraduate course in biopsychology. I could not imagine anything more interesting than a field of science dedicated to studying the relation between psychological processes and the brain. My initial fascination led to a long career as a student, researcher, and teacher of biopsychological science. *Biopsychology* is my attempt to share this fascination with you.

I have tried to make *Biopsychology* a different kind of textbook, a textbook that includes clear, concise, and well-organized explanations of the key points but is still interesting to read—a book from which you might suggest a suitable chapter to an interested friend or relative. To accomplish this goal, I thought about what kind of textbook I would have liked when I was a student, and I decided immediately to avoid the stern formality and ponderous style of conventional textbook writing.

I wanted *Biopsychology* to have a relaxed and personal style. In order to accomplish this, I imagined that you and I were chatting as I wrote, and that I was telling you—usually over a glass of something—about the interesting things that go on in the field of biopsychology. Imagining these chats kept my writing from drifting back into conventional "textbookese," and it never let me forget that I was writing this book for you, the student.

I was particularly excited, and a bit nervous, about the fifth edition of *Biopsychology* because it was the first one to have an accompanying CD. I was particularly concerned about students' reactions to the animations and film clips because designing them was a new experience for my partner, Maggie, and me. However, the CD proved to be a smashing success with students, and thus it has been greatly expanded in this edition. I hope that you like the new material. As for me, I may never recover from the shock of seeing and hearing myself on my own computer monitor.

I hope that *Biopsychology* teaches you much, and that reading it generates in you the same personal feeling that writing it did in me. If you are so inclined, I welcome your comments and suggestions. You can contact me at the Department of Psychology, University of British Columbia, Vancouver, BC, Canada, V6T 1Z4, or at the following e-mail address:

jpinel@psych.ubc.ca

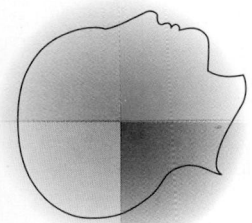

About the Author

John Pinel, the author of *Biopsychology*, obtained his PhD from McGill University in Montreal. He worked briefly at the Massachusetts Institute of Technology before taking up his current position at the University of British Columbia in Vancouver. Professor Pinel is an award-winning teacher and the author of over 200 scientific papers; however, he feels that *Biopsychology* is his major career-related accomplishment. "It ties together everything that I love about my job: students, teaching, writing, and research."

When we asked him about his personal interests, Professor Pinel spoke glowingly of his partner, Maggie, and son, Greg. The high quality of the illustrations in *Biopsychology* is largely attributable to the effort and talent of Maggie, who is an artist and technical writer. Greg is currently completing his PhD at the London School of Economics, specializing in social and educational programs for indigenous peoples.

"I get most of my exercise by rehearsing and performing West African drum rhythms," Pinel says. "For a peak mental and physical experience, a bit of Kpanlogo with my friend Nigerian drum master Kwasi Iruoje is hard to beat." (Be sure to view *The Beat Goes On* video clip on the *Beyond the Brain & Behavior* CD-ROM—free with the purchase of a new text.) "Most of my rest and relaxation comes from cuddling our cats, Sambala and Rastaman."

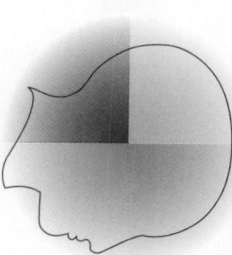

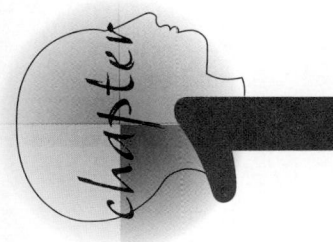
chapter 1

Biopsychology as a Neuroscience

What Is Biopsychology, Anyway?

1.1 What Is Biopsychology?

1.2 What Is the Relation between Biopsychology and the Other Disciplines of Neuroscience?

1.3 What Types of Research Characterize the Biopsychological Approach?

1.4 What Are the Divisions of Biopsychology?

1.5 Converging Operations: How Do Biopsychologists Work Together?

1.6 Scientific Inference: How Do Biopsychologists Study the Unobservable Workings of the Brain?

1.7 Critical Thinking about Biopsychological Claims

The appearance of the human brain is far from impressive (see Figure 1.1). The human brain is a squishy, wrinkled, walnut-shaped hunk of tissue weighing about 1.3 kilograms. It looks more like something that you might find washed up on a beach than like one of the wonders of the world—which it surely is. Despite its disagreeable external appearance, the human brain is an amazingly intricate network of neurons (cells that receive and transmit electrochemical signals). Contemplate for a moment the complexity of your own brain's neural circuits. Consider the 100 billion neurons in complex array, the estimated 100 trillion connections among them, and the almost infinite number of paths that neural signals can follow through this morass.

The complexity of the human brain is hardly surprising, considering what it can do. An organ capable of creating a *Mona Lisa*, an artificial limb, and a supersonic aircraft; of traveling to the moon and to the depths of the sea; and of experiencing the wonders of an alpine sunset, a newborn infant, and a reverse slam dunk *must* be complex. Paradoxically, **neuroscience** (the scientific study of the nervous system) may prove to be the brain's ultimate challenge: Does the brain have the capacity to understand something as complex as itself?

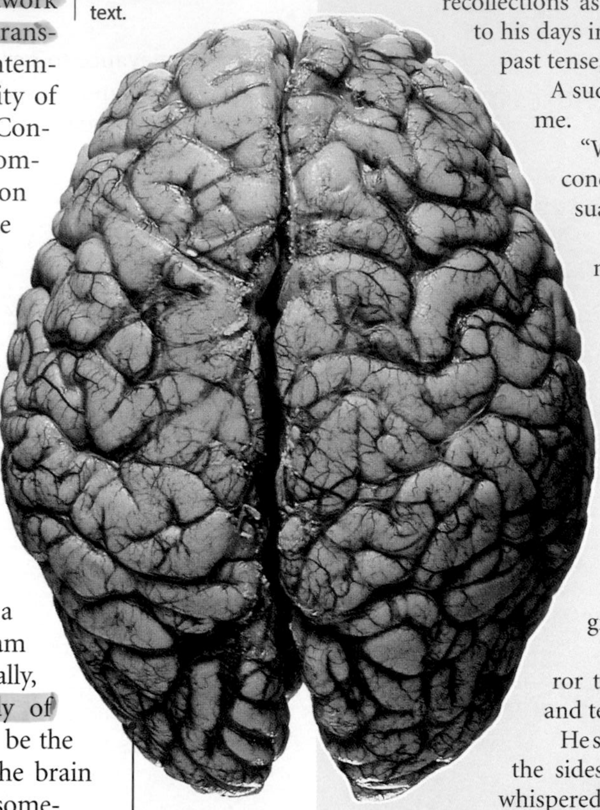

Neuroscience comprises several related disciplines. The primary purpose of this chapter is to introduce you to one of them: biopsychology. Each of this chapter's seven sections characterizes biopsychology from a different perspective.

Before you proceed to the body of this chapter, I would like to tell you about two things: (1) the case of Jimmie G., which will give you a taste of the interesting things that lie ahead, and (2) the major themes of this book.

ON THE CD

Visit the *Greetings from the Author* module. Pinel welcomes you personally and explains an often overlooked aspect of biopsychology he has included in this text.

FIGURE 1.1
The human brain.

The Case of Jimmie G., the Man Frozen in Time

[In 1975] Jimmie was a fine-looking man, with a curly bush of grey hair, a healthy and handsome forty-nine-year-old. He was cheerful, friendly, and warm.

He was quick-witted, observant, and logical, and had no difficulty solving complex problems and puzzles—no difficulty, that is, if they could be done quickly. If much time was required, he forgot what he was doing....

On intelligence testing he showed excellent ability. He was quick-witted, observant, and logical, and had no

"I see these beds, and these patients everywhere. Looks like a sort of hospital to me. But hell, what would I be doing in a hospital—and with all these old people, years older than me.... Maybe I work here.... If I don't work here, I've been put here. Am I a patient, am I sick and don't know it, Doc? It's crazy, it's scary...."

"... 'Where do you think you are?'

"I wouldn't forget you, Doc?"

"No, I can't say we have. Quite a beard you got there."

"Haven't we met before, Mr. G.?" I asked casually.

do I take this chair here?' There was no sign of recognition on his frank, open face.

Two minutes later I re-entered the room.... "Hiya, Doc!" he said. "Nice morning! You want to talk to me—

... I stole away, taking the hateful mirror with me.

happened to me? Is this a nightmare? Am I crazy? Is this a joke?"—and he became frantic, panicked.

whispered. "Christ, what's going on? What's happened to me? Is this a nightmare? Am I crazy? Is this a joke?"—and he became frantic, panicked.

the sides of the chair. "Jesus Christ," he whispered. "Christ, what's going on? What's

He suddenly turned ashen and gripped the sides of the chair. "Jesus Christ," he whispered.

ror toward him. "Look in the mirror and tell me what you see...."

"Here," I said, and thrust a mirror toward him. "Look in the mirror

given myself....

man before me, I had an impulse for which I have never forgiven myself....

Looking at the grey-haired man before me, I had an impulse for which I have never forgiven myself....

Doc. I'll be twenty next birthday."

"Why, I guess I'm nineteen, Doc. I'll be twenty next birthday."

"And you, Jimmie, how old would you be?"...

the war, FDR's dead, Truman's at the helm. There are great times ahead."

"Forty-five, man. What do you mean?" He went on, "We've won the war, FDR's dead, Truman's at

"What year is this, Mr. G.?" I asked, concealing my perplexity under a casual manner.

A sudden, improbable suspicion seized me.

... I was very struck by the change of tense in his recollections as he passed from his school days to his days in the navy. He had been using the past tense, but now used the present....

some reason his reminiscences stopped....

stationed, the names of his shipmates.... But there for

which he had served, their missions, where they were

remembered the names of the various submarines on

from high school when he was seventeen, had just graduated

ics and science ... he was seventeen, had just graduated

friends he'd had, and his special fondness for mathemat-

ly had lived.... He spoke of school and school days, the

chair here?" ... He spoke of the houses where his fami-

"Hiya, Doc!" he said. "Nice morning! Do I take this

Homing in on his memory, I found an extreme and extraordinary loss of recent memory—so that whatever was said or shown to him was apt to be forgotten in a few seconds' time. Thus I laid out my watch, my tie, and my glasses on the desk, covered them, and asked him to remember these. Then, after a minute's chat, I asked him what I had put under the cover. He remembered none of them—or indeed that I had even asked him to remember. I repeated the test, this time getting him to write down the names of the three objects; again he forgot, and when I showed him the paper with his writing on it he was astounded....

"What is this?" I asked, showing him a photo in the magazine I was holding.

"It's the moon," he replied.

"No, it's not," I answered. "It's a picture of the earth taken from the moon."

"Doc, you're kidding! Someone would've had to get a camera up there!... how the hell would you do that?"....

He was becoming fatigued, and somewhat irritable and anxious, under the continuing pressure of anomaly and contradiction, and their fearful implications.... And I myself was wrung with emotion—it was heartbreaking... to think of his life lost in limbo, dissolving.

He is, as it were... isolated in a single moment of being, with a moat... of forgetting all round him.... He is a man without a past (or future), stuck in a constantly changing, meaningless moment.

(Reprinted with the permission of Simon & Schuster Adult Publishing Group from *The Man Who Mistook His Wife for a Hat and Other Clinical Tales* by Oliver Sacks. Copyright © 1970, 1981, 1983, 1984, 1985 by Oliver Sacks.)

Remember Jimmie G.; you will encounter him again, later in this chapter.

Four Major Themes of This Book

You will learn many new facts in this book—new findings, concepts, brain structures, and the like. But more importantly, many years from now, long after you have forgotten most of those facts, you will still be carrying with you productive new ways of thinking. I have selected four new ideas for special emphasis: They are the major themes of this book.

To help you give these themes the special attention they deserve and to help you follow their development as you progress though the book, I have marked relevant passages with tabs. The following are the four major themes and their related tabs.

Thinking about Biopsychology Because many biopsychological topics are so interesting (as you have already seen in the case of Jimmie G.) and often relevant to everyday life, we are fed a steady diet of biopsychological information and opinion—by television, newspapers, the Internet, friends, relatives, books, teachers, etc. One major purpose of this book is to help you make the transition from being a passive consumer of biopsychological claims to being an effective, critical thinker, a person who takes nothing at face value, judges the reasonableness of various claims, and assesses their relevance to her or his own social views and lifestyle. To help you achieve this goal, I have marked each directly relevant passage in this book with a thinking-about-biopsychology tab.

Thinking Critically

ON THE CD

Visit the *Themes of Biopsychology* module. Hear Pinel explain how and why the themes of *Biopsychology* have been highlighted for your convenience.

Clinical Implications Clinical (pertaining to illness or treatment) considerations are woven through the fabric of biopsychology. Much of what biopsychologists learn about the functioning of the normal brain comes from studying the diseased or damaged brain; and, conversely, much of what biopsychologists discover has relevance for the treatment of brain disorders. This book focuses on the interplay between brain dysfunction and biopsychology, and each major example of that interplay is highlighted by a clinical implications tab.

Clinical Implications

The Evolutionary Perspective Although the events that led to the evolution of the human species can never be determined with certainty, thinking of the environmental pressures that likely led to the evolution of our brains and behavior often leads to important biopsychological insights. This approach is called the **evolutionary perspective**. An important aspect of the evolutionary perspective is the *comparative approach* (trying to understand biological phenomena by comparing them in different species). You will learn throughout the text that we humans have learned much about ourselves by studying species that are related to us through evolution. The evolutionary approach has proven to be one of the cornerstones of modern biopsychological inquiry. Each discussion that relates to the evolutionary perspective is marked by an evolutionary perspective tab.

Evolutionary Perspective

Cognitive Neuroscience The advances in any field of science are driven to a large degree by technological innovation: The development of an effective new research instrument is often followed by a series of discoveries. There is no better example of this than *cognitive neuroscience*, a relatively new field of biopsychology

that has been fueled by the development of methods for creating images of the activity of the living human brain. Using these functional brain-imaging methods, cognitive neuroscientists study the areas of the human brain that become active while subjects engage in particular *cognitive* (pertaining to thinking) processes, such as memory, attention, and perception. Each discussion involving this type of research is highlighted by a cognitive neuroscience tab.

1.1   What Is Biopsychology?

Biopsychology is the scientific study of the biology of behavior—see Dewsbury (1991). Some refer to this field as *psychobiology, behavioral biology,* or *behavioral neuroscience;* but I prefer the term *biopsychology* because it denotes a biological approach to the study of psychology rather than a psychological approach to the study of biology: Psychology commands center stage in this text. *Psychology is the scientific study of behavior*—the scientific study of all overt activities of the organism as well as all the internal processes that are presumed to underlie them (e.g., learning, memory, motivation, perception, and emotion).

The study of the biology of behavior has a long history, but biopsychology did not develop into a major neuroscientific discipline until the 20th century. Although it is not possible to specify the exact date of biopsychology's birth, the publication of *The Organization of Behavior* in 1949 by D. O. Hebb played a key role in its emergence (see Brown & Milner, 2003; Milner, 1993;

Milner & White, 1987). In his book, Hebb developed the first comprehensive theory of how complex psychological phenomena, such as perceptions, emotions, thoughts, and memories, might be produced by brain activity. Hebb's theory did much to discredit the view that psychological functioning is too complex to have its roots in the physiology and chemistry of the brain. Hebb based his theory on experiments involving both humans and laboratory animals, on clinical case studies, and on logical arguments developed from his own insightful observations of daily life. This eclectic approach has become a hallmark of biopsychological inquiry.

In comparison to physics, chemistry, and biology, biopsychology is an infant—a healthy, rapidly growing infant, but an infant nonetheless. In this book, you will reap the benefits of biopsychology's youth. Because biopsychology does not have a long and complex history, you will be able to move directly to the excitement of current research.

1.2   What Is the Relation between Biopsychology and the Other Disciplines of Neuroscience?

Neuroscience is a team effort, and biopsychologists are important members of the team (see Albright, Kandel, & Posner, 2000; Kandel & Squire, 2000). This section of the chapter further defines biopsychology by discussing its relation to other neuroscientific disciplines.

Biopsychologists are neuroscientists who bring to their research a knowledge of behavior and of the methods of behavioral research. It is their behavioral orientation and expertise that make their contribution to neuroscience unique. You will be able to better appreciate the importance of this contribution if you consider that the ultimate purpose of the nervous system is to produce and control behavior (see Doupe & Heisenberg, 2000; Grillner & Dickson, 2002).

Biopsychology is an integrative discipline. Biopsychologists draw together knowledge from the other neuroscientific disciplines and apply it to the study of behavior.

The following are a few of the disciplines of neuroscience that are particularly relevant to biopsychology:

Neuroanatomy. The study of the structure of the nervous system (see Chapter 3).

Neurochemistry. The study of the chemical bases of neural activity (see Chapter 4).

Neuroendocrinology. The study of interactions between the nervous system and the endocrine system (see Chapters 13 and 17).

Neuropathology. The study of nervous system disorders (see Chapter 10).

Neuropharmacology. The study of the effects of drugs on neural activity (see Chapters 4, 15, and 18).

Neurophysiology. The study of the functions and activities of the nervous system (see Chapter 4).

1.3　What Types of Research Characterize the Biopsychological Approach?

Although biopsychology is only one of many disciplines that contribute to neuroscience, it is itself broad and diverse. Biopsychologists study many different phenomena, and they approach their research in many different ways. In order to characterize biopsychological research, this section discusses three major dimensions along which approaches to biopsychological research vary. Biopsychological research can involve either human or nonhuman subjects; it can take the form of either formal experiments or nonexperimental studies; and it can be either pure or applied.

Human and Nonhuman Subjects

Both human and nonhuman animals are the subject of biopsychological research. Of the nonhumans, rats are the most common subjects; however, mice, cats, dogs, and nonhuman primates are also widely studied.

Humans have several advantages over other animals as experimental subjects of biopsychological research: They can follow instructions, they can report their subjective experiences, and their cages are easier to clean. Of course, I am joking about the cages, but the joke does serve to draw attention to one advantage that humans have over other species of experimental subjects: Humans are often cheaper. Because only the highest standards of animal care are acceptable, the cost of maintaining an animal laboratory can be prohibitive for all but the most well-funded researchers.

Of course, the greatest advantage that humans have as subjects in a field aimed at understanding the intricacies of human brain function is that they have human brains. In fact, you might wonder why biopsychologists would bother studying nonhuman subjects at all. The answer lies in the evolutionary continuity of the brain. The brains of humans differ from the brains of other mammals primarily in their overall size and the extent of their cortical development. In other words, the differences between the brains of humans and those of related species are more quantitative than qualitative, and thus many of the principles of human brain function can be derived from the study of nonhumans (e.g., Nakahara et al., 2002).

Conversely, nonhuman animals have three advantages over humans as subjects in biopsychological research. The first is that the brains and behavior of nonhuman subjects are simpler than those of human subjects. Hence, the study of nonhuman species is more likely to reveal fundamental brain–behavior interactions. The second advantage is that insights frequently arise from the **comparative approach**, the study of biological processes by comparing different species. For ex-

ample, comparing the behavior of species that do not have a cerebral cortex with the behavior of species that do can provide valuable clues about cortical function. The third advantage is that it is possible to conduct research on laboratory animals that, for ethical reasons, is not possible with human subjects. This is not to say that the study of nonhuman animals is not governed by a strict code of ethics (see Institute of Laboratory Animal Resources, 1996)—it is. However, there are fewer ethical constraints on the study of laboratory species than on the study of humans.

In my experience, most biopsychologists display considerable concern for their subjects, whether they are of their own species or not; however, ethical issues are not left to the discretion of the individual researcher. All biopsychological research, whether it involves human or nonhuman subjects, is regulated by independent committees according to strict ethical guidelines: "Researchers cannot escape the logic that if the animals we observe are reasonable models of our own most intricate actions, then they must be respected as we would respect our own sensibilities" (Ulrich, 1991, p. 197).

Experiments and Nonexperiments

Biopsychological research involves both experiments and nonexperimental studies. Two common types of nonexperimental studies are quasiexperimental studies and case studies.

Experiments　The experiment is the method used by scientists to find out what causes what, and, as such, it is almost single-handedly responsible for our modern way of life. It is paradoxical that a method capable of such complex feats is itself so simple. To conduct an experiment involving living subjects, the experimenter first designs two or more conditions under which the subjects will be tested. Usually, a different group of subjects is tested under each condition (**between-subjects design**), but sometimes it is possible to test the same group of subjects under each condition (**within-subjects design**). The experimenter assigns the subjects to conditions, administers the treatments, and measures the outcome in such a way that there is only one relevant difference between the conditions that are being compared. This difference between the conditions is called the **independent variable**. The variable that is measured by the experimenter to assess the effect of the independent variable is called the **dependent variable**.

Why is it critical that there be no differences between conditions other than the independent variable? The reason is that when there is more than one difference that could affect the dependent variable, it is difficult to

Evolutionary Perspective

determine whether it was the independent variable or the unintended difference—called a **confounded variable**—that led to the observed effects on the dependent variable.

difficult. Readers of research papers must be constantly on the alert for confounded variables that have gone unnoticed by the experimenters themselves.

Although the experimental method is conceptually simple, eliminating all confounded variables can be quite

An experiment by Lester and Gorzalka (1988) illustrates the experimental method in action. The experiment was a demonstration of the Coolidge effect. The **Coolidge effect** is the fact that a copulating male who becomes incapable of continuing to copulate with one sex partner can often recommence copulating with a new sex partner (see Figure 1.2). Before your imagination starts running wild, I should mention that the subjects in Lester and Gorzalka's experiment were hamsters, not students from the undergraduate subject pool.

Lester and Gorzalka argued that the Coolidge effect had not been demonstrated in females because it is more difficult to conduct well-controlled Coolidge-effect experiments with females—not because females do not display a Coolidge effect. The confusion, according to Lester and Gorzalka, stemmed from the fact that the males of most mammalian species become sexually fatigued more readily than do the females. As a result, attempts to demonstrate the Coolidge effect in females are often confounded by the fatigue of the males. When, in the midst of copulation, a female is provided with a new sex partner, the increase in her sexual receptivity could be either a legitimate Coolidge effect or a reaction to the greater vigor of the new male. Because female mammals usually display little sexual fatigue, this confounded variable is not a serious problem in demonstrations of the Coolidge effect in males.

Lester and Gorzalka devised a clever procedure to control for this confounded variable. At the same time that a female subject was copulating with one male (the familiar male), the other male to be used in the test (the unfamiliar male) was copulating with another female. Then, both males were given a rest while the female was copulating with a third male. Finally, the female subject was tested with either the familiar male or the unfamiliar male. The dependent variable was the amount of time that the female displayed **lordosis** (the arched-back, rump-up, tail-diverted posture of female rodent sexual receptivity) during each sex test. As Figure 1.3 illustrates, the females responded more vigorously to the unfamiliar males than they did to the familiar males during the third test, despite the fact that both the unfamiliar and familiar males were equally fatigued and both mounted the females with equal vigor. This experiment illustrates the importance of good experimental design as well as a point made in Chapter 13: that males and females are more similar than most people appreciate.

FIGURE 1.2   President Calvin Coolidge and Mrs. Grace Coolidge. Many students think that the Coolidge effect is named after a biopsychologist named Coolidge. In fact, it is named after President Calvin Coolidge, of whom the following story is told. (If the story isn't true, it should be.) During a tour of a poultry farm, Mrs. Coolidge inquired of the farmer how his farm managed to produce so many eggs with such a small number of roosters. The farmer proudly explained that his roosters performed their duty dozens of times each day.

"Perhaps you could point that out to Mr. Coolidge," replied the First Lady in a pointedly loud voice.

The President, overhearing the remark, asked the farmer, "Does each rooster service the same hen each time?"

"No," replied the farmer, "there are many hens for each rooster."

"Perhaps you could point that out to Mrs. Coolidge," replied the President.

Quasiexperimental Studies   It is not possible for biopsychologists to bring the experimental method to bear on all problems of interest to them. There are frequently physical or ethical impediments that make it impossible to assign subjects to particular conditions or to administer the conditions once the subjects have been assigned to them. For example, experiments on the causes of brain damage in human alcoholics are not feasible bethe neuroanatomical or intellectual differences that were observed between them? There are several. For example, alcoholics as a group tend to be more poorly educated, more prone to accidental head injury, more likely to use other drugs, and more likely to have poor diets. Accordingly, quasiexperimental studies have revealed that alcoholics tend to have more brain damage than nonalcoholics, but they have not indicated why.

Have you forgotten Jimmie G.? He was a product of long-term alcohol consumption.

Case Studies Studies that focus on a single case or subject are called **case studies.** Because they focus on a single case, they often provide a more in-depth picture than that provided by an experiment or a quasiexperimental study, and they are an excellent source of testable hypotheses. However, there is a major problem with all case studies: their **generalizability**—the degree to which their results can be applied to other cases. Because humans differ from one another in both brain function and behavior, it is important to be skeptical of any biopsychological theory based entirely on a few case studies.

Pure and Applied Research

Biopsychological research can be either pure or applied. Pure research and applied research differ in a number of respects, but they are distinguished less by their own attributes than by the motives of the individuals involved in their pursuit. **Pure research** is research motivated primarily by the curiosity of the researcher—it is done solely for the purpose of acquiring knowledge. In contrast, **applied research** is research intended to bring about some direct benefit to humankind.

Many scientists believe that pure research will ultimately prove to be of more practical benefit than applied research. Their view is that applications flow readily from an understanding of basic principles and that attempts to move directly to application without first gaining a basic understanding are shortsighted. Of course, it is not necessary for a research project to be completely pure or completely applied; many research programs have elements of both approaches.

One important difference between pure and applied research is that pure research is more vulnerable to the vagaries of political regulation because politicians and the voting public have difficulty understanding why research of no immediate practical benefit should be supported. If the decision were yours, would you be willing to grant hundreds of thousands of dollars to support the study of squid *motor neurons* (neurons that control muscles), learning in recently hatched geese, the activity of single nerve cells in the visual systems of monkeys, the hormones released by the *hypothalamus* (a small neural structure at the base of the brain) of pigs and sheep, or the function of the *corpus callosum* (the large neural

cause it would not be ethical to assign a subject to a condition that involves years of alcohol consumption. (Some of you may be more concerned about the ethics of assigning subjects to a control condition that involves years of sobriety.) In such prohibitive situations, biopsychologists sometimes conduct **quasiexperimental studies**—studies of groups of subjects who have been exposed to the conditions of interest in the real world. These studies have the appearance of experiments, but they are not true experiments because potential confounded variables have not been controlled—for example, by the random assignment of subjects to conditions.

In one quasiexperimental study, a team of researchers compared 100 detoxified male alcoholics from an alcoholism treatment unit with 50 male nondrinkers obtained from various sources (Acker et al., 1984). The alcoholics as a group performed more poorly on various tests of perceptual, motor, and cognitive ability, and their brain scans revealed extensive brain damage. Although this quasiexperimental study seems like an experiment, it is not. Because the subjects themselves decided which group they would be in—by drinking alcohol or not—the researchers had no means of ensuring that exposure to alcohol was the only variable that distinguished the two groups. Can you think of differences other than exposure to alcohol that could reasonably be expected to exist between a group of alcoholics and a group of abstainers—differences that could have contributed to

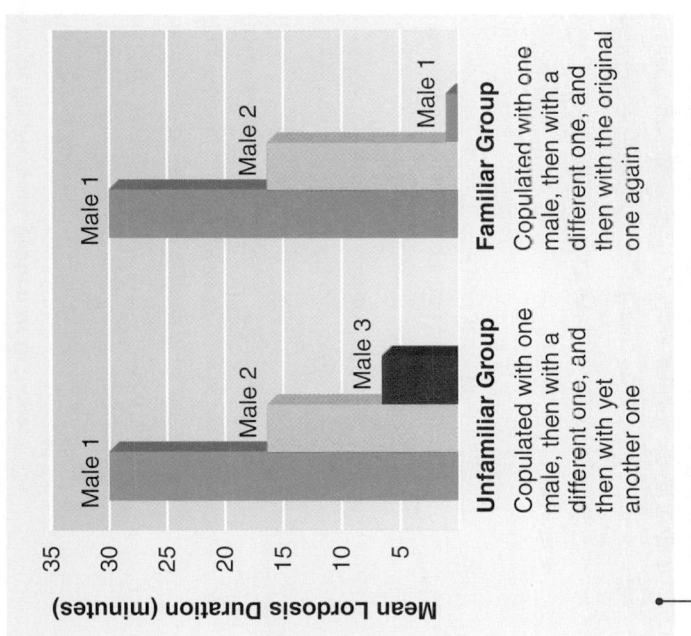

Mean Lordosis Duration (minutes)

Unfamiliar Group
Copulated with one male, then with a different one, and then with yet another one

Familiar Group
Copulated with one male, then with a different one, and then with the original one again

FIGURE 1.3 The experimental design and results of Lester and Gorzalka (1988). On the third test, the female hamsters were more sexually receptive to unfamiliar males than they were to the males with which they had copulated on the first test.

TABLE 1.1 Some of the Nobel Prizes Awarded for Studies Related to the Nervous System or Behavior

NOBEL WINNER	DATE	ACCOMPLISHMENT
Ivan Pavlov	1904	Research on the physiology of digestion
Camillo Golgi and Santiago Ramón y Cajal	1906	Research on the structure of the nervous system
Charles Sherrington and Edgar Adrian	1932	Discoveries about the functions of neurons
Henry Dale and Otto Loewi	1936	Discoveries about the transmissions of nerve impulses
Joseph Erlanger and Herbert Gasser	1944	Research on the functions of single nerve fibers
Walter Hess	1949	Research on the role of the brain in controlling behavior
Egas Moniz	1949	Development of prefrontal lobotomy
Georg von Békésy	1961	Research on the auditory system
John Eccles, Alan Hodgkin, and Andrew Huxley	1963	Research on the ionic basis of neural transmission
Ragnor Granit, Haldan Hartline, and George Wald	1967	Research on the chemistry and physiology of vision
Bernard Katz, Ulf von Euler, and Julius Axelrod	1970	Discoveries related to synaptic transmission
Karl Von Frisch, Konrad Lorenz, and Nikolass Tinbergen	1973	Studies of animal behavior
Roger Guillemin and Andrew Schally	1977	Discoveries related to hormone production by the brain
Herbert Simon	1979	Research on human cognition
Roger Sperry	1981	Research on differences between the cerebral hemispheres
David Hubel and Torsten Wiesel	1981	Research on information processing in the visual system
Rita Levi-Montalcini and Stanley Cohen	1986	Discovery and study of nerve and epidermal growth factors
Erwin Neher and Bert Sakmann	1991	Research on ion channels
Alfred Gilman and Martin Rodbell	1994	Discovery of G-protein–coupled receptors
Arvid Carlsson, Paul Greengard, and Eric Kandel	2000	Discoveries related to synaptic transmission

pathway that connects the left and right halves of the brain)? Which, if any, of these projects would you consider worthy of support? Each of these seemingly esoteric projects was supported, and each earned a Nobel Prize for its author.

Table 1.1 lists some of the Nobel Prizes awarded for research related to the brain and behavior (see Benja-

min, 2003). The purpose of this list is to give you a general sense of the official recognition that behavioral and brain research has received, not to have you memorize the list. You will learn later in the chapter that, when it comes to evaluating science, the Nobel committee has not been infallible.

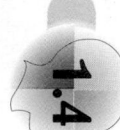

1.4 What Are the Divisions of Biopsychology?

As you have just learned, biopsychologists conduct their research in a variety of fundamentally different ways. Biopsychologists who take the same approaches to their research tend to publish their research in the same journals, attend the same scientific meetings, and belong to the same professional societies. The particular approaches to biopsychology that have flourished and grown have gained wide recognition as separate divisions of biopsychological research. The purpose of this section of the chapter is to give you a clearer sense of biopsychology and its diversity by describing six of its major divisions: (1) physiological psychology, (2) psychopharmacology,

(3) neuropsychology, (4) psychophysiology, (5) cognitive neuroscience, and (6) comparative psychology. For simplicity, they are presented as distinct approaches; but there is much overlap among them, and many biopsychologists regularly follow more than one approach.

Physiological Psychology

Physiological psychology is the division of biopsychology that studies the neural mechanisms of behavior through the direct manipulation of the brain in controlled experiments—surgical and electrical methods of brain manipulation are most common. The subjects of physiological psychology research are almost always laboratory animals, because the focus on direct brain manipulation and controlled experiments precludes the use of human subjects in most instances. There is also a tradition of pure research in physiological psychology; the emphasis is usually on research that contributes to the development of theories of the neural control of behavior rather than on research that is of immediate practical benefit.

Psychopharmacology

Psychopharmacology is similar to physiological psychology, except that it focuses on the manipulation of neural activity and behavior with drugs. In fact, many of the early psychopharmacologists were simply physiological psychologists who moved into drug research, and many of today's biopsychologists identify closely with both approaches. However, the study of the effects of drugs on the brain and behavior has become so specialized that psychopharmacology is regarded as a separate discipline.

A substantial portion of psychopharmacological research is applied (see Brady, 1993). Although drugs are **[Clinical Implications]** sometimes used by psychopharmacologists to study the basic principles of brain–behavior interaction, the purpose of many psychopharmacological experiments is to develop therapeutic drugs (see Chapter 18) or to reduce drug abuse (see Chapter 15). Psychopharmacologists study the effects of drugs on laboratory species—and on humans, if the ethics of the situation permits it.

Neuropsychology

Neuropsychology is the study of the psychological effects of brain damage in human patients. Obviously, human subjects cannot ethically be exposed to experimental treatments that endanger normal brain function. Consequently, neuropsychology deals almost exclusively with case studies and quasiexperimental studies of patients with brain damage resulting from disease, accident, or neurosurgery. The outer layer of the cerebral hemispheres—the **cerebral cortex**—is most likely to be damaged by accident or surgery; this is one reason why neuropsychology has focused on this important part of the human brain.

Neuropsychology is the most applied of the biopsychological subdisciplines; the neuropsychological assessment of human patients, even when **[Clinical Implications]** part of a program of pure research, is always done with an eye toward benefiting them in some way. Neuropsychological tests facilitate diagnosis and thus help the attending physi-

cian prescribe effective treatment (see Benton, 1994). They can also be an important basis for patient care and counseling; Kolb and Whishaw (1990) described such an application.

The Case of Mr. R., the Brain-Damaged Student Who Switched to Architecture

Mr. R., a 21-year-old left-handed man, struck his head on the dashboard in a car accident. . . . Prior to his accident Mr. R. was an honor student at a university. . . . However, a year after the accident he had become a mediocre student who had particular trouble completing his term papers. . . . He was referred to us for neuropsychological assessment, which revealed several interesting facts.

First, Mr. R. was one of about one-third of left-handers whose language functions are represented in the right rather than left hemisphere. . . . In addition, although Mr. R. had a superior IQ, his verbal memory and reading speed were only low-average, which is highly unusual for a person of his intelligence and education. These deficits indicated that his right temporal lobe may have been slightly damaged in the car accident, resulting in an impairment of his language skills. On the basis of our neuropsychological investigation we were able to recommend vocations to Mr. R. that did not require superior verbal memory skills, and he is currently studying architecture.

(From *Fundamentals of Human Neuropsychology*, 3rd Edition, by Bryan Kolb and Ian Q. Whishaw, p. 128. Copyright © 1980, 1985, 1990 W. H. Freeman and Company. Reprinted with permission.)

Psychophysiology

Psychophysiology is the division of biopsychology that studies the relation between physiological activity and psychological processes in human subjects (Coles, 2003; Gratton & Fabiani, 2003). Because the subjects of psychophysiological research are human, psychophysiological recording procedures are typically noninvasive; that is, the physiological activity is recorded from the surface of the body. The usual measure of brain activity is the scalp **electroencephalogram (EEG)**. Other common psychophysiological measures are muscle tension, eye movement, and several indicators of autonomic nervous system activity (e.g., heart rate, blood pressure, pupil dilation, and electrical conductance of the skin). The **autonomic nervous system (ANS)** is the division of the nervous system that regulates the body's inner environment.

Most psychophysiological research focuses on understanding the physiology of psychological processes,

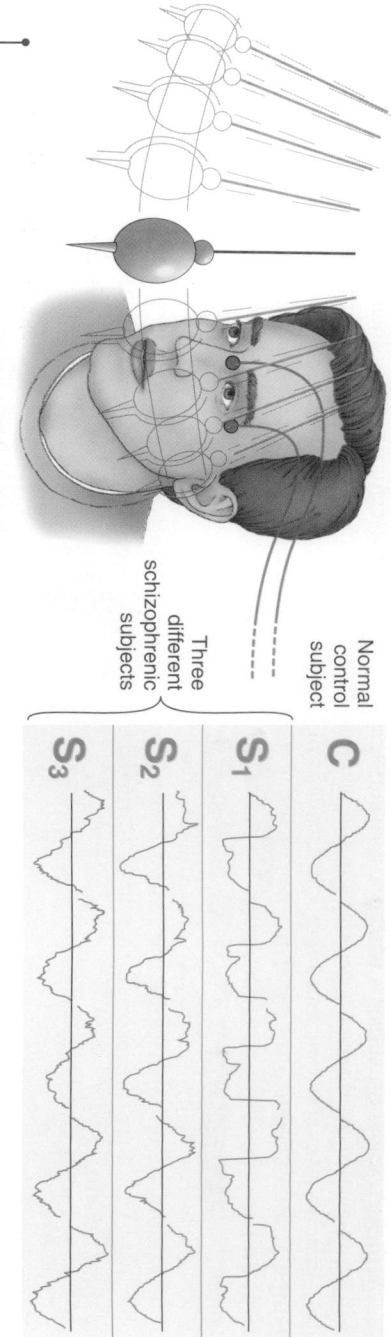

FIGURE 1.4   Visual tracking of a pendulum by a normal control subject (top) and three schizophrenics. (Adapted from Iacono & Koenig, 1983.)

such as attention, emotion, and information processing, but there have also been a number of interesting clinical applications of the psychophysiological method. For example, psychophysiological experiments have indicated that schizophrenics have difficulty smoothly tracking a moving object such as a pendulum (Avila et al., 2003; Holzman, 2000; Hong et al., 2003)—see Figure 1.4.

Cognitive Neuroscience

Cognitive neuroscience is the youngest division of biopsychology, but it is currently among the most active and exciting. Cognitive neuroscientists study the neural bases **of cognition,** a term that generally refers to higher intellectual processes such as thought, memory, attention, and complex perceptual processes (see Albright, Kandel, & Posner, 2000; Cabeza & Kingston, 2002). Because of its focus on cognition, most cognitive neuroscience research involves human subjects; and because of its focus on human subjects, its major method is noninvasive recording rather than the direct manipulation of the brain.

The major method of cognitive neuroscience is functional brain imaging (recording images of the activity of the living human brain; see Chapter 5) while the subjects are engaged in particular cognitive activities. For example, Figure 1.5 shows that the visual areas of the left and right cerebral cortex at the back of the brain became active when the subject viewed a flashing light.

Because the theory and methods of cognitive neuroscience are so complex and interesting to people in so many fields (see Cacioppo et al., 2003; Ochsner & Lieberman, 2001), most cognitive neuroscientific research is an interdisciplinary collaboration among individuals with different types of training. For example, in addition

to conventionally trained biopsychologists, cognitive psychologists, computing and mathematics experts, and various types of neuroscientists commonly contribute to the field. Cognitive neuroscience research sometimes involves noninvasive electrophysiological recording, and

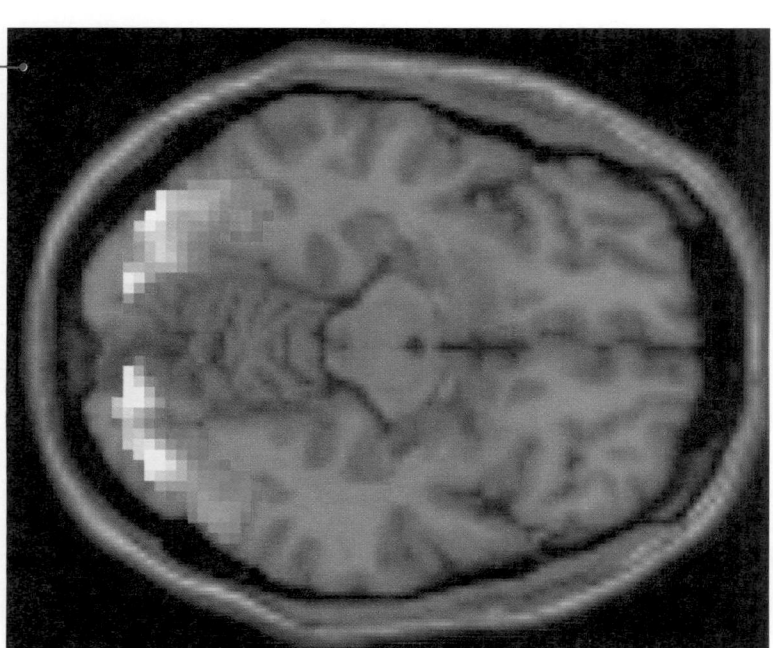

FIGURE 1.5   Functional brain imaging is the major method of cognitive neuroscience. This image—taken from the top of the head with the subject lying on her back—reveals the locations of high levels of neural activity at one level of the brain as the subject views a flashing light. The red and yellow areas indicate high levels of activity in the visual cortex at the back of the brain. (Courtesy of Todd Handy, Department of Psychology, University of British Columbia.)

it sometimes focuses on subjects with brain pathology; in these cases, the boundaries between cognitive neuroscience and psychophysiology and neuropsychology, respectively, are blurry.

Comparative Psychology

Although most biopsychologists study the neural mechanisms of behavior, there is more to biopsychology than this. As Dewsbury (1991) asserted:

> The "biology" in "psychobiology" should include the whole-animal approaches of ethology, ecology, evolution . . . as well as the latest in physiological methods and thought. . . . The "compleat psychobiologist" should use whatever explanatory power can be found with modern physiological techniques, but never lose sight of the problems that got us going in the first place: the integrated behavior of whole, functioning, adapted organisms. (p. 198)

The division of biopsychology that deals generally with the biology of behavior, rather than specifically with the neural mechanisms of behavior, is **comparative psychology.** Comparative psychologists compare the behavior of different species in order to understand the evolution, genetics, and adaptiveness of behavior. Some comparative psychologists study behavior in the laboratory; others engage in **ethological research**—the study of animal behavior in its natural environment.

Because two important areas of biopsychological research often employ comparative analysis, I have included them as part of comparative psychology. One of these is *evolutionary psychology* (a subfield that focuses on understanding behavior by considering its likely evolutionary origins; see Caporael, 2001; Duchaine, Cosmides, & Tooby, 2001; Kenrick, 2001). The other is *behavioral genetics* (the study of genetic influences on behavior; see Carson & Rothstein, 1999; Plomin et al., 2002).

In case you have forgotten, the purpose of this section has been to demonstrate the diversity of biopsychology by describing its six major divisions. These are summarized for you in Table 1.2. You will learn about the progress being made in each of these divisions in subsequent chapters.

Evolutionary Perspective

TABLE 1.2   The Six Major Divisions of Biopsychology, with Examples of How They Have Approached the Study of Memory

THE SIX DIVISIONS OF BIOPSYCHOLOGY	EXAMPLES OF HOW THE SIX APPROACHES HAVE PURSUED THE STUDY OF MEMORY
Physiological psychology: study of the neural mechanisms of behavior by manipulating the nervous systems of nonhuman animals in controlled experiments.	**Physiological psychologists** have studied the contributions of the hippocampus to memory by surgically removing the hippocampus in rats and assessing their ability to perform various memory tasks.
Psychopharmacology: study of the effects of drugs on the brain and behavior.	**Psychopharmacologists** have tried to improve the memory of Alzheimer's patients by administering drugs that increase the levels of the neurotransmitter acetylcholine.
Neuropsychology: study of the psychological effects of brain damage in human patients.	**Neuropsychologists** have shown that patients with alcohol-produced brain damage have particular difficulty in remembering recent events.
Psychophysiology: study of the relation between physiological activity and psychological processes in human subjects by noninvasive physiological recording.	**Psychophysiologists** have shown that familiar faces elicit the usual changes in autonomic nervous system activity even when patients with brain damage report that they do not recognize a face.
Cognitive neuroscience: study of the neural mechanisms of human cognition, largely through the use of functional brain imaging.	**Cognitive neuroscientists** have used brain-imaging technology to observe the changes that occur in various parts of the brain while human volunteers perform memory tasks.
Comparative psychology: study of the evolution, genetics, and adaptiveness of behavior, largely through the use of the comparative method.	**Comparative psychologists** have shown that species of birds that cache their seeds tend to have big hippocampi, thus confirming that the hippocampus is involved in memory for location.

SCAN YOUR BRAIN

To see if you are ready to proceed to the next section of the chapter, scan your brain by filling in each of the following blanks with one of the six divisions of biopsychology. The correct answers are provided at the bottom of the page. Before proceeding, review material related to your errors and omissions.

1. A biopsychologist who studies the memory deficits of human patients with brain damage would likely identify with the division of biopsychology termed _____.

2. Psychologists who study the physiological correlates of psychological processes by recording physiological signals from the surface of the human body are often referred to as _____.

3. The biopsychological research of _____ frequently involves the direct manipulation or recording of the neural activity of laboratory animals by various invasive surgical, electrical, and chemical means.

4. The division of biopsychology that focuses on the study of the effects of drugs on behavior is often referred to as _____.

5. Although _____ can be considered to be a division of biopsychology because it focuses on the neural bases of cognition, it is a collaborative interdisciplinary field.

6. _____ are biopsychologists who study the genetics, evolution, and adaptiveness of behavior, often by using the comparative approach.

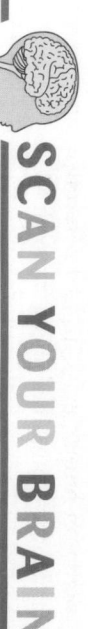

1.5 Converging Operations: How Do Biopsychologists Work Together?

Because none of the six biopsychological approaches to research is without its shortcomings and because of the complexity of the brain and its role in psychological processes, major biopsychological issues are rarely resolved by a single experiment or even by a single series of experiments taking the same general approach. Progress is most likely when different approaches are focused on a single problem in such a way that the strengths of one approach compensate for the weaknesses of the others; this combined approach is called **converging operations**.

Consider, for example, the relative strengths and weaknesses of neuropsychology and physiological psychology in the study of the psychological effects of damage to the human cerebral cortex. In this instance, the strength of the neuropsychological approach is that it deals directly with human patients; its weakness is that its focus on human patients precludes experiments. In contrast, the strength of the physiological psychology approach is that it can bring the power of the experimental method and neuroscientific technology to bear through research on nonhuman animals; its weakness is that the relevance of research on laboratory animals to human neuropsychological deficits is always open to question. Clearly these two approaches complement each other well; together they can answer questions that neither can answer individually.

To examine converging operations in action, let's return to the case of Jimmie G. The neuropsychologi-

cal disorder from which Jimmie G. suffered was first described in the late 19th century by S. S. Korsakoff, a Russian physician, and subsequently became known as **Korsakoff's syndrome**. The primary symptom of Korsakoff's syndrome is severe memory loss, which is made all the more heartbreaking—as you have seen in Jimmie G.'s case—by the fact that its sufferers are often otherwise quite capable. Because Korsakoff's syndrome commonly occurs in alcoholics, it was initially believed to be a direct consequence of the toxic effects of alcohol on the brain. This conclusion proved to be a good illustration of the inadvisability of basing causal conclusions on quasiexperimental research. Subsequent research showed that Korsakoff's syndrome is largely caused by the brain damage associated with *thiamine* (vitamin B₁ deficiency (see Heap et al., 2002; Thomson, 2000).

The first support for the thiamine-deficiency interpretation of Korsakoff's syndrome came from the discovery of the syndrome in malnourished persons who consumed little or no alcohol. Additional support came from experiments in which thiamine-deficient rats were

Clinical Implications

compared with otherwise identical groups of control rats. The thiamine-deficient rats displayed memory deficits and patterns of brain damage similar to those observed in human alcoholics (see Mumby, Cameli, & Glenn, 1999). Alcoholics often develop Korsakoff's syndrome because most of their caloric intake comes in the form of alcohol, which lacks vitamins, and because alcohol interferes with the metabolism of what little thiamine they do consume. However, alcohol has been shown to accelerate the development of brain damage in thiamine-deficient rats, so it may have a direct toxic effect on the brain as well (Zimitat et al., 1990).

The point of all this (in case you have forgotten) is that progress in biopsychology typically comes from converging operations—in this case, from the convergence of neuropsychological case studies, quasiexperi-

Thinking Critically

ments on human subjects, and controlled experiments on laboratory animals. The strength of biopsychology lies in the diversity of its methods and approaches. This means that, in evaluating biopsychological claims, it is rarely sufficient to consider the results of one study or even of one line of experiments using the same method or approach.

So what has all the research on Korsakoff's syndrome done for Jimmie G. and others like him? Today, alcoholics are often counseled to stop drinking and are treated with massive doses of thiamine. The thiamine limits the development of further brain damage and often leads to a slight improvement in the patient's condition; but, unfortunately, brain damage, once produced, is largely permanent. In some parts of the world, the fortification of alcoholic beverages with thiamine has been considered. What do you think of this idea?

1.6 Scientific Inference: How Do Biopsychologists Study the Unobservable Workings of the Brain?

Scientific inference is the fundamental method of biopsychology and of most other sciences—it is what makes being a scientist fun. This section provides further insight into the nature of biopsychology by defining, illustrating, and discussing scientific inference.

The scientific method is a system for finding things out by careful observation, but many of the processes studied by scientists cannot be observed. For example, scientists use empirical (observational) methods to study ice ages, gravity, evaporation, electricity, and nuclear fission—none of which can be directly observed; their effects can be observed, but the processes themselves cannot. Biopsychology is no different from other sciences in this respect. One of its main goals is to characterize, through empirical methods, the unobservable processes by which the nervous system controls behavior.

The empirical method that biopsychologists and other scientists use to study the unobservable is called **scientific inference.** The scientists carefully measure key events that they can observe and then use these measures as a basis for logically inferring the nature of events that they cannot observe. Like a detective carefully gathering clues from which to recreate an unwitnessed crime, a biopsychologist carefully gathers relevant measures of behavior and neural activity from which to infer the nature of the neural processes that regulate behavior. The fact that the neural mechanisms of behavior cannot be directly observed and must be studied through scientific inference is what makes biopsychological research such a challenge—and, as I said before, so much fun.

To illustrate scientific inference, I have selected a research project in which you can participate. By making a few simple observations about your own visual abili-

ties under different conditions, you will be able to discover the principle by which your brain translates the movement of images on your retinas into perceptions of movement (see Figure 1.6 on page 14). One feature of the mechanism is immediately obvious. Hold your hand in front of your face, and then move its image across your retinas by moving your eyes, by moving your hand, or by moving both at once. You will notice that only those movements of the retinal image that are produced by the movement of your hand are translated into the sight of motion; movements of the retinal image that are produced by your own eye movements are not. Obviously, there must be a part of your brain that monitors the movements of your retinal image and subtracts from the total those image movements that are produced by your own eye movements, leaving the remainder to be perceived as motion.

Now, let's try to characterize the nature of the information about your eye movements that is used by your brain in its perception of motion (see Schlag & Schlag-Rey, 2002; Sommer & Wurtz, 2002). Try the following. Shut one eye, then rotate your other eye slightly upward by gently pressing on your lower eyelid with your fingertip. What do you see? You see all of the objects in your visual field moving downward. Why? It seems that the brain mechanism that is responsible for the perception of motion does not consider eye movement per se. It considers only those eye movements that are actively produced by neural signals from the brain to the eye muscles, not those that are passively produced by exter-

ON THE CD

Visit the *Perception of Motion* module. As you protect the earth from interstellar invasion, you demonstrate to yourself how your brain perceives motion.

nal means (e.g., by your finger). Thus, when your eye was moved passively, your brain assumed that it had remained still and attributed the movement of your retinal image to the movement of objects in your visual field.

It is possible to trick the visual system in the opposite way; instead of the eyes being moved when no active signals have been sent to the eye muscles, the eyes can be held stationary despite the brain's attempts to move them. Because this experiment involves paralyzing the eye muscles, you cannot participate. Hammond, Merton, and Sutton (1956) injected the active ingredient of *curare*, the paralytic substance with which some South American natives coat their blow darts, into the eye muscles of their subject—who was Merton himself. What do you think Merton saw when he tried to move his eyes? He saw the stationary visual world moving in the same direction as his attempted eye movements. If a visual object is focused on part of your retina, and it

Conclusion
Therefore, the brain sees as movement the total movement of an object's image on the retina minus that portion produced by active movement of the eyes: It does not subtract passive movement of the eyes.

FIGURE 1.6   The perception of motion under four different conditions.

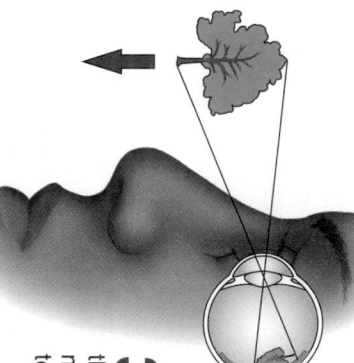

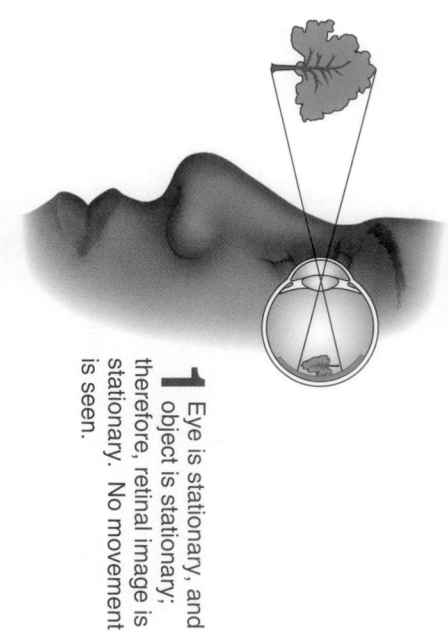

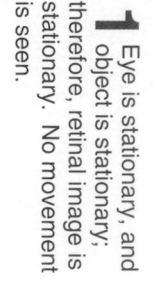

1 Eye is stationary, and object is stationary; therefore, retinal image is stationary. No movement is seen.

2 Eye actively rotates upward, and object is stationary; therefore, retinal image moves up. No movement is seen.

3 Eye is stationary, and object moves down; therefore, retinal image moves up. Object is seen to move down.

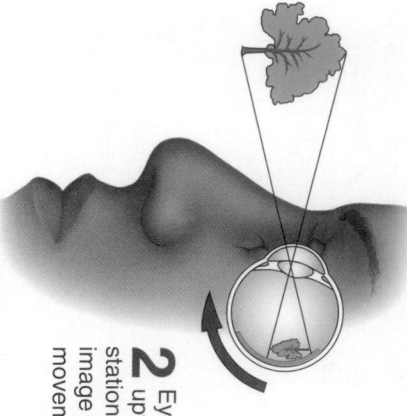

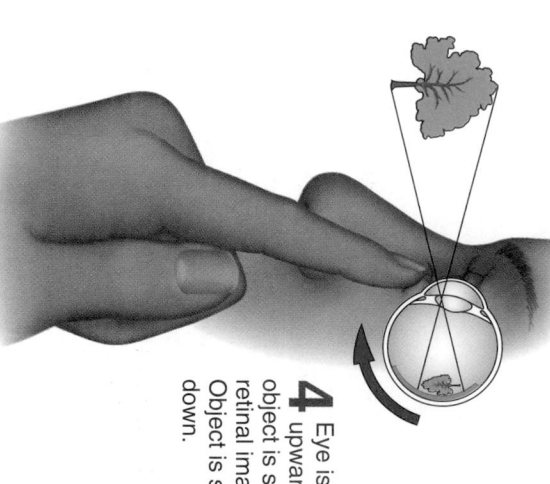

4 Eye is passively rotated upward by finger, and object is stationary; therefore, retinal image moves up. Object is seen to move down.

stays focused there despite the fact that you have moved your eyes to the right, it too must have moved to the right. Consequently, when Merton sent signals to his eye muscles to move his eyes to the right, his brain assumed that the movement had been carried out, and it perceived stationary objects as moving to the right.

The point of the eye-movement example is that biopsychologists can learn much about the activities of the brain without directly observing them—and so can you. Understanding that biopsychology, like most sciences, is based on scientific inference is a critical early step in developing your ability to think about it. By the way, an experiment that recorded the responses of visual system neurons in monkeys to active and passive movement of retinal images provided direct evidence for just the type of feedback mechanism that we have inferred here (Thiele et al., 2002).

Thinking Critically

1.7 Critical Thinking about Biopsychological Claims

We have all heard or read that we use only a small portion of our brains, that it is important to eat three meals a day, that intelligence is inherited, that everybody needs at least 8 hours of sleep per night, that there is a gene for schizophrenia, that morphine is a particularly dangerous (hard) drug, that neurological diseases can now be cured by genetic engineering, and that homosexuality is caused by inappropriate upbringing—to name just a few claims about biopsychological phenomena that have been widely disseminated. You may believe some of these claims. But are they true? How does one find out? And if they are not true, why do so many people believe them?

As you have already learned, one of the major goals of this book is to teach you how to think effectively about biopsychological information. The purpose of this final section of the chapter is to begin the development

Thinking Critically

of your *critical thinking ability*, the ability to evaluate scientific claims by identifying potential omissions or weaknesses in the evidence. Accordingly, the chapter concludes with two claims that were once widely accepted but were subsequently shown to be unfounded. Notice that if you keep your wits about you, you do not have to be an expert to spot the weaknesses.

The first step in judging the validity of any scientific claim is to determine whether or not the claim and the research on which it is based were published in a reputable scientific journal (Rensberger, 2000). The reason is that, in order to be published in a reputable scientific journal, an article must first be reviewed by experts in the field—usually three or four of them—and judged to be of good quality. Indeed, the best scientific journals publish only a small proportion of the manuscripts submitted to them. You should be particularly skeptical of scientific claims that have not gone through this review process, but, as you are about to learn, the review process is not a guarantee that scientific papers are free of unrecognized flaws.

The first case that follows deals with an unpublished claim that was largely dispensed through the news media. The second deals with a claim that was initially supported by published research. Because both of these cases are part of the history of biopsychology, we have the advantage of 20/20 hindsight in evaluating their claims.

Case 1: José and the Bull

José Delgado demonstrated to a group of newspaper reporters a remarkable new procedure for controlling aggression. Delgado strode into a Spanish

bull ring carrying only a red cape and a small radio transmitter. With the transmitter, he could activate a battery-powered stimulator that had previously been mounted on the horns of the other inhabitant of the ring. As the raging bull charged, Delgado calmly activated the stimulator and sent a weak train of electrical current from the stimulator through an electrode that had been implanted in the caudate nucleus, a structure deep in the bull's brain. The bull immediately veered from its charge. After a few such interrupted charges, the bull stood tamely as Delgado swaggered about the ring. According to Delgado, this demonstration marked a significant scientific breakthrough—the discovery of a caudate taming center and the fact that stimulation of this structure could eliminate aggressive behavior, even in bulls specially bred for their ferocity.

To those present at this carefully orchestrated event and to most of the millions who subsequently read about it, Delgado's conclusion was compelling. Surely, if caudate stimulation could stop the charge of a raging bull, the caudate must be a taming center. It was even suggested that caudate stimulation through implanted electrodes might be an effective treatment for human psychopaths. What do you think?

Analysis of Case 1   The fact of the matter is that Delgado's demonstration provided little or no support for his conclusion. It should have been obvious to anyone who did not get caught up in the provocative nature of Delgado's media event that there are numerous ways in which brain stimulation can abort a bull's charge, most of which are simpler or more direct, and thus more probable, than the one suggested by Delgado. For example, the stimulation may have simply rendered the bull confused, dizzy, nauseous, sleepy, or temporarily blind rather than nonaggressive; or the stimulation could have been painful. Clearly, any observation that can be interpreted in so many different ways provides little support for any one interpretation. When there are several possible interpretations for a behavioral observation, the rule is to give precedence to the simplest one; this rule is called **Morgan's Canon.** The following comments of Valenstein (1973) provide a reasoned view of Delgado's demonstration:

> Actually there is no good reason for believing that the stimulation had any direct effect on the bull's aggressive tendencies. An examination of the film record makes it apparent that the charging bull was stopped because as long as the stimulation was on it was forced to turn around in the same direction continuously. After examining the film, any scientist with knowledge in this field could conclude only that the stimulation had been activating a neural pathway controlling movement. (p. 98)

... he [Delgado] seems to capitalize on every individual effect his electrodes happen to produce and presents little, if any, experimental evidence that his impression of the underlying cause is correct. (p. 103)

... his propensity for dramatic, albeit ambiguous, demonstrations has been a constant source of material for those whose purposes are served by exaggerating the omnipotence of brain stimulation. (p. 99)

Case 2: Becky, Moniz, and Prefrontal Lobotomy

In 1949, Dr. Egas Moniz was awarded the Nobel Prize in Physiology and Medicine for the development of **prefrontal lobotomy**—a surgical procedure in which the connections between the prefrontal lobes and the rest of the brain are cut—as a treatment for mental illness. The **prefrontal lobes** are the large areas, left and right, at the very front of the brain (see Figure 1.7). Moniz's discovery was based on the report that Becky, a chimpanzee that frequently became upset when she made errors during the performance of a food-rewarded task, did not do so following the creation of a large *bilateral lesion* (an area of damage to both sides of the brain) of her prefrontal lobes. After hearing about this isolated observation at a scientific meeting in 1935, Moniz persuaded neurosurgeon Almeida Lima to operate on a series of psychiatric patients; Lima cut out six large cores of prefrontal tissue

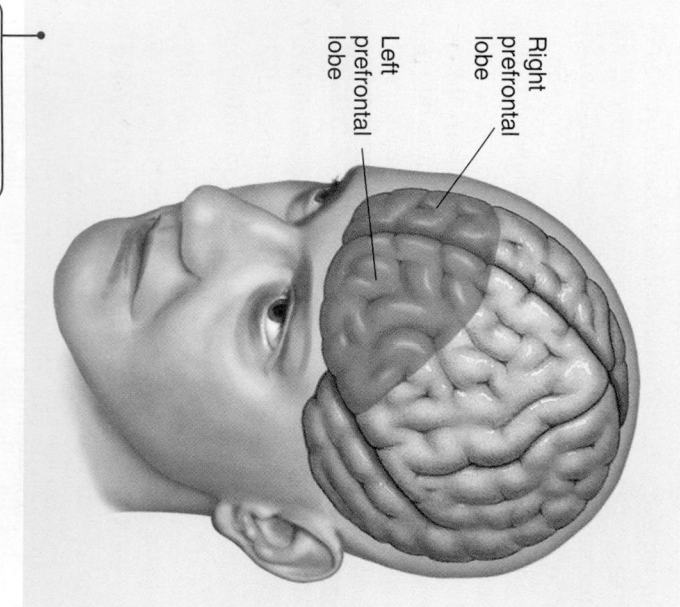

Right prefrontal lobe

Left prefrontal lobe

FIGURE 1.7   The right and left prefrontal lobes, whose connections to the rest of the brain are disrupted by prefrontal lobotomy.

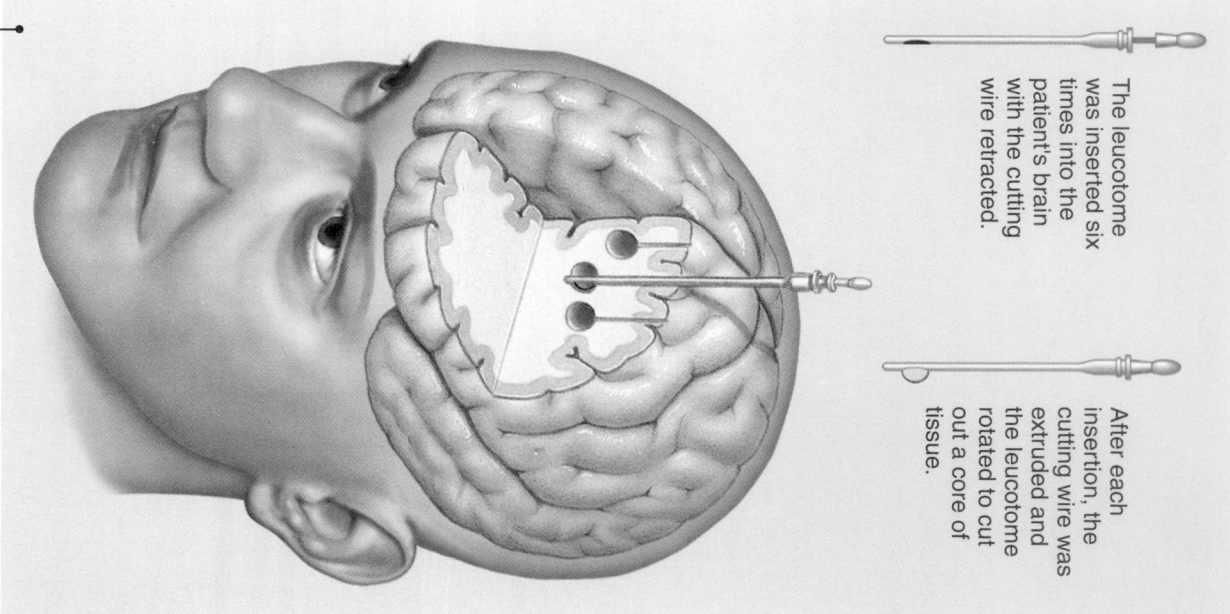

The leucotome was inserted six times into the patient's brain with the cutting wire retracted.

After each insertion, the cutting wire was extruded and the leucotome rotated to cut out a core of tissue.

FIGURE 1.8   The prefrontal lobotomy procedure developed by Moniz and Lima.

with a surgical device called a **leucotome** (see Figure 1.8).

Following Moniz's claims that prefrontal surgery was therapeutically successful and had no significant side effects, there was a rapid proliferation of various forms of prefrontal psychosurgery (see O'Callaghan & Carroll, 1982; Valenstein, 1980, 1986). One such variation was **transorbital lobotomy**, which was developed in Italy and then popularized in the United States by Walter Freeman in the late 1940s. It involved inserting an ice-pick–like device under the eyelid, driving it through the orbit (the eye socket) with a few taps of a mallet, and pushing it into the frontal lobes, where it was waved back and forth to sever the connections between the prefrontal lobes and the rest of the brain (see Figure 1.9). This operation was frequently performed in the surgeon's office.

Analysis of Case 2 Incredible as it may seem, Moniz's program of psychosurgery was largely based on the observation of a single chimpanzee in a single situation, thus displaying a complete lack of appreciation for the diversity of brain and behavior, both within and between species. No program of psychosurgery should ever be initiated without a thorough assessment of the effects of the surgery on a large sample of subjects from various nonhuman mammalian species.

A second major weakness in the scientific case for prefrontal psychosurgery was the failure of Moniz and others to carefully evaluate the consequences of the surgery in the first patients to undergo the operation. The early reports that the operation was therapeutically successful were based on the impressions of the individuals who were the least objective—the physicians who had prescribed the surgery and their colleagues. Patients were frequently judged as improved if they were more manageable, and little effort was made to evaluate more important aspects of their psychological adjustment or to document the existence of adverse side effects.

Eventually, it became clear that prefrontal lobotomies are of little therapeutic benefit and that they produce a wide range of undesirable side effects, such as amorality, lack of foresight, emotional unresponsiveness, epilepsy, and urinary incontinence. This led to the abandonment of prefrontal lobotomy in many parts of the world—but not before over 40,000 patients had been lobotomized in the United States alone. Still, prefrontal lobotomies continue to be performed in some countries.

Some regard sound scientific methods as unnecessary obstacles in the paths of patients seeking treatment and therapists striving to provide it. However, the unforeseen consequences of prefrontal lobotomy should caution us against abandoning science for expediency. Only by observing the rules of science can

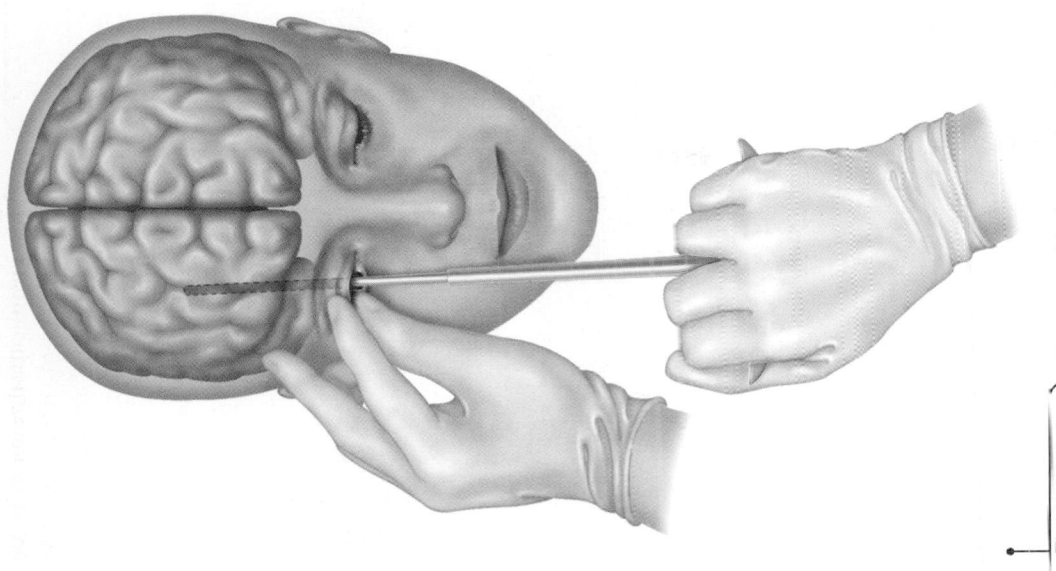

FIGURE 1.9 The transorbital procedure for performing prefrontal lobotomy.

scientists protect the public from bogus scientific claims (Carroll, 1984).

There is a somber postscript to this story. Moniz was shot by one of his patients. The bullet became lodged in his spine, rendering him *paraplegic* (paralyzed below the waist).

Themes Revisited

The seeds for all four major themes of this book were planted in this chapter, but the thinking-about-biopsychology theme predominated. You learned three important ideas that will help you think about many scientific claims: (1) the experimental method, (2) converging operations, and (3) scientific inference. You were then introduced to two biopsychological claims that were widely believed, even though the evidence for them was weak, and you saw critical thinking in action as the weaknesses were identified and the claims dismissed.

You also learned that the three other major themes of the book—clinical implications, the evolutionary perspective, and cognitive neuroscience—tend to be associated with particular divisions of biopsychology.

Clinical implications most commonly emerge from neuropsychological and psychopharmacological research; the evolutionary perspective is a defining feature of comparative psychology; and, of course, modern cognitive neuroscientific research is a product of the burgeoning field of cognitive neuroscience.

You are about to enter a world of amazing discovery and intriguing ideas: the world of biopsychology. I hope that your brain enjoys learning about itself.

ON THE CD

See Hard Copy for additional readings for Chapter 1.

Evolutionary Perspective

Cognitive Neuroscience

Think about It

1. This chapter tells you in general conceptual terms what biopsychology is. Another, and perhaps better, way of defining biopsychology is to describe what biopsychologists do. Ask your instructor what she or he did to become a biopsychologist and what she or he does each workday. I think that you will be surprised. Is your instructor predominantly a physiological psychologist, a psychopharmacologist, a neuropsychologist, a psychophysiologist, a cognitive neuroscientist, or a comparative psychologist?

2. What ethical considerations should guide biopsychological research on nonhuman animals? How should

these ethical considerations differ from those that should guide biopsychological research on humans?

3. In retrospect, the entire story of prefrontal lobotomies is shocking. How could physicians, who are generally intelligent, highly educated, and dedicated to helping their patients, participate in such a travesty? How could somebody win a Nobel Prize for developing a form of surgery that left over 40,000 mental cripples in the United States alone? Why did this happen? Could it happen today?

ON THE CD

Studying for an exam? Try the Practice Tests for Chapter 1.

Key Terms

Applied research (p. 7)
Autonomic nervous system (p. 9)
Between-subjects design (p. 9)
Biopsychology (p. 4)
Case studies (p. 7)
Cerebral cortex (p. 9)
Clinical (p. 3)
Cognition (p. 10)
Cognitive neuroscience (p. 10)
Comparative approach (p. 5)
Comparative psychology (p. 11)
Confounded variable (p. 6)

Converging operations (p. 12)
Coolidge effect (p. 6)
Dependent variable (p. 5)
Electroencephalogram (EEG) (p. 9)
Ethological research (p. 11)
Evolutionary perspective (p. 3)
Generalizability (p. 7)
Independent variable (p. 5)
Korsakoff's syndrome (p. 12)
Leucotome (p. 16)
Lordosis (p. 6)
Morgan's Canon (p. 15)
Neuroanatomy (p. 4)

Neurochemistry (p. 4)
Neuroendocrinology (p. 4)
Neurons (p. 2)
Neuropathology (p. 4)
Neuropharmacology (p. 4)
Neurophysiology (p. 4)
Neuropsychology (p. 9)
Neuroscience (p. 2)
Physiological psychology (p. 8)
Prefrontal lobes (p. 16)
Prefrontal lobotomy (p. 16)
Psychopharmacology (p. 9)
Psychophysiology (p. 7)
Pure research (p. 7)

Quasiexperimental studies (p. 7)
Scientific inference (p. 7)
Transorbital lobotomy (p. 16)
Within-subjects design (p. 5)

ON THE CD

Need some help studying the key terms for this chapter? Check out the electronic flash cards for Chapter 1.

chapter 2

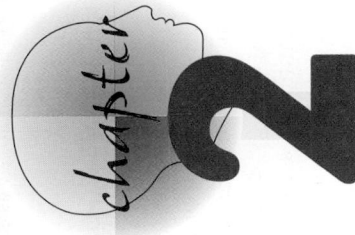

Evolution, Genetics, and Experience

Thinking about the Biology of Behavior

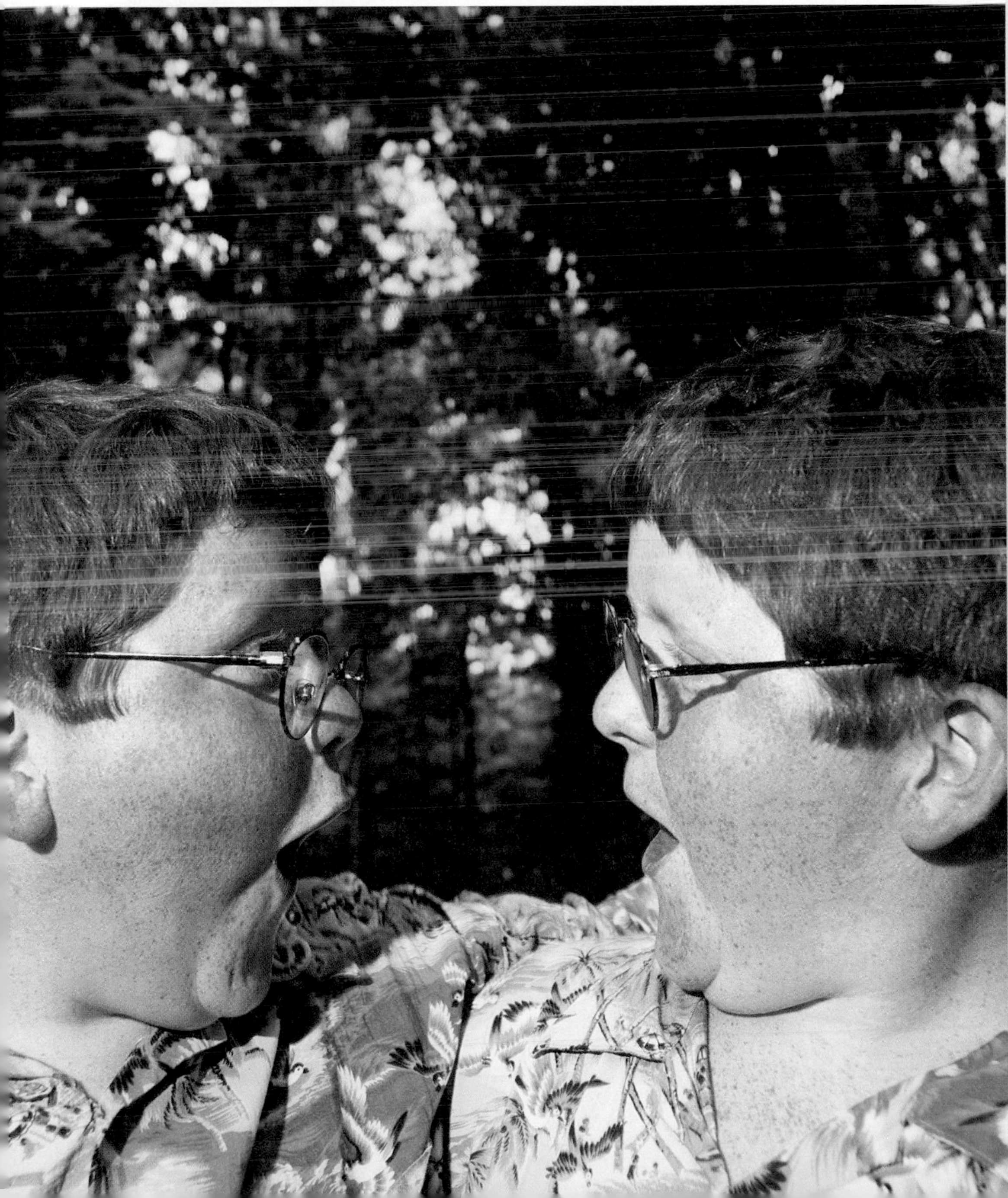

2.1 Thinking about the Biology of Behavior: From Dichotomies to Relations and Interactions

2.2 Human Evolution

2.3 Fundamental Genetics

2.4 Behavioral Development: The Interaction of Genetic Factors and Experience

2.5 The Genetics of Human Psychological Differences

2.1   Thinking about the Biology of Behavior: From Dichotomies to Relations and Interactions

We all tend to think about things in ways that have been ingrained in us by our **Zeitgeist** (pronounced "ZYTE-gyste"), the general intellectual climate of our culture. That is why this is a particularly important chapter for you. You see, you are the intellectual product of a Zeitgeist that promotes ways of thinking about the biological bases of behavior that are inconsistent with the facts. The primary purpose of this chapter is to help you bring your thinking about the biology of behavior in line with modern biopsychological science.

We tend to ignore the subtleties, inconsistencies, and complexities of our existence and to think in terms of simple, mutually exclusive dichotomies: right–wrong, good–bad, attractive–unattractive, and so on. The allure of this way of thinking is its simplicity.

The tendency to think about behavior in terms of dichotomies is illustrated by two kinds of questions that people commonly ask about behavior: (1) Is it physiological, or is it psychological? (2) Is it inherited, or is it learned? Both questions have proved to be misguided; yet they are among the most common kinds of questions asked in biopsychology classrooms. That is why I am dwelling on them here.

Is It Physiological, or Is It Psychological?

The idea that human processes fall into one of two categories, physiological or psychological, grew out of a 17th-century conflict between science and the Roman Church. For much of the history of Western civilization, truth was whatever was decreed to be true by the Church. Then, in about 1400, things started to change. The famines, plagues, and marauding armies that had repeatedly swept Europe during the Middle Ages subsided, and interest turned to art, commerce, and scholarship—this was the period of the *Renaissance*, or rebirth (1400 to 1700). Some Renaissance scholars were not content to follow the dictates of the Church; instead, they started to study things directly by observing them—and so it was that modern science was born.

Much of the scientific knowledge that accumulated during the Renaissance was at odds with Church dictates. However, the conflict was resolved by the prominent French philosopher René Descartes (pronounced "day-CART"). Descartes (1596–1650) proposed a philosophy that, in a sense, gave one part of the universe to science and the other part to the Church. He argued that the universe is composed of two elements: (1) physical matter, which behaves according to the laws of nature and is thus a suitable object of scientific investigation; and (2) the human mind (soul, self, or spirit), which lacks physical substance, controls human behavior, obeys no natural laws, and is thus the appropriate purview of the

Church. The human body, including the brain, was assumed to be entirely physical, and so were nonhuman animals.

Cartesian dualism, as Descartes's philosophy became known, was sanctioned by the Roman Church, and so the idea that the human brain and the mind are separate entities became widely accepted. It has survived to this day, despite the intervening centuries of scientific progress. Most people now understand that human behavior has a physiological basis, but many still cling to the dualistic assumption that there is a category of human activity that somehow transcends the human brain (Searle, 2000).

Is It Inherited, or Is It Learned?

The tendency to think in terms of dichotomies extends to the way people think about the development of behavioral capacities. For centuries, scholars have debated whether humans and other animals inherit their behavioral capacities or whether they acquire them through learning. This debate is commonly referred to as the **nature–nurture issue.**

Most of the early North American experimental psychologists were totally committed to the nurture (learning) side of the nature–nurture issue (de Waal, 1999). The degree of this commitment is illustrated by the oft-cited words of John B. Watson, the father of *behaviorism:*

> We have no real evidence of the inheritance of [behavioral] traits. I would feel perfectly confident in the ultimately favorable outcome of careful upbringing of a healthy, well-formed baby born of a long line of crooks, murderers and thieves, and prostitutes. Who has any evidence to the contrary?
>
> . . . Give me a dozen healthy infants, well-formed, and my own specified world to bring them up in and I'll guarantee to take any one at random and train him to become any type of specialist I might select—doctor, lawyer, artist, merchant-chief and, yes even beggar-man and thief. (Watson, 1930, pp. 103–104)

At the same time that experimental psychology was taking root in North America, **ethology** (the study of animal behavior in the wild) was becoming the domi-

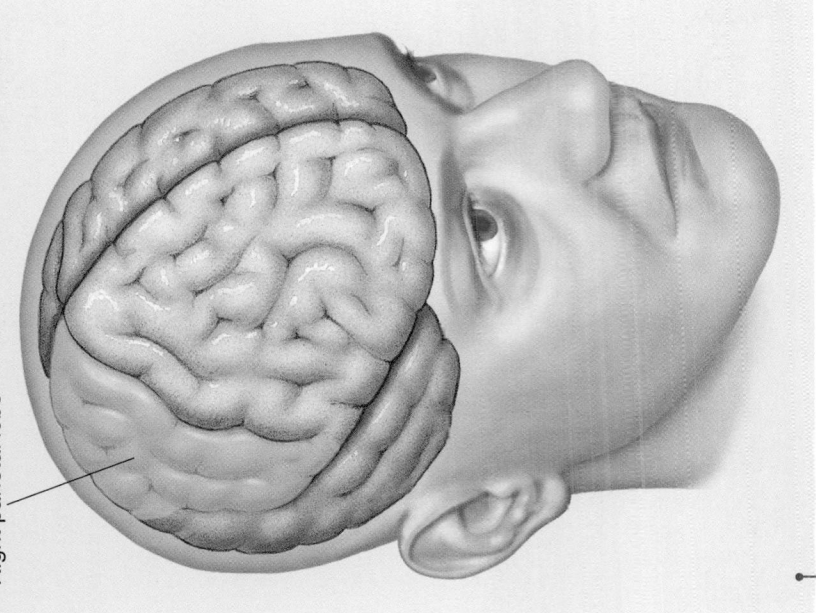

Right parietal lobe

FIGURE 2.1 Asomatognosia typically involves damage to the right parietal lobe.

nant approach to the study of behavior in Europe. European ethology, in contrast to North American experimental psychology, focused on the study of **instinctive behaviors** (behaviors that occur in all like members of a species, even when there seems to have been no opportunity for them to have been learned), and it emphasized the role of nature, or inherited factors, in behavioral development. Because instinctive behaviors do not seem to be learned, the early ethologists assumed that they are entirely inherited. They were wrong, but then so were the early experimental psychologists.

Problems with Thinking about the Biology of Behavior in Terms of Traditional Dichotomies

Thinking Critically The physiological-or-psychological and nature-or-nurture debates are based on incorrect ways of thinking about the biology of behavior, and a new generation of questions is directing the current boom in biopsychological research (Churchland, 2002). What is wrong with these old ways of thinking about the biology of behavior, and what are the new ways?

Physiological-or-Psychological Thinking Runs into Difficulty Not long after Descartes's mind–brain dualism was officially sanctioned by the Roman Church, it started to come under public attack.

In 1747, Julien Offroy de la Mettrie anonymously published a pamphlet that scandalized Europe.... la Mettrie fled to Berlin, where he was forced to live in exile for the rest of his life. His crime? He had argued that thought was produced by the brain—a dangerous assault, in the eyes of his contemporaries. (Corsi, 1991; cover)

There are two lines of evidence against *physiological-or-psychological thinking* (the assumption that some aspects of human psychological functioning are so complex that they could not possibly be the product of a physical brain). The first line is composed of the many demonstrations that even the most complex psychological changes (e.g., changes in self-awareness, memory, or emotion) can be effected by damage to, or stimulation of, parts of the brain (see Kosslyn & Andersen, 1992). The second line of evidence is composed of the many demonstrations that some nonhuman species possess abilities that were once assumed to be purely psychological and thus purely human (see Clayton, Bussey, & Dickinson, 2003; Hauser, 2000). The following two cases illustrate these two kinds of evidence. Both cases deal with self-awareness, which is widely regarded as the hallmark of the human mind (see Damasio, 1999).

The first case is Oliver Sacks's (1985) account of "the man who fell out of bed." He—the patient, not Sacks—

was suffering from **asomatognosia**, a deficiency in the awareness of parts of one's own body. Asomatognosia typically involves the left side of the body and usually results from damage to the *right parietal lobe* (see Figure 2.1). The second case describes G. G. Gallup's (1983) research on self-awareness in chimpanzees (see Parker, Mitchell, & Boccia, 1994; and Figure 2.2).

Clinical Implications

The Case of the Man Who Fell Out of Bed

He had felt fine all day, and fallen asleep towards evening. When he woke up he felt fine too, until he moved in the bed. Then he found, as he put it, "someone's leg" in the bed—*a severed human leg, a horrible thing!* He was stunned, at first, with amazement and disgust.... [Then] he had a brainwave.... Obviously one of the nurses ... had stolen into the Dissecting Room and nabbed a leg, and then slipped it under his bedclothes as a joke.... *When he threw it out of bed, he somehow came after it—and now it was attached to him.*

"Look at it!" he cried.... "Have you ever seen such a creepy, horrible thing?"...

"Easy!" I said. "Be calm! Take it easy!"...

"...why..." he asked irritably, belligerently. "Because it's *your* leg," I answered. "Don't you know your own leg?"...

"...Ah Doc!" he said. "You're fooling me! You're in cahoots with that nurse."...

"Listen," I said. "I don't think you're well. Please allow us to return you to bed. But I want to ask you one final question. If this—this thing—is *not* your left leg... then where is your own left leg?"

Once more he became pale—so pale that I thought he was going to faint. "I don't know," he said. "I have no idea. It's disappeared. It's gone. It's nowhere to be found."

Evolutionary Perspective

The Case of the Chimps and the Mirrors

An organism is self-aware to the extent that it can be shown capable of becoming the object of its own attention.... One way to assess an organism's capacity to become the object of its own attention is to confront it with a mirror.

...I gave a number of group-reared, preadolescent chimpanzees individual exposure to themselves in mirrors.... Invariably, their first reaction to the mirror was to respond as if they were seeing another chimpanzee.... After about two days, however,... they... started to use the mirror to groom and inspect parts of their bodies they had not seen before, and progressively began to experiment with the reflection by making faces, looking at themselves upside down, and assuming unusual postures while monitoring the results in the mirror....

So in an attempt to provide a more convincing demonstration of self-recognition, I devised an unobtrusive and more rigorous test.... [E]ach chimpanzee was anesthetized.... I carefully painted the uppermost portion of an eyebrow ridge and the top half of the opposite ear with a bright red, odorless, alcohol soluble dye....

Following recovery from anesthesia... the mirror was then reintroduced as an explicit test of self-recognition. Upon seeing their painted faces in the mirror, all the chimpanzees showed repeated mark-directed responses, consisting of attempts to touch and inspect marked areas on their eyebrow and ear while watching the image. In addition, there was over a three-fold increase in viewing time.... Several chimpanzees also showed noteworthy attempts to visually examine and smell the fingers which had been used to touch these facial marks. I suspect that you would respond pretty much the same way, if upon awakening one morning you saw yourself in the mirror with red spots on your face.

(From "Toward a Comparative Psychology of Mind" by G. G. Gallup, Jr., *American Journal of Primatology* 2:237–248, 1983.)

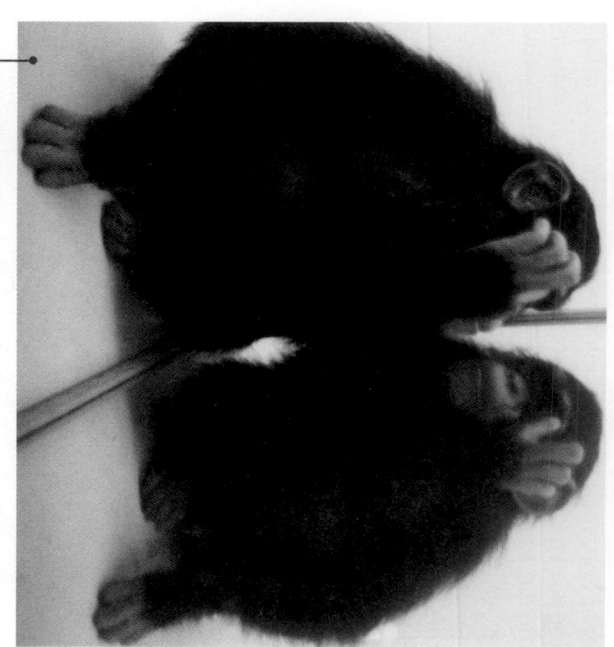

FIGURE 2.2 The reactions of chimpanzees to their own images indicate that they are self-aware. In this photo, the chimpanzee is reacting to the bright red, odorless dye that was painted on its eyebrow ridge while it was anesthetized. (Photograph by Donna Bierschwale, courtesy of the New Iberia Research Center.)

Nature-or-Nurture Thinking Runs into Difficulty

The history of nature-or-nurture thinking can be summed up by paraphrasing Mark Twain: "Reports of its death have been greatly exaggerated." Each time it has been discredited, it has resurfaced in a slightly modified form. First, factors other than genetics and learning were shown to influence behavioral development; factors such as the fetal environment, nutrition, stress, and sensory stimulation also proved to be influential. This led to a broadening of the concept of nurture to include a variety of experiential factors in addition to learning. In effect, it changed the nature-or-nurture dichotomy from "genetic factors or learning" to "genetic factors or experience."

Next, it was argued convincingly that behavior always develops under the combined control of both nature and nurture (see Johnston, 1987; Rutter, 1997), not under the control of one or the other. Faced with this discovery, many people merely substituted one kind of nature-or-nurture thinking for another. They stopped asking, "Is it genetic, or is it the result of experience?" and started asking, "How much of it is genetic, and how much of it is the result of experience?"

Like earlier versions of the nature-or-nurture question, the how-much-of-it-is-genetic-and-how-much-of-it-is-the-result-of-experience version is fundamentally flawed. The problem is that it is based on the premise that genetic factors and experiential factors combine in an additive fashion—that a behavioral capacity, such as intelligence, is created through the combination or mixture of so many parts of genetics and so many parts of experience, rather than through the interaction of genetics and experience. Once you learn more about how genetic factors and experience interact, you will better appreciate the folly of this assumption. For the time being, however, let me illustrate its weakness with a metaphor embedded in an anecdote.

to try to find how much comes from genes and how much comes from experience."

"And the same is true of any other behavioral trait," I added.

Several days later, the student strode into my office, reached into her pack, and pulled out a familiar object. "I believe that this is your mystery musical instrument," she said. "It's a Peruvian panpipe." She was right . . . again.

The point of this metaphor, in case you have forgotten, is to illustrate why it is nonsensical to try to understand interactions between two factors by asking how much each factor contributes. We would not ask how much the musician and how much the panpipe contributes to panpipe music; we would not ask how much the water and how much the temperature contributes to evaporation; and we would not ask how much the male and how much the female contributes to copulation. Similarly, we shouldn't ask how much genetic and experiential factors contribute to behavioral development. In each case, the answers lie in understanding the nature of the interactions (see Lederhendler & Schulkin, 2000; Newcombe, 2002; Rutter & Silberg, 2002). The importance of thinking in this interactive way about development will become obvious to you in Chapter 9, which focuses on the mechanisms of neural development. At this point, however, it is sufficient for you to realize that neurons become active long before they are fully developed and that the subsequent course of their development (e.g., the number of connections they form or whether or not they survive) depends greatly on their activity, much of which is triggered by external experience.

A Model of the Biology of Behavior

So far in this section, you have learned why people tend to think about the biology of behavior in terms of dichotomies, and you have learned some of the reasons why this way of thinking is inappropriate. Now, let's look at the way of thinking about the biology of behavior that has been adopted by many biopsychologists (see Kimble, 1989). It is illustrated in Figure 2.3 on page 24. Like other powerful ideas, it is simple and logical. This model boils down to the single premise that all behavior is the product of interactions among three factors: (1) the organism's genetic endowment, which is a product of its evolution; (2) its experience; and (3) its perception of the current situation. Please examine the model carefully, and consider its implications.

The next three sections of this chapter deal with three elements of this model of behavior: evolution, genetics, and the interaction of genetics and experience in behavioral development. The final section deals with the genetics of human psychological differences.

Thinking Critically

The Case of the Thinking Student

Thinking Critically

One of my students told me that she had read that intelligence was one-third genetic and two-thirds experience, and she wondered whether this was true. She must have been puzzled when I began my response by describing an alpine experience. "I was lazily wandering up a summit ridge when I heard an unexpected sound. Ahead, with his back to me, was a young man sitting on the edge of a precipice, blowing into a peculiar musical instrument. I sat down behind him on a large sun-soaked rock, ate my lunch, and shared his experience with him. Then, I got up and wandered back down the ridge, leaving him undisturbed."

I put the following question to my student: "If I wanted to get a better understanding of this music, would it be reasonable for me to begin by asking how much of it came from the musician and how much of it came from the instrument?"

"That would be dumb," she said. "The music comes from both; it makes no sense to ask how much comes from the musician and how much comes from the instrument. Somehow the music results from the interaction of the two together. You would have to ask about the interaction."

"That's exactly right," I said. "Now, do you see why . . . ."

"Don't say any more," she interrupted. "I see what you're getting at. Intelligence is the product of the interaction of genes and experience, and it is dumb

1 Evolution influences the pool of behavior-influencing genes available to the members of each species.

2 Each individual's genes initiate a unique program of neural development.

3 The development of each individual's nervous system depends on its interactions with its environment (i.e., on its experience).

4 Each individual's current behavioral capacities and tendencies are determined by its unique patterns of neural activity, some of which are experienced as thoughts, feelings, memories, etc.

5 Each individual's current behavior arises out of interactions among its ongoing patterns of neural activity and its perception of the current situation.

6 The success of each individual's behavior influences the likelihood that its genes will be passed on to future generations.

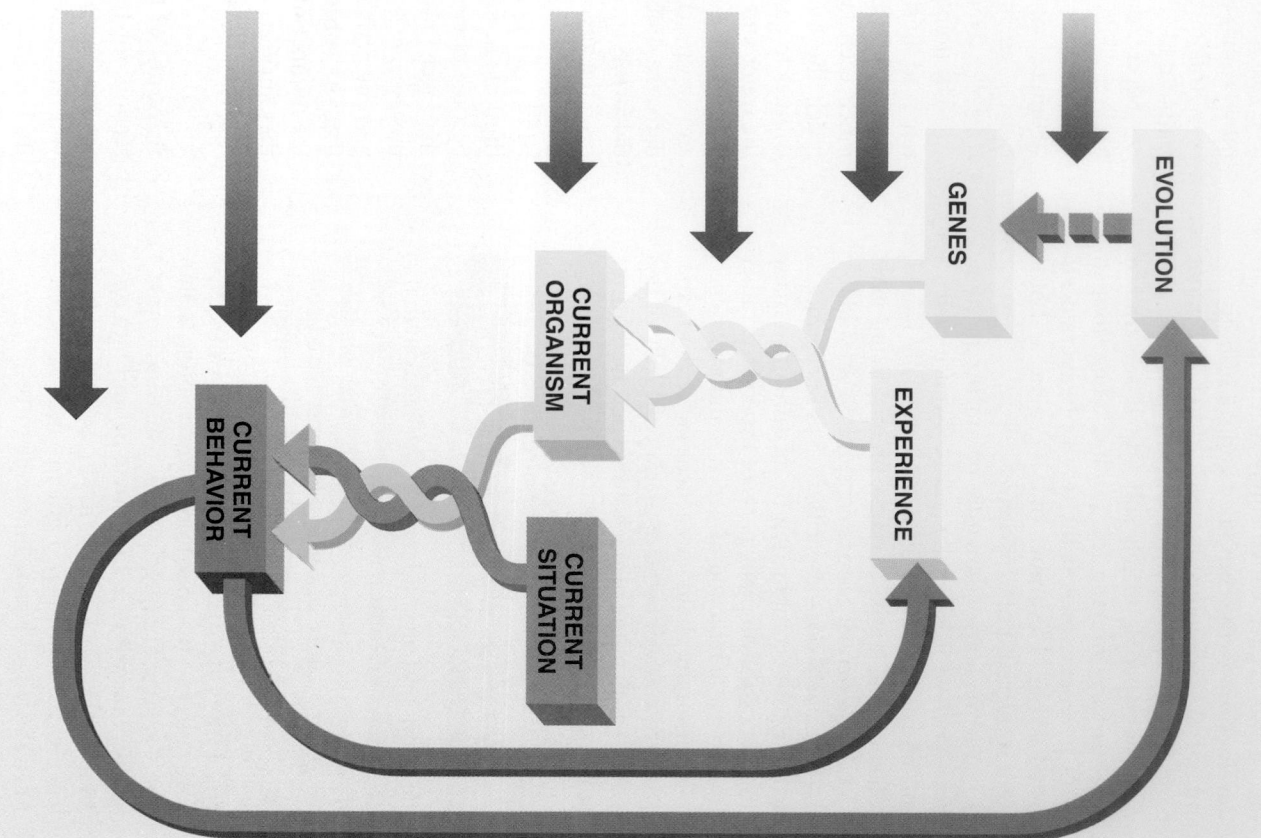

FIGURE 2.3   A schematic illustration of the way in which many biopsychologists think about the biology of behavior.

2.2

Human Evolution

Modern biology began in 1859 with the publication of Charles Darwin's *On the Origin of Species*. In this monumental work, Darwin described his theory of evolution—the single most influential theory in the biological sciences. Darwin was not the first to suggest that species evolve (undergo gradual orderly change) from preexisting species, but he was the first to amass a large body of supporting evidence and the first to suggest how evolution occurs.

Darwin presented three kinds of evidence to support his assertion that species evolve: (1) He documented the evolution of fossil records through progressively more recent geological layers, (2) He described striking structural similarities among living species (e.g., a human's

FIGURE 2.4 Four kinds of evidence supporting the theory that species evolve.

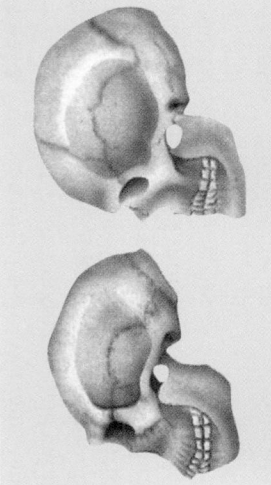

Fossil records change systematically through geological layers. Illustrated here is the evolution of the hominid skull.

Major changes have been created in domestic plants and animals by programs of selective breeding.

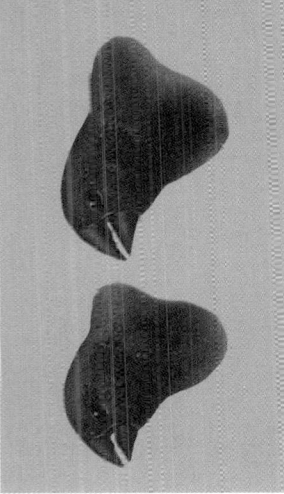

Evolution has been observed in progress. For example, an 18-month drought on one of the Galápagos Islands left only large, difficult-to-eat seeds and increased the beak size in one species of finch.

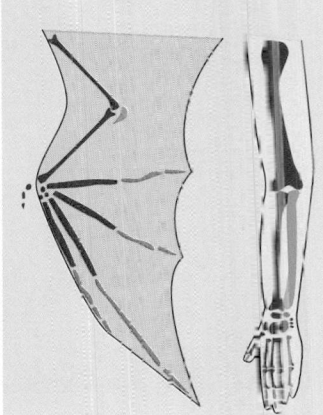

There are striking structural similarities among diverse living species (e.g., between a human arm and a bat's wing).

with high rates of survival and reproduction are the most likely ones to be passed on to future generations. He argued that natural selection, when repeated for generation after generation, leads to the evolution of species that are better adapted to surviving and reproducing in their particular environmental niche. Darwin called this process *natural selection* to emphasize its similarity to the artificial selective breeding practices employed by breeders of domestic animals. Just as horse breeders create faster horses by selectively breeding the fastest of their existing stock, nature creates fitter animals by selectively breeding the fittest. **Fitness,** in the Darwinian sense, is the ability of an organism to survive and contribute its genes to the next generation.

The theory of evolution was at odds with the various dogmatic views that were embedded in the 19th-century Zeitgeist, so it met with initial resistance. Although traces of this resistance still exist, virtually none comes from people who understand the evidence (*see* Mayr, 2000):

Evolution by natural selection meets no significant opposition within biological science. The principle of natural selection has a logical necessity to it; indeed, some have argued that it is a tautology rather than an empirical law . . . [S]ubsequent development of biology in major new areas like genetics and biochemistry has only reinforced Darwin's conclusion that the facts make a belief in the theory of evolution by natural selection "inescapable." (Daly & Wilson, 1983, p. 7)

Evolution and Behavior

Some behaviors play an obvious role in evolution. For example, the ability to find food, avoid predation, or defend one's young obviously increases an animal's ability to pass on its genes to future generations. Other behaviors play a role that is less obvious but no less important (e.g., Bergman et al., 2003; Dunbar, 2003; Silk, Alberts,

hand, a bird's wing, and a cat's paw), which suggested that they had evolved from common ancestors. (3) He pointed to the major changes that had been brought about in domestic plants and animals by programs of selective breeding. However, the most convincing evidence of evolution comes from direct observations of evolution in progress. For example, Grant (1991) observed evolution of the finches of the Galápagos Islands—a population studied by Darwin himself—after only a single season of drought. Figure 2.4 illustrates these four kinds of evidence.

Darwin argued that evolution occurs through **natural selection.** He pointed out that the members of each species vary greatly in their structure, physiology, and behavior, and that the heritable traits that are associated

Evolutionary Perspective

& Altmann, 2003). Two examples are social dominance and courtship display.

Social Dominance

The males of many species establish a stable *hierarchy of social dominance* through combative encounters with other males. In some species, these encounters often involve physical damage; in others, they involve mainly posturing and threatening until one of the two combatants backs down. The dominant male usually wins encounters with all other males of the group; the number 2 male usually wins encounters with all males except the dominant male; and so on down the line. Once a hierarchy is established, hostilities diminish because the low-ranking males learn to avoid or quickly submit to the dominant males. Because most of the fighting goes on between males competing for positions high in the social hierarchy, low-ranking males fight little; thus, the lower levels of the hierarchy tend to be only vaguely recognizable.

Why is social dominance an important factor in evolution? One reason is that in some species dominant males copulate more than nondominant males and thus are more effective in passing on their characteristics to future generations. McCann (1981) studied the effect of social dominance on the rate of copulation in 10 bull elephant seals that cohabited the same breeding beach. Figure 2.5 illustrates how these massive animals challenge each other by raising themselves to full height and pushing chest to chest. Usually, the smaller of the two backs down; if it does not, a vicious neck-biting battle ensues. McCann found that the dominant male accounted for about 37% of the copulations during the study, whereas poor number 10 accounted for only about 1% (see Figure 2.5).

Another reason why social dominance is an important factor in evolution is that in some species dominant females are more likely to produce more, and more

healthy, offspring. For example, Pusey, Williams, and Goodall (1997) found that high-ranking female chimpanzees produced more offspring and that these offspring were more likely to survive to sexual maturity. They attributed these advantages to the fact that higher-ranking female chimpanzees are more likely to maintain access to productive food foraging areas.

Courtship Display

An intricate series of courtship displays precedes copulation in many species. The male approaches the female and signals his interest. His signal (which may be olfactory, visual, auditory, or tactual) may elicit a signal in the female, which may elicit another response in the male, and so on until copulation ensues. But copulation is unlikely to occur if one of the pair fails to react appropriately to the signals of the other.

Courtship displays are thought to promote the evolution of new species. Let me explain. A **species** is a group of organisms that is reproductively isolated from other organisms; that is, the members of one species can produce fertile offspring only by mating with members of the same species. A new species begins to branch off from an existing species when some barrier discourages breeding between a subpopulation of the existing species and the remainder of the species (Peterson, Soberón, & Sánchez-Cordero, 1999). Once such a reproductive barrier forms, the subpopulation evolves independently of the remainder of the species until cross-fertilization becomes impossible.

The reproductive barrier may be geographic; for example, a few birds may fly together to an isolated island, where many generations of their offspring breed among themselves and evolve into a separate species. Alternatively—to get back to the main point—the reproductive barrier may be behavioral. A few members of a species may develop different courtship displays, and these may

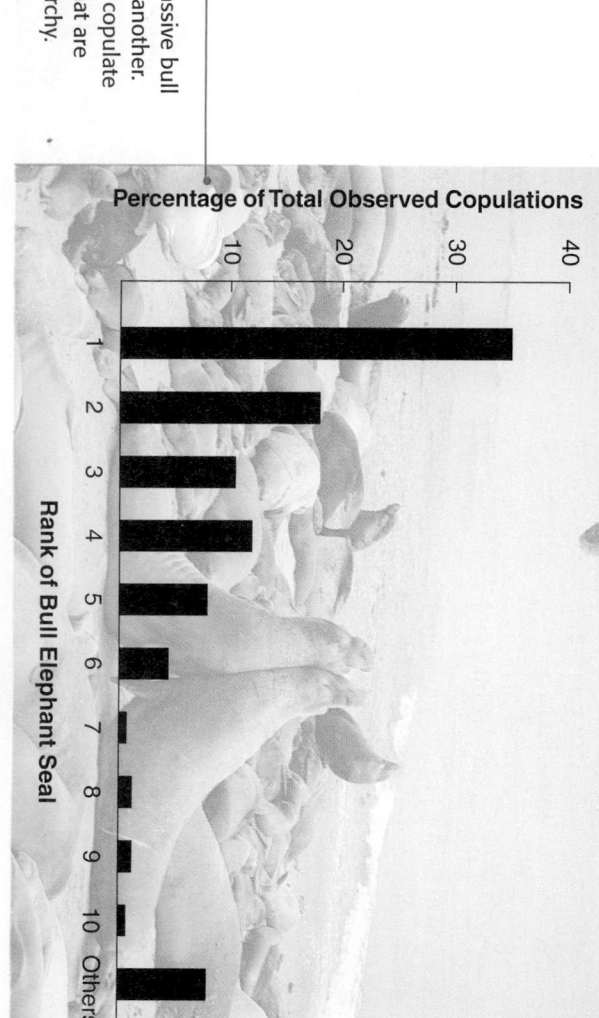

Percentage of Total Observed Copulations

Rank of Bull Elephant Seal

FIGURE 2.5   Two massive bull elephant seals challenge one another. Dominant bull elephant seals copulate more frequently than those that are lower in the dominance hierarchy. (Adapted from McCann, 1981.)

form a reproductive barrier between themselves and the rest of their **conspecifics** (members of the same species).

Course of Human Evolution

By studying fossil records and comparing current species, we humans have looked back in time and pieced together the evolutionary history of our species—although some of the details are still controversial. Human evolution, as it is currently understood, is summarized in this section.

Evolution of Vertebrates Complex multicellular water-dwelling organisms first appeared on earth about 600 million years ago (Vermeij, 1996). About 150 million years later, the first chordates evolved. **Chordates** (pronounced "KOR-dates") are animals with dorsal nerve cords (large nerves that run along the center of the back, or *dorsum*); they are 1 of the 20 or so large categories, or *phyla* (pronounced "FY-la"), into which zoologists group animal species. The first chordates with spinal bones to protect their dorsal nerve cords evolved about 25 million years later. The spinal bones are called *vertebrae* (pronounced "VERT-eh-bray"), and the chordates that possess them are called **vertebrates.** The first vertebrates were primitive bony fishes. Today, there are seven classes of vertebrates: three classes of fishes, plus amphibians, reptiles, birds, and mammals.

Evolution of Amphibians About 410 million years ago, the first bony fishes ventured out of the water. Fishes that could survive on land for brief periods of time had two great advantages: They could escape from stagnant pools to nearby fresh water, and they could take advantage of terrestrial food sources. The advantages of life on land were so great that natural selection transformed the fins and gills of bony fishes to legs and lungs, respectively—and so it was that the first **amphibians** evolved about 400 million years ago. Amphibians (e.g., frogs, toads, and salamanders) in their larval form must live in the water; only adult amphibians can survive on land.

Evolution of Reptiles About 300 million years ago, reptiles (e.g., lizards, snakes, and turtles) evolved from amphibians. Reptiles were the first vertebrates to lay shell-covered eggs and to be covered by dry scales. Both of these adaptations reduced the reliance of reptiles on watery habitats. A reptile does not have to spend the first stage of its life in the watery environment of a pond or lake; instead, it spends the first stage of its life in the watery environment of a shell-covered egg. And once hatched, a reptile can live far from water, because its dry scales greatly reduce water loss through its water-permeable skin.

Evolution of Mammals About 180 million years ago, during the height of the age of dinosaurs, a new class of vertebrates evolved from one line of small reptiles. The females of this new class fed their young with secretions from special glands called *mammary glands*, and the members of the class are called **mammals** after these glands. Eventually, mammals stopped laying eggs; instead, the females nurtured their young in the watery environment of their bodies until the young were mature enough to be born. The duck-billed platypus is one surviving mammalian species that lays eggs.

Spending the first stage of life inside one's mother proved to have considerable survival value; it provided the long-term security and environmental stability necessary for complex programs of development to unfold. The one to which we belong is the order **primates.** We humans—in our usual humble way—named our order after the Latin *primus*, which means "first" or "foremost." There are five families of primates: prosimians, New-World monkeys, Old-World monkeys, apes, and hominids. Examples of the five primate families appear in Figure 2.6 on page 28.

Apes (gibbons, orangutans, gorillas, and chimpanzees) are thought to have evolved from a line of Old-World monkeys. Like Old-World monkeys, apes have long arms and grasping hind feet that are specialized for arboreal travel, and they have opposable thumbs that are not long enough to be of much use for precise manipulation (see Figure 2.7 on page 29). Unlike Old-World monkeys, though, apes have no tails and can walk upright for short distances. Chimpanzees are the closest living relatives of humans; approximately 99% of the genetic material is identical in the two species (see O'Neill, Murphy, & Gallager, 1994).

Emergence of Humankind The family of primates that includes humans is the **hominids.** According to one simple view, this family is composed of two genera (the plural of genus): *Australopithecus* and *Homo* (*Homo erectus* and *Homo sapiens*). However, humans (*Homo sapiens*) are the only surviving hominid species. The *taxonomy* (classification) of the human species is illustrated in Figure 2.8 on page 29.

The fossil and genetic evidence of human evolution is currently the subject of much debate among experts (see Cann, 2001; Wong, 2003). However, most believe that the Australopithecines evolved about 6 million years ago in Africa from a line of apes (*australo* means "southern," and *pithecus* means "ape"). Several species of *Australopithecus* are thought to have roamed the African plains for about 5 million years before becoming extinct (see Tattersall & Matternes, 2000). Australopithecines were only about 1.3 meters (4 feet) tall, and they had small brains; but analysis of their pelvis and leg bones indicates that their posture was as upright as yours or mine. Any doubts about their upright posture were erased by the discovery of the fossilized footprints pictured in Figure 2.9 (Agnew & Demas, 1998).

The first *Homo* species are thought to have evolved from a species of *Australopithecus* about 2 million years ago (Wood & Collard, 1999). The most distinctive feature of the early *Homo* species was their large brain cavity (about 850 cubic centimeters), larger than that of *Australopithecus* (about 500 cubic centimeters), but smaller than that of modern humans (about 1,330 cubic centimeters). The early *Homo* species used fire and tools (see Ambrose, 2001), coexisted in Africa with various species of *Australopithecus* for about a half-million years until *Australopithecus* died out, and began to move out of Africa into Europe and Asia in large numbers about 1.7 million years ago (see Vekua et al., 2002).

About 200,000 years ago (Pääbo, 1995), early *Homo* species were gradually replaced in the fossil record by

FIGURE 2.6   Examples of the five different families of primates.

OLD-WORLD MONKEY
Hussar Monkey

NEW-WORLD MONKEY
Squirrel Monkey

APE
Silver-Backed Lowland Gorilla

PROSIMIAN
Tarsus Monkey

HOMINID
Human

Thinking Critically

FIGURE 2.9 Fossilized footprints of Australopithecine hominids who strode across African volcanic ash about 3.6 million years ago. They left a 70-meter trail. There were two adults and a child; the child often walked in the footsteps of the adults.

modern humans (*Homo sapiens*). Paradoxically, although the big three human attributes—large brain, upright posture, and free hands with an opposable thumb—have been evident for hundreds of thousands of years, most human accomplishments are of recent origin. Artistic products (e.g., wall paintings and carvings) did not appear until about 40,000 years ago, ranching and farming were not established until about 10,000 years ago (e.g., Denham et al., 2003), and writing was not invented until about 3,500 years ago.

Thinking about Human Evolution

Figure 2.10 on page 30 illustrates the main branches of vertebrate evolution. As you examine it, put human

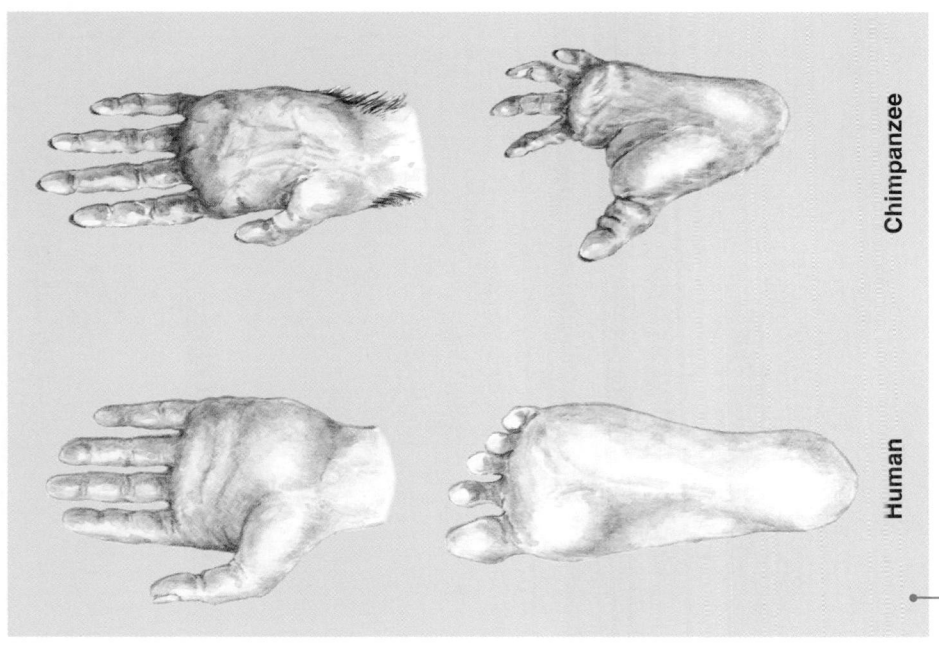

FIGURE 2.7 A comparison of the feet and hands of a human and a chimpanzee.

Human   Chimpanzee

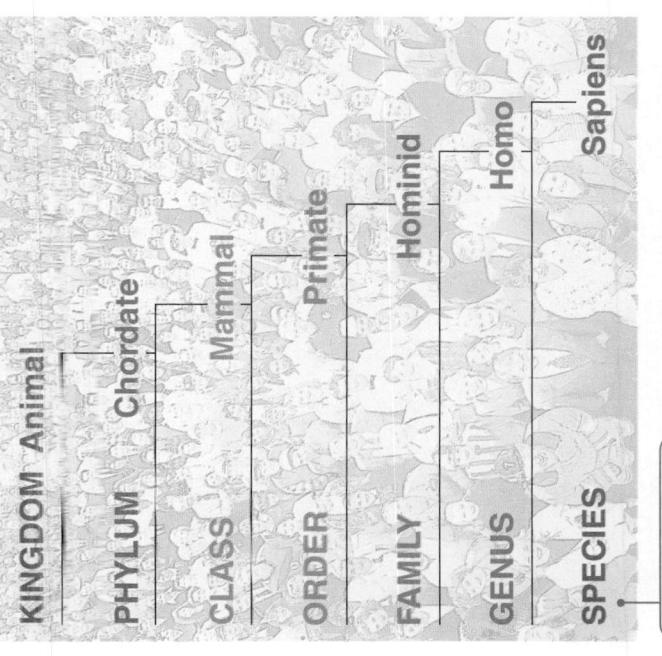

KINGDOM Animal
PHYLUM Chordate
CLASS Mammal
ORDER Primate
FAMILY Hominid
GENUS Homo
SPECIES Sapiens

FIGURE 2.8 The taxonomy of the human species.

evolution into perspective by considering the following eight often-misunderstood points about evolution:

1. Evolution does not proceed in a single line. Although it is common to think of an evolutionary ladder or scale, a far better metaphor for evolution is a dense bush.

2. We humans have little reason to claim evolutionary supremacy. We are the last surviving species of a family (i.e., hominids) that has existed for only a blip of evolutionary time.

3. Evolution does not always proceed slowly and gradually. Rapid evolutionary changes (i.e., in a few generations) can be triggered by sudden changes in the environment (see Becker, 2002) or by adaptive genetic mutations (see Elena, Cooper, & Lenski, 1996). Whether human evolution occurred gradually or suddenly is still a matter of intense debate among paleontologists (those who scientifically study fos-

sils)—see Kerr (1996). About the time that hominids evolved, there was a sudden cooling of the earth leading to a decrease in African forests and an increase in African grasslands. This may have accelerated human evolution.

4. Few products of evolution have survived to the present day—only the tips of the evolutionary bush have survived. Fewer than 1% of all known species are still in existence.

5. Evolution does not progress to preordained perfection—evolution is a tinkerer, not an architect. Increases in adaptation occur through changes to existing programs of development; and the results, although improvements in their particular environmental context, are never perfect designs (see Nesse & Williams, 1998). For example, the fact that mammalian sperm do not develop effectively at body temperature led to the evolution of the scrotum—hardly a perfect solution to any design problem.

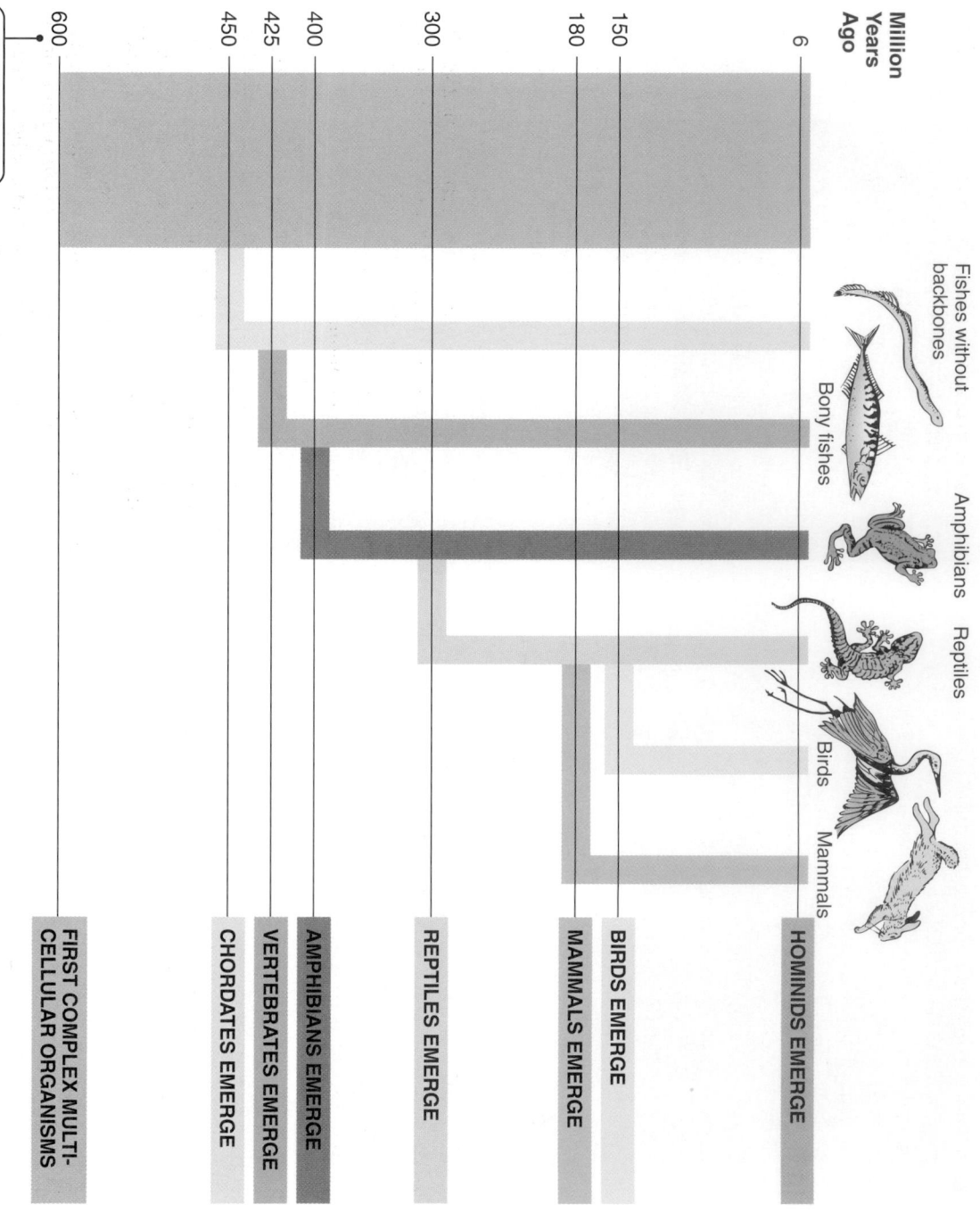

FIGURE 2.10 Vertebrate evolution.

6. Not all existing behaviors or structures are adaptive. Evolution often occurs through changes in developmental programs that lead to several related characteristics, only one of which might be adaptive—the incidental nonadaptive evolutionary by-products are called **spandrels.** Also, behaviors or structures that were once adaptive might become nonadaptive, or even maladaptive, if the environment changes. The human belly button is a spandrel; it serves no adaptive function and is merely the by-product of the umbilical cord.

7. Not all existing adaptive characteristics evolved to perform their current function. Some characteristics, called **exaptations,** evolved to perform one function and were later co-opted to perform another (Buss et al., 1998; Tattersall, 2001). For example, bird wings are exaptations—they are limbs that first evolved for the purpose of walking.

8. Similarities among species do not necessarily mean that the species have common evolutionary origins. Structures that are similar because they have a common evolutionary origin are termed **homologous,** structures that are similar but do not have a common evolutionary origin are termed **analogous.** The similarities between analogous structures result from **convergent evolution,** the evolution in unrelated species of similar solutions to the same environmental demands. Deciding whether a structural similarity is analogous or homologous depends on a careful analysis of the similarity. For example, a bird's wing and a human's arm have a basic underlying commonality of skeletal structure that suggests a common ancestor (see Burke & Feduccia, 1997); in contrast, a bird's wing and a bee's wing have few structural similarities, although they do serve the same function.

Evolution of the Human Brain

Early research on the evolution of the human brain focused on size. This research was stimulated by the assumption that brain size and intellectual capacity are closely related—an assumption that quickly ran into two problems. First, it was shown that modern humans, whom modern humans believe to be the most intelligent of all creatures, do not have the biggest brains. With brains weighing about 1,350 grams, humans rank far behind whales and elephants, whose brains weigh between 5,000 and 8,000 grams (Harvey & Krebs, 1990). Second, the sizes of the brains of acclaimed intellectuals (e.g., Einstein) were found to be unremarkable, certainly no match for their gigantic intellects. It is now clear that, although healthy adult human brains vary greatly in size—between about 1,000 and 2,000 grams—there is no clear relationship between brain size and intelligence.

One obvious problem in relating brain size to intelligence is the fact that larger animals tend to have larger brains, presumably because larger bodies require more brain tissue to control and regulate them. Thus, the facts that large men tend to have larger brains than small men, that men tend to have larger brains than women, and that elephants have larger brains than humans do not suggest anything about the relative intelligence of these populations. This problem led to the proposal that brain weight expressed as a percentage of total body weight might be a better measure of intellectual capacity. This measure allows humans (2.33%) to take their rightful place ahead of elephants (0.20%), but it also allows both humans and elephants to be surpassed by that intellectual giant of the animal kingdom, the shrew (3.33%).

A more reasonable approach to the study of brain evolution has been to compare the evolution of different brain regions (Finlay & Darlington, 1995; Killacky, 1995). For example, it has been informative to consider the evolution of the **brain stem** separately from the evolution of the **cerebrum** (cerebral hemispheres). In general, the brain stem regulates reflex activities that are critical for survival (e.g., heart rate, respiration, and blood glucose level), whereas the cerebrum is involved in more complex adaptive processes such as learning, perception, and motivation.

Figure 2.11 on page 32 is a schematic representation of the relative size of the brain stems and cerebrums of several species that are living descendants of species from which humans evolved. This figure makes three important points about the evolution of the human brain: The first is that it has increased in size during evolution; the second is that most of the increase in size has occurred in the cerebrum; and the third is that there has been an increase in the number of convolutions—folds on the cerebral surface—that has greatly increased the volume of cerebral tissue.

More significant than the differences among the brains of various related species are the similarities. All brains are constructed of neurons, and the neural structures that compose the brains of one species can almost always be found in the brains of related species. For example, the brains of humans, monkeys, rats, and mice contain the same gross (major) structures connected in the same way. Moreover, similar structures tend to perform similar functions. For example, neurons that respond to the number of objects in a display, independent of the identity of the objects, have been found in the *parietal cortex* of humans, monkeys, and cats (see Dehaene, 2002; Nieder, Freedman, & Miller, 2002).

Evolutionary Psychology: Understanding Mate Bonding

The evolutionary approach has been embraced by many psychologists. Indeed, a new field of psychology, termed *evolutionary psychology*, has coalesced around it. Evolutionary psychologists try to understand human behaviors through a consideration of the pressures that

Evolutionary Perspective

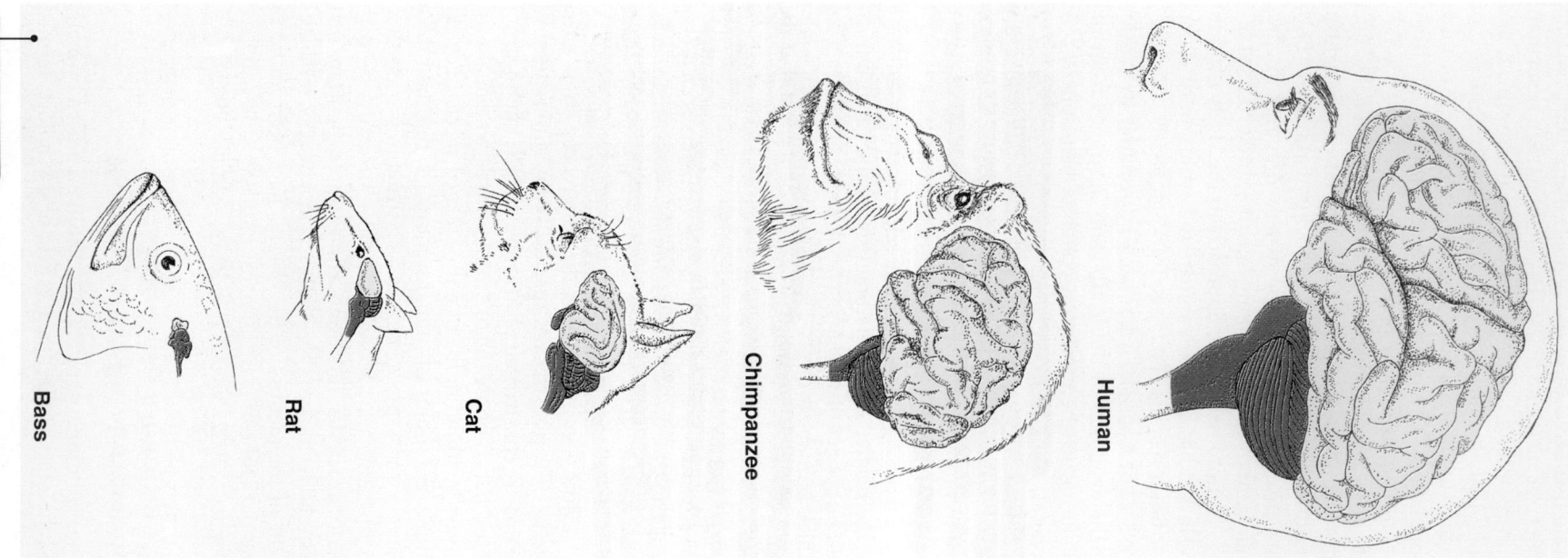

Bass

Rat

Cat

Chimpanzee

Human

FIGURE 2.11 The brains of animals of different evolutionary age. Cerebrums are shown in beige; brain stems are shown in blue.

led to their evolution. Some of the most interesting and controversial work in this field has focused on questions of sex differences in mate bonding, questions you may be dealing with in your own life (see Geary, 1999).

In most species, mating is totally promiscuous. *Promiscuity* is a mating arrangement in which the members of both sexes indiscriminately copulate with many different partners during each mating period. Although such indiscriminate copulation is the predominant mode of reproduction (see Small, 1992), the males and females of some species form *mating bonds* (enduring mating relationships) with members of the other sex.

Most mammals tend to form mating bonds. Why? An influential theory, originally proposed by Trivers (1972), attributes the evolution of mating-bond formation in mammals to the fact that female mammals give birth to relatively small numbers of helpless, slow-developing young. As a result, it is adaptive for mammalian males to stay with the females who are carrying their offspring and to promote the successful development of those offspring. A male mammal that behaves in this way is more likely to pass his heritable characteristics on to future generations. Thus, natural selection has promoted the evolution in mammalian males of the tendency to bond with the females with which they have copulated. Similarly, there is selection pressure on female mammals to behave in ways that will induce males to bond to them because this improves their ability to pass on their own heritable characteristics to future generations. In many species, mating bonds last a lifetime.

The pattern of mate bonding that is most prevalent in mammals is **polygyny** (pronounced "pol-IG-in-ee"), an arrangement in which one male forms mating bonds with more than one female. Why did polygyny evolve in so many mammalian species? The evidence suggests that polygyny evolved as the predominant mating system in mammals because female mammals make a far greater contribution to the rearing of their young than do males (Trivers, 1972). Mammalian mothers carry their developing young in their bodies, sometimes for many months, and then suckle and care for them after they are born. In contrast, mammalian fathers often do not contribute much more to reproduction than sperm. One major consequence of this one-sided mammalian parenting arrangement is that female mammals can produce only a few offspring during their lifetimes, whereas males have the capacity to sire many offspring.

Because each female mammal can produce only a few offspring, she must make the best of her chances if her heritable characteristics are going to be passed on to future generations in significant numbers. In particular, it is important that she mate with particularly fit males. Mating with fit males increases the likelihood that her offspring will be fit and will pass on her genes, along with those of her mate, to the next generation; it also increases the likelihood that what little parental support her offspring will receive from their father will be effective.

in which enduring bonds are formed between one male and one female. Although monogamy is the most common human mate-bonding system, it is important to remember that it is not the predominant mammalian system.

Monogamy is thought to have evolved in those mammalian species in which each female could raise more young, or more fit young, if she had undivided help (see Dewsbury, 1988). In such species, any change in the behavior of a female that would encourage a male to bond exclusively with her would increase the likelihood that her heritable characteristics would be passed on to future generations. One such behavioral change is for each female to drive other females of reproductive age away from her mate. This strategy is particularly effective if a female will not copulate with a male until he has stayed with her for a period of time. Once this pattern of behavior evolved in the females of a particular species, the optimal mating strategy for males would change. It would become difficult for each male to bond with many females, and a male's best chance of producing many fit offspring would be for him to bond with a fit female and to put most of his reproductive effort into her and their offspring. Of course, in a monogamous relationship, it is important that males select fertile females and that females select males that can effectively protect them and their offspring.

It is important not to lose sight of the fact that the significance of evolutionary psychology does not lie in the many theories it has generated. It is easy to speculate about how particular human behaviors evolved without ever having one's theories disproved, because it is not possible to know for sure how an existing behavior evolved. Good theories of behavioral evolution have predictions about current behaviors built into them so that the predictions—and thus the theory—can be tested. Theories that cannot be tested have little use.

The foregoing evolutionary theory of mate selection is one that has led to many predictions about current aspects of human mate selection. Buss (1992) has confirmed several of them: (1) Men in most cultures value youth and attractiveness (both indicators of fertility) in their mates more than women do; in contrast, women value power and earning capacity more than men do. (2) Physical attractiveness best predicts which women will bond with men of high occupational status. (3) The major mate-attraction strategy of women is increasing their physical attractiveness; in men, it is displaying their power and resources. (4) Men are more likely than women to commit adultery.

The foregoing evolutionary psychological analysis—and others like it—drives home three key points. First, it illustrates the ability of evolutionary analysis to generate insights into even the most complex psychological processes. Second, it emphasizes that we humans are products of over 600 million years of adaptation. And

---

Thus, according to current theory, the tendency to establish mating bonds with only the fittest males evolved in females of many mammalian species. In contrast, because male mammals can sire so many offspring, there has been little evolutionary pressure on them to become selective in their bonding—the males of most mammalian species will form mating bonds with as many females as possible. The inevitable consequence of the selective bonding of female mammals and the nonselective bonding of male mammals is polygyny—see Figure 2.12.

The strongest evidence in support of the theory that polygyny evolves when females make a far greater contribution to reproduction and parenting than males do comes from the studies of **polyandry** (pronounced "pol-ee-AN-dree"). Polyandry is a mating arrangement in which one female forms mating bonds with more than one male. Polyandry does not occur in mammals; it occurs only in species in which the contributions of the females to reproduction are greater than those of the males. For example, in one polyandrous species, the sea horse, the female deposits her eggs in the male's pouch, and he fertilizes them and carries them until they are mature enough to venture out on their own (see Daly & Wilson, 1983).

The current thinking is that both large body size and the tendency to engage in aggression evolved in male mammals because female mammals tend to be more selective in their reproductive bonding. Because of the selectivity of the females, the competition among the males for reproductive partners becomes fierce, with only the successful competitors passing on their genes. In contrast, the females of most species have little difficulty finding reproductive partners.

Although most mammals are polygynous, 3% of mammalian species, including humans, are primarily monogamous. **Monogamy** is a mate-bonding pattern

FIGURE 2.12 Horses, like most mammals, are polygynous. The stallion breeds with all the mares in the herd by virtue of his victories over other males.

Thinking Critically

third, it stresses the fact that we humans are related to all other animal species—in some cases, more closely than we like to admit (see Dess & Chapman, 1998; Whiten & Boesch, 2001).

Even our most personal hopes and desires are products of evolution. It is extremely important, however, to appreciate that the behavioral tendencies stamped in by evolution exist in humans without any need for our understanding or even awareness, and that all inherited tendencies are modulated by experience (see Eagly & Wood, 1999). Think about it.

Thinking Critically   www.ablongman.com/pinel6e

2.3   Fundamental Genetics

Darwin did not understand two of the key facts on which his theory of evolution was based. He did not understand why conspecifics differ from one another, and he did not understand how anatomical, physiological, and behavioral characteristics are passed from parent to offspring. While Darwin puzzled over these questions, there was an unread manuscript in his files that contained the answers. It had been sent to him by an unknown Augustinian monk, Gregor Mendel (1822–1884). Unfortunately for Darwin (1809–1882), the significance of Mendel's research was not recognized until the early part of the 20th century, well after both of their deaths.

Mendelian Genetics

Mendel studied inheritance in pea plants. In designing his experiments, he made two wise decisions. He decided to study dichotomous traits, and he decided to begin his experiments by crossing the offspring of true-breeding lines. **Dichotomous traits** are traits that occur in one form or the other, never in combination. For example, seed color is a dichotomous pea plant trait. Every pea plant has either brown seeds or white seeds. **True-breeding lines** are breeding lines in which interbred members always produce offspring with the same trait (e.g., brown seeds), generation after generation.

In one of his early experiments, Mendel studied the inheritance of seed color: brown or white. He began by crossing the offspring of a line of pea plants that had bred true for brown seeds with the offspring of a line of pea plants that had bred true for white seeds. The offspring of this cross all had brown seeds. Then, Mendel bred these first-generation offspring with one another, and he found that about three-quarters of the resulting second-generation offspring had brown seeds and about one-quarter had white seeds. Mendel repeated this experiment many times with various pairs of dichotomous pea plant traits, and each time the result was the same. One trait, which Mendel called the **dominant trait,** appeared in all of the first-generation offspring; the other trait, which he called the **recessive trait,** appeared in about one-quarter of the second-generation offspring. Mendel would have obtained a similar result if he had conducted an experiment with true-breeding lines of brown-eyed (dominant) and blue-eyed (recessive) humans.

The results of Mendel's experiment challenged the central premise upon which all previous ideas about inheritance had rested: that offspring inherit the traits of their parents. Somehow, the recessive trait (white seeds) was passed on to one-quarter of the second-generation pea plants by first-generation pea plants that did not themselves possess it. An organism's observable traits are referred to as its **phenotype;** the traits that it can pass on to its offspring through its genetic material are referred to as its **genotype.**

Mendel devised a theory to explain his results. It comprised four ideas. First, Mendel proposed that there are two kinds of inherited factors for each dichotomous trait—for example, that a brown-seed factor and a white-seed factor control seed color. Today, we call each inherited factor a **gene.** Second, Mendel proposed that each organism possesses two genes for each of its dichotomous traits; for example, each pea plant possesses either two brown-seed genes, two white-seed genes, or one of each. The two genes that control the same trait are called **alleles** (pronounced "a-LEELZ"). Organisms that possess two identical genes for a trait are said to be **homozygous** for that trait; those that possess two different genes for a trait are said to be **heterozygous** for that trait. Third, Mendel proposed that one of the two kinds of genes for each dichotomous trait dominates the other in heterozygous organisms. For example, pea plants with a brown-seed gene and a white-seed gene always have brown seeds because the brown-seed gene always dominates the white-seed gene. And fourth, Mendel proposed that for each trait each organism randomly inherits one of its "father's" two factors and one of its "mother's" two factors. Figure 2.13 illustrates how Mendel's theory accounts for the result of his experiment on the inheritance of seed color in pea plants.

Chromosomes, Reproduction, and Linkage

It was not until the early 20th century that genes were found to be located on **chromosomes**—the threadlike structures in the *nucleus* of each cell. Chromosomes oc-

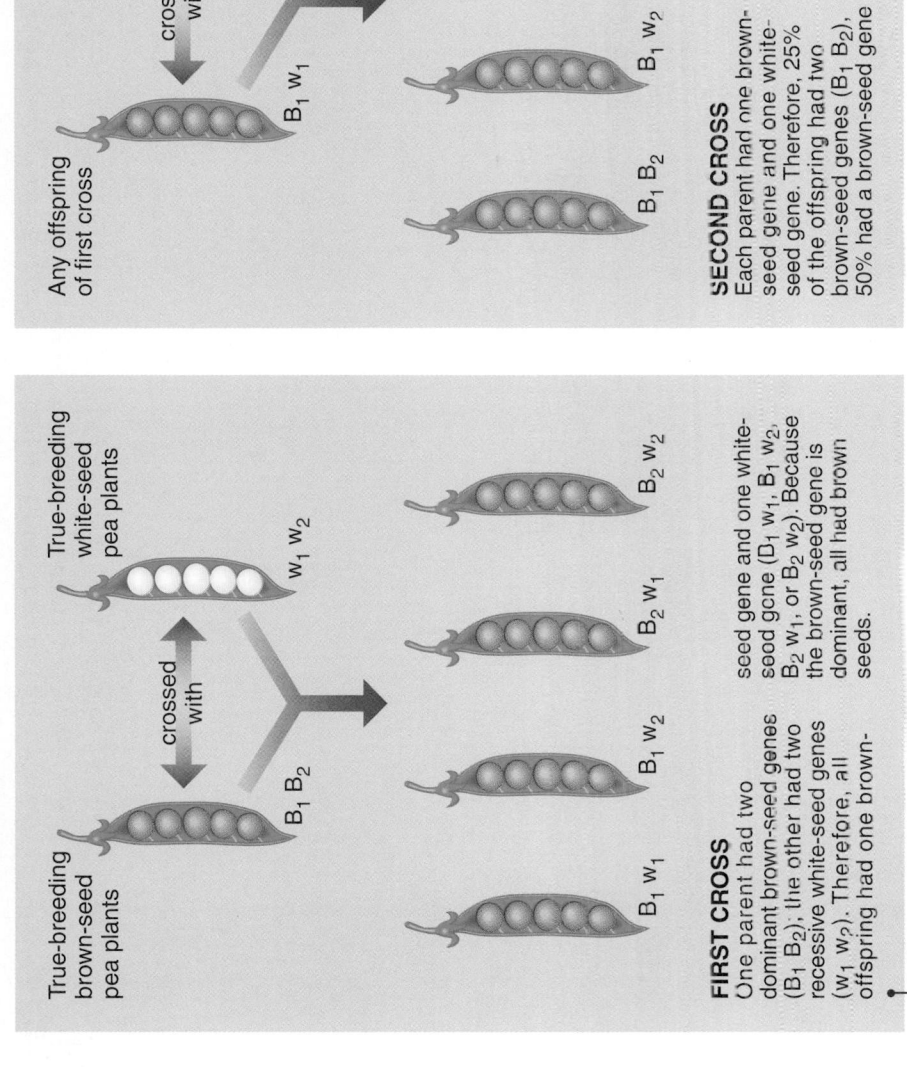

FIRST CROSS

True-breeding brown-seed pea plants

$B_1 B_2$

crossed with

True-breeding white-seed pea plants

$w_1 w_2$

$B_1 W_1$

$B_1 W_2$

$B_2 W_1$

$B_2 W_2$

One parent had two dominant brown-seed genes ($B_1 B_2$); the other had two recessive white-seed genes ($w_1 w_2$). Because the brown-seed gene is dominant, all offspring had one brown-seed gene and one white-seed gene ($B_1 w_1$, $B_1 w_2$, $B_2 w_1$, or $B_2 w_2$). Therefore, all offspring had brown-seeds.

Any offspring of first cross

$B_1 W_1$

crossed with

Any offspring of first cross

$B_2 W_2$

$B_1 B_2$

$B_1 W_2$

$B_2 W_1$

$w_1 w_2$

SECOND CROSS

Each parent had one brown-seed gene and one white-seed gene. Therefore, 25% of the offspring had two brown-seed genes ($B_1 B_2$), 50% had a brown-seed gene and a white-seed gene ($B_1 w_2$ or $B_2 w_1$), and 25% had two white-seed genes ($w_1 w_2$). Because the brown-seed gene is dominant, 75% had brown seeds.

FIGURE 2.13 How Mendel's theory accounts for the results of his experiment on the inheritance of seed color in pea plants.

cur in matched pairs, and each species has a characteristic number of pairs in each of its body cells; humans have 23 pairs. The two genes (alleles) that control each trait are situated at the same locus, one on each chromosome of a particular pair.

The process of cell division that produces **gametes** (egg cells and sperm cells) is called **meiosis** (pronounced "my-OH-sis")—see Sluder and McCollum (2000). In meiosis, the chromosomes divide, and one chromosome of each pair goes to each of the two gametes that results from the division. As a result, each gamete has only half the usual number of chromosomes (23 in humans); and when a sperm cell and an egg cell combine during fertilization (see Figure 2.14), a **zygote** (a fertilized egg cell) with the full complement of chromosomes is produced. All other cell division in the body occurs by **mitosis** (pronounced "my-TOE-sis"). Just prior to mitotic division, the number of chromosomes doubles so that, when the division occurs, both daughter cells end up with the full complement of chromosomes. Figure 2.15 on page 36 illustrates meiosis, fertilization, and mitosis.

Meiosis accounts for much of the genetic diversity within each species. In humans, for example, each meiotic division produces two gametes; each gamete contains one chromosome from each of the 23 pairs contained in

ON THE CD

Visit the *Mitosis* module to see how this type of cell division works.

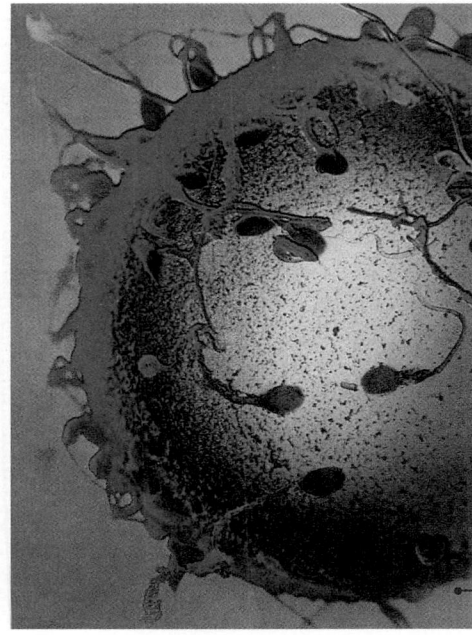

FIGURE 2.14 During fertilization, sperm cells attach themselves to the surface of an egg cell; only one will enter the egg cell and fertilize it.

Sperm Cells Are Created by Meiotic Division

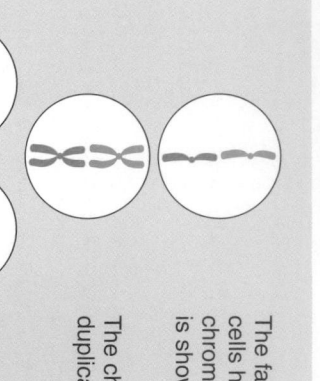

The father's body cells have 23 pairs of chromosomes; 1 pair is shown here.

The chromosomes duplicate themselves.

The cell divides to create two cells, each with 23 duplicated chromosomes.

Each cell divides again to create 4 sperm cells, each with 23 chromosomes, half the normal number.

Egg Cells Are Created by Meiotic Division

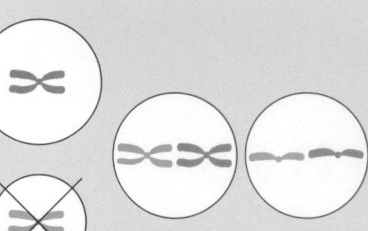
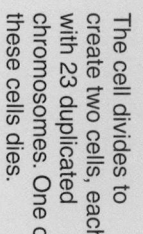

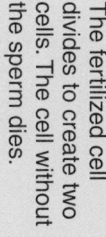

The mother's body cells have 23 pairs of chromosomes; 1 pair is shown here.

The chromosomes duplicate themselves.

The cell divides to create two cells, each with 23 duplicated chromosomes. One of these cells dies.

Bingo! Fertilization.

The fertilized cell divides to create two cells. The cell without the sperm dies.

The sperm and the egg combine to form a zygote with 23 pairs of chromosomes.

The Zygote Grows by Mitotic Division

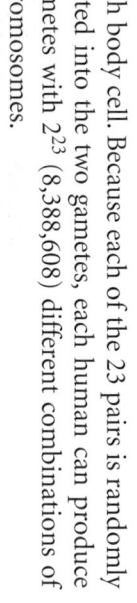

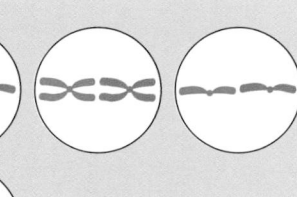
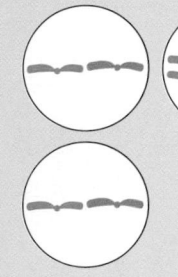
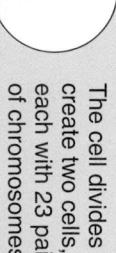

The zygote has 23 pairs of chromosomes.

The chromosomes duplicate.

The cell divides to create two cells, each with 23 pairs of chromosomes.

Mitotic division occurs over and over until an adult organism is created.

FIGURE 2.15 Meiotic cell division, fertilization, and mitotic cell division.

each body cell. Because each of the 23 pairs is randomly sorted into the two gametes, each human can produce gametes with 2^{23} (8,388,608) different combinations of chromosomes.

The first comprehensive study of **linkage** was conducted in the early 20th century by Morgan and his colleagues (1915). They found that there are four different clusters of fruit fly genes. If the gene for one trait in a cluster was inherited from one parent, that fruit fly had a higher probability (greater than 0.5) of inheriting genes for other traits in the cluster from the same parent. Because fruit flies have four pairs of chromosomes, Morgan and his colleagues concluded that linkage occurs between traits that are encoded on the same chromosome. They were correct; in every species in which linkage has been assessed, the number of clusters of linked traits has been found to equal the number of pairs of chromosomes.

If genes are passed from generation to generation on chromosomes, why are the genes on the same chromosome not always inherited together? The linkage between pairs of genes on a single chromosome varies from almost complete (close to 1.0) to just above chance (just over 0.5).

Sex Chromosomes and Sex-Linked Traits

There is one exception to the rule that chromosomes always come in matched pairs. That exception is the **sex chromosomes**—the pair of chromosomes that determines an individual's sex. There are two types of sex chromosomes, X and Y, and the two look different and carry different genes. Female mammals have two X chromosomes, and male mammals have an X and a Y. Traits that are influenced by genes on the sex chromosomes are referred to as **sex-linked traits.** Virtually all sex-linked traits are controlled by genes on the X chromosome because the Y chromosome is small and carries few genes (see Jegalian & Lahn, 2001).

Traits that are controlled by genes on the X chromosome occur more frequently in one sex than the other. If the trait is dominant, it occurs more frequently in females. Females have twice the chance of inheriting the dominant gene because they have twice the number of X chromosomes. In contrast, recessive sex-linked traits occur more frequently in males. The reason is that recessive sex-linked traits are manifested only in females who possess two of the recessive genes—one on each of their X chromosomes—whereas the traits are manifested in all males who possess the gene because they have only one X chromosome. The classic example of a recessive sex-linked trait is color blindness. Because the color-blindness gene is quite rare, females almost never inherit two of them and thus almost never possess the disorder; in contrast, every male who possesses one color-blindness gene is color blind.

Chromosome Structure and Replication

Each chromosome is a double-stranded molecule of **deoxyribonucleic acid (DNA)**. Each strand is a sequence of **nucleotide bases** attached to a chain of *phosphate* and *deoxyribose;* there are four nucleotide bases: *adenine, thymine, guanine,* and *cytosine.* It is the sequence of these bases on each chromosome that constitutes the genetic code—just as the sequence of letters constitutes the code of our language.

The two strands that compose each chromosome are exact complements of each other. For example, the sequence of adenine, guanine, thymine, cytosine, and guanine on one strand is always attached to the complementary sequence of thymine, cytosine, adenine, guanine, and cytosine on the other. Figure 2.17 on page 38 illustrates the structure of DNA.

Morgan and his colleagues proposed that **crossing over** provided the solution to the puzzle of partial linkage. Figure 2.16 illustrates how crossing over works. During the first stage of meiosis, after the chromosomes have replicated, they line up in their pairs. Then they usually cross over one another at random points, break apart at the points of contact, and exchange sections of themselves. As a result, parents rarely pass on intact chromosomal clusters of genes to their children. Each of your gametes contains chromosomes that are unique spliced-together combinations of chromosomes inherited from your mother and father.

The phenomenon of crossing over is important for two reasons. First, by ensuring that chromosomes are not passed intact from generation to generation, crossing over shuffles the genetic deck before the chromosomes are randomly dealt out to the next generation. Second, the study of crossovers was the first means by which geneticists could construct **gene maps.** Because each crossover occurs at a random point along the length of a chromosome, the degree of linkage between two genes indicates how close they are together on the chromosome. Crossovers rarely occur between adjacent genes, and they frequently occur between genes at opposite ends of a chromosome.

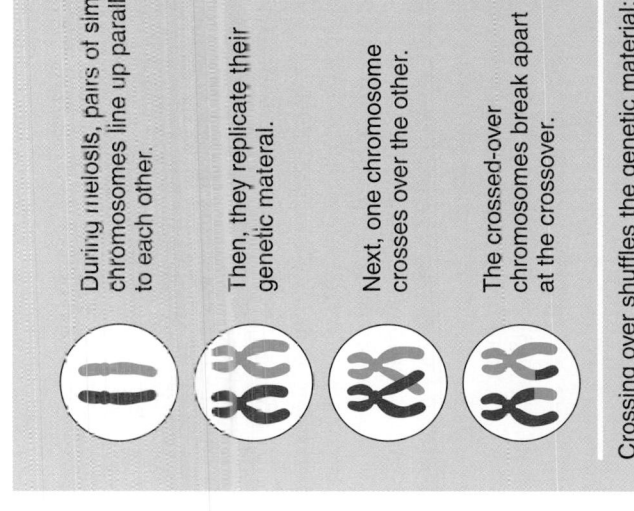

During meiosis, pairs of similar chromosomes line up parallel to each other.

Then, they replicate their genetic material.

Next, one chromosome crosses over the other.

The crossed-over chromosomes break apart at the crossover.

Crossing over shuffles the genetic material; it is why all the genes on a chromosome are not always inherited together.

FIGURE 2.16   Crossing over.

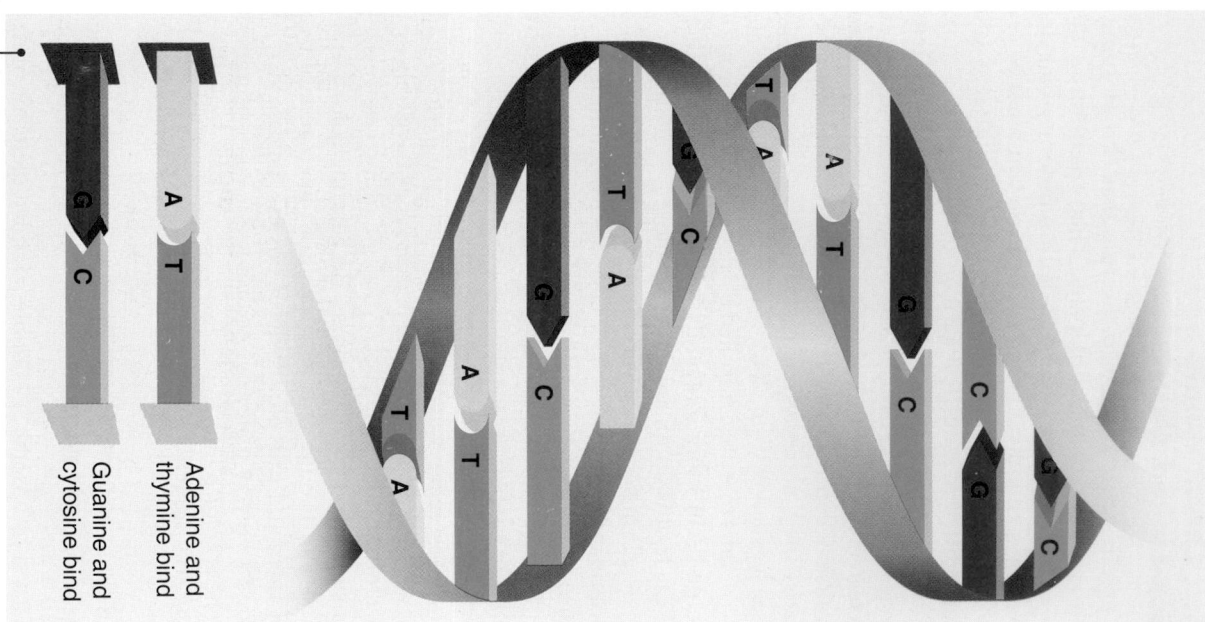

FIGURE 2.17 A schematic illustration of the structure of a DNA molecule. Notice the complementary binding of nucleotide bases: thymine to adenine, and guanine to cytosine.

Adenine and thymine bind

Guanine and cytosine bind

Chromosome replication does not always go according to plan; there may be errors. Sometimes, these errors are gross errors. For example, in *Down syndrome*, which you will learn about in Chapter 10, there is an extra chromosome in each cell. But more commonly, errors in duplication take the form of **mutations**—accidental alterations in individual genes. In most cases, mutations disappear from the genetic pool within a few generations because the organisms that inherit them are less fit. However, in rare instances, mutations increase fitness and in so doing contribute to rapid evolution.

The Genetic Code and Gene Expression

There are several different kinds of genes. The most well understood are the **structural genes**—genes that contain the information necessary for the synthesis of a single protein. **Proteins** are long chains of **amino acids;** they control the physiological activities of cells and are important components of cellular structure. All the cells in the body (e.g., brain cells, hair cells, and bone cells) contain exactly the same structural genes. How then do different kinds of cells develop? The answer lies in a complex category of genes, often called the **operator genes.**

Each operator gene controls a structural gene or a group of related structural genes. The function of an operator gene is to determine whether or not each of its structural genes initiates the synthesis of a protein (i.e., whether or not the structural gene will be *expressed*) and at what rate.

The control of **gene expression** by operator genes is an important process because it determines how a cell will develop and how it will function once it reaches maturity. Operator genes are like switches; and, like switches, they can be regulated in two ways. Some operator genes are normally off, and they are regulated by **DNA-binding proteins** that turn them on; others are normally on, and they are regulated by DNA-binding proteins that turn them up, down, or off. Many of the DNA-binding proteins that control operator genes are influenced by signals received by the cell from its environment (see Darnell, 1997). This, then—if it has not already occurred to you—is the major mechanism by which experience interacts with genes to influence development.

The expression of a structural gene is illustrated in Figure 2.19 on page 40. First, the small section of the chromosome that contains the structural gene unravels, and the unraveled section of one of the DNA strands serves as a template for the transcription of a short strand of **ribonucleic acid (RNA).** RNA is like DNA except that it contains the nucleotide base uracil instead of thymine and has a phosphate and ribose backbone instead of a phosphate and deoxyribose backbone. The

Replication is a critical process of the DNA molecule. Without it, mitotic cell division would not be possible. Figure 2.18 illustrates how DNA replication is thought to work (see Losick & Shapiro, 1998). The two strands of DNA start to unwind. Then the exposed nucleotide bases on each of the two strands attract loose complementary bases from the fluid of the nucleus. Thus, when the unwinding is complete, two double-stranded DNA molecules, both of which are identical to the original, have been created.

FIGURE 2.18 DNA replication. As the two strands of the original DNA molecule unwind, the nucleotide bases on each strand attract loose complementary bases. Once the unwinding is complete, two DNA molecules, each identical to the first, will have been created.

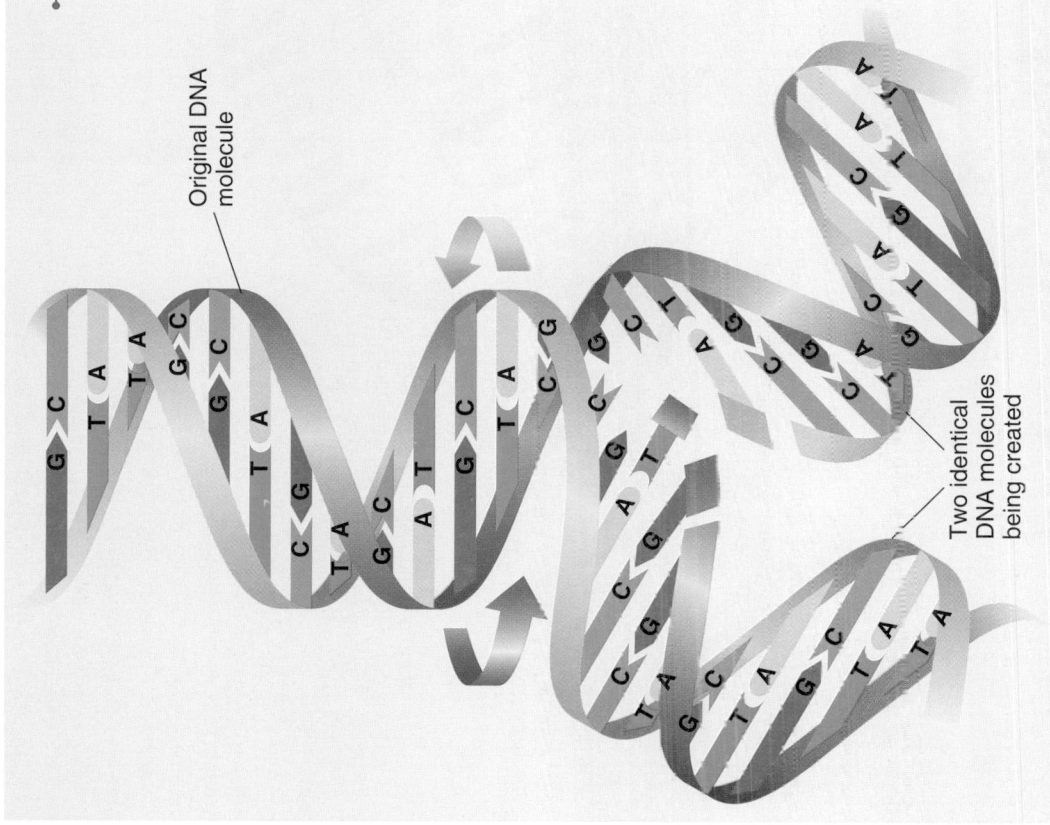

Original DNA molecule

Two identical DNA molecules being created

strand of transcribed RNA is called **messenger RNA** because it carries the genetic code from the nucleus of the cell. Once it has left the nucleus, the messenger RNA attaches itself to one of the many **ribosomes** in the cell's *cytoplasm* (the clear fluid within the cell). The ribosome then moves along the strand of messenger RNA, translating the genetic code as it proceeds.

Each group of three consecutive nucleotide bases on the messenger RNA strand is called a **codon.** Each codon instructs the ribosome to add 1 of the 20 different kinds of amino acids to the protein that it is constructing; for example, the sequence guanine-guanine-adenine instructs the ribosome to add the amino acid glycine. Each kind of amino acid is carried to the ribosome by molecules of **transfer RNA;** as the ribosome reads a codon, it attracts a transfer RNA molecule that is attached to the appropriate amino acid. The ribosome reads codon after codon and adds amino acid after amino acid until it reaches a codon that tells it the protein is com-

plete, whereupon the completed protein is released into the cytoplasm. Thus, the process of gene expression involves two phases: the *transcription* of the DNA base-sequence code to an RNA base-sequence code and the *translation* of the RNA base-sequence code into a sequence of amino acids.

Mitochondrial DNA

So far, we have discussed only the DNA that composes the chromosomes in the cell nucleus. Indeed, you may have the impression that all the DNA is in the nucleus. It isn't. The cells' mitochondria also contain DNA—*mitochondrial DNA.* **Mitochondria** are the energy-generating structures located in the cytoplasm of every cell. All mitochondrial genes are inherited from one's mother.

Mitochondrial DNA is of great interest to scientists for two reasons. The first is that mutations in mitochondrial DNA have been implicated in the cause of several disorders. The second is that because mutations seem to develop in mitochondrial DNA at a reasonably consistent rate, mitochondrial DNA can be used as an evolutionary clock (see Kaessmann & Pääbo, 2002). Analysis of mutations of mitochondrial DNA have confirmed paleontological evidence that hominids evolved in Africa and spread over the earth (Wallace, 1997)—see Figure 2.20 on page 41.

Evolutionary Perspective

Human Genome Project: What's Next?

Arguably, the most ambitious scientific project of all time began in 1990. Known as the **human genome project,** it was a loosely knit collaboration of major research institutions and individual research teams in several countries. The purpose of this collaboration was to compile a map of all 3 billion bases that compose human

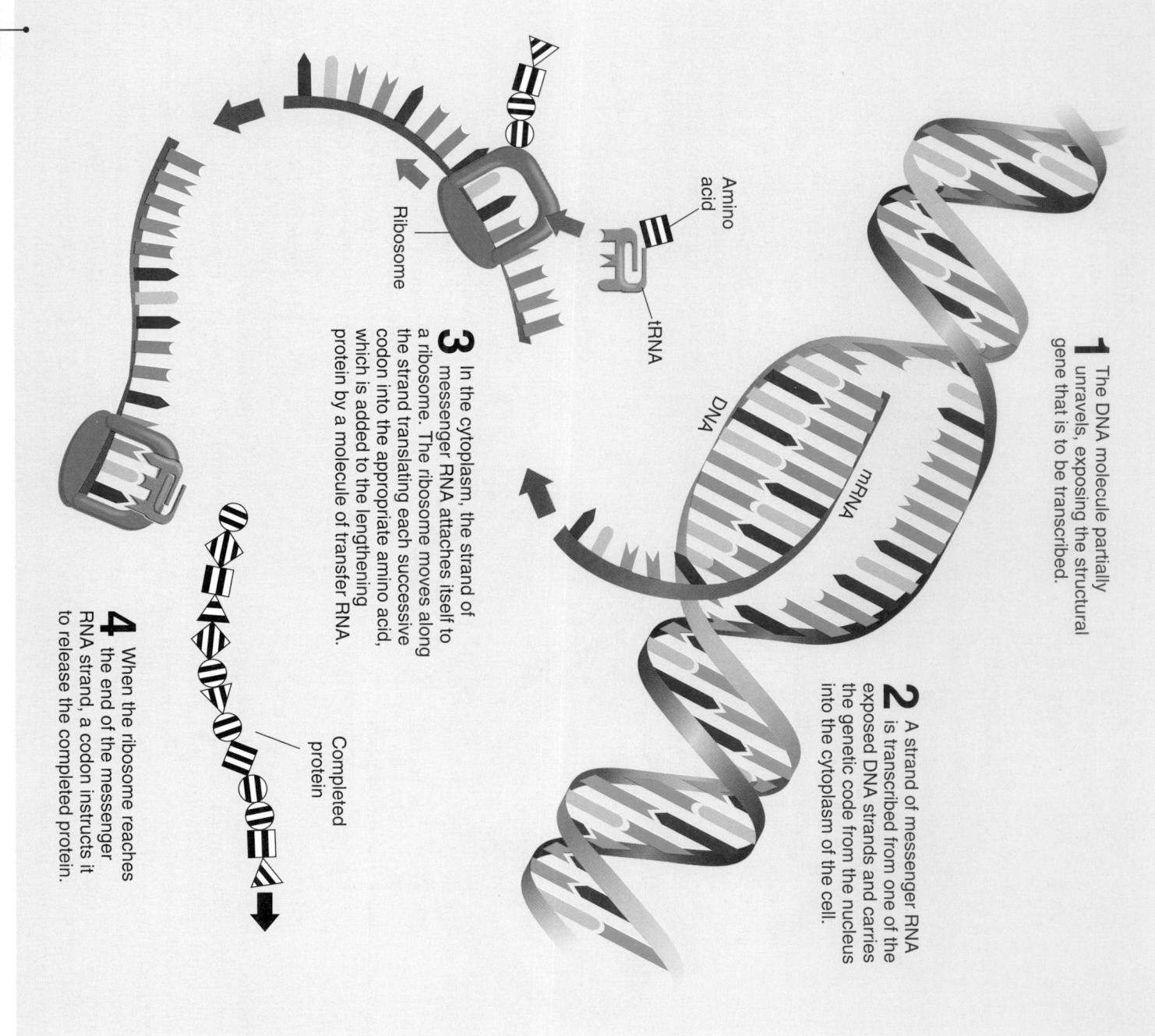

1 The DNA molecule partially unravels, exposing the structural gene that is to be transcribed.

2 A strand of messenger RNA is transcribed from one of the exposed DNA strands and carries the genetic code from the nucleus into the cytoplasm of the cell.

DNA

mRNA

Amino acid

tRNA

Ribosome

3 In the cytoplasm, the strand of messenger RNA attaches itself to a ribosome. The ribosome moves along the strand translating each successive codon into the appropriate amino acid, which is added to the lengthening protein by a molecule of transfer RNA.

4 When the ribosome reaches the end of the messenger RNA strand, a codon instructs it to release the completed protein.

Completed protein

FIGURE 2.19 Gene expression. Transcription of a section of DNA into a complementary strand of messenger RNA is followed by the translation of the messenger RNA strand into a protein.

chromosomes. This ambitious task was completed in 2001 with the simultaneous publication of the first draft of the human genome in *Nature* and *Science*, two of the most respected scientific journals.

Perhaps the most surprising attribute of the human genome is the relatively small number of genes it includes—only a fraction of the bases in the human genome are components of classic protein-coding genes.

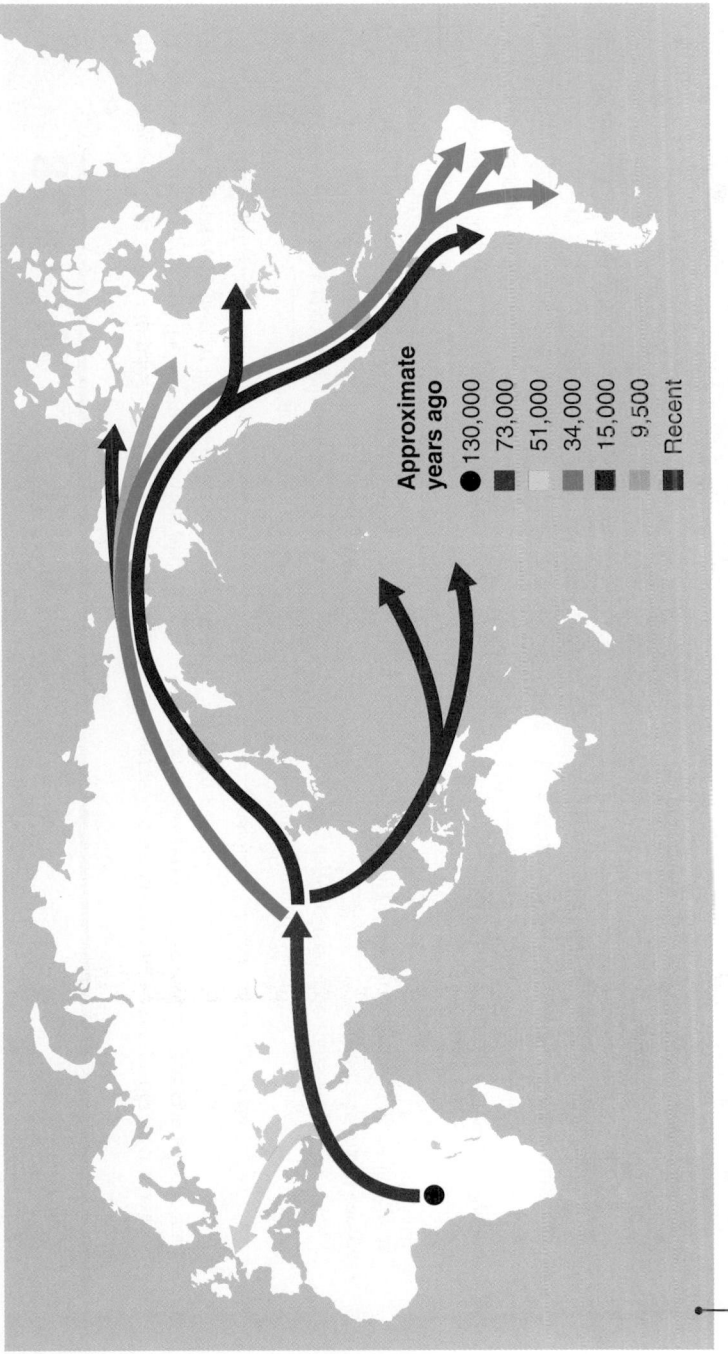

FIGURE 2.20 The analysis of mitochondrial DNA indicates that hominids evolved in Africa and spread over the earth in a series of migrations. (Adapted from Wallace, 1997.)

Approximate
years ago
● 130,000
73,000
51,000
34,000
15,000
9,500
Recent

Current estimates of the total number of these classic genes tend to range around 34,000, only about half again as many as in the mouse genome and only three times as many as in the fruit fly genome. The function of the many bases that are not involved in protein synthesis remains a mystery.

The relatively small number of human genes indicates that human complexity is the product of a relatively small number of genetic changes and that biological complexity evolves more through refinements in gene expression than through increases in gene number (Claverie, 2001). This will provide us with a whole new set of biological puzzles and philosophical issues (Pääbo, 2001).

Many people overestimate the degree to which deciphering the human genome will contribute to the understanding of human development. It is a major step, but it still leaves us a great distance from the ultimate goal: understanding genetic contributions to human behavior, in all its complexity and variety.

So, now that a draft of the human genome exists, what's next? Genome research is currently focusing on five important lines of inquiry (see Plomin & McGuffin,

2003). First, efforts are being made to characterize the genomes of more species; this research is progressing rapidly, and it will provide a comparative context for interpreting the human findings. Second, previous research has focused on parts of the human genome that are common to all humans; now, the focus is switching to the many variations among humans. Third, differences in patterns of gene expression in different parts of the human body are being characterized. Fourth, the protein encoded by each human gene is being identified. And fifth, the function of each gene-encoded protein is being investigated.

Although the achievement of these five objectives will be an amazing accomplishment, their attainment will still leave the ultimate goal in the distance. To understand how genes influence human behavioral development will require an understanding of how the products of many genes interact with one another and with experience—thinking that each behavioral attribute is controlled by a single dedicated gene is a big, but common, mistake (see Kosik, 2003). A few years ago, I would have asserted that attaining such understanding is impossible, but now, after identification of the human genome, I am not so sure. What do you think?

Thinking
Critically

Thinking
Critically

SCAN YOUR BRAIN

This is a good place for you to pause to scan your brain to see if you are ready to proceed. Fill in the following blanks with the most appropriate terms from the first three sections of the chapter. The correct answers are provided at the bottom of the page. Before proceeding, review material related to your errors and omissions.

1. The _____ side of the nature–nurture controversy is that all behavior is learned.

2. Physiological-or-psychological thinking was given official recognition in the 17th century when the Roman Church sanctioned _____.

3. In the Darwinian sense, _____ refers to the ability of an organism to survive and produce large numbers of fertile offspring.

4. A _____ is a group of reproductively isolated organisms.

5. Mammals are thought to have evolved from _____ about 180 million years ago.

6. There are five different families of primates: prosimians, New-World monkeys, Old-World monkeys, _____, and _____.

7. _____ are the closest living relatives of humans; they have about 99% of the same genetic material.

8. The first hominids were _____.

9. An organism's observable traits are its _____; the traits that it can pass to its offspring through its genetic material are its _____.

10. The degree of _____ between two genes is a measure of how close they are together on a chromosome.

11. Each structural gene contains the information for the production of a single _____.

12. Structural genes can be turned off or on by _____ genes.

13. The massive international research effort to physically map human chromosomes was the _____ project.

Scan Your Brain answers: (1) nurture, (2) Cartesian dualism, (3) fitness, (4) species, (5) reptiles, (6) apes, hominins, (7) Chimpanzees, (8) Australopithecines, (9) phenotype, (10) linkage, (11) protein, (12) operator, (13) human genome.

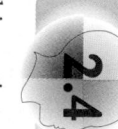

2.4   Behavioral Development: The Interaction of Genetic Factors and Experience

This section of the chapter provides three classic examples of how genetic factors and experience interact to direct behavioral ontogeny. **Ontogeny** is the development of individuals over their life span; **phylogeny**, in contrast, is the evolutionary development of species through the ages. These three examples have been particularly influential in shaping modern views of behavioral ontogenetic development. In each example, you will see that this development is a product of gene–experience interaction.

Selective Breeding of "Maze-Bright" and "Maze-Dull" Rats

You have already learned in this chapter that most early psychologists assumed that behavior develops largely through learning. Tryon (1934) undermined this assumption by showing that behavioral traits can be selectively bred.

Tryon focused his selective-breeding experiments on the behavior that had been the focus of early psychologists in their investigations of learning: the maze running of laboratory rats. Tryon began by training a large heterogeneous group of laboratory rats to run a complex maze; the rats received a food reward when they reached the goal box. Tryon then mated the females and males that least frequently entered incorrect alleys during training—he referred to these rats as *maze-bright*. And he bred the females and males that most frequently entered incorrect alleys during training—he referred to these rats as *maze-dull*.

When the offspring of both the maze-bright and the maze-dull rats matured, their maze-learning performance was assessed. Then, the brightest of the maze-bright offspring were mated with one another and so were the dullest of the maze-dull offspring. This selective breeding procedure was continued for 21 generations (and the descendants of Tryon's original strains are

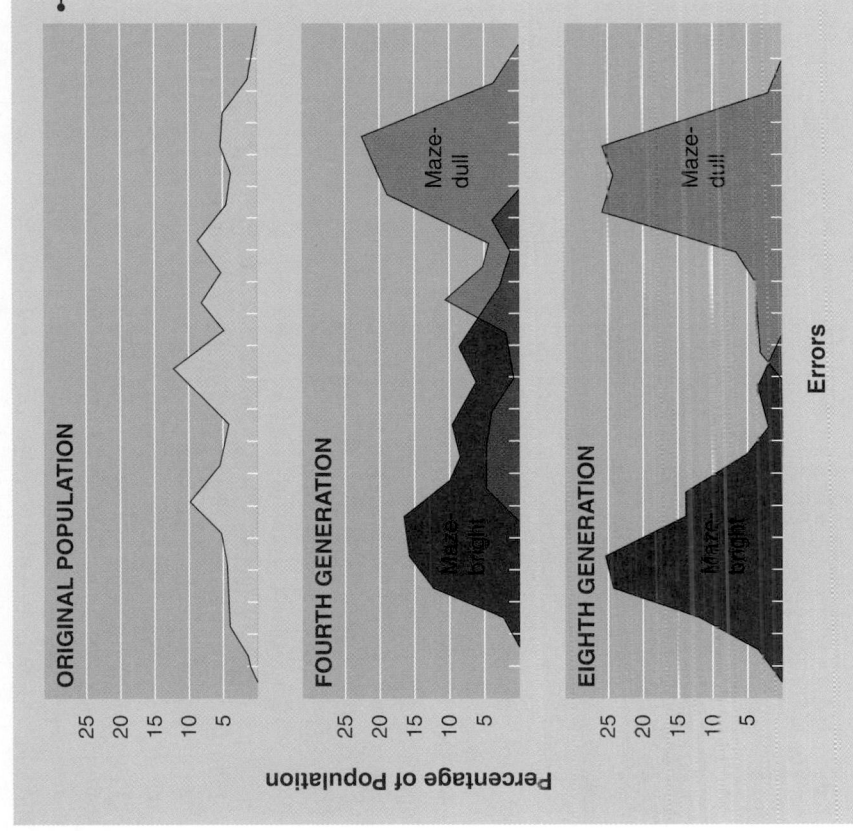

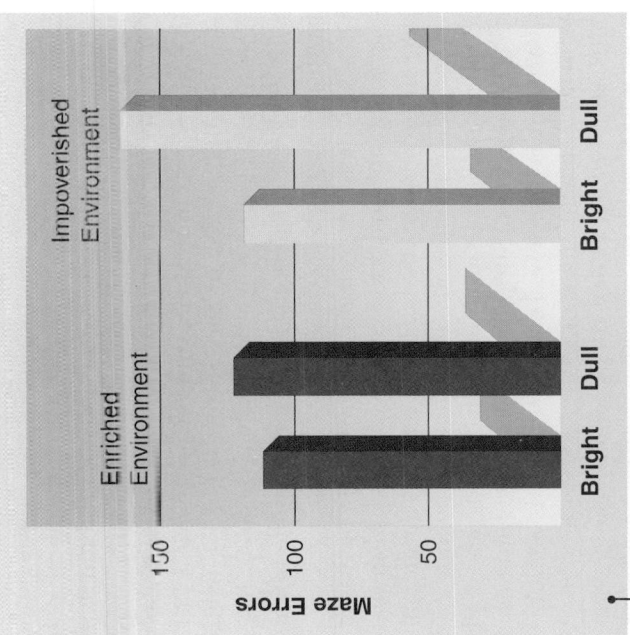

FIGURE 2.22   Maze-dull rats did not make significantly more errors than maze-bright rats when both groups were reared in an enriched environment. (Adapted from Cooper & Zubek, 1958.)

of differences suggested that the maze-bright rats were superior maze learners not because they were more intelligent but because they were less emotional.

Selective-breeding studies have proved that genes influence the development of behavior. This conclusion in no way implies that experience does not. This point was driven home by Cooper and Zubek (1958) in a classic study of maze-bright and maze-dull rats. The researchers reared maze-bright and maze-dull rats in one of two environments: (1) an impoverished environment (a barren wire-mesh group cage) or (2) an enriched environment (a wire-mesh group cage that contained tunnels, ramps, visual displays, and other objects designed to stimulate interest). When the maze-dull rats reached maturity, they made significantly more errors than the maze-bright rats only if they had been reared in the impoverished environment (see Figure 2.22). Apparently,

still available today). By the eighth generation, there was almost no overlap in the maze-learning performance of the two strains. With a few exceptions, the worst of the maze-bright strain made fewer errors than the best of the maze-dull strain (see Figure 2.21).

To control for the possibility that good maze-running performance was somehow being passed from parent to offspring through learning, Tryon used a *cross-fostering control procedure:* He tested maze-bright offspring that had been reared by maze-dull parents and maze-dull offspring that had been reared by maze-bright parents. However, the offspring of maze-bright rats made few errors even when they were reared by maze-dull rats, and the offspring of maze-dull rats made many errors even when they were reared by maze-bright rats.

Since Tryon's seminal selective-breeding experiments, many behavioral traits have been selectively bred. Indeed, it appears that any measurable behavioral trait that varies among members of a species can be selectively bred.

An important general point made by studies of selective breeding is that selective breeding based on one behavioral trait usually brings a host of other behavioral traits along with it. This indicates that the behavioral trait used as the criterion for selective breeding is not the only behavioral trait that is influenced by the genes segregated by the breeding. Indeed, Searle (1949) compared maze-dull and maze-bright rats on 30 different behavioral tests and found that they differed on many of them; the pattern

enriched early environments can overcome the negative effects of disadvantaged genes. Indeed, rats reared in enriched environments develop thicker cerebral cortexes than those reared in impoverished environments (Bennett et al., 1964); these experience-induced differences in cortical development appear to be mediated by changes in gene expression (Rampon et al., 2000).

Phenylketonuria: A Single-Gene Metabolic Disorder

It is often easier to understand the genetics of a behavioral disorder than it is to understand the genetics of normal behavior. The reason is that many genes influence the development of a normal behavioral trait, but it often takes only one abnormal gene to screw it up. A good example of this point is the neurological disorder **phenylketonuria (PKU)**.

Clinical Implications

PKU was discovered in 1934 when a Norwegian dentist, Asbjörn Fölling, noticed a peculiar odor in the urine of his two mentally retarded children. He correctly assumed that the odor was related to their disorder, and he had their urine analyzed. High levels of **phenylpyruvic acid** were found in both samples. Spurred on by his discovery, Fölling identified other retarded children who had abnormally high levels of urinary phenylpyruvic acid, and he concluded that this subpopulation of retarded children was suffering from the same disorder. In addition to mental retardation, the symptoms of PKU include vomiting, seizures, hyperactivity, hyperirritability, and brain damage (Antshel & Waisbren, 2003; Sener, 2003).

The pattern of transmission of PKU through the family trees of afflicted individuals indicates that it is transmitted by a single gene mutation. About 1 in 100 people of European descent carry the PKU gene; but because the gene is recessive, PKU develops only in homozygous individuals (those who inherit a PKU gene from both their mother and their father). In the United States, about 1 in 10,000 white infants is born with PKU; the incidence is much lower among infants of African heritage.

The biochemistry of PKU turned out to be reasonably straightforward. PKU homozygotes lack *phenylalanine hydroxylase*, an enzyme that is required for the conversion of the amino acid *phenylalanine* to *tyrosine*. As a result, phenylalanine accumulates in the body; and levels of *dopamine*, a neurotransmitter normally synthesized from tyrosine, are low. The consequence is abnormal brain development.

Like other behavioral traits, the behavioral symptoms of PKU result from an interaction between genetic and environmental factors: between the PKU gene and diet. Accordingly, in most modern hospitals, the blood of each newborn infant is routinely screened for a high phenylalanine level (Saxena, 2003; Wall et al., 2003). If the level is high, the infant is immediately placed on a special phenylalanine-restricted diet; this diet reduces both the amount of phenylalanine in the blood and the development of mental retardation—however, it does not prevent the development of subtle cognitive deficits (Huijbregts et al., 2002). The timing of this treatment is extremely important. The phenylalanine-restricted diet does not significantly reduce the development of mental retardation in PKU homozygotes unless it is initiated within the first few weeks of life; conversely, the restriction of phenylalanine in the diet is usually relaxed in late childhood, with few obvious adverse consequences. The period, usually early in life, during which a particular experience must occur to have a major effect on the development of a trait is the **sensitive period** for that trait.

Development of Birdsong

In the spring, the songs of male songbirds threaten conspecific male trespassers and attract potential mates (Mennill, Ratcliffe, & Boag, 2002). The males of each species sing similar songs that are readily distinguishable from the songs of other species, and there are recognizable local dialects within each species (see Ball & Hulse, 1998).

Studies of the ontogenetic development of birdsong suggest that this behavior develops in two phases (see Mooney, 1999). The first phase, called the **sensory phase**, begins several days after hatching. Although the young birds do not sing during this phase, they form memories of the adult songs they hear—usually sung by their own male relatives—that later guide the development of their own singing. The young males of many songbird species are genetically prepared to acquire the songs of their own species during the sensory phase. They cannot readily acquire the songs of other species; nor can they acquire the songs of their own species if they do not hear them during the sensory phase. Males who do not hear the songs of their own species early in their lives may later develop a song, but it is likely to be highly abnormal with only a few recognizable features of their species' mature songs.

The second phase of birdsong development, the **sensorimotor phase**, begins when the juvenile males begin to twitter *subsongs* (the immature songs of young birds), usually when they are several months old. During this phase, the rambling vocalizations of subsongs are gradually refined until they resemble the songs of the birds' earlier adult tutors. Auditory feedback is necessary for the development of singing during the sensorimotor phase; unless the young birds are able to hear themselves sing, their subsongs do not develop into adult songs (Troyer & Bottjer, 2001). However, once stable adult song has crystallized, songbirds are much less dependent

Shackleton & Ball, 1999). Third, each spring, as the male canary prepares its new repertoire of songs for the summer seduction, the song-control structures of its brain double in size, only to shrink back in the fall; this springtime burst of brain growth and singing is triggered by elevated levels of the hormone testosterone that result from the increasing daylight (Tramontin & Brenowitz, 2000). Fourth, the seasonal increase in size of the song-control brain structures results from the growth of new neurons, not from an increase in the size of existing ones (Tramontin, Hartman, & Brenowitz, 2000)—this finding was one of the first documented examples of adult *neurogenesis* (growth of new neurons).

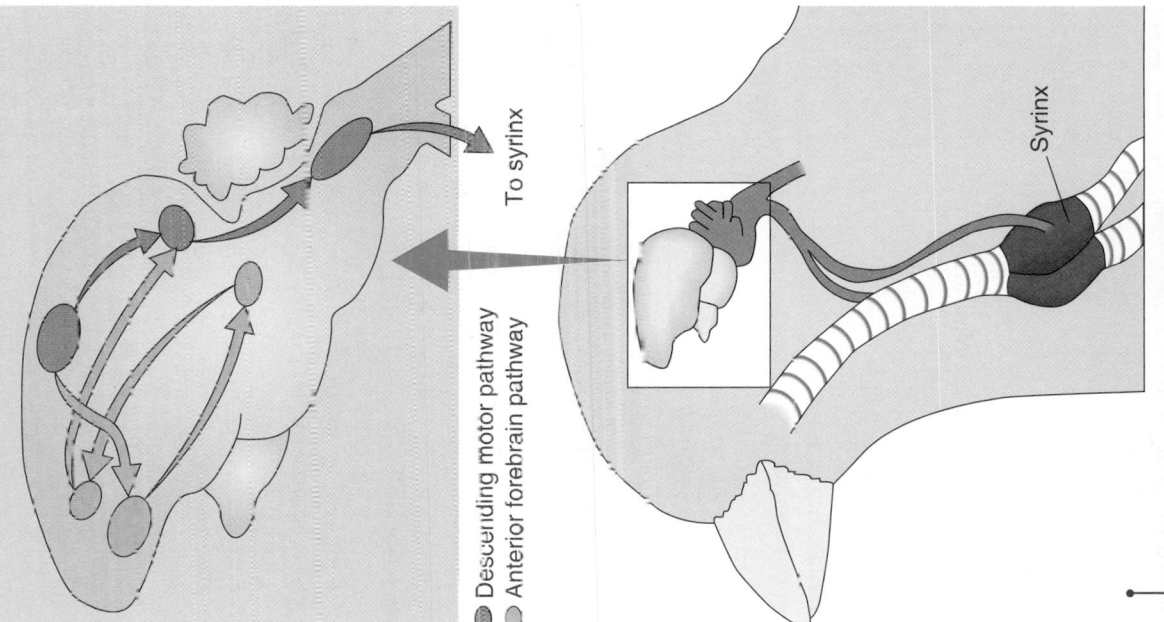

To syrinx

● Descending motor pathway
● Anterior forebrain pathway

Syrinx

FIGURE 2.24 The neural pathway responsible for the production and learning of song in the male canary.

FIGURE 2.23 Male zebra finches (age-limited song learners) and male canaries (open-ended song learners) are common subjects of research on birdsong development. (Illustration kindly provided by *Trends in Neuroscience*; original photograph by Arturo Alvarez-Buylla.)

on hearing for normal song production; the disruptive effects of deafening on adult song are usually less severe, and they require several months to be fully realized (Lombardino & Nottebohm, 2000).

When it comes to the retention of their initial crystallized adult songs, there are two common patterns among songbird species. Most songbird species, such as the widely studied zebra finches and white-crowned sparrows, are *age-limited learners*; in these species, adult songs, once crystallized, remain unchanged for the rest of the birds' lives. In contrast, some species are *open-ended learners*; they are able to add new songs to their repertoire throughout their lives. For example, at the end of each mating season, male canaries return from a period of stable song to a period of plastic song—a period during which they can add new songs for the next mating season. Male zebra finches (age-limited learners) and male canaries (open-ended learners) are shown in Figure 2.23.

Figure 2.24 is a simplified version of the neural circuit that controls birdsong in the canary. It has two major components: the descending motor pathway and the anterior forebrain pathway. The *descending motor pathway* descends from the high vocal center on each side of the brain to the syrinx (voice box) on the same side; it mediates song production. The *anterior forebrain pathway* mediates song learning (Doupe, 1993; Vicario, 1991).

The canary song circuit is remarkable in four respects (see Mooney, 1999). First, the left descending motor pathway plays a more important role in singing than the right descending motor pathway (which duplicates the left-hemisphere dominance for language in humans). Second, the high vocal center is four times larger in male canaries than in females (see MacDougall-

This chapter has focused on three topics—human evolution, genetics, and the interaction of genetics and experience in the ontological development of psychological traits. All three topics converge on one fundamental question: Why are we the way we are? You have learned that each of us is a product of gene–experience interactions and that the effects of genes and experience on individual development are inseparable—remember the metaphor of the musical mountaineer and the panpipe. In view of the fact that I have emphasized these points at every opportunity throughout the chapter, I am certain that you appreciate them by now. However, I am raising them one last time because this final section of the chapter focuses on a developmental issue that is fundamentally different from the ones that we have been discussing.

Thinking Critically

Development of Individuals versus Development of Differences among Individuals

So far, this chapter has dealt with the development of individuals. The remainder of the chapter deals with the development of differences among individuals. In the development of the individual, the effects of genes and experience are inseparable. In the development of differences among individuals, they are separable. This distinction is extremely important, but it confuses many people. Let me return to the mountaineer-and-panpipe metaphor to explain it.

The music of an individual panpipe player is the product of the interaction of the musician and the panpipe, and it is nonsensical to ask what proportion of the music is produced by the musician and what proportion by the panpipe. However, if we measured the panpipe playing of a large sample of subjects, we could statistically estimate the degree to which the differences among them in the quality of their music resulted from differences in the subjects themselves as opposed to differences in their instruments. For example, if we selected 100 Peruvians at random and gave each a test on a professional-quality panpipe, we would likely find that most of the variation in the quality of the music resulted from differences in the subjects, some being experienced players and some never having played before. In the same way, researchers can select a group of subjects and ask what proportion of the variation among them in some attribute (e.g., intelligence) results from genetic differences as opposed to experiential differences.

To assess the relative contributions of genes and experience to the development of differences in psychological attributes, behavioral geneticists study individuals of known genetic similarity. For example, they often compare **identical twins** (monozygotic twins), who developed from the same zygote and thus are genetically identical, with **fraternal twins** (dizygotic twins), who developed from two zygotes and thus are no more similar than any pair of siblings. Studies of pairs of identical and fraternal twins who have been separated at infancy by adoption are particularly informative about differences in human psychological development. The most extensive of such studies is the Minnesota Study of Twins Reared Apart (see Bouchard & Pedersen, 1998).

Minnesota Study of Twins Reared Apart

The Minnesota Study of Twins Reared Apart involved 59 pairs of identical twins and 47 pairs of fraternal twins who had been reared apart, as well as many pairs of identical and fraternal twins who had been reared together. Their ages ranged from 19 to 68 years. Each twin was brought to the University of Minnesota for approximately 50 hours of testing, which focused on the assessment of intelligence and personality. Would the adult identical twins reared apart prove to be similar because they were genetically identical, or would they prove to be different because they had been brought up in different family environments?

The results of the Minnesota Study of Twins Reared Apart proved to be remarkably consistent—both internally, between the various cognitive and personality dimensions that were studied, and externally, with the findings of other, similar studies. In general, adult identical twins were substantially more similar to one another on all psychological dimensions than were adult fraternal twins, whether or not both twins of a pair were raised in the same family environment (see Turkheimer, 2000). General intelligence (as measured by the Wechsler Adult Intelligence Scale) has been the most widely studied psychological attribute of twins; Figure 2.25 illustrates the general pattern of findings (see Bouchard, 1998).

The results of the Minnesota study have been widely disseminated by the popular press. Unfortunately, the meaning of the results has often been distorted. Sometimes, the misrepresentation of science by the popular press does not matter—at least not much. This is not one of those times. People's misbeliefs about the origins of human intelligence and personality are often translated into inappropriate and discriminatory social attitudes and practices. The following newspaper story illustrates how the results of the Minnesota study have been misrepresented to the public.

ON THE CD

Visit the *Twin Studies* module to learn about twin research.

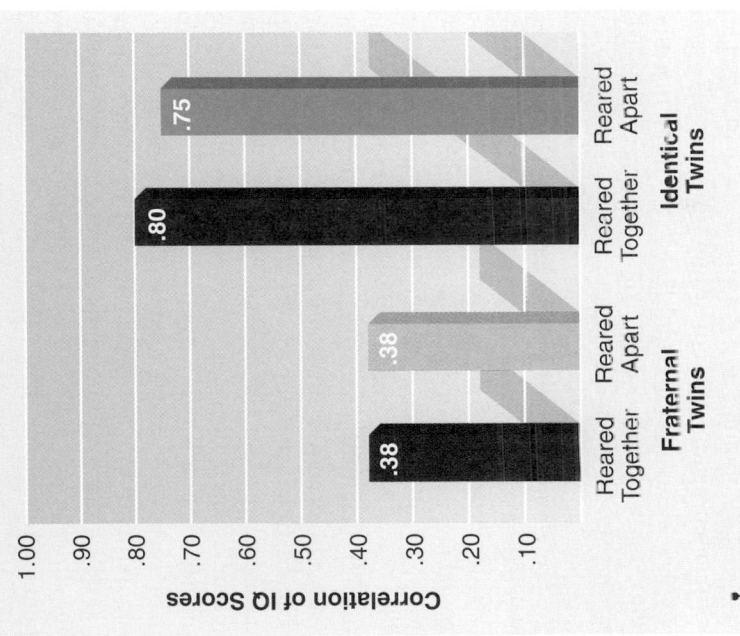

FIGURE 2.25 The correlations of the intelligence quotients (IQs) of identical and fraternal twins, reared together or apart.

any two people if one asks them enough questions and ignores the dissimilarities. Third, the story creates the impression that the results of the Minnesota study are revolutionary. On the contrary, the importance of the Minnesota study lies mainly in the fact that it constitutes a particularly thorough confirmation of the results of previous adoption studies. Fourth, and most important, the story creates the false impression that the results of the Minnesota study make some general point about the relative contributions of genes and experience to the development of intelligence and personality in individuals. They do not, and neither do the results of any other adoption study. True, Bouchard and his colleagues estimated the heritability of IQ to be .70, but they did not conclude that IQ is 70% genetic. A **heritability estimate** is not about individual development; it is a numerical estimate of the proportion of variability that occurred in a particular trait in a particular study as a result of the genetic variation in that study (see Plomin & DeFries, 1998). Thus, heritability estimates tell us about the contribution of genetic differences to phenotypic differences among subjects; they have nothing to say about the relative contributions of genes and experience to the development of individuals.

The concept of heritability estimates can be quite confusing. I suggest that you pause here and carefully think through the definition. The panpipe metaphor will help.

Thinking Critically

This story is misleading in four ways. You should have no difficulty spotting the first: it oozes nature-or-nurture thinking and all of the misconceptions associated with it. Second, by focusing on the similarities of Bob and Bob, the story creates the impression that Bob and Bob (and the other monozygotic pairs of twins reared apart) are cognitively identical. They are not. It is easy to come up with a long list of similarities between

The magnitude of a study's heritability estimate depends on the amount of genetic and environmental variation from which it was calculated, and it cannot be applied to other kinds of situations. For example, in the Minnesota study, there was relatively little environmental variation. All subjects were raised in industrialized countries (e.g., Great Britain, Canada, and the United States) by parents who could meet the strict standards required for adoption. Accordingly, most of the variation in the subjects' intelligence and personality resulted from genetic variation. If the twins had been separately adopted by European royalty, African Bushmen, Hungarian Gypsies, Los Angeles rap stars, London advertising executives, and Argentinian army officers, the resulting heritability estimates for IQ and personality would likely have been lower. Bouchard and his colleagues emphasize this point in their papers. Still, selective-breeding studies in laboratory animals and twin studies in humans have revealed no psychological differences that do not have a significant genetic component—even in twins over 80 years old (Dick & Rose, 2002; McGuffin, Riley, & Plomin, 2001). Indeed, between childhood and adolescence, adopted children grow more and more similar to their biological parents in cognitive ability (Plomin et al., 1997).

A commonly overlooked point about the role of genetic factors in the development of human psychological differences is that genetic differences promote

psychological differences by influencing experience (see Plomin & Neiderhiser, 1992). At first, this statement seems paradoxical because we have been conditioned to think of genes and experience as separate developmental influences. However, there is now ample evidence that individuals of similar genetic endowment tend to seek out similar environments and experiences. For example, individuals whose genetic endowments promote aggression are likely to become involved in aggressive activities (e.g., football or competitive fighting), and these experiences are likely to further contribute to the development of aggressive tendencies.

Before I finish this chapter, I have one more study to tell you about, one by Turkheimer and colleagues (2003). I hope that you take some time to ponder its implications. Its findings challenge fuzzy thinking about the meaning of heritability estimates in such a simple and compelling way that considering them is certain to sharpen your own understanding. Turkheimer and colleagues studied the heritability of IQ in a sample of 7-year-old twins. Unlike the other studies that you have encountered in this chapter, this study focused on the heritability of IQ as a function of socioeconomic status. Remarkably, among the very poor twins in the sample, the heritability estimate for IQ was close to 0, whereas among the affluent twins, it was close to 1.00. What do you make of these findings and of their implications for social policy?

Themes Revisited

This chapter introduced the topics of evolution, genetics, and development, but its unifying focus was thinking clearly about the biology of behavior. Not surprisingly, then, of this book's four major themes, the thinking-about-biopsychology theme received the most atten-

tion. This chapter singled out several biopsychological issues about which there tends to be a lot of fuzzy think-

ing and tried to convince you that there are better ways to think about them. Thinking-about-biopsychology tabs marked points in the chapter where you were encouraged to sharpen up your thinking about the physiological-or-psychological dichotomy, the nature–nurture issue, human evolution, the biopsychological implications of the human genome project, and the genetics of human psychological differences.

Two of this book's other themes also received coverage in this chapter and were marked by the appropriate tabs. The evolutionary perspective was illustrated by comparative research on self-awareness in chimps, by efforts to understand human mate bonding, and by the use of mitochondrial DNA to study human evolution. The clinical implications theme was illustrated by the case of the man who fell out of bed and the discussion of phenylketonuria (PKU).

Think about It

for some genetic diseases. But what constitutes a disease? Should genetic testing be used to select a child's characteristics? If so, what characteristics?

1. Nature-or-nurture thinking about intelligence is sometimes used as an excuse for racial discrimination. How can the interactionist approach, which is championed in this chapter, be used as a basis for arguing against discriminatory practices?

4. In the year 2030, a major company demands that all prospective executives take a gene test. As a result, some lose their jobs, and others fail to qualify for health insurance. Discuss.

2. Imagine that you are a biopsychology instructor. One of your students asks you whether depression is physiological or psychological. What would you say?

5. "All men are created equal." Discuss.

3. Modern genetics can prevent the tragedy of a life doomed by heredity; embryos can now be screened

Key Terms

Alleles (p. 34)
Amino acids (p. 38)
Amphibians (p. 27)
Analogous (p. 31)
Asomatognosia (p. 21)
Brain stem (p. 31)
Cartesian dualism (p. 20)
Cerebrum (p. 31)
Chordates (p. 27)
Chromosomes (p. 34)
Codon (p. 39)
Conspecifics (p. 27)
Convergent evolution (p. 31)
Convolutions (p. 31)
Crossing over (p. 37)
Deoxyribonucleic acid (DNA) (p. 37)
Dichotomous traits (p. 34)
DNA-binding proteins (p. 38)
Dominant trait (p. 34)
Ethology (p. 20)
Evolve (p. 24)

Exaptation (p. 31)
Fitness (p. 25)
Fraternal twins (p. 46)
Gametes (p. 35)
Gene (p. 34)
Gene expression (p. 38)
Gene maps (p. 37)
Genotype (p. 34)
Heritability estimate (p. 47)
Heterozygous (p. 34)
Hominids (p. 27)
Homologous (p. 31)
Homozygous (p. 34)
Human genome project (p. 39)
Identical twins (p. 46)
Instinctive behaviors (p. 21)
Linkage (p. 36)
Mammals (p. 27)
Meiosis (p. 35)
Messenger RNA (p. 39)
Mitochondria (p. 39)
Mitosis (p. 35)

Monogamy (p. 33)
Mutations (p. 38)
Natural selection (p. 25)
Nature–nurture issue (p. 20)
Nucleotide bases (p. 37)
Ontogeny (p. 42)
Operator genes (p. 38)
Phenotype (p. 34)
Phenylketonuria (PKU) (p. 44)
Phenylpyruvic acid (p. 44)
Phylogeny (p. 42)
Polyandry (p. 33)
Polygyny (p. 32)
Primates (p. 27)
Proteins (p. 38)
Recessive trait (p. 34)
Replication (p. 38)
Ribonucleic acid (RNA) (p. 38)
Ribosomes (p. 39)
Sensitive period (p. 44)
Sensorimotor phase (p. 44)
Sensory phase (p. 44)

Sex chromosomes (p. 37)
Sex-linked traits (p. 37)
Spandrels (p. 31)
Species (p. 26)
Structural genes (p. 38)
Transfer RNA (p. 39)
True-breeding lines (p. 34)
Vertebrates (p. 27)
Zeitgeist (p. 20)
Zygote (p. 35)

The Anatomy of the Nervous System

The Systems, Structures, and Cells That Make Up Your Nervous System

chapter

3

3.1 General Layout of the Nervous System

3.2 Cells of the Nervous System

3.3 Neuroanatomical Techniques and Directions

3.4 The Spinal Cord

3.5 The Five Major Divisions of the Brain

3.6 Major Structures of the Brain

n order to understand what the brain does, it is first necessary to understand what it is—to know the names and locations of its major parts and how they are connected to one another. This chapter introduces you to these fundamentals of brain anatomy.

Before you begin this chapter, I want to apologize for the lack of foresight displayed by early neuroanatomists in their choice of names for neuroanatomical structures—but, then, how could they have anticipated that Latin and Greek, universal languages of the educated in their day, would not be compulsory university fare in our time? To help you, I have provided the literal English meanings of many of the neuroanatomical terms, and I have kept this chapter as brief and to the point as possible by covering only the most important structures. Still, there is no denying that learning their names and locations will require considerable effort.

3.1 General Layout of the Nervous System

Divisions of the Nervous System

The vertebrate nervous system is composed of two divisions: the central nervous system and the peripheral nervous system (see Figure 3.1). Roughly speaking, the **central nervous system (CNS)** is the division of the nervous system that is located within the skull and spine; the **peripheral nervous system (PNS)** is the division that is located outside the skull and spine.

The central nervous system is composed of two divisions: the brain and the spinal cord. The *brain* is the part of the CNS that is located in the skull; the *spinal cord* is the part that is located in the spine.

The peripheral nervous system is also composed of two divisions: the somatic nervous system and the autonomic nervous system. The **somatic nervous system (SNS)** is the part of the PNS that interacts with the external environment. It is composed of **afferent nerves** that carry sensory signals from the skin, skeletal muscles, joints, eyes, ears, and so on, to the central nervous system, and **efferent nerves** that carry motor signals from the central nervous system to the skeletal muscles. The **autonomic nervous system (ANS)** is the part of the peripheral nervous system that regulates the body's internal environment. It is composed of afferent nerves that carry sensory signals from internal organs to the CNS and efferent nerves that carry motor signals from the CNS to internal organs. You will not confuse the terms *afferent* and *efferent* if you remember that many words that involve the idea of going toward something—in this case, going toward the CNS—begin with an *a* (e.g., advance, approach, arrive) and that many words that involve the idea of going away from something begin with an *e* (e.g., exit, embark, escape).

The autonomic nervous system has two kinds of efferent nerves: sympathetic nerves and parasympathetic nerves. The **sympathetic nerves** are those autonomic motor nerves that project from the CNS in the *lumbar* (small of the back) and *thoracic* (chest area) regions of the spinal cord. The **parasympathetic nerves** are those autonomic motor nerves that project from the brain and *sacral* (lower back) region of the spinal cord. See Appendix I. (Ask your instructor to specify the degree to which

ON THE CD

You can review the differences between the efferent branches of the somatic and autonomic divisions of the PNS in the module titled *The Nervous System.* In particular, note the different transmitters used by the two divisions.

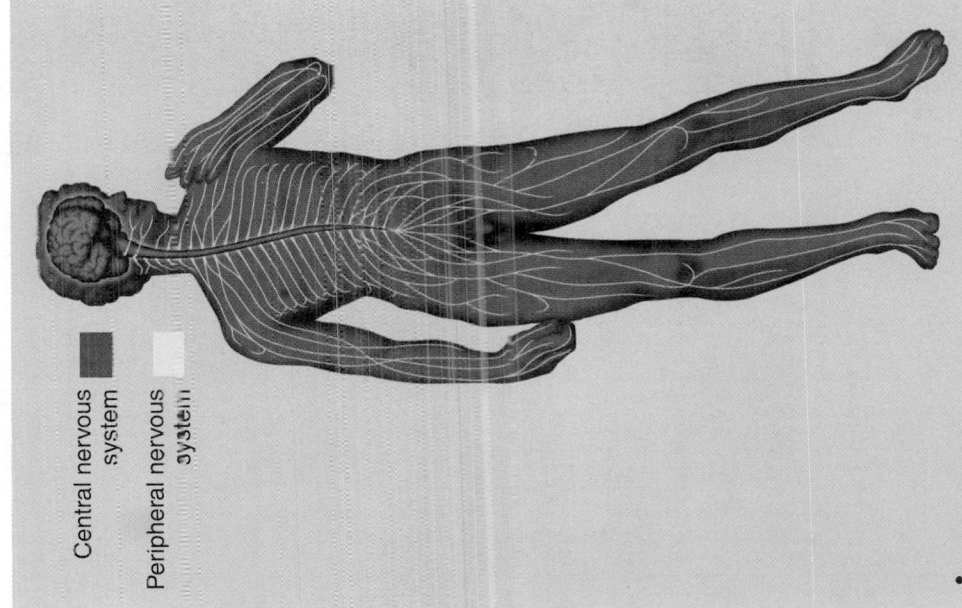

Central nervous system

Peripheral nervous system

FIGURE 3.1 The human central nervous system (CNS) and peripheral nervous system (PNS). The CNS is represented in red; the PNS in yellow. Notice that even those portions of nerves that are within the spinal cord are considered to be part of the PNS.

you are responsible for material in the appendices.) All sympathetic and parasympathetic nerves are two-stage neural paths: The sympathetic and parasympathetic neurons project from the CNS and go only part of the way to the target organs before they *synapse* on other neurons (second-stage neurons) that carry the signals the rest of the way. However, the sympathetic and parasympathetic systems differ in that the sympathetic neurons that project from the CNS synapse on second-stage neurons at a substantial distance from their target organs, whereas the parasympathetic neurons that project from the CNS synapse near their target organs on very short second-stage neurons (see Appendix I).

The conventional view of the respective functions of the sympathetic and parasympathetic systems stresses three important principles: (1) that sympathetic nerves stimulate, organize, and mobilize energy resources in threatening situations, whereas parasympathetic nerves act to conserve energy; (2) that each autonomic target organ receives opposing sympathetic and parasympathetic input, and its activity is thus controlled by relative levels of sympathetic and parasympathetic activity; and (3) that sympathetic changes are indicative of psychological arousal, whereas parasympathetic changes are indicative of psychological relaxation. Although these principles are gener-

ally correct, there are significant exceptions to each of them (see Blessing, 1997; Hugdahl, 1996)—see Appendix II.

Most of the nerves of the peripheral nervous system project from the spinal cord, but there are 12 pairs of exceptions: the 12 pairs of **cranial nerves,** which project from the brain. They are numbered in sequence from front to back. The cranial nerves include purely sensory nerves such as the olfactory nerves (I) and the optic nerves (II), but most contain both sensory and motor fibers. The longest cranial nerves are the vagus nerves (X), which contain motor and sensory fibers traveling to and from the gut. The 12 pairs of cranial nerves and their targets are illustrated in Appendix III; the functions of these nerves are listed in Appendix IV. The autonomic motor fibers of the cranial nerves are parasympathetic.

The functions of the various cranial nerves are commonly assessed by neurologists as a basis for diagnosis. Because the functions and locations of the cranial nerves are specific, disruptions of particular cranial nerve functions provide excellent clues about the location and extent of tumors and other kinds of brain pathology.

Figure 3.2 summarizes the major divisions of the nervous system. Notice that the nervous system is a "system of twos."

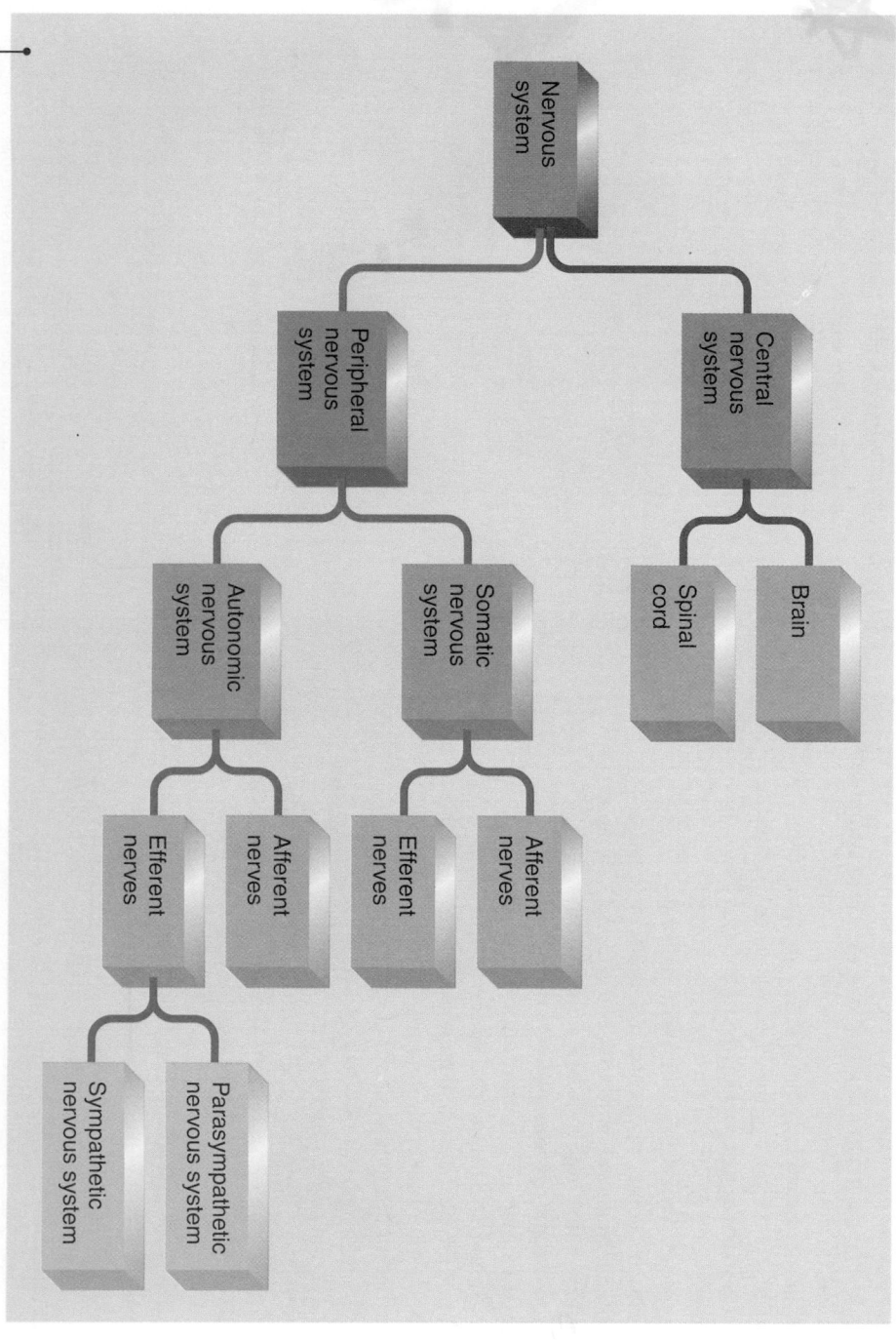

FIGURE 3.2   The major divisions of the nervous system.

Meninges, Ventricles, and Cerebrospinal Fluid

The brain and spinal cord (the CNS) are the most protected organs in the body. They are encased in bone and covered by three protective membranes, the three **meninges** (pronounced "men-IN-gees"). The outer *meninx* (which, believe it or not, is the singular of *meninges*) is a tough membrane called the **dura mater** (tough mother). Immediately inside the dura mater is the fine **arachnoid membrane** (spiderweblike membrane). Beneath the arachnoid membrane is a space called the **subarachnoid space,** which contains many large blood vessels and cerebrospinal fluid; then comes the innermost meninx, the delicate **pia mater** (pious mother), which adheres to the surface of the CNS.

Also protecting the CNS is the **cerebrospinal fluid (CSF),** which fills the subarachnoid space, the central canal of the spinal cord, and the cerebral ventricles of the brain. The **central canal** is a small central channel that runs the length of the spinal cord; the **cerebral ventricles** are the four large internal chambers of the brain: the two lateral ventricles, the third ventricle, and the fourth ventricle (see Figure 3.3). The subarachnoid space, central canal, and cerebral ventricles are interconnected by a series of openings and thus form a single reservoir.

The cerebrospinal fluid supports and cushions the brain. These functions are all too apparent to patients who have had some of their cerebrospinal fluid drained away; they suffer raging headaches and experience stabbing pain each time they jerk their heads.

Cerebrospinal fluid is continuously produced by the **choroid plexuses**—networks of capillaries (small blood vessels) that protrude into the ventricles from the pia mater lining. The excess cerebrospinal fluid is continuously absorbed from the subarachnoid space into large blood-filled spaces, or *dural sinuses,* which run through the dura mater and drain into the large jugular veins of the neck. Figure 3.4 on page 54 illustrates the absorption of cerebrospinal fluid from the subarachnoid space into the large sinus that runs along the top of the brain between the two cerebral hemispheres.

Occasionally, the flow of cerebrospinal fluid is blocked by a tumor near one of the narrow channels that link the ventricles—for example, near the *cerebral aqueduct,* which connects the third and fourth ventricles. The resulting buildup of fluid in the ventricles causes the walls of the ventricles, and thus the entire brain, to expand, producing a condition called *hydrocephalus* (water head). Hydrocephalus is treated by draining the excess fluid from the ventricles and trying to remove the obstruction.

Clinical Implications

Blood–Brain Barrier

The brain is a finely tuned electrochemical organ whose function can be severely disturbed by the introduction of certain kinds of chemicals. Fortunately, there is a mechanism that impedes the passage of many toxic substances from the blood into the brain: the **blood–brain barrier.** This barrier is a consequence of the special structure of cerebral blood vessels. In the rest of the

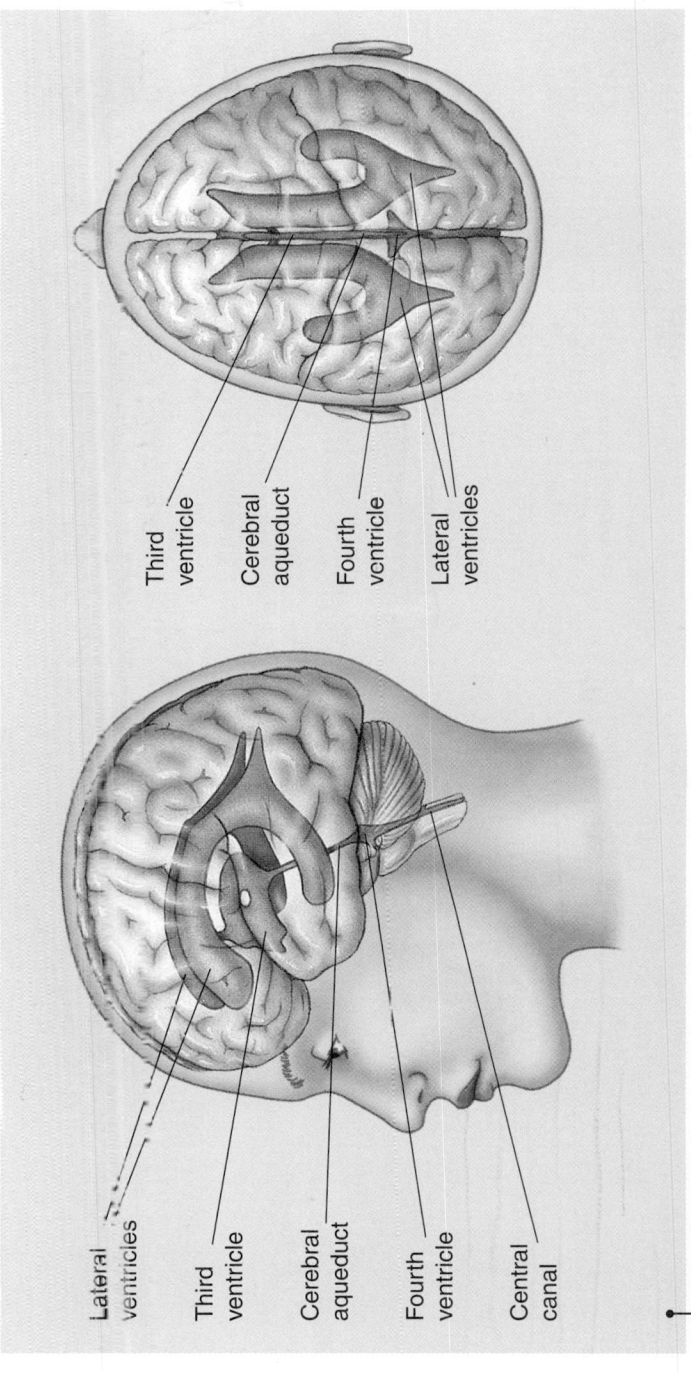

Lateral
ventricles

Third
ventricle

Cerebral
aqueduct

Fourth
ventricle

Central
canal

Third
ventricle

Cerebral
aqueduct

Fourth
ventricle

Lateral
ventricles

FIGURE 3.3   The cerebral ventricles.

3.2 Cells of the Nervous System

Most of the cells of the nervous system are of two fundamentally different types: neurons and glial cells. Their anatomy is discussed in the following two subsections.

Anatomy of Neurons

Neurons are cells that are specialized for the reception, conduction, and transmission of electrochemical signals. They come in an incredible variety of shapes and sizes (see Macaferri & Lacaille, 2003; Mott & Dingledine, 2003; Silberberg, Gupta, & Markram, 2002); however, many are similar to the one illustrated in Figures 3.5 and 3.6.

External Anatomy of Neurons   Figure 3.5 is an illustration of the major external features of one type of neuron.

ON THE CD

Want some help with the anatomy of neurons? Visit the *Learning the External Parts of a Neuron* module.

For your convenience, the definition of each feature is included in the illustration.

Internal Anatomy of Neurons   Figure 3.6 on page 56 is an illustration of the major internal features of one type of neuron. Again, the definition of each feature is included in the illustration.

Neuron Cell Membrane   The neuron cell membrane is composed of a *lipid bilayer*—two layers of fat molecules (see Figure 3.7 on page 57). Embedded in the lipid bilayer are numerous protein molecules that are the basis of many of the cell membrane's functional properties. Some membrane proteins are *channel proteins*, through which certain molecules can pass; others are *signal proteins*, which transfer a signal to the inside of the neuron when particular molecules bind to them on the outside of the membrane.

---

body, the cells that compose the walls of blood vessels are loosely packed; as a result, most molecules pass readily through them into surrounding tissue. In the brain, however, the cells of the blood vessel walls are tightly packed, thus forming a barrier to the passage of many molecules—particularly proteins and other large molecules. The degree to which psychoactive drugs influence psychological processes depends on the ease with which they penetrate the blood–brain barrier.

The blood–brain barrier does not impede the passage of all large molecules. Some large molecules that are critical for normal brain function (e.g., glucose) are actively transported through cerebral blood vessel walls. Also, the blood vessel walls in some areas of the brain allow certain large molecules to pass through them unimpeded; for example, sex hormones, which readily enter those parts of the brain involved in sexual behavior.

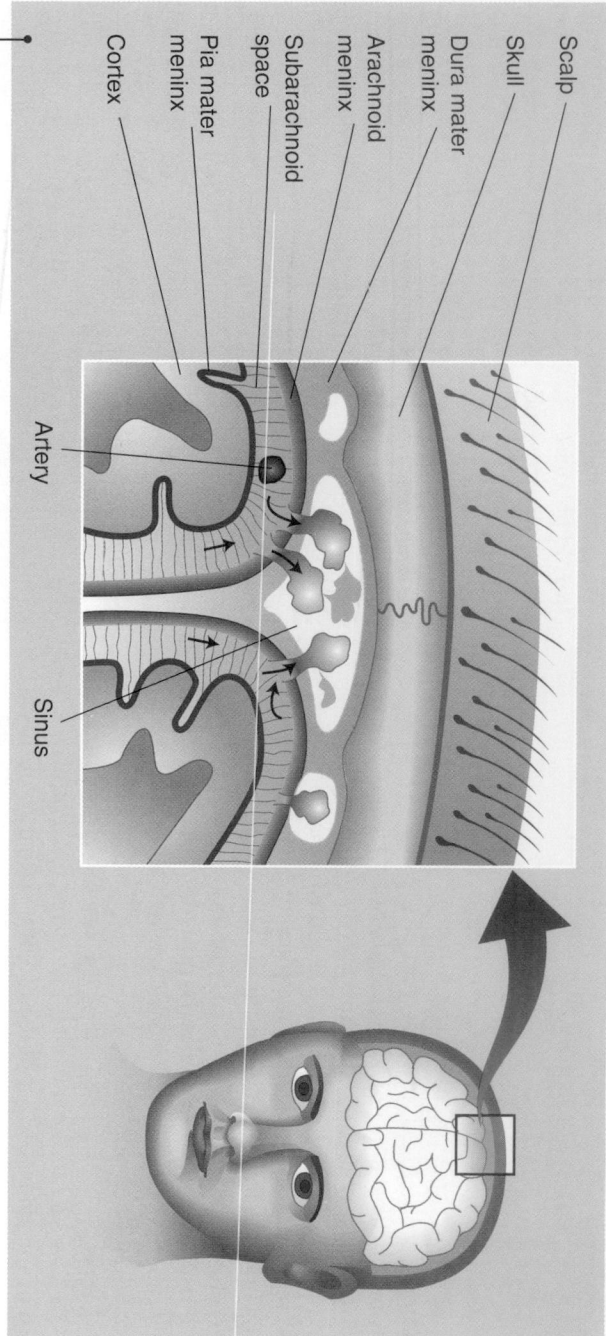

FIGURE 3.4   The absorption of cerebrospinal fluid from the subarachnoid space (blue) into a major sinus. Note the three meninges.

Scalp
Skull
Dura mater meninx
Arachnoid meninx
Subarachnoid space
Cortex
Artery
Sinus
Pia mater meninx

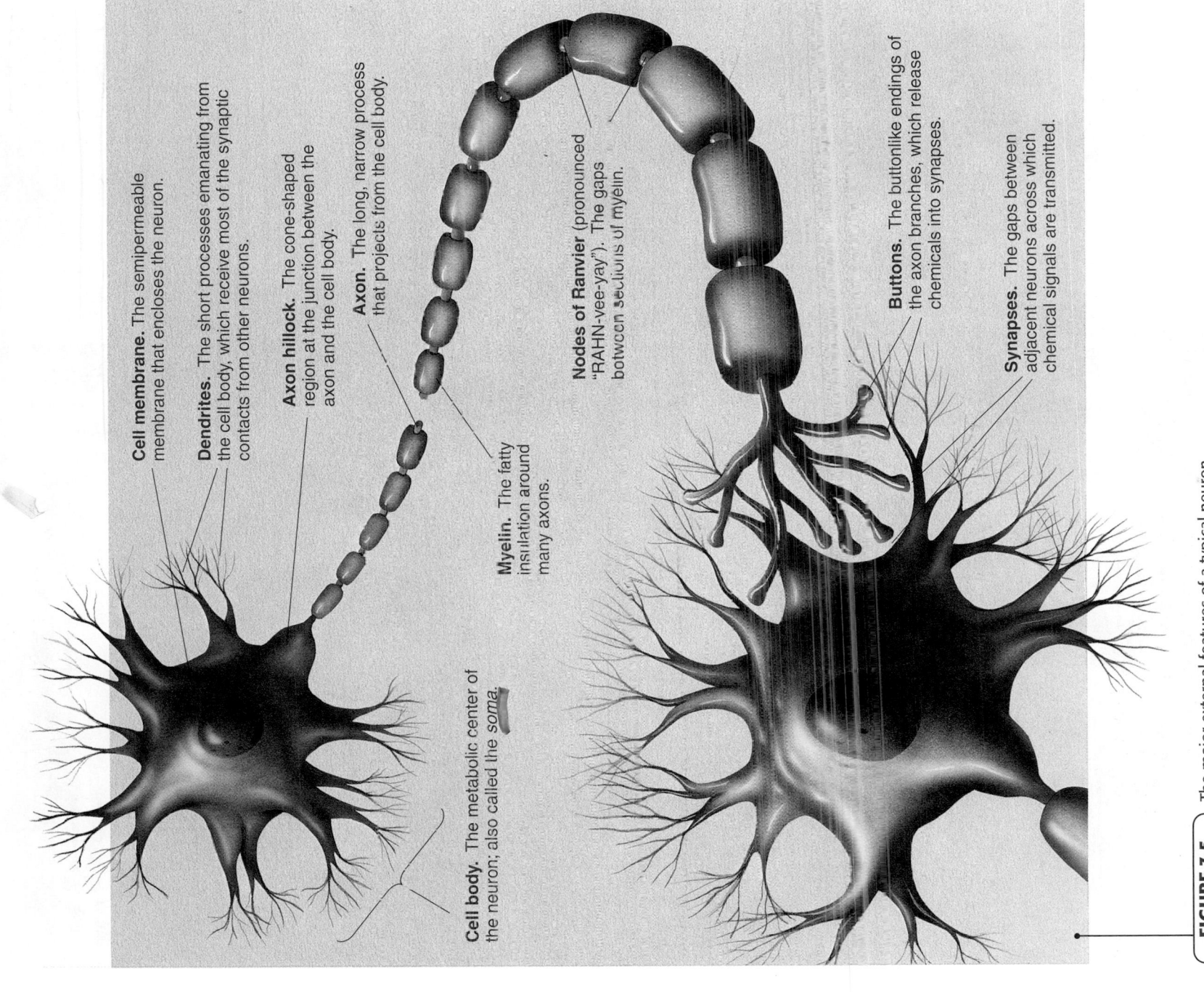

Cell membrane. The semipermeable membrane that encloses the neuron.

Dendrites. The short processes emanating from the cell body, which receive most of the synaptic contacts from other neurons.

Axon hillock. The cone-shaped region at the junction between the axon and the cell body.

Axon. The long, narrow process that projects from the cell body.

Nodes of Ranvier (pronounced "RAHN-vee-yay"). The gaps between sections of myelin.

Myelin. The fatty insulation around many axons.

Cell body. The metabolic center of the neuron; also called the *soma*.

Buttons. The buttonlike endings of the axon branches, which release chemicals into synapses.

Synapses. The gaps between adjacent neurons across which chemical signals are transmitted.

FIGURE 3.5 The major external features of a typical neuron.

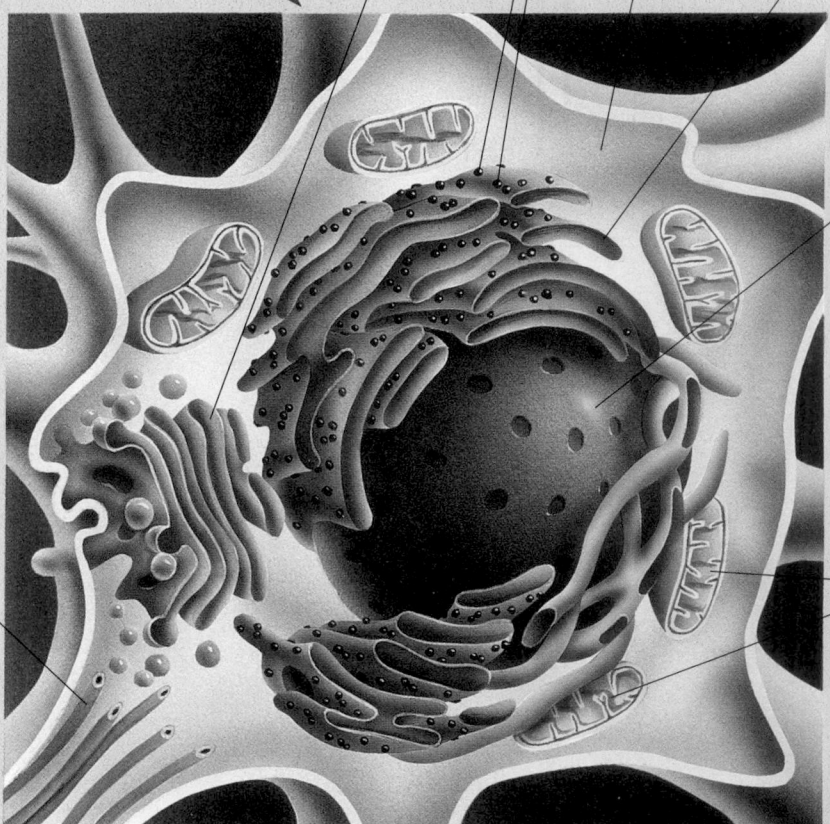
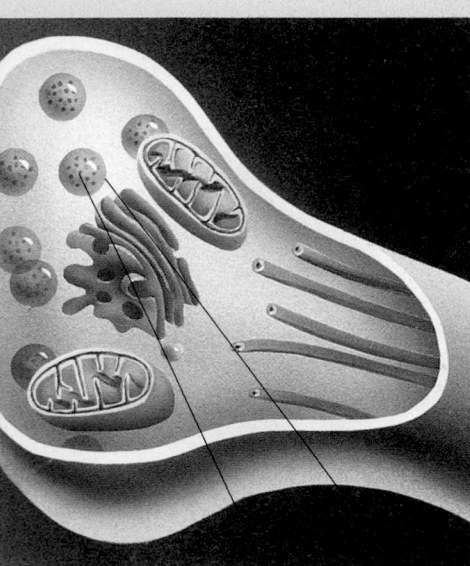
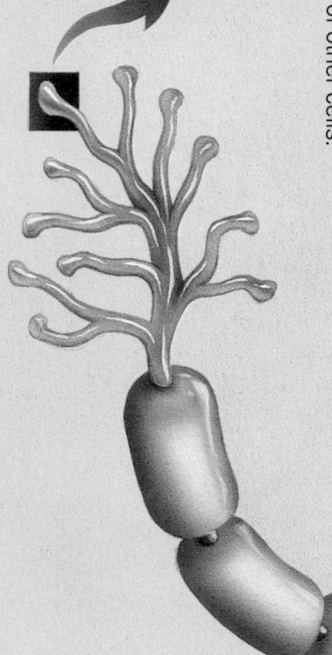

FIGURE 3.6 The major internal features of a typical neuron.

Endoplasmic reticulum. A system of folded membranes in the cell body; rough portions (those with ribosomes) play a role in the synthesis of proteins; smooth portions (those without ribosomes) play a role in the synthesis of fats.

Cytoplasm. The clear internal fluid of the cell.

Ribosomes. Internal cellular structures on which proteins are synthesized; they are located on the endoplasmic reticulum.

Golgi complex. A system of membranes that packages molecules in vesicles.

Nucleus. The spherical DNA-containing structure of the cell body.

Mitochondria. Sites of aerobic (oxygen-consuming) energy release.

Microtubules. Tubules responsible for the rapid transport of material throughout neurons.

Synaptic vesicles. Spherical membrane packages that store neurotransmitter molecules ready for release near synapses.

Neurotransmitters. Molecules that are released from active neurons and influence the activity of other cells.

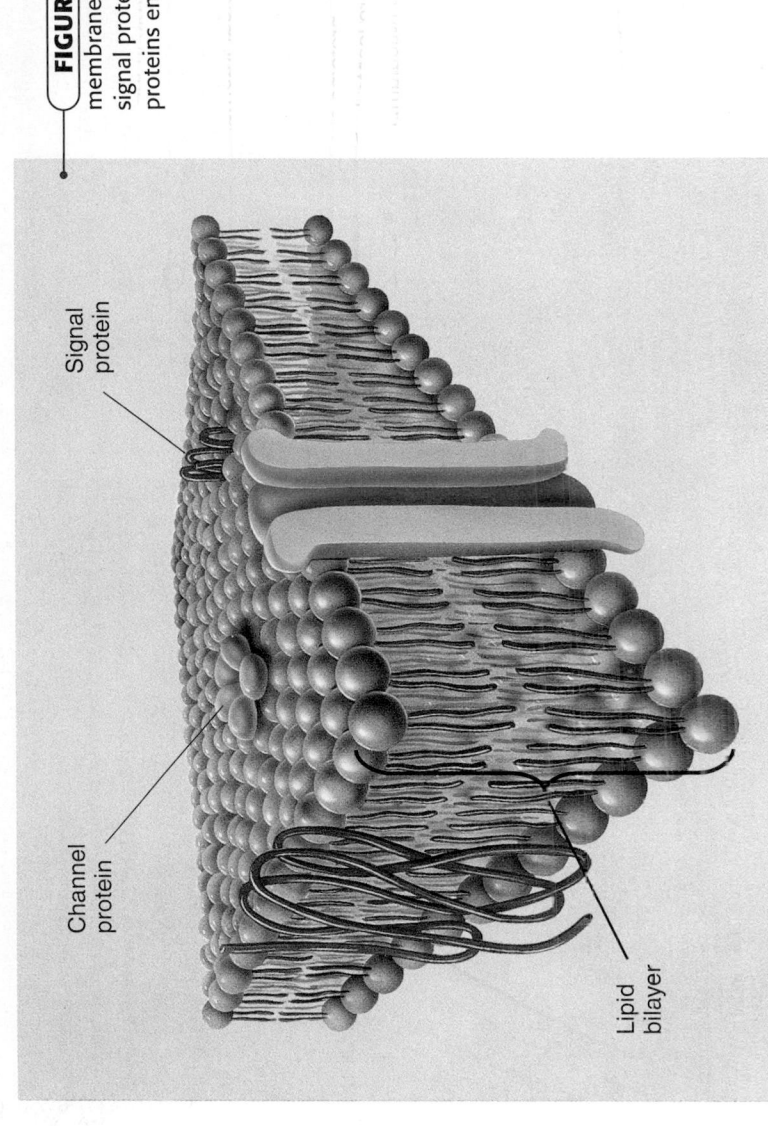

FIGURE 3.7 The cell membrane is a lipid bilayer with signal proteins and channel proteins embedded in it.

Signal protein

Channel protein

Lipid bilayer

Classes of Neurons Figure 3.8 illustrates a way of classifying neurons that is based on the number of processes (i.e., projections) emanating from their cell bodies. A neuron with more than two processes extending from its cell body is classified as a **multipolar neuron;** most neurons are multipolar. A neuron with one process extending from its cell body is classified as a **unipolar neuron,** and a neuron with two processes extending from its cell body is classified as a **bipolar neuron.** Neurons with short axons or no axon at all are called

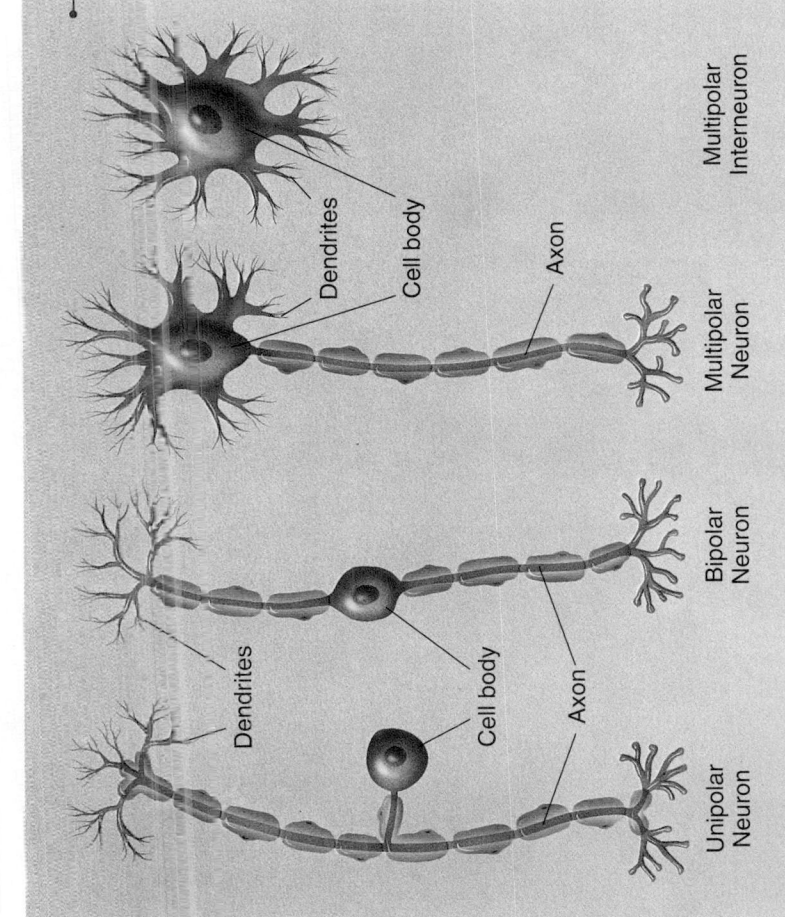

FIGURE 3.8 A unipolar neuron, a bipolar neuron, a multipolar neuron, and an interneuron.

Dendrites

Cell body

Axon

Multipolar Interneuron

Multipolar Neuron

Dendrites

Cell body

Axon

Bipolar Neuron

Unipolar Neuron

interneurons; their function is to integrate the neural activity within a single brain structure, not to conduct signals from one structure to another.

In general, there are two kinds of gross neural structures in the nervous system: those composed primarily of cell bodies and those composed primarily of axons. In the central nervous system, clusters of cell bodies are called **nuclei** (singular *nucleus*); in the peripheral nervous system, they are called **ganglia** (singular *ganglion*). (Note that the word *nucleus* has two different neuroanatomical meanings; it is a structure in the neuron cell body and a cluster of cell bodies in the CNS.) In the central nervous system, bundles of axons are called **tracts;** in the peripheral nervous system, they are called **nerves.**

Glial Cells: The Forgotten Majority

Neurons are not the only cells in the nervous system; others are called **glial cells.** Glial cells outnumber neurons by 10 to 1.

There are four kinds of glial cells (Fields & Stevens-Graham, 2002). **Oligodendrocytes** are one class of glial cells; they send out extensions that wrap around the axons of some neurons of the central nervous system. These extensions are rich in *myelin*, a fatty insulating substance, and the myelin sheaths that they form increase the speed and efficiency of axonal conduction. A similar function is performed in the peripheral nervous system by **Schwann cells,** a second class of glial cells. Oligodendrocytes and Schwann cells are illustrated in Figure 3.9. Notice that each Schwann cell constitutes one myelin segment, whereas each oligodendrocyte provides several myelin segments, often on more than one axon. Another important difference between Schwann cells and oligodendrocytes is that only Schwann cells can guide axonal *regeneration* (regrowth) after damage. That is why effective axonal regeneration in the mammalian nervous system is restricted to the PNS.

Astrocytes are a third class of glial cells. They are the largest glial cells, and they are so-named because

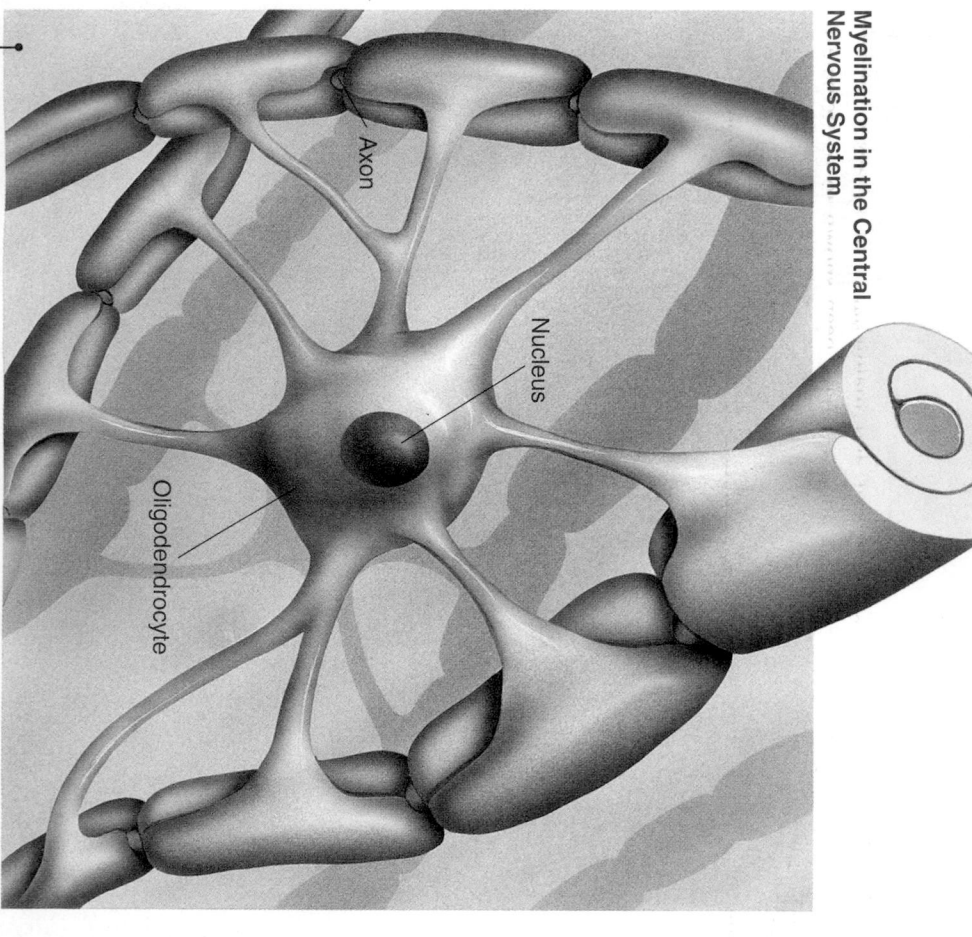

Axon

Nucleus

Oligodendrocyte

Myelination in the Central Nervous System

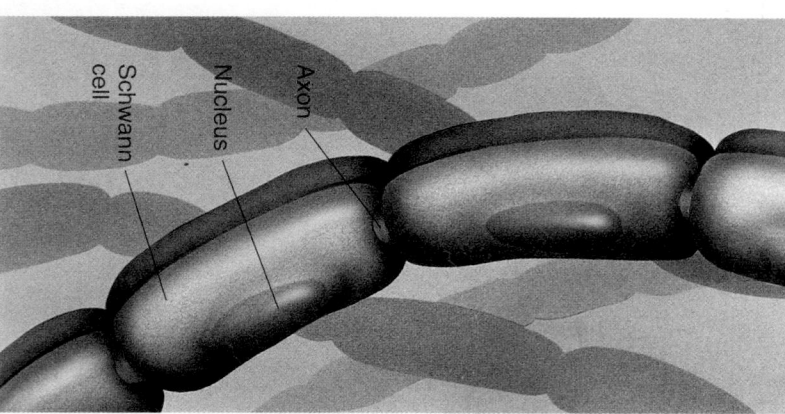

Schwann cell

Nucleus

Axon

Myelination in the Peripheral Nervous System

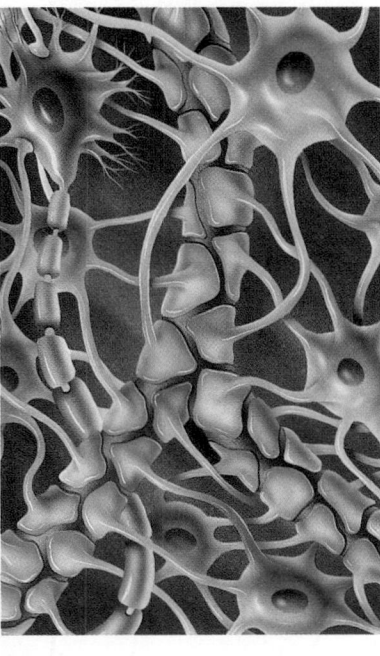

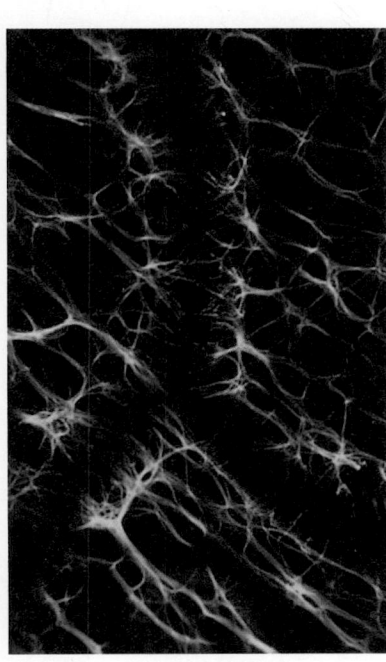

FIGURE 3.10 Astrocytes have an affinity for blood vessels, and they form a supportive matrix for neurons. The photograph on the left is of a slice of brain tissue stained with a glial stain; the unstained channels are blood vessels. The illustration on the right is a three-dimensional representation of the image on the left showing how the feet of astrocytes cover blood vessels and contact neurons. Compare the two panels. (Photograph courtesy of T. Chan-Ling.)

they are star-shaped (*astron* means "star"). The armlike extensions of some astrocytes cover the outer surfaces of blood vessels that course through the brain; they also make contact with neuron cell bodies (see Figure 3.10). These particular astrocytes play a role in the passage of chemicals from the blood into CNS neurons, but other astrocytes perform a variety of different functions.

Microglia are a fourth class of glial cells. Microglia respond to injury or disease by engulfing cellular debris and triggering inflammatory responses.

For decades, it was assumed that the function of glial cells was merely to provide support for neurons—providing them with nutrition, clearing waste, and forming

a physical matrix to hold neural circuits together (*glia* means "glue"). But this limited view of the role of glial cells is rapidly disappearing. In the last few years, glial cells have been shown to participate in the transmission of signals by sending signals to neurons and receiving signals from them; they have been shown to control the establishment and maintenance of synapses between neurons; and they have been shown to participate in glial circuits (Haydon, 2001). Now that this first wave of discoveries has focused neuroscientific attention on glial cells, appreciation of their role in nervous system function should increase quickly. These underappreciated supporting players are moving closer to center stage.

3.3 Neuroanatomical Techniques and Directions

This section of the chapter first describes a few of the most common neuroanatomical techniques. Then, it explains the system of directions that neuroanatomists use to describe the location of structures in vertebrate nervous systems.

Neuroanatomical Techniques

The major problem in visualizing neurons is not their minuteness. The major problem is that neurons are so tightly packed and their axons and dendrites so intricately intertwined that looking through a microscope at unprepared neural tissue reveals almost nothing about them. The key to the study of neuroanatomy lies in preparing neural tissue in a variety of ways, each of which permits a clear view of a different aspect of neuronal

structure, and then combining the knowledge obtained from each of the preparations. This point is illustrated by the following neuroanatomical techniques.

Golgi Stain The greatest blessing to befall neuroscience in its early years was the accidental discovery of the Golgi stain by Camillo Golgi (pronounced "GOLE-jee"), an Italian physician, in the early 1870s. Golgi was trying to stain the meninges, by exposing a block of neural tissue to potassium dichromate and silver nitrate, when he noticed an amazing thing. For some unknown reason, the silver chromate created by the chemical reaction of the two substances Golgi was using invaded a few neurons in each slice of tissue and stained each invaded neuron entirely black. This discovery made it possible to see individual neurons for the first time, although only

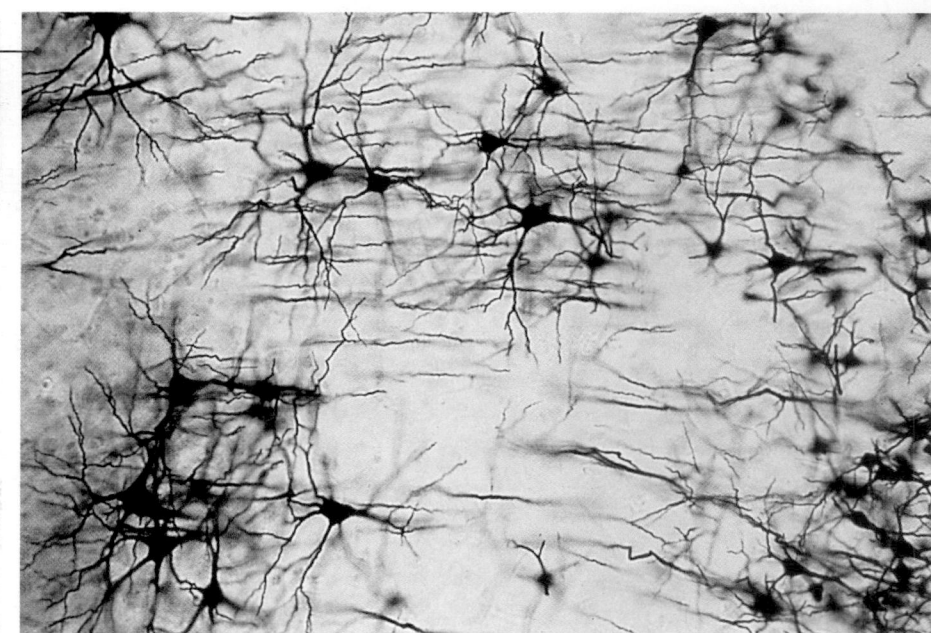

FIGURE 3.11 Neural tissue that has been stained by the Golgi method. Because only a few neurons take up the stain, their silhouettes are revealed in great detail, but their internal details are invisible. Usually, only part of a neuron is captured in a single slice. (Ed Reschke © Peter Arnold, Inc.)

in silhouette (see Figure 3.11). Stains that totally dye all neurons on a slide reveal nothing of their structure because the neurons are so tightly packed.

Nissl Stain

Although the Golgi stain permits an excellent view of the silhouettes of the few neurons that take up the stain, it provides no indication of the number of neurons in an area or the nature of their inner structure. The first neural staining procedure to overcome these shortcomings was the **Nissl stain,** which was developed by Franz Nissl, a German psychiatrist, in the 1880s. The most common dye used in the Nissl method is cresyl violet. Cresyl violet and other Nissl dyes penetrate all cells on a slide, but they bind effectively only to structures in neuron cell bodies. Thus, one can estimate the number of cell bodies in an area by counting the number of Nissl-stained dots. Figure 3.12 is a photograph of a slice of brain tissue stained with cresyl violet. Notice that only the layers composed mainly of neuron cell bodies are densely stained.

Electron Microscopy

A neuroanatomical technique that provides information about the details of neuronal

structure is **electron microscopy** (pronounced "my-CROSS-cuh-pee"). Because of the nature of light, the limit of magnification in light microscopy is about 1,500 times, a level of magnification that is insufficient to reveal the fine anatomical details of neurons. Greater detail can be obtained by first coating thin slices of neural tissue with an electron-absorbing substance that is taken up by different parts of neurons to different degrees, then passing a beam of electrons through the tissue onto a photographic film. The result is an *electron micrograph,* which captures neuronal structure in exquisite detail (see Figure 4.10). A *scanning electron microscope* provides spectacular electron micrographs in three dimensions (see Figure 3.13), but is not capable of as much magnification as a conventional electron microscope.

Neuroanatomical Tracing Techniques

Neuroanatomical tracing techniques are of two types: anterograde

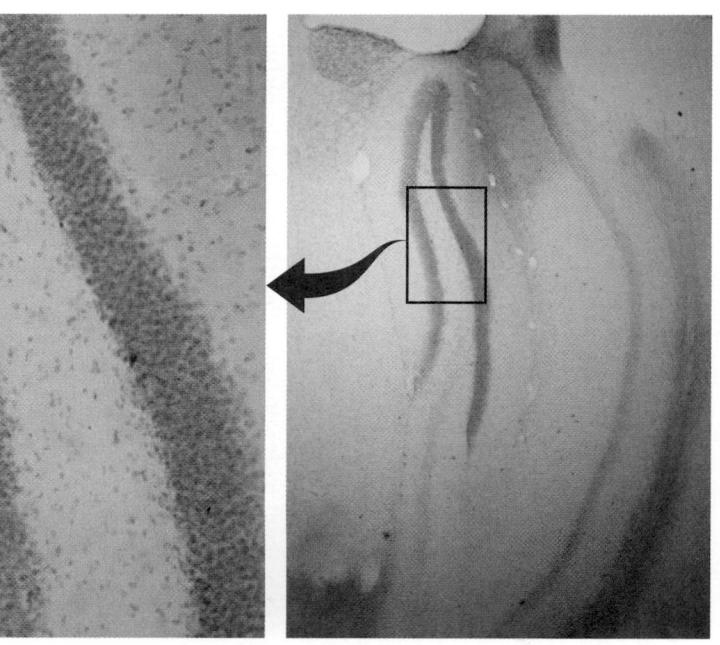

FIGURE 3.12 The Nissl stain. Presented here is a Nissl-stained coronal section through the rat hippocampus, at two levels of magnification to illustrate two uses of Nissl stains. Under low magnification (top panel), Nissl stains provide a gross indication of brain structure by selectively staining groups of neural cell bodies—in this case, the layers of the hippocampus. Under higher magnification (bottom panel), one can distinguish individual neural cell bodies and thus count the number of neurons in various areas. (Courtesy of my good friends Carl Ernst and Brian Christie, Department of Psychology, University of British Columbia.)

Directions in the Vertebrate Nervous System

It would be difficult for you to develop an understanding of the layout of an unfamiliar city without a system of directional coordinates: north–south, east–west. The same goes for the nervous system. Thus, before introducing you to the locations of major nervous system structures, I will describe the three-dimensional system of directional coordinates used by neuroanatomists.

Directions in the vertebrate nervous system are described in relation to the orientation of the spinal cord. This system is straightforward for most vertebrates, as Figure 3.14 indicates. The vertebrate nervous system has three axes: anterior–posterior, dorsal–ventral, and medial–lateral. First, **anterior** means toward the nose end (the anterior end), and **posterior** means toward the tail end (the posterior end); these same directions are sometimes referred to as *rostral* and *caudal*, respectively. Second, **dorsal** means toward the surface of the back or the top of the head (the dorsal surface), and **ventral** means toward the surface of the chest or the bottom of the head (the ventral surface). Third, **medial** means toward the midline of the body, and **lateral** means away from the midline toward the body's lateral surfaces.

We humans complicate this simple three-axis (anterior–posterior, ventral–dorsal, medial–lateral) system of neuroanatomical directions by insisting on walking around on our hind legs. This changes the orientation of our cerebral hemispheres in relation to our spines and brain stems.

You can save yourself a lot of confusion if you remember that the system of vertebrate neuroanatomical directions was adapted for use in humans in such a way that the terms used to describe the positions of various body surfaces are the same in humans as they are in more typical, non-upright vertebrates. Specifically, notice that the top of the human head and the back of the human body are both referred to as *dorsal* even though they are in different directions, and the bottom of the human head and the front of the human body are both referred to as *ventral* even though they are in different directions

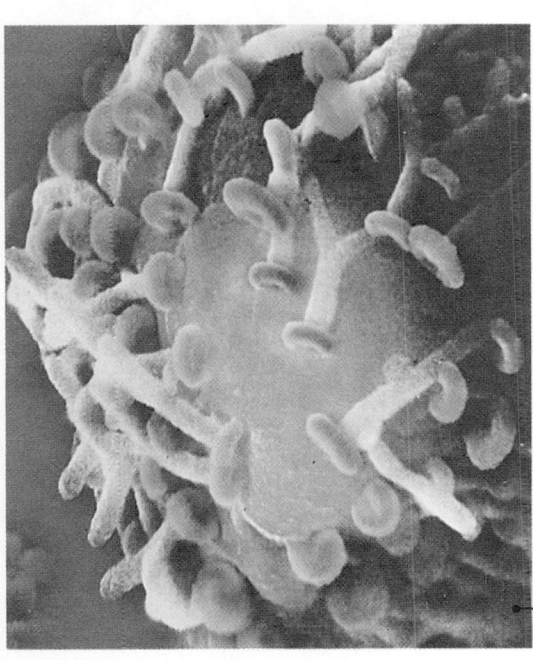

FIGURE 3.13 A color-enhanced scanning electron micrograph of a neuron cell body (green) studded with terminal buttons (orange). Each neuron receives numerous synaptic contacts. (Courtesy of Jerold J. M. Chun, M.D., Ph.D.)

(forward) tracing methods and retrograde (backward) tracing methods. *Anterograde tracing methods* are used when an investigator wants to trace the paths of axons projecting away from cell bodies located in a particular area. The investigator injects into the area one of several chemicals commonly used for anterograde tracing—chemicals that are taken up by cell bodies and then transported forward along their axons to their terminal buttons. After a few days, the brain is removed and sliced; the slices are then treated to reveal the locations of the injected chemical. *Retrograde tracing methods* work in reverse; they are used when an investigator wants to trace the paths of axons projecting into a particular area. The investigator injects into the area one of several chemicals commonly used for retrograde tracing—chemicals that are taken up by terminal buttons and then transported backward along their axons to their cell bodies. After a few days, the brain is removed and sliced; the slices are then treated to reveal the locations of the injected chemical.

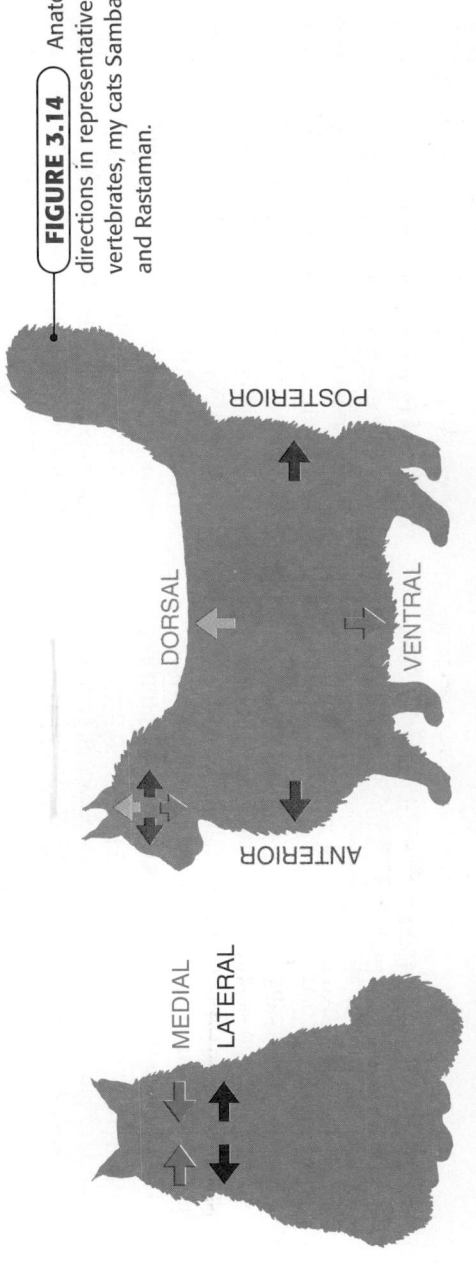

FIGURE 3.14 Anatomical directions in representative vertebrates, my cats Sambala and Rastaman.

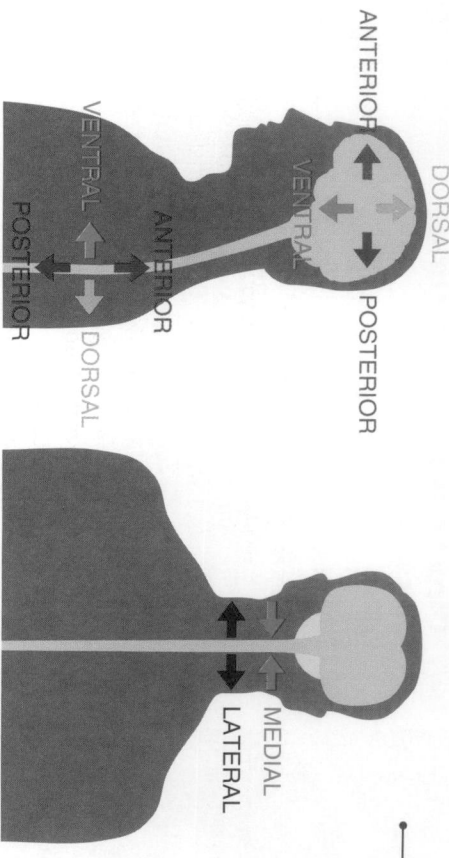

ANTERIOR

ANTERIOR

POSTERIOR

DORSAL

VENTRAL

VENTRAL

ANTERIOR

POSTERIOR

DORSAL

MEDIAL

LATERAL

FIGURE 3.15 Anatomical directions in a human. Notice that the directions in the cerebral hemispheres are rotated by 90° in comparison to those in the spinal cord and brain stem because of the unusual upright posture of humans.

(see Figure 3.15). To circumvent this complication, the terms **superior** and **inferior** are often used to refer to the top and bottom of the primate head, respectively.

Proximal and distal are two other common directional terms. In general, *proximal* means "close," and *distal* means "far." Specifically, with regard to the nervous system, *proximal* means closer to the CNS, and *distal* means farther from the CNS—for example, the nerve terminals of the shoulders are proximal to those of the fingers.

In the next few pages, you will be seeing drawings of sections (slices) of the brain cut in one of three different planes: **horizontal sections, frontal** (also termed *coronal*) **sections,** and **sagittal sections.** These three planes are illustrated in Figure 3.16. A section cut down the center of the brain, between the two hemispheres, is called a *midsagittal section.* A section cut at a right angle to any long, narrow structure, such as the spinal cord or a nerve, is called a **cross section.**

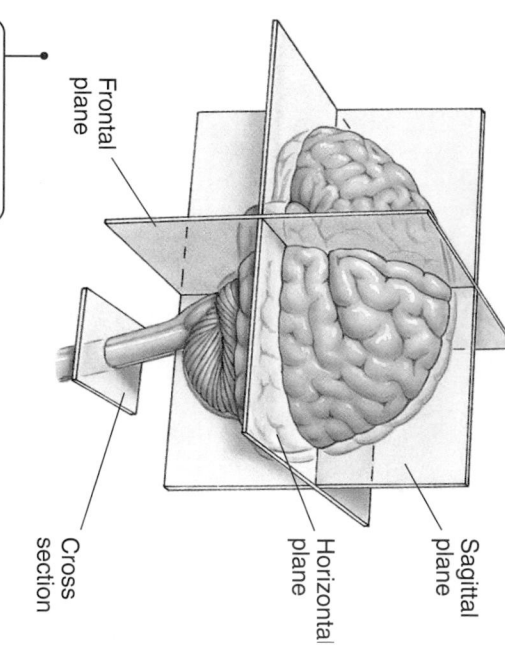

Frontal plane

Horizontal plane

Sagittal plane

Cross section

FIGURE 3.16 Horizontal, frontal (coronal), and sagittal planes in the human brain and a cross section of the human spinal cord.

3.4 The Spinal Cord

In the first three sections of this chapter, you learned about the divisions of the nervous system, the cells that compose it, and some of the neuroanatomical techniques that are used to study it. This section begins your ascent of the human CNS by focusing on the spinal cord. The final two sections of the chapter focus on the brain.

In cross section, it is apparent that the spinal cord comprises two different areas (see Figure 3.17): an inner H-shaped core of gray matter and a surrounding area of white matter. *Gray matter* is composed largely of cell bodies and unmyelinated interneurons, whereas *white matter* is composed largely of myelinated axons. (It is

the myelin that gives the white matter its glossy white sheen.) The two dorsal arms of the spinal gray matter are called the **dorsal horns,** and the two ventral arms are called the **ventral horns.**

Pairs of *spinal nerves* are attached to the spinal cord—one on the left and one on the right—at 31 different levels of the spine. Each of these 62 spinal nerves divides as it nears the cord (see Figure 3.17), and its axons are joined to the cord via one of two roots: the *dorsal root* or the *ventral root.*

All dorsal root axons, whether somatic or autonomic, are sensory (afferent) unipolar neurons with their cell

SCAN YOUR BRAIN

This is a good place for you to pause to scan your brain. Are you ready to proceed to the structures of the brain and spinal cord? Test your grasp of the preceding sections of this chapter by drawing a line between each term in the left column

1. Autonomic nervous system
2. Cerebral aqueduct
3. Axon hillock
4. Dorsal
5. Cell membrane
6. Cranial nerves
7. Superior or dorsal
8. Cell body
9. Synaptic vesicles
10. Oligodendrocytes
11. Nissl
12. Dura mater
13. Midsagittal section
14. Golgi

and the appropriate phrase in the right column. The correct answers are provided at the bottom of this page. Before proceeding, review material related to your incorrect answers.

a. Packets of neurotransmitter molecules
b. PNS minus the somatic nervous system
c. Connects the third and fourth ventricles
d. Stains cell bodies
e. Top of a vertebrate's head
f. Outer meninx
g. Between the cell body and axon
h. Contains the nucleus of a neuron
i. Olfactory, visual, and vagus
j. Myelinate CNS axons
k. A slice down the center of the brain
l. Top of the primate head
m. Silhouette
n. Lipid bilayer

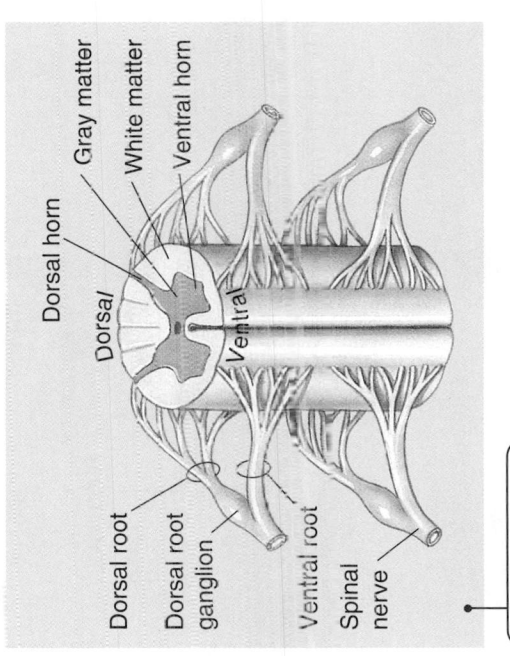

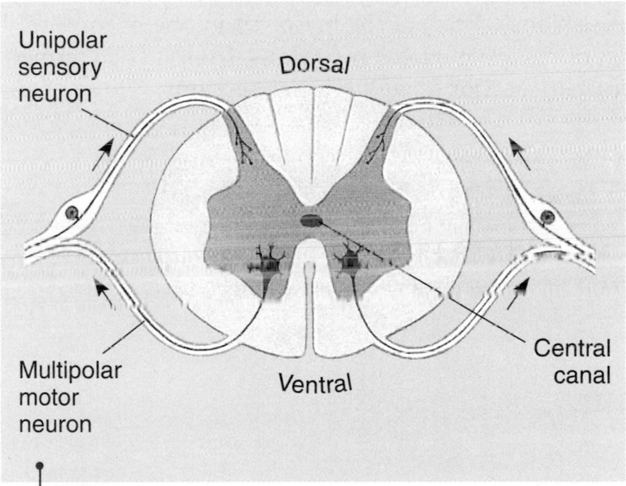

FIGURE 3.18 A schematic cross section of the spinal cord.

FIGURE 3.17 The dorsal and ventral roots of the spinal cord.

bodies grouped together just outside the cord to form the *dorsal root ganglia*. Many of their synaptic terminals are in the dorsal horns of the spinal gray matter (see Figure 3.18). In contrast, the neurons of the ventral root are motor (efferent) multipolar neurons with their cell bodies in the ventral horns. Those that are part of the somatic nervous system project to skeletal muscles; those that are part of the autonomic nervous system project

to ganglia, where they synapse on neurons that in turn project to internal organs (heart, stomach, liver, etc.). See Appendix I.

Scan Your Brain answers: (1) b, (2) c, (3) g, (4) e, (5) n, (6) i, (7) l, (8) h, (9) a, (10) j, (11) d, (12) f, (13) k, (14) m.

3.5 The Five Major Divisions of the Brain

A necessary step in learning to live in an unfamiliar city is learning the names and locations of its major neighborhoods or districts. Those who possess this information can easily communicate the general location of any destination in the city. This section of the chapter introduces you to the five "neighborhoods," or divisions, of the brain—for much the same reason.

To understand why the brain is considered to be composed of five divisions, it is necessary to understand its early development (see Swanson, 2000). In the vertebrate embryo, the tissue that eventually develops into the CNS is recognizable as a fluid-filled tube (see Figure 3.19). The first indications of the developing brain are three swellings that occur at the anterior end of this tube. These three swellings eventually develop into the adult *forebrain, midbrain,* and *hindbrain*.

Before birth, the initial three swellings in the neural tube become five (see Figure 3.19). This occurs because the forebrain swelling grows into two different swellings, and so does the hindbrain swelling. From anterior to posterior, the five swellings that compose the developing brain at birth are the *telencephalon,* the *diencephalon,* the *mesencephalon* (or midbrain), the *metencephalon,* and the *myelencephalon* (enceph-

alon means "within the head"). These swellings ultimately develop into the five divisions of the adult brain. As a student, I memorized their order by remembering that the telencephalon is on the top and the other four divisions are arrayed below it in alphabetical order.

Figure 3.20 illustrates the locations of the telencephalon, diencephalon, mesencephalon, metencephalon, and myelencephalon in the adult human brain. Notice that in humans, as in other higher vertebrates, the telencephalon (the left and right *cerebral hemispheres*) undergoes the greatest growth during development. The other four divisions of the brain are often referred to collectively as the **brain stem**—the stem on which the cerebral hemispheres sit. The myelencephalon is often referred to as the *medulla*.

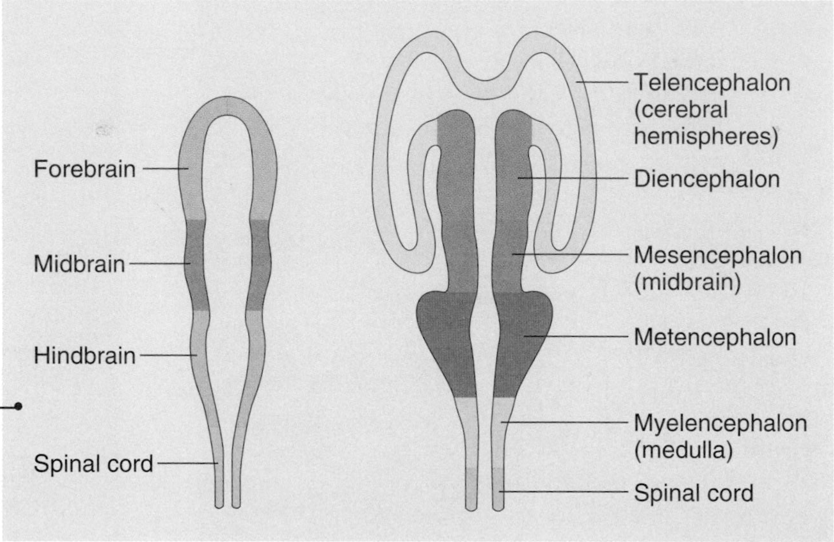

FIGURE 3.19   The early development of the mammalian brain illustrated in schematic horizontal sections. Compare with the adult human brain in Figure 3.20.

Forebrain
Midbrain
Hindbrain
Spinal cord

Telencephalon
(cerebral
hemispheres)
Diencephalon
Mesencephalon
(midbrain)
Metencephalon
Myelencephalon
(medulla)
Spinal cord

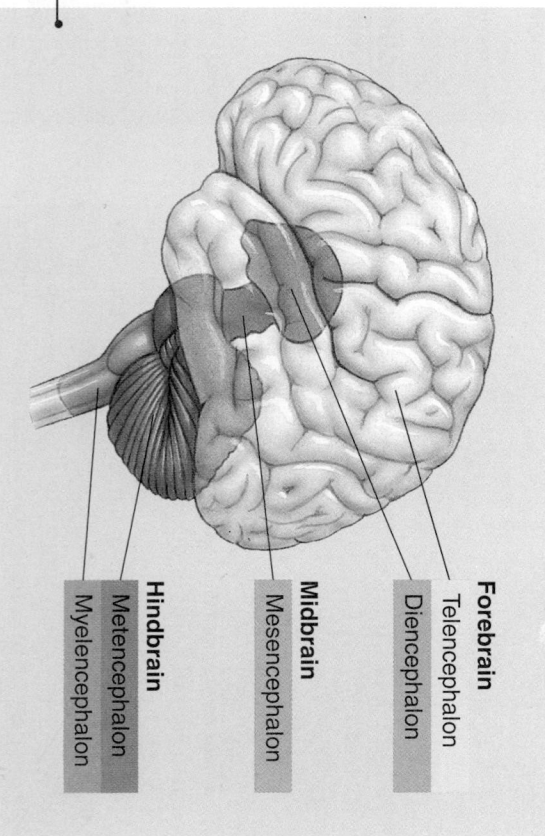

FIGURE 3.20   The divisions of the adult human brain.

Forebrain
Telencephalon
Diencephalon

Midbrain
Mesencephalon

Hindbrain
Metencephalon
Myelencephalon

3.6 Major Structures of the Brain

Now that you have learned the five major divisions of the brain, it is time to introduce you to their major structures. This section of the chapter begins its survey of brain structures in the myelencephalon, then ascends through the other divisions to the telencephalon. The boldfaced brain structures introduced and defined in this section are not included in the Key Terms list at the end of the chapter. Rather, they are arranged according to their locations in the brain in Figure 3.30 on page 73.

Here is a reminder before you delve into the anatomy of the brain: The directional coordinates are the same for the brain stem as for the spinal cord, but they are rotated by 90° for the forebrain.

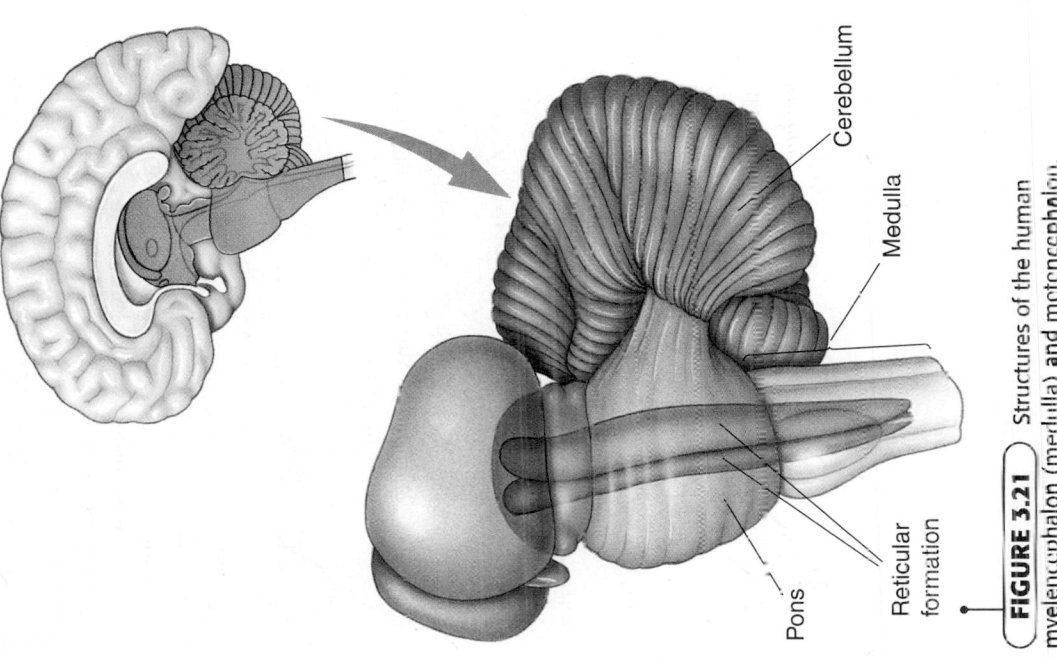

FIGURE 3.21 Structures of the human myelencephalon (medulla) and metencephalon.

Labels: Cerebellum, Medulla, Reticular formation, Pons

Myelencephalon

Not surprisingly, the **myelencephalon** (or **medulla**), the most posterior division of the brain, is composed largely of tracts carrying signals between the rest of the brain and the body. An interesting part of the myelencephalon from a psychological perspective is the **reticular formation** (see Figure 3.21). It is a complex network of about 100 tiny nuclei that occupies the central core of the brain stem from the posterior boundary of the myelencephalon to the anterior boundary of the midbrain. It is so named because of its netlike appearance (*reticulum* means "little net"). Sometimes, the reticular formation is referred to as the *reticular activating system* because parts of it seem to play a role in arousal. However, the various nuclei of the reticular formation are involved in a variety of functions—including sleep, attention, movement, the maintenance of muscle tone, and various cardiac, circulatory, and respiratory reflexes. Accordingly, referring to this collection of nuclei as a system can be misleading.

Metencephalon

The **metencephalon**, like the myelencephalon, houses many ascending and descending tracts and part of the reticular formation. These structures create a bulge, called the **pons**, on the brain stem's ventral surface. The pons is one major division of the metencephalon; the other is the cerebellum (little brain)—see Figure 3.21. The **cerebellum** is the large, convoluted structure on the brain stem's dorsal surface. It is an important sensorimotor structure; cerebellar damage eliminates the ability to precisely control one's movements and to adapt them to changing conditions. However, the fact that cerebellar damage also produces a variety of cognitive deficits suggests that the functions of the cerebellum are not restricted to sensorimotor control.

Mesencephalon

The **mesencephalon**, like the metencephalon, has two divisions. The two divisions of the mesencephalon are the tectum and the tegmentum (see Figure 3.22 on page 66). The **tectum** (roof) is the dorsal surface of the midbrain. In mammals, the tectum is composed of two pairs of bumps, the *colliculi* (little hills). The posterior pair, called the **inferior colliculi**, have an auditory function; the anterior pair, called the **superior colliculi**, have a visual function. In lower vertebrates, the function of the tectum is entirely visual; thus, the tectum is referred to as the *optic tectum*.

The **tegmentum** is the division of the mesencephalon ventral to the tectum. In addition to the reticular formation and tracts of passage, the tegmentum contains three colorful structures that are of particular interest to biopsychologists: the periaqueductal gray, the substantia

FIGURE 3.22 The human mesencephalon (midbrain).

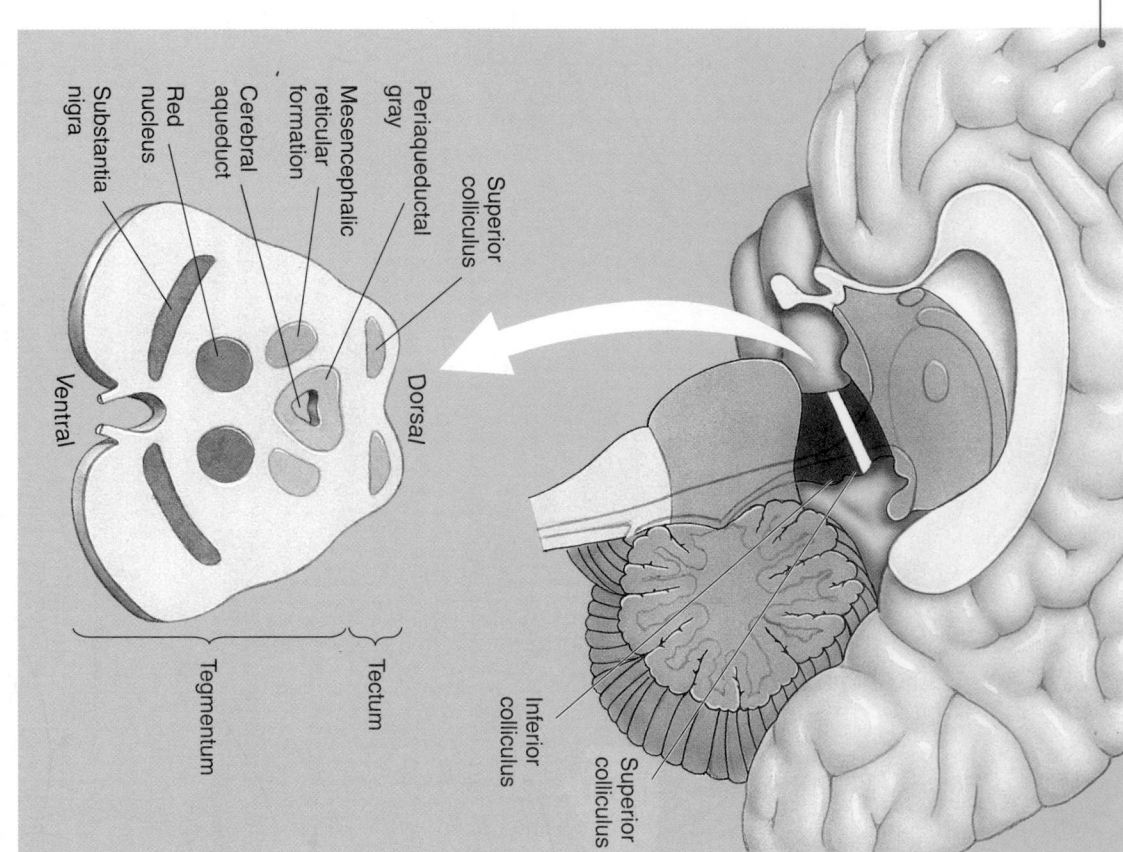

Superior colliculus

Inferior colliculus

Superior colliculus

Periaqueductal gray

Mesencephalic reticular formation

Cerebral aqueduct

Red nucleus

Substantia nigra

Dorsal

Ventral

Tectum

Tegmentum

nigra, and the red nucleus (see Figure 3.22). The **peri-aqueductal gray** is the gray matter situated around the **cerebral aqueduct,** the duct connecting the third and fourth ventricles; it is of special interest because of its role in mediating the analgesic (pain-reducing) effects of opiate drugs. The **substantia nigra** (black substance) and the **red nucleus** are both important components of the sensorimotor system.

Diencephalon

The **diencephalon** is composed of two structures: the thalamus and the hypothalamus (see Figure 3.23). The **thalamus** is the large, two-lobed structure that constitutes the top of the brain stem. One lobe sits on each side of the third ventricle, and the two lobes are joined by the

massa intermedia, which runs through the ventricle. Visible on the surface of the thalamus are white *lamina* (layers) that are composed of myelinated axons.

The thalamus comprises many different pairs of nuclei, most of which project to the cortex. Some are *sensory relay nuclei*—nuclei that receive signals from sensory receptors, process them, and then transmit them to the appropriate areas of sensory cortex. For example, the **lateral geniculate nuclei,** the **medial geniculate nuclei,** and the **ventral posterior nuclei** are important relay stations in the visual, auditory, and somatosensory systems, respectively. The organization of the thalamus is illustrated in Appendix V.

The **hypothalamus** is located just below the anterior thalamus (*hypo* means "below")—see Figure 3.24 on page 68. It plays an important role in the regulation

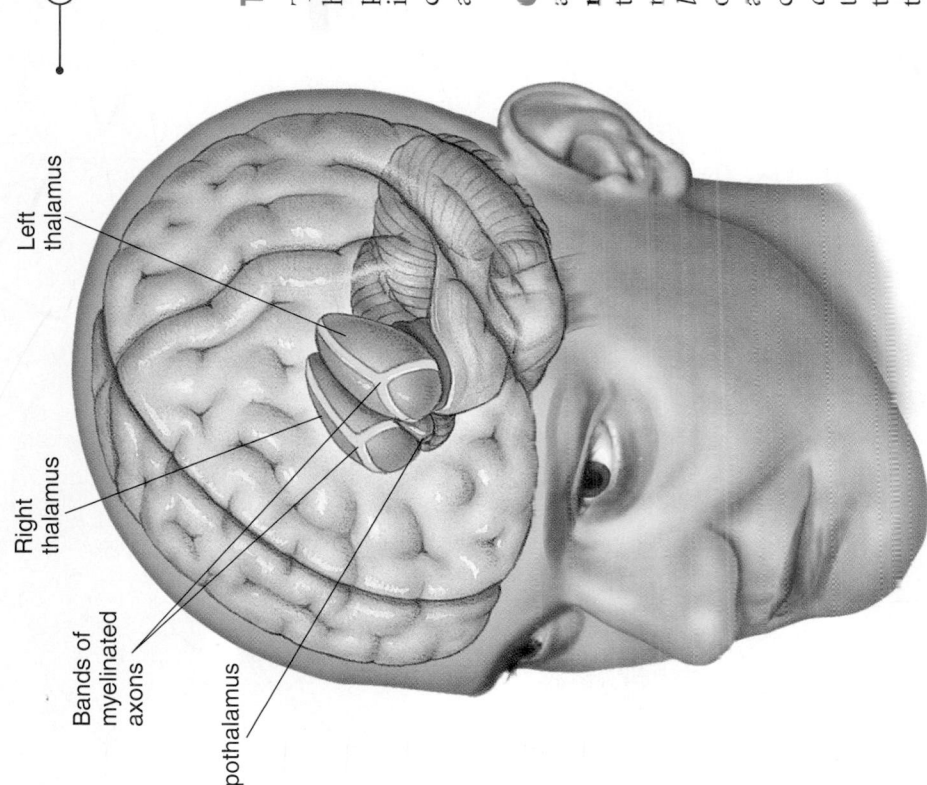

Right
thalamus

Bands of
myelinated
axons

Hypothalamus

Left
thalamus

FIGURE 3.23   The human diencephalon.

Telencephalon

The **telencephalon,** the largest division of the human brain, mediates the brain's most complex functions. It initiates voluntary movement, interprets sensory input, and mediates complex cognitive processes such as learning, speaking, and problem solving.

Cerebral Cortex   The cerebral hemispheres are covered by a layer of tissue called the **cerebral cortex** (cerebral bark). In humans, the cerebral cortex is deeply convoluted (furrowed)—see Figure 3.25 on page 69. The *convolutions* have the effect of increasing the amount of cerebral cortex without increasing the overall volume of the brain. Not all mammals have convoluted cortexes; most mammals are *lissencephalic* (smooth-brained). It was once believed that the number and size of cortical convolutions determined a species' intellectual capacities; however, the number and size of cortical convolutions appear to be related more to body size. Every large mammal has an extremely convoluted cortex.

The large furrows in a convoluted cortex are called **fissures,** and the small ones are called *sulci* (singular *sulcus*). The ridges between fissures and sulci are called **gyri** (singular *gyrus*). It is apparent in Figure 3.25 that the cerebral hemispheres are almost completely separated by the largest of the fissures: the **longitudinal fissure.** The cerebral hemispheres are directly connected by only a few tracts spanning the longitudinal fissure; these hemisphere-connecting tracts are called **cerebral commissures.** The largest cerebral commissure, the **corpus callosum,** is clearly visible in Figure 3.25.

As Figure 3.26 on page 69 indicates, the two major landmarks on the lateral surface of each hemisphere are the **central fissure** and the **lateral fissure.** These fissures partially divide each hemisphere into four lobes: the **frontal lobe,** the **parietal lobe** (pronounced "pa-RYE-e-tal"), the **temporal lobe,** and the **occipital lobe** (pronounced "ok-SIP-i-tal"). Among the largest gyri are the **precentral gyri,** which contain motor cortex; the **postcentral gyri,** which contain somatosensory (body-sensation) cortex; and the **superior temporal gyri,** which contain auditory cortex. The function of occipital cortex is entirely visual.

of several motivated behaviors. It exerts its effects in part by regulating the release of hormones from the **pituitary gland,** which dangles from it on the ventral surface of the brain. The literal meaning of *pituitary gland* is "snot gland"; it was discovered in a gelatinous state behind the nose of an unembalmed cadaver and was incorrectly assumed to be the main source of nasal mucus.

In addition to the pituitary gland, two other structures appear on the inferior surface of the hypothalamus: the optic chiasm and the mammillary bodies (see Figure 3.24). The **optic chiasm** is the point at which the *optic nerves* from each eye come together. The X shape is created because some of the axons of the optic nerve **decussate** (cross over to the other side of the brain) via the optic chiasm. The decussating fibers are said to be **contralateral** (projecting from one side of the body to the other), and the nondecussating fibers are said to be **ipsilateral** (staying on the same side of the body). The **mammillary bodies,** which are often considered to be part of the hypothalamus, are a pair of spherical nuclei located on the inferior surface of the hypothalamus, just behind the pituitary. The mammillary bodies and the other nuclei of the hypothalamus are illustrated in Appendix VI.

FIGURE 3.24 The human hypothalamus (in color) in relation to the optic chiasm and the pituitary gland.

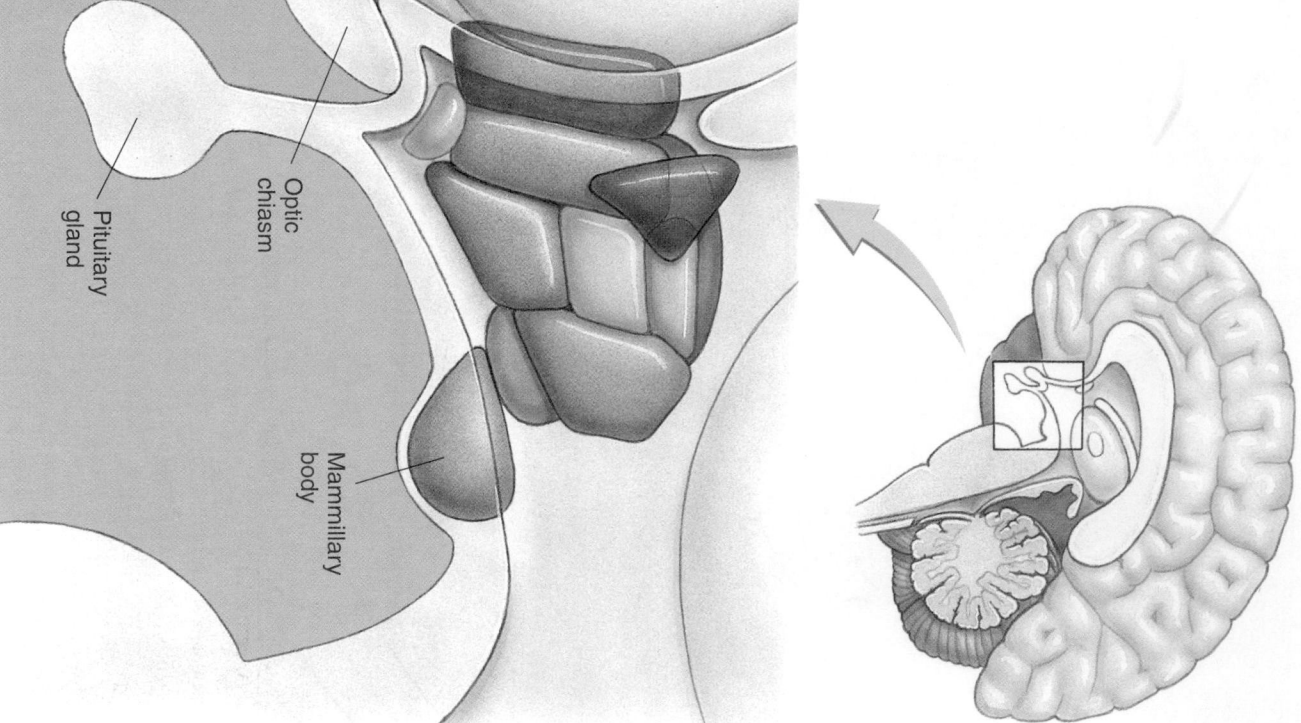

Pituitary gland

Optic chiasm

Mammillary body

About 90% of human cerebral cortex is **neocortex** (new cortex); that is, it is six-layered cortex of relatively recent evolution (Northcutt & Kaas, 1995). By convention, the layers of neocortex are numbered I through VI, starting at the surface. Figure 3.27 on page 70 illustrates two adjacent sections of neocortex. One has been stained with a Nissl stain to reveal the number and shape of its cell bodies; the other has been stained with a Golgi stain to reveal the silhouettes of a small proportion of its neurons.

Three important characteristics of neocortical anatomy are apparent from the sections in Figure 3.27. First, it is apparent that there are two fundamentally different kinds of cortical neurons: pyramidal (pyramid-shaped) cells and stellate (star-shaped) cells. **Pyramidal cells** are large multipolar neurons with pyramid-shaped cell bodies, a large dendrite called an *apical dendrite* that extends from the apex of the pyramid straight toward the cortex surface, and a very long axon. In contrast, **stellate cells** are small star-shaped interneurons (neurons with short axons or no axon). Second, it is apparent that the six layers of neocortex differ from one another in terms of the size and density of their cell bodies and the relative proportion of pyramidal and stellate cell bodies they contain. Third, it is apparent that many long axons and dendrites course vertically (i.e., at right angles to the cortical layers) through the neocortex. This vertical flow of information is the basis of the neocortex's **colum-**

The Limbic System and the Basal Ganglia   Although much of the subcortical portion of the telencephalon is taken up by axons projecting to and from the neocortex, there are several large subcortical nuclear groups. Some of them are considered to be part of either the *limbic system* or the *basal ganglia motor system*. Don't be misled by the word *system* in these contexts; it implies a level of certainty that is unwarranted. It is not entirely

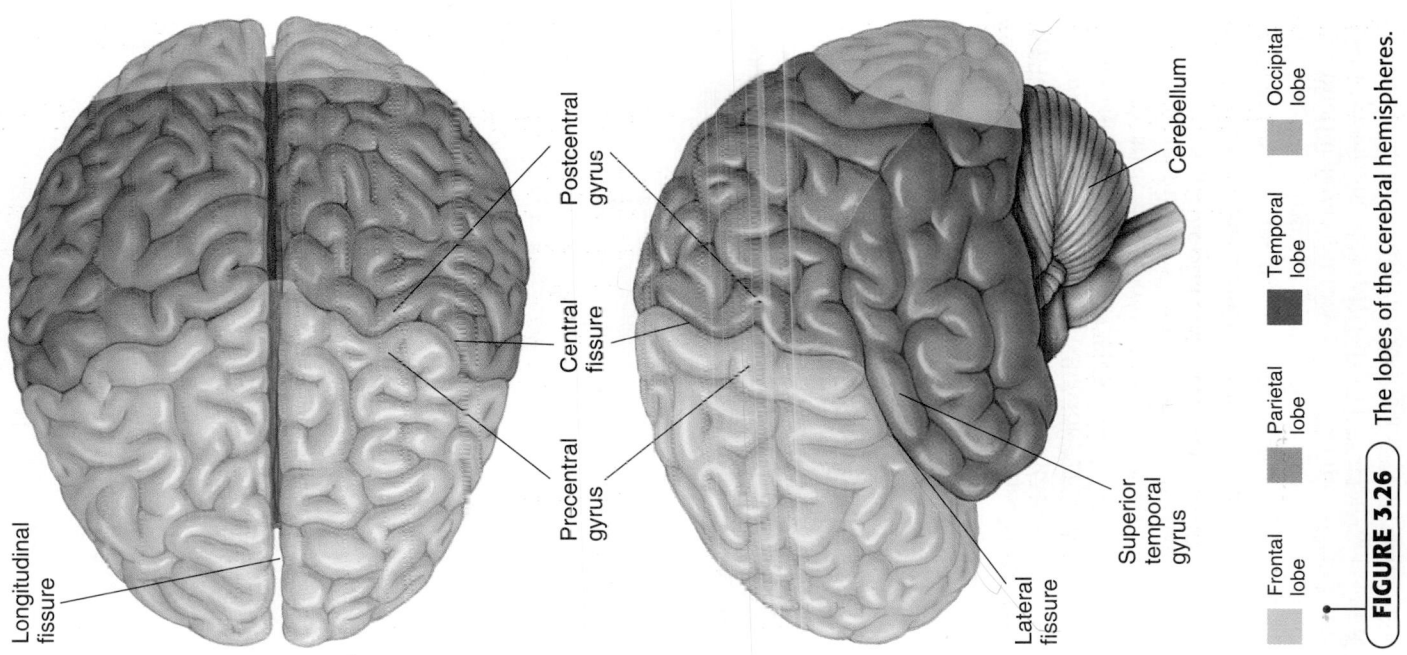

FIGURE 3.26   The lobes of the cerebral hemispheres.

Frontal lobe   Parietal lobe   Temporal lobe

Occipital lobe

Longitudinal fissure

Postcentral gyrus

Central fissure

Procentral gyrus

Lateral fissure

Superior temporal gyrus

Cerebellum

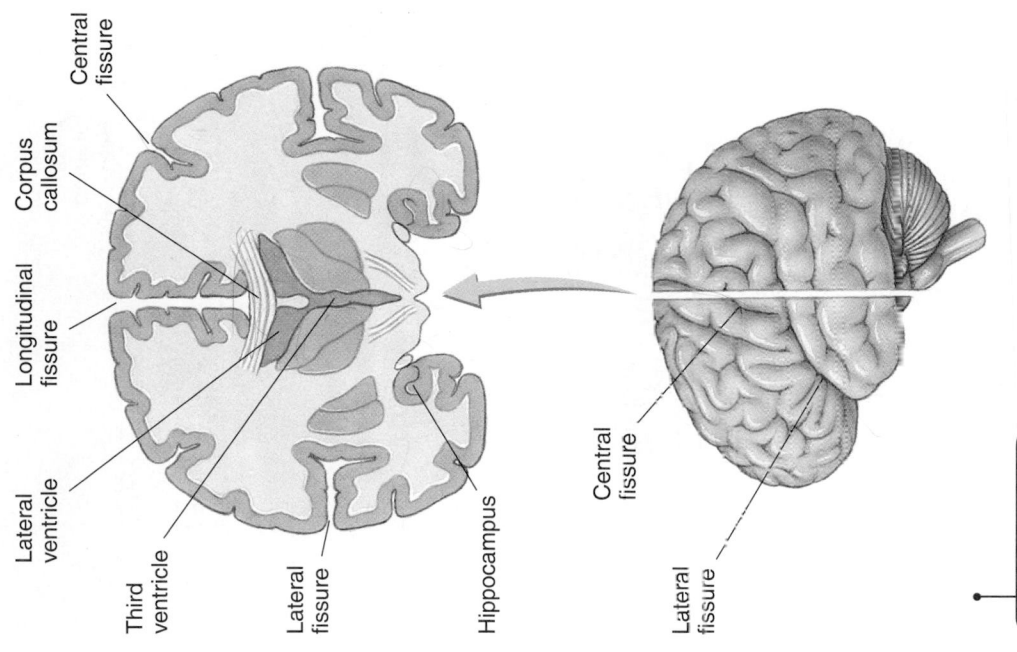

FIGURE 3.25   The major fissures of the human cerebral hemispheres.

Lateral ventricle   Longitudinal fissure   Corpus callosum   Central fissure

Third ventricle

Lateral fissure

Hippocampus

Central fissure

Lateral fissure

nar organization; neurons in a given vertical column of neocortex often form a mini-circuit that performs a single function (Laughlin & Sejnowski, 2003).

A fourth important characteristic of neocortical anatomy is not apparent in Figure 3.27: Although all neocortex is six-layered, there are variations in the layers from area to area (Brown & Bowman, 2002; Passingham, Stephan, & Kotter, 2002). For example, because the stellate cells of layer IV are specialized for receiving sensory signals from the thalamus, layer IV is extremely thick in areas of sensory cortex. Conversely, because the pyramidal cells of layer V conduct signals from the neocortex to the brain stem and spinal cord, layer V is extremely thick in areas of motor cortex.

The **hippocampus** is one important area of cortex that is not neocortex—it has only three layers. The hippocampus is located at the medial edge of the cerebral cortex as it folds back on itself in the medial temporal lobe (see Figure 3.25). This folding produces a shape that is, in cross section, somewhat reminiscent of a sea horse (*hippocampus* means "sea horse").

clear exactly what these hypothetical systems do, exactly which structures should be included in them, or even whether it is appropriate to view them as unitary systems. Nevertheless, if not taken too literally, the concepts of *limbic system* and *basal ganglia motor system* provide a useful means of conceptualizing the organization of the subcortex.

The **limbic system** is a circuit of midline structures that circle the thalamus (*limbic* means "ring"). The limbic system is involved in the regulation of motivated behaviors—including the four Fs of motivation: fleeing, feeding, fighting, and sexual behavior. (This joke is as old as biopsychology itself, but it is a good one.) In addition to several structures about which you have already read (e.g., the mammillary bodies and the hippocampus), major structures of the limbic system include the amygdala, the fornix, the cingulate cortex, and the septum.

Let's begin tracing the limbic circuit (see Figure 3.28) at the **amygdala**—the almond-shaped nucleus in the anterior temporal lobe (*amygdala* means "almond" and is pronounced "a-MIG-dah-lah")—see Swanson & Petrovich (1998). Posterior to the amygdala is the hip-

pocampus, which runs beneath the thalamus in the medial temporal lobe. Next in the ring are the cingulate cortex and the fornix. The **cingulate cortex** is the large area of neocortex in the cingulate gyrus on the medial surface of the cerebral hemispheres, just superior to the corpus callosum; it encircles the dorsal thalamus (*cingulate* means "encircling"). The **fornix**, the major tract of the limbic system, also encircles the dorsal thalamus; it leaves the dorsal end of the hippocampus and sweeps forward in an arc coursing along the superior surface of the third ventricle and terminating in the septum and mammillary bodies (*fornix* means "arc"). The **septum** is a midline nucleus that is located at the anterior tip of the cingulate cortex. Several tracts connect the septum and mammillary bodies with the amygdala and hippocampus, thereby completing the limbic ring.

The **basal ganglia** are illustrated in Figure 3.29. As we did with the limbic system, let's begin our examination of the basal ganglia with the amygdala, which is considered to be part of both systems. Sweeping out of each amygdala, first in a posterior direction and then in an anterior direction, is the long tail-like **caudate** (*caudate*

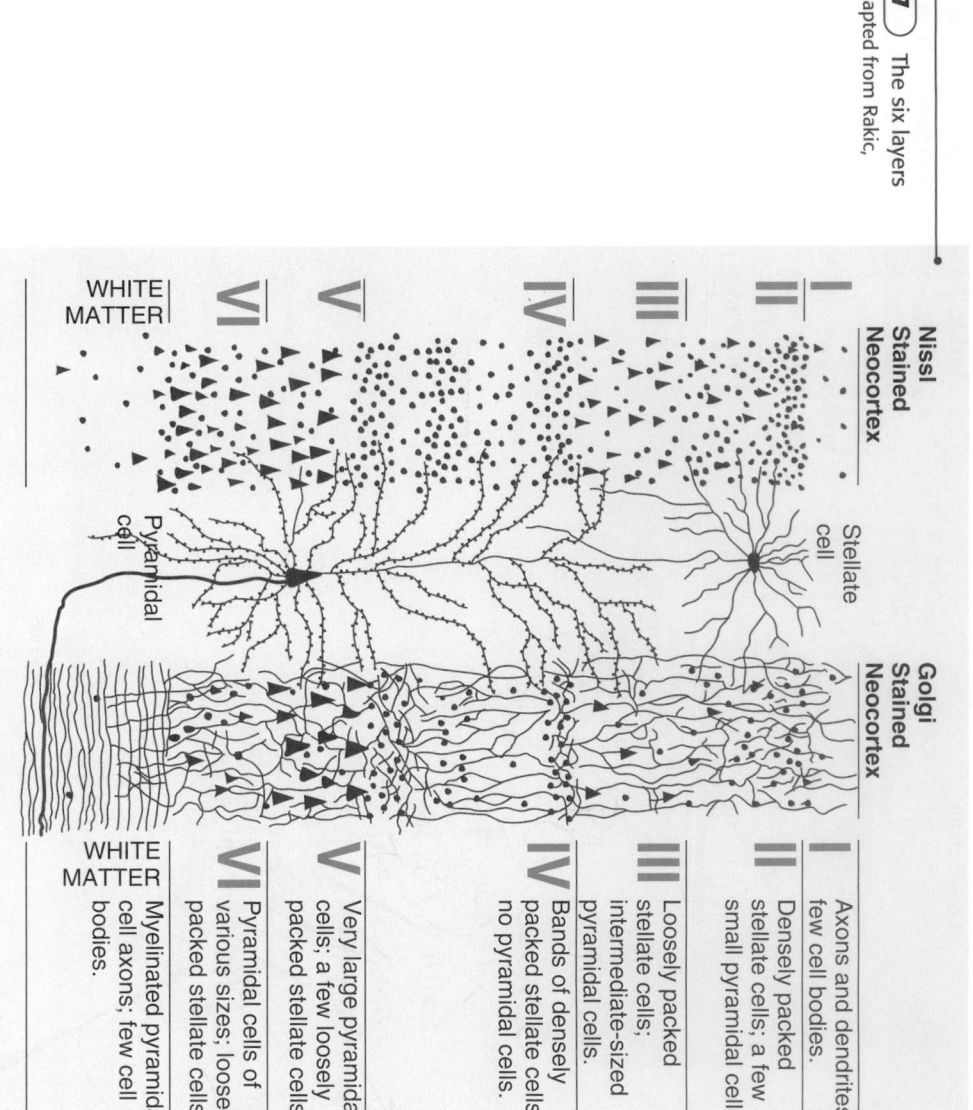

FIGURE 3.27 The six layers of neocortex. (Adapted from Rakic, 1979.)

Nissl Stained Neocortex

WHITE MATTER

I II III IV V VI

Golgi Stained Neocortex

Pyramidal cell

Stellate cell

WHITE MATTER

I — Axons and dendrites; few cell bodies.

II — Densely packed stellate cells; a few small pyramidal cells.

III — Loosely packed stellate cells; intermediate-sized pyramidal cells.

IV — Bands of densely packed stellate cells; no pyramidal cells.

V — Very large pyramidal cells; a few loosely packed stellate cells.

VI — Pyramidal cells of various sizes; loosely packed stellate cells.

Myelinated pyramidal cell axons; few cell bodies.

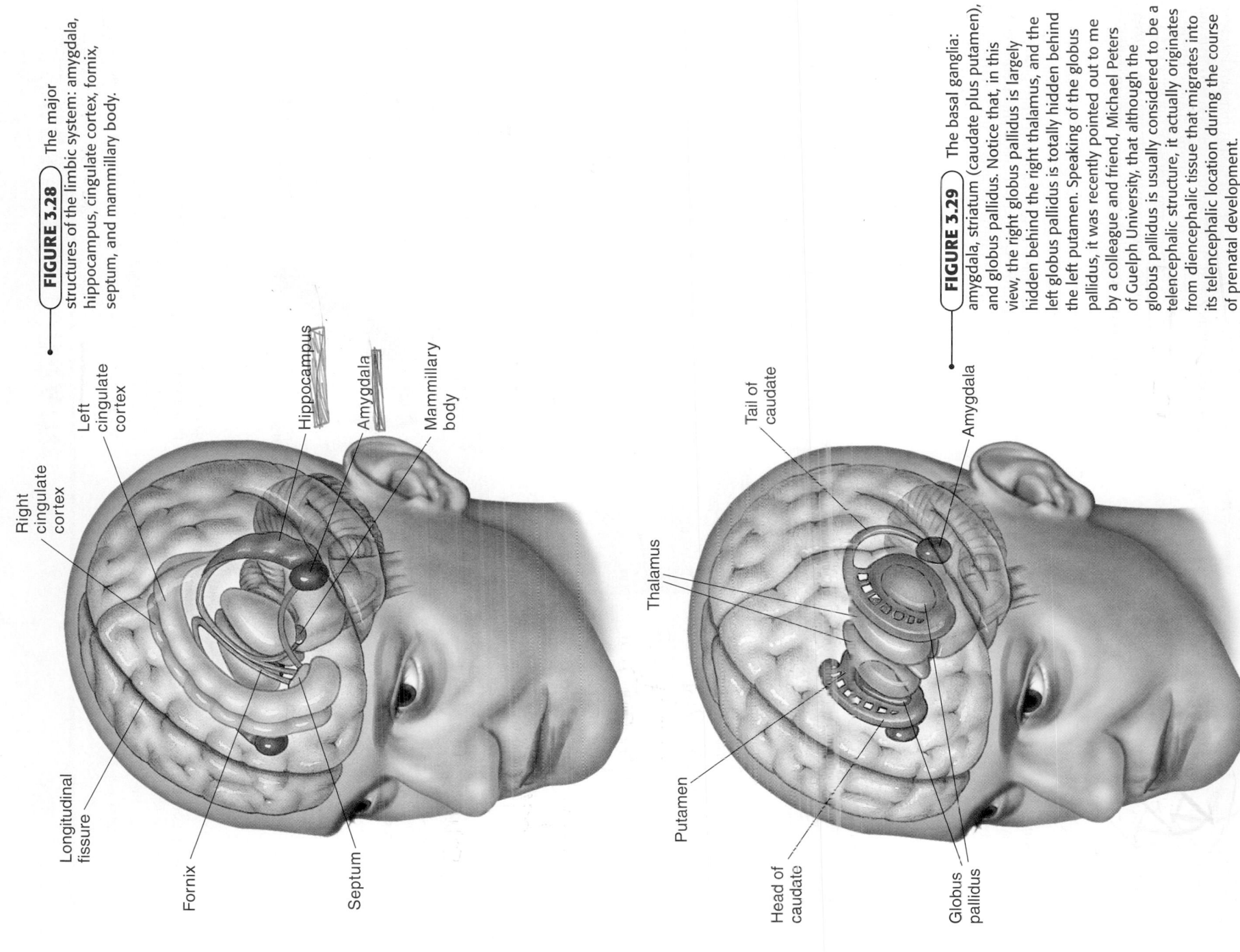

FIGURE 3.28   The major structures of the limbic system: amygdala, hippocampus, cingulate cortex, fornix, septum, and mammillary body.

Right cingulate cortex

Left cingulate cortex

Hippocampus

Amygdala

Mammillary body

Longitudinal fissure

Fornix

Septum

FIGURE 3.29   The basal ganglia: amygdala, striatum (caudate plus putamen), and globus pallidus. Notice that, in this view, the right globus pallidus is largely hidden behind the right thalamus, and the left globus pallidus is totally hidden behind the left putamen. Speaking of the globus pallidus, it was recently pointed out to me by a colleague and friend, Michael Peters of Guelph University, that although the globus pallidus is usually considered to be a telencephalic structure, it actually originates from diencephalic tissue that migrates into its telencephalic location during the course of prenatal development.

Tail of caudate

Amygdala

Thalamus

Putamen

Head of caudate

Globus pallidus

SCAN YOUR BRAIN

If you have not previously studied the gross anatomy of the brain, your own brain is probably straining under the burden of new terms. To determine whether or not you are ready to proceed, scan your brain by labeling the following midsagittal view of a real human brain. (It will be challenging to switch from color-coded diagrams to a photograph.)

The correct answers are provided at the bottom of the page. Before proceeding, review material related to your errors and omissions. Notice that Figure 3.30 includes all the brain anatomy terms that have appeared in bold type in this section and thus is an excellent review tool.

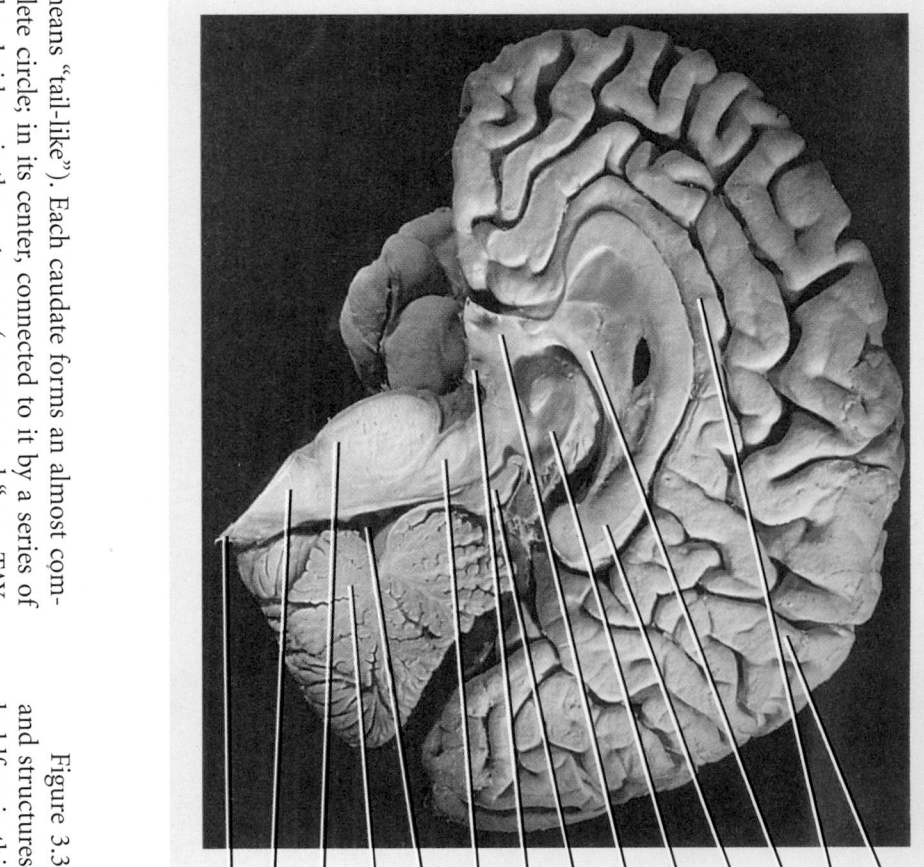

1. PARIETAL _____ lobe
2. CINGULATE _____ gyrus
3. FORNIX
4. CORPUS CALLOSUM
5. THALAMUS
6. HYPOTHALAMUS
7. SUPERIOR _____ colliculus
8. MAMMILLARY _____ body
9. TEGMENTUM
10. FOURTH _____ ventricle
11. CEREBELLUM
12. PONS
13. MEDULLA
14. SPINAL CORD

means "tail-like"). Each caudate forms an almost complete circle; in its center, connected to it by a series of fiber bridges, is the **putamen** (pronounced "pew-TAY-men"). Together, the caudate and the putamen, which both have a striped appearance, are known as the **striatum** (striped structure). The remaining structure of the basal ganglia is the pale circular structure known as the **globus pallidus** (pale globe). The globus pallidus is located medial to the putamen, between the putamen and the thalamus.

The basal ganglia play a major role in the performance of voluntary motor responses. Of particular interest is a pathway that projects to the striatum from the substantia nigra of the midbrain. *Parkinson's disease*, a disorder that is characterized by rigidity, tremors, and poverty of voluntary movement, is associated with the deterioration of this pathway.

Figure 3.30 summarizes the major brain divisions and structures—those key terms that have appeared in boldface in this section.

Figure 3.31 on page 74 concludes this chapter for reasons that too often get lost in the shuffle of neuroanatomical terms and technology. I have included it here to illustrate the beauty of the brain and the art of those who study its structure. I hope you are inspired by it. I wonder what thoughts its neural circuits once contained.

Scan Your Brain answers: (1) parietal, (2) cingulate, (3) fornix, (4) corpus callosum, (5) thalamus, (6) hypothalamus, (7) superior, (8) mammillary, (9) tegmentum, (10) fourth, (11) cerebellum, (12) pons, (13) medulla, (14) spinal cord.

Division	Structure	Components
Telencephalon	Cerebral cortex	Neocortex Hippocampus
	Major fissures	Central fissure Lateral fissure Longitudinal fissure
	Major gyri	Precentral gyrus Postcentral gyrus Superior temporal gyrus Cingulate gyrus
	Four lobes	Frontal lobe Temporal lobe Parietal lobe Occipital lobe
	Limbic system	Amygdala Hippocampus Fornix Cingulate cortex Septum Mammillary bodies
	Basal ganglia	Amygdala Caudate } Striatum Putamen } Globus pallidus
	Cerebral commissures	Corpus callosum
Diencephalon	Thalamus	Massa intermedia Lateral geniculate nuclei Medial geniculate nuclei Ventral posterior nuclei
	Hypothalamus	Mammillary bodies
	Optic chiasm	
	Pituitary gland	
Mesencephalon	Tectum	Superior colliculi Inferior colliculi
	Tegmentum	Reticular formation Cerebral aqueduct Periaqueductal gray Substantia nigra Red nucleus
Metencephalon	Reticular formation Pons Cerebellum	
Myelencephalon or Medulla	Reticular formation	

FIGURE 3.30 Summary of major brain structures. This display contains all the brain anatomy key terms that appear in boldface in Section 3.6.

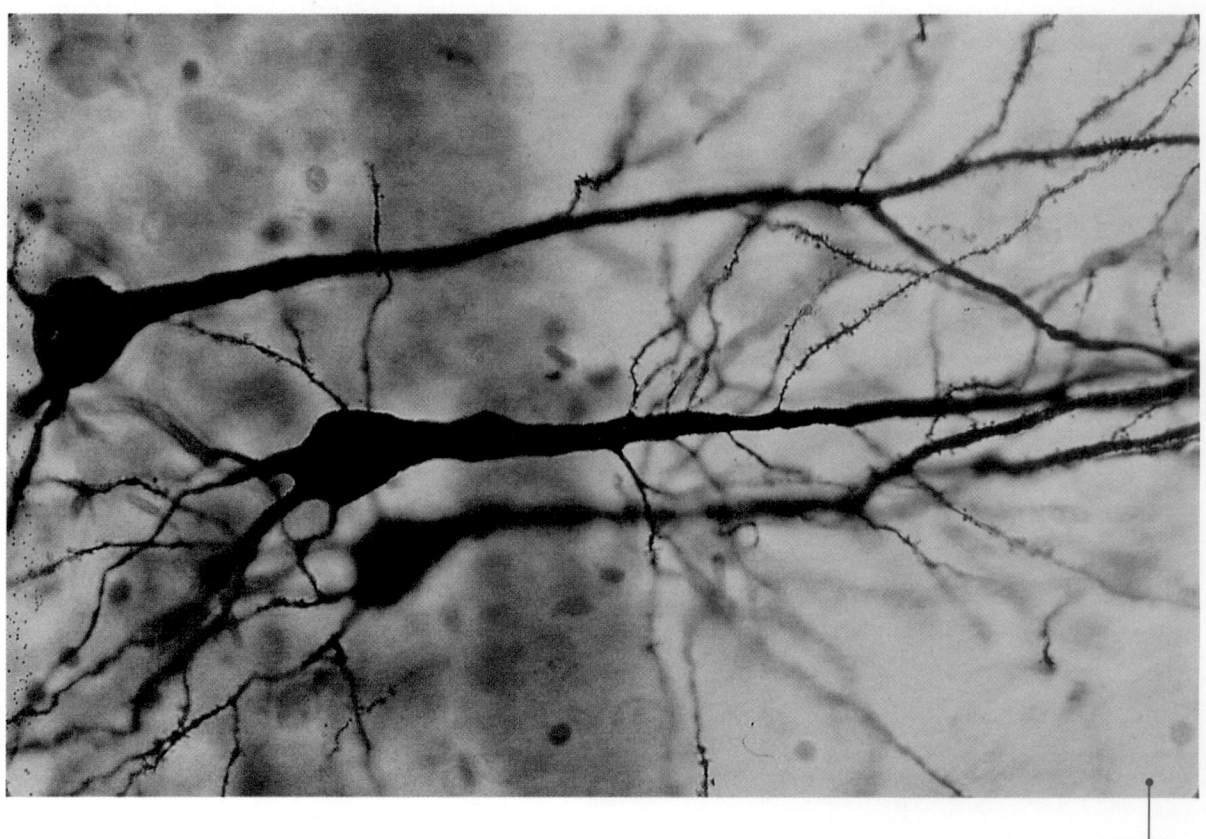

FIGURE 3.31 The art of neuroanatomical staining. This slide was stained with both a Golgi stain and a Nissl stain. Clearly visible on the Golgi-stained pyramidal neurons are the pyramid-shaped cell bodies, the large apical dendrites, and numerous dendritic spines. Each pyramidal cell has a long, narrow axon, which projects off the bottom of the slide. (Courtesy of Miles Herkenham, Unit of Functional Neuroanatomy, National Institute of Mental Health, Bethesda, MD.)

ON THE CD See Hard Copy for additional readings for Chapter 3.

Themes Revisited

This chapter contributed relatively little to the development of the book's themes; that development was temporarily slowed while you were being introduced to the key areas and structures of the human brain. A knowledge of fundamental neuroanatomy will serve as the foundation of discussions of brain function in subsequent chapters.

However, the clinical implications theme did arise three times: the importance of the cranial nerves in neurological diagnosis, the role of blockage of cerebral aqueducts in hydrocephalus, and the involvement of damage to the pathway from the substantia nigra to the striatum in Parkinson's disease.

Clinical Implications

Think about It

1. Which of the following extreme positions do you think is closer to the truth? (a) The primary goal of all psychological research should be to relate psychological phenomena to the anatomy of neural circuits. (b) Psychologists should leave the study of neuroanatomy to neuroanatomists.

2. Perhaps the most famous mistake in the history of biopsychology was made by Olds and Milner (see Chapter 15). They botched an electrode implantation in the brain of a rat, and the tip of the stimulation electrode ended up in an unknown structure. When they subsequently tested the effects of electrical stimulation of this unknown structure, they made a fantastic discovery: The rat seemed to find the brain stimulation extremely pleasurable. In fact, the rat would press a lever for hours at an extremely high rate if every press produced a brief stimulation to its brain through the electrode. If you had accidentally stumbled on this intracranial self-stimulation phenomenon, what neuroanatomical procedures would you have used to identify the stimulation site and the neural circuits involved in the pleasurable effects of the stimulation?

ON THE CD

Studying for an exam? Try the Practice Tests for Chapter 3.

Key Terms

Afferent nerves (*p. 51*)
Anterior (*p. 61*)
Arachnoid membrane (*p. 53*)
Astrocytes (*p. 58*)
Autonomic nervous system (ANS) (*p. 51*)
Bipolar neuron (*p. 57*)
Blood–brain barrier (*p. 53*)
Brain stem (*p. 64*)
Central canal (*p. 53*)
Central nervous system (CNS) (*p. 51*)
Cerebral ventricles (*p. 53*)
Cerebrospinal fluid (CSF) (*p. 53*)
Choroid plexuses (*p. 53*)
Columnar organization (*p. 68*)
Contralateral (*p. 67*)
Cranial nerves (*p. 52*)

Cross sections (*p. 62*)
Decussate (*p. 67*)
Dorsal (*p. 61*)
Dorsal horns (*p. 62*)
Dura mater (*p. 53*)
Efferent nerves (*p. 51*)
Electron microscopy (*p. 60*)
Frontal sections (*p. 62*)
Ganglia (*p. 58*)
Glial cells (*p. 58*)
Golgi stain (*p. 59*)
Horizontal sections (*p. 62*)
Inferior (*p. 62*)
Interneurons (*p. 58*)
Ipsilateral (*p. 67*)
Lateral (*p. 61*)
Medial (*p. 61*)
Meninges (*p. 53*)
Microglia (*p. 59*)

Multipolar neuron (*p. 57*)
Nerves (*p. 58*)
Nissl stain (*p. 60*)
Nuclei (*p. 58*)
Oligodendrocytes (*p. 58*)
Parasympathetic nerves (*p. 51*)
Peripheral nervous system (PNS) (*p. 51*)
Pia mater (*p. 53*)
Posterior (*p. 61*)
Pyramidal cells (*p. 68*)
Sagittal sections (*p. 62*)
Schwann cells (*p. 58*)
Somatic nervous system (SNS) (*p. 51*)
Stellate cells (*p. 68*)
Subarachnoid space (*p. 53*)
Superior (*p. 62*)
Sympathetic nerves (*p. 51*)

Tracts (*p. 58*)
Unipolar neuron (*p. 57*)
Ventral (*p. 61*)
Ventral horns (*p. 62*)

ON THE CD

Need some help studying the key terms for this chapter? Check out the electronic flash cards for Chapter 3.

Neural Conduction and Synaptic Transmission

How Neurons Send and Receive Signals

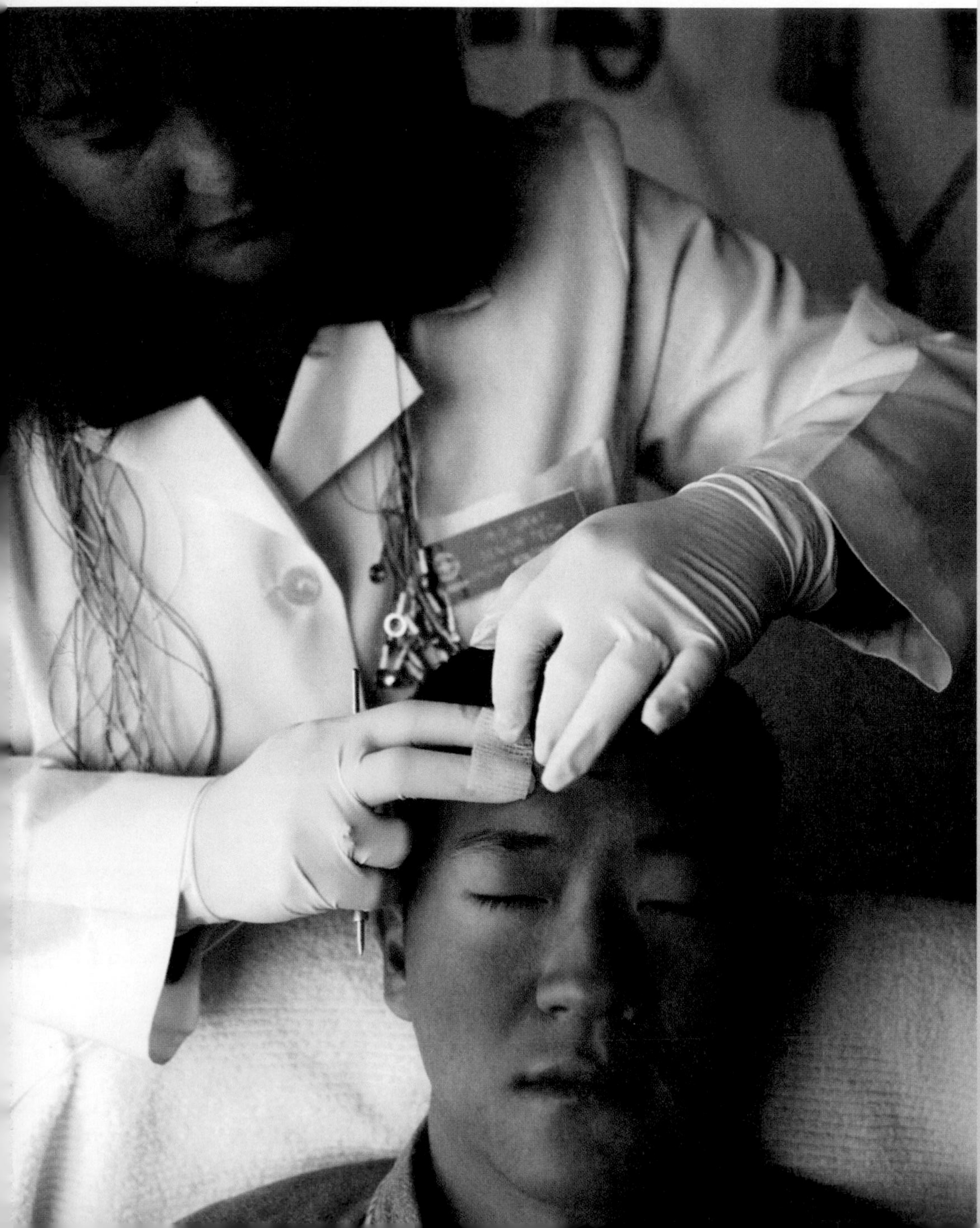

4.1 The Neuron's Resting Membrane Potential

4.2 Generation and Conduction of Postsynaptic Potentials

4.3 Integration of Postsynaptic Potentials and Generation of Action Potentials

4.4 Conduction of Action Potentials

4.5 Synaptic Transmission: Chemical Transmission of Signals from One Neuron to Another

4.6 The Neurotransmitters

4.7 Pharmacology of Synaptic Transmission

4

chapter

Chapter 3 introduced you to the anatomy of neurons. This chapter introduces you to their function—it is about how neurons conduct and transmit electrochemical signals. It begins with a description of how signals are generated in resting neurons; then, it follows the signals as they are conducted through neurons and transmitted across synapses to other neurons.

"The Lizard," a case study of a patient with Parkinson's disease, Roberto Garcia d'Orta, will help you appreciate why a knowledge of neural conduction and synaptic transmission is an integral part of biopsychology.

Clinical Implications

The Lizard, a Case of Parkinson's Disease

"I have become a lizard," he began. "A great lizard frozen in a dark, cold, strange world."

His name was Roberto Garcia d'Orta. He was a tall thin man in his sixties, but like most patients with Parkinson's disease, he appeared to be much older than his actual age. Not many years before, he had been an active, vigorous business man. Then it happened—not all at once, not suddenly, but slowly, subtly, insidiously. Now he turned like a piece of granite, walked in slow shuffling steps, and spoke in a monotonous whisper. What had been his first symptom?

A tremor.

Had his tremor been disabling?

"No," he said. "My hands shake worse when they are doing nothing at all"—a symptom called *tremor-at-rest*.

The other symptoms of Parkinson's disease are not quite so benign. They can change a vigorous man into a lizard. These include rigid muscles, a marked poverty of spontaneous movements, difficulty in starting to move, and slowness in executing voluntary movements once they have been initiated.

The term "reptilian stare" is often used to describe the characteristic lack of blinking and the widely opened eyes gazing out of a motionless face, a set of features that seems more reptilian than human. Truly a lizard in the eyes of the world.

What was happening in Mr. d'Orta's brain? A small group of nerve cells called the *substantia nigra* (black substance) were unaccountably dying. These neurons make a particular chemical neurotransmitter called dopamine, which they deliver to another part of the brain, known as the striatum. As the cells of the substantia nigra die, the amount of dopamine they can deliver goes down. The striatum helps control movement, and to do that normally, it needs dopamine.

(Paraphrased from *Newton's Madness: Further Tales of Clinical Neurology* by Harold L. Klawans, pp. 53–57. New York: Harper & Row, © Harold Klawans, 1990.)

Dopamine is not an effective treatment for Parkinson's disease because it does not readily penetrate the blood–brain barrier. However, knowledge of dopaminergic transmission has led to the development of an effective treatment: L-dopa, the chemical precursor of dopamine, which readily penetrates the blood–brain barrier and is converted to dopamine once inside the brain.

Mr. d'Orta's neurologist prescribed L-dopa, and it worked. He still had a bit of tremor; but his voice became stronger, his feet no longer shuffled, his reptilian stare faded away, and he was once again able to perform with ease many of the activities of daily life (e.g., eating, bathing, writing, speaking, and even making love with his wife). Mr. d'Orta had been destined to spend the rest of his life trapped inside a body that was becoming increasingly difficult to control, but his life sentence was repealed.

Mr. d'Orta's story does not end here. You will read more about him in a later chapter, and you should keep him in mind as you read this one. His situation will remind you that normal neural activity is necessary for normal psychological function. A knowledge of neural conduction and synaptic transmission is a major asset for any psychologist; it is a must for any biopsychologist.

4.1 The Neuron's Resting Membrane Potential

One key to understanding neural function is the **membrane potential**, the difference in electrical charge between the inside and the outside of a cell.

Recording the Membrane Potential

To record a neuron's membrane potential, it is necessary to position the tip of one electrode inside the neuron and the tip of another electrode outside the neuron in the extracellular fluid. Although the size of the extracellular electrode is not critical, it is paramount that the tip of the intracellular electrode be fine enough to pierce the neural membrane without severely damaging it. The intracellular electrodes are called **microelectrodes**; their tips are less than one-thousandth of a millimeter in diameter—much too small to be seen by the naked eye.

The Resting Membrane Potential

When both electrode tips are in the extracellular fluid, the voltage difference between them is zero. However, when the tip of the intracellular electrode is inserted into a neuron, a steady potential of about –70 millivolts (mV) is recorded. This indicates that the potential inside the resting neuron is about 70 mV less than that outside the neuron. This steady membrane potential of about –70 mV is called the neuron's **resting potential**. In its resting state, with the –70 mV charge built up across its membrane, a neuron is said to be *polarized*.

The Ionic Basis of the Resting Potential

Why are resting neurons polarized? Like all salts in solution, the salts in neural tissue separate into positively and negatively charged particles called **ions**. The resting potential results from the fact that the ratio of negative to positive charges is greater inside the neuron than outside. Why this unequal distribution of charges occurs can be understood in terms of the interaction of four factors: two factors that act to distribute ions equally throughout the intracellular and extracellular fluids of the nervous system and two features of the neural membrane that counteract these homogenizing effects.

The first of the two homogenizing factors is *random motion*. The ions in neural tissue are in constant random motion, and particles in random motion tend to become evenly distributed because they are more likely to move down their *concentration gradients* than up them; that is, they are more likely to move from areas of high concentration to areas of low concentration than vice versa. The second factor that promotes the even distribution of ions is *electrostatic pressure*. Any accumulation of charges, positive or negative, in one area tends to be dispersed by the repulsion among the like charges in the vicinity and the attraction of opposite charges concentrated elsewhere.

Despite the continuous homogenizing effects of random movement and electrostatic pressure, no single class of ions is distributed equally on the two sides of the neural membrane. Four kinds of ions contribute significantly to the resting potential: sodium ions (Na⁺), potassium ions (K⁺), chloride ions (Cl⁻), and various negatively charged protein ions. The concentrations of both Na⁺ and Cl⁻ ions are greater outside a resting neuron than inside, whereas K⁺ ions are more concentrated on the inside. The negatively charged protein ions are synthesized inside the neuron and, for the most part, stay there. See Figure 4.1. By the way, the symbols for sodium and potassium were derived from their Latin names: *natrium* (Na⁺) and *kalium* (K⁺), respectively.

Two properties of the neural membrane are responsible for the unequal distribution of Na⁺, K⁺, Cl⁻, and protein ions in resting neurons. One of these properties is passive; that is, it does not involve the consumption of energy. The other is active and does involve the consumption of energy. The passive property of the neural membrane that contributes to the unequal disposition of Na⁺, K⁺, Cl⁻, and protein ions is its differential permeability to those ions. In resting neurons, K⁺ and Cl⁻ ions pass

readily through the neural membrane, Na⁺ ions pass through it with difficulty, and the negatively charged protein ions do not pass through it at all. Ions pass through the neural membrane at specialized pores called **ion channels**, each type of which is specialized for the passage of particular ions.

In the 1950s, the classic experiments of neurophysiologists Alan Hodgkin and Andrew Huxley provided the first evidence that an energy-consuming process is involved in the maintenance of the resting potential. Hodgkin and Huxley began by wondering why the high extracellular concentrations of Na⁺ and Cl⁻ ions and the high intracellular concentration of K⁺ ions were not eliminated by the tendency for them to move down their concentration gradients to the side of lesser concentration. Could the electrostatic pressure of –70 mV across the membrane be the countering force that maintained the unequal distribution of ions? To answer this question, Hodgkin and Huxley calculated for each of the three ions the electrostatic charge that would be

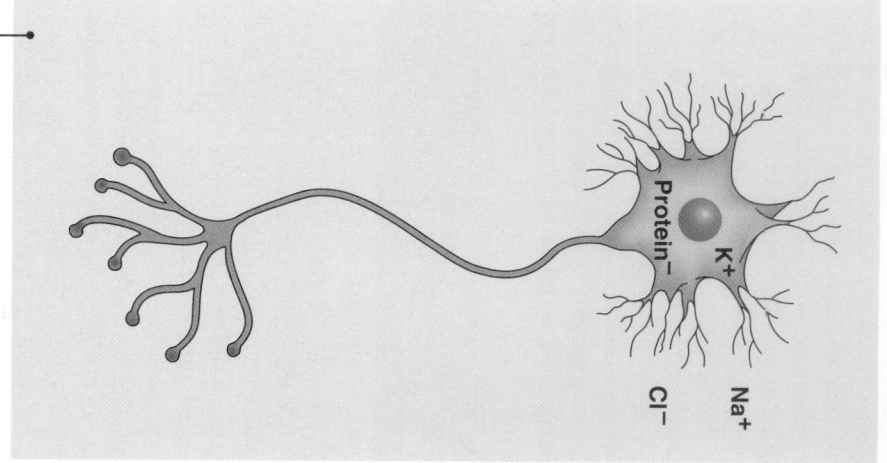

FIGURE 4.1   In its resting state, more Na⁺ and Cl⁻ ions are outside the neuron than inside, and more K⁺ ions and negatively charged protein ions are inside the neuron than outside.

ON THE CD

The *Ion Channels* module illustrates the locations and functions of different types of ion channels.

required to offset the tendency for them to move down their concentration gradients.

For Cl⁻ ions, this calculated electrostatic charge was −70 mV, the same as the actual resting potential. Hodgkin and Huxley thus concluded that when neurons are at rest, the unequal distribution of Cl⁻ ions across the neural membrane is maintained in equilibrium by the balance between the tendency for Cl⁻ ions to move down their concentration gradient into the neuron and the 70 mV of electrostatic pressure driving them out.

The situation turned out to be different for the K⁺ ions. Hodgkin and Huxley calculated that 90 mV of electrostatic pressure would be required to keep intracellular K⁺ ions from moving down their concentration gradient and leaving the neuron—some 20 mV more than the actual resting potential.

In the case of Na⁺ ions, the situation was much more extreme because the effects of both the concentration gradient and the electrostatic gradient act in the same direction. The concentration of Na⁺ ions that exists outside of a resting neuron is such that 50 mV of outward pressure would be required to keep Na⁺ ions from mov-

ing down their concentration gradient into the neuron, which is added to the 70 mV of electrostatic pressure acting to move them in the same direction. Thus, the equivalent of a whopping 120 mV of pressure is trying to force Na⁺ ions into resting neurons.

Subsequent experiments confirmed Hodgkin and Huxley's calculations. They showed that K⁺ ions are continuously being driven out of resting neurons by 20 mV of pressure and that, despite the high resistance of the cell membrane to the passage of Na⁺ ions, those ions are continuously being driven in by the equivalent of 120 mV of pressure. Why, then, do the intracellular and extracellular concentrations of Na⁺ and K⁺ remain constant in resting neurons? Hodgkin and Huxley discovered that there are active mechanisms in the cell membrane to counteract the *influx* (inflow) of Na⁺ ions by pumping Na⁺ ions out as rapidly as they pass in and to counteract the *efflux* (outflow) of K⁺ ions by pumping K⁺ ions in as rapidly as they pass out. Figure 4.2 summarizes Hodgkin and Huxley's findings and conclusions.

It was subsequently discovered that the transport of Na⁺ ions out of neurons and the transport of K⁺ ions into

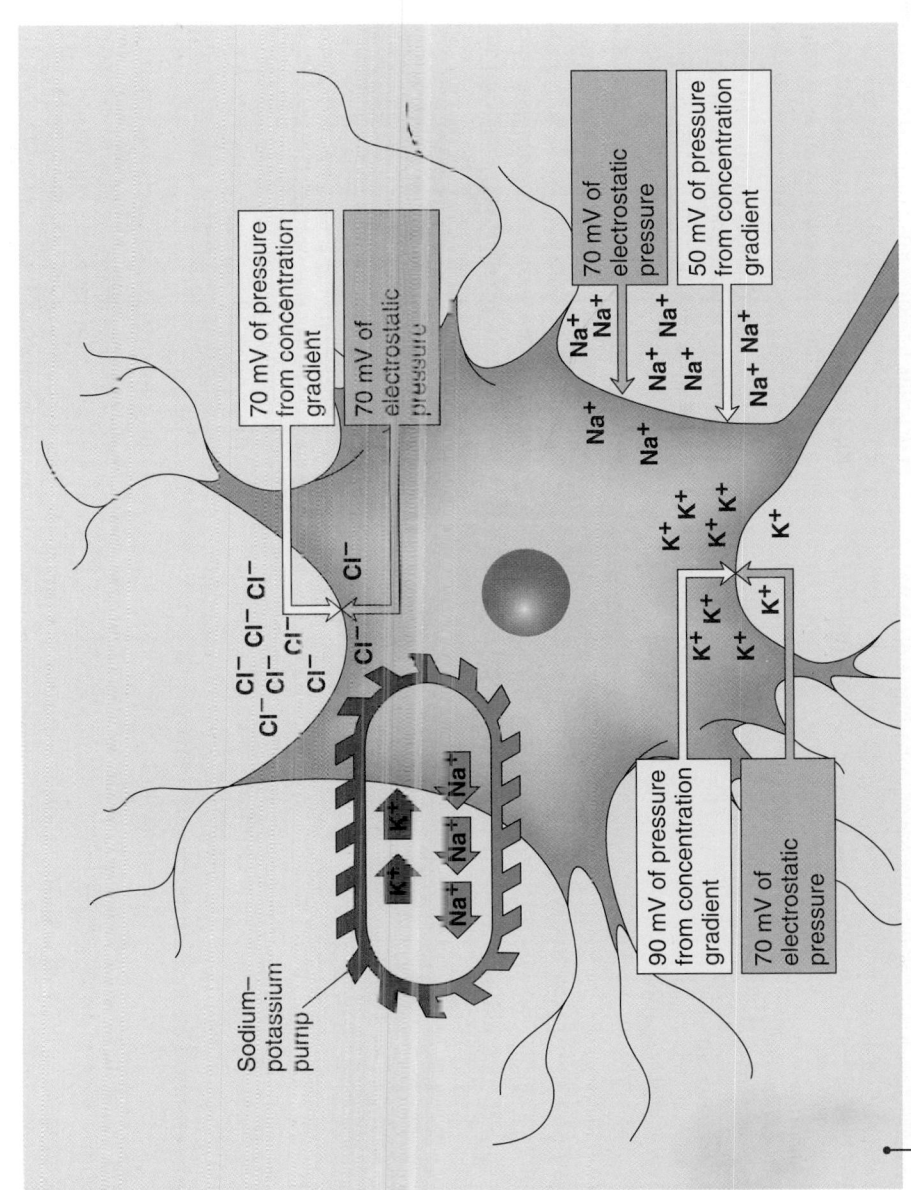

FIGURE 4.2   The passive and active factors that influence the distribution of Na⁺, K⁺, and Cl⁻ ions across the neural membrane. Passive factors continuously drive K⁺ ions out of the resting neuron and Na⁺ ions in; therefore, K⁺ ions must be actively pumped in and Na⁺ ions must be actively pumped out to maintain the resting equilibrium. These factors can be thought of in terms of the interaction of forces that push ions into and out of neurons.

Sodium—potassium pump

Cl⁻ Cl⁻ Cl⁻
Cl⁻ Cl⁻
Cl⁻ Cl⁻
Cl⁻

70 mV of pressure from concentration gradient

70 mV of electrostatic pressure

Na⁺ Na⁺
Na⁺ Na⁺
Na⁺ Na⁺
Na⁺
Na⁺ Na⁺

70 mV of electrostatic pressure

50 mV of pressure from concentration gradient

K⁺ K⁺
K⁺ K⁺
K⁺ K⁺
K⁺

90 mV of pressure from concentration gradient

70 mV of electrostatic pressure

TABLE 4.1 **The Factors Responsible for Maintaining the Differences in the Intracellular and Extracellular Concentrations of Na+, K+, and Cl- Ions in Resting Neurons**

Na+	Na+ ions tend to be driven into the neurons by both the high concentration of Na+ ions outside the neuron and the negative internal resting potential of −70 mV. However, the membrane is resistant to the passive diffusion of Na+, and the sodium–potassium pump is thus able to maintain the high external concentration of Na+ ions by pumping them out at the same slow rate as they move in.
K+	K+ ions tend to move out of the neuron because of their high internal concentration, although this tendency is partially offset by the internal negative potential. Despite the tendency for the K+ ions to leave the neuron, they do so at a substantial rate because the membrane offers little resistance to their passage. To maintain the high internal concentration of K+ ions, mechanisms in the cell membrane pump K+ ions into neurons at the same rate as they move out.
Cl-	There is little resistance in the neural membrane to the passage of Cl- ions. Thus, Cl- ions are readily forced out of the neuron by the negative internal potential. As chloride ions begin to accumulate on the outside, there is an increased tendency for them to move down their concentration gradient back into the neuron. When the point is reached where the electrostatic pressure for Cl- ions to move out of the neuron is equal to the tendency for them to move back in, the distribution of Cl- ions is held in equilibrium. This point of equilibrium occurs at −70 mV.

them are not independent processes. Such ion transport is performed by energy-consuming mechanisms in the cell membrane that continually exchange three Na+ ions inside the neuron for two K+ ions outside. These transport mechanisms are commonly referred to as **sodium–potassium pumps.**

Table 4.1 summarizes the major factors that are responsible for maintaining the differences between the intracellular and extracellular concentrations of Na+, K+, and Cl- ions in resting neurons. These differences plus the negative charges of the various protein ions, which are trapped inside the neuron, are largely responsible for the resting membrane potential.

Now that you understand these basic properties of the resting neuron, you are prepared to consider how neurons respond to input.

4.2 Generation and Conduction of Postsynaptic Potentials

When neurons fire, they release from their terminal buttons chemicals called *neurotransmitters*, which diffuse across the synaptic clefts and interact with specialized receptor molecules on the receptive membranes of the next neurons in the circuit. When neurotransmitter molecules bind to postsynaptic receptors, they typically have one of two effects, depending on the structure of both the neurotransmitter and the receptor in question. They may **depolarize** the receptive membrane (decrease the resting membrane potential, from −70 to −67 mV, for example) or they may **hyperpolarize** it (increase the resting membrane potential, from −70 to −72 mV, for example).

Postsynaptic depolarizations are called **excitatory postsynaptic potentials (EPSPs)** because, as you will soon learn, they increase the likelihood that the neuron will fire. Postsynaptic hyperpolarizations are called **in-** **hibitory postsynaptic potentials (IPSPs)** because they decrease the likelihood that the neuron will fire. Both EPSPs and IPSPs are **graded responses.** This means that the amplitudes of EPSPs and IPSPs are proportional to the intensity of the signals that elicit them: Weak signals elicit small postsynaptic potentials, and strong signals elicit large ones.

EPSPs and IPSPs travel passively from their sites of generation at synapses, usually on the dendrites or cell body, in much the same way that electrical signals travel through a cable. Accordingly, the transmission of postsynaptic potentials has two important characteristics. First, it is rapid—so rapid that it can be assumed to be instantaneous for most purposes. It is important not to confuse the duration of EPSPs and IPSPs with their rate of transmission; although the duration of EPSPs and IPSPs varies considerably, all postsynaptic potentials, whether brief or enduring, are transmitted at great speed. Second, the transmission of EPSPs and IPSPs is *decremental*: EPSPs and IPSPs decrease in amplitude as they travel through the neuron, just as a sound wave grows fainter as it travels through air.

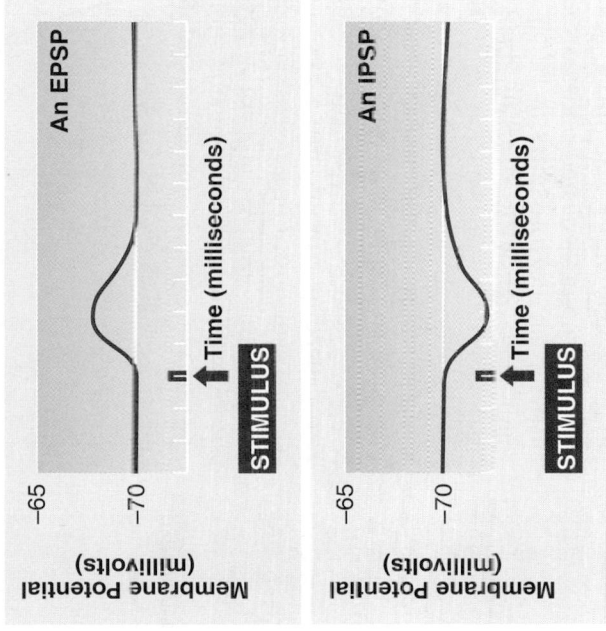

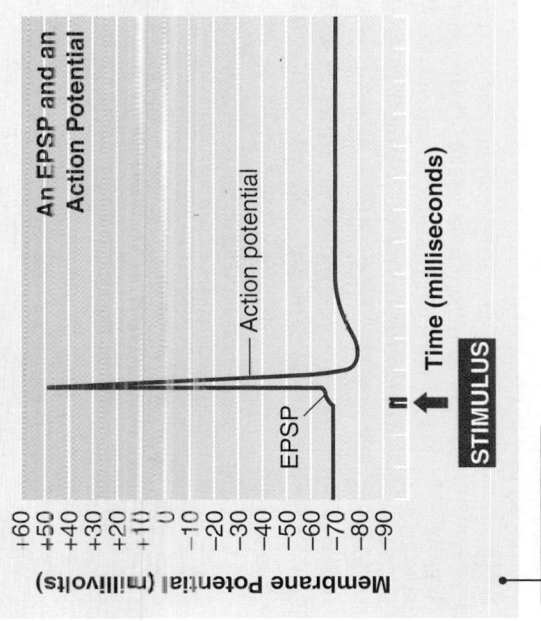

4.3 Integration of Postsynaptic Potentials and Generation of Action Potentials

The postsynaptic potentials created at a single synapse typically have little effect on the firing of the postsynaptic neuron. The receptive areas of most neurons are covered with thousands of synapses, and whether or not a neuron fires is determined by the net effect of their activity. More specifically, whether or not a neuron fires depends on the balance between the excitatory and inhibitory signals reaching its axon. Until recently, it was believed that action potentials were generated at the **axon hillock** (the conical structure at the junction between the cell body and the axon), but they are actually generated in the adjacent section of the axon.

The graded EPSPs and IPSPs created by the action of neurotransmitters at particular receptive sites on a neuron's membrane are conducted instantly and decrementally to the axon hillock. If the sum of the depolarizations and hyperpolarizations reaching the section of the axon adjacent to the axon hillock at any time is sufficient to depolarize the membrane to a level referred to as its **threshold of excitation**—usually about –65 mV—an action potential is generated near the axon hillock. The **action potential (AP)** is a massive momentary—lasting for 1 millisecond—reversal of the membrane potential from about –70 to about +50 mV. Unlike postsynaptic potentials, action potentials are not graded responses; their magnitude is not related in any way to the intensity of the stimuli that elicit them. To the contrary, they are **all-or-none responses**; that is, they either occur to their full extent or do not occur at all. See Figure 4.3 for an illustration of an EPSP, an IPSP, and an AP.

In effect, each multipolar neuron adds together all the graded excitatory and inhibitory postsynaptic potentials reaching its axon and decides to fire or not to fire on the basis of their sum. Adding or combining a number of individual signals into one overall signal is called **integration.** Neurons integrate incoming signals in two ways: over space and over time.

Figure 4.4 on page 82 illustrates the three possible combinations of **spatial summation.** It shows how local EPSPs that are produced simultaneously on different parts of the receptive membrane sum to form a greater EPSP, how

ON THE CD

Visit the *Summation of EPSPs* module for an illustration of how temporal summation or spatial summation of EPSPs can elicit an action potential.

FIGURE 4.3 An EPSP, an IPSP, and an EPSP followed by an AP.

simultaneous IPSPs sum to form a greater IPSP, and how simultaneous EPSPs and IPSPs sum to cancel each other out.

FIGURE 4.4 The three possible combinations of spatial summation.

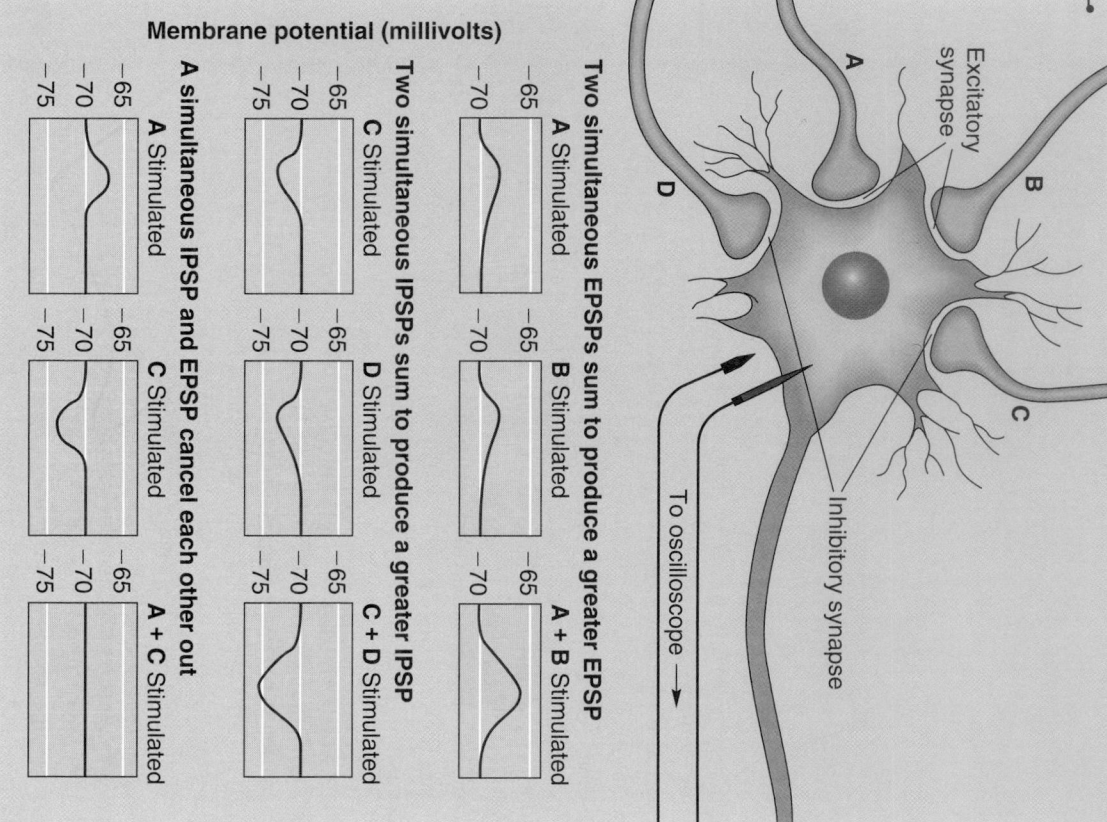

Two simultaneous EPSPs sum to produce a greater EPSP

A Stimulated   B Stimulated   A + B Stimulated

Two simultaneous IPSPs sum to produce a greater IPSP

C Stimulated   D Stimulated   C + D Stimulated

A simultaneous IPSP and EPSP cancel each other out

A Stimulated   C Stimulated   A + C Stimulated

Membrane potential (millivolts)

Excitatory synapse

Inhibitory synapse

To oscilloscope →

Figure 4.5 on page 83 illustrates **temporal summation**. It shows how postsynaptic potentials produced in rapid succession at the same synapse sum to form a greater signal. The reason that stimulations of a neuron can add together over time is that the postsynaptic potentials they produce often outlast them. Thus, if a particular synapse is activated and then activated again before the original postsynaptic potential has completely dissipated, the effect of the second stimulus will be superimposed on the lingering postsynaptic potential produced by the first. Accordingly, it is possible for a brief subthreshold excitatory stimulus to fire a neuron if it is administered twice in rapid succession. In the same way, an inhibitory synapse activated twice in rapid succession can produce a greater IPSP than that produced by a single stimulation.

Each neuron continuously integrates signals over both time and space as it is continually bombarded with stimuli through the thousands of synapses covering its dendrites and cell body. Remember that, although schematic diagrams of neural circuitry rarely show neurons with more than a few representative synaptic contacts, most neurons receive thousands of such contacts.

The location of a synapse on a neuron's receptive membrane has long been assumed to be an important factor in determining its potential to influence the neuron's firing. Because EPSPs and IPSPs are transmitted decrementally, synapses near the axon trigger zone have been assumed to have the most influence on the firing of the neuron (see Mel, 2002). However, it has recently been demonstrated that some neurons have

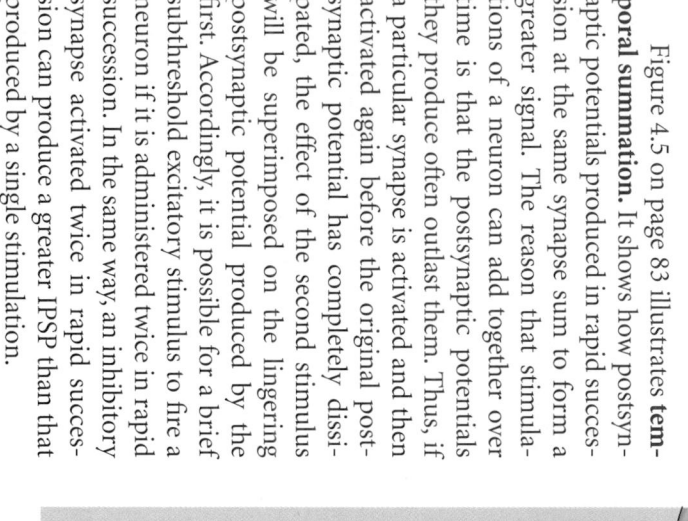

ON THE CD

For more about how the interactions between EPSPs and IPSPs determine whether a neuron will fire, take a look at the *Integration of Postsynaptic Potentials* module.

Thinking Critically

a mechanism for amplifying dendritic signals that originate far from their cell bodies; thus, all dendritic signals reaching the cell body of such a neuron have a similar amplitude, regardless of where they originate (Williams & Stuart, 2002, 2003).

In some ways, the firing of a neuron is like the firing of a gun. Both are all-or-none reactions triggered by graded responses. As a trigger is squeezed, it gradually moves back until it causes the gun to fire; as a neuron is stimulated, it becomes less polarized until the threshold of excitation is reached and firing occurs. Furthermore, the firing of a gun and neural firing are both all-or-none events. Just as squeezing a trigger harder does not make the bullet travel faster or farther, stimulating a neuron more intensely does not increase the speed or amplitude of the resulting action potential.

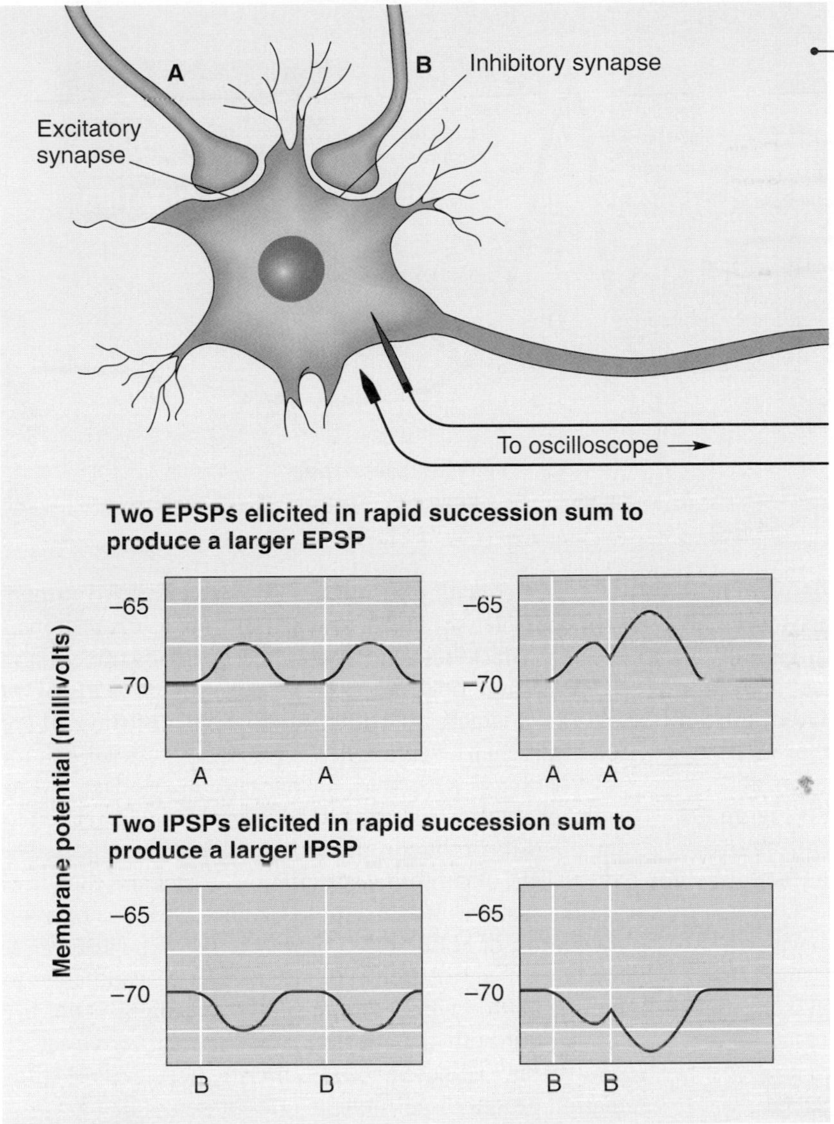

FIGURE 4.5 The two possible combinations of temporal summation.

Excitatory synapse

A

B Inhibitory synapse

To oscilloscope →

Membrane potential (millivolts)

Two EPSPs elicited in rapid succession sum to produce a larger EPSP

−65
−70
A A   A A

Two IPSPs elicited in rapid succession sum to produce a larger IPSP

−65
−70
B B   B B

4.4 Conduction of Action Potentials

The Ionic Basis of Action Potentials

How are action potentials produced, and how are they conducted along the axon? The answer to both questions is basically the same: through the action of **voltage-activated ion channels**—ion channels that open or close in response to changes in the level of the membrane potential (see McCormick, 1999).

Recall that the membrane potential of a neuron at rest is relatively constant despite the high pressure acting to drive Na^+ ions into the cell. This is because the resting membrane is relatively impermeable to Na^+ ions and because those few that do pass in are pumped out. But things suddenly change when the membrane potential of the axon is reduced to the threshold of excitation. The voltage-activated sodium channels in the axon membrane open wide, and Na^+ ions rush in, suddenly driving the membrane potential from about −70 to about +50 mV. The rapid change in the membrane potential that is associated with the *influx* of Na^+ ions then triggers the opening of voltage-activated potassium channels. At this point, K^+ ions near the membrane are driven out of the cell through these channels—first by their relatively high internal concentration and then, when the action potential is

ON THE CD

The *Generation of the Action Potential* module explains the threshold of activation of voltage-activated ion channels.

near its peak, by the positive internal charge. After about 1 millisecond, the sodium channels close. This marks the end of the *rising phase* of the action potential and the beginning of *repolarization* by the continued efflux of K+ ions. Once repolarization has been achieved, the potassium channels gradually close. Because they close gradually, too many K+ ions flow out of the neuron, and it is left hyperpolarized for a brief period of time. Figure 4.6 illustrates the timing of the opening and closing of the sodium and potassium channels during an action potential.

The number of ions that flow through the membrane during an action potential is extremely small in relation to the total number inside and around the neuron. The action potential involves only those ions right next to the membrane. Therefore, a single action potential has little effect on the relative concentrations of various ions inside and outside the neuron, and the resting ion concentrations next to the membrane are rapidly reestablished by the random movement of ions. The sodium–potassium pump plays only a minor role in the reestablishment of the resting potential.

ON THE CD

For a detailed review of the ionic basis of the action potentials, see the *Ionic Basis of the Action Potential* module.

Refractory Periods

There is a brief period of about 1 to 2 milliseconds after the initiation of an action potential during which it is impossible to elicit a second one. This period is called the **absolute refractory period.** The absolute refractory period is followed by the **relative refractory period**—the period during which it is possible to fire the neuron again, but only by applying higher-than-normal levels of stimulation. The end of the relative refractory period is the point at which the amount of stimulation necessary to fire a neuron returns to baseline.

The refractory period is responsible for two important characteristics of neural activity. First, it is responsible for the fact that action potentials normally travel along axons in only one direction. Because the portions of an axon over which an action potential has just traveled are left momentarily refractory, an action potential cannot reverse direction. Second, the refractory period is responsible for the fact that the rate of neural firing is related to the intensity of the stimulation. If a neuron is subjected to a high level of continual stimulation, it fires and then fires again as soon as its absolute refractory period is over—a maximum of about 1,000 times per second. However, if the level of stimulation is of an intensity just sufficient to fire the neuron when it is at rest, the neuron does not fire again until both the absolute and the relative refractory periods have run their course. Intermediate levels of stimulation produce intermediate rates of neural firing.

Axonal Conduction of Action Potentials

The conduction of action potentials along an axon differs from the conduction of EPSPs and IPSPs in two important ways. First, the conduction of action potentials along an axon is *nondecremental*; action potentials do not grow weaker as they travel along the axonal membrane. Second, action potentials are conducted more slowly than postsynaptic potentials.

The reason for these two differences is that the conduction of EPSPs and IPSPs is passive, whereas the axonal conduction of action potentials is largely active. Once an action potential has been generated, it travels passively along the axonal membrane to the adjacent voltage-activated sodium channels, which have yet to open. The arrival of the electrical signal opens these channels, thereby allowing Na+ ions to rush into the neuron and generate a full-blown action potential on this portion of the membrane. This signal is then conducted passively to the next sodium channels, where another action poten-

FIGURE 4.6 The opening and closing of voltage-activated sodium and potassium channels during the three phases of the action potential: rising phase, repolarization, and hyperpolarization.

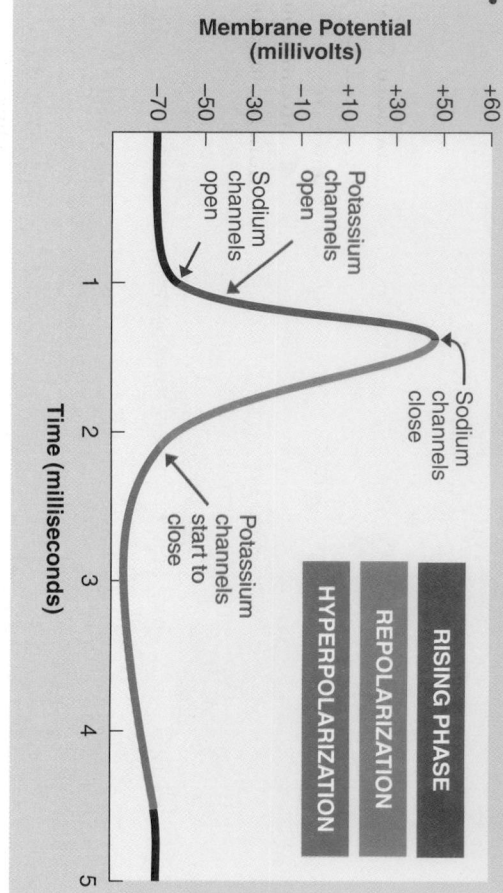

Membrane Potential (millivolts)

RISING PHASE · REPOLARIZATION · HYPERPOLARIZATION

Sodium channels open · Potassium channels open · Sodium channels close · Potassium channels start to close

Time (milliseconds)

tial is actively triggered. These events are repeated again and again until a full-blown action potential is triggered in all the terminal buttons (Huguenard, 2000). However, because there are so many ion channels on the axonal membrane and they are so close together, it is usual to think of axonal conduction as a single wave of excitation spreading actively at a constant speed along the axon, rather than as a series of discrete events.

The wave of excitation triggered by the generation of an action potential near the axon hillock also spreads back through the cell body and dendrites of the neuron. Although little is yet known about the functions of these backward action potentials, they are currently the subject of intensive investigation.

The following analogy may help you appreciate the major characteristics of axonal conduction. Consider a row of mousetraps on a wobbly shelf, all of them set and ready to be triggered. Each trap stores energy by holding back its striker against the pressure of the spring, in the same way that each sodium channel stores energy by holding back Na$^+$ ions, which are under pressure to move down their concentration and electrostatic gradients into the neuron. When the first trap in the row is triggered, the vibration is transmitted passively through the shelf, and the next trap is sprung—and so on down the line.

The nondecremental nature of action potential conduction is readily apparent from this analogy; the last trap on the shelf strikes with no less intensity than did the first. This analogy also illustrates the refractory period: A trap cannot respond again until it has been reset, just as a section of axon cannot fire again until it has been repolarized. Furthermore, the row of traps can transmit in either direction, just like an axon. If electrical stimulation of sufficient intensity is applied to the terminal end of an axon, an action potential will be generated and will travel along the axon back to the cell body; this is called **antidromic conduction**. Axonal conduction in the natural direction—from cell body to terminal buttons—is called **orthodromic conduction.**

Conduction in Myelinated Axons

In Chapter 3, you learned that the axons of many neurons are insulated from the extracellular fluid by segments of fatty tissue called *myelin*. In myelinated axons, ions can pass through the axonal membrane only at the nodes of Ranvier—the gaps between adjacent myelin segments. Indeed, in myelinated axons, sodium channels are concentrated at the nodes of Ranvier (Salzer, 2002). How, then, are action potentials transmitted in myelinated axons?

When an action potential is generated in a myelinated axon, the signal is conducted passively—that is, instantly and decrementally—along the first segment of myelin to the next node of Ranvier. Although the signal

is somewhat diminished by the time it reaches that node, it is still strong enough to open the voltage-activated sodium channels at the node and to generate another full-blown action potential. This action potential is then conducted passively along the axon to the next node, where another full-blown action potential is elicited, and so on.

Myelination increases the speed of axonal conduction. Because conduction along the myelinated segments of the axon is passive, it occurs instantly, and the signal thus "jumps" along the axon from node to node. There is, of course, a slight delay at each node of Ranvier while the action potential is actively generated, but conduction is still much faster in myelinated axons than in unmyelinated axons, in which passive conduction plays a less prominent role. The transmission of action potentials in myelinated axons is called **saltatory conduction** (*saltare* means "to skip or jump").

The Velocity of Axonal Conduction

At what speed are action potentials conducted along an axon? The answer to this question depends on two properties of the axon. Conduction is faster in large-diameter axons, and—as you have just learned—it is faster in those that are myelinated. Mammalian *motor neurons* (neurons that synapse on skeletal muscles) are large and myelinated; thus, some can conduct at speeds of 100 meters per second (about 224 miles per hour). In contrast, small, unmyelinated axons conduct action potentials at about 1 meter per second.

There is a misconception about the velocity of motor neuron action potentials in humans. The maximum velocity of motor neuron action potentials was found to be about 100 meters per second in cats and was then assumed to be the same in humans; It is not. The maximum velocity of conduction in human motor neurons is about 60 meters per second (Peters & Brooke, 1998).

Conduction in Neurons without Axons

Action potentials are the means by which axons conduct all-or-none signals nondecrementally over relatively long distances. Thus, to keep what you have just learned about action potentials in perspective, it is important for you to remember that many neurons in mammalian brains do not have axons and thus do not display action potentials. Neural conduction in these *interneurons* is typically by graded, decrementally conducted potentials (Juusola et al., 1996).

The Hodgkin-Huxley Model and the Changing View of Dendritic Function

The preceding account of neural conduction is based heavily on the *Hodgkin-Huxley model*, the theory

Structure of Synapses

Most communication among neurons occurs across synapses such as the one illustrated in Figure 4.7. Neurotransmitter molecules are released from buttons into synaptic clefts, where they induce EPSPs or IPSPs in other neurons by binding to receptors on their postsynaptic membranes. The synapses featured in Figure 4.7 are *axodendritic synapses*—synapses of axon terminal buttons on dendrites. As you have just

You have learned in this chapter how postsynaptic potentials are generated on the receptive membrane of a resting neuron, how these graded potentials are conducted passively to the axon, how the sum of these graded potentials can trigger action potentials, and how these all-or-none potentials are actively conducted down the axon to the terminal buttons. In the remaining sections of this chapter, you will learn how action potentials arriving at terminal buttons trigger the release of neurotransmitters into synapses and how neurotransmitters carry signals to other cells. This section provides an overview of five aspects of synaptic transmission: (1) the structure of synapses; (2) the synthesis, packaging, and transport of neurotransmitter molecules; (3) the release of neurotransmitter molecules; (4) the activation of receptors by neurotransmitter molecules; and (5) the reuptake, enzymatic degradation, and recycling of neurotransmitter molecules.

4.5 Synaptic Transmission: Chemical Transmission of Signals from One Neuron to Another

proposed by Hodgkin and Huxley in the early 1950s (see Huxley, 2002). Although this theory does a good job of accounting for the fundamental characteristics of neural conduction, it fails to explain many complexities of neural conduction that have been subsequently discovered (see Meunier & Segev, 2002).

Arguably, the greatest shortcoming of the Hodgkin-Huxley model is its failure to account for three recently discovered abilities of dendrites, which have long been assumed to be merely passive conductors of postsynaptic potentials (see Häusser, Spruston, & Stuart, 2000). The first of these recent discoveries is that some dendrites are capable of generating action potentials, which can be actively conducted away from the site of generation in either direction (e.g., Chen, Midtgaard, & Shepherd, 1997). The second and third discoveries both involve **dendritic**

ON THE CD

Visit the *Synaptic Transmission* animation. See synaptic transmission in action.

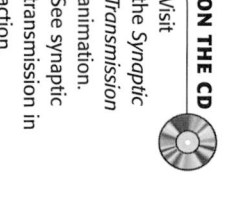

ON THE CD

The *Action at the Synapse* module presents diagrams, explanations, and exercises that will help you understand and remember the mechanisms of synaptic function.

spines, nodules of various shapes that are located on the surfaces of many dendrites (see Yuste, Majewska, & Holthoff, 2000) and are the sites of most excitatory synapses (typically one synapse per spine) in the mature mammalian brain. The second discovery is that dendritic spines *compartmentalize* a dendrite; that is, they tend to keep postsynaptic chemical changes restricted to the immediate area of the synapse (Segal, 2001). The third is that dendritic spines change rapidly (within minutes to hours) in shape and number in response to neural stimulation (Hering & Sheng, 2001; Kasai et al., 2003).

It is not yet well understood how these newly recognized dendritic capabilities affect neural conduction. Still, their discovery will surely prove to be a critical step toward improved understanding of neural conduction.

learned, many excitatory synapses terminate on *dendritic spines* (see Figure 3.31). Also common are *axosomatic synapses*—synapses of axon terminal buttons on *somas* (cell bodies).

Although axodendritic and axosomatic synapses are the most common synaptic arrangements, there are several others (Shepherd & Erulkar, 1997). For example, there are *dendrodendritic synapses*, which are interesting because they are capable of transmission in either direction; and there are *axoaxonal synapses*, which are interesting because some of them mediate presynaptic inhibition (see Wu & Saggau, 1997). **Presynaptic inhibition** is compared with **postsynaptic inhibition** in Figure 4.8 on page 88.

The synapses depicted in Figure 4.7 are **directed synapses**—synapses at which the site of neurotransmitter release and the site of neurotransmitter reception are in close proximity. This is a common arrangement, but there are also many nondirected synapses in the mammalian nervous system. **Nondirected synapses** are synapses at which the site of release is at some distance from the site of reception. One type of nondirected synapse is depicted in Figure 4.9 on page 90. In this type of arrangement, neurotransmitter molecules are released from a series of varicosities along the axon and its branches and thus are widely dispersed to surrounding targets. Because of their appearance, these synapses are often referred to as *string-of-beads synapses*.

Synthesis, Packaging, and Transport of Neurotransmitter Molecules

There are two basic categories of neurotransmitter molecules: small and large. The small neurotransmitters are

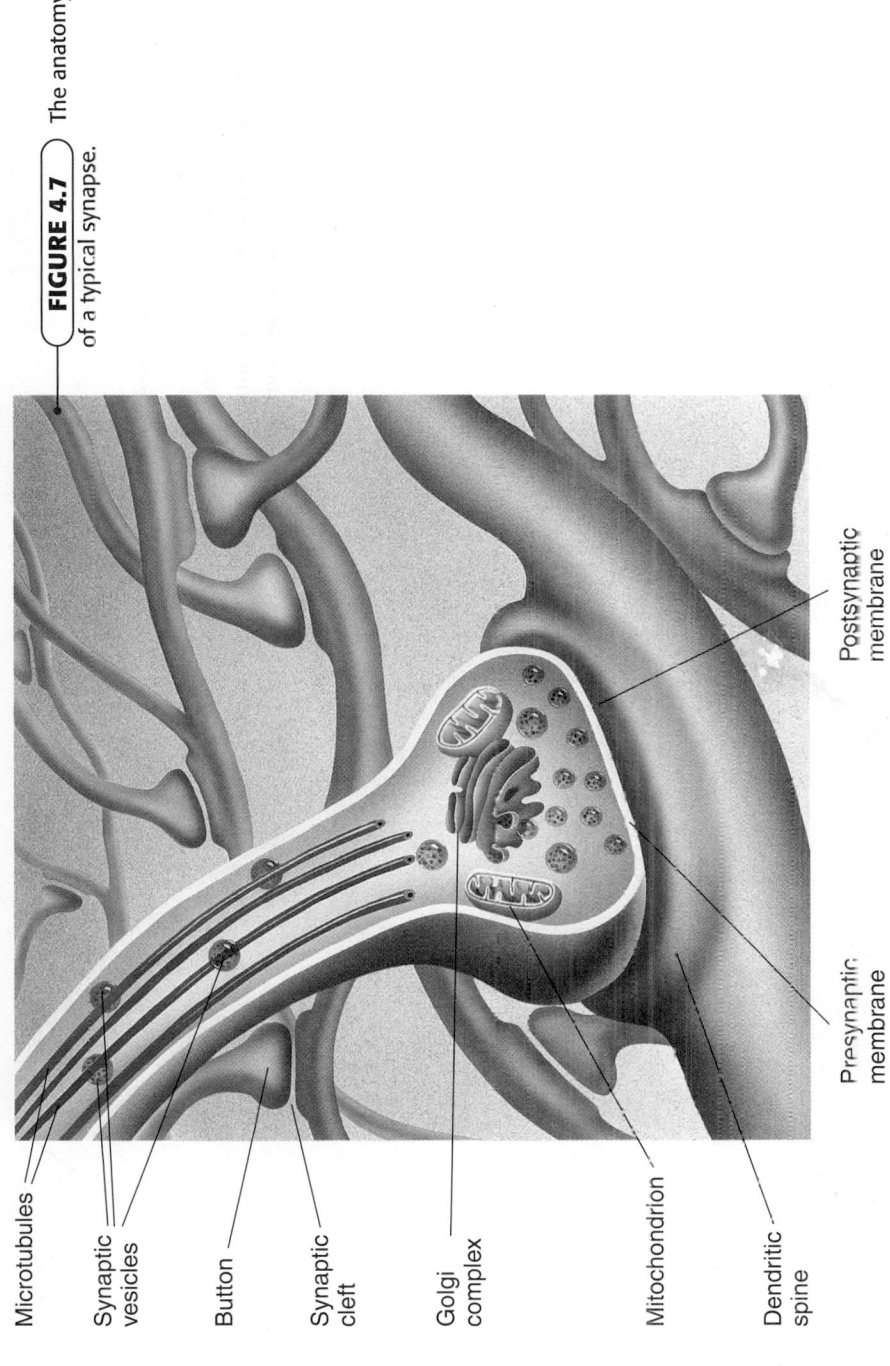

Microtubules

Synaptic
vesicles

Button

Synaptic
cleft

Golgi
complex

Mitochondrion

Dendritic
spine

Presynaptic
membrane

Postsynaptic
membrane

FIGURE 4.7   The anatomy
of a typical synapse.

of several types; large neurotransmitters are all peptides. **Peptides** are amino acid chains that are composed of 10 or fewer amino acids; in effect, they are short proteins. They may be small for proteins, but they are large for neurotransmitters.

Small-molecule neurotransmitters are typically synthesized in the cytoplasm of the terminal button and packaged in **synaptic vesicles** by the button's **Golgi complex** (see Brittle & Waters, 2000). Once filled with neurotransmitter, the vesicles are stored in clusters next to the presynaptic membrane. In contrast, peptide neurotransmitters, like other proteins, are assembled in the cytoplasm of the cell body on *ribosomes*; they are then packaged in vesicles by the cell body's Golgi complex and transported by *microtubules* to the terminal buttons at a rate of about 40 centimeters per day. The vesicles that contain large-molecule neurotransmitters are larger than those that contain small-molecule neurotransmitters, and they do not congregate as closely as the other vesicles to the presynaptic membrane.

It may have escaped your notice that the button illustrated in Figure 4.7 contains synaptic vesicles of two sizes. This means that it contains two neurotransmitters: a peptide neurotransmitter in the larger vesicles and a small-molecule neurotransmitter in the smaller vesicles. It was once believed that each neuron synthesizes and

releases only one neurotransmitter; but it is now clear that many neurons contain two neurotransmitters—a situation that is referred to as **coexistence.** So far, almost all documented cases of coexistence have involved one small-molecule neurotransmitter and one peptide neurotransmitter.

Release of Neurotransmitter Molecules

Exocytosis—the process of neurotransmitter release—is illustrated in Figure 4.10 on page 90 (see Zucker, Kullman, & Bennett, 1999). When a neuron is at rest, synaptic vesicles that contain small-molecule neurotransmitters congregate next to sections of the presynaptic membrane that are particularly rich in *voltage-activated calcium channels.* When stimulated by action potentials, these channels open, and Ca^{2+} ions enter the button. The entry of the Ca^{2+} ions causes the synaptic vesicles to fuse with the presynaptic membrane and empty their contents into the synaptic cleft (see Rettig & Neher, 2002).

The exocytosis of small-molecule neurotransmitters differs from the exocytosis of peptide neurotransmitters in one important respect. Small-molecule neurotransmitters are typically released in a pulse each time an action potential triggers a momentary influx of Ca^{2+} ions through the presynaptic membrane; in contrast, peptide

FIGURE 4.8   Postsynaptic
and presynaptic inhibition.

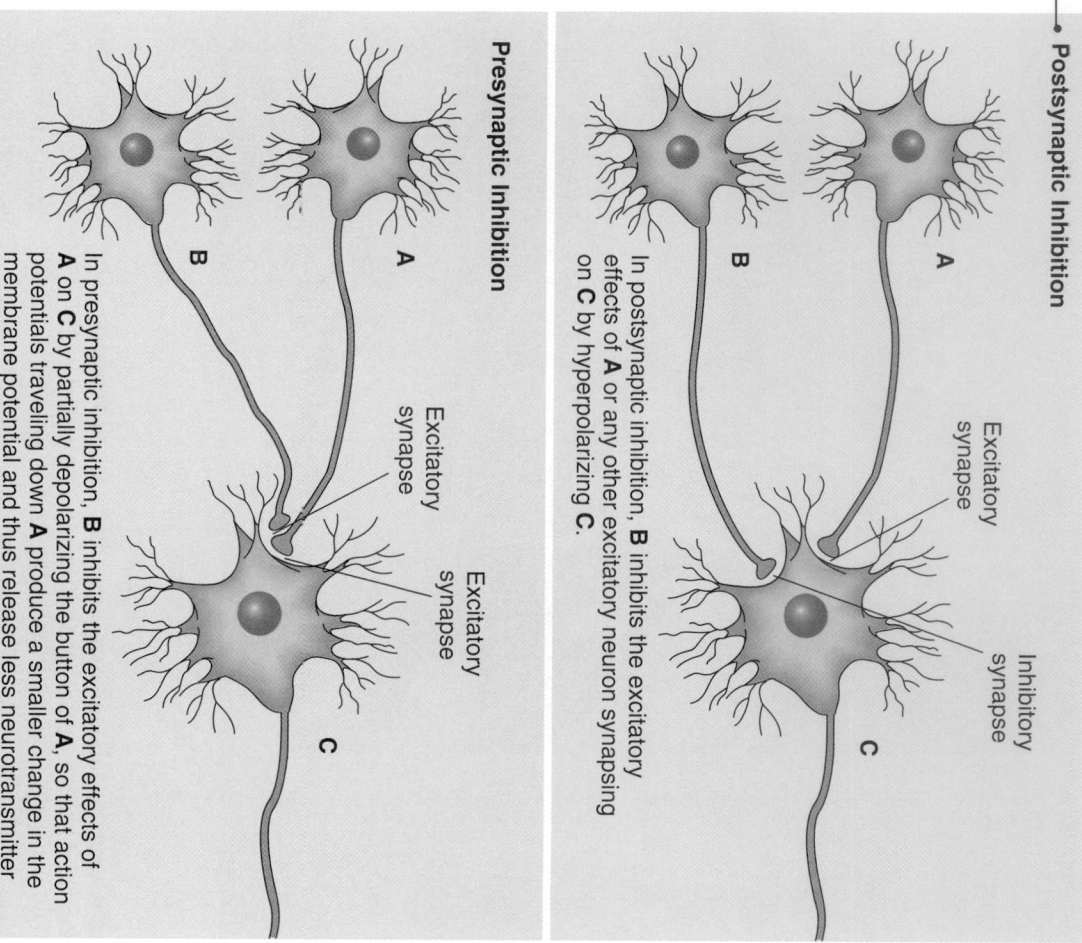

Postsynaptic Inhibition

In postsynaptic inhibition, **B** inhibits the excitatory effects of **A** or any other excitatory neuron synapsing on **C** by hyperpolarizing **C**.

Excitatory synapse

Inhibitory synapse

Presynaptic Inhibition

In presynaptic inhibition, **B** inhibits the excitatory effects of **A** on **C** by partially depolarizing the button of **A**, so that action potentials traveling down **A** produce a smaller change in the membrane potential and thus release less neurotransmitter onto **C**. Notice that presynaptic inhibition occurs in the absence of inhibitory neurotransmitters or IPSPs.

Excitatory synapse

neurotransmitters are typically released gradually in response to general increases in the level of intracellular Ca²⁺ ions, such as might occur during a general increase in the rate of neuron firing.

Activation of Receptors by Neurotransmitter Molecules

Once released, neurotransmitter molecules produce signals in postsynaptic neurons by binding to **receptors** in the postsynaptic membrane. Each receptor is a protein that contains binding sites for only particular neurotransmitters; thus, a neurotransmitter can influence only those cells that have receptors for it. Any molecule that binds to another is referred to as its **ligand**, and a neurotransmitter is thus said to be a ligand of its receptor.

It was initially assumed that there is only one type of receptor for each neurotransmitter, but this has not proved to be the case. As more receptors have been identified, it has become clear that most neurotransmitters bind to several different types of receptors. The different types of receptors to which a particular neurotransmitter can bind are called the **receptor subtypes** for that neurotransmitter. The various receptor subtypes for a neurotransmitter are typically located in different brain areas, and they typically respond to the neurotransmitter in different ways (see Darlison & Richter, 1999). Thus, one advantage of receptor subtypes is that they enable a neurotransmitter to transmit different kinds of messages to different parts of the brain.

The binding of a neurotransmitter to one of its receptor subtypes can influence a postsynaptic neuron

Ca^{2+}

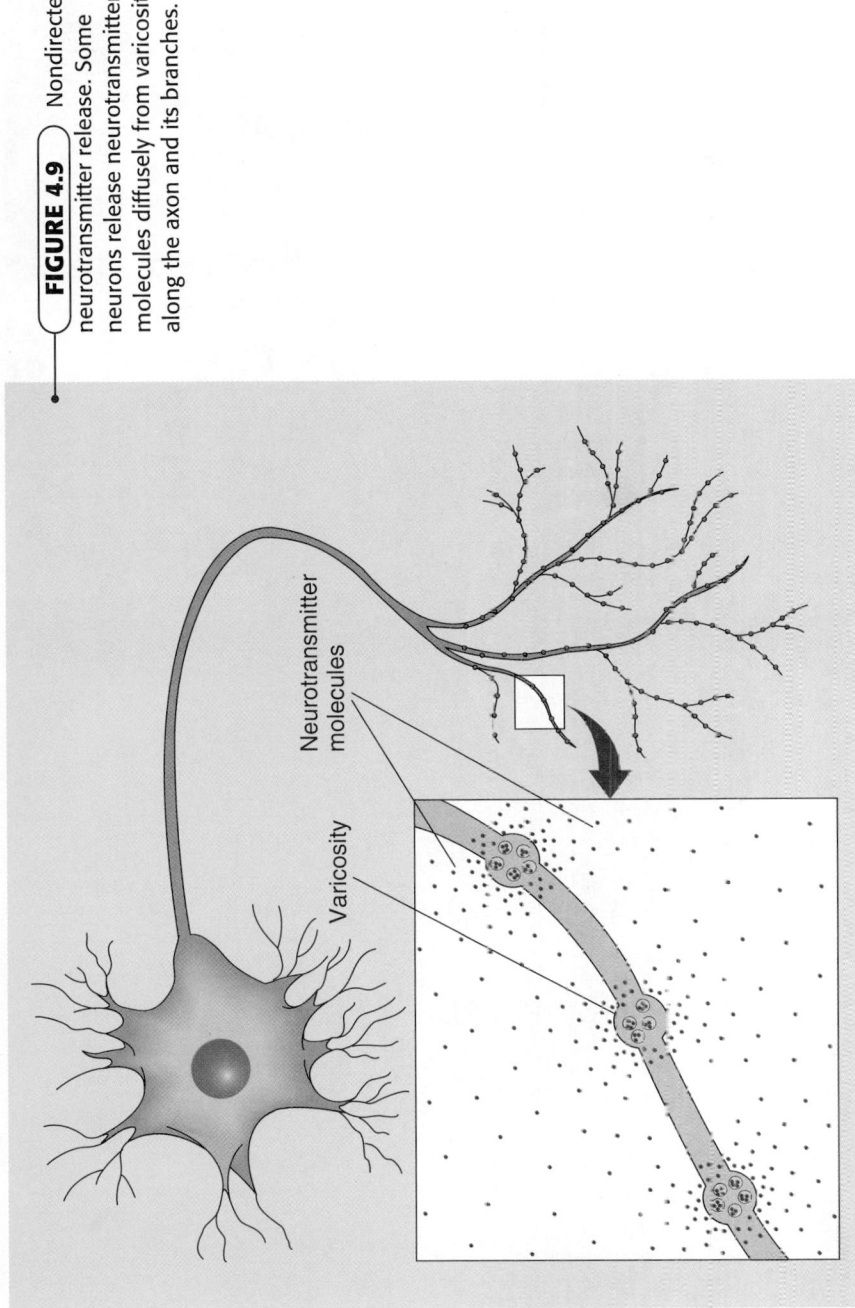

Neurotransmitter molecules

Varicosity

FIGURE 4.9 Nondirected neurotransmitter release. Some neurons release neurotransmitter molecules diffusely from varicosities along the axon and its branches.

in one of two fundamentally different ways, depending on whether the receptor is ionotropic or metabotropic (Heuss & Gerber, 2000; Waxham, 1999). **Ionotropic receptors** are those receptors that are associated with ligand-activated ion channels; **metabotropic receptors** are those receptors that are associated with signal proteins and G proteins (*guanosine-triphosphate-sensitive proteins*)—see Figure 4.11 on page 91.

When a neurotransmitter molecule binds to an ionotropic receptor, the associated ion channel usually opens or closes immediately, thereby inducing an immediate postsynaptic potential. For example, in some neurons, EPSPs (depolarizations) occur because the neurotransmitter opens sodium channels, thereby increasing the flow of Na$^+$ ions into the neuron. In contrast, IPSPs (hyperpolarizations) often occur because the neurotransmitter opens potassium channels or chloride channels, thereby increasing the flow of K$^+$ ions out of the neuron or the flow of Cl$^-$ ions into it, respectively.

Metabotropic receptors are more prevalent than ionotropic receptors, and their effects are slower to develop, longer-lasting, more diffuse, and more varied. There are many different kinds of metabotropic receptors, but each is attached to a signal protein that winds its way back and forth through the cell membrane seven

times. The metabotropic receptor is attached to a portion of the signal protein outside the neuron; the G protein is attached to a portion of the signal protein inside the neuron.

When a neurotransmitter binds to a metabotropic receptor, a subunit of the associated G protein breaks away. Then, one of two things happens, depending on the particular G protein: The subunit may move along the inside surface of the membrane and bind to a nearby ion channel, thereby inducing an EPSP or IPSP; or it may trigger the synthesis of a chemical called a **second messenger** (neurotransmitters are considered to be the *first messengers*). Once created, a second messenger diffuses through the cytoplasm and may influence the activities of the neuron in a variety of ways (Neves, Ram, & Iyengar, 2002)—for example, it may enter the nucleus and bind to the DNA, thereby influencing genetic expression (see Noselli & Perrimon, 2000). Thus, a neurotransmitter's binding to a metabotropic receptor can have radical, long-lasting effects.

One type of metabotropic receptors—autoreceptors—warrants special mention (see Parnas et al., 2000). **Autoreceptors** are metabotropic receptors that have two unconventional characteristics: They bind to their neuron's own neurotransmitter molecules; and they are located on the presynaptic, rather than the postsynaptic, membrane. Their usual function is to monitor the number of neurotransmitter molecules in the synapse, to reduce subsequent release when the levels are high, and to increase subsequent release when they are low.

Differences between small-molecule and peptide neurotransmitters in patterns of release and receptor binding suggest that they serve different functions. Small-molecule neurotransmitters tend to be released into directed synapses and to activate either ionotropic receptors or metabotropic receptors that act directly on ion channels. In contrast, peptide neurotransmitters tend to be released diffusely and bind to metabotropic receptors that act through second messengers. Consequently, the function of small-molecule

neurotransmitters appears to be the transmission of rapid, brief excitatory or inhibitory signals to adjacent cells; and the function of peptide neurotransmitters appears to be the transmission of slow, diffuse, long-lasting signals.

Reuptake, Enzymatic Degradation, and Recycling

If nothing intervened, a neurotransmitter molecule would remain active in the synapse, in effect clogging that channel of communication. However, two mechanisms terminate synaptic messages and keep that from happening. These two message-terminating mechanisms are **reuptake** and **enzymatic degradation** (see Figure 4.12 on page 92).

Reuptake is the more common of the two deactivating mechanisms. The majority of neurotransmitters,

ON THE CD

The Review of Synaptic Transmission module takes an in-depth look at the different stages of synaptic transmission.

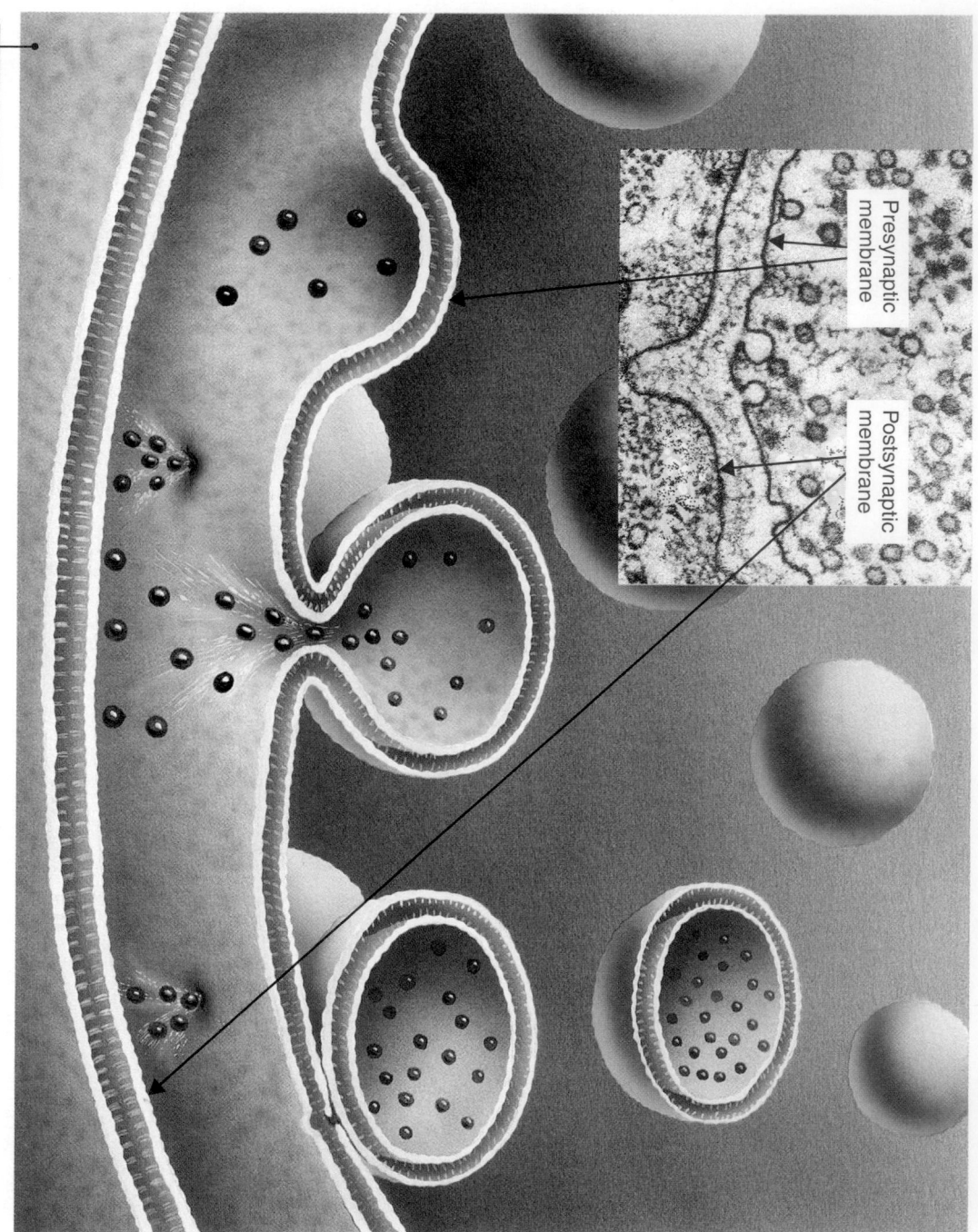

FIGURE 4.10   Schematic and photographic illustrations of exocytosis.

(The photomicrograph was reproduced from J. E. Heuser et al., *Journal of Cell Biology*, 1979, *81*, 275–300, by copyright permission of The Rockefeller University Press.)

Presynaptic membrane

Postsynaptic membrane

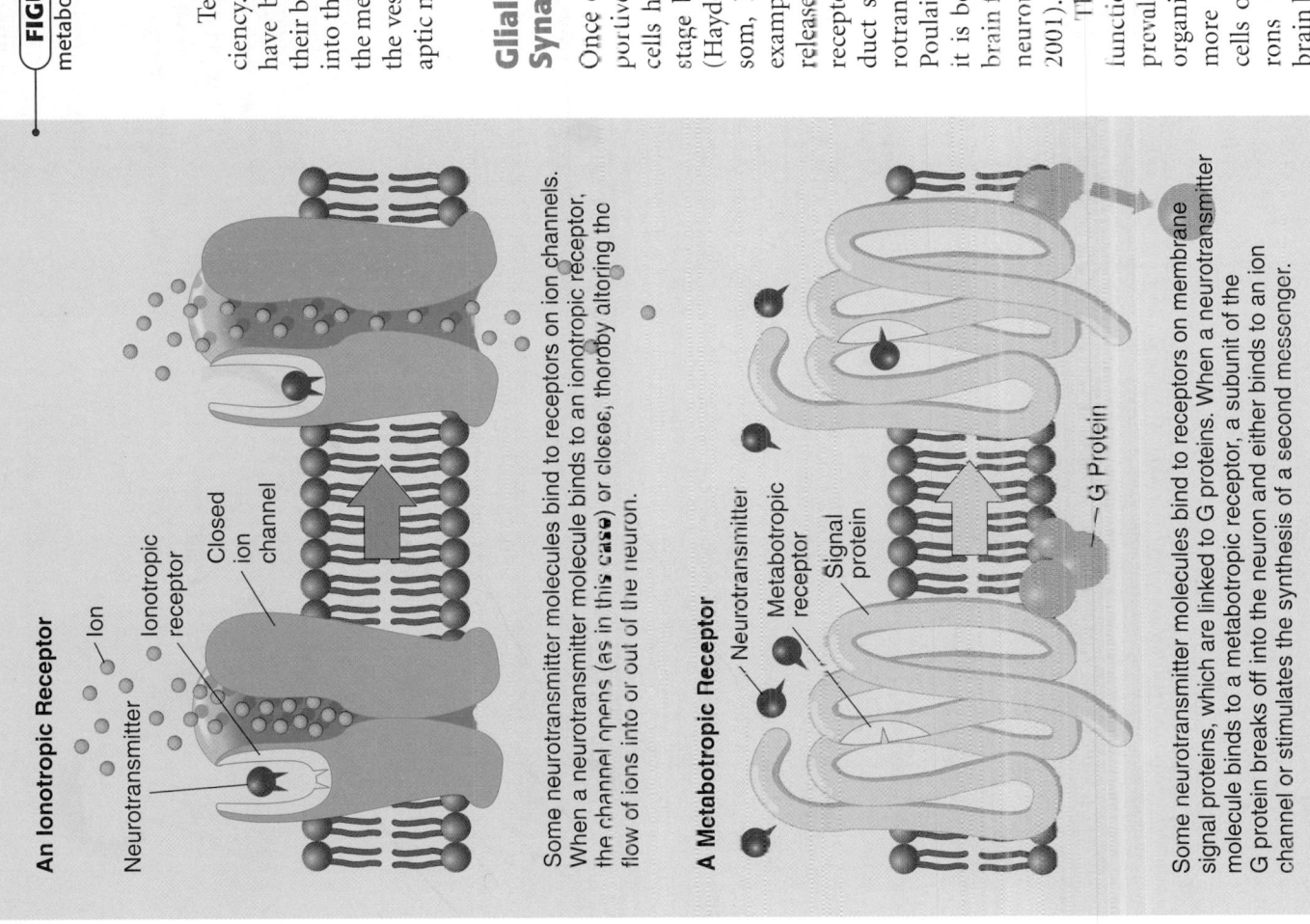

FIGURE 4.11 Ionotropic and metabotropic receptors.

An Ionotropic Receptor

Ion
Ionotropic receptor
Closed ion channel
Neurotransmitter

Some neurotransmitter molecules bind to receptors on ion channels. When a neurotransmitter molecule binds to an ionotropic receptor, the channel opens (as in this case) or closes, thereby altering the flow of ions into or out of the neuron.

A Metabotropic Receptor

Neurotransmitter
Metabotropic receptor
Signal protein
G Protein

Some neurotransmitter molecules bind to receptors on membrane signal proteins, which are linked to G proteins. When a neurotransmitter molecule binds to a metabotropic receptor, a subunit of the G protein breaks off into the neuron and either binds to an ion channel or stimulates the synthesis of a second messenger.

Terminal buttons are models of efficiency. Neurotransmitter molecules that have been released into the synapse or their breakdown products are drawn back into the button and recycled, regardless of the mechanism of their deactivation. Even the vesicles are recycled from the presynaptic membrane (Harata et al., 2001).

Glial Function and Synaptic Transmission

Once overlooked as playing merely supportive roles in the nervous system, glial cells have recently been thrust to center stage by a wave of remarkable findings (Haydon, 2001; Newman, 2003; Ransom, Behar, & Nedergaard, 2003). For example, astrocytes have been shown to release chemical transmitters, to contain receptors for neurotransmitters, to conduct signals, and to participate in neurotransmitter reuptake (see Oliet, Piet, & Poulain, 2001; Iino et al., 2001). Indeed, it is becoming inappropriate to think of brain function solely in terms of neuron-neuron connections (Gallo & Chittajallu, 2001). Neurons are only part of the story.

The importance of glial cells in brain function may be reflected in the greater prevalence of these cells in intelligent organisms. Many simple organisms have more neurons than glial cells, but glial cells outnumber neurons in the human brain by about 10 to 1. Will *neuroscience* prove to be a misnomer? Anybody for "gliascience"?

Evolutionary Perspective

once released, are almost immediately drawn back into the presynaptic buttons (see Clements et al., 1992).

In contrast, other neurotransmitters are degraded (broken apart) in the synapse by the action of **enzymes**—proteins that stimulate or inhibit biochemical reactions without being affected by them. For example, *acetylcholine*, one of the few neurotransmitters for which enzymatic degradation is the main mechanism of synaptic deactivation, is broken down by the enzyme **acetylcholinesterase.**

Gap Junctions Interest in gap junctions has recently been rekindled. **Gap junctions** are narrow spaces between adjacent neurons that are bridged by fine tubular channels that contain cytoplasm. Consequently, the cytoplasm is continuous, allowing electrical signals and small molecules to pass readily from one neuron to the next. Gap junctions are sometimes called *electrical synapses.*

Gap junctions are commonplace in invertebrate nervous systems, but their existence was more difficult

Two Mechanisms of Neurotransmitter Deactivation

Reuptake

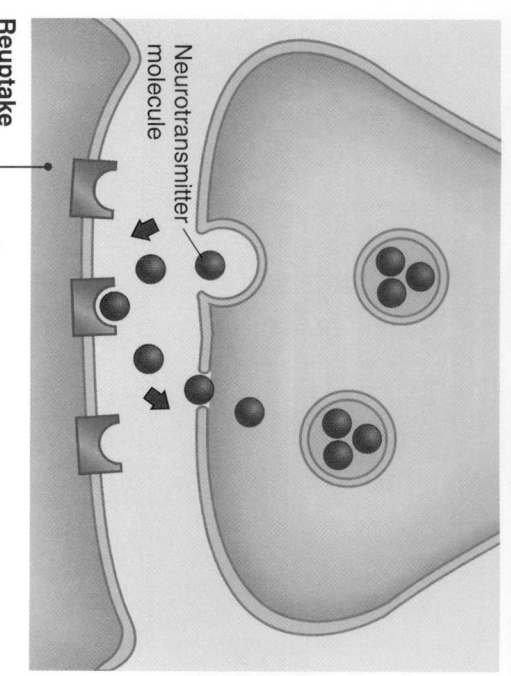

Neurotransmitter
molecule

Enzymatic Degradation

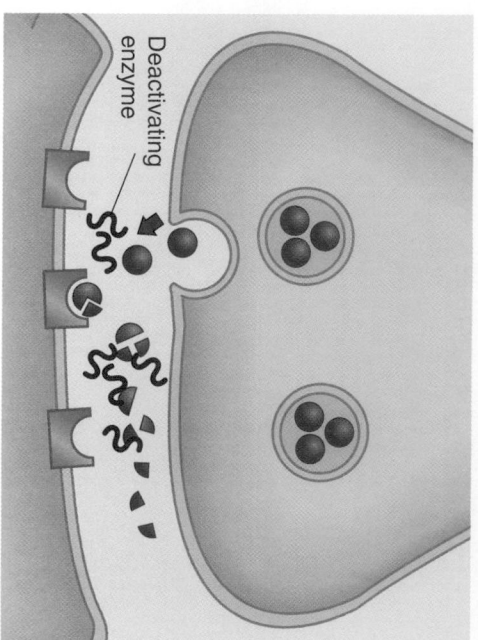

Deactivating
enzyme

FIGURE 4.12   The two mechanisms for terminating neurotransmitter action in the synapse: reuptake and enzymatic degradation.

to establish in mammals (see Bennett, 2000). They were first demonstrated in mammals in the 1970s, but few mammalian examples accumulated over the ensuing years—that is, until recently.

Recent technological developments have led to the discovery of gap junctions throughout the mammalian brain; they seem to be an integral feature of local neural inhibitory circuits (Galarreta & Hestrin, 2001). In addi-

tion, astrocytes have been shown to communicate with neurons and other cells through gap junctions (Bennett et al., 2003). Thus, the recent focus on glial function is reviving interest in gap junctions. Clearly, gap junctions play important roles in human brain function. The next few years should see major advances in our appreciation and understanding of this means of cellular communication.

4.6   The Neurotransmitters

Now that you understand the basics of neurotransmitter function, let's take a closer look at some of the neurotransmitter substances (see Deutch & Roth, 1999). There are four classes of small-molecule neurotransmitters: the *amino acids*, the *monoamines*, the *soluble gases*, and *acetylcholine*. In addition, there is the one class of large-molecule neurotransmitter: the *neuropeptides*. Most neurotransmitters produce either excitation or inhibition, not both; but a few produce excitation when they bind to some of their receptor subtypes and inhibition when they bind to others. All of the neurotransmitter classes and individual neurotransmitters that appear in this section in boldface type are outlined in Figure 4.15 later in this section.

Amino Acid Neurotransmitters

The neurotransmitters in the vast majority of fast-acting, directed synapses in the central nervous system

are **amino acids**—the molecular building blocks of proteins. The four most widely acknowledged amino acid neurotransmitters are **glutamate, aspartate, glycine,** and **gamma-aminobutyric acid (GABA).** The first three are common in the proteins we consume, whereas GABA is synthesized by a simple modification of the structure of glutamate. Glutamate is the most prevalent excitatory neurotransmitter in the mammalian central nervous system; GABA is the most prevalent inhibitory neurotransmitter.

ON THE CD

The *Amino Acid Synapses* module summarizes the effects of three amino acid neurotransmitters—glutamate, GABA, and glycine.

Monoamine Neurotransmitters

Monoamines are another class of small-molecule neurotransmitters. Each is synthesized from a single amino acid—hence the name *monoamine* (one amine). Monoamine neurotransmitters are slightly larger than amino acid neurotransmitters, and their effects tend to be more diffuse (see Bunin & Wightman, 1999). The monoamines are present in small groups of neurons whose cell bodies are, for the most part, located in the brain stem. These neurons often have highly branched axons with many varicosities (string-of-beads synapses), from which monoamine neurotransmitters are diffusely released into the extracellular fluid (see Figures 4.9 and 4.13).

There are four monoamine neurotransmitters: **dopamine, epinephrine, norepinephrine,** and **serotonin.** They are subdivided into two groups, **catecholamines** and **indolamines,** on the basis of their structures. Dopamine, norepinephrine, and epinephrine are catecholamines. Each is synthesized from the amino acid *tyrosine.* Tyrosine is converted to *L-dopa,* which in turn is converted to dopamine. Neurons that release norepinephrine have an extra enzyme (one that is not present in dopaminergic neurons), which converts the dopamine in them to norepinephrine. Similarly, neurons that release epinephrine have all the enzymes present in

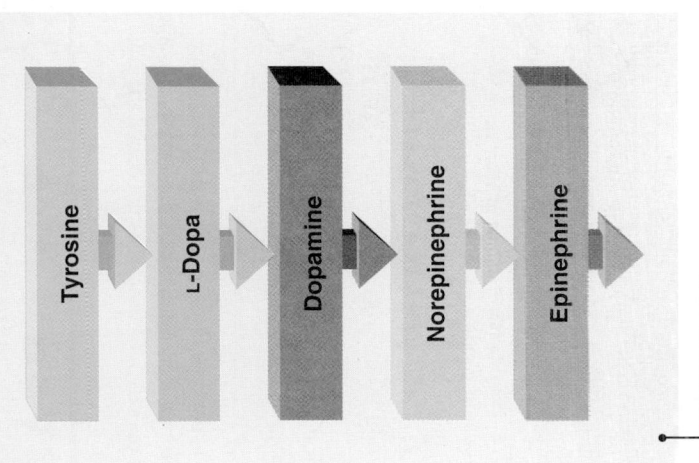

neurons that release norepinephrine, along with an extra enzyme that converts norepinephrine to epinephrine (see Figure 4.14). In contrast to the other monoamines, *serotonin* (also called *5-hydroxytryptamine,* or *5-HT*) is synthesized from the amino acid *tryptophan* and is classified as an indolamine.

Neurons that release norepinephrine are called *noradrenergic;* those that release epinephrine are called *adrenergic.* There are two reasons for this naming. One is that epinephrine and norepinephrine used to be called *adrenaline* and *noradrenaline,* respectively, by many scientists, until a drug company registered *Adrenalin* as a brand name. The other reason will become apparent to you if you try to say *norepinephrinergic.*

Soluble-Gas Neurotransmitters

Another class of small-molecule neurotransmitters, the **soluble gases,** includes **nitric oxide** and **carbon monoxide.** The soluble gases do not act like the other neurotransmitters (Boehning & Snyder, 2003). They are produced in the neural cytoplasm; and once produced, they immediately diffuse through the cell membrane into the extracellular fluid and then into nearby cells. They easily pass through cell membranes because they are soluble in lipids. Once in other cells, they stimulate the production of a second messenger and in a few seconds are deactivated by being converted to other molecules. They are difficult to study because they exist for only a few seconds.

FIGURE 4.14 The steps in the synthesis of catecholamines from tyrosine.

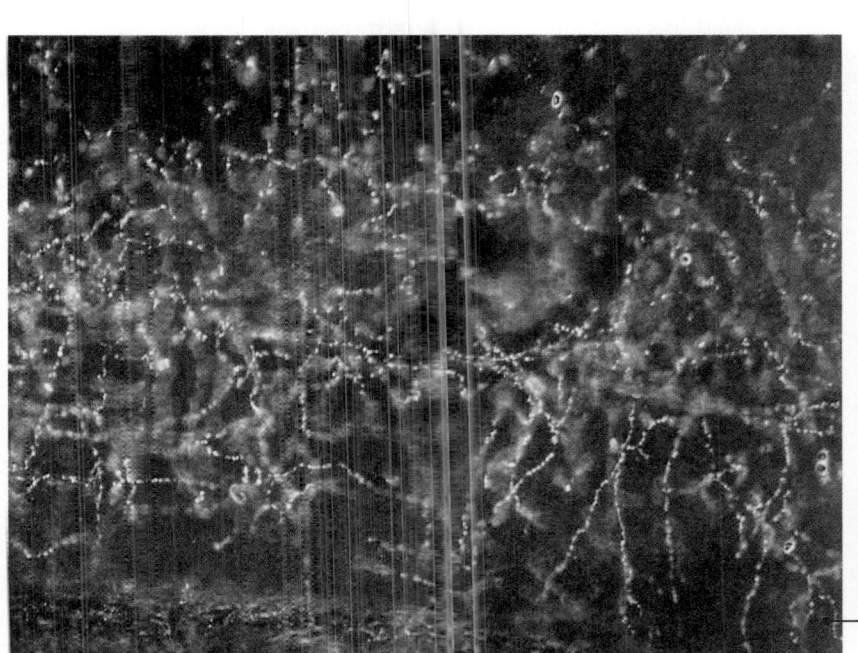

FIGURE 4.13 String-of-beads noradrenergic nerve fibers in rat cerebellar cortex. The bright beaded structures represent sites in these multiply branched axons where the monoamine neurotransmitter norepinephrine is stored in high concentration and released into the surrounding extracellular fluid. (Courtesy of Floyd E. Bloom, M.D., The Scripps Research Institute, La Jolla, California.)

SCAN YOUR BRAIN

This is a good place for you to pause to scan your brain to see if you are ready to proceed. Are you familiar with the neurotransmitters to which you have just been introduced? Find out by filling in the blanks. The correct answers are provided at the bottom of this page. Before proceeding, review material related to your errors and omissions.

Amino acids are the neurotransmitters in the vast majority of (1) _____ - acting, directed synapses. Four amino acids are widely recognized neurotransmitters: (2) _____ , (3) _____ , (4) _____ , and (5) _____ . In contrast to the amino acid neurotransmitters, the (6) _____ are small-molecule neurotransmitters with slower, more diffuse effects; they belong to one of two categories: (7) _____ or indolamines. Belonging to the former category are epinephrine, (8) _____ , and (9) _____ ; (10) _____ is the only neurotransmitter belonging to the latter category. The neuropeptides, which are short chains of (11) _____ , are the only class of large-molecule neurotransmitters. (12) _____ , the neurotransmitter at neuromuscular junctions, is a neurotransmitter in a class by itself. Finally, there are the (13) _____ neurotransmitters, such as nitric oxide and carbon monoxide.

Acetylcholine

Soluble-gas neurotransmitters have been shown to be involved in *retrograde transmission*. At some synapses, they transmit feedback signals from the postsynaptic neuron back to the presynaptic neuron. The function of the retrograde transmission seems to be to regulate the activity of presynaptic neurons (Ludwig & Pittman, 2003). Retrograde transmission by other neurotransmitters has been documented but seems to be less prevalent (Blakely, 2001; Falkenburger, Barstow, & Mintz, 2001).

Acetylcholine

Acetylcholine (abbreviated Ach) is a small-molecule neurotransmitter that is in one major respect like a professor who is late for a lecture: It is in a class by itself. It is created by adding an *acetyl group* to a *choline molecule*. Acetylcholine is the neurotransmitter at neuromuscular junctions, at many of the synapses in the autonomic nervous system, and at synapses in several parts of the central nervous system. As you learned in the last section, acetylcholine is broken down in the synapse by the enzyme *acetylcholinesterase*. Neurons that release acetylcholine are said to be *cholinergic*.

Neuropeptides

Peptides that play a role in neurotransmission are referred to as **neuropeptides.** Close to 100 have been identified (Greengard, 2001).

Among the most interesting neuropeptides are the **endorphins** (see Stefano et al., 2000); endorphins are endogenous opiates (opiumlike chemicals that are produced within the body). The existence of endorphins was first suggested by the discovery that opiate drugs (e.g., opium, morphine, and heroin) bind to receptors in the brain; presumably, there would not be receptors in the brain for substances that are not themselves produced by the body. This suggestion was subsequently confirmed by the discovery of several different endorphins and several subtypes of the endorphin receptor. Endorphins activate neural systems that produce *analgesia* (pain supression) and neural systems that mediate the experience of pleasure. These effects are presumably why opiate drugs are so addictive.

Figure 4.15 summarizes the neurotransmitters that were introduced in this section. Consequently, they do not appear in the list of key terms at the end of the chapter.

Amino acids	Glutamate _excitatory_ _smooth muscle constriction_ Aspartate Glycine GABA _inhibitory_	
Monoamines	Catecholamines	Dopamine _pleasure, concentration_ Epinephrine _(or Adrenalin)_ Norepinephrine _mood_
	Indolamines	Serotonin _sleep, appetite, mood_
Soluble gases	Nitric oxide Carbon monoxide	
Acetylcholine	Acetylcholine _movement learn/memory_	
Neuropeptides _large molecules_	Endorphins _pleasure, pain suppression_ Other neuropeptides	

FIGURE 4.15 Classes of neurotransmitters and the particular neurotransmitters that have been introduced, and appear in boldface, in this chapter.

4.7 Pharmacology of Synaptic Transmission

The more neuroscientists have discovered about synaptic transmission, the greater has been their ability to develop drugs to modify it in specific ways. The effects of synaptic-transmission–altering drugs on psychological processes is currently one of the most productive topics of biopsychological research. This research has taught us a great deal about the neural bases of psychological processes. Also, it has led to the development of effective pharmacological treatments for psychological disorders—recall the improvement of Roberto García d'Orta. This section completes the chapter by explaining some of the ways drugs influence psychological processes through their effects on synaptic transmission.

Drugs have two fundamentally different kinds of effects on synaptic transmission: They facilitate it or they inhibit it. Drugs that facilitate the effects of a particular neurotransmitter are said to be **agonists** of that neurotransmitter. Drugs that inhibit the effects of a particular neurotransmitter are said to be its **antagonists.**

How Drugs Influence Synaptic Transmission

Although synthesis, release, and action vary from neurotransmitter to neurotransmitter (see Walmsley, Alvarez, & Fyffe, 1998), the following seven general steps are common to most neurotransmitters: (1) synthesis of the neurotransmitter, (2) storage in vesicles, (3) breakdown in the cytoplasm of any neurotransmitter that leaks from the vesicles, (4) exocytosis, (5) inhibitory feedback via

autoreceptors, (6) activation of postsynaptic receptors, and (7) deactivation. Figure 4.16 on page 96 illustrates these seven steps, and Figure 4.17 on page 97 illustrates some ways that agonistic and antagonistic drugs influence them. For example, some agonists bind to postsynaptic receptors and activate them, whereas some antagonistic drugs, called **receptor blockers**, bind to postsynaptic receptors without activating them and, in so doing, block the access of the usual neurotransmitter.

Psychoactive Drugs: Five Examples

You will encounter many psychoactive drugs, their psychological effects, and their mechanisms of action in future chapters. Here are five examples to complete this section: two agonists, cocaine and the benzodiazepines; and three antagonists, atropine, curare, and Botox.

Cocaine Cocaine is a potent catecholamine agonist that is highly addictive. It increases the activity of both dopamine and norepinephrine by blocking their reuptake from the synapse into the presynaptic button. Accordingly, when there are high levels of cocaine in the brain, molecules of dopamine and norepinephrine, once released into the synapse, continue to activate postsynaptic receptors because their primary method of deactivation has been blocked. This produces a variety of psychological effects, including euphoria, loss of appetite, and insomnia. It is also responsible for the addictive potential of cocaine (see Chapter 15).

Seven Steps in Neurotransmitter Action

1 Neurotransmitter molecules are synthesized from precursors under the influence of enzymes.

2 Neurotransmitter molecules are stored in vesicles.

3 Neurotransmitter molecules that leak from their vesicles are destroyed by enzymes.

4 Action potentials cause vesicles to fuse with the presynaptic membrane and release their neurotransmitter molecules into the synapse.

5 Released neurotransmitter molecules bind with autoreceptors and inhibit subsequent neurotransmitter release.

6 Released neurotransmitter molecules bind to postsynaptic receptors.

7 Released neurotransmitter molecules are deactivated by either reuptake or enzymatic degradation.

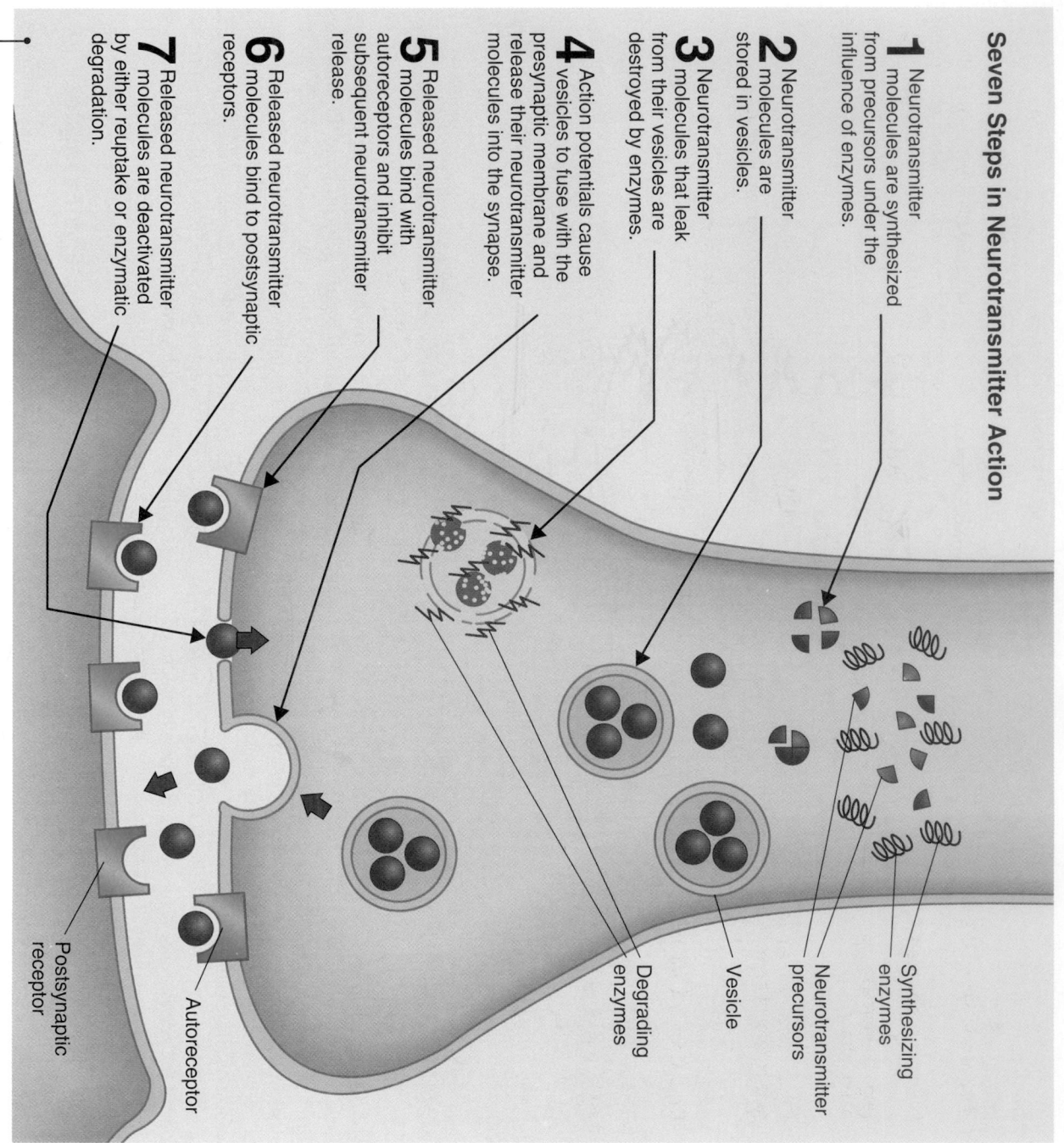

FIGURE 4.16   Seven steps in neurotransmitter action: (1) synthesis, (2) storage in vesicles, (3) breakdown of any neurotransmitter leaking from the vesicles, (4) exocytosis, (5) inhibitory feedback via autoreceptors, (6) activation of postsynaptic receptors, and (7) deactivation.

Synthesizing enzymes

Neurotransmitter precursors

Vesicle

Degrading enzymes

Autoreceptor

Postsynaptic receptor

Clinical Implications

Benzodiazepines   *Chlordiazepoxide* (marketed under the name *Librium*) and *diazepam* (marketed under the name *Valium*) belong to a class of drugs called *benzodiazepines*. **Benzo-diazepines** have *anxiolytic* (anxiety-reducing), *sedative* (sleep-inducing), and *anticonvulsant* effects. They appear to exert their anxiolytic effects by serving as GABA agonists. Benzodiazepines bind to one subtype of the GABA receptor, the ionotropic GABA$_A$ receptor (see Macdonald & Olsen, 1994), but they do not exert their agonistic effect by mimicking GABA's actions.

Benzodiazepine molecules do not bind to the GABA$_A$ receptor at the same site at which GABA molecules bind. Instead they bind to another part of the molecule; by so doing, they increase the binding of GABA molecules to the receptor and thus increase GABA's inhibitory effects by increasing the influx of Cl$^-$ ions and hyperpolarizing the neuron (see Figure 4.18 on page 98).

Atropine   Many of the drugs that are used in research and in medicine are extracts of plants that have long been used for medicinal and recreational purposes. For exam-

Some Mechanisms of Drug Action

Agonistic Drug Effects

Drug increases the synthesis of neurotransmitter molecules (e.g., by increasing the amount of precursor).

Drug increases the number of neurotransmitter molecules by destroying degrading enzymes.

Drug increases the release of neurotransmitter molecules from terminal buttons.

Drug binds to autoreceptors and blocks their inhibitory effect on neurotransmitter release.

Drug binds to postsynaptic receptors and either activates them or increases the effect on them of neurotransmitter

Drug blocks the deactivation of neurotransmitter molecules by blocking degradation or reuptake.

Antagonistic Drug Effects

Drug blocks the synthesis of neurotransmitter molecules (e.g., by destroying synthesizing enzymes).

Drug causes the neurotransmitter molecules to leak from the vesicles and be destroyed by degrading enzymes.

Drug blocks the release of the neurotransmitter molecules from terminal buttons.

Drug activates autoreceptors and inhibits neurotransmitter release.

Drug is a receptor blocker; it binds to the postsynaptic receptors and blocks the effect of the neurotransmitter.

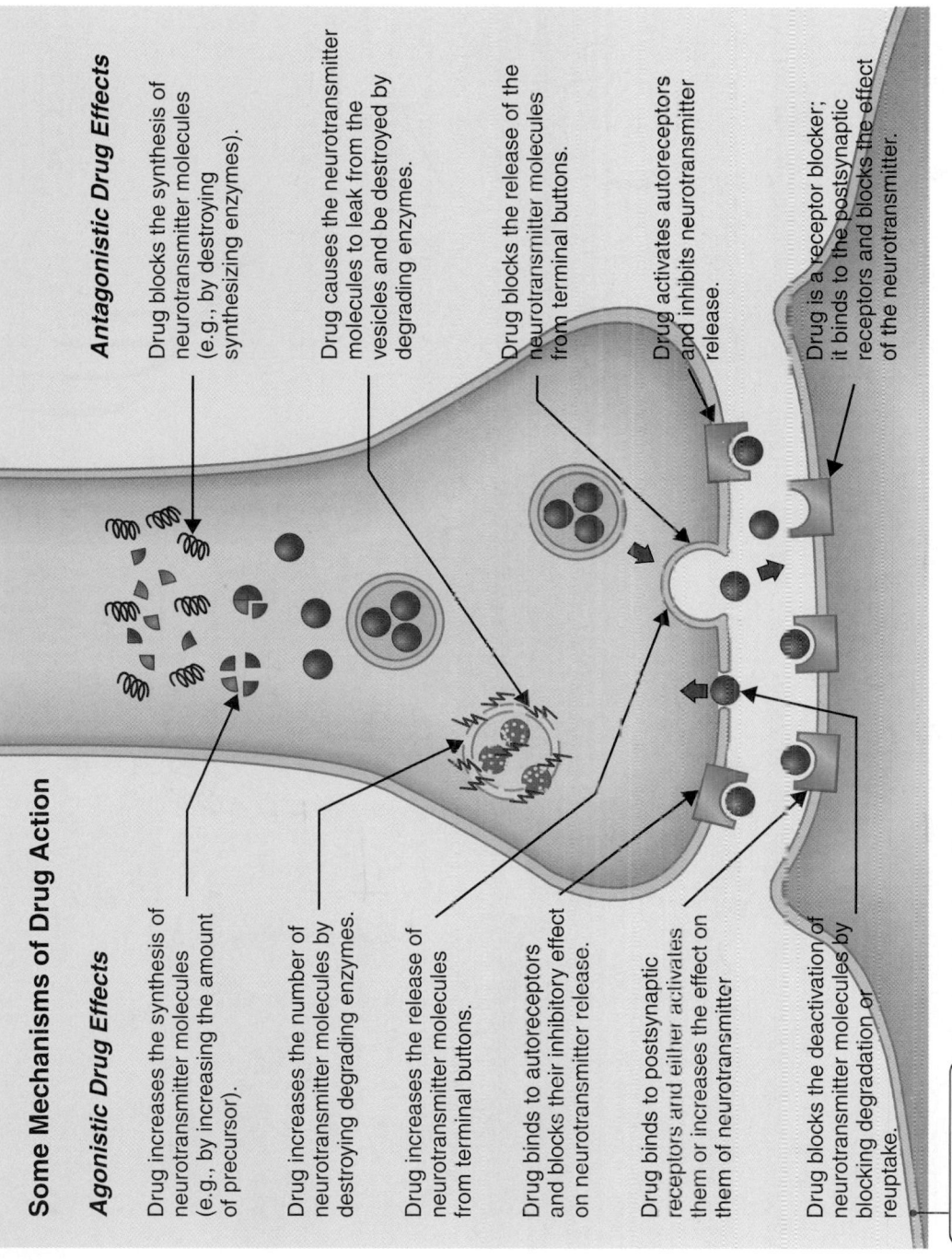

FIGURE 4.17 Some mechanisms of agonistic and antagonistic drug effects.

ple, in the time of Hippocrates, the Greeks consumed extracts of the belladonna plant to treat stomach ailments and to make themselves more attractive. Greek women believed that its pupil-dilating effects enhanced their beauty (*belladonna* means "beautiful lady"). **Atropine** is the active ingredient of belladonna. It is a receptor blocker that exerts its antagonist effect by binding to a metabotropic subtype of acetylcholine receptors called *muscarinic receptors*, thereby blocking the effects of acetylcholine on them. Many muscarinic receptors are located in the brain; the disruptive effect of high doses of atropine on memory was one of the earliest clues that cholinergic mechanisms play a role in memory (see Chapter 11).

Curare South American Indians have long used curare—an extract of a certain class of woody vines—to kill their game and occasionally their enemies. Like atropine, curare is a receptor blocker at cholinergic syn-

apses, but it acts at a different subtype of acetylcholine receptors: an ionotropic subtype called *nicotinic receptors*. By binding to nicotinic receptors, curare blocks transmission at **neuromuscular junctions**, thus paralyzing its recipients and killing them by blocking their respiration.

You may be surprised, then, to learn that the active ingredient of curare is sometimes administered to human patients during surgery to ensure that their muscles do not contract during an incision. When curare is used for this purpose, the patient's breathing must be artificially maintained by a respirator.

Botox *Botox* (short for *Botulinum toxin*), a neurotoxin released by a bacterium often found in spoiled food, is also a nicotinic antagonist: It blocks the release of acetylcholine at neuromuscular junctions and is thus a deadly poison. However, injected in minute doses at specific sites, it has applications in medicine (e.g., reduction of tremors) and cosmetics (e.g., reduction of wrinkles).

Clinical Implications

FIGURE 4.18 The GABA$_A$–benzodiazepine receptor complex.

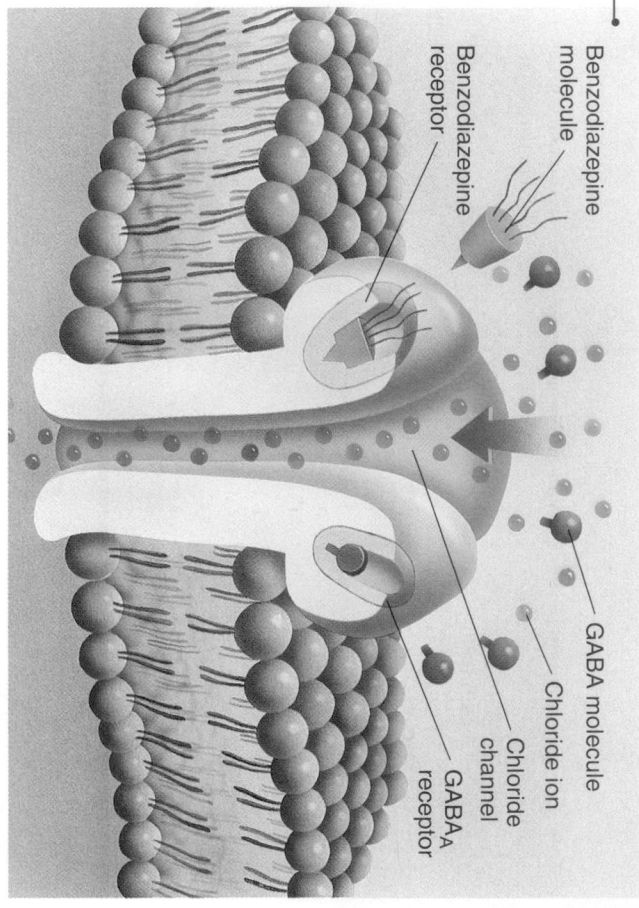

Benzodiazepine molecule

Benzodiazepine receptor

GABA molecule

Chloride ion

Chloride channel

GABA$_A$ receptor

You may be wondering about the differences between muscarinic and nicotinic receptors and about the significance of their names. The existence of these cholinergic receptor subtypes was inferred from the discovery that some of the receptors to which acetylcholine binds also bind to *muscarine*, whereas others bind to *nicotine*.

Themes Revisited

The function of the nervous system, like the function of any circuit, depends on how signals travel through it. The primary purpose of this chapter was to introduce you to neural conduction and transmission. This introduction touched on three of the book's four themes.

Clinical Implications

The clinical implications theme was illustrated by the opening case of the Lizard, Roberto Garcia d'Orta, whose symptoms resulted from a disruption of dopaminergic transmission. Also, there were discussions of the therapeutic use of anxiolytic drugs and curare.

Evolutionary Perspective

The evolutionary perspective theme was implicit throughout the entire chapter because almost all neu-

rophysiological research is conducted on the neurons and synapses of nonhuman subjects. However, the evolutionary perspective received explicit emphasis from the particularly high glial-cell-to-neuron ratio (10:1) of human brains.

Thinking Critically

The thinking-about-biopsychology theme arose in two metaphors: the firing-gun metaphor of action potentials and the mouse-traps-on-a-wobbly-shelf metaphor of axonal conduction. Metaphors are useful in teaching, and scientists find them useful for thinking about the phenomena they study and for generating hypotheses about them.

ON THE CD

See Hard Copy for additional readings for Chapter 4.

Think about It

1. Just as computers operate on binary (yes–no) signals, the all-or-none action potential is the basis of neural communication. The human brain is thus nothing more than a particularly complex computer. Discuss.

2. How have the findings described in this chapter changed your understanding of brain function?

3. Why is it important for biopsychologists to understand neural conduction and synaptic transmission? Is it important for all psychologists to have such knowledge? Discuss.

4. The discovery that neurotransmitters can act directly on DNA via G proteins uncovered a mechanism through which experience and genes can interact (see Chapter 2). Discuss.

5. Dendrites and glial cells are currently "hot" subjects of neuroscientific research. Discuss.

ON THE CD

Studying for an exam? Try the Practice Tests for Chapter 4.

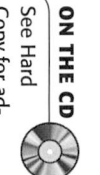

Key Terms

Absolute refractory period (p. 84)
Acetylcholinesterase (p. 91)
Action potential (AP) (p. 81)
Agonists (p. 95)
All-or-none responses (p. 81)
Antagonists (p. 95)
Antidromic conduction (p. 85)
Atropine (p. 97)
Autoreceptors (p. 89)
Axon hillock (p. 81)
Benzodiazepines (p. 96)
Cocaine (p. 95)
Coexistence (p. 87)
Curare (p. 97)
Dendritic spines (p. 86)
Depolarize (p. 80)
Directed synapses (p. 86)

Enzymatic degradation (p. 90)
Enzymes (p. 91)
Excitatory postsynaptic
 potentials (EPSPs) (p. 80)
Exocytosis (p. 87)
Gap junctions (p. 91)
Golgi complex (p. 87)
Graded responses (p. 80)
Hyperpolarize (p. 80)
Inhibitory postsynaptic
 potentials (IPSPs) (p. 80)
Integration (p. 81)
Ion channels (p. 78)
Ionotropic receptors (p. 89)
Ions (p. 78)
Ligand (p. 88)
Membrane potential (p. 77)
Metabotropic receptors (p. 89)

Microelectrodes (p. 77)
Neuromuscular junctions
 (p. 97)
Nodes of Ranvier (p. 85)
Nondirected synapses (p. 86)
Orthodromic conduction
 (p. 85)
Peptides (p. 87)
Postsynaptic inhibition (p. 86)
Presynaptic inhibition (p. 86)
Receptor blockers (p. 95)
Receptors (p. 88)
Receptor subtypes (p. 88)
Relative refractory period
 (p. 84)
Resting potential (p. 78)
Reuptake (p. 90)
Saltatory conduction (p. 85)

Second messenger (p. 89)
Sodium–potassium pumps
 (p. 80)
Spatial summation (p. 81)
Synaptic vesicles (p. 87)
Temporal summation (p. 82)
Threshold of excitation (p. 81)
Voltage-activated ion channels
 (p. 83)

ON THE CD

Need some
help studying
the key terms
for this chapter?
Check out the
electronic flash
cards for Chap-
ter 4.

The Research Methods of Biopsychology

Understanding What Biopsychologists Do

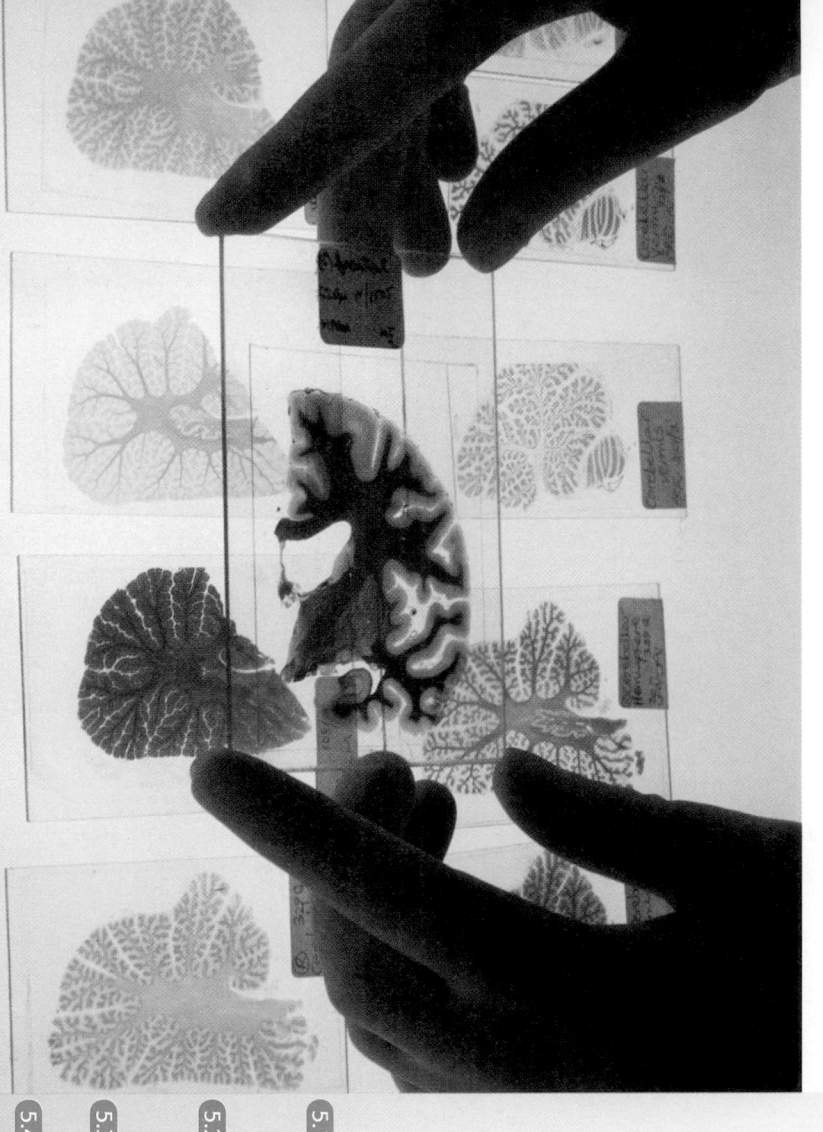

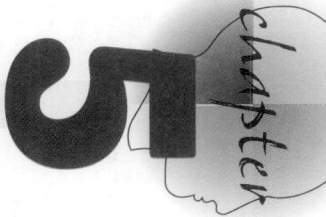

5 chapter

PART ONE
Methods of Studying the Nervous System

5.1 Methods of Visualizing and Stimulating the Living Human Brain

5.2 Recording Human Psychophysiological Activity

5.3 Invasive Physiological Research Methods

5.4 Pharmacological Research Methods

5.5 Genetic Engineering

PART TWO
Behavioral Research Methods of Biopsychology

5.6 Neuropsychological Testing

5.7 Behavioral Methods of Cognitive Neuroscience

5.8 Biopsychological Paradigms of Animal Behavior

Chapters 1 and 2 introduced you to the general interests, ideas, and approaches that characterize biopsychology. In Chapters 3 and 4, your introduction to biopsychology was temporarily curtailed while background material in neuroanatomy, neurophysiology, and neurochemistry was presented. This chapter gets down to the nitty-gritty of biopsychology; it describes the specific day-to-day activities of the biopsychology laboratory. It is intended to prepare you for later chapters and to sharpen your understanding of biopsychology by describing how biopsychologists do their research.

The organization of this chapter reflects biopsychology's intrinsic duality. The chapter has two major parts: one dealing with methods of studying the nervous system and the other dealing with methods of studying behavior.

As you read through this chapter, you should keep in mind that most of the methods that are used to study the human brain are also used for clinical purposes, for either diagnosis or treatment. The case of Professor P. makes this point.

The Ironic Case of Professor P.

Clinical Implications

Two weeks before his brain surgery, Professor P. reported to the hospital for a series of tests. What amazed Professor P. most about these tests was how familiar they seemed. No, Professor P. was not a psychic; he was a behavioral neuroscientist, and he was struck by how similar the tests performed on him were to the tests he had seen in his department.

Professor P. had a brain tumor on his right auditory-vestibular cranial nerve (cranial nerve VIII; see Appendices III and IV), and he had to have it *excised* (cut out). First, Professor P.'s auditory abilities were assessed by measuring his ability to detect sounds of various volumes and pitches and then by measuring the magnitude of the EEG signals evoked in his auditory cortex by clicks in his right ear.

Next, Professor P.'s vestibular function (balance) was tested by injecting cold water into his ear.

"Do you feel anything, Professor P.?"

"Well, a cold ear."

"Nothing else?"

"No."

So colder and colder water was tried with no effect until the final, coldest test was conducted. "Ah, that feels weird," said Professor P. "It's kind of like the bed is tipping."

The results of the tests were bad, or good, depending on your perspective. Professor P.'s hearing in his right ear was poor, and his right vestibular nerve was barely functioning. "At the temperatures we flushed down there, most people would have been on their hands and knees puking their guts out." Professor P. smiled at the technical terminology.

Of course, he was upset that his brain had deteriorated so badly, but he sensed that his neurosurgeon was secretly pleased: "We won't have to try to save the nerve; we'll just cut it."

There was one last test. The skin of his right cheek was lightly pricked while the EEG responses of his somatosensory cortex were recorded from his scalp. "This is just to establish a baseline for the surgery," it was explained. "One main risk of removing tumors on the auditory-vestibular cranial nerve (VIII), is damaging the facial cranial nerve (VII), and that would make the right side of your face sag. So during the surgery, electrodes will be inserted in your cheek, and your cheek will be repeatedly stimulated with tiny electrical pulses. The cortical responses will be recorded and fed into a loudspeaker so that the surgeon can immediately hear changes in the activity if his scalpel starts to stray into the area."

As Professor P. was driving home, his mind wandered from his own plight to his day at the hospital. "Quite interesting," he thought to himself. There were biopsychologists everywhere, doing biopsychological things. In all three labs he had visited, there were people who began their training as biopsychologists.

Two weeks later, Professor P. was rolled into the preparation room. "Sorry to do this, Professor P., you were one of my favorite instructors," the nurse said, as she inserted a large needle into Professor P.'s face and left it there.

Professor P. didn't mind; he was barely conscious. He did not know that he wouldn't regain consciousness for several days—at which point he would be incapable of talking, eating, or even breathing.

Don't forget Professor P.; you will learn more about his case in Chapter 10. For now, this case has demonstrated to you that many of the research methods of biopsychology are also used in clinical settings. Let's move on to the methods themselves.

5.1   Methods of Visualizing and Stimulating the Living Human Brain

Prior to the early 1970s, biopsychological research was impeded by the inability to obtain images of the organ of primary interest: the living human brain. Conventional X-ray photography is next to useless for this purpose. For an X-ray photograph to be taken, an X-ray beam is passed through an object and then onto a photographic plate. Each of the molecules through which the beam passes absorbs some of the radiation; thus, only the unabsorbed portions of the beam reach the photographic plate. X-ray photography is therefore effective in characterizing internal structures that differ substantially from their surroundings in the degree to which they absorb X-rays—for example, a revolver in a suitcase full of clothes or a bone in flesh. However, by the time an X-ray beam has passed through the numerous overlapping structures of the brain, which differ only slightly from one another in their ability to absorb X-rays, it carries little information about the shape of the individual structures through which it has passed.

Contrast X-Rays

Although conventional X-ray photography is not useful for visualizing the brain, contrast X-ray techniques are. **Contrast X-ray techniques** involve injecting into one compartment of the body a substance that absorbs X-rays either less than or more than the surrounding tissue. The injected substance then heightens the contrast between the compartment and the surrounding tissue during X-ray photography.

 **Clinical Implications**

One contrast X-ray technique, **cerebral angiography**, uses the infusion of a radio-opaque dye into a cerebral artery to visualize the cerebral circulatory system during X-ray photography (see Figure 5.1). Cerebral angiograms are most useful for localizing vascular damage, but the displacement of blood vessels from their normal position also can indicate the location of a tumor.

X-Ray Computed Tomography

In the early 1970s, the study of the living human brain was revolutionized by the introduction of computed tomography. **Computed tomography (CT)** is a computer-assisted X-ray procedure that can be used to visualize the brain and other internal structures of the living body. During cerebral computed tomography, the neurological patient lies with his or her head positioned in the center of a large cylinder, as depicted in Figure 5.2. On one side of the cylinder is an X-ray tube that projects an X-ray

beam through the head to an X-ray detector mounted on the other side. The X-ray tube and detector automatically rotate around the head of the patient at one level of the brain, taking many individual X-ray photographs as they rotate. The meager information in each X-ray photograph is combined by a computer to generate a CT scan of one horizontal section of the brain. Then, the X-ray tube and detector are moved along the axis of the patient's body to another level of the brain, and the process is repeated. Scans of eight or nine horizontal brain sections are typically obtained from a patient; combined, they provide a three-dimensional representation of the brain.

Magnetic Resonance Imaging

The success of computed tomography stimulated the development of other techniques for obtaining images of the inside of the living body. Among these techniques is **magnetic resonance imaging (MRI)**—a procedure in which high-resolution images are constructed from the measurement of waves that hydrogen atoms emit when they are activated by radio-frequency waves in a magnetic field. MRI provides clearer images of the brain than does CT. A color-coded two-dimensional MRI scan of the midsagittal brain is presented in Figure 5.3.

In addition to providing relatively high **spatial resolution** (the ability to detect differences in spatial location), MRI can produce images in three dimensions. Figure 5.4 is a three-dimensional MRI scan.

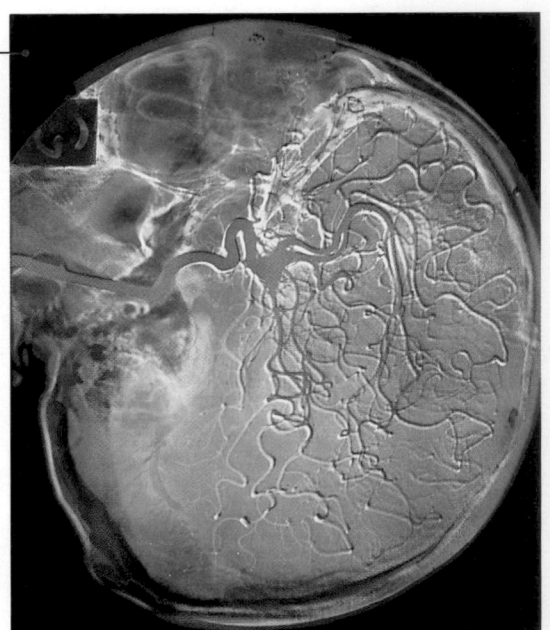

FIGURE 5.1   A cerebral angiogram of a healthy subject.

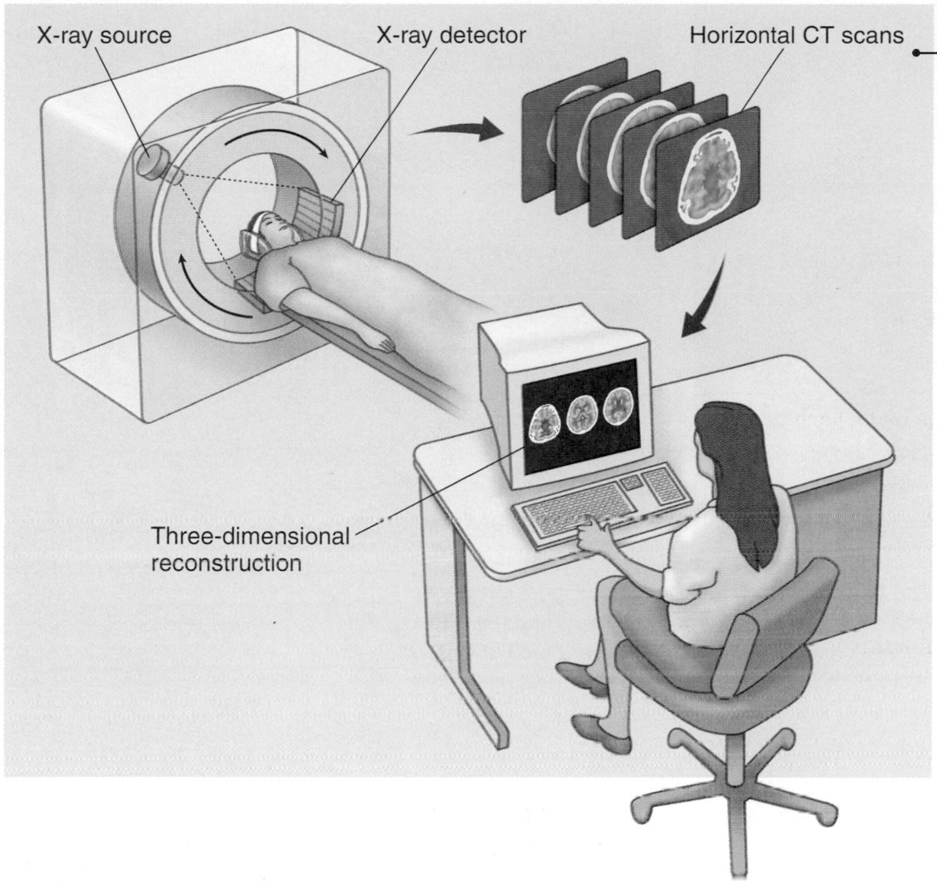

FIGURE 5.2 Computed tomography (CT) uses X-rays to create a CT scan of the brain.

Horizontal CT scans

X-ray detector

X-ray source

Three-dimensional reconstruction

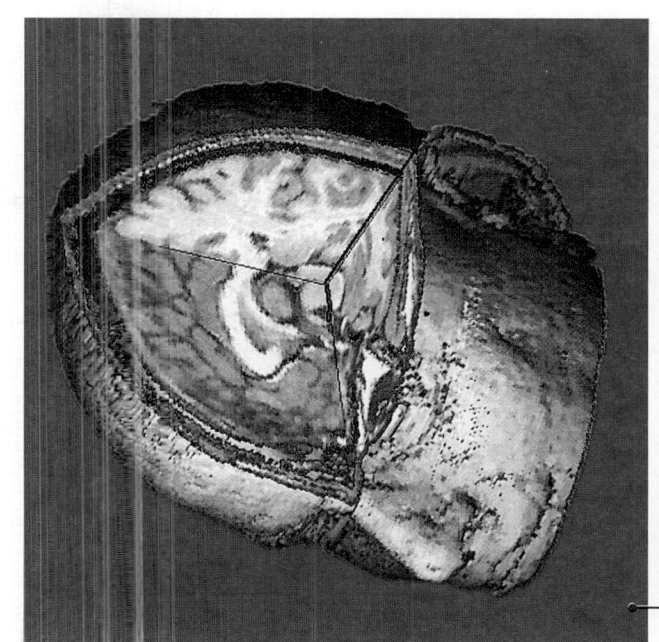

FIGURE 5.4 Structural MRI can be used to provide three-dimensional images of the entire brain. (Courtesy of Bruce Foster and Robert Hare, University of British Columbia.)

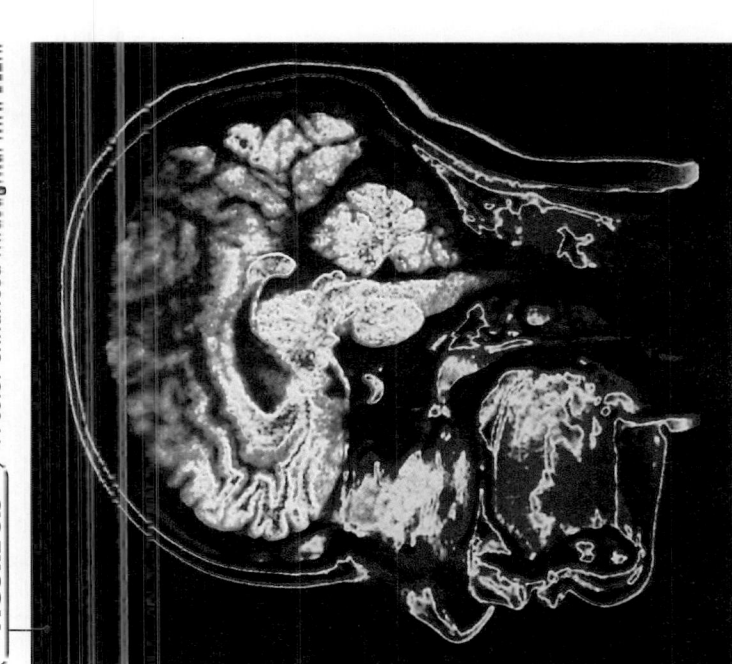

FIGURE 5.3 A color-enhanced midsagittal MRI scan.

Figure 5.5 shows two-dimensional MRI scans of a slice of a brain.

Positron Emission Tomography

Positron emission tomography (PET) is a brain-imaging technique that has been widely used in biopsychological research because it provides images of brain activity rather than brain structure. In one common version of PET, radioactive **2-deoxyglucose (2-DG)** is injected into the patient's *carotid artery* (an artery of the neck that feeds the ipsilateral cerebral hemisphere). Because of its similarity to glucose, the primary metabolic fuel of the brain, 2-deoxyglucose is rapidly taken up by active (energy-consuming) neurons. However, unlike glucose, 2-deoxyglucose cannot be metabolized; it therefore accumulates in active neurons until it is gradually broken down. Each PET scan is an image of the levels of radioactivity (indicated by color coding) in various parts of one horizontal level of the brain. Thus, if a PET scan is taken of a patient who engages in an activity such as reading for about 30 seconds after the 2-DG injection, the resulting scan will indicate the areas at that brain level that were most active during the 30 seconds of activity (see Figure 5.6). Usually, several different levels of the brain are scanned so that the extent of brain activity can be better assessed.

Notice from Figure 5.6 that PET scans are not images of the brain. Each PET scan is merely a colored map of the amount of radioactivity in each of the tiny cubic voxels (volume pixels) that compose the scan. One can

Cognitive Neuroscience

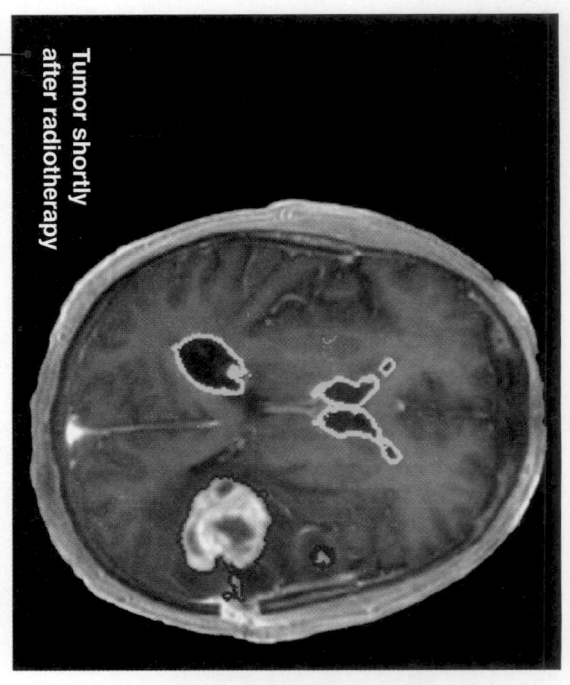

FIGURE 5.5 Structural MRI can also be used to provide two-dimensional images of brain slices. The MRI scan on the left shows a tumor shortly after radiotherapy, and the MRI scan on the right shows the same tumor several weeks later. Ventricles are outlined in yellow; the tumor is outlined in red. (Adapted from Calmon et al., 1998; courtesy of Neil Roberts, University of Liverpool.)

Tumor shortly after radiotherapy

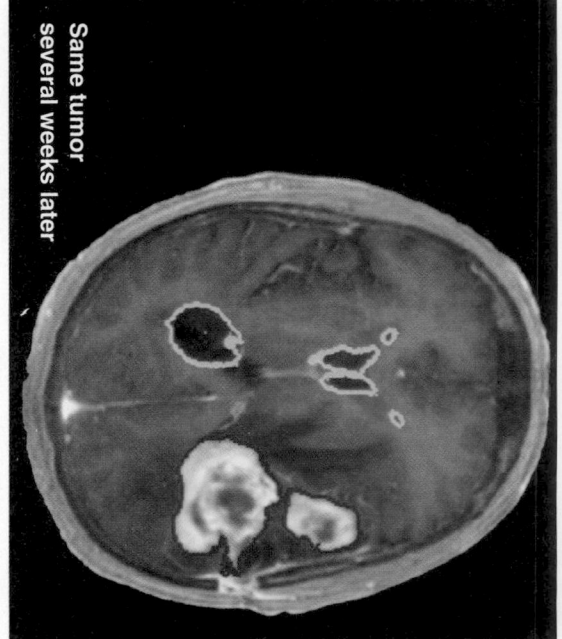

Same tumor several weeks later

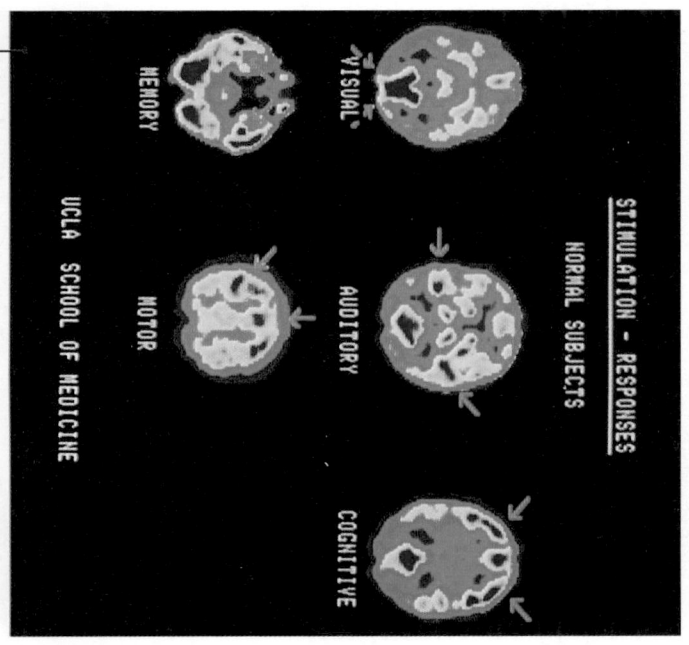

FIGURE 5.6 A series of PET scans. Each scan is a horizontal section recorded during a different psychological activity. Areas of high activity are indicated by reds and yellows. For example, notice the high level of activity in the visual cortex of the occipital lobe when the subject scanned a visual display. (From "Positron Tomography: Human Brain Function and Biochemistry" by Michael E. Phelps and John C. Mazziotta, *Science*, 228 [9701], May 17, 1985, p. 804. Copyright 1985 by the AAAS. Reprinted by permission. Courtesy of Drs. Michael E. Phelps and John Mazziotta, UCLA School of Medicine.)

only estimate exactly how each voxel maps onto a particular brain structure.

Functional MRI

Cognitive Neuroscience

MRI technology has been applied with great success to the measurement of brain activity (see Cabeza & Nyberg, 2000). Conventional techniques of **functional**

MRI (fMRI) produce images of the increase in oxygen flow in the blood to active areas of the brain.

Functional MRI has four advantages over PET: (1) Nothing has to be injected into the subject; (2) it provides both structural and functional information in the same image; (3) its spatial resolution is better; and (4) it can be used to produce three-dimensional images of activity over the entire brain. Functional MRIs are shown in Figure 5.7.

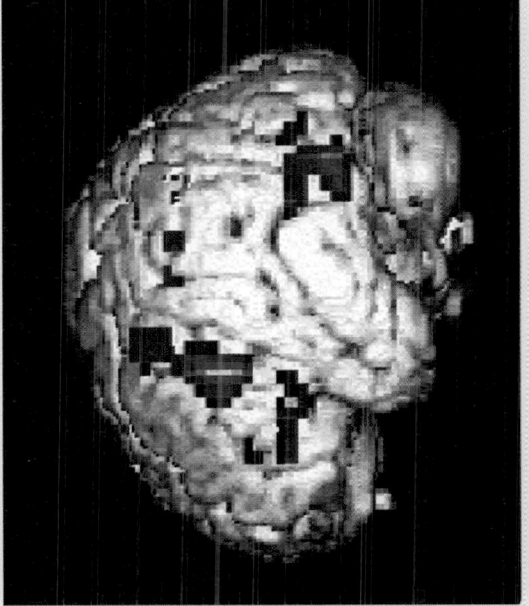
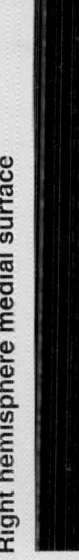

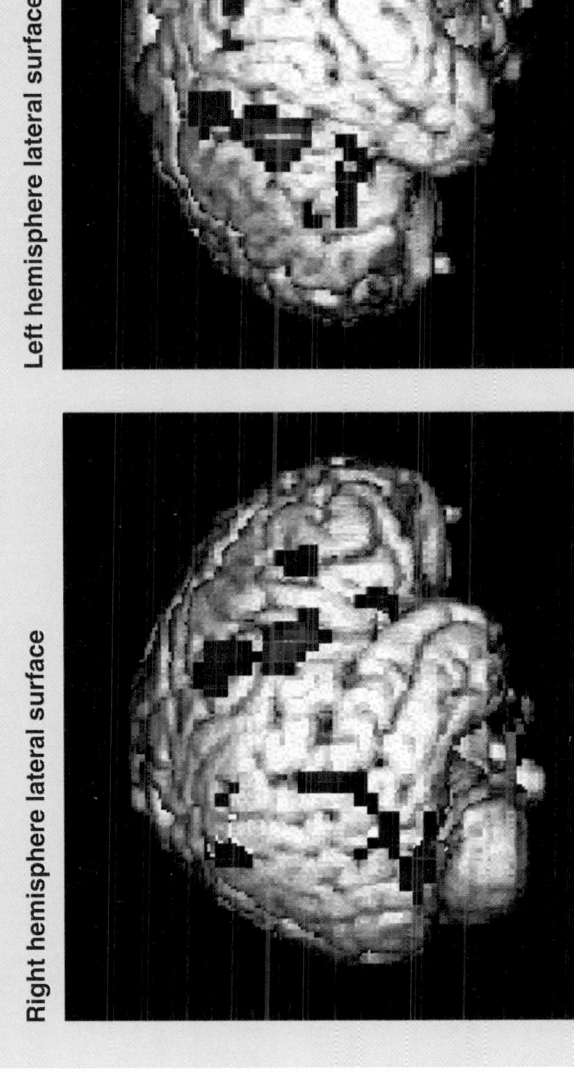
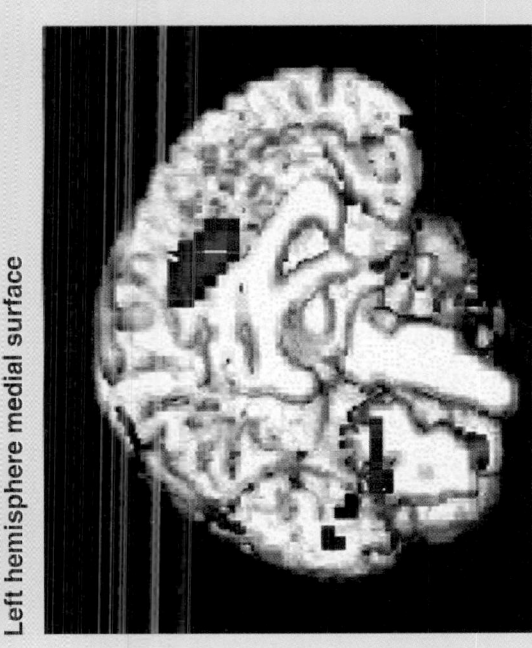

Right hemisphere lateral surface

Left hemisphere lateral surface

Left hemisphere medial surface

Right hemisphere medial surface

FIGURE 5.7 Functional magnetic resonance images (fMRIs). These images illustrate the areas of cortex that became more active when the subjects observed strings of letters and were asked to specify which strings were words; in the control condition, subjects viewed strings of asterisks (Kiehl et al., 1999). These fMRIs illustrate surface activity; but images of sections through the brain can also be displayed. (Courtesy of Kent Kiehl and Peter Liddle, Department of Psychiatry, University of British Columbia.)

Magnetoencephalography

Another technique that is used to monitor the brain activity of human subjects is magnetoencephalography (MEG). MEG measures changes in magnetic fields on the surface of the scalp that are produced by changes in underlying patterns of neural activity. Its major advantage over fMRI is its temporal resolution; it can record fast changes in neural activity.

Brain-Image Archives

One important recent development in brain-imaging research is not a new technique, but rather the establishment of *brain-image archives*. Only a few summary images are published in each research paper, and the countless complex variations in data processing make it virtually impossible for researchers to compare the results of a published study with their own findings. However, many researchers who study brain images now submit their raw data to a brain-image archive to which other researchers have access (see Roland et al.,2001; Van Horn & Gazzaniga, 2002). Cognitive neuroscientists can often obtain the raw data collected in a particular study from a brain-image archive and compare those data to, or combine them with, their own.

5.2 Recording Human Psychophysiological Activity

The preceding section introduced you to functional brain imaging, the cornerstone of cognitive neuroscience research. This section deals with *psychophysiological recording methods* (methods of recording physiological activity from the surface of the human body). Five of the most widely studied psychophysiological measures are described: one measure of brain activity (the scalp EEG), two measures of somatic nervous system activity (muscle tension and eye movement), and two measures of autonomic nervous system activity (skin conductance and cardiovascular activity).

Scalp Electroencephalography

The *electroencephalogram* (EEG) is a measure of the gross electrical activity of the brain. It is recorded through large electrodes by a device called an *electroencephalograph* (EEG machine), and the technique is called **electroencephalography**. In EEG studies of human subjects, each channel of EEG activity is usually recorded from disk-shaped electrodes, about half the size of a dime, which are taped to the scalp.

The scalp EEG signal reflects the sum of electrical events throughout the head. These events include action potentials and postsynaptic potentials, as well as electrical signals from the skin, muscles, blood, and eyes. Thus, the utility of the scalp EEG does not lie in its ability to provide an unclouded view of neural activity. Its value as a research and diagnostic tool rests on the fact that some EEG wave forms are associated with particular states of consciousness or particular types of cerebral pathology (e.g., epilepsy). For example, **alpha waves** are regular, 8- to 12-per-second, high-amplitude waves that are associated with relaxed wakefulness. A few examples of EEG wave forms and their psychological correlates are presented in Figure 5.8.

Because EEG signals decrease in amplitude as they spread from their source, a comparison of signals recorded from various sites on the scalp can sometimes indicate the origin of particular waves. This is why it is usual to record EEG activity from many sites simultaneously.

Psychophysiologists are often more interested in the EEG waves that accompany certain psychological events than they are in the background EEG signal.

Transcranial Magnetic Stimulation

PET, fMRI, and magnetoencephalography have allowed cognitive neuroscientists to create images of the activity of the human brain. But these methods all have the same weakness: They can be used to show a correlation between brain activity and cognitive activity, but they can't prove that brain activity and cognitive activity are causally related. For example, a brain-imaging technique may show that the cingulate cortex becomes active when human subjects view disturbing photographs, but it can't prove that activity in the cingulate cortex causes the emotional reaction. Transcranial magnetic stimulation may provide a way of studying causal relations between human cortical activity and cognition.

Transcranial magnetic stimulation (TMS) is a technique for disrupting the activity in an area of the cortex by creating a magnetic field under a coil positioned next to the skull (see Fitzpatrick & Rothman, 2000; Pascual-Leone, Walsh, & Rothwell, 2000). In effect, the magnetic stimulation temporarily turns off part of the brain while the effects on cognition and behavior are assessed.

Although TMS is currently being used to study the neural mechanisms of cognition, its full potential will not be realized until fundamental questions about safety, depth of effect, and mechanisms of neural disruption are answered.

These accompanying EEG waves are generally referred to as **event-related potentials (ERPs)**. One commonly studied type of event-related potential is the **sensory evoked potential**—the change in the cortical EEG signal that is elicited by the momentary presentation of a sensory stimulus. As Figure 5.9 illustrates, the cortical EEG that follows a sensory stimulus has two components: the response to the stimulus (the signal) and the ongoing background EEG activity (the noise). The *signal* is the part of any recording that is of interest; the *noise* is the part that isn't. The problem in recording sensory evoked potentials is that the noise of the background EEG is often so great that the sensory evoked potential is masked. Measuring a sensory evoked potential can be like detecting a whisper at a rock concert.

A method used to reduce the noise of the background EEG is **signal averaging.** First, a subject's response to a stimulus, such as a click, is recorded many let's say 1,000 times. Then, a computer identifies the millivolt value of each of the 1,000 traces at their starting points (i.e., at the click) and calculates the mean of these

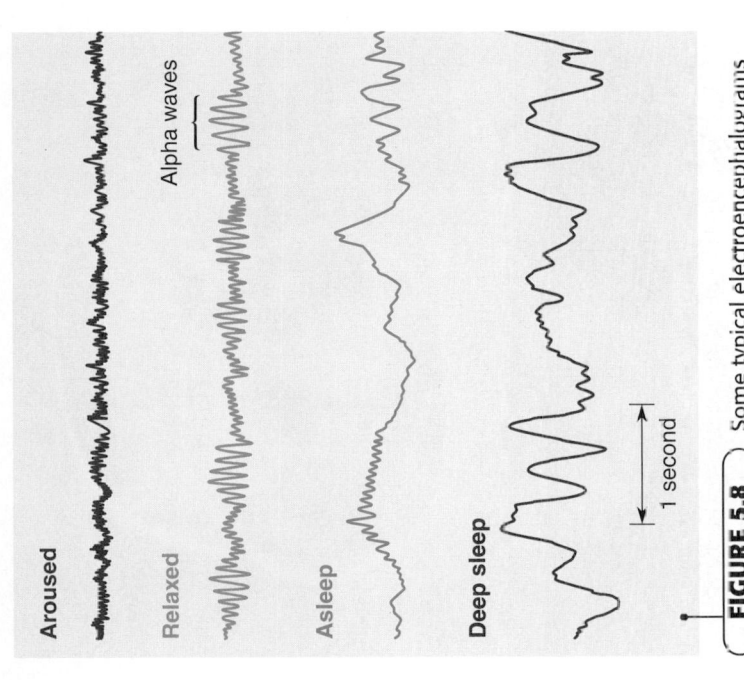

FIGURE 5.8   Some typical electroencephalograms and their psychological correlates.

Aroused

Relaxed

Alpha waves

Asleep

Deep sleep

1 second

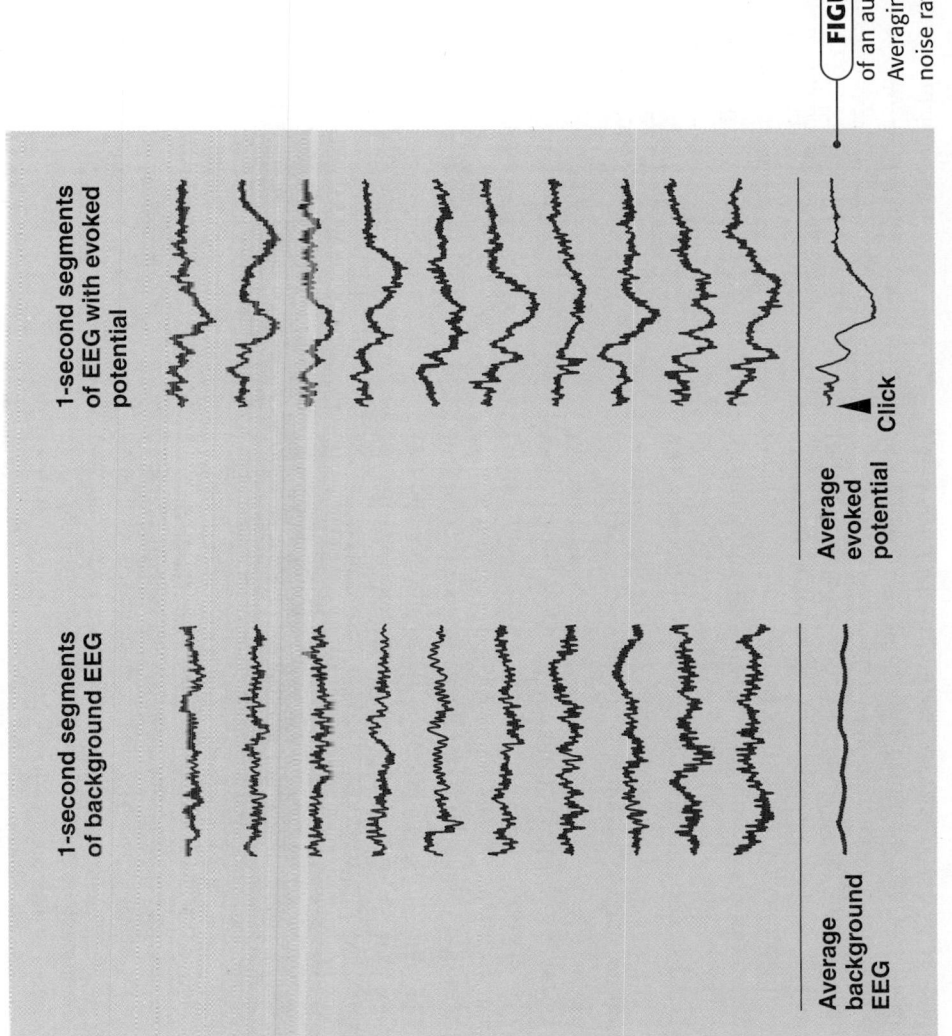

1-second segments of background EEG

1-second segments of EEG with evoked potential

Average background EEG

Average evoked potential

Click

FIGURE 5.9   The averaging of an auditory evoked potential. Averaging increases the signal-to-noise ratio.

1,000 scores. Next, it considers the value of each of the 1,000 traces 1 millisecond (msec) from their start, for example, and calculates the mean of these values. It repeats this process at the 2-msec mark, the 3-msec mark, and so on. When these averages are plotted, the average response evoked by the click is more apparent because the random background EEG is canceled out by the averaging. See Figure 5.9, which illustrates the averaging of an auditory evoked potential.

The analysis of *average evoked potentials* (AEPs) focuses on the various waves in the averaged signal. Each wave is characterized by its direction, positive or negative, and by its latency. For example, the **P300 wave** illustrated in Figure 5.10 is the positive wave that occurs about 300 milliseconds after a momentary stimulus that has meaning for the subject (e.g., a stimulus to which the subject must respond)—see Friedman, Cycowicz, and Gaeta (2001). In contrast, the portions of an evoked potential recorded in the first few milliseconds after a stimulus are not influenced by the meaning of the stimulus for the subject. These small waves are called **far-field potentials** because, although they are recorded from the scalp, they originate far away in the sensory nuclei of the brain stem.

Although electroencephalography scores high on temporal resolution, it initially failed miserably on spatial resolution. With conventional electroencephalographic procedures, one can only roughly estimate the source of a particular signal. However, newer techniques employing sophisticated computer software and many electrodes can accurately locate the source of signals. The spatial resolution of these techniques is sufficient to enable the amplitude of evoked EEG signals recorded on the cortex to be color-coded and plotted on the surface of a three-dimensional MRI scan (Gevins et al, 1995). This useful marriage of techniques is illustrated in Figure 5.11.

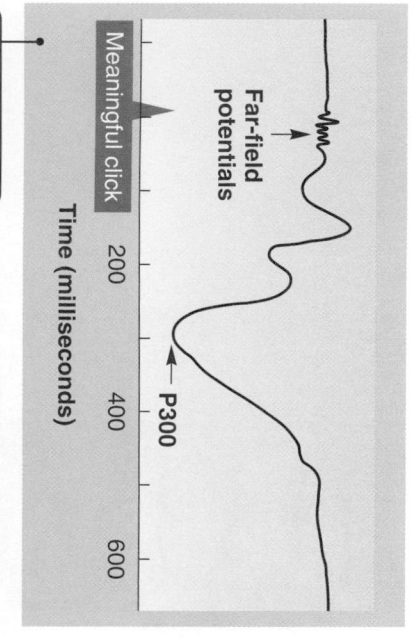

FIGURE 5.10 An average auditory evoked potential. Notice the P300 wave. This wave occurs only if the stimulus has meaning for the subject; in this case, the click signals the imminent delivery of a reward. By convention, positive EEG waves are always shown as downward deflections.

Meaningful click

Far-field potentials

P300

Time (milliseconds)

200   400   600

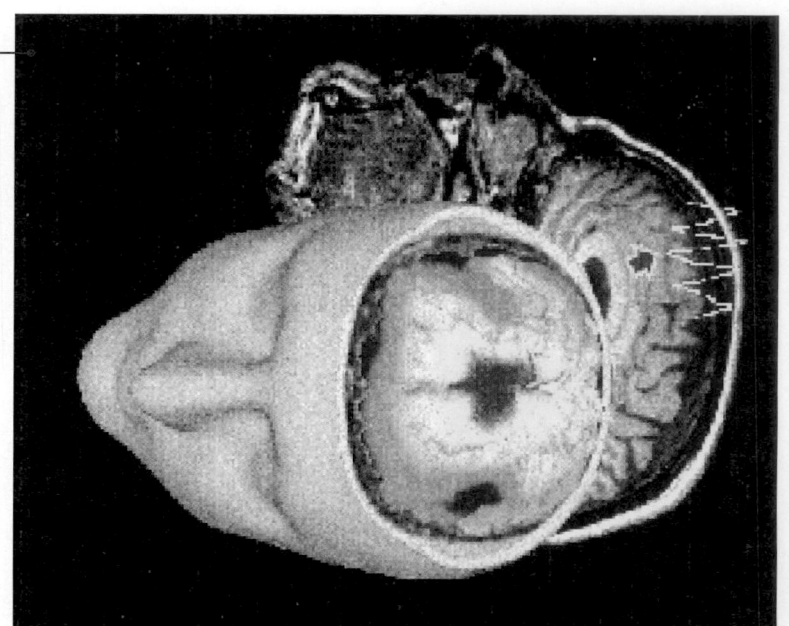

FIGURE 5.11 The marriage of electroencephalography and magnetic resonance imaging: The distribution of EEG signals can be represented on a structural cerebral MRI. Plotted in this illustration is the distribution of theta waves recorded while the subjects worked on a memory task. The highest incidence of theta waves (indicated by red in the three-dimensional MRI of the dorsal brain surface and by blue on the midsagittal section) occurred in the anterior cingulate cortex. (Alan Gevins, EEG Systems Laboratory & SAM Technology, San Francisco.)

Muscle Tension

Each skeletal muscle is composed of millions of thread-like muscle fibers. Each muscle fiber contracts in an all-or-none fashion when activated by the motor neuron that innervates it. At any given time, a few fibers in each resting muscle are likely to be contracting, thus maintaining the overall tone (tension) of the muscle. Movement results when a large number of fibers contract at the same time.

In everyday language, anxious people are commonly referred to as "tense." This usage acknowledges the fact that anxious, or otherwise aroused, individuals typically display high resting levels of tension in their muscles. This is why psychophysiologists are interested in this measure; they use it as an indicator of psychological arousal.

Electromyography is the usual procedure for measuring muscle tension. The resulting record is called an *electromyogram* (EMG). EMG activity is usually recorded between two electrodes taped to the surface of the skin over the muscle of interest. An EMG record is presented

Skin Conductance

Emotional thoughts and experiences are associated with increases in the ability of the skin to conduct electricity. The two most commonly employed indexes of *electrodermal activity* are the **skin conductance level (SCL)** and the **skin conductance response (SCR)**. The SCL is a measure of the background level of skin conductance that is associated with a particular situation, whereas the SCR is a measure of the transient changes in skin conductance that are associated with discrete experiences.

The physiological bases of skin conductance changes are not fully understood, but there is considerable evidence implicating the sweat glands (see Boucsein, 1992). Although the main function of sweat glands is to cool the body, these glands tend to become active in emotional situations. Sweat glands are distributed over most of the body surface; but, as you are almost certainly aware, those of the hands, feet, armpits, and forehead are particularly responsive to emotional stimuli.

Cardiovascular Activity

The presence in our language of phrases such as *chicken hearted, white with fear,* and *blushing bride* indicates that modern psychophysiologists were not the first to recognize the relationship between *cardiovascular activity* and emotion. The cardiovascular system has two parts: the blood vessels and the heart. It is a system for distributing oxygen and nutrients to the tissues of the body, removing metabolic wastes, and transmitting chemical messages. Three different measures of cardiovascular activity are frequently employed in psychophysiological research: heart rate, arterial blood pressure, and local blood volume.

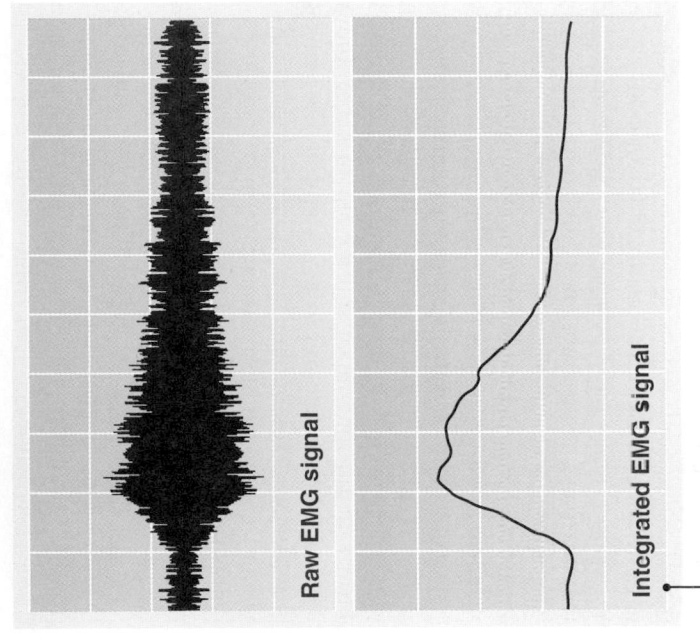

Raw EMG signal

Integrated EMG signal

FIGURE 5.12   The relation between a raw EMG signal and its integrated version. The subject tensed the muscle beneath the electrodes and then gradually relaxed it.

in Figure 5.12. You will notice from this figure that the main correlate of an increase in muscle contraction is an increase in the amplitude of the raw EMG signal, which reflects the number of muscle fibers contracting at any one time.

Most psychophysiologists do not work with raw EMG signals; they convert them to a more workable form. The raw signal is fed into a computer that calculates the total amount of EMG spiking per unit of time—in consecutive 0.1-second intervals, for example. The integrated signal (i.e., the total EMG activity per unit of time) is then plotted. The result is a smooth curve, the amplitude of which is a simple, continuous measure of the level of muscle tension (see Figure 5.12).

Eye Movement

The electrophysiological technique for recording eye movements is called **electrooculography**, and the resulting record is called an *electrooculogram (EOG)*. Electrooculography is based on the fact that there is a steady potential difference between the front (positive) and back (negative) of the eyeball. Because of this steady potential, when the eye moves, a change in the electrical potential between electrodes placed around the eye can be recorded. It is usual to record EOG activity between two electrodes placed on each side of the eye to measure its horizontal movements and between two electrodes placed above and below the eye to measure its vertical movements (see Figure 5.13).

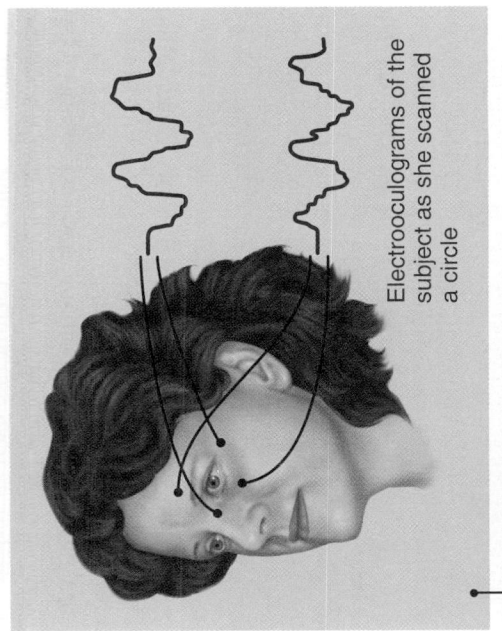

Electrooculograms of the subject as she scanned a circle

FIGURE 5.13   The typical placement of electrodes around the eye for electrooculography. The two electrooculogram traces were recorded as the subject scanned a circle.

Heart Rate The electrical signal that is associated with each heartbeat can be recorded through electrodes placed on the chest. The recording is called an **electrocardiogram** (abbreviated either ECG, for obvious reasons, or **EKG**, from the original German). The average resting heart rate of a healthy adult is about 70 beats per minute, but it increases abruptly at the sound, or thought, of a dental drill.

Blood Pressure Measuring arterial blood pressure involves two independent measurements: a measurement of the peak pressure during the periods of heart contraction, the *systoles*, and a measurement of the minimum pressure during the periods of relaxation, the *diastoles*. Blood pressure is usually expressed as a ratio of systolic over diastolic blood pressure in millimeters of mercury (mmHg). The normal resting blood pressure for an adult is about 130/70 mmHg. A chronic blood pressure of more than 140/90 mmHg is viewed as a serious health hazard and is called **hypertension.**

You have likely had your blood pressure measured with a *sphygmomanometer*—a crude device composed of a hollow cuff, a rubber bulb for inflating it, and a pressure gauge for measuring the pressure in the cuff (*sphygmos* means "pulse"). More reliable, fully automated methods are used in research.

Blood Volume Changes in the volume of blood in particular parts of the body are associated with psychological events. The best-known example of such a change is the engorgement of the genitals that is associated with sexual arousal in both males and females. **Plethysmography** refers to the various techniques for measuring changes in the volume of blood in a particular part of the body (*plethysmos* means "an enlargement").

One method of measuring these changes is to record the volume of the target tissue by wrapping a strain gauge around it. Although this method has utility in measuring blood flow in fingers or similarly shaped organs, the possibilities for employing it are somewhat limited. Another plethysmographic method is to shine a light through the tissue under investigation and to measure the amount of the light that is absorbed by it. The more blood there is in a structure, the more light it will absorb.

5.3 Invasive Physiological Research Methods

Efforts to study brain–behavior relations in human subjects are impeded by the ethical requirement of adhering to lines of research that involve no direct interaction with the organ of interest: the brain. We turn now from a consideration of the noninvasive techniques employed in research on living human brains to a consideration of more direct techniques, which are commonly employed in biopsychological studies of laboratory animals.

Most physiological techniques used in biopsychological research on laboratory animals fall into one of three categories: lesion methods, electrical stimulation methods, and invasive recording methods. Each of these three methods is discussed in this section of the chapter, but it begins with a description of *stereotaxic surgery*.

Stereotaxic Surgery

Stereotaxic surgery is the first step in many biopsychological experiments. *Stereotaxic surgery* is the means by which experimental devices are precisely positioned in the depths of the brain. Two things are required in stereotaxic surgery: an atlas to provide directions to the target site and an instrument for getting there.

The **stereotaxic atlas** is used to locate brain structures in much the same way that a geographic atlas is used to locate geographic landmarks. There is, however, one important difference. In contrast to the surface of the earth, which has only two dimensions, the brain has three. Accordingly, the brain is represented in a stereotaxic atlas by a series of individual maps, one per page, each representing the structure of a single, two-dimensional frontal brain slice. In stereotaxic atlases, all distances are given in millimeters from a designated reference point. In some rat atlases, the reference point is **bregma**—the point on the top of the skull where two of the major *sutures* (seams in the skull) intersect.

The **stereotaxic instrument** has two parts: a *head-holder*, which firmly holds each subject's brain in the prescribed position and orientation; and an *electrode holder*, which holds the device to be inserted. A system of precision gears allows the electrode holder to be moved in three dimensions: anterior–posterior, dorsal–ventral, and lateral–medial. The implantation by stereotaxic surgery of an electrode in the amygdala of a rat is illustrated in Figure 5.14.

Lesion Methods

Those of you with an unrelenting drive to dismantle objects to see how they work will appreciate the lesion methods. In those methods, a part of the brain is removed, damaged, or destroyed; then, the behavior of the subject is carefully assessed in an effort to determine the functions of the lesioned structure. Four types of lesions are discussed here: aspiration lesions, radio-frequency lesions, knife cuts, and cryogenic blockade.

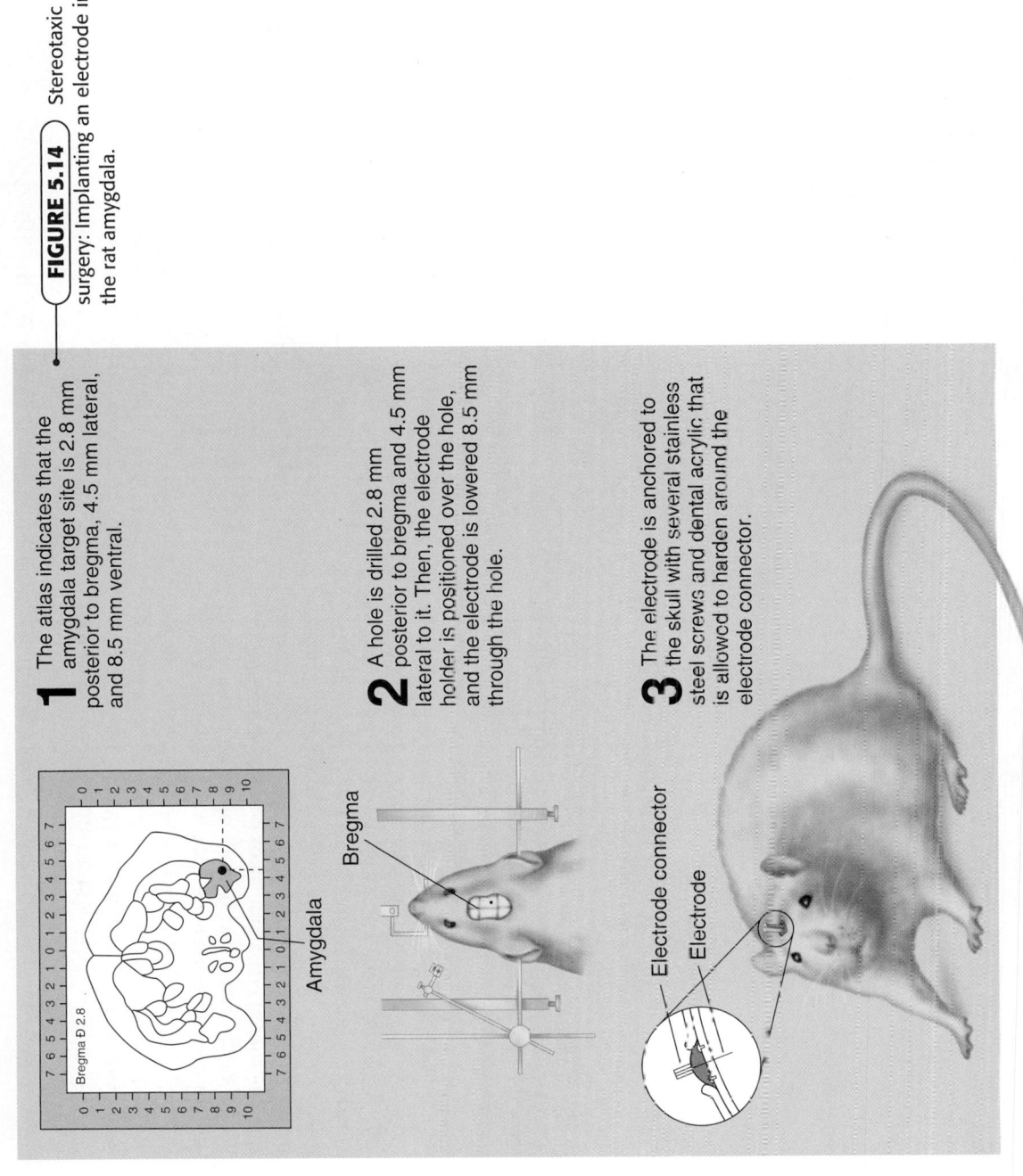

1 The atlas indicates that the amygdala target site is 2.8 mm posterior to bregma, 4.5 mm lateral, and 8.5 mm ventral.

Amygdala

Bregma

2 A hole is drilled 2.8 mm posterior to bregma and 4.5 mm lateral to it. Then, the electrode holder is positioned over the hole, and the electrode is lowered 8.5 mm through the hole.

3 The electrode is anchored to the skull with several stainless steel screws and dental acrylic that is allowed to harden around the electrode connector.

Electrode connector

Electrode

FIGURE 5.14 Stereotaxic surgery: Implanting an electrode in the rat amygdala.

Aspiration Lesions When a lesion is to be made in an area of cortical tissue that is accessible to the eyes and instruments of the surgeon, **aspiration** is frequently the method of choice. The cortical tissue is drawn off by suction through a fine-tipped handheld glass pipette. Because the underlying white matter is slightly more resistant to suction than the cortical tissue itself, a skilled surgeon can delicately peel off the layers of cortical tissue from the surface of the brain, leaving the underlying white matter and major blood vessels undamaged.

Radio-Frequency Lesions Small subcortical lesions are commonly made by passing *radio-frequency current* (high-frequency current) through the target tissue from the tip of a stereotaxically positioned electrode. The heat from the current destroys the tissue. The size and shape of the lesion are determined by the duration and intensity of the current and the configuration of the electrode tip.

Knife Cuts *Sectioning* (cutting) is used to eliminate conduction in a nerve or tract. A tiny, well-placed cut can unambiguously accomplish this task without producing extensive damage to surrounding tissue. How does one insert a knife into the brain to make a cut without severely damaging the overlying tissue? One method is depicted in Figure 5.15 on page 112.

Cryogenic Blockade An alternative to destructive lesions is **cryogenic blockade.** When coolant is pumped through an implanted *cryoprobe,* such as the one depicted in Figure 5.16, neurons near the tip are cooled until they stop firing. The temperature is maintained above the freezing level, so there is no structural damage. Then, when the tissue is allowed to warm up, normal neural activity returns. A cryogenic blockade is functionally similar to a lesion in that it eliminates the contribution of a particular area of the brain to the ongoing behavior

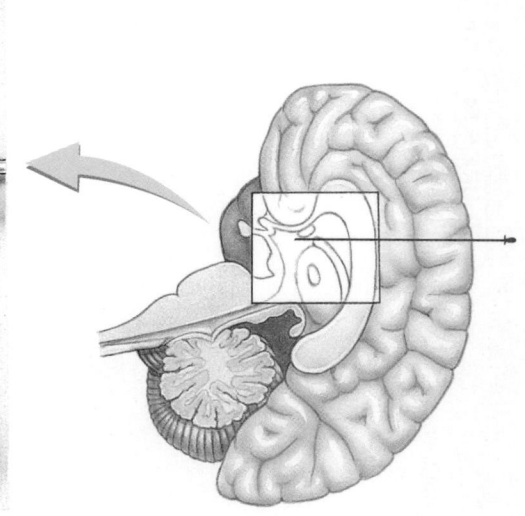

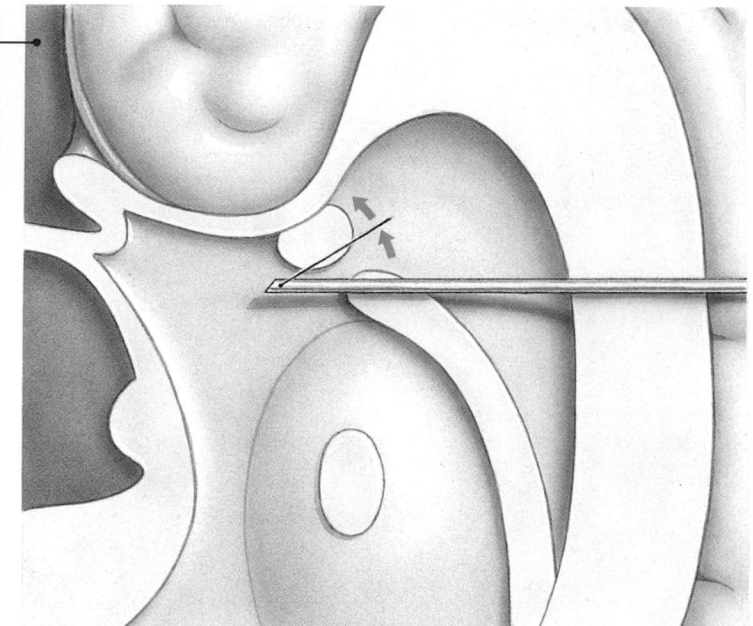

FIGURE 5.15   A device for performing subcortical knife cuts. The device is stereotaxically positioned in the brain; then, the blade swings out to make the cut. Here, the anterior commissure is being sectioned.

of the subject. This is why cryogenic blockades are sometimes referred to as *reversible lesions*. Reversible lesions can also be produced with microinjections into the brain of local anesthetics such as lidocaine (see Floresco, Seamans, & Phillips, 1997).

Interpreting Lesion Effects   Before you leave this section on lesions, a word of caution is in order. Lesion effects are deceptively difficult to interpret. Because the structures of the brain are small, convoluted, and tightly packed together, even a highly skilled surgeon cannot completely destroy a structure without producing signif-

icant damage to adjacent structures. There is, however, an unfortunate tendency to lose sight of this fact. For example, a lesion that leaves major portions of the amygdala intact and damages an assortment of neighboring structures comes to be thought of simplistically as an *amygdala lesion*. Such an apparently harmless abstraction can be misleading in two ways. If you believe that all lesions referred to as "amygdala lesions" include damage to no other brain structure, you may incorrectly attribute all of their behavioral effects to amygdala damage; conversely, if you believe that all lesions referred to as "amygdala lesions" include the entire amygdala, you may incorrectly conclude that the amygdala does not participate in behaviors uninfluenced by the lesion.

Bilateral and Unilateral Lesions   As a general principle—but one with several notable exceptions—the behavioral effects of *unilateral lesions* (lesions restricted

Thinking Critically

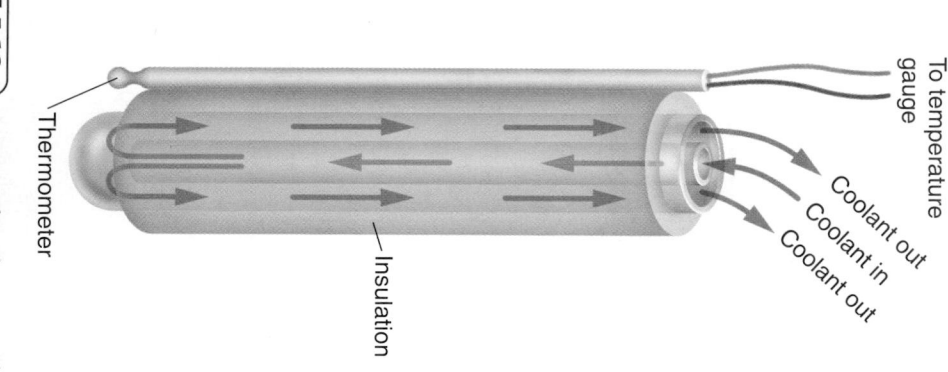

FIGURE 5.16   A cryoprobe. The cryoprobe is implanted in the brain; then, the brain area at the uninsulated tip of the cryoprobe is cooled while the effects on behavior are assessed. Cryoprobes are slender so that they can be implanted in the brain without causing substantial damage; they are typically constructed of hypodermic tubing of two gauges.

To temperature gauge

Thermometer

Insulation

Coolant out

Coolant in

Coolant out

to one half of the brain) are much milder than those of symmetrical *bilateral lesions* (lesions involving both sides of the brain), particularly in nonhuman species. Indeed, behavioral effects of unilateral lesions to some brain structures can be difficult to detect. As a result, most experimental studies of lesion effects are studies of bilateral, rather than unilateral, lesions.

Electrical Stimulation

Clues about the function of a neural structure can be obtained by stimulating it electrically. Electrical brain stimulation is usually delivered across the two tips of a *bipolar electrode*—two insulated wires wound tightly together and cut at the end. Weak pulses of current produce an immediate increase in the firing of neurons near the tip of the electrode.

Electrical stimulation of the brain is an important biopsychological research tool because it often has behavioral effects, usually opposite to those produced by a lesion to the same site. It can elicit a number of behavioral sequences, including eating, drinking, attack-

ing, copulating, and sleeping. The particular behavioral response that is elicited depends on the location of the electrode tip, the parameters of the current, and the test environment in which the stimulation is administered.

Invasive Electrophysiological Recording Methods

This section describes four invasive electrophysiological recording methods: intracellular unit recording, extracellular unit recording, multiple-unit recording, and invasive EEG recording. See Figure 5.17 for an example of each method.

Intracellular Unit Recording   A method whose findings were discussed at length in Chapter 4, *intracellular unit recording* provides a moment-by-moment record of the graded fluctuations in one neuron's membrane potential. Most experiments using this recording procedure are performed on chemically immobilized animals because it is next to impossible to keep the tip of a microelectrode positioned inside a neuron of a freely moving animal.

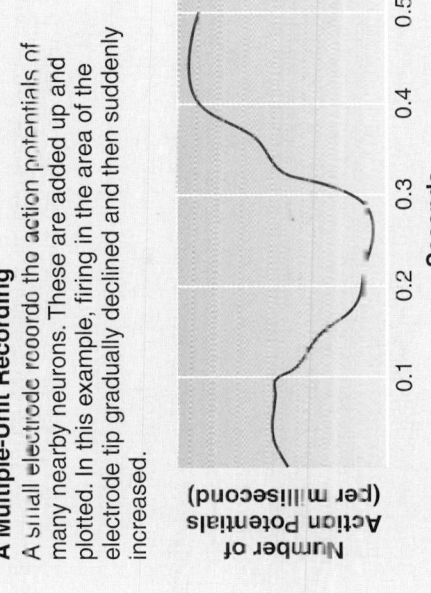

A Multiple-Unit Recording
A small electrode records the action potentials of many nearby neurons. These are added up and plotted. In this example, firing in the area of the electrode tip gradually declined and then suddenly increased.

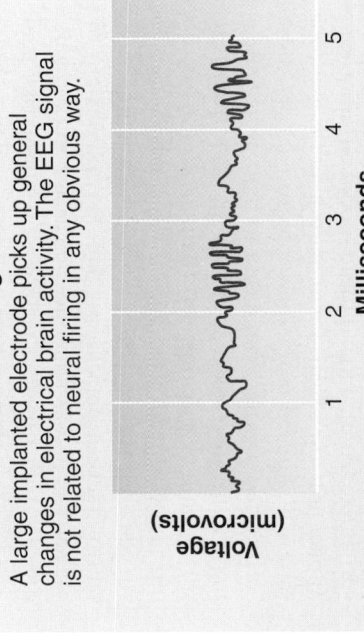

An Invasive EEG Recording
A large implanted electrode picks up general changes in electrical brain activity. The EEG signal is not related to neural firing in any obvious way.

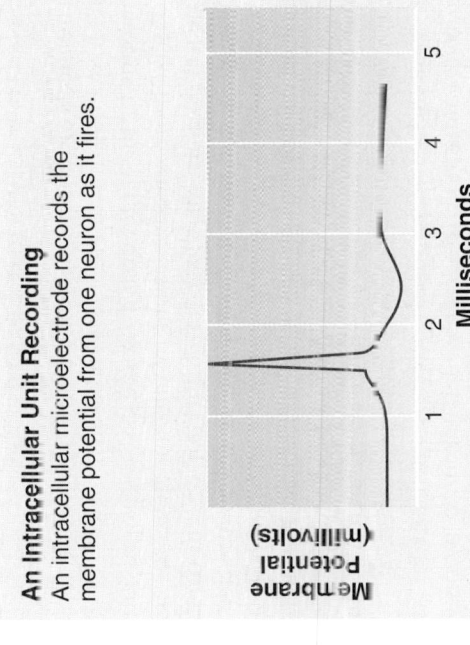

An Intracellular Unit Recording
An intracellular microelectrode records the membrane potential from one neuron as it fires.

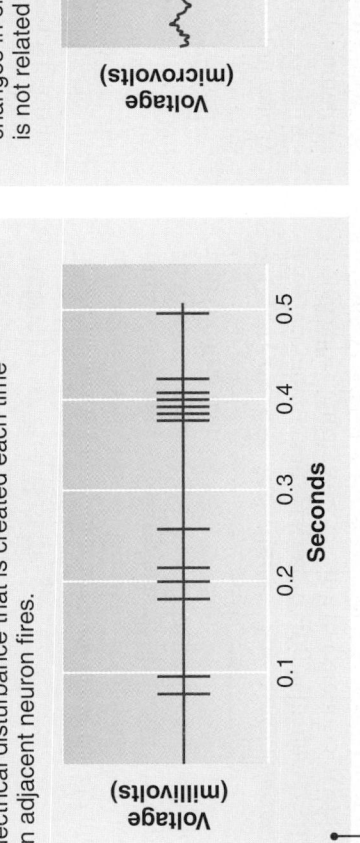

An Extracellular Unit Recording
An extracellular microelectrode records the electrical disturbance that is created each time an adjacent neuron fires.

FIGURE 5.17   Four methods of recording electrical activity of the nervous system.

Extracellular Unit Recording   It is possible to record the action potentials of a neuron through a microelectrode whose tip is positioned in the extracellular fluid next to it. Each time the neuron fires, a blip is recorded on the oscilloscope. Accordingly, *extracellular unit recording* provides a record of the firing of a neuron but no information about the neuron's membrane potential. It is difficult to record extracellularly from a single neuron in a freely moving animal without the electrode tip shifting away from the neuron, but it can be accomplished with special flexible microelectrodes that can shift slightly with the brain. Initially, extracellular unit recording involved recording from one neuron at a time, each at the tip of a separately implanted electrode. However, it is now possible to simultaneously record extracellular signals from up to 100 or so neurons by analyzing the correlations among the signals picked up through several different electrodes implanted in the same general area.

Multiple-Unit Recording   In *multiple-unit recording*, the electrode tip is larger than that of a microelectrode; thus, it picks up signals from many neurons. (The larger the electrode, the more neurons contribute to the signal.) The action potentials picked up by the electrode are fed into an integrating circuit, which adds them together. A multiple-unit recording is a graph of the total number of recorded action potentials per unit of time (e.g., per 0.1 second).

Invasive EEG Recording   In laboratory animals, EEG signals are recorded through large implanted electrodes rather than through scalp electrodes. Cortical EEG signals are frequently recorded through stainless steel skull screws, whereas subcortical EEG signals are typically recorded through stereotaxically implanted wire electrodes.

5.4   Pharmacological Research Methods

In the preceding section, you learned how physiological psychologists study the brain by manipulating it and recording from it using surgical and electrical methods. In this section, you will learn how psychopharmacologists manipulate and record from the brain using chemical methods.

The major research strategy of psychopharmacology is to administer drugs that either increase or decrease the effects of particular neurotransmitters and to observe the behavioral consequences. You learned in Chapter 4 how *agonists* and *antagonists* affect neurotransmitter systems. Described here are routes of drug administration, methods of using chemicals to make selective brain lesions, methods of measuring the chemical activity of the brain that are particularly useful in biopsychological research, and methods for locating neurotransmitter systems.

Routes of Drug Administration

In most psychopharmacological experiments, drugs are administered in one of the following ways: (1) They are fed to the subject; (2) they are injected through a tube into the stomach (*intragastrically*); or (3) they are injected hypodermically into the peritoneal cavity of the abdomen (*intraperitonally, IP*), into a large muscle (*intramuscularly, IM*), into the fatty tissue beneath the skin (*subcutaneously, SC*), or into a large surface vein (*intravenously, IV*). A problem with these peripheral routes of administration is that many drugs do not readily pass through the blood–brain barrier. To overcome this problem, drugs can be administered in small amounts through a fine, hollow tube, called a **cannula**, that has been stereotaxically implanted in the brain.

Selective Chemical Lesions

The effects of surgical, electrolytic, and cryogenic lesions are frequently difficult to interpret because they affect all neurons in the target area. In some cases, it is possible to make more selective lesions by injecting **neurotoxins** (neural poisons) that have an affinity for certain components of the nervous system. There are many selective neurotoxins. For example, when either *kainic acid* or *ibotenic acid* is administered by microinjection, it is preferentially taken up by cell bodies at the tip of the cannula and destroys those neurons, while leaving neurons with axons passing through the area largely unscathed.

Another widely used selective neurotoxin is *6-hydroxydopamine (6-OHDA)*. It is taken up by only those neurons that release the neurotransmitter *norepinephrine* or *dopamine*, and it leaves other neurons at the injection site undamaged.

Measuring Chemical Activity of the Brain

There are many procedures for measuring the chemical activity of the brains of laboratory animals. Two techniques that have proved particularly useful in biopsychological research are the 2-deoxyglucose technique and cerebral dialysis.

2-Deoxyglucose Technique   The *2-deoxyglucose (2-DG)* technique entails placing an animal that has been injected with radioactive 2-DG in a test situation in which it engages in the behavior of interest. Because 2-DG is similar in structure to glucose—the brain's main source of energy—neurons active during the test absorb it at a high rate but do not metabolize it. After the subject engages in the behavior, it is killed, and its brain is removed and sliced. The slices are then subjected to **autoradiography;** they are coated with a photographic emulsion, stored in the dark for a few days, and then developed much like film. Areas of the brain that absorbed high levels of the radioactive 2-DG during the test appear as black spots on the slides. The density of the spots in various regions of the brain can then be color-coded (see Figure 5.18).

Cerebral Dialysis Cerebral dialysis is a method of measuring the extracellular concentration of specific neurochemicals in behaving animals (see Robinson & Justice, 1991)—most other techniques for measuring neurochemicals require that the animals be killed so that tissue can be extracted. Cerebral dialysis involves the implantation in the brain of a fine tube with a short semipermeable section. The semipermeable section is positioned in the brain structure of interest so that extracellular chemicals from the structure will diffuse into the tube. Once in the tube, they can be collected for freezing, storage, and later analysis; or they can be carried in solution directly to a *chromatograph* (a device for measuring the chemical constituents of liquids or gases).

Locating Neurotransmitters and Receptors in the Brain

A key step in trying to understand the psychological function of a particular neurotransmitter or receptor is finding out where it is located in the brain. Two of the techniques available for this purpose are immuno-

cytochemistry and in situ hybridization. Each involves exposing brain slices to a labeled *ligand* of the molecule under investigation (the ligand of a molecule is another molecule that binds to it).

Immunocytochemistry When a foreign protein (an *antigen*) is injected into an animal, the animal creates *antibodies* that bind to it and then help the body remove or destroy it; this is known as the body's *immune reaction*. Neurochemists have created stocks of antibodies to most of the brain's peptide neurotransmitters and receptors. **Immunocytochemistry** is a procedure for locating particular neuroproteins in the brain by labeling their antibodies with a dye or radioactive element and then exposing slices of brain tissue to the labeled antibodies. Regions of dye or radioactivity accumulation in the brain slices mark the locations of the target neuroprotein.

Because all enzymes are proteins and because only those neurons that release a particular neurotransmitter are likely to contain all the enzymes required for its synthesis, immunocytochemistry can be used to locate neurotransmitters by binding to their enzymes. This is done by exposing brain slices to labeled antibodies that bind to enzymes located in only those neurons that contain the neurotransmitter of interest (see Figure 5.19 on page 116).

In Situ Hybridization Another technique for locating peptides and other proteins in the brain is **in situ hybridization.** This technique takes advantage of the fact that all peptides and proteins are transcribed from sequences of nucleotide bases on strands of messenger RNA (see Chapter 2). The nucleotide base sequences

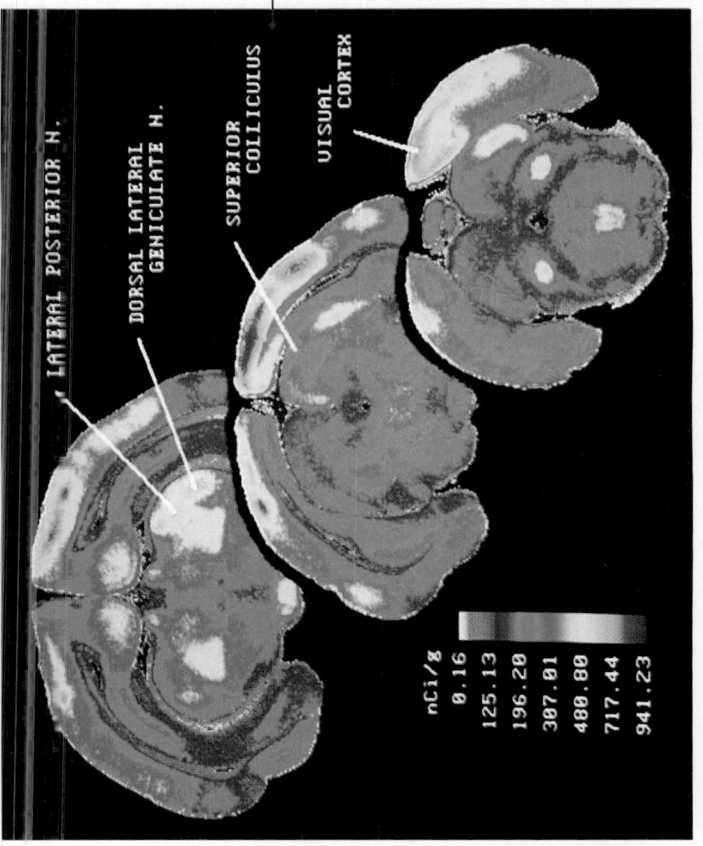

FIGURE 5.18 The 2-deoxyglucose technique. The accumulation of radioactivity is shown in three frontal sections taken from the brain of a Richardson's ground squirrel. The subject was injected with radioactive 2-deoxyglucose; then, for 45 minutes, it viewed brightly illuminated black and white stripes through its left eye while its right eye was covered. Because the ground squirrel visual system is largely crossed, most of the radioactivity accumulated in the visual structures of the right hemisphere (the hemisphere on your right). (Courtesy of Rod Cooper, Department of Psychology, University of Calgary.)

SCAN YOUR BRAIN

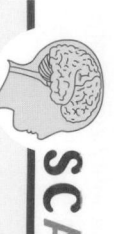

The research methods of biopsychology illustrate a psychological disorder suffered by many scientists. I call it "unabreviaphobia"—the fear of leaving any term unabbreviated. To determine whether you have mastered Part One of this chapter

and are ready for Part Two, supply the full term for each of the following abbreviations. The correct answers are provided at the bottom of the page. Before proceeding, review material related to your incorrect answers and omissions.

1. CT: _____
2. MRI: _____
3. PET: _____
4. 2-DG: _____
5. fMRI: _____
6. MEG: _____
7. TMS: _____

8. EEG: _____
9. ERP: _____
10. AEP: _____
11. EMG: _____
12. EOG: _____
13. SCL: _____
14. SCR: _____

15. ECG: _____
16. EKG: _____
17. IP: _____
18. IM: _____
19. IV: _____
20. SC: _____
21. 6-OHDA: _____

Scan Your Brain answers: (1) computed tomography, (2) magnetic resonance imaging, (3) positron emission tomography, (4) 2-deoxyglucose, (5) functional MRI, (6) magnetoencephalography, (7) transcranial magnetic stimulation, (8) electroencephalogram, (9) event-related potential, (10) average evoked potential, (11) electromyogram, (12) electrooculogram, (13) skin conductance level, (14) skin conductance response, (15) electrocardiogram, (16) electrocardiogram, (17) intraperitoneal, (18) intramuscular, (19) intravenous, (20) subcutaneous, (21) 6-hydroxydopamine.

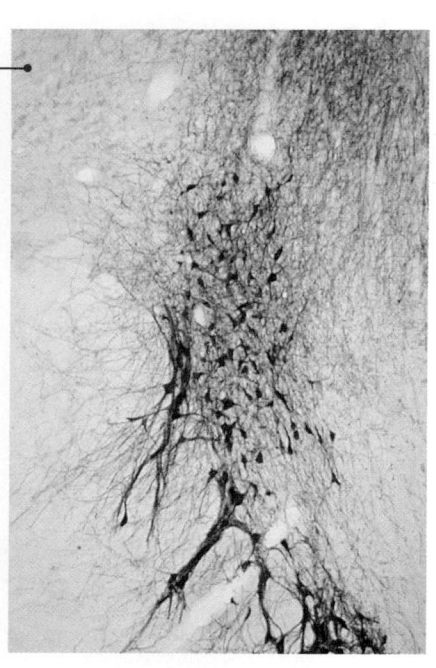

FIGURE 5.19 Immunocytochemistry. This section through a rat's substantia nigra reveals dopaminergic neurons that have taken up the antibody for tyrosine hydroxylase, the enzyme that converts tyrosine to L-dopa. (Courtesy of Mark Klitenick and Chris Fibiger, Department of Psychiatry, University of British Columbia.)

that direct the synthesis of many neuroproteins have been identified, and hybrid strands of mRNA with the complementary base sequences have been artificially created. In situ hybridization (see Figure 5.20) involves the following steps. First, hybrid RNA strands with the base sequence complementary to that of the mRNA that directs the synthesis of the target neuroprotein are obtained. Next, the hybrid RNA strands are labeled with a dye or radioactive element. Finally, the brain slices are exposed to the labeled hybrid RNA strands; they bind to the complementary mRNA strands, marking the location of neurons that release the target neuroprotein.

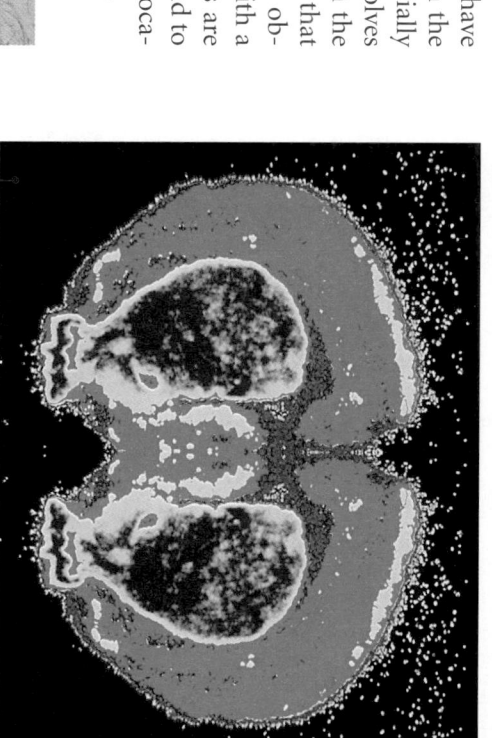

FIGURE 5.20 In situ hybridization. This color-coded frontal section through a rat brain reveals high concentrations of mRNA expression for an endorphin in the striatum (in red and yellow). (Courtesy of Ningning Guo and Chris Fibiger, Department of Psychiatry, University of British Columbia.)

5.5   Genetic Engineering

Genetics is a science that has made amazing progress in the last decade, and biopsychologists are reaping the benefits. Modern genetic methods are now widely used in biopsychological research. Gene knockout and gene replacement techniques are two of them.

Gene Knockout Techniques

Gene knockout techniques are procedures for creating organisms that lack a particular gene under investigation. Once these subjects have been created, efforts are made to identify and then investigate any observable neural or behavioral anomalies they might possess. Mice (the favored mammalian subjects of genetic research), that are the products of gene knockout techniques are referred to as *knockout mice*. This term often makes me smile, as images of little mice with boxing gloves flit through my mind.

There has been much enthusiasm for gene knockout technology, and many gene knockout studies are in progress. However, behavioral studies of knockout mice may be more difficult to interpret than first anticipated (e.g., Cook et al., 2002; Phillips & Belknap, 2002). At least three warnings have been issued. First, most behavioral traits are influenced by the activities of many interacting genes; consequently, the elimination of a behavioral trait by knockout of a gene can at best identify only one small genetic contribution to the behavior. Second, elimination of a gene often influences the expression of other genes; as a result, any observed change in the behavior of knockout mice may be only indirectly related to the knocked-out gene, or, conversely, the effects of a knocked-out gene can be masked by compensatory changes in other genes (Mogil, Yu, & Basbaum, 2000). And, third, the expression of genes can be influenced by experience; thus, gene knockouts are likely to interact in complex ways with the mice's experiences (Crabbe, Wahlsten, & Dudek, 1999).

Antisense drugs potentially circumvent some of the problems with gene knockout techniques. Think of the

potential medical applications of a research technique that allows organisms to develop normally but then reaches into their brains and blocks the expression of a particular gene. The concept underlying such a technique is simple and elegant: Molecules with a complementary sequence of nucleic acids to that of the messenger RNA (mRNA) associated with a target gene can deactivate the mRNA and block the expression of the gene. However, turning this simple antisense concept into practice is proving to be difficult. Ideal antisense drugs must be resistant to breakdown by the body, nontoxic, and specific to the mRNA they are targeting; also, techniques must be available for delivering the antisense drugs to particular neural systems. However, these and other related difficulties are being resolved, and antisense research is starting to gain momentum. Its potential is huge.

Gene Replacement Techniques

It is now possible to replace one gene with another in mice (Tsien, 2000). **Gene replacement techniques** are creating some interesting possibilities for developmental research and therapy. For example, scientists have removed pathological genes from human cells and inserted them in mice (mice that contain the genetic material of another species are called **transgenic mice**). It is also possible to replace a gene with one that is identical except for the addition of a few bases that can act as a switch, turning the gene off or on in response to particular chemicals. These chemicals can be used to activate or suppress a gene at a particular point in development or in a particular brain structure (see Gingrich & Roder, 1998).

Gene knockout and gene replacement technologies are now the focus of intensive investigation. How much they will teach us about the neural basis of behavior and how useful they will be in the treatment of brain disorders remain to be determined.

BEHAVIORAL RESEARCH METHODS OF BIOPSYCHOLOGY

We turn now from methods used by biopsychologists to study the nervous system to those that deal with the behavioral side of biopsychology. Because of the inherent invisibility of neural activity, the primary objective of the methods used in its investigation is to render the

unobservable observable. In contrast, the major objectives of behavioral research methods are to control, to simplify, and to objectify.

A single set of procedures developed for the investigation of a particular behavioral phenomenon is commonly referred to as a **behavioral paradigm**. Each behavioral paradigm normally comprises a method for producing the behavioral phenomenon under investigation and a method for objectively measuring it.

5.6 Neuropsychological Testing

A patient suspected of suffering from some sort of nervous system dysfunction is usually referred to a *neurologist*, who assesses simple sensory and motor functions. More subtle changes in perceptual, emotional, motivational, or cognitive functions are the domain of the *neuropsychologist*.

Because neuropsychological testing is so time consuming, it is typically prescribed for only a small portion of brain-damaged patients. This is unfortunate; the results of neuropsychological testing can help brain-damaged patients in three important ways: (1) by assisting in the diagnosis of neural disorders, particularly in cases in which brain imaging, EEG, and neurological testing have proved equivocal; (2) by serving as a basis for counseling and caring for the patients; or (3) by providing a basis for objectively evaluating the effectiveness of the treatment and the seriousness of its side effects.

Modern Approach to Neuropsychological Testing

The nature of neuropsychological testing has changed radically since the 1950s (see Stuss & Levine, 2002). Indeed, the dominant approach to psychological testing has evolved through three distinct phases: the *single-test approach*, the *standardized-test-battery approach*, and the *modern customized-test-battery approach*.

Single-Test Approach   Before the 1950s, the few existing neuropsychological tests were designed to detect the presence of brain damage; in particular, the goal of these early tests was to discriminate between patients with psychological problems resulting from structural brain damage and those with psychological problems resulting from functional, rather than structural, changes to the brain. This approach proved unsuccessful, in large part because no single test could be developed that would be sensitive to all the varied and complex psychological symptoms that could potentially occur in a brain-damaged patient.

Standardized-Test-Battery Approach   The standardized-test-battery approach to neuropsychological testing grew out of the failures of the single-test approach, and by the 1960s, it was predominant. The objective stayed the same—to identify brain-damaged patients—but the testing involved standardized batteries

(sets) of tests rather than a single test. The most widely used standardized test battery has been the *Halstead-Reitan Neuropsychological Test Battery*. The Halstead-Reitan is a set of tests that tend to be performed poorly by brain-damaged patients in relation to other patients or healthy control subjects; the scores on each test are added together to form a single aggregate score. An aggregate score below the designated cutoff leads to a diagnosis of brain damage. The standardized-test-battery approach has proved only marginally successful; standardized test batteries discriminate effectively between neurological patients and healthy patients, but they are not so good at discriminating between neurological patients and psychiatric patients.

The Customized-Test-Battery Approach   The customized-test-battery approach began to be used routinely in a few elite neuropsychological research institutions in the 1960s. This approach proved highly successful in research, and it soon spread to clinical practice. It now predominates in both the research laboratory and the neurological ward (see Lezak, 1997; Strub & Black, 1997).

The objective of current neuropsychological testing is not merely to identify patients with brain damage; the objective is to characterize the nature of the psychological deficits of each brain-damaged patient. So how does the customized-test-battery approach to neuropsychological testing work? It usually begins in the same way for all patients: with a common battery of tests selected by the neuropsychologist to provide an indication of the general nature of the neuropsychological symptoms. Then, depending on the results of the common test battery, the neuropsychologist selects a series of tests customized to each patient in an effort to characterize in more detail the general symptoms revealed by the common battery. For example, if the results of the test battery indicated that a patient had a memory problem, subsequent tests would include those designed to reveal the specific nature of the memory problem.

The tests used in the customized-test-battery approach differ in three respects from earlier tests. First, the newer tests are specifically designed to measure aspects of psychological function that have been spotlighted by modern theories and data. For example, modern theories, and the evidence on which they are based, suggest that the mechanisms of short-term and long-term memory are totally different; thus, the testing of patients with memory problems virtually always involves specific tests of both short-term and long-term memory. Second, the interpretation of the tests often does not rest entirely on how well the patient does; unlike early neuropsychological tests, currently used tests often require the neuropsychologist to assess the cognitive strategy that the patient employs in performing the test. Brain damage often changes the strategy that a neuropsychological patient uses to perform a test without lowering the overall score. Third, the customized-test-battery approach requires more skillful examination. Skill and knowledge are often required to select just the right battery of tests to expose a patient's deficits and to identify qualitative differences in cognitive strategy.

Tests of the Common Neuropsychological Test Battery

Clinical Implications

Because the customized-test-battery approach to neuropsychological testing typically involves two phases—a battery of general tests given to all patients followed by a series of specific tests customized to each patient—the following examples of neurological tests are presented in two subsections. First are some tests that are often administered as part of the initial common test battery, and second are some tests that might be used by a neuropsychologist to investigate in more depth particular problems revealed by the common battery.

Intelligence   Although the overall *intelligence quotient* (IQ) is a notoriously poor measure of brain damage, a test of general intelligence is nearly always included in the battery of neuropsychological tests routinely given to all patients. Many neuropsychological assessments begin with the *Wechsler Adult Intelligence Scale* (WAIS). This is because knowing a patient's IQ can help the neuropsychologist interpret the results of other tests. Also, a skilled neuropsychologist can sometimes draw inferences about a patient's neuropsychological dysfunction from the pattern of deficits on the various subtests of the WAIS. For example, low scores on subtests of verbal ability tend to be associated with left hemisphere damage, whereas right hemisphere damage tends to reduce scores on performance subtests. The 11 subtests of the WAIS are described in Table 5.1.

Memory   One weakness of the WAIS is that it often fails to detect memory deficits, despite including two subtests specifically designed to test memory function. The information subtest of the WAIS assesses memory for general knowledge (e.g., "Who is Queen Elizabeth?"), and the subtest focusing on **digit span** identifies the longest sequence of random digits that can be correctly repeated 50% of the time by the patient—most people have

a digit span of 7. However, these two forms of memory are among the least likely to be disrupted by brain damage—patients with seriously disturbed memories often show no deficits on either the information or digit-span subtests of the WAIS. Be that as it may, memory problems rarely escape unnoticed. If present, they may be detected by other tests that are included in the common test battery; they may be noticed by the neuropsychologist during discussions with the patient; or they may be reported by the patient or the family of the patient.

TABLE 5.1   The 11 Subtests of the Wechsler Adult Intelligence Scale (WAIS)

VERBAL SUBTESTS

Information   Read to the subject are 29 questions of general information—for example "Who is the president of the United States?"

Digit-span   Three digits are read to the subject at 1-second intervals, and the subject is asked to repeat them in the same order. Two trials are given at three digits, four digits, five digits, and so on until the subject fails both trials at one level.

Vocabulary   The subject is asked to define a list of 35 words that range in difficulty.

Arithmetic   The subject is presented with 14 arithmetic questions and must answer them without the benefit of pencil and paper.

Comprehension   The subject is asked 16 questions that test the ability to understand general principles—for example, "Why should people vote?"

Similarities   The subject is presented with pairs of items and is asked to explain how the items in each pair are similar.

PERFORMANCE SUBTESTS

Picture-completion   The subject must identify the important part missing from 20 drawings—for example, a drawing of a squirrel with no tail.

Picture-arrangement   The subject is presented with 10 sets of cartoon drawings and is asked to arrange each set so that it tells a sensible story.

Block-design   The subject is presented with blocks that are red on two sides, white on two sides, and half red and half white on the other two. The subject is shown pictures of nine patterns and is asked to duplicate them by arranging the blocks appropriately.

Object-assembly   The subject is asked to put together the pieces of four simple jigsaw puzzles to form familiar objects.

Digit-symbol   The subject is presented with a key that matches each of a series of symbols with a different digit. On the same page is a series of digits, and the subject is given 90 seconds to write the correct symbol, according to the key, next to as many digits as possible.

Language If a neuropsychological patient has taken the WAIS, deficits in the use of language can be inferred from a low aggregate score on the six verbal subtests. If the WAIS has not been taken, patients can be quickly screened for language-related deficits with the **token test**. Twenty tokens of two different sizes (large and small), and five different colors (white, black, yellow, green, and red) are placed on a table in front of the subject. The test begins with the examiner reading simple instructions—for example, "Touch a red square"—and the subject trying to follow them. Then, the test progresses to more difficult instructions, such as "Touch the small, red circle and then the large, green square." Finally, the subject is asked to read the instructions aloud and follow them.

Language Lateralization It is usual for one hemisphere to participate more than the other in language-related activities. In most people, the left hemisphere is dominant for language, but in some, the right hemisphere is dominant. A test of language lateralization is often included in the common test battery because knowing which hemisphere is dominant for language is often useful in interpreting the results of other tests. Furthermore, a test of language lateralization is virtually always given to patients before any surgery that might encroach on the cortical language areas. The results are used to plan the surgery, trying to avoid the language areas if possible.

There are two widely used tests of language lateralization. The sodium amytal test (Wada, 1949) is one, and the dichotic listening test (Kimura, 1973) is the other.

The **sodium amytal test** involves injecting the anesthetic sodium amytal into either the left or right carotid artery in the neck. This temporarily anesthetizes the *ipsilateral* (same-side) hemisphere while leaving the *contralateral* (opposite-side) hemisphere largely unaffected. Several tests of language function are quickly administered while the ipsilateral hemisphere is anesthetized. Later, the process is repeated for the other side of the brain. When the injection is on the side dominant for language, the patient is completely mute for about 2 minutes. When the injection is on the nondominant side, there are only a few minor speech problems. Because the sodium amytal test is invasive, it can be administered only for medical reasons—usually to determine the dominant language hemisphere prior to brain surgery.

In the standard version of the **dichotic listening test**, sequences of spoken digits are presented to subjects through stereo headphones. Three digits are presented to one ear at the same time that three different digits are presented to the other ear. Then the subjects are asked to report as many of the six digits as they can. Kimura found that subjects correctly report more of the digits heard by the ear contralateral to their dominant hemisphere for language, as determined by the sodium amytal test.

Tests of Specific Neuropsychological Function

Following analysis of the results of a neuropsychological patient's performance on the common test battery, the neuropsychologist selects a series of specific tests to clarify the nature of the general problems exposed by the common battery. There are thousands of tests that might be selected. This section describes a few of them and mentions some of the considerations that might influence their selection.

Clinical Implications

Memory Following the discovery of a memory impairment by the common test battery, at least four fundamental questions about the memory impairment must be answered: (1) Does the memory impairment involve *short-term memory*, *long-term memory*, or both? (2) Are any deficits in long-term memory *anterograde* (affecting the retention of things learned after the damage), *retrograde* (affecting the retention of things learned before the damage), or both? (3) Do any deficits in long-term memory involve *semantic memory* (memory for knowledge of the world) or *episodic memory* (memory for personal experiences)? (4) Are any deficits in long-term memory deficits of *explicit memory* (memories of which the patient is aware and can thus express verbally), *implicit memory* (memories that are demonstrated by the improved performance of the patient without the patient being conscious of them), or both?

Many amnesic patients display severe deficits in explicit memory with no deficits at all in implicit memory (Curran & Schacter, 1997). **Repetition priming tests** have proven instrumental in the assessment and study of this pattern. Patients are first shown a list of words and asked to study them; they are not asked to remember them. Then, at a later time, they are asked to complete a list of word fragments, many of which are fragments of words from the initial list. For example, if "purple" had been in the initial test, "pu__p___" could be one of the test word fragments. Amnesic patients often complete the fragments as well as healthy control subjects. But—and this is the really important part—they often have no conscious memory of any of the words in the initial list or even of ever having seen the list. In other words, they display good implicit memory of experiences without explicit memories of them.

Language If a neuropsychological patient turns out to have language-related deficits on the common test battery, a complex series of tests is administered to clarify the nature of the problem. For example, if there is a speech

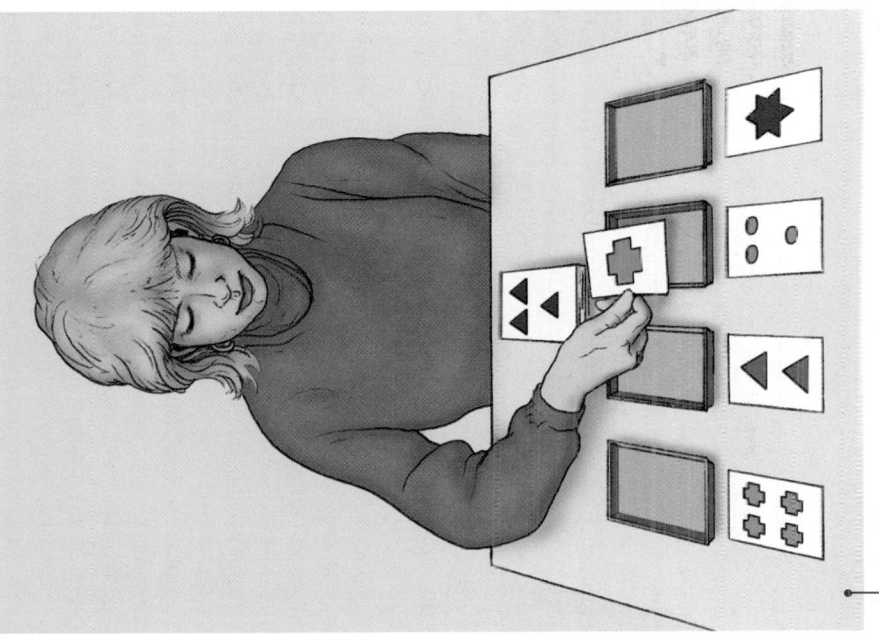

FIGURE 5.21 The Wisconsin Card Sorting Test. This woman is just starting the test. If she places her first card in front of the stimulus card with the three green circles, she is sorting on the basis of color. She must guess until she can learn which principle—color, shape, or number—should guide her sorting. After she has placed a card, she is told whether or not her placement is correct.

problem, there may be one of three fundamentally different problems: problems of *phonology* (the rules governing the sounds of the language), problems of *syntax* (the grammar of the language), or problems of *semantics* (the meanings of the language). Because brain-damaged patients may have one of these problems but not the others, it is imperative that the testing of all neuropsychological patients with speech problems include tests of each of these three capacities (Saffran, 1997).

Reading aloud can be disrupted in different ways by brain damage, and follow-up tests must be employed that can differentiate between the different patterns of disruption (Coslett, 1997). Some *dyslexic* patients (those with reading problems) remember the rules of pronunciation but have difficulties pronouncing words that do not the follow these rules, words such as *come* and *tongue*, whose pronunciation must be remembered. Other dyslexic patients pronounce simple familiar words based on memory but have lost the ability to apply the rules of pronunciation—they cannot pronounce nonwords such as *trapple* or *fleeming*.

Frontal-Lobe Function

Injuries to the frontal lobes are common, and the **Wisconsin Card Sorting Test** (see Figure 5.21) is a component of many customized test batteries because it is sensitive to frontal-lobe damage. On each Wisconsin card is either one symbol or two, three, or four identical symbols. The symbols are all either triangles, stars, circles, or crosses; and they are all either red, green, yellow, or blue. At the beginning of the test, the patient is confronted with four stimulus cards that differ from one another in form, color, and number. The task is to correctly sort cards from a deck into piles in front of the stimulus cards. However, the patient does not know whether to sort by form, by color, or by number. The patient begins by guessing and is told after each card has been sorted whether it was sorted correctly or incorrectly. At first, the task is to learn to sort by color. But as soon as the patient makes several consecutive correct responses, the sorting principle is changed to shape or number without any indication other than the fact that responses based on color become incorrect. Thereafter, each time a new sorting principle is learned, the principle is changed.

Patients with damage to their frontal lobes often continue to sort on the basis of one sorting principle for 100 or more trials after it has become incorrect. They seem to have great difficulty learning and remembering that previously appropriate guidelines for effective behavior are no longer appropriate, a problem called *perseveration*.

5.7 Behavioral Methods of Cognitive Neuroscience

Cognitive neuroscience is predicated on two related assumptions. The first premise is that each complex cognitive process results from the combined activity of simple cognitive processes called **constituent cognitive processes.** The second premise is that each constituent cognitive process is mediated by neural activity in a particular area of the brain. One of the main goals of cognitive neuroscience is to identify the parts of the brain that mediate various constituent cognitive processes.

With the central role played by PET and fMRI in cutting-edge cognitive neuroscience research, the **paired-image subtraction technique** has become one of the key behavioral research methods in cognitive neuroscience research (see Posner & Raichle, 1994). Let me illustrate this technique with an example from a PET study of single-word processing by Petersen and colleagues (1988). Petersen and his colleagues were interested in locating the parts of the brain that enable a subject to make a word association (to respond to a printed word by saying a related word). You might think this would be an easy task to accomplish by having a subject perform a word-association task while a PET image of the subject's brain is recorded. The problem with this approach is that many parts of the brain that would be active during the test period would have nothing to do with the constituent cognitive process of forming a word association; much of the activity recorded would be associated with other processes such as seeing the words, reading the words, and speaking. The paired-image subtraction technique was developed to deal with this problem.

The paired-image subtraction technique involves obtaining PET or fMRI images during several different cognitive tasks. Ideally, the tasks are designed so that pairs of them differ from each other in terms of only a single constituent cognitive process. Then, the brain activity associated with that process can be estimated by subtracting the activity in the image associated with one of the two tasks from the activity in the image associated with the other. For example, in one of the tasks in the study by Petersen and colleagues, subjects spent a minute reading aloud printed nouns as they appeared on a screen; in another, they observed the same nouns on the screen but responded to each of them by saying aloud an associated verb (e.g., *truck—drive*). Then, Petersen and his colleagues subtracted the activity in the images that they recorded during the two tasks to obtain a *difference image*. The difference image illustrated the areas of the brain that were specifically involved in the constituent cognitive process of forming the word association; the activity associated with fixating on the screen, seeing the nouns, saying the words, and so on was eliminated by the subtraction (see Figure 5.22).

Another problem involved in using PET and fMRI to locate constituent cognitive processes is the *noise* associated with random cerebral events that occur during the test—for example, thinking about a sudden pang of hunger, noticing a fly on the screen, or wondering whether the test will last much longer. The noise created by such events can be significantly reduced with a technique discussed earlier in this chapter: *signal averaging*. By averaging the difference images obtained from repetitions of the same tests, the researchers can greatly increase the *signal-to-noise ratio*. It is standard practice to average the images obtained from several subjects; the resulting mean (averaged) difference image emphasizes areas of activity that are common to most of the subjects and deemphasizes areas of activity that are peculiar to a few of them (see Figure 5.22). However, this averaging procedure can lead to a serious problem: If two subjects had specific but different patterns of cortical activity, the averaged image would reveal little about either.

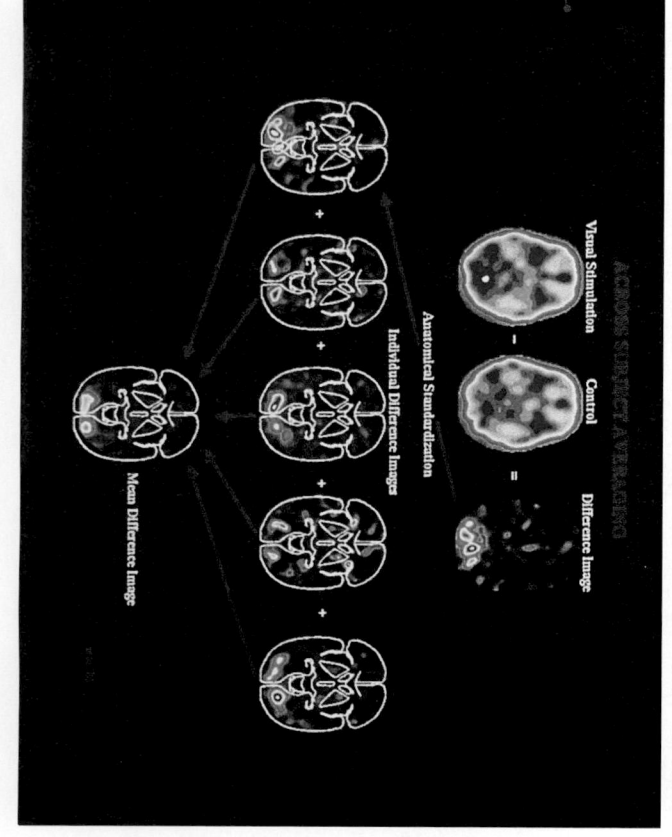

FIGURE 5.22   The paired-image subtraction technique, which is commonly employed in cognitive neuroscience. Here we see that the brain of a subject is generally active when the subject looks at a flickering checkerboard pattern (visual stimulation condition). However, if the activity that occurred when the subject stared at a blank screen (control situation) is subtracted, it becomes apparent that the perception of the flashing checkerboard pattern was associated with an increase in activity that was largely restricted to the occipital lobe. The individual difference images of five subjects were averaged to produce the mean difference image. (PET scans courtesy of Marcus Raichle, Mallinckrodt Institute of Radiology, Washington University Medical Center.)

5.8 Biopsychological Paradigms of Animal Behavior

Noteworthy examples of the behavioral paradigms used to study the biopsychology of laboratory species are provided here under three headings: (1) paradigms for the assessment of species-common behaviors, (2) traditional conditioning paradigms, and (3) seminatural animal learning paradigms. In each case, the focus is on methods used to study the behavior of the laboratory rat, the most common subject of biopsychological research.

Paradigms for Assessment of Species-Common Behaviors

Many of the behavioral paradigms that are used in biopsychological research are used to study species-common behaviors. **Species-common behaviors** are those that are displayed by virtually all members of a species, or at least by all those of the same age and sex. Commonly studied species-common behaviors include grooming, swimming, eating, drinking, copulating, fighting, and nest building. Described here are the open-field test, tests of aggressive and defensive behavior, and tests of sexual behavior.

Open-Field Test   In the **open-field test**, the subject is placed in a large, barren chamber, and its activity is recorded. It is usual to measure general activity either with an automated activity recorder or by drawing lines on the floor of the chamber and counting the number of line-crossings during the test. It is also common in the open-field test to count the number of *boluses* (pieces of excrement) that were dropped by an animal during the test. Low activity scores and high bolus counts are frequently used as indicators of fearfulness. Fearful rats are highly **thigmotaxic**; that is, they rarely venture away from the walls of the test chamber and rarely engage in such activities as rearing and grooming. Rats are often fearful when they are first placed in a strange open field, but this fearfulness usually declines with repeated exposure to the same open field.

Tests of Aggressive and Defensive Behavior   Typical patterns of aggressive and defensive behavior can be observed and measured during combative encounters between the dominant male rat of an established colony and a smaller male intruder (see Blanchard & Blanchard, 1988). This is called the **colony-intruder paradigm.** The behaviors of the dominant male are considered to be aggressive and those of the hapless intruder defensive. The dominant male of the colony (the *alpha male*) moves sideways toward the intruder, with its hair erect. When it nears the intruder, it tries to push the intruder off balance and to deliver bites to its back and flanks. The defender tries to protect its back and flanks by rearing up on its hind legs

and pushing the attacker away with its forepaws or by rolling onto its back. Thus, piloerection, lateral approach, and flank- and back-biting indicate conspecific aggression in the rat; freezing, boxing (rearing and pushing away), and rolling over indicate defensiveness.

Some tests of rat defensive behavior assess reactivity to the experimenter rather than to another rat. For example, it is common to rate the resistance of a rat to being picked up—no resistance being the lowest category and biting the highest—and to use the score as one measure of defensiveness (Kalynchuk et al., 1997).

The **elevated plus maze**, a four-armed, plus-sign-shaped maze that is typically mounted 50 centimeters above the floor, is a test of defensiveness that is commonly used to study in rats the *anxiolytic* (anxiety-reducing) effects of drugs. Two of the arms of the maze have sides, and two do not. The measure of defensiveness, or anxiety, is the proportion of time the rats spend in the protected closed arms rather than on the exposed arms. Many established anxiolytic drugs significantly increase the proportion of time that rats spend on the open arms (see Pellow et al., 1985), and, conversely, many new drugs that prove to be effective in reducing rats' defensiveness on the maze often turn out to be effective in the treatment of human anxiety.

Clinical Implications

Tests of Sexual Behavior   Most attempts to study the physiological bases of rat sexual behavior have focused on the copulatory act itself. The male mounts the female from behind and clasps her hindquarters. If the female is receptive, she responds by assuming the posture called **lordosis;** that is, she sticks her hindquarters in the air, she bends her back in a U, and she deflects her tail to the side. During some mounts, the male inserts his penis into the female's vagina; this act is called **intromission.** After intromission, the male dismounts by jumping backwards. He then returns a few seconds later to mount and intromit once again. Following about 10 such cycles of mounting, intromitting, and dismounting, the male mounts, intromits, and **ejaculates** (ejects his sperm).

Three common measures of male rat sexual behavior are the number of mounts required to achieve intromission, the number of intromissions required to achieve ejaculation, and the interval between ejaculation and the reinitiation of mounting. The most common measure of female rat sexual behavior is the **lordosis quotient** (the proportion of mounts that elicit lordosis).

Traditional Conditioning Paradigms

Learning paradigms play a major role in biopsychological research for three reasons. The first is that learning is a phenomenon of primary interest to psychologists. The second is that learning paradigms provide an effective technology for producing and controlling animal behavior. Because animals cannot follow instructions from the experimenter, it is often necessary to train them to behave in a fashion consistent with the goals of the experiment. The third reason is that it is possible to infer much about the sensory, motor, motivational, and cognitive state of an animal from its ability to learn and perform various responses.

If you have taken a previous course in psychology, you will likely be familiar with the Pavlovian and operant conditioning paradigms. In the **Pavlovian conditioning paradigm**, the experimenter pairs an initially neutral stimulus called a *conditional stimulus* (e.g., a tone or a light) with an *unconditional stimulus* (e.g., meat powder)—a stimulus that elicits an *unconditional* (reflexive) *response* (e.g., salivation). As a result of these pairings, the conditional stimulus eventually acquires the capacity, when administered alone, to elicit a *conditional response* (e.g., salivation)—a response that is often, but not always, similar to the unconditional response.

In the **operant conditioning paradigm**, the rate at which a particular voluntary response (such as a lever press) is emitted is increased by *reinforcement* or decreased by *punishment*. One of the most widely used operant conditioning paradigms in biopsychology is the self-stimulation paradigm. In the **self-stimulation paradigm**, animals press a lever to deliver electrical stimulation to particular sites in their own brains; those structures in the brain that support self-stimulation are often called *pleasure centers*.

Seminatural Animal Learning Paradigms

In addition to Pavlovian and operant conditioning paradigms, biopsychologists use animal learning paradigms that have been specifically designed to mimic situations that an animal might encounter in its natural environ-

Evolutionary Perspective

ment (see Gerlai & Clayton, 1999). Development of these paradigms stemmed in part from the reasonable assumption that forms of learning tending to benefit an animal's survival in the wild are likely to be more highly developed and more directly related to innate neural mechanisms. The following are four common seminatural learning paradigms: the conditioned taste aversion, radial arm maze, Morris water maze, and conditioned defensive burying.

Conditioned Taste Aversion   A **conditioned taste aversion** is the avoidance response that develops to tastes of food whose consumption has been followed by illness (see Garcia & Koelling, 1966). In the standard conditioned taste aversion experiment, rats receive an *emetic* (a nausea-inducing drug) after they consume a

food with an unfamiliar taste. On the basis of this single conditioning trial, the rats learn to avoid the taste.

The ability of rats to readily learn the relationship between a particular taste and subsequent illness unquestionably increases their chances of survival in their natural environment, where potentially edible substances are not routinely screened by government agencies. Rats and many other animals are *neophobic* (afraid of new things); thus, when they first encounter a new food, they consume it in only small quantities. If they subsequently become ill, they will not consume it again. Conditioned aversions also develop to familiar tastes, but these typically require more than a single trial to be learned.

Humans also develop conditioned taste aversions. Cancer patients have been reported to develop aversions to foods consumed before nausea-inducing chemotherapy (Bernstein & Webster, 1980). Many of you will be able to testify on the basis of personal experience about the effectiveness of conditioned taste aversions. I still have vivid memories of a long-ago batch of red laboratory punch that I overzealously consumed after eating two pieces of blueberry pie. But that is another story—albeit a particularly colorful one.

The following words communicate just how much the study of conditioned taste aversion changed the thinking of psychologists about conditioning:

> The 1950s was a time of sock hops, sodas at Al's, crewcuts, and drive-in movies. In the animal-behavior laboratory, it was a time of lever presses, key pecks, and shuttles made in response to flashing lights, tones, and geometric patterns. Then, along came rock 'n' roll and the discovery of conditioned taste aversion: Things have not been the same since.

The discovery of conditioned taste aversion challenged three widely accepted principles of learning (see Revusky & Garcia, 1970) that had grown out of research on traditional operant and Pavlovian conditioning paradigms. First, it challenged the view that animal conditioning is always a gradual step-by-step process; robust taste aversions can be established in only a single trial. Second, it showed that *temporal contiguity* is not essential for conditioning; rats acquire taste aversions even when they do not become ill until several hours after eating. Third, it challenged the *principle of equipotentiality*—the view that conditioning proceeds in basically the same manner regardless of the particular stimuli and responses under investigation. Rats appear to have evolved to readily learn associations between tastes and illness; it is only with great difficulty that they learn relations between the color of food and nausea or between taste and footshock.

Radial Arm Maze   The radial arm maze taps the well-developed spatial abilities of rodents. The survival of rats in the wild depends on their ability to navigate quickly and accurately through their environment and

to learn which locations in it are likely to contain food and water. This task is much more complex for a rodent than it is for us. Most of us obtain food from locations where the supply is continually replenished; we go to the market confident that we will find enough food to satisfy our needs. In contrast, the foraging rat must learn, and retain, a complex pattern of spatially coded details. It must not only learn where morsels of food are likely to be found but must also remember which of these sites it has recently stripped of their booty so as not to revisit them too soon. Designed by Olton and Samuelson (1976) to study these spatial abilities, the **radial arm maze** (see Figure 5.23) is an array of arms—usually eight or more—radiating from a central starting area. At the end of each arm is a food cup, which may or may not be baited, depending on the purpose of the experiment.

In one version of the radial arm maze paradigm, rats are placed each day in a maze that has the same arms baited each day. After a few days of experience, rats rarely visit unbaited arms at all, and they rarely visit baited arms more than once in the same day—even when control procedures make it impossible for them to recognize odors left during previous visits to an arm or to make their visits in a systematic sequence. Because the arms are identical, rats must orient themselves in the maze with reference to external room cues; thus, their performance can be disrupted by rotation of the maze or by changes in the appearance of the room.

Morris Water Maze Another seminatural learning paradigm that has been designed to study the spatial abilities of rats is the **Morris water maze** (Morris, 1981). The rats are placed in a circular, featureless pool of cool milky water, in which they must swim until they discover the escape platform—which is invisible just beneath the surface of the water. The rats are allowed to rest on the platform before being returned to the water for another trial. Despite the fact that the starting point is varied from trial to trial, the rats learn after only a few trials to swim directly to the platform, presumably by using spatial cues from the room as a reference. The Morris water maze has proved extremely useful for assessing the navigational skills of lesioned or drugged animals (e.g., D'Hooge & De Deyn, 2001).

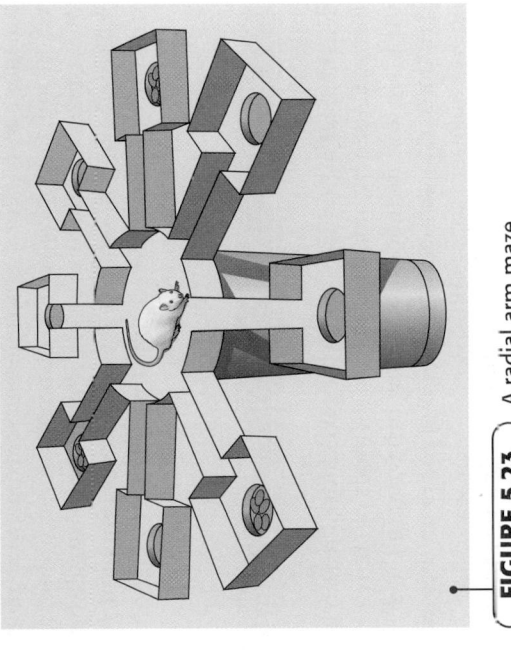

FIGURE 5.23 A radial arm maze.

Conditioned Defensive Burying Yet another seminatural learning paradigm that is useful in biopsychological research is conditioned defensive burying (e.g., Pinel & Mana, 1989; Pinel & Treit, 1978). In studies of **conditioned defensive burying,** rats receive a single aversive stimulus (e.g., a shock, airblast, or noxious odor) from an object mounted on the wall of the chamber just above the floor, which is littered with bedding material. After a single trial, almost every rat learns that the test object is a threat and responds by spraying bedding material at the test object with its head and forepaws (see Figure 5.24). Antianxiety drugs reduce the amount of conditioned defensive burying, and thus the paradigm is used to study the neurochemistry of anxiety (e.g., Treit, 1987).

Before moving on to the next chapter, you need to appreciate that to be effective these research methods must be used together. Seldom, if ever, is an important biopsychological issue resolved by a single method. The reason for this is that neither the methods used to manipulate the brain nor the methods used to assess the behavioral consequences of these manipulations are totally selective; there are no methods of manipulating the brain that change only a single aspect of brain

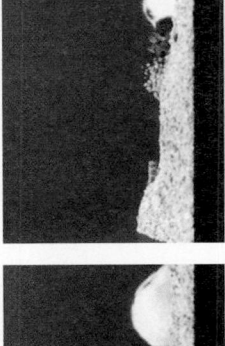
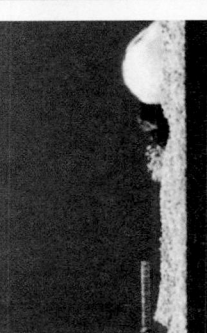

FIGURE 5.24 A rat burying a test object from which it has just received a single mild shock. (Photograph by Jack Wong.)

function, and there are no measures of behavior that reflect only a single psychological process. Accordingly, the lines of research that use a single method can usually be interpreted in more than one way and thus cannot provide unequivocal evidence for any one interpretation.

Typically, important research questions are resolved only when several methods are brought to bear on a single problem. This general approach, as you learned in Chapter 1, is called *converging operations*.

Themes Revisited

This chapter introduced you to the two kinds of research methods used by biopsychologists: methods of studying the brain and methods of studying behavior. In the descriptions of these methods, all four of the main themes of the book were apparent.

Clinical Implications

The clinical implications theme was most evident in the chapter-opening case of Professor P. This case alerted you to the fact that many of the methods used by biopsychologists to study the human brain are also used clinically, in either diagnosis or treatment. In addition, the clinical implications theme was repeatedly emphasized during the discussion of neuropsychological methods; all neuropsychological methods have direct clinical implications because the subjects of neuropsychological research are patients with brain damage.

Predictably, the cognitive neuroscience theme emerged repeatedly in the two sections dealing with the methods of that field. In contrast, the evolutionary perspective theme was evident only in the subsection that discussed seminatural paradigms of animal learning.

The thinking-about-biopsychology theme came up frequently in the chapter. Because the subject matter of biopsychology is so complex, all biopsychological research methods require thoughtful application. It is very important for both scientists and consumers of science to understand the weaknesses, as well as the strengths, of the various methods.

Cognitive Neuroscience

Evolutionary Perspective

Thinking Critically

Think about It

1. The current rate of progress in the development of new and better brain-scanning devices will soon render behavioral tests of brain damage obsolete. Discuss.

2. You are taking a physiological psychology course, and your laboratory instructor gives you two rats: one rat with a lesion in an unknown brain structure and one normal rat. How would you test the rats to determine which one has the lesion? How would you determine the behavioral effects of the lesion? How would your approach differ from one that you might use to test a human patient suspected of having brain damage?

3. The search for the neural mechanisms of learning should focus on forms of learning necessary for survival in the wild. Discuss.

4. All patients should complete a battery of neuropsychological tests both before and after neurosurgery. Discuss.

5. The methods that biopsychologists use to study behavior are fundamentally different from the methods that they use to study the brain, and these fundamental differences lead to an underappreciation of behavioral methods by those who lack expertise in their use. Discuss.

ON THE CD
Studying for an exam? Try the Practice Tests for Chapter 5.

ON THE CD
See Hard Copy for additional readings for Chapter 5.

Key Terms

Alpha waves (p. 106)
Aspiration (p. 111)
Autoradiography (p. 115)
Behavioral paradigm (p. 118)
Bregma (p. 110)
Cannula (p. 114)

Cerebral angiography (p. 102)
Cerebral dialysis (p. 115)
Cognitive neuroscience (p. 121)
Colony–intruder paradigm (p. 123)

Computed tomography (CT) (p. 102)
Conditioned defensive burying (p. 125)
Conditioned taste aversion (p. 124)

Constituent cognitive processes (p. 121)
Contrast X-ray techniques (p. 102)
Cryogenic blockade (p. 111)
2-deoxyglucose (2-DG) (p. 104)

Dichotic listening test (p. 120)
Digit span (p. 119)
Ejaculates (p. 123)
Electrocardiogram (ECG or EKG) (p. 110)
Electroencephalography (p. 106)
Electromyography (p. 108)
Electrooculography (p. 109)
Elevated plus maze (p. 123)
Event-related potentials (ERPs) (p. 107)
Far-field potentials (p. 108)
Functional MRI (fMRI) (p. 105)
Gene knockout techniques (p. 117)
Gene replacement techniques (p. 117)
Hypertension (p. 110)
Immunocytochemistry (p. 115)

In situ hybridization (p. 115)
Intromission (p. 123)
Lordosis (p. 123)
Lordosis quotient (p. 123)
Magnetic resonance imaging (MRI) (p. 102)
Magnetoencephalography (MEG) (p. 106)
Morris water maze (p. 125)
Neurotoxins (p. 114)
Open-field test (p. 123)
Operant conditioning paradigm (p. 124)
P300 wave (p. 108)
Paired-image subtraction technique (p. 122)
Pavlovian conditioning paradigm (p. 124)
Plethysmography (p. 110)

Positron emission tomography (PET) (p. 104)
Radial arm maze (p. 125)
Repetition priming tests (p. 120)
Self-stimulation paradigm (p. 124)
Sensory evoked potential (p. 107)
Signal averaging (p. 107)
Skin conductance level (SCL) (p. 109)
Skin conductance response (SCR) (p. 109)
Sodium amytal test (p. 120)
Spatial resolution (p. 102)
Species-common behaviors (p. 123)
Stereotaxic atlas (p. 110)
Stereotaxic instrument (p. 110)

Temporal resolution (p. 106)
Thigmotaxic (p. 123)
Token test (p. 120)
Transcranial magnetic stimulation (TMS) (p. 106)
Transgenic mice (p. 117)
Wechsler Adult Intelligence Scale (WAIS) (p. 119)
Wisconsin Card Sorting Test (p. 121)

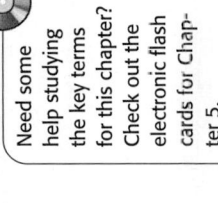

ON THE CD

Need some help studying the key terms for this chapter? Check out the electronic flash cards for Chapter 5.

The Visual System

From Your Eyes to Your Cortex

6 chapter

6.1 Light Enters the Eye and Reaches the Retina

6.2 The Retina and Translation of Light into Neural Signals

6.3 From Retina to Primary Visual Cortex

6.4 Seeing Edges

6.5 Seeing Color

This chapter is about the visual system. Most people think that their visual system has evolved to respond as accurately as possible to the patterns of light that enter their eyes. They recognize the obvious limitations in their visual system's accuracy, of course; and they appreciate those curious instances, termed *visual illusions*, in which it is "tricked" into seeing things the way they aren't. But such shortcomings are generally regarded as minor imperfections in a system that responds as faithfully as possible to the external world.

Despite its intuitive appeal, this way of thinking about the visual system is wrong. The visual system does not produce an accurate internal copy of the external world. It does much more. From the tiny, distorted, upside-down, two-dimensional retinal images projected on the visual receptors that line the backs of the eyes, the visual system creates an accurate, richly detailed, three-dimensional perception that is—and this is the really important part—in some respects even better than the external reality from which it was created.

Regardless of what you may have heard to the contrary, "what you see is not necessarily what you get." One of my primary goals in this chapter is to help you recognize and appreciate the inherent creativity of your own visual system.

This chapter is composed of five sections. The first three sections take you on a journey from the external visual world to the visual receptors of the retina and from there over the major visual pathway to the primary visual cortex. The last two sections describe how the neurons of this pathway mediate the perception of two particularly important features of the visual world: edges and color.

You will learn in this chapter that understanding the visual system requires the integration of two types of research: (1) research that probes the visual system with sophisticated neuroanatomical, neurochemical, and neurophysiological techniques; and (2) research that focuses on the assessment of what we see. Both types of research receive substantial coverage in this chapter, but it is the second type that provides you with a unique educational opportunity: the opportunity to participate in the very research you are studying. Throughout this chapter, you will be encouraged to participate in demonstrations designed to give you a taste of the excitement of scientific discovery and to illustrate the relevance of what you are learning in this text to life outside its pages.

Before you begin the first section of the chapter, I'd like you to consider an interesting clinical case. Have you ever wondered whether one person's subjective experiences are like those of others? This case provides evidence that at least some of them are. It was reported by Whitman Richards (1971), and his subject was Mrs. Richards. Mrs. Richards suffered from migraine headaches, and like 20% of migraine sufferers, she often experienced visual displays, called *fortification illusions*, prior to her attacks (see Pietrobon & Striessnig, 2003).

The Case of Mrs. Richards: Fortification Illusions and the Astronomer

Evolutionary Perspective

Each fortification illusion began with a gray area of blindness near the center of her visual field—see Figure 6.1. During the next few minutes, the gray area would

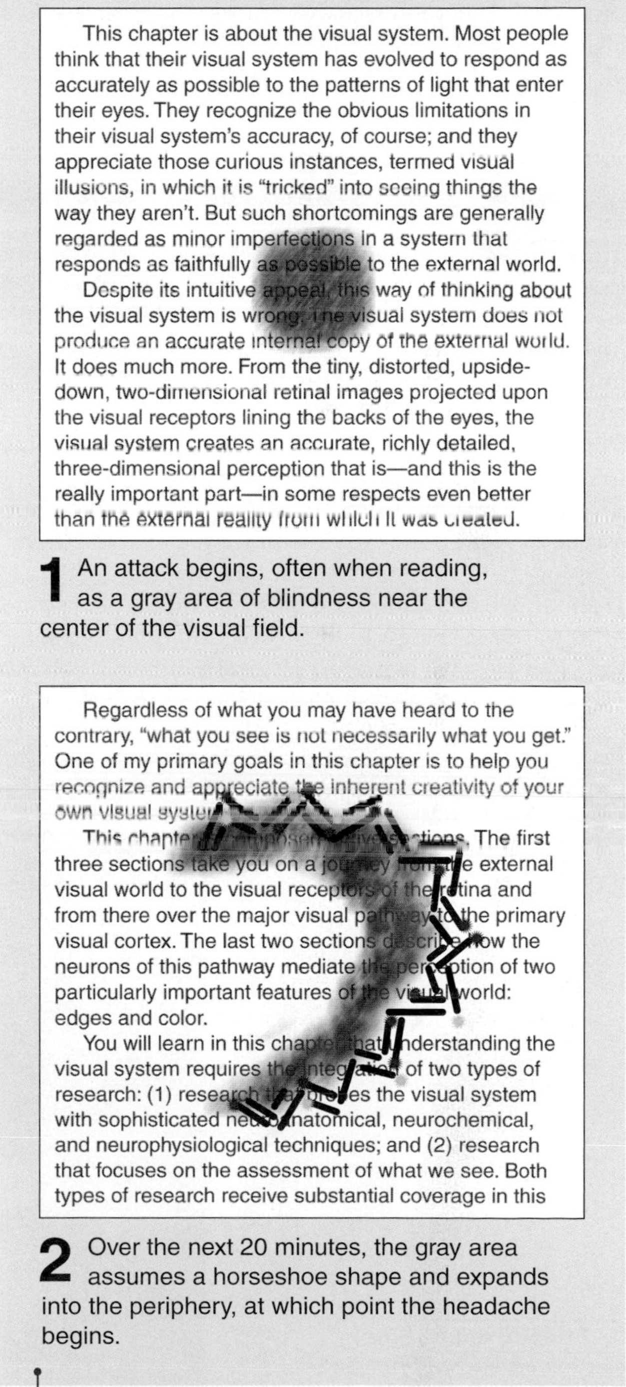

This chapter is about the visual system. Most people think that their visual system has evolved to respond as accurately as possible to the patterns of light that enter their eyes. They recognize the obvious limitations in their visual system's accuracy, of course; and they appreciate those curious instances, termed visual illusions, in which it is "tricked" into seeing things the way they aren't. But such shortcomings are generally regarded as minor imperfections in a system that responds as faithfully as possible to the external world.

Despite its intuitive appeal, this way of thinking about the visual system is wrong. The visual system does not produce an accurate internal copy of the external world. It does much more. From the tiny, distorted, upside-down, two-dimensional retinal images projected upon the visual receptors lining the backs of the eyes, the visual system creates an accurate, richly detailed, three-dimensional perception that is—and this is the really important part—in some respects even better than the external reality from which it was created.

1 An attack begins, often when reading, as a gray area of blindness near the center of the visual field.

Regardless of what you may have heard to the contrary, "what you see is not necessarily what you get." One of my primary goals in this chapter is to help you recognize and appreciate the inherent creativity of your own visual system.

This chapter is composed of five sections. The first three sections take you on a journey from the external visual world to the visual receptors of the retina and from there over the major visual pathway to the primary visual cortex. The last two sections describe how the neurons of this pathway mediate the perception of two particularly important features of the visual world: edges and color.

You will learn in this chapter that understanding the visual system requires the integration of two types of research: (1) research that probes the visual system with sophisticated neuroanatomical, neurochemical, and neurophysiological techniques; and (2) research that focuses on the assessment of what we see. Both types of research receive substantial coverage in this

2 Over the next 20 minutes, the gray area assumes a horseshoe shape and expands into the periphery, at which point the headache begins.

FIGURE 6.1 The fortification illusions associated with migraine headaches.

begin to expand into a horseshoe shape, with a zigzag pattern of flickering lines at its advancing edge. It normally took about 20 minutes for the lines and the trailing area of blindness to reach the periphery of her visual field. At this point, her headache would usually begin.

Because the illusion expanded so slowly, Mrs. Richards was able to stare at a point on the center of a blank sheet of paper and periodically trace on the sheet the details of her illusion. This method made it apparent that the lines became thicker and the expansion of the area of blindness occurred faster as the illusion spread into the periphery.

The features of fortification illusions are quite interesting, but they are not the most intriguing aspect of this case. Dr. Richards discovered that a similar set of drawings was published in 1870 by the famous British astronomer George Biddell Airy, and they were virtually identical to those done by Mrs. Richards. (By the way, the illusions got their name because their advancing edges reminded people of the plans for a fortification.)

We will return to fortification illusions after we have learned a bit about the visual system. At that point, you will be able to appreciate the significance of their features.

6.1 Light Enters the Eye and Reaches the Retina

Everybody knows that cats, owls, and other nocturnal animals can see in the dark. Right? Wrong! Some animals have special adaptations that allow them to see under very dim illumination, but no animal can see in complete darkness. The light reflected into your eyes from the objects around you is the basis for your ability to see them; if there is no light, there is no vision.

You may recall from high-school physics that light can be thought of in two different ways: as discrete particles of energy, called *photons*, traveling through space at about 300,000 kilometers (186,000 miles) per second or as waves of energy. Both theories are useful; in some ways light behaves like a particle, and in others it behaves like a wave. Physicists have learned to live with this nagging inconsistency, and we must do the same.

Light is sometimes defined as waves of electromagnetic energy that are between 380 and 760 nanometers (billionths of a meter) in length (see Figure 6.2). There is nothing special about these wavelengths except that the human visual system responds to them. In fact, some animals can see wavelengths that we cannot (see Fernald, 2000). For example, rattlesnakes can see *infrared waves*, which are too long for humans to see; as a result, they can see warm-blooded prey in what for us would be complete darkness. Accordingly, if I were writing this book for rattlesnakes, I would be forced to provide another, equally arbitrary, definition of light.

Wavelength and intensity are two properties of light that are of particular interest—wavelength because it

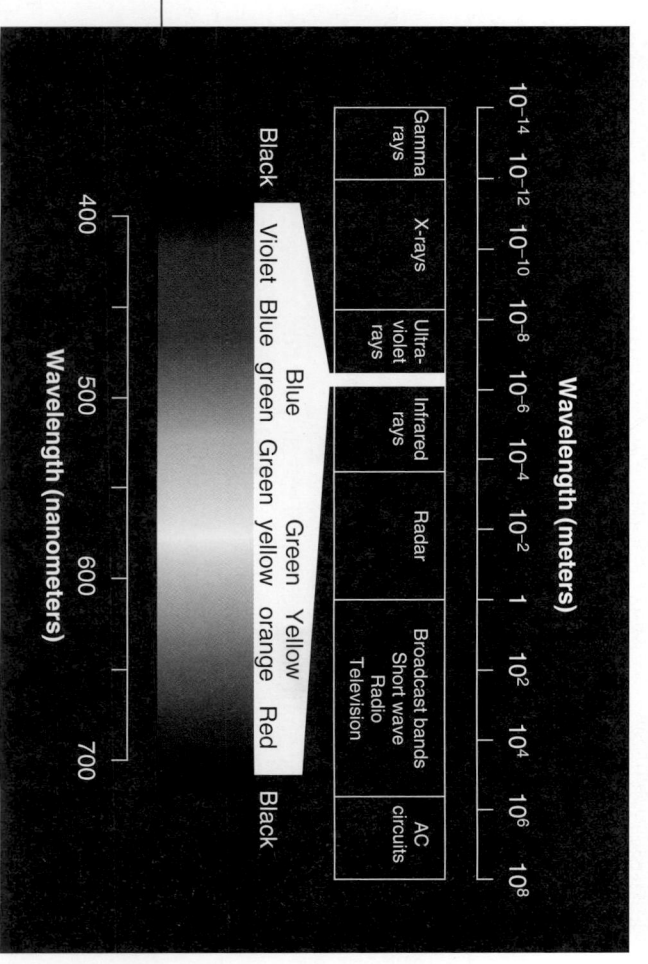

FIGURE 6.2 The electromagnetic spectrum and the colors associated with the wavelengths that are visible to humans.

plays an important role in the perception of color, and intensity because it plays an important role in the perception of brightness. The concepts of *wavelength* and *color* are typically regarded as interchangeable, and so are *intensity* and *brightness*. For example, we commonly refer to an intense light with a wavelength of 700 nanometers as being a bright red light (see Figure 6.2), when in fact it is our perception of the light, not the light itself, that is bright and red. I know that these distinctions may seem trivial to you now, but by the end of the chapter you will appreciate their importance.

The amount of light reaching the retinas is regulated by the donut-shaped bands of contractile tissue, the *irises*, which give our eyes their characteristic color (see Figure 6.3). Light enters the eye through the *pupil*, the hole in the iris. The adjustment of pupil size in response to changes in illumination represents a compromise between **sensitivity** (the ability to detect the presence of dimly lit objects) and **acuity** (the ability to see the details of objects). When the level of illumination is high and sensitivity is thus not important, the visual system takes advantage of the situation by constricting the pupils. When the pupils are constricted, the image falling on each retina is sharper and there is a greater *depth of focus*; that is, a greater range of depths are simultaneously kept in focus on the retinas. However, when the

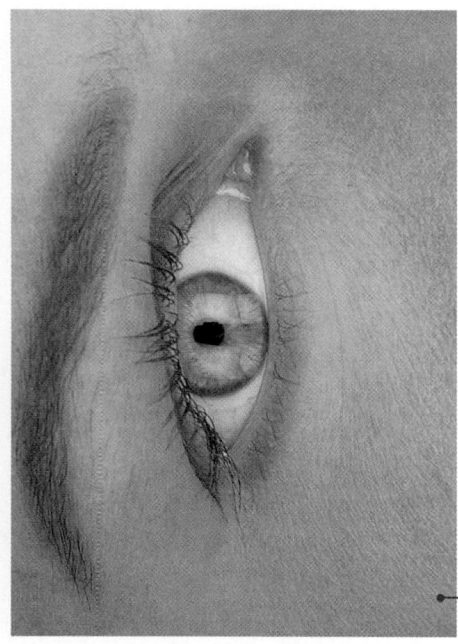

FIGURE 6.3 The human eye. Light enters the eye through the pupil, whose size is regulated by the iris. The iris gives the eye its characteristic color—blue, brown, or other.

level of illumination is too low to adequately activate the receptors, the pupils dilate to let in more light, thereby sacrificing acuity and depth of focus.

Behind each pupil is a *lens*, which focuses incoming light on the retina (see Figure 6.4). When we direct our gaze at something near, the tension on the ligaments

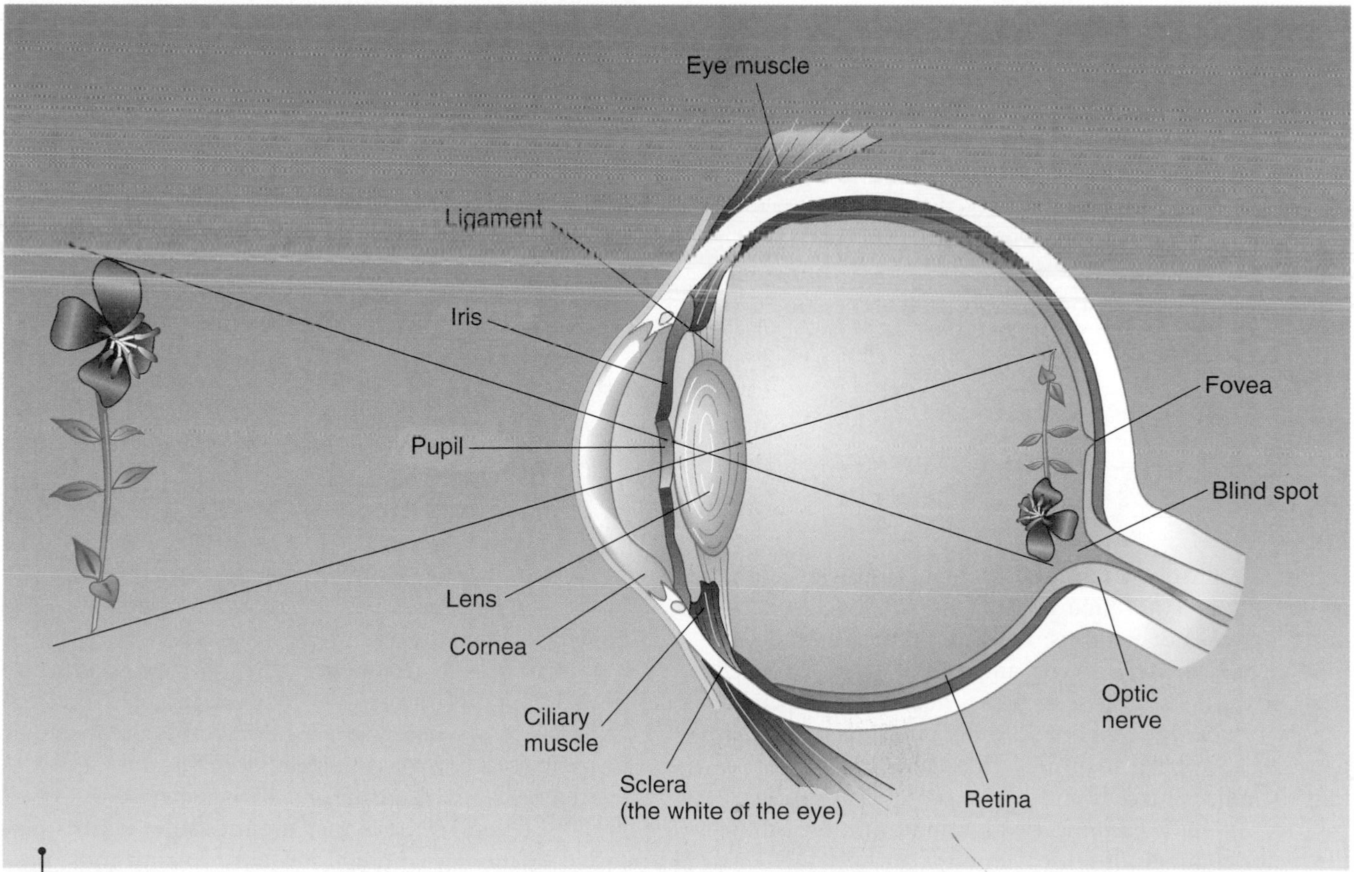

FIGURE 6.4 A diagram of the human eye.

Eye muscle

Ligament

Iris

Pupil

Lens

Cornea

Ciliary muscle

Sclera (the white of the eye)

Retina

Optic nerve

Blind spot

Fovea

holding each lens in place is reduced by the contraction of the **ciliary muscles**, and the lens assumes its natural cylindrical shape. (Be alert here: The fact that the tension on the lens is reduced by muscle contraction is counterintuitive.) This increases the ability of the lens to *refract* (bend) light and thus brings close objects into sharp focus. When we focus on a distant object, the ciliary muscles relax, and the lens is flattened. The process of adjusting the configuration of the lenses to bring images into focus on the retina is called **accommodation**.

No description of the eyes of vertebrates would be

Evolutionary Perspective

6.2

complete without a discussion of their most obvious feature: the fact that they come in pairs. One reason vertebrates have two eyes is that vertebrates have two sides: left and right. By having one eye on each side, which is by far the most common arrangement, vertebrates can see in almost every direction without moving their heads. But then why do some mammals, including humans, have their eyes mounted side by side on the front of their heads? This arrangement sacrifices the ability to see behind so that what is in front can be viewed through both eyes simultaneously—an arrangement that is an important basis for our visual system's ability to create three-dimensional perceptions (to see depth) from two-dimensional retinal images. Why do you think the two-eyes-on-the-front arrangement has evolved in some species but not in others?

The movements of your eyes are coordinated so that each point in your visual world is projected to corresponding points on your two retinas. To accomplish this, your eyes must *converge* (turn slightly inward); convergence is greatest when you are inspecting things that are close. But the positions of the retinal images on your two eyes can never correspond exactly because your two eyes do not view the world from exactly the same position (see the accompanying demonstration). **Binocular disparity**—the difference in the position of the same im-

age on the two retinas—is greater for close objects than for distant objects; therefore, your visual system can use the degree of binocular disparity to construct one three-dimensional perception from two two-dimensional retinal images.

Demonstration

The demonstration of binocular disparity and convergence is the first of the demonstrations that punctuate this chapter. If you compare the views from each eye (by quickly closing one eye and then the other) of objects at various distances in front of you—for example, your finger held at different distances—you will notice that the disparity between the two views is greater for closer objects. Now try the mysterious demonstration of the cocktail sausage. Face the farthest wall (or some other distant object) and bring the tips of your two pointing fingers together at arm's length in front of you—with the backs of your fingers away from you, unless you prefer sausages with fingernails. Now, with both eyes open, look through the notch between your touching fingertips, but focus on the wall. Do you see the cocktail sausage between your fingertips? Where did it come from? To prove to yourself that the sausage is a product of binocularity, make it disappear by shutting one eye. Warning: Do not eat this sausage.

6.2 The Retina and Translation of Light into Neural Signals

Figure 6.5 illustrates the fundamental cellular structure of the retina. The retina is composed of five layers of different types of neurons: **receptors, horizontal cells, bipolar cells, amacrine cells,** and **retinal ganglion cells.** Each of these five types of retinal neurons comes in a variety of subtypes. About 55 different kinds of retinal neurons have been identified (Masland, 2001). Notice that the amacrine cells and horizontal cells are specialized for *lateral communication* (communication across the major channels of sensory input).

Also notice in Figure 6.5 that the retina is in a sense inside-out: Light reaches the receptor layer only after passing through the other four layers. Then, once the receptors have been activated, the neural message is transmitted back out through the retinal layers to the retinal ganglion cells, whose axons project across the inside of the retina before gathering together in a bundle and exiting the eyeball. This inside-out arrangement creates two visual problems. One is that the incoming light is distorted by the retinal tissue through which it must pass

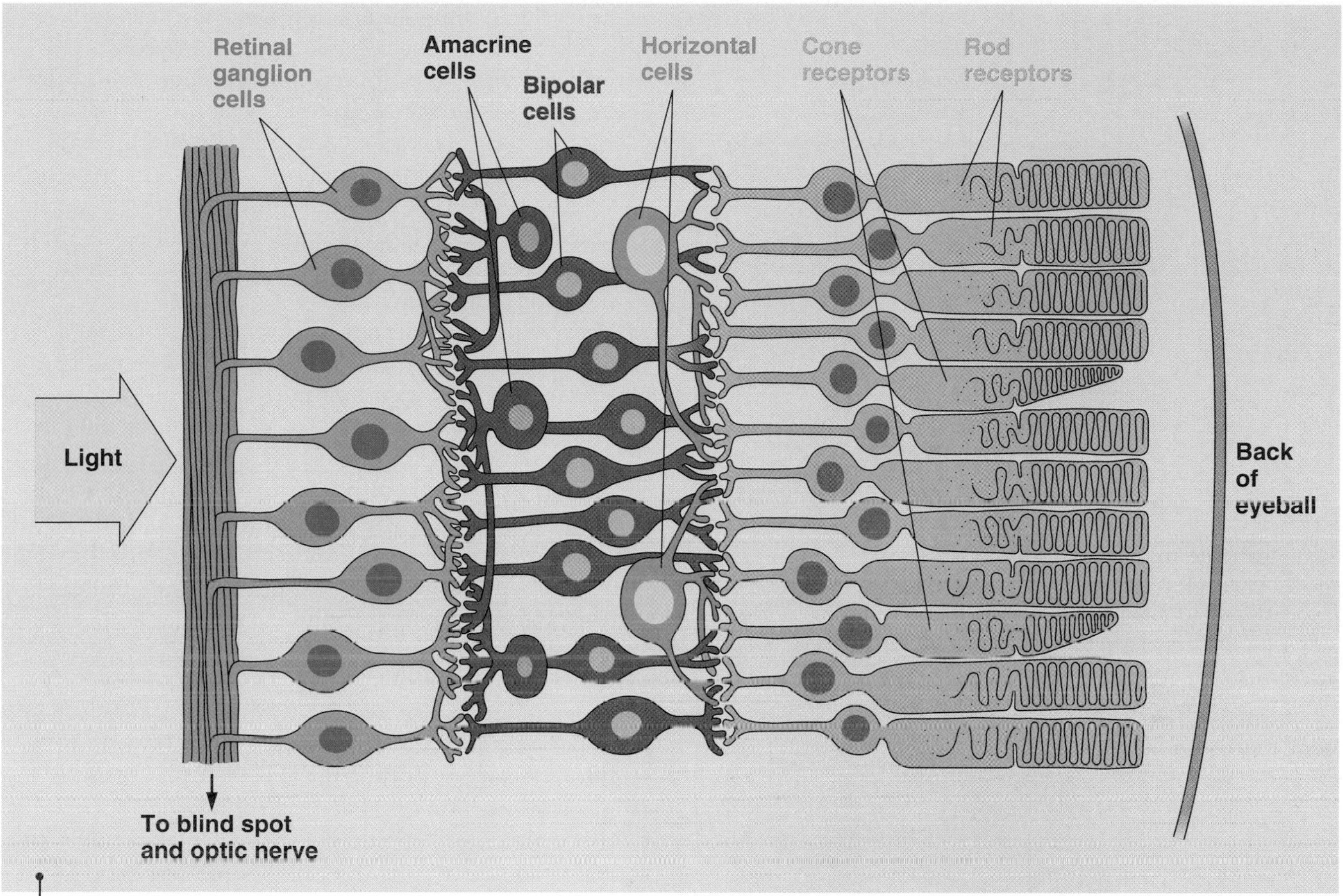

Retinal
ganglion
cells

**Amacrine
cells**

Horizontal
cells

Cone
receptors

Rod
receptors

**Bipolar
cells**

Back
of
eyeball

To blind spot
and optic nerve

Light

FIGURE 6.5 The cellular structure of the mammalian retina.

before reaching the receptors. The other is that for the bundle of retinal ganglion cell axons to leave the eye, there must be a gap in the receptor layer; this gap is called the **blind spot.**

The first of these two problems is minimized by the fovea (see Figure 6.6 on page 134). The **fovea** is an indentation, about 0.33 centimeter in diameter, at the center of the retina; it is the area of the retina that is specialized for high-acuity vision (for seeing fine details). The thinning of the retinal ganglion cell layer at the fovea reduces the distortion of incoming light. The blind spot, the second of the two visual problems created by the inside-out structure of the retina, requires a more creative solution—which is illustrated in the demonstration on page 135.

In this demonstration, you will experience **completion.** The visual system uses information provided by the receptors around the blind spot to fill in the gaps in your retinal images. When the visual system detects a straight bar going into one side of the blind spot and another straight bar leaving the other side, it fills in the missing bit for you; and what you see is a continuous straight bar, regardless of what is actually there. The completion phenomenon is one of the most compelling demonstrations that the visual system does much more than create a faithful copy of the external world.

It is a mistake to think that completion is merely a response to blind spots (see Ramachandran, 1992; Spillman & Werner, 1996). Indeed, completion is a fundamental visual system function. When you look at an object, your visual system does not conduct an image of that object from your retina to your cortex. Instead, it extracts key information about the object—primarily information about its edges and their location—and conducts that information to the cortex, where a perception of the entire object is created from that partial information. For example, the color and brightness of large unpatterned surfaces are not directly perceived but are filled in (completed) by a completion process, in this case called surface interpolation.

**Thinking
Critically**

ON THE CD

Visit the
Surface Interpolation module.
The Cornsweet
Illusion demonstrates that
much of what
you "see" is actually a creation
of your visual
system.

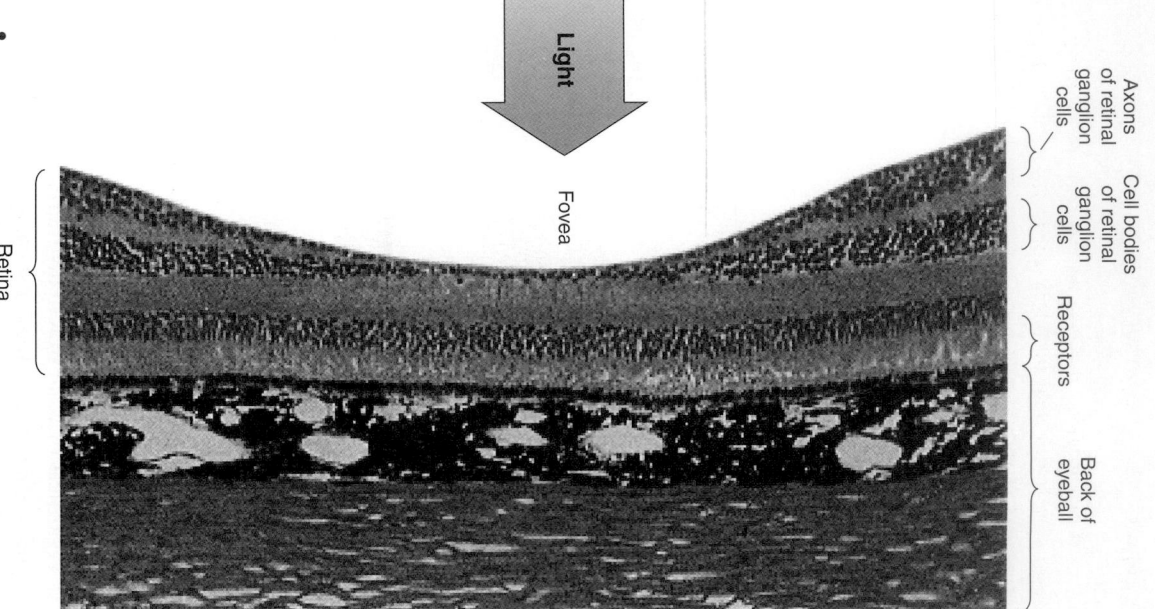

Light

Fovea

Axons
of retinal
ganglion
cells

Cell bodies
of retinal
ganglion
cells

Receptors

Back of
eyeball

Retina

FIGURE 6.6   A section of the retina. The fovea is the indentation at the center of the retina; it is specialized for high-acuity vision.

Cone and Rod Vision

You likely noticed in Figure 6.5 that there are two different types of receptors in the human retina: cone-shaped receptors called **cones**, and rod-shaped receptors called **rods** (see Figure 6.7). The existence of these two types of receptors puzzled researchers until 1866, when it was first noticed that species active only in the day tend to have cone-only retinas and that species active only at night tend to have rod-only retinas.

From this observation emerged the **duplexity theory** of vision—the theory that cones and rods mediate different kinds of vision. Cone-mediated vision (**photopic vision**) predominates in good lighting and provides high-acuity (finely detailed) colored perceptions of

the world. In dim illumination, there is not enough light to reliably excite the cones, and the more sensitive rod-mediated vision (**scotopic vision**) predominates. However, the sensitivity of scotopic vision is not achieved without cost: Scotopic vision lacks both the detail and the color of photopic vision.

The differences between photopic (cone) and scotopic (rod) vision result in part from a difference in the way the two systems are "wired." As Figure 6.8 illustrates, there is a large difference in *convergence* between the two systems. The output of several hundred rods may ultimately converge on a single retinal ganglion cell, whereas it is not uncommon for a retinal ganglion cell to receive input from only a few cones. As a result, the effects of dim light simultaneously stimulating many rods can summate (add) to influence the firing of a retinal ganglion cell onto which the output of the stimulated rods converges, whereas the effects of the same dim light applied to a sheet of cones cannot summate to the same degree, and the retinal ganglion cells may not respond to the light.

The convergent scotopic system pays for its high degree of sensitivity with a low level of acuity. When a retinal ganglion cell that receives input from hundreds of rods changes its firing, the brain has no way of knowing which portion of the rods contributed to the change. Although a more intense light is required to change the firing of a retinal ganglion cell that receives signals from cones, when such a retinal ganglion cell does react, there is less ambiguity about the location of the stimulus that triggered the reaction.

Cones and rods differ in their distribution on the retina. As Figure 6.9 on page 136 illustrates, there are no rods at all in the fovea, only cones. At the boundaries of the foveal indentation, the proportion of cones declines markedly, and there is an increase in the number of rods. The density of rods reaches a maximum at 20° from the

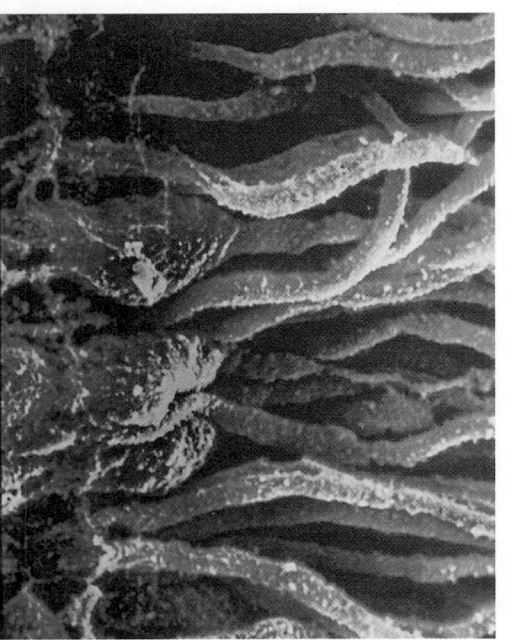

FIGURE 6.7   Cones and rods. The smaller, conical cells are cones; the larger, cylindrical cells are rods.

Demonstration

First, prove to yourself that you do have areas of blindness that correspond to your retinal blind spots. Close your left eye and stare directly at the A below, trying as hard as you can to not shift your gaze. While keeping the gaze of your right eye fixed on the A, hold the book at different distances from you until the black dot to the right of the A becomes focused on your blind spot and disappears (at about 20 centimeters, or 8 inches).

(A)

If each eye has a blind spot, why is there not a black hole in your perception of the world when you look at it with one eye? You will discover the answer by focusing on B with your right eye while holding the book at the same distance as before. Suddenly, the broken line to the right of B will become whole. Now focus on C at the same distance with your right eye. What do you see?

(B)

(C)

Low Convergence in Cone-Fed Circuits

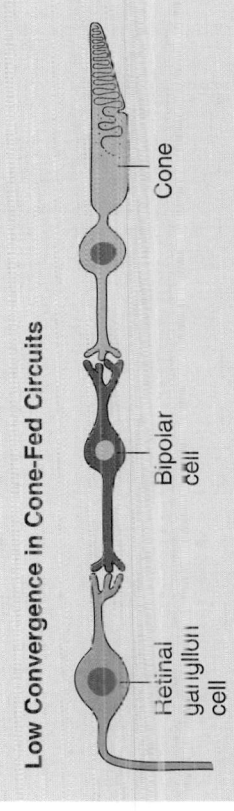

Cone

Bipolar cell

Retinal ganglion cell

High Convergence in Rod-Fed Circuits

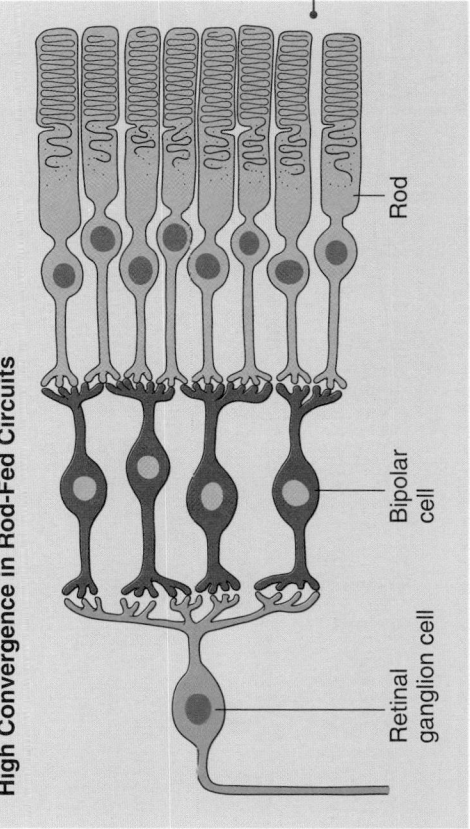

Rod

Bipolar cell

Retinal ganglion cell

FIGURE 6.8 A schematic representation of the convergence of cones and rods on retinal ganglion cells. There is a low degree of convergence in cone-fed pathways and a high degree of convergence in rod-fed pathways.

center of the fovea. Notice that there are many more rods in the **nasal hemiretina** (the half of each retina next to the nose) than in the **temporal hemiretina** (the half next to the temples).

Generally speaking, more intense lights appear brighter. However, wavelength also has a substantial effect on the perception of brightness. Because our visual systems are not equally sensitive to all wavelengths in the visible spectrum, lights of the same intensity but of different wavelengths can differ markedly in brightness. A graph of the relative brightness of lights of the same intensity presented at different wavelengths is called a *spectral sensitivity curve*.

By far the most important thing to remember about spectral sensitivity curves is that humans and other animals with both cones and rods have two of them: a **photopic spectral sensitivity curve** and a **scotopic spectral sensitivity curve**. The photopic spectral sensitivity of humans can be determined by having subjects judge the relative brightness of different wavelengths of light shone on the fovea. Their scotopic spectral sensitivity can be determined by asking subjects to judge the relative brightness of different wavelengths of light shone on the periphery of the retina at an intensity too low to activate the few peripheral cones that are located there.

The photopic and scotopic spectral sensitivity curves of human subjects are plotted in Figure 6.10. Notice that under photopic conditions, the visual system is maximally sensitive to wavelengths of about 560 nanometers; thus, under photopic conditions, a light at 500 nanometers would have to be much more intense than one at 560 nanometers to be seen as equally bright. In contrast, under scotopic conditions, the visual system is maximally sensitive to wavelengths of about 500 nanometers; thus, under scotopic conditions, a light of 560 nanometers would have to be much more intense than one at 500 nanometers to be seen as equally bright.

Because of the difference in photopic and scotopic spectral sensitivity, an interesting visual effect can be observed during the transition from photopic to scotopic vision. In 1825, Jan Purkinje described the following occurrence, which has become known as the **Purkinje effect** (pronounced "pur-KIN-jee"). One evening, just before dusk, while Purkinje was walking in his garden, he noticed how bright most of his yellow and red flowers appeared in relation to his blue ones. What amazed him was that just a few minutes later the relative brightness of his flowers had somehow been reversed; the entire scene, when viewed at night, appeared completely in shades of gray, but most of the blue flowers appeared as brighter grays than did the yellow and red ones. Can you explain this shift in relative brightness by referring to the photopic and scotopic spectral sensitivity curves in Figure 6.10?

Eye Movement

If cones are in fact responsible for mediating high-acuity color vision under photopic conditions, how can they accomplish their task when most of them are crammed into the fovea? Look around you. What you see is not a few colored details at the center of a grayish scene. You seem to see an expansive, richly detailed, lavishly colored visual world. How can such a perception be the product of a photopic system that, for the most part, is restricted to a few degrees in the center of your visual field? The next demonstration provides a clue.

What this demonstration shows is that what we see is determined not just by what is projected on the retina at that instant. Although we are not aware of it, the eye continually scans the visual field by making a series of brief fixations. About three fixations occur every second, and they are connected by very quick eye movements called **saccades**. The visual system *integrates* (adds to-

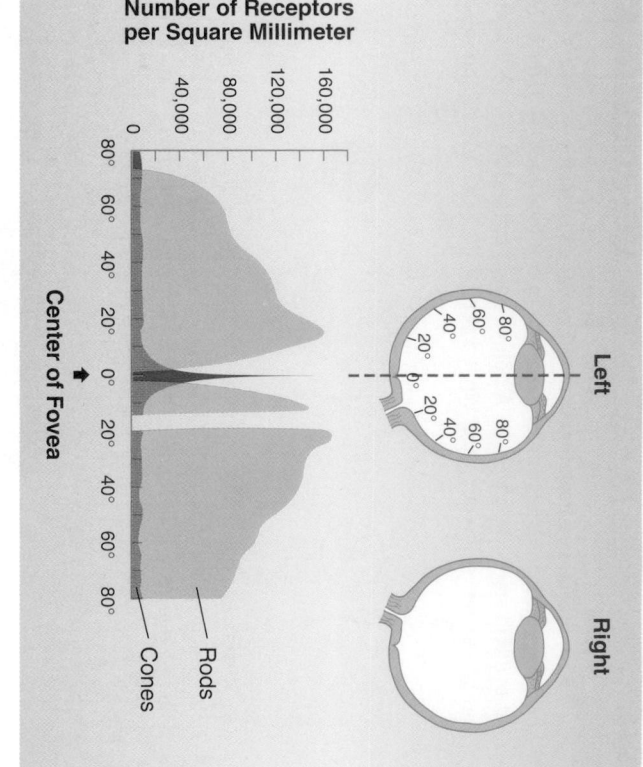

FIGURE 6.9 The distribution of cones and rods over the human retina. The figure illustrates the number of cones and rods per square millimeter as a function of distance from the center of the fovea. (Adapted from Lindsay & Norman, 1977.)

Number of Receptors per Square Millimeter

160,000 120,000 80,000 40,000 0

Center of Fovea

80° 60° 40° 20° 0 20° 40° 60° 80°

Rods   Cones

Left   Right

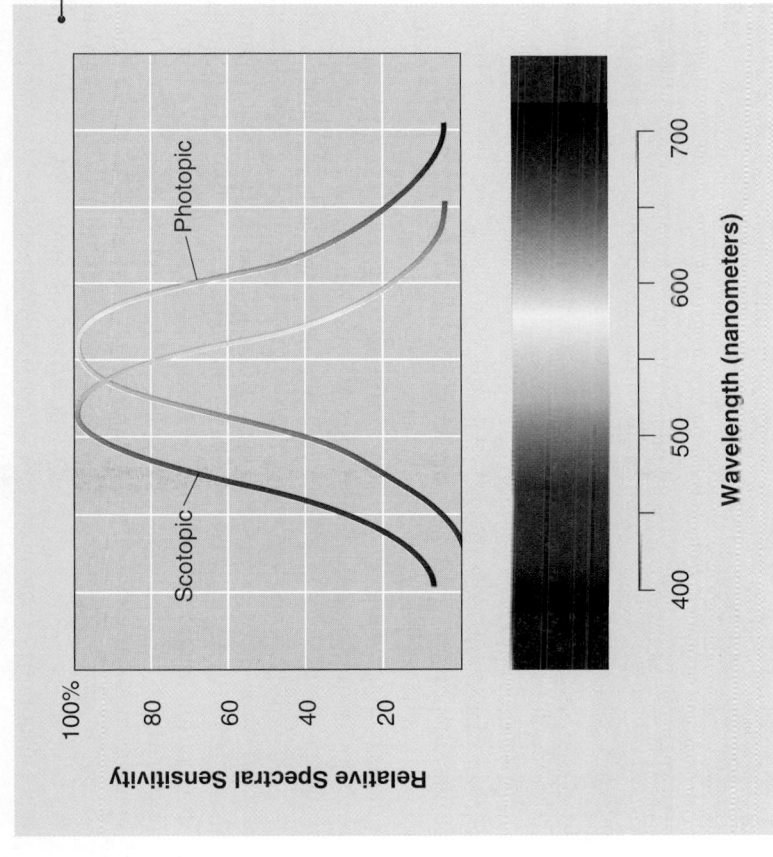

FIGURE 6.10 Human photopic (cone) and scotopic (rod) spectral sensitivity curves. The peak of each curve has been arbitrarily set at 100%.

gether) some of the information from the preceding fixations to produce a wide-angled, high-acuity, richly colored perception (see Irwin, 1996). It is because of this *temporal integration* that the world does not vanish momentarily each time we blink.

One way of demonstrating the critical role played by eye movement in vision is to study what happens to vision when all eye movement is stopped. However, because of the risks inherent in paralyzing the eye muscles,

researchers have taken an alternative approach. Rather than stopping eye movement, they have stopped the primary consequence of eye movement—the movement of the retinal image across the retina. They have accomplished this by projecting test stimuli from a tiny projector mounted on a contact lens. Each time the eye moves, the lens and the projector move with it; this keeps the retinal image fixed on the same receptors, as if the eye had remained still.

The effect on vision of stabilizing the retinal image is dramatic (e.g., Pritchard, 1961). After a few seconds of viewing, a simple **stabilized retinal image** disappears, leaving a featureless gray field. The movements of the eyes then increase, presumably in an attempt to bring the image back. However, such movements are futile in this situation because the stabilized retinal image simply moves with the eyes. In a few seconds, the stimulus pattern, or part of it, spontaneously reappears, only to disappear once again.

Why do stabilized images disappear? The answer lies in the fact that the neurons of the visual system respond

Demonstration

Close your left eye, and with your right eye stare at the fixation point ◆ at a distance of about 12 centimeters (4.75 inches) from the page. Be very careful that your gaze does not shift. You will notice when your gaze is totally fixed that it is difficult to see detail and color at 20° or more

from the fixation point because there are so few cones there. Now look at the page again with your right eye, but this time without fixing your gaze. Notice the difference that eye movement makes to your vision.

W	F	D	M	E	A	◆
50°	40°	30°	20°	10°	5°	0°

to change rather than to steady input. Most visual system neurons respond vigorously when a stimulus is presented, moved, or terminated; they respond only weakly to a continuous, unchanging stimulus. Apparently, one function of eye movements is to keep the retinal image moving back and forth across the receptors, thus ensuring that the receptors and the neurons to which they are connected receive a continually changing pattern of stimulation. When a retinal image is stabilized, parts of the visual system stop responding to the image, and it disappears.

Visual Transduction: The Conversion of Light to Neural Signals

Transduction is the conversion of one form of energy to another. *Visual transduction* is the conversion of light to neural signals by the visual receptors. A breakthrough in the study of visual transduction came in 1876, when a red *pigment* (a pigment is any substance that absorbs light) was extracted from the predominantly rod retina of the frog. This pigment had a curious property. When exposed to continuous intense light, it was *bleached* (lost its color) and lost its ability to absorb light; but when it was returned to the dark, it regained both its redness and its light-absorbing capacity.

It is now clear that the absorption and bleaching of rhodopsin by light is the first step in rod-mediated vision. Evidence comes from demonstrations that the degree to which rhodopsin absorbs light in various situations predicts how humans see under the very same conditions. For example, it has been shown that the degree to which rhodopsin absorbs lights of different wavelengths is related to the ability of humans and other animals with rods to detect the presence of different wavelengths of light under scotopic conditions. Figure 6.11 illustrates the relationship between the **absorption spectrum** of rhodopsin and the human scotopic spectral sensitivity curve. The goodness of the fit leaves little doubt that, in dim light, our sensitivity to various

wavelengths is a direct consequence of rhodopsin's ability to absorb them.

Rhodopsin is a G-protein–linked receptor that responds to light rather than to neurotransmitter molecules (see Koutalos & Yau, 1993; Molday & Hsu, 1995). Rhodopsin receptors, like other G-protein–linked receptors, initiate a cascade of intracellular chemical events when they are activated (see Figure 6.12). When rods are in darkness, an intracellular chemical called *cyclic GMP* (guanosine monophosphate) keeps sodium channels partially open, thus keeping the rods slightly depolarized and a steady flow of excitatory glutamate neurotransmitter molecules emanating from them. However, when rhodopsin receptors are bleached by light, the resulting cascade of intracellular chemical events deactivates the cyclic GMP; and in so doing, it closes the sodium channels, hyperpolarizes the rods, and reduces the release of glutamate. The transduction of light by rods makes an important point: Signals are often transmitted through neural systems by inhibition.

Less is known about the cone photopigments than about rhodopsin. However, their structure and function appear to be similar to those of rhodopsin. For example, when stimulated, cones become hyperpolarized and reduce their release of glutamate (see Hendry & Calkins, 1998).

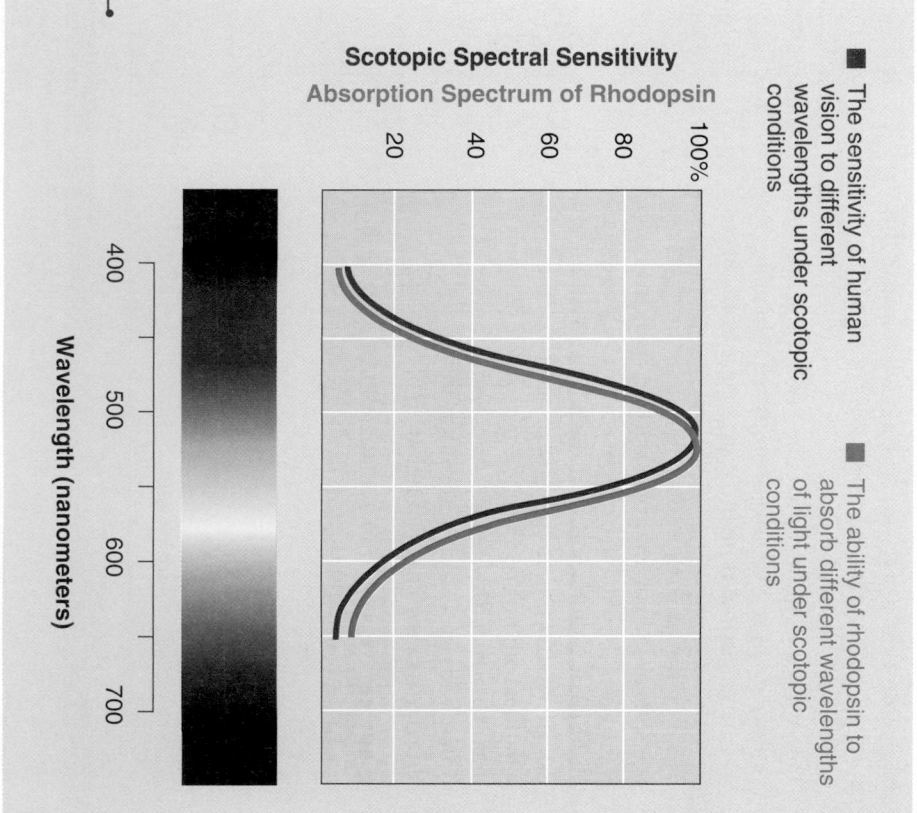

■ The sensitivity of human vision to different wavelengths under scotopic conditions

■ The ability of rhodopsin to absorb different wavelengths of light under scotopic conditions

Scotopic Spectral Sensitivity
Absorption Spectrum of Rhodopsin

FIGURE 6.11   The absorption spectrum of rhodopsin compared with the human scotopic spectral sensitivity curve.

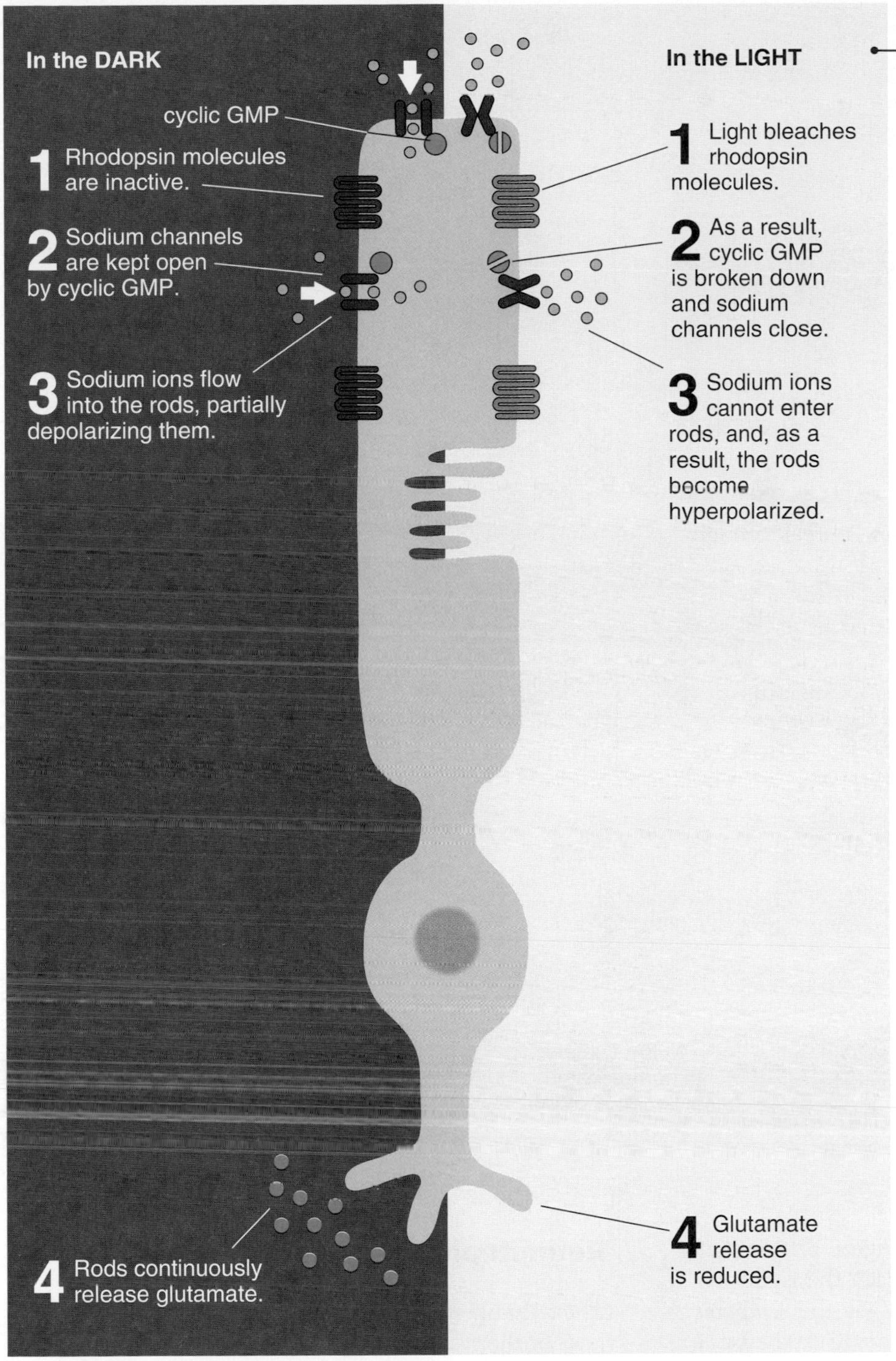

In the LIGHT

FIGURE 6.12   The inhibitory response of rods to light. When light bleaches rhodopsin molecules, the rods' sodium channels close; as a result, the rods become hyperpolarized and release less glutamate.

1 Light bleaches rhodopsin molecules.

2 As a result, cyclic GMP is broken down and sodium channels close.

3 Sodium ions cannot enter rods, and, as a result, the rods become hyperpolarized.

4 Glutamate release is reduced.

In the DARK

cyclic GMP

1 Rhodopsin molecules are inactive.

2 Sodium channels are kept open by cyclic GMP.

3 Sodium ions flow into the rods, partially depolarizing them.

4 Rods continuously release glutamate.

6.3 From Retina to Primary Visual Cortex

Many pathways in the brain carry visual information. By far the largest and most thoroughly studied visual pathways are the **retina-geniculate-striate pathways,** which conduct signals from each retina to the **primary visual cortex,** or *striate cortex,* via the **lateral geniculate nuclei** of the thalamus.

About 90% of the axons of retinal ganglion cells become part of the retina-geniculate-striate pathways (see Tong, 2003). No other sensory system has such a predominant pair (left and right) of pathways to the cortex. The organization of these visual pathways is illustrated in Figure 6.13 on page 140. Examine it carefully.

FIGURE 6.13 The retina-geniculate-striate system: The neural projections from the retinas through the lateral geniculate nuclei to the left and right primary visual cortex (striate cortex). The colors indicate the flow of information from various parts of the receptive fields of each eye to various parts of the visual system. (Adapted from Netter, 1962.)

The main thing to notice from Figure 6.13 is that all signals from the left visual field reach the right primary visual cortex, either ipsilaterally via the *temporal hemiretina* of the right eye or contralaterally via the *nasal hemiretina* of the left eye—and that the opposite is true of all signals from the right visual field. Each lateral geniculate nucleus has six layers, and each layer of each nucleus receives input from all parts of the contralateral visual field of one eye. In other words, each lateral geniculate nucleus receives visual input only from the contralateral visual field; three layers receive input from one eye, and three from the other. Most of the lateral geniculate neurons that project to the primary visual cortex terminate in the lower part of cortical layer IV (see Figure 3.27), producing a characteristic stripe, or striation, when viewed in cross section—hence the name *striate cortex*.

Retinotopic Organization

The retina-geniculate-striate system is **retinotopic**; each level of the system is organized like a map of the retina. This means that two stimuli presented to adjacent areas of the retina excite adjacent neurons at all levels of the system. The retinotopic layout of the primary visual cortex has a disproportionate representation of the fovea; although the fovea is only a small part of the retina, a relatively large proportion of the primary visual cortex (about 25%) is dedicated to the analysis of its input.

A dramatic demonstration of the retinotopic organization of the primary visual cortex was provided by Dobelle, Mladejovsky, and Girvin (1974). They implanted an array of electrodes in the primary visual

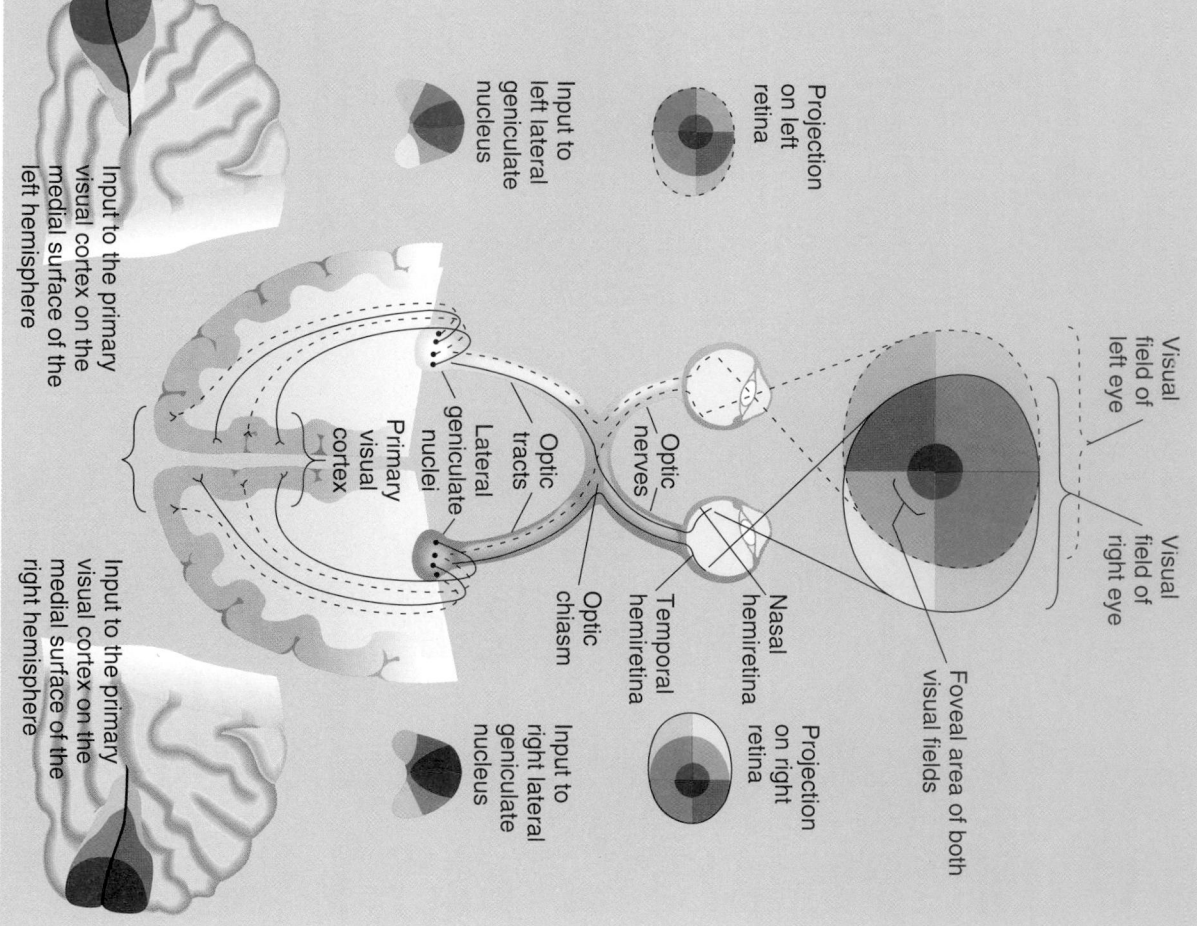

Visual field of left eye

Visual field of right eye

Foveal area of both visual fields

Nasal hemiretina

Temporal hemiretina

Projection on left retina

Projection on right retina

Input to left lateral geniculate nucleus

Input to right lateral geniculate nucleus

Optic nerves

Optic chiasm

Optic tracts

Lateral geniculate nuclei

Primary visual cortex

Input to the primary visual cortex on the medial surface of the left hemisphere

Input to the primary visual cortex on the medial surface of the right hemisphere

Clinical Implications

SCAN YOUR BRAIN

This is a good place to pause to scan your brain. Are you ready to proceed to the last two sections of the chapter, which describe how the visual system mediates the perception of edges and color? Find out by filling in the following blanks.

1. Neural signals are carried from the retina to the lateral geniculate nuclei by the axons of _____ cells.

2. The axons of retinal ganglion cells leave the eyeball at the _____.

3. The area of the retina that mediates high-acuity vision is the _____.

4. Cones are the receptors of the _____ system, which functions only in good lighting.

5. The retinal ganglion cells from the nasal hemiretinas decussate (cross over to the other side of the brain) via the _____.

The correct answers are provided at the bottom of the page. Before proceeding, review material related to your errors and omissions.

6. The photopigment of rods is _____.

7. The most important organizational principle of the retina-geniculate-striate system is that it is laid out _____.

8. Evidence that rhodopsin is the scotopic photopigment is provided by the fit between the _____ spectrum of rhodopsin and the scotopic spectral sensitivity curve.

9. The high degree of _____ characteristic of the scotopic system increases its sensitivity but decreases its acuity.

---

cortex of patients who were blind because of damage to their eyes. If electrical current was administered simultaneously through an array of electrodes forming a shape, such as a cross, on the surface of a patient's cortex, the patient reported "seeing" a glowing image of that shape.

The M and P Channels

Not apparent in Figure 6.13 is the fact that at least two independent channels of communication flow through each lateral geniculate nucleus (see Hendry & Calkins, 1998). One channel runs through the top four layers. These layers are called the **parvocellular layers** (or *P layers*) because they are composed of neurons with small cell bodies (*parvo* means "small"). The other channel runs through the bottom two layers, which are called

---

the **magnocellular layers** (or *M layers*) because they are composed of neurons with large cell bodies (*magno* means "large").

The parvocellular neurons are particularly responsive to color, to fine pattern details, and to stationary or slowly moving objects. In contrast, the magnocellular neurons are particularly responsive to movement. Cones provide the majority of the input to the P layers, whereas rods provide the majority of the input to the M layers.

The parvocellular and magnocellular neurons project to slightly different sites in the lower part of layer IV of the striate cortex. The magnocellular neurons terminate just above the parvocellular neurons (see Yabuta & Callaway, 1998). In turn, these M and P portions of lower layer IV project to different parts of visual cortex (Levitt, 2001; Yabuta, Sawatari, & Callaway, 2001).

6.4 Seeing Edges

Evolutionary Perspective

Edge perception (seeing edges) does not sound like a particularly important topic, but it is. Edges are the most informative features of any visual display because they define the extent and position of the various objects in it. Given the importance of perceiving visual edges and the unrelenting pressure of natural selection, it is not surprising that the visual systems of many species are particularly good at edge perception.

Before considering the visual mechanisms underlying edge perception, it is important to appreciate exactly what a visual edge is. In a sense, a visual edge is nothing: It is merely the place where two different areas of a visual image meet. Accordingly, the perception of an edge is really the perception of a *contrast* between two adjacent areas of the visual field. This section of the chapter reviews the perception of edges (the perception of contrast) between areas that differ from one another in brightness. Color contrast is discussed in the following section.

Lateral Inhibition and Contrast Enhancement

Carefully examine the stripes in Figure 6.14. The intensity graph in the figure indicates what is there—a series of homogeneous stripes of different intensity. But this is not exactly what you see, is it? What you see is indicated in the brightness graph. Adjacent to each edge, the brighter stripe looks brighter than it really is and the darker stripe looks darker than it really is (see the demonstration). The nonexistent stripes of brightness and darkness running adjacent to the edges are called *Mach bands*; they enhance the contrast at each edge and make the edge easier to see.

It is important to appreciate that **contrast enhancement** is not something that occurs just in books. Although we are normally unaware of it, every edge

ON THE CD

Visit the Contrast Enhancement module. View the important Mach band demonstration in a particularly compelling way.

we look at is highlighted for us by the contrast-enhancing mechanisms of our nervous systems. In effect, our perception of edges is better than the real thing.

The classic studies of the physiological basis of contrast enhancement were conducted on the eyes of an unlikely subject: the *horseshoe crab* (e.g., Ratliff, 1972). The *lateral eyes* of the horseshoe crab are ideal for certain types of neurophysiological research. Unlike mammalian eyes, they are composed of very large receptors, called **ommatidia**, each with its own large axon. The axons of the ommatidia are interconnected by a lateral neural network.

In order to understand the physiological basis of contrast enhancement in the horseshoe crab, you must know two things. The first is that if a single ommatidium is illuminated, it fires at a rate that is proportional to the intensity of the light striking it; more intense lights produce more firing. The second is that when a receptor fires, it inhibits its neighbors via the lateral neural network; this inhibition is called **lateral inhibition** because it spreads laterally across the array of receptors (or *mutual inhibition*, because neighboring receptors inhibit one another). The amount of lateral inhibition produced by a receptor is greatest when it is most intensely illuminated, and it has its greatest effect on its immediate neighbors.

The neural basis of contrast enhancement can be understood in terms of the firing rates of the receptors on each side of an edge, as indicated in Figure 6.15. Notice that the receptor adjacent to the edge on the more intense side (receptor D) fires more than the other intensely illuminated receptors (A, B, C), while the receptor adjacent to the edge on the less well-illuminated side (receptor E) fires less than the other receptors on that side (E, G, H). Lateral inhibition accounts for these differences. Receptors A, B, and C all fire at the same rate, because they are all receiving the same high level of stimulation and the same high degree of lateral inhibition from all their highly stimulated neighbors. Receptor D fires more than A, B, and C, because it receives less inhibition as they do but less inhibition from

www.ablongman.com/pinel6e

Demonstration

The Mach band demonstration is so compelling that you may be confused by it. You many think that the Mach bands in Figure 6.14 have been created by the printers of the book, rather than by your own visual system. To prove to yourself that the Mach bands are a creation of your visual system, view each stripe individually by covering the adjacent ones with two pieces of paper. You will see at once that each stripe is completely homogeneous. Then, take the paper away, and the Mach bands will suddenly reappear.

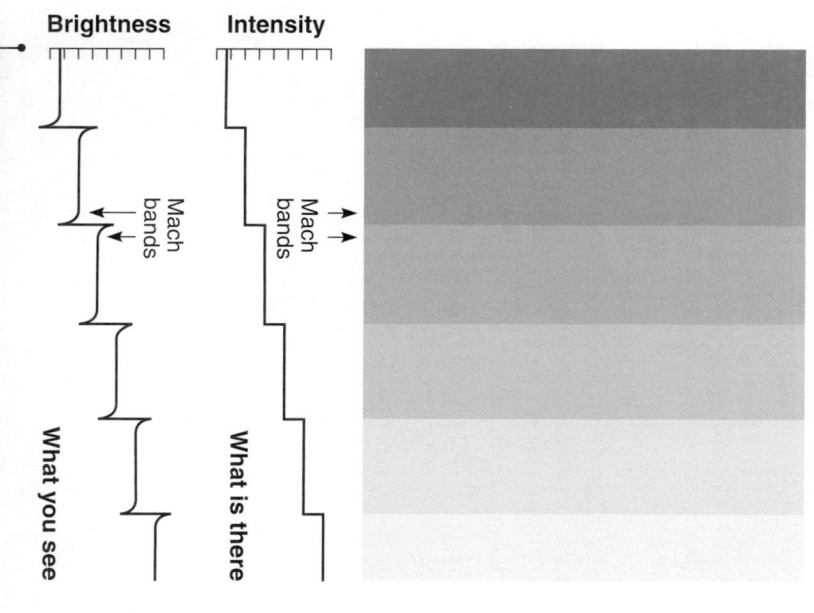

Intensity

Mach bands

What is there

Brightness

Mach bands

Mach bands

What you see

FIGURE 6.14   The illusory bands visible in this figure are often called Mach bands although Mach used a different figure to generate them in his studies (see Eagleman, 2001).

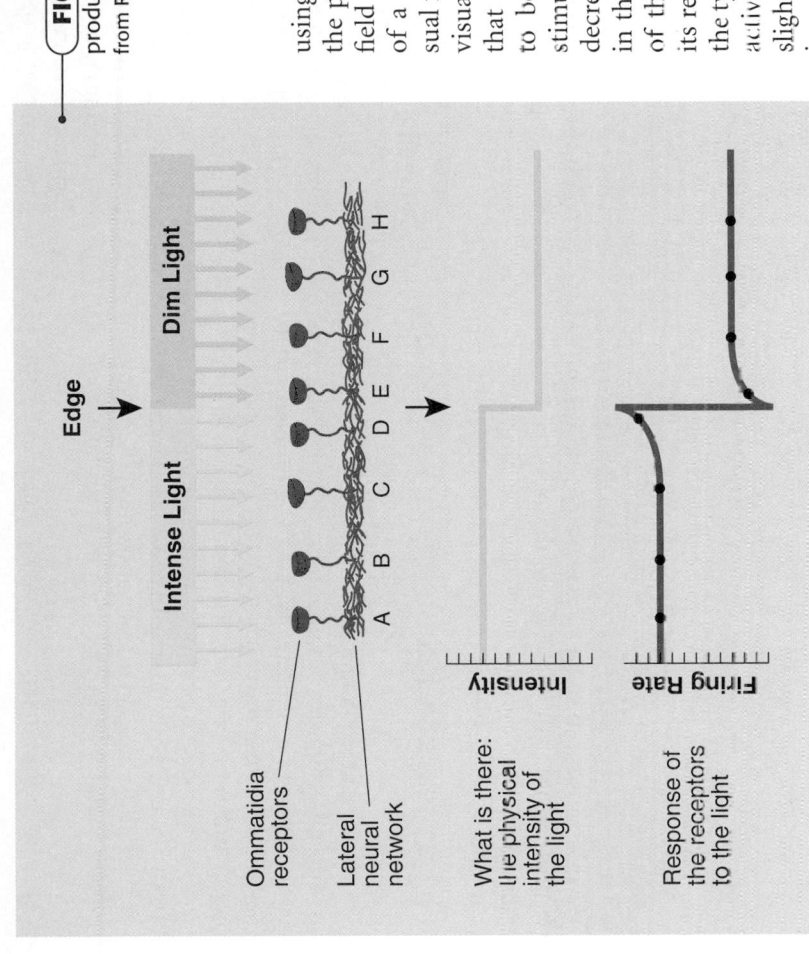

FIGURE 6.15 How lateral inhibition produces contrast enhancement. (Adapted from Ratliff, 1972.)

its neighbors, many of whom are on the dimmer side of the edge. Now consider the receptors on the dimmer side. Receptors F, G, and H fire at the same rate, because they are all being stimulated by the same low level of light and receiving the same low level of inhibition from their neighbors. However, receptor E fires even less, because it is receiving the same excitation but more inhibition from its neighbors, many of which are on the more intense side of the edge. Now that you understand the neural basis of contrast enhancement, take another look at Figure 6.14.

Receptive Fields of Visual Neurons

The Nobel Prize–winning research of David Hubel and Torsten Wiesel is the fitting climax to this discussion of brightness contrast. Their research has revealed much about the neural mechanisms of vision, and their methods have been adopted by a generation of sensory neurophysiologists. Hubel and Wiesel's subjects are single neurons in the visual systems of cats and monkeys; because it is invasive, their technique cannot be employed on human subjects.

First, the tip of a microelectrode is positioned near a single neuron in the visual area of interest. During testing, eye movements are blocked by *curare* (see Chapter 4), and the images on a screen in front of the subject are focused sharply on the retina by an experimenter using an adjustable lens. The next step in the procedure is to identify the receptive field of the neuron. The **receptive field** of a visual neuron is the area of the visual field within which it is possible for a visual stimulus to influence the firing of that neuron. Visual system neurons tend to be continually active; thus, effective stimuli are those that either increase or decrease the rate of firing. The final step in the method is to record the responses of the neuron to various stimuli within its receptive field in order to characterize the types of stimuli that most influence its activity. Then, the electrode is advanced slightly, and the entire process of identifying and characterizing the receptive field properties is repeated for another neuron, and then for another, and another, and so on. The general strategy is to begin by studying neurons near the receptors and gradually working up through "higher" and "higher" levels of the system in an effort to understand the increasing complexity of the neural responses at each level.

Receptive Fields: Neurons of the Retina–Geniculate–Striate System

Hubel and Wiesel (e.g., 1979) began their studies of visual system neurons by recording from the three levels of the retina-geniculate-striate system: first from retinal ganglion cells, then from lateral geniculate neurons, and finally from the striate neurons of lower layer IV, the terminus of the system. They found little change in the receptive fields as they worked their way along the left and right pathways.

When Hubel and Wiesel compared the receptive fields recorded from retinal ganglion cells, lateral geniculate nuclei, and lower layer IV neurons, four commonalities were readily apparent. First, at each level, the receptive fields in the foveal area of the retina were smaller than those at the periphery; this is consistent with the fact that the fovea mediates fine-grained (high-acuity) vision. Second, all the neurons (retinal ganglion cells, lateral geniculate neurons, and lower layer IV neurons) had receptive fields that were circular. Third, all the neurons were **monocular;** that is, each neuron had a receptive field in one eye but not the

ON THE CD

The *How the Receptive Fields of Visual Systems Neurons Are Studied* module is definitely worth a visit.

Evolutionary Perspective

other. And fourth, many neurons at each of the three levels of the retina-geniculate-striate system had receptive fields that comprised an excitatory area and an inhibitory area separated by a circular boundary. It is this fourth point that is most important and most complex. Let me explain.

When Hubel and Wiesel shone a spot of white light onto the various parts of the receptive fields of neurons in the retina-geniculate-striate pathway, they discovered two different responses. The neuron responded with either "on" firing or "off" firing, depending on the location of the spot of light in the receptive field. That is, the neuron either displayed a burst of firing when the light was turned on ("on" firing), or it displayed an inhibition of firing when the light was turned on and a burst of firing when it was turned off ("off" firing).

For most neurons in the retina-geniculate-striate system, their reaction—"on" firing or "off" firing—to a light in a particular part of the receptive field was quite predictable. It depended on whether they were on-center or off-center cells, as illustrated in Figure 6.16.

On-center cells respond to lights shone in the central region of their receptive fields with "on" firing and to lights shone in the periphery of their receptive fields with inhibition, followed by "off" firing when the light is turned off. **Off-center cells** display the opposite pattern: They respond with inhibition and "off" firing in response to lights in the center of their receptive fields and with "on" firing to lights in the periphery of their receptive fields.

In effect, on-center and off-center cells respond best to contrast. Figure 6.17 illustrates this point. The most effective way to influence the firing rate of an on-center or off-center cell is to maximize the contrast between the center and the periphery of its receptive field by illuminating either the entire center or the entire surround (periphery), while leaving the other region completely dark. Diffusely illuminating the entire receptive field has little effect on firing. Hubel and Wiesel thus concluded that one function of many neurons in the retina-geniculate-striate system is to respond to the degree of brightness contrast between the two areas

FIGURE 6.16   The receptive fields of an on-center cell and an off-center cell.

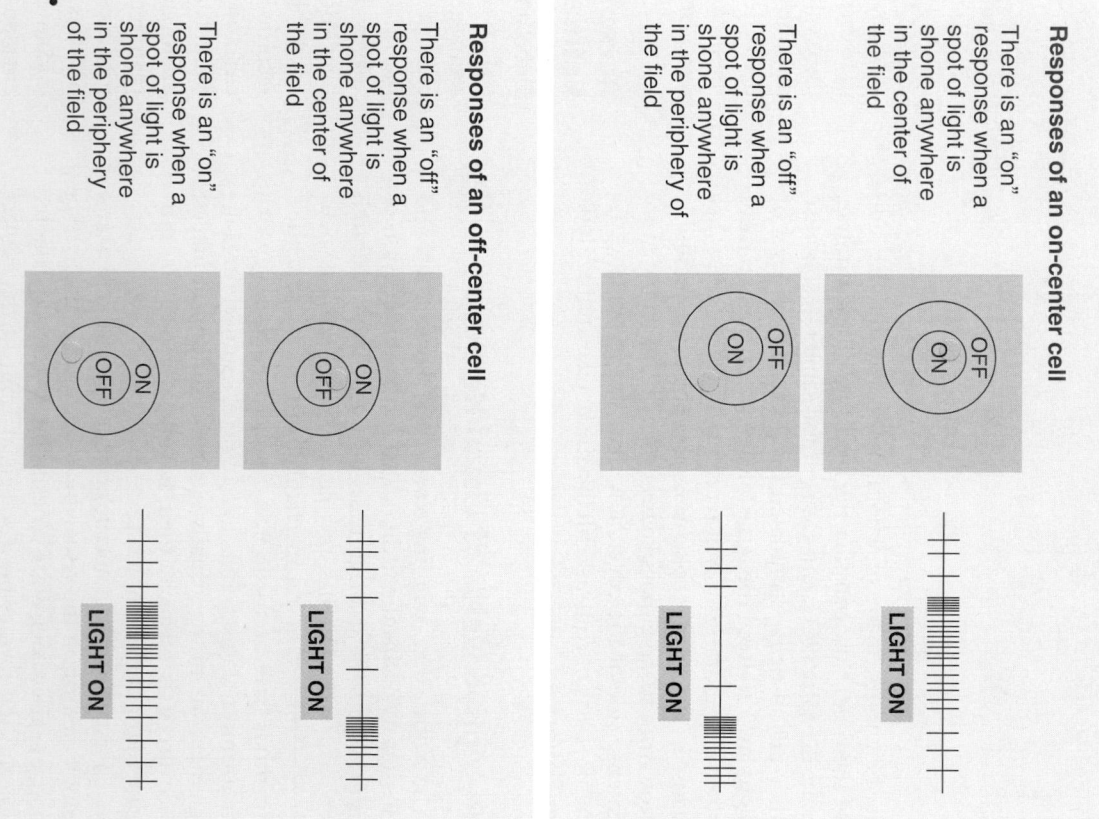

Responses of an on-center cell

There is an "on" response when a spot of light is shone anywhere in the center of the field

There is an "off" response when a spot of light is shone anywhere in the periphery of the field

LIGHT ON

Responses of an off-center cell

There is an "off" response when a spot of light is shone anywhere in the center of the field

There is an "on" response when a spot of light is shone anywhere in the periphery of the field

LIGHT ON

of their receptive fields (see Livingstone & Hubel, 1988).

Before leaving Figures 6.16 and 6.17, notice one important thing about visual system neurons: Most are continually active, even when there is no visual input (Tsodyks et al., 1999). Indeed, spontaneous activity is a characteristic of most cerebral neurons. Arieli and colleagues (1996) have shown that the level of activity of visual cortical neurons at the time that a visual stimulus is presented influences how the cells respond to the stimulus—this may be the means by which cognition influences perception.

Receptive Fields: Simple Cortical Cells

The striate cortex neurons that you just read about—that is, the neurons of lower layer IV—are exceptions. Their receptive fields are unlike those of the vast majority of striate neurons. The receptive fields of most primary visual cortex neurons fall into one of two classes: simple or

of a particular orientation regardless of its position within the receptive field of that cell. Thus, if a stimulus (e.g., a 45° bar of light) that produces "on" firing in a particular complex cell is swept across its receptive field, the cell will respond continuously to it as it moves across the field. Many complex cells respond more robustly to the movement of a straight line across their receptive fields in a particular direction. Third, unlike simple cortical cells, which are all monocular (respond to stimulation of only one of the eyes), many complex cells are **binocular** (respond to stimulation of either eye). Indeed, in monkeys, over half the complex cortical cells are binocular.

If the receptive field of a binocular complex cell is measured through one eye and then through the other, the receptive fields in each eye turn out to have almost exactly the same position in the visual field, as well as the same orientation preference. In other words, what you learn about the cell by stimulating one eye is confirmed by stimulating the other. What is more, if the appropriate stimulation is applied through both eyes simultaneously, a binocular cell usually fires more robustly than if only one eye is stimulated.

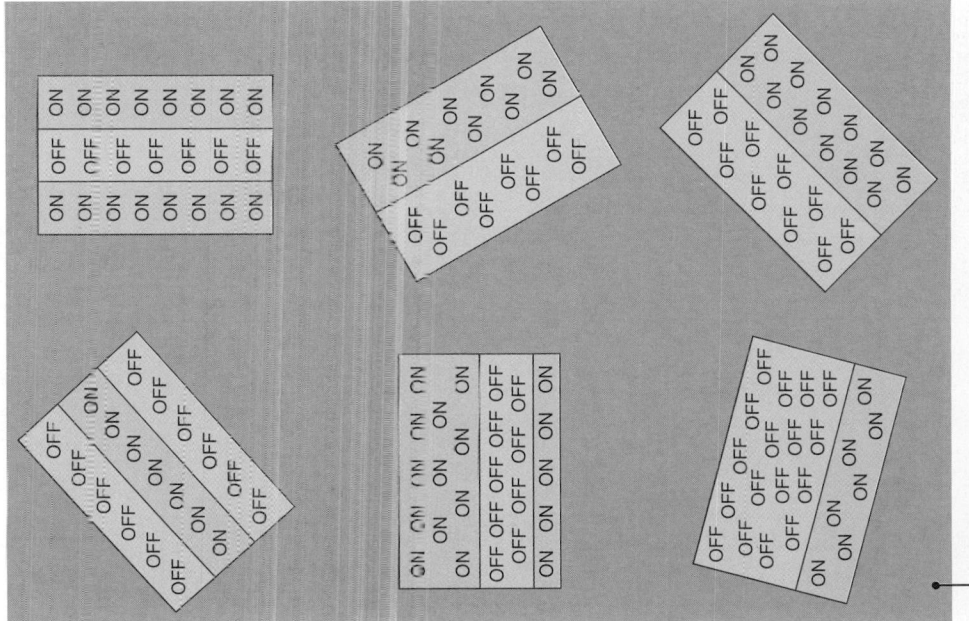

FIGURE 6.18 Examples of visual fields of simple cortical cells.

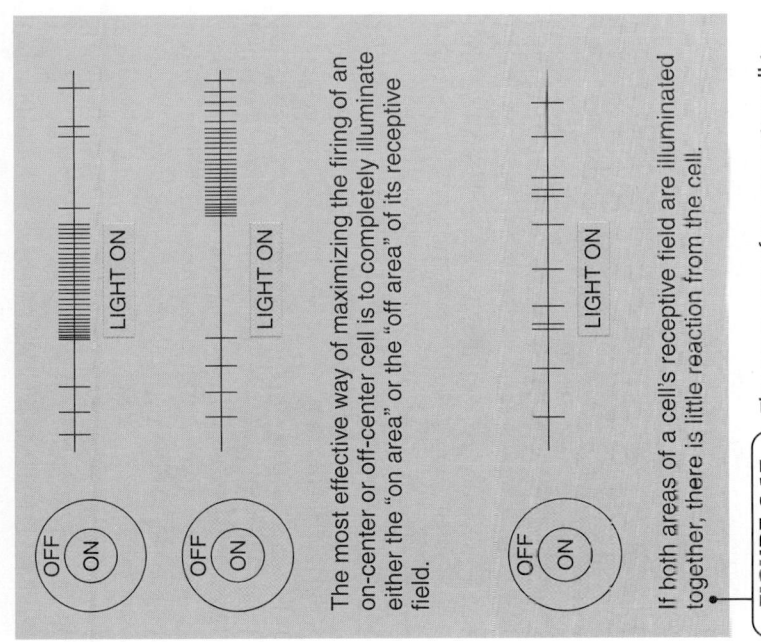

The most effective way of maximizing the firing of an on-center or off-center cell is to completely illuminate either the "on area" or the "off area" of its receptive field.

If both areas of a cell's receptive field are illuminated together, there is little reaction from the cell.

FIGURE 6.17 The responses of an on-center cell to contrast.

complex. Neither of these classes includes the neurons of lower layer IV.

Simple cells, like lower layer IV neurons, have receptive fields that can be divided into antagonistic "on" and "off" regions and are thus unresponsive to diffuse light. And like lower layer IV neurons, they are all monocular. The main difference is that the borders between the "on" and "off" regions of the cortical receptive fields of simple cells are straight lines rather than circles. Several examples of receptive fields of simple cortical cells are presented in Figure 6.18. Notice that simple cells respond best to bars of light in a dark field, dark bars in a light field, or single straight edges between dark and light areas; that each simple cell responds maximally only when its preferred straight-edge stimulus is in a particular position and in a particular orientation; and that the receptive fields of simple cortical cells are rectangular rather than circular.

Receptive Fields: Complex Cortical Cells

Complex cells are more numerous than simple cells. Like simple cells, complex cells have rectangular receptive fields, respond best to straight-line stimuli in a specific orientation, and are unresponsive to diffuse light. However, complex cells differ from simple cells in three important ways. First, they have larger receptive fields. Second, it is not possible to divide the receptive fields of complex cells into static "on" and "off" regions: A complex cell responds to a particular straight-edge stimulus

Most of the binocular cells in the primary cortex of monkeys display some degree of *ocular dominance*; that is, they respond more robustly to stimulation of one eye than they do to the same stimulation of the other. In addition, some binocular cells fire best when the preferred stimulus is presented to both eyes at the same time but in slightly different positions on the two retinas (e.g., Ohzawa, 1998). In other words, these cells respond best to *retinal disparity* and thus are likely to play a role in depth perception (e.g., Livingstone & Tsao, 1999).

Columnar Organization of Primary Visual Cortex

The study of the receptive fields of primary visual cortex neurons has led to two important conclusions. The first conclusion is that the characteristics of the receptive fields of visual cortex neurons are attributable to the flow of signals from neurons with simpler receptive fields to those with more complex fields (see Reid & Alonso, 1996). Specifically, it seems that signals flow from on-center and off-center cells in lower layer IV to simple cells and from simple cells to complex cells.

The second conclusion is that primary visual cortex neurons are grouped in functional vertical columns (in this context, *vertical* means at right angles to the cortical layers). Much of the evidence for this conclusion comes from studies of the receptive fields of neurons along various vertical and horizontal electrode tracks (see Figure 6.19). If an electrode is advanced vertically through the layers of the visual cortex, with stops to plot the receptive fields of many neurons along the way, the results show that each cell in the column has a receptive field in the same area of the visual field. In addition, all the cells in

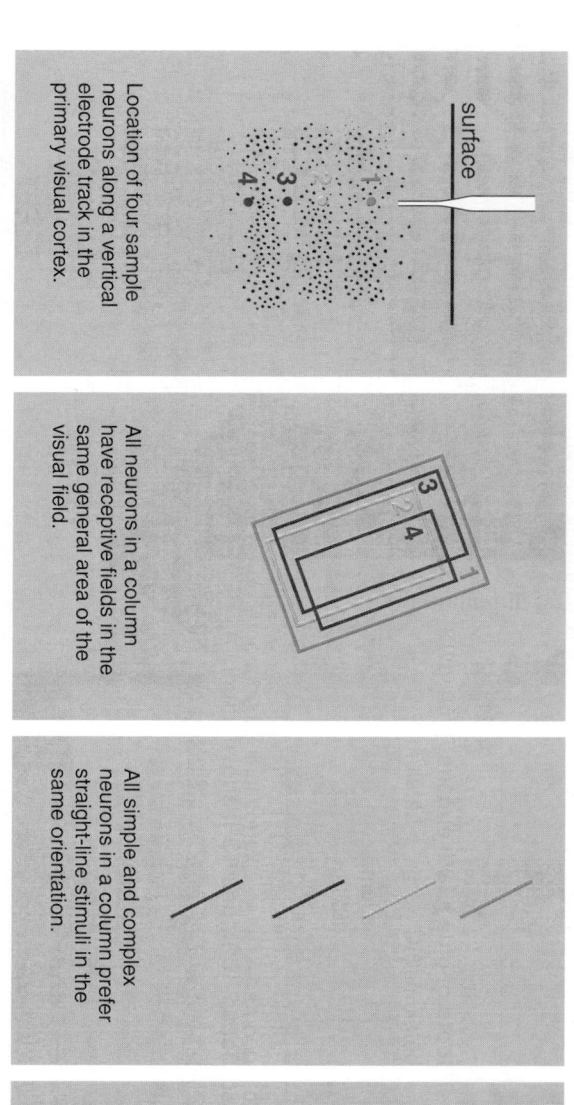

surface

Location of four sample neurons along a vertical electrode track in the primary visual cortex.

All neurons in a column have receptive fields in the same general area of the visual field.

All simple and complex neurons in a column prefer straight-line stimuli in the same orientation.

1 right-eye dominant

2 right-eye dominant

3 right-eye dominant

4 right-eye dominant

In a given column, all monocular neurons and all binocular neurons that display ocular dominance are dominated by the same eye.

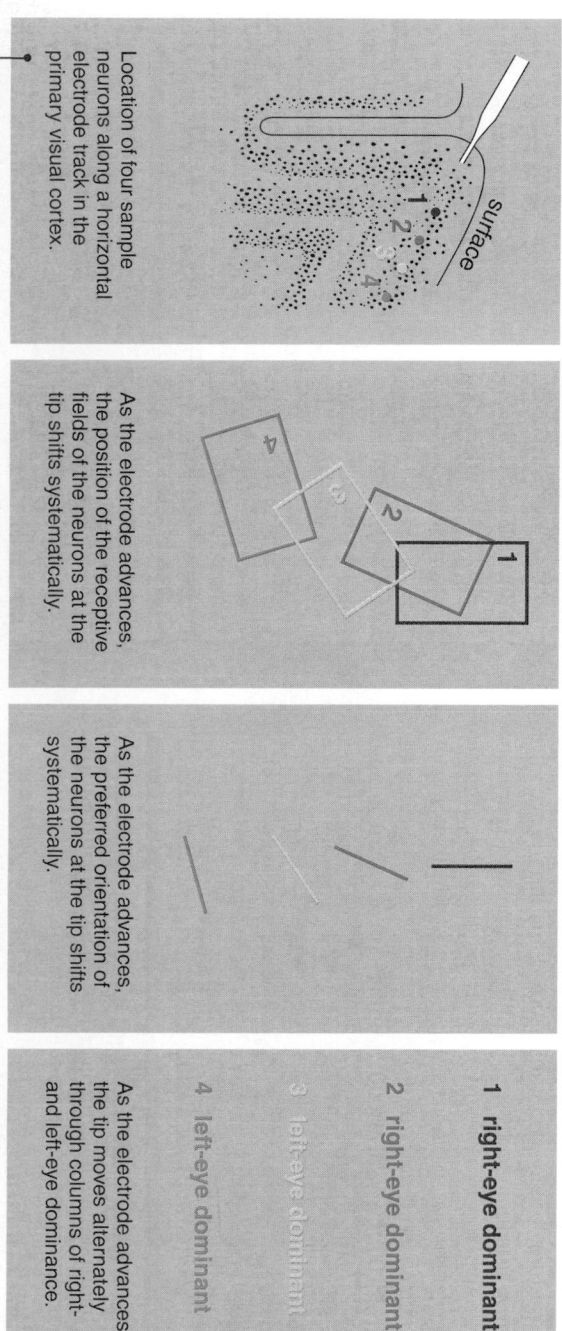

surface

Location of four sample neurons along a horizontal electrode track in the primary visual cortex.

As the electrode advances, the position of the receptive fields of the neurons at the tip shifts systematically.

As the electrode advances, the preferred orientation of the neurons at the tip shifts systematically.

1 right-eye dominant

2 right-eye dominant

3 left-eye dominant

4 left-eye dominant

As the electrode advances, the tip moves alternately through columns of right- and left-eye dominance.

FIGURE 6.19 The organization of the primary visual cortex: The receptive-field properties of cells encountered along typical vertical and horizontal electrode tracks in the primary visual cortex.

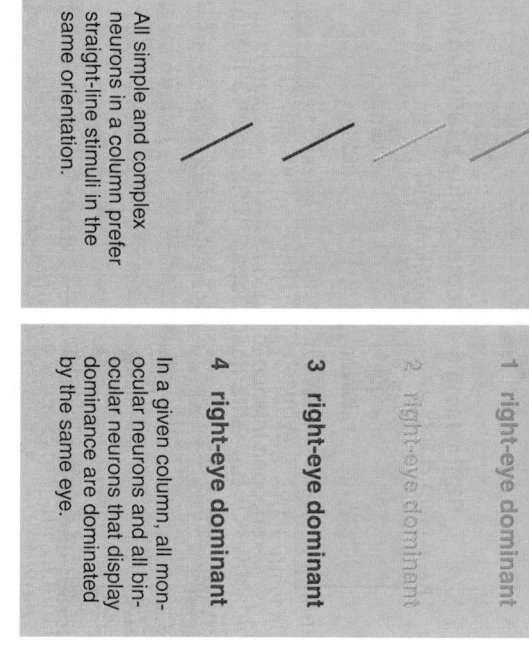

a column respond best to straight lines in the very same orientation, and those neurons in a column that are either monocular or binocular with ocular dominance are all most sensitive to light in the same eye, left or right.

In contrast, if an electrode is advanced horizontally through the tissue of the primary visual cortex, each successive cell encountered is likely to have a receptive field in a slightly different location and to be maximally responsive to straight lines of a slightly different orientation. And during a horizontal electrode pass, the tip passes alternately through areas of left-eye dominance and right-eye dominance—commonly referred to as *ocular dominance columns.*

All of the functional columns in the primary visual cortex that analyze input from one area of the retina are

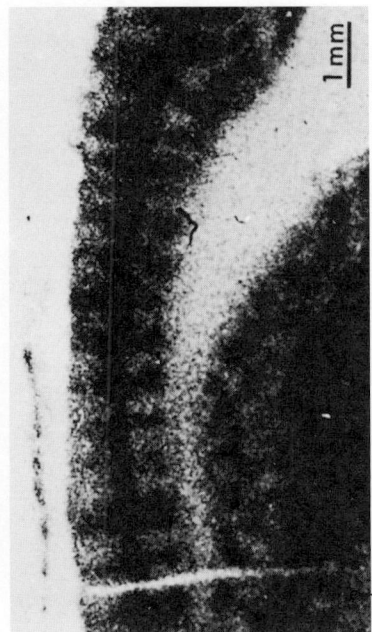

clustered together. Half of a cluster receives input primarily from the left eye, and half receives input primar-

Cognitive Neuroscience

ily from the right eye. Indeed, input from the eyes has been found to enter layer IV in alternating patches. The best kind of evidence of this alternating arrangement first came from a study (LeVay, Hubel, & Wiesel, 1975) in which a radioactive amino acid was injected into one eye in sufficient quantities to cross the synapses of the retina-geniculate-striate system and show up in lower layer IV of the primary visual cortex, and to a lesser degree in the layers just above and below it. The alternating patches of radioactivity and nonradioactivity in the autoradiograph in Figure 6.20 mark the alternating patches of input from the two eyes.

All of the clusters of functional columns that analyze input from one area of the retina are thought to include neurons with preferences for straight-line stimuli of various orientations. The columns of orientation specificity were visualized in a study (Hubel, Wiesel, &

Stryker, 1977) in which radioactive 2-DG was injected into monkeys that then spent 45 minutes viewing a pattern of vertical stripes moving back and forth. As you know from Chapter 5, radioactive 2-DG is taken up by active neurons and accumulates in them, thus identifying the location of neurons that are particularly active during the test period. The autoradiograph in Figure 6.21 reveals the columns of cells in the primary visual cortex that were activated by exposure to the moving vertical stripes. Notice that the neurons in lower layer IV show no orientation specificity—because they do not respond to straight-line stimuli. High-powered MRI techniques have been developed for visualizing columns of orientation specificity in human subjects (Kim, Duong, & Kim, 2000).

Figure 6.22 on page 148 summarizes Hubel and Wiesel's theory of how the vertical columns of the primary visual cortex are organized (see Martinez & Alonso, 2003).

Spatial-Frequency Theory

Hubel and Wiesel barely had time to place their Nobel Prize medals on their mantels before an important qualification to their theory was proposed. DeValois, DeValois, and their colleagues (see DeValois & DeValois, 1988) proposed that the visual cortex operates on a code of spatial frequency, not on the code of straight lines and edges hypothesized by Hubel and Wiesel.

In support of the **spatial-frequency theory** is the observation that visual cortex neurons respond even more robustly to sine-wave gratings that are placed at specific angles in their receptive fields than they do to bars or edges. A **sine-wave grating** is a set of equally spaced, parallel, alternating light and dark stripes that is created by varying the light across the grating in a

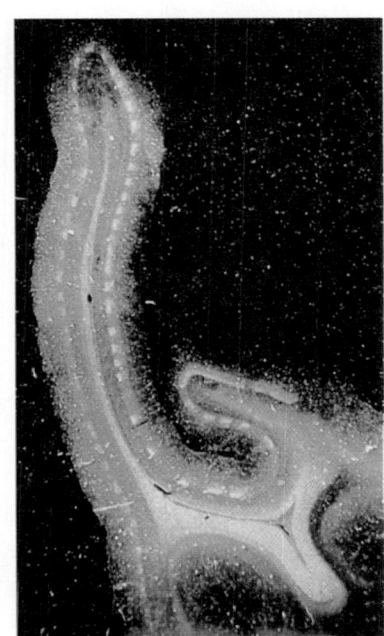

FIGURE 6.20 The alternation of input into lower layer IV of the primary visual cortex from the left and right eyes. Radioactive amino acids that were injected into one eye were subsequently revealed on autoradiographs of the visual cortex as patches of radioactivity alternating with patches of nonradioactivity. (From "Brain Mechanisms of Vision" by D. H. Hubel and T. N. Wiesel. Reprinted by permission of *Scientific American,* vol. 241, p. 151. Copyright © 1979 by Scientific American, Inc.)

FIGURE 6.21 The columns of orientation specificity in the primary visual cortex of a monkey as revealed by 2-DG autoradiography. (From "Orientation Columns in Macaque Monkey Visual Cortex Demonstrated by the 2-Deoxyglucose Autoradiographic Technique" by D. H. Hubel, T. N. Wiesel, and M. P. Stryker. Reprinted by permission from *Nature,* vol. 269, p. 329. Copyright © 1977 by Macmillan Magazines Ltd.)

1 mm

A block of tissue such as this is assumed to analyze visual signals from one area of the visual field.

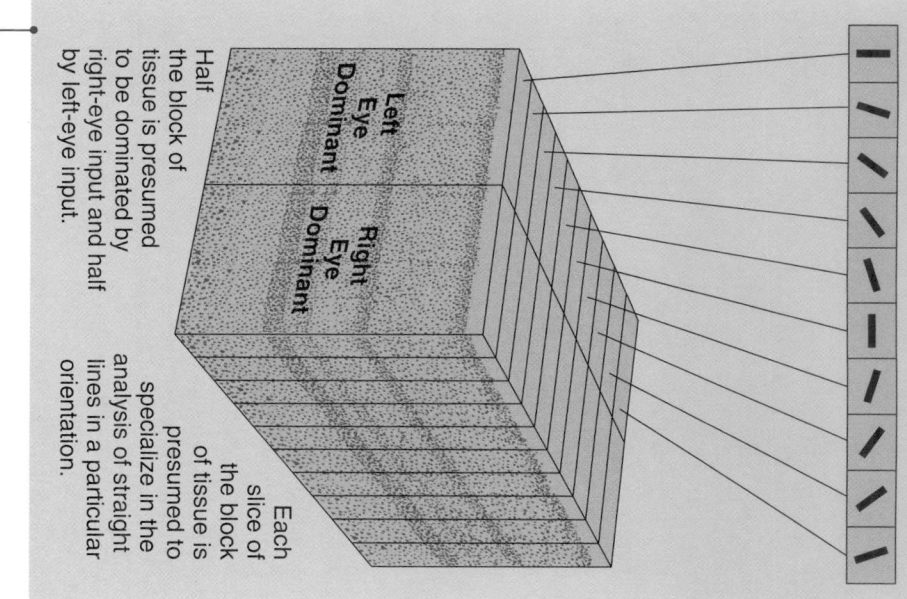

FIGURE 6.22 Hubel and Wiesel's model of the organization of functional columns in the primary visual cortex.

Left Eye Dominant

Right Eye Dominant

Half the block of tissue is presumed to be dominated by right-eye input and half by left-eye input.

Each slice of the block of tissue is presumed to specialize in the analysis of straight lines in a particular orientation.

Intensity of light across the gradient

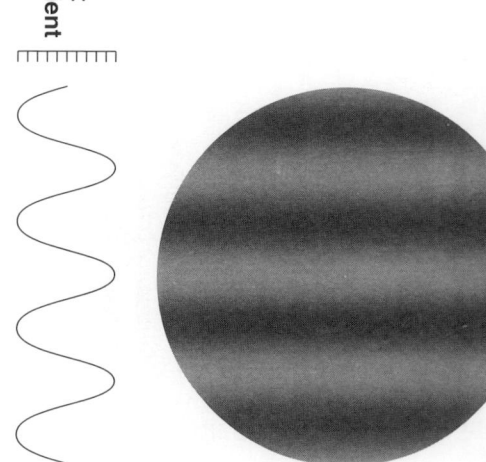

FIGURE 6.23 A sine-wave grating. (Adapted from DeValois & DeValois, 1988.)

sine-wave pattern—see Figure 6.23. Sine-wave gratings differ from one another in frequency (the width of their stripes), amplitude (the magnitude of the difference in intensity between the dark and light stripes), and angle.

The spatial-frequency theory is based on two physical principles. The first is that any visual stimulus can be represented by a plotting of the intensity of light along lines running through it (see Figure 6.24). The second is that any curve, no matter how irregular, can be broken down into constituent sine waves by a mathematical procedure called **Fourier analysis** (see Figure 6.25).

The spatial-frequency theory of visual cortex function (see DeValois & DeValois, 1988) is that each functional module of the visual cortex performs a sort of

FIGURE 6.24 A visual stimulus represented by the plotting of changes in the intensity of light along slices running through it. For example, plotted here are the changes in intensity along one slice of a scene that would interest any hungry lion.

Intensity

Low

High

lar location of the visual field (see Issa, Trepel, & Stryker, 2000). However, straight-edge stimuli, which have been used in most studies of visual cortex neurons, can readily be translated into component sine-wave gratings of the same orientation. Thus, the research on spatial-frequency detection by visual neurons extends and complements previous research rather than refuting it.

This is a good point in the chapter to reconsider the case of Mrs. Richards, the woman who sketched her premigraine fortification illusions so that her husband could study them. Now that you have learned some of the fundamentals of visual system organization and function, you are in a better position to understand Mrs. Richards's symptoms.

Clinical Implications

The Case of Mrs. Richards, Revisited

There was obviously a disturbance in Mrs. Richards's visual system: But where? And what kind of disturbance? And why the straight lines? A simple test located the disturbance. Mrs. Richards was asked to shut one eye and then the other and to report what happened to her illusion. The answer was, "Nothing." This suggested that the disturbance was cortical, because the visual cortex is the first part of the retina-geniculate-striate system that contains neurons that receive input from both eyes.

This hypothesis was confirmed by a few simple calculations: The gradual acceleration of the illusion as it spread out to the periphery is consistent with a wave of disturbance expanding from the "foveal area" of the primary visual cortex to its boundaries at a constant rate of about 3 millimeters per minute—the illusion accelerated because proportionally less visual cortex is dedicated to receiving signals from the periphery of the visual field.

And why the lines? Would you expect anything else from an area of the cortex whose elements appear to be specialized for coding straight-line stimuli?

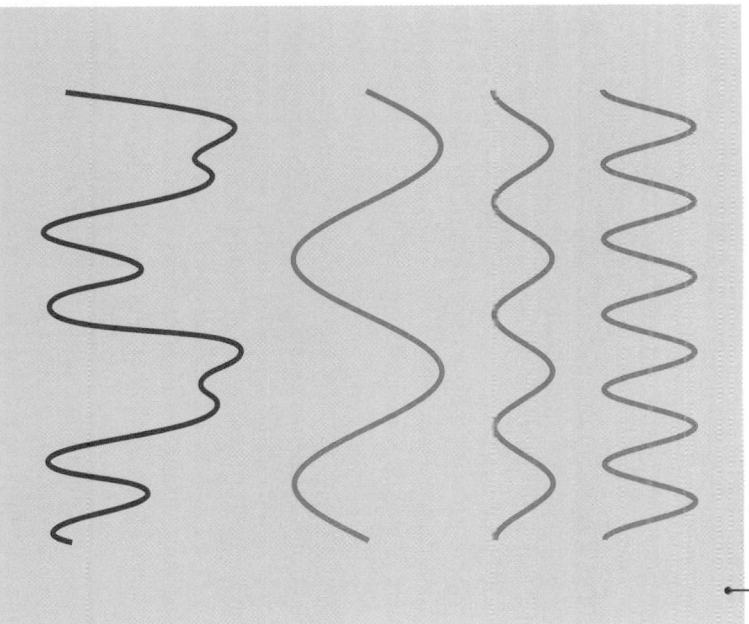

FIGURE 6.25 Any wave can be broken down into component sine waves by Fourier analysis. For example, the complex wave at the top is the sum of the sine waves shown beneath it. (Adapted from DeValois & DeValois, 1988.)

Fourier analysis on the visual pattern in its receptive field; the neurons in each module are thought to respond selectively to various frequencies and orientations of sine-wave gratings. When all of the visual cortex neurons that are influenced by a particular scene respond together, a perception of the scene is created by the summation of its various constituent sine-wave gratings.

As I said before, the primary support for the spatial-frequency theory is that primary visual cortex neurons are more responsive to sine-wave gratings than they are to straight lines. Most neurons in the primary visual cortex respond best when a sine-wave grating of a particular frequency is presented at a particular angle in a particu-

6.5 Seeing Color

Color is one of the most obvious qualities of human visual experience. So far in this chapter, we have largely limited our discussion of vision to the so-called **achromatic colors:** black, white, and gray. Black is experienced when there is an absence of light, the perception of white is produced by an intense mixture of a wide range of wavelengths in roughly equal proportion, and the perception of gray is produced by the same mixture at lower

intensities. In this section, we deal with the perception of **chromatic colors**—colors such as blue, green, and yellow. The correct term for chromatic colors is *hues*, but in everyday language they are referred to as colors; and for the sake of simplicity, I will do the same.

What is there about a visual stimulus that determines the color we perceive? To a large degree, the perception of an object's color depends on the wavelengths of light that it reflects into the eye. Figure 6.2 is an illustration of the colors associated with individual wavelengths; however, outside the laboratory, one never encounters objects that reflect single wavelengths. Sunlight and most sources of artificial light contain complex mixtures of most visible wavelengths. Most objects absorb the different wavelengths of light that strike them to varying degrees and reflect the rest. The mixture of wavelengths that objects reflect influences our perception of their color.

With the development and refinement of methods for studying the responses of individual receptors and neurons in the visual system, an impressive amount has been learned in the last four decades about how the visual system responds to different wavelengths. However, in some ways, it is even more impressive that the basic mechanisms of color vision were derived in the 19th century by behavioral scientists whose research technology was limited to their own ingenuity and observational skills. Through careful observation of the perceptual abilities of their subjects, these scientists were able to infer some of the major features of the physiological basis of color vision.

Component and Opponent Processing

The **component theory** (trichromatic theory) of color vision was proposed by Thomas Young in 1802 and refined by Hermann von Helmholtz in 1852. According to this theory, there are three different kinds of color receptors (cones), each with a different spectral sensitivity, and the color of a particular stimulus is presumed to be encoded by the ratio of activity in the three kinds of receptors. Young and Helmholtz derived their theory from the observation that any color of the visible spectrum can be matched by a mixing together of three different wavelengths of light in different proportions. This can be accomplished with any three wavelengths, provided that the color of any one of them cannot be matched by a mixing of the other two. The fact that three is normally the minimum number of different wavelengths necessary to match every color suggested that there were three types of receptors.

Another theory of color vision, the **opponent-process theory** of color vision, was proposed by Ewald Hering in 1878. He suggested that there are two different classes of cells in the visual system for encoding color and another class for encoding brightness. Hering hypothesized that each of the three classes of cells encoded two complementary color perceptions. One class of color-coding cells signaled red by changing its activity in one direction (e.g., hyperpolarization) and signaled red's complementary color, green, by changing its activity in the other direction (e.g., hypopolarization). Another class of color-coding cells was hypothesized to signal blue and its complement, yellow, in the same opponent fashion; and a class of brightness-coding

cells was hypothesized to similarly signal both black and white. **Complementary colors** are pairs of colors that produce white or gray when combined in equal measure (e.g., green light and red light).

Hering based his opponent-process theory of color vision on several behavioral observations. One was that complementary colors cannot exist together: There is no such thing as bluish yellow or reddish green. Another was that the afterimage produced by staring at red is green and vice versa, and the afterimage produced by staring at yellow is blue and vice versa (see the following demonstration).

A somewhat misguided debate raged for many years between supporters of the component (trichromatic) and opponent theories of color vision. I say "misguided" because it was fueled more by the adversarial predisposition of scientists than by the incompatibility of the two theories. In fact, research subsequently proved that both color-coding mechanisms coexist in our visual systems (see DeValois et al., 2000).

It was the development in the early 1960s of **microspectrophotometry**—a technique for measuring the absorption spectrum of the photopigment contained in a single cone—that allowed researchers (e.g., Wald, 1964) to confirm the conclusion that had been reached by Young over a century and a half before. They found that there are indeed three different kinds of cones in the retinas of those vertebrates with good color vision, and they found that each of the three has a different photopigment with its own characteristic absorption spectrum. As Figure 6.26 illustrates, some cones are most sensitive to short wavelengths, some are most sensitive

Demonstration

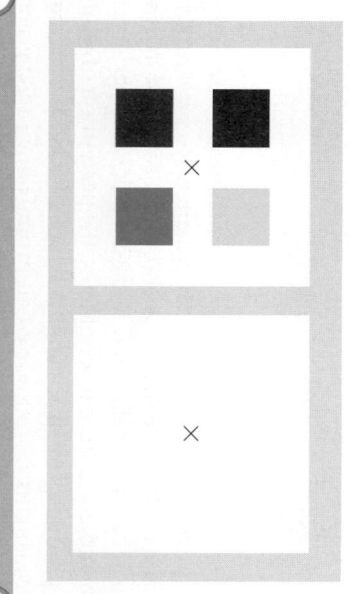

Have you ever noticed complementary afterimages? To see them, stare at the fixation point in the left panel for 1 minute without moving your eyes; then quickly shift your gaze to the fixation point in the right panel. In the right panel, you will see four squares whose colors are complementary to those in the left panel.

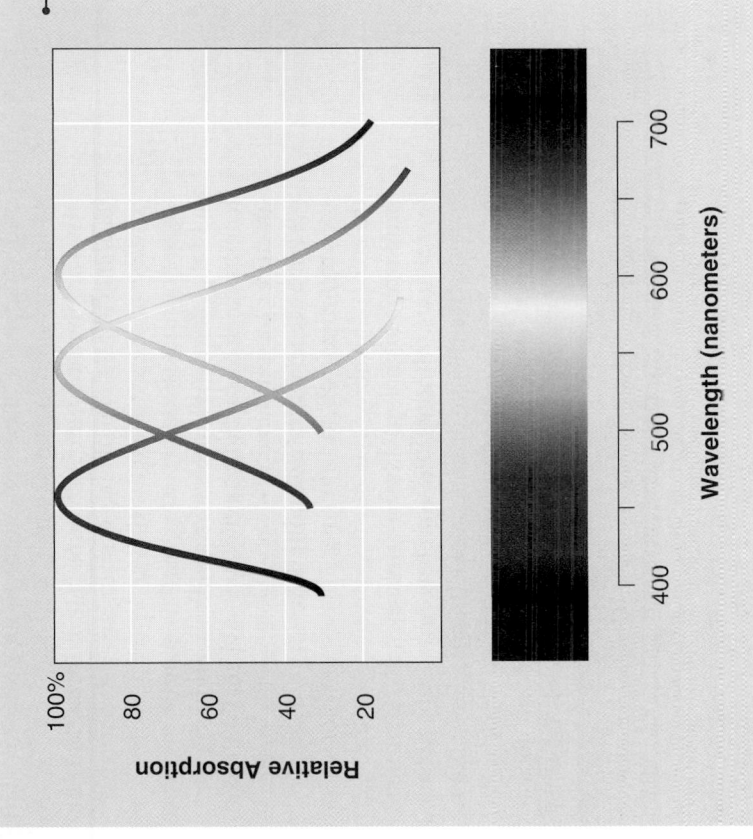

FIGURE 6.26 The absorption spectra of the three classes of cones.

to medium wavelengths, and some are most sensitive to long wavelengths.

Although the coding of color by cones seems to operate on a purely component basis (see Jameson, Highnote, & Wasserman, 2001), there is evidence of opponent processing of color at all subsequent levels of the retina-geniculate-striate system. That is, at all subsequent levels, there are cells that respond in one direction (e.g., increased firing) to one color and in the opposite direction (e.g., decreased firing) to its complementary color (see Chatterjee & Callaway, 2003; Gegenfurtner & Kiper, 2003).

Color Constancy and the Retinex Theory

Neither component nor opponent processing can account for the single most important characteristic of color vision: color constancy. **Color constancy** refers to the fact that the perceived color of an object is not a simple function of the wavelengths reflected by it.

As I write this at 7:15 on a December morning, it is dark outside, and I am working in my office by the light of a tiny incandescent desk lamp. Later in the morning, when students start to arrive, I turn on my nasty fluorescent office lights; and then, in the afternoon, when the sun has shifted to my side of the building, I turn off the lights and work by natural light. The point is that because these light sources differ markedly in the wavelengths they contain, the wavelengths reflected by vari-

ous objects in my office—my blue shirt, for example—change substantially during the course of the day. However, although the wavelengths reflected by my shirt change markedly, its color does not. My shirt will be just as blue in midmorning and in late afternoon as it is now. Color constancy is the tendency for an object to stay the same color despite major changes in the wavelengths of light that it reflects.

Although the phenomenon of color constancy is counterintuitive, its advantage is obvious. Color constancy improves our ability to tell objects apart in a memorable way so that we can respond appropriately to them; our ability to recognize objects would be greatly lessened if their color changed every time there was a change in illumination. In essence, if it were not for color constancy, color vision would have little survival value.

Although color constancy is an important feature of our vision, we are normally unaware of it. Under everyday conditions, we have no way of appreciating just how much the wavelengths reflected by an object can change without the object changing its color. It is only in the controlled environment of the laboratory that one can fully appreciate that color constancy is more than an important factor in color vision: It is the essence of color vision.

Edwin Land (1977), the inventor of the Polaroid camera, developed several dramatic laboratory demonstrations of color constancy. The following is one of them. First, Land asked subjects to adjust the intensity of light coming from each of three different projectors until they judged the mixture to be a pure white when viewed in an otherwise dark room. Each projector emitted only one wavelength of light: one a short-wavelength light, one a medium-wavelength light, and one a long-wavelength light. Next, Land shone the three projectors on a test display like the one in Figure 6.27 on page 152. (These displays are called *Mondrians* because they resemble the paintings of the Dutch master painter Piet Mondrian.) Land himself adjusted the three projectors so that the mixture of the three that was being reflected from one particular area of the Mondrian—let's say the blue rectangular shape—was the exact mixture that had been judged as white by subjects in the first stage of the demonstration. To accomplish this, Land used a

Evolutionary Perspective

Thinking Critically

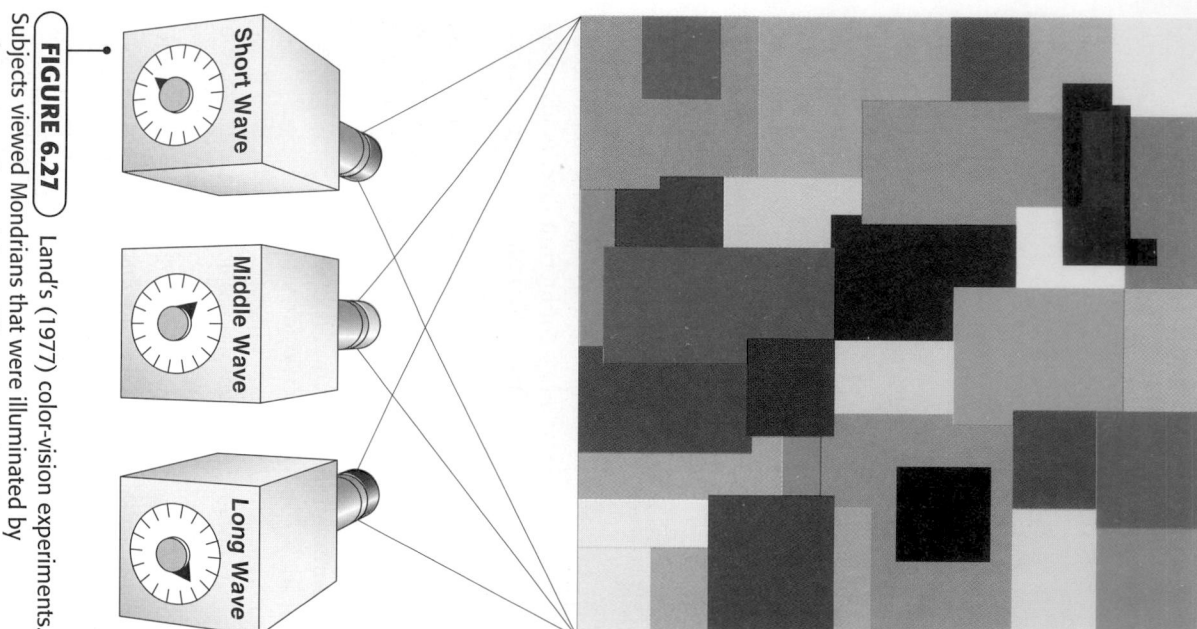

Short Wave **Middle Wave** **Long Wave**

FIGURE 6.27 Land's (1977) color-vision experiments. Subjects viewed Mondrians that were illuminated by various proportions of three different wavelengths: a short wavelength, a middle wavelength, and a long wavelength.

photometer to measure the amounts of the three wavelengths being reflected by the blue rectangle. Next, he repeated this process but this time for another area of the Mondrian—let's say the green rectangle—that is, he adjusted the three projectors until the mixture that had previously been judged as white was being reflected by the green rectangle.

What color was the blue rectangle when it was reflecting a pure white mixture of light, and what color was the green rectangle when it was reflecting the very same mixture of light? The answers to these questions astound many students: The blue rectangle appeared blue, and the green rectangle appeared green, even though they were reflecting the exact same mixture of white light. However, when the blue and green rectangles were viewed in isolation (not as part of a Mondrian)

under the same illumination but in an otherwise dark room, they both appeared white.

The point of Land's demonstration is that blue objects stay blue, green objects stay green, and so forth, regardless of the wavelengths they reflect. This color constancy occurs as long as the object is illuminated with light that contains some short, medium, and long wavelengths (such as daylight, firelight, and virtually all manufactured lighting) and as long as the object is viewed as part of a scene, not in isolation.

According to Land's **retinex theory** of color vision, the color of an object is determined by its *reflectance*—the proportion of light of different wavelengths that a surface reflects. Although the wavelengths of light reflected by a surface change dramatically with changes in illumination, the efficiency with which a surface absorbs each wavelength and reflects the unabsorbed portion does not change. According to the retinex theory, the visual system calculates the reflectance of surfaces, and thus perceives their colors, by comparing the light reflected by adjacent surfaces in at least three different wavelength bands (short, medium, and long)—see Hurlbert and Wolf (2004).

Why is Land's research so critical for neuroscientists trying to discover the neural mechanisms of color vision? It is important because it suggests one type of cortical neuron that is likely to be involved in color vision (see Shapely & Hawken, 2002). If the perception of color depends on the analysis of contrast between adjacent areas of the visual field, then the critical neurons should be responsive to color contrast (see Hurlbert, 2003). And they are. For example, **dual-opponent color cells** in the monkey visual cortex respond with vigorous "on" firing when the center of their circular receptive field is illuminated with one wavelength, such as green, and the surround (periphery) is simultaneously illuminated with another wavelength, such as red. And the same cells display vigorous "off" firing when the pattern of illumination is reversed—for example, red in the center and green in the surround. In essence, dual-opponent color cells respond to the contrast between wavelengths reflected by adjacent areas of their receptive field.

A major breakthrough in the understanding of the organization of the primary visual cortex came with the discovery that dual-opponent color cells are not distributed evenly throughout the primary visual cortex of monkeys (see Zeki, 1993a). Livingstone and Hubel (1984) found that these neurons are concentrated in the primary visual cortex in peglike columns that penetrate the layers of the monkey primary visual cortex, with the exception of lower layer IV. Many neurons in these peglike columns are particularly rich in the mitochondrial enzyme **cytochrome oxidase;** thus, their distribution in the primary visual cortex can be visualized if one stains slices of tissue with stains that have an affinity for this enzyme.

When a section of monkey striate tissue is cut parallel to the cortical layers and stained in this way, the

Evolutionary Perspective

pegs are seen as "blobs" of stain scattered over the cortex (unless the section is cut from lower layer IV). To the relief of instructors and students alike, the term **blobs** has become the accepted scientific label for peglike, cytochrome oxidase–rich, dual-opponent color columns. The blobs were found to be located in the middle of ocular dominance columns (see Figure 6.28, and compare it with Figure 6.22). Functional MRI studies have provided evidence of dual-opponent color cells in the human visual cortex (Engel, 1999).

A key goal of this chapter was to help you understand that vision is a creative process. The retina-geniculate-striate system does not conduct intact visual images to the cortex. It conducts information about a few critical features of the visual field—for example, information about location, movement, brightness contrast, and color contrast—and from these bits of information, it creates a perception that is better than the retinal image in all respects and better than the external reality in some. The study of the visual system is arguably the best example of the use of converging operations in biopsychology—significant insights into the neural bases of psychological processes have resulted from the convergence of neuroanatomical, neurochemical, neurophysiological, and behavioral research.

In this chapter, there were opportunities for you to experience firsthand the important principles of the

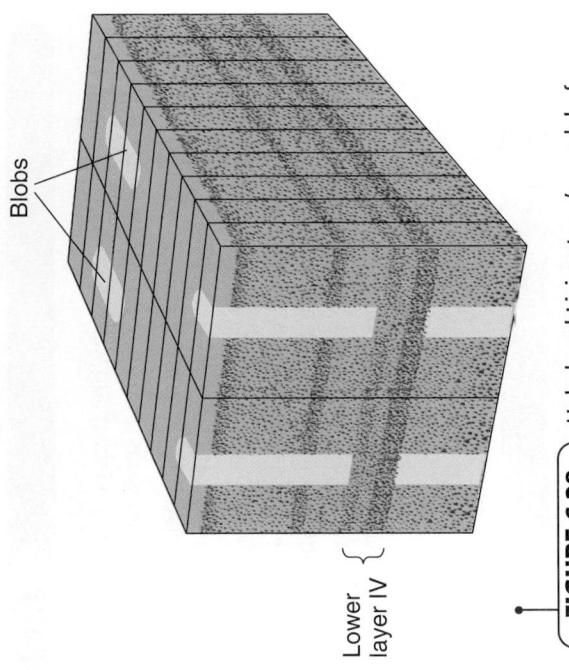

Blobs

Lower
layer IV }

FIGURE 6.28 Hubel and Livingstone's model of primary visual cortex organization. The blobs are peglike columns that contain dual-opponent color cells.

visual process. I hope these demonstrations made you more aware of the amazing abilities of your own visual system and the relevance of what you have learned in this chapter to your everyday life.

Themes Revisited

All four major themes of this book were developed in this chapter, but two of them—the evolutionary perspective and thinking about biopsychology—predominated. The evolutionary perspective theme was emphasized for two reasons: because the vast majority of research on the neural mechanisms of human vision is comparative, and because evolutionary analyses have been important in developing an appreciation of the key roles played by edge perception and color constancy in human vision. The thinking-about-biopsychology theme was emphasized because many people think about their own visual systems in a way that is fundamentally incorrect: The visual system does not passively provide images of the external world; it actively extracts some features of the external visual world and from these it creates visual perceptions.

The cognitive neuroscience and clinical implications themes played lesser, but still significant, roles in this chapter. You learned that, although most of the research on the neural mechanisms of vision has been invasive and thus has involved nonhuman subjects, technological developments have made it possible for cognitive neuroscientists to study the neural mechanisms of vision in human subjects. Finally, you learned about two clinical implications that were based on the finding that the visual cortex is organized retinotopically: a better understanding of the fortification illusions associated with migraine headaches and the demonstration that brain stimulation can be used to produce images in patients who are blind but still have a functional visual cortex.

Think about It

1. In vision, as in photography, one frequently has to sacrifice sharpness (acuity) to increase sensitivity. Discuss.

2. Why is it important to distinguish between intensity and brightness and between wavelength and color?

3. If you mix equal proportions of red and green light, you get something close to white or gray light, depending on the exact wavelengths of red and green. However, if you mix equal portions of red and green paint, you get an approximation of black paint. Explain this paradox.

4. Is it appropriate to refer to the light being reflected by a red object as a red light? Why or why not?

5. The study of the neural mechanisms of human vision could not have progressed without research on other species. Discuss.

6. It is difficult to define *illusion* rigorously because in a sense all of what we see is an illusion. Explain and discuss.

ON THE CD

Studying for an exam? Try the Practice Tests for Chapter 6.

Key Terms

Absorption spectrum (p. 138)
Accommodation (p. 132)
Achromatic colors (p. 149)
Acuity (p. 131)
Amacrine cells (p. 132)
Binocular (p. 132)
Binocular disparity (p. 145)
Bipolar cells (p. 132)
Blind spot (p. 133)
Blobs (p. 153)
Chromatic colors (p. 149)
Ciliary muscles (p. 132)
Color constancy (p. 151)
Complementary colors (p. 150)
Completion (p. 133)
Complex cells (p. 145)
Component theory (p. 150)
Cones (p. 134)
Contrast enhancement (p. 142)
Cytochrome oxidase (p. 152)

Dual-opponent color cells (p. 152)
Duplexity theory (p. 134)
Fourier analysis (p. 148)
Fovea (p. 133)
Horizontal cells (p. 132)
Lateral geniculate nucleus (p. 139)
Lateral inhibition (p. 142)
Magnocellular layers (p. 141)
Microspectrophotometry (p. 150)
Monocular (p. 143)
Nasal hemiretina (p. 136)
Off-center cells (p. 144)
Ommatidia (p. 142)
On-center cells (p. 144)
Opponent-process theory (p. 150)

Parvocellular layers (p. 141)
Photopic spectral sensitivity curve (p. 136)
Photopic vision (p. 134)
Primary visual cortex (p. 139)
Purkinje effect (p. 136)
Receptive field (p. 143)
Receptors (p. 132)
Retina-geniculate-striate pathway (p. 139)
Retinal ganglion cells (p. 132)
Retinex theory (p. 152)
Retinotopic (p. 140)
Rhodopsin (p. 138)
Rods (p. 134)
Saccades (p. 136)
Scotopic spectral sensitivity curve (p. 136)
Scotopic vision (p. 134)
Sensitivity (p. 131)

Simple cells (p. 145)
Sine-wave grating (p. 147)
Spatial-frequency theory (p. 147)
Stabilized retinal image (p. 137)
Temporal hemiretina (p. 136)
Transduction (p. 138)

ON THE CD

Need some help studying the key terms for this chapter? Check out the electronic flash cards for Chapter 6.

chapter 7

Mechanisms of Perception, Conscious Awareness, and Attention

How You Know the World

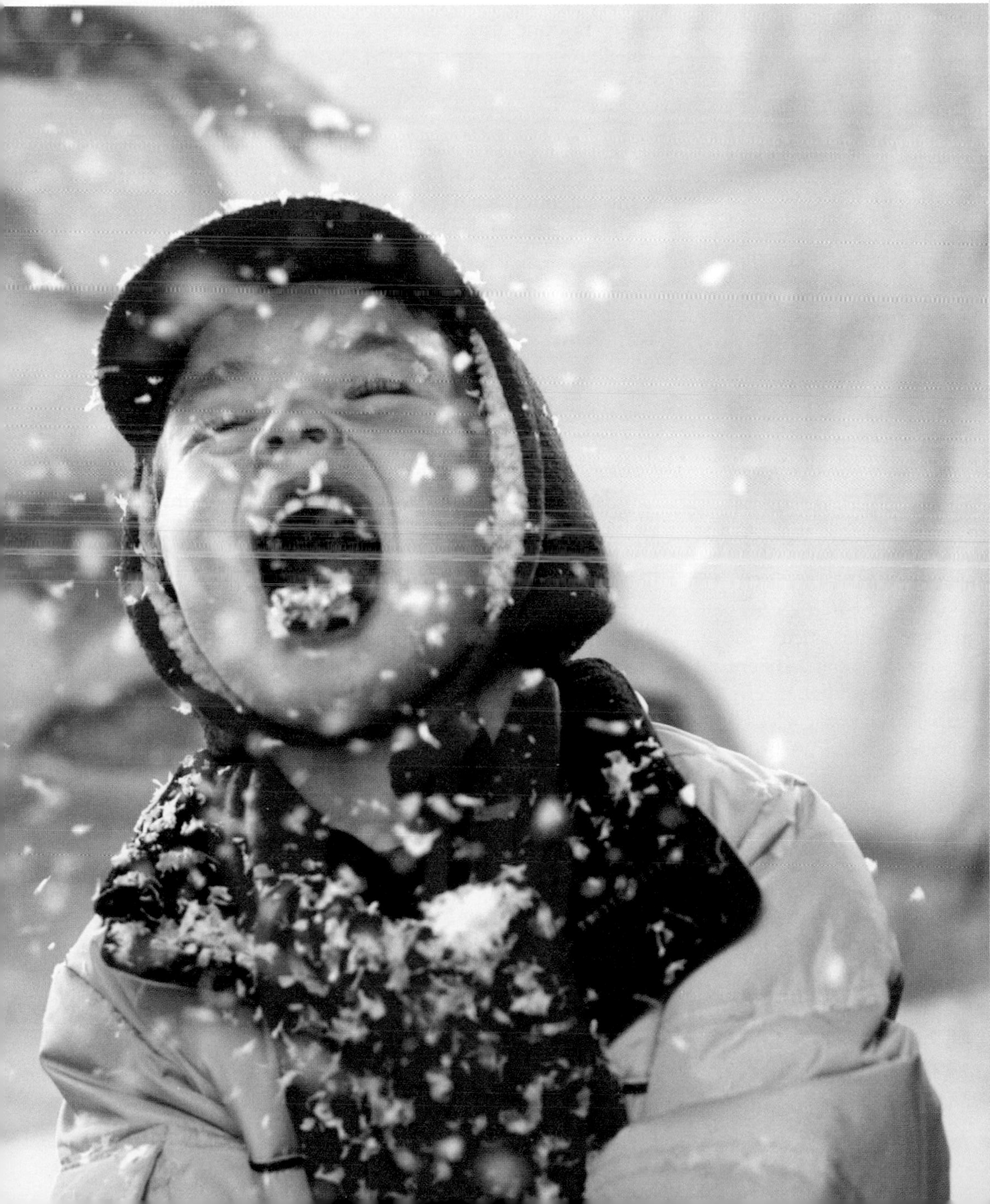

7.1 Principles of Sensory System Organization

7.2 Cortical Mechanisms of Vision

7.3 Audition

7.4 Somatosensation: Touch and Pain

7.5 The Chemical Senses: Smell and Taste

7.6 Selective Attention

There are two chapters in this text whose primary focus is sensory: Chapter 6 was the first, and this is the second. Chapter 6 described how visual signals are translated into neural signals by cones and rods and how these neural signals are conducted by the retina-geniculate-striate system to the primary visual cortex.

This chapter differs from Chapter 6 in two major respects. First, rather than focusing on one sensory system, it discusses all five **exteroceptive sensory systems**, the five sensory systems that interpret stimuli from outside the body: vision, hearing, touch, smell, and taste. Second, rather than focusing on the conduction of sensory signals from receptors to cortex, this chapter focuses on cortical mechanisms and phenomena.

Before you begin the first section of this chapter, consider the following case from Williams (1970). By the time you have reached the final section, you will be prepared to diagnose the patient and interpret the case.

Clinical Implications

The Case of the Man Who Could See Only One Thing at a Time

A 68-year-old patient was referred because he had difficulty finding his way around—even around his own home. The patient attributed his problems to his "inability to see properly."

"It was found that if two objects (e.g., two pencils) were held in front of him at the same time, he could see only one of them, whether they were held side by side, one above the other, or even one partially behind the other. Pictures of single objects or faces could be identified, even when quite complex; but if a picture included two objects, only one object could be identified, whereupon the other would enter the patient's perception. If a sentence were presented in a line, only the rightmost word could be read, but if one word were presented spread over the entire area covered by the previous sentence, the word could be read in its entirety. If the patient was shown overlapping drawings (i.e., one drawn on top of another), he would see one but deny the existence of the other."

As you read this chapter, think about this patient. Think about the nature of his deficit and the likely location of his brain damage.

7.1 Principles of Sensory System Organization

To understand the organization of the sensory areas of the cortex, it is important that you appreciate that they are of three fundamentally different types: primary, secondary, and association. The **primary sensory cortex** of a system is the area of sensory cortex that receives most of its input directly from the thalamic relay nuclei of that system. For example, as you learned in Chapter 6, the primary visual cortex is the area of the cerebral cortex that receives most of its input from the lateral geniculate nucleus of the thalamus. The **secondary sensory cortex** of a system comprises the areas of the sensory cortex that receive most of their input from the primary sensory cortex of that system or from other areas of the secondary cortex of the same system. **Association cortex** is any area of cortex that receives input from more than one sensory system. Most input to areas of association cortex comes via areas of secondary sensory cortex.

The interactions among these three types of sensory cortex are characterized by three major principles: hierarchical organization, functional segregation, and parallel processing.

Hierarchical Organization

Sensory systems are characterized by **hierarchical organization**. A *hierarchy* is a system whose members can be

assigned to specific levels or ranks in relation to one another. For example, the army is a hierarchical system because all soldiers are ranked with respect to their authority. In the same way, sensory structures are organized in a hierarchy on the basis of the specificity and complexity of their function (see Figure 7.1). As one moves through a sensory system from receptors, to thalamic nuclei, to primary sensory cortex, to secondary sensory cortex, to association cortex, one finds neurons that respond optimally to stimuli of greater and greater specificity and complexity. Each level of a sensory hierarchy receives its input from lower levels and adds another layer of analysis before passing it on up the hierarchy (see Rees, Kreiman, & Koch, 2002).

The hierarchical organization of sensory systems is apparent from a comparison of the effects of damage to various levels: The higher the level of damage, the more specific and complex the deficit. For example, destruction of a sensory system's receptors produces a complete loss of ability to perceive in that sensory modality (e.g., total blindness or deafness); in contrast, destruction of an area of association or secondary sensory cortex typically produces complex and specific sensory deficits, while leaving fundamental sensory abilities intact. Dr. P., the man who mistook his wife for a hat (Sacks, 1985), displayed such a pattern of deficits.

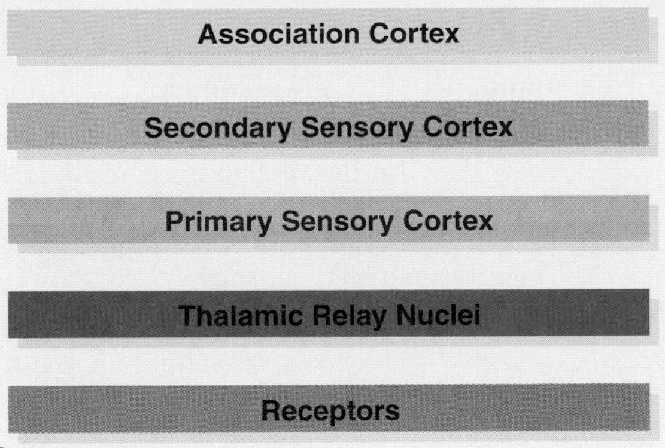

In recognition of the hierarchical organization of sensory systems, psychologists sometimes divide the general process of perceiving into two general phases: sensation and perception. **Sensation** is the process of detecting the presence of stimuli, and **perception** is the higher-order process of integrating, recognizing, and interpreting complete patterns of sensations. Dr. P.'s problem was clearly one of visual perception, not visual sensation.

Functional Segregation

It was once assumed that the primary, secondary, and association areas of a sensory system were each *functionally homogeneous*. That is, it was assumed that all areas of cortex at any given level of a sensory hierarchy acted together to perform the same function. However, research has shown that **functional segregation**, rather than functional homogeneity, characterizes the organization of sensory systems. It is now clear that each of the three levels of cerebral cortex—primary, secondary, and association—in each sensory system contains functionally distinct areas that specialize in different kinds of analysis.

FIGURE 7.1 The hierarchical organization of the sensory systems. The receptors perform the simplest and most general analyses, and the association cortex performs the most complex and specific analyses.

Association Cortex

Secondary Sensory Cortex

Primary Sensory Cortex

Thalamic Relay Nuclei

Receptors

The Case of the Man Who Mistook His Wife for a Hat

Clinical Implications

Dr. P. was a musician of distinction, well-known for many years as a singer . . . and as a teacher. . . . It was obvious within a few seconds of meeting him that there was no trace of dementia [intellectual deterioration]. . . . He was a man of great cultivation and charm who talked well and fluently, with imagination and humour. . . .

"What seems to be the matter?" I asked him at length.

"Nothing that I know of," he replied with a smile, "but people seem to think that there's something wrong with my eyes."

"But *you* don't recognise any visual problems?"

"No, not directly, but I occasionally make mistakes," . . . .

It was while examining his reflexes . . . that the first bizarre experience occurred. I had taken off his left shoe and scratched the sole of his foot with a key—a frivolous-seeming but essential test of a reflex—and then, excusing myself to screw my ophthalmoscope together, left him to put on the shoe himself. To my surprise, a minute later, he had not done this.

"Can I help?" I asked.

"Help what? Help whom?" . . .

"Your shoe," I repeated. "Perhaps you'd put it on."

He continued to look downwards, though not at the shoe, with an intense but misplaced concentration. Finally his gaze settled on his foot.

"That is my shoe, yes?" Did I mis-hear? Did he mis-see?

"My eyes," he explained, and put his hand to his foot. "This is my shoe, no?"

"No, it is not. That is your foot. *There* is your shoe."

"Ah! I thought that was my foot. *There* is your shoe."

Was he joking? Was he mad? Was he blind? If this was one of his "strange mistakes," it was the strangest mistake I had ever come across.

I helped him on with his shoe (his foot), to avoid further complication. . . . I resumed my examination. His visual acuity was good; he had no difficulty seeing a pin on the floor. . . .

He saw all right, but what did he see? . . .

"What is this?" I asked, holding up a glove.

"May I examine it?" he asked, taking it from me.

"A continuous surface," he announced at last, "infolded on itself. It appears to have"—he hesitated—"five outpouchings, if this is the word."

"Yes," I said cautiously. "You have given me a description. Now tell me what it is."

"A container of some sort?"

"Yes," I said, "and what would it contain?"

"It would contain its contents!" said Dr. P., with a laugh. "There are many possibilities. It could be a change purse, for example, for coins of five sizes. It could . . ."

"Does it not look familiar? Do you think it might contain, might fit, a part of the body?"

No light of recognition dawned on his face. . . .

I must have looked aghast, but he seemed to think he had done rather well. There was a hint of a smile on his face. He also appeared to have decided the examination was over and started to look around for his hat. He reached out his hand and took hold of his wife's head, tried to lift it off, to put it on. He had apparently mistaken his wife for a hat! His wife looked as if she was used to such things.

(Reprinted with the permission of Simon & Schuster Adult Publishing Group from *The Man Who Mistook His Wife for a Hat and Other Clinical Tales* by Oliver Sacks. Copyright © 1970, 1981, 1983, 1984, 1985 by Oliver Sacks).

Parallel Processing

It was once believed that the different levels of a sensory hierarchy were connected in a serial fashion. A *serial system* is a system in which information flows among the components over just one pathway, like a string through a strand of beads. However, there is now evidence that sensory systems are *parallel systems*—systems in which information flows through the components over multiple pathways. Parallel systems feature **parallel processing**—the simultaneous analysis of a signal in different ways by the multiple parallel pathways of a neural network.

There appear to be two fundamentally different kinds of parallel streams of analysis in our sensory systems: one that is capable of influencing our behavior without our conscious awareness and one that influences our behavior by engaging our conscious awareness. The existence of these two kinds of parallel streams is as counterintuitive as it is important. Pause for a moment to consider its implications. What do you think would happen if a lesion disrupted the conscious stream without disrupting its parallel unconscious stream? You will encounter patients in this chapter who have such damage: They can reach out and deftly pick up objects that they do not consciously see.

The Current Model of Sensory System Organization

Figure 7.2 summarizes the information in this section of the chapter by illustrating how thinking about the organization of sensory systems has changed. In the 1960s, sensory systems were believed to be hierarchical, functionally homogeneous, and serial. However, subsequent research has established that sensory systems are hierarchical, functionally segregated, and parallel (see Tong, 2003).

Sensory systems are characterized by a division of labor: multiple specialized areas, at multiple levels, interconnected by multiple parallel pathways. Yet, complex stimuli are normally perceived as integrated wholes, not as combinations of independent attributes. How does the brain combine individual sensory attributes to produce integrated perceptions? This is called the *binding problem* (see Bernstein & Robertson, 1998; De Gelder, 2000; Friedman-Hill, Robertson, & Treisman, 1995).

One possible solution to the binding problem is that there is a single area of the cortex at the top of the sensory hierarchy that receives signals from all other areas of the sensory system and puts them together to form perceptions; however, there are no areas of cortex to which all areas of a single sensory system report. It seems, then,

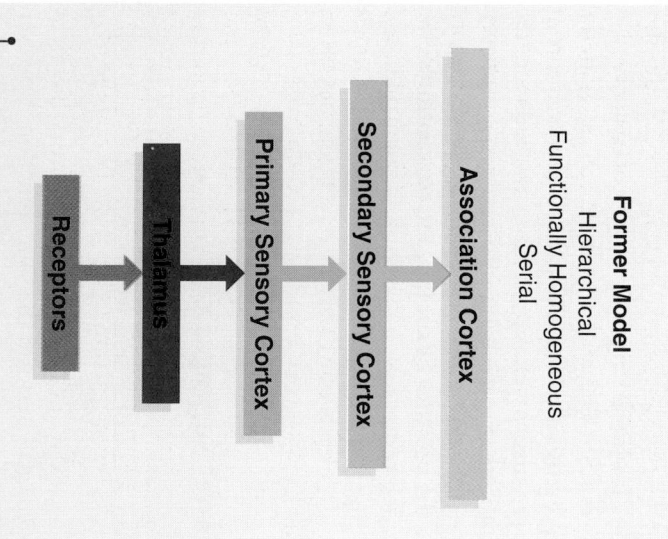

Former Model
Hierarchical
Functionally Homogeneous
Serial

Receptors
Thalamus
Primary Sensory Cortex
Secondary Sensory Cortex
Association Cortex

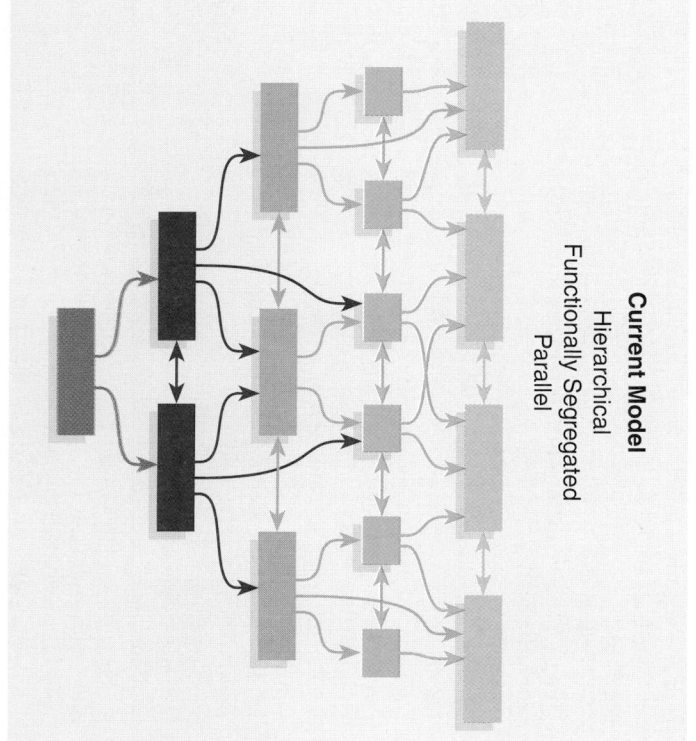

Current Model
Hierarchical
Functionally Segregated
Parallel

FIGURE 7.2   Two models of sensory system organization: The former model was hierarchical, functionally homogeneous, and serial; the current model, which is more consistent with the evidence, is hierarchical, functionally segregated, and parallel. Not shown in the current model are descending pathways that provide feedback from higher levels to lower levels.

that perceptions must be a product of the combined activity of the many interconnected cortical areas.

Not shown in Figure 7.2 are the many pathways that descend through the sensory hierarchies. Although most sensory neurons carry information from lower to higher levels of their respective sensory hierarchies, some conduct in the opposite direction (from higher to lower lev-

els). For example, groups of neurons that conduct information from cortical sensory areas to subcortical areas are called **corticofugal pathways.** Corticofugal pathways are one of the means by which cognitive processes, such as attention, can influence perception—this is termed *top-down influence* (see Engel, Fries, & Singer, 2001; Gao & Suga, 2000).

7.2 Cortical Mechanisms of Vision

We humans are visual animals. The entire occipital cortex as well as large areas of temporal cortex and parietal cortex are involved in vision (see Figure 7.3). The *primary visual cortex* is located in the posterior region of the occipital lobes, much of it hidden from view in the longitudinal fissure. The areas of *secondary visual cortex* are located in two general regions: in the prestriate cortex and in the inferotemporal cortex. The **prestriate cortex** is the band of tissue in the occipital lobe that surrounds the primary visual cortex. The **inferotemporal cortex** is the cortex of the inferior temporal lobe. Areas of association cortex that receive visual input are located in several parts of the cerebral cortex, but the largest single area is in the **posterior parietal cortex.**

In keeping with the general hierarchical organization of the sensory cortex, the major flow of visual information is from the primary visual cortex to the various areas of secondary visual cortex to the areas of association cortex. As one moves up this visual hierarchy, the neurons have larger receptive fields and the stimuli to which the neurons respond are more specific and more complex (see Zeki, 1993b).

Scotomas: Completion

Damage to an area of the primary visual cortex produces a **scotoma**—an area of blindness—in the corresponding area of the contralateral visual field of both eyes (see Figure 6.13). Neurological patients with suspected damage to the primary visual cortex are usually given a **perimetry test.** While the patient's head is held motionless on a chin rest, the patient stares with one eye at a fixation point on a screen. A small dot of light is then flashed on various parts of the screen, and the patient presses a button to record when the dot is seen. Then, the entire process is repeated for the other eye. The result is a map of the visual field of each eye, which indicates any areas of blindness. Figure 7.4 on page 160 illustrates the perimetric maps of the visual fields of a man with a bullet wound in his left primary visual cortex. Notice the massive scotoma in the right visual field of each eye.

Many patients with extensive scotomas are unaware of their deficits. One of the factors that contributes to this lack of awareness is the phenomenon of **completion** (see Chapter 6). A patient with a scotoma who looks at a complex figure, part of which lies in the scotoma, often reports seeing a complete image (Zur & Ullman, 2003). In some cases, this completion may depend on residual visual capacities in the scotoma; however, completion also occurs in cases in which this explanation can be ruled out. For example, patients who are **hemianopsic** (having a scotoma covering half of the visual field) may see an entire face when they focus on a person's nose, even when the side of the face in the scotoma has been covered by a blank card.

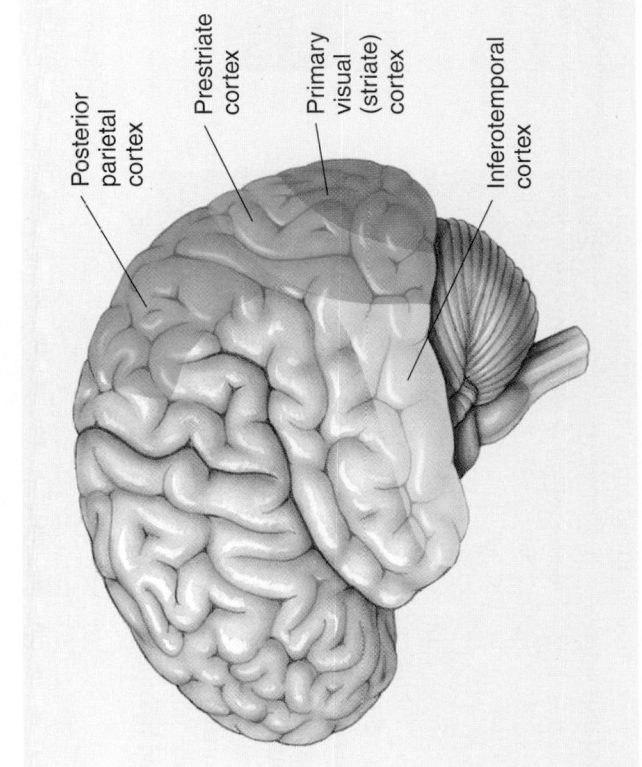

FIGURE 7.3 The visual areas of the human cerebral cortex.

Posterior parietal cortex

Prestriate cortex

Primary visual (striate) cortex

Inferotemporal cortex

The Case of the Physiological Psychologist Who Made Faces Disappear

Consider the completion phenomenon experienced by the esteemed physiological psychologist Karl Lashley (1941). He often developed a large scotoma next to his fovea during a migraine attack (see Figure 7.5).

Talking with a friend I glanced just to the right of his face wherein his head disappeared. His shoulders and necktie were still visible but the vertical stripes on the wallpaper behind him seemed to extend down to the necktie. It was impossible to see this as a blank area when projected on the striped wallpaper of uniformly patterned surface although any intervening object failed to be seen. (Lashley, 1941, p. 338)

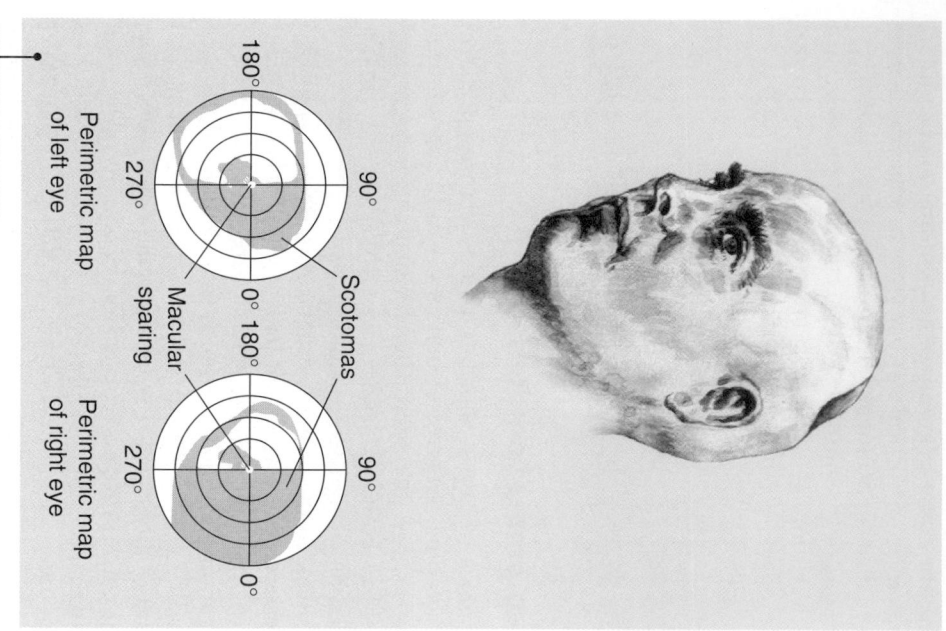

FIGURE 7.4   The perimetric maps of a subject with a bullet wound in his left primary visual cortex. The scotomas (areas of blindness) are indicated in gray. (Adapted from Teuber, Battersby, & Bender, 1960.)

Perimetric map of left eye

180°

270°   90°

0°   180°

Scotomas

Macular sparing

Perimetric map of right eye

90°

270°

0°

Scotomas: Blindsight

Blindsight is another phenomenon displayed by patients with scotomas resulting from damage to primary visual cortex. **Blindsight** is the ability of such patients to respond to visual stimuli in their scotomas even though they have no conscious awareness of the stimuli (Weiskrantz, 2004). Of all visual abilities, perception of motion is most likely to survive damage to primary visual cortex (Intriligator, Xie, & Barton, 2002). For example, a subject might reach out and grab a moving object in her scotoma, all the while claiming not to see it.

If blindsight confuses you, imagine how it confuses people who experience it. Consider, for example, the reactions to blindsight of D.B., a patient who was blind in his left visual field following surgical removal of his right occipital lobe (Weiskrantz, 2002; Weiskrantz et al., 1974).

The Case of D.B., the Man Confused by His Own Blindsight

Even though the patient had no awareness of "seeing" in his blind [left] field, evidence was obtained that (a) he could reach for visual stimuli [in his left field] with considerable accuracy; (b) could differentiate the orientation of a vertical line from a horizontal or diagonal line; (c) could differentiate the letters "X" and "O."

Needless to say, he was questioned repeatedly about his vision in his left half-field, and his most common response was that he saw nothing at all. . . . When he was shown his results [through his good, right-half field] he expressed surprise and insisted several times that he thought he was just "guessing." When he was shown a video film of his reaching and judging orientation of lines, he was openly astonished. (Weiskrantz et al., 1974, pp. 721, 726)

Two neurological interpretations of blindsight have been proposed. One is that the striate cortex is not completely destroyed and the remaining islands of functional cells are capable of mediating some visual abilities in the absence of conscious awareness (see Wüst, Kasten, & Sabel, 2002). The other is that those visual pathways that ascend directly to the secondary visual cortex from subcortical visual structures without passing through the primary visual cortex are capable of maintaining some visual abilities in the absence of cognitive awareness (see Kentridge, Heywood, & Weiskrantz, 1997). There is some support for both theories, but the evidence is not conclusive for either (see Gross, Moore, & Rodman, 2004; Rosa, Tweedale, & Elston, 2000; Schärli, Harman, & Hogben, 1999a, 1999b). Indeed, it is possible that both mechanisms contribute to the phenomenon.

areas of secondary visual cortex and 7 areas of association visual cortex have been identified. The neurons in each functional area respond most vigorously to different aspects of visual stimuli (e.g., to their color, movement, or shape); selective lesions to the different areas produce different visual losses; and there are anatomical differences among the areas.

The various functional areas of secondary and association visual cortex in the macaque are prodigiously interconnected. Anterograde and retrograde tracing studies have identified over 300 interconnecting pathways (Van Essen, Anderson, & Felleman, 1992). Although connections between areas are virtually always reciprocal, the major flow of information is up the hierarchy, from more simple to more complex areas.

PET (positron emission tomography) and fMRI have been used to identify various areas of visual cortex in humans. The activity of the subjects' brains has been monitored while they inspect various types of visual stimuli (e.g., Grossman et al., 2000; Kourtzi & Kanwisher, 2000). By identifying the areas of activation associated with various visual properties (e.g., movement or color), researchers have so far delineated about a dozen different functional areas of human visual cortex. A map of these areas is shown in Figure 7.8 on page 163. Most are similar in terms of location, anatomical characteristics, and function to areas in the macaque (Courtney & Ungerleider, 1997), but there are some differences (see Vanduffel et al., 2002).

Dorsal and Ventral Streams

You learned in Chapter 6 that most visual information enters the primary visual cortex via the lateral geniculate nuclei. In the primary visual cortex, the information from the two lateral geniculate nuclei is received, combined, and then segregated into multiple pathways that project separately to the various functional areas of secondary, and then association, visual cortex (see Cabeza & Nyberg, 1997; Logothetis, 1998).

Many pathways that conduct information from the primary visual cortex through various specialized areas

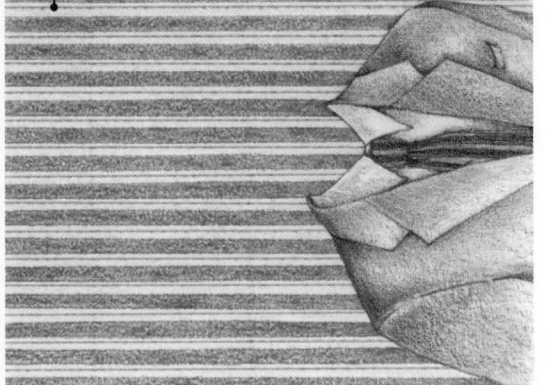

FIGURE 7.5 The completion of a migraine-induced scotoma as described by Karl Lashley (1941).

Visual Awareness and Neural Activity

Do you recall the key point stressed in Chapter 6—that our visual perceptions are often different from the physical reality of visual input? This occurs because the activity of visual cortical neurons is often associated with the properties of the perception rather than the physical stimulus (Albright & Stoner, 2002; Eysel, 2003; Zettran, 2004).

Figure 7.6 on page 162 illustrates this point by showing that we often see visual contours where none exist (Albright, 1995); these are called **subjective contours.** Why do we see subjective contours? The reason is that prestriate neurons (Peterhans & von der Heydt, 1991), and even a few primary visual cortex neurons (Sheth et al., 1996), respond as if real contours are present when subjective contours of the appropriate orientation appear in their receptive fields (see Figure 7.7 on page 162).

A similar point was made by an fMRI (functional magnetic resonance imaging) study of subjects who were viewing a color illusion (Humphrey et al., 1999). Activity in areas of prestriate cortex was more closely related to the perceived colors than to the wavelengths of the actual stimuli.

Functional Areas of Secondary and Association Visual Cortex

Secondary visual cortex and the portions of association cortex that are involved in visual analysis are both composed of different areas, each specialized for a particular type of visual analysis. For example, in the macaque monkey, whose visual cortex has been thoroughly mapped, there are at least 30 different functional areas of visual cortex; in addition to primary visual cortex, 24

FIGURE 7.6 Subjective contours. You see the white bar in the top pattern and the white triangle in the middle pattern even though they do not physically exist—they are subjective contours. Your ability to see subjective contours helps you see boundaries between objects of similar brightness, color, and pattern—for example, look at the bottom pattern.

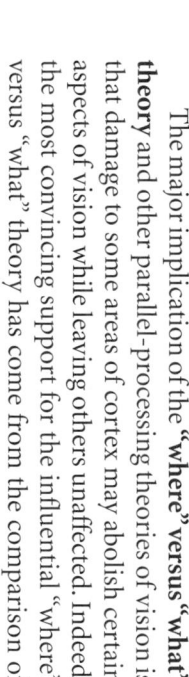

of secondary and association cortex are parts of two major streams: the dorsal stream and the ventral stream (Courtney & Ungerleider, 1997; Ungerleider & Mishkin, 1982). The **dorsal stream** flows from the primary visual cortex to the dorsal prestriate cortex to the posterior parietal cortex, and the **ventral stream** flows from the primary visual cortex to the ventral prestriate cortex to the inferotemporal cortex—see Figure 7.9.

Ungerleider and Mishkin (1982) proposed that the dorsal and ventral visual streams perform different visual functions. They suggested that the dorsal stream is involved in the perception of "where" objects are and the ventral stream is involved in the perception of "what" objects are.

The major implication of the **"where" versus "what" theory** and other parallel-processing theories of vision is that damage to some areas of cortex may abolish certain aspects of vision while leaving others unaffected. Indeed, the most convincing support for the influential "where" versus "what" theory has come from the comparison of

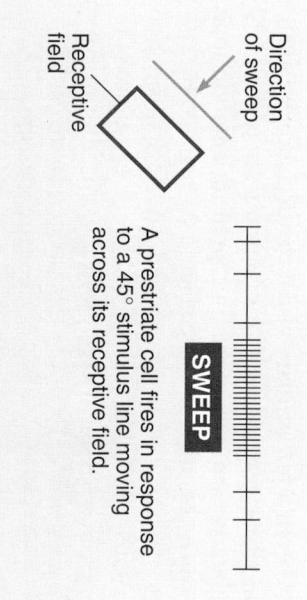

SWEEP

A prestriate cell fires in response to a 45° stimulus line moving across its receptive field.

Receptive field

Direction of sweep

SWEEP

The same cell fires in response to a 45° subjective contour moving across its field in the same direction.

FIGURE 7.7 Neurons of the monkey prestriate cortex and primary visual cortex respond to subjective contours of a particular orientation. (Adapted from Peterhans & von der Heydt, 1991.)

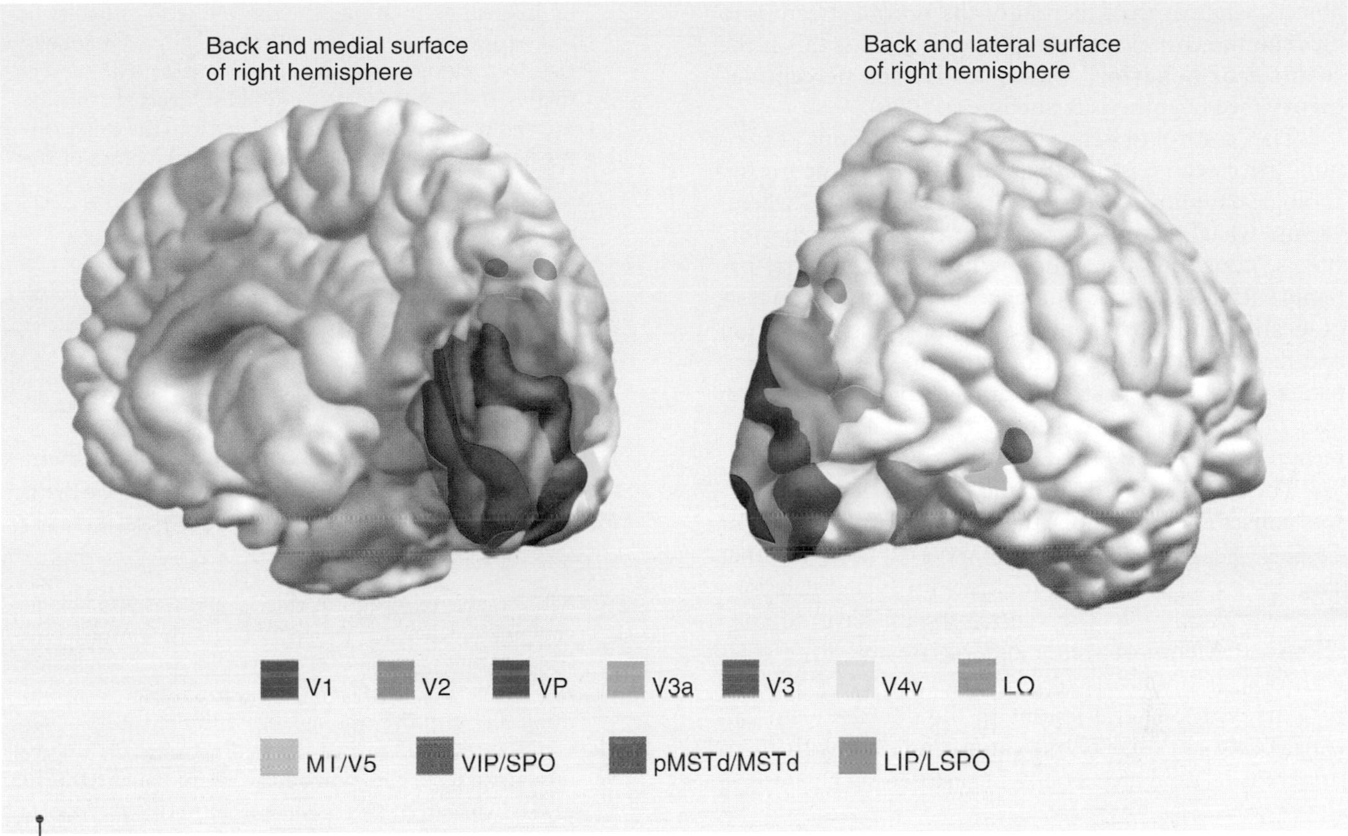

Back and medial surface
of right hemisphere

Back and lateral surface
of right hemisphere

V1 V2 VP V3a V3 V4v LO

M1/V5 VIP/SPO pMSTd/MSTd LIP/LSPO

FIGURE 7.8 Areas of visual cortex so far discovered in humans. Their names are based on similarities to areas of visual cortex in the more thoroughly studied macaque monkey. (Based on Tootell et al., 1996.)

the specific effects of damage to the dorsal and ventral streams (see Ungerleider & Haxby, 1994). Patients with damage to the posterior parietal cortex often have difficulty reaching accurately for objects that they have no difficulty describing; conversely, patients with damage to the inferotemporal cortex often have no difficulty reaching accurately for objects that they have difficulty describing.

Although the "where" versus "what" theory has many advocates, there is an alternative interpretation for the same evidence (Goodale, 1993; Milner & Goodale, 1993). Goodale and Milner argued that the key difference between the dorsal and ventral streams is not the kinds of information they carry but the use to which that information is put. They suggested that the function of the dorsal stream is to direct behavioral interactions with

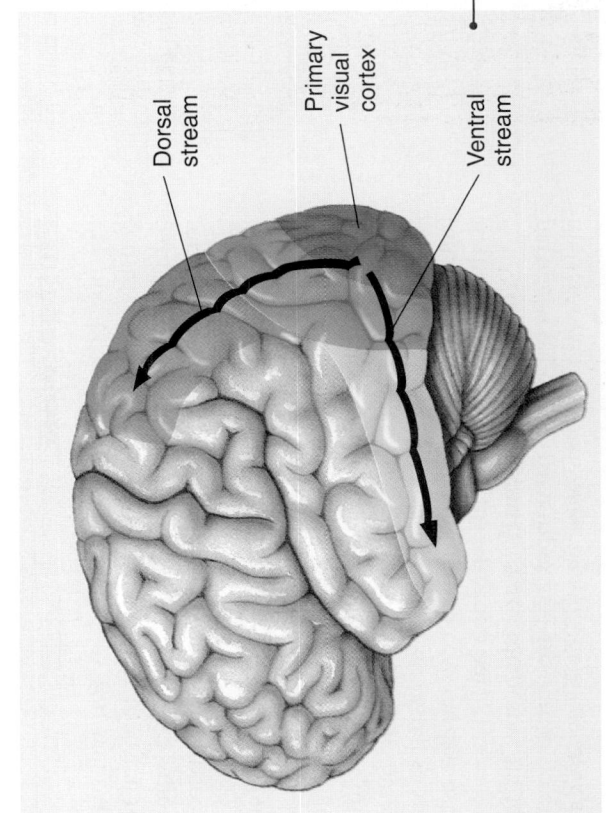

Dorsal
stream

Primary
visual
cortex

Ventral
stream

FIGURE 7.9 Information about particular aspects of a visual display flow out of the primary visual cortex over many pathways. The pathways can be grouped into two general streams: dorsal and ventral.

objects, whereas the function of the ventral stream is to mediate the conscious perception of objects; this is the **"control of behavior" versus "conscious perception" theory** (see Logothetis & Sheinberg, 1996).

The "control of behavior" versus "conscious perception" theory can readily explain the two major neuropsychological findings that are the foundation of the "where" versus "what" theory. Namely, the "control of behavior" versus "conscious perception" theory suggests that patients with dorsal stream damage may do poorly on tests of location and movement because most tests of location and movement involve performance measures, and that patients with ventral stream damage may do poorly on tests of visual recognition because most tests of visual recognition involve verbal, and thus conscious, report.

The major strength of the "control of behavior" versus "conscious perception" theory is the confirmation of its two primary assertions: (1) that some patients with bilateral lesions to the ventral stream have no conscious experience of seeing and yet are able to interact with objects under visual guidance, and (2) that some patients with bilateral lesions to the dorsal stream can consciously see objects but cannot interact with them under visual guidance. Following are two such cases.

Clinical Implications

The Case of D.F., the Woman Who Could Grasp Objects She Did Not Consciously See

D.F. has bilateral damage to her ventral prestriate cortex, thus interrupting the flow of the ventral stream (Goodale et al., 1991). Amazingly, she can respond accurately to visual stimuli that she does not consciously see. Goodale and Milner (1992) describe her thusly:

Despite her profound inability to recognize the size, shape and orientation of visual objects, D.F. showed strikingly accurate guidance of hand and finger movements directed at the very same objects. Thus, when she was presented with a pair of rectangular blocks of the same or different dimensions, she was unable to distinguish between them. When she was asked to indicate the width of a single block by means of her index finger and thumb, her matches bore no relationship to the dimensions of the object and showed considerable trial to trial variability. However, when she was asked simply to reach out and pick up the block, the aperture between her index finger and thumb changed systematically with the width of the object, just as in normal subjects. In other words, D.F. scaled her grip to the dimensions of the objects she was about to pick up, even though she appeared to be unable to [consciously] "perceive" those dimensions.

A similar dissociation was seen in her responses to the orientation of stimuli. Thus, when presented with a large slot that could be placed in one of a number of different orientations, she showed great difficulty in indicating the orientation either verbally or manually (i.e., by rotating her hand or a hand-held card). Nevertheless, she was as good as normal subjects at reaching out and placing her hand or the card into the slot, turning her hand appropriately from the very onset of the movement. (p. 22)

The Case of A.T., the Woman Who Could Not Accurately Grasp Unfamiliar Objects That She Saw

The case of A.T. is in major respects complementary to that of D.F. The patient A.T. is a woman with a lesion of the occipitoparietal region, which likely interrupts her dorsal route.

A.T. was able to recognize objects, and was also able to demonstrate their size with her fingers. By contrast, preshape of the hand during object-directed movements was incorrect. Correlation between object size and maximum grip size was lacking, with the consequence that objects could not be grasped between the fingertips; instead, the patient made awkward palmar grasps. The schema framework offers a compelling explanation for this deficit. Because the grasp schemas were destroyed by the lesion, or disconnected from visual input, the grip aperture did not stop at the required size, grip closure was delayed and the transport was prolonged in order to remain co-ordinated with the grasp.

A.T. cannot preshape her hand for neutral objects like plastic cylinders, yet, when faced with a familiar object whose size is a semantic property, like a lipstick, she can grasp it with reasonable accuracy. This interaction reflects the role of the abundant anatomical interconnections between the two cortical systems. (Jeannerod et al., 1995, p. 320)

Prosopagnosia

Prosopagnosia is an interesting and, as you will learn, controversial neuropsychological disorder of visual recognition. Its investigation has provided further support for the "control of behavior" versus "conscious perception" theory.

What is prosopagnosia? **Prosopagnosia**, briefly put, is visual agnosia for faces. Let me explain. **Agnosia** is a failure of recognition (*gnosis* means "to know") that is not attributable to a sensory deficit or to verbal or intellectual impairment; **visual agnosia** is a specific agnosia for visual stimuli. Visual agnosics can see visual stimuli, but they don't know what they are. (Recall the case of Dr. P., the man who mistook his wife for a hat.)

Visual agnosias themselves are often specific to a particular aspect of visual input and are named accordingly; for example, *movement agnosia, object agnosia, and color agnosia* are difficulties in recognizing movement, objects, and color, respectively. It is presumed that each specific visual agnosia results from damage to an area of secondary visual cortex that mediates the recognition of that particular attribute. Prosopagnosics are visual agnosics with a specific difficulty in recognizing faces.

Prosopagnosics can usually recognize a face as a face, but they have problems recognizing whose face it is. They often report seeing a jumble of individual facial parts (e.g., eyes, nose, chin, cheeks) that for some reason are never fused, or bound, into an easy-to-recognize whole. In extreme cases, prosopagnosics cannot recognize themselves: Imagine what it would be like to stare in the mirror every morning and not recognize the face that is looking back.

The belief that prosopagnosia is a deficit specific to the recognition of faces has been challenged. To understand this challenge, you need to know that the diagnosis of prosopagnosia is typically applied to neuropsychological patients who have difficulty recognizing particular faces, but can readily identify other test objects (e.g., a chair, a dog, or a tree). Surely, this is powerful evidence that prosopagnosics have recognition difficulties specific to faces: Not so. Pause for a moment, and think about this evidence: It is seriously flawed.

Because prosopagnosics have no difficulty recognizing faces as faces, the fact that they can recognize chairs as chairs, pencils as pencils, and doors as doors is not relevant. The critical question is whether they can recognize which chair, which pencil, and which door. Careful testing of many prosopagnosics has revealed that their recognition deficits are not restricted to faces: A farmer lost his ability to recognize particular cows when he became prosopagnosic, and a bird-watcher lost his ability to distinguish species of birds. These cases suggest that

many prosopagnosics have a general problem recognizing specific objects that belong to complex classes of objects (e.g., particular automobiles or particular houses), not a specific problem recognizing faces (see Dixon, Bub, & Arguin, 1998; Gauthier, Behrmann, & Tarr, 1999). Although it is now well established that the recognition deficits of most prosopagnosics are not restricted to faces, there are a few cases of prosopagnosia in which thorough testing has failed to detect recognition deficits unrelated to faces (De Renzi, 1997; Farah, 1990).

testing had stopped there, it would have been concluded that R.P. is an agnosic with recognition problems specific to human faces. However, more thorough testing suggested that R.P. is deficient in recognizing all objects with complex curved surfaces (e.g., amoeboid shapes), not just faces.

The diagnosis of prosopagnosia is usually associated with damage to the ventral stream in the area of the boundary between the occipital and temporal lobes. This area of cortex has become known as the *fusiform face area.*

An interesting hypothesis about prosopagnosia can be derived from the "control of behavior" versus "conscious perception" theory. (Remember that I told you that the study of prosopagnosia has lent support to this theory.) The fact that prosopagnosia results from bilateral damage to the ventral stream suggests that dorsal-stream function may be intact. In other words, it suggests that prosopagnosics may be able to unconsciously recognize faces that they cannot recognize consciously. Remarkably, this is, indeed, the case.

Tranel and Damasio (1985) were the first to demonstrate unconscious facial recognition in prosopagnosics. They presented a series of photographs to each patient, some familiar to the patient, some not. The subjects claimed not to recognize any of the faces. However, when familiar, but not unfamiliar, faces were presented, the subjects displayed a large skin conductance response, thus indicating that the faces were being unconsciously recognized by undamaged portions of the brain.

Areas of the Ventral Stream Specialized for Recognizing Specific Classes of Objects

Claims that some neuropsychological patients have specific deficits in facial recognition stimulated a search for particular brain areas involved in the recognition of faces. Indeed, functional brain imaging has revealed pronounced increases in activity in the fusiform face area during recognition of faces but not during recognition of other objects (Gauthier et al., 2000; Ishai et al., 2000).

The discovery that there are areas in the human cortex that seem to be specialized for facial recognition has stimulated the search for areas of cortex that might be specialized for the perception of other classes of objects. Several have been reported. For example, studies using functional brain imaging have identified different areas of the human ventral stream whose activation

R.P., a Typical Case of Prosopagnosia

R.P. is a typical prosopagnosic. With routine testing, he displayed a severe deficit in recognizing faces and in identifying facial expressions (Laeng & Caviness, 2001) but no other recognition problems. If

seems to be specific to the sight of humans (Downing et al., 2001), cats (Haxby et al., 2001), or houses (Epstein & Kanwisher, 1998).

There are two important things you need to know about these class-specific areas for visual object recognition (see Grill-Spector, 2003): First, more than one area of the ventral stream responds to each class of objects; and second, there is great overlap among the areas that respond to various classes of objects. Thus, if there are neural circuits in the human cortex that are specific to the visual recognition of particular classes of objects, such as faces, they appear to be interspersed with circuits for recognizing other objects. Perhaps this is why brain damage is unlikely to produce cases of agnosia that are specific to any one class of objects.

Interim Conclusion

Before leaving this section on visual perception, review in your mind the topics that we have discussed: completion, blindsight, subjective contours, prosopagnosia, dorsal and ventral streams, and the cases of D.B., D.F., A.T., and R.P. This discussion should have reinforced your understanding of the three principles of perceptual processing that introduced the chapter: hierarchical organization, functional segregation, and parallel processing.

7.3 Audition

The function of the auditory system is the perception of sound—or, more accurately, the perception of objects and events through the sounds that they make. Sounds are vibrations of air molecules that stimulate the auditory system; humans hear only those molecular vibrations between about 20 and 20,000 hertz (cycles per second). Figure 7.10 illustrates how sounds are commonly recorded in the form of waves and the relation between the physical dimensions of sound vibrations and our perceptions of them. The *amplitude*, *frequency*, and *complexity* of the molecular vibrations are perceived as *loudness*, *pitch*, and *timbre*, respectively.

Pure tones (sine wave vibrations) exist only in laboratories and sound recording studios; in real life, sound is always associated with complex patterns of vibrations. For example, Figure 7.11 illustrates the complex sound wave associated with one note of a clarinet. The figure also illustrates that any complex sound wave can be broken down mathematically into a series of sine waves of various frequencies and amplitudes; these component sine waves produce the original sound when they are added together. As you learned in Chapter 6, *Fourier analysis* is the mathematical procedure for breaking down complex waves into their component sine waves. One theory of audition is that the auditory system performs a Fourier-like analysis of complex sounds in terms of their component sine waves.

The Ear

The ear is illustrated in Figure 7.12. Sound waves travel down the *auditory canal* and cause the **tympanic membrane** (the eardrum) to vibrate. These vibrations are then transferred to the three **ossicles**—the small bones of the middle ear: the *malleus* (the hammer), the *incus* (the anvil), and the *stapes* (the stirrup). The vibrations of the stapes trigger vibrations of the membrane called the **oval window**, which in turn transfers the vibrations to the **fluid** of the snail-shaped **cochlea** (*kokhlos* means "land snail"). The cochlea is a long, coiled tube with an internal membrane running almost to its tip. This internal membrane is the auditory receptor organ, the **organ of Corti**.

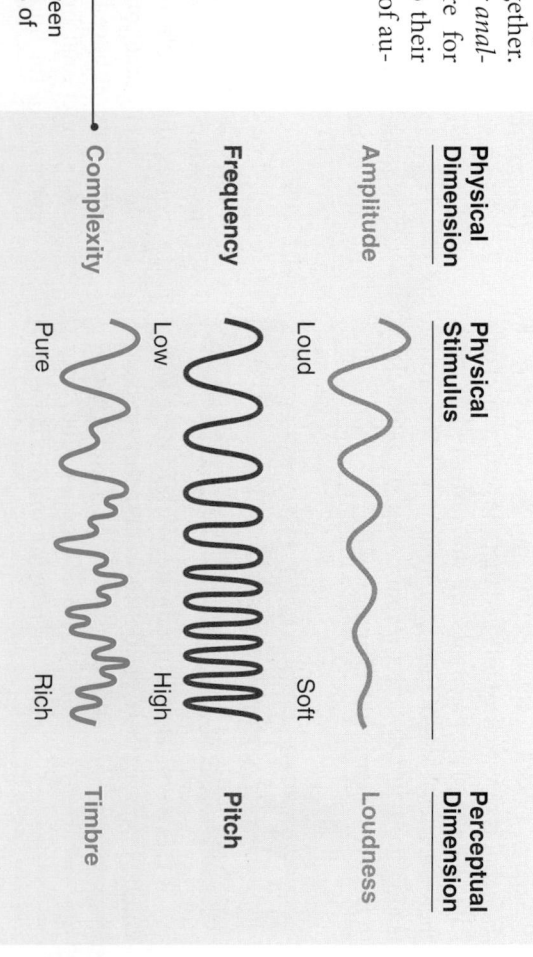

FIGURE 7.10 The relation between the physical and perceptual dimensions of sound.

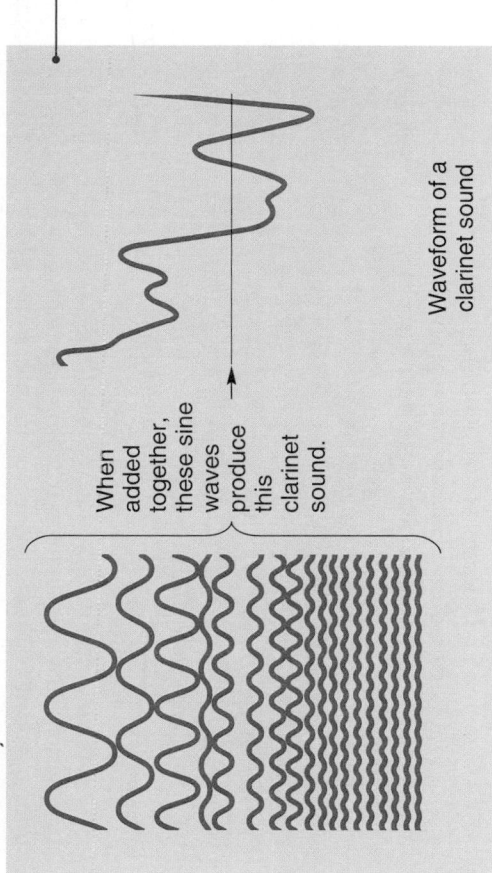

When added together, these sine waves produce this clarinet sound.

Waveform of a clarinet sound

FIGURE 7.11 The breaking down of a sound-in this case, the sound of a clarinet-into its component sine waves by Fourier analysis. When added together, the sine waves produce the complex sound wave.

FIGURE 7.12 Anatomy of the ear.

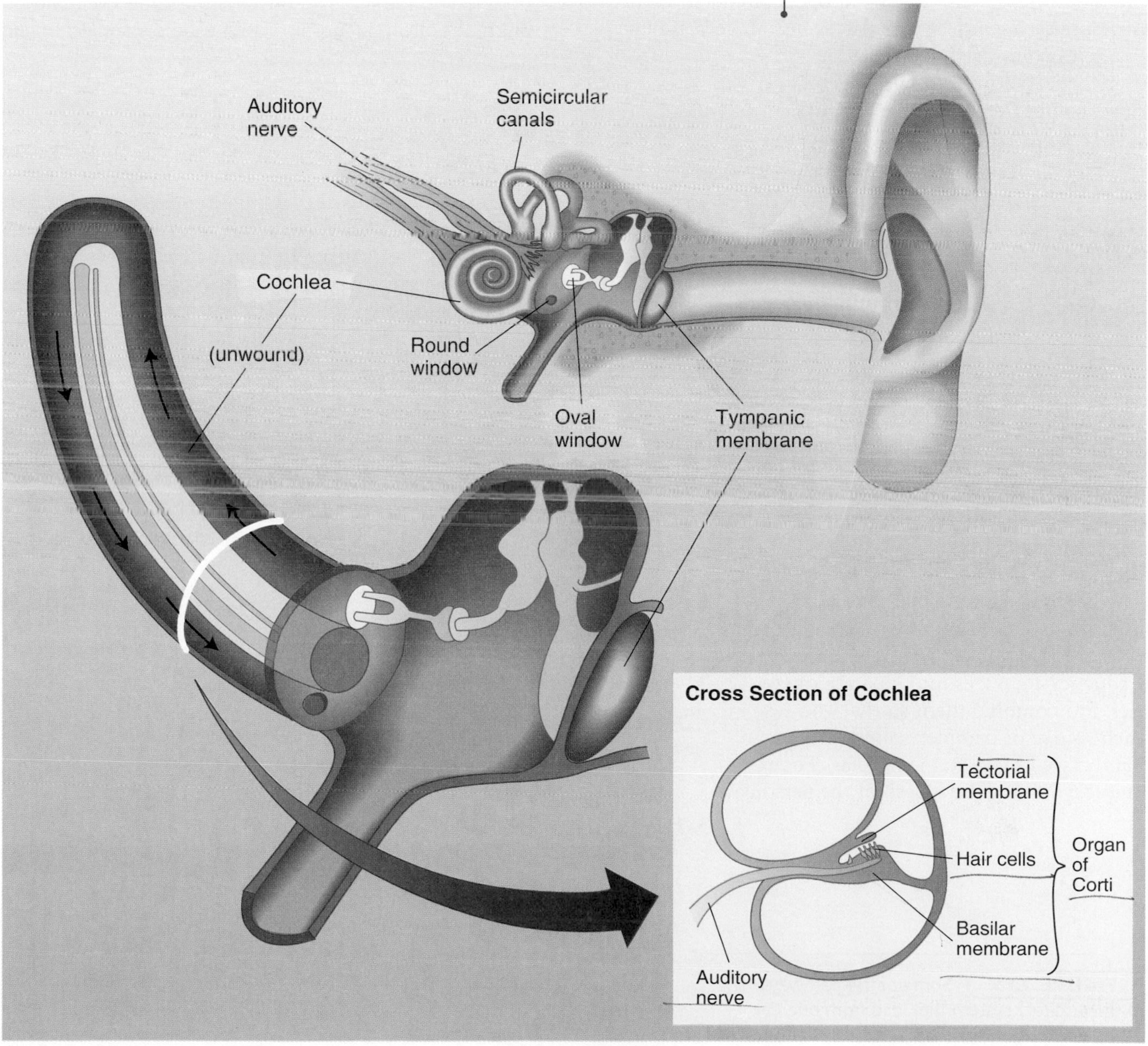

Semicircular canals

Auditory nerve

Cochlea (unwound)

Round window

Oval window

Tympanic membrane

Cross Section of Cochlea

Tectorial membrane

Hair cells

Organ of Corti

Basilar membrane

Auditory nerve

Each pressure change at the oval window travels along the organ of Corti as a wave. The organ of Corti is composed of two membranes: the basilar membrane and the tectorial membrane. The auditory receptors, the **hair cells**, are mounted in the **basilar membrane**, and the **tectorial membrane** rests on the hair cells. Accordingly, a deflection of the organ of Corti at any point along its length produces a shearing force on the hair cells at the same point (Corwin & Warchol, 1991). This force stimulates the hair cells and thereby triggers action potentials in axons of the **auditory nerve**—a branch of cranial nerve VIII (the *auditory-vestibular nerve*). The vibrations of the cochlear fluid are ultimately dissipated by the *round window*, an elastic membrane in the cochlea wall.

The major principle of cochlear coding is that different frequencies produce maximal stimulation of hair cells at different points along the basilar membrane—with higher frequencies producing greater activation closer to the windows. Thus, the many component frequencies that compose each complex sound activate hair cells at many different points along the basilar membrane, and the many signals created by a single complex sound are carried out of the ear by many different auditory neurons. Like the cochlea, most other structures of the auditory system are arrayed according to frequency. Thus, in the same way that the organization of the visual system is primarily **retinotopic**, the organization of the auditory system is primarily **tonotopic**.

This brings us to the major unsolved mystery of auditory processing. Imagine yourself in a complex acoustic environment such as a party. The music is playing; people are dancing, eating, and drinking; and numerous conversations are going on around you. Because the component frequencies in each individual sound activate many sites along your basilar membrane, the number of sites simultaneously activated at any one time by the party noises is enormous. But somehow your auditory system manages to sort these individual frequency messages into separate categories and combine them so that you hear each source of complex sounds independently (see Feng & Ratnam, 2000). For example, you hear the speech of the person

standing next to you as a separate sequence of sounds, despite the fact that it contains many of the same component frequencies coming from other sources.

Figure 7.12 also shows the **semicircular canals**—the receptive organs of the vestibular system. The **vestibular system** carries information about the direction and intensity of head movements, which helps us maintain our balance.

From the Ear to the Primary Auditory Cortex

There is no major auditory pathway to the cortex comparable to the retina-geniculate-striate pathway of the visual system. Instead, there is a network of auditory pathways (see Masterton, 1992), some of which are illustrated in Figure 7.13. The axons of each *auditory nerve* synapse in the ipsilateral *cochlear nuclei*, from which many projections lead to the **superior olives** at the same level. The axons of the olivary neurons project via the *lateral lemniscus*

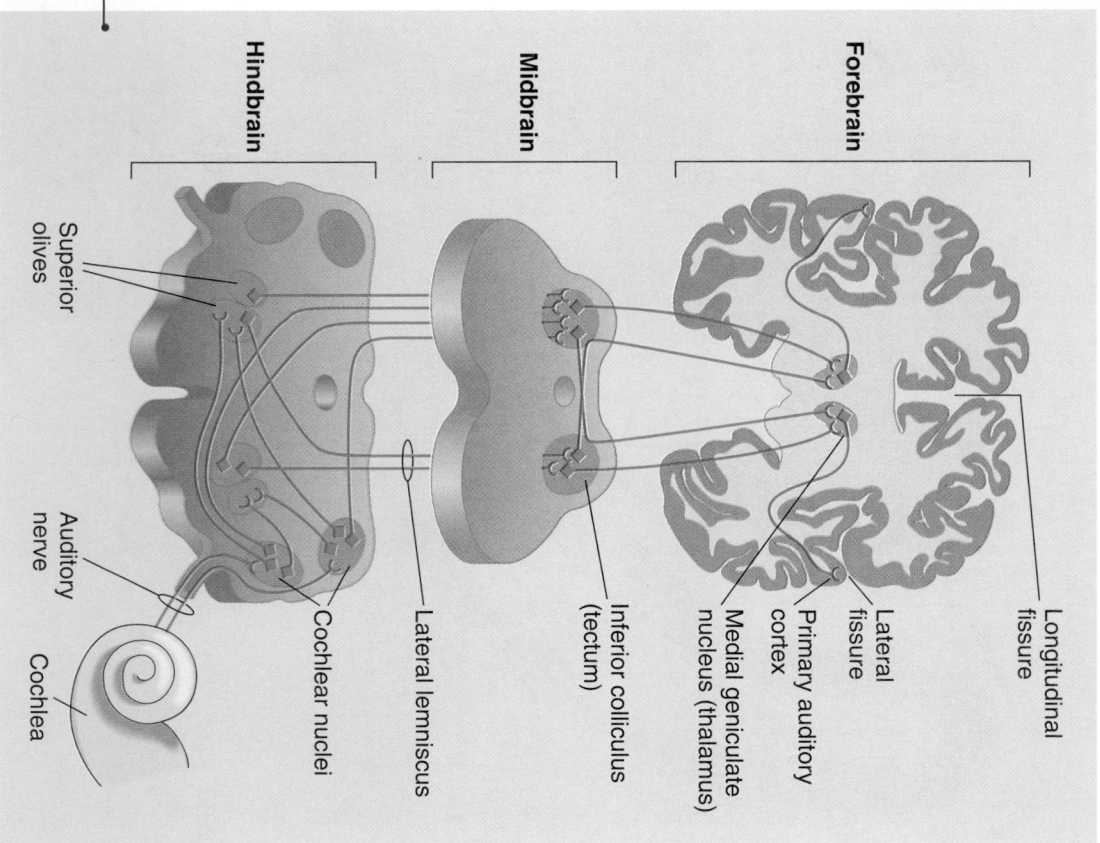

Forebrain
- Longitudinal fissure
- Lateral fissure
- Primary auditory cortex
- Medial geniculate nucleus (thalamus)

Midbrain
- Inferior colliculus (tectum)
- Lateral lemniscus

Hindbrain
- Superior olives
- Auditory nerve
- Cochlear nuclei
- Cochlea

FIGURE 7.13 Some of the pathways of the auditory system that lead from one ear to the cortex.

to the **inferior colliculi,** where they synapse on neurons that project to the **medial geniculate nuclei** of the thalamus, which in turn project to the *primary auditory cortex.* Notice that signals from each ear are transmitted to both ipsilateral and contralateral auditory cortex.

Primary Auditory Cortex

In humans, the primary auditory cortex is located in the temporal lobe, hidden from view within the *lateral fissure* (see Figure 7.14). Adjacent to the primary auditory cortex are two bands of secondary auditory cortex. There are thought to be two or three areas of primary auditory cortex and about seven areas of secondary auditory cortex (see Semple & Scott, 2003).

Two important principles of organization of the primary auditory cortex have been identified. First, like other areas of the cerebral cortex, the primary auditory cortex is organized in functional columns (see Schreiner, 1992): All of the neurons encountered during a vertical microelectrode penetration of primary auditory cortex (i.e., a penetration at right angles to the cortical layers) respond optimally to sounds in the same frequency range. Second, like the cochlea, primary auditory cortex is organized tonotopically (see Schreiner, Read, & Sutter, 2000): Posterior regions are more sensitive to higher frequencies.

Little is known about the neurons in primate secondary auditory cortex because they respond weakly and inconsistently to the pure tones typically used by researchers. Rauschecker, Tian, and Hauser (1995) reasoned on the basis of what was known about the neurons of secondary visual cortex that they might have more success in studying the neurons of secondary auditory cortex if they used more complex stimuli—secondary visual cortex neurons respond to complex visual stimuli but show little response to dots of light. These research-

ers found that pure tones are more effective in activating neurons in monkeys' primary auditory cortex, but monkey calls are more effective in activating neurons in their secondary auditory cortex. A similar pattern of preferential activation of human primary and secondary auditory cortex by pure and complex sounds, respectively, has been documented using fMRI (Wessinger et al., 2001). This suggests that auditory cortex is organized hierarchically in humans and other primates (Semple & Scott, 2003).

Sound Localization

Localization of sounds in space is mediated by the lateral and medial superior olives, but in different ways. When a sound originates to a person's left, it reaches the left ear first, and it is louder at the left ear. Some neurons in the *medial superior olives* respond to slight differences in the time of arrival of signals from the two ears, whereas some neurons in the *lateral superior olives* respond to slight differences in the amplitude of sounds from the two ears (see Heffner & Masterton, 1990).

The medial and lateral superior olives project to the *superior colliculus* (not shown in Figure 7.13), as well as to the inferior colliculus. In contrast to the general tonotopic organization of the auditory system, the deep layers of the superior colliculi, which receive auditory input, are laid out according to a map of auditory space (King, Schnupp, & Thompson, 1998). The superficial layers of the superior colliculi, which receive visual input, are organized retinotopically. Thus, it appears that the general function of the superior colliculi is locating sources of sensory input in space.

Many researchers interested in sound localization have studied barn

owls because these owls can locate sources of sounds better than any other animal whose hearing has been tested (see Konishi, 2003). They are nocturnal hunters and must be able to locate field mice solely by the rustling sounds the mice make in the dark. Not surprisingly, the auditory neurons of the barn owl's superior colliculus region are very finely tuned; that is, each neuron responds only to those sounds from a particular location near the owl (see Cohen & Knudsen, 1999).

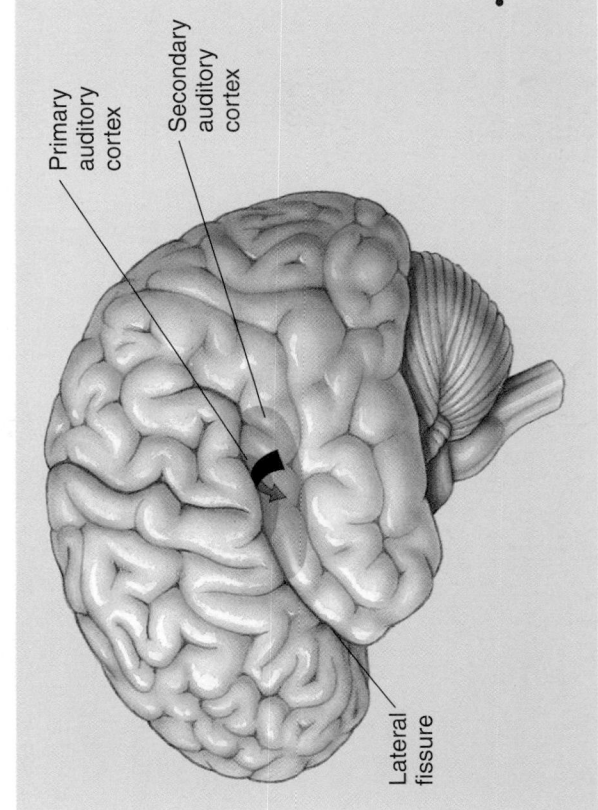

FIGURE 7.14 Location of the primary and secondary auditory cortex in the temporal cortex. Most of the auditory cortex is hidden in the lateral fissure.

Primary auditory cortex

Secondary auditory cortex

Lateral fissure

Effects of Auditory Cortex Damage

Efforts to characterize the effects of damage to the auditory cortex have been complicated by the fact that most 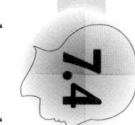 human auditory cortex is deep in the lateral fissure. Consequently, it is rarely destroyed in its entirety; and if it is, there is inevitably extensive damage to surrounding tissue. As a result of this problem, efforts to understand the effects of auditory cortex damage have relied largely on the study of nonhumans.

Evolutionary Perspective

Surprisingly, complete bilateral lesions of the primary auditory cortex in laboratory mammals produce no permanent deficits in their ability to detect the presence of sounds (e.g., Kavanagh & Kelly, 1988), even when the lesions include substantial secondary auditory cortex. However, such lesions do disrupt the abilities to localize brief sounds and to recognize rapid complex sequences of sound.

7.4 Somatosensation: Touch and Pain

You have undoubtedly experienced a wide variety of sensations emanating from your body. These are generally referred to as *somatosensations*. The system that mediates these bodily sensations—the *somatosensory system*—is, in fact, three separate but interacting systems: (1) an *exteroceptive system*, which senses external stimuli that are applied to the skin; (2) a *proprioceptive system*, which monitors information about the position of the body that comes from receptors in the muscles, joints, and organs of balance; and (3) an *interoceptive system* (see Craig, 2002), which provides general information about conditions within the body (e.g., temperature and blood pressure). This discussion deals almost exclusively with the exteroceptive system, which itself comprises three somewhat distinct divisions: a division for perceiving *mechanical stimuli* (touch), one for *thermal stimuli* (temperature), and one for *nociceptive stimuli* (pain).

Cutaneous Receptors

There are several different kinds of receptors in the skin (see Johnson, 2001). Figure 7.15 illustrates four that are found in both hairy skin and hairless skin, such as that on the palms of your hands. The simplest cutaneous receptors are the **free nerve endings** (neuron endings with no specialized structures on them), which are particularly sensitive to temperature change and pain.

The largest and deepest cutaneous receptors are the onionlike **Pacinian corpuscles;** because they adapt rapidly, they respond best to sudden displacements of the skin. In contrast, *Merkel's disks* and *Ruffini endings* both adapt slowly and respond best to gradual skin indentation and gradual skin stretch, respectively.

To appreciate the functional significance of fast and slow receptor adaptation, consider what happens when

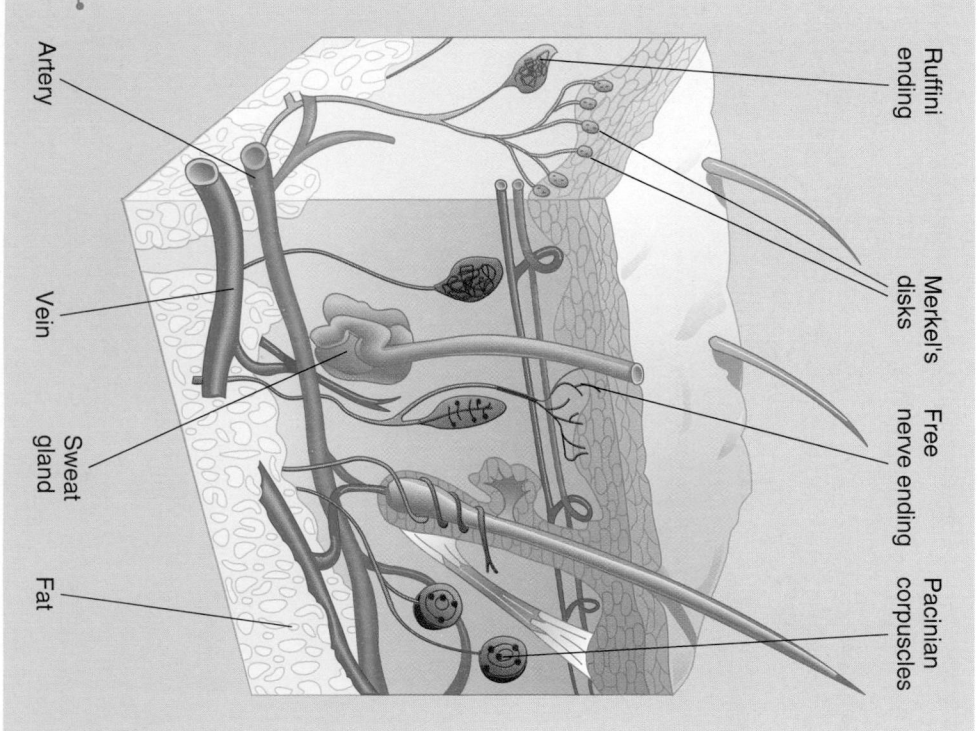

FIGURE 7.15   Four cutaneous receptors that occur in both hairy and hairless skin.

Artery — Vein — Sweat gland — Fat

Ruffini ending

Merkel's disks

Free nerve ending

Pacinian corpuscles

a constant pressure is applied to the skin. The pressure evokes a burst of firing in all receptors, which corresponds to the sensation of being touched; however, after a few hundred milliseconds, only the slowly adapting receptors remain active, and the quality of the sensation changes. In fact, you are often totally unaware of constant skin pressure; for example, you are usually unaware of the feeling of your clothes against your body until you focus attention on it. As a consequence, when you try to identify objects by touch, you manipulate them in your hands so that the pattern of stimulation continually changes. The identification of objects by touch is called **stereognosis.**

Dermatomes

The neural fibers that carry information from cutaneous receptors and other somatosensory receptors gather together in nerves and enter the spinal cord via the *dorsal roots.* The area of the body that is innervated by the left and right dorsal roots of a given segment of the spinal cord is called a **dermatome.** Figure 7.16 is a dermatomal map of the human body. Because there is considerable overlap between adjacent dermatomes, destruction of a single dorsal root typically produces little somatosensory loss.

The Two Major Ascending Somatosensory Pathways

Somatosensory information ascends to the human cortex over two major somatosensory pathways: the dorsal-column medial-lemniscus system and the anterolateral system. The **dorsal-column medial-lemniscus system** carries information about touch and proprioception. The **anterolateral system** carries information about pain and temperature.

The dorsal-column medial-lemniscus system is illustrated in Figure 7.17 on page 172. The sensory neurons of this system enter the spinal cord via a dorsal root, ascend ipsilaterally in the **dorsal columns,** and synapse in the *dorsal column nuclei* of the medulla. The axons of dorsal column nuclei neurons *decussate* (cross over to the other side of the brain) and then ascend in the **medial lemniscus** to the contralateral **ventral posterior nucleus** of the thalamus. The ventral posterior nuclei also receive input via the three branches of the *trigeminal nerve,* which carry somatosensory information from the contralateral areas of the face. Most neurons of the ventral posterior nucleus project to the *primary somatosensory cortex (SI);* others project to the *secondary somatosensory cortex (SII)* or the *posterior parietal cortex.* Neuroscience trivia buffs will almost certainly want to add to their collection the fact that the dorsal column neurons that originate in the toes are the longest neurons in the human body.

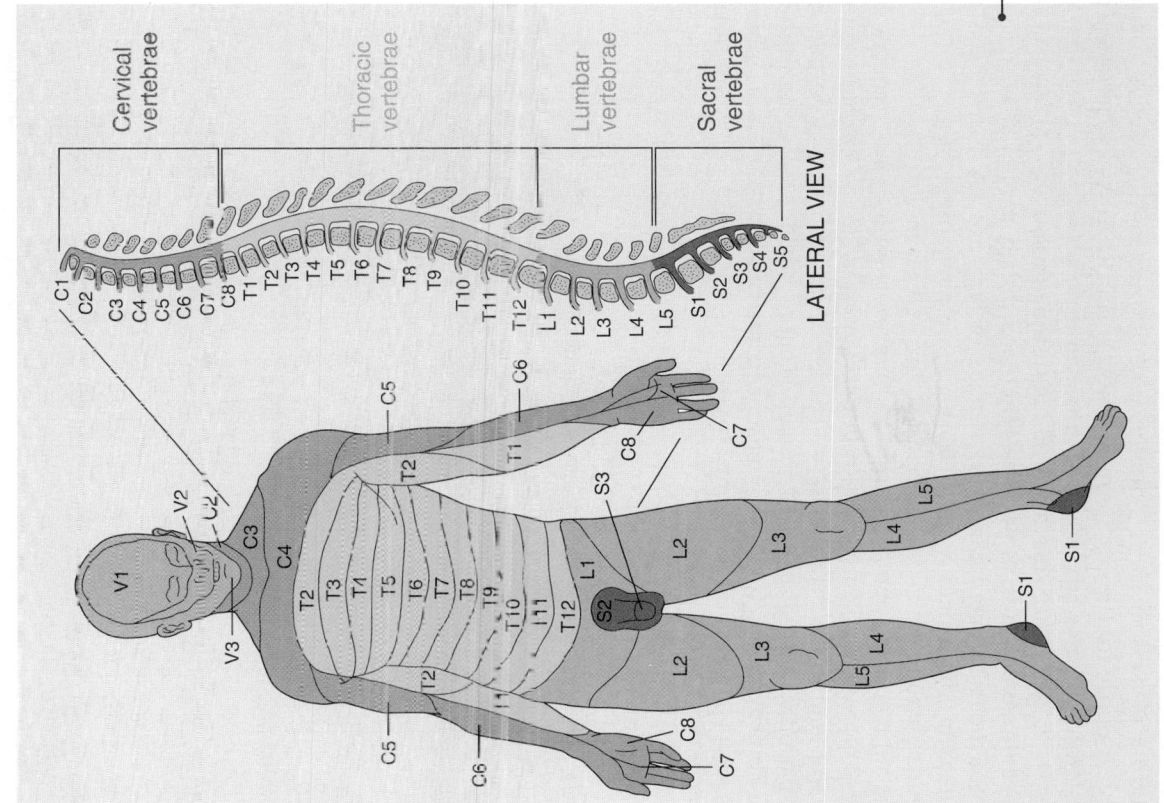

Cervical vertebrae

Thoracic vertebrae

Lumbar vertebrae

Sacral vertebrae

LATERAL VIEW

FIGURE 7.16 The dermatomes of the human body. S, L, T, and C refer respectively to the *sacral, lumbar, thoracic,* and *cervical* regions of the spinal cord. V1, V2, and V3 stand for the three branches of the trigeminal nerve.

FIGURE 7.17 The dorsal-column medial-lemniscus system.

The anterolateral system is illustrated in Figure 7.18. Most dorsal root neurons of the anterolateral system synapse as soon as they enter the spinal cord. The axons of most of the second-order neurons decussate but then ascend to the brain in the contralateral anterolateral portion of the spinal cord; however, some do not decussate but ascend ipsilaterally. The anterolateral system comprises three different tracts: the *spinothalamic tract*, which projects to the *ventral posterior nucleus of the thalamus* (as does the dorsal-column medial-lemniscus system); the *spinoreticular tract*, which projects to the *reticular formation* (and then to the *parafascicular nuclei* and *intralaminar nuclei of the thalamus*); and the *spinotectal tract*, which projects to the *tectum* (colliculi). The three branches of the trigeminal nerve carry pain and temperature information from the face to the same thalamic sites. The pain and temperature information that reaches the thalamus is then distributed to SI, SII, posterior parietal cortex, and other parts of the brain.

Mark, Ervin, and Yakolev (1962) assessed the effects of lesions to the thalamus on the chronic pain of patients in the advanced stages of cancer. Lesions to the ventral posterior nuclei, which receive input from both the spinothalamic tract and the dorsal-column medial-lemniscus system, produced some loss of cutaneous

sensitivity to touch, to temperature change, and to sharp pain; but the lesions had no effect on deep, chronic pain. In contrast, lesions of the parafascicular and intralaminar nuclei, both of which receive deep chronic pain input from the spinoreticular tract, reduced deep chronic pain without disrupting cutaneous sensitivity.

Cortical Areas of Somatosensation

In 1937, Penfield and his colleagues mapped the primary somatosensory cortex of patients during neurosurgery (see Figure 7.19 on page 174) Penfield applied electrical stimulation to various sites on the cortical surface, and

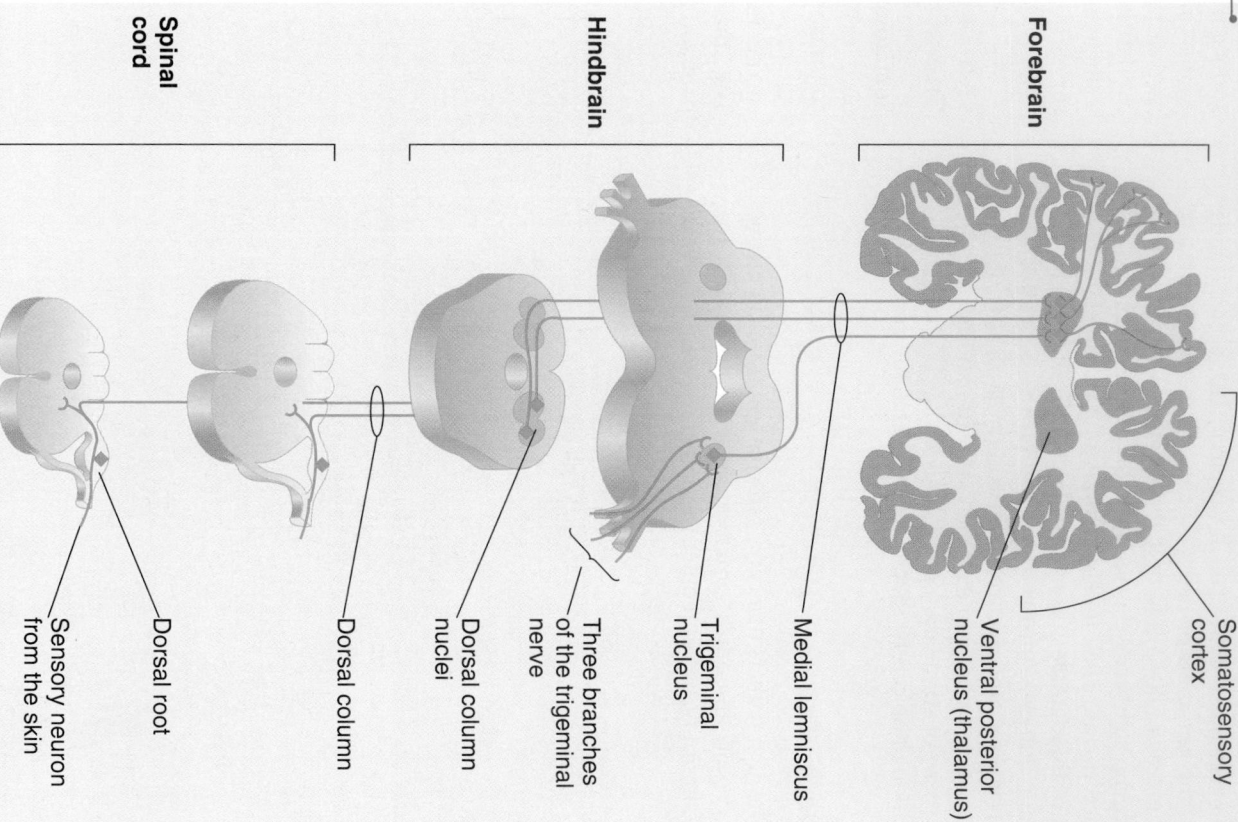

Forebrain

Hindbrain

Spinal cord

Somatosensory cortex

Ventral posterior nucleus (thalamus)

Medial lemniscus

Trigeminal nucleus

Three branches of the trigeminal nerve

Dorsal column nuclei

Dorsal column

Dorsal root

Sensory neuron from the skin

the patients, who were fully conscious under a local anesthetic, described what they felt. When stimulation was applied to the *postcentral gyrus*, the patients reported somatosensory sensations in various parts of their bodies. When Penfield mapped the relation between each site of stimulation and the part of the body in which the sensation was felt, he discovered that the human primary somatosensory cortex (SI) is **somatotopic**—organized according to a map of the body surface. This somatotopic map is commonly referred to as the **somatosensory homunculus** (*homunculus* means "little man").

Notice in Figure 7.19 that the somatosensory homunculus is distorted; the greatest proportion of SI is dedicated to receiving input from the parts of the body

There are several other areas of secondary somatosensory cortex in humans (see Kaas & Collins, 2001). For example, there are two narrow bands, one on either side of SI, and there is another adjacent to SII. Each is somatotopically organized, but the function of each is unclear.

Kaas and others (1981) found that the primary somatosensory cortex is composed of four functional strips, each with a similar, but separate, somatotopic organization. Each strip of primary somatosensory cortex is most sensitive to a different kind of somatosensory input (e.g., to light touch or temperature). Thus, if one were to record from neurons in a horizontal line across the four strips, one would find neurons that "preferred" four different kinds of tactile stimulation, all to the same part of the body. Also, one would find that as one moved from anterior to posterior, the preferences of the neurons would tend to become more complex and specific (see Caselli, 1997), suggesting an anterior-to-posterior hierarchical scheme (Iwamura, 1998).

The receptive fields of many neurons in the primary somatosensory cortex, like those of visual system neurons, can be divided into antagonistic excitatory and inhibitory areas (DiCarlo & Johnson, 2000; DiCarlo, Johnson, & Hsaio, 1998). Figure 7.20 on page 175 illustrates the receptive field of a neuron of the primary somatosensory cortex that is responsive to light touch (Mountcastle & Powell, 1959).

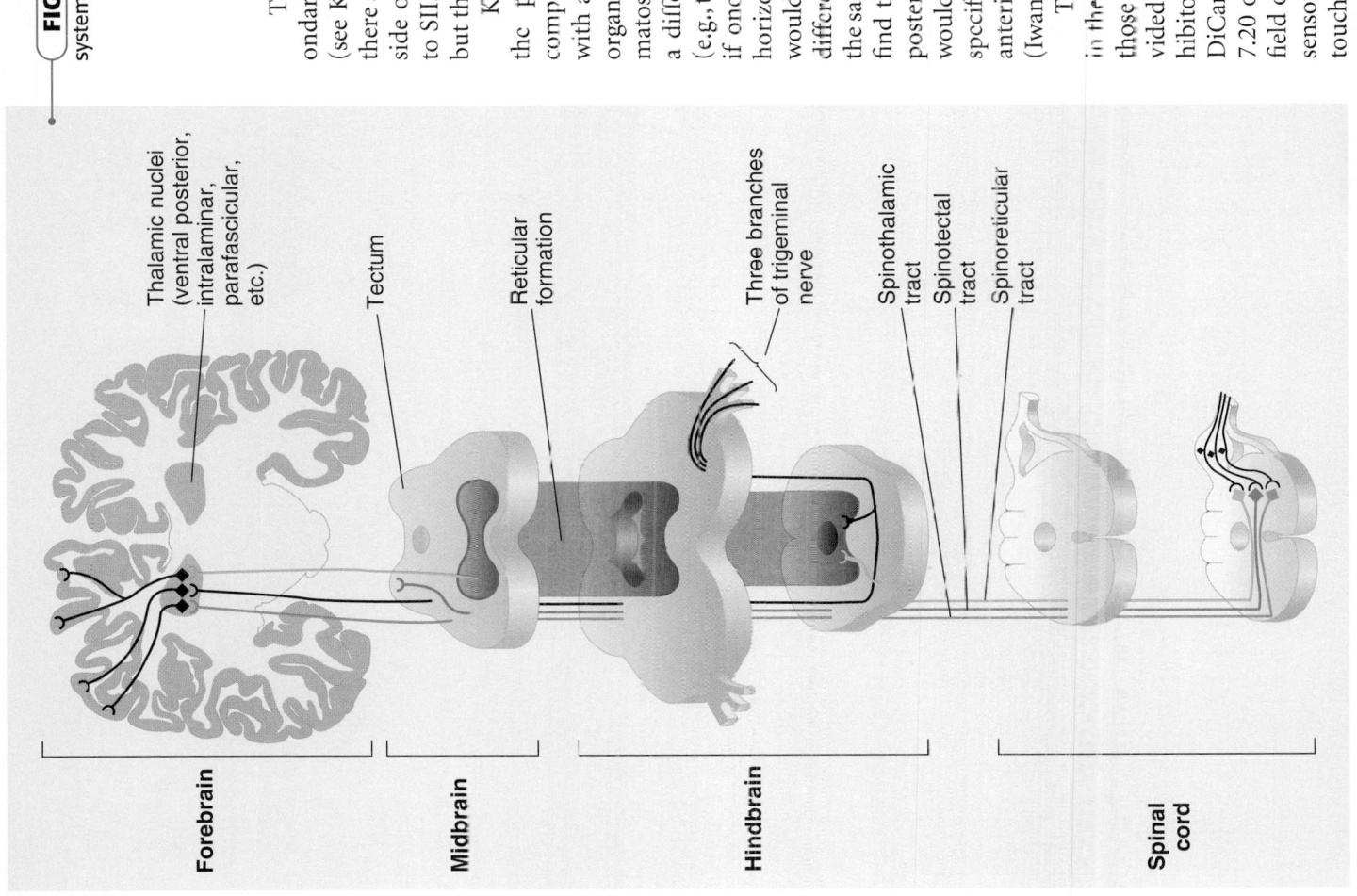

FIGURE 7.18   The anterolateral system.

Forebrain
Thalamic nuclei (ventral posterior, intralaminar, parafascicular, etc.)

Midbrain
Tectum

Hindbrain
Reticular formation
Three branches of trigeminal nerve

Spinothalamic tract
Spinotectal tract
Spinoreticular tract

Spinal cord

that are capable of the finest tactile discriminations (e.g., hands, lips, and tongue).

A second somatotopically organized area, SII, lies just ventral to SI in the postcentral gyrus, and much of it extends into the lateral fissure. SII receives most of its input from SI and is thus regarded as secondary somatosensory cortex. In contrast to SI, whose input is largely contralateral, SII receives substantial input from both sides of the body. Much of the output of SI and SII goes to the association cortex of the *posterior parietal lobe*.

Effects of Damage to the Primary Somatosensory Cortex

Like the effects of damage to the primary auditory cortex, the effects of damage to the primary somatosensory cortex are often remarkably mild. Corkin, Milner, and Rasmussen (1970) assessed the somatosensory abilities of epileptic patients both before and after a unilateral excision that included SI. Following surgery, the patients displayed two minor contralateral deficits: a reduced

FIGURE 7.19 The locations of human primary somatosensory cortex (SI) and one area of secondary somatosensory cortex (SII) with the conventional portrayal of the somatosensory homunculus. Something has always confused me about this portrayal of the somatosensory homunculus: The body is upside-down, while the head is right side up. It now appears that this conventional portrayal is wrong. The results of an fMRI study suggest that the face representation is also inverted. (Servos et al, 1999).

ability to detect light touch and a reduced ability to identify objects by touch (i.e., a deficit in stereognosis). These deficits were bilateral only in those cases in which the unilateral lesion encroached on SII.

Somatosensory Agnosias

There are two major types of somatosensory agnosia. One is **asterognosia**—the inability to recognize objects by touch. Cases of pure asterognosia—those that occur in the absence of simple sensory deficits—are rare (Corkin, Milner, & Rasmussen, 1970). The other type of somatosensory agnosia is **asomatognosia**—the failure to recognize parts of one's own body. Asomatognosia is usually unilateral, affecting only the left side of the body; and it is usually associated with extensive damage to the right posterior parietal lobe. You have already encountered one example of asomatognosia in this book, the case of the man who fell out of bed; the case of Aunt Betty is another.

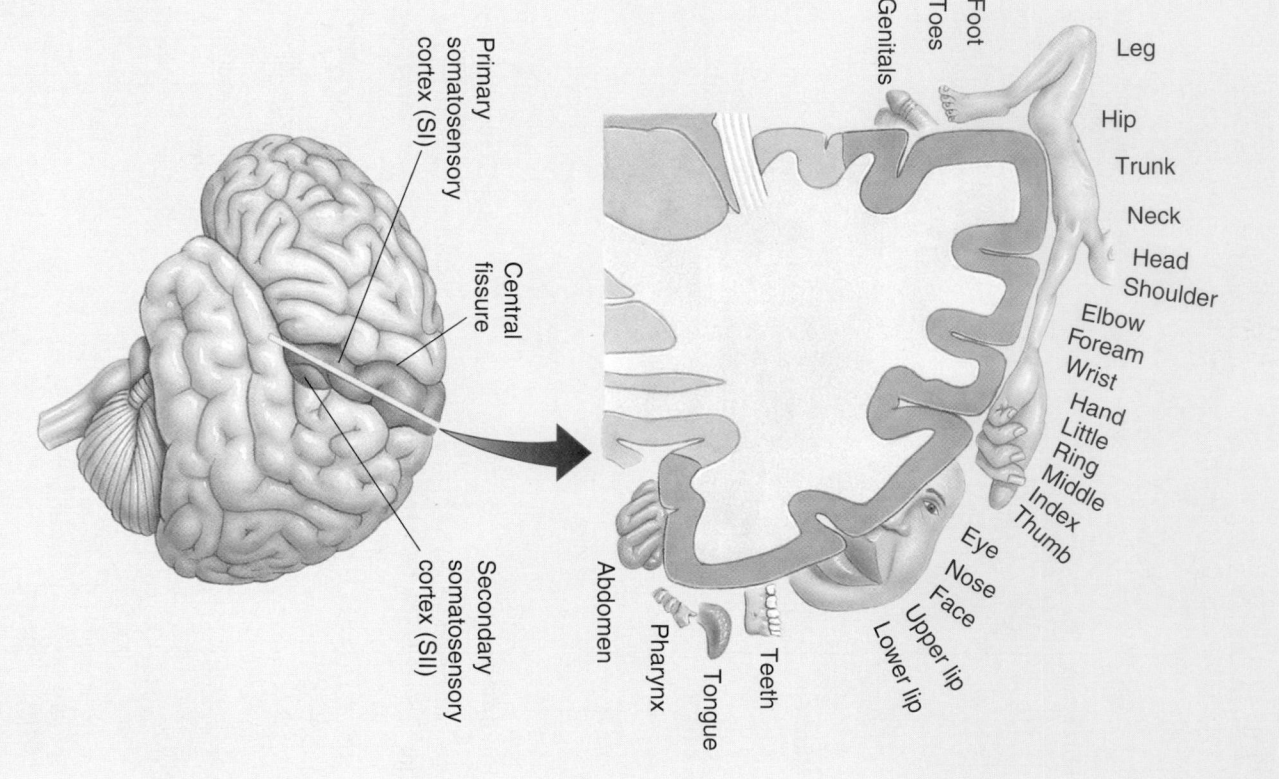

Primary somatosensory cortex (SI)

Central fissure

Secondary somatosensory cortex (SII)

Leg
Hip
Trunk
Neck
Head
Shoulder
Elbow
Foream
Wrist
Hand
Little
Ring
Middle
Index
Thumb
Eye
Nose
Face
Upper lip
Lower lip
Teeth
Tongue
Pharynx
Abdomen

Foot
Toes
Genitals

The Case of Aunt Betty, Who Lost Half of Her Body

Clinical Implications

It was time to see Aunt Betty—she wasn't really my aunt, but I grew up thinking that she was. She was my mother's best friend. She had had a stroke in her right hemisphere.

As we walked to her room, one of the medical students described the case. "Left hemiplegia [left-side paralysis]," I was told.

Aunt Betty was lying on her back with her head and eyes turned to the right. "Betty," I called out. Not

Aunt Betty, but Betty. I was 37; I'd dropped the "Aunt" long ago—at least 2 years earlier.

I approached her bed from the left, but Aunt Betty did not turn her head or even her eyes to look towards me.

"Hal," she called out. "Where are you?" I turned her head gently toward me. We talked. It was clear that she had no speech problems, no memory loss, and no confusion. She was as bright as ever. But her eyes still looked to the right as if the left side of her world did not exist.

I picked up her right hand and held it in front of her eyes. "What's this?" I asked.

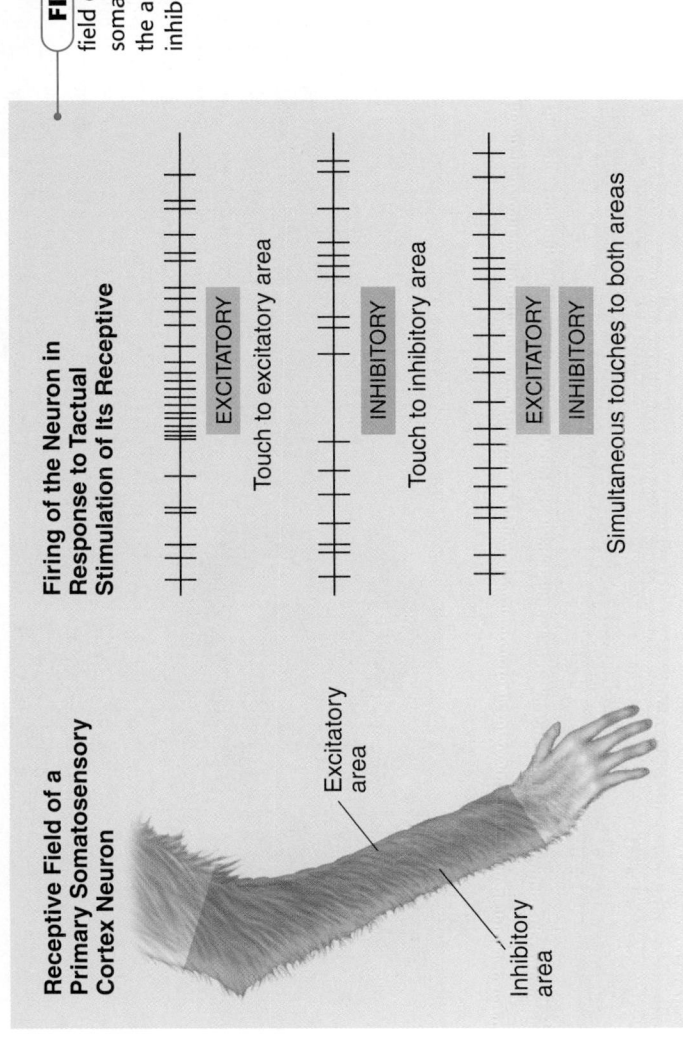

Receptive Field of a Primary Somatosensory Cortex Neuron

Firing of the Neuron in Response to Tactual Stimulation of Its Receptive

Excitatory area

Inhibitory area

EXCITATORY

Touch to excitatory area

INHIBITORY

Touch to inhibitory area

EXCITATORY

INHIBITORY

Simultaneous touches to both areas

FIGURE 7.20 The receptive field of a neuron of the primary somatosensory cortex. Notice the antagonistic excitatory and inhibitory areas.

The Paradoxes of Pain

A paradox is a logical contradiction. The perception of pain is paradoxical in three important respects, which is why I have singled out pain for special discussion. The three paradoxes of pain are explained in the following three subsections.

Adaptiveness of Pain   One paradox of pain is that an experience that seems in every respect to be so bad is in fact extremely important for our survival. There is no special stimulus for pain; it is a response to excessive (potentially harmful) stimulation of any type (see Craig, 2003). The value of pain is best illustrated by the case of a person who does not experience it.

"My hand, of course," she said with an intonation that suggested what she thought of my question.

"Well then, what's this?" I said, as I held up her limp left hand where she could see it.

"A hand."

"Whose hand?"

"Your hand, I guess," she replied. She seemed genuinely puzzled. I carefully placed her hand on the bed.

"Why have you come to this hospital?" I asked.

"To see you," she replied hesitantly. I could tell that she didn't really know the answer.

"Is there anything wrong with you?"

"No."

"How about your left hand and leg?"

"They're fine," she said. "How are yours?"

"They're fine too," I replied. There was nothing else to do. Aunt Betty was in trouble.

(Paraphrased from pp. 12–14 of *Newton's Madness: Further Tales of Clinical Neurology* by Harold L. Klawans. New York: Harper & Row, 1990.)

As in the case of Aunt Betty, asomatognosia is often accompanied by **anosognosia**—the failure of neuropsychological patients to recognize their own symptoms. Asomatognosia may also be accompanied by **contralateral neglect**—the tendency not to respond to stimuli that are contralateral to a right-hemisphere injury. (You will learn more about contralateral neglect in Chapter 8).

The Case of Miss C., the Woman Who Felt No Pain

Clinical Implications

The best documented of all cases of congenital insensitivity to pain is Miss C., a young Canadian girl who was a student at McGill University in Montreal. . . . The young lady was highly intelligent and seemed normal in every way except that she had never felt pain. As a child, she had bitten off the tip of her tongue while chewing food, and had suffered third-degree burns after kneeling on a radiator to look out of the window. . . . She felt no pain when parts of her body were subjected to strong electric shock, to hot water at temperatures that usually produce reports of burning pain, or to a prolonged ice-bath. Equally astonishing was the fact that she showed no changes in blood pressure, heart rate, or respiration when these stimuli were presented. Furthermore, she could not remember ever sneezing or coughing, the gag reflex could be elicited only with great difficulty, and corneal reflexes (to protect the eyes) were absent. A variety of other stimuli, such as insert-ing a stick up through the nostrils, pinching tendons, or injections of histamine under the skin—which are normally considered as forms of torture—also failed to produce pain.

Miss C. had severe medical problems. She exhibited pathological changes in her knees, hip, and spine, and underwent several orthopaedic operations. The sur-geon attributed these changes to the lack of protection to joints usually given by pain sensation. She apparently failed to shift her weight when standing, to turn over in her sleep, or to avoid certain postures, which normally prevent inflammation of joints....

Miss C. died at the age of twenty-nine of massive infections... and extensive skin and bone trauma.

(From *The Challenge of Pain*, pp. 16–17, by Ronald Melzack and Patrick D. Wall, 1982, London: Penguin Books Ltd. Copyright © Ronald Mel-zack and Patrick D. Wall, 1982.)

Cognitive Neuroscience

Lack of Clear Cortical Representation of Pain The second paradox of pain is that it has no obvious cortical representation (Rainville, 2002). Painful stimuli often activate areas of cortex, but the areas of activation have varied greatly from study to study (Apkarian, 1995).

Painful stimuli usually elicit responses in SI and SII. However, removal of SI and SII in humans is not associ-ated with any change in the threshold for pain. Indeed, *hemispherectomized patients* (those with one cerebral hemisphere removed) can still perceive pain from both sides of their bodies.

The cortical area that has been most frequently linked to the experience of pain is the **anterior cingu-late cortex** (the cortex of the anterior cingulate gyrus; see Figure 7.21). For example, using PET, Craig and col-leagues (1996) demonstrated increases in anterior cin-gulate cortex activity when subjects placed a hand on painfully cold bars, painfully hot bars, or even on a series of alternating cool and warm bars, which produce an il-lusion of painful stimulation.

Evidence suggests that the anterior cingulate cortex is involved in the emotional reaction to pain rather than to the perception of pain itself (Panksepp, 2003; Price, 2000). For example, *prefrontal lobotomy*, which dam-ages the anterior cingulate cortex and its connections, typically reduces the emotional reaction to pain without changing the threshold for pain.

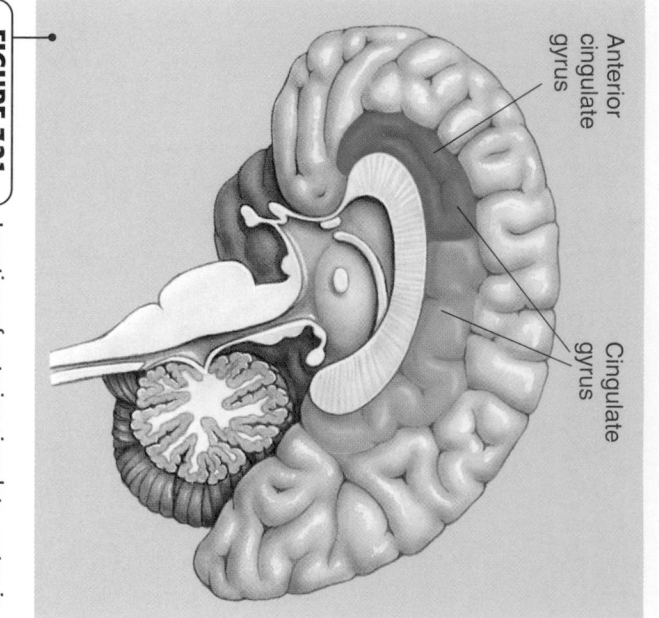

FIGURE 7.21 Location of anterior cingulate cortex in the cingulate gyrus.

Anterior cingulate gyrus

Cingulate gyrus

Descending Pain Control The third paradox of pain is that this most compelling of all sensory experi-ences can be so effectively suppressed by cognitive and emotional factors. For example, men participating in a certain religious ceremony swing from ropes attached to giant meat hooks in their backs with little evidence of pain; severe wounds suffered by soldiers in battle are often associated with little pain; and people injured in life-threatening situations frequently feel no pain until the threat is over.

Melzack and Wall (1965) proposed the **gate-control theory** to account for the ability of cognitive and emo-tional factors to block pain. They theorized that signals descending from the brain can activate neural gating cir-cuits in the spinal cord to block incoming pain signals.

Three discoveries led to the identification of a de-scending pain-control circuit. First was the discovery that electrical stimulation of the **periaqueductal gray (PAG)** has analgesic (pain-blocking) effects: Reynolds (1969) was able to perform surgery on rats with no an-algesia other than that provided by PAG stimulation. Second was the discovery that the PAG and other areas of the brain contain specialized receptors for opiate an-algesic drugs such as morphine. And third was the isola-tion of several endogenous (internally produced) opiate analgesics, the **endorphins**, which you learned about in Chapter 4. These three findings together suggested that analgesic drugs and psychological factors might block pain through an endorphin-sensitive circuit that de-scends from the PAG.

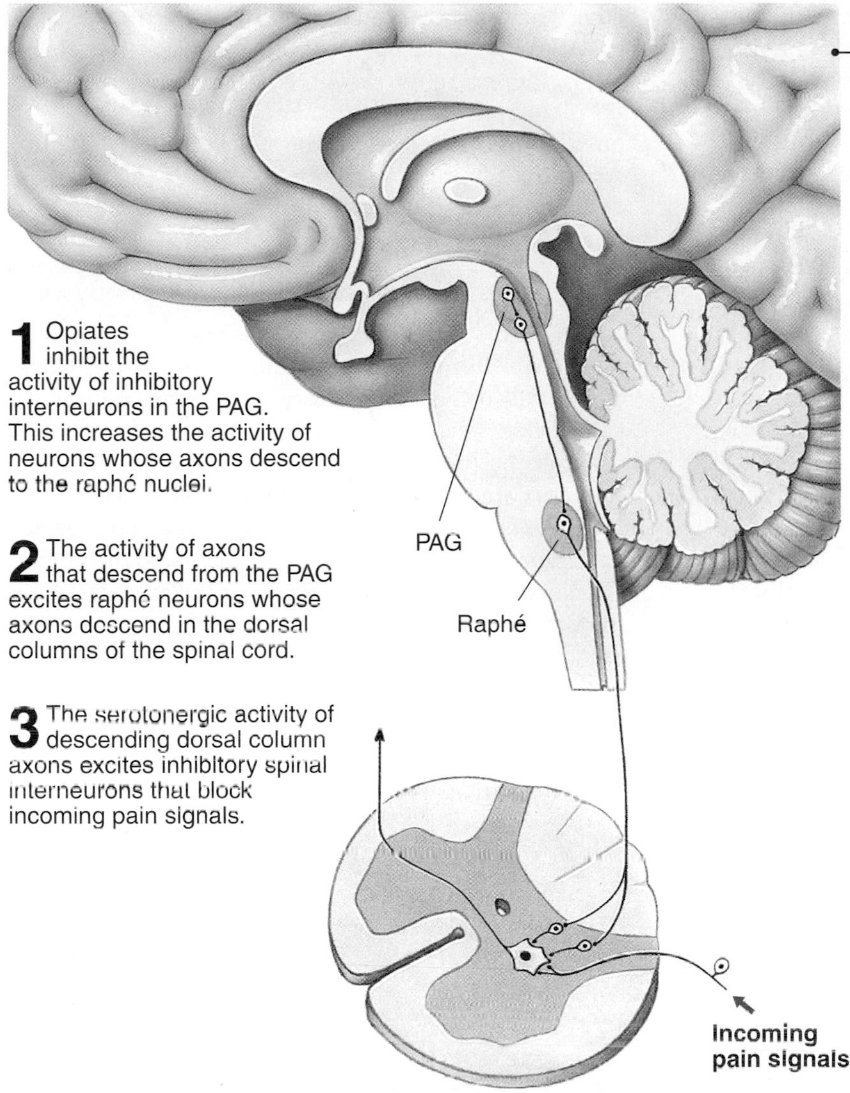

FIGURE 7.22 Basbaum and Fields's (1978) model of the descending analgesia circuit.

1 Opiates inhibit the activity of inhibitory interneurons in the PAG. This increases the activity of neurons whose axons descend to the raphé nuclei.

2 The activity of axons that descend from the PAG excites raphé neurons whose axons descend in the dorsal columns of the spinal cord.

3 The serotonergic activity of descending dorsal column axons excites inhibitory spinal interneurons that block incoming pain signals.

PAG

Raphé

Incoming pain signals

Figure 7.22 illustrates the descending analgesia circuit first hypothesized by Basbaum and Fields (1978). They proposed that the output of the PAG excites the serotonergic neurons of the *raphé nuclei (a cluster of serotonergic nuclei in the core of the medulla)*, which in turn project down the dorsal columns of the spinal cord and excite interneurons that block incoming pain signals in the dorsal horn.

Descending analgesia pathways have been the subject of intensive investigation since the first model was proposed by Basbaum and Fields in 1978. In order to incorporate the mass of accumulated data, models of the descending analgesia circuits have grown much more complex (see Borszcz, 1999; McNally, 1999). Still, a descending component involving opiate activity in the PAG and serotonergic activity in the raphé nuclei remains a key part of most of these models.

7.5 The Chemical Senses: Smell and Taste

Olfaction (smell) and *gustation* (taste) are referred to as the chemical senses because their function is to monitor the chemical content of the environment. Smell is the response of the olfactory system to airborne chemicals that are drawn by inhalation over receptors in the nasal passages, and taste is the response of the gustatory system to chemicals in solution in the oral cavity.

When we are eating, smell and taste act in concert. Molecules of food excite both smell and taste receptors and produce an integrated sensory impression termed **flavor.** The contribution of olfaction to flavor is often underestimated, but you won't make this mistake if you remember that people with no sense of smell have difficulty distinguishing the flavors of apples and onions.

Arguably, the single most interesting aspect of the chemical senses is their role in the social lives of many species (e.g., DeCatanzaro et al., 2000; Luo, Fee, & Katz, 2003). The members of many species release **pheromones**—chemicals that influence the physiology and behavior of *conspecifics* (members of the same species). For example, Murphy and Schneider (1970) showed that the sexual and aggressive behavior of hamsters is under pheromonal control. Normal male hamsters attack and kill unfamiliar males that are placed in their colonies, whereas they mount and impregnate unfamiliar sexually receptive females. However, male hamsters that are unable to smell the intruders engage in neither aggressive nor sexual behavior. Murphy and Schneider confirmed the olfactory basis of hamsters' aggressive and sexual behavior in a particularly devious fashion. They swabbed a male intruder with the vaginal secretions of a

Evolutionary Perspective

sexually receptive female before placing it in an unfamiliar hamster colony; in so doing, they converted it from an object of hamster assassination to an object of hamster lust.

The possibility that humans may release sexual pheromones has received considerable attention because of its financial and recreational potential. There have been many suggestive findings. For example, (1) the olfactory sensitivity of women is greatest when they are ovulating; (2) the menstrual cycles of women living together tend to become synchronized; (3) humans—particularly women—can tell the sex of a person from the breath or the underarm odor; and (4) men can judge the stage of a woman's menstrual cycle on the basis of her vaginal odor. However, there is still no direct evidence that human odors can serve as sex attractants. Most subjects do not find the aforementioned body odors to be particularly attractive.

Another feature of the chemical senses that has attracted attention is that they are involved in some interesting forms of learning. As you discovered in Chapter 5, animals that suffer from gastrointestinal upset after consuming a particular food develop a *conditioned aversion* to that taste. Conversely, it has been shown that rats develop preferences for flavors they encounter in their mother's milk or on the breath of conspecifics (Galef, 1989). And adult male rats that were nursed as pups by lemon-scented mothers copulate more effectively with females that smell of lemons (Fillion & Blass, 1986)—a phenomenon that has been aptly referred to as the *I-want-a-girl-just-like-the-girl-who-married-dear-old-dad phenomenon* (Diamond, 1986).

The Olfactory System

The olfactory system is illustrated in Figure 7.23. The olfactory receptors are located in the upper part of the nose, embedded in a layer of mucus-covered tissue called the **olfactory mu-**

cosa. They have their own axons, which pass through a porous portion of the skull (the *cribriform plate*) and enter the **olfactory bulbs**, where they synapse on neurons that project via the *olfactory tracts* to the brain.

About one thousand kinds of receptor proteins have been identified, each sensitive to different odors (see Gibson & Garbers, 2000). In mammals, each olfactory receptor cell contains one type of receptor protein molecule (Serizawa et al., 2003). This is called the *one-olfactory-receptor-one-neuron rule* (Lewcock & Reed, 2003). Researchers have attempted to discover the functional principle by which the various receptors are distributed through the olfactory mucosa. If there is such a principle, it has not yet been discovered: Each type of receptor appears to be scattered throughout the mucosa, providing no clue about the organization of the system.

Despite the fact that each kind of olfactory receptor seems to be scattered throughout the olfactory mucosa, somehow all the olfactory receptors with the same re-

ON THE CD

Visit *Investigating Olfaction: The Nose Knows.* This module will provide you with everything you ever wanted to know about olfaction and the olfactory system.

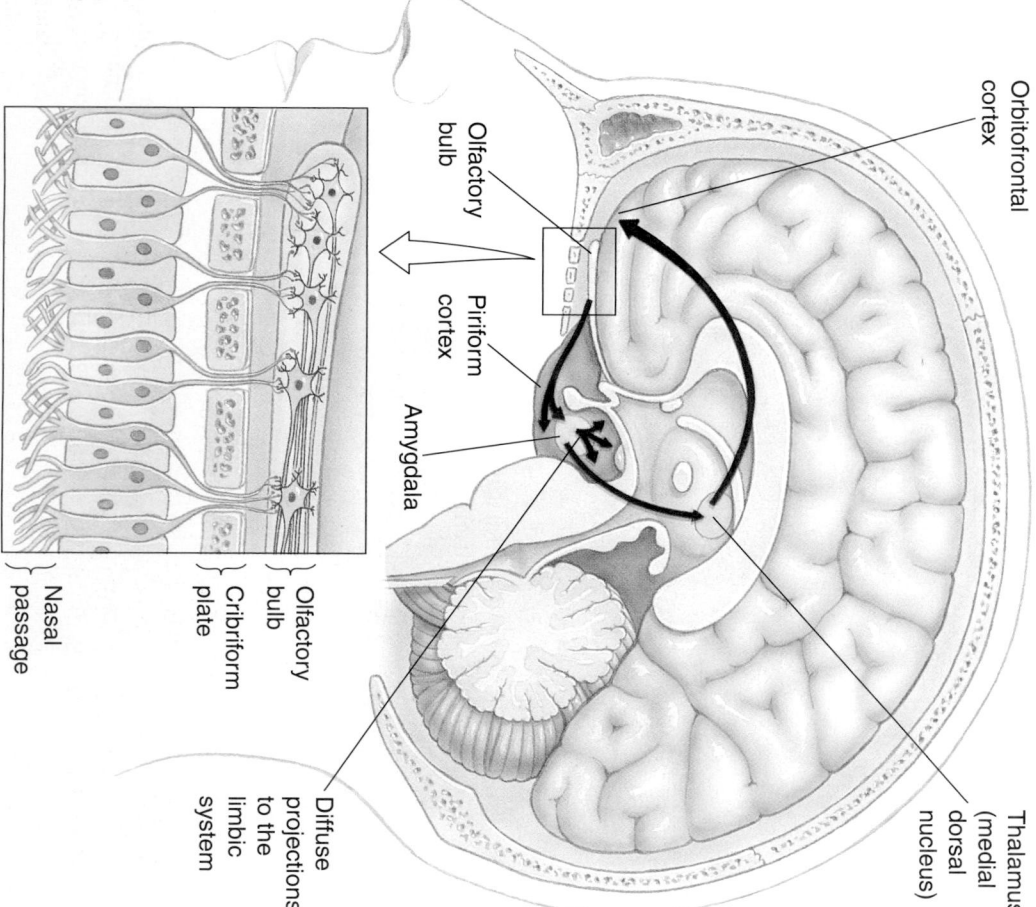

FIGURE 7.23   The human olfactory system.

Orbitofrontal cortex

Olfactory bulb

Piriform cortex

Amygdala

Thalamus (medial dorsal nucleus)

Diffuse projections to the limbic system

Olfactory bulb

Cribriform plate

Nasal passage

ceptor protein project to the same general location in the olfactory bulb (see Lewcock & Reed, 2003). Accordingly, different odors produce different spatial patterns of activity on the olfactory bulbs, patterns that can be detected with the 2-deoxyglucose technique (Leon & Johnson, 2003). Because each type of receptor responds in varying degrees to a wide variety of odors, each odor seems to be encoded by component processing—that is, by the pattern of activity across many receptor types (Doty, 2001).

The olfactory receptor cells differ from the receptor cells of other sensory systems in one important way. New olfactory receptor cells are created throughout each individual's life, to replace those that have deteriorated (Doty, 2001). Once created, the new receptor cells develop axons, which grow until they reach appropriate sites in the olfactory bulb.

Each olfactory tract projects to several structures of the medial temporal lobes, including the amygdala and the **piriform cortex**—an area of medial temporal cortex adjacent to the amygdala. The piriform cortex is considered to be primary olfactory cortex. The olfactory system is the only sensory system whose major sensory pathway reaches the cerebral cortex without first passing through the thalamus.

Two major olfactory pathways leave the amygdala-piriform area. One projects diffusely to the limbic system, and the other projects via the **medial dorsal nuclei** of the thalamus to the **orbitofrontal cortex**—the area of cortex on the inferior surface of the frontal lobes, next to the *orbits* (eye sockets). The limbic projection is thought to mediate the emotional response to odors; the thalamic-orbitofrontal projection is thought to mediate the conscious perception of odors. Little is known about how neurons receptive to different odorants are organized in the cortex (see Savic, 2002).

The Gustatory System

Taste receptors are found on the tongue and in parts of the oral cavity; they typically occur in clusters of about 50, called **taste buds.** On the tongue, taste buds are often located around small protuberances called *papillae* (singular *papilla*). The relation between taste receptors, taste buds, and papillae is illustrated in Figure 7.24 (see Gilbertson, Damak, & Margolskee, 2000). Unlike olfactory receptors, taste receptors do not have their own axons; each neuron that carries impulses away from a taste bud receives input from many receptors.

It was once believed that there are four primary tastes—sweet, sour, bitter, and salty—and four kinds of taste receptors, one for each primary taste. The perception of any taste was assumed to be a product of the relative amounts of activity produced in these four kinds of receptors.

This simple component-processing theory of taste has several major problems (see Smith & Margolskee, 2001). One is that it is now clear that there are at least five primary tastes; *umami* (meaty or savory) is the fifth. Another problem is that many tastes cannot be created by combinations of the primary tastes (Schiffman & Erickson, 1980). Yet another is that some

Surface of Tongue

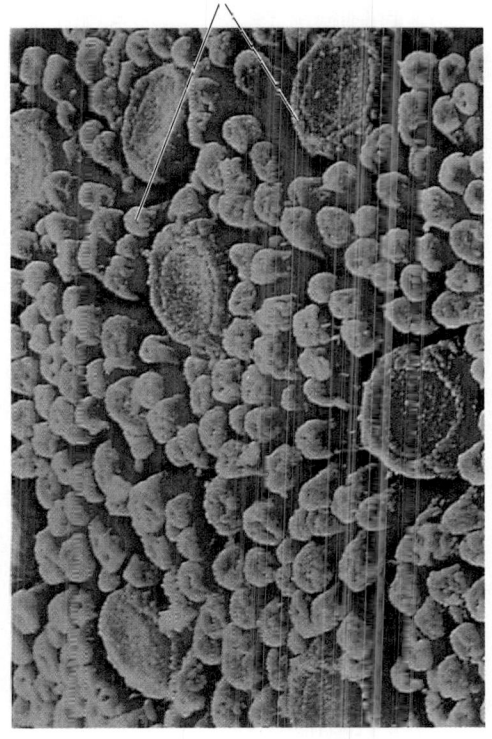

Papillae

Cross Section of a Papilla

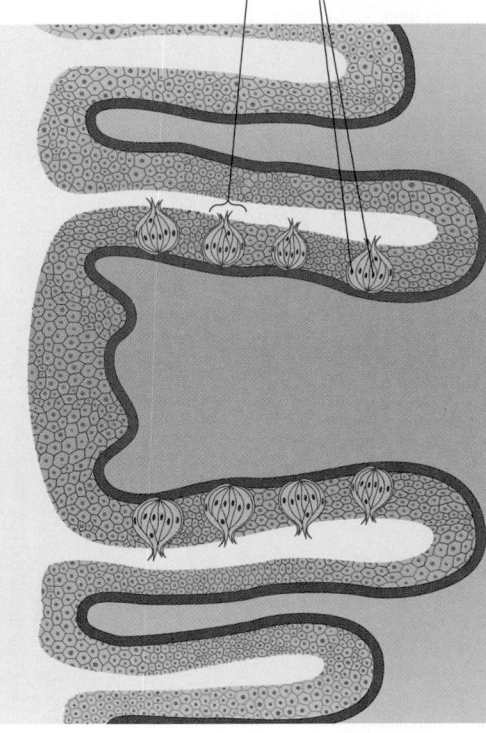

Taste
bud

Taste
receptors

FIGURE 7.24 Taste receptors, taste buds, and papillae on the surface of the tongue. Two sizes of papillae are visible in the photograph; only the larger papillae contain taste buds and receptors.

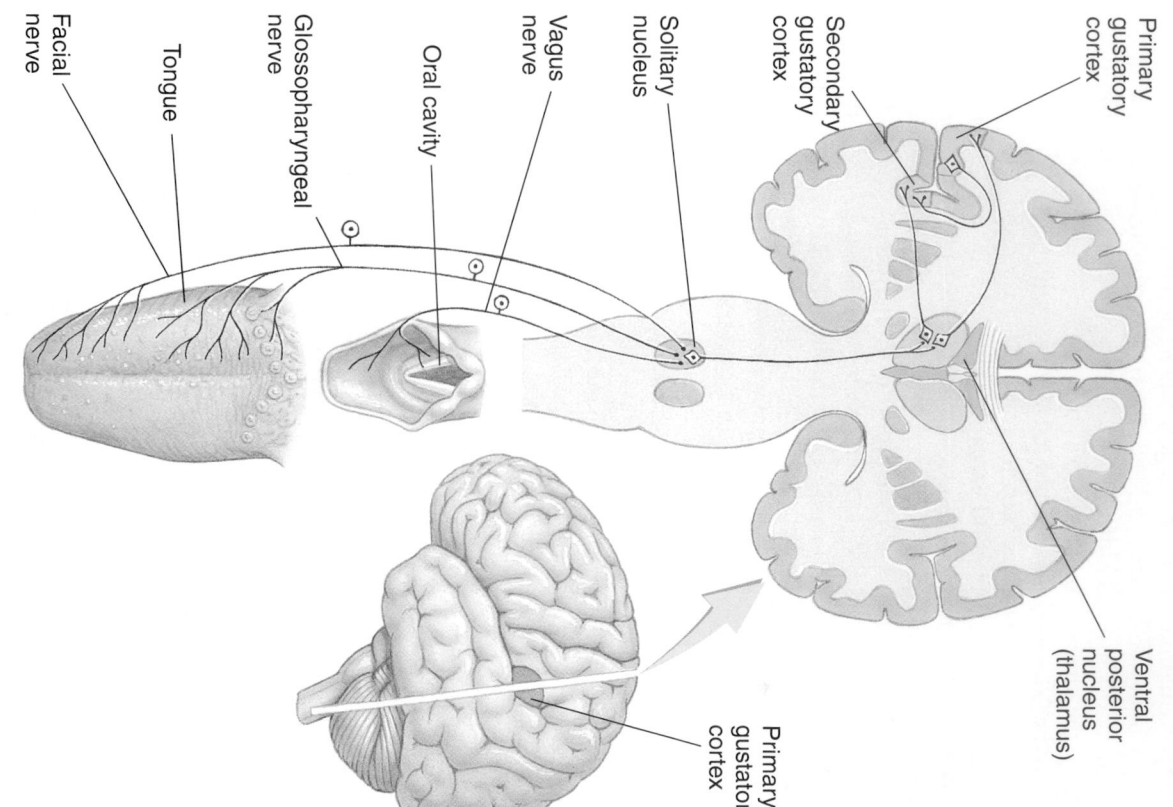

FIGURE 7.25 The human gustatory system.

tastes (salty and sour) seem to have no receptors specific to them; instead, they have been shown to influence the activity of some taste receptors by acting directly on their ion channels (see Montmayeur & Matsunami, 2002).

The major pathways over which gustatory signals are conducted to the cortex are illustrated in Figure 7.25. Gustatory afferent neurons leave the mouth as part of the *facial* (VII), *glossopharyngeal* (IX), and *vagus* (X) *cranial nerves*, which carry information from the front of the tongue, back of the tongue, and back of the oral cavity, respectively. These fibers all terminate in the **solitary nucleus** of the medulla, where they synapse on neurons that project to the *ventral posterior nucleus* of the thalamus. The gustatory axons of the ventral posterior nucleus project to the *primary gustatory cortex*, which is near the face area of the somatosensory homunculus, and to the *secondary gustatory cortex*, which is hidden from view in the lateral fissure (Sewards & Sewards, 2001). Unlike the projections of other sensory systems, the projections of the gustatory system are primarily ipsilateral.

Although evidence for simple component processing of taste at the receptor level is still lacking, electrophysiological recordings of both peripheral and central neurons in the gustatory system suggest that some type of component processing is occurring (see Smith & Margolskee, 2001). Most gustatory neurons respond to a variety of dissimilar tastes, and particular tastes seem to be encoded in the brain by profiles of activity in groups of neurons (e.g., high in some and low in others).

Brain Damage and the Chemical Senses

The inability to smell is called **anosmia;** the inability to taste is called **ageusia.** The most common neurologi-

cal cause of anosmia is a blow to the head that causes a displacement of the brain within the skull and shears the olfactory nerves where they pass through the cribriform plate. Less complete deficits in olfaction have been linked to a wide variety of neurological disorders including Alzheimer's disease, Down syndrome, epilepsy, multiple sclerosis, Korsakoff's disease, and Parkinson's disease (see Doty, 2001).

Ageusia is rare, presumably because sensory signals from the mouth are carried via three separate pathways. However, partial ageusia, limited to the anterior two-thirds of the tongue on one side, is sometimes observed after damage to the ear on the same side of the body. This is because the branch of the facial nerve (VII) that carries gustatory information from the anterior two-thirds of the tongue passes through the middle ear.

Labels in figure: Primary gustatory cortex; Secondary gustatory cortex; Ventral posterior nucleus (thalamus); Primary gustatory cortex; Solitary nucleus; Vagus nerve; Oral cavity; Glossopharyngeal nerve; Facial nerve; Tongue

Clinical Implications

SCAN YOUR BRAIN

Now that you have reached this chapter's final section, on selective attention, you should scan your brain to test your knowledge of the sensory systems. Complete each sentence with the name of the appropriate system. The correct answers are provided at the bottom of this page. Before proceeding, review material related to your incorrect answers and omissions.

1. The inferotemporal cortex is an area of secondary _____ cortex.

2. The dorsal and ventral streams are part of the _____ system.

3. The primary _____ cortex is organized tonotopically.

4. The inferior colliculi and medial geniculate nuclei are components of the _____ system.

5. The dorsal-column medial-lemniscus system and the anterolateral system are pathways of the _____ system.

6. The ventral posterior nuclei, the intralaminar nuclei, and the parafascicular nuclei are all thalamic nuclei of the _____ system.

7. The periaqueductal gray and the raphé nuclei are involved in blocking the perception of _____.

8. One pathway of the _____ system projects from the amygdala and piriform cortex to the orbitofrontal cortex.

9. Parts of the ventral posterior nuclei are thalamic relay nuclei of both the somatosensory and _____ systems.

10. Unlike the projections of all other sensory systems, the projections of the _____ system are primarily ipsilateral.

7.6 Selective Attention

We consciously perceive only a small subset of the many stimuli that excite our sensory organs at any one time and largely ignore the rest. The process by which this occurs is **selective attention.**

There are two aspects to selective attention: It improves the perception of the stimuli that are its focus, and it interferes with the perception of the stimuli that are not its focus. For example, if you focus your attention on a potentially important announcement in a noisy airport, your chances of understanding it increase; but your chances of understanding a simultaneous comment from a traveling companion decrease.

Attention can be focused in two different ways: by internal cognitive processes (*endogenous attention*) or by external events (*exogenous attention*)—see Treue (2003). For example, your attention can be focused on a table top because you are searching for your keys (endogenous attention), or it can be drawn there because your cat tipped over a lamp (exogenous attention). Endogenous attention is thought to be mediated by *top-down* (from higher to lower levels) neural mechanisms, whereas exogenous attention is thought to be mediated by *bottom-up* (from lower to higher levels) neural mechanisms.

Attention is an extremely important aspect of perception. There is no better illustration of its importance than the phenomenon of **change blindness** (Rensink,

2002). To study change blindness, a subject is shown a photographic image on a computer screen and is asked to report any change in the image as soon as it is noticed. In fact, the image is composed of two images that alternate with a delay of less than 0.1 second between. The two photographic images are identical except for one gross feature. For example, the two images in Figure 7.26 on page 182 are identical except that the picture in the center of the wall is missing from one. You might think that any subject would immediately notice the picture disappearing and reappearing. But this is not what happens—most subjects spend many seconds staring at the image—searching, as instructed, for some change—before they notice the disappearing and reappearing picture. When this finally happens, they wonder in amazement why it took them so long.

<0.1 second

FIGURE 7.26 The change blindness phenomenon. These two illustrations were continually alternated, with a brief (less than 0.1 second) interval between each presentation, and the subjects were asked to report any changes that they noticed. Amazingly, it took most of them many seconds to notice the disappearing and reappearing picture in the center of the wall. (Photographs prepared by James Enns, Department of Psychology, University of British Columbia.)

Why does change blindness occur? It occurs because, contrary to our impression, when we view a scene, we have absolutely no memory for parts of the scene that are not the focus of our attention. When viewing the scene in Figure 7.26, most subjects attend to the two people and do not notice when the picture disappears from the wall between them. Because they have no memory of the parts of the image to which they did not attend, they are not aware when those parts change.

The change blindness phenomenon does not occur without the brief (i.e., less than 0.1 second) intervals between images, although they barely produce a flicker. Without the intervals, no memory is required and the changes are immediately perceived.

Moran and Desimone (1985) were the first to demonstrate the effects of attention on neural activity in the visual system. They trained monkeys to stare at a fixation point on the screen while they recorded the activity of neurons in a prestriate area that was part of the ventral stream and particularly sensitive to color. In one experiment, they recorded from individual neurons that responded to either red or green bars of light in their receptive fields. When the monkey was trained to perform a task that required attention to the red cue, the response to the red cue was increased, and the response to the green cue was reduced. The opposite happened when the monkey attended to green.

Experiments paralleling those in monkeys have been conducted in humans using functional brain-imaging techniques. For example, Corbetta and colleagues (1990) presented a collection of moving, colored stimuli of various shapes and asked their subjects to discriminate among the stimuli based on their movement, color, or shape. At-

tention to shape or color produced increased activity in areas of the ventral stream; attention to movement produced increased activity in an area of the dorsal stream.

In another study of attention in human subjects, Ungerleider and Haxby (1994) showed subjects a series of faces. The subjects were asked whether the faces belonged to the same person or whether they were located in the same position relative to the frame. When the subjects were attending to identity, regions of the ventral stream were more active; when the subjects were attending to position, regions of the dorsal stream were more active.

How do the mechanisms of selective attention work? According to current theories, neural representations of various aspects of a visual display compete with one another. Selective attention is thought to work by strengthening the representations of the attended-to aspects and by weakening the others (Chun & Marois, 2002). In general, anticipation of a stimulus increases neural activity in the same circuits affected by the stimulus itself (Carlsson et al., 2000).

Cognitive Neuroscience

A cognitive neuroscience experiment by Kastner and colleagues (1998) illustrates the type of evidence on which these theories are based. The researchers used fMRI to measure activity in various areas of visual cortex during the visual presentation of one and then four objects. First, they showed that the activity produced by the presence of the single object declined markedly when the other three objects were presented along with it. Second, they showed that the magnitude of this decline was less if subjects were instructed to attend to the first object.

Demonstration

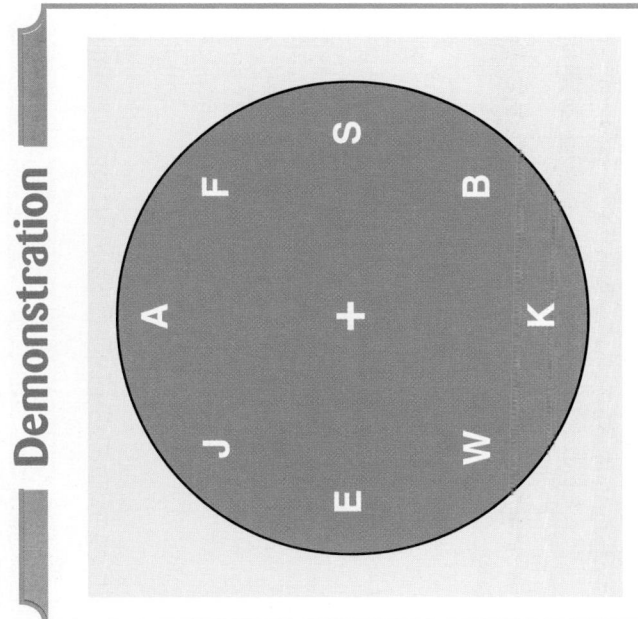

Fix your gaze on the +, concentrate on it. Next, shift your attention to one of the letters without shifting your gaze from +. Now, shift your attention to other letters, again without shifting your gaze from the +. You have experienced *covert attention*—a shift of visual attention without corresponding eye movement. A change in visual attention that involves a shift in gaze is called *overt attention*.

Eye movements often play an important role in visual attention, but it is important to realize that visual attention can be shifted without shifting the direction of visual focus (Rees et al., 1999). To prove this to yourself, see the Demonstration.

One last important characteristic of selective attention is the cocktail-party phenomenon (see Feng & Ratnam, 2000). The **cocktail-party phenomenon** is the fact that even when you are focusing so intently on one conversation that you are totally unaware of the content of other conversations going on around you, the mention of your name in one of the other conversations will immediately gain access to your consciousness. This phenomenon suggests that your brain can block from conscious awareness all stimuli except those of a particular kind while still unconsciously monitoring the blocked-out stimuli just in case something comes up that requires attention.

No, I have not forgotten that I asked you to think about the patient whose case opened this chapter. He could iden-

Clinical Implications

tify objects in any part of his visual field if they were presented individually; thus, he was not suffering from blindness or other visual field defects. His was a disorder of visual attention. He suffered from visual **simultanagnosia,** a difficulty in attending to more than one visual object at a time. Because the dorsal stream is responsible for localizing objects in space, you may have hypothesized that the patient's problem was associated with damage to this area. If you did, you were correct. The damage associated with simultagnosia is typically bilateral.

Themes Revisited

The clinical implications theme was the dominant one in this chapter, but you saw it in a different light. Previous chapters focused on how biopsychological research is leading to the development of new treatments; this chap-

Clinical Implications

ter focused on what particular clinical cases reveal about the organization of healthy sensory systems. The fol-

lowing cases played a key role in this chapter: the patient with visual simultanagnosia; Dr. P., the visual agnosic who mistook his wife for a hat; Karl Lashley, the physiological psychologist who used his scotoma to turn a friend's head into a wallpaper pattern; D. B., the man with blindsight; D.F., who showed by her accurate reaching that she perceived the size, shape, and orientation of objects that she could not describe; A. T., who could describe the size and shape of objects that she could not accurately reach for; R. P., a typical prosopagnosic; Aunt Betty, the asomatognosic who lost the left side of her body; and Miss C., the student who felt no pain and died as a result.

The other three major themes were also developed in this chapter. You learned how the study of the neural organization of the sensory systems has been extended to healthy human subjects by using the functional brain-imaging techniques of cogni-

Cognitive Neuroscience

tive neuroscience. You learned that the comparative study of some species has been particularly informative because of their evolutionary specializations (e.g., the auditory localiza-

Evolutionary Perspective

tion abilities of the barn owl and the tendency of the secondary auditory cortex of monkeys to respond to monkey calls). And you learned how critical thinking has

Thinking Critically

led to a re-evaluation of the concept of prosopagnosia.

ON THE CD

See Hard Copy for additional readings for Chapter 7.

Think about It

1. How has this chapter changed your concept of perception?

2. Some sensory pathways control behavior directly without producing conscious perceptions, whereas others control behavior by mediating conscious perceptions. Discuss the evolutionary implications of this fact. Why did consciousness evolve?

3. Comparative biopsychological research often focuses on species that are similar to humans in key respects;

however, such research sometimes focuses productively on species that differ from humans in key respects. Explain and discuss.

4. One purpose of biopsychological research is to help neuropsychological patients, but neuropsychological research also helps biopsychologists understand the neural mechanisms of psychological processes. Explain.

Key Terms

Ageusia (p. 180)
Agnosia (p. 164)
Anosmia (p. 180)
Anosognosia (p. 175)
Anterior cingulate cortex (p. 176)
Anterolateral system (p. 171)
Asomatognosia (p. 174)
Association cortex (p. 156)
Astereognosia (p. 174)
Auditory nerve (p. 168)
Basilar membrane (p. 168)
Blindsight (p. 160)
Change blindness (p. 181)
Cochlea (p. 166)
Cocktail-party phenomenon (p. 183)
Completion (p. 159)
Contralateral neglect (p. 175)
"Control of behavior" versus "conscious perception" theory (p. 164)
Corticofugal pathways (p. 164)
Dermatome (p. 171)
Dorsal columns (p. 171)

Dorsal stream (p. 162)
Dorsal-column medial-lemniscus system (p. 171)
Endorphins (p. 176)
Exteroceptive sensory systems (p. 156)
Flavor (p. 177)
Free nerve endings (p. 170)
Functional segregation (p. 157)
Gate-control theory (p. 176)
Hair cells (p. 168)
Hemianopsic (p. 159)
Hierarchical organization (p. 156)
Inferior colliculi (p. 169)
Inferotemporal cortex (p. 159)
Medial dorsal nuclei (p. 179)
Medial geniculate nuclei (p. 169)
Medial lemniscus (p. 171)
Olfactory bulbs (p. 178)
Olfactory mucosa (p. 178)
Orbitofrontal cortex (p. 179)
Organ of Corti (p. 166)
Ossicles (p. 166)

Oval window (p. 166)
Pacinian corpuscles (p. 170)
Parallel processing (p. 158)
Perception (p. 158)
Periaqueductal gray (PAG) (p. 176)
Perimetry test (p. 159)
Pheromones (p. 177)
Piriform cortex (p. 179)
Posterior parietal cortex (p. 159)
Prestriate cortex (p. 159)
Primary sensory cortex (p. 156)
Prosopagnosia (p. 164)
Retinotopic (p. 168)
Scotoma (p. 159)
Secondary sensory cortex
Selective attention (p. 181)
Semicircular canals (p. 168)
Sensation (p. 157)
Simultanagnosia (p. 183)
Solitary nucleus (p. 180)
Somatosensory homunculus (p. 172)

Somatotopic (p. 172)
Stereognosis (p. 171)
Subjective contours (p. 161)
Superior olives (p. 168)
Taste buds (p. 179)
Tectorial membrane (p. 168)
Tonotopic (p. 168)
Tympanic membrane (p. 166)
Ventral posterior nucleus (p. 171)
Ventral stream (p. 162)
Vestibular system (p. 168)
Visual agnosia (p. 164)
"Where" versus "what" theory (p. 162)

chapter

8

The Sensorimotor System

How You Do What You Do

8.1 Three Principles of Sensorimotor Function

8.2 Sensorimotor Association Cortex

8.3 Secondary Motor Cortex

8.4 Primary Motor Cortex

8.5 Cerebellum and Basal Ganglia

8.6 Descending Motor Pathways

8.7 Sensorimotor Spinal Circuits

8.8 Central Sensorimotor Programs

The evening before I started to write this chapter, I was standing in a checkout line at the local market. As I waited, I furtively scanned the headlines on the prominently displayed magazines—WOMAN GIVES BIRTH TO CAT; FLYING SAUCER LANDS IN CLEVELAND SHOPPING MALL; HOW TO LOSE 20 POUNDS IN 2 DAYS. Then, my mind began to wander, and I started to think about beginning to write this chapter. That is when I began to watch Rhonda's movements and to wonder about the neural system that controlled them. Rhonda is the cashier—the best in the place.

The Case of Rhonda, the Dexterous Cashier

I was struck by the complexity of even Rhonda's simplest movements. As she deftly transferred a bag of tomatoes to the scale, there was a coordinated adjustment in almost every part of her body. In addition to her obvious finger, hand, arm, and shoulder movements, coordinated movements of her head and eyes tracked her hand to the tomatoes; and there were adjustments in the muscles of her feet, legs, trunk, and other arm, which kept her from lurching forward. The accuracy of these responses suggested that they were guided in part by the patterns of visual, somatosensory, and vestibular changes they produced. The term *sensorimotor* in the title of this chapter formally recognizes the critical contribution of sensory input to guiding motor output.

As my purchases flowed through her left hand, Rhonda registered the prices with her right hand and bantered with Rick, the bagger. I was intrigued by how little of what Rhonda was doing appeared to be under her conscious control. She made general decisions about which items to pick up and where to put them, but she seemed to give no thought to the exact means by which these decisions were carried out. Each of her responses could have been made with an infinite number of different combinations of finger, wrist, elbow, shoulder, and body adjustments; but somehow she unconsciously picked one. The higher parts of her sensorimotor system—perhaps her cortex—seemed to issue conscious general commands to other parts of the system, which unconsciously produced a specific pattern of muscular responses that carried them out.

The automaticity of Rhonda's performance was a far cry from the slow, effortful responses that had characterized her first days at the market. Somehow, experience had integrated her individual movements into smooth sequences, and it seemed to have transferred the movements' control from a mode that involved conscious effort to one that did not.

I was suddenly jarred from my contemplations by a voice. "Sir, excuse me, sir, that will be $18.65," Rhonda said, with just a hint of delight at catching me in mid-daydream. I hastily paid my bill, muttered "thank you," and scurried out of the market.

As I write this, I am smiling both at my own embarrassment and at the thought that Rhonda has unknowingly introduced you to three principles of sensorimotor control that are the foundations of this chapter: (1) The sensorimotor system is hierarchically organized. (2) Motor output is guided by sensory input. (3) Learning can change the nature and the locus of sensorimotor control.

8.1 Three Principles of Sensorimotor Function

Before getting into the details of the sensorimotor system, let's take a closer look at the three principles of sensorimotor function introduced by Rhonda. You will better appreciate these principles if you recognize that they are the very same principles that govern the operation of a large, efficient company—perhaps because both are systems of controlling output that have evolved in a competitive environment.

The Sensorimotor System Is Hierarchically Organized

The operation of both the sensorimotor system and a large, efficient company is directed by commands that cascade down through the levels of a hierarchy (see Koechlin, Ody, & Kouneiher, 2003)—from the association cortex or the company president (the highest levels) to the muscles or the workers (the lowest levels). Like the orders that are issued from the office of a company president, the commands that emerge from the association cortex specify general goals rather than specific plans of action. Neither the association cortex nor the company president routinely gets involved in the details. The main advantage of this *hierarchical organization* is that the higher levels of the hierarchy are left free to perform more complex functions.

Both the sensorimotor system and large, efficient companies are parallel hierarchical systems; that is, they are hierarchical systems in which signals flow between

Thinking Critically

levels over multiple paths (see Darian-Smith, Burman, & Darian-Smith, 1999). This parallel structure enables the association cortex or company president to exert control over the lower levels of the hierarchy in more than one way. For example, the association cortex may directly inhibit an eyeblink reflex to allow the insertion of a contact lens, and a company president may personally organize a delivery to an important customer.

The sensorimotor and company hierarchies are also characterized by *functional segregation*. That is, each level of the sensorimotor and company hierarchies tends to be composed of different units (neural structures or departments), each of which performs a different function.

In summary, the sensorimotor system—like the sensory systems you read about in Chapter 7—is a parallel, functionally segregated, hierarchical system. The main difference between the sensory systems and the sensorimotor system is the primary direction of information flow. In sensory systems, information mainly flows up through the hierarchy; in the sensorimotor system, information mainly flows down.

Motor Output Is Guided by Sensory Input

Efficient companies continuously monitor the effects of their own activities, and they use this information to fine-tune those activities. The sensorimotor system does the same (Dietz, 2002b). The eyes, the organs of balance, and the receptors in skin, muscles, and joints all monitor the body's responses; and they feed their information back into sensorimotor circuits. In most instances, this **sensory feedback** plays an important role in directing the continuation of the responses that produced it. The only responses that are not normally influenced by sensory feedback are *ballistic movements*—brief, all or none, high-speed movements, such as swatting a fly.

Behavior in the absence of just one kind of sensory feedback—the feedback that is carried by the somatosensory nerves of the arms—was studied in G.O., a former darts champion.

not keep from spilling a cup of coffee if somebody brushed against him. However, G.O.'s greatest problem was his inability to maintain a constant level of muscle contraction:

> The result of this deficit was that even in the simplest of tasks requiring a constant motor output to the hand, G.O. would have to keep a visual check on his progress. For example, when carrying a suitcase, he would frequently glance at it to reassure himself that he had not dropped it some paces back. However, even visual feedback was of little use to him in many tasks. These tended to be those requiring a constant force output such as grasping a pen while writing or holding a cup. Here, visual information was insufficient for him to be able to correct any errors that were developing in the output since, after a period, he had no indication of the pressure that he was exerting on an object; all he saw was either the pen or cup slipping from his grasp. (Rothwell et al., 1982, p. 539)

Many adjustments in motor output that occur in response to sensory feedback are controlled unconsciously by the lower levels of the sensorimotor hierarchy without the involvement of the higher levels (see Poppele & Bosco, 2003). In the same way, large companies run more efficiently if the clerks do not have to check with the company president each time they encounter a minor problem.

Learning Changes the Nature and Locus of Sensorimotor Control

When a company is just starting up, each individual decision is made by the company president after careful consideration. However, as the company develops, many individual actions are coordinated into sequences of prescribed procedures that are routinely carried out by personnel at lower levels of the hierarchy.

Similar changes occur during sensorimotor learning (see Willingham, 1999). During the initial stages of motor learning, each individual response is performed under conscious control; then, after much practice, individual responses become organized into continuous integrated sequences of action that flow smoothly and are adjusted by sensory feedback without conscious regulation. If you think for a moment about the sensorimotor skills you have acquired (e.g., typing, swimming, knitting, basketball playing, dancing, piano playing), you will appreciate that the organization of individual responses into continuous motor programs and the transfer of their control to lower levels of the nervous system characterizes most sensorimotor learning.

ON THE CD

Visit *The Beat Goes On.* In this module, Pinel demonstrates an important feature of the sensorimotor system.

The Case of G.O., the Man with Too Little Feedback

Clinical Implications

An infection had selectively destroyed the somatosensory nerves of G.O.'s arms. He had great difficulty performing intricate responses such as doing up his buttons or picking up coins, even under visual guidance. Other difficulties resulted from his inability to adjust his motor output in the light of unanticipated external disturbances; for example, he could

FIGURE 8.1 A general model of the sensorimotor system. Notice its hierarchical structure, its functional segregation, its parallel descending pathways, and its feedback circuits.

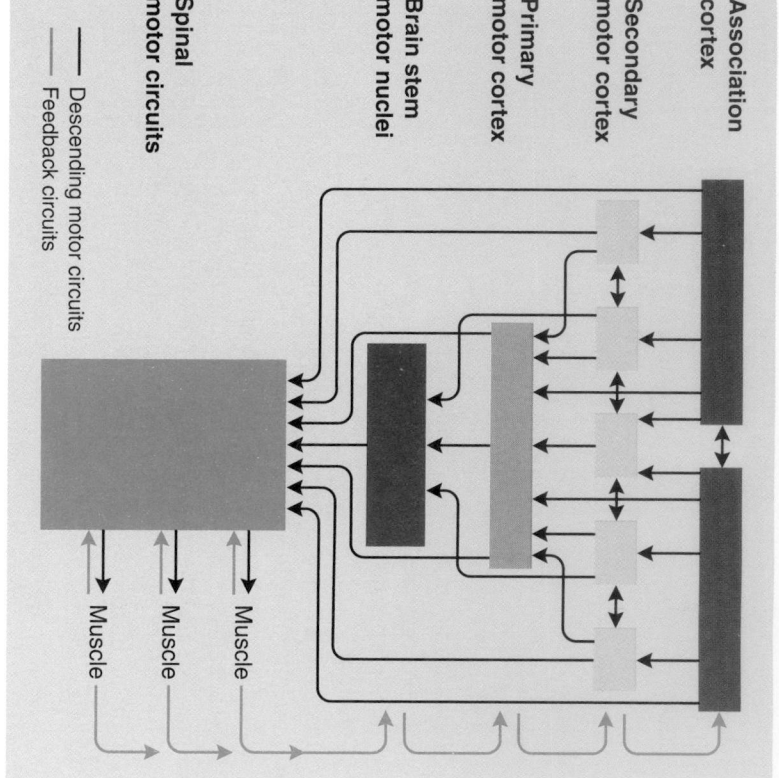

Association
cortex

Secondary
motor cortex

Primary
motor cortex

Brain stem
motor nuclei

Spinal
motor circuits

—— Descending motor circuits
—— Feedback circuits

Muscle

Muscle

Muscle

A General Model of Sensorimotor System Function

Figure 8.1 is a model that illustrates several principles of sensorimotor system organization; it is the framework of this chapter. Notice its hierarchical structure, the functional segregation of the levels (e.g., of secondary motor cortex), the parallel connections between levels, and the numerous feedback pathways.

This chapter focuses on the neural structures that play important roles in the control of voluntary behavior (e.g., picking up an apple). It begins at the level of association

cortex and traces major motor signals as they descend the sensorimotor hierarchy to the skeletal muscles that ultimately perform the movements.

8.2 Sensorimotor Association Cortex

Association cortex is at the top of your sensorimotor hierarchy. There are two major areas of sensorimotor association cortex: the posterior parietal association cortex and the dorsolateral prefrontal association cortex (see Barash, 2003; Szametiat et al., 2002). Experts agree that the posterior parietal cortex and the dorsolateral prefrontal cortex are each composed of several different areas, each of which has a different function (see Culham & Kanwisher, 2001; Fuster, 2000); however, they do not yet agree on how best to divide them up (see Rushworth, 2000).

Posterior Parietal Association Cortex

Before an effective movement can be initiated, certain information is required. The nervous system must know the original positions of the parts of the body that are to be moved, and it must know the positions of any external objects with which the body is going to interact. The **posterior parietal association cortex** plays an important role in integrating these two kinds of information

and in directing attention (see Andersen & Buneo, 2003; Assad, 2003; Cohen & Andersen, 2002).

You learned in Chapter 7 that the posterior parietal cortex is classified as *association cortex* because it receives input from more than one sensory system. It receives information from the three sensory systems that play roles in the localization of the body and external objects in space: the visual system, the auditory system, and the somatosensory system (see Andersen & Buneo, 2003; Macaluso, Driver, & Frith, 2003). In turn, much of the output of the posterior parietal cortex goes to areas of motor cortex, which are located in the frontal cortex: to the *dorsolateral prefrontal association cortex*, to the various areas of *secondary motor cortex*, and to the **frontal eye field**—a small area of prefrontal cortex that controls eye movements (see Figure 8.2).

Damage to the posterior parietal cortex can produce a variety of sensorimotor deficits, including deficits in the perception and memory of spatial relationships, in accurate reaching and grasping, in the control of eye

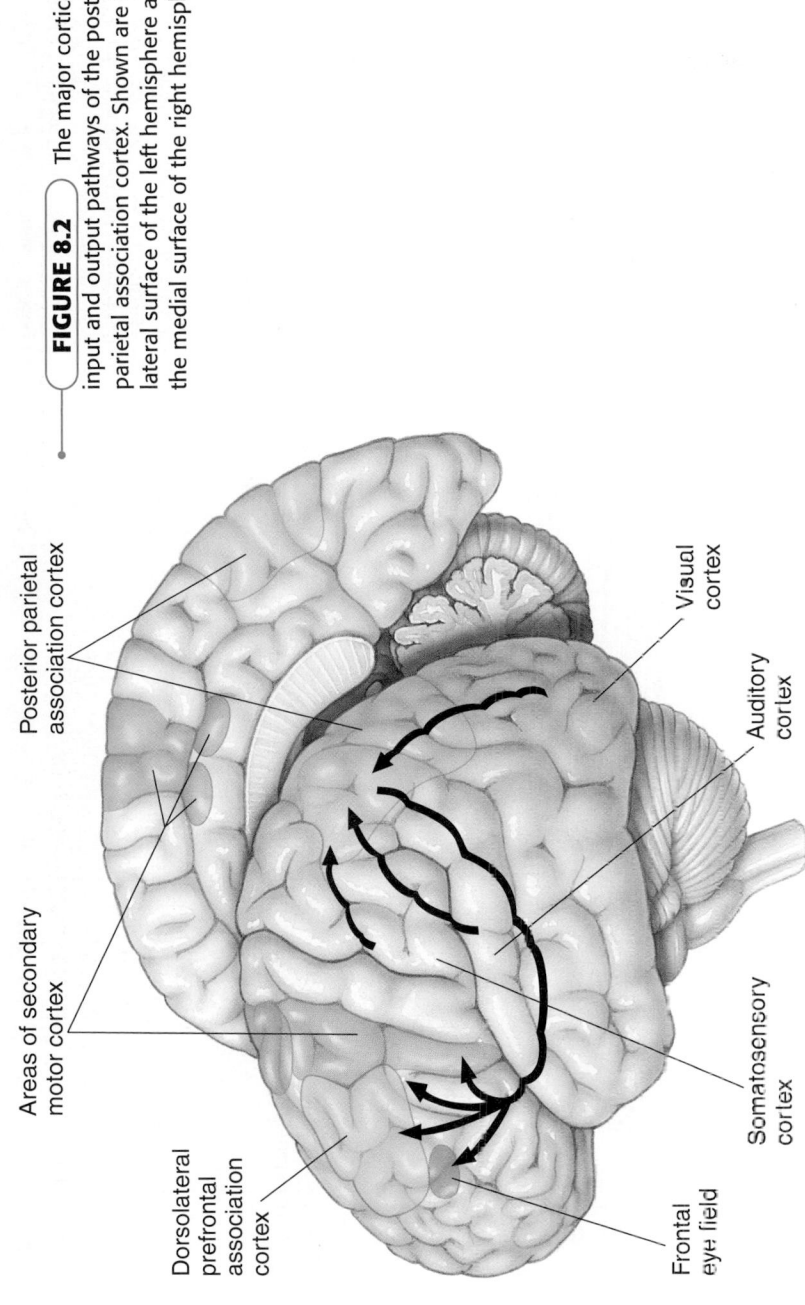

FIGURE 8.2 The major cortical input and output pathways of the posterior parietal association cortex. Shown are the lateral surface of the left hemisphere and the medial surface of the right hemisphere.

Posterior parietal association cortex

Areas of secondary motor cortex

Dorsolateral prefrontal association cortex

Frontal eye field

Somatosensory cortex

Auditory cortex

Visual cortex

movement, and in attention (Freund, 2003). However, apraxia and contralateral neglect are the two most striking consequences of posterior parietal cortex damage.

Apraxia is a disorder of voluntary movement that is not attributable to a simple motor deficit (e.g., not to paralysis or weakness) or to any deficit in comprehension or motivation (see Heilman, Watson, & Rothi, 1997). Remarkably, apraxic patients have difficulty making specific movements when they are requested to do so, particularly when the movements are out of context; however, they can often readily perform the very same movements under natural conditions, when they are not thinking about doing so. For example, an apraxic carpenter who has no difficulty at all hammering a nail during the course of her work might not be able to demonstrate hammering movements when requested to make them, particularly in the absence of a hammer. Although its symptoms are bilateral, apraxia is often caused by unilateral damage to the left posterior parietal lobe or its connections.

Contralateral neglect is a disturbance of a patient's ability to respond to stimuli on the side of the body opposite (contralateral) to the side of a brain lesion, in the absence of simple sensory or motor deficits (see Heilman, Watson, & Valenstein, 1997).

The disturbance is often associated with large lesions of the right posterior parietal lobe (see Mort et al., 2003). For example, Mrs. S. suffered from contralateral neglect after a mas-

sive stroke to the posterior portions of her right hemisphere. Like many other neuropsychological patients, she developed ways of dealing with her deficiency.

The Case of Mrs. S., the Woman Who Turned in Circles

She has totally lost the idea of "left," with regard to both the world and her own body. Sometimes she complains that her portions are too small, but this is because she only eats from the right half of the plate—it does not occur to her that it has a left half as well. Sometimes, she will put on lipstick, and make up the right half of her face, leaving the left half completely neglected: it is almost impossible to treat these things, because her attention cannot be drawn to them....

. . . She has worked out strategies for dealing with her [problem]. She cannot look left, directly, she cannot turn left, so what she does is turn right—and right through a circle. Thus she requested, and was given, a rotating wheelchair. And now if she cannot find something which she knows should be there, she swivels to the right, through a circle, until it comes into view.... If her portions seem too small, she will swivel to the right, keeping her eyes to the right, until the previously missed half now comes into view; she will eat this, or rather half of this, and feel less hungry than before. But if she is still hungry, or if she thinks on the matter, and realises that she may have perceived only half of the missing half, she will make a second rotation till the remaining quarter comes into view.

sive investigation (see Bartholmeo & Chokron, 2002; Kerkoff, 2001; Palovskaya et al., 2002). For most patients with contralateral neglect, the deficits in responding occur for stimuli to the left of their own bodies, referred to as *egocentric left*. Egocentric left is partially defined by gravitational coordinates because when patients tilt their heads, their field of neglect is not normally tilted with it (see the top panel of Figure 8.3).

In addition to failing to respond to objects on their egocentric left, many patients tend not to respond to the

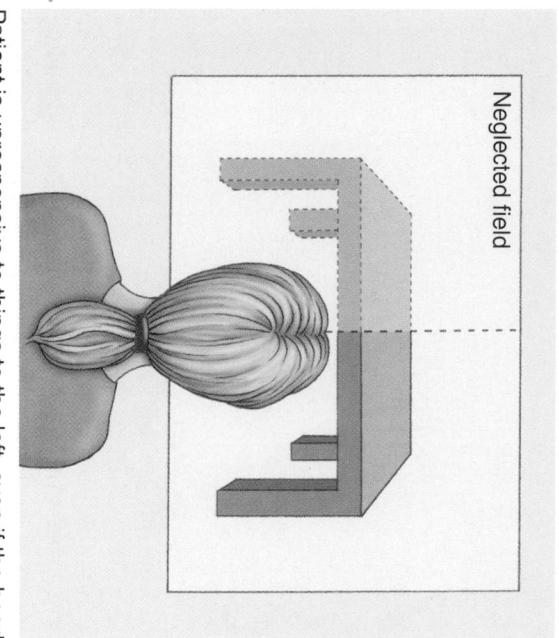

Neglected field

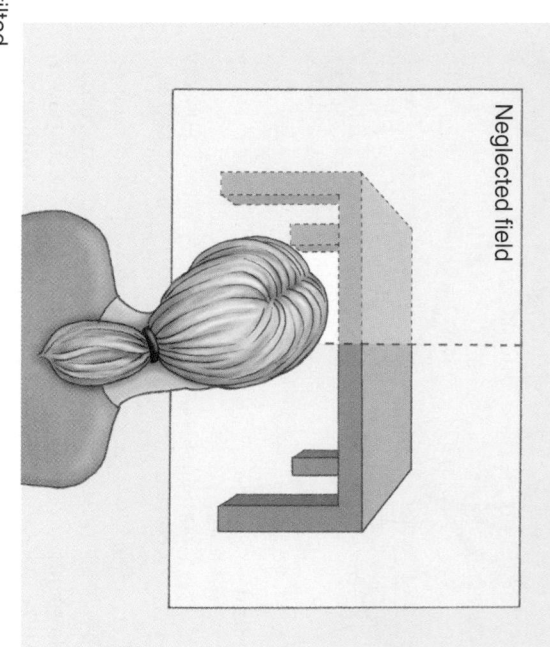

Neglected field

Patient is unresponsive to things to the left, even if the head is tilted.

Most patients with contralateral neglect have difficulty responding to things to the left. But to the left of what? This question is currently the subject of inten-

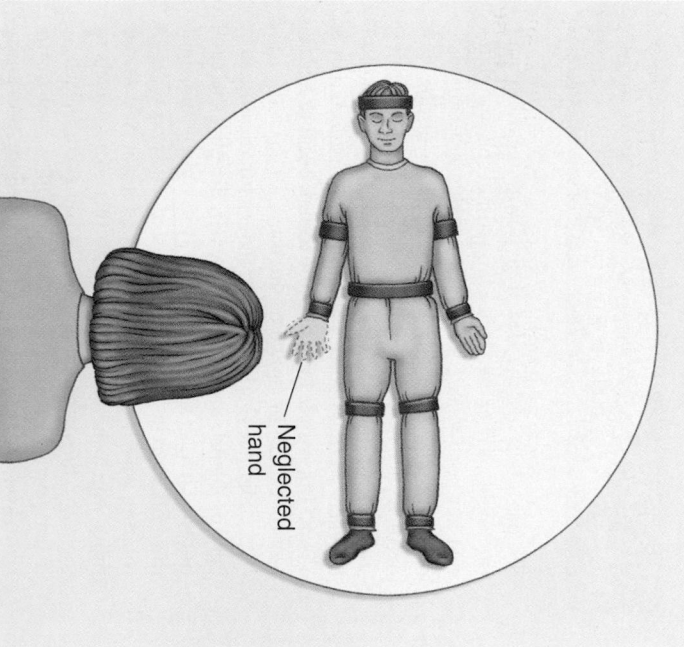

Neglected hand

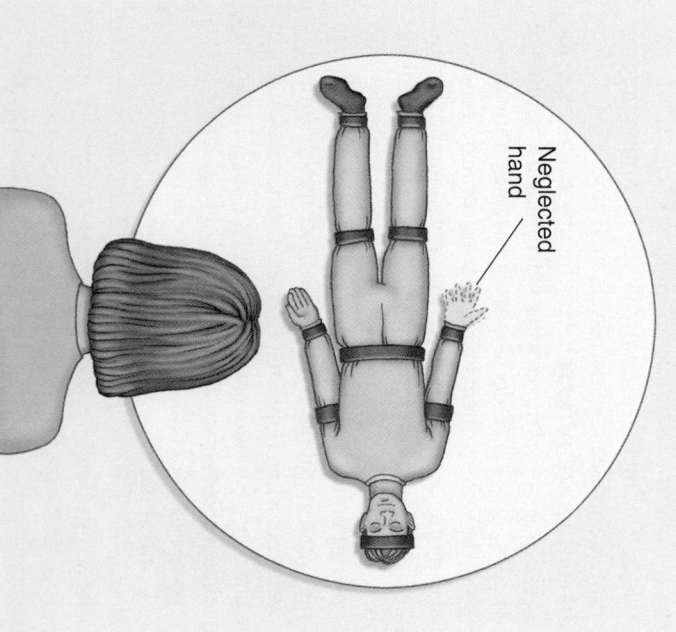

Neglected hand

FIGURE 8.3   Contralateral neglect is sometimes manifested in terms of gravitational coordinates, sometimes in terms of object-based coordinates.

Contralateral neglect is sometimes manifested in terms of object-based coordinates.

left sides of objects, regardless of where the objects are in their visual fields. Neurons that have egocentric receptive fields and others with object-based receptive fields have been found in primate parietal cortex (Olson, 2003; Pouget & Driver, 2000).

Object-based contralateral neglect is demonstrated in the lower panel of Figure 8.3. In this demonstration, patients with contralateral neglect had deficits in responding to the right hand of an experimenter who was facing them, regardless of its specific location in the patients' visual field.

A somatosensory study of contralateral neglect also demonstrated that it is not a straightforward matter to define the field of neglect. Patients were found to be more responsive to touches on their neglected left hand if their arms were crossed (Aglioti, Smania, & Peru, 1999).

Patients with contralateral neglect often fail to report visual stimuli presented to the left of their bodies. However, you have already learned in the preceding chapters that the failure to consciously perceive an object does not necessarily mean that the object was not perceived. Indeed, two types of evidence suggest that information about objects that are not noticed by patients with contralateral neglect is, in fact, unconsciously perceived. First, when objects were repeatedly presented at the same spot to the left of patients with contralateral neglect, they tended to look to the same spot on future trials although they were unaware of the objects (Geng & Behrmann, 2002). Second, patients could more readily identify fragmented (partial) drawings viewed to

their right if complete versions of the drawings had previously been presented to the left, where they were not consciously perceived (Vuilleumier et al., 2002).

Dorsolateral Prefrontal Association Cortex

The other large area of association cortex that has important sensorimotor functions is the **dorsolateral prefrontal association cortex.** It receives projections from the posterior parietal cortex, and it sends projections to areas of *secondary motor cortex,* to *primary motor cortex,* and to the *frontal eye field.* These projections are shown in Figure 8.4. Not shown are the major projections back from dorsolateral prefrontal cortex to posterior parietal cortex.

Dorsolateral prefrontal cortex seems to play a role in the evaluation of external stimuli and the initiation of voluntary reactions to them (Christoff & Gabrieli, 2000; Ohbayashi, Ohki, & Miyashita, 2003). This view is supported by the response characteristics of neurons in this area of association cortex. Several studies have characterized the activity of monkey dorsolateral prefrontal neurons as the monkeys identify and respond to objects (e.g., Rao, Rainer, & Miller, 1997). The activity of some neurons depends on the characteristics of objects; the activity of others depends on the locations of objects; and the activity of still others depends on a combination of both. The activity of other dorsolateral prefrontal neurons is related to the response, rather than to the object. These neurons typically begin to fire before the response and continue to fire until the response is complete. There are neurons in all cortical motor areas that begin to fire in anticipation of a motor activity, but those in the dorsolateral prefrontal association cortex fire first.

The response properties of dorsolateral prefrontal neurons and the pattern of connections between this area and other areas of sensorimotor cortex suggest that decisions to initiate voluntary

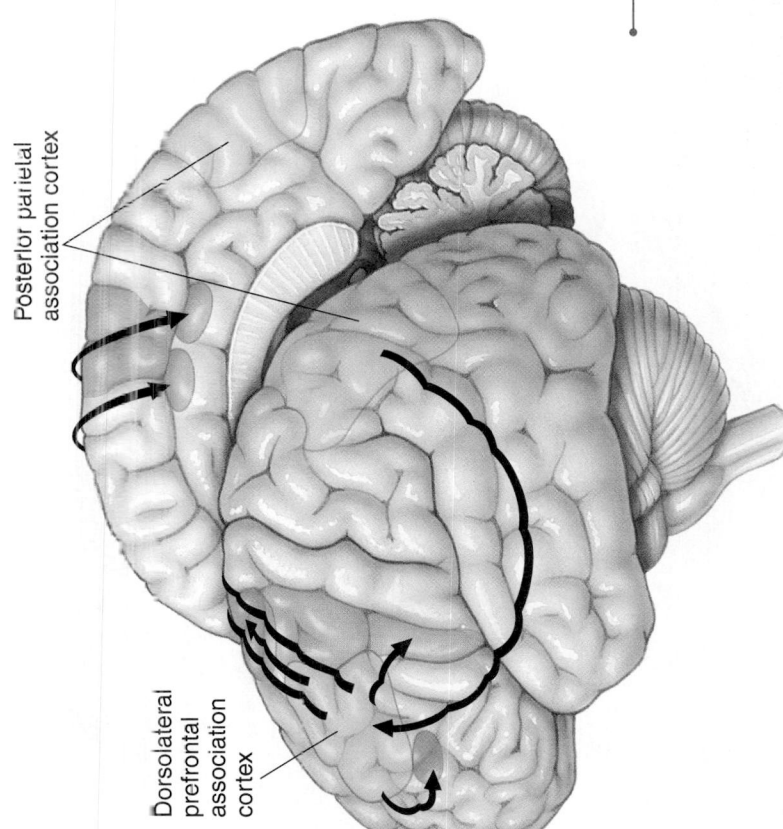

Posterior parietal association cortex

Dorsolateral prefrontal association cortex

FIGURE 8.4 The major cortical input and output pathways of the dorsolateral prefrontal association cortex. Shown are the lateral surface of the left hemisphere and the medial surface of the right hemisphere.

Evolutionary Perspective

movements may be made in this area of cortex (Rowe et al., 2000; Tanji & Hoshi, 2001). However, it is more likely that such decisions arise from the interaction of

dorsolateral prefrontal cortex and posterior parietal cortex (Connolly, Andersen, & Goodale, 2003; Jeannerod & Farne, 2003; Rushworth et al., 2003).

8.3   Secondary Motor Cortex

Areas of **secondary motor cortex** are those that receive much of their input from association cortex and send much of their output to primary motor cortex (see Figure 8.5). For many years, only two areas of secondary motor cortex were known: the supplementary motor area and the premotor cortex. Both of these large areas are clearly visible on the lateral surface of the frontal lobe, just anterior to the *primary motor cortex*. The **supplementary motor area** wraps over the top of the frontal lobe and extends down its medial surface into the longitudinal fissure, and the **premotor cortex** runs in a strip from the supplementary motor area to the lateral fissure.

In the past few years, this simple two-area conception of secondary motor cortex has become more complex. Neuroanatomical and neurophysiological research with monkeys has made a case for at least seven different areas in each hemisphere: two different supplementary

motor areas (SMA and preSMA), two premotor areas (dorsal and ventral), and three small areas—the **cingulate motor areas**—in the cortex of the cingulate gyrus.

Recent functional brain-imaging studies have suggested that human secondary motor cortex is similar to that of other primates (see Rizzolatti, Fogassi, & Gallese, 2002). There is evidence of at least two cingulate motor areas in humans, and a strong case can be made for subdividing both the supplementary motor area and the premotor cortex. However, there is still no general consensus about the exact boundaries of these newly identified areas or even whether they are better classified as secondary motor cortex or association cortex (see Kollias et al., 2001; Picard & Strick, 2001).

The various unresolved issues regarding secondary motor cortex are currently the focus of a major research

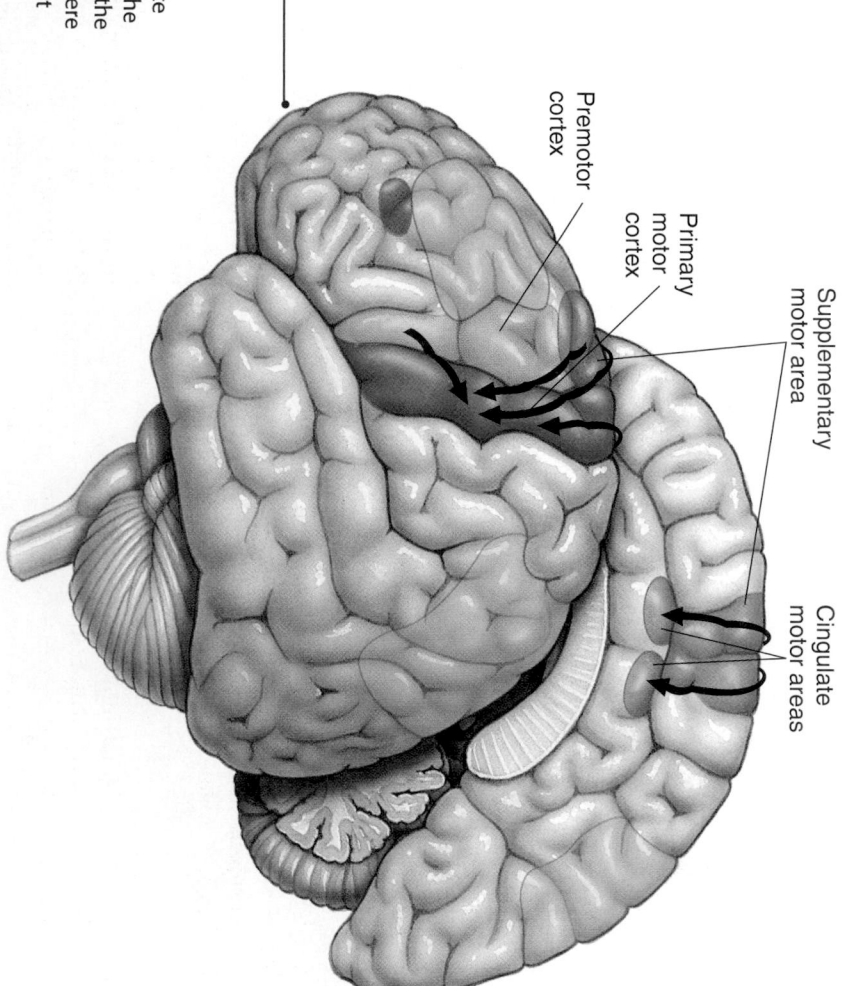

Premotor cortex

Primary motor cortex

Supplementary motor area

Cingulate motor areas

FIGURE 8.5   Four areas of secondary motor cortex—the supplementary motor area, the premotor cortex, and two cingulate motor areas—and their output to the primary motor cortex. Shown are the lateral surface of the left hemisphere and the medial surface of the right hemisphere.

effort. To qualify as secondary motor cortex, an area must be appropriately connected with other sensorimotor areas (see Figure 8.5). From a functional perspective, electrical stimulation of an area of secondary motor cortex typically elicits complex movements, often involving both sides of the body; and neurons in an area of secondary motor cortex often become more active just prior to the initiation of a voluntary movement and continue to be active throughout the movement.

In general, areas of secondary motor cortex are thought to be involved in the programming of specific patterns of movements after taking general instructions from dorsolateral prefrontal cortex. Evidence of such a function comes from brain-imaging studies in which the patterns of activity in the brain have been measured while the subject is either imagining his or her own performance of a particular series of movements or planning the performance of the same movements (see Kosslyn, Ganis, & Thompson, 2001; Sirigu & Duhamel, 2001). For example, Parsons and colleagues (1995) found that there was increased PET activity in the supplementary motor area, premotor cortex, and cingulate motor areas while subjects imagined grasping and picking up an object.

Despite evidence of similarities among areas of secondary motor cortex, substantial effort has been put into discovering their differences. Until recently, this research has focused on differences between the supplementary motor area and the premotor cortex as originally defined. Although several theories have been proposed to explain functional differences between these areas, none has received consistent support. Once the number and location of the various areas of human secondary motor cortex have been established, it should prove easier to determine the function of each area.

One interesting line of research on premotor cortex neurons has focused on how they encode spatial relations (Graziano & Gross, 1998). Many premotor neurons respond to touch, and each of these has a somatosensory receptive field on a particular part of the body. Many of these neurons also respond to visual input and are thus referred to as *bimodal neurons* (neurons that can be affected by stimuli in two different stimulus modalities). The visual receptive field of a bimodal neuron is always adjacent to its somatosensory receptive field. For example, if a bimodal neuron has its somatosensory receptive field on the left hand, its visual receptive field is usually in the space adjacent to the left hand. Remarkably, the visual receptive field remains next to the left hand regardless of where the left hand is or where the eyes are focused. Clearly, such a neuron is dedicated to the programming of movements of the left hand.

8.4 Primary Motor Cortex

The **primary motor cortex** is located in the *precentral gyrus* of the frontal lobe (see Figures 8.5 and 8.6, on page 194). It is the major point of convergence of cortical sensorimotor signals, and it is the major point of departure of sensorimotor signals from the cerebral cortex.

In 1937, Penfield and Boldrey mapped the primary motor cortex of conscious human patients during neurosurgery by applying electrical stimulation to various points on the cortical surface and noting which part of the body moved in response to each stimulation. They found that the primary motor cortex is somatotopically organized. The **somatotopic** (organized according to a map of the body) layout of the human primary motor cortex is commonly referred to as the **motor homunculus** (see Figure 8.6). Notice that most of the primary motor cortex is dedicated to controlling parts of the body that are capable of intricate movements, such as the hands and mouth.

More recent research has necessitated an important revision to the original motor homunculus proposed by Penfield and Boldrey, with respect to the hand areas. Recordings from individual primary motor cortex neurons in monkeys while they performed individual finger movements revealed that the control of any individual finger movement depended on the activity of a network of neurons that was widely distributed throughout the primary motor cortex hand area rather than being located in one somatotopically segregated finger area (Schieber & Hibbard, 1993). A similar pattern in the hand area of the human primary motor cortex has also been documented using fMRI (Sanes et al., 1995). Furthermore, small lesions in the hand area of the primary motor cortex of humans (Schieber, 1999) and monkeys (Schieber & Poliakov, 1998) never selectively disrupt the activity of a single finger. It is now clear that the area of primary motor cortex that controls any particular finger is large and overlaps areas controlling other fingers.

Each general area in the primary motor cortex controls the movements of particular groups of muscles, and each receives somatosensory feedback, via somatosensory cortex, from receptors in these muscles and in the joints that they influence. One interesting exception to this general pattern of feedback has been described in monkeys: Monkeys have two different hand areas in the primary motor cortex of each hemisphere, and one receives input from receptors in the skin rather than

FIGURE 8.6 The motor homunculus: the somatotopic map of the human primary motor cortex. Stimulation of sites in the primary motor cortex elicits simple movements in the indicated parts of the body. (Adapted from Penfield & Rasmussen, 1950.)

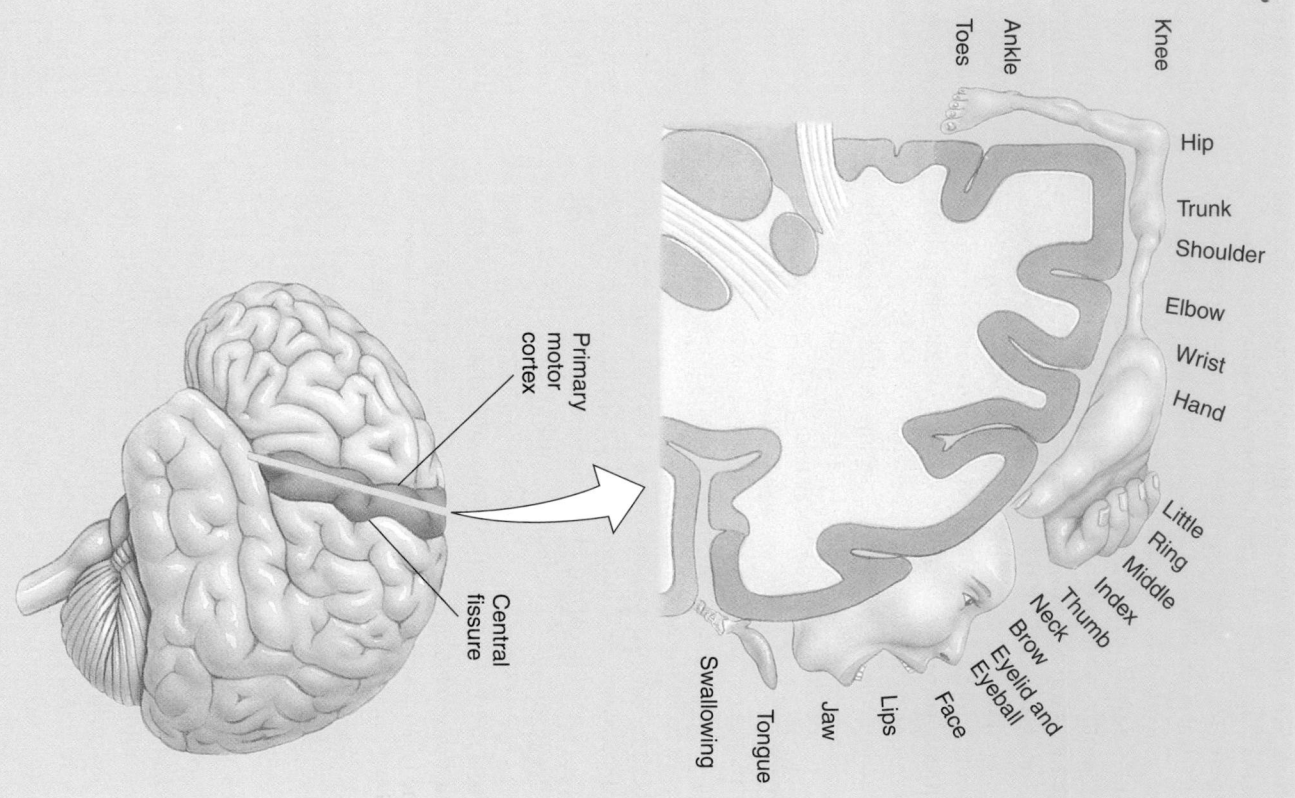

Knee
Hip
Trunk
Shoulder
Elbow
Wrist
Hand
Little
Ring
Middle
Index
Thumb
Neck
Brow
Eyelid and Eyeball
Face
Lips
Jaw
Tongue
Swallowing
Ankle
Toes

Primary motor cortex

Central fissure

from receptors in the muscles and joints. Presumably, this adaptation facilitates **stereognosis**—the process of identifying objects by touch. Close your eyes and explore an object with your hands; notice how stereognosis depends on a complex interplay between motor responses and the somatosensory stimulation produced by them.

Neurons in the arm area of the primary motor cortex fire maximally when the arm reaches in a particular direction; each neuron has a different preferred direction. Georgopoulos (1995) dissociated the direction of force and the direction of movement by applying external forces to monkeys' arms while the arms reached in various directions. The firing of primary motor cortex neurons was correlated with the direction of the resulting movement rather than with the direction of the force that was generated to produce the movement. Each neuron fired most during and just before movements in a preferred direction but also fired to movements in other directions; the closer to the preferred direction, the more it fired.

Belle: The Monkey That Controlled a Robot with Her Mind

The neurons of the primary motor cortex play a major role in initiating body movements and controlling their direction. With an appropriate interface, could they control the movements of a machine (see Craelius, 2002; König & Verschure, 2002; Taylor, Tillery, & Schwartz, 2002)? Belle says, "yes."

In the laboratory of Miguel Nicolesis and John Chapin (2002), a tiny owl monkey called Belle watched a series of lights on a control panel. Belle had learned

that if she moved the joystick in her right hand in the direction of a light, she would be rewarded with a drop of fruit juice. On this particular day, Nicolesis and Chapin demonstrated an amazing feat. As a light flashed on the panel, 100 microelectrodes recorded extracellular unit activity from neurons in Belle's primary motor cortex. This activity moved Belle's arm toward the light, but at the same time, the signals were analyzed by a computer, which fed the output to a laboratory several hundred kilometers away, at the Massachusetts Institute of Technology. At MIT, the signals from Belle's brain entered the circuits of a robotic arm. On each trial, the activity of Belle's primary motor cortex moved her arm toward the test light, and it moved the robotic arm in the same direction. Belle's neural signals were directing the activity of a robot.

This truly remarkable feat raises a possibility. Perhaps one day injured people will be able to control wheelchairs, prosthetic limbs, or even their own paralyzed limbs through the power of their own thoughts.

Extensive damage to the human primary motor cortex has less effect than you might expect, given that this

cortex is the major point of departure of motor fibers from the cerebral cortex. Large lesions to the primary motor cortex may disrupt a patient's ability to move one body part (e.g., one finger) independently of others; may produce **astereognosia** (deficits in stereognosis), and may reduce the speed, accuracy, and force of a patient's movements. They do not, however, eliminate voluntary movement, presumably because there are pathways that descend directly from secondary motor areas to subcortical motor circuits without passing through primary motor cortex.

8.5 Cerebellum and Basal Ganglia

The cerebellum and the basal ganglia (see Figures 3.21 and 3.29) are both important sensorimotor structures, but neither is a major part of the pathway by which signals descend through the sensorimotor hierarchy; instead, both the cerebellum and the basal ganglia interact with different levels of the sensorimotor hierarchy, and in so doing, they coordinate and modulate its activities. The interconnections between sensory and motor areas via the cerebellum and basal ganglia are thought to be the reason why damage to cortical connections between visual cortex and frontal motor areas does not abolish visually guided responses (Glickstein, 2000).

Cerebellum

The complexity of the cerebellum is suggested by its structure. Although it constitutes only 10% of the mass of the brain, it contains more than half of its neurons (see Goldowitz & Hamre, 1998; Voogd & Glickstein, 1998). The cerebellum receives information from primary and secondary motor cortex, information about descending motor signals from brain stem motor nuclei, and feedback from motor responses via the somatosensory and vestibular systems. The cerebellum is thought to compare these three sources of input and correct ongoing movements that deviate from their intended course (see Garwicz, 2002; Ohyama et al., 2003). By performing this function, it is believed to play a major role in motor learning, particularly in the learning of sequences of movements in which timing is a critical factor (Medina et al., 2000; Spencer et al., 2003).

The consequences of diffuse cerebellar damage for motor function are devastating. The patient loses the ability to control precisely the direction, force, velocity, and amplitude of movements and the ability to adapt patterns of motor output to changing conditions. It is difficult to maintain steady postures (e.g., standing), and at-

tempts to do so frequently lead to tremor. There are also severe disturbances in balance, gait, speech, and the control of eye movement. Learning new motor sequences is very difficult (Shin & Ivry, 2003; Thach & Bastian, 2004).

The traditional view that the function of the cerebellum is limited to the fine-tuning and learning of motor responses has been challenged. The basis for this challenge has come from the observation of activity in the cerebellum by functional brain imaging during the performance of a variety of nonmotor cognitive tasks by healthy human subjects (e.g., Lotze et al., 1999) and from the documentation of cognitive deficits in patients with cerebellar damage (e.g., Fabbro et al., 2004; Townsend et al., 1999). Various alternative theories have been proposed, but the most parsimonious of them tend to argue that the cerebellum functions in the fine-tuning and learning of cognitive responses in the same way that it functions in the fine-tuning and learning of motor responses (e.g., Doya, 2000).

Basal Ganglia

The basal ganglia do not contain as many neurons as the cerebellum, but in one sense they are more complex. Unlike the cerebellum, which is organized systematically in lobes, columns, and layers, the basal ganglia are a complex heterogeneous collection of interconnected nuclei.

The anatomy of the basal ganglia suggests that, like the cerebellum, they perform a modulatory function. They contribute no fibers to descending motor pathways; instead, they are part of neural loops that receive cortical input from various cortical areas and transmit it back via the thalamus to the various areas of motor cortex (see Bar-Gad & Bergman, 2001; Groenewegen, 2003).

Theories of basal ganglia function have evolved—in much the same way that theories of cerebellar function have changed. The traditional view of the basal ganglia was that they, like the cerebellum, play a role in the

SCAN YOUR BRAIN

Are you ready to continue your descent into the sensorimotor circuits of the spinal cord? This is a good place for you to pause to scan your brain to evaluate your knowledge of the sensorimotor circuits of the cortex, cerebellum, and basal ganglia by

completing the following statements. The correct answers are provided at the bottom of this page. Before proceeding, review material related to your incorrect answers and omissions.

1. Visual, auditory, and somatosensory input converges on the _____ association cortex.

2. A small area of frontal cortex called the frontal _____ plays a major role in the control of eye movement.

3. Contralateral neglect is often associated with large lesions of the right _____ lobe.

4. The _____ prefrontal cortex seems to play an important role in initiating complex voluntary responses.

5. The secondary motor area that is just dorsal to the premotor cortex and is largely hidden from view on the medial surface of each hemisphere is the _____.

6. Most of the direct sensory input to the supplementary motor area comes from the _____ system.

7. Most of the direct sensory input to the premotor cortex comes from the _____ system.

8. The _____ cortex is the main point of departure of motor signals from the cerebral cortex to lower levels of the sensorimotor hierarchy.

9. The foot area of the motor homunculus is in the _____ fissure.

10. Although the _____ constitutes only 10% of the mass of the brain, it contains more than half of its neurons.

11. The _____ are part of neural loops that receive input from various cortical areas and transmit it back to various areas of motor cortex via the thalamus.

12. Although both are considered to be motor structures, damage to the _____ or the _____ produces cognitive deficits.

In experiments on rats, the basal ganglia have been shown to participate in learning to respond correctly to learned associations, a type of response learning which characteristically progresses gradually, trial by trial (e.g., McDonald & White, 1993). However, the basal ganglia's cognitive functions do not appear to be limited to this form of response learning (e.g., Ravizza & Ivry, 2001).

8.6 Descending Motor Pathways

Neural signals are conducted from the primary motor cortex to the motor neurons of the spinal cord over four different pathways. Two pathways descend in the *dorsolateral* region of the spinal cord, and two descend in the *ventromedial* region of the spinal cord. These pathways act together in the control of voluntary movement (see Iwaniuk & Whishaw, 2000).

Dorsolateral Corticospinal Tract and Dorsolateral Corticorubrospinal Tract

One group of axons that descends from the primary motor cortex descends through the *medullary pyramids*—two bulges on the ventral surface of the medulla—then decussates and continues to descend in the contralateral

dorsolateral spinal white matter. This group of axons constitutes the **dorsolateral corticospinal tract**. Most notable among its neurons are the **Betz cells**—extremely large pyramidal neurons of the primary motor cortex. Their axons terminate in the lower regions of the spinal cord on motor neurons that project to the muscles of the legs. They are thought to be the means by which we exert rapid and powerful voluntary control over our legs.

modulation of motor output. Now, the basal ganglia are thought to be involved in a variety of cognitive functions in addition to their role in the modulation of motor output (see Perkel & Farries, 2000). This expanded view of the function of the basal ganglia is consistent with the fact that they project to cortical areas known to have cognitive functions (e.g., the prefrontal lobes).

Most axons of the dorsolateral corticospinal tract synapse on small interneurons of the spinal gray matter, which synapse on the motor neurons of distal muscles of the wrist, hands, fingers, and toes. Primates and the few other mammals that are capable of moving their digits independently (e.g., hamsters and raccoons) have dorsolateral corticospinal tract neurons that synapse directly on digit motor neurons (see Porter & Lemon, 1993).

A second group of axons that descends from the primary motor cortex synapses in the *red nucleus* of the midbrain. The axons of neurons in the red nucleus then decussate and descend through the medulla, where some

of them terminate in the nuclei of the cranial nerves that control the muscles of the face. The rest continue to descend in the dorsolateral portion of the spinal cord. This pathway is called the **dorsolateral corticorubrospinal tract** (*rubro* refers to the red nucleus). The axons of the dorsolateral corticorubrospinal tract synapse on interneurons that in turn synapse on motor neurons that project to the distal muscles of the arms and legs.

The two divisions of the dorsolateral motor pathway—the direct dorsolateral corticospinal tract and the indirect dorsolateral corticorubrospinal tract—are illustrated schematically in Figure 8.7.

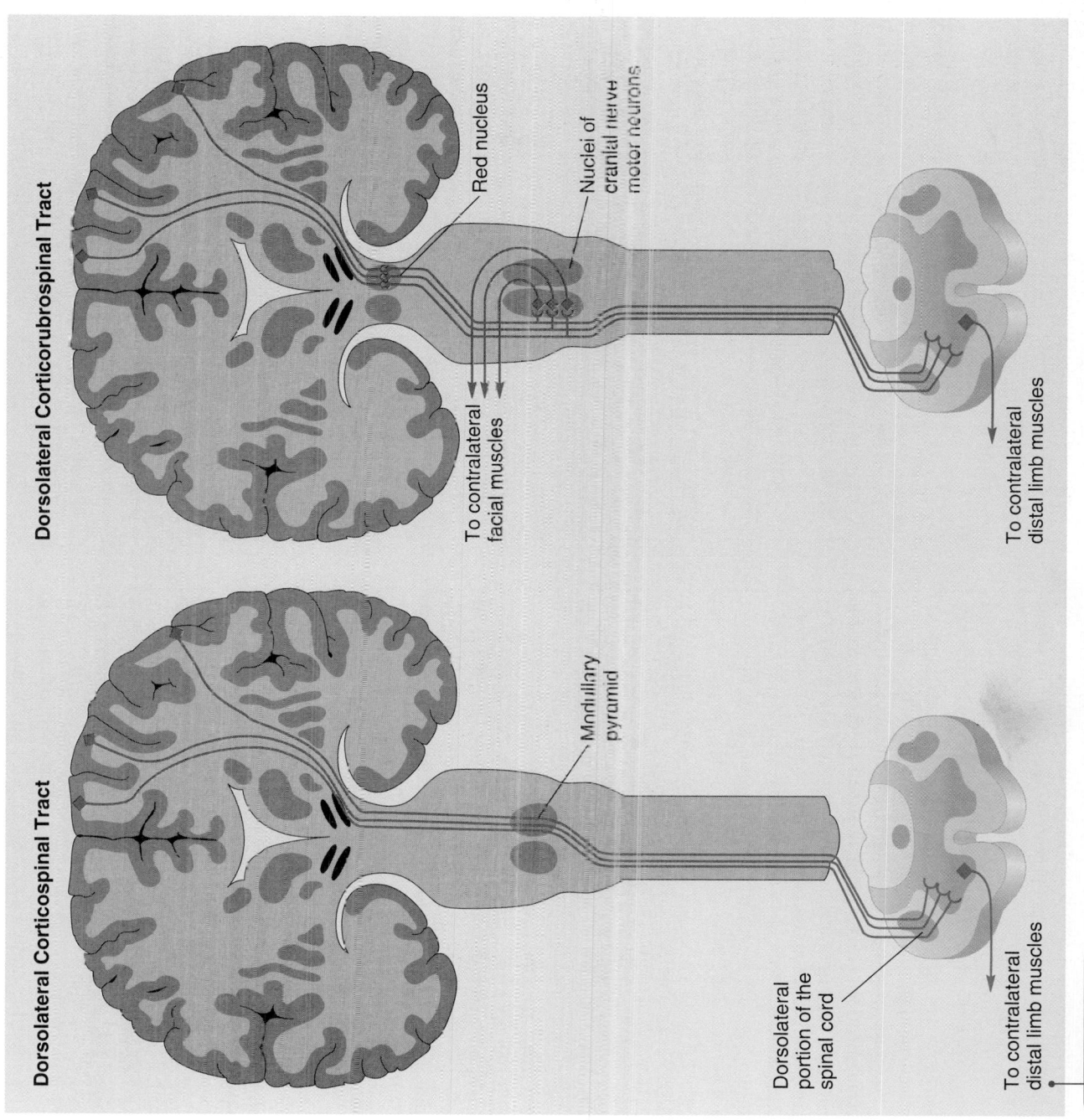

Dorsolateral Corticospinal Tract

Dorsolateral Corticorubrospinal Tract

Medullary pyramid

Dorsolateral portion of the spinal cord

To contralateral distal limb muscles

Red nucleus

Nuclei of cranial nerve motor neurons

To contralateral facial muscles

To contralateral distal limb muscles

FIGURE 8.7   The two divisions of the dorsolateral motor pathway: the dorsolateral corticospinal tract and the dorsolateral corticorubrospinal tract. The projections from only one hemisphere are shown.

Ventromedial Corticospinal Tract and Ventromedial Cortico-brainstem-spinal Tract

Just as there are two major divisions of the dorsolateral motor pathway, one direct (the corticospinal tract) and one indirect (the corticorubrospinal tract), there are two major divisions of the ventromedial motor pathway, one direct and one indirect. The direct ventromedial pathway is the **ventromedial corticospinal tract**, and the indirect one—as you might infer from its cumbersome but descriptive name—is the **ventromedial cortico-brainstem-spinal tract**.

The long axons of the ventromedial corticospinal tract descend ipsilaterally from the primary motor cortex directly into the ventromedial areas of the spinal white matter. As each axon of the ventromedial corticospinal tract descends, it branches diffusely and innervates the interneuron circuits in several different spinal segments on both sides of the spinal gray matter.

The ventromedial cortico-brainstem-spinal tract comprises motor cortex axons that feed into a complex network of brain stem structures. The axons of some of the neurons in this complex brain stem motor network then descend bilaterally in the ventromedial portion of the spinal cord. Each side carries signals from both hemispheres, and each neuron synapses on the interneurons of several different spinal cord segments that control the proximal muscles of the trunk and limbs.

Which brain stem structures interact with the ventromedial cortico-brainstem-spinal tract? There are four major ones: (1) the **tectum**, which receives auditory and visual information about spatial location; (2) the **vestibular nucleus**, which receives information about balance from receptors in the semicircular canals of the inner ear; (3) the **reticular formation**, which, among other things, contains motor programs that regulate complex species-common movements such as walking, swimming, and jumping; and (4) the motor nuclei of the cranial nerves that control the muscles of the face.

The two divisions of the descending ventromedial pathway—the direct ventromedial corticospinal tract and the indirect ventromedial cortico-brainstem-spinal tract—are illustrated in Figure 8.8.

Comparison of the Two Dorsolateral Motor Pathways and the Two Ventromedial Motor Pathways

The descending dorsolateral and ventromedial pathways are similar in that each is composed of two major tracts, one whose axons descend directly to the spinal cord and another whose axons synapse in the brain stem on neurons that in turn descend to the spinal cord. However, the two dorsolateral tracts differ from the two ventromedial tracts in two major respects:

1. The two ventromedial tracts are much more diffuse. Many of their axons innervate interneurons on both sides of the spinal gray matter and in several different segments, whereas the axons of the two dorsolateral tracts terminate in the contralateral half of one spinal cord segment, sometimes directly on a motor neuron.

2. The motor neurons that are activated by the two ventromedial tracts project to proximal muscles of the trunk and limbs (e.g., shoulder muscles), whereas the motor neurons that are activated by the two dorsolateral tracts project to distal muscles (e.g., finger muscles).

Because all four of the descending motor tracts originate in the cerebral cortex, all are presumed to mediate voluntary movement; however, major differences in their routes and destinations suggest that they have different functions. This difference was first demonstrated in two experiments that were reported by Lawrence and Kuypers in 1968.

In their first experiment, Lawrence and Kuypers (1968a) transected (cut through) the left and right dorsolateral corticospinal tracts of their monkey subjects in the medullary pyramids, just above the decussation of the tracts. Following surgery, these monkeys could stand, walk, and climb quite normally; however, their ability to use their limbs for other activities was impaired. For example, their reaching movements were weak and poorly directed, particularly in the first few days following the surgery. Although there was substantial improvement in the monkeys' reaching ability over the ensuing weeks, two other deficits remained unabated. First, the monkeys never regained the ability to move their fingers independently of one another; when they picked up pieces of food, they did so by using all of their fingers as a unit, as if they were glued together. And second, they never regained the ability to release objects from their grasp; as a result, once they picked up a piece of food, they often had to root for it in their hand like a pig rooting for truffles in the ground. In view of this latter problem, it is remarkable that they had no difficulty releasing their grasp on the bars of their cage when they were climbing. This point is important because it shows that the same response performed in different contexts can be controlled by different parts of the central nervous system.

In their second experiment, Lawrence and Kuypers (1968b) made additional transections in the monkeys whose dorsolateral corticospinal tract had already been transected in the first experiment. The dorsolateral corticorubrospinal tract was transected in one group of these monkeys. The monkeys could stand, walk, and climb after this second transection; but when they were sitting, their arms hung limply by their sides (remember that monkeys normally use their arms for standing and walking). In those few instances in which the monkeys did use an arm

Evolutionary Perspective

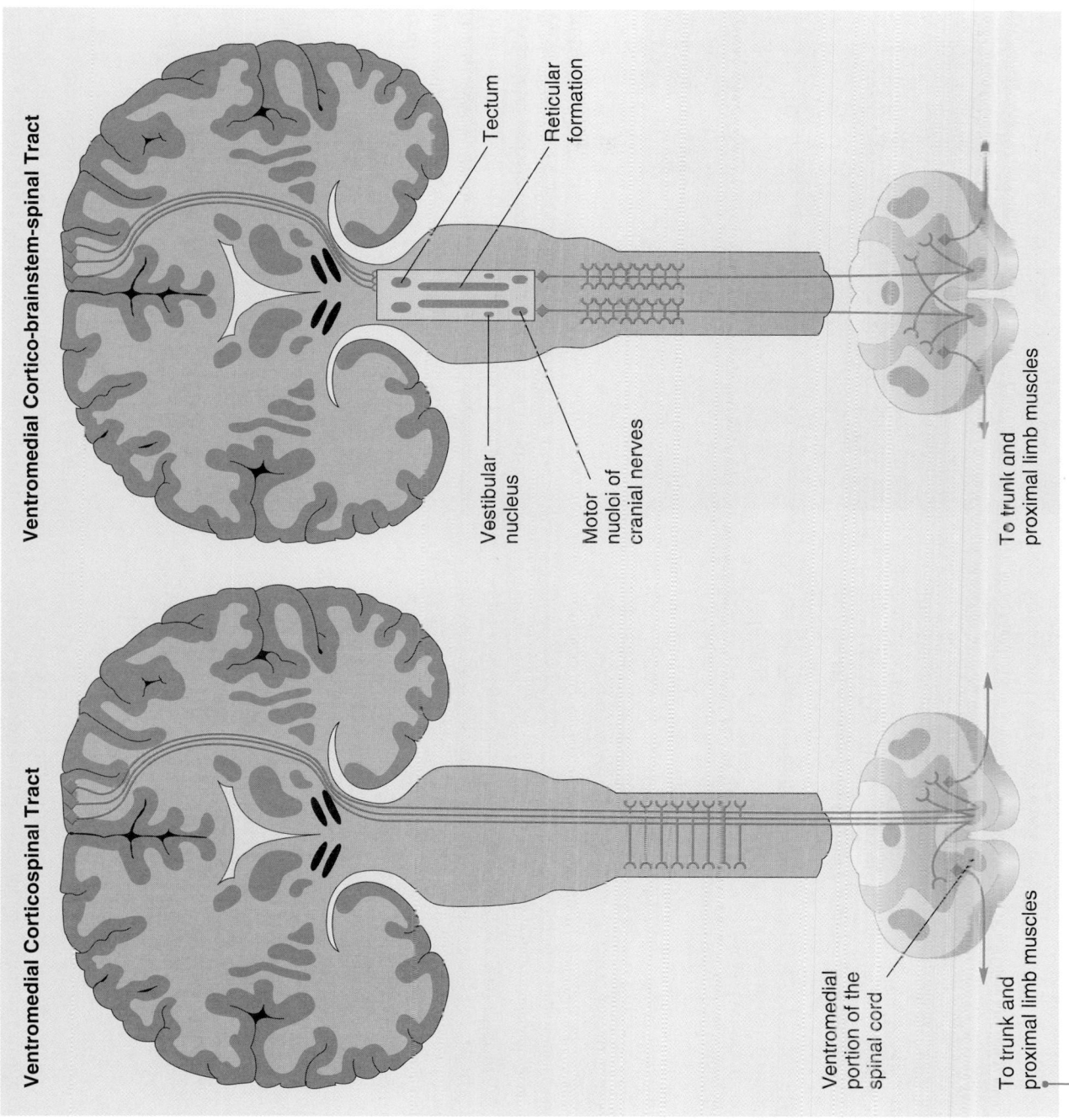

Ventromedial Corticospinal Tract

Ventromedial Cortico-brainstem-spinal Tract

Tectum

Reticular formation

Vestibular nucleus

Motor nucloi of cranial nerves

To trunk and proximal limb muscles

Ventromedial portion of the spinal cord

To trunk and proximal limb muscles

FIGURE 8.8   The two divisions of the ventromedial motor pathway: the ventromedial corticospinal tract and the ventromedial cortico-brainstem-spinal tract. The projections from only one hemisphere are shown.

for reaching, they used it like a rubber-handled rake—throwing it out from the shoulder and using it to draw small objects of interest back along the floor.

The other group of monkeys in the second experiment had both of their ventromedial tracts transected. In contrast to the first group, these subjects had severe postural abnormalities: They had great difficulty walking or sitting. If they did manage to sit or stand without clinging to the bars of their cages, the slightest disturbance, such as a loud noise, frequently made them fall. Although they had some use of their arms, the additional transection of the two ventromedial tracts elimi-

nated their ability to control their shoulders. When they fed, they did so with elbow and whole-hand movements while their upper arms hung limply by their sides.

What do these experiments tell us about the roles of the various descending sensorimotor tracts in the control of movement? They suggest that the two ventromedial tracts are involved in the control of posture and whole-body movements (e.g., walking and climbing) and that they can exert control over the limb movements involved in such activities. In contrast, both dorsolateral tracts—the corticospinal tract and the corticorubrospinal tract—control the movements of the limbs. This redundancy was presumably the basis for the good recovery of limb movement after the initial lesions of the corticospinal dorsolateral tract. However, only the corti-

cospinal division of the dorsolateral system is capable of mediating independent movements of the digits.

8.7 Sensorimotor Spinal Circuits

Muscles

Motor units are the smallest units of motor activity. Each motor unit comprises a single motor neuron and all of the individual skeletal muscle fibers that it innervates (see Figure 8.9). When the motor neuron fires, all the muscle fibers of its unit contract together. Motor units differ appreciably in the number of muscle fibers they contain; the units with the fewest fibers—those of the fingers and face—permit the highest degree of selective motor control.

A skeletal muscle comprises hundreds of thousands of threadlike muscle fibers bound together in a tough membrane and attached to a bone by a *tendon. Acetyl-*

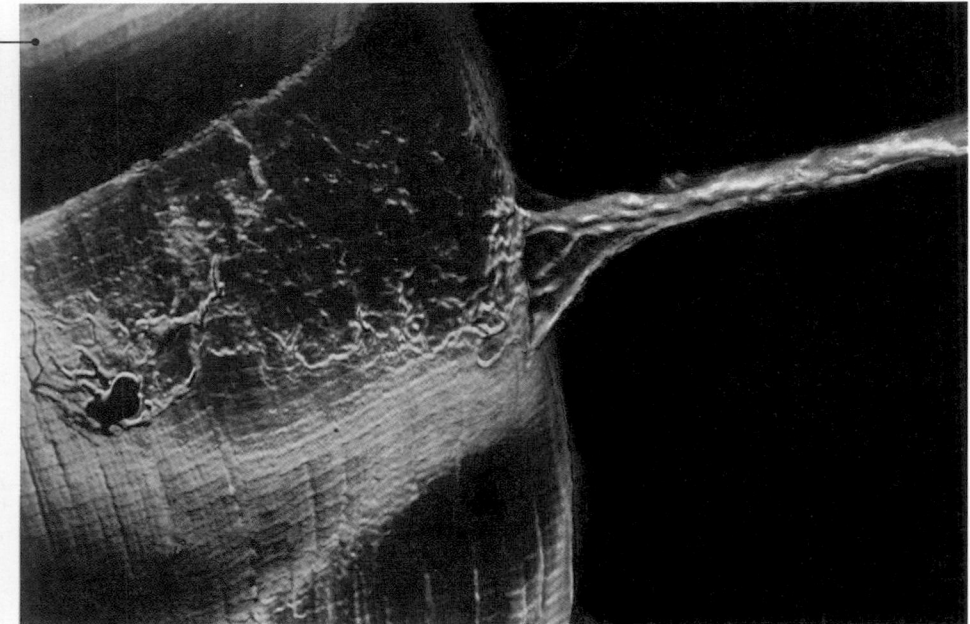

FIGURE 8.9 An electron micrograph of a motor unit: a motor neuron (pink) and the muscle fibers that it innervates.

choline, which is released by motor neurons at *neuromuscular junctions,* activates the **motor end-plate** on each muscle fiber and causes the fiber to contract. All of the motor neurons that innervate the fibers of a single muscle are called its **motor pool.**

Although it is an oversimplification (see Gollinick & Hodgson, 1986), skeletal muscle fibers are often considered to be of two basic types: fast and slow. *Fast muscle fibers,* as you might guess, are those that contract and relax quickly. Although they are capable of generating great force, they fatigue quickly because they are poorly vascularized (which gives them a pale color). In contrast, *slow muscle fibers,* although slower and weaker, are capable of more sustained contraction because they are more richly vascularized (and hence much redder). Depending on their function, muscles have different proportions of fast and slow fibers.

Many skeletal muscles belong unambiguously to one of two categories: flexors or extensors. **Flexors** act to bend or flex a joint, and **extensors** act to straighten or extend it. Figure 8.10 illustrates the *biceps* and *triceps*—the flexor and extensor, respectively, of the elbow joint. Any two muscles whose contraction produces the same movement, be it flexion or extension, are said to be **synergistic muscles;** those that act in opposition, like the biceps and the triceps, are said to be **antagonistic muscles.**

To understand how muscles work, it is important to realize that muscles have elastic, rather than inflexible, cablelike, properties. If you think of an increase in muscle tension as being analogous to an increase in the tension of an elastic band joining two bones, you will appreciate that muscle contraction can be of two types. Activation of a muscle can increase the tension that it exerts on two bones without shortening and pulling them together; this is termed **isometric contraction.** Or it can shorten and pull them together; this is termed **dynamic contraction.** The tension in a muscle can be increased by increasing the number of neurons in its motor pool that are firing, by increasing the firing rates of those that are already firing, or more commonly by a combination of the two.

Receptor Organs of Tendons and Muscles

The activity of skeletal muscles is monitored by two kinds of receptors: Golgi tendon organs and muscle spindles. **Golgi tendon organs** are embedded in the *tendons,* which connect each skeletal muscle to bone; **muscle spindles**

muscle length, but they do not respond to changes in muscle tension.

Under normal conditions, the function of Golgi tendon organs is to provide the central nervous system with information about muscle tension, but they also serve a protective function. When the contraction of a muscle is so extreme that there is a risk of damage, the Golgi tendon organs excite inhibitory interneurons in the spinal cord that cause the muscle to relax.

Figure 8.11 is a schematic diagram of the *muscle-spindle feedback circuit.* Examine it carefully. Notice that each muscle spindle has its own threadlike **intrafusal muscle,** which is innervated by its own **intrafusal motor neuron.** Why would a receptor have its own muscle and motor neuron? The reason becomes apparent when you

are embedded in the muscle tissue itself. Because of their different locations, Golgi tendon organs and muscle spindles respond to different aspects of muscle contraction. Golgi tendon organs respond to increases in muscle tension (i.e., to the pull of the muscle on the tendon), but they are completely insensitive to changes in muscle length. In contrast, muscle spindles respond to changes in

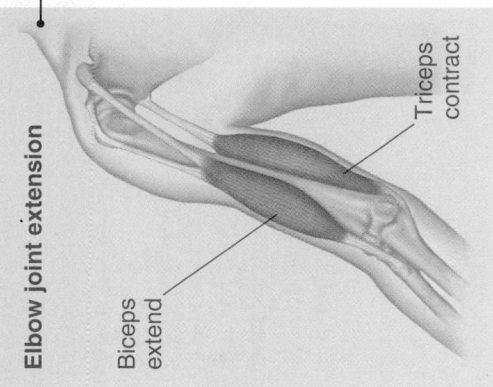

Elbow joint flexion

Biceps contract

Triceps extend

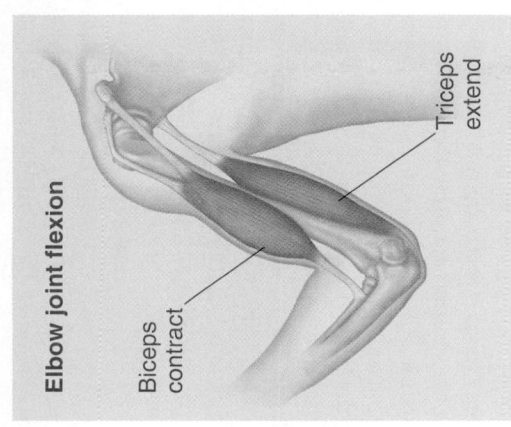

Elbow joint extension

Biceps extend

Triceps contract

FIGURE 8.10 The biceps and triceps, which are the flexor and extensor, respectively, of the elbow joint.

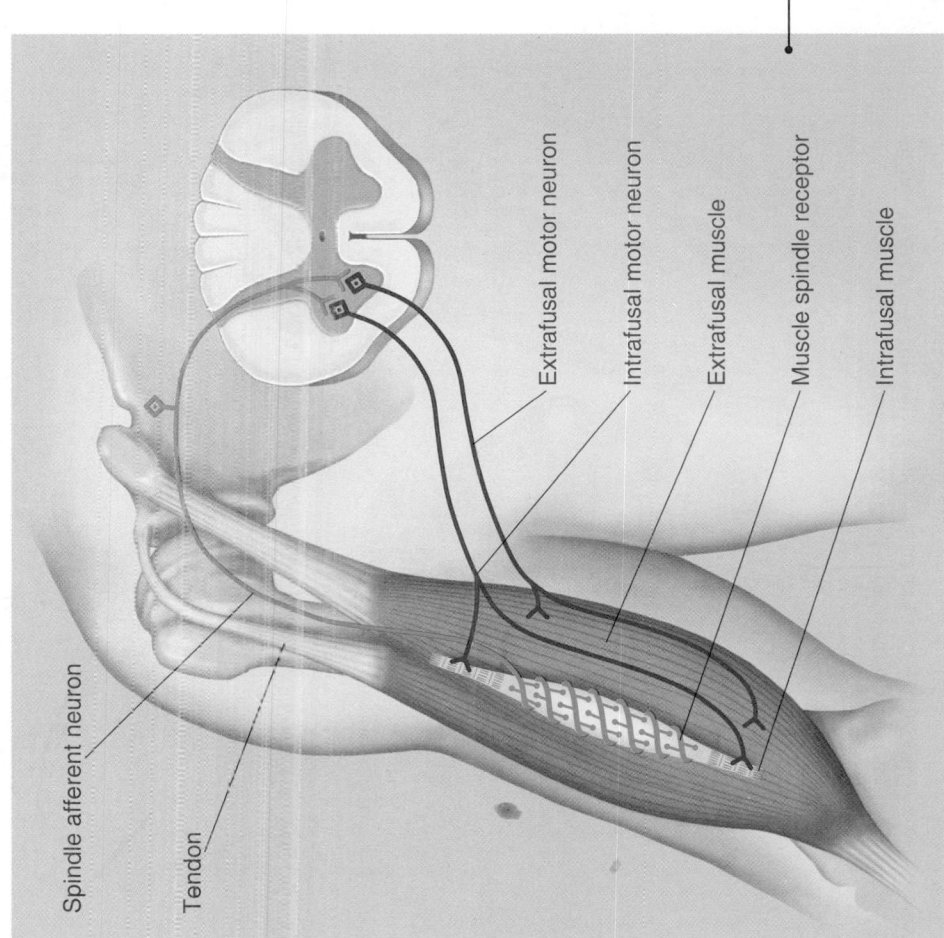

Spindle afferent neuron

Tendon

Extrafusal motor neuron

Intrafusal motor neuron

Extrafusal muscle

Muscle spindle receptor

Intrafusal muscle

FIGURE 8.11 The muscle-spindle feedback circuit. There are many muscle spindles in each muscle; for clarity, only one much-enlarged muscle spindle is illustrated here.

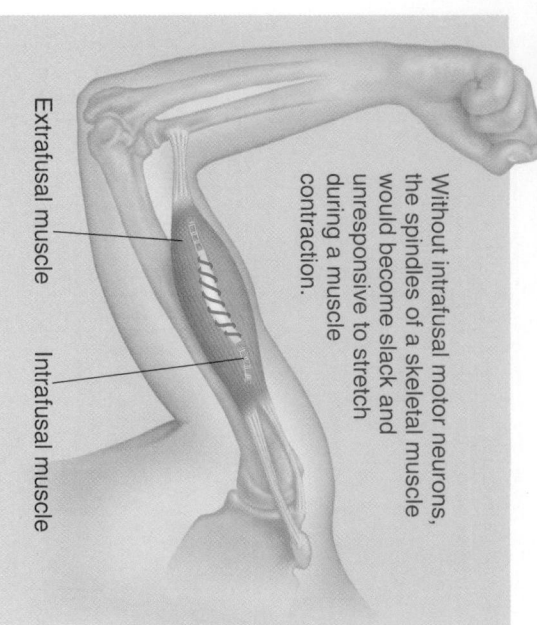

Without intrafusal motor neurons, the spindles of a skeletal muscle would become slack and unresponsive to stretch during a muscle contraction.

Extrafusal muscle

Intrafusal muscle

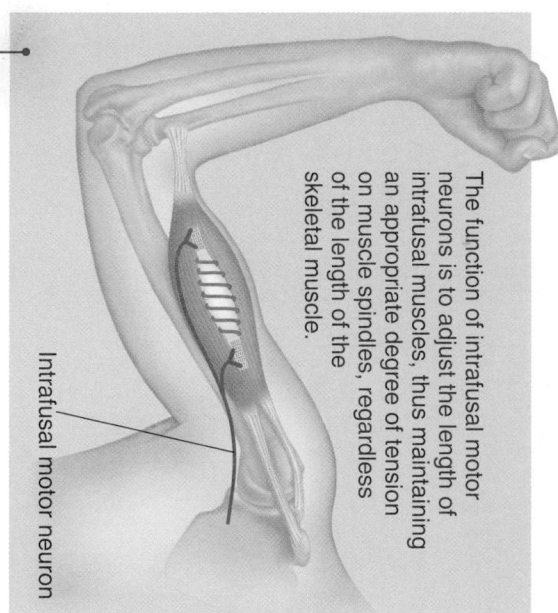

The function of intrafusal motor neurons is to adjust the length of intrafusal muscles, thus maintaining an appropriate degree of tension on muscle spindles, regardless of the length of the skeletal muscle.

Intrafusal motor neuron

FIGURE 8.12   The function of intrafusal motor neurons.

consider what would happen to a muscle spindle without them. Without its intrafusal motor input, a muscle spindle would fall slack each time its **skeletal muscle (extrafusal muscle)** contracted. In this slack state, the muscle spindle could not do its job, which is to respond to slight changes in extrafusal muscle length. As Figure 8.12 illustrates, the intrafusal motor neuron solves this problem by shortening the intrafusal muscle each time the extrafusal muscle becomes shorter, thus keeping enough tension on the middle, stretch-sensitive portion of the muscle spindle to keep it responsive to slight changes in the length of the extrafusal muscle.

Stretch Reflex

When the word *reflex* is mentioned, many people think of themselves sitting on the edge of their doctor's examination table having their knees rapped with a little

rubber-headed hammer. The resulting leg extension is called the **patellar tendon reflex** (*patella* means "knee"). This reflex is a **stretch reflex**—a reflex that is elicited by a sudden external stretching force on a muscle.

When your doctor strikes the tendon of your knee, the extensor muscle running along your thigh is stretched. This initiates the chain of events that is depicted in Figure 8.13. The sudden stretch of the thigh muscle stretches its muscle-spindle stretch receptors, which in turn initiates a volley of action potentials that is carried from the stretch receptors into the spinal cord by **spindle afferent neurons** via the *dorsal root*. This volley of action potentials excites motor neurons in the *ventral horn* of the spinal cord, which respond by sending action potentials back to the muscle whose stretch originally excited them (see Illert & Kummel, 1999). The arrival of these impulses back at the starting point results in a compensatory muscle contraction and a sudden leg extension.

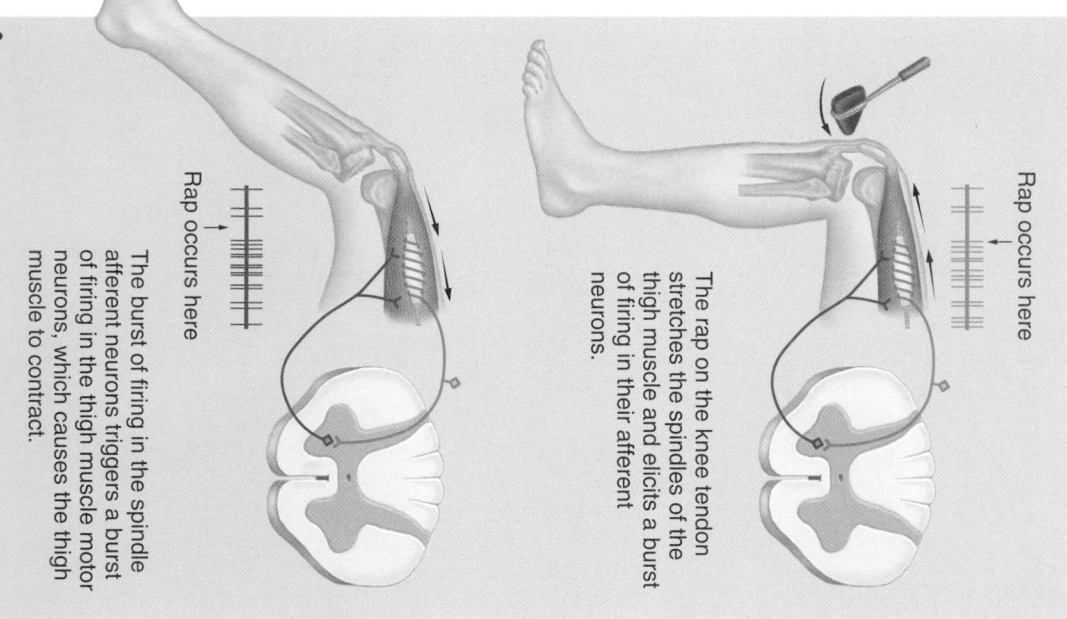

Rap occurs here

The rap on the knee tendon stretches the spindles of the thigh muscle and elicits a burst of firing in their afferent neurons.

Rap occurs here

The burst of firing in the spindle afferent neurons triggers a burst of firing in the thigh muscle motor neurons, which causes the thigh muscle to contract.

FIGURE 8.13   The elicitation of a stretch reflex. All of the muscle spindles in a muscle are activated during a stretch reflex, but only a single muscle spindle is depicted here.

The method by which the patellar tendon reflex is typically elicited in a doctor's office—that is, by a sharp blow to the tendon of a completely relaxed muscle—is designed to make the reflex readily observable. However, it does little to communicate its functional significance. In real-life situations, the function of the stretch reflex is to keep external forces from altering the intended position of the body. When an external force, such as a push on your arm while you are holding a cup of coffee, causes an unanticipated extrafusal muscle stretch, the muscle-spindle feedback circuit produces an immediate compensatory contraction of the muscle that counteracts the force and keeps you from spilling the coffee—unless, of course, you are wearing your best clothes.

The mechanism by which the stretch reflex maintains limb stability is illustrated in Figure 8.14. Examine

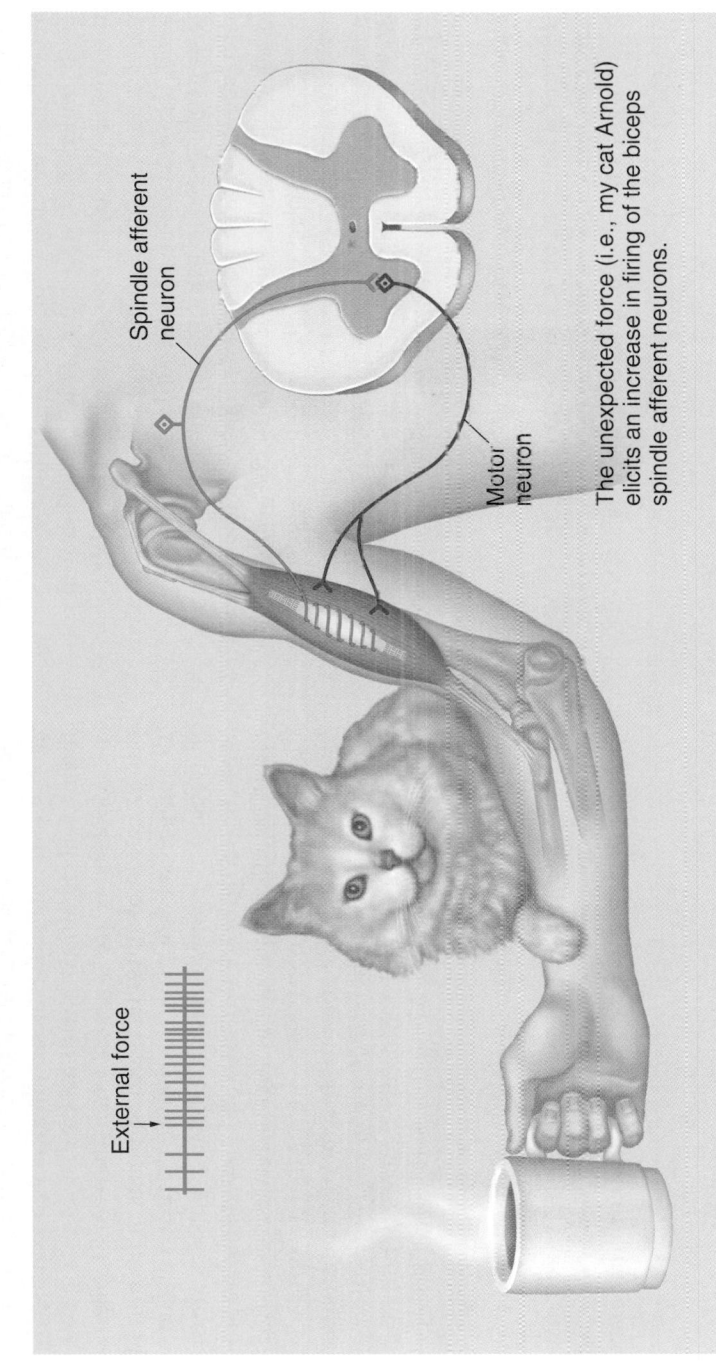

External force

Spindle afferent neuron

Motor neuron

The unexpected force (i.e., my cat Arnold) elicits an increase in firing of the biceps spindle afferent neurons.

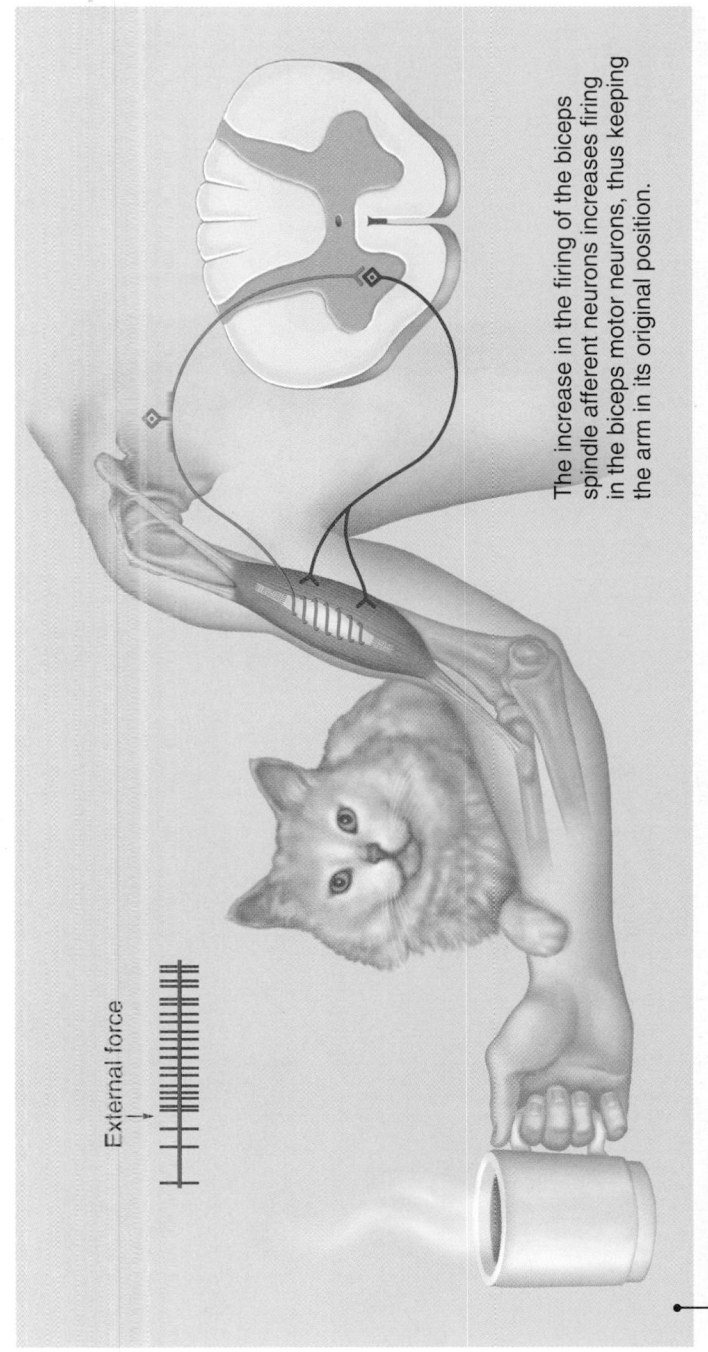

External force

The increase in the firing of the biceps spindle afferent neurons increases firing in the biceps motor neurons, thus keeping the arm in its original position.

FIGURE 8.14 The automatic maintenance of limb position by the muscle-spindle feedback system.

it carefully because it illustrates two of the principles of sensorimotor system function that are the focus of this chapter: the important role played by sensory feedback in the regulation of motor output and the ability of lower circuits in the motor hierarchy to take care of "business details" without the involvement of higher levels.

Withdrawal Reflex

I am sure that, at one time or another, you have touched something painful—a hot pot, for example—and suddenly pulled back your hand. This is a **withdrawal reflex.** Unlike the stretch reflex, the withdrawal reflex is *not monosynaptic.* When a painful stimulus is applied to the hand, the first responses are recorded in the motor neurons of the arm flexor muscles about 1.6 milliseconds later, about the time it takes a neural signal to cross two synapses. Thus, the shortest route in the withdrawal-reflex circuit involves one interneuron. Other responses are recorded in the motor neurons of the arm flexor muscles after the initial volley; these responses are triggered by signals that have traveled over multisynaptic pathways—some involving the cortex. See Figure 8.15.

Reciprocal Innervation

Reciprocal innervation is an important principle of spinal cord circuitry. It refers to the fact that antagonistic muscles are innervated in a way that permits a smooth,

unimpeded motor response: When one is contracted, the other relaxes. Figure 8.15 illustrates the role of reciprocal innervation in the withdrawal reflex. "Bad news" of a sudden painful event in the hand arrives in the dorsal horn of the spinal cord and has two effects: The signals excite both excitatory and inhibitory interneurons. The excitatory interneurons excite the motor neurons of the elbow flexor; the inhibitory interneurons inhibit the motor neurons of the elbow extensor. Thus, a single sensory input produces a coordinated pattern of motor output; the activities of agonists and antagonists are automatically coordinated by the internal circuitry of the spinal cord.

Movements are quickest when there is simultaneous excitation of all agonists and complete inhibition of all antagonists; however, this is not the way voluntary movement is normally produced. Most muscles are always contracted to some degree, and movements are produced by adjustment in the level of relative cocontraction between antagonists. Movements that are produced by **cocontraction** are smooth, and they can be stopped with precision by a slight increase in the contraction of the antagonistic muscles. Moreover, cocontraction insulates us from the effects of unexpected external forces.

Recurrent Collateral Inhibition

Like most workers, muscle fibers and the motor neurons that innervate them need an occasional break, and there are inhibitory neurons in the spinal cord that make

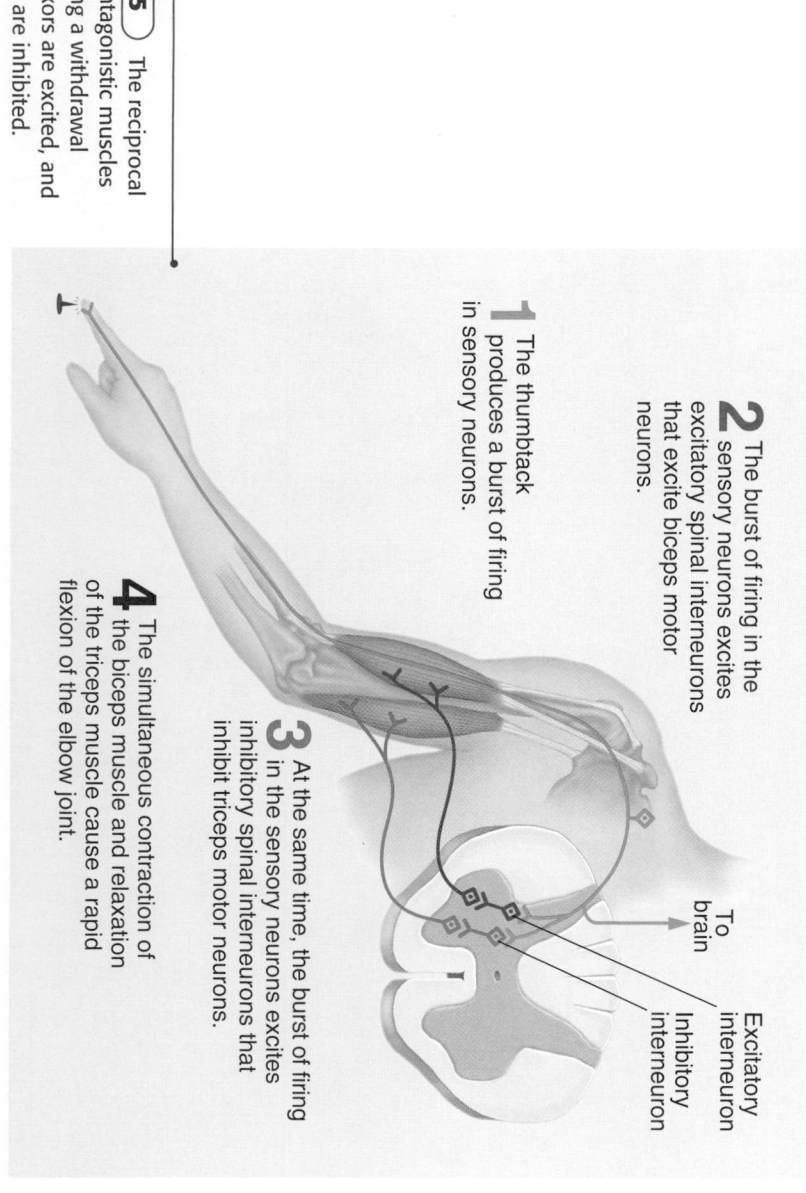

1 The thumbtack produces a burst of firing in sensory neurons.

2 The burst of firing in the sensory neurons excites excitatory spinal interneurons that excite biceps motor neurons.

3 At the same time, the burst of firing in the sensory neurons excites inhibitory spinal interneurons that inhibit triceps motor neurons.

4 The simultaneous contraction of the biceps muscle and relaxation of the triceps muscle cause a rapid flexion of the elbow joint.

To brain

Excitatory interneuron

Inhibitory interneuron

FIGURE 8.15 The reciprocal innervation of antagonistic muscles in the arm. During a withdrawal reflex, elbow flexors are excited, and elbow extensors are inhibited.

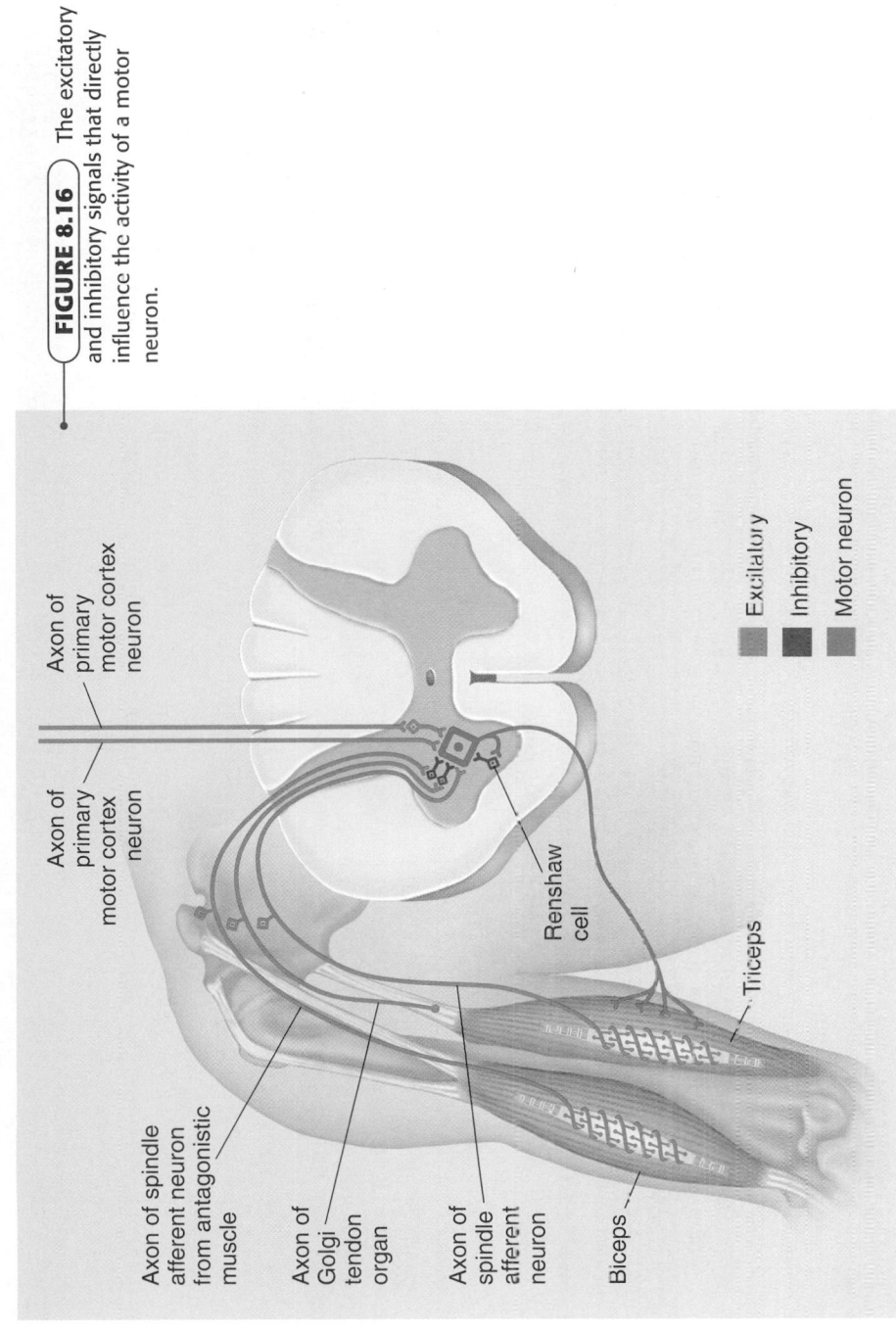

Axon of primary motor cortex neuron

Axon of primary motor cortex neuron

Axon of spindle afferent neuron from antagonistic muscle

Axon of Golgi tendon organ

Axon of spindle afferent neuron

Biceps

Triceps

Renshaw cell

■ Excitatory
■ Inhibitory
■ Motor neuron

FIGURE 8.16 The excitatory and inhibitory signals that directly influence the activity of a motor neuron.

sure they get it. Each motor neuron branches just before it leaves the spinal cord, and the branch synapses on a small inhibitory interneuron, which inhibits the very motor neuron from which it receives its input (see Illert & Kümmel, 1999). The inhibition produced by these local feedback circuits is called **recurrent collateral inhibition,** and the small inhibitory interneurons that mediate recurrent collateral inhibition are called *Renshaw cells.* As a consequence of recurrent collateral inhibition, each time a motor neuron fires, it momentarily inhibits itself and shifts the responsibility for the contraction of a particular muscle to other members of the muscle's motor pool.

Figure 8.16 provides a summary; it illustrates recurrent collateral inhibition and other factors that directly excite or inhibit motor neurons.

Walking: A Complex Sensorimotor Reflex

Most reflexes are much more complex than withdrawal and stretch reflexes. Think for a moment about the complexity of the program of reflexes that is needed to control an activity such as walking (see Capaday, 2002;

Dietz, 2002a; Nielsen, 2002). Such a program must integrate visual information from the eyes; somatosensory information from the feet, knees, hips, arms, and so on; and information about balance from the semicircular canals of the inner ears. And it must produce, on the basis of this information, an integrated series of movements that involves the muscles of the trunk, legs, feet, and upper arms. This program of reflexes must also be incredibly flexible; it must be able to adjust its output immediately to changes in the slope of the terrain, to instructions from the brain, or to external forces such as a bag of groceries. Nobody has yet managed to build a robot that can come close to duplicating these feats.

Grillner (1985) showed that walking can be controlled by circuits in the spinal cord. Grillner's subjects were cats whose spinal cords had been separated from their brains by transection. He suspended the cats in a sling over a treadmill; amazingly, when the treadmill was started so that the cats received sensory feedback of the sort that normally accompanies walking, they began to walk. Similar effects have been observed in other species, but in humans the descending motor pathways play a greater role in walking (see Drew, Jiang, & Widajewicz, 2002).

In this chapter, you have learned that the sensorimotor system is like the hierarchy of a large efficient company. You have learned how the executives—the dorsolateral prefrontal cortex, the supplementary motor area, and the premotor cortex—issue commands based on information supplied to them by the posterior parietal cortex. And you have learned how these commands are forwarded to the director of operations (the primary motor cortex) for distribution over four main channels of communication (the two dorsolateral and the two ventromedial spinal motor pathways) to the metaphoric office managers of the sensorimotor hierarchy (the spinal sensorimotor circuits). Finally, you have learned how spinal sensorimotor circuits direct the activities of the workers (the muscles).

One theory of sensorimotor function is that the sensorimotor system comprises a hierarchy of **central sensorimotor programs** (see Brooks, 1986; Georgopoulos, 1991). The central sensorimotor program theory suggests that all but the highest levels of the sensorimotor system have certain patterns of activity programmed into them and that complex movements are produced by activating the appropriate combinations of these programs (See Swinnen, 2002; Tresch et al., 2002). Accordingly, if your association cortex decides that you might like to look at a magazine, it activates high-level cortical programs that in turn activate lower-level programs—perhaps in your brain stem—for walking, bending over, picking up, and thumbing through. These programs in turn activate specific spinal programs that control the various elements of the sequences and cause your muscles to complete the objective.

Once activated, each level of the sensorimotor system is capable of operating on the basis of current sensory feedback, without the direct control of higher levels. Thus, although the highest levels of your sensorimotor system retain the option of directly controlling your activities, most of the individual responses that you make are performed without direct cortical involvement, and you are barely aware of them.

In much the same way, a company president who wishes to open a new branch office simply issues the command to one of the executives, and the executive responds in the usual fashion by issuing a series of commands to the appropriate people lower in the hierarchy, who in turn do the same. Each of the executives and workers of the company knows how to complete many different tasks and executes them in the light of current conditions when instructed to do so. Good companies have mechanisms for ensuring that the programs of action at different levels of the hierarchy are well coordinated and effective. In the sensorimotor system, these mechanisms seem to be the responsibility of the cerebellum and basal ganglia.

Central Sensorimotor Programs Are Capable of Motor Equivalence

Like a large, efficient company, the sensorimotor system does not always accomplish a particular task in exactly the same way. The fact that the same basic movement can be carried out in different ways involving different muscles is called **motor equivalence**. For example, you have learned to sign your name with stereotypical finger and hand movements, yet if you signed your name with your toe on a sandy beach, your signature would still retain many of its typical characteristics. This example of motor equivalence suggests that the central sensorimotor programs for signing your name are not stored in the neural circuits that directly control your preferred hand, but higher in your sensorimotor hierarchy. Where?

In an fMRI study, Rijntjes and others (1999) showed that the central sensorimotor programs for signing one's name seem to be stored in areas of secondary motor cortex that control the preferred hand. Remarkably, these same hand areas were also activated when the signature was made with a toe.

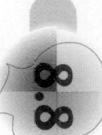

Cognitive Neuroscience

Sensory Information That Controls Central Sensorimotor Programs Is Not Necessarily Conscious

In Chapter 7, you learned that the neural mechanisms of conscious visual perception (ventral stream) are not necessarily the same as those that mediate the visual control of behavior (dorsal stream). Initial evidence for this theory came from neuropsychological patients who could respond to visual stimuli of which they had no conscious awareness and from others who could not effectively interact with objects that they consciously perceived.

Is there evidence for the separation of conscious perception and sensory control of behavior in intact subjects? Haffenden and Goodale (1998) supplied such evidence. They showed healthy subjects a three-dimensional version of the visual illusion in Figure 8.17—notice that the two central disks appear to be different sizes, even though they are identical. Remarkably, when subjects were asked to indicate the size of each central disk with their right thumb and pointing finger, they judged the disk on the left to be bigger than the one on the right; however, when they were asked to reach out and pick up the disks with the same two digits, the preparatory gap

shoulder movements that would have swept their fore-paws across their eyes. Fentress's study also demonstrated the importance of sensory feedback in the operation of central sensorimotor programs. The forelimbless mice, deprived of normal tongue–forepaw contact during face grooming, would often interrupt ostensible grooming se-quences to lick a cage-mate or even the floor.

Practice Can Create Central Sensorimotor Programs

Although central sensorimotor programs for many spe-cies-typical behaviors develop without practice, practice is a certain way to generate or modify such programs. Theories of sensorimotor learning emphasize two kinds of processes that influence the learning of central senso-rimotor programs: response chunking and shifting con-trol to lower levels of the sensorimotor system.

Response Chunking According to the **response-chunking hypothesis**, practice combines the central sensorimotor programs that control individual response into programs that control sequences (chunks) of be-havior. In a novice typist, each response necessary to type a word is individually triggered and controlled; in a skilled typist, sequences of letters are activated as a unit, with a marked increase in speed and continuity.

An important principle of chunking is that chunks can themselves be combined into higher-order chunks. For example, the responses needed to type the individual letters and digits of one's address may be chunked into longer sequences necessary to produce the individual words and numbers, and these chunks may in turn be combined so that the entire address can be typed as a unit.

Shifting Control to Lower Levels In the process of learning a central sensorimotor program, control is shifted from higher levels of the sensorimotor hierar-chy to lower levels (see Ramnani & Passingham, 2001; Sanes, 2003). Shifting the level of control to lower levels of the sensorimotor system during training (see Seitz et al., 1990) has two advantages. One is that it frees up the higher levels of the system to deal with more esoteric as-pects of performance. For example, skilled pianists can concentrate on interpreting a piece of music because they do not have to consciously focus on pressing the right keys. The other advantage of shifting the level of control is that it permits great speed because different circuits at the lower levels of the hierarchy can act si-multaneously, without interfering with one another. It is possible to type 120 words per minute only because the circuits responsible for activating each individual key press can become active before the preceding response has been completed.

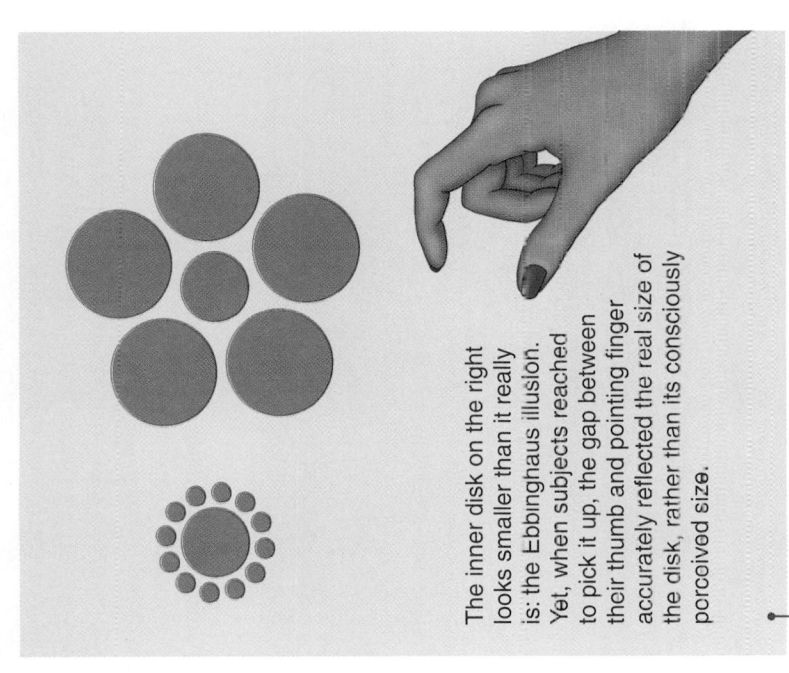

The inner disk on the right looks smaller than it really is: the Ebbinghaus illusion. Yet, when subjects reached to pick it up, the gap between their thumb and pointing finger accurately reflected the real size of the disk, rather than its consciously perceived size.

FIGURE 8.17 The Ebbinghaus illusion. Notice that the central disk on the left appears larger than the one on the right. Haffenden and Goodale (1998) found that when subjects reached out to pick up either of the central disks, the position of their fingers as they approached the disks indicated that their responses were being controlled by the actual sizes of the disks, not their consciously perceived sizes.

between the digits was a function of the actual size of each disk rather than its perceived size.

Central Sensorimotor Programs Can Develop without Practice

What type of experience is necessary for the normal de-velopment of central sensorimotor programs? In partic-ular, is it necessary to practice a particular behavior for its central sensorimotor program to develop?

Although central sensorimotor programs for some behaviors can be established by practicing the behaviors, the central sensorimotor programs for many species-typical behaviors are established without explicit practice of the behaviors. This point was made clear by the clas-sic study of Fentress (1973). Fentress showed that adult mice raised from birth without forelimbs still made the patterns of shoulder movements typi-cal of grooming in their species—and that these movements were well coor-dinated with normal tongue, head, and eye movements. For example, the mice blinked each time they made the

> **Evolutionary Perspective**

Functional Brain Imaging of Sensorimotor Learning

Functional brain-imaging techniques have provided opportunities for studying the neural correlates of sensorimotor learning. By recording the brain activity of human subjects as they learn to perform new motor sequences, researchers can develop hypotheses about the roles of various structures in sensorimotor learning. A good example of this approach is the

PET study of Jenkins and colleagues (1994). These researchers re-

corded PET activity from human subjects who performed two different sequences of key presses. There were four different keys, and each sequence was four presses long. The presses were performed with the right hand, one every 3 seconds, and tones indicated when to press and whether or not a press was correct. There were three conditions: a rest control condition, a condition in which the subjects performed a newly learned sequence, and a condition in which the subjects performed a well-practiced sequence.

The following are six major findings of this study (see Figure 8.18). They recapitulate important points that have already been made in this chapter.

Finding 1: Posterior parietal cortex was activated during the performance of both the newly learned sequence and the well-practiced sequence, but it was more active during the newly learned sequence. This finding is consistent with the hypothesis that the posterior parietal cortex integrates sensory stimuli (in this case, the tones) that are used to guide motor sequences, and it is consistent with the finding that the posterior parietal cortex is more active when subjects are attending more to the stimuli, as is often the case during the early stages of motor learning.

Finding 2: Dorsolateral prefrontal cortex was activated during the performance of the newly learned sequence but not the well-practiced sequence. This suggests that the dorsolateral prefrontal cortex plays a particularly important role when motor sequences are being performed

Sensorimotor areas activated by performing a newly learned sequence of finger movements

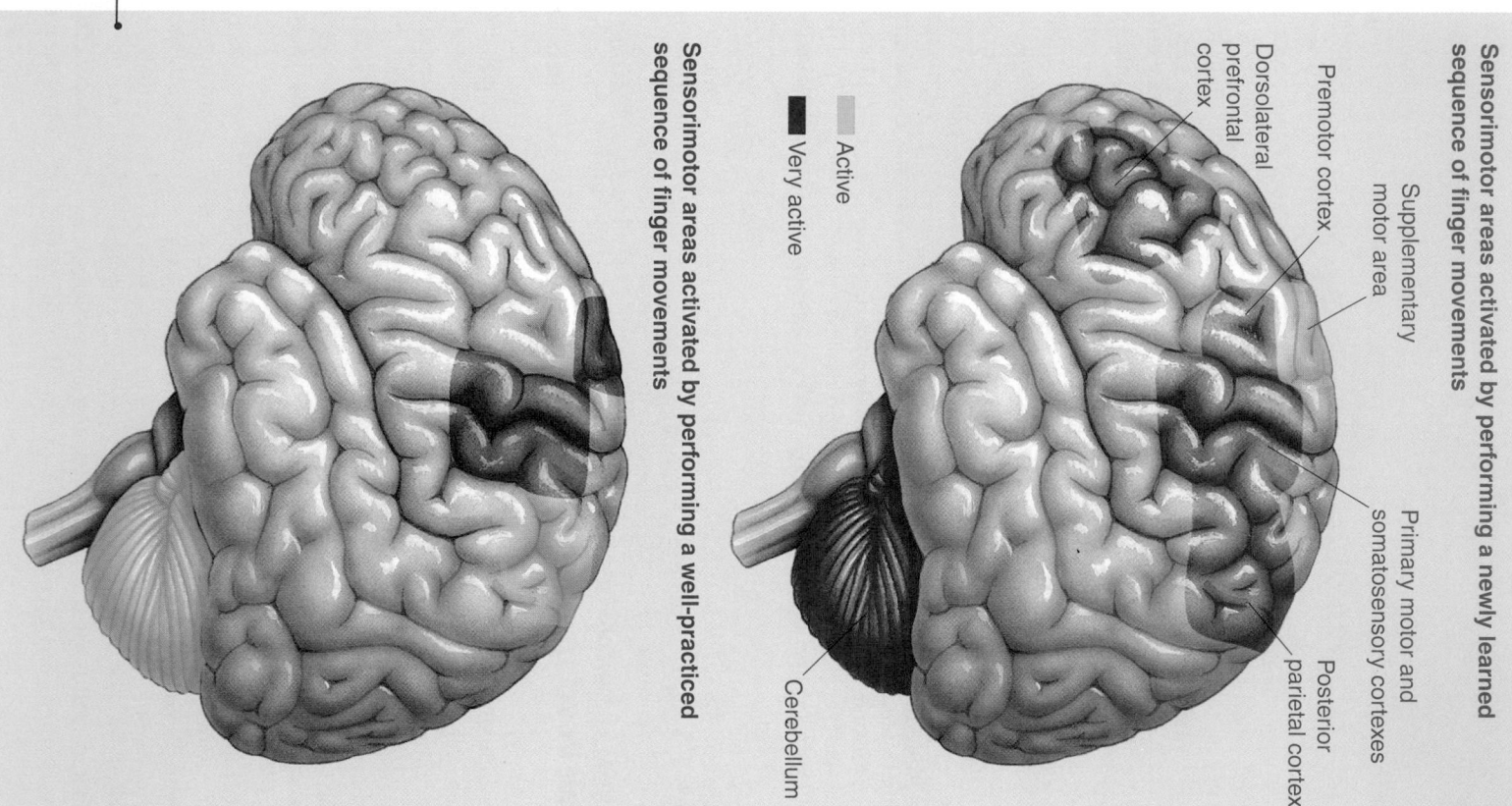

- Supplementary motor area
- Premotor cortex
- Dorsolateral prefrontal cortex
- Primary motor and somatosensory cortexes
- Posterior parietal cortex

☐ Active
■ Very active

Sensorimotor areas activated by performing a well-practiced sequence of finger movements

- Cerebellum

FIGURE 8.18 The activity recorded by PET scans during the performance of newly learned and well-practiced sequences of finger movements. (Adapted from Jenkins et al., 1994.)

largely under conscious control, as is often the case during the early stages of motor learning.

Finding 3: The areas of secondary motor cortex responded differently. The contralateral premotor cortex was more active during the performance of the newly learned sequence, whereas the supplementary motor area was more active bilaterally during the well-practiced sequence. This finding is consistent with the hypothesis that the premotor cortex plays a more prominent role when performance is being guided largely by sensory stimuli, as is often the case in the early stages of motor learning, and that the supplementary motor area plays a more prominent role when performance is largely independent of sensory stimuli, as is often the case for well-practiced motor sequences, which can be run off automatically with little sensory feedback.

Finding 4: Contralateral primary motor and somatosensory cortexes were equally activated during the performance of both the newly learned and well-practiced motor sequences. This finding is consistent with the fact that the motor elements were the same during both sequences.

Finding 5: The contralateral basal ganglia were equally activated during the performance of the newly learned sequence and the well practiced sequence. Jenkins and colleagues speculated that different subpopulations of basal ganglia neurons may have been active during the two conditions, but this could not be detected because of the poor spatial resolution of PET.

Finding 6: The cerebellum was activated bilaterally during the performance of both the newly learned and the well-practiced sequences, but it was more active during the newly learned sequence. This is consistent with the idea that the cerebellum plays a prominent role in motor learning.

The Case of Rhonda, Revisited

A few days after I finished writing this chapter, I stopped off to pick up a few fresh vegetables and some fish for dinner, and I once again found myself waiting in Rhonda's line. It was the longest line, but I am a creature of habit. This time, I felt rather smug as I watched her. All of the reading and thinking that had gone into the preparation of this chapter had provided me with some new insights into what she was doing and how she was doing it. I wondered whether she appreciated her own finely tuned sensorimotor system as much as I did. Then I hatched my plot—a little test of Rhonda's muscle-spindle feedback system. How would Rhonda's finely tuned sensorimotor system react to a bag that looked heavy but was in fact extremely light? Next time, I would get one of those paper bags at the mushroom counter, blow it up, drop one mushroom in it, and then fold the top so it looked completely full. I smiled at the thought. But I wasn't the only one smiling. My daydreaming ended abruptly, and the smile melted from my face, as I noticed Rhonda's extended hand and her amused grin. Will I never learn?

Themes Revisited

All four of this book's major themes were addressed in this chapter. Most prominent were the clinical implications and cognitive neuroscience themes: You learned how the convergence of research on neuropsychological patients with sensorimotor deficits and studies of functional brain images of human subjects engaging in sensorimotor activities has contributed to current theories of sensorimotor functioning.

The evolutionary perspective theme was evident in the discussion of several comparative experiments on the sensorimotor system, largely in nonhuman primates. An important point to keep in mind is that although the sensorimotor functions of nonhuman primates are similar to those of humans, they are not identical (e.g., monkeys walk on both their hands and feet).

Finally, you learned how the conmetaphors can be used to think productively about science—in particular, how a large, efficient company can serve as a useful metaphor for the sensorimotor system.

Clinical Implications

Cognitive Neuroscience

Evolutionary Perspective

Thinking Critically

ON THE CD

See Hard Copy for additional readings for Chapter 8.

Think about It

1. Both sensorimotor systems and large businesses are complex systems trying to survive in a competitive milieu. It is no accident that they function in similar ways. Discuss.

2. We humans tend to view cortical mechanisms as preeminent, presumably because we are the species with the largest cortexes. However, one might argue from several perspectives that the lower sensorimotor functions are more important. Discuss.

3. This chapter has presented more evidence of parallel processing: Some neural circuits perform their function under conscious awareness, and other circuits perform the same function in the absence of consciousness. Discuss.

4. Belle, the owl monkey, controlled a robotic arm with her brain. How might the technology that allowed her to do this be used to improve the lives of paralyzed patients?

Key Terms

Antagonistic muscles (p. 200)
Apraxia (p. 189)
Asterognosia (p. 195)
Betz cells (p. 196)
Central sensorimotor programs (p. 206)
Cingulate motor areas (p. 192)
Cocontraction (p. 204)
Contralateral neglect (p. 189)
Dorsolateral corticorubrospinal tract (p. 197)
Dorsolateral corticospinal tract (p. 196)
Dorsolateral prefrontal association cortex (p. 196)
Dynamic contraction (p. 200)
Extensors (p. 200)

Flexors (p. 200)
Frontal eye field (p. 188)
Golgi tendon organs (p. 200)
Intrafusal motor neuron (p. 201)
Intrafusal muscle (p. 201)
Isometric contraction (p. 200)
Motor end-plate (p. 200)
Motor equivalence (p. 206)
Motor homunculus (p. 193)
Motor pool (p. 200)
Motor units (p. 200)
Muscle spindles (p. 200)
Patellar tendon reflex (p. 202)
Posterior parietal association cortex (p. 188)
Premotor cortex (p. 192)
Primary motor cortex (p. 193)

Reciprocal innervation (p. 204)
Recurrent collateral inhibition (p. 205)
Response-chunking hypothesis (p. 207)
Reticular formation (p. 198)
Secondary motor cortex (p. 192)
Sensory feedback (p. 187)
Skeletal muscle (extrafusal muscle) (p. 202)
Somatotopic (p. 193)
Spindle afferent neurons (p. 202)
Stereognosis (p. 194)
Stretch reflex (p. 202)
Supplementary motor area (p. 192)

Synergistic muscles (p. 200)
Tectum (p. 198)
Ventromedial cortico-brainstem-spinal tract (p. 198)
Ventromedial corticospinal tract (p. 198)
Vestibular nucleus (p. 198)
Withdrawal reflex (p. 204)

chapter

9

Development of the Nervous System

From Fertilized Egg to You

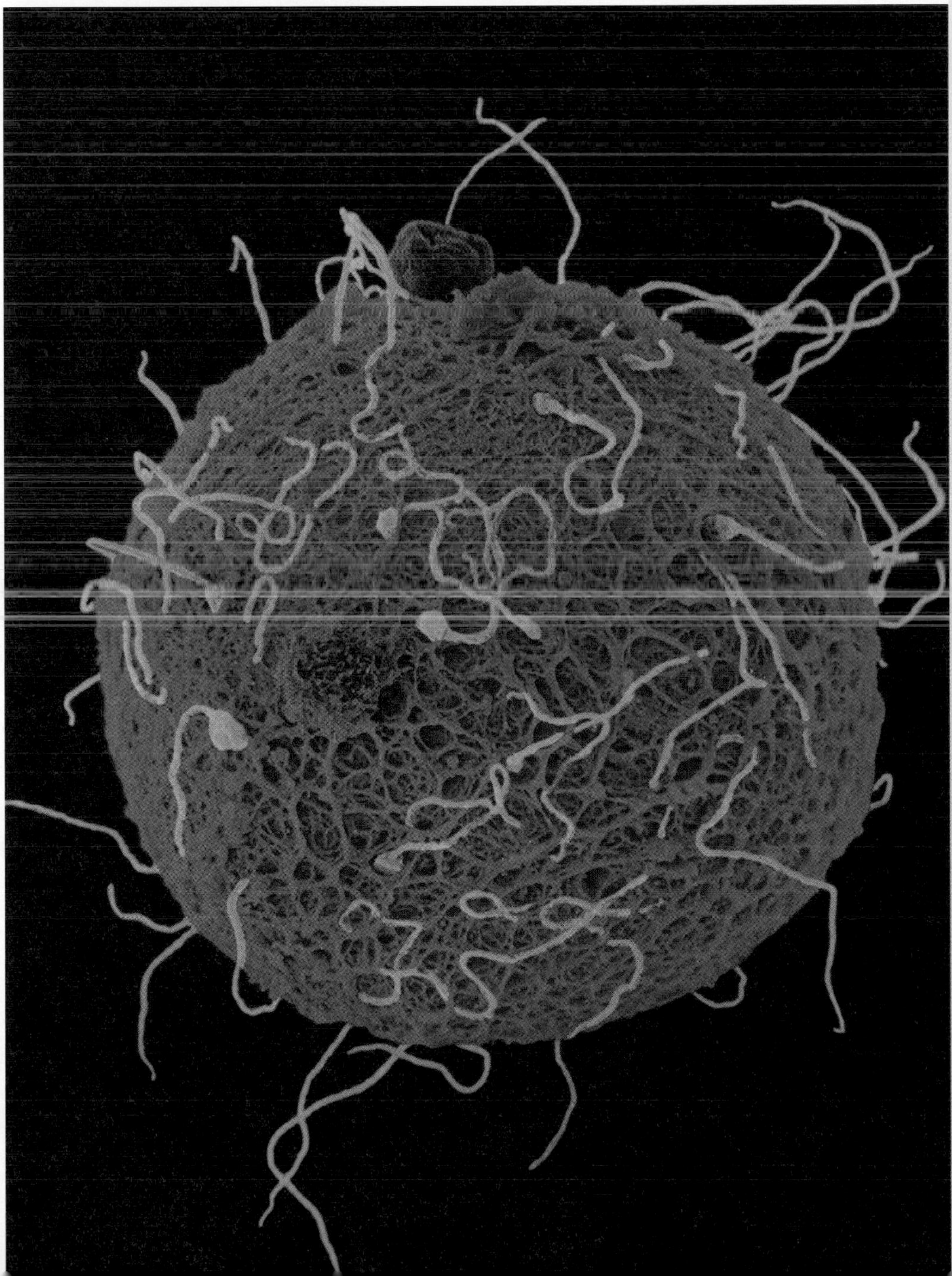

9.1 Phases of Neurodevelopment

9.2 Postnatal Cerebral Development in Human Infants

9.3 Effects of Experience on the Early Development, Maintenance, and Reorganization of Neural Circuits

9.4 Neuroplasticity in Adults

9.5 Disorders of Neurodevelopment: Autism and Williams Syndrome

Most of us tend to think of the nervous system as a three-dimensional array of neural elements "wired" together in a massive network of circuits. The sheer magnitude and complexity of such a wiring diagram would be staggering, but the analogy sells the nervous system short by failing to capture one of its most important features. The nervous system is not a static network of interconnected elements, as is implied by the wiring-diagram model; rather, it is a *plastic* (changeable), living organ that grows and changes continuously in response to its genetic programs and its interactions with its environment.

This chapter focuses on the amazing process of *neurodevelopment* (neural development), which begins with a single fertilized egg cell (see the chapter-opening photo) and ends with a functional adult brain. There are three key points: (1) the complexity and wonder of neurodevelopment, (2) the important role experience plays in neurodevelopment, and (3) the dire consequences when neurodevelopment goes wrong. This chapter progresses through these three points, culminating in a discussion of two devastating disorders of human neurodevelopment: autism and Williams disorder.

But first is the sad case of Genie. People tend to underestimate the role of experience in human neural and psychological development. One of the reasons is that most of us are reared in similar environments. Because there is so little variation in most people's early experience, the critical role of experience in human cerebral and psychological development is not obvious. This misconception can be corrected by considering cases in which children have been reared in grossly abnormal environments. Genie is such a case (Curtiss, 1977; Rymer, 1993).

Thinking Critically

The Case of Genie

Clinical Implications

When Genie was admitted to the hospital at the age of 13, she was only 1.35 meters (4 feet, 5 inches) tall and weighed only 28.1 kilograms (62 pounds). She could not stand erect, chew solid food, or control her bladder or bowels. Since the age of 20 months, Genie had spent most days tied to a potty in a small, dark, closed room. Her only clothing was a cloth harness, which kept her from moving anything other than her feet and hands. In the evening, Genie was transferred to a covered crib and a straitjacket. Her father was intolerant of noise, and he beat Genie if she made any sound whatsoever. According to her mother, who was almost totally blind, Genie's father and brother rarely spoke to Genie, although they sometimes barked at her like dogs. The mother was permitted only a few minutes with Genie each day, during which time she fed Genie cereal or baby food—Genie was allowed no solid food. Genie's severe childhood deprivation left her seriously scarred. When she was admitted to hospital, she made almost no sounds and was totally incapable of speech.

After Genie's discovery, a major effort was made to get her development back on track and to document her problems and improvements; however, after a few years, Genie "disappeared" in a series of legal proceedings, foster homes, and institutions. (Rymer, 1993)

Although Genie did show some improvement in the years after her rescue, during which time she was receiving special care, it was readily apparent that she would never achieve anything approximating normal psychological development. The following were a few of her continuing problems: She did not react to extremes of warmth and cold; she tended to have silent tantrums during which she would flail, spit, scratch, urinate, and rub her own "snot" all over herself; she was easily terrified (e.g., of dogs and men wearing khaki); she could not chew; she could speak only short, poorly pronounced utterances. Genie is currently living in a home for retarded adults. Clearly, experience plays a major role in the processes of neurodevelopment, processes to which you are about to be introduced.

9.1 Phases of Neurodevelopment

In the beginning, there is a *zygote*, a single cell formed by the amalgamation of an *ovum* and a *sperm*. The zygote divides to form two daughter cells. These two divide to form four, the four divide to form eight, and so on, until a mature organism is produced. Of course, there must be more to development than this; if there were not, each of us would have ended up like a bowl of rice pudding: an amorphous mass of homogeneous cells.

To save us from this fate, three things other than cell multiplication must occur. First, cells must *differentiate*; some must become muscle cells, some must become multipolar neurons, some must become glial cells, and so on. Second, cells must make their way to appropriate sites and align themselves with the cells around them to form particular structures. And third, cells must establish appropriate functional relations with other cells (see Kozloski, Hamzei-Sichani, & Yuste, 2001). This section describes how developing neurons accomplish these things in five phases: (1) induction of the neural plate, (2) neural proliferation, (3) migration and aggregation, (4) axon growth and synapse formation, and (5) neuron death and synapse rearrangement.

Induction of the Neural Plate

Three weeks after conception, the tissue that is destined to develop into the human nervous system becomes recognizable as the **neural plate**—a small patch of ectodermal tissue on the dorsal surface of the developing embryo. The ectoderm is the outermost of the three layers of embryonic cells: *ectoderm, mesoderm,* and *endoderm.* The development of the neural plate is the first major stage of neurodevelopment in all vertebrates.

The development of the neural plate seems to be *induced* by chemical signals from an area of the underlying **mesoderm layer**—an area that is consequently referred to as an *organizer* (see Dodd, Jessel, & Placzek, 1998). Tissue taken from the dorsal mesoderm of one embryo (i.e., the *donor*) and implanted beneath the ventral ectoderm of another embryo (i.e., the *host*) induces the development of an extra neural plate on the ventral surface of the host.

The search for the particular substance that is released by the organizer and induces the development of the neural plate is in full swing (see Muñoz-Sanjuán & Brivanlou, 2002). A key event in induction appears to be

inhibition of a class of proteins that normally suppress neural development, the bone morphogenetic proteins (BMPs). However, the means by which this inhibition is initiated is not yet known.

An important change occurs to the cells of the developing nervous system at about the time that the neural plate becomes visible. The earliest cells of the human embryo are **totipotent**—that is, they have the ability to develop into any type of cell in the body if transplanted to the appropriate site. However, as the embryo develops, the destiny of various cells becomes more *specified*. With the development of the neural plate, its cells lose much of their potential to become different kinds of cells. Each cell of the neural plate still has the potential to develop into any type of mature nervous system cell, but it cannot normally develop into other kinds of cells. Cells like these are said to be **multipotent,** rather than totipotent.

The cells of the neural plate are often referred to as embryonic **stem cells.** Stem cells are cells that meet two specific criteria (see Brivanlou et al., 2003; Seaberg & van der Kooy, 2003): (1) They have a seemingly unlimited capacity for self-renewal, and (2) they have the ability to develop into different types of mature cells. The cells of

the neural plate meet both of these criteria: If maintained in an appropriate cell culture, they will continue to multiply; and, as you have just learned, they have the capacity to develop into any type of cell in the adult nervous system. However, as the neural tube develops, some of its cells become specified as future glial cells of various types, and others become specified as future neurons of various types. Because these cells still have the capacity for unlimited self-renewal and are still multipotent, these cells are termed *glial stem cells* and *neural stem cells,* respectively.

Because of the ability of embryonic stem cells to develop into different types of mature cells, their therapeutic potential is currently under intensive investigation. Will embryonic stem cells injected into a damaged part of a mature brain develop into the appropriate brain structure and improve function? You will learn about the potential of stem-cell therapy in Chapter 10.

As Figure 9.1 illustrates, the neural plate folds to form the *neural groove,* and then the lips of the neural groove fuse

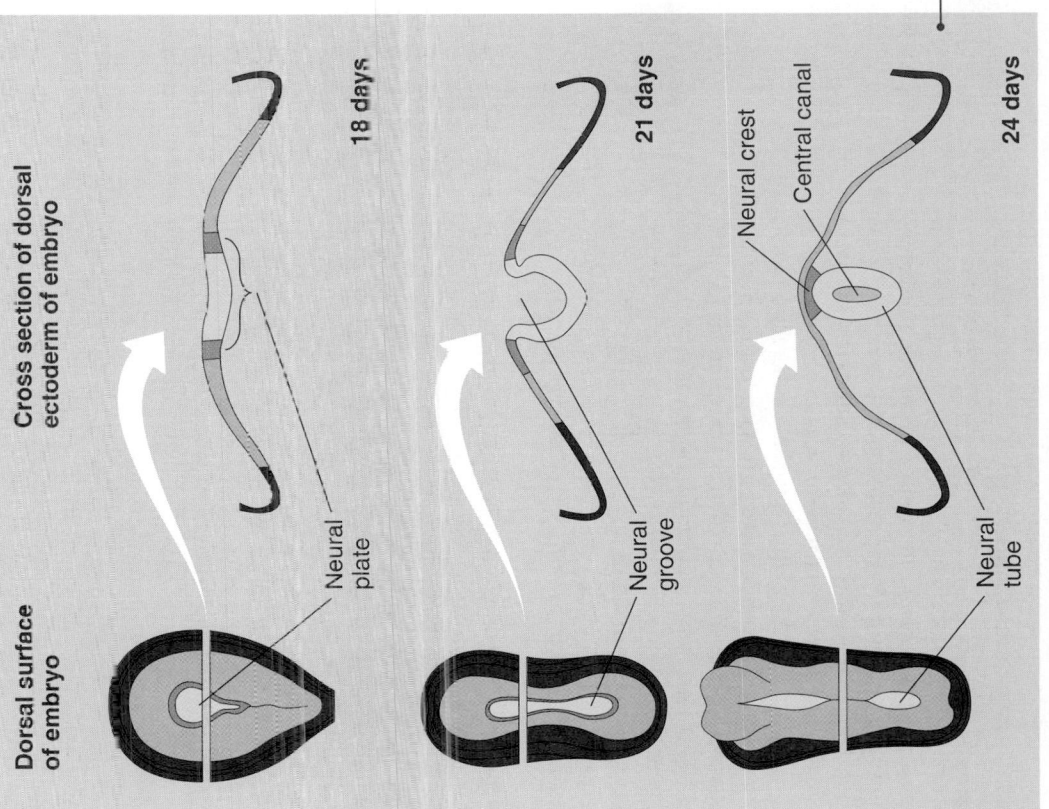

FIGURE 9.1 How the neural plate develops into the neural tube during the third and fourth weeks of human embryological development. (Adapted from Cowan, 1979.)

to form the **neural tube**. The inside of the neural tube eventually becomes the *cerebral ventricles* and *spinal canal*. By 40 days after conception, three swellings are visible at the anterior end of the human neural tube; these swellings ultimately develop into the *forebrain*, *midbrain*, and *hindbrain* (see Figure 3.19).

Neural Proliferation

Once the lips of the neural groove have fused to create the neural tube, the cells of the tube begin to *proliferate* (increase greatly in number). This **neural proliferation** does not occur simultaneously or equally in all parts of the tube. In each species, the cells in different parts of the neural tube proliferate in a characteristic sequence that is responsible for the pattern of swelling and folding that gives the brain its species-characteristic shape. Most cell division in the neural tube occurs in the **ventricular zone**—the region adjacent to the *ventricle* (the fluid-filled center of the tube).

Migration and Aggregation

Migration   Once cells have been created through cell division in the ventricular zone of the neural tube, they migrate to the appropriate target location. During this period of **migration**, the cells are still in an immature form, lacking the processes (i.e., axons and dendrites) that characterize mature neurons.

Cell migration in the developing neural tube is considered to be of two kinds (see Figure 9.2): **Radial migration** proceeds from the ventricular zone in a straight line outward toward the outer wall of the tube; **tangential migration** occurs at a right angle to radial migration—that is, parallel to the tube's walls. Most cells engage in both radial and tangential migration to get from their

point of origin in the ventricular zone to their target destination (see Hatten, 2002).

There are two methods by which developing cells migrate (see Figure 9.3). One is somal translocation. In **somal translocation**, an extension grows from the developing cell in the general direction of the migration; the extension seems to explore the immediate environment for attractive and repulsive cues as it grows. Then, the cell body itself moves into and along the extending process, and trailing processes are retracted (see Nadarajah & Parnavelas, 2002; Ridley et al., 2003).

The second method of migration is **glia-mediated migration** (see Figure 9.3). Once the period of neural proliferation is well underway and the walls of the neural tube are thickening, a temporary network of glial cells, called **radial glial cells**, appears in the developing neural tube (Campbell & Gotz, 2002). At this point, most cells engaging in radial migration do so by moving along the radial glial network (see Nadarajah & Parnavelas, 2002).

Most research on migration in the developing neural tube has focused on the cortex (see Marin & Rubenstein, 2001; Qi, Stapp, & Qiu, 2002). This line of research makes an important point about migration: Timing is everything. The neurons of each of the six layers of the cortex are created and migrate at six different times, and then they develop layer-specific anatomical and functional characteristics (Hanashima et al., 2004; Levitt, 2004).

Most studies of the migration of cortical neurons have focused on radial patterns. These studies have revealed orderly waves of migrating cells, progressing from deeper to more superficial layers. Because each wave of cortical cells migrates through the already formed lower layers of cortex before stopping, this radial pattern of cortical development is referred to as an **inside-out pattern**. However, it is clear that cortical migration patterns are much more complex than first thought; many cortical cells engage in lengthy tangential migration to reach their final destinations. Developing interneurons and glial cells are the most likely to take long tangential journeys.

The **neural crest** is a structure that is situated just dorsal to the neural tube (see Figure 9.1). It is formed from cells that break off from the neural tube as it is being formed. Neural crest cells develop into the neurons and glial cells of the peripheral nervous system, and thus many of them must migrate over considerable distances. For this reason, they are favored subjects of research on neural migration.

Numerous chemicals that guide migrating neurons by either attracting or repelling them have been discovered (Marin & Rubenstein, 2003). Some of these substances are released by glial cells (see Auld, 2001; Marin et al., 2001).

Aggregation   Once developing neurons have migrated, they must align themselves with other developing

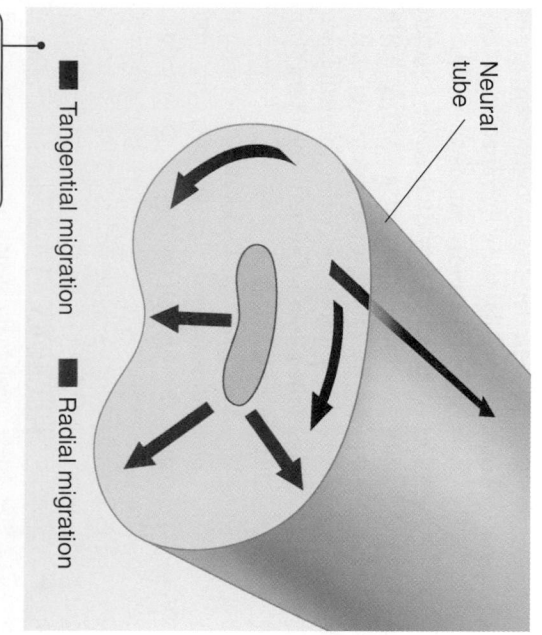

■ Tangential migration   ■ Radial migration

FIGURE 9.2   Two types of neural migration: radial migration and tangential migration.

Somal Translocation (Radial or Tangential)

Glia-Mediated Migration (Radial Only)

Radial glial cells

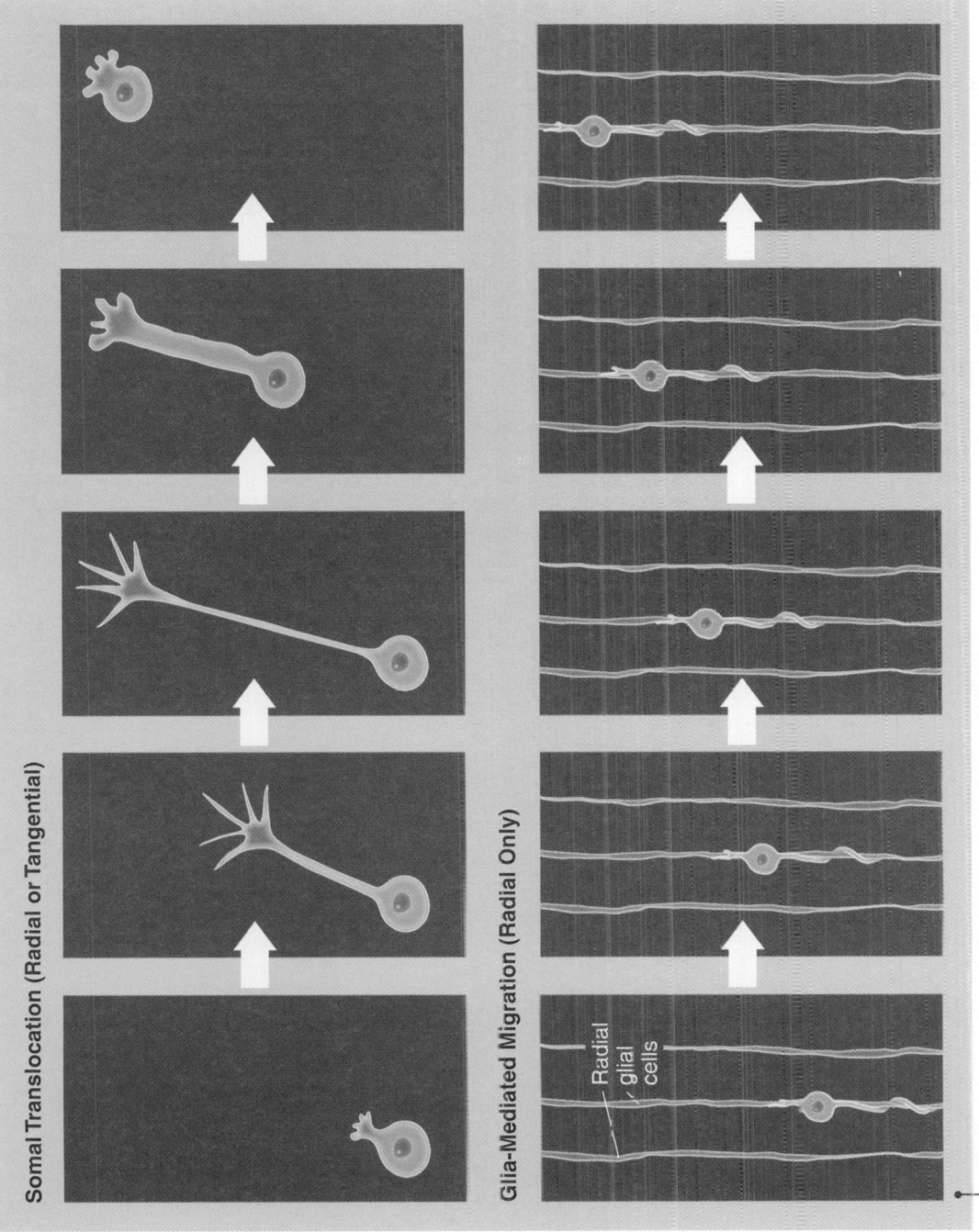

FIGURE 9.3 Two methods by which cells migrate in the developing neural tube: somal translocation and glia-mediated migration.

neurons that have migrated to the same area to form the structures of the nervous system. This process is called **aggregation**.

Both migration and aggregation are thought to be mediated by **cell-adhesion molecules (CAMs)**, which are located on the surface of neurons and other cells. Cell-adhesion molecules have the ability to recognize molecules on other cells and adhere to them.

Axon Growth and Synapse Formation

Axon Growth Once neurons have migrated to their appropriate positions and aggregated into neural structures, axons and dendrites begin to grow from them. For the nervous system to function, these projections must grow to appropriate targets. At each growing tip of an axon or dendrite is an amoebalike structure called a **growth cone**, which extends and retracts fingerlike cy-

toplasmic extensions called *filopodia* (see Figure 9.4 on page 216), as if searching for the correct route.

Remarkably, most growth cones reach their correct targets, even when they must travel a considerable distance. A series of studies of neural regeneration by Roger Sperry in the early 1940s first demonstrated that axons are capable of precise growth and suggested how the precise growth occurs.

In one study, Sperry cut the optic nerves of frogs, rotated their eyeballs 180°, and waited for the axons of the **retinal ganglion cells**, which compose the optic nerve, to *regenerate* (grow again). (Frogs, unlike mammals, have retinal ganglion cells that regenerate.) Once regeneration was complete, Sperry used a convenient behavioral test to assess the frogs' visual capacities (see

ON THE CD

The module *Roger Sperry's Classic Study of Axonal Regeneration* provides a vivid look at this remarkable study.

Evolutionary Perspective

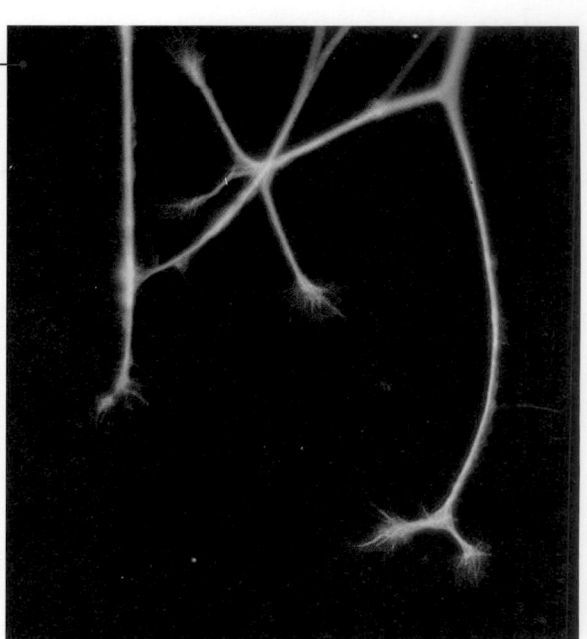

FIGURE 9.4   Growth cones. The cytoplasmic fingers (the filopodia) of growth cones seem to grope for the correct route. (Courtesy of Naweed I. Syed, Ph.D., Departments of Anatomy and Medical Physiology, the University of Calgary.)

Figure 9.5). When he dangled a lure behind the frogs, they struck forward, thus indicating that their visual world, like their eyes, had been rotated 180°. Frogs whose eyes had been rotated, but whose optic nerves had not been cut, responded in exactly the same way. This was strong behavioral evidence that each retinal ganglion cell had grown back to the same point of the **optic tectum** (called the superior colliculus in mammals) to which it had originally been connected. Neuroanatomical investigations have confirmed that this is exactly what happens (see Guo & Udin, 2000).

On the basis of his studies of regeneration, Sperry proposed the **chemoaffinity hypothesis** of axonal development (see Sperry, 1963). He hypothesized that each postsynaptic surface in the nervous system releases a specific chemical label and that each growing axon is attracted by the label to its postsynaptic target during both neural development and regeneration. Indeed, it is difficult to imagine another mechanism by which an axon growing out from a rotated eyeball could find its precise target on the optic tectum.

Although the chemoaffinity hypothesis was a major first step toward understanding the mechanisms of accurate axonal growth in the developing nervous system, it fails to account for one of the major features of such growth. The chemoaffinity hypothesis does not account for the fact that some axons follow exactly the same circuitous route to reach their target in every member of a species, rather than growing directly to it (see Araújo & Tear, 2003).

Since Sperry's groundbreaking research, much has been learned about the processes of accurate axonal

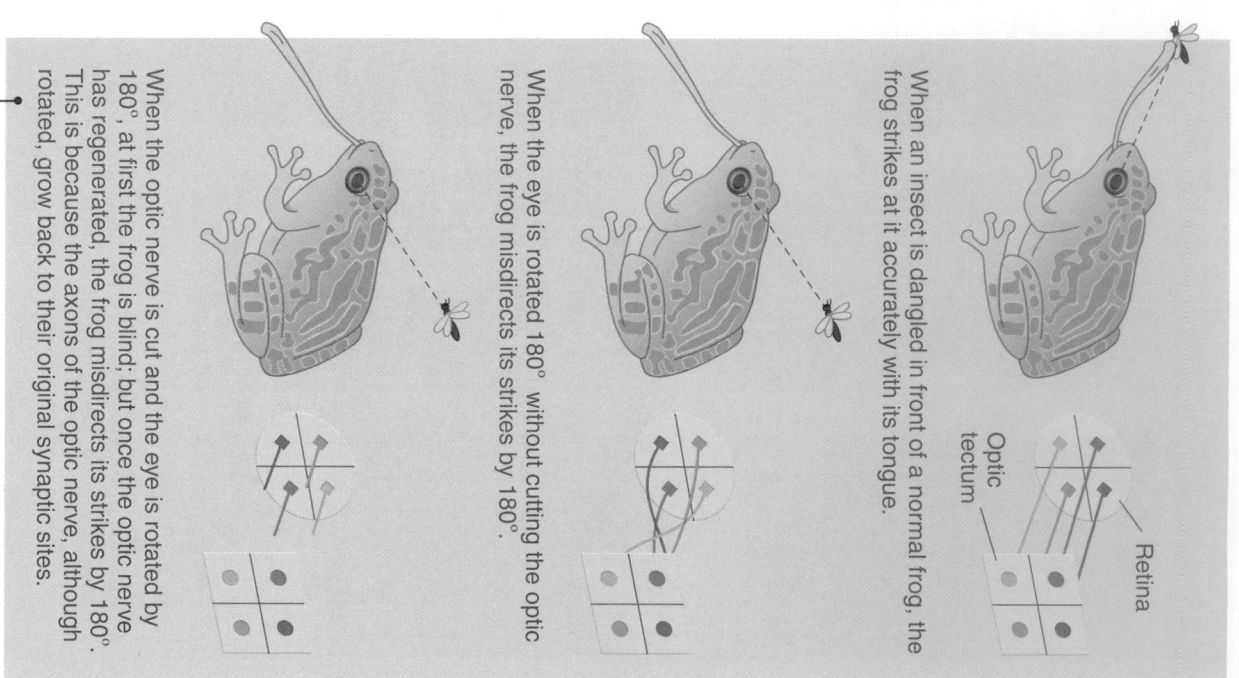

FIGURE 9.5   Sperry's classic study of eye rotation and regeneration.

When an insect is dangled in front of a normal frog, the frog strikes at it accurately with its tongue.

Optic tectum

Retina

When the eye is rotated 180° without cutting the optic nerve, the frog misdirects its strikes by 180°.

When the optic nerve is cut and the eye is rotated by 180°, at first the frog is blind; but once the optic nerve has regenerated, the frog misdirects its strikes by 180°. This is because the axons of the optic nerve, although rotated, grow back to their original synaptic sites.

growth. Key to advances in our understanding of these processes is the fact that the mechanisms that guide growing axons in simple invertebrates (e.g., worms and flies) have been found to perform the same functions in vertebrates (see Jessell & Sanes, 2000). A revised notion of how growing axons reach their specific targets is emerging from this comparative research. This new notion is an elaboration of Sperry's original chemoaffinity hypothesis.

According to the new hypothesis, a growing neuron is not attracted to its target by a single specific attractant released by the target, as Sperry thought. Instead, axonal growth seems to be influenced by a series of chemical signals along the route. Some of these *guidance molecules* attract the growing axons, whereas others repel them (see Guan & Rao, 2003). Several families of guidance molecules have been identified; even neurotransmitters can serve as guidance molecules in the developing nervous system (see Holmberg & Frisén, 2002; Inantani et al., 2003; Markus, Patel, & Snider, 2002; Owens & Kriegstein, 2002). It is noteworthy that several guidance molecules are released by glia (Lemke, 2001).

Guidance molecules are not the only signals that guide growing axons to their targets. Other signals come from adjacent growing axons. **Pioneer growth cones**—the first growth cones to travel along a particular route in a developing nervous system—are presumed to follow the correct trail by interacting with guidance molecules along the route. Then, subsequent growth cones embarking on the same journey follow the routes blazed by the pioneers. The tendency of developing axons to grow along the paths established by preceding axons is called **fasciculation.** When pioneer axons in the fish spinal cord were destroyed with a laser, subsequent axons of the same nerves did not reach their usual destinations.

Much of the axonal development in complex nervous systems involves growth from one topographic array of neurons to another. The neurons on one array project to another, maintaining the same topographic relation they had on the first; for example, the topographic map of the retina is maintained on the optic tectum.

At first, it was assumed that the integrity of topographical relations in the developing nervous system was maintained by a point-to-point chemoaffinity, with each retinal ganglion cell growing toward a specific chemical label. However, evidence indicates that the mechanism must be more complex. In most species, the synaptic connections between retina and optic tectum are established long before either reaches full size. Then, as the retinas and the optic tectum grow at different rates, the initial synaptic connections shift to other tectal neurons so that the retina is always faithfully mapped onto the tectum, regardless of their relative sizes.

Studies of the regeneration (rather than the development) of retinal-tectum projections tell a similar story. In one informative series of studies, the optic nerves of mature frogs or fish were cut

and their pattern of regeneration was assessed after parts of either the retina or the optic tectum had been destroyed. In both cases, the axons did not grow out to their original points of connection (as the chemoaffinity hypothesis predicted they would); instead, they grew out to fill the available space in an orderly fashion. Axons growing from the remaining portion of a lesioned retina "spread out" in an orderly fashion to fill all of the space on an intact tectum. Conversely, axons growing from an intact retina "squeeze in" in an orderly fashion to fill the remaining space on a lesioned tectum. These results are illustrated schematically in Figure 9.6.

The **topographic gradient hypothesis** has been proposed to explain accurate axonal growth involving topographic

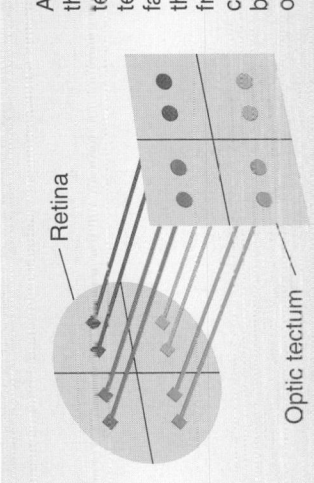

Axons normally grow from the frog retina and terminate on the optic tectum in an orderly fashion. The assumption that this orderliness results from point-to-point chemoaffinity is challenged by the following two observations.

Retina

Optic tectum

1 When half the retina was destroyed and the optic nerve cut, the retinal ganglion cells from the remaining half retina projected systematically over the entire tectum.

Lesioned half retina

2 When half the optic tectum was destroyed and the optic nerve cut, the retinal ganglion cells from the retina projected systematically over the remaining half retina.

Lesioned half tectum

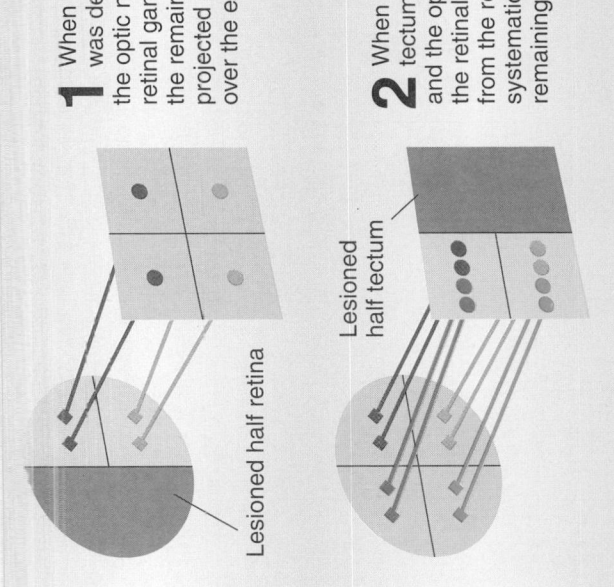

FIGURE 9.6 The regeneration of the optic nerve of the frog after portions of either the retina or the optic tectum have been destroyed. These phenomena support the topographic gradient hypothesis.

mapping in the developing brain (see Debski & Cline, 2002; Grove & Fukuchi-Shimogori, 2003; McLaughlin, Hindges, & O'Leary, 2003). According to this hypothesis, axons growing from one topographic surface (e.g., the retina) to another (e.g., the optic tectum) are guided to specific targets that are arranged on the terminal surface in the same way as the axons' cell bodies are arranged on the original surface. The key part of this hypothesis is that the growing axons are guided to their destinations by two intersecting signal gradients (e.g., an anterior-posterior gradient and a medial-lateral gradient). The mechanism is illustrated in Figure 9.7.

Synapse Formation   Once axons have reached their intended sites, they must establish an appropriate pattern of synapses. A single neuron can grow an axon on its own, but it takes coordinated activity in at least two neurons to create a synapse between them (see Yuste & Bonhoeffer, 2004). This is one reason why our understanding of how axons connect to their targets has lagged behind our understanding of how they reach them (see Benson, Colman, & Huntley, 2001; Lee & Sheng, 2000). Still, some exciting recent breakthroughs have been made.

Perhaps the most exciting recent discovery about **synaptogenesis** (the formation of new synapses) is that

it depends on the presence of glial cells, particularly astrocytes (see Barres & Smith, 2001; Fields, 2004; Slezak & Pfrieger, 2003). Retinal ganglion cells maintained in culture formed seven times more synapses when astrocytes were present. Moreover, synapses formed in the presence of astrocytes were quickly lost when those cells were removed. Other research has suggested that developing neurons need high levels of cholesterol during the period of synapse formation and that this extra cholesterol is supplied by astrocytes (Mauch et al., 2001; Pfrieger, 2002).

Most current research on synaptogenesis is focusing on elucidating the chemical signals that must be exchanged between presynaptic and postsynaptic neurons for a synapse to be created (see Scheiffele, 2003). One complication this research faces is the promiscuity developing neurons display when it comes to synaptogenesis. On one hand, it seems that in order to function, the brain must be wired-up according to a specific plan; however, in vitro, any type of neuron will form synapses with any other type. This suggests that any given synapse is not created under the control of a single set of chemical signals. Rather, a more hierarchical process, in which each presynaptic and postsynaptic neuron weighs a variety of synapse-promoting and synapse-inhibiting signals before

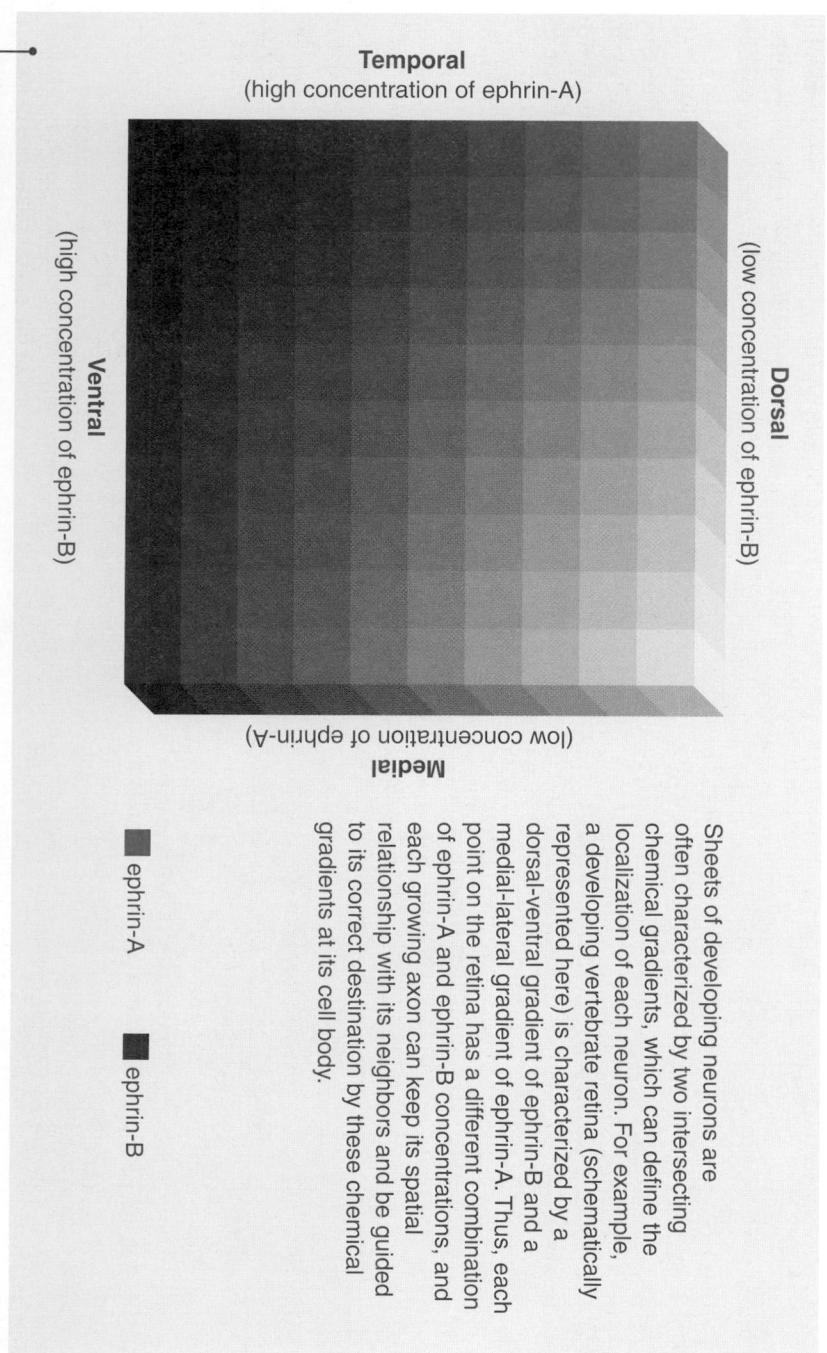

FIGURE 9.7   The topographic gradient hypothesis. Gradients of ephrin-A and ephrin-B on the developing retina (see McLaughlin et al., 2003).

Temporal
(high concentration of ephrin-A)

Dorsal
(low concentration of ephrin-B)

Ventral
(high concentration of ephrin-B)

Medial
(low concentration of ephrin-A)

ephrin-A   ephrin-B

Sheets of developing neurons are often characterized by two intersecting chemical gradients, which can define the localization of each neuron. For example, a developing vertebrate retina (schematically represented here) is characterized by a dorsal-ventral gradient of ephrin-B and a medial-lateral gradient of ephrin-A. Thus, each point on the retina has a different combination of ephrin-A and ephrin-B concentrations, and each growing axon can keep its spatial relationship with its neighbors and be guided to its correct destination by these chemical gradients at its cell body.

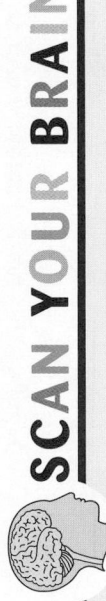

SCAN YOUR BRAIN

Are you ready to focus on neurodevelopment in the human brain after birth? To find out, scan your brain by filling in the blanks in the following chronological list of stages of neuro-

development. The correct answers are provided at the bottom of this page. Before proceeding, review material related to your errors and omissions.

1. Induction of the neural _____
2. Formation of the _____ tube
3. Neural _____
4. Neural _____
5. _____ aggregation
6. Growth of neural _____
7. Formation of _____
8. Neuron _____ and synapse _____

---

forming synapses with the best available cells, must be operating. This will not be an easy problem to solve.

Neuron Death and Synapse Rearrangement

Neuron Death   Neuron death is a normal and important part of neurodevelopment. Such development seems to operate on the principle of survival of the fittest: Many more neurons—about 50% more—are produced than are required, and only the fittest survive. Large-scale death is not a time-limited stage of development; it occurs in waves in various parts of the brain throughout development.

Three findings suggest that developing neurons die because of their failure to compete successfully for life-preserving chemicals that are supplied to them by their targets. First, the implantation of extra target sites decreases neuron death. For example, grafting an extra limb on one side of a chick embryo reduces motor neuron death on that side. Second, destroying some of the neurons growing into an area before the period of cell death increases the survival rate of the remaining neurons. Third, increasing the number of axons that initially innervate a target decreases the proportion that survive.

Several life-preserving chemicals that are supplied to developing neurons by their targets have been identified. The most prominent class of these chemicals is the **neurotrophins. Nerve growth factor (NGF)** was the first neurotrophin to be isolated (see Levi-Montalcini, 1952, 1975), but since then three others have been identified in mammals. The neurotrophins perform a variety of functions: For example, they promote the growth and survival of neurons, function as axon guidance molecules, and stimulate synaptogenesis (see Huang & Reichardt, 2001; Vicario-Abejón et al., 2002).

Neuron death during development was initially assumed to be a passive process. It was assumed that the appropriate neurotrophins are needed for the survival of neurons and that without them neurons passively de-

generate and die. However, it is now clear that cell death during development is usually an active process: The absence of the appropriate neurotrophins can trigger a genetic program inside neurons that causes them to actively commit suicide. Passive cell death is called **necrosis** (ne-KROE-sis); active cell death is called **apoptosis** (A-poe-toc-sis).

Apoptosis is safer than necrosis. Necrotic cells break apart and spill their contents into extracellular fluid, and the consequence is potentially harmful inflammation. In contrast, in apoptotic cell death, DNA and other internal structures are cleaved apart and packaged in membranes before the cell breaks apart. These membranes contain molecules that attract scavenger cells and others that prevent inflammation (Li et al., 2003; Savill, Gregory, & Haslett, 2003; Wang et al., 2003).

During the phase of neuron death, apoptosis removes excess neurons—for example, neurons that do not obtain enough neurotrophins—in a safe, neat, and orderly way. But apoptosis has a dark side as well. If genetic programs for apoptotic cell death are inhibited, the consequence can be cancer; if the programs are inappropriately activated, the consequence can be neurodegenerative disease.

Synapse Rearrangement   During the period of cell death, neurons that have established incorrect connections are particularly likely to die. As they die, the space they vacate on postsynaptic membranes is filled by the sprouting axon terminals of surviving neurons. Thus, cell death results in a massive rearrangement of synaptic connections. This phase of synapse rearrangement tends to focus the output of each neuron on a smaller number of postsynaptic cells, thus increasing the selectivity of transmission (see Figure 9.8 on page 220).

FIGURE 9.8 The effect of neuron death and synapse rearrangement on the selectivity of synaptic transmission. The synaptic contacts of each axon become focused on a smaller number of cells.

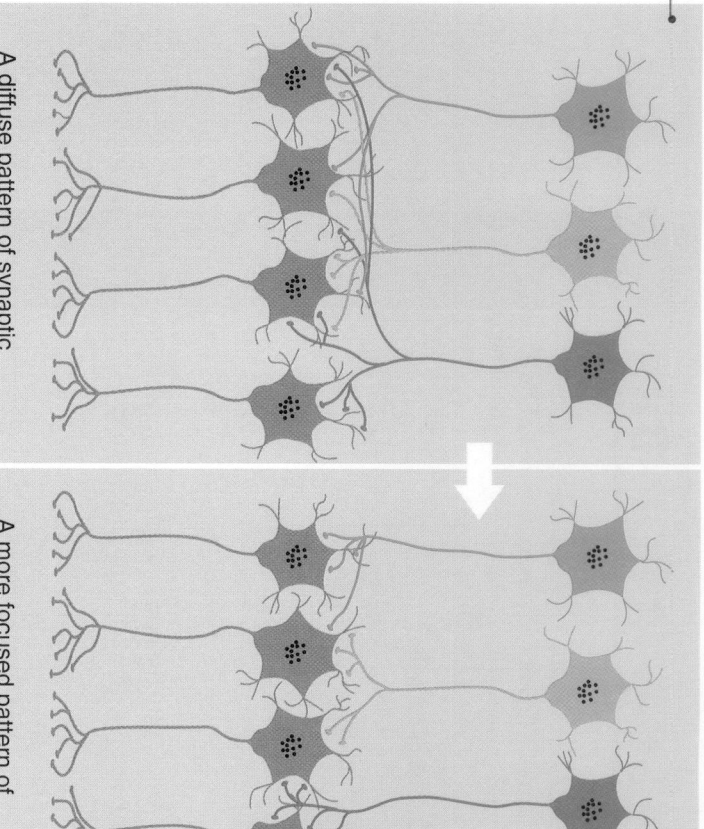

A diffuse pattern of synaptic contact is characteristic of early stages of development.

A more focused pattern of synaptic contact is present after synapse rearrangement.

9.2   Postnatal Cerebral Development in Human Infants

Most of our knowledge of neurodevelopment comes from the study of nonhuman species. This fact emphasizes the value of the comparative approach and the evolutionary perspective. There is, however, one way in which the development of the human brain is unique: The human brain develops far more slowly than that of other species, not achieving full maturity until late adolescence (Spear, 2000).

This section deals with that part of the development of the human brain that occurs after birth. It focuses on the development of the prefrontal cortex (see Figure 1.7). The prefrontal cortex is the last part of the brain to reach maturity, and it is thought to mediate many higher cognitive abilities.

Postnatal Growth of the Human Brain

The human brain grows substantially after birth: Its volume quadruples between birth and adulthood (see Johnson, 2001). This increase in size does not, however, result from the development of additional neurons. With the exception of a few structures (e.g., the olfactory bulb and the hippocampus) in which many new neurons continue to be created during the adult years, all of the

neurons that will compose the adult human brain have developed and migrated to their appropriate locations by the seventh month of prenatal development. The postnatal growth of the human brain seems to result from three other kinds of growth: *synaptogenesis*, myelination of many axons, and increased branching of dendrites.

There has been particular interest in the postnatal formation of synapses because the number of connections between neurons in a particular region of the brain is assumed to be an indicator of the analytic ability of that region. There seems to be an increase in the rate of formation of synapses throughout the human cortex shortly after birth, but there are differences among the cortical regions in the course of this development (Huttenlocher, 1994). For example, in the primary visual and auditory cortexes, there is a major burst of synaptogenesis in the fourth postnatal month, and maximum synapse density (150% of adult levels) is achieved in the seventh or eighth month; whereas synaptogenesis in the prefrontal cortex occurs at a relatively steady rate, reaching maximum synapse density in the second year.

Myelination increases the speed of axonal conduction, and the myelination of various areas of the human brain during development roughly parallels their functional development. Myelination of sensory areas occurs in the first few months after birth, and myelination of the motor areas follows soon after that, whereas myelination of prefrontal cortex continues into adolescence.

In general, the pattern of dendritic branching duplicates the original pattern of neural migration. Just as the cells of the deeper layers are first to migrate into position, and the cells of progressively more superficial layers migrate through them to assume their positions, dendritic branching progresses from deeper to more superficial layers. For example, the growth of dendritic trees in layer V always seems to precede that in layers II and III, regardless of the cortical area.

Postnatal human brain development is not a one-way street; there are regressive changes as well as growth (Huttenlocher, 1994). For example, once maximum synaptic density has been achieved, there are periods of synaptic loss. Like periods of synaptogenesis, periods of synaptic loss occur at different times in different parts of the brain. For example, synaptic density in primary visual cortex declines to adult levels by about 3 years of age, whereas its decline to adult levels in prefrontal cortex is not achieved until adolescence. It has been suggested that the overproduction of synapses may underlie the greater plasticity of the young brain.

Development of the Prefrontal Cortex

As you have just learned, the prefrontal cortex displays the most prolonged period of development of any brain region. Its development is believed to be largely responsible for the course of human cognitive development, which occurs over the same period.

Given the size, complexity, and heterogeneity of the prefrontal cortex, it is hardly surprising that there is no single widely accepted theory explaining its function. Nevertheless, three types of cognitive functions have consistently been linked to this area in studies of adults with prefrontal damage. The prefrontal cortex seems to play a role in (1) *working memory*, that is, keeping relevant information accessible for short periods of time while a task is being completed; (2) planning and carrying out sequences of actions; and (3) inhibiting respons-

es that are inappropriate in the current context but not in others (see Hauser, 1999).

One interesting line of research on prefrontal cortex development is based on Piaget's classic studies of psychological development in human babies. In his studies of 7-month-old children, Piaget noticed an intriguing error. A small toy was shown to an infant; then it was placed, as the child watched, behind one of two screens, left or right. After a brief delay period, the infant was allowed to reach for the toy. Piaget found that almost all 7-month-old infants reached for the screen behind which they had seen the toy being placed. However, if, after being placed behind the same screen on several consecutive trials, the toy was placed behind the other screen (as the infant watched), most of the 7-month-old infants kept reaching for the previously correct screen, rather than the screen that currently hid the toy. Children tend to make this *perseverative error* between about 7 and 12 months, but not thereafter (Diamond, 1985). **Perseveration** is the tendency to continue making a formerly correct response when it is currently incorrect.

Diamond (1991) hypothesized that this perseverative error occurred in infants between 7 and 12 months because the neural circuitry of the prefrontal cortex is not yet fully developed during that period. Synaptogenesis in the prefrontal cortex is not maximal until early in the second year, and correct performance of the task involved two of the major functions of this brain area: holding information in working memory and suppressing previously correct, but currently incorrect, responses.

In support of her hypothesis, Diamond conducted a series of comparative experiments. First, she showed that infant, but not adult, monkeys make the same perseverative error as 7-to-12-month-old human infants on Piaget's test. Then, she tested adult monkeys with bilateral lesions to their dorsolateral prefrontal cortex (see Figure 8.2 for the location of this area of cortex), and she found that the lesioned adult monkeys made perseverative errors similar to those made by the infant monkeys. Control monkeys with lesions in the hippocampus or posterior parietal cortex did not make such errors.

9.3 Effects of Experience on the Early Development, Maintenance, and Reorganization of Neural Circuits

Genetic programs of neurodevelopment do not act in a vacuum. Neurodevelopment unfolds through interactions between neurons and their environment. You learned in the first section of this chapter how factors (e.g., neurotrophins and CAMs) in neurons' immediate environment can influence their migration, aggregation, and growth. This section focuses on how the experiences of the developing organism influence the development,

Evolutionary Perspective

maintenance, and reorganization of neural circuits. The main principle that governs the effects of early experience on neural circuits is simple: Neurons and synapses that are not activated by experience do not usually survive (see Hockfield & Kalb, 1993; Kalil, 1989). That is, use it or lose it.

You have just learned that humans are uniquely slow in their neural development. One advantage of this slowness

may be that it offers many opportunities for experience to fine-tune developing systems (Johnson, 2001).

Early Studies of Experience and Neurodevelopment

Many of the first demonstrations of the impact of early
experience on neurodevelopment came from two lines
of research: the study of the effects of early visual deprivation and the study of early exposure to enriched environments. For example, rats reared from birth in the
dark were found to have fewer synapses and fewer dendritic spines in their primary visual cortexes, and they
were found to have deficits in depth and pattern vision
as adults. Conversely, rats that were raised in enriched
(complex) group cages rather than by themselves in barren cages were found to have thicker cortexes with more
dendritic spines and more synapses per neuron.

Competitive Nature of Experience and Neurodevelopment

Experience promotes the development of active neural
circuits and the maintenance or reorganization of existing ones, but there seems to be a competitive aspect to
this. This competitive aspect is clearly illustrated by the
disruptive effects of early monocular deprivation.

Depriving one eye of input for a few days early in life
has a lasting adverse effect on vision in the deprived eye,
but this does not happen if the other eye is also blindfolded. When only one eye is blindfolded, the ability of that eye
to activate the visual cortex is reduced, whereas the ability
of the other eye is increased. Both these effects occur because early monocular deprivation changes the pattern of
synaptic input into layer IV of the primary visual cortex.

In many species, ocular dominance columns (see
Figure 6.22) in layer IV of the primary visual cortex are

almost fully developed at birth (see Katz & Crowley,
2002). However, if just one eye is deprived of light for
several days at some point during the first few months of
life, the system is reorganized: The width of the columns
of input from the deprived eye is
decreased, and the width of the columns of input from the nondeprived
eye is increased (Hata & Stryker, 1994; Hubel, Wiesel, &
LeVay, 1977). The exact timing of the *sensitive period* for
this effect is specific to each species.

Because the adverse effects of early monocular deprivation manifest themselves so quickly (i.e., in a few
days), it was believed that they could not be mediated
by structural changes. However, Antonini and Stryker
(1993) found that a few days of monocular deprivation
produces a massive decrease in the axonal branching
of the lateral geniculate nucleus neurons that normally
carry signals from the deprived eye to layer IV of the primary visual cortex (see Figure 9.9).

The competitive nature of the effects of neural activity on synapse rearrangement has also been demonstrated
in experiments on motor neurons and muscle cells. In
neonates (newborns), each muscle cell is normally innervated by several motor neurons, and then all but one
are eliminated during the course of development. Lo and
Poo (1991) studied an *in vitro* preparation in which one
developing muscle cell was innervated by two developing
motor neurons. Applying pulses of electrical stimulation
to one of these neurons caused a rapid degradation in the
synaptic contacts of the other. Apparently, motor neurons
compete with one another for synaptic contacts on muscle cells, and active synapses take precedence.

Effects of Experience on Topographic Sensory Cortex Maps

Some of the most remarkable demonstrations of the effects of experience on the organization of the nervous sys-

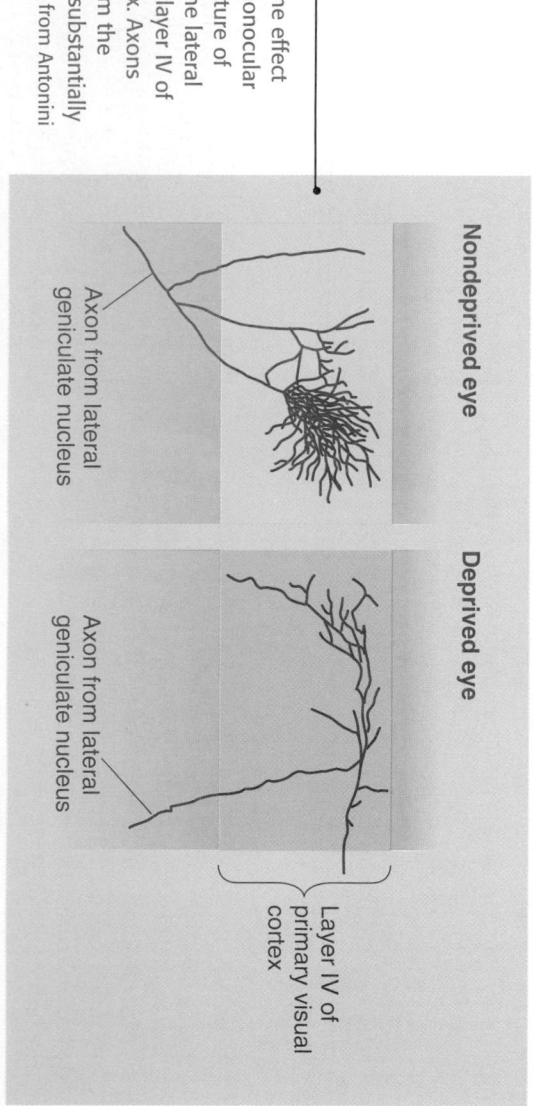

FIGURE 9.9   The effect
of a few days of early monocular
deprivation on the structure of
axons projecting from the lateral
geniculate nucleus into layer IV of
the primary visual cortex. Axons
carrying information from the
deprived eye displayed substantially
less branching. (Adapted from Antonini
& Stryker, 1993.)

Nondeprived eye

Axon from lateral
geniculate nucleus

Deprived eye

Axon from lateral
geniculate nucleus

Layer IV of
primary visual
cortex

tem come from studies of cortical topographic maps of the sensory systems. The following are four such studies.

First, Roe and colleagues (1990) surgically altered the course of developing axons of ferrets' retinal ganglion cells so that the axons synapsed in the medial geniculate nucleus of the auditory system instead of in the lateral geniculate nucleus of the visual system. Remarkably, the experience of visual input caused the auditory cortex of the ferrets to become organized retinotopically (laid out like a map of the retina). See Pallas (2001) for a review of cross-modal rewiring experiments.

Second, Knudsen and Brainard (1991) raised barn owls with vision-displacing prisms over their eyes. This led to a corresponding change in the auditory spatial map in the tectum. For example, an owl that was raised wearing prisms that shifted its visual world 23° to the right had an auditory map that was also shifted 23° to the right, so that objects were heard to be where they were seen to be (see Gutfreund, Zheng, & Knudsen, 2002; Miller & Knudsen, 1999).

Third, Weliky and Katz (1997) periodically disturbed the spontaneous optic nerve activity of neonatal ferrets that had yet to open their eyes. This disrupted the orientation and direction selectivity of the ferrets' primary visual cortex neurons. Thus, it appears that patterns of spontaneous neural activity emanating from fetal eyes prior to the onset of vision play a role in the development or maintenance of the visual cortex (see Katz & Shatz, 1996).

Fourth, several studies have shown that early music training influences the organization of human auditory cortex (see Münte, Altenmüller, & Jäncke, 2002). In particular, fMRI studies have shown that early musical training tends to expand the area of auditory cortex that responds to complex musical tones, and behavioral studies have shown that early musical training leads to the development of *absolute pitch* (the ability to identify the pitch of any tone).

Mechanisms by Which Experience Might Influence Neurodevelopment

It is well established that experience has major effects on the development and maintenance of neural circuits, but the mechanisms through which experience exerts these effects are not well understood. The problem is not the lack of possible mechanisms, but rather that there are so many (see Gottlieb, 2000). The following are three of the possibilities.

First, neural activity has been shown to regulate the expression of genes that direct the synthesis of cell-adhesion molecules (CAMs). Thus, by influencing neural activity, experience could produce changes in cell adhesion.

Second, neural activity has been shown to influence the release of neurotrophins (Thoenen, 1995). Thus, by influencing neural activity, experience could promote and direct the growth of neurons and influence their survival.

Third, some neural circuits are spontaneously active early in the course of brain development, and the activity of these circuits is necessary for the normal progression of some aspects of brain development (Huberman et al., 2003). Thus, by influencing the activity of spontaneously active neural circuits, experience could influence the course of brain development.

Evolutionary Perspective

9.4 Neuroplasticity in Adults

If this book were a road trip that you and I were taking together, at this point, the following highway sign would appear: SLOW, IMPORTANT VIEWPOINT AHEAD. You see, you are about to encounter an idea that is currently one of the most influential in all of neuroscience, one that is changing how neuroscientists are thinking about the human brain.

Until the last decade, neuroplasticity was thought to be restricted to the brain's developmental period. Mature brains were considered to be set in their ways, incapable of substantial reorganization. Now, it is apparent that mature brains are also plastic. It has become clear that the mature brain is not a static organ, but is continually changing and adapting. Discovering the nature of these changes is currently a top priority of neuroscientific research (see Kolb, Gibb, & Robinson, 2003). Many lines of research are con-

tributing to neuroscientists' excitement about adult neuroplasticity. For now, consider the following two. You will encounter more in the next two chapters.

Neurogenesis in Adult Mammals

When I was a student, I learned two important principles of brain development. The first I learned through experience: The human brain starts to function in the womb and never stops working until one stands up to speak in public. The second I learned in a course on brain development: **Neurogenesis** (the growth of new neurons) does not occur in adults. The first principle appears to be fundamentally correct, at least when applied to me, but the second has been proved to be wrong (see Kempermann & Gage, 1999; Ormerod & Galea, 2001a).

Prior to the early 1980s, all neurons were thought to be created during early stages of development. Accordingly, subsequent brain development was seen as a downhill slope: Neurons continually die throughout a person's life, and it was assumed that the lost cells are never replaced by new ones. Although researchers began to chip away at this misconception in the early 1980s, it persisted until recently as one of the central principles of neurodevelopment.

The first serious challenge to the assumption that neurogenesis is restricted to early stages of development came in the early 1980s, with the discovery of the growth of new neurons in the brains of adult birds. Nottebohm and colleagues (e.g., Goldman & Nottebohm, 1983) found that brain structures involved in singing begin to grow in

Evolutionary Perspective

songbirds just before each mating season and that this growth results from an increase in the number of neurons.

This finding stimulated the re-examination of earlier unconfirmed claims that new neurons are created in the adult rat hippocampus.

Then, in the 1990s, researchers, armed with newly developed immunohistochemical markers that had a selective affinity for recently created neurons, convincingly showed that adult neurogenesis does indeed occur in the rat hippocampus (Cameron et al., 1993)—see Figure 9.10. And shortly thereafter, it was discovered that new neurons are also continually added to adult olfactory bulbs. Subsequently, it was reported that new neurons are added to adult monkeys' association cortex (Gould et al., 1999); this claim created quite a stir, but apparently it was made in error (Kornack & Rakic, 2001). Hence, in adult mammals, neurogenesis seems to be restricted to the olfactory bulbs and hippocampuses.

At first, reports of adult neurogenesis were not embraced by a generation of neuroscientists who had been trained to think of the adult brain as fixed, but acceptance grew as confirmatory reports accumulated. Particularly influential were the findings that new neurons are added to the hippocampuses of primates (e.g., Kornack & Rakic, 1999), including humans (Eriksson et al., 1998) and that the number of new neurons added to the adult hippocampus is substantial, an estimated 2,000 per hour (West, Slomianka, & Gunderson, 1991).

Where do the neurons created by adult neurogenesis come from? *Adult neural stem cells* are created at certain sites in the *ependymal layer* lining the ventricles and in the adjacent layer of neural tissue (Momma, Johansson, & Frisén, 2000; Morshead & van der Kooy, 2001); from there, they migrate to the olfactory bulbs. In contrast, new hippocampal cells appear to be created near their final location.

Many lines of research are focused on adult neural stem cells, and you will learn about some of these in later chapters. One particularly promising line began with a study of the effects on adult rodents of living in enriched environments. It turned out that adult rats living in enriched environments (changing environments, with toys,

running wheels, and other rats) produced 60% more new hippocampal neurons than did adult rats living in nonenriched environments (Kempermann & Gage, 1999). However, before you start enriching your apartment, you should be aware that the observed positive effect on neurogenesis in the adult rat hippocampus is not a direct consequence of the enriched environments. The effect depends largely, if not entirely, on the increases in exercise that typically occur in enriched environments (Farmer et al., 2004; Van Praag et al., 1999). This finding has a provocative implication: In view of the fact that the hippocampus is involved in some kinds of memory (see Duffy et al., 2001; Rhodes et al., 2002), perhaps exercise can be used as a treatment for those with memory problems (Cottman & Berchtold, 2002).

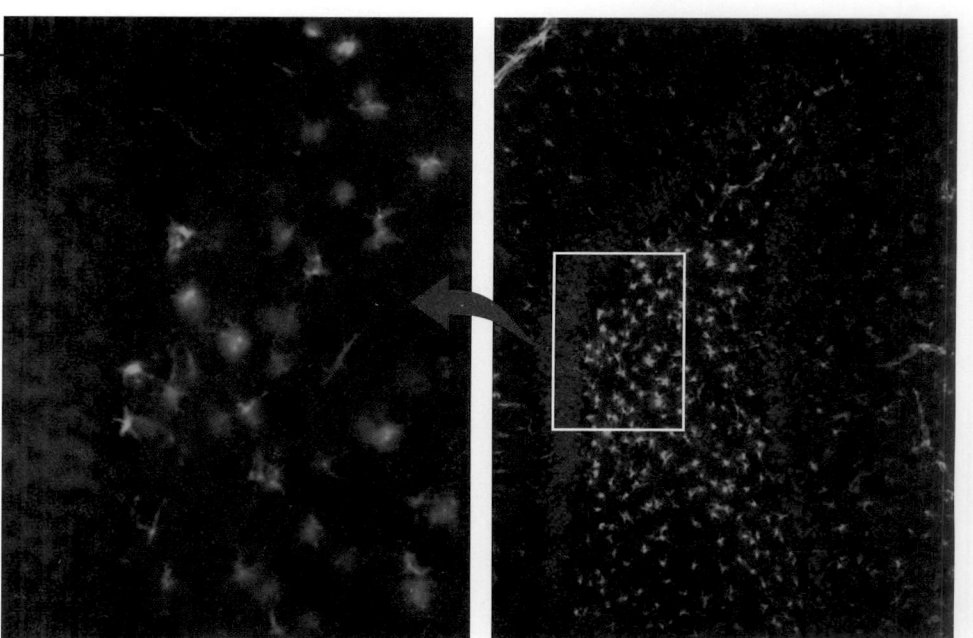

FIGURE 9.10   Adult neurogenesis. The top panel shows new cells in the dentate gyrus of the hippocampus—the cell bodies of neurons are stained blue, mature glial cells are stained green, and new cells are stained red. The bottom panel shows the new cells from the top panel under higher magnification, which makes it apparent that the new cells have taken up both blue and red stain and are thus new neurons. (Courtesy of my friends Carl Ernst and Brian Christie, Department of Psychology, University of British Columbia.)

Effects of Experience on the Reorganization of the Adult Cortex

I said that we would consider two current lines of research on adult neuroplasticity. You have just learned about the research on adult neurogenesis; the second line of research focuses on the effects of experience on the reorganization of adult cortex (see Elbert & Rockstroh, 2004).

Surprisingly, experience in adulthood can lead to reorganization of sensory and motor cortical maps (e.g., Jones, 2000; Sanes & Donoghue, 2000). For example, Mühlnickel and colleagues (1998) found that *tinnitus* (ringing in the ears) produces a major reorganization of primary auditory cortex, and Elbert and colleagues (1995) showed that adult musicians who play stringed instruments that are fingered with the left hand (e.g., violin) have an enlarged hand-representation area in their right somatosensory cortex. Evidence suggests that it is skill training rather than strength or endurance training that leads to reorganization of the motor cortex (Remple et al., 2001).

In a more controlled demonstration of the ability of experience to reorganize the adult human brain, healthy human volunteers received 1 hour of tactual experience for 20 days (Braun et al., 2000). For the 20 hours, the subjects experienced patterns of touch simultaneously delivered to the tips of their left thumb and left little finger. There were two conditions: In one, the subjects sat passively while the stimuli were delivered; in the other, the subjects were required to identify the patterns. The areas of the right somatosensory cortex activated by stimulation of the tip of either the left thumb or the left little finger were measured by high-resolution EEG evoked potentials. The results differed with the experimental condition. In the passive condition, the areas of somatosensory cortex responding to touches of the thumb and little finger moved closer together as the experiment progressed. In the active identification condition, the areas of somatosensory cortex responding to touches of the thumb and little finger moved farther apart.

The discovery of adult neuroplasticity is changing the way that we humans think about ourselves. More importantly for those with brain disorders, it has suggested some promising new treatment options. You will learn about these in the next chapter.

9.5 Disorders of Neurodevelopment: Autism and Williams Syndrome

I have tried to keep this chapter focused on fundamentals rather than on details. Still, I hope you have managed to get a sense of the incredible complexity of neurodevelopment. Like all complex processes, neurodevelopment is easily thrown off track; and, unfortunately, one tiny screw-up can have far-reaching and tragic consequences because it can disrupt all subsequent stages. This fact will become apparent to you in this, the final section of the chapter, which focuses on two disorders of neurodevelopment: autism and Williams syndrome.

Autism

Autism is a complex neurodevelopmental disorder that typically occurs in about 4 of every 10,000 individuals. It usually becomes apparent before the age of 3 and changes little thereafter (Happé & Frith, 1996). The diagnosis of autism is based on the presence of three core symptoms: (1) a reduced ability to interpret the emotions and intentions of others (see Aldolphs, Sears, & Piven, 2001); (2) a reduced capacity for social interaction and communication; and (3) a preoccupation with a single subject or activity (Pierce & Courchesne, 2001). Although this triad of symptoms defines the disorder, other signs are commonly, but not universally, associated with it. For example, about 75% of those with autism are male, about 75% suffer from mental retardation, and about 35% suf-

fer from epilepsy. Most people with autism have difficulty mimicking the gestures of others (Williams et al., 2001).

Autism is a difficult disorder to treat. Intensive behavioral therapy can improve the lives of some individuals, but it is rarely possible for a person with autism to live independently, even if he or she represents one of those few cases in which intelligence is reasonably normal. How is a person who has no appreciation for the feelings and motivations of others, who has difficulty communicating, who compulsively bangs his head against the wall, and who is obsessed by bus schedules going to function in society?

Autism Is a Heterogeneous Disorder Although many scientists who study autism do so in an effort to help those who have the disorder, many are interested in it because of one of its major features—its heterogeneity (Happé & Frith, 1996). In autism, some functions are severely impaired, whereas others are normal or even superior. It is these "spotty" patterns of neuropsychological deficits that have the most potential to teach us about the neural bases of psychological functions.

Unfortunately, not all autistic patients display the same pattern of deficits and spared abilities, which greatly complicates the study of this disorder. This suggests that autism has no single cause and that it is best regarded as a group of related disorders (Eigsti & Shapiro, 2004; Trottier, Srivastava, & Walker, 1999).

Despite the heterogeneity of autism, there are some common patterns. For example, most autistic individuals—even those who are severely retarded—display the following preserved abilities: rote memory, the ability to complete jigsaw puzzles, musical ability, and artistic ability.

Even within the single category of speech disability, there is often a heterogeneous pattern of deficits. Many autistic individuals have sizable vocabularies, are good spellers, and can read aloud even those things they do not understand. However, the same individuals are often unable to use intonation to communicate emotion, to coordinate eye gaze and facial expression with speech, and to speak metaphorically. About a quarter of autistic individuals have little or no language ability.

Autistic Savants   Perhaps the single most remarkable aspect of autism is the tendency for autistic individuals to be savants. **Savants** are intellectually handicapped individuals who nevertheless display amazing and specific cognitive or artistic abilities. About 1 in 10 autistic individuals display savant abilities. Savant abilities can take many forms, but the following are common among these rare individuals: feats of memory, naming the day of the week for any future or past date, identifying prime numbers (any number divisible only by itself and 1), drawing, and playing musical instruments (see Bonnel et al., 2003).

Savant abilities may be the most puzzling phenomena in all of neuroscience. Consider the following cases (Ramachandran & Blackeslee, 1998; Sacks, 1985).

Some Cases of Amazing Savants

Clinical Implications

Nadia suffered from severe autism; her IQ was between 60 and 70. She could barely put two words together. Yet, by the time she reached the age of 6, she could draw gallery-quality pictures of people, animals, and other complex subjects.

One savant could tell the time of day to the exact second without ever referring to his watch. Even when he was asleep, he would mumble the correct time.

Another savant could specify the width of objects. For example, she was asked the width of a rock that lay on the ground about 20 feet away. "Exactly two feet, eleven and three-quarter inches," she replied. She was right; indeed, she was always right.

Tom was a blind, autistic 13-year-old who could not tie his own shoes. He had never had any musical training, but he could play the most difficult piano piece after hearing it just once, even if he was playing with his back to the piano. Once, he played one song

with one hand and a second with the other, while singing a third.

One pair of autistic twins had difficulty doing simple addition and subtraction and could not even comprehend multiplication and division. Yet, if given any date in the last or next 40,000 years, they could specify the day of week that it would fall on. Their short-term memory for digits was amazing: They were able to correctly repeat a list of 300 digits after hearing it only once. A box of matches fell on the floor: "One hundred and eleven," they immediately cried out together. There were 111.

These and many other well-documented savant cases remain a mystery. Savant abilities do not develop through rote learning or practice; they seem to emerge spontaneously. Even the savants with language abilities cannot explain their own feats. They seem naturally to recognize implicit patterns and relations that escape others. We can only regard these cases with wonder and speculate that somehow damage to certain parts of their brains has led to compensatory overdevelopment in other parts. For example, it has been suggested that savant abilities are created when damage to the left hemisphere triggers compensatory functional improvement in the right hemisphere (Treffert & Wallace, 2002).

Neural Basis of Autism   Two lines of research show that genetic factors influence the development of autism (see Rodier, 2000). First, autism has been found to run in families; various studies have shown that siblings of people with autism have about a 5% chance of being diagnosed with the disorder. This is well above the rate in the general population, but well below the 50% chance that would be expected if autism were caused solely by a single dominant gene or the 25% chance that would be expected if autism were caused solely by a single recessive gene. Second, several studies have shown that the development of autism is highly related in monozygotic twins; if one twin is diagnosed as autistic, the other has a 60% chance of receiving the same diagnosis. Although this high correlation shows that autism has a genetic basis, it also shows that it is not entirely genetic. If it were, the concordance rate would be 100% in individuals with identical genes. Together, these two lines of research suggest that autism is triggered by several genes interacting with the environment (see Zoghbi, 2003).

Given the patient-to-patient variability of both the symptoms and the genetics of autism, it is not surprising that the brain damage associated with the disorder is also variable. Damage has been most commonly observed in the cerebellum and related parts of the brain, but it generally tends to be widespread throughout the brain (see Machado et al., 2003; Müller et al., 2001; Müller et al., 2003).

Given the diffuse and variable pattern of autism-related brain damage, it is clear that any line of research focusing on one area of the brain will not provide ultimate answers about the the disorder. Nevertheless, the following line of experiments was a promising beginning. Strömland and colleagues (1994) discovered that a pregnant woman's taking *thalidomide*, the morning-sickness pill that caused an epidemic of birth defects in the 1960s, greatly increased the probability that the child would be born with autism. Because a prescription for thalidomide was restricted to the early weeks of pregnancy, this relationship suggests that autism is created by a neurodevelopmental error occurring at this time.

Knowing when something happens provides *embryologists* (scientists who study embryos) with important clues. Knowing that thalidomide-induced autism develops in the first few weeks of embryological development has focused attention on the motor neurons of the cranial nerves that control the face, mouth, and eyes, because few neurons other than these are formed by the fourth week. Indeed, it was shown that both thalidomide-induced and typical autism are associated with various deficits in face, mouth, and eye control (e.g., Strömland et al., 1994).

Another clue came from analysis of the physical appearance of individuals with autism—whether or not the disorder was thalidomide-induced. Their appearance is typically good; however, there are a few minor anomalies of ear structure: square shape, positioned too low on the head, rotated slightly backward, tops flopped over (see Figure 9.11). This suggested that autism is triggered by an abnormal event occurring between 20 and 24 days after conception, when the ears are developing. Remarkably, most of the cases of thalidomide-induced autism did not display the stunted and misshapen limbs typical of most cases of thalidomide-induced birth defects; they did, however, display anomalies of external ear structure.

Rodier (2000) had the opportunity to conduct an autopsy examination of the brain of an autistic woman,

and influenced by the research on thalidomide-induced autism, she focused her examination on the brain stem. She made a remarkable finding: The woman's brain stem was shortened, as if a slice had failed to develop. Nuclei in the slice were either underdeveloped (facial nucleus) or totally missing (superior olive) (see Figure 9.12 on page 228).

As Rodier examined the shortened brain stem of the autistic woman, she experienced a "powerful shock of recognition." She had seen this pattern before. From the stacks of papers on her office floor, she retrieved an article about the brains of knockout

mice, engineered to lack the expression of a gene known as *Hoxa 1*. These mice exhibited shortening of the brain stem, an underdeveloped facial nucleus, and no superior olive. Moreover, the mice had ear malformations and abnormal eye movements. Rodier (2000) subsequently discovered that some people have a variant form of Hoxa 1, which is located on chromosome 7, and that the variant form is prevalent in people with autism—it is found in 40% of autistic persons, compared with 20% of the general population.

Let's put this series of findings in perspective. First, it is unlikely that the developmental distortions in the midbrain are responsible for all, or even most, of the symptoms of autism. Second, the Hoxa 1 gene has been implicated in only some cases of autism.

Williams Syndrome

Williams syndrome, like autism, is a neurodevelopmental disorder associated with mental retardation and a strikingly uneven pattern of abilities and disabilities. Williams syndrome occurs in approximately 1 of every 20,000 births (see Rourke et al., 2002).

In contrast to the withdrawn, emotionally insensitive, uncommunicative person with autism, people with Williams syndrome are sociable, empathetic, and talkative. It is their language abilities that have attracted the most attention. Although they display a delay in language development and language deficits in adulthood (Bishop, 1999; Paterson et al., 1999), their language skills are remarkable considering their characteristically poor IQs—which average around 60. For example, when asked about his infantile scribble on a piece of paper, one severely retarded Williams teenager, with an IQ of 49, identified it as an elephant and offered the following verbal commentary (Bellugi et al., 1999):

And what an elephant is it is one of the animals. And what the elephant does, it lives in the jungle. It can also live in the zoo. And what it has, it has long gray ears, fan ears, ears that can blow in the wind. It has a long trunk that can pick up grass, or pick up hay . . . if they're in a bad mood it can be terrible. . . . If the elephant gets mad it could

FIGURE 9.11 A boy with autism shows the typical anomalies of ear structure.

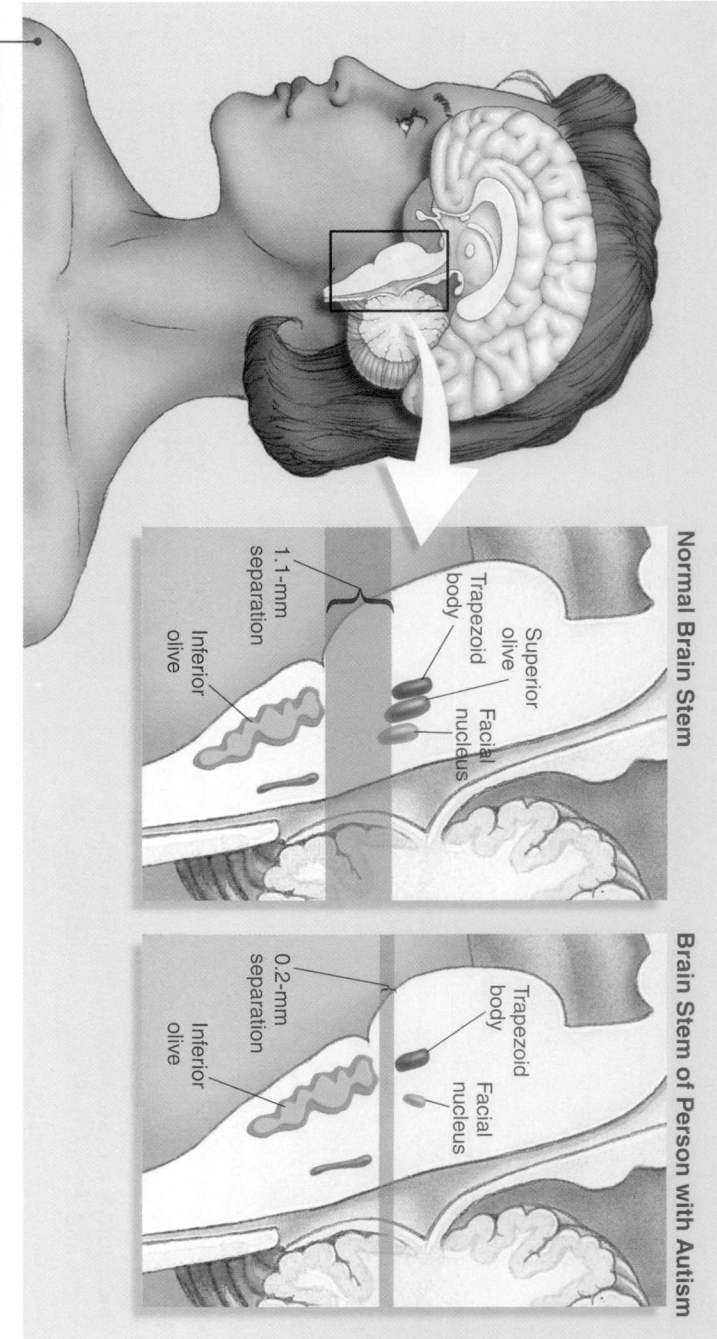

FIGURE 9.12 The brain stem of a woman with autism was found to be shortened, missing a band of tissue at the junction of the pons and medulla. (Adapted from Rodier, 2000.)

Normal Brain Stem

Superior olive
Trapezoid body
Facial nucleus
1.1-mm separation
Inferior olive

Brain Stem of Person with Autism

Trapezoid body
Facial nucleus
0.2-mm separation
Inferior olive

stomp; it could charge. Sometimes elephants can charge. They have long tusks. You don't want an elephant as a pet. You want a cat or a dog or a bird. . . (p. 199)

The remarkable language skills of Williams children have also been demonstrated by objective tests (Bellugi et al., 1999). For example, in one test, Williams children were asked to name as many animals as they could in 60 seconds. Answers included koala, yak, ibex, condor, chihuahua, brontosaurus, and hippopotamus. When asked to look at a picture and tell a story about it, Williams children often produced an animated narrative. As they told the story, the children altered the pitch, volume, rhythm, and vocabulary of their speech to engage the audience. Sadly, the verbal and social skills of these children often lead teachers to overestimate their cognitive abilities, and thus they do not always receive the extra academic support they need.

Williams people have other cognitive strengths, several of which involve music (Lennoff et al., 1997). Although most cannot learn to read music, some have perfect or near-perfect pitch and an uncanny sense of rhythm. Many retain melodies for years, and some are professional musicians. As a group, Williams people show more interest in, and emotional reaction to, music than does the general population. One Williams child said, "Music is my favorite way of thinking." Yet another

cognitive strength of Williams people is their remarkable ability to recognize faces.

Like any group of individuals with an average IQ of 60, Williams people display many severe cognitive deficits. Against this background, their strengths tend to stand out. However, there is one class of cognitive problems that is noteworthy because it is even more severe in them than it is in other people with similar IQs: They have a profound impairment in spatial cognition. For example, they have great difficulty remembering the location of a few blocks placed on a test board, their spatial-related speech is poor, and their ability to draw objects is almost nonexistent (Jordan et al., 2002).

Williams syndrome is also associated with a variety of health problems, including several involving the heart. Ironically, the study of one of these disorders in people who did not have the syndrome led to the identification of a major genetic factor in the syndrome. This heart disorder was found to result from a mutation in a gene on chromosome 7 that controls the synthesis of *elastin*, a protein that imparts elasticity to many organs and tissues. Aware that the same cardiac problem is prevalent in Williams people, investigators assessed the status of this gene in that group. Remarkably, they found that the gene on one of the two copies of chromosome 7

Clinical Implications

was absent in 95% of Williams people. Other genes were missing as well; through an accident of reproduction, an entire region of chromosome 7 had been deleted. Once the other genes in this region have been identified and their functions determined, there will be a much fuller understanding of the etiology of Williams syndrome.

In general, Williams people display gross underdevelopment of occipital and parietal cortex, which could account for their poor spatial abilities; normal frontal and temporal cortex, which could account for their preserved speech; and abnormalities in the limbic system, which could account for their heightened friendliness (see Bellugi et al., 1999).

You may have unknowingly encountered stories of Williams people. Many cultures feature tales involving magical little people: pixies, elves, leprechauns, etc. Remarkably, descriptions and drawings of these creatures portray them as virtually identical to Williams people, who are often described as elfin in appearance. Williams people tend to be short, and they have small upturned noses, oval ears, broad mouths with full lips, puffy eyes, and small chins (see Figure 9.13). Accordingly, many believe that folk tales about elves may have originally been

FIGURE 9.13   Williams people are characterized by their elfin appearance.

based on Williams people. Even the typical behavioral characteristics of elves—engaging storytellers, talented musicians, loving, trusting, and sensitive to the feelings of others—match those of Williams people.

Themes Revisited

The clinical implications and evolutionary perspective themes were heavily emphasized in this chapter. One

of the best ways to understand the principles of normal neurodevelopment is to consider what happens when it goes wrong: Accordingly, the chapter began with the tragic case of Genie and ended with a discussion

of autism and Williams syndrome. The evolutionary perspective theme was emphasized because much of the information that we have about normal human neurodevelopment and human neurodevelopmental disorders has come from studying other species.

The thinking-about-biopsychology tab appeared infrequently in this chapter, but the theme was pervasive.

Thinking-about-biopsychology tabs highlighted discussions that made two general points. First, neurodevelopment always proceeds from gene-experience interactions rather than from either genetics or environment alone. Second, it is important not to overreact to the impressive recent advances in the study of neurodevelopment: Important steps have been taken, but we are still a long way from a complete understanding.

The cognitive neuroscience theme came up infrequently in this chapter. Only recently has the power of brain-imaging techniques been brought to bear on the study of neurodevelopment and neurodevelopmental disorders.

ON THE CD

See Hard Copy for additional readings for Chapter 9.

Think about It

1. What does the case of Genie teach us about normal development?

2. Neuron death is a necessary stage in neurodevelopment. Discuss.

3. Even the adult brain displays plasticity. What do you think is the evolutionary significance of this ability?

4. Discuss the evolutionary significance of the slow development of the human brain.

5. Autism and Williams syndrome are opposites in several ways and could be fruitfully studied together. Discuss.

ON THE CD

Studying for an exam? Try the Practice Tests for Chapter 9.

Key Terms

Aggregation (p. 215)
Apoptosis (p. 219)
Autism (p. 225)
Cell-adhesion molecules
    (CAMs) (p. 215)
Chemoaffinity hypothesis
    (p. 216)
Fasciculation (p. 217)
Glia-mediated migration
    (p. 214)
Growth cone (p. 214)
Inside-out pattern (p. 214)
Mesoderm layer (p. 213)

Migration (p. 214)
Multipotent (p. 213)
Necrosis (p. 219)
Nerve growth factor (NGF)
    (p. 219)
Neural crest (p. 214)
Neural plate (p. 213)
Neural proliferation
    (p. 214)
Neural tube (p. 214)
Neurogenesis (p. 223)
Neurotrophins (p. 219)
Optic tectum (p. 216)

Perseveration (p. 221)
Pioneer growth cones (p. 217)
Radial glial cells (p. 214)
Radial migration (p. 214)
Retinal ganglion cells (p. 215)
Savants (p. 227)
Somal translocation (p. 214)
Stem cells (p. 213)
Synaptogenesis (p. 218)
Tangential migration (p. 214)
Topographic gradient
    hypothesis (p. 217)
Totipotent (p. 213)

Ventricular zone (p. 214)
Williams syndrome (p. 227)

ON THE CD

Need some help studying the key terms for this chapter? Check out the electronic flash cards for Chapter 9.

chapter 10

Brain Damage and Neuroplasticity

Can the Brain Recover from Damage?

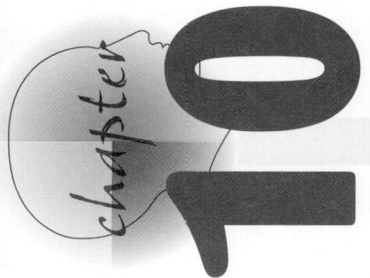

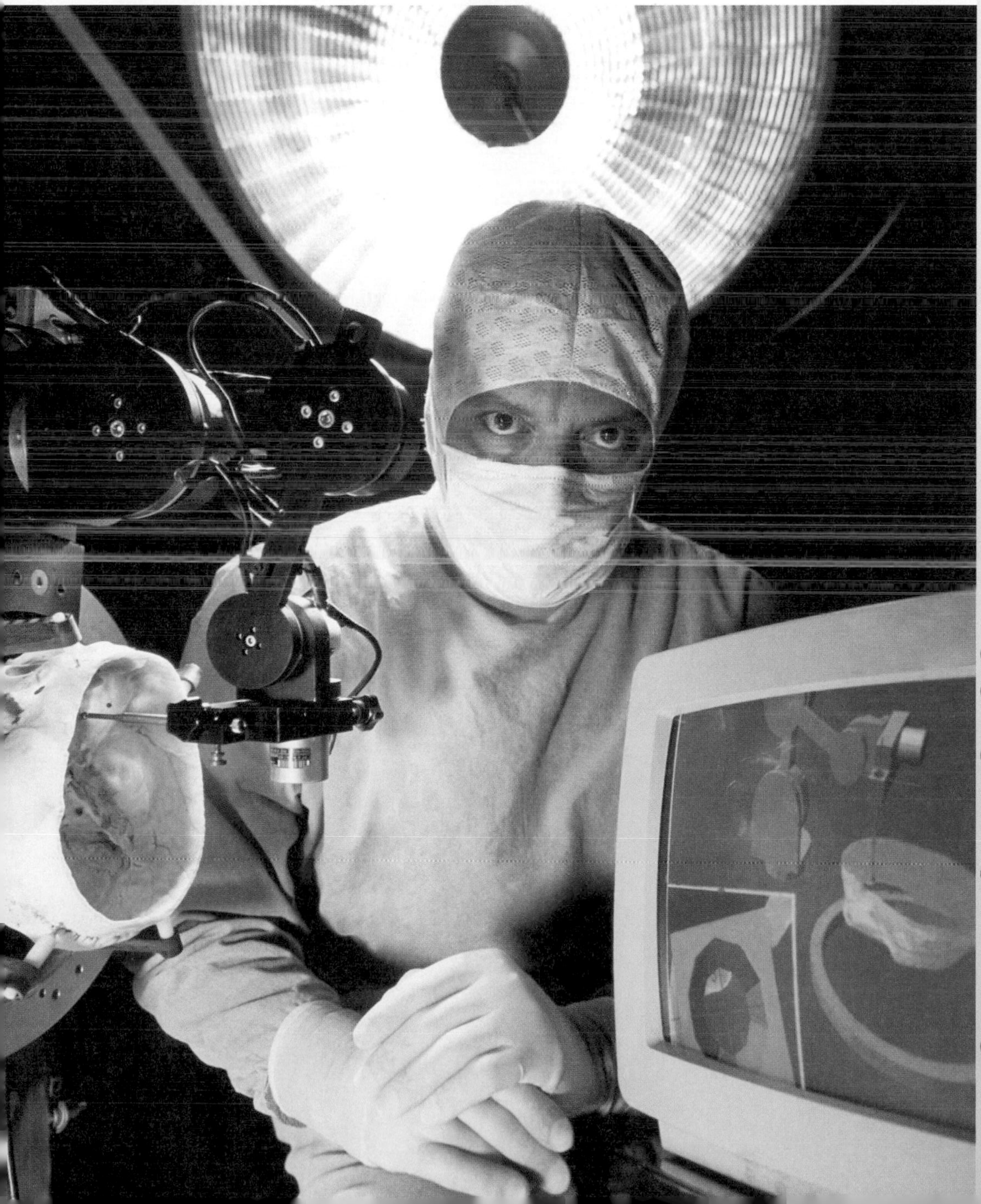

10.1 Causes of Brain Damage

10.2 Neuropsychological Diseases

10.3 Animal Models of Human Neuropsychological Diseases

10.4 Neuroplastic Responses to Nervous System Damage: Degeneration, Regeneration, Reorganization, and Recovery

10.5 Neuroplasticity and the Treatment of Nervous System Damage

The study of human brain damage serves two purposes: It increases our understanding of the healthy brain, and it serves as a basis for the development of new treatments. The first three sections of this chapter focus on brain damage itself. The last two sections continue the neuroplasticity theme that was introduced in Chapter 9: The fourth focuses on the recovery and reorganization of the brain after damage, and the fifth discusses exciting new neuroplasticity-promoting treatments. But first, the continuation of the ironic case of Professor P., whom you first met in Chapter 5, relates the personal tragedy of brain damage.

The Ironic Case of Professor P.

Clinical Implications

One night Professor P. sat at his desk staring at a drawing of the cranial nerves, much like the one in Appendix III of this book. As he mulled over the location and function of each cranial nerve (see Appendix IV), the painful truth became impossible for him to deny. The irony of the situation was that Professor P. was a neuroscientist, all too familiar with what he was experiencing.

His symptoms started subtly, with slight deficits in balance. He probably wouldn't have even noticed them except that his experience as a mountaineer had taught him to pay attention to such things. Professor P. chalked these occasional lurches up to aging—after all, he thought to himself, he was past his prime, and things like this happen. Similarly, his doctor didn't seem to think that it was a problem worth looking into, but Professor P. monitored his symptoms carefully nevertheless. Three years later, his balance problems still unabated, Professor P. really started to worry. He was trying to talk with a colleague on the phone but was not having much success because of what he thought was a bad connection. Then, he changed the phone to his other ear, and all of a sudden, the faint voice on the other end became louder. He tried this switch several times over the ensuing days, and the conclusion became inescapable: Professor P. was going deaf in his right ear.

Professor P. immediately made an appointment with his doctor, who referred him to a specialist. After a cursory and poorly controlled hearing test, the specialist gave him good news. "You're fine, Professor P.; lots of people experience hearing loss when they reach middle age, and your problems are not serious enough to worry about." To this day, Professor P. regrets that he did not insist on a second opinion; his problem would have been so much easier to deal with at that stage.

It was about a year later that Professor P. sat staring at the illustration of the cranial nerves. By then he had begun to experience numbness on the right side of his mouth; he was having minor problems swallowing; and his right tear ducts were not releasing enough tears. There he sat staring at the point where the auditory and vestibular nerves come together to form cranial nerve VIII (the auditory-vestibular nerve). He knew it was there, and he knew that it was large enough to be affecting cranial nerves V through X as well, but he didn't know what it was: a tumor, a stroke, an angioma, an infection? Was he going to die? Was his death going to be terrible and lingering as his brain and intellect gradually deteriorated?

He didn't make an appointment with his doctor right away. A friend of his was conducting a brain MRI study, and Professor P. volunteered to be a control subject, knowing that his problem would show up on the scan. It did: a large tumor sitting, as predicted, on the right cranial nerve VIII.

Then, MRI in hand, Professor P. went back to his doctor, who referred him to a neurologist, who in turn referred him to a neurosurgeon. Several stressful weeks later, Professor P. found himself on life support in the intensive care unit of his local hospital, hands tied to the bed and tubes emanating seemingly from every part of his body. You see, the tumor was so convoluted that it took 6 hours to remove; and during the 6 hours that Professor P.'s brain was exposed, air entered his circulatory system, and he developed pneumonia. Near death and hallucinating from the morphine, Professor P. thought he heard his wife, Maggie, calling for help and tried to go to her assistance: That is why he was tied down. One gentle morphine-steeped professor was no match for five burly nurses intent on saving his life.

Professor P.'s auditory-vestibular nerve was transected during his surgery, which has left him permanently deaf and without vestibular function on the right side. He was also left with partial hemifacial paralysis, including serious blinking and tearing problems, but these facial symptoms have largely cleared up.

Professor P. has now returned to his students, his research, and his writing, hoping that the tumor was completely removed and that he will not have to endure another surgery. Indeed, at the very moment that I am writing these words, Professor P. is working on the forthcoming edition of this textbook. . . . If it has not yet occurred to you, I am Professor P.

ON THE CD

Visit the module *My Tumor and Welcome To It.* Pinel, relaxing in his own garden, describes his struggle with a brain tumor.

10.1 Causes of Brain Damage

This section provides an introduction to six causes of brain damage: brain tumors, cerebrovascular disorders, closed-head injuries, infections of the brain, neurotoxins, and genetic factors. It concludes with a discussion of programmed cell death, which mediates many forms of brain damage.

Brain Tumors

A **tumor,** or **neoplasm** (literally, "new growth"), is a mass of cells that grows independently of the rest of the body (see Wechsler-Reya & Scott, 2001). In other words, it is a cancer.

About 20% of tumors found in the human brain are **meningiomas** (see Figure 10.1)—tumors that grow between the *meninges,* the three membranes that cover the central nervous system. All meningiomas are **encapsulated tumors**—tumors that grow within their own membrane. As a result, they are particularly easy to identify on a CT scan, they can influence the function of the brain only by the pressure they exert on surrounding tissue, and they are almost always **benign tumors**—tumors that are surgically removable with little risk of further growth in the body (see Grimson et al., 1999).

Unfortunately, encapsulation is the exception rather than the rule when it comes to brain tumors. Aside from meningiomas, most brain tumors are infiltrating. **Infiltrating tumors** are those that grow diffusely through surrounding tissue. As a result, they are usually **malignant tumors;** it is difficult to remove or destroy them completely, and any cancerous tissue that remains after surgery continues to grow.

About 10% of brain tumors do not originate in the brain. They grow from infiltrating tumor fragments carried to the brain by the bloodstream from some other part of the body. (The brain is a particularly fertile ground for tumor growth.) These tumors are called **metastatic tumors;** *metastasis* refers to the transmission of disease from one organ to another. Most metastatic brain tumors originate as cancers of the lungs. Obviously, the chance of recovering from a cancer that has already attacked two or more separate sites is slim at best. Figure 10.2 on page 234 illustrates the ravages of metastasis.

Fortunately, my tumor was encapsulated. Encapsulated tumors that grow on cranial nerve VIII are referred to as *acoustic neuromas* (neuromas are tumors that grow on nerves or tracts). Figure 10.3 on page 234 is an MRI scan of my acoustic neuroma, the very same scan that I took to my doctor.

Cerebrovascular Disorders

Strokes are sudden-onset cerebrovascular disorders that cause brain damage. There are two major types of strokes: those resulting from cerebral hemorrhage and those resulting from cerebral ischemia (pronounced "iss-KEEM-ee-a"). In the United States, stroke is the third leading cause of death and the most common cause of adult disability (Janardhan & Qureshi, 2004). Common consequences of stroke are amnesia, aphasia (language difficulties), paralysis, and coma. The area of dead or dying tissue produced by a stroke is called an *infarct.*

Cerebral Hemorrhage Cerebral hemorrhage (bleeding in the brain) occurs when a cerebral blood vessel ruptures and blood seeps into the surrounding neural tissue and damages it. Bursting aneurysms are a common cause of intracerebral hemorrhage. An **aneurysm** is a pathological balloonlike dilation that forms in the wall of a blood vessel at a point where the elasticity of the vessel wall is defective. Aneurysms can be **congenital** (present at birth) or can result from exposure to vascular poisons or infection (see Kalaria, 2001). Individuals who have aneurysms should make every effort to avoid high blood pressure.

Cerebral Ischemia Cerebral ischemia is a disruption of the blood supply to an area of the brain. The three main causes of cerebral ischemia are thrombosis, embolism, and arteriosclerosis. In **thrombosis,** a plug called a *thrombus* is formed and blocks blood flow at the site of its formation. A thrombus may be composed of a blood clot, fat, oil, an air bubble, tumor cells, or any

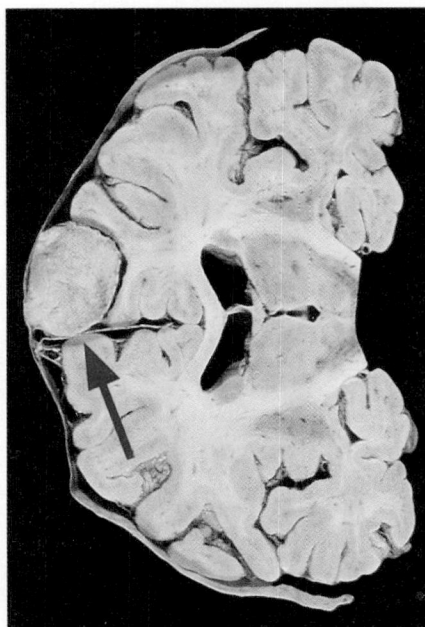

FIGURE 10.1 A meningioma. (Courtesy of Kenneth Berry, Head of Neuropathology, Vancouver General Hospital.)

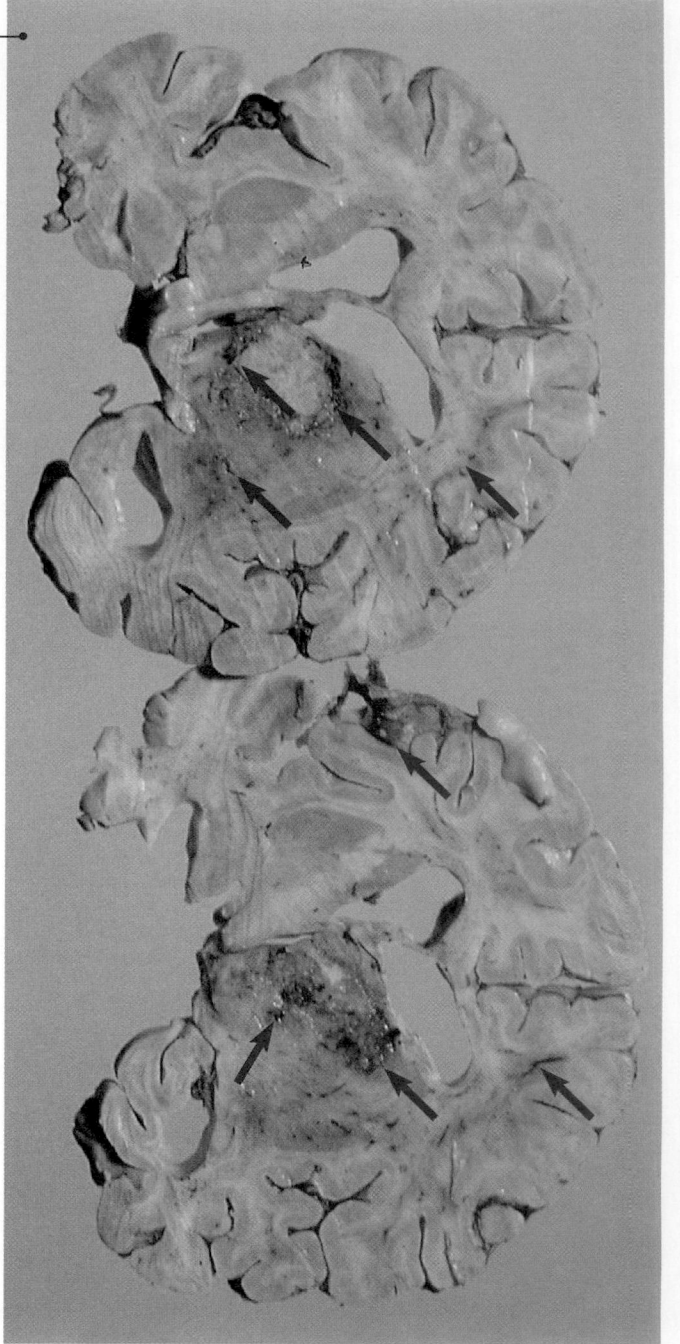

FIGURE 10.2   Multiple metastatic brain tumors. The arrows indicate some of the more advanced areas of metastatic tumor development.

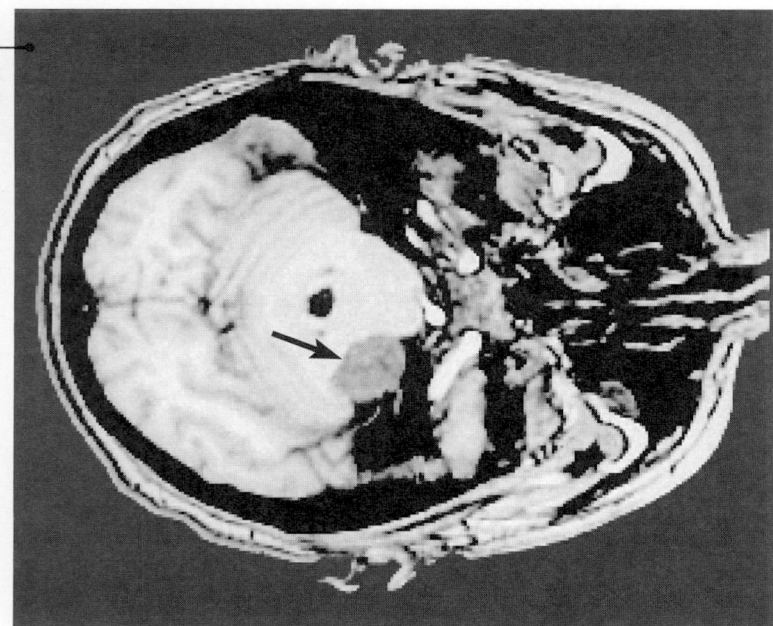

FIGURE 10.3   An MRI of Professor P's acoustic neuroma. The arrow indicates the tumor.

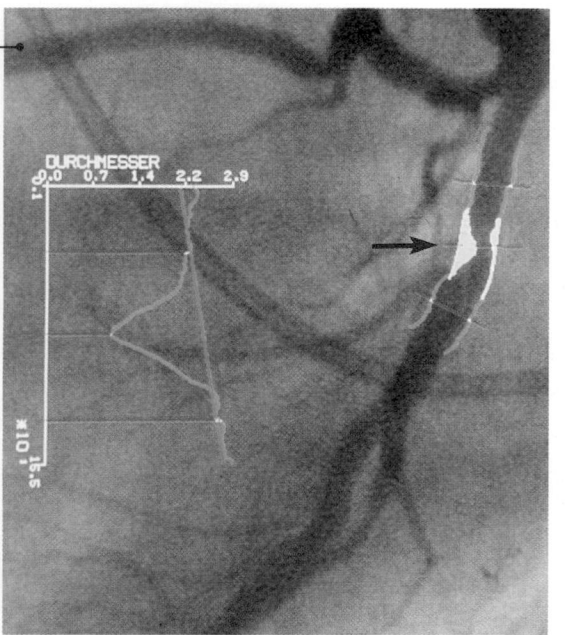

FIGURE 10.4   An angiogram that illustrates narrowing of the carotid artery (see arrow), the main pathway of blood to the brain. Compare this angiogram with the normal angiogram in Figure 5.1.

combination thereof. **Embolism** is similar except that the plug, called an *embolus* in this case, is carried by the blood from a larger vessel, where it was formed, to a smaller one, where it becomes lodged; in essence, an

embolus is just a thrombus that has taken a trip. In **arteriosclerosis,** the walls of blood vessels thicken and the channels narrow, usually as the result of fat deposits; this narrowing can eventually lead to complete blockage of the blood vessels (Libby, 2002). The *angiogram* in Figure 10.4 illustrates partial blockage of one carotid artery.

Much of the damage produced by cerebral ischemia takes a day or two to develop fully; and, paradoxically, some of the brain's own neurotransmitters play a key role in its development (Wahlgren & Ahmed, 2004). Much of the brain damage associated with stroke is a consequence of excessive release of excitatory amino acid neurotransmitters, in particular **glutamate,** the brain's most prevalent excitatory neurotransmitter.

Here is how this mechanism is thought to work (see Dirnagl, Iadecola, & Moskowitz, 1999). After a blood vessel becomes blocked, many of the blood-deprived neurons become overactive and release excessive quantities of glutamate. The glutamate in turn overactivates glutamate receptors in the membranes of postsynaptic neurons; the glutamate receptors that are most involved in this reaction are the **NMDA (N-methyl-D-aspartate)**

receptors. As a result, large numbers of Na^+ and Ca^{2+} ions enter the postsynaptic neurons.

The excessive internal concentrations of Na^+ and Ca^{2+} ions affect the postsynaptic neurons in two ways: They trigger the release of excessive amounts of glutamate from them, thus spreading the toxic cascade to yet other neurons; and they trigger a sequence of internal reactions that ultimately kill the postsynaptic neurons. (See Figure 10.5.)

Ischemia-induced brain damage has three important properties (Krieglstein, 1997). First, it takes a while to develop. Soon after a temporary cerebral ischemic episode, say, one 10 minutes in duration, there usually is little or no evidence of brain damage; however,

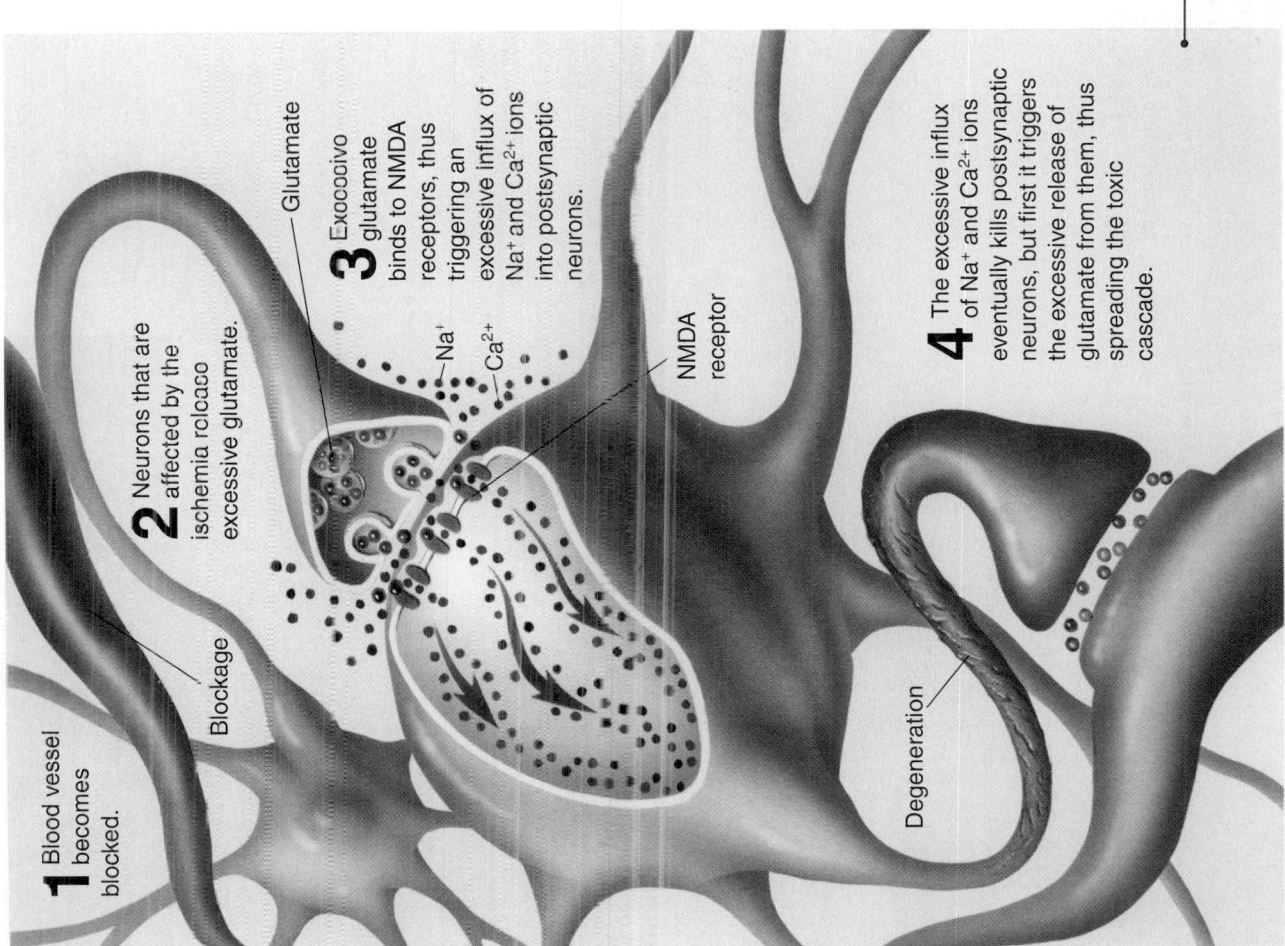

1 Blood vessel becomes blocked.

Blockage

2 Neurons that are affected by the ischemia release excessive glutamate.

Glutamate

3 Excessive glutamate binds to NMDA receptors, thus triggering an excessive influx of Na^+ and Ca^{2+} ions into postsynaptic neurons.

Na^+

Ca^{2+}

NMDA receptor

4 The excessive influx of Na^+ and Ca^{2+} ions eventually kills postsynaptic neurons, but first it triggers the excessive release of glutamate from them, thus spreading the toxic cascade.

Degeneration

FIGURE 10.5 The cascade of events by which the stroke-induced release of glutamate kills neurons.

substantial neuron loss can often be detected a day or two later. Second, ischemia-induced brain damage does not occur equally in all parts of the brain; particularly susceptible are neurons in certain areas of the hippocampus (Ohtaki et al., 2003). Third, the mechanisms of ischemia-induced damage vary somewhat from structure to structure within the brain.

An exciting implication of the discovery that excessive glutamate release causes much of the brain damage associated with stroke is the possibility of preventing stroke-related brain damage by blocking the glutaminergic cascade. The search is on for a glutamate antagonist that is effective and safe for use in human stroke victims (Leker & Shohami, 2002; Lo, Dalkara, & Moskowitz, 2003). Several have proved to be effective in laboratory animals, but so far none has been shown to limit brain damage from strokes in humans. Wahlgren and Ahmed (2004) have argued that if such treatments are to be effective, they need to be initiated in the ambulance, not hours later in the hospital.

Closed-Head Injuries

It is not necessary for the skull to be penetrated for the brain to be seriously damaged. In fact, any blow to the head should be treated with extreme caution, particularly when confusion, sensorimotor disturbances, or loss of consciousness ensues. Brain injuries produced by blows that do not penetrate the skull are called *closed-head injuries*.

Contusions are closed-head injuries that involve damage to the cerebral circulatory system. Such damage produces internal hemorrhaging, which results in a hematoma. A **hematoma** is a localized collection of clotted blood in an organ or tissue—in other words, a bruise.

It is paradoxical that the very hardness of the skull, which protects the brain from penetrating injuries, is the major factor in the development of contusions. Contusions from closed-head injuries occur when the brain slams against the inside of the skull. As Figure 10.6 illustrates, blood from such injuries can accumulate in the *subdural space*—the space between the dura mater and arachnoid membrane—and severely distort the surrounding neural tissue.

It may surprise you to learn that contusions frequently occur on the side of the brain opposite the side struck by a blow. The reason for such so-called **contrecoup injuries** is that the blow causes the brain to strike the inside of the skull on the other side of the head.

When there is a disturbance of consciousness following a blow to the head and there is no evidence of a contusion or other structural damage, the diagnosis is **concussion**. It is commonly assumed that concussions entail a temporary disruption of normal cerebral function with no long-term damage. However, the punch-drunk syndrome suggests otherwise. The **punch-**

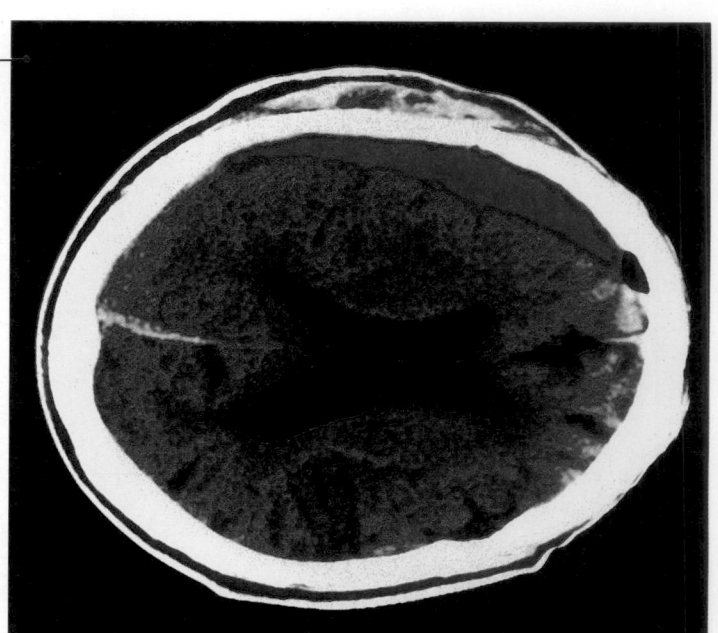

FIGURE 10.6 A CT scan of a subdural hematoma. Notice that the subdural hematoma has displaced the left lateral ventricle.

drunk syndrome is the **dementia** (general intellectual deterioration) and cerebral scarring that is observed in boxers and other individuals who experience repeated concussions. If there were no damage associated with a single concussion, the effects of many concussions could not summate to produce severe damage (McCrory & Berkovic, 1998).

One of the most dangerous aspects of concussion is the complacency with which it is regarded. Flippant references to it, such as "having one's bell rung," do little to communicate its hazards.

The Case of Jerry Quarry, Ex-Boxer

Jerry Quarry thumps his hard belly with both fists. Smiles at the sound. Like a stone against a tree.

"Feel it," he says proudly, punching himself again and again.

He pounds big, gnarled fists into meaty palms. Cocks his head. Stares. Vacant blue eyes. Punch-drunk at 50. Medical name: *Dementia pugilistica* [punch-drunk syndrome]. Cause: Thousands of punches to the head.

A top heavyweight contender in the 1960s and '70s, Quarry now needs help shaving, showering, putting on shoes and socks. Soon, probably, diapers. His older brother, James, cuts meat into little pieces so he won't choke. Jerry smiles like a kid. Shuffles like an old man.

Slow, slurred speech. Random thoughts snagged on branches in a dying brain. Memories twisted. Voices no one else hears. (Steve Wiltstein, Associated Press, 1995)

Infections of the Brain

An invasion of the brain by microorganisms is a *brain infection*, and the resulting inflammation is **encephalitis.** There are two common types of brain infections: bacterial infections and viral infections.

Bacterial Infections   When bacteria infect the brain, they often lead to the formation of *cerebral abscesses*—pockets of pus in the brain. They also often attack and inflame the meninges, creating a disorder known as **meningitis,** which is fatal in 25% of adults (Nau & Brück, 2002). Penicillin and other antibiotics sometimes eliminate the infection, but they cannot reverse brain damage that has already been produced.

Syphilis is one bacterial brain infection you have likely heard about. Syphilis bacteria are passed from infected to noninfected individuals through contact with genital sores. The infecting bacteria then go into a dormant stage for several years before they become virulent and attack many parts of the body, including the brain. The syndrome of insanity and dementia that results from a syphilitic infection is called **general paresis.**

Syphilis has a particularly interesting history (see Klawans, 1990). The first Europeans to visit America stripped the natives of their gold and left smallpox in return. But the deal was not totally one-sided; the booty carried back to Europe by Columbus's sailors and the adventurers that followed included a cargo of syphilis bacteria. Until then, syphilis had been restricted to the Americas, but it quickly spread to the rest of the world.

Viral Infections   There are two types of viral infections of the nervous system: those that have a particular affinity for neural tissue and those that attack neural tissue but have no greater affinity for it than for other tissues.

Rabies, which is usually transmitted through the bite of a rabid animal, is a well-known example of a viral infection that has a particular affinity for the nervous system. The fits of rage caused by the virus's effects on the brain increase the probability that rabid animals that normally attack by biting (e.g, dogs, cats, raccoons, bats, and mice) will spread the disorder. Although the effects of the rabies virus on the brain are ultimately lethal, the virus does have one redeeming feature: It does not usually attack the brain for at least a month after it has been contracted, thus allowing time for a preventive vaccination.

The *mumps* and *herpes* viruses are common examples of viruses that can attack the nervous system but have no special affinity for it. Although these viruses sometimes spread into the brain, they typically attack other tissues of the body.

Viruses may play a far greater role in neuropsychological disorders than is currently thought. Their involvement in the *etiology* (cause) of disorders is often difficult to recognize because they may lie dormant for many years before producing symptoms.

Neurotoxins

The nervous system can be damaged by exposure to any one of a variety of toxic chemicals, which can enter general circulation from the gastrointestinal tract, from the lungs, or through the skin. For example, heavy metals such as mercury and lead can accumulate in the brain and permanently damage it, producing a **toxic psychosis** (chronic insanity produced by a neurotoxin). Have you ever wondered why Alice in Wonderland's Mad Hatter was a mad hatter and not a mad something else? In 18th- and 19th-century England, hatmakers were commonly driven mad by the mercury employed in the preparation of the felt used to make hats. In a similar vein, the word *crackpot* originally referred to the toxic psychosis observed in some people in England—primarily the poor—who steeped their tea in cracked ceramic pots with lead cores.

Sometimes, the very drugs used to treat neurological disorders prove to have toxic effects. For example, some of the antipsychotic drugs introduced in the early 1950s produced effects of distressing scope. By the late 1950s, millions of psychotic patients were being maintained on these new drugs. However, after several years of treatment, many of the patients developed a motor disorder termed **tardive dyskinesia (TD)**. Its primary symptoms are involuntary smacking and sucking movements of the lips, thrusting and rolling of the tongue, lateral jaw movements, and puffing of the cheeks. Safer antipsychotic drugs have since been developed.

Brain damage from the effects of recreational drugs is also a serious problem. You learned in Chapter 1 that alcohol produces brain damage through a combination of its direct neurotoxic effects and its effects on thiamine metabolism. Do you remember the case of Jimmie G.?

Some neurotoxins are *endogenous* (produced by the patient's own body). For example, the body can produce antibodies that attack particular components of the nervous system (see Newsom-Davis & Vincent, 1991).

Genetic Factors

Normal human cells have 23 pairs of chromosomes; however, sometimes accidents of cell division occur, and the fertilized egg ends up with an abnormal chromosome or with an abnormal number of normal chromosomes. Then, as the fertilized egg divides and redivides, these chromosomal anomalies are duplicated in every cell of the body.

Most neuropsychological diseases of genetic origin are caused by abnormal recessive genes that are passed from parent to offspring. (In Chapter 2, you learned about one such disorder, *phenylketonuria.*) Inherited neuropsychological disorders are rarely associated with dominant genes because dominant genes that disturb neuropsychological function tend to be eliminated from the gene pool—every individual who carries one is at a major survival and reproductive disadvantage. In contrast, individuals who inherit one abnormal recessive gene do not develop the disorder, and the gene is passed on to future generations.

There are, however, two possible situations in which neurological disorders can be associated with dominant genes. One is the case in which an abnormal dominant gene manifests itself only in rare environmental circumstances. The other is the case in which an abnormal dominant gene is not expressed until the individual is well past puberty.

Down syndrome is a genetic disorder that is caused not by a faulty gene, but by a genetic accident, which occurs in 0.15% of births. The usual cause is an accident that happens during ovulation. During ovulation an extra chromosome 21 is created in the egg; thus, when the egg is fertilized, there are three rather than two in the zygote. The consequences of the superfluous chromosome 21 are unfortunate. In addition to characteristic disfigurement—flattened skull and nose, folds of skin over the inner corners of the eyes, and short fingers (see Figure 10.7)—intellectual development is retarded, and there are often serious medical complications. The probability of giving birth to a child with Down syndrome increases with advancing maternal age (Carothers et al., 2001).

Rapid progress is being made in locating and characterizing the faulty genes that are associated with some neuropsychological disorders. Once this goal is achieved, it will open up a variety of new treatment and prevention strategies, such as splicing in healthy genes to replace faulty ones and developing specific DNA-binding proteins that can enter neurons and block the expression of faulty genes.

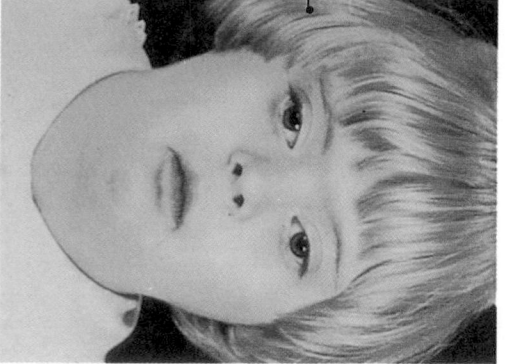

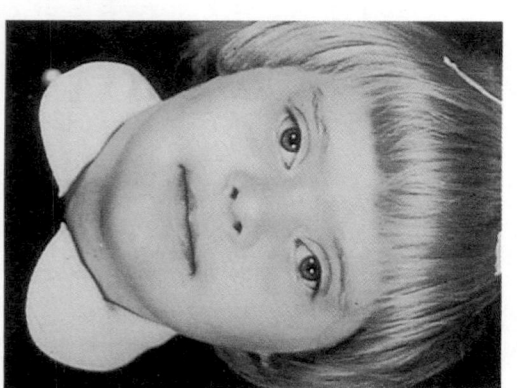

FIGURE 10.7 A child with Down syndrome before and after plastic surgery. The purpose of these photographs is not to promote cosmetic surgery but to challenge our culture's reaction to patients with Down syndrome. The little girl on the left and the little girl on the right are the same girl; they deserve the same respect and consideration. (Courtesy of Kenneth E. Salyer, Director, International Craniofacial Institute.)

You learned in Chapter 9 that neurons and other cells have genetic programs for suicide, that the death of neurons can be triggered, and that apoptosis plays a critical role in early development by eliminating some of the excessive neurons that are initially created. Apoptosis also plays a role in brain damage. Indeed, each of the six causes of brain damage that have already been discussed in this chapter (tumors, cerebrovascular disorders, closed-head injuries, infections, toxins, and genetic factors) appears to produce its effect, in part, by activating apoptotic programs of self-destruction (Allsop & Fazakerley, 2000; Dirnagl, Simon, & Hallenbeck, 2003; Nijhawan, Honarpour, & Wang, 2000).

It was once assumed that the death of neurons following brain damage was totally necrotic—*necrosis* is passive cell death resulting from injury. It now seems that if cells are not damaged too severely, they will attempt to marshal enough resources to commit suicide. However, cell death is not an either-or situation: Some damaged and dying cells display signs of both necrosis and apoptosis (see Elibol et al., 2001).

It is easy to understand why apoptotic mechanisms have evolved: Apoptosis is clearly more adaptive than necrosis. In necrosis, the damaged neuron swells and breaks apart, beginning in the axons and dendrites and ending in the cell body. This fragmentation leads to inflammation, which can damage other cells in the vicinity. Necrotic cell death is quick, it is typically complete in a few hours. In contrast, apoptotic cell death is slow, typically requiring a day or two. Apoptosis of a neuron proceeds gradually, starting with shrinkage of the cell body. Then, as parts of the neuron die, the resulting debris is packaged in vesicles. As a result, there is no inflammation, and damage to nearby cells is kept to a minimum.

Programmed Cell Death

10.2 Neuropsychological Diseases

The preceding section focused on the causes of human brain damage. This section considers five diseases that are associated with brain damage: epilepsy, Parkinson's disease, Huntington's disease, multiple sclerosis, and Alzheimer's disease.

Clinical Implications

Epilepsy

The primary symptom of **epilepsy** is the epileptic seizure, but not all persons who suffer seizures are considered to have epilepsy. It is not uncommon for an otherwise healthy person to have a seizure during temporary illness or following exposure to a convulsive agent. The label *epilepsy* is applied to only those patients whose seizures appear to be generated by their own chronic brain dysfunction. About 1% of the population are diagnosed as epileptic at some point in their lives.

In view of the fact that epilepsy is characterized by epileptic seizures—or, more accurately, by spontaneously recurring epileptic seizures—you might think that the task of diagnosing this disorder would be an easy one. But you would be wrong. The task is made difficult by the diversity and complexity of epileptic seizures. You are probably familiar with seizures that take the form of **convulsions** (motor seizures); these often involve tremors (*clonus*), rigidity (*tonus*), and loss of both balance and consciousness. But many seizures do not take this form; instead, they involve subtle changes of thought, mood, or behavior that are not easily distinguishable from normal ongoing activity.

There are many causes of epilepsy. Indeed, all of the causes of brain damage that have been described in this chapter—including viruses, neurotoxins, tumors, and blows to the head—can cause epilepsy, and over 70 different faulty genes have been linked to it (Noebels, 2003). Many cases of epilepsy appear to be associated with faults at inhibitory synapses that cause large numbers of neurons to fire in synchronous bursts (Köhling, 2002).

The diagnosis of epilepsy rests heavily on evidence from electroencephalography (EEG). The value of scalp electroencephalography in confirming suspected cases of epilepsy stems from the fact that epileptic seizures are associated with bursts of high-amplitude EEG spikes, which are often apparent in the scalp EEG during an attack (see Figure 10.8), and from the fact that individual spikes often punctuate the scalp EEGs of epileptics between attacks. (Cohen et al., 2002). Although the observation of spontaneous epileptic discharges is incontrovertible evidence of epilepsy, the failure to observe them does not always mean that the patient is not epileptic. It could mean that the patient is epileptic but did not happen to experience epileptic discharges during the test or

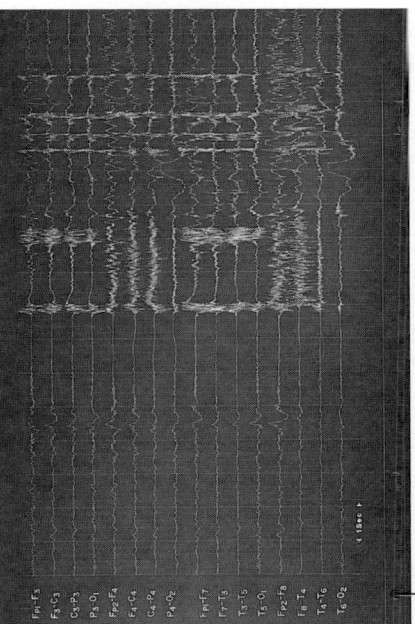

FIGURE 10.8 Cortical electroencephalogram (EEG) record from various locations on the scalp during the beginning of a complex partial seizure. The letters and numbers to the left of each trace indicate the conventional locations of the electrodes over the frontal (F), temporal (T), parietal (P), and occipital (O) lobes.

that epileptic discharges did occur during the test but were not recorded through the scalp electrodes.

Some epileptics experience peculiar psychological changes just before a convulsion. These changes, called **epileptic auras,** may take many different forms—for example, a bad smell, a specific thought, a vague feeling of familiarity, a hallucination, or a tightness of the chest. Epileptic auras are important for two reasons. First, the nature of the auras provides clues concerning the location of the epileptic focus. Second, because the epileptic auras experienced by a particular patient are often similar from attack to attack, they warn the patient of an impending convulsion.

Once an individual has been diagnosed as epileptic, it is usual to assign the epilepsy to one of two general categories—*partial epilepsy* or *generalized epilepsy*—and then to one of their respective subcategories. The various seizure types are so different from one another that epilepsy is best viewed not as a single disease but as a number of different, but related, diseases. Supporting this view is the fact that epilepsy has no single cause; almost any kind of brain disturbance can cause seizures.

Partial Seizures A **partial seizure** is a seizure that does not involve the entire brain. The epileptic neurons at a focus begin to discharge together in bursts, and it is this synchronous bursting of neurons (see Figure 10.9 on page 240) that produces epileptic spiking in the EEG. The synchronous activity may stay restricted to the focus until the seizure is over, or it may spread to other areas of the brain—but, in the case of partial seizures, not to

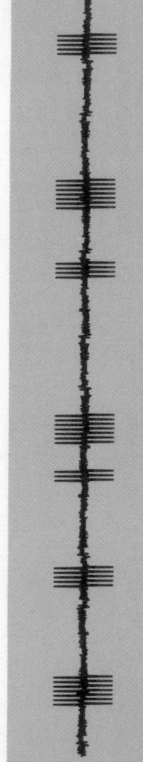

FIGURE 10.9 The bursting of an epileptic neuron, recorded by extracellular unit recording.

the entire brain. The specific behavioral symptoms of a partial epileptic seizure depend on where the disruptive discharges begin and into what structures they spread. Because partial seizures do not involve the entire brain, they are not usually accompanied by a total loss of consciousness or equilibrium.

There are two major categories of partial seizures: simple and complex. **Simple partial seizures** are partial seizures whose symptoms are primarily sensory or motor or both; they are sometimes called *Jacksonian seizures* after the famous 19th-century neurologist Hughlings Jackson. As the epileptic discharges spread through the sensory or motor areas of the brain, the symptoms spread systematically through the body.

In contrast, **complex partial seizures** are often restricted to the temporal lobes, and those who experience them are often said to have *temporal lobe epilepsy*. During a complex partial seizure, the patient engages in compulsive, repetitive, simple behaviors commonly referred to as *automatisms* (e.g., doing and undoing a button) and in more complex behaviors that appear almost normal. The diversity of complex partial seizures is illustrated by the following four cases.

The Subtlety of Complex Partial Seizures: Four Cases

Clinical Implications

A war veteran subject to many automatisms read in the newspaper about a man who had embraced a woman in a park, followed her into a women's toilet, and then boarded a bus. From the description given, he realized he was the man.

One morning a doctor left home to answer an emergency call from the hospital and returned several hours later, a trifle confused, feeling as though he had experienced a bad dream. At the hospital he had performed a difficult . . . [operation] with his usual competence, but later had done and said things deemed inappropriate.

A young man, a music teacher, when listening to a concert, walked down the aisle and onto the platform, circled the piano, jumped to the floor, did a hop, skip, and jump up the aisle, and regained his senses when part way home. He often found himself on a trolley [bus] far from his destination.

A man in an attack went to his employer and said, "I have to have more money or [I] quit." Later, to his surprise, he found that his salary had been raised. (Lennox, 1960, pp. 237–238.)

Although patients appear to be conscious throughout their complex partial seizures, they usually have little or no subsequent recollection of them. About half of all cases of epilepsy are of the complex partial variety—the temporal lobes are particularly susceptible to epileptic discharges.

Generalized Seizures

Generalized seizures involve the entire brain. Some begin as focal discharges that gradually spread through the entire brain. In other cases, the discharges seem to begin almost simultaneously in all parts of the brain. Such sudden-onset generalized seizures may result from diffuse pathology or may begin focally in a structure, such as the thalamus, that projects to many parts of the brain.

Like partial seizures, generalized seizures occur in many forms. One is the **grand mal** (literally, "big trouble") **seizure**. The primary symptoms of a grand mal seizure are loss of consciousness, loss of equilibrium, and a violent *tonic-clonic convulsion*—a convulsion involving both tonus and clonus. Tongue biting, urinary incontinence, and *cyanosis* (turning blue from excessive extraction of oxygen from the blood during the convulsion) are common manifestations of grand mal convulsions. The **hypoxia** (shortage of oxygen supply to tissue, for example, to the brain) that accompanies a grand mal seizure can itself cause brain damage, some of which develops slowly after the attack and is mediated by the excessive release of excitatory amino acid neurotransmitters.

A second major category of generalized seizure is the **petit mal** (literally, "small trouble") **seizure** (see Crunelli & Leresche, 2002). Petit mal seizures are not associated with convulsions; their primary behavioral symptom is the *petit mal absence*—a disruption of consciousness that is associated with a cessation of ongoing behavior, a vacant look, and sometimes fluttering eyelids. The EEG of a petit mal seizure is different from that of other seizures; it is a bilaterally symmetrical **3-per-second spike-and-wave discharge** (see Figure 10.10). Petit mal seizures are most common in children, and they frequently cease at puberty. They often go undiagnosed; thus, children with petit mal epilepsy are sometimes considered to be "daydreamers" by their parents and teachers.

Although there is no cure for epilepsy, the frequency and severity of seizures can often be reduced by anti-major neurotransmitter released by most neurons of the substantia nigra, there is little dopamine in the substantia nigra and striatum of long-term Parkinson's patients.

As you saw in the case of d'Orta, the symptoms of Parkinson's disease can be alleviated by injections of L-**dopa**—the chemical from which dopamine is synthesized. However, L-dopa is rarely a permanent solution; it typically becomes less and less effective with continued use, until its side effects (e.g., involuntary movements; see Bezard, Brotchie, & Gross, 2001) outweigh its benefits. This is exactly what happened to d'Orta. L-Dopa therapy gave him a 3-year respite from his disease, but ultimately it became totally ineffective. His prescription was then changed to another dopamine agonist, and again his condition improved—but again the improvement was only temporary. We will return to d'Orta's roller-coaster case later in this chapter.

About 10 different gene mutations have been linked to Parkinson's disease (see Dawson & Dawson, 2003; Le & Appel, 2004). This has led many people to believe that a cure is just around the corner. However, it is important to realize that each of these gene mutations has been discovered in a different family, each of which had members suffering from a rare form of *early-on-set* Parkinson's disease that runs in families. Thus, these mutations are unlikely to be factors in typical forms of the disease. Still, the study of the effects of these gene mutations may eventually lead to a better understanding of the physiological changes that underlie the symptoms of the disorder (see Vila, Wu, & Przedborski, 2001).

Huntington's Disease

Like Parkinson's disease, **Huntington's disease** is a progressive motor disorder of middle and old age; but, unlike Parkinson's disease, it is rare. It has a strong genetic basis, and it is associated with severe dementia.

The first motor signs of Huntington's disease are often increased fidgetiness; as the disorder develops, rapid, complex, jerky movements of entire limbs (rather than individual muscles) begin to predominate. Eventually the motor and intellectual deterioration become so severe that sufferers are incapable of feeding themselves, controlling their bowels, or recognizing their own children. There is no cure; death typically occurs about 15 years after the appearance of the first symptoms.

Huntington's disease is passed from generation to generation by a single dominant gene; thus, all of the individuals carrying the gene develop the disorder, as do about half their offspring. The Huntington's gene is readily passed from parent to child because the first symptoms of the disease do not appear until the parent is well past the peak reproductive years (at about age 40).

The abnormal dominant gene that causes Huntington's disease was identified and characterized in 1993.

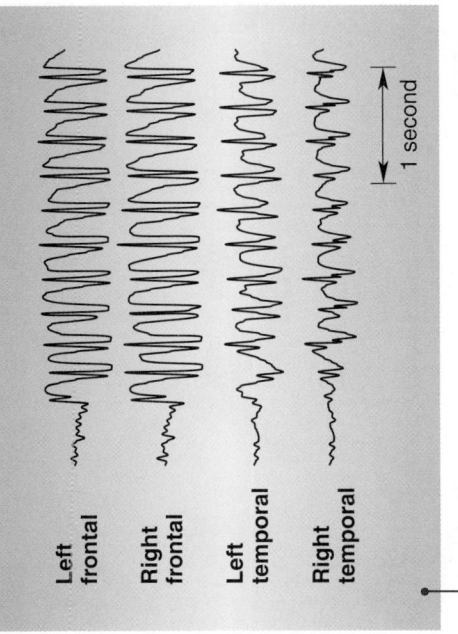

FIGURE 10.10   The bilaterally symmetrical, 3-persecond spike-and-wave EEG discharge that is associated with petit mal epileptic seizures.

Left frontal

Right frontal

Left temporal

Right temporal

1 second

convulsant medication. Brain surgery is sometimes prescribed in life-threatening situations.

Parkinson's Disease

Parkinson's disease is a movement disorder of middle and old age that affects about 0.5% of the population (see Strickland & Bertoni, 2004). It is about 2.5 times more prevalent in males than in females (see Sawada & Shimohama, 2000; Wooten et al., 2004).

The initial symptoms of Parkinson's disease are mild—perhaps no more than a slight stiffness or tremor of the fingers—but they inevitably increase in severity with advancing years. The most common symptoms of the full-blown disorder are a tremor that is pronounced during inactivity but not during voluntary movement or sleep, muscular rigidity, difficulty initiating movement, slowness of movement, and a masklike face. Pain and depression often develop before the motor symptoms become severe.

Although Parkinson's patients often display some cognitive deficits, dementia is not typically associated with the disorder. In essence, Parkinson's disease victims are thinking people trapped inside bodies they cannot control. Do you remember from Chapter 4 the case of "The Lizard"—Roberto Garcia d'Orta?

Like epilepsy, Parkinson's disease seems to have no single cause; faulty genes, brain infections, strokes, tumors, traumatic brain injury, and neurotoxins have all been implicated in specific cases (see Greenamyre & Hastings, 2004). However, in the majority of cases, no cause is obvious, and there is no family history of the disorder (see Calne et al., 1987).

Parkinson's disease is associated with degeneration of the **substantia nigra**—the midbrain nucleus whose neurons project via the **nigrostriatal pathway** to the **striatum** of the basal ganglia. Although *dopamine* is normally the

The abnormal protein produced by the Huntington's gene has also been isolated and characterized. However, the precise effect of this protein, which has been named *huntingtin*, has not yet been determined (see McMurray, 2001). Curiously, huntingtin is produced in all parts of the brains of Huntington's sufferers, yet brain damage is largely restricted to the striatum and cerebral cortex (see DiFiglia et al., 1997; Jakel & Maragos, 2000).

If one of your parents were to develop Huntington's disease, the chance would be 50/50 that you too would develop it. If you were in such a situation, would you want to know whether or not you would suffer the same fate? Medical geneticists have developed a test that can tell relatives of Huntington's patients whether they are carrying the gene (Gilliam, Gusella, & Lehrach, 1987; Martin, 1987). Some choose to take the test, and some do not. One advantage of the test is that it permits the relatives of Huntington's patients who have not inherited the gene to have children without the fear of passing on the disorder.

Clinical Implications

Shortly after the first edition of this textbook appeared in print, I received the letter reproduced on the next page. I have altered it slightly to protect the identity of its author and his family. It speaks for itself.

Multiple Sclerosis

Multiple sclerosis (MS), is a progressive disease that attacks the myelin of axons in the CNS. It is particularly disturbing because it typically attacks young people just as they are beginning their adult life. First, there are microscopic areas of degeneration on myelin sheaths; but eventually there is a breakdown of both the myelin and the associated axons, along with the development of many areas of hard scar tissue (*sclerosis* means "hardening"). Figure 10.11 illustrates degeneration in the white matter of a patient with multiple sclerosis.

Diagnosing multiple sclerosis is difficult because the nature and severity of the disorder depend on the number, size, and position of the sclerotic lesions. Furthermore, in some cases, there are lengthy periods of remission (up to 2 years), during which the patient seems almost normal; however, these are usually just oases in the progression of the disorder. Common symptoms of advanced multiple sclerosis are visual disturbances, muscular weakness, numbness, tremor, and **ataxia** (loss of motor coordination).

Epidemiological studies of multiple sclerosis have provided evidence of the environmental and genetic factors that influence its development. **Epidemiology** is the study of the various factors, such as diet, geographic location, age, sex, and race, that influence the distribution of a disease in the general population.

Evidence that environmental factors influence the development of multiple sclerosis comes from the finding that the incidence of multiple sclerosis is far greater in

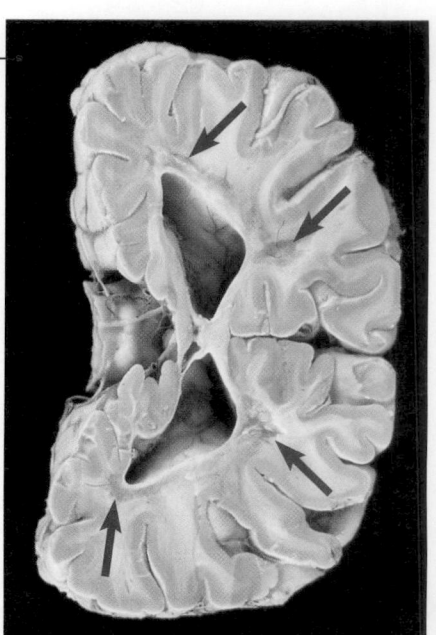

FIGURE 10.11 Areas of sclerosis (see arrows) in the white matter of a patient with MS.

people who spent their childhood in a cool climate, even if they subsequently moved to a warm climate. In contrast, evidence of genetic involvement comes from the finding that multiple sclerosis is rare among certain groups, such as Africans and Asians, even when they live in environments in which the incidence of the disease is high in other groups. The disorder occurs in 0.15% of Caucasians and is about twice as common in females (Steinman et al., 2002). Research indicates that there is a strong genetic predisposition to multiple sclerosis, with involvement of a large number of different genes, each making a small contribution (Hemmer, Archelos, & Hartung, 2002).

Multiple sclerosis is an *autoimmune disorder*—a disorder in which the body's immune system attacks part of the body, as if it were a foreign substance. In multiple sclerosis, myelin is the focus of the faulty immune reaction. Indeed, an animal model of multiple sclerosis, termed **experimental autoimmune encephalomyelitis**, can be induced by injecting laboratory animals with myelin and a preparation that stimulates the immune system. One of the puzzles of multiple sclerosis is that the healing response of *remyelination*, which occurs in animal models and in the early stages of most human cases, eventually fails (Franklin, 2002).

There are a number of drugs that retard the progression of multiple sclerosis or block some of its symptoms. However, there is no cure.

Alzheimer's Disease

Alzheimer's disease is the most common cause of *dementia*. It sometimes appears in individuals as young as 40, but the likelihood of its development becomes greater with advancing years. About 10% of the general population over the age of 65 suffer from the disease, and the proportion is about 35% in those over 85 (St. George-Hyslop, 2000).

Alzheimer's disease is progressive. Its early stages are often characterized by a selective decline in memory; its

Mr. Walter S. Miller
1500 N. Severn-Langdon Rd.
Manchester, Connecticut 22022
Z9/900-854
August 5, 1991

Dr. John P. J. Pinel
Department of Psychology
University of British Columbia
Vancouver, B. C. Canada V6T., 1Y7.

Dear Dr. Pinel:

I am worried about my children and their future. In fact, I am worried sick. After reading your book I feel that you are my friend and I have nowhere else to turn.

My wife came down with Huntington's disease 7 years ago, and today she can't walk or take care of herself. I have three young children. Where can I take them to see if they have inherited my wife's infected cells? I am presently incarcerated, and could take my psychological pain. I look to be released soon, and get answers. my wife and kids just about any where to find help and get any

Any kind of advice that you could give us would be greatly appreciated by me and my family. I wish to thank you for any assistance that you can give.

God bless you and give you and yours His love and peace! I remain with warmest personal regards.

Very truly yours,

Walter S. Miller

Walter S. Miller

WSM:

THE UNIVERSITY OF BRITISH COLUMBIA

Department of Psychology
2136 West Mall
Vancouver, B. C. Canada V6T 1Z4
Tel: (604) 822–2755
Fax: (604) 822–6923

November 25, 1991

Mr. Walter S. Miller
1500 N. Severn-Langdon Road
Manchester, Connecticut 22022
U.S.A.

Dear Mr. Miller:

I was saddened to learn of your unhappy state of affairs. In requesting my advice, I hope that you understand that I am a scientist, not a physician. In any case, the following, is my assessment.

If your wife does in fact have Huntington's disease and not some other neurological disorder, each of your children has a 50/50 chance of developing Huntington's disease in adulthood. I am sure that you are aware that there is currently no cure.

I advise you to seek the advice of a local neurologist, who can explain your options to you and provide you with the advice and support that you sorely need. You must decide whether or not to subject your children to the tests that are required to determine whether or not they are carrying the Huntington's gene. One option would be to wait for your children to reach legal age and then allow them to make the decision for themselves. Some people whose parents develop Huntington's disease decide to take the test; others decide not to. In either case, it is extremely important for them not to risk passing on the Huntington's gene to future generations.

I am sorry that I cannot provide you with a more optimistic assessment, but your children's situation is too serious for me to be less than totally frank. Again, please consult a neurologist as soon as possible.

Do not lose hope. There is a chance (1/8) that none of your children is carrying the Huntington's gene. I wish you, your wife, and your children good fortune.

Cordially,

John P. J. Pinel
Professor

intermediate stages are marked by confusion, irritability, anxiety, and deterioration of speech; and in its advanced stages, the patient deteriorates to the point that even simple responses such as swallowing and controlling the bladder are difficult. Alzheimer's disease is terminal.

Because Alzheimer's disease is not the only cause of dementia, it cannot be diagnosed with certainty on the basis of its behavioral symptoms—definitive diagnosis of Alzheimer's disease must await autopsy. The two defining characteristics of the disease are neurofibrillary tangles and amyloid plaques. *Neurofibrillary tangles* are threadlike tangles of protein in the neural cytoplasm, and *amyloid plaques* are clumps of scar tissue composed of degenerating neurons and a protein called **amyloid**, which is present in normal brains in only very small amounts. In addition, there is substantial neuron loss. The presence of amyloid plaques in the brain of a patient who died of Alzheimer's disease is illustrated in Figure 10.12.

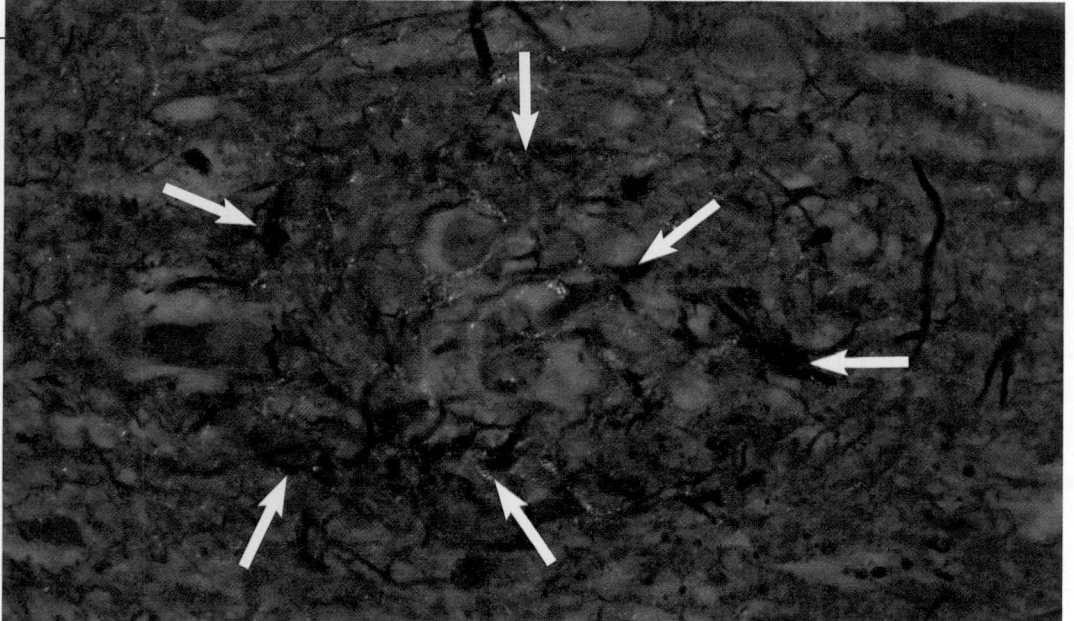

FIGURE 10.12   Amyloid plaques (see arrows) in the brain of a patient with Alzheimer's disease.

Although neurofibrillary tangles, amyloid plaques, and neuron loss tend to occur throughout the brains of Alzheimer's patients, they are more prevalent in some areas than in others. For example, they are particularly prevalent in medial temporal lobe structures such as the *entorhinal cortex, amygdala,* and *hippocampus*—all structures that are involved in various aspects of memory (see Collie & Maruff, 2000; Selkoe, 2002). They are also prevalent in the inferior temporal cortex, posterior parietal cortex, and prefrontal cortex—all areas that mediate complex cognitive functions. (See Figure 10.13.)

There is a difficulty in studying the genetics of Alzheimer's disease: Its carriers often die of natural causes before their Alzheimer's symptoms can be manifested. Nevertheless, it is clear that Alzheimer's disease has a major genetic component. People with an Alzheimer's victim in their immediate family have a 50% chance of being stricken by the disease if they survive into their 80s (Breitner, 1990).

Much of the research on the genetics of Alzheimer's disease has focused on rare early-onset *familial* forms of the disease. Several gene mutations have been found to be associated with early-onset Alzheimer's disease, and all of them have been implicated in the synthesis of amyloid or *tau,* a protein found in neurofibrillary tangles (see St. George-Hyslop, 2000).

The massive research effort currently aimed at developing a cure for Alzheimer's disease is fueled by a combination of two factors. One is the severity of the problem. The other is that a major advance seems feasible—because Alzheimer's is a disease of old age, the number of cases could be halved by a treatment that would slow its development by even 5 years.

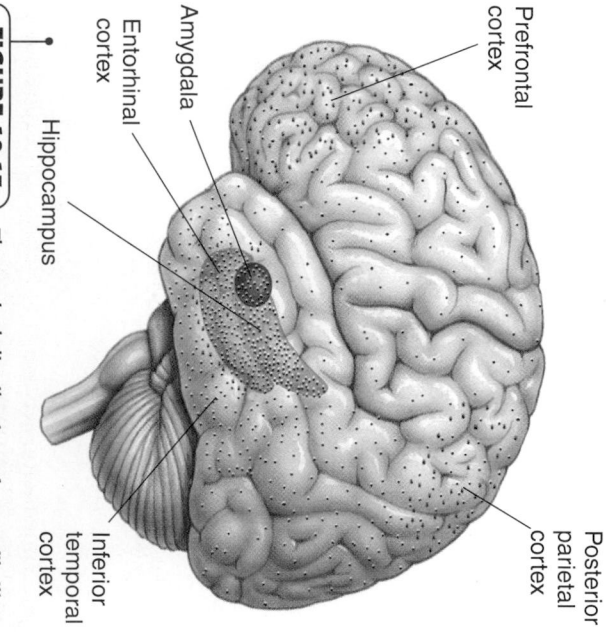

Prefrontal cortex

Amygdala

Entorhinal cortex

Hippocampus

Posterior parietal cortex

Inferior temporal cortex

FIGURE 10.13   The typical distribution of neurofibrillary tangles and amyloid plaques in the brains of patients with advanced Alzheimer's disease. (Based on Goedert, 1993, and Selkoe, 1991.)

SCAN YOUR BRAIN

This is a good place for you to pause to scan your brain. Are you ready to progress to the following section, which discusses animal models of some of the disorders that you have just learned about? Fill in the following blanks. The correct answers are provided at the bottom of this page. Before proceeding, review material related to your errors and omissions.

1. The two major categories of epileptic seizures are _____ and _____.

2. _____ are simple repetitive responses that occur during complex partial seizures.

3. The disorder characterized by tremor at rest is _____ disease.

4. Parkinson's disease is associated with degeneration in the _____ dopamine pathway.

5. _____ disease is passed from generation to generation by a single dominant gene.

6. Genetic studies of Parkinson's disease and Alzheimer's disease have focused on early-onset _____ forms of the disorder.

7. Experimental autoimmune encephalomyelitis is an animal model of _____.

8. The most common cause of dementia is _____ disease.

9. Two major neuropathological symptoms of Alzheimer's disease are _____ tangles and _____ plaques.

One factor complicating the search for a treatment or cure for Alzheimer's disease is that it is still not clear which symptom is primary (see Lee, 2001; Mudher & Lovestone, 2002). This is a key issue because an effective treatment is most likely to be developed only by research focusing on the primary symptom. The most popular candidate is the amyloid plaques; the *amyloid hypothesis* holds that the development of these plaques is the primary symptom of the disorder, which causes all other symptoms (see Hardy & Selkoe, 2002). However, others believe that the development of tau and neurofibrillary tangles is the primary symptom, and still others support other contenders—for example, a disruption of calcium regulation—for this role (see LaFerla, 2002).

The first efforts to develop treatments for Alzheimer's disease focused on the fact that declines in ace-tylcholine levels were among the earliest neurochemical changes appearing in patients. Cholinergic agonists are still sometimes prescribed, but, except for a few minor benefits early in the disorder, they have proven ineffective. Several other treatment approaches are currently under development (see Hardy & Selkoe, 2002). Arguably, the most promising of these is the *immunotherapeutic approach* (see Ingram, 2001; Schenk, 2002). This approach has used an amyloid vaccine to reduce plaque deposits and improve performance on memory tasks in a transgenic mouse model of Alzheimer's disease (which we'll discuss further in the next section). Human trials have been mixed: Therapeutic effects have been observed, but dangerous inflammation occurred in the CNSs of 5% of the patients (see Monsonego & Weiner, 2003).

10.3 Animal Models of Human Neuropsychological Diseases

The first two sections of this chapter focused on neuropsychological diseases and their causes, but they also provided some glimpses into the ways in which researchers have attempted to solve the many puzzles of neurological dysfunction. This section focuses on one of these ways: the experimental investigation of animal models. Because the experimentation necessary to identify the neuropathological basis of human neuropsychological diseases is seldom possible on the patients themselves, animal models of the diseases play an important role in such investigation (see Cenci, Whishaw, & Schallert, 2002).

It is important to appreciate that even the best animal models of neuropsychological diseases display only some of the features of the diseases they are modeling (see Maries et al., 2003). Consequently, animal models must be employed with caution. Studying an animal model is

Scan Your Brain answers: (1) partial and generalized, in either order, (2) Automatisms, (3) Parkinson's, (4) nigrostriatal, (5) Huntington's, (6) familial, (7) multiple sclerosis, (8) Alzheimer's, (9) neurofibrillary and amyloid.

like exploring a section of an unknown maze. One enters an unfamiliar section with little more than a hope that its exploration will prove fruitful, and it is only after each of its arms has been carefully explored that it is possible to know whether the decision to enter the section was wise. In the same way, it is not possible to evaluate animal models of neuropsychological dysfunction that are currently under investigation until each has been thoroughly explored. Surely, only a few animal models will lead toward the goals of understanding and prevention, but only time and effort can tell which ones these are.

This section of the chapter discusses three animal models that are currently the focus of intensive investigation: the kindling model of epilepsy, the transgenic mouse model of Alzheimer's disease, and the MPTP model of Parkinson's disease.

Kindling Model of Epilepsy

In 1969, Goddard, McIntyre, and Leech delivered one mild electrical stimulation per day to rats through implanted amygdalar electrodes. There was no behavioral response to the first few stimulations, but soon each stimulation began to elicit a convulsive response. The first convulsions were mild, involving only a slight tremor of the face. However, with each subsequent stimulation, the elicited convulsions became more generalized, until each convulsion involved the entire body. The progressive development and intensification of convulsions elicited by a series of periodic brain stimulations became known as the **kindling phenomenon.**

Although kindling is most frequently studied in rats subjected to repeated amygdalar stimulation, it is a remarkably general phenomenon. For example, kindling has been reported in mice (Leech & McIntyre, 1976), rabbits (Tanaka, 1972), cats (Adamec, 1990), dogs (Wauquier, Ashton, & Melis, 1979), and various primates (Wada, 1990a). Moreover, kindling can be produced by the repeated stimulation of many brain sites other than the amygdala, and it can be produced by the repeated application of initially subconvulsive doses of convulsive chemicals (Cain, 1986; Mori & Wada, 1990; Post et al., 1990).

There are many interesting features of kindling (see Racine & Burnham, 1984; Wada, 1990b), but two warrant emphasis. The first is that the neural changes underlying kindling are permanent. A subject that has been kindled and then left unstimulated for several months still responds to each low-intensity stimulation with a generalized convulsion (Goddard, McIntyre, & Leech, 1969; Wada & Sato, 1974). The second is that kindling is produced by distributed, as opposed to massed, stimulations. If the intervals between successive stimulations are shorter than an hour or two, it usually requires many more stimulations to kindle a subject; and under normal circumstances, no kindling at all occurs at intervals of less than about 20 minutes (Racine et al., 1973).

Much of the interest in kindling stems from the fact that it models epilepsy in two ways. First, the convulsions elicited in kindled animals are similar in many respects to those observed in some types of human epilepsy. Second, the kindling phenomenon itself is comparable to the **epileptogenesis** (the development, or genesis, of epilepsy) that can follow a head injury: Some individuals who at first appear to have escaped serious injury after a blow to the head begin to experience convulsions a few weeks later, and these convulsions sometimes begin to recur more and more frequently and with greater and greater intensity.

It must be stressed that the kindling model as it is applied in most laboratories is different from epilepsy in one important respect. You will recall from earlier in this chapter that epilepsy is a disease in which epileptic attacks recur spontaneously; in contrast, kindled convulsions are elicited. However, a model that overcomes this shortcoming has been developed in several species. If subjects are kindled for a very long time—about 300 stimulations in rats—a syndrome can be induced that is truly epileptic, in the sense that the subjects begin to display spontaneous seizures and continue to display them even after the regimen of stimulation is curtailed (e.g., Pinel, 1981; Shouse et al., 1990; Wada, Sato, & Corcoran, 1974).

One interesting and potentially important development in the study of kindling is that some researchers have started to focus on *interictal behavior* (behavior that occurs in epileptics between their seizures). For some human epileptics, particularly those who suffer from complex partial seizures, pathological changes in interictal behavior are more distressing and more difficult to treat than the seizures themselves (Leung, Ma, & McLachlan, 2000). Several studies of kindling have shown that kindled subjects display a variety of changes in interictal emotional behavior that are similar to those observed in human epileptics (Kalynchuk, 2000; Wintink et al., 2003).

Transgenic Mouse Model of Alzheimer's Disease

Perhaps the most exciting development in the study of Alzheimer's disease has been the transgenic model of the disorder. **Transgenic** refers to animals into which the genes of another species have been introduced (see Carter et al., 1999).

One difficulty in studying Alzheimer's disease is that only humans and a few related primates develop amyloid plaques, considered by many to be the primary symptom of the disorder. As a result, experimental studies of Alzheimer's disease have been difficult to conduct, and fundamental questions of causation have been difficult to address. For example, the causal role of amyloid plaques in Alzheimer's disease has not yet been sorted out: Some investigators believe that amyloid deposition triggers neuron degeneration, thereby causing the

or **MPTP**. . . . There has been no sign of remission, and most are becoming increasingly severe management problems. (Langston, 1985, p. 79)

Researchers immediately turned the misfortune of these few to the advantage of many by developing a much-needed animal model of Parkinson's disease (Langston, 1986). It was quickly established that nonhuman primates respond like humans to MPTP. The brains of primates exposed to MPTP have cell loss in the substantia nigra similar to that observed in the brains of Parkinson's patients. Considering that the substantia nigra is the major source of the brain's dopamine, it is not surprising that the level of dopamine is greatly reduced in both the MPTP model and in the naturally occurring disorder. However, it is curious that in a few monkeys MPTP produces a major depletion of dopamine without producing any gross motor symptoms (Taylor et al., 1990).

The MPTP animal model has already benefitted patients with Parkinson's disease. For example, it was discovered that **deprenyl**, a monoamine agonist, blocks the effects of MPTP in an animal model, and it was subsequently shown that deprenyl administered to early Parkinson's patients retards the progression of the disease (Tetrud & Langston, 1989)—see Figure 10.14

Several transgenic mouse models of Parkinson's disease have been developed. However, the MPTP model is still regarded as the best (Beal, 2001).

behavioral symptoms; others believe that the amyloid plaques are the result, not the cause, of the neural degeneration (Neve & Robakis, 1998). This lack of progress in answering fundamental causal questions about Alzheimer's disease is why the development of the transgenic mouse model of the disorder is such an important contribution.

There are several forms of the transgenic mouse model. In one (Hsiao et al., 1996), genes that accelerate the synthesis of human amyloid are injected into newly fertilized mouse eggs, which are then injected into a foster mother to develop. When the transgenic mice mature, their brains contain many amyloid plaques like those of human Alzheimer's patients. Moreover, the distribution of the amyloid plaques is comparable to that observed in human Alzheimer's patients, with the highest concentrations occurring in structures of the medial temporal lobes (e.g., hippocampus, amygdala, and entorhinal cortex).

Although the transgenic mice of Hsiao and her colleagues arguably provide the best animal model of Alzheimer's disease, the model is not without its problems. For example, the mice show no neurofibrillary tangles, and the degree of memory impairment changes little as the mice mature and develop more plaques. However, an animal model does not have to mimic the human disorder in every respect to be useful. As you learned in the preceding section, the transgenic mouse model of Alzheimer's disease has been used to develop an amyloid vaccine that is being tested on human patients.

MPTP Model of Parkinson's Disease

The preeminent animal model of Parkinson's disease grew out of an unfortunate accident, which resulted in the following anomalous cases of Parkinson's disease.

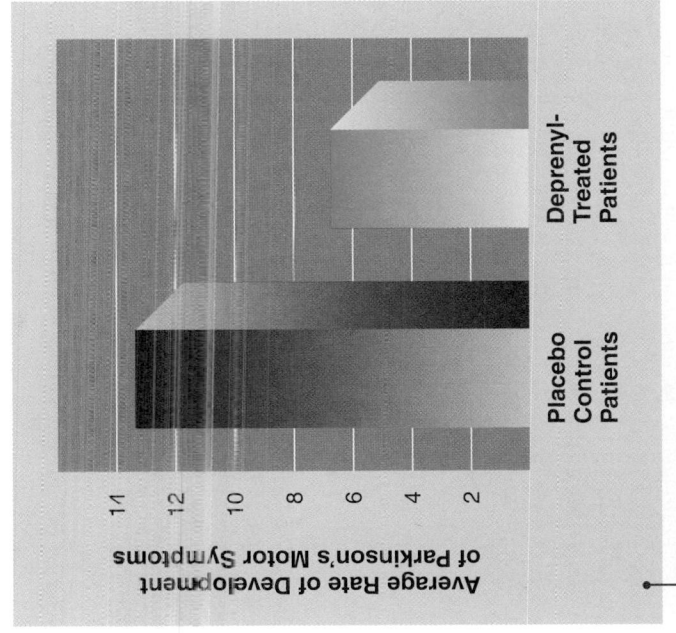

FIGURE 10.14 Average rate of motor symptom development in early Parkinson's patients treated with deprenyl (a monoamine oxidase inhibitor) or with a placebo. Deprenyl slowed the progression of the disease by 50%. (Based on Tetrud and Langston, 1989.)

The Case of the Frozen Addicts

Clinical Implications

Parkinson's disease . . . rarely occurs before the age of 50. It was somewhat of a surprise then to see a group of young drug addicts at our hospital in 1982 who had developed symptoms of severe and what proved to be irreversible parkinsonism. The only link between these patients was the recent use of a new "synthetic heroin." They exhibited virtually all of the typical motor features of Parkinson's disease, including the classic triad of bradykinesia (slowness of movement), tremor and rigidity of their muscles. Even the subtle features, such as seborrhea (oiliness of the skin) and micrographia (small handwriting), that are typical of Parkinson's disease were present. After tracking down samples of this substance, the offending agent was tentatively identified as 1-methyl-4-phenyl-1,2,3,6-tetrahydropyridine

Damage to the nervous system may trigger four neuroplastic responses: degeneration, regeneration, reorganization, and recovery of function. Each of these four responses is discussed in this section.

Neural Degeneration

A widely used method for the controlled study of the responses of neurons to damage is to cut their axons. Two kinds of neural degeneration (deterioration) ensue: anterograde degeneration and retrograde degeneration (see Coleman & Perry, 2002; Raff, Whitmore, & Finn, 2002). **Anterograde degeneration** is the degeneration of the **distal segment**—the segment of a cut axon between the cut and the synaptic terminals. **Retrograde degeneration** is the degeneration of the **proximal segment**—the segment of a cut axon between the cut and the cell body.

Anterograde degeneration occurs quickly following *axotomy*, because the cut separates the distal segment of the axon from the cell body, which is the metabolic center of the neuron. The entire distal segment becomes badly swollen within a few hours, and it breaks into fragments within a few days.

The course of retrograde degeneration is different; it progresses gradually back from the cut to the cell body. In about 2 or 3 days, major changes become apparent in the cell bodies of most axotomized neurons. These early cell body changes are either degenerative or regenerative in nature. Early degenerative changes to the cell body (e.g., a decrease in size) suggest that the neuron will ultimately die—usually by apoptosis but sometimes by necrosis or a combination of both (Syntichaki & Tavernarakis, 2003). Early regenerative changes (e.g., an increase in size) indicate that the cell body is involved in a massive synthesis of the proteins that will be used to replace the degenerated axon. But early regenerative changes in the cell body do not guarantee the long-term survival of the neuron; if the regenerating axon does not manage to make synaptic contact with an appropriate target, the neuron eventually dies.

Sometimes, degeneration spreads from damaged neurons to neurons that are linked to them by synapses; this is called **transneuronal degeneration**. In some cases, transneuronal degeneration spreads from damaged neurons to the neurons on which they synapse; this is called *anterograde transneuronal degeneration*. And in some cases, it spreads from damaged neurons to the neurons that synapse on them; this is called *retrograde transneuronal degeneration*. Neural and transneuronal degeneration are illustrated in Figure 10.15.

Neural Regeneration

Neural regeneration—the regrowth of damaged neurons—does not proceed as successfully in mammals and other higher vertebrates as it does in most invertebrates and lower vertebrates. The capacity for accurate axonal growth, which is possessed by higher vertebrates during their original development, is lost once they reach maturity. Regeneration is virtually nonexistent in the CNS of adult mammals, and is at best a hit-or-miss affair in the PNS.

In the mammalian PNS, regrowth from the proximal stump of a damaged nerve usually begins 2 or 3 days after axonal damage. What happens next depends on the nature of the injury (see Tonge & Golding, 1993); there are three possibilities. First, if the original Schwann cell myelin sheaths remain intact, the regenerating peripheral axons grow through them to their original targets at a rate of a few millimeters per day. Second, if the peripheral nerve is severed and the cut ends become separated by a few millimeters, regenerating axon tips often grow into incorrect sheaths and are guided by them to incorrect destinations; that is why it is often difficult to regain the coordinated use of a limb affected by nerve damage even if there has been substantial regeneration. And third, if the cut ends of a severed mammalian peripheral nerve become widely separated or if a lengthy section of the nerve is damaged, there may be no meaningful regeneration at all; regenerating axon tips grow in a tangled mass around the proximal stump, and the neurons ultimately die. These three patterns of mammalian peripheral nerve regeneration are illustrated in Figure 10.16 on page 250.

Why do mammalian PNS neurons regenerate, and mammalian CNS neurons do not? The obvious answer is that PNS neurons are inherently capable of regeneration while CNS neurons are not, but this answer has proved to be incorrect. CNS neurons are capable of regeneration if they are transplanted to the PNS, whereas PNS neurons are not capable of regeneration if they are transplanted to the CNS. Clearly, there is something about the environment of the PNS that promotes regeneration and something about the environment of the CNS that does not (Goldberg & Barres, 2000). Schwann cells are the key.

Schwann cells, which myelinate PNS axons, promote regeneration in the mammalian PNS by producing both neurotrophic factors and cell-adhesion molecules (CAMs). The neurotrophic factors released by Schwann cells stimulate the growth of new axons, and the cell-adhesion molecules on the cell membranes of Schwann cells provide the paths along which regenerating PNS

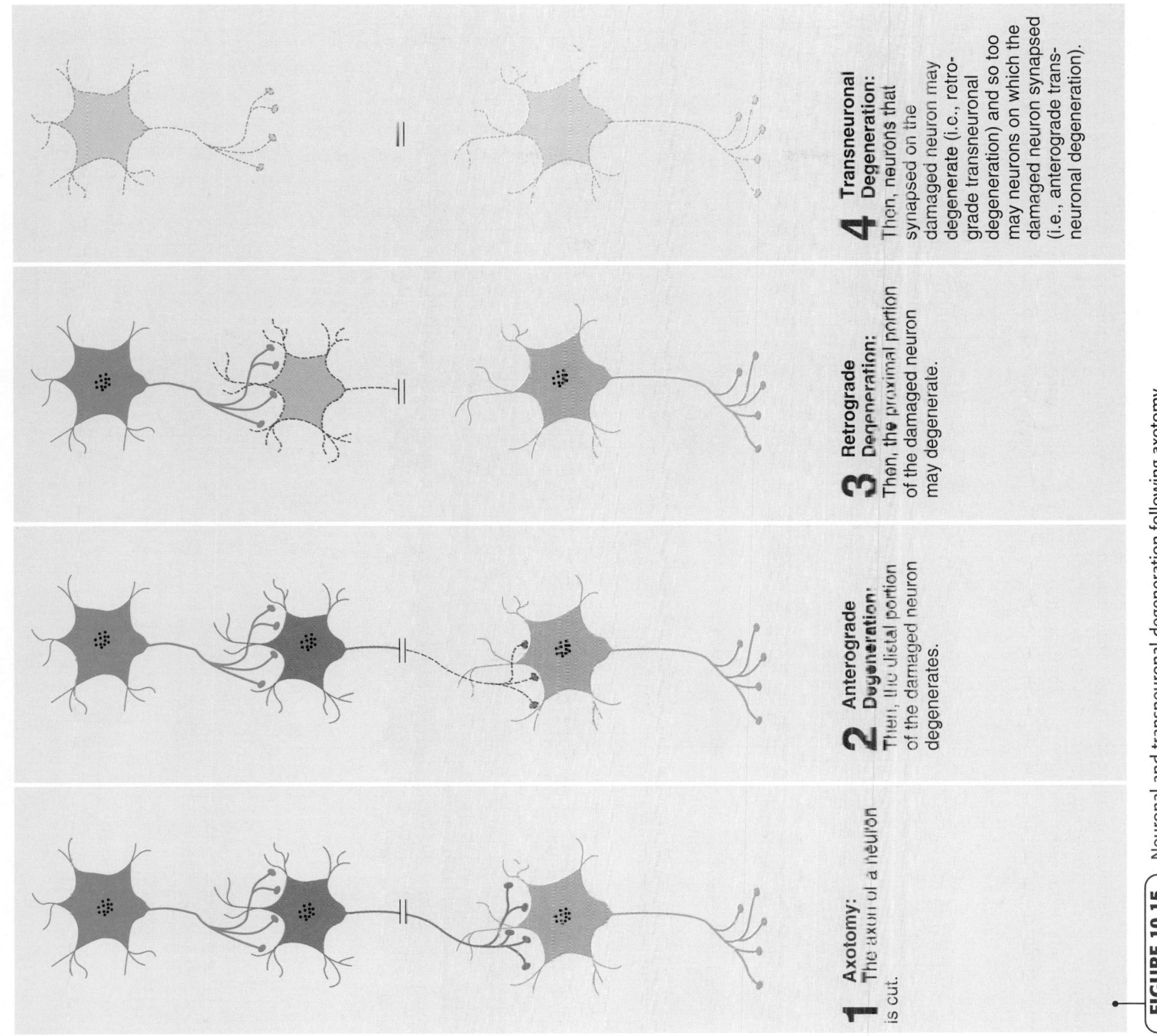

1 Axotomy: The axon of a neuron is cut.

2 Anterograde Degeneration: Then, the distal portion of the damaged neuron degenerates.

3 Retrograde Degeneration: Then, the proximal portion of the damaged neuron may degenerate.

4 Transneuronal Degeneration: Then, neurons that synapsed on the damaged neuron may degenerate (i.e., retrograde transneuronal degeneration) and so too may neurons on which the damaged neuron synapsed (i.e., anterograde transneuronal degeneration).

FIGURE 10.15 Neuronal and transneuronal degeneration following axotomy.

axons grow. In contrast, **oligodendroglia,** which myelinate CNS axons, do not stimulate or guide regeneration; indeed, they release factors that actively block regeneration (Filbin, 2003; Fournier & Strittmatter, 2001).

In contrast to neural regeneration in mammals, that in lower vertebrates is extremely accurate. It is accurate

in both the CNS and the PNS, and it is accurate even when the regenerating axons do not grow into remnant Schwann cell myelin sheaths. The accuracy of regeneration in lower vertebrates offers hope of a medical breakthrough: If the factors that promote accurate regeneration

Evolutionary Perspective

FIGURE 10.16   Three patterns of axonal regeneration in mammalian peripheral nerves.

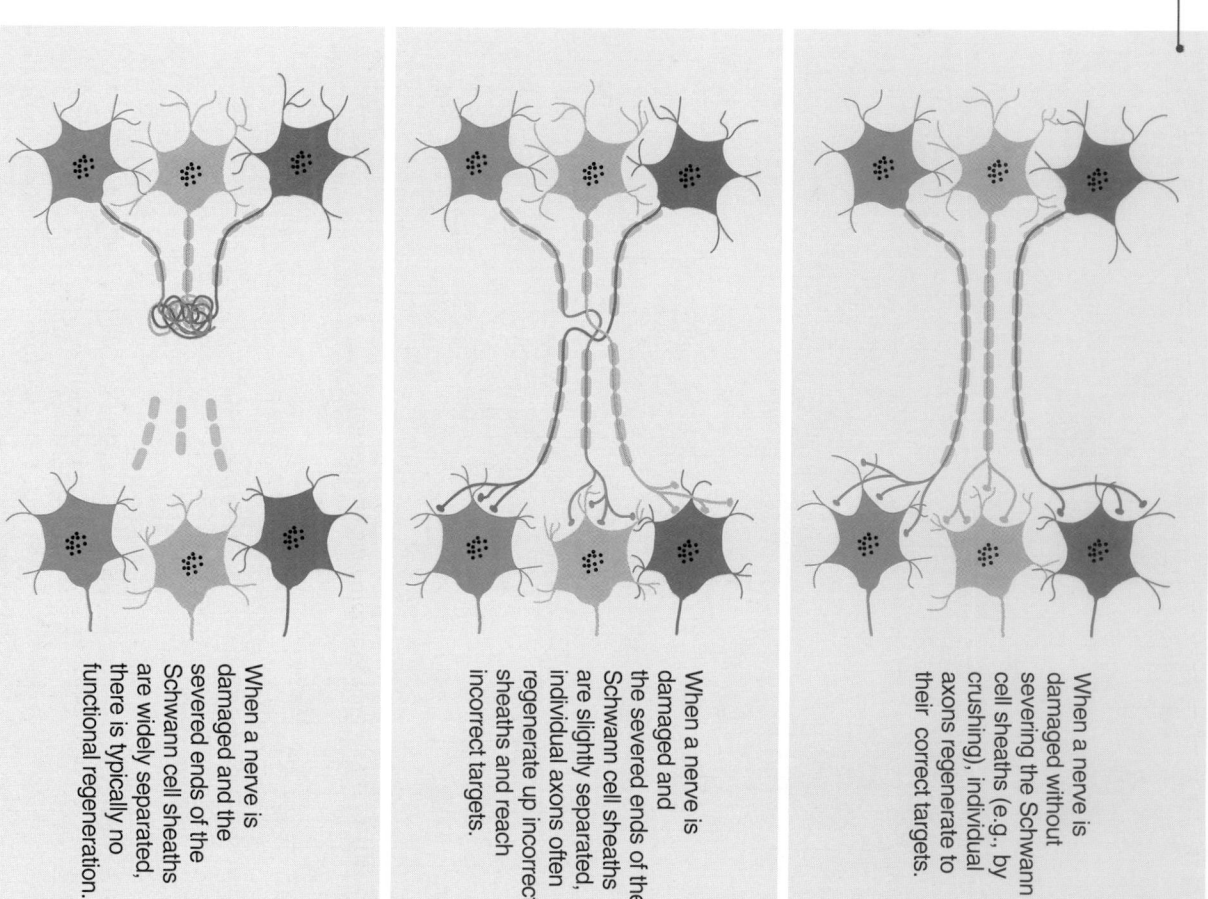

When a nerve is damaged without severing the Schwann cell sheaths (e.g., by crushing), individual axons regenerate to their correct targets.

When a nerve is damaged and the severed ends of the Schwann cell sheaths are slightly separated, individual axons often regenerate up incorrect sheaths and reach incorrect targets.

When a nerve is damaged and the severed ends of the Schwann cell sheaths are widely separated, there is typically no functional regeneration.

in lower vertebrates can be identified and applied to the human brain, it might be possible to cure currently untreatable brain injuries.

When an axon degenerates, axon branches grow out from adjacent healthy axons and synapse at the sites vacated by the degenerating axon; this is called **collateral sprouting.** Collateral sprouts may grow out from the axon terminal branches or the nodes of Ranvier on adjacent neurons. Collateral sprouting is illustrated in Figure 10.17.

Neural Reorganization

It has long been assumed that major changes in mammalian nervous systems were limited to the period of early development: Adult mammalian nervous systems were

thought to be limited to the subtle functional changes that mediate learning and memory. However, as you learned in Chapter 9, it was recently discovered that adult mammalian brains retain the ability to reorganize themselves in response to experience. They also retain the ability to reorganize themselves in response to damage.

Examples of Cortical Reorganization Following Nervous System Damage   Most studies of neural reorganization following damage have focused on adult sensory and motor systems (see Donoghue, 1995; Wall, Xu, & Wang, 2002). Sensory and motor systems are ideally suited to the study of neural reorganization because of their topographic layout. The damage-induced reorganization of the primary sensory and motor systems has been studied in two fundamentally different condi-

Working with rats, Sanes, Suner, and Donoghue (1990) transected the motor neurons that controlled the muscles of the rats' *vibrissae* (whiskers). A few weeks later, stimulation of the area of motor cortex that had previously elicited vibrissae movement now activated other muscles of the face. This result is illustrated in Figure 10.18.

Mechanisms of Neural Reorganization   Two kinds of mechanisms have been proposed to account for the reorganization of neural circuits: a strengthening of existing connections, possibly through release from inhibition, and the establishment of new connections by collateral sprouting (see O'Leary, Ruff, & Dyck, 1994). Support for the first mechanism comes from two observations: Reorganization often occurs too quickly to be explained by neural growth, and rapid reorganization never involves changes of more than 2 millimeters of cortical surface. Support for

tions: following damage to peripheral nerves and following damage to the primary cortical areas (Buonomano & Merzenich, 1998). Let's consider some studies that illustrate these two approaches.

Kaas and colleagues (1990) assessed the effect of making a small lesion in one retina and removing the other. Several months after the retinal lesions were made, primary visual cortex neurons that originally had receptive fields in the lesioned area of the retina were found to have receptive fields in the area of the retina next to the lesion; remarkably, this change began within minutes of the lesion (Gilbert & Wiesel, 1992).

Pons and colleagues (1991) mapped the primary somatosensory cortex of monkeys whose contralateral arm sensory neurons had been cut 10 years before. They found that the cortical face representation had systematically expanded into the original arm area. This study created a stir because the scale of the reorganization was far greater than had been assumed to be possible: The primary somatosensory cortex face area had expanded its border by well over a centimeter, likely as a consequence of the particularly long (10-year) interval between surgery and testing.

Jenkins and Merzenich (1987) removed the area of monkey somatosensory cortex that responded to touches of the palm of the contralateral hand. Several weeks later, they found that neurons adjacent to the lesion now responded to touches of the palm.

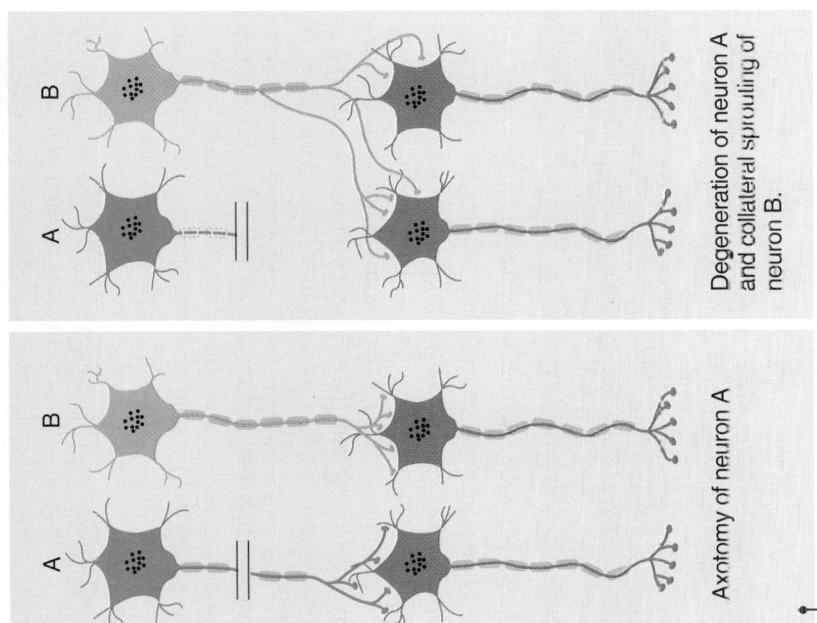

FIGURE 10.17   Collateral sprouting after neural degeneration.

A   B

Anatomy of neuron A

A   B

Degeneration of neuron A and collateral sprouting of neuron B.

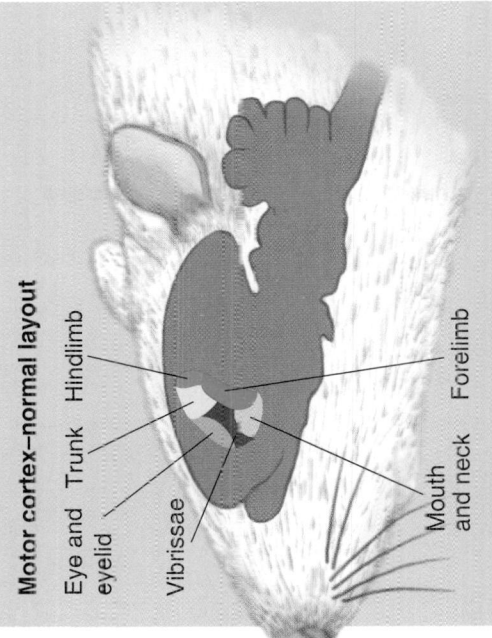

Motor cortex–normal layout

Eye and eyelid
Vibrissae
Trunk
Hindlimb
Forelimb
Mouth and neck

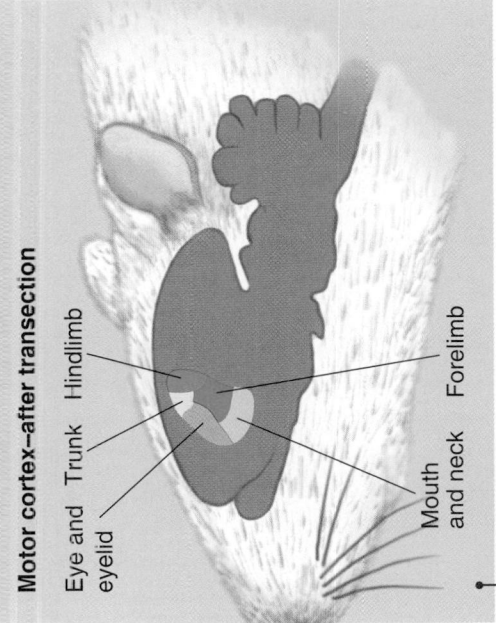

Motor cortex–after transection

Eye and eyelid
Trunk
Hindlimb
Forelimb
Mouth and neck

FIGURE 10.18   Reorganization of the rat motor cortex following transection of the motor neurons that control movements of the vibrissae. The motor cortex was mapped by brain stimulation before transection and then again a few weeks after. (Adapted from Sanes, Suner, & Donoghue, 1990.)

the second mechanism comes from the observation that the magnitude of long-term reorganization can be too great to be explained by changes in existing connections. Figure 10.19 illustrates how these two mechanisms might account for the reorganization that occurs after damage to a peripheral somatosensory nerve.

Recovery of Function after Brain Damage

Understanding the mechanisms that underlie the recovery of function after nervous system damage is a high priority for neuroscientists. If these mechanisms were understood, steps could be taken to promote recovery. However, recovery of function after nervous system damage is a poorly understood phenomenon.

Little is known about recovery of function after nervous system damage for two reasons. The first is that it is difficult to conduct controlled experiments on populations of brain-damaged patients. The second is that nervous system damage may result in a variety of compensatory changes that can easily be confused with true recovery of function. For example, any improvement in the week or two after damage could reflect a decline in *cerebral edema* (brain swelling) rather than a recovery from the neural damage itself, and any gradual improvement in the months after damage could reflect the learning of new cognitive and behavioral strategies (i.e., substitution of functions) rather than the return of lost functions (see Wilson, 1998). Consequently, true recovery of function is less common than most believe (see

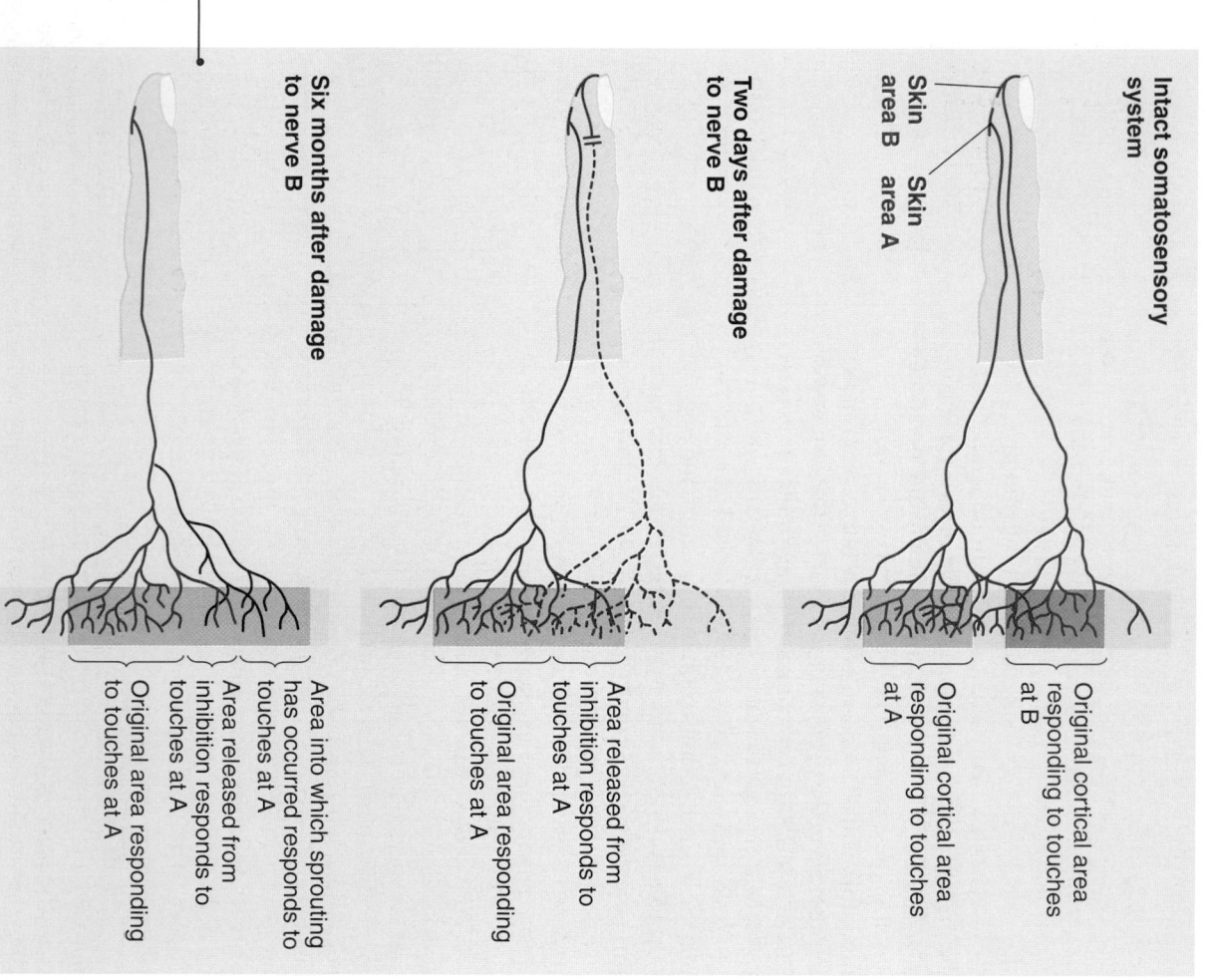

Intact somatosensory system

Skin area B   Skin area A

Original cortical area responding to touches at B

Original cortical area responding to touches at A

Two days after damage to nerve B

Area released from inhibition responds to touches at A

Original area responding to touches at A

Six months after damage to nerve B

Area into which sprouting has occurred responds to touches at A

Area released from inhibition responds to touches at A

Original area responding to touches at A

FIGURE 10.19 The two-stage model of neural reorganization: (1) strengthening of existing connections through release from inhibition and (2) establishment of new connections by collateral sprouting.

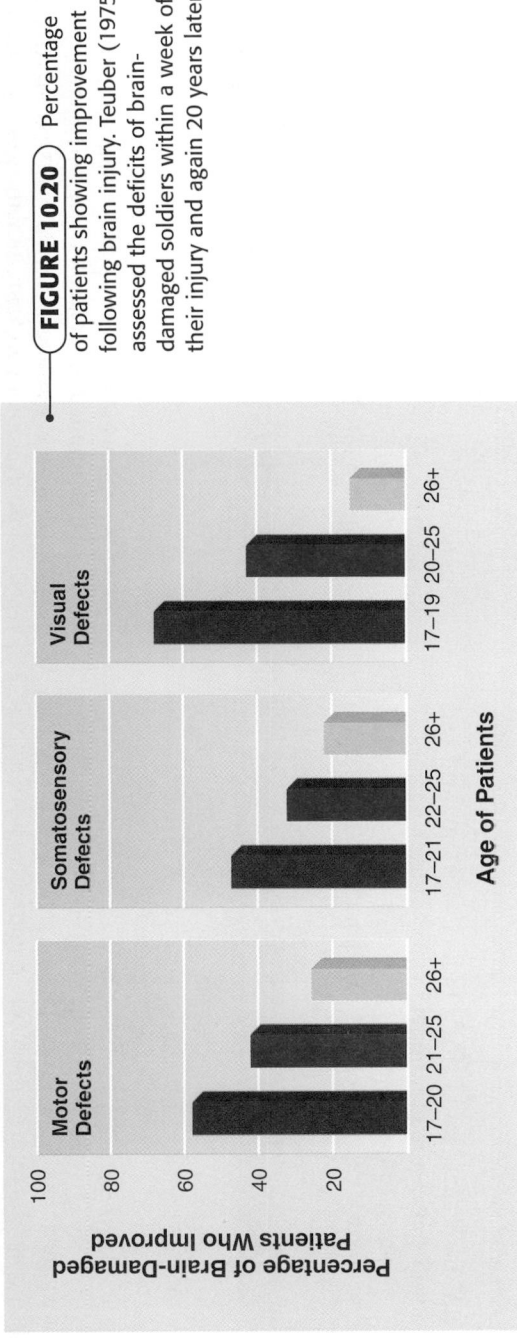

Figure 10.20). However, substantial recovery of function is most likely when lesions are small and the patient is young (see Payne & Lomber, 2001).

Cognitive reserve (roughly equivalent to education and intelligence) is thought to play an important role in the apparent recovery of cognitive function after brain damage. Kapur (1997) conducted a biographical study of doctors and neuroscientists with brain damage, and he observed a great deal of cognitive recovery. He concluded that the observed improvement did not occur because these patients had actually recovered lost cognitive function but because their cognitive reserve allowed them to accomplish cognitive tasks in alternative ways.

The mechanisms of recovery of function remain unknown. It seems likely that neural reorganization contributes to recovery, but so far most of the evidence

for this hypothesis has been indirect (see Hallett, 2001). The strongest evidence comes from a study in which the degree of motor recovery in stroke patients was found to be correlated with the degree of motor cortex reorganization (Lipert et al., 2000).

For years, neural reorganization seemed to be the only explanation for recovery from CNS damage. However, the discovery of adult neurogenesis raised another possibility: Perhaps the growth of new neurons plays a role in such recovery, particularly when the damage affects the hippocampus. It has recently been shown (see Kokaia & Lindvall, 2003) that cerebral ischemia, which preferentially damages the hippocampus, increases adult neurogenesis; that many of the new cells become part of the hippocampus; and that these new cells establish synapses and develop into mature neurons—see Figure 10.21.

FIGURE 10.21 Increased neurogenesis in the dentate gyrus following damage. The left panel shows (1) an electrolytic lesion in the dentate gyrus (damaged neurons are stained turquoise) and (2) the resulting increase in the formation of new cells (stained red), many of which develop into mature neurons (stained dark blue). The right panel displays the comparable control area in the unlesioned hemisphere, showing the normal number of new cells (stained red). (These beautiful images are courtesy of my good friends Carl Ernst and Brian Christie, Department of Psychology, University of British Columbia.)

It is thus possible that an increase in adult neurogenesis contributes to recovery from stroke, but there is currently no direct evidence for this attractive hypothesis. However, if this hypothesis is proven, exercise—which has been shown to increase adult neurogenesis (Holmes et al., 2004; Van Praag et al., 2002)—could prove to be therapeutic for patients with hippocampal damage.

10.5 Neuroplasticity and the Treatment of Nervous System Damage

The study of neuroplasticity is currently one of the most active and exciting areas of research in neuroscience. This section reveals the major reason for all the excitement: The dream that recent discoveries about neuroplasticity—with which you are now familiar—can be applied to the treatment of brain damage in human patients.

The following four subsections describe research on some major new treatment approaches. Most of this research has focused on animal models, but some of it has progressed to clinical trials with human patients.

Evolutionary Perspective

Reducing Brain Damage by Blocking Neurodegeneration

Several studies have shown that it may be possible to reduce brain damage by blocking neural degeneration in human patients. For example, in one study, Xu and colleagues (1999) induced cerebral ischemia in rats by limiting blood flow to the brain. This had two major effects in the control group of rats: It produced damage in the hippocampus, a structure that is particularly susceptible to ischemic damage, and it produced deficits in the rats' performance in the Morris water maze (see Chapter 5). The hippocampuses of rats in the experimental group were treated with viruses genetically engineered to release *apoptosis inhibitor protein*. Amazingly, the apoptosis inhibitor protein prevented both the loss of hippocampal neurons and the deficits in Morris water maze performance.

In addition to apoptosis inhibitor protein, several other neurochemicals have been shown to block the degeneration of damaged neurons. The most widely studied of these is *nerve growth factor* (see Sofroniew, Howe, & Mobley, 2001). You may be surprised to learn that estrogens have a similar effect (see Behl, 2002; Sawada & Shimohama, 2000; Stein, 2001; Wise et al., 2001). **Estrogens** are a class of steroid hormones that are released in large amounts by the *ovaries* (the female gonads). These hormones have several important effects on the maturation of the female body, which you will learn about in Chapter 13, but they also have a variety of influences on the brain. Estrogens have been shown to limit or delay neuron death in animal models and in cell cultures, and there are also some supportive findings from human patients. These neuroprotective effects of estrogens may explain why several brain disorders (e.g., Parkinson's disease) are more prevalent in males than in females.

In general, molecules that limit neural degeneration also promote regeneration. This point leads us to the next subsection.

Promoting Recovery from CNS Damage by Promoting Regeneration

Although regeneration does not normally occur in the mammalian CNS, several studies have shown that it can be induced. The following three studies are particularly promising because they have shown that such regeneration can be associated with functional recovery.

Eitan and colleagues (1994) transected the left optic nerves of rats. In the control rats, the retinal ganglion cells, which compose the left optic nerve, permanently degenerated. The experimental rats received injections of an agent that is toxic to oligodendrocytes, thus eliminating these cells' ability to block regeneration. In these experimental subjects, the optic nerves regenerated, and 6 weeks after the injury, evoked potentials could be recorded from the optic nerve in response to light flashes presented to the left eye.

Cheng, Cao, and Olson (1996) transected the spinal cords of rats, thus rendering them *paraplegic* (paralyzed in the posterior portion of their bodies). The researchers then transplanted sections of myelinated peripheral nerve across the transection. As a result, spinal cord neurons regenerated through the implanted Schwann cell myelin sheaths, and the regeneration allowed the rats to regain use of their hindquarters.

A similar study involved transplanting *olfactory ensheathing cells* rather than Schwann cells. Olfactory ensheathing cells, which are similar to Schwann cells, were selected because the olfactory system is unique in its ability to support continual growth of axons from new PNS neurons into the CNS (i.e., into the olfactory bulbs). Li, Field, and Raisman (1998) made lesions in the corticospinal tract of rats and then implanted bridges of olfactory ensheathing cells across the lesion. Axons grew through the lesion, and the motor function of the affected paw was partially restored. Although it is not yet clear how this recovery occurs, these findings have generated considerable optimism (see Barnett & Chang, 2004; Edgerton & Roy, 2002; Keyvan-Fouladi, Li, & Raisman, 2002).

large-scale clinical trial was premature. Researchers do not yet know how to maximize the survival and growth of neurotransplants and how to minimize their side effects. It is important to achieve a balance between the pressure to develop new treatments quickly and the need to base treatments on a carefully constructed foundation of scientific understanding (see Döbrössy & Dunnett, 2001).

In Chapter 4, you were introduced to Roberto Garcia d'Orta—the Lizard. D'Orta, who suffered from Parkinson's disease, initially responded to L-dopa therapy; but, after 3 years of therapy, his condition worsened. Then he responded to treatment with a dopamine agonist, but again the improvement was only temporary. D'Orta, was in a desperate state when he heard about *adrenal medulla autotransplantation* (transplanting a patient's own adrenal medulla cells into her or his striatum, usually for the treatment of Parkinson's disease). Adrenal medulla cells release small amounts of dopamine, and there were some early indications that adrenal medulla autotransplantation might alleviate the symptoms of Parkinson's disease.

D'Orta demanded adrenal medulla autotransplantation from his doctor. When his doctor refused, on the grounds that the effectiveness of the treatment was still in doubt, d'Orta found himself another doctor—a neurosurgeon who was not nearly so cautious.

The Case of Roberto Garcia d'Orta: The Lizard Gets an Autotransplant

Roberto flew to Juarez. The neurosurgeon there greeted him with open arms. As long as Roberto could afford the cost, he'd be happy to do an adrenal implant on him....

Were there any dangers?

The neurosurgeon seemed insulted by the question. If Señor d'Orta didn't trust him, he could go elsewhere....

Roberto underwent the procedure.

He flew back home two weeks later. He was no better. He was told that it took time for the cells to grow and make the needed chemicals....

Then I received an unexpected call from Roberto's wife. Roberto was dead....

He'd died of a stroke.... Had the stroke been a complication of his surgery? It was more than a mere possibility. (Klawans, 1990, pp. 63–64)

Transplanting Stem Cells In Chapter 9, you learned about *embryonic neural stem cells*, which are *multipotent* (having the capacity to develop into many types of mature neurons). Investigators are trying to develop procedures for repairing brain damage by injecting embryonic neural stem cells into the damaged site. Once

Promoting Recovery from CNS Damage by Neurotransplantation

A few years ago, the idea of brain transplantation was little more than science fiction. Today, the treatment of brain damage by transplanting neural tissue is approaching reality. Efforts to treat CNS damage by neurotransplantation have taken two different approaches (see Björklund & Lindvall, 2000). The first is to transplant fetal tissue; the second is to transplant stem cells.

Transplanting Fetal Tissue The first approach to neurotransplantation was to replace a damaged structure with fetal tissue that would develop into the same structure. Could the *donor* tissue develop and become integrated into the *host* brain, and in so doing alleviate the symptoms? This approach focused on Parkinson's disease. Parkinson's patients lack the dopamine-releasing cells of the nigrostriatal pathway. Could they be cured by transplanting the appropriate fetal tissue into the site?

Early signs were positive. Bilateral transplantation of fetal substantia nigra cells was successful in treating the MPTP monkey model of Parkinson's disease (Bankie wicz et al., 1990; Sladek et al., 1987). Fetal substantia nigra transplants survived in the MPTP-treated monkeys; they innervated adjacent striatal tissue, released dopamine, and, most importantly, alleviated the severe poverty of movement, tremor, and rigidity produced by the MPTP.

Soon after the favorable effects of neurotransplants in the MPTP monkey model were reported, neurotransplantation was offered as a treatment for Parkinson's disease at major research hospitals. The results of the first case studies were promising. The fetal substantia nigra implants survived, and they released dopamine into the host striatum (see Sawle & Myers, 1993). More importantly, some of the patients improved.

The results of these case studies triggered a large-scale double-blind evaluation study of patients suffering from advanced Parkinson's disease. The study was extremely thorough; it even included placebo controls—patients who received surgery but no implants. The initial results were encouraging: Although control patients showed no improvement, the implants survived in the experimental patients, and some displayed a modest improvement. Unfortunately, however, about 15% of these patients started to display a variety of uncontrollable writhing and chewing movements about a year after the surgery (Greene et al., 1999).

The results of this first double-blind placebo-controlled clinical trial of the effectiveness of fetal tissue transplants created widespread debate (see Dunnett, Björklund, & Lindvall, 2001).The incidence of adverse motor side effects is likely to stifle future attempts to develop neurotransplantation as a treatment for Parkinson's disease. However, many still believe that this is an extremely promising therapeutic approach, but that the

injected, the stem cells could develop and replace the damaged cells, under guidance from surrounding tissue. This line of research received a major boost from the development of renewable cultures of stem cells (see Wakayama et al., 2001), which can serve as a source for transplantation and research (Gage, 2000). The study by McDonald and colleagues (1999) illustrates the potential of this method.

McDonald and colleagues injected embryonic neural stem cells into an area of spinal damage. Their subjects were rats that had been rendered paraplegic by a blow. The stem cells migrated to different areas around the damaged area, where they developed into mature neurons. Remarkably, the rats receiving the implants became capable of supporting their weight with their hindlimbs and walking, albeit awkwardly.

The study by McDonald and colleagues and several similar ones triggered widespread media attention and a frenzy of research activity. Effective treatment for severe CNS damage appeared to be within reach. However, it quickly became apparent that much research still needs to be done (see Rossi & Cattaneo, 2002; Wexler & Palmer, 2002). First, effective methods of propagating populations of neural stem cells must be developed (see Gottlieb, 2002). Because sources of embryonic stem cells have been limited by law in some parts of the world, efforts have focused on harvesting neural stem cells from adult brains or on trying to cause other types of adult stem cells (e.g., blood stem cells) to develop into neural stem cells. Neither approach has as yet achieved unqualified success (see Temple, 2001; Wagers et al., 2002). Second, techniques for promoting the survival and appropriate maturation of the neural stem cells once they have been implanted need to be developed. Third, the factors that promote the establishment of correct connections with surviving cells need to be identified. And fourth, methods for encouraging functional recovery have to be developed. For example, little attention has been paid to the behavioral treatment of patients with neural stem cell implants, which is likely to be an important factor in their recovery. In short, although therapeutic neural stem cell transplantation is one of the most exciting subjects of investigation in all of neuroscience, the ultimate goal is an ambitious one whose achievement will take longer than once thought (see Zoghbi, Gage, & Choi, 2000).

Clinical Implications

Promoting Recovery from CNS Damage by Rehabilitative Training

Several demonstrations of the important role of experience in the organization of the developing and adult brain kindled a renewed interest in the use of rehabilitative training to promote recovery from CNS damage.

The following innovative rehabilitative training programs were derived from such findings.

Strokes   Small strokes produce a core of brain damage, which is often followed by a gradually expanding loss of neural function around this core. Nudo and colleagues (1996) produced small *ischemic lesions* (lesions produced by an interruption of blood supply) in the hand area of the motor cortex of monkeys. Then, 5 days later, a program of hand training and practice was initiated. During the ensuing 3 or 4 weeks, the monkeys plucked hundreds of tiny food pellets from food wells of different sizes. This practice substantially reduced the expansion of cortical damage. The monkeys that received the rehabilitative training also showed greater recovery in the use of their affected hand.

One of the principles that has emerged from the study of neurodevelopment is that neurons seem to be in a competitive situation: They compete with other neurons for synaptic sites and neurotrophins, and the losers die. Weiller and Rijntjes (1999) designed a rehabilitative program based on this principle, tested it on monkeys, and then tested it on unilateral stroke patients who had difficulty using one arm. Their procedure, called *constraint-induced therapy* (Taub, Uswatte, & Elbert, 2002), was to tie down the functioning arm for 2 weeks while the affected arm received markedly intensive training. Performance with the affected arm improved markedly over the 2 weeks, and there was an increase in the area of motor cortex controlling that arm.

Spinal Injury   In one approach to treating patients with spinal injuries (see Rossignol, 2000; Wolpaw & Tennissen, 2001), patients incapable of walking were supported by a harness over a moving treadmill. With most of their weight supported and the treadmill providing appropriate feedback, the patients gradually learned to make walking movements. Then, as they improved, the amount of support was gradually reduced. In one study using this technique, over 90% of the trained patients eventually became independent walkers, compared with only 50% of those receiving conventional physiotherapy.

Phantom Limbs   Most amputees continue to experience limbs that have been amputated—a condition referred to as **phantom limbs**. The most striking feature of phantom limbs is their reality. Their existence is so compelling that a patient may try to jump out of bed onto a nonexistent leg or to lift a cup with a nonexistent hand. In most cases, the amputated limb behaves like a normal limb; for example, as an amputee walks, a phantom arm seems to swing back and forth in perfect coordination with the intact arm. However, sometimes an amputee feels that the amputated limb is stuck in a peculiar position. For example, one amputee felt that his phantom arm extended straight out from the shoulder, and as a result, he turned sideways whenever he passed through doorways (Melzack, 1992).

About 50% of amputees experience chronic severe pain in their phantom limbs. A typical complaint is that an amputated hand is clenched so tightly that the fingernails are digging into the palm of the hand. Occasionally, phantom limb pain can be treated by having the amputee concentrate on opening the amputated hand. However, when this does not work, the pain can become so intense that desperate measures are attempted.

Based on the premise that phantom limb pain results from irritation at the stump, many efforts to control it involved cutting off the stump or surgical destruction of various parts of the neural pathway between the stump and the cortex. Unfortunately, none of these surgical interventions provided patients with relief from the pain or eliminated the phantom limb (see Melzack, 1992). Still, the idea that phantom limbs and phantom limb pain result from irritation of nerves in the stump persisted. There seemed to be no other possibility.

This chapter ends with the stories of two patients suffering from phantom limb pain and their exceptional doctor. The patients were Tom and Philip, and their physician was the neuropsychologist V. S. Ramachandran. In the process of treating Tom and Philip, Dr. Ramachandran solved a long-standing neuropsychological puzzle and developed a new treatment to boot.

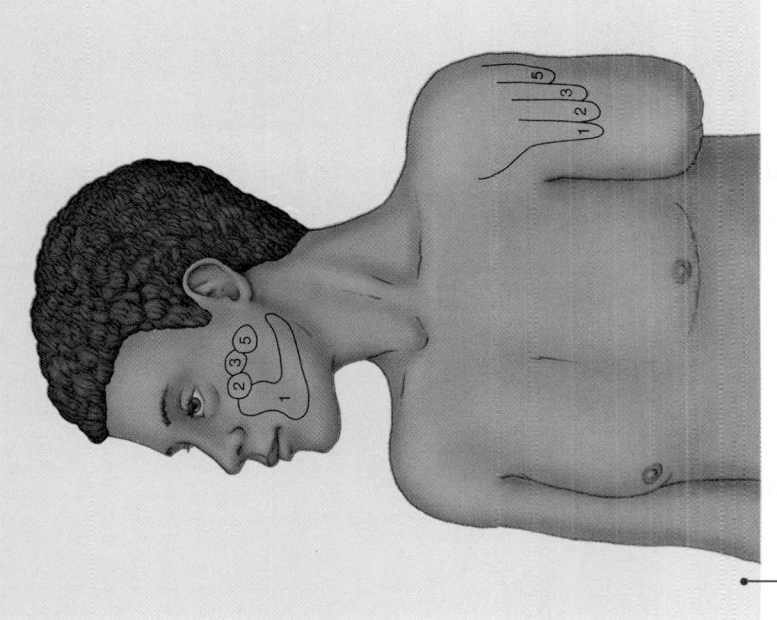

FIGURE 10.22 The places on Tom's body where touches elicited sensations in his phantom hand. (Adapted from Ramachandran & Blakeslee, 1998.)

The Cases of Tom and Philip: Phantom Limbs and Ramachandran

Dr. Ramachandran read an article about a study you have already encountered in this chapter, the study by Pons and colleagues (1991). In this study, severing the sensory neurons in the arms of monkeys led to a reorganization of somatosensory cortex. The area of somatosensory cortex that originally received input from the damaged arm now received input from areas of the body normally mapped onto adjacent areas of somatosensory cortex. Ramachandran was struck by a sudden insight: Perhaps phantom limbs were not in the stump at all, but in the brain; perhaps the perception of a phantom arm originated from parts of the body that now innervated the original

arm area of the somatosensory cortex (see Ramachandran & Blakeslee, 1998).

Excited by his hypothesis, Dr. Ramachandran asked one of his patients, Tom, if he would participate in a simple test. He touched various parts of Tom's body and asked Tom what he felt. Remarkably, when he touched the side of Tom's face on the same side as his amputated arm, Tom felt sensations from various parts of his phantom hand as well as his face. Indeed, when

some warm water was dropped on his face, he felt it running down his phantom hand. A second map of his hand was found on his shoulder (see Figure 10.22).

Philip, another patient of Dr. Ramachandran, suffered from severe chronic pain in his phantom arm. For a decade, Philip had been unable to move the joints of the phantom arm; it was frozen in an awkward position (Ramachandran & Rogers-Ramachandran, 2000), and Philip suffered great pain in all of its joints, particularly the elbow.

Dr. Ramachandran applied a bit of biopsychological ingenuity to the problem. Could he relieve Philip's pain by teaching him to move his phantom arm? Knowing how important feedback is in movement (see Chapter 8), Dr. Ramachandran constructed a special feedback apparatus for Philip. This was a box divided in two by a vertical mirror. Philip was instructed to put his good right hand into the box through a hole in the front and view it through a hole in the top. When he looked at his hand, he could see it and its mirror image. He was instructed to put his phantom limb in the box and try to position it, as best he could, so that it corresponded to the mirror image of his good hand. Then, he was instructed to make synchronous, bilaterally symmetrical movements of his arms—his actual right arm and his phantom left arm—while viewing his good arm and its mirror image.

"Oh my God! Oh my God, doctor! This is unbelievable. It's mind-boggling." He was jumping up and down like a kid. "My left arm is plugged in again. It's as if I'm in the past.... I can move my arm again. I can feel my elbow moving, my wrist moving. It's all moving again. (Ramachandran & Blakeslee, 1998, pp. 47–48)

But when Philip shut his eyes or removed his arms from the apparatus, his phantom limb was frozen once again . . . and the pain was as bad as ever. So, Ramachandran sent Philip home with the box and instructions to use it. Three weeks later, Philip phoned.

"Doctor," he exclaimed, "it's gone!"

"What's gone?" (I thought maybe he had lost the mirror box.)

"My phantom is gone."

"What are you talking about?"

"You know, my phantom arm, which I had for 10 years. It doesn't exist anymore. All I have is my phantom fingers and palm dangling from my shoulder."

" . . . "Philip—does this bother you?"

"No, no, no.... On the contrary. You know the excruciating pain that I always had in my elbow? . . . Well, now I don't have an elbow and I don't have that pain anymore." (Ramachandran & Blakeslee, 1998, p. 49)

I hope that I have managed to communicate to you some of the excitement that is being generated by the discovery that the adult human brain is plastic. The possibilities of applying neuroplastic processes to repair brain damage are truly exciting. I am optimistic that there will soon be a breakthrough because, as you have just learned, progress is being made on so many different fronts.

Themes Revisited

Because this entire chapter dealt with clinical issues, the clinical implications tab made numerous appearances. In particular, it drew attention to the many cases that appeared in the chapter: the ironic case of Professor P.; Jerry Quarry, the punch-drunk ex-boxer; the cases of complex partial epilepsy; Walter S. Miller, the man whose wife had Huntington's disease; the cases of MPTP poisoning; and Tom and Philip, the amputees with phantom limbs.

The chapter stressed clear thinking about biopsychology in several places. Attention was drawn to thinking about the cumulative effects of concussions, about the relation between genes and Parkinson's disease, about animal models of disease, about the identity of

See Hard Copy for additional readings for Chapter 10.

Clinical Implications

Thinking Critically

the primary symptom of Alzheimer's disease, and about recovery of function. Particularly interesting were the insightful approaches that Dr. Ramachandran took in treating Tom and Philip, who suffered from phantom limb pain.

The evolutionary perspective was also highlighted at several points. You were introduced to the concept of animal models, which is based on the comparative approach, and you learned that most of the research on neural regeneration and reorganization following brain damage has been done with animal models. Finally, you learned that research into the mechanisms of neural regeneration has been stimulated by the fact that this process occurs accurately in some species.

Evolutionary Perspective

ON THE CD
Studying for an exam? Try the Practice Tests for Chapter 10.

Think about It

1. An epileptic is brought to trial for assault. The lawyer argues that her client is not a criminal and that the assaults in question were psychomotor attacks. She points out that her client takes her medication faithfully, but that it does not help. The prosecution lawyer argues that the defendant has a long history of violent assault and must be locked up. What do you think the judge should do?

2. Describe a bizarre incident you have observed that you think in retrospect might have been a complex partial or petit mal seizure.

3. The more that is known about a disease, the easier it is to diagnose; and the more accurately it can be diagnosed, the easier it is to find things out about it. Explain and discuss.

4. Total dementia often creates less suffering than partial dementia. Discuss.

5. In order to be useful, animal models do not have to have all of the features of the disorder they are modeling. Discuss.

6. Major breakthroughs in the treatment of CNS damage are on the horizon. Discuss.

7. The first evaluation of the effectiveness of neurotransplantation in the treatment of Parkinson's disease suggested that the treatment, as administered, was not effective. What do you think should be the next step?

Key Terms

Alzheimer's disease (p. 242)
Amyloid (p. 244)
Aneurysm (p. 233)
Anterograde degeneration (p. 248)
Apoptosis (p. 238)
Arteriosclerosis (p. 234)
Ataxia (p. 242)
Benign tumors (p. 233)
Cerebral hemorrhage (p. 233)
Cerebral ischemia (p. 233)
Collateral sprouting (p. 250)
Complex partial seizures (p. 240)
Concussion (p. 236)
Congenital (p. 233)
Contrecoup injuries (p. 236)
Contusions (p. 236)
Convulsions (p. 239)
Dementia (p. 236)
Deprenyl (p. 242)
Distal segment (p. 248)

Down syndrome (p. 238)
Embolism (p. 234)
Encapsulated tumors (p. 233)
Encephalitis (p. 237)
Epidemiology (p. 242)
Epilepsy (p. 239)
Epileptic auras (p. 239)
Epileptogenesis (p. 246)
Estrogens (p. 254)
Experimental autoimmune encephalomyelitis (p. 242)
General paresis (p. 237)
Generalized seizures (p. 240)
Glutamate (p. 235)
Grand mal seizure (p. 240)
Hematoma (p. 236)
Huntington's disease (p. 241)
Hypoxia (p. 240)
Infiltrating tumors (p. 233)
Kindling phenomenon (p. 246)
L-Dopa (p. 241)
MPTP (p. 242)

Malignant tumors (p. 233)
Meningiomas (p. 233)
Meningitis (p. 237)
Metastatic tumors (p. 233)
Multiple sclerosis (MS) (p. 242)
NMDA (N-methyl-D-aspartate) receptors (p. 235)
Neural regeneration (p. 248)
Nigrostriatal pathway (p. 241)
Oligodendroglia (p. 249)
Parkinson's disease (p. 241)
Partial seizures (p. 239)
Petit mal seizure (p. 240)
Phantom limb (p. 256)
Proximal segment (p. 248)
Punch-drunk syndrome (p. 236)
Retrograde degeneration (p. 248)
Schwann cells (p. 248)
Simple partial seizures (p. 240)
Striatum (p. 241)

Strokes (p. 233)
Substantia nigra (p. 241)
Tardive dyskinesia (TD) (p. 237)
3-per-second spike-and-wave discharge (p. 240)
Thrombosis (p. 233)
Toxic psychosis (p. 237)
Transgenic (p. 246)
Transneuronal degeneration (p. 248)
Tumor (neoplasm) (p. 233)

ON THE CD

Need some help studying the key terms for this chapter? Check out the electronic flash cards for Chapter 10.

Learning, Memory, and Amnesia

How Your Brain Stores Information

chapter 11

11.1 Amnesic Effects of Bilateral Medial Temporal Lobectomy

11.2 Amnesia of Korsakoff's Syndrome

11.3 Amnesia of Alzheimer's Disease

11.4 Amnesia after Concussion: Evidence for Consolidation

11.5 Neuroanatomy of Object-Recognition Memory

11.6 The Hippocampus and Memory for Spatial Location

11.7 Where Are Memories Stored?

11.8 Synaptic Mechanisms of Learning and Memory

11.9 Conclusion: Infantile Amnesia and the Biopsychologist Who Remembered H.M.

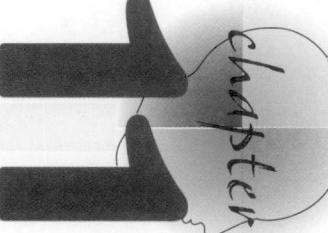

earning and memory are two ways of thinking about the same thing: Both deal with the ability of the brain to change its functioning in response to experience. **Learning** deals with how experience changes the brain, and **memory** deals with how these changes are stored and subsequently reactivated. Without the ability to learn and remember, we would experience every moment as if waking from a lifelong sleep—each person

would be a stranger, each act a new challenge, and each word incomprehensible.

The chapter focuses on the roles played by various brain structures in the processes of learning and memory. Knowledge of these roles is largely based on the study of amnesic patients with brain damage and on animal models of brain-damage–produced amnesia.

11.1   Amnesic Effects of Bilateral Medial Temporal Lobectomy

Ironically, the person who has contributed more than any other to our understanding of the neuropsychology of memory is not a neuropsychologist. In fact, although he has collaborated on dozens of studies of memory, he has no formal research training and not a single degree to his name. He is H.M., a man who in 1953, at the age of 27, had the medial portions of his temporal lobes removed for the treatment of a severe case of epilepsy. Just as the Rosetta Stone provided archaeologists with important clues to the meaning of Egyptian hieroglyphics, H.M.'s memory deficits have been instrumental in the achievement of our current understanding of the neural bases of memory (see Corkin, 2002).

dividual with normal perceptual and motor abilities and superior intelligence, and he left it in the same condition. Indeed, H.M.'s IQ increased from 104 to 118 as a result of his surgery, presumably because of the decline in the incidence of his seizures. Be that as it may, H.M. was the last patient to receive a bilateral medial temporal lobectomy—because of its devastating amnesic effects.

In assessing the amnesic effects of brain surgery, it is usual to administer tests of the patient's ability to remember things learned before the surgery and tests of the patient's ability to remember things learned after the surgery. Deficits on the former tests lead to a diagnosis of **retrograde** (backward-acting) **amnesia;**

The Case of H.M., the Man Who Changed the Study of Memory

During the 11 years preceding his surgery, H.M. suffered an average of one generalized convulsion each week and many partial convulsions each day, despite massive doses of anticonvulsant medication. Electroencephalography suggested that H.M.'s convulsions arose from foci in the medial portions of both his left and right temporal lobes. Because the removal of one medial temporal lobe had proved to be an effective treatment for patients with a unilateral temporal lobe focus, the decision was made to perform a **bilateral medial temporal lobectomy**—the removal of the medial portions of both temporal lobes, including most of the **hippocampus, amygdala,** and adjacent cortex (see Figure 11.1). (A **lobectomy** is an operation in which a lobe, or a major part of one, is removed from the brain; a **lobotomy** is an operation in which a lobe, or a major part of one, is separated from the rest of the brain by a large cut but is not removed.)

In several respects, H.M.'s bilateral medial temporal lobectomy was an unqualified success. His generalized convulsions were all but eliminated, and the incidence of his minor seizures was reduced to one or two per day, even though the level of his anticonvulsant medication was substantially reduced. Furthermore, H.M. entered surgery a reasonably well-adjusted in-

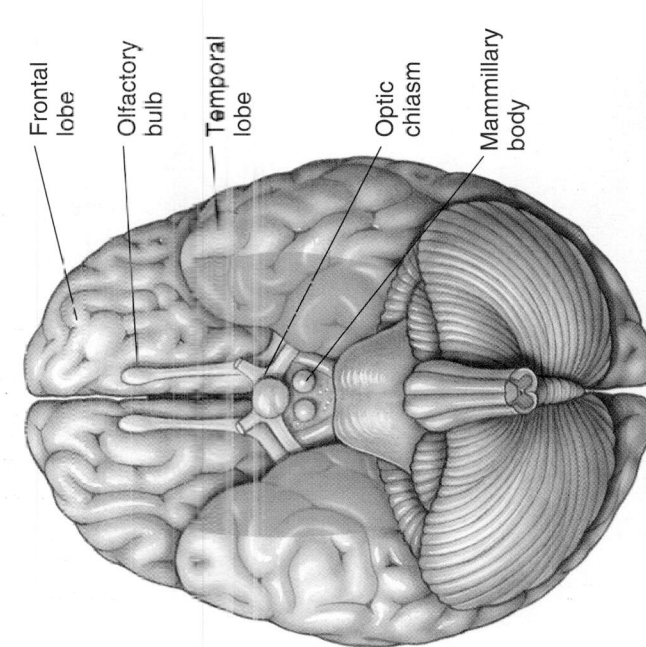

Frontal lobe

Olfactory bulb

Temporal lobe

Optic chiasm

Mammillary body

Tissue typically excised in medial temporal lobectomy

FIGURE 11.1   Medial temporal lobectomy. The portions of the medial temporal lobes that were removed from H.M.'s brain are illustrated in a view of the inferior surface of the brain.

those on the latter tests lead to a diagnosis of **antero-grade** (forward-acting) **amnesia.**

Like his intellectual abilities, H.M.'s memory for events predating his surgery remains largely intact. Although he has a mild retrograde amnesia for those events that occurred in the 2 years before his surgery, his memory for more remote events (e.g., for the events of his childhood) is reasonably normal.

In contrast, H.M. suffers from a severe anterograde amnesia. His ability to hold information in short-term storage is well within the normal range—he has a **digit span** of six digits (Wickelgren, 1968); however, he has great difficulty forming new long-term memories. Once he stops thinking about a new experience, it is usually lost forever. In effect, H.M. became suspended in time on that day in 1953 when he regained his health but lost his future:

As far as we can tell, this man has retained little if anything of events subsequent to the operation.... Ten months before I examined him, his family had moved from their old house to a new one a few blocks away on the same street. He still had not learned the new address (though remembering the old one perfectly), nor could he be trusted to find his way home alone. He did not know where objects in constant use were kept, and his mother stated that he would read the same magazines over and over again without finding their contents familiar.... [F]orgetting occurred the instant the patient's focus of attention shifted. (Milner, 1965, pp. 104–105)

During three of the nights at the Clinical Research Center, the patient rang for the night nurse, asking her, with many apologies, if she would tell him where he was and how he came to be there. He clearly realized that he was in a hospital but seemed unable to reconstruct any of the events of the previous day. On another occasion he remarked "Every day is alone in itself, whatever enjoyment I've had, and whatever sorrow I've had." Our own impression is that ... events fade for him long before the day is over. He often volunteers stereotyped descriptions of his own state, by saying that it is "like waking from a dream." His experience seems to be that of a person who is just becoming aware of his surroundings without fully comprehending the situation, because he does not remember what went before.

He still fails to recognize people who are close neighbours or family friends but who got to know him only after the operation. When questioned, he tries to use accent as a clue to a person's place of origin and weather as a clue to the time of year. Although he gives his date of birth unhesitatingly and accurately, he always underestimates his own age and can only make wild guesses as to the date. (Milner, Corkin, & Teuber, 1968, pp. 216–217)

H.M. has lived in a nursing home for many years. He spends much of each day doing crossword puzzles; his progress on a crossword puzzle is never lost because it is written down.

Formal Assessment of H.M.'s Anterograde Amnesia

This subsection describes H.M.'s performance on several objective tests of memory.

Digit Span + 1 Test   H.M.'s inability to form long-term memories is illustrated by his performance on the *digit span + 1 test*. H.M. was asked to repeat 5 digits that were read to him at 1-second intervals. He repeated the sequence correctly. On the next trial, the same 5 digits were presented in the same sequence with 1 new digit added to the end. This same 6-digit sequence was presented a few times until he got it right, and then another digit was added to the end of it, and so on. After 25 trials, H.M. had not managed to repeat the 8-digit sequence. Normal subjects can repeat about 15 digits after 25 digit span + 1 trials (Drachman & Arbit, 1966).

Block-Tapping Memory-Span Test   Milner (1971) demonstrated that H.M.'s amnesia was not restricted to verbal material by assessing his performance on the + 1 version of the *block-tapping memory-span test*. An array of 9 blocks was spread out on a board in front of H.M., and he was asked to watch the neuropsychologist touch a sequence of them and then to repeat the same sequence of touches. H.M. had a *block-tapping span* of 5 blocks, which is in the normal range; but he could not learn to correctly touch a sequence of 6 blocks, even when the same sequence was repeated 12 times. H.M. has **global amnesia**—amnesia for information presented in all sensory modalities.

Mirror-Drawing Test   The first indication that H.M.'s anterograde amnesia does not involve all long-term memories came from the results of a *mirror-drawing test* (Milner, 1965). H.M.'s task was to draw a line within the boundaries of a star-shaped target by watching his hand in a mirror. H.M. was asked to trace the star 10 times on each of 3 consecutive days, and the number of times he went outside the boundaries on each trial was recorded. As Figure 11.2 shows, H.M.'s performance improved over the 3 days, which indicates retention of the task. However, despite his improved performance, H.M. could not recall ever having seen the task before.

Rotary-Pursuit Test   In the *rotary-pursuit test* (see Figure 11.3 on page 264), the subject tries to keep the tip of a stylus in contact with a target that rotates on a revolving turntable. Corkin (1968) found that H.M.'s performance on the rotary-pursuit test improved significantly over 9 daily practice sessions, despite the fact that H.M. claimed each day that he had never seen the rotary-pursuit rotor before. His improved performance was retained over a 7-day retention interval.

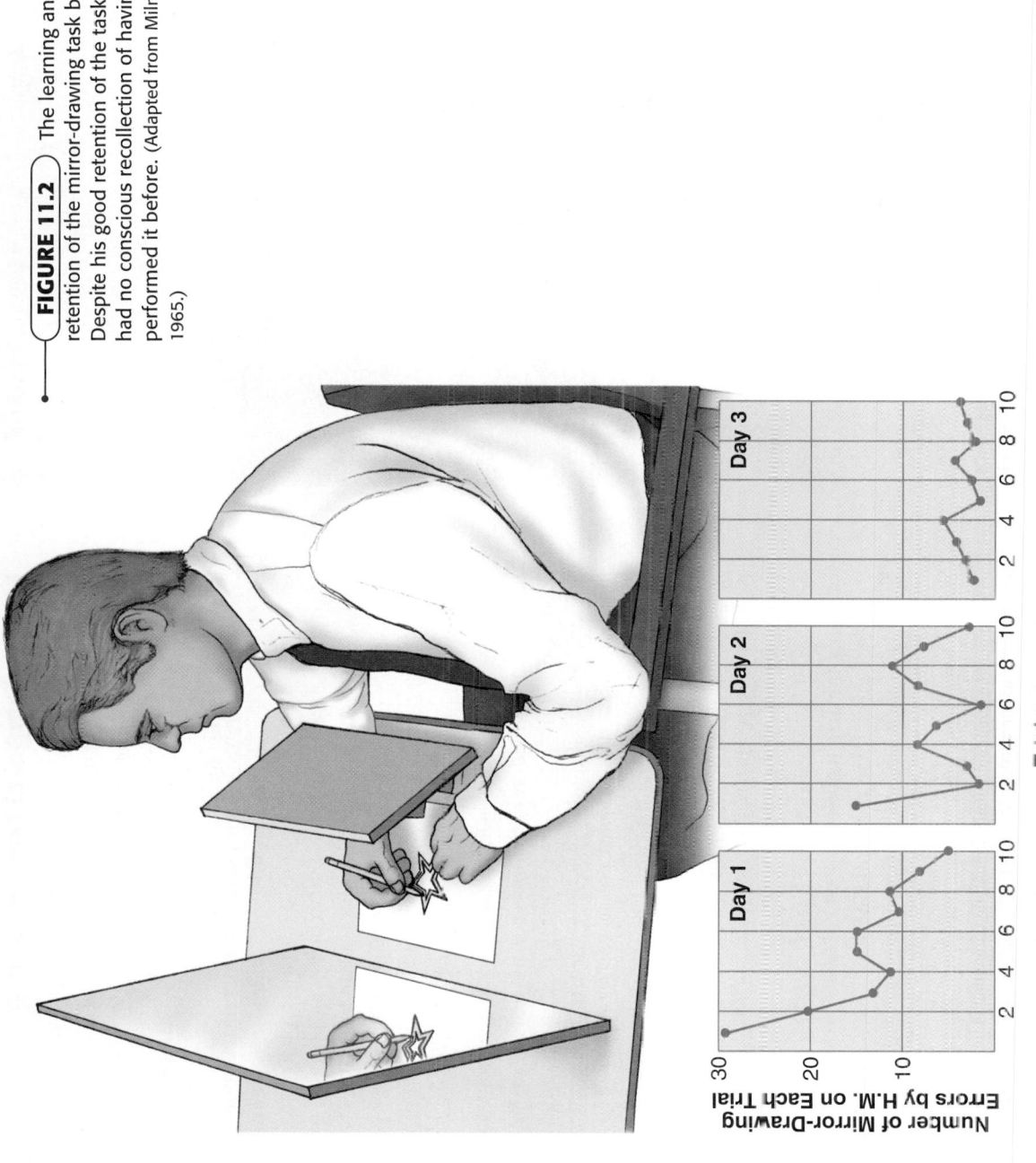

FIGURE 11.2 The learning and retention of the mirror-drawing task by H.M. Despite his good retention of the task, H.M. had no conscious recollection of having performed it before. (Adapted from Milner, 1965.)

Number of Mirror-Drawing Errors by H.M. on Each Trial

Trials

Day 1 Day 2 Day 3

Incomplete-Pictures Test The discovery that H.M. is capable of forming long-term memories for mirror drawing and rotary pursuit suggested that sensorimotor tasks were the one exception to his inability to form long-term memories. However, this view was challenged by the demonstration that H.M. could also form new long-term memories for the **incomplete-pictures test** (Gollin, 1960)—a nonsensorimotor test of memory that employs five sets of fragmented drawings. Each set contains drawings of the same 20 objects, but they differ in their degree of sketchiness: Set 1 contains the most fragmented drawings, and set 5 contains the complete drawings. The subject is asked to identify the 20 objects from the sketchiest set (set 1); then, those objects that go unrecognized are presented in their set 2 versions, and so on, until all 20 items have been identified. Figure 11.4 on page 265 illustrates the performance of H.M. on this test and his

improved performance 1 hour later (Milner, Corkin, & Teuber, 1968). Despite his improved performance, H.M. could not recall previously performing the task.

Pavlovian Conditioning H.M. learned an eye-blink Pavlovian conditioning task, albeit at a retarded rate (Woodruff-Pak, 1993). A tone was sounded just before a puff of air was administered to his eye, until the tone alone elicited an eyeblink. Two years later, H.M. retained this conditioned response almost perfectly, although he had no conscious recollection of the training.

Scientific Contributions of H.M.'s Case

H.M.'s case is a story of personal tragedy, but his contributions to the study of the neural basis of memory have

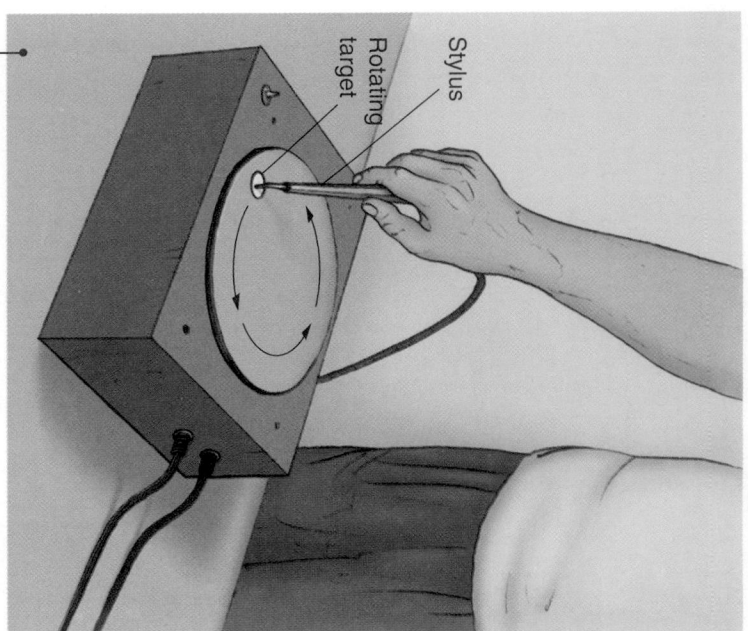

Stylus

Rotating
target

FIGURE 11.3 The rotary-pursuit task. The subject tries to keep the stylus in contact with the rotating target, and time-on-target is automatically recorded. H.M. learned and retained this task, although he had no conscious recollection of the learning trials.

been immense. By showing that the medial temporal lobes play an especially important role in memory, H.M.'s case challenged the then prevalent view that memory functions are diffusely and equivalently distributed throughout the brain. In so doing, H.M.'s case renewed efforts to relate individual brain structures to specific mnemonic processes. Particularly, H.M.'s case spawned a massive research effort aimed at clarifying the *mnemonic* (memory-related) functions of the hippocampus and other medial temporal lobe structures.

The discovery that bilateral medial temporal lobectomy abolished H.M.'s ability to form certain kinds of long-term memories without disrupting his performance on tests of short-term memory supported the theory that there are different modes of storage for short-term and long-term memory. H.M.'s specific problem appears to be a difficulty in **memory consolidation** (the transfer of short-term memories to long-term storage).

Finally, H.M.'s case was the first to reveal that an amnesic patient might claim no recollection of a previous experience, while demonstrating memory for it by improved performance. Conscious memories are called **explicit memories**, whereas memories that are expressed by improved test performance without conscious awareness are called **implicit memories**.

Medial Temporal Lobe Amnesia

Neuropsychological patients with a profile of mnemonic deficits similar to those of H.M., with preserved intellectual functioning, and with evidence of medial temporal lobe damage are said to suffer from **medial temporal lobe amnesia.**

Research on medial temporal lobe amnesia has shown that H.M.'s difficulty in forming explicit long-term memories while retaining the ability to form implicit long-term memories of the same experiences is not unique to him (see Eichenbaum, 1999). This problem has proved to be a symptom of medial temporal lobe amnesia, as well as many other amnesic disorders. As a result, the assessment of implicit long-term memories has played an important role in the study of human amnesia.

Tests that have been developed to assess implicit memory are called **repetition priming tests.** The incomplete-pictures test is an example, but repetition priming tests that involve memory for words are more common. First, the subjects are asked to examine a list of words; they are not asked to learn or remember anything. Later, they are shown a series of word fragments (e.g., _ _ O _ B _ S _ _ _ E _ R _) of words from the original list, and they are simply asked to complete them. Control subjects who have seen the original words perform well. Surprisingly, amnesic subjects often perform equally well, even though they have no explicit memory of seeing the original list.

Most medial temporal lobe amnesics have difficulty forming explicit long-term memories, but, unlike H.M., they do not completely lose this ability. Consequently, medial temporal lobe amnesics have been studied to determine whether particular kinds of explicit long-term memories are more susceptible to disruption by medial temporal lobe damage. Indeed, research on medial temporal lobe amnesics has shown that not all of their explicit long-term memories are equally effected. The semantic long-term memories of medial temporal lobe amnesics are often quite normal, but their episodic memories are largely absent (see Baddeley, Vargha-Khadem, & Mishkin, 2002; Tulving, 2002). **Semantic memories** are explicit memories for general facts or information, whereas **episodic memories** are explicit memories for the particular events or experiences of one's life. For example, Vargha-Khadem and colleagues (1997) identified three individuals who had experienced bilateral medial temporal lobe damage early in life and then assessed the memory problems experienced by these amnesics as they matured. Remarkably, despite the fact that they remembered few of the experiences that they had during their daily lives (episodic memory), they progressed through mainstream schools and acquired reasonable levels of language ability and factual knowledge (semantic memory).

The symptoms of medial temporal lobe amnesia raise an important question: Why do we have two par-

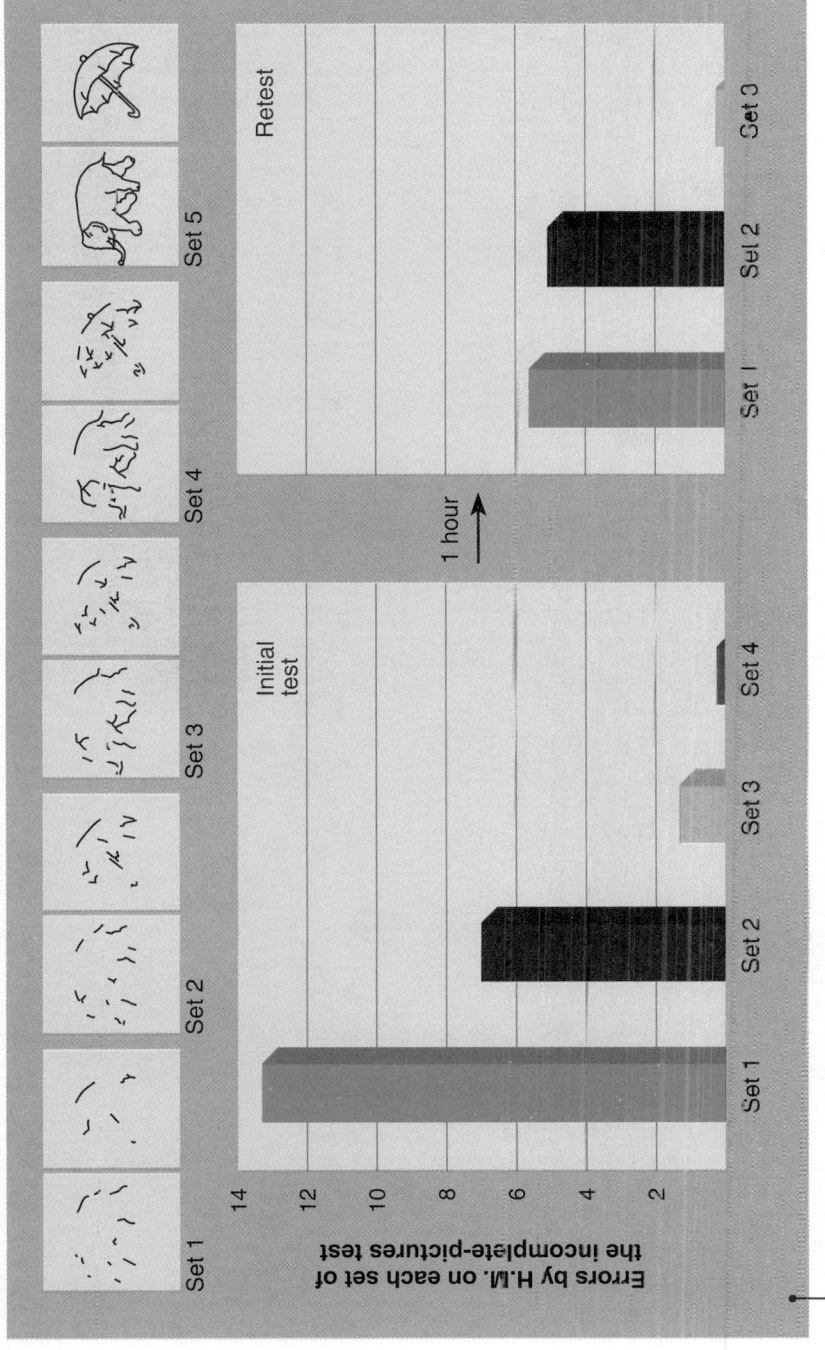

FIGURE 11.4 Two items from the incomplete-pictures test. H.M.'s memory for the 20 items on the test was indicated by his ability to recognize the more fragmented versions of them when he was retested. Nevertheless, he had no conscious awareness of having previously seen the items.

allel memory systems, one conscious (explicit) and one unconscious (implicit)? Presumably, the implicit system was the first to evolve, so the question is actually this: What advantage is there in having a second, conscious system?

Two experiments, one in amnesic patients (Reber, Knowlton, & Squire, 1996) and one in amnesic monkeys with medial temporal lobe lesions (Buckley & Gaffan, 1998), suggest that the answer is "flexibility." In both experiments, the amnesic subjects learned an implicit learning task as well as control subjects did; however, if they were asked to use their implicit knowledge in a different way or in a different context, they failed miserably. Presumably, the evolution of explicit memory systems provided for the flexible use of information.

Effects of Cerebral Ischemia on the Hippocampus and Memory

Patients who have experienced **cerebral ischemia**—that is, have experienced an interruption of blood supply to their brains—often suffer from medial temporal lobe amnesia. R.B. is one such individual (Zola-Morgan, Squire, & Amaral, 1986).

The Case of R.B., the Product of a Bungled Operation

At the age of 52, R.B. underwent cardiac bypass surgery. The surgery was bungled, and, as a consequence, R.B. suffered brain damage. The pump that was circulating R.B.'s blood to his body while his heart was disconnected broke down, and it was several minutes before a replacement arrived from another part of the hospital. R.B. lived, but the resulting ischemic brain damage left him amnesic.

Although R.B.'s amnesia was not as severe as H.M.'s, it was comparable in many aspects. R.B. died in 1983 of a heart attack, and a detailed postmortem examination of his brain was carried out with the permission of his family. Obvious brain damage was restricted largely to the **pyramidal cell layer** of just one part of the hippocampus—the CA1 subfield (see Figure 11.5 on page 266).

R.B.'s case suggested that hippocampal damage by itself can produce amnesia; however, this conclusion has been challenged—as you will learn later in this chapter.

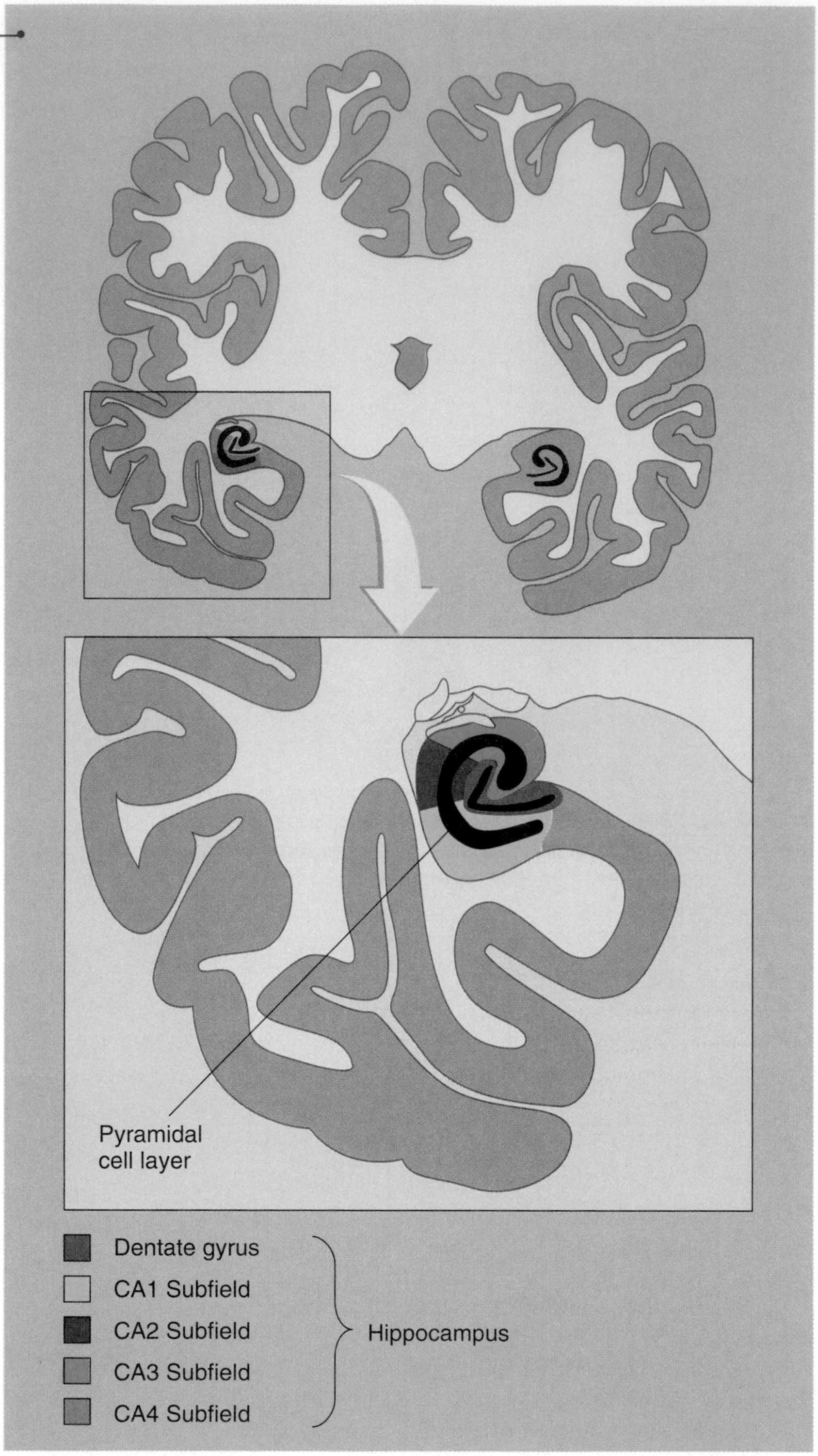

FIGURE 11.5 The major components of the hippocampus: CA1, CA2, CA3, and CA4 subfields and the dentate gyrus. R.B.'s brain damage appeared to be restricted largely to the pyramidal cell layer of the CA1 subfield. (CA stands for *cornu ammonis*, another name for hippocampus.)

11.2 Amnesia of Korsakoff's Syndrome

As you learned in Chapter 1, **Korsakoff's syndrome** is a disorder of memory that is common in people who have consumed large amounts of alcohol. In its advanced stages, it is characterized by a variety of sensory and mo-

tor problems, extreme confusion, personality changes, and a risk of death from liver, gastrointestinal, or heart disorders. Postmortem examination typically reveals lesions to the *medial diencephalon* (the medial thalamus

Pyramidal cell layer

Dentate gyrus
CA1 Subfield
CA2 Subfield
CA3 Subfield
CA4 Subfield

Hippocampus

Clinical Implications

The Up-Your-Nose Case of N.A.

After a year of junior college, N.A. joined the U.S. Air Force; he served as a radar technician until his accident in December of 1960. On that fateful day, N.A.

was assembling a model airplane in his barracks room. His roommate had removed a miniature fencing foil from the wall and was making thrusts behind N.A.'s chair. N.A. turned suddenly and was stabbed through the right nostril. The foil penetrated the cribriform plate [the thin bone around the base of the frontal lobes], taking an upward course to the left into the forebrain. (Squire, 1987, p. 177)

The examiners . . . noted that at first he seemed to be unable to recall any significant personal, national or international events for the two years preceding the accident, but this extensive retrograde amnesia appeared to shrink. . . . Two-and-a-half years after the accident, the retrograde amnesia was said to involve a span of perhaps two weeks immediately preceding the injury, but the exact extent of this retrograde loss was (and remains) impossible to determine. . . .

During . . . convalescence (for the first six to eight months after the accident), the patient's recall of day-to-day events was described as extremely poor, but "occasionally some items sprang forth uncontrollably; he suddenly recalled something he seemed to have no business recalling." His physicians thus gained the impression that his memory was patchy; he appeared to have difficulty in calling up at will many things that at other times emerged spontaneously. . . .

Since his injury, he has been unable to return to any gainful employment, although his memory has continued to improve, albeit slowly. (Teuber, Milner, & Vaughan, 1968, pp. 268–269)

An MRI of N.A.'s brain was taken in the late 1980s (Squire et al., 1989). It revealed extensive medial diencephalic damage, including damage to the mediodorsal nuclei and mammillary bodies.

ON THE CD

Interested in the case of N.A.? Visit the *Memory Deficit* module to see him being tested.

---

and the medial hypothalamus) and diffuse damage to several other brain structures, most notably the neocortex, hippocampus, and cerebellum (e.g., Sullivan & Marsh, 2003).

The amnesia of Korsakoff's syndrome is similar to medial temporal lobe amnesia in some respects. For example, during the early stages of the disorder, anterograde amnesia for explicit episodic memories is the most prominent symptom. However, as the disorder progresses, severe retrograde amnesia, which can extend back into childhood, also develops.

The gradual, insidious onset and progressive development of Korsakoff's syndrome complicate the study of the resulting retrograde amnesia. It is never entirely clear to what extent Korsakoff amnesia for recent events reflects the retrograde disruption of existing memories or the gradually increasing anterograde blockage of the formation of new ones.

Thinking Critically

Because the brain damage associated with Korsakoff's syndrome is diffuse, it has not been easy to identify the portion of it that is specifically responsible for the amnesia. The first hypothesis, which was based on several small postmortem studies, was that damage to the *mammillary bodies* of the hypothalamus was responsible for the memory deficits of Korsakoff patients; however, subsequent studies revealed cases of Korsakoff amnesia with no mammillary body damage. But in all of these exceptional cases, there was damage to another pair of medial diencephalic nuclei: the **mediodorsal nuclei** of the thalamus. The occurrence of **medial diencephalic amnesia** (amnesia, such as Korsakoff amnesia and similar memory disorders, associated with damage to the medial diencephalon) in stroke patients with small ischemic lesions to the mediodorsal nuclei provides additional evidence of the importance of these structures to mnemonic function (e.g., Graff-Radford et al., 1985; Winocur et al., 1984). However, it is unlikely that the memory deficits of Korsakoff patients are attributable to the damage of any single diencephalic structure (see Vann & Aggleton, 2004).

11.3 Amnesia of Alzheimer's Disease

Clinical Implications

Alzheimer's disease is another major cause of amnesia. The first sign of Alzheimer's disease is often a mild deterioration of memory. However, the disorder is progressive: Eventually, *dementia* develops and becomes so severe that the patient is incapable of even simple activities (e.g., eating, speaking, recognizing a spouse, or bladder control). Alzheimer's disease is terminal.

Efforts to understand the neural basis of Alzheimer's amnesia have focused on *predementia Alzheimer's patients* (Alzheimer's patients who have yet to develop dementia). The memory deficits of these patients are more general than those associated with medial temporal lobe damage, medial diencephalic damage, or Korsakoff's syndrome (see Butters & Delis, 1995). In addition to major anterograde and retrograde deficits in tests of explicit memory; predementia Alzheimer's patients often display deficits in short-term memory and in some types of implicit memory: Implicit memory for verbal and perceptual material is often deficient, whereas implicit memory for sensorimotor learning is not (see Gabrieli et al., 1993; Postle, Corkin, & Growdon, 1996).

The level of acetylcholine is greatly reduced in the brains of Alzheimer's patients. This reduction results from the degeneration of the **basal forebrain** (a midline area located just above the hypothalamus; see Figure 11.16 on page 279), which is the brain's main source of acetylcholine. This finding, coupled with the finding that strokes in the basal forebrain area can cause amnesia (Morris et al., 1992), led to the view that acetylcholine depletion is the cause of Alzheimer's amnesia. However, although acetylcholine depletion resulting from damage to the basal forebrain may contribute to Alzheimer's amnesia, it is unlikely to be the only factor. The brain damage associated with Alzheimer's disease is extremely diffuse (see Figure 10.13) and involves areas such as the medial temporal lobe and prefrontal cortex, which play major roles in memory. Furthermore, damage to some structures of the basal forebrain produces attentional deficits, which can easily be mistaken for memory problems (see Baxter & Chiba, 1999; Everitt & Robbins, 1997).

11.4 Amnesia after Concussion: Evidence for Consolidation

Blows to the head that do not penetrate the skull but are severe enough to produce *concussion* (a temporary disturbance of consciousness produced by a nonpenetrating head injury) are the most common causes of amnesia (see Levin, 1989). Amnesia following a nonpenetrating blow to the head is called **posttraumatic amnesia (PTA).**

Clinical Implications

Posttraumatic Amnesia

The *coma* (pathological state of unconsciousness) following a severe blow to the head usually lasts a few seconds or minutes, but in severe cases it can last weeks.

Then, once the patient regains consciousness, there is a period of confusion. Victims of concussion are typically not tested by a neuropsychologist until after the period of confusion—if they are tested at all. Testing usually reveals that the patient has a permanent retrograde amnesia for the events that led up to the blow and a permanent anterograde amnesia for many of the events that occurred during the subsequent period of confusion.

The anterograde memory deficits that follow a nonpenetrating head injury are often quite puzzling to the friends and relatives who have talked to the patient during the period of confusion—for example, during a hospital visit. The patient may seem reasonably lucid at the time, because short-term memory is normal, but later may have no recollection whatsoever of the conversation.

Figure 11.6 summarizes the effects of a closed-head injury on memory. Note that the duration of the period of confusion and anterograde amnesia is typically longer than that of the coma, which is typically longer than the period of retrograde amnesia. More severe blows to the head tend to produce longer comas, longer periods of confusion, and longer periods of amnesia (Levin, Papanicolaou, & Eisenberg, 1984). Not illustrated in Figure 11.6 are *islands of memory*—memories that sometimes survive for isolated events that occurred during periods that have otherwise been wiped out.

Gradients of Retrograde Amnesia and Memory Consolidation

Gradients of retrograde amnesia after concussion seem to provide evidence for *memory consolidation* (see Riccio, Millin, & Gisquet-Verrier, 2003). The fact that concussions preferentially disrupt recent memories suggests that the storage of older memories has been strengthened (i.e., consolidated).

The most prominent theory of memory consolidation is Hebb's theory. He argued that memories of experiences are stored in the short term by neural activity *reverberating* (circulating) in closed circuits. These reverberating patterns of neural activity are susceptible to disruption—for example, by a blow to the head—but eventually they induce structural changes in the involved synapses, which provide stable long-term storage.

Electroconvulsive shock seemed to provide a controlled method of studying memory consolidation. **Electroconvulsive shock (ECS)** is an intense, brief, diffuse, seizure-inducing current that is administered to the brain through large electrodes attached to the scalp. The rationale was that by disrupting neural activity, ECS would erase from storage only those memories that had not yet been converted to structural synaptic changes; the length of the period of retrograde amnesia produced by an ECS would thus provide an estimate of the amount of time needed for memory consolidation.

Many studies have employed ECS to study consolidation. Some studies have been conducted on human patients, who receive ECS for the treatment of depression. However, the most well-controlled studies have been conducted with laboratory animals.

In one such study, thirsty rats were placed for 10 minutes on each of 5 consecutive days in a test box that con-

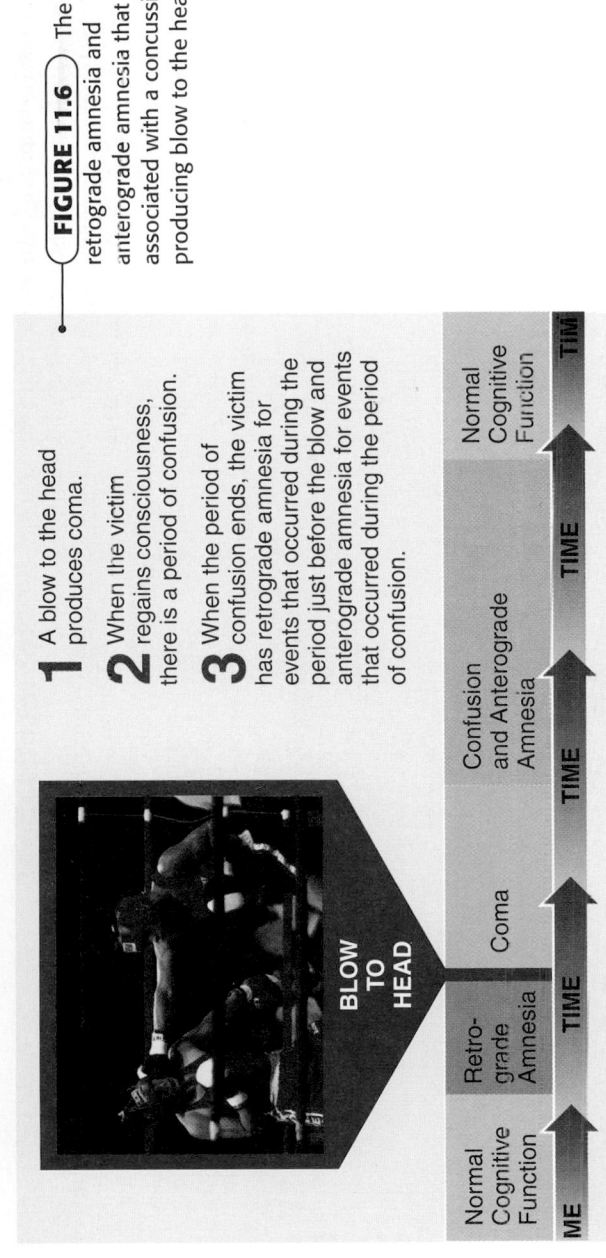

1 A blow to the head produces coma.

2 When the victim regains consciousness, there is a period of confusion.

3 When the period of confusion ends, the victim has retrograde amnesia for events that occurred during the period just before the blow and anterograde amnesia for events that occurred during the period of confusion.

| Normal Cognitive Function | Retrograde Amnesia | Coma | Confusion and Anterograde Amnesia | Normal Cognitive Function |
| ME TIME | TIME | TIME | TIME | TIME |

BLOW TO HEAD

Evolutionary Perspective

tained a small niche. By the 5th of these habituation sessions, most rats explored the niche only 1 or 2 times per session. On the 6th day, a water spout was placed in the niche, and each rat was allowed to drink for 15 seconds after it discovered the spout. This was the learning trial. Then, 10 seconds, 1 minute, 10 minutes, 1 hour, or 3 hours later, each experimental rat received a single ECS. The next day, the retention of all subjects was assessed on the basis of how many times each explored the niche when the water spout was not present. The control rats that experi-

enced the learning trial but received no ECS explored the empty niche an average of 10 times during the 10-minute test session, thereby indicating that they remembered their discovery of water the previous day. The rats that had received ECS 1 hour or 3 hours after the learning trial also explored the niche about 10 times. In contrast, the rats that received the ECS 10 seconds, 1 minute, or 10 minutes after the learning trial explored the empty niche significantly less on the test day. This result suggested that the consolidation of the memory of the learning trial took between 10 minutes and 1 hour (see Figure 11.7).

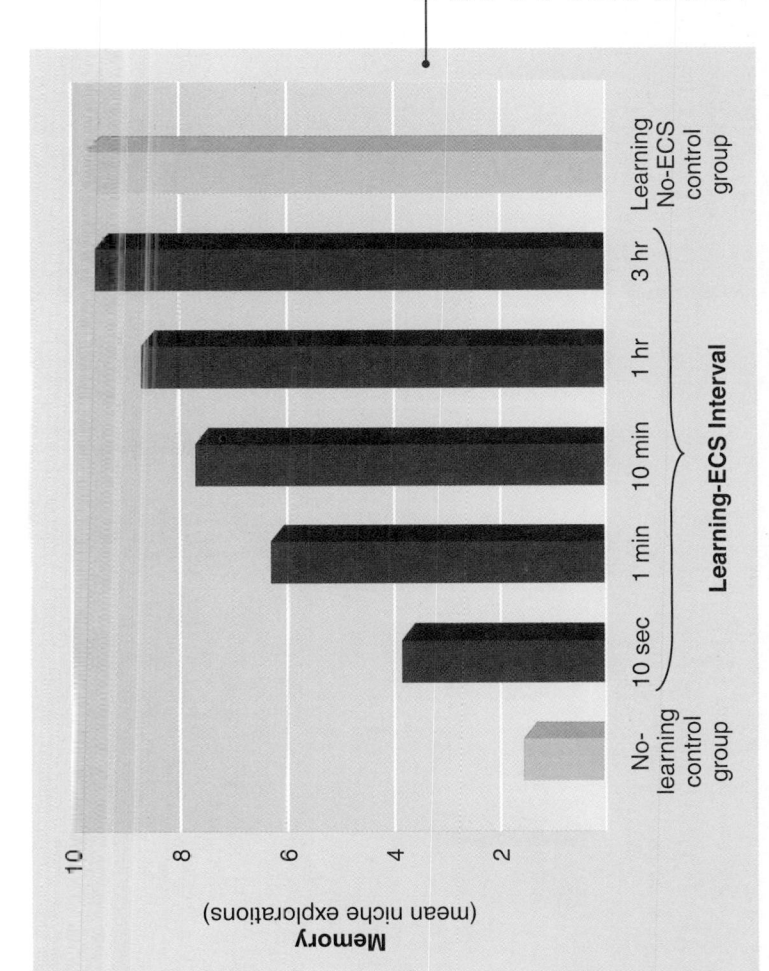

FIGURE 11.7 A short gradient of ECS-produced retrograde amnesia. Retention of one-trial appetitive learning by a control group of rats and by groups of rats that received ECS at various intervals after the learning trial. Only the rats that received ECS within 10 minutes of the learning trial displayed significant retrograde amnesia for it. (Adapted from Pinel, 1969.)

Memory (mean niche explorations)

No-learning control group   10 sec   1 min   10 min   1 hr   3 hr   Learning No-ECS control group

Learning-ECS Interval

Numerous variations of this experiment were conducted in the 1950s and 1960s, with different learning tasks, different species, and different numbers and intensities of electroconvulsive shocks. Initially, there was some consistency in the findings: Most seemed to suggest a rather brief consolidation time of a few minutes or less (e.g., Chorover & Schiller, 1965). But some researchers observed very long gradients of ECS-produced retrograde amnesia. For example, Squire, Slater, and Chace (1975) measured the memory of a group of ECS-treated patients for television shows that had played for only one season in different years prior to their electroconvulsive therapy. They tested each subject twice on different forms of the test: once before they received a series of five electroconvulsive shocks and once after. The difference between the before-and-after scores served as an estimate of memory loss for the events of each year. Figure 11.8 illustrates that five electroconvulsive shocks disrupted the retention of television shows that had played in the 3 years prior to treatment but not those that had played earlier.

Long gradients of retrograde amnesia are incompatible with Hebb's theory of consolidation. It is reasonable to think of the neural activity resulting from an experience reverberating through the brain for a few seconds or even a few minutes; but gradients of retrograde amnesia covering days, weeks, or years cannot be easily accounted for by the disruption of reverberatory neural activity (e.g., Squire & Spanis, 1984). Long gradients of retrograde amnesia indicate that memory consolidation can continue for a very long time after learning, perhaps indefinitely.

Reconsolidation

One theoretical construct that has attracted attention recently is *reconsolidation* (see Dudai, 2002). According to this notion, each time a memory is retrieved from long-term storage, it is temporarily held in labile short-term memory, where it is once again susceptible to posttraumatic amnesia before it is reconsolidated.

Interest in the process of reconsolidation originated with several studies in the 1960s but then faded. A key study by Nader, Schafe, and LeDoux (2000) rekindled this interest. These researchers infused the protein-synthesis inhibitor *anisomycin* into the amygdalae of rats shortly after the rats had been required to recall a fear conditioning trial. The infusion produced retrograde amnesia for the fear conditioning, even though the original conditioning trial had occurred days before.

The Hippocampus and Consolidation

The discovery that H.M. seemed to be suffering from a temporally graded retrograde amnesia led Scoville and Milner (1957) to conclude that the hippocampus and related structures play a role in consolidation. To account for the fact that the bilateral medial temporal lobectomy disrupted only those retrograde memories acquired in the period just before H.M.'s surgery, they suggested that memories are temporarily stored in the hippocampus until they can be transferred to a more stable cortical storage system. This theory has been supported by several demonstrations that medial temporal lobe lesions produce

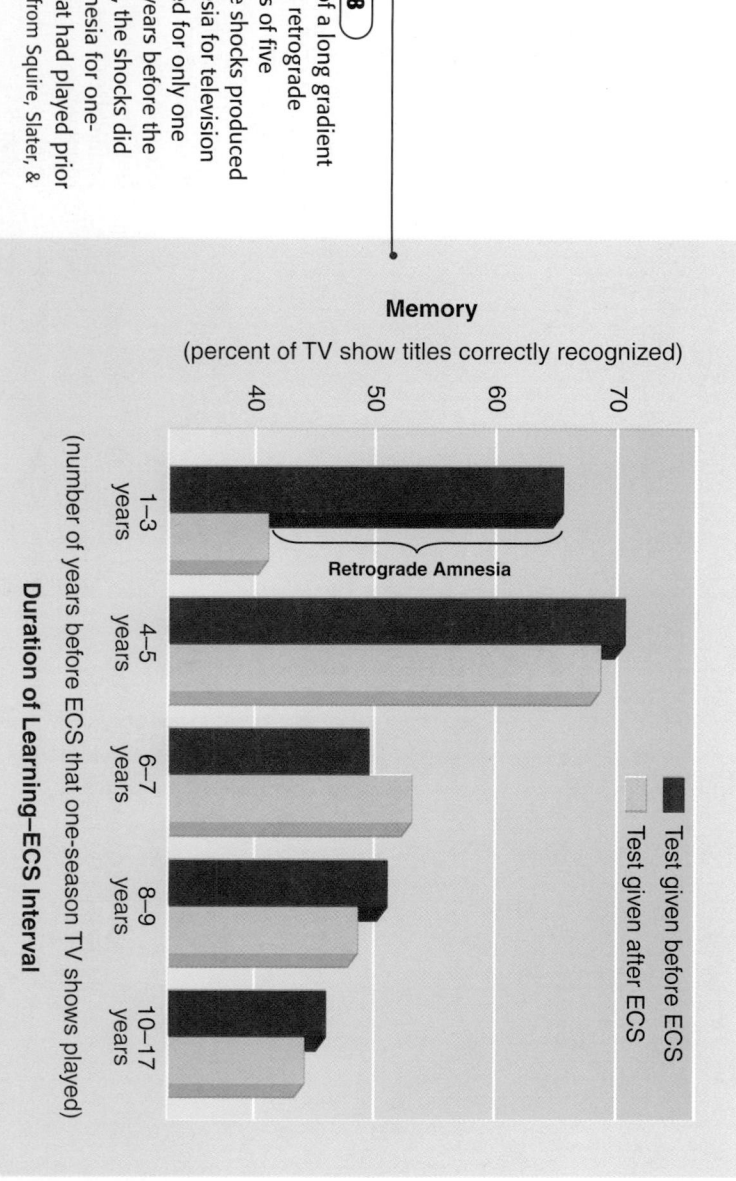

FIGURE 11.8

Demonstration of a long gradient of ECS-produced retrograde amnesia. A series of five electroconvulsive shocks produced retrograde amnesia for television shows that played for only one season in the 3 years before the shocks; however, the shocks did not produce amnesia for one-season shows that had played prior to that. (Adapted from Squire, Slater, & Chace, 1975.)

Memory

(percent of TV show titles correctly recognized)

40   50   60   70

Retrograde Amnesia

1–3 years   4–5 years   6–7 years   8–9 years   10–17 years

(number of years before ECS that one-season TV shows played)

Duration of Learning–ECS Interval

■ Test given before ECS
□ Test given after ECS

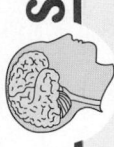

SCAN YOUR BRAIN

This chapter is about to move from discussion of human memory disorders to consideration of animal models of human memory disorders. Are you ready? Scan your brain to assess your knowledge of human memory disorders by filling in the blanks in the following sentences. The correct answers are provided at the bottom of this page. Before proceeding, review the material related to your errors and omissions.

1. H.M. had his _____ temporal lobes removed.

2. The mirror-drawing test, the rotary pursuit test, the incomplete-pictures test, and the repetition priming test are all test of _____ memory.

3. H.M. appears incapable of forming new long-term _____ memories.

4. Support for the view that hippocampal damage can by itself cause amnesia comes from the study or R.B., who suffered _____ damage to the pyramidal cells of his CA1 hippocampal subfield.

5. The current view is that damage to the diencephalon _____ is responsible for most of the memory deficits of people with Korsakoff's disease.

6. The gradual onset of Korsakoff's syndrome complicates the study of the resulting _____ amnesia.

7. The _____ nuclei are the medial diencephalic nuclei that have been most frequently implicated in memory.

8. Alzheimer's disease is associated with degeneration of _____ neurons in the basal forebrain.

9. Posttraumatic amnesia can be induced with _____ shock, which is used in the treatment of depression.

10. The transfer of a memory from short-term storage to long-term storage is termed _____.

11. Because some gradients of retrograde amnesia are extremely long, it is unlikely that memory consolidation is mediated by _____ neural activity, as hypothesized by Hebb.

12. The changes in the brain that store memories are called _____.

---

temporally graded retrograde amnesia in experimental animals (e.g., Haist, Bowden, & Mao, 2001; Hanson, Bunsey, & Riccio, 2002; Squire, Clark, & Knowlton, 2001).

Several alternative theories of memory consolidation have been proposed (see James & MacKay, 2001). The theory of Nadel and Moscovitch (1997) is particularly compatible with the finding that gradients of retrograde amnesia are often very long. Nadel and Moscovitch proposed that the hippocampus and other structures involved in memory storage store memories for as long as they exist—not just during the period im-

mediately after learning. When a conscious experience occurs, it is rapidly and sparsely encoded in a distributed fashion throughout the hippocampus and other involved structures. According to Nadel and Moscovitch, retained memories become progressively more resistant to disruption by hippocampal damage because each time a similar experience occurs or the original memory is recalled, a new **engram** (a change in the brain that stores a memory) is established and linked to the original engram, making the memory easier to recall and the original engram more difficult to disrupt.

11.5 Neuroanatomy of Object-Recognition Memory

Thinking Critically

As interesting and informative as the study of amnesic patients can be, it has major limitations. Many important questions about the neural bases of amnesia can be answered only by controlled experiments. For example, in order to identify the particular structures of the brain that participate in various kinds of memory, it is necessary to make precise lesions in various structures and to control what and when the subjects learn, and how and when their retention is tested. Because such experiments are not feasible with human subjects, there

has been a major effort to develop animal models of human brain-damage-produced amnesia.

The first reports of H.M.'s case in the 1950s triggered a massive effort to develop an animal model of his disorder so that it could be subjected to experimental

---

Scan Your Brain answers: (1) medial, (2) implicit, (3) explicit, (4) ischemic, (5) medial, (6) retrograde, (7) mediodorsal, (8) cholinergic, (9) electroconvulsive, (10) consolidation, (11) reverberating, (12) engrams.

analysis. In its early years, this effort was a dismal failure; lesions of medial temporal lobe structures did not produce severe anterograde amnesia in rats, monkeys, or other nonhuman species.

In retrospect, there were two reasons for the initial difficulty in developing an animal model of medial temporal lobe amnesia. First, it was not initially apparent that H.M.'s anterograde amnesia did not extend to all kinds of long-term memory—that is, that it was specific to explicit long-term memories—and most animal memory tests that were widely used in the 1950s and 1960s were tests of implicit memory (e.g., Pavlovian and operant conditioning). Second, it was incorrectly assumed that the amnesic effects of medial temporal lobe lesions were largely, if not entirely, attributable to hippocampal damage; and most efforts to develop animal models of medial temporal lobe amnesia thus focused on hippocampal lesions.

Monkey Model of Object-Recognition Amnesia: The Delayed Nonmatching-to-Sample Test

Finally, in the mid 1970s, over two decades after the first reports of H.M.'s remarkable case, an animal model of his disorder was developed. It was hailed as a major breakthrough because it opened up the neuroanatomy of medial temporal lobe amnesia to experimental investigation.

In separate laboratories, Gaffan (1974) and Mishkin and Delacour (1975) showed that monkeys with bilateral medial temporal lobectomies have major problems forming long-term memories for objects encountered in the **delayed nonmatching-to-sample test**. In this test, a monkey is presented with a distinctive object (the *sample object*), under which it finds food (e.g., a banana pellet). Then, after a delay, the monkey is presented with two test objects: the sample object and an unfamiliar object. The monkey must remember the sample object so that it can select the unfamiliar object to obtain food concealed beneath it. The correct performance of a trial is illustrated in Figure 11.9.

Intact, well-trained monkeys performed correctly on about 90% of the delayed nonmatching-to-sample trials when the retention intervals were a few minutes or less. In contrast, monkeys with bilateral medial temporal lobe lesions had major object-recognition deficits (see Figure 11.10). These deficits modeled those of H.M. in key respects. For example, the monkeys' performance was normal at delays of a few seconds but fell off to near chance levels at delays of several minutes, and their performance was extremely susceptible to the disruptive effects of distraction (Squire & Zola-Morgan, 1985). In fact, human medial temporal lobe amnesics have been tested on the delayed nonmatching-to-sample test—their re-

wards were coins rather than banana pellets—and their performance mirrored the performance of monkeys with similar brain damage.

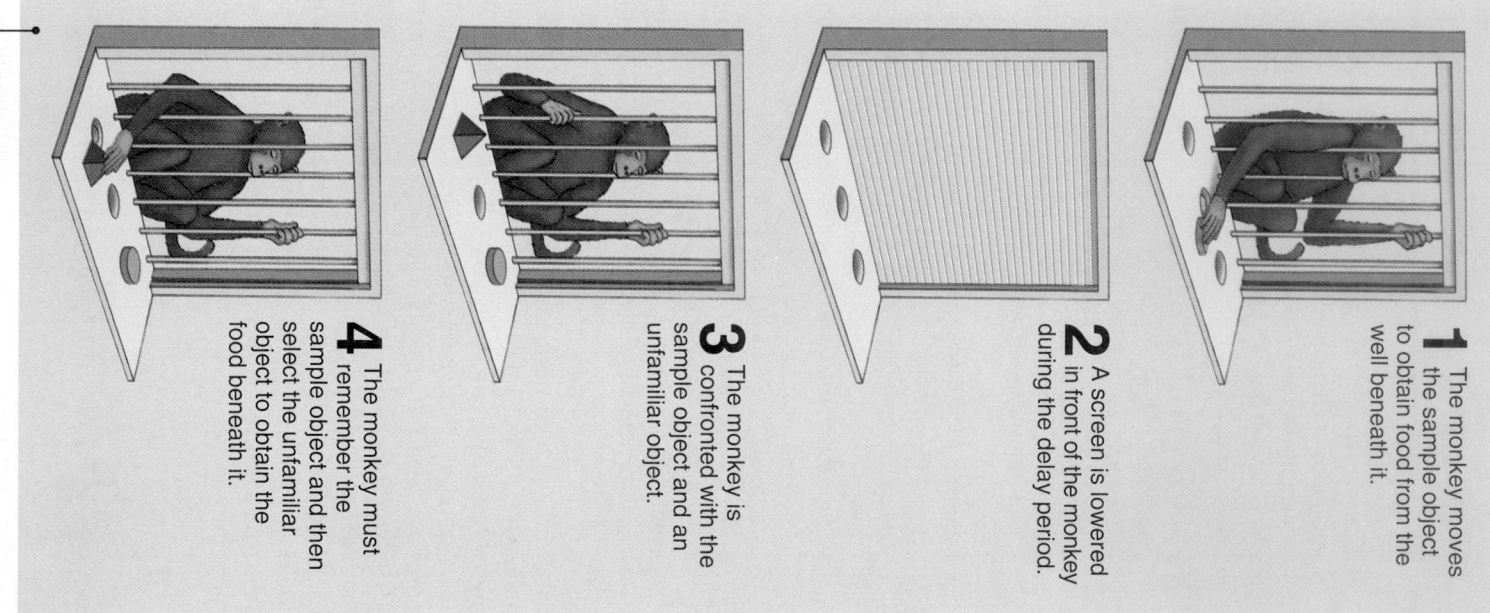

FIGURE 11.9   The correct performance of a delayed nonmatching-to-sample trial. (Adapted from Mishkin & Appenzeller, 1987.)

1 The monkey moves the sample object to obtain food from the well beneath it.

2 A screen is lowered in front of the monkey during the delay period.

3 The monkey is confronted with the sample object and an unfamiliar object.

4 The monkey must remember the sample object and then select the unfamiliar object to obtain the food beneath it.

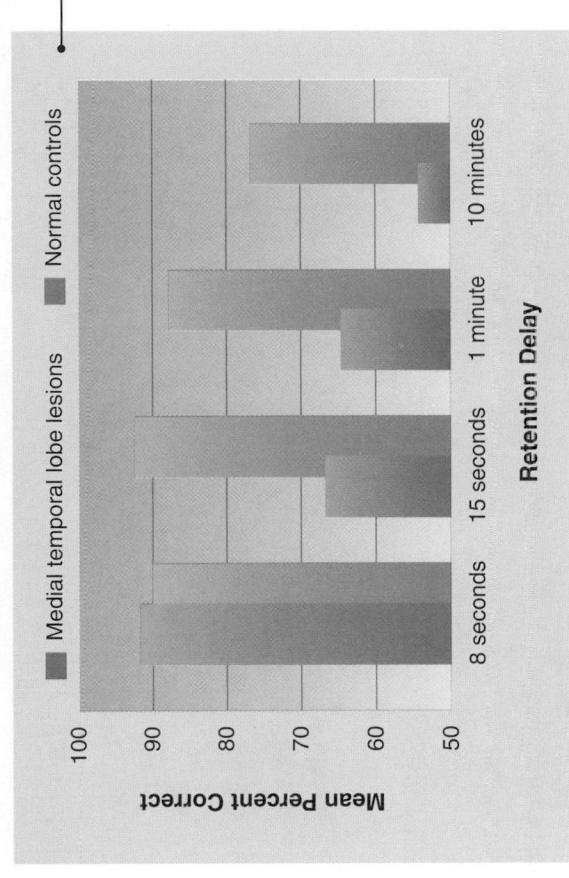

FIGURE 11.10 The performance deficits of monkeys with large bilateral medial temporal lobe lesions on the delayed nonmatching-to-sample test. There were significant deficits at all but the shortest retention interval. These deficits parallel the memory deficits of human medial temporal lobe amnesics on the same task. (Adapted from Squire & Zola-Morgan, 1991.)

The development of the delayed nonmatching-to-sample test for monkeys provided a means of testing the assumption that the amnesia resulting from medial temporal lobe damage is entirely the consequence of hippocampal damage—Figure 11.11 illustrates the locations in the monkey brain of the three major temporal lobe structures: hippocampus, amygdala, and adjacent **rhinal cortex**. But before we consider this important line of research, we need to look at another important method-

ological development: the rat version of the delayed nonmatching-to-sample test.

The Delayed Nonmatching-to-Sample Test for Rats

In order to understand why the development of the rat version of the delayed nonmatching-to-sample test

Evolutionary Perspective

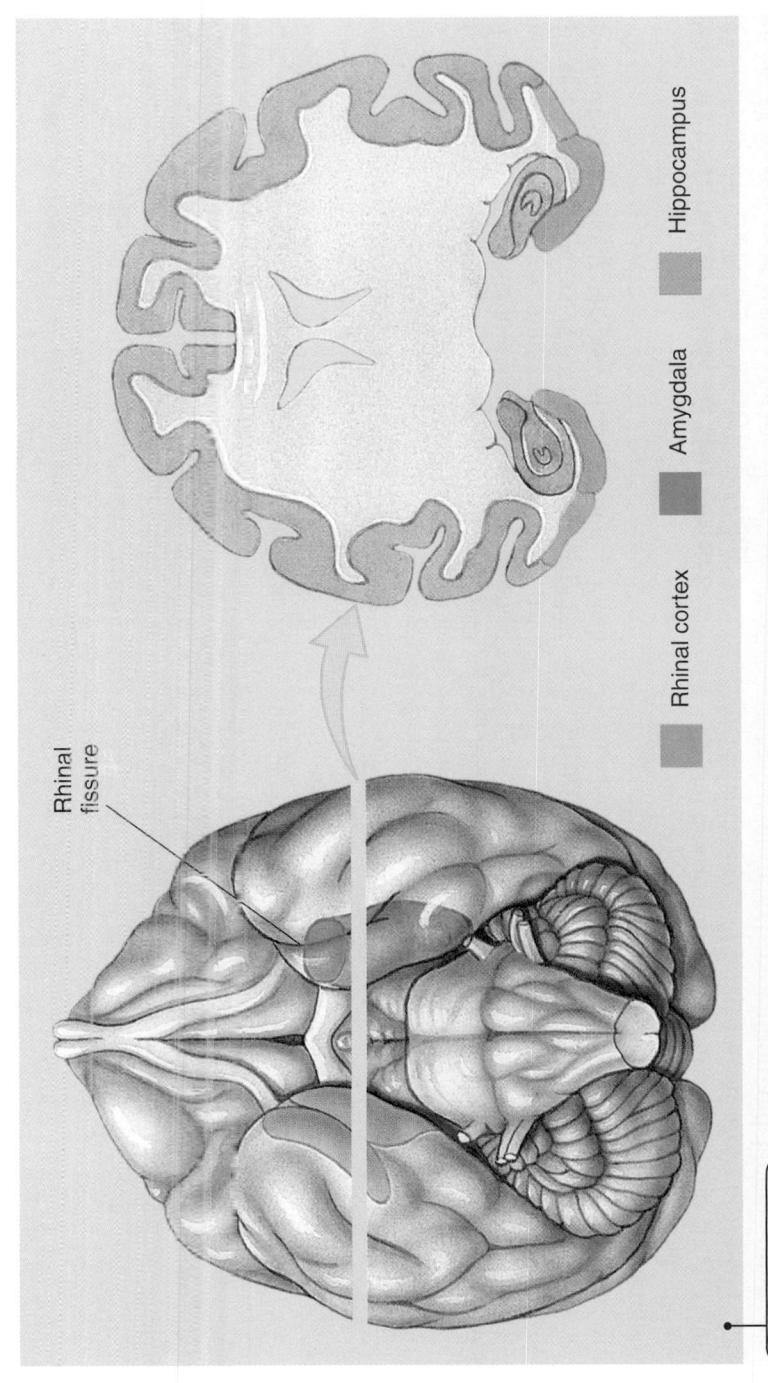

FIGURE 11.11 The three major structures of the medial temporal lobe, illustrated in the monkey brain: the hippocampus, the amygdala, and the rhinal cortex.

FIGURE 11.12 Aspiration lesions of the hippocampus in monkeys and rats. Because of differences in the size and location of the hippocampus in monkeys and in rats, hippocampectomy typically involves the removal of large amounts of rhinal cortex in monkeys, but not in rats.

played an important role in assessing the specific role of hippocampal damage in medial temporal lobe amnesia, examine Figure 11.12, which illustrates the usual methods of making hippocampal lesions in monkeys and rats. Because of the size and location of the hippocampus, almost all studies of hippocampal lesions in monkeys have involved *aspiration* (suction) of large portions of the rhinal cortex in addition to the hippocampus. However, in rats the extraneous damage associated with aspiration lesions of the hippocampus is typically limited to a small area of parietal neocortex. Furthermore, the rat hippocampus is small enough that it can readily be lesioned electrolytically or with intracerebral neurotoxin injections; in either case, there is little extraneous damage.

The version of the delayed nonmatching-to-sample test for rats that most closely resembles that for monkeys was developed by David Mumby using an apparatus that has become known as the **Mumby box.** This rat version of the test is illustrated in Figure 11.13

It was once assumed that rats could not perform a task as complex as that required for the delayed nonmatching-to-sample test; Figure 11.14 on page 276 indicates otherwise. Rats perform almost as well as monkeys with delays of up to 1 minute (Mumby, Pinel, & Wood, 1989).

The validity of the rat version of the delayed nonmatching-to-sample test has been established by studies of the effects of medial temporal lobe lesions. Combined bilateral lesions of rats' hippocampus, amygdala, and rhinal cortex produce major retention deficits at all but the shortest retention intervals (Mumby, Wood, & Pinel, 1992).

Neuroanatomical Basis of the Object-Recognition Deficits Resulting from Medial Temporal Lobectomy

To what extent are the object-recognition deficits following bilateral medial temporal lobectomy a consequence of hippocampal damage? In the early 1990s, researchers began assessing the relative effects on performance in the delayed nonmatching-to-sample test of lesions to various medial temporal lobe structures in both monkeys and rats. Early challenges to the preeminence of the hippocampus (Meunier et al., 1990; Mumby, Wood, & Pinel, 1992; Zola-Morgan et al., 1989) attracted the interest of other researchers and yielded many relevant findings. Reviewers of this research (Brown & Aggleton, 2001; Duva, Kornecook, & Pinel, 2000; Mumby, 2001; Murray, 1996; Murray & Richmond, 2001) have all reached similar conclusions: Bilateral surgical removal of the rhinal cortex consistently produces severe and permanent deficits in performance on the delayed nonmatching-to-sample test and other tests of object recognition. In contrast, bilateral surgical removal of the hippocampus produces either moderate deficits or none at all, and bilateral destruction of the amygdala has no effect. Figure 11.15 on page 276 compares the effects of rhinal cortex lesions on object recognition and hippocampus-plus-amygdala lesions on object recognition in rats.

The reports that object-recognition memory is severely disrupted by rhinal cortex lesions but only mod-

The Location of the Hippocampus

Monkeys

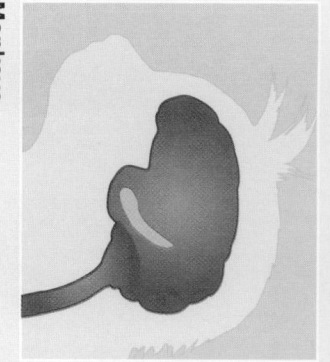

In monkeys, the hippocampus is usually removed by aspiration via the inferior surface of the brain, thus destroying substantial amounts of rhinal cortex.

Rats

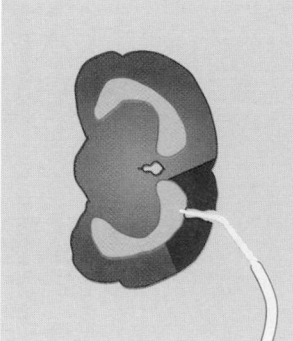
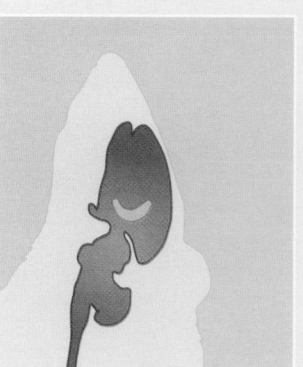

In rats, the hippocampus is usually removed by aspiration from the superior surface of the brain, thus destroying small amounts of parietal neocortex.

Evolutionary Perspective

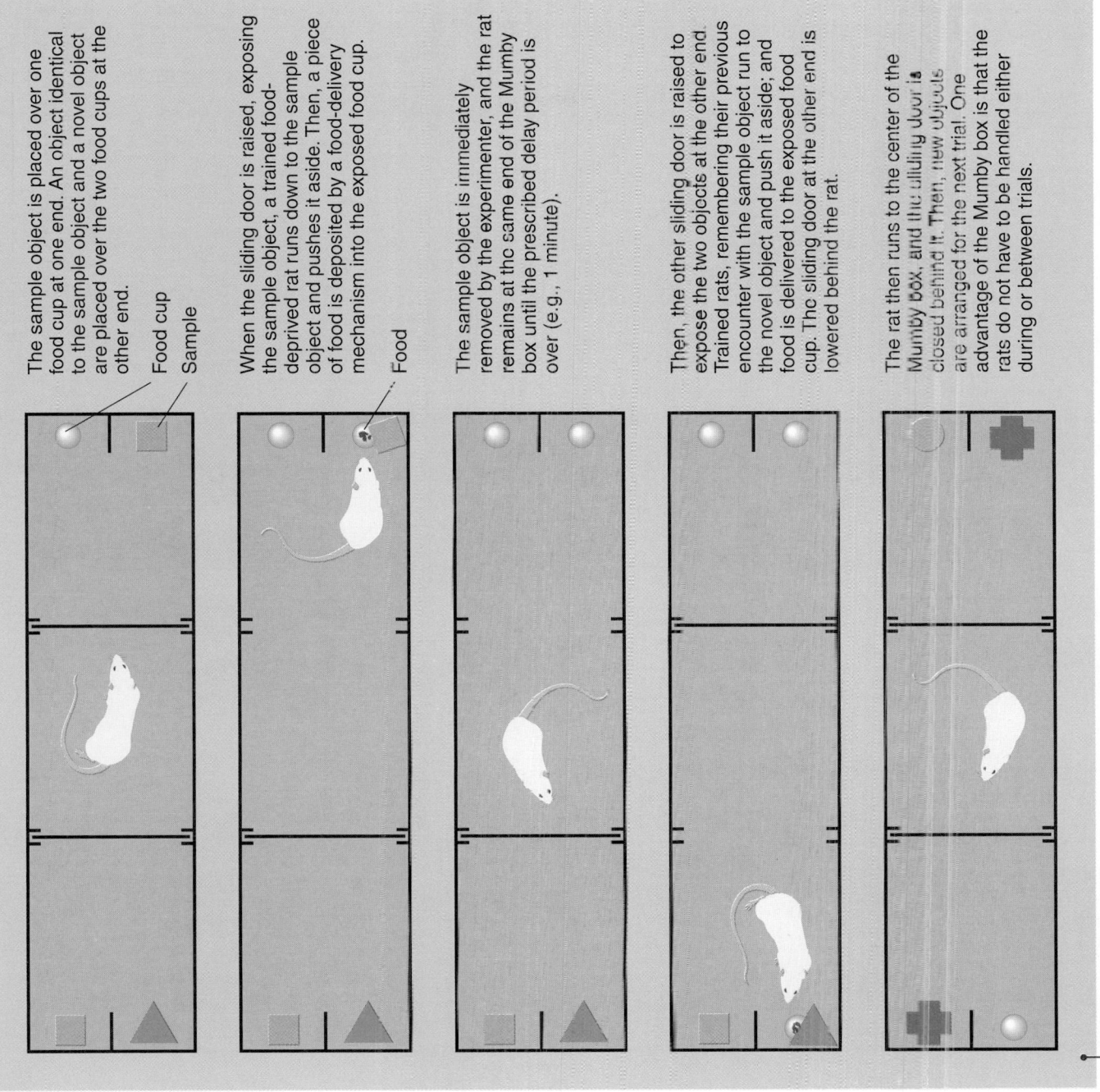

FIGURE 11.13 The Mumby box and the rat version of the delayed nonmatching-to-sample test.

The sample object is placed over one food cup at one end. An object identical to the sample object and a novel object are placed over the two food cups at the other end.

Food cup
Sample

When the sliding door is raised, exposing the sample object, a trained food-deprived rat runs down to the sample object and pushes it aside. Then, a piece of food is deposited by a food-delivery mechanism into the exposed food cup.

Food

The sample object is immediately removed by the experimenter, and the rat remains at the same end of the Mumby box until the prescribed delay period is over (e.g., 1 minute).

Then, the other sliding door is raised to expose the two objects at the other end. Trained rats, remembering their previous encounter with the sample object run to the novel object and push it aside; and food is delivered to the exposed food cup. The sliding door at the other end is lowered behind the rat.

The rat then runs to the center of the Mumby box, and the sliding door is closed behind it. Then, new objects are arranged for the next trial. One advantage of the Mumby box is that the rats do not have to be handled either during or between trials.

erately by hippocampal lesions led to a resurgence of interest in the case of R.B. and others like it. Earlier in this chapter, you learned that R.B. was left amnesic following an ischemic accident that occurred during heart surgery and that subsequent analysis of his brain revealed that obvious cell loss was restricted largely to the pyramidal cell layer of his CA1 hippocampal subfield (see Figure 11.5). This result has been replicated in both monkeys and rats. In both monkeys (Zola-Morgan et al., 1992) and rats (Wood et al., 1993), cerebral ischemia leads to

a loss of CA1 hippocampal pyramidal cells and severe deficits in the delayed nonmatching-to-sample task.

The relation between ischemia-produced hippocampal damage and object-recognition deficits in humans, monkeys, and rats seems to provide strong support for the theory that the hippocampus plays a key role in object-recognition memory. But there is a gnawing problem with this line of evidence: How can ischemia-produced lesions to one small part of the hippocampus

Thinking Critically

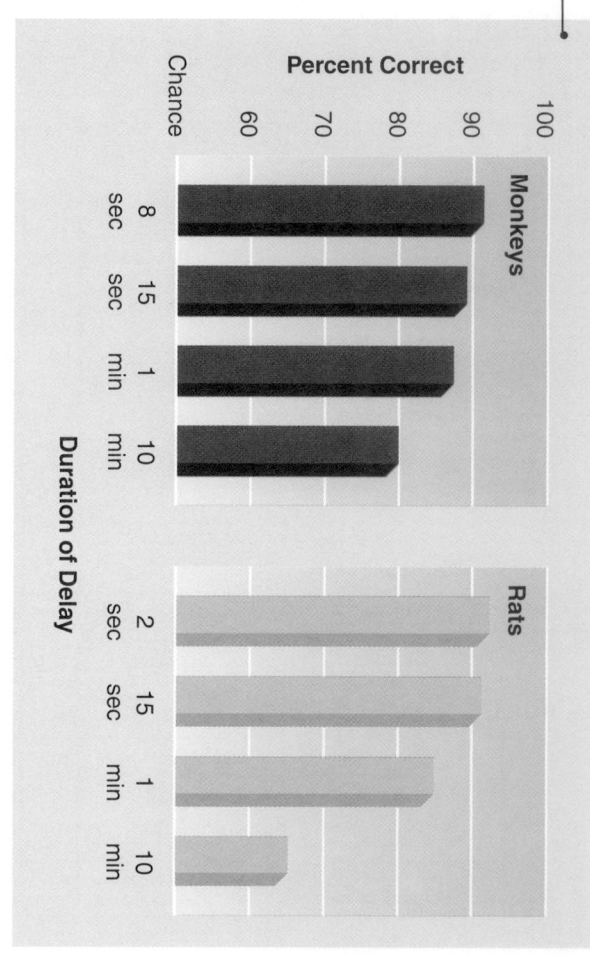

FIGURE 11.14 A comparison of the performance of intact monkeys (Zola-Morgan, Squire, & Mishkin, 1982) and intact rats (Mumby, Pinel, & Wood, 1989) on the delayed nonmatching-to-sample test.

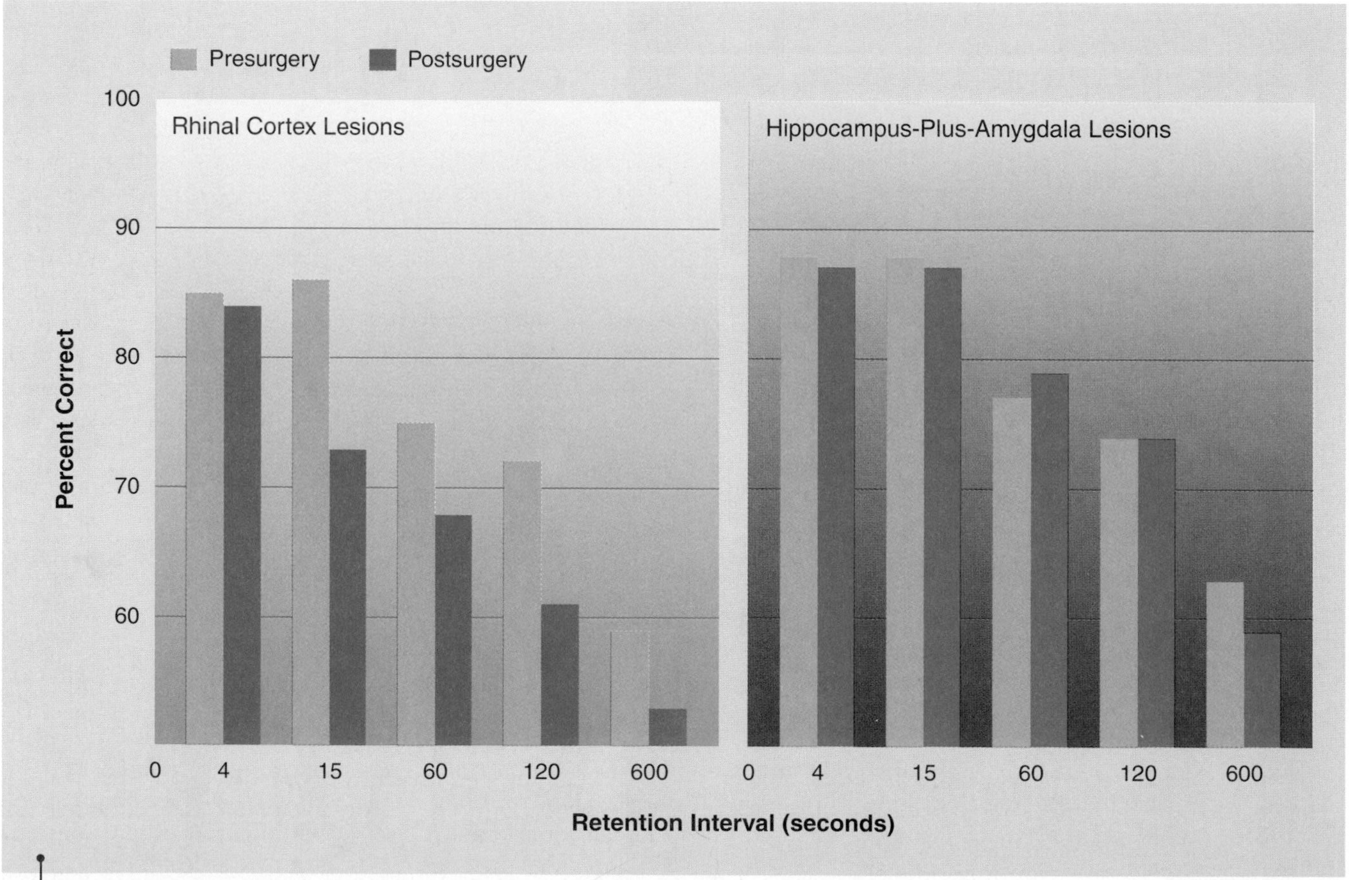

FIGURE 11.15 Effects of rhinal cortex lesions and hippocampus-plus-amygdala lesions in rats. Lesions of the rhinal cortex, but not of the hippocampus and amygdala combined, produced severe deficits in performance of the delayed nonmatching-to-sample test in rats. (Adapted from Mumby & Pinel, 1994; Mumby, Wood, & Pinel, 1992.)

Percent Correct

Presurgery

Postsurgery

Rhinal Cortex Lesions

Hippocampus-Plus-Amygdala Lesions

Retention Interval (seconds)

be associated with severe deficits in performance on the delayed nonmatching-to-sample test when the deficits associated with total removal of the hippocampus are only moderate?

Mumby and his colleagues (1996) conducted an experiment that appears to resolve this paradox. They hypothesized the following: (1) that the ischemia-produced hyperactivity of CA1 pyramidal cells damages neurons outside the hippocampus, possibly through the excessive release of excitatory amino acid neurotransmitters; (2) that this extrahippocampal damage is not readily detectable by conventional histological analysis (i.e., it does not involve concentrated cell loss); and (3) that this extrahippocampal damage is largely responsible for the object-recognition deficits that are produced by cerebral ischemia. Mumby and colleagues supported their hypothesis by showing that bilateral hippocampectomy actually blocks the development of ischemia-produced deficits in performance on the delayed nonmatching-to-sample test. First, they produced cerebral ischemia in rats by temporarily tying off their carotid arteries. Then, one group of the ischemic rats received a bilateral hip-

pocampectomy 1 hour later, a second group received a bilateral hippocampectomy 1 week later, and a third group received no bilateral hippocampectomy. Following recovery, the latter two groups of ischemic rats displayed severe object-recognition deficits, whereas the rats whose hippocampus had been removed 1 hour after ischemia did not. Explaining how hippocampectomy can prevent the development of the object-recognition deficits normally produced by cerebral ischemia is a major problem for the theory that the hippocampus plays a critical role in object-recognition memory.

Support for the theory that the object-recognition deficits of ischemic patients result from extrahippocampal disturbances comes from functional brain-imaging studies. Widespread cerebral dysfunction is commonly observed in neuro-anatomically intact areas distant from sites of ischemic cell loss (e.g., Baron, 1989; Fazio et al., 1992). Consequently, cases of ischemia-produced amnesia with hippocampal cell loss (cases such as that of R.B.) provide only equivocal evidence that the hippocampus plays the major role in object recognition.

Cognitive Neuroscience

11.6 The Hippocampus and Memory for Spatial Location

The discovery that the rhinal cortex plays a more important role than the hippocampus in object recognition does not mean that the hippocampus plays no significant role in memory. Indeed, the hippocampus plays a key role in memory for spatial location.

Hippocampal Lesions Disrupt Spatial Memory

Bilateral lesions of the hippocampus in laboratory animals often have little or no effect on performance on memory tests. But there is one exception to this general result: Hippocampal lesions consistently disrupt the performance of tasks that involve the memory for spatial location (e.g., Kaut & Bunsey, 2001; McDonald & White, 1993; O'Keefe, 1993). For example, hippocampal lesions disrupt performance on the *Morris water maze test* and the *radial arm maze test*.

In the **Morris water maze test**, intact rats placed at various locations in a circular pool of murky water rapidly learn to swim to a stationary platform hidden just below the surface. Rats with hippocampal lesions learn this simple task with great difficulty.

In the **radial arm maze test**, several arms (e.g., eight arms) radiate out from a central starting chamber, and the same few arms are baited with food each day. Intact

Evolutionary Perspective

rats readily learn to visit only those arms that contain food, without visiting the same arm more than once each day. The ability to visit only the baited arms of the radial arm maze is a measure of **reference memory** (memory for the general principles and skills that are required to perform a task), and the ability to refrain from visiting an arm more than once in a given day is a measure of **working memory** (temporary memory that is necessary for the successful performance of a task on which one is currently working). Rats with hippocampal lesions display major deficits on both the reference memory and the working memory measures of radial arm maze performance.

Hippocampal Place Cells

Consistent with the observation that hippocampal lesions disrupt spatial memory is the fact that many hippocampal neurons are **place cells** (Best, White, & Minai, 2001; Brun et al., 2002; Moser and Paulsen, 2001)—neurons that respond only when a subject is in specific locations (i.e., in the *place fields* of the neurons). For example, when a rat is first placed in an unfamiliar test environment, none of its hippocampal neurons have a place field in that environment; then, as the rat familiarizes itself with the environment, many hippocampal neurons acquire a place field in it—that is, each fires only when the rat is in a particular part of the test environment. Each place cell has a place field in a different part of the environment.

By placing a rat in an ambiguous situation in a familiar test environment, it is possible to determine where the rat thinks it is from the route it takes to get to the location in the environment where it has previously been rewarded. Using this strategy, researchers (O'Keefe & Speakman, 1987; Wilson & McNaughton, 1993) have shown that the firing of a rat's place cells indicates where the rat "thinks" it is in the test environment, not necessarily where it actually is.

Comparative Studies of the Hippocampus and Spatial Memory

Although most of the evidence that the hippocampus plays a role in spatial memory comes from research on rats, the hippocampus seems to perform a similar function in many other species (see Colombo & Broadbent, 2000). Most noteworthy has been the research in food-caching birds. Food-caching birds must have remarkable spatial memories, because in order to survive, they must remember the locations of hundreds of food caches scattered around their territories. In one study, Sherry and Vaccarino (1989) found that food-caching species tended to have larger hippocampuses than related non–food-caching species. Indeed, Clayton (2001) found that caching and retrieving are required to trigger hippocampal growth and maintain its size in mountain chickadees.

Although research on a variety of species indicates that the hippocampus does play a role in spatial memory, the evidence from primate studies has been less consistent. The hippocampal pyramidal cells of primates do have place fields (Rolls, Robertson, & Georges-François, 1995), but the effects of hippocampal damage on the performance of spatial memory tasks have been mixed

(e.g., Henke et al., 1999; Maguire et al., 1998; Kessels et al., 2001; Maguire et al., 1998). The problem may be that spatial memory in humans and monkeys is typically tested with subjects remaining stationary and making judgments of locations on computer screens, whereas spatial memory in rats, mice, and birds is typically studied as subjects navigate through controlled test environments (see Suzuki & Clayton, 2000). The results of two studies by Maguire and colleagues suggest that this is the case.

First, Maguire and colleagues (1998) used positron emission tomography (PET) to record the brain activity of subjects as they learned to find their way around a virtual-reality town. Activation of the right hippocampus was strongly associated with knowing where places were

and navigating accurately to them. Second, Maguire and colleagues (2000) used structural magnetic resonance imaging (MRI) to estimate hippocampal volume in a group of humans who had intensive spatial training—London taxi drivers. They found that London taxi drivers with more than 20 years of experience had significantly more posterior hippocampal gray matter than usual.

Theories of Hippocampal Function

There are many theories of hippocampal function, all of which acknowledge the important role of the hippocampus in spatial memory. Let's take a look at three of these theories.

O'Keefe and Nadel (1978) proposed the **cognitive map theory** of hippocampal function. According to this theory, there are several systems in the brain that specialize in the memory for different kinds of information, and the specific function of the hippocampus is the storage of memories for spatial location. Specifically, Nadel and O'Keefe proposed that the hippocampus constructs and stores allocentric maps of the external world from the sensory input that it receives. *Allocentric* refers to representations of space based on relations among external objects and landmarks; in contrast, *egocentric* refers to representations of space based on relations to one's own position.

Another influential theory of hippocampal function is the *configural association theory* (Rudy & Sutherland, 1992). The configural association theory is based on the premise that spatial memory is one specific manifestation of the hippocampus's more general function. The configural association theory is that the hippocampus plays a role in the retention of the behavioral significance of combinations of stimuli but not of individual stimuli. For example, according to this theory, the hippocampus is involved in remembering that a flashing light in a particular context (i.e., at a particular location or time) signals food but not that a flashing light signals food irrespective of the context. There is substantial support for this theory; however, there have also been some failures to disrupt the performance of nonspatial configural tasks with hippocampal lesions (e.g., Bussey et al., 1998).

Finally, Brown and Aggleton (2001) have proposed a specific theory of the role of the hippocampus in object recognition and its relation to that of the rhinal cortex. They concur with the evidence that the rhinal cortex, not the hippocampus, plays a role in most object-recognition tasks. However, they suggest that the hippocampus plays a role in recognizing spatial arrangements of objects, as in a visual scene, for example (see Wan, Aggleton, & Brown, 1999).

11.7 Where Are Memories Stored?

Evidence suggests that each memory is stored diffusely throughout the structures of the brain that participated in its original experience (see Fries, Fernández, & Jensen, 2003; Nyberg et al., 2000; Wheeler, Petersen, & Buckner, 2000). This chapter has focused on two structures of the medial temporal lobes—the hippocampus and the rhinal cortex—and their roles in spatial location and object recognition, respectively. Attention was also given to the mediodorsal nucleus and basal forebrain; the mnemonic functions of these structures is less well understood, but they have been implicated in memory by studies of Korsakoff's and Alzheimer's patients, respectively. In this section, we take a brief look at five other areas of the brain that have been implicated in memory storage: inferotemporal cortex, amygdala, prefrontal cortex, cerebellum, and striatum. See Figure 11.16.

Inferotemporal Cortex

Areas of secondary sensory cortex are presumed to play an important role in storing sensory memories. For example, because the **inferotemporal cortex** (the cortex of the inferior temporal lobe) is involved in the visual perception of objects, it is thought to participate in storing memories of visual patterns (see Rossion et al., 2001). In support of this view, Naya, Yoshida, and Miyashita (2001) recorded the responses of neurons in inferotemporal cortex and rhinal cortex while monkeys learned the relation between the two items in pairs of visual images. When a pair was presented, responses were first recorded in inferotemporal neurons and then in rhinal neurons; however, when the monkeys were required to recall the same pair, activity was recorded in rhinal neurons before inferotemporal neurons. Naya and colleagues concluded that this reversed pattern of activity reflected the retrieval of visual memories from inferotemporal cortex.

Amygdala

The amygdala seems to play a role in memory for the emotional significance of experiences. Rats with amygdalar lesions, unlike intact rats, do not respond with fear to a neutral stimulus that has been repeatedly followed by electric footshocks (see McGaugh, 2002; Medina et al., 2002). Also, Bechara and colleagues (1995)

Clinical Implications

reported the case of a neuropsychological patient with bilateral damage to the amygdala who could not acquire conditioned autonomic startle responses to various visual or auditory stimuli but had good explicit memory for them.

Prefrontal Cortex

Patients with damage to the *prefrontal cortex* are not grossly amnesic; they often display no deficits at all on conventional tests of memory (see Müller, Machado, & Knight, 2002; Petrides, 1996). They do, however, display deficits in memory for the temporal order of events, even when they can remember the events themselves, as well as deficits in *working memory* (the

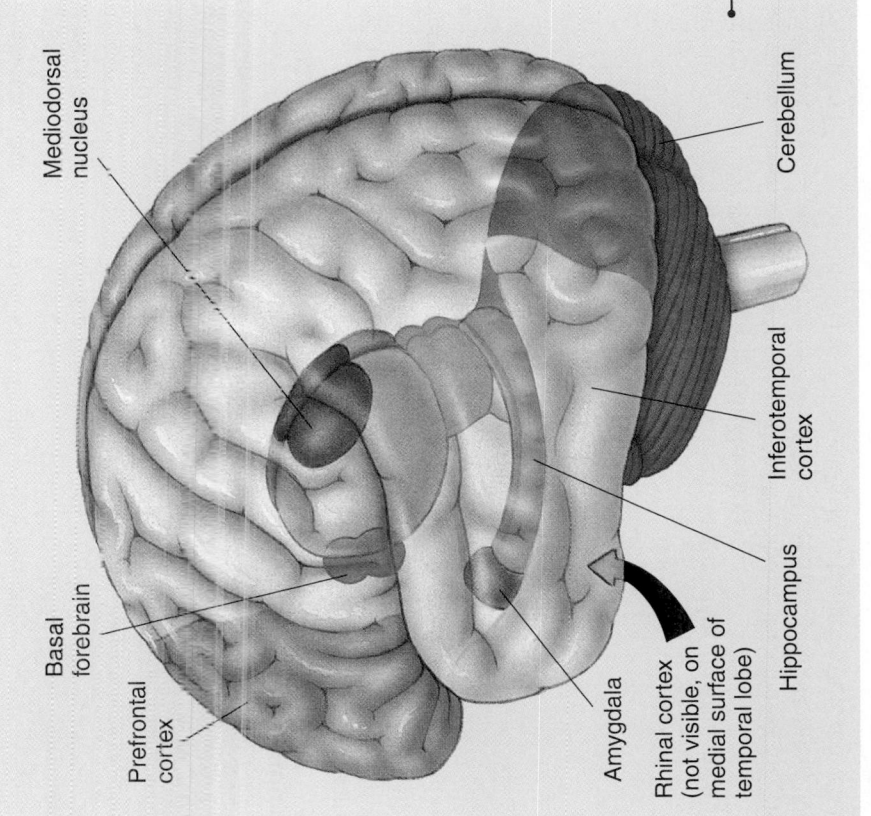

Mediodorsal nucleus

Basal forebrain

Prefrontal cortex

Hippocampus

Amygdala

Rhinal cortex (not visible, on medial surface of temporal lobe)

Inferotemporal cortex

Cerebellum

FIGURE 11.16 The structures of the brain that have been shown to play a role in memory. Because it would have blocked the view of other structures, the striatum is not included. (See Figure 3.29.)

ability to maintain relevant memories while a task is being completed)—see Kimberg, D'Esposito, and Farah (1998) and Smith (2000). As a result of these two deficits, patients with prefrontal cortex damage have particular difficulty performing tasks that involve a series of responses (see Colvin, Dunbar, & Grafman, 2001).

The Case of the Cook Who Couldn't

Clinical Implications

The story of one patient with prefrontal cortex damage is very well known because she was the sister of Wilder Penfield, the famous Montreal neurosurgeon. Before her brain damage, she had been an excellent cook; and afterward, she retained all the prerequisite knowledge. She remembered her favorite recipes, and she remembered how to perform each individual cooking technique. However, she was incapable of preparing even simple meals because she could not carry out the various steps in proper sequence (Penfield & Evans, 1935).

The prefrontal cortex is a large heterogeneous structure; it is composed of numerous anatomically distinct areas that have different connections and, presumably, different functions. Do different areas of prefrontal cortex mediate different kinds of working memory—spatial, visual, verbal, and so forth? The answer seems to be, "yes and no." Functional brain-imaging studies suggest that

Cognitive Neuroscience

some regions of prefrontal cortex perform fundamental cognitive processes (e.g., attention and task management) during all working memory tasks; however, there are other regions of prefrontal cortex that seem to mediate specific kinds of working memory (Collette & Van der Linden, 2002; Petrides, 2000; Rämä et al., 2001).

Cerebellum and Striatum

Just as explicit memories of experiences are presumed to be stored in the circuits of the brain that mediated their

original perception, implicit memories of sensorimotor learning are presumed to be stored in sensorimotor circuits (see Ohyama et al., 2003). Most research on the neural mechanisms of memory for sensorimotor tasks have focused on two structures: the *cerebellum* and the *striatum*.

Evolutionary Perspective

The **cerebellum** is thought to store memories of learned sensorimotor skills. Its role in the Pavlovian conditioning of the eyeblink response of rabbits has been most intensively investigated (see Linden, 2003). In this paradigm, a tone (conditional stimulus) is sounded just before a puff of air (unconditional stimulus) is delivered to the eye. After several trials, the tone comes to elicit an eyeblink. The convergence of evidence from stimulation, recording, and lesion studies suggests that the effects of this conditioning are stored in the form of changes in the way that cerebellar neurons respond to the tone (see Koekkoek et al., 2003).

The **striatum** is thought to store memories for consistent relationships between stimuli and responses—the type of memories that develop incrementally over many trials (see White, 1997). Sometimes this striatum-based form of learning is referred to as *habit formation* (Packard & Knowlton, 2002; Schultz, Tremblay, & Hollerman, 2003).

Clinical Implications

One study of striatal function compared Parkinson's patients, who all have striatal damage, with patients suffering from medial temporal lobe damage. Knowlton, Mangels, and Squire (1996) found that the Parkinson's patients could not solve a probabilistic discrimination problem. The problem was a computer "weather forecasting" game, and the task of the subjects was to correctly predict the weather by pressing one of two keys, rain or shine. They based their predictions on stimulus cards presented on the screen—each card had a different probability of leading to sunshine. The Parkinson's patients did not improve over 50 trials, although they displayed normal explicit (conscious) memory for the training episode. In contrast, amnesic patients with medial temporal lobe or medial diencephalic damage displayed marked improvement in performance but had no explicit memory of their training.

11.8 Synaptic Mechanisms of Learning and Memory

So far, this chapter has focused on the particular structures of the human brain that are involved in learning and memory and what happens when these structures are damaged. In this section, the level of analysis changes; the focus shifts to the neuroplastic mechanisms within these structures that are thought to be the fundamental bases of learning and memory.

Most modern thinking about the neural mechanisms of memory began with Hebb (1949). Hebb argued so convincingly that enduring changes in the efficiency of synaptic transmission were the basis of long-term memory that the search for the neural bases of learning and memory has focused almost exclusively on the synapse (see Kandel, 2001; Malenka, 2003).

Long-Term Potentiation

Because Hebb's hypothesis that enduring facilitations of synaptic transmission are the neural basis of learning and memory was so influential, there was great excitement when such an effect was discovered. In 1973, Bliss and Lømo showed that there is a facilitation of synaptic transmission following high-frequency electrical stimulation applied to presynaptic neurons. This phenomenon has been termed **long-term potentiation (LTP)**.

LTP has been demonstrated in many species and in many parts of their brains, but it has been most frequently studied in the rat hippocampus. Figure 11.17 illustrates the three hippocampal synapses at which LTP is commonly studied.

Figure 11.18 on page 282 is a demonstration of LTP in the granule cell layer of the rat hippocampal dentate gyrus. First, a single low-intensity pulse of current was delivered to the perforant path (the major input to the dentate gyrus), and the response was recorded through an extracellular multiple-unit electrode in the granule cell layer of the hippocampal dentate gyrus; the purpose of this initial stimulation was to determine the initial response baseline. Second, high-intensity, high-frequency

Evolutionary Perspective

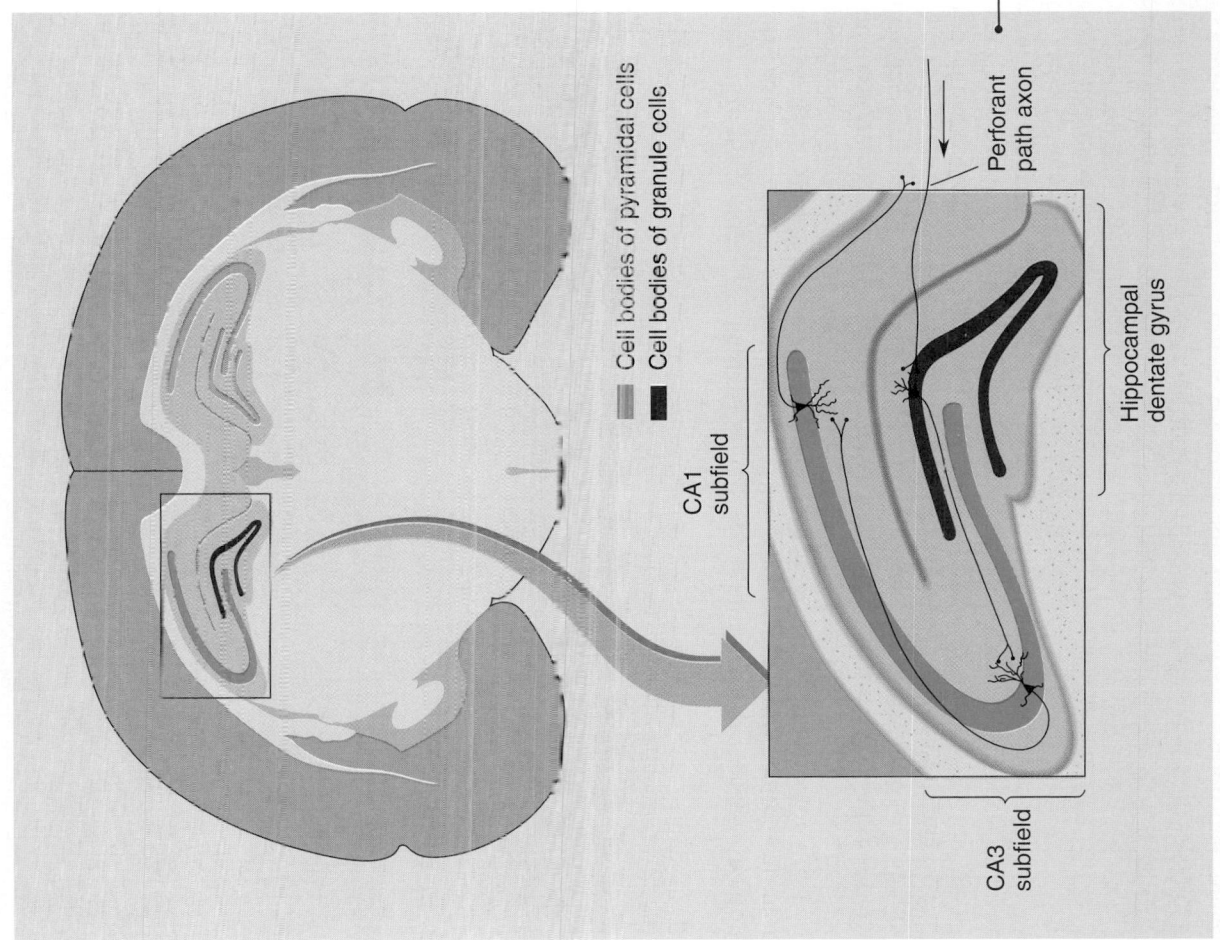

FIGURE 11.17 A slice of rat hippocampal tissue that illustrates the three synapses at which LTP is most commonly studied: (1) the dentate granule cell synapse, (2) the CA3 pyramidal cell synapse, and (3) the CA1 pyramidal cell synapse.

Cell bodies of pyramidal cells
Cell bodies of granule cells

CA1 subfield

CA3 subfield

Hippocampal dentate gyrus

Perforant path axon

stimulation lasting 10 seconds was delivered to the perforant path to induce the LTP. Third, the granule cells'
responses to single pulses of low-intensity current were
measured again after various delays. It is apparent in Figure 11.18 that transmission at the granule cells' synapses
was still potentiated 1 week after the high-frequency
stimulation.

LTP is among the most widely studied neuroscientific phenomena. Why? The reason goes back to 1949
and Hebb's influential theory of memory. The synaptic changes that were hypothesized by Hebb to underlie long-term memory seemed to be the same kind of
changes that underlie LTP.

LTP has two key properties that Hebb proposed as
characteristics of the physiological mechanisms of learning and memory. First, LTP can last for a long time—for
many weeks after multiple stimulations. Second, LTP

develops only if the firing of the presynaptic neuron
is followed by the firing of the postsynaptic neuron; it
does not develop when the presynaptic neuron fires and
the postsynaptic neuron does not, and it does not develop when the presynaptic neuron does not fire and the
postsynaptic neuron does (see Bi & Poo, 2001). The *co-
occurrence of firing in presynaptic and postsynaptic cells*
is now recognized as the critical factor in LTP, and the assumption that co-occurrence is a physiological necessity
for learning and memory is often referred to as *Hebb's
postulate for learning.*

Additional support for the idea that LTP is related
to the neural mechanisms of learning and memory has
come from several observations (see Lisman, Lichtman,
& Sanes, 2003; Lynch, 2004; Morris et al., 2003): (1) LTP
can be elicited by low levels of stimulation that mimic
normal neural activity; (2) LTP effects are most promi-

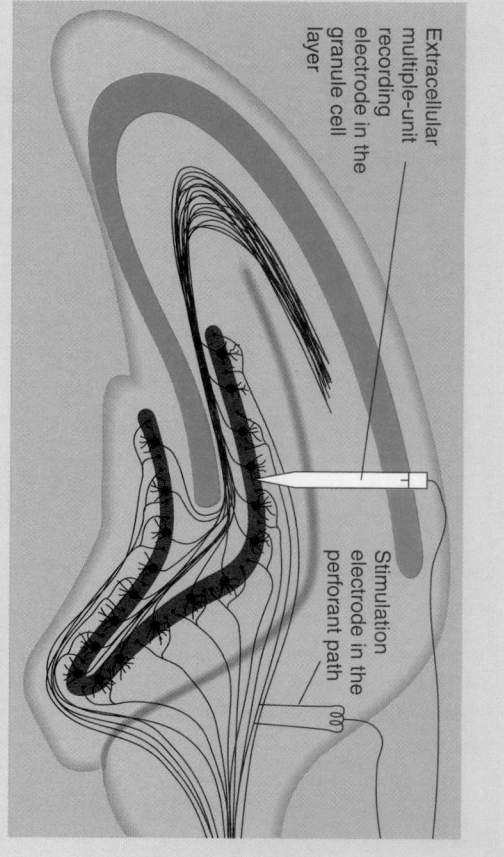

Extracellular
multiple-unit
recording
electrode in the
granule cell
layer

Stimulation
electrode in the
perforant path

A single pulse of stimulation was
administered to the perforant path,
and the baseline response was
recorded by an extracellular
electrode in the granule cell layer.
Then, several trains of intense high-
frequency stimulation were applied
to the perforant path to induce the
LTP.

A single pulse of stimulation was
administered 1 day later and again
1 week later to assess the
magnitude of and duration of the
potentiation. The usual measure of
LTP is the increased amplitude of
the *population spike*, in this case,
the spike created by the firing of a
greater number of granule cells.

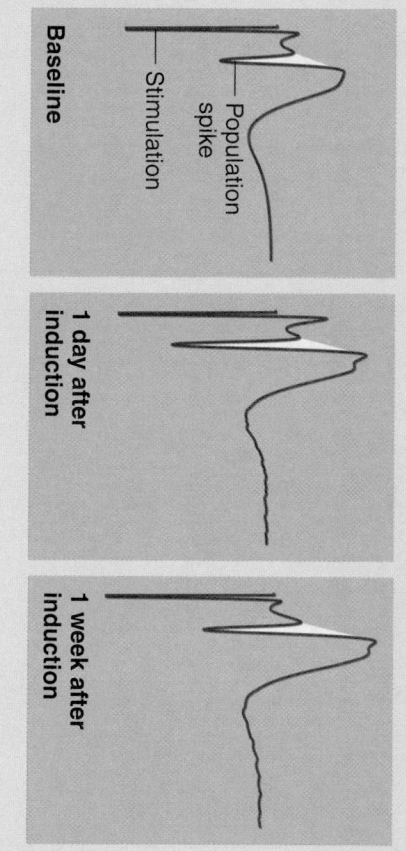

Baseline

— Population
   spike
— Stimulation

1 day after
induction

1 week after
induction

FIGURE 11.18   Long-term
potentiation in the granule cell layer
of the rat hippocampal dentate
gyrus. (Traces courtesy of Michael
Corcoran, Department of Psychology,
University of Saskatchewan.)

nent in structures that have been implicated in learning and memory, such as the hippocampus; (3) behavioral conditioning can produce LTP-like changes in the hippocampus; (4) many drugs that influence learning and memory have parallel effects on LTP; (5) the induction of maximal LTP blocks the learning of a Morris water maze until the LTP has subsided; (6) mutant mice that display little hippocampal LTP have difficulty learning the Morris water maze; and (7) LTP occurs at specific synapses that have been shown to participate in learning and memory in simple invertebrate nervous systems. Still, it is important to keep in mind that all of this evidence is indirect and that LTP as induced in the laboratory by electrical stimulation is at best a caricature of the subtle cellular events that underlie learning and memory (see Cain, 1997; Eichenbaum, 1996).

Conceiving of LTP as a three-part process, many researchers are investigating the mechanisms of *induction*, *maintenance*, and *expression*, that is, the processes by which high-frequency stimulations induce LTP (learning), the changes responsible for storing LTP (memory), and the changes that allow it to be expressed during the test (recall).

Induction of LTP: Learning

LTP has been studied most extensively at synapses at which the NMDA (N-methyl-D-aspartate) receptor is prominent. The **NMDA receptor** is a receptor for **glutamate**—the main excitatory neurotransmitter of the brain. The NMDA receptor has a special property. It does not respond maximally unless two events occur simultaneously: Glutamate must bind to it, and the postsynaptic neuron must already be partially depolarized. This dual requirement stems from the fact that the calcium channels that are linked to NMDA receptors allow only small numbers of calcium ions to enter the neuron unless the neuron is already depolarized when glutamate binds to the receptor; it is the influx of calcium ions that triggers action potentials and the cascade of events in the postsynaptic neuron that induces LTP. The study of calcium influx has been greatly facilitated by the devel-

opment of *optical imaging techniques* for visualizing it (see Figure 11.19).

An important characteristic of the induction of LTP at glutaminergic synapses stems from the nature of the NMDA receptor and LTP's requirement for co-occurrence. This characteristic is not obvious under the usual, but unnatural, experimental condition in which LTP is induced by high-intensity, high-frequency stimulation, which always activates the postsynaptic neurons through massive temporal and spatial summation. However, when a more natural, low-intensity stimulation is applied, the postsynaptic neurons do not fire and thus LTP is not induced—unless the postsynaptic neurons are already partially depolarized so that their calcium channels open wide when glutamate binds to their NMDA receptors.

The requirement for the postsynaptic neurons to be partially depolarized when the glutamate binds to them is an extremely important characteristic of LTP because it permits neural networks to learn associations. Let me explain. If one glutaminergic neuron were to fire by itself and release its glutamate neurotransmitter across a synapse onto the NMDA receptors of a postsynaptic neuron, there would be no potentiation of transmission at that synapse because the postsynaptic cell would not fire. However, if the postsynaptic neuron were partially depolarized by input from other neurons when the presynaptic neuron fired, the binding of the glutamate to the NMDA receptors would open wide the calcium channels, calcium ions would flow into the postsynaptic neuron, and transmission across the synapses between the presynaptic and postsynaptic neuron would be potentiated. Accordingly, the requirement for co-occurrence and the dependence of NMDA receptors on simultaneous binding and partial depolarization mean that, under natural conditions, synaptic facilitation records the fact that there has been simultaneous activity in at least two converging inputs to the postsynaptic neuron—as would be produced by the "simultaneous" presentation of a conditional stimulus and an unconditional stimulus.

The exact mechanisms by which calcium influx induces LTP are complex and unclear (see Lisman, 2003);

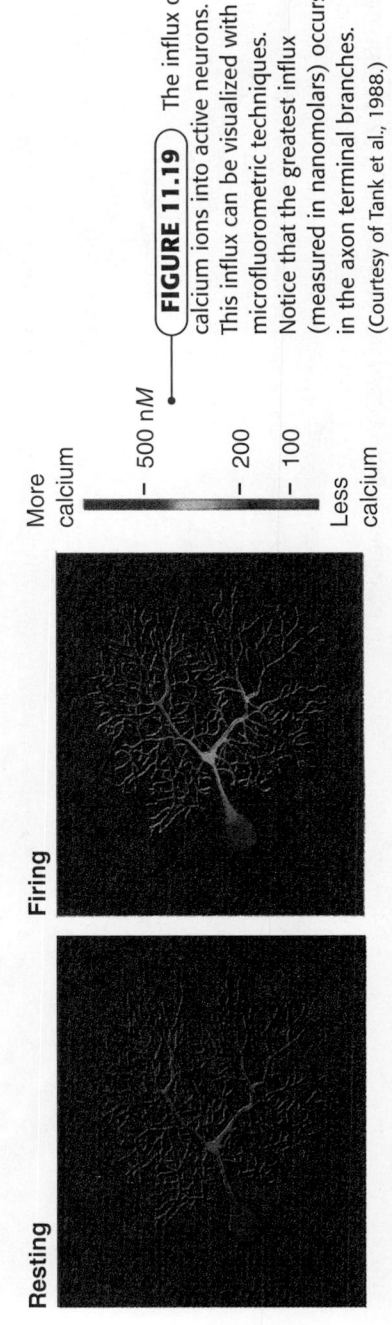

FIGURE 11.19 The influx of calcium ions into active neurons. This influx can be visualized with microfluorometric techniques. Notice that the greatest influx (measured in nanomolars) occurs in the axon terminal branches. (Courtesy of Tank et al., 1988.)

More calcium

— 500 nM

— 200

— 100

Less calcium

Resting   Firing

however, there is substantial evidence that calcium exerts some of its effects by activating *protein kinases* (a class of enzymes that influence many chemical reactions of the cell) in the neural cytoplasm (see Kind & Neumann, 2001). A consistent finding has been that protein kinase inhibitors block the induction of LTP (see Bashir & Collingridge, 1992). Figure 11.20 summarizes the induction of NMDA-receptor–mediated LTP. Although it is well established that the induction of LTP at synapses with NMDA receptors depends on the influx of calcium ions into the postsynaptic neuron, the next stages of the induction process are not well understood. This is prob-

ably because several mechanisms are involved (see Sheng & Kim, 2002).

Maintenance and Expression of LTP: Storage and Recall

The search for the mechanisms underlying the maintenance and expression of LTP began with attempts to determine whether these mechanisms occur in presynaptic or postsynaptic neurons. This question has been answered: The maintenance and expression of LTP involve changes in both presynaptic and postsynaptic neu-

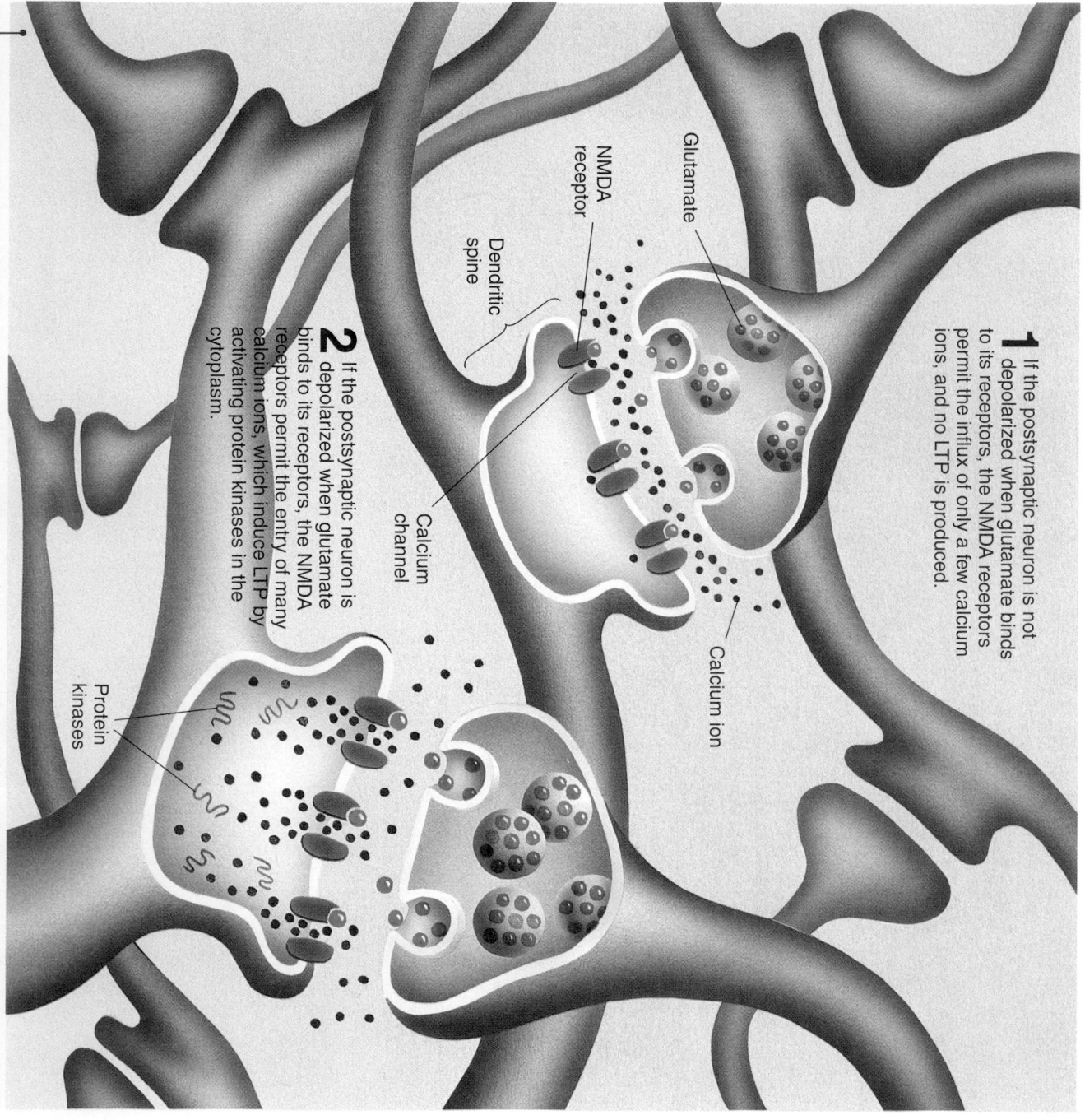

1 If the postsynaptic neuron is not depolarized when glutamate binds to its receptors, the NMDA receptors permit the influx of only a few calcium ions, and no LTP is produced.

2 If the postsynaptic neuron is depolarized when glutamate binds to its receptors, the NMDA receptors permit the entry of many calcium ions, which induce LTP by activating protein kinases in the cytoplasm.

Glutamate

NMDA receptor

Dendritic spine

Calcium channel

Calcium ion

Protein kinases

FIGURE 11.20   The induction of NMDA-receptor–mediated LTP.

rons. This discovery has complicated the identification of the mechanisms of maintenance and expression (see Lisman, 2003). Nevertheless, five particularly important advances have been made.

First, once it became apparent that only those synapses that were depolarized before the high-frequency stimulation were involved in LTP (other synapses on the same postsynaptic neurons were unaffected), it was clear that there must be a mechanism for keeping the events at one set of synapses on a postsynaptic neuron from affecting other synapses on the same neuron. This specificity appears to be due to the **dendritic spines**; the calcium ions that enter one dendritic spine do not readily diffuse out of it, and thus they exert their effects locally (see Harris & Kater, 1994).

Second, it has become apparent that the changes that occur immediately and maintain the experience of the high-frequency stimulation for a time are not the same as those that maintain the experience weeks later. Specifically, the long-term maintenance, because of its permanence, is likely to involve structural changes, which depend on protein synthesis. Protein synthesis cannot be responsible for the short-term maintenance because it does not occur rapidly enough.

Third, there is direct evidence that presynaptic changes are involved in the maintenance and expression of LTP at synapses having NMDA receptors. LTP at these synapses has been shown to be associated with a long-lasting increase in the extracellular levels of glutamate and with an increase in the degree to which extracellular glutamate is increased by subsequent electrical stimulation (Errington, Galley, & Bliss, 2003).

Fourth, given that the induction of LTP begins in the postsynaptic neurons and that its maintenance and expression involve presynaptic changes, there must be some type of signal that passes from the postsynaptic neurons back to the presynaptic neurons. Evidence suggests that at NMDA synapses, this signal takes the form of the soluble-gas neurotransmitter **nitric oxide**. Nitric oxide is synthesized in the postsynaptic neurons in response to calcium influx and then diffuses back into the terminal buttons of the presynaptic neurons (e.g., Harris, 1995).

And fifth, it is now well-established that structural changes occur at NMDA synapses in association with long-lasting LTP. There are increases in the number and size of synapses, in the number and size of dendritic spines, and in the number of postsynaptic NMDA receptors (see Harris, Fiala, & Ostroff, 2003; Lüscher & Frerking, 2001; Yuste & Bonhoeffer, 2001).

Variability of LTP

When I first started reading about research on LTP, I was excited at the potential. If LTP were the key to understanding the neural basis of learning and memory, then important discoveries would soon be forthcoming. A generation of neuroscientists has shared my view, and LTP has become the most researched topic in all of neuroscience. With such a massive effort, it seemed that identifying the mechanisms underlying the induction, maintenance, and expression of LTP should be relatively straightforward.

As I read the current literature on LTP, however, it seems that researchers are further from ultimate answers than I naively thought they were about a quarter-century ago. What has happened? Many important discoveries have been made, but rather than leading to ultimate solutions, they have often simply revealed what a complex and varied phenomenon LTP is and led to more questions.

Most of the research on LTP has focused on NMDA-receptor–mediated LTP in the hippocampus. It is now clear that NMDA-receptor–mediated LTP involves a complex array of changes that are difficult to sort out. In addition, LTP has been documented in many other parts of the CNS where it tends to be mediated by different mechanisms (e.g., Gaiarsa, Caillard, & Ben-Ari, 2002; Ikeda et al., 2003). And then there is LTD (long-term depression), the flip side of LTP; LTD occurs in response to prolonged low-frequency stimulation of presynaptic neurons (Bliss & Schoepfer, 2004; Lui et al., 2004). Presumably, a full understanding of LTP will require an understanding of LTD (Christie, Kerr, & Abraham, 1994).

The dream of discovering the neural basis or learning and memory is what has attracted so many neuroscientists to focus on LTP. Although this dream has not yet been fulfilled, the study of LTP has led to many important discoveries about the function and plasticity of neural systems. By this criterion, this massive research effort should be judged as worthwhile.

11.9 Conclusion: Infantile Amnesia and the Biopsychologist Who Remembered H.M.

Thinking Critically

We tend to think of memory as a unitary ability. Nevertheless, brain-damaged individuals often display severe deficits in one memory process but not others. Because this chapter has so far focused on the amnesic affects of brain damage, you may have been left with the impression that the dissociations among various kinds of memory have little direct relevance to individuals with intact healthy brains. This, the final, section emphasizes that such is not the case. It makes the point with one interesting line of experiments and one provocative case study.

We all experience *infantile amnesia*; that is, we remember virtually nothing of the events of our infancy (Howe, 2003). Newcombe and her colleagues (2000) addressed the following question: Do normal children who fail explicitly to recall or recognize things from their early childhood display preserved implicit memory for these things? The results of two experiments indicate that the answer is "yes."

In one study of infantile amnesia (Newcombe & Fox, 1994), children were shown a series of photographs of preschool-aged children, some of whom had been their preschool classmates. The subjects recognized a few of their former preschool classmates. However, whether they explicitly remembered a former classmate or not, they consistently displayed a large skin conductance response to the photographs of those classmates.

In a second study of infantile amnesia, Drummey and Newcombe (1995) used a modern version of the incomplete-pictures test. They showed a series of drawings to 3-year-olds, 5-year-olds, and adults. Three months later, subjects' memory for these drawings was assessed by asking them to identify them and some control drawings as quickly as they could. The drawings were initially badly out of focus, but became progressively sharper. Following this test of implicit memory, the subjects were asked which of the drawings they remembered seeing before. The 5-year-olds and adults showed better explicit memory than the 3-year-olds did; that is, they were more likely to recall seeing drawings from the original series. However, all three groups displayed substantial implicit memory: All subjects were able to identify more quickly the drawings they had seen before, even when they had no conscious recollection of having seen them before.

This chapter began with the case of H.M.; it ends with the case of R.M. The case of R.M. is one of the most ironic that I have encountered, which is why I have saved it for a chapter-ending treat. R.M. is a biopsychologist, and, as you will learn, his vocation played an important role in one of his symptoms.

The Case of R.M., the Biopsychologist Who Remembered H.M.

R.M. fell on his head while skiing; when he regained consciousness, he was suffering from both retrograde and anterograde amnesia. For several hours, he could recall few of the events of his previous life. He could not remember if he was married, where he lived, or where he worked. He had lost most of his episodic memory.

Also, many of the things that happened to him in the hours after his accident were forgotten as soon as his attention was diverted from them. For example, in the car on his way to the hospital, R.M. chatted with the person sitting next to him—a friend of a friend with whom he had skied all day. But each time his attention was drawn elsewhere—for example, by the mountain scenery—he completely forgot this person and their previous conversations, and subsequently reintroduced himself.

This was a classic case of posttraumatic amnesia. Like H.M., R.M. was trapped in the present, with only a cloudy past and seemingly no future. The irony of the situation was that during those few hours, when R.M. could recall few of the events of his own life, his thoughts repeatedly drifted to one semantic memory—his memory of a person he remembered learning about somewhere in his muddled past. Through the haze, he remembered H.M., his fellow prisoner of the present and wondered if the same fate lay in store for him.

R.M. recovered fully and looks back on what he can recall of his experience with relief and a feeling of empathy for H.M. Unlike H.M., R.M. received a reprieve, but his experience left him with a better appreciation for the situation of those amnesics, like H.M., who are serving life sentences.

Themes Revisited

Because this chapter was based almost entirely on the study of human memory disorders and animal models of them, the clinical implications and evolutionary perspective themes predominated. The clinical study of memory disorders has so far been a one-way street: We have learned much about memory and its neural mechanisms from studying amnesic patients, but we have not yet learned enough to treat their memory problems.

Clinical Implications

Evolutionary Perspective

The cognitive neuroscience theme emerged infrequently in this chapter. However, modern functional brain-imaging methods are starting to play a major role in the study of brain-damage–produced memory disorders.

Cognitive Neuroscience

Finally, the thinking-about-biopsychology tab marked several points in the chapter where it was particularly important for you to think clearly and carefully. It warned you to (1) appreciate the limitations of case studies, (2) not think about memory as a unitary process, (3) appreciate the difficulty in distinguishing anterograde and retrograde effects when disorders have a gradual onset (e.g., Korsakoff's disease), (4) recognize that cases of cerebral ischemia (e.g., that of R.B.) do not provide conclusive evidence of the role of the hippocampus in memory, and (5) appreciate that, although most research has focused on NMDA-receptor–mediated LTP in the hippocampus, LTP is a complex and varied phenomenon.

Thinking Critically

ON THE CD

See Hard Copy for additional readings for Chapter 11.

Think about It

1. The study of the anatomy of memory has come a long way since H.M.'s misfortune. What kind of advances do you think will be made in the next decade?

2. Using examples from your own experience, compare implicit and explicit memory.

3. What are the advantages and shortcomings of animal models of amnesia? Compare the usefulness of monkey and rat models.

4. LTP is one of the most intensely studied of all neuroscientific phenomena. Why? Has the effort been successful?

5. Case studies have played a particularly important role in the study of memory. Discuss.

ON THE CD

Studying for an exam? Try the Practice Tests for Chapter 11.

Key Terms

Amygdala (p. 261)
Anterograde amnesia (p. 262)
Basal forebrain (p. 268)
Bilateral medial temporal lobectomy (p. 261)
CA1 subfield (p. 265)
Cerebellum (p. 280)
Cerebral ischemia (p. 265)
Cognitive map theory (p. 278)
Delayed nonmatching-to-sample test (p. 272)
Dendritic spines (p. 285)
Digit span (p. 262)
Electroconvulsive shock (ECS) (p. 268)
Engram (p. 271)

Episodic memories (p. 264)
Explicit memories (p. 264)
Global amnesia (p. 262)
Glutamate (p. 283)
Hippocampus (p. 261)
Implicit memories (p. 264)
Incomplete-pictures test (p. 263)
Inferotemporal cortex (p. 279)
Korsakoff's syndrome (p. 266)
Learning (p. 261)
Lobectomy (p. 261)
Lobotomy (p. 261)
Long-term potentiation (LTP) (p. 281)

Medial diencephalic amnesia (p. 267)
Medial temporal lobe amnesia (p. 264)
Mediodorsal nuclei (p. 267)
Memory (p. 261)
Memory consolidation (p. 264)
Morris water maze test (p. 277)
Mumby box (p. 274)
Nitric oxide (p. 285)
NMDA receptor (p. 283)
Place cells (p. 277)
Posttraumatic amnesia (PTA) (p. 268)
Pyramidal cell layer (p. 265)
Radial arm maze test (p. 277)

Reference memory (p. 277)
Repetition priming tests (p. 264)
Retrograde amnesia (p. 261)
Rhinal cortex (p. 273)
Semantic memories (p. 264)
Striatum (p. 280)
Working memory (p. 277)

ON THE CD

Need some help studying the key terms for this chapter? Check out the electronic flash cards for Chapter 11.

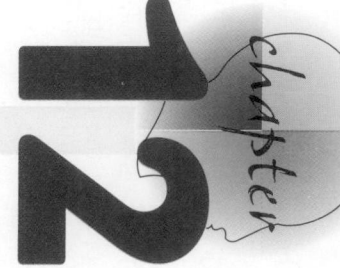

Hunger, Eating, and Health

Why Do Many People Eat Too Much?

chapter

12

12.1 Digestion and Energy Flow

12.2 Theories of Hunger and Eating: Set Points versus Positive Incentives

12.3 Factors That Determine What, When, and How Much We Eat

12.4 Physiological Research on Hunger and Satiety

12.5 Body Weight Regulation: Set Points versus Settling Points

12.6 Human Obesity

12.7 Anorexia Nervosa

Eating is a behavior that is of interest to virtually everyone. We all do it, and most of us derive great pleasure from it. But for many of us, it becomes a source of serious personal and health problems.

Most eating-related health problems are associated with eating too much (see Kopelman, 2000). For example, by one estimate, over half of the adult U.S. population meets the current criteria of clinical obesity, qualifying this problem for epidemic status. The resulting financial and personal costs are huge. Each year in the United States, $45 billion is spent treating obesity-related disorders; missed work costs another $23 billion; and $33 billion is spent on weight-loss products and services. Moreover, each year an estimated 300,000 U.S. citizens die from disorders caused by their excessive eating (e.g., diabetes, hypertension, cardiovascular diseases, and some cancers). Although the United States is the trend-setter when it comes to overeating and obesity, many other countries are not far behind.

Ironically, as overeating and obesity have reached epidemic proportions, there has been a related increase in disorders associated with eating too little (see Polivy & Herman, 2002). For example, about 3% of U.S. adolescents currently suffer from *anorexia nervosa*, which is life-threatening in extreme cases.

The message is clear: At some time in your life, you or somebody you care about will almost certainly suffer from an eating-related disorder.

The massive increases in obesity and other eating-related disorders that have occurred over the last few decades in many countries stand in stark contrast to most people's thinking about hunger and eating. Most people—and I assume that they include you—believe that hunger and eating are normally triggered when the body's energy resources fall below a prescribed optimal level, or **set point**. Most people appreciate that many factors influence hunger and eating, but they assume that the hunger and eating system has evolved to supply the body with just the right amount of energy.

The incompatibility of set-point thinking with the current epidemic of eating disorders is the focus of this chapter. If we all have hunger and eating systems whose primary function is to maintain energy resources at optimal levels, then eating disorders should be rare. The fact that they are so prevalent suggests that hunger and eating are regulated in some other way.

The first sections of this chapter examine some of the fundamental characteristics of hunger and eating; from this examination, a different way of thinking about hunger, eating, and health is derived. Armed with this new perspective, we will reexamine the clinical problems of obesity and anorexia nervosa in the final sections. This chapter will provide you with new insights of major personal relevance—I guarantee it.

Before you move on to the body of the chapter, I would like you to pause to consider a case study. What would a severely amnesic patient do if offered a meal shortly after finishing one? If his hunger and eating were controlled by energy set points, he would refuse the second meal. Did he?

ON THE CD

In the module *Thinking about Hunger,* Pinel welcomes you to this chapter and talks about a common misconception about meal-time hunger.

The Case of the Man Who Forgot Not to Eat

Clinical Implications

R.H. was a 48-year-old male whose progress in graduate school was interrupted by the development of severe amnesia for long-term explicit memory. His amnesia was similar in pattern and severity to that of H.M., whom you met in Chapter 11, and an MRI examination revealed bilateral damage to the medial temporal lobes.

The meals offered to R.H. were selected on the basis of interviews with him about the foods he liked: veal parmigiana (about 750 calories) plus all the apple juice he wanted. On one occasion, he was offered a second meal about 15 minutes after he had eaten the first, and he ate it. When offered a third meal 15 minutes later, he ate that, too. When offered a fourth meal he rejected it, claiming that his "stomach was a little tight."

Then, a few minutes later, R.H. announced that he was going out for a good walk and a meal. When asked what he was going to eat, his answer was "veal parmigiana." Clearly, R.H.'s hunger (i.e., motivation to eat) did not result from an energy deficit (Rozin et al., 1998).

12.1 Digestion and Energy Flow

The primary purpose of eating is to supply the body with the energy it needs to survive and function. This section provides a brief overview of the processes by which food is digested, stored, and converted to energy.

The *gastrointestinal tract* and the process of digestion are illustrated in Figure 12.1 on page 290. **Digestion** is the gastrointestinal process of breaking down food and absorbing its constituents into the body. In order to appreciate the basics of digestion, it is useful to consider the body without its protuberances, as a simple living tube with a hole at each end. To supply itself with energy and other nutrients, the tube puts food into one of its two holes—typically the one with teeth—and passes the food along its internal canal so that it can be broken down and partially absorbed from the canal into the body. The leftovers are jettisoned from the other end. Although this is not a particularly appetizing description of eating, it does serve to illustrate that, strictly speaking, food has not been consumed until it has been digested.

As a consequence of digestion, energy is delivered to the body in three forms: (1) **lipids** (fats), (2) **amino**

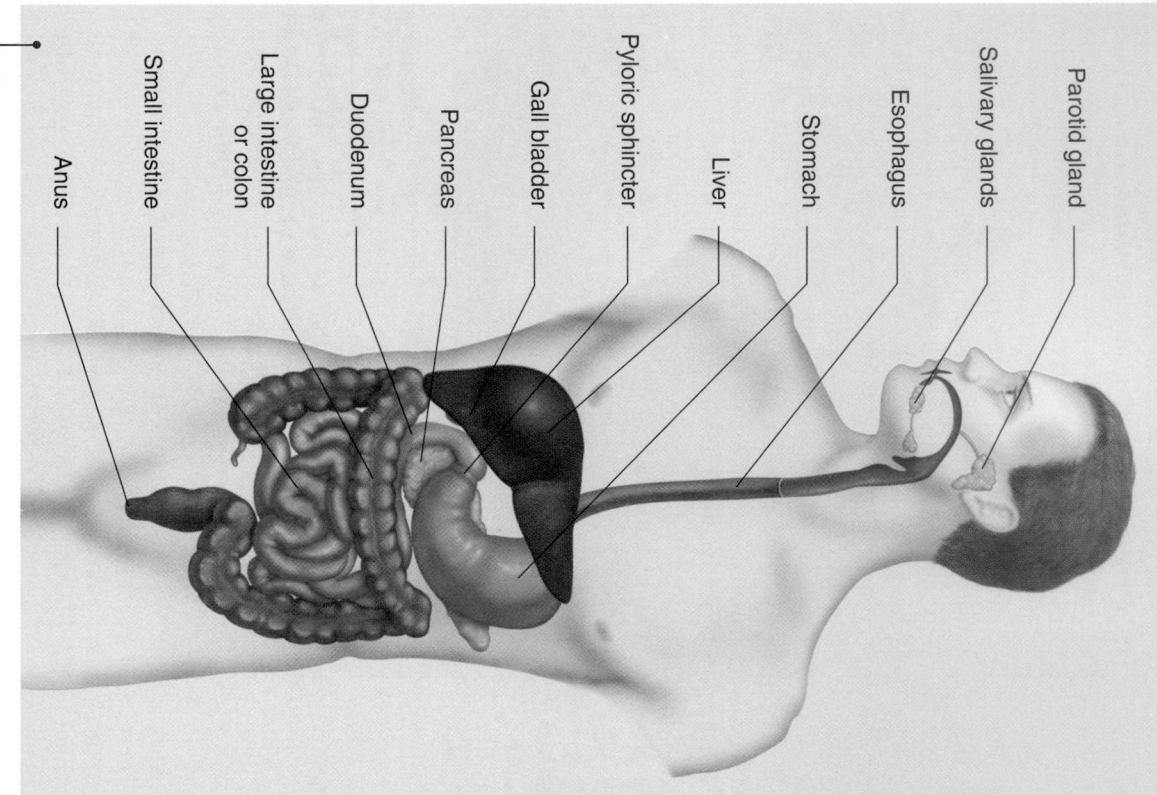

FIGURE 12.1   The gastrointestinal tract and the process of digestion.

Parotid gland

Salivary glands

Esophagus

Stomach

Liver

Pyloric sphincter

Gall bladder

Pancreas

Duodenum

Large intestine or colon

Small intestine

Anus

Steps in Digestion

1 Chewing breaks up food and mixes it with saliva.

2 Saliva lubricates food and begins its digestion.

3 Swallowing moves food and drink down the esophagus to the stomach.

4 The primary function of the stomach is to serve as a storage reservoir. The hydrochloric acid in the stomach breaks food down into small particles, and pepsin begins the process of breaking down protein molecules to amino acids.

5 The stomach gradually empties its contents through the pyloric sphincter into the duodenum, the upper portion of the intestine, where most of the absorption takes place.

6 Digestive enzymes in the duodenum, many of them from the gall bladder and pancreas, break down protein molecules to amino acids, and starch and complex sugar molecules to simple sugars. Simple sugars and amino acids readily pass through the duodenum wall into the bloodstream and are carried to the liver.

7 Fats are emulsified (broken into droplets) by bile, which is manufactured in the liver and stored in the gall bladder until it is released into the duodenum. Emulsified fat cannot pass through the duodenum wall and is carried by small ducts in the duodenum wall into the lymphatic system.

8 Most of the remaining water and electrolytes are absorbed from the waste in the large intestine, and the remainder is ejected from the anus.

acids (the breakdown products of proteins), and (3) **glucose** (a simple sugar that is the breakdown product of complex *carbohydrates*, that is, complex starches and sugars).

The body uses energy continuously, but its consumption is intermittent; therefore, it must store energy for use in the intervals between meals. Energy is stored in three forms: *fats, glycogen,* and *proteins*. Most of the body's energy reserves are stored as fats, relatively little as glycogen and proteins (see Figure 12.2). Thus, changes in the body weights of adult humans are largely a consequence of changes in the amount of body fat.

Because glycogen, which is largely stored in the liver, is readily converted to glucose—the body's main directly

an organism's use): the cephalic phase, the absorptive phase, and the fasting phase. The **cephalic phase** is the preparatory phase; it often begins with the sight, smell, or even just the thought of food, and it ends when the food starts to be absorbed into the bloodstream. The **absorptive phase** is the period during which the energy absorbed into the bloodstream from the meal is meeting the body's immediate energy needs. The **fasting phase** is the period during which all of the unstored energy from the previous meal has been used and the body is withdrawing energy from its reserves to meet its immediate energy requirements; it ends with the beginning of the next cephalic phase. During periods of rapid weight gain, people often go directly from one absorptive phase into the next cephalic phase, without experiencing an intervening fasting phase.

The flow of energy during the three phases of energy metabolism is controlled by two pancreatic hormones: insulin and glucagon. During the cephalic and absorptive phases, the pancreas releases a great deal of insulin into the bloodstream and very little glucagon. The **insulin** does three things: (1) It promotes the use of glucose as the primary source of energy by the body. (2) It promotes the conversion of bloodborne fuels to forms that can be stored: glucose to glycogen and fat, and amino acids to proteins. (3) It promotes the storage of glycogen in liver and muscle, fat in adipose tissue, and proteins in muscle. In short, the function of insulin during the cephalic phase is to lower the levels of bloodborne fuels, primarily glucose, in anticipation of the impending influx; and its function during the absorptive phase is to minimize the increasing levels of bloodborne fuels by utilizing and storing them.

In contrast to the cephalic and absorptive phases, the fasting phase is characterized by high blood levels of **glucagon and low levels of insulin.** Without high levels of insulin, glucose has difficulty entering most body cells; thus, glucose stops being the body's primary fuel. In effect, this saves the body's glucose for the brain, because insulin is not required for glucose to enter most brain cells. The low levels of insulin also promote the conversion of glycogen and protein to glucose. (The conversion of protein to glucose is called **gluconeogenesis.**)

On the other hand, the high levels of fasting-phase glucagon promote the release of **free fatty acids** from adipose tissue and their use as the body's primary fuel. The high glucagon levels also stimulate the conversion of free fatty acids to **ketones,** which are used by muscles as a source of energy during the fasting phase. After a prolonged period without food, however, the brain also starts to use ketones, thus further conserving the body's resources of glucose.

Figure 12.3 on page 292 summarizes the major metabolic events associated with the three phases of energy metabolism.

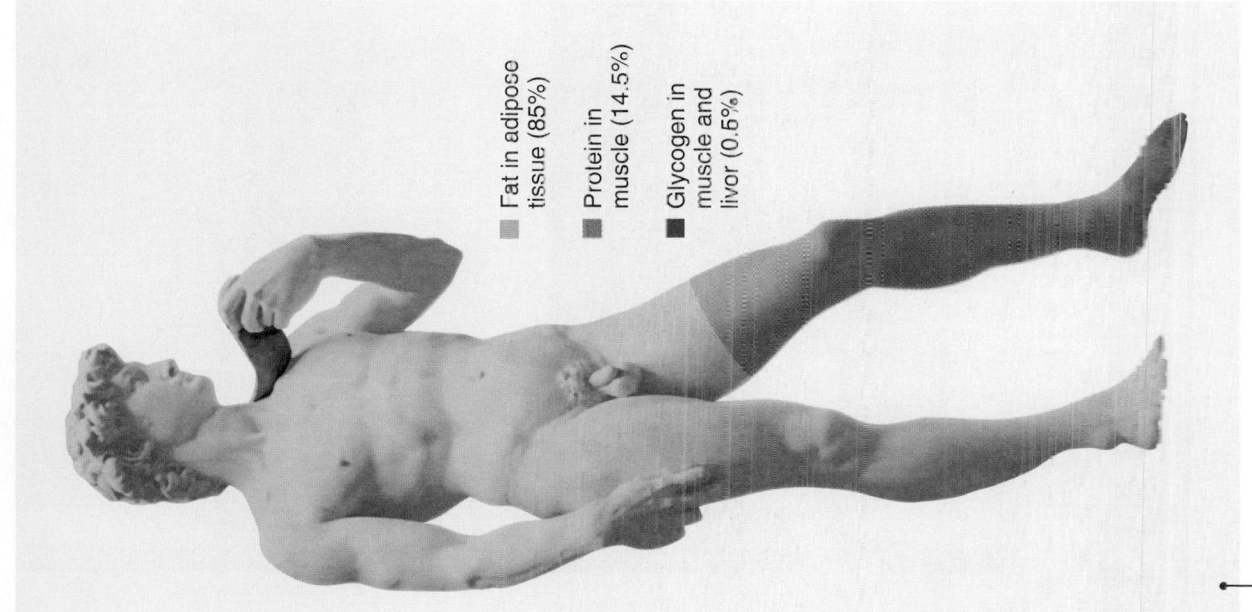

- Fat in adipose tissue (85%)
- Protein in muscle (14.5%)
- Glycogen in muscle and liver (0.5%)

FIGURE 12.2 Distribution of stored energy in an average person.

utilizable source of energy—one might expect that glycogen would be the body's preferred mode of energy storage. There are two main reasons why fat, rather than glycogen, is the primary mode of energy storage. One is that a gram of fat can store twice as much energy as a gram of glycogen; the other is that glycogen, unlike fat, attracts and holds substantial quantities of water. Consequently, if your weight is reasonably normal and all your fat calories were stored as glycogen, you would likely weigh well over 275 kilograms (600 pounds).

There are three phases of *energy metabolism* (the chemical changes by which energy is made available for

FIGURE 12.3 The major events associated with the three phases of energy metabolism: the cephalic, absorptive, and fasting phases.

Cephalic Phase
Preparatory phase, which is initiated by the sight, smell, or expectation of food

Insulin levels high
Glucagon levels low

Promotes
- Utilization of blood glucose as a source of energy
- Conversion of excess glucose to glycogen and fat
- Conversion of amino acids to proteins
- Storage of glycogen in liver and muscle, fat in adipose tissue, and protein in muscle

Inhibits
- Conversion of glycogen, fat, and protein into directly utilizable fuels (glucose, free fatty acids, and ketones)

Absorptive Phase
Nutrients from a meal meeting the body's immediate energy requirements, with the excess being stored

Glucagon levels high
Insulin levels low

Promotes
- Conversion of fats to free fatty acids and the utilization of free fatty acids as a source of energy
- Conversion of glycogen to glucose, free fatty acids to ketones, and protein to glucose

Inhibits
- Utilization of glucose by the body but not by the brain
- Conversion of glucose to glycogen and fat, and amino acids to protein
- Storage of fat in adipose tissue

Fasting Phase
Energy being withdrawn from stores to meet the body's immediate needs

---

12.2 Theories of Hunger and Eating: Set Points versus Positive Incentives

One of the main difficulties I have in teaching the fundamentals of hunger, eating, and body weight regulation is the **set-point assumption.** Although it dominates most people's thinking about hunger and eating (Assanand, Pinel, & Lehman, 1998a, 1998b), whether they realize it or not, it is inconsistent with the bulk of the evidence. What exactly is the set-point assumption?

Set-Point Assumption

Most people attribute *hunger* (the motivation to eat) to the presence of an energy deficit, and they view eating as the means by which the energy resources of the body are returned to their optimal level—that is, to their *energy set point.* Figure 12.4 summarizes this set-point

assumption. After a *meal* (a bout of eating), a person's energy resources are thought to be near their set point and to decline thereafter as the body uses energy to fuel its physiological processes. When the level of the body's energy resources falls far enough below the set point, a person becomes motivated by hunger to initiate another meal. The meal continues, according to the set-point assumption, until the energy level returns to its set point and the person feels *satiated* (no longer hungry).

The set-point model of hunger and eating works in much the same way as a thermostat-regulated heating system in a cool climate. The heater increases the house temperature until it reaches its set point (the thermostat setting). This turns off the heat, and then the temperature of the house gradually declines until the decline is

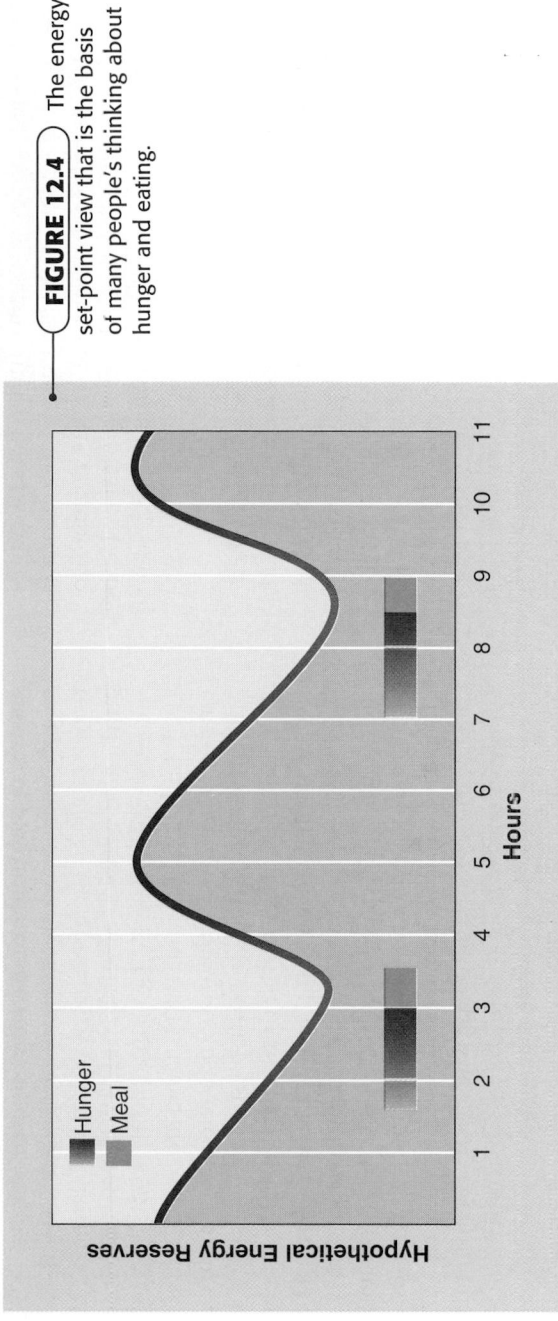

FIGURE 12.4 The energy set-point view that is the basis of many people's thinking about hunger and eating.

large enough to turn the heater back on. All set-point systems have three components: a set-point mechanism, a detector mechanism, and an effector mechanism. The *set-point mechanism* defines the set point, the *detector mechanism* detects deviations from the set point, and the *effector mechanism* acts to eliminate the deviations. For example, the set-point, detector, and effector mechanisms of a heating system are the thermostat, the thermometer, and the heater, respectively.

All set-point systems are **negative feedback systems**—systems in which feedback from changes in one direction elicit compensatory effects in the opposite direction. Negative feedback systems are common in mammals because they act to maintain **homeostasis**—a constant internal environment—which is critical for mammals' survival (see Wenning, 1999).

Glucostatic and Lipostatic Set-Point Theories of Hunger and Eating

In the 1940s and 1950s, researchers working under the assumption that eating is regulated by some type of set-point system speculated about the nature of the regulation. Several researchers suggested that eating is regulated by a system that is designed to maintain a blood glucose set point—the idea being that we become hungry when our blood glucose levels drop significantly below their set point and that we become satiated when eating returns our blood glucose levels to their set point. Various versions of this theory are referred to as the **glucostatic theory.** It seemed to make good sense that the main purpose of eating is to defend a blood glucose set point, because glucose is the brain's primary fuel.

The **lipostatic theory** is another set-point theory that was proposed in various forms in the 1940s and 1950s. According to this theory, every person has a set point for body fat, and deviations from this set point

produce compensatory adjustments in the level of eating that return levels of body fat to their set point. The most frequently cited support for the theory is the fact that the body weights of adults stay relatively constant.

The glucostatic and lipostatic theories were viewed as complementary, not mutually exclusive. The glucostatic theory was thought to account for meal initiation and termination, whereas the lipostatic theory was thought to account for long-term regulation. Thus, the dominant view in the 1950s was that eating is regulated by the interaction between two set-point systems: a short-term glucostatic system and a long-term lipostatic system. The simplicity of these 1950s theories is appealing. Remarkably, they are still being presented as the latest word in some textbooks; perhaps you have encountered them.

Problems with Set-Point Theories of Hunger and Eating

Set-point theories of hunger and eating have several serious weaknesses (see de Castro & Plunkett, 2002). You have already learned one fact that undermines these theories: the current epidemic of obesity and other eating disorders. Let's look at three more.

First, set-point theories of hunger and eating are inconsistent with basic eating-related evolutionary pressures as we understand them. The major eating-related problem faced by our ancestors was the inconsistency and unpredictability of the food supply. Thus, in order to survive, it was important for them to eat large quantities of good food when it was available so that calories could be banked in the form of body fat. Any ancestor—human or otherwise—that stopped feeling hungry as soon as immediate energy needs were met would not have survived the first hard winter or prolonged drought. For any

Evolutionary Perspective

warm-blooded species to survive under natural conditions, it needs a hunger and eating system that prevents energy deficits, rather than one that merely responds to them once they have developed. From this perspective, it is difficult to imagine how a set-point hunger and feeding system could have evolved in mammals (see Pinel, Assanand, & Lehman, 2000).

Second, major predictions of the set-point theories of hunger and eating have not been confirmed. Early studies seemed to support the set-point theories by showing that large reductions in body fat, produced by starvation, or large reductions in blood glucose, produced by insulin injections, induce increases in eating in laboratory animals. The problem is that reductions of the magnitude needed to reliably induce eating rarely occur naturally. Indeed, as you have already learned in this chapter, over 50% of the U.S. adult population have a significant excess of fat deposits when they begin a meal. Conversely, efforts to reduce meal size by having subjects consume a high-calorie drink before eating have been largely unsuccessful; indeed, beliefs about the caloric content of a premeal drink often influence the size of a subsequent meal more than does its actual caloric content (see Lowe, 1993).

Third, set-point theories of hunger and eating are deficient because they fail to recognize the major influences on hunger and eating of such important factors as taste, learning, and social factors. To convince yourself

Thinking Critically

of the importance of these factors, pause for a minute and imagine the sight, smell, and taste of your favorite food. Perhaps it is a succulent morsel of lobster meat covered with melted garlic butter, a piece of chocolate cheesecake, or a plate of sizzling homemade french fries. Are you starting to feel a bit hungry? If the homemade french fries—my personal weakness—were sitting in front of you right now, wouldn't you reach out and have one, or maybe the whole plateful? Have you not on occasion felt discomfort after a large main course, only to polish off a substantial dessert? The usual positive answers to these questions lead unavoidably to the conclusion that hunger and eating are not rigidly controlled by deviations from energy set points. This same point can be easily demonstrated in laboratory rats by adding a small amount of saccharin to their laboratory chow; saccharin increases the sweetness of the chow without adding calories, and it produces a major increase in both eating and body weight.

Positive-Incentive Perspective

The inability of set-point theories to account for the basic phenomena of eating and hunger has led to the development of an alternative theoretical perspective (see Berridge, 2004). The central assertion of this new theoretical perspective, commonly referred to as **positive-incentive**

theory, is that humans and other animals are not normally driven to eat by internal energy deficits but are drawn to eat by the anticipated pleasure of eating—the anticipated pleasure of a behavior is called its **positive-incentive value** (see Bolles, 1980; Booth, 1981; Collier, 1980; Rolls, 1981; Toates, 1981). There are several different positive-incentive theories, and I refer generally to all of them as the *positive-incentive perspective*.

The major tenet of the positive-incentive perspective on eating is that eating is controlled in much the same way as sexual behavior: We engage in sexual behavior not because we have an internal deficit, but because we have evolved to crave it. The evolutionary pressures of unexpected food shortages have shaped us and all other warm-blooded animals, who need a continuous supply of energy to maintain their body temperatures, to take advantage of good food when it is present and eat it. According to the positive-incentive perspective, it is the presence of good food, or the anticipation of it, that normally makes us hungry, not an energy deficit.

According to the positive-incentive perspective, the degree of hunger you feel at any particular time depends on the interaction of all the factors that influence the positive-incentive value of eating. These include the following: the flavor of the food you are likely to consume, what you have learned about the effects of this food either from eating it previously or from other people, the amount of time since you last ate, the type and quantity of food in your gut, whether or not other people are present and eating, whether or not your blood glucose levels are within the normal range. This partial list illustrates one strength of the positive-incentive perspective. Unlike set-point theories, positive-incentive theories do not single out one factor as the major determinant of hunger and ignore the others; they acknowledge that many factors interact to determine a person's hunger at any time, and they suggest that this interaction occurs through the influence of these various factors on the positive-incentive value of eating (see Cabanac, 1971).

In this section, you learned that most people think about hunger and eating in terms of energy set points, and you were introduced to an alternative: the positive-incentive perspective. Which is correct? If you are like most people, you will have an attachment to familiar ways of thinking and a resistance to new ones. The principles of clear thinking, however, require that you put these tendencies aside and base your views about this important issue entirely on the evidence.

Thinking Critically

You have already learned about some of the major weaknesses of set-point theories of hunger and eating. In the next section, you will learn some of the things that biopsychological research has taught us about eating. As you progress through the section, notice the superiority of the positive-incentive theories over set-point theories in accounting for the basic facts of hunger and eating.

12.3 Factors That Determine What, When, and How Much We Eat

This section describes major factors that commonly determine what we eat, when we eat, and how much we eat. Notice that energy deficits are not included among these factors. Although major energy deficits clearly increase hunger and eating, they are not a common factor in the eating behavior of people like us, who live in food-replete societies. Although you may believe that your body is short of energy just before a meal, it is not. This misconception is one that is addressed in this section. Also, notice that research on nonhumans has played an important role in furthering understanding of eating by our species.

Factors That Determine What We Eat

Certain tastes have a high positive-incentive value for virtually all members of a species. For example, most humans have a special fondness for sweet, fatty, and salty tastes. This species-typical pattern of human taste preferences is adaptive because in nature sweet and fatty tastes are typically characteristic of high-energy foods that are rich in vitamins and minerals, and salty tastes are characteristic of sodium-rich foods. In contrast, bitter tastes, for which most humans have an aversion, are often associated with toxins. Superimposed on our species-typical taste preferences and aversions, each of us has the ability to learn specific taste preferences and aversions (see Rozin & Shulkin, 1990).

Learned Taste Preferences and Aversions Animals learn to prefer tastes that are followed by an infusion of calories, and they learn to avoid tastes that are followed by illness (e.g., Baker & Booth, 1989; Lucas & Sclafani, 1989; Sclafani, 1990). In addition, humans and other animals learn what to eat from their conspecifics. For example, rats learn to prefer flavors that they experience in mother's milk and those that they smell on the breaths of other rats (see Galef, 1995, 1996; Galef, Whishkin, & Bielavska, 1997). Similarly, in humans, many food preferences are culturally specific—for example, in some cultures, various nontoxic insects are considered to be a delicacy. Galef and Wright (1995) have shown that rats reared in groups, rather than in isolation, are more likely to learn to eat a healthy diet.

Learning to Eat Vitamins and Minerals How do animals select a diet that provides all of the vitamins and minerals they need? To answer this question, researchers have studied how dietary deficiencies influence diet selection. Two patterns of results have emerged: one for sodium and one for the other essential vitamins and minerals. When an animal is deficient in sodium, it de-

velops an immediate and compelling preference for the taste of sodium salt (see Rowland, 1990). In contrast, an animal that is deficient in some vitamin or mineral other than sodium must learn to consume foods that are rich in the missing nutrient by experiencing their positive effects; this is because vitamins and minerals other than sodium normally have no detectable taste in food. For example, rats maintained on a diet deficient in *thiamine* (vitamin B$_1$) develop an aversion to the taste of that diet; and if they are offered two new diets, one deficient in thiamine and one rich in thiamine, they often develop a preference for the taste of the thiamine-rich diet over the ensuing days.

If we, like rats, are capable of learning to select diets that are rich in the vitamins and minerals we need, why are dietary deficiencies so prevalent in our society (see Willett, 1994)? One reason is that, in order to maximize profits, manufacturers produce foods with the tastes that we prefer but with most of the essential nutrients extracted from them. (Even rats prefer chocolate chip cookies to nutritionally complete rat chow.) The second reason is illustrated by the classic study of Harris and associates (1933). When thiamine-deficient rats were offered two new diets, one with thiamine and one without, almost all of them learned to eat the complete diet and avoid the deficient one. However, when they were offered ten new diets, only one of which contained the badly needed thiamine, few developed a preference for the complete diet. The number of different substances consumed each day by most people in industrialized societies is immense, and this makes it difficult, if not impossible, for their bodies to learn which foods are beneficial and which are not.

There is not much about nutrition in this chapter. Although it is certainly important to eat a nutritious diet, nutrition has little direct effect on our hunger and eating. However, while I am on the topic, I would like to direct you to a good source of information about nutrition: Many popular books on nutrition are of questionable validity, and even governments, inordinately influenced by economic considerations and special-interest groups, often do not provide the best nutritional advice (see Nestle, 2003). For sound research-based advice on nutrition, check out an article by Willett and Stampfer (2003) and the book on which it is based (Willett, Skerrett, & Giovannucci, 2001).

Factors That Influence When We Eat

Collier and his colleagues (see Collier, 1986) found that most mammals choose to eat many small meals (snacks) each day if they have ready access to a continuous supply of food. Only when there are physical costs involved in initiating meals—for example, having to travel a considerable distance—does an animal opt for a few large meals.

The number of times humans eat each day is influenced by cultural norms, work schedules, family routines, personal preferences, wealth, and a variety of other factors. However, in contrast to the usual mammalian preference, most people, particularly those living in family groups, tend to eat a few large meals each day at regular times. Interestingly, each person's regular mealtimes are the very same times at which that person is likely to feel most hungry; in fact, many people experience attacks of malaise (headache, nausea, and an inability to concentrate) when they miss a regularly scheduled meal.

Premeal Hunger I am sure that you have experienced attacks of premeal hunger. Subjectively, they seem to provide compelling support for set-point theories. Your body seems to be crying out: "I need more energy. I cannot function without it. Please feed me." But things are not always the way they seem. Woods has straightened out the confusion (see Woods, 1991; Woods & Ramsay, 2000; Woods & Strubbe, 1994).

According to Woods, the key to understanding hunger is to appreciate that eating meals stresses the body. Before a meal, the body's energy reserves are in reasonable homeostatic balance; then, as a meal is consumed, there is a homeostasis-disturbing influx of fuels into the bloodstream. The body does what it can to defend its homeostasis. At the first indication that a person will soon be eating—for example, when the usual mealtime approaches—the body enters the cephalic phase and takes steps to soften the impact of the impending homeostasis-disturbing influx by releasing insulin into the blood and thus reducing blood glucose. Woods's message is that the strong, unpleasant feelings of hunger that you may experience at mealtimes are not cries from your body for food; they are the sensations of your body's preparations for the expected homeostasis-disturbing meal. Mealtime hunger is caused by the expectation of food, not by an energy deficit.

As a high school student, I ate lunch at exactly 12:05 every day and was overwhelmed by hunger as the time approached. Now, my eating schedule is different, and I never experience noontime hunger pangs; I now get hungry just before the time at which I usually eat. Have you had a similar experience?

Thinking Critically

Pavlovian Conditioning of Hunger In a clever series of Pavlovian conditioning experiments on laboratory rats, Weingarten (1983, 1984, 1985) provided strong support for the view that hunger is often caused by the expectation of food, not by an energy deficit. During the conditioning phase of one of his experiments, Weingarten presented rats with six meals per day at irregular intervals, and he signaled the impending delivery of each meal with a buzzer-and-light conditional stimulus. This conditioning procedure was continued for 11 days. Throughout the ensuing test phase of the experiment, the food was continuously available. Despite the fact that the subjects were never deprived during the test phase, the rats started to eat each time the buzzer and light were presented—even if they had recently completed a meal.

Factors That Influence How Much We Eat

The motivational state that causes us to stop eating a meal when there is food remaining is **satiety**. Satiety mechanisms play a major role in determining how much we eat.

Satiety Signals As you will learn in the next section of the chapter, food in the gut and glucose entering the blood can induce satiety signals, which inhibit subsequent consumption. These signals depend on both the volume and the **nutritive density** (calories per unit volume) of the food.

Evolutionary Perspective

The effects of nutritive density have been demonstrated in studies in which laboratory rats have been maintained on a single diet. Once a stable baseline of consumption has been established, the nutritive density of the diet is changed. Many rats learn to adjust the volume of food they consume to keep their caloric intake and body weights relatively stable. However, there are limits to this adjustment: Rats often do not increase their intake sufficiently to maintain their body weights if the nutritive density of their conventional laboratory feed is reduced by more than 50%, and they do not maintain the constancy of their caloric intake if there are major changes in the diet's palatability.

Sham Eating The study of **sham eating** indicates that satiety signals from the gut or blood are not necessary to terminate a meal. In sham-eating experiments, food is chewed and swallowed by the subject; but rather than passing down the subject's esophagus into the stomach, it passes out of the body through an implanted tube (see Figure 12.5).

Because sham eating adds no energy to the body, set-point theories predict that all sham-eaten meals should be huge. But this is not the case. Weingarten and Kulikovsky (1989) sham fed rats one of two differently flavored diets: one that the rats had naturally eaten many times before and one that they had never eaten before. The first sham meal of the rats that had previously eaten the diet was the same size as the previously eaten meals of that diet; then, on ensuing days they began to sham eat more and more (see Figure 12.6). In contrast, the rats that were presented with the unfamiliar diet sham ate large quantities right from the start. Weingarten and

Kulikovsky concluded that the amount we eat is influenced largely by our previous experience with the particular food's postingestive effects, not by the immediate effect of the food on the body.

Appetizer Effect and Satiety   The next time you attend a dinner party, you may experience a major weakness of the set-point theory of satiety. If appetizers are served, you will experience the fact that small amounts of food consumed before a meal actually increase hunger rather than reducing it. This is the **appetizer effect.** Presumably, it occurs because the consumption of a small amount of food is particularly effective in eliciting cephalic-phase responses.

Social Influences and Satiety   Feelings of satiety depend on whether we are eating alone or with others. Redd and de Castro (1992) found that their subjects consumed 60% more when eating with others. Laboratory rats also eat substantially more when fed in groups.

In humans, social factors have also been shown to reduce consumption. Many people eat less than they would like in order to achieve their society's ideal of slenderness, and others refrain from eating large amounts in front of others so as not to appear gluttonous. Unfortunately, in our culture, females are greatly influenced by such pressures, and, as you will learn later in the chapter, some develop serious eating disorders as a result.

Sensory-Specific Satiety   The number of different tastes available at each meal has a major effect on meal size. For example, the effect of offering a laboratory rat a varied diet of highly palatable foods—a **cafeteria diet**—is dramatic. Adults rats that were offered bread and chocolate in addition to their usual laboratory diet increased their average intake of calories by 84%, and after 120 days they had increased their average body weights by 49% (Rogers & Blundell, 1980). The spectacular effects of cafeteria diets on consumption and

> **Thinking Critically**

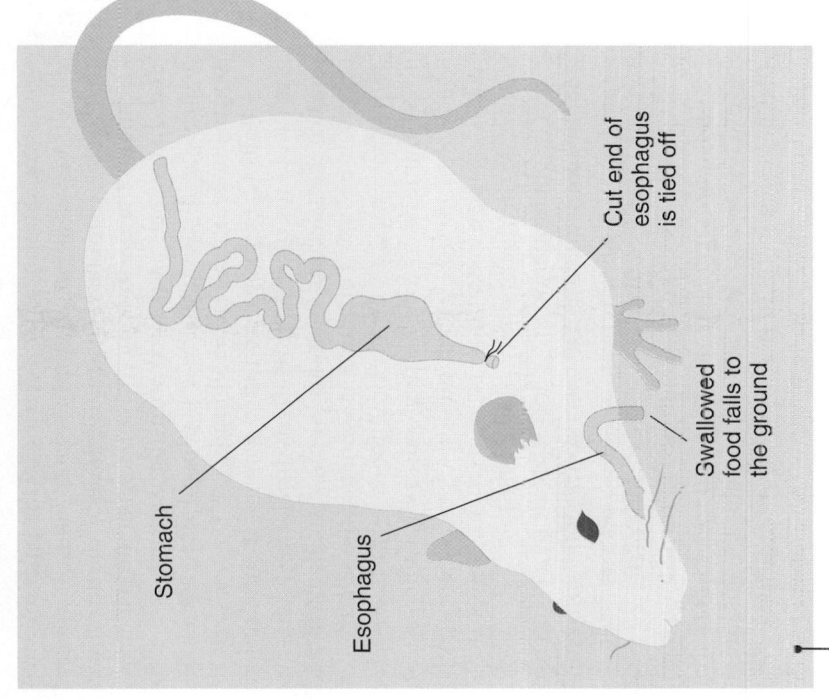

FIGURE 12.5   The sham-eating preparation.

Stomach

Esophagus

Cut end of esophagus is tied off

Swallowed food falls to the ground

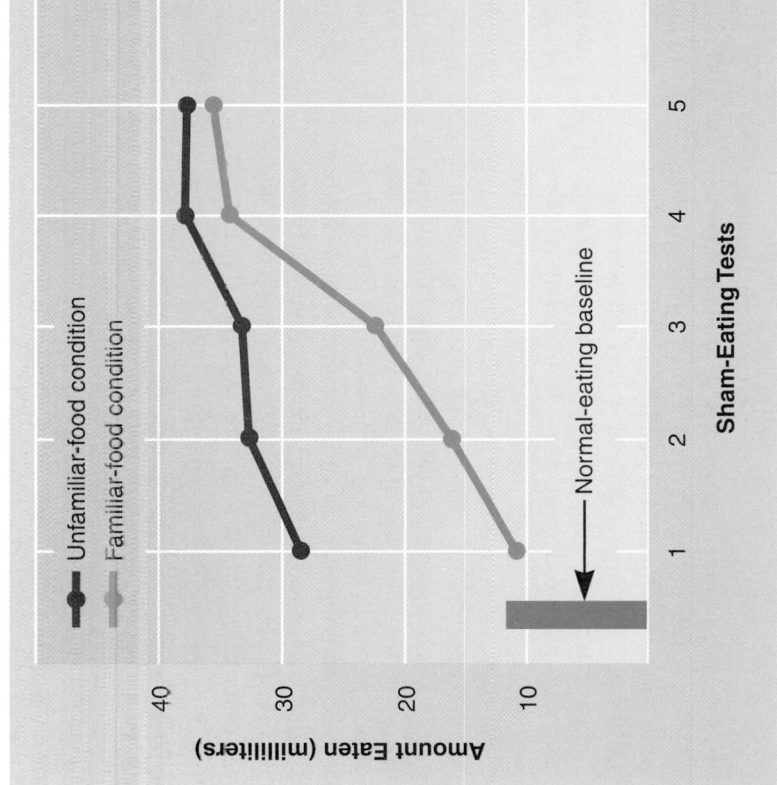

FIGURE 12.6   Change in the magnitude of sham eating over repeated sham-eating trials. The rats in one group sham ate the same diet they had eaten before the sham-eating phase; the rats in another group sham ate a diet different from the one they had previously eaten. (Adapted from Weingarten, 1990.)

Amount Eaten (milliliters)

40

30

20

10

1   2   3   4   5

Sham-Eating Tests

Unfamiliar-food condition

Familiar-food condition

Normal-eating baseline

body weight clearly run counter to the idea that satiety is rigidly controlled by internal energy set points.

The effect on meal size of cafeteria diets results from the fact that satiety is to a large degree taste-specific. As you eat one food, the positive-incentive value of all foods declines slightly, but the positive-incentive value of that particular food plummets. As a result, you soon become satiated on that food and stop eating it. However, if another food is offered to you, you will often begin eating again.

In one study of **sensory-specific satiety** (Rolls et al., 1981), human subjects were asked to rate the palatability of eight different foods, and then they ate a meal of one of them. After the meal, they were asked to rate the palatability of the eight foods once again, and it was found that their rating of the food they had just eaten had declined substantially more than had their ratings of the other seven foods. Moreover, when the subjects were offered an unexpected second meal, they consumed most of it unless it was the same as the first.

Booth (1981) asked subjects to rate the momentary pleasure produced by the flavor, the smell, the sight, or just the thought of various foods at different times after consuming a large, high-calorie, high-carbohydrate liquid meal. There was an immediate sensory-specific decrease in the palatability of foods of the same or similar flavor as soon as the liquid meal was consumed. This was followed by a general decrease in the palatability of all substances about 30 minutes later. Thus, it appears that signals from taste receptors produce an immediate decline in the positive-incentive value of similar tastes and that signals associated with the postingestive consequences of eating produce a general decrease in the positive-incentive value of all foods.

Rolls (1990) suggested that sensory-specific satiety has two kinds of effects: relatively brief effects that influence the selection of foods within a single meal and relatively enduring effects that influence the selection of foods from meal to meal. Some foods seem to be relatively immune to long-lasting sensory-specific satiety; foods such as rice, bread, potatoes, sweets, and green salads can be eaten almost every day with only a slight decline in their palatability (Rolls, 1986).

The phenomenon of sensory-specific satiety has two adaptive consequences. First, it encourages the consumption of a varied diet. If there were no sensory-specific satiety, a person would tend to eat her or his preferred food and nothing else, and the result would be malnutrition. Second, sensory-specific satiety encourages animals that have access to a variety of foods to eat a lot; an animal that has eaten its fill of one food will often begin eating again if it encounters a different one (Raynor & Epstein, 2001). This encourages animals to take full advantage of times of abundance, which are all too rare in nature.

12.4 Physiological Research on Hunger and Satiety

Now that you have been introduced to the set-point theory, the positive-incentive perspective, and some basic eating-related facts, this section introduces you to five prominent lines of research on the physiology of hunger and satiety.

Role of Blood Glucose Levels in Hunger and Satiety

As I have already explained, efforts to link blood glucose levels to eating have been largely unsuccessful. However, there was a renewed interest in the role of glucose in the regulation of eating in the 1990s, following the development of methods of continually monitoring blood glucose levels. In the classic experiment of Campfield and Smith (1990), rats were housed individually, with free access to a mixed diet and water, and their blood glucose levels were continually monitored via a chronic intravenous catheter (i.e., a hypodermic needle located in a vein). In this situation, baseline blood glucose levels rarely fluctuated more than 2%. However, about 10 minutes before a meal was initiated, the levels suddenly dropped about 8% (see Figure 12.7).

Does the finding of Campfield and Smith lend support to the glucostatic theory of hunger? I think not, for three reasons. The first is that it is a simple matter to construct a situation in which drops in blood glucose levels do not precede eating (e.g., Strubbe & Steffens, 1977)—for example, by unexpectedly serving a food with a high positive-incentive value. The second reason is that the premeal decreases in blood glucose observed by Campfield and Smith seemed to be a response to the animals' intention to start eating, not the other way round. The premeal decreases in blood glucose were preceded by increases in blood insulin levels: This indicates that the decreases did not occur because the rats were running out of energy, but rather that the rats lowered their own blood glucose levels by releasing insulin. Also, the suddenness of the drop in blood glucose suggests that the drop was actively produced rather than being a consequence of a gradual decline in the body's energy reserves (see Figure 12.7). The third reason why I think that Campfield and Smith's data do not support the glucostatic theory is that if the expected meal was not served, blood glucose levels returned to their previous homeostatic levels.

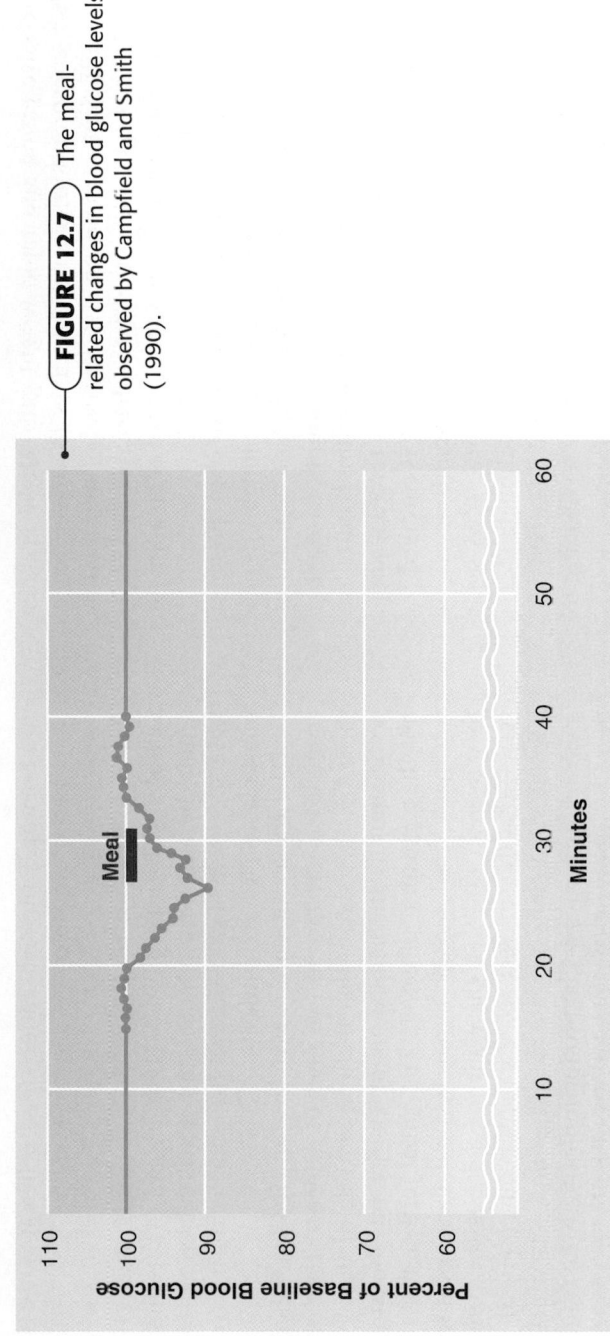

FIGURE 12.7 The meal-related changes in blood glucose levels observed by Campfield and Smith (1990).

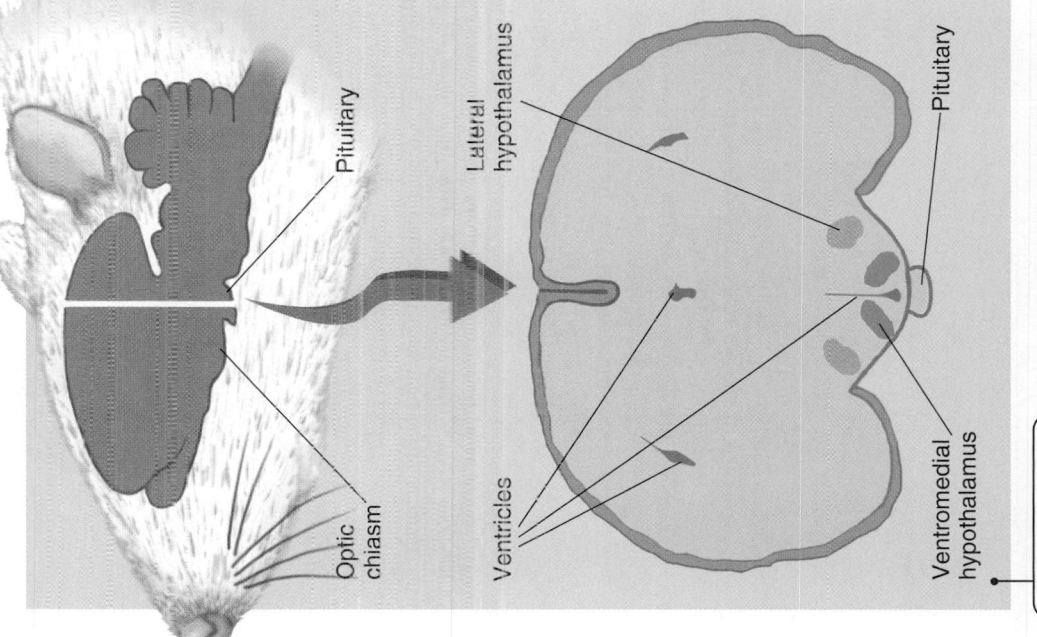

FIGURE 12.8 The locations in the rat brain of the ventromedial hypothalamus and the lateral hypothalamus.

The fact that injections of insulin do not reliably induce eating in experimental subjects unless the injections are sufficiently great to reduce blood glucose levels by 50% (see Rowland, 1981) and the fact that large premeal infusions of glucose often do not suppress eating (see Geiselman, 1987) indicate that glucose deficits are not the primary cause of hunger. However, some results suggest that decreases in blood glucose can contribute to feelings of hunger. For example, Smith and Campfield (1993) used drugs to induce in rats a slight reduction in blood glucose similar to that which occurs spontaneously prior to meals, and they found that the reduction increased subsequent food consumption. Conversely, Campfield, Brandon, and Smith (1985) delayed the onset of meals by infusing glucose into the blood of rats at the first sign of a premeal decline in blood glucose.

Myth of Hypothalamic Hunger and Satiety Centers

In the 1950s, experiments on rats seemed to suggest that eating behavior is controlled by two different regions of the hypothalamus: satiety by the **ventromedial hypothalamus (VMH)** and feeding by the **lateral hypothalamus (LH)**—see Figure 12.8. This theory turned out to be wrong, but it stimulated several important discoveries.

VMH Satiety Center In 1940, it was discovered that large bilateral electrolytic lesions to the ventromedial hypothalamus produce **hyperphagia** (excessive eating) and extreme obesity in rats (Hetherington & Ranson, 1940). This *VMH syndrome* has two different phases: dynamic and static. The **dynamic phase**, which begins as soon as the subject regains consciousness after the operation, is characterized by several weeks of grossly excessive eating and rapid weight gain. However, after that, consumption gradually declines to a level that is just sufficient to maintain a stable level of obesity; this marks the beginning of the **static phase**. Figure 12.9 illustrates the weight gain and food intake of an adult rat with bilateral VMH lesions.

The most important feature of the static phase of the VMH syndrome is that the animal maintains its new body weight. If a rat in the static phase is deprived of food until it has lost a substantial amount of weight, it will regain the lost weight once deprivation is curtailed; conversely, if it is made to gain weight by forced feeding, it will lose the excess once forced feeding is curtailed.

Paradoxically, despite their prodigious levels of consumption, VMH-lesioned rats in some ways seem less hungry than unlesioned controls. Although VMH-lesioned rats eat much more than normal rats when palatable food is readily available, they are less willing to work for it (Teitelbaum, 1957) or to consume it if it is slightly unpalatable (Miller, Bailey, & Stevenson, 1950). Weingarten, Chang, and Jarvie (1983) showed that the finicky eating of VMH-lesioned rats is a consequence of their obesity, not a primary effect of their lesion; they are no less likely to consume unpalatable food than are unlesioned rats of equal obesity.

LH Feeding Center   In 1951, Anand and Brobeck reported that bilateral electrolytic lesions to the *lateral hypothalamus* produce **aphagia**—a complete cessation of eating. Even rats that were first made hyperphagic by VMH lesions were rendered aphagic by the addition of LH lesions. Anand and Brobeck concluded that the lateral region of the hypothalamus is a feeding center. Teitelbaum and Epstein (1962) subsequently discovered two important features of the *LH syndrome*. First, they found that the aphagia was accompanied by **adipsia**—a complete cessation of drinking. Second, they found that LH-lesioned rats partially recover if they are kept alive by tube feeding. First, they begin to eat wet, palatable foods, such as chocolate chip cookies soaked in milk,

and eventually they will eat dry food pellets if water is concurrently available.

Reinterpretation of the Effects of VMH and LH Lesions

The theory of VMH satiety and LH feeding centers became very popular, and it was served up to wave after wave of students as if the evidence for it were unassailable. However, little about it is true.

The theory that the VMH is a satiety center has crumbled in the face of two lines of evidence. One of these lines has shown that the primary role of the hypothalamus is the regulation of energy metabolism, not the regulation of eating. The initial interpretation was that VMH-lesioned animals become obese because they overeat; however, the evidence suggests the converse—that they overeat because they become obese. Bilateral VMH lesions increase blood insulin levels, which increases **lipogenesis** (the production of body fat) and decreases **lipolysis** (the breakdown of body fat to utilizable forms of energy)—see Powley et al. (1980). Both are likely to be the result of the increases in insulin levels that occur following the lesion. Because the calories

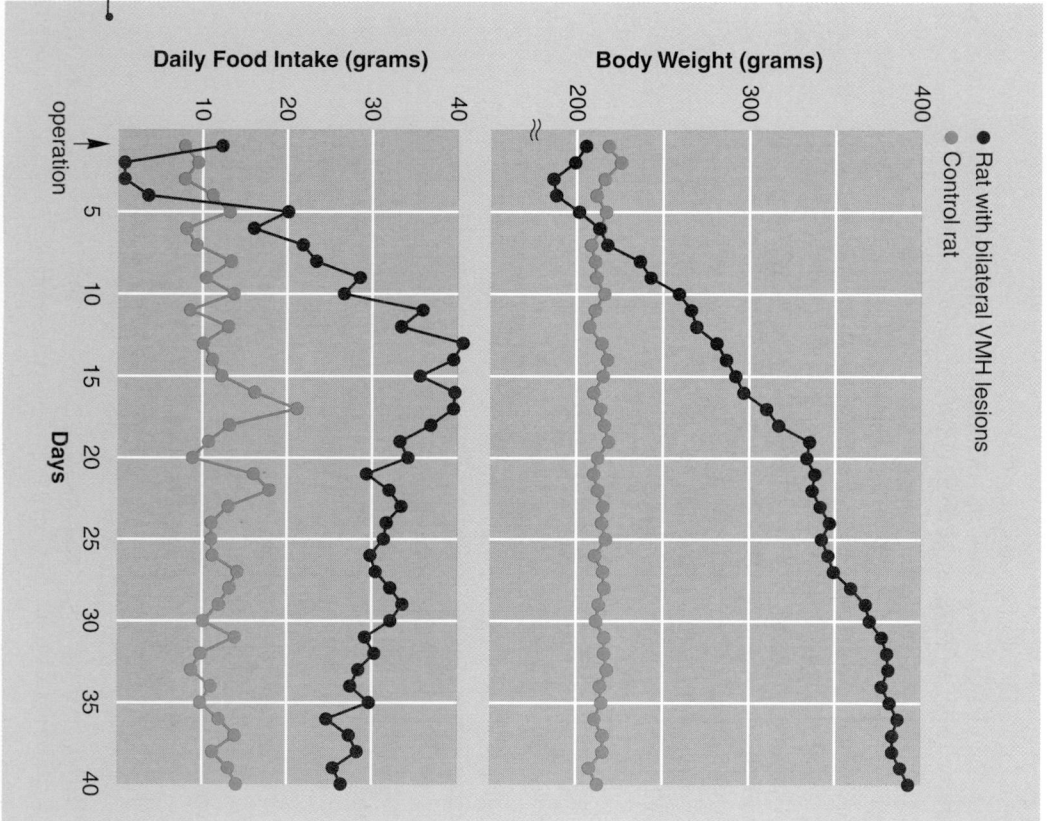

Daily Food Intake (grams)

Body Weight (grams)

Days

● Rat with bilateral VMH lesions
● Control rat

FIGURE 12.9   Postoperative hyperphagia and obesity in a rat with bilateral VMH lesions. (Adapted from Teitelbaum, 1961.)

Most of the evidence against the notion that the LH is a feeding center has come from a thorough analysis of the effects of bilateral LH lesions. Early research focused exclusively on the aphagia and adipsia that are produced by LH lesions, but subsequent research has shown that LH lesions produce a wide range of severe motor disturbances and a general lack of responsiveness to sensory input (of which food and drink are but two examples). Consequently, the idea that the LH is a center specifically dedicated to feeding no longer warrants serious consideration.

ingested by VMH-lesioned rats are converted to fat at a high rate, the rats must keep eating to ensure that they have enough calories in their blood to meet their immediate energy requirements (e.g., Hustvedt & Løvø, 1972); they are like misers who run to the bank each time they make a bit of money and deposit it in a savings account from which withdrawals cannot be made.

The second line of evidence that has undermined the theory of a VMH satiety center has shown that many of the effects of VMH lesions are not attributable to VMH damage. A large fiber bundle, the *ventral noradrenergic bundle*, courses past the VMH and is thus inevitably damaged by large electrolytic VMH lesions; in particular, fibers that project from the nearby **paraventricular nuclei** of the hypothalamus are damaged (see Figure 12.10). Bilateral lesions of the noradrenergic bundle (e.g., Gold et al., 1977) or the paraventricular nuclei (Leibowitz, Hammer, & Chang, 1981) produce hyperphagia and obesity similar to those produced by VMH lesions.

Role of the Gastrointestinal Tract in Satiety

One of the most influential early studies of hunger was published by Cannon and Washburn in 1912. It was a perfect collaboration: Cannon had the ideas, and Washburn had the ability to swallow a balloon. First, Washburn swallowed an empty balloon tied to the end of a thin tube. Then, Cannon pumped some air into the balloon and connected the end of the tube to a water-filled glass U-tube so that Washburn's stomach contractions produced a momentary increase in the level of the water at the other end of the U-tube. Washburn reported a "pang" of hunger each time that a large stomach contraction was recorded (see Figure 12.11 on page 302).

Cannon and Washburn's finding led to the theory that hunger is the feeling of contractions caused by an empty stomach, whereas satiety is the feeling of stomach distention. However, support for this theory and interest in the role of the gastrointestinal tract in hunger and satiety quickly waned with the discovery that human patients whose stomachs had been surgically removed and whose esophaguses had been hooked up directly to their **duodenums** continued to report feelings of hunger and satiety and continued to maintain their normal body weights by eating more meals of smaller size.

In the 1980s, there was a resurgence of interest in the role of the gastrointestinal tract in eating. It was stimulated by a series of experiments that indicated that the gastrointestinal tract is the source of satiety signals. For example, Koopmans (1981) transplanted an extra stomach and length of intestine into rats and then joined the major arteries and veins of the implants to the recipients' circulatory systems (see Figure 12.12 on page 303). Koopmans found that food injected into the transplanted stomach and kept there by a noose around the *pyloric sphincter* decreased eating in proportion to both its caloric content and volume. Because the transplanted stomach had no functional nerves, the gastrointestinal satiety signal had to be reaching the brain through the blood. And because nutrients are not absorbed from the stomach, the blood-borne satiety signal could not have been a nutrient. It had to be some chemical or chemicals that were released from the stomach in response to the caloric value and volume of the food—which leads us nicely into the next subsection.

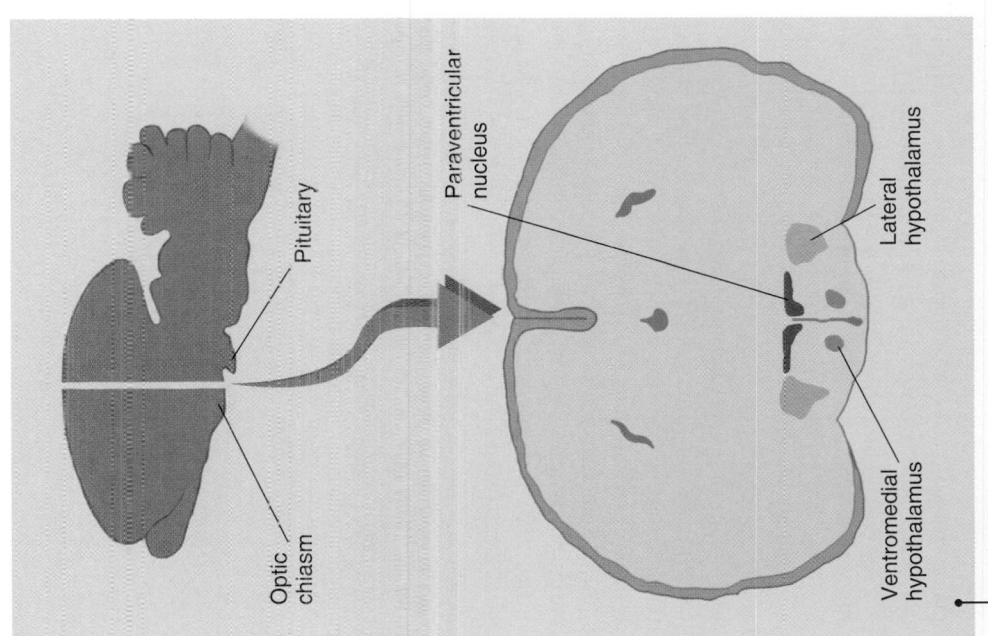

FIGURE 12.10   Location of the paraventricular nucleus in the rat hypothalamus. Note that the section through the hypothalamus is slightly different than the one in Figure 12.8.

Paraventricular nucleus

Pituitary

Optic chiasm

Lateral hypothalamus

Ventromedial hypothalamus

Hunger and Satiety Peptides

Soon after the discovery that the stomach and other parts of the gastrointestinal tract release chemicals, evidence began to accumulate that these were *peptides*, short chains of amino acids that function as hormones and neurotransmitters. Ingested food interacts with receptors in the gastrointestinal tract and in so doing causes the tract to release peptides into the bloodstream. In 1973, Gibbs, Young, and Smith injected one of these gut peptides, **cholecystokinin (CCK)**, into hungry rats and found that they ate smaller meals. This led to the hypothesis that circulating gut peptides provide the brain with information about the quantity and nature of food in the gastrointestinal tract and that this information plays a role in satiety.

There has been considerable support for the hypothesis that peptides can function as satiety signals (see Ritter, 2004). Several gut peptides have been shown to bind to receptors in the brain, and a dozen or so (e.g., CCK, bombesin, glucagon, alpha-melanocyte-stimulating hormone, and somatostatin) have been reported to reduce food intake (see Beck, 2001; Halford & Blundell, 2000; Strubbe & van Dijk, 2002).

Evolutionary Perspective

In studying the appetite-reducing effects of peptides, researchers had to rule out the possibility that these effects are not merely the consequence of illness (see Moran, 2004). Indeed, there is evidence that CCK induces illness: CCK administered to rats after they have eaten an unfamiliar substance induces a *conditioned taste aversion* for that substance, and CCK induces nausea in human subjects. However, CCK reduces appetite and eating at doses substantially below those that are required to induce taste aversion in rats, and thus it qualifies as a legitimate *satiety peptide* (a peptide that decreases appetite).

Several *hunger peptides* (peptides that increase appetite) have also been discovered. These peptides tend to be synthesized in the brain, particularly in the hypothalamus. The most widely studied of these are neuropeptide Y, galanin, orexin-A, and ghrelin (e.g., Inui, 2001; Williams et al., 2004).

The discovery of the hunger and satiety peptides has had two major effects on the search for the neural mechanisms of hunger and satiety. First, the sheer number of these hunger and satiety peptides indicates that the neural system that controls eating likely reacts to many different signals (see Berthoud, 2002; Schwartz & Azzara,

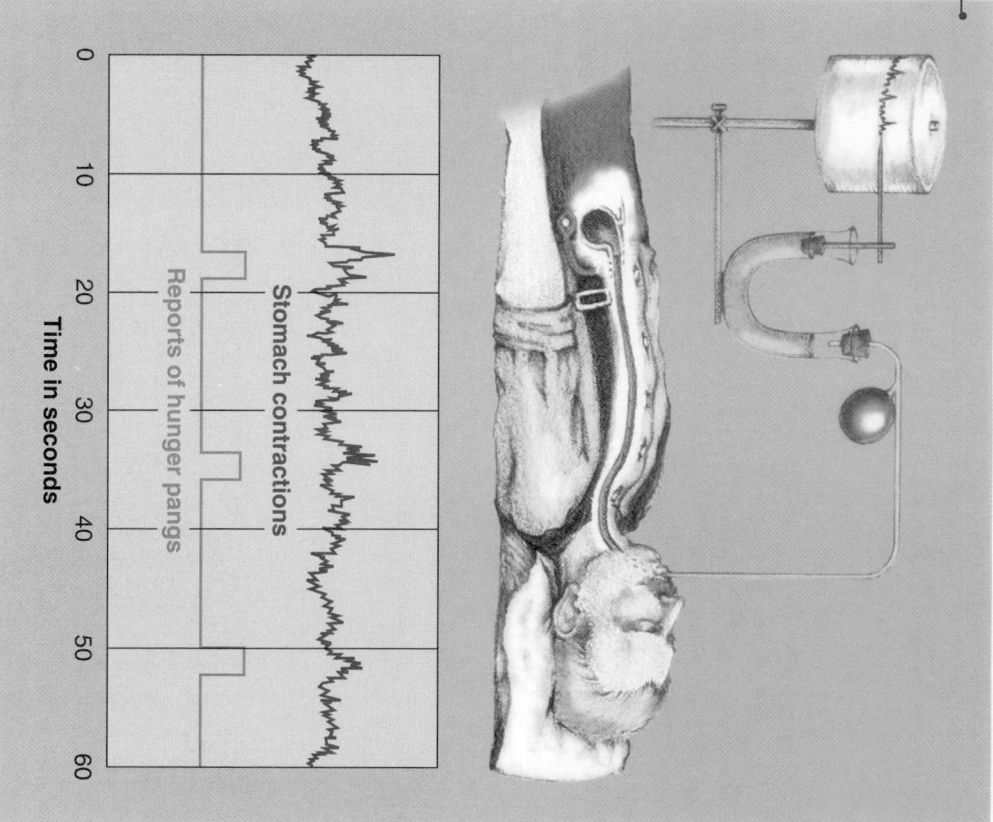

Stomach contractions

Reports of hunger pangs

Time in seconds

0   10   20   30   40   50   60

2004), not just to one or two (e.g., not just to glucose and fat). Second, the discovery that many of the hunger and satiety peptides have receptors in the hypothalamus has renewed interest in the role of the hypothalamus in the control of eating (Mercer & Speakman, 2001). The strongest support for this role comes from demonstrations that microinjections of particular gut peptides into certain sites in the hypothalamus have major effects on eating. Still, there is a general acceptance that hypothalamic circuits are only one part of a much larger system.

Serotonin and Satiety

The monoaminergic neurotransmitter serotonin plays a role in satiety. The initial evidence for this role came from a line of research on rats that was initiated in the 1970s. In these studies, serotonin agonists consistently reduced rats' food intake.

In rats, the satiety-inducing effects of serotonin have three major characteristics (see Blundell & Halford, 1998). First, they are powerful: They can even overcome the powerful attraction of highly palatable cafeteria diets. Second, they reduce the amount of food that is consumed during each meal rather than reducing the number of meals (see Clifton, 2000). And third, they are associated with a shift in food preferences away from fatty foods.

In humans, serotonin agonists (e.g., fenfluramine, dexfenfluramine, fluoxetine) have been shown to reduce hunger, eating, and body weight under a variety of conditions (see Blundell & Halford, 1998). Later in this chapter, you will learn about the use of serotonin in the treatment of obesity (see De Vry & Schreiber, 2000).

Evolutionary Perspective

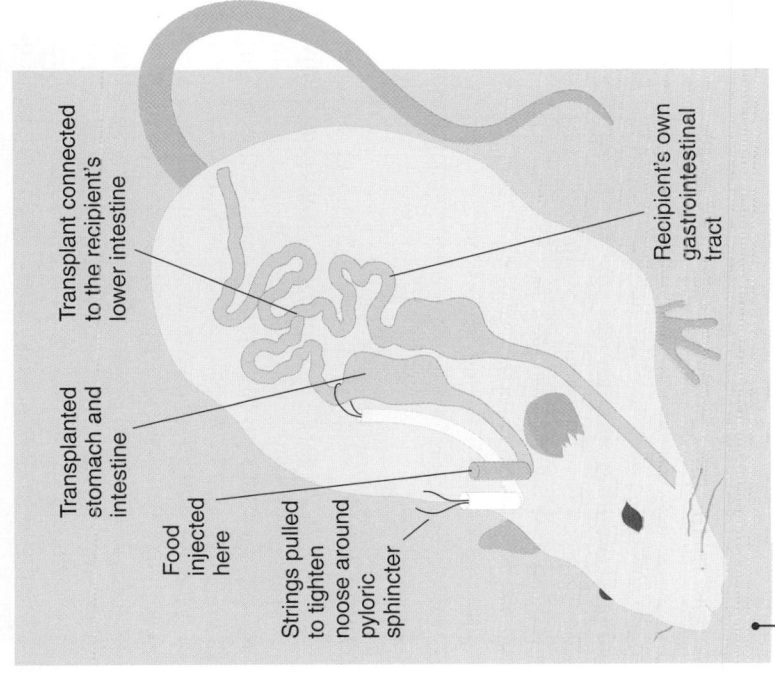

FIGURE 12.12 Transplantation of an extra stomach and length of intestine in a rat. Koopmans (1981) implanted an extra stomach and length of intestine in each of his experimental subjects. He then connected the major blood vessels of the implanted stomachs to the circulatory systems of the recipients. Food injected into the extra stomach and kept there by a noose around the pyloric sphincter decreased eating in proportion to its volume and caloric value.

Transplanted stomach and intestine

Transplant connected to the recipient's lower intestine

Food injected here

Strings pulled to tighten noose around pyloric sphincter

Recipient's own gastrointestinal tract

12.5 Body Weight Regulation: Set Points versus Settling Points

One strength of set-point theories of eating is that they also explain body-weight regulation. You have already learned that set-point theories are largely inconsistent with the facts of eating, but how well do they account for the regulation of body weight? Certainly, most people in our culture believe that body weight is regulated by a body-fat set point (Assanand, Pinel, & Lehman, 1998a, 1998b). They believe that when fat deposits are below a person's set point, a person becomes hungrier and eats more, which results in a return of body-fat levels to that person's set point; and, conversely, they believe that when fat deposits are above a person's set point, a person becomes less hungry and eats less, which results in a return of body fat levels to their set point.

Set-Point Assumptions about Body Weight and Eating

You have already learned that set-point theories do a poor job of predicting the major properties of hunger and eating. Do they do a better job of accounting for the facts of body-weight regulation? Let's begin by looking at three lines of evidence that challenge fundamental aspects of many set-point theories of body weight regulation.

Variability of Body Weight The set-point model was expressly designed to explain why adult body weights remain constant. Indeed, a set-point mechanism should make it virtually impossible for an adult to gain or lose large amounts of weight. Yet, many adults experience large and lasting changes in body weight. Moreover, set-point thinking crumbles in the face of the epidemic of obesity that is currently sweeping fast-food societies.

Set-point theories of body weight regulation suggest that the best method of maintaining a constant body weight is to eat each time there is a motivation to eat—because the main function of these hunger motivations is to defend the set point. However, as I am sure many of you know from personal experience, many people avoid obesity only by resisting their urges to eat.

Set Points and Health

One implication of set-point theories of body weight regulation is that each person's set point is optimal for that person's health—or at least not incompatible with good health. This is why media psychologists commonly advise people to "listen to the wisdom of their bodies" and eat as much as they need to satisfy their hunger. Experimental results indicate that this common prescription for good health could not be further from the truth.

Two kinds of evidence suggest that *ad libitum* (free-feeding) levels of consumption are unhealthy (see Brownell & Rodin, 1994). First are the results of studies of humans who consume fewer calories than others. For example, people living on the Japanese island of Okinawa seemed to eat so few calories that it was of concern to health officials. When they took a closer look, here is what they found (see Kagawa, 1978). Adult Okinawans were found to consume, on average, 20% fewer calories than other adult Japanese, and Okinawan schoolchildren were found to consume 38% fewer calories than recommended by public health officials. It was somewhat surprising then that rates of morbidity and mortality and of all aging-related diseases were found to be substantially lower in Okinawa than in other parts of Japan, a country in which overall levels of caloric intake and obesity are far below Western norms. For example, the death rates from stroke, cancer, and heart disease in Okinawa were only 59%, 69%, and 59%, respectively, of those in the rest of Japan. Indeed, the proportion of Okinawans living to be over 100 years of age was up to 40 times greater than that of inhabitants of various other regions of Japan.

The Okinawan study and the other studies that have reported major health benefits in humans who eat less (e.g., Manson et al., 1995; Walford & Walford, 1994) are not controlled experiments; therefore they must be interpreted with caution. For example, perhaps it is not the consumption of fewer calories per se that leads to the health and longevity; perhaps people who eat less tend to eat healthier diets. Fortunately, calorie-restriction experiments conducted in over a dozen different species, including monkeys, do not have these problems of interpretation.

The effects of calorie restriction are the second kind of evidence that *ad libitum* levels of consumption are un-

Thinking Critically

healthy. In *calorie-restriction experiments*, one group of subjects is allowed to eat as much as they choose, while other groups of subjects have their caloric intake of the same diets substantially reduced (by between 25% and 65% in various studies). Results of such experiments have been remarkably consistent (see Bucci, 1992; Masoro, 1988; Weindruch, 1996; Weindruch & Walford, 1988): In experiment after experiment, substantial reductions in the caloric intake of balanced diets have improved numerous indices of health and increased longevity. For example, in one experiment (Weindruch et al., 1986), groups of mice had their caloric intake of a well-balanced commercial diet reduced by either 25%, 55%, or 65% after weaning. All levels of dietary restriction substantially improved health and increased longevity but the benefits were greatest in the mice whose intake was reduced the most. Those mice that consumed the least had the lowest incidence of cancer, the best immune responses, and the greatest maximum life span—they lived 67% longer than did mice that ate as much as they liked.

Evolutionary Perspective

One surprising point about the results of the calorie-restriction experiments: They suggested that the health benefits of restricted diets are not entirely attributable to loss of body fat (see Weindruch, 1996). The subjects were not frankly obese when they commenced their calorie-reduced diets, and thus they did not lose a lot of weight; moreover, there was no correlation between the amount of weight loss and degree of improved health. The current thinking is that some by-product of energy consumption accumulates in cells and accelerates aging with all its attendant health problems (Lane, Ingram, & Roth, 2002; Prolla & Mattson, 2001).

Please stop and think about the implications of these amazing calorie-restriction experiments. How much do you eat?

Thinking Critically

Regulation of Body Weight by Changes in the Efficiency of Energy Utilization

Implicit in many set-point theories is the premise that body weight is largely a function of how much a person eats. Of course, how much someone eats plays a role in his or her body weight, but it is now clear that the body controls its fat levels, to a large degree, by changing the efficiency with which it uses energy. As a person's level of body fat declines, that person starts to use energy resources more efficiently, which limits further weight loss (see Martin, White, & Hulsey, 1991); conversely, weight gain is limited by a progressive decrease in the efficiency of energy utilization. Rothwell and Stock (1982) created a group of obese rats by maintaining them on a cafeteria diet, and they found that the resting level of energy expenditure in these obese rats was 45% greater than in control rats.

This point is illustrated by the progressively declining effectiveness of weight-loss programs. Initially, low-calorie diets produce substantial weight loss. But the rate

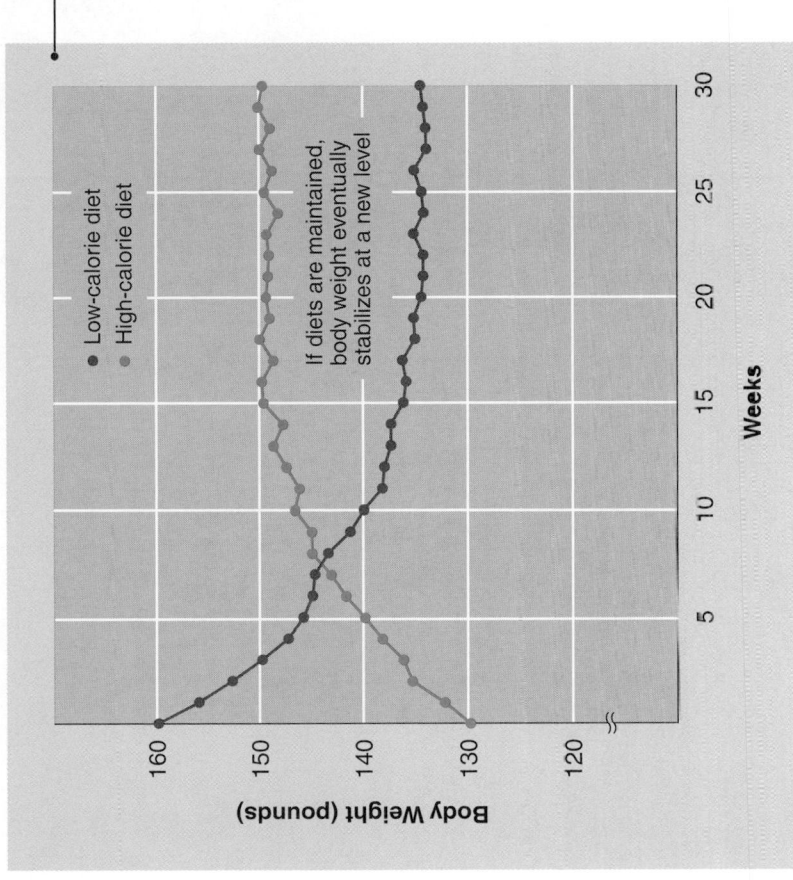

FIGURE 12.13 The diminishing effects on body weight of a low-calorie diet and a high-calorie diet.

of weight loss diminishes with each successive week on the diet, until an equilibrium is achieved and little or no further weight loss occurs. Most dieters are familiar with this disappointing trend. A similar effect occurs with weight-gain programs (see Figure 12.13).

The mechanism by which the body adjusts the efficiency of its energy utilization in response to its levels of body fat has been termed **diet-induced thermogenesis.** Increases in the levels of body fat produce increases in body temperature, which require additional energy to maintain them—and decreases in the level of body fat have the opposite effects.

There are major differences among subjects both in their **basal metabolic rate** (the rate at which they utilize energy to maintain bodily processes when resting) and in their ability to adjust their metabolic rate in response to changes in the levels of body fat. We all know people who remain slim even though they eat gluttonously. However, the research on calorie-restricted diets suggests that these people may not eat with impunity: There may be a health cost to pay for overeating even in the absence of obesity.

Set Points and Settling Points in Weight Control

The theory that eating is part of a system designed to defend a body-fat set point has long had its critics (see Booth, Fuller, & Lewis, 1981; Wirtshafter & Davis, 1977); but for many years their arguments were largely ignored

and the set-point assumption ruled. This situation is changing: Several recent prominent reviews of research on hunger and weight regulation generally acknowledge that a strict set-point model cannot account for the facts of weight regulation, and they argue for a more flexible model (see Berthoud, 2002; Mercer & Speakman, 2001; Woods et al., 2000). Because body-fat set points still dominate the thinking of many people—presumably including you—I want to review the main advantages of one such flexible regulatory model: the settling-point model.

According to the settling-point model, body weight tends to drift around a natural **settling point**—the level at which the various factors that influence body weight achieve an equilibrium. The idea is that as body-fat levels increase, changes occur that tend to limit further increases until a balance is achieved between all factors that encourage weight gain and all those that discourage it.

The settling-point model provides a loose kind of homeostatic regulation, without a set-point mechanism or mechanism to return body weight to a set point. According to the settling-point model, body weight remains stable as long as there are no long-term changes in the factors that influence it; and if there are such changes, their impact is limited by negative feedback. In the settling-point model, the feedback merely limits further changes in the same direction, whereas in the set-point model, negative feedback triggers a return to the set point. A neuron's resting potential is a well-known biological settling point—see Chapter 4.

The seductiveness of the set-point mechanism is attributable in no small part to the existence of the thermostat model, which provides a vivid means of thinking about it. Figure 12.14 on page 306 presents an analogy I like to use to think about the settling-point mechanism. I call it the **leaky-barrel model:** (1) The amount of water entering the hose is analogous to the amount of food available to the subject; (2) the water pressure at the nozzle is analogous to the positive-incentive value of the available food; (3) the amount of water entering the barrel is analogous to the amount of energy consumed;

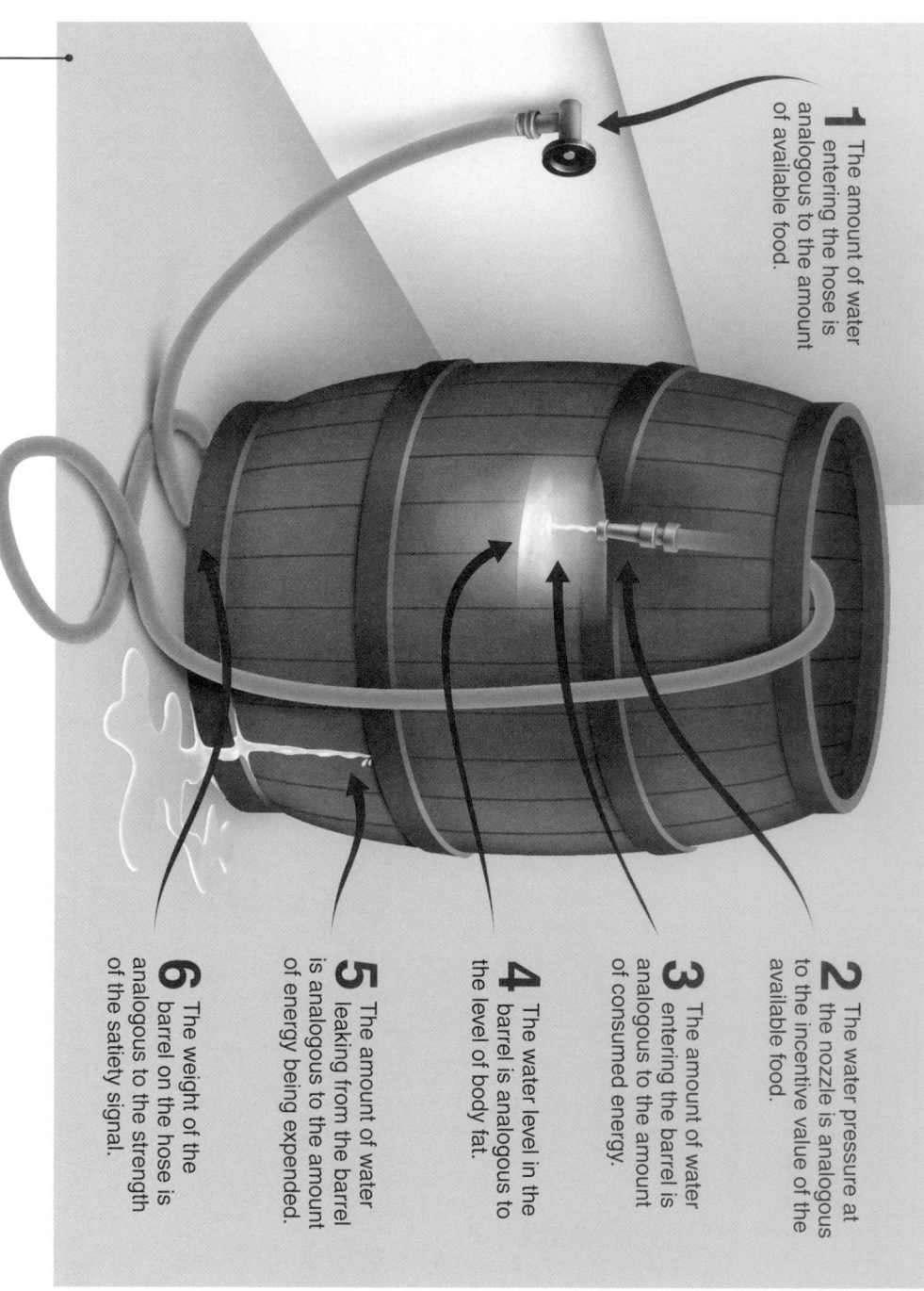

1 The amount of water entering the hose is analogous to the amount of available food.

2 The water pressure at the nozzle is analogous to the incentive value of the available food.

3 The amount of water entering the barrel is analogous to the amount of consumed energy.

4 The water level in the barrel is analogous to the level of body fat.

5 The amount of water leaking from the barrel is analogous to the amount of energy being expended.

6 The weight of the barrel on the hose is analogous to the strength of the satiety signal.

FIGURE 12.14 The leaky-barrel model: a settling-point model of eating and body weight homeostasis.

(4) the water level in the barrel is analogous to the level of body fat; (5) the amount of water leaking from the barrel is analogous to the amount of energy being expended; and (6) the weight of the barrel on the hose is analogous to the strength of the satiety signal.

The main advantage of the settling-point model of body weight regulation over the body-fat set-point model is that it is more consistent with the data. Another advantage is that in those cases in which both models make the same prediction, the settling-point model does so more parsimoniously—that is, with a simpler mechanism that requires fewer assumptions. Let's use the leaky-barrel analogy to see how the two models account for four key facts of weight regulation.

Fact 1: Body weight remains relatively constant in many adult animals. On the basis of this fact, it has been argued that body fat must be regulated around a set point. However, constant body

weight does not require, or even imply, a set point. Consider the leaky-barrel model. As water from the tap begins to fill the barrel, the weight of the water in the barrel increases. This increases the amount of water leaking out of the barrel and decreases the amount of water entering the barrel by increasing the pressure of the barrel on the hose. Eventually, this system settles into an equilibrium where the water level stays constant; but because this level is neither predetermined nor actively defended, it is a settling point, not a set point.

Fact 2: Many adult animals experience enduring changes in body weight. Set-point systems are designed to maintain internal constancy in the face of fluctuations of the external environment. Thus, the fact that many adult animals experience long-term changes in body weight is a strong argument against the set-point model. In contrast, the settling-point model predicts that when there is an enduring change in one of the parameters that affect body weight—for example, a major increase in the positive-incentive value of avail-

SCAN YOUR BRAIN

Are you ready to move on to the final two sections of the chapter, which deal with eating disorders? This is a good place to pause and scan your brain to see if you understand the biopsychological principles of eating and weight regulation.

1. The primary function of the _____ is to serve as a storage reservoir for undigested food.

2. Most of the absorption of nutrients into the body takes place through the wall of the _____, or upper intestine.

3. The phase of energy metabolism that is triggered by the expectation of food is the _____ phase.

4. During the absorptive phase, the pancreas releases a great deal of _____ into the bloodstream.

5. During the fasting phase, the primary fuels of the body are _____.

6. During the fasting phase, the primary fuel of the brain is _____.

Complete the following sentences by filling in the blanks. The correct answers are provided at the bottom of this page. Before proceeding, review material related to your incorrect answers and omissions.

7. The three components of a set-point system are a set-point mechanism, a detector, and an _____.

8. The theory that hunger and satiety are regulated by a blood glucose set point is the _____ theory.

9. Evidence suggests that hunger is a function of the expected _____ value of food.

10. The _____ hypothalamus was once believed to be the satiety center.

11. Evidence suggests that the monoaminergic neurotransmitter _____ plays a role in satiety.

12. Research evidence supports a _____ model of body weight regulation rather than a set-point model.

able food—body weight will drift to a new settling point.

Fact 3: If a subject's intake of food is reduced, metabolic changes that limit the loss of weight occur; the opposite happens when the subject overeats. This fact is often cited as evidence for set-point regulation of body weight; however, because the metabolic changes merely limit further weight changes rather than eliminating those that have occurred, they are more consistent with a settling-point model. For example, when water intake in the leaky-barrel model is reduced, the water level in the barrel begins to drop; but the drop is limited by a decrease in leakage and an increase in inflow attributable to the falling water pressure in the barrel. Eventually, a new settling point is achieved, but the reduction in water level is not as great as one might expect because of the loss-limiting changes.

Fact 4: After an individual has lost a substantial amount of weight (by dieting, exercise, or the surgical removal of fat), there is a tendency for the original weight to be regained once the subject returns to the previous eating- and energy-related lifestyle. Although this finding is often offered as irrefutable evidence of a body-weight set point, the settling-point model readily accounts for it. When the water level in the leaky-barrel model is reduced—by temporarily decreasing input (dieting), by temporarily increasing out-

put (exercising), or by scooping out some of the water (surgical removal of fat)—only a temporary drop in the settling point is produced. When the original conditions are reinstated, the water level inexorably drifts back to the original settling point.

Does it really matter whether we think about body weight regulation in terms of set points or settling points—or is it just splitting hairs? It certainly matters to biopsychologists: Understanding that body weight is regulated by a settling-point system helps them better understand, and more accurately predict, the changes in body weight that are likely to occur in various situations; it also indicates the kinds of physiological mechanisms that are likely to mediate these changes. And it should matter to you. If the set-point model is correct, attempting to change your body weight would be a waste of time; you would inevitably be drawn back to your body-weight set point. On the other hand, the leaky-barrel model suggests that it is possible to permanently change your body weight by permanently changing any of the factors that influences energy intake and output.

Thinking Critically

You have already learned that obesity is currently a major health problem in many parts of the world. What is more distressing is the rate at which the problem is growing: in the United States, for example, its incidence more than doubled during the 20th century (see Kuczmarski, 1992) and continues to rise. This rapid rate of increase indicates that environmental factors play a significant role in obesity.

Genetic factors also contribute to obesity. For example, it was estimated from a sample of U.S. twins that environmental and genetic factors contribute equally to individual differences in body fat in this population (see Price & Gottesman, 1991). However, the current surge in obesity is occurring too rapidly to be a product of genetic changes. Also, set-point theories are of no help in trying to understand the epidemic of obesity; according to that view, permanent weight gain should not occur in healthy adults.

Why Is There an Epidemic of Obesity?

Let's begin our analysis of obesity by considering the pressures that are likely to have led to the evolution of our eating and weight-regulation systems (see Pinel et al., 2000). During the course of evolution, inconsistent food supplies were one of the main threats to survival. As a result, the fittest individuals were those who preferred high-calorie foods, ate to capacity when food was available, stored as many excess calories as possible in the form of body fat, and used their stores of calories as efficiently as possible. Individuals who did not have these characteristics were unlikely to survive a food shortage, and so these characteristics were passed on to future generations.

Augmenting the effects of evolution has been the development of numerous cultural practices and beliefs that promote consumption. For example, in my culture, it is commonly believed that one should eat three meals per day at regular times, whether one is hungry or not; that food should be the focus of most social gatherings; that meals should be served in courses of progressively increasing palatability; and that salt, sweets (e.g., sugar), and fats (e.g., butter) should be added to foods to improve their flavor and thus increase their consumption.

Each of us possesses an eating and weight-regulation system that evolved to deal effectively with periodic food shortages, and many of us live in cultures whose eating-related practices evolved for the same purpose. However, our current environment differs from our "natural" environment in critical food-related ways. We live in an environment in which an endless variety of foods of the highest positive-incentive value are readily and continuously available. The consequence is an appallingly high level of consumption.

Why Do Some People Become Obese While Others Do Not?

Why do some people become obese while others living under the same obesity-promoting conditions do not? At a superficial level, the answer is obvious: Those who are obese are those whose energy intake has grossly exceeded their energy output; those who are slim are those whose energy intake has not grossly exceeded their energy output. Although this answer provides little insight, it does serve to emphasize that two kinds of individual differences play a role in obesity: those that lead to differences in energy input and those that lead to differences in energy output. Let's consider examples of each kind.

There are many factors that lead some people to eat more than others who have comparable access to food. For example, some people consume more energy because they have strong preferences for the taste of high-calorie foods (see Blundell & Finlayson, 2004); some consume more because they were raised in families and/or cultures that promote excessive eating; and some consume more because they have particularly large cephalic-phase responses to the sight or smell of food (Rodin, 1985).

With respect to energy output, people differ markedly from one another in the degree to which they can dissipate excess consumed energy. The most obvious difference is that people differ substantially in the amount of exercise they get; however, there are others. You have already learned about two of them: differences in *basal metabolic rate* and in the ability to react to fat increases by *diet-induced thermogenesis*. The third factor is called **NEAT**, or *nonexercise activity thermogenesis*, which is generated by activities such as fidgeting and the maintenance of posture and muscle tone (Ravussin & Danforth, 1999). Although the effects of NEAT on body weight have not been investigated systematically, evidence suggests that it plays a significant role in dissipating excess energy (Levine, Eberhardt, & Jensen, 1999).

Why Are Weight-Loss Programs Typically Ineffective?

Figure 12.15 describes the course of the typical dietary weight-loss program. Most weight-loss programs are unsuccessful in the sense that, as predicted by the set-tling-point model, most of the lost weight is regained once the program is terminated and the original conditions are reestablished. Clearly, the key to permanent weight loss is a permanent lifestyle change.

People who have difficulty controlling their weight may receive some solace by understanding that the tendency to eat large amounts of food, to accumulate body fat, and to use energy efficiently would all be highly

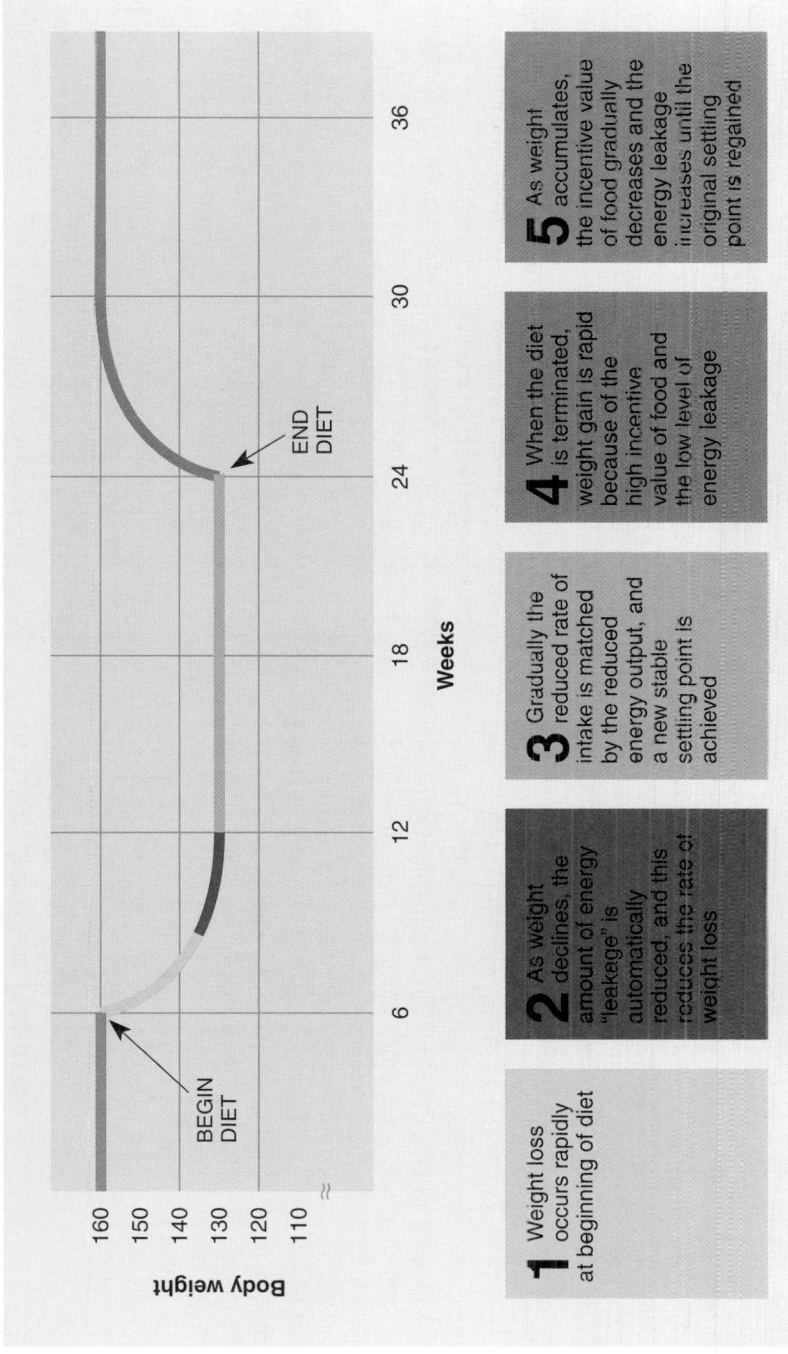

FIGURE 12.15 The five stages of a typical weight loss program.

1 Weight loss occurs rapidly at beginning of diet

2 As weight declines, the amount of energy "leakage" is automatically reduced, and this reduces the rate of weight loss

3 Gradually the reduced rate of intake is matched by the reduced energy output, and a new stable setting point is achieved

4 When the diet is terminated, weight gain is rapid because of the high incentive value of food and the low level of energy leakage

5 As weight accumulates, the incentive value of food gradually decreases and the energy leakage increases until the original settling point is regained

adaptive tendencies in a natural environment. It is our current environment that is "pathological," not the people with weight problems.

Exercise has many health-promoting effects; however, despite the general belief that exercise is the most effective method of losing weight, several studies have shown that it often contributes little to weight loss (e.g., Sweeney et al., 1993). One reason is that physical exercise normally accounts for only a small proportion of total energy expenditure: About 80% of the energy you expend is used to maintain the resting physiological processes of your body and to digest your food (Calles-Escandon & Horton, 1992). Another reason is that after exercise, many people consume extra drinks and foods that contain more calories than the relatively small number that were expended during the exercise.

Severe cases of obesity are sometimes treated by wiring the jaw shut to limit consumption to liquid diets, stapling part of the stomach together to reduce the size of meals, or cutting out a section of the duodenum to reduce the absorption of nutrients from the gastrointestinal tract. Unfortunately, some patients do not lose weight on a liquid diet, and those who do typically regain it once the wires are removed. Problems with both of the other two aforementioned methods of weight reduction include diarrhea, flatulence, and vitamin and mineral deficiencies.

Mutant Obese Mice and Leptin

In 1950, a genetic mutation occurred spontaneously in the mouse colony being maintained in the Jackson Laboratory at Bar Harbor, Maine. It was thought that this fortuitous development might prove to be the key to understanding and treating extreme forms of human obesity. You see, the mice that were *homozygous* for this mutant gene (ob) were grossly obese, weighing up to three times as much as typical mice (see Figure 12.16). These homozygous obese mice are commonly referred to as **ob/ob mice.**

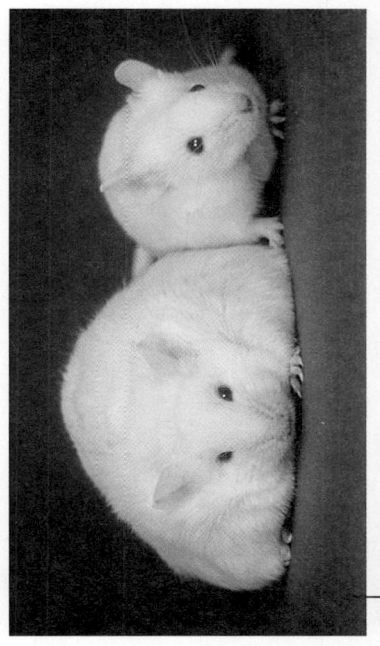

FIGURE 12.16 An ob/ob mouse and a control mouse.

Evolutionary Perspective

calories more efficiently. Coleman (1979) hypothesized that ob/ob mice lack a critical hormone that normally inhibits fat production.

In 1994, Friedman and his colleagues characterized and cloned the gene that is mutated in ob/ob mice (Zhang et al., 1994). They found that this gene is *expressed* only in fat cells, and they characterized the protein hormone that it encodes. They named this protein **leptin**.

Research has shown that leptin satisfies three criteria for a negative feedback fat signal (Ahima & Osei, 2004; Seeley & Schwartz, 1997): (1) Levels of leptin in the blood have been found to be positively correlated with fat deposits in humans and other animals (Schwartz et al., 1996a); (2) injections of leptin at doses too low to be aversive have been shown to reduce eating and body fat in ob/ob mice (Campfield et al., 1995); and (3) receptors for leptin have been found in the brain (Schwartz et al., 1996b).

Do obese humans, like ob/ob mice, have a mutation to the ob gene, and do they have low levels of the satiety signal, leptin? The answer to both these questions is "not usually." Genetic mutations are rare in obese humans, and most have high levels of circulating leptin. Moreover, injections of leptin have not reliably reduced the body fat of obese individuals (Heymsfield et al., 1999). Although few obese humans have a genetic mutation to the ob gene, leptin may prove to be a panacea for those few who do. Consider the following case.

The Case of the Child with No Leptin

The patient was of normal weight at birth, but soon it began to increase at an excessive rate. She demanded food continually and was disruptive when denied food. As a result of her extreme obesity, deformities of her legs developed, and surgery was required.

She was 9 when she was referred for treatment. At this point, she weighed 94.4 kilograms (about 210 pounds), and her weight was still increasing at an alarming rate. She was found to be homozygous for the ob gene and had no detectable leptin. Thus, leptin therapy was commenced.

The leptin therapy immediately curtailed the weight gain. She began to eat less, and she lost weight steadily over the 12-month period of the study, a total of 16.5 kilograms (about 36 pounds), almost all in the form of fat. There were no obvious side effects (Farooqi et al., 1999).

Clinical Implications

Ob/ob mice eat more and convert calories to fat more efficiently than controls, and they use their fat more efficiently. Coleman (1979) hypothesized that leptin is not the only hormone to satisfy the three criteria for a negative feedback fat signal—it wasn't even the first (see Schwartz, 2000; Woods, 2004).

Insulin: Another Negative Feedback Fat Signal

Although the discovery of leptin received substantial publicity, leptin is not the only hormone to satisfy the three criteria for a negative feedback fat signal—it wasn't even the first (see Schwartz, 2000; Woods, 2004). The pancreatic peptide hormone insulin was identified as being such a signal more than 25 years ago by Woods and colleagues (1979).

At first, the suggestion that insulin serves as a negative feedback fat signal was viewed with a great deal of skepticism. After all, how could the level of insulin in the body, which goes up and then comes back down to normal following each meal, provide the brain with information about gradually changing levels of body fat? It turns out that insulin does not readily penetrate the blood–brain barrier, and its levels in the brain were found to stay relatively stable. More importantly, brain levels of insulin were found to be positively correlated with levels of body fat (Seeley et al., 1996); receptors for it were found in the brain (Baura et al., 1993); and infusions of insulin into the brains of laboratory animals, at doses too low to be aversive and too low to affect blood glucose levels, were found to reduce eating and body weight (Campfield et al., 1995; Chavez, Seeley, & Woods, 1995).

Unlike leptin-deficient individuals, insulin-deficient individuals are not obese (see Woods et al., 2000). Despite their extreme hyperphagia, they remain slim because they cannot convert food to fat without insulin. Most of the excess calories they consume remain in the blood and are then excreted.

Serotonergic Drugs and the Treatment of Obesity

Because—as you have already learned—serotonin agonists have been shown to reduce food consumption in both human and nonhuman subjects, they have considerable potential in the treatment of obesity (Halford & Blundell, 2000a). Serotonin agonists seem to act by a mechanism different from that for leptin and insulin, which produce long-term satiety signals based on fat stores. Serotonin agonists seem to increase short-term satiety signals associated with the consumption of a meal (Halford & Blundell, 2000b).

Serotonin agonists have been found in various studies of obese patients to reduce the following: the urge to eat high-calorie foods, the consumption of fat, the subjective intensity of hunger, the size of meals, the number of between-meal snacks, and bingeing. Because of this extremely positive profile of effects and the severity of the obesity problem, serotonin agonists (fenfluramine and dexfenfluramine) were rushed into clinical use. However, they

Clinical Implications

were subsequently withdrawn from the market because chronic use was found to be associated with heart disease in a small, but significant, number of users. Currently, the search is on for serotonergic weight-loss medications that do not have dangerous side effects. There is reason for optimism. The variety of different serotonin receptor subtypes means that it may be possible to develop serotonin agonists that selectively promote weight loss.

12.7 Anorexia Nervosa

Clinical Implications

In contrast to obesity, **anorexia nervosa** is a disorder of underconsumption of food (see Klein & Walsh, 2004).

Anorexics eat so little that they experience health-threatening weight loss; and despite their grotesquely emaciated appearance, they often perceive themselves as fat. About 50% of anorexics periodically engage in binges of eating, which are usually followed by purging with large doses of laxatives or by self-induced vomiting. Individuals who display the cycles of fasting, bingeing, and purging without the extreme weight loss are said to suffer from **bulimia nervosa.**

The incidence of anorexia nervosa among North American student populations is about 2.5%, with the vast majority of sufferers being female. Unfortunately, there are currently no proven effective treatments. Few sufferers display complete recovery, and those who respond to treatment often relapse.

Anorexics are ambivalent about food. On the one hand, they display a higher than normal cephalic-phase insulin response (Broberg & Bernstein, 1989), and they are often preoccupied with the discussion, purchase, and preparation of food. However, eating food is a different matter; they are often disgusted by sweet and fatty tastes, and they often feel ill after a meal.

Anorexia and Dieting

Although some degree of dietary restraint appears to be essential for the maintenance of optimal health by most people in wealthy, fast-food cultures, the practice of restrained eating is associated with risks. Virtually all patients with eating disorders have a history of strict dieting prior to the onset of the disorder. For example, in one study (Patton, 1988), 21% of teenage girls who were dieting at the time of their initial interview had developed an eating disorder 1 year later, compared with only 3% of nondieters.

Evidence suggests that people—primarily adolescent females—under great pressure from a cultural emphasis on slenderness begin dieting, and those who are highly controlled, rigid, and obsessive overcome the attraction of food and develop the disorder (see Wilson, Heffernan, & Black, 1996). However, the new ideas about hunger and eating that you have encountered in this chapter point to another factor in the etiology of anorexia nervosa. Consider the following hypothesis.

Anorexia and Positive Incentives

Thinking Critically

The positive-incentive perspective on eating suggests that the decline in eating that defines anorexia nervosa is likely a consequence of a corresponding decline in the positive-incentive value of food. However, the positive incentive value of food for anorexia patients has received little attention—in part, because anorexic patients often display substantial interest in food. The fact that many anorexic patients are obsessed with food—continually talking about it, thinking about it, and preparing it for others (Crisp, 1983)—seems to suggest that it still holds a high positive-incentive value for them. However, to avoid confusion, it is necessary to keep in mind that the positive-incentive value of interacting with food is not necessarily the same as the positive-incentive value of eating food—and it is the positive-incentive value of eating food that is critical when considering anorexia nervosa.

A few studies have examined the positive-incentive value of various tastes in anorexic patients (see, e.g., Drewnowski et al., 1987; Sunday & Halmi, 1990). In general, these studies have found that the positive-incentive value of various tastes is lower in anorexic patients than in control participants. However, these studies grossly underestimate the importance of reductions in the positive-incentive value of food in the etiology of anorexia nervosa because the anorexic participants and the normal-weight control participants were not matched for weight.

People who have had starvation imposed on them—although difficult to find—are the suitable equal-weight comparison subjects for anorexic participants. Starvation normally triggers a radical increase in the positive-incentive value of food. This has been best documented by the descriptions and behavior of participants voluntarily undergoing experimental semistarvation. When asked how it felt to starve, one participant replied:

I wait for mealtime. When it comes I eat slowly and make the food last as long as possible. The menu never gets monotonous even if it is the same each day or is of poor quality. It is food and all food tastes good. Even dirty crusts of bread in the street look appetizing. (Keys et al., 1950, p. 852)

The Puzzle of Anorexia

The domination of set-point theories over research into the regulation of hunger and eating has resulted in

widespread inattention to one of the major puzzles of anorexia: Why does the adaptive massive increase in the positive-incentive value of eating that occurs in victims of starvation not occur in starving anorexics? The positive-incentive value of eating normally increases to such high levels under conditions of starvation that it is difficult to imagine how anybody who is starving—no matter how controlled, rigid, obsessive, and motivated—could refrain from eating in the presence of palatable food. Why this protective mechanism is not activated in severe anorexics is a pressing question about the etiology of anorexia nervosa. The answer will have to explain how anyone can overcome food's attraction enough to reach the level of starvation characteristic of extreme anorexia.

I believe that part of the answer lies in the research of Woods and his colleagues on the physiological effects of meals. At the beginning of meals, people are normally in reasonably homeostatic balance, and this homeostasis is disrupted by the sudden infusion of calories. The other part of the answer lies in the finding that the aversive effects of meals are much greater in people who have been eating little (Brooks & Melnik, 1995). Meals, which produce adverse, but tolerable, effects in healthy individuals, may be extremely aversive for individuals who have undergone food deprivation. Evidence for the extremely noxious effects that eating meals has on starving humans is found in the reactions of World War II concentration camp victims to refeeding—many were rendered ill and some were even killed by the very food given to them by their liberators (Keys et al., 1950; see also Soloman & Kirby, 1990).

So why do severe anorexics not experience a massive increase in the positive-incentive value of eating, similar to the increase experienced by other starving individuals? The answer may be *meals*—meals forced on these patients as a result of the misconception of our society that meals are the healthy way to eat. Each meal consumed by an anorexic may produce a variety of conditioned taste aversions that reduce the motivation to eat. This hypothesis needs to be addressed because of its implication for treatment: Anorexic patients—or anybody else who is severely undernourished—should not be encouraged, or even permitted, to eat meals. They should be fed—or infused with—small amounts of food intermittently throughout the day.

I have described the preceding hypothesis to show you the value of the new ideas that you have encountered in this chapter: The major test of a new theory is whether it leads to innovative hypotheses. A few months ago, as I was perusing an article on global famine and malnutrition, I noticed an intriguing comment: One of the clinical complications that results from feeding meals to famine victims is anorexia (Blackburn, 2001).

Thinking Critically

What do you make of this?

The Case of the Anorexic Student

Clinical Implications

In a society in which obesity is the main disorder of consumption, anorexics are out of step. People who are struggling to eat less have difficulty understanding those who have to struggle to eat. Still, when you stare anorexia in the face, it is difficult not to be touched by it.

She began by telling me how much she had been enjoying the course and how sorry she was to be dropping out of the university. She was articulate and personable, and her grades were high. Her problem was anorexia; she weighed only 82 pounds, and she was about to be hospitalized.

"But don't you want to eat?" I asked naively. "Don't you see that your plan to go to medical school will go up in smoke if you don't eat?"

"Of course I want to eat. I know I am terribly thin—my friends tell me I am. Believe me, I know this is wrecking my life. I try to eat, but I just can't force myself. In a strange way, I am pleased with my thinness."

She was upset, and I was embarrassed by my insensitivity. "It's too bad you're dropping out of the course before we cover the chapter on eating," I said, groping for safer ground.

"Oh, I've read it already," she responded. "It's the first chapter I looked at. It had quite an effect on me; a lot of things started to make more sense. The bit about positive incentives and learning was really good. I think my problem began when eating started to lose its positive-incentive value for me—in my mind, I kind of associated eating with being fat and all the boyfriend problems I was having. This made it easy to diet, but every once in a while I would get hungry and binge, or my parents would force me to eat a big meal. I would eat so much that I would feel ill. So I would put my finger down my throat and make myself throw up. This kept me from gaining weight, but I think it also taught my body to associate my favorite foods with illness—kind of a conditioned taste aversion. What do you think of my theory?"

Her insightfulness impressed me; it made me feel all the more sorry that she was going to discontinue her studies. How could such a bright, personable, young woman knowingly risk her health and everything that she had worked for?

After a lengthy chat, she got up to leave, and I walked her to the door of my office. I wished her luck and made her promise to come back for a visit. I never saw her again. The image of her emaciated body walking down the hallway from my office has stayed with me.

Themes Revisited

Three of the book's four themes played prominent roles in this chapter. The thinking-about-biopsychology theme was common as you were challenged to critically evaluate your own beliefs and ambiguous research findings, to consider the scientific implications of your own experiences, and to think creatively about the personal and clinical implications of the new ideas you encountered. The chapter ended by using these new ideas to develop a potentially important hypothesis about the etiology of anorexia nervosa. Because of its emphasis on thinking, this chapter is my personal favorite.

 **Thinking Critically**

 **Evolutionary Perspective**

Both aspects of the evolutionary theme were emphasized repeatedly.

First, you saw how thinking about hunger and eating from an evolutionary perspective leads to important insights. Second, you saw how controlled research on nonhuman species has contributed to our current understanding of human hunger and eating.

Finally, the clinical implications theme was featured in the case of the man who forgot not to eat, near the beginning of the chapter, and in two more cases in the section on the eating disorders obesity and anorexia nervosa: those of the child with no leptin and the anorexic student.

ON THE CD
See Hard Copy for additional readings for Chapter 12.

Clinical Implications

Think about It

1. Set-point theories suggest that attempts at permanent weight loss are a waste of time. On the basis of what you have learned in this chapter, design an effective weight-loss program.

2. Most of the eating-related health problems that people in our society face occur because the conditions in which we live are different from those in which our species evolved. Discuss.

3. On the basis of what you have learned in this chapter, develop a feeding program for laboratory rats

that would lead to obesity. Compare this program with the eating habits prevalent in those cultures in which obesity is a serious problem.

4. What causes anorexia nervosa? Summarize the evidence that supports your view.

ON THE CD
Studying for an exam? Try the Practice Tests for Chapter 12.

Key Terms

Absorptive phase (p. 291)
Adipsia (p. 300)
Amino acids (p. 290)
Anorexia nervosa (p. 311)
Aphagia (p. 300)
Appetizer effect (p. 297)
Basal metabolic rate (p. 305)
Bulimia nervosa (p. 311)
Cafeteria diet (p. 297)
Cephalic phase (p. 291)
Cholecystokinin (CCK) (p. 302)
Diet-induced thermogenesis (p. 305)
Digestion (p. 289)
Duodenum (p. 301)
Dynamic phase (p. 299)

Fasting phase (p. 291)
Free fatty acid (p. 291)
Glucagon (p. 291)
Gluconeogenesis (p. 291)
Glucose (p. 290)
Glucostatic theory (p. 293)
Homeostasis (p. 293)
Hyperphagia (p. 299)
Insulin (p. 291)
Ketones (p. 291)
Lateral hypothalamus (LH) (p. 299)
Leaky-barrel model (p. 305)
Leptin (p. 310)
Lipids (p. 290)
Lipogenesis (p. 300)

Lipolysis (p. 300)
Lipostatic theory (p. 293)
NEAT (p. 308)
Negative feedback systems (p. 293)
Nutritive density (p. 296)
Ob/ob mice (p. 309)
Paraventricular nuclei (p. 301)
Positive-incentive theory (p. 294)
Positive-incentive value (p. 294)
Satiety (p. 296)
Sensory-specific satiety (p. 298)
Set point (p. 289)
Set-point assumption (p. 292)

Settling point (p. 305)
Sham eating (p. 296)
Static phase (p. 300)
Ventromedial hypothalamus (VMH) (p. 299)

ON THE CD
Need some help studying the key terms for this chapter? Check out the electronic flash cards for Chapter 12.

Hormones and Sex

What's Wrong with the Mamawawa?

chapter

13

13.1 The Neuroendocrine System

13.2 Hormones and Sexual Development

13.3 Three Cases of Exceptional Human Sexual Development

13.4 Effects of Gonadal Hormones on Adults

13.5 Neural Mechanisms of Sexual Behavior

13.6 Sexual Orientation, Hormones, and the Brain

This chapter is about hormones and sex, a topic that fascinates most people. Perhaps it is because we hold our sexuality in such high esteem that we are intrigued by the fact that it is influenced by the secretions of a pair of glands that some regard as unfit topics of conversation. Perhaps it is because we each think of our gender as fundamental and immutable that we are fascinated by the fact that it can be altered with a snip or two and a few hormone injections. Perhaps what fascinates us is the idea that our sex lives might be enhanced by the application of a few hormones. For whatever reason, the topic of hormones and sex is always a hit. Some remarkable things await you in this chapter; let's go directly to them.

The Developmental and Activational Effects of Sex Hormones

Hormones influence sex in two ways: (1) by influencing the development from conception to sexual maturity of the anatomical, physiological, and behavioral characteristics that distinguish one as female or male; and (2) by activating the reproduction-related behavior of sexually mature adults. Both the *developmental* and *activational* effects of sex hormones are discussed in this chapter.

The Men-Are-Men-and-Women-Are-Women Assumption

Almost everybody brings to the topic of hormones and sex a piece of excess baggage: the men-are-men-and-women-are-women assumption—or the "mamawawa." This assumption is seductive; it seems so right that we are continually drawn to it without considering alternative views. Unfortunately, it is fundamentally flawed.

The men-are-men-and-women-are-women assumption is the tendency to think about femaleness and maleness as discrete, mutually exclusive, complementary categories. In thinking about hormones and sex, this general attitude leads one to assume that females have female sex hormones that give them female bodies and make them do female things, and that males have male sex hormones that give them male bodies and make them do opposite male things. Despite the fact that this approach to hormones and sex is totally wrong, its simplicity, symmetry, and comfortable social implications draw us to it. That's why this chapter grapples with it throughout.

13.1 The Neuroendocrine System

This section introduces the general principles of neuroendocrine function. It introduces these principles by focusing on the glands and hormones that are directly involved in sexual development and behavior.

The endocrine glands are illustrated in Figure 13.1 on page 316. By convention, only the organs whose primary function appears to be the release of hormones are referred to as endocrine glands. However, other organs (e.g., the stomach, liver, and intestine) also release hormones into general circulation (see Chapter 12), and they are thus, strictly speaking, also part of the endocrine system.

Glands

There are two types of glands: exocrine glands and endocrine glands. **Exocrine glands** (e.g., sweat glands) release their chemicals into ducts, which carry them to their targets, mostly on the surface of the body. **Endocrine glands** (ductless glands) release their chemicals, which are called **hormones,** directly into the circulatory system. Once released by an endocrine gland, a hormone travels via the circulatory system until it reaches the target on which it normally exerts its effect (e.g., other endocrine glands or sites in the nervous system).

Hormones

Most hormones fall into one of three categories: (1) amino acid derivatives, (2) peptides and proteins, and (3) steroids. **Amino acid derivative hormones** are hormones that are synthesized in a few simple steps from an amino acid molecule; an example is *epinephrine*, which is released from the *adrenal medulla* and synthesized from *tyrosine*. **Peptide hormones** and **protein hormones** are chains of amino acids—peptide hormones are short chains, and protein hormones are long chains. **Steroid hormones** are hormones that are synthesized from *cholesterol*, a type of fat molecule.

Steroid hormones play the major role in sexual development and behavior. Most other hormones produce their effects by binding to receptors in cell membranes. Steroid molecules can influence cells in this fashion; however, because they are small and fat-soluble, they can readily penetrate cell membranes and often affect cells in a second way. Once inside a cell, the steroid molecules can bind to receptors in the cytoplasm or nucleus and, by so doing, directly influence gene expression—amino acid derivative and peptide hormones can also affect gene expression, but they do so less commonly and by less direct mechanisms because they cannot penetrate cell membranes. Consequently, of all the hormones,

Thinking Critically

steroid hormones tend to have the most diverse and long-lasting effects on cellular function (Brown, 1994).

Gonads

Central to any discussion of hormones and sex are the **gonads**—the male **testes** (pronounced TEST-eez) and the female **ovaries** (see Figure 13.1). The primary function of the testes and ovaries is the production of *sperm cells* and *ova*, respectively. After **copulation** (sexual intercourse), a single sperm cell may combine with an *ovum* to form a cell called a **zygote**, which contains all of the information necessary for the normal growth of a complete adult organism in its natural environment. The amalgamation of sperm and egg is called *fertilization* (see Primakoff & Myles, 2002).

With the exception of ova and sperm cells, each cell of the human body has 23 pairs of chromosomes. In contrast, the ova and sperm cells contain only half that number, one member of each of the 23 pairs. Thus, when a sperm cell fertilizes an ovum, the resulting zygote ends up with the full complement of 23 pairs of chromosomes, one of each pair from the father and one of each pair from the mother.

Of particular interest in the context of this chapter is the pair of chromosomes called the **sex chromosomes,** so named because they contain the genetic programs that direct sexual development. The cells of females have two large sex chromosomes, called *X chromosomes.* In males, one sex chromosome is an X chromosome, and the other is a small X-shaped chromosome called a *Y chromosome.* Consequently, the sex chromosome of every ovum is

an X chromosome, whereas half the sperm cells have X chromosomes and half have Y chromosomes. Your gender with all its social, economic, and personal ramifications was determined by which of your mother's ovum cells won the dash to your father's sperm cells: with an X sex chromosome won, you are a female; if one with a Y sex chromosome won, you are a male.

Many texts claim that X chromosomes are X-shaped and Y chromosomes are Y-shaped, but this is incorrect. Once a chromosome has duplicated, the two products remain joined at one point, producing an X shape. This is true of all chromosomes, including Y chromosomes. Because Y chromosomes are much smaller than X chromosomes, early investigators failed to discern one small arm.

Writing this section reminded me of my grade 7 basketball team, the "Nads." The name puzzled our teacher because it was not at all like the names usually favored by pubescent boys—names such as the "Avengers," the "Marauders," and the "Vikings." Her puzzlement ended abruptly at our first game as our fans began to chant their support. You guessed it: "Go Nads, Go! Go Nads, Go!" My 14-year-old spotted-faced teammates and I considered this to be humor of the most mature and sophisticated sort. The teacher didn't.

Sex Steroids

The gonads do more than create sperm and egg cells; they also produce and release steroid hormones. Most people are surprised to learn that the testes and ovaries release the very same hormones. The two main classes

FIGURE 13.1   The endocrine glands.

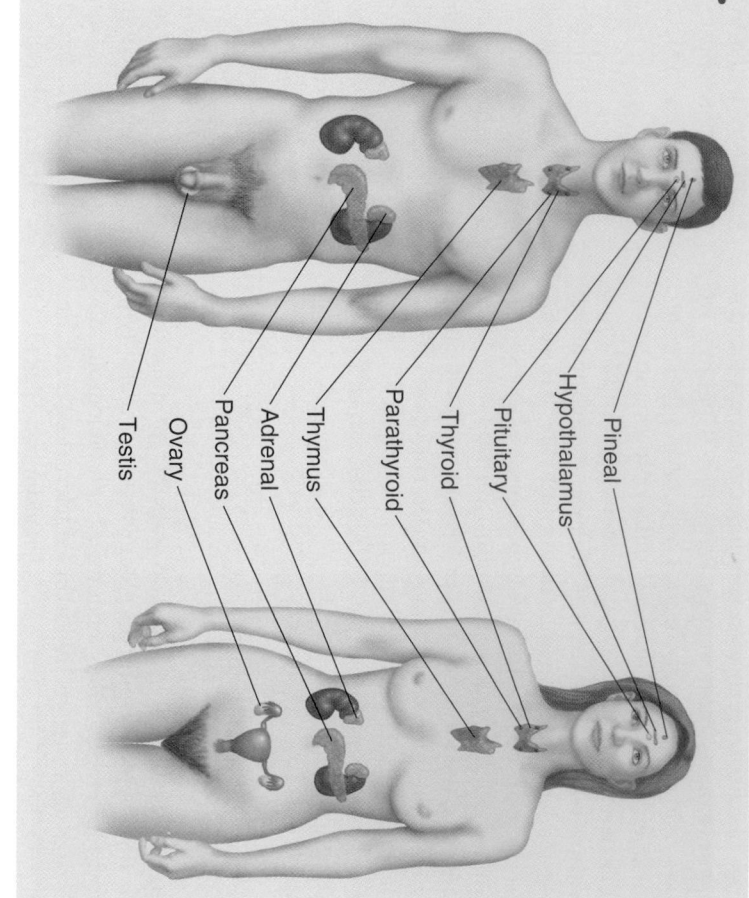

Pineal
Hypothalamus
Pituitary
Thyroid
Parathyroid
Thymus
Adrenal
Pancreas
Ovary
Testis

of gonadal hormones are **androgens** and **estrogens; testosterone** is the most common androgen, and **estradiol** is the most common estrogen. The fact that adult ovaries tend to release more estrogens than they do androgens and that adult testes release more androgens than they do estrogens has led to the common, but misleading, practice of referring to androgens as "the *male* sex hormones" and to estrogens as "the *female* sex hormones." This practice should be avoided because of its men-are-men-and-women-are-women implication that androgens produce maleness and estrogens produce femaleness. They don't.

The ovaries and testes also release a third class of steroid hormones called **progestins.** The most common progestin is **progesterone,** which in females prepares the uterus and the breasts for pregnancy. Its function in males is unclear.

Because the primary function of the **adrenal cortex**—the outer layer of the *adrenal glands* (see Figure 13.1)—is the regulation of glucose and salt levels in the blood, it is not generally thought of as a sex gland. However, in addition to its principal steroid hormones, it does release small amounts of all of the sex steroids that are released by the gonads.

Hormones of the Pituitary

The pituitary gland is frequently referred to as the *master gland* because most of its hormones are tropic hormones. *Tropic hormones* are hormones whose primary function is to influence the release of hormones from other glands (*tropic* is an adjective that describes things

that stimulate or change other things). For example, **gonadotropin** is a pituitary tropic hormone that travels through the circulatory system to the gonads, where it stimulates the release of gonadal hormones.

The pituitary gland is really two glands, the posterior pituitary and the anterior pituitary, which fuse during the course of embryological development. The **posterior pituitary** develops from a small outgrowth of hypothalamic tissue that eventually comes to dangle from the *hypothalamus* on the end of the **pituitary stalk** (see Figure 13.2). In contrast, the **anterior pituitary** begins as part of the same embryonic tissue that eventually develops into the roof of the mouth; during the course of development, it pinches off and migrates upward to assume its position next to the posterior pituitary. It is the anterior pituitary that releases tropic hormones; thus, it is the anterior pituitary in particular, rather than the pituitary in general, that qualifies as the master gland.

Female Gonadal Hormone Levels Are Cyclic; Male Gonadal Hormone Levels Are Steady

The major difference between the endocrine function of women and men is that in women the levels of gonadal and gonadotropic hormones go through a cycle that repeats itself every 28 days or so (see Appendix VIII). It is these more-or-less regular hormone fluctuations that control the female **menstrual cycle.** In contrast, human males are, from a neuroendocrine perspective, rather dull creatures; the levels of their gonadal and gonadotropic hormones change little from day to day.

Because the anterior pituitary is the master gland, many early scientists assumed that an inherent difference between the male and female anterior pituitary was the basis for the difference in their patterns of gonadotropic and gonadal hormone release. However, this hypothesis was discounted by a series of clever transplant studies conducted by Geoffrey Harris in the 1950s (see Raisman, 1997). In these studies, a cycling pituitary removed from a mature female rat became a steady-state pituitary when transplanted at the appropriate site in a male, and a

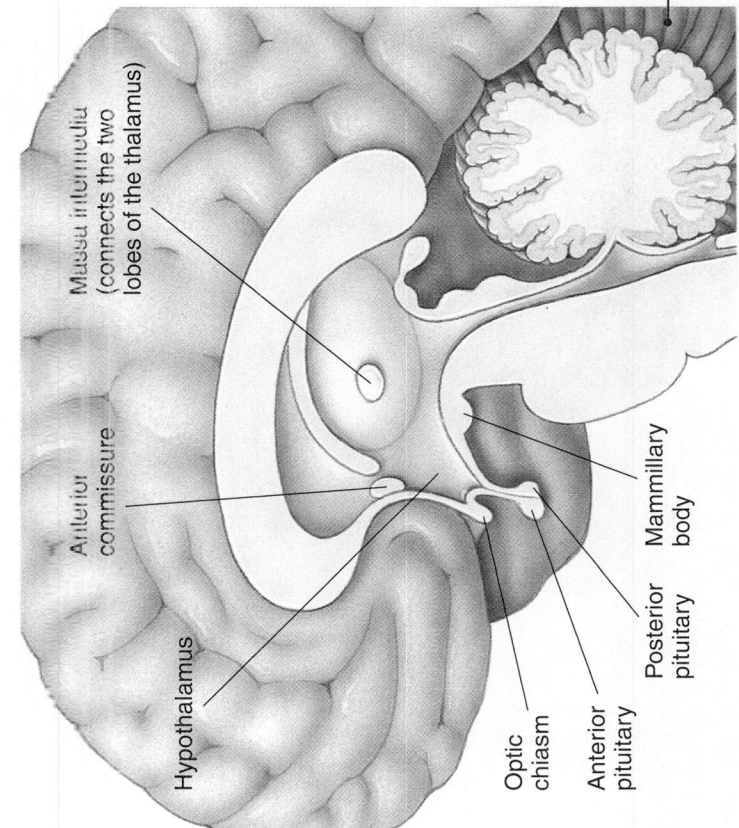

Evolutionary Perspective

FIGURE 13.2   A midline view of the posterior and anterior pituitary and surrounding structures.

Massa intermedia (connects the two lobes of the thalamus)

Anterior commissure

Hypothalamus

Optic chiasm

Anterior pituitary

Posterior pituitary

Mammillary body

steady-state pituitary removed from a mature male rat began to cycle once transplanted in a female. What these studies established was that anterior pituitaries are not inherently female (cyclical) or male (steady-state); their patterns of hormone release are controlled by some other part of the body. The master gland seemed to have its own master. Where was it?

Neural Control of the Pituitary

The nervous system was implicated in the control of the anterior pituitary by behavioral research on birds and other animals that breed only during a specific time of the year. It was found that the seasonal variations in the light–dark cycle triggered many of the breeding-related changes in hormone release. If the lighting conditions under which the animals lived were reversed, for example, by having the animals transported across the equator, the breeding seasons were also reversed. Somehow, visual input to the nervous system was controlling the release of tropic hormones from the anterior pituitary.

The search for the particular neural structure that controlled the anterior pituitary turned, naturally enough, to the *hypothalamus*, the structure from which the pituitary is suspended. Hypothalamic stimulation and lesion experiments quickly established that the hypothalamus is the regulator of the anterior pituitary, but how the hypothalamus carries out this role remained a mystery. You see, the anterior pituitary, unlike the posterior pituitary, receives no neural input whatsoever from

Evolutionary Perspective

the hypothalamus, or from any other neural structure (see Figure 13.3).

Control of the Anterior and Posterior Pituitary by the Hypothalamus

There are two different mechanisms by which the hypothalamus controls the pituitary: one for the posterior pituitary and one for the anterior pituitary. The two major hormones of the posterior pituitary, **vasopressin** and **oxytocin**, are peptide hormones that are synthesized in the cell bodies of neurons in the **paraventricular nuclei** and **supraoptic nuclei** of the hypothalamus (see Figure 13.3). They are then transported along the axons of these neurons to their terminals in the posterior pituitary and are stored there until the arrival of action potentials causes them to be released into the bloodstream. (Neurons that release hormones into general circulation are called *neurosecretory cells*.) Oxytocin stimulates contractions of the uterus during labor and the ejection of milk during suckling. Vasopressin (also called *antidiuretic hormone*) facilitates the reabsorption of water by the kidneys.

The means by which the hypothalamus controls the release of hormones from the neuron-free anterior pituitary was more difficult to explain. Harris (1955) suggested that the release of hormones from the anterior pituitary was itself regulated by hormones released from the hypothalamus. Two findings provided early support for this hypothesis. The first was the discovery of a vascular network, the **hypothalamopituitary portal**

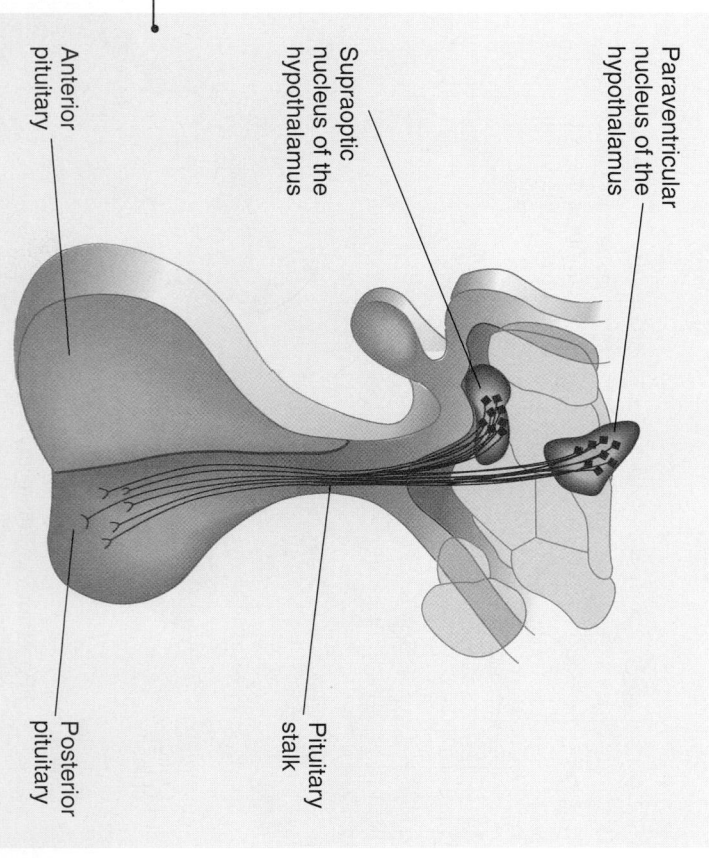

FIGURE 13.3 The neural connections between the hypothalamus and the pituitary. All neural input to the pituitary goes to the posterior pituitary; the anterior pituitary has no neural connections.

Anterior pituitary

Supraoptic nucleus of the hypothalamus

Paraventricular nucleus of the hypothalamus

Pituitary stalk

Posterior pituitary

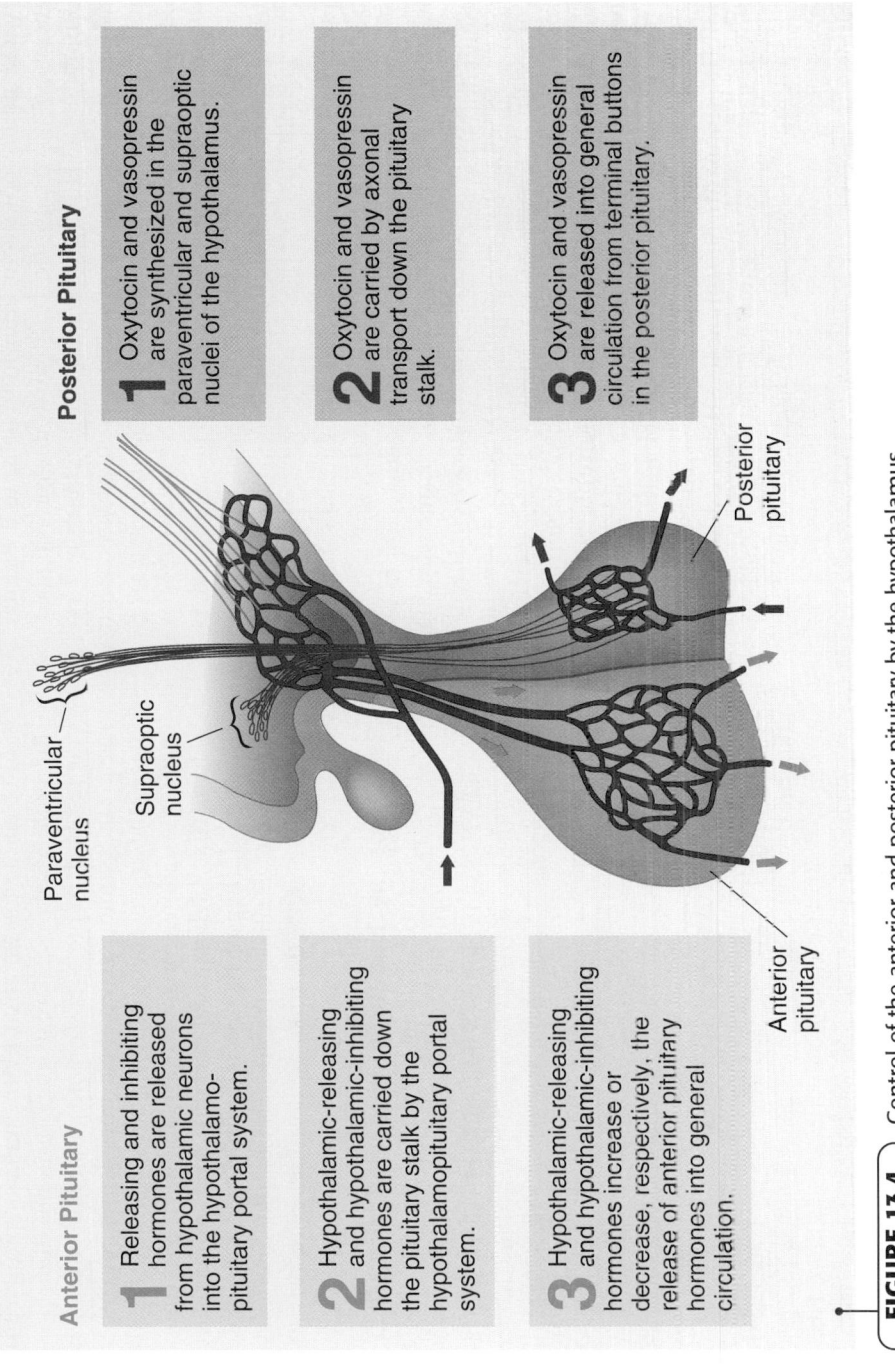

Anterior Pituitary

1 Releasing and inhibiting hormones are released from hypothalamic neurons into the hypothalamo-pituitary portal system.

2 Hypothalamic-releasing and hypothalamic-inhibiting hormones are carried down the pituitary stalk by the hypothalamopituitary portal system.

3 Hypothalamic-releasing and hypothalamic-inhibiting hormones increase or decrease, respectively, the release of anterior pituitary hormones into general circulation.

Paraventricular nucleus

Supraoptic nucleus

Posterior pituitary

Anterior pituitary

Posterior Pituitary

1 Oxytocin and vasopressin are synthesized in the paraventricular and supraoptic nuclei of the hypothalamus.

2 Oxytocin and vasopressin are carried by axonal transport down the pituitary stalk.

3 Oxytocin and vasopressin are released into general circulation from terminal buttons in the posterior pituitary.

FIGURE 13.4   Control of the anterior and posterior pituitary by the hypothalamus.

system, that seemed well suited to the task of carrying hormones from the hypothalamus to the anterior pituitary. As Figure 13.4 illustrates, a network of hypothalamic capillaries feeds a bundle of portal veins that carries blood down the pituitary stalk into another network of capillaries in the anterior pituitary. (A *portal vein* is a vein that connects one capillary network with another.) The second finding was the discovery that cutting the portal veins of the pituitary stalk disrupts the release of anterior pituitary hormones until the damaged veins regenerate (Harris, 1955).

Discovery of Hypothalamic Releasing Hormones

It was hypothesized that the release of each anterior pituitary hormone is controlled by a different hypothalamic hormone. The hypothalamic hormones that were thought to stimulate the release of an anterior pituitary hormone were referred to as **releasing factors;** those thought to inhibit the release of an anterior pituitary hormone were referred to as **inhibitory factors.**

Efforts to isolate the putative (hypothesized) hypothalamic-releasing and inhibitory factors led to a major break-through in the late 1960s. Guillemin and his colleagues isolated **thyrotropin-releasing hormone** from the hypothalamus of sheep, and Schally and his colleagues isolated the same hormone from the hypothalamus of pigs. Thyrotropin-releasing hormone triggers the release of **thyrotropin** from the anterior pituitary, which in turn stimulates the release of hormones from the *thyroid gland.*

It is difficult to appreciate the effort that went into the initial isolation of thyrotropin-releasing hormone. Releasing and inhibiting factors exist in such small amounts that a mountain of hypothalamic tissue was required to extract even minute quantities. Schally reported that the work of his group required over 1 million pig hypothalami. And where did Schally get such a quantity of pig hypothalami? From Oscar Mayer & Company—where else?

Why would two research teams dedicate over a decade of their lives to accumulate a pitifully small quantity of thyrotropin-releasing hormone? The reason was

Evolutionary Perspective

that it enabled both Guillemin and Schally to determine the chemical composition of thyrotropin-releasing hormone and then to develop methods of synthesizing larger quantities of the hormone for research and clinical use. For their efforts, Guillemin and Schally were awarded Nobel Prizes in 1977.

You may have noticed a change in terminology during the preceding discussion: from *releasing factors* to **releasing hormones.** This shift reflects the usual practice of referring to a hormone as a "factor" or "substance" until it has been isolated and its chemical structure has been identified.

Schally's and Guillemin's isolation of thyrotropin-releasing hormone confirmed that hypothalamic releasing hormones control the release of hormones from the anterior pituitary and thus provided the major impetus for the isolation and synthesis of several other releasing hormones. Of direct relevance to the study of sex hormones was the subsequent isolation of **gonadotropin-releasing hormone** by Schally and his group (Schally, Kastin, & Arimura, 1971). This releasing hormone stimulates the release of both of the anterior pituitary's gonadotropins: **follicle-stimulating hormone (FSH)** and **luteinizing hormone (LH).** All hypothalamic releasing hormones, like all tropic hormones, have proven to be peptides.

Regulation of Hormone Levels

Hormone release is regulated by three different kinds of signals: signals from the nervous system, signals from other hormones, and signals from nonhormonal chemicals in the blood (Brown, 1994).

Neural Regulation All endocrine glands, with the exception of the anterior pituitary, are directly regulated by signals from the nervous system. Endocrine glands located in the brain (i.e., pituitary and pineal) are regulated by cerebral neurons; those located outside the CNS are innervated by the *autonomic nervous system*—usually by both the *sympathetic* and *parasympathetic* branches, which often have opposite effects on hormone release.

The effects of experience on hormone release are usually mediated by signals from the nervous system. It is extremely important to remember that hormone release is regulated by experience. This **Thinking Critically** means that hormonal explanations do not in any way rule out experiential explanations; in fact, they may be different parts of the same mechanism.

Hormonal Regulation Signals from the hormones themselves also influence hormone release. You have already learned, for example, that the tropic hormones of the anterior pituitary influence the release of hormones from their respective target glands. However, the regula-

tion of endocrine function by the anterior pituitary is not a one-way street. Circulating hormones often provide feedback to the very structures that influence their release: the pituitary gland, the hypothalamus, and other sites in the brain. The function of most hormonal feedback is the maintenance of stable blood levels of the hormones. Thus, high gonadal hormone levels usually have effects on the hypothalamus and pituitary that decrease subsequent gonadal hormone release, and low levels usually have effects that increase hormone release.

Regulation by Nonhormonal Chemicals Circulating chemicals other than hormones can play a role in regulating hormone levels. Glucose, calcium, and sodium levels in the blood all influence the release of particular hormones. For example, you learned in Chapter 12 that increases in blood glucose increase the release of *insulin* from the *pancreas,* and insulin, in turn, reduces blood glucose levels.

Pulsatile Hormone Release

Hormones tend to be released in pulses (Karsch, 1987); they are discharged several times per day in large surges, which typically last no more than a few minutes. Hormone levels in the blood are regulated by changes in the frequency and duration of the hormone pulses (Reame et al., 1984). One consequence of **pulsatile hormone release** is that there are often large minute-to-minute fluctuations in the levels of circulating hormones (e.g., Koolhaas, Schuurman, & Wiepkema, 1980). Accordingly, when the pattern of human male gonadal hormone release is referred to as "steady," it means that there are no major systematic changes in circulating gonadal hormone levels from day to day, not that the levels never vary.

A Summary Model of Gonadal Endocrine Regulation

Figure 13.5 is a summary model of the regulation of gonadal hormones. According to this model, the brain controls the release of gonadotropin-releasing hormone from the hypothalamus into the hypothalamopituitary portal system, which carries it to the anterior pituitary. In the anterior pituitary, the gonadotropin-releasing hormone stimulates the release of gonadotropin, which is carried by the circulatory system to the gonads. In response to the gonadotropin, the gonads release androgens, estrogens, and progestins, which feed back into the pituitary and hypothalamus to regulate subsequent gonadal hormone release.

Armed with this general perspective of neuroendocrine function, you are ready to consider how gonadal hormones direct sexual development and activate adult sexual behavior.

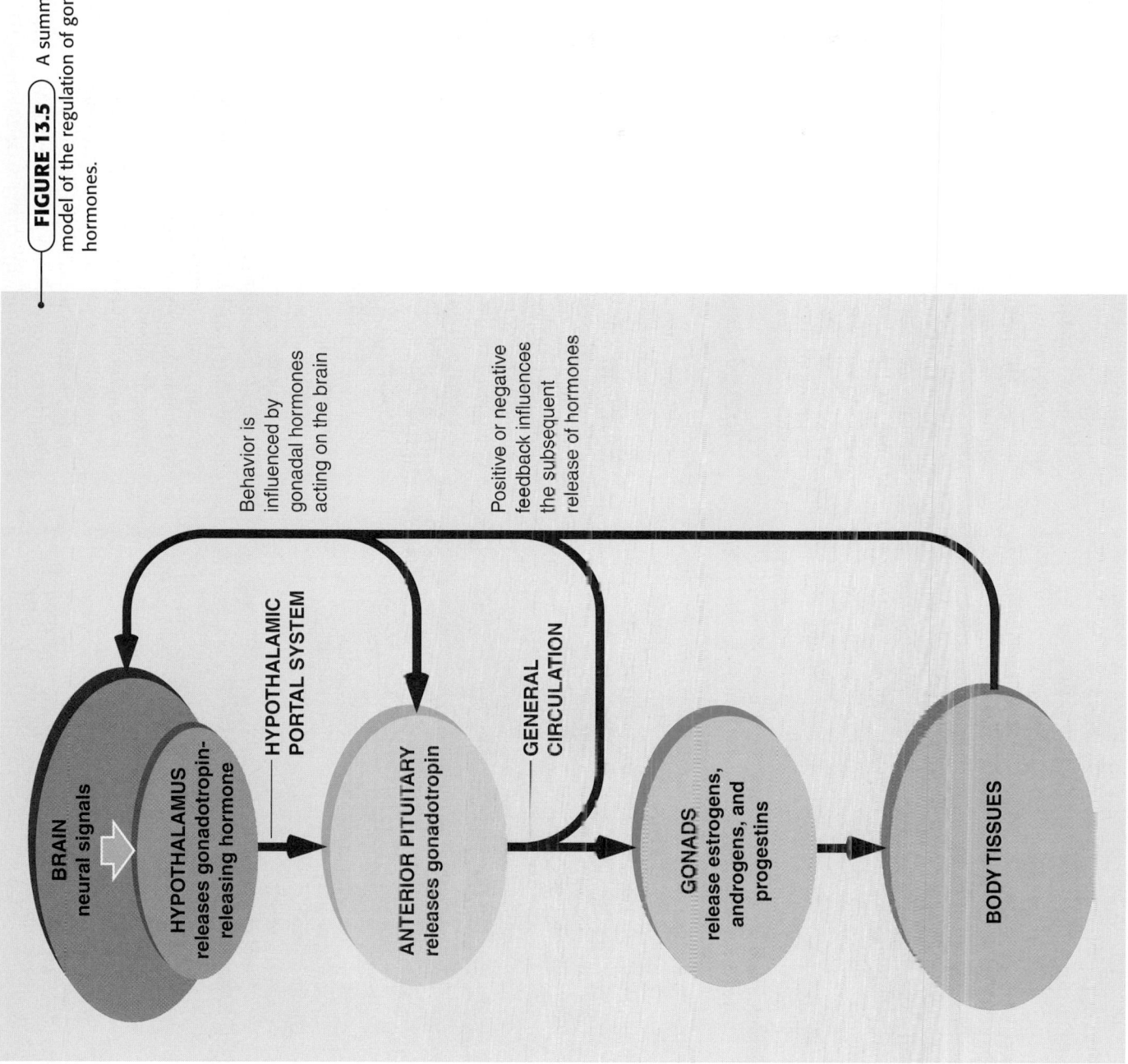

FIGURE 13.5 A summary model of the regulation of gonadal hormones.

13.2 Hormones and Sexual Development

You have undoubtedly noticed that humans are *dimorphic*—that is, they come in two standard models: female and male. This section describes how the development of female and male characteristics is directed by hormones.

The next section discusses three cases of exceptional sexual development. I am sure you will be intrigued by these three cases, but that is not the only reason why I have chosen to include them. My main reason is expressed by

a proverb: The exception proves the rule. Most people think this proverb means that the exception "proves" the rule in the sense that it establishes its truth, but this is nonsense: The truth of a rule is challenged by, not confirmed by, exceptions to it. The word *proof* comes from the Latin *probare*, which means "to test"—as in *proving ground* or printer's *proof*—and this is the sense in which it is used in the proverb. Hence, the proverb means that the explanation of exceptional cases is a major challenge for any theory. Accordingly, the primary purpose of discussing the three cases of exceptional sexual development is to test the theories presented in this section.

Sexual differentiation in mammals begins at fertilization with the production of one of two different kinds of zygotes: either one with an XX (female) pair of sex chromosomes or one with an XY (male) pair. (The opening photograph for Chapter 9 shows fertilization in progress.) It is the genetic information on the sex chromosomes that normally determines whether development will occur along female or male lines. But be cautious here: Do not fall into the seductive embrace of the men-are-men-and-women-are-women assumption. Do not begin by assuming that there are two parallel but opposite genetic programs for sexual development, one for female development and one for male development. As you are about to learn, sexual development unfolds according to an entirely different principle, one that many males—particularly those who still stubbornly adhere to notions of male preeminence—find unsettling. This principle is that we are all genetically programmed to develop female bodies; genetic males develop male bodies only because their fundamentally female program of development is overruled.

Thinking Critically

Fetal Hormones and the Development of Reproductive Organs

Gonads   Figure 13.6 illustrates the structure of the gonads as they appear 6 weeks after fertilization. Notice that at this stage of development, each fetus, regardless of its genetic sex, has the same pair of gonadal structures, called *primordial gonads* (*primordial* means "existing at the beginning"). Each primordial gonad has an outer covering, or *cortex*, which has the potential to develop into an ovary; and each has an internal core, or *medulla*, which has the potential to develop into a testis.

Six weeks after conception, the Y chromosome of the male triggers the synthesis of **H-Y antigen** (see Haqq et al., 1994; Wang et al., 1995), and this protein causes the medulla of each primordial gonad to grow and to develop into a testis. There is no female counterpart of H-Y antigen; in the absence of H-Y antigen, the cortical cells of the primordial gonads automatically develop into ovaries. Accordingly, if H-Y antigen is injected into a genetic female fetus 6 weeks after conception, the result is a genetic female with testes; or if drugs that block the effects of H-Y antigen are injected into a male fetus, the result is a genetic male with ovaries. Such "mixed-gender" individuals expose in a dramatic fashion the weakness of the "mamawawa."

Internal Reproductive Ducts   Six weeks after fertilization, both males and females have two complete sets of reproductive ducts. They have a male **Wolffian system,** which has the capacity to develop into the male

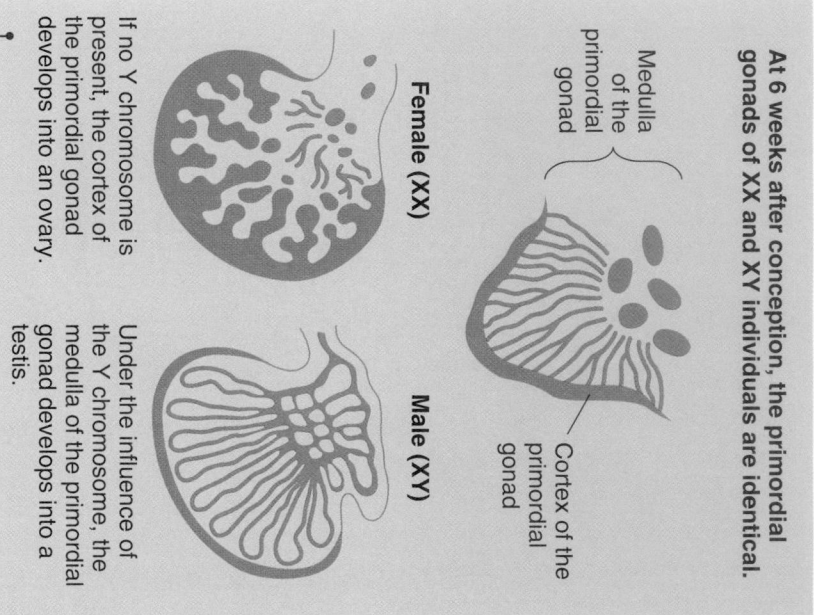

At 6 weeks after conception, the primordial gonads of XX and XY individuals are identical.

Medulla of the primordial gonad

Cortex of the primordial gonad

Female (XX)   Male (XY)

If no Y chromosome is present, the cortex of the primordial gonad develops into an ovary.

Under the influence of the Y chromosome, the medulla of the primordial gonad develops into a testis.

FIGURE 13.6   The development of an ovary and a testis from the cortex and the medulla, respectively, of the primordial gonadal structure that is present 6 weeks after conception.

reproductive ducts (e.g., the *seminal vesicles,* which hold the fluid in which sperm cells are ejaculated; and the *vas deferens,* through which sperm cells travel to the seminal vesicles). And they have a female **Müllerian system,** which has the capacity to develop into the female ducts (e.g., the *uterus;* the upper part of the *vagina;* and the *fallopian tubes,* through which ova travel from the ovaries to the uterus, where they can be fertilized).

In the third month of male fetal development, the testes secrete testosterone and **Müllerian-inhibiting substance.** As Figure 13.7 illustrates, the testosterone stimulates the development of the Wolffian system, and the Müllerian-inhibiting substance causes the Müllerian system to degenerate and the testes to descend into the **scrotum**—the sac that holds the testes outside the body cavity. Because it is testosterone—not the sex chromosomes—that triggers Wolffian development, genetic females who are injected with testosterone during the appropriate fetal period develop male reproductive ducts along with their female ones.

The differentiation of the internal ducts of the female reproductive system (see Figure 13.7) is not under the control of ovarian hormones; the ovaries are almost completely inactive during fetal development. The development of the Müllerian system occurs in any fetus

both male and female **genitals**—external reproductive organs—develop from the same precursor. This *bipotential precursor* and its subsequent differentiation are illustrated in Figure 13.8 on page 324.

In the second month of pregnancy, the bipotential precursor of the external reproductive organs consists of four parts: the glans, the lateral bodies, the urethral folds, and the labioscrotal swellings. Then it begins to differentiate. The *glans* grows into the head of the *penis* in the male or the *clitoris* in the female, the *urethral folds* fuse in the male or enlarge to become the *labia minora* in the female, the *lateral bodies* form the shaft of the penis in the male or the hood of the clitoris in the female, and the *labioscrotal swellings* form the *scrotum* in the male or the *labia majora* in the female.

Like the development of the internal reproductive ducts, the development of the external genitals is controlled by the presence or absence of testosterone. If testosterone is present at the appropriate stage of fetal development, male external genitals develop from the bipotential precursor; if testosterone is not present, the development of the external genitals proceeds along female lines.

ON THE CD

The *Differentiation of the External Genitals* module will help you visualize this process.

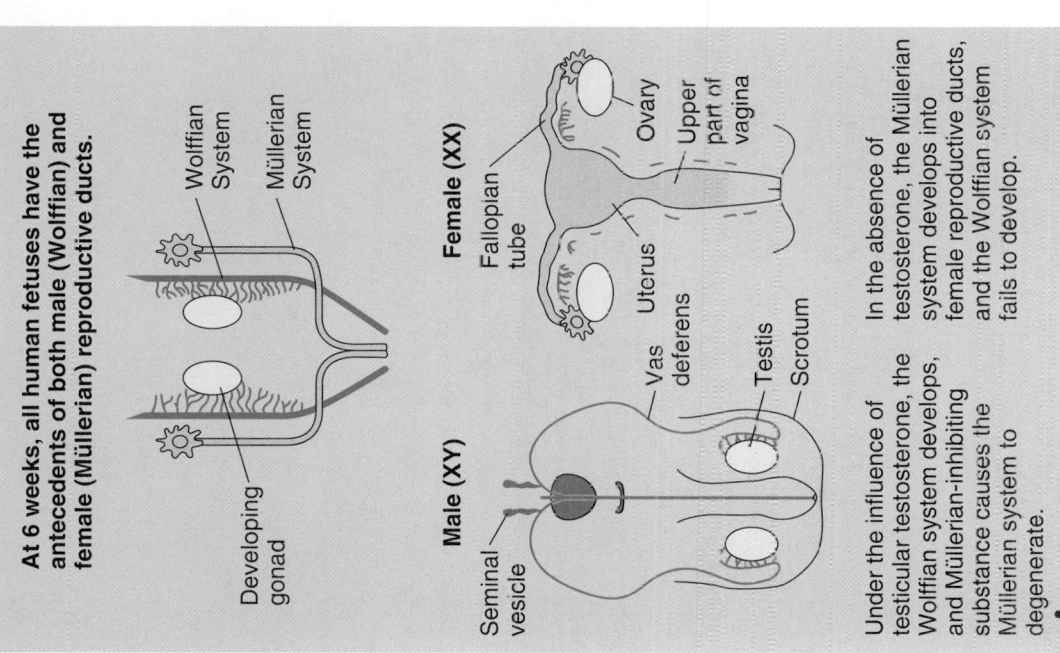

At 6 weeks, all human fetuses have the antecedents of both male (Wolffian) and female (Müllerian) reproductive ducts.

Developing gonad

Wolffian System

Müllerian System

Male (XY)

Seminal vesicle

Vas deferens

Testis

Scrotum

Under the influence of testicular testosterone, the Wolffian system develops, and Müllerian-inhibiting substance causes the Müllerian system to degenerate.

Female (XX)

Fallopian tube

Uterus

Ovary

Upper part of vagina

In the absence of testosterone, the Müllerian system develops into female reproductive ducts, and the Wolffian system fails to develop.

FIGURE 13.7 The development of the internal ducts of the male and female reproductive systems from the Wolffian and Müllerian systems, respectively.

Sex Differences in the Brain

The brains of men and women may look the same on casual inspection, and it may be politically correct to believe that they are. But they are not. The brains of men tend to be about 15% larger than those of women, and numerous other anatomical differences exist. There are major sex differences in the volumes of various nuclei and fiber tracts, in the numbers and types of neural and glial cells that compose various structures, and in the numbers and types of synapses that connect the cells in various structures. *Sexual dimorphisms* (male–female structural differences) of the brain are typically studied in nonhuman mammals, but many have also been documented in humans (see Simerly, 2002; Stone, 1996; Woodson & Gorski, 2000).

Research on sexual dimorphisms of mammalian brains is in transition. Initially, neuroscientists focused on identifying and describing examples, but now that so many have been documented, they are trying to understand the cause and function of these differences. Before I can describe this important area of current research, I need to tell you how the first brain sexual dimorphism was identified and studied. It set the stage for everything that followed.

Discovery of the First Mammalian Sexual Dimorphism of the Brain The first attempts to discover sex differences in the mammalian brain focused on the factors that control the development of the steady and cyclic patterns of gonadotropin release in males and females, respectively. The seminal experiments were conducted by Pfeiffer in 1936. In his experiments, some neonatal rats (males and females) were gonadectomized

that is not exposed to testicular hormones during the critical fetal period. Accordingly, normal female fetuses, ovariectomized female fetuses, and orchidectomized male fetuses all develop female reproductive ducts (Jost, 1972). **Ovariectomy** is the removal of the ovaries, and **orchidectomy** is the removal of the testes (*orchis* means "testicle"). **Gonadectomy,** or *castration,* is the surgical removal of gonads—either ovaries or testes.

External Reproductive Organs There is a basic difference between the differentiation of the external reproductive organs and the differentiation of the internal reproductive organs (i.e., the gonads and reproductive ducts). As you have just read, every normal fetus develops separate precursors for the male (medulla) and female (cortex) gonads and for the male (Wolffian system) and female (Müllerian system) reproductive ducts; then, only one set, male or female, develops. In contrast,

and some were not, and some received gonad transplants (ovaries or testes) and some did not.

Remarkably, Pfeiffer found that gonadectomizing neonatal rats of either genetic sex caused them to develop into adults with the female cyclic pattern of gonadotropin release. In contrast, transplantation of testes into gonadectomized or intact female neonatal rats caused them to develop into adults with the steady male pattern of gonadotropin release. Transplantation of ovaries had no effect on the pattern of hormone release. Pfeiffer concluded that the female cyclic pattern of gonadotropin release develops unless the preprogrammed female cyclicity is overridden by testosterone during perinatal development (see Harris & Levine, 1965).

Pfeiffer incorrectly concluded that the presence or absence of testicular hormones in neonatal rats influenced the development of the pituitary because he was not aware of something we know today: that the release of gonadotropins from the anterior pituitary is controlled by the hypothalamus. Once this was discovered, it became apparent that Pfeiffer's experiments had provided the first evidence of the role of *perinatal* (around the time of birth) androgens in the sexual differentiation of the hypothalamus.

Soon a complication to the simple androgen theory of hypothalamic differentiation was discovered. You see, all gonadal and adrenal sex hormones are steroid hormones, and because all steroid hormones are derived from cholesterol, they have similar structures and are readily converted from one to the other. For example, a slight change to one ring of the testosterone molecule changes that ring to a benzene ring and in so doing, converts testosterone to estradiol; this process is called **aromatization** (see Balthazart & Ball, 1998). There is good evidence that aromatization is a critical step in the masculinization of the brain by testosterone in some species.

According to this aromatization hypothesis, perinatal testosterone does not directly masculinize the brain; the brain is masculinized by estradiol that has been aromatized from perinatal testosterone. Although the idea

that estradiol—the alleged female hormone—masculinizes the brain is counterintuitive, there is strong evidence for it in several species. In the rat, for example, (1) neonatal injections of estradiol masculinize the brain; (2) **dihydrotestosterone**—an androgen that cannot be converted to estrogen—has no masculinizing effect on the brain; and (3) agents that block the aromatization of testosterone or block estradiol receptors interfere with the masculinizing effects of testosterone on the brain.

How do genetic females of species whose brains are masculinized by estradiol keep from being masculinized by their mothers' estradiol, which circulates through the fetal blood supply? In the rat, alpha fetoprotein is the answer. **Alpha fetoprotein** is present in the blood of rats during the perinatal period, and it deactivates circulating estradiol by binding to it. How, then, does estradiol masculinize the brain of the male fetus in the presence of the deactivating effects of alpha fetoprotein? Because

Evolutionary Perspective

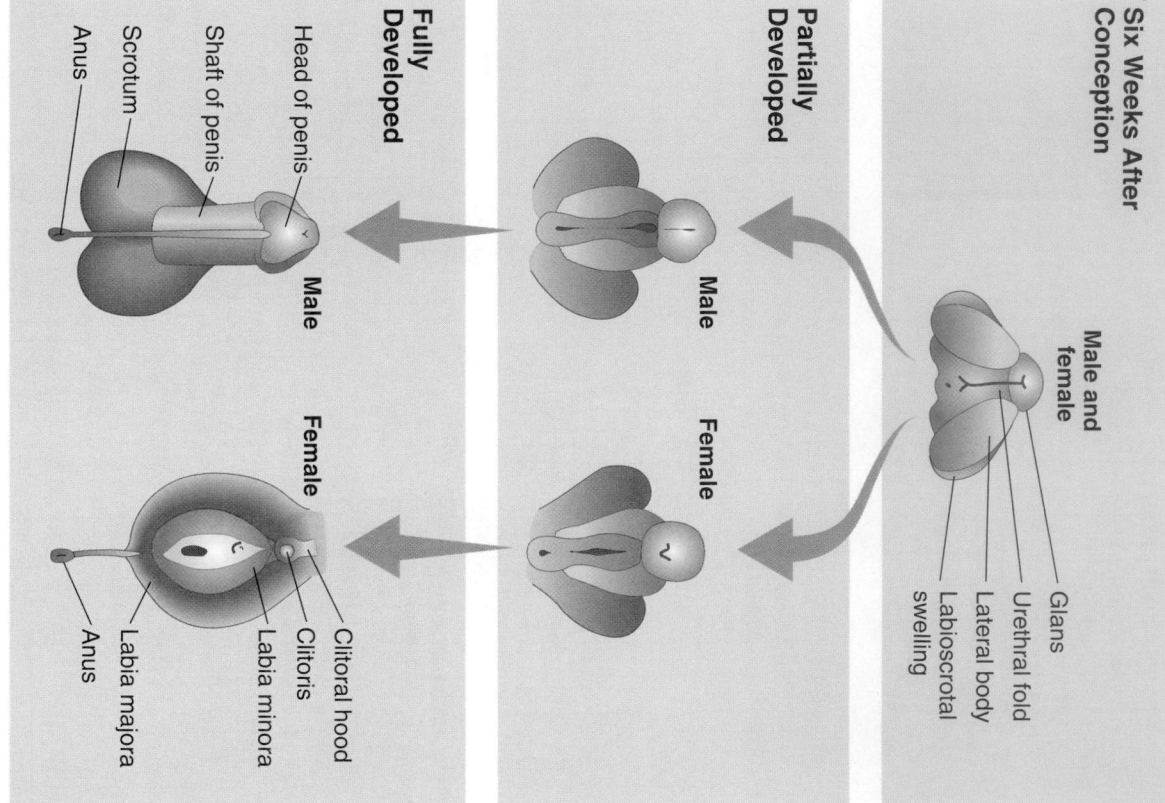

Six Weeks After Conception

Male and female
- Glans
- Urethral fold
- Lateral body
- Labioscrotal swelling

Partially Developed
Male   Female

Fully Developed

Male
- Head of penis
- Shaft of penis
- Scrotum
- Anus

Female
- Clitoral hood
- Clitoris
- Labia minora
- Labia majora
- Anus

Evolutionary Perspective

FIGURE 13.8 The development of male and female external reproductive organs from the same bipotential precursor.

testosterone is immune to alpha fetoprotein, it can travel unaffected from the testes to the brain, where it enters cells and is converted there to estradiol. The estradiol is not broken down in the brain because alpha fetoprotein does not readily penetrate the blood–brain barrier.

In humans, aromatization does not appear to be necessary for testosterone to have masculinizing effects on the brain; nevertheless, estradiol is capable of masculinizing effects similar to those of testosterone. How then are female fetuses protected from the masculinizing effects of the mother's estrogens? They are protected by the *placental barrier.* Unfortunately, this barrier is not as effective against some synthetic estrogens (e.g., *diethylstilbestrol*). As a result, the female offspring of mothers who have been exposed to synthetic estrogens while pregnant may display a variety of male characteristics (see McEwen, 1983).

Modern Research on Sexual Dimorphisms of the Mammalian Brain   Early research on the development of sexual dimorphisms in the mammalian brain suggested that the same general mechanism that guides the differentiation of the reproductive organs guides the differentiation of the brain—that is, that the default program is female and the male program is activated by early exposure to testosterone (e.g., Guillamón, Segovia, & Del Abril, 1988). However, this theory has been attacked on three fronts. First, there is now substantial evidence that the sex chromosomes contribute directly to brain dimorphism: XX and XY cells differ from one another even before they have been exposed to testosterone or estradiol, and differences between XX and XY cells persist even after the cells have been exposed to the same controlled doses of these hormones (Arnold, 2003; Arnold et al., 2004). Second, recent evidence suggests that the female program of brain development may not unfold automatically in the absence of estrogens: Various methods (e.g., gene knockouts) have been used to interfere with estradiol receptors, and this interference has disrupted normal female patterns of brain development (Bakker et al., 2003). The third challenge to the conventional view of the development of brain sexual dimorphisms focuses on the premise that there is a single mechanism that accounts for the development of all differences between male and female brains. There is now overwhelming evidence that various sexual dimorphisms of the brain emerge at different stages of development under different influences (see McCarthy, Auger, & Perrot-Sinal, 2002; Woodson & Gorski, 2000). Thus, although the conventional view of the development of sexual dimorphisms does an excellent job of explaining differentiation of the reproductive organs, it falters when it comes to the brain.

One cellular mechanism of the development of brain dimorphisms is well understood. Volumetric differences between particular structures in male and female brains develop by preferential apoptotic cell loss, not by preferential cell growth. Typically, males and females begin with the same number of neurons in a particular brain structure, and then programs of apoptotic cell death become more active in that structure in one sex (see McCarthy et al., 2002).

Perinatal Hormones and Behavioral Development

Evolutionary Perspective

In view of the fact that perinatal hormones influence the development of the brain, it should come as no surprise that they also influence the development of behavior. Much of the research on hormones and behavioral development has focused on the role of perinatal hormones in the development of sexually dimorphic copulatory behaviors in laboratory animals.

Phoenix and colleagues (1959) were among the first to demonstrate that the perinatal injection of testosterone **masculinizes** and **defeminizes** a genetic female's adult copulatory behavior. First, they injected pregnant guinea pigs with testosterone. Then, when the litters were born, they ovariectomized the female offspring. Finally, when these ovariectomized female guinea pigs reached maturity, they injected them with testosterone and assessed their copulatory behavior. Phoenix and his colleagues found that the females that had been exposed to perinatal testosterone displayed more malelike mounting behavior in response to testosterone injections in adulthood than did adult females that had not been exposed to perinatal testosterone. And when as adults they were injected with progesterone and estradiol and mounted by males, they displayed less **lordosis**—the intromission facilitating arched-back posture that signals female rodent receptivity.

In a study complementary to that of Phoenix and colleagues, Grady, Phoenix, and Young (1965) found that the lack of early exposure of male rats to testosterone both **feminizes** and **demasculinizes** their copulatory behavior as adults. Male rats castrated shortly after birth failed to display the normal male copulatory pattern of mounting, **intromission** (penis insertion), and **ejaculation** (ejection of sperm) when they were treated with testosterone and given access to a sexually receptive female; and when they were injected with estrogen and progesterone as adults, they exhibited more lordosis than did uncastrated controls. The aromatization of perinatal testosterone to estradiol seems to be important for both the defeminization and the masculinization of rodent copulatory behavior (Goy & McEwen, 1980; Shapiro, Levine, & Adler, 1980).

Because much of the research on hormones and behavioral development has focused on the copulatory act itself, we know less about the development of **proceptive behaviors** (solicitation behaviors) and in the development of gender-related behaviors that are not directly related to reproduction. However, perinatal testosterone has been reported to disrupt the proceptive hopping, darting, and ear wiggling of receptive female rats; to increase the aggressiveness of female mice; to disrupt the maternal behavior of female rats; and to increase rough social play in female monkeys and rats.

In thinking about hormones and behavioral development, it is important to remember two things. First, feminizing and demasculinizing effects do not always go together; nor do defeminizing and masculinizing effects. Hormone treatments can enhance or disrupt female behavior without affecting male behavior, and vice versa (Bloch, Mills, & Gale, 1995). Second, timing is important. The ability of single injections of testosterone to masculinize and defeminize the rat brain seems to be restricted to the first 11 days after birth. However, large multiple doses of testosterone can have masculinizing effects outside this *sensitive period* (Bloch & Mills, 1995).

Puberty: Hormones and the Development of Secondary Sex Characteristics

During childhood, levels of circulating gonadal hormones are low, reproductive organs are immature, and

males and females differ little in general appearance. This period of developmental quiescence ends abruptly with the onset of *puberty*—the transitional period between childhood and adulthood during which fertility is achieved, the adolescent growth spurt occurs, and the **secondary sex characteristics** develop. **Secondary sex characteristics** are those features other than the reproductive organs that distinguish sexually mature men and women. The body changes that occur during puberty are illustrated in Figure 13.9; you are undoubtedly familiar with at least half of them.

Puberty is associated with an increase in the release of hormones by the anterior pituitary (see Grumbach, 2002). The increase in the release of **growth hormone**—the only anterior pituitary hormone that does not have a gland as its primary target—acts directly on bone and muscle tissue to produce the pubertal growth spurt. Increases in gonadotropic hormone and **adrenocorticotropic hormone** release cause the gonads and adrenal cortex to increase their release of gonadal and adrenal hormones, which in turn initiate the maturation of the genitals and the development of secondary sex characteristics.

The general principle guiding normal pubertal sexual maturation is a simple one: In pubertal males, androgen levels are higher than estrogen levels, and mascu-

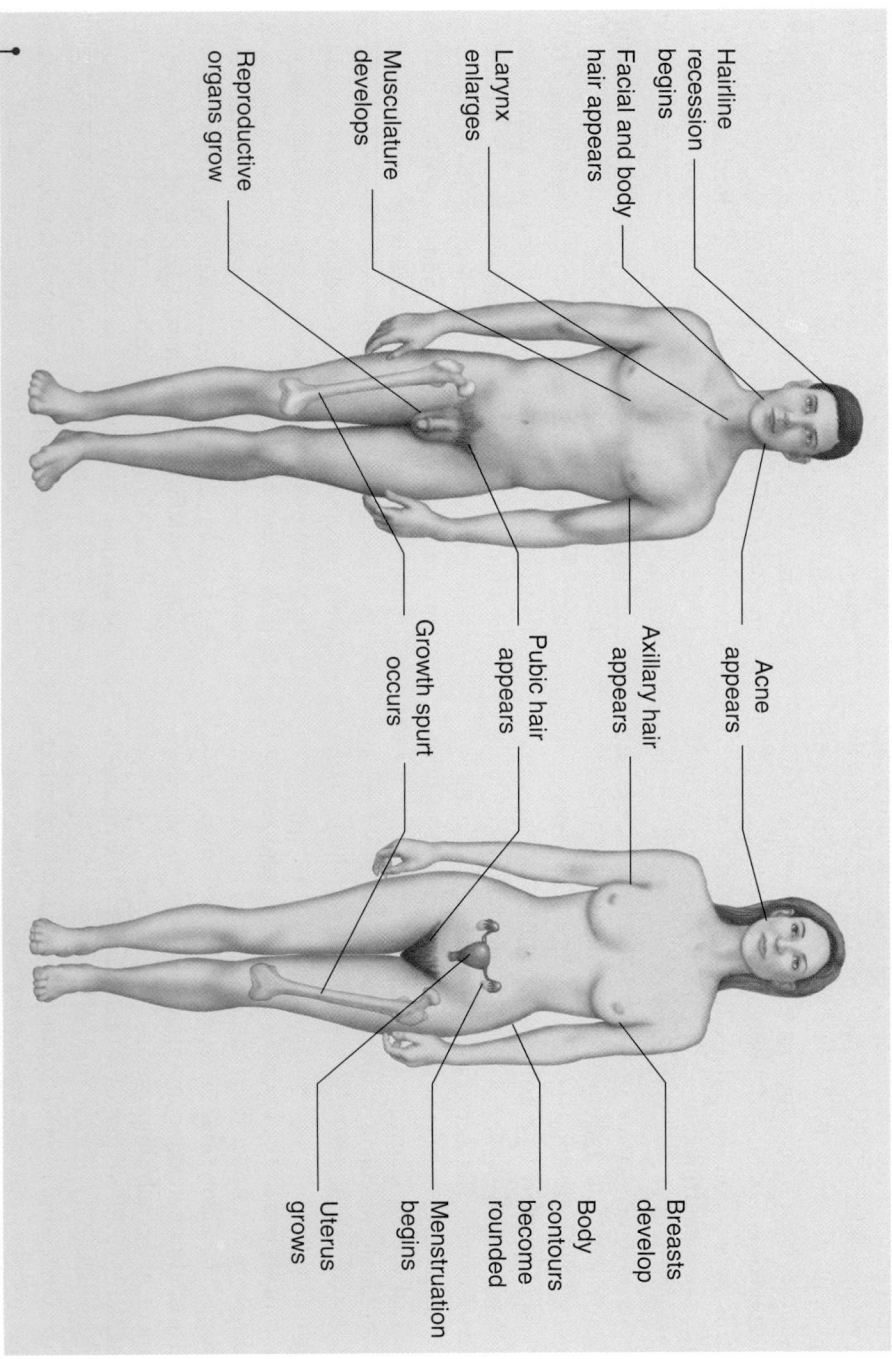

Hairline recession begins

Facial and body hair appears

Larynx enlarges

Musculature develops

Reproductive organs grow

Acne appears

Axillary hair appears

Pubic hair appears

Growth spurt occurs

Breasts develop

Body contours become rounded

Menstruation begins

Uterus grows

SCAN YOUR BRAIN

Before you proceed to a consideration of three cases of exceptional human sexual development, scan your brain to see whether you understand the basics of normal sexual development by completing the following exercise. The correct answers are provided at the bottom of this page. Review material related to your errors and omissions before proceeding.

1. Six weeks after conception, the Y chromosome of the human male triggers the production of _____.

2. In the absence of H-Y antigen, the cortical cells of the primordial gonads develop into _____.

3. In the third month of male fetal development, the testes secrete testosterone and _____ substance.

4. The hormonal factor that triggers the development of the human Müllerian system is the lack of _____ around the third month of fetal development.

5. The scrotum and the _____ develop from the same bipotential precursor.

6. The female pattern of cyclic release from the anterior pituitary develops in adulthood unless androgens are present in the body during the perinatal period.

7. It has been hypothesized that perinatal testosterone must first be changed to estradiol before it can masculinize the male rat brain. This is called the _____ hypothesis.

8. _____ is normally responsible for pubic and axillary hair growth in human females during puberty.

9. Girls usually begin puberty _____ boys do.

linization is the result; in pubertal females, the estrogens predominate, and the result is feminization. Individuals castrated prior to puberty do not become sexually mature unless they receive replacement injections of androgens or estrogens.

But even during puberty, its only major time of relevance, the men-are-men-and-women-are-women assumption stumbles badly. You see, **androstenedione,** an androgen that is released primarily by the adrenal cortex, is normally responsible for the growth of pubic hair and *axillary hair* (underarm hair) in females. It is hard to take seriously the practice of referring to androgens as "male hormones" when one of them is respon-

 **Thinking Critically**

sible for the development of the female pattern of pubic hair growth. The male pattern is a pyramid, and the female pattern is an inverted pyramid (see Figure 13.9).

Do you remember how old you were when you started to go through puberty? In most North American and European countries, puberty begins at about 10.5 years of age for girls and 11.5 years for boys. I am sure that you would have been unhappy if you had not started puberty until you were 15 or 16, but this was the norm in North America and Europe just a century and a half ago. Presumably, this acceleration of puberty has resulted from an improvement in dietary, medical, and socioeconomic conditions.

13.3 Three Cases of Exceptional Human Sexual Development

So far in this chapter, you have learned the "rules" according to which hormones seem to influence normal sexual development. Now, three exceptional cases are offered to prove (to test) these rules.

The Case of Anne S., the Woman Who Wasn't

Anne S., an attractive 26-year-old female, sought treatment for two sex-related disorders: lack of men-

struation and pain during sexual intercourse (Jones & Park, 1971). She sought help because she and her husband of 4 years had been trying without success to have children, and she correctly surmised that her

Clinical Implications

lack of a menstrual cycle was part of the problem. A physical examination revealed that Anne was a healthy young woman. Her only readily apparent peculiarity was the sparseness and fineness of her pubic and axillary hair. Examination of her external genitals revealed no abnormalities; however, there were some problems with her internal genitals. Her vagina was only 4 centimeters long, and her uterus was underdeveloped.

At the start of this chapter, I said that you would encounter some remarkable things, and the diagnosis of Anne's case certainly qualifies as one of them. Anne's doctors concluded that her sex chromosomes were those of a man. No, this is not a misprint; they concluded that Anne, the attractive young housewife, had the genes of a genetic male. Three lines of evidence supported their diagnosis. First, analysis of cells scraped from the inside of Anne's mouth revealed that they were of the male XY type. Second, a tiny incision in Anne's abdomen, which enabled Anne's physicians to look inside, revealed a pair of internalized testes but no ovaries. Finally, hormone tests revealed that Anne's hormone levels were those of a male.

Anne suffers from **androgenic insensitivity syndrome**; all her symptoms stem from a mutation to the androgen receptor gene that rendered her androgen receptors defective (see Fink et al., 1999; Goldstein, 2000). During development, Anne's testes released normal amounts of androgens for a male, but her body could not respond to them, and her development thus proceeded as if no androgens had been released. Her external genitals, her brain, and her behavior developed along female lines, without the effects of androgens to override the female program, and her testes could not descend from her body cavity with no scrotum for them to descend into. Furthermore, Anne did not develop normal internal female reproductive ducts because, like other genetic males, her testes released Müllerian-inhibiting substance; that is why her vagina was short and her uterus undeveloped. At puberty, Anne's testes released enough estrogens to feminize her body in the absence of the counteracting effects of androgens; however, adrenal androstenedione was not able to stimulate the growth of pubic and axillary hair.

Money and Ehrhardt (1972) studied the psychosexual development of 10 androgen-insensitive patients and concluded that the placidity of their childhood play, their goals, their fantasies, their sexual behavior, and their maternal tendencies—several had adopted children—all conformed to the idealized stereotype of what constitutes femininity in our culture. Apparently, without the masculinizing effects of androgens, infants who look like females and are raised as females come to think and act like females—even when they are genetic males.

An interesting issue of medical ethics is raised by the androgenic insensitivity syndrome. Many people be-

lieve that physicians should always disclose all relevant findings to their patients. If you were Anne's physician, would you tell her that she is a man? Would you tell her husband? Anne's vagina was surgically enlarged, she was counseled to consider adoption, and, as far as I know, she is still happily married and unaware of her genetic sex. On the other hand, I have heard from several women with androgenic insensitivity who recommend full disclosure: They had faced a variety of problems throughout their lives and learning the cause helped them.

Clinical Implications

The Case of the Little Girl Who Grew into a Boy

The patient—let's call her Elaine—sought treatment in 1972. Elaine was born with somewhat ambiguous external genitals, but she was raised by her parents as a girl without incident, until the onset of puberty, when she suddenly began to develop male secondary sex characteristics. This was extremely distressing. Her treatment had two aspects: surgical and hormonal. Surgical treatment was used to increase the size of her vagina and decrease the size of her clitoris; hormonal treatment was used to suppress androgen release so that her own estrogen could feminize her body. Following treatment, Elaine developed into an attractive young woman—narrow hips and a husky voice being the only signs of her brush with masculinity. Fifteen years later, she was married and enjoying a normal sex life (Money & Ehrhardt, 1972).

Elaine suffered from adrenogenital syndrome. **Adrenogenital syndrome** is a disorder of sexual development caused by **congenital adrenal hyperplasia**—a congenital deficiency in the release of the hormone *cortisol* from the adrenal cortex, which results in compensatory adrenal hyperactivity and the excessive release of adrenal androgens. This has little effect on the development of males, other than accelerating the onset of puberty, but it has major effects on the development of genetic females. Females who suffer from the adrenogenital syndrome are usually born with an enlarged clitoris and partially fused labia. Their gonads and internal ducts are usually normal because the adrenal androgens are released too late to stimulate the development of the Wolffian system.

Most female cases of adrenogenital syndrome are diagnosed at birth. In such cases, the abnormalities of the external genitals are immediately corrected, and cortisol is administered to reduce the levels of circulating adrenal androgens. Following early treatment, adrenogenital females grow up to be physically normal except that the onset of menstruation is likely to be later than normal. This makes them good subjects for studies of the effects of fetal androgen exposure on psychosexual development.

Adrenogenital teenage girls who have received early treatment typically display a high degree of tomboyishness and little interest in maternity (e.g., Hines, 2003). They prefer boys' clothes and toys, play mainly with boys, show little interest in handling babies, and tend to daydream about future careers rather than motherhood. It is important not to lose sight of the fact that many teenage girls display similar characteristics—and why not? Accordingly, the behavior of treated adrenogenital females, although perhaps tending toward the masculine, is well within the range considered normal by the current standards of our culture.

The most interesting questions about the development of females with adrenogenital syndrome concern their romantic and sexual preferences as adults. They seem to lag behind normal females in dating and marriage—perhaps because of the delayed onset of their menstrual cycle—but in other respects their sexual interests appear normal. Most are heterosexual, although it has been suggested that they have a slight tendency toward bisexuality. However, Zucker and others (1996) found that although females with adrenogenital syndrome had fewer heterosexual experiences and fantasies, they had no more homosexual experiences or fantasies.

Prior to the development of cortisol therapy in 1950, genetic females with adrenogenital syndrome were left untreated. Some were raised as boys and some as girls, but the direction of their pubertal development was unpredictable. In some cases, adrenal androgens predominated and masculinized their bodies; in others, ovarian estrogens predominated and feminized their bodies. Thus, some who were raised as boys were transformed at puberty into women, and some who were raised as girls were transformed into men, with devastating emotional consequences. Elaine was such a case.

The Case of the Twin Who Lost His Penis

Clinical Implications

One of the most famous cases in the literature on sexual development is that of a male identical twin whose penis was accidentally destroyed during circumcision at the age of 7 months. Because there was no satisfactory way of surgically replacing the lost penis, a respected expert in such matters, John Money, recommended that the boy be castrated, that an artificial vagina be created, that the boy be raised as a girl, and that estrogen be administered at puberty to feminize the body. After a great deal of consideration and anguish, the parents followed Money's advice.

Money's (1975) report of this case of **ablatio penis** has been influential. It has been seen by some as

the ultimate test of the *nature–nurture controversy* (see Chapter 2) with respect to the development of sexual identity and behavior. It seemed to pit the masculinizing effects of male genes and male prenatal hormones against the effects of being reared as a female. And the availability of a genetically identical control subject, the twin brother, made the case all the more interesting.

According to Money, the outcome of this case strongly supports the *social-learning theory* of sexual identity. Money reported in 1975, when the patient was 12, that "she" had developed as a normal female, thus confirming his prediction that being gonadectomized, having the genitals surgically altered, and being raised as a girl would override the masculinizing effects of male genes and early androgens. Because it is such an interesting case, Money's description of it continues to be featured in some textbooks, each time carrying with it the message that the sexual identity and sexual behavior of men and women are largely a matter of upbringing.

However, a long-term follow-up study published by experts other than those who initially prescribed the treatment tells an entirely different story (Diamond & Sigmundson, 1997). Despite having female genitalia and being treated as a female, John/Joan developed along male lines. Apparently, the organ that determines the course of psychosocial development is the brain, not the genitals (Reiner, 1997). The following paraphrases from Diamond and Sigmundson's report give you a glimpse of John/Joan's life:

From a very early age, Joan tended to act in a masculine way. She preferred boys' activities and games and displayed little interest in dolls, sewing, or other conventional female activities. When she was four, she was watching her father shave and her mother put on lipstick, and she began to put shaving cream on her face. When she was told to put makeup on like her mother, she said, "No, I don't want no makeup, I want to shave."

"Things happened very early. As a child, I began to see that I felt different about a lot of things than I was supposed to. I suspected I was a boy from the second grade on."

Despite the absence of a penis, Joan often tried to urinate while standing, and she would sometimes go to the boys' lavatory.

Joan was attractive as a girl, but as soon as she moved or talked her masculinity became apparent. She was teased incessantly by the other girls, and she often retaliated violently, which resulted in her expulsion from school.

Joan was put on an estrogen regimen at the age of 12 but rebelled against it. She did not want to feminize; she hated her developing breasts and refused to wear a bra.

At 14, Joan decided to live as a male and switched to John. At that time, John's father tearfully revealed John's entire early history to him. "All of a sudden everything clicked. For the first time I understood who and what I was."

John requested androgen treatment, a *mastectomy* (surgical removal of breasts), and *phalloplasty* (surgical creation of a penis). He became a handsome and popular young man. He married at the age of 25 and adopted his wife's children. He is strictly heterosexual.

John's ability to ejaculate and experience orgasm returned following his androgen treatments. However, his early castration permanently eliminated his reproductive capacity.

John remained bitter about his early treatment and his inability to produce offspring. To save others from his experience, he cooperated in writing his biography, *As Nature Made Him* (Colapinto, 2000). But John never recovered from his emotional scars. On May 4, 2004, he committed suicide.

John's case suggests that the clinical practice of surgically modifying a person's sex at birth should be curtailed. Any such irrevocable treatments should await early puberty and the emergence of the patient's sexual identity and sexual attraction. Then, a compatible course of treatment can be selected.

13.4 Effects of Gonadal Hormones on Adults

Once an individual reaches sexual maturity, gonadal hormones begin to play a role in activating reproductive behavior. These activational effects are the focus of the first two parts of this section, which has four parts. The first deals with the role of hormones in activating the reproduction-related behavior of men, and the second deals with the role of hormones in activating reproduction-related behavior of women. The third and fourth parts of this section deal with the clinical effects of gonadal hormone administration in adults. The third discusses the epidemic of anabolic steroid use, and the fourth describes the neuroprotective effects of estradiol.

Male Reproduction–Related Behavior and Testosterone

The important role played by gonadal hormones in the activation of male sexual behavior is clearly demonstrated by the asexualizing effects of orchidectomy. Bremer (1959) reviewed the cases of 157 orchidectomized Norwegians. Many had committed sex-related offenses and had agreed to castration to reduce the length of their prison terms.

Two important generalizations can be drawn from Bremer's study. The first is that orchidectomy leads to a reduction in sexual interest and behavior; the second is that the rate and degree of the loss is variable. About half the men became completely asexual within a few weeks of the operation; others quickly lost their ability to achieve an erection but continued to experience some sexual interest and pleasure; and a few continued to copulate successfully, although somewhat less enthusiastically, for the duration of the study. There were also body changes; a reduction of hair on the trunk, extremities, and face; the deposition of fat on the hips and chest; a softening of the skin; and a reduction in strength.

Of the 102 sex offenders in Bremer's study, only 3 were reconvicted of sex offenses. Accordingly, he recommended castration as an effective treatment of last resort for male sex offenders.

Why do some men remain sexually active for months after orchidectomy, despite the fact that testicular hormones are cleared from their bodies within days? It has been suggested that adrenal androgens may play some role in the maintenance of sexual activity in some castrated men, but there is no direct evidence for this hypothesis.

Orchidectomy, in one fell swoop—or, to put it more precisely, in two fell swoops—removes a pair of glands that release many hormones. Because testosterone is the major testicular hormone, the major symptoms of orchidectomy have been generally attributed to the loss of tes-

Do the Exceptional Cases Prove the Rule?

Do current theories of hormones and sexual development pass the test imposed by the three preceding cases of exceptional sexual development? In my view, the answer is an emphatic yes. Although current theories do not supply all of the answers, especially when it comes to brain dimorphisms and behavior, they have contributed greatly to the understanding of exceptional sexual development.

For centuries, cases of abnormal sexual development have befuddled scholars, but now, armed with a basic understanding of the role of hormones in sexual development, they have been able to make sense of even the most puzzling of such cases. Moreover, the study of sexual development has pointed the way to effective treatments. Judge these contributions for yourself by comparing your current understanding of these three cases with the understanding that you would have had if you had encountered them before beginning this chapter.

Notice one more thing about the three cases: Each of the three subjects was male in some respects and female in others. Accordingly, each case is a serious challenge to the men-are-men-and-women-are-women assumption.

tosterone, rather than to the loss of some other testicular hormone or to some nonhormonal consequence of the surgery. The therapeutic effects of **replacement injections** of testosterone have confirmed this assumption.

The Case of the Man Who Lost and Regained His Manhood

Clinical Implications

The very first case report of the effects of testosterone replacement therapy concerned an unfortunate 38-year-old World War I veteran, who was castrated in 1918 at the age of 19 by a shell fragment that removed his testes but left his penis undamaged.

His body was soft; it was as if he had almost no muscles at all; his hips had grown wider and his shoulders seemed narrower than when he was a soldier. He had very little drive....

Just the same this veteran had married, in 1924, and you'd wonder why, because the doctors had told him he would surely be **impotent** [unable to achieve an erection]....he made some attempts at sexual intercourse "for his wife's satisfaction" but he confessed that he had been unable to satisfy her at all....

Dr. Foss began injecting it [testosterone] into the feeble muscles of the castrated man....

After the fifth injection, erections were rapid and prolonged....But that wasn't all. During twelve weeks of treatment he had gained eighteen pounds, and all his clothes had become too small. Originally, he wore fourteen-and-a-half inch collars. Now fifteen-and-a-half were too tight....testosterone had resurrected a broken man to a manhood he had lost forever. (de Kruif, 1945, pp. 97–100)

Since this first clinical trial, testosterone has breathed sexuality into the lives of many men. Testosterone does not, however, eliminate the *sterility* (inability to reproduce) of males who lack functional testes.

The fact that testosterone is necessary for male sexual behavior has led to two widespread assumptions: (1) that the level of a man's sexuality is a function of the amount of testosterone he has in his blood, and (2) that a man's sex drive can be increased by increasing his testosterone levels. Both assumptions are incorrect. Sex drive and testosterone levels are uncorrelated in healthy men, and testosterone injections do not increase their sex drive.

It seems that each healthy male has far more testosterone than is required to activate the neural circuits that produce his sexual behavior and that having more than the minimum is of no advantage in this respect (Sherwin, 1988). A classic experiment by Grunt and Young (1952) clearly illustrates this point.

First, Grunt and Young rated the sexual behavior of each of the male guinea pigs in their experiment. Then, on the basis of the ratings, the researchers divided the male guinea pigs into three experimental groups: low, medium, and high sex drive. Following castration, the sexual behavior of all of the guinea pigs fell to negligible levels within a few weeks (see Figure 13.10), but it recovered after the initiation of a series of testosterone replacement injections. The important point is that although each subject received the same, very large replacement injections of testosterone, the injections simply returned each to its previous level of copulatory activity. The conclusion is clear: With respect to the effects of testosterone on sexual behavior, more is not necessarily better.

Evolutionary Perspective

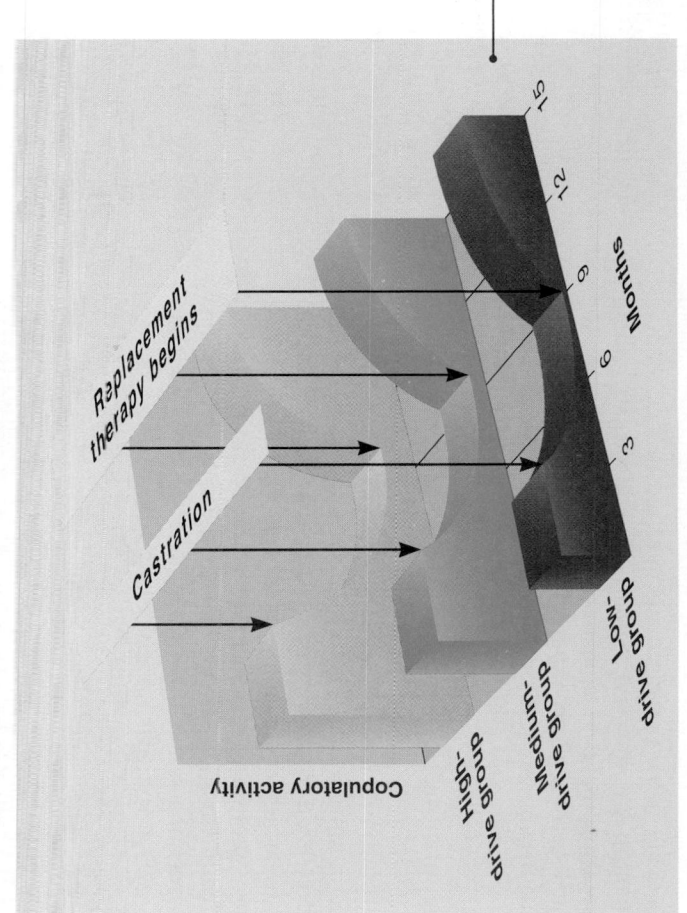

FIGURE 13.10 The sexual behavior of male guinea pigs with low, medium, and high sex drive. Sexual behavior was disrupted by castration and returned to its original level by very large replacement injections of testosterone. (Adapted from Grunt & Young, 1952.)

Dihydrotestosterone, a nonaromatizable androgen, has failed to reactivate the copulatory behavior of castrated male rats in several studies (see MacLusky & Naftolin, 1981). This suggests that in male rats the activation effects of testosterone on sexual behavior may be produced by estradiol that has been aromatized from the testosterone. However, dihydrotestosterone has proved effective in activating sexual behavior in orchidectomized primates (e.g., Davidson, Kwan, & Greenleaf, 1982).

Female Reproduction–Related Behavior and Gonadal Hormones

Sexually mature female rats and guinea pigs display 4-day cycles of gonadal hormone release. There is a gradual increase in the secretion of estrogens by the developing follicle in the 2 days prior to ovulation, followed by a sudden surge in progesterone as the egg is released. These surges of estrogens and progesterone initiate **estrus**—a period of 12 to 18 hours during which the female is *fertile*, *receptive* (likely to assume the lordosis posture when mounted), *proceptive* (likely to engage in behaviors that serve to attract the male), and *sexually attractive* (smelling of chemicals that attract males).

The close relation between the cycle of hormone release and the **estrous cycle**—the cycle of sexual receptivity—in female rats and guinea pigs and in many other mammalian species suggests that female sexual behavior in these species is under hormonal control. The effects of ovariectomy confirm this conclusion; ovariectomy of female rats and guinea pigs produces a rapid decline of both proceptive and receptive behaviors. Furthermore, estrus can be induced in ovariectomized rats and guinea pigs by an injection of estradiol followed about a day and a half later by an injection of progesterone.

Women are different from female rats and guinea pigs when it comes to the hormonal control of their sexual behavior. Neither the sexual motivation nor the sexual behavior of women is inextricably linked with their menstrual cycles (see Sanders & Bancroft, 1982). Moreover, ovariectomy has surprisingly little direct effect on either their sexual motivation or sexual behavior (e.g., Martin, Roberts, & Clayton, 1980). Other than sterility, the major consequence of ovariectomy in women is a decrease in vaginal lubrication.

Paradoxically, there is evidence that the sex drive of women is under the control of androgens, not estrogens (see Sherwin, 1988). Apparently, enough androgens are released from the human adrenal glands to maintain the sexual motivation of women even after their ovaries have been removed. Support for the theory that androgens control human female sexuality has come from three sources:

1. Experiments in nonhuman female primates: Replacement injections of testosterone, but not estradiol, increase the proceptivity of ovariectomized and adrenalectomized rhesus monkeys (see Everitt & Herbert, 1972; Everitt, Herbert, & Hamer, 1971).

2. Correlational studies in healthy women: Various measures of sexual motivation are correlated with testosterone levels but not with estradiol levels (see Bancroft et al., 1983; Morris et al., 1987).

3. Clinical studies of women following ovariectomy and adrenalectomy: Replacement injections of testosterone, but not of estradiol, rekindle their sexual motivation (see Sherwin, 1985; Sherwin, Gelfand, & Brender, 1985).

Anabolic Steroid Abuse

Anabolic steroids are steroids, such as testosterone, that have *anabolic* (growth-promoting) effects. Testosterone itself is not very useful as an anabolic drug because it is broken down soon after injection and because it has undesirable side effects. Chemists have managed to synthesize a number of potent anabolic steroids that are long-acting, but they have not managed to synthesize one that does not have side effects.

We are currently in the midst of an epidemic of anabolic steroid abuse. Many competitive athletes and bodybuilders are self-administering appallingly large doses to increase their muscularity and strength, but the problem is even more extensive than this. In recent years, the cosmetic use of steroids has reached troubling proportions. For example, studies indicate that over a million young American males have used steroids (see Pope, Kouri, & Hudson, 2000).

Because steroids are illegal in most parts of the United States, it has been difficult to document their effects. Research is tightly regulated, and users are not forthcoming.

Effects of Anabolic Steroids on Athletic Performance

Do anabolic steroids really increase the muscularity and strength of the athletes who use them? Surprisingly, the scientific evidence is inconsistent (see Yesalis & Bahrke, 1995), even though many athletes and coaches believe that it is impossible to compete successfully at the highest levels of their sports without an anabolic steroid boost. The failure of science to confirm the benefits that have been experienced by many athletes likely results from two shortcomings of the scientific research. First, the experimental studies have tended to use doses of steroids smaller than those used by athletes and for shorter periods of time. Second, the experimental studies have often been conducted on subjects who are not involved in intense anabolic training. However, despite the lack of firm scientific evidence, it is difficult to ignore the successes of steroid users such as the man pictured in Figure 13.11.

Evolutionary Perspective

Clinical Implications

used by human athletes (Bronson & Matherne, 1997). None of the mice died during the period of steroid exposure; however, by 20 months of age, 52% of the steroid-exposed mice had died, whereas only 12% of the controls had died.

Behavioral Effects of Anabolic Steroids Most of the research on the behavioral effects of anabolic steroids, aside from that focusing on athletic performance, has focused on aggression. There have been numerous anecdotal reports that steroid use increases aggression. However, these reports must be treated with caution for at least three reasons. First, because many people believe that testosterone is linked to aggression, reports of aggressive behavior in steroid users might be a consequence of expectation. Second, many individuals (e.g., professional fighters or football players) who use steroids are likely to have been aggressive before they started treatment. And third, aggressive behavior might be an indirect consequence of increased size and muscularity.

Despite the need for experimental assessment of the effects of anabolic steroids on aggression, few such experiments have been conducted. The best is one by Pope and colleagues (2000). They administered either testosterone or placebo injections in a double-blind study of 53 men. The subjects completed tests of aggression, as well as keeping daily aggression-related diaries—a similar diary was also kept by a "significant other" of each subject. Pope and colleagues found large increases in aggression in some of the subjects.

There is no indication that the chronic use of high doses of steroids increases, improves, or redirects sexual motivation or sexual behavior. However, there are a few reports of disruptive effects in human steroid users, and some anabolic steroids have been shown to disrupt the copulatory behavior of both male and female rodents (see Clark & Henderson, 2003).

One last important point about the behavioral effects of anabolic steroids: So far, research on the effects of anabolic steroids in humans has focused on adults. The use of anabolic steroids in puberty, before developmental programs of sexual differentiation are complete, has the potential to produce lasting deleterious effects (see Farrell & McGinnis, 2003).

The Neuroprotective Effects of Estradiol

Although estradiol is best known for its sex-related organizational and activational effects, this hormone also can reduce the brain damage associated with stroke and various neurodegenerative disorders. For example, Yang and colleagues (2003) showed that estradiol administered just before, during, or just after the induction of *cerebral hypoxia* (reduction of oxygen to the brain) substantially reduced subsequent brain damage (see Chapter 10).

FIGURE 13.11 An athlete who used anabolic steroids to augment his training program.

Physiological Effects of Anabolic Steroids There is general agreement (see Yesalis & Bahrke, 1995) that people who take high doses of anabolic steroids risk several sex-related physiological side effects. In men, the negative feedback from high levels of anabolic steroids reduces gonadotropin release; this leads to a reduction in testicular activity, which can result in *testicular atrophy* (wasting away of the testes) and sterility. *Gynecomastia* (breast growth in men) can also occur, presumably as the result of the aromatization of anabolic steroids to estrogens. In women, anabolic steroids can produce *amenorrhea* (cessation of menstruation), sterility, *hirsutism* (excessive growth of body hair), growth of the clitoris, development of a masculine body shape, baldness, shrinking of the breasts, and deepening and coarsening of the voice. Unfortunately, many of the sex-related effects on women appear to be irreversible.

Both men and women who use anabolic steroids can suffer muscle spasms, muscle pains, blood in the urine, acne, general swelling from the retention of water, bleeding of the tongue, nausea, vomiting, and a variety of psychotic behaviors, including fits of depression and anger (Pope & Katz, 1987). Oral anabolic steroids produce cancerous liver tumors.

A controlled evaluation of the effects of exposure to anabolic steroids was conducted in adult male mice. Mice were exposed for 6 months to a cocktail of four anabolic steroids at relative levels comparable to those

Estradiol has been shown to have several neurotrophic effects that might account for its neuroprotective properties (see Chapter 10). For example, estradiol has been shown to reduce inflammation, encourage axonal regeneration, and promote synaptogenesis (see Stein & Hoffman, 2003; Zhang et al., 2004). Brandi Ormerod and Liisa Galea conducted an interesting line of experiments on yet another neurotrophic effect of estradiol: increasing adult neurogenesis (see Chapter 10). They showed that an injection of estradiol initially increased the number of new neurons created in the dentate gyri of the hippocampi of adult female rats and then, about 48 hours later, suppressed neurogenesis for a period (Ormerod, Falconer, & Galea, 2003; Ormerod, Lee, & Galea, 2001). They also found that estradiol, as well as increasing adult neurogenesis, increased the survival rate of the new neurons (Ormerod & Galea, 2001b).

Several recent studies have assessed the effects of estradiol on cognitive ability. Unfortunately, there has been no consistent pattern of effects. A study by Holmes, Wide, and Galea (2002) suggests that the confusion about the effects of estradiol on cognition may be due

to the specificity and dose-dependency of such effects. They trained ovariectomized female rats daily on a *radial arm maze* (see Chapter 5), after giving the rats an injection of estradiol. The rats' memory for the location of the food, which was at the end of the same arm each day (reference memory), was unaffected by the injection, whereas the rats' memory for the arms previously visited on that day (working memory) was affected. Replacement injections of estradiol at low doses facilitated working memory, whereas high doses disrupted it.

The discovery of estradiol's neuroprotective properties is creating a lot of excitement among neuroscientists. These properties may account for the greater longevity of women, the lower incidence of several common neuropsychological disorders such as Parkinson's disease among women, and the decline in some cognitive functions experienced by postmenopausal women (see Bisagno, Bowman, & Luine, 2003; Gandy, 2003). Furthermore, estradiol-like compounds may prove to be effective as preventive and therapeutic agents (see Gooren & Toorians, 2003; Sherwin, 2003).

Clinical Implications

13.5 Neural Mechanisms of Sexual Behavior

Major differences among cultures in sexual practices and preferences indicate that the control of human sexual behavior involves the highest levels of the nervous system (e.g., association cortex), and the same point is made by controlled demonstrations of the major role played by experience in the sexual preferences and behaviors of nonhuman animals (see Woodson, 2002; Woodson & Balleine, 2002; Woodson, Balleine, & Gorski, 2002). Nevertheless, research on the neural mechanisms of sexual behavior has focused almost exclusively on hypothalamic circuits. Consequently, I am forced to do the same here: When it comes to the study of the neural regulation of sexual behavior, the hypothalamus is virtually the only game in town.

Why has research on the neural mechanisms of sexual behavior focused almost exclusively on hypothalamic circuits? There are three obvious reasons. First, because of the difficulty of studying the neural mechanisms of complex human sexual behaviors, researchers have focused on the relatively simple, controllable copulatory behaviors (e.g., ejaculation, mounting, and lordosis) of laboratory animals (see Agmo & Ellingsen, 2003), which tend to be controlled by the hypothalamus. Second, because the hypothalamus controls gonadotropin release, it was the obvious place to look for sexually dimorphic structures and circuits that might control copulation. And third, early studies confirmed that the hypothalamus does play a major role in sexual behavior, and this

finding led subsequent neuroscientific research on sexual behavior to focus on that brain structure.

Structural Differences between the Male Hypothalamus and the Female Hypothalamus

You have already learned that the male hypothalamus and the female hypothalamus are functionally different in their control of anterior pituitary hormones (steady versus cyclic release, respectively). In the 1970s, structural differences between the male and female hypothalamus were discovered in rats (Raisman & Field, 1971), suggesting that the hypothalamus is involved in the regulation of reproductive behavior. Most notably, Gorski and his colleagues (1978) discovered a nucleus in the **medial preoptic area** of the rat hypothalamus that was several times larger in males (see Figure 13.12). They called this nucleus the **sexually dimorphic nucleus.**

At birth, the sexually dimorphic nuclei of male and female rats are the same size. In the first few days after birth, the male sexually dimorphic nuclei grow at a high rate and the female sexually dimorphic nuclei do not. The growth of the male sexually dimorphic nuclei is triggered by estradiol, which has been aromatized from testosterone (see McEwen, 1987). Accordingly, castrating day-old (but not 4-day-old) male rats significantly

Evolutionary Perspective

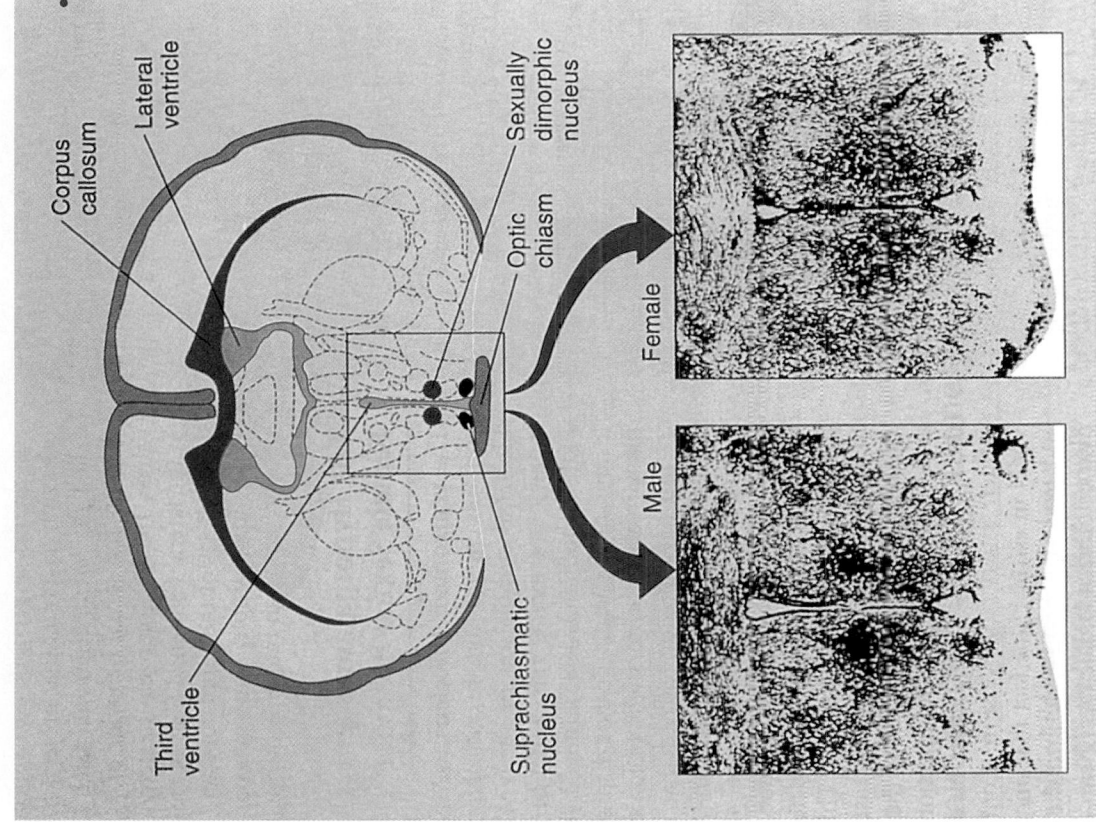

FIGURE 13.12 Nissl-stained coronal sections through the preoptic area of male and female rats. The sexually dimorphic nuclei are larger in male rats than in female rats. (Adapted from Gorski et al., 1978.)

(Allen et al., 1989) regions of the hypothalamus that differ in men and women.

The Hypothalamus and Male Sexual Behavior

The medial preoptic area (which includes the sexually dimorphic nucleus) is one area of the hypothalamus that plays a key role in male sexual behavior. Destruction of the entire area abolishes sexual behavior in the males of all mammalian species that have been studied (see Hull et al., 1999). In contrast, medial preoptic area lesions do not eliminate the female sexual behaviors of females, but they do eliminate the male sexual behaviors (e.g., mounting) that are often observed in females (Singer, 1968). Thus, bilateral medial preoptic lesions appear to abolish male copulatory behavior in both sexes. On the other side of the coin, electrical stimulation of the medial preoptic area elicits copulatory behavior in male rats (Malsbury, 1971; Rodríguez-Manzo et al., 2000), and copulatory behavior can be reinstated in castrated male rats by medial preoptic implants of testosterone (Davidson, 1980).

It is not clear why males with medial preoptic lesions stop copulating. One possibility is that the lesions disrupt the ability of males to copulate; another is that the lesions reduce the motivation of the males to engage in sexual behavior. The evidence is mixed, but it strongly favors the hypothesis that the medial preoptic area is involved in the motivational aspects of male sexual behavior (Paredes, 2003).

The medial preoptic area appears to control male sexual behavior via a tract that projects to an area of the midbrain called the *lateral tegmental field*. Destruction of this tract disrupts the sexual behavior of male rats (Brackett & Edwards, 1984). Moreover, the activity of individual neurons in the lateral tegmental field of male rats is often correlated with aspects of the copulatory act (Shimura & Shimokochi, 1990); for example, some neurons in the lateral tegmental field fire at a high rate only during intromission.

Neuropharmacological approaches are being used to study the medial preoptic area's control of male sexual

reduces the size of their sexually dimorphic nuclei as adults, whereas injecting neonatal (newborn) female rats with testosterone significantly increases the size of theirs (Gorski, 1980)—see Figure 13.13 on page 336. Although the overall size of the sexually dimorphic nucleus diminishes only slightly in male rats that are castrated in adulthood, specific areas of the nucleus do display significant degeneration (Bloch & Gorski, 1988).

The size of a male rat's sexually dimorphic nucleus is correlated with the rat's testosterone levels and aspects of its sexual activity (Anderson et al., 1986). However, bilateral lesions of the sexually dimorphic nucleus have only slight disruptive effects on male rat sexual behavior (e.g., De Jonge et al., 1989; Turkenburg et al., 1988), and the specific function of this nucleus is unclear.

Since the discovery of the sexually dimorphic nuclei in rats, other sex differences in hypothalamic anatomy have been identified in rats and in other species (see Swaab & Hofman, 1995; Witelson, 1991). In humans, for example, there are nuclei in the preoptic (Swaab & Fliers, 1985), suprachiasmatic (Swaab et al., 1994), and anterior

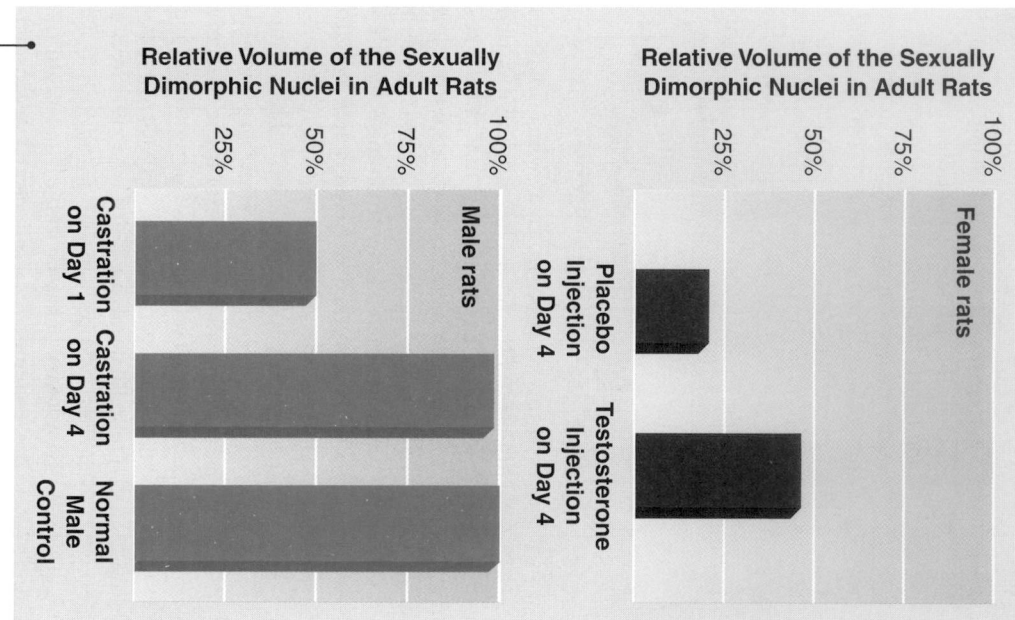

Relative Volume of the Sexually Dimorphic Nuclei in Adult Rats

Female rats

Placebo Injection on Day 4 | Testosterone Injection on Day 4

Relative Volume of the Sexually Dimorphic Nuclei in Adult Rats

Male rats

Castration on Day 1 | Castration on Day 4 | Normal Male Control

25% 50% 75% 100%

FIGURE 13.13 The effects of neonatal testosterone exposure on the size of the sexually dimorphic nuclei in male and female adult rats. (Adapted from Gorski, 1980.)

Evolutionary Perspective

The Hypothalamus and Female Sexual Behavior

The **ventromedial nucleus (VMN)** of the rat hypothalamus contains circuits that appear to be critical for female sexual behavior. Female rats with bilateral lesions of the VMN do not display lordosis, and they are likely to attack suitors who become too ardent.

The following are three recent findings: (1) Extracellular levels of dopamine increase in the male medial preoptic area before and during copulation (Putnam, Sato, & Hull, 2003). (2) Copulatory activity reduces the number of androgen receptors in the male medial preoptic area (Fernández-Guasti, Swaab, & Rodríguez-Manzo, 2003), and blocking androgen receptors in this area prevents copulation (Harding & McGinnis, 2004). (3) Endogenous opioids appear to be released in the male medial preoptic area during copulation (Coolen et al., 2004).

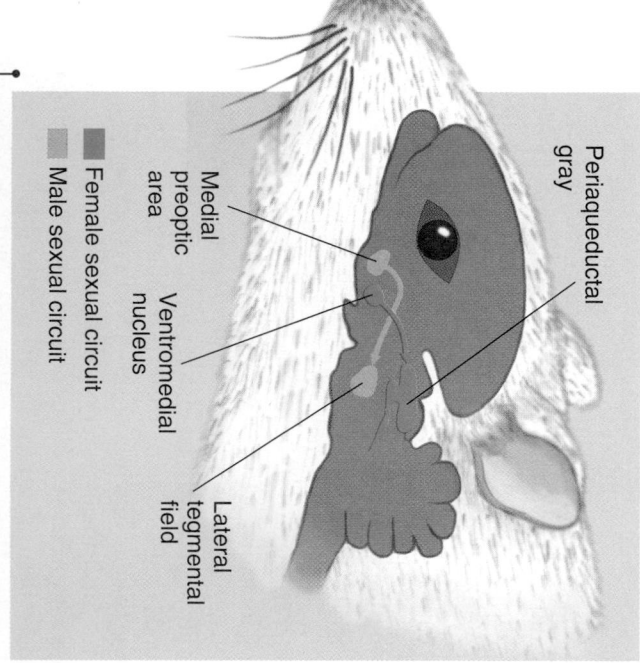

Periaqueductal gray

Medial preoptic area

Ventromedial nucleus

Lateral tegmental field

■ Female sexual circuit
■ Male sexual circuit

FIGURE 13.14 The hypothalamus-tegmentum circuits that play a role in female and male sexual behavior in rats.

You have already learned that an injection of progesterone brings into estrus an ovariectomized female rat that received an injection of estradiol about 36 hours before. Because the progesterone by itself does not induce estrus, the estradiol must in some way prime the nervous system so that the progesterone can exert its effect. This priming effect appears to be mediated by the large increase in the number of *progesterone receptors* that occurs in the VMN and surrounding area following an estradiol injection (Blaustein et al., 1988); the estradiol exerts this effect by entering VMN cells and influencing gene expression. Confirming the role of the VMN in estrus is the fact that microinjections of estradiol and progesterone directly into the VMN induce estrus in ovariectomized female rats (Pleim & Barfield, 1988).

The influence of the VMN on the sexual behavior of female rats appears to be mediated by a tract that descends to the *periaqueductal gray (PAG)* of the tegmentum. Destruction of this tract eliminates female sexual behavior (Hennessey et al., 1990), as do lesions of the PAG itself (Sakuma & Pfaff, 1979).

In conclusion, although many parts of the brain play a role in sexual behavior, much of the research has focused on the role of the hypothalamus in the copulatory behavior of rats. Several areas of the hypothalamus influence this copulatory behavior, and several hypothalamic nuclei are sexually dimorphic in rats, but the medial preoptic area and the ventromedial nucleus are two of the most widely studied. Male rat sexual behavior is influenced by a tract that runs from the medial preoptic area to the lateral tegmental field, and female rat sexual behavior is influenced by a tract that runs from the ventromedial nucleus to the periaqueductal gray (see Figure 13.14).

So far, this chapter has not addressed the topic of sexual orientation. As you know, some people are **heterosexual** (sexually attracted to members of the other sex), some are **homosexual** (sexually attracted to members of the same sex), and some are **bisexual** (sexually attracted to members of both sexes). A discussion of research on sexual orientation is a fitting conclusion to this chapter because it brings together the exception-proves-the-rule and anti-"mamawawa" messages.

Sexual Orientation and Genes

Research has shown that differences in sexual orientation have a genetic basis. For example, Bailey and Pillard (1991) studied a group of male homosexuals who had twin brothers, and they found that 52% of the monozygotic twin brothers and 22% of the dizygotic twin brothers were homosexual. In a comparable study of female twins by the same group of researchers (Bailey et al., 1993), the concordance rates for homosexuality were 48% for monozygotic twins and 16% for dizygotic twins.

Considerable excitement was created by the claim that a gene for male homosexuality had been localized on one end of the X chromosome (Hamer et al., 1993). However, subsequent research has not confirmed this claim.

Sexual Orientation and Early Hormones

Many people mistakenly assume that homosexuals have lower levels of sex hormones. They don't: Heterosexuals and homosexuals do not differ in their levels of circulating hormones. Moreover, orchidectomy reduces the sexual behavior of both heterosexual and homosexual males, but it does not redirect it; and replacement injections simply reactivate the preferences that existed prior to surgery.

Many people also assume that sexual preference is a matter of choice. It isn't: People discover their sexual preferences; they don't choose them. Sexual preferences seem to develop very early, and a child's first indication of the direction of sexual attraction usually does not change as he or she matures. Could perinatal hormone exposure be the early event that shapes sexual orientation?

Efforts to determine whether perinatal hormone levels influence the development of sexual orientation have focused on nonhuman species. A consistent pattern of findings has emerged from this research (see Ellis & Ames, 1987). In rats, hamsters, ferrets, pigs, zebra finches, and dogs, perinatal castration of males and

testosterone treatment of females have been shown to induce same-sex preferences (see Adkins-Regan, 1988; Baum et al., 1990; Hrabovszky & Hutson, 2002).

On the one hand, prudence should be exercised in applying the results of experiments on laboratory species to the development of sexual preferences in humans; it would be a mistake to ignore the profound cognitive and emotional components of human sexuality, which have no counterpart in laboratory animals. On the other hand, it would also be a mistake to think that a pattern of results that runs so consistently through so many mammalian species has no relevance to humans.

Do perinatal hormone levels influence the sexual orientation of adult humans? Although directly relevant evidence is sparse, there are some indications that the answer is yes. The strongest support for this view comes from the quasiexperimental study of Ehrhardt and her colleagues (1985). They interviewed adult women whose mothers had been exposed to *diethylstilbestrol* (a synthetic estrogen) during pregnancy. The subjects' responses indicated that they were significantly more sexually attracted to women than was a group of matched control subjects. Ehrhardt and her colleagues concluded that perinatal estrogen exposure does encourage homosexuality and bisexuality in women but that its effect is relatively weak: The sexual behavior of all but 1 of the 30 subjects was still primarily heterosexual.

What Triggers the Development of Sexual Attraction?

The evidence indicates that most girls and boys living in Western countries experience their first feelings of sexual attraction at about 10 years of age, whether they are heterosexual or homosexual (see Quinsey, 2003). This finding is at odds with the usual assumption that sexual interest is triggered by puberty, which, as you have learned, currently tends to occur at 10.5 years of age in girls and at 11.5 years in boys.

McClintock and Herdt (1996) have suggested that the emergence of sexual attraction may be stimulated by adrenal cortex steroids. Unlike gonadal maturation, adrenal maturation occurs at about the age of 10.

Is There a Difference in the Brains of Homosexuals and Heterosexuals?

The brains of homosexuals and heterosexuals must differ in some way, but how? There have been several reports of neuroanatomical, neuropsychological, and hormonal response differences between homosexuals and heterosexuals (see Gladue, 1994). Most studies have compared

Evolutionary Perspective

male heterosexuals and homosexuals; studies of lesbians are scarce.

In the highly publicized study of LeVay (1991), the structure of one hypothalamic nucleus in male homosexuals was found to be intermediate between that in female heterosexuals and that in male heterosexuals. This study has not been consistently replicated, however. Indeed, no consistent difference between the brains of heterosexuals and homosexuals has been discovered.

Transsexualism

Transsexualism is a disorder of sexual identity in which the individual believes that he or she is trapped in a body of the other sex. To put it mildly, the transsexual faces a bizarre conflict: "I am a woman (or man). Help!" It is important to appreciate the desperation of these individuals; they do not merely think that life might be better if their gender were different. Although many transsexuals do seek *surgical sexual reassignment* (surgery to change their sex), the desperation of these people is better captured by the ways in which some of them dealt with their problem before surgical sexual reassignment was an option: Some biological males (psychological females) attempted self-castration, and others consumed copious quantities of estrogen-containing face creams in order to feminize their bodies.

How does surgical sexual reassignment work? I will describe the male-to-female procedure: The female-to-male procedure is much more complex (because a penis

must be created) and far less satisfactory (for example, because a surgically created penis has no erectile potential), and male-to-female sexual reassignment is three times more prevalent.

The first step in male-to-female reassignment is thorough psychiatric assessment and counseling to establish that the individual is a true transsexual and to prepare "her" for what will follow. Second, a lifelong regimen of estrogen is initiated to feminize the body and maintain the changes. Third, the penis and testes are removed, and female external genitalia and vagina are constructed. The vagina is lined with skin from the penis so that it will have sensory nerve endings that will respond to sexual stimulation. Finally, some patients have cosmetic surgery to feminize the face (e.g., to reduce the size of the Adam's apple). Generally, the adjustment of transsexuals after surgical sexual reassignment is good.

The causes of transsexualism are unknown. Transsexualism was once thought to be a product of social learning, that is, of inappropriate child-rearing practices (e.g., mothers dressing their little boys in dresses). The occasional case that is consistent with this view can be found, but in most cases, there is no obvious cause.

The Independence of Sexual Orientation and Sexual Identity

To complete this chapter, I would like to remind you of two of its main messages and show you how useful they are in thinking about one of the puzzles of human sexuality. One of the two messages is that a knowledge of the mechanisms of a behavior frequently provides us with a greater understanding of that behavior. I hope that you now have a greater understanding of, and acceptance of, differences in human sexuality.

This analysis exemplifies a point I make many times in this book. The study of biopsychology often has important personal and social implications: The search for the neural basis of a behavior frequently provides us with a greater understanding of that behavior. I hope that you now have a greater understanding of, and acceptance of, differences in human sexuality.

Here, I want to focus on the puzzling fact that sexual attraction, sexual identity, and body type are sometimes unrelated. For example, consider transsexuals: They, by definition, have the body type of one sex and the sexual identity of the other sex, but the orientation of their sexual attraction is an independent matter. Some transsexuals with a male body type are sexually attracted to females, others are sexually attracted to males, and others are sexually attracted to neither—and this is not changed by sexual reassignment (see Van Goozen et al., 2002).

Obviously, the mere existence of homosexuality and transsexualism is a challenge to the "mamawawa," the assumption that males and females belong to distinct and opposite categories. Many people tend to think of "femaleness" and "maleness" as being at opposite ends of a continuum, with a few abnormal cases somewhere between the two ideals. Perhaps this is how you tend to think. However, the fact that body type, sexual orientation, and sexual identity are often independent constitutes a serious attack on any assumption that femaleness and maleness lie at opposite ends of a single scale. Clearly, femaleness and maleness each comprise several different attributes (e.g., body type, sexual orientation, and sexual identity), each of which can develop quite independently. This is a real puzzle for many people, including scientists, but what you have learned in this chapter suggests a solution.

Think back to the section on brain differentiation. Until recently, it was assumed that the differentiation of the human brain into its female and male forms occurred through a single testosterone-based mechanism. However, a different notion has developed from recent evidence. Now, it is clear that male and female brains differ in many ways and that the differences develop at different times and by different mechanisms. If you keep this developmental principle in mind, you will have no difficulty understanding how one individual can be female in some ways and male in others.

To put it mildly, the transsexual faces a conflict. Although many transsexuals do seek surgical sexual reassignment, the desperation of these people is better captured by the ways in which some of them dealt with their problem.

Themes Revisited

Three of the book's four major themes were repeatedly emphasized in this chapter: the evolutionary perspective, clinical implications, and thinking-about-biopsychology themes.

The evolutionary theme was pervasive. It received frequent attention because most of the experimental studies of hormones and sex have been conducted in nonhuman species. The other major source of information about hormones and sex has been the study of human clinical cases, which is why the clinical implications theme was prominent in the cases of the woman who wasn't, the little girl who grew into a

boy, the twin who lost his penis, and the man who lost and regained his manhood.

The thinking-about-biopsychology theme was emphasized throughout the chapter because conventional ways of thinking about hormones and sex have often been at odds with the results of biopsychological research. If you are now better able to resist the seductive appeal of the men-are-men-and-women-are-women assumption, you are leaving this chapter a more broadminded and understanding person than when you began it. I hope you have gained an abiding appreciation of the fact that maleness and femaleness are multidimensional and, at times, ambiguous variations of each other.

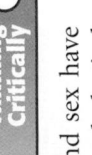

Thinking Critically

ON THE CD

See Hard Copy for additional readings for Chapter 13.

Think about It

ON THE CD

Studying for an exam? Try the Practice Tests for Chapter 13.

1. Over the last century and a half, the onset of puberty has changed from age 15 or 16 to age 10 or 11, but there has been no corresponding acceleration in psychological and intellectual development. Precocious puberty is like a loaded gun in the hand of a child. Discuss.

2. Do you think adult sex change operations should be permitted? Explain.

3. What should be done about the current epidemic of anabolic steroid abuse? Would you make the same recommendation if a safe anabolic steroid were de-

veloped? If a safe drug that would dramatically improve your memory were developed, would you take it?

4. Heterosexuality cannot be understood without studying homosexuality. Discuss.

5. What treatment should be received by infants born with ambiguous external genitals? Why?

6. Sexual orientation, sexual identity, and body type are not always related. Discuss.

Key Terms

Ablatio penis (p. 329)
Adrenal cortex (p. 317)
Adrenocorticotropic hormone (p. 326)
Adrenogenital syndrome (p. 328)
Alpha fetoprotein (p. 324)
Amino acid derivative hormones (p. 315)
Anabolic steroids (p. 332)
Androgenic insensitivity syndrome (p. 328)
Androgens (p. 317)
Androstenedione (p. 327)
Anterior pituitary (p. 317)
Aromatization (p. 324)
Bisexual (p. 337)

Congenital adrenal hyperplasia (p. 328)
Copulation (p. 316)
Defeminizes (p. 325)
Demasculinizes (p. 325)
Dihydrotestosterone (p. 324)
Ejaculation (p. 325)
Endocrine glands (p. 315)
Estradiol (p. 317)
Estrogens (p. 317)
Estrous cycle (p. 332)
Estrus (p. 332)
Exocrine glands (p. 315)
Feminizes (p. 325)
Follicle-stimulating hormone (FSH) (p. 320)

Genitals (p. 323)
Gonadectomy (p. 323)
Gonadotropin-releasing hormone (p. 320)
Gonadotropins (p. 317)
Gonads (p. 316)
Growth hormone (p. 326)
H-Y antigen (p. 321)
Heterosexual (p. 337)
Homosexual (p. 337)
Hormones (p. 315)
Hypothalamopituitary portal system (p. 318)
Impotent (p. 331)
Inhibitory factors (p. 319)
Intromission (p. 325)
Lordosis (p. 325)

Luteinizing hormone (LH) (p. 320)
Masculinizes (p. 325)
Medial preoptic area (p. 334)
Menstrual cycle (p. 317)
Müllerian-inhibiting substance (p. 322)
Müllerian system (p. 322)
Orchidectomy (p. 323)
Ovariectomy (p. 323)
Ovaries (p. 316)
Oxytocin (p. 318)
Paraventricular nuclei (p. 318)
Peptide hormones (p. 315)
Pituitary stalk (p. 317)
Posterior pituitary (p. 317)
Proceptive behaviors (p. 325)

Progesterone (p. 317)
Progestins (p. 317)
Protein hormones (p. 315)
Pulsatile hormone release (p. 320)
Releasing factors (p. 319)
Releasing hormones (p. 320)
Replacement injections (p. 331)
Scrotum (p. 322)

Secondary sex characteristics (p. 326)
Sex chromosomes (p. 316)
Sexually dimorphic nucleus (p. 334)
Steroid hormones (p. 315)
Supraoptic nuclei (p. 318)
Testes (p. 316)
Testosterone (p. 317)

Thyrotropin (p. 319)
Thyrotropin-releasing hormone (p. 319)
Transsexualism (p. 338)
Vasopressin (p. 318)
Ventromedial nucleus (VMN) (p. 336)
Wolffian system (p. 322)
Zygote (p. 316)

www.ablongman.com/pinel6e

ON THE CD

Need some help studying the key terms for this chapter? Check out the electronic flash cards for Chapter 13.

chapter

14

Sleep, Dreaming, and Circadian Rhythms

How Much Do You Need to Sleep?

14.1 The Physiological and Behavioral Events of Sleep

14.2 REM Sleep and Dreaming

14.3 Why Do We Sleep, and Why Do We Sleep When We Do?

14.4 Comparative Analysis of Sleep

14.5 Circadian Sleep Cycles

14.6 Effects of Sleep Deprivation

14.7 Four Areas of the Brain Involved in Sleep

14.8 The Circadian Clock: Neural and Molecular Mechanisms

14.9 Drugs That Affect Sleep

14.10 Sleep Disorders

14.11 The Effects of Long-Term Sleep Reduction

Most of us have a fondness for eating and sex—the two highly esteemed motivated behaviors discussed in Chapters 12 and 13. But the amount of time devoted to these behaviors by even the most amorous gourmands pales in comparison to the amount of time spent sleeping: Most of us will sleep for well over 175,000 hours in our lifetimes.

This extraordinary commitment of time implies that sleep fulfills a critical biological function. But what is it? And what about dreaming: Why do we spend so much time dreaming? And why do we tend to get sleepy at about the same time every day? Answers to these questions await you in this chapter.

Almost every time I give a lecture about sleep, somebody asks "How much sleep do we need?" and each time, I provide the same unsatisfying answer. I explain that there are two fundamentally different answers to this question, but that neither has emerged a clear winner. One answer stresses the presumed health-promoting and recuperative powers of sleep and suggests that people need as much sleep as they can comfortably get. The other answer is that many of us sleep more than we need to and are consequently sleeping part of our lives away. Just think how your life could change if you slept 5 hours per night instead of 8. You would have an extra 21 waking hours each week, a mind-boggling 10,952 hours each decade.

As I prepared to write this chapter, I began to think of some of the personal implications of the idea that we get more sleep than we need. That is when I decided to do something a bit unconventional. While I write this chapter, I am going to be your subject in a sleep-reduction experiment. I am going to try to get no more than 5 hours of sleep per night—11:00 P.M. to 4:00 A.M.—until this chapter is written. As I begin, I am excited by the prospect of having more time to write, but a little worried that this extra time might be obtained at a personal cost that is too dear.

It is now the next day—4:50 Saturday morning to be exact—and I am just beginning to write. There was a party last night, and I didn't make it to bed by 11:00; but considering that I slept for only 3 hours and 35 minutes, I feel quite good. I wonder what I will feel like later in the day. In any case, I will report my experiences to you at the end of the chapter.

The following case study challenges several common beliefs about sleep. Ponder its implications before proceeding into the body of the chapter.

The Case of the Woman Who Wouldn't Sleep

Miss M . . . is a busy lady who finds her ration of twenty-three hours of wakefulness still insufficient for her needs. Even though she is now retired she is still busy in the community; helping sick friends whenever requested. She is an active painter and . . . writer. Although she becomes tired physically, when she needs to sit down to rest her legs, she does not ever report feeling sleepy. During the night she sits on her bed . . . reading, writing, crocheting or painting. At about 2:00 A.M. she falls asleep without any preceding drowsiness often while still holding a book in her hands. When she wakes about an hour later, she feels as wide awake as ever. It would be wrong to say that she woke refreshed because she did not complain of tiredness in the first place.

To test her claim we invited her along to the laboratory. She came willingly but on the first evening we hit our first snag. She announced that she did not sleep at all if she had interesting things to do, and by her reckoning a visit to a university sleep laboratory counted as very interesting. Moreover, for the first time in years, she had someone to talk to for the whole of the night. So we talked.

In the morning we broke into shifts so that some could sleep while at least one person stayed with her and entertained her during the next day. The second night was a repeat performance of the first night. . . . Things had not gone according to plan. So far we were very impressed by her cheerful response to two nights of sleep deprivation, but we had very little by way of hard data to show others.

In the end we prevailed upon her to allow us to apply EEG electrodes and to leave her sitting comfortably on the bed in the bedroom. She had promised that she would co-operate by not resisting sleep although she claimed not to be especially tired. . . . At approximately 1:30 A.M., the EEG record showed the first signs of sleep even though . . . she was still sitting with the book in her hands. . . .

The only substantial difference between her sleep and what we might have expected from any other . . . lady was that it was of short duration. . . . [After 99 minutes], she had no further interest in sleep and asked to . . . join our company again.

(From *The Sleep Instinct*, pp. 42–44, by R. Meddis. Copyright © 1977, Routledge & Kegan Paul, London. Reprinted by permission of the Taylor & Francis Group.)

14.1 The Physiological and Behavioral Events of Sleep

Many changes occur in the body during sleep. This section introduces you to the major ones.

The Three Standard Psychophysiological Measures of Sleep

There are major changes in the human EEG during the course of a night's sleep (Loomis, Harvey, & Hobart, 1936). Although the EEG waves that accompany sleep are generally high-voltage and slow, there are periods throughout the night that are dominated by low-voltage, fast waves similar to those in nonsleeping subjects. In 1953, Aserinsky and Kleitman discovered that *rapid eye movements* (*REMs*) occur under the closed eyelids of sleeping subjects during these periods of low-voltage, fast EEG activity. And in 1962, Berger and Oswald discovered that there is also a loss of electromyographic activity in the neck muscles during these same sleep periods. Subsequently, the **electroencephalogram** (**EEG**), the **electrooculogram** (**EOG**), and the neck **electromyogram** (**EMG**) became the three standard psychophysiological bases for defining stages of sleep (Rechtschaffen & Kales, 1968).

Figure 14.1 depicts a subject participating in a sleep experiment. A subject's first night's sleep in a sleep laboratory is often fitful. That's why it is the usual practice to have each subject sleep several nights in the laboratory before commencing a study. The disturbance of sleep observed during the first night in a sleep laboratory is called the *first-night phenomenon*. It is well known to markers of introductory psychology examinations, because of the creative definitions of it that are offered by students who forget that it is a sleep-related, rather than a sex-related, phenomenon.

Four Stages of Sleep EEG

There are four stages of sleep EEG: stage 1, stage 2, stage 3, and stage 4. Examples of these are presented in Figure 14.2 on page 344.

After the eyes are shut and a person prepares to go to sleep, **alpha waves**—waxing and waning bursts of 8- to 12-Hz EEG waves—begin to punctuate the low-voltage, high-frequency waves of active wakefulness. Then, as the person falls asleep, there is a sudden transition to a period of stage 1 sleep EEG. The stage 1 sleep EEG is a low-voltage, high-frequency signal that is similar to, but slower than, that of active wakefulness.

There is a gradual increase in EEG voltage and a decrease in EEG frequency as the person progresses from stage 1 sleep through stages 2, 3, and 4. Accordingly, the stage 2 sleep EEG has a slightly higher amplitude and a lower frequency than the stage 1 EEG; in addition, it is punctuated by two characteristic wave forms: K complexes and sleep spindles. Each *K complex* is a single large negative wave (upward deflection) followed immediately by a single large positive wave (downward deflection). Each *sleep spindle* is a 1- to 2-second waxing and waning burst of 12- to 14-Hz waves. The stage 3 sleep EEG is defined by the occasional presence of **delta waves**—the largest and slowest EEG waves, with a frequency of 1 to 2 Hz—whereas the stage 4 sleep EEG is defined by a predominance of delta waves.

Once subjects reach stage 4 EEG sleep, they stay there for a time, and then they retreat back through the stages of sleep to stage 1. However, when they return to stage 1, things are not at all the same as they were the first time through. The first period of stage 1 EEG during a night's sleep (**initial stage 1 EEG**) is not marked by any striking electromyographic or electrooculographic changes, whereas subsequent periods of stage 1 sleep EEG (**emergent stage 1 EEG**) are accompanied by REMs and by a loss of tone in the muscles of the body core.

After the first cycle of sleep EEG—from initial stage 1 to stage 4 and back to emergent stage 1—the rest of the night is spent going back and forth through the stages. Figure 14.3 on page 344 illustrates the EEG cycles of a typical night's sleep and the close relation between

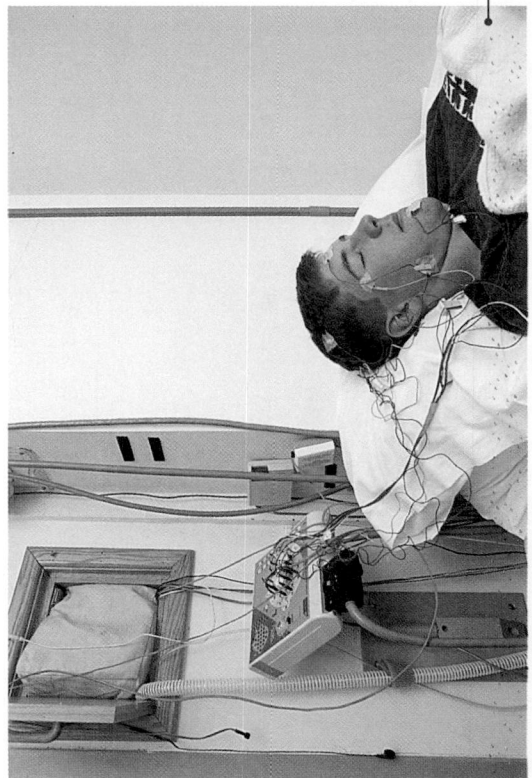

FIGURE 14.1 A subject participating in a sleep experiment.

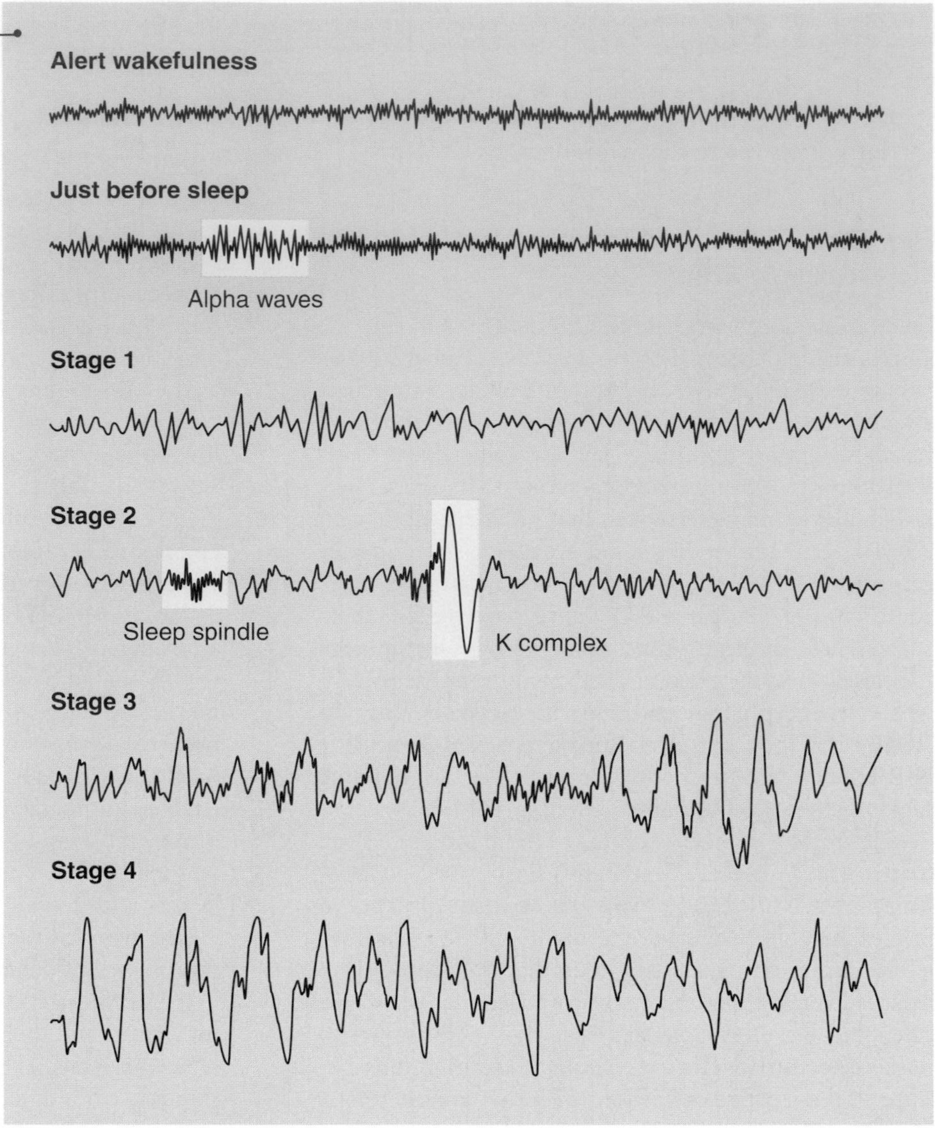

FIGURE 14.2 The EEG of alert wakefulness, the EEG that precedes sleep onset, and the four stages of sleep EEG. Each trace is about 10 seconds long.

Alert wakefulness

Just before sleep

Alpha waves

Stage 1

Stage 2

Sleep spindle

K complex

Stage 3

Stage 4

www.ablongman.com/pinel6e

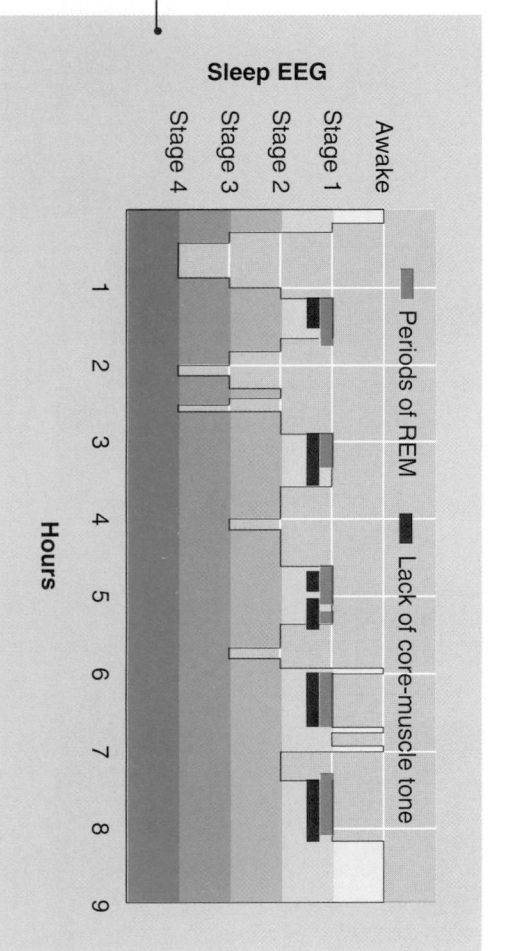

FIGURE 14.3 The course of EEG stages during a typical night's sleep and the relation of emergent stage 1 EEG to REMs and lack of tone in core muscles.

Sleep EEG

Awake
Stage 1
Stage 2
Stage 3
Stage 4

Periods of REM

Lack of core-muscle tone

Hours

1   2   3   4   5   6   7   8   9

emergent stage 1 sleep, REMs, and the loss of tone in core muscles. Notice that each cycle tends to be about 90 minutes long and that, as the night progresses, more and more time is spent in emergent stage 1 sleep, and less and less time is spent in the other stages, particularly stage 4. Notice also that there are brief periods during the night when the subject is awake; these periods of wakefulness are usually not remembered in the morning.

Let's pause here to get some sleep-stage terms straight. The sleep associated with emergent stage 1 EEG is usually called **REM sleep**, (pronounced "rehm"), after the associated rapid eye movements; whereas all other stages of sleep together are called *NREM sleep* (non-REM sleep). Stages 3 and 4 together are referred to as **slow-wave sleep (SWS)**, after the delta waves that characterize them.

REMs, loss of core-muscle tone, and a low-amplitude, high-frequency EEG are not the only physiological correlates of REM sleep. Cerebral activity (e.g., oxygen consumption, blood flow, and neural firing) increases to waking levels in many brain structures, and there is a general increase in autonomic nervous system activity (e.g., in blood pressure, pulse, and respiration). Also, the muscles of the extremities occasionally twitch, and there is always some degree of clitoral or penile erection.

14.2 REM Sleep and Dreaming

Nathaniel Kleitman's laboratory was an exciting place in 1953. Kleitman's students had just discovered REM sleep, and they were driven by the fascinating implication of their discovery. With the exception of the loss of tone in the core muscles, all of the other measures suggested that REM sleep episodes were emotion-charged. Could REM sleep be the physiological correlate of dreaming? Could it provide researchers with a window into the subjective inner world of dreams? The researchers began by waking a few subjects in the middle of REM episodes and asking them if they had been dreaming. The results were remarkable:

The vivid recall that could be elicited in the middle of the night when a subject was awakened while his eyes were moving rapidly was nothing short of miraculous. It [seemed to open] ... an exciting new world to the subjects whose only previous dream memories had been the vague morning-after recall. Now, instead of perhaps some fleeting glimpse into the dream world each night, the subjects could be tuned into the middle of as many as ten or twelve dreams every night. (From *Some Must Watch While Some Must Sleep* by William E. Dement, Portable Stanford Books, Stanford Alumni Association, Stanford University, 1978, p. 37.)

Strong support for the theory that REM sleep is the physiological correlate of dreaming came from the observation that 80% of awakenings from NREM (non-REM) sleep led to dream recall. The dreams recalled from NREM sleep tended to be individual experiences (e.g., "I was falling"), unlike the stories associated with REM sleep. The phenomenon of dreaming, which for centuries had been the subject of wild speculation, was finally rendered accessible to scientific investigation. The following anecdote related by Dement (1978) communicates some of the excitement felt by those involved in the discovery:

I decided to be a subject primarily out of envy; having listened with amazement and awe as many subjects recounted their dreams, I wished to enjoy the experience myself....

A hastily trained medical student ... was monitoring the EEG and supervising my arousals. I went to sleep prepared for an exciting night and woke up with a certain urgency.... I searched my mind.... I could remember nothing.... So I went back to sleep and was suddenly aware of being wrenched from the void once again. This time I could remember nothing except a very, very vague feeling of a name or a person....

The next time I was jolted awake—still unable to recall anything—I began to worry. Why didn't I remember a dream? I had expected to dazzle the medical student with my brilliant recall! After a fourth and fifth awakening with exactly the same results, I was really upset....

The experience had left me exhausted and extremely puzzled, and I was anxious to look at the polygraphic record of my miserable night. Upon examining the record I discovered, to my utter delight and relief, that the medical student had been mistakenly arousing me in NREM. Not once had I awakened during a REM period....

The next night, with additional instruction ... the medical student hit the REM periods right on the button, and vivid recall flooded my mind with each awakening. (From *Some Must Watch While Some Must Sleep* by William E. Dement, Portable Stanford Books, Stanford Alumni Association, Stanford University, 1978, pp. 38–39.)

Testing Common Beliefs about Dreaming

The high correlation between REM sleep and dream recall provided an opportunity to test some common beliefs about dreaming. The following are five such beliefs that have been subjected to empirical tests.

1. Many people believe that external stimuli can become incorporated into their dreams. Dement and Wolpert (1958) sprayed water on sleeping subjects after they had been in REM sleep for a few minutes, and a few seconds after the spray, each subject was awakened. In 14 of 33 cases, the water was incorporated into the

dream report. The following narrative was reported by a subject who had been dreaming that he was acting in a play:

> I was walking behind the leading lady when she suddenly collapsed and water was dripping on her. I ran over to her and water was dripping on my back and head. The roof was leaking... I looked up and there was a hole in the roof. I dragged her over to the side of the stage and began pulling the curtains. Then I woke up. (p. 550)

2. Some people believe that dreams last only an instant, but research suggests that dreams run on "real time." In one study (Dement & Kleitman, 1957), subjects were awakened 5 or 15 minutes after the beginning of a REM episode and asked to decide on the basis of the duration of the events in their dreams whether they had been dreaming for 5 or 15 minutes. They were correct in 92 of 111 cases.

3. Some people claim that they do not dream. However, these people have just as much REM sleep as normal dreamers. Moreover, they report dreams if they are awakened during REM episodes (Goodenough et al., 1959), although they do so less frequently than do normal dreamers.

4. Penile erections are commonly assumed to be indicative of dreams with sexual content. However, erections are no more complete during dreams with frank sexual content than during those without it (Karacan et al., 1966). Even babies have REM-related penile erections.

5. Most people believe that sleeptalking and **somnambulism** (sleepwalking) occur during dreams. This is not so; sleeptalking and somnambulism occur least frequently during dreaming, when core muscles tend to be totally relaxed. They occur most frequently during stage 4 sleep.

The Interpretation of Dreams

The idea that dreams are disguised messages has a long history. For example, the Bible describes how a dream of seven lean cattle following and devouring seven fat cattle warned that seven years of famine would follow seven years of plenty. It was Freud's theory of dreams that refined this view of dreams and gave it legitimacy.

Freud believed that dreams are triggered by unacceptable repressed wishes, often of a sexual nature. He argued that because dreams represent unacceptable wishes, the dreams we experience (our *manifest dreams*) are merely disguised versions of our real dreams (our *latent dreams*): An unconscious censor disguises and subtracts information from our real dreams so that we can endure them. Freud thus concluded that one of the keys to understanding people and dealing with their psychological problems is to expose the meaning of their latent dreams through the interpretation of their manifest dreams.

There is no convincing evidence for the Freudian theory of dreams; indeed, the brain science of the 1890s, which served as its foundation, is now obsolete. Nevertheless, the Freudian theory of dreams has been the basis for many interesting stories; as a result, it continues to be widely disseminated to the general public through the entertainment and communication media as if it were fact. Consequently, even today, the Freudian theory of dreams is deeply ingrained in many people's thinking. Many accept the notion that dreams bubble up from a troubled subconscious and that they represent repressed thoughts and wishes.

The modern alternative to the Freudian theory of dreams is Hobson's (1989) activation-synthesis theory. It is based on the observation that, during REM sleep, many brain-stem circuits become active and bombard the cerebral cortex with neural signals. The essence of the **activation-synthesis theory** is that the information supplied to the cortex during REM sleep is largely random and that the resulting dream is the cortex's effort to make sense of these random signals.

Activation-synthesis theory does not deny that dreams have meaning, but it differs from Freudian theory in terms of where that meaning lies. Hobson's dreamers reveal themselves by what they add to the random jumble of brain-stem signals in order to create a coherent story, not by the painful hidden messages contained in their dreams.

Lucid Dreams

The reality of dreams is usually quite distinct from the reality of consciousness (see Williams et al., 1992). However, some people claim that they have dreams, called **lucid dreams**, in which this distinction becomes blurred. These are dreams in which the dreamer is aware at the time that she or he is dreaming and can influence the course of the dream. The experience of a lucid dream is something like being awake in a dream (see Blackmore, 1991).

Support for the existence of lucid dreams has come from demonstrations in which a few sleeping subjects have purportedly signaled to the experimenter from their dreams (by a prearranged signal). For example, in one study, the subject was instructed to draw large triangles with his right arm as soon as he got into a dream and to signal to the experimenter with eye movements just before he drew each triangle. EMG activity that was consistent with triangle drawing was recorded from the right forearm each time the eye-movement signal was received (Schatzman, Worsley, & Fenwick, 1988). In another study, a woman who could create various positive sexual encounters in her lucid dreams was found to experience real physiological orgasms during some dream encounters (LaBerge, Greenleaf, & Kedzierski, 1983). However, the evidence for the existence of lucid dreams remains sparse, and I remain skeptical, but interested, until more evidence emerges.

14.3 Why Do We Sleep, and Why Do We Sleep When We Do?

Now that you have been introduced to the properties of sleep and its various stages, the focus of this chapter shifts to a consideration of two fundamental questions about sleep: Why do we sleep? And why do we sleep when we do? The first question deals with the functions of sleep; the second deals with its timing and duration.

Two kinds of theories for sleep have been proposed: *recuperation theories* and *circadian theories*. The differences between these two theoretical approaches are revealed by the answers they offer to the two fundamental questions about sleep.

The essence of **recuperation theories of sleep** is that being awake disrupts the *homeostasis* (internal physiological stability) of the body in some way and sleep is required to restore it. Various recuperation theories differ in terms of the particular physiological disruption they propose as the trigger for sleep—for example, it is commonly believed that the function of sleep is to restore energy levels. However, regardless of the particular function postulated by restoration theories of sleep, they all imply that sleepiness is triggered by a deviation from homeostasis caused by wakefulness and that sleep is terminated by a return to homeostasis.

The essence of **circadian theories of sleep** is that sleep is not a reaction to the disruptive effects of being awake but the result of an internal timing mechanism— that is, we humans are all programmed to sleep at night regardless of what happens to us during the day. According to these theories, we have evolved to sleep at night because sleep protects us from accident and predation during the night. (Remember that humans evolved long before the advent of artificial lighting.)

Circadian theories of sleep focus more on when we sleep than on the function of sleep. However, one extreme version of a circadian theory proposes that sleep plays no role in the efficient physiological functioning of the body. According to this theory, early humans had enough time to get their eating, drinking, and reproducing out of the way during the daytime, and their strong motivation to sleep at night evolved to conserve their energy resources and to make them less susceptible to mishap (e.g., predation) in the dark. This theory suggests that sleep is like reproductive behavior in the sense that we are highly motivated to engage in it, but we don't need it to stay healthy.

Some metaphors may help you think about the difference between the recuperation and circadian approaches to sleep. In essence, recuperation theories view sleep as a nightly repairperson who fixes damage produced by wakefulness, while circadian theories regard sleep as a strict parent who demands inactivity because it keeps us out of trouble.

Choosing between the recuperation and circadian approaches is the logical first step in the search for the physiological basis of sleep. Is the sleep system run by a biological clock that produces compelling urges to sleep at certain times of the day, perhaps to conserve energy and protect us from mishap; or is it a homeostatic system whose function is to correct some adverse consequence of staying awake? Several lines of research that have a bearing on the answer to this question will be discussed in the sections that follow.

14.4 Comparative Analysis of Sleep

All mammals and birds sleep, and their sleep is much like ours—characterized by high-amplitude, low-frequency EEG waves punctuated by periods of low-amplitude, high-frequency waves (see Winson, 1993). Even fish, reptiles, amphibians, and insects go through periods of inactivity and unresponsiveness that are similar to mammalian sleep (e.g., Shaw et al., 2000). Table 14.1 on page 348 gives the average number of hours per day that various mammalian species spend sleeping.

The comparative investigation of sleep has led to several important conclusions. Let's consider four of these.

First, the fact that all mammals and birds sleep suggests that sleep serves some important physiological function, rather than merely protecting animals from

mishap and conserving energy. The evidence is strongest in species that are at increased risk of predation when they sleep (e.g., antelopes) and in species that have evolved complex mechanisms that enable them to sleep. For example, some marine mammals, such as dolphins, sleep with only half of their brain at a time so that the other half can control resurfacing for air (see Rattenborg, Amlaner, & Lima, 2000). It is against the logic of natural selection for some animals to risk predation while sleeping and for others to have evolved complex mechanisms to permit them to sleep unless sleep itself serves some critical function (Rechtschaffen, 1998).

Second, the fact that all mammals and birds sleep suggests that the function of sleep is not some special, higher-order human function. For example, suggestions that sleep helps humans reprogram our complex brains

TABLE 14.1 The Average Number of Hours Slept per Day by Various Mammalian Species

MAMMALIAN SPECIES	HOURS OF SLEEP PER DAY
Giant sloth	20
Opossum, brown bat	19
Giant armadillo	18
Owl monkey, nine-banded armadillo	17
Arctic ground squirrel	16
Tree shrew	15
Cat, golden hamster	14
Mouse, rat, gray wolf, ground squirrel	13
Arctic fox, chinchilla, gorilla, raccoon	12
Mountain beaver	11
Jaguar, vervet monkey, hedgehog	10
Rhesus monkey, chimpanzee, baboon, red fox	9
Human, rabbit, guinea pig, pig	8
Gray seal, gray hyrax, Brazilian tapir	6
Tree hyrax, rock hyrax	5
Cow, goat, elephant, donkey, sheep	3
Roe deer, horse	2

or that it permits some kind of emotional release to maintain our mental health seem to be ruled out by the comparative evidence.

Third, the large between-species differences in sleep time suggest that although sleep may be essential for survival, it is not necessarily needed in large quantities (refer to Table 14.1). Horses and many other animals get by quite nicely on 2 or 3 hours of sleep per day.

Fourth, many studies have tried to identify some characteristic that identifies various species as long sleepers or short sleepers. Why do cats tend to sleep about 14

hours a day and horses only about 2? Under the influence of recuperation theories, researchers have focused on energy-related factors in their efforts. However, there is no clear relationship between a species' sleep time and its level of activity, its body size, or its body temperature. The fact that giant sloths sleep 20 hours per day is a strong argument against the theory that sleep is a compensatory reaction to energy expenditure. In contrast, circadian theories correctly predict that the daily sleep time of each species is related to how vulnerable it is while it is asleep and how much time it must spend each day to feed itself and to take care of its other survival requirements. For example, zebras must graze almost continuously to get enough to eat and are extremely vulnerable to predatory attack when they are asleep—and they sleep only about 2 hours per day. In contrast, African lions often sleep more or less continuously for 2 or 3 days after they have gorged themselves on a kill. Figure 14.4 says it all.

FIGURE 14.4 After gorging themselves on a kill, African lions often sleep almost continuously for 2 or 3 days. And where do they sleep? Anywhere they want!

14.5 Circadian Sleep Cycles

The world in which we live cycles from light to dark and back again once every 24 hours, and most surface-dwelling species have adapted to this regular change in their environment by developing a variety of so-called **circadian rhythms** (see Foster & Kreitzman, 2004). (*Circadian* means "lasting about 1 day.") For example, most species display a regular circadian sleep-wake cycle. Humans take advantage of the light of day to take care of their biological needs, and then they sleep for much of the night; *nocturnal animals*, such as rats, sleep for much of the day and stay awake at night.

Although the sleep-wake cycle is the most obvious circadian rhythm, it is virtually impossible to find a physiological, biochemical, or behavioral process in animals that does not display some measure of circadian rhythmicity. Each day, our bodies adjust themselves in a variety of ways to meet the demands of the two environments in which we live: light and dark.

Our circadian cycles are kept on their once-every-24-hours schedule by temporal cues in the environment. The most important of these cues for the regulation of mammalian circadian rhythms is the daily cycle of light and dark. Environmental cues, such as the light–dark cycle, that can *entrain* (control the timing of) circadian rhythms are called **zeitgebers** (pronounced "ZITE-gay-bers"), a German word that means "time givers." In controlled laboratory environments, it is possible to lengthen or shorten circadian cycles by adjusting the duration of the light–dark cycle; for example, when exposed to alternating 10-hour periods of light and 10-hour periods of dark, subjects' circadian cycles begin to conform to a 20-hour day. In a world without 24-hour cycles of light and dark, other *zeitgebers* can entrain circadian cycles. For example, the circadian sleep–wake cycles of hamsters living in continuous darkness or in continuous light can be entrained by regular daily bouts of social interaction, hoarding, eating, or exercise (see Mistlberger, 1994; Mistlberger et al., 1996; Sinclair & Mistlberger, 1997). Hamsters display particularly clear circadian cycles and thus are frequent subjects of research on circadian rhythms.

Free-Running Circadian Sleep–Wake Cycles

The study of sleep in the absence of *zeitgebers* provides a powerful method for studying regulation of the temporal pattern of sleep. What happens to sleep–wake cycles and other circadian rhythms in an environment that is devoid of *zeitgebers*? Remarkably, under conditions in which there are absolutely no temporal cues, humans and other animals maintain all of their circadian rhythms. Circadian rhythms in constant environments are said to be **free-running rhythms,** and their duration is called the **free-running period.** Free running periods vary in length from subject to subject, are of relatively constant duration within a given subject, and are usually longer than 24 hours—about 25 hours in most humans (see Lavie, 2001). It seems that we all have an internal *biological clock* that habitually runs a little slow unless it is entrained by time-related cues in the environment. A typical free-running circadian sleep–wake cycle is illustrated in Figure 14.5. Notice its regularity. Without any external cues, this man fell asleep approximately every 25.3 hours for an entire month.

Perhaps the most remarkable characteristic of free-running circadian cycles is that they do not have to be learned. Even rats that are born and raised in an unchanging laboratory environment (in continuous light or in continuous darkness) display regular free-running sleep–wake cycles of about 25 hours (Richter, 1971).

Many animals display a circadian cycle of body temperature that is related to their circadian sleep–wake cycle: They tend to sleep during the falling phase of their circadian body temperature cycle and awaken during its rising phase. However, when subjects are housed in constant laboratory environments, their sleep–wake and body temperature cycles sometimes break away from one another. This phenomenon is called **internal desynchronization.**

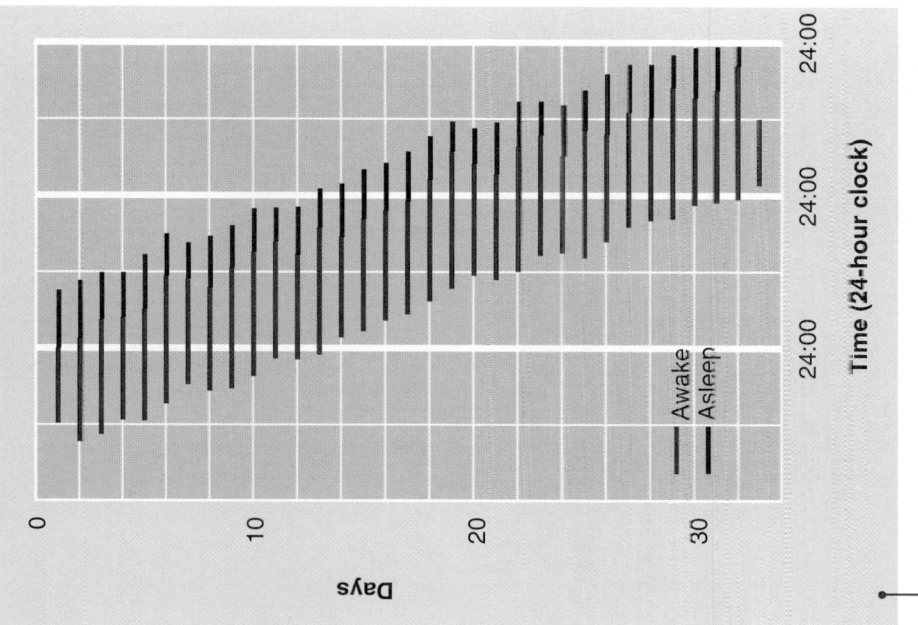

FIGURE 14.5 A free-running circadian sleep–wake cycle 25.3 hours in duration. Despite living in an unchanging environment with no time cues, the subject went to sleep each day approximately 1.3 hours later than he had the day before. (Adapted from Wever, 1979, p. 30.)

For example, in one case, the free running periods of *both* the sleep–wake and body temperature cycles of a human subject were initially 25.7 hours; then, for some unknown reason, there was an increase in the free-running period of the sleep–wake cycle to 33.4 hours and a decrease in the free-running period of the body temperature cycle to 25.1 hours. The potential for the simultaneous existence of two different free-running periods suggests that there is more than one circadian timing mechanism, and that sleep is not causally related to the decreases in body temperature that are normally associated with it.

So, what has research on circadian sleep–wake cycles taught us about the function of sleep? The fact that the regularity of the free-running period of such cycles is maintained despite day-to-day variations in physical and mental activity provides strong support for the dominance of circadian factors over recuperative factors in the regulation of sleep. Indeed, there have been several attempts to change the timing of sleep in both human and nonhuman subjects by having them engage in intensive physical or mental activity or by exposing them to infectious physical or mental agents, but these attempts have had little, if any, effect on the subjects' subsequent sleep (see Rechtschaffen, 1998).

There is another point about free-running circadian sleep–wake cycles that is incompatible with recuperative theories of sleep. On occasions when subjects stay awake longer than usual, the following sleep time is shorter rather than longer (Wever, 1979). Humans and other animals are programmed to have sleep–wake cycles of approximately 24 hours; hence, the more wakefulness there is during a cycle, the less time there is for sleep.

Jet Lag and Shift Work

People in modern industrialized societies are faced with two different disruptions of circadian rhythmicity: jet lag and shift work. **Jet lag** occurs when the *zeitgebers* that control the phases of various circadian rhythms are accelerated during east-bound flights (*phase advances*) or decelerated during west-bound flights (*phase delays*). In *shift work*, the *zeitgebers* stay the same, but workers are forced to adjust their natural sleep–wake cycles in order to meet the demands of changing work schedules. Both of these disruptions produce sleep disturbances, fatigue, general malaise, and deficits on tests of physical and cognitive function. The disturbances can last for many days; for example, it typically takes about 10 days to complete-

ly adjust to a Tokyo-to-Boston flight—a phase advance of 10.5 hours.

What can be done to reduce the disruptive effects of jet lag and shift work? Two behavioral approaches have been proposed for the reduction of jet lag. One is gradually shifting one's sleep–wake cycle in the days prior to the flight. The other is administering treatments after the flight that promote the required shift in the circadian rhythm. For example, exposure to intense light early in the morning following an east-bound flight accelerates adaptation to the phase advance. Similarly, the results of a study of hamsters (Mrosovsky & Salmon, 1987) suggest that a good workout early in the morning of the first day after an east-bound flight might accelerate adaptation to the phase advance; hamsters that engaged in one 3-hour bout of wheel running 7 hours before their usual period of activity adapted quickly to an 8-hour advance in their light-dark cycle (see Figure 14.6).

Companies that employ shift workers have had great success in improving the productivity and job satisfaction of those workers by scheduling phase delays rather than phase advances; whenever possible, shift workers are transferred from their current schedule to one that begins later in the day. It is much more difficult to go to sleep 4 hours earlier and get up 4 hours earlier (a phase advance) than it is to go to sleep 4 hours later and get up 4 hours later (a phase delay). That is why east-bound flights tend to be more problematic for travelers than west-bound flights.

14.6 Effects of Sleep Deprivation

Recuperation theories of sleep make specific predictions about the effects of sleep deprivation. Because recuperation theories are based on the premise that sleep is a response to the accumulation of some debilitating effect of wakefulness, they predict (1) that long periods of wakefulness will produce physiological and behavioral disturbances, (2) that these disturbances will grow steadily worse as the sleep deprivation continues, and (3) that after a period of deprivation has ended, much of the missed sleep will be regained. Have these predictions been confirmed?

This section begins with a cautionary note about the personal experience of sleep deprivation. It next presents two classic sleep-deprivation case studies. Then, the major findings of sleep-deprivation studies in humans and laboratory animals are summarized. Finally, the evidence that sleep tends to become more efficient as a result of sleep deprivation is reviewed.

Personal Experience of Sleep Deprivation: A Cautionary Note

I am sure that you have experienced the negative effects of sleep deprivation. When you sleep substantially less

than you are used to, the next day you feel crabby and unable to function as well as you usually do. Although such experiences of sleep deprivation are compelling, you need to be cautious in interpreting your own experiences and the similar experiences of others. Let me illustrate this point by referring to a recurring news story.

Every few months, I see on the television news or read in the newspaper that most people need more sleep. To support this contention, an "expert" explains that many people in modern society work such long, irregular hours that they do not sleep enough and suffer all kinds of adverse effects as a result. To make this point, there are typically a few interviews with people such as long-distance truck drivers and shift workers who describe their sleep-related experiences. Two things never seem to occur to the news reporters or to the "expert." First, it never occurs to them that people who sleep little or irregularly do so because they are under stress. Second, it never occurs to them that most people who are forced to change their schedule of sleep also experience a major disruption of their circadian rhythms. Accordingly, stress and circadian disruptions might be responsible for, or at least contrib-

Thinking Critically

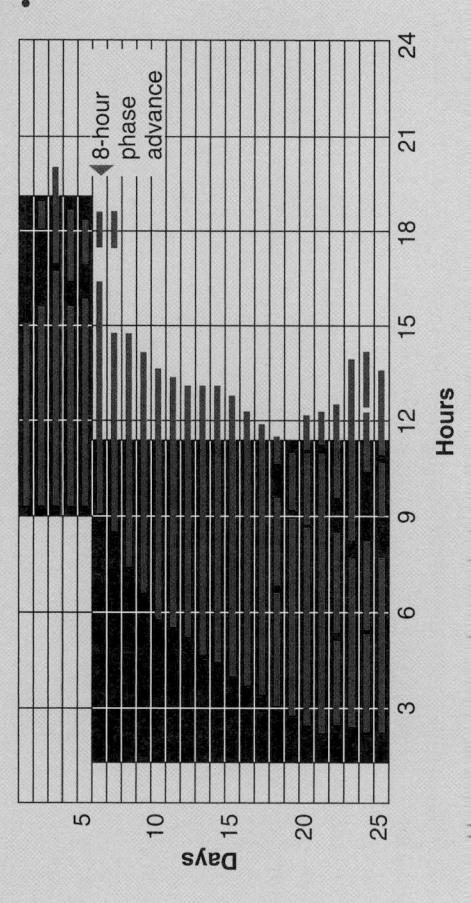

Hamsters were active each day during the 10-hour dark phase of their light-dark cycle (activity shown in red and darkness shown in black). Then, the light-dark cycle was advanced by 8 hours. The hamster circadian activity cycle gradually adapted to the phase advance over the ensuing 10 days.

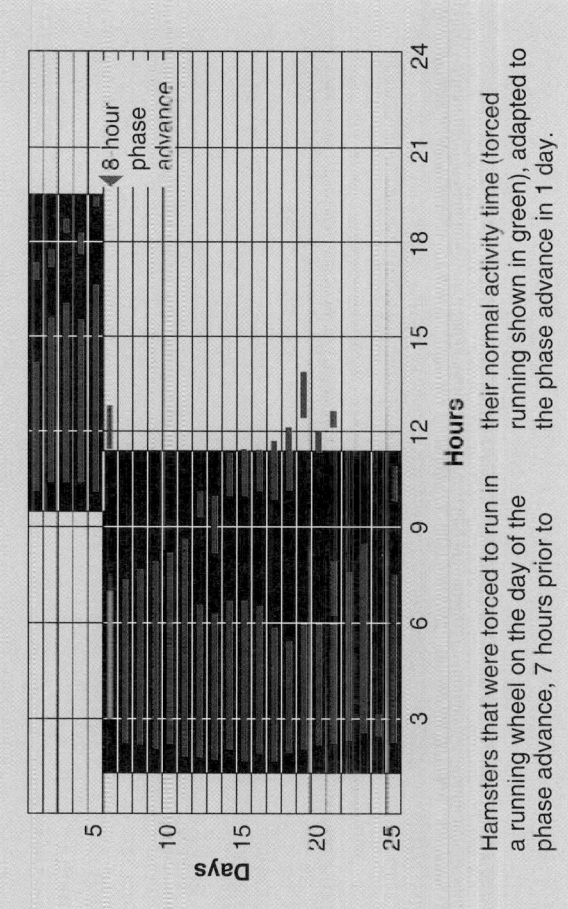

Hamsters that were forced to run in a running wheel on the day of the phase advance, 7 hours prior to their normal activity time (forced running shown in green), adapted to the phase advance in 1 day.

FIGURE 14.6 A period of forced exercise accelerates adaptation to an 8-hour phase advance in the circadian light-dark cycle. Daily activity is shown in red; periods of darkness are shown in black; and the period of forced exercise is shown in green. (Adapted from Mrosovsky & Salmon, 1987.)

ute to, many of the adverse effects commonly attributed to loss of sleep (see Taub & Berger, 1973).

Compounding these two possible causes is the fact that people have proven to be poor judges of the impact of sleep deprivation on their performance. Both types of errors have been reported: In some cases, people claim that they cannot function after sleep loss but perform without decrement; in other cases, people claim that sleep loss has not adversely affected their performance when the data tell a different story.

Consequently, your own experiences of sleep loss and the testimonials of others who have experienced sleep loss need to be interpreted cautiously. Documenting the effects of sleep loss requires systematic research.

Two Classic Sleep-Deprivation Case Studies

Let's begin our consideration of the research on sleep deprivation by looking at two classic case studies. First is the case study of a group of sleep-deprived students, described by Kleitman (1963); second is the case of Randy Gardner, described by Dement (1978).

The Case of the Sleep-Deprived Students

While there were differences in the many subjective experiences of the sleep-evading persons, there were several features common to most. . . . [D]uring the first night the subject did not feel very tired or sleepy. He could read or study or do laboratory work, without much attention from the watcher, but usually felt an attack of drowsiness between 3 A.M. and 6 A.M. . . . Next morning the subject felt well, except for a slight malaise which always appeared on sitting down and resting for any length of time. However, if he occupied himself with his ordinary daily tasks, he was likely to forget having spent a sleepless night. During the second night . . . reading or study was next to impossible because sitting quietly was conducive to even greater sleepiness. As during the first night, there came a 2–3 hour period in the early hours of the morning when the desire for sleep was almost overpowering. . . . Later in the morning the sleepiness diminished once more, and the subject could perform routine laboratory work, as usual. It was not safe for him to sit down, however, without danger of falling asleep, particularly if he attended lectures. . . .

The third night resembled the second, and the fourth day was like the third. . . . At the end of that time the individual was as sleepy as he was likely to be. Those who continued to stay awake experienced the wavelike increase and decrease in sleepiness with the greatest drowsiness at about the same time every night. (Kleitman, 1963, pp. 220–221)

The Case of Randy Gardner

As part of a 1965 science fair project, Randy Gardner and two classmates, who were entrusted with keeping him awake, planned to break the then world record of 260 hours of consecutive wakefulness. Dement read about the project in the newspaper and, seeing an opportunity to collect some important data, joined the team, much to the comfort of Randy's worried parents. Randy proved to be a friendly and cooperative subject, although he did complain vigorously when his team would not permit him to close his eyes for more than a few seconds at a time. However, in no sense could Randy's behavior be considered abnormal or disturbed. Near the end of his vigil, Randy held a press conference attended by reporters and television crews from all over the United States, and he conducted himself impeccably. When asked how he had managed to stay awake for 11 days, he replied politely, "It's just mind over matter." Randy went to sleep exactly 264 hours and 12 minutes after his alarm clock

had awakened him 11 days before. And how long did he sleep? Only 14 hours the first night, and thereafter he returned to his usual 8-hour schedule. Although it may seem amazing that Randy did not have to sleep longer to "catch up" on his lost sleep, the lack of substantial recovery sleep is typical of such cases (Dement, 1978).

Mrs. Maureen Weston later supplanted Randy Gardner in the *Guinness Book of World Records*. During a rocking-chair marathon in 1977, Mrs. Weston kept rocking for 449 hours (18 days, 17 hours)—an impressive bit of "rocking around the clock." By the way, my own modest program of sleep reduction is now in its 10th day.

Experimental Studies of Sleep Deprivation in Humans

Investigations have assessed the effects on human subjects of sleep-deprivation schedules ranging from a slightly reduced amount of sleep during one night to total sleep deprivation for several nights, and they have assessed the effects of these schedules on dozens of different objective measures: measures of sleepiness, mood, cognition, motor performance, and physiological function.

Even moderate amounts of sleep deprivation—for example, 3 or 4 hours in one night—have been found to have three consistent effects. First, sleep-deprived subjects display an increase in sleepiness: They report being more sleepy, and they fall asleep more quickly if given the opportunity. Second, sleep-deprived subjects display disturbances on various written tests of mood. And third, they perform poorly on tests of vigilance, such as listening to a series of tones and responding when one differs slightly from the rest.

After 2 or 3 days of continuous sleep deprivation, subjects experience microsleeps. **Microsleeps** are brief periods of sleep, typically about 2 or 3 seconds long, during which the eyelids droop and the subjects become less responsive to external stimuli, even though they remain sitting or standing. Microsleeps disrupt performance on passive tests, such as tests of vigilance, but they are not necessary for such performance deficits to occur (Dinges et al., 1997; Ferrara, De Gennaro, & Bertini, 1999).

Remarkably, the effects of sleep deprivation on complex cognitive function, motor performance, and physiological function have been much less consistent. Deficits have been observed in some studies but not in others, even after lengthy periods of deprivation (e.g., Bonnet & Arand, 1996; Harrison & Horne, 1997; Dinges et al., 1997; Gillberg et al., 1996; Mar-tin, 1986) concluded that adverse physiological changes following sleep deprivation have yet to be convincingly documented; VanHelder and Radomski (1989) found that periods of sleep deprivation lasting up to 72 hours had no effect on physical strength or motor performance, except for reducing time to exhaustion; and active tests of complex cognitive ability (such as IQ tests) have proven to be largely immune to disruption by sleep deprivation (Binks, Waters, & Hurry, 1999; Percival, Horne, & Tilley, 1983). It should be pointed out, however, that although performance on intelligence tests is influenced little by sleep deprivation, Horne (1983) found that 32 hours of sleep deprivation greatly disrupted subjects' performance on several tests expressly designed to measure creativity.

To put sleep deprivation in context, I like to compare it to deprivation of the motivated behaviors discussed in Chapters 12 and 13. If subjects were deprived of the opportunity to eat or engage in sexual activity, the effects would be severe and unavoidable: In the first case, starvation and death would ensue; in the second, there would be a total loss of reproductive capacity. There have been no such dramatic effects reported in sleep-deprivation studies. Indeed, as you are about to learn, none of the three major predictions of the recuperation approach to understanding sleep has been confirmed.

Sleep-Deprivation Studies with Laboratory Animals

Studies using a **carousel apparatus** (see Figure 14.7) to deprive rats of sleep suggest that sleep deprivation may not be as inconsequential as the research on human sub-

jects suggests. Two rats, an experimental rat and its *yoked control*, are placed in separate chambers of the

apparatus. Each time the EEG activity of the experimental rat indicates that it is sleeping, the disk, which serves as the floor of half of both chambers, starts to slowly rotate. As a result, if the sleeping experimental rat does not awaken immediately, it gets shoved off the disk into a shallow pool of water. The yoked control is exposed to exactly the same pattern of disk rotations; but if it is not sleeping, it can easily avoid getting dunked by walking in the direction opposite to the direction of disk rotation. The experimental rats typically died after several days, while the yoked controls stayed reasonably healthy (see Rechtschaffen & Bergmann, 1995).

The fact that human subjects have been sleep-deprived for similar periods of time without dire consequences argues for caution in interpreting the results of the carousel sleep-deprivation experiments. It may be that repeatedly being awakened by the moving platform or, worse yet, being plunged into water while sleeping kills the experimental rats not because it keeps them from sleeping but because it is stressful and physically damaging. This interpretation is consistent with the pathological symptoms that were revealed in the experimental rats by postmortem examination: for example, swollen adrenal glands, gastric ulcers, and internal bleeding. Indeed, it may not be possible to study the effects of sleep deprivation in nonhumans adequately because of the unavoidable confounding effects of extreme stress (see Benington & Heller, 1999; D'Almeida et al., 1997; Horne, 2000).

REM-Sleep Deprivation

Because of its association with dreaming, REM sleep has been the subject of intensive investigation. In an effort to reveal the particular functions of REM sleep, sleep researchers have specifically deprived sleeping subjects of REM sleep by waking them up each time a bout of REM sleep begins.

REM-sleep deprivation has been shown to have two consistent effects (see Figure 14.8). First, with each successive night of deprivation, there is a greater tendency for subjects to initiate REM sequences. Thus, as REM-sleep deprivation proceeds, subjects have to be awakened more and more frequently to keep them from accumulating significant amounts of REM sleep. For example, during the first night of REM-sleep deprivation in one experiment (Webb & Agnew, 1967), the subjects had to be awakened 17 times to keep them from having extended periods of REM sleep; but during the seventh night of deprivation, they had to be awakened 67 times. Second, following REM-sleep deprivation, subjects display a *REM rebound*; that is, they have more than their usual amount of REM sleep for the first two or three nights (Brunner et al., 1990).

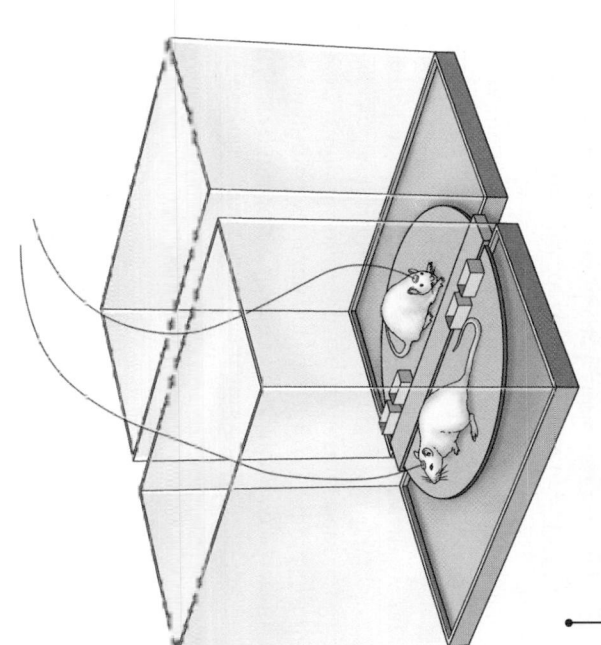

FIGURE 14.7 The carousel apparatus used to deprive an experimental rat of sleep while a yoked control rat is exposed to the same number and pattern of disk rotations. The disk on which both rats rest rotates every time the experimental rat has a sleep EEG. If the sleeping rat does not awaken immediately, it is deposited in the water. (Adapted from Rechtschaffen et al., 1983.)

FIGURE 14.8   The two effects of REM-sleep deprivation.

The compensatory increase in REM sleep following a period of REM-sleep deprivation suggests that the amount of REM sleep is regulated separately from the amount of slow-wave sleep and that REM sleep serves a special function. Numerous theories of the functions of REM sleep have been proposed (see Webb, 1973; Winson, 1993). Most of them fall into one of three categories: (1) those that hypothesize that REM sleep is necessary for the maintenance of an individual's mental health, (2) those that hypothesize that REM sleep is necessary for the maintenance of normal levels of motivation, and (3) those that hypothesize that REM sleep is necessary for the processing of memories. None of these theories has emerged a clear winner. Reports that REM-sleep deprivation produces a variety of personality and motivational problems (e.g., Dement, 1960) have not proved replicable, and more recent reports that REM-sleep deprivation produces memory deficits for certain kinds of material learned the preceding day (see Hobson & Pace-Schott, 2002), while promising, are still controversial (see Maquet, 2001; Siegel, 2001).

One challenge faced by any theory of the function of REM sleep is to explain why **tricyclic antidepressant drugs** are not severely debilitating. Because tricyclic antidepressants selectively block REM sleep, patients who regularly take large doses (e.g., for depression) get little REM sleep for months at a time—and yet they experience no serious side effects from this REM-sleep loss. Another finding that is inconsistent with most theories of REM sleep is that it is most prevalent in the weeks before and after birth.

One recent theory about REM sleep is based on the premise that this type of sleep serves no critical function: This is the *default theory of REM sleep* (Horne, 2000). According to this theory, it is difficult to stay continuously in NREM sleep, so the brain periodically switches to one of two other states. If there is any immediate bodily need to take care of (e.g., eating or drinking), the brain switches to wakefulness; if there are no immediate needs, it switches to the default state—REM sleep. According to

the default theory, REM sleep and wakefulness are similar states, but REM sleep is more adaptive when there are no immediate bodily needs. Indirect support for this theory comes from the many similarities between REM sleep and wakefulness. For example, you have already learned about the high levels of neural activity, rapid heart rate, and high blood pressure that characterize REM sleep, and it has been found that subjects awaken easily and quickly from REM sleep (see Horne, 2000).

A study by Nycamp and colleagues (1998) provides more direct support for the default theory of REM sleep. These researchers awakened subjects every time they entered REM sleep, but instead of letting them go back to sleep immediately, the researchers substituted a 15-minute period of wakefulness for each lost REM period. Under these conditions, the subjects, unlike the controls, were not tired the next day, despite getting only 5 hours of sleep, and they displayed no REM rebound. In other words, there seemed to be no need for REM sleep if peri-

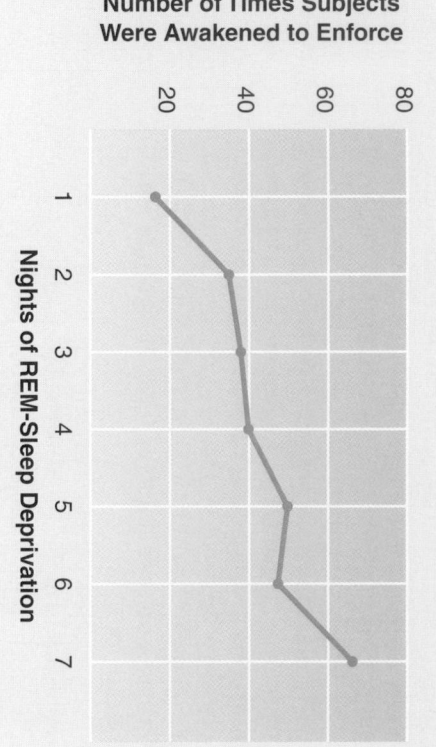

Number of Times Subjects Were Awakened to Enforce

Nights of REM-Sleep Deprivation

The number of awakenings required to deprive a subject of REM sleep increases as the period of deprivation ensues.

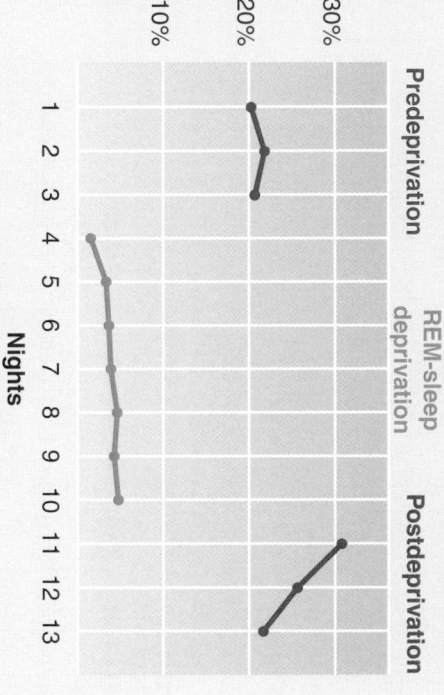

Percent of Total Sleep Time Spent in REM Sleep

Predeprivation   REM-sleep deprivation   Postdeprivation

Nights

After a period of REM-sleep deprivation, subjects spend a greater than usual portion of their sleep time in REM sleep.

SCAN YOUR BRAIN

Before continuing with this chapter, scan your brain by completing the following exercise to make sure you understand the fundamentals of sleep. The correct answers are provided at the bottom of this page. Before proceeding, review material related to your errors and omissions.

1. The three most commonly studied psychophysiological correlates of sleep are the EEG, EMG, and _____.

2. Stage 4 sleep EEG is characterized by a predominance of _____ waves.

3. _____ stage 1 EEG is accompanied by neither REM nor loss of core-muscle tone.

4. Dreaming occurs predominantly during _____ sleep.

5. The modern alternative to Freud's theory of dreaming is Hobson's _____ theory.

6. Environmental cues that can entrain circadian rhythms are called _____ or time givers.

7. In contrast to the prediction of the recuperation theories of sleep, when a subject stays awake longer than usual under free-running conditions, the following period of sleep tends to be _____.

8. The most convincing evidence that REM-sleep deprivation is not seriously debilitating comes from the study of patients taking _____.

9. After a lengthy period of sleep deprivation (e.g., several days), a subject's first night of sleep is only slightly longer than usual, but it contains a much higher proportion of _____ waves.

10. _____ sleep in particular, rather than sleep in general, appears to play the major recuperative role.

Sleep Deprivation Increases the Efficiency of Sleep

One of the most important findings of human sleep-deprivation research is that individuals who are deprived of sleep become more efficient sleepers. In particular, their sleep has a higher proportion of slow-wave sleep (stages 3 and 4), which seems to serve the main restorative function. Because this is such an important finding, let's take a look at six major pieces of evidence that support it.

First, although subjects regain only a small proportion of their total lost sleep after a period of sleep deprivation, they regain most of their lost stage 4 sleep (e.g., Borbély et al., 1981; De Gennaro, Ferrara, & Bertini, 2000; Lucidi et al., 1997). Second, after sleep deprivation, the slow-wave sleep EEG of humans is characterized by an even higher proportion than usual of slow waves (Borbély, 1981; Borbély et al., 1981). Third, short sleepers normally get as much slow-wave sleep as long sleepers do (e.g., Jones & Oswald, 1966; Webb & Agnew, 1970). Fourth, if subjects take an extra nap in the morn-

ods of wakefulness were substituted for it. This is consistent with the finding that as antidepressants reduce REM sleep, the number of nighttime awakenings increases (see Horne, 2000).

ing after a full night's sleep, their naptime EEG shows few slow waves, and the nap does not reduce the duration of the following night's sleep (e.g., Åkerstedt & Gillberg, 1981; Hume & Mills, 1977; Karacan et al., 1970). Fifth, subjects who gradually reduce their usual sleep time get less stage 1 and stage 2 sleep, but the duration of their slow-wave sleep remains about the same as before (Mullaney et al., 1977; Webb & Agnew, 1975). And sixth, repeatedly waking subjects up during REM sleep produces little, if any, increase in the sleepiness they experience the next day, whereas repeatedly waking subjects up during slow-wave sleep has major effects (Nykamp et al., 1998).

The fact that sleep becomes more efficient in people who sleep less means that conventional sleep-deprivation studies are virtually useless for discovering how much humans need to sleep. The negative consequences of sleep loss in inefficient sleepers do not indicate whether the lost sleep was really needed; the true need for sleep can be assessed only by experiments in which sleep is regularly reduced for many weeks, to give the subjects an opportunity to adapt to less sleep by increasing their sleep to its maximum efficiency. Only when people are sleeping at their maximal efficiency is it possible to

ON THE CD

In the *Good Morning* module, the camera catches Pinel arriving at his office at 6:00 A.M. He discusses a common misconception about sleep.

Thinking Critically

Scan Your Brain answers: (1) EOG, (2) delta, (3) initial, (4) REM, (5) activation-synthesis, (6) *zeitgebers*, (7) shorter, (8) tricyclic antidepressants, (9) slow (or delta), (10) Slow-wave (or Stage 3 and 4).

determine how much sleep they really need. Such sleep-reduction studies are discussed later in the chapter, but please pause here to think about this point—it is extremely important, and it is totally consistent with the new appreciation of the plasticity and adaptiveness of the adult mammalian brain.

It is an appropriate time, here at the end of the section on sleep deprivation, for me to file a brief progress report. It has now been 2 weeks since I began my 5-hours-per-night sleep schedule. Generally, things are going well. My progress on this chapter has been faster than usual. I am not having any difficulty getting up on time or getting my work done, but I am finding that it takes a major effort to stay awake in the evening. If I try to read or watch a bit of television after 10:30, I experience microsleeps. Luckily for me, my so-called friends delight in making sure that my transgressions last no more than a few seconds.

14.7 Four Areas of the Brain Involved in Sleep

In this section, you will be introduced to four areas of the brain that are involved in sleep. You will learn more about them in the later section on sleep disorders.

Two Areas of the Hypothalamus Involved in Sleep

It is remarkable that two areas of the brain that are involved in the regulation of sleep were discovered early in the 20th century, long before the advent of modern behavioral neuroscience. The discovery was made by Baron Constantin von Economo, a Viennese neurologist.

The Case of Constantin von Economo, the Insightful Neurologist

During World War I, the world was swept by a serious viral infection of the brain: *encephalitis lethargica*. Many of its victims slept almost continuously. Baron Constantin von Economo discovered that the brains of deceased victims who had problems with excessive sleep all had damage in the *posterior hypothalamus* and adjacent parts of the midbrain. He then turned his attention to the brains of a small group of victims of encephalitis lethargica who had had the opposite sleep-related problem: In contrast to most victims, they had difficulty sleeping. He found that the brains of the deceased victims in this minority always had damage in the *anterior hypothalamus* and adjacent parts of the basal forebrain. On the basis of these clinical observations, von Economo concluded that the posterior hypothalamus promotes wakefulness, whereas the preoptic area promotes sleep.

Since von Economo's discovery of the involvement of the posterior hypothalamus and the anterior hypothalamus in human wakefulness and sleep, respectively, that involvement has been confirmed by lesion studies in experimental animals (see Saper, Chou, & Scammell, 2001). The locations of the posterior and anterior hypothalamus are shown in Figure 14.9.

Evolutionary Perspective

Reticular Activating System and Sleep

Another area involved in sleep was discovered through the comparison of the effects of two different brain-stem transections in cats. First, in 1936, Bremer severed the brain stems of cats between their *inferior colliculi* and *superior colliculi* in order to disconnect their forebrains from ascending sensory input (see Figure 14.10). This surgical preparation is called a **cerveau isolé preparation** (pronounced "ser-VOE ees-o-LAY"—literally, "isolated forebrain").

Bremer found that the cortical EEG of the isolated cat forebrains was indicative of almost continuous slow-wave sleep. Only when strong visual or olfactory stimuli were presented (the cerveau isolé has intact visual and olfactory input) could the continuous high-amplitude, slow-wave activity be changed to a **desynchronized EEG**—a low-amplitude, high-frequency EEG. However, this arousing effect barely outlasted the stimuli.

Next, for comparison purposes, Bremer (1937) transected (cut through) the brain stems of a different group of cats. These transections were located in the caudal brain stem, and thus, they disconnected the brain from the rest of the nervous system (see Figure 14.10). This experimental preparation is called the **encéphale isolé preparation** (pronounced "on-say-FELL ees-o-LAY").

Although it cut most of the same sensory fibers as the cerveau isolé transection, the encéphale isolé transection did not disrupt the normal cycle of sleep EEG and wakefulness EEG. This suggested that a structure for maintaining wakefulness was located somewhere in the brain stem between the two transections.

Later, two important findings suggested that this wakefulness structure in the brain stem was the *reticular formation*. First, it was shown that partial transections at the cerveau isolé level disrupted normal sleep-wake

Evolutionary Perspective

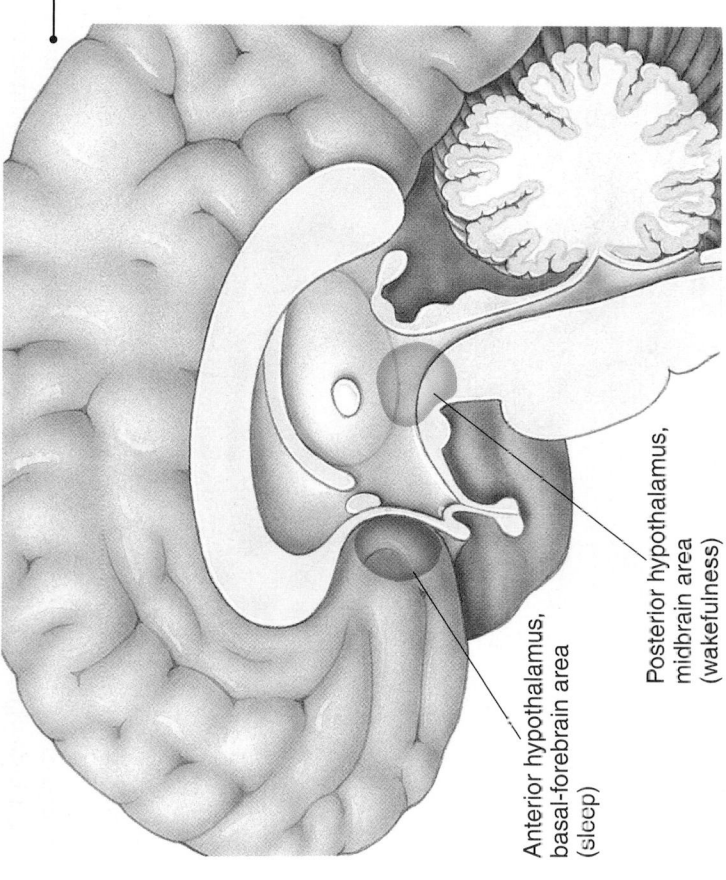

Anterior hypothalamus,
basal-forebrain area
(sleep)

Posterior hypothalamus,
midbrain area
(wakefulness)

FIGURE 14.9 Two regions of the brain involved in sleep. The anterior hypothalamus and adjacent basal forebrain are thought to promote sleep; the posterior hypothalamus and adjacent midbrain are thought to promote wakefulness.

on the cortical EEG (Lindsey, Bowden, & Magoun, 1949). Second, it was shown that electrical stimulation of the reticular formation of sleeping cats awakened them and produced a lengthy period of EEG desynchronization (Moruzzi & Magoun, 1949).

In 1949, Moruzzi and Magoun considered these four findings together: (1) the effects on cortical EEG of the cerveau isolé preparation, (2) the effects on cortical EEG of the encéphale isolé preparation, (3) the effects of reticular formation lesions, and (4) the effects on sleep of stimulation of the reticular formation. From these four key findings, Moruzzi and Magoun proposed that low levels of activity in the reticular formation produce sleep and that high levels produce wakefulness. Indeed, this

cycles of cortical EEG only when they severed the reticular formation core of the brain stem; when the partial transections were restricted to more lateral areas, which contain the ascending sensory tracts, they had little effect

Four Pieces of Evidence That the Reticular Activating System Is Involved in Sleep

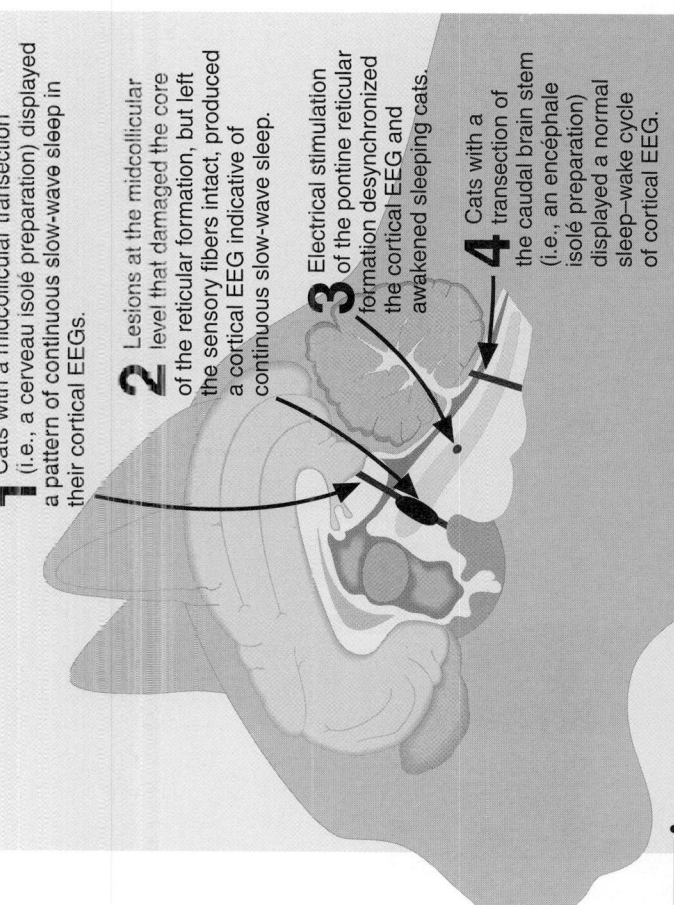

1 Cats with a midcollicular transection (i.e., a cerveau isolé preparation) displayed a pattern of continuous slow-wave sleep in their cortical EEGs.

2 Lesions at the midcollicular level that damaged the core of the reticular formation, but left the sensory fibers intact, produced a cortical EEG indicative of continuous slow-wave sleep.

3 Electrical stimulation of the pontine reticular formation desynchronized the cortical EEG and awakened sleeping cats.

4 Cats with a transection of the caudal brain stem (i.e., an encéphale isolé preparation) displayed a normal sleep–wake cycle of cortical EEG.

Together, these four findings suggested that a wakefulness-producing area was located in the reticular formation between the cerveau isolé and the encéphale isolé transections.

FIGURE 14.10 Four pieces of evidence that the reticular activating system is involved in sleep.

theory is so widely accepted that the reticular formation is commonly referred to as the **reticular activating system**, even though maintaining wakefulness is only one of the functions of the many nuclei that it comprises.

Reticular REM-Sleep Nuclei

The fourth area of the brain that is involved in sleep controls REM sleep and is included in the brain area I have just described—it is part of the caudal reticular formation. It makes sense that an area of the brain involved in maintaining wakefulness would also be involved in the production of REM sleep because of the similarities between the two states. Indeed, REM sleep is controlled by a variety of nuclei scattered throughout the caudal reticular formation. Each site is responsible for control-

ling one of the major indices of REM sleep (Siegel, 1983; Vertes, 1983)—a site for the reduction of core-muscle tone, a site for EEG desynchronization, a site for rapid eye movements, and so on. The approximate location in the caudal brain stem of each of these REM-sleep nuclei is illustrated in Figure 14.11.

Please think for a moment about the broad implications of these various REM-sleep nuclei. In thinking about the brain mechanisms of behavior, many people assume that if there is one name for a behavior, there must be a single structure for it in the brain: In other words, they assume that evolutionary pressures have acted to shape the human brain according to our current language and theories. Here we see the weakness of this assumption: The brain is organized along differ-

Thinking Critically

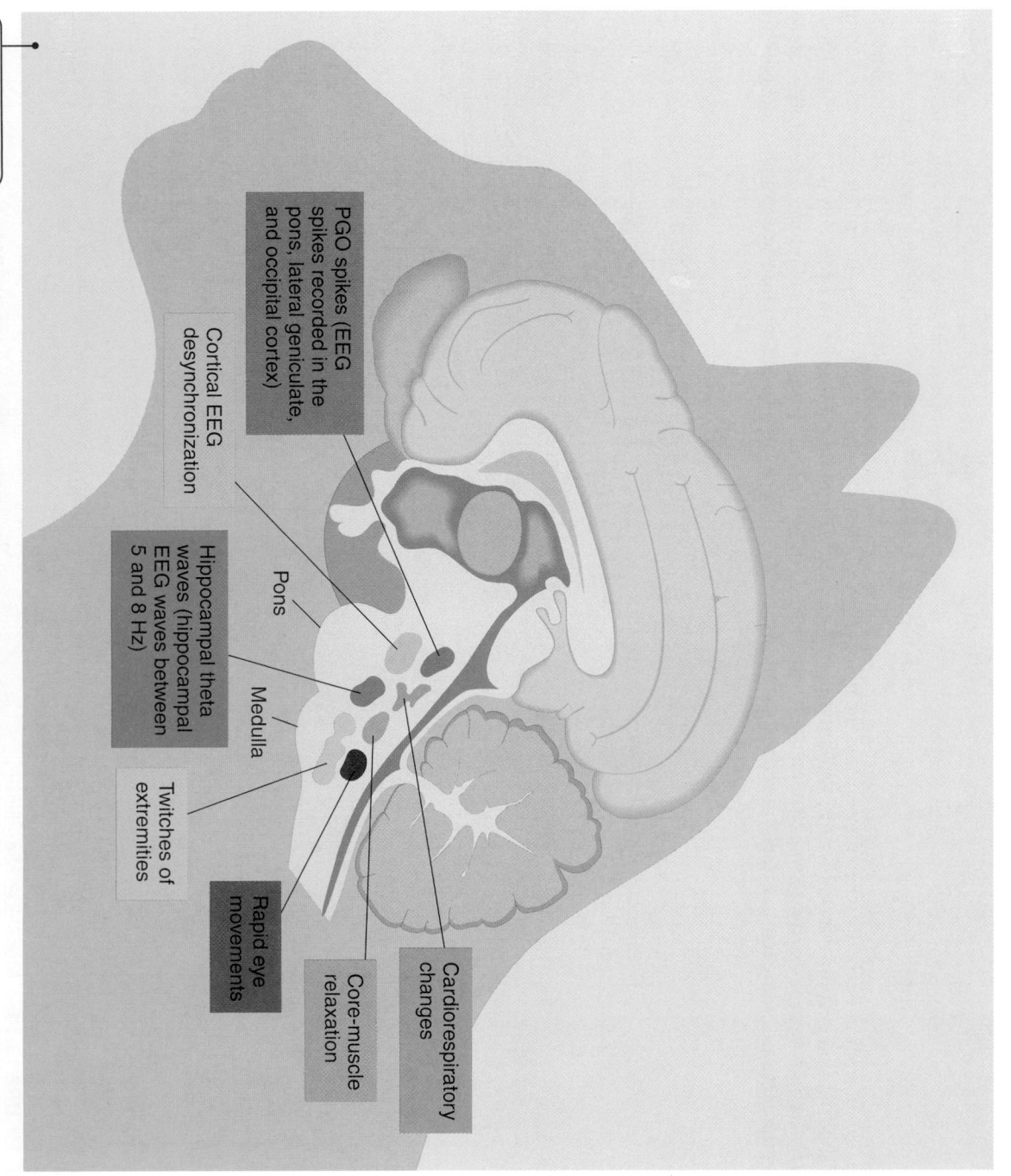

FIGURE 14.11 A sagittal section of the brain stem of the cat illustrating the areas that control the various physiological indexes of REM sleep. (Adapted from Vertes, 1983.)

PGO spikes (EEG spikes recorded in the pons, lateral geniculate, and occipital cortex)

Cortical EEG desynchronization

Hippocampal theta waves (hippocampal EEG waves between 5 and 8 Hz)

Pons

Medulla

Twitches of extremities

Core-muscle relaxation

Rapid eye movements

Cardiorespiratory changes

ent principles, and REM sleep occurs only when a network of independent structures becomes active together. Relevant to this is the fact that the physiological changes that go together to define REM sleep sometimes break apart and go their separate ways—and the same is true of the changes that define slow-wave sleep. For example, during REM-sleep deprivation, penile erections, which normally occur during REM sleep, begin to occur during slow-wave sleep. And during total sleep deprivation, slow waves, which normally occur only during slow-wave sleep, begin to occur during wakefulness. This suggests that REM sleep, slow-wave sleep, and wakefulness are not each controlled by a single mechanism. Each state seems to result from the interaction of several mechanisms that are capable under certain conditions of operating independently of one another.

14.8 The Circadian Clock: Neural and Molecular Mechanisms

The fact that circadian sleep–wake cycles persist in the absence of temporal cues from the environment indicates that the physiological systems that regulate sleep are controlled by an internal timing mechanism—the **circadian clock**. The circadian clock has been the subject of such intensive investigation that it warrants its own section of this chapter.

Location of the Circadian Clock in the Suprachiasmatic Nuclei

The first breakthrough in the search for the circadian clock was Richter's 1967 discovery that large medial hypothalamic lesions disrupt circadian cycles of eating, drinking, and activity in rats. Next, specific lesions of the **suprachiasmatic nuclei (SCN)** of the medial hypothalamus were shown to disrupt various circadian cycles, including sleep–wake cycles. Although SCN lesions do not reduce the amount of time mammals spend sleeping, they do abolish its circadian periodicity. Further support for the conclusion that the suprachiasmatic nuclei contain a circadian timing mechanism comes from the observation that the nuclei display circadian cycles of electrical, metabolic, and biochemical activity that can be entrained by the light–dark cycle (see Buijs & Kalsbeek, 2001; Van Esseveldt, Lehman, & Boer, 2000).

If there was any lingering doubt about the location of the circadian clock, it was eliminated by the brilliant experiment of Ralph and his colleagues (1990). They removed the SCN from the fetuses of a strain of mutant hamsters that had an abnormally short (20-hour) free-running sleep–wake cycle. Then, they transplanted the SCN into normal adult hamsters whose free-running sleep–wake cycles of 25 hours had been abolished by SCN lesions. These transplants restored free-running sleep–wake cycles in the recipients; but, remarkably, the cycles were about 20 hours long rather than the original 25 hours. Transplants in the other direction—that is, from normal hamster fetuses to SCN-lesioned adult mutants—had the complementary effect: They restored free-running sleep–wake cycles that were about 25 hours long rather than the original 20 hours.

Although the suprachiasmatic nuclei are unquestionably the major circadian clocks in mammals, they are not the only ones. Three lines of experiments, largely conducted in the 1980s and 1990s, pointed to the existence of other circadian timing mechanisms in the body. First, under certain conditions, bilateral SCN lesions have been shown to leave some circadian rhythms unaffected while abolishing others. Second, bilateral SCN lesions do not eliminate the ability of all environmental stimuli to entrain circadian rhythms; for example, SCN lesions can block entrainment by light but not by food or water availability. Third, just as suprachiasmatic neurons do, cells from other parts of the body display free-running circadian cycles of activity when maintained in tissue culture.

Mechanisms of Entrainment

How does the 24-hour light–dark cycle entrain the sleep–wake cycle and other circadian rhythms? To answer this question, researchers began at the obvious starting point: the eyes. They tried to identify and track the specific neurons that left the eyes and carried the information about light and dark that entrained the biological clock. Cutting the *optic nerves* before they reached the *optic chiasm* eliminated the ability of the light–dark cycle to entrain circadian rhythms; however, when the *optic tracts* were cut at the point where they left the optic chiasm, the ability of the light–dark cycle to entrain circadian rhythms was unaffected. As Figure 14.12 on page 359 illustrates, these two findings indicated that visual axons critical for the entrainment of circadian rhythms branch off from the optic nerve in the vicinity of the optic chiasm. This finding led to the discovery of the *retinohypothalamic tracts*, which leave the optic chiasm and project to the adjacent suprachiasmatic nuclei.

Surprisingly, although the retinohypothalamic tracts mediate the ability of light to entrain photoreceptors, neither rods or cones are necessary for the entrainment. *Transgenic mice* lacking both rods and cones still show light-entrained circadian cycles (Freedman et al., 1999; Lucas et al., 1999). This finding suggested that the SCN must be getting information about light and dark from other receptors. These receptors were recently discovered, creating considerable excitement among neuroscientists.

Surprisingly, these mystery photoreceptors have proven to be neurons, a rare type of *retinal ganglion cells* with distinctive functional properties (see Berson, 2003; Hattar et al., 2002). During the course of evolution, these photoreceptors seem to have sacrificed the ability to respond quickly and briefly to rapid changes of light in favor of the ability to respond consistently to slowly changing levels of background illumination. These photoreceptors also play a role in the adjustment of pupillary size in response to changes in background illumination (Lucas et al., 2003; Van Gelder et al., 2003). Their photopigment appears to be *melanopsin*.

Genetics of Circadian Rhythms

An important breakthrough in the study of the genetic basis of circadian rhythms came in 1988 when routine screening of a shipment of hamsters revealed that some of them had abnormally short 20-hour free-running circadian rhythms. Subsequent breeding experiments showed that the abnormality was the result of a genetic mutation, and the gene that was found was named *tau* (Ralph & Menaker, 1988).

Although *tau* was the first mammalian circadian gene to be identified, it was not the first to have its molecular structure characterized. This honor went to *clock*, a mammalian circadian gene discovered in mice. The structure of the clock gene was characterized in 1997, and that of the tau gene was characterized in 2000 (Lowrey et al., 2000). The molecular structures of several other mammalian circadian genes have now been specified (see Morse & Sassone-Corsi, 2002).

The identification of circadian genes has led to two important discoveries. First, the same or similar circa-

dian genes have been found in many species of different evolutionary ages (e.g., bacteria, flies, fish, frogs, mice, and humans). It seems that circadian rhythms evolved early in evolutionary history, and the same genes have been conserved in various descendant species (see Cermakian & Sassone-Corsi, 2002). Second, the identification of circadian genes provided a more direct method of exploring the circadian timing capacities of parts of the body other than the SCN. Although the existence of extra-SCN circadian timing mechanisms had been inferred from the results of research conducted in the 1980s and 1990s (as I have already described to you), direct evidence was lacking. Once researchers established that the circadian genes within SCN neurons transcribed their protein products on a circadian cycle, they began to examine the same genes in other cells of the body and were amazed by what they found: Circadian timing mechanisms similar to those in the SCN exist in most cells of the body (see Green & Menaker, 2003; Hastings, Reddy, & Maywood, 2003; Yamaguchi et al., 2003). Although most cells contain a genetic circadian clock, these cellular clocks are normally entrained by neural and hormonal signals from the SCN.

www.ablongman.com/pinel6e

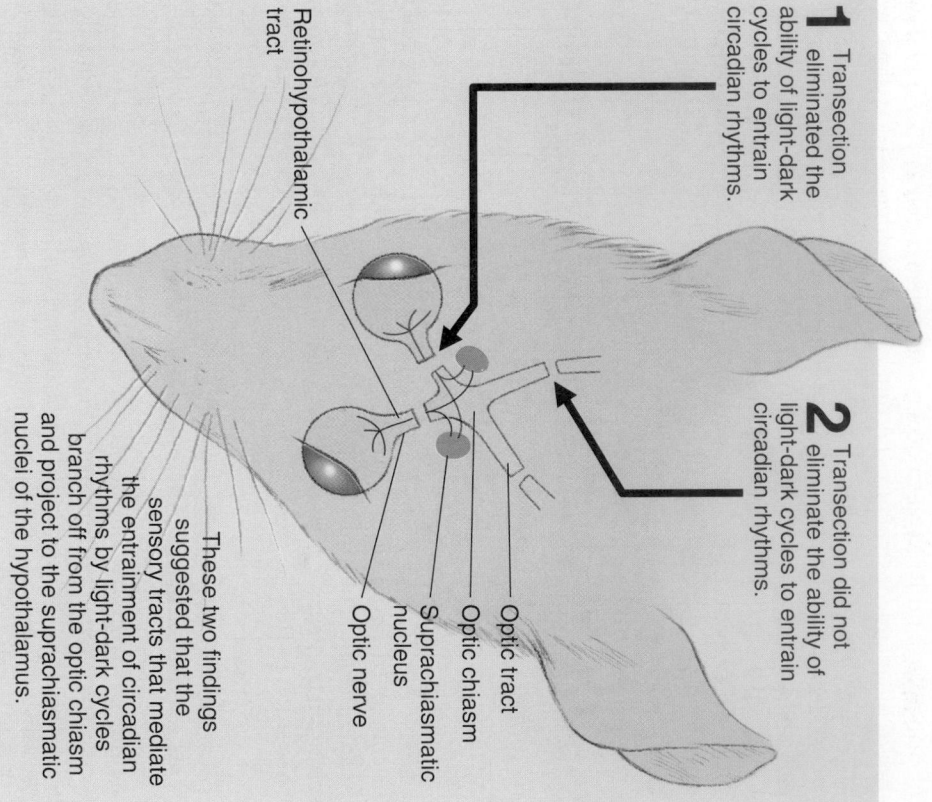

FIGURE 14.12 The discovery of the retinohypothalamic tracts. Neurons from each retina project to both suprachiasmatic nuclei.

1 Transection eliminated the ability of light-dark cycles to entrain circadian rhythms.

2 Transection did not eliminate the ability of light-dark cycles to entrain circadian rhythms.

Retinohypothalamic tract

Optic tract
Optic chiasm
Suprachiasmatic nucleus
Optic nerve

These two findings suggested that the sensory tracts that mediate the entrainment of circadian rhythms by light-dark cycles branch off from the optic chiasm and project to the suprachiasmatic nuclei of the hypothalamus.

14.9   Drugs That Affect Sleep

Most drugs that influence sleep fall into two different classes: hypnotic and antihypnotic. **Hypnotic drugs** are drugs that increase sleep; **antihypnotic drugs** are drugs that reduce sleep. A third class of sleep-influencing drugs comprises those that influence its circadian rhythmicity; the main drug of this class is **melatonin.**

Hypnotic Drugs

The **benzodiazepines** (e.g., Valium and Librium) were developed and tested for the treatment of anxiety, yet

Clinical Implications

they are the most commonly prescribed hypnotic medications. In the short term, they increase drowsiness, decrease the time it takes to fall asleep, reduce the number of awakenings during a night's sleep, and increase total sleep time. Thus, they can be effective in the treatment of occasional difficulties in sleeping.

Although benzodiazepines can be effective therapeutic hypnotic agents in the short term, their prescription for the treatment of chronic sleep difficulties is ill-advised. Still, they are commonly prescribed for this purpose—primarily by general practitioners. Following are four complications associated with the chronic use of benzodiazepines as hypnotic agents: First, tolerance develops to the hypnotic effects of benzodiazepines; thus, patients must take larger and larger doses to maintain the drugs' efficacy. Second, cessation of benzodiazepine therapy after chronic use causes *insomnia* (sleeplessness), which can exacerbate the very problem that the benzodiazepines were intended to correct. Third, chronic benzodiazepine use is addictive. Fourth, benzodiazepines distort the normal pattern of sleep; they increase the duration of sleep by increasing the duration of stage 2 sleep, while actually decreasing the duration of stage 4 and REM sleep.

Evidence that the raphé nuclei play a role in sleep suggested that serotonergic drugs might be effective hypnotics. Efforts to demonstrate the hypnotic effects of such drugs have focused on **5-hydroxytryptophan (5-HTP)**—the precursor of serotonin—because 5-HTP, but not serotonin, readily passes through the blood–brain barrier. Injections of 5-HTP do reverse the insomnia produced in both cats and rats by the serotonin antagonist PCPA; however, they are of no therapeutic benefit in the treatment of human insomnia (see Borbély, 1983).

Antihypnotic Drugs

There are two main classes of antihypnotic drugs: *stimulants* (e.g., cocaine and amphetamine) and *tricyclic antidepressants*. Both stimulants and antidepressants increase the activity of catecholamines (norepinephrine, epineph-

rine, and dopamine) by either increasing their release or blocking their reuptake from the synapse, or both.

From the perspective of the treatment of sleep disorders, the most important property of antihypnotic drugs is that they act preferentially on REM sleep. They can totally suppress REM sleep even at doses that have little ef-

Clinical Implications

fect on total sleep time.

Using stimulant drugs to treat chronic excessive sleepiness is a risky proposition. Most stimulants are highly addictive, and they produce a variety of adverse side effects, such as loss of appetite. Moreover, unless these drugs are taken at just the right doses and at just the right times, there is a danger that they will interfere with normal sleep.

Melatonin

Melatonin is a hormone that is synthesized from the neurotransmitter serotonin in the **pineal gland** (see Moore, 1996). The pineal gland is an inconspicuous gland that René Descartes, whose dualistic philosophy was discussed in Chapter 2, once believed to be the seat of the soul. The pineal gland is located on the midline of the brain just ventral to the rear portion of the corpus callosum (see Figure 14.13 on page 362).

The pineal gland has important

Evolutionary Perspective

functions in birds, reptiles, amphibians, and fish (see Cassone, 1990). The pineal gland of these species has inherent timing properties and regulates circadian rhythms and seasonal changes in reproductive behavior through its release of melatonin. In humans and other mammals, however, the functions of the pineal gland and melatonin are not as apparent.

In humans and other mammals, circulating levels of melatonin display circadian rhythms under control of the suprachiasmatic nuclei (see Gillette & McArthur, 1996), with the highest levels being associated with darkness and sleep (see Foulkes et al., 1997). On the basis of this correlation, it has long been assumed that melatonin plays a role in promoting sleep or in regulating its timing in mammals.

In order to put the facts about melatonin in perspective, it is important to keep one significant point firmly in mind. In adult mammals, pinealectomy and the consequent elimination of melatonin have little effect. The pineal gland plays a role in the development of mammalian sexual maturity, but its functions after puberty are not at all obvious.

Does *exogenous* (externally produced) melatonin improve sleep, as widely believed? The evidence is mixed. Several studies have shown that large doses of melatonin during the day, when levels of *endogenous* (internally produced) melatonin are low, produce quicker and

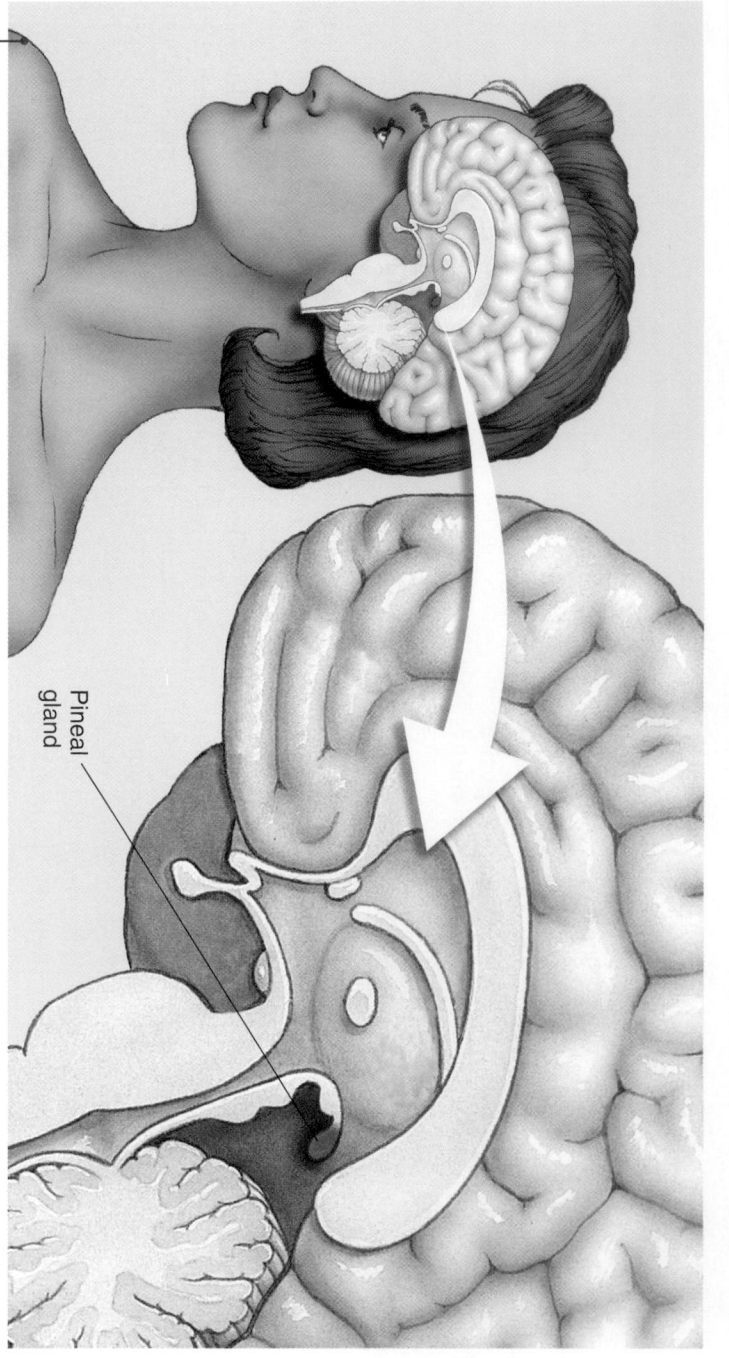

Pineal gland

FIGURE 14.13   The location of the pineal gland, the source of melatonin.

better sleep during subsequent nap tests (e.g., Haimov & Lavie, 1996). However, the effects of melatonin taken at bedtime have been inconsistent: A few studies have found subsequent sleep to be longer and more efficient (e.g., Attenburrow, Cowen, & Sharpely, 1996), but others have not (Baskett et al., 2003; Dawson & Encel, 1993).

In contrast to the controversy over the soporific (sleep-promoting) effects of exogenous melatonin in mammals, there is good evidence that it can influence mammalian circadian cycles (see Beaumont et al., 2004; Lewy, Ahmed, & Sack, 1996; Rajaratnam et al., 2003). Exposure to exogenous melatonin acts much like exposure to a period of darkness, which makes sense because high levels of endogenous melatonin are associated with darkness. Thus, a dose of melatonin before dusk may

help jet-lagged travelers adapt to east-bound flights, whereas a dose after dawn can help with adaptation to west-bound flights. The shift in circadian rhythms is, however, typically slight—less than an hour.

Exogenous melatonin has been shown to have a therapeutic potential in the treatment of two types of sleep problems. Melatonin before bedtime has been shown to improve the sleep of those insomniacs who are melatonin-deficient (e.g., Haimov et al., 1995) and of blind patients who have sleep problems attributable to the lack of the synchronizing effects of the light–dark cycle (e.g., Sack & Lewy, 2001). Melatonin's effectiveness in the treatment of other sleep disorders remains controversial (see Almeida et al., 2003; Serfaty et al., 2002).

14.10   Sleep Disorders

Many sleep disorders fall into one of two complementary categories: insomnia and hypersomnia. **Insomnia** includes all disorders of initiating and maintaining sleep, whereas **hypersomnia** includes disorders of excessive sleep or sleepiness. A third major class of sleep disorders includes all those disorders that are specifically related to REM-sleep dysfunction.

In various surveys, approximately 30% of the respondents report significant sleep-related problems.

However, it is important to recognize that complaints of sleep problems often come from people whose sleep appears normal in laboratory sleep tests. For example, many people who complain of insomnia actually sleep a reasonable amount (e.g., 6 hours a night), but they believe that they should sleep more (e.g., 8 hours a night). As a result, they spend more time in bed than they should and have difficulty getting to sleep. Often, the anxiety associated with their inability to sleep makes it even more difficult for them to sleep (see Espie, 2002). Such patients can often be helped by counseling that convinces them to go to bed only when they are very sleepy (see Anch et al., 1988). Others with disturbed sleep have more serious problems.

Insomnia

Many cases of insomnia are **iatrogenic** (physician-created). Paradoxically, sleeping pills (e.g., benzodiazepines) prescribed by well-intentioned physicians are a major cause of insomnia. At first, hypnotic drugs are effective in increasing sleep, but soon the patient is trapped in a rising spiral of drug use, as *tolerance* to the drug develops and progressively more of it is required to produce its original hypnotic effect. Soon, the patient cannot stop taking the drug without running the risk of experiencing *withdrawal symptoms*, which include insomnia. The case of Mr. B. illustrates this problem.

Mr. B., the Case of Iatrogenic Insomnia

Mr. B. was studying for a civil service exam, the outcome of which would affect his entire future. He was terribly worried about the test and found it difficult to get to sleep at night. Feeling that the sleep loss was affecting his ability to study, he consulted his physician for the express purpose of getting "something to make me sleep." His doctor prescribed a moderate dose of barbiturate at bedtime, and Mr. B. found that this medication was very effective . . . for the first several nights. After about a week, he began having trouble sleeping again and decided to take two sleeping pills each night. Twice more the cycle was repeated, until on the night before the exam he was taking four times as many pills as his doctor had prescribed. The next night, with the pressure off, Mr. B. took no medication. He had tremendous difficulty falling asleep, and when he did, his sleep was terribly disrupted. . . . Mr. B. now decided that he had a serious case of insomnia, and returned to his sleeping pill habit. By the time he consulted our clinic several years later, he was taking approximately 1,000 mg sodium amytal every night, and his sleep was more disturbed than ever. . . . Patients may go on for years and years—from one sleeping pill to another—never realizing that their troubles are caused by the pills.

(From *Some Must Watch While Some Must Sleep* by William E. Dement, Portable Stanford Books, Stanford Alumni Association, Stanford University, 1978, p. 80.)

leads to a sense of having slept poorly and is thus often diagnosed as insomnia. However, some patients are totally unaware of their multiple awakenings and instead complain of excessive sleepiness during the day, which leads to a diagnosis of *hypersomnia* (Stepanski et al., 1984).

Sleep apnea disorders are thought to be of two types: (1) those resulting from obstruction of the respiratory passages by muscle spasms or *atonia* (lack of muscle tone), and (2) those resulting from the failure of the central nervous system to stimulate respiration. Sleep apnea is more common in males, in the overweight, and in the elderly.

Two other causes of insomnia—nocturnal myoclonus and restless legs—both involve the legs. **Nocturnal myoclonus** is a periodic twitching of the body, usually the legs, during sleep. Most patients suffering from this disorder complain of poor sleep and daytime sleepiness but are unaware of the nature of their problem. In contrast, people with **restless legs** are all too aware of their problem. They complain of a hard-to-describe tension or uneasiness in their legs that keeps them from falling asleep. Benzodiazepines are often prescribed in cases of nocturnal myoclonus and restless legs because of their hypnotic, *anxiolytic* (antianxiety), muscle-relaxant, and anticonvulsant properties; however, they are rarely effective.

In one study, insomniacs claimed to take an average of 1 hour to fall asleep and to sleep an average of only 4.5 hours per night; but when they were tested in a sleep laboratory, they were found to have an average *sleep latency* (time to fall asleep) of only 15 minutes and an average nightly sleep duration of 6.5 hours. It used to be common medical practice to assume that people who claimed to suffer from insomnia but slept more than 6.5 hours per night were neurotic. However, this practice stopped when some of those diagnosed as *neurotic pseudoinsomniacs* were subsequently found to be suffering from sleep apnea, nocturnal myoclonus, or other sleep-disturbing problems. Insomnia is not necessarily a problem of too little sleep; it is often a problem of too little undisturbed sleep (Stepanski et al., 1987).

Remarkably, one of the most effective treatments for insomnia is *sleep restriction therapy*. First, the amount of time that an insomniac is allowed to spend in bed is substantially reduced. Then, after a period of sleep restriction, the amount of time spent in bed is gradually increased in small increments, as long as sleep latency remains in the normal range. Even severe insomniacs benefit from this treatment (Morin, Kowatch, & O'Shanick, 1990; Spielman, Saskin, & Thorpy, 1987).

Hypersomnia

Narcolepsy is the most widely studied disorder in the hypersomnia category. It occurs in 1 out of 2000 individuals (Takahashi, 1999) and has two prominent symptoms (see Siegel, 2000). First, narcoleptics experience severe daytime sleepiness and repeated, brief (10- to

Sleep apnea is another common cause of insomnia. In sleep apnea, the patient stops breathing many times each night. Each time, the patient awakens, begins to breathe again, and drifts back to sleep. Sleep apnea usually

15-minute) daytime sleep episodes. Narcoleptics typically sleep only about an hour per day more than average; it is the inappropriateness of their sleep episodes that most clearly defines their condition. Most of us occasionally fall asleep on the beach, in front of the television, or in that most *soporific* (sleep-promoting) of all daytime sites—the large, dimly lit lecture hall. But narcoleptics fall asleep in the middle of a conversation, while eating, while making love, or even while scuba diving.

The second prominent symptom of narcolepsy is cataplexy. **Cataplexy** is characterized by recurring losses of muscle tone during wakefulness, often triggered by an emotional experience. In its mild form, it may simply force the patient to sit down for a few seconds until it passes. In its extreme form, the patient drops to the ground as if shot and remains there for a minute or two, fully conscious.

In addition to the two prominent symptoms of narcolepsy (daytime sleep attacks and cataplexy), narcoleptics often experience two other symptoms: sleep paralysis and hypnagogic hallucinations. **Sleep paralysis** is the inability to move (paralysis) when falling asleep or waking up. **Hypnagogic hallucinations** are dreamlike experiences during wakefulness. Sleep paralysis and hypnagogic hallucinations are occasionally experienced by many people. Have you experienced them?

Three lines of evidence suggested to early researchers that narcolepsy results from an abnormality in the mechanisms that trigger REM sleep. First, unlike normal people, narcoleptics often go directly into REM sleep when they fall asleep. Second and third, narcoleptics often experience dreamlike states and loss of muscle tone during wakefulness.

Some of the most exciting current research on the neural mechanisms of sleep in general and narcolepsy in particular began with the study of a strain of narcoleptic dogs. After 10 years of studying the genetics of these

narcoleptic dogs, Lin and colleagues (1999) finally isolated the gene that causes the disorder. The gene encodes a receptor protein that binds to a neuropeptide called **orexin**, which exists in two forms: orexin-A and orexin-B (see Taheri, Zeitzer, & Mignot, 2002). In response to this discovery, Chemielli and colleagues (1999) bred *knockout mice* whose gene coding for the orexin-binding protein is dysfunctional. These mice display the symptoms of narcolepsy. This finding led other researchers to focus on the role of orexin in human narcoleptics: Several studies have documented reduced levels in the cerebrospinal fluid of living narcoleptics and in the brains of deceased narcoleptics (see Mieda & Yanagisawa, 2002).

Where is orexin synthesized in the brain? As you might have anticipated from an earlier section of this chapter, orexin is synthesized by neurons in the region of the hypothalamus that has been linked to the promotion of wakefulness: the posterior hypothalamus (mainly its lateral regions). The orexin-producing neurons project

diffusely throughout the brain, but they show many connections with neurons of the other wakefulness-promoting area of the brain: the reticular formation (see Pace-Schott & Hobson, 2002; Sucliffe & De Lecea, 2002).

When narcolepsy occurs in an identical twin, the probability that the other twin will be narcoleptic is only 25%. This finding suggests that environmental factors normally play a major role in the brain damage associated with narcolepsy. Perhaps exposure to a neurotoxin initiates an autoimmune reaction against some component of the orexin system.

REM-Sleep–Related Disorders

Several sleep disorders are specific to REM sleep; these are classified as *REM-sleep–related disorders*. Even narcolepsy, which is usually classified as a hypersomnic disorder, can reasonably be considered to be a REM-sleep–related disorder—for reasons you have just encountered.

Occasionally, patients are discovered who have little or no REM sleep. Although this disorder is rare, it is important because of its theoretical implications. Lavie and others (1984) described a patient who had suffered a brain injury that presumably involved damage to the REM-sleep controllers in the caudal reticular formation. The most important finding of this case study was that the patient did not appear to be adversely affected by his lack of REM sleep. After receiving his injury, he completed high school, college, and law school and established a thriving law practice.

Some patients experience REM sleep without coremuscle atonia. It has been suggested that the function of REM-sleep atonia is to prevent the acting out of dreams. This theory receives support from case studies of people who suffer from this disorder.

I was a halfback playing football, and after the quarterback received the ball from the center he lateraled it sideways to me and I'm supposed to go around and cut back over tackle and—this is very vivid—as I cut back over tackle there is this big 280-pound tackle waiting, so I, according to football rules, was to give him my shoulder and bounce him out of the way.... [W]hen I came to I was standing in front of our dresser and I had [gotten up out of bed and run and] knocked lamps, mirrors and everything off the dresser, hit my head against the wall and my knee against the dresser. (Schenck et al., 1986, p. 294)

Presumably, REM sleep without atonia is caused by damage to the nucleus magnocellularis or to an interruption of its output. The **nucleus magnocellularis** is a

Evolutionary Perspective

structure of the caudal reticular formation that controls muscle relaxation during REM sleep. In normal dogs, it is active only during REM sleep; in narcoleptic dogs, it is active during their narcoleptic attacks. Lesions of the caudal reticular formation often induce a similar REM-sleep–related disorder in cats.

The cat, which is standing . . . may attack unknown enemies, play with an absent mouse, or display flight behavior. There are orienting movements of the head or eyes toward imaginary stimuli, although the animal does not respond to visual or auditory stimuli. (Jouvet, 1972, pp. 236–237)

14.11   The Effects of Long-Term Sleep Reduction

You have already learned in this chapter that when people sleep less than they are used to sleeping, they do not feel or function well. I am sure that you have experienced these effects. But what do they mean? Most people—nonexperts and experts alike—believe that the adverse effects of sleep loss indicate that we need the sleep we typically get. However, there is an alternative interpretation, one that is consistent with the new awareness of the plasticity of the adult human brain. Perhaps the brain slowly adapts to the amount of sleep it usually gets—even though this amount may be far more than it needs—and is disturbed when there is a sudden reduction in the expected amount of sleep.

Fortunately, there is a way to determine which of these two interpretations of the effects of sleep loss is correct and to find out how much sleep people really need. The key is to study the effects of systematic programs of long-term sleep reduction. For example, if you reduced your regular amount of sleep from 8.5 hours per night to 6.5 hours per night, you would initially have some problems. But what if you regularly slept 6.5 hours per night for a couple of months, would you eventually become comfortable with sleeping 6.5 hours each night? And what if you then further reduced your nightly sleep time to 6.0 hours? The major point here is that if it is possible for you to adapt to a regular schedule of 6 hours of sleep per night without adverse consequences, then it is ludicrous to believe that you need 8.5 hours.

Let's see what has happened in studies of long-term sleep reduction. Because they are so time-consuming, few of these critical studies have been conducted; but there have been enough of them for a clear pattern of results to have emerged. I think you will by amazed by the results.

There have been two kinds of long-term sleep-reduction studies: studies in which the subjects sleep nightly and studies in which subjects sleep by napping. Following a brief discussion of these two kinds of studies and my own personal experience of long-term sleep reduction, the chapter concludes with an important, and somewhat disturbing, recent finding that is sure to challenge your thinking about sleep.

Long-Term Reduction of Nightly Sleep

There have been two studies in which healthy subjects have reduced their nightly sleep for several weeks or longer. In one (Webb & Agnew, 1974), a group of 16 subjects slept for only 5.5 hours per night for 60 days, with only one detectable deficit on an extensive battery of mood, medical, and performance tests: a slight deficit on a test of auditory vigilance.

In the other systematic study of long-term nightly sleep reduction (Friedman et al., 1977; Mullaney et al., 1977), 8 subjects reduced their nightly sleep by 30 minutes every 2 weeks until they reached 6.5 hours per night, then by 30 minutes every 3 weeks until they reached 5 hours, and then by 30 minutes every 4 weeks thereafter. After a subject indicated a lack of desire to reduce sleep further, the person slept for 1 month at the shortest duration of nightly sleep that was achieved, then for 2 months at the shortest duration plus 30 minutes. Finally, each subject slept each night for 1 year for however long the person preferred. The minimum duration of nightly sleep achieved during this experiment was 5.5 hours for 2 subjects, 5.0 hours for 4 subjects, and an impressive 4.5 hours for 2 subjects. In each of the subjects, a reduction in sleep time was associated with an increase in sleep efficiency: a decrease in the amount of time it took the subjects to fall asleep after going to bed, a decrease in the number of nighttime awakenings, and an increase in the proportion of stage 4 sleep. After the subjects had reduced their sleep to 6 hours per night, they began to experience daytime sleepiness, and this became a problem as sleep time was further reduced. Nevertheless, there were no deficits on any of the mood, medical, or performance tests given to the subjects throughout the experiment. The most encouraging result was that during a follow-up 1 year later, all subjects were sleeping less than they had previously—between 7 and 18 hours less each week—with no excessive sleepiness.

Long-Term Sleep Reduction by Napping

Most mammals and human infants display **polyphasic sleep cycles;** that is, they regularly sleep more than once per day. In contrast, most adult humans display **mono-phasic sleep cycles;** that is, they sleep once per day. Nevertheless, most adult humans do display polyphasic cycles of sleepiness, with periods of sleepiness occurring in late afternoon and late morning (Stampi, 1992a). Have you ever experienced them?

Do adult humans need to take sleep in one continuous period per day, or can they sleep effectively in several naps as human infants and other mammals do? Research has shown that naps have recuperative powers out of proportion with their brevity (e.g., Gillberg et al., 1996; Horne & Reyner, 1996; Naitoh, 1992), suggesting that polyphasic sleep might be particularly efficient.

Interest in the value of polyphasic sleep was stimulated by the legend that Leonardo da Vinci managed to generate a steady stream of artistic and engineering accomplishments during his life by napping for 15 minutes every 4 hours, thereby limiting his sleep to 1.5 hours per day. As unbelievable as this may seem, it has been replicated in several experiments (see Stampi, 1992b). Here are the main findings of these truly mind-boggling experiments. First, the subjects required a long time, about 2 weeks, to adapt to a polyphasic sleep schedule. Second, once adapted to polyphasic sleep, the subjects were content and displayed no deficits on the performance tests that they received. Third, Leonardo's 4-hour schedule works quite well, but in unstructured working situations (e.g., as in around-the-world solo sailboat races), subjects often vary the duration of the cycle without feeling negative consequences. Fourth, most subjects display a strong preference for particular sleep durations (e.g., 25 minutes) and refrain from sleeping too little, which leaves them unrefreshed, or too much, which leaves them groggy for several minutes when they awake—an effect called *sleep inertia.* Fifth, at first most of the sleep is slow-wave sleep, but eventually the subjects return to their usual relative proportions of REM and slow-wave sleep; however, REM and slow-wave sleep seldom occur during the same nap.

The following are the words of artist Giancarlo Sbragia, who adopted Leonardo's sleep schedule:

This schedule was difficult to follow at the beginning.... It took about 3 wk to get used to it. But I soon reached a point at which I felt a natural propensity for sleeping at this rate, and it turned out to be a thrilling and exciting experience.

... How beautiful my life became! I discovered dawns, I discovered silence, and concentration. I had more time for studying and reading—far more than I did before. I had more time for myself, for painting, and for developing my career. (Sbragia, 1992, p. 181)

Long-Term Sleep Reduction: A Personal Case Study

I began this chapter 4 weeks ago with both zeal and trepidation. I was fascinated by the idea that I could wring 2 or 3 extra hours of living out of each day by sleeping

---

The Case of the Author Who Reduced His Sleep

Rather than using the gradual stepwise reduction method of Friedman and his colleagues, I jumped directly into my 5-hours-per-night sleep schedule. This proved to be less difficult than you might think. I took advantage of a trip to the East Coast from my home on the West Coast to reset my circadian clock. While I was in the East, I got up at 7:00 A.M., which is 4:00 A.M. on the West Coast, and I just kept on the same schedule when I got home. I decided to add my extra waking hours to the beginning of my day rather than to the end so there would be no temptation for me to waste them; there are not too many distractions around this university at 5:00 A.M.

Figure 14.14 is a record of my sleep times for the 4-week period that it took me to write a first draft of this chapter. I didn't quite meet my goal of sleeping less than 5 hours every night, but I didn't miss by much: My overall mean was 5.05 hours per night. Notice that in the last week, there was a tendency for my circadian clock to run a bit slow; I began sleeping in until 4:30 A.M. and staying up until 11:30 P.M.

What were the positives and negatives of my experience? The main positive was the added time to do things: Having an extra 21 hours per week was wonderful. Furthermore, because my daily routine was out of synchrony with everybody else's, I spent little time sitting in rush-hour traffic. The only negative of the experience was sleepiness. It was no problem during the day, when I was active. However, staying awake during the last hour before I went to bed—an hour during which I usually engaged in sedentary activities, such as reading—was at times a problem. This is when I became personally familiar with the phenomenon of microsleeps, and it was then that I required some assistance in order to stay awake. Going to bed and falling asleep each night became a fleeting but satisfying experience.

I began this chapter with this question: How much sleep do we need? Then, I gave you my best professorial it-could-be-this, it-could-be-that answer. However, that was a month ago. Now, after experiencing sleep reduction firsthand, I am less inclined toward wishy-washiness on the topic of sleep. The fact that most committed subjects who are active during the day can reduce their sleep to about 5.5 hours per night without great difficulty or ma-

---

less, and I hoped that adhering to a sleep-reduction program while writing about sleep would create an enthusiasm for the subject that would color my writing and be passed on to you. On the other hand, I was more than a little concerned about the negative effect that losing 3 hours of sleep per night might have on me.

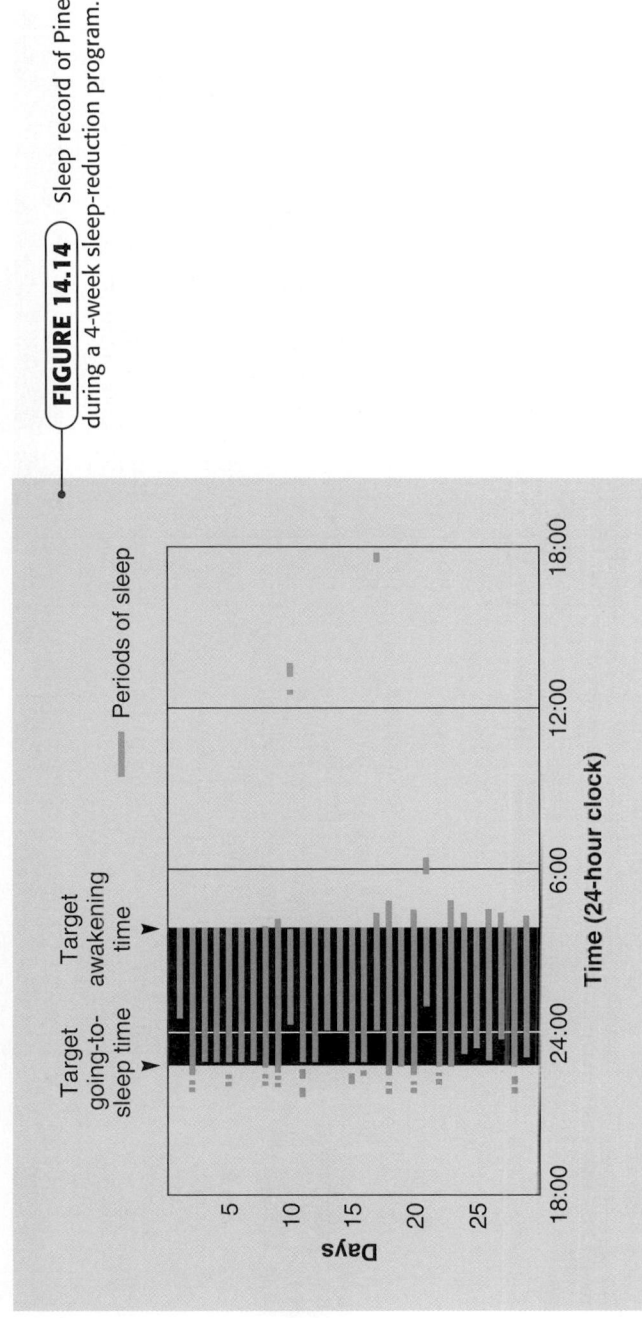

FIGURE 14.14 Sleep record of Pinel during a 4-week sleep-reduction program.

jor adverse consequences suggested to me that the answer is 5.5 hours of sleep. But that was before I reviewed the research on napping and polyphasic sleep schedules. Now, I must revise my estimate downward—substantially.

Earlier, I said that this chapter would end with an important new finding about sleep that would challenge your thinking on this topic. Here it is.

For decades, it has been reported that sleeping 8 hours or more per night is associated with health and longevity. Now a series of large-scale studies conducted in both the United States and Japan tell a different story (e.g., Ayas et al., 2003; Kripke et al., 2002; Patel et al.,

2003; Tamakoshi & Ohno, 2004). Unlike older studies, these new studies did not include subjects who were a potential source of bias, for example, people who slept little because they were ill, depressed, or under stress. The results of these new studies are remarkably uniform (Kripke, 2004). For example, Figure 14.15 presents data from Tamakoshi and Ohno (2004), who followed 104,010 subjects for 10 years. You will immediately see that sleeping 8 hours per night is not the healthy ideal that we have assumed it to be: The fewest deaths occurred among people sleeping between 5 and 7 hours per night, far fewer than among those who slept 8 hours.

Thinking Critically

Clinical Implications

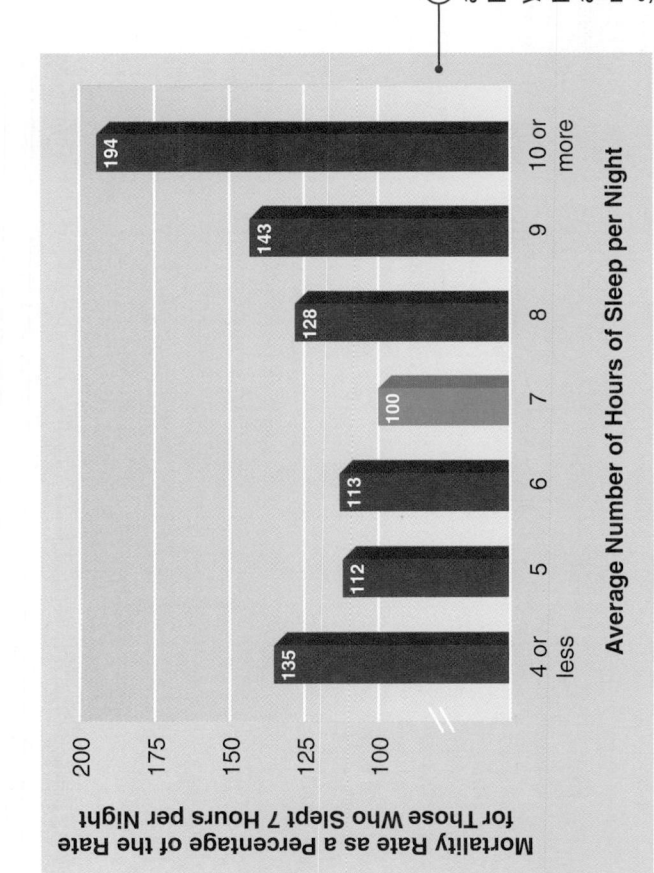

FIGURE 14.15 The mortality rates associated with different amounts of sleep, based on 104,010 subjects followed over 10 years. The mortality rate at 7 hours of sleep per night has been arbitrarily set at 100%, and the other mortality rates are presented in relation to it. [Adapted from Tamakoshi & Ohno, *Sleep* 2004, 27(1):51–4.]

Themes Revisited

The evolutionary perspective theme played a prominent role in this chapter. You learned how thinking about the adaptive function of sleep and comparing sleep in different species have led to interesting insights. Also, you saw how research into the physiology and genetics of sleep has been conducted on nonhuman species.

The thinking-about-biopsychology theme pervaded this chapter. The major purpose of the chapter was to

encourage you to reevaluate conventional ideas about sleep. Has this chapter changed your thinking about sleep? Writing it changed mine.

Finally, the clinical implications theme received emphasis in the section on sleep disorders. Perhaps most exciting and interesting were the recent breakthroughs in the understanding of the genetics and physiology of narcolepsy.

ON THE CD

See Hard Copy for additional readings for Chapter 14.

Think about It

1. Do you think your life could be improved by changing when or how long you sleep each day? In what ways? What negative effects do you think such changes might have on you?

2. Some people like to stay up late, some people like to get up early, others like to do both, and still others like to do neither. Design a sleep-reduction program that is tailored to your own preferences and lifestyle and that is consistent with the research literature on circadian cycles and sleep deprivation. The program should produce the greatest benefits for you with the least discomfort.

3. How has reading about sleep research changed your views about sleep? Give three specific examples.

4. Given the evidence that the long-term use of benzodiazepines actually contributes to the problems of insomnia, why are they so commonly prescribed for its treatment?

5. Your friend tells you that everybody needs 8 hours of sleep per night; she points out that every time she stays up late to study, she feels lousy the next day. Convince her that she is wrong.

ON THE CD

Studying for an exam? Try the Practice Tests for Chapter 14.

Key Terms

Activation-synthesis theory (p. 346)

Alpha waves (p. 346)

Antihypnotic drugs (p. 361)

Benzodiazepines (p. 361)

Carousel apparatus (p. 353)

Cataplexy (p. 364)

Cerveau isolé preparation (p. 356)

Circadian clock (p. 359)

Circadian rhythms (p. 348)

Circadian theories of sleep (p. 347)

Delta waves (p. 343)

Desynchronized EEG (p. 356)

Electroencephalogram (EEG) (p. 343)

Electromyogram (EMG) (p. 343)

Electrooculogram (EOG) (p. 343)

Emergent stage 1 EEG (p. 343)

Encéphale isolé preparation (p. 356)

5-Hydroxytryptophan (5-HTP) (p. 361)

Free-running period (p. 349)

Free-running rhythms (p. 349)

Hypersomnia (p. 362)

Hypnagogic hallucinations (p. 364)

Hypnotic drugs (p. 361)

Iatrogenic (p. 363)

Initial stage 1 EEG (p. 343)

Insomnia (p. 362)

Internal desynchronization (p. 349)

Jet lag (p. 350)

Lucid dreams (p. 346)

Melatonin (p. 361)

Microsleeps (p. 352)

Monophasic sleep cycles

Narcolepsy (p. 363)

Nocturnal myoclonus (p. 363)

Nucleus magnocellularis (p. 364)

Orexin (p. 364)

Pineal gland (p. 361)

Polyphasic sleep cycles (p. 365)

Recuperation theories of sleep

REM sleep (p. 345)

Restless legs (p. 363)

Reticular activating system (p. 358)

Sleep apnea (p. 363)

Sleep paralysis (p. 364)

Slow-wave sleep (SWS) (p. 345)

Somnambulism (p. 346)

Suprachiasmatic nuclei (SCN) (p. 359)

Tricyclic antidepressant drugs (p. 354)

Zeitgebers (p. 349)

ON THE CD

Need some help studying the key terms for this chapter? Check out the electronic flash cards for Chapter 14.

chapter

15

Drug Addiction and the Brain's Reward Circuits

Chemicals That Harm with Pleasure

15.1 Basic Principles of Drug Action

15.2 Role of Learning in Drug Tolerance and Drug Withdrawal

15.3 Five Commonly Abused Drugs

15.4 Biopsychological Theories of Addiction

15.5 Intracranial Self-Stimulation and the Pleasure Centers of the Brain

15.6 Neural Mechanisms of Motivation and Addiction

15.7 A Noteworthy Case of Addiction

D rug addiction is a serious problem in most parts of the world. For example, in the United States alone, over 60 million people are addicted to nicotine, alcohol, or both; 5.5 million are addicted to illegal drugs; and many millions more are addicted to prescription drugs. Pause for a moment and think about the sheer magnitude of the grief represented by such figures—hundreds of millions of sick and suffering people worldwide. Think about what these figures may mean for you personally. The incidence of drug addiction is so high that it is almost certain that you, or somebody dear to you, will be adversely affected by drugs. Perhaps it has happened already.

This chapter introduces you to some basic pharmacological principles and concepts, compares the effects of five common addictive drugs, and reviews the research on the neural mechanisms of addiction. You likely already have strong views about drug addiction; thus, as

Thinking Critically

you progress through this chapter, it is particularly important that you do not let your thinking be clouded by preconceptions. In particular, it is important that you do not fall into the trap of assuming that a drug's legal status has much to say about its safety. You will be less likely to assume that legal drugs are safe and illegal drugs are

dangerous if you remember that most laws governing drug abuse in various parts of the world were enacted in the early part of the 20th century, long before there was any scientific research on the topic.

People's tendency to equate drug legality with drug safety was recently conveyed to me in a particularly ironic fashion: I was invited to address a convention of high school teachers on the topic of drug abuse. When I arrived at the convention center to give my talk, I was escorted to a special suite, where I was encouraged to join the executive committee in a round of drug taking—the drug being a special high-proof single-malt whiskey. Later, the irony of the situation had its full impact. As I stepped to the podium under the influence of a psychoactive drug (the whiskey), I looked out through the haze of cigarette smoke at an audience of educators who had invited me to speak to them because they were concerned about the unhealthy impact of drugs on their students. The welcoming applause gradually gave way to the melodic tinkling of ice cubes in liquor glasses, and I began. They did not like what I had to say.

15.1 Basic Principles of Drug Action

This section focuses on the basic principles of drug action, with an emphasis on **psychoactive drugs**—drugs that influence subjective experience and behavior by acting on the nervous system.

Drug Administration and Absorption

Drugs are usually administered in one of four ways: by oral ingestion, by injection, by inhalation, or by absorption through the mucous membranes of the nose, mouth, or rectum. The route of administration influences the rate at which and the degree to which the drug reaches its sites of action.

Ingestion   The oral route is the preferred route of administration for many drugs. Once they are swallowed, drugs dissolve in the fluids of the stomach and are carried to the intestine, where they are absorbed into the bloodstream. However, some drugs readily pass through the stomach wall (e.g., alcohol), and these take effect sooner because they do not have to reach the intestine to be absorbed. Drugs that are not readily absorbed from the digestive tract or that are broken down into inactive metabolites before they can be absorbed must be taken by some other route.

The two main advantages of the oral route of administration over other routes are its ease and relative safety. Its main disadvantage is its unpredictability: Absorption from the digestive tract into the bloodstream can be greatly influenced by such difficult-to-gauge factors as the amount and type of food in the stomach.

Injection   Drug injection is common in medical practice because the effects of injected drugs are strong, fast, and predictable. Drug injections are typically made *subcutaneously* (SC), into the fatty tissue just beneath the skin; *intramuscularly* (IM), into the large muscles; or *intravenously* (IV), directly into veins at points where they run just beneath the skin. Many addicts prefer the intravenous route because the bloodstream delivers the drug directly to the brain. However, the speed and directness of the intravenous route are mixed blessings; after an intravenous injection, there is little or no opportunity to counteract the effects of an overdose, an impurity, or an allergic reaction. Furthermore, many addicts develop scar tissue, infections, and collapsed veins at the few sites on their bodies where there are large accessible veins.

Inhalation   Some drugs can be absorbed into the bloodstream through the rich network of capillaries in the lungs. Many anesthetics are typically administered by *inhalation*, as are tobacco and marijuana. The two main shortcomings of this route are that it is difficult to precisely regulate the dose of inhaled drugs, and many substances damage the lungs if they are inhaled chronically.

Absorption through Mucous Membranes   Some drugs can be administered through the mucous membranes of the nose, mouth, and rectum. Cocaine, for example, is commonly self-administered through the nasal membranes (snorted)—but not without damaging them.

Drug Penetration of the Central Nervous System

Once a drug enters the bloodstream, it is carried in the blood to the blood vessels of the central nervous system. Fortunately, a protective filter, the *blood–brain barrier*, makes it difficult for many potentially dangerous bloodborne chemicals to pass from the blood vessels of the CNS into its neurons.

Mechanisms of Drug Action

Psychoactive drugs influence the nervous system in many ways (see Kuob & Bloom, 1988). Some drugs (e.g., alcohol and many of the general anesthetics) act diffusely on neural membranes throughout the CNS. Others act in a more specific way: by binding to particular synaptic receptors; by influencing the synthesis, transport, release, or deactivation of particular neurotransmitters; or by influencing the chain of chemical reactions elicited in postsynaptic neurons by the activation of their receptors (see Chapter 4).

Drug Metabolism and Elimination

The actions of most drugs are terminated by enzymes synthesized by the *liver*. These liver enzymes stimulate the conversion of active drugs to nonactive forms—a process referred to as **drug metabolism.** In many cases, drug metabolism eliminates a drug's ability to pass through lipid membranes of cells so that it can no longer penetrate the blood–brain barrier. In addition, small amounts of some psychoactive drugs are deactivated by being passed from the body in urine, sweat, feces, breath, and mother's milk.

Drug Tolerance

Drug tolerance is a state of decreased sensitivity to a drug that develops as a result of exposure to it. Drug tolerance can be demonstrated in two ways: by showing that a given dose of the drug has less effect than it had before drug exposure or by showing that it takes more of the drug to produce the same effect. In essence, what this means is that drug tolerance is a shift in the *dose-response curve* (a graph of the magnitude of the effect of different doses of the drug) to the right (see Figure 15.1).

There are three important points to remember about the specificity of drug tolerance. The first is that exposure to one drug can produce tolerance to other drugs that act by the same mechanism; this is known as **cross tolerance.** The second is that drug tolerance often develops to some effects of a drug but not to others. Failure to understand this second point can have tragic consequences for people who think that because they have become tolerant to some effects of a drug (e.g., to the nauseating effects of alcohol or tobacco), they are tolerant to all of them. In fact, tolerance may develop to some effects of a drug while sensitivity to other effects of the same drug increases—increases in the sensitivity to a drug is called **drug sensitization** (Robinson, 1991). The third important point about the specificity of drug tolerance is that it is not a unitary phenomenon; that is, there is no single mechanism that underlies all examples of it. When a drug is administered at active doses, many kinds of adaptive changes can occur to reduce its effects.

Thinking Critically

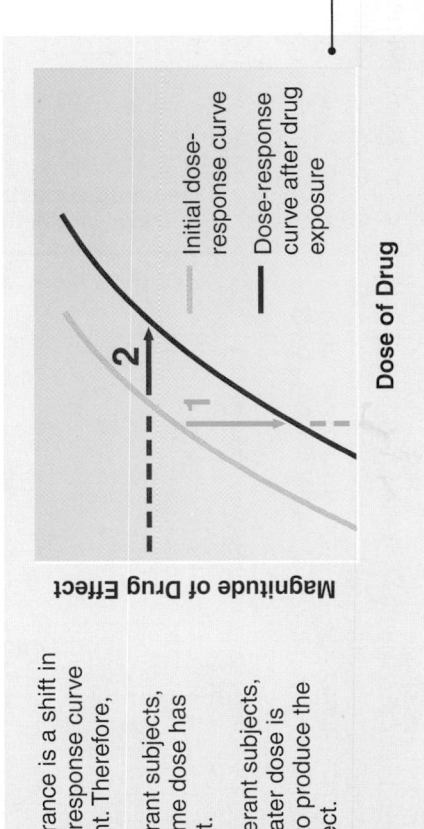

Drug tolerance is a shift in the dose-response curve to the right. Therefore,

1 In tolerant subjects, the same dose has less effect.

2 In tolerant subjects, a greater dose is required to produce the same effect.

Magnitude of Drug Effect

— Initial dose-response curve

— Dose-response curve after drug exposure

Dose of Drug

FIGURE 15.1   Drug tolerance: A shift in the dose-response curve to the right as a result of exposure to the drug.

Two categories of changes underlie drug tolerance: metabolic and functional. Drug tolerance that results from changes that reduce the amount of the drug getting to its sites of action is called **metabolic tolerance.** Drug tolerance that results from changes that reduce the reactivity of the sites of action to the drug is called **functional tolerance.**

Tolerance to psychoactive drugs is largely functional. Functional tolerance to psychoactive drugs can result from several different types of neural changes. For example, exposure to a psychoactive drug can reduce the number of receptors for it, decrease the efficiency with which it binds to existing receptors, or diminish the impact of receptor binding on the activity of the cell.

Drug Withdrawal Effects and Physical Dependence

After significant amounts of a drug have been in the body for a period of time (e.g., several days), its sudden elimination can trigger an adverse physiological reaction called a **withdrawal syndrome.** The effects of drug withdrawal are virtually always opposite to the initial effects of the drug. For example, the withdrawal of anticonvulsant drugs often triggers convulsions, and the withdrawal of sleeping pills often produces insomnia. Individuals who suffer withdrawal reactions when they stop taking a drug are said to be **physically dependent** on that drug.

The fact that withdrawal effects are frequently opposite to the initial effects of the drug suggests that withdrawal effects may be produced by the same neural changes that produce drug tolerance (see Figure 15.2). According to this theory, exposure to a drug produces compensatory changes in the nervous system that offset the drug's effects and produce drug tolerance. Then, when the drug is eliminated from the body, these compensatory neural changes, without the

drug to offset them, manifest themselves as withdrawal symptoms opposite to the initial effects of the drug.

The severity of withdrawal symptoms depends on the particular drug in question, on the duration and degree of the preceding drug exposure, and on the speed with which the drug is eliminated from the body. In general, longer exposure to greater doses followed by more rapid elimination produces greater withdrawal effects.

Addiction: What Is It?

Addicts are habitual drug users, but not all habitual drug users are addicts. **Addicts** are those habitual drug users who continue to use a drug despite its adverse effects on their health and social life and despite their repeated efforts to stop using it (see Hyman & Malenka, 2001).

The greatest confusion about the nature of addiction concerns its relation to physical dependence. Many people equate the two: They see addicts as people who are trapped on a merry-go-round of drug taking, withdrawal symptoms, and further drug taking to combat the withdrawal symptoms. Although appealing in its simplicity, this conception of drug addiction is wrong. Addicts sometimes take drugs to prevent or alleviate withdrawal symptoms, but this is rarely the primary motivating

---

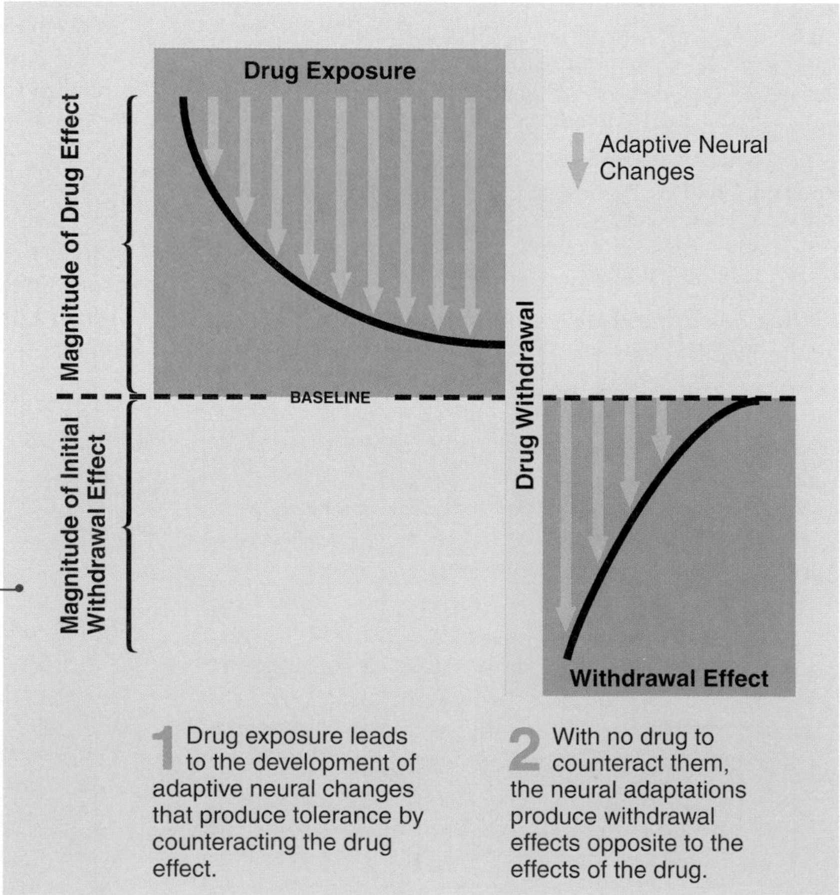

FIGURE 15.2   The relation between drug tolerance and withdrawal effects. The same adaptive neurophysiological changes that develop in response to drug exposure and produce drug tolerance manifest themselves as withdrawal effects once the drug is removed. As the neurophysiological changes develop, tolerance increases; as they subside, the severity of the withdrawal effects decreases.

Magnitude of Initial Withdrawal Effect   **Magnitude of Drug Effect**

BASELINE

Drug Exposure

Drug Withdrawal

Withdrawal Effect

← Adaptive Neural Changes

1 Drug exposure leads to the development of adaptive neural changes that produce tolerance by counteracting the drug effect.

2 With no drug to counteract them, the neural adaptations produce withdrawal effects opposite to the effects of the drug.

factor in their addiction. If it were, addicts could be easily cured by hospitalizing them for a few days, until their withdrawal symptoms subsided. However, most addicts renew their drug taking even after months of enforced abstinence. This is an important issue, and it will be revisited later in the chapter.

When physical dependence was believed to be the major cause of addiction, the term *psychological depen-*

dence was coined to refer to exceptions to this general rule. **Psychological dependence** was said to be the cause of any compulsive drug taking that occurred in the absence of physical dependence. However, now that it is clear that physical dependence is not the major motivating factor in addiction, there is little need for a special category of psychological dependence (see Leshner, 1997).

15.2   Role of Learning in Drug Tolerance and Drug Withdrawal

An important line of psychopharmacologic research has shown that learning plays a major role in both drug tolerance and drug withdrawal. This research has contributed substantially to an understanding of tolerance and withdrawal, but its impact has been more far-reaching: It has established that efforts to understand the effects of psychoactive drugs without considering the experience and behavior of the subjects will provide only partial answers.

Research on the role of learning in drug tolerance has focused on three phenomena: contingent drug tolerance, conditioned drug tolerance, and conditioned withdrawal effects. These phenomena are discussed in the following subsections.

Contingent Drug Tolerance

Contingent drug tolerance refers to demonstrations that tolerance develops only to drug effects that are actually experienced. Most studies of contingent drug tolerance employ the **before-and-after design.** In before-and-after experiments, two groups of subjects receive the same series of drug injections and the same series of repeated tests, but the subjects in one group receive the drug before each test of the series and those in the other group receive the drug after each test. At the end of the experiment, all subjects receive the same dose of the drug followed by the test so that the degree to which the drug disrupts test performance in the two groups can be compared.

My colleagues and I (e.g., Pinel, Mana, & Kim, 1989) have used the before-and-after design to study contingent tolerance to the anticonvulsant effect of alcohol. In one study, two groups of rats received exactly the same regimen of alcohol injections: one injection every 2 days for the duration of the experiment. During the tolerance development phase, the rats in one group received each alcohol injection 1 hour before a mild convulsive amygdala stimulation so that the anticonvulsant effect of the alcohol could be experienced on each trial. The rats in the other group received their injections 1 hour after each convulsive stimulation so that the anticonvul-

sant effect could not be experienced. At the end of the experiment, all of the subjects received a test injection of alcohol, followed 1 hour later by a convulsive stimulation so that the amount of tolerance to the anticonvulsant effect of alcohol could be compared in the two groups. As Figure 15.3 on page 374 illustrates, the rats that received alcohol on each trial before a convulsive stimulation became almost totally tolerant to alcohol's anticonvulsant effect, whereas those that received the same injections and stimulations in the reverse order developed no tolerance whatsoever to alcohol's anticonvulsant effect. Contingent drug tolerance has been demonstrated for many other drug effects in many species (see Poulos & Cappell, 1991; Wolgin & Jakubow, 2003).

Conditioned Drug Tolerance

Whereas studies of contingent drug tolerance focus on what subjects do while they are under the influence of drugs, studies of conditioned drug tolerance focus on the situations in which drugs are taken. **Conditioned drug tolerance** refers to demonstrations that tolerance effects are maximally expressed only when a drug is administered in the same situation in which it has previously been administered (see Mitchell, Basbaum, & Fields, 2000; Siegel, 2004; Weise-Kelley & Siegel, 2001).

In one demonstration of conditioned drug tolerance (Crowell, Hinson, & Siegel, 1981), two groups of rats received 20 alcohol and 20 saline injections in an alternating sequence, 1 injection every other day. The only difference between the two groups was that the rats in one group received all 20 alcohol injections in a distinctive test room and the 20 saline injections in their colony room, while the rats in the other group received the alcohol in the colony room and the saline in the distinctive test room. At the end of the injection period, the tolerance of all rats to the *hypothermic* (temperature-reducing) effects of alcohol was assessed in both environments. As Figure 15.4 on page 374 illustrates, tolerance was observed only when the rats were injected in the environment that had previously been paired with alcohol administration. There have been dozens of other demonstrations of the

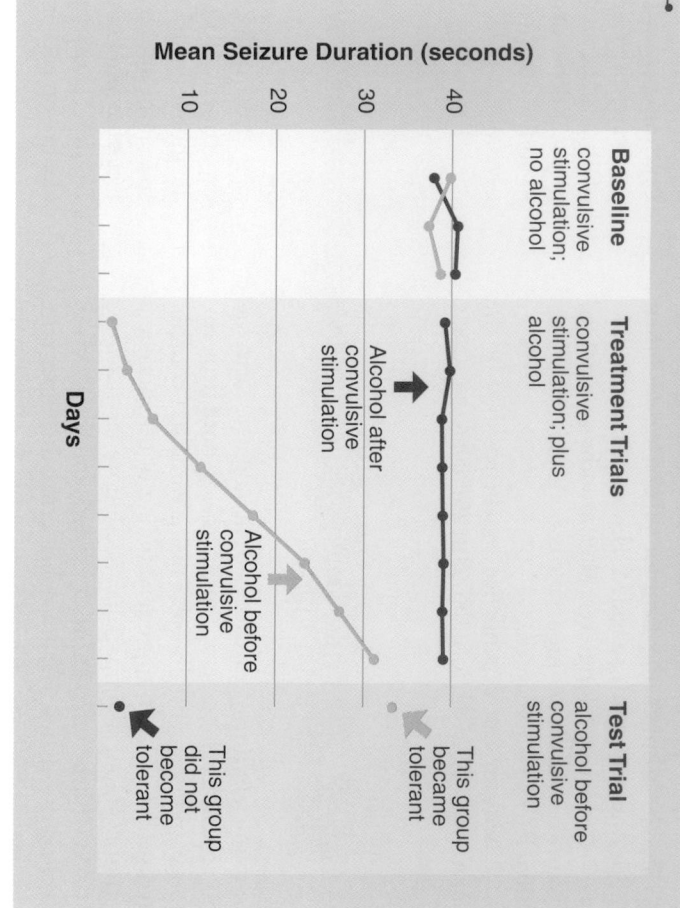

FIGURE 15.3   Contingent tolerance to the anticonvulsant effect of alcohol. The rats that received alcohol on each trial *before* a convulsive stimulation became tolerant to its anticonvulsant effect; those that received the same injections *after* a convulsive stimulation on each trial did not become tolerant. (Adapted from Pinel, Mana, & Kim, 1989.)

situational specificity of drug tolerance: The effect is large, reliable, and general.

The situational specificity of drug tolerance led Siegel and his colleagues to propose that addicts may be particularly susceptible to the lethal effects of a drug *overdose* when the drug is administered in a new context. Their hypothesis is that addicts become tolerant

when they repeatedly self-administer their drug in the same environment and, as a result, begin taking larger and larger doses to counteract the diminution of drug effects. Then, if the addict administers the usual massive dose in an unusual situation, tolerance effects are not present to counteract the effects of the drug, and there is a greater risk of death from overdose. In support of

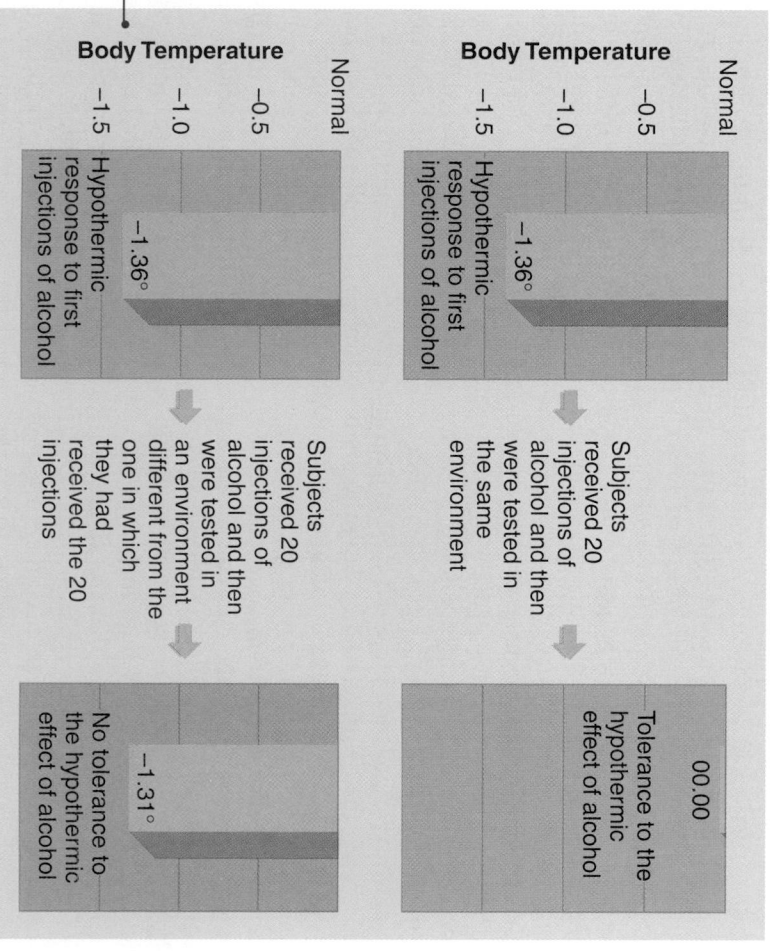

FIGURE 15.4   The situational specificity of tolerance to the hypothermic effects of alcohol. (Adapted from Crowell et al., 1981.)

this hypothesis, Siegel and colleagues (1982) found that many more heroin-tolerant rats died following a high dose of heroin administered in a novel environment than in their usual injection environment. Heroin kills by suppressing respiration.

Siegel views each incidence of drug administration as a Pavlovian conditioning trial in which various environmental stimuli that regularly predict the administration of the drug (e.g., pubs, washrooms, needles, other addicts) are conditional stimuli and the drug effects are unconditional stimuli. The central assumption of the theory is that conditional stimuli that predict drug administration come to elicit conditional responses opposite to the unconditional effects of the drug. Siegel has termed these hypothetical opposing conditional responses **conditioned compensatory responses.** The theory is that as the stimuli that repeatedly predict the effects of a drug come to elicit greater and greater conditioned compensatory responses, they increasingly counteract the unconditional effects of the drug and produce situationally specific tolerance.

Although tolerance develops to many drug effects, sometimes the opposite—sensitization—occurs. *Drug sensitization*, like drug tolerance, can be situationally specific (see Arvanitogiannis, Sullivan, & Amir, 2000). For example, Anagnostaras and Robinson (1996) demonstrated the situational specificity of sensitization to the motor stimulant effects of amphetamine. They found that 10 amphetamine injections, 1 every 3 or 4 days, greatly increased the ability of amphetamine to activate the motor activity of rats—but only when the rats were injected and tested in the same environment in which they had experienced the previous amphetamine injections.

Conditioned Withdrawal Effects

As you have just learned, Siegel's conditioned compensatory response theory suggests that when a drug is repeatedly administered in the same environment, that environment begins to elicit responses that counteract the drug effects and lead to the development of tolerance. One prediction of this theory is that in the absence of the drug, the drug environment should elicit effects opposite to the original effects of the drug. Withdrawal effects that are elicited by the drug environment or by other drug-associated cues are **conditioned withdrawal effects.**

There have been many demonstrations of conditioned withdrawal effects. For example, Krank and Perkins (1993) administered two injections each day to three groups of rats. One group of rats received a morphine injection each day in a distinctive test environment and a saline injection in their home cages; another group received saline injections in the test environment and morphine injections in their home cages; and the third group received saline injections in both the test environment and their home cages. After 10 injection days (i.e., after 20 injections), all

Evolutionary Perspective

injections ceased, the rats were placed in the distinctive test environment, and the morphine withdrawal reactions were assessed. The results are presented in Figure 15.5 on page 376. The rats that had received morphine injections in the distinctive test environment displayed substantially more morphine withdrawal symptoms than did the rats that had received morphine injections in their home cages and the rats that had received only saline injections.

Thinking about Drug Conditioning

In any situation in which drugs are repeatedly administered, conditioned effects are inevitable. That is why it is particularly important to understand them. However, most theories of drug conditioning have a serious problem: They have difficulty predicting the direction of the conditioned effects. For example, Siegel's conditioned compensatory response theory predicts that conditioned drug effects will always be opposite to the unconditioned effects of the drug, but there are many documented instances in which conditional stimuli elicit responses similar to those of the drug.

Ramsay and Woods (1997) contend that much of the confusion about conditioned drug effects stems from a misunderstanding of Pavlovian conditioning. In particular, they criticize the common assumption that the unconditional stimulus in a drug-tolerance experiment is the drug and that the unconditional response is whatever change in physiology or behavior the experimenter happens to be recording. They argue instead that the unconditional stimulus (i.e., the stimulus to which the subject reflexively reacts) is the disruption of neural functioning that has been directly produced by the drug, and that the unconditional responses are the various neurally mediated compensatory reactions to the unconditional stimulus.

Thinking Critically

This change in perspective makes a big difference. For example, in the previously described alcohol tolerance experiment by Crowell and others (1981), alcohol was designated as the unconditional stimulus and the resulting hypothermia as the unconditional response. Instead, Ramsay and Woods would argue that the unconditional stimulus was the hypothermia directly produced by the exposure to alcohol, whereas the compensatory changes that tended to counteract the reductions in body temperature were the unconditional responses.

The important point about all of this is that once one determines the unconditional stimulus and unconditional response, it is easy to predict the direction of the conditional response in any drug-conditioning experiment: The conditional response is always similar to the unconditional response. Moreover, Ramsay and Woods would argue that when the unconditional response counteracts the unconditional stimulus, as is usually the case, conditioning produces tolerance; whereas when the unconditional response augments the unconditional stimulus, conditioning produces sensitization.

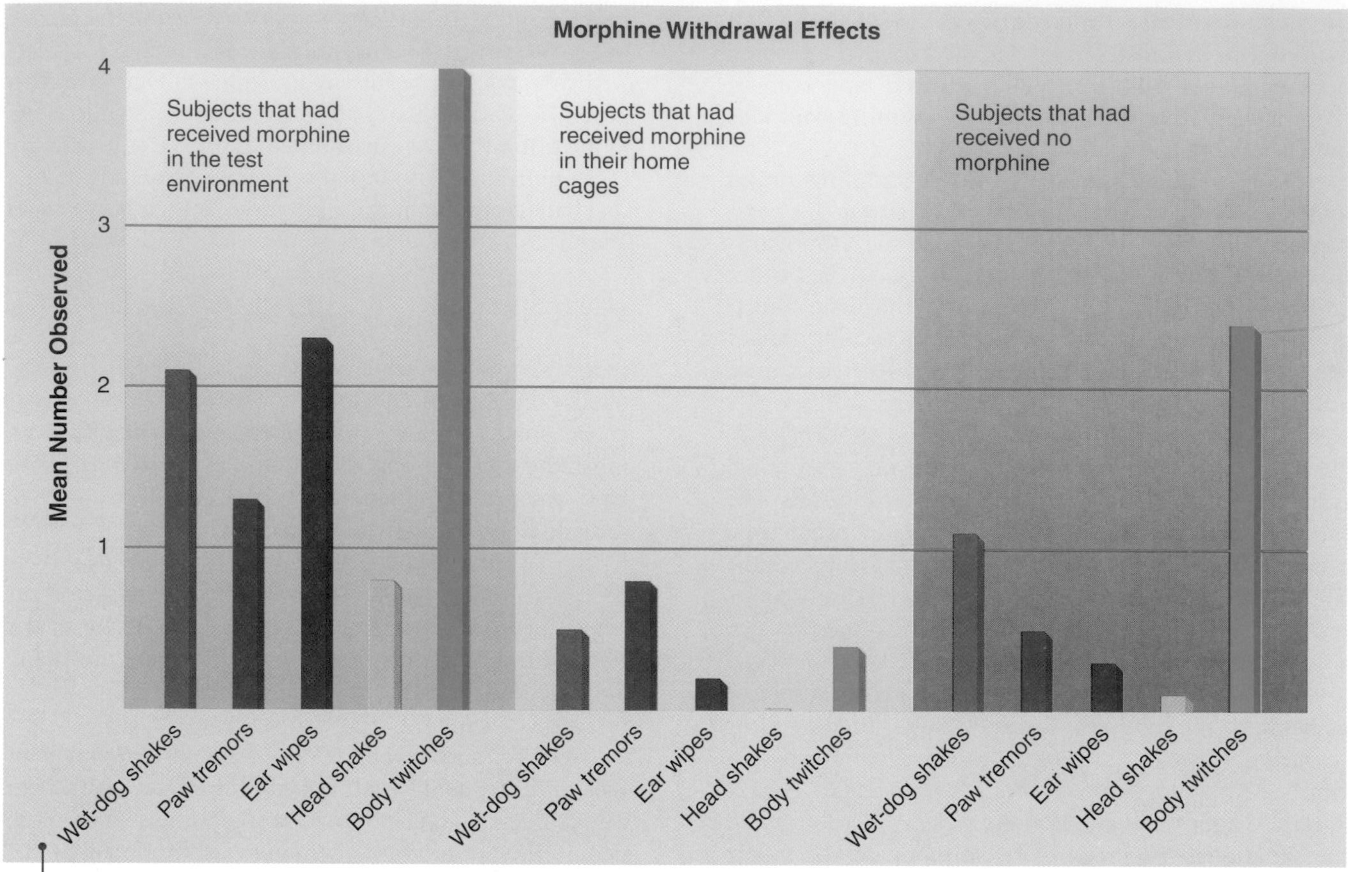

15.3 Five Commonly Abused Drugs

This section focuses on the hazards of chronic use of five commonly abused drugs: tobacco, alcohol, marijuana, cocaine, and the opiates.

Tobacco

When a cigarette is smoked, **nicotine**—the major psychoactive ingredient of tobacco—and some 4,000 other chemicals, collectively referred to as *tar*, are absorbed through the lungs. Each year, tobacco is responsible for over 3 million deaths worldwide, 450,000 in the United States alone, and it contributes to about 20% of all deaths in Western countries (see Laviolette & Van der Kooy, 2004).

Because considerable tolerance develops to some of the immediate effects of tobacco, the effects of smoking a cigarette on nonsmokers and smokers can be quite different. Nonsmokers often respond to a few puffs of a cigarette with various combinations of nausea, vomiting, coughing, sweating, abdominal cramps, dizziness, flushing, and diarrhea. In contrast, smokers report that they are more relaxed, more alert, and less hungry after a cigarette.

There is no question that heavy smokers are drug addicts in every sense of the word (Jones, 1987). The compulsive drug craving, which is the major defining feature of addiction, is readily apparent in any habitual smoker who has run out of cigarettes or who is forced by

FIGURE 15.5 ▸ Conditioned morphine withdrawal effects in rats. Being placed in an environment in which they had previously experienced the effects of morphine elicited morphine withdrawal effects in rats. (Adapted from Krank & Perkins, 1993.)

Morphine Withdrawal Effects

Mean Number Observed

Subjects that had received morphine in the test environment
- Wet-dog shakes
- Paw tremors
- Ear wipes
- Head shakes
- Body twitches

Subjects that had received morphine in their home cages
- Wet-dog shakes
- Paw tremors
- Ear wipes
- Head shakes
- Body twitches

Subjects that had received no morphine
- Wet-dog shakes
- Paw tremors
- Ear wipes
- Head shakes
- Body twitches

circumstance to refrain from smoking for several hours. Furthermore, habitual smokers who stop smoking experience a variety of withdrawal effects, such as depression, anxiety, restlessness, irritability, constipation, and difficulties in sleeping and concentrating.

About 70% of all people who experiment with smoking become addicted—this figure compares unfavorably with 10% for alcohol and 30% for heroin. Moreover, only about 20% of all attempts to stop smoking are successful for 2 years or more (Schelling, 1992). Can you think of any other psychoactive drug that is self-administered almost continually—even while the addicts are walking along the street?

Twin studies (Lerman et al., 1999; True et al., 1999) indicate that nicotine addiction has a major genetic component. The heritability estimate is about 65%.

The consequences of long-term tobacco use are alarming. **Smoker's syndrome** is characterized by chest pain, labored breathing, wheezing, coughing, and a heightened susceptibility to infections of the respiratory tract. Chronic smokers are highly susceptible to a variety of potentially lethal lung disorders, including pneumonia, *bronchitis* (chronic inflammation of the bronchioles of the lungs), *emphysema* (loss of elasticity of the lung from chronic irritation), and lung cancer. Although the increased risk of lung cancer receives the greatest publicity, smoking also increases the risk of cancer of the larynx (voice box), mouth, esophagus, kidneys, pancreas, bladder, and stomach. Smokers also run a greater risk of developing a variety of cardiovascular diseases, which may culminate in heart attack or stroke.

Many smokers claim that they smoke despite the adverse effects because smoking reduces tension. However, smokers are actually more tense than nonsmokers. Their levels of tension are reasonably normal while they are smoking, but they increase markedly between cigarettes. Thus, the apparent relaxant effect of smoking merely reflects the temporary reversal of the stress caused by the smoker's addiction (see Parrott, 1999).

Sufferers from Buerger's disease provide a shocking illustration of the addictive power of nicotine. **Buerger's disease** is a condition in which the blood vessels, especially those supplying the legs, are constricted whenever nicotine enters the bloodstream:

If a patient with this condition continues to smoke, gangrene may eventually set in. First a few toes may have to be amputated, then the foot at the ankle, then the leg at the knee, and ultimately at the hip. Somewhere along this gruesome progression gangrene may also attack the other leg. Patients are strongly advised that if they will only stop smoking, it is virtually certain that the otherwise inexorable march of gangrene up the legs will be curbed. Yet surgeons report that it is not at all uncommon to find a patient with Buerger's disease vigorously puffing away in his hospital bed following a second or third amputation operation. (Brecher, 1972, pp. 215–216)

Clinical Implications

The adverse effects of tobacco smoke are unfortunately not restricted to those who smoke. There is now strong evidence that individuals who live or work with smokers are more likely to develop heart disease and cancer than those who don't. Even the unborn are vulnerable: Smoking during pregnancy increases the likelihood of miscarriage, stillbirth, and early death of the child. The levels of nicotine in the blood of breastfed infants are often as great as those in the blood of their smoking mothers.

Alcohol

Approximately 104 million Americans have consumed alcohol in the last month, 13 million of these are heavy users, and over 100,000 die each year from alcohol-related diseases and accidents. Alcohol is involved in roughly 3% of all deaths in the United States, including deaths from birth defects, ill health, accidents, and violence.

Because alcohol molecules are small and soluble in both fat and water, they invade all parts of the body. Alcohol is classified as a **depressant** because at moderate-to-high doses it depresses neural firing; however, at low doses it can stimulate neural firing and facilitate social interaction. Alcohol addiction has a major genetic component (McGue, 1999): Heritability estimates are about 55%.

With moderate doses, the alcohol drinker experiences various degrees of cognitive, perceptual, verbal, and motor impairment, as well as a loss of control that can lead to a variety of socially unacceptable actions. High doses result in unconsciousness; and if blood levels reach 0.5%, there is a risk of death from respiratory depression. The telltale red facial flush of alcohol intoxication is produced by the dilation of blood vessels in the skin; this dilation increases the amount of heat that is lost from the blood to the air and leads to a decrease in body temperature (*hypothermia*). Alcohol is also a *diuretic*; that is, it increases the production of urine by the kidneys.

Alcohol, like many addictive drugs, produces both tolerance and physical dependence. The livers of heavy drinkers metabolize alcohol more quickly than do the livers of nondrinkers, but this increase in metabolic

efficiency contributes only slightly to overall alcohol tolerance; most alcohol tolerance is functional. Alcohol withdrawal often produces a mild syndrome of headache, nausea, vomiting, and tremulousness, which is euphemistically referred to as a *hangover.*

A full-blown alcohol withdrawal syndrome comprises three phases (see De Witte et al., 2003). The first phase begins about 5 or 6 hours after the cessation of a long bout of heavy drinking and is characterized by severe tremors, agitation, headache, nausea, vomiting, abdominal cramps, profuse sweating, and sometimes hallucinations. The defining feature of the second phase, which typically occurs between 15 and 30 hours after cessation of drinking, is convulsive activity. The third phase, which usually begins a day or two after the cessation of drinking and lasts for 3 or 4 days, is called **delirium tremens (DTs)**. The DTs are characterized by disturbing hallucinations, bizarre delusions, agitation, confusion, *hyperthermia* (high temperature), and *tachycardia* (rapid heartbeat). The convulsions and the DTs produced by alcohol withdrawal can be lethal.

Alcohol attacks almost every tissue in the body (see Anderson et al., 1993). Chronic alcohol consumption produces extensive brain damage (Hayakawa et al., 1992) and, as you learned in Chapter 1, **Korsakoff's syndrome**—a neuropsychological disorder that is characterized by severe memory loss, sensory and motor dysfunction, and severe *dementia* (intellectual deterioration). Chronic alcohol consumption also causes extensive scarring, or **cirrhosis,** of the liver, which is the major cause of death among heavy alcohol users. Alcohol erodes the muscles of the heart and thus increases the risk of heart attack. It irritates the lining of the digestive tract and, in so doing, increases the risk of oral and liver cancer, stomach ulcers, *pancreatitis* (inflammation of the pancreas), and *gastritis* (inflammation of the stomach). And not to be forgotten is the carnage that alcohol produces on our highways and in our homes. (The devastating effect of alcohol on the families of addicts was emphasized to me by a student who had grown up with an alcoholic parent and who asked me to stress this adverse effect.)

Like nicotine, alcohol readily penetrates the placental membrane and affects the fetus. The result is that the offspring of mothers who consume substantial quantities of alcohol during pregnancy can develop **fetal alcohol syndrome (FAS)**. The FAS child suffers from some or all of the following symptoms (O'Leary, 2004): brain damage, mental retardation, poor coordination, poor muscle tone, low birth weight, retarded growth, and/or physical deformity. Because alcohol can disrupt brain development in so many ways (e.g., by disrupting neurotrophic support, by disrupting the production of cell-adhesion molecules, or by disrupting normal patterns of apoptosis), there is no time during pregnancy when alcohol consumption is safe (see Guerri, 2002; Farber & Olney, 2003). Moreover, there seems to be no safe

Clinical Implications

amount. Although full-blown FAS is rarely seen in the babies of mothers who never had more than one drink a day during pregnancy, children of mothers who drank only moderately while pregnant are sometimes found to have a variety of cognitive problems, even though they are not diagnosed with FAS (see Korkman, Kettunen, & Autti-Ramo, 2003).

Alcohol affects the brain function of drinkers in many ways. For example, it reduces the flow of calcium ions into neurons by acting on ion channels; it interferes with the function of second messengers inside neurons; it disrupts GABAergic and glutaminergic transmission; and it triggers apoptosis (see Farber & Olney, 2003; Ikonomidou et al., 2000).

Marijuana

Marijuana is the name commonly given to the dried leaves and flowers of **Cannabis sativa**—the common hemp plant. Approximately 2 million Americans have used marijuana in the last month. The usual mode of consumption is to smoke these leaves in a *joint* (a cigarette of marijuana) or a pipe; but marijuana is also effective when ingested orally, if first baked into an oil-rich substrate, such as a chocolate brownie, to promote absorption from the gastrointestinal tract.

The psychoactive effects of marijuana are largely attributable to a constituent called **THC** (delta-9-tetrahydrocannabinol). However, marijuana contains over 80 *cannabinoids* (chemicals of the same chemical class as THC), which may also be psychoactive. Most of the cannabinoids are found in a sticky resin covering the leaves and flowers of the plant, which can be extracted and dried to form a dark corklike material called **hashish.** Hashish can be further processed into an extremely potent product called *hash oil.*

Written records of marijuana use go back 6,000 years in China, where its stems were used to make rope, its seeds were used as a grain, and its leaves and flowers were used for their psychoactive and medicinal effects.

In the Middle Ages, cannabis cultivation spread from the Middle East into Western Europe; however, in

Europe, the plant was grown primarily for the manufacture of rope, and its psychoactive properties were largely forgotten. During the period of European imperialism, rope was in high demand for sailing vessels. In 1611, the American colonies responded to this demand by growing cannabis as a cash crop; George Washington was one of the more notable cannabis growers.

The practice of smoking the leaves of *Cannabis sativa* and the word *marijuana* itself seem to have been introduced to the southern United States in the early part of the 20th century by Mexican immigrants; and the drug gradually became popular among certain subgroups, such as the poor in city ghettos and jazz musicians. In 1926, an article appeared in a New Orleans newspaper exposing the "menace of marijuana," and soon similar stories were appearing in newspapers all over the United States under titles such as "The Evil Weed," "The Killer Drug," and "Marijuana Madness." The population was told that marijuana turns normal people into violent, drug-crazed criminals who rapidly become addicted to heroin.

The result of the misrepresentation of the effects of marijuana by the U.S. news media was the enactment of many laws against the drug. In many states, marijuana was legally classified a **narcotic** (a legal term used to refer to opiates), and punishment for its use was dealt out accordingly. However, the structure of the active constituents of marijuana and their physiological and behavioral effects bear no resemblance to those of the other narcotics; thus, legally classifying marijuana as a narcotic was akin to passing a law that red is green.

The popularization of marijuana smoking among the middle and upper classes in the 1960s stimulated a massive program of research; yet there is still considerable confusion about marijuana among the general population. One of the difficulties in characterizing the effects of marijuana is that they are subtle, difficult to measure, and greatly influenced by the social situation:

At low, usual "social" doses, the intoxicated individual may experience an increased sense of well-being; initial restlessness and hilarity followed by a dreamy, carefree state of relaxation; alteration of sensory perceptions including expansion of space and time; and a more vivid sense of touch, sight, smell, taste, and sound; a feeling of hunger, especially a craving for sweets; and subtle changes in thought formation and expression. To an unknowing observer, an individual in this state of consciousness would not appear noticeably different. (National Commission on Marijuana and Drug Abuse, 1972, p. 68)

Although the effects of typical social doses of marijuana are subtle, high doses do impair psychological functioning. Short-term memory is impaired, and the ability to carry out tasks involving multiple steps to reach a specific goal declines. Speech becomes slurred, and meaningful conversation becomes difficult. A sense of unreality, emotional intensification, sensory distortion, and motor impairment are also common. However, even after high doses, an unexpected knock at the door can often bring about the return of a reasonable semblance of normal behavior.

In the light of the documented effects of marijuana, the earlier claims that its use would trigger a wave of violent crimes in the youth of America seem absurd. It is difficult to imagine how anybody could believe that the red-eyed, gluttonous, sleepy, giggling products of common social doses of marijuana would be likely to commit violent criminal acts. In fact, marijuana actually curbs aggressive behavior (Tinklenberg, 1974).

The addiction potential of marijuana is low. Most people who use marijuana do so only occasionally, and most who use it as youths curtail their use in their 30s and 40s. Tolerance to marijuana develops during periods of sustained use; however, obvious withdrawal symptoms (e.g., nausea, diarrhea, sweating, chills, tremor, sleep disturbance) are rare, except in contrived laboratory situations in which massive oral doses are administered.

What are the health hazards of marijuana use? This is a difficult question to answer because there have been so many claims based on so little convincing evidence. However, most scientists who have carefully scrutinized the evidence have reached the same general conclusion: The occasional use of small amounts of marijuana, the pattern of use favored by most users, has few, if any, permanent adverse effects (Jacques et al., 2004). Even long-term heavy use of marijuana has effects that are far less severe than those of its legal cousins: nicotine and alcohol.

Two adverse effects of heavy marijuana use have been well documented. First, the minority of marijuana smokers who smoke it regularly tend to develop respiratory problems (see Zimmer & Morgan, 1997): cough, bronchitis, and asthma. Second, because marijuana produces *tachycardia* (elevated heart rate), single large doses can trigger heart attacks in susceptible individuals (e.g., elderly men who have previously suffered a heart attack).

A third effect of heavy marijuana use relates to the brain. Many people believe that marijuana use causes brain damage, in particular, damage to those areas of the brain involved in memory: Is this true? Rogers and Robbins (2001) reviewed the evidence. There is no convincing evidence that marijuana use causes brain damage, but the evidence pertaining to deficits in memory function is more complex. Some reviewers (e.g., Pope, Gruber, & Yurgelun-Todd, 1995) have concluded that there is no good evidence of neurocognitive deficits that outlast the period of marijuana exposure. Two studies have found slight memory deficits in particularly heavy long-term users (Block & Ghoneim, 1993; Fletcher et al., 1996), but there is no evidence that these effects are permanent. Indeed, a study by Pope and colleagues (2001) indicates that they are not permanent.

Some effects of marijuana have been shown to be of clinical benefit. It has been used, often illegally, to block the nausea of cancer patients undergoing chemotherapy and to stimulate the appetites of patients who have lost their appetites. Marijuana has also been shown to block seizures (Corcoran, McCaughran, & Wada, 1978), to dilate the bronchioles of asthmatics, to decrease the severity of *glaucoma* (a disorder characterized by an increase in the pressure of the fluid inside the eye), and to reduce some kinds of pain.

Because THC is fat-soluble, it was initially assumed that it influenced the brain by inserting itself directly into neural membranes. However, we now know that THC binds to receptors that are particularly dense in the basal ganglia, hippocampus, cerebellum, and neocortex (Howlett et al., 1990), and presumably, it exerts most of its effects by binding to cannabinoid receptors (see Piomelli, 2003; Wilson & Nicoll, 2002). The cloning of the gene for the THC receptor (Matsuda et al., 1990) triggered a search for an endogenous THC-like chemical that binds to this receptor. Such a chemical has been isolated, its structure has been characterized (Devane et al., 1992) and named *anandamide* (which means "internal bliss"), but its function is still unknown (Di Marzo et al., 1998).

Evolutionary Perspective

What might the function of anandamide be? One study has shown that it might protect the brain from excitotoxicity. Knockout mice with no type 1 cannabinoid receptors are more susceptible to seizures produced by *excitotoxins* (chemicals that kill neurons by overactivating them) (see Wilson & Nicoll, 2002).

I cannot end this discussion of marijuana (*Cannabis sativa*) without telling you the following story:

> You can imagine how surprised I was when my colleague went to his back door, opened it, and yelled, "Sativa, here Sativa, dinner time."
>
> "What was that you called your dog?" I asked as he returned to his beer.
>
> "Sativa," he said. "The kids picked it. I think they learned about it at school; a Greek goddess or something. Pretty, isn't it? And catchy too: Every kid on the street seems to remember her name."
>
> "Yes," I said. "Very pretty."

Cocaine and Other Stimulants

Stimulants are drugs whose primary effect is to produce general increases in neural and behavioral activity. Although stimulants all have a similar profile of effects, they differ greatly in their potency. Coca-Cola is a mild commercial stimulant preparation consumed by many people around the world. Today, its stimulant action is attributable to *caffeine*, but when it was first introduced, "the pause that refreshes" packed a real wallop in the form of small amounts of cocaine. **Cocaine** and its derivatives are the most commonly abused stimulants, and thus they are the focus of this discussion.

Cocaine is prepared from the leaves of the coca bush, which is found primarily in Peru and Bolivia. For centuries, a crude extract called *coca paste* has been made

Clinical Implications

directly from the leaves and eaten. Today, it is more common to treat the coca paste and extract *cocaine hydrochloride*, the nefarious white powder that is referred to simply as *cocaine* and typically consumed by snorting or by injection. Cocaine hydrochloride may be converted to its base form by boiling it in a solution of baking soda until the water has evaporated. The impure residue of this process is **crack**, which is a potent, cheap, smokable form of cocaine. Crack has rapidly become the preferred form of the drug for many cocaine users. However, because crack is impure, variable, and consumed by smoking, it is difficult to study and most research on cocaine derivatives has thus focused on pure cocaine hydrochloride. Approximately 1.5 million Americans used cocaine or crack in the last month.

Cocaine hydrochloride is an effective local anesthetic and was once widely prescribed as such until it was supplanted by synthetic analogues such as *procaine* and *lidocaine*. It is not, however, cocaine's anesthetic actions that are of interest to users. People eat, smoke, snort, or inject cocaine or its derivatives in order to experience its psychological effects. Users report being swept by a wave of well-being; they feel self-confident, alert, energetic, friendly, outgoing, fidgety, and talkative; and they have less than their usual desire for food and sleep.

Like alcohol, cocaine hydrochloride is frequently consumed in *binges* (see Gawin, 1991). Cocaine addicts tend to go on so-called **cocaine sprees**, binges in which extremely high levels of intake are maintained for periods of a day or two. During a cocaine spree, users become increasingly tolerant to the euphoria-producing effects of cocaine. Accordingly, larger and larger doses are often administered. The spree usually ends when the cocaine is gone or when it begins to have serious toxic effects.

Extremely high blood levels of cocaine are reached during cocaine sprees. The results commonly include sleeplessness, tremors, nausea, hyperthermia, and psychotic behavior. The syndrome of psychotic behavior observed during cocaine sprees is called **cocaine psychosis.** It is similar to, and has often been mistakenly diagnosed as, *paranoid schizophrenia*.

During cocaine sprees, there is a risk of loss of consciousness, seizures, respiratory arrest, heart attack, or stroke (Kokkinos & Levine, 1993). Although tolerance develops to most effects of cocaine (e.g., to the euphoria), repeated cocaine exposure sensitizes subjects (i.e., makes them even more responsive) to its motor and convulsive effects (see Robinson & Berridge, 1993).

Cocaine snorting can damage the nasal membranes, and cocaine smoking can damage the lungs; but both routes are safer than IV injection. Fatalities from cocaine overdose are most likely to follow IV injection.

Although cocaine is extremely addictive, the withdrawal effects triggered by abrupt termination of a cocaine spree are mild (Miller, Summers, & Gold, 1993). Common cocaine withdrawal symptoms include a negative mood swing and insomnia.

Cocaine facilitates catecholaminergic transmission. It does this by blocking the reuptake of *catecholamines* (dopamine, norepinephrine, and epinephrine) into presynaptic neurons. Its effects on dopaminergic transmission seem to play the major role in mediating its euphoria-inducing effects.

Cocaine and its various derivatives are not the only commonly abused stimulants. **Amphetamine** (speed) and its relatives also present major health problems. Amphetamine has been in wide illicit use since the 1960s—it is usually consumed orally in the potent form called *d-amphetamine* (dextroamphetamine). The effects of *d*-amphetamine are comparable to those of cocaine; for example, it produces a syndrome of psychosis called *amphetamine psychosis.*

In the 1990s, *d*-amphetamine was supplanted as the favored amphetaminelike drug by several more potent relatives. One is *methamphetamine* (see Cho, 1990). Methamphetamine (meth) is commonly used in its even more potent, smokable, crystalline form (ice or crystal). Another potent relative of amphetamine is *3,4-methylenedioxymethamphetamine* (MDMA, or ecstasy), which is taken orally. Because it is widely used in the "rave" culture, ecstasy commonly interacts with the adverse consequences of overexercise on the dance floor, leading to dehydration, exhaustion, muscle breakdown, overheating, and convulsions.

Do stimulants have long-term adverse effects on the health of habitual users? Mounting evidence suggests that stimulants are neurotoxins (see Davidson et al., 2001). Recent research has focused on the effects of MDMA (ecstasy) because of its powerful effects and current prevalence (see Cole & Sumnall, 2003). The results of experiments on nonhuman animals are cause for concern: There is good evidence from experiments on laboratory animals that MDMA can have toxic effects on both serotonergic and dopaminergic neurons (see Ricaurte et al., 2002). The question is whether the high doses used in these laboratory experiments limit the relevance of the findings for human users.

Correlational studies in human users of MDMA support the hypothesis that the drug can cause brain damage: There are several reports that habitual users display abnormalities of serotonergic function and deficits in the performance of tests of memory, psychomotor function, and mood (e.g., McCardle et al., 2004). It has not yet been established that these effects in humans are caused by the MDMA and are permanent, but considering the results of the correlational studies on humans along with the results of experiments in laboratory animals clearly provides cause for concern. Women who use stimulants while they are pregnant tend to have children who score poorly on IQ tests (see Singer et al., 2002).

Clinical Implications

The Opiates: Heroin and Morphine

Opium—the sap that exudes from the seeds of the opium poppy—has several psychoactive ingredients. Most notable are **morphine** and **codeine,** its weaker relative. Morphine, codeine, and other drugs that have similar structures or effects are commonly referred to as the **opiates.** The opiates have a clear Jekyll and Hyde character. On their Dr. Jekyll side, the opiates are unmatched as **analgesics** (painkillers), and they are also extremely effective in the treatment of cough and diarrhea. But, unfortunately, the kindly Dr. Jekyll brings with him the evil Mr. Hyde—the risk of addiction.

Archeological evidence suggests that the practice of eating opium became popular in the Middle East sometime before 4000 B.C., and then it spread throughout Africa, Europe, and Asia (see Berridge & Edwards, 1981; Latimer & Goldberg, 1981). Three historic events fanned the flame of opiate addiction. First, in 1644, the Emperor of China banned tobacco smoking, and many Chinese tobacco smokers tried smoking opium and liked it. Because smoking opium has a greater effect on the brain than does eating it, many more people became addicted

Evolutionary Perspective

to opium as the practice of opium smoking slowly spread to other countries. Second, morphine, the most potent constituent of opium, was first isolated in 1803, and it became available commercially in the 1830s. Third, the hypodermic needle was invented in 1856, and soon injured soldiers (e.g., those of the American Civil War) were introduced to morphine through a needle; during this era, morphine addiction was known as *soldiers' disease*.

Most people are surprised to learn that until the early part of the 20th century, opium was legally available and consumed in great quantity in many parts of the world, including Europe and North America. Opium was available in cakes, candies, and wines, as well as in a variety of over-the-counter medicinal offerings. Opium potions such as *laudanum* (a very popular mixture of opium and alcohol), *Godfrey's Cordial*, and *Dalby's Carminative* were very popular. (The word *carminative* should win first prize for making a sow's ear at least sound like a silk purse: A carminative is a drug that expels gas from the digestive tract, thereby reducing stomach cramps and flatulence. *Flatulence* is the obvious pick for second prize.) There were even over-the-counter opium potions just for baby. Potions such as *Mrs. Winslow's Soothing Syrup* and the aptly labeled *Street's Infant Quietness* were popular in many households. Although pure morphine could not be purchased without a prescription at the time, it was so frequently prescribed by physicians for so many different maladies that morphine addiction was common among those who could afford doctors.

The **Harrison Narcotics Act,** passed in 1914, made it illegal to sell or use opium, morphine, or cocaine in the United States. However, the act did not include the semisynthetic opiate **heroin.** Heroin had been synthesized in 1870 by the addition of two acetyl groups to the morphine molecule, which greatly increased its ability to penetrate the blood–brain barrier. In 1898, heroin was marketed by the Bayer Drug Company; it was freely available without prescription and was widely advertised as a super aspirin. Tests showed that it was a more potent analgesic than morphine and that it was less likely to induce nausea and vomiting. Moreover, the Bayer Drug Company, on the basis of flimsy evidence, claimed that heroin was not addictive; this is why it was not covered by the Harrison Narcotics Act.

The consequence of this omission was that opiate addicts in the United States, forbidden by law to use opium or morphine, turned to the readily available and much more potent heroin; and the flames of addiction were further fanned. In 1924, the U.S. Congress made it illegal for anybody to possess, sell, or use heroin. Unfortunately, the laws enacted to stamp out opiate addiction in the United States have been far from successful: An estimated 130,000 Americans currently use heroin, and organized crime flourishes on the proceeds.

The effect of opiates most valued by addicts is the *rush* that follows intravenous injection. The *heroin rush* is a wave of intense abdominal, orgasmic pleasure that evolves into a state of serene, drowsy euphoria. Many opiate users, drawn by these pleasurable effects, begin to use the drug more and more frequently. Then, once they reach a point where they keep themselves drugged much of the time, tolerance and physical dependence develop and contribute to the problem. Opiate tolerance encourages addicts to progress to higher doses, to more potent drugs (e.g., heroin), and to more direct routes of administration (e.g., IV injection); and physical dependence adds to the already high motivation to take the drug.

Although opiates are highly addictive, the direct health hazards of chronic exposure are surprisingly minor. The main risks are constipation, pupil constriction, menstrual irregularity, and reduced libido (sex drive). Many opiate addicts have taken pure heroin or morphine for years with no serious ill effects. In fact, opiate addiction is more prevalent among doctors, nurses, and dentists than among other professionals (e.g., Brewster, 1986):

Clinical Implications

An individual tolerant to and dependent upon an opiate who is socially or financially capable of obtaining an adequate supply of good quality drug, sterile syringes and needles, and other paraphernalia may maintain his or her proper social and occupational functions, remain in fairly good health, and suffer little serious incapacitation as a result of the dependence. (Julien, 1981, p. 117)

One such individual was Dr. William Steward Halsted, one of the founders of Johns Hopkins Medical School and one of the most brilliant surgeons of his day . . . . known as "the father of modern surgery." And yet, during his career he was addicted to morphine, a fact that he was able to keep secret from all but his closest friends. In fact, the only time his habit caused him any trouble was when he was attempting to reduce his dosage. (McKim, 1986, p. 197)

The classic opiate withdrawal syndrome usually begins 6 to 12 hours after the last dose. The first withdrawal sign is typically an increase in restlessness; the addict begins to pace and fidget. Watering eyes, running nose, yawning, and sweating are also common during the early stages of opiate withdrawal. Then, the addict often falls into a fitful sleep, which typically lasts for several hours. After the sleep is over, the original symptoms may be joined in extreme cases by chills, shivering, profuse sweating, gooseflesh, nausea, vomiting, diarrhea, cramps, pains, dilated pupils, tremor, and muscle spasms. The gooseflesh skin and leg spasms of the opiate withdrawal syndrome are the basis for the expressions "going cold turkey" and "kicking the habit." The symptoms of opiate withdrawal are typically most severe in the second or third day after the last injection, and by the seventh day they have all but disappeared.

The symptoms of opiate withdrawal are not trivial, but their severity has been widely exaggerated. Opiate withdrawal is about as serious as a bad case of the flu—a far cry from the convulsions, delirium, and risk of death associated with alcohol withdrawal:

> Opiate withdrawal is probably one of the most misunderstood aspects of drug use. This is largely because of the image of withdrawal that has been portrayed in the movies and popular literature for many years. . . . Few addicts . . . take enough drug to cause the . . . severe withdrawal symptoms that are shown in the movies. Even in its most severe form, however, opiate withdrawal is not as dangerous or terrifying as withdrawal from barbiturates or alcohol. (McKim, 1986, p. 199)

Most risks of opiate addiction are indirect—that is, not attributable to the drug itself. Many are risks that

Thinking Critically

arise out of the battle between the relentless addictive power of opiates and the attempts of governments to eradicate addiction by making drugs illegal. The opiate addicts who cannot give up their habit—treatment programs report success rates of only 10%—are caught in the middle. Because most opiate addicts must purchase their morphine and heroin from illicit dealers at greatly inflated prices, those who are not wealthy become trapped in a life of poverty and petty crime. They are poor, they are undernourished, they receive poor medical care, they are often driven to prostitution, and they run great risk of contracting AIDS and other infections (e.g., hepatitis, syphilis, gonorrhea) from unsafe sex and unsterile needles. Moreover, they never know for sure what they are injecting: Some street drugs are poorly processed, and virtually all will have been *cut* (stretched by the addition of some similar-appearing substance) to some unknown degree.

One particularly serious risk associated with heroin that is largely indirect is death from overdose. (Overdose deaths are a risk any time addictive drugs are routinely administered via the intravenous route, but it is clear that the very laws designed to prevent heroin addiction

are complicit in heroin-overdose deaths. The laws force addicts to buy their drugs from unreliable sources, and, as a result, waves of overdose deaths occur when shipments of contaminated drugs hit the street. Paradoxically, similar waves of deaths occur when shipments of particularly pure heroin hit the street—because addicts select doses on the basis of their previous experience with heroin that has been heavily cut.

The opiates, like marijuana, seem to exert their effects by binding to particular receptors whose normal function is to bind to endogenous chemicals. The endogenous chemicals that bind to opiate receptors are called *endorphins*, and about 20 different kinds have been identified.

The primary treatment for heroin addiction has been methadone. Ironically, methadone is itself an opiate with many of the same effects as heroin. However, because methadone produces less pleasure than heroin, the strategy has been to block heroin withdrawal effects with methadone and then maintain addicts on methadone until they can be weaned from it. Although methadone replacement therapy has been only marginally effective, it has been the sole option available to many heroin addicts. Recently, however, *buprenorphine* was approved for the treatment of heroin addiction. Buprenorphine has a high and long-lasting affinity for opiate receptors and thus blocks the effects on the brain of other opiates, without producing powerful euphoria. Early studies suggest that it has some promise (see Davids & Gaspar, 2004; Gerra et al., 2004).

Comparison of the Hazards of Tobacco, Alcohol, Marijuana, Cocaine, and Heroin

Thinking Critically

One way of comparing the adverse effects of tobacco, alcohol, marijuana, cocaine, and heroin is to compare the prevalence of their use in society as a whole. In terms of this criterion, it is clear that tobacco and alcohol have a far greater negative impact than do marijuana, cocaine, and heroin (see Figure 15.6). Another method of comparison is to base it on death rates: Tobacco has been implicated in the deaths of approximately 450,000 Americans per year; alcohol, in approximately 100,000 per year; and all other drugs combined, in about 40,000 per year.

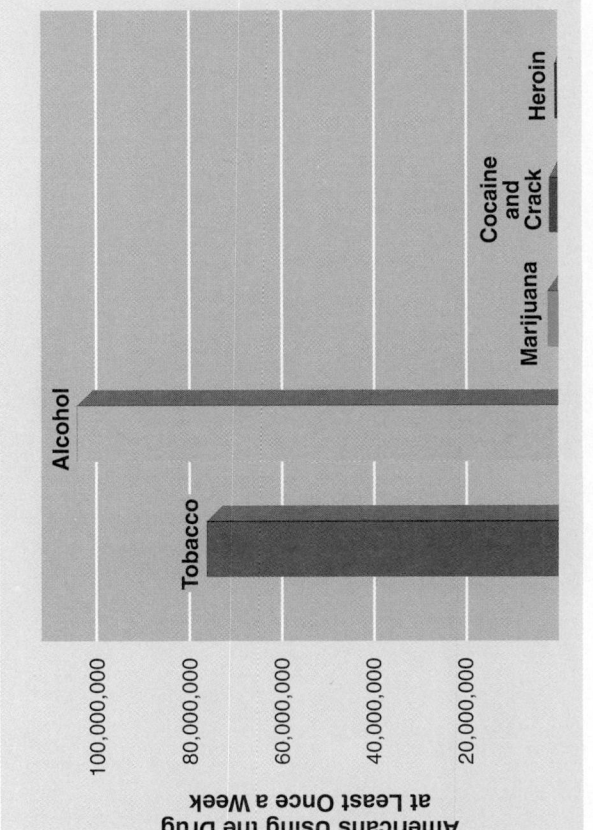

FIGURE 15.6 Prevalence of drug use in the United States. Figures are based on a recent survey of people 12 years of age and over who live in households and used the drug in question at least once in the last month.

But what about the individual drug user? Who is taking greater health risks: the cigarette smoker, the alcohol drinker, the marijuana smoker, the cocaine user, or the heroin user? You now have the information to answer this question. Complete the Demonstration, which will help you appreciate the positive impact that studying biopsychology is having on your understanding of important issues. Would you have ranked the health risks of these drugs in the same way before you began this chapter?

The Drug Dilemmas: Striking the Right Balance

Drug abuse is currently a serious problem. In the United States alone, recreational drugs contribute to several

hundred thousand deaths each year, and the public must bear the brunt of the crime and violence that is perpetrated by addicts who are forced to steal and prostitute themselves to fuel their expensive habits. Also, the public must bear the economic burdens of increased medical care, increased law enforcement, and decreased productivity—close to $100 billion annually.

Several eminent psychopharmacologists and political scientists evaluated the U.S. approach to drug control; they all recommended sweeping changes (see Goldstein & Kalant, 1990; Jarvik, 1990; Nadelmann, 1989). Each of these experts concluded that the system of drug control in the United States is both poorly conceived and ineffective. The following quotes provide glimpses of

Thinking Critically

Demonstration

List the major direct health hazards of the following five drugs. Omit the indirect hazards that result from the drugs' legal or social status.

Tobacco
1. _____
2. _____
3. _____
4. _____
5. _____
6. _____

Alcohol
1. _____
2. _____
3. _____
4. _____
5. _____
6. _____

Marijuana
1. _____
2. _____
3. _____
4. _____
5. _____
6. _____

Cocaine
1. _____
2. _____
3. _____
4. _____
5. _____
6. _____

Heroin
1. _____
2. _____
3. _____
4. _____
5. _____
6. _____

On the basis of comparisons among your lists, rank the five drugs in terms of their overall health risks.

Most Hazardous
1. _____
2. _____
3. _____
4. _____
5. _____

Least Hazardous

their disenchantment with a system that treats addiction as a crime, rather than a disease, and that tries to combat it by reducing the supply and punishing the users:

> The investment of more than 70% of the federal [U.S.] drug control money into supply reduction seems misplaced.... Curtailing the supply of demanded drugs has been compared to squeezing a balloon: constrict it in one place and it expands somewhere else.... An example is the expansion of the California marijuana crop after the availability of Mexican marijuana was reduced. (Jarvik, p. 339)

> The greatest beneficiaries of the drug laws are ... drug traffickers. More than half of all organized crime revenues are believed to derive from the illicit drug business. (Nadelmann, p. 941)

> Drug treatment programs remain notoriously underfunded, turning away tens of thousands of addicts seeking help even as increasing billions of dollars are spent to arrest, prosecute, and imprison illegal drug ... users. (Nadelmann, p. 942)

Thinking Critically

The experts recommend solutions to the drug problem that are different from those preferred by the American public. The experts say (1) that there is no way of stopping the supply—every major drug bust merely increases the street prices of drugs and encourages more illicit suppliers to enter the market; (2) that it makes little sense to persecute and punish the sick and the weak; and (3) that it is hypocritical to take severe measures against some drugs while allowing others that are more dangerous to be openly advertised. In contrast to the views of the experts, surveys suggest that the U.S. public, frustrated with the drug problem and not understanding the issues, wants even more money to be spent on the approaches that have proven to be so ineffective.

Here are some of the specific recommendations that have been made by the experts:

1. The only way of reducing recreational drug use is by reducing the demand. Some of the billions that are currently being spent on arresting and supporting drug users in crowded jails would be better spent on education, research, and social programs.

2. More emphasis should be placed on caring for addicts than on persecuting them.

3. Unlike the current laws, the laws that govern drug use should be enforceable and should be tailored to the hazards of each drug.

4. Judges should be given greater discretion in sentencing. For example, the current 5-year minimum sentence for anybody caught sharing a small amount of heroin or cocaine with a friend is unduly harsh.

5. All cigarette and alcohol advertising should be curtailed.

6. The possession of small amounts of marijuana for personal use has been legalized in some parts of the United States and in many other countries (see Booth, 2004). Because legalization in some states has not led to a significant increase in use, clearly other states should follow suit to allow the legal system to focus on more serious problems.

7. Lessons should be learned from countries that have taken alternative approaches to drug control. For example, in 1976, Holland removed criminal penalties for possession and small-scale sales of marijuana, with no resulting increases in the use of marijuana or more dangerous drugs (see MacCoun & Reuter, 1997; Reinarman, Cohen, & Kaal, 2004).

8. Finally, experimental clinics should be established. In them, addicts, as a first step in their treatment, should be provided with their drug. The potential advantages of such programs are many: They would encourage addicts to enter treatment; they would bring addicts in contact with health care professionals who are experienced in dealing with the health problems of addicts (e.g., AIDS and malnutrition); they would allow some addicts who have not been able to shake their habits to live reasonably normal, productive lives; and they would reduce the amount of drug-related crime.

Clinical Implications

The most important current research effort on the treatment of heroin addiction is the Swiss experiment. In 1994, the Swiss government established—despite substantial opposition from the public—a series of clinics in which, as part of a total treatment package, resident heroin addicts are supplied with heroin injections on request (doses are checked for safety by physicians). The Swiss government also funded a major research program to evaluate the clinics (see Gschwend et al., 2002). The first wave of research reports have been published, and the results have been uniformly positive: Addicts are no longer a presence in the streets and parks; drug-related crime has substantially declined; the physical and social well-being of the addicts has improved; there has been a decrease in heroin use by the addicts; and the number of new heroin addicts has declined (see Brehmer & Iten, 2001; De Preux, Dubois-Arber, & Zobel, 2004; Guttinger et al., 2003; Rehm et al., 2001).

One does not normally find a discussion of legal and social policy in a biopsychology textbook. Please excuse my digression, but I believe that the drug problem is a serious one and that biopsychologists have important things to say about it. They have a responsibility to bring the relevant research literature to the attention of policy makers and the educated public. Unfortunately, although scientists have been speaking out against the so-called war on drugs for over a decade, little has changed in the United States and many other countries.

This section of the chapter introduces two diametrically different ways of thinking about an addiction: Are addicts driven to take drugs by an internal need, or are they drawn to take drugs by their anticipated positive effects? I am sure you will recognize from preceding chapters that this is the same fundamental question that has been the focus of biopsychological research on the motivation to eat and sleep.

Physical-Dependence and Positive-Incentive Perspectives of Addiction

Early attempts to explain the phenomenon of drug addiction attributed it to physical dependence. According to various **physical-dependence theories of addiction,** physical dependence traps addicts in a vicious circle of drug taking and withdrawal symptoms. The idea was that drug users whose intake has reached a level sufficient to induce physical dependence are driven by their withdrawal symptoms to self-administer the drug each time they attempt to curtail their intake.

Early drug addiction treatment programs were based on the physical-dependence perspective. They attempted to break the vicious circle of drug taking by gradually withdrawing drugs from addicts in a hospital environment. Unfortunately, once discharged, almost all detoxified addicts return to their former drug-taking habits—**detoxified addicts** are addicts who have no drugs in their bodies and who are no longer experiencing withdrawal symptoms.

The failure of detoxification as a treatment for addiction is not surprising, for two reasons. First, some highly addictive drugs, such as cocaine and amphetamines, do not produce severe withdrawal distress (see Gawin, 1991). Second, the pattern of drug taking routinely displayed by many addicts involves an alternating cycle of binges and detoxification (Mello & Mendelson, 1972). There are a variety of reasons for this pattern of drug use. For example, some addicts adopt it because weekend binges are compatible with their work schedules, others adopt it because they do not have enough money to use drugs continuously, others have it forced on them because their binges often land them in jail, and others have it forced on them by their repeated unsuccessful efforts to shake their habit. However, whether detoxification is by choice or necessity, it does not stop addicts from renewing their drug-taking habits (see Leshner, 1997).

One physical-dependence theory of drug addiction attempts to account for the fact that addicts frequently relapse after lengthy drug-free periods by pointing to the fact that withdrawal symptoms can be conditioned. According to this theory, when addicts who have remained drug-free for a considerable period of time return to a situation in which they have previously experienced the drug, conditioned withdrawal effects opposite to the effects of the drug (conditioned compensatory responses) are elicited. These effects are presumed to result in a powerful craving for the drug to counteract them.

The failure of physical-dependence theories to account for some aspects of addiction has lent support to explanations that hold that most addicts take drugs not to escape or avoid the unpleasant consequences of withdrawal or conditioned withdrawal, but rather primarily to obtain the drugs' positive effects. These **positive-incentive theories of addiction** hold that the primary factor in most cases of addiction is the craving for the positive-incentive (pleasure-producing) properties of the drugs. Consider the following statement of one addict:

> I'm just trying to get high as much as possible.... If I could get more money, I would spend it all on drugs. All I want is to get loaded. I just really like shooting dope. I don't have any use for sex; I'd rather shoot dope. I like to shoot dope better than anything else in the world.

One positive-incentive theory of addiction is based on the idea that the positive-incentive value of addictive drugs increases (i.e., is sensitized) with drug use. Robinson and Berridge (2003) have suggested that in addiction-prone individuals, the use of drugs sensitizes their positive-incentive value, thus rendering the user highly motivated to consume drugs and to seek drug-associated stimuli. A key point of Robinson and Berridge's **incentive-sensitization theory** deserves emphasis: They argue that it isn't the pleasure (liking) of drug taking per se that is the basis of addiction; it is the anticipated pleasure (wanting) of drug taking (i.e., the drug's positive-incentive value). Initially, a drug's positive-incentive value is closely tied to its pleasurable effects; but tolerance often develops to the pleasurable effects, whereas the addict's wanting for the drug is sensitized. Thus, in chronic addicts, the positive-incentive value of the drug is often out of proportion with the pleasure actually derived from it: Many addicts are miserable, their lives are in ruins, and the drug effects are not that great anymore; but they crave the drug more than ever.

So which perspective on addiction is correct, the physical-dependence view or the positive-incentive view? Although there is no question that the alleviation of withdrawal symptoms is a significant factor in the drug use of many addicts, most evidence suggests that the positive-incentive value of addictive drugs *is* the primary factor in addiction (see Cardinal & Everitt, 2004; Everitt, Dickinson, & Robbins, 2001; Martin-Soelch et al., 2001).

Causes of Relapse

Virtually all addicts have stopped taking the drug they abuse at some point, but they eventually *relapse* (start taking the drug again). Thus, understanding the causes of relapse is the key to understanding addiction and its treatment.

Three fundamentally different causes of relapse have been identified. The first is stress. Most therapists and patients point to stress as the major factor in relapse. The impact of stress on drug taking was illustrated in a dramatic fashion by the marked increases in cigarette and alcohol consumption that occurred among New Yorkers following the attacks of September 11, 2001. The second cause of relapse is *priming* (a single exposure to the formerly abused drug). Many addicts who have abstained for many weeks, and thus feel that they have their addic-

tion under control, sample their formerly abused drug just once and are immediately plunged back into full-blown addiction. The third cause of relapse is exposure to environmental cues (e.g., people, times, places, or objects) that have previously been associated with drug taking (see Di Ciano & Everitt, 2003; Kruzich, Congleton, & See, 2001). Such environmental cues have been shown to precipitate relapse. The fact that the many U.S. soldiers who became addicted to heroin while fighting in the Vietnam War easily shed their addiction when they returned home has been attributed to their removal from that drug-associated environment.

15.5 Intracranial Self-Stimulation and the Pleasure Centers of the Brain

Rats, humans, and many other species will administer brief bursts of weak electrical stimulation to specific sites in their own brains (see Figure 15.7). This phenomenon is known as **intracranial self-stimulation (ICSS)**, and the brain sites capable of mediating the phenomenon are often called *pleasure centers*.

Olds and Milner (1954), the discoverers of intracranial self-stimulation, argued that the specific brain sites that mediate self-stimulation are those that normally mediate the pleasurable effects of natural rewards (e.g., food, water, and sex). Accordingly, researchers have studied the self-stimulation of various brain sites in order to map the neural circuits that mediate the experience of pleasure. Because the pleasure-producing effects of drugs are now believed to play a major causal role in addiction, this section focuses on these cerebral pleasure circuits.

Fundamental Characteristics of Intracranial Self-Stimulation

It was initially assumed that intracranial self-stimulation was a unitary phenomenon—that is, that its fundamental properties were the same regardless of the site of stimulation. Most early studies of intracranial self-stimulation involved septal or lateral hypothalamic stimulation because the rates of self-stimulation from these sites are spectacularly high: Rats typically press a lever thousands of times per hour for stimulation of these sites, stopping only when they become exhausted. However, the self-stimulation of many other brain structures has been documented.

Early studies of intracranial self-stimulation suggested that lever pressing for brain stimulation was fundamentally different from lever pressing for natural reinforcers such as food or water. Two puzzling observations

Evolutionary Perspective

contributed to this view. First, despite their extremely high response rates, many rats stopped pressing the self-stimulation lever almost immediately when the current delivery mechanism was shut off. This finding was puzzling because high rates of operant responding are generally assumed to indicate that the reinforcer is particularly pleasurable, whereas rapid rates of extinction are usually assumed to indicate that it is not. Would you stop pressing a lever that had been delivering $100 bills the first few times that a press did not produce one? Second, experienced self-stimulators often did not recommence lever pressing when they were returned to the apparatus after being briefly removed from it. In such cases, the rats had to be **primed** to get them going again: The experimenter simply pressed the lever a couple of times, to deliver a few free stimulations, and the hesitant rat immediately began to self-stimulate at a high rate once again.

These differences between lever pressing for reward-ing lateral hypothalamic or septal stimulation and lever

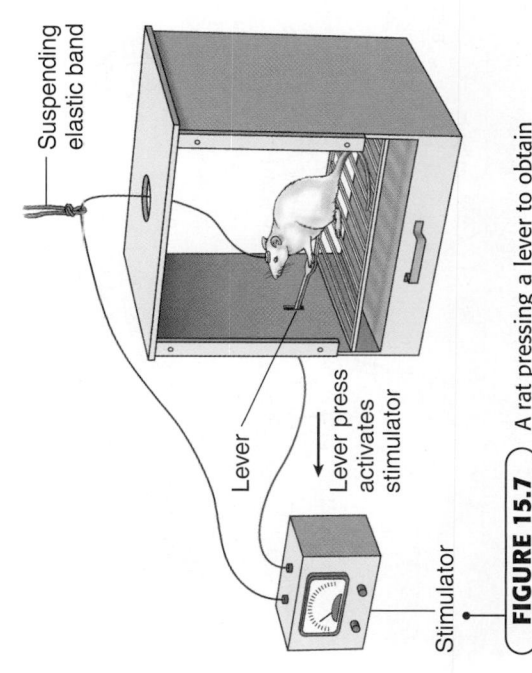

FIGURE 15.7 A rat pressing a lever to obtain rewarding brain stimulation.

Stimulator

Suspending elastic band

Lever

Lever press activates stimulator

Stimulator

pressing for food or water seemed to discredit Olds and Milner's original theory that intracranial self-stimulation involves the activation of natural reward circuits in the brain. However, several lines of research indicate that the circuits mediating intracranial self-stimulation are natural reward circuits. Let's consider three of these.

First, brain stimulation through electrodes that mediate self-stimulation often elicits a natural motivated behavior such as eating, drinking, maternal behavior, or copulation in the presence of the appropriate goal object.

Second, producing increases in natural motivation (for example, by food or water deprivation, by hormone injections, or by the presence of prey objects) often increases self-stimulation rates (e.g., Caggiula, 1970).

And third, it became clear that differences between the situations in which the rewarding effects of brain stimulation and those of natural rewards were usually studied contribute to the impression that these effects are qualitatively different. For example, comparisons between lever pressing for food and lever pressing for brain stimulation are usually confounded by the fact that subjects pressing for food and lever pressing for brain stimulation are nondeprived and by the fact that the lever press delivers the reward directly and immediately. In contrast, in studies of lever pressing for natural rewards, subjects are often deprived, and they press a lever for a food pellet or drop of water that they then must approach and consume to experience rewarding effects. This point was illustrated by a clever experiment (Panksepp & Trowill, 1967) that compared lever pressing for brain stimulation and lever pressing for a natural reinforcer in a situation in which the usual confounds were absent. In the absence of the confounds, some of the major differences between lever

pressing for food and lever pressing for brain stimulation disappeared. When nondeprived rats pressed a lever to inject a small quantity of chocolate milk directly into their mouths through an intraoral tube, they behaved remarkably like self-stimulating rats: They quickly learned to lever press, they pressed at high rates, they extinguished quickly, and some even had to be primed.

Mesotelencephalic Dopamine System and Intracranial Self-Stimulation

The mesotelencephalic dopamine system plays an important role in intracranial self-stimulation. The **mesotelencephalic dopamine system** is a system of dopaminergic neurons that projects from the mesencephalon (the midbrain) into various regions of the telencephalon. As Figure 15.8 indicates, the neurons that compose the mesotelencephalic dopamine system have their cell bodies in two midbrain nuclei—the **substantia nigra** and the **ventral tegmental area.** Their axons project to a variety of telencephalic sites, including specific regions of the prefrontal neocortex, the limbic cortex, the olfactory tubercle, the amygdala, the septum, the dorsal striatum, and, in particular, the **nucleus accumbens** (nucleus of the ventral striatum)—see Zahm, 2000.

Most of the axons of dopaminergic neurons that have their cell bodies in the substantia nigra project to the dorsal striatum; this component of the mesotelencephalic dopamine system is called the *nigrostriatal pathway.* It is degeneration in this pathway that is associated with Parkinson's disease.

Most of the axons of dopaminergic neurons that have their cell bodies in the ventral tegmental area pro-

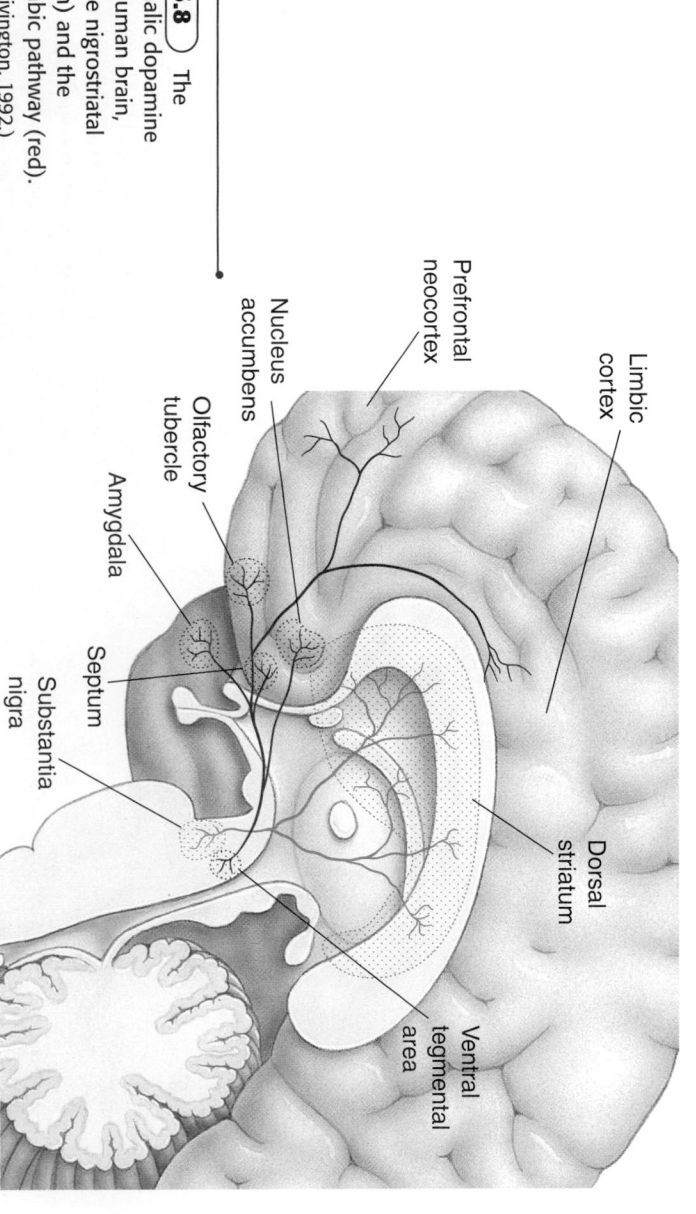

www.ablongman.com/pinel6e

FIGURE 15.8   The mesotelencephalic dopamine system in the human brain, consisting of the nigrostriatal pathway (green) and the mesocorticolimbic pathway (red). (Adapted from Klivington, 1992.)

Prefrontal neocortex

Nucleus accumbens

Olfactory tubercle

Amygdala

Septum

Substantia nigra

Limbic cortex

Dorsal striatum

Ventral tegmental area

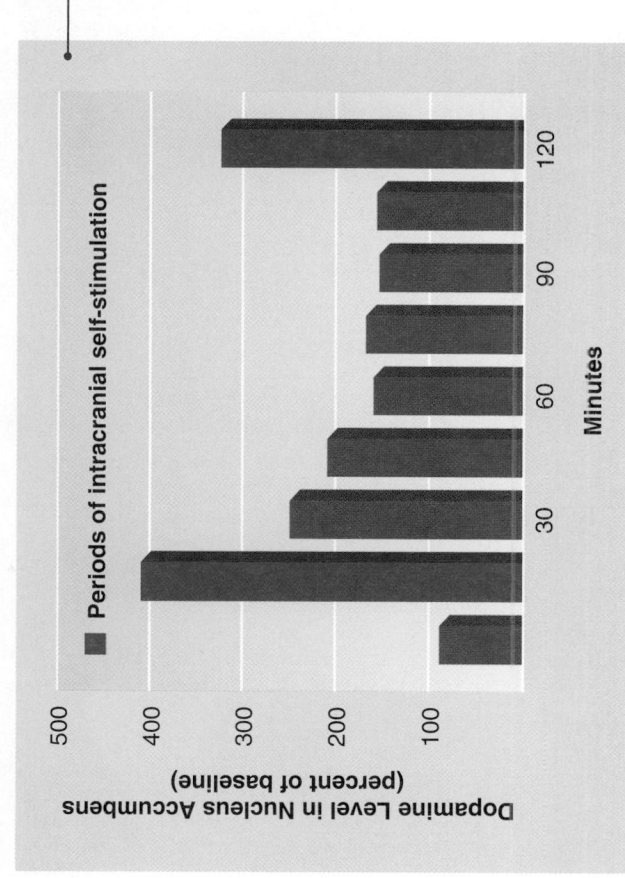

FIGURE 15.9 The increase in dopamine release from the nucleus accumbens during consecutive periods of intracranial self-stimulation. (Adapted from Phillips et al., 1992.)

ject to various cortical and limbic sites. This component of the mesotelencephalic dopamine system is called the *mesocorticolimbic pathway*. Although there is some intermingling of the neurons between these two dopaminergic pathways, it is the particular neurons that project from the ventral tegmental area to the nucleus accumbens that have been most frequently implicated in the rewarding effects of brain stimulation, natural rewards, and addictive drugs.

The results of several kinds of studies have supported the view that the mesocorticolimbic pathway plays an important role in mediating intracranial self-stimulation. The following are four general supportive findings:

1. Many of the brain sites at which self-stimulation occurs are part of the mesotelencephalic dopamine system. Some self-stimulation sites that do not contain dopaminergic neurons project directly to the mesotelencephalic dopamine system.

2. In *cerebral dialysis studies*, microsamples of extracellular fluid are continuously drawn from a particular area of the brain as the subject behaves, and the fluid is later subjected to chemical analysis. Such studies have shown that intracranial self-stimulation is often associated with an increase in dopamine release in the mesocorticolimbic pathway—see Figure 15.9.

3. Dopamine agonists tend to increase intracranial self-stimulation, and dopamine antagonists, tend to decrease self-stimulation.

4. Lesions of the mesocorticolimbic pathway tend to disrupt intracranial self-stimulation.

15.6 Neural Mechanisms of Motivation and Addiction

The search for the neural mechanisms of drug addiction has focused on the mesocorticolimbic pathway. This focus evolved from three influences: (1) from the increasing appreciation that the pleasurable effects of drugs, rather than the alleviation of withdrawal effects, are the major factors in addiction; (2) from the finding that the mesocorticolimbic pathway plays a principal role in intracranial self-stimulation; and (3) from the discovery that the mesocorticolimbic pathway is involved in the effects of natural rewards (e.g., food and sex). Brain mechanisms certainly did not evolve for the purpose of mediating addiction; therefore, the key to understanding the neural mechanisms of addiction lies in understand-

ing natural motivational mechanisms and how they are co-opted and warped by addictive drugs (Nesse & Berridge, 1997).

Two Key Methods for Measuring Drug-Produced Reinforcement

Most of the research on the neural mechanisms of addiction has been conducted in nonhumans. Because of the presumed role of the positive-incentive value of drugs in addiction, methods used to measure the rewarding effects of drugs in nonhumans have played a key role in this research. Two such methods have played

Drug Self-Administration

Conditioned Place Preference

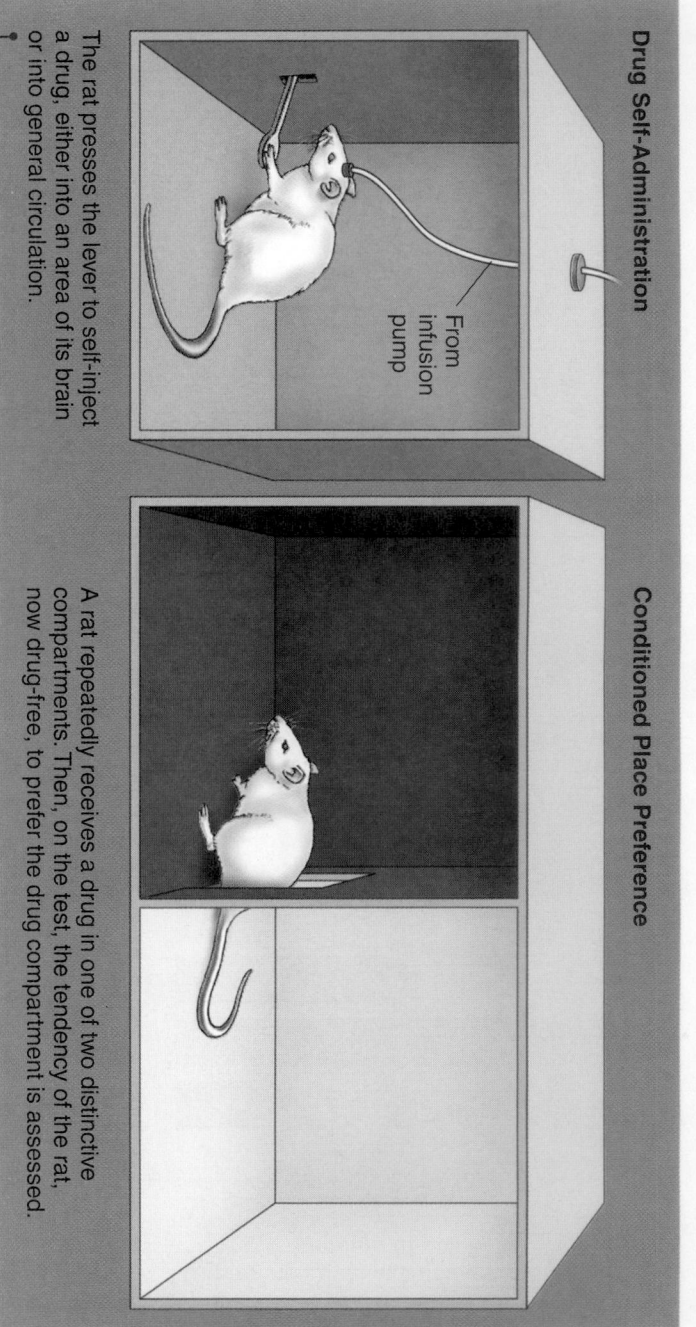

The rat presses the lever to self-inject a drug, either into an area of its brain or into general circulation.

From infusion pump

A rat repeatedly receives a drug in one of two distinctive compartments. Then, on the test, the tendency of the rat, now drug-free, to prefer the drug compartment is assessed.

FIGURE 15.10   Two behavioral paradigms that are used extensively in the study of the neural mechanisms of addiction: the drug self-administration paradigm and the conditioned place-preference paradigm.

---

particularly important roles: the drug self-administration paradigm and the conditioned place-preference paradigm. They are illustrated in Figure 15.10.

In the **drug self-administration paradigm**, laboratory rats or primates press a lever to inject drugs into themselves through implanted *cannulas* (thin tubes). They readily learn to self-administer intravenous injections of drugs to which humans become addicted. Furthermore, once they have learned to self-administer an addictive drug, their drug taking often mimics in major respects the drug taking of human addicts (Deroche-Gamonet, Belin, & Piazza, 2004; Louk, Vanderschuren, & Everitt, 2004; Robinson, 2004). Studies in which microinjections have been self-administered directly into particular brain structures have proved particularly enlightening.

In the **conditioned place-preference paradigm**, rats repeatedly receive a drug in one compartment (the *drug compartment*) of a two-compartment box. Then, during the test phase, the rat is placed in the box drug-free, and the proportion of time it spends in the drug compartment, as opposed to the equal-sized but distinctive *control compartment*, is measured. Rats usually prefer the drug compartment over the control compartment when the drug compartment has been associated with the effects of drugs to which humans become addicted. The main advantage of the conditioned place-preference paradigm is that the subjects are tested drug-free, which means that the mea-

sure of the incentive value of a drug is not confounded by other effects the drug might have on behavior.

Early Evidence of the Involvement of Dopamine in Drug Addiction

In the 1970s, following much research on the role of dopamine in intracranial self-stimulation, experiments began to implicate dopamine in the rewarding effects of natural reinforcers and addictive drugs. For example, in rats, dopamine antagonists blocked the self-administration of, or conditioned preference for, several different addictive drugs; and they reduced the reinforcing effects of food. These findings suggested that dopamine signaled something akin to reward value or pleasure.

The Nucleus Accumbens and Drug Addiction

Once evidence had accumulated linking dopamine to natural reinforcers and drug-induced reward, investigators began to explore particular sites in the mesocorticolimbic dopamine pathway by conducting experiments on laboratory animals. Their findings soon focused attention on the nucleus accumbens. Events occurring in the nucleus accumbens and dopaminergic input to it from the ventral tegmental area were most clearly related to the experience of reward and pleasure.

ON THE CD

Visit the *Drug Self-Administration Paradigm* module to see a rat taking cocaine.

Evolutionary Perspective

The following are four kinds of findings from research on laboratory animals that focused attention on the nucleus accumbens (see Ikemoto & Panksepp, 1999; Spanagel & Weiss, 1999):

1. Laboratory animals self-administered microinjections of addictive drugs (e.g., cocaine, amphetamine, and morphine) directly into the nucleus accumbens.
2. Microinjections of addictive drugs into the nucleus accumbens produced a conditioned place preference for the compartment in which they were administered.
3. Lesions to either the nucleus accumbens or the ventral tegmental area blocked the self-administration of drugs into general circulation or the development of drug-associated conditioned place preferences.
4. Both the self-administration of addictive drugs and the experience of natural reinforcers were found to be associated with elevated levels of extracellular dopamine in the nucleus accumbens.

Evolutionary Perspective

Support for the Involvement of Dopamine in Addiction: Evidence from Imaging Human Brains

With the development of brain-imaging techniques for measuring dopamine in human brains, considerable evidence began to emerge that dopamine is involved in human reward in general and human addiction in particular (see Volkow et al., 2004). One of the strongest of the early brain-imaging studies linking dopamine to addiction was published by Volkow and colleagues (1997). They administered various doses of radioactively labeled cocaine to addicts and asked the addicts to rate the resulting "high." They also used positron emission tomography (PET) to measure the degree to which the labeled cocaine bound to dopamine transporters.

Cognitive Neuroscience

Dopamine transporters are molecules in the presynaptic membrane of dopaminergic neurons that attract dopamine molecules in the synaptic cleft and deposit them back inside the neuron—cocaine has its agonistic effects on dopamine by binding to these transporters, blocking reuptake, and thus increasing extracellular dopamine levels. The intensity of the "highs" experienced by the addicts was correlated with the degree to which cocaine bound to the dopamine transporters—no high at all was experienced unless the drug bound to 50% of the dopamine transporters.

Brain-imaging studies have also indicated that the nucleus accumbens plays an important role in mediating the rewarding effects of addictive behavior. For example, in one study, healthy (i.e., nonaddicts) human subjects were given an IV injection of amphetamine (Dre-vets et al., 2001). As dopamine levels in the nucleus accumbens increased in response to the amphetamine injection, the subjects reported a parallel increase in their experience of euphoria.

In general, brain-imaging studies have shown that dopamine function is markedly diminished in human addicts. However, when addicts are exposed to their drug or to stimuli associated with their drug, the nucleus accumbens and some of the other parts of the mesocorticolimbic dopamine pathway tend to become hyperactive.

Dopamine, Nucleus Accumbens, and Addiction: Current View

As you have just learned, there is a great deal of evidence linking dopamine release, particularly in the nucleus accumbens, to the rewarding effects of addictive drugs and natural reinforcers (see Nestler & Malenka, 2004). The weight of this evidence might lead you to conclude that the neural mechanisms of addiction are well understood—certainly, I often see reports to this effect in the popular press. However, most of the top researchers in this held do not voice the same degree of certainty (see Wise, 2004).

There is little doubt that dopamine and the nucleus accumbens are involved in reward and addiction (see Kelley, 2004): The evidence for this involvement is very strong. However, researchers currently have little idea *how* they are involved. Consider the following important questions about the involvement of dopamine and the nucleus accumbens in reward and addiction.

What exactly is the reward-related function of the release of dopamine in the nucleus accumbens? Reward is a complex cognitive process, with many different psychological components (see Berridge & Robinson, 2003). Although it is often assumed that dopamine release in the nucleus accumbens is responsible for the experience of reward, this seems not to be the case. Several studies on laboratory animals have shown that neutral stimuli that signal the impending delivery of a reward (e.g., food or an addictive drug) themselves trigger dopamine release in the nucleus accumbens (e.g., Fiorino, Coury, & Phillips, 1997; Weiss et al., 2000).

A similar point has been made through the study of dopaminergic neurons in the ventral tegmental area. Schultz (1997) recorded the activity of individual dopaminergic neurons in the ventral tegmental area of monkeys. He found that these neurons responded to rewards only when the rewards were presented unpredictably—as in the early stages of a conditioning experiment. If a reward was expected—as in the late stages of a conditioning experiment—the reward itself did not increase the activity of dopaminergic neurons, but the conditional stimulus that predicted the reward did.

Evolutionary Perspective

In a subsequent study, Schultz and his colleagues (Fiorillo, Tobler, & Schultz, 2003) varied the certainty with which a conditional stimulus predicted reward, and the response of the dopaminergic neurons to that stimulus was greater when the reward was more certain to follow. These studies suggest that dopamine is involved in the expectation of reward, rather than in reward itself.

Does dopamine release in the nucleus accumbens occur selectively to reward or to its expectation? Joseph, Datla, and Young (2003) reviewed all of the cerebral dialysis studies of dopamine release in the nucleus accumbens. They concluded that reward or the expectation of reward has been shown to increase dopamine release in virtually every study that has tried to demonstrate this effect. More problematic is the fact that a variety of other stimuli (including some aversive stimuli) have also been found to trigger dopamine release in the nucleus accumbens.

Is the nucleus accumbens the only brain structure involved in reward? No (Wise, 2004). Although most research on the neural basis of reward has focused on the nucleus accumbens, several of the structures of the mesotelencephalic dopamine system (e.g., prefrontal cortex, dorsal striatum, and amygdala) show susceptibility to electrical self-stimulation and chemical self-administration in laboratory animals. Moreover, brain-imaging studies often reveal low cell density and hypoactivity in the anterior cingulate cortex of addicts (see Peoples, 2002). Arguably, the strongest evidence that the nucleus accumbens is not the only neural structure involved in reward and addiction is the dismal failure of lesions to this structure to block relapse in opiate addicts (Gao et al., 2003).

Is dopamine the only neurotransmitter involved in reward and addiction? Recent evidence has pointed to glutamate as another candidate for such involvement (Kalivas, 2004)—of special interest have been the projections of glutamatergic neurons from prefrontal cortex back into the nucleus accumbens. Conclusive evidence that dopamine is not the only neurotransmitter involved in reward comes from the study of knockout mice that lack dopamine: They display no deficits in their ability to identify sweet solutions or to be rewarded by them (Cannon & Bseikri, 2004).

So, what's the take-home message on current theories of reward and addiction? There are three important points: (1) A great deal of evidence implicates dopamine and the nucleus accumbens in reward and addiction, and thus there is little question that they are somehow involved. (2) On the other hand, considerable evidence indicates that establishing the involvement of dopamine is merely a simplistic first step in understanding the neural mechanisms of reward and addiction. (3) The discovery of many links between the mechanisms of reward and addiction has lent support to the positive-incentive perspective of addiction.

15.7 A Noteworthy Case of Addiction

To illustrate in a more personal way some of the things you have learned about addiction, this chapter concludes with a case study of one addict. The addict was Sigmund Freud, a man of great significance to psychology.

Freud's case is particularly important for two reasons. First, it shows that nobody, no matter how powerful their intellect, is immune to the addictive effects of drugs. Second, it allows comparisons between the two drugs of addiction with which Freud had problems.

Clinical Implications

The Case of Sigmund Freud

In 1883, a German army physician prescribed cocaine, which had recently been isolated, to Bavarian soldiers to help them deal with the demands of military maneuvers. When Freud read about this, he decided to procure some of the drug.

In addition to taking cocaine himself, Freud pressed it on his friends and associates, both for themselves and for their patients. He even sent some to his fiancée. In short, by today's standards, Freud was a public menace.

Freud's famous essay "Song of Praise" was about cocaine and was published in July 1884. Freud wrote in such glowing terms about his own personal experiences with cocaine that he created a wave of interest in the drug. But within a year, there was a critical reaction to Freud's premature advocacy of the drug. As evidence accumulated that cocaine was highly addictive and produced a psychosis-like state at high doses, so too did published criticisms of Freud.

Freud continued to praise cocaine until the summer of 1887, but soon thereafter he suddenly stopped all use of cocaine—both personally and professionally. Despite the fact that he had used cocaine for 3 years, he seems to have had no difficulty stopping.

Some 7 years later, in 1894, when Freud was 38, his physician and close friend ordered him to stop smoking because it was causing a heart arrhythmia. Freud was a heavy smoker; he smoked approximately 20 cigars per day.

Freud did stop smoking, but 7 weeks later he started again. On another occasion, Freud stopped for 14 months, but at the age of 58, he was still smoking 20 cigars a day—and still struggling against his addiction. He wrote to friends that smoking was adversely affecting his heart and making it difficult for him to work . . . yet he kept smoking.

In 1923, at the age of 67, Freud developed sores in his mouth. They were cancerous. When he was recovering from oral surgery, he wrote to a friend that smoking was the cause of his cancer . . . yet he kept smoking.

In addition to the cancer, Freud began to experience severe heart pains (tobacco angina) whenever he smoked . . . still he kept smoking.

At 73, Freud was hospitalized for his heart condition and stopped smoking. He made an immediate recovery. But 23 days later, he started to smoke again.

In 1936, at the age of 79, Freud was experiencing more heart trouble, and he had had 33 operations to deal with his recurring oral cancer. His jaw had been entirely removed and replaced by an artificial one. He was in constant pain, and he could swallow, chew, and talk only with difficulty . . . yet he kept smoking.

Freud died of cancer in 1939. Imagine his many years of suffering and its effect on his family and friends. Do you smoke? Do people you love smoke?

Themes Revisited

Two of this book's themes received strong emphasis in this chapter because they are integral to its major objective: to sharpen your thinking about the effects of addiction on health. These two themes are the

Thinking Critically

Clinical Implications

thinking-about-biopsychology and the clinical implications themes.

The evolutionary perspective theme was also highlighted frequently in this chapter, largely because of the nature of biopsychological research on drug addiction. Because of the risks associated with the administration of addictive drugs and with the direct manipulation of brain structures, the majority of biopsychological studies of drug addiction involve nonhumans—mostly

Evolutionary Perspective

rats and monkeys. Also, in studying the neural mechanisms of addiction, there is a need to maintain an evolutionary perspective. It is important not to lose sight of the fact that brain mechanisms did not evolve to support addiction; they evolved to serve natural adaptive functions and have somehow been co-opted by addictive drugs.

Some of the most exciting recent research on the mechanisms of addiction has employed the methods of cognitive neuroscience. Highlighting the cognitive neuroscience theme in this chapter was the use of functional brain-imaging techniques to measure cocaine binding and dopamine release in the living human brain. This research has confirmed the results of experiments on other species.

Cognitive Neuroscience

ON THE CD
See Hard Copy for additional readings for Chapter 15.

Think about It

1. There are many misconceptions about drug abuse. Describe three. What do you think are the reasons for these misconceptions?

2. A man who had been a heroin user for many years was found dead of an overdose at a holiday resort. He appeared to have been in good health, and no foul play was suspected. What factors might have led to his death?

3. If you had an opportunity to redraft the current legislation related to drug abuse in the light of what you have learned in this chapter, what changes would you make? Explain.

4. Speculate. How might recent advances in the study of the mesotelencephalic dopamine system eventually lead to effective treatments?

5. Does somebody you love use a hard drug such as nicotine or alcohol? Now that you know the truth about these drugs, do you feel ethically obligated to help? What should you do?

6. Although my primary purpose in writing this chapter was to explain the biopsychology of addiction, it was not my only purpose. My other purpose was to provide you with a way of thinking about addiction that might be of benefit to you and those around you. Imagine my dismay, then, when I received an e-mail message suggesting that this chapter was making things worse for addicts. According to this message, explicit photographs and discussion of addiction induce craving in addicts who have stopped taking drugs (perhaps by inducing conditioned compensatory responses), thus encouraging them to recommence their drug taking. Discuss this argument, and consider its implications for the design of televised antidrug campaigns.

ON THE CD
Studying for an exam? Try the Practice Tests for Chapter 15.

Key Terms

Addicts (p. 372)
Amphetamine (p. 381)
Analgesics (p. 381)
Before-and-after design (p. 373)
Buerger's disease (p. 377)
Cannabis sativa (p. 378)
Cirrhosis (p. 378)
Cocaine (p. 380)
Cocaine psychosis (p. 380)
Cocaine sprees (p. 380)
Codeine (p. 381)
Conditioned compensatory responses (p. 375)
Conditioned drug tolerance (p. 373)
Conditioned place-preference paradigm (p. 390)
Conditioned withdrawal effects (p. 375)

Contingent drug tolerance (p. 373)
Crack (p. 373)
Cross tolerance (p. 380)
Delirium tremens (DTs) (p. 371)
Depressant (p. 378)
Detoxified addicts (p. 386)
Dopamine transporters (p. 391)
Drug metabolism (p. 371)
Drug self-administration paradigm (p. 371)
Drug sensitization (p. 390)
Drug tolerance (p. 371)
Fetal alcohol syndrome (FAS) (p. 378)
Functional tolerance (p. 372)
Harrison Narcotics Act (p. 382)
Hashish (p. 378)

Heroin (p. 382)
Incentive-sensitization theory (p. 386)
Intracranial self-stimulation (ICSS) (p. 387)
Korsakoff's syndrome (p. 378)
Mesotelencephalic dopamine system (p. 388)
Metabolic tolerance (p. 372)
Morphine (p. 381)
Narcotic (p. 379)
Nicotine (p. 376)
Nucleus accumbens (p. 388)
Opiates (p. 381)
Opium (p. 381)
Physical-dependence theories of addiction (p. 386)
Physically dependent (p. 372)
Positive-incentive theories of addiction (p. 386)

Primed (p. 387)
Psychoactive drugs (p. 370)
Psychological dependence (p. 373)
Smoker's syndrome (p. 377)
Stimulants (p. 380)
Substantia nigra (p. 388)
THC (p. 378)
Ventral tegmental area (p. 388)
Withdrawal syndrome (p. 372)

ON THE CD

Need some help studying the key terms for this chapter? Check out the electronic flash cards for Chapter 15.

chapter

16

Lateralization, Language, and the Split Brain

The Left Brain and the Right Brain of Language

16.1 Cerebral Lateralization of Function: Introduction

16.2 The Split Brain

16.3 Differences between the Left and Right Hemispheres

16.4 Cortical Localization of Language: The Wernicke-Geschwind Model

16.5 Evaluation of the Wernicke-Geschwind Model

16.6 The Cognitive Neuroscience Approach to Language

16.7 The Cognitive Neuroscience Approach and Dyslexia

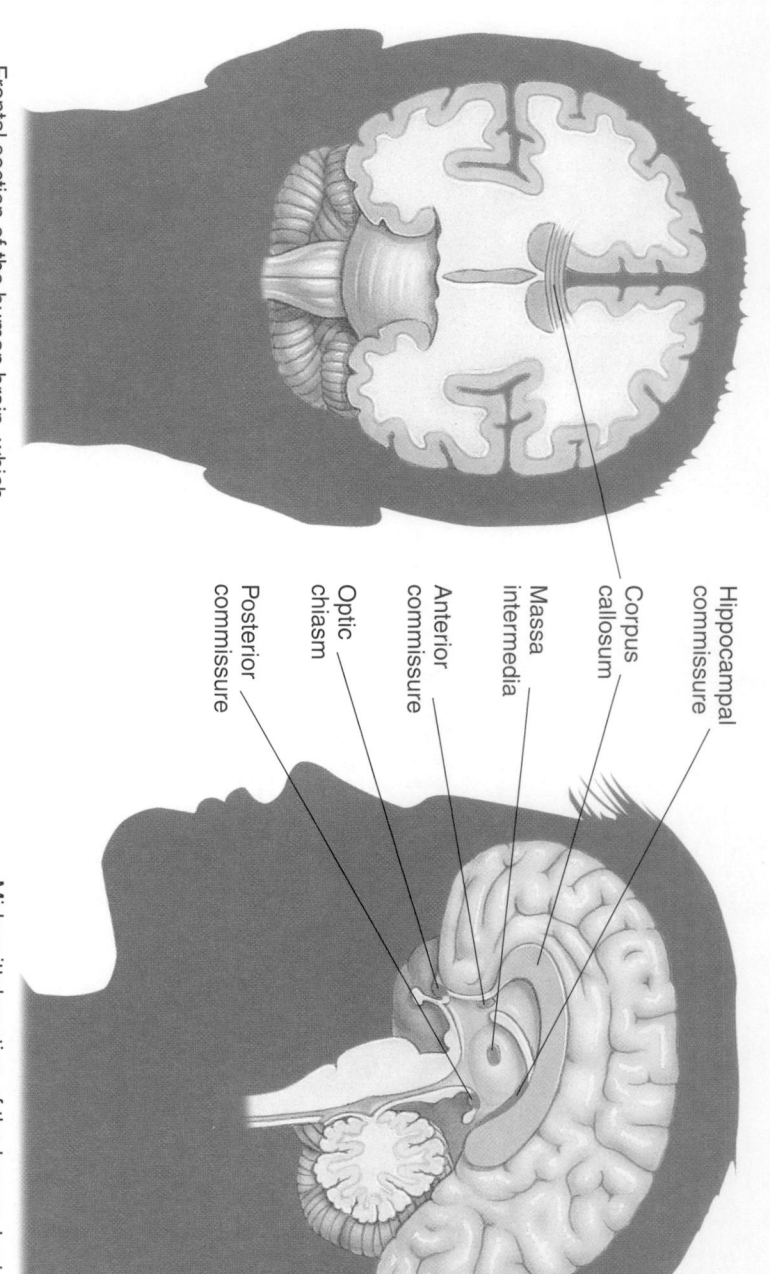

Frontal section of the human brain, which illustrates the fundamental duality of the human forebrain.

FIGURE 16.1   The cerebral hemispheres and cerebral commissures.

Hippocampal commissure

Corpus callosum

Massa intermedia

Anterior commissure

Optic chiasm

Posterior commissure

Midsagittal section of the human brain, which illustrates the corpus callosum and other commissures.

16.1 Cerebral Lateralization of Function: Introduction

With the exception of a few midline orifices, we have two of almost everything—one on the left and one on the right. Even the brain, which most people view as the unitary and indivisible basis of self, reflects this general principle of bilateral duplication. In its upper reaches, the brain comprises two structures, the left and right cerebral hemispheres, which are entirely separate except for the **cerebral commissures**, which connect them. The fundamental duality of the human forebrain and the locations of the cerebral commissures are illustrated in Figure 16.1.

Although the left and right hemispheres are similar in appearance, there are major differences between them in function. This chapter is about these differences, a topic commonly referred to as **lateralization of function**. The study of **split-brain patients**—patients whose left and right hemispheres have been separated by **commissurotomy**—is a major focus of discussion. Another focus is the cortical localization of language abilities in the left hemisphere; language abilities are the most highly lateralized of all cognitive abilities.

You will learn in this chapter that your left and right hemispheres have different abilities and that they have the capacity to function independently—to have different thoughts, memories, and emotions. Accordingly, this chapter will challenge the concept you have of yourself as a unitary being. I hope you both enjoy it.

In 1836, Marc Dax, an unknown country doctor, presented a short report at a medical society meeting in France. It was his first and only scientific presentation. Dax was struck by the fact that of the 40 or so brain-

damaged patients with speech problems whom he had seen during his career, not a single one had damage restricted to the right hemisphere. His report aroused little interest, and Dax died the following year unaware that he had anticipated one of the most important areas of modern neuropsychological research.

Aphasia, Apraxia, and Left-Hemisphere Damage

One reason Dax's paper had little impact was that most of his contemporaries believed that the brain acted as a whole and that specific functions could not be attributed to particular parts of it. This view began to change 25 years later, when Paul Broca reported his postmortem examination of two aphasic patients. **Aphasia** is a brain-damage-produced deficit in the ability to produce or comprehend language.

Both of Broca's patients had a left-hemisphere lesion that involved an area in the frontal cortex just in front of the face area of the primary motor cortex. Broca at first

did not realize that there was a relation between aphasia and the side of the brain damage; he had not heard of Dax's report. However, by 1864, Broca had performed postmortem examinations on seven more aphasic patients, and he was struck by the fact that, like his first two, they all had damage to the *inferior prefrontal cortex* of the left hemisphere—which by then had become known as **Broca's area** (see Figure 16.2).

In the early 1900s, another example of *cerebral lateralization of function* was discovered. Hugo-Karl Liepmann found that **apraxia**, like aphasia, is almost always

associated with left-hemisphere damage, despite the fact that its symptoms are *bilateral* (involving both sides of the body). Apraxic patients have difficulty performing movements when asked to perform them out of context, even though they often have no difficulty performing the same movements when they are not thinking about doing so.

The combined impact of the evidence that the left hemisphere plays a special role in both language and voluntary movement led to the concept of *cerebral dominance*. According to this concept, one hemisphere—usually the left—assumes the dominant role in the control of all complex behavioral and cognitive processes, and the other plays only a minor role. This concept led to the practice of referring to the left hemisphere as the **dominant hemisphere** and the right hemisphere as the **minor hemisphere.**

Tests of Cerebral Lateralization

Early research on the cerebral lateralization of function compared the effects of left-hemisphere and right-hemisphere lesions. Now, however, other techniques are also used for this purpose. The sodium amytal test, the dichotic listening test, and functional brain imaging are three of them.

Sodium Amytal Test   The **sodium amytal test** of language lateralization (Wada, 1949) is often given to patients prior to neurosurgery. The neurosurgeon uses the results of the test to plan the surgery; every effort is made to avoid damaging areas of the cortex that are likely to be involved in language. The sodium amytal test involves the injection of a small amount of sodium amytal into the carotid artery on one side of the neck. The injection anesthetizes the hemisphere on that side for a few minutes, thus allowing the capacities of the other hemisphere to be assessed. During the test, the patient is asked to recite well-known series (e.g., letters of the alphabet, days of the week, months of the year) and to name pictures of common objects. Then, an injection is administered to the other side, and the test is repeated. When the hemisphere that is dominant for speech, usually the left hemisphere, is anesthetized, the patient is rendered completely mute for a minute or two; then once the ability to talk returns, there are errors of serial order and naming. In contrast, when the minor speech hemisphere, usually the right, is anesthetized, mutism often does not occur at all, and errors are few.

Dichotic Listening Test   Unlike the sodium amytal test, the **dichotic listening test** is noninvasive; thus, it can be administered to healthy subjects. In the standard dichotic listening test (Kimura, 1961), three pairs of

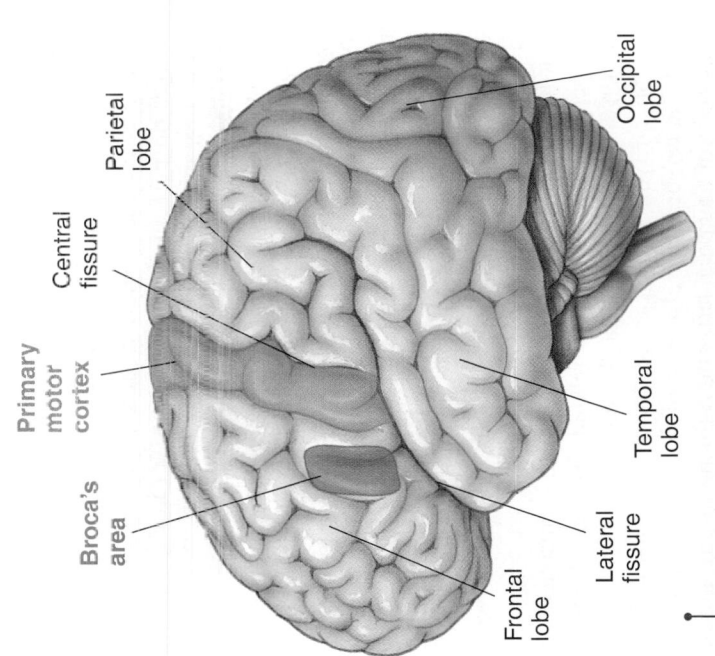

Primary motor cortex

Central fissure

Parietal lobe

Occipital lobe

Broca's area

Frontal lobe

Lateral fissure

Temporal lobe

FIGURE 16.2   The location of Broca's area: in the inferior left prefrontal cortex, just anterior to the face area of the left primary motor cortex.

spoken digits are presented through earphones; the digits of each pair are presented simultaneously, one to each ear. For example, a subject might hear the sequence 3, 9, 2 through one ear and at the same time 1, 6, 4 through the other. The subject is then asked to report all of the digits. Kimura found that most people report slightly more of the digits presented to the right ear than the left, which is indicative of left-hemisphere dominance for language. In contrast, Kimura found that all the patients who had been identified by the sodium amytal test as right-hemisphere dominant for language performed better with the left ear than the right.

Why does the superior ear on the dichotic listening test indicate the dominance of the contralateral hemisphere? Kimura argued that although the sounds from each ear are projected to both hemispheres, the contralateral connections are stronger and take precedence when two different sounds are simultaneously competing for access to the same cortical auditory centers.

Cognitive Neuroscience

Functional Brain Imaging Lateralization of function has also been studied using functional brain-imaging techniques. While the subject engages in some activity, such as reading, the activity of the brain is monitored by positron emission tomography (PET) or functional magnetic resonance imaging (fMRI). On language tests, functional brain-imaging techniques typically reveal far greater activity in the left hemisphere than in the right hemisphere (see Martin, 2003).

Clinical Implications

Speech Laterality and Handedness

Two early large-scale lesion studies clarified the relation between the cerebral lateralization of speech and handedness. One study involved military personnel who suffered brain damage in World War II (Russell & Espir, 1961), and the other focused on neurological patients who underwent unilateral excisions for the treatment of neurological disorders (Penfield & Roberts, 1959). In both studies, approximately 60% of **dextrals** (right-handers) with left-hemisphere lesions and 2% of those with right-hemisphere lesions were diagnosed as aphasic; the comparable figures for **sinestrals** (left-handers) were about 30% and 24%, respectively. These results indicate that the left hemisphere is dominant for language-related abilities in almost all dextrals and in the majority of sinestrals; they also indicate that sinestrals are more variable than dextrals with respect to language lateralization.

Results of the sodium amytal test have confirmed the relation between handedness and language lateralization that was first observed in early lesion studies. For example, Milner (1974) found that almost all right-handed

Clinical Implications

patients without early left-hemisphere damage were left-hemisphere dominant for speech (92%), that most left-handed and ambidextrous patients without early left-hemisphere damage were left-hemisphere dominant for speech (69%), and that early left-hemisphere damage decreased left-hemisphere dominance for speech in left-handed and ambidextrous patients (30%).

In interpreting Milner's figures, it is important to remember that sodium amytal tests are administered only to people who are experiencing brain dysfunction, that early brain damage can cause the lateralization of speech to shift to the other hemisphere (see Maratsos & Matheny, 1994; Stiles, 1998), and that many more people are left-hemisphere dominant to start with. Considered together, these points suggest that Milner's findings likely underestimate the proportion of left-hemisphere dominant individuals among healthy members of the general population.

Thinking Critically

Sex Differences in Brain Lateralization

Interest in the possibility that the brains of females and males differ in their degree of lateralization was stimulated by McGlone's (1977, 1980) studies of unilateral stroke victims. McGlone found that male victims of unilateral strokes were three times more likely to suffer from aphasia than female victims. She found that male victims of left-hemisphere strokes had deficits on the Wechsler Adult Intelligence Scale (WAIS) verbal subtests, whereas male victims of right-hemisphere strokes had deficits on the WAIS performance subtests. In contrast, in female victims, there were no significant differences between the disruptive effects of left and unilateral strokes on performance on the WAIS. On the basis of these three findings, McGlone concluded that the brains of males are more lateralized than the brains of females.

McGlone's hypothesis of a sex difference in brain lateralization has been widely embraced, and it has been used to explain almost every imaginable behavioral difference between the sexes. But support for McGlone's hypothesis has been mixed. Some researchers have failed to confirm her report of a sex difference in the effects of unilateral brain lesions (see Inglis & Lawson, 1982). However, several brain-imaging studies have suggested that females, more than males, use both hemispheres in the performance of language-related tasks (e.g., Jaeger et al., 1998; Kansaku, Yamaura, & Kitazawa, 2000).

So far, you have learned about four methods of studying cerebral lateralization of function: comparing the effects of unilateral left- and right-hemisphere lesions, the sodium amytal test, the dichotic listening test, and functional brain imaging. The next section describes a fifth method.

Clinical Implications

Cognitive Neuroscience

16.2 The Split Brain

In the early 1950s, the **corpus callosum**—the largest cerebral commissure—constituted a paradox of major proportions. Its size, an estimated 200 million axons, and its central position, right between the two cerebral hemispheres, implied that it performed an extremely important function; yet research in the 1930s and 1940s seemed to suggest that it did nothing at all. The corpus callosum had been cut in monkeys and in several other laboratory species, but the animals seemed no different after the surgery than they had been before. Similarly, human patients who were born without a corpus callosum seemed perfectly normal. In the early 1950s, Roger Sperry and his colleagues were intrigued by this paradox.

Groundbreaking Experiment of Myers and Sperry

Evolutionary Perspective

The solution to the puzzle of the corpus callosum was provided in 1953 by an experiment on cats by Myers and Sperry. The experiment made two astounding theoretical points. First, it showed that one function of the corpus callosum is to transfer learned information from one hemisphere to the other. Second, it showed that when the corpus callosum is cut, each hemisphere can function independently; each split-brain cat appeared to have two brains. If you find the thought of a cat with two brains provocative, you will almost certainly be bowled over by similar observations about split-brain humans.

But I am getting ahead of myself. Let's first consider the research on cats.

In their experiment, Myers and Sperry trained cats to perform a simple visual discrimination. On each trial, each cat was confronted by two panels, one with a circle on it and one with a square on it. The relative positions of the circle and square (right or left) were varied randomly from trial to trial, and the cats had to learn which symbol to press in order to get a food reward. Myers and Sperry correctly surmised that the key to split-brain research was to develop procedures for teaching and testing one hemisphere at a time. Figure 16.3 illustrates the method they used to isolate visual-discrimination learning in one hemisphere of the cats. There are two routes by which visual information can cross from one eye to the contralateral hemisphere: via the corpus callosum or via the optic chiasm. Accordingly, in their key experimental group, Myers and Sperry *transected* (cut completely through) both the optic chiasm and the corpus callosum of each cat and put a patch on one eye. This restricted all incoming visual information to the hemisphere ipsilateral to the uncovered eye.

The results of Myers and Sperry's experiment are illustrated in Figure 16.4 on page 400. In the first phase of the study, all cats learned the task with a patch on one eye. The cats in the key experimental group (those with both the optic chiasm and the corpus callosum transected) learned the simple discrimination as rapidly as did unlesioned control cats or control cats with either the corpus

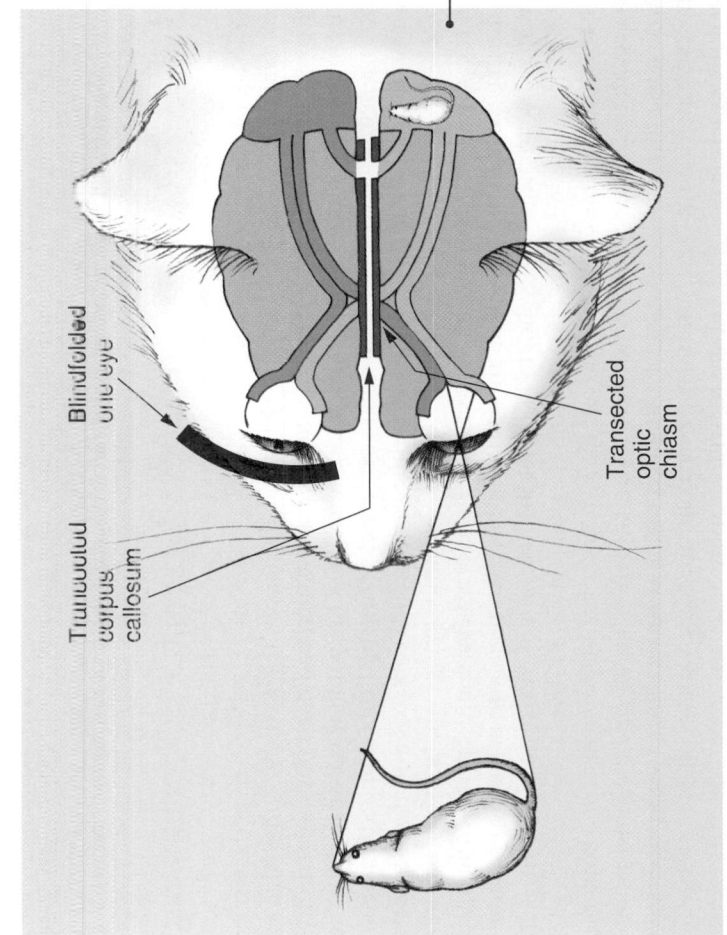

Transected corpus callosum

Blindfolded one eye

Transected optic chiasm

FIGURE 16.3 Restricting visual information to one hemisphere in cats. To restrict visual information to one hemisphere, Myers and Sperry (1) cut the corpus callosum, (2) cut the optic chiasm, and (3) blindfolded one eye. This restricted the visual information to the hemisphere ipsilateral to the uncovered eye.

Control groups

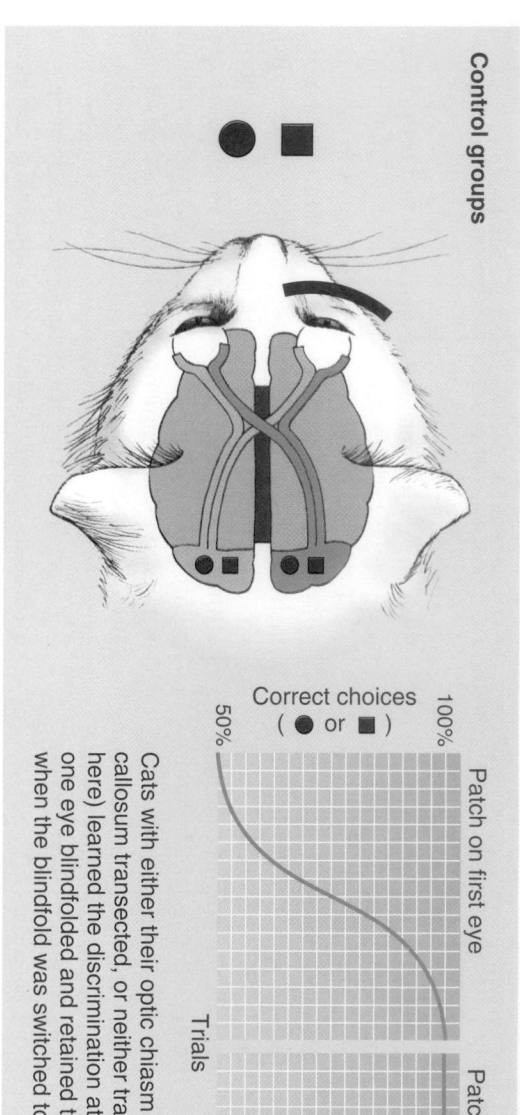

Cats with either their optic chiasm transected, corpus callosum transected, or neither transected (shown here) learned the discrimination at a normal rate with one eye blindfolded and retained the task perfectly when the blindfold was switched to the other eye.

Correct choices
(● or ■)
100%
50%

Patch on first eye   Patch on second eye

Trials

Experimental group

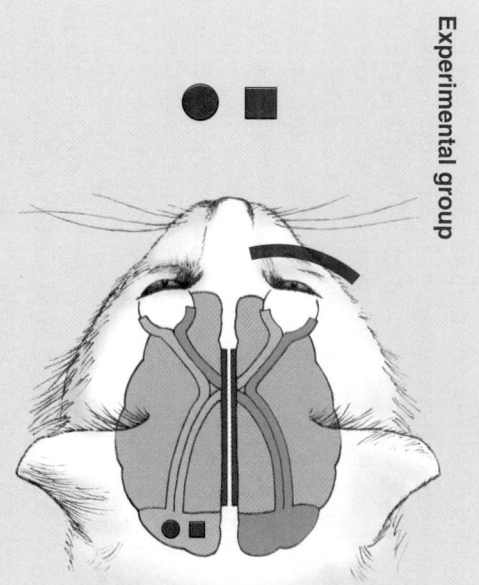

Cats with both their optic chiasms and corpus callosums transected learned the discrimination at a normal rate with one eye blindfolded, but they showed no retention whatsoever when the blindfold was switched to the other eye.

Correct choices
(● or ■)
100%
50%

Patch on first eye   Patch on second eye

Trials

FIGURE 16.4 Schematic illustration of Myers and Sperry's (1953) groundbreaking split-brain experiment. There were four groups: (1) the key experimental group with both the optic chiasm and corpus callosum transected, (2) a control group with only the optic chiasm transected, (3) a control group with only the corpus callosum transected, and (4) an unlesioned control group. The performance of the three control groups did not differ, so they are illustrated here together.

callosum or the optic chiasm transected, despite the fact that cutting the optic chiasm produced a **scotoma**—an area of blindness—involving the entire medial half of each retina. This result suggested that one hemisphere working alone can learn simple tasks as rapidly as two hemispheres working together.

More surprising were the results of the second phase of Myers and Sperry's experiment, during which the patch was transferred to each cat's other eye. The transfer of the patch had no effect on the performance of the intact control cats or of the control cats with either the optic chiasm or the corpus callosum transected; these subjects continued to perform the task with close to 100% accuracy. In contrast, transferring the eye patch had a devastating effect on the performance of the experimental cats. In effect, it blindfolded the hemisphere that had

originally learned the task and tested the knowledge of the other hemisphere, which had been blindfolded during initial training. When the patch was transferred, the performance of the experimental cats dropped immediately to baseline (i.e., to 50% correct); and then the cats relearned the task with no savings whatsoever, as if they had never seen it before. Myers and Sperry concluded that the cat brain has the capacity to act as two separate brains and that the function of the corpus callosum is to transmit information between them.

Myers and Sperry's startling conclusions about the fundamental duality of the cat brain and the information-transfer function of the corpus callosum have been confirmed in a variety of species with a variety of test procedures. For example, split-brain monkeys cannot perform tasks requiring fine tactual discriminations (e.g., rough versus smooth) or fine motor responses (e.g., unlocking a puzzle) with one hand if they have learned them with the other—provided that they are not allowed to watch their hands, which would allow the information to enter both hemispheres. There is no transfer of fine tactual and motor information in split-brain monkeys because the somatosensory and motor fibers involved in fine sensory and motor discriminations are all contralateral.

Commissurotomy in Human Epileptics

In the first half of the 20th century, when the normal function of the corpus callosum was still a mystery, it was known that epileptic discharges often spread from one hemisphere to the other through the corpus callosum. This fact and the fact that cutting the corpus callosum had proven in numerous studies to have no obvious effect on performance outside the contrived conditions of Sperry's laboratory led two neurosurgeons, Vogel and Bogen, to initiate a program of *commissurotomy* for the treatment of severe intractable cases of epilepsy.

The rationale underlying therapeutic commissurotomy—which typically involves transecting the corpus callosum and leaving the smaller commissures intact—was that the severity of the patient's convulsions might

be reduced if the discharges could be limited to the hemisphere of their origin. The therapeutic benefits of commissurotomy turned out to be even greater than anticipated: Despite the fact that commissurotomy is performed in only the most severe cases, many commissurotomized patients do not experience another major convulsion.

The evaluation of the split-brain patient's neuropsychological status was placed in the capable hands of Sperry and his associate Gazzaniga. They began by developing a battery of tests based on the same methodological strategy that had proved so informative in their studies of laboratory animals: delivering information to one hemisphere while keeping it out of the other.

They could not use the same visual-discrimination procedure that had been used in studies of split-brain laboratory animals (i.e., cutting the optic chiasm and blindfolding one eye) because cutting the optic chiasm produces a scotoma. Instead, they employed the procedure illustrated in Figure 16.5. Each patient was asked to fixate on the center of a display screen; then, visual stimuli were flashed onto the left or right side of the screen for 0.1 second. The 0.1 second exposure time was long enough for the subjects to perceive the stimuli but short enough to preclude the confounding effects of eye movement. All stimuli thus presented in the left visual

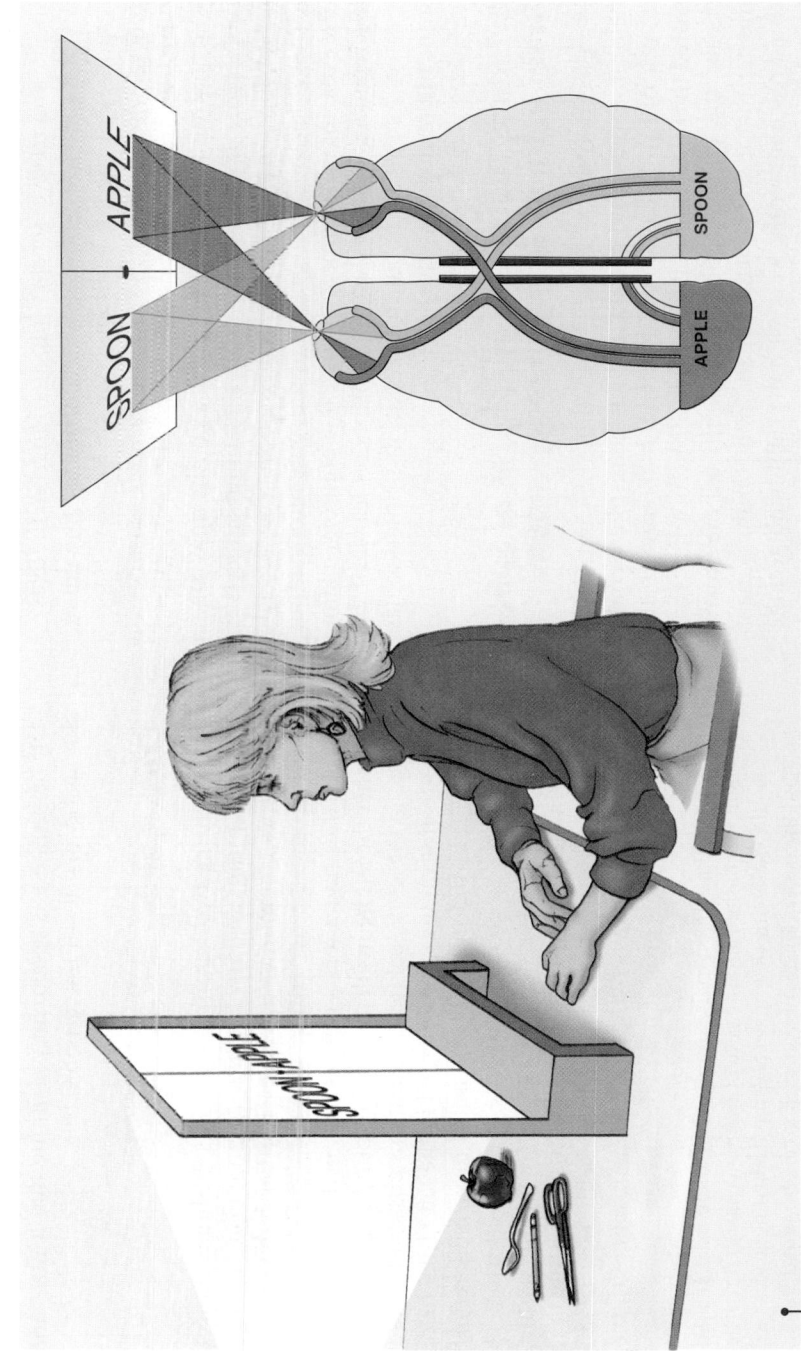

FIGURE 16.5 The testing procedure that was used to evaluate the neuropsychological status of split-brain patients. Visual input goes from each visual field to the contralateral hemisphere; fine tactile input goes from each hand to the contralateral hemisphere; and each hemisphere controls the fine motor movements of the contralateral hand.

field were transmitted to the right visual cortex, and all stimuli thus presented in the right visual field were transmitted to the left visual cortex.

Fine tactual and motor tasks were performed by each hand under a ledge. This procedure was used so that the nonperforming hemisphere, that is, the ipsilateral hemisphere, could not monitor the performance via the visual system.

The results of the tests on split-brain patients have confirmed the findings in split-brain laboratory animals in one major respect, but not in another. Like split-brain laboratory animals, human split-brain patients seem to have two independent brains, each with its own stream of consciousness, abilities, memories, and emotions (e.g., Gazzaniga, 1967; Gazzaniga & Sperry, 1967; Sperry, 1964). But unlike the hemispheres of split-brain laboratory animals, the hemispheres of split-brain patients are far from equal in their ability to perform certain tasks. Most notably, the left hemisphere of most split-brain patients is capable of speech, whereas the right hemisphere is not.

Before I recount some of the key results of the tests on split-brain humans, let me give you some advice. Some students become confused by the results of these tests because their tendency to think of the human brain as a single unitary organ is deeply engrained. If you become confused, think of each split-brain patient as two separate subjects: Ms. or Mr. Right Hemisphere, who understands a few simple instructions but cannot speak, who receives sensory information from the left visual field and left hand, and who controls the fine motor responses of the left hand; and Ms. or Mr. Left Hemisphere, who is verbally adept, who receives sensory information from the right visual field and right hand, and who controls the fine motor responses of the right hand.

Evidence That the Hemispheres of Split-Brain Patients Function Independently

If a picture of an apple were flashed in the right visual field of a split-brain patient, the left hemisphere could do one of two things to indicate that it had received and stored the information. Because it is the hemisphere that speaks, the left hemisphere could simply tell the experimenter that it saw a picture of an apple. Or the patient could reach under the ledge with the right hand, feel the test objects that are there, and pick out the apple. Similarly, if the apple were presented to the left hemisphere by being placed in the patient's right hand, the left hemisphere could indicate to the experimenter that it was an apple either by saying so or by putting the apple down

and picking out another apple with the right hand from the test objects under the ledge. If, however, the nonspeaking right hemisphere were asked to indicate the identity of an object that had previously been presented to the left hemisphere, it could not do so. Although objects that have been presented to the left hemisphere can be accurately identified with the right hand, performance is no better than chance with the left hand.

When test objects are presented to the right hemisphere either visually (in the left visual field) or tactually (in the left hand), the pattern of responses is entirely different. A split-brain patient asked to name an object flashed in the left visual field is likely to claim that nothing appeared on the screen. (Remember that it is the left hemisphere who is talking and the right hemisphere who has seen the stimulus.) A patient asked to name an object placed in the left hand is usually aware that something is there, presumably because of the crude tactual information carried by ipsilateral somatosensory fibers, but is unable to say what it is (see Fabri et al., 2001). Amazingly, all the while the patient is claiming (i.e., all the while that the left hemisphere is claiming) the inability to identify a test object presented in the left visual field or left hand, the left hand (i.e., the right hemisphere) can identify the correct object. Imagine how confused the patient must become when, in trial after trial, the left hand can feel an object and then fetch another just like it from a collection of test items under the ledge, while the left hemisphere is vehemently claiming that it does not know the identity of the test object.

Cross-Cuing

Although the two hemispheres of a split-brain subject have no means of direct neural communication, they sometimes communicate with each other indirectly by a process called **cross-cuing**. An example of cross-cuing occurred during a series of tests designed to determine whether the left hemisphere could respond to colors presented in the left visual field. To test this possibility, a red or a green stimulus was presented in the left visual field, and the split-brain subject was asked to verbally report the color: red or green. At first, the patient performed at a chance level on this task (50% correct); but after a time, performance improved appreciably, thus suggesting that the color information was somehow being transferred over neural pathways from the right hemisphere to the left. However, this proved not to be the case:

We soon caught on to the strategy the patient used. If a red light was flashed and the patient by chance guessed red, he would stick with that answer. If the flashed light was red, and the patient by chance guessed green, he would frown, shake his head and then say, "Oh no, I meant red." What was happening was that the right hemisphere saw the red light and heard the left hemisphere make the guess "green." Knowing that the answer was wrong, the right hemisphere precipitated a frown and a shake of the head, which in turn cued in the left hemisphere to the fact that the answer was wrong and that it had better correct itself.... The realization that the neurological patient has various strategies at his command emphasizes how difficult it is to obtain a clear neurological description of a human being with brain damage. (Gazzaniga, 1967, p. 27)

Learning Two Things at Once

In most of the classes I teach, there is a student who fits the following stereotype. He sits—or rather sprawls—near the back of the class; and despite good grades, he tries to create the impression that he is above it all by making sarcastic comments. I am sure you recognize him—and it is almost always a him. Such a student inadvertently triggered an interesting discussion in one of my classes. His comment went something like this: "If getting my brain cut in two could create two separate brains, perhaps I should get it done so that I could study for two different exams at the same time."

The question raised by this comment is a good one. If the two hemispheres of a split-brain patient are capable of total independence, then they should be able to learn two different things at the same time. Can they? Indeed they can. For example, in one test, two different visual stimuli appeared simultaneously on the test screen—let's say a pencil in the left visual field and an orange in the right visual field. The split-brain patient was asked to simultaneously reach into two bags—one with each hand—and grasp in each hand the object that was on the screen. After grasping the objects, but before withdrawing them, the subject was asked to tell the experimenter what was in the two hands; the subject (i.e., the left hemisphere) replied, "Two oranges." Much to the bewilderment of the verbal left hemisphere, when the hands were withdrawn, there was an orange in the right hand and a pencil in the left. The two hemispheres of the split-brain subject had learned two different things at exactly the same time.

In another test in which two visual stimuli were presented simultaneously—again, let's say a pencil to the left visual field and an orange to the right—the split-brain subject was asked to pick up the presented object from an assortment of objects on a table, this time in full view. As the right hand reached out to pick up the orange under the direction of the left hemisphere, the right hemisphere saw what was happening and thought an error was being made (remember that the right hemisphere saw a pencil). On some trials, the right hemisphere dealt with this problem in the only way that it could: The left hand shot out, grabbed the right hand away from the orange, and redirected it to the pencil. This response is called the **helping-hand phenomenon.**

Yet another example of simultaneous learning in the two hemispheres involves the phenomenon of **visual completion.** As you may recall from Chapter 7, individuals with scotomas are often unaware of them because their brains have the capacity to fill them in (to complete

them) by using information from the surrounding areas of the visual field. In a sense, each hemisphere of a split-brain patient is a subject with a scotoma covering the entire ipsilateral visual field.

The ability of each hemisphere of a split-brain patient to simultaneously and independently engage in completion has been demonstrated in studies using the **chimeric figures test**—named after *Chimera*, a mythical monster composed of the combined parts of different animals. Levy, Trevarthen, and Sperry (1972) flashed photographs composed of fused together half faces of two different people onto the center of a screen in front of their split-brain subjects. The subjects were then asked to describe what they saw or to indicate what they saw by pointing to it in a series of photographs of intact faces. Amazingly, each subject (i.e., each left hemisphere) reported seeing a complete, bilaterally symmetrical face, even when asked such leading questions as "Did you notice anything peculiar about what you just saw?" When the subjects were asked to describe what they saw, they usually described a completed version of the half that had been presented to the right visual field (i.e., the left hemisphere).

The Z Lens

Once it was firmly established that the two hemispheres of each split-brain patient can function independently, it became clear that the study of split-brain patients provided a unique opportunity to compare the abilities of left and right hemispheres. However, early studies of the lateralization of function in split-brain patients were limited by the fact that visual stimuli requiring more than 0.1 second to perceive could not be studied using the conventional method for restricting visual input to one hemisphere. This methodological barrier was eliminated by Zaidel in 1975. Zaidel developed a lens, called the **Z lens,** that limits visual input to one hemisphere of split-brain patients while they scan complex visual material such as the pages of a book. As Figure 16.6 on page 404 illustrates, the Z lens is a contact lens that is opaque on one side (left or right). Because it moves with the eye, it permits visual input to enter only one hemisphere, irrespective of eye movement. Zaidel used the Z lens to compare the ability of the left and right hemispheres of split-brain patients to perform various tests.

The usefulness of the Z lens is not restricted to purely visual tests. For example, here is how it has been used to compare the ability of the left and right hemispheres to comprehend speech. Because each ear projects to both hemispheres, it is not possible to present spoken words to only one hemisphere. Thus, to assess the ability of a hemisphere to comprehend spoken words or sentences, Zaidel presented them to both ears, and then he asked the subject to pick the correct answer or to perform the correct response under the direction of visual input to only that hemisphere. For example, to test the ability of the right hemisphere to understand oral commands, the

So far in this chapter, you have learned about five methods of studying cerebral lateralization of function: unilateral lesions, the sodium amytal test, the dichotic listening test, functional brain imaging, and studies of

16.3 Differences between the Left and Right Hemispheres

Dual Mental Functioning and Conflict in Split-Brain Patients

In most split-brain patients, the right hemisphere does not seem to have a strong will of its own; the left hemisphere seems to control most everyday activities. However, in

split-brain patients. This section takes a look at some of the major functional differences between the left and right cerebral hemispheres that have been discovered using these methods. Because the verbal and motor abilities

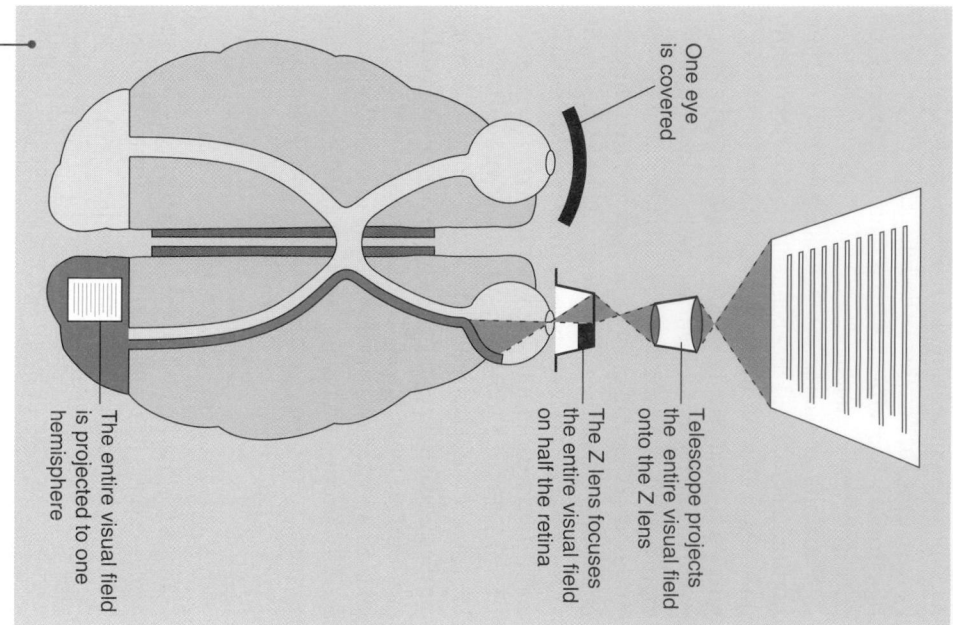

FIGURE 16.6 The Z lens, which was developed by Zaidel to study functional asymmetry in split-brain patients. It is a contact lens that is opaque on one side (left or right), so that visual input reaches only one hemisphere.

One eye is covered

Telescope projects the entire visual field onto the Z lens

The Z lens focuses the entire visual field on half the retina

The entire visual field is projected to one hemisphere

subjects were given an oral instruction (such as "Put the green square under the red circle"), and then the right hemisphere's ability to comprehend the direction was tested by allowing only the right hemisphere to observe the colored tokens while the task was being completed.

other patients, the right hemisphere takes a more active role in controlling behavior. In these latter cases, there can be serious conflicts between the left and right hemispheres. Patient 2C (let's call him Peter) was such a case.

The Case of Peter, the Split-Brain Patient Tormented by Conflict

At the age of 8, Peter began to suffer from complex partial seizures. Antiepileptic medication was ineffective, and at 20, he received a commissurotomy, which greatly improved his condition but did not completely block his seizures. A sodium amytal test administered prior to surgery showed that he was left-hemisphere dominant for language.

Following surgery, Peter, unlike most other split-brain patients, was not able to respond with the left side of his body to verbal input. When asked to make whole-body movements (e.g., "Stand like a boxer") or movements of the left side of his body (e.g., "Touch your left ear with your left hand"), he could not respond correctly. Apparently, his left hemisphere could not, or would not, control the left side of his body via ipsilateral fibers. During such tests, Peter—or, more specifically, Peter's left hemisphere—often remarked that he hated the left side of his body.

The independent, obstinate, and sometimes mischievous behavior of Peter's right hemisphere often caused him (his left hemisphere) considerable frustration. He (his left hemisphere) complained that his left hand would turn off television shows that he was enjoying, that his left leg would not always walk in the intended direction, and that his left arm would sometimes perform embarrassing, socially unacceptable acts (e.g., striking a relative).

In the laboratory, he (his left hemisphere) sometimes became angry with his left hand, swearing at it, striking it, and trying to force it with his right hand to do what he (his left hemisphere) wanted. In these cases, his left hand usually resisted his right hand and kept performing as directed by his right hemisphere. In these instances, it was always clear that the right hemisphere was behaving with intent and understanding and that the left hemisphere had no clue why the despised left hand was doing what it was doing (Joseph, 1988).

of the left hemisphere are readily apparent (see Beeman & Chiarello, 1998; Reuter-Lorenz & Miller, 1998), most research on the lateralization of function has focused on uncovering the special abilities of the right hemisphere.

Slight Biases versus All-or-None Hemispheric Differences

Before I introduce you to some of the differences between the left and right hemispheres, I need to clear up a common misconception: For many functions, there are no differences between the hemispheres; and when functional differences do exist, these tend to be slight biases in favor of one hemisphere or the other—not absolute differences (see Brown & Kosslyn, 1993). Disregarding these facts, the popular media inevitably portray left–right cerebral differences as absolute. As a result, it is widely believed that various abilities reside exclusively in one hemisphere or the other. For example, it is widely believed that the left hemisphere has exclusive control over language and the right hemisphere has exclusive control over emotion and creativity. The most disturbing thing about this misrepresentation is that educational programs are sometimes inspired by it.

Language-related abilities provide a particularly good illustration of the fact that lateralization of function is statistical rather than absolute. Language is the most lateralized of all cognitive abilities. Yet, even in this most extreme case, lateralization is far from total; there is substantial language-related activity in the right hemisphere. Following are three illustrations of this point: First, on the dichotic listening test, subjects who are left-hemisphere dominant for language tend to identify more digits with the right ear than the left ear, but this right-ear advantage is only slight, 55% to 45%. Second, in most split-brain patients, the left hemisphere is dominant for language, but the right hemisphere can understand many spoken or written words and simple sentences (see Baynes & Gazzaniga, 1997; Zaidel, 1987). And third, although there is considerable variability among split-brain patients in their right-hemisphere performance on tests of language comprehension (Gazzaniga, 1998), the language abilities of their right hemispheres tend to be comparable to those of a preschool child.

Some Examples of Lateralization of Function

Table 16.1 lists some of the abilities that have been shown to be lateralized. They are arranged in two columns:

TABLE 16.1   Abilities That Display Cerebral Lateralization of Function

GENERAL FUNCTION	Left-Hemisphere Dominance	Right-Hemisphere Dominance
VISION	Words Letters	Faces Geometric patterns Emotional expression
AUDITION	Language sounds	Nonlanguage sounds Music
TOUCH		Tactile patterns Braille
MOVEMENT	Complex movement Ipsilateral movement	Movement in spatial patterns
MEMORY	Verbal memory Finding meaning in memories	Nonverbal memory Perceptual aspects of memories
LANGUAGE	Speech Reading Writing Arithmetic	Emotional content
SPATIAL ABILITY		Mental rotation of shapes Geometry Direction Distance

those that are controlled more by the left hemisphere and those that are controlled more by the right hemisphere. The study of lateralization of function has put the archaic notion of left-hemisphere dominance to rest. The right hemisphere has been shown to be functionally superior to the left in several respects. The three best-documented domains of right-hemisphere superiority are spatial ability, emotion, and musical ability. Also, the right hemisphere is superior in performing some memory tasks. Before discussing these four superiorities of the right hemisphere, let's take a look at an unexpected superiority of the left hemisphere.

Superiority of the Left Hemisphere in Controlling Ipsilateral Movement

One interesting and unexpected lateralized function was revealed by functional brain-imaging studies (see Haaland & Harrington, 1996). When complex, cognitively driven movements are made by one hand, most of the activity is observed in the *contralateral* hemisphere, as expected. However, some activation is also observed in the *ipsilateral* hemisphere, and these ipsilateral effects are substantially greater in the left hemisphere than in the right (Kim et al., 1993). Consistent with this observation is the fact that left-hemisphere lesions are more likely than right-hemisphere lesions to be associated with ipsilateral motor problems.

Superiority of the Right Hemisphere in Spatial Ability

In a classic early study, Levy (1969) placed a three-dimensional block of a particular shape in either the right hand or the left hand of her split-brain subjects. Then, after they had thoroughly *palpated* (tactually investigated) it, she asked them to point to the two-dimensional test stimulus that best represented what the three-dimensional block would look like if it were made of cardboard and unfolded. She found a right-hemisphere superiority on this task, and she found that the two hemispheres seemed to go about the task in different ways. The performance of the left hand and right hemisphere was rapid and silent, whereas the performance of the right hand and left hemisphere was hesitant and often accompanied by a running verbal commentary that was difficult for the subjects to inhibit. Levy concluded that the right hemisphere is superior to the left at spatial tasks. This conclusion has been frequently confirmed (e.g., Funnell, Corballis, & Gazzaniga, 1999; Kaiser et al., 2000), and it is consistent with the finding that disorders of spatial perception (e.g., contralateral neglect—see Chapters 7 and 8) tend to be associated with right-hemisphere damage.

Superiority of the Right Hemisphere in the Experience of Emotion

According to the old concept of left-hemisphere dominance, the right hemisphere is uninvolved in emotion. This presumption has been proven false. Indeed, analysis of the effects of unilateral brain lesions indicates that the right hemisphere is superior to

the left at perceiving both facial expression of emotions (Bowers et al., 1985) and mood (Tompkins & Mateer, 1985).

Sperry, Zaidel, and Zaidel (1979) used the Z lens to assess the behavioral reactions of the right hemispheres of split-brain patients to various emotion-charged images: photographs of relatives; of pets; of themselves; and of political, historical, and religious figures and emblems. Their behavioral reactions were appropriate, thus indicating that right hemispheres are capable of emotional expression. In addition, there was an unexpected finding: The emotional content of images presented to the right hemisphere was reflected in the patients' speech as well as in their nonverbal behavior. This suggested that emotional information was somehow being passed from the right to the verbal left hemisphere of the split-brain subjects. The ability of emotional reactions, but not visual information, to be passed from the right hemisphere to the left hemisphere created a bizarre situation. A subject's left hemisphere often reacted with the appropriate emotional verbal response to an image that had been presented to the right hemisphere, even though it did not know what the image was.

Consider the following remarkable exchange (paraphrased from Sperry, Zaidel, & Zaidel, 1979, pp. 161–162). The patient's right hemisphere was presented with an array of photos, and the patient was asked if one was familiar. He pointed to the photo of his aunt.

Experimenter: "Is this a neutral, a thumbs-up, or a thumbs-down person?"
Patient: With a smile, he made a thumbs-up sign and said, "This is a happy person."
Experimenter: "Do you know him personally?"
Patient: "Oh, it's not a him, it's a her."
Experimenter: "Is she an entertainment personality or an historical figure?"
Patient: "No, just . . ."
Experimenter: "Someone you know personally?"
Patient: He traced something with his left index finger on the back of his right hand, and then he exclaimed, "My aunt, my Aunt Edie."
Experimenter: "How do you know?"
Patient: "By the E on the back of my hand."

Pause and think about the experiences and thoughts of these two hemispheres as each struggled to perform the task.

Superiority of the Right Hemisphere in Musical Ability

Kimura (1964) compared the performance of 20 right-handers on the standard, digit version of the dichotic listening test with their performance on a version of the test involving the dichotic presentation of melodies. In the melody version of the test, Kimura simultaneously played two different melodies—one to each ear—and then asked the subjects to identify the two that were subsequently played to them through both ears. The right ear (i.e., the left hemisphere) was superior in the perception of digits, whereas the left ear (i.e., the right hemisphere) was superior in the perception of melodies. This is consistent with the observation that right temporal lobe lesions are more likely to disrupt music discriminations than are left temporal lobe lesions.

Hemispheric Difference in Memory   Both the left and right hemispheres have the ability to remember, but they seem to go about the task of remembering in different ways (see Gazzaniga, 1998). Although this hemispheric difference in memory style has been demonstrated in several ways, it is particularly well illustrated by the performance of split-brain patients on the following task. In this task, the left or right hemispheres of split-brain patients are tested separately. The task is to guess which of two lights—top or bottom—will come on next, based on the hemisphere's memory of recent trials. The top light comes on 80% of the time in random sequence, but the subjects are not given this information. The fact that the top light comes on more than the bottom is quickly discovered by intact control subjects; however, because they try to figure out the nonexistent rule that predicts the exact sequence, they are correct only 68% of the time—even though they could score 80% if they always selected the top light.

The left hemispheres of split-brain subjects perform like intact controls: They attempt to find deeper meaning in their memories and as a result perform poorly on this task. In contrast, right hemispheres, like rats, do not try to interpret their memories and readily learn to maximize their correct responses by always selecting the top light. The left hemisphere attempts to place its experiences in a larger context, while the right hemisphere attends strictly to the perceptual aspects of the stimulus (see Metcalfe, Funnell, & Gazzaniga, 1995; Roser & Gazzaniga, 2004).

The two hemispheres also seem to differ somewhat with respect to what types of information they remember. In general, the left hemisphere plays the greater role in memory for verbal material, whereas the right hemisphere plays the greater role in memory for nonverbal material (e.g., Kelley et al., 2002).

What Is Lateralized—Broad Clusters of Abilities or Individual Cognitive Processes?

Take another look at Table 16.1, which summarizes major examples of cerebral lateralization of function. I have already alerted you to one way in which examples of cerebral lateralization are commonly misinterpreted: They reflect slight hemispheric biases, not all-or-none differences. Now that you have had the opportunity to digest the information in Table 16.1, I want to issue a second warning about it.

You have undoubtedly encountered some of this information before: Is there a single educated person in this society who does not know that the left hemisphere is the logical language hemisphere and the right hemisphere is the emotional spatial hemisphere? Information like that in Table 16.1 summarizes the results of many studies and thus serves a useful function if it is not taken too literally. The problem is that such information is almost always taken too literally. Let me explain.

Early theories of cerebral laterality tended to ascribe complex clusters of mental abilities to one hemisphere or the other. The left hemisphere tended to perform better on language tests, so it was presumed to be dominant for language-related abilities; the right hemisphere tended to perform better on some spatial tests, so it was presumed to be dominant for space-related abilities; and so on. Perhaps this was a reasonable first step, but now the general view among researchers is that this approach is simplistic, illogical, and inconsistent with the evidence.

The problem is that categories such as language, emotion, musical ability, and spatial ability are each composed of dozens of different individual cognitive activities, and there is no reason to assume that all those activities associated with a general English label (e.g., spatial ability) will necessarily be lateralized in the same hemisphere. The inappropriateness of broad categories of cerebral lateralization has been confirmed. How is it possible to argue that all language-related abilities are lateralized in the left hemisphere, when the right hemisphere has proved superior in perceiving the intonation of speech and the identity of the speaker (Beeman & Chiarello, 1998)? Indeed, notable exceptions to all broad categories of cerebral lateralization have emerged (see Vogel, Bowers, & Vogel, 2003).

As a result of mounting evidence of the inappropriateness of broad categories of cerebral lateralization, many researchers are taking a different approach. They are basing their studies of cerebral lateralization on the work of cognitive psychologists, who have broken down complex cognitive tasks—such as reading, judging space, and remembering—into their *constituent cognitive processes*. Once the laterality of the individual cognitive elements has been determined, it is possible to predict the laterality of cognitive tasks based on the specific cognitive elements that compose them. The research of Chabris and Kosslyn (1998) is an excellent example of this approach:

Consider the problems of (a) assessing whether one object is above or below another and (b) assessing whether two objects are greater or less than 1 foot apart. Both are spatial tasks, so early theories might have predicted that the right hemisphere would be superior at both. Yet both require a verbal response . . . , so perhaps the left hemisphere would be better . . . in each case. But if the left hemisphere is better, could this instead be because of the "analytical" processing required to compare two elements? It is clear that the coarse conceptualizations offered by early theories shed little light on even such apparently similar tasks as these.

Chabris and Kosslyn therefore took a different approach to predicting the laterality of these two simple spatial judgments. They based their research on the cognitive theory of Kosslyn (1994). Kosslyn found evidence that separate processes in the visual system judge different types of spatial relations between objects: There is a process for making *categorical* judgments about the spatial relations (e.g., left/right, above/below) and one for making precise judgments of the spatial relations between objects in terms of their distance and angle from each other. Because the process for making *categorical spatial judgments* is dominant in the left hemisphere and the process for making *coordinate* (distance and angles) *spatial judgments* is dominant in the right hemisphere, Chabris and Kosslyn predicted that the left hemisphere would be superior in judging whether an object is above or below another and that the right hemisphere would be better in judging whether two objects are greater or less than a foot apart. They were right.

Anatomical Asymmetries of the Brain

Casual inspection suggests that the left and right hemispheres are mirror images of one another, but they are not; many anatomical differences between them have been documented. Most of the research effort has been expended trying to document anatomical asymmetries in areas of cortex that are important for language (see Figure 16.7). Three of these areas are the planum temporale, Heschl's gyrus, and the frontal operculum. The **planum temporale** is the area of temporal lobe cortex that lies in the posterior region of the lateral fissure; it is

thought to play a role in the comprehension of language and is often referred to as *Wernicke's area*. **Heschl's gyrus** is located in the lateral fissure just anterior to the planum temporale in the temporal lobe; it is the location of primary auditory cortex. The **frontal operculum** is the area of frontal lobe cortex that lies just in front of the face area of the primary motor cortex; in the left hemisphere, it is the location of Broca's area.

Because the planum temporale, Heschl's gyrus, and the frontal operculum are all involved in language-related activities, one might expect that they would all be larger in the left hemisphere than in the right in most subjects; but they aren't. The left planum temporale does tend to be larger on the left, but in only 65% of human brains (Geschwind & Levitsky, 1968). In contrast, the cortex of Heschl's gyrus tends to be larger on the right, primarily because there are often two Heschl's gyri in the right hemisphere and only one in the left. The laterality of the frontal operculum is less clear. The area of the frontal operculum that is visible on the surface of the brain tends to be larger on the right; but when the cortex buried within sulci of the frontal operculum is considered, there tends to be a greater volume of frontal operculum cortex on the left (Falzi, Perrone, & Vignolo, 1982).

A word of caution is in order. It is tempting to conclude that the tendency for the planum temporale to be larger in the left hemisphere predisposes the left hemisphere for language dominance. Indeed, the finding that the left planum temporale is larger than the right in fetal brains (Wada, Clarke, & Hamm, 1975) is consistent with this view. However, because most studies of neuroanatomical asymmetry are conducted at autopsy, there is no evidence that people with well-developed anatomical asymmetries tend to have more lateralized language functions. In fact, there is a substantial discrepancy between the proportion of the population that has been reported to have a larger left planum temporale (about 65%) and the proportion that is left-hemisphere dominant for language (over 90%).

Techniques for imaging the living human brain have made it easier to look for correlations between particular neuroanatomical asymmetries and particular performance measures. Such studies are important because they have the potential for revealing the functional advantages of cerebral lateralization. One such study is that of Schlaug and colleagues (1995). They used structural magnetic resonance imaging (MRI) to measure the asymmetry of the planum temporale and relate it to the presence of *perfect pitch* (the ability to identify the pitch of individual musical notes). The planum temporale was found to be more lateralized to the left hemisphere in musicians with perfect pitch than in nonmusicians or in musicians without perfect pitch (see Figure 16.8).

Most studies of anatomical asymmetries of the brain have measured differences in gross neuroanatomy, comparing the sizes of particular gross structures in the left

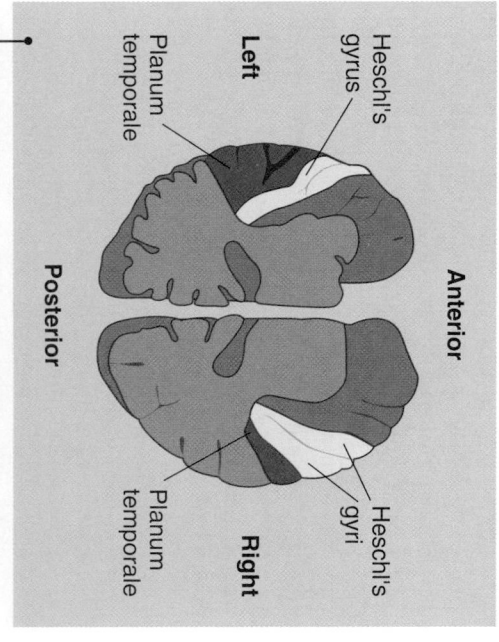

Anterior

Heschl's
gyrus

Left

Planum
temporale

Posterior

Heschl's
gyri

Right

Planum
temporale

FIGURE 16.7 Two language areas of the cerebral cortex that display neuroanatomical asymmetry: the planum temporale (Wernicke's area) and Heschl's gyrus (primary auditory cortex).

Cognitive Neuroscience

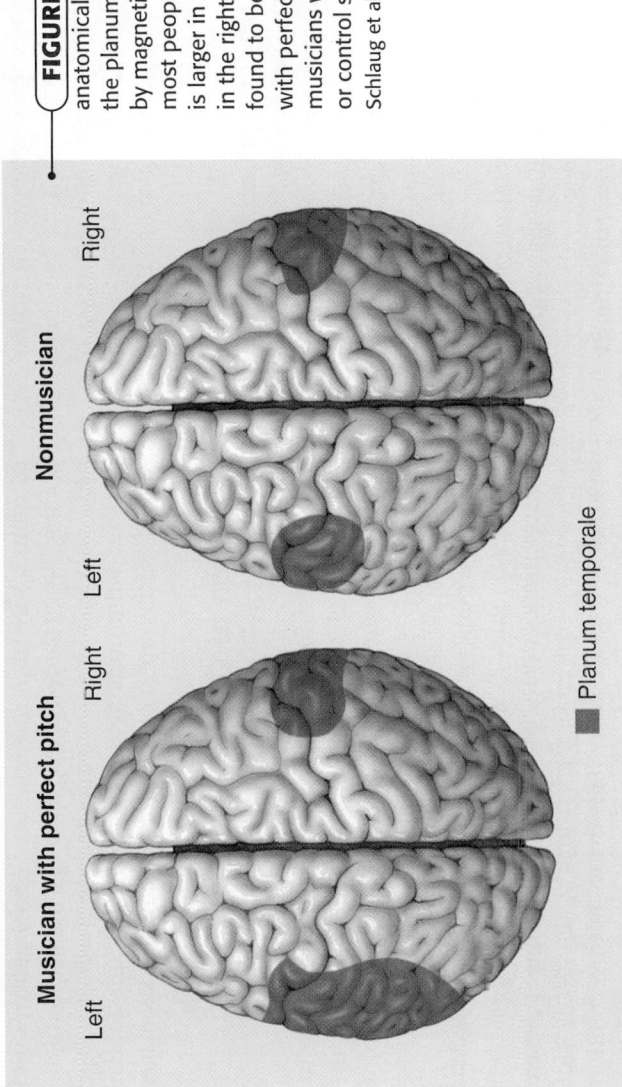

Musician with perfect pitch

Left   Right   Left   Right

Nonmusician

■ Planum temporale

FIGURE 16.8 The anatomical asymmetry detected in the planum temporale of musicians by magnetic resonance imaging. In most people, the planum temporale is larger in the left hemisphere than in the right; this difference was found to be greater in musicians with perfect pitch than in either musicians without perfect pitch or control subjects. (Adapted from Schlaug et al., 1995.)

and right hemispheres. Recently, however, anatomists have started to study differences in cellular structure between corresponding areas of the two hemispheres that have been found to differ in function (see Gazzaniga, 2000; Hutsler & Galuske, 2003). One such study was conducted by Galuske and colleagues (2000). They compared the organization of the microcircuitry in part of Wernicke's area with its organization in the same part of the right hemisphere. They found that the areas in both hemispheres are organized into regularly spaced columns of interconnected neurons and that the columns are interconnected by medium range axons. The columns are the same diameter in both hemispheres, but they are about 20% further apart in the left hemisphere and are interconnected by longer axons. Presumably, the particular way in which the columns are organized in Wernicke's area is an adaptation for the processing of language signals.

A similar pattern of findings has emerged from research on asymmetries in the hand area of human primary motor cortex (see Hammond, 2002). The hand area in the hemisphere contralateral to the person's preferred hand tends to be larger and have more lateral connections.

Theories of Cerebral Asymmetry

Several theories have been proposed to explain why cerebral asymmetry evolved. All of them are based on the same general premise: that it is advantageous for areas of the brain that perform similar functions to be located in the same hemisphere. However, each theory of cerebral asymmetry postulates a different fundamental distinction between left and right hemisphere function. The following are three prominent theories of cerebral asymmetry.

Analytic–Synthetic Theory One theory of cerebral asymmetry is the analytic–synthetic theory. The *analytic synthetic theory of cerebral asymmetry* holds that there are two basic modes of thinking, an analytic mode and a synthetic mode, which have become segregated during the course of evolution in the left and right hemispheres, respectively. According to this theory,

...the left hemisphere operates in a more logical, analytical, computerlike fashion, analyzing stimulus information input sequentially and abstracting the relevant details, to which it attaches verbal labels; the right hemisphere is primarily a synthesizer, more concerned with the overall stimulus configuration, and organizes and processes information in terms of gestalts, or wholes. (Harris, 1978, p. 463)

Although the analytic–synthetic theory has been the darling of pop psychology, its vagueness is a problem. Because it is not possible to specify the degree to which any task requires either analytic or synthetic processing, it has been difficult to subject the analytic–synthetic theory to empirical tests.

Motor Theory A second theory of cerebral asymmetry is the motor theory (see Kimura, 1979). According to the *motor theory of cerebral asymmetry*, the left hemisphere is specialized not for the control of speech per se but for the control of fine movements, of which speech is only one category. Support for this theory comes from reports that lesions that produce aphasia also produce other motor deficits. For example, Kimura (1987) found a correlation between the disruption of language abilities by lesions and the disruption of voluntary nonspeech oral movements by the same lesions; Kimura and Watson (1989) found that left frontal lesions produced deficits in the ability to make both individual speech sounds and individual facial movements, whereas left temporal and parietal lesions produced deficits in the ability to make sequences of speech sounds and sequences of facial movements; and Wolff and others (1990) found that subjects with reading disabilities also had difficulty performing a finger-tapping test.

Linguistic Theory

A third theory of cerebral asymmetry is the linguistic theory. The *linguistic theory of cerebral asymmetry* posits that the primary role of the left hemisphere is language—in contrast to the analytic-synthetic and motor theories, which view language as a secondary specialization residing in the left hemisphere because of its primary specialization for analytic thought and skilled motor activity, respectively.

The linguistic theory of cerebral asymmetry is based to a large degree on the study of deaf people who use American Sign Language (a sign language with a structure similar to spoken language) and then suffer unilateral brain damage (see Hickok, Bellugi, & Klima, 2001).

W.L. was such a case.

The Case of W.L., the Man Who Experienced Aphasia for Sign Language

Clinical Implications

W.L. is a congenitally deaf, right-handed male. He has two deaf, signing brothers and grew up using American Sign Language. Until his stroke, he had relied on sign language as his primary means of communication with his spouse, relatives, and friends.

W.L. has a history of cardiovascular disease; and 7 months prior to testing, he was admitted to hospital complaining of right-side weakness and motor problems. A CT scan revealed a large frontotemporoparietal lesion. At that time, W.L.'s wife noticed that he was making many uncharacteristic errors in signing and was having difficulty understanding the signs of others.

Fortunately, W.L.'s neuropsychologists managed to obtain a 2-hour videotape of an interview with him recorded 10 months before his stroke, which served as a valuable source of prestroke performance measures. Formal poststroke neuropsychological testing confirmed that W.L. had suffered a specific loss in his ability to use and understand sign language. The fact that he could produce and understand complex pantomime gestures suggested that his sign-language aphasia was not the result of motor or sensory deficits, and the results of cognitive tests suggested that it was not the result of general cognitive deficits (Corina et al., 1992).

The case of W.L. is particularly important because it illustrates a striking dissociation between two kinds of

communicative gestures: linguistic (sign) gestures and nonlinguistic (pantomime) gestures. The fact that left-hemisphere damage can disrupt the use of sign language but not pantomime gestures suggests that the fundamental specialization of the left hemisphere is language.

Evolution of Cerebral Lateralization of Function

Evolutionary Perspective

Cerebral lateralization is often assumed to be an exclusive feature of the hominid brain. One theory of the evolution of cerebral asymmetry is based on the motor theory of cerebral asymmetry: Left-hemisphere dominance for motor control is thought to have evolved in early hominids in response to their use of tools, and then the propensity for vocal language is thought to have subsequently evolved in the left hemisphere because of its greater motor dexterity. This theory of the evolution of cerebral lateralization of function is challenged by reports of cerebral lateralization in nonhuman primates.

The first studies of hand preference in nonhuman primates found that some individual monkeys tended to use one hand more than the other but that there was no general tendency for the right to be preferred over the left (Colell, Segarra, & Sabater-Pi, 1995). However, more recently, there have been several reports that the nonhuman primates most closely related to humans display a right-hand preference for certain tasks (see Hopkins, 1996). For example, Hopkins (1995) found that chimpanzees tend to use their right hands to extract peanut butter from a transparent tube. Subsequently, Hopkins, Dahl, and Pilcher (2001) found that hand preference (left or right) is under genetic influence in chimpanzees, and Hopkins and Pilcher (2001) found the hand area to be larger in the left primary motor cortex than in the right primary motor cortex in a mixed sample of apes (e.g., gorillas, orangutans, and chimpanzees). Evidence of handedness in nonhuman primates rules out the possibility that tool use by early hominids was the major factor in the evolution of cerebral lateralization of function.

Hand preference is not the only evidence of cerebral lateralization of function in nonhuman primates. In some nonhuman primate species, the left hemispheres have been found to be dominant for the production (see Owren, 1990) and discrimination (Heffner & Heffner, 1984) of communicative vocalizations, and the cortical area homologous to Wernicke's area has been found to be larger in the left hemisphere (Gannon et al., 1998). Moreover, in some nonhuman primate species, the right hemisphere has proven to be superior in the discrimination of facial identity and expression (Vermeire, Hamilton, & Erdmann, 1998). All these findings suggest that the evolution of cerebral laterality preceded the evolution of humans.

Interestingly, the motor circuit controlling singing in male canaries is more developed on the left side of their brains (see Mooney, 1999). Because birds are not part of the evolutionary lineage of humans—birds evolved from reptiles in a separate branch—this finding indicates either that cerebral laterality evolved prior to the branching or that the advantages of cerebral laterality led to its independent evolution in more than one species.

16.4 Cortical Localization of Language: The Wernicke-Geschwind Model

So far, this chapter has focused on the functional asymmetry of the brain, with an emphasis on the lateralization of language-related functions. At this point, it shifts its focus from language lateralization to language localization. In contrast to language lateralization, which refers to the relative control of language-related functions by the left and right hemispheres, *language localization* refers to the location within the hemispheres of the circuits that participate in language-related activities.

Like most introductions to language localization, the following discussion begins with the *Wernicke-Geschwind model*, the predominant theory of language localization. Because most of the research on the localization of language has been conducted and interpreted within the context of this model, reading about the localization of language without a basic understanding of the Wernicke-Geschwind model would be like watching a game of chess without knowing the rules—not a very fulfilling experience.

ON THE CD

See the *Wernicke-Geschwind Model of Language* module for a clear and vivid explanation of the model.

Historical Antecedents of the Wernicke-Geschwind Model

The history of the localization of language and the history of the lateralization of function began at the same point, with Broca's assertion that a small area in the inferior portion of the left prefrontal cortex (Broca's area) is the center for speech production. Broca hypothesized that programs of articulation are stored within this area and that speech is produced when these programs activate the adjacent area of the precentral gyrus, which controls the muscles of the face and oral cavity. According to Broca, damage restricted to Broca's area should disrupt speech production without producing deficits in language comprehension.

The next major event in the study of the cerebral localization of language occurred in 1874, when Carl Wernicke (pronounced "VER-ni-key") concluded on the basis of 10 clinical cases that there is a language area in the left temporal lobe just posterior to the primary auditory cortex (i.e., in the left planum temporale). This second language area, which Wernicke argued was the cortical area of language comprehension, subsequently became known as **Wernicke's area.**

Wernicke suggested that selective lesions of Broca's area produce a syndrome of aphasia whose symptoms are primarily **expressive**—characterized by normal comprehension of both written and spoken language and by speech that retains its meaningfulness despite being slow, labored, disjointed, and poorly articulated. This hypothetical form of aphasia became known as **Broca's aphasia.** In contrast, Wernicke suggested that selective lesions of Wernicke's area produce a syndrome of aphasia whose deficits are primarily **receptive**—characterized by poor comprehension of both written and spoken language and speech that is meaningless but still retains the superficial structure, rhythm, and intonation of normal speech. This hypothetical form of aphasia became known as **Wernicke's aphasia,** and the normal-sounding but nonsensical speech of Wernicke's aphasia became known as **word salad.**

The following are examples of the kinds of speech that are presumed to be associated with selective damage to Broca's and Wernicke's areas (Geschwind, 1979, p. 183):

> **Broca's aphasia:** A patient who was asked about a dental appointment replied haltingly and indistinctly: "Yes. . . . Monday. . . Dad and Dick. . . . Wednesday nine o'clock. . . 10 o'clock. . . . doctors. . . . and . . . . teeth."

> **Wernicke's aphasia:** A patient who was asked to describe a picture that showed two boys stealing cookies reported smoothly: "Mother is away here working her work to get her better, but when she's looking the two boys looking in the other part. She's working another time."

Wernicke reasoned that damage to the pathway connecting Broca's and Wernicke's areas—the **arcuate fasciculus**—would produce a third type of aphasia, one he called **conduction aphasia.** He contended that comprehension and spontaneous speech would be largely intact in patients with damage to the arcuate fasciculus but that they would have difficulty repeating words that had just been heard.

The left **angular gyrus**—the area of left temporal and parietal cortex just posterior to Wernicke's area—is another cortical area that has been implicated in language. Its role in language was recognized in 1892 by Dejerine on the basis of the postmortem examination of one special patient. The patient suffered from **alexia** (the inability to read) and **agraphia** (the inability to write). What made this case special was that the alexia and agraphia were exceptionally pure: Although the patient could not read or write, he had no difficulty speaking

FIGURE 16.9 The seven components of the Wernicke-Geschwind model.

or understanding speech. Dejerine's post-mortem examination revealed damage in the pathways connecting the visual cortex with the left angular gyrus. He concluded that the left angular gyrus is responsible for comprehending language-related visual input, which is received directly from the adjacent left visual cortex and indirectly from the right visual cortex via the corpus callosum.

During the era of Broca, Wernicke, and Dejerine, many influential scholars (e.g., Freud, Head, and Marie) opposed their

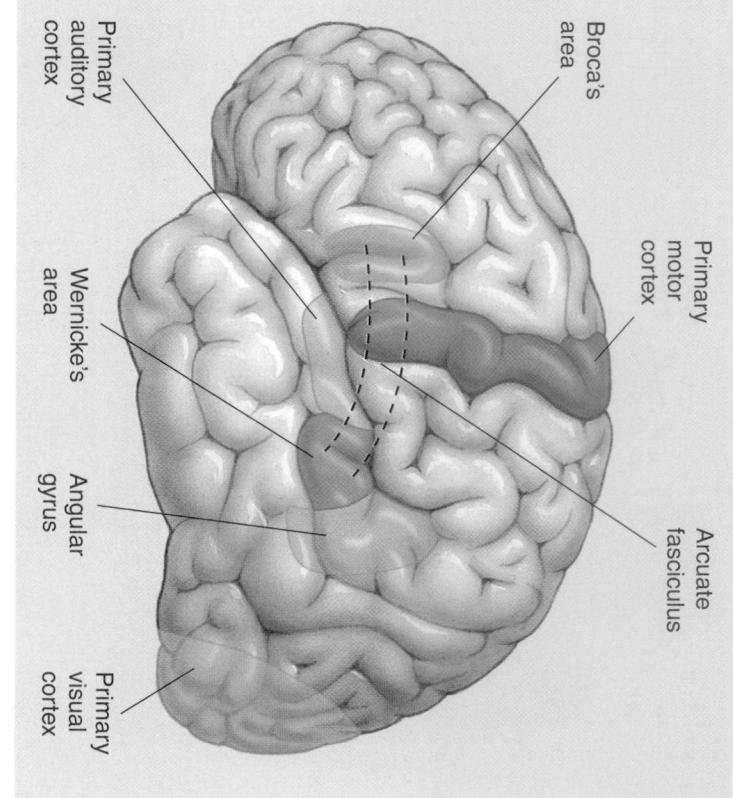

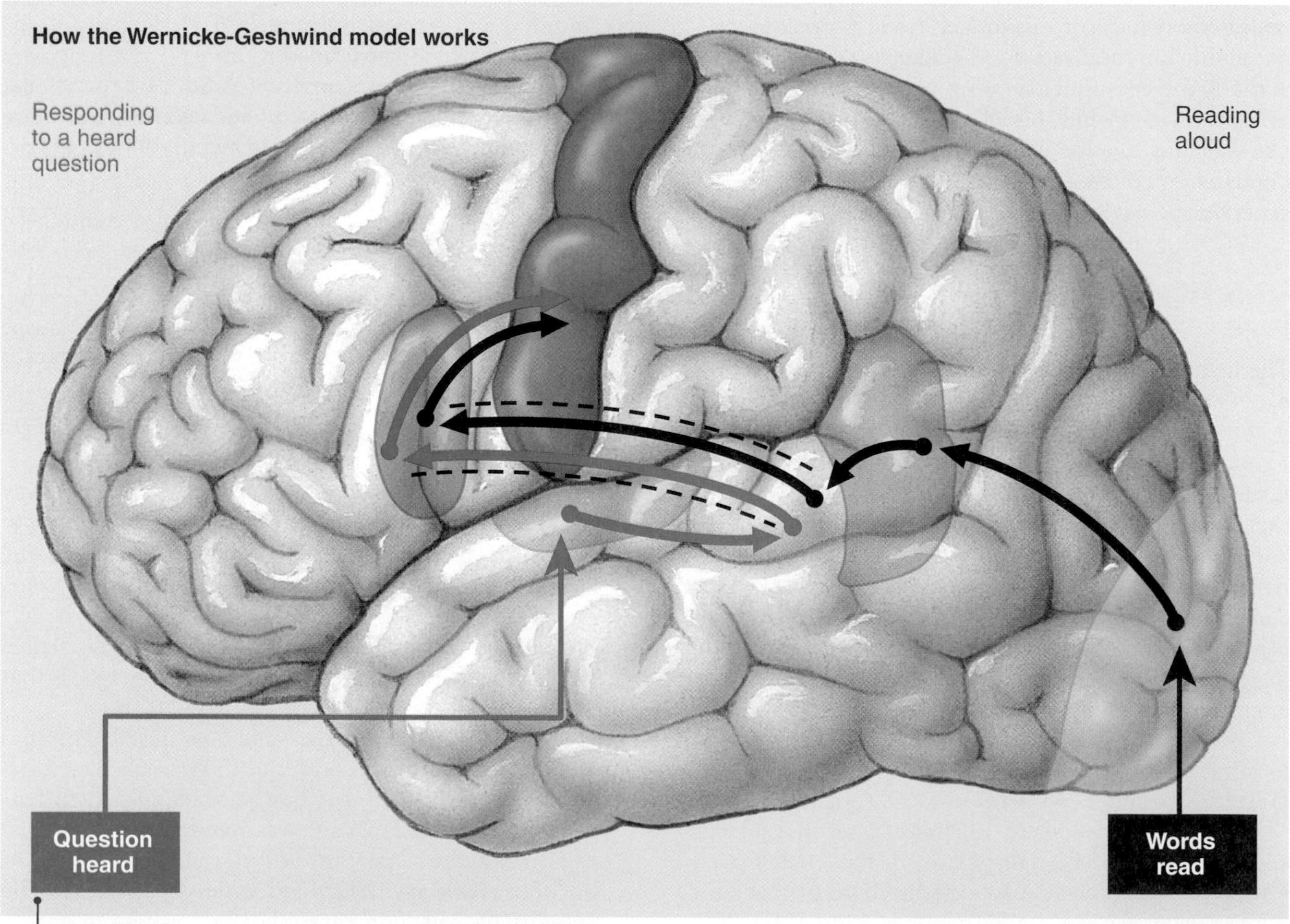

Broca's area

Primary motor cortex

Arcuate fasciculus

Primary auditory cortex

Wernicke's area

Angular gyrus

Primary visual cortex

How the Wernicke-Geschwind model works

Question heard

Responding to a heard question

Words read

Reading aloud

FIGURE 16.10 How the Wernicke-Geschwind model works in a person who is responding to a heard question and reading aloud. The hypothetical circuit that allows the person to respond to heard questions is in green; the hypothetical circuit that allows the person to read aloud is in black.

SCAN YOUR BRAIN

Before proceeding to the following evaluation of the Wernicke-Geschwind model, scan your brain to confirm that you understand its fundamentals. The correct answers are provided near the bottom of this page. Review material related to your errors and omissions before proceeding.

According to the Wernicke-Geschwind model, the following seven areas of the left cerebral cortex play a role in language-related activities:

1. The _____ gyrus translates the visual form of a read word into an auditory code.

2. The _____ cortex controls the muscles of articulation.

3. The _____ cortex perceives the written word.

4. _____ area is the center for language comprehension.

5. The _____ cortex perceives the spoken word.

6. _____ area contains the programs of articulation.

7. The left _____ carries signals from Wernicke's area to Broca's area.

---

attempts to localize various language-related abilities to specific neocortical areas. In fact, advocates of the holistic approach to brain function gradually gained the upper hand, and interest in the cerebral localization of language waned. However, in the mid-1960s, Norman Geschwind (1970) revived the old localizationist ideas of Broca, Wernicke, and Dejerine, added some new data and insightful interpretation, and melded the mix into a powerful theory: the Wernicke-Geschwind model.

The Wernicke-Geschwind Model

The following are the seven components of the Wernicke-Geschwind model: primary visual cortex, angular gyrus, primary auditory cortex, Wernicke's area, arcuate fasciculus, Broca's area, and primary motor cortex—all in the left hemisphere. They are shown in Figure 16.9.

The following two examples illustrate how the Wernicke-Geschwind model is presumed to work (see Figure 16.10). First, when you are having a conversation, the auditory signals triggered by the speech of the other person are received by your primary auditory cortex and

conducted to Wernicke's area, where they are comprehended. If a response is in order, Wernicke's area generates the neural representation of the thought underlying the reply, and it is transmitted to Broca's area via the left arcuate fasciculus. In Broca's area, this signal activates the appropriate program of articulation that drives the appropriate neurons of your primary motor cortex and ultimately your muscles of articulation. Second, when you are reading aloud, the signal received by your primary visual cortex is transmitted to your left angular gyrus, which translates the visual form of the word into its auditory code and transmits it to Wernicke's area for comprehension. Wernicke's area then triggers the appropriate responses in your arcuate fasciculus, Broca's area, and motor cortex, respectively, to elicit the appropriate speech sounds.

Scan Your Brain answers: (1) angular, (2) primary motor, (3) primary visual, (4) Wernicke's, (5) primary auditory, (6) Broca's, (7) arcuate fasciculus

---

16.5 Evaluation of the Wernicke-Geschwind Model

Thinking Critically

Unless you are reading this text from back to front, you should have read the preceding description of the Wernicke-Geschwind model with some degree of skepticism. By this point in the text, you will almost certainly recognize that any model of a complex cognitive process

that involves a few localized neocortical centers joined in a serial fashion by a few arrows is sure to have major shortcomings, and you will appreciate that the neocortex is not divided into neat compartments whose cognitive functions conform to vague concepts such as language comprehension, speech motor programs, and conversion of written language to auditory language. Initial skepticism aside, the ultimate test of a theory's validity is the degree to which its predictions are consistent with the empirical evidence.

Before we examine this evidence, I want to emphasize one point. The Wernicke-Geschwind model was initially based on case studies of aphasic patients with strokes, tumors, and penetrating brain injuries. Damage in such cases is often diffuse, and it inevitably encroaches on subcortical fibers coursing through the lesion site to other areas of the brain (see Bogen & Bogen, 1976). For example, illustrated in Figure 16.11 is the extent of the cortical damage in one of Broca's two original cases (see Mohr, 1976).

Effects of Damage to Various Areas of Cortex on Language-Related Abilities

In view of the fact that the Wernicke-Geschwind model grew out of the study of patients with cortical damage, it is appropriate to begin evaluating it by assessing its ability to predict the language-related deficits produced by damage to various parts of the cortex.

Surgical Removal of Cortical Tissue   The study of patients in whom discrete areas of cortex have been surgically removed has proved particularly informative with regard to understanding the cortical localization of language. This is because the location and extent of these patients' lesions can be derived with reasonable accuracy from the surgeon's report. The study of neurosurgical patients has not confirmed the predictions of

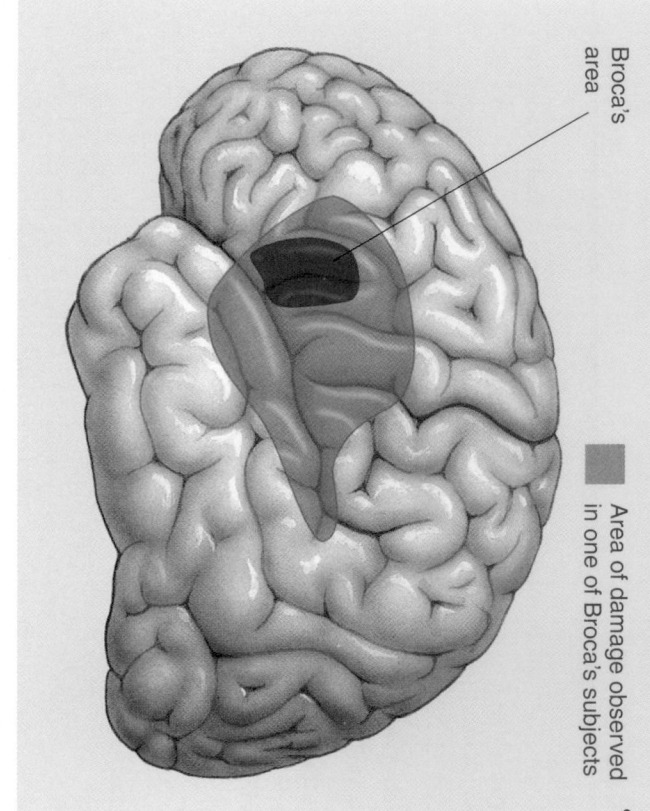

Broca's area

■ Area of damage observed in one of Broca's subjects

FIGURE 16.11 The extent of brain damage in one of Broca's two original patients. Like this patient, most aphasic patients have diffuse brain damage. It is thus difficult to determine from studying them the precise location of particular cortical language areas. (Adapted from Mohr, 1976.)

www.ablongman.com/pinel6e

Clinical Implications

the Wernicke-Geschwind model by any stretch of the imagination. See the six cases summarized in Figure 16.12.

Surgery that destroys all of Broca's area but little surrounding tissue typically has no lasting effects on speech (Penfield & Roberts, 1959; Rasmussen & Milner, 1975; Zangwill, 1975). Some speech problems were observed after the removal of Broca's area, but their temporal course suggested that they were products of postsurgical edema (swelling) in the surrounding neural tissue rather than of the excision (cutting out) of Broca's area per se. Prior to the use of effective anti-inflammatory drugs, patients with excisions of Broca's area often regained consciousness with their language abilities fully intact only to have serious language-related problems develop over the next few hours and then subside in the following weeks. Similarly, permanent speech difficulties were not produced by discrete surgical lesions to the arcuate fasciculus, and permanent alexia and agraphia were not produced by surgical lesions restricted to the cortex of the angular gyrus (Rasmussen & Milner, 1975).

The consequences of surgical removal of Wernicke's area are less well documented; surgeons have been hesitant to remove it in light of Wernicke's dire predictions. Nevertheless, in some cases, a good portion of Wernicke's area has been removed without lasting language-related deficits (e.g., Ojemann, 1979; Penfield & Roberts, 1959).

Supporters of the Wernicke-Geschwind model argue that, despite the precision of surgical excision, negative evidence obtained from the study of the effects of brain surgery should be discounted. They argue that the brain pathology that warranted the surgery may have reorganized the control of language by the brain.

Accidental or Disease-Related Brain Damage   Hécaen and Angelergues (1964) rated the articulation, fluency, comprehension, naming ability, ability to repeat spoken sentences, reading, and writing of 214 right-handed patients with small, medium, or large accidental or disease-related lesions to the left hemisphere. The

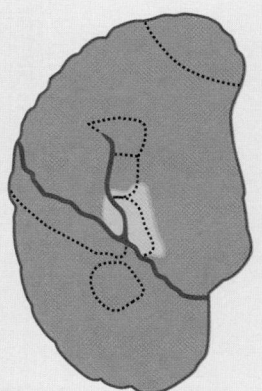

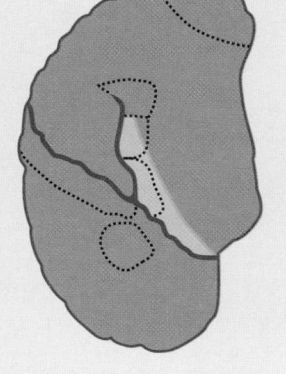

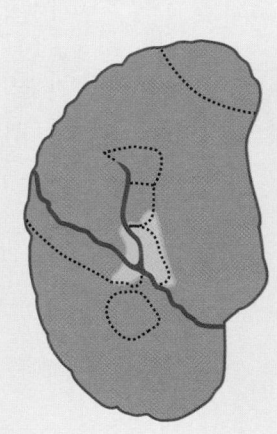

Case J.M. No speech difficulties for 2 days after his surgery, but by Day 3 he was almost totally aphasic; 18 days after his operation he had no difficulty in spontaneous speech, naming, or reading, but his spelling and writing were poor.

Case H.N. After his operation, he had a slight difficulty in spontaneous speech, but 4 days later he was unable to speak; 23 days after surgery, there were minor deficits in spontaneous speech, naming, and reading aloud, and a marked difficulty in oral calculation.

Case J.C. There were no immediate speech problems; 18 hours after his operation he became completely aphasic, but 21 days after surgery, only mild aphasia remained.

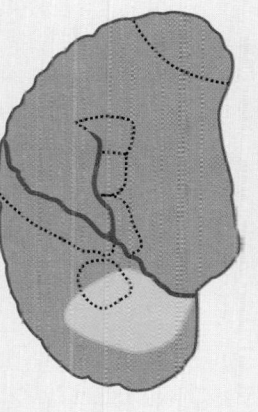

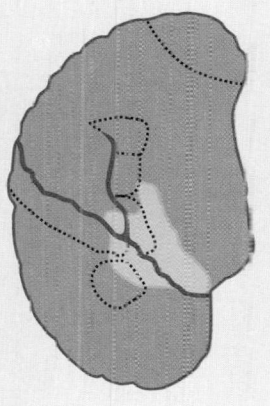

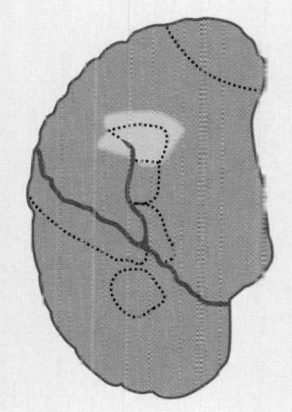

Case P.R. He had no immediate speech difficulties; 2 days after his operation, he had some language-related problems, but they cleared up.

Case D.H. This operation was done in two stages; following completion of the second stage, no speech-related problems were reported.

Case A.D. He had no language-related problems after his operation, except for a slight deficit in silent reading and writing.

FIGURE 16.12   The lack of permanent disruption of language-related abilities after surgical excision of the classic Wernicke-Geschwind language areas. (Adapted from Penfield & Roberts, 1959.)

extent and location of the damage in each case were estimated by either postmortem histological examination or visual inspection during subsequent surgery. Figure 16.13 on page 416 summarizes the deficits found by Hécaen and Angelergues in patients with relatively localized damage to one of five different regions of left cerebral cortex.

Hécaen and Angelergues found that small lesions to Broca's area seldom produced lasting language deficits and that those restricted to Wernicke's area sometimes did not produce such deficits. Medium-sized lesions did produce some deficits; but in contrast to the predictions of the Wernicke-Geschwind model, problems of articulation were just as likely to occur following medium-sized parietal or temporal lesions as they were following comparable lesions in the vicinity of Broca's area. All

other symptoms that were produced by medium-sized lesions were more likely to appear following parietal or temporal lesions than following frontal damage.

Consistent with the Wernicke-Geschwind model, large lesions (those involving three lobes) in the anterior areas of the brain were more likely to be associated with articulation problems than were large lesions in the posterior areas of the brain. It is noteworthy that none of the 214 subjects displayed syndromes of aphasia that were either totally expressive (Broca's aphasia) or totally receptive (Wernicke's aphasia).

CT and Structural MRI Scans of Aphasic Patients

Since the development of computed tomography (CT) and structural magnetic resonance imaging (MRI), it has been possible to visualize the brain damage of living aphasic patients (see Damasio, 1989). In early CT

FIGURE 16.13 The relative effects on language-related abilities of damage to one of five general areas of left-hemisphere cortex. (Adapted from Hécaen & Angelergues, 1964.)

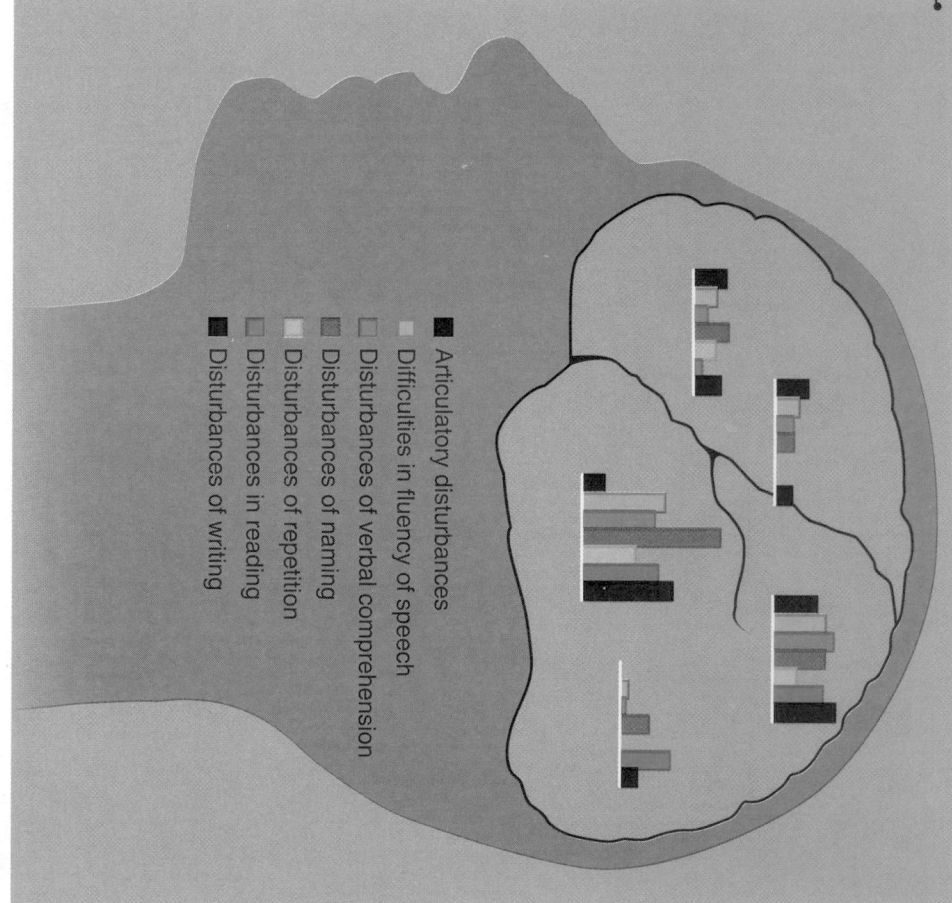

■ Articulatory disturbances
▨ Difficulties in fluency of speech
▨ Disturbances of verbal comprehension
▨ Disturbances of naming
▨ Disturbances of repetition
▨ Disturbances in reading
■ Disturbances of writing

studies by Mazzocchi and Vignolo (1979) and Naeser and colleagues (1981), none of the aphasic patients had cortical damage restricted to Broca's and Wernicke's areas, and all had extensive damage to subcortical white matter. Consistent with the Wernicke-Geschwind model, large anterior lesions of the left hemisphere were more likely to produce deficits in language expression than were large posterior lesions, and large posterior lesions were more likely to produce deficits in language comprehension than were large anterior lesions. Also, in both studies, **global aphasia**—a severe disruption of all language-related abilities—was associated with very large left-hemisphere lesions that involved both anterior and posterior cortex as well as substantial portions of subcortical white matter.

The findings of Damasio's (1989) structural MRI study were similar to those of the aforementioned CT studies, with one important addition. Damasio found a few aphasic patients whose damage was restricted to the medial frontal lobes (to the supplementary motor area and the anterior cingulate cortex), an area not included in the Wernicke-Geschwind model. Similarly, several CT and MRI studies have found cases of aphasia resulting from damage to subcortical structures (see Alexander,

1989)—for example, to the left subcortical white matter, the left basal ganglia, or the left thalamus (e.g., Naeser et al., 1982).

Electrical Stimulation of the Cortex and Localization of Language

The first large-scale electrical brain-stimulation studies of humans were conducted by Penfield and his colleagues in the 1940s at the Montreal Neurological Institute (see Feindel, 1986). One purpose of the studies was to map the language areas of each patient's brain so that tissue involved in language could be avoided during the surgery. The mapping was done by assessing the responses of conscious patients who were under local anesthetic to stimulation applied to various points on the cortical surface. The description of the effects of each stimulation were dictated to a stenographer—this was before the days of tape recorders—and then a tiny numbered card was dropped on the stimulation site for subsequent photography.

Figure 16.14 illustrates the responses to stimulation of a 37-year-old right-handed epileptic patient. He had started to have seizures about 3 months after receiv-

Clinical Implications

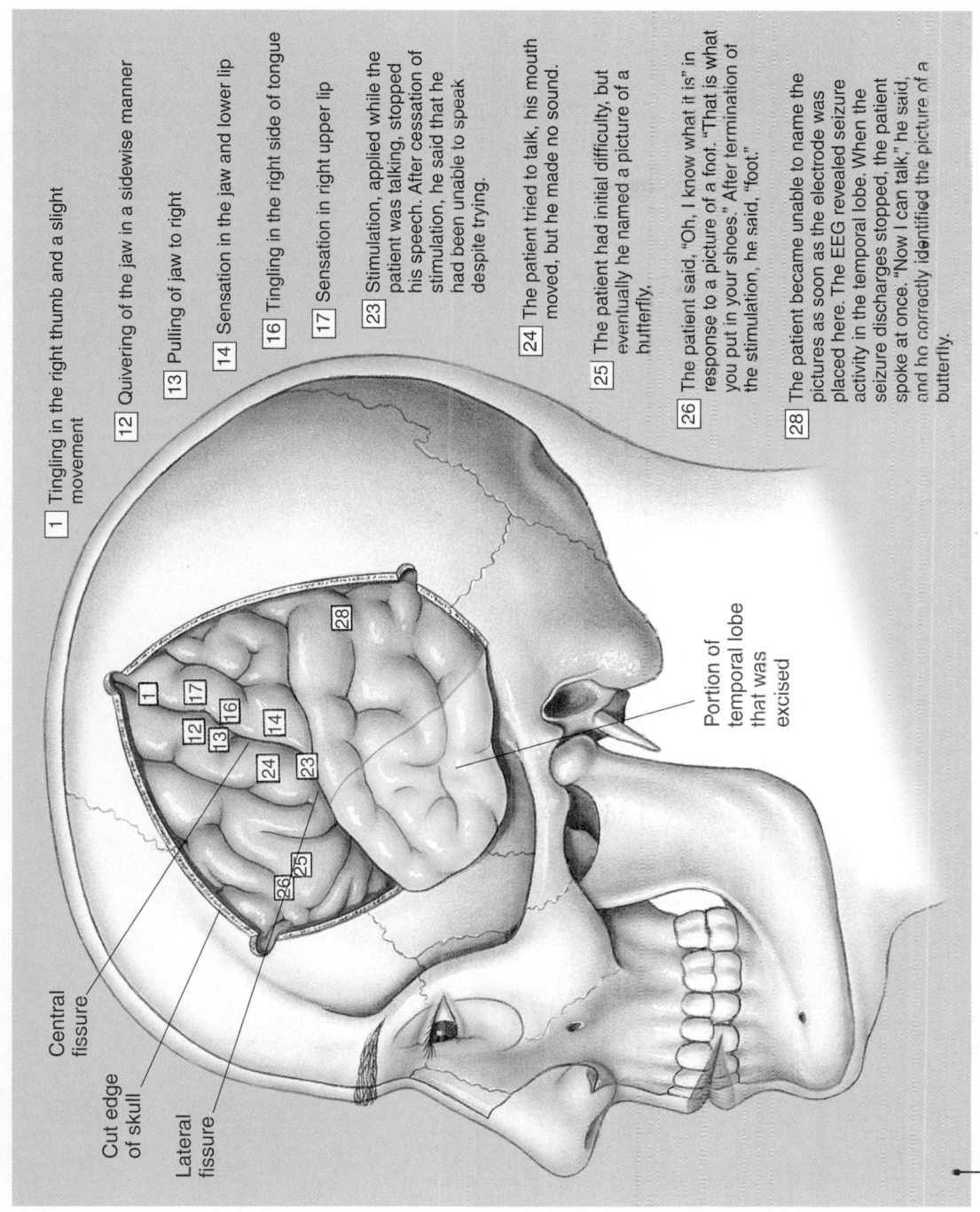

FIGURE 16.14 The responses of the left hemisphere of a 37-year-old epileptic to electrical stimulation. Numbered cards were placed on the brain during surgery to mark the sites where brain stimulation had been applied. (Adapted from Penfield & Roberts, 1959.)

ing a blow to the head; at the time of his operation, in 1948, he had been suffering from seizures for 6 years, despite efforts to control them with medication. In considering his responses, remember that the cortex just posterior to the central fissure is primary somatosensory cortex and that the cortex just anterior to the central fissure is primary motor cortex.

Because electrical stimulation of the cortex is much more localized than a brain lesion, it has been a useful method for testing predictions of the Wernicke-Geschwind model. Penfield and Roberts (1959) published the first large-scale study of the effects of cortical stimulation on speech. They found that sites at which stimulation blocked or disrupted speech in conscious neurosurgical patients were scattered throughout a large expanse of frontal, temporal, and parietal cortex, rather than being restricted to the Wernicke-Geschwind language areas (see Figure 16.15 on page 418). They also

found no tendency for particular kinds of speech disturbances to be elicited from particular areas of the cortex: Sites at which stimulation produced disturbances of pronunciation, confusion of counting, inability to name objects, or misnaming of objects were pretty much intermingled. Right-hemisphere stimulation almost never disrupted speech.

In a more recent series of cortical stimulation studies, Ojemann and his colleagues (see Ojemann, 1983) assessed naming, reading of simple sentences, short-term verbal memory, ability to mimic movements of the face and mouth, and ability to recognize **phonemes**—individual speech sounds—during cortical stimulation. They found (1) that the areas of cortex at which stimulation could disrupt language extended far beyond the boundaries of the Wernicke-Geschwind language areas, (2) that each of the language tests was disrupted by stimulation at widely scattered sites, and (3) that there were

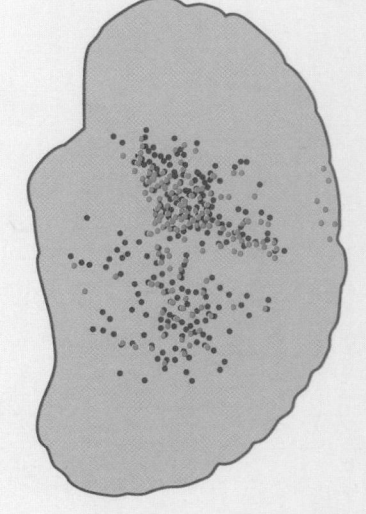

● Sites at which stimulation produced a complete arrest of speech

● Sites at which stimulation disrupted speech but did not block it completely

FIGURE 16.15 The wide distribution of left hemisphere sites where cortical stimulation either blocked speech or disrupted it. (Adapted from Penfield & Roberts, 1959.)

major differences among the subjects in the organization of language abilities.

Because the disruptive effects of stimulation at a particular site were frequently quite specific (i.e., disrupting only a single test), Ojemann suggested that the language cortex is organized like a mosaic, with the discrete columns of tissue that perform a particular function widely distributed throughout the language areas of cortex.

Current Status of the Wernicke-Geschwind Model

Empirical evidence has supported the Wernicke-Geschwind model in two general respects. First, the evidence has confirmed that important roles are played in language by Broca's and Wernicke's areas; many aphasics have diffuse cortical damage that involves one or both of these areas. Second, there is a tendency for aphasias associated with anterior damage to involve deficits that are more expressive and those associated with posterior damage to involve deficits that are more receptive.

However, the evidence has not been supportive of the specific predictions of the Wernicke-Geschwind model. First, damage restricted to the boundaries of the Wernicke-Geschwind cortical areas often has little last-

ing effect on the use of language. Second, brain damage that does not include any of the Wernicke-Geschwind areas can produce aphasia. Third, Broca's and Wernicke's aphasias rarely exist in the pure forms implied by the Wernicke-Geschwind model; aphasia virtually always involves both expressive and receptive symptoms (see Benson, 1985). Fourth, there seem to be major differences in the localization of cortical language areas in different individuals.

Despite these problems, the Wernicke-Geschwind model has been an extremely important theory. It guided the study and clinical diagnosis of aphasia for more than four decades. Indeed, clinical neuropsychologists still use *Broca's aphasia* and *Wernicke's aphasia* as diagnostic categories, but with an understanding that the syndromes are much less selective and the precipitating damage much more diffuse and variable than implied by the model (Alexander, 1997).

Because of the lack of empirical support for its major predictions, the Wernicke-Geschwind model has been largely abandoned by researchers, but it is still prominent in the classroom and clinic. The last two sections of this chapter focus on an alternative to the Wernicke-Geschwind perspective on the neural mechanisms of language: the *cognitive neuroscience approach.*

16.6 The Cognitive Neuroscience Approach to Language

The cognitive neuroscience approach is currently dominating research on language and its disorders. What is this approach, and how does it differ from the traditional perspective?

The following are three related ideas that define the cognitive neuroscience approach to language. Although these ideas were originally premises, or assumptions, that directed cognitive neuroscience research on language, each one has been supported by a

substantial amount of evidence (see Patterson & Ralph, 1999; Saffran, 1997).

Premise 1: Language-related behaviors are mediated by activity in those particular areas of the brain that are involved in the specific cognitive processes required for the behaviors. The Wernicke-Geschwind model theorized that particular areas of the brain involved in language were each dedicated to a specific, but complex, activity such as speech, comprehension, or reading. But cognitive neuroscience research has found that each of these activities can itself be broken down into *constituent cognitive processes*, which may be organized in different parts of the brain (Neville & Bavelier, 1998). Accordingly, these constituent cognitive processes, not the general Wernicke-Geschwind activities, appear to be the appropriate level at which to conduct analysis. Cognitive neuroscientists typically divide the cognitive processes involved in language into three categories of activity: **phonological analysis** (analysis of the sound of language), **grammatical analysis** (analysis of the structure of language), and **semantic analysis** (analysis of the meaning of language).

Premise 2: The areas of the brain involved in language are not dedicated solely to that purpose (Nobre & Plunkett, 1997). In the Wernicke-Geschwind model, large areas of left cerebral cortex were thought to be dedicated solely to language, whereas the cognitive neuroscience approach assumes that many of the constituent cognitive processes involved in language also play roles in other behaviors (see Bischoff-Grethe et al., 2000). For example, some of the areas of the brain that participate in short-term memory and visual pattern recognition are clearly involved in reading as well.

Premise 3: Because many of the areas of the brain that perform specific language functions are also parts of other functional systems, these areas are likely to be small, widely distributed, and specialized (Neville & Bavelier, 1998). In contrast, the language areas of the Wernicke-Geschwind model are assumed to be large, circumscribed, and homogeneous.

In addition to these three premises, the cognitive neuroscience approach to language is distinguished from the traditional approach by its methodology. The Wernicke-Geschwind model rested heavily on the analysis of brain-damaged patients, whereas researchers using the cognitive neuroscience approach also have at their disposal an increasing array of techniques—most notably, functional brain imaging—for studying the localization of language in healthy subjects.

Functional Brain Imaging and Language

Functional brain-imaging techniques have revolutionized the study of the localization of language. In the last decade, there have been numerous PET and fMRI studies of subjects engaging in various language-related activities (see Bookheimer, 2002; Gernsbacher & Kaschak, 2003; Martin, 2003). I have selected two to describe to you. As you are about to learn, I selected them because they are of high quality, have interesting findings, and feature two different approaches. The first is the fMRI study of silent reading by Bavelier and colleagues (1997); the second is the PET study of object naming by Damasio and colleagues (1996).

Bavelier's fMRI Study of Reading Bavelier and colleagues used fMRI to measure the brain activity of healthy subjects while they read silently. The researchers' general purpose was not to break down reading into its constituent cognitive processes or elements but to get a sense of the extent of cortical involvement in reading.

The methodology of Bavelier and colleagues was noteworthy in two respects. First, they used a particularly sensitive fMRI machine that allowed them to identify areas of activity with more accuracy than in most previous studies and without having to average the scores of several subjects (see Chapter 5). Second, they recorded activity during the reading of sentences—rather than during the simpler, controllable, and unnatural activities most often used in functional brain-imaging studies of language (e.g., listening to individual words).

The subjects in Bavelier and colleagues' study viewed sentences displayed on a screen. Interposed between periods of silent reading were control periods, during which the subjects were presented with strings of consonants. The differences in activity during the reading and control periods served as the basis for calculating the areas of cortical activity associated with reading. Because of the computing power required for the detailed analyses, only the lateral cortical surfaces were monitored.

Let's begin by considering the findings observed in individual subjects on individual trials, before any averaging took place. Three important points emerged from this analysis. First, the areas of activity were patchy; that is, they were tiny areas of activity separated by areas of inactivity. Second, the patches of activity were variable; that is, the areas of activity differed from subject to subject and even from trial to trial in the same subject. Third, although some activity was observed in the classic Wernicke-Geschwind areas, it was widespread over the lateral surfaces of the brain. The widespread, spotty activity over the left cortex is consistent with the basic premises of the cognitive neuroscience approach and with previous research—in particular, with brain stimulation studies of language.

Figure 16.16 on page 420 illustrates the reading-related increases of activity averaged over all the trials and subjects in the study by Bavelier and colleagues—as they are typically reported. The averaging creates the false impression that large, homogeneous expanses of tissue were active during reading, whereas the patches of activity induced on any given trial comprised only between 5% and 10% of the illustrated areas. Still, two points are

Cognitive Neuroscience

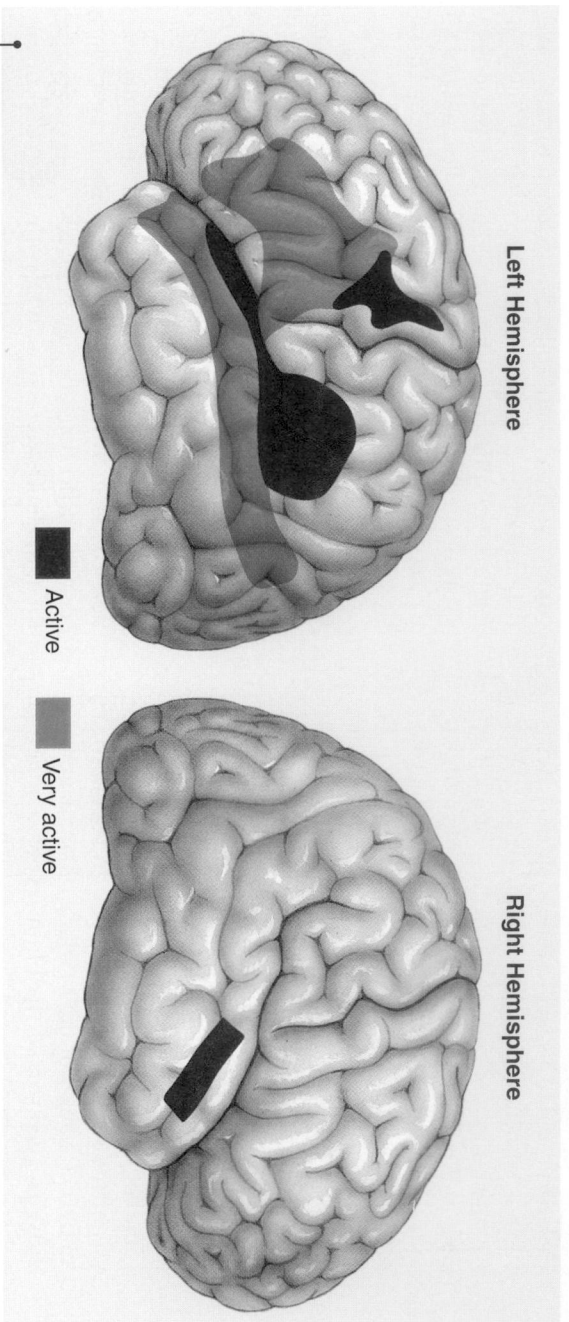

FIGURE 16.16 The areas in which reading-associated increases in activity were observed in the fMRI study of Bavelier and colleagues (1997). These maps were derived by averaging the scores of all subjects, each of whom displayed patchy increases of activity in 5–10% of the indicated areas on any particular trial.

Left Hemisphere

Right Hemisphere

■ Active   ■ Very active

clear: First, although there was significant activity in the right hemisphere, there was far more activity in the left hemisphere; second, the activity extended far beyond those areas predicted by the Wernicke-Geschwind model to be involved in silent reading (e.g., activity in Broca's area and motor cortex would not have been predicted).

Cognitive Neuroscience

Damasio's PET Study of Naming   In contrast to the purpose of the study by Bavelier and colleagues, which was to assess the extent of activity associated with silent reading, the objective of Damasio and colleagues (1996) was to look selectively at the temporal-lobe activity involved in naming objects within particular categories.

Damasio and colleagues recorded the PET activity in the left temporal lobes of healthy subjects while they named images presented on a screen. The images were

of three different types: famous faces, animals, and tools. To get a specific measure of the temporal-lobe activity involved in naming, they subtracted from the activity recorded during this task the activity recorded while the subjects judged the orientation of the images. The researchers focused on the left temporal lobes of the subjects to permit a more fine-grained PET analysis.

Naming objects activated the left temporal lobe outside the classic Wernicke's language area. Remarkably, the precise area that was activated by the naming depended on the category: Famous faces, animals, and tools each activated a slightly different area. In general, the areas for naming famous faces, animals, and tools

are arrayed from anterior to posterior along the middle portions of the left temporal lobe.

Damasio and colleagues have not been the only ones to report category-specific naming-related activity in the left temporal lobes (see Gerlach, Law, & Paulson, 2002; Löw et al., 2003; Martin et al., 1996; Nobre & Plunkett, 1997). Moreover, the existence of category-specific lexical areas in the left temporal lobes has been supported by the analysis of aphasic patients with damage in that area. Some patients have naming difficulties that are specific to particular categories (see Kurbat & Farah, 1998), and specific deficits in naming famous faces, animals, and tools have been shown to correspond to the three areas of the left temporal lobe that were identified by the PET study (Damasio et al., 1996).

One last point about the cognitive neuroscience approach to language: There has been so much enthusiasm for the use of new functional brain-imaging technology to study language that there has been a tendency for knowledge gained from the study of brain lesions to be ignored. But this is not how science works best: Science works best when new data are added to past data rather than supplanting them. For example, significant right-hemisphere activity is virtually always recorded by functional brain imaging during language-related activities, suggesting that the right hemisphere plays a significant role in language; yet lesions of the right hemisphere rarely disrupt the same activities, suggesting that its role is not critical. Clearly, a consideration of both types of research is needed to solve this puzzle (see Price et al., 1999).

16.7 The Cognitive Neuroscience Approach and Dyslexia

This, the final section of the chapter, looks further at the cognitive neuroscience approach introduced in the preceding section. It focuses on dyslexia, one of the major subjects of cognitive neuroscience research.

Dyslexia is a pathological difficulty in reading, one that does not result from general visual, motor, or intellectual deficits. There are two fundamentally different types of dyslexias: *developmental dyslexias*, dyslexias that become apparent when a child is learning to read; and *acquired dyslexias*, dyslexias that are caused by brain damage in individuals who were already capable of reading. Developmental dyslexia is a widespread problem; for example, approximately 15% of English-speaking males and 5% of English-speaking females fail to learn to read despite reasonably normal visual, motor, and intellectual abilities (Nicolson, Fawcett, & Dean, 2001; Shaywitz, 1996).

Although the causes of acquired dyslexia are usually apparent, the causes of developmental dyslexia are not. The problem in discovering the causes of developmental dyslexia is not that no abnormalities have been discovered in the brains of individuals suffering from the disorder. Many differences between the brains of dyslexics and normal readers have been reported (see Farmer & Klein, 1995). For example, dyslexics often do not display the usual left-larger-than-right asymmetry in the size of the planum temporale, and they often have cerebellar abnormalities.

Although many structural abnormalities have been identified in the brains of patients suffering from developmental dyslexia, three problems have impeded the discovery of the neural basis of this disorder. First, although many abnormalities have been reported in the brains of developmental dyslexics, none seems to play a critical role in the disorder. Second, there are several types of developmental dyslexia, and these are likely to have different causes. Third, it is difficult to rule out the possibility that particular brain "abnormalities" observed in developmental dyslexics are the result, rather than the cause, of the disorder; perhaps the lack of reading experience causes the brains of dyslexics to develop differently than those of normal readers.

In the last decade, it has become apparent that patients with developmental dyslexias often display a variety of subtle visual, auditory, and motor deficits (Nicolson, Fawcett, & Dean, 2001; Wilmer et al., 2004). A debate regarding these deficits is ongoing (see Ramus, 2003). Some experts believe that the sensory and motor deficits are primary and that developmental dyslexia results from them (McCandliss & Noble, 2003; Renvall & Hari, 2002). Others believe that the sensory and motor deficits are too slight to account for the reading dif-

ficulties and that the primary deficit in developmental dyslexia is language-related (Ramus, 2003).

There is a genetic component to developmental dyslexia; it has a heritability estimate of about 50% (Fisher & DeFries, 2002). It has been suggested that the disorder may be caused by the early exposure of genetically susceptible individuals to a virus or a toxin, but there is no strong evidence for this notion.

Developmental Dyslexia: Cultural Diversity and Biological Unity

Although it is established that developmental dyslexia is influenced by genetic factors and is associated with abnormalities of brain function, it has long been considered by many to be a psychological rather than a neural disorder. Paulesu and colleagues (2001) recently used the cognitive neuroscience approach to drive the final nail into the coffin of this misguided way of thinking about dyslexia.

For many years, those whose thinking was warped by the physiology-or-psychology dichotomy (see Chapter 2) assumed that because developmental dyslexia is influenced by culture, it could not possibly be a brain disorder. Why? Because developmental dyslexia is influenced by culture.

The work of Paulesu and colleagues is based on the remarkable finding that about twice as many English speakers as Italian speakers are diagnosed as dyslexic. This fact has to do with the complexity of the respective languages. English consists of 40 phonemes (individual speech sounds), which can be spelled, by one count, in 1120 different ways. In contrast, Italian is composed of 25 phonemes, which can be spelled in 33 different ways. As a result, Italian-speaking children learn to read much more quickly than English-speaking children and are less likely to develop reading disorders.

Paulesu and colleagues (2000) began by comparing PET activity in the brains of normal English-speaking and Italian-speaking adults. These researchers hypothesized that since the cognitive demands of reading aloud are different for Italian- and English-speaking subjects, they should use different parts of their brains while reading. That is exactly what the researchers found. Although the same general areas were active during reading in both groups, Italian readers displayed more activity in the left superior temporal lobe, whereas English readers displayed more activity in the left inferior temporal and frontal lobes.

Next, Paulesu and colleagues (2001) turned their attention to developmental dyslexia. They recorded

PET scans of the brains of normal and dyslexic British, French, and Italian university students while the sub-

Cognitive Neuroscience

jects read individual words in their own language. (University students were used to rule out lack of access to education as a possible confounding factor.) Despite the fact that the Italian dyslexics had less severe reading problems, all three groups of dyslexics displayed the same pattern of abnormal PET activity when reading: less than normal reading-related activity in the posterior region of the temporal lobe, near its boundary with the occipital lobe. Thus, although dyslexia can manifest itself differently in people who speak different languages, the underlying neural pathology appears to be the same.

Cognitive Neuroscience Analysis of Reading Aloud: Deep and Surface Dyslexia

Cognitive psychologists have long recognized that reading aloud can be accomplished in two entirely different ways. One is by a **lexical procedure**, which is based on specific stored information that has been acquired about written words: The reader simply looks at the word, recognizes it, and says it. The other way reading can be accomplished is by a **phonetic procedure:** The reader looks at the word, recognizes the letters, sounds them out, and says the word. The lexical procedure dominates in the reading of familiar words; the phonetic procedure dominates in the reading of unfamiliar words.

This simple cognitive analysis of reading aloud has proven useful in understanding the symptoms of two different kinds of dyslexia resulting from brain damage. These two different classes of acquired dyslexia are observed for developmental dyslexia, but they tend to be less severe.

Clinical Implications

In cases of **surface dyslexia,** patients have lost their ability to pronounce words based on their specific memories of the words (i.e., they have lost the *lexical procedure*), but they can still apply rules of pronunciation in their reading (i.e., they can still use the *phonetic procedure*). Accordingly, they retain their ability to pronounce words whose pronunciation is consistent with common rules (e.g., *fish, river,* or *glass*) and their ability to pronounce nonwords according to common rules of pronunciation (e.g., *spleener* or *twipple*); but they have great difficulty pronouncing words that do not follow common rules of pronunciation (e.g., *have, lose,* or *steak*). The errors they make often involve the misapplication of common rules of pronunciation; for example, *have, lose,* and *steak* are typically pronounced as if they rhyme with *cave, hose,* and *beak.*

In cases of **deep dyslexia,** patients have lost their ability to apply rules of pronunciation in their reading (i.e.,

they have lost the *phonetic procedure*), but they can still pronounce familiar concrete words based on their specific memories of them (i.e., they can still use the *lexical procedure*). Accordingly, they are completely incapable of pronouncing nonwords and words whose meaning is abstract. In attempting to pronounce words, patients with deep dyslexia try to react to them by using various lexical strategies, such as responding to the overall look of the word, the meaning of the word, or the derivation of the word. This leads to a characteristic pattern of errors. A patient with deep dyslexia might say "quill" for *quail* (responding to the overall look of the word), "hen" for *chicken* (responding to the meaning of the word), or "wise" for *wisdom* (responding to the derivation of the word).

Clinical Implications

I used to have difficulty keeping these two syndromes straight. Now I remember which is which by reminding myself that surface dyslexics have difficulty reacting to the overall shape of the word, which is metaphorically more superficial (less deep) than a problem in applying rules of pronunciation, which is experienced by deep dyslexics.

Where are the lexical and phonetic procedures performed in the brain? Much of the research attempting to answer this question has focused on the study of deep dyslexia. Deep dyslexics most often have extensive damage to the left-hemisphere language areas, suggesting that the disrupted phonetic procedure is widely distributed in the frontal and temporal areas of the left hemisphere. But which part of the brain maintains the lexical procedure in deep dyslexics? There have been two theories, both of which have received some support.

Cognitive Neuroscience

One theory is that the surviving lexical abilities of deep dyslexics are mediated by activity in surviving parts of the left-hemisphere language areas. Evidence for this theory comes from the observation of such activity during reading (Laine et al., 2000; Price et al., 1998). The other theory is that the surviving lexical abilities of deep dyslexics are mediated by activity in the right hemisphere. Support for this view comes from the following remarkable case study.

The Case of N.I., the Woman Who Read with Her Right Hemisphere

Prior to the onset of her illness, N.I. was a healthy girl. At the age of 13, she began to experience periods of aphasia, and several weeks later, she suffered a generalized convulsion. She subsequently had many convulsions, and her speech and motor abilities deteriorated badly. CT scans indicated ischemic brain damage to the left hemisphere.

Clinical Implications

Two years after the onset of her disorder, N.I. was experiencing continual seizures and blindness in her right visual field, and there was no meaningful movement or perception in her right limbs. In an attempt to relieve these symptoms, a total left **hemisherectomy** was performed; that is, her left hemisphere was totally removed. Her seizures were totally arrested by this surgery.

The reading performance of N.I. is poor, but she displays a pattern of retained abilities strikingly similar to those displayed by deep dyslexics or split-brain patients reading with their right hemispheres. For example, she recognizes letters but is totally incapable of translating them into sounds; she can read concrete familiar words; she cannot pronounce even simple nonsense words (e.g., *neg*); and her reading errors indicate that she is reading on the basis of the meaning and appearance of words rather than by translating letters into sounds (e.g., when presented with the word *fruit*, she responded, "Juice. . . . it's apples and pears and. . . . fruit"). In other words, she suffers from a severe case of deep dyslexia (Patterson, Vargha-Khadem, & Polkey, 1989).

The case of N.I. completes the circle: The chapter began with a discussion of language and lateralization of function, and the case of N.I. concludes it on the same note.

Themes Revisited

In positioning the themes tabs throughout this chapter, I learned something; I learned why this is one of my favorite chapters. This chapter has more themes tabs than any other chapter—it contributes most to developing the themes of the book. Indeed, several passages in this chapter are directly relevant to more than one of the themes, which made placing the tabs difficult.

Clinical Implications The clinical implications theme is the most prevalent because much of what we know about the lateralization of function and the localization of language in the brain comes from the study of neuropsychological patients. However, the cognitive neuroscience approach is now playing a particularly prominent role in the study of the localization of language, which is why the cognitive neuroscience theme was also **Cognitive Neuroscience** prevalent, particularly in the second half of the chapter.

Because lateralization of function and language localization are often covered by the popular media, they have become integrated into pop culture, and many widely held ideas about these subjects are overly simplistic. In this chapter, the thinking-about-biopsychology tabs mark aspects of laterality and language about which it is particularly important that you think clearly. **Thinking Critically**

Evolutionary analysis has not played a major role in the study of the localization of language, largely because humans are the only species with well-developed language. However, it has played a key role in trying to understand why cerebral lateralization of function evolved in the first place, and the major breakthrough in understanding the split-brain phenomenon came from comparative research. **Evolutionary Perspective**

ON THE CD

See Hard Copy for additional readings for Chapter 16.

Think about It

1. Design an experiment to show that it is possible for a split-brain student to study for an English exam and a geometry exam at the same time by using a Z lens.

2. The decision to perform commissurotomies on epileptic patients turned out to be a good one; the decision to perform prefrontal lobotomies on mental patients (see Chapter 1) turned out to be a bad one. Was this just the luck of the draw? Discuss.

3. Design a fMRI study to identify the areas of the brain involved in comprehending speech.

4. Why do you think cerebral lateralization of function evolved?

ON THE CD

Studying for an exam? Try the Practice Tests for Chapter 16.

Key Terms

Agraphia (p. 411)
Alexia (p. 411)
Angular gyrus (p. 411)
Aphasia (p. 397)
Apraxia (p. 397)
Arcuate fasciculus (p. 411)
Broca's aphasia (p. 411)
Broca's area (p. 397)
Cerebral commissures (p. 396)
Chimeric figures test (p. 403)
Commissurotomy (p. 396)
Conduction aphasia (p. 411)
Corpus callosum (p. 399)
Cross-cuing (p. 402)
Deep dyslexia (p. 422)

Dextrals (p. 398)
Dichotic listening test (p. 397)
Dominant hemisphere (p. 397)
Dyslexia (p. 421)
Expressive (p. 411)
Frontal operculum (p. 408)
Global aphasia (p. 416)
Grammatical analysis (p. 419)
Helping-hand phenomenon
    (p. 403)
Hemispherectomy (p. 423)
Heschl's gyrus (p. 408)
Lateralization of function
    (p. 396)
Lexical procedure (p. 422)

Minor hemisphere (p. 397)
Phonemes (p. 417)
Phonetic procedure (p. 422)
Phonological analysis (p. 419)
Planum temporale (p. 408)
Receptive (p. 411)
Scotoma (p. 400)
Semantic analysis (p. 419)
Sinestrals (p. 398)
Sodium amytal test (p. 397)
Split-brain patients (p. 396)
Surface dyslexia (p. 422)
Visual completion (p. 403)
Wernicke's aphasia (p. 411)
Wernicke's area (p. 411)

Wernicke-Geschwind model
    (p. 413)
Word salad (p. 411)
Z lens (p. 403)

ON THE CD

Need some
help studying
the key terms
for this chapter?
Check out the
electronic flash
cards for Chap-
ter 16.

chapter 17

Biopsychology of Emotion, Stress, and Health

Fear, the Dark Side of Emotion

17.1 Biopsychology of Emotion: Introduction

17.2 Fear, Defense, and Aggression

17.3 Stress and Health

17.4 Fear Conditioning

17.5 Brain Mechanisms of Human Emotion

17.1 Biopsychology of Emotion: Introduction

This chapter is about the biopsychology of emotion, stress, and health. It begins with a general introduction to the biopsychology of emotion and gradually focuses on the dark end of the emotional spectrum: fear. Biopsychological research on emotions has concentrated on fear not because biopsychologists are a scary bunch, but because fear has three important qualities: It is the easiest emotion to infer from behavior; it

plays an important adaptive function in motivating the avoidance of threatening situations; and the stress associated with chronic fear increases our susceptibility to a wide range of disorders. These include physical disorders such as ulcers and infections, which you will learn about in this chapter, and numerous psychological disorders, which you will learn about in the next.

This section provides a general introduction to the biopsychology of emotion by reviewing several of the classic early discoveries, the role of the autonomic nervous system in emotional experience, and the facial expression of emotion.

Early Landmarks in the Biopsychological Investigation of Emotion

This subsection describes, in chronological sequence, six early landmarks in the biopsychological investigation of emotion. It begins with the 1848 case of Phineas Gage.

The Mind-Blowing Case of Phineas Gage

In 1848, Phineas Gage, a 25-year-old construction foreman for the Rutland and Burlington Railroad, was the victim of a tragic accident. In order to lay new tracks, the terrain had to be leveled, and Gage was in charge of the blasting. His task involved drilling holes in the rock, pouring some gun powder into each hole, covering it with sand, and tamping the material down with a large tamping iron before detonating it with a fuse. On the fateful day, the gunpowder exploded while Gage was tamping it, launching the 3-cm-thick, 90-cm-long tamping iron through his face, skull, and brain and out the other side.

Amazingly, Gage survived his accident, but he survived it a changed man. Before the accident, Gage had been a responsible, intelligent, socially well-adapted person, who was well liked by his friends and fellow workers. Once recovered, he appeared to be as able-bodied and intellectually capable as before, but his personality and emotional life had totally changed. Formerly a religious, respectful, reliable man, Gage became irreverent and impulsive. In particular, his abundant profanity offended many. He became so unreliable and undependable that he soon lost his job, and was never again able to hold a responsible position.

Gage became an itinerant, roaming the country for a dozen years until his death in San Francisco. His bizarre accident and apparently successful recovery made headlines around the world, but his death went largely unnoticed and unacknowledged.

Gage was buried next to the offending tamping iron. Five years later, neurologist John Harlow was granted permission from Gage's family to exhume the body and tamping iron to study them. Since then, Gage's skull and the tamping iron have been on display in the Warren Anatomical Medical Museum at Harvard University.

In 1994, Damasio and her colleagues brought the power of computerized reconstruction to bear on Gage's classic case. They began by taking an X-ray of the skull and measuring it precisely, paying particular attention to the position of the entry and exit holes. From these measurements, they reconstructed the accident and determined the likely region of Gage's brain damage (see Figure 17.1). It was apparent that the damage to Gage's brain affected both *medial prefrontal lobes*, which we now know are involved in planning and emotion.

Darwin's Theory of the Evolution of Emotion

The first major event in the study of the biopsychology of emotion was the publication in 1872 of Darwin's book *The Expression of Emotions in Man and Animals*. In it, Darwin argued, largely on the basis of anecdotal evidence, that particular emotional responses, such as human facial expressions, tend to accompany the same emotional states in all members of a species.

Darwin believed that expressions of emotion, like other behaviors, are products of evolution; he therefore tried to understand them by comparing them in different species. From such interspecies comparisons, Darwin developed a theory of the evolution of emotional expression that was composed of three main ideas: (1) Expressions of emotion evolve from behaviors that indicate what an animal is likely to do next; (2) if the signals provided by such behaviors benefit the animal that displays them, they will evolve in ways that enhance

James-Lange theory, emotion-inducing sensory stimuli are received and interpreted by the cortex, which triggers changes in the visceral organs via the autonomic nervous system and in the skeletal muscles via the somatic nervous system. Then, the autonomic and somatic responses trigger the experience of emotion in the brain. In effect, what the James-Lange theory did was to reverse the usual common-sense way of thinking about the causal relation between the experience of emotion and its expression. James and Lange argued that the autonomic activity and behavior that are triggered by the emotional event (e.g., rapid heartbeat and running away) produce the feeling of emotion, not vice versa.

Around 1915, Cannon proposed an alternative to the James-Lange theory of emotion, and it was subsequently extended and promoted by Bard. According to the **Cannon-Bard theory**, emotional stimuli have two indepen-

Aggression

Submission

FIGURE 17.2   Two woodcuts from Darwin's 1872 book, *The Expression of Emotions in Man and Animals*, that he used to illustrate the principle of antithesis. The aggressive posture of dogs features ears forward, back up, hair up, and tail up; the submissive posture features ears back, back down, hair down, and tail down.

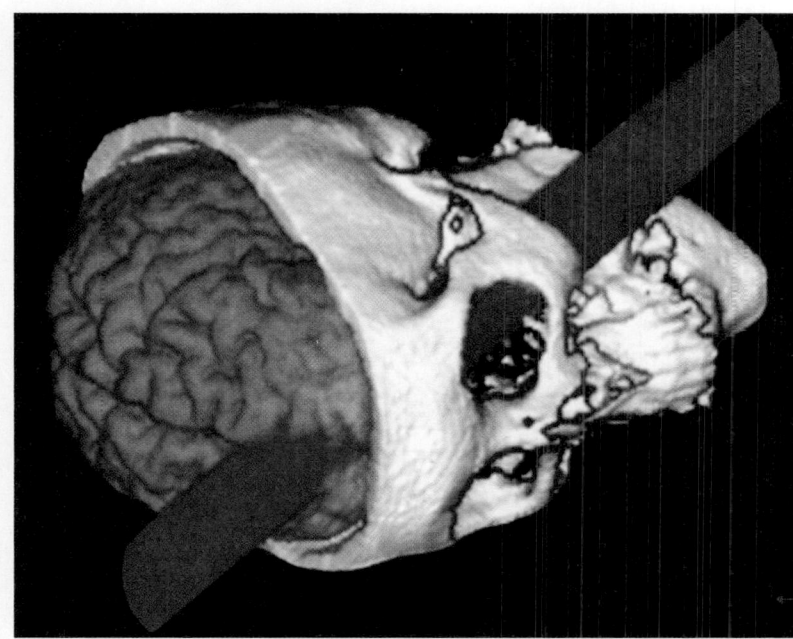

FIGURE 17.1   A reconstruction of the brain injury of Phineas Gage. The damage focused on the medial prefrontal lobes. (Adapted from Damasio et al., 1994.)

their communicative function, and their original function may be lost; and (3) opposite messages are often signaled by opposite movements and postures (the *principle of antithesis*).

Consider how Darwin's theory accounts for the evolution of *threat displays*. Originally, facing one's enemies, rising up, and exposing one's weapons were the components of the early stages of combat. But once enemies began to recognize these behaviors as signals of impending aggression, a survival advantage accrued to attackers that could communicate their aggression most effectively and intimidate their victims without actually fighting. As a result, elaborate threat displays evolved, and actual combat declined.

To be most effective, signals of aggression and submission must be clearly distinguishable; thus, they tended to evolve in opposite directions. For example, gulls signal aggression by pointing their beaks at one another and submission by pointing their beaks away from one another; primates signal aggression by staring and submission by averting their gaze. Figure 17.2 is a reproduction of the actual woodcuts that Darwin used in his 1872 book to illustrate this principle of antithesis in dogs.

James-Lange and Cannon-Bard Theories   The first physiological theory of emotion was proposed independently by James and Lange in 1884. According to the

dent excitatory effects: They excite both the feeling of emotion in the brain and the expression of emotion in the autonomic and somatic nervous systems. That is, the Cannon-Bard theory, in contrast to the James-Lange theory, views emotional experience and emotional expression as parallel processes that have no direct causal relation.

The James-Lange and Cannon-Bard theories make different predictions about the role of feedback from autonomic and somatic nervous system activity in emotional experience. According to the James-Lange theory, emotional experience depends entirely on feedback from autonomic and somatic nervous system activity; according to the Cannon-Bard theory, emotional experience is totally independent of such feedback. Both extreme positions have proved to be incorrect. On the one hand, it seems that the autonomic and somatic feedback is not necessary for the experience of emotion: Human patients whose autonomic and somatic feedback has been largely eliminated by a broken neck are capable of a full range of emotional experiences (e.g., Lowe & Carroll, 1985). On the other hand, there have been numerous reports—some of which you will soon encounter—that autonomic and somatic responses to emotional stimuli can influence emotional experience.

Failure to find unqualified support for either the James-Lange or the Cannon-Bard theory led to a third theory. According to this theory, each of the three principal factors in an emotional response—the perception of the emotion-inducing stimulus, the autonomic and somatic responses to the stimulus, and the experience of the emotion—influences the other two (see Figure 17.3).

Sham Rage In the late 1920s, Bard (1929) discovered that **decorticate** cats—cats whose cortex has been removed—respond aggressively to the slightest provocation: After a light touch, they arch their backs, erect their hair, growl, hiss, and expose their teeth.

The aggressive responses of decorticate animals are abnormal in two respects: They are inappropriately severe, and they are not directed at particular targets. Bard referred to the exaggerated, poorly directed aggressive responses of decorticate animals as **sham rage.**

Sham rage can be elicited in cats whose cerebral hemispheres have been removed down to, but not including, the hypothalamus; but it cannot be elicited if the hypothalamus is also removed. On the basis of this observation, Bard concluded that the hypothalamus is critical for the expression of aggressive responses and that the function of the cortex is to inhibit and direct these responses.

Evolutionary Perspective

Limbic System and Emotion In 1937, Papez (pronounced "Payps") proposed that emotional expression is controlled by several interconnected neural structures that he referred to as the limbic system. The **limbic system** is a collection of nuclei and tracts that borders the thalamus (*limbic* means "border"). Figure 17.4 on page 730 illustrates some of its key structures: the amygdala, mammillary body, hippocampus, fornix, cortex of the cingulate gyrus, septum, olfactory bulb, and hypothalamus (see Macchi, 1989). Papez proposed that emotional states are expressed through the action of the other limbic structures on the hypothalamus and that they are experienced through the action of the limbic structures on the cortex.

Kluver-Bucy Syndrome In 1939, Kluver and Bucy observed a striking *syndrome* (pattern of behavior) in monkeys that had had their anterior temporal lobes removed. This syndrome, which is commonly referred to as the **Kluver-Bucy syndrome,** includes the following behaviors: the consumption of almost anything that is edible, increased sexual activity often directed at inappropriate objects, a tendency to repeatedly investigate familiar objects, a tendency to investigate objects with the mouth, and a lack of fear. Monkeys that could not be handled before surgery were transformed by bilateral anterior temporal lobectomy into tame subjects that showed no fear whatsoever—even in response to snakes, which terrify normal monkeys. In primates, most of the symptoms of the Kluver-Bucy syndrome appear to result from amygdala damage.

The Kluver-Bucy syndrome has been observed in several species. Following is a description of the syndrome in a human patient with a brain infection.

Evolutionary Perspective

A Human Case of Kluver-Bucy Syndrome

Clinical Implications

He exhibited a flat affect, and although originally restless, ultimately became remarkably placid. He appeared indifferent to people or situations. He spent much time gazing at the television, but never learned to turn it on; when the set was off, he tended to watch reflections of others in the room on the glass screen. On occasion he became facetious, smiling inappropriately and mimicking the gestures and actions of others. Once initiating an imitative series, he would perseverate copying all movements made by another for extended periods of time.... He engaged in oral exploration of all objects within his grasp, appearing unable to gain information via tactile or visual means alone. All objects that he could lift were placed in his mouth and sucked or chewed....

Although vigorously heterosexual prior to his illness, he was observed in hospital to make advances toward other male patients.... [H]e never made advances toward women, and, in fact, his apparent re-

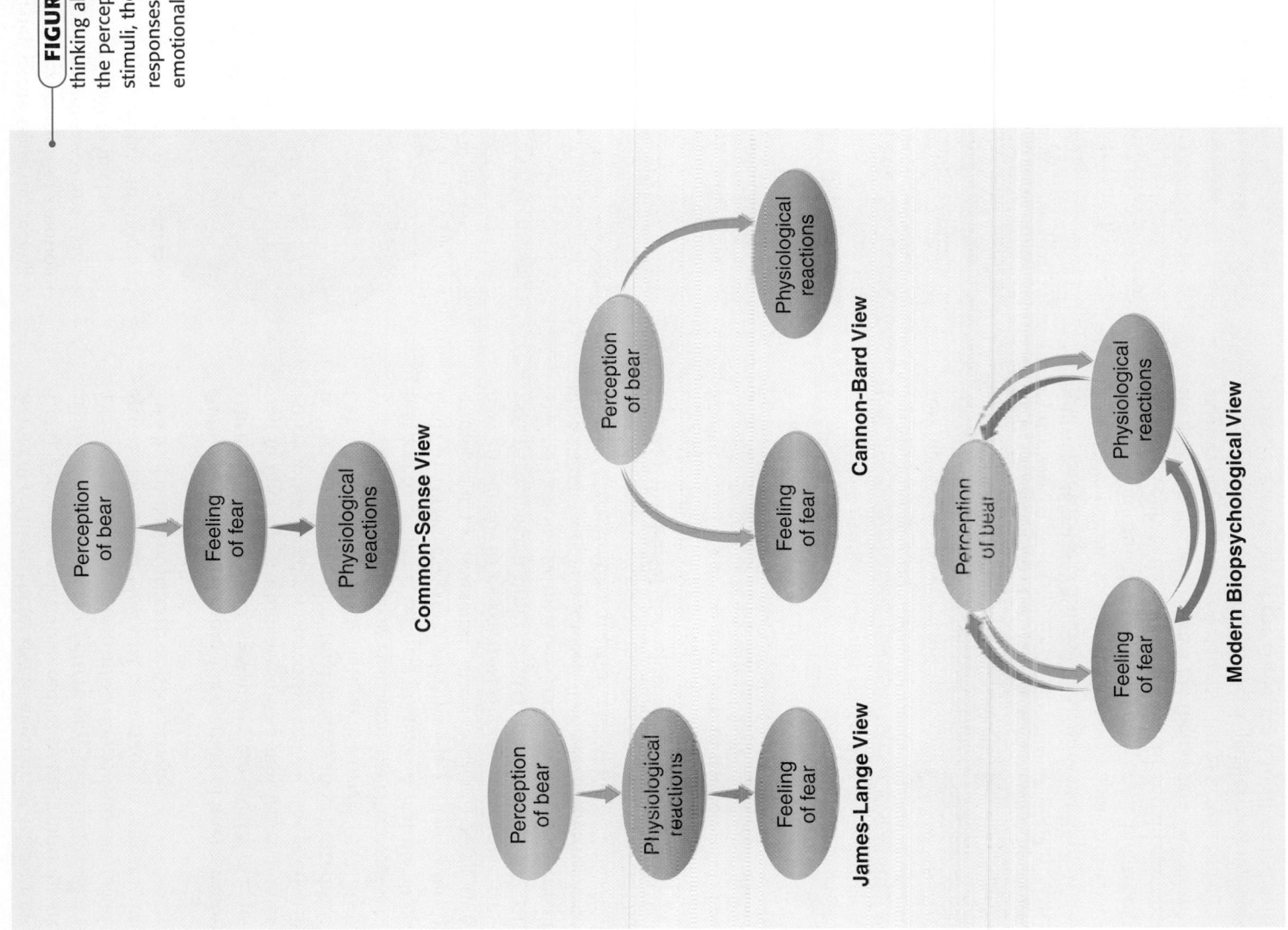

FIGURE 17.3   Four ways of thinking about the relations among the perception of emotion-inducing stimuli, the autonomic and somatic responses to the stimuli, and the emotional experience.

versal of sexual polarity prompted his fiancée to sever their relationship. (Marlowe, Mancall, & Thomas, 1985, pp. 55–56)

The six early landmarks in the study of brain mechanisms of emotion just reviewed are listed in Table 17.1 on page 430.

Emotions and the Autonomic Nervous System

Research on the role of the autonomic nervous system (ANS) in emotion has focused on two issues: the degree to which specific patterns of ANS activity are associated with specific emotions and the effectiveness of ANS measures in polygraphy (lie detection).

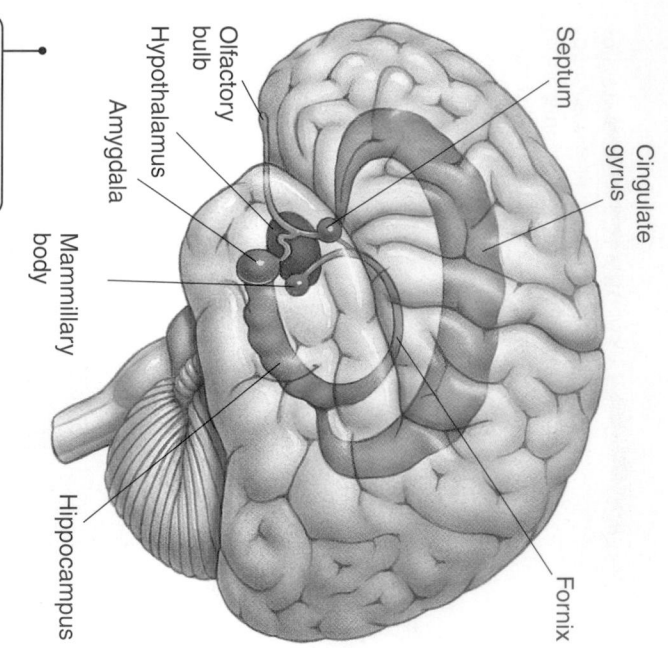

Cingulate
gyrus

Septum

Olfactory
bulb

Hypothalamus

Amygdala

Mammillary
body

Hippocampus

Fornix

FIGURE 17.4   The location of the major limbic system structures. In general, they are arrayed near the midline in a ring around the thalamus. (See also Figure 3.28.)

TABLE 17.1   Biopsychological Investigation of Emotion: Six Early Landmarks

EVENT	DATE
Case of Phineas Gage	1848
Darwin's theory of the evolution of emotion	1872
James-Lange and Cannon-Bard theories	about 1900
Discovery of sham rage	1929
Limbic system theory of emotion	1937
Discovery of Kluver–Bucy syndrome	1939

Emotional Specificity of the Autonomic Nervous System

The James-Lange and Cannon-Bard theories differ in their views of the emotional specificity of the autonomic nervous system. The James-Lange theory says that different emotional stimuli induce different patterns of ANS activity and that these different patterns produce different emotional experiences. In contrast, the Cannon-Bard theory claims that all emotional stimuli produce the same general pattern of sympathetic activation, which prepares the organism for action (i.e., increased heart rate, increased blood pressure, pupil dilation, increased flow of blood to the muscles, increased respiration, and increased release of epinephrine and norepinephrine from the adrenal medulla).

The experimental evidence suggests that the specificity of ANS reactions lies somewhere between the extremes of total specificity and total generality (Levenson, 1994). There is ample evidence that not all emotions are associated with the same pattern of ANS activity (see Ax, 1955.); however, there is insufficient evidence to make a strong case for the view that each emotion is characterized by a different pattern of ANS activity.

Polygraphy   Polygraphy is a method of interrogation that employs autonomic nervous system indexes of emotion to infer the truthfulness of the subject's responses. Polygraph tests administered by skilled examiners can be useful additions to normal interrogation procedures, but they are not infallible (Iacono & Patrick, 1987).

The main problem in evaluating the effectiveness of polygraphy is that it is rarely possible in real-life situations to know for certain whether the suspect is guilty or innocent. Consequently, many studies of polygraphy have employed the *mock-crime procedure:* Volunteer subjects participate in a mock crime and are then subjected to a polygraph test by an examiner who is unaware of their "guilt" or "innocence." The usual interrogation method is the **control-question technique,** in which the physiological response to the target question (e.g., "Did you steal that purse?") is compared with the physiological responses to control questions whose answers are known (e.g., "Have you ever been in jail before?"). The assumption is that lying will be associated with greater sympathetic activation. The average success rate in various mock-crime studies using the control-question technique is about 80%.

Despite being commonly referred to as *lie detection,* polygraphy detects emotions, not lies. Consequently, it is less likely to successfully identify lies in real life than in experiments. In real-life situations, questions such as "Did you steal that purse?" are likely to elicit a reaction from all suspects, regardless of their guilt or innocence, making it difficult to detect deception. Lykken (1959) developed the **guilty-knowledge technique** to circumvent this problem. In order to use this technique, the polygrapher must have a piece of information concerning the crime that would be known only to the guilty person. Rather than attempting to catch the suspect in a lie, the polygrapher simply assesses the suspect's reaction to a list of actual and contrived details of the crime. Innocent parties, because they have no knowledge of the crime, react to all such details in the same way; the guilty react differentially.

In one study of the guilty-knowledge technique (Lykken, 1959), subjects waited until the occupant of an office went to the washroom. Then, they entered her office, stole her purse from her desk, removed the money, and left the purse in a locker. The critical part of the interrogation went something like this: "Where do you think we found the purse? In the washroom? . . . In a locker? . . . Hanging on a coat rack? . . . Even though electrodermal activity was the only measure of ANS ac-

Thinking Critically

tivity used in this study, 88% of the mock criminals were correctly identified; more importantly, none of the in-nocent parties was judged guilty.

Emotions and Facial Expression

Ekman and his colleagues have been preeminent in the study of facial expression (see Ekman, 2003). They began in the 1960s by analyzing hundreds of films and pho-tographs of people experiencing various real emotions. From these, they compiled an atlas of the facial expres-sions that are normally associated with different emo-tions (Ekman & Friesen, 1975). The facial expressions in Ekman and Friesen's atlas are not photographs of people experiencing genuine emotions. They are photographs of models who were instructed to contract specific facial muscles on the basis of Ekman and Friesen's analysis. For example, to produce the facial expression for sur-prise, models were instructed to pull their brows upward so as to wrinkle their forehead, to open their eyes wide so as to reveal white above the iris, to slacken the muscles around their mouth, and to drop their jaw. Try it.

Universality of Facial Expression   Despite Darwin's assertion that people in all parts of the world make simi-lar facial expressions, it was widely believed that facial ex-pressions are learned and culturally variable. Then, several empirical studies showed that people of different cultures do indeed make similar facial expressions in similar situ-ations and that they can correctly identify the emotional significance of facial expressions displayed by people from cultures other than their own (e.g., Ekman, Sorenson, & Friesen, 1969, Hejmadi, Davidson, & Rozin, 2000; Izard, 1971). The most convincing of these studies was a study of the members of an isolated New Guinea tribe who had had little or no contact with the outside world (Ekman & Friesen, 1971). Although these findings support Darwin's view of the universality of facial expressions, they do not deny the possibility of cultural differences (see Russell, Bachorowski, & Fernandez-Dols, 2003).

Primary Facial Expressions   Ekman and Friesen concluded that the facial expressions of the following six emotions are primary: surprise, anger, sadness, dis-gust, fear, and happiness (however, see Tracy & Robbins, 2004). They further concluded that all other facial ex-pressions of genuine emotion are composed of predict-able mixtures of these six primaries. In Figure 17.5, Ekman himself illustrates his six primary facial expressions and the combination of two of them to form a nonprimary expression.

Facial Feedback Hypothesis   Is there any truth to the old idea that putting on a happy face can make you feel better? Research suggests that there is (see Adelmann & Zajonc, 1989). The hypothesis that our facial expres-

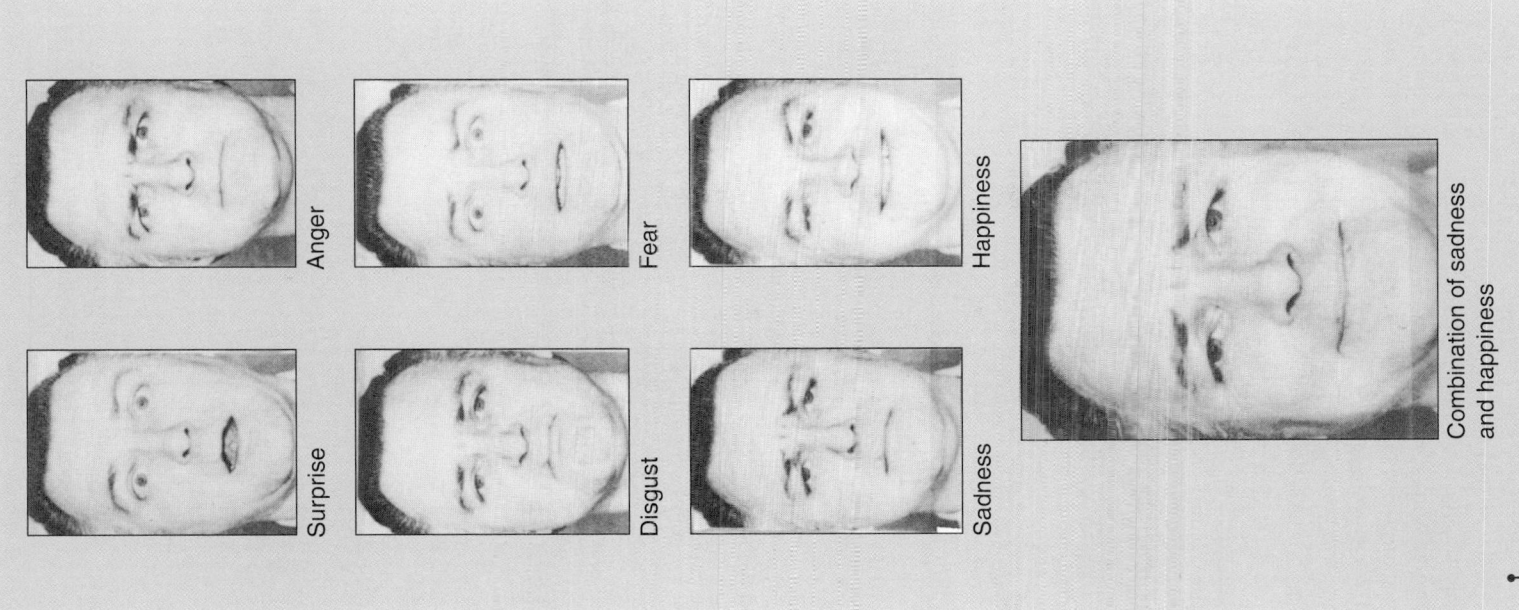

Surprise

Anger

Disgust

Fear

Sadness

Happiness

Combination of sadness and happiness

FIGURE 17.5   Examples of the six facial expressions that Ekman and Friesen (1975) considered to be primary: surprise, anger, sadness, disgust, fear, and happiness. All other emotional facial expressions were considered to be combinations of these six. For example, shown at the bottom here is an expression you might make while visiting a sick friend; it is a combination of sadness in the upper half of the face and happiness in the lower half.

FIGURE 17.6 The effects of facial expression on the experience of emotion. Subjects reported feeling more happy and less angry when they viewed slides while making a happy face, and less happy and more angry when they viewed slides while making an angry face. (Adapted from Rutledge & Hupka, 1985.)

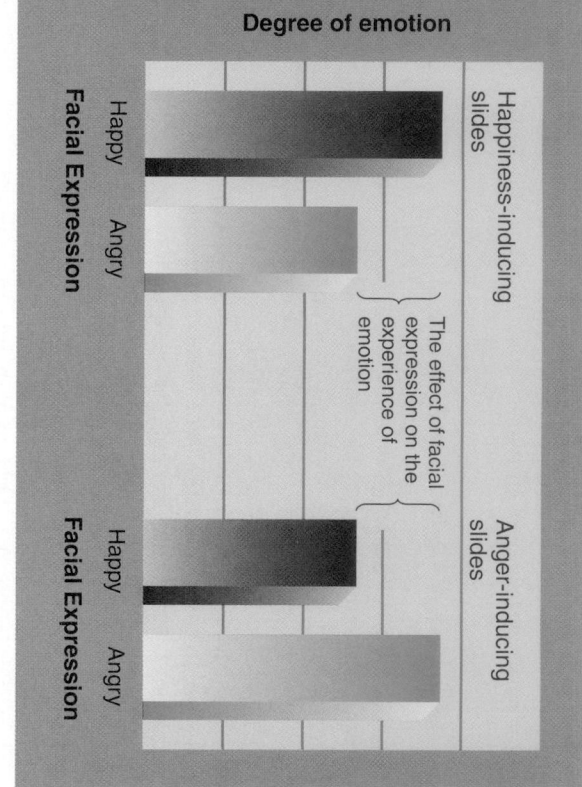

sions influence our emotional experience is called the **facial feedback hypothesis.**

In a test of the facial feedback hypothesis, Rutledge and Hupka (1985) instructed subjects to assume one of two patterns of facial contractions while they viewed a series of slides; the patterns corresponded to happy or angry faces, although the subjects were unaware of it. The subjects reported that the slides made them feel more happy and less angry when they were making happy faces, and less happy and more angry when they were making angry faces (see Figure 17.6). Why don't you try it? Pull your eyebrows down and together; raise your upper eyelids and tighten your lower eyelids, and narrow your lips and press them together. Now, hold this expression for a few seconds. If it makes you feel slightly angry, you have just experienced the effect of facial feedback.

Voluntary Control of Facial Expression   Because we can exert voluntary control over our facial muscles, it is possible to inhibit true facial expressions and to substitute false ones. There are many reasons for choosing to put on a false facial expression. Some of them are positive (e.g., putting on a false smile to reassure a worried friend), and some are negative (e.g., putting on a false smile to disguise a lie). In either case, it is difficult to fool an expert.

There are two ways of distinguishing true expressions from false ones (Ekman, 1985). First, *microexpressions* (brief facial expressions) of the real emotion often break through the false one. Such microexpressions last only about 0.05 second, but with practice they can be detected without the aid of slow-motion photography. Second, there are often subtle differences between genuine facial expressions and false ones that can be detected by skilled observers.

The most widely studied difference between a genuine and a false facial expression was first described by the French anatomist Duchenne in 1862. Duchenne said that the smile of enjoyment could be distinguished from deliberately produced smiles by consideration of the two facial muscles that are contracted during genuine smiles: *orbicularis oculi*, which encircles the eye and pulls the skin from the cheeks and forehead toward the eyeball,

and *zygomaticus major*, which pulls the lip corners up (see Figure 17.7). According to Duchenne, the zygomaticus major can be controlled voluntarily, whereas the orbicularis oculi is normally contracted only by genuine pleasure. Thus, inertia of the orbicularis oculi in smiling unmasks a false friend—a fact you would do well to remember. Ekman named the genuine smile the **Duchenne smile** (see Ekman & Davidson, 1993).

Not all emotions are accompanied by changes in facial expression—as any good poker player will tell you. However, *facial electromyography (EMG)* can detect changes in the motor input to facial muscles that are too slight to produce observable changes in muscle contraction (see Tassinary & Cacioppo, 1992). For example, Cacioppo and colleagues (1986) recorded the EMG activity of several facial muscles while the subjects viewed slides. Although facial expressions were seldom evoked, the EMG activity was related to how much the subjects reported they liked each slide. For example, the smile muscles—the orbicularis oculi and the zygomaticus major—tended to be more active while the subjects were viewing slides that they judged to be pleasant.

A study by Dimberg, Thunberg, and Elmehed (2000) assessed the effect of the observation of facial expressions on the facial muscles of the observer. These researchers found that people tend to mimic the facial expressions they see in others, even if they are not consciously aware of what they are seeing. The researchers presented either a happy or an angry face for 30 milliseconds and then immediately replaced the target expression with a neutral expression. None of the subjects reported being aware of the briefly presented target expression; they were aware of only the neutral expression. Yet, facial EMG revealed that those who had been presented with a happy face as the target expression made subtle happy faces, whereas those who had been presented with an angry face made subtle angry faces.

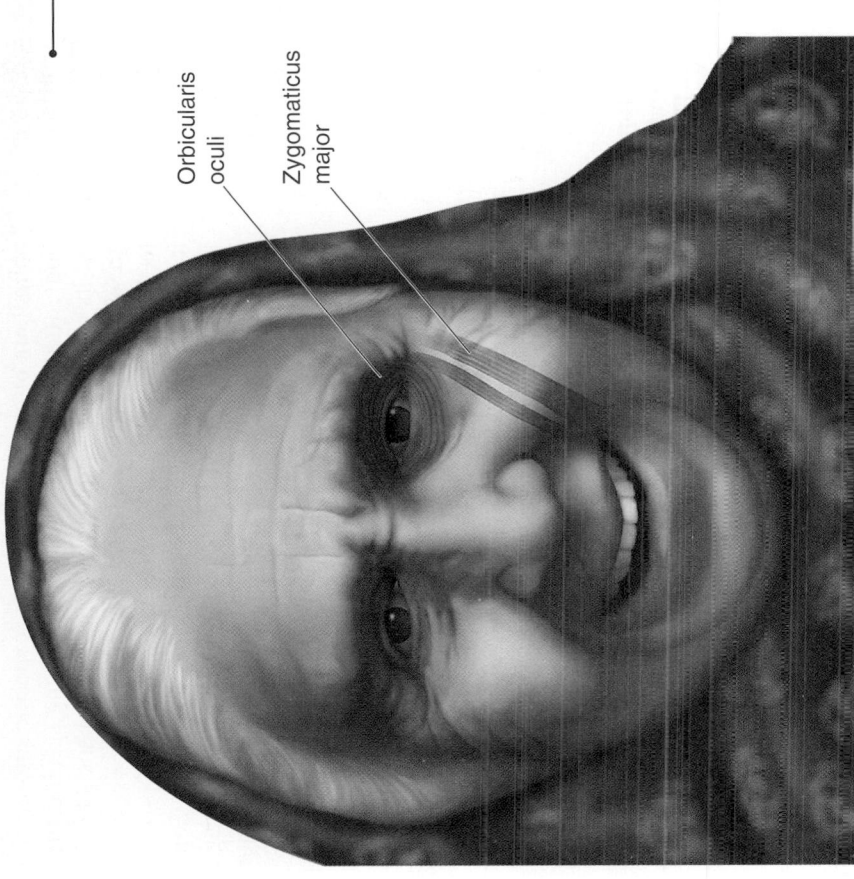

Orbicularis
oculi

Zygomaticus
major

FIGURE 17.7 The orbicularis oculi and zygomaticus major, two muscles that contract during genuine (Duchenne) smiles. Because the lateral portion of the orbicularis oculi is difficult for most people to contract voluntarily, fake smiles usually lack this component.

Biopsychological research on emotion has focused to a large degree on fear and defensive behaviors. One reason for this focus—which will become more apparent as the chapter progresses—is the major role played by the stressful effects of chronic fear in the development of disease (see Blanchard et al., 2001). **Fear** is the emotional reaction to threat; it is the motivating force for defensive behaviors. **Defensive behaviors** are behaviors whose primary function is to protect the organism from threat or harm. In contrast, **aggressive behaviors** are behaviors whose primary function is to threaten or harm.

Types of Aggressive and Defensive Behaviors

Evolutionary Perspective

Considerable progress in the understanding of aggressive and defensive behaviors has come from the research of Blanchard and Blanchard (see 1989, 1990) on the *colony-intruder model of aggression and defense* in rats. Blanchard and Blanchard have derived rich descriptions of rat intraspecific aggressive and defensive behaviors by studying the interactions between the **alpha male**—the dominant male—of an established mixed-sex colony and a small male intruder:

> The alpha approaches the stranger and sniffs at its perianal area.... If the intruder is an adult male, the alpha's sniff leads to piloerection [involuntary bristling of hairs]....
>
> Shortly after piloerecting, the alpha male usually bites the intruder, and the intruder runs away. The alpha chases after it, and after one or two additional bites, the intruder stops running and turns to face its attacker. It rears up on its hind legs, using its forelimbs to push off the alpha.... However, rather than standing nose to nose with the "boxing" intruder, the attacking rat abruptly moves to a lateral orientation, with the long axis of its body perpendicular to the front of the defending rat.... It moves sideways toward the intruder, crowding and sometimes pushing it off balance. If the defending rat stands solid against this "lateral attack" movement, the alpha may make a quick lunge forward and around the defender's body to bite at its back. In response to such a lunge, the defender usually pivots on its hind feet, in the same direction as the attacker is moving, continuing its frontal orientation to the attacker. If the defending rat moves quickly enough, no bite will be made.
>
> However, after a number of instances of the lateral attack, and especially if the attacker has succeeded in biting

the intruder, the stranger rat may roll backward slowly from the boxing position, to lie on its back. The attacker then takes up a position on top of the supine animal, digging with its forepaws at the intruder's sides. If the attacker can turn the other animal over, or expose some portion of its back, . . . it bites. In response to these efforts, the defender usually moves in the direction of the attacker's head, rolling slightly on its back to continue to orient its ventrum [front] toward the alpha, and continuing to push off with both forelimbs and hindlimbs. Although all four legs and abdomen of the defending rat are exposed, the attacker does not bite them. This sequence of bites, flight, chasing, boxing, lateral attack, lying on the back, and standing on top is repeated . . . until the stranger rat is removed. (From "Affect and Aggression," by D. C. Blanchard and R. J. Blanchard, pp. 8–9, in *Advances in the Study of Aggression*, Vol. 1, 1984, edited by D. C. Blanchard and R. J. Blanchard. San Diego: Academic Press. Copyright 1984 by Academic Press. Reprinted by permission.)

Another excellent example of gaining insight from careful observation of defensive and aggressive behaviors is the study of Pellis and colleagues (1988). They began by videotaping interactions between cats and mice. They found that different cats reacted to mice in different ways: Some were efficient mouse killers, some reacted defensively, and some seemed to play with the mice. Careful analysis of the "play" sequences led to two important conclusions. The first conclusion was that, in contrast to the common belief, cats do not play with their prey; the cats that appeared to be playing with the mice were simply vacillating between attack and defense. The second conclusion was that one can best understand each cat's interactions with mice by locating the interactions on a linear scale, with total aggressiveness at one end, total defensiveness at the other, and various proportions of the two in between.

Pellis and colleagues tested their conclusions by reducing the defensiveness of the cats with an antianxiety drug. As predicted, the drug moved each cat along the scale toward more efficient killing. Cats that avoided mice before the injection played with them after the injection, those that played with them before the injection killed them after the injection, and those that killed them before the injection killed them more quickly after the injection. The next time you play with a cat, take the opportunity to analyze the cat's behavior in the light of Pellis's observations.

The defensive and aggressive behaviors of rats have been divided into categories on the basis of three different criteria: (1) their *topography* (form), (2) the situations that elicit them, and (3) their apparent function. Several of these categories are described in Table 17.2 (see also Blanchard et al., 2001; Kavaliers & Choleris, 2001).

The analysis of aggressive and defensive behaviors has led to the development of the **target-site concept**—the idea that the aggressive and defensive behaviors of an animal are often designed to attack specific sites on the body of another animal while protecting specific sites on its own. For example, the behavior of a socially aggressive rat (e.g., lateral attack) appears to be designed to deliver bites to the defending rat's back and to protect its own face, the likely target of a defensive attack. Conversely, most of the maneuvers of the defending rat (e.g., boxing) appear to be designed to protect the target site on its back.

The discovery that aggressive and defensive behaviors occur in a variety of stereotypical species-common forms was the necessary first step in the identification of their neural bases. Because the different categories of aggressive and defensive behaviors are mediated by different neural circuits, little progress was made in identifying these circuits before the categories were delineated. For example, the lateral septum was once believed to inhibit all aggression, because lateral septal lesions rendered laboratory rats notoriously difficult to handle—the behavior of the lesioned rats was commonly referred to as *septal aggression* or *septal rage*. However, we now know that lateral septal lesions do not increase aggression: Rats with lateral septal lesions do not initiate more attacks at the experimenter if they are left undisturbed. These lesioned rats are more defensive, not more aggressive.

Aggression and Testosterone

The fact that social aggression in many species occurs more commonly among males than among females is usually explained with reference to the organizational and activational effects of testosterone. The brief period of testosterone release that occurs around birth in genetic males is thought to organize their nervous systems along masculine lines and hence to create the potential for male patterns of social aggression to be activated by the high testosterone levels that are present after puberty. These organizational and activational effects have been demonstrated in many nonprimate mammalian species. For example, neonatal castration of male mice eliminates the ability of testosterone injections to induce social aggression in adulthood, and adult castration eliminates social aggression in males that do not receive testosterone replacement injections.

In contrast to the research on nonprimates, attempts to demonstrate the organizational and activational effects of testosterone on the aggressive behavior of humans have been mixed. In human males, aggressive behavior does not increase at puberty as testosterone levels increase, it is not eliminated by castration, and it is not increased by testosterone injections that raise blood levels of testosterone to high, but normal, levels. However, a few studies have found that violent male criminals and aggressive male athletes tend to have slightly higher testosterone levels than normal (see Bernhardt, 1997). This weak correlation may indicate that aggressive encoun-

Evolutionary Perspective

TABLE 17.2 Categories of Aggressive and Defensive Behaviors in Rats

AGGRESSIVE BEHAVIORS		
	PREDATORY AGGRESSION	The stalking and killing of members of other species for the purpose of eating them. Rats kill prey, such as mice and frogs, by delivering bites to the back of the neck.
	SOCIAL AGGRESSION	Unprovoked aggressive behavior that is directed at a conspecific (member of one's own species) for the purpose of establishing, altering, or maintaining a social hierarchy. In mammals, social aggression occurs primarily among males. In rats, it is characterized by piloerection, lateral attack, and bites directed at the defender's back.
DEFENSIVE BEHAVIORS	INTRASPECIFIC DEFENSE	Defense against social aggression. In rats, it is characterized by freezing and flight and by various behaviors, such as boxing, that are specifically designed to protect the back from bites.
	DEFENSIVE ATTACKS	Attacks that are launched by animals when they are cornered by threatening members of their own or other species. In rats, they include lunging, shrieking, and biting attacks that are usually directed at the face of the attacker.
	FREEZING AND FLIGHT	Responses that many animals use to avoid attack. For example, if a human approaches a wild rat, it will often freeze until the human penetrates its safety zone, whereupon it will explode into flight.
	MATERNAL DEFENSIVE BEHAVIORS	The behaviors by which mothers protect their young. Despite their defensive function, they are similar to male social aggression in appearance.
	RISK ASSESSMENT	Behaviors that are performed by animals in order to obtain specific information that helps them defend themselves more effectively. For example, rats that have been chased by a cat into their burrow do not emerge until they have spent considerable time at the entrance scanning the surrounding environment.
	DEFENSIVE BURYING	Rats and other rodents spray sand and dirt ahead with their forepaws to bury dangerous objects in their environment, to drive off predators, and to construct barriers in burrows.

ters increase testosterone, rather than vice versa (see Archer, 1991).

The fact that human aggression is not strongly related to testosterone levels could mean that its hormonal and neural regulation differs from that in nonprimate mammalian species. However, Albert, Walsh, and Jonik (1993) argued that the evidence favors a different conclusion. They suggested that the confusion has arisen because the researchers who study human aggres-

Thinking Critically

sion often fail to appreciate the difference between social aggression, which is related to testosterone in many species, and defensive aggression, which is not. Most aggressive outbursts in humans are overreactions to real or perceived threat, and they are thus appropriately viewed as defensive attack, not social aggression. Consequently, the failure to find positive correlations between human aggressive behavior and testosterone levels is consistent with the failure to find positive correlations between defensive attack and testosterone levels in other species.

ed in ill health (see Kiecolt-Glaser et al., 2002; Krantz & McCeney, 2002; Natelson, 2004).

The Stress Response

Hans Selye (pronounced "SELL-yay") first described the stress response in the 1950s, and he quickly recognized its dual nature. In the short term, it produces adaptive

17.3 Stress and Health

When the body is exposed to harm or threat, the result is a cluster of physiological changes that is generally referred to as *the stress response*—or just **stress.** All *stressors*, whether psychological (e.g., dismay at the loss of one's job) or physical (e.g., long-term exposure to cold), produce a similar core pattern of physiological changes; however, it is *chronic psychological stress* (e.g., in the form of chronic fear) that has been most frequently implicat-

changes that help the animal respond to the stressor (e.g., mobilization of energy resources, inhibition of inflammation, and resistance to infection); in the long term, however, it produces changes that are maladaptive (e.g., enlarged adrenal glands).

Selye attributed the stress response to the activation of the *anterior-pituitary adrenal-cortex system*. He concluded that stressors acting on neural circuits stimulate the release of **adrenocorticotropic hormone (ACTH)** from the anterior pituitary, that the ACTH in turn triggers the release of **glucocorticoids** from the **adrenal cortex**, and that the glucocorticoids produce many of the effects of the stress response (see Erickson, Drevets, & Schulkin, 2003; Korte, 2001). The level of circulating glucocorticoids is the most commonly employed physiological measure of stress.

With his emphasis on the role of the anterior-pituitary adrenal-cortex system in stress, Selye largely ignored the contributions of the sympathetic nervous system. Stressors also activate the sympathetic nervous system, thereby increasing the amounts of epinephrine and norepinephrine released from the **adrenal medulla.** Most modern theories of stress (see Stanford & Salmon, 1993) acknowledge the major roles of both systems (see Figure 17.8).

The magnitude of the stress response depends not only on the stressor and the individual; it also depends on the strategies the individual adopts to cope with the stress (McEwen, 1994). For example, in a study of women awaiting surgery for possible breast cancer, the levels of stress were lower in those who had convinced themselves to think about their problem in certain ways. Those who had convinced themselves that they could not possibly have cancer, that their prayers were certain to be answered, or that it was counterproductive to worry about it experienced less stress (Katz et al., 1970).

From the perspective of psychological science, the major contribution of Selye's stress response was that it suggested a mechanism by which psychological factors can influence physical illness. All kinds of common psychological stressors (e.g., losing a job, preparing for an examination, ending a relationship) are associated with high circulating levels of glucocorticoids, epinephrine, and norepinephrine; and these in turn have been implicated in many physical disorders (Salovey et al., 2000). For example, fear or stress prior to surgery has been associated with slower postsurgical recovery, including delays in wound healing (Kiecolt-Glaser et al., 1998).

Clinical Implications

Evolutionary Perspective

The relation between chronic fear, stress, and ill health is readily apparent in animals undergoing subordination stress. Virtually all mammals—particularly males—experience threats from con-*specifics* (members of the same species) at certain points in their lives.

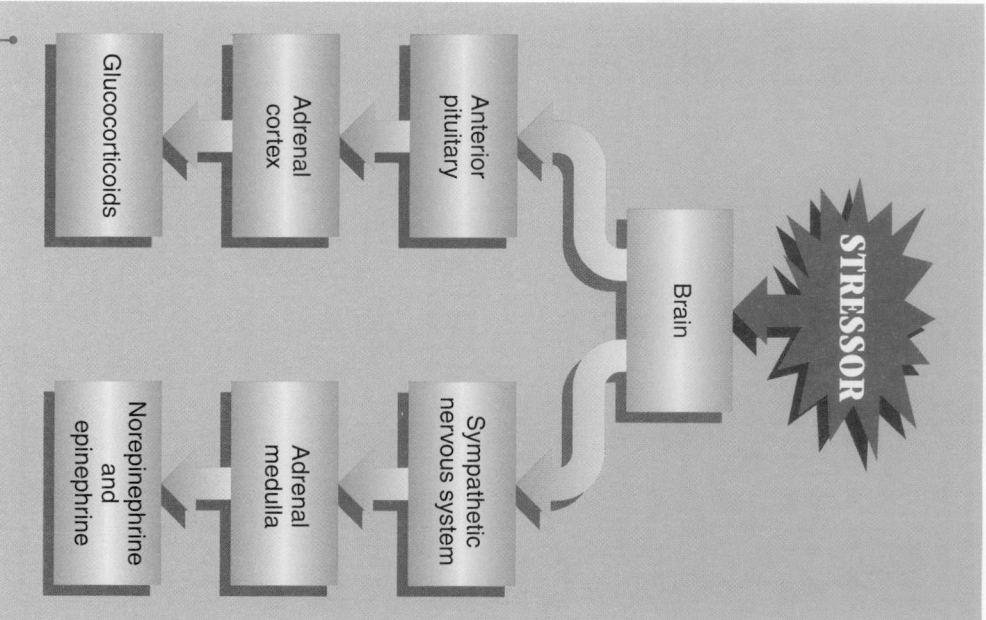

FIGURE 17.8   The two-system view of the stress response.

Brain

STRESSOR

Anterior pituitary

Sympathetic nervous system

Adrenal cortex

Adrenal medulla

Glucocorticoids

Norepinephrine and epinephrine

When conspecific threat becomes an enduring feature of daily life, the result is **subordination stress.** Subordination stress is most readily studied in social species that form stable *dominance hierarchies* (pecking orders). What do you think happens to subordinate male rodents who are continually attacked by more dominant males? Several studies (see Blanchard et al., 1993; Delville, Melloni, & Ferris, 1998) have reported that animals exposed to subordination stress are more likely to attack juveniles, to have testes that are reduced in size, to have shorter life spans, and to have lower levels of testosterone and higher levels of corticosterone (a glucocorticoid).

Stress and Gastric Ulcers

Stress has long been implicated in the development of gastric ulcers. **Gastric ulcers** are painful lesions to the lining of the stomach and duodenum, which in extreme cases can be life-threatening. In the United States alone, about 500,000 new cases are reported each year (see Livingston & Guth, 1992). Gastric ulcers occur more

Clinical Implications

commonly in people living in stressful situations, and stressors (e.g., confinement to a restraint tube for a few hours) can produce these ulcers in laboratory animals.

For decades, gastric ulcers were regarded as the prototypical *psychosomatic disease* (physical disease with incontrovertible evidence of a psychological cause). However, this view seemed to change with the report that gastric ulcers are caused by bacteria. Indeed, it has been claimed that the ulcer-causing bacteria (*Helicobacter pylori*) are responsible for all cases of gastric ulcers except those caused by nonsteroidal anti-inflammatory agents such as aspirin (Blaser, 1996). This seemed to rule out stress as a causal factor in such ulcers, but a careful consideration of the evidence suggests otherwise (Overmier & Murison, 1997).

The facts do not deny that *H. pylori* damages the stomach wall or that antibiotic treatment of gastric ulcers helps many sufferers. The facts do, however, suggest that *H. pylori* infection alone is insufficient to produce the disorder in most people. Although it is true that most patients with gastric ulcers display signs of *H. pylori* infection, so too do 75% of healthy control subjects. Also, although it is true that antibiotics improve the condition of many patients with gastric ulcers, so do psychological treatments—and they do it without reducing signs of *H. pylori* infection. Apparently, there is another factor that increases the susceptibility of the stomach wall to damage from *H. pylori*, and this factor is likely to be stress.

Psychoneuroimmunology: Stress, the Immune System, and the Brain

A major change in the study of stress and health came in the 1970s with the accumulation of reports that stress might reduce a person's resistance to infection. These reports had a great impact on the field of psychology, because they suggested that stress could play a role in infectious diseases, which up to that point had been regarded as "strictly physical."

The theoretical and clinical implications of the suggestion that stress can increase susceptibility to infection were so great that they led in the early 1980s to the emergence of a new field of biopsychological research. That field is **psychoneuroimmunology**—the study of interactions among psychological factors, the nervous system, and the immune system.

Psychoneuroimmunological research is the focus of this subsection. Let's begin, however, with an introduction to the immune system.

Immune System Microorganisms of every description revel in the warm, damp, nutritive climate of your body (see Ploegh, 1998). Your **immune system** keeps your body from being overwhelmed by these invaders. Before it can take any action against an invading micro-

organism, the immune system must have some way of distinguishing foreign cells from body cells. That is why **antigens**—protein molecules on the surface of a cell that identify it as native or foreign—play a major role in specific immune reactions (see Matzinger, 2002; Medzhitov & Janeway, 2002).

Immune system barriers to infection are often considered to be of two sorts (see Banchereau, 2002). First, there are nonspecific barriers, those that act generally and quickly against most invaders. These barriers include mucous membranes, which destroy many foreign microorganisms, and **phagocytosis,** the process by which foreign microorganisms and debris are consumed and destroyed by *phagocytes* (specialized body cells such as microglia that consume foreign microorganisms and debris)—see Figure 17.9.

Second, there are specific barriers, those that act specifically against particular strains of invaders. The specific barriers are of two types—cell-mediated and antibody-mediated—each defended by a different class of lymphocytes. **Lymphocytes** are specialized white blood cells that are produced in bone marrow and are stored in the lymphatic system. **Cell-mediated immunity** is directed by **T cells** (T lymphocytes); **antibody-mediated immunity** is directed by **B cells** (B lymphocytes).

The cell-mediated immune reaction begins when a **macrophage**—a type of large phagocyte—ingests a foreign microorganism. The macrophage then displays the microorganism's antigens on the surface of its cell

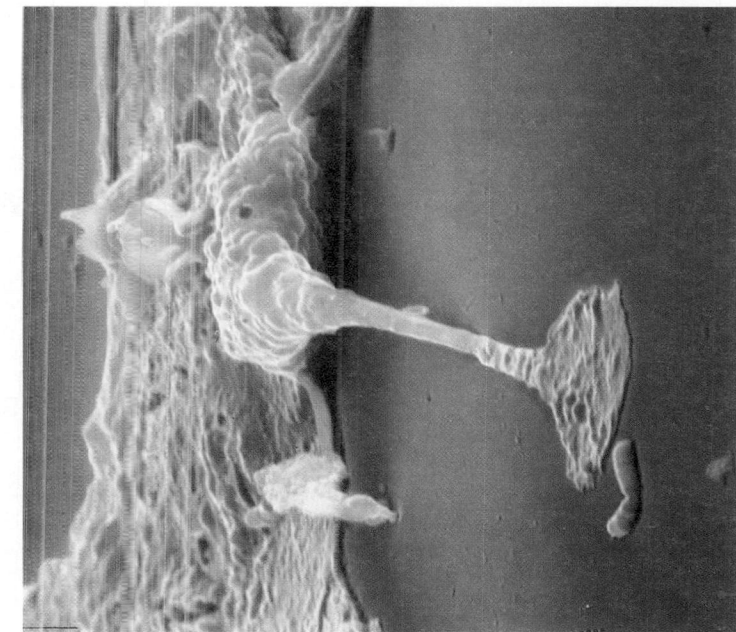

FIGURE 17.9 Phagocytosis: A macrophage hunts down and destroys a bacterium.

Cell-Mediated Immunity

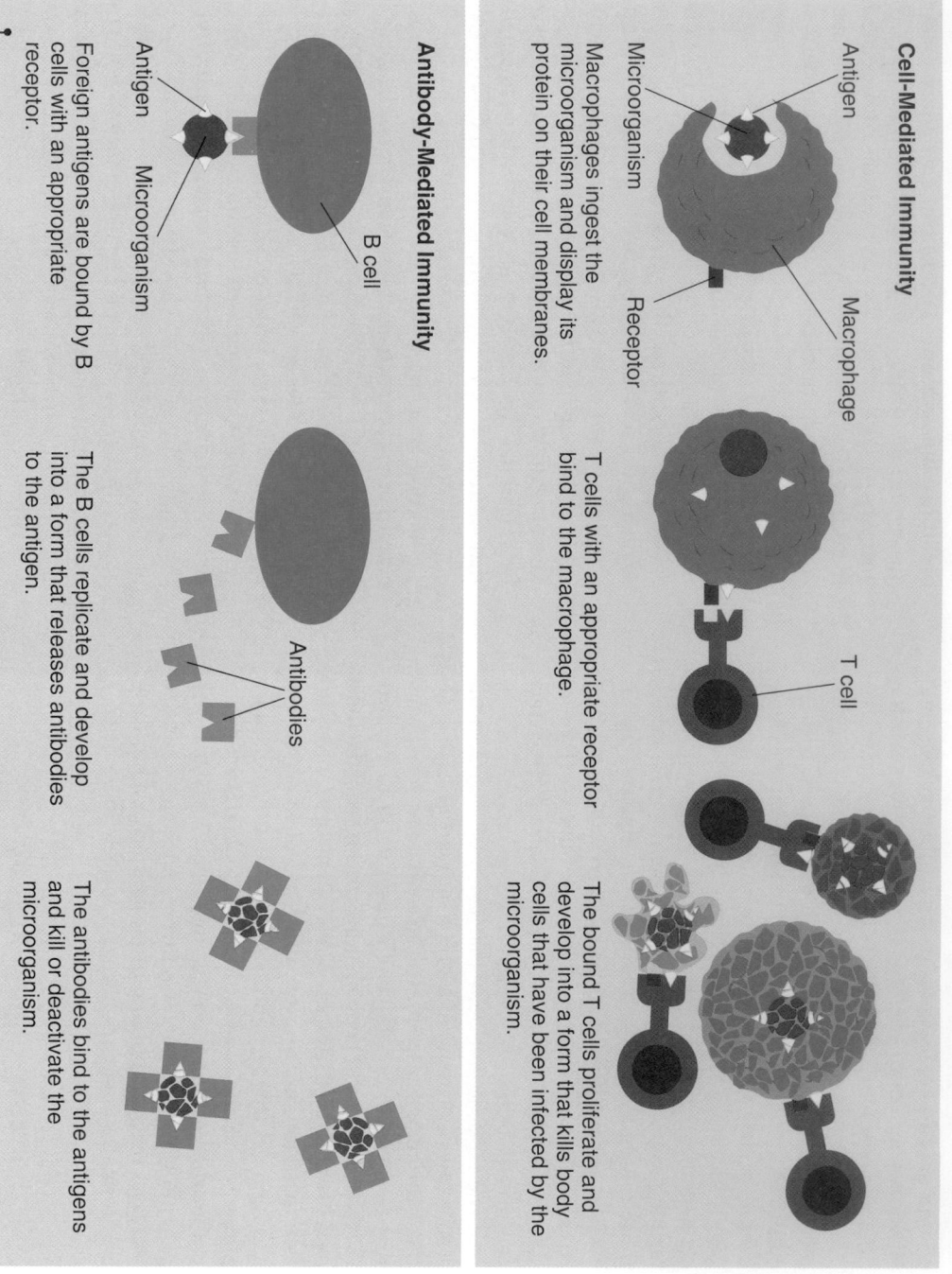

Macrophage

Antigen

Microorganism

Receptor

Macrophages ingest the microorganism and display its protein on their cell membranes.

T cells with an appropriate receptor bind to the macrophage.

T cell

The bound T cells proliferate and develop into a form that kills body cells that have been infected by the microorganism.

Antibody-Mediated Immunity

Antigen

Microorganism

B cell

Foreign antigens are bound by B cells with an appropriate receptor.

The B cells replicate and develop into a form that releases antibodies to the antigen.

Antibodies

The antibodies bind to the antigens and kill or deactivate the microorganism.

FIGURE 17.10   Specific barriers to infection: Cell-mediated immunity and antibody-mediated immunity. In cell-mediated immunity, microorganisms or body cells that they have invaded are killed by T cells; in antibody-mediated immunity, microorganisms are killed by antibodies produced by B cells.

---

membrane (see Figure 17.10), and this attracts T cells. Each T cell has two kinds of receptors on its surface, one for molecules that are normally found on the surface of macrophages and other body cells, and one for a specific foreign antigen. There are millions of different receptors for foreign antigens on T cells, but there is only one kind on each T cell, and there are only a few T cells with each kind of receptor. After the microorganism has been ingested and its antigens have been displayed, a T cell with a receptor for the foreign antigen binds to the surface of the infected macrophage, which initiates a series of reactions (Grakoui et al., 1999; Malissen, 1999). Among these reactions is the multiplication of the bound T cell, creating more T cells with the specific receptor necessary to destroy all invaders that contain the target antigens and all body cells that have been infected by the invaders.

The antibody-mediated immune reaction begins when a B cell binds to a foreign antigen for which it contains an appropriate receptor. This causes the B cell to

multiply and to synthesize a lethal form of its receptor molecules. These lethal receptor molecules, called **antibodies**, are released into the intracellular fluid, where they bind to the foreign antigens and destroy or deactivate the microorganisms that possess them. Memory B cells for the specific antigen are also produced during the process; these cells have a long life and accelerate antibody-mediated immunity if there is a subsequent infection by the same organism (see Ahmed & Gray, 1996).

Cell-mediated immunity and antibody-mediated immunity are illustrated in Figure 17.10. Both processes take several days the first time a particular foreign antigen is recognized, but responses to subsequent invasions of microorganisms with the same antigen are much faster thanks to the memory T cells and B cells. This is why *inoculation* (the injection of small samples of an infective microorganism into healthy individuals) is often an effective preventive measure against the effects of subsequent infection.

If you have not previously learned about the immune system, the preceding description of its function may seem a bit complex. However, in order to keep things in perspective, you need to realize that the preceding introduction is much simplified. Immune function is extremely complex, and this complexity plays an important role in the following discussion.

What Effect Does Stress Have on Immune Function? It is widely believed that stress disrupts immune function. I am sure that you have heard this point made by family members, friends, and even by physi-

Thinking Critically

cians. But is this true? By this point in the book, I am sure you appreciate that common beliefs are not necessarily true: that the ultimate criterion of truth is empirical evidence, not popular opinion.

The following view of the relation between stress and immune function is based on a meta-analysis by Segerstrom and Miller (2004). What is a meta-analysis? A *meta-analysis* is a study that analyzes and combines the results of a group of previously published studies. For example, the meta-analysis of Segerstrom and Miller is a combined analysis of the 300 or so empirical studies of the relationship between stress and immune function in humans that have been published since the advent of the field of psychoneuroimmunology. In short, the findings of Segerstrom and Miller are currently the ultimate word on this matter.

One of the most important contributions of Segerstrom and Miller's meta-analysis is that their results rec-

Evolutionary Perspective

onciled the seeming incompatibility of psychoneuroimmunological research findings and evolutionary psychology principles. Virtually every individual organism encounters many stressors during the course of its life, and it is difficult to see how a maladaptive response to stress, such as a disruption of immune function, could have evolved—or could have survived if it had been created by a genetic accident or as a *spandrel* (a nonadaptive by-product of an adaptive evolutionary change).

Segerstrom and Miller found that the effects of stress on immune function depended on the kind of stress. They found that acute (brief) stressors (i.e., those lasting less than 100 minutes, such as public speaking, athletic competitions, or musical performances) actually led to improvements in immune function. Not surprisingly, the improvements in immune function following acute stress occurred mainly in nonspecific barriers, which can be marshaled quickly. In contrast, chronic (long-lasting) stressors, such as caring for a demented loved one, living with a handicap, or experiencing unemployment, adversely affected more complex immune system processes.

How Does Stress Influence Immune Function? The mechanisms by which stress influences immune function have been difficult to specify because there

are so many possibilities (see Dustin & Colman, 2002). Stress produces widespread changes in the body through its effects on the anterior-pituitary adrenal-cortex system and the sympathetic adrenal-medulla system, and there are innumerable mechanisms by which these systems could influence immune function. For example, both T cells and B cells have receptors for glucocorticoids; and lymphocytes have receptors for epinephrine, norepinephrine, and glucocorticoids. In addition, many of the neuropeptides that are released by neurons are also released by cells of the immune system. Conversely, *cytokines*, a class of signaling chemicals originally thought to be produced only by cells of the immune system, have been found to be produced in the nervous system (Salzet, Vieau, & Day, 2000). In short, the physiological mechanisms by which the nervous system and the immune system can interact are innumerable.

It is important not to forget that there are also behavioral routes by which stress may affect immune function. For example, people under severe stress often display changed patterns of diet, exercise, sleep, and drug use, all of which could influence immune function.

Does Stress Affect Susceptibility to Infectious Disease? It has proven difficult to show unequivocally that stress causes increases in susceptibility to infectious diseases in human subjects. One reason for this difficulty is that only correlational studies are

Thinking Critically

possible. Numerous studies have reported *positive* correlations between stress and ill health in human subjects; for example, students in one study reported more respiratory infections during final exams (Glaser et al., 1987). However, interpretation of such correlations is never straightforward: Subjects may report more illness during times of stress because they expect to be more ill, because their experience of illness during times of stress is more unpleasant, or because the stress caused changes in their behavior that increased their susceptibility to infection.

Another reason why it has proven difficult to show that stress causes increases in susceptibility to infectious diseases is that adverse effects of stress on immune function are not necessarily reflected in more illness. There are three reasons why particular decreases in immune function may not be reflected in increased infectious disease: (1) The immune system seems to have many redundant components; thus, disruption of one of them may have little or no effect on vulnerability to infection. (2) In young healthy individuals, the subjects of most psychoneuroimmunological investigations, stress-produced changes in immune function may be too short-lived to have substantial effects on the probability of infection. (3) Declines in some aspects of immune function may induce compensatory increases in others.

Despite the difficulties of proving a causal link between stress and infectious disease in humans, the evidence for such a link now seems incontrovertible. Fortunately, research on stress, immune function, and infectious disease in humans is complemented by the re-

sults of research with laboratory animals. Several controlled experiments conducted on laboratory animals have convincingly demonstrated that chronic exposure to stressors can indeed disrupt immune function and increase susceptibility to infection (see Ben-Eliyahu et al., 2000; Quan et al., 2001). Accordingly, considered together, correlational studies on humans and experiments on laboratory animals have provided strong support for the basic tenets of psychoneuroimmunology.

Early Experience of Stress

Early exposure to severe stress can have a variety of adverse effects on subsequent development. Children subjected to maltreatment or other forms of severe stress display a variety of brain and endocrine system abnormalities (Teicher, 2002; Teicher et al., 2003). As you will learn in the next chapter, some psychiatric disorders are thought to result from an interaction between an inherited susceptibility to a disorder and early exposure to severe stress. Because early exposure to stress often increases the intensity of subsequent stress responses (e.g., increases the subsequent release of glucocorticoids in response to stressors), such exposure likely amplifies the adverse effects of subsequent stressors.

It is important to understand that the developmental window during which early stress can adversely affect neural and endocrine development begins before birth.

Many experiments have demonstrated the adverse effects of prenatal stress in laboratory animals. In experiments on prenatal stress, pregnant females are exposed to stressors, and the adverse effects of that exposure on their offspring are subsequently assessed (see Avishai-Eliner et al., 2002; Kofman, 2002; Maccari et al., 2003).

One particularly interesting line of research on the role of early experience in the development of the stress response began with the observation that handling of rat pups by researchers for a few minutes per day during the first few weeks of their lives has a variety of salutary (health-promoting) effects (see Sapolsky, 1997). The majority of these effects seemed to result from a decrease in the magnitude of the handled pups' responses to stressful events. As adults, rats that were handled as pups displayed smaller increases in circulating glucocorticoids in response to stressors (see Francis & Meaney, 1999). It seemed remarkable that a few hours of handling early in life could have such a significant and lasting effect. In fact, evidence supports an alternative interpretation.

Liou and colleagues (1997) found that handled rat pups are groomed (licked) more by their mothers, and they hypothesized that the salutary effects of early handling resulted from the extra grooming, rather than from

the handling itself. They confirmed this hypothesis by showing that unhandled rat pups that received a lot of grooming from their mothers developed the same profile of increased glucocorticoid release that was observed in handled pups. This effect seems to have been produced by decreased negative feedback from greater numbers of glucocorticoid receptors in the hippocampus.

In general, early separation of rat pups from their mothers seems to have effects opposite to those of high levels of early grooming (see Cirulli, Berry, & Alleva, 2003; Pryce & Feldon, 2003; Rhees, Lephart, & Eliason, 2001). As adults, rats that are separated from their mothers in infancy display elevated behavioral and hormonal responses to stress.

Those mother rats that are most reactive to stress provide the poorest maternal care to their offspring. This poor care has lasting adverse effects on the stress responses of the offspring (Meaney, 2001). Think about the significance of this sequence of events: It constitutes a nongenetic mechanism by which behavioral tendencies can be passed from generation to generation.

Stress and the Hippocampus

Many studies of the effects of stress on the brain suggest that the hippocampus is particularly susceptible to stress-induced effects. The reason for this susceptibility seems to be the particularly dense population of glucocorticoid receptors in the hippocampus (see McEwen, 2000b).

Two particular effects of stress on the structure of the hippocampus have been observed in several species of laboratory animals (McEwen, 2000a). Following exposure to a period of stress, the dendrites of pyramidal cells are shorter and show less branching, and the rate of adult neurogenesis of granule cells is reduced.

The effects of stress on the hippocampus are being investigated intensively because of their possible involvement in stress-related psychiatric problems. Five important findings have been reported. First, the effects of stress on the hippocampus appear to be mediated by stress-induced increases in the release of corticosteroids—the effects can be blocked by adrenalectomy (Tanapat et al., 2001) and can be produced by corticosteroid injections (McEwen, 2000a). Second, even a period of stress lasting only a few hours can induce structural changes in the hippocampus that last a month or more (Kim & Diamond, 2000). Third, natural stressors (e.g., threat from dominant conspecifics or from predators) tend to produce more hippocampal pathology than do artificial stressors (e.g., restraint). Fourth, the effects of stress on the hippocampus are great enough to disrupt behavior mediated by hippocampal activity (e.g., radial arm maze performance). And, fifth, the effects of stress

SCAN YOUR BRAIN

This chapter is about to change direction: The remaining sections focus on those structures of the brain that mediate the experience of emotion. Accordingly, this is an appropriate point at which to pause and scan your brain to see whether it has retained the introductory material on emotion, fear, and stress. Fill in each of the following blanks with the most appropriate term. The correct answers are provided near the bottom of this page. Before continuing, review material related to your errors and omissions.

1. The theory that the subjective experience of emotion is triggered by ANS responses is called the _____ theory.

2. The pattern of aggressive responses observed in decorticate animals is called _____.

3. Between the amygdala and the fornix in the limbic ring is the _____.

4. A Duchenne smile, but not a false smile, involves contraction of the _____.

5. Aggression directed by the alpha male of a colony at a male intruder is called _____ aggression.

6. The usual target site of rat defensive attacks is the _____ of the attacking rat.

7. Testosterone increases _____ aggression.

8. Glucocorticoids are released from the _____ as part of the stress response.

9. Stressors increase the release of epinephrine and norepinephrine from the _____.

10. When threats from conspecifics become an enduring feature of daily life, the result is _____.

11. The study of the interactions among psychological factors, the nervous system, and the immune system is called _____.

12. T cells and B cells are involved in cell-mediated _____ and _____ immune reactions, respectively.

13. As adults, rats groomed intensely by their mothers as pups display decreased _____ release in response to stressors.

14. In laboratory animals, stress has been shown to shrink _____ hippocampal _____ and blocks hippocampal _____.

Scan Your Brain answers: (1) James–Lange, (2) sham rage, (3) hippocampus, (4) orbicularis oculi, (5) social, (6) face, (7) social, (8) adrenal cortex, (9) adrenal medulla, (10) subordination stress, (11) psychoneuroimmunology, (12) antibody-mediated, (13) glucocorticoid, (14) dendrites, neurogenesis.

The implications for better understanding of stress-related psychiatric disorders are immense.

on the hippocampus tend to be greater in males. Falconer and Galea (2003) found a stress-induced disruption of hippocampal neurogenesis in male rats but not in females—the reason for this sex difference may lie in the fact that *estradiol* has been shown to promote adult neurogenesis (Ormerod & Galea, 2001) and recovery from brain damage (Garcia-Segura, Azcoitia, & DonCarlos, 2001).

Research on the adverse effects of stress on the brain is in its early stages, but rapid progress is being made.

17.4 Fear Conditioning

In the past decade, much of the research on the neural mechanisms of emotion has focused on fear conditioning, largely in rats. **Fear conditioning** is the establishment of fear in response to a previously neutral stimulus (the *conditional stimulus*) by presenting it, usually several times, before the delivery of an aversive stimulus (the *unconditional stimulus*). Fear conditioning has been the preferred method of studying fear because the source of fear is always unambiguous (the unconditional stimulus) with this method and because the development of

the fear response can be investigated systematically (see Maren, 2001).

In the usual fear-conditioning experiment, the subject, typically a rat, hears a tone (conditional stimulus) and then receives a mild electric shock to its feet (unconditional stimulus). After several pairings of the tone and the shock, the rat responds to the tone with a variety of defensive behaviors (e.g., freezing and increased susceptibility to startle) and sympathetic nervous system responses (e.g., increased heart rate and blood pressure).

LeDoux and his colleagues have mapped the neural mechanism that mediates this form of auditory fear conditioning (see LeDoux, 2000a, 2000b).

Amygdala and Fear Conditioning

LeDoux and his colleagues began their search for the neural mechanisms of auditory fear conditioning by making lesions in the auditory pathways of rats. They found that bilateral lesions to the *medial geniculate nucleus* (the auditory relay nucleus of the thalamus) blocked fear conditioning to a tone, but bilateral lesions to the auditory cortex did not. This indicated that for auditory fear conditioning to occur, it is necessary for signals elicited by the tone to reach the medial geniculate nucleus but not the auditory cortex. It also indicated that a pathway from the medial geniculate nucleus to a structure other than the auditory cortex plays a key role in fear conditioning. This pathway proved to be the pathway from the medial geniculate nucleus to the amygdala. Lesions of the amygdala, like lesions of the medial geniculate nucleus, blocked fear conditioning. The amygdala receives input from all sensory systems, and it is believed to be the structure in which the emotional significance of sensory signals is learned and retained.

Several pathways carry signals from the amygdala to brain-stem structures that control the various emotional responses. For example, a pathway to the periaqueductal gray of the midbrain elicits appropriate defensive responses (see Bandler & Shipley, 1994), whereas another pathway to the lateral hypothalamus elicits appropriate sympathetic responses.

The fact that auditory cortex lesions do not disrupt fear conditioning to simple tones does not mean that the auditory cortex is not involved in auditory fear conditioning. There are two pathways from the medial geniculate nucleus to the amygdala: the direct one, which you have already learned about, and an indirect one that

Evolutionary Perspective

projects via the auditory cortex (Romanski & LeDoux, 1992). Both routes are capable of mediating fear conditioning to simple sounds; if only one is destroyed, conditioning progresses normally. However, only the cortical route is capable of mediating fear conditioning to complex sounds (Jarrell et al., 1987).

Figure 17.11 illustrates the circuit of the brain that is thought to mediate fear conditioning to auditory conditional stimuli (see LeDoux, 1994). Sound signals from the medial geniculate nucleus of the thalamus reach the amygdala either directly or via the auditory cortex. The amygdala assesses the emotional significance of the sound on the basis of previous encounters with it, and then the amygdala activates the appropriate response circuits—for example, behavioral circuits in the periaqueductal gray and sympathetic circuits in the hypothalamus.

Anatomy of the Amygdala: A General Comment

The preceding discussion has probably left you with the impression that the amygdala is a single brain structure; it isn't. It is actually a cluster of many nuclei, often referred to as the *amygdala complex*. The amygdala is composed of a dozen or so major regions, which are themselves divided into subregions. Each of these subregions is structurally distinct and has different connections. Making things potentially even more confusing is the fact that the anatomy of the amygdala is so complex

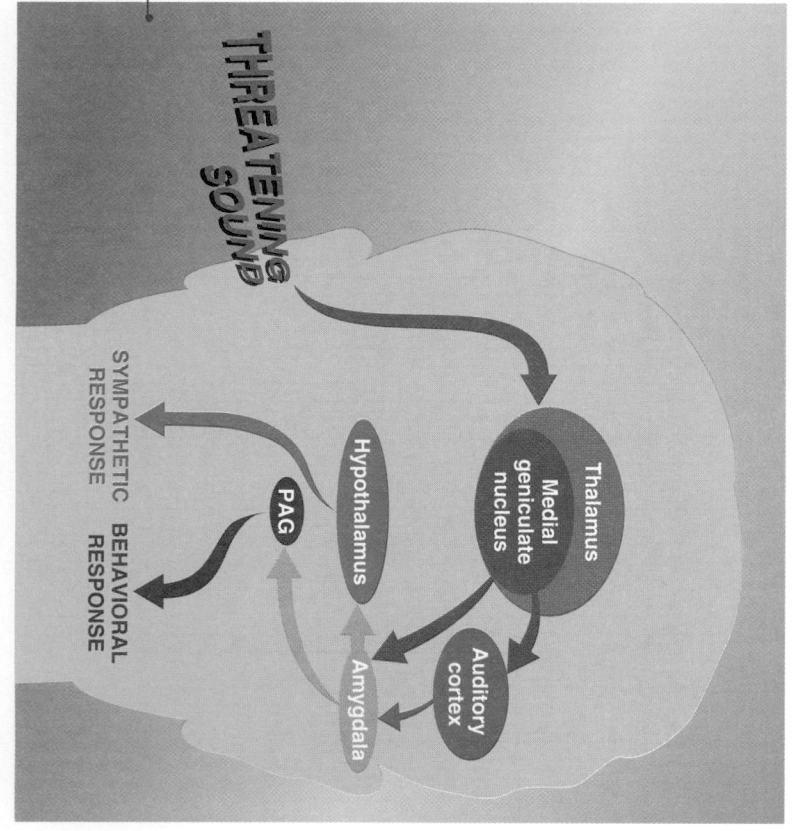

FIGURE 17.11 The structures that are thought to mediate the sympathetic and behavioral responses conditioned to an auditory conditional stimulus.

that there is no general consensus about how to divide it into its components (see LeDoux, 2000b).

Thinking Critically

Don't worry! I have not raised this issue here because I expect you to master the intricacies of amygdalar anatomy. I merely want you to be able to put what you have learned about the amygdala in context. So far, all evidence suggests that the amygdala plays a critical role in fear conditioning; thus, researchers are focusing on its internal circuitry. Researchers are tracing the pathways by which sensory input signaling the presence of a conditional stimulus enters the amygdala and studying how, through conditioning, this input activates circuits within the amygdala that trigger pathways to structures outside the amygdala that ultimately produce the fear response (see Maren, 1999; Schettino & Otto, 2001).

Contextual Fear Conditioning and the Hippocampus

Environments, or *contexts*, in which fear-inducing stimuli are encountered can themselves come to elicit fear. For example, if you repeatedly encountered a bear on a particular trail in the forest, the trail itself would elicit fear in you. The process by which benign contexts come to elicit fear through their association with fear-inducing stimuli is called **contextual fear conditioning.**

Evolutionary Perspective

Contextual fear conditioning has been produced in the laboratory in two ways. First, it has been produced by the conventional fear-conditioning procedure, which we just discussed. For example, if a rat repeatedly receives a footshock following a conditional stimulus, such as a tone, the rat will become fearful of the conditional context (the test chamber) as well as the tone. Second, contextual fear conditioning has been produced by delivering aversive stimuli in a particular context in the absence of any other conditional stimulus. For example, if a rat receives footshocks in a distinctive test chamber, the rat will become fearful of that chamber.

In view of the fact that the hippocampus plays a key role in memory for spatial location, it is reasonable to expect that it would be involved in contextual fear conditioning. This seems to be the case (see Antoniadis & McDonald, 2000). Two kinds of lesion studies have implicated the hippocampus in contextual fear conditioning. First, bilateral hippocampal lesions made *before* conditioning block the development of a fear response to the context without blocking the development of a fear response to the explicit conditional stimulus (e.g., a tone). Second, bilateral hippocampal lesions made shortly *after* conditioning block the retention of the fear response to the context without disrupting retention of the fear response to the explicit conditional stimulus.

The study of fear conditioning has entered a new phase. Fear conditioning has been studied in human subjects as their brain activity was being monitored by functional MRI. Although such research is still in its infancy, there is already substantial evidence from these functional brain-imaging studies that both the amygdala and the hippocampus are involved in human fear responses (see Büchel & Dolan, 2000; Cheng et al., 2003).

17.5 Brain Mechanisms of Human Emotion

So far in this chapter, you have been introduced to various prominent lines of biopsychological research on emotion. These lines of research have provided you with glimpses of the neural mechanisms of emotion, often in nonhuman species. This, the final section of the chapter, focuses exclusively on the brain mechanisms of emotion in humans.

Most studies of the brain mechanisms of emotion in humans are of two types: neuropsychological studies of emotional changes in brain-damaged patients (see Kolb & Taylor, 2000) and functional brain-imaging studies of healthy subjects (see Dolen & Morris, 2000; Whalen, 1998). The strength of this contemporary research is that it generally confirms and extends the research conducted on nonhuman species. Specifically, studies of the brain mechanisms of human emotion have repeatedly confirmed the involvement of the amygdala and the prefrontal cortex—although they have not been so kind to the limbic system theory (see LeDoux, 2000b; Calder, Lawrence, & Young, 2001).

The study of the brain mechanisms of human emotion is in its early stages. Consequently, most of the progress that has been made is in discovering the complexities of the problem, rather than providing simple answers. In the following subsections, three such advances are described. Notice that in each case, the amygdala and the prefrontal cortex have been implicated (see Cardinal et al., 2002).

Specific Brain Structures Play Specific Roles in Emotion

Early theories of the neural mechanisms of emotion (e.g., the limbic system theory) were based on the premise that the activity of a single neural circuit mediates all emotional experience. The results of two lines of research challenge this premise (see Calder, Lawrence, & Young, 2001). First, particular brain structures appear to be involved in only some human emotions; for example, the amygdala appears to be particularly involved in fear and to some extent in other negative emotions (Adolphs, 2002; Adolphs, Baron-Cohen, & Tranel, 2002; Ohman, 2002). Second, a particular brain structure found to be involved in a single emotion is not necessarily involved in all aspects of that emotion. For example, effective social behavior depends on the ability to perceive (receive) emotional social signals and the ability to produce (send) them; however, the human amygdala seems to be more involved in the perception of social fear than in its production. Consider the following case.

The Case of S.P., the Woman Who Couldn't Perceive Fear

At the age of 48, S.P. had her right amygdala and adjacent tissues removed for the treatment of epilepsy. Because her left amygdala had been damaged, she in effect had a bilateral amygdalar lesion.

Following her surgery, S.P. had an above average I.Q., and her perceptual abilities were generally normal. Of particular relevance was the fact that she had no difficulty in identifying faces or extracting information from them (e.g., information about age or gender). However, S.P. did have a severe postsurgical deficit in recognizing facial expressions of fear and less striking deficits in recognizing facial expressions of disgust, sadness, and happiness.

In contrast, S.P. had no difficulty specifying which emotion would go with particular sentences. Also, she had no difficulty expressing various emotions using facial expressions upon request (Anderson & Phelps, 2000).

This case is consistent with previous reports that the human amygdala is specifically involved in perceiving facial expressions of emotion, particularly of fear (e.g., Broks et al., 1998; Calder et al., 1996). Because S.P. had damage to structures other than her amygdala, it was not possible to determine the extent to which that other damage contributed to the disruption in her perception of facial expressions other than fear.

Clinical Implications

The case of S.P. is similar to reported cases of Urbach-Wiethe disease (see Aggleton & Young, 2000). **Urbach-Wiethe disease** is a genetic disorder that often results in *calcification* (hardening by conversion to calcium carbonate, the main component of bone) of the amygdala and surrounding anterior medial temporal-lobe structures in both hemispheres. One Urbach-Wiethe patient with bilateral amygdala damage was found to have lost the ability to recognize facial expressions of fear (Adolphs et al., 1994). Indeed, she could not describe fear-inducing situations or draw fearful expressions although she had no difficulty on tests involving other emotions.

Although recent research has focused on the role of the amygdala in the recognition of negative facial expressions, subjects with bilateral amygdalar damage also have difficulty recognizing a variety of other stimuli (e.g., patterns, landscapes), particularly those stimuli that the subjects report liking the least (Adolphs & Tranel, 1999). There is also evidence that the amygdala participates in positive emotions (see Hamann et al., 2002); several experiments on nonhuman animals suggest that the amygdala plays a role in learning about the beneficial value of stimuli and in the expression of positive emotions associated with such judgments (Baxter & Murray, 2002).

Evolutionary Perspective

Evidence for the involvement of specific brain structures in particular emotions has also come from research on the prefrontal cortex. For example, Northoff and colleagues (2000) found that the medial and lateral portions of prefrontal cortex respond differently to pictures designed to elicit different emotions. Functional MRIs indicated that negative emotions produce strong medial prefrontal activation, whereas positive emotions produce strong lateral prefrontal activation.

Cognitive Neuroscience

The Right Hemisphere Is More Involved Than the Left in Human Emotion

The investigation of neuropsychological brain damage provides a means of studying the cerebral lateralization of human emotion, and so does whole-brain functional brain imaging. Both of these types of research often find a general tendency for structures in the right hemisphere to play a greater role in emotion than structures in the left hemisphere do. However, whether or not there is right-hemisphere dominance depends on the structures under consideration and the particular aspect of emotion under study. Consider the following lines of research.

There are many reports that the right hemisphere is dominant for the perception of emotion—from both facial expression and **prosody** (emotional tone of voice). However, this does not mean that the left hemisphere does not play a role or that all structures of the right hemisphere play a greater role than their corresponding structures in the left hemisphere. For example, Kolb and Taylor (1988) found that the perception of emotion from facial expression was disrupted by right temporal lesions but not at all by left temporal lesions, whereas right and left frontal lesions produced equivalent dis-

Clinical Implications

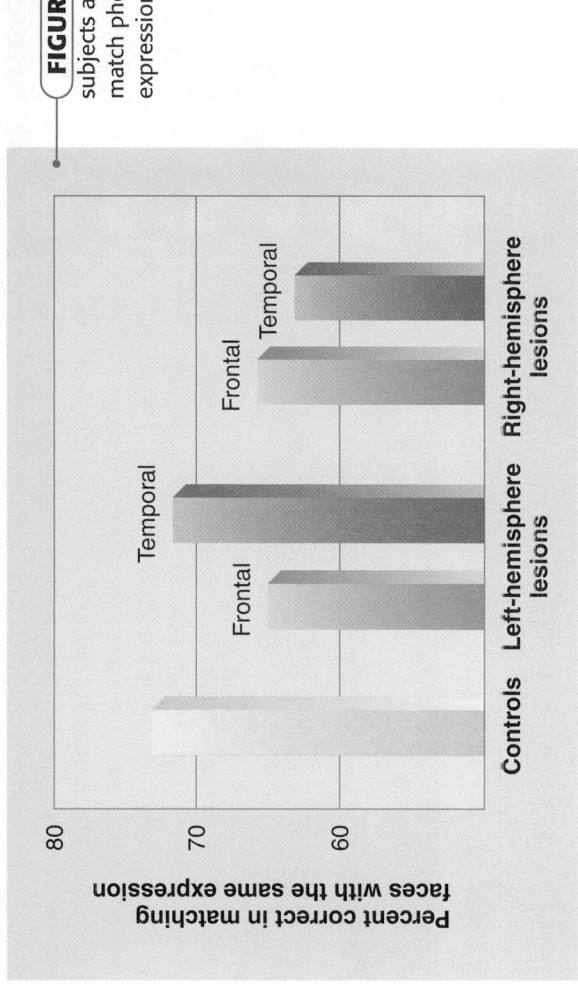

FIGURE 17.12 The ability of control subjects and patients with cortical damage to match photographs of faces on the basis of expression. (Adapted from Kolb & Taylor, 1988.)

ruption (see Figure 17.12). Similarly, there seems to be no difference in the contributions of left and right amygdalae to the recognition of fearful facial expressions (Anderson & Phelps, 2002; Zald, 2003).

The study of lateralization in the production of emotional expression tells a similarly complex story: Whether or not there is right-hemisphere dominance depends on the part of the hemisphere under consideration. For example, although there is a general right-hemisphere dominance for the production of emotional facial expressions, right frontal and left frontal lesions have been found to have an equivalent disruptive effect on such expression (Kolb & Taylor, 2000).

The general right-hemisphere dominance for producing emotional facial expressions is also suggested by a careful study of the emotional expressions themselves. Facial expressions appear to develop sooner and to be of greater magnitude on the left side of the face, which is controlled by the right hemisphere. Remarkably, the same asymmetry of facial expressions has been documented in monkeys (Hauser, 1993)—see Figure 17.13 on page 446.

Clinical Implications

Individual Differences in the Neural Mechanisms of Emotion

Unlike those parts of the brain that play major sensory and motor roles, the parts that play a role in emotion seem to vary substantially from person to person. This, of course, greatly complicates the search for the neural mechanisms of emotion. Let's consider two lines of research and one case study that illustrate individual differences in the organization of the neural mechanisms of emotion.

First, Adolphs and colleagues (1999) tested the ability of nine neuropsychological patients with bilateral amygdalar damage to correctly identify facial expressions of emotion. As others had reported, these researchers found that the group of patients as a whole had difficulty identifying facial expressions of fear. However, there were substantial differences among the subjects: Some also had difficulty identifying other negative emotions, but two had no deficits whatsoever in identifying facial expressions. Remarkably, structural MRIs revealed that both of these two subjects had total bilateral amygdalar lesions. Subsequent testing of these two subjects showed that, in addition to having no deficits in identifying facial expressions of emotion, they had no deficits in judging the similarity of pairs of emotional expressions (Hamann & Adolphs, 1999).

Second, Canli and colleagues (2001) used functional MRIs to compare the reactions of healthy subjects who scored high on *extraversion* with those of healthy subjects who scored high on *neuroticism*. These personality dimensions were selected because of their relation to emotion—people high on the extraversion scale have a tendency toward positive emotional reaction; people high on the neuroticism scale have a tendency toward negative emotional reaction. The reactivity of various parts of the brain to pleasant images was found to be correlated with the degree of extraversion; reactivity to negative images was correlated with the degree of neuroticism. In particular, although all subjects displayed increased activity in the amygdalae when viewing fearful faces, only the extraverts displayed increased amygdalar activity when viewing happy faces (Canli et al., 2002). The finding that the brains of people with different

FIGURE 17.13 A frame-by-frame illustration of a fear grimace in a rhesus monkey (redrawn with permission of Hauser, 1993). Notice that the expression begins on the left side and is of greater magnitude there, thus suggesting right-side dominance for facial expression.

personalities react differently to emotional stimuli suggests that efforts to identify brain reactions to emotional stimuli must consider differences among the subjects.

The following case study ends the chapter by emphasizing the point that the brain mechanisms of emotion differ from person to person. Fortunately, the reactions of Charles Whitman to brain damage are atypical.

The Case of Charles Whitman, the Texas Tower Sniper

Clinical Implications

After having lunch with his wife and his mother, Charles Whitman went home and typed a letter of farewell—perhaps as an explanation for what would soon happen.

He stated in his letter that he was having many compelling and bizarre ideas. Psychiatric care had been no help. He asked that his brain be autopsied after he was through; he was sure that they would find the problem.

By all reports, Whitman had been a good person. An Eagle Scout at 12 and a high school graduate at 17, he then enlisted in the Marine Corps, where he established himself as expert marksman. After his discharge, he entered the University of Texas to study architectural engineering.

Nevertheless, in the evening of August 1, 1966, Whitman killed his wife and mother. He professed love for both of them, but he did not want them to face the aftermath of what was to follow.

The next morning, at about 11:30, Whitman went to the Tower of the University of Texas, carrying six guns, ammunition, several knives, food, and water. He clubbed the receptionist to death and shot four more people on his way to the observation deck. Once on the deck, he opened fire on people crossing the campus and on nearby streets. He was deadly, killing people as far as 300 meters away—people who assumed they were out of range.

At 1:24 that afternoon, the police fought their way to the platform and shot Whitman to death. All told, 17 people, including Whitman, had been killed, and another 31 had been wounded (Helmer, 1986).

An autopsy was conducted. Whitman was correct: They found a walnut-sized tumor in his right amygdala.

Themes Revisited

All four of the book's themes were prevalent in this chapter. The clinical implications theme appeared frequently because brain-damaged patients have taught us much about the neural mechanisms of emotion and because emotions have a major impact on health. The evolutionary perspective theme also occurred frequently because comparative research and the consideration of evolutionary pressures have also had a major impact on current thinking about the biopsychology of emotion.

Clinical Implications

Evolutionary Perspective

Cognitive Neuroscience

Current understanding of the biopsychology of emotion is largely the result of the convergence of evolutionary and comparative approaches with clinical research; however, the cognitive neuroscience approach is starting to play a major role in the study of the neural mechanisms of emotion. Accordingly, the cognitive neuroscience theme came up several times late in the chapter.

The thinking-about-biopsychology theme appeared where the text emphasized the importance of thinking clearly about the use of polygraphy in lie detection, about the relation between testosterone and aggression in men, about the critical interpretation of reports of correlations between stress and ill health, about the possibility of susceptibility to stress being communicated from generation to generation by maternal care, and about the complex structure of the amygdala.

Thinking Critically

ON THE CD

See Hard Copy for additional readings for Chapter 17.

Think about It

1. With practice, you could become an expert in the production and recognition of facial expressions. How could you earn a living with these skills?

2. Does the target-site concept have any relevance to human aggression, defense, and play fighting?

3. Genes are not the only means by which behavioral tendencies can be passed from generation to generation. Discuss, with reference to maternal care and susceptibility to stress.

4. The amygdala is not a single structure. Discuss.

5. Evidence suggests that emotion is a right-hemisphere phenomenon. Discuss.

6. Research on emotion has focused on fear. Why?

ON THE CD

Studying for an exam? Try the Practice Tests for Chapter 17.

Key Terms

Adrenal cortex (p. 436)
Adrenal medulla (p. 436)
Adrenocorticotropic hormone (ACTH) (p. 436)
Aggressive behaviors (p. 433)
Alpha male (p. 433)
Antibodies (p. 438)
Antibody-mediated immunity (p. 437)
Antigens (p. 437)
B cells (p. 437)
Cannon-Bard theory (p. 427)
Cell-mediated immunity (p. 437)

Contextual fear conditioning (p. 443)
Control-question technique (p. 430)
Decorticate (p. 428)
Defensive behaviors (p. 433)
Duchenne smile (p. 432)
Facial feedback hypothesis (p. 432)
Fear (p. 433)
Fear conditioning (p. 441)
Gastric ulcers (p. 436)
Glucocorticoids (p. 436)

Guilty-knowledge technique (p. 430)
Immune system (p. 437)
James-Lange theory (p. 427)
Kluver-Bucy syndrome (p. 428)
Limbic system (p. 428)
Lymphocytes (p. 437)
Macrophage (p. 437)
Phagocytosis (p. 437)
Polygraphy (p. 430)
Prosody (p. 444)
Psychoneuroimmunology (p. 437)
Sham rage (p. 428)

Stress (p. 435)
Subordination stress (p. 436)
Target-site concept (p. 434)
T cells (p. 437)
Urbach-Wiethe disease (p. 444)

ON THE CD

Need some help studying the key terms for this chapter? Check out the electronic flash cards for Chapter 17.

Biopsychology of Psychiatric Disorders

The Brain Unhinged

chapter

18

18.1 Schizophrenia

18.2 Affective Disorders: Depression and Mania

18.3 Anxiety Disorders

18.4 Tourette Syndrome

18.5 Clinical Trials: Development of New Psychotherapeutic Drugs

This chapter is about the biopsychology of *psychiatric disorders*. Before we begin, let's consider the answers to two fundamental questions: What are psychiatric disorders? How do they differ from neuropsychological disorders, which you learned about in Chapter 10?

Defining psychiatric disorders is fairly straightforward: A **psychiatric disorder** (or psychological disorder) is a disorder of psychological function sufficiently severe to require treatment by a psychiatrist or clinical psychologist. Explaining how psychiatric disorders differ from neuropsychological disorders is more difficult because there really are no clear-cut differences between the two types of disorders.

The convention of viewing psychological disorders as being of two fundamentally different types—psychiatric or neuropsychological—is the product of the archaic mind–brain (psychology–biology) dichotomy, discussed in Chapter 2. Neuropsychological disorders are those that were assumed to be products of dysfunctional brains; psychiatric disorders are those that were assumed to be products of dysfunctional minds in the absence of brain pathology. As you will learn in this chapter, there is now plenty of evidence that psychiatric disorders are disorders of dysfunctional brains, and thus the main basis for distinguishing between psychiatric and neuropsychological disorders no longer exists (see Hyman, 2000).

Still, the conventional categories of neuropsychological and psychiatric disorders persist, and there tend to be some differences between them. For example, psychiatric disorders tend to be influenced more by experiential factors (e.g., stress), tend to be the product of more subtle forms of brain pathology, and tend to be less well understood.

This chapter begins with discussion of the biopsychological research on four psychiatric disorders: schizophrenia, affective (emotional) disorders, anxiety disorders, and Tourette syndrome. In each case, you will learn how advances in understanding the neural mechanisms of the disorder have gone hand in hand with the development of therapeutic drugs. For each of the four disorders, the initial breakthrough was the fortuitous discovery of an effective drug; then, study of the drug's mechanisms led to theories of the disorder's neural mechanisms and the development of drugs that are even more effective. The chapter ends with a discussion of the steps involved in establishing the efficacy of new *psychotherapeutic drugs*.

Schizophrenia

The term *schizophrenia* means the splitting of psychic functions. The term was coined in the early years of the 20th century to describe what was assumed at that time to be the primary symptom of the disorder: the breakdown of integration among emotion, thought, and action.

Schizophrenia is the disease that is most commonly associated with the concept of madness. It attacks about 1% of individuals of all races and cultural groups, typically beginning in adolescence or early adulthood. Schizophrenia occurs in many forms, but the case of Lena introduces you to some of its common features.

The Case of Lena, the Catatonic Schizophrenic

Clinical Implications

Lena's mother was hospitalized with schizophrenia when Lena was 2. She died in the hospital under peculiar circumstances, a suspected suicide. As a child, Lena displayed periods of hyperactivity; as an adolescent, she was viewed by others as odd. Although she enjoyed her classes and got good grades, she seldom established relationships with her fellow students. Lena rarely dated. However, she married her husband only a few months after meeting him. He was a quiet man who tried to avoid fuss or stress at all costs and who was attracted to Lena because she was quiet and withdrawn.

Shortly after their marriage, Lena's husband noticed that Lena was becoming even more withdrawn. She would sit for hours barely moving a muscle. He also found her having lengthy discussions with nonexistent persons.

About 2 years after he first noticed her odd behavior, Lena's husband found her sitting on the floor in an odd posture staring into space. She was totally unresponsive. When he tried to move her, Lena displayed *waxy flexibility*—that is, she reacted like a mannequin, not resisting movement but holding her new position until she was moved again. At that point, he took her to the hospital, where her disorder was immediately diagnosed as *stuporous catatonic schizophrenia* (schizophrenia characterized by long periods of immobility and waxy flexibility).

In the hospital, Lena displayed a speech pattern that is displayed by many schizophrenics; *echolalia* (a speech pattern characterized by repetition of some or all of what has just been heard).

Doctor: How are you feeling today?
Lena: I am feeling today, feeling the feelings today.
Doctor: Are you still hearing the voices?
Lena: Am I still hearing the voices, voices?

(Meyer & Salmon, 1988)

What Is Schizophrenia?

The major difficulty in studying and treating schizophrenia is accurately defining it (Andreasen, 2000; Peralta & Cuesta, 2000). Its symptoms are complex and diverse; they overlap greatly with those of other psychiatric disorders, and they frequently change during the progression of the disorder (see Andreasen, 1994; Heinrichs, 1993). As a result, there have been many attempts to break schizophrenia down into several disorders, but none of these attempts has proved successful.

The following are common symptoms of schizophrenia, but none of them appears in all cases. Indeed, the recurrence of only one of these symptoms for 8 months is grounds for the diagnosis of schizophrenia:

Bizarre delusions. Delusions of being controlled (e.g., "Martians are making me think evil thoughts"), delusions of persecution (e.g., "My mother is trying to poison me"), delusions of grandeur (e.g., "Michael Jordan admires my sneakers").

Inappropriate affect. Failure to react with an appropriate level of emotionality to positive or negative events (Keltner, Kring, & Bonanno, 1999; Kring, 1999).

Hallucinations. Imaginary voices telling the person what to do or commenting negatively on the person's behavior.

Incoherent thought. Illogical thinking, peculiar associations among ideas, or belief in supernatural forces.

Odd behavior. Long periods with no movement (*catatonia*), a lack of personal hygiene, talking in rhymes, avoiding social interaction, echolalia.

Causal Factors in Schizophrenia

In the first half of the 20th century, the cloak of mysticism began to be removed from mental illness by a series of studies that established schizophrenia's genetic basis. First, it was discovered that although only 1% of the population develops schizophrenia, the probability of schizophrenia's occurring in a close biological relative (i.e., in a parent, child, or sibling) of a schizophrenic is about 10%, even if the relative was adopted shortly after birth by a healthy family (e.g., Kendler & Gruenberg, 1984; Rosenthal et al., 1980). Then, it was discovered that the concordance rates for schizophrenia are higher in identical twins (45%) than in fraternal twins (10%)—see Holzman and Matthyse (1990) and Kallman (1946). Finally, adoption studies have shown that the risk of schizophrenia is increased by the presence of the disorder in biological parents but not by its presence in adoptive parents (Gottesman & Shields, 1982).

The fact that the concordance rate for schizophrenia in identical twins is substantially less than 100% suggests that differences in experience contribute significantly to

differences among people in the development of schizophrenia. The current view is that some people inherit a potential for schizophrenia, which may or may not be activated by experience. Supporting this view is a recent comparison of the offspring of a large sample of identical twins who were themselves discordant for schizophrenia (i.e., one had the disorder and one did not); the incidence of schizophrenia was as great in the offspring of the nonschizophrenic twins as in the offspring of the schizophrenic twins (Gottesman & Bertelsen, 1989).

It is clear that schizophrenia has multiple causes. Regions on several different chromosomes have been implicated in the vulnerability to schizophrenia (see Cowan, Kopnisky, & Hyman, 2002; Kennedy et al., 2003; Torrey & Yoken, 2000). Also, a variety of early experiential factors have been implicated in the development of schizophrenia—for example, early infections, autoimmune reactions, toxins, traumatic injury, and stress. These early experiences are thought to alter the normal course of neurodevelopment, leading to schizophrenia in individuals with a genetic susceptibility (see Conklin & Iacono, 2002; Lewis & Levitt, 2002).

Discovery of the First Antischizophrenic Drugs

The first major breakthrough in the study of the biochemistry of schizophrenia was the accidental discovery in the early 1950s of the first antischizophrenic drug, **chlorpromazine.** Chlorpromazine was developed by a French drug company as an antihistamine. Then, in 1950, a French surgeon noticed that chlorpromazine given prior to surgery to counteract swelling had a calming effect on some of his patients, and he suggested that it might have a calming effect on difficult-to-handle psychotic patients. His suggestion proved to be incorrect, but the research it triggered led to the discovery that chlorpromazine alleviates schizophrenic symptoms: Agitated schizophrenics were calmed by chlorpromazine, and emotionally blunted schizophrenics were activated by it. Don't get the idea that chlorpromazine cures schizophrenia. It doesn't. But in many cases it reduces the severity of schizophrenic symptoms enough to allow institutionalized patients to be discharged.

Shortly after the antischizophrenic action of chlorpromazine was first documented, an American psychiatrist became interested in reports that the snakeroot plant had long been used in India for the treatment of mental illness. He gave **reserpine**—the active ingredient of the snakeroot plant—to his schizophrenic patients and confirmed its antischizophrenic action. Reserpine is no longer used in the treatment of schizophrenia because it produces a dangerous decline in blood pressure at the doses needed for the treatment.

Although the chemical structures of chlorpromazine and reserpine are dissimilar, their antischizophrenic effects are similar in two major respects. First, the antischizophrenic effect of both drugs is manifested only after a patient has been medicated for 2 or 3 weeks. Second, the onset of the antischizophrenic effect of the medication is usually associated with motor effects similar to the the symptoms of Parkinson's disease: tremors at rest, muscular rigidity, and a general decrease in voluntary movement. These similarities suggested to researchers that chlorpromazine and reserpine were acting through the same mechanism, one that was related to Parkinson's disease.

Dopamine Theory of Schizophrenia

Clinical Implications

Paradoxically, the next major breakthrough in the study of schizophrenia came from research on Parkinson's disease. In 1960, it was reported that the *striatums* (caudates plus putamens) of persons dying of Parkinson's disease had been depleted of dopamine (Ehringer & Hornykiewicz, 1960). This finding suggested that a disruption of dopaminergic transmission might produce Parkinson's disease and, because of the relation between Parkinson's disease and the antischizophrenic effects of chlorpromazine and reserpine, also suggested that antischizophrenic drug effects might be produced in the same way. Thus was born the *dopamine theory of schizophrenia*—the theory that schizophrenia is caused by too much dopamine and, conversely, that antischizophrenic drugs exert their effects by decreasing dopamine levels.

Lending instant support to the dopamine theory of schizophrenia were two already well-established facts.

First, the antischizophrenic drug reserpine was known to deplete the brain of dopamine and other monoamines by breaking down their synaptic vesicles. Second, drugs such as amphetamine and cocaine, which can trigger schizophrenic episodes in normal subjects, were known to increase the extracellular levels of dopamine and other monoamines in the brain.

An important step in the evolution of the dopamine theory of schizophrenia came in 1963, when Carlsson and Lindqvist assessed the effects of chlorpromazine on extracellular levels of dopamine and its *metabolites* (molecules that are created when another molecule is broken down). Although they expected to find that chlorpromazine, like reserpine, depletes the brain of dopamine, they didn't. The extracellular levels of dopamine were unchanged by chlorpromazine, and the extracellular levels of its metabolites were increased. The researchers concluded that both chlorpromazine and reserpine antagonize transmission at dopamine synapses but that they do it in different ways—reserpine by depleting the brain of dopamine and chlorpromazine by binding to dopamine receptors. Carlsson and Lindqvist argued that chlorpromazine is a *receptor blocker* at dopamine synapses—that is, that it binds to dopamine receptors without activating them and, in so doing, keeps dopamine from activating them (see Figure 18.1 on page 452). We now know that many psychoactive drugs are receptor blockers, but chlorpromazine was the first to be identified as such.

Carlsson and Lindqvist further postulated that the lack of activity at postsynaptic dopamine receptors sent a feedback signal to the presynaptic cells that increased their release of dopamine, which was broken down in the synapses. This explained why dopaminergic activity was reduced while extracellular levels of dopamine stayed about the same and extracellular levels of its metabolites were increased. Carlsson and Lindqvist's findings led to an important revision of the dopamine theory of schizophrenia: Rather than high dopamine levels per se, the main factor in schizophrenia was presumed to be high levels of activity at dopamine receptors.

In the mid-1970s, Snyder and his colleagues (Creese, Burt, & Snyder, 1976) assessed the degree to which the various antischizophrenic drugs that had been developed by that time bind to dopamine receptors. First, they added radioactively labeled dopamine to samples of dopamine-receptor-rich neural membrane obtained from calf striatums. Then, they rinsed away the unbound dopamine molecules from the samples and measured the amount of radioactivity left in them to obtain a measure of the number of dopamine receptors. Next, in other samples, they measured each drug's ability to block the binding of radioactive dopamine to the sample, the assumption being that the drugs with a high affinity for dopamine receptors would leave fewer sites available for the dopamine. In general, they found that chlorpromazine and the other effective antischizophrenic drugs had

FIGURE 18.1

Chlorpromazine is a receptor blocker at dopamine synapses. Chlorpromazine was the first receptor blocker to be identified, and its discovery changed psychopharmacology.

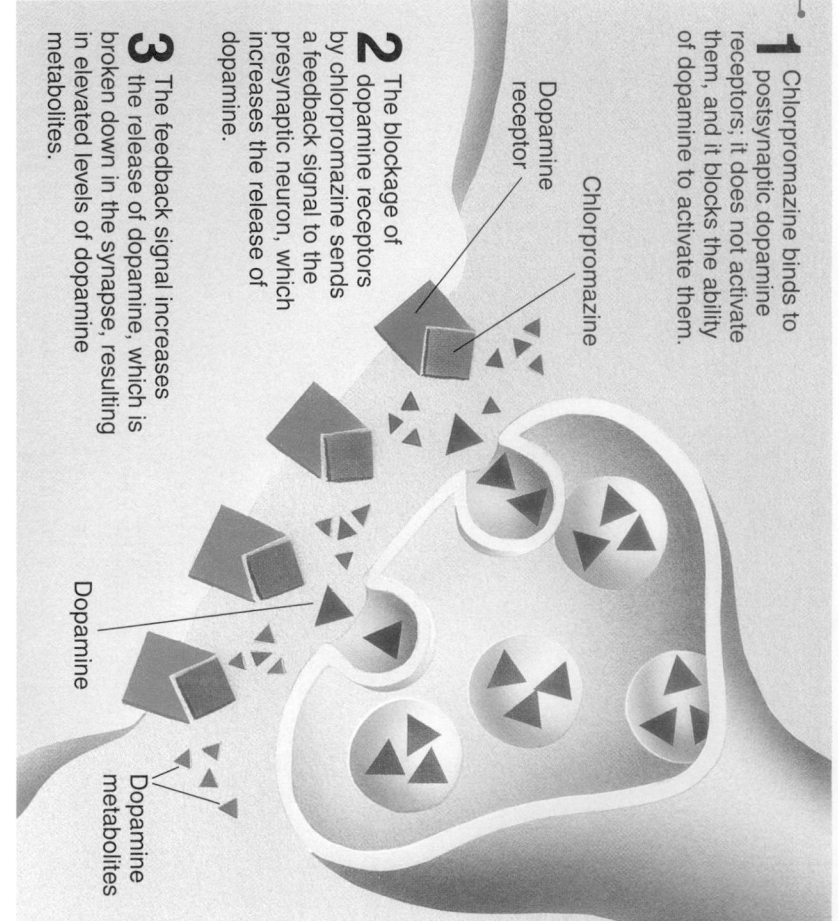

1 Chlorpromazine binds to postsynaptic dopamine receptors; it does not activate them, and it blocks the ability of dopamine to activate them.

Dopamine receptor

Chlorpromazine

2 The blockage of dopamine receptors by chlorpromazine sends a feedback signal to the presynaptic neuron, which increases the release of dopamine.

3 The feedback signal increases the release of dopamine, which is broken down in the synapse, resulting in elevated levels of dopamine metabolites.

Dopamine

Dopamine metabolites

a high affinity for dopamine receptors, whereas ineffective antischizophrenic drugs had a low affinity. There were, however, several major exceptions, one of them being haloperidol. Although **haloperidol** was one of the most potent antischizophrenic drugs of its day, it had a relatively low affinity for dopamine receptors.

A solution to the haloperidol puzzle came with the discovery that dopamine binds to more than one receptor subtype—five have been identified (Hartmann & Civelli, 1997). It turns out that chlorpromazine and the other antischizophrenic drugs in the same chemical class (the **phenothiazines**) all bind effectively to both D_1 and D_2 receptors, whereas haloperidol and the other antischizophrenic drugs in its chemical class (the **butyrophenones**) all bind effectively to D_2 receptors but not to D_1 receptors.

This discovery of the selective binding of butyrophenones to D_2 receptors led to an important revision in the dopamine theory of schizophrenia. It suggested that schizophrenia is caused by hyperactivity specifically at D_2 receptors, rather than at dopamine receptors in general. Snyder and his colleagues (see Snyder, 1978) subsequently confirmed that the degree to which **neuroleptics**—antischizophrenic drugs—bind to D_2 receptors is highly correlated with their effectiveness in

suppressing schizophrenic symptoms (see Figure 18.2). For example, the butyrophenone *spiroperidol* had the greatest affinity for D_2 receptors and the most potent antischizophrenic effect.

ON THE CD

The *Dopamine Theory* module illustrates the main support for this theory by showing how typical neuroleptics block activity at D_2 receptors.

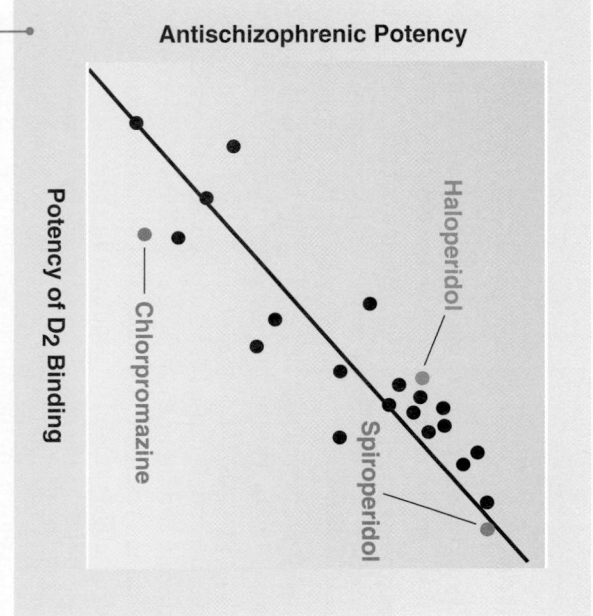

Antischizophrenic Potency

Haloperidol

Chlorpromazine

Spiroperidol

Potency of D₂ Binding

FIGURE 18.2   The positive correlation between the ability of various neuroleptics to bind to D_2 receptors and their clinical potency. (Adapted from Snyder, 1978.)

Current Research on the Neural Basis of Schizophrenia

Although the evidence implicating D_2 receptors in schizophrenia is strong, it has become apparent that the D_2 version of the dopamine theory of schizophrenia cannot explain several key findings. Appreciation of these limitations has led to the current version of the theory. This version holds that excessive activity at D_2 receptors is involved in the disorder but that there are other, as yet unidentified, causal factors. The major events in the development of the dopamine theory are summarized in Table 18.1.

The following are four key discoveries about schizophrenia that cannot be resolved by a strict interpretation of the D_2 version of the dopamine theory. These four discoveries are key to the current view that although overactivity at D_2 receptors plays a major role in schizophrenia, other factors are yet to be identified.

Receptors Other Than D_2 Receptors Are Involved in Schizophrenia

Recent research has implicated neurotransmitters other than dopamine in schizophrenia (see Tallman, 2000). These include glutamate (Javitt & Coyle, 2004; Konradi & Heckers, 2003; Moghaddam,

2003), GABA (Benes & Berretta, 2001), and serotonin (Sawa & Snyder, 2002). The most compelling evidence that D_2 receptors are not the sole mechanism underlying schizophrenia came from the development of *atypical neuroleptics* (antischizophrenic drugs that are not primarily D_2 receptor blockers). For example, **clozapine**, the most effective atypical neuroleptic for the treatment of schizophrenia, has an affinity for D_1 receptors, D_4 receptors, and several serotonin receptors, but only a slight affinity for D_2 receptors.

Clozapine has some promising therapeutic properties. It is often effective in treating schizophrenics who have not responded to typical neuroleptics, and it does not produce Parkinsonian side effects. Unfortunately, the therapeutic utility of clozapine is limited because it produces a severe blood disorder in about 1% of patients who use it (see Wong & Van Tol, 2003).

The discovery of atypical neuroleptics led to qualification of the D_2 theory of schizophrenia rather than its abandonment, for two reasons. First, all of the atypical neuroleptics have been found to bind weakly to D_2 receptors. Second, evidence of the involvement of D_2 receptors in schizophrenia does not rest entirely on the relation between the therapeutic efficacy of drugs and the strength with which they bind to those receptors. For example, recently diagnosed schizophrenics who have not been exposed to neuroleptics have more D_2 receptors and more extracellular dopamine than do nonschizophrenics (Abi-Dargham et al., 2000).

It Takes Several Weeks of Neuroleptic Therapy to Alleviate Schizophrenic Symptoms

As you have already learned, it takes several weeks of neuroleptic therapy to alleviate schizophrenic symptoms. However, neuroleptics effectively block activity at D_2 receptors within hours. This time lag indicates that the blockage of D_2 receptors is not the specific mechanism of the neuroleptics' therapeutic effect. It appears that blocking D_2 receptors triggers some slow-developing compensatory change in the brain that is the key factor in the therapeutic effect. One theory is that this critical slow-acting change is the *dopamine-cell depolarization block* (Grace et al., 1997). Neuroleptics initially increase the firing of dopaminergic neurons, but eventually, at about the time that the therapeutic effects are manifested, there is a general decrease in their firing. This decrease is the dopamine-cell depolarization block.

Schizophrenia Is Associated with Widespread Brain Damage

Brain-imaging studies of schizophrenic patients typically reveal widespread abnormalities, including an abnormally small cerebral cortex and abnormally large cerebral ventricles (see Frith & Dolan, 1998). However, although the brain damage is widespread, it is not evenly distributed. For example, cortical damage is most prevalent in prefrontal, cingulate, and

---

TABLE 18.1   The Key Events That Led to the Development and Refinement of the Dopamine Theory of Schizophrenia

Early 1950s	The antischizophrenic effects of both chlorpromazine and reserpine were documented and related to their Parkinsonian side effects.
Late 1950s	The brains of recently deceased Parkinson's patients were found to be depleted of dopamine.
Early 1960s	It was hypothesized that schizophrenia was associated with excessive activity at dopaminergic synapses.
1960s and early 1970s	Chlorpromazine and other clinically effective neuroleptics were found to act as receptor blockers at dopamine synapses.
Mid-1970s	The affinity of neuroleptics for dopamine receptors was found to be only roughly correlated with their antischizophrenic potency.
Late 1970s	The binding of existing antischizophrenic drugs to D_2 receptors was found to be highly correlated with their antischizophrenic potency.
1980s and 1990s	It became clear that a strict interpretation of the D_2 version of the dopamine theory of schizophrenia cannot account for all of the research findings.

---

medial temporal areas of the cortex. Two things about the pattern of brain damage observed in many schizophrenics are problematic for the dopamine theory: One is that there is little evidence of structural damage to dopaminergic circuits (see Egan & Weinberger, 1997; Nopoulis et al., 2001); the other is that the dopamine theory provides no rationale for the diffuse pattern of brain damage that is often observed.

One major question about the brain pathology of schizophrenics is whether or not it is developmental: Do the brains of schizophrenics develop abnormally, or do they develop normally and then suffer some type of damage? One important finding suggests that schizophrenia is a result of disordered early brain development: The brain pathology associated with schizophrenia tends to be extensive when the disorder is first diagnosed, and there is little evidence of subsequent damage (see Wong, Buckle, & Van Tol, 2000).

Several reports have suggested that normal brain laterality does not develop in the brains of schizophrenics (Rockstroh et al., 1998, 2001; Shapleske et al., 2001). Again, the dopamine theory provides no explanation for this effect.

Neuroleptics Help Only Some Schizophrenics
Typical neuroleptics (i.e., D_2 receptor blockers) do not help all schizophrenics (see Wong & Van Tol, 2003): About 30% are not helped at all, and the remaining usu-

ally gain relief from only some of the symptoms. In general, neuroleptics are more effective in treating *positive schizophrenic symptoms* (such as incoherence, hallucinations, and delusions), which are assumed to be caused by increased neural activity, than they are in treating *negative schizophrenic symptoms* (such as lack of affect, cognitive deficits, and poverty of speech), which are assumed to be caused by brain damage. Many patients who are initially helped by neuroleptics soon develop tolerance to their therapeutic effects and relapse.

The point is that if schizophrenia results from excessive activity at D_2 receptors, then blockers of those receptors should alleviate all symptoms in all schizophrenics. The fact that these drugs do not do so is a challenge to a strict interpretation of the D_2 version of the dopamine theory of schizophrenia.

The fact that neuroleptics help only some patients suggests that the diagnosis of schizophrenia currently encompasses a variety of patients with different disorders. Indeed, many researchers in the field prefer to use "the schizophrenias" to acknowledge that the current diagnostic category undoubtedly includes several related disorders. Until this problem of diagnosis is solved, the development of a better theory and more effective treatments for those diagnosed with schizophrenia will be difficult.

18.2 Affective Disorders: Depression and Mania

All of us have experienced depression. Depression is a normal reaction to grievous loss such as the loss of a loved one, the loss of self-esteem, the loss of personal possessions, or the loss of health. However, there are people whose tendency toward depression is out of proportion. These people repeatedly fall into the depths of despair, and lose the capacity to experience pleasure, often for no apparent reason; and their depression can be so extreme that it is almost impossible for them to meet the essential requirements of their daily lives—to keep a job, to maintain social contacts, or even to maintain an acceptable level of personal hygiene. It is these people who are said to be suffering from clinical **depression.** The case of P.S. introduces you to some of the main features of clinical depression.

The Case of P.S., the Weeping Widow

P.S. was a 57-year-old widow and mother of four. She was generally cheerful and friendly and known for

her meticulous care of her home and children. She took great pride in having reared her children by herself following the death of her husband 14 years earlier.

For no apparent reason, her life began to change. She suddenly appeared more fatigued, less cheerful, and more lackadaisical about her housework. Over the ensuing weeks, she stopped going to church and cancelled all of her regular social engagements, including the weekly family dinner, which she routinely hosted. She started to spend all her time sleeping or rocking back and forth and sobbing in her favorite chair. She wasn't eating, bathing, or changing her clothes. And her house was rapidly becoming a garbage dump. She woke up every morning at about 3:00 A.M. and was unable to get back to sleep.

Things got so bad that her two children who were still living with her called her oldest son for advice. He drove from the nearby town where he lived. What he found reminded him of an episode about 10 years earlier, when his mother had attempted suicide by slitting her wrists.

At the hospital, P.S. answered few questions. She cried throughout the admission interview and sat rocking in her chair wringing her hands and rolling her head up towards the ceiling. When asked to explain what was bothering her, she just shook her head no.

She was placed on a regimen of antidepressant medication. Several weeks later, she was discharged, much improved (Spitzer et al., 1983).

Major Categories of Affective Disorders

Clinical Implications

Depression is not the only *affective disorder* (psychotic disorder of emotion). The other major type is **mania,** which is in many respects the opposite of depression. Mania is an affective disorder characterized by overconfidence, impulsivity, distractibility, and high energy.

During periods of mild mania, people are talkative, energetic, impulsive, positive, and very confident. In this state, they can be very effective at certain jobs and can be great fun to be with. But when mania becomes extreme, it is a serious clinical problem. The florid manic often awakens in a state of unbridled enthusiasm, with an outflow of incessant chatter that careens nonstop from topic to topic. No task is too difficult. No goal is unattainable. This confidence and grandiosity, coupled with high energy, distractibility, and a leap-before-you-look impulsiveness, result in a continual series of disasters. Mania often leaves behind it a trail of unfinished projects, unpaid bills, and broken relationships.

Many depressive patients experience periods of mania. Those who do are said to suffer from **bipolar affective disorder.** Those depressives who do not experience periods of mania are said to suffer from **unipolar affective disorder.**

Depression is often divided into two categories. Depression triggered by a negative experience (e.g., the death of a friend, the loss of a job) is called **reactive depression;** depression with no apparent cause is called **endogenous depression.**

The high incidence of affective disorders in industrialized Western societies has been well documented. About 6% of people suffer from unipolar affective disorder at some point in their lives, and about 1% suffer from bipolar affective disorder. Unipolar affective disorder tends to be twice as prevalent in women as in men, but there is no sex difference in the incidence of bipolar affective disorder. About 10% of those suffering from affective disorders commit suicide (see Culbertson, 1997; Weissman & Olfson, 1995).

Although there is less information about the incidence of affective disorders in nonindustrialized societies, there are indications that culture may play a major role in the disorders—or at least in the tendency to seek treatment for them. For example, in Chile and China, many times more women than men seek treatment for depression (see Kleinman & Cohen, 1997).

Causal Factors in Affective Disorders

Clinical Implications

Genetic factors contribute to differences among people in the development of affective disorders (see MacKinnon, Jamison, & DePaulo, 1997). Twin studies of affective disorders suggest a concordance rate of about 60% for identical twins and 15% for fraternal twins, whether they are reared together or apart. Although there are many exceptions, there is a tendency for affected twins to suffer from the same type of disorder, unipolar or bipolar; and the concordance rates for bipolar disorders tend to be higher than those for unipolar disorders.

Most of the research on the causal role of experience in affective disorders has focused on the role of stress in the etiology of depression. Several studies have shown that stressful experiences can trigger attacks of depression in already depressed individuals. For example, Brown (1993) found that over 84% of a large sample of patients seeking treatment for depression had experienced severe stress in the preceding year, in comparison to 32% of a group of control subjects. However, it has been more difficult to confirm the hypothesis that early exposure to stress increases the likelihood of developing depression in adulthood (Kessler, 1997).

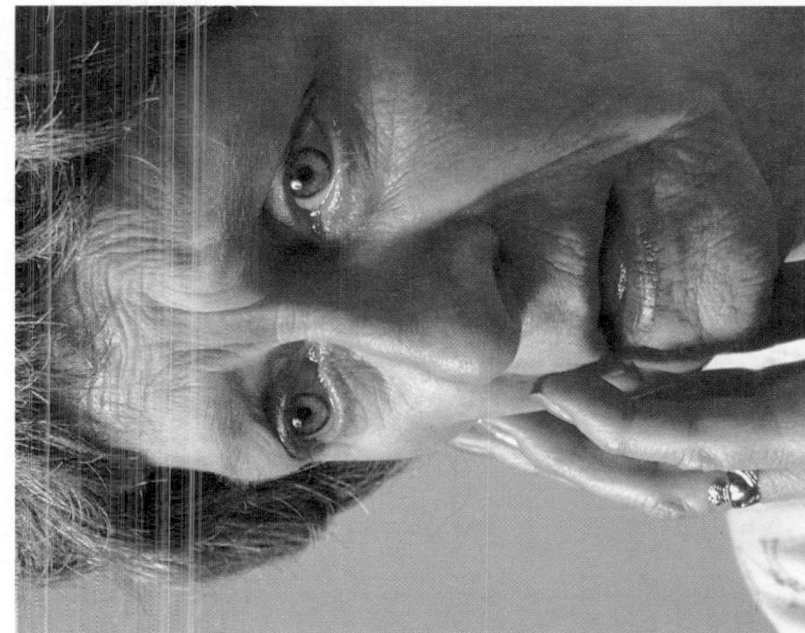

ON THE CD

The module called *Recognizing Mood Disorders (Affective Disorders)* includes a general overview of affective disorders and a 45-second audio clip of a patient describing one such disorder.

Discovery of Antidepressant Drugs

Clinical Implications

Four major classes of drugs are used in the treatment of affective disorders: monoamine oxidase inhibitors, tricyclic antidepressants, lithium, and selective monoamine-reuptake inhibitors.

Monoamine Oxidase Inhibitors *Iproniazid,* the first antidepressant drug, was originally developed for the treatment of tuberculosis, for which it proved to be a dismal flop. However, interest in the antidepressant potential of the drug was kindled by the observation that it left patients with tuberculosis less depressed about their disorder. As a result, iproniazid was tested on a mixed group of psychiatric patients and was found to be effective against depression. It was first marketed as an antidepressant drug in 1957.

Iproniazid is a monoamine agonist; it increases the levels of monoamines (e.g., norepinephrine and serotonin) by inhibiting the activity of *monoamine oxidase* (*MAO*), the enzyme that breaks down monoamine neurotransmitters in the cytoplasm of the neuron. However, people who take MAO inhibitors and consume tyramine-rich foods run the risk of strokes caused by surges in blood pressure.

MAO inhibitors have several side effects; the most dangerous is known as the **cheese effect.** Foods such as cheese, wine, and pickles contain an amine called *tyramine,* which is a potent elevator of blood pressure. Normally, these foods have little effect on blood pressure, because tyramine is rapidly metabolized in the liver by MAO. However, people who take MAO inhibitors and consume tyramine-rich foods run the risk of strokes caused by surges in blood pressure.

Tricyclic Antidepressants The **tricyclic antidepressants** are so named because of their chemical structures include three rings of atoms. **Imipramine,** the first tricyclic antidepressant, was initially thought to be an antischizophrenic drug. However, when its effects on a mixed sample of psychiatric patients were assessed, its antidepressant effect was immediately obvious. Tricyclic antidepressants block the reuptake of both serotonin and norepinephrine, thus increasing their levels in the brain. They are a safer alternative to MAO inhibitors.

Lithium The discovery of the ability of **lithium**—a simple metallic ion—to block mania is yet another important pharmacological breakthrough that was made by accident. John Cade, an Australian psychiatrist, mixed the urine of manic patients with lithium to form a soluble salt; then he injected the salt into a group of guinea pigs to see if it would induce mania. As a control, he injected lithium into another group. Instead of inducing mania, the urine solution seemed to calm the guinea pigs; and Cade concluded that lithium, not uric acid, was the calm-

ing agent. In retrospect, Cade's conclusion was incredibly foolish. We now know that at the doses he used, lithium salts produce extreme nausea. To Cade's untrained eye, his subjects' inactivity may have looked like calmness. But the subjects weren't calm; they were sick. In any case, flushed with what he thought was the success of his guinea pig experiments, in 1954 Cade tried lithium on a group of 10 manic patients, and it proved remarkably effective.

There was little immediate reaction to Cade's report. Few scientists were impressed by Cade's scientific credentials, and few drug companies were interested in spending millions of dollars to evaluate the therapeutic potential of a metallic ion that could not be protected by a patent. Accordingly, the therapeutic potential of lithium was not fully appreciated until the late 1960s, when it was discovered that the ion—in addition to acting against mania—reduced the depression of a few bipolar patients.

Lithium is considered to be a **mood stabilizer,** a drug that blocks the rapid transition between depression and mania rather than treating depression. Until recently, lithium was the treatment of choice for bipolar affective disorder, but it has largely been supplanted by mood stabilizers that are also effective against depression.

Selective Monoamine-Reuptake Inhibitors In the late 1980s, a new class of drugs—the selective serotonin-reuptake inhibitors (SSRIs)—was introduced for treating depression. Selective serotonin-reuptake inhibitors exert agonistic effects on serotonergic transmission by blocking the reuptake of serotonin from synapses—see Figure 18.3.

Fluoxetine, which is marketed as **Prozac,** was the first SSRI to be developed. Now there are many more (e.g., Paxil, Zoloft, Luvox, Remeron). Prozac's structure is a slight variation of that of imipramine and other tricyclic antidepressants; in fact, Prozac is no more effective than imipramine in treating depression. Nevertheless, it was immediately embraced by the psychiatric community and has been prescribed in many millions of cases.

The remarkable popularity of Prozac and other SSRIs is attributable to two things: First, they have few side effects; second, they are effective against a wide range of psychological disorders in addition to depression. Because SSRIs are so effective against disorders that were once considered to be the exclusive province of psychotherapy (e.g., lack of self-esteem, fear of failure, excessive sensitivity to criticism, and inability to experience pleasure), they have had a major impact on psychiatry and clinical psychology.

The success of the SSRIs spawned the introduction of a similar class of drugs, the *selective norepinephrine-reuptake inhibitors* (SNRIs). These (e.g., Reboxetine) have proven to be as effective as the SSRIs in the treatment of depression. Also effective against depression are

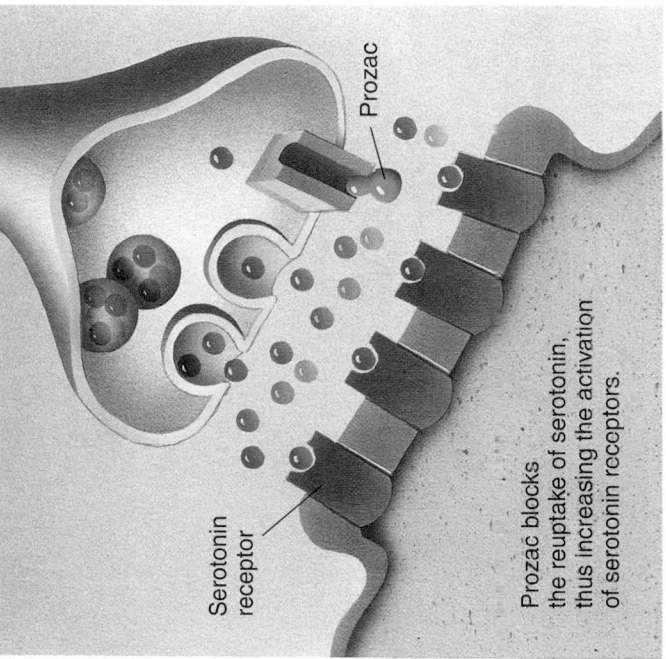

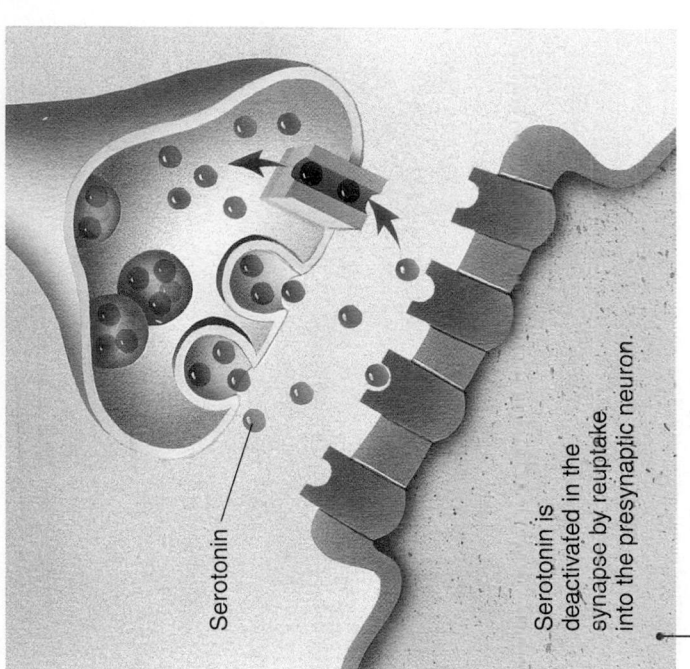

Prozac

Serotonin
receptor

Prozac blocks
the reuptake of serotonin,
thus increasing the activation
of serotonin receptors.

Serotonin

Serotonin is
deactivated in the
synapse by reuptake
into the presynaptic neuron.

FIGURE 18.3 Blocking of serotonin reuptake by fluoxetine (Prozac).

drugs (e.g., Wellbutrin, Effexor) that block the reuptake of more than one monoamine neurotransmitter.

Effectiveness of Drugs in the Treatment of Depression Hollon, Thase, and Markowitz (2002) compared the efficacies of the various pharmacological treatments for depression. The results were about the same for MAO inhibitors, tricyclic antidepressants, and selective monoamine-reuptake inhibitors: About 50% of depressed subjects improved, compared to 25% of the placebo controls. Although all three categories of drugs benefit some patients experiencing attacks of depression, they seem to have little or no effect with regard to prevention of the recurrence of attacks.

Theories of Depression

The search for the neural mechanisms of affective disorders has focused on depression. However, the fact that depression and mania often occur in the same patients—that is, in those with bipolar affective disorder—and the fact that some drugs act against both of these disorders suggest that the mechanisms of the two are closely related.

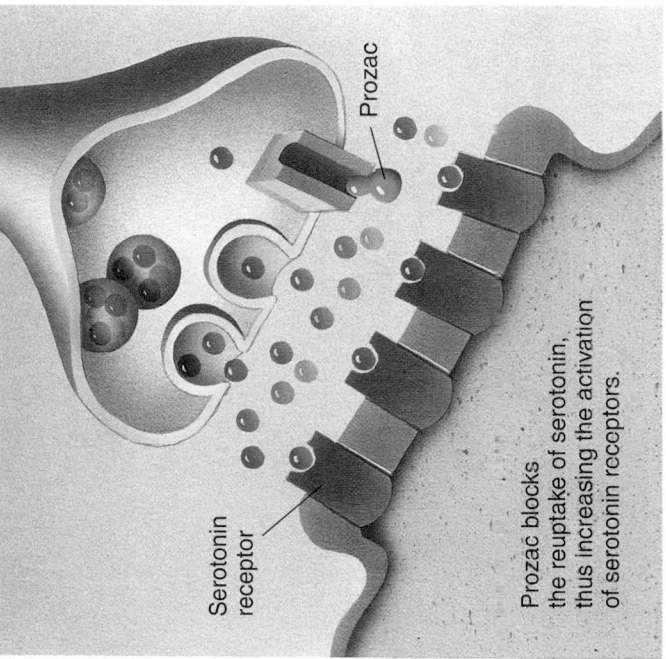

Clinical Implications

Monoamine Theory of Depression The most widely accepted theory of depression is the *monoamine theory*. The monoamine theory of depression holds that depression is associated with underactivity at serotoner-

gic and noradrenergic synapses. It is based on the fact that monoamine oxidase inhibitors, tricyclic antidepressants, selective serotonin-reuptake inhibitors, and selective norepinephrine-reuptake inhibitors are all agonists of serotonin, norepinephrine, or both.

The monoamine theory of depression has been supported by the results of some autopsy studies (see Nemeroff, 1998). Certain subtypes of norepinephrine and serotonin receptors have been found to be elevated in depressed individuals who have not received pharmacological treatment. This implicates a deficit in monoamine release: When an insufficient amount of a neurotransmitter is released at a synapse, there are usually compensatory increases in the number of receptors for that neurotransmitter. This process of compensatory proliferation of receptors is called **up-regulation.**

Overall, support for the monoamine theory of depression is weak. The main problem is that it is largely based on the fact that monoamine agonists are used to treat depressed patients, but this evidence is not so convincing when one considers that only about 25% of patients are actually helped by these treatments.

Diathesis–Stress Model of Depression A second theory of depression is the *diathesis–stress model.* According to this theory (see Nemeroff, 1998), some people inherit a **diathesis** (genetic susceptibility) which is incapable of initiating the disorder by itself. The central idea of the diathesis–stress model is that if susceptible individuals are exposed to stress early in life, their systems become permanently sensitized, and they overreact to mild stressors for the rest of their lives.

Support for the diathesis–stress model of depression is largely indirect: It is based on the finding that depressed people tend to release more stress hormones (see Brown, Rush, & McEwen, 1999; Holsboer, 2000; Young et al., 2000). Depressed individuals synthesize more hypothalamic *corticotropin-releasing hormone*, release more *adrenocorticotropic hormone* from the anterior pituitary, and release more *glucocorticoids* from the adrenal cortex. Moreover, injections of *dexamethasone*, a synthetic glucocorticoid, do not reduce the release of glucocorticoids through negative feedback in many depressed patients, though they do in normal subjects.

Antidepressant Effect of Sleep Deprivation

I would be remiss if I did not point out one of the most puzzling findings about the treatment of depression:

Clinical Implications

More than 50% of depressed patients display dramatic improvements after one night of sleep deprivation (Demet et al., 1999). The antidepressant action of sleep deprivation cannot be explained by current theories of depression. Also, the finding is of little therapeutic relevance because the depression returns once the patients return to their normal sleep pattern. However, studying how sleep deprivation reduces depression may lead to a better understanding of the neural mechanism of depression and to the development of new antidepressant drugs.

Brain Pathology and Affective Disorders

Individuals diagnosed with depression display damage to many parts of their brains (see Kaufman et al., 2001); however, damage is most frequently observed in three areas (see Drevets, 2001). Two of these three areas are the amygdala and the prefrontal cortex, which, as you learned in Chapter 17, play roles in the perception and experience of emotion. The third area comprises several of the terminal sites of the mesotelencephalic dopamine system, which, as you learned in Chapter 15, is involved in the experience of pleasure. Because depressed patients often suffer from **anhedonia**, the inability to experience pleasure, it is not surprising that they would display abnormalities in the striatal and limbic structures of the mesotelencephalic dopamine system.

Cognitive Neuroscience

The discovery—made possible by brain-imaging technology—of structural changes in the brains of patients with unipolar affective disorder is changing the way that people are thinking of the disorder (see Drevets, 2001). It has long been assumed that affective disorders are associated with abnormal brain activity but without structural brain damage. As evidence of structural abnormalities in the brains of depressed patients accumulates, it is becoming more difficult to defend this view.

18.3 Anxiety Disorders

Anxiety—chronic fear that persists in the absence of any direct threat—is a common psychological correlate of stress. Anxiety is adaptive if it motivates effective coping behaviors; however, when it becomes so severe that it disrupts normal functioning, it is referred to as an **anxiety disorder**. All anxiety disorders are associated with feelings of anxiety (e.g., fear, worry, despondency) and with a variety of physiological stress reactions—for example, *tachycardia* (rapid heartbeat), *hypertension* (high blood pressure), nausea, breathing difficulty, sleep disturbances, and high glucocorticoid levels.

Anxiety disorders are the most prevalent of all psychiatric disorders; in Great Britain, for example, 1 in 5 women and 1 in 10 men take antianxiety medication each year (Dunbar, Perera, & Jenner, 1989). An estimated 25% of people suffer from an anxiety disorder at some point in their lives.

The case of M.R., a woman who was afraid to leave her home, serves to introduce anxiety.

The Case of M.R., the Woman Who Was Afraid To Go Out

Clinical Implications

M.R. was a 35-year-old woman who developed a pathological fear of leaving home. The onset of her problem was sudden. Following an argument with her husband, she went out to mail a letter and cool off, but before she could accomplish her task, she was overwhelmed by dizziness and fear. She immediately struggled back to her house and rarely left it again, for about 2 years. Then, she gradually started to improve.

Her recovery was abruptly curtailed, however, by the death of her sister and another argument with her husband. Following the argument, she tried to go shopping, panicked, and had to be escorted home by a stranger. Following that episode, she was not able to leave her house by herself without experiencing an

disorders are characterized by frequently recurring, uncontrollable, anxiety-producing thoughts (obsessions) and impulses (compulsions). Responding to them—for example, by repeated compulsive hand washing—is a means of dissipating the anxiety associated with them. **Posttraumatic stress disorder** is a persistent pattern of psychological distress following exposure to extreme stress (McNally, 2003; McNally, Bryant, & Ehlers, 2003; Newport & Nemeroff, 2000).

M.R., the woman who was afraid to go out, suffered from a common phobic anxiety disorder: agoraphobia. **Agoraphobia** is the pathological fear of public places and open spaces.

Etiology of Anxiety Disorders

Because anxiety disorders are often triggered by identifiable stressful events and because the anxiety is often focused on particular objects or situations, the role of experience in shaping the disorder is often readily apparent (see Anagnostaras, Craske, & Fanselow, 1999). For example, in addition to having agoraphobia, M.R. was obsessed by her health—particularly by high blood pressure, although hers was in the normal range. The fact that both her grandfather and father suffered from high blood pressure and died of heart attacks clearly shaped this component of her disorder.

Like other psychiatric disorders, anxiety disorders have a significant genetic component. The concordance rates for various anxiety disorders are substantially higher for identical twins than for fraternal twins. Still, although identical twins have the same genetic susceptibility to anxiety disorders, the timing and focus of their attacks often reflect their individual experiences (see Gross & Hen, 2004).

Pharmacological Treatment of Anxiety Disorders

Two major classes of drugs are effective against anxiety disorders: benzodiazepines and serotonin agonists.

Benzodiazepines Benzodiazepines such as *chlordiazepoxide* (Librium) and *diazepam* (Valium) are widely prescribed for the treatment of anxiety disorders. They are also prescribed as hypnotics (sleep-inducing drugs), anticonvulsants, and muscle relaxants. Indeed, benzodiazepines are the most widely prescribed psychoactive drugs; approximately 10% of adult North Americans are currently taking them. The benzodiazepines have several adverse side effects: sedation, ataxia (disruption of motor activity), tremor, nausea, addiction, and a withdrawal reaction that includes rebound anxiety. Another serious problem with benzodiazepines is that they are highly

anxiety attack. Shortly after leaving home by herself, she would feel dizzy and sweaty, and her heart would start to pound; at that point, she would flee home to avoid a full-blown panic attack.

Although M.R. could manage to go out if she was escorted by her husband or one of her children, she felt anxious the entire time. Even with an escort, she was terrified of crowds—crowded stores, restaurants, or movie theaters were out of the question.

Five Classes of Anxiety Disorders

There are five major classes of anxiety disorders: generalized anxiety disorders, phobic anxiety disorders, panic disorders, obsessive-compulsive disorders, and posttraumatic stress disorder.

Generalized anxiety disorders are characterized by stress responses and extreme feelings of anxiety that occur in the absence of any obvious precipitating stimulus. **Phobic anxiety disorders** are similar to generalized anxiety disorders except that they are triggered by exposure to particular objects (e.g., birds, spiders) or situations (e.g., crowds, darkness). **Panic disorders** are characterized by rapid-onset attacks of extreme fear and severe symptoms of stress (e.g., choking, heart palpitations, shortness of breath); they are often components of generalized anxiety and phobic disorders, but they also occur as separate disorders. **Obsessive-compulsive**

addictive. Consequently, they should be prescribed only for short-term use (see Gray & McNaughton, 2000).

The behavioral effects of benzodiazepines are thought to be mediated by their agonistic action on $GABA_A$ receptors. Benzodiazepines bind to a $GABA_A$ receptor at a different site than the one at which GABA molecules bind and, in so doing, increase the binding of GABA molecules to the receptor (see Figure 4.18). $GABA_A$ receptors are distributed widely throughout the brain.

Serotonin Agonists Serotonin agonists are also widely used in the treatment of anxiety disorders. For example, *buspirone*, which is often prescribed for the treatment of anxiety, has selective agonist effects at one subtype of serotonin receptor, the 5-HT_{1A} receptor. The main advantage of buspirone over the benzodiazepines is its specificity: It produces *anxiolytic* (antianxiety) effects without producing ataxia, muscle relaxation, and sedation, the common side effects of the benzodiazepines. Buspirone does, however, have other side effects (e.g., dizziness, nausea, headache, and insomnia).

The serotonin agonists that are used to treat depression (i.e., monoamine oxidase inhibitors, tricyclic antidepressants, and selective serotonin-reuptake inhibitors) also tend to have anxiolytic effects. Indeed, SSRIs are also commonly used in the treatment of anxiety disorders.

Animal Models of Anxiety

Evolutionary Perspective

Animal models have played an important role in the study of anxiety and in the assessment of the anxiolytic potential of new drugs (see Gray & McNaughton, 2000; Green, 1991; Treit, 1985). These models typically involve animal defensive behaviors, the implicit assumption being that defensive behaviors are motivated by fear and that fear and anxiety are similar states. Three animal behaviors that model anxiety are elevated-plus-maze performance, defensive burying, and risk assessment.

In the *elevated-plus-maze test*, rats are placed on a four-armed plus-sign–shaped maze that is 50 centimeters above the floor. Two arms have sides and two arms have no sides, and the measure of anxiety is the proportion of time the rats spend in the enclosed arms, rather than venturing onto the exposed arms (see Pellow et al., 1985).

In the *defensive-burying test* (see Figure 5.24), rats are shocked by a wire-wrapped wooden dowel mounted on the wall of a familiar test chamber. The measure of anxiety is the amount of time the rats spend spraying bedding material from the floor of the chamber at the source of the shock with forward thrusting movements of their head and forepaws (see Treit et al., 1993).

In the *risk-assessment test*, after a single brief exposure to a cat on the surface of a laboratory burrow system, rats flee to their burrows and freeze. Then, they engage in a variety of risk-assessment behaviors (e.g., scanning et al., 2000).

the surface from the mouth of the burrow or exploring the surface in a cautious stretched posture) before their behavior returns to normal (see Blanchard, Blanchard, & Rodgers, 1991; Blanchard et al., 1990). The measures of anxiety are the amounts of time that the rats spend in freezing and in risk assessment.

The elevated-plus-maze, defensive-burying, and risk-assessment tests of anxiety have all been validated by demonstrations that benzodiazepines reduce the various indexes of anxiety used in the tests, whereas nonanxiolytic drugs usually do not. There is a potential problem with this line of evidence, however. The potential problem stems from the fact that many cases of anxiety do not respond well to benzodiazepine therapy. Accordingly, existing animal models of anxiety may be models of benzodiazepine-sensitive anxiety rather than of anxiety in general, and thus the models may not be sensitive to anxiolytic drugs that act by a different (i.e., a non-GABA-ergic) mechanism. For example, the serotonin agonist *buspirone* does not have a reliable anxiolytic effect in the elevated-plus-maze test.

Neural Bases of Anxiety Disorders

Clinical Implications

Like current theories of the neural bases of schizophrenia and depression, current theories of the neural bases of anxiety disorders rest heavily on the analysis of therapeutic drug effects. The fact that many anxiolytic drugs are agonists at either $GABA_A$ receptors (e.g., the benzodiazepines) or serotonin receptors (e.g., buspirone and Prozac) has focused attention on the possible role in anxiety disorders of deficits in both GABAergic and serotonergic transmission.

Speculations about the brain structures involved in anxiety disorders have focused on the amygdala because of the central role it plays in fear and defensive behavior (see LeDoux, 1995). In support of the involvement of the amygdala in anxiety disorders are the following findings: The amygdala has a high concentration of $GABA_A$ receptors, local infusion of benzodiazepines into the amygdala produces anxiolytic effects in laboratory animals, and local injections of GABA antagonists into the amygdala can block the anxiolytic effects of *systemic* (into general circulation) injections of benzodiazepines (see Davis, Rainie, & Cassell, 1994).

Cognitive Neuroscience

Brain-imaging studies of patients suffering from anxiety have not revealed obvious structural pathology in the amygdala or any other brain structure. In contrast, many functional brain changes have been reported, but so far none has been consistently replicated. The likely problem is that anxiety is such a broad diagnostic category that brain images that are obtained by averaging observations from several subjects are inevitably clouded by variability among subjects (Reiman

18.4 Tourette Syndrome

Tourette syndrome is the last of the four psychiatric disorders discussed in this chapter. It differs from the first three (schizophrenia, affective disorders, and anxiety) in the specificity of its effects. And they are as interesting as they are specific. The case of R.G. introduces you to Tourette syndrome.

Clinical Implications

The Case of R.G.—Barking Mad

Clinical Implications

When R.G. was 15, he developed *tics* (involuntary, repetitive, stereotyped movements or vocalizations). For the first week, his tics took the form of involuntary blinking, but after that they started to involve other parts of the body, particularly his arms and legs.

R.G. and his family were religious, so it was particularly distressing when his tics became verbal. He began to curse repeatedly and involuntarily. Involuntary cursing is a common symptom of Tourette syndrome and of several other psychiatric and neurological disorders (Van Lancke & Cummings, 1999). R.G. also started to bark like a dog. Finally, he developed echolalia: When his mother said, "Dinner is ready," he responded, "Is ready, is ready?"

Prior to the onset of R.G.'s symptoms, he was an A student, apparently happy and with an outgoing, engaging personality. Once his symptoms developed, he was jeered at, imitated, and ridiculed by his schoolmates. He responded by becoming anxious, depressed, and withdrawn. His grades plummeted.

Once R.G. was taken to a psychiatrist by his parents, his condition was readily diagnosed—the symptoms of Tourette syndrome are unmistakable. Medication eliminated 99% of his symptoms, and once his disorder was explained to him and he realized he was not mad, he resumed his former outgoing manner (Spitzer et al., 1983).

(Jankovic, 2001; Leckman et al., 2001). It typically begins in childhood with simple motor tics, such as eye blinking or head movements, but the symptoms develop over time, becoming more complex and severe. Common complex motor tics include making lewd gestures, hitting, touching objects, squatting, hopping, and twirling. Common verbal tics include inarticulate sounds (e.g., barking, coughing, grunting), *coprolalia* (uttering obscenities), *echolalia* (repetition of another's words), and *palilalia* (repetition of one's own words).

Tourette syndrome develops in approximately 0.7% of children and is three times more frequent in males than in females. There is a major genetic component: Concordance rates are 55% for identical twins and 8% for fraternal twins (see Pauls, 2001).

Some patients with Tourette syndrome also display signs of *attention-deficit/hyperactivity disorder*, obsessive-compulsive disorder, or both (Sheppard et al., 1999). For example, R.G. was obsessed by odd numbers and refused to sit in even-numbered seats.

Many people with Tourette syndrome experience no symptoms other than tics. Accordingly, if their friends, family members, and colleagues are understanding and supportive, these people can live happy, productive lives—for example, Tim Howard (shown in the photo) is goalkeeper for Manchester United, one of the top soccer teams in the world.

What Is Tourette Syndrome?

Tourette syndrome is a disorder of **tics** (involuntary, repetitive, stereotyped movements or vocalizations)

Although the tics of Tourette syndrome are involuntary, they can be suppressed for brief periods of time with great concentration and effort from the patient. However, if they are suppressed, a discomfort or tension builds up in the body, which is eventually released in the form of a bout of particularly frequent and intense tics.

Imagine how difficult it would be to get on with your life if you suffered from an extreme form of Tourette syndrome—for example if you frequently grabbed your genitals and started barking like a dog. No matter how intelligent, capable, and kind you were inside, not many people would be willing to socialize with or employ you (see Kushner, 1999).

Impediments to the Study of the Neuropathology of Tourette Syndrome

Little is known about the neural mechanisms of Tourette syndrome, in part because of several major impediments that make studying them difficult (see Swerdlow & Young, 2001). The following are three of these: First, there are no animal models of Tourette syndrome; as a result, controlled experiments are difficult, and studies that involve direct manipulation of the brain are impossible. Second, no particular genes have yet been implicated in the development of the disorder, and thus a potentially important source of clues about its neurochemical basis is absent. Third, because of the involuntary movements that characterize the disorder, brain imaging is difficult and must be restricted to brief periods during which patients are capable of controlling their tics.

Brain Mechanisms of Tourette Syndrome

Little information can be gleaned about Tourette syndrome from published postmortem neuropathological investigations. Remarkably, this literature describes only seven cases, and all of these are complicated by ambiguities of diagnosis and the coexistence of other disorders, such as epilepsy (see Swerdlow & Young, 2001).

This shortage of postmortem studies of the brains of Tourette patients is not a chance situation. Tourette patients typically receive most of their medical care in

childhood, when they first display signs of the disorder and the symptoms are most severe. Thus, when they die, they are usually no longer in contact with the specialists who treated them as children, and thus their brains are rarely examined for links to Tourette syndrome. Consequently, the few brains that have been subjected to postmortem study have been brains of atypical Tourette patients who were receiving neurological care just prior to their death.

Many abnormalities have been reported in functional brain images of Tourette patients who are actively

suppressing their tics. However, most of these abnormalities have not been replicated—with two exceptions (Peterson, 2001). First, abnormalities are almost always observed in the basal ganglia. Second, abnormalities are commonly observed in the cortex, particularly in areas of limbic and association cortex. You may recall that the basal ganglia are part of a major feedback circuit: They receive input from many areas of the cortex, and much of their output goes to the thalamus, which in turn projects back to many areas of the cortex. The results of functional brain-imaging studies suggest that the neuropathology of Tourette syndrome lies in this circuit.

Treatment of Tourette Syndrome

Although tics are the defining feature of Tourette syndrome, treatment typically begins by focusing on other aspects of the disorder. First, the patient, family members, friends, and teachers are educated about the nature of the syndrome. Second, the treatment focuses on the ancillary emotional problems (e.g., anxiety and depression). Once these first two steps have been taken, attention turns to treating the symptoms.

The tics of Tourette syndrome are usually treated with *neuroleptics* (the D_2 receptor blockers that are used in the treatment of schizophrenia). However, there have been few controlled studies demonstrating the effectiveness of these drugs against Tourette syndrome (Lang, 2001; Riddle & Carlson, 2001).

The apparent success of D_2 receptor blockers in the treatment of Tourette syndrome is consistent with the hypothesis that the disorder is related to an abnormality of the basal ganglia–thalamus–cortex feedback circuit. In particular, the efficacy of these drugs implicates the *striatum*, which is the target of many of the dopaminergic projections into the basal ganglia. The current hypothesis is that Tourette syndrome is a neurodevelopmental disorder that results from excessive dopaminergic innervation of the striatum and the associated limbic cortex (see Jankovic, 2001).

Tourette syndrome has been P.H.'s problem for more than three decades (Hollenbeck, 2001). Taking advantage of his position as a medical school faculty member, he regularly offers a series of lectures on the topic. Along with students, many other Tourette patients and their families are attracted to his lectures.

Encounters with Tourette patients of his own generation taught P.H. a real lesson. He was astounded to learn that most of them did not have his thick skin. About half of them were still receiving treatment for psychological wounds inflicted during childhood.

For the most part, these patients' deep-rooted pain and anxiety did not result from the tics themselves. They derived from being ridiculed and tormented by others and from the self-righteous advice repeatedly offered by well-meaning "clods." "The malfunction may be in the basal ganglia, but in reality this is more a disorder of the onlooker than of the patient.

There is no character, howsoever good and fine, but it can be destroyed by ridicule, howsoever poor and witless.

MARK TWAIN

18.5 Clinical Trials: Development of New Psychotherapeutic Drugs

Almost daily, there are news reports of exciting discoveries that appear to be pointing to effective new therapeutic drugs or treatments. But most often, the promise does not materialize. For example, almost 50 years after the revolution in molecular biology began, not a single form of gene therapy is yet in use. The reason is that the journey of a drug or other medical treatment from promising basic research to useful reality is excruciatingly complex, time-consuming, and expensive.

You have no true appreciation of the difficulties of developing psychotherapeutic drugs after reading the preceding sections of this chapter because, so far, the chapter has focused on early drug discoveries and their role in the development of theories of psychiatric dysfunction. In the early years, the development of psychotherapeutic drugs was largely a hit-or-miss process. New drugs were tested on patient populations with little justification and then quickly marketed to an unsuspecting public, often before it was discovered that they were ineffective for their original purpose.

Things have changed. The testing of experimental drugs on human subjects and their subsequent release for sale are now strictly regulated by government agencies.

The process of gaining permission from the government to market a new psychotherapeutic drug begins with the synthesis of the drug, the development of procedures for synthesizing it economically, and the collection of evidence from nonhuman subjects showing that the drug is likely safe for human consumption and has potential therapeutic benefits. These initial steps take a long time—at least 5 years—and only if the evidence is sufficiently promising is permission granted to proceed to clinical trials. **Clinical trials** are studies conducted on human subjects to assess the therapeutic efficacy of an untested drug or other treatment. This entire process is summarized in Table 18.2 on page 464.

This final section of the chapter focuses on the process of conducting clinical trials. But before we begin, I want to emphasize the critical role played by research on nonhuman subjects in the development of effective therapeutic drugs for human patients. Without a solid foundation of comparative research, it is extremely difficult to gain governmental permission to begin clinical trials.

Clinical Trials: The Three Phases

Once approval has been obtained from the appropriate government agencies, clinical trials of a new drug with therapeutic potential can commence. Clinical trials are conducted in three separate phases: (1) screening for safety, (2) establishing the testing protocol, and (3) the final tests (see Zivin, 2000).

Screening for Safety The purpose of the first phase of a clinical trial is to determine whether the drug is safe for human use and, if it is, to determine how much of the drug can be tolerated. Administering the drug to humans for the first time is always a risky process because there is no way of knowing for certain how they will respond. The subjects in phase 1 are typically healthy paid volunteers. Phase 1 clinical trials always begin with tiny injections, which are gradually increased as the tests proceed. The reactions of the subjects are meticulously monitored, and once strong adverse reactions are observed, phase 1 is curtailed. It usually requires about 1.5 years and about $10 million to complete phase 1.

Establishing the Testing Protocol The purpose of the second phase of a clinical trial is to establish the *protocol* (the conditions) under which the final tests are likely to provide a clear result. For example, in phase 2, researchers hope to discover which doses are likely to be therapeutically effective, how frequently they should be administered, how long they need to be administered to have a therapeutic effect, what benefits are likely to occur, and which patients are likely to be helped. Phase 2 tests are conducted on patients suffering from the target disorder; the tests usually include *placebo-control groups*

TABLE 18.2 Phases of Drug Development

TABLE 18.2 Phases of Drug Development

TIME		BASIC RESEARCH	COST
At least 5 years		Discovery of the drug, development of efficient methods of synthesis, and testing with animal models	
About 1 year		Application to begin clinical trials and the review of basic research by government agency	
		HUMAN CLINICAL TRIALS	
About 1.5 years	**Phase I**	Screening for safety and finding the maximum safe dose	About $10 million
About 2 years	**Phase II**	Establishing most effective doses and schedules of treatment	About $20 million
About 3.5 years	**Phase III**	Clear demonstrations that the drug is therapeutic	About $45 million
About 1.5 years		**Application to begin marketing and reviews of results of clinical trials by government agency**	
		SELLING TO THE PUBLIC	
Ongoing		Recovering development costs and continuing to monitor the safety of the drug	

Source: Adapted from Zivin (2000).

(groups of subjects who receive a control substance rather than the drug), and their designs are *double-blind*—that is, the tests are conducted so that neither the patients nor the physicians interacting with them know which treatment (drug or placebo) each patient has received. It typically requires about 2 years and about $20 million to complete phase 2.

The Final Tests   Phase 3 of a clinical trial is typically a double-blind, placebo-control study on large numbers—often, many thousands—of patients suffering from the target disorder. The design of the phase 3 tests is based on the results of phase 2 so that the final tests are likely to demonstrate positive therapeutic effects, if these exist. The first test of the final phase is often not conclusive, but if it is promising, a second test based on a redesigned protocol may be conducted. In most cases, two independent successful tests are required to convince government regulatory agencies. A successful test is one in which the beneficial effects are substantially greater than the adverse side effects. The typical length of the final test phase is about 3.5 years, and the typical cost is about $45 million.

Controversial Aspects of Clinical Trials

The clinical trial process is not without controversy, as is clear from the following major focuses of criticism and debate (Zivin, 2000).

Requirement for Double-Blind Design and Placebo Controls   In most clinical trials, patients are assigned to drug or placebo groups randomly and do not know for sure which treatment they are receiving (see Woods et al., 2001). Accordingly, some patients whose only hope for recovery may be the latest experimental treatment will, without knowing it, receive the placebo. Drug companies and government agencies concede that this is true, but they argue that there can be no convincing evidence that the experimental treatment is effective until a double-blind, placebo-control trial is complete. Because psychiatric disorders often improve after a placebo, a double-blind, placebo-control procedure is essential in the evaluation of any psychotherapeutic drug.

The Need for Active Placebos   The double-blind, placebo-control procedure seems perfect for clinical testing, but it isn't (see Salamone, 2000). At therapeutic doses, many drugs have side effects that are obvious to people taking them, and thus the subjects in double-blind, placebo-control studies who receive the drug can be certain that they are not in the placebo group. This knowledge may greatly contribute to the positive effects of the drug, independent of any real therapeutic effect. Accordingly, it is now widely recognized that an active placebo is better than an inert placebo as the control drug. **Active placebos** are control drugs that have

Thinking Critically

Thinking Critically

no therapeutic effect but produce side effects similar to those produced by the drug under evaluation.

Length of Time Required Patients desperately seeking new treatments are frustrated by the amount of time needed for clinical trials. Accordingly, researchers, drug companies, and government agencies are striving to speed up the evaluation process, but without sacrificing the quality of the procedures designed to protect patients from ineffective treatments.

Financial Issues The drug companies pay the scientists, physicians, technicians, assistants, and patients involved in drug trials. Considering the millions they spend and the fact that only 20% of the candidate drugs entering phase 1 testing ever gain final approval (Zivin, 2000), it should come as no surprise that drug companies are anxious to recoup their costs. In view of this pressure, many have questioned the impartiality of those conducting the trials. The scientists themselves have often complained that drug companies make them sign agreements that prohibit them from publishing or discussing negative findings without the consent of the sponsoring company.

Another financial issue is the fact that drug companies seldom develop drugs to treat rare disorders because such treatments will not be profitable. Drugs for which the market is too small for them to be profitable are called *orphan drugs*. Acts have been passed by governments in Europe and North America to promote the development of orphan drugs (see Maeder, 2003).

Effectiveness of Clinical Trials

Despite the controversy that surrounds the clinical trial process, there is no question that it works.

A long, dismal history tells of charlatans who make unfounded promises and take advantage of people at the time when they are least able to care for themselves. The clinical trial process is the most objective method ever devised to assess the efficacy of a treatment. It is expensive and slow, and in need of constant refinements, and oversight, but the process is trustworthy. (Zivin, 2000, p.75)

Certainly, the clinical trial process is far from perfect. For example, concerns about the ethics of randomized double-blind, placebo-control studies are often warranted. Still, the vast majority of those in the medical and research professions accept that these studies are the essential critical test of any new therapy. This is particularly true of psychotherapeutic drugs because psychiatric disorders often respond to placebo treatments and because assessment of their severity is subjective and can be greatly influenced by the expectations of the therapist.

Everybody agrees that clinical trials are too expensive and take too long. But one expert responds to this concern in the following way: Clinical trials can be trustworthy, fast, or cheap; but in any one trial, only two of the three are possible (Zivin, 2000). Think about it.

It is important to realize that every clinical trial is carefully monitored as it is being conducted. Any time the results warrant it, changes to the research protocol are made to reduce costs and the time required to deliver an effective treatment to patients in need—particularly to the placebo subjects who participated in the clinical trials.

Conclusion The chapter, and indeed the book, ends with the case of S.B., who suffers from bipolar affective disorder. S.B.'s case is appropriate here because S.B. benefited greatly from the clinical trial process and because S.B.'s case demonstrates the value of a biopsychological education that stresses clear thinking and the importance of taking responsibility for one's own health. You see, S.B. took a course similar to the one that you are currently taking, and the things that he learned in the course enabled him to steer his own treatment to a positive outcome.

The Case of S.B., the Biopsychology Student Who Took Control

I met S.B. when he was a third-year undergraduate. That year, he was a student in my biopsychology course, and he also volunteered to work in my laboratory. S.B. is a quiet, pleasant, shy person; he has an unassuming manner, but he is kind, knowledgeable, and intelligent, with broad interests. For example, I was surprised to learn that he was a skilled artist, interested in medical illustration, so we chatted at length about the illustrations in this book.

I was delighted to discover that S.B.'s grades confirmed my positive impression of him. He had the highest grades in the program. In addition, it soon became apparent that he had a real "touch" for research, so I invited him to become my graduate student. He accepted and has been truly exceptional. As you can tell, I am very proud of him.

S.B. is now going to describe his case to you in his own words. I wanted to tell you about him myself so that you would have a clear picture of his situation. As you are about to discover, S.B.'s view of himself, obscured by a black cloud of depression, often bears little relation to reality.

As an undergraduate student, I suffered from depression. Although my medication improved things somewhat, I still felt stupid, disliked, and persecuted. There were some positives in my undergraduate years. Dr.

Pinel was very good to me, and I liked his course. He always emphasized that the most important part of his course was learning to be an independent thinker, and I was impressed by how he had been able to diagnose his own brain tumor. I did not appreciate at the time just how important these lessons would be.

A few months after beginning graduate school, my depression became so severe that I could not function. My psychiatrist advised me to take a leave of absence, which I did. I returned a few months later, filled with antipsychotics and antidepressants, barely capable of keeping things together.

You can appreciate how pleased I was 2 years later, when I started to snap out of it. It occurred to me that I was feeling better than I had ever felt. My productivity and creativity increased. I read, wrote, and drew, and new ideas for experiments flooded into my head. Things were going so well that I found that I was sleeping only 2 or 3 hours a night, and my brain was so energized that my friends sometimes begged me to talk more slowly so that they could follow what I was saying.

But my euphoria soon came to an abrupt end. I was still energetic and creative, but the content of my ideas changed. My consciousness was again dominated by feelings of inferiority, stupidity, and persecution. Thoughts of suicide were a constant companion.

As a last resort, I called my psychiatrist, and when she saw me, she immediately had me committed. My diagnosis was bipolar affective disorder with a *mixed episode*. As she explained, mixed episodes are transition states between mania and depression and are associated with particularly high suicide rates.

Heavily sedated, I slept for much of the first week. When I came out of my stupor, two resident psychiatrists informed me that I would be placed on a mood stabilizer and would likely have to take it for the rest of my life. Two things made me feel uncomfortable about this. First, many patients in the ward were taking this drug, and they seemed like bloated zombies; second, my physicians seemed to know less about this drug and its mechanisms than I did. So I requested that they give me access to the hospital library so I could learn about my disorder and drug. In effect, I was pulling a "Pinel."

I was amazed by what I found. The drug favored by the residents had been shown several months before to be no more effective in the treatment of bipolar affective disorder than an active placebo. Moreover, a new drug that had recently cleared clinical trials was proving very effective with few side effects.

When I confronted my psychiatrists with this evidence, they were astounded and agreed to prescribe the new drug. Today, I am feeling well and am enjoying graduate school. I still find it difficult to believe that I had enough nerve to question my physicians and prescribe for myself. I never imagined that the lessons learned from this book would have such a positive impact on my life. I am glad that I could tell you my story, and I hope that you benefit from it.

(Used by permission of Steven Barnes.)

Themes Revisited

This entire chapter focused on psychiatric disorders, so it should come as no surprise that the clinical implications theme was predominant. Nevertheless, the other three major themes of this book also received substantial coverage.

Clinical Implications

The thinking-about-biopsychology theme arose during the discussions of the differences between psychiatric and neuropsychological disorders, the diagnosis of schizophrenia, and the reasons why postmortem studies of typical Tourette patients are rare. The thinking-about-biopsychology theme also arose several times during the description of clinical trials.

Thinking Critically

The cognitive neuroscience theme was apparent in the discussion of functional brain-imaging studies of affective disorders, anxiety disorders, and Tourette syndrome. Functional brain-imaging studies have been important in the study of these particular disorders because structural correlates have not been identified.

Cognitive Neuroscience

The evolutionary perspective theme came up twice: in the section on animal models of anxiety and in the discussion of the important role played by research on nonhuman subjects in gaining official clearance to commence human clinical trials.

Evolutionary Perspective

ON THE CD
See Hard Copy for additional readings for Chapter 18.

ON THE CD
Studying for an exam? Try the Practice Tests for Chapter 18.

Think about It

1. Blunders often play an important role in scientific progress. Discuss this with respect to the development of drugs for the treatment of psychiatric disorders.

2. The mechanism by which a disorder is alleviated is not necessarily opposite to the mechanism by which it was caused. Discuss this with respect to the evidence supporting current theories of schizophrenia, depression, and anxiety.

3. Discuss the diathesis-stress model of depression. Design an experiment to test the model.

4. Judge people by what they do, not by what they say. Discuss this recommendation with respect to Tourette syndrome.

5. Tourette syndrome is a disorder of onlookers. Explain and discuss.

6. Clinical trials are no more than excessive government bureaucracy. The prescription of drugs should be left entirely to the discretion of physicians. Discuss.

Key Terms

Active placebos (p. 464)
Agoraphobia (p. 459)
Anhedonia (p. 458)
Anxiety (p. 458)
Anxiety disorder (p. 458)
Benzodiazepines (p. 459)
Bipolar affective disorder (p. 455)
Butyrophenones (p. 452)
Cheese effect (p. 456)
Chlorpromazine (p. 450)
Clinical trials (p. 463)
Clozapine (p. 453)

Depression (p. 454)
Diathesis (p. 457)
Endogenous depression (p. 455)
Generalized anxiety disorders (p. 459)
Haloperidol (p. 452)
Imipramine (p. 456)
Iproniazid (p. 456)
Lithium (p. 456)
Mania (p. 455)
MAO inhibitors (p. 456)
Mood stabilizer (p. 456)

Neuroleptics (p. 452)
Obsessive-compulsive disorders (p. 459)
Panic disorders (p. 459)
Phenothiazines (p. 452)
Phobic anxiety disorders (p. 459)
Posttraumatic stress disorder (p. 459)
Prozac (p. 456)
Psychiatric disorder (p. 449)
Reactive depression (p. 455)
Reserpine (p. 451)

Tics (p. 461)
Tricyclic antidepressants (p. 456)
Unipolar affective disorder (p. 455)
Up-regulation (p. 457)

ON THE CD

Need some help studying the key terms for this chapter? Check out the electronic flash cards for Chapter 18.

Epilogue

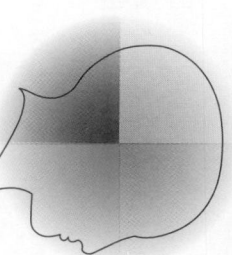

feel relieved to be finishing the edition that I began almost 2 years ago, and I am excited by the prospect of being able to speak to so many students like you through this edition and its CD. You must also feel relieved to be finishing this book; still, I hope that you feel a tiny bit of regret that our time together is over.

Like good friends, we have shared good times and bad. We have shared the fun and wonder of Rhonda, the dexterous cashier; the Nads basketball team; people who rarely sleep; the "mamawawa"; split brains; and brain transplantation. But we have also been touched by many personal tragedies: for example, the victims of Alzheimer's disease and MPTP poisoning; the lost mariner; H.M.; the man who mistook his wife for a hat; Professor P., the biopsychologist who experienced brain surgery from the other side of the knife; and his graduate student, S.B., who guided the treatment of his own disease. Thank you for allowing me to share *Biopsychology* with you. I hope you have found it to be an enriching experience.

Our mutual experiences have transcended space and time. Right now, I am sitting at my desk looking out over my garden and the Pacific Ocean, as the neighborhood finches celebrate the completion of this edition and the first wave of spring flowers with a song. It is 7:00 A.M. on Saturday, April 30, 2005. Where and when are you?

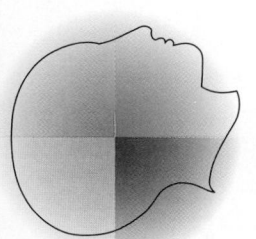

Appendixes

Appendix I   The Autonomic Nervous System

Appendix II   Some Functions of Sympathetic and Parasympathetic Neurons

Appendix III   The Cranial Nerves

Appendix IV   Functions of the Cranial Nerves

Appendix V   Nuclei of the Thalamus

Appendix VI   Nuclei of the Hypothalamus

Appendix I
The Autonomic Nervous System

Parasympathetic Pathways

Sympathetic Pathways

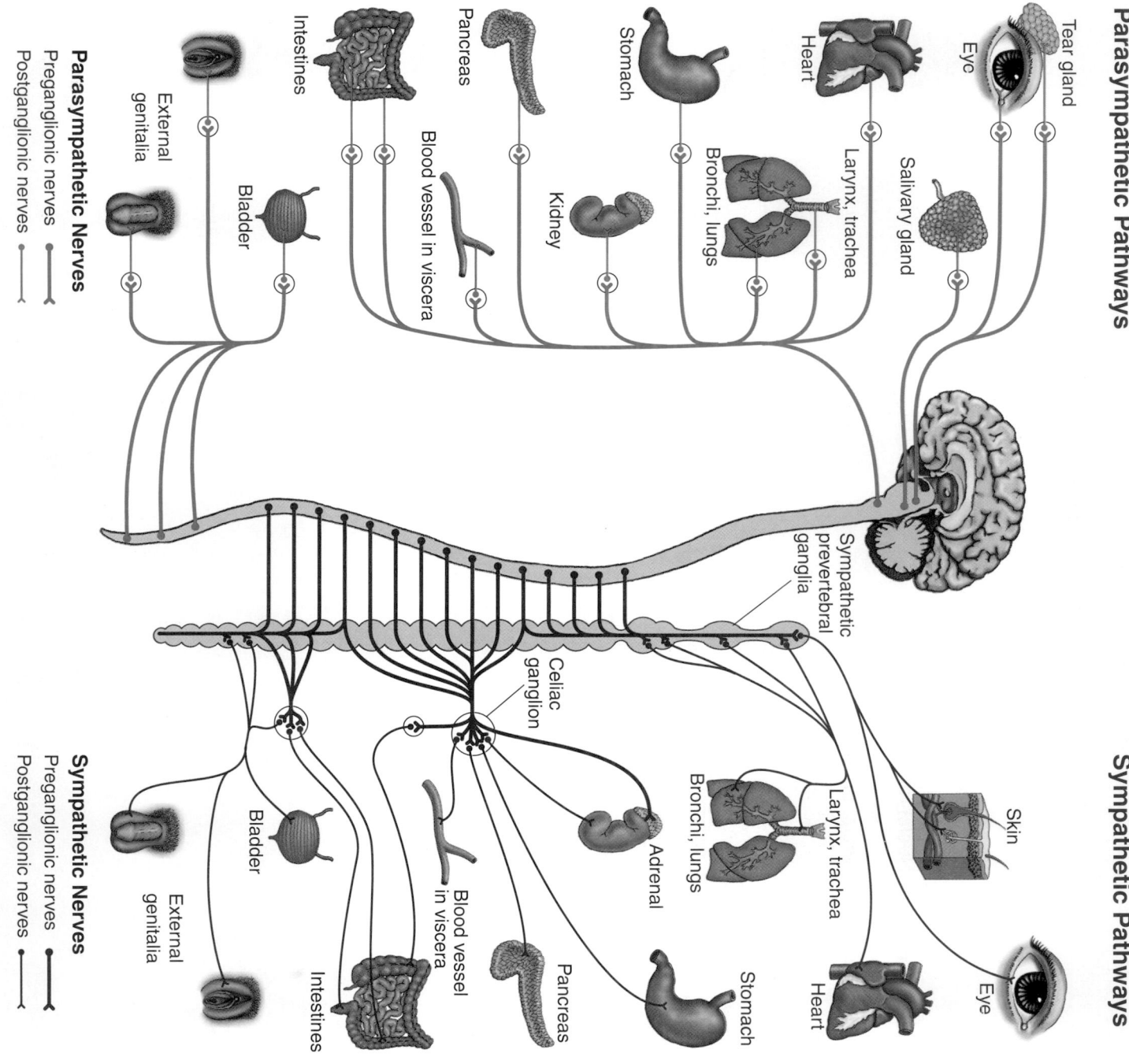

Tear gland

Eye

Salivary gland

Heart

Larynx, trachea

Stomach

Bronchi, lungs

Pancreas

Kidney

Blood vessel in viscera

Intestines

External genitalia

Bladder

Sympathetic prevertebral ganglia

Celiac ganglion

Skin

Larynx, trachea

Bronchi, lungs

Heart

Eye

Adrenal

Stomach

Pancreas

Blood vessel in viscera

Intestines

External genitalia

Bladder

Parasympathetic Nerves
Preganglionic nerves
Postganglionic nerves

Sympathetic Nerves
Preganglionic nerves
Postganglionic nerves

Appendix II

Some Functions of Sympathetic and Parasympathetic Activation

ORGAN	SYMPATHETIC EFFECT	PARASYMPATHETIC EFFECT
Salivary gland	Decreases secretion	Increases secretion
Heart	Increases heart rate	Decreases heart rate
Blood vessels	Constricts blood vessels in most organs	Dilates blood vessels in a few organs
Penis	Ejaculation	Erection
Iris radial muscles	Dilates pupils	No effect
Iris sphincter muscles	No effect	Constricts pupils
Tear gland	No effect	Stimulates secretion
Sweat gland	Stimulates secretion	No effect
Stomach and intestine	No effect	Stimulates secretion
Lungs	Dilates bronchioles; inhibits mucous secretion	Constricts bronchioles; stimulates mucous secretion
Arrector pili muscles	Erects hair and creates gooseflesh	No effect

Appendix III
The Cranial Nerves

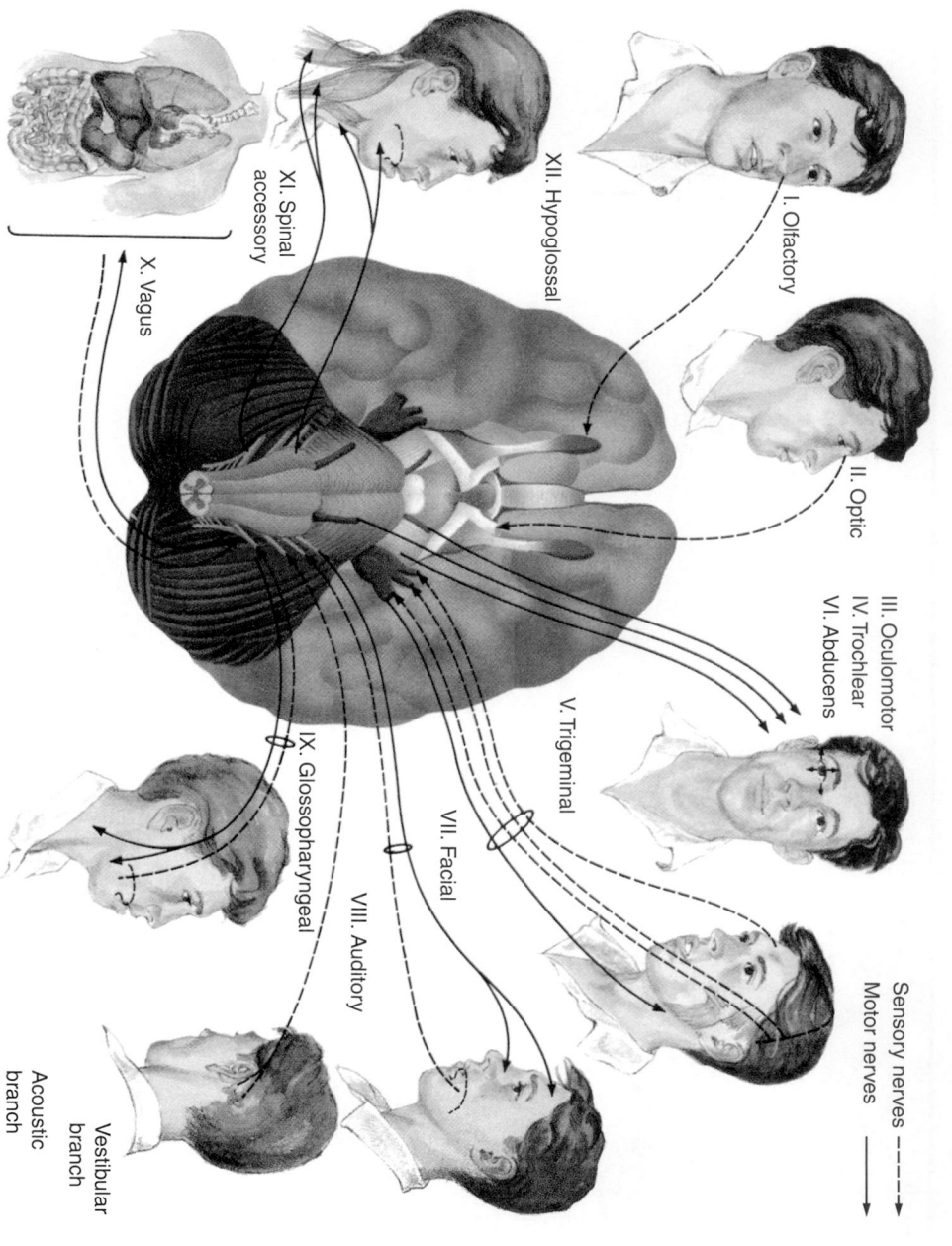

I. Olfactory

II. Optic

III. Oculomotor
IV. Trochlear
VI. Abducens

V. Trigeminal

VII. Facial

VIII. Auditory

Vestibular branch

Acoustic branch

IX. Glossopharyngeal

X. Vagus

XI. Spinal accessory

XII. Hypoglossal

Sensory nerves --------
Motor nerves ------

Appendix IV

Functions of the Cranial Nerves

NUMBER	NAME	GENERAL FUNCTION	SPECIFIC FUNCTIONS
I	Olfactory	Sensory	Smell
II	Optic	Sensory	Vision
III	Oculomotor	Motor	Eye movement and pupillary constriction
		Sensory	Sensory signals from certain eye muscles
IV	Trochlear	Motor	Eye movement
		Sensory	Sensory signals from certain eye muscles
V	Trigeminal	Sensory	Facial sensations
		Motor	Chewing
VI	Abducens	Motor	Eye movement
		Sensory	Sensory signals from certain eye muscles
VII	Facial	Sensory	Taste from anterior two-thirds of tongue
		Motor	Facial expression, secretion of tears, salivation, cranial blood vessel dilation
VIII	Auditory-Vestibular	Sensory	Audition; sensory signals from the organs of balance in the inner ear
IX	Glossopharyngeal	Sensory	Taste from posterior third of tongue
		Motor	Salivation, swallowing
X	Vagus	Sensory	Sensations from abdominal and thoracic organs
		Motor	Control over abdominal and thoracic organs and muscles of the throat
XI	Spinal Accessory	Motor	Movement of neck, shoulders, and head
		Sensory	Sensory signals from muscles of the neck
XII	Hypoglossal	Motor	Tongue movements
		Sensory	Sensory signals from tongue muscles

Appendix V
Nuclei of the Thalamus

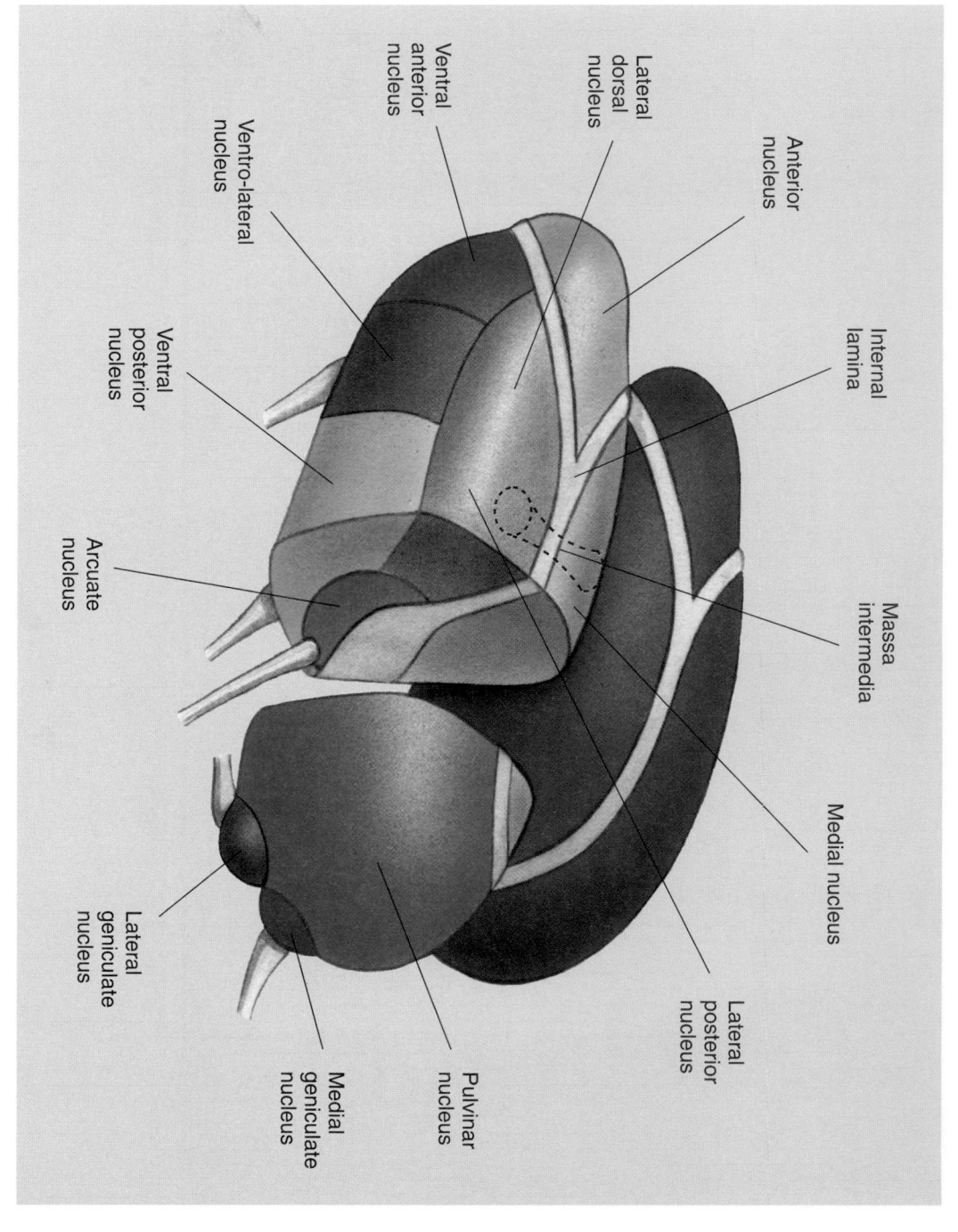

Ventral
anterior
nucleus

Lateral
dorsal
nucleus

Ventro-lateral
nucleus

Anterior
nucleus

Ventral
posterior
nucleus

Internal
lamina

Massa
intermedia

Arcuate
nucleus

Medial nucleus

Lateral
posterior
nucleus

Lateral
geniculate
nucleus

Medial
geniculate
nucleus

Pulvinar
nucleus

Appendix VI
Nuclei of the Hypothalamus

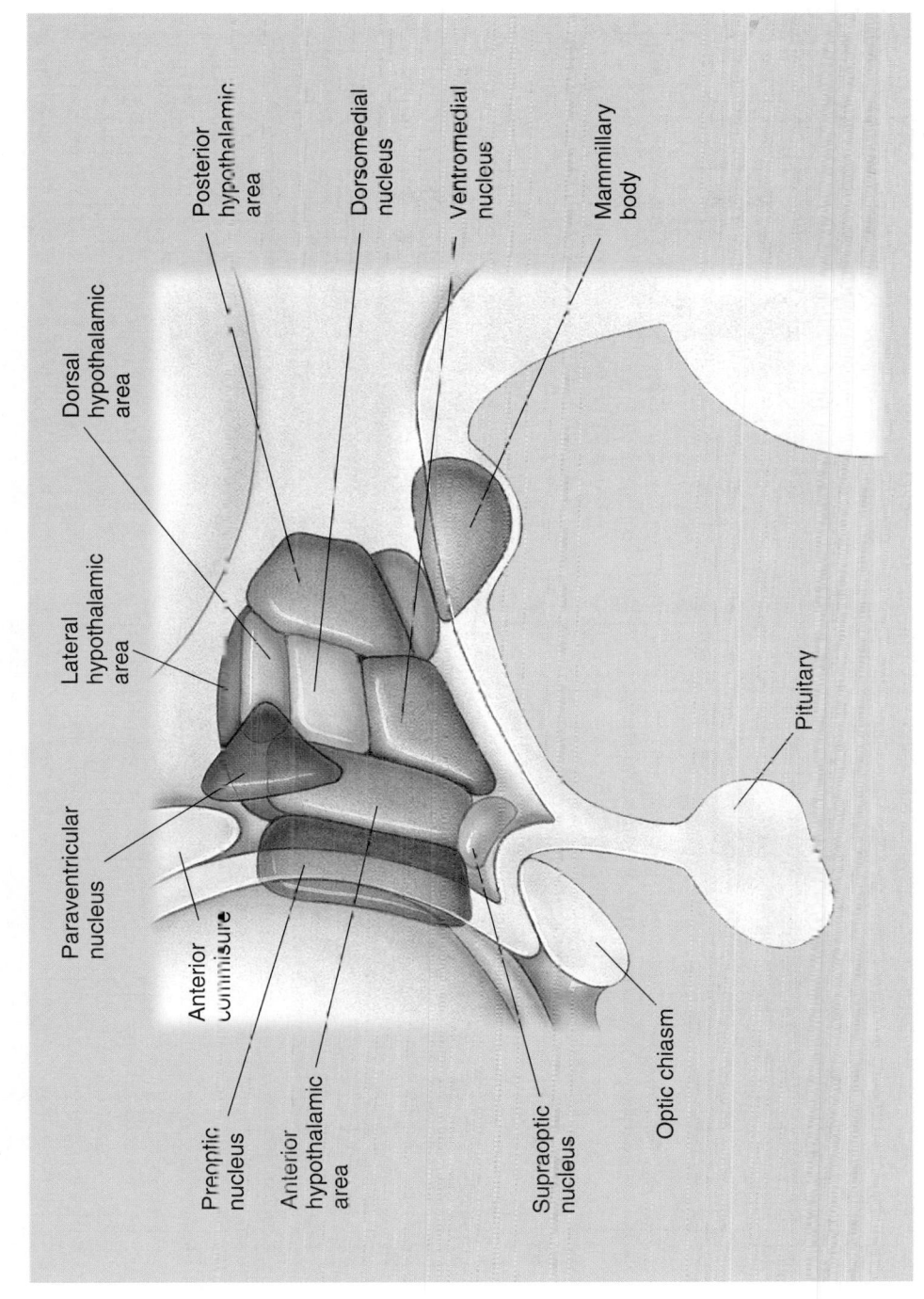

Posterior hypothalamic area

Dorsomedial nucleus

Ventromedial nucleus

Mammillary body

Dorsal hypothalamic area

Lateral hypothalamic area

Paraventricular nucleus

Anterior commisure

Preoptic nucleus

Anterior hypothalamic area

Supraoptic nucleus

Optic chiasm

Pituitary

Glossary

Ablatio penis. Accidental destruction of the penis.

Absolute refractory period. A brief period (typically 1 to 2 milliseconds) after the initiation of an action potential during which it is impossible to elicit another action potential in the same neuron.

Absorption spectrum. A graph of the ability of a substance to absorb light of different wavelengths.

Absorptive phase. The metabolic phase during which the body is operating on the energy from a recently consumed meal and is storing the excess as body fat, glycogen, and proteins.

Accommodation. The process of adjusting the configuration of the lenses to bring images into focus on the retina.

Achromatic colors. Black, white, and gray.

Acetylcholinesterase. The enzyme that breaks down the neurotransmitter acetylcholine.

Action potential (AP). A massive momentary reversal of a neuron's membrane potential from about −70 mV to about +50 mV.

Activation-synthesis theory. The theory that dream content reflects the cerebral cortex's inherent tendency to make sense of, and give form to, the random signals it receives from the brain stem during REM sleep.

Active placebos. Control drugs that have no therapeutic effect but produce side effects similar to those produced by the drug under evaluation in a clinical trial.

Acuity. The ability to see the details of objects.

Addicts. Habitual drug users who continue to use a drug despite its adverse effects on their health and social life and despite their repeated efforts to stop using it.

Adipsia. Complete cessation of drinking.

Adrenal cortex. The outer layer of the adrenal glands, which releases glucocorticoids in response to stressors as well as steroid hormones in small amounts.

Adrenal medulla. The core of each adrenal gland, which releases epinephrine and norepinephrine in response to stressors.

Adrenocorticotropic hormone (ACTH). The anterior pituitary hormone that triggers the release of gonadal and adrenal hormones from the adrenal cortices.

Adrenogenital syndrome. A sexual developmental disorder in which high levels of adrenal androgens, resulting from congenital adrenal hyperplasia, masculinize the bodies of genetic females.

Afferent nerves. Nerves that carry sensory signals to the central nervous system; sensory nerves.

Ageusia. The inability to taste.

Aggregation. The alignment of cells within different areas of the embryo during development to form various structures.

Aggressive behaviors. Behaviors whose primary function is to threaten or harm other organisms.

Agnosia. An inability to consciously recognize sensory stimuli of a particular class that is not attributable to a sensory deficit or to verbal or intellectual impairment.

Agonists. Drugs that facilitate the effects of a particular neurotransmitter.

Agraphia. A specific inability to write; one that does not result from general visual, motor, or intellectual deficits.

Agoraphobia. Pathological fear of public places and open spaces.

Alexia. A specific inability to read; one that does not result from general visual, motor, or intellectual deficits.

Alleles. The two genes that control the same trait.

All-or-none responses. Responses that are not graded, that either occur to their full extent or not at all.

Alpha fetoprotein. A protein that is present in the blood of rats during the perinatal period and that deactivates circulating estradiol by binding to it.

Alpha male. The dominant male of a colony.

Alpha waves. Regular, 8- to 12-per-second, high-amplitude EEG waves that typically occur during relaxed wakefulness and just before falling asleep.

Alzheimer's disease. The major cause of dementia in old age, characterized by neurofibrillary tangles, amyloid plaques, and neuron loss.

Amacrine cells. A type of retinal neurons whose specialized function is lateral communication.

Amino acid derivative hormones. Hormones that are synthesized in a few simple steps from amino acids.

Amino acids. The building blocks and breakdown products of proteins.

Amphetamine. A stimulant drug whose effects are similar to those of cocaine.

Amphibians. Species that spend their larval phase in water and their adult phase on land.

Amygdala. A structure of the medial temporal lobe that plays a role in the memory for the emotional significance of experiences.

Amyloid. A protein that is normally present in small amounts in the human brain but is a major constituent of the numerous plaques in the brains of Alzheimer's patients.

Anabolic steroids. Steroid drugs that are similar to testosterone and have powerful anabolic (growth-promoting) effects.

Analgesics. Drugs that reduce pain.

Analogous. Having a similar structure because of convergent evolution (e.g., a bird's wing and a bee's wing are analogous).

Androgenic insensitivity syndrome. The developmental disorder of genetic males in which a mutation to the androgen receptor gene renders the androgen receptors defective and causes the development of a female body.

Androgens. The class of steroid hormones that includes testosterone.

Androstenedione. The adrenal androgen that triggers the growth of pubic and axillary hair in human females.

Aneurysm. A pathological balloonlike dilation that forms in the wall of a blood vessel at a point where the elasticity of the vessel wall is defective.

Angular gyrus. The gyrus of the posterior cortex at the boundary between the temporal and parietal lobes, which in the left hemisphere is thought to play a role in reading.

Anhedonia. The inability to experience pleasure.

Anorexia nervosa. An eating disorder that is characterized by a pathological fear of obesity and that results in health-threatening weight loss.

Anosmia. The inability to smell.

Anosognosia. The common failure of neuropsychological patients to recognize their own symptoms.

Antagonistic muscles. Pairs of muscles that act in opposition.

Antagonists. Drugs that inhibit the effects of a particular neurotransmitter.

Anterior. Toward the nose end of a vertebrate.

Anterior cingulate cortex. The cortex of the anterior cingulate gyrus, which is involved in the emotional reaction to painful stimulation.

Anterior pituitary. The part of the pituitary gland that releases tropic hormones.

Anterograde amnesia. Loss of memory for events occurring after the amnesia-inducing brain injury.

Anterograde degeneration. The degeneration of the distal segment of a cut axon.

Anterolateral system. The division of the somatosensory system that ascends in the anterolateral portion of spinal white matter and carries signals related to pain and temperature.

Antibodies. Proteins that bind specifically to antigens on the surface of invading micro-organisms and in so doing promote the destruction of the micro-organisms.

Antibody-mediated immunity. The immune reaction by which B cells destroy invading micro-organisms.

Antidromic conduction. Axonal conduction opposite to the normal direction; conduction from axon terminals back toward the cell body.

Antigens. Proteins on the surface of cells that identify them as native or foreign.

Antihypnotic drugs. Sleep-reducing drugs.

Anxiety. Chronic fear that persists in the absence of any direct threat.

Anxiety disorder. Anxiety that is so extreme and so pervasive that it disrupts normal functioning.

Aphagia. Complete cessation of eating.

Aphasia. A brain-damage-produced deficit in the ability to use or comprehend language.

Apoptosis. Cell death that is actively induced by genetic programs; programmed cell death.

Appetizer effect. The increase in hunger that is produced by the consumption of small amounts of palatable food.

Applied research. Research that is intended to bring about some direct benefit to humankind.

Apraxia. A disorder in which patients have great difficulty performing movements when asked to do so out of con-

text but can readily perform them spontaneously in natural situations.

Arachnoid membrane. The meninx that is located between the dura mater and the pia mater and has the appearance of a gauzelike spiderweb.

Arcuate fasciculus. The major neural pathway between Broca's area and Wernicke's area.

Aromatization. The chemical process by which testosterone is converted to estradiol.

Arteriosclerosis. A condition in which blood vessels are blocked by the accumulation of fat deposits on their walls.

Asomatognosia. A deficiency in the awareness of parts of one's own body that is typically produced by damage to the parietal lobe.

Aspiration. A lesion technique in which tissue is drawn off by suction through the fine tip of a glass pipette.

Association cortex. Any area of the cortex that receives input from more than one sensory system.

Astereognosia. An inability to recognize objects by touch that is not attributable to a simple sensory deficit or to general intellectual impairment.

Astrocytes. Large, star-shaped glial cells that play a role in the passage of chemicals from the blood into CNS neurons and perform several other important functions that are not yet well understood.

Ataxia. Loss of motor coordination.

Atropine. A receptor blocker that exerts an antagonistic effect at muscarinic receptors.

Auditory nerve. The branch of cranial nerve VIII that carries auditory signals from the hair cells in the basilar membrane.

Autism. A neurodevelopmental disorder characterized by (1) a reduced ability to interpret the emotions and intentions of others, (2) a reduced capacity for social interaction and communication, and (3) a preoccupation with a single subject or activity.

Autonomic nervous system (ANS). The part of the peripheral nervous system that participates in the regulation of the body's internal environment.

Autoradiography. The technique of photographically developing brain slices that have been exposed to a radioactively labeled substance such as 2-DG so that regions of high uptake are visible.

Autoreceptors. A type of metabotropic receptor located on the presynaptic membrane and sensitive to a neuron's own neurotransmitter.

Axon hillock. The conical structure at the junction between the axon and cell body.

B cells. B lymphocytes; lymphocytes that manufacture antibodies against antigens they encounter.

Basal forebrain. A midline area of the forebrain, which is located just in front of and above the hypothalamus and is the brain's main source of acetylcholine.

Basal metabolic rate. The rate at which an individual utilizes energy to maintain bodily processes.

Basilar membrane. The membrane of the organ of Corti in which the hair cell receptors are embedded.

Before-and-after design. The experimental design used to demonstrate contingent drug tolerance; the experimental

Behavioral paradigm. A single set of procedures developed for the investigation of a particular behavioral phenomenon.

Benign tumors. Tumors that are surgically removable with little risk of further growth in the body.

Benzodiazepines. A class of GABA agonists with anxiolytic, sedative, and anticonvulsant properties; drugs such as chlordiazepoxide (Librium) and diazepam (Valium).

Between-subjects design. An experimental design in which a different group of subjects is tested under each condition.

Betz cells. Large pyramidal neurons of the primary motor cortex that synapse directly on motor neurons in the lower regions of the spinal cord.

Bilateral medial temporal lobectomy. The removal of the medial portions of both temporal lobes, including the hippocampus, the amygdala, and the adjacent cortex.

Binocular. Involving both eyes.

Binocular disparity. The difference in the position of the retinal image of the same object on the two retinas.

Biopsychology. The scientific study of the biology of behavior.

Bipolar affective disorder. A disorder of emotion in which the patient experiences periods of mania interspersed with periods of depression.

Bipolar cells. Bipolar neurons that form the middle layer of the retina.

Bipolar neuron. A neuron with two processes extending from its cell body.

Bisexual. Sexually attracted to members of both sexes.

Blind spot. The area on the retina where the bundle of axons of the retinal ganglion cells penetrate the receptor layer and leave the eye as the optic nerve.

Blindsight. The ability of some patients who are blind as a consequence of cortical damage to unconsciously see some aspects of their visual environments.

Blobs. Peglike, cytochrome oxidase–rich, dual-opponent columns or columns.

Blood–brain barrier. The mechanism that keeps certain toxic substances in the blood from passing into brain tissue.

Brain stem. The part of the brain on which the cerebral hemispheres rest; in general, it regulates reflex activities that are critical for survival (e.g., heart rate and respiration).

Bregma. The point on the surface of the skull where two of the major sutures intersect, commonly used as a reference point in stereotaxic surgery on rodents.

Broca's aphasia. A hypothetical disorder of speech production with no associated deficits in language comprehension.

Broca's area. The area of the inferior prefrontal cortex of the left hemisphere hypothesized by Broca to be the center of speech production.

Buerger's disease. A condition in which the blood vessels, especially those supplying the legs, are constricted whenever nicotine enters the bloodstream, the ultimate result being gangrene and amputation.

Bulimia nervosa. An eating disorder that is characterized by recurring cycles of fasting, bingeing, and purging without dangerous weight loss.

Butyrophenones. A class of antischizophrenic drugs that bind primarily to D_2 receptors.

CA1 subfield. The region of the hippocampus that is commonly damaged by cerebral ischemia.

Cafeteria diet. A diet offered to experimental animals that is composed of a wide variety of palatable foods.

Cannabis sativa. The common hemp plant, which is the source of marijuana.

Cannon–Bard theory. The theory that emotional experience and emotional expression are parallel processes that have no direct causal relation.

Cannula. A fine, hollow tube that is implanted in the body for the purpose of introducing or extracting substances.

Carousel apparatus. An apparatus used to study the effects of sleep deprivation in laboratory rats.

Cartesian dualism. The philosophical position of René Descartes, who argued that the universe is composed of two elements: physical matter and the human mind.

Case studies. Studies that focus on a single case, or subject.

Cataplexy. A disorder that is characterized by recurring losses of muscle tone during wakefulness and is often seen in cases of narcolepsy.

Cell-adhesion molecules (CAMs). Molecules on the surface of cells that have the ability to recognize specific molecules on the surface of other cells and bind to them.

Cell-mediated immunity. The immune reaction by which T cells destroy invading micro-organisms.

Central canal. The small CSF-filled channel that runs the length of the spinal cord.

Central nervous system (CNS). The portion of the nervous system within the skull and spine.

Central sensorimotor programs. Patterns of activity that are programmed into the sensorimotor system.

Cephalic phase. The metabolic phase during which the body prepares for food that is about to be absorbed.

Cerebellum. The metencephalic structure that has been shown to mediate the retention of Pavlovian eyeblink conditioning.

Cerebral angiography. A contrast X-ray technique for visualizing the cerebral circulatory system by infusing a radio-translucent dye into a cerebral artery.

Cerebral aqueduct. The narrow channel that connects the third and fourth ventricles.

Cerebral commissures. Tracts that connect the left and right cerebral hemispheres.

Cerebral cortex. The layer of neural tissue covering the cerebral hemispheres of humans and other mammals.

Cerebral dialysis. A method for recording changes in brain chemistry in behaving animals in which a fine tube with a short semipermeable section is implanted in the brain, and extracellular neurochemicals are continuously drawn off for analysis.

Cerebral hemorrhage. Bleeding in the brain.

Cerebral ischemia. An interruption of the blood supply to an area of the brain; a common cause of medial temporal lobe amnesia.

Cerebral ventricles. The four CSF-filled internal chambers of the brain: the two lateral ventricles, the third ventricle, and the fourth ventricle.

Cerebrospinal fluid (CSF). The colorless fluid that fills the subarachnoid space, the central canal, and the cerebral ventricles.

Cerebrum. The portion of the brain that sits on the brain stem; in general, it plays a role in complex adaptive processes (e.g., learning, perception, and motivation).

Cerveau isolé preparation. An experimental preparation in which the forebrain is disconnected from the rest of the brain by a midcollicular transection.

Change blindness. The difficulty perceiving major changes to unattended-to parts of a visual image when the changes are introduced during brief interruptions in the presentation of the image.

Cheese effect. The surges in blood pressure that occur when individuals taking MAO inhibitors consume tyramine-rich foods, such as cheese.

Chemoaffinity hypothesis. The hypothesis that growing axons are attracted to the correct targets by different chemicals released by the target sites.

Chimeric figures test. A test of visual completion in split-brain subjects that uses pictures composed of the left and right halves of two different faces.

Chlorpromazine. The first antischizophrenic drug.

Cholecystokinin (CCK). A peptide that is released by the gastrointestinal tract and is thought to function as a satiety signal.

Chordates. Animals with dorsal nerve cords.

Choroid plexuses. The networks of capillaries that protrude into the ventricles from the pia mater and continuously produce cerebrospinal fluid.

Chromatic colors. The hues—colors such as blue, green, and yellow.

Chromosomes. Threadlike structures in the cell nucleus that contain the genes; each chromosome is a DNA molecule.

Ciliary muscles. The eye muscles that control the shape of the lenses.

Cingulate motor areas. Two small areas of secondary motor cortex located in the cortex of the cingulate gyrus of each hemisphere.

Circadian clock. An internal timing mechanism that is capable of maintaining daily cycles of physiological functions, even when there are no temporal cues from the environment.

Circadian rhythms. Diurnal (daily) cycles of body functions.

Circadian theories of sleep. Theories based on the premise that sleep is controlled by an internal timing mechanism and is not a reaction to the adverse effects of wakefulness.

Cirrhosis. Scarring, typically of the liver.

Clinical. Pertaining to illness or treatment.

Clinical trials. Studies conducted on human subjects to assess the therapeutic efficacy of an untested drug or other treatment.

Clozapine. An atypical neuroleptic that is used to treat schizophrenia, does not produce Parkinsonian side effects, and does not have a high affinity for D_2 receptors.

Cocaine. A potent catecholamine agonist and stimulant that is highly addictive.

Cocaine psychosis. Psychotic behavior observed during a cocaine spree, similar in many respects to paranoid schizophrenia.

Cocaine sprees. Binges of cocaine use.

Cochlea. The long, coiled tube in the inner ear that is filled with fluid and contains the organ of Corti and its auditory receptors.

Cocktail-party phenomenon. The ability to unconsciously monitor the contents of one conversation while consciously focusing on another.

Cocontraction. The simultaneous contraction of antagonistic muscles.

Codeine. A relatively weak psychoactive ingredient of opium.

Codon. A group of three consecutive nucleotide bases on a DNA or messenger RNA strand; each codon specifies the particular amino acid that is to be added to an amino acid chain during protein synthesis.

Coexistence The presence of more than one neurotransmitter in the same neuron.

Cognition. Higher intellectual processes such as thought, memory, attention, and complex perceptual processes.

Cognitive map theory. The theory that the main function of the hippocampus is to store memories of spatial location.

Cognitive neuroscience. A division of biopsychology that focuses on the use of functional brain imaging to study the neural bases of human cognition.

Collateral sprouting. The growth of axon branches from mature neurons, usually to postsynaptic sites abandoned by adjacent axons that have degenerated.

Colony–intruder paradigm. A paradigm for the study of aggressive and defensive behaviors in male rats; a small male intruder rat is placed in an established colony in order to study the aggressive responses of the colony's alpha male and the defensive responses of the intruder.

Color constancy. The tendency of an object to appear the same color even when the wavelengths of light that it reflects change.

Columnar organization. The functional organization of the neocortex in vertical columns; the cells in each column form a mini-circuit that performs a single function.

Commissurotomy. Surgical severing of the cerebral commissures.

Comparative approach. The study of biological processes by comparing different species—usually from the evolutionary perspective.

Comparative psychology. The division of biopsychology that studies the evolution, genetics, and adaptiveness of behavior, often by using the comparative approach.

Complementary colors. Pairs of colors that produce white or gray when combined in equal measure; every color has a complementary color.

Completion. The visual system's automatic use of information obtained from receptors around the blind spot, or scotoma, to create a perception of the missing portion of the retinal image.

Complex cells. Neurons in the visual cortex that respond optimally to straight-edge stimuli in a certain orientation in any part of their receptive field.

Complex partial seizures. Seizures that are characterized by various complex psychological phenomena and are thought to result from temporal lobe discharges.

Component theory. The theory that the relative amount of activity produced in three different classes of cones by light determines its perceived color (also called *trichromatic theory*).

Computed tomography (CT). A computer-assisted X-ray procedure that can be used to visualize the brain and other internal structures of the living body.

Concussion. Disturbance of consciousness following a blow to the head with no cerebral bleeding or obvious structural damage.

Conditioned compensatory responses. Physiological responses opposite to the effects of a drug that are thought to be elicited by stimuli that are regularly associated with experiencing the drug effects.

Conditioned defensive burying. The burial of a source of aversive stimulation by rodents.

Conditioned drug tolerance. Tolerance effects that are maximally expressed only when a drug is administered in the situation in which it has previously been administered.

Conditioned place-preference paradigm. A test that assesses a laboratory animal's preference for environments in which it has previously experienced drug effects.

Conditioned taste aversion. An avoidance response developed by animals to the taste of food whose consumption has been followed by illness.

Conditioned withdrawal effects. Withdrawal effects that are elicited by the drug environment or by other drug-associated cues.

Conduction aphasia. Aphasia that is thought to result from damage to the neural pathway between Broca's area and Wernicke's area.

Cones. The visual receptors in the retina that mediate high-acuity color vision in good lighting.

Confounded variable. An unintended difference between the conditions of an experiment that could have affected the dependent variable.

Congenital. Present at birth.

Congenital adrenal hyperplasia. A congenital deficiency in the release of cortisol from the adrenal cortex, which leads to the excessive release of adrenal androgens.

Conspecifics. Members of the same species.

Constituent cognitive processes. Simple cognitive processes that combine to produce complex cognitive processes and that are assumed to be mediated by neural activity in particular parts of the brain.

Contextual fear conditioning. The process by which benign contexts (situations) come to elicit fear through their association with fear-inducing stimuli.

Contingent drug tolerance. Drug tolerance that develops as a reaction to the experience of the effects of drugs rather than to drug exposure alone.

Contralateral. Projecting from one side of the body to the other.

Contralateral neglect. A disturbance of the patient's ability to respond to visual, auditory, and somatosensory stimuli on the side of the body opposite to a site of brain damage, usually the left side of the body following damage to the right parietal lobe.

Contrast enhancement. The intensification of the perception of edges.

Contrast X-ray techniques. X-ray techniques that involve the injection into one compartment of the body a substance that absorbs X-rays either less than or more than the surrounding tissue.

Contrecoup injuries. Contusions that occur on the side of the brain opposite to the side of a blow.

"Control of behavior" versus "conscious perception" theory. The theory that the dorsal stream mediates behav-

ioral interactions with objects and the ventral stream mediates conscious perception of objects.

Control-question technique. A lie-detection interrogation method in which the polygrapher compares the physiological responses to target questions with the responses to control questions.

Contusions. Closed-head injuries that involve damage to the cerebral circulatory system, which produces internal hemorrhaging.

Convergent evolution. The evolution in unrelated species of similar solutions to the same environmental demands.

Converging operations. The use of several research approaches to solve a single problem.

Convolutions. Folds on the surface of the cerebral hemispheres.

Convulsions. Motor seizures.

Coolidge effect. The fact that a copulating male who becomes incapable of continuing to copulate with one sex partner can often recommence copulating with a new sex partner.

Copulation. Sexual intercourse.

Corpus callosum. The largest cerebral commissure.

Corticofugal pathways. Descending pathways that conduct information from cortical sensory areas to subcortical areas.

Crack. A potent, cheap, smokable form of cocaine.

Cranial nerves. The 12 pairs of nerves extending from the brain (e.g., the optic nerves, the olfactory nerves, and the vagus nerves).

Cross-cuing. Nonneural communication between hemispheres that have been separated by commissurotomy.

Cross section. Section cut at a right angle to any long, narrow structure of the CNS.

Cross tolerance. Tolerance to the effects of one drug that develops as the result of exposure to another drug that acts by the same mechanism.

Crossing over. The exchange of sections between pairs of chromosomes during the first stage of meiosis.

Cryogenic blockade. The temporary elimination of neural activity in an area of the brain by cooling the area with a cryoprobe.

Curare. A receptor blocker of cholinergic synapses that acts at nicotinic receptors and produces paralysis by blocking transmission at neuromuscular junctions.

Cytochrome oxidase. An enzyme present in particularly high concentrations in the mitochondria of dual-opponent color cells of the visual cortex.

Decorticate. Lacking a cortex.

Decussate. To cross over to the other side of the brain.

Deep dyslexia. A reading disorder in which the phonetic procedure is disrupted while the lexical procedure is not.

Defeminizes. Suppresses or disrupts female characteristics.

Defensive behaviors. Behaviors whose primary function is protection from threat or harm.

Delayed nonmatching-to-sample test. A test in which the subject is presented with an unfamiliar sample object and then, after a delay, is presented with a choice between the sample object and an unfamiliar object, where the correct choice is the unfamiliar object.

Delirium tremens (DTs). The phase of alcohol withdrawal syndrome characterized by hallucinations, delusions, agitation, confusion, hyperthermia, and tachycardia.

Delta waves. The largest and slowest EEG waves.

Demasculinizes. Suppresses or disrupts male characteristics.

Dementia. General intellectual deterioration.

Dendritic spines. Tiny nodules of various shapes that are located on the surfaces of many dendrites and are the sites of most excitatory synapses in the mature mammalian brain.

2-Deoxyglucose (2-DG). A substance similar to glucose that is taken up by active neurons in the brain and accumulates in them because, unlike glucose, it cannot be metabolized.

Deoxyribonucleic acid (DNA). The double-stranded, coiled molecule of genetic material; a chromosome.

Dependent variable. The variable measured by the experimenter to assess the effect of the independent variable.

Depolarize. To decrease the resting membrane potential.

Deprenyl. A monoamine agonist that has been shown to retard the development of Parkinson's disease.

Depressant. A drug that depresses neural activity.

Depression. A normal reaction to grievous loss; when depression is excessive, disruptive, and recurring, it is classified as a psychiatric disorder.

Dermatome. An area of the body that is innervated by the left and right dorsal roots of one segment of the spinal cord.

Desynchronized EEG. Low-amplitude, high-frequency EEG.

Detoxified addicts. Addicts who have none of the drug to which they are addicted in their body and who are no longer experiencing withdrawal symptoms.

Dextrals. Right-handers

Diathesis. A genetic susceptibility to a disorder, as in the diathesis–stress model of depression.

Dichotic listening test. A test of language lateralization in which two different sequences of three spoken digits are presented simultaneously, one to each ear, and the subject is asked to report all of the digits heard.

Dichotomous traits. Traits that occur in one form or the other, never in combination.

Diet-induced thermogenesis. The homeostasis-defending increases in body temperature that are associated with increases in body fat.

Digestion. The process by which food is broken down and absorbed through the lining of the gastrointestinal tract.

Digit span. The longest sequence of random digits that can be repeated correctly 50% of the time—most people have a digit span of 7.

Dihydrotestosterone. An androgen that cannot be aromatized to estrogen.

Directed synapses. Synapses at which the site of neurotransmitter release and the site of neurotransmitter reception are in close proximity.

Distal segment. The segment of a cut axon between the cut and the axon terminals.

DNA-binding proteins. Proteins that bind to DNA molecules and in so doing either induce or block gene expression.

Dominant hemisphere. A term used in the past to refer to the left hemisphere, based on the incorrect assumption that the left hemisphere is dominant in all complex behavioral and cognitive activities.

Dominant trait. The trait of a dichotomous pair that is expressed in the phenotypes of heterozygous individuals.

Dopamine transporters. Molecules in the presynaptic membrane of dopaminergic neurons that attract dopamine

molecules in the synaptic cleft and deposit them back inside the neuron.

Dorsal. Toward the surface of the back of a vertebrate or toward the top of the head.

Dorsal-column medial-lemniscus system. The division of the somatosensory system that ascends in the dorsal portion of the spinal white matter and carries signals related to touch and proprioception.

Dorsal columns. The somatosensory tracts that ascend in the dorsal portion of the spinal cord white matter.

Dorsal horns. The two dorsal arms of the spinal gray matter.

Dorsal stream. The group of visual pathways that flows from the primary visual cortex to the dorsal prestriate cortex to the posterior parietal cortex; according to one theory, its function is the control of visually guided behavior.

Dorsolateral corticorubrospinal tract. The descending motor tract that synapses in the red nucleus of the midbrain, decussates, and descends in the dorsolateral spinal white matter.

Dorsolateral corticospinal tract. The motor tract that leaves the primary motor cortex, descends to the medullary pyramids, decussates, and then descends in the contralateral dorsolateral spinal white matter.

Dorsolateral prefrontal association cortex. The area of the prefrontal association cortex that plays a role in the evaluation of external stimuli and the initiation of complex voluntary motor responses.

Down syndrome. A disorder associated with the presence of an extra chromosome 21, resulting in disfigurement and mental retardation.

Drug metabolism. The conversion of a drug from its active form to a nonactive form.

Drug self-administration paradigm. A test of the addictive potential of drugs in which laboratory animals can inject drugs into themselves by pressing a lever.

Drug sensitization. An increase in the sensitivity to a drug effect that develops as the result of exposure to the drug.

Drug tolerance. A state of decreased sensitivity to a drug that develops as a result of exposure to the drug.

Dual-opponent color cells. Neurons that respond to the differences in the wavelengths of light stimulating adjacent areas of their receptive field.

Duchenne smile. A genuine smile, one that includes contraction of the facial muscles called the *orbicularis oculi*.

Duodenum. The upper portion of the intestine through which most of the glucose and amino acids are absorbed into the bloodstream.

Duplexity theory. The theory that cones and rods mediate photopic and scotopic vision, respectively.

Dura mater. The tough outer meninx.

Dynamic contraction. Contraction of a muscle that causes the muscle to shorten.

Dynamic phase. The first phase of the VMH syndrome, characterized by grossly excessive eating and rapid weight gain.

Dyslexia. A pathological difficulty in reading, one that does not result from general visual, motor, or intellectual deficits.

Efferent nerves. Nerves that carry motor signals from the central nervous system to the skeletal muscles or internal organs.

Ejaculate. To eject sperm from the penis.

Ejaculation. Ejection of sperm.

Electrocardiogram (ECG or EKG). A recording of the electrical signals associated with heartbeats.

Electroconvulsive shock (ECS). An intense, brief, diffuse, seizure-inducing current administered to the brain via large electrodes attached to the scalp.

Electroencephalogram (EEG). A measure of the gross electrical activity of the brain, commonly recorded through scalp electrodes.

Electroencephalography. A technique for recording the gross electrical activity of the brain through disk-shaped electrodes, which in humans are usually taped to the surface of the scalp.

Electromyogram (EMG). A measure of the electrical activity of muscles.

Electromyography. A procedure for measuring muscle tension by recording the gross electrical discharges of muscles.

Electron microscopy. A neuroanatomical technique used to study the fine details of cellular structure.

Electrooculogram (EOG). A measure of eye movement.

Electrooculography. A technique for recording eye movements through electrodes placed around the eye.

Elevated plus maze. An apparatus for recording defensiveness or anxiety in rats by assessing their tendency to avoid the two open arms of a plus-sign-shaped maze mounted some distance above the floor of a lab.

Embolism. The blockage of blood flow in a smaller blood vessel by a plug that was formed in a larger blood vessel and carried by the bloodstream to the smaller one.

Emergent stage 1 EEG. All periods of stage 1 sleep EEG except initial stage 1; each is associated with REMs.

Encapsulated tumors. Tumors that grow within their own membrane.

Encéphale isolé preparation. An experimental preparation in which the brain is separated from the rest of the nervous system by a transection of the caudal brain stem.

Encephalitis. The inflammation associated with brain infection.

Endocrine glands. Ductless glands that release chemicals called hormones directly into the circulatory system.

Endogenous depression. Depression that occurs with no apparent cause.

Endorphins. Endogenous (internally produced) opiate analgesics.

Engram. A change in the brain that stores a memory.

Enzymatic degradation. The breakdown of chemicals by enzymes—one of the two mechanisms for deactivating released neurotransmitters.

Enzymes. Proteins that stimulate or inhibit biochemical reactions without being affected by them.

Epidemiology. The study of the factors that influence the distribution of a disease in the general population.

Epilepsy. A neurological disorder characterized by spontaneously recurring seizures.

Epileptic auras. Psychological symptoms that precede the onset of a convulsion.

Epileptogenesis. Development of epilepsy.

Episodic memories. Explicit memories for the particular events and experiences of one's life.

Estradiol. The most common estrogen.

Estrogens. The class of steroid hormones that are released in large amounts by the ovaries; an example is estradiol.

Estrous cycle. The cycle of sexual receptivity displayed by many female mammals.

Estrus. The portion of the estrous cycle characterized by proceptivity, sexual receptivity, and fertility (*estrus* is a noun and *estrous* an adjective).

Ethological research. The study of animal behavior in its natural environment.

Ethology. The study of the behavior of animals in their natural environments.

Event-related potentials (ERPs). The EEG waves that regularly accompany certain psychological events.

Evolutionary perspective. The approach that focuses on the environmental pressures that likely led to the evolution of the characteristics (e.g., of brain and behavior) of current species.

Evolve. To undergo gradual orderly change.

Exaptation. A characteristic that evolved because it performed one function but was later co-opted to perform another.

Excitatory postsynaptic potentials (EPSPs). Graded postsynaptic depolarizations, which increase the likelihood that an action potential will be generated.

Exocrine glands. Glands that release chemicals into ducts that carry them to targets, mostly on the surface of the body.

Exocytosis. The process of releasing a neurotransmitter.

Experimental autoimmune encephalomyelitis. A model of multiple sclerosis that can be induced in laboratory animals by injecting them with myelin and a preparation that stimulates the immune system.

Explicit memories. Conscious memories.

Expressive. Pertaining to the generation of language; that is, pertaining to writing or talking.

Extensors. Muscles that act to straighten or extend a joint.

Exteroceptive sensory systems. The five sensory systems that interpret stimuli from outside the body: vision, hearing, touch, smell, and taste.

Extrafusal muscle. Skeletal muscle.

Facial feedback hypothesis. The hypothesis that our facial expressions can influence how we feel.

Far-field potentials. EEG signals recorded in attenuated form at the scalp because they originate far away—for example, in the brain stem.

Fasciculation. The tendency of developing axons to grow along the paths established by preceding axons.

Fasting phase. The metabolic phase that begins when energy from the preceding meal is no longer sufficient to meet the immediate needs of the body and during which energy is extracted from fat and glycogen stores.

Fear. The emotional reaction that is normally elicited by the presence or expectation of threatening stimuli.

Fear conditioning. Establishing fear of a previously neutral conditional stimulus by pairing it with an aversive unconditional stimulus.

Feminizes. Enhances or produces female characteristics.

Fetal alcohol syndrome (FAS). A syndrome produced by prenatal exposure to alcohol and characterized by brain damage, mental retardation, poor coordination, poor muscle tone, low birth weight, retarded growth, and/or physical deformity.

Fitness. According to Darwin, the ability of an organism to survive and contribute its genes to the next generation.

Flavor. The combined impression of taste and smell.

Flexors. Muscles that act to bend or flex a joint.

Follicle-stimulating hormone (FSH). The gonadotropic hormone that stimulates development of ovarian follicles.

Fourier analysis. A mathematical procedure for breaking down a complex wave form (e.g., an EEG signal) into component sine waves of varying frequency.

Fovea. The central indentation of the retina, which is specialized for high-acuity vision.

Fraternal twins. Twins that develop from different zygotes and thus are no more similar than any pair of siblings; dizygotic twins.

Free fatty acids. The main source of the body's energy during the fasting phase; released from adipose tissue in response to high levels of glucagon.

Free nerve endings. Neuron endings that lack specialized structures on them and that detect cutaneous pain and changes in temperature.

Free-running period. The duration of one cycle of a free-running rhythm.

Free-running rhythms. Circadian rhythms that do not depend on environmental cues to keep them on a regular schedule.

Frontal eye field. A small area of prefrontal cortex that controls eye movements.

Frontal operculum. The area of prefrontal cortex that in the left hemisphere is the location of Broca's area.

Frontal sections. Any slices of brain tissue cut in a plane that is parallel to the face; also termed *coronal sections*.

Functional MRI (fMRI). A magnetic resonance imaging technique for inferring brain activity by measuring increased oxygen flow into particular areas.

Functional segregation. Organization into different areas, each of which performs a different function; for example, in sensory systems, different areas of secondary and association cortex analyze different aspects of the same sensory stimulus.

Functional tolerance. Tolerance resulting from a reduction in the reactivity of the nervous system (or other sites of action) to a drug.

Gametes. Egg cells and sperm cells.

Ganglia. Clusters of neuronal cell bodies in the peripheral nervous system (singular *ganglion*).

Gap junctions. Narrow spaces between adjacent neurons that are bridged by fine tubular channels containing cytoplasm, through which electrical signals and small molecules can pass readily.

Gastric ulcers. Painful lesions to the lining of the stomach or duodenum.

Gate-control theory. The theory that signals descending from the brain can activate neural gating circuits in the spinal cord to block incoming pain signals.

Gene. A unit of inheritance; for example, the section of a chromosome that controls the synthesis of one protein.

Gene expression. The production of the protein specified by a particular gene.

Gene knockout techniques. Procedures for creating organisms that lack a particular gene.

Gene maps. Maps that indicate the relative positions of genes along a chromosome.

Gene replacement techniques. Procedures for creating organisms in which a particular gene has been replaced with another.

General paresis. The insanity and intellectual deterioration resulting from syphilitic infection.

Generalizability. The degree to which the results of a study can be applied to other individuals or situations.

Generalized anxiety disorders. Anxiety disorders that are not precipitated by any obvious event.

Generalized seizures. Seizures that involve the entire brain.

Genitals. The external reproductive organs.

Genotype. The traits that an organism can pass on to its offspring through its genetic material.

Glia-mediated migration. One of two major modes of neural migration during development, by which immature neurons move out from the central canal along radial glial cells.

Glial cells. Several classes of nonneural cells of the nervous system, whose important contributions to nervous system function are just starting to be understood.

Global amnesia. Amnesia for information presented in all sensory modalities.

Global aphasia. Severe disruption of all language-related abilities.

Glucagon. A pancreatic hormone that promotes the release of free fatty acids from adipose tissue, their conversion to ketones, and the use of both as sources of energy.

Glucocorticoids. Steroid hormones that are released from the adrenal cortex in response to stressors.

Gluconeogenesis. The process by which protein is converted to glucose.

Glucose. A simple sugar that is the breakdown product of complex carbohydrates; it is the body's primary, directly utilizable source of energy.

Glucostatic theory. The theory that eating is controlled by deviations from a hypothetical blood glucose set point.

Glutamate. The brain's most prevalent excitatory neurotransmitter, whose excessive release causes much of the brain damage resulting from cerebral ischemia.

Golgi complex. Structures in the cell bodies and terminal buttons of neurons that package neurotransmitters and other molecules in vesicles.

Golgi stain. A neural stain that completely darkens a few of the neurons in each slice of tissue, thereby revealing their silhouettes.

Golgi tendon organs. Receptors that are embedded in tendons and are sensitive to the amount of tension in the skeletal muscles to which their tendons are attached.

Gonadectomy. The surgical removal of the gonads (testes or ovaries); castration.

Gonadotropin. The pituitary tropic hormone that stimulates the release of hormones from the gonads.

Gonadotropin-releasing hormone. The hypothalamic releasing hormone that controls the release of the two gonadotropic hormones from the anterior pituitary.

Gonads. The testes and the ovaries.

Graded responses. Responses whose magnitude is indicative of the magnitude of the stimuli that induce them.

Grammatical analysis. Analysis of the structure of language.

Grand mal seizure. A seizure whose symptoms are loss of consciousness, loss of equilibrium, and a violent tonic-clonic convulsion.

Growth cone. Amoebalike structure at the tip of each growing axon or dendrite that guides growth to the appropriate target.

Growth hormone. The anterior pituitary hormone that acts directly on bone and muscle tissue to produce the pubertal growth spurt.

Guilty-knowledge technique. A lie-detection method in which the polygrapher records autonomic nervous system responses to a list of control and crime-related information known only to the guilty person and the examiner.

Hair cells. The receptors of the auditory system.

Haloperidol. A butyrophenone that was used as an antischizophrenic drug.

Harrison Narcotics Act. The act, passed in 1914, that made it illegal to sell or use opium, morphine, or cocaine in the United States.

Hashish. Dark corklike material extracted from the resin on the leaves and flowers of *Cannabis sativa.*

Hematoma. A bruise.

Helping-hand phenomenon. The redirection of one hand of a split-brain patient by the other hand.

Hemianopsic. Having a scotoma that covers half of the visual field.

Hemispherectomy. The removal of one cerebral hemisphere.

Heritability estimate. A numerical estimate of the proportion of variability that occurred in a particular trait in a particular study and that resulted from the genetic variation among the subjects in that study.

Heroin. A powerful semisynthetic opiate.

Heschl's gyrus. The temporal lobe gyrus that is the location of primary auditory cortex.

Heterosexual. Sexually attracted to members of the other sex.

Heterozygous. Possessing two different genes for a particular trait.

Hierarchical organization. Organization into a series of levels that can be ranked with respect to one another; for example, primary cortex, secondary cortex, and association cortex perform progressively more detailed analyses.

Hippocampus. A structure of the medial temporal lobes that plays a role in memory for spatial location.

Homeostasis. The stability of an organism's constant internal environment.

Hominids. The family of primates that includes *Homo sapiens* (humans), *Homo erectus,* and *Australopithecus.*

Homologous. Having a similar structure because of a common evolutionary origin (e.g., a human's arm and a bird's wing are homologous).

Homosexual. Sexually attracted to members of the same sex.

Homozygous. Possessing two identical genes for a particular trait.

Horizontal cells. Type of retinal neurons whose specialized function is lateral communication.

Horizontal sections. Any slices of brain tissue cut in a plane that is parallel to the top of the brain.

Hormones. Chemicals released by the endocrine system directly into the circulatory system.

Human genome project. The international research effort to construct a detailed map of the human chromosomes.

Huntington's disease. A progressive terminal disorder of motor and intellectual function that is produced in adulthood by a dominant gene.

H-Y antigen. The protein that stimulates the cells of the medullary portion of the primordial gonads to proliferate and develop into testes.

5-Hydroxytryptophan (5-HTP). The precursor of serotonin.

Hyperphagia. Excessive eating.

Hyperpolarize. To increase the resting membrane potential.

Hypersomnia. Disorders characterized by excessive sleep or sleepiness.

Hypertension. Chronically high blood pressure.

Hypnagogic hallucinations. Dreamlike experiences that occur during wakefulness.

Hypnotic drugs. Sleep-promoting drugs.

Hypothalamopituitary portal system. The vascular network that carries hormones from the hypothalamus to the anterior pituitary.

Hypoxia. Shortage of oxygen supply to tissue—for example, to the brain.

Iatrogenic. Physician-created.

Identical twins. Twins that develop from the same zygote and are thus genetically identical; monozygotic twins.

Imipramine. The first tricyclic antidepressant drug.

Immune system. The system that protects the body against infectious micro-organisms.

Immunocytochemistry. A procedure for locating particular proteins in the brain by labeling their antibodies with a dye or radioactive element and then exposing slices of brain tissue to the labeled antibodies.

Implicit memories. Memories that are expressed by improved performance without conscious recall or recognition.

Impotent. Unable to achieve a penile erection.

In situ hybridization. A technique for locating particular proteins in the brain; molecules that bind to the mRNA that directs the synthesis of the target protein are synthesized and labeled, and brain slices are exposed to them.

Incentive-sensitization theory. Theory that addictions develop when drug use sensitizes the neural circuits mediating wanting of the drug—not necessarily liking for the drug.

Incomplete-pictures test. A test of memory measuring the improved ability to identify fragmented figures that have been previously observed.

Independent variable. The difference between experimental conditions that is arranged by the experimenter.

Inferior. Toward the bottom of the primate head or brain.

Inferior colliculi. The structures of the tectum that receive auditory input from the superior olives.

Inferotemporal cortex. The cortex of the inferior temporal lobe, in which is located an area of secondary visual cortex that is involved in object recognition.

Infiltrating tumors. Tumors that grow diffusely through surrounding tissue.

Inhibitory factors. Hypothalamic hormones thought to regulate anterior pituitary hormones by inhibiting their release.

Inhibitory postsynaptic potentials (IPSPs). Graded postsynaptic hyperpolarizations, which decrease the likelihood that an action potential will be generated.

Initial stage 1 EEG. The period of the stage 1 EEG that occurs at the onset of sleep; it is not associated with REM.

Inside-out pattern. The pattern of cortical development in which orderly waves of tangential migrations progress systematically from deeper to more superficial layers.

Insomnia. Disorders of initiating and maintaining sleep.

Instinctive behaviors. Behaviors that occur in all like members of a species, even when there seems to have been no opportunity for them to have been learned.

Insulin. A pancreatic hormone that facilitates the entry of glucose into cells and the conversion of bloodborne fuels to forms that can be stored.

Integration. Adding or combining a number of individual signals into one overall signal.

Internal desynchronization. The cycling on different schedules of the free-running circadian rhythms of two different processes.

Interneurons. Neurons with short axons or no axons at all, whose function is to integrate neural activity within a single brain structure.

Intracranial self-stimulation (ICSS). The repeated performance of a response that delivers electrical stimulation to certain sites in the animal's brain.

Intrafusal motor neuron. A motor neuron that innervates an intrafusal muscle.

Intrafusal muscle. A threadlike muscle that adjusts the tension on a muscle spindle.

Intromission. Insertion of the penis into the vagina.

Ion channels. Pores in neural membranes through which specific ions pass.

Ionotropic receptors. Receptors that are associated with ligand-activated ion channels.

Ions. Positively or negatively charged particles.

Iproniazid. The first antidepressant drug; a monoamine oxidase inhibitor.

Ipsilateral. On the same side of the body.

Isometric contraction. Contraction of a muscle that increases the force of its pull but does not shorten the muscle.

James-Lange theory. The theory that emotional experience results from the brain's perception of the pattern of autonomic and somatic nervous system responses elicited by emotion-inducing sensory stimuli.

Jet lag. The adverse effects on body function of the acceleration of zeitgebers during east-bound flights or their deceleration during west-bound flights.

Ketones. Breakdown products of free fatty acids that are used by muscles as a source of energy during the fasting phase.

Kindling phenomenon. The progressive development and intensification of convulsions elicited by a series of periodic low-intensity brain stimulations—most commonly by daily electrical stimulations to the amygdala.

Kluver-Bucy syndrome. The syndrome of behavioral changes (e.g., lack of fear and hypersexuality) that is induced in primates by bilateral damage to the anterior temporal lobes.

Korsakoff's syndrome. A neuropsychological disorder that is common in alcoholics and whose primary symptom is severe memory loss.

Lateral. Away from the midline of the body of a vertebrate, toward the body's lateral surfaces.

Lateral geniculate nuclei. The six-layered thalamic structures that receive input from the retinas and transmit their output to the primary visual cortex.

Lateral hypothalamus (LH). The area of the hypothalamus once thought to be the feeding center.

Lateral inhibition. Inhibition of adjacent neurons or receptors in a topographic array.

Lateralization of function. The unequal representation of various psychological function in the two hemispheres of the brain.

L-Dopa. The chemical precursor of dopamine, which is used in the treatment of Parkinson's disease.

Leaky-barrel model. A settling-point model of body-fat regulation.

Learning. The brain's ability to change in response to experience.

Leptin. A protein normally synthesized in fat cells; it is thought to act as a negative feedback fat signal, reducing consumption.

Leucotome. Any of the various surgical devices used for performing lobotomies—*leucotomy* is another word for lobotomy.

Lexical procedure. A procedure for reading aloud that is based on specific stored information acquired about written words.

Ligand. A molecule that binds to another molecule; neurotransmitters are ligands of their receptors.

Limbic system. A collection of interconnected nuclei and tracts that borders the thalamus and is widely assumed to play a role in emotion.

Linkage. The tendency for traits that are encoded on the same chromosome to be inherited together.

Lipids. Fats.

Lipogenesis. The production of body fat.

Lipolysis. The breakdown of body fat.

Lipostatic theory. The theory that eating is controlled by deviations from a hypothetical body-fat set point.

Lithium. A metallic ion that is used in the treatment of bipolar affective disorder.

Lobectomy. An operation in which a lobe, or a major part of one, is removed from the brain.

Lobotomy. An operation in which a lobe, or a major part of one, is separated from the rest of the brain by a large cut but is not removed.

Long-term potentiation (LTP). The enduring facilitation of synaptic transmission that occurs following activation of synapses by high-intensity, high-frequency stimulation of the presynaptic neurons.

Lordosis. The arched-back, rump-up, tail-to-the-side posture of female rodent sexual receptivity, which serves to facilitate intromission.

Lordosis quotient. The proportion of mounts that elicit lordosis.

Lucid dreams. Dreams in which the dreamer is aware that she or he is dreaming and can influence the course of the dream.

Luteinizing hormone (LH). The gonadotropic hormone that causes the developing ovum to be released from its follicle.

Lymphocytes. Specialized white blood cells that are produced in bone marrow and play important roles in the body's immune reactions.

Macrophage. A large phagocyte that plays a role in cell-mediated immunity.

Magnetic resonance imaging (MRI). A procedure in which high-resolution images of the structures of the living brain are constructed from the measurement of waves that hydrogen atoms emit when they are activated by radio-frequency waves in a magnetic field.

Magnetoencephalography (MEG). A technique for recording changes produced in magnetic fields on the surface of the scalp by changes in underlying patterns of neural activity.

Magnocellular layers. The layers of the lateral geniculate nuclei that are composed of neurons with large cell bodies; the bottom two layers (also called *M layers*).

Malignant tumors. Tumors that may continue to grow in the body even after attempted surgical removal.

Mammals. Species whose young are fed from mammary glands.

Mania. An affective disorder in which the patient is overconfident, impulsive, distractible, and highly energetic.

MAO inhibitors. Antidepressant drugs that increase the level of monoamine neurotransmitters by inhibiting the action of monoamine oxidase.

Masculinizes. Enhances or produces male characteristics.

Medial. Toward the midline of the body of a vertebrate.

Medial diencephalic amnesia. Amnesia that is associated with damage to the medial diencephalon (e.g., Korsakoff's amnesia).

Medial dorsal nuclei. The thalamic relay nuclei of the olfactory system.

Medial geniculate nuclei. The auditory thalamic nuclei that receive input from the inferior colliculi and project to primary auditory cortex.

Medial lemniscus. The somatosensory pathway between the dorsal column nuclei and the ventral posterior nucleus of the thalamus.

Medial preoptic area. The area of the hypothalamus that includes the sexually dimorphic nuclei and that plays a key role in the control of male sexual behavior.

Medial temporal lobe amnesia. Amnesia associated with bilateral damage to the medial temporal lobes; its major feature is anterograde amnesia for explicit memories in combination with preserved intellectual functioning.

Mediodorsal nuclei. A pair of medial diencephalic nuclei in the thalamus, damage to which is thought to be responsible for many of the memory deficits associated with Korsakoff's syndrome.

Meiosis. The process of cell division that produces cells (e.g., egg cells and sperm cells) with half the chromosomes of the parent cell.

Melatonin. A hormone that is synthesized from serotonin in the pineal gland and influences the circadian rhythm of sleep.

Membrane potential. The difference in electrical charge between the inside and the outside of a cell.

Memory. The brain's ability to store and access the learned effects of experiences.

Memory consolidation. The transfer of short-term memories to long-term storage.

Meninges. The three protective membranes that cover the brain and spinal cord (singular *meninx*).

Meningiomas. Tumors that grow between the meninges.

Meningitis. Inflammation of the meninges, usually caused by bacterial infection.

Menstrual cycle. The hormone-regulated cycle in women of follicle growth, egg release, buildup of the uterus lining, and menstruation.

Mesoderm layer. The middle of the three cell layers in the developing embryo.

Mesotelencephalic dopamine system. The ascending projections of dopamine-releasing neurons from the substantia nigra and ventral tegmental area of the mesencephalon (midbrain) into various regions of the telencephalon.

Messenger RNA. A strand of RNA that is transcribed from DNA and carries the genetic code out of the cell nucleus to direct the synthesis of a protein.

Metabolic tolerance. Tolerance that results from a reduction in the amount of a drug getting to its sites of action.

Metabotropic receptors. Receptors that are associated with signal proteins and G proteins.

Metastatic tumors. Tumors that originate in one organ and spread to another.

Microelectrodes. Extremely fine recording electrodes, which are used for intracellular recording.

Microglia. Glial cells that respond to injury or disease by engulfing cellular debris and triggering inflammatory responses.

Microsleeps. Brief periods of sleep that occur in sleep-deprived subjects while they remain sitting or standing.

Microspectrophotometry. A technique for measuring the absorption spectrum of the photopigment contained in a single cone.

Migration. The movement of cells from their site of creation in the ventricular zone of the neural tube to their ultimate location in the mature nervous system.

Minor hemisphere. A term used in the past to refer to the right hemisphere, based on the incorrect assumption that the left hemisphere is dominant.

Mitochondria. The energy-generating, DNA-containing structures in each cell's cytoplasm.

Mitosis. The process of cell division that produces cells with the same number of chromosomes as the parent cell.

Monocular. Involving only one eye.

Monogamy. A pattern of mate bonding in which one male and one female form an enduring bond.

Monophasic sleep cycles. Sleep cycles that regularly involve only one period of sleep per day, typically at night.

Mood stabilizer. A drug that blocks the rapid transition between depression and mania.

Morgan's Canon. The rule that the simplest possible interpretation for a behavioral observation should be given precedence.

Morphine. The major psychoactive ingredient in opium.

Morris water maze. A pool of milky water that has a goal platform invisible just beneath its surface and is used to study the ability of rats to learn spatial locations.

Morris water maze test. A widely used test of spatial memory in which rats must learn to swim directly to a platform hidden just beneath the surface of a circular pool of murky water.

Motor end-plate. The receptive area on a muscle fiber at a neuromuscular junction.

Motor equivalence. The ability of the sensorimotor system to carry out the same basic movement in different ways that involve different muscles.

Motor homunculus. The somatotopic map of the human primary motor cortex.

Motor pool. All of the motor neurons that innervate the fibers of a given muscle.

Motor units. A single motor neuron and all of the skeletal muscle fibers that are innervated by it.

MPTP. A neurotoxin that produces a disorder in primates that is similar to Parkinson's disease.

Müllerian-inhibiting substance. The testicular hormone that causes the precursor of the female reproductive ducts (the Müllerian system) to degenerate and the testes to descend.

Müllerian system. The embryonic precursor of the female reproductive ducts.

Multiple sclerosis (MS). A progressive disease that attacks the myelin of axons in the CNS.

Multipolar neuron. A neuron with more than two processes extending from its cell body.

Multipotent. Capable of developing into a limited number of types of mature body cell.

Mumby box. An apparatus that is used in a rat version of the delayed nonmatching-to-sample test.

Muscle spindles. Receptors that are embedded in skeletal muscle tissue and are sensitive to changes in muscle length.

Mutations. Accidental alterations in individual genes that arise during chromosome duplication.

Narcolepsy. A disorder in the hypersomnia category that is characterized by repeated, brief daytime sleep attacks and cataplexy.

Narcotic. A legal category of drugs, mostly opiates.

Nasal hemiretina. The half of each retina next to the nose.

Natural selection. The idea that heritable traits that are associated with high rates of survival and reproduction are preferentially passed on to future generations.

Nature–nurture issue. The debate about the relative contributions of nature (genes) and nurture (experience) to the behavioral capacities of individuals.

NEAT. Nonexercise activity thermogenesis, which is generated by activities such as fidgeting and the maintenance of posture and muscle tone.

Necrosis. Passive cell death, which is characterized by inflammation.

Negative feedback systems. Systems in which feedback from changes in one direction elicit compensatory effects in the opposite direction.

Nerve growth factor (NGF). A neurotrophin that attracts the growing axons of the sympathetic nervous system and promotes their survival.

Nerves. Bundles of axons in the peripheral nervous system.

Neural crest. The structure that is formed by cells breaking off from the neural groove during the formation of the neural tube and that develops into the peripheral nervous system.

Neural plate. A small patch of ectodermal tissue on the dorsal surface of the vertebrate embryo, from which the neural groove, the neural tube, and, ultimately, the mature nervous system develop.

Neural proliferation. The rapid increase in the number of neurons that follows the formation of the neural tube.

Neural regeneration. The regrowth of damaged neurons.

Neural tube. The tube that is formed in the vertebrate embryo when the edges of the neural groove fuse and that develops into the central nervous system.

Neuroanatomy. The study of the structure of the nervous system.

Neurochemistry. The study of the chemical bases of neural activity.

Neuroendocrinology. The study of the interactions between the nervous system and the endocrine system.

Neurogenesis. The growth of new neurons.

Neuroleptics. Drugs that alleviate schizophrenic symptoms.

Neuromuscular junctions. The synapses of a motor neuron on a muscle.

Neurons. Cells of the nervous system that are specialized for receiving and transmitting electrochemical signals.

Neuropathology. The study of nervous system disorders.

Neuropharmacology. The study of the effects of drugs on neural activity.

Neurophysiology. The study of the functions and activities of the nervous system.

Neuropsychology. The division of biopsychology that studies the psychological effects of brain damage in human patients.

Neuroscience. The scientific study of the nervous system.

Neurotoxins. Neural poisons.

Neurotrophins. Chemicals that are supplied to developing neurons by their targets and that promote their survival.

Nicotine. The major psychoactive ingredient of tobacco.

Nigrostriatal pathway. The pathway along which axons from the substantia nigra project to the striatum.

Nissl stain. A neural stain that has an affinity for structures in neuron cell bodies.

Nitric oxide. A soluble-gas neurotransmitter that is thought to serve as a signal from postsynaptic neurons to presynaptic neurons in the maintenance of LTP.

NMDA (N-methyl-D-aspartate) receptors. Glutamate receptors that play key roles in the development of stroke-induced brain damage and long-term potentiation at glutaminergic synapses.

Nocturnal myoclonus. Periodic sleep-disrupting twitching of body, usually the legs, during sleep.

Nodes of Ranvier. The gaps between adjacent myelin segments on an axon.

Nondirected synapses. Synapses at which the site of neurotransmitter release and the site of neurotransmitter reception are not close together.

Nuclei. The DNA-containing structures of cells; also, clusters of neuronal cell bodies in the central nervous system (singular *nucleus*).

Nucleotide bases. A class of chemical substances that includes adenine, thymine, guanine, and cytosine—the constituents of the genetic code.

Nucleus accumbens. Nucleus of the ventral striatum and a major terminal of the mesocorticolimbic dopamine pathway.

Nucleus magnocellularis. The nucleus of the caudal reticular formation that promotes relaxation of the core muscles during REM sleep and during cataplectic attacks.

Nutritive density. Calories per unit volume of a food.

Ob/ob mice. Mice that are homozygous for the mutant ob gene; their body fat produces no leptin, and they become very obese.

Obsessive-compulsive disorders. Anxiety disorders characterized by recurring uncontrollable, anxiety-producing thoughts and impulses.

Off-center cells. Visual neurons that respond to lights shone in the center of their receptive fields with "off" firing and to lights shone in the periphery of their fields with "on" firing.

Olfactory bulbs. The first cranial nerves, whose output goes primarily to the amygdala and piriform cortex.

Olfactory mucosa. The mucous membrane that lines the upper nasal passages and contains the olfactory receptor cells.

Oligodendrocytes. Glial cells that myelinate axons of the central nervous system; also known as *oligodendroglia.*

Ommatidia. The visual receptors of the horseshoe crab.

On-center cells. Visual neurons that respond to lights shone in the center of their receptive fields with "on" firing and to lights shone in the periphery of their fields with "off" firing.

Ontogeny. The development of individuals over their life span.

Open-field test. A method for recording and scoring the general activity of an animal in a large, barren chamber.

Operant conditioning paradigm. A paradigm in which the rate of a particular voluntary response is increased by reinforcement or decreased by punishment.

Operator genes. Short segments of DNA that determine whether or not messenger RNA will be transcribed from associated structural genes.

Opiates. Morphine, codeine, heroin, and other chemicals with similar structures or effects.

Opium. The sap that exudes from the seed pods of the opium poppy.

Opponent-process theory. The theory that a visual receptor or a neuron signals one color when it responds in one way (e.g., by increasing its firing rate) and signals its complementary color when it responds in the opposite way (e.g., by decreasing its firing rate).

Optic tectum. The main destination of retinal ganglion cells in lower vertebrates.

Orbitofrontal cortex. The cortex of the inferior frontal lobes, which receives olfactory input from the thalamus.

Orchidectomy. The removal of the testes.

Orexin. A neuropeptide that has been implicated in narcolepsy in dogs and in knockout mice.

Organ of Corti. The auditory receptor organ, comprising the basilar membrane, the hair cells, and the tectorial membrane.

Orthodromic conduction. Axonal conduction in the normal direction—from the cell body toward the terminal buttons.

Ossicles. The three small bones of the middle ear: the malleus, the incus, and the stapes.

Oval window. The membrane that transfers vibrations from the ossicles to the fluid of the cochlea.

Ovariectomy. The removal of the ovaries.

Ovaries. The female gonads.

Oxytocin. One of the two major peptide hormones of the posterior pituitary, which in females stimulates contractions of the uterus during labor and the ejection of milk during suckling.

Pacinian corpuscles. The largest and most deeply positioned cutaneous receptors, which are sensitive to sudden displacements of the skin.

Paired-image subtraction technique. The use of PET or fMRI to locate constituent cognitive processes in the brain by producing an image of the difference in brain activity associated with two cognitive tasks that differ in terms of a single constituent cognitive process.

Panic disorders. Anxiety disorders characterized by recurring rapid-onset attacks of extreme fear and severe symptoms of stress (choking, heart palpitations, and shortness of breath).

Parallel processing. The simultaneous analysis of a signal in different ways by the multiple parallel pathways of a neural network.

Parasympathetic nerves. Those motor nerves of the autonomic nervous system that project from the brain (as components of cranial nerves) or from the sacral region of the spinal cord.

Paraventricular nuclei. Hypothalamic nuclei that play a role in eating and synthesize hormones released by the posterior pituitary.

Parkinson's disease. A movement disorder that is associated with degeneration of dopaminergic neurons in the nigrostriatal pathway.

Partial seizures. Seizures that do not involve the entire brain.

Parvocellular layers. The layers of the lateral geniculate nuclei that are composed of neurons with small cell bodies; the top four layers (also called *P layers*).

Patellar tendon reflex. The stretch reflex that is elicited when the patellar tendon is struck.

Pavlovian conditioning paradigm. A paradigm in which the experimenter pairs an initially neutral stimulus (conditional stimulus) with a stimulus (unconditional stimulus) that elicits a reflexive response (unconditional response); after several pairings, the neutral stimulus elicits a response (conditional response).

Peptide hormones. Hormones that are short chains of amino acids.

Peptides. Short chains of amino acids, some of which function as neurotransmitters.

Perception. The higher-order process of integrating, recognizing, and interpreting complex patterns of sensations.

Periaqueductal gray (PAG). The gray matter around the cerebral aqueduct, which contains opiate receptors and activates a descending analgesia circuit.

Perimetry test. The procedure used to map scotomas.

Peripheral nervous system (PNS). The portion of the nervous system outside the skull and spine.

Perseveration. The tendency to continue making a formerly correct response that is currently incorrect.

Petit mal seizure. A generalized seizure that is characterized by a disruption of consciousness and a 3-per-second spike-and-wave EEG discharge.

Phagocytosis. The consumption and destruction of dead tissue and foreign micro-organisms by specialized body cells (phagocytes).

Phantom limb. The vivid perception that an amputated limb still exists.

Phenothiazines. A class of antischizophrenic drugs that bind effectively to both D_1 and D_2 receptors.

Phenotype. An organism's observable traits.

Phenylketonuria (PKU). A neurological disorder whose symptoms are vomiting, seizures, hyperactivity, hyperirritability, mental retardation, brain damage, and high levels of phenylpyruvic acid in the urine.

Phenylpyruvic acid. A substance that is found in abnormally high concentrations in the urine of those suffering from phenylketonuria.

Pheromones. Chemicals that are released by an animal and elicit through their odor specific patterns of behavior in its conspecifics.

Phobic anxiety disorders. Anxiety disorders characterized by extreme, largely irrational fears of specific objects or situations.

Phonemes. Individual speech sounds.

Phonetic procedure. A procedure for reading aloud that involves the recognition of letters and the application of a language's rules of pronunciation.

Phonological analysis. Analysis of the sound of language.

Photopic spectral sensitivity curve. The graph of the sensitivity of cone-mediated vision to different wavelengths of light.

Photopic vision. Cone-mediated vision, which predominates when lighting is good.

Phylogeny. The evolutionary development of species.

Physical-dependence theories of addiction. Theories holding that the main factor that motivates drug addicts to keep taking drugs is the prevention or termination of withdrawal symptoms.

Physically dependent. Being in a state in which the discontinuation of drug taking will induce withdrawal reactions.

Physiological psychology. The division of biopsychology that studies the neural mechanisms of behavior through direct manipulation of the brains of nonhuman animal subjects in controlled experiments.

Pia mater. The delicate, innermost meninx.

Pineal gland. The endocrine gland that is the human body's sole source of melatonin.

Pioneer growth cones. The first growth cones to travel along a particular route in the developing nervous system.

Piriform cortex. An area of medial temporal cortex that is adjacent to the amygdala and that receives direct olfactory input.

Pituitary stalk. The structure connecting the hypothalamus and the pituitary gland.

Place cells. Neurons that develop place fields—that is, that respond only when the subject is in a particular place in a familiar test environment.

Planum temporale. An area of temporal lobe cortex that lies in the posterior region of the lateral fissure and, in the left hemisphere, roughly corresponds to Wernicke's area.

Plethysmography. Any technique for measuring changes in the volume of blood in a part of the body.

Polyandry. A pattern of mate bonding in which one female bonds with more than one male.

Polygraphy. A method of interrogation in which autonomic nervous system indexes of emotion are used to infer the truthfulness of the responses.

Polygyny. A pattern of mate bonding in which one male bonds with more than one female; the most prevalent pattern of mate bonding in mammals.

Polyphasic sleep cycles. Sleep cycles that regularly involve more than one period of sleep per day.

Positive-incentive theory. The idea that behaviors (e.g., eating and drinking) are motivated by their anticipated pleasurable effects.

Positive-incentive theories of addiction. Theories holding that the primary factor in most cases of addiction is a craving for the pleasure-producing properties of drugs.

Positive-incentive value. The anticipated pleasure involved in the performance of a particular behavior, such as eating a particular food or drinking a particular beverage.

Positron emission tomography (PET). A technique for visualizing brain activity, usually by measuring the accumulation of radioactive 2-deoxyglucose (2-DG) or radioactive water in the various areas of the brain.

Posterior. Toward the tail end of a vertebrate or toward the back of the head.

Posterior parietal (association) cortex. An area of association cortex that receives input from the visual, auditory, and somatosensory systems and is involved in the perception of spatial location and guidance of voluntary behavior.

Posterior pituitary. The part of the pituitary gland that contains the terminals of hypothalamic neurons.

Postsynaptic inhibition. A form of inhibition that reduces a neuron's responsiveness to all excitatory synaptic inputs.

Posttraumatic amnesia (PTA). Amnesia produced by a nonpenetrating head injury (a blow to the head that does not penetrate the skull).

Posttraumatic stress disorder. An anxiety disorder exhibited as a persistent pattern of psychological distress that follows a period of exposure to extreme stress.

Prefrontal lobes. The large areas, left and right, at the very front of the brain.

Prefrontal lobotomy. A surgical procedure in which the connections between the prefrontal lobes and the rest of the brain are cut, as a treatment for mental illness.

Premotor cortex. The area of secondary motor cortex that lies between the supplementary motor area and the lateral fissure.

Prestriate cortex. The band of tissue in the occipital lobe that surrounds the primary visual cortex and contains areas of secondary visual cortex.

Presynaptic inhibition. A form of inhibition that reduces a neuron's responsiveness to specific synaptic input and is mediated by excitatory axoaxonal synapses.

Primary motor cortex. The cortex of the precentral gyrus, which is the major point of departure for motor signals descending from the cerebral cortex into lower levels of the sensorimotor system.

Primary sensory cortex. An area of sensory cortex that receives most of its input directly from the thalamic relay nuclei of one sensory system.

Primary visual cortex. The area of the cortex that receives direct input from the lateral geniculate nuclei (also called *striate cortex*).

Primates. One of 14 different orders of mammals; there are five families of primates: prosimians, New-World monkeys, Old-World monkeys, apes, and hominids.

Primed. Induced to resume self-stimulation by the delivery of a few free stimulations.

Proceptive behaviors. Behaviors that solicit the sexual advances of members of the other sex.

Progesterone. A progestin that prepares the uterus and breasts for pregnancy.

Progestins. The class of steroid hormones that includes progesterone.

Prosody. Emotional tone of voice.

Prosopagnosia. Visual agnosia for faces.

Protein hormones. Hormones that are long chains of amino acids.

Proteins. Long chains of amino acids.

Proximal segment. The segment of a cut axon between the cut and the cell body.

Prozac. The trade name of fluoxetine, the first selective serotonin-reuptake inhibitor developed for treating depression.

Psychiatric disorder. A disorder of psychological function sufficiently severe to require treatment by a psychiatrist or clinical psychologist.

Psychoactive drugs. Drugs that influence subjective experience and behavior by acting on the nervous system.

Psychological dependence. Presumed cause of any compulsive drug taking that occurs in the absence of physical dependence.

Psychoneuroimmunology. The study of interactions among psychological factors, the nervous system, and the immune system.

Psychopharmacology. The division of biopsychology that studies the effects of drugs on the brain and behavior.

Psychophysiology. The division of biopsychology that studies the relation between physiological activity and psychological processes in human subjects by noninvasive methods.

P300 wave. The positive EEG wave that usually occurs about 300 milliseconds after a momentary stimulus that has meaning for the subject.

Pulsatile hormone release. The typical pattern of hormone release, which occurs in large surges several times a day.

Punch-drunk syndrome. The dementia and cerebral scarring that result from repeated concussions.

Pure research. Research motivated primarily by the curiosity of the researcher and done solely for the purpose of acquiring knowledge.

Purkinje effect. In intense light, red and yellow wavelengths look brighter than blue or green wavelengths of equal intensity; in dim light, blue and green wavelengths look brighter than red and yellow wavelengths of equal intensity.

Pyramidal cell layer. The major layer of cell bodies in the hippocampus.

Pyramidal cells. Large multipolar cortical neurons with a pyramid-shaped cell body, an apical dendrite, and a very long axon.

Quasiexperimental studies. Studies of groups of subjects who have been exposed to the conditions of interest in the real world; such studies have the appearance of experiments but are not true experiments because potential confounded variables have not been controlled.

Radial arm maze. A maze in which several arms radiate out from a central starting chamber, commonly used to study spatial learning in rats.

Radial arm maze test. A widely used test of rats' spatial ability in which the same arms are baited on each trial, and the rats must learn to visit only the baited arms only one time on each trial.

Radial glial cells. Glial cells that exist in the neural tube only during the period of neural migration and that form a network along which radial migration occurs.

Radial migration. Movement of cells in the developing neural tube from the ventricular zone in a straight line outward toward the tube's outer wall.

Reactive depression. Depression that is triggered by a negative experience.

Receptive. Pertaining to the comprehension of language and speech.

Receptive field. The area of the visual field within which it is possible for the appropriate stimulus to influence the firing of a visual neuron.

Receptor blockers. Antagonistic drugs that bind to postsynaptic receptors without activating them and block the access of the usual neurotransmitter.

Receptor subtypes. The different types of receptors to which a particular neurotransmitter can bind.

Receptors. Cells that are specialized to receive chemical, mechanical, or radiant signals from the environment; also proteins that contain binding sites for particular neurotransmitters.

Recessive trait. The trait of a dichotomous pair that is not expressed in the phenotype of heterozygous individuals.

Reciprocal innervation. The principle of spinal cord circuitry that causes a muscle to automatically relax when a muscle that is antagonistic to it contracts.

Recovery theories of sleep. Theories based on the premise that being awake disturbs the body's homeostasis and the function of sleep is to restore it.

Recurrent collateral inhibition. The inhibition of a neuron that is produced by its own activity via a collateral branch of its axon and an inhibitory interneuron.

Reference memory. Memory for the general principles and skills that are required to perform a task.

Relative refractory period. A period after the absolute refractory period during which a higher-than-normal amount of stimulation is necessary to make a neuron fire.

Releasing factors. Hypothesized hypothalamic releasing hormones that have not yet been isolated.

Releasing hormones. Hypothalamic hormones that stimulate the release of hormones from the anterior pituitary.

REM sleep. The stage of sleep characterized by rapid eye movements, loss of core muscle tone, and emergent stage 1 EEG.

Repetition priming tests. Tests of implicit memory; in one example, a list of words is presented, then fragments of the original words are presented and the subject is asked to complete them.

Replacement injections. Injections of a hormone whose natural release has been curtailed by the removal of the gland that normally releases it.

Replication. The process by which the DNA molecule duplicates itself.

Reserpine. The first monoamine antagonist to be used in the treatment of schizophrenia; the active ingredient of the snakeroot plant.

Response-chunking hypothesis. The idea that practice combines the central sensorimotor programs that control individual responses into programs that control sequences of responses (chunks of behavior).

Resting potential. The steady membrane potential of a neuron at rest, usually about −70 mV.

Restless legs. Tension or uneasiness in the legs that keeps people from falling asleep.

Reticular activating system. The hypothetical arousal system in the reticular formation.

Reticular formation. A complex network of nuclei in the core of the brain stem that contains, among other things, motor programs that regulate complex species-common movements such as walking and swimming.

Retina-geniculate-striate pathway. The major visual pathway from each retina to the striate cortex (primary visual cortex) via the lateral geniculate nuclei of the thalamus.

Retinal ganglion cells. Retinal neurons whose axons leave the eyeball and form the optic nerve.

Retinex theory. Land's theory that the color of an object is determined by its reflectance, which the visual system calculates by comparing the ability of adjacent surfaces to reflect short, medium, and long wavelengths.

Retinotopic. Organized, like the primary visual cortex, according to a map of the retina.

Retrograde amnesia. Loss of memory for events or information learned before the amnesia inducing brain injury.

Retrograde degeneration. Degeneration of the proximal segment of a cut axon.

Reuptake. The drawing back into the terminal button of neurotransmitter molecules after their release into the synapse; the more common of the two mechanisms for deactivating a released neurotransmitter.

Rhinal cortex. An area of medial temporal cortex adjacent to the amygdala and hippocampus.

Rhodopsin. The photopigment of rods.

Ribonucleic acid (RNA). A molecule that is similar to DNA except that it has the nucleotide base uracil and a phosphate and ribose backbone.

Ribosome. A structure in the cell's cytoplasm that translates the genetic code from strands of messenger RNA.

Rods. The visual receptors in the retina that mediate achromatic, low-acuity vision under dim light.

Saccades. The rapid movements of the eyes between fixations.

Sagittal sections. Any slices of brain tissue cut in a plane that is parallel to the side of the brain.

Saltatory conduction. Conduction of an action potential from one node of Ranvier to the next along a myelinated axon.

Satiety. The motivational state that terminates a meal when there is food remaining.

Savants. Intellectually handicapped individuals who nevertheless display amazing and specific cognitive or artistic abilities; savant abilities are sometimes associated with autism.

Schwann cells. The glial cells that compose the myelin sheaths of PNS axons and promote their regeneration.

Scientific inference. The logical process by which observable events are used to infer the properties of unobservable events.

Scotoma. An area of blindness produced by damage to, or disruption of, an area of the visual system.

Scotopic spectral sensitivity curve. The graph of the sensitivity of rod-mediated vision to different wavelengths of light.

Scotopic vision. Rod-mediated vision, which predominates in dim light.

Scrotum. The sac that holds the male testes outside the body cavity.

Second messenger. A chemical synthesized in a neuron in response to the binding of a neurotransmitter to a metabotropic receptor in its cell membrane.

Secondary motor cortex. Areas of the cerebral cortex that receive much of their input from association cortex and send much of their output to primary motor cortex.

Secondary sensory cortex. Areas of sensory cortex that receive most of their input from the primary sensory cortex of one sensory system or from other areas of secondary cortex of the same system.

Secondary sex characteristics. Body features, other than the reproductive organs, that distinguish men from women.

Selective attention. The ability to focus on a small subset of the multitude of stimuli that are being received at any one time.

Self-stimulation paradigm. A paradigm in which animals press a lever to administer reinforcing electrical stimulation to their own brains.

Semantic analysis. Analysis of the meaning of language.

Semantic memories. Explicit memories for general facts and knowledge.

Semicircular canals. The receptive organs of the vestibular system.

Sensation. The process of detecting the presence of stimuli.

Sensitive period. The period during the development of a particular trait, usually early in life, when a particular experience is likely to change the course of that development.

Sensitivity. In vision, the ability to detect the presence of dimly lit objects.

Sensorimotor phase. The second of the two phases of birdsong development, during which juvenile birds progress from subsongs to adult songs.

Sensory evoked potential. A change in the electrical activity of the brain (e.g., in the cortical EEG) that is elicited by the momentary presentation of a sensory stimulus.

Sensory feedback. Sensory signals that are produced by a response and are often used to guide the continuation of the response.

Sensory phase. The first of the two phases of birdsong development, during which young birds do not sing but form memories of the adult songs they hear.

Sensory-specific satiety. The fact that the consumption of a particular food produces increased satiety for foods of the same taste than for other foods.

Set point. The value of a physiological parameter that is maintained constantly by physiological or behavioral mechanisms; for example, the body's energy resources are often assumed to be maintained at a constant optimal level by compensatory changes in hunger.

Set-point assumption. The assumption that hunger is typically triggered by the decline of the body's energy reserves below their set point.

Settling point. The point at which various factors that influence the level of some regulated function (such as body weight) achieve an equilibrium.

Sex chromosomes. The pair of chromosomes that determine an individual's sex: XX for a female and XY for a male.

Sex-linked traits. Traits that are influenced by genes on the sex chromosomes.

Sexually dimorphic nucleus. The nucleus in the medial preoptic area of rats that is larger in males than in females.

Sham eating. The experimental protocol in which an animal chews and swallows food, which immediately exits its body through a tube implanted in its esophagus.

Sham rage. The exaggerated, poorly directed aggressive responses of decorticate animals.

Signal averaging. A method of increasing the signal-to-noise ratio by reducing background noise.

Simple cells. Neurons in the visual cortex that respond maximally to straight-edge stimuli in a certain position and orientation.

Simple partial seizures. Partial seizures in which the symptoms are primarily sensory or motor or both.

Simultanagnosia. A disorder characterized by the inability to attend to more than one thing at a time.

Sinestrals. Left-handers.

Sine-wave grating. An array of equally spaced, parallel, alternating dark and light stripes that is created by varying the light across the grating in a sine-wave pattern.

Skeletal muscle (extrafusal muscle). Striated muscle that is attached to the skeleton and is usually under voluntary control.

Skin conductance level (SCL). The steady level of skin conductance associated with a particular situation.

Skin conductance response (SCR). The transient change in skin conductance associated with a brief experience.

Sleep apnea. A condition in which sleep is repeatedly disturbed by momentary interruptions in breathing.

Sleep paralysis. A sleep disorder characterized by the inability to move (paralysis) just as a person is falling asleep or waking up.

Slow-wave sleep (SWS). Stages 3 and 4 of sleep, which are characterized by the largest and slowest EEG waves.

Smoker's syndrome. The chest pain, labored breathing, wheezing, coughing, and heightened susceptibility to infections of the respiratory tract commonly observed in tobacco smokers.

Sodium amytal test. A test involving the anesthetization of first one cerebral hemisphere and then the other to determine which hemisphere plays the dominant role in language.

Sodium–potassium pumps. Active transport mechanisms that pump Na$^+$ ions out of neurons and K$^+$ ions in.

Solitary nucleus. The medullary relay nucleus of the gustatory system.

Somal translocation. One of two major modes of neural migration, in which an extension grows out from the undeveloped neuron and draws the cell body up into it.

Somatic nervous system (SNS). The part of the peripheral nervous system that interacts with the external environment.

Somatosensory homunculus. The somatotopic map that corresponds to the primary somatosensory cortex.

Somatotopic. Organized, like the primary somatosensory cortex, according to a map of the surface of the body.

Somnambulism. Sleepwalking.

Spandrels. Nonadaptive characteristics that evolve because they are related to evolutionary changes that are adaptive.

Spatial-frequency theory. The theory that the visual cortex encodes visual patterns in terms of their component sine waves.

Spatial resolution. Ability of a recording technique to detect differences in spatial location (e.g., to pinpoint a location in the brain).

Spatial summation. The integration of signals that occur at different sites on the neuron's membrane.

Species. A group of organisms that is reproductively isolated from other organisms; the members of one species cannot produce fertile offspring by mating with members of other species.

Species-common behaviors. Behaviors that are displayed in the same manner by virtually all like members of a species.

Spindle afferent neurons. Neurons that carry signals from muscle spindles into the spinal cord via the dorsal root.

Split-brain patients. Commissurotomized patients.

Stabilized retinal image. A retinal image that does not shift across the retina when the eye moves.

Static phase. The second phase of the VMH syndrome, during which the grossly obese animal maintains a stable level of obesity.

Stellate cells. Small star-shaped cortical interneurons.

Stem cells. Developing cells that have the capacity for self-renewal and the potential to develop into various types of mature cells.

Stereognosis. The process of identifying objects by touch.

Stereotaxic atlas. A series of maps representing the three-dimensional structure of the brain that is used to determine coordinates for stereotaxic surgery.

Stereotaxic instrument. A device for performing stereotaxic surgery, composed of two parts: a head holder and an electrode holder.

Steroid hormones. Hormones that are synthesized from cholesterol.

Stimulants. Drugs that produce general increases in neural and behavioral activity.

Stress. The physiological response to physical or psychological threat.

Stretch reflex. A reflexive countering reaction to an unanticipated external stretching force on a muscle.

Striatum. A structure of the basal ganglia that is the terminal of the dopaminergic nigrostriatal pathway and is damaged in Parkinson's patients; it seems to play a role in memory for consistent relationships between stimuli and responses in multiple-trial tasks.

Strokes. Sudden-onset cerebrovascular disorders that cause brain damage.

Structural genes. Genes that contain the information required for the synthesis of a particular protein.

Subarachnoid space. The space beneath the arachnoid membrane, which contains many large blood vessels and cerebrospinal fluid.

Subjective contours. Perceived visual contours that do not exist.

Subordination stress. Stress experienced by animals, typically males, that are continually attacked by higher-ranking conspecifics.

Substantia nigra. The midbrain nucleus whose neurons project via the nigrostriatal pathway to the striatum of the basal ganglia; it is part of the mesotelencephalic dopamine system and degenerates in cases of Parkinson's disease.

Superior. Toward the top of the primate head.

Superior olives. Medullary nuclei that play a role in sound localization.

Supplementary motor area. The area of secondary motor cortex that is within and adjacent to the longitudinal fissure.

Suprachiasmatic nuclei (SCN). Nuclei of the medial hypothalamus that control the circadian cycles of various body functions.

Supraoptic nuclei. Hypothalamic nuclei in which the hormones of the posterior pituitary are synthesized.

Surface dyslexia. A reading disorder in which the lexical procedure is disrupted while the phonetic procedure is not.

Sympathetic nerves. Those motor nerves of the autonomic nervous system that project from the CNS in the lumbar and thoracic areas of the spinal cord.

Synaptic vesicles. Small spherical membranes that store neurotransmitter molecules and release them into the synaptic cleft.

Synaptogenesis. The formation of new synapses.

Synergistic muscles. Pairs of muscles whose contraction produces a movement in the same direction.

T cells. T lymphocytes; lymphocytes that bind to foreign micro-organisms and cells that contain them and, in so doing, destroy them.

Tangential migration. Movement of cells in the developing neural tube in a direction parallel to the tube's walls.

Tardive dyskinesia (TD). A motor disorder that results from chronic use of certain antipsychotic drugs.

Target-site concept. The idea that aggressive and defensive behaviors of an animal are often designed to attack specific sites on the body of another animal while protecting specific sites on its own.

Taste buds. Clusters of taste receptors found on the tongue and in parts of the oral cavity.

Tectorial membrane. The cochlear membrane that rests on the hair cells.

Tectum. The division of the midbrain that comprises the superior and inferior colliculi and receives auditory and visual information about spatial location.

Temporal hemiretina. The half of each retina next to the temple.

Temporal resolution. Ability of a recording technique to detect differences in time (i.e., to pinpoint when an event occurred).

Temporal summation. The integration of neural signals that occur at different times at the same synapse.

Testes. The male gonads.

Testosterone. The most common androgen.

THC. Delta-9-tetrahydrocannabinol, the main psychoactive constituent of marijuana.

Thigmotaxic. Tending to stay near the walls of an open space such as a test chamber.

3-per-second spike-and-wave discharge. The characteristic EEG pattern of the petit mal seizure.

Threshold of excitation. The level of depolarization necessary to generate an action potential, usually about −65 mV.

Thrombosis. The blockage of blood flow by a plug (a thrombus) at the site of its formation.

Thyrotropin. The anterior pituitary hormone that stimulates the release of hormones from the thyroid gland.

Thyrotropin-releasing hormone. The hypothalamic hormone that stimulates the release of thyrotropin from the anterior pituitary.

Tics. Involuntary, repetitive, stereotyped movements or vocalizations; the defining feature of Tourette syndrome.

Token test. A preliminary test for language-related deficits that involves following verbal instructions to touch or move tokens of different shapes, sizes, and colors.

Tonotopic. Organized, like the primary auditory cortex, according to the frequency of sound.

Topographic gradient hypothesis. The hypothesis that axonal growth is guided by the relative position of the cell bodies on intersecting gradients, rather than by point-to-point coding of neural connections.

Totipotent. Capable of developing into any type of mature body cell.

Toxic psychosis. A chronic psychiatric disorder produced by exposure to a neurotoxin.

Tracts. Bundles of axons in the central nervous system.

Transcranial magnetic stimulation (TMS). A technique for disrupting the activity in an area of the cortex by creating a magnetic field under a coil positioned next to the skull; the effect of the disruption on cognition is assessed to clarify the function of the affected area of cortex.

Transduction. The conversion of one form of energy to another.

Transfer RNA. Molecules of RNA that carry amino acids to ribosomes during protein synthesis; each kind of amino acid is carried by a different kind of transfer RNA molecule.

Transgenic. Containing the genes of another species, which have been implanted there for research purposes.

Transgenic mice. Mice into which the genetic material of another species has been introduced.

Transneuronal degeneration. Degeneration of a neuron caused by damage to another neuron to which it is linked by a synapse.

Transorbital lobotomy. A prefrontal lobotomy performed with a cutting instrument inserted through the eye socket.

Transsexualism. A disorder of sexual identity in which the individual believes that he or she is trapped in a body of the other sex.

Tricyclic antidepressant drugs, or tricyclic antidepressants. Drugs with an antidepressant action and a three-ring molecular structure; they selectively suppress REM sleep.

True-breeding lines. Breeding lines in which interbred members always produce offspring with the same trait, generation after generation.

Tumor (neoplasm). A mass of cells that grows independently of the rest of the body.

Tympanic membrane. The eardrum.

Unipolar affective disorder. A disorder of emotion in which a patient experiences depression but no periods of mania.

Unipolar neuron. A neuron with one process extending from its cell body.

Up-regulation. An increase in the number of receptors for a neurotransmitter in response to decreased release of that neurotransmitter.

Urbach-Wiethe disease. A genetic disorder that often results in the calcification of the amygdala and surrounding brain structures.

Vasopressin. One of the two major peptide hormones of the posterior pituitary; it facilitates reabsorption of water by kidneys and is thus also called *antidiuretic hormone.*

Ventral. Toward the chest surface of a vertebrate or toward the bottom of the head.

Ventral horns. The two ventral arms of the spinal gray matter.

Ventral posterior nucleus. A thalamic relay nucleus in both the somatosensory and gustatory systems.

Ventral stream. The group of visual pathways that flows from the primary visual cortex to the ventral prestriate cortex to the inferotemporal cortex; according to one theory, its function is conscious visual perception.

Ventral tegmental area. The midbrain nucleus of the mesotelencephalic dopamine system that is a major source of the mesocorticolimbic pathway.

Ventricular zone. The region adjacent to the ventricle in the developing neural tube; the zone where neural proliferation occurs.

Ventromedial cortico-brainstem-spinal tract. The indirect ventromedial motor pathway, which descends bilaterally from the primary motor cortex to several interconnected brain stem motor structures and then descends in the ventromedial portions of the spinal cord.

Ventromedial corticospinal tract. The direct ventromedial motor pathway, which descends ipsilaterally from the primary motor cortex directly into the ventromedial areas of the spinal white matter.

Ventromedial hypothalamus (VMH). The area of the hypothalamus that was once thought to to contain the satiety center.

Ventromedial nucleus (VMN). A hypothalamic nucleus that is thought to be involved in female sexual behavior.

Vertebrates. Chordates that possess spinal bones.

Vestibular nucleus. The brain stem nucleus that receives information about balance from receptors in the semicircular canals.

Vestibular system. The sensory system that detects changes in the direction and intensity of head movements and that contributes to the maintenance of balance through its output to the motor system.

Visual agnosia. A failure to recognize visual stimuli that is not attributable to sensory, verbal, or intellectual impairment.

Visual completion. The completion or filling in of a scotoma by the brain.

Voltage-activated ion channels. Ion channels that open and close in response to changes in the level of the membrane potential.

Wechsler Adult Intelligence Scale (WAIS). A widely used test of general intelligence that includes 11 subtests.

Wernicke-Geschwind model. An influential model of cortical language localization in the left hemisphere.

Wernicke's aphasia. A hypothetical disorder of language comprehension with no associated deficits in speech production.

Wernicke's area. The area of the left temporal cortex hypothesized by Wernicke to be the center of language comprehension.

"Where" versus "what" theory. The theory that the dorsal stream mediates the perception of where things are and the ventral stream mediates the perception of what things are.

Williams syndrome. A neurodevelopmental disorder characterized by severe mental retardation, accompanied by preserved language and social skills.

Wisconsin Card Sorting Test. A neuropsychological test that evaluates a patient's ability to remember that previously learned rules of behavior are no longer effective and to learn to respond to new rules.

Withdrawal reflex. The reflexive withdrawal of a limb when it comes in contact with a painful stimulus.

Withdrawal syndrome. The illness brought on by the elimination from the body of a drug on which the person is physically dependent.

Within-subjects design. An experimental design in which the same subjects are tested under each condition.

Wolffian system. The embryonic precursor of the male reproductive ducts.

Word salad. Speech that has the overall sound and flow of normal speech but is totally incomprehensible.

Working memory. Temporary memory necessary for the successful performance of a task on which one is currently working.

Z lens. A contact lens that is opaque on one side (left or right) and thus allows visual input to enter only one hemisphere of a split-brain subject, irrespective of eye movement.

Zeitgebers. Environmental cues, such as the light–dark cycle, that entrain circadian rhythms.

Zeitgeist. The general intellectual climate of a culture.

Zygote. The cell formed from the amalgamation of a sperm cell and an ovum.

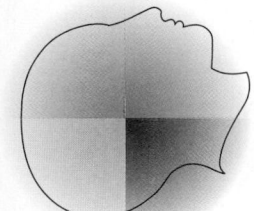

References

Abi-Dargham, A., Rodenhiser, J., Printz, D., Zea-Ponce, Y., Gil, R., Kegeles, L. S., et al. (2000). Increased baseline occupancy of D2 receptors by dopamine in schizophrenia. *Proceedings of the National Academy of Science, U.S.A., 97,* 8104–8109.

Acker, W., Ron, M. A., Lishman, W. A., & Shaw, G. K. (1984). A multivariate analysis of psychological, clinical and CT scanning measures in detoxified chronic alcoholics. *British Journal of Addiction, 79,* 293–301.

Adamec, R. (1990). Kindling, anxiety and limbic epilepsy: Human and animal perspectives. In J. A. Wada (Ed.), *Kindling 4* (pp. 329–341). New York: Plenum Press.

Adelmann, P. K., & Zajonc, R. B. (1989). Facial efference and the experience of emotion. *Annual Review of Psychology, 40,* 249–280.

Adkins-Regan, E. (1988). Sex hormones and sexual orientation in animals. *Psychobiology, 16,* 335–347.

Adolphs, R. (2002). Neural systems for recognizing emotion. *Current Opinion in Neurobiology, 12,* 169–177.

Adolphs, R., Baron-Cohen, S., & Tranel, D. (2002). Impaired recognition of social emotions following amygdala damage. *Journal of Cognitive Neuroscience, 14,* 1264–1274.

Adolphs, R., Sears, L., & Piven, J. (2001). Abnormal processing of social information from faces in autism. *Journal of Cognitive Neuroscience, 13,* 232–240.

Adolphs, R., & Tranel, D. (1999). Preferences for visual stimuli following amygdala damage. *Journal of Cognitive Neuroscience, 11,* 610–616.

Adolphs, R., Tranel, D., Damasio, H., & Damasio, A. (1994). Impaired recognition of emotion in facial expressions following bilateral damage to the human amygdala. *Nature, 3/2,* 669–672.

Adolphs, R., Tranel, D., Hamann, S., Young, A. W., Calder, A. J., Phelps, E. A., et al. (1999). Recognition of facial emotion in nine individuals with bilateral amygdala damage. *Neuropsychologia, 37,* 1111–1117.

Aggleton, J. P., & Young, A. W. (2000). The enigma of the amygdala: On its contribution to human emotion. In R. D. Lane & L. Nadel (Eds.), *Cognitive neuroscience of emotion* (pp. 106–128). New York: Oxford University Press.

Agmo, A., & Ellingsen, E. (2003). Relevance of non-human animal studies to the understanding of human sexuality. *Scandinavian Journal of Psychology, 44,* 293–301.

Agnew, N., & Demas, M. (1998, September). Preserving the Laetoli footprints. *Scientific American, 279,* 46–55.

Ahima, R. S., & Osei, S. Y. (2004). Leptin signaling. *Physiology and Behavior, 81,* 223–241.

Ahmed, R., & Gray, D. (1996). Immunological memory and protective immunity: Understanding their relation. *Science, 272,* 54–60.

Akerstedt, T., & Gillberg, M. (1981). The circadian variation of experimentally displaced sleep. *Sleep, 4,* 159–169.

Albert, D. J., Walsh, M. L., & Jonik, R. H. (1993). Aggression in humans: What is its biological foundation? *Neuroscience and Biobehavioural Reviews, 17,* 405–425.

Albright, T. D. (1995). "My most true mind thus makes mine eye untrue." *Trends in Neurosciences, 18,* 331–333.

Albright, T. D., Kandel, E. R., & Posner, M. I. (2000). Cognitive neuroscience. *Current Opinion in Neurobiology, 10,* 612–624.

Albright, T. D., & Stoner, G. R. (2002). Contextual influences on visual processing. *Annual Review of Neuroscience, 25,* 339–379.

Alexander, M. P. (1989). Clinical-anatomical correlations of aphasia following predominantly subcortical lesions. In H. Goodglass (Ed.), *Handbook of neuropsychology* (Vol. II, Pt. 2, pp. 47–66). New York: Elsevier.

Alexander, M. P. (1997). Aphasia: Clinical and anatomic aspects. In T. E. Feinberg & M. J. Farah, (Eds.), *Behavioral neurology and neuropsychology* (pp. 133–149). New York: McGraw-Hill.

Allen, L. S., Hines, M., Shryne, J. E., & Gorski, R. A. (1989). Two sexually dimorphic cell groups in the human brain. *Journal of Neuroscience, 9,* 497–506.

Allsop, T. E., & Fazakerley, J. K. (2000). Altruistic cell suicide and the specialized case of the virus-infected nervous system. *Trends in Neurosciences, 23,* 284–290.

Almeida, M. L. G., Ontiveros, U. M. P., Cortes, S. J., & Heinze, M. G. (2003). Treatment of primary insomnia with melatonin: A double blind, placebo-controlled, crossover study. *Journal of Psychiatry & Neuroscience, 28,* 191–196.

Ambrose, S. H. (2001). Paleolithic technology and human evolution. *Science, 291,* 1748–1753.

Anagnostaras, S. G., Craske, M. G., & Fanselow, M. S. (1999). Anxiety: At the intersection of genes and experience. *Nature Neuroscience, 2,* 780–782.

Anagnostaras, S. G., & Robinson, T. E. (1996). Sensitization to the psychomotor stimulant effects of amphetamine: Modulation by associative learning. *Behavioral Neuroscience, 110*(6), 1397–1414.

Anand, B. K., & Brobeck, J. R. (1951). Localization of a "feeding center" in the hypothalamus of the rat. *Proceedings of the Society for Experimental Biology and Medicine, 77,* 323–324.

Arch, A. M., Browman, G. P., Miller, M. M., & Walsh, J. K. (1988). *Sleep: A scientific perspective.* Englewood Cliffs, NJ: Prentice Hall.

Andersen, R. A., & Buneo, C. A. (2003). Sensorimotor integration in posterior parietal cortex. *Advances in Neurology, 93,* 159–177.

Anderson, P., Cremona, A., Paton, A., Turner, C., & Wallace, P. (1993). The risk of alcohol. *Addiction, 88,* 1493–1508.

Anderson, R. H., Fleming, D. E., Rhees, R. W., & Kinghorn, E. (1986). Relationships between sexual activity, plasma testosterone, and the volume of the sexually dimorphic nucleus of the preoptic area in prenatally stressed and non-stressed rats. *Brain Research, 370,* 1–10.

Anderson, A. K., & Phelps, E. A. (2000). Expression without recognition: Contributions of the human amygdala to emotional communication. *Psychological Science, 11,* 106–111.

Anderson, A. K., & Phelps, E. A. (2002). Is the human amygdala critical for the subjective experience of emotions? Evidence of intact dispositional affect in patients with amygdala lesions. *Journal of Cognitive Neuroscience, 14,* 709–720.

Andreasen, N. C. (1994). The mechanisms of schizophrenia. *Current Opinion in Neurobiology, 4,* 245–251.

Andreasen, N. C. (2000). Schizophrenia: The fundamental questions. *Brain Research Reviews, 31,* 106–112.

Antoniadis, E. A., & McDonald, R. J. (2000). Amygdala, hippocampus, and discriminative fear conditioning to context. *Behavioural Brain Research, 108,* 1–19.

Antonini, A., & Stryker, M. P. (1993). Rapid remodeling of axonal arbors in the visual cortex. *Science, 260,* 1819–1821.

Antshel, K. M., & Waisbren, S. E. (2003). Timing is everything: Executive functions in children exposed to elevated levels of phenylalanine. *Neuropsychology, 17,* 458–468.

Apkarian, A. V. (1995). Functional imaging of pain: New insights regarding the role of the cerebral cortex in human pain perception. *Seminars in the Neurosciences, 7,* 279–293.

Araújo, S. J., & Tear, G. (2003). Axon guidance mechanisms and molecules: Lessons from invertebrates. *Nature Reviews Neuroscience, 4,* 910–922.

Archer, J. (1991). The influence of testosterone on human aggression. *British Journal of Psychology, 82,* 1–28.

Arieli, A., Sterkin, A., Grinvald, A., & Aertsen, A. (1996). Dynamics of ongoing activity: Explanation of the large variability in evoked cortical responses. *Science, 273,* 1868–1870.

Arnold, A. P. (2003). The gender of the voice within: The neural origin of sex differences in the brain. *Current Opinion in Neurobiology, 13,* 759–764.

Arnold, A. P., Xu, J., Grisham, W., Chen, X., Kim, Y. H., & Itoh, Y. (2004). Sex chromosomes and brain sexual differentiation [Minireview]. *Endocrinology, 145,* 1057–1062.

Arvanitogiannis, A., Sullivan, J., & Amir, S. (2000). Time acts as a conditioned stimulus to control behavioral sensitization to amphetamine in rats. *Neuroscience, 101,* 1–3.

Aserinsky, E., & Kleitman, N. (1953). Regularly occurring periods of eye motility and concomitant phenomena, during sleep. *Science, 118,* 273–274.

Assad, J. A. (2003). Neural coding of behavioral relevance in parietal cortex. *Current Opinion in Neurobiology, 13,* 194–197.

Assanand, S., Pinel, J. P. J., & Lehman, D. R. (1998a). Personal theories of hunger and eating. *Journal of Applied Social Psychology, 28,* 998–1015.

Assanand, S., Pinel, J. P. J., & Lehman, D. R. (1998b). Teaching theories of hunger and eating: Overcoming students' misconceptions. *Teaching Psychology, 25,* 44–46.

Attenburrow, M. E. J., Cowen, P. J., & Sharpely, A. L. (1996). Low dose melatonin improves sleep in healthy middle-aged subjects. *Psychopharmacology, 126,* 179–181.

Auld, V. J. (2001). Why didn't the glia cross the road? *Trends in Neurosciences, 24,* 309–311.

Avila, M. T., Adami, H. M., McMahon, R. P., & Thaker, G. K. (2003). Using neurophysiological markers of genetic risk to define the boundaries of the schizophrenia spectrum phenotype. *Schizophrenia Bulletin, 29*(2), 299–309.

Avishai-Eliner, S., Kristen, L. B., Sandman, C. A., & Baram, T. Z. (2002). Stressed-out, or in (*utero*)? *Trends in Neurosciences, 25,* 518–524.

Ax, A. F. (1955). The physiological differentiation between fear and anger in humans. *Psychosomatic Medicine, 15,* 433–442.

Ayas, N. T., White, D. P., Manson, J. E., Stampfer, M. J., Speizer, F. E., Malhotra, A. & Hu, F. B. (2003). A prospective study of sleep duration and coronary heart disease in women. *Archives of Internal Medicine, 163,* 205–209.

Baddeley, A., Vargha-Khadem, F., & Mishkin, M. (2002). Preserved recognition in a case of developmental amnesia: Implications for the acquisition of semantic memory? *Journal of Cognitive Neuroscience, 13,* 357–369.

Bailey, J. M., Pillard, R. C., Neale, M. C., & Agyei, Y. (1993). Heritable factors influence sexual orientation in women. *Archives of General Psychiatry, 50,* 217–223.

Bailey, M. J., & Pillard, R. C. (1991). A genetic study of male sexual orientation. *Archives of General Psychiatry, 48,* 1089–1096.

Baker, B. J., & Booth, D. A. (1989). Preference conditioning by concurrent diets with delayed proportional reinforcement. *Physiology & Behavior, 46,* 585–590.

Bakker, J., Honda, S., Harada, N., & Balthazart, J. (2003, December). The aromatase knockout (ArKO) mouse provides new evidence

that estrogens are required for the development of the female brain. *Annals of the New York Academy of Science, 1007,* 251–262.

Ball, G. F., & Hulse, S. H. (1998). Birdsong. *American Psychologist, 53,* 37–58.

Balthazart, J., & Ball, G. F. (1998). New insights into the regulation and function of brain estrogen synthase (aromatase). *Trends in Neurosciences, 21,* 243–249.

Banchereau, J. (2002, November). The long arm of the immune system. *Scientific American, 287,* 52–59.

Bancroft, J., Sanders, D., Davidson, D., & Warner, P. (1983). Mood, sexuality, hormones and the menstrual cycle: III. Sexuality and the role of androgens. *Psychosomatic Medicine, 45,* 509–516.

Bandler, R., & Shipley, M. T. (1994). Columnar organization in the midbrain periaqueductal gray: Modules for emotional expression? *Trends in Neuroscience, 17,* 379–389.

Bankiewicz, K .S., Plunkett, R. J., Jaconowitz, D. M., Porrino, L., di Porzio, U., London, W. T., et al. (1990). The effect of fetal mesencephalon implants on primate MPTP-induced Parkinsonism: Histochemical and behavioral studies. *Journal of Neuroscience, 72,* 231–244.

Barash, S. (2003). Paradoxical activities: Insight into the relationship of parietal and prefrontal cortices. *Trends in Neurosciences, 26,* 582–589.

Bard P. (1929). The central representation of the sympathetic system. *Archives of Neurology and Psychiatry, 22,* 230–246.

Bar-Gad, I., & Bergman, H. (2001). Stepping out of the box: Information processing in the neural networks of the basal ganglia. *Current Opinion in Neurobiology, 11,* 689–695.

Barnett, S. C., & Chang, L. (2004). Olfactory ensheathing cells and CNS repair: Going solo or in need of a friend? *Trends in Neurosciences, 27,* 54–60.

Baron, J. C. (1989). Depression of energy metabolism in distant brain structures: Studies with positron emission tomography in stroke patients. *Seminars in Neurology, 9,* 281–285.

Barres, B. A., & Smith, S. J. (2001). Cholesterol—making or breaking the synapse. *Science, 294,* 1296–1297.

Bartholmeo, P., & Chokron, S. (2002). Orienting of attention in left unilateral neglect. *Neuroscience and Biobehavioural Reviews, 26,* 217–234.

Basbaum, A. I., & Fields, H. L. (1978). Endogenous pain control mechanisms: Review and hypothesis. *Annals of Neurology, 4,* 451–462.

Bashir, Z. I., & Collingridge, G. L. (1992). Synaptic plasticity: Long-term potentiation in the hippocampus. *Current Opinion in Neurobiology, 2,* 328–335.

Baskett, J. J., Broad, J. B., Wood, P. C., Duncan, J. R., Pledger, M. J., English, J., & Arendt, J. (2003). Does melatonin improve sleep in older people? A randomized crossover trial. *Age and Ageing, 32,* 164–170.

Baum, M. J., Erskine, M. S., Kornberg, E., & Weaver, C. E. (1990). Prenatal and neonatal testosterone exposure interact to affect differentiation of sexual behavior and partner preference in female ferrets. *Behavioral Neuroscience, 104,* 183–198.

Baura, G., Foster, D., Porte, D., Kahn, S. E., Bergman, R. N., Cobelli, C., & Schwartz, M. W. (1993). Saturable transport of insulin from plasma into the central nervous system of dogs *in vivo*: A mechanism for regulated insulin delivery to the brain. *Journal of Clinical Investigations, 92,* 1824–1830.

Bavelier, D., Corina, D., Jessard, P., Padmanabhan, S., Clark, V. P., Karni, A., et al. (1997). Sentence reading: A functional MRI study at 4 tesla. *Journal of Cognitive Neuroscience, 9,* 664–686.

Baxter, M. G., & Chiba, A. A. (1999). Cognitive functions of the basal forebrain. *Current Opinion in Neurobiology, 9,* 178–183.

Baxter, M. G., & Murray, E. A. (2002). The amygdala and reward. *Nature Reviews Neuroscience, 3,* 563–573.

Baynes, K., & Gazzaniga, M. S. (1997). Callosal disconnection. In T. E. Feinberg & M. J. Farah (Eds.), *Behavioral neurology and neuropsychology* (pp. 419–425). New York: McGraw-Hill.

Beal, M. F. (2001). Experimental models of Parkinson's disease. *Nature Reviews Neuroscience, 2*, 325–332.

Beaumont, M., Batejat, D., Pierard, C., Van Beers, P., Denis, J., Coste, O., et al. (2004). Caffeine or melatonin effects on sleep and sleepiness after rapid eastward transmeridian travel. *Journal of Applied Physiology, 96*, 50–58.

Bechara, A., Tranel, D., Damasio, H., Adolphs, R., Rockland, C., & Damasio, A. R. (1995). Double dissociation of conditioning and declarative knowledge relative to the amygdala and hippocampus in humans. *Science, 269*, 1115–1118.

Beck, B. (2001). KO's and organization of peptidergic feeding behavior mechanisms. *Neuroscience and Biobehavioral Reviews, 25*, 143–158.

Becker, L. (2002, March). Repeated blows. *Scientific American, 286*, 77–83.

Beeman, M. J., & Chiarello, C. (1998). Complementary right- and left-hemisphere language comprehension. *Current Directions in Psychological Science, 7*, 2–8.

Behl, C. (2002). Oestrogen as a neuroprotective hormone. *Nature Reviews Neuroscience, 3*, 433–442.

Bellugi, U., Lichtenberger, L., Mills, D., Galaburda, A., & Korenberg, J. R. (1999). Bridging cognition, the brain and molecular genetics: Evidence from Williams syndrome. *Trends in Neurosciences, 22*, 197–207.

Ben-Eliyahu, S., Shakhar, G., Page, G. G., Stefanski, V., & Shakhar, K. (2000). Suppression of NK cell activity and of resistance to metastasis by stress: A role for adrenal catecholamines and beta-adrenoceptors. *Neuroimmunomodulation, 8*, 154–164.

Benes, F. M., & Berretta, S. (2001). GABAergic interneurons: Implications for understanding schizophrenia and bipolar disorder. *Neuropsychopharmacology, 25*, 1–27.

Benington, J. H., & Heller, H. C. (1999). Implications of sleep deprivation experiments for our understanding of sleep homeostasis. *Sleep, 22*, 1033–1043.

Benjamin, L. T., Jr. (2003). Behavioral science and Nobel Prize: A history. *American Journal of Psychology, 58*, 731–741.

Bennett, E. L., Diamond, M. C., Krech, D., & Rosenzweig, M. R. (1964). Chemical and anatomical plasticity of brain. *Science, 146*, 610–619.

Bennett, M. V. L. (2000). Electrical synapses, a personal perspective (or history). *Brain Research Reviews, 32*, 16–28.

Bennett, M. V. L., Contreras, J. E., Bukauskas, F. F., & Saez, J. C. (2003). New roles for astrocytes: Gap junction hemichannels have something to communicate. *Trends in Neurosciences, 26*, 610–617.

Benson, D. F. (1985). Aphasia. In K. M. Heilman & E. Valenstein (Eds.), *Clinical neuropsychology* (pp. 17–47). New York: Oxford University Press.

Benson, D. L., Colman, D. R., & Huntley, G. W. (2001). Molecules, maps and synapse specificity. *Nature Reviews Neuroscience, 2*, 899–908.

Benton, A. L. (1994). Neuropsychological assessment. *Annual Review of Psychology, 45*, 1–23.

Bergman, T. J., Beehner, J. C., Cheney, D. L., & Seyfarth, R. M. (2003). Hierarchical classification by rank and kinship in baboons. *Science, 302*, 1234–1236.

Bernhardt, P. C. (1997). Influences of serotonin and testosterone in aggression and dominance: Convergence with social psychology. *Current Directions in Psychological Science, 6*, 44–48.

Bernstein, I. L., & Webster, M. M. (1980). Learned taste aversion in humans. *Physiology & Behavior, 25*, 363–366.

Bernstein, L. J., & Robertson, L. C. (1998). Illusory conjunctions of color and motion with shape following bilateral parietal lesions. *Psychological Science, 9*, 167–175.

Berridge, K. C. (2004). Motivation concepts in behavioral neuroscience. *Physiology and Behavior, 81*, 179–209.

Berridge, K. C., & Robinson, T. E. (2003). Parsing reward. *Trends in Neurosciences, 26*, 507–513.

Berridge, V., & Edwards, G. (1981). *Opiate use in nineteenth-century England.* New York: St. Martin's Press.

Berson, D. M. (2003). Strange vision: Ganglion cells as circadian photoreceptors. *Trends in Neurosciences, 26*, 314–320.

Berthoud, H.-R. (2002). Multiple neural systems controlling food intake and body weight. *Neuroscience and Biobehavioural Reviews, 26*, 393–428.

Best, P. J., White, A. M., & Minai, A. (2001). Spatial processing in the brain: The activity of hippocampal place cells. *Annual Review of Neuroscience, 24*, 459–486.

Bezard, E., Brotchie, J. M., & Gross, C. E. (2001). Pathophysiology of levodopa-induced dyskinesia: Potential for new therapies. *Nature Reviews Neuroscience, 2*, 577–588.

Bi, G.-Q., & Poo, M.-M. (2001). Synaptic modification by correlated activity: Hebb's postulate revisited. *Annual Review of Neuroscience, 24*, 139–166.

Binks, P. G., Waters, W. F., & Hurry, M. (1999). Short-term total sleep deprivation does not selectively impair higher cortical functioning. *Sleep, 22*, 328–334.

Bisagno, V., Bowman, R., & Luine, V. (2003). Functional aspects of estrogen neuroprotection. *Endocrine, 21*, 33–41.

Bischoff-Grethe, A., Proper, S. M., Mao, H., Daniels, K. A., & Berns, G. S. (2000). Conscious and unconscious processing of nonverbal predictability in Wernicke's area. *Journal of Neuroscience, 20*, 1975–1981.

Bishop, D. V. M. (1999). An innate basis for language? *Science, 286*, 2283–2255.

Björklund, A., & Lindvall, O. (2000). Cell replacement therapies for central nervous system disorders. *Nature, 3*, 537–544.

Blackburn, G. L. (2001). Pasteur's quadrant and malnutrition. *Nature, 409*, 397–401.

Blackmore, S. (1991). Lucid dreaming: Awake in your sleep? *Skeptical Inquirer, 15*, 362–370.

Blakely, R. D. (2001). Dopamine's reversal of fortune. *Science, 293*, 2408–2409.

Blanchard, D. C., & Blanchard, R. J. (1984). Affect and aggression: An animal model applied to human behavior. In D. C. Blanchard & R. J. Blanchard (Eds.), *Advances in the study of aggression* (pp. 1–62). Orlando, FL: Academic Press.

Blanchard, D. C., & Blanchard, R. J. (1988). Ethoexperimental approaches to the biology of emotion. *Annual Review of Psychology, 39*, 43–68.

Blanchard, D. C., & Blanchard, R. J. (1990). Behavioral correlates of chronic dominance-subordination relationships of male rats in a seminatural situation. *Neuroscience and Biobehavioural Reviews, 14*, 455–462.

Blanchard, D. C., Blanchard, R. J., & Rodgers, R. J. (1991). Risk assessment and animal models of anxiety. In J. Olivier, J. Mos, & J. L. Slangen (Eds.), *Animal models in psychopharmacology* (pp. 117–134). Basel, Switzerland: Birkhauser Verlag.

Blanchard, D. C., Blanchard, R. J., Tom, P., & Rodgers, R. J. (1990). Diazepam changes risk assessment in an anxiety/defense test battery. *Psychopharmacology, 101*, 511–518.

Blanchard, D. C., Sakai, R. R., McEwen, B., Weiss, S. M., & Blanchard, R. J. (1993). Subordination stress: Behavioral, brain, and neuroendocrine correlates. *Behavioral Brain Research, 58*, 113–121.

Blanchard, D. C., Hynd, A. L., Minke, K. A., Minemoto, T., & Blanchard, R. J. (2001). Human defensive behaviors to threat scenarios show parallels to fear and anxiety-related defense patterns of non-human mammals. *Neuroscience and Biobehavioural Reviews, 25*, 761–770.

Blanchard, R. J., & Blanchard, D. C. (1989). Anti-predator defensive behaviors in a visible burrow system. *Journal of Comparative Psychology, 103*, 70–82.

Blaser, M. J. (1996, February). The bacteria behind ulcers. *Scientific American, 275*, 104–107.

Blaustein, J. D., King, J. C., Toft, D. O., & Turcotte, J. (1988). Immunocytochemical localization of estrogen-induced progestin receptors in guinea pig brain. *Brain Research, 474*, 1–15.

Blessing, W. W. (1997). Inadequate frameworks for understanding bodily homeostasis. *Trends in Neurosciences, 20,* 235–239.

Bliss, T., & Schoepfer, R. (2004). Controlling the ups and downs of synaptic strength. *Science, 304,* 973–974.

Bliss, T. V. P., & Lømo, T. (1973). Long-lasting potentiation of synaptic transmission in the dentate area of the anaesthetized rabbit following stimulation of the perforant path. *Journal of Physiology, 232,* 331–356.

Bloch, G. J., & Gorski, R. A. (1988). Cytoarchitectonic analysis of the SDN-POA of the intact and gonadectomized rat. *Journal of Comparative Neurology, 275,* 604–612.

Bloch, G. J., & Mills, R. (1995). Prepubertal testosterone treatment of neonatally gonadectomized male rats: Defeminization and masculinization of behavioral and endocrine function in adulthood. *Neuroscience and Behavioural Reviews, 19,* 187–200.

Bloch, G. J., Mills, R., & Gale, S. (1995). Prepubertal testosterone treatment of female rats: Defeminization of behavioral and endocrine function in adulthood. *Neuroscience and Biobehavioural Reviews, 19,* 177–186.

Block, R. I., & Ghoneim, M. M. (1993). Effects of chronic marijuana use on human cognition. *Psychopharmacology, 110,* 219–228.

Blundell, J. E., & Finlayson, G. (2004). Is susceptibility to weight gain characterized by homeostatic or hedonic risk factors for overconsumption? *Physiology and Behavior, 82,* 21–25.

Blundell, J. E., & Halford, J. C. G. (1998). Serotonin and appetite regulation. *CNS Drugs, 9,* 473–495.

Boehning, D., & Snyder, S. H. (2003). Novel neural modulators. *Annual Review of Neuroscience, 26,* 105–131.

Bogen, J. G., & Bogen, G. M. (1976). Wernicke's region—where is it? *Annals of the New York Academy of Science, 280,* 834–843.

Bolles, R. C. (1980). Some functionalistic thought about regulation. In F. M. Toates & T. R. Halliday (Eds.), *Analysis of motivational processes* (pp. 63–75). London: Academic Press.

Bonnel, A., Mottron, L., Peretz, I., Trudel, M., Gallun, E., & Bonnel, A. M. (2003). Enhanced pitch sensitivity in individuals with autism: A signal detection analysis. *Journal of Cognitive Neuroscience, 15,* 226–235.

Bonnet, M. H., & Arand, D. L. (1996). Insomnia—nocturnal sleep disruption—daytime fatigue: The consequences of a week of insomnia. *Sleep, 19,* 453–461.

Bookheimer, S. (2002). Functional MRI of language: New approaches to understanding the cortical organization of semantic processing. *Annual Review of Neuroscience 25,* 151–188.

Booth, D. A. (1981). The physiology of appetite. *British Medical Bulletin, 37,* 135–140.

Booth, D. A., Fuller, J., & Lewis, V. (1981). Human control of body weight: Cognitive or physiological? Some energy-related perceptions and misperceptions. In L. A. Cioffi (Ed.), *The body weight regulatory system: Normal and disturbed systems* (pp. 305–314). New York: Raven Press.

Booth, M. (2004). *Cannabis: A history.* London: Bantam Books.

Borbély, A. A. (1981). The sleep process: Circadian and homeostatic aspects. *Advances in Physiological Sciences, 18,* 85–91.

Borbély, A. A. (1983). Pharmacological approaches to sleep regulation. In A. R. Mayes (Ed.), *Sleep mechanisms and functions in humans and animals* (pp. 232–261). Wokingham, England: Van Nostrand Reinhold.

Borbély, A. A., Baumann, F., Brandeis, D., Strauch, I., & Lehmann, D. (1981). Sleep deprivation: Effect on sleep stages and EEG power density in man. *Electroencephalography and Clinical Neurophysiology, 51,* 483–493.

Borszcz, G. S. (1999). Differential contributions of medullary, thalamic, and amygdaloid serotonin to the antinociceptive action of morphine administered into the periaqueductal gray: A model of morphine analgesia. *Behavioural Neuroscience, 113,* 612–631.

Bouchard, T. J., Jr. (1998). Genetic and environmental influences on adult intelligence and special mental abilities. *Human Biology, 70,* 257–279.

Bouchard, T. J., Jr., & Pedersen, N. (1998). Twins reared apart: Nature's double experiment. In E. L. Grigorenko & S. Scarr (Eds.), *On the way to individuality: Current methodological issues in behavioral genetics.* Commack, NY: Nova Science Publishers.

Boucsein, W. (1992). *Electrodermal activity.* New York: Plenum Press.

Bowers, D., Bauer, R. M., Coslett, H. B., & Heilman, K. M. (1985). Processing of face by patients with unilateral hemisphere lesions. I. Dissociations between judgements of facial affect and facial identity. *Brain and Cognition, 4,* 258–272.

Brackett, N. L., & Edwards, D. A. (1984). Medial preoptic connections with the midbrain tegmentum are essential for male sexual behavior. *Physiology & Behavior, 32,* 79–84.

Brady, J. V. (1993). Behavior analysis applications and interdisciplinary research strategies. *American Psychologist, 48,* 435–440.

Braun, C., Schweizer, R., Elbert, T., Birbaumer, N., & Taub, E. (2000). Differential activation in somatosensory cortex for different discrimination tasks. *Journal of Neuroscience, 20,* 446–450.

Brecher, E. M. (1972). *Licit and illicit drugs.* Boston: Little, Brown & Co.

Bremer, F. (1936). Nouvelles recherches sur le mécanisme du sommeil. *Comptes rendus de la Société de Biologie, 22,* 460–464.

Bremer, F. L. (1937). L'activité cérébrale au cours du sommeil et de la narcose. Contribution à l'étude du mécanisme du sommeil. *Bulletin de l'Académie Royale de Belgique, 4,* 68–86.

Bremner, J. (1959). *Asexualization.* New York: Macmillan.

Brewster, J. M. (1986). Prevalence of alcohol and other drug problems among physicians. *Journal of the American Medical Association, 255,* 1913–1920.

Breitner, J. C. S. (1990). Life table methods and assessment of familial risk in Alzheimer's disease. *Archives of General Psychiatry, 47,* 395–396.

Brehmer, C., & Iten, P. X. (2001). Medical prescription of heroin to chronic heroin addicts in Switzerland—a review. *Forensic Science International, 121,* 23–26.

Brittle, E. R., & Waters, M. G. (2000). ER-to-Golgi traffic—this bud's for you. *Science, 289,* 403–448.

Brivanlou, A. H., Gage, F. H., Jaenisch, R., Jessell, T., Melton, D., & Rossant, J. (2003). Setting standards for human embryonic stem cells. *Science, 300,* 913–916.

Broberg, D. J., & Bernstein, I. L. (1989). Cephalic insulin release in anorexic women. *Physiology & Behavior, 45,* 871–875.

Broks, P., Young, A. W., Maratos, E. J., Coffey, P. J., Calder, A. J., Isaac, C. L., et al. (1998). Face processing impairments after encephalitis: Amygdala damage and recognition of fear. *Neuropsychologia, 36,* 59–70.

Brooks, M. J., & Melnik, G. (1995). The refeeding syndrome: An approach to understanding its complications and preventing its occurrence. *Pharmacotherapy, 15,* 713–726.

Brooks, V. B. (1986). *The neural basis of motor control.* New York: Oxford University Press.

Bronson, F. H., & Matherne, C. M. (1997). Exposure to anabolic-androgenic steroids shortens life span of male mice. *Medicine and Science in Sports and Exercise, 29,* 615–619.

Brown, E. S., Rush, A. J., & McEwen, B. S. (1999). Hippocampal remodeling and damage by corticosteroids: Implications for mood disorders. *Neuropsychopharmacology, 21,* 474–484.

Brown, G. W. (1993). The role of life events in the aetiology of depressive and anxiety disorders. In S. C. Stanford & S. Salmon (Eds.), *Stress: From synapse to syndrome* (pp. 23–50). San Diego: Academic Press.

Brown, H. D., & Kosslyn, S. M. (1993). Cerebral lateralization. *Current Opinion in Neurobiology, 3,* 183–186.

Brown, M. W., & Aggleton, J. P. (2001). Recognition memory: What are the roles of the perirhinal cortex and hippocampus? *Nature Reviews Neuroscience, 2,* 51–61.

Brown, R. E. (1994). *An introduction to neuroendocrinology.* Cambridge, England: Cambridge University Press.

Brown, R. E., & Milner, P. M. (2003). The legacy of Donald Hebb: More than the Hebb Synapse. *Nature Reviews Neuroscience, 4,* 1013–1019.

Brown, V. J., & Bowman, E. M. (2002). Rodent models of prefrontal cortical function. *Trends in Neurosciences, 25*(7), 340–343.

Brownell, K. D., & Rodin, J. (1994). The dieting maelstrom: Is it possible and advisable to lose weight? *American Psychologist, 49,* 781–791.

Brun, V. H., Otnaes, M. K., Molden, S., Steffenach, H.-A., Witter, M. P., Moser, M.-B., & Moser, E. I. (2002). Place cells and place recognition maintained by direct entorhinal-hippocampal circuitry. *Science, 296,* 2243–2246.

Brunner, D. P., Dijk, D-J., Tobler, L., & Borbély, A. A. (1990). Effect of partial sleep deprivation on sleep stages and EEG power spectra: Evidence for non-REM and REM sleep homeostasis. *Electroencephalography and Clinical Neurophysiology, 75,* 492–499.

Bucci, T. J. (1992). Dietary restriction: Why all the interest? An overview. *Laboratory Animal, 21,* 29–34.

Büchel, C., & Dolan, R. J. (2000). Classical fear conditioning in functional neuroimaging. *Current Opinion in Neurobiology, 10,* 219–223.

Buckley, M. J., & Gaffan, D. (1998). Perirhinal cortex ablation impairs visual object identification. *Journal of Neuroscience, 18*(6), 2268–2275.

Buijs, R. M., & Kalsbeek, A. (2001). Hypothalamic integration of central and peripheral clocks. *Nature Reviews Neuroscience, 2,* 521–526.

Bunin, M. A., & Wightman, R. M. (1999). Paracrine neurotransmission in the CNS: Involvement of 5-HT. *Trends in Neurosciences, 22,* 377–382.

Buonomano, D. V., & Merzenich, M. M. (1998). Cortical plasticity: From synapses to maps. *Annual Reviews of Neuroscience, 21,* 149–186.

Burke, A. C., & Feduccia, A. (1997). Developmental patterns and the identification of homologies in the avian hand. *Science, 278,* 666–668.

Buss, D. M. (1992). Mate preference mechanisms: Consequences for partner choice and intrasexual competition. In J. M. Barkow, L. Cosmides, & J. Tooby (Eds.), *The adapted mind* (pp. 249–265). New York: Oxford University Press.

Buss, D. M., Haselton, M. G., Shackelford, T. K., Bleske, A. L., & Wakefield, J. C. (1998). Adaptations, exaptations, and spandrels. *American Psychologist, 53,* 533–548.

Bussey, T. J., Warburton, E. C., Aggleton, J. P., & Muir, J. L. (1998). Fornix lesions can facilitate acquisition of the transverse patterning task: A challenge for "configural" theories of hippocampal function. *Journal of Neuroscience, 18*(4), 1622–1631.

Butters, N., & Delis, D. C. (1995). Clinical assessment of memory disorders in amnesia and dementia. *Annual Review of Psychology, 46,* 493–523.

Cabanac, M. (1971). Physiological role of pleasure. *Science, 173,* 1103–1107.

Cabeza, R., & Kingstone, A. (2002). Cognitive neuroimaging for all! *Trends in Neurosciences, 25*(5), 275.

Cabeza, R., & Nyberg, L. (1997). Imaging cognition: An empirical review of PET studies with normal subjects. *Journal of Cognitive Neuroscience, 9*(1), 1–26.

Cabeza, R., & Nyberg, L. (2000). Imaging cognition II: An empirical review of 275 PET and fMRI studies. *Journal of Cognitive Neuroscience, 12*(1), 1–47.

Cacioppo, J. T., Berntson, G. G., Lorig, T. S., Norris, C. J., Rickett, E., & Nusbaum, H. (2003). Just because you're imaging the brain doesn't mean you can stop using your head: A primer and set of first principles. *Journal of Personality and Social Psychology, 85,* 650–661.

Cacioppo, J. T., Petty, R. E., Losch, M., & Kim, H. S. (1986). Electromyographic activity over facial muscle regions can differentiate the valence and intensity of emotional reactions. *Journal of Personality and Social Psychology, 50,* 260–268.

Caggiula, A. R. (1970). Analysis of the copulation-reward properties of posterior hypothalamic stimulation in male rats. *Journal of Comparative and Physiological Psychology, 70,* 399–412.

Cain, D. P. (1986). The transfer phenomenon in kindling. In J. A. Wada (Ed.), *Kindling 3* (pp. 231–245). New York: Raven Press.

Cain, D. P. (1997). LTP, NMDA, genes and learning. *Current Opinion in Neurobiology, 7,* 235–242.

Calder, A. J., Lawrence, A. D., & Young, A. W. (2001). Neuropsychology of fear and loathing. *Nature Reviews Neuroscience, 2,* 352–363.

Calder, A. J., Young, A. W., Rowland, D., Perrett, D. I., Hodges, J. R., & Etcoff, N. L. (1996). Facial emotion recognition after bilateral amygdala damage: Differentially severe impairment of fear. *Cognitive Neuropsychology, 13,* 699–745.

Calles-Escandon, J., & Horton, E. S. (1992). The thermogenic role of exercise in the treatment of morbid obesity: A critical evaluation. *American Journal of Clinical Nutrition, 55,* 533S–537S.

Calmon, G., Roberts, N., Eldridge, P., & Thirion, J-P. (1998). Automatic quantification of changes in the volume of brain structures. *Lecture Notes in Computer Science, 1496,* 761–769.

Calne, S., Schoenberg, B., Martin, W., Uitti, J., Spencer, P., & Calne, D. B. (1987). Familial Parkinson's disease: Possible role of environmental factors. *Canadian Journal of Neurological Sciences, 14,* 303–305.

Cameron, H. A., Woolley, C. S., McEwen, B. S., & Gould, E. (1993). Differentiation of newly born neurons and glia in the dentate gyrus of the adult rat. *Neuroscience, 56,* 337–344.

Campbell, K., & Gotz, M. (2002). Radial glia: Multi-purpose cells for vertebrate brain development. *Trends in Neurosciences, 25,* 235–238.

Campfield, L. A., Brandon, P., & Smith, F. J. (1985). On-line continuous measurement of blood glucose and meal pattern in free feeding rats: The role of glucose in meal initiation. *Brain Research Bulletin, 14,* 605–616.

Campfield, L. A., & Smith, F. J. (1990). Transient declines in blood glucose signal meal initiation. *International Journal of Obesity, 14*(Suppl. 3), 15–33.

Campfield, L. A., Smith, F. J., Gulsez, Y., Devos, R., & Burn, P. (1995). Mouse Ob protein: Evidence for a peripheral signal linking adiposity and central neural networks. *Science, 269,* 546–550.

Canli, T., Sivers, H., Whitfield, S. L., Gotlib, I. H., & Gabrieli, J. D. E. (2002). Amygdala response to happy faces as a function of extraversion. *Science, 296,* 2191.

Canli, T., Zhao, Z., Desmond, J. E., Kang, E., Gross, J., & Gabrieli, J. D. E. (2001). An fMRI study of personality influences on brain reactivity to emotional stimuli. *Behavioral Neuroscience, 115,* 33–42.

Cann, R. (2001). Genetic clues to dispersal in human populations: Retracing the past from the present. *Science, 291,* 1742–1748.

Cannon, C. M., & Bseikri, M. R. (2004). Is dopamine required for natural reward? *Physiology and Behaviour, 81,* 741–748.

Cannon, W. B., & Washburn, A. L. (1912). An explanation of hunger. *American Journal of Physiology, 29,* 441–454.

Capaday, C. (2002). The special nature of human walking and its neural control. *Trends in Neurosciences, 25,* 370–376.

Caporael, L. R. (2001). Evolutionary psychology: Toward a unifying theory and a hybrid science. *Annual Review of Psychology, 52,* 607–628.

Cardinal, R. N., & Everitt, B. J. (2004). Neural and psychological mechanisms underlying appetitive learning: Links to drug addiction. *Current Opinion in Neurobiology, 14,* 156–162.

Cardinal, R. N., Parkinson, J. A., Hall, J., & Everitt, B. J. (2002). Emotion and motivation: The role of the amygdala, ventral striatum, and prefrontal cortex. *Neuroscience and Biobehavioural Reviews, 26,* 321–352.

Carlsson, A., & Lindqvist, M. (1963). Effect of chlorpromazine or haloperidol on formation of 3-methoxytyramine and normetanephrine in mouse brains. *Acta Pharmacologica et Toxicologica, 20,* 140–144.

Carlsson, K., Petrovic, P., Skare, S., Petersson, K. M., & Ingvar, M. (2000). Tickling expectations: Neural processing in anticipation of a sensory stimulus. *Journal of Cognitive Neuroscience, 12,* 691–703.

Carothers, A. D., Castilla, E. E., Dutra, M. G., & Hook, E. B. (2001). Search for ethnic, geographic, and other factors in the epidemiology of Down syndrome in South America: Analysis of data from the ECLAMC project, 1967–1997. *American Journal of Medical Genetics, 103,* 149–156.

Carroll, D. (1984). *Biofeedback in practice.* New York: Longman Group.

Carson, R. A. & Rothstein, M. A. (1999). *Behavioral genetics: The clash of culture and biology.* New York: Worth Publishers.

Carter, R. J., Lione, L. A., Humby, T., Mangiarini, L., Mahal, A., Bates, G. P., et al. (1999). Characterization of progressive motor deficits in mice transgenic for the human Huntington's disease mutation. *Journal of Neuroscience, 19,* 3248–3257.

Caselli, R. J. (1997). Tactile agnosia and disorders of tactile perception. In T. E. Feinberg & M. J. Farah (Eds.), *Behavioral neurology and neuropsychology* (pp. 277–288). New York: McGraw-Hill.

Cassone, V. M. (1990). Effects of melatonin on vertebrate circadian systems. *Trends in Neurosciences, 13*(11), 457–467.

Cenci, M. A., Whishaw, I. Q., & Schallert, T. (2002). Animal models of neurological deficits: How relevant is the rat? *Nature Reviews Neuroscience, 3,* 574–579.

Cermakian, N., & Sassone-Corsi, P. (2002). Environmental stimulus perception and control of circadian clocks. *Current Opinion in Neurobiology, 12,* 359–365.

Chabris, C. F., & Kosslyn, S. M. (1998). How do the cerebral hemispheres contribute to encoding spatial relations? *Current Directions in Psychological Science, 7,* 8–14.

Chatterjee, S., & Callaway, E. M. (2003). Parallel colour-opponent pathways to primary visual cortex. *Nature, 426,* 668–671.

Chavez, M., Seeley, R. J., & Woods, S. C. (1995). A comparison between the effects of intraventricular insulin and intraperitoneal LiCl on three measures sensitive to emetic agents. *Behavioral Neuroscience, 109,* 547–550.

Chemielli, R. M., Willie, J. T., Sinton, C. M., Elmquist, J. K., Scammell, T., Lee, C., et al. (1999). Narcolepsy in orexin knockout mice: Molecular genetics of sleep regulation. *Cell, 98,* 427–451.

Chen, W. R., Midtgaard, J., & Shepherd, G. M. (1997). Forward and backward propagation of dendritic impulses and their synaptic control in mitral cells. *Science, 278,* 463–466.

Cheng, J., Cao, Y., & Olson, L. (1996). Spinal cord repair in adult paraplegic rats: Partial restoration of hind limb function. *Science, 273,* 510–513.

Cheng, D. T., Knight, D. C., Smith, C. N., Stein, E. A., & Helmstetter, F. J. (2003). Functional MRI of human amygdala activity during Pavlovian fear conditioning: Stimulus processing versus response expression. *Behavioral Neuroscience, 117,* 3–10.

Cho, A. K. (1990). Ice: A new dosage form of an old drug. *Science, 249,* 631–634.

Chorover, S. L., & Schiller, P. H. (1965). Short-term retrograde amnesia in rats. *Journal of Comparative and Physiological Psychology, 59,* 73–78.

Christie, B. R., Kerr, D. S., & Abraham, W. C. (1994). Flip side of synaptic plasticity: Long-term depression mechanisms in the hippocampus. *Hippocampus, 4,* 127–135.

Christoff, K., & Gabrieli, J. D. E. (2000). The frontopolar cortex and human cognition: Evidence for a rostrocaudal hierarchical organization within the human prefrontal cortex. *Psychobiology, 28,* 168–186.

Chun, M. M., & Marois, R. (2002). The dark side of visual attention. *Current Opinion in Neurobiology, 12,* 184–189.

Churchland, P. C. (2002). Self representation in nervous systems. *Science, 296,* 308–310.

Cirulli, F., Berry, A., & Alleva, E. (2003). Early disruption of the mother–infant relationship: Effects on brain plasticity and implications for psychopathology. *Neuroscience and Biobehavioural Reviews, 27,* 73–82.

Clark, A. S., & Henderson, L. P. (2003). Behavioral and physiological responses to anabolic-androgenic steroids. *Neuroscience and Biobehavioural Reviews, 27,* 413–436.

Claverie, J. M. (2001). What if there are only 30,000 human genes? *Science, 291,* 1255–1257.

Clayton, N. S. (2001). Hippocampal growth and maintenance depend on food-caching experience in juvenile mountain chickadees (*Poecile gambeli*). *Behavioral Neuroscience, 115,* 614–625.

Clayton, N. S., Bussey, T. J., & Dickinson, A. (2003). Can animals recall the past and plan for the future? *Nature Reviews Neuroscience, 4,* 685–691.

Clements, J. D., Lester, R. A. J., Tong, G., Jahr, C. E., & Westbrook, G. L. (1992). The time course of glutamate in the synaptic cleft. *Science, 258,* 1498–1501.

Clifton, P. G. (2000). Meal patterning in rodents: Psychopharmacological and neuroanatomical studies. *Neuroscience and Biobehavioural Reviews, 24,* 213–222.

Cohen, L., Navarro, V., Clemenceau, S., Baulac, M., & Miles, R. (2002). On the origin of interictal activity in human temporal lobe epilepsy *in vitro*. *Science, 298,* 1418–1421.

Cohen, Y. E., & Andersen, R. A. (2002). A common reference name for movement plans in the posterior parietal cortex. *Nature Reviews Neuroscience, 3,* 553–562.

Cohen, Y. E., & Knudsen, E. I. (1999). Maps versus clusters: Different representations of auditory space in the midbrain and forebrain. *Trends in Neuroscience, 22,* 128–135.

Colapinto, J. (2000). *As nature made him: The boy who was raised as a girl.* New York: HarperCollins.

Cole, J. C., & Sumnall, H. R. (2003). The pre-clinical behavioral pharmacology of 3,4-methylenedioxymethamphetamine (MDMA). *Neuroscience and Biobehavioural Reviews, 27,* 199–217.

Colell, M., Segarra, M. D., & Sabater-Pi, J. (1995). Manual laterality in chimpanzees (*Pan troglodytes*) in complex tasks. *Journal of Comparative Psychology, 109,* 298–307.

Coleman, D. L. (1979). Obesity genes: Beneficial effects in heterozygous mice. *Science, 203,* 663–665.

Coleman, M. P., & Perry, V. H. (2002). Axon pathology in neurological disease: A neglected therapeutic target. *Trends in Neurosciences, 25,* 532–537.

Coles, M. G. (2003). Thirty years of cognitive psychophysiology: Retrospective, current state, and prospective. *Biological Psychology, 64*(1–2), 211–216.

Collier, G. (1986). The dialogue between the house economist and the resident physiologist. *Nutrition and Behavior, 3,* 9–26.

Collier, G. H. (1980). An ecological analysis of motivation. In F. M. Toates & T. R. Halliday (Eds.), *Analysis of motivational processes* (pp. 125–151). London: Academic Press.

Collette, F., & Van der Linden, M. (2002). Brain imaging of the central executive component of working memory. *Neuroscience and Biobehavioural Reviews, 26,* 105–125.

Collie, A., & Maruff, P. (2000). The neuropsychology of preclinical Alzheimer's disease and mild cognitive impairment. *Neuroscience and Biobehavioural Reviews, 24,* 365–374.

Colombo, M., & Broadbent, N. (2000). Is the avian hippocampus a functional homologue of the mammalian hippocampus? *Neuroscience and Biobehavioural Reviews, 24,* 465–484.

Colvin, M. K., Dunbar, K., & Grafman, J. (2001). The effects of frontal lobe lesions on goal achievement in the water jug task. *Journal of Cognitive Neuroscience, 13,* 1129–1147.

Conklin, H. M., & Iacono, W. G. (2002). Schizophrenia: A neurodevelopmental perspective. *Current Directions in Psychological Science, 11,* 33–37.

Connolly, J. D., Andersen, R. A., & Goodale, M. A. (2003). fMRI evidence for a "parietal reach region" in the human brain. *Experimental Brain Research, 153,* 140–145.

Cook, M. N., Bolivar, V. J., McFadyen, M. P., & Flaherty, L. (2002). Behavioral differences among 129 substrains: Implications for knockout and transgenic mice. *Behavioral Neuroscience, 116,* 600–611.

Coolen, L. M., Fitzgerald, M. E., Yu, L., & Lehman, M. N. (2004). Activation of mu opioid receptors in the medial preoptic area following copulation in male rats. *Neuroscience, 124,* 11–21.

Cooper, R. M., & Zubek, J. P. (1958). Effects of enriched and restricted early environments on the learning ability of bright and dull rats. *Canadian Journal of Psychology, 12,* 159–164.

Corbetta, M., Miezin, F. M., Dobmeyer, S., Shulman, G. L., & Petersen, S. E. (1990). Attentional modulation of neural processing of shape, color, and velocity in humans. *Science, 248,* 1556–1559.

Corcoran, M., McCaughran, J. A., Jr., & Wada, J. A. (1978). Antiepileptic and prophylactic effects of tetrahydrocannabinols in amygdaloid kindled rats. *Epilepsia, 19,* 47–55.

Corina, D. P., Poizner, H., Bellugi, U., Feinberg, T., Dowd, D., & O'Grady-Batch, L. (1992). Dissociation between linguistic and nonlinguistic gestural systems: A case for compositionality. *Brain and Language, 43,* 414–447.

Corkin, S. (1968). Acquisition of motor skill after bilateral medial temporal-lobe excision. *Neuropsychologia, 6,* 255–265.

Corkin, S. (2002). What's new with the amnesic patient H.M.? *Nature Reviews Neuroscience, 3,* 153–160.

Corkin, S., Milner, B., & Rasmussen, R. (1970). Somatosensory thresholds. *Archives of Neurology, 23,* 41–59.

Corsi, P. L. (1991). *The enchanted loom: Chapters in the history of neuroscience.* New York: Oxford University Press.

Corwin, J. T., & Warchol, M. E. (1991). Auditory hair cells. *Annual Review of Neuroscience, 14,* 301–333.

Coslett, H. B. (1997). Acquired dyslexia. In T. E. Feinberg & M. J. Farah (Eds.), *Behavioral neurology and neuropsychology* (pp. 209–218). New York: McGraw-Hill.

Cotman, C. W., & Berchtold, N. C. (2002). Exercise: A behavioral intervention to enhance brain health and plasticity. *Trends in Neurosciences, 25,* 295–301.

Courtney, S. M., & Ungerleider, L. G. (1997). What fMRI has taught us about human vision. *Current Opinion in Neurobiology, 7,* 554–561.

Cowan, W. M. (1979, September). The development of the brain. *Scientific American, 241,* 113–133.

Cowan, W. M., Kopnisky, K. L., & Hyman, S. E. (2002). The human genome project and its impact on psychiatry. *Annual Review of Neuroscience, 25,* 1–50.

Crabbe, J. C., Wahlsten, D., & Dudek, B. C. (1999). Genetics of mouse behavior: Interactions with laboratory environment. *Science, 284,* 1670–1672.

Craelius, W. (2002). The bionic man: Restoring mobility. *Science, 295,* 1018–1019.

Craig, A. D. (2002). How do you feel? Interoception: The sense of the physiological condition of the body. *Nature Reviews Neuroscience, 3,* 655–666.

Craig, A. D. (2003). Pain mechanisms: Labeled lines versus convergence in central processing. *Annual Review of Neuroscience, 26,* 1–30.

Craig, A. D., Reiman, E. M., Evans, A., & Bushnell, M. C. (1996). Functional imaging of an illusion of pain. *Nature, 384,* 258–260.

Creese, I., Burt, D. R., & Snyder, S. H. (1976). Dopamine receptor binding predicts clinical and pharmacological potencies of antischizophrenic drugs. *Science, 192,* 481–483.

Crisp, A. H. (1983). Some aspects of the psychopathology of anorexia nervosa. In P. L. Darby, P. E. Garfinkel, D. M. Garner, & D. V. Coscina (Eds.), *Anorexia nervosa: Recent developments in research* (pp. 15–28). New York: Alan R. Liss.

Crowell, C. R., Hinson, R. E., & Siegel, S. (1981). The role of conditional drug responses in tolerance to the hypothermic effects of ethanol. *Psychopharmacology, 73,* 51–54.

Crunelli, V., & Leresche, N. (2002). Childhood absence epilepsy: Genes, channels, neurons and networks. *Nature Reviews Neuroscience, 3,* 371–382.

Culbertson, F. M. (1997). Depression and gender. *American Psychologist, 52,* 25–31.

Culham, J. C., & Kanwisher, N. G. (2001). Neuroimaging of cognitive functions in human parietal cortex. *Current Opinion in Neurobiology, 11,* 157–163.

Curran, T., & Schacter, D. L. (1997). Amnesia: Cognitive neuropsychological aspects. In T. E. Feinberg & M. J. Farah (Eds.), *Behavioral neurology and neuropsychology* (pp. 463–472) New York: McGraw-Hill.

Curtiss, S. (1977). *Genie: A psycholinguistic study of a modern-day "wild child."* New York: Academic Press

D'Almeida, V., Hipólide, D. C., Azzalis, L. A., Lobo, L. L., Junqueira, V. B. C., & Tufik, S. (1997). Absence of oxidative stress following paradoxical sleep deprivation in rats. *Neuroscience Letters, 235,* 25–28.

Daly, M., & Wilson, M. (1983). *Sex, evolution, and behavior.* Boston: Allard Grant Press.

Damasio, A. R. (1999, December). How the brain creates the mind. *Scientific American, 281,* 112–117.

Damasio, H. (1989) Neuroimaging contributions to the understanding of aphasia. In F. Boller & J. Grafman (Eds.), *Handbook of neuropsychology* (Vol. 2, pp. 3–46). New York: Elsevier.

Damasio, H., Grabowski, T., Frank, R., Galaburda, A. M., & Damasio, A. R. (1994). The return of Phineas Gage: Clues about the brain from the skull of a famous patient. *Science, 264,* 1102–1105.

Damasio, H., Grabowski, T. J., Tranel, D., Hichwa, R. D., & Damasio, A. R. (1996). A neural basis for lexical retrieval. *Nature, 380,* 499–505.

Darian-Smith, I., Burman, K., & Darian-Smith, C. (1999). Parallel pathways mediating manual dexterity in the macaque. *Experimental Brain Research, 128,* 101–108.

Darlison, M. G., & Richter, D. (1999). Multiple genes for neuropeptides and their receptors: Co-evolution and physiology. *Trends in Neurosciences, 22,* 81–88.

Darnell, J. E., Jr. (1997). STATS and gene regulation. *Science, 277,* 1630–1635.

Davids, E., & Gaspar, M. (2004). Buprenorphine in the treatment of opioid dependence. *European Neuropsychopharmacology, 14,* 209–216.

Davidson, C., Gow, A. J., Lee, T. H., & Ellinwood, E. H. (2001). Methamphetamine neurotoxicity: Necrotic and apoptotic mechanisms and relevance to human abuse and treatment. *Brain Research Reviews, 36,* 1–22.

Davidson, J. M. (1980). Hormones and sexual behavior in the male. In D. T. Krieger & J. C. Hughes (Eds.), *Neuroendocrinology* (pp. 232–238). Sunderland, MA: Sinauer Associates.

Davidson, J. M., Kwan, M., & Greenleaf, W. J. (1982). Hormonal replacement and sexuality in men. *Clinics in Endocrinology and Metabolism, 11,* 599–623.

Davis, M., Rainie, D., & Cassell, M. (1994). Neurotransmission in the rat amygdala related to fear and anxiety. *Trends in Neuroscience, 17,* 208–214.

Dawson, D., & Encel, N. (1993). Melatonin and sleep in humans. *Journal of Pineal Research, 15,* 1–2.

Dawson, T. M., & Dawson, V. L. (2003). Molecular pathways of neurodegenerations in Parkinson's disease. *Science, 302,* 819–822.

Debski, E. A., & Cline, H. T. (2002). Activity-dependent mapping in the retinotectal projection. *Current Opinion in Neurobiology, 12,* 93–99.

de Castro, J. M., & Plunkett, S. (2002). A general model of intake regulation. *Neuroscience and Biobehavioural Reviews, 26,* 581–595.

DeCatanzaro, D., Muir, C., Spironello, E., Binger, T., & Thomas, J. (2000). Intense arousal of novel male mice in proximity to previously inseminated females: Inactivation of males via chlorpromazine does not diminish the capacity to disrupt pregnancy. *Psychobiology, 28,* 110–114.

de Gelder, B. (2000). Neuroscience. More to seeing than meets the eye. *Science, 289,* 1148–1208.

De Gennaro, L., Ferrara, M., & Bertini, M. (2000). Muscle twitch activity during REM sleep: Effect of sleep deprivation and relation with rapid eye movement activity. *Psychobiology, 28,* 432–436.

Dehaene, S. (2002). Single-neuron arithmetic. *Science, 297,* 1652–1653.

De Jonge, F. H., Louwerse, A. L., Ooms, M. P., Evers, P., Endert, E., & van de Poll, N. E. (1989). Lesions of the SDN-POA inhibit sexual behavior of male Wistar rats. *Brain Research Bulletin, 23,* 483–492.

de Kruif, P. (1945). *The male hormone.* New York: Harcourt, Brace.

Delville, Y., Melloni, R. H., Jr., & Ferris, C. F. (1998). Behavioral and neurobiological consequences of social subjugation during puberty in golden hamsters. *Journal of Neuroscience, 18,* 2667–2672.

Dement, W. C. (1960). The effect of dream deprivation. *Science, 131,* 1705–1707.

Dement, W. C. (1978). *Some must watch while some must sleep.* New York: W. W. Norton.

Dement, W. C., & Kleitman, N. (1957). The relation of eye movement during sleep to dream activity: An objective method for the study of dreaming. *Journal of Experimental Psychology, 53,* 339 553.

Dement, W. C., & Wolpert, E. A. (1958). The relation of eye movements, body motility and external stimuli to dream content. *Journal of Experimental Psychology, 55,* 543–553.

Demet, E. M., Chicz-Demet, A., Fallon, J. H., & Sokolski, K. N. (1999). Sleep deprivation therapy in depressive illness and Parkinson's disease. *Progressive Neuro-Psychopharmacology & Biological Psychiatry, 23,* 753–784.

Denham, T. P., Haberle, S. G., Lentfer, C., Fullagar, R., Field, J., Therin, M., et al. (2003). Origins of agriculture at Kuk Swamp in the highlands of New Guinea. *Science, 301,* 189–193.

De Preux, E., Dubois-Arber, F., & Zobel, F. (2004). Current trends in illegal drug use and drug related health problems in Switzerland. *Swiss Medical Weekly, 134,* 313–321.

De Renzi, E. (1997). Visuospatial and constructional disorders. In T. E. Feinberg & M. J. Farah (Eds.), *Behavioral neurology and neuropsychology* (pp. 297–308). New York: McGraw-Hill.

Deroche-Gamonet, V., Belin, D., & Piazza, P. V. (2004). Evidence for addiction-like behavior in the rat. *Science, 305,* 1014–1017.

Dess, N. K., & Chapman, C. D. (1998). "Humans and animals"? On saying what we mean. *Psychological Science, 9(2),* 156–157.

Deutch, A. Y., & Roth, R. H. (1999). Neurotransmitters. In M. J. Zigmond, F. E. Bloom, S. C. Landis, J. L. Roberts, & L. R. Squire (Eds.), *Fundamental neuroscience* (pp. 193–234). New York: Academic Press.

De Valois, R. L., Cottaris, N. P., Elfar, S. D., Mahon, L. E., & Wilson, J. A. (2000). Some transformations of color information from lateral geniculate nucleus to striate cortex. *Proceedings of the National Academy of Science, U.S.A., 97,* 4997–5002.

De Valois, R. L., & De Valois, K. K. (1988). *Spatial vision.* New York: Oxford University Press.

Devane, W. A., Hanus, L., Breuer, A., Pertwee, R. G., Stevenson, L. A., Griffin, G., et al. (1992). Isolation and structure of a brain constituent that binds to the cannabinoid receptor. *Science, 258,* 1946–1949.

De Vry, J., & Schreiber, R. (2000). Effects of selected serotonin 5-HT1 and 5-HT2 receptoragonists on feeding behavior: Possible mechanisms of action. *Neuroscience and Biobehavioural Reviews, 24,* 341–353.

de Waal, F. B. M. (1999, December). The end of nature versus nurture. *Scientific American, 281,* 94–99.

De Witte, P., Pinto, E., Ansseau, M., & Verbanck, P. (2003). Alcohol and withdrawal: From animal research to clinical issues. *Neuroscience and Biobehavioural Reviews, 27,* 189–197.

Dewsbury, D. A. (1988). The comparative psychology of monogamy. In D. W. Leger (Ed.), *Comparative perspectives in modern psychology: Nebraska Symposium on Motivation* (Vol. 35, pp. 1–50). Lincoln: University of Nebraska Press.

Dewsbury, D. A. (1991). Psychobiology. *American Psychologist, 46,* 198–205.

D'Hooge, R., & De Deyn, P. P. (2001). Applications of the Morris water maze in the study of learning and memory. *Brain Research Reviews, 36,* 60–90.

Diamond, A. (1985). Development of the ability to use recall to guide action, as indicated by infants' performance on AB. *Child Development, 56,* 868–883.

Diamond, A. (1991). Neuropsychological insights into the meaning of object concept development. In S. Carey & R. Gelman (Eds.), *The epigenesis of mind: Essays on biology and cognition* (pp. 67–110). Hillsdale, NJ: Lawrence Erlbaum.

Diamond, M., & Sigmundson, H. K. (1997). Sex reassignment at birth: Long-term review and clinical implications. *Archives of Pediatric and Adolescent Medicine, 151,* 298–304.

Diamond, M. C. (1986). I want a girl just like the girl . . . . *Discover, 7,* 65–68.

DiCarlo, J. J., & Johnson, K. O. (2000). Spatial and temporal structure of receptive fields in primate somatosensory area 3b: Effects of stimulus scanning direction and orientation. *Journal of Neuroscience, 20,* 495–510.

DiCarlo, J. J., Johnson, K. O., & Hsaio, S. S. (1998). Structure of receptive fields in area 3b of primary somatosensory cortex in the alert monkey. *Journal of Neuroscience, 18,* 2626–2645.

Di Ciano, P., & Everitt, B. J. (2003). Differential control over drug-seeking behavior by drug-associated conditioned reinforcers and discriminative stimuli predictive of drug availability. *Behavioral Neuroscience, 117,* 952–960.

Dick, D. M., & Rose, R. J. (2002). Behavior genetics: What's new? What's next? *Current Directions in Psychological Science, 11(2),* 70–74.

Dielenberg, R. A., & McGregor, I. S. (2001). Defensive behavior in rats towards predatory odors: A review. *Neuroscience and Biobehavioural Reviews, 25,* 597–609.

Dietz, V. (2002b). Proprioception and locomotor disorders. *Nature Reviews Neuroscience, 3,* 781–790.

DiFiglia, M., Sapp, E., Chase, K. O., Davies, S. W., Bates, G. P., Vonsattel, J. P., & Aronin, N. (1997). Aggregation of Huntingtin in neuronal intranuclear inclusions and dystrophic neurites in brain. *Science, 277,* 1990–1993.

Di Marzo, V., Melck, D., Bisogno, T., & De Petrocellis, L. (1998). Endocannabinoids: Endogenous cannabinoid receptor ligands with neuromodulatory action. *Trends in Neurosciences, 21,* 521–528.

Dimberg, U., Thunberg, M., & Elmehed, K. (2000). Unconscious facial reactions to emotional facial expressions. *Psychological Science, 11,* 86–89.

Dinges, D. F., Pack, F., Williams, K., Gillen, K. A., Powell, J. W., Ott, G. E., et al. (1997). Cumulative sleepiness, mood disturbance, and psychomotor vigilance performance decrements during a week of sleep restricted to 4–5 hours per night. *Sleep, 20,* 267–277.

Dirnagl, U., Iadecola, C., & Moskowitz, M. A. (1999). Pathobiology of ischaemic stroke: An integrated view. *Trends in Neurosciences, 22,* 391–397.

Dirnagl, U., Simon, R. P., & Hallenbeck, J. M. (2003). Ischemic tolerance and endogenous neuroprotection. *Trends in Neurosciences, 24,* 248–254.

Dixon, M. J., Bub, D. N., & Arguin, M. (1998). Semantic and visual determinants of face recognition in a prosopagnosic patient. *Journal of Cognitive Neuroscience, 10,* 362–376.

Dobelle, W. H., Mladejovsky, M. G., & Girvin, J. P. (1974). Artificial vision for the blind: Electrical stimulation of visual cortex offers hope for a functional prosthesis. *Science, 183,* 440–444.

Döbrössy, M., & Dunnett, S. B. (2001). The influence of environment and experience on neural grafts. *Nature Reviews Neuroscience, 2,* 871–909.

Dodd, J., Jessel, T. M., & Placzek, M. (1998). The when and where of floor plate induction. *Science, 282,* 1654–1658.

Dolen, R. J., & Morris, J. S. (2000). The functional anatomy of innate and acquired fear: Perspectives from neuroimaging. In R. D. Lane & L. Nadel (Eds.), *Cognitive neuroscience of emotion* (pp. 225–241). New York: Oxford University Press.

Donoghue, J. P. (1995). Plasticity of adult sensorimotor representations. *Current Opinion in Neurobiology, 5,* 749–754.

Doty, R. L. (2001). Olfaction. *Annual Review of Psychology, 52,* 423–452.

Doupe, A. J. (1993). A neural circuit specialized for vocal learning. *Current Opinion in Neurobiology, 3,* 104–110.

Doupe, A. J., & Heisenberg, M. (2000). Neurobiology of behaviour. Old principles and new approaches. *Current Opinion in Neurobiology, 10,* 755–756.

Downing, P. E., Jiang, Y., Shuman, M., & Kanwisher, N. (2001). A cortical area selective for visual processing of the human body. *Science, 293,* 2470–2473.

Doya, K. (2000). Complementary roles of basal ganglia and cerebellum in learning and motor control. *Current Opinion in Neurobiology, 10,* 732–739.

Drachman, D. A., & Arbit, J. (1966). Memory and the hippocampal complex. *Archives of Neurology, 15,* 52–61.

Drevets, W. C. (2001). Neuroimaging and neuropathological studies of depression: Implications for the cognitive-emotional features of mood disorders. *Current Opinion in Neurobiology, 11,* 210–249.

Drewnowski, A., Halmi, K. A., Pierce, B., Gibbs, J., & Smith, G. P. (1987). Taste and eating disorders. *American Journal of Clinical Nutrition, 46,* 442–450.

Drummey, A. B., & Newcombe, N. (1995). Remembering versus knowing the past: Children's explicit and implicit memories for pictures. *Journal of Experimental Child Psychology, 59,* 540–565.

Duchaine, B., Cosmides, L., & Tooby, J. (2001). Evolutionary psychology and the brain. *Current Opinion in Neurobiology, 11,* 225–230.

Dudai, Y. (2002). Molecular bases of long-term memories: A question of persistence. *Current Opinion in Neurobiology, 12,* 211–216.

Duffy, S. N., Craddock, K. J., Abel, T., & Nguyen, P. V. (2001). Environmental enrichment modifies the PKA-dependence of hippocampal LTP and improves hippocampus-dependent memory. *Learning and Memory, 8,* 26–34.

Dunbar, G. C., Perera, M. H., & Jenner, F. A. (1989). Patterns of benzodiazepine use in Great Britain as measured by a general population survey. *British Journal of Psychiatry, 155,* 836–841.

Dunbar, R. (2003). Evolution of the social brain. *Science, 302,* 1160–1161.

Dunnett, S. B., Björklund, A., & Lindvall, O. (2001). Cell therapy in Parkinson's disease—stop or go? *Nature Reviews Neuroscience, 2,* 365–368.

Durtin, M. I., & Colman, D. R. (2002). Neural and immunological synaptic relations. *Science, 298,* 785–789.

Duva, C. A., Kornecook, T. J., & Pinel, J. P. J. (2000). Animal models of medial temporal lobe amnesia: The myth of the hippocampus. In M. Haug & R. E. Whalen (Eds.), *Animal models of human emotion and cognition* (pp. 197–214). Washington, DC: American Psychological Association.

Eagleman, D. M. (2001). Visual illusions and neurobiology. *Nature Reviews Neuroscience, 2,* 920–926.

Eagly, A. H., & Wood, W. (1999). The origins of sex differences in human behavior. *American Psychologist, 54*(6), 408–423.

Edgerton, V. R., & Roy, R. R. (2002). Paralysis recovery in humans and model systems. *Current Opinion in Neurobiology, 12,* 658–667.

Egan, M. F., & Weinberger, D. R. (1997). Neurobiology of schizophrenia. *Current Opinion in Neurobiology, 7,* 701–707.

Ehrhardt, A. A., Meyer-Bahlburg, H. F. L., Rosen, L. R., Feldman, J. F., Veridiano, N. P., Zimmerman, I., & McEwen, B. S. (1985). Sexual orientation after prenatal exposure to exogenous estrogen. *Archives of Sexual Behavior, 14,* 57–77.

Ehringer, H., & Hornykiewicz, O. (1960). Verteilung von Noradrenalin und Dopamin (3-Hydroxytyramin) im gehirn des Menschen und ihr Verhalten bei Erkrankungen des Extrapyramidalen Systems. *Klinische Wochenschrift, 38,* 1236–1239.

Eichenbaum, H. (1996). Learning from LTP: A comment on recent attempts to identify cellular and molecular mechanisms of memory. *Learning & Memory, 3,* 61–73.

Eichenbaum, H. (1999). Conscious awareness, memory and the hippocampus. *Nature, 2,* 775–776.

Eigsti, I. M., & Shapiro, T. (2004). A systems neuroscience approach to autism: Biological, cognitive, and clinical perspectives. *Mental Retardation and Developmental Disabilities Research Reviews, 9,* 205–215.

Eitan, S., Solomon, A., Lavie, V., Yoles, E., Hirschberg, D. L., Belkin, M., & Schwartz, M. (1994). Recovery of visual response of injured adult rat optic nerves treated with transglutaminase. *Science, 264,* 1764–1768.

Ekman, P. (1985). *Telling lies.* New York: Norton.

Ekman, P. (2003). *Emotions revealed: Recognizing faces and feelings to improve communication and emotional life.* New York: Times Books, Henry Holt.

Ekman, P., & Davidson, R. J. (1993). Voluntary smiling changes regional brain activity. *Psychological Science, 4,* 342–345.

Ekman, P., & Friesen, W. V. (1971). Constants across cultures in the face and emotion. *Journal of Personality and Social Psychology, 17,* 124–129.

Ekman, P., & Friesen, W. V. (1975). *Unmasking the face: A guide to recognizing emotions from facial clues.* Englewood Cliffs, NJ: Prentice-Hall.

Ekman, P., Sorenson, E. R., & Friesen, W. V. (1969). Pan cultural elements in facial displays of emotions. *Science, 164,* 86–88.

Elbert, T., Pantev, C., Wienbruch, C., Rockstroh, B., & Taub, E. (1995). Increased cortical representation of the fingers of the left hand in string players. *Science, 270,* 305–307.

Elbert, T., & Rockstroh, B. (2004). Reorganization of human cerebral cortex: The range of changes following use and injury. *The Neuroscientist, 10,* 129–141.

Elena, S. F., Cooper, V. S., & Lenski, R. E. (1996). Punctuated evolution caused by selection of rare beneficial mutations. *Science, 272,* 1802–1807.

Eliboi, B., Söylemezoglu, F., Ünal, I., Fujii, M., Hirt, L., Huang, P. L., et al. (2001). Nitric oxide is involved in ischemia-induced apoptosis in brain. A study in neuronal nitric oxide synthase null mice. *Neuroscience, 105,* 79–86.

Ellis, L., & Ames, M. A. (1987). Neurohormonal functioning and sexual orientation: A theory of homosexuality-heterosexuality. *Psychological Bulletin, 101,* 233–258.

Engel, A. K., Fries, P., & Singer, W. (2001). Dynamic predictions: Oscillations and synchrony in top-down processing. *Nature Reviews Neuroscience, 2,* 704–716.

Engel, S. A. (1999). Using neuroimaging to measure mental representations: Finding color-opponent neurons in visual cortex. *Current Directions in Psychological Science, 8,* 23–27.

Epstein, R., & Kanwisher, N. (1998). A cortical representation of the local visual environment. *Nature, 392,* 598–601.

Erickson, K., Drevets, W., & Schulkin, J. (2003). Glucocorticoid regulation of diverse cognitive functions in normal and pathological emotional states. *Neuroscience and Biobehavioural Reviews, 27,* 233–246.

Eriksson, P. S., Perfilieva, E., Björk-Eriksson, T., Alborn, A., Nordberg, C., Peterson, D. A., & Gage, F. H. (1998). Neurogenesis in the adult human hippocampus. *Nature Medicine, 4,* 1313–1317.

Errington, M. L., Galley, P. T., & Bliss, T. V. P. (2003). Long-term potentiation in the dentate gyrus of the anaesthetized rat is accompanied by an increase in extracellular glutamate: Real-time measurements using a novel dialysis electrode. *Philosophical Transactions of the Royal Society of London, 358,* 675–687.

Espie, C. A. (2002). Insomnia: Conceptual issues in the development, persistence, and treatment of sleep disorder in adults. *Annual Review of Neuroscience, 53,* 215–243.

Everitt, B. J., Dickinson, A., & Robbins, T. W. (2001). The neuropsychological basis of addictive behaviour. *Brain Research Reviews, 36,* 129–138.

Everitt, B. J., & Herbert, J. (1972). Hormonal correlates of sexual behavior in sub-human primates. *Danish Medical Bulletin, 19,* 246–258.

Everitt, B. J., Herbert, J., & Hamer, J. D. (1971). Sexual receptivity of bilaterally adrenalectomized female rhesus monkeys. *Physiology & Behavior, 8,* 409–415.

Everitt, B. J., & Robbins, T. W. (1997). Central cholinergic systems and cognition. *Annual Review of Psychology, 48,* 649–684.

Eysel, U. T. (2003). Illusions and perceived images in the primate brain. *Science, 302,* 789–791.

Fabbro, F., Tavano, A., Corti, S., Bresolin, N., De Fabritis, P., & Borgatti, R. (2004). Long-term neuropsychological deficits after cerebellar infarctions in two young adult twins. *Neuropsychologia, 42,* 536–545.

Fabri, M., Polonara, G., Del Pesce, M., Quattrini, A., Salvolini, U., & Manzoni, T. (2001). Posterior corpus callosum and interhemispheric transfer of somatosensory information: An fMRI and neuropsychological study of a partially callosotomized patient. *Journal of Cognitive Neuroscience, 13,* 1071–1079.

Falconer, E. M., & Galea, L. A. M. (2003). Sex differences in cell proliferation, cell death and defensive behavior following acute predator stress in adult rats. *Brain Research, 975,* 22–36.

Falkenburger, B. H., Barstow, K. L., & Mintz, I. M. (2001). Dendrodendritic inhibition through reversal of dopamine transport. *Science, 293,* 2465–2470.

Falzi, G., Perrone, P., & Vignolo, L. A. (1982). Right-left asymmetry in anterior speech region. *Archives of Neurology, 39,* 239–240.

Farah, M. J. (1990). *Visual agnosia: Disorders of object recognition and what they tell us about normal vision.* Cambridge, MA: MIT Press.

Farber, N. B., & Olney, J. W. (2003). Drugs of abuse that cause developing neurons to commit suicide. *Developmental Brain Research, 147,* 37–45.

Farmer, M. E., & Klein, R. M. (1995). The evidence for a temporal processing deficit linked to dyslexia: A review. *Psychonomic Bulletin and Review, 2,* 460–493.

Farmer, J., Zhao, X., Van Praag, H., Wodke, K., Gage, F. H., & Christie, B. R. (2004). Effects of voluntary exercise on synaptic plasticity and gene expression in the dentate gyrus of adult male Sprague-Dawley rats in vivo. *Neuroscience, 124,* 71–79.

Farooqi, I. S., Jebb, S. A., Langmack, G., Lawrence, E., Cheetham, C. H., Prentice, A. M., et al. (1999). Effects of recombinant leptin therapy in a child with congenital leptin deficiency. *New England Journal of Medicine, 341,* 879–884.

Farrell, S. E., & McGinnis, M. Y. (2003). Effects of pubertal anabolic-androgenic steroid (AAS) administration on reproductive and aggressive behaviors in male rats. *Behavioral Neuroscience, 117,* 904–911.

Fazio, F., Perani, D., Gilardi, M. C., Colombo, F., Cappa, S. F., Vallar, G., et al. (1992). Metabolic impairment in human amnesia: A PET study of memory networks. *Journal of Cerebral Blood Flow and Metabolism, 12,* 353–358.

Feindel, W. (1986). Electrical stimulation of the brain during surgery for epilepsy—historical highlights. In G. P. Varkey (Ed.), *Anesthetic considerations for craniotomy in awake patients* (pp. 75–87). Boston: Little, Brown.

Feng, A. S., & Ratnam, R. (2000). Neural basis of hearing in real-world situations. *Annual Review of Psychology, 51,* 699–725.

Fentress, J. C. (1973). Development of grooming in mice with amputated forelimbs. *Science, 179,* 704–705.

Fernald, R. D. (2000). Evolution of eyes. *Current Opinion in Neurobiology, 10,* 444–450.

Fernández-Guasti, A., Swaab, D., & Rodríguez-Manzo, G. (2003). Sexual behavior reduces hypothalamic androgen receptor immunoreactivity. *Psychoneuroendocrinology, 28,* 501–512.

Ferrara, M., De Gennaro, L., & Bertini, M. (1999). The effects of slow-wave sleep (SWS) deprivation and time of night on behavioral performance upon awakening. *Physiology & Behavior, 68,* 55–61.

Fields, R. D. (2004, April). The other half of the brain. *Scientific American, 290,* 55–61.

Fields, R. D., & Stevens-Graham, B. (2002). New insights into neuron-glia communication. *Science, 298,* 556–562.

Filbin, M. T. (2003). Myelin-associated inhibitors of axonal regeneration in the adult mammalian CNS. *Nature Reviews Neuroscience, 4,* 703–712.

Fillion, T. J., & Blass, E. M. (1986). Infantile experience with suckling odors determines adult sexual behavior in male rats. *Science, 231,* 729–731.

Fink, G., Sumner, B., Rosie, R., Wilson, H., & McQueen, J. (1999). Androgen actions on central serotonin neurotransmission: Relevance for mood, mental state and memory. *Behavioural Brain Research, 105,* 53–68.

Finlay, B. L., & Darlington, R. B. (1995). Linked regularities in the development and evolution of mammalian brains. *Science, 268,* 1578–1584.

Fiorillo, C. D., Tobler, P. N., & Schultz, W. (2003). Discrete coding of reward probability and uncertainty by dopamine neurons. *Science, 299,* 1898–1902.

Fiorino, D. F., Coury, A., & Phillips, A. G. (1997). Dynamic changes in nucleus accumbens dopamine efflux during the Coolidge effect in male rats. *Journal of Neuroscience, 17,* 4849–4855.

Fisher, S. E., & DeFries, J. C. (2002). Developmental dyslexia: Genetic dissection of a complex cognitive trait. *Nature Reviews Neuroscience, 3,* 767–780.

Fitzpatrick, S. M., & Rothman, D. L. (2000). Meeting report: Transcranial magnetic stimulation and studies of human cognition. *Journal of Cognitive Neuroscience, 12,* 704–709.

Fletcher, J. M., Page, J. B., Francis, D. J., Copeland, K., Naus, M. J., Davis, C. M., et al. (1996). Cognitive correlates of long-term cannabis use in Costa Rican men. *Archives of General Psychiatry, 53,* 1051–1057.

Floresco, S. B., Seamans, J. K., & Phillips, A. G. (1997). Selective roles for hippocampal, prefrontal cortical, and ventral striatal circuits in radial-arm maze tasks with or without a delay. *Journal of Neuroscience, 17*(5), 1880–1890.

Foster, R. G., & Kreitzman, L. (2004). *Rhythms of life.* London: Profiles.

Foulkes, N. S., Borjigin, J., Snyder, S. H., & Sassone-Corsi, P. (1997). Rhythmic transcription: The molecular basis of circadian melatonin synthesis. *Trends in Neurosciences, 20,* 487–492.

Fournier, A. E., & Strittmatter, S. M. (2001). Repulsive factors and axon regeneration in the CNS. *Current Opinion in Neurobiology, 11,* 89–94.

Francis, D. D., & Meaney, M. J. (1999). Maternal care and the development of stress responses. *Current Opinion in Neurobiology, 9,* 128–134.

Franklin, R. J. M. (2002). Why does remyelination fail in multiple sclerosis? *Nature Reviews Neuroscience, 3,* 705–714.

Freedman, M. S., Lucas, R. J., Soni, B., von Schantz, M., Muñoz, M., David-Gray, Z., & Foster, R. (1999). Regulation of mammalian circadian behavior by non-rod, non-cone, ocular photoreceptors. *Science, 284,* 502–504.

Freund, H. J. (2003). Somatosensory and motor disturbances in patients with parietal lobe lesions. *Advances in Neurology, 93,* 179–193.

Friedman, D. Cycowicz, Y. M., & Gaeta, H. (2001). The novelty P3: An event-related brain potential (ERP) sign of the brain's evaluation of novelty. *Neuroscience and Biobehavioural Reviews, 25,* 355–373.

Friedman, J., Globus, G., Huntley, A., Mullaney, D., Naitoh, P., & Johnson, L. (1977). Performance and mood during and after gradual sleep reduction. *Psychophysiology, 14,* 245–250.

Friedman-Hill, S. R., Robertson, L. C., & Treisman, A. (1995). Parietal contributions to visual feature binding: Evidence from a patient with bilateral lesions. *Science, 269,* 853–855.

Fries, P., Fernández, G., & Jensen, O. (2003). When neurons form memories. *Trends in Neurosciences, 26,* 123–124.

Frith, C., & Dolan, R. J. (1998). Images of psychopathology. *Current Opinion in Neurobiology, 8*, 259–262.

Funnell, M. G., Corballis, P. M., & Gazzaniga, M. S. (1999). A deficit in perceptual matching in the left hemisphere of a callostomy patient. *Neuropsychologia, 37*, 1143–1154.

Fuster, J. M. (2000). The prefrontal cortex of the primate: A synopsis. *Psychobiology, 28*, 125–131.

Gabrieli, J. D. E., Corkin, S., Mickel, S. F., & Growdon, J. H. (1993). Intact acquisition and long-term retention of mirror-tracing skill in Alzheimer's disease and in global amnesia. *Behavioral Neuroscience, 107*, 899–910.

Gaffan, D. (1974). Recognition impaired and association intact in the memory of monkeys after transection of the fornix. *Journal of Comparative and Physiological Psychology, 86*, 1100–1109.

Gage, F. H. (2000). Mammalian neural stem cells. *Science, 287*, 1433–1438.

Gaiarsa, J.-L., Caillard, O., & Ben-Ari, Y. (2002). Long-term plasticity at GABAergic and glycenergic synapses: Mechanisms and functional significance. *Trends in Neurosciences, 25*, 561 570.

Galarreta, M., & Hestrin, S. (2001). Electrical synapses between GABA-releasing interneurons. *Nature Reviews Neuroscience, 2*, 425–433.

Galef, B. G. (1989). Laboratory studies of naturally-occurring feeding behaviors: Pitfalls, progress and problems in ethoexperimental analysis. In R. J. Blanchard, P F Brain, D. C. Blanchard, & S. Parmigiani (Eds.), *Ethoexperimental approaches to the study of behavior* (pp. 51–77). Dordrecht, The Netherlands: Kluwer Academic Publishers.

Galef, B. G. (1995). Food selection: Problems in understanding how we choose foods to eat. *Neuroscience and Biobehavioural Reviews, 20*, 67–73.

Galef, B. G. (1996). Social enhancement of food preferences in Norway rats: A brief review. In C. M. Heyes & B. G. Galef, Jr. (Eds.), *Social learning in animals: The roots of culture* (pp. 49 64). New York: Academic Press.

Galef, B. G., Whishkin, E. E., & Bielavska, E. (1997). Interaction with demonstrator rats changes observer rats' affective responses to flavors. *Journal of Comparative Psychology, 111*, 393–398.

Galef, B. G., & Wright, T. J. (1995). Groups ot naive rats learn to select nutritionally adequate foods faster than do isolated naive rats. *Animal Behavior, 49*, 403–409.

Gallo, V., & Chittajallu, R. (2001). Unwrapping glial cells from the synapse: What lies inside? *Science, 292*, 872–873.

Gallup, G. G., Jr. (1983). Toward a comparative psychology of mind. In R. L. Mellgren (Ed.), *Animal cognition and behavior* (pp. 473–505). New York: North-Holland Publishing.

Galuske, R. A. W., Schlote, W., Bratzke, H., & Singer, W. (2000). Interhemispheric asymmetries of the modular structure in human temporal cortex. *Science, 289*, 1946–1949.

Gandy, S. (2003). Estrogen and neurodegeneration. *Neurochemical Research, 28*, 1003–1008.

Gannon, P. J., Holloway, R. L., Broadfield, D. C., & Braun, A. R. (1998). Asymmetry of chimpanzee planum temporale: Humanlike pattern of Wernicke's brain language area homolog. *Science, 279*, 220–222.

Gao, E., & Suga, N. (2000). Experience-dependent plasticity in the auditory cortex and the inferior colliculus of bats: Role of the corticofugal system. *Proceedings of the National Academy of Sciences U.S.A., 97*, 8081–8086.

Gao, G., Wang, X., He, S., Li, W., Wang, Q., Liang, Q., et al. (2003). Clinical study for alleviating opiate drug psychological dependence by a method of ablating the nucleus accumbens with stereotactic surgery. *Stereotactic and Functional Neurosurgery, 81*, 96–104.

Garcia, J., & Koelling, R. A. (1966). Relation of cue to consequence in avoidance learning. *Psychonomic Science, 4*, 123–124.

Garcia-Segura, L. M., Azcoitia, I., & DonCarlos, L. L. (2001). Neuroprotection by estradiol. *Progress in Neurobiology, 63*, 29–60.

Garwicz, M. (2002). Spinal reflexes provide motor error signals to cerebellar modules—relevance for motor coordination. *Brain Research Reviews, 40*, 152–165.

Gauthier, I., Behrmann, M., & Tarr, M. J. (1999). Can face recognition really be dissociated from object recognition? *Journal of Cognitive Neuroscience, 11*, 349–370.

Gauthier, I., Skudlarski, P., Gore, J. C., & Anderson, A. W. (2000). Expertise for cars and birds recruits brain areas involved in face recognition. *Nature, 3*, 191–197.

Gawin, F. H. (1991). Cocaine addiction: Psychology and neurophysiology. *Science, 251*, 1580–1586.

Gazzaniga, M. S. (1967, August). The split brain in man. *Scientific American, 217*, 24–29.

Gazzaniga, M. S. (1998, July). The split brain revisited. *Scientific American, 278*, 51–55.

Gazzaniga, M. S. (2000). Regional differences in cortical organization. *Science, 289*, 1887–1888.

Gazzaniga, M. S., & Sperry, R. W. (1967). Language after section of the cerebral commissure. *Brain, 90*, 131–148.

Geary, D. C. (1999). Evolution and developmental sex differences. *Current Directions in Psychological Science, 8*(4), 115–120.

Gegenfurtner, K. R., & Kiper, D. C. (2003) Color vision. *Annual Review of Neuroscience, 26*, 181–206.

Geiselman, P. J. (1987). Carbohydrates do not always produce satiety: An explanation of the appetite- and hunger-stimulating effects of hexoses. *Progress in Psychobiology and Physiological Psychology, 12*, 1–46.

Geng, J. J., & Behrmann, M. (2002). Probability cuing of target location facilitates visual search implicitly in normal participants and patients with hemispatial neglect. *Psychological Science, 13*, 520–525.

Georgopoulos, A. P. (1991). Higher order motor control. *Annual Review of Neuroscience, 14*, 361–377.

Georgopoulos, A. P. (1995). Current issues in directional motor control. *Trends in Neurosciences, 18*, 506–510.

Gerlach, C., Law, I., & Paulson, O. B. (2002). When action turns into words. Activation of motor-based knowledge during categorization of manipulable objects. *Journal of Cognitive Neuroscience, 14*, 1230–1239.

Gerlai, R., & Clayton, N. S. (1999). Analyzing hippocampal function in transgenic mice: An ethological perspective. *Trends in Neurosciences, 22*, 47–51.

Gernsbacher, M. A., & Kaschak, M. P. (2003). Neuroimaging studies of language production and comprehension. *Annual Review of Psychology, 54*, 91–114.

Gerra, G., Borella, F., Zaimovic, A., Moi, G., Bussandri, M., Bubici, C., & Bertacca, S. (2004). Buprenorphine versus methadone for opioid dependence. Predictor variables for treatment outcome. *Drug and Alcohol Dependence, 75*, 37–45.

Geschwind, N. (1970). The organization of language and the brain. *Science, 170*, 940–944.

Geschwind, N. (1979, September). Specializations of the human brain. *Scientific American, 241*, 180–199.

Geschwind, N., & Levitsky, W. (1968). Human brain: Left-right asymmetries in temporal speech region. *Science, 161*, 186–187.

Gevins, A., Leong, H., Smith, M. E., Le, J., & Du, R. (1995). Mapping cognitive brain function with modern high-resolution electroencephalography. *Trends in Neurosciences, 18*, 429–436.

Gibbs, J., Young, R. C., & Smith, G. P. (1973). Cholecystokinin decreases food intake in rats. *Journal of Comparative and Physiological Psychology, 84*, 488–495.

Gibson, A. D., & Garbers, D. L. (2000). Guanylyl cyclases as a family of putative odorant receptors. *Annual Review of Neuroscience, 23*, 417–439.

Gilbert, C. D., & Wiesel, T. N. (1992). Receptive field dynamics in adult primary visual cortex. *Nature, 356*, 150–152.

Gilbertson, T., Damak, S., & Margolskee, R. F. (2000). The molecular physiology of taste transduction. *Current Opinion in Neurobiology, 10*, 519–527.

Gillberg, M., Kecklund, G., Axelsson, J., & Åkerstedt, T. (1996). The effects of a short daytime nap after restricted night sleep. *Sleep, 19*, 570–575.

Gillette, M. U., & McArthur, A. J. (1996). Circadian actions of melatonin at the suprachiasmatic nucleus. *Behavioural Brain Research, 73,* 135–139.

Gilliam, T. C., Gusella, J. F., & Lehrach, H. (1987). Molecular genetic strategies to investigate Huntington's disease. *Advances in Neurology, 48,* 17–29.

Gingrich, J. R., & Roder, J. (1998). Inducible gene expression in the nervous system of transgenic mice. *Annual Review of Neuroscience, 21,* 377–405.

Gladue, B. A. (1994). The biopsychology of sexual orientation. *Current Directions in Psychological Science, 3,* 150–154.

Glaser, R., Rice, J., Sheridan, J., Fertel, R., Stout, J., Speicher, C., et al. (1987). Stress-related immune suppression: Health implications. *Brain, Behavior, and Immunity, 1,* 7–20.

Glickstein, M. (2000). How are visual areas of the brain connected to motor areas for the sensory guidance of movement? *Trends in Neurosciences, 23,* 613–617.

Goddard, G. V., McIntyre, D. C., & Leech, C. K. (1969). A permanent change in brain function resulting from daily electrical stimulation. *Experimental Neurology, 25,* 295–330.

Goedert, M. (1993). Tau protein and the neurofibrillary pathology of Alzheimer's disease. *Trends in Neurosciences, 16,* 460–465.

Gold, R. M., Jones, A. P., Sawchenko, P. E., & Kapatos, G. (1977). Paraventricular area: Critical focus of a longitudinal neurocircuitry mediating food intake. *Physiology & Behavior, 18,* 1111–1119.

Goldberg, J. L., & Barres, B. A. (2000). The relationship between neuronal survival and regeneration. *Annual Review of Neuroscience, 23,* 576–612.

Goldman, S. A., & Nottebohm, F. (1983). Neuronal production, migration, and differentiation in a vocal control nucleus of the adult female canary brain. *Proceedings of the National Academy of Sciences, U.S.A., 80,* 2390–2394.

Goldowitz, D., & Hamre, K. (1998). The cells and molecules that make a cerebellum. *Trends in Neurosciences, 21,* 375–382.

Goldstein, A., & Kalant, H. (1990). Drug policy: Striking the right balance. *Science, 249,* 1513–1521.

Goldstein, I. (2000, August). Male sexual circuitry. *Scientific American, 283,* 70–75.

Gollin, E. S. (1960). Developmental studies of visual recognition of incomplete objects. *Perceptual Motor Skills, 11,* 289–298.

Gollnick, P. D., & Hodgson, D. R. (1986). The identification of fiber types in skeletal muscle: A continual dilemma. *Exercise and Sport Sciences Reviews, 14,* 81–104.

Goodale, M. A. (1993). Visual pathways supporting perception and action in the primate cerebral cortex. *Current Opinion in Neurobiology, 3,* 578–585.

Goodale, M. A. & Milner, A. D. (1992). Separate visual pathways for perception and action. *Trends in Neurosciences, 15,* 20–25.

Goodale, M. A., Milner, A. D., Jakobson, L. S., & Carey, D. P. (1991). A neurological dissociation between perceiving objects and grasping them. *Nature, 349,* 154–156.

Goodenough, D. R., Shapiro, A., Holden, M., & Steinschriber, L. (1959). A comparison of "dreamers" and "nondreamers": Eye movements, electroencephalograms, and the recall of dreams. *Journal of Abnormal and Social Psychology, 59,* 295–303.

Gooren, L. J., & Toorians, A. W. (2003). Significance of estrogens in male (patho)physiology. *Annales d'endocrinologie, 64,* 126–135.

Gorski, R. A. (1980). Sexual differentiation in the brain. In D. T. Krieger & J. C. Hughes (Eds.), *Neuroendocrinology* (pp. 215–222). Sunderland, MA: Sinauer.

Gorski, R. A., Gordon, J. H., Shryne, J. E., & Southam, A. M. (1978). Evidence for a morphological sex difference within the medial preoptic area of the rat brain. *Brain Research, 148,* 333–346.

Gottesman, I. I., & Bertelsen, A. (1989). Confirming unexpressed genotypes for schizophrenia. *Archives of General Psychiatry, 46,* 867–872.

Gottesman, I. I., & Shields, J. (1982). *Schizophrenia: The epigenetic puzzle.* Cambridge, England: Cambridge University Press.

Gottlieb, D. I. (2002). Large-scale sources of neural stem cells. *Annual Review of Neuroscience, 25,* 381–407.

Gottlieb, R. A. (2000). Role of mitochondria in apoptosis. *Critical Reviews in Eukaryotic Gene Expression, 10,* 231–239.

Gould, E., Reeves, A. J., Graziano, M. S. A., & Gross, C. G. (1999). Neurogenesis in the neocortex of adult primates. *Science, 286,* 548–552.

Goy, R. W., & McEwen, B. S. (1980). *Sexual differentiation of the brain.* Cambridge, MA: MIT Press.

Grace, A., Bunney, B. S., Moore, H., & Todd, C. L. (1997). Dopamine-cell depolarization block as a model for the therapeutic actions of antipsychotic drugs. *Trends in Neurosciences, 20,* 31–37.

Grady, K. L., Phoenix, C. H., & Young, W. C. (1965). Role of the developing rat testis in differentiation of the neural tissues mediating mating behavior. *Journal of Comparative and Physiological Psychology, 59,* 176–182.

Graff-Radford, N., Damasio, H., Yamada, T., Eslinger, P. J., & Damasio, A. R. (1985). Nonhaemorrhagic thalamic infarction. *Brain, 108,* 485–516.

Grakoui, A., Bromley, S. K., Sumen, C., Davis, M. M., Shaw, A. S., Allen, P. M., & Dustin, M. L. (1999). The immunological synapse: A molecular machine controlling T cell activation. *Science, 285,* 221–227.

Grant, P. R. (1991, October). Natural selection and Darwin's finches. *Scientific American, 265,* 82–87.

Gratton, G., & Fabiani, M. (2003). Michael G. H. Coles: Thirty years of psychophysiology. *Biological Psychology, 64(1–2),* 1–5.

Gray, J. A., & McNaughton, N. (2000). *The neuropsychology of anxiety.* London: Oxford University Press.

Graziano, M. S. A., & Gross, C. G. (1998). Spatial maps for the control of movement. *Current Opinion in Neurobiology, 8,* 195–201.

Green, C. B., & Menaker, M. (2003). Clock on the brain. *Science, 301,* 319–320.

Green, S. (1991). Benzodiazepines, putative anxiolytics and animal models of anxiety. *Trends in Neuroscience, 14,* 101–103.

Greenamyre, J. T., & Hastings, T. G. (2004). Parkinson's—divergent causes, convergent mechanisms. *Science, 304,* 1120–1122.

Greene, P. E., Fahn, S., Tsai, W. Y., Winfield, H., Dillon, S., Kao, R., et al. (1999). Double-blind controlled trial of human embryonic dopaminergic tissue transplants in advanced Parkinson's disease: Long-term unblinded follow-up phase. *Neurology, 52(Suppl. 2).*

Greengard, P. (2001). The neurobiology of slow synaptic transmission. *Science, 294,* 1024–1030.

Grillner, S. (1985). Neurobiological bases of rhythmic motor acts in vertebrates. *Science, 228,* 143–149.

Grillner, S., & Dickinson, M. (2002). Motor systems. *Current Opinion in Neurobiology, 12,* 629–632.

Grill-Spector, K. (2003). The neural basis of object perception. *Current Opinion in Neurobiology, 13,* 159–166.

Grimson, W. E. L., Kikinis, R., Jolesz, F. A., & Black, P. M. (1999, June). Virtual-reality technology. *Scientific American, 280,* 63–69.

Groenewegen, H. J. (2003). The basal ganglia and motor control. *Neural Plasticity, 10,* 107–120.

Gross, C., & Hen, R. (2004). The developmental origins of anxiety. *Nature Reviews Neuroscience, 5,* 545–552.

Gross, C. G., Moore, T., & Rodman, H. R. (2004). Visually guided behavior after V1 lesions in young and adult monkeys and its relation to blindsight in humans. *Progress in Brain Research, 144,* 279–294.

Grossman, E., Donnelly, M., Price, R., Pickens, D., Morgan, V., Neighbor, G., & Blake, R. (2000). Brain areas involved in perception of biological motion. *Journal of Cognitive Neuroscience, 12,* 711–720.

Grove, E. A., & Fukuchi-Shimogori, T. (2003). Generating the cerebral cortical area map. *Annual Review of Neuroscience, 26,* 355–380.

Grumbach, M. M. (2002). The neuroendocrinology of human puberty revisited. *Hormone Research, 57,* S2–S14.

Grunt, J. A., & Young, W. C. (1952). Differential reactivity of individuals and the response of the male guinea pig to testosterone propionate. *Endocrinology, 51,* 237–248.

Gschwend, P., Rehm, J., Lezzi, S., Blättler, R., Steffen, T., Gutzwiller, F., & Uchtenhagen, A. (2002). Development of a monitoring system for heroin-assisted substitution treatment in Switzerland. *Sozial und Praventivmedizin, 47*, 33–38.

Guan, K-L., & Rao, Y. (2003). Signalling mechanisms mediating neuronal responses to guidance cues. *Nature Reviews Neuroscience, 4*, 941–956.

Guerri, C. (2002). Mechanisms involved in central nervous system dysfunctions induced by prenatal ethanol exposure. *Neurotoxicity Research, 4*, 327–335.

Guillamón, A., Segovia, S., & Del Abril, A. (1988). Early effects of gonadal steroids on the neuron number in the medial posterior region and the lateral division of the bed nucleus of the *stria terminalis* in the rat. *Developmental Brain Research, 44*, 281–290.

Guo, Y., & Udin, S. B. (2000). The development of abnormal axon trajectories after rotation of one eye in *Xenopus. Journal of Neuroscience, 20*, 4189–4197.

Gutfreund, Y., Zheng, W., & Knudsen, E. I. (2002). Gated visual input to the central auditory system. *Science, 297*, 1556–1559.

Guttinger, F., Gschwend, P., Schulte, B., Rehm, J., & Uchtenhagen, A. (2003). Evaluating long-term effects of heroin-assisted treatment: The results of a 6-year follow-up. *European Addiction Research, 9*, 73–79.

Haaland, K. Y., & Harrington, D. L. (1996). Hemispheric asymmetry of movement. *Current Opinion in Neurobiology, 6*, 796–800.

Haffenden, A. M., & Goodale, M. A. (1998). The effect of pictorial illusion on prehension and perception. *Journal of Cognitive Neuroscience, 10*, 122–136.

Haimov, I., & Lavie, P. (1996). Melatonin—a soporific hormone. *Current Directions in Psychological Science, 5*(4), 106–111.

Haimov, I., Lavie, P., Laudon, M., Herer, P., & Zisapel, N. (1995). Melatonin replacement therapy of elderly insomniacs. *Sleep, 18*, 598–603.

Haist, F., Bowden, G. J., & Mao, H. (2001). Consolidation of human memory over decades revealed by functional magnetic resonance imaging. *Nature Neuroscience, 4*, 1057–1058.

Halford, J. C. G., & Blundell, J. E. (2000a). Pharmacology of appetite suppression. In E. Jucker (Ed.). *Progress in drug research* (Vol. 54, 25–58). Basel: Birkhäuser, Verlag.

Halford, J. C. G., & Blundell, J. E. (2000b). Separate systems for serotonin and leptin in appetite control. *Annals of Medicine, 32*, 222–232.

Hallett, M. (2001). Plasticity of the human motor cortex and recovery from stroke. *Brain Research Review, 36*, 169–174.

Hamann, S. B., & Adolphs, R. (1999). Normal recognition of emotional similarity between facial expressions following bilateral amygdala damage. *Neuropsychologia, 37*, 1135–1141.

Hamann, S. B., Ely, T. D., Hoffman, J. M., & Kilts, C. D. (2002). Ecstasy and agony: Activation of the human amygdala in positive and negative emotion. *Psychological Science, 13*, 135–141.

Hamer, D. H., Hu, S., Magnuson, V. L., Hu, N., & Pattatucci, A. M. L. (1993). A linkage between DNA markers on the chromosome and male sexual orientation. *Science, 261*, 321–327.

Hammond, G. (2002). Correlates of human handedness in primary motor cortex: A review and hypothesis. *Neuroscience and Biobehavioural Reviews, 26*, 285–292.

Hammond, P. H., Merton, P. A., & Sutton, G. G. (1956). Nervous gradation of muscular contraction. *British Medical Bulletin, 12*, 214–218.

Hanashima, C., Li, S. C., Shen, L., Lai, E., & Fishell, G. (2004). *Foxg1* suppresses early cortical cell fate. *Science, 303*, 56–59.

Hanson, G. R., Bunsey, M. D., & Riccio, D. C. (2002). The effects of pretraining and reminder treatments on retrograde amnesia in rats: Comparison of lesions to the fornix or perirhinal and entorhinal cortices. *Neurobiology Learning & Memory, 78*, 365–378.

Happé, F., & Frith, U. (1996). The neuropsychology of autism. *Brain, 119*, 1377–1400.

Haqq, C. M., King, C.-Y., Ukiyama, E., Falsafi, S., Haqq, T. N., Donahoe, P. K., & Weiss, M. A. (1994). Molecular basis of mamma-

lian sexual determination: Activation of Müllerian inhibiting substance gene expression by SRY. *Science, 266*, 1494–1500.

Harata, N., Pyle, J. L., Aravanis, A. M., Mozhayeva, M., Kavalali, E. T., & Tsien, R. W. (2001). Limited numbers of recycling vesicles in small CNS nerve terminals: Implications for neural signaling and vesicular cycling. *Trends in Neurosciences, 24*, 637–643.

Harding, S. M., & McGinnis, M. Y. (2004). Androgen receptor blockade in the MPOA or VMN: Effects on male sociosexual behaviors. *Physiology & Behavior, 81*, 671–680.

Hardy, J., & Selkoe, D. J. (2002). The amyloid hypothesis of Alzheimer's disease: Progress and problems on the road to therapeutics. *Science, 297*, 353–356.

Harris, G. W. (1955). *Neural control of the pituitary gland.* London: Edward Arnold.

Harris, G. W., & Levine, S. (1965). Sexual differentiation of the brain and its experimental control. *Journal of Physiology; 181*, 379–400.

Harris, K. M. (1995). How multiple-synapse boutons could preserve input specificity during an interneuronal spread of LTP. *Trends in Neurosciences, 18*, 365–369.

Harris, K. M., Fiala, J. C., & Ostroff, L. (2003). Structural changes at dendritic spine synapses during long-term potentiation. *Philosophical Transactions of the Royal Society of London, 358*, 745–748.

Harris, K. M., & Kater, S. B. (1994). Dendritic spines: Cellular specializations imparting both stability and flexibility to synaptic function. *Annual Review of Neuroscience, 17*, 341–371.

Harris, L. J. (1978). Sex differences in spatial ability: Possible environmental, genetic, and neurological factors. In M. Kinsbourne (Ed.), *Asymmetrical function of the brain* (p. 463). Cambridge, England: Cambridge University Press.

Harris, L. I., Clay, J., Hargreaves, F. J., & Ward, A. (1933). Appetite and choice of diet. The ability of the vitamin B deficient rat to discriminate between diets containing and lacking the vitamin. *Proceedings of the Royal Society of London (B), 113*, 161–190.

Harrison, Y., & Horne, J. A. (1997). Sleep deprivation affects speech. *Sleep, 20*, 871–877.

Hartmann, D. S., & Civelli, O. (1997). Dopamine receptor diversity: Molecular and pharmacological perspectives. *Progressive Drug Research, 48*, 173–194.

Harvey, P. H., & Krebs, J. R. (1990). Comparing brains. *Science, 249*, 140–145.

Hastings, M. H., Reddy, A. B., & Maywood, E. S. (2003). A clockwork web: Circadian timing in brain and periphery, in health and disease. *Nature Reviews Neuroscience, 4*, 649–661.

Hata, Y., & Stryker, M. P. (1994). Control of thalamocortical afferent rearrangement by postsynaptic activity in developing visual cortex. *Science, 265*, 1732–1735.

Hattar, S., Liao, H.-W., Takao, M., Berson, D. M., & Yau, K.-W. (2002). Melanopsin-containing retinal ganglion cells: Architecture, projections, and intrinsic photosensitivity. *Science, 295*, 1065–1070.

Hatten, M. E. (2002). New directions in neural migration. *Science, 297*, 1660–1665.

Häuser, M., Spruston, N., & Stuart, G. J. (2000). Diversity and dynamics of dendritic signaling. *Science, 290*, 739–743.

Hauser, M. D. (1993). Right hemisphere dominance for the production of facial expression in monkeys. *Science, 261*, 475–478.

Hauser, M. D. (1999). Perseveration, inhibition and the prefrontal cortex: A new look. *Current Opinion in Neurobiology, 9*, 214–222.

Hauser, M. D. (2000). *Wild minds: What animals really think.* New York: Henry Holt.

Haxby, J. V., Gobbini, M. I., Furey, M. L., Ishai, A., Schouten, J. L., & Pietrini, P. (2001). Distributed and overlapping representations of faces and objects in ventral temporal cortex. *Science, 293*, 2405–2407.

Hayakawa, K., Kumagai, H., Suzuki, Y., Furusawa, N., Haga, T., Hoshi, T., et al. (1992). MRI imaging of chronic alcoholism. *Acta Radiologica, 33*, 201–206.

Haydon, P. G. (2001). Glia: Listening and talking to the synapse. *Nature Reviews Neuroscience, 2*, 185–193.

Heap, L. C., Pratt, O. E., Ward, R. J., Waller, S., Thomson, A. D., Shaw, G. K., & Peters, T. J. (2002). Individual susceptibility to Wernicke-Korsakoff syndrome and alcoholism-induced cognitive deficit: Impaired thiamine utilization found in alcoholics and alcohol abusers. *Psychiatric Genetics, 12,* 217–224.

Hebb, D. O. (1949). *The organization of behavior.* New York: John Wiley & Sons.

Hécaen, H., & Angelergues, R. (1964). Localization of symptoms in aphasia. In A. V. S. de Reuck & M. O'Connor (Eds.), *CIBA foundation symposium on the disorders of language* (pp. 222–256). London: Churchill Press.

Heffner, H. E., & Heffner, R. S. (1984). Temporal lobe lesions and perception of species-specific vocalizations by macaques. *Science, 226,* 75–76.

Heffner, H. E., & Masterton, R. B. (1990). Sound localization in mammals: Brainstem mechanisms. In M. Berkley & W. Stebbins (Eds.), *Comparative perception, Vol. 1: Discrimination.* New York: John Wiley & Sons.

Heilman, K. M., Watson, R. T., & Rothi, L. J. G. (1997). Disorders of skilled movements: Limb apraxia. In T. E. Feinberg & M. J. Farah (Eds.), *Behavioral neurology and neuropsychology* (pp. 227–236). New York: McGraw-Hill.

Heilman, K. M., Watson, R. T., & Valenstein, E. (1997). Neglect: Clinical and anatomic aspects. In T. E. Feinberg & M. J. Farah (Eds.), *Behavioral neurology and neuropsychology* (pp. 309–317). New York: McGraw-Hill.

Heinrichs, R. W. (1993). Schizophrenia and the brain. *American Psychologist, 48,* 221–233.

Hejmadi, A., Davidson, R. J., & Rozin, P. (2000). Exploring Hindu Indian emotion expressions: Evidence for accurate recognition by Americans and Indians. *Psychological Science, 11,* 183–187.

Helmer, W. J. (1986, February). The madman in the tower. *Texas Monthly.*

Hemmer, B., Archelos, J. J., & Hartung, H.-P. (2002). New concepts in the immunopathogenesis of multiple sclerosis. *Nature Reviews Neuroscience, 3,* 291–301.

Hendry, S. H. C., & Calkins, D. J. (1998). Neuronal chemistry and functional organization in the primate visual system. *Trends in Neurosciences, 21*(8), 344–349.

Henke, K., Kroll, N. E. A., Behniea, H., Amaral, D. G., Miller, M. B., Rafal, R., & Gazzaniga, M. S. (1999). Memory lost and regained following bilateral hippocampal damage. *Journal of Cognitive Neuroscience, 11,* 682–697.

Hennessey, A. C., Camak, L., Gordon, F., & Edwards, D. A. (1990). Connections between the pontine central gray and the ventromedial hypothalamus are essential for lordosis in female rats. *Behavioral Neuroscience, 104,* 477–488.

Hering, H., & Sheng, M. (2001). Dendritic spines: Structure, dynamics and regulation. *Nature Reviews Neuroscience, 2,* 880–888.

Hetherington, A. W., & Ranson, S. W. (1940). Hypothalamic lesions and adiposity in the rat. *Anatomical Record, 78,* 149–172.

Heuser, J. E., Reese, T. S., Dennis, M. J., Jan, Y., Jan, L., & Evans, L. (1979). Synaptic vesicle exocytosis captured by quick freezing and correlated with quantal transmitter release. *Journal of Cell Biology, 81,* 275–300.

Heuss, C., & Gerber, U. (2000). G-protein-independent signaling by G-protein-coupled receptors. *Trends in Neurosciences, 23,* 469–474.

Heymsfield, S. N., Greenberg, A. S., Fujioka, K., Dixon, R. M., Kushner, R., Hunt, T., et al. (1999). Recombinant leptin for weight loss in obese and lean adults. *Journal of the American Medical Association, 282,* 1568–1575.

Hickok, G., Bellugi, U., & Klima, E. S. (2001, June). Sign language in the brain: How does the human brain process language? New studies of deaf signers hint at an answer. *Scientific American, 284,* 58–65.

Hines, M. (2003). Sex steroids and human behavior: Prenatal androgen exposure and sex-typical play behavior in children. *Annals of the New York Academy of Sciences, 1007,* 272–282.

Hobson, J. A. (1989). *Sleep.* New York: Scientific American Library.

Hobson, J. A., & Pace-Schott, E. F. (2002). The cognitive neuroscience of sleep: Neuronal systems, consciousness and learning. *Nature Reviews Neuroscience, 3,* 679–693.

Hockfield, S., & Kalb, R. G. (1993). Activity-dependent structural changes during neuronal development. *Current Opinion in Neurobiology, 3,* 87–92.

Hollenbeck, P. J. (2001). Insight and hindsight into Tourette syndrome. In D. J. Cohen, C. G. Goetz, & J. Jankovic (Eds.), *Tourette syndrome* (pp. 363–367). Philadelphia: Lippincott Williams & Wilkins.

Hollon, S. D., Thase, M. E., & Markowitz, J. C. (2002). Treatment and prevention of depression. *Psychological Science in the Public Interest, 3,* 39–77.

Holmberg, J., & Frisén, J. (2002). Ephrins are not only unattractive. *Trends in Neurosciences, 25,* 239–243.

Holmes, M. M., Galea, L. A. M., Mistlberger, R. E., & Kempermann, G. (2004). Adult hippocampal neurogenesis and voluntary running activity: Circadian and dose-dependent effects. *Journal of Neuroscience Research, 76*(2), 216–222.

Holmes, M. M., Wide, J. K., & Galea, L. A. M. (2002). Low levels of estradiol facilitate, whereas high levels of estradiol impair, working memory performance on the radial arm maze. *Behavioral Neuroscience, 116,* 928–934.

Holsboer, F. (2000). The corticosteroid receptor hypothesis of depression. *Neuropsychopharmacology, 23,* 477–501.

Holzman, P. S. (2000). Eye movements and the search for the essence of schizophrenia. *Brain Research Reviews, 31,* 350–356.

Holzman, P. S., & Matthyse, S. (1990). The genetics of schizophrenia: A review. *Current Directions in Psychological Science, 1,* 279–286.

Hong L. E., Avila, M. T., Adami, H., Elliot, A., & Thaker, G. K. (2003). Components of the smooth pursuit function in deficit and non-deficit schizophrenia. *Schizophrenia Research, 63,* 39–48.

Hopkins, W. D. (1995). Chimpanzee handedness revisited: 55 years since Finch (1941). *Psychonomic Bulletin & Review, 3,* 449–457.

Hopkins, W. D. (1996). Hand preferences for a coordinated bimanual task in 110 chimpanzees (*Pan troglodytes*): Cross-sectional analysis. *Journal of Comparative Psychology, 109*(3), 291–297.

Hopkins, W. D., & Pilcher, D. L. (2001). Neuroanatomical localization of the motor hand area with magnetic resonance imaging: The left hemisphere is larger in great apes. *Behavioral Neuroscience, 115,* 1159–1164.

Hopkins, W. D., Dahl, J. F., & Pilcher, D. (2001). Genetic influence on the expression of hand preferences in chimpanzees (*Pan troglodytes*): Evidence in support of the right-shift theory and developmental instability. *Psychological Science, 12,* 299–303.

Horne, J. A. (1983). Sleep loss and "divergent" thinking ability. *Sleep, 11,* 528–536.

Horne, J. A. (2000). REM sleep—by default? *Neuroscience and Biobehavioural Reviews, 24,* 777–797.

Horne, J. A., & Reyner, L. A. (1996). Counteracting driver sleepiness: Effects of napping, caffeine, and placebo. *Psychophysiology, 33,* 306–309.

Howe, M. L. (2003). Memories from the cradle. *Current Directions in Psychological Science, 12,* 62–65.

Howlett, A. C., Bidaut-Russell, M., Devane, W. A., Melvin, L. S., Johnson, M. R., & Herkenham, M. (1990). The cannabinoid receptor: Biochemical, anatomical and behavioral characterization. *Trends in Neurosciences, 13,* 420–423.

Hrabovszky, Z., & Hutson, J. M. (2002). Androgen imprinting of the brain in animal models and humans with intersex disorders: Review and recommendations. *The Journal of Urology, 168,* 2142–2148.

Hsiao, K., Chapman, P., Nilsen, S., Eckman, C., Harigaya, Y., Younkin, S., et al. (1996). Correlative memory deficits, Aβ elevation, and amyloid plaques in transgenic mice. *Science, 274,* 99–102.

Huang, E. J., & Reichardt, L. F. (2001). Neurotrophins: Roles in neuronal development and function. *Annual Review of Neuroscience, 24,* 677–736.

Hubel, D. H., & Wiesel, T. N. (1979, September). Brain mechanisms of vision. *Scientific American, 241,* 150–162.

Hubel, D. H., Wiesel, T. N., & LeVay, S. (1977). Plasticity of ocular dominance columns in the monkey striate cortex. *Philosophical Transactions of the Royal Society of London, 278,* 377–409.

Hubel, D. H., Wiesel, T. N., & Stryker, M. P. (1977). Orientation columns in macaque monkey visual cortex demonstrated by the 2-deoxyglucose autoradiographic technique. *Nature, 269,* 328–330.

Huberman, A. D., Wang, G. Y., Liets, L. C., Collins, O. A., Chapman, B., & Chalupa, L. M. (2003). Eye-specific retinogeniculate segregation independent of normal neuronal activity. *Science, 300,* 994–998.

Hugdahl, K. (1996). Cognitive influences on human autonomic nervous system function. *Current Opinion in Neurobiology, 6,* 252–258.

Huguenard, J. R. (2000). Reliability of axonal propagation: The spike doesn't stop here. *Proceedings of the National Academy of Science, U.S.A., 97,* 9349–9350.

Huijbregts, S. C. J., de Sonneville, L. M. J., van Spronsen, F. J., Licht, R., & Sergeant, J. A. (2002). The neuropsychological profile of early and continuously treated phenylketonuria: Orienting, vigilance, and maintenance versus manipulation-functions of working memory. *Neuroscience and Biobehavioural Reviews, 26,* 697–712.

Hull, E. M., Lorrain, D. S., Du, J., Matuszewich, L., Lumley, L. A., Putnam, S. K., & Moses, J. (1999). Hormone neurotransmitter interaction in the control of sexual behavior. *Behavioural Brain Research, 105,* 105–116.

Hume, K. I., & Mills, J. N. (1977). Rhythms of REM and slow wave sleep in subjects living on abnormal time schedules. *Waking and Sleeping, 1,* 291–296.

Humphrey, K. G., James, T. W., Gati, J. S., Menon, R. S., & Goodale, M. A. (1999). Perception of the McCollough effect correlates with activity in extrastriate cortex: A functional magnetic resonance imaging study. *Psychological Science, 10,* 444–448.

Hurlbert, A. (2003). Colour vision: Primary visual cortex shows its influence. *Current Biology, 13,* 270–272.

Hurlbert, A., & Wolf, K. (2004). Color contrast: A contributory mechanism to color constancy. *Progress in Brain Research, 144,* 147–160.

Hustvedt, B. E., & Lovo, A. (1972). Correlation between hyperinsulinemia and hyperphagia in rats with ventromedial hypothalamic lesions. *Acta Physiologica Scandinavica, 84,* 29–33.

Hutsler, J., & Galuske, R. A. W. (2003). Hemispheric asymmetries in cerebral cortical networks. *Trends in Neurosciences, 26,* 429–435.

Huttenlocher, P. R. (1994). Synaptogenesis, synapse elimination, and neural plasticity in human cerebral cortex. In C. A. Nelson (Ed.), *Threats to optimal development: The Minnesota symposium on child psychology* (Vol. 27, 35–54). Hillsdale, NJ: Lawrence Erlbaum.

Huxley, A. (2002). From overshoot to voltage clamp. *Trends in Neurosciences, 25*(11), 553–558.

Hyman, S. (2000). Mental illness: Genetically complex disorders of neural circuitry and neural communication. *Neuron, 28,* 321–323.

Hyman, S. E., & Malenka, R. C. (2001). Addiction and the brain: The neurobiology of compulsion and its persistence. *Nature Reviews Neuroscience, 2,* 695–703.

Iacono, W. G., & Koenig, W. G. R. (1983). Features that distinguish the smooth-pursuit eye-tracking performance of schizophrenic, affective-disorder, and normal individuals. *Journal of Abnormal Psychology, 92,* 29–41.

Iacono, W. G., & Patrick, C. J. (1987). What psychologists should know about lie detection. In I. B. Weiner & A. K. Hess (Eds.), *Handbook of forensic psychology* (pp. 460–489). New York: John Wiley & Sons.

Iino, M., Goto, K., Kakegawa, W., Okado, H., Sudo, M., Ishiuchi, S., et al. (2001). Glia-synapse interaction through calcium-permeable AMPA receptors in Bergmann glia. *Science, 292,* 926–929.

Ikeda, H., Heinke, B., Ruscheweyh, R., & Sandkuhler, J. (2003). Synaptic plasticity in spinal lamina I projection neurons that mediate hyperalgesia. *Science, 299,* 1237–1240.

Ikemoto, S., & Panksepp, J. (1999). The role of nucleus accumbens dopamine in motivated behavior: A unifying interpretation with special reference to reward-seeking. *Brain Research Reviews, 31,* 6–41.

Ikonomidou, C., Bittigau, P., Ishimaru, M. J., Wozniak, D. F., Koch, C., Geenz, K., et al. (2000). Ethanol-induced apoptotic neurodegeneration and fetal alcohol syndrome. *Science, 287,* 1056–1060.

Illert, M., & Kümmel, H. (1999). Reflex pathways from large muscle spindle afferents and recurrent axon collaterals to motoneurones of wrist and digit muscles: A comparison in cats, monkeys and humans. *Experimental Brain Research, 128,* 13–19.

Inatani, M., Irie, F., Plump, A. S., Tessier-Lavigne, M., & Yamaguchi, Y. (2003). Mammalian brain morphogenesis and midline axon guidance require heparin sulfate. *Science, 302,* 1044–1046.

Inglis, J., & Lawson, J. S. (1982). A meta-analysis of sex differences in the effects of unilateral brain damage on intelligence test results. *Canadian Journal of Psychology, 36,* 670–683.

Ingram, D. K. (2001). Vaccine development for Alzheimer's disease: A shot of good news. *Trends in Neurosciences, 24,* 305–307.

Institute of Laboratory Animal Resources: Commission on Life Sciences (1996). *Guide for the care and use of laboratory animals.* Washington: National Academy Press.

Intriligator, J. M., Xie, R., & Barton, J. J. S. (2002). Blindsight modulation of motion perception. *Journal of Cognitive Neuroscience, 14,* 1174–1183.

Inui, A. (2001). Ghrelin: An orexigenic and somatotrophic signal from the stomach. *Nature Reviews Neuroscience, 2,* 551–560.

Irwin, D. E. (1996). Integrating information across saccadic eye movements. *Current Directions in Psychological Science, 5,* 94–100.

Ishai, A., Ungerleider, L. G., Martin, A., & Haxby, J. V. (2000). The representation of objects in the human occipital and temporal cortex. *Journal of Cognitive Neuroscience, 12*(Suppl. 2), 35–51.

Issa, N. P., Trepel, C., & Stryker, M. P. (2000). Spatial frequency maps in cat visual cortex. *The Journal of Neuroscience, 20,* 8504–8514.

Iwamura, Y. (1998). Hierarchical somatosensory processing. *Current Opinion in Neurobiology, 8,* 522–528.

Iwaniuk, A. N., & Whishaw, I. Q. (2000). On the origin of skilled forelimb movements. *Trends in Neurosciences, 23,* 372–376.

Izard, C. E. (1971). *The face of emotion.* New York: Appleton-Century-Crofts.

Jacques, J. P., Zombek, S., Guillain, C., & Duez, P. (2004). Cannabis: Experts agree more than they admit. *Revue medicale de Bruxelles, 25,* 87–92.

Jaeger, J. J., Lockwood, A. H., Van Valin, R. D., Kemmerer, D. L., Murphy, B. W., & Wack, D. S. (1998). Sex differences in brain regions activated by grammatical and reading tasks. *NeuroReport, 9,* 2803–2807.

Janardhan, V., & Qureshi, A. I. (2004). Mechanisms of ischemic brain injury. *Current Cardiology Reports, 6,* 117–123.

Jankovic, J. (2001). Tourette's syndrome. *New England Journal of Medicine, 345,* 1184–1192.

James, L. E., & MacKay, D. G. (2001). H.M., word knowledge, and aging: Support for a new theory of long-term retrograde amnesia. *Current Directions in Psychological Science, 12,* 485–492.

Jameson, K. A., Highnote, S. M., & Wasserman, L. M. (2001). Richer color experience in observers with multiple photopigment opsin genes. *Psychonomic Bulletin & Review, 8*(2), 244–261.

Jakel, R. J., & Maragos, W. F. (2000). Neuronal cell death in Huntington's disease: A potential role for dopamine. *Trends in Neurosciences, 23,* 239–245.

Jarrell, T. W., Gentile, C. G., Romanski, L. M., McCabe, P. M., & Schneiderman, N. (1987). Involvement of cortical and thalamic auditory regions in retention of differential bradycardia conditioning to acoustic conditioned stimuli in rabbits. *Brain Research, 412,* 285–294.

Jarvik, M. E. (1990). The drug dilemma: Manipulating the demand. *Science, 250,* 387–392.

Javitt, D. C., & Coyle, J. T. (2004, January). Decoding schizophrenia. A fuller understanding of signaling in the brain of people with this disorder offers new hope for improved therapy. *Scientific American, 290*, 48–55.

Jeannerod, M., Arbib, M. A., Rizzolatti, G., & Sakarta, H. (1995). Grasping objects: The cortical mechanisms of visuomotor transformation. *Trends in Neurosciences, 18*(7), 314–327.

Jeannerod, M., & Farne, A. (2003). The visuomotor functions of posterior parietal areas. *Advances in Neurology, 93*, 205–217.

Jegalian, K., & Lahn, B. T. (2001, February). Why the Y is so weird. *Scientific American, 284*, 56–61.

Jenkins, I. H., Brooks, D. J., Bixon, P. D., Frackowiak, R. S. J., & Passingham, R. E. (1994). Motor sequence learning: A study with positron emission tomography. *Journal of Neuroscience, 14*(6), 3775–3790.

Jenkins, W. M., & Merzenich, M. M. (1987). Reorganization of neocortical representations after brain injury: A neurophysiological model of the bases of recovery from stroke. *Progressive Brain Research, 71*, 249–266.

Jessell, T. M., & Sanes, J. R. (2000). Development. The decade of the developing brain. *Current Opinion in Neurobiology, 10*, 599–611.

Johnson, K. O. (2001). The roles and functions of cutaneous mechanoreceptors. *Current Opinion in Neurobiology, 11*, 455–461.

Johnson, M. H. (2001). Functional brain development in humans. *Nature Reviews Neuroscience, 2*, 475–483.

Johnston, T. D. (1987). The persistence of dichotomies in the study of behavioral development. *Developmental Review, 7*, 149–182.

Jones, E. G. (2000). Cortical and subcortical contributions to activity-dependent plasticity in primate somatosensory cortex. *Annual Review of Neuroscience, 23*, 1–37.

Jones, H. S., & Oswald, I. (1966). Two cases of healthy insomnia. *Electroencephalography and Clinical Neurophysiology, 24*, 378–380.

Jones, H. W., & Park, I. J. (1971). A classification of special problems in sex differentiation. In D. Bergsma (Ed.), *The clinical delineation of birth defects. Part X: The endocrine system* (pp. 113–121). Baltimore: Williams and Wilkins.

Jones, R. T. (1987). Tobacco dependence. In H. Y. Meltzer (Ed.), *Psychopharmacology: The third generation of progress* (pp. 1589–1596). New York: Raven Press.

Jordan, H., Reis, J. E., Hoffman, J. E., & Landau, B. (2002). Intact perception of biological motion in the face of profound spatial deficits: Williams syndrome. *Psychological Science, 13*, 162–167.

Joseph, M. H., Datla, K., & Young, A. M. J. (2003). The interpretation of the measurement of nucleus accumbens dopamine by in vivo dialysis: The kick, the craving or the cognition? *Neuroscience and Biobehavioural Reviews, 27*, 527–541.

Joseph, R. (1988). Dual mental functioning in a split-brain patient. *Journal of Clinical Psychology, 44*, 771–779.

Jost, A. (1972). A new look at the mechanisms controlling sex differentiation in mammals. *Johns Hopkins Medical Journal, 130*, 38–53.

Jouvet, M. (1972). The role of monoamines and acetylcholine-containing neurons in the regulation of the sleep-waking cycle. *Ergebnisse der Physiologie, 64*, 166–307.

Julien, R. M. (1981). *A primer of drug action.* San Francisco: W. H. Freeman.

Juusola, M., French, A. S., Uusitalo, R. O., & Weckström, M. (1996). Information processing by graded-potential transmission through tonically active synapses. *Trends in Neurosciences, 19*, 292–297.

Kaas, J. H., & Collins, C. E. (2001). The organization of sensory cortex. *Current Opinion in Neurobiology, 11*, 498–504.

Kaas, J. H., Krubitzer, L. A., Chino, Y. M., Langston, A. L., Polley, E. H., & Blair, N. (1990). Reorganization of retinotopic cortical maps in adult mammals after lesions of the retina. *Science, 248*, 229–231.

Kaas, J. H., Nelson, R. J., Sur, M., & Merzenich, M. M. (1981). Organization of somatosensory cortex in primates. In F. O. Schmitt, F. G. Worden, G. Adelman, & S. G. Dennis (Eds.), *The organization of the cerebral cortex* (pp. 237–261). Cambridge, MA: MIT Press.

Kaessmann, H., & Pääbo, S. (2002). The genetical history of humans and the great apes. *Journal of Internal Medicine, 251*, 1–18.

Kagawa, Y. (1978). Impact of Westernization on the nutrition of Japanese: Changes in physique, cancer, longevity, and centenarians. *Preventive Medicine, 7*, 205–217.

Kaiser, J., Lutzenberger, W., Preissl, H., Ackermann, H., & Birbaumer, N. (2000). Right-hemisphere dominance for the processing of sound-source lateralization. *Journal of Neuroscience, 20*, 6631–6639.

Kalaria, R. N. (2001). Advances in molecular genetics and pathology of cerebrovascular disorders. *Trends in Neurosciences, 24*, 392–400.

Kalil, R. E. (1989, December). Synapse formation in the developing brain. *Scientific American, 261*, 76–85.

Kalivas, P. W. (2004). Glutamate systems in cocaine addiction. *Current Opinion in Pharmacology, 4*, 23–29.

Kallman, F. J. (1946). The genetic theory of schizophrenia: An analysis of 691 schizophrenic twin index families. *American Journal of Psychiatry, 103*, 309–322.

Kalynchuk, L. E. (2000). Long-term amygdala kindling in rats as a model for the study of interictal emotionality in temporal lobe epilepsy. *Neuroscience and Biobehavioural Reviews, 24*, 691–704.

Kalynchuk, L. E., Pinel, J. P. J., Treit, D., & Kippin, T. E. (1997). Changes in emotional behavior produced by long-term amygdala kindling in rats. *Biological Psychiatry, 41*, 438–451.

Kandel, E. R. (2001). The molecular biology of memory storage: A dialogue between genes and synapses. *Science, 294*, 1030–1038.

Kandel, E. R., & Squire, L. R. (2000). Neuroscience: Breaking down barriers to the study of brain and mind. *Science, 290*, 1113–1120.

Kansaku, K., Yamaura, A., & Kitazawa, S. (2000). Sex differences in lateralization revealed in the posterior language areas. *Cerebral Cortex, 10*, 866–872.

Kapur, N. (1997). *Injured brains of medical minds.* Oxford, England: Oxford University Press.

Karacan, I., Goodenough, D. R., Shapiro, A., & Starker, S. (1966). Erection cycle during sleep in relation to dream anxiety. *Archives of General Psychiatry, 15*, 183–189.

Karacan, I., Williams, R. L., Finley, W. W., & Hursch, C. J. (1970). The effects of naps on nocturnal sleep: Influence on the need for stage-1 REM and stage-4 sleep. *Biological Psychiatry, 2*, 391–399.

Karsch, F. J. (1987). Central actions of ovarian steroids in the feedback regulation of pulsatile secretion of luteinizing hormone. *Annual Review of Physiology, 49*, 365–382.

Kasai, H., Matsuzaki, M., Noguchi, J., Yasumatsu, N., & Nakahara, H. (2003). Structure-stability-function relationships of dendritic spines. *Trends in Neurosciences, 26*(7), 360–368.

Kastner, S., De Weerd, P., Desimone, R., & Ungerleider, L. G. (1998). Mechanisms of directed attention in the human extrastriate cortex as revealed by functional MRI. *Science, 282*, 108–112.

Katz, J. L., Ackman, P., Rothwax, Y., Sachar, E. J., Weiner, H., Hellman, L., & Gallagher, T. F. (1970). Psychoendocrine aspects of cancer of the breast. *Psychosomatic Medicine, 32*, 1–18.

Katz, L. C., & Crowley, J. C. (2002). Development of cortical circuits: Lessons from ocular dominance columns. *Nature Reviews Neuroscience, 3*, 34–42.

Katz, L. C., & Shatz, C. J. (1996). Synaptic activity and the construction of cortical circuits. *Science, 274*, 1133–1138.

Kaufman, J., Martin, A., King, R. A., & Charney, D. (2001). Are child-, adolescent-, and adult-onset depression one and the same disorder? *Biological Psychiatry, 49*, 980–1001.

Kaut, K. P., & Bunsey, M. D. (2001). The effects of lesions to the rat hippocampus or rhinal cortex on olfactory and spatial memory: Retrograde and anterograde findings. *Cognitive, Affective, & Behavioral Neuroscience, 1*, 270–286.

Kavaliers, M., & Choleris, E. (2001). Antipredator responses and defensive behavior: Ecological and ethological approaches for the neurosciences. *Neuroscience and Biobehavioural Reviews, 25*, 577–586.

Kavanagh, G. L., & Kelly, J. B. (1988). Hearing in the ferret (*Mustela putorius*): Effects of primary auditory cortical lesions on thresholds for pure tone detection. *Journal of Neurophysiology, 60*, 879–888.

Kelley, A. E. (2004). Ventral striatal control of appetitive motivation: Role in ingestive behavior and reward-related learning. *Neuroscience and Biobehavioural Reviews, 27,* 765–776.

Kelley, W. M., Ojemann, J. G., Wetzel, R. D., Derdeyn, C. P., Moran, C. J., Cross, D. T., et al. (2002). Wada testing reveals frontal lateralization for the memorization of words and faces. *Journal of Cognitive Neuroscience, 14,* 116–125.

Keltner, D., Kring, A. M., & Bonanno, G. A. (1999). Fleeting signs of the course of life: Facial expression and personal adjustment. *Current Directions in Psychological Science, 8,* 18–22.

Kempermann, G., & Gage, F. H. (1999, May). New nerve cells for the adult brain. *Scientific American, 282,* 48–53.

Kendler, K. S., & Gruenberg, A. M. (1984). An independent analysis of the Danish adoption study of schizophrenia: VI. The relationship between psychiatric disorders as defined by DSM-III in the relatives and adoptees. *Archives of General Psychiatry, 41,* 555–564.

Kennedy, J. L., Farrer, L. A., Andreasen, N. C., Mayeux, R., & St. George-Hyslop, P. (2003). The genetics of adult-onset neuropsychiatric disease: Complexities and conundra? *Science, 302,* 822–826.

Kenrick, D. T. (2001). Evolutionary psychology, cognitive science, and dynamical systems: Building an integrative paradigm. *Current Directions in Psychological Science, 10*(1), 13–17.

Kentridge, R. W., Heywood, C. A., & Weiskrantz, L. (1997). Residual vision in multiple retinal locations within a scotoma: Implications for blindsight. *Journal of Cognitive Neuroscience, 9,* 191–202.

Kerkoff, G. (2001). Spatial hemineglect in humans. *Progress in Neurobiology, 63,* 1–27.

Kerr, R. A. (1996). New mammal data challenge evolutionary pulse theory. *Science, 273,* 431–432.

Kessels, R. P. C., De Haan, E. H. F., Kappelle, L. J., & Postma, A. (2001). Varieties of human spatial memory: A meta-analysis on the effects of hippocampal lesions. *Brain Research Reviews, 35,* 295–303.

Kessler, R. C. (1997). The effects of stressful life events on depression. *Annual Review of Psychology, 48,* 191–214.

Keys, A., Brož, J., Henschel, A., Mickelsen, O., & Taylor H. L. (1950). *The biology of human starvation.* Minneapolis: The University of Minnesota Press.

Keyvan-Fouladi, N., Li, Y., & Raisman, G. (2002). How do transplanted olfactory ensheathing cells restore function? *Brain Research Review, 40,* 325–327.

Kiecolt-Glaser, J. K., McGuire, L., Robles, T. F., & Glaser, R. (2002). Emotions, morbidity, and mortality: New perspectives from psychoneuroimmunology. *Annual Review of Psychology, 53,* 83–107.

Kiehl, K. A., Liddle, P. F., Smith, A. M., Mendrek, A., Forster, B. B., & Hare, R. D. (1999). Neural pathways involved in the processing of concrete and abstract words. *Human Brain Mapping, 7,* 225–233.

Killackey, H. P. (1995). Evolution of the human brain: A neuroanatomical perspective. In M. S. Gazzaniga (Ed.), *The cognitive neurosciences.* Cambridge, MA: MIT Press.

Kim, D-S., Duong, T. Q., & Kim, S-G. (2000). High-resolution mapping of iso-orientation columns by fMRI. *Nature, 3*(2), 164–169.

Kim, J. J., & Diamond, D. M. (2002). The stressed hippocampus, synaptic plasticity and lost memories. *Nature Reviews Neuroscience, 3,* 453–462.

Kim, J. J., & Yoon, K. S. (1998). Stress: Metaplastic effects in the hippocampus. *Trends in Neurosciences, 21,* 505–509.

Kim, S-G., Ashe, J., Hendrich, K., Ellermann, J. M., Merkle, H., Ugurbil, K., & Georgopoulos, A. P. (1993). Functional magnetic resonance imaging of motor cortex: Hemispheric asymmetry and handedness. *Science, 261,* 615–617.

Kimberg, D. Y., D'Esposito, M., & Farah, M. J. (1998). Cognitive functions in the prefrontal cortex—working memory and executive control. *Current Directions in Psychological Science, 6,* 185–192.

Kimble, G. A. (1989). Psychology from the standpoint of a generalist. *American Psychologist, 44,* 491–499.

Kimura, D. (1961). Some effects of temporal-lobe damage on auditory perception. *Canadian Journal of Psychology, 15,* 156–165.

Kimura, D. (1964). Left-right differences in the perception of melodies. *Quarterly Journal of Experimental Psychology, 16,* 355–358.

Kimura, D. (1973, March). The asymmetry of the human brain. *Scientific American, 228,* 70–78.

Kimura, D. (1979). Neuromotor mechanisms in the evolution of human communication. In H. E. Steklis & M. J. Raleigh (Eds.), *Neurobiology of social communication in primates* (pp. 197–219). New York: Academic Press.

Kimura, D. (1987). Sex differences, human brain organization. In G. Adelman (Ed.), *Encyclopedia of neuroscience* (Vol. II, pp. 1084–1085). Boston: Birkhäuser.

Kimura, D., & Watson, N. (1989). The relation between oral movement control and speech. *Brain and Language, 37,* 565–590.

Kind, P. C., & Neumann, P. E. (2001). Plasticity: Downstream of glutamate. *Trends in Neurosciences, 24,* 553–555.

King, A. J., Schnupp, J. W. H., & Thompson, I. D. (1998). Signals from the superficial layers of the superior colliculus enable the development of the auditory space map in the deeper layers. *Journal of Neuroscience, 18,* 9394–9408.

Klawans, H. L. (1990) *Newton's madness: Further tales of clinical neurology.* New York: Harper & Row.

Klein, D. A., & Walsh, T. B. (2004). Eating disorders: Clinical features and pathophysiology. *Physiology and Behavior, 81,* 359–374.

Kleinman, A., & Cohen, A. (1997, March). Psychiatry's global challenge: An evolving crisis in the developing world signals the need for a better understanding of the links between culture and mental disorders. *Scientific American, 276,* 86–89.

Kleitman, N. (1963). *Sleep and wakefulness.* Chicago: University of Chicago Press.

Klivington, K. A. (Ed.). (1992). *Gehirn und Geist.* Heidelberg, Germany: Spektrum Akademischer Verlag.

Kluver, H., & Bucy, P. C. (1939). Preliminary analysis of the temporal lobes in monkeys. *Archives of Neurology and Psychiatry, 42,* 979–1000.

Knowlton, B. J., Mangels, J. A., & Squire, L. R. (1996). A neostriatal habit learning system in humans. *Science, 273,* 1399–1402.

Knudsen, E. I., & Brainard, M. S. (1991). Visual instruction of the neural map of auditory space in the developing optic tectum. *Science, 253,* 85–87.

Koechlin, E., Ody, C., & Kouneiher, F. (2003). The architecture of cognitive control in the human prefrontal cortex. *Science, 302,* 1181–1185.

Koekkoek, S. K. E., Hulscher, H. C., Dortland, B. R., Hensbroek, R. A., Elgersma, Y., Ruigrok, T. J. H., & De Zeeuw, C. I. (2003). Cerebellar LTD and learning-dependent timing of conditioned eyelid responses. *Science, 301,* 1736–1739.

Kofman, O. (2002). The role of prenatal stress in the etiology of developmental behavioural disorders. *Neuroscience and Biobehavioural Reviews, 26,* 457–470.

Köhling, R. (2002). GABA becomes exciting. *Science, 298,* 1350–1351.

Kokaia, Z., & Lindvall, O. (2003). Neurogenesis after ischaemic brain insults. *Current Opinion in Neurobiology, 13,* 127–132.

Kokkinos, J., & Levine, S. R. (1993). Stroke. *Neurologic Complications of Drug and Alcohol Abuse, 11,* 577–590.

Kolb, B., Gibb, R., & Robinson, T. E. (2003). Brain plasticity and behavior. *Current Directions in Psychological Science, 12,* 1–5.

Kolb, B., & Taylor, L. (1988). Facial expression and the neocortex. *Society for Neuroscience Abstracts, 14,* 219.

Kolb, B., & Taylor, L. (2000). Facial expression, emotion, and hemispheric organization. In R. D. Lane & L. Nadel (Eds.), *Cognitive neuroscience of emotion* (pp. 62–83). New York: Oxford University Press.

Kolb, B., & Whishaw, I. Q. (1990). *Fundamentals of human neuropsychology* (3rd ed.). New York: Freeman.

Kollias, S. S., Alkadhi, H., Jaermann, T., Crelier, G., & Hepp-Reymond, M.-C. (2001). Identification of multiple nonprimary motor cortical areas with simple movements. *Brain Research Reviews, 36,* 185–195.

König, P., & Verschure, P. F. M. J. (2002). Neurons in action. *Science, 296,* 1817–1818.

Konishi, M. (2003). Coding of auditory space. *Annual Review of Neuroscience, 26,* 31–35.

Konradi, C., & Heckers, S. (2003). Molecular aspects of glutamate dysregulation: Implications for schizophrenia and its treatment. *Pharmacology and Therapeutics, 97,* 153–179.

Koob, G. F., & Bloom, F. E. (1988). Cellular and molecular mechanisms of drug dependence. *Science, 242,* 715–723.

Koolhaas, J. M., Schuurman, T., & Wiepkema, P. R. (1980). The organization of intraspecific agonistic behaviour in the rat. *Progress in Neurobiology, 15,* 247–268.

Koopmans, H. S. (1981). The role of the gastrointestinal tract in the satiation of hunger. In L. A. Cioffi, W. B. T. James, & T. B. Van Italie (Eds.), *The body weight regulatory system: Normal and disturbed mechanisms* (pp. 45–55). New York: Raven Press.

Kopelman, P. G. (2000). Obesity as a medical problem. *Nature, 404,* 635–648.

Korkman, M., Kettunen, S., & Autti-Ramo, I. (2003). Neurocognitive impairment in early adolescence following prenatal alcohol exposure of varying duration. *Neuropsychology, Development, and Cognition. Section C, Child Neuropsychology, 9,* 117–128.

Kornack, D. R., & Rakic, P. (1999). Continuation of neurogenesis in the hippocampus of the adult macaque monkey. *Proceedings of the National Academy of Sciences, U.S.A. 96,* 5768–5773.

Kornack, D. R., & Rakic, P. (2001). Cell proliferation without neurogenesis in adult primate neocortex. *Science, 294,* 2127–2129.

Korte, S. M. (2001). Corticosteroids in relation to fear, anxiety and psychopathology. *Neuroscience and Biobehavioural Reviews, 25,* 117–142.

Kosik, K. S. (2003). Beyond phrenology, at last. *Nature Reviews Neuroscience, 4,* 234–239.

Kosslyn, S. M. (1994). *Image and brain: The resolution of the imagery debate.* Cambridge, MA: MIT Press.

Kosslyn, S. M., & Andersen, R. A. (1992). *Frontiers in cognitive neuroscience.* Cambridge, MA: MIT Press.

Kosslyn, S. M., Ganis, G., & Thompson, W. L. (2001). Neural foundations of imagery. *Nature Reviews Neuroscience, 2,* 635–642.

Kourtzi, Z., & Kanwisher, N. (2000). Activation in human MT/MST by static images with implied motion. *Journal of Cognitive Neuroscience 12,* 48–55.

Koutalos, Y., & Yau, K.-W. (1993) A rich complexity emerges in phototransduction. *Current Opinion in Neurobiology, 3,* 513–519.

Kozloski, J., Hamzei-Sichani, F., & Yuste, R. (2001). Stereotyped position of local synaptic targets in neocortex. *Science, 293,* 868–870.

Krank, M. D., & Perkins, W. L. (1993). Conditioned withdrawal signs elicited by contextual cues for morphine administration. *Psychobiology, 21,* 113–119.

Krantz, D. S., & McCeney, M. K. (2002). Effects of psychological and social factors on organic disease: A critical assessment of research on coronary heart disease. *Annual Review of Psychology, 53,* 341–369.

Krieglstein, J. (1997). Mechanisms of neuroprotective drug actions. *Clinical Neuroscience, 4,* 184–193.

Kring, A. M. (1999). Emotion in schizophrenia: Old mystery, new understanding. *Current Directions in Psychological Science, 8,* 160–163.

Kripke, D. F. (2004). Do we sleep too much? *Sleep, 27,* 13–14.

Kripke, D. F., Garfinkel, L., Wingard, D. L., Klauber, M. R., & Marler, M. R. (2002). Mortality associated with sleep duration and insomnia. *Archives of General Psychiatry, 59,* 131–136.

Kruzich, P. J., Congleton, K. M., & See, R. E. (2001). Conditioned reinstatement of drug-seeking behavior with a discrete compound

stimulus classically conditioned with intravenous cocaine. *Behavioral Neuroscience, 115,* 1086–1092.

Kuczmarski, R. J. (1992). Prevalence of overweight and weight gain in the United States. *American Journal of Clinical Nutrition, 55,* 495S–502S.

Kurbat, M. A., & Farah, M. J. (1998). Is the category-specific deficit for living things spurious? *Journal of Cognitive Neuroscience, 10,* 355–361.

Kushner, H. I. (1999). *A cursing brain? The histories of Tourette syndrome.* Cambridge, MA: Harvard University Press.

LaBerge, S., Greenleaf, W., & Kedzierski, B. (1983). Physiological responses to dreamed sexual activity during lucid REM sleep. *Psychophysiology, 20,* 454–455.

Laeng, B., & Caviness, V. S. (2001). Prosopagnosia as a deficit in encoding curved surface. *Journal of Cognitive Neuroscience, 13,* 556–576.

LaFerla, F. M. (2002). Calcium dyshomeostasis and intracellular signalling in Alzheimer's disease. *Nature Reviews Neuroscience, 3,* 862–872.

Laine, M., Salmelin, R., Helenius, P., & Marttila, R. (2000). Brain activation during reading in deep dyslexia: An MEG study. *Journal of Cognitive Neuroscience, 12,* 622–634.

Land, E. H. (1977, April). The retinex theory of color vision. *Scientific American, 237,* 108–128.

Lane, M. A., Ingram, D. K., & Roth, G. S. (2002, August). The serious search for an anti-aging pill. *Scientific American, 287,* 36–41.

Lang, A. E. (2001). Update on the treatment of tics. *Advances in Neurology, 85,* 355–362.

Langston, J. W. (1985). MPTP and Parkinson's disease. *Trends in Neurosciences, 8,* 79–83.

Langston, J. W. (1986). MPTP-induced Parkinsonism: How good a model is it? In S. Fahn, C. P. Marsden, P. Jenner, & P. Teychenne (Eds.), *Recent developments in Parkinson's disease* (pp. 119–126). New York: Raven Press.

Lashley, K. S. (1941). Patterns of cerebral integration indicated by the scotomas of migraine. *Archives of Neurology and Psychiatry, 46,* 331–339.

Latimer, D., & Goldberg, J. (1981). *Flowers in the blood.* New York: Franklin Watts.

Laughlin, S. B., & Sejnowski, T. J. (2003). Communication in some neuronal networks. *Science, 301,* 1870–1874.

Lavie, P. (2001). Sleep–wake as a biological rhythm. *Annual Review of Psychology, 52,* 277–303.

Laviolette, S. R., & Van der Kooy, D. (2004). The neurobiology of nicotine addiction: Bridging the gap from molecules to behaviour. *Nature Reviews Neuroscience, 5,* 55–65.

Lawrence, D. G., & Kuypers, H. G. J. M. (1968a). The functional organization of the motor system in the monkey: I. The effects of bilateral pyramidal lesions. *Brain, 91,* 1–14.

Lawrence, D. G., & Kuypers, H. G. J. M. (1968b). The functional organization of the motor system in the monkey: II. The effects of lesions of the descending brain-stem pathways. *Brain, 91,* 15–36.

Le, W., & Appel, S. H. (2004). Mutant genes responsible for Parkinson's disease. *Current Opinion in Pharmacology, 4,* 79–84.

Leckman, J. F., Peterson, B. S., King, R. A., Scahill, L., & Cohen, D. J. (2001). Phenomenology of tics and natural history of tic disorders. In D. J. Cohen, C. G. Goetz, & J. Jankovic (Eds.), *Tourette syndrome* (pp. 1–14). Philadelphia: Lippincott Williams & Wilkins.

Lederhendler, I., & Schulkin, J. (2000). Behavioral neuroscience: Challenges for the era of molecular biology. *Trends in Neurosciences, 23,* 451–453.

LeDoux, J. E. (1994, June). Emotion, memory and the brain. *Scientific American, 270,* 50–57.

LeDoux, J. E. (1995). Emotion: Clues from the brain. *Annual Review of Psychology, 46,* 209–235.

LeDoux, J. E. (2000a). Cognitive-emotional interactions: Listen to the brain. In R. D. Lane & L. Nadel (Eds.), *Cognitive neuroscience of emotion* (pp. 129–155). New York: Oxford University Press.

LeDoux, J. E. (2000b). Emotion circuits in the brain. *Annual Review of Neuroscience, 23,* 155–184.

Lee, S. H., & Sheng, M. (2000). Development of neuron–neuron synapse. *Current Opinion in Neurobiology, 10,* 125–131.

Lee, V. M. (2001). Tauists and βaptists united—well almost! *Science, 293,* 1446–1495.

Leech, C. K., & McIntyre, D. C. (1976). Kindling rates in inbred mice: An analog to learning? *Behavioral Biology, 16,* 439–452.

Leibowitz, S. F., Hammer, N. J., & Chang, K. (1981). Hypothalamic paraventricular nucleus lesions produce overeating and obesity in the rat. *Physiology & Behavior, 27,* 1031–1040.

Leker, R. R., & Shohami, E. (2002). Cerebral ischemia and trauma—different etiologies yet similar mechanisms: Neuroprotective opportunities. *Brain Research Reviews, 39,* 55–73.

Lemke, G. (2001). Glial control of neuronal development. *Annual Review of Neuroscience, 24,* 87–105.

Lennoff, H. M., Wang, P. P., Greenberg, F., & Bellugi, U. (1997, December). Williams syndrome and the brain. *Scientific American, 279,* 68–73.

Lennox, W. G. (1960). *Epilepsy and related disorders.* Boston: Little, Brown.

Leon, M., & Johnson, B. A. (2003). Olfactory coding in the mammalian olfactory bulb. *Brain Research Reviews, 42,* 23–32.

Lerman, C., Caporaso, N. E., Audrain, J., Main, D., Bowman, E. D., Lukshin, B., et al. (1999). Evidence suggesting the role of specific genetic factors in cigarette smoking. *Health Psychology, 18,* 14–20.

Leshner, A. I. (1997). Addiction is a brain disease, and it matters. *Science, 278,* 45–46.

Lester, G. L. L., & Gorzalka, B. B. (1988). Effect of novel and familiar mating partners on the duration of sexual receptivity in the female hamster. *Behavioral and Neural Biology, 49,* 398–405.

Leung, L. S., Ma, J., & McLachlan, R. S. (2000). Behaviors induced or disrupted by complex partial seizures. *Neuroscience and Biobehavioural Reviews, 24,* 763–775.

LeVay, S. (1991). A difference in hypothalamic structure between heterosexual and homosexual men. *Science, 253,* 1034–1037.

LeVay, S., Hubel, D. H., & Wiesel, T. N. (1975). The pattern of ocular dominance columns in macaque visual cortex revealed by a reduced silver stain. *Journal of Comparative Neurology, 159,* 559–576.

Levenson, R. W. (1994). The search for autonomic specificity. In P. Ekman & R. J. Davidson (Eds.), *The nature of emotion: Fundamental questions* (pp. 252–257). New York: Oxford University Press.

Levi-Montalcini, R. (1952). Effects of mouse motor transplantation on the nervous system. *Annals of the New York Academy of Sciences, U.S.A., 55,* 330–344.

Levi-Montalcini, R. (1975). NGF: An uncharted route. In F. G. Worden, J. P. Swazey, & G. Adelman (Eds.), *The neurosciences: Paths of discovery* (pp. 245–265). Cambridge, MA: MIT Press.

Levin, H. S. (1989). Memory deficit after closed-head injury. *Journal of Clinical and Experimental Neuropsychology, 12,* 129–153.

Levin, H. S., Papanicolaou, A., & Eisenberg, H. M. (1984). Observations on amnesia after non-missile head injury. In L. R. Squire & N. Butters (Eds.), *Neuropsychology of memory* (pp. 247–257). New York: Guilford Press.

Levine, J. A., Eberhardt, N. L., & Jensen, M. D. (1999). Role of nonexercise activity thermogenesis in resistance to fat gain in humans. *Science, 283,* 212–214.

Levitt, J. B. (2001). Function following form. *Science, 292,* 232–234.

Levitt, P. (2004). Sealing cortical cell fate. *Science, 303,* 48–49.

Levy, J. (1969). Possible basis for the evolution of lateral specialization of the human brain. *Nature, 224,* 614–615.

Levy, J., Trevarthen, C., & Sperry, R. W. (1972). Perception of bilateral chimeric figures following hemispheric deconnection. *Brain, 95,* 61–78.

Lewcock, J. W., & Reed, R. R. (2003). ORs rule the roost in the olfactory system. *Science, 302,* 2078–2079.

Lewis, D. A., & Levitt, P. (2002). Schizophrenia as a disorder of neurodevelopment. *Annual Review of Neuroscience, 25,* 409–432.

Lewy, A. J., Ahmed, S., & Sack, R. L. (1996). Phase shifting the human circadian clock using melatonin. *Behavioural Brain Research, 73,* 131–134.

Lezak, M. D. (1997). Principles of neuropsychological assessment. In T. E. Feinberg & M. J. Farah (Eds.), *Behavioral neurology and neuropsychology* (pp. 43–54). New York: McGraw-Hill.

Li, M. O., Sarkisian, M. R., Mehal, W. Z., Rakic, P., & Flavell, R. A. (2003). Phosphatidylserine receptor is required for clearance of apoptotic cells. *Science, 302,* 1560–1562.

Li, Y., Field, P. M., & Raisman, G. (1998). Regeneration of adult rat corticospinal axons induced by transplanted olfactory ensheathing cells. *Journal of Neuroscience, 18,* 10514–10524.

Libby, P. (2002, May). Atherosclerosis: The new view. *Scientific American, 286,* 5, 47–55.

Lin, L., Faraco, J., Li, R., Kadotani, H., Rogers, W., Lin, X., et al. (1999). The sleep disorder canine narcolepsy is caused by a mutation in the hypocretin (orexin) receptor 2 gene. *Cell, 98,* 365–376.

Linden, D. J. (2003). From molecules to memory in the cerebellum. *Science, 301,* 1682–1683.

Lindsay, P. H., & Norman, D. A. (1977). *Human information processing* (2nd ed.). New York: Academic Press.

Lindsey, D. B., Bowden, J., & Magoun, H. W. (1949). Effect upon the EEG of acute injury to the brain stem activating system. *Electroencephalography and Clinical Neurophysiology, 1,* 475–486.

Liou, J. D., Ma, Y. Y., Gibson, L. H., Su, H., Charest, N., Lau, Y. F., & Yang-Feng, T. L. (1997). Cytogenetic and molecular studies of a familial paracentric inversion of Y chromosome present in a patient with ambiguous genitalia. *American Journal of Medical Genetics, 16(70),* 131–137.

Lipert, J., Bauder, H., Miltner, W. H. R., Taub, E., & Weiller, C. (2000). Treatment-induced cortical reorganization after stroke in humans. *Stroke, 31,* 1210–1216.

Lisman, J. (2003). Long-term potentiation: Outstanding questions and attempted synthesis. *Philosophical Transactions of the Royal Society of London, 358,* 829–842.

Lisman, J., Lichtman, J. W., & Sanes, J. R. (2003). LTP: Perils and progress. *Nature Reviews Neuroscience, 4,* 926–929.

Liu, D., Dorio, J., Tannenbaum, B., Caldji, C., Francis, D., Freedman, A., et al. (1997). Maternal care, hippocampal glucocorticoid receptors, and hypothalamic-pituitary-adrenal responses to stress. *Science, 277,* 1659–1662.

Liu, L., Wong, T. P., Pozza, M. F., Lingenhoehl, K., Wang, Y., Sheng, M., et al. (2004). Role of NMDA receptor subtypes in governing the direction of hippocampal synaptic plasticity. *Science, 304,* 1021–1024.

Livingston, K. E., & Guth, P. H. (1992). Peptic ulcer disease: Wounds in the walls of the stomach develop only after elaborate cellular and molecular defensive mechanisms are breached. *American Scientist, 80,* 592–598.

Livingstone, M. S., & Hubel, D. H. (1984). Anatomy and physiology of a color system in the primate visual cortex. *Journal of Neuroscience, 4,* 309–356.

Livingstone, M. S., & Hubel, D. S. (1988). Segregation of form, color, movement, and depth: Anatomy, physiology, and perception. *Science, 240,* 740–749.

Livingstone, M. S., & Tsao, D. Y. (1999). Receptive fields of disparity-selective neurons in macaque striate cortex. *Nature Reviews Neuroscience, 2,* 825–832.

Lo, E. H., Dalkara, T., & Moskowitz, M. A. (2003). Mechanisms, challenges and opportunities in stroke. *Nature Reviews Neuroscience, 4,* 399–415.

Lo, Y-J., & Poo, M-M. (1991). Activity-dependent synaptic competition in vitro: Heterosynaptic suppression of developing synapses. *Science, 254,* 1019–1022.

Logothetis, N. (1998). Object vision and visual awareness. *Current Opinion in Neurobiology, 8,* 536–544.

Logothetis, N. K., & Sheinberg, D. L. (1996). Visual object recognition. *Annual Review of Neuroscience, 19*, 577–621.

Lombardino, A. J., & Nottebohm, F. (2000). Age at deafening affects the stability of learned song in adult male zebra finches. *Journal of Neuroscience, 20*, 5054–5064.

Loomis, A. L., Harvey, E. N., & Hobart, G. (1936). Electrical potentials of the human brain. *Journal of Experimental Psychology, 19*, 249–279.

Losick, R., & Shapiro, L. (1998). Bringing the mountain to Mohammed. *Science, 282*, 1430–1431.

Lotze, M., Montoya, P., Erb, M., Hülsmann, E., Flor, H., Klose, U., et al. (1999). Activation of cortical and cerebellar motor areas during executed and imagined hand movements: An fMRI study. *Journal of Cognitive Neuroscience, 11*, 491–501.

Louk Vanderschuren, J. M. J., & Everitt, B. J. (2004). Drug seeking becomes compulsive after prolonged cocaine self-administration. *Science, 305*, 1017–1019.

Löw, A., Bentin, S., Rockstroh, B., Silberman, Y., Gomolla, A., Cohen, R., & Elbert, T. (2003). Semantic categorization in the human brain: Spatiotemporal dynamics revealed by magnetoencephalography. *Psychological Science, 14*, 367–372.

Lowe, J., & Carroll, D. (1985). The effects of spinal injury on the intensity of emotional experience. *The British Journal of Clinical Psychology, 24*, 135–136.

Lowe, M. R. (1993). The effects of dieting on eating behavior: A three-factor model. *Psychological Bulletin, 114*, 100–121.

Lowrey, P. L., Shimomura, K., Antoch, M. P., Yamazaki, S., Zemenides, P. D., Ralph, M. R., et al. (2000). Positional syntenic cloning and functional characterization of the mammalian circadian mutation *tau*. *Science, 288*, 483–491.

Lucas, F., & Sclafani, A. (1989). Flavor preferences conditioned by intragastric fat infusions in rats. *Physiology & Behavior, 46*, 403–412.

Lucas, R. J., Freedman, M. S., Muñoz, M., Garcia-Fernández, J. M., & Foster, R. G. (1999). Regulation of the mammalian pineal by non-rod, non-cone, ocular photoreceptors. *Science, 284*, 505–507.

Lucas, R. J., Hattar, S., Takao, M., Berson, D. M., Foster, R. G., & Yau, K.-W. (2003). Diminished pupillary light reflex at high irradiances in melanopsin-knockout mice. *Science, 299*, 245–247.

Lucidi, F., Devoto, A., Violani, C., Mastracci, P., & Bertini, M. (1997). Effects of different sleep duration on delta sleep in recovery nights. *Psychophysiology, 34*, 227–233.

Ludwig, M., & Pittman, Q. J. (2003). Talking back: Dendritic neurotransmitter release. *Trends in Neurosciences, 26*, 255–261.

Luo, M., Fee, M. S., & Katz, L. C. (2003). Encoding pheromonal signals in the accessory olfactory bulb of behaving mice. *Science, 299*, 1196–1201.

Lüscher, C., & Frerking, M. (2001). Restless AMPA receptors: Implications for synaptic transmission and plasticity. *Trends in Neurosciences, 24*, 665–670.

Lykken, D. T. (1959). The GSR in the detection of guilt. *Journal of Applied Psychology, 43*, 385–388.

Lynch, M. A. (2004). Long-term potentiation and memory. *Physiological Review, 84*, 87–136.

Macaluso, E., Driver, J., & Frith, C. D. (2003). Multimodal spatial representations engaged in human parietal cortex during both saccadic and manual spatial orienting. *Current Biology, 13*, 990–999.

Macaferri, G., & Lacaille, J. C. (2003). Hippocampal interneuron classifications—making things as simple as possible, not simpler. *Trends in Neurosciences, 26*(10), 564–571.

Maccari, S., Darnaudery, M., Morley-Fletcher, S., Zuena, A. R., Cinque, C., & Van Reeth, O. (2003). Prenatal stress and long-term consequences: Implications of glucocorticoid hormones. *Neuroscience and Biobehavioural Reviews, 27*, 119–127.

Macchi, G. (1989). Anatomical substrate of emotional reactions. In F. Boller & J. Grafman (Eds.), *Handbook of neuropsychology* (Vol. 3, pp. 283–304). New York: Elsevier.

MacCoun, R., & Reuter, P. (1997). Interpreting Dutch cannabis policy: Reasoning by analogy in the legalization debate. *Science, 278*, 47–52.

Macdonald, R. L., & Olsen, R. (1994). GABA$_A$ receptor channels. *Annual Review of Neuroscience, 17*, 569–602.

MacDougall-Shackleton, S. A., & Ball, G. F. (1999). Comparative studies of sex differences in the song-control system of songbirds. *Trends in Neurosciences, 22*(10), 432–436.

Machado, M. G., Oliveira, H. A., Cipolotti, R., Santos, C. A., Oliveira, E. F., Donald, R. M., & Krauss, M. P. (2003). Anatomical and functional abnormalities of central nervous system in autistic disorder: A MRI and SPECT study. *Archives of Neurology, 61*, 957–961.

MacKinnon, D. F., Jamison, K. R., & DePaulo, J. R. (1997). Genetics of manic depressive illness. *Annual Review of Neurosciences, 20*, 355–373.

Maclusky, N. J., & Naftolin, F. (1981). Sexual differentiation of the central nervous system. *Science, 211*, 1294–1302.

Maeder, T. (2003, May). The orphan drug backlash. *Scientific American, 288*, 81–87.

Maguire, A. A., Burgess, N., Donnett, J. G., Frackowiak, R. S. J., Frith, C. D., & O'Keefe, J. (2000). Knowing where and getting there: A human navigation network. *Science, 280*, 921–924.

Maguire, E. A., Frith, C. D., Burgess, N., Donnett, J. G., & O'Keefe, J. (1998). Knowing where things are: Parahippocampal involvement in encoding object locations in virtual large-scale space. *Journal of Cognitive Neuroscience, 19*, 61–76.

Malenka, R. C. (2003). The long-term potential of LTP. *Nature Reviews Neuroscience, 4*, 923–926.

Malissen, B. (1999). Dancing the immunological two-step. *Science, 285*, 207–208.

Malsbury, C. W. (1971). Facilitation of male rat copulatory behavior by electrical stimulation of the medial preoptic area. *Physiology & Behavior, 7*, 797–805.

Manson, J. E., Willett, W. C., Stampfer, M. J., Colditz, G. A., Hunter, D. J., Hankinson, S. E., et al. (1995). Body weight and mortality among women. *New England Journal of Medicine, 333*, 677–685.

Maquet, P. (2001). The role of sleep in learning and memory. *Science, 294*, 1048–1052.

Maratsos, M., & Matheny, L. (1994). Language specificity and elasticity: Brain and clinical syndrome studies. *Annual Review of Psychology, 45*, 487–516.

Maren, S. (1999). Neurotoxic basolateral amygdala lesions impair learning and memory but not the performance of conditional fear in rats. *The Journal of Neuroscience, 19*, 8696–8703.

Maren, S. (2001). Neurobiology of Pavlovian fear conditioning. *Annual Review of Neuroscience, 24*, 897–931.

Maries, E., Dass, B., Collier, T. J., Kordower, J. H., & Steece-Collier, K. (2003). The role of α-synuclein in Parkinson's disease: Insights from animal models. *Nature Reviews Neuroscience, 4*, 727–738.

Marin, O., & Rubenstein, J. L. R. (2001). A long, remarkable journey: Tangential migration in the telencephalon. *Nature Reviews Neuroscience, 2*, 780–790.

Marin, O., & Rubenstein, J. L. R. (2003). Cell migration in the forebrain. *Annual Review of Neuroscience, 26*, 441–483.

Marin, O., Yaron, A., Bagri, A., Tessier-Lavigne, M., & Rubenstein, J. L. R. (2001). Sorting of striatal and cortical interneurons regulated by semaphorin-neuropilin interactions. *Science, 293*, 872–875.

Mark, V. H., Ervin, F. R., & Yakolev, P. I. (1962). The treatment of pain by stereotaxic methods. First International Symposium on Stereoencephalotomy (Philadelphia, 1961). *Confinia Neurologica, 22*, 238–245.

Markus, A., Patel, T. D., & Snider, W. (2002). Neurotrophic factors and axonal growth. *Current Opinion in Neurobiology, 12*, 523–531.

Marlowe, W. B., Mancall, E. L., & Thomas, J. J. (1985). Complete Kluver-Bucy syndrome in man. *Cortex, 11*, 53–59.

Martin, A., Wiggs, C. L., Ungerleider, L. G., & Haxby, J. V. (1996). Neural correlates of category-specific knowledge. *Nature, 379*, 649–652.

Martin, J. B. (1986). Sleep deprivation and exercise. In K. B. Pandolf (Ed.), *Exercise and sport sciences reviews* (pp. 213–229). New York: Macmillan.

Martin, J. B. (1987). Molecular genetics: Applications to the clinical neurosciences. *Science, 238,* 765–772.

Martin, R. C. (2003). Language processing: Functional organization and neuroanatomical basis. *Annual Review of Psychology, 54,* 55–89.

Martin, R. J., White, B. D., & Hulsey, M. G. (1991). The regulation of body weight. *American Scientist, 79,* 528–541.

Martin, R. L., Roberts, W. V., & Clayton, P. J. (1980). Psychiatric status after a one-year prospective follow-up. *Journal of the American Medical Association, 244,* 350–353.

Martinez, L. M., & Alonso, J. M. (2003). Complex receptive fields in primary visual cortex. *The Neuroscientist, 9,* 317–331.

Martin-Soelch, C., Leenders, K. L., Chevalley, A.-F., Missimer, J., König, G., Magyar, S., et al. (2001). Reward mechanisms in the brain and their role in dependence: Evidence from neurophysiological and neuroimaging studies. *Brain Research Reviews, 36,* 139–149.

Masland, R. H. (2001). Neuronal diversity in the retina. *Current Opinion in Neurobiology, 11,* 431–436.

Masoro, E. J. (1988). Food restriction in rodents: An evaluation of its role in the study of aging [Minireview]. *Journal of Gerontology, 43,* 59–64.

Masterton, R. B. (1992). Role of the central auditory system in hearing: The new direction. *Trends in Neurosciences, 15,* 280–285.

Matsuda, L. A., Lolait, S. J., Brownstein, M. J., Young, A. C., & Bonner, T. I. (1990). Structure of a cannabinoid receptor and functional expression of the cloned DNA. *Nature, 346,* 561–564.

Matzinger, P. (2002). The danger model: A renewed sense of self. *Science, 296,* 301–305.

Mauch, D. H., Nagler, K., Schumacher, S., Goritz, C., Muller, E.-C., Otto, A., & Pfrieger, F. W. (2001). CNS synaptogenesis promoted by glia-derived cholesterol. *Science, 294,* 1354–1357.

Mayr, E. (2000, July). Darwin's influence on modern thought. *Scientific American, 283,* 70–83.

Mazzocchi, F., & Vignolo, L. A. (1979). Localisation of lesions in aphasia: Clinical–CT scan correlations in stroke patients. *Cortex, 15,* 627–654.

McCandliss, B. D., & Noble, K. G. (2003). The development of reading impairment: A cognitive neuroscience model. *Mental Retardation and Developmental Disabilities Research Reviews, 9,* 196–204.

McCann, T. S. (1981). Aggression and sexual activity of male southern elephant seals, *Mirounga leonina. Journal of Zoology, 195,* 295–310.

McCardle, K., Luebbers, S., Carter, J. D., Croft, R. J., & Stough, C. (2004). Chronic MDMA (Ecstasy) use, cognition and mood. *Psychopharmacology, 173,* 434–439.

McCarthy, M. M., Auger, A. P., & Perrot-Sinal, T. S. (2002). Getting excited about GABA and sex differences in the brain. *Trends in Neurosciences, 25,* 307–313.

McClintock, M. K., & Herdt, G. (1996). Rethinking puberty: The development of sexual attraction. *Current Directions in Psychological Sciences, 5,* 178–183.

McCormick, D. A. (1999). Membrane potential and action potential. In M. J. Zigmond, F. E. Bloom, S. C. Landis, J. L. Roberts, & L. R. Squire (Eds.), *Fundamental neuroscience* (pp. 129–154). New York: Academic Press.

McCrory, P. R., & Berkovic, S. F. (1998). Second impact syndrome. *Neurology, 50,* 677–683.

McDonald, J. W., Liu, X-Z., Qu, Y., Liu, S., Mickey, S. K., Turetsky, D., et al. (1999). Transplanted embryonic stem cells survive, differentiate and promote recovery in injured rat spinal cord. *Nature Medicine, 5,* 1410–1412.

McDonald, R. J., & White, N. M. (1993). Triple dissociation of memory systems: Hippocampus, amygdala, and dorsal striatum. *Behavioral and Neural Biology, 59,* 107–119.

McEwen, B. (1994). Introduction: Stress and the nervous system. *Seminars in the Neurosciences, 6,* 195–196.

McEwen, B. S. (1983). Gonadal steroid influences on brain development and sexual differentiation. In R. O. Greep (Ed.), *Reproductive physiology IV.* Baltimore: University Park Press.

McEwen, B. S. (1987). Sexual differentiation. In G. Adelman (Ed.), *Encyclopedia of neuroscience* (Vol. II, pp. 1086–1088). Boston: Birkhäuser.

McEwen, B. S. (2000a). Effects of adverse experiences for brain structure and function. *Biological Psychiatry, 48,* 721–731.

McEwen, B. S. (2000b). The neurobiology of stress: From serendipity to clinical relevance. *Brain Research, 886,* 172–189.

McGaugh, J. L. (2002). Memory consolidation and the amygdala: A systems perspective. *Trends in Neuroscience, 25,* 456–461.

McGlone, J. (1977). Sex differences in the cerebral organization of verbal functions in patients with unilateral brain lesions. *Brain, 100,* 775–793.

McGlone, J. (1980). Sex differences in human brain asymmetry: A critical survey. *Behavioral and Brain Sciences, 3,* 215–263.

McGue, M. (1999). The behavioral genetics of alcoholism. *Current Directions in Psychological Science, 8,* 109–115.

McGuffin, P., Riley, B., & Plomin, R. (2001). Toward behavioral genomics. *Science, 291,* 1232–1249.

McKim, W. A. (1986). *Drugs and behavior: An introduction to behavioral pharmacology.* Englewood Cliffs, NJ: Prentice-Hall.

McLaughlin, T., Hindges, R., & O'Leary, D. D. M. (2003). Regulation of axial patterning of the retina and its topographic mapping in the brain. *Current Opinion in Neurobiology, 13,* 57–69.

McMurray, C. T. (2001). Huntington's disease: New hope for therapeutics. *Trends in Neurosciences, 24,* 832–838.

McNally, G. P. (1999). Pain facilitatory circuits in the mammalian central nervous system: Their behavioral significance and role in morphine analgesic tolerance. *Neuroscience and Biobehavioural Reviews, 23,* 1059–1078.

McNally, R. J. (2003). Progress and controversy in the study of posttraumatic stress disorder. *Annual Review of Psychology, 54,* 229–252.

McNally, R. J., Bryant, R. A., & Ehlers, A. (2003). Does early psychological intervention promote recovery from posttraumatic stress? *Psychological Science in the Public Interest, 4,* 45–79.

Meaney, M. J. (2001). Maternal care, gene expression, and the transmission of individual differences in stress reactivity across generations. *Annual Review of Neuroscience, 24,* 1161–1192.

Meddis, R. (1977). *The sleep instinct.* London: Routledge & Kegan Paul.

Medina, J. F., Nores, W. L., Ohyama, T., & Mauk, M. D. (2000). Mechanisms of cerebellar learning suggested by eyelid conditioning. *Current Opinion in Neurobiology, 10,* 717–724.

Medina, J. F., Repa, J. C., Mauk, M. D., & LeDoux, J. E. (2002). Parallels between cerebellum- and amygdala-dependent conditioning. *Nature Reviews Neuroscience, 3,* 122–131.

Medzhitov, R., & Janeway, C. A., Jr., (2002). Decoding the patterns of self and nonself by the innate immune system. *Science, 296,* 298–301.

Mel, B. W. (2002). What the synapse tells the neuron. *Science, 295,* 1845–1846.

Mello, N. K., & Mendelson, J. H. (1972). Drinking patterns during work-contingent and noncontingent alcohol acquisition. *Psychosomatic Medicine, 34,* 139–165.

Melzack, R. (1992, April). Phantom limbs. *Scientific American, 266,* 120–126.

Melzack, R., & Wall, P. D. (1965). Pain mechanisms: A new theory. *Science, 150,* 971–979.

Melzack, R., & Wall, P. D. (1982). *The challenge of pain.* London: Penguin Books.

Mennill, D. J., Ratcliffe, L. M., & Boag, P. T. (2002). Female eavesdropping on male song contests in songbirds. *Science, 296,* 873.

Mercer, J. G., & Speakman, J. R. (2001). Hypothalamic neuropeptide mechanisms for regulating energy balance: From rodent models to human obesity. *Neuroscience and Biobehavioural Reviews, 25,* 101–116.

Metcalfe, J., Funnell, M., & Gazzaniga, M. S. (1995). Right hemisphere memory veridicality: Studies of a split-brain patient. *Psychological Science, 6,* 157–165.

Meunier, C., & Segev, I. (2002). Playing the devil's advocate: Is the Hodgkin-Huxley model useful? *Trends in Neurosciences, 25*(11), 558–563.

Meunier, M., Murray, E. A., Bachevalier, J., & Mishkin, M. (1990). Effects of perirhinal cortical lesions on visual recognition memory in rhesus monkeys. *Society for Neuroscience Abstracts, 17,* 337.

Meyer, R. G., & Salmon, P. (1988). *Abnormal psychology* (2nd ed.). Boston: Allyn & Bacon.

Mieda, M., & Yanagisawa, M. (2002). Sleep, feeding, and neuropeptides: Roles of orexins and orexin receptors. *Current Opinion in Neurobiology, 12,* 339–345.

Miller, G. L., & Knudsen, E. I. (1999). Early visual experience shapes the representation of auditory space in the forebrain gaze fields of the barn owl. *Journal of Neuroscience, 19,* 2326–2336.

Miller, N. E., Bailey, C. J., & Stevenson, J. A. F. (1950). Decreased "hunger" but increased food intake resulting from hypothalamic lesions. *Science, 112,* 256–259.

Miller, N. S., Summers, G. L., & Gold, M. S. (1993). Cocaine dependence: Alcohol and other drug dependence and withdrawal characteristics. *Journal of Addictive Diseases, 12,* 25–35.

Milner, B. (1965). Memory disturbances after bilateral hippocampal lesions. In P. Milner & S. Glickman (Eds.), *Cognitive processes and the brain* (pp. 104–105). Princeton, NJ: D. Van Nostrand.

Milner, B. (1971). Interhemispheric differences in the localization of psychological processes in man. *British Medical Bulletin, 27,* 272–277.

Milner, B. (1974). Hemispheric specialization: Scope and limits. In F. O. Schmitt & F. G. Worden (Eds.), *The neurosciences: Third study program* (pp. 75–89). Cambridge, MA: MIT Press.

Milner, B., Corkin, S., & Teuber, H. L. (1968). Further analysis of the hippocampal amnesic syndrome: 14-year follow-up study of H.M. *Neuropsychologia, 6,* 317–338.

Milner, D., & Goodale, M. A. (1993). Visual pathways to perception and action. *Progress in Brain Research, 95,* 317–337.

Milner, P. M. (1993, January). The mind and Donald O. Hebb. *Scientific American, 268,* 124–129.

Milner, P. M., & White, N. M. (1987). What is physiological psychology? *Psychobiology, 15,* 2–6.

Mishkin, M., & Appenzeller, T. (1987, June). The anatomy of memory. *Scientific American, 256,* 80–89.

Mishkin, M., & Delacour, J. (1975). An analysis of short-term visual memory in the monkey. *Journal of Experimental Psychology: Animal Behavior Processes, 1,* 326–334.

Mistlberger, R. E. (1994). Circadian food-anticipatory activity: Formal models and physiological mechanisms. *Neuroscience and Biobehavioural Reviews, 18,* 171–195.

Mistlberger, R. E., de Groot, M. H. M., Bossert, J. M., & Marchant, E. G. (1996). Discrimination of circadian phase in intact and suprachiasmatic nuclei-ablated rats. *Brain Research, 739,* 12–18.

Mitchell, J. M., Basbaum, A. I., & Fields, H. L. (2000). A locus and mechanism of action for associative morphine tolerance. *Nature Neuroscience, 3,* 47–53.

Moghaddam, B. (2003). Bringing order to the glutamate chaos in schizophrenia. *Neuron, 40,* 881–884.

Mogil, J. S., Yu, L. & Basbaum, A. I. (2000). Pain genes? Natural variation and transgenic mutants. *Annual Review of Neuroscience 23,* 777–811.

Mohr, J. P. (1976). Broca's area and Broca's aphasia. In H. Whitaker & H. A. Whitaker (Eds.), *Studies in neurolinguistics* (Vol. 1, pp. 201–235). New York: Academic Press.

Molday, R. S., & Hsu, Y-T. (1995). The cGMP-gated channel of photoreceptor cells: Its structural properties and role in phototransduction. *Behavioral and Brain Sciences, 18,* 441–451.

Momma, S., Johansson, C. B., & Frisén, J. (2000). Get to know your stem cells. *Current Opinion in Neurobiology, 10,* 45–49.

Money, J. (1975). Ablatio penis: Normal male infant sex-reassigned as a girl. *Archives of Sexual Behavior, 4*(1), 65–71.

Money, J., & Ehrhardt, A. A. (1972). *Man & woman, boy & girl.* Baltimore: Johns Hopkins University Press.

Monsonego, A., & Weiner, H. L. (2003). Immunotherapeutic approaches to Alzheimer's disease. *Science, 302,* 834–838.

Montmayeur, J. P., & Matsunami, H. (2002). Receptors for bitter and sweet taste. *Current Opinion in Neurobiology, 12,* 366–371.

Mooney, R. (1999). Sensitive periods and circuits for learned birdsong. *Current Opinion in Neurobiology, 9,* 121–127.

Moore, R. Y. (1996). Neural control of the pineal gland. *Behavioural Brain Research, 73,* 125–130.

Moran, J., & Desimone, R. (1985). Selective attention gates visual processing in the extrastriate cortex. *Science, 229,* 782–784.

Moran, M. H. (2004). Gut peptides in the control of food intake: 30 years of ideas. *Physiology and Behavior, 82,* 175–180.

Morgan, T. H., Sturtevant, A. H., Muller, H. J., & Bridges, C. B. (1915). *The mechanism of Mendelian heredity.* New York: Henry Holt.

Mori, N., & Wada, J. A. (1990). Does electrical and excitatory amino acid kindling share a common neurobiological mechanism? In J. A. Wada, (Ed.), *Kindling 4* (pp. 209–222). New York: Plenum Press.

Morin, C. M., Kowatch, R. A, & O'Shanick, G. (1990). Sleep restriction for the inpatient treatment of insomnia. *Sleep, 13,* 183–186.

Morris, M. K., Bowers, D., Chatterjee, A., & Heilman, K. M. (1992). Amnesia following a discrete basal forebrain lesion. *Brain, 115,* 1827–1847.

Morris, N. M., Udry, J. R., Khan-Dawood, F., & Dawood, M. Y. (1987). Marital sex frequency and midcycle female testosterone. *Archives of Sexual Behavior, 16,* 27–37.

Morris, R. G. M. (1981). Spatial localization does not require the presence of local cues. *Learning and Motivation, 12,* 239–260.

Morris, R. G. M., Moser, E. I., Riedel, G., Martin, S. J., Sandin, J., Day, M., & O'Carroll, C. O. (2003). Elements of a neurobiological theory of the hippocampus: The role of activity-dependent synaptic plasticity in memory. *Philosophical Transactions of the Royal Society of London, 358,* 773–786.

Morse, D., & Sassone-Corsi, P. (2002). Time after time: Inputs to and outputs from the mammalian circadian oscillators. *Trends in Neurosciences 25,* 632–637.

Morshead, C. M., & van der Kooy, D. (2001). A new "spin" on neural stem cells? *Current Opinion in Neurobiology, 11,* 59–65.

Mort, D. J., Malhotra, P., Mannan, S. K., Rorden, C., Pambakian, A., Kennard, C., & Husain, M. (2003). The anatomy of visual neglect. *Brain, 126,* 1986–1997.

Moruzzi, G., & Magoun, H. W. (1949). Brain stem reticular formation and activation of the EEG. *Electroencephalography and Clinical Neurophysiology, 1,* 455–473.

Moser, E. I., & Paulsen, O. (2001). New excitement in cognitive space: Between place cells and spatial memory. *Current Opinion in Neurobiology, 11,* 745–751.

Mott, D. D., & Dingledine, R. (2003). Interneuron research—challenges and strategies. *Trends in Neurosciences, 26*(9), 484–488.

Mountcastle, V. B., & Powell, T. P. S. (1959). Neural mechanisms subserving cutaneous sensibility with special references to the role of afferent inhibition in sensory perception and discrimination. *Bulletin of Johns Hopkins Hospital, 105,* 201–232.

Mrosovsky, N., & Salmon, P. A. (1987). A behavioral method for accelerating re-entrainment of rhythms to new light-dark cycles. *Nature, 330,* 372–373.

Mudher, A., & Lovestone, S. (2002). Alzheimer's disease—do tauists and baptists finally shake hands? *Trends in Neurosciences, 25,* 22–26.

Mühlnickel, W., Elbert, T., Taub, E., & Flor, H. (1998). Reorganization of auditory cortex in tinnitus. *Proceedings of the National Academy of Sciences, U.S.A., 95,* 10340–10343.

Mullaney, D. J., Johnson, L. C., Naitoh, P., Friedman, J. K., & Globus, G. G. (1977). Sleep during and after gradual sleep reduction. *Psychophysiology, 14,* 237–244.

Müller, N. G., Machado, L., & Knight, R. T. (2002). Contributions of the prefrontal cortex to working memory: Evidence from brain lesions in humans. *Journal of Cognitive Neuroscience, 14,* 673–686.

Müller, R-A., Kleinhans, N., Kemmotsu, N., Pierce, K., & Courchesne, E. (2003). Abnormal variability and distribution of functional maps in autism: An fMRI study of visuomotor learning. *The American Journal of Psychiatry, 160,* 1847–1862.

Müller, R-A., Pierce, K., Ambrose, J. B., Allen, G., & Courchesne, E. (2001). Atypical patterns of cerebral motor activation in autism: A functional magnetic resonance study. *Biological Psychiatry, 49,* 665–676.

Mumby, D. G. (2001). Perspectives on object-recognition memory following hippocampal damage: Lessons from studies in rats. *Behavioral Brain Research, 14,* 159–181.

Mumby, D. G., Cameli, L., & Glenn, M. J. (1999). Impaired allocentric spatial working memory and intact retrograde memory after thalamic damage caused by thiamine deficiency in rats. *Behavioral Neuroscience, 113,* 42–50.

Mumby, D. G., & Pinel, J. P. J. (1994). Rhinal cortex lesions impair object recognition in rats. *Behavioral Neuroscience, 108,* 11–18.

Mumby, D. G., Pinel, J. P. J., & Wood, E. R. (1989). Nonrecurring items delayed nonmatching-to-sample in rats: A new paradigm for testing nonspatial working memory. *Psychobiology, 18,* 321–326.

Mumby, D. G., Wood, E. R., Duva, C. A., Kornecook, T. J., Pinel, J. P. J., & Phillips, A. G. (1996). Ischemia-induced object-recognition deficits in rats are attenuated by hippocampal ablation before or soon after ischemia. *Behavioral Neuroscience, 110*(2), 266–281.

Mumby, D. G., Wood, E. R., & Pinel, J. P. J. (1992). Object-recognition memory is only mildly impaired in rats with lesions of the hippocampus and amygdala. *Psychobiology, 20,* 18–27.

Muñoz-Sanjuán, I., & Brivanlou, A. H. (2002). Neural induction, the default model and embryonic stem cells. *Nature Reviews Neuroscience, 3,* 271–280.

Münte, T. F., Altenmüller, E., & Jänke, L. (2002). The musician's brain as a model of neuroplasticity. *Nature Reviews Neuroscience, 3,* 473–478.

Murphy, M. R., & Schneider, G. E. (1970). Olfactory bulb removal eliminates mating behavior in the male golden hamster. *Science, 157,* 302–304.

Murray, E. A. (1996). What have ablation studies told us about the neural substrates of stimulus memory? *Seminars in the Neurosciences, 8,* 13–22.

Murray, E. A., & Richmond, B. J. (2001). Role of perirhinal cortex in object perception, memory, and associations. *Current Opinion in Neurobiology, 11,* 188–193.

Myers, R. E., & Sperry, R. W. (1953). Interocular transfer of a visual form discrimination habit in cats after section of the optic chiasma and corpus callosum. In *Abstracts of Papers from Platform* (p. 351), American Association of Anatomists.

Nadarajah, B., & Parnavelas, J. G. (2002). Modes of neuronal migration in the developing cerebral cortex. *Nature Reviews Neuroscience, 3,* 423–432.

Nadel, L., & Moscovitch, M. (1997). Memory consolidation, retrograde amnesia and the hippocampal complex. *Current Opinion in Neurobiology, 7,* 217–227.

Nadelmann, E. A. (1989). Drug prohibition in the United States: Costs, consequences, and alternatives. *Science, 245,* 939–947.

Nader, K., Schafe, G. E., & LeDoux, J. E. (2000). Fear memories require protein synthesis in the amygdala for reconsolidation after retrieval. *Nature, 406,* 722–726.

Naeser, M. A., Alexander M. P., Helm-Estabrooks, N., Levine, H. L., Laughlin, S. A., & Geschwind, N. (1982). Aphasia with predominantly subcortical lesion sites. *Archives of Neurolinguistics, 39,* 2–14.

Naeser, M. A., Hayward, R. W., Laughlin, S. A., & Zatz, L. M. (1981). Quantitative CT scan studies in aphasia. *Brain and Language, 12,* 140–164.

Naitoh, P. (1992). Minimal sleep to maintain performance: The search for sleep quantum in sustained operations. In C. Stampi (Ed.), *Why we nap: Evolution, chronobiology, and functions of polyphasic and ultrashort sleep.* Boston: Birkhaüser.

Nakahara, K., Hayashi, T., Konishi, S., & Miyashita, Y. (2002). Functional MRI of macaque monkeys performing a cognitive set-shifting task. *Science, 295,* 1532–1536.

Natelson, B. H. (2004). Stress, hormones and disease. *Physiology and Behavior, 82,* 139–143.

National Commission on Marijuana and Drug Abuse. (1972). *Marijuana: A signal of misunderstanding.* New York: New American Library.

Nau, R., & Brück, W. (2002). Neuronal injury in bacterial meningitis: Mechanisms and implications for therapy. *Trends in Neurosciences, 25,* 38–45.

Naya, Y., Yoshida, M., & Miyashita, Y. (2001). Backward spreading of memory-retrieval signal in the primate temporal cortex. *Science, 291,* 661–664.

Nemeroff, C. B. (1998, June). The neurobiology of depression. *Scientific American, 278,* 42–49.

Nesse, R. M., & Berridge, K. C. (1997). Psychoactive drug use in evolutionary perspective. *Science, 278,* 63–66.

Nesse, R. M., & Williams, G. C. (1998, November). Evolution and the origins of disease. *Scientific American, 278,* 86–93.

Nestle, M. (2003). The ironic politics of obesity. *Science, 299,* 781.

Nestler, E. J., & Malenka, R. C. (2004, March). The addicted brain. *Scientific American, 290,* 78–85.

Netter, F. H. (1962). *The CIBA collection of medical illustrations. Vol. 1, The nervous system.* New York: CIBA.

Neve, R. L., & Robakis, N. K. (1998). Alzheimer's disease: A reexamination of the amyloid hypothesis. *Trends in Neurosciences, 21,* 15–19.

Neves, S. R., Ram, P. T., & Iyengar, R. (2002). G protein pathways. *Science, 296,* 1636–1639.

Neville, H., & Bavelier, D. (1998). Neural organization and plasticity of language. *Current Opinion in Neurobiology, 8,* 254–258.

Newcombe, N., & Fox, N. (1994). Infantile amnesia: Through a glass darkly. *Child Development, 65,* 31–40.

Newcombe, N. S. (2002). The nativst-empiricist controversy in the context of recent research on spatial and quantitative development. *Psychological Science, 13*(5), 395–400.

Newcombe, N. S., Drummey, A. B., Fox, N. A., Lie, E., & Ottinger-Alberts, W. (2000). Remembering early childhood. How much, how, and why (or why not). *Current Directions in Psychological Science, 9,* 55–58.

Newman, E. A. (2003). New roles for astrocytes: Regulation of synaptic transmission. *Trends in Neurosciences, 26,* 536–542.

Newport, D. J., & Nemeroff, C. B. (2000). Neurobiology of posttraumatic stress disorder. *Current Opinion in Neurobiology, 10,* 211–218.

Newsom-Davis, J., & Vincent, A. (1991). Antibody-mediated neurological disease. *Current Opinion in Neurobiology, 1,* 430–435.

Nicolesis, M. A. L., & Chapin, J. K. (October, 2002). People with nerve or limb injuries may one day be able to command wheelchairs, prosthetics and even paralyzed arms and legs by "thinking them through" the motions. *Scientific American, 287,* 47–53.

Nicolson, I. R., Fawcett, A. J., & Dean, P. (2001). Developmental dyslexia: The cerebellar deficit hypothesis. *Trends in Neurosciences, 24,* 508–516.

Nieder, A., Freedman, D. J., & Miller, E. K. (2002). Representation of the quantity of visual items in the primate prefrontal cortex. *Science, 297,* 1708–1711.

Nielsen, J. B. (2002). Motoneuronal drive during human walking. *Brain Research Reviews, 40,* 192–201.

Nijhawan, D., Honarpour, N., & Wang, X. (2000). Apoptosis in neural development and disease. *Annual Review of Neuroscience, 23,* 73–89.

Nobre, A. C., & Plunkett, K. (1997). The neural system of language: Structure and development. *Current Opinion in Neurobiology, 7,* 262–268.

Noebels, J. L. (2003). The biology of epilepsy genes. *Annual Review of Neuroscience, 26,* 599–625.

Nopoulis, P. C., Ceilley, J. W., Gailis, E. A., & Andreasen, N. C. (2001). An MRI study of midbrain morphology in patients with schizophrenia: Relationship to psychosis, neuroleptics, and cerebellar neural circuitry. *Biological Psychiatry, 49,* 13–19.

Northcutt, R. G., & Kaas, J. H. (1995). The emergence and evolution of mammalian neocortex. *Trends in Neurosciences, 18*(9), 373–418.

Northoff, G., Richter, A., Gessner, M., Schlagenhauf, F., Fell, J., Baumgart, F., et al. (2000). Functional dissociation between medial and lateral prefrontal cortical spatiotemporal activation in negative and positive emotions: A combined fMRI/MEG study. *Cerebral Cortex, 10,* 93–107.

Noselli, S., & Perrimon, N. (2000). Are there close encounters between signaling pathways? *Science, 290,* 68–69.

Nudo, R. J., Jenkins, W. M., & Merzenich, M. M. (1996). Repetitive microstimulation alters the cortical representation of movements in adult rats. *Somatosensory Motor Research, 7,* 463–483.

Nyberg, L., Habib, R., McIntosh, A. R., & Tulving, E. (2000). Reactivation of encoding-related brain activity during memory retrieval. *Proceedings of the National Academy of Sciences, U.S.A., 97,* 11120–11124.

Nykamp, K., Rosenthal, L., Folkerts, M., Roehrs, T., Guido, P., & Roth, T. (1998). The effects of REM sleep deprivation on the level of sleepiness/alertness. *Sleep, 21,* 609–614.

O'Callaghan, M. A. J., & Carroll, D. (1982). *Psychosurgery: A scientific analysis.* Ridgewood, NJ: George A. Bogdaen & Son.

Ochsner, K. O., & Lieberman, M. D. (2001). The emergence of social cognitive neuroscience. *American Psychologist, 56*(9), 717–734.

Ohbayashi, M., Ohki, K., & Miyashita, Y. (2003). Conversion of working memory to motor sequence in the monkey premotor cortex. *Science, 301,* 233–236.

Ohman, A. (2002). Automaticity and the amygdala: Nonconscious responses to emotional faces. *Current Directions in Psychological Science, 11,* 62–66.

Ohtaki, H., Mori, S., Nakamachi, T., Dohi, K., Yin, L., Endo, S., et al. (2003). Evaluation of neuronal cell death after a new global ischemia model in infant mice. *Acta Neurochirurgica Suppl., 86,* 97–100.

Ohyama, T., Nores, W. L., Murphy, M., & Mauk, M. D. (2003). What the cerebellum computes. *Trends in Neurosciences, 26,* 222–227.

Ohzawa, I. (1998). Mechanisms of stereoscopic vision: The disparity energy model. *Current Opinion in Neurobiology, 8,* 509–515.

Ojemann, G. A. (1979). Individual variability in cortical localization of language. *Journal of Neurosurgery, 50,* 164–169.

Ojemann, G. A. (1983). Brain organization for language from the perspective of electrical stimulation mapping. *Behavioral and Brain Sciences, 2,* 189–230.

O'Keefe, J. (1993). Hippocampus, theta, and spatial memory. *Current Opinion in Neurobiology, 3,* 917–924.

O'Keefe, J., & Nadel, L. (1978). *The hippocampus as a cognitive map.* Oxford, England: Clarendon Press.

O'Keefe, J., & Speakman, A. (1987). Single unit activity in the rat hippocampus during a spatial memory task. *Experimental Brain Research, 68,* 1–27.

Olds, J., & Milner, P. (1954). Positive reinforcement produced by electrical stimulation of septal area and other regions of rat brain. *Journal of Comparative and Physiological Psychology, 47,* 419–427.

O'Leary, C. M. (2004) Fetal alcohol syndrome: Diagnosis, epidemiology, and developmental outcomes. *Journal of Paediatrics and Child Health, 40,* 2–7.

O'Leary, D. D. M., Ruff, N. L. & Dyck, R. H. (1994). Development, critical period plasticity, and adult reorganization of mamma-

lian somatosensory systems. *Current Opinion in Neurobiology, 4,* 535–544.

Oliet, S. H. R., Piet, R., & Poulain, A. (2001). Control of glutamate clearance and synaptic efficacy by glial coverage of neurons. *Science, 292,* 923–925.

Olson, C. R. (2003). Brain representations of object-centered space in monkeys and humans. *Annual Review of Neuroscience, 26,* 331–354.

Olton, D. S., & Samuelson, R. J. (1976). Remembrance of places: Spatial memory in rats. *Journal of Experimental Psychology: Animal Behavior Processes, 2,* 97–116.

O'Neill, L., Murphy, M., & Gallager, R. B. (1994). What are we? Where did we come from? Where are we going? *Science, 263,* 181–184.

Ormerod, B. K., Falconer, E. M., & Galea, L. A. M. (2003). N-methyl-D-aspartate receptor activity and estradiol: Separate regulation of cell proliferation in the dentate gyrus of adult female meadow vole. *Journal of Endocrinology, 179,* 155–163.

Ormerod, B. K., Lee, T. T.-Y., & Galea, L. A. M. (2001a). Mechanism and function of adult neurogenesis. In C. A. Shaw & J. C. McEachern (Eds.), *Towards a theory of neuroplasticity* (pp. 85–100). Philadelphia: Taylor & Francis.

Ormerod, B. K., & Galea, L. A. M. (2001b). Reproductive status influences cell proliferation and cell survival in the dentate gyrus of adult female meadow voles: A possible regulatory role for estradiol. *Neuroscience, 102,* 369–379.

Overmier, J. B., & Murison, R. (1997). Animal models reveal the "psych" in the psychosomatics of peptic ulcers. *Current Directions in Psychological Science, 6,* 180–184.

Owens, D. F., & Kriegstein, A. R. (2002). Is there more to GABA than synaptic inhibition? *Nature Reviews Neuroscience, 3,* 715–727.

Owren, M. J. (1990). Acoustic classification of alarm calls by vervet monkeys (*Ceropithecus aethiops*) and humans (*Homo sapiens*): II. Synthetic calls. *Journal of Comparative Psychology, 104,* 29–40.

Pace-Schott, E. F., & Hobson, J. A. (2002). The neurobiology of sleep: Genetics, cellular physiology and subcortical networks. *Nature Reviews Neuroscience, 3,* 591–605.

Pääbo, S. (1995). The Y chromosome and the origin of all of us (men). *Science, 268,* 1141–1142.

Pääbo, S. (2001). The human genome and our view of ourselves. *Science, 291,* 1219–1220.

Packard, M. G., & Knowlton, B. J. (2002). Learning and memory functions of the basal ganglia. *Annual Review of Neuroscience, 25,* 563–593.

Pallas, S. P. (2001). Intrinsic and extrinsic factors that shape neocortical specification. *Trends in Neurosciences, 24,* 417–423.

Palovskaya, M., Ring, H., Groswasser, Z., & Hochstein, S. (2002). Searching with unilateral neglect. *Journal of Cognitive Neuroscience, 14,* 745–756.

Panksepp, J. (2003). Feeling the pain of social loss. *Science, 302,* 237–239.

Panksepp, J., & Trowill, J. A. (1967). Intraoral self-injection: II. The simulation of self-stimulation phenomena with a conventional reward. *Psychonomic Science, 9,* 407–408.

Papez, J. W. (1937). A proposed mechanism of emotion. *Archives of Neurology and Psychiatry, 38,* 725–743.

Paredes, R. G. (2003). Medial preoptic area/anterior hypothalamus and sexual motivation. *Scandinavian Journal of Psychology, 44,* 203–212.

Parker, S. T., Mitchell, R. W., & Boccia, M. L. (1994). *Self-awareness in animals and humans: Developmental perspectives.* New York: Cambridge University Press.

Parnas, H., Segel, L., Dudel, J., & Parnas, I. (2000). Autoreceptors, membrane potential and the regulation of transmitter release. *Trends in Neurosciences, 23,* 60–68.

Parrott, A. C. (1999). Does cigarette smoking *cause* stress? *American Psychologist, 54,* 817–820.

Parsons, L. M., Fox, P. T., Downs, J. H., Glass, T., Hirsch, T. B., Martin, C. C., et al. (1995). Use of implicit motor imagery for visual shape discrimination as revealed by PET. *Nature, 375,* 54–58.

Pascual-Leone, A., Walsh, V., & Rothwell, J. (2000). Transcranial magnetic stimulation in cognitive neuroscience—virtual lesion, chronometry, and functional connectivity. *Current Opinion in Neurobiology, 10,* 232–237.

Passingham, R. E., Stephan, K. E., & Kotter, R. (2002). The anatomical basis of functional localization in the cortex. *Nature Reviews Neuroscience, 3,* 606–616.

Patel, S. R., Ayas, N. T., White, D. P., Speizer, F. E., Stampfer, M. J., & Hu, F. B. (2003). A prospective study of sleep duration and mortality risk in women. *Sleep, 26,* A184.

Paterson, S. J., Brown, J. H., Gsödl, M. K., Johnson, M. H., & Karmiloff-Smith, A. (1999). Cognitive modularity and genetic disorders. *Science, 286,* 2355–2358.

Patterson, K., & Ralph, M. A. L. (1999). Selective disorders of reading? *Current Opinion in Neurobiology, 9,* 235–239.

Patterson, K., Vargha-Khadem, F., & Polkey, C. E. (1989). Reading with one hemisphere. *Brain, 112,* 39–63.

Patton, G. C. (1988). The spectrum of eating disorders in adolescence. *Journal of Psychosomatic Research, 32,* 579–584.

Paulesu, E., Démonet, J.-F., Fazio, F., McCrory, E., Chanoine, V., Brunswick, N., et al. (2001). Dyslexia: Cultural diversity and biological unity. *Science, 291,* 2165–2167.

Paulesu, E., McCrory, E., Fazio, F., Menoncello, L., Brunswick, N., Cappa, S. F., et al. (2000). A cultural effect on brain function. *Nature Neuroscience, 3,* 91–96.

Paus, D. L. (2001). Update on the genetics of Tourette syndrome. In D. J. Cohen, C. G. Goetz, & J. Jankovic (Eds.), *Tourette syndrome* (pp. 281–293). Philadelphia: Lippincott Williams & Wilkins.

Payne, B. R., & Lomber, S. G. (2001). Reconstructing functional systems after lesions of cerebral cortex. *Nature Reviews Neuroscience, 2,* 911–919.

Pellis, S. M., O'Brien, D. P., Pellis, V. C., Teitelbaum, P., Wolgin, D. L., & Kennedy, S. (1988). Escalation of feline predation along a gradient from avoidance through "play" to killing. *Behavioral Neuroscience, 102,* 760–777.

Pellow, S., Chopin, P., File, S. E., & Briley, M. (1985). Validation of open:closed arm entries in an elevated plus-maze as a measure of anxiety in the rat. *Journal of Neuroscience Methods, 14,* 149–167.

Penfield, W., & Boldrey, E. (1937). Somatic motor and sensory representations in cerebral cortex of man as studied by electrical stimulation. *Brain, 60,* 389–443.

Penfield, W., & Evans, J. (1935). The frontal lobe in man: A clinical study of maximum removals. *Brain, 58,* 115–133.

Penfield, W., & Rasmussen, T. (1950). *The cerebral cortex of man: A clinical study of the localization of function.* New York: Macmillan.

Penfield, W., & Roberts, L. (1959). *Speech and brain mechanisms.* Princeton, NJ: Princeton University Press.

Peoples, L. L. (2002). Will, anterior cingulated cortex, and addiction. *Science, 296,* 1623–1624.

Peralta, V., & Cuesta, M. J. (2000). Clinical models of schizophrenia: A critical approach to competing conceptions. *Psychopathology, 33,* 252–258.

Percival, J. E., Horne, J. A., & Tilley, A. J. (1983). Effects of sleep deprivation on tests of higher cerebral functioning. In *Sleep 1982* (pp. 390–391). Sixth European Congress on Sleep Research, Zurich. Basel, Switzerland: Karger.

Perkel, D. J., & Farries, M. A. (2000). Complementary "bottom-up" and "top-down" approaches to basal ganglia function. *Current Opinion in Neurobiology, 10,* 725–731.

Peterhans, E., & von der Heydt, R. (1991). Subjective contours—bridging the gap between psychophysics and physiology. *Trends in Neurosciences, 14,* 112–119.

Peters, M., & Brooke, J. (1998). Conduction velocity in muscle and cutaneous afferents in humans. *Journal of Motor Behavior, 30,* 285–287.

Petersen, S. E., Fox, P. T., Posner, M. I., Mintun, M., & Raichle, M. E. (1988). Positron emission tomographic studies of the cortical anatomy of single-word processing. *Nature, 331,* 585–589.

Peterson, A. T., Soberón, J., & Sánchez-Cordero, V. (1999). Conservatism of ecological niches in evolutionary time. *Science, 285,* 1265–1267.

Peterson, B. S. (2001). Neuroimaging studies of Tourette syndrome: A decade of progress. In D. J. Cohen, C. G. Goetz, & J. Jankovic (Eds.), *Tourette syndrome* (pp. 179–196). Philadelphia: Lippincott Williams & Wilkins.

Petrides, M. (1996). Lateral frontal cortical contribution to memory. *Seminars in the Neurosciences, 8,* 57–63.

Petrides, M. (2000). Dissociable roles of mid-dorsolateral prefrontal and anterior inferotemporal cortex in visual working memory. *Journal of Neuroscience, 20,* 7496–7503.

Pfeiffer, C. A. (1936). Sexual differences of the hypophyses and their determination by the gonads. *American Journal of Anatomy, 58,* 195–225.

Pfrieger, F. W. (2002). Role of glia in synapse development. *Current Opinion in Neurobiology, 12,* 486–490.

Phelps, M. E., & Mazziotta, J. (1985). Positron tomography: Human brain function and biochemistry. *Science, 228,* 804.

Phillips, A. G., Coury, A., Fiorino, D., LePiane, F. G., Brown, E., & Fibiger, H. C. (1992). Self-stimulation of the ventral tegmental area enhances dopamine release in the nucleus accumbens: A microdialysis study. *Annals of the New York Academy of Sciences, 654,* 199–206.

Phillips, T., & Belknap, J. K. (2002). Complex-trait genetics: Emergence of multivariate strategies. *Nature Reviews Neuroscience, 3,* 478–485.

Phoenix, C. H., Goy, R. W., Gerall, A. A., & Young, W. C. (1959). Organizing action of prenatally administered testosterone proprionate on the tissues mediating mating behavior in the female guinea pig. *Endocrinology, 65,* 369–382.

Picard, N., & Strick, P. L. (2001). Imaging the premotor areas. *Current Opinion in Neurobiology, 11,* 663–672.

Pierce, K., & Courchesne, E. (2001). Evidence for a cerebellar role in reduced exploration and stereotyped behavior in autism. *Biological Psychiatry, 49,* 655–664.

Pietrobon, D., & Striessnig, J. (2003). Neurobiology of migraine. *Nature Reviews Neuroscience, 4,* 386–398.

Pinel, J. P. J. (1969). A short gradient of ECS produced amnesia in a one trial appetitive learning situation. *Journal of Comparative and Physiological Psychology, 68,* 650–655.

Pinel, J. P. J. (1981). Spontaneous kindled motor seizures in rats. In J. A. Wada (Ed.), *Kindling 2* (pp. 179–192). New York: Raven Press.

Pinel, J. P. J., Assanand, S., & Lehman, D. R. (2000). Hunger, eating, and ill health. *American Psychologist, 55,* 1105–1116.

Pinel, J. P. J., & Mana, M. J. (1989). Adaptive interactions of rats with dangerous inanimate objects: Support for a cognitive theory of defensive behavior. In R. J. Blanchard, P. F. Brain, D. C. Blanchard, & S. Parmigiani (Eds.), *Ethoexperimental approaches to the study of behavior* (pp. 137–150). Dordrecht, The Netherlands: Kluwer Academic Publishers.

Pinel, J. P. J., Mana, M. J., & Kim, C. K. (1989). Effect-dependent tolerance to ethanol's anticonvulsant effect on kindled seizures. In R. J. Porter, R. H. Mattson, J. A. Cramer, & I. Diamond (Eds.), *Alcohol and seizures: Basic mechanisms and clinical implications* (pp. 115–125). Philadelphia: F. A. Davis.

Pinel, J. P. J., & Treit, D. (1978). Burying as a defensive response in rats. *Journal of Comparative and Physiological Psychology, 92,* 708–712.

Piomelli, D. (2003). The molecular logic of endocannabinoid signaling. *Nature Reviews Neuroscience, 4,* 873–884.

Pleim, E. T., & Barfield, R. J. (1988). Progesterone versus estrogen facilitation of female sexual behavior by intracranial administration to female rats. *Hormones and Behavior, 22,* 150–159.

Ploegh, H. L. (1998). Viral strategies of immune evasion. *Science, 280,* 248–252.

Plomin, R., & DeFries, J. C. (1998, May). The genetics of cognitive abilities and disabilities. *Scientific American, 278,* 62–69.

Plomin, R., DeFries, J. C., McGuffin, P., & Craig, I. W. (2002). *Behavioral genetics in the postgenomic era.* Washington, DC: American Psychological Association.

Plomin, R., Fulker, D. W., Corley, R., & DeFries, J. C. (1997). Nature, nurture, and cognitive development from 1 to 16 years: A parent-offspring adoption study. *Psychological Science, 8*(6), 442–447.

Plomin, R., & McGuffin, P. (2003). Psychopathology in the postgenomic era. *Annual Review of Psychology, 54,* 205–228.

Plomin, R., & Neiderhiser, J. M. (1992). Genetics and experience. *Current Directions in Psychological Science, 1,* 160–163.

Polivy, J., & Herman, P. C. (2002). Causes of eating disorders. *Annual Review of Neuroscience, 53,* 187–213.

Pons, T. P., Garraghty, P. E., Ommaya, A. K., Kaas, J. H., Taub, E., & Mishkin, M. (1991). Massive cortical reorganization after sensory deafferentation in adult macaques. *Science, 252,* 1857–1860.

Pope, H. G., Gruber, A. J., Hudson, J. I., Huestis, M. A., & Yurgelun-Todd, D. (2001). Neuropsychological performance in long-term cannabis users. *Archives of General Psychiatry, 58,* 909–915.

Pope, H. G., Gruber, A. J., & Yurgelun-Todd, D. (1995). The residual neuropsychological effects of cannabis: The current status of research. *Drug and Alcohol Dependence, 38,* 25–34.

Pope, H. G., & Katz, D. L. (1987). Bodybuilder's psychosis. *Lancet, 1*(8537), 863.

Pope, H. G., Jr., Kouri, E. M., & Hudson, J. I. (2000). Effects of supraphysiologic doses of testosterone on mood and aggression in normal men. *Archives of General Psychiatry, 57,* 133–140.

Poppele, R., & Bosco, G. (2003). Sophisticated spinal contributions to motor control. *Trends in Neurosciences, 26,* 269–276.

Porter, R., & Lemon, R. N. (1993). Corticospinal function and voluntary movement. *Monographs of the Physiological Society, No. 45.* Oxford University Press.

Posner, M. I., & Raichle, M. E. (1994). *Images of the mind.* New York: Scientific American Library.

Post, R. M., Weiss, S. R. B., Clark, M., Nakajima, T., & Pert, A. (1990). Amygdala versus local anesthetic kindling: Differential anatomy, pharmacology, and clinical implications. In J. A. Wada (Ed.), *Kindling 4* (pp. 357–369). New York: Plenum Press.

Postle, B. R., Corkin, S., & Growdon, J. H. (1996). Intact implicit memory for novel patterns in Alzheimer's disease. *Learning & Memory, 3,* 305–312.

Pouget, A., & Driver, J. (2000). Relating unilateral neglect to the neural coding of space. *Current Opinion in Neurobiology, 10,* 242–249.

Poulos, C. X., & Cappell, H. (1991). Homeostatic theory of drug tolerance: A general model of physiological adaptation. *Psychological Review, 98,* 390–408.

Powley, T. L., Opsahl, C. A., Cox, J. E., & Weingarten, H. P. (1980). The role of the hypothalamus in energy homeostasis. In P. J. Morgane & J. Panksepp (Eds.), *Handbook of the hypothalamus, 3A: Behavioral studies of the hypothalamus* (pp. 211–298). New York: Marcel Dekker.

Price, C. J., Howard, D., Patterson, K., Warburton, E. A., Friston, K. J., & Frackowiak, R. S. J. (1998). A functional neuroimaging description of two deep dyslexic patients. *Journal of Cognitive Neuroscience, 10,* 303–315.

Price, C. J., Mummery, C. J., Moore, C. J., Frackowiak, R. S. J., & Friston, K. J. (1999). Delineating necessary and sufficient neural systems with functional imaging studies of neuropsychological patients. *Journal of Cognitive Neuroscience, 11,* 371–382.

Price, D. D. (2000). Psychological and neural mechanisms of the affective dimension of pain. *Science, 288,* 1769–1772.

Price, J., & Williams, B. P. (2001). Neural stem cells. *Current Opinion in Neurobiology, 11,* 564–567.

Price, R. A., & Gottesman, I. I. (1991). Body fat in identical twins reared apart: Roles for genes and environment. *Behavioral Genetics, 21,* 1–7.

Primakoff, P., & Myles, D. G. (2002). Penetration, adhesion, and fusion in mammalian sperm–egg interaction. *Science, 296,* 2183–2185.

Pritchard, R. M. (1961, June). Stabilized images on the retina. *Scientific American, 204,* 72–78.

Prolla, T. A., & Mattson, M. P. (2001). Molecular mechanisms of brain aging and neurodegenerative disorders: Lessons from dietary restriction. *Trends in Neurosciences, 24,* S21–S31.

Pryce, C. R., & Feldon, J. (2003). Long-term neurobehavioural impact of the postnatal environment in rats: Manipulations, effects, and mediating mechanisms. *Neuroscience and Biobehavioural Reviews, 27,* 57–71.

Pusey, A., Williams, J., & Goodall, J. (1997). The influence of dominance rank on the reproductive success of female chimpanzees. *Science, 277,* 828–830.

Putnam, S. K., Sato, S., & Hull, E. M. (2003). Effects of testosterone metabolites on copulation and medial preoptic dopamine release in castrated male rats. *Hormones and Behavior, 44,* 419–426.

Qi, Y., Stapp, D., & Qiu, M. (2002). Origin and molecular specification of oligodendrocytes in the telencephalon. *Trends in Neurosciences, 25,* 223–225.

Quan, N., Avitsur, R., Stark, J. L., He, L., Shah, M., & Caligiuri, M. (2001). Social stress increases the susceptibility to endotoxic shock. *Journal of Neuroimmunology, 115,* 36–45.

Quinsey, V. L. (2003). The etiology of anomalous sexual preferences in men. *Annals of the New York Academy of Sciences, 989,* 105–117.

Racine, R. J., & Burnham, W. M. (1984). The kindling model. In P. A. Schwartzkroin & H. Wheal (Eds.), *Electrophysiology of epilepsy* (pp. 153–171). London: Academic Press.

Racine, R. J., Burnham, W. M., Gartner, J. G., & Levitan, D. (1973). Rates of motor seizure development in rats subjected to electrical brain stimulation: Strain and interstimulation interval effects. *Electroencephalography and Clinical Neurophysiology, 35,* 553–556.

Raff, M. C., Whitmore, A. V., & Finn, J. T. (2002). Axonal self-destruction and neurodegeneration. *Science, 296,* 868–871.

Rainville, P. (2002). Brain mechanisms of pain affect and pain modulation. *Current Opinion in Neurobiology, 12,* 195–204.

Raisman, G. (1997). An urge to explain the incomprehensible: Geoffrey Harris and the discovery of the neural control of the pituitary gland. *Annual Review of Neuroscience, 20,* 533–566.

Raisman, G., & Field, P. M. (1971). Sexual dimorphism in the neuropil of the preoptic area of the rat and its dependence on neonatal androgens. *Brain Research, 54,* 1–29.

Rajaratnam, S. M., Dijk, D. J., Middleton, B., Stone, B. M., & Arendt, J. (2003). Melatonin phase-shifts human circadian rhythms with no evidence of changes in the duration of endogenous melatonin secretion or the 24-hour production of reproductive hormones. *The Journal of Clinical Endocrinology and Metabolism, 88,* 4303–4309.

Rakic, P. (1979). Genetic and epigenetic determinants of local neuronal circuits in the mammalian central nervous system. In F. O. Schmitt & F. G. Worden (Eds.), *The neurosciences: Fourth study program.* Cambridge, MA: MIT Press.

Ralph, M. R., Foster, T. G., Davis, F. C., & Menaker, M. (1990). Transplanted suprachiasmatic nucleus determines circadian period. *Science, 247,* 975–978.

Ralph, M. R., & Menaker, M. (1988). A mutation of the circadian system in golden hamsters. *Science, 241,* 1225–1227.

Rämä, P., Sala, J. B., Gillen, J. S., Pekar, J. J., & Courtney, S. M. (2001). Dissociation of the neural systems for working memory maintenance of verbal and nonspatial visual information. *Cognitive, Affective, & Behavioral Neuroscience, 1,* 161–171.

Ramachandran, V. S. (1992, May). Blind spots. *Scientific American, 260,* 86–91.

Ramachandran, V. S., & Blackeslee, S. (1998). *Phantoms in the brain.* New York: William Morrow.

Ramachandran, V. S., & Rogers-Ramachandran, D. (2000). Phantom limbs and neuronal plasticity. *Archives of Neurology, 57*, 317–320.

Ramnani, N., & Passingham, R. E. (2001). Changes in the human brain during rhythm learning. *Journal of Cognitive Neuroscience, 13*, 952–966.

Rampon, C., Jiang, C. H., Dong, H., Tang, Y. P., Lockhart, D. J., Schultz, P. G., et al. (2000). Effects of environmental enrichment on gene expression in the brain. *Proceedings of the National Academy of Sciences, U.S.A., 97*(23), 12880–12884.

Ramsay, D. S., & Woods, S. C. (1997). Biological consequences of drug administration: Implications for acute and chronic tolerance. *Psychological Review, 104*(1), 170–193.

Ramus, F. (2003). Developmental dyslexia: Specific phonological deficit or general sensorimotor dysfunction? *Current Opinion in Neurobiology, 13*, 212–218.

Ranson, B., Behar, T., & Nedergaard, M. (2003). New roles for astrocytes (stars at last). *Trends in Neurosciences, 26*, 520–530.

Rao, S. C., Rainer, G., & Miller, E. K. (1997). Integration of what and where in the primate prefrontal cortex. *Science, 276*, 821–824.

Rasmussen, T., & Milner, B. (1975). Clinical and surgical studies of the cerebral speech areas in man. In K. J. Zulch, O. Creutzfeldt, & G. C. Galbraith (Eds.), *Cerebral localization* (pp. 238–257). New York: Springer-Verlag.

Ratliff, F. (1972, June). Contour and contrast. *Scientific American, 226*, 90–101.

Rattenborg, N. C., Amlaner, C. J., & Lima, S. L. (2000). Behavioral, neurophysiological and evolutionary perspectives on unihemispheric sleep. *Neuroscience and Biobehavioural Reviews, 24*, 817–842.

Raynor, H. A., & Epstein, L. H. (2001). Dietary variety, energy regulation, and obesity. *Psychological Bulletin, 127*, 325–341.

Reame, N., Sauder, S. E., Kelch, R. P., & Marshall, J. C. (1984). Pulsatile gonadotropin secretion during the human menstrual cycle: Evidence for altered frequency of gonadotropin releasing hormone secretion. *Journal of Clinical Endocrinology and Metabolism, 59*, 328.

Reber, P. J., Knowlton, B. J., & Squire, L. R. (1996). Dissociable properties of memory system: Differences in the flexibility of declarative and nondeclarative knowledge. *Behavioral Neuroscience, 110*(5), 861–871.

Rechtschaffen, A. (1998). Current perspectives on the function of sleep. *Perspectives in Biology and Medicine, 41*(3), 359–390.

Rechtschaffen, A., & Bergmann, B. M. (1995). Sleep deprivation in the rat by the disk-over-water method. *Behavioural Brain Research, 69*, 55–63.

Rechtschaffen, A., Gilliland, M. A., Bergmann, B. M., & Winter, J. B. (1993). Physiological correlates of prolonged sleep deprivation in rats. *Science, 221*, 182–184.

Rechtschaffen, A., & Kales, A. (1968). *A manual of standardized terminology, techniques and scoring systems for sleep stages of human subjects.* Washington, DC: U.S. Government Printing Office.

Redd, M., & de Castro, J. M. (1992). Social facilitation of eating: Effects of social instruction on food intake. *Physiology & Behavior, 52*, 749–754.

Rees, G., Kreiman, G., & Koch, C. (2002). Neural correlates of consciousness in humans. *Nature Reviews Neuroscience, 3*, 261–270.

Rees, G., Russell, C., Frith, C. D., & Driver, J. (1999). Inattentional blindness versus inattentional amnesia for fixated but ignored words. *Science, 286*, 2504–2507.

Rehm, J., Gschwend, P., Steffen, T., Gutzwiller, F., Dobler-Mikola, A., & Uchtenhagen, A. (2001). Feasibility, safety, and efficacy of inject-

able heroin prescription for refractory opioid addicts: A follow-up study. *Lancet, 358*, 1417–1423.

Reid, R. C., & Alonso, J-M. (1996). The processing and encoding of information in the visual cortex. *Current Opinion in Neurobiology, 6*, 475–480.

Reiman, E. M., Lane, R. D., Ahern, G. L., Schwartz, G. E., & Davidson, R. J. (2000). Positron emission tomography in the study of emotion, anxiety, and anxiety disorders. In R. D. Lane & L. Nadel (Eds.), *Cognitive neuroscience of emotion* (pp. 389–406). New York: Oxford University Press.

Reinarman, C., Cohen, P. D., & Kaal, H. L. (2004). The limited relevance of drug policy: Cannabis in Amsterdam and in San Francisco. *American Journal of Public Health, 94*, 836–842.

Reiner, W. (1997). To be male or female—that is the question. *Archives of Pediatrics and Adolescent Medicine, 151*, 224–225.

Remple, M. S., Bruneau, R. M., VandenBerg, P. M., Goertzen, C., & Kleim, J. A. (2001). Sensitivity of cortical movement representations to motor experience: Evidence that skill learning but not strength training induces cortical reorganization. *Behavioral Brain Research, 123*, 133–141.

Rensberger, B. (2000). The nature of evidence. *Science, 289*, 61.

Rensink, R. A. (2002). Change detection. *Annual Review of Psychology, 53*, 245–277.

Renvall, R., & Hari, R. (2002). Auditory cortical responses to speech-like stimuli in dyslexic adults. *Journal of Cognitive Neuroscience, 14*, 757–768.

Rettig, J., & Neher, E. (2002). Emerging roles of presynaptic proteins in calcium-triggered exocytosis. *Science, 298*, 781–785.

Reuter-Lorenz, P. A., & Miller, A. C. (1998). The cognitive neuroscience of human laterality: Lessons from the bisected brain. *Current Directions in Psychological Science, 7*, 15–20.

Kevusky, S. H., & Garcia, J. (1970). Learned associations over long delays. In G. H. Bower & J. T. Spence (Eds.), *The psychology of learning and motivation* (Vol. 4, pp. 1–85). New York: Academic Press.

Reynolds, D. V. (1969). Surgery in the rat during electrical analgesia induced by focal brain stimulation. *Science, 164*, 444–445.

Rhees, R. W., Lephart, E. D., & Eliason, D. (2001). Effects of maternal separation during early postnatal development on male sexual behavior and female reproductive function. *Behavioural Brain Research, 123*, 1–10.

Rhodes, J. S., Van Praag, H., Jeffrey, S., Girard, I., Mitchell, G. S., Garland, T., Jr., & Gage, F. H. (2002). Exercise increases hippocampal neurogenesis to high levels but does not improve spatial learning in mice bred for increased voluntary wheel running. *Behavioral Neuroscience, 117*, 1006–1016.

Ricaurte, G. A., Yuan, J., Hatzidimitriou, G., Cord, B. J., & McCann, U. D. (2002). Severe dopaminergic neurotoxicity in primates after a common recreational dose regimen of MDMA ("Ecstasy"). *Science, 297*, 2260–2263.

Riccio, D. C., Millin, P. M., & Gisquet-Verrier, P. (2003). Retrograde amnesia: Forgetting back. *Current Directions in Psychological Science, 12*, 41–44.

Richards, W. (1971, May). The fortification illusions of migraines. *Scientific American, 224*, 89–97.

Richter, C. P. (1967). Sleep and activity: Their relation to the 24-hour clock. *Proceedings of the Association for Research on Nervous and Mental Disorders, 45*, 8–27.

Richter, C. P. (1971). Inborn nature of the rat's 24-hour clock. *Journal of Comparative and Physiological Psychology, 75*, 1–14.

Riddle, M. A., & Carlson, J. (2001). Clinical psychopharmacology for Tourette syndrome and associated disorders. In D. J. Cohen, C. G. Goetz, & J. Jancovic (Eds), *Tourette syndrome*. Philadelphia: Lippincott Williams & Wilkins.

Ridley, A. J., Schwartz, M. A., Burridge, K., Firtel, R. A., Ginsberg, M. H., Borisy, G., et al. (2003). Cell migration: Integrating signals from front to back. *Science, 302*, 1704–1711.

Rijntjes, M., Dettmers, C., Büchel, C., Kiebel, S., Frackowiak, R. S. J., & Weiller, C. (1999). A blueprint for movement: Functional and anatomical representations in the human motor system. *Journal of Neuroscience, 19,* 8043–8048.

Ritter, R. C. (2004). Gastrointestinal mechanisms of satiation for food. *Physiology and Behavior, 81,* 249–273.

Rizzolatti, G., Fogassi, L., & Gallese, V. (2002). Motor and cognitive functions of the ventral premotor cortex. *Current Opinion in Neurobiology, 12,* 149–154.

Robinson, T. E. (1991). Persistent sensitizing effects of drugs on brain dopamine systems and behavior: Implications for addiction and relapse. In J. Barchas & S. Korenman (Eds.), *The biological basis of substance abuse and its therapy.* New York: Oxford University Press.

Robinson, T. E. (2004). Addicted rats. *Science, 305,* 951–953.

Robinson, T. E., & Berridge, K. C. (1993). The neural basis of drug craving: An incentive-sensitization theory of addiction. *Brain Research Reviews, 18,* 247–291.

Robinson, T. E., & Justice, J. B. (Eds.). (1991). *Microdialysis in the neurosciences, Vol. 7, Techniques in the neural and behavioral sciences.* Amsterdam: Elsevier.

Rockstroh, B., Clementz, B. A., Pantev, C., Blumenfeld, L. D., Sterr, A., & Elbert, T. (1998). Failure of dominant left-hemispheric activation to right-ear stimulation in schizophrenia. *Neuroreport, 9,* 3819–3822.

Rockstroh, B., Kissler, J., Mohr, B., Eulitz, C., Lommen, U., Wienbruch, C., et al. (2001). Altered hemispheric asymmetry of auditory magnetic fields to tones and syllables in schizophrenia. *Biological Psychiatry, 49,* 694–703.

Rodgers, R. J., Halford, J. C. G., Nunes de Souza, R. L., Canto de Souza, A. L., Piper, D. C., Arch, J. R. S., et al. (2001). SB-334867, a selective orexin-1 receptor antagonist, enhances behavioural satiety and blocks the hyperphagic effect of orexin-A in rats. *European Journal of Neuroscience, 13,* 1444–1452.

Rodier, P. M. (2000, February). The early origins of autism. *Scientific American, 284,* 56–63.

Rodin, J. (1985). Insulin levels, hunger, and food intake: An example of feedback loops in body weight regulation. *Health Psychology, 4,* 1–24.

Rodriguez-Manzo, G., Pellicer, F., Larsson, K., & Fernández-Guasti, A. (2000). Stimulation of the medial preoptic area facilitates sexual behavior but does not reverse sexual satiation. *Behavioral Neuroscience, 114,* 553–560.

Roe, A. W., Pallas, S. L., Hahm, J-O., & Sur, M. (1990). A map of visual space induced in primary auditory cortex. *Science, 250,* 818–820.

Rogers, P. J., & Blundell, J. E. (1980). Investigation of food selection and meal parameters during the development of dietary induced obesity. *Appetite, 1,* 85–88.

Rogers, R. D., & Robbins, T. W. (2001). Investigating the neurocognitive deficits associated with chronic drug misuse. *Current Opinion in Neurobiology, 11,* 250–257.

Roland, P., Svensson, G., Lindeberg, T., Risch, T., Baumann, P., Dehmel, A., et al. (2001). A database generator for human brain imaging. *Trends in Neurosciences, 24,* 562–564.

Rolls, B. J. (1986). Sensory-specific satiety. *Nutrition Reviews, 44,* 93–101.

Rolls, B. J. (1990). The role of sensory-specific satiety in food intake and food selection. In E. D. Capaldi & T. L. Powley (Eds.), *Taste, experience, and feeding* (pp. 28–42). Washington, DC: American Psychological Association.

Rolls, B. J., Rolls, E. T., Rowe, E. A., & Sweeney, K. (1981). Sensory specific satiety in man. *Physiology & Behavior, 27,* 137–142.

Rolls, E. T. (1981). Central nervous mechanisms related to feeding and appetite. *British Medical Bulletin, 37,* 131–134.

Rolls, E. T., Robertson, R. G., & Georges-François, P. (1995). The representation of space in the primate hippocampus. *Society for Neuroscience Abstracts, 21,* 1492.

Romanski, L. M., & LeDoux, J. E. (1992). Equipotentiality of thalamocortico-amygdala projections as auditory conditioned stimulus pathways. *Journal of Neuroscience, 12,* 4501–4509.

Rosa, M. G. P., Tweedale, R., & Elston, G. N. (2000). Visual responses of neurons in the middle temporal area of New World monkeys after lesions of striate cortex. *Journal of Neuroscience, 20,* 5552–5563.

Rosenthal, D., Wender, P. H., Kety, S. S., Welner, J., & Schulsinger, F. (1980). The adopted-away offspring of schizophrenics. *American Journal of Psychiatry, 128,* 87–91.

Roser, M., & Gazzaniga, M. S. (2004). Automatic brains—interpretive minds. *Current Directions in Psychological Science, 13,* 56–59.

Rossi, F., & Cattaneo, E. (2002). Neural stem cell therapy for neurological diseases: Dreams and reality. *Nature Reviews Neuroscience, 3,* 401–409.

Rossignol, S. (2000). Locomotion and its recovery after spinal injury. *Current Opinion in Neurobiology, 10,* 708–716.

Rossion, B., Schiltz, C., Robaye, L., Pirenne, D., & Crommelinck, M. (2001). How does the brain discriminate familiar and unfamiliar faces? A PET study of face categorical perception. *Journal of Cognitive Neuroscience, 13,* 1019–1034.

Rothwell, J. C., Traub, M. M., Day, B. L., Obeso, J. A., Thomas, P. K., & Marsden, C. D. (1982). Manual motor performance in a deafferented man. *Brain, 105,* 515–542.

Rothwell, N. J., & Stock, M. J. (1982). Energy expenditure derived from measurements of oxygen consumption and energy balance in hyperphagic, "cafeteria"-fed rats. *Journal of Physiology, 324,* 59–60.

Rourke, B. P., Ahmad, S. A., Collins, D. W., Hayman-Abello, B. A., Hayman-Abello, S. E., & Warriner, E. M. (2002). Child clinical/pediatric neuropsychology: Some recent advances. *Annual Review of Psychology, 53,* 309–339.

Rowe, J. B., Toni, I., Josephs, O., Frackowiak, R. S., & Pasingham, R. E. (2000). The prefrontal cortex: Response selection or maintenance within working memory? *Science, 288,* 1656–1660.

Rowland, N. (1981). Glucoregulatory feeding in cats. *Physiology & Behavior, 26,* 901–903.

Rowland, N. E. (1990). Sodium appetite. In E. D. Capaldi & T. L. Powley (Eds.), *Taste, experience, and feeding* (pp. 94–104). Washington, DC: American Psychological Association.

Rozin, P., Dow, S., Moscovitch, M., & Rajaram, S. (1998). What causes humans to begin and end a meal? A role for memory for what has been eaten, as evidenced by a study of multiple meal eating in amnesic patients. *Psychological Science, 9,* 392–396.

Rozin, P. N., & Schulkin, J. (1990). Food selection. In E. M. Stricker (Ed.), *Handbook of behavioral neurobiology* (pp. 297–328). New York: Plenum Press.

Rudy, J. W., & Sutherland, R. J. (1992). Configural and elemental associations and the memory coherence problem. *Journal of Cognitive Neuroscience, 4,* 208–216.

Rushworth, M. F., Johansen-Berg, H., Gobel, S. M., & Devlin, J. T. (2003). The left parietal and premotor cortices: Motor attention and selection. *Neuroimage, 20,* 89–100.

Rushworth, M. F. S. (2000). Anatomical and functional subdivision within the primate lateral prefrontal cortex. *Psychobiology, 28,* 187–196.

Russell, J. A., Bachorowski, J.-A., & Fernandez-Dols, J.-M. (2003). Facial and vocal expressions of emotion. *Annual Review of Psychology, 54,* 329–349.

Russell, W. R., & Espir, M. I. E. (1961). *Traumatic aphasia—a study of aphasia in war wounds of the brain.* London: Oxford University Press.

Rutledge, L. L., & Hupka, R. B. (1985). The facial feedback hypothesis: Methodological concerns and new supporting evidence. *Motivation and Emotion, 9,* 219–240.

Rutter, M. L. (1997). Nature-nurture integration: The example of antisocial behavior. *American Psychologist, 52,* 390–398.

Rutter, M., & Silberg, J. (2002). Gene-environment interplay in relation to emotional and behavioral disturbance. *Annual Review of Psychology, 53,* 463–490.

Rymer, R. (1993). *Genie.* New York: HarperCollins

Sack, R. L., & Lewy, A. J. (2001). Circadian rhythm sleep disorders: Lessons from the blind. *Sleep Medicine Reviews, 5,* 189–206.

Sacks, O. (1985). *The man who mistook his wife for a hat and other clinical tales.* New York: Summit Books.

Saffran, E. M. (1997). Aphasia: Cognitive neuropsychological aspects. In T. E. Feinberg & M. J. Farah (Eds.), *Behavioral neurology and neuropsychology* (pp. 151–166). New York: McGraw-Hill.

Sakuma, Y., & Pfaff, D. W. (1979). Mesencephalic mechanisms for the integration of female reproductive behavior in the rat. *American Journal of Physiology, 237,* 285–290.

Salamone, J. D. (2000). A critique of recent studies on placebo effects of antidepressants: Importance of research on active placebos. *Psychopharmacology, 152,* 1–6.

Salovey, P., Rothman, A. J., Detweiler, J. B., & Steward, W. T. (2000). Emotional states and physical health. *American Psychologist, 55,* 110–121.

Salzer, J. L. (2002). Nodes of Ranvier come of age. *Trends in Neurosciences, 25*(1), 2–5.

Salzet, M., Vieau, D., & Day, R. (2000). Crosstalk between nervous and immune systems through the animal kingdom: Focus on opioids. *Trends in Neuroscience, 23,* 550–555.

Sanders, D., & Bancroft, J. (1982). Hormones and the sexuality of women—the menstrual cycle. *Clinics in Endocrinology and Metabolism, 11,* 639–659.

Sanes, J. N. (2003). Neocortical mechanisms in motor learning. *Current Opinion in Neurobiology, 13,* 225–231.

Sanes, J. N., & Donoghue, J. P. (2000). Plasticity and primary motor cortex. *Annual Review of Neuroscience,* 393–415.

Sanes, J. N., Donoghue, J. P., Thangaraj, V., Edelman, R. R., & Warach, S. (1995). Shared neural substrates controlling hand movements in human motor cortex. *Science, 268,* 1775–1777.

Sanes, J. N., Suner, S., & Donoghue, J. P. (1990). Dynamic organization of primary motor cortex output to target muscles in adult rats. I. Long-term patterns of reorganization following motor or mixed peripheral nerve lesions. *Experimental Brain Research, 79,* 479–491.

Saper, C. B., Chou, T. C., & Scammell, T. E. (2001). The sleep switch: Hypothalamic control of sleep and wakefulness. *Trends in Neurosciences, 24,* 726–731.

Sapolsky, R. M. (1997). The importance of a well-groomed child. *Science, 277,* 1620–1622.

Savic, I. (2002). Imaging of brain activation by odorants in humans. *Current Opinion in Neurobiology, 12,* 455–461.

Savill, J., Gregory, C., & Haslett, C. (2003). Eat me or die. *Science, 302,* 1516–1517.

Sawa, A., & Snyder, S. H. (2002). Schizophrenia: Diverse approaches to a complex disease. *Science, 296,* 692–695.

Sawada, H., & Shimohama, S. (2000). Neuroprotective effects of estradiol in mesencephalic dopaminergic neurons. *Neuroscience and Biobehavioural Reviews, 24,* 143–147.

Sawle, G. V., & Myers, R. (1993) The role of positron emission tomography in the assessment of human neurotransplantation. *Trends in Neurosciences, 16,* 172–176.

Saxena, A. (2003). Issues in newborn screening. *Genetic Testing, 7,* 131–134.

Sbragia, G. (1992). Leonardo da Vinci and ultrashort sleep. In C. Stampi (Ed.), *Why we nap: Evolution, chronobiology, and functions of polyphasic and ultrashort sleep.* Boston: Birkhäuser.

Schärli, H., Harman, A. M., & Hogben, J. H. (1999a). Blindsight in subjects with homonymous visual field defects. *Journal of Cognitive Neuroscience, 11,* 52–66.

Schärli, H., Harman, A. M., & Hogben, J. H. (1999b). Residual vision in a subject with damaged visual cortex. *Journal of Cognitive Neuroscience, 11,* 502–510.

Schatzman, M., Worsley, A., & Fenwich, P. (1988). Correspondence during lucid dreams between dreamed and actual events. In J. Gackenbach & S. LaBerge (Eds.), *Conscious mind, sleeping brain* (pp. 67–103). New York: Plenum.

Scheiber, M. H. (1999). Somatotopic gradients in the distributed organization of the human primary motor cortex hand area: Evidence from small infarcts. *Experimental Brain Research, 128,* 139–148.

Scheiber, M. H., & Poliakov, A. V. (1998). Partial inactivation of the primary motor cortex hand area: Effects on individuated finger movements. *Journal of Neuroscience, 18,* 9038–9054.

Scheffele, P. (2003). Cell–cell signaling during synapse formation in the CNS. *Annual Review of Neuroscience, 26,* 485–508.

Schelling, T. C. (1992). Addictive drugs: The cigarette experience. *Science, 255,* 430–433.

Schenck, C. H., Bundlie, S. R., Ettinger, M. G., & Mahowald, M. W. (1986). Chronic behavioral disorders of human REM sleep: A new category of parasomnia. *Sleep, 9,* 293–308.

Schenk, D. (2002). Amyloid-β immunotherapy for Alzheimer's disease: The end of the beginning. *Nature Reviews Neuroscience, 3,* 824–828.

Schettino, L. F., & Otto, T. (2001). Patterns of expression in the amygdala and ventral perirhinal cortex induced by training in an olfactory fear conditioning paradigm. *Behavioral Neuroscience, 115,* 1257–1272.

Schieber, M. H., & Hibbard, L. S. (1993). How somatotopic is the motor cortex hand area? *Science, 261,* 489–492.

Schiffman, S. S., & Erickson, R. P. (1980). The issue of primary tastes versus a taste continuum. *Neuroscience and Biobehavioural Reviews, 4,* 109–117.

Schlag, J., & Schlag-Rey, M. (2002). Through the eye, slowly: Delays and localization errors in the visual system. *Nature Reviews Neuroscience, 3,* 191–200.

Schlaug, G., Jäncke, L., Huang, Y., & Steinmetz, H. (1995). *In vivo* evidence of structural brain asymmetry in musicians. *Science, 267,* 699–701.

Schreiner, C. E. (1992). Functional organization of the auditory cortex: Maps and mechanisms. *Current Opinion in Neurobiology, 2,* 516–521.

Schreiner, C. E., Read, H. L., & Sutter, M. L. (2000). Modular organization of frequency integration in primary auditory cortex. *Annual Review of Neuroscience, 23,* 501–529.

Schultz, W. (1997). Dopamine neurons and their role in reward mechanisms. *Current Opinion in Neurobiology, 7,* 191–197.

Schultz, W., Tremblay, L., & Hollerman, J. R. (2003). Changes in behavior-related neuronal activity in the striatum during learning. *Trends in Neurosciences, 26,* 321–328.

Schwartz, G. J., & Azzara, A.V. (2004). Sensory neurobiological analysis of neuropeptide modulation of meal size. *Physiology and Behavior, 82,* 81–87.

Schwartz, M. W. (2000). Staying slim with insulin in mind. *Science, 289,* 2066–2067.

Schwartz, M. W., Peskind, E., Raskind, M., Nicolson, M., Moore, J., Morawiecki, A., et al. (1996a). Cerebrospinal fluid leptin levels: Relationship to plasma levels and to adiposity in humans. *Nature Medicine, 2,* 589–593.

Schwartz, M. W., Seeley, R. J., Campfield, L. A., Burn, P., & Baskin, D. G. (1996b). Identification of hypothalamic targets of leptin action. *Journal of Clinical Investigation, 98,* 1101–1106.

Sclafani, A. (1990). Nutritionally based flavor preferences in rats. In E. D. Capaldi & T. L. Powley (Eds.), *Taste, experience, and feeding* (pp. 139–156). Washington, DC: American Psychological Association.

Scoville, W. B., & Milner, B. (1957). Loss of recent memory after bilateral hippocampal lesions. *Journal of Neurology, Neurosurgery and Psychiatry, 20,* 11–21.

Seaberg, R. M., & van der Kooy, D. (2003). Stem and progenitor cells: The premature desertion of rigorous definitions. *Trends in Neurosciences, 26,* 125–131.

Searle, J. R. (2000). Consciousness. *Annual Review of Neuroscience, 23,* 557–578.

Searle, L. V. (1949). The organization of hereditary maze-brightness and maze-dullness. *Genetic Psychology Monographs, 39,* 279–325.

Seeley, R. J., & Schwartz, M. W. (1997). The regulation of energy balance: Peripheral hormonal signals and hypothalamic neuropeptides. *Current Directions in Psychological Science, 6,* 39–44.

Seeley, R. J., van Dijk, G., Campfield, L. A., Smith, F. J., Nelligan, J. A., Bell, S. M., et al. (1996). The effect of intraventricular administration of leptin (Ob protein) on food intake and body weight in the rat. *Hormone and Metabolic Research, 28,* 664–668.

Segal, M. (2001). Rapid plasticity of dendritic spine: Hints to possible functions? *Progress in Neurobiology, 63,* 61–70.

Segerstrom, S. C., & Miller, G. E. (2004). Psychological stress and the human immune system: A meta-analytic study of 30 years of inquiry. *Psychological Bulletin, 130,* 601–630.

Seitz, R. J., Roland, P. E., Bohm, C., Greitz, T., & Stone-Elanders, S. (1990). Motor learning in man: A positron emission tomographic study. *NeuroReport, 1,* 17–20.

Selkoe, D. J. (1991, November). Amyloid protein and Alzheimer's. *Scientific American, 265,* 68–78.

Selkoe, D. J. (2002). Alzheimer's disease is a synaptic failure. *Science, 298,* 789–791.

Semple, M. N., & Scott, B. H. (2003). Cortical mechanisms in hearing. *Current Opinion in Neurobiology, 13,* 167–173.

Sener, R. N. (2003). Phenylketonuria: Diffusion magnetic resonance imaging and proton magnetic resonance spectroscopy. *Computer Assisted Tomography, 27,* 541–543.

Serfaty, M., Kennell-Webb, S., Warner, J., Blizard, R., & Raven, P. (2002). Double blind randomized placebo controlled trial of low dose melatonin for sleep disorders in dementia. *International Journal of Geriatric Psychiatry, 17,* 1120–1127.

Serizawa, S, Miyamichi, K., Nakatani, H., Suzuki, M., Saito, M., Yoshihara, Y., & Sakano, H. (2003). Negative feedback regulation ensures the one receptor—one olfactory neuron rule in mouse. *Science, 302,* 2088–2094.

Servos, P., Engel, S. A., Gati, J., & Menon, R. (1999). fMRI evidence for an inverted face representation in human somatosensory cortex. *Neuroreport, 1007,* 1393–1395.

Sewards, T. V., & Sewards, M. A. (2001). Cortical association areas in the gustatory system. *Neuroscience and Biobehavioural Reviews, 25,* 395–407.

Shapely, R., & Hawken, M. (2002). Neural mechanisms for color perception in the primary visual cortex. *Current Opinion in Neurobiology, 12,* 426–432.

Shapiro, B. H., Levine, D. C., & Adler, N. T. (1980). The testicular feminized rat: A naturally occurring model of androgen independent brain masculinization. *Science, 209,* 418–420.

Shapleske, J., Rossell, S. L., Simmons, A., David, A. S., & Woodruff, P. W. R. (2001). Are auditory hallucinations the consequence of abnormal cerebral lateralization? A morphometric MRI study of the sylvian fissure and planum temporale. *Biological Psychiatry, 49,* 685–693.

Shaw, P. J., Cirelli, C., Greenspan, R. J., & Tononi, G. (2000). Correlates of sleep and waking in *Drosophila melanogaster. Science, 287,* 1834–1837.

Shaywitz, S. E. (1996, November). Dyslexia. *Scientific American, 275,* 98–104.

Sheng, M., & Kim, M. J. (2002). Postsynaptic signaling and plasticity mechanisms. *Science, 298,* 776–780.

Shepherd, G. M., & Erulkar, S. D. (1997). Centenary of the synapse: From Sherrington to the molecular biology of the synapse and beyond. *Trends in Neurosciences, 20,* 385–392.

Sheppard, D. M., Bradshaw, J. L., Purcell, R., & Pantelis, C. (1999), Tourette's and comorbid syndromes: Obsessive compulsive and attention deficit hyperactivity disorder. A common etiology? *Clinical Psychology Review, 19,* 531–552.

Sherry, D. F., & Vaccarino, A. L. (1989). Hippocampus and memory for food caches in black-capped chickadees. *Behavioral Neuroscience, 103,* 308–318.

Sherwin, B. B. (1985). Changes in sexual behavior as a function of plasma sex steroid levels in post-menopausal women. *Maturitas, 7,* 225–233.

Sherwin, B. B. (1988). A comparative analysis of the role of androgen in human male and female sexual behavior: Behavioral specificity, critical thresholds, and sensitivity. *Psychobiology, 16,* 416–425.

Sherwin, B. B. (2003). Estrogen and cognitive functioning in women. *Endocrine Reviews, 24,* 133–151.

Sherwin, B. B., Gelfand, M. M., & Brender, W. (1985). Androgen enhances sexual motivation in females: A prospective cross-over study of sex steroid administration in the surgical menopause. *Psychosomatic Medicine, 47,* 339–351.

Sheth, B. R., Sharma, J., Chenchal Rao, S., & Sur, M. (1996). Orientation maps of subjective contours in visual cortex. *Science, 274,* 2110–2115.

Shimura, T., & Shimokochi, M. (1990). Involvement of the lateral mesencephalic tegmentum in copulatory behavior of male rats: Neuron activity in freely moving animals. *Neuroscience Research, 9,* 173–183.

Shin, J. C., & Ivry, R. B. (2003). Spatial and temporal sequence learning in patients with Parkinson's disease or cerebellar lesions. *Journal of Cognitive Neuroscience, 15,* 1232–1243.

Shouse, M. N., King, A., Langer, J., Vreeken, T., King, K., & Richkind, M. (1990). The ontogeny of feline temporal lobe epilepsy: Kindling a spontaneous seizure disorder in kittens. *Brain Research, 525,* 215–224.

Siegel, J. M. (1983). A behavioral approach to the analysis of reticular formation unit activity. In T. E. Robinson (Ed.), *Behavioral approaches to brain research* (pp. 94–116). New York: Oxford University Press.

Siegel, J. M. (2000, January). Narcolepsy. *Scientific American, 282,* 77–81.

Siegel, J. M. (2001). The REM sleep-memory consolidation hypothesis. *Science, 294,* 1058–1063.

Siegel, S. (2004). Intra-administration associations and withdrawal symptoms: Morphine-elicited morphine withdrawal. *Experimental and Clinical Psychopharmacology, 10,* 162–183.

Siegel, S., Hinson, R. E., Krank, M. D., & McCully, J. (1982). Heroin "overdose" death: Contribution of drug-associated environmental cues. *Science, 216,* 436–437.

Silberberg, G., Gupta, A., & Markram, H. (2002). Stereotypy in neocortical microcircuits. *Trends in Neurosciences, 25*(5), 227–230.

Silk, J. B., Alberts, S. C., & Altmann, J. (2003). Social bonds of female baboons enhance infant survival. *Science, 302,* 1231–1233.

Simerly, R. B. (2002). Wired for reproduction: Organization and development of sexually dimorphic circuits in the mammalian forebrain. *Annual Review of Neuroscience, 25,* 507–536.

Sinclair, S. V., & Mistlberger, R. E. (1997). Scheduled activity reorganizes circadian phase of Syrian hamsters under full and skeleton photoperiods. *Behavioural Brain Research, 87,* 127–137.

Singer, J. (1968). Hypothalamic control of male and female sexual behavior. *Journal of Comparative and Physiological Psychology, 66,* 738–742.

Singer, L. T., Arendt, R., Minnes, S., Farkas, K., Salvator, A., Kirchner, K. L., & Kliegman, R. (2002). Cognitive and motor outcomes of cocaine-exposed infants. *Journal of the American Medical Association, 287,* 1952–1960.

Sirigu, A., & Duhamel, J. R. (2001). Motor and visual imagery as two complementary but neurally dissociable mental processes. *Journal of Cognitive Neuroscience, 13,* 910–919.

Sladek, J. R., Jr., Redmond, D. E., Jr., Collier, T. J., Haber, S. N., Elsworth, J. D., Deutch, A.Y., & Roth, R. H. (1987). Transplantation of fetal dopamine neurons in primate brain reverses MPTP induced Parkinsonism. In F. J. Seil, E. Herbert, & B. M. Carlson (Eds.), *Progress in brain research* (Vol. 71, pp. 309–323). New York: Elsevier.

Slezak, M., & Pfrieger, F. W. (2003). New roles for astrocytes: Regulation of CNS synaptogenesis. *Trends in Neurosciences, 26,* 531–535.

Sluder, G., & McCollum, D. (2000). The mad ways of meiosis. *Science, 289,* 254–255.

Small, M. F. (1992). Female choice in mating. *American Scientist, 80,* 142–151.

Smith, D. V., & Margolskee, R. F. (March, 2001). Making sense of taste. *Scientific American, 284,* 32–39.

Smith, E. E. (2000). Neural bases of human working memory. *Current Directions in Psychological Science, 9,* 45–49.

Smith, F. J., & Campfield, L. A. (1993). Meal initiation occurs after experimental induction of transient declines in blood glucose. *American Journal of Physiology, 265,* 1423–1429.

Snyder, S. H. (1978). Neuroleptic drugs and neurotransmitter receptors. *Journal of Clinical and Experimental Psychiatry, 133,* 21–31.

Sofroniew, M. V., Howe, C. L., & Mobley, W. C. (2001). Nerve growth factor signaling, neuroprotection, and neural repair. *Annual Review of Neuroscience, 24,* 1217–1281.

Soloman, S. M., & Kirby, D. F. (1990). The refeeding syndrome: A review. *Journal of Parenteral and Enteral Nutrition, 14,* 90–97.

Sommer, M. A., & Wurtz, R. H. (2002). A pathway in primate brain for internal monitoring of movements. *Science, 296,* 1480–1482.

Spanagel, R., & Weiss, F. (1999). The dopamine hypothesis of reward: Past and current status. *Trends in Neurosciences, 22,* 521–527.

Spear, L. P. (2000). Neurobehavioral changes in adolescence. *Current Directions in Psychological Science, 9,* 111–114.

Spencer, R. M. C., Zelaznik, H. N., Diedrichsen, J., & Ivry, R. B. (2003). Disrupted timing of discontinuous but not continuous movements by cerebellar lesions. *Science, 300,* 1437–1440.

Sperry, R. W. (1943). Effect of 180° rotation of the retinal field on visuomotor coordination. *Journal of Experimental Zoology, 92,* 263–279.

Sperry, R. W. (1963). Chemoaffinity in the orderly growth of nerve fiber patterns and connections. *Proceedings of the National Academy of Sciences, U.S.A., 50,* 703–710.

Sperry, R. W. (1964, January). The great cerebral commissure. *Scientific American, 210,* 42–52.

Sperry, R. W., Zaidel, E., & Zaidel, D. (1979). Self recognition and social awareness in the deconnected minor hemisphere. *Neuropsychologia, 17,* 153–166.

Spielman, A. J., Saskin, P., & Thorpy, M. J. (1987). Treatment of chronic insomnia by restriction of time in bed. *Sleep, 10,* 45–56.

Spillman, L., & Werner, J. S. (1996). Long-range interactions in visual perception. *Trends in Neurosciences, 19,* 428–434.

Spitzer, R. L., Skodol, A. E., Gibbon, M., & Williams, J. B. W. (1983). *Psychopathology: A case book.* New York: McGraw-Hill.

Squire, L. R. (1987). *Memory and brain.* New York: Oxford University Press.

Squire, L. R., Amaral, D. G., Zola-Morgan, S., Kritchevsky, M., & Press, G. (1989). Description of brain injury in the amnesic patient N.A. based on magnetic resonance imaging. *Experimental Neurology, 105,* 23–35.

Squire, L. R., Clark, R. E., & Knowlton, B. J. (2001). Retrograde amnesia. *Hippocampus, 11,* 50–55.

Squire, L. R., Slater, P. C., & Chace, P. M. (1975). Retrograde amnesia: Temporal gradient in very long term memory following electroconvulsive therapy. *Science, 187,* 77–79.

Squire, L. R., & Spanis, C. W. (1984). Long gradient of retrograde amnesia in mice: Continuity with the findings in humans. *Behavioral Neuroscience, 98,* 345–348.

Squire, L. R., & Zola-Morgan, S. (1985). The neuropsychology of memory: New links between humans and experimental animals. *Annals of the New York Academy of Sciences, 444,* 137–149.

Squire, L. R. & Zola-Morgan, S. (1991). The medial temporal lobe memory system. *Science, 253,* 1380–1386.

St. George-Hyslop, P. H. (2000, December). Piecing together Alzheimer's. *Scientific American, 283,* 76–83.

Stampi, C. (1992a). Evolution, chronobiology, and functions of polyphasic and ultrashort sleep: Main issues. In C. Stampi (Ed.), *Why we nap: Evolution, chronobiology, and functions of polyphasic and ultrashort sleep.* Boston: Birkhäuser.

Stampi, C. (Ed.). (1992b). *Why we nap: Evolution, chronobiology, and functions of polyphasic and ultrashort sleep.* Boston: Birkhäuser.

Stanford, S. C., & Salmon, P. (1993). *Stress: From synapse to syndrome.* London: Academic Press.

Stefano, G. B., Goumon, Y., Casares, F., Cadet, P., Frichione, G. L., Rialas, C., et al. (2000). Endogenous morphine. *Trends in Neurosciences, 23,* 436–442.

Stein, D. G. (2001). Brain damage, sex hormones and recovery: A new role for progesterone and estrogen? *Trends in Neurosciences, 24,* 386–391.

Stein, D. G., & Hoffman, S. W. (2003). Estrogen and progesterone as neuroprotective agents in the treatments of acute brain injuries. *Pediatric Rehabilitation, 6,* 13–22.

Steinman, L., Martin, R., Bernard, C., Conlon, P., & Oksenberg, J. R. (2002). Multiple sclerosis: Deeper understanding of its pathogenesis reveals new targets for therapy. *Annual Review of Neuroscience, 25,* 491–505.

Stepanski, E., Lamphere, J., Badia, P., Zorick, F., & Roth, T. (1984). Sleep fragmentation and daytime sleepiness. *Sleep, 7,* 18–26.

Stepanski, E., Lamphere, J., Roelus, T., Zorick, F., & Roth, T. (1987). Experimental sleep fragmentation in normal subjects. *International Journal of Neuroscience, 33,* 207–214.

Stiles, J. (1998). The effects of early focal brain injury on lateralization of cognitive function. *Current Directions in Psychological Science, 7,* 21–26.

Stone, T. W. (1996). *CNS neurotransmitters and neuromodulators. Neuroactive steroids.* Boca Raton, FL: CRC Press.

Strickland, D., & Bertoni, J. M. (2004). Parkinson's prevalence estimated by a state registry. *Movement Disorders, 19,* 318–323.

Strömland, K., Nordin, V., Miller, M., Åkerström, B., & Gillberg, C. (1994). Autism in thalidomide embryopathy: A population study. *Developmental Medicine and Child Neurology, 36,* 351–356.

Strubbe, J. H., & Van Dijk, G. (2002). The temporal organization of ingestive behaviour and its interaction with regulation of energy balance. *Neuroscience and Biobehavioural Reviews, 26,* 485–498.

Strubbe, J. H., & Steffens, A. B. (1997). Blood glucose levels in portal and peripheral circulation and their relation to food intake in the rat. *Physiology & Behavior, 19,* 303–307.

Stuss, D. T., & Levine, B. (2002). Adult clinical neuropsychology: Lessons from studies of the frontal lobes. *Annual Review of Psychology, 53,* 401–433.

Strub, R. L., & Black, F. W. (1997). The mental status exam. In T. E. Feinberg & M. J. Farah (Eds.), *Behavioral neurology and neuropsychology* (pp. 25–42). New York: McGraw-Hill.

Sutcliffe, J. G., & De Lecca, L. (2002). The hypocretins: Setting the arousal threshold. *Nature Reviews Neuroscience, 3,* 339–349.

Sullivan, E. V., & Marsh, L. (2003). Hippocampal volume deficits in alcoholic Korsakoff's syndrome. *Neurology, 61,* 1716–1719.

Sunday, S. R., & Halmi, K. A. (1990). Taste perceptions and hedonicas in eating disorders. *Physiology and Behavior, 48,* 587–594.

Suzuki, W. A., & Clayton, N. S. (2000). The hippocampus and memory: A comparative and ethological perspective. *Current Opinion in Neurobiology, 10,* 768–773.

Swaab, D. F., & Fliers, E. (1985). A sexually dimorphic nucleus in the human brain. *Science, 188,* 1112–1115.

Swaab, D. F., & Hofman, M. A. (1995). Sexual differentiation of the human hypothalamus in relation to gender and sexual orientation. *Trends in Neuroscience, 18,* 264–270.

Swaab, D. F., Zhou, J. N., Ehlhart, T., & Hofman, M. A. (1994). Development of vasoactive intestinal polypeptide neurons in the human suprachiasmatic nucleus in relation to birth and sex. *Developmental Brain Research, 79,* 249–259.

Swanson, L. W. (2000). What is the brain? *Trends in Neurosciences, 23,* 519–527.

Swanson, L. W., & Petrovich, G. D. (1998). What is the amygdala? *Trends in Neurosciences, 21,* 323–331.

Sweeney, M. E., Hill, P. A., Baney, R., & DiGirolamo, M. (1993). Severe vs. moderate energy restriction with and without exercise in the treatment of obesity: Efficiency of weight loss. *American Journal of Clinical Nutrition, 57,* 127–134.

Swerdlow, N. R., & Young, A. B. (2001). Neuropathology in Tourette syndrome: An update. In D. J. Cohen, C. G. Goetz, & J. Jankovic (Eds.), *Tourette syndrome* (pp. 151–161). Philadelphia: Lippincott Williams & Wilkins.

Swinnen, S. P. (2002). Intermanual coordination: From behavioral principles to neural-network interactions. *Nature Reviews Neuroscience, 3,* 350–361.

Syntichaki, P., & Tavernarakis, N. (2003). The biochemistry of neuronal necrosis: Rogue biology? *Nature Reviews Neuroscience, 4,* 672–684.

Szameitat, A. J., Schubert, T., Muller, K., & Von Cramon, D. Y. (2002). Localization of executive functions in dual-task performance with fMRI. *Journal of Cognitive Neuroscience, 14,* 1184–1199.

Taheri, S., Zeitzer, J. M., & Mignot, E. (2002). The role of hypocretins (orexins) in sleep regulation and narcolepsy. *Annual Review of Neuroscience, 25,* 283–313.

Takahashi, J. S. (1999). Narcolepsy genes wake up the sleep field. *Science, 285,* 2076–2077.

Tallman, J. F. (2000). Development of novel antipsychotic drugs. *Brain Research Interactive, 31,* 385–390.

Tamakoshi, A., & Ohno, Y. (2004). Self-reported sleep duration as a predictor of all-cause mortality: Results from the JACC study, Japan. *Sleep, 27,* 51–54.

Tanaka, A. (1972). A progressive change of behavioral and electroencephalographic response to daily amygdaloid stimulations in rabbits. *Fukuoka Acta Medica, 63,* 152–163.

Tanji, J., & Hoshi, E. (2001). Behavioral planning in the prefrontal cortex. *Current Opinion in Neurobiology, 11,* 164–170.

Tank, D. W., Sugimori, M., Connor, J. A., & Llinás, R. R. (1998). Spatially resolved calcium dynamics of mammalian Purkinje cells in cerebellar slice. *Science, 242,* 7733–7777.

Tassinary, L. G., & Cacioppo, J. T. (1992). Unobservable facial actions and emotion. *Psychological Science, 3,* 28–33.

Tatersall, I., & Matternes, J. H. (2000, January). Once we were not alone. *Scientific American, 282,* 56–62.

Tattersall, J. (2001, December). How we came to be human. *Scientific American, 285,* 56–63.

Taub, E. Uswatte, G., & Elbert, T. (2002). New treatments in neurorehabilitation founded on basic research. *Nature Reviews Neuroscience, 3,* 228–236.

Taub, J. M., & Berger, R. J. (1973). Performance and mood following variations in the length and timing of sleep. *Psychophysiology, 10,* 559–570.

Taylor, D. M., Tillery, S. I. H., & Schwartz, A. B. (2002). Direct cortical control of 3D neuroprosthetic devices. *Science, 296,* 1829–1832.

Taylor, J. R., Elsworth, J. D., Roth, J. R., Sladek, J. R., Jr., & Redmond, D. E., Jr. (1990). Cognitive and motor deficits in the acquisition of an object retrieval/detour task in MPTP-treated monkeys. *Brain, 113,* 617–637.

Teicher, M. H. (2002, March). Scars that won't heal: The neurobiology of child abuse. *Scientific American, 286,* 68–75.

Teicher, M. H., Andersen, S. L., Polcari, A., Anderson, C. M., Navalta, C. P., & Kim, D. M. (2003). The neurobiological consequences of early stress and childhood maltreatment. *Neuroscience and Biobehavioural Reviews, 27,* 33–44.

Teitelbaum, P. (1957). Random and food-directed activity in hyperphagic and normal rats. *Journal of Comparative and Physiological Psychology, 50,* 486–490.

Teitelbaum, P. (1961). Disturbances in feeding and drinking behavior after hypothalamic lesions. In M. R. Jones (Ed.), *Nebraska Symposium on Motivation* (pp. 39–69). Lincoln: University of Nebraska Press.

Teitelbaum, P., & Epstein, A. N. (1962). The lateral hypothalamic syndrome: Recovery of feeding and drinking after lateral hypothalamic lesions. *Psychological Review, 69,* 74–90.

Temple, S. (2001). Stem cell plasticity—building the brain of our dreams. *Nature Reviews Neuroscience, 2,* 513–520.

Tetrud, J. W., & Langston, J. W. (1989). The effect of deprenyl (Selegiline) on the natural history of Parkinson's disease. *Science, 245,* 519–522.

Teuber, H.-L. (1975). Recovery of function after brain injury in man. In *Outcomes of severe damage to the nervous system. Ciba Foundation Symposium 34.* Amsterdam: Elsevier North-Holland.

Teuber, H.-L., Battersby, W. S., & Bender, M. B. (1960). Recovery of function after brain injury in man. In *Outcome of severe damage to the nervous system. Ciba Foundation Symposium 34.* Amsterdam: Elsevier North-Holland.

Teuber, H.-L., Milner, B., & Vaughan, H. G., Jr. (1968). Persistent anterograde amnesia after stab wound of the basal brain. *Neuropsychologia, 6,* 267–282.

Thach, W. T., & Bastian, A. J. (2004). Role of the cerebellum in the control and adaptation of gait in health and disease. *Progress in Brain Research, 143,* 353–366.

Thiele, A., Henning, P., Kubischik, M., & Hoffmann, K. P. (2002). Neural mechanisms of saccadic suppression. *Science, 295,* 2460–2462.

Thoenen, H. (1995). Neurotrophins and neuronal plasticity. *Science, 270,* 593–598.

Thomson, A. D. (2000). Mechanisms of vitamin deficiency in chronic alcohol misusers and the development of the Wernicke-Korsakoff syndrome. *Alcohol and Alcoholism Supplement, 35,* 2–7.

Tinklenberg, J. R. (1974). Marijuana and human aggression. In L. L. Miller (Ed.), *Marijuana, effects on human behavior* (pp. 339–358). New York: Academic Press.

Toates, F. M. (1981). The control of ingestive behaviour by internal and external stimuli—a theoretical review. *Appetite, 2,* 35–50.

Tompkins, C. A., & Mateer, C. A. (1985). Right hemisphere appreciation of intonational and linguistic indications of affect. *Brain and Language, 24,* 185–203.

Tong, F. (2003). Primary visual cortex and visual awareness. *Nature Reviews Neuroscience, 4,* 219–229.

Tonge, D. A., & Golding, J. P. (1993). Regeneration and repair of the peripheral nervous system. *Seminars in the Neurosciences, 5,* 385–390.

Tootell, R. B. H., Dale, A. M., Sereno, M. I., & Malach, R. (1996). New images from human visual cortex. *Trends in Neurosciences, 19,* 481–489.

Torrey, E. F., & Yolken, R. H. (2002). Familial and genetic mechanisms in schizophrenia. *Brain Research Interactive, 31,* 113–117.

Townsend, J., Courchesne, E., Covington, J., Westerfield, M., Singer Harris, N., Lyden, P., et al. (1999). Spatial attention deficits in patients with acquired or developmental cerebellar abnormality. *Journal of Neuroscience, 19,* 5632–5643.

Tracy, J. L., & Robbins, R. W. (2004). Show your pride. Evidence for a discrete emotion expression. *Psychological Science, 15,* 194–197.

Tramontin, A. D., & Brenowitz, E. A. (2000). Seasonal plasticity in the adult brain. *Trends in Neurosciences, 23(6),* 251–258.

Tramontin, A. D., Hartman, V. N., & Brenowitz, E. A. (2000). Breeding conditions induce rapid and sequential growth in adult avian song control circuits: A model of seasonal plasticity in the brain. *Journal of Neuroscience, 20(2),* 854–861.

Tranel, D., & Damasio, A. R. (1985). Knowledge without awareness: An autonomic index of facial recognition by prosopagnosics. *Science, 228,* 1453–1454.

Treffert, D. A., & Wallace, G. L. (2002, June). Islands of genius. *Scientific American*, 286, 76–85.

Treit, D. (1985). Animal models for the study of anti-anxiety agents: A review. *Neuroscience and Biobehavioural Reviews*, 9, 203–222.

Treit, D. (1987). RO 15-1788, CGS 8216, picrotoxin, pentylenetetrazol: Do they antagonize anxiolytic drug effects through an anxiogenic action? *Brain Research Bulletin*, 19, 401–405.

Treit, D., Robinson, A., Rotzinger, S., & Pesold, C. (1993). Anxiolytic effects of serotonergic interventions in the shock-probe burying test and the elevated plus-maze test. *Behavioural Brain Research*, 54, 23–34.

Tresch, M. C., Saltiel, P., d'Avella, A., & Bizzi, E. (2002). Coordination and localization in spinal motor systems. *Brain Research Reviews*, 40, 66–79.

Treue, S. (2003). Visual attention: The where, what and why of saliency. *Current Opinion in Neurobiology*, 13, 428–432.

Trivers, R. L. (1972). Parental investment and sexual selection. In B. Campbell (Ed.), *Sexual selection and the descent of man* (pp. 136–179). Chicago: Aldine.

Trottier, G., Srivastava, L., & Walker, C. D. (1999). Etiology of infantile autism: A review of recent advances in genetic and neurobiological research. *Journal of Psychiatry and Neuroscience*, 24, 103–115.

Troyer, T. W., & Bottjer, S. W. (2001). Birdsong: Models and mechanisms. *Current Opinion in Neurobiology*, 11, 721–726.

True, W. R., Xian, H., Scherrer, J. F., Madden, P. A. F., Bucholz, K. K., Heath, A. C., et al. (1999). Common genetic vulnerability for nicotine and alcohol dependence in men. *Archives of General Psychiatry*, 56, 655–661.

Tryon, R. C. (1934). Individual differences. In F. A. Moss (Ed.), *Comparative psychology* (pp. 409–448). New York: Prentice-Hall.

Tsien, J. Z. (2000, April). Building a brainier mouse. *Scientific American*, 282, 62–68.

Tsodyks, M., Kenet, T., Grinvald, A., & Arieli, A. (1999). Linking spontaneous activity of single cortical neurons and the underlying functional architecture. *Science*, 286, 1943–1946.

Tulving, E. (2002). Episodic memory: From mind to brain. *Annual Review of Neuroscience*, 53, 1–25.

Turkheimer, E. (2000). Three laws of behavior genetics and what they mean. *Current Directions in Psychological Science*, 9(5), 160–164.

Turkheimer, E., Haley, A., Waldron, M., D'Onofrio, B., & Gottesman, I. (2003). Socioeconomic status modifies heritability of IQ in young children. *Psychological Science*, 14(6), 623–628.

Ulrich, R. E. (1991). Commentary: Animal rights, animal wrongs and the question of balance. *Psychological Science*, 2, 197–201.

Ungerleider, L. G., & Haxby, J. V. (1994). "What" and "where" in the human brain. *Current Opinion in Neurobiology*, 4, 157–165.

Ungerleider, L. G., & Mishkin, M. (1982). Two cortical visual systems. In D. J. Ingle, M. A. Goodale, & R. J. W. Mansfield (Eds.), *Analysis of visual behavior* (pp. 549–586). Cambridge, MA: MIT Press.

Valenstein, E. S. (1973). *Brain control*. New York: John Wiley & Sons.

Valenstein, E. S. (1980). *The psychosurgery debate: Scientific, legal, and ethical perspectives*. San Francisco: W. H. Freeman.

Valenstein, E. S. (1986). *Great and desperate cures: The rise and decline of psychosurgery and other radical treatments for mental illness*. New York: Basic Books.

Vanduffel, W., Fize, D., Peuskens, H., Denys, K., Sunaert, S., Todd, J. T., & Orban, G. A. (2002). Extracting 3D from motion: Differences in human and monkey intraparietal cortex. *Science*, 298, 413–415.

Van Essen, D. C., Anderson, C. H., & Felleman, D. J. (1992). Information processing in the primate visual system: An integrated systems perspective. *Science*, 255, 419–423.

Van Essevelt, L. E., Lehman, M. N., & Boer, G. J. (2000). The suprachiasmatic nucleus and the circadian time-keeping system revisited. *Brain Research Review*, 33, 34–77.

Van Gelder, R. N., Wee, R., Lee, J. A., & Tu, D. C. (2003). Reduced pupillary light responses in mice lacking cryptochromes. *Science*, 299, 222.

Van Goozen, S. H. M., Slabbekoorn, D., Gooren, L. J. G., Sanders, G., & Cohen-Kettenis, P. T. (2002). Organizing and activating effects of sex hormones in homosexual transsexuals. *Behavioral Neuroscience*, 116, 982–988.

VanHelder, T., & Radomski, M. W. (1989). Sleep deprivation and the effect on exercise performance. *Sports Medicine*, 7, 235–247.

Van Horn, J. D., & Gazzaniga, M. S. (2002). Databasing fMRI studies—towards a 'discovery science' of brain function. *Nature Reviews Neuroscience*, 3, 314–318.

Van Lancker, D., & Cummings, J. L. (1999). Expletives: Neurolinguistic and neurobehavioral perspectives on swearing. *Brain Research Reviews*, 31, 83–104.

Vann, S. D., & Aggleton, J. P. (2004). The mammillary bodies: Two memory systems in one? *Nature Reviews Neuroscience*, 5, 35–43.

Van Praag, H., Christie, B. R., Sejnowski, T. J., & Gage, F. H. (1999). Running enhances neurogenesis, learning, and long-term potentiation in mice. *Proceedings of the National Academy of Sciences, U.S.A.*, 19, 13427–13431.

Van Praag, H., Schinder, A. F., Christie, B. R., Toni, N., Palmer, T. D., & Gage, F. H. (2002). Functional neurogenesis in the adult hippocampus. *Nature*, 415, 1030–1034.

van Vactor, D. (1998). Adhesion and signaling in axonal fasciculation. *Current Opinion in Neurobiology*, 8, 80–86.

Vargha-Khadem, F., Gadian, D. G., Watkins, K. E., Connelly, A., van Paesschen, W., & Mishkin, M. (1997). Differential effects of early hippocampal pathology on episodic and semantic memory. *Science*, 277, 376–380.

Vekua, A., Lordkipanidze, D., Rightmire, G. P., Agusti, J., Ferring, R., Maisuradze, G., et al. (2002). A new skull of early *Homo* from Dmanisi, Georgia. *Science*, 297, 85–89.

Vermeij, G. J. (1996). Animal origins. *Science*, 274, 525–526.

Vermeire, B. A., Hamilton, C. R., & Erdmann, A. L. (1998). Right-hemisphere superiority in split-brain monkeys for learning and remembering facial discriminations. *Behavioral Neuroscience*, 112, 1048–1061.

Vertes, R. P. (1983). Brainstem control of the events of REM sleep. *Progress in Neurobiology*, 22, 241–288.

Vicario, D. S. (1991). Neural mechanisms of vocal production in songbirds. *Current Opinion in Neurobiology*, 1, 595–600.

Vicario-Abejón, C., Owens, D., McKay, R., & Segal, M. (2002). Role of neurotrophins in central synapse formation and stabilization. *Nature Reviews Neuroscience*, 3, 965–974.

Vila, M., Wu, D. C., & Przedborski, S. (2001). Engineered modeling and the secrets of Parkinson's disease. *Trends in Neurosciences*, 24, S49–S55.

Vogel, J. J., Bowers, C. A., & Vogel, D. S. (2003). Cerebral lateralization of spatial abilities: A meta-analysis. *Brain and Cognition*, 52, 197–204.

Volkow, N. D., Fowler, J. S., Wang, G. J., & Swanson, J. M. (2004). Dopamine in drug abuse and addiction: Results from imaging studies and treatment implications. *Molecular Psychiatry*, 9, 557–569.

Volkow, N. D., Wang, G. J., Fischman, M. W., Foltin, R. W., Fowler, J. S., Abumrad, N. N., et al. (1997). Relationship between subjective effects of cocaine and dopamine transporter occupancy. *Nature*, 386, 827–830.

Voogd, J., & Glickstein, M. (1998). The anatomy of the cerebellum. *Trends in Neurosciences*, 21, 370–374.

Vuilleumier, P., Schwartz, S., Clarke, K., Husain, M., & Driver, J. (2002). Testing memory for unseen visual stimuli in patients with extinction and spatial neglect. *Journal of Cognitive Neuroscience*, 14, 875–886.

Wada, J. A. (1949). A new method for the determination of the side of cerebral speech dominance. *Igaku to Seibutsugaku, 14,* 221–222.

Wada, J. A. (1990a). Erosion of kindled epileptogenesis and kindling-induced long-term seizure suppressive effect in primates. In J. A. Wada (Ed.), *Kindling 4* (pp. 382–394). New York: Plenum Press.

Wada, J. A. (Ed.). (1990b). *Kindling 4.* New York: Plenum Press.

Wada, J. A., Clarke, R., & Hamm, A. (1975). Cerebral hemispheric asymmetry in humans. *Archives of Neurology, 32,* 239–246.

Wada, J. A., & Sato, M. (1974). Generalized convulsive seizures induced by daily electrical stimulation of the amygdala in cats: Correlative electrographic and behavioral features. *Neurology, 24,* 565–574.

Wada, J. A., Sato, M., & Corcoran, M. E. (1974). Persistent seizure susceptibility and recurrent spontaneous seizures in kindled cats. *Epilepsia, 15,* 465–478.

Wagers, A. J., Sherwood, R. I., Christensen, J. L., & Weissman, I. L. (2002). Little evidence for developmental plasticity of adult hematopoietic stem cells. *Science, 297,* 2256–2267.

Wahlgren, N. G., & Ahmed, N. (2004). Neuroprotection in cerebral ischaemia: Facts and fancies—the need for new approaches. *Cerebrovascular Diseases, 17,* 153–166.

Wakayama, T., Tabar, V., Rodriguez, I., Perry, A. C. F., Studer, L., & Mombaerts, P. (2001). Differentiation of embryonic stem cell lines generated from adult somatic cells by nuclear transfer. *Science, 292,* 740–743.

Wald, G. (1964). The receptors of human color vision. *Science, 145,* 1007–1016.

Walford, R. L., & Walford, L. (1994) *The anti-aging plan.* New York: Four Walls Eight Windows.

Wall, J. T., Xu, J., & Wang, X. (2002). Human brain plasticity: An emerging view of the multiple substrates and mechanisms that cause cortical changes and related sensory dysfunctions after injuries of sensory inputs from the body. *Brain Research Review, 39,* 181–215.

Wall, T. C., Brumfield, C. G., Cliver, S. P., Hou, J., Ashworth, C. S., & Norris, M. J. (2003). Does early discharge with nurse home visits affect adequacy of newborn metabolic screening? *The Journal of Pediatrics, 143,* 213–218.

Wallace, D. C. (1997, August). Mitochondrial DNA in aging and disease. *Scientific American, 277,* 40–47.

Walmsley, B., Alvarez, F. I., & Fyffe, E. W. (1998). Diversity of structure and function at mammalian central synapses. *Trends in Neurosciences, 21,* 81–88.

Wan, H., Aggleton, J. P., & Brown, M. W. (1999). Different contributions of the hippocampus and perirhinal cortex to recognition memory. *Journal of Neuroscience, 19,* 1142–1148.

Wang, W., Meadows, L. R., den Haan, J. M. M., Sherman, N. E., Chen, Y., Blokland, E., et al. (1995). Human H-Y: A male-specific histocompatibility antigen derived from the SMCY protein. *Science, 269,* 1588–1590.

Wang, X., Wu, Y.-C., Fadok, V. A., Lee, M.-C., Gengyo-Ando, K., Cheng, L.-C., et al. (2003). Cell corpse engulfment mediated by C. elegans phosphatidylserine receptor through CED-5 and CED-12. *Science, 302,* 1563–1566.

Watson, J. B. (1930). *Behaviorism.* New York: W.W. Norton.

Wauquier, A., Ashton, D., & Melis, W. (1979). Behavioral analysis of amygdaloid kindling in beagle dogs and the effects of clonazepam, diazepam, phenobarbital, diphenylhydantoin, and flunarizine on seizure manifestation. *Experimental Neurology, 64,* 579–586.

Waxham, M. N. (1999). Neurotransmitter receptors. In M. J. Zigmond, F. E. Bloom, S. C. Landis, J. L. Roberts, & L. R. Squire (Eds.), *Fundamental neuroscience* (pp. 235–268). New York: Academic Press.

Webb, W. B. (1973). Selective and partial deprivation of sleep. In W. P. Koella & P. Levin (Eds.), *Sleep: Physiology, biochemistry, psychology; pharmacology; clinical implications* (pp. 176–204). Basel, Switzerland: Karger.

Webb, W. B., & Agnew, H. W. (1967). Sleep cycling within the twenty-four hour period. *Journal of Experimental Psychology, 74,* 167–169.

Webb, W. B., & Agnew, H. W. (1970). Sleep stage characteristics of long and short sleepers. *Science, 163,* 146–147.

Webb, W. B., & Agnew, H. W. (1974). The effects of a chronic limitation of sleep length. *Psychophysiology, 11,* 265–274.

Webb, W. B., & Agnew, H. W. (1975). The effects on subsequent sleep of an acute restriction of sleep length. *Psychophysiology, 12,* 367–370.

Wechsler-Reya, R., & Scott, M. P. (2001). The developmental biology of brain tumors. *Annual Review of Neuroscience, 24,* 385–428.

Weiller, C., & Rijntjes, M. (1999). Learning, plasticity, and recovery in the central nervous system. *Experimental Brain Research, 128,* 134–138.

Weindruch, R. (1996, January). Caloric restriction and aging. *Scientific American, 274,* 46–52.

Weindruch, R., & Walford, R. L. (1988). *The retardation of aging and disease by dietary restriction.* Springfield, IL: Charles C. Thomas.

Weindruch, R., Walford, R. L., Fligiel, S., & Guthrie, D. (1986). The retardation of aging in mice by dietary restriction: Longevity, cancer, immunity, and lifetime energy intake. *Journal of Nutrition, 116,* 641–654.

Weingarten, H. P. (1983) Conditioned cues elicit feeding in sated rats: A role for learning in meal initiation. *Science, 220,* 431–433.

Weingarten, H. P. (1984). Meal initiation controlled by learned cues: Basic behavioral properties. *Appetite, 5,* 147–158.

Weingarten, H. P. (1985). Stimulus control of eating: Implications for a two-factor theory of hunger. *Appetite, 6,* 387–401.

Weingarten, H. P. (1990). Learning, homeostasis, and the control of feeding behavior. In E. D. Capaldi & T. L. Powley (Eds.), *Taste, experience, and feeding* (pp. 14–27). Washington, DC: American Psychological Association.

Weingarten, H. P., Chang, P. K., & Jarvie, K. R. (1983). Reactivity of normal and VMH-lesion rats to quinine-adulterated foods: Negative evidence for negative finickiness. *Behavioral Neuroscience, 97,* 221–233.

Weingarten H. P., & Kulikovsky, O. T. (1989). Taste-to-postingestive consequence conditioning: Is the rise in sham feeding with repeated experience a learning phenomenon? *Physiology & Behavior, 45,* 471–476.

Weise-Kelley, L., & Siegel, S. (2001). Self-administration cues as signals: Drug self-administration and tolerance. *Journal of Experimental Psychology, 27,* 125–136.

Weiskrantz, L. (2004). Roots of blindsight. *Progress in Brain Research, 144,* 229–241.

Weiskrantz, L., Warrington, E. K., Sanders, M. D., & Marshall, J. (1974). Visual capacity in the hemianopic field following a restricted occipital ablation. *Brain, 97,* 709–728.

Weiss, F., Maldonado-Vlaar, C. S., Parsons, L. H., Kerr, T. M., Smith, D. L., & Ben-Shahar, O. (2000). Control of cocaine-seeking behavior by drug-associated stimuli in rats: Effects on recovery of extinguished operant-responding and extracellular dopamine levels in amygdala and nucleus accumbens. *Proceedings of the National Academy of Sciences U.S.A., 97,* 4321–4326.

Weissman, M.M, & Olfson, M. (1995). Depression in women: Implications for health care research. *Science, 269,* 799–801.

Weliky, M., & Katz, C. (1997). Disruption of orientation tuning in visual cortex by artificially correlated neuronal activity. *Nature, 386,* 680–685.

Wenning, A. (1999). Sensing effectors make sense. *Trends in Neurosciences, 22,* 550–555.

Wessinger, C. M., VanMeter, J., Tian, B., Van Lare, J., Pekar, J., & Rauschecker, J. P. (2001). Hierarchical organization of the human auditory cortex revealed by functional magnetic resonance imaging. *Journal of Cognitive Neuroscience, 13,* 1–7.

West, M.J., Slomianka, L., & Gunderson, H.J.G. (1991). Unbiased stereological estimation of the total number of neurons in the subdivisions of the rat hippocampus using the optical fractionator. *Anatomical Record, 231,* 482–497.

Wever, R. A. (1979). *The circadian system of man.* Seewiesen-Andechs, Germany: Max-Planck-Institut für Verhaltensphysiologie.

Wexler, E., & Palmer, T. (2002). Where, oh where, have my stem cells gone? *Trends in Neurosciences, 25,* 225–227.

Whalen, P. J. (1998). Fear, vigilance, and ambiguity: Initial neuroimaging studies of the human amygdala. *Current Directions in Psychological Science, 7,* 177–188.

Wheeler, M. E., Petersen, S. E., & Buckner, R. L. (2000). Memory's echo: Vivid remembering reactivates sensory-specific cortex. *Proceedings of the National Academy of Sciences, U.S.A., 97,* 11125–11129.

White, N. M. (1997). Mnemonic functions of the basal ganglia. *Current Opinion in Neurobiology, 7,* 164–169.

Whiten, A., & Boesch, C. (2001, January). The cultures of chimpanzees. *Scientific American, 284,* 61–67.

Wickelgren, W. A. (1968). Sparing of short-term memory in an amnesic patient: Implications for strength theory of memory. *Neuropsychologia, 6,* 31–45.

Wieskrantz, L. (2002). Prime-sight and blindsight. *Consciousness and Cognition, 11,* 568–581.

Willett, W. C. (1994). Diet and health: What should we eat? *Science, 264,* 532–537.

Willet, W. C., Skerrett, P. J., & Giovannucci, E. L. (2001). *Eat, drink, and be healthy: The Harvard Medical School guide to healthy eating.* New York: Simon & Schuster.

Willett, W. C., & Stampfer, M. J. (2003, January). Rebuild the food pyramid. *Scientific American, 288,* 65–71.

Williams, G., Cai, X. J., Elliot, J. C., & Harrold, J. A. (2004). Anabolic neuropeptides. *Physiology and Behavior, 81,* 211–222.

Williams, J., Merritt, J., Rittenhouse, C., & Hobson, J. A. (1992). Bizarreness in dreams and fantasies: Implications for the activation synthesis hypothesis. *Consciousness and Cognition, 1,* 172–185.

Williams, J. H. G., Whiten, A., Suddendorf, T., & Perret, D. I. (2001). Imitation, mirror neurons and autism. *Neuroscience and Biobehavioural Reviews, 25,* 287–295.

Williams, M. (1970). *Brain damage and the mind.* Baltimore: Penguin Books.

Williams, S. R., & Stuart, G. J. (2002). Dependence of EPSP efficacy on synapse location in neocortical pyramidal neurons. *Science, 295,* 1907–1910.

Williams, S. R., & Stuart, G. J. (2003). Role of dendritic synapse location in the control of action potential output. *Trends in Neurosciences, 26*(3), 147–154.

Willingham, D. B. (1999). The neural basis of motor-skill learning. *Current Directions in Psychological Science, 8,* 178–182.

Wilmer, J. B., Richardson, A. J., Chen, Y., & Stein, J. F. (2004). Two visual motion processing deficits in developmental dyslexia associated with different reading skills deficits. *Journal of Cognitive Neuroscience, 16,* 528–540.

Wilson, B. A. (1998). Recovery of cognitive functions following nonprogressive brain injury. *Current Opinion in Neurobiology, 8,* 281–287.

Wilson, G. T., Heffernan, K., & Black, C. M. D. (1996). Eating disorders. In E. J. Mash & R. A. Barkley (Eds.), *Child psychopathology* (pp. 541–571). New York: Guilford Press.

Wilson, M. A., & McNaughton, B. L. (1993). Dynamics of the hippocampal ensemble code for space. *Science, 261,* 1055–1058.

Wilson, R. I., & Nicoll, R. A. (2002). Endocannabinoid signaling in the brain. *Science, 296,* 678–682.

Wittstein, S. (1995, October 26). Quarry KO'd by dementia. *The Vancouver Sun,* 135.

Winocur, G., Oxbury, S., Roberts, R., Agnetti, V., & Davis, C. (1984). Amnesia in a patient with bilateral lesions to the thalamus. *Neuropsychologia, 22,* 123–143.

Winson, J. (1993). The biology and function of rapid eye movement sleep. *Current Opinion in Neurobiology, 3,* 243–248.

Wintink, A. J., Young, N. A., Davis, A. C., Gregus, A., & Kalynchuck, L. E. (2003). Kindling-induced emotional behavior in male and female rats. *Behavioral Neuroscience, 117,* 632–640.

Wirtshafter, D., & Davis, J. D. (1977). Set points, settling points, and the control of body weight. *Physiology & Behavior, 19,* 75–78.

Wise, P. M., Dubal, D. B., Wilson, M. E., Shane, W. R., Böttner, M., & Rosewell, K. L. (2001). Estradiol is a protective factor in the adult and aging brain: Understanding of mechanisms derived from *in vivo* and *in vitro* studies. *Brain Research Review, 37,* 313–319.

Wise, R. A. (2004). Dopamine, learning and motivation. *Nature Reviews Neuroscience, 5,* 483–493.

Witelson, S. F. (1991). Neural sexual mosaicism: Sexual differentiation of the human temporo-parietal region for functional asymmetry. *Psychoneuroendocrinology, 16,* 133–153.

Wolff, P. H., Michel, G. F., Ovrut, M., & Drake, C. (1990). Rate and timing precision of motor coordination in developmental dyslexia. *Developmental Psychology, 26,* 349–359.

Wolgin, D. L., & Jakubow, J. J. (2003). Tolerance to amphetamine hypophagia: A microstructural analysis of licking behavior in the rat. *Behavioral Neuroscience, 117,* 95–104.

Wolpaw, J. R., & Tennissen, A. (2001). Activity-dependent spinal cord plasticity in health and disease. *Annual Review of Neuroscience, 24,* 807–843.

Wong, A. H., Buckle, C. E., & Van Tol, H. H. (2000). Dopamine receptor and gene transfer into rat striatum using a recombinant adenoviral vector: Rotational behaviour. *Neuroscience Letters, 291,* 135–138.

Wong, A. H. C., & Van Tol, H. H. M. (2003). Schizophrenia: From phenomenology to neurobiology. *Neuroscience and Biobehavioural Reviews, 27,* 269–306.

Wong, K. (2003, January). An ancestor to call our own. *Scientific American, 288,* 54–63.

Wood, B., & Collard, M. (1999). The human genus. *Science, 284,* 65–71.

Wood, E. R., Mumby, D. G., Pinel, J. P. J., & Phillips, A. G. (1993). Impaired object recognition memory in rats following ischemia-induced damage to the hippocampus. *Behavioral Neuroscience, 107,* 51–62.

Woodruff Pak, D. S. (1993). Eyeblink classical conditioning in H.M.: Delay and trace paradigms. *Behavioral Neuroscience, 107,* 911–925.

Woods, S. C. (1991). The eating paradox: How we tolerate food. *Psychological Review, 98,* 488–505.

Woods, S. C. (2004). Lessons in the interactions of hormones and ingestive behavior. *Physiology & Behavior, 82*(1), 187–190.

Woods, S. C., Lotter, E. C., McKay, L. D., & Porte, D., Jr. (1979). Chronic intracerebroventricular infusion of insulin reduces food intake and body weight of baboons. *Nature, 282,* 503–505.

Woods, S. C., & Ramsay, D. S. (2000). Pavlovian influences over food and drug intake. *Behavioural Brain Research, 110,* 175–182.

Woods, S. C., Schwartz, M. W., Baskin, D. G., & Seeley, R. J. (2000). Food intake and the regulation of body weight. *Annual Review of Neuroscience, 51,* 255–277.

Woods, S. W., Stolar, M., Sernyak, M. J., & Charney, D. S. (2001). Consistency of atypical antipsychotic superiority to placebo in recent clinical trials. *Biological Psychiatry, 49,* 64–70.

Woods, S. C., & Strubbe, J. H. (1994). The psychology of meals. *Psychonomic Bulletin & Review, 1,* 141–155.

Woodson, J. C. (2002). Including "learned sexuality" in the organization of sexual behavior. *Neuroscience and Biobehavioural Reviews, 26,* 69–80.

Woodson, J. C., & Balleine, B. W. (2002). An assessment of factors contributing to instrumental performance for sexual reward in the rat. *The Quarterly Journal of Experimental Psychology, 55*(B), 75–88.

Woodson, J. C., Balleine, B. W., & Gorski, R. A. (2002). Sexual experience interacts with steroid exposure to shape the partner preferences of rats. *Hormones and Behavior, 42,* 148–157.

Woodson, J. C., & Gorski, R. A. (2000). Structural sex differences in the mammalian brain: Reconsidering the male/female dichotomy. In A. Matsumoto (Ed.), *Sexual differentiation of the brain* (pp. 229–255). Boca Raton, FL: CRC Press.

Wooten, G. F., Currie, L. J., Bovbjerg, V. E., Lee, J. K., & Patrie, J. (2004). Are men at greater risk for Parkinson's disease than women? *Journal of Neurology, Neurosurgery, and Psychiatry, 75,* 637–639.

Wu, L-G., & Saggau, P. (1997). Presynaptic inhibition of elicited neurotransmitter release. *Trends in Neurosciences, 20,* 204–212.

Wüst, S., Kasten, E., & Sabel, A. (2002). Blindsight after optic nerve injury indicates functionality of spared fibers. *Journal of Cognitive Neuroscience, 14,* 243–253.

Xu, D., Bureau, Y., McIntyre, D. C., Nicholson, D. W., Liston, P., Zhu, Y., et al. (1999). Attenuation of ischemia-induced cellular and behavioral deficits by X chromosome–linked inhibitor of apoptosis protein overexpression in the rat hippocampus. *Journal of Neuroscience, 19,* 5026–5033.

Yabuta, N. H., & Callaway, E. M. (1998). Functional streams and local connections of layer 4 neurons in primary visual cortex of the macaque monkey. *Journal of Neuroscience, 18(22),* 9489–9499.

Yabuta, N. H., Sawatari, A., & Callaway, E. M. (2001). Two functional channels from primary visual cortex to dorsal visual cortical areas. *Science, 292,* 297–301.

Yamaguchi, S., Isejima, H., Matsuo, T., Okura, R., Yagita, K., Kobayashi, M., & Okamura, H. (2003). Synchronization of cellular clocks in the suprachiasmatic nucleus. *Science, 302,* 1408–1412.

Yang, S. H., Liu, R., Wu, S. S., & Simpkins, J. W. (2003). The use of estrogens and related compounds in the treatment of damage from cerebral ischemia. *Annals of the New York Academy of Sciences, 1007,* 101–107.

Yesalis, C. E., & Bahrke, M. S. (1995). Anabolic-androgenic steroids: Current issues. *Sports Medicine, 19,* 326–340.

Young, E. A., Lopez, J. F., Murphy-Weinberg, V., Watson, S. J., & Akil, H. (2000). Hormonal evidence for altered responsiveness to social stress in major depression. *Neuropsychopharmacology, 23,* 411–418.

Yuste, R., & Bonhoeffer, T. (2001). Morphological changes in dendritic spines associated with long-term synaptic plasticity. *Annual Review of Neuroscience, 24,* 1071–1089.

Yuste, R., & Bonhoeffer, T. (2004). Genesis of dendritic spines: Insights from ultrastructural and imaging studies. *Nature Reviews Neuroscience, 5,* 24–34.

Yuste, R., Majewska, A., & Holthoff, K. (2000). From form to function: Calcium compartmentalization in dendritic spines. *Nature, 3(7),* 653–659.

Zahm, D. S. (2000). An integrative neuroanatomical perspective on some subcortical substrates of adaptive responding with emphasis on the nucleus accumbens. *Neuroscience and Biobehavioural Reviews, 24,* 85–105.

Zaidel, E. (1975). A technique for presenting lateralized visual input with prolonged exposure. *Vision Research, 15,* 283–289.

Zaidel, E. (1987). Language in the disconnected right hemisphere. In G. Adelman (Ed.), *Encyclopedia of neuroscience* (pp. 563–564). Cambridge, MA: Birkhäuser.

Zald, D. H. (2003). The human amygdala and the emotional evaluation of sensory stimuli. *Brain Research Reviews, 41,* 88–123.

Zangwill, O. L. (1975). Excision of Broca's area without persistent aphasia. In K. J. Zulch, O. Creutzfeldt, & G. C. Galbraith (Eds.), *Cerebral localization* (pp. 258–263). New York: Springer-Verlag.

Zeki, S. M. (1993a). *A vision of the brain.* Oxford: Blackwell Scientific.

Zeki, S. M. (1993b). The visual association cortex. *Current Opinion in Neurobiology, 3,* 155–159.

Zeman, A. (2004). Theories of visual awareness. *Progress in Brain Research, 144,* 321–329.

Zhang, L., Nair, A., Krady, K., Corpe, C., Bonneau, R. H., Simpson, I. A., & Vannucci, S. J. (2004). Estrogen stimulates microglia and brain recovery from hypoxia-ischemia in normoglycemic but not diabetic female mice. *Journal of Clinical Investigations, 113,* 85–95.

Zhang, Y., Proenca, R., Maffie, M., Barone, M., Leopold, L., & Friedman, J. M. (1994). Positional cloning of the mouse obese gene and its human homologue. *Nature, 372,* 425–432.

Zimitat, C., Kril, J., Harper, C. G., & Nixon, P. F. (1990). Progression of neurological disease in thiamin-deficient rats is enhanced by ethanol. *Alcohol, 7,* 493–501.

Zimmer, L., & Morgan, J. P. (1997). *Marijuana myths, marijuana facts: A review of the scientific evidence.* New York: Lindesmith Center.

Zivin, J. A. (2000, April). Understanding clinical trials. *Scientific American, 282,* 69–75.

Zoghbi, H. Y. (2003). Postnatal neurodevelopmental disorders: Meeting at the synapse? *Science, 302,* 826–830.

Zoghbi, H. Y., Gage, F. H., & Choi, D. W. (2000). Neurobiology of disease. *Current Opinion in Neurobiology, 10,* 655–660.

Zola-Morgan, S., Squire, L. R., & Amaral, D. G. (1986). Human amnesia and the medial temporal region: Enduring memory impairment following a bilateral lesion limited to field CA1 of the hippocampus. *Journal of Neuroscience, 6,* 2950–2967.

Zola-Morgan, S. M., Squire, L. R., Amaral, D. G., & Suzuki, W. A. (1989). Lesions of perirhinal and parahippocampal cortex that spare the amygdala and hippocampal formation produce severe memory impairment. *Journal of Neuroscience, 9,* 4355–4370.

Zola-Morgan, S., Squire, L. R., & Mishkin, M. (1982). The neuroanatomy of amnesia: Amygdala-hippocampus versus temporal stem. *Science, 218,* 1337–1339.

Zola-Morgan, S., Squire, L. R., Rempel, N. L., Clower, R. P., & Amaral, D. G. (1992). Enduring memory impairment in monkeys after ischemic damage to the hippocampus. *Journal of Neuroscience, 12,* 2582–2596.

Zucker, K. J., Bradley, S. J., Oliver, G., Blake, J., Fleming, S., & Hood, J. (1996). Psychosexual development of women with congenital adrenal hyperplasia. *Hormones and Behavior, 30,* 300–318.

Zucker, R. S., Kullman, D. M., & Bennett, M. (1999). Release of neurotransmitters. In M. J. Zigmond, F. E. Bloom, S. C. Landis, J. L. Roberts, & L. R. Squire (Eds.), *Fundamental neuroscience* (pp. 155–192). New York: Academic Press.

Zur, D., & Ullman, S. (2003). Filling-in of retinal scotomas. *Vision Research, 43,* 971–982.

Credits

Photo Credits

p. 1, © Chris Falkenstein/Photodisc Green/Getty Images. **Fig. 1.1,** © Med. Ills. SBHA/Getty Images/Stone. **Fig. 1.2,** © Bettmann/CORBIS. **Fig. 1.5,** Courtesy of Todd Handy, Department of Psychology, University of British Columbia. **p. 19,** © Seth Kuschner/Getty Images/Stone. **Fig. 2.2,** Photograph by Donna Bierschwale, Courtesy of the New Iberia Research Center. **Fig. 2.5,** © Dale and Marion Zimmerman/Animals, Animals. **Fig. 2.6, top left,** © Kevin Shafer/Peter Arnold, Inc.; **top right,** © PhotoDisc; **bottom left and center,** © Erwin & Peggy Bauer/Bruce Coleman, Inc.; **bottom right,** © A. Comoost/Peter Arnold, Inc. **Fig. 2.8,** © Ken Fisher/Getty Images/Stone. **Fig. 2.9,** © John Reader/Photo Researchers, Inc. **Fig. 2.12,** © Fastcott/Momatiuk/Getty Images/Stone. **Fig. 2.14,** © David Phillips/Photo Researchers, Inc. **Fig. 2.23,** Original photograph by Arturo Alvarez-Buylla; illustration kindly provided by *Trends in Neuroscience.* **p. 47,** © K. Wanstall/The Image Works. **p. 50,** © Stephen Wilkes/Getty Images/The Image Bank. **Fig. 3.10, left,** Courtesy of T. Chan-Ling. **Fig. 3.11,** © Ed Reschke/Peter Arnold, Inc. **Fig. 3.12,** Courtesy of Carl Ernst and Brian Christie, Department of Psychology, University of British Columbia. **Fig. 3.13,** Courtesy of Jerold J. M. Chun, M.D., Ph.D. **p. 72,** © Manfred Kage/Peter Arnold, Inc. **Fig. 3.31,** Courtesy of Miles Herkenham, Unit of Functional Neuroanatomy, N.I.M.H., Bethesda, MD. **p. 76,** © Keith Brofky/Photodisc Green/Getty Images. **Fig. 4.10, upper left,** photomicrograph from J. E. Heuser et al., *Journal of Cell Biology,* 1979, *81,* 275–300 by copyright permission of The Rockefeller University Press. **Fig. 4.13,** Courtesy of Floyd E. Bloom, M.D., The Scripps Research Institute, La Jolla, California. **p. 100,** © S. Fraser/Photo Researchers, Inc. **Fig. 5.1,** © Science Photo Library/Photo Researchers, Inc. **Fig. 5.3,** © Scott Camazine/Photo Researchers, Inc. **Fig. 5.4,** Courtesy of Bruce Foster and Robert Hare, University of British Columbia. **Fig. 5.5,** Courtesy of Neil Roberts, University of Liverpool. **Fig. 5.6,** Courtesy of Drs. Michael E. Phelps and John Mazziotta, UCLA School of Medicine. **Fig. 5.7,** Courtesy of Peter Liddle, Department of Psychiatry, University of British Columbia. **Fig. 5.11,** Alan Gevins, EEG Systems Laboratory & SAM Technology, San Francisco. **Fig. 5.18,** Courtesy of Rod Cooper, Department of Psychology, University of Calgary. **Fig. 5.19,** Courtesy of Mark Klitenick and Chris Fibiger, Department of Psychiatry, University of British Columbia. **Fig. 5.20,** Courtesy of Ningning Guo and Chris Fibiger, Department of Psychiatry, University of British Columbia. **Fig. 5.22,** PET scans courtesy of Marcus Raichle, Mallinckrodt Institute of Radiology, Washington University Medical Center. **Fig. 5.24,** Photographs by Jack Wong. **p. 128,** © Coneyl Jay/Getty Images/The Image Bank. **Fig. 6.3,** © Oscar Burriel/Science Photo Library/Photo Researchers, Inc. **Fig. 6.6,** © Science Photo Library/Photo Researchers, Inc. **Fig. 6.7,** © Ralph C. Eagle/Photo Researchers, Inc. **Fig. 6.20,** From "Brain Mechanisms of Vision" by D.H. Hubel and T.N. Wiesel. Reprinted by permission of *Scientific American,* vol. 241, p 151. ©1979 by Scientific American, Inc. **Fig. 6.21,** From "Orientation Columns in Macaque Monkey Visual Cortex Demonstrated by the 2-Deoxyglucose Autoradiographic Technique" by D. H. Hubel, T. N. Wiesel, and M. P. Stryker. Reprinted by permission from *Nature,* vol. 269, p. 329. Copyright ©1977 by Macmillan Magazines Ltd. **Fig. 6.24, left,** © M. Bruce/Index Stock Imagery. **p. 155,** © Michael Kelley/Getty Images. **Fig. 7.24, top,** © Omikron/Photo Researchers, Inc. **Fig. 7.26,** Both photographs prepared by James Enns, Department of Psychology, University of British Columbia. **p. 185,** © Peter Adams/Getty Images. **Fig. 8.9,** © Science Photo Library/Photo Researchers, Inc. **p. 211,** © Dr. Y. Nikas/PhotoTake. **Fig. 9.4,** Courtesy of Naweed I. Syed, Ph.D., Departments of Anatomy and Medical Physiology, the University of Calgary. **Fig. 9.10,** Courtesy of Carl Ernst and Brian Christie, Department of Psychology, University of British Columbia. **Fig. 9.11,** AP/Wide World Photos. **Fig. 9.13,** Courtesy of the Williams Syndrome Association, Inc. **p. 231,** © Klaus Guldbrandsen/Photo Researchers, Inc. **Fig. 10.1,** Courtesy of Kenneth Berry, Head of Neuropathology, Vancouver General Hospital. **Fig. 10.2,** © CMSP/Custom Medical Stock. **Fig. 10.3,** Courtesy of Dr. John P. J. Pinel. **Fig. 10.4,** © Volker Steger/Peter Arnold, Inc. **Fig. 10.6,** ©1996 Scott Camazine. **Fig. 10.7,** Courtesy of Kenneth E. Salyer, Director, International Craniofacial Institute. **Fig. 10.8,** © Dr. David Rosenbaum/ PhotoTake. **Fig. 10.11,** © James Stevens/Science Photo Library/Photo Researchers, Inc. **Fig. 10.12,** © Cecil Fox/Photo Researchers, Inc. **Fig. 10.21,** Courtesy of Carl Ernst and Brian Christie, Department of Psychology, University of British Columbia. **p. 260,** Photolibrary.com. **Fig. 11.6, upper left,** © Kevin R. Morris/CORBIS. **Fig. 11.19,** Both images courtesy of Tank et al., 1988. **p. 288,** © Rhydian Lewis/Getty Images/Stone. **Fig. 12.2,** photo of David © Richard Reinauer/Color-Pic, Inc. **Fig. 12.16,** The Jackson Lab, Bar Harbor, ME. **p. 314,** © Photodisc Blue/Getty Images. **Fig. 13.11,** © Gabo/Focus/Trivel/Woodfin Camp & Associates. **p. 341,** © Dana Edmunds/Getty Images/Taxi. **Fig. 14.1,** © Hank Morgan/Photo Researchers, Inc. **Fig. 14.4,** © Animals/Animals. **p. 369,** © James Darrell/Getty Images/Stone. **p. 376,** © Skjold Photographs/The Image Works. **p. 377,** © Royalty-Free/CORBIS. **p. 378,** © Jeffrey L. Rotman/CORBIS. **p. 380,** © The Cover Story/CORBIS. **p. 381,** © Mark Peterson/CORBIS. **p. 384,** Courtesy of Maggie Edwards. **p. 395,** © Robin Sachs/PhotoEdit. **p. 425,** © David Madison/CORBIS. **Fig. 17.1,** From Damasio H, Grabowski T, Frank R, Galaburda AM, Damasio AR: The return of Phineas Gage: Clues about the brain from a famous patient. *Science,* 264:1102–1105, 1994. Department of Neurology and Image Analysis Facility, University of Iowa. **Fig. 17.5,** Reprinted by permission of the Human Interaction Laboratory/Dr. Ekman and Dr. Friesen (1975). **Fig. 17.9,** Lennert Nillson/Bonnierforlagen AB. **p. 448,** © Color Day Production/Getty Images/The Image Bank. **p. 450,** © Jan Halaska/Photo Researchers, Inc. **p. 455,** © SIU School of Medicine/Bruce Coleman, Inc. **p. 459,** © Will Hart. **p. 461,** © Paul J. Sutton/CORBIS.

Illustration Credits

Figs. 1.3, 2.3, 2.4, 2.10, 2.11, 2.13, 2.15, 2.16, 2.21, 2.22, 2.24, 3.2, 3.4, 3.5, 3.7, 3.15, 3.17, 3.20, 4.2, 4.3, 4.4, 4.5, 4.6, 4.7, 4.14, 5.8, 5.9, 5.10, 5.15, 5.17, 5.24, 6.2, 6.9, 6.12, 6.13, 6.14, 6.15, 6.16, 6.17, 6.18, 6.19, 6.23, 6.24, 6.25, 7.7, 7.17, 7.18, 7.22, 8.7, 8.8, 8.15, 9.6, 10.13, 10.14, 10.19, 10.20, 11.4, 11.6, 11.7, 11.8, 11.10, 11.13, 11.14, 11.15, 11.16, 11.17, 11.18, 12.2, 12.3, 12.4, 12.5, 12.6, 12.7, 12.9, 12.13, 12.15, 13.1, 13.7, 13.10, 13.13, 14.2, 14.6, 14.8, 14.10, 14.11, 14.14, 15.1, 15.2, 15.3, 15.4, 15.5, 15.6, 15.9, 16.8, 16.12, 16.14, 16.15, 17.2, 17.3, 17.6, 17.8, 17.10, 17.12, 18.2, Schneck-DePippo Graphics.

Figs. 1.4, 1.6, 1.7, 1.8, 1.9, 2.1, 2.17, 2.18, 2.19, 2.20, 3.1, 3.3, 3.14, 3.23, 3.28, 3.29, 4.8, 4.9, 4.11, 4.12, 4.16, 4.17, 5.2, 5.13, 5.14, 5.16,

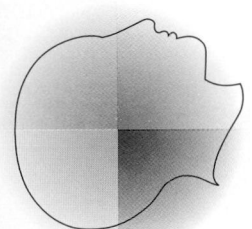

Name Index

Abi-Dargham, A., 453
Abraham, W. C., 285
Acker, W., 7
Adamec, R., 246
Adelmann, P. K., 431
Aderson, A. K., 445
Adkins-Regan, E., 337
Adler, N. T., 325
Adolphs, R., 225, 444, 445
Adrian, E., 8
Aggleton, J. P., 267, 274, 278, 444
Aglioti, S., 191
Agmo, A., 334
Agnew, H. W., 353, 355, 365
Agnew, N., 28
Ahima, R. S., 310
Ahmed, N., 235, 236
Ahmed, R., 438
Ahmed, S., 362
Airy, G. B., 130
Åkerstedt, R., 355
Albert, D. J., 435
Alberts, S. C., 25
Albright, T. D., 4, 10, 161
Alexander, M. P., 416, 418
Allen, G., 226
Allen, L. S., 335
Alleva, E., 440
Allsop, T. E., 238
Almelda, M. L. G., 362
Alonso, J-M., 146, 147
Altenmüller, E., 223
Altmann, J., 26
Alvarez, F. J., 95
Alvarez-Buylla, A., 45
Amaral, D. G., 265
Ambrose, J. B., 226
Ambrose, S. H., 28
Ames, M. A., 337
Amir, S., 375
Amlaney, C. J., 347
Anagnostaras, S. G., 375, 459
Anand, B. K., 300
Anch, A. M., 363
Andersen, R. A., 21, 188, 192
Anderson, A. K., 444
Anderson, C. H., 161
Anderson, P., 378
Anderson, R. H., 335
Andreasen, N. C., 450
Angelergues, R., 414, 415
Antoniadis, E. A., 443
Antonini, A., 222
Antshel, K. M., 44
Apkarian, A. V., 176

Appel, S. H., 241
Appenzeller, T., 272
Arand, D. L., 352
Araújo, S. J., 216
Arbit, J., 262
Archelos, J. J., 242
Archer, J., 435
Arguin, M., 165
Arieli, A., 144
Arimura, A., 320
Arnold, A. P., 325
Arvanitogiannis, A., 375
Aserinsky, E., 343
Ashton, D., 246
Assad, J. A., 188
Assanand, S., 292, 294, 303
Attenburrow, M. E. J., 362
Auger, A. P., 325
Auld, V. J., 214
Autti-Rämö, I., 378
Avila, M. T., 10
Avishai-Eliner, S., 440
Ax, A. F., 430
Axelrod, J., 8
Ayas, N. T., 367
Azcoitia, I., 441
Azzara, A. V., 302

Bachorowski, J.-A., 431
Baddeley, A., 264
Baluke, M. S., 332, 333
Bailey, C. J., 300
Dailey, J. M., 337
Bakker, R. J., 295
Bakker, J., 325
Ball, G. F., 44, 45, 324
Balleine, B. W., 334
Balthazart, J., 177, 324
Banchereau, J., 437
Bancroft, J., 332
Bandler, R., 442
Bankiewicz, K. S., 255
Barash, S., 188
Bard, P., 427, 428
Barfield, R. J., 336
Bar-Gad, I., 195
Barnes, B. A., 218
Barnett, S. C., 254
Baron, J. C., 277
Baron-Cohen, S., 444
Barres, B. A., 248
Barstow, K. L., 94
Bartholmeo, P., 190
Barton, J. J. S., 160
Basbaum, A. I., 117, 177, 373
Bashir, Z. I., 284
Baskett, J. J., 362

Bastian, A. J., 195
Battersby, W. S., 160
Baum, M. J., 337
Baura, G., 310
Bavelier, D., 419, 420
Baxter, M. G., 268, 444
Baynes, K., 405
Beal, M. F., 247
Beaumont, M., 362
Bechara, A., 279
Beck, B., 302
Becker, L., 30
Beeman, M. J., 405, 407
Behar, T., 91
Behl, C., 254
Behrmann, M., 165, 191
Belin, D., 390
Belknap, J. K., 117
Bellugi, U., 227, 228, 229, 410
Ben-Ari, Y., 285
Bender, M. B., 160
Ben-Eliyahu, S., 440
Benes, F. M., 453
Benington, J. H., 353
Benjamin, L. T., Jr., 8
Bennet, M. V. L., 92
Bennett, E. L., 44
Bennett, M., 87
Benson, D. F., 418
Benson, D. I., 218
Benton, A. L., 9
Berchtold, N. C., 224
Berger, R. J., 343, 351
Bergman, T. J., 25
Bergmann, B. M., 353
Berkovic, S. F., 236
Bernhardt, P. C., 434
Bernstein, I. L., 124, 311
Bernstein, L. J., 158
Berretta, S., 453
Berridge, K. C., 294, 381, 386, 389, 391
Berridge, V., 381
Berry, A., 440
Berry, K., 233
Berson, D. M., 360
Bertelsen, A., 450
Berthoud, H.-R., 302, 305
Bertini, M., 352, 355
Bertoni, J. M., 241
Best, P. J., 277
Bezard, E., 241
Bi, G.-Q., 282
Bielavska, E., 295
Bierschwale, D., 22

Binger, T., 177
Binks, P. G., 353
Bisagno, V., 334
Bischoff-Grethe, A., 419
Bishop, D. V. M., 227
Björklund, A., 255
Black, C. M. D., 311
Black, F. W., 118
Blackburn, G. L., 312
Blackeslee, S., 226
Blackmore, S., 346
Blakely, R. D., 94
Blakeslee, S., 257, 258
Blanchard, D. C., 123, 433, 434, 436, 460
Blanchard, R. J., 123, 433, 434, 460
Blaser, M. J., 437
Blass, E. M., 178
Blaustein, J. D., 336
Blessing, W. W., 52
Bliss, T. V. P., 281, 285
Bloch, G. J., 326, 335
Block, R. I., 379
Bloom, F. E., 93, 371
Blundell, J. E., 297, 302, 303, 308, 310

Boag, P. T., 44
Boccia, M. L., 21
Boehning, D., 93
Boer, G. J., 359
Boesch, C., 34
Bogen, G. M., 401, 414
Bogen, J. G., 401, 414
Bolles, R. C., 294
Bonanno, G. A., 450
Bonhoeffer, T., 218, 285
Bonnel, A., 226
Bonnet, M. H., 352
Bookheimer, S., 419
Booth, D. A., 294, 295, 298, 305
Borbély, A. A., 355, 361
Borszcz, G. S., 177
Bosco, G., 187
Botjer, S. W., 44
Bouchard, T. J., Jr., 46, 47, 48
Boucsein, W., 109
Bowden, G. J., 271
Bowden, J., 357
Bowers, C. A., 407
Bowers, D., 406
Bowman, E. M., 69
Bowman, R., 334
Brackett, N. L., 335
Brady, J. V., 9
Brainard, M. S., 223

Brandon, P., 299
Braun, C., 225
Brecher, E. M., 377
Brehmer, C., 385
Breitner, J. C. S., 244
Bremer, F., 356
Bremer, J., 330
Brenowitz, E. A., 45
Brewster, J. M., 382
Brittle, E. R., 87
Brivanlou, A. H., 213
Broadbent, N., 278
Brobeck, J. R., 300
Broberg, D. J., 311
Broca, P., 397, 412
Broks, P., 444
Bronson, F. H., 333
Brooke, J., 85
Brooks, M. J., 312
Brooks, V. B., 206
Brotchie, J. M., 241
Brown, E. S., 458
Brown, G. W., 455
Brown, H. D., 405
Brown, M. W., 274, 278
Brown, R. E., 4, 316, 320
Brown, V. J., 69
Brownell, K. D., 304
Brück, W., 237
Brun, V. H., 277
Brunner, D. P., 353
Bryant, R. A., 459
Bseikri, M. R., 392
Bub, D. N., 165
Bucci, T. J., 304
Büchel, C., 443
Buckle, C. E., 454
Buckley, M. J., 265
Buckner, R. L., 279
Bucy, P. C., 428
Buijs, R. M., 359
Buneo, C. A., 188
Bunin, M. A., 93
Bunsey, M. D., 271, 277
Buonomano, D. V., 251
Burke, A. C., 31
Burman, K., 187
Burt, D. R., 451
Buss, D. M., 31, 33
Bussey, T. J., 21, 278
Butters, N., 267

Cabanac, M., 294
Cabeza, R., 10, 105, 161
Cacioppo, J. T., 10, 432
Cade, J., 456
Caggiula, A. R., 388

Caillard, O., 285
Cain, D. P., 246, 283
Calder, A. J., 443, 444
Calkins, D. J., 138, 141
Callaway, E. M., 141, 151
Calles-Escandon, J., 309
Calmon, G., 104
Calne, S., 8
Cameli, L., 13
Cameron, H. A., 224
Campbell, K., 214
Campbell, L. A., 298, 299
Canli, T., 445
Cann, R., 27
Cannon, C., 392
Cannon, W. B., 301, 302, 427
Cao, Y., 254
Capaday, C., 205
Caporael, L. R., 11
Cappell, H., 373
Cardinal, R. N., 386, 443
Carlson, J., 462
Carlson, K., 182
Carlson, A., 8, 451
Carothers, A. D., 238
Carroll, D., 16, 17, 428
Carson, R. A., 11
Carter, R. J., 246
Caselli, R. J., 173
Cassell, M., 460
Cassone, V. M., 361
Cattaneo, E., 256
Caviness, V. S., 165
Cenci, M. A., 245
Cermakian, N., 360
Chabris, C. F., 407, 408
Chace, P. M., 270
Chang, K., 301
Chang, L., 254
Chang, P. K., 300
Chapin, J. K., 194
Chapman, C. D., 34
Chatterjee, S., 151
Chavez, M., 310
Chemelli, R. M., 364
Chen, W. R., 86
Cheng, D. T., 443
Cheng, J., 254
Chiarello, C., 405, 407
Chiba, A. A., 268
Chittajallu, R., 91
Cho, A. K., 381
Choi, D. W., 256
Chokron, S., 190
Choleris, E., 434
Chorover, S. L., 270
Chou, T. C., 356
Christie, B., 60, 224
Christie, B. R., 285
Christoff, K., 191
Chun, J. J. M., 61
Chun, M. M., 182
Churchland, P. C., 21
Cirulli, F., 440
Civelli, O., 452
Clark, A. S., 333
Clarke, R., 408
Claverie, J. M., 41
Clayton, N. S., 21, 124, 278
Clayton, P. J., 332

Clements, J. D., 91
Clifton, P. G., 303
Cline, H. T., 218
Cohen, A., 455
Cohen, I., 239
Cohen, P. D., 385
Cohen, S., 8
Cohen, Y. E., 169, 188
Colapinto, J., 330
Cole, J. C., 381
Colell, M., 410
Coleman, D. L., 310
Coleman, M. P., 248
Coles, M. G., 9
Collard, M., 28
Collette, F., 280
Collie, A., 244
Collier, G., 295
Collier, G. H., 294
Collingridge, G. L., 284
Collins, C. E., 173
Colman, D. R., 439
Colombo, M., 278
Colvin, M. K., 280
Coman, D. R., 218
Congleton, K. M., 387
Conklin, H. M., 450
Connolly, J. D., 192
Cook, N. J., 117
Coolidge, C., 6
Coolidge, G., 6
Cooper, R., 115
Cooper, R. M., 43
Cooper, V. S., 30
Corballis, P. M., 406
Corbetta, M., 182
Corcoran, M., 282, 380
Corcoran, M. E., 246
Corina, D. P., 410
Corkin, S., 173, 174, 261,
     262, 263, 268
Corsi, P. I., 21
Corwin, J. T., 166
Coslett, H. B., 121
Cosmides, L., 11
Cottman, C. W., 224
Courchesne, E., 225, 226
Courtney, S. M., 161, 162
Coury, A., 391
Cowan, W. M., 213, 450
Cowen, P. J., 362
Coyle, J. T., 453
Crabbe, J. C., 117
Craelius, W., 194
Craig, A. D., 170, 175, 176
Craske, M. G., 459
Creese, I., 451
Crisp, A. H., 311
Crowell, C. R., 373, 374, 375
Crowley, J. C., 222
Crunelli, V., 240
Cuesta, M. J., 450
Culbertson, F. M., 455
Culham, J. C., 188
Cummings, J. L., 461
Curran, T., 120
Curtiss, S., 212
Cycowicz, Y. M., 108

Dahl, J. E., 410
Dale, H., 8

Dalkara, T., 236
D'Almeida, V., 353
Daly, M., 25, 33
Damak, S., 179
Damasio, H., 21, 165, 415,
     416, 419, 420, 426, 427
Danforth, E., Jr., 308
Darian-Smith, C., 187
Darian-Smith, I., 187
Darlington, R. B., 31
Darlison, M. G., 88
Darnell, J. E., Jr., 38
Darwin, C., 24, 25, 34, 426,
     427, 430, 431
Datla, K., 392
Davids, E., 383
Davidson, C., 381
Davidson, J. M., 332, 335
Davidson, R. J., 431, 432
da Vinci, L., 366
Davis, J. D., 305
Davis, M., 460
Dawson, D., 362
Dawson, T. M., 241
Dawson, V. L., 241
Dax, M., 396, 397
Day, R., 439
Dean, P., 421
Debski, E. A., 218
de Castro, J. M., 293, 297
DeCatanzaro, D., 177
De Deyn, P. P., 125
De Lecea, L., 364
Delgado, J., 15
Delis, D. C., 267
Delville, Y., 436
Demas, M., 28
Dement, W. C., 345, 346,
     351, 352, 354, 363
Demet, E. M., 458
Denham, T. P., 29
DePaulo, J. R., 455
De Preux, E., 385
De Renzi, E., 165
Deroche-Gamonet, V., 390
Descartes, R., 20, 21
Desimone, R., 182
D'Esposito, M., 280
Dess, N. K., 34
Deutch, A. Y., 92
De Valois, K. K., 147,
     148, 149
De Valois, R. L., 147,
     148, 149, 150
Devane, W. A., 380
DeVry, J., 303
de Waal, F. B. M., 20
De Witte, P., 378
Dewsbury, D. A., 4, 11, 33
D'Hooge, R., 125
Diamond, A., 221
Diamond, D. M., 440

Diamond, M., 329
Diamond, M. C., 178
Di Cano, P., 387
DiCarlo, J. J., 173
Dick, D. M., 48
Dickinson, A., 21, 386
Dielenberg, R. A., 434
Dietz, V., 187, 205
DiFiglia, M., 242
Di Marzo, V., 380
Dinges, D. F., 352
Dingledine, R., 54
Dirnagl, U., 235, 238
Dixon, M. J., 165
Dobelle, W. H., 140
Döbrössy, M., 255
Dodd, J., 213
Dolan, R. J., 443, 453
DonCarlos, L. L., 441
Donoghue, J. P., 225,
     250, 251
d'Orta, R. G., 77, 95, 98,
     241, 255
Doty, R. L., 179, 180
Doupe, A. J., 4, 45
Downing, P. E., 166
Doya, K., 195
Drachman, D. A., 262
Drevets, W., 436
Drevets, W. C., 391, 458
Drew, T., 205
Drewnowski, A., 311
Driver, J., 188, 191
Drummey, A. B., 286
Dubois-Arber, E., 385
Duchaine, B., 11
Dudai, Y., 270
Dudek, B. C., 117
Duffy, S. N., 224
Duhamel, J. R., 193
Dunbar, G. C., 458
Dunbar, K., 280
Dunbar, R., 25
Dunnett, S. B., 255
Duong, T. Q., 147
Dustin, M. L., 439
Duva, C. A., 274
Dyck, R. H., 251

Eagleman, D. M., 142
Eagly, A. H., 34
Eberhardt, N. L., 308
Eccles, J., 8
Edgerton, V. R., 254
Edwards, D. A., 335
Egan, M. F., 381
Ehlers, A., 459
Ehrhardt, A. A., 328, 337
Ehringer, H., 451
Eichenbaum, H., 264, 283
Eigsti, I. M., 225
Einstein, A., 31
Eisenberg, H. M., 268
Eitan, S., 254
Ekman, P., 431, 432
Elbert, T., 225, 256
Elena, S. F., 30
Eliason, D., 440

Elibol, B., 238
Ellingsen, E., 334
Ellis, L., 337
Elmehed, K., 432
Elston, G. N., 160
Encel, N., 362
Engel, A. K., 159
Engel, S. A., 153
Enns, J., 182
Epstein, L. H., 298, 300
Epstein, R., 166
Erdmann, A. L., 410
Erickson, K., 436
Erickson, R. P., 179
Erikkson, P. S., 224
Erlanger, J., 8
Ernst, C., 60, 224
Ernst, M. L., 285
Errington, M. L., 285
Erulkar, S. D., 86
Ervin, F. R., 172
Espie, C. A., 362
Espir, M. I. E., 398
Evans, J., 280
Everitt, B. J., 268, 332, 386,
     387, 390
Eysel, U. T., 161

Fabbro, F., 195
Fabiani, M., 9
Fabri, M., 402
Falconer, E. M., 334, 440
Falkenburger, B. H., 94
Falzi, G., 408
Fanselow, M. S., 459
Farah, M. J., 165, 280, 420
Farber, N. B., 378
Farmer, J., 224
Farmer, M. E., 421
Farne, A., 192
Farooqi, I. S., 310
Farrell, S. F., 333
Farries, M. A., 196
Fawcett, A. J., 421
Fazakerley, J. K., 238
Fazio, F., 277
Feduccia, A., 31
Fee, M. S., 177
Feindel, W., 416
Feldon, J., 440
Felleman, D. J., 161
Feng, A. S., 168, 183
Fentress, J. C., 207
Fenwick, P., 346
Fernald, R. D., 130
Fernández, G., 279
Fernandez-Dols, J-M., 431
Fernández-Guasti, A., 336
Ferrara, M., 352, 355
Ferris, C. F., 436
Fiala, J. C., 285
Fibiger, C., 116
Field, P. M., 254, 334
Fields, H. L., 177, 373
Fields, R. D., 58, 218
Fillion, T. J., 178
Filbin, M. T., 249
Fink, G., 328
Finlay, B. L., 31
Finlayson, G., 308
Finn, J. T., 248
Fiorillo, C. D., 392

Fiorino, D. F., 391
Fisher, S. E., 421
Fitzpatrick, S. M., 106
Fletcher, J. M., 379
Fliers, E., 335
Floresco, S. B., 112
Fogassi, L., 192
Fölling, A., 44
Foster, R. G., 348
Foulkes, N. S., 361
Fournier, A. E., 249
Fox, N., 286
Francis, D. D., 440
Franklin, R. J. M., 242
Freedman, D. J., 31
Freedman, M. S., 359
Frerking, M., 285
Freud, S., 346, 392, 393, 412
Freund, H. J., 189
Friedman, D., 108
Friedman, J., 365
Friedman, J. M., 310
Friedman-Hill, S. R., 158
Fries, P., 159, 279
Friesen, W. V., 431
Frisén, J., 217, 224
Frith, C., 453
Frith, C. D., 188
Frith, U., 225
Fukuchi-Shimogori, T., 218
Fuller, J., 305
Funnell, M. G., 406, 407
Fuster, J. M., 188
Fyffe, F. W., 95

Gabrieli, J. D. E., 191, 268
Gaeta, H., 108
Gaffan, D., 265, 272
Gage, F. H., 223, 224, 256
Gage, P., 426, 430
Gaiarsa, J. L., 285
Galarreta, M., 92
Gale, S., 326
Galea, L. A. M., 223, 334, 440, 441
Galef, B. G., 178, 295
Gallager, R. B., 27
Gallese, V., 192
Galley, P. T., 285
Gallo, V., 91
Gallup, G. G., Jr., 21, 22
Galuske, R. A. W., 409
Gandy, S., 334
Ganis, G., 193
Gannon, P. J., 410
Gao, E., 159
Gao, G., 392
Garbers, D. L., 178
Garcia, J., 124
Gardner, R., 351, 352
Garcia-Segura, L. M., 441
Garwicz, M., 195
Gaspar, M., 383
Gasser, H., 8
Gauthier, I., 165
Gawin, F. H., 380, 386
Gazzaniga, M. S., 106, 401, 402, 403, 405, 406, 407, 409
Geary, D. C., 32
Gegenfurtner, K. R., 151

Geiselman, P. J., 299
Geng, J. J., 191
Georges-François, P., 278
Georgopoulos, A. P., 194, 206
Gerber, U., 89
Gerlach, C., 420
Gerlai, R., 124
Gernsbacher, M. A., 419
Gerra, G., 383
Geschwind, N., 408, 411, 413
Gevins, A., 108
Ghoneim, M. M., 379
Gibb, R., 223
Gibbs, J., 302
Gibson, A. D., 178
Gilbert, C. D., 251
Gilbertson, T., 179
Gillberg, M., 352, 355, 366
Gillette, M. U., 361
Gilliam, T. C., 242
Gilman, A., 8
Gingrich, J. R., 117
Giovannucci, E. L., 295
Girvin, J. P., 140
Gisquet-Verrier, P., 268
Gladue, B. A., 337
Glaser, R., 439
Glenn, M. J., 13
Glickstein, M., 195
Goddard, G. V., 246
Goedert, M., 244
Gold, M. S., 381
Gold, R. M., 301
Goldberg, J., 381
Goldberg, J. L., 248
Goldberg, J. P., 248
Goldman, S. A., 224
Goldowitz, D., 195
Goldstein, J., 328
Golgi, C., 8, 59
Gollin, E. S., 263
Gollnick, P. D., 200
Goodale, M. A., 163, 164, 192, 206, 207
Goodall, J., 26
Goodcnough, D. R., 346
Gooren, L. J., 334
Gorski, R. A., 323, 325, 334, 335, 336
Gorzalka, B. B., 6, 7
Gottesman, I. I., 308, 450
Gottlieb, D. I., 256
Gottlieb, R. A., 223
Gotz, M., 214
Gould, E., 224
Goy, R. W., 325
Grace, A., 453
Grady, K. L., 325
Graff-Radford, N., 267
Grafman, J., 280
Grakoui, A., 438
Granit, R., 8
Grant, P. R., 25
Gratton, G., 9
Gray, D., 438
Gray, J. A., 460
Graziano, M. S. A., 193
Green, S., 460

Greenamyre, J. T., 241
Greene, P. E., 255
Greengard, P., 8, 94
Greenleaf, W., 346
Greenleaf, W. J., 332
Gregory, C., 219
Grillner, S., 4, 205
Grill-Spector, K., 166
Grimson, W. E. L., 233
Groenewegen, H. J., 195
Gross, C., 459
Gross, C. E., 241
Gross, C. G., 160, 193
Grossman, E., 161
Grove, E. A., 218
Growdon, J. H., 268
Gruber, A. J., 379
Gruenberg, A. M., 450
Grumbach, M. M., 326
Grunt, J. A., 331
Gschwend, P., 385
Guan, K.-L., 217
Guerri, C., 378
Guillamón, A., 325
Guillemin, R., 8, 319, 320
Gunderson, H. J. G., 224
Guo, N., 116
Guo, Y., 216
Gupta, A., 54
Gusella, J. F., 242
Gutfreund, Y., 223
Guth, P. H., 436
Guttinger, F., 385

Haaland, K. Y., 406
Haffenden, A. M., 206, 207
Haimov, I., 362
Haist, F., 271
Halford, J. C. G., 302, 303, 310
Hallenbeck, J. M., 238
Hallett, M., 253
Halmi, K. A., 311
Hamann, S. B., 444, 445
Hamer, D. H., 337
Hamer, J. D., 352
Hamilton, C. R., 410
Hamm, A., 408
Hammer, N. J., 301
Hammond, P., 409
Hammond, P. H., 14
Hamre, K., 195
Hamzei-Sichani, F., 212
Hanashima, C., 214
Handi, T., 10
Hanson, G. R., 271
Happé, F., 225
Haqq, C. M., 322
Harada, N., 177
Harata, N., 91
Hardy, J., 245
Hari, R., 421
Harlow, J., 426
Harman, A. M., 160
Harrington, D. L., 406
Harris, G. W., 317, 318, 319, 324
Harris, K. M., 285
Harris, L. J., 295, 409
Harrison, Y., 352
Hartline, H., 8

Hartman, V. N., 45
Hartmann, D. S., 452
Hartung, H.-P., 242
Harvey, E. N., 343
Harvey, P. H., 31
Haslett, C., 219
Hastings, M. H., 360
Hastings, T. G., 241
Hata, Y., 222
Hattar, S., 360
Hatten, M. E., 214
Hauser, M., 86, 169
Hauser, M. D., 21, 221, 445, 446
Hawken, M., 152
Haxby, J. V., 163, 166, 182
Hayakawa, K., 378
Haydon, P. G., 59, 91
Heap, L. C., 12
Hebb, D. O., 4, 270, 280, 281, 282
Hécaen, H., 414, 415
Heckers, S., 453
Heffernan, K., 311
Heffner, H. E., 169, 410
Heffner, R. S., 410
Heilman, K. M., 189
Heinrichs, R. W., 450
Heisenberg, M., 4
Hejmadi, A., 431
Heller, H. C., 353
Helmer, W. J., 446
Hemmer, B., 242
Hen, R., 459
Hendersen, L. P., 333
Hendry, S. H. C., 138, 141
Henke, K., 278
Hennessey, A. C., 336
Herbert, J., 332
Herdt, G., 337
Hering, E., 150
Hering, H., 86
Herkenham, M., 74
Herman, P. C., 289
Hess, W., 8
Hestrin, S., 92
Hetherington, A. W., 299
Heuss, C., 89
Heymsfield, S. N., 310
Heywood, C. A., 160
Hibbard, L. S., 193
Hickok, G., 410
Highnote, S. M., 151
Hindges, R., 218
Hines, M., 329
Hinson, R. E., 373, 374
Hobart, G., 343
Hobson, J. A., 346, 354, 364
Hockfield, S., 221
Hodgkin, A., 8, 78, 79, 86
Hodgson, D. R., 200
Hoffman, S. W., 334
Hofman, M. A., 335
Hogben, J. H., 160
Hollenbeck, P. J., 462
Hollerman, J. R., 280
Holloway, S. D., 457
Holmberg, J., 217
Holmes, M. M., 254

Holsboer, F., 458
Holthoff, K., 86
Holzman, P. S., 10, 450
Homes, M. M., 334
Honarpour, N., 238
Honda, S., 177
Hong, L. E., 10
Hopkins, W. D., 410
Horne, J. A., 352, 353, 354, 355, 366
Hornykiewicz, O., 451
Horton, E. S., 309
Hoshi, E., 192
Howe, C. L., 254
Howe, M. L., 286
Howlett, A. C., 380
Hrabovszky, Z., 337
Hsiao, K., 247
Hsiao, S. S., 173
Hsu, Y-T., 138
Huang, E. J., 219
Hubel, D., 8
Hubel, D. H., 113, 144, 147, 148, 152, 153, 222
Hubel, D. S., 144
Huberman, A. D., 223
Hudson, J. I., 332
Hugdahl, K., 52
Huguenard, J. R., 85
Huijbregts, S. C. J., 44
Hull, E. M., 335, 336
Hulst, S. H., 44
Hulsey, M. G., 304
Hume, K. I., 355
Humphrey, K. G., 161
Huntley, G. W., 218
Hupka, R. B., 432
Hurlbert, A., 152
Hurry, M., 353
Hustvedt, B. E., 301
Hutsler, J., 409
Hutson, J. M., 337
Huttenlocher, P. R., 220, 221
Huxley, A., 8, 78, 79, 86
Hyman, S., 410
Hyman, S. E., 372, 450

Iacono, W. G., 10, 430, 450
Iadecola, C., 235
Iino, M., 91
Ikeda, H., 285
Ikemoto, S., 391
Ikonomidou, C., 378
Illert, M., 202, 205
Inantani, M., 217
Inglis, J., 398
Ingram, D. K., 245, 304
Institute of Laboratory Animal Resources, 5
Intriligator, J. M., 160
Inui, A., 302
Irwin, D. E., 137
Ishai, A., 165
Issa, N. P., 149
Iten, P. X., 385
Ivry, R. B., 195, 196
Iwamura, Y., 173
Iwaniuk, A. N., 196
Iyengar, R., 89
Izard, C. E., 431

Jackson, H., 240
Jacques, J. P., 379
Jaeger, J. J., 398
Jakel, R. J., 242
Jakubow, J. J., 373
James, L. E., 271
James, W., 427
Jameson, K. A., 151
Jamison, K. R., 455
Janardhan, V., 233
Janeway, C. A., Jr., 437
Jänke, L., 223
Jankovic, J., 461,462
Jarell, T. W., 442
Jarvie, K. R., 300
Jarvik, M. E., 384, 385
Javitt, D. C., 453
Jeannerod, M., 164, 192
Jegalian, K., 37
Jenkins, J. H., 208
Jenkins, W. M., 251
Jenner, F. A., 458
Jensen, M. D., 308
Jensen, O., 279
Jessell, T. M., 213,216
Jiang, W., 205
Johansson, C. B., 224
Johnson, B. A., 179
Johnson, K. O., 170,173
Johnson, M. H., 220, 222
Johnston, T. D., 23
Jones, E. G., 225
Jones, H. S., 355
Jones, H. W., 327
Jones, R. T., 376
Jonik, R. H., 435
Jordan, H., 228
Joseph, M. H., 392
Joseph, R., 404
Jost, A., 323
Jouvet, M., 365
Julien, R. M., 382
Justice, J. B., 115
Juusola, M., 85

Kaal, H. L., 385
Kaas, J. H., 68, 173, 251
Kaessmann, H., 39
Kagawa, Y., 304
Kaiser, J., 406
Kalant, H., 384
Kalaria, R. N., 233
Kalb, R. G., 221
Kales, A., 343
Kalil, R. E., 221
Kalivas, P. W., 392
Kallman, F. J., 450
Kalsbeek, A., 359
Kalynchuk, L. E., 123,246
Kandel, E. R., 4, 8, 10,281
Kansaku, K., 398
Kanwisher, N., 161, 166, 188
Kapur, N., 253
Karacan, I., 346
Karsch, F. J., 320
Kasai, H., 86
Kaschak, M. P., 419
Kasten, E., 160
Kastin, A. J., 320
Kastner, S., 182
Kater, S. B., 285

Katz, B., 8
Katz, D. L., 333
Katz, J. L., 436
Katz, L. C., 177, 222
Kaufman, J., 458
Kaut, K. P., 277
Kavaliers, M., 434
Kavanagh, G. L., 170
Koppitsky, K. L., 450
Kedzerski, B., 346
Kelley, W. M., 407
Kelly, J. B., 170
Keltner, D., 450
Kempermann, G., 223, 224
Kendler, K. S., 450
Kennedy, J. L., 450
Kenrick, D. T., 11
Kentridge, R. W., 160
Kerkoff, G., 190
Kerr, D. S., 285
Kerr, R. A., 30
Kessels, R. P. C., 278
Kessler, R. C., 455
Kettunen, S., 378
Keys, A., 311, 312
Keyvan-Fouladi, N., 254
Kiecolt-Glaser, J. K.,
   407,408
Kiehl, K. A., 105
Killacky, H. P., 31
Kim, C. K., 373, 374
Kim, D.-S., 147
Kim, J. J., 440
Kim, M. J., 284
Kim, S.-G., 147, 406
Kimberg, D. Y., 280
Kimble, G. A., 23
Kimura, D., 120, 397, 398,
   406, 409
Kind, P. C., 284
King, A. J., 169
Kingston, A., 10
Kiper, D. C., 151
Kirby, D. F., 312
Kitazawa, S., 398
Klawans, H. L., 77, 175,
   237,255
Klein, D. A., 311
Klein, R. M., 421
Kleinman, A., 455
Kleitman, N., 343, 345, 346,
   351,352
Klima, E. S., 410
Klitenick, M., 116
Klivington, K. A., 388
Kluver, H., 428
Knight, R. T., 279
Knowlton, B. J., 265,
   271,280
Knudsen, E. I., 169, 223
Koch, C., 156
Koechlin, E., 186
Koekkoek, S. K. E., 280
Koelling, R. A., 124
Koenig, W. G. R., 10
Kofman, O., 440
Köhling, R., 239
Kokaia, Z., 253
Kokinos, J., 381
Kolb, B., 9, 223, 443,
   444, 445
Kollias, S. S., 192

König, P., 194
Konishi, M., 169
Konradi, C., 453
Koob, G. E., 371
Koolhaas, J. M., 320
Koopmans, H. S., 301, 303
Kopelman, P. G., 289
Koppitsky, K. L., 450
Korkman, M., 378
Kornack, D. R., 224
Kornecook, T. J., 274
Korsakoff, S. S., 12, 13
Korte, S. M., 436
Kosik, K. S., 41
Kosslyn, S. M., 21, 193, 405,
   407, 408
Kotter, R., 69
Kouneiher, F., 186
Kouri, E. M., 332
Koutalos, Y., 161
Kourtzi, Z., 161
Kring, A. M., 450
Kripke, D. F., 367
Kruzich, P. J., 387
Kowatch, R. A., 363
Kozloski, J., 212
Krank, M. D., 376
Krantz, D. S., 435
Krebs, J. R., 31
Kreiman, G., 156
Kreitzman, L., 348
Kriegstein, A. R., 217
Kriegstein, J., 235
Kubat, M. A., 420
Kümmel, H., 202, 205
Kullman, D. M., 87
Kulikovsky, O. T., 296, 297
Kuczmarski, R. J., 308
Kümmel, H., 202, 205
Kurbat, M. A., 420
Kushner, H. I., 462
Kuypers, H. G. J. M., 198
Kwan, M., 332

LaBerge, S., 346
Lacaille, J. C., 54
Laeng, B., 165
LaFerla, F. M., 245
Lahn, B. T., 37
Laine, M., 422
Land, E. H., 151, 152
Lane, M. A., 304
Lang, A. E., 462
Lange, C. G., 427
Langston, J. W., 247
Lashley, K. S., 160, 161, 183
Latimer, D., 381
Laughlin, S. B., 69
Lavie, P., 349, 362, 364
Laviolette, S. R., 376
Law, I., 420
Lawrence, A. D., 443, 444
Lawrence, D. G., 198
Lawson, J. S., 398
Le, W., 241
Leckman, J. F., 461
Lederhendler, I., 23
LeDoux, J. E., 270, 442,
   443, 460
Lee, S. H., 218
Lee, T. T.-Y., 334
Lee, V. M., 245
Leech, C. K., 246

Lehman, D. R., 292, 294, 303
Lehman, M. N., 359
Lehrach, H., 242
Leibowitz, S. F., 301
Leker, R. R., 236
Lemke, G., 217
Lemon, R. N., 197
Lennoff, H. M., 228
Lennox, W. G., 240
Lenski, R. E., 30
Leon, M., 179
Lephart, E. D., 440
Leresche, N., 240
Lerman, C., 377
Leshner, A. I., 373, 386
Lester, G. L. L., 6, 7
Leung, L. S., 246
LeVay, S., 147, 222, 337
Levenson, R. W., 430
Levi-Montalcini, R., 8, 219
Levin, H. S., 268
Levine, B., 118
Levine, D. C., 325
Levine, J. A., 308
Levine, S., 324
Levinsky, W., 408
Levitt, J. B., 141
Levitt, P., 214, 450
Levy, J., 403, 406
Lewcock, J. W., 178, 179
Lewis, D. A., 450
Lewis, V., 305
Lewy, A. J., 362
Lezak, M. D., 118
Li, M. O., 219
Li, Y., 254
Libby, P., 234
Lichtman, J. W., 282
Liddle, P. F., 105
Lieberman, M. D., 10
Liepmann, H.-K., 397
Lima, A., 16
Lima, S. L., 347
Lin, L., 364
Linden, D. J., 280
Lindqvist, M., 451
Lindsay, P. H., 136
Lindsey, D. B., 357
Lindvall, O., 253, 255
Liou, J. D., 440
Lipert, J., 253
Lisman, J., 282, 283, 284
Livingston, E. H., 436
Livingstone, M. S., 144, 146,
   152, 153
Lo, E. H., 236
Lo, Y.-J., 222
Loewi, O., 8
Logothetis, N., 161, 164
Lombardino, A. J., 45
Lomber, S. G., 253
Lømo, T., 281
Loomis, A. L., 343
Lorenz, K., 8
Losick, R., 38
Lotze, M., 195
Louk Vanderschuren, J. M.
   J., 390

Löw, A., 420
Lowe, J., 428
Lowe, M. R., 294
Lowrey, P. L., 360
Lucas, F., 295
Lucas, R. J., 359, 360
Lucidi, F., 355
Ludwig, M., 94
Lui, L., 285
Luine, V., 334
Luo, M., 177
Lüscher, C., 285
Lykken, D. T., 430
Lynch, M. A., 282

Ma, J., 246
Macaluso, E., 188
Machado, M. G., 226
Maccaferri, G., 54
Maccari, S., 440
MacLusky, N. J., 332
Maeder, T., 465
Magoun, H. W., 357
Maguire, E. A., 278
Majewska, A., 86
Malenka, R. C., 281,
   372, 391
Mallissen, B., 438
Malsbury, C. W., 335
Mana, M. J., 125, 373, 374
Mancall, E. L., 429
Mangels, J. A., 280
Manson, J. E., 304
Mao, H., 271
Maquet, P., 354
Maragos, W. F., 242
Maratsos, M., 398
Maren, S., 441, 443
Margolskee, R. F., 179
Maries, E., 245
Martin, O., 214
Mark, V. H., 172
Markowitz, J. C., 457
Markram, H., 54
Markus, A., 217
Marlowe, W. B., 429
Marois, R., 182
Marsh, L., 267
Martin, A., 420
Martin, J. B., 242, 352
Martin, R. C., 398, 419
Martin, R. J., 304
Martin, R. L., 332
Martinez, L. M., 147
Martin-Soelch, C., 386
Maruff, P., 244
Masland, R. H., 132
Masoro, E. J., 304
Masterton, R. B., 168, 169
Mateer, C. A., 406
Matheny, L., 398
Matherne, C. M., 333
Matsuda, L. A., 380

Matsunami, H., 180
Matternes, J. H., 27
Matthyse, S., 450
Mattson, M. P., 304
Matzinger, P., 437
Mauch, D. H., 218
Mayr, E., 25
Maywood, E. S., 360
Mazziotta, J., 104
Mazzocchi, F., 416
McArthur, A. J., 361
McCandliss, B. D., 421
McCann, T. S., 26
McCardle, K., 381
McCarthy, M. M., 325
McCaughran, J. A., Jr., 380
McCeney, M. K., 435
McClintock, M. K., 337
McCollum, D., 35
McCormick, D. A., 83
McCrory, P. R., 236
McDonald, J. W., 256
McDonald, R. J., 196, 277, 443
McEwen, B., 436
McEwen, B. S., 325, 334, 440, 458
McGaugh, J. L., 279
McGinnis, M. Y., 333, 336
McGlone, J., 398
McGregor, I. S., 434
McGue, M., 377
McGuffin, P., 41, 48
McIntyre, D. C., 246
McKim, W. A., 382, 383
McLachlan, R. S., 246
McLaughlin, T., 218
McMurray, C. T., 242
McNally, G. P., 177
McNally, R. J., 459
McNaughton, B. L., 278
McNaughton, N., 460
Meaney, M. J., 440
Meddis, R., 342
Medina, J. F., 195, 279
Medzhitov, R., 437
Mel, B. W., 82
Melis, W., 216
Mello, N. K., 386
Melloni, R. H., Jr., 436
Melnik, G., 312
Melzack, R., 176, 256, 257
Menaker, M., 360
Mendel, G., 34, 35
Mendelson, J. H., 386
Mennill, D. J., 44
Mercer, J. G., 303, 305
Merton, P. A., 14
Merzenich, M. M., 251
Metcalfe, J., 407
Meunier, C., 86
Meunier, M., 274
Meyer, R. G., 449
Midtgaard, J., 86
Mieda, M., 364
Mignot, E., 364
Miller, A. C., 405
Miller, E. K., 31, 191
Miller, G. E., 439
Miller, G. L., 223
Miller, N. E., 300

Miller, N. S., 381
Miller, W. S., 243, 258
Millin, P. M., 268
Mills, J. N., 355
Mills, R., 326
Milner, B., 173, 174, 262, 263, 267, 270, 398, 414
Milner, D., 163
Milner, P. M., 4
Minai, A., 277
Mintz, I. M., 94
Mishkin, M., 162, 264, 272, 276
Mistlberger, R. E., 349
Mitchell, J. M., 373
Mitchell, R. W., 21
Miyashita, Y., 191, 279
Mladejovsky, M. G., 140
Mobley, W. C., 254
Moghaddam, B., 453
Mogil, J. S., 117
Mohr, J. P., 414
Molday, R. S., 138
Momma, S., 224
Mondrian, P., 151
Money, J., 328, 329
Moniz, E., 8, 16, 17
Mousonego, A., 245
Montmayeur, J. P., 180
Mooney, R., 44, 45, 411
Moore, R. Y., 361
Moore, T., 160
Morau, J., 182
Moran, M. H., 302
Morgan, J. P., 379
Morgan, T. H., 36
Mori, N., 246
Morin, C. M., 363
Morris, J. S., 413
Morris, M. K., 268
Morris, N. M., 332
Morris, R. G. M., 125, 282
Morse, D., 360
Morshead, C. M., 224
Mort, D. J., 189
Moruzzi, G., 357
Moscovitch, M., 271
Moser, E. I., 277
Moskowitz, M. A., 235, 236
Mott, D. D., 54
Mountcastle, V. B., 173
Mrosovsky, N., 350, 351
Mudher, A., 245
Mühlnickel, W., 225
Muir, C., 177
Mullaney, D. J., 355, 365
Muller, N. G., 279
Muller, R-A., 226
Mumby, D. G., 13, 274, 276, 277
Muñoz-Sanjuán, L., 213
Münte, T. F., 223
Murison, R., 437
Murphy, M., 27
Murphy, M. R., 177, 178
Murray, E. A., 274, 444
Myers, R., 255
Myers, R. E., 399, 400
Myles, D. G., 316

Nadarjah, B., 214
Nadel, L., 271, 278
Nadelmann, E. A., 384, 385
Nader, K., 270
Naeser, M. A., 416
Naftolin, F., 332
Naitoh, P., 366
Nakahara, K., 5
Natelson, B. H., 435
National Commission on Marijuana and Drug Abuse, 379
Nau, R., 237
Naya, Y., 279
Nedergaard, M., 91
Neher, E., 8, 87
Neiderhiser, J. M., 48
Nemeroff, C. B., 457, 459
Nesse, R. M., 30, 389
Nestle, M., 295
Nestler, E. J., 391
Netter, F. H., 140
Neumann, P. E., 284
Neve, R. L., 247
Neves, S. R., 89
Neville, H., 419
Newcombe, N. S., 23, 286
New Iberia Research Center, 22
Newman, E. A., 91
Newport, D. J., 459
Newsom-Davis, J., 237
Nicolelis, M. A. L., 194
Nicoll, R. A., 380
Nicolson, I. R., 421
Nieder, A., 31
Nielsen, J. B., 205
Nijhawan, D., 238
Nissl, F., 60
Noble, K. G., 421
Nobre, A. C., 419, 420
Noebels, J. L., 239
Nopoulis, P. C., 454
Norman, D. A., 136
Northcutt, R. G., 68
Northoff, G., 444
Noselli, S., 89
Nottebohm, F., 45, 224
Nudo, R. J., 256
Nyberg, L., 105, 161, 279
Nycamp, K., 354, 355

O'Callaghan, M. A. J., 16
Ochsner, K. O., 10
Ody, C., 186
Ohbayashi, M., 191
Ohki, K., 191
Ohman, A., 444
Ohno, Y., 367
Ohtaki, H., 236
Ohyama, T., 195, 280
Ohzawa, I., 146
Ojemann, G. A., 414, 417
O'Keefe, J., 277, 278
O'Leary, A. T., 26
O'Leary, C. M., 378
O'Leary, D. D. M., 218, 251
Olfson, M., 455
Oliet, S. H. R., 91
Olney, J. W., 378
Olsen, R., 96
Olson, C. R., 191

Olson, L., 254
Olton, D. S., 125
O'Neill, L., 27
Ormerod, B. K., 223, 334, 441
Osei, S. Y., 310
O'Shanick, G., 363
Ostroff, L., 285
Oswald, L., 343
Otto, T., 443
Overmier, J. B., 437
Overney, D. F., 217
Owens, M. J., 410

Pääbo, S., 28, 39, 41
Pace-Schott, E. E., 354, 364
Packard, M. G., 280
Pallas, S. P., 223
Palmer, T., 256
Palovskaya, M., 190
Pankseep, J., 176, 388, 391
Papez, J. W., 428
Papnicolaou, A., 268
Paredes, R. G., 335
Park, I. J., 327
Parker, S. T., 21
Parnas, I., 89
Parnavelas, J. G., 214
Parrott, A. C., 377
Parsons, L. M., 193
Pascual-Leone, A., 106
Passingham, R. E., 69, 207
Patel, S. R., 367
Patel, T. D., 217
Paterson, S. J., 227
Patrick, C. J., 430
Patterson, K., 418, 423
Patton, G. C., 311
Paulesu, E., 421
Pauls, D. L., 461
Paulsen, O., 277
Paulson, O. B., 420
Pavlov, I., 8
Payne, B. R., 253
Pedersen, N., 46
Pellis, S. M., 434
Pellow, S., 123, 460
Penfield, W., 172, 194, 280, 398, 414, 415, 416, 417
Peoples, L. L., 392
Peralta, V., 450
Percival, J. E., 353
Perera, M. H., 458
Perkel, D. J., 196
Perkins, W. L., 376
Perrimon, N., 89
Perrone, P., 408
Perrot-Sinal, T. S., 325
Perry, V. H., 248
Peru, A., 191
Peterhaus, E., 161
Peters, M., 71, 85
Petersen, S. E., 122, 279
Peterson, A. T., 26
Peterson, B. S., 462
Petrides, M., 279, 280
Petrovich, G. D., 70
Pfaff, D. W., 336
Pfeiffer, C. A., 323, 324
Pfrieger, F. W., 218
Phelps, E. A., 444, 445

Phelps, M. E., 104
Phillips, A. G., 112, 389, 391
Phillips, T., 117
Phoenix, C. H., 325
Piazza, P. V., 390
Picard, N., 192
Pierce, K., 225, 226
Piet, R., 91
Pietrobon, D., 129
Pilcher, D., 410
Pillard, R. C., 337
Pinel, J. P. J., 125, 243, 246, 269, 274, 276, 292, 294, 303, 308, 373, 374
Piomelli, D., 380
Pittman, Q. J., 94
Piven, J., 225
Placzek, M., 213
Pleim, E. T., 336
Ploegh, H. L., 437
Plomin, R., 11, 41, 47, 48
Plunkett, K., 419, 420
Plunkett, S., 293
Poliakov, A. V., 193
Polivy, J., 289
Polkey, C. E., 423
Pons, T. P., 251, 257
Poo, M.-M., 222, 282
Pope, H. G., 333, 379
Pope, H. G., Jr., 332, 333
Poppele, R., 187
Porter, R., 197
Posner, M. I., 4, 10, 122
Post, R. M., 246
Postle, B. R., 268
Pouget, A., 191
Poulain, A., 91
Poulos, C. X., 373
Powell, T. P. S., 173
Powley, T. L., 300
Price, C. J., 420, 422
Price, D. D., 176
Price, R. A., 308
Primakoff, P., 316
Pritchard, R. M., 137
Prolla, T. A., 304
Pryce, C. R., 440
Przedborski, S., 241
Pusey, A., 26
Putnam, S. K., 335

Qi, Y., 214
Qiu, M., 214
Quan, N., 440
Quarry, J., 236, 258
Queen Elizabeth, 119
Quinsey, V. L., 337
Qureshi, A. I., 233

Racine, R. J., 246
Radomski, M. W., 352
Raff, M. C., 248
Raichle, M. E., 122
Rainer, G., 191
Rainie, D., 460
Rainville, P., 176
Raisman, G., 254, 317, 334
Rajaratnam, S. M., 362
Rakic, P., 70, 224
Ralph, M. A. L., 418

Ralph, M. R., 359, 360
Ram, P. T., 89
Rämä, P., 280
Ramachandran, V. S., 133, 226, 257, 258
Rammani, N., 207
Ramón y Cajal, S., 8
Rampon, C., 44
Ramsay, D. S., 296, 375
Ramus, F., 421
Ranson, B., 91
Ranson, S. W., 299
Rao, S. C., 191
Rao, Y., 217
Rasmussen, R., 173, 174
Rasmussen, T., 194, 414
Ratcliffe, L. M., 44
Ratliff, F., 142
Ratnam, R., 168, 183
Rattenborg, N. C., 347
Rauschecker, J. P., 169
Ravizza, S. M., 196
Ravussin, E., 308
Raynor, H. A., 298
Read, H. L., 169
Reame, N., 320
Reber, P. J., 265
Rechtschaffen, A., 343, 347, 350, 353
Redd, M., 297
Reddy, A. B., 360
Reed, R. R., 178, 179
Rees, G., 156, 182
Rehm, J., 385
Reichardt, L. F., 219
Reid, R. C., 146
Reiman, E. M., 460
Reinarman, C., 385
Reiner, W., 329
Remple, M. S., 225
Rensberger, B., 15
Rensink, R. A., 181
Renvall, R., 421
Reschke, E., 60
Rettig, J., 87
Reuter, P., 385
Reuter-Lorenz, P. A., 405
Revusky, S. H., 124
Reynolds, D. V., 176
Rhees, R. W., 440
Rhodes, J. S., 224
Ricaurte, G. A., 381
Riccio, D. C., 268, 271
Richards, W., 129, 130
Richardson, B. J., 274
Richmond, C. P., 349, 359
Richter, D., 88
Riddle, M. A., 462
Ridley, A. J., 214
Rijntjes, M., 206, 256
Riley, B., 48
Ritter, R. C., 302
Rizzolatti, G., 192
Robakis, N. K., 247
Robbins, R. W., 431
Robbins, T. W., 268, 379, 386
Roberts, L., 398, 414, 415, 417
Roberts, N., 104
Roberts, W. V., 332
Robertson, L. C., 158

Robertson, R. G., 278
Robinson, T. E., 115, 223, 371, 375, 381, 386, 390, 391
Rockstroh, B., 225, 454
Rodbell, M., 8
Roder, J., 117
Rodgers, R. J., 302, 460
Rodier, P. M., 226, 227
Rodin, J., 304, 308
Rodman, H. R., 160
Rodriguez-Manzo, G., 335, 336
Roe, A. W., 223
Rogers, P. J., 297
Rogers, R. D., 379
Rogers-Ramachandran, D., 257
Roland, P., 106
Rolls, B. J., 298
Rolls, E. T., 278, 294
Romanski, L. M., 442
Rosa, M. G. P., 160
Rose, R. J., 48
Rosenthal, D., 450
Roser, M., 407
Rossi, E., 256
Rossignol, S., 256
Rossion, B., 279
Roth, G. S., 304
Roth, R. H., 92
Rothi, L. J. G., 189
Rothman, D. L., 106
Rothstein, M. A., 11
Rothwell, J. C., 106
Rothwell, N. J., 304
Rourke, B. P., 227
Rowe, J. B., 192
Rowland, N., 295, 299
Roy, R. R., 254
Rozin, P., 289, 295, 431
Rubenstein, J. L. R., 214
Rudy, J. W., 278
Ruff, N. L., 251
Rush, A. J., 458
Rushworth, M. F., 188, 192
Russell, J. A., 431
Russell, W. R., 398
Rutledge, L. L., 432
Rutter, M., 23
Rymer, R., 212
Ryner, L. A., 366

Sabater-Pi, J., 410
Sabel, A., 160
Sack, R. L., 362
Sacks, O., 3, 21, 22, 156, 157, 190, 226
Saffran, E. M., 121
Sagau, P., 86
Sakmann, B., 8
Sakuma, Y., 336
Salamone, J. D., 464
Salmon, P., 436, 449
Salmon, D. P., 350, 351
Salovey, P., 436
Salyer, K. E., 238
Salzer, J. L., 85
Salzet, M., 439
Samuelson, R. J., 125

Sánchez-Cordero, V., 26
Sanders, D., 332
Serizawa, S., 178
Sanes, J. N., 193, 207, 225, 251
Sanes, J. R., 216, 282
Saper, C. B., 356
Sapolsky, R. M., 440
Saskin, P., 363
Sassone-Corsi, P., 360
Sato, M., 246
Sato, S., 335
Savic, I., 179
Savill, J., 219
Sawa, A., 453
Sawada, H., 241, 254
Sawatari, A., 141
Sawle, G. V., 255
Saxena, A., 44
Sbragia, G., 366
Scammell, T. E., 356
Schacter, D. L., 120
Schafe, G. E., 270
Schallert, T., 245
Schall, A., 8
Schally, A. V., 319, 320
Schärli, H., 160
Schatzman, M., 346
Scheffele, P., 218
Schelling, T. C., 377
Schenck, C. H., 364
Schenk, F., 245
Schettino, L. F., 443
Schieber, M. H., 193
Schiffman, S. S., 179, 180
Schiller, P. H., 270
Schlag, J., 13
Schlag-Rey, M., 13
Schlaug, G., 408, 409
Schneider, G. E., 177, 178
Schnupp, J. W. H., 169
Schoepfer, R., 285
Schreiber, C. E., 169
Schreiner, C. E., 169
Schulkin, J., 23, 295, 436
Schultz, W., 280, 391, 392
Schurman, T., 320
Schwartz, A. B., 194
Schwartz, G. J., 302
Schwartz, M. W., 310
Sclafani, A., 295
Scott, B. H., 169
Scott, M. P., 233
Scoville, W. B., 270
Seaberg, R. M., 213
Seamans, J. K., 112
Searle, J. R., 20
Searle, L. V., 43
Sears, L., 225
See, R. E., 387
Seeley, R. J., 310
Segal, M., 86
Segarra, M. D., 410
Segerstrom, S. C., 439
Segev, I., 86
Segovia, S., 325
Seitz, R. J., 207
Sejnowski, T. J., 69
Selkoe, D. J., 244, 245
Selye, H., 435, 436
Semple, M. N., 169
Sener, R. N., 44

Serfaty, M., 362
Servos, P., 174
Sewards, M. A., 180
Sewards, T. V., 180
Shapely, R., 152
Shapiro, B. H., 325
Shapiro, L., 38
Shapiro, T., 225
Shapleske, J., 454
Sharpey, A. L., 362
Shaw, P. J., 347
Shaywitz, S. E., 421
Sheinberg, D. L., 164
Sheng, M., 86, 218, 284
Shepherd, G. M., 86
Sheppard, D. M., 461
Sherrington, C., 8
Sherry, D. F., 278
Sherwin, B. B., 331, 332, 334
Sheth, B. R., 161
Shields, J., 450
Shimohama, S., 241, 254
Shimokochi, M., 335
Shimura, T., 335
Shin, J. C., 195
Shipley, M. T., 442
Shohami, E., 236
Shouse, M. N., 246
Siegel, J. M., 354, 358, 363
Siegel, S., 373, 374, 375
Sigmundson, H. K., 329
Silberberg, G., 54
Silberg, J., 23
Silk, J. B., 25
Simerly, R. B., 323
Simon, H., 8
Simon, R. P., 238
Sinclair, S. V., 349
Singer, J., 335
Singer, L. T., 381
Singer, W., 159
Sirigu, A., 193
Skerrett, P. J., 295
Sladek, J. R., Jr., 255
Slater, P. C., 270
Slezak, M., 218
Slomianka, L., 224
Sluder, G., 35
Small, M. F., 32
Smania, N., 191
Smith, D. V., 179, 180
Smith, E. E., 280
Smith, F. J., 298, 299
Smith, G. P., 302
Smith, S. J., 218
Snider, W., 217
Snyder, S. H., 93, 451, 452, 453
Soberón, J., 26
Sofroniew, M. V., 254
Soloman, S. M., 312
Sommer, M. A., 13
Sorenson, E. R., 431
Spanagel, R., 391
Spanis, C. W., 270
Speakman, A., 278
Speakman, J. R., 303, 305
Spear, L. P., 220
Spencer, R. M. C., 195

Sperry, R. W., 8, 215, 216, 399, 400, 401, 402, 403, 406
Spielman, A. J., 363
Spillman, L., 133
Spironello, E., 177
Spitzer, R. L., 455, 461
Spruston, N., 86
Squire, L. R., 4, 265, 267, 270, 271, 272, 273, 276, 280
Srivastava, L., 225
St. George-Hyslop, P. H., 242, 244
Stampfer, M. J., 295
Stampi, C., 366
Stanford, S. C., 436
Stapp, D., 214
Stefano, G. B., 94
Steffens, A. B., 298
Stein, D. G., 254, 334
Steinman, L., 242
Stepanski, E., 363
Stephan, K. E., 69
Stevens-Graham, B., 58
Stevenson, J. A. F., 300
Stiles, J., 398
Stock, M. J., 304
Stone, T. W., 323
Stoner, G. R., 161
Strick, P. L., 192
Strickland, D., 241
Striessnig, J., 129
Strittmatter, S. M., 249
Strömland, K., 227
Strub, R. L., 118
Strubbe, J. H., 296, 298, 302
Stryker, M. P., 147, 149, 222
Stuart, G. J., 82, 86
Stuss, D. T., 118
Sucliffe, J. G., 364
Suga, N., 159
Sullivan, E. V., 267
Sullivan, J., 375
Summers, G. L., 381
Sunnall, H. R., 381
Sunday, S. R., 311
Suner, S., 251
Sutherland, R. J., 278
Sutter, M. L., 169
Sutton, G. G., 14
Suzuki, W. A., 278
Swaab, D. E., 335, 336
Swanson, L. W., 64, 70
Sweeney, M. E., 309
Swerdlow, N. R., 462
Swinnen, S. P., 206
Syed, N. I., 216
Syntichaki, P., 248
Szameitat, A. J., 188

Taheri, S., 364
Takahashi, J. S., 363
Tallman, J. F., 453
Tamakoshi, A., 367
Tanaka, K., 246
Tanapat, P., 440
Tanji, J., 192
Tank, D. W., 283
Tarr, M. J., 165
Tassinary, L. G., 432

Tattersall, I., 27
Tattersall, J., 31
Taub, E., 256
Taub, J. M., 351
Tavernarakis, N., 248
Taylor, D. M., 194
Taylor, J. R., 247
Taylor, L., 443, 444, 445
Tear, G., 216
Teicher, M. H., 440
Teitelbaum, P., 300
Temple, S., 256
Tennissen, A., 256
Tetrud, J. W., 247
Teuber, H.-L., 160, 253, 262, 263, 267
Thach, W. T., 195
Thase, M. E., 457
Thiele, A., 14
Thoenen, H., 223
Thomas, J., 177
Thomas, J. J., 429
Thompson, I. D., 169
Thompson, W. L., 193
Thomson, A. D., 12
Thorpy, M. J., 363
Thunberg, M., 432
Tian, B., 169
Tilley, S. I. II., 194
Tinbergen, N., 8
Tinklenberg, J. R., 379
Toates, F. M., 294
Tobler, P. N., 392
Tompkins, C. A., 406
Tong, E., 139, 158
Tonge, D. A., 248
Tooby, J., 11
Toorians, A. W., 334
Tootell, R. B. H., 163
Torrey, E. F., 450
Townsend, J., 195
Tracy, J. L., 431
Thunomiu, A. D., 15
Tranel, D., 165, 444
Treffert, D. A., 226
Treisman, A., 158
Treit, D., 125, 460
Tremblay, L., 280
Trepel, C., 149
Tresch, M. C., 206
Treue, S., 181
Trevarthen, C., 403
Trivers, R. L., 32
Trottier, G., 225
Trowill, J. A., 388
Troyer, T. W., 44
True, W. R., 377
Tryon, R. C., 42, 43

Tsao, D. Y., 146
Tsien, J. Z., 117
Tsodyks, M., 144
Tulving, E., 264
Turkenburg, J. L., 335
Turkheimer, E., 46, 48
Twain, M., 22
Tweedale, R., 160

Udin, S. B., 216
Ullman, S., 159
Ulrich, R. E., 5
Ungerleider, L. G., 161, 162, 163, 182
Uswatte, G., 256

Vaccarino, A. L., 278
Valenstein, E., 189
Valenstein, E. S., 16
van der Kooy, D., 213, 224, 376
Van der Linden, M., 280
van Dijk, G., 302
Vanduffel, W., 161
Van Essen, D. C., 161
Van Essevelt, L. E., 359
Van Gelder, R. N., 360
Van Goozen, S. H. M., 337
VanIelder, T., 352
Van Horn, J. D., 106
Van Lancke, D., 461
Vann, S. D., 267
Van Praag, H., 224, 254
Van Tol, H. H. M., 453, 454
Vargha-Khadem, F., 264, 423
Vaughan, H. G., Jr., 267
Vekua, A., 28
Vermeij, G. J., 27
Vermeire, B. A., 410
Verschure, P. F. M. J., 194
Vertes, R. P., 358
Vicario, D. S., 15
Vicario-Abejón, C., 219
Vieau, D., 439
Vignolo, L. A., 408, 416
Vila, M., 241
Vincent, A., 237
Vogel, D. S., 401, 407
Vogel, J. J., 407
Volkow, N. D., 391
von Békésy, G., 8
von der Heydt, R., 161
von Economo, B. C., 356
von Euler, U., 8
Von Frisch, K., 8
von Helmholtz, H., 150
Voogd, J., 195

Vuilleumier, P., 191

Wada, J. A., 120, 246, 380, 397, 408
Wagers, A. J., 256
Wahlgren, N. G., 235, 236
Wahlsten, D., 117
Waisbren, S. E., 44
Wakayama, T., 256
Wald, G., 8, 150
Walford, L., 304
Walford, R. L., 304
Walker, C. D., 225
Wall, J. T., 250
Wall, P. D., 176
Wall, T. C., 44
Wallace, D. C., 39, 41
Wallace, G. L., 226
Walmsley, B., 95
Walsh, M. L., 435
Walsh, T. B., 311
Walsh, V., 106
Wan, H., 278
Wang, W., 322
Wang, X., 219, 238, 250
Warchol, M. E., 168
Washburn, A. L., 301, 302
Washington, G., 379
Wasserman, L. M., 151
Waters, M. G., 87
Waters, W. F., 353
Watson, J. B., 20
Watson, N., 409
Watson, R. T., 189
Wauqier, A., 246
Waxham, M. N., 89
Webb, W. B., 353, 354, 355, 365
Webster, M. M., 124
Wechsler-Reya, R., 233
Weiller, C., 256
Wemberger, D. R., 454
Weinfurth, R., 304
Weiner, H. L., 245
Weingarten, H. P., 296, 297, 300
Weise-Kelley, L., 373
Weiskrantz, L., 160
Weiss, F., 391
Weissman, M. M., 455
Wenning, A., 293
Werner, J. S., 133
Wermicke, C., 411, 412
Wessinger, C. M., 169
West, M. J., 224
Weston, M., 352
Wever, R. A., 349, 350
Wexler, E., 256

Whalen, P. J., 443
Wheeler, M. E., 279
Whishaw, I. Q., 9, 196, 245
Whishkin, E. E., 295
White, A. M., 277
White, B. D., 304
White, N. M., 4, 196, 277, 280
Whiten, A., 34
Whitman, C., 446
Whitmore, A. V., 248
Wicklegren, W. A., 262
Widajewicz, W., 205
Wide, J. K., 334
Wierpkema, P. R., 320
Wiesel, T. N., 8, 143, 144, 147, 148, 222, 251
Wightman, R. M., 93
Willett, W. C., 295
Williams, G., 302
Williams, G. C., 30
Williams, I., 26, 346
Williams, J. H. G., 225
Williams, M., 156
Williams, S. R., 82
Willingham, D. B., 187
Wilmer, J. B., 421
Wilson, B. A., 252
Wilson, G. T., 311
Wilson, M., 25, 33
Wilson, M. A., 278
Wilson, R. I., 380
Wiltstein, S., 237
Winocur, G., 267
Winson, J., 347, 354
Wintink, A. J., 246
Wirtshafter, D., 305
Wise, P. M., 254
Wise, R. A., 391, 392
Witelson, S. F., 335
Wolf, K., 152
Wolff, P. H., 410
Wolgin, D. L., 373
Wolpaw, J. R., 256
Wolpert, F. A., 315
Wong, A. H. C., 453, 454
Wong, J., 125
Wong, K., 27
Wood, B., 28
Wood, E. R., 274, 275, 276
Wood, W., 34
Woodruff-Pak, D. S., 263
Woods, S. C., 296, 305, 310, 375
Woods, S. W., 464
Woodson, J. C., 323, 325, 334

Wooten, G. F., 241
Worsley, A., 346
Wright, T. I., 295
Wu, D. C., 241
Wu, L.-G., 86
Wurtz, R. H., 13
Wüst, S., 160

Xie, R., 160
Xu, D., 254
Xu, J., 250

Yabuta, N. H., 141
Yakolev, P. I., 172
Yamaguchi, S., 360
Yamura, A., 398
Yanagisawa, M., 364
Yang, S. H., 333
Yau, K-W., 138
Yesalis, C. E., 332, 333
Yoken, R. H., 450
Yoshida, M., 279
Young, A. B., 462
Young, A. M. J., 392
Young, A. W., 443, 444
Young, E. A., 458
Young, R. C., 302
Young, T., 150
Young, W. C., 325, 331
Yu, L., 117
Yurgelin-Todd, D., 379
Yuste, R., 86, 212, 218, 285

Zahm, D. S., 388
Zaidel, D., 406
Zaidel, E., 403, 405, 406
Zajonc, R. B., 431
Zald, D. H., 445
Zaugwill, O. L., 414
Zeitzer, J. M., 364
Zeki, S., 152, 159
Zemnn, A., 161
Zhang, I., 334
Zhang, Y., 310
Zheng, W., 223
Zimitat, C., 13
Zimmer, L., 379
Zivin, J. A., 463, 464, 465
Zobel, E., 385
Zoghbi, H. Y., 226, 256
Zola-Morgan, S., 265, 272, 273, 274, 275, 276
Zubek, J. P., 43
Zucker, K. J., 329
Zucker, R. S., 87
Zur, D., 159

Subject Index

Abducens cranial nerve, 472, 473
Ablatio penis, 329–330
Abscesses, cerebral, 237
Absolute pitch, 223
Absolute refractory period, 84
Absorption spectrum, 138
Absorptive phase, of energy metabolism, 291–292
Accommodation, 132
Acetylcholine, 91, 92, 94, 95, 200, 245, 268
Acetylcholinesterase, 91, 94
Achromatic colors, 149
Acoustic neuromas, 233, 234
Acquired dyslexias, 421, 422–423
ACTH, 326, 436, 458
Action potential (AP), 81–86, 96
Activational effects, of sex hormones, 315, 330–338
Activation-synthesis theory, 346
Active placebos, 464–465
Acuity, 131
Adipose tissue, 291
Ad libitum levels of consumption, 304
Addict(s), drug, 372–373
Freud as, 392–393
Parkinson's disease in, 247
relapse of, 386–387
Addiction. *See* Drug addiction
Adenine, 37–38, 39
Adipsia, 300
Adrenal cortex, 317, 436
Adrenal glands, 316, 317
Adrenal medulla, 436, 439
autotransplantation of, 255
Adrenalectomy, 332, 440
Adrenergic neurons, 93
Adrenocorticotropic hormone (ACTH), 326, 436, 458
Adrenogenital syndrome, 328–329
AEPs, 107, 108
Affective disorders, 454–458, 465–466
Afferent nerves, 51, 52
Age-limited learners, 45
Ageusia, 180
Aggregation, 214–215
Aggressive behaviors, 123, 427, 428, 433–435
anabolic steroids and, 333
controlling, 15–16
Agnosia, 164–165
Agonists, 95, 97
serotonin, 460
Agoraphobia, 459
Agraphia, 411
Alcohol, 377–378, 383–384, 387
anticonvulsant effect of, 373, 374
hypothermic effects of, 373–375
Alcoholism, 2–3, 6–7
Korsakoff's syndrome and, 12–13
Alexia, 411
Alleles, 34–37
Allocentric maps, 436
All-or-none responses, 81, 82
Alpha fetoprotein, 324–325

Alpha male, 123, 433–434
Alpha waves, 106–107, 343, 344
Alzheimer's disease, 242, 244–245
amnesia of, 267–268
transgenic mouse model of, 246–247
Amacrine cells, 132
Amenorrhea, 333
American Sign Language, 410
Amino acid derivative hormones, 315
Amino acids, 38, 39, 92, 95, 290, 315. *See also*
Gamma-aminobutyric acid; Glutamate
Amnesia
of Alzheimer's disease, 267–268
bilateral medial temporal lobes and, 244,
261–266, 272–277, 280
after concussion, 268–271
infantile, 285–286
ischemia-produced, 277
of Korsakoff's syndrome, 267
for long-term explicit memory, 289
object-recognition, 272–273, 274–276
retrograde, 261–262, 267, 268–271
Amphetamine, 375, 381
Amphetamine psychosis, 381
Amphibians, evolution of, 27
Amplitude, 166
Amputees, rehabilitative training of, 256–258
Amygdala, 70, 112, 244, 428, 430
anxiety and, 460
depression and, 458
facial expressions and, 445–446
fear conditioning and, 442–443, 444
lesions of, 112
memory and, 273, 274, 276, 279
removal of, 261–264
Amygdala complex, 442–443
Amyloid, 244, 245, 246–247
Amyloid plaques, 244, 245, 246–247
Anabolic steroids, 332–334
Analgesia, 94
Analgesia circuit, descending, 176–177
Analgesics, 381
Analogous, 31
Analytic-synthetic theory of cerebral
asymmetry, 409
Anandamide, 380
Androgenic insensitivity syndrome, 328
Androgens, 317, 320–321, 324, 326–328, 330, 332,
336. *See also* Testosterone
Androstenedione, 327
Aneurysm, 233
Angiogram, 233
Angiography, cerebral, 102
Angular gyrus, 411–412, 413
Anhedonia, 458
Animal models
of Alzheimer's disease, 246–247
of anxiety, 460
of neuropsychological diseases, 245–247
of object-recognition amnesia, 272–277
Animals, as research subjects, 5, 110–114, 391. *See
also specific animals*

Anisomycin, 270
Anorexia nervosa, 289, 311–312
Anosmia, 180
Anosognosia, 175
ANS. *See* Autonomic nervous system
Antagonistic muscles, 200
Antagonists, 95, 97
Anterior, 61
Anterior cingulate cortex, 176
Anterior forebrain pathway, 45
Anterior hypothalamus, 356, 357
Anterior pituitary, 317, 318, 319–320, 321, 324
Anterior-pituitary adrenal-cortex system, 436, 439
Anterior-posterior axis, 61, 62
Anterograde amnesia, 262–264, 267, 268, 269, 272
Anterograde degeneration, 248, 249
Anterograde memory deficits, 120
Anterograde tracing methods, 61
Anterograde transneuronal degeneration,
248, 249
Anterolateral system, 171–172, 173
Antidiuretic hormone, 318
Antidromic conduction, 85
Antigens, 115, 437–438
Antibodies, 115, 437–438
Antibody-mediated immunity, 437–438
Anticonvulsants, 96, 459
Antidepressants, 354–355, 373, 374, 455,
456–457
Antihypnotic drugs, 361
Antisense drugs, 117
Antithesis, principle of, 427
Anus, 290, 324
Anxiety, 125, 362–363, 458–460
Anxiety disorders, 458–460
Anxiolytic, 96, 123, 363
Apes, 27, 28, 410
Aphagia, 300
Aphasia, 397, 398, 409, 410, 411–418
Apical dendrite, 68, 74
Apnea, sleep, 363
Apoptosis, 219, 238, 378
Apoptosis inhibitor protein, 254
Appetizer effect, 297
Applied research, 7–8
Apraxia, 189, 397
Aqueduct, cerebral, 53, 66
Arachnoid membrane, 53
Archives, brain-image, 106
Arcuate fasciculus, 411–413
Arithmetic subset of WAIS, 119
Aromatization, 324–325
Arteriosclerosis, 234
As Nature Made Him, 330
Asomatognosia, 21–22, 174–175
Aspartate, 92
Aspiration, 111, 274
Association cortex, 156, 157, 158, 161–164, 173,
208–209
sensorimotor, 188–192
Asteroagnosia, 174, 195
Asthma, 380

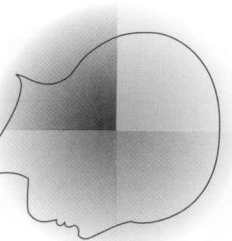

Astrocytes, 58–59, 91, 218
Asymmetry, cerebral, 408–410
Ataxia, 242
Atonia, 363, 364
Atropine, 96–97
Attention
  covert vs. overt, 183
  endogenous, 181
  selective, 159, 181–183
Attention-deficit hyperactivity disorder, 461
Atypical neuroleptics, 453
Audition, 166–170, 223, 403–404, 405
Auditory canal, 166
Auditory cortex, 223
Auditory nerve, 167, 168
Auditory-vestibular nerve, 168, 472, 473
Auras, epileptic, 239
Australopithecus, 27–29
Autism, 225–227, 228
Autoimmune disorder, 242
Automatisms, 240
Autonomic nervous system (ANS), 9, 51, 52, 470
  emotion and, 427–428, 429–431
  endocrine glands and, 320
  REM sleep and, 345
Autoradiography, 115, 147
Autoreceptors, 89–90, 96, 97
Autotransplantation, of adrenal medulla, 255
Average evoked potentials (AEPs), 107, 108
Aversions, taste, 124, 295, 302, 312
Awareness, conscious, 158, 160, 161, 264
Axillary hair, 326, 327
Axoaxonal synapses, 86
Axodendritic synapses, 86
Axon(s), 55, 58, 70, 215–218
Axon hillock, 55, 81
Axonal conduction, 83–85
Axosomatic synapses, 86
Axotomy, 248, 249

B cells, 437–438, 439
Backward action potentials, 85
Ballistic movements, 187
Basal forebrain, 268
Basal ganglia, 15–16, 73, 195–196
  Parkinson's disease and, 241
  Tourette syndrome and, 462
Basal ganglia motor system, 69–70
Basal metabolic rate, 305, 308
Bases, nucleotide, 37, 39
Basilar membrane, 167, 168
Bayer Drug Company, 382
Before-and-after design, 373, 374
Behavior. See also Sexual behavior
  aggressive, 123, 333, 427, 428, 433–435
  biology of, 20–24
  brain lateralization and. See Lateralization of function
  evolution and, 25–27
  instinctive, 11, 21
  interictal, 246
  ontogenetic development of, 42–45
  paradigms of animal, 123–126
  perinatal hormones and, 325–326
Behavioral biology, 4. See also Biopsychology
Behavioral genetics, 11, 34–41
Behavioral neuroscience, 4. See also Biopsychology
Behavioral paradigm(s), 117–118, 123–126
Behavioral research methods, 117–126
Behaviorism, 20
Belladonna, 97

Benign tumors, 233
Benzodiazepines, 96, 98, 361, 363, 459–460
Between-subjects design, 5
Betz cells, 196
Biceps, 200, 201, 205
Bilateral hippocampectomy, 274, 277
Bilateral lesion, 16, 113
Bilateral medial temporal lobectomy
  amnesia and, 261–264
  object-recognition deficits and, 274–277
Bile, 290
Bimodal neurons, 193
Binding problem, 158–159
Binges, 380–381, 386
Binocular, 145
Binocular cells, 145–146
Binocular disparity, 132
Biological clock, 349, 359–361
Biopsychology, 4
  converging operations and, 12–13
  divisions of, 8–11
  research in, 5–8. See also Research methods
  scientific inference and, 13–14
Bipolar affective disorder, 455, 457, 465, 466
Bipolar cells, 132
Bipolar electrode, 113
Bipolar neuron, 57, 132
Bipotential precursor, 323, 324
Birdsong, 44–45, 410–411
Bisexual, 329, 337
Blind spot, 133, 135
Blindness, 159–160. See also Scotoma
  change, 181–182
  color, 37
  melatonin and, 362
Blindsight, 160
Blobs, 153
Block-design subtest of WAIS, 119
Block-tapping memory-span test, 262
Blood–brain barrier, 53–54, 77, 371
Blood glucose levels, 293, 294, 298–299, 320
Blood pressure, 110
Body weight, 289, 308, 309, 311–312. See also Obesity
  brain weight and, 31
  regulation of, 292–294, 296–298, 303–307
Boluses, 123
Botox, 97
Bottom-up mechanisms, 181
Botulinum toxin, 97
Boxing, 433–434, 435
Brain, 2, 51–54. See also Brain damage; Brain imaging
  asymmetries of, 408–410
  evolution of, 5, 31
  frontal section of, 62
  infections of, 237
  locating neurotransmitters and receptors in, 115–116
  major divisions of, 64
  major structures of, 65–73
  measuring chemical activity in, 114–115
  postnatal growth of, 220–221
  sex differences in, 323–324
  sexual orientation and, 337–338
  tumors of, 101, 233
Brain damage. See also specific brain areas
  causes of, 233–238
  chemical senses and, 180
  disease-related, 239–247, 378, 414–415, 453–454, 458
  drug related, 12–13, 381
  dyslexia and, 422–423
  estradiol and, 333–334, 441

  neuroplasticity and, 248–258
  research on, 9, 11
  sensorimotor function and, 188–191
  testing for, 118–121
Brain-image archives, 106
Brain imaging, 3–4, 10–11, 102–106. See also Computed tomography; Functional MRI; Magnetic resonance imaging; Positron emission tomography
  and anxiety, 460
  and brain lateralization, 398
  and depression, 458
  and object recognition, 165–166, 277
  and prefrontal cortex, 280
  and secondary motor cortex, 192
  and selective attention, 182
  and Tourette syndrome, 462
Brain stem, 64, 65–67
  and autism, 227, 228
  evolution of, 31, 32
  truncation of, 356–357, 358
Bregma, 110
Brightness, 130–131
Broca's aphasia, 411
Broca's area, 397, 411–418
Bronchitis, 377
Buerger's disease, 377
Bulimia nervosa, 311
Bulls, controlling aggression in, 15
Buprenorphine, 383
Buspirone, 460
Buttons, terminal, 55, 61, 91, 97
Butyrophenones, 452

CA1 subfield, 265–266, 275, 276
Cafeteria diet, 297, 298, 301
Caffeine, 380
Calcium ions, 87–88, 235, 283–284, 378
Calorie-restriction experiments, 304–305
Calories, 301, 304–305, 312
CAMs, 215, 223
Canaries, singing of, 45, 410–411
Cancer, oral, 393
Cannabinoids, 378
Cannabis sativa, 376, 378–380, 383–386
Cannon-Bard theory, of emotion, 427–428, 429, 430
Cannula, 114, 390
Carbohydrates, 290
Carbon monoxide, 93
Cardiovascular activity, 109–110
Carotid artery, 104, 234
Carousel apparatus, 353
Cartesian dualism, 20, 21
Case studies, 7
  of abnormal psychological development, 212
  of abnormal sexual development, 327–328, 329–330
  of affective disorders, 454–455, 465–466
  of amnesia, 261–262, 265, 267, 286, 289
  of anorexia, 312
  of aphasia, 458–459
  of aphasia for sign language, 410
  of asomatognosia, 21–22, 174–175
  of blindsight, 160
  of brain damage consequences, 426, 446
  of brain tumor diagnosis and treatment, 101, 232
  of complex partial seizures, 240
  of contralateral neglect, 189–190
  of deep dyslexia, 422–423
  of drug addiction, 392–393
  of evaluating scientific claims, 15–16
  of fear perception, 444

Case studies, (continued)
of flaw in nature-or-nurture thinking, 23
of fortification illusions, 129, 149
of leptin deficiency, 310
of lesions to ventral/dorsal stream, 164
of motor output disruption, 187
of neural control of robot, 194–195
of neuropsychological assessment, 9
of Kluver-Bucy syndrome, 428–429
of Korsakoff's syndrome, 2–3
of pain insensitivity, 175–176
of Parkinson's disease, 77, 247, 255
of phantom limb pain, 257–258
of prosopagnosia, 165
of punch-drunk syndrome, 236–237
of savants, 226
of schizophrenia, 449
of scotoma, 160
of self-awareness in chimps, 22
of sensorimotor control, 186, 208
of simultanagnosia, 156
of sleep, 342, 351–352, 356, 363, 364, 366
of split-brain patient, 404
of testosterone replacement, 331
of Tourette syndrome, 461, 462–463
of visual agnosia, 157
Castration. See Gonadectomy
Cataplexy, 364
Catecholamines, 93, 95, 381. See also Dopamine;
  Epinephrine; Norepinephrine
Categorical spatial judgments, 408
Catonia, 449, 450
Cats
  aggressive behavior of, 428, 434
  sleep in, 356–358, 365
  speed of action potential in, 85
  spinal cord control of walking in, 205
  split brain in, 399–400
  visual system of, 143–144, 146, 148
Caudal, 61, 62
Caudate, 70–72
Caudate nucleus, 15–16
CCK, 302
Cell-adhesion molecules (CAMs), 215, 223
Cell body, 55, 61
Cell-mediated immunity, 437–438
Cell membrane, of neuron, 54, 55, 57
Central canal, 53
Central fissure, 67, 69
Central nervous system (CNS), 51–53. See also
  Brain; Spinal cord
  drug penetration of, 371
  myelination in, 58
  neurotransplantation and, 255–256
  regeneration in, 248–249
  rehabilitative training and, 256–257
  sleep apnea and, 363
Central sensorimotor programs, 206–209
Cephalic phase, of energy metabolism,
  291–292, 296, 297, 308, 311
Cerebellum, 65, 69, 73, 195
  learning and, 209
  memory and, 280
Cerebral abscesses, 237
Cerebral angiography, 102
Cerebral aqueduct, 53, 66
Cerebral commissures, 67, 73, 396, 399
Cerebral cortex, 9, 12, 67–69, 73, 121
  experience and, 225
  language and, 397, 411–418
  removal of, 428
  Tourette syndrome and, 462
Cerebral dialysis, 115, 389
Cerebral dominance, 397
Cerebral edema, 252, 414

Cerebral hemispheres, 64, 67–73, 214, 396,
  399–411. See also Lateralization of function;
  Left hemisphere; Right hemisphere
Cerebral hemorrhage, 233
Cerebral hypoxia, 240, 333
Cerebral ischemia, cerebral, 233–236, 253, 254
Cerebral lesions, cerebral, 265–266
  object-recognition deficits and, 277
Cerebral ventricles, 53, 214
Cerebrospinal fluid (CSF), 53, 54
Cerebrovascular disorders, 233–236
Cerebrum. See Cerebral hemispheres
  asymmetry of, 409
  postnatal development of, 31, 32
Cerveau isolé preparation, 356–357
Change blindness, 181–182
Channel proteins, 54, 57
Cheese effect, 456
Chemical lesions, selective, 114
Chemical senses. See Smell; Taste
Chemoaffinity hypothesis, 216–217
Chemotherapy, 379–380
Chimera, 403
Chimeric figures test, 403
Chimpanzees, 27, 29
  hand preferences of, 410
  prefrontal lobotomy in, 16
  self-awareness in, 22
Chlordiazepoxide, 96, 459
Chloride ions, 78–80, 89
Cholinergic neurons, 94
Cholecystokinin (CCK), 302
Cholesterol
  in neurodevelopment, 218
  steroid hormones and, 315, 324
Chordates, 27
Choroid plexuses, 53
Chromatic colors, 148–149
Chromatograph, 115
Chromosome(s) 34–38, 316, 322, 325, 328
  number 7, 227–228
  number 21, 238
Chronic stress, 435
Chunking, 207
Cigarettes, 376–377. See also Tobacco
Ciliary muscles, 132
Cingulate cortex, 70, 176
Cingulate gyrus, 70, 428, 430
Cingulate motor areas, 193
Circadian clock, 349, 359–361
Circadian rhythms, 348–350, 359, 360
Circadian theories of sleep, 347, 348
Cirrhosis, 378
Clinical, 3
Clinical implications theme, 3
Clinical trials, 463–466
Clitoral hood, 324
Clitoris, 323, 324, 333, 345
Clock, biological, 349, 359–361
Clock gene, 360
Clonus, 239, 240
Clozapine, 453
Closed-head injuries, 236–237, 268, 269
CNS. See Central nervous system
Coca-Cola, 380
Coca paste, 380
Cocaine, 95, 376, 380–381, 383–386, 392
Cocaine hydrochloride, 380
Cocaine psychosis, 380
Cocaine sprees, 380–381
Cochlea, 166–168
Cocktail-party phenomenon, 183
Cocontraction, 204

Codeine, 381
Codon, 39
Coexistence, 87
Cognition, 10, 121–122, 419. See also Awareness;
  Learning; Memory
  brain lateralization and, 407–408
  estradiol and, 334
  spatial, 228, 405, 408
  sleep deprivation and, 352–353
Cognitive map theory, of hippocampal function,
  278
Cognitive neuroscience, 3–4, 10–11
  behavioral methods of, 121–122
  and language, 418–423
Cognitive reserve, 253
Collateral sprouting, 250, 251
Colliculi, 65, 66, 168, 169, 356
Colon, 290
Colony–intruder paradigm, 123, 433–434
Color, 37, 130–131, 149–153, 161, 165
Color agnosia, 105
Color blindness, 37
Color constancy, 151–153
Columnar organization, 68–69, 147, 148
Coma, 268, 269
Commissures, cerebral, 67, 73, 396, 399–404
Commissurotomy, 396, 399–404
Common-sense view of emotion, 429
Comparative approach, 3, 5
Comparative psychology, 11
Compartmentalization, 86
Compensatory responses, conditioned, 375, 386
Complementary colors, 150–151
Completion, in visual system, 133, 159–160, 161
Complex cells, 145–146
Complex partial seizures, 240
Component theory, of color vision, 150
Comprehension subtest of WAIS, 119
Compulsions, 459
Computed tomography (CT), 102, 103, 415–416
Concentration camp victims, 312
Concentration gradients, 78
Concussion, 236–237, 268–271
Conditional response, 124
Conditional stimulus, 124
Conditioned aversion, 124, 178, 295, 302, 312
Conditioned compensatory responses, 375, 386
Conditioned defensive burying, 125
Conditioned drug tolerance, 373–375
Conditioned place-preference paradigm, 390
Conditioned taste aversion, 124, 295, 312, 302
Conditioned withdrawal effects, 375, 376, 386
Conditioning
  of fear, 441–443, 444
  of hunger, 296
  paradigms of, 123–126
  Pavlovian, 124, 263, 280, 375
Conduction
  of action potential, 83–86
  of postsynaptic potential, 80–81
Conduction aphasia, 411
Cones, 134–139, 150–151, 215–216, 217, 359–360
Configural association theory, 278
Confounded variable, 6
Congenital, 233
Congenital adrenal hyperplasia, 328–329
Congenital aneurysms, 233
Conscious awareness, 158, 160, 161, 264
Conspecifics, 27, 177
  eating and, 295
  stress and, 436
Constituent cognitive processes, 121–122,
  407–408, 419
Constraint-induced therapy, 256
Contexts. See Environmental factors

Contextual fear conditioning, 443
Contingent drug tolerance, 373, 374
Contralateral, 67
Contralateral movement, 405, 406
Contralateral neglect, 175, 189–191
Contrast enhancement, 142–143
Contrast X-ray techniques, 102
Contrecoup injuries, 236
Control compartment, 390
"Control of behavior" versus "conscious perception" theory, 164, 165
Control-question technique, 430
Contusions, 236
Convergence, 132, 134, 135
Convergent evolution, 31
Converging operations, 12–13, 126
Convolutions, 31, 67
Convulsions, 239–241, 401–402
Co-occurrence, of neuronal firing, 282
Coolidge effect, 6
Coordinate spatial judgments, 408
Coprolalia, 461
Copulation, 316, 325–326, 330, 335, 336
Coronal sections, of brain, 62
Corpus callosum, 7–8, 67, 396, 399–404
Cortex, adrenal, 317, 416
Cortex, cerebral. See Cerebral cortex
Cortex, of primordial gonad, 322
Corticofugal pathways, 159
Corticosteroids, 440
Corticotropin-releasing hormone, 458
Cortisol, 328, 329
Courtship display, 26–27
Covert attention, 183
Crack, 380
Cranial nerves, 52, 472, 473
Cresyl violet, 60
Critical thinking, 3, 15–17
Cross-cuing, 402–403
Cross-fostering control procedure, 43–44
Cross section, of brain, 62, 63
Cross tolerance, 371
Crossing over, 37
Cryogenic blockade, 111–112
Cryoprobe, 111–112
Crystal meth, 381
CSF, 53, 54
CT, 102, 103, 415–416
Cultural factors
  dyslexia and, 421–422
  obesity and, 308
Curare, 14, 97
Customized-test-battery approach, 118–119
Cut drugs, 383
Cutaneous receptors, 170–171
Cyclic GMP, 138
Cytochrome oxidase, 152
Cytokines, 439
Cytoplasm, 39, 56, 91
Cytosine, 37–38

Dalby's Carminative, 382
d-Amphetamine, 381
Deafness, 410
Decorticate, 428
Decremental transmission, 81
Decussate, 67
Deep dyslexia, 422–423
Default theory of REM sleep, 354–355
Defeminization, 325–326
Defensive behaviors, 123, 125, 433–435, 441, 460
Defensive burying, 125, 435, 460
Degeneration, neural, 248, 249, 254
Delayed nonmatching-to-sample test, 272–274, 275, 276

Delirium tremens (DTs), 378
Delta waves, 343, 345
Delusions, 450
Demasculinization, 325, 326
Dementia, 236–237, 241–242, 244–245, 267–268, 378
Dementia pugilistic, 236–237
Dendrites, 55, 68, 70, 74, 80, 82, 85–86, 220, 221
Dendritic spines, 74, 86, 285
Dendrodendritic synapses, 86
2-Deoxyglucose (2-DG) technique, 104, 114–115, 147
Deoxyribonucleic acid (DNA), 37–41
Deoxyribose, 37
Dependent variable, 5–6
Depolarization, 80
Deprenyl, 247
Depressant, 377
Depression, 454–458
Depth of focus, 131
Dermatome, 171
Descending analgesic pathway, 176–177
Descending motor pathways, 45, 196–200
Desynchronization, internal, 349
Desynchronized EEG, 356, 357, 358
Detector mechanism, 293
Detoxified addicts, 386
Developmental dyslexias, 421–422
Developmental effects, of sex hormones, 315–330
Dexamethasone, 458
Dexfenfluramine, 310–311
Dextrals, 398
Dialysis, cerebral, 115, 389
Diastoles, 110
Diathesis, 457–458
Diathesis–stress model, of depression, 457–458
Diazepam, 96, 459
Dichotic listening test, 120, 397–398, 405, 406–407
Dichotomous traits, 34
Diencephalon, 64, 66–67, 73, 266–267. See also Hypothalamus; Thalamus
Diet-induced thermogenesis, 305, 308
Diethylstilbestrol, 337
Dieting, 311. See also Weight-loss programs
Difference image, 122
Differentiation, of cells, 212–214
Digestion, 289–292
Digit span, 119, 262
Digit span + 1 test, 262
Digit-span subtest of WAIS, 119
Digit-symbol subtest of WAIS, 119
Dihydrotestosterone, 324, 332
Dimorphic, 321
Dimorphisms, sexual, 323
Directed synapses, 86
Directional coordinates, for vertebrate anatomy, 61–62
Distal, 62
Distal segment, 248, 249
Diuretic, 377
Dizygotic twins, 46–48. See also Twin studies
DNA, 37–41
DNA-binding proteins, 38
Dogs
  principle of antithesis and, 427
  narcolepsy in, 364, 365
Dominance
  cerebral, 397
  ocular, 146, 147
  social, 26, 436
Dominance hierarchies, 26, 436
Dominant hemisphere, 396
Dominant trait, 34, 37
Dopamine transporters, 391

Dopamine, 44, 93, 114, 336, 389
  and addiction, 390, 391–392
  and Parkinson's disease, 77, 241, 247
  and schizophrenia, 451–454
Dopamine-cell depolarization block, 453
Dorsal, 61
Dorsal-column medial-lemniscus system, 171–172
Dorsal columns, 171–172
Dorsal horns, 62–63
Dorsal root, of spinal cord, 62–63
Dorsal root ganglia, 63
Dorsal stream, 161–165, 182
Dorsal-ventral axis, 61, 62
Dorsolateral corticorubrospinal tract, 197, 198–200
Dorsolateral corticospinal tract, 196–197, 198–200
Dorsolateral prefrontal association cortex, 188, 191–192, 208–209
Dorsum, 27
Dose-response curve, 371
Double-blind design, 464, 465
Down syndrome, 38, 238
Dreaming, 345–347
Drinking
  cessation of, 300
  premeal, 294
Drug addiction, 370, 372–373
  biopsychological theories of, 386–387
  Freud and, 392–393
  neural mechanisms of, 389–392
  Parkinson's disease and, 247
  treatment programs for, 385, 386–387
Drug compartment, 390
Drug metabolism, 371
Drug self-administration paradigm, 390
Drug sensitization, 371, 375, 381
Drug tolerance, 363, 371–372, 373–376, 378, 379, 381
Drugs, 9, 370–373
  antidepressant, 354–355, 361, 373, 374, 455, 456–457
  antischizophrenic, 450–451
  antisense, 117
  anxiolytic, 96, 123, 363, 459–460
  clinical trials of, 463–466
  commonly abused, 376–385
  psychoactive, 95–98, 370, 371, 372, 459–460
  in research, 9, 11, 114–116
  sleep and, 361–362
DTs, 378
Dual-opponent color cells, 152, 153
Dualism, Cartesian, 20, 21
Duchenne smile, 432–433
Duck-billed platypus, 27
Duodenum, 290, 301
Duplexity theory, of vision, 134
Dura mater, 53, 54
Dural sinuses, 53
Dynamic contraction, 200–204
Dynamic phase, of VMH syndrome, 299–300
Dyslexia, 121, 421–423

Ear, 166–168
Eardrum, 166, 167
Eating. See also Hunger; Satiety
  cessation of, 300
  disorders of, 289, 293–294
  energy and, 289–292
  factors in, 295–298
  theories of, 292–294
Ebbinghaus illusion, 207
ECG, 110
ECS, 268–270
Echolalia, 449, 461

Ecstasy (MDMA), 381
Ectoderm, 213
Edema, 252, 414
Edge perception, 141–149
EEG. See Electroencephalogram
Effector mechanism, 293
Efferent nerves, 51, 52, 320, 436, 441
Efflux, of ions, 79–80
Egg cells, 35–37, 212, 316
Egocentric, 278
Egocentric left, 190
Ejaculation, 123, 325
EKG, 110
Electrical stimulation, 113
Electrical synapses, 91–92
Electrocardiogram (ECG or EKG), 110
Electroconvulsive shock (ECS), 268–270
Electrodermal activity, 109
Electroencephalogram (EEG), 9
    desynchronized, 356, 357, 358
    epilepsy and, 239–241, 261, 416–417
    scalp, 106–108
    stages of sleep on, 343–345
Electroencephalography, 106–108, 261
    invasive, 113, 114
Electromyogram (EMG), 108–109, 343, 346
Electromyography, 108–109, 343, 346, 432
Electron micrograph, 60, 61, 200
Electron microscopy, 60
Electrooculogram (EOG), 109, 343
Electrooculography, 109, 343
Electrophysiological recording methods, 113–114
Electrostatic pressure, of ions, 78–80
Elevated plus maze, 123, 460
Embolism, 233, 234
Embryologists, 227
Embryonic neural stem cells, 255–256
Emergent stage 1 EEG, 343–345
Emetic, 124
EMG, 108–109, 343, 346
Emotions
    autonomic nervous system and, 429–431
    brain mechanisms and, 443–446
    cardiovascular activity and, 109, 110
    evolution of, 426–427
    facial expressions and, 431–433, 444–446
    lateralization of brain function and, 406
    theories of, 427–428
Emphysema, 377
Empirical methods, 13
Encapsulated tumors, 233
Encéphale isolé preparation, 356–357
Encephalitis, 237
Encephalitis lethargica, 356
Endocrine glands, 315–321. See also specific glands
Endoderm, 213
Endogenous attention, 181
Endogenous depression, 455
Endogenous melatonin, 361–362
Endogenous neurotoxins, 237
Endoplasmic reticulum, 56
Endorphins, 94, 95, 176, 383
Energy metabolism
    body weight and, 304–307, 308, 309, 311
    digestion and, 289–292
    food supply and, 293–294
    satiety and, 296, 297
Energy set point, 292
Engram, 271
Entorhinal cortex, 244
Entrainment, 349, 359–360
Environmental factors
    circadian rhythms and, 348–349
    drug tolerance/addiction and, 374–376, 387
    fear and, 443

intelligence and, 46–48
multiple sclerosis and, 242
narcolepsy and, 364
obesity and, 308
Enzymatic degradation, 90, 91, 92, 96, 97
Enzymes, 91, 92, 96, 371
EOG, 109, 343
Ephrin-A and -B, 218
Epidemiology, 242
Epilepsy, 239–241
    commissurotomy and, 401–402, 404
    cortical stimulation and, 416–417
    kindling model of, 246
Epileptic auras, 239
Epileptogenesis, 246
Epinephrine, 93, 436, 439
Episodic memories, 120, 264
EPSPs, 80–83
Equipotentiality, principle of, 124
ERPs, 107–108
Esophagus, 290, 301, 303
Estradiol, 317, 324–325, 332, 333–334
    adult neurogenesis and, 441
    progesterone and, 336
Estrogens, 254, 317, 320–321, 326–327. See also
    Estradiol
    female sexual behavior and, 332
    in surgical sexual reassignment, 338
Estrous cycle, 332
Estrus, 332
Ethical issues, in biopsychological research, 5, 6–7
Ethological research, 11
Ethology, 20–21
Event-related potentials (ERPs), 107–108
Evolution, 24
    behavior and, 25–27
    Darwin's theory of, 24–25, 426–427
    of humans, 27–31
Evolutionary perspective, 3
Evolutionary psychology, 11, 31–34
Exaptations, 31
Excision, 414, 415
Excitatory postsynaptic potentials (EPSPs), 80–83
Excitotoxins, 380
Exercise
    jet lag and, 350, 351
    neuroplasticity and, 224
    obesity and, 308, 309
Exocrine glands, 315
Exocytosis, 87–88, 90, 96
Exogenous attention, 181
Exogenous melatonin, 361–362
Experience
    behavior and, 42–45
    hormone release and, 320
    neurodevelopment and, 221–223
    neuroplasticity and, 225
Experimental autoimmune encephalomyelitis, 242
Experiments, 5–6
Explicit memories, 120, 264–265, 272
Expression, of genes. See Gene expression
Expression, of long-term potentiation, 283,
    284–285
Expression of Emotions in Man and Animals, The,
    426, 427
Expressive, 411
Extensors, 200, 201
Exteroceptive sensory systems, 156, 170
Extracellular unit recording, 113, 114
Extrafusal muscle, 202
Extraversion, 445
Extraversion/neuroticism, 445–446
Eyeblink response, 263, 280
Eyes, 130–141
    movements of, 13–14, 109, 132, 136–138, 183,
    188–189, 215–216, 217, 222–223, 343

Facial cranial nerves, 180, 472, 473
Facial electromyography, 432
Facial expressions, 431–433, 444–446
Facial feedback hypothesis, 431–432
Facial recognition, 157, 164–166, 410
Fallopian tubes, 322–323
Far-field potentials, 108
FAS, 378
Fasciculation, 217
Fast muscle fibers, 200
Fasting phase, of energy metabolism,
    291–292
Fats, 290–291, 294, 300–301
Fear, 433. See also Anxiety
Fear conditioning, 441–443, 444
Feminization, 325–326, 327
Fenfluramine, 310–311
Ferrets, neurodevelopment in, 223
Fertility, 332
Fertilization, 35–37, 316, 322
Fetal alcohol syndrome (FAS), 378
Fetal hormones, 322–323
Fetal tissue, transplantation of, 255
Filopodia, 215, 216
Finches
    evolution of, 25
    song development in, 45
Firing, of neurons, 80–83, 144–145, 282
First messengers, 89. See also Neurotransmitters
First-night phenomenon, 343
Fissures, 67, 69, 73, 169–170
Fitness, 67, 69, 73, 169–170
Flatulence, 382
Flavor, 177
Flexors, 200, 201
Flight, 435
Fluoxetine, 456, 457
fMRI. See Functional MRI
Follicle-stimulating hormone (FSH), 320
Food supply, consistency of, 293–294, 308
Forebrain, 64, 214
    basal, 268
Fornix, 70, 428, 430
Fortification illusions, 129–130, 149
Fossil records, 24–25, 27–29
Fourier analysis, 148–149, 166, 167
Fovea, 133, 134, 136
Fraternal twins, 46–48. See also Twin studies
Free fatty acids, 291
Free-feeding levels, 304
Free nerve endings, 170
Free-running period, 349–350
Free-running rhythms, 349–350
Freezing, 435, 460
Frequency, 166, 168, 223, 408, 409
Frogs, axon regeneration in, 215–216, 217
Frontal eye field, 188, 191
Frontal lobe, 67, 69, 121
Frontal operculum, 408
Frontal sections, of brain, 62
Fruit fly genes, 36
FSH, 320
Functional brain imaging, 4, 10, 104–106, 165,
    208–209, 398, 419. See also Functional MRI;
    Positron emission tomography
Functional columns, 147, 148
Functional homogeneity, 157, 158
Functional MRI (fMRI), 105
    and auditory cortex, 223
    and emotions, 444
    and extraversion/neuroticism, 445–446
    and fear, 443
    and motor equivalence, 206
    and paired-image subtraction technique, 122
    and reading, 419–420

and selective attention, 182
and vision, 161
Functional segregation, 157, 158, 187
Functional tolerance, 372, 378
Fusiform face area, 165

G proteins, 89
GABA. *See* Gamma-aminobutyric acid
GABA$_A$ receptors, 96, 460
Galápagos Islands, 25
Gall bladder, 290
Gametes, 35–37, 316. *See also* Ova; Sperm
Gamma-aminobutyric acid (GABA), 92, 96, 98
alcohol and, 378
schizophrenia and, 453
Ganglia, 58. *See also* Basal ganglia
dorsal root, 63
Gap junctions, 91–92
Gases, soluble, 92, 93–94, 95, 285
Gastric ulcers, 436–437
Gastritis, 378
Gastrointestinal tract, 289–290, 301–302, 303
Gate-control theory, of pain, 176
Gene(s), 34–41. *See also* Genetics
dominant, 238
mutations of, 38, 39, 241, 328
Gene expression, 38–39, 40, 41, 223, 238, 310, 315–316
Gene knockout techniques, 117
Gene maps, 37
Gene replacement techniques, 117
General paresis, 237
Generalizability, 7
Generalized anxiety disorders, 459
Generalized epilepsy, 239, 240–241
Generalized seizures, 240–241, 261
Genetic code, 38–39
Genetic engineering, 117
Genetics, 34–41, 117. *See also* Heritability
and affective disorders, 455
and Alzheimer's disease, 244
and autism, 226
and behavioral development, 42–45
and brain damage, 237–238
of circadian rhythms, 360
and multiple sclerosis, 242
and obesity, 308
of psychological differences, 16–18
and sexual orientation, 337
Genitals, 323
Genotype, 34
Gland(s)
endocrine, 315–321
exocrine, 315
mammary, 27
parotid, 290
pineal, 316, 361–362
pituitary, 67, 68, 73, 316, 317–320, 321, 324
Glans, 323, 324
Glaucoma, and marijuana, 380
Glia-mediated migration, 214, 215
Glial cells, 54, 58–59, 217
functions of, 91–92, 218, 248–249
radial, 214
Glial stem cells, 213
Global amnesia, 262
Global aphasia, 416
Globus pallidus, 72
Glossopharyngeal cranial nerve, 180, 472, 473
Glucagon, 291–292
Glucocorticoids, 436, 439, 440, 458
Gluconeogenesis, 291
Glucose, 290, 291, 317
blood levels of, 293, 294, 298–299, 320
Glucostatic theory, 293

Glutamate, 92, 235–236
addiction and, 378, 392
long-term potentiation and, 283–285
schizophrenia and, 453
Glycine, 92
Glycogen, 290–291
Godfrey's Cordial, 382
Golgi complex, 56, 87
Golgi stain, 59–60
of neocortex, 70
of pyramidal neurons, 74
Golgi tendon organs, 200–202, 205
Gonadectomy, 323, 324, 329–332, 334–335, 336, 434
Gonadotrophic hormone, 326
Gonadotropin, 317, 320–321
Gonadotropin-releasing hormone, 320–321, 323–324
Gonads, 316–318, 320–323. *See also* Ovaries; Testes
Graded responses, 80
Grammatical analysis, 419
Grand mal seizure, 240
Granule cells, 440
Gray matter, 62
Growth cones, 215–216, 217
Growth hormone, 326
Guanine, 37–38, 39
Guidance molecules, 217
Guilty-knowledge technique, 430, 431
Guinea pigs
lithium and, 456
sexual behavior in, 325, 332
Guinness Book of World Records, 352
Gulls, aggression in, 427
Gustation. *See* Taste
Gynecomastia, 353
Gyrus (gyri), 67, 73
angular, 411–412, 413
cingulate, 70, 73, 428, 430
Heschl's, 408
postcentral, 67, 69, 73, 172, 411
precentral, 67, 69, 73
superior temporal, 67, 69, 73

Habit formation, 280
Hair, 326, 327, 333
Hair cells, 167, 160
Hallucinations, 364, 450
Haloperidol, 452
Halstead-Reitan Neuropsychological Test Battery, 118
Hamsters
circadian rhythms in, 359, 360
jet lag in, 350, 351
pheromones and, 177–178
Handedness, 410
Hangover, 378
Harrison Narcotics Act, 382
Hash oil, 378
Hashish, 378
Headaches, migraine, 129–130
Hearing, 166–170, 223, 403–404, 405
Heart attack, 378, 379
Heart rate, 110
Hebb's postulate for learning, 282
Helicobacter pylori, 437
Helping-hand phenomenon, 403
Hematoma, 236
Hemianopsic patients, 159
Hemispherectomy, 176, 423
Hemispheres, cerebral. *See* Cerebral hemispheres
Heritability, 31–34, 47–48, 421. *See also* Genetics
Heritability estimate, 47–48
Heroin, 375, 376, 377, 382–386, 387

Heroin rush, 382
Herpes, 237
Heschl's gyrus, 408
Heterosexual, 337–338
Heterozygous, 34
Hierarchical organization, 156
of auditory cortex, 169
of sensorimotor system, 186–187
of sensory systems, 156–157
Hierarchy, 156
of social dominance, 26
Hindbrain, 64, 214
Hippocampus, 69, 273–274, 276
Alzheimer's disease and, 244
cerebral ischemia and, 254, 265–266
contextual fear conditioning and, 443
emotion and, 428, 430
long-term potentiation and, 281–282
memory consolidation and, 270–271
removal of, 261–264, 274, 277
spatial memory and, 277–278
stress and, 440–441
Hirsutism, 333
Hodgkin-Huxley model, 85–86
Homeostasis, 293, 296
of body weight, 305–306
sleep and, 347
Hominids, 27–31, 39, 41
Homo erectus, 27–29
Homo sapiens, 27–29
Homologous, 31
Homosexual, 337–338
Homozygous, 34
Homozygous mice, 309–310
Horizontal cells, 132
Horizontal sections, of brain, 62, 64
Hormone(s), 315–316
corticotropin-releasing, 458
gonadal, 317–318, 320–321, 330–334. *See also* Androgens; Estrogens; Progestins
hypothalamic releasing, 319, 320
peptide, 315, 318, 319
protein, 315
regulation of, 320–321
sexual development and, 321–330
steroid, 315–317, 324, 332–334
tropic, 317, 318
Horses, mating in, 33
Horseshoe crab, contrast enhancement in, 142
Hoxa 1 gene, 227
Hues, 148–149
Human evolution, 27–31
Human genome project, 39–41
Human research subjects, 5
Hunger, 289
blood glucose levels and, 298–299
body weight and, 304
factors in, 295–298
gastrointestinal tract and, 301
hypothalamus and, 299–301, 303
Pavlovian conditioning of, 296
peptides and, 302–303
serotonin and, 303
theories of, 292–294
Hunger peptides, 302–303
Huntingtin, 242
Huntington's disease, 241–242, 243
H-Y antigen, 322
Hydrocephalus, 53
Hydrochloric acid, 290
6-Hydroxydopamine (6-OHDA), 114
5-Hydroxytryptamine (5-HT), 93. *See also* Serotonin
5-Hydroxytryptophan (5-HTP), 361

Hyperphagia, 299–300, 301, 310
Hyperplasia, congenital adrenal, 328–329
Hyperpolarization, 80, 84
Hypersomnia, 362, 363–364
Hypertension, 110, 458
Hypnagogic hallucinations, 364
Hypnotic drugs, 361, 363, 459
Hypoglossal cranial nerve, 472, 473
Hypothalamic releasing hormones, 319–320
Hypothalamopituitary portal system, 319
Hypothalamus, 7, 66–67, 68, 73, 316
  control of pituitary by, 318–320
  emotion and, 428, 430
  gonadotropin release and, 321, 324
  hunger and, 299–301, 303
  nuclei of, 475
  sexual behavior and, 334–337
  sleep and, 356, 357
Hypothermia, 373–375, 377, 378
Hypoxia, 240, 333

Iatrogenic, 363
Ibotenic acid, 114
Ice, 381
ICSS, 387–389
Identical twins, 46–48. See also Twin studies
Illusions, 129–130
IM injections, 114, 370
Imipramine, 456
Immune reaction, 115
Immune system, 437–440
Immunocytochemistry, 115, 116
Immunotherapeutic approach, 245
Implicit memories, 120, 264–265, 267–268
Impotent, 331
In situ hybridization, 115–116
Inappropriate affect, 450
Incentive-sensitization theory, 386
Incomplete-pictures test, 263, 265
Incus, 166
Independent variable, 5–6
Indolamines, 93, 95
Induction, of long-term potentiation, 283–284
Infantile amnesia, 285–286
Infants, brain growth in, 220–221
Infarct, 233
Infectious disease, stress and, 439–440
Inferior, 62
Inferior colliculi, 65, 66, 168, 169, 356
Inferior olives, 228
Inferior prefrontal cortex, 397, 411–418
Inferotemporal cortex, 159, 244, 279
Infiltrating tumors, 233
Influx, of ions, 79–80, 83
Information subtest of WAIS, 119
Infrared waves, 130
Ingestion, of drugs, 370
Inhalation, of drugs, 370–371
Inhibitory factors, 319–320
Inhibitory postsynaptic potentials (IPSPs), 80–83
Initial stage 1 EEG, 343–344
Injection(s), 114, 370, 381, 383
Inoculation, 438
Inside-out pattern, 214
Insomnia, 361, 362–363, 381
Instinctive behaviors, 11, 21
Insulin, 291–292, 298–299, 300–301, 310
Integration, of signals, 81
Intelligence quotient (IQ), 46–48, 119
Intelligence tests, 119, 353, 381
Intensity, of light, 130–131
Interictal behavior, 246
Internal desynchronization, 349
Internal lamina, of thalamus, 474
Interneurons, 57, 58, 85

Interoceptive somatosensory system, 170
Intracellular unit recording, 113
Intracranial self-stimulation (ICSS), 387–389
Intrafusal motor neuron, 201–202
Intrafusal muscle, 201–202
Intragastric injections, 114
Intramuscular (IM) injections, 114, 370
Intraperitoneal (IP) injections, 114
Intraspecific defense, 433–434, 435
Intravenous (IV) injection, 114, 370, 381, 383
Intromission, 123, 325
Invasive physiological research methods, 110–114
Ion channels, 78–80, 83–84, 87, 89, 378
Ionotropic receptors, 89, 91
Ions, 78–80, 83–84. See also specific types
IP injections, 114
Iproniazid, 456
Ipsilateral, 67
Ipsilateral movement, 405, 406
IPSPs, 80–83
IQ, 46–48, 119
Iris, 131
Ischemia. See Cerebral ischemia
Ischemic lesions, 256
Islands of memory, 268
Isometric contraction, 200–204
IV injections, 114, 370, 381, 383
I-want-a-girl-just-like-the-girl-who-married-dear-old-dad phenomenon, 178

Jacksonian seizures, 240
James-Lange theory, of emotion, 427, 428, 429, 430
Jet lag, 350, 351, 362
Joint (marijuana), 378

K complex, 343, 344
Kainic acid, 114
Ketones, 291
Kindling phenomenon, 246
Kluver-Bucy syndrome, 428–429
Knife cuts, 111, 112
Knockout mice, 117, 227, 364, 380, 392
Korsakoff's syndrome, 12–13, 266–267, 378

Labia majora, 323, 324
Labia minora, 323, 324
Labioscrotal swellings, 323, 324
Language
  cerebral cortex and, 397, 411–418
  cognitive neuroscience approach to, 418–423
  localization of, 411–418
  sign, 410
  testing of, 120–121
  Williams syndrome and, 227–228
Language lateralization, 120, 396–411
Large intestine, 290
Large-molecule neurotransmitters, 86–87
Latent dreams, 346
Lateral, 61
Lateral attack, 433–434, 435
Lateral bodies, 323, 324
Lateral communication, 132
Lateral fissure, 67, 69, 169–170
Lateral geniculate nuclei, 66, 139–141, 474
Lateral hypothalamus (LH), 299, 300–301
Lateral inhibition, 142–143
Lateral lemniscus, 168–169
Lateral tegmental field, 335, 336
Lateralization of function, 396–398. See also Cerebral hemispheres
  brain asymmetries and, 408–410
  and emotions, 444–445
  evolution of, 410–411
  examples of, 405–407

LH syndrome, 300
Librium, 96, 459
Lidocaine, 380
Lie detection, 430–431
Ligand, 88, 115
Light, 130–139, 151–152
Light-dark cycle, 348–349, 350, 351, 359–360
Limbic system, 69–72, 73, 428, 430, 434
Limbs, phantom, 256–258
Linguistic gestures, 410
Linguistic theory of cerebral asymmetry, 410
Linkage, 36–37
Lipid bilayer, 54, 57
Lipids, 290–291, 294, 300–301
Lipogenesis, 300
Lipolysis, 300
Lipostatic theory, 293
Lissencephalic, 67
Lithium, 456
Liver, 290, 291
Liver enzymes, 371
Lizard, the, 77, 255
Lobectomy, 261–264, 274–277
Lobotomy, 16–17, 261
Longitudinal fissure, 67, 69
Long-term potentiation (LTP), 281–285
Lordosis, 6, 123, 325
Lordosis quotient, 123
Loudness, 166
LTP, 281–285
Lucid dreams, 346
Luteinizing hormone (LH), 320
Lymphocytes, 437, 439

M channel, 141
Macaque monkey, visual cortex in, 161, 163
Mach bands, 142
Macrophage, 437–438
Magnetic resonance imaging (MRI), 102–104, 108

Language and, 411–418
  split-brain studies and, 399–404
Laudanum, 382
L-dopa, 77, 93, 241
Leaky-barrel model, 305–307
Learners, of birdsong, 45
Learning, 261. See also Conditioning
  basal ganglia and, 209
  drug tolerance/withdrawal and, 373–376
  eating and, 294
  Hebb's postulate for, 282
  neuroplasticity and, 280–285
  sensorimotor, 187, 208–209
Left-handers, 398
Left hemisphere, 396, 404–411
Lens, of eye, 131–132
Leptin, 310
Lesion research methods, 110–113
Lesions, 16, 110–113, 253
  bilateral, to dorsal vs. ventral stream, 164
  of hippocampus, 277
  of hypothalamus, 300–301, 335
  ischemic, 256
  of medial temporal lobe, 265, 270
  of mesocorticolimbic pathway, 389
  of primary auditory cortex, 170
  of primary motor cortex, 193, 195
  selective chemical, 114
  sleep and, 356
  of thalamus, 172
Leucotome, 16
Lexical procedure, 422
LH. See Lateral hypothalamus; Luteinizing hormone

www.ablongman.com/pinel6e

and aphasia, 415–416
and asymmetry of planum temporale, 408, 409
and damage to amygdala, 445
and hippocampal volume, 278
Magnetoencephalography (MEG), 106
Magnocellular layers, 141
Maintenance, of LTP, 283, 284–285
Malaise, 296
Malignant tumors, 233
Malleus, 166
"Mamawawa," 315, 317, 322, 327, 330, 338
Mammals, 27, 67, 347–348. See also specific species
Mammary glands, 27
Mammillary bodies, 67, 261, 267, 428, 430
Mania, 455, 456, 457
Manifest dreams, 346
MAO inhibitors, 456
Marijuana, 376, 378–380, 383–386
Masculinization, 325–326, 327
Massa intermedia, 66, 474
Mastectomy, 330
Master gland, 317. See also Pituitary gland
Maternal defensive behaviors, 435
Mating bonds, 32–34, 177
Maze(s), 42–44
  Morris water, 125, 254, 277
  radial arm, 124–125, 277, 334
MDMA, 381
Meals, 292, 312
Mechanical stimuli, 170. See also Touch
Medial, 61
Medial diencephalic amnesia, 267
Medial diencephalon, 266–267
Medial dorsal (mediodorsal) nuclei, 179, 267
Medial geniculate nuclei, 66, 168, 169, 442, 474
Medial-lateral axis, 61, 62
Medial lemniscus, 171–172
Medial prefrontal lobes, damage to, 426, 427
Medial preoptic area, 334, 335–336
Medial temporal lobe amnesia, 244, 264–266, 272–277, 280
Medial temporal lobectomy, 261–264, 274–277
Medulla, 64, 65, 73
  of adrenal gland, 436, 439
  of primordial gonad, 322
Medullary pyramids, 196, 197, 198
MEG, 106
Meiosis, 35–37
Melanopsin, 360
Melatonin, 361–362
Membrane potential, 77. See also Action potential; Postsynaptic potential; Resting potential
Memory, 2–3, 11, 261
  atropine and, 97
  brain damage and, 2–3, 9, 268, 269
  brain lateralization and, 405, 407
  conscious, 264
  consolidation of, 264, 268–271
  deficits in, 120
  episodic, 120, 264
  explicit, 120, 264–265, 267–268
  Korsakoff's syndrome and, 12–13
  marijuana use and, 379
  neuroplasticity and, 280–285
  object-recognition, 271–277
  reference, 277
  REM sleep and, 354
  social development and, 321–326
  for spatial location, 277–278
  testing of, 119, 120
  working, 221, 277, 279–280
Memory consolidation, 264, 268–271
Men-are-men-and-women-are-women
  assumption ("mamawawa"), 315, 317, 322, 327, 330, 338

Mendelian genetics, 34
Meninges, 53, 54
Meningiomas, 233
Meningitis, 237
Menstrual cycle, 317–318
Menstruation, 327–329, 332
Merkel's disks, 170
Mesencephalon, 64, 65–66, 73
Mesocorticolimbic pathway, 388–389
Mesoderm layer, 213
Mesotelencephalic dopamine system, 388–389, 392, 458
Messenger RNA, 115–116, 117
Meta-analysis, 439
Metabolic rate, 305, 308
Metabolic tolerance, 372
Metabolism, drug, 371
Metabolism, energy. See Energy metabolism
Metabolites, 451–452
Metabotropic receptors, 89–90, 91
Metastatic tumors, 233, 234
Metencephalon, 64, 65, 73
Methadone, 383
Methamphetamine (meth), 381
3,4-Methylenedioxymethamphetamine
  (MDMA), 381
Mice
  anabolic steroids and, 333
  caloric restriction and, 301
  castration of, 434
  grooming in, 207
  knockout, 117, 227, 364, 380, 392
  obese, 309–310
  transgenic, 117, 246, 247, 359
Microelectrodes, 77
Microexpressions, 432
Microfluorometric techniques, 283
Microglia, 59
Microscope, electron, 60
Microsleeps, 352, 356, 366
Microspectrophotometry, 150–151
Microtubules, 56, 87
Midbrain, 64, 214. See also Mesencephalon
Midsagittal section, of brain, 62
Migraine headaches, 129–130
Migration, of developing neurons, 214, 215
Minerals, 295
Minnesota Study of Twins Reared Apart, 46–48
Mirror hemisphere, 397
Mirror-drawing test, 262, 263
Mitochondria, 39, 41, 56
Mitochondrial DNA, 39, 41
Mitosis, 35–37, 38
Mixed episode, 466
Mixed-gender individuals, 322
Mnemonic, 264
Mock-crime procedure, 430–431
Mondrians, 151–152
Monkeys, 27, 28
  amnesia in, 265, 272–273, 274–276
  fear grimace in, 446
  hand preferences among, 410
  Kluver-Bucy syndrome in, 428
  neural reorganization in, 251
  perseverative errors by, 221
  proceptivity of, 332
  rehabilitative training and, 256
  sensorimotor system of, 193–195, 198–199
  split-brain, 400–401
  visual system of, 143, 145–146, 147, 152–153, 161, 162, 182

Monocular, 143
Monocular deprivation, 222
Monogamy, 33
Monophasic sleep cycles, 366
Monozygotic twins, 46–48. See also Twin studies
Montreal Neurological Institute, 416
Mood
  brain lateralization and, 406
  cocaine use and, 381
  sleep deprivation and, 352
Mood stabilizer, 456
Morgan's Canon, 15
Morphine, 375, 376, 381–386
Morris water maze test, 125, 254, 277
Mortality rates, 304, 367
Motion, perception of, 13–14
Motivation
  limbic system and, 70
  neural mechanisms of, 389–392
  REM sleep and, 354
Motor cortex
  neural reorganization and, 251
  primary, 191, 193–195, 208, 209, 412–413
  secondary, 188, 191, 192–193, 209
Motor discrimination, and split brain, 401, 402
Motor end-plate, 200
Motor equivalence, 206
Motor homunculus, 193–194
Motor neurons, 7, 85, 200, 201–202, 205
Motor pathways, descending, 45, 196, 200
Motor pool, 200
Motor theory of cerebral asymmetry, 409, 410
Motor units, 200
Movement(s), 187, 193–195, 198–199, 405, 406
  of eyes, 13–14, 109, 152, 156–158, 185, 188–189, 215–216, 217, 222, 223, 343
Movement agnosia, 164–165
MPTP, 247
MPTP model of Parkinson's disease, 247, 255
MRI. See Magnetic resonance imaging
Mrs. Winslow's Soothing Syrup, 382
MS, 242
Mucous membranes, 371, 437–438
Mullerian inhibiting substance, 322–323
Mullerian system, 322–323
Multiple sclerosis (MS), 242
Multiple-unit recording, 113, 114
Multipolar neuron, 57
Multipotent, 213, 255
Mumby box, 274, 275
Mumps, 237
Muscarinic receptors, 97, 98
Muscle(s), 200–205
  ciliary, 132
  energy storage in, 291
Muscle relaxants, 459
Muscle-spindle feedback circuit, 201–202, 203
Muscle spindles, 200–202
Muscle tension, 108–109
Muscle tone, and sleep, 343–345, 346, 358, 363, 364
Musical ability, 406–407
Mutations, 38, 39, 241, 328
Mutism, 397
Mutual inhibition, 142
Myelencephalon, 64, 65, 73
Myelin, 55, 58, 62, 85
Myelinated axons, 85, 220–221, 242
Myelination, 58, 85, 220–221

Napping, 365–366
Narcolepsy, 363–364
Narcotic, 379
Nasal hemiretina, 136, 140
Natural selection, 25, 32–33

Nature, 40
Nature–nurture issue, 20–21, 22–23, 329–330. *See also* Behavior, biology of; Environmental factors
NEAT, 308
Necrosis, 219, 238
Negative feedback systems, 293, 310
Negative schizophrenic symptoms, 454
Neocortex, 68–69, 70
Neonates, 222
Neophobic animals, 124
Neoplasm, 233
Nerve growth factor (NGF), 219, 254
Nerves, 51, 52, 58, 67, 167, 168, 170, 171, 172, 173, 180, 215–216, 217, 320, 359–360, 436, 441
Nervous system, 61–62. *See also* Central nervous system; Peripheral nervous system
  damage to, 219, 248–258
  endocrine glands and, 318–321
  layout of, 51–54
  methods of studying, 102–117
  sexual behavior and, 334–336
Neural crest, 214
Neural groove, 213
Neural plate, 213–214
Neural proliferation, 214
Neural regeneration, 215–216, 217, 248–250, 254
Neural reorganization, 222–223, 250–252
Neural stem cells, 213
Neural tube, 213, 214
Neuroanatomy, 4, 59–62
Neurochemistry, 4
Neurodevelopment
  disorders of, 225–229
  experience and, 221–223
  phases of, 212–220
Neuroendocrinology, 4, 315–321
Neurofibrillary tangles, 244, 245
Neurogenesis, 45, 223–224, 253–254, 441
Neuroleptics, 451–452, 453, 454, 462
Neurologist, 118
Neuromas, acoustic, 233, 234
Neuromuscular junctions, 97
Neurons, 2, 59–62
  anatomy of, 54–58
  bimodal, 193
  bipolar, 57, 132
  cholinergic, 94
  death of, 219, 220, 238, 248
  developing, 45, 212–214. *See also* Neurodevelopment
  inter-, 57, 58, 85
  intrafusal motor, 201–202
  motor, 7, 85, 200, 201–202, 205
  multipolar, 57
  noradrenergic, 93
  as photoreceptors, 360
  pyramidal, 68, 70, 74, 265–266, 440
  regrowth of, 248–250
  somatosensory, 173, 175
  spindle afferent, 202–204, 205
  in visual system, 143–149
Neuropathology, 4
Neuropeptides, 94, 95, 176, 383, 439
Neuropharmacology, 4
Neurophysiology, 4
Neuroplasticity. *See also* Neural regeneration; Neurogenesis
  Neural reorganization; Neurogenesis in adult mammals, 223–225
  experience and, 225
  in response to nervous system damage, 248–254
  sleep reduction and, 365

and treatment of brain damage, 254–258
Neuropsychological diseases, 239–245
Neuropsychological testing, 118–121
Neuropsychology, 9, 11, 12
Neuroscience, 2, 4
Neurosecretory cells, 318
Neurotic pseudoinsomniacs, 363
Neuroticism, 445
Neurotoxins, 114, 237, 381
Neurotransmitters, 56, 80. *See also specific types*
  brain locations of, 115–116
  classes of, 92–95
  large-molecule, 86–87
  peptide, 87–88, 90
  small-molecule, 87, 90
Neurotrophins, 219
New-World monkeys, 27, 28
Newborns, 222
NGF, 219, 254
Nicotine, 376–377. *See also* Tobacco
Nicotinic receptors, 97, 98
Nigrostriatal pathway, 241, 388
Nissl stain, 60
  of neocortex, 70
  of pyramidal neurons, 74
Nitric oxide, 93, 285
NMDA (N-methyl-D-aspartate) receptors, 235, 283–285
Nobel Prizes, 8
Nociceptive stimuli, 170. *See also* Pain
Nocturnal animals, 348
Nocturnal myoclonus, 363
Nodes of Ranvier, 55, 85
Noise, 107–108, 122
Nondecremental conduction, 84–85
Nondirected synapses, 86
Nonexercise activity thermogenesis (NEAT), 308
Nonexperimental studies, 6–7
Nonhuman research subjects, 5. *See also* Animals, as research subjects
Nonlinguistic gestures, 410
Noradrenergic neurons, 93
Norepinephrine, 93, 114
  depression and, 456, 457
  stress and, 436, 439
NREM sleep, 345
Nuclei, 56, 58
  of hypothalamus, 475
  lateral geniculate, 66, 139–141, 474
  medial dorsal (mediodorsal), 179, 267
  medial geniculate, 66, 168, 169, 442, 474
  paraventricular, 301, 318
  raphé, 177, 361
  red, 66, 197
  reticular REM-sleep, 358–359
  sensory relay, 66
  sexually dimorphic, 334–336
  solitary, 180
  of thalamus, 474
  ventral posterior, 66, 171–172, 180
  ventromedial, 336
  vestibular, 198, 199
Nucleotide bases, 37, 39
Nucleus accumbens, 388, 389, 390–392
Nucleus magnocellularis, 364–365
Nurture. *See* Experience; Nature–nurture issue
Nutrition, 295
Nutritive density, 296

Obesity, 289, 308–311
  set-point theories and, 293–294
  ventromedial hypothalamus and, 299–301
Object agnosia, 164–165
Object-assembly subtest of WAIS, 119
Object-recognition memory, 271–277, 278

Ob/ob mice, 309–310
Observational methods, 13
Obsessions, 459
Obsessive–compulsive disorders, 459, 461
Occipital lobe, 67, 69
Ocular dominance, 146, 147
Ocular dominance columns, 147
Oculomotor cranial nerve, 472, 473
Off-center cells, 144
Old-World monkeys, 27, 28
Olfaction, 177–179, 180, 294
Olfactory bulbs, 178–179, 261, 428, 430
Olfactory cranial nerve, 472, 473
Olfactory ensheathing cells, 254
Olfactory mucosa, 178
On-center cells, 144, 145
Ommatidia, 142, 143
"On"/"off" firing, 144–145
On the Origin of Species, 24
Ontogeny, 42–45
Open-ended learners, 45
Open-field test, 123
Opiates, 66, 94, 176, 177, 381–386
Opium, 381
Opponent-process theory, of color vision, 150–151
Optic chiasm, 67, 68, 73, 261, 359–360
Optic nerves, 67, 215–216, 217, 359–360, 472, 473
Optic tectum, 65, 216, 217
Optic tracts, 359–360
Optical imaging techniques, 283
Oral cancer, 393
Orbicularis oculi, 432–433
Orbitofrontal cortex, 179
Orchidectomy, 323, 330, 337
Orexin, 364
Organ of Corti, 166–168
Organization of Behavior, The, 4
Orphan drugs, 465
Orthodromic conduction, 85
Ossicles, 166
Ova, 212, 316
Oval window, 166–168
Ovariectomy, 323, 332, 334
Ovaries, 254, 316–317, 322–323, 324
Overdose, drug, 374–375, 383
Overt attention, 183
Owls, barn
  neurodevelopment in, 223
  sound localization by, 169
Oxytocin, 318–319

P channel, 141
PAG. *See* Periaqueductal gray
Pacinian corpuscles, 170
Pain, 170, 172, 175–177
Paired-image subtraction technique, 121
Palatability, 298
Paleontologists, 30
Palilalia, 461
Palpation, 406
Pancreas, 290, 316
Pancreatitis, 378
Panic disorders, 459
Pantomime, 410
Papillae, 179
Paradigms, behavioral, 117–118, 123–126, 280, 390, 433–434
Parallel processing, 158, 162–164

Paranoid schizophrenia, 380
Paraplegic, 17
Paraplegic rats, 254, 256
Parasympathetic nerves, 51–52, 320, 470
Parathyroid gland, 316
Paraventricular nuclei, 301, 318
Parietal cortex, 31
Parietal lobe, 67, 69
Parkinson's disease, 72, 77, 241, 388
  in drug addicts, 247
  MPTP model of, 247, 255
  neurotransplantation and, 255
  striatal damage and, 280, 451
Parotid gland, 290
Partial epilepsy, 239
Partial seizure, 239–240
Parvocellular layers, 141
Patellar tendon reflex, 202–204
Pavlovian conditioning, 263, 296, 375
Pavlovian conditioning paradigm, 124, 280
Pea plants, inheritance in, 34, 35
Penis, 323, 324, 325, 329–330, 338, 345, 346, 359
Pepsin, 290
Peptide hormones, 315, 318, 319
Peptide neurotransmitters, 87–88, 90
Peptides, 87
  hunger and satiety, 302 303
Perception, 157. See also Attention; Audition;
  Pain; Smell; Taste; Touch; Vision
  edge, 141–149
  of motion, 13 14
Perfect pitch, 408, 409
Performance subtest of WAIS, 119
Periaqueductal gray (PAG), 66, 176–177, 336, 442
Perimetry test, 159, 160
Perinatal, 324
Perinatal hormones, behavioral development and,
  324, 325–326
Peripheral nervous system (PNS), 51–52. See
  also Autonomic nervous system; Somatic
  nervous system
  myelination in, 58
  regeneration in, 248–250
Perseveration, 121, 221
Perseverative errors, 221
PET. See Positron emission tomography
Petit mal seizure, 240
Phagocytes, 437
Phagocytosis, 437
Phalloplasty, 330
Phantom limbs, 256–258
Pharmacological research methods, 114–116
Phase advances/delays, 350
Phenothiazines, 452
Phenotype, 34
Phenylketonuria (PKU), 44, 238
Phenylpyruvic acid, 44
Pheromones, 177
Phobic anxiety disorders, 459
Phonemes, 417
Phonetic procedure, 422
Phonological analysis, 419
Phonology, 121
Phosphate, 37
Photons, 130
Photopic spectral sensitivity curve, 136, 137
Photopic vision, 134, 136, 137
Photoreceptors, 360. See also Cones; Rods
Phyla, 27
Phylogeny, 42
Physical-dependence theories of addiction, 386
Physically dependent, 372
Physiological-or-psychological thinking, 20,
  21–22
Physiological psychology, 8–9, 11, 12

Pia mater, 53
Picture-arrangement subtest of WAIS, 119
Picture-completion subtest of WAIS, 119
Pigment, 138
Pigs, thyrotropin-releasing hormone and,
  319–320
Piloerection, 433, 435
Pineal gland, 316, 361–362
Pioneer growth cones, 217
Piriform cortex, 179
Pitch, 166, 168, 223, 408, 409
Pituitary gland, 67, 68, 73, 316, 317–320, 321, 324
Pituitary stalk, 317, 318, 319
PKU, 44, 238
Place cells, 277–278
Place fields, 277
Placebo-control groups, 463–464, 465
Placebos, 463–465
Placental barrier, 325
Place-reference paradigm, 390
Planum temporale, 408, 409, 411
Plasticity, of nervous system, 212. See also
  Neuroplasticity
Platypus, duck-billed, 27
Pleasure, anticipated, 294,
Pleasure centers, 124, 387–389
Plethysmography, 110
PNS. See Peripheral nervous system
Polarization, 78
Polyandry, 33
Polygraphy, 430–431
Polygyny, 32–33
Polyphasic sleep cycles, 365 366
Pons, 65, 73
Population spike, 282
Portal vein, 319
Positive-incentive theories, 294, 311, 386, 392
Positive-incentive value, 294, 298, 308, 311
Positive schizophrenic symptoms, 454
Positron emission tomography (PET), 104–105
  and dopamine involvement in addiction, 391
  and dyslexia, 421–422
  and naming, 420
  and pain, 176
  and paired-image subtraction technique, 122
  and programmed movements, 193
  and sensorimotor learning, 208
  and spatial memory, 278
  and visual cortex, 161
Postcentral gyri, 67, 69, 172, 411
Posterior, 61
Posterior hypothalamus, 356, 357
Posterior parietal (association) cortex, 159,
  188–191, 208, 244
Posterior parietal lobe, 173
Posterior pituitary, 317
Postsynaptic inhibition, 86
Postsynaptic potentials, 80–83
Posttraumatic amnesia (PTA), 268
Posttraumatic stress disorder, 459
Potassium ions, 78–80, 83–84, 89
Precentral gyri, 67, 69
Predatory aggression, 434, 435
Predementia Alzheimer's patients, 267–268
Preferences, taste, 295
Prefrontal cortex
  depression and, 458
  development of, 220–221
  language and, 397, 411–418
  memory and, 244, 279–280
Prefrontal lobes, 16–17, 176
Prefrontal lobotomy, 16–17, 176, 426, 427
Premeal hunger, 296
Premotor cortex, 192–193, 208
Prenatal stress, 440

Prestriate cortex, 159
Presynaptic inhibition, 86
Primary auditory cortex, 168–170, 412–413
Primary gustatory cortex, 180
Primary motor cortex, 191, 193–195, 208, 209,
  412–413
Primary sensory cortex, 156–159
Primary somatosensory cortex (SI), 171–174,
  208–209
Primary visual cortex, 139–141, 412–413
  damage to, 159–161
  organization of, 146–147, 148, 152–153
  pathways from, 161–166
Primates, 27–31, 39, 41, 247
Primed, 387
Primordial gonads, 322–323
Principle of antithesis, 427
Principle of equipotentiality, 124
Procaine, 380
Proceptive behaviors, 325–326, 332
Progesterone, 332, 336
Progesterone receptors, 336
Progestins, 317, 320–321. See also Progesterone
Proliferation, of neural tube cells, 214
Promiscuity, 32
Proof, 321–322
Proprioceptive somatosensory system, 170
Prosimians, 27, 28
Prosody, 444
Prosopagnosia, 157, 164–166
Protein hormones, 315
Protein kinases, 284
Proteins, 38, 41, 54, 57, 89, 254, 290–291
Protocol, for clinical trial, 463–464
Proximal, 62
Proximal segment, 248, 249
Prozac, 456, 457
Psychiatric disorder, 449. See also specific disorders
Psychoactive drugs, 95–98, 370, 371, 372, 459–460
Psychobiology, 4. See also Biopsychology
Psychological dependence, 373
Psychological differences, and genetics, 46–48
Psychology, 4, 11
Psychoneuroimmunology, 437–440
Psychopharmacology, 9, 11. See also Drugs
Psychophysiological recording methods, 106 110
Psychophysiology, 9–10
Psychosomatic disease, 157
Psychotherapeutic drugs, 463–466
PTA, 268
P300 wave, 108
Puberty, 326–327
Pubic hair, 326, 327
Pulsatile hormone release, 320
Punch-drunk syndrome, 236–237
Punishment, 124
Pupil, of eye, 131
Pure research, 7–8, 9
Purkinje effect, 136
Putamen, 72
Pyloric sphincter, 290, 301, 303
Pyramidal cell layer, 265, 266
Pyramidal cells, 68, 70, 74, 440

Quasiexperimental studies, 6–7

Rabbits, eyeblink response of, 280
Rabies, 237
Radial arm maze test, 124–125, 277, 334
Radial glial cells, 214
Radial migration, 214
Radio-frequency current, 111
Random motion, of ions, 78–80
Raphé nuclei, 177, 361
Rapid eye movements (REMs), 343, 358

Rats
  aggressive behavior of, 433–434, 435
  anticonvulsant effect of alcohol on, 373, 374
  and anxiety, 460
  behavioral paradigms and, 123–126
  circadian cycles in, 359
  dopamine and, 390
  drug tolerance and withdrawal effects in, 375
  eating and, 294, 296, 297, 298, 300, 301, 303, 304–305
  epilepsy and, 246
  fear conditioning of, 441
  hormones in, 324, 334
  long-term potentiation in, 281–282
  mazes and, 42–44, 124–125
  memory consolidation in, 251
  neural reorganization in, 222
  neurodevelopment in, 254
  neuroplasticity in, 254
  object-recognition amnesia in, 273–277
  pleasure centers in, 387–388
  response learning in, 196
  sexual behavior in, 332, 334–335, 336
  sleep deprivation in, 353
  spatial memory in, 124–125, 277, 278
  stem cell transplantation in, 256
  stress response in, 440
  taste aversion in, 295
Reactive depression, 455
Reading, 419–423
Recall, 284–285
Receptive, 411
Receptive field
  of somatosensory neuron, 173, 175
  of visual neuron, 143–149
Receptiveness, 332
Receptor blockers, 95, 451–452. See also
  Antagonists
Receptor subtypes, 88
Receptors, 88–90, 91, 96, 97, 98. See also Cones;
  Rods
  brain locations of, 115
  cutaneous, 170–171
  NMDA, 235, 283–285
  progesterone, 336
Recessive trait, 34, 37
Reciprocal innervation, 204
Reconsolidation, 270
Recovery, from nervous system damage, 252–258
Recuperation theories of sleep, 347, 348, 350
Recurrent collateral inhibition, 204–205
Recycling, of neurotransmitters, 91
Red nucleus, 66, 197
Reference memory, 277
Reflectance, 152
Reflexes, 202–204
Relapse, 386–387
Relative refractory period, 84
Refractory periods, 84
Refraction, 132
Regeneration, neural, 215–216, 217, 248–250, 254
Rehabilitative training, 256–258
Reinforcement, 124
Releasing factors, 319
Releasing hormones, 320
REM rebound, 353
REM sleep, 345
  deprivation of, 353–355
  disorders related to, 364–365
  dreaming and, 345–346
  narcolepsy and, 364
REMs, 343, 358
Remyelination, 242
Renaissance, 20
Renshaw cells, 205

Reorganization, neural, 222–223, 250–252
Repetition priming tests, 120, 264
Replacement injections, 331–332, 337
Replication, of chromosome, 38
Repolarization, in action potential, 84
Repression, dreams and, 346
Reproductive barrier, 26–27
Reproductive organs, development of, 322–325, 327–330
Reptiles, 27
Reptilian stare, 77
Research
  characteristics of, 5–8
  ethological, 11
  Research methods. See also Brain imaging
    behavioral, 117–126
    ethological, 11, 20–21
    genetic, 117
    invasive physiological, 110–114
    pharmacological, 114–116
    psychophysiological recording, 106–110
Reserpine, 451
Response-chunking hypothesis, 207
Resting potential, 77–80, 305
Restless legs, 363
Reticular activating system, 358. See also Reticular
  formation
Reticular formation, 65, 66, 73, 173, 198, 199
  orexin and, 364
  sleep and, 356–359
Reticular REM-sleep nuclei, 358–359
Retina, 132–141
Retina-geniculate-striate pathway, 139–141, 143–144
Retinal disparity, 146
Retinal ganglion cells, 132, 133, 135, 215–216, 360
Retinex theory, of color vision, 152–153
Retinohypothalamic tracts, 359–360
Retinotopic, 140, 168
Retrograde amnesia, 261–262, 267, 268–271
Retrograde degeneration, 248, 249
Retrograde memory deficits, 120
Retrograde tracing methods, 61
Retrograde transmission, 94
Retrograde transneuronal degeneration, 248, 249
Reuptake, 90–91, 92, 96, 97
Reversible lesions, 112
Rhesus monkey, fear grimace in, 446
Rhinal cortex, 273–274, 276, 278
Rhodopsin, 138–139
Ribonucleic acid (RNA), 38–39, 115–116, 117
Ribosomes, 39, 56, 87
Richardson's ground squirrel, brain activity
  in, 115
Right-handers, 398
Right hemisphere, 396, 404–411, 444–445
Right parietal lobe, 21–22
Rising phase, of action potential, 84
Risk assessment, 435
Risk-assessment test, 435
RNA, 38–39, 115–116, 117
Robotics, brain signals and, 194–195
Rods, 134–139, 359–360
Roman Church, and science, 20
Rostral, 61, 62
Rotary-pursuit test, 262, 264
Round window, 168
Ruffini endings, 170

Saccades, 136–138
Saccharin, eating and, 294
Sagittal sections, of brain, 62
Saliva, 290
Salutary conduction, 85
Salutary effects, 440

Satiety, 292–294, 296–298, 303
Satiety peptides, 302–303
Savants, 226
SC injections, 114, 370
Scalp electroencephalography, 106–108, 239
Scanning electron microscope, 60
Schizophrenia, 380, 449–454
Schwann cells, 58, 248–250
  Science, 40
Scientific inference, 13–14
Scientific journals, 15
Scientific method, 13
SCL, 109
Sclerosis, 242
SCN, 359–361
Scotoma, 159–160, 161, 400, 403
Scotopic spectral sensitivity curve, 136, 137, 138
Scotopic vision, 134, 136, 137, 138
SCR, 109
Scrotum, 322–323, 324
Sea horses, mating of, 33
Seals, social dominance among, 26
Second messenger, 89, 378
Secondary gustatory cortex, 180
Secondary motor cortex, 188, 191, 192–193, 209
Secondary sensory cortex, 156–159, 279
Secondary sex characteristics, 326–327, 328–329
Secondary somatosensory cortex (SII), 171–172, 173, 209
Secondary visual cortex, 159
  damage to, 164–165
  functional areas of, 161–166
Sectioning, 111, 112
Sedative, 96
Seizures
  generalized, 240–241
  marijuana and, 380
  partial, 239–240
Selective attention, 159, 181–183
Selective breeding, 25
Selective norepinephrine-reuptake inhibitors
  (SNRIs), 456
Selective serotonin-reuptake inhibitors (SSRIs),
  456–457, 460
Self-awareness, in chimpanzees, 22
Self-stimulation, intracranial, 387–389
Self-stimulation paradigm, 124
Semantic analysis, 419
Semantic memory, 120, 264
Semantics, 121
Semicircular canals, 167, 168
Seminal vesicles, 322–323
Sensation, 157. See also Audition; Pain; Smell;
  Taste; Touch; Vision
Sensitive period, 44, 222, 326
Sensitivity, in vision, 131, 136, 137, 138
Sensorimotor association cortex, 188–192
Sensorimotor learning, 187, 208–209
Sensorimotor phase, of birdsong development,
  44–45
Sensorimotor spinal circuits, 200–205
Sensorimotor system, 186–188
  association cortex in, 188–192
  basal ganglia in, 195–196
  central programs in, 206–209
  cerebellum in, 195
  descending motor pathways in, 196–200
  motor cortex in, 192–195
  spinal circuits in, 200–205
Sensory cortex, 156, 157, 158, 279
Sensory discrimination, and split brain, 401, 402
Sensory evoked potential, 107–108
Sensory feedback, 187
Sensory phase, of birdsong development, 44
Sensory relay nuclei, 66

Sensory-specific satiety, 297–298
Sensory systems, 156–159. See also Audition; Smell; Taste; Touch; Vision
Septal aggression, 434
Septal rage, 434
Septum, 70, 428, 430, 434
Serial system, 158
Serotonin, 93
  depression and, 456–457
  obesity and, 310–311
  satiety and, 303
  schizophrenia and, 453
  sleep and, 361–362
Serotonin agonists, 460
Set point, 289, 292–294, 303–307
Set-point assumption, 292–294, 303–307
Set-point mechanism, 293
Settling point, 305–307
Sex chromosomes, 37, 316, 322, 325, 328
Sex hormones, 315, 330–338
Sex-linked traits, 37
Sex offenders, 330–331
Sexual arousal, measurement of, 110
Sexual attractiveness, 332
Sexual behavior, 6, 294, 325, 330–332
  measurement of, 123
  neural mechanisms of, 334–336
Sexual development, 321–330
Sexual differentiation, 322–326, 338
Sexual dimorphisms, 323
Sexual identity, 329–330, 338
Sexual intercourse, 123, 316, 325
Sexual orientation, 337–338
Sexually dimorphic nucleus, 334–336
Sham eating, 296
Sham rage, 428
Sheep, thyrotropin releasing hormone in, 319–320
Shift work, 350
Sign language, 410
Signal averaging, 107–108, 122
Signal proteins, 54, 57, 89
Signal, 81, 107–108, 122
Signal gradients, 217–218
Signal-to-noise ratio, 122
Signature, motor equivalence and, 206
Similarities subtest of WAIS, 119
Simple cells, 144–145
Simple partial seizure, 210
Simultanagnosia, 183
Sinestrals, 398
Sine-wave grating, 147–149
Sine waves, 147–149, 166, 167
Single-test approach, 118
Situational specificity of drug tolerance, 373–375
Skeletal muscle, 202
Skill training, neuroplasticity and, 225
Skin conductance level (SCL), 109
Skin conductance response (SCR), 109
Skin receptors, 170–171
Sleep
  in animals, 347–348
  brain areas involved in, 356–359
  circadian cycles of, 348–350, 359–360
  deprivation of, 350–356, 458
  disorders of, 361, 362–365, 381
  drugs and, 361–362
  long-term reduction of, 342, 365–367
  NREM, 345
  psychophysiological measures of, 343–345
  REM, 345–346, 353–355, 364–365
  slow-wave, 345, 366
  theories of, 347
Sleep apnea, 363
Sleep EEG waves, 342–345, 347–348

Sleep inertia, 366
Sleep laboratory, 342, 343, 345, 363
Sleep latency, 363
Sleep paralysis, 364
Sleep restriction therapy, 363
Sleep spindle, 343, 344
Sleep-wake cycle, 348–350, 359–360
Sleeptalking, 346
Sleepwalking, 346
Slow muscle fibers, 200
Slow-wave sleep (SWS), 345, 366
Small intestine, 290
Small-molecule neurotransmitters, 87, 90
Smell, 177–179, 180, 294
Smiling, 432–433
Smoker's syndrome, 377
Smoking, 376–377, 381. See also Tobacco
Snacking, 295
Snakeroot, 451
Snorting, of cocaine, 381
SNRIs, 456
SNS, 51, 52, 427–428
Social aggression, 433, 434, 435
Social dominance, 26, 436
Social factors, eating and, 294, 297
Social-learning theory of sexual identity, 329–330
Sodium amytal test, 120, 397, 398, 404
Sodium deficiency, 295
Sodium ions, 78–80, 83–84, 89, 235, 302
Sodium–potassium pumps, 80, 84
Soldiers' disease, 382
Solitary nucleus, 180
Soluble gases, 92, 93–94, 95, 285
Soma, 55, 61
Somal translocation, 214, 215
Somatic nervous system (SNS), 51, 52, 427–428
Somatosensations, 170
Somatosensory homunculus, 172, 174
Somatosensory neurons, 173, 175
Somatosensory system, 170–177, 208–209, 251, 252. See also Pain; Touch
Somatotopic, 172, 193
Somnambulism, 346
"Song of Praise," 393
Songbirds, 44–45, 224
Soporific, 364
Sound, 166–170
Spandrels, 31, 459
Sparrows, white-crowned, as age-limited learners, 45
Spatial cognition
  brain lateralization and, 405, 408
  Williams syndrome and, 228
Spatial-frequency theory, 147–149
Spatial memory, 277–278
Spatial resolution, 102–104
Spatial summation, 81–82
Species, 26, 27–29
Species-common behaviors, 123
Spectral sensitivity curve, 136, 137, 138
Speed, 375, 381
Sperm, 35–37, 212, 316, 325
Sphygmomanometer, 110
Spinal accessory nerve, 472, 473
Spinal canal, 214
Spinal cord, 51, 52, 53, 62–63, 256
Spindle afferent neurons, 202–204, 205
Spinoreticular tract, 172, 173
Spinotectal tract, 172, 173
Spinothalamic tract, 172, 173
Spiroperidol, 452
Split-brain experiments, 399–401
Split-brain patients, 396, 401–404
Squirrel, Richardson's ground, brain activity in, 115

SSRIs, 456–457, 460
Stabilized retinal image, 137–138
Staining, of neural tissue, 59–60, 70, 74
Standardized-test-battery approach, 118
Stapes, 166
Starvation, 289, 311–312
Static phase, of VMH syndrome, 300
Stellate cells, 68, 70
Stem cells, 213, 255–256
Stereognosis, 170–175, 194
Stereotaxic atlas, 110, 111, 112
Stereotaxic instrument, 110, 111
Stereotaxic surgery, 110, 111
Sterility, 331–332, 333
Steroid hormones, 315, 316–317, 324, 332–334
Stimulants, 361, 380–381, 383–386. See also Amphetamines; Cocaine
Stomach, 290, 301–303
Street's Infant Quietness, 382
Stress, 435–441
  depression and, 455
  extreme, 459
  relapse and, 387
  sleep deprivation and, 353
  smoking and, 377
Stressors, 435–436, 439
Stretch reflex, 202–204
Striate cortex, 139. See also Primary visual cortex
Striatum, 72, 241
  memory and, 280
  Parkinson's disease and, 451
  Tourette syndrome and, 462
String of beads synapses, 86, 93
Strokes, 233, 235–236, 253, 256, 265–266, 398, 410
Structural genes, 38
Stuporous catatonic schizophrenia, 449
Subarachnoid space, 53, 54
Subcutaneous (SC) injections, 114, 370
Subdural hematoma, 236
Subjective contours, 161, 162
Subordination stress, 436
Subsongs, bird, 44
Substantia nigra, 66, 77, 241, 247, 388
Suicide, affective disorders and, 455
Sulci, 67
Superior, 62
Superior colliculi, 65, 66, 169, 356
Superior olives, 168–169, 228
Superior temporal gyri, 67, 69
Supplementary motor area, 192–193
Suprachiasmatic nuclei (SCN), 359–361
Supraoptic nuclei, 318
Surface dyslexia, 422
Surface interpolation, 133
Surgical sexual reassignment, 338
Sweat glands, 109
SWS, 345, 366
Sympathetic nerves, 51–52, 320, 436, 441, 470
Synapses, 52, 55. See also Synaptic transmission
  formation of new, 218–219
  rearrangement of, 219–220
  structure of, 86, 93
Synaptic clefts, 86
Synaptic transmission, 86–92
  learning and, 280–285
  pharmacology of, 95–98
Synaptic vesicles, 56, 95
Synaptogenesis, 218–219, 220, 221
Synergistic muscles, 200
Syntax, 121
Synthesis, 95, 96
Syphilis, 237
Systemic injections, 460
Systoles, 110

T cells, 437–438, 439
Tachycardia, 378, 379, 458
Tangential migration, 214
Tar, 376
Tardive dyskinesia (TD), 237
Target-site concept, 434
Taste, 124, 177, 179–180, 295, 298
Taste aversions, 124, 295, 302, 312
Taste buds, 179–180
Tau, 244, 245, 360
Taxonomy, of the human species, 27, 29
TD, 237
Tectorial membrane, 167, 168
Tectum, 65, 66, 73, 173, 198, 199, 216, 217, 218
Tegmentum, 65–66, 73
Telencephalon, 64, 67–73, 214
Temporal hemiretina, 136, 140
Temporal integration, in vision, 137
Temporal lobe, 67, 69, 261
Temporal lobe epilepsy, 240
Temporal resolution, 106
Temporal summation, 82, 83
Tendons, 200–202
Terminal buttons, 55, 61, 91, 97
Testes, 316–317, 322–323, 324, 338
Testicular atrophy, 333
Testosterone, 317, 322–323, 324–326, 330–332, 334, 335–336
    aggression and, 434–435
    birdsong and, 45
    injections of, 326, 331–332, 337

Texas tower sniper, 446
Thalamic lesions, 172
Thalamus, 66, 73, 172, 173, 474
Thalidomide, 227
THC, 378, 380
Thermal stimuli, 170, 172
Thermogenesis, diet-induced, 305, 308
Theta waves, hippocampal, 358
Thiamine, 12–13, 295
Thigmotaxic, 123
Thinking, critical, 3, 15–17
Thinking-about-biopsychology theme, 3
Threat displays, 427
3-per-second spike-and-wave discharge, 240–241
Threshold of excitation, 81
Thrombosis, 233
Thrombus, 233–234
Thymine, 37–38
Thymus, 316
Thyroid gland, 316, 319–320
Thyrotropin, 319–320
Thyrotropin-releasing hormone, 319–320
Tics, 461–462
Timbre, 166
Tinnitus, 225
TMS, 106
Tobacco, 376–377, 383–386, 387, 392–393
Token test, 120
Tolerance, drug, 363, 371–372, 373–376, 378, 379, 381
Tongue, 179–180
Tonic-clonic convulsion, 240
Tonotopic, 168, 169
Tonus, 239, 240
Top-down mechanisms, 159, 181
Topographic gradient hypothesis, 217–218
Topographic sensory cortex maps, 222–223
Topography, 434
Totipotent, 213
Touch, 170–175, 405
Tourette syndrome, 461–463
Toxic psychosis, 237
Tracing techniques, 60–61
Tracts, 58

Traits, 34–37
Transcranial magnetic stimulation (TMS), 106
Transcription, 138–139
Transcription, of DNA code, 39, 40
Transduction, 198, 205, 356, 357, 358, 399
Transfer RNA, 39
Transgenic, 246
Transgenic mice, 117, 246–247, 359
Translation, of RNA code, 39, 40
Transneuronal degeneration, 248, 249
Transorbital lobotomy, 16–17
Transplantation
    of extra stomach, 303
    of fetal tissue, 255
    of ovaries, 324
    of stem cells, 255–256
Transsexualism, 338
Tremor-at-rest, 77
Triceps, 200, 201, 205
Trichromatic theory, of color vision, 150
Tricyclic antidepressants, 354–355, 361, 456
Trigeminal cranial nerve, 171, 172, 173, 472, 473
Trochlear cranial nerve, 472, 473
Tropic hormones, 317, 318
True-breeding lines, 34
Tumor, 233
    brain, 101, 233, 234
Twin studies. See also Heritability
    on affective disorders, 455
    on anxiety disorders, 459
    on autism, 226
    on intelligence, 46–48
    on narcolepsy, 364
    on nicotine addiction, 377
    on obesity, 308
    on schizophrenia, 450
    on sexual orientation, 337
    on Tourette syndrome, 461
Tympanic membrane, 166, 167
Tyramine, 44, 93
Tyrosine, 44, 456

Ulcers, gastric, 436–437
Unconditional response, 124
Unconditional stimulus, 124
Unilateral lesions, 112–113
Unipolar affective disorder, 455, 458
Unipolar neuron, 57
Up-regulation, 457
Urbach-Wiethe disease, 444
Urethral folds, 323, 324
Uterus, 322–323, 328

Vagina, 322–323, 328, 338
Vagus cranial nerve, 180, 472, 473
Valium, 96, 459
Vas deferens, 322–323
Vasopressin, 318–319
Ventral, 61
Ventral horns, 62, 63
Ventral noradrenergic bundle, 301
Ventral posterior nucleus, 301
Ventral root, of spinal cord, 62
Ventral stream, 161–166, 182
Ventral tegmental area, 388, 391
Ventricle, 214
Ventricles, cerebral, 53
Ventricular zone, 214
Ventromedial cortico-brainstem-spinal tract, 198–200
Ventromedial corticospinal tract, 198–200
Ventromedial hypothalamus (VMH), 299–301
Ventromedial nucleus (VMN), 336
Verbal subtest of WAIS, 119
Vertebrae, 27

Vertebrates, evolution of, 27, 30
Vesicles, 87, 96, 97
    seminal, 322–323
Vestibular nucleus, 198, 199
Vestibular system, 168
Vibrissae, 251
Vietnam War, addiction and, 387
Viral infections of brain, 237
Vision, 130–141. See also Eyes
    brain lateralization and, 399–403, 405
    color, 149–153
    cortical mechanisms of, 159–166
    edge perception in, 141–149
Visual agnosia, 157, 164–165
Visual completion, 403
Visual cortex, 159–166
Visual discrimination, and split brain, 399–400, 401–402
Visual illusions, 129
Vitamin B_1, 12–13, 295
Vitamins, 295
VMH, 299–301
VMH syndrome, 299–300
VMN, 336
Vocabulary subtest of WAIS, 119
Voltage-activated ion channels, 83–84, 87

WAIS. See Wechsler Adult Intelligence Scale
Wakefulness, 356, 357
Walking, 205
Wavelength, of light, 130–131, 151–152
Waves
    alpha, 106–107, 343, 344
    delta, 343, 345
    infrared, 130
    light, 130
    sine, 147–149, 166, 167
    theta, 358
Waxy flexibility, 449
Weather forecasting game, 280
Wechsler Adult Intelligence Scale (WAIS), 46, 119–120, 398
Weight, body, 289, 291, 293, 303–307, 311–312. See also Obesity
Weight-loss programs, 308–309
Wernicke-Geschwind model, 411–418
Wernicke's aphasia, 411
Wernicke's area, 408, 409, 411, 412, 413
"Where" versus "what" theory, 162–164
White-crowned sparrows, as age-limited learners, 45
White matter, 62, 416
Williams syndrome, 227–229
Wisconsin Card Sorting Test, 121
Withdrawal reflex, 204
Withdrawal symptoms, 363, 377, 378, 379
Withdrawal syndrome, 372, 373, 375, 376, 382–383
Within-subjects design, 5
Wolffian system, 322–323, 328
Word salad, 411
Working memory, 221, 277, 279–280

X chromosomes, 316
X-ray, 102

Y chromosome, 316, 322
Yoked control rat, 353

Z lens, 403–404, 406
Zebra finches, song development in, 45
Zeitgebers, 349, 350
Zeitgeist, 20, 25
Zygomaticus major, 432–433
Zygote, 35–37, 212, 316, 322

America's
TEST KITCHEN

BEST AMERICAN SIDE DISHES

A BEST RECIPE CLASSIC

A BEST RECIPE CLASSIC

Best American
Side Dishes

BY THE EDITORS OF

COOK'S ILLUSTRATED

PHOTOGRAPHY

CARL TREMBLAY

DANIEL J. VAN ACKERE

ILLUSTRATIONS

JOHN BURGOYNE

America's
TEST KITCHEN

AMERICA'S TEST KITCHEN

BROOKLINE, MASSACHUSETTS

Copyright © 2005 by the Editors of *Cook's Illustrated*

America's Test Kitchen
17 Station Street
Brookline, MA 02445

0-936184-85-X
Library of Congress Cataloging-in-Publication Data
The Editors of *Cook's Illustrated*

Best American Side Dishes: Tired of fussy salads, boring side dishes, and appetizers that take all day?
Here are 500 practical recipes for everything but the main course.

1st Edition

ISBN 0-936184-85-X (hardcover): $35.00
I. Cooking. I. Title
2005

Manufactured in the United States of America

10 9 8 7 6 5 4 3 2 1

Distributed by America's Test Kitchen, 17 Station Street, Brookline, MA 02445.

Senior Editor: Lori Galvin
Senior Food Editor: Julia Collin Davison
Test Cook: Jeremy Sauer
Editorial Assistant: Elizabeth Wray
Series Designer: Amy Klee
Jacket Designer: Richard Oriolo
Book Production Specialist: Ronald Bilodeau
Photographers: Carl Tremblay, Daniel J. van Ackere
Illustrator: John Burgoyne
Senior Production Manager: Jessica Lindheimer Quirk
Copyeditor: India Koopman
Proofreader: Holly Hartman
Indexer: Cathy Dorsey

Pictured on front of jacket: Greek-Style Garlic-Lemon Potatoes with Sun-Dried Tomatoes and Scallions (page 280)
Pictured on back of jacket: Cheese Tray with Whipped Goat Cheese with Chives and Lemon (page 11), Marinated Black and Green Olives (page 5), Toasted Almonds (page 4), and Cheese Straws (page 16); Green Goddess Dip, Smoked Salmon Dip with Dill and Horseradish, and Smoky, Spicy Avocado Dip with Cilantro (page 26–27); Salad with Herbed Baked Goat Cheese, Apples, Walnuts, and Dried Cherries (page 102); Pommes Anna (page 294); Skillet Green Beans with Orange Essence and Toasted Maple Pecans (page 213); Faster Acorn Squash with Brown Sugar (page 234)

CONTENTS

WELCOME TO AMERICA'S TEST KITCHEN   x

PREFACE BY CHRISTOPHER KIMBALL   xi

CHAPTER 1   Appetizers   1

CHAPTER 2   Salads   81

CHAPTER 3   Vegetable Sides and Casseroles   159

CHAPTER 4   Potato Sides and Casseroles   261

CHAPTER 5   Rice, Grain, and Bean Sides and Casseroles   303

INDEX   341

WELCOME TO AMERICA'S TEST KITCHEN

THIS BOOK HAS BEEN TESTED, WRITTEN, AND edited by the folks at America's Test Kitchen, a very real 2,500-square-foot kitchen located just outside of Boston. It is the home of *Cook's Illustrated* magazine and is the Monday through Friday destination for close to two dozen test cooks, editors, food scientists, tasters, and cookware specialists. Our mission is to test recipes over and over again until we understand how and why they work and until we arrive at the "best" version.

We start the process of testing a recipe with a complete lack of conviction, which means that we accept no claim, no theory, no technique, and no recipe at face value. We simply assemble as many variations as possible, test a half dozen of the most promising, and taste the results blind. We then construct our own hybrid recipe and continue to test it, varying ingredients, techniques, and cooking times until we reach a consensus. The result, we hope, is the "best" version of a particular recipe, but we realize that only you can be the final judge of our success (or failure). As we like to say in the test kitchen, "We make the mistakes, so you don't have to."

All of this would not be possible without a belief that good cooking, much like good music, is indeed based on a foundation of objective technique. Some people like spicy foods and others don't, but there is a right way to sauté, there is a "best" way to cook a pot roast, and there are measurable scientific principles involved in producing perfectly beaten, stable egg whites. This is our ultimate goal: to investigate the fundamental principles of cooking so that you become a better cook. It is as simple as that.

You can watch us work (in our actual test kitchen) by tuning in to *America's Test Kitchen* (www.americastestkitchen.com) on public television or by subscribing to *Cook's Illustrated* magazine (www.cooksillustrated.com), which is published every other month. We welcome you into our kitchen, where you can stand by our side as we test our way to the "best" recipes in America.

PREFACE

I AM ONE OF THE FEW COOKS IN AMERICA who doesn't have a problem with side dishes. This is because for most of the year our family eats from the root cellar, which is filled with potatoes: Green Mountains, Yukon Golds, fingerlings, and whatever seed red potatoes I could find down at Whitman's in North Bennington in the spring. That quickly translates into mashed, baked, boiled, steamed, casseroled, and the odd fancier recipe, such as pommes Anna. Beets and Brussels sprouts are a close second (at least for the adults) and, in the summer, a fresh salad is our "go to" side dish. Our pantry is also packed with cellophane packages of dried beans that are eminently suited to side dishes as well.

But even I admit a lack of expertise and range when it comes to what to serve with the main course. I do spruce things up for the holidays, but the rest of the time I cook more like an Italian—one, perhaps two, items on the plate at a time. It's just my flimsy excuse to remain ignorant about what I know I should be doing.

This reminds me of the classic Vermont story about the flatlander who moves into town. After a few years, he finally makes the time to visit his neighbor, a farmer who lives a half-mile down the road. He starts to chat up the farmer and his wife and, after a bit, says, "You know, I should have stopped by years ago!" The farmer pauses, looks him in the eye, and says very slowly, "Well, we weren't waiting on yuh."

So, perhaps like you, I've gotten along just fine by sticking with a few old standbys, but that leaves so much fertile culinary ground unplowed. Sure, this book contains "best recipes" for dips, cheese courses, potato salads, nachos, coleslaws, stuffed mushrooms, green bean casseroles, and stir-fries, but there is also more interesting fare, including Mexican Rice, Braised Cauliflower (with anchovies, garlic, and white wine), Glazed Root Vegetables, Arugula and Roasted Pear Salad,

Homemade Spring Rolls, and Saffron Couscous Pilaf. Indeed, life (and your diet) can be a whole lot more interesting with a modicum of good recipes for side dishes, appetizers, and salads.

Being a throwback, I am loath to accept change, even when it demonstrably offers a better mousetrap. We still boil sap using an arch fired with wood, not oil; grow our own apples (even though store-bought specimens often make better pies); press our own cider; collect our own eggs; and raise our own pork and beef. We also can our own jams and applesauce (even our wormy apples are great for applesauce) and raise our own bees.

I had always complained about those "four-wheelers" up in the woods, the ATVs (all-terrain vehicles) that hunters and joy riders use on old logging roads all over town. Well, about a year ago I finally gave in and bought a Polaris to use around the farm. Among other things, it's good for bringing grain out to the beefers, moving empty water tubs, and carrying a chain saw to clean up the mountain trails. One day last August I took Charlie, my 9-year-old son, for a ride in the late afternoon. We went up by the hunting cabin to the top of the mountain and then headed down past our tree stand and the new pastures by the ponds.

I pretended it was all work, but I knew better. Although no real Vermonter will ever admit it, riding around on a four-wheeler is fun. When we got home, I related the results of our trip to my wife, Adrienne, as if I had been checking fence line in Australia. Then I asked her what was for dinner and she said something about a new recipe for roasted baby artichokes. I said, just under my breath, that I would be perfectly happy with mashed potatoes, but then I smiled, thinking that those artichokes actually sounded pretty darn good.

Christopher Kimball
Founder and Editor
Cook's Illustrated

1

APPETIZERS

WHETHER AS HOMEY AS A BOWL OF SPICED nuts or as elegant as an enticing array of cheese, appetizers are the beginning to any great meal. There's no need for fussy, time-consuming dishes here—leave those to the restaurants. The appetizers we've chosen to include in this chapter are all relatively quick and easy, from American classics like deviled eggs (page 44) and spinach dip (page 29) to international favorites like frico (page 13) and olivada (page 48) that are destined to become part of your repertoire. Spicy and casual or refined and sophisticated, the recipes in this chapter are many and various; we're sure you'll find one suitable for any occasion.

When choosing appetizers, you may want to think about the meal as a whole. How do the flavors of the appetizer(s) relate to the main course? Is the meal complementary from start to finish, or do the different dishes conflict? Asian-style appetizers, for example, might not mesh harmoniously with a Mexican-flavored main course. Also look for balance in richness and spiciness. Appetizers are designed to "tease" the palate, not overload it. For cocktail parties, however, feel free to mix and match a wide variety of different styles of appetizers to keep things interesting.

Cheese plates and crudité platters yield maximum impact with minimal effort. See page 14 for information on assembling a cheese selection. Dips for vegetables can be whirled together in moments and the vegetables themselves—raw or blanched—are a breeze to trim and slice. See page 21 for suggestions on preparing crudités.

While many of the recipes in this chapter can be assembled quickly, with a little advance planning most can be prepared ahead of time, leaving you free to focus on your guests and your main course. Some of the recipes, like the cheese straws (page 16), can even be prepared weeks ahead and frozen.

And because presentation is almost as important to an appetizer's appeal as taste, arranging foods on interesting platters or in decorative bowls goes far in adding charm, as does a sprinkling of fresh chopped herbs. Simple garnishes like lemon slices, sprigs of herbs, or colorful lettuce leaves (such as endive, watercress, or radicchio) easily gussy up the simplest items.

SPICED NUTS

AT PARTIES, SPICED NUTS USUALLY DISAPPEAR faster than the host can replenish the bowl. But most spiced nuts are made with a heavy sugar syrup, which can leave your hands sticky and cause the nuts to clump together in unappealing, indelicate clusters.

Finding the right coating method required a good deal of testing on our part. The most common technique, boiling the nuts in a thick, sweetened, seasoned syrup, was not even an option because it made the nuts sticky. Another popular method, toasting or sautéing the nuts in butter or oil before tossing them with spices, dulled the finish of the nuts and made them taste bland or oily. A third possibility, coating the nuts with a spiced egg white mixture, created such a chunky, candylike coating that the nuts themselves were barely visible.

Our answer came when we made a light glaze for the nuts from very small amounts of liquid, sugar, and butter. It worked like a charm. This treatment left the nuts shiny and just tacky enough for a dry spice coating to stick perfectly, giving the nuts both a consistent, beautiful appearance and plenty of flavor.

Kosher salt is important here because it adds crunch and has a clean flavor. If you can, make the nuts ahead of time; as they sit they will better absorb the flavorings.

Spiced Pecans with Rum Glaze

MAKES ABOUT 2 CUPS

We like the crunch and clean flavor of kosher salt in this recipe, but table salt can be substituted—just reduce the amount used by half.

2   cups (8 ounces) raw pecan halves

SPICE MIX

2   tablespoons sugar

³/₄ teaspoon kosher salt

¹/₂ teaspoon ground cinnamon

¹/₈ teaspoon ground cloves

¹/₈ teaspoon ground allspice

RUM GLAZE

1	tablespoon rum, preferably dark
1	tablespoon unsalted butter
2	teaspoons vanilla extract
1	teaspoon light or dark brown sugar

1. Adjust an oven rack to the middle position and heat the oven to 350 degrees. Line a rimmed baking sheet with parchment paper and spread the pecans on it in an even layer. Toast for 4 minutes, rotate the pan, and continue to toast until fragrant and the color deepens slightly, about 4 minutes longer. Transfer the baking sheet with the nuts to a wire rack.

2. FOR THE SPICE MIX: While the nuts are toasting, stir the sugar, salt, cinnamon, cloves, and allspice together in a medium bowl; set aside.

3. FOR THE GLAZE: Bring the rum, butter, vanilla, and brown sugar to a boil in a medium saucepan over medium-high heat, whisking constantly. Stir in the toasted pecans and cook, stirring constantly with a wooden spoon, until the nuts are shiny and almost all the liquid has evaporated, about 1½ minutes.

4. Transfer the glazed pecans to the bowl with the spice mix; toss well to coat. Return the glazed and spiced pecans to the parchment-lined baking sheet to cool. (The nuts can be stored in an airtight container for up to 5 days.)

Mexican-Spiced Almonds, Peanuts, and Pumpkin Seeds
MAKES ABOUT 2 CUPS

If substituting table salt for kosher, reduce the amount specified by half.

1¼	cups (4½ ounces) sliced almonds
⅔	cup (3 ounces) unsalted roasted peanuts
¼	cup (1 ounce) raw pumpkin seeds

MEXICAN SPICE MIX

1	tablespoon sugar
1	teaspoon kosher salt
¼	teaspoon ground cinnamon
¼	teaspoon ground cumin
¼	teaspoon ground coriander

⅛	teaspoon cayenne pepper
⅛	teaspoon garlic powder

SIMPLE GLAZE

2	tablespoons water
1	tablespoon unsalted butter
1	teaspoon light or dark brown sugar

1. Adjust an oven rack to the middle position and heat the oven to 350 degrees. Line a rimmed baking sheet with parchment paper and spread the almonds on it in an even layer. Toast for 4 minutes and rotate the pan; add the peanuts and pumpkin seeds. Continue to toast until fragrant and the color deepens slightly, about 4 minutes longer. Transfer the baking sheet with the nuts and seeds to a wire rack.

2. FOR THE SPICE MIX: While the nuts and seeds are toasting, stir the sugar, salt, cinnamon, cumin, coriander, cayenne, and garlic powder together in a medium bowl; set aside.

3. FOR THE GLAZE: Bring the water, butter, and brown sugar to a boil in a medium saucepan over medium-high heat, whisking constantly. Stir in the toasted nuts and seeds and cook, stirring constantly with a wooden spoon, until the nuts are shiny and almost all the liquid has evaporated, about 1½ minutes.

4. Transfer the glazed mixture to the bowl with the spice mix; toss well to coat. Return the glazed and spiced nuts to the parchment-lined baking sheet to cool. (The nuts can be stored in an airtight container for up to 5 days.)

Indian-Spiced Cashews and Pistachios with Currants
MAKES ABOUT 2 CUPS

If substituting table salt for kosher, reduce the amount specified by half.

1¼	cups (6 ounces) raw unsalted cashews
½	cup (2 ounces) raw unsalted shelled pistachios
2	tablespoons currants

INDIAN SPICE MIX

1   tablespoon sugar
1   teaspoon kosher salt
1   teaspoon curry powder
1/4 teaspoon ground cumin
1/4 teaspoon ground coriander

SIMPLE GLAZE

2   tablespoons water
1   tablespoon unsalted butter
1   teaspoon light or dark brown sugar

1. Adjust an oven rack to the middle position and heat the oven to 350 degrees. Line a rimmed baking sheet with parchment paper and spread the cashews on it in an even layer. Toast for 4 minutes, rotate the pan, and toast for 4 minutes more. Add the pistachios, spreading them in an even layer; continue to toast until fragrant and the color deepens slightly, about 2 minutes. Transfer the baking sheet with the nuts to a wire rack; add the currants.

2. FOR THE SPICE MIX: While the nuts are toasting, stir the sugar, salt, curry powder, cumin, and coriander together in a medium bowl; set aside.

3. FOR THE GLAZE: Bring the water, butter, and brown sugar to a boil in a medium saucepan over medium-high heat, whisking constantly. Stir in the nut mix and cook, stirring constantly with a wooden spoon, until the nuts are shiny and almost all the liquid has evaporated, about 1½ minutes.

4. Transfer the glazed nuts and currants to the bowl with the spice mix; toss well to coat. Return the glazed and spiced nuts and currants to the parchment-lined baking sheet to cool. (The nuts can be stored in an airtight container for up to 5 days.)

QUICK TOASTED ALMONDS

CANNED ALMONDS ARE ALMOST ALWAYS TOO salty, never mind that they usually taste less than fresh. Luckily, you can easily toast your own in about 8 minutes in a skillet on the stovetop. Not only do these toasted almonds have an incredibly fresh flavor, but you can season them with a variety of herbs and spices more appetizing than the ubiquitous store-bought smoked variety. Bottom line: You simply can't buy almonds this good.

BASIC TOASTED ALMONDS

Heat 1 tablespoon extra-virgin olive oil or butter in a large nonstick skillet. Add 2 cups skin-on raw almonds, 1 teaspoon salt, ¼ teaspoon ground black pepper, and, if desired, one of the flavor combinations below. Toast the almonds over medium-low heat, stirring often, until fragrant and the color deepens slightly, about 8 minutes. Transfer to a plate lined with paper towels and allow to cool before serving. The almonds can be stored in an airtight container for up to 5 days.

ROSEMARY ALMONDS

Add ½ teaspoon dried rosemary to the skillet with the almonds.

LEMON-GARLIC ALMONDS

Add ½ teaspoon grated lemon zest and 1 minced garlic clove to the skillet with the almonds. Just before serving, toss with another ½ teaspoon grated lemon zest.

WARM SPICED ALMONDS

Use unsalted butter rather than olive oil, add 2 tablespoons sugar, ½ teaspoon ground cinnamon, ⅛ teaspoon ground cloves, and ⅛ teaspoon ground allspice to the skillet with the almonds.

SPANISH-STYLE ALMONDS

Add ¾ teaspoon smoked Spanish paprika to the skillet with the almonds.

CHINESE FIVE-SPICE ALMONDS

Add 1 teaspoon Chinese five-spice powder to the skillet with the almonds.

ORANGE-FENNEL ALMONDS

Add 1 teaspoon grated orange zest and ½ teaspoon ground fennel seeds to the skillet with the almonds. Just before serving, toss with another 1 teaspoon grated orange zest.

MARINATED OLIVES

IF YOU START WITH GOOD OLIVES (AND THAT can be a big if) and good olive oil, it's pretty hard to make bad marinated olives. That said, some olive mixes are better than others, with more complex flavors. We wanted to make a mixture of marinated olives that would be easy to put together and worth the wait.

Good olives are the right place to begin, and that means olives with their pits and packed in brine. (Oil-cured olives can be added in small quantities, but in large quantities we find their flavors too potent for this dish.) Pitted olives generally have little flavor, and you can't expect marinating to make them taste better. Our tasters liked a mix of black and green olives. We tested half a dozen varieties of each color and didn't find a bad olive.

In addition to the olive oil, the marinade typically includes garlic, herbs (our tasters liked thyme best), and red pepper flakes (we found that more heat was better than less and opted for a full teaspoon). We liked thinly sliced shallots as well; they softened in the marinade and added their gentle allium flavor to the mix. Grated orange zest (rather than the more traditional lemon zest) won the day in the test kitchen for its fresh, lively citrus kick.

The real surprise was the addition of sambuca, an Italian after-dinner liqueur that tastes like licorice. The heady anise flavor worked wonders on the olives and made the mix much more interesting.

The final issue to resolve was how long to marinate the olives. Tasters found that the olives required 12 hours to pick up sufficient flavor and were even better after a day or two. In fact, we held marinated olives in the refrigerator for several weeks and concluded that time only served to improve the flavor.

Marinated Black and Green Olives

MAKES ABOUT 3 CUPS

These olives will keep in the refrigerator for at least a month and are perfect to have on hand for impromptu entertaining. (Remember to put out a small bowl for the pits.) Sambuca is a sweet, licorice-flavored Italian spirit. You can substitute ouzo.

8	ounces large, brine-cured green olives with pits
8	ounces large, brine-cured black olives with pits
5	large garlic cloves, crushed
3	large shallots, sliced thin
½	cup sambuca (see note)
¼	cup extra-virgin olive oil
1	teaspoon grated zest from 1 orange
1	teaspoon minced fresh thyme leaves
1	teaspoon red pepper flakes
¾	teaspoon salt
	Pinch cayenne pepper

1. Drain the olives in a colander and rinse them well under cold running water. Drain the olives of excess water.

2. Combine the remaining ingredients in a glass or plastic bowl. Add the olives and toss to combine. Cover and refrigerate for at least 12 hours. Remove from the refrigerator at least 30 minutes before serving.

INGREDIENTS: Olives

There are literally hundreds of varieties of olives, but all can be categorized by two factors: their ripeness when picked and the manner in which they are cured. Green olives, picked before they are fully ripe, tend to have fruitier and somewhat lighter flavors, while ripe olives—which range in color from dark brown to purple to deep black—have deeper, more fully developed flavors.

Most olives are brine-cured in a process that involves fermenting them in a strong salt solution. Others are oil-cured in a process that gives them a wrinkled appearance and sharper flavor. Both types are sold loose and should be kept refrigerated. It almost goes without saying that canned (or jarred) pitted olives (which are not refrigerated and reside in the condiment aisle of the supermarket) are to be avoided. We find them devoid of flavor, and the black olives are in truth green olives that have been colored with a chemical additive.

Olives may be named after the type of cure, their place of origin, or their varietal name. The most important thing to remember about these little fruits (yes, olives are technically a fruit) is that they vary widely from batch to batch and year to year. Tasting is the only way to judge the quality of any particular batch.

➤ VARIATION

Warm Marinated Olives

The ingredients in this variation are similar to those in our traditional cold marinated olives, but warming the olives mellows and softens their briny flavor.

Follow the recipe for Marinated Black and Green Olives. In step 2, in a medium saucepan, heat ¼ cup extra-virgin olive oil. Omit the shallots and add 3 garlic cloves (in place of the 5 crushed garlic cloves), minced or pressed through a garlic press, to the warm oil and heat until fragrant, about 2 minutes. Stir in the olives. Omit the sambuca and salt; in addition to the orange zest, thyme, red pepper flakes, and cayenne, add 1 teaspoon minced fresh rosemary. Cook until warmed through, about 3 minutes. Serve immediately.

JAZZING UP POPCORN WITH FLAVORED BUTTERS

MICROWAVING A BAG OF POPCORN IS FINE FOR MOVIE NIGHT ON THE COUCH, BUT when company is coming, consider giving your corn some serious punch by using one of our flavored butters. If using microwave popcorn, follow the instructions for popping the corn on the package (see our tasting on the facing page for recommended brands) or use our stovetop method.

PERFECT POPPED CORN
MAKES ABOUT 4 QUARTS

Add 2 tablespoons vegetable oil and ½ cup popcorn to a large saucepan or wok, cover, and place over medium-high heat, shaking occasionally, until the first few kernels begin to pop. Continue to cook, shaking vigorously, until the popping has mostly stopped. Pour immediately into a large bowl, toss with one of the flavored butters below, and season with salt and ground black pepper.

FLAVORED BUTTERS

Before popping the corn, melt 3 tablespoons unsalted butter in a small skillet and add one of the following flavor combinations:

SUPER-GARLIC BUTTER: Add 4 minced garlic cloves to the melted butter and sauté until fragrant, about 1 minute. Season with salt and pepper. Cover and keep warm until ready to toss with the popcorn.

GARLIC AND HERB BUTTER: Add 2 minced garlic cloves and 1 tablespoon chopped fresh herbs such as rosemary, thyme leaves, and/or dill to the melted butter and sauté until fragrant, about 1 minute. Season with salt and pepper. Cover and keep warm until ready to toss with the popcorn.

PARMESAN AND BLACK PEPPER BUTTER: Add ½ teaspoon ground black pepper to the melted butter. Season with salt. Cover and keep warm until ready to toss with the popcorn. When ready to serve, add 1 cup grated Parmesan cheese with the melted butter to the popcorn. Toss thoroughly to distribute the cheese evenly.

CAJUN-SPICED BUTTER: Add 1 teaspoon red pepper flakes, ¾ teaspoon hot sauce, ½ teaspoon each garlic powder and paprika, and ¼ teaspoon each onion powder and dried thyme to the melted butter and sauté until fragrant, about 1 minute. Cover and keep warm until ready to toss with the popcorn.

WARM SPICED BUTTER: Add 2 minced garlic cloves, ½ teaspoon each ground cumin, coriander, and paprika, and ¼ teaspoon cayenne pepper to the melted butter. Cover and keep warm until ready to toss with the popcorn.

HOT AND SWEET BUTTER: Add 2 tablespoons sugar, 1 teaspoon ground cinnamon, and ½ teaspoon chili powder to the melted butter and sauté until fragrant, about 1 minute. Cover and keep warm until ready to toss with the popcorn.

Supermarket shelves are overrun with more than a dozen brands of microwave popcorn in countless permutations of flavors, from "movie theater butter" to "butter blast" to natural to kettle corn. Would we prefer any of these brands to our own homemade? We narrowed the field to nine popular brands and selected the most basic butter flavor each brand offered—no "butter light" or "butter bonanza." For "homemade" microwave popcorn, we popped kernels in a paper bag in the microwave and then doused them with fresh melted butter.

Tasters were asked to give each sample an overall score, as well as to score the popcorns on the following characteristics: butteriness, artificiality, and corniness. We discovered what tasters looked for in popcorn: good corn flavor, nothing artificial, and a moderate amount of butter flavor—not too much, and not too little. Our top two overall finishers, the homemade and Newman's Own, were ranked among the lowest for artificiality and the highest for corniness, and they were right in the middle of the pack when it came to butteriness. Ironically, the two brands deemed the most buttery, Orville Redenbacher and Pop Secret, were also deemed the most artificial and ranked at the bottom of the tasting.

The real surprise of the tasting was the showing of the homemade popcorn, which barely squeaked a victory over Newman's Own. Though many tasters praised the real butter flavor of the homemade, several described that popcorn as soggy or greasy. Most of the commercial popcorns were flavored with a dry butter powder, which lent a buttery flavor (sometimes) but not a buttery texture. That real-butter texture was more appealing when the popcorn was warm, but when the popcorns cooled (we sampled them all at room temperature because they cooled off too quickly to taste them all warm) they became soft and greasy. For that reason, only half a point separated our homemade popcorn from the second-place finisher, Newman's Own.

The benefit of popping your own, other than the monetary savings (kernels cost about half as much as packaged microwave popcorn), is that you control the flavor and can add as much butter, salt, or any other seasoning you wish. However, when you're looking for true convenience and a taste that's almost as good as homemade, choose Newman's Own Butter Flavor.

MARINATED MUSHROOMS

MARINATED MUSHROOMS SHOULD TASTE good. As a classic Italian antipasto, foraged wild mushrooms are potent with earthy flavor. Blended with the right combination of bright acidity, heady herbs, and the nap of a fine olive oil, each bite packs a punch. But today most marinated mushrooms have morphed into little more than white button mushrooms soaked in bottled Italian dressing for days on end. The result is slimy, rubbery, brown orbs—hardly the life of the party.

Be that as it may, marinated mushrooms are still inexplicably popular (just try to find an hors d'oeuvres tray without them), and so it was time to get to work. Our goals were clear: We wanted to get rid of that slippery, rubbery texture; we wanted a balance of flavor from oil and vinegar; and, above all, we wanted to make the mushrooms taste like mushrooms again.

Wild mushrooms aren't a produce-case regular, so we tested what was readily available—namely, portobellos, cremini (baby portobellos), and the ubiquitous white button mushrooms. When all was said and done, we had eliminated the portobellos because of their spongy texture. Cremini got the thumbs up for flavor, and because we wanted to be practical, we also included the white button mushrooms.

Simply marinating raw mushrooms for any length of time was a no-go—they ended up slippery and slimy, with no mushroom flavor. Boiling the mushrooms in a vinegar bath only compounded the problem; these mushrooms were not only slimy but tough, too. Poaching the mushrooms in oil worked a bit better, but the whole dish was watery and bland.

It was clear that we would have to think outside the box, so we tried a few dry heat methods instead, hoping the excess moisture would have a chance to evaporate. Spread out on a sheet pan and roasted in a hot oven, the mushrooms expelled their liquid and began to intensify in flavor. But we still felt that the flavor could be bigger.

And so we turned to a 12-inch skillet. The mushrooms were crowded in the pan and exuded a lot of liquid—so much so that we worried that this flood wouldn't reduce sufficiently, but we were wrong. With the heat cranked up, the liquid reduced down until it formed a potent glaze with concentrated mushroom flavor. And if that wasn't good enough, the seven or so minutes that it took to reduce the liquid produced a tender yet "al dente" mushroom, with no slime in sight.

Now we turned to marinating the mushrooms. For our base ingredients, olive oil—the fruitier the better—and lemon juice, with its fresh zing, fit the bill perfectly. Simply soaking the sautéed mushrooms in this simple vinaigrette wasn't cutting it; days passed before the mushrooms fully absorbed its flavors. We went back to sautéing and added a little lemon juice, which reduced nicely into the mushroom glaze. What a difference! Now the mushrooms started to take on a marinated flavor in only minutes instead of days. But if lemon juice was good, how about additional ingredients like garlic and shallots? Tasters liked the shallots and garlic, along with the sweet flavor from a red bell pepper, but sautéing the vegetables gave the whole dish a dull, stewed flavor.

We decided to add the vegetables to the cooled mushrooms. We tossed the whole lot together and came back to taste an hour later. Not bad, but two hours was better, three hours even better, and six hours turned out mushrooms with optimal flavor. The only thing left to do was to add a final shot of fresh lemon juice and olive oil as well as a chopped herb to brighten the flavors.

Marinated Mushrooms

MAKES ABOUT 3 1/2 CUPS

Skillet size limits the yield of this recipe; if you would like to double it, cook the mushrooms in two separate batches but marinate them together. Thyme, parsley, or basil makes a good last-minute addition—use only one, however, not all three.

3 tablespoons extra-virgin olive oil, plus
   1 tablespoon for finishing
1/8 teaspoon red pepper flakes
   Salt

1 pound cremini or white button mushrooms, wiped clean, left whole if small, halved if medium, quartered if large
2 tablespoons juice from 1 lemon, plus 1 tablespoon for finishing
1 medium garlic clove, sliced very thin
1 large shallot, chopped fine
1/4 small red bell pepper, chopped fine
1 teaspoon minced fresh thyme leaves or 1 tablespoon chopped fresh parsley or basil leaves
   Ground black pepper

1. Heat 3 tablespoons of the oil, the red pepper flakes, and ½ teaspoon salt in a 12-inch skillet over medium-high heat until shimmering but not smoking. Add the mushrooms and 2 tablespoons of the lemon juice; cook, stirring frequently, until the mushrooms release liquid, the liquid evaporates, and the mushrooms have browned around the edges, about 10 minutes. Spread the mushrooms in a single layer on a large plate or rimmed baking sheet; cool to room temperature, about 20 minutes. When cooled, transfer the mushrooms to a medium bowl, leaving behind any juices. Stir the garlic, shallot, and bell pepper into the mushrooms, cover with plastic wrap, and refrigerate at least 6 or up to 24 hours.

2. Before serving, allow the mushrooms to stand at room temperature about 1 hour. Stir in the remaining 1 tablespoon olive oil, 1 tablespoon lemon juice, and thyme and adjust seasonings with salt and pepper just before serving.

ROASTED BELL PEPPERS

WHEN ROASTED, SWEET RED BELL PEPPERS assume a whole new layer of complex, smoky flavor. In testing the various methods of roasting peppers— including flaming (over a gas burner), oven-roasting, and broiling—we sought the most efficient way to achieve a tender but not mushy flesh, smoky flavor, and skin that would peel off easily.

The first method we tested was the stovetop gas burner. The one benefit of this method is that whole peppers retain the liquid released during roasting. The disadvantages, however, are many. The peppers require constant tending and must be turned with tongs after each exposed area of flesh has charred. The clever tong manipulation doesn't end there, as both ends of the pepper need to be charred to promote even peeling. Also, only two peppers can be roasted at a time, unless you want to try to double this number by using two burners at a time. That, however, requires two pairs of tongs and deft eye-hand coordination, and it invites both scorched arms and overroasted peppers. Forget about using a long-handled fork instead of tongs. After three or four minutes, we found that the softened pepper fell off the fork right onto the burner flame.

The second approach we tested was oven-roasting at 550 degrees. Whether the peppers are kept whole or split open and flattened, this method takes a while, usually from 12 to 15 minutes, which in turn creates overcooked, soggy flesh. Lower oven temperatures also yielded overcooked peppers and required even longer cooking times—up to 1 hour at 325 degrees.

Next up was broiling, which also presented some challenges. The broiler element in most ovens is approximately 3 inches away from the upper rack, which means that whole peppers usually touch the element. A lower rack level takes too long and cooks the flesh too much. After some trial and error, we found that the answer was to cut the peppers. Broiling then took eight to 10 minutes, with the baking sheet turned back

PREPARING BELL PEPPERS FOR ROASTING

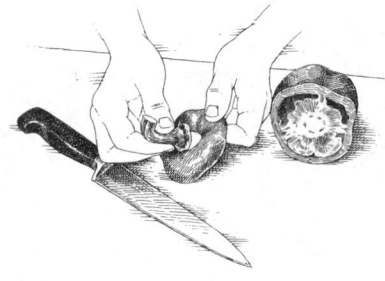 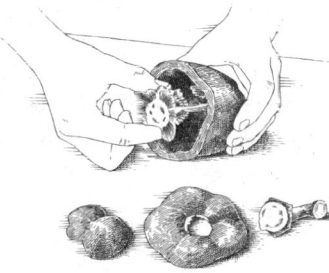 

1. Slice ¼ inch from the top and bottom of the bell pepper, then gently remove the stem from the top lobe.

2. Pull the core out of the pepper.

3. Make a slit down one side of the pepper, then lay it flat, skin-side down, in one long strip. Slide a sharp knife along the inside of the pepper to remove all ribs and seeds.

4. Arrange the strips of pepper and the top and bottom lobes skin-side up on a foil-lined baking sheet. Flatten the strips with the palm of your hand.

5. Adjust an oven rack to the top position. If the rack is more than 3½ inches from the heating element, set another rimmed baking sheet, bottom up, on the rack under the baking sheet with the peppers. Roast until the skin of the peppers is charred and puffed up like a balloon but the flesh is still firm.

6. Remove the baking sheet from the oven. You may steam the peppers at this point or not, as you wish. When the peppers are cool enough to handle, start peeling where the skin has charred and bubbled the most. The skin will come off in large strips.

to front halfway through cooking. We found that this method yielded less juice than flaming or oven roasting (although some does collect in the bowl later as the peppers steam), but we decided that this was an easy trade-off given the many benefits of this method, which was far and away our favorite. Primary among these benefits is the fact that the peppers consistently achieved a meaty texture and rich flavor. In addition, peppers that have been cut open and roasted under the broiler are easier to peel than peppers roasted by any other method. The skin blackens and swells up like a balloon and lifts off in whole sections. By comparison, flaming and, to a lesser degree, roasting result in small patches of skin peeling off at best. We did find that with broiling you must take care not to overroast the peppers. When the skin of the pepper just puffs up and turns black, you have reached the point at which flavor is maximized and the texture of the flesh is soft but not mushy. After this point, continued exposure to heat will result in darkened flesh that is thinner, flabbier, and slightly bitter.

Peppers should not be rubbed with oil before they are roasted. The skins will char and blister faster without the oil. It does, however, help to line the baking pan with foil. Without foil, sticky, dark spots formed on the baking sheet where the juices dripped and evaporated during roasting.

Unless you have asbestos fingers, roasted peppers need time to cool before handling, and steaming during this time does make the charred skin a bit easier to peel off. The ideal steaming time is 15 minutes—any less and the peppers are still too hot to work with comfortably. Any more time (we tested lengths up to one hour) provided no discernible advantage. The best method is to use a heat-resistant bowl (glass, ceramic, or metal) with a piece of plastic wrap secured over the top to trap the steam. The wrap holds in the heat, creating intense steam.

Seeding the peppers before roasting makes it possible to peel the peppers without having to rinse them to wash away the seeds. If you are still tempted to rinse, notice the rich oils that accumulate on your fingers as you work. It seems silly to rinse away those oils rather than savoring them later with your meal.

The way peppers are treated after they are peeled will determine how long they will keep. Unadorned and wrapped in plastic wrap, peppers will keep their full, meaty texture for only about two days in the refrigerator. Drizzled with a generous amount of olive oil and kept in an airtight container, peppers will keep about one week without losing texture or flavor.

Roasted Red Bell Peppers

MAKES 4 ROASTED PEPPERS, SERVING 8

Cooking times vary, depending on the broiler, so watch the peppers carefully as they roast. You will need to increase the cooking time slightly if your peppers are just out of the refrigerator instead of at room temperature. Yellow and orange peppers roast faster than red ones, so decrease their cooking time by 2 to 4 minutes. Do not roast green or purple peppers—their flavor is bitter and not worth the effort.

4   medium-to-large red bell peppers (6 to 9 ounces each), prepared according to illustrations 1 through 4 on page 9
     Extra-virgin olive oil
     Salt

1. Adjust an oven rack to the top position. The oven rack should be 2½ to 3½ inches from the heating element. If it is not, set a rimmed baking sheet, turned upside down, on the oven rack to elevate the pan (see illustration 5 on page 9). Turn the broiler on and heat for 5 minutes. Broil the peppers until spotty brown, about 5 minutes. Reverse the pan in the oven and roast until the skin is charred and puffed but the flesh is still firm, 3 to 5 minutes longer.

2. Remove the pan from the oven and let the peppers sit until cool enough to handle. (To facilitate peeling, transfer the peppers straight from the oven to a large heat-resistant bowl, cover it with plastic wrap, and steam for 15 minutes.) Peel and discard the skin from each piece (see illustration 6 on page 9).

3. To serve, slice the peppers and arrange them on a platter. Drizzle with oil just until lightly moistened and sprinkle with salt to taste.

CHEESE HORS D'OEUVRES

IN LIEU OF, OR IN ADDITION TO, A CHEESE tray (page 15), consider the following recipes, which highlight some of our favorite cheeses in appetizer form. Fresh goat cheese can be marinated to enliven its flavor, or whipped to transform its texture. Parmesan, when paired with dried dates and walnuts, is an instant elegant bite to serve with drinks. Another great complement to cocktails is the Italian favorite, frico, which is simply grated cheese toasted into lacy crackers. If you're looking for an appetizer to serve at table, warm figs with goat cheese and honey will make an elegant beginning to a special meal.

Marinated Goat Cheese

SERVES 4

The garlic should be broken down into a fine puree for this recipe. After you mince it, sprinkle the garlic with the salt, mash the garlic-salt mixture with the side of a chef's knife, and then continue to mince until the garlic forms a smooth puree (see the illustrations at right). Serve this marinated goat cheese with bread or crackers.

1	(8-ounce) log goat cheese, chilled
1/4	cup extra-virgin olive oil
3/4	teaspoon chopped fresh thyme leaves
3/4	teaspoon minced fresh chives
1/4	teaspoon minced fresh rosemary
1	small garlic clove, minced to a puree with 1/8 teaspoon salt (see illustrations at right)
	Ground black pepper

1. Following the illustration on page 100, use a piece of dental floss to cut the cheese crosswise into slices 1/3 inch thick.

2. Whisk the oil, thyme, chives, rosemary, garlic-salt puree, and pepper to taste together in a small bowl.

3. Pour the oil mixture over the cheese. Serve immediately or cover and refrigerate for up to 1 day.

Whipped Goat Cheese with Chives and Lemon

MAKES ABOUT 1 CUP, SERVING 4

Serve with pita chips (see Easy Homemade Crackers in box on page 33), Crostini Toasts (page 47), or any good crackers.

8	ounces fresh goat cheese
1/3	cup heavy cream
1	tablespoon minced fresh chives
1/2	teaspoon grated zest from 1 lemon
	Pinch salt
1/8	teaspoon ground black pepper

Whip all the ingredients with an electric mixer until soft and uniform, about 1 minute. Transfer the cheese mixture to a serving bowl; serve. (The whipped cheese can be refrigerated for up to 1 day.)

MINCING GARLIC TO A PASTE

There are times when you want minced garlic to be absolutely smooth. A garlic press yields a smooth paste easily. To obtain the same effect with a chef's knife, you will need some salt. If possible, use kosher or coarse salt; the larger crystals do a better job of breaking down the garlic than fine table salt.

1. Mince the garlic as you normally would on a cutting board. Sprinkle the minced garlic with a pinch of salt.

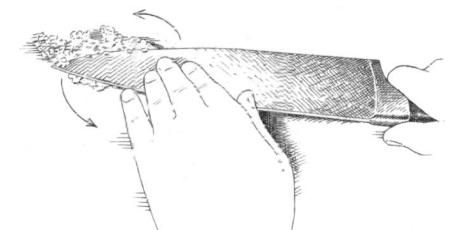

2. Drag the side of the chef's knife over the garlic-salt mixture to form a fine paste. Continue to mince and drag the knife as necessary until the paste is smooth.

➤ VARIATION
Whipped Goat Cheese with Garlic and Mint

Follow the recipe for Whipped Goat Cheese with Chives and Lemon, replacing the chives, zest, and pepper with 2 teaspoons minced fresh mint leaves, 1 small garlic clove minced with the pinch of salt to form a smooth paste, and ¼ teaspoon red pepper flakes.

Dates Stuffed with Parmesan

MAKES 16 PIECES, SERVING 4 TO 6

Use high-quality dates (such as Medjools) and only the finest Parmigiano-Reggiano in this exotic pairing.

  16   large dates
   1   piece (3 ounces) Parmesan cheese
  16   walnut halves, toasted in a small dry skillet over medium heat until fragrant, about 4 minutes

1. Slit the dates lengthwise with a paring knife and remove the pits.

2. Following the illustrations below, cut the cheese into thin shards about 1 inch long. Place a piece of cheese and 1 walnut half in each date and close the date around the cheese to seal. Place the dates on a platter and serve. (The stuffed dates can be wrapped in plastic and kept at room temperature for several hours.)

Warm Figs with Goat Cheese and Honey

MAKES 16 PIECES, SERVING 4 TO 6

The figs should be baked briefly—just long enough to soften the cheese and warm the figs.

  16   walnut halves (about ½ cup)
   1   tablespoon brown sugar
  ⅛   teaspoon salt
  ⅛   teaspoon ground cinnamon
 1½   ounces goat cheese (about 3 tablespoons)
   8   fresh figs, halved lengthwise
   2   tablespoons honey

1. Combine the walnuts, brown sugar, salt, and cinnamon in a small, heavy-bottomed skillet. Cook over medium-high heat until the sugar melts and coats the nuts evenly, about 3 minutes. Remove the nuts from the pan, separating them from each other. Cool.

2. Adjust the oven rack to the middle position and heat the oven to 500 degrees. Spoon a heaping ½ teaspoon goat cheese onto each fig half and place on a parchment-lined rimmed baking sheet. Bake the figs for 4 minutes. Transfer the warm figs to a serving platter.

3. Place a candied walnut half on each fig half and drizzle the honey over the figs. Serve immediately.

CUTTING PARMESAN INTO SHARDS

1. Use a chef's knife to remove the rind from a square block of Parmesan cheese. Cut the trimmed block in half on the diagonal.

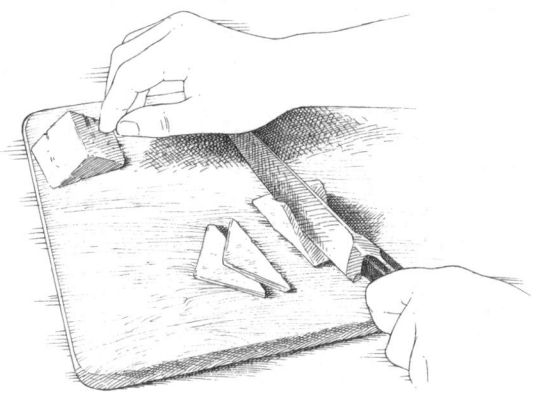

2. Place each half cut-side down on a cutting board and slice the cheese into thin triangles, about 1/16 inch wide. These thin shards should be about the size of a date.

Frico

MAKES 8 LARGE WAFERS

Frico, a thin, golden, flavorful cheese crisp, is probably the simplest and most addictive snack you'll ever eat. Frico can be left as flat wafers or draped, straight from the pan, over an inverted glass to form an attractive bowl shape to hold salad. Serve frico with drinks and perhaps with a bowl of Marinated Olives (page 5).

1   pound Montasio, Asiago (aged), or
     Parmigiano-Reggiano cheese, finely grated

Sprinkle 2 ounces (about 1 cup) grated cheese over the bottom of a medium nonstick skillet set over medium-high heat. Use a heat-resistant rubber spatula or wooden spoon to tidy the lacy outer edges of the cheese. Cook, shaking the pan occasionally to ensure an even distribution of the cheese over the pan bottom, until the edges are lacy and toasted, about 4 minutes. Remove the pan from the heat and allow the cheese to set for about 30 seconds. Using a fork and a heatproof spatula (see the illustration below), carefully flip the cheese wafer over and return the pan to medium heat. Cook until the second side is golden brown, about 2 minutes. Slide the cheese wafer out of the pan and transfer it to a plate, or drape it over an inverted glass to form a fluted bowl. Repeat with the remaining cheese. Serve the frico within 1 hour.

MAKING FRICO

Once the first side is browned, remove the pan from the heat and let cool for 30 seconds so the frico firms slightly. Using a fork and a heatproof spatula, carefully flip over the cheese wafer and return the pan to medium heat to cook the second side.

INGREDIENTS: Cheese

A cheese's flavor is dependent on a long list of factors, including the type of milk, the fodder fed to the animals that produced that milk, the age and salt content of the cheese, the mold strain (for blue cheeses), and the region of the world where the cheese originated. A Danish-made fontina has little in common with an Italian-made fontina (save its name); the same can be said for American and Alsatian Muenster as well as many other cheeses.

All cheeses, however, start with just three components: milk, a starter culture, and rennet. The milk, unpasteurized (rare in the United States because of U.S. Department of Agriculture regulations) or pasteurized, is combined with a culture that converts the milk sugars into lactic acid, which in turn prompts the proteins in the milk to convert to curds. Rennet, an enzyme extracted from either animal (the stomachs of calves, kids, or lambs) or plant sources, causes the curds to clump. From here on, the treatment of the cheese depends on the style being made. Fresh, soft cheeses are ready to eat; some hard cheeses are aged for years before they will be consumed.

Like fruits and vegetables, cheeses have a period of peak "ripeness," at which time their flavor and texture are at their very best. Creamy cheeses, like Brie, become runny and more distinct in flavor as they age; blue cheeses grow earthier and more pungent. For highly processed, commercial cheeses, such as the shrink-wrapped cheddar or Swiss found in the dairy case, ripeness is less of a concern, though mold and age are. Small patches of mold can be trimmed away, and the cheese is still perfectly edible. Large patches of mold (especially new mold on blue cheeses) or dried, cracked patches suggest the cheese is well past its prime.

When storing cheese, it is crucial to keep it tightly wrapped. Air will dry it out and prompt the development of mold. In a perfect world, cheese should first be wrapped tightly in parchment or waxed paper and then sealed in plastic wrap, aluminum foil, or a zipper-lock bag. Cheese can absorb off flavors and odors from plastic wrap or plastic containers. If the cheese has a rind, as do Parmesan, Brie, and Gouda, make sure to leave it on the cheese until serving time; the rind provides an extra layer of protection. And buy cheese in reasonable amounts that can be consumed within a couple of weeks. We've tested freezing cheese and have found that in most cases, freezing dries out and mutes a cheese's flavor.

TIPS FOR PREPARING A CHEESE TRAY

LONG HAILED AS AN ESSENTIAL COCKTAIL PARTY CENTERPIECE, A CHEESE TRAY IS EASILY assembled well ahead of serving time, yielding maximum impact with minimal effort. Two or three different cheeses, crackers or bread, and fruit take just minutes to plate yet look elegant and offer a little something for everyone.

Although cheese trays once meant cubes of processed cheese impaled with toothpicks, surrounded by mediocre crackers and stacks of less-than-ripe grapes, cooks today have more options. We're not suggesting that you line your tray with chestnut leaves and spend exorbitant amounts of money on the cheese, but you can assemble a company-worthy cheese tray with modest effort and expense. There are no hard and fast rules, but here are some guidelines that we find most helpful.

First, keep it simple. Choose from two to four varieties of cheese. (Any more will be overkill.) Choose cheeses based on a variety of factors, including intensity (mild to strong), texture (soft to hard), or type of milk (cow, goat, or sheep). We think it's best to include cheeses with a variety of characteristics. Country of origin is another factor to consider. You might want to assemble a cheese tray of all American cheeses, or perhaps you want your selection to come from several countries. Some of our favorite combinations include a creamy Brie served with a sharp cheddar and a rich blue, or a pungent goat cheese matched with a dry, aged Parmesan and a nutty, firm Gruyère. See page 15 for more ideas on cheese pairings and accompaniments.

CHOOSING ACCOMPANIMENTS

BREADS AND CRACKERS are the classic accompaniments to cheese. Slices from a crusty French loaf or Italian bread are always good, as are thin, sturdy slices from a hearty nut-studded whole wheat bread. Choose simple breads and crackers. Because you want the cheese to take center stage, it's best to avoid heavily seasoned breads. Water crackers are especially nice served with cheese, and you don't need to buy expensive European brands. Domestic "store brands" are just as good.

NUTS: Toasted almonds, walnuts, or hazelnuts make a great addition to a cheese plate. Purchase your nuts raw and toast them yourself for optimal flavor. Allow the nuts to cool completely before assembling your tray.

FRUIT: Fresh fruit cuts the richness of some cheeses and softens the pungency of strongly flavored cheeses. Although sweet grapes are the most popular choice, thin slices of apple, pear, or melon are equally good. Dried fruits, such as apricots, figs, and dates, are also welcome additions. Likewise, fruit chutneys such as Quick Apricot Chutney (page 72) or hot pepper jelly provide a flavorful counterpoint to cheese.

MEAT: Paper-thin slices of Italian-style sausage such as sopressata or pungent, salt-cured prosciutto go well with Italian fresh mozzarella or the more pronounced taste of Pecorino. In Spain, thin pieces of Serrano ham are commonly served with such Spanish cheeses as Manchego and Cabrales. French meat pâtés, either coarse or smooth, make a rich and luxurious accompaniment to cheese.

ASSEMBLY AND SERVING

You don't need a fancy marble slab and special cheese knives for serving. A simple, clean cutting board makes a rustic and attractive tray—not to mention a practical base. Sharp knives are all you need to slice servings (allow one knife per cheese). If you're serving a full meal after the cheese, allow 2 ounces of cheese per person. Diners will be eating accompaniments as well, so you don't want to overload your tray. If you are serving several cheeses on one tray, space them as far apart as possible. You don't want a runny cheese oozing into its neighbor.

Because cold mutes the flavor and aroma of cheese, allow time for it to come to room temperature before serving (at least 30 minutes and up to 2 hours). And keep cheeses wrapped until serving to keep them from drying out.

OUR FAVORITE CHEESE TRAYS

HERE ARE SOME OF OUR FAVORITE CHEESE tray combinations. Many of these cheeses are widely available in well-stocked supermarkets. You may find the less familiar cheeses in gourmet or specialty cheese shops.

AMERICAN
Vermont or Wisconsin Cheddar
Maytag Blue or Fresh Goat Cheese
Sliced Apples
Cheese Straws (page 16) and Hearty Crackers
Spiced Pecans (page 2)

FRENCH
Brie or Camembert
Roquefort or Morbier
Pâté
French Bread
Warm Figs with Goat Cheese and Honey (page 12)
Gougères (page 19) or Pissaladière (page 57)

ITALIAN
Gorgonzola or Taleggio
Italian Fontina
Dates Stuffed with Parmesan (page 12)
Focaccia (page 52)
Melon and Prosciutto (page 33)
Warm Marinated Olives (page 6)

SPANISH
Manchego
Cabrales
Rustic Bread
Dried Cured Chorizo or Serrano Ham
Spanish-Style Almonds (page 4)
Roasted Red Pepper Spread (page 35)

CHEESE STRAWS

CHEESE STRAWS ARE AN OLD-FASHIONED appetizer that never fail to impress. In fact, a recipe for them, called Parmesan Cheese Pastry Twists, is usually printed on the back of the Pepperidge Farm Puff Pastry box. After making this old standby as the box suggested, we knew we could do better.

First, we wanted more cheese flavor. While the back-of-the-box recipe called for only ¼ cup cheese, we found it took a full cup of grated Parmesan to produce cheese straws with a good, hearty flavor. We then tried a few other cheeses, including Asiago, smoked cheddar, and manchego. While all of the cheeses melted just fine, only the Parmesan and Asiago retained their full-flavored punch after baking. The other cheeses, although potent on their own, tasted bland against the rich dough. We also tried adding various herbs and spices, such as fresh thyme, smoked paprika, and chili powder, but tasters preferred the batches seasoned only with a little salt and black pepper.

To form the straws, we found it much easier to work with pastry that wasn't fully thawed. When left just a bit icy, the dough came to room temperature as we rolled it out. The recipe on the box forms the straws by cutting the dough into two pieces and sandwiching the cheese between them. We tried pressing the cheese into just one side of a single piece of dough, but there was simply not enough surface area to hold a cup of cheese. In the end, we found it was better (and simpler) to press the grated cheese onto both sides of a single piece of dough. The exposed cheese then melted and toasted as the pastry puffed in the oven.

Many recipes call for the dough to be put back into the freezer for several minutes before baking to maximize the height of the puff. We found this wasn't necessary, as the dough was still relatively cool after rolling it out with the cheese. At 425 degrees, the straws took only 10 minutes to bake through. They emerged from the oven with a crisp, airy texture and an undeniable cheese flavor that is a classic.

Cheese Straws

MAKES 14 STRAWS

For an attractive presentation, stand the baked cheese straws straight up in a tall glass and serve with drinks and olives.

Thaw the puff pastry on the counter as you preheat the oven and grate the cheese. See the illustrations below for tips on shaping cheese straws. Note that this recipe requires parchment paper.

½	box (1 sheet) frozen puff pastry (Pepperidge Farm), thawed on the counter for 10 minutes
2	ounces grated Parmesan or Asiago cheese (about 1 cup)
¼	teaspoon salt
¼	teaspoon ground black pepper

1. Adjust the oven racks to the upper-middle and lower-middle positions and heat the oven to 425 degrees. Line 2 baking sheets with parchment paper and set them aside. Place the puff pastry on a sheet of parchment and sprinkle with ½ cup of the cheese and ⅛ teaspoon each of salt and pepper. Place a sheet of parchment over the cheese and, using a rolling pin, press the cheese into the dough by gently rolling the pin back and forth. Without removing the parchment, carefully flip the dough over, cheese-side down. Remove the top layer of parchment and sprinkle with the remaining cheese, salt, and pepper. Cover the pastry with the parchment. Measure the piece of dough and continue to roll it out, if necessary, to form a 10½-inch square.

2. Remove the top sheet of parchment and, using a sharp knife or pizza cutter, and following the illustrations at left, cut the dough into fourteen ¾-inch-wide strips. Gently twist each strip of dough and transfer it to a parchment-lined baking sheet, spacing the strips about 1 inch apart.

3. Bake immediately until fully puffed and golden brown, about 10 minutes, reversing the positions of the baking sheets from top to bottom halfway through the baking time. Remove the straws from the oven and cool on a wire rack for 5 minutes before serving. (The cheese straws, completely cooled, can be stored in an airtight container at room temperature for up to 3 days.)

MAKING CHEESE STRAWS

1. Using a sharp knife or pizza cutter, cut the dough into fourteen ¾-inch-wide strips.

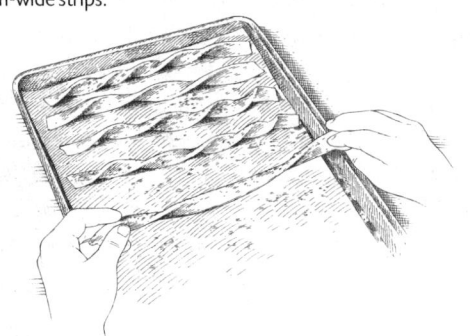

2. Holding 1 strip of dough at each end, gently twist the dough in opposite directions and transfer it to a parchment-lined baking sheet. Repeat with the remaining pieces of dough, spacing the dough strips about 1 inch apart.

➤ VARIATIONS

Cheddar-Adobo Cheese Straws

Follow the recipe for Cheese Straws, substituting 1 cup shredded sharp cheddar (about 3 ounces) for the Parmesan. In step 2, just before cutting the pastry into strips, brush with 1 tablespoon of adobo sauce from a can of chipotle chiles packed in adobo sauce.

Blue Cheese-Walnut Cheese Straws

Follow the recipe for Cheese Straws, substituting ½ cup crumbled blue cheese (about 2 ounces) and ¼ cup finely chopped walnuts for the Parmesan.

Fines Herbes Straws

Follow the recipe for Cheese Straws, substituting 1 tablespoon each of minced parsley, chervil, tarragon, and chives for the Parmesan.

Pistachio–Golden Raisin Straws with Cardamom

Follow the recipe for Cheese Straws, omitting the salt and substituting ¼ cup finely chopped pistachios, ¼ cup roughly chopped, rehydrated golden raisins, and ¼ teaspoon ground cardamom for the Parmesan.

Ancho–Cinnamon Sugar Straws

Follow the recipe for Cheese Straws, omitting the salt and pepper and substituting 1 tablespoon sugar, 2 teaspoons ancho chili powder, and ⅛ teaspoon ground cinnamon for the Parmesan.

Kalamata Olive, Feta, and Oregano Cheese Straws

Follow the recipe for Cheese Straws, substituting ½ cup finely chopped kalamata olives, ¼ cup crumbled feta, and 1 tablespoon minced fresh oregano leaves for the Parmesan.

Sun-Dried Tomato, Caper, and Garlic Straws

Follow the recipe for Cheese Straws, substituting ¼ cup finely chopped sun-dried tomatoes (oil-packed), 2 tablespoons finely chopped capers, 2 medium garlic cloves, minced or pressed through a garlic press, and 1 tablespoon minced fresh basil for the Parmesan.

Horseradish and Grainy Mustard Straws

Follow the recipe for Cheese Straws, substituting 2 tablespoons well-drained prepared horseradish and 2 tablespoons whole-grain mustard for the Parmesan.

Everything Straws

Follow the recipe for Cheese Straws, substituting 1 teaspoon sesame seeds, ½ teaspoon poppy seeds, ½ teaspoon dehydrated minced garlic, ½ teaspoon coarse salt, and ¼ teaspoon caraway seeds for the Parmesan.

GOUGÈRES

GOUGÈRES ARE GOLDEN BROWN, AIRY PASTRY puffs flavored with nutty Gruyère cheese and a hint of cayenne. A perfect gougère has a crisp, caramel-colored exterior that yields to a tender, slightly moist interior. It should taste nutty from the browned cheese and a little eggy—not unlike the custardy interior of a popover. Unfortunately, most are either dry, brittle, and bitter or squishy, soft, and gooey. What's the trick to a perfect gougère?

Gougères are prepared from pâte à choux, the same dough used for cream puffs, éclairs, and profiteroles. The traditional method for preparing pâte à choux (or choux paste) involves bringing water or milk, salt, and butter to a boil in a saucepan. When the mixture reaches a rolling boil, flour is vigorously beaten in to make a paste. The paste is continuously stirred over low heat to develop stringy strands of gluten, which will give the dough elasticity and strong oven spring once baked. Once the paste is shiny and smooth, it is removed from the heat and eggs are beaten in one at a time until incorporated. This dough is then piped onto baking sheets and baked until well puffed, darkly browned, and crisp.

How long must the paste be stirred and cooked for optimum gluten development? We prepared four batches and cooked each to a different degree—from not at all up to five minutes—over low heat. The uncooked batch and the batch cooked for only a minute rose little when baked. The batches made from paste cooked for three and five minutes, however, ballooned once baked. There was little difference between these two batches, so we opted for the three-minute method.

As for adding the eggs, this is conventionally done off the heat with a wooden spoon. This is serious grunt work, requiring feverish stirring so that the eggs don't cook as they hit the hot paste. Lazy cooks that we are, we tried using both a standing mixer and a food processor to stir the mixture. Unsurprisingly, both options worked better than the wooden spoon, but it was the food processor that won our vote because its whirling blade incorporated the eggs in record time. Best of all, the choux prepared in the food processor rose higher in the oven than the hand-mixed version.

With our basic mixing technique in hand, we

could focus on the ingredients. Beginning with the liquid, choux paste made exclusively with milk baked up with a caramel gold color, but it was too soft; a batch made with water alone was light and crisp but ashen pale. Equal parts of each made for an acceptable color and texture, but 2 parts water to 1 part milk was the best yet.

Whole eggs are the most common option in choux, but we decided to follow the lead of food writer/scientist Shirley Corriher and tried adding a higher proportion of egg whites to yolks. After a good deal of playing with the ratio, we found that 2 whole eggs to 1 egg white yielded the most delicate texture, rich flavor, and golden color.

Butter is added to choux paste for both flavor and texture. The fat helps to keep the dough tender. We tried amounts ranging from 3 to 5 tablespoons and found that the latter yielded the richest flavor and most delicately crisp texture.

Last but not least, we tackled the flour. After attempts with bread and pastry flour proved insignificant, we decided to stick with all-purpose flour. With its moderate levels of protein, the pastry developed just the right texture.

We quickly realized that proper baking of choux paste was as key to the pastry's success as the mixing technique and the ingredients. Small variations in temperature led to wildly different results in both color and texture. A 400-degree oven proved too cool, as the puffs barely puffed, but a 425-degree oven proved too warm, burning the puffs before the interior had set. Trial and error led us to hit upon a combination method that yielded perfect results: 425 degrees for 15 minutes, then 375 degrees for another 12 minutes or so.

After baking, the exterior was crisp, but the interior was still moist from trapped steam. Lancing each puff with a paring knife was the easy solution. Some recipes leave the puffs in the cooling oven to dry further for up to an hour, but we found that this method yielded overly crisp puffs (perfect for puffs destined to be filled with pastry cream or ice cream, but not to be eaten on their own). Removing the puffs from the oven after just 10 minutes kept the interior a little soft—just the way we wanted it.

As we baked batch after batch, we realized that the choux paste was sticky enough to be intractable outside of a pastry bag. No matter how tidy we tried to be with spoons or a scoop, the puffs turned out messy and lopsided. A pastry bag was simply unavoidable.

With a basic choux paste recipe, we were finally ready to make gougères. Traditionally, gougères are flavored with nothing but Gruyère, a pinch of cayenne, and a touch of dried mustard. It took just a few tests to settle on the right amount of cheese and cayenne pepper (just a pinch). Three ounces of cheese (or about 1 cup grated) added a rich nuttiness to the puffs without affecting their texture. Good-quality Gruyère made all the difference in flavor, but if you have trouble locating it, Emmental or Swiss cheese can work just fine. We opted to skip the dried mustard—it muddied the flavor.

The simple, clean flavor of the gougères begged for variations. After experimenting with a few

---

FAVORITE HOLIDAY APPETIZERS

WE PULL OUT ALL THE STOPS DURING the holidays, but we like to keep things simple, too. Here are some of our favorite appetizers, quick to prepare yet special enough for company.

- Frico (page 13)
- Gougères (page 19)
- Cheese Straws (page 16)
- Roasted Red Pepper Spread (page 35)
- Smoked Salmon Mousse (page 37)
- Smoked Trout Mousse (page 37)
- Shrimp Cocktail (page 40)
- Broiled Bacon-Wrapped Shrimp (page 80)
- Broiled Bacon-Wrapped Sea Scallops (page 80)
- Cocktail Crab Cakes (page 42)

options, we realized that we couldn't add much volume to the paste without affecting its texture and rise. Any additions needed to pack a punch in a small package. Garlic was one of the first flavors that came to mind. Added raw, the pungent allium obliterated the mild nuttiness of the Gruyère. Sautéing muted the garlic flavor to a more palatable level. The garlic and Gruyère combination tasted good but needed something sweet and rich to round it out. Bacon proved the perfect touch, and easy, too: We cooked the bacon and garlic together until both were golden brown. A little thyme added a much-needed hint of freshness and a woodsy flavor to accent the pork.

For a second variation, we wanted to swap out the Gruyère for something distinctly untraditional: Parmesan. To accent its nutty flavor, we quickly chose sautéed scallions. And to replace the heat of the cayenne, we chose to add a healthy spoonful of black pepper. The mild burn honed the Parmesan and tempered the scallions.

Gougères

MAKES SIXTEEN 3-INCH PUFFS

If you prefer smaller gougères, simply use a smaller tip on the piping bag. Pay close attention as they bake because smaller puffs may require a shorter baking time. Gougères are best served warm, although they can be made in advance and reheated as needed.

2	large eggs plus 1 large egg white
6	tablespoons water
5	tablespoons unsalted butter, cut into 10 pieces
2	tablespoons whole milk
¼	teaspoon salt
½	cup (2½ ounces) unbleached all-purpose flour, sifted
3	ounces Gruyère cheese, shredded (about 1 cup)
	Pinch cayenne pepper

1. Beat the eggs and egg white in a measuring cup or small bowl; you should have ½ cup (discard the excess). Set aside.

2. Bring the water, butter, milk, and salt to a boil in a small saucepan over medium heat, stirring once or twice. When the mixture reaches a full boil (the butter should be fully melted), immediately remove the saucepan from the heat and stir in the flour with a heatproof spatula or wooden spoon until combined and the mixture clears the sides of the pan. Return the saucepan to low heat and cook, stirring constantly, using a smearing motion, until the mixture is slightly shiny and looks like wet sand, and tiny beads of fat appear on the bottom of the saucepan, about 3 minutes (the paste should register 175 to 180 degrees on an instant-read thermometer).

3. Immediately transfer the mixture to a food processor and process with the feed tube open for 10 seconds to cool slightly. With the machine

MAKING CHOUX PASTE FOR GOUGÈRES

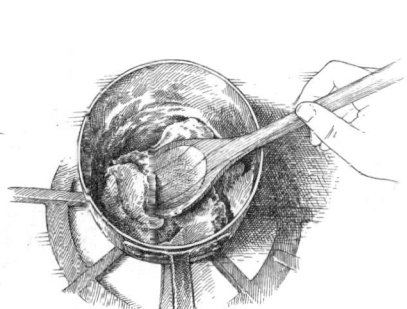

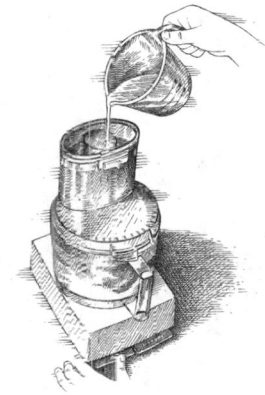

1. Occasionally stir the butter mixture until it comes to a full boil. Remove the pan from the heat.

2. Add the flour, return the pan to low heat and cook the paste for 3 minutes, stirring constantly and using a smearing motion.

3. With the feed tube open, process the paste for 10 seconds, then add the eggs in a steady stream.

running, gradually add the eggs in a steady stream. When all the eggs have been added, scrape down the sides of the bowl and add the cheese and cayenne to the food processor. Process for 30 seconds until a smooth, thick, sticky paste forms. (If not using immediately in one of the following recipes, transfer the paste to a medium bowl, press a sheet of plastic wrap that has been sprayed lightly with nonstick cooking spray directly on the surface, and store at room temperature for up to 2 hours.)

4. Adjust an oven rack to the middle position and heat the oven to 425 degrees. Spray a large (18 by 12-inch) baking sheet with nonstick cooking spray and line with parchment paper; set the pan aside.

5. Fold down the top 3 or 4 inches of a large pastry bag fitted with a ½-inch plain tip to form a cuff. Hold the bag open with one hand in the cuff and fill the bag with the paste. Unfold the cuff, place the bag on the work surface, and, using your hands or a bench scraper, push the paste toward the tip of the pastry bag. Twist the top of the bag and pipe the paste onto the prepared baking sheet into 16 evenly spaced 2-inch mounds. Use the back of a teaspoon dipped in a bowl of cold water to even out the shape and smooth the surface of the piped mounds.

6. Bake 15 minutes (do not open the oven door), then reduce the oven temperature to 375 degrees and continue to bake until golden brown and fairly firm (the puffs should not be soft and squishy), 12 to 14 minutes longer. Remove the baking sheet from the oven. With a paring knife, cut a ¾-inch slit into the side of each puff to release steam; return to the oven, turn off the oven, and prop the oven door open with the handle of a wooden spoon. After 10 minutes, transfer the puffs to a wire rack. Serve warm. (The gougères can be cooled completely and stored at room temperature for up to 24 hours or frozen in a zipper-lock plastic bag for up to 1 month. Before serving, crisp room-temperature gougères in a 300-degree oven for 5 to 8 minutes; crisp frozen gougères for 8 to 10 minutes.)

➤ VARIATIONS

Bacon, Garlic, and Thyme Gougères

Mince 7 ounces (about 7 slices) thinly sliced bacon. Transfer to a small skillet and fry until almost crisp, about 8 minutes. Add 4 medium garlic cloves, minced or pressed through a garlic press, to the skillet and stir until fragrant, about 30 seconds. Drain the mixture through a small strainer, reserving 2 tablespoons bacon fat. Set aside the bacon-garlic mixture. Follow the recipe for Gougères, replacing 2 tablespoons of the butter with the bacon fat in step 2. In step 3, after the eggs, cheese, and cayenne have been added to the food processor, add the reserved bacon-garlic mixture along with ½ teaspoon minced fresh thyme leaves.

PIPING GOUGÈRES

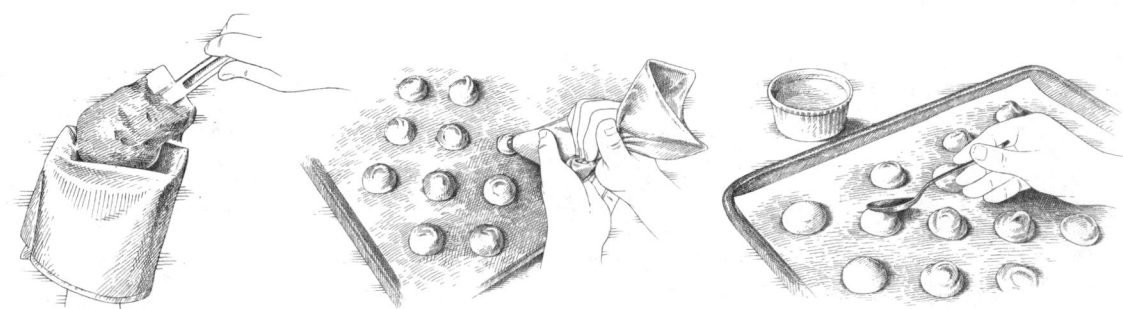

1. Fill a pastry bag with the paste, push the paste to the bottom of the bag using your hands or a bench scraper, and twist the top of the bag to seal.

2. Pipe the paste into 1¼- to 1½-inch mounds on the prepared baking sheet.

3. Use the back of a teaspoon dipped in cold water to even out the shape and smooth the surface of the piped mounds.

Scallion, Parmesan, and Black Pepper Gougères

Make sure to use freshly ground black pepper and good-quality, imported Parmesan.

Cook 8 thinly sliced scallions (white and green parts) with 1 tablespoon unsalted butter and a pinch of salt in a small skillet over medium-high heat until wilted and browned about the edges, about 3 minutes; cool slightly. Follow the recipe for Gougères, substituting 2 ounces grated Parmesan cheese (about 1 cup) for the Gruyère. Pulse the scallions and 1 teaspoon ground black pepper into the batter in step 3 after the cheese has been processed.

CRUDITÉS

WITH AN EXTENSIVE SELECTION OF vegetables now available year-round in most markets, a platter of crudités should be downright tempting, if not exotic, and offer a colorful variety of flavors and textures. But the key to good crudités doesn't lie only in the selection and arrangement of good-looking vegetables. We have found that if you want vegetables that actually taste good, some of them must first be prepared—beyond rinsing and being cut, that is.

Not all vegetables are meant to be eaten raw (unless you're a rabbit), and after extensive kitchen tests we concluded that many require a quick dunk in boiling, salted water (blanching) before being added to the platter. This crucial step is often overlooked for the sake of convenience, but we found it makes all the difference between mediocre and great crudités. Not only does blanching render tough vegetables toothsome, but the salty water also seasons the vegetables as they cook, enhancing their natural flavors.

Here are three keys to successfully blanched vegetables.

First, to keep carrots from tasting like asparagus or cauliflower from turning green, blanch each vegetable separately. Being mindful of the order in which you blanch them, begin with the bland and pale ones and finish with the bold-flavored and dark. The vegetables listed in the

cooking chart on page 24 are organized in the order in which they should be blanched.

Second, use a large pot that allows the vegetables to cook in ample water and become seasoned. A large volume of water—we use 6 quarts—ensures quick cooking times and brightly colored vegetables.

Third, once the vegetables are crisp-tender, transfer them from the boiling water to an ice-water bath immediately. This process, called shocking, prevents residual heat in the vegetables from cooking them further, which compromises their final color, texture, and flavor.

ARRANGING CRUDITÉS

Height is an important visual element in an appealing crudités presentation. Even with an assortment as simple as cherry tomatoes and carrot and celery sticks, we use the following two tricks to create a little height in our displays.

A. To elevate a small bowl of bite-size items such as cherry tomatoes or trimmed broccoli florets, overturn a small glass or ceramic bowl to use as a stand for the bowl holding the tomatoes. Put a small piece of folded plastic wrap between the two to keep the top bowl from sliding off the bottom one.

B. Give celery and carrot sticks extra lift (and freshness) by standing them up in glasses or cups with a few ice cubes in the bottom.

Preparing Vegetables for Crudités

To make vegetables more palatable and a lot easier to swipe through a dip, prepare them according to the following tips:

ASPARAGUS

1. To trim a bunch of asparagus efficiently, gently bend one stalk until the tough portion of the stem breaks off.

2. Place this broken asparagus alongside the still untrimmed ones. Using the shorter stalk as a guide, cut the tough ends off the remaining asparagus.

BROCCOLI AND CAULIFLOWER

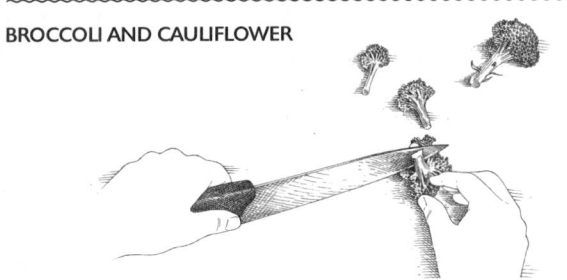

To cut attractive, bite-size florets, slice down through the main stem and out through the buds to produce 1-inch florets with 2-inch stems.

CARROTS

Although it is tempting to use bagged, prewashed baby carrots, their stubby stature makes it all too easy for dippers' fingers or knuckles to graze the surface of the dip when swiping. For long, elegant lengths of carrot, slice peeled carrots in half lengthwise. Then, with the cut side flat to the board, slice each half into 3 long pieces.

CELERY

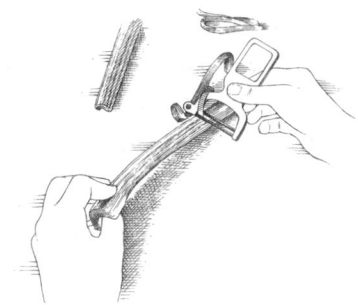

Celery often tastes harsh and vegetal, but its flavors can quickly turn sweet and mellow after its bitter skin and stringy fibers are removed with a vegetable peeler.

GREEN BEANS

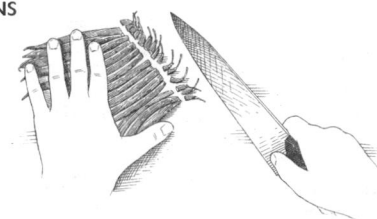

Instead of trimming the stem from one green bean at a time, line the beans up on the counter and trim off all the ends at one time with just one slice.

SNOW AND SNAP PEAS

Delicate snow and snap peas taste best when the fibrous string that runs along the straight edge of the pod has been removed. Use a paring knife to remove this string.

ENDIVE

Pull the leaves off gently, one at a time, continuing to trim the root end as you work your way toward the center.

BELL PEPPERS

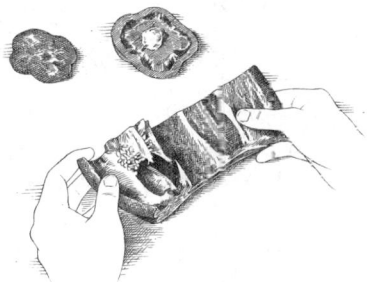

1. To turn this unusually shaped vegetable into uniform pieces, first slice a ½-inch section off both the tip and stem ends. Make one slit in the trimmed shell, place it skin-side down, and press the flesh flat against the cutting board.

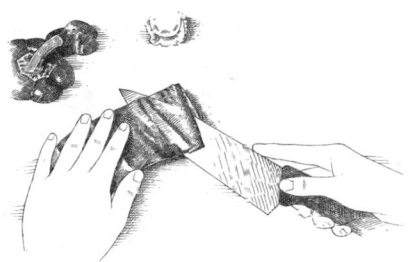

2. After removing the seeds and core, use a sharp knife to remove a ⅛-inch-thick piece of the tasteless inner membrane, then cut the pepper into ½-inch-wide lengths.

ZUCCHINI, SUMMER SQUASH, AND DAIKON RADISHES

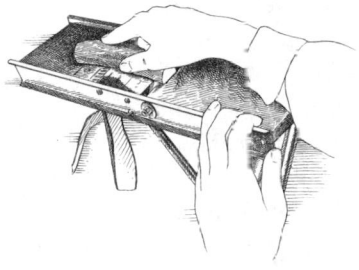

1. Though somewhat unusual for crudités, these vegetables can easily be added to the platter. Using a mandoline, cut them into ⅛-inch-thick slices.

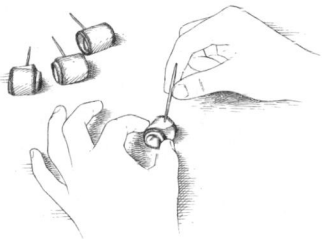

2. To make the thin slices easy to dip and eat, roll them into tidy cylinders and secure with a toothpick.

JÍCAMA

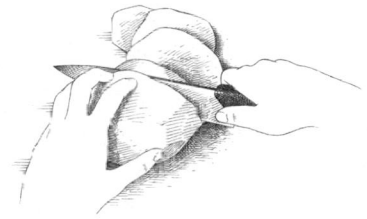

1. After peeling the jícama, slice it into ½-inch-thick disks.

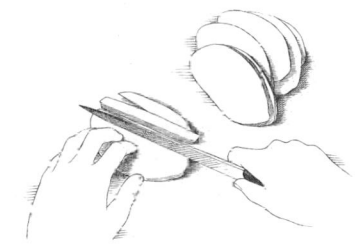

2. Cut each disk into ½-inch-thick strips.

FENNEL

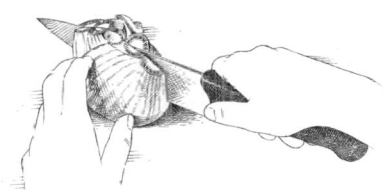

1. After trimming the base and removing the upper stalks and fronds, slice the oval bulb in half lengthwise.

2. Remove the layers of fennel from each half, then cut them into ½-inch-thick strips.

RADISHES

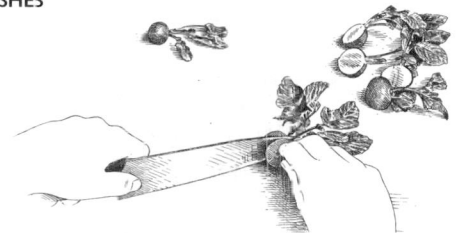

Choose radishes with their green tops still attached so that each half has a leafy handle for grasping and dipping. Slice each radish in half through the stem.

BLANCHED VEGETABLES FOR CRUDITÉS

CELERY, BELL PEPPERS, ENDIVE, JÍCAMA, tomatoes, and radishes taste best raw, but the vegetables listed below are best served by a quick blanch-and-shock before joining the rest on the platter. Blanch the vegetables in the order given, which starts with the mildest in flavor and ends with the strongest. See the illustrations on pages 22–23 for tips on preparing some of these vegetables. We found that 2 pounds of prepared vegetables and 1½ cups of dip are sufficient for a group of 8 to 10 people.

CARROTS	15 seconds
SNOW/SNAP PEAS	15 seconds
CAULIFLOWER	1 to 1½ minutes
GREEN BEANS	1 minute
FENNEL	1 minute
BROCCOLI	1 to 1½ minutes
ASPARAGUS	30 to 60 seconds

KEY STEPS FOR BLANCHING VEGETABLES

1. Bring 6 quarts water to a boil in a large pot over high heat and season with 2 tablespoons salt. Cook the vegetables, one variety at a time, until slightly softened but still crunchy (crisp-tender), following the times recommended in the chart above.

2. Using tongs or a strainer, transfer the blanched vegetables to a bowl of ice water and soak until completely cool, about 1 minute. Place on several layers of paper towels and pat dry. Blanch and shock the next vegetable on your list.

SWEET POTATO CHIPS

EVERYONE LOVES POTATO CHIPS, BUT MAKING them at home never really seems worth the trouble. An exception to this rule is sweet potato chips—they are crunchy and subtly sweet, and they marry well with both savory and sweet seasonings.

Our first challenge in developing a worthy chip was in getting potato slices of the appropriate thickness. We first tried hand-slicing the sweet potatoes but realized pretty quickly that this was a foolhardy path. It was impossible to achieve slices of consistent thickness. Our first batch yielded a basket of chips both raw and burnt. We next turned to the food processor, which produced slices that were consistent in thickness but that were still, overall, too thick; when cooked they had a texture more like that of French fries than chips. Not bad, but not what we were looking for. Recalling that we used a mandoline to slice potatoes for our scalloped potatoes (page 297), we gave it a try. The mandoline did the trick (a V-slicer also worked; see the equipment reviews on page 296). In a pinch, we found that a good vegetable peeler can do a decent job of making thin potato slices, although your chips will be more strip-shaped than traditional chip slices. The choice is up to you. Next we turned to the cooking method.

Potato chips are typically fried, but a couple of recipes called for baking them, and we wanted to explore this option. We consulted a few of these recipes and then placed the potato slices on a well-oiled baking sheet and popped them in the oven. We tested temperatures from 375 to 450 degrees, but no matter what temperature, the chips didn't have the crunch we were seeking, and they browned unevenly. We realized then that we weren't going to get out of frying these chips.

We chose peanut oil as our frying medium, both for its high smoke point and its mild but toasty flavor. Vegetable oil works well, too, but it lacks the rich flavor of peanut oil. In any kind of deep frying, getting the oil to the proper temperature is key to a good outcome. The only way to guarantee that the proper temperature has been reached—in this case, 375 degrees—is to use an instant-read or candy thermometer. Frying the chips in batches is also important. When we added too many slices at once, the chips clumped together and cooked unevenly. We recommend using a spider (see below) for skimming batches of chips from the oil. Its long handle protects hands and forearms from any hot splattering oil.

Sweet Potato Chips
SERVES 6

The oil will bubble up when you add the chips, so be sure you have at least 3 inches of room at the top of the pot. In lieu of a mandoline or V-slicer (see page 296), you can use a vegetable peeler to make sweet potato strips.

2   quarts peanut or vegetable oil
3   pounds sweet potatoes (about 4 large), peeled and cut into $1/16$-inch-thick slices using a mandoline or V-slicer
     Salt and ground black pepper

1. Heat the oil in a Dutch oven over medium heat until it reaches 375 degrees. (Use an instant-read thermometer that registers high temperatures or clip a candy/deep-fat thermometer onto the side of the pan.)

2. Carefully add just a handful (about a sixth) of the sweet potatoes and fry until lightly browned, 2 to 3 minutes, adjusting the heat as necessary to maintain the cooking temperature.

3. Using a slotted spoon or spider, transfer the chips to a baking sheet lined with several layers of paper towels and sprinkle them lightly with salt and pepper. Repeat with the remaining potato slices, allowing the oil to come back to 375 degrees after cooking each batch. The chips can be stored for up to 2 days in a resealable plastic bag.

VARIATIONS
Spicy Sweet Potato Chips
Follow the recipe for Sweet Potato Chips. Along with the salt and pepper, sprinkle the freshly fried chips with ⅛ teaspoon cayenne pepper.

Chinese Five-Spice Sweet Potato Chips
You can find Chinese five-spice powder in the spice aisle of most supermarkets. The spices lend the chips an exotic flavor.

Follow the recipe for Sweet Potato Chips. Along with the salt and pepper, sprinkle the freshly fried chips with ¼ teaspoon Chinese five-spice powder.

Rosemary Sweet Potato Chips
Thyme can be substituted for the rosemary in this variation.

Follow the recipe for Sweet Potato Chips. Along with the salt and pepper, sprinkle the freshly fried chips with 1 teaspoon finely minced rosemary.

Dilly Sweet Potato Chips
Dill and onion give the chips a pleasant tang.

Follow the recipe for Sweet Potato Chips. Along with the salt and pepper, sprinkle the freshly fried chips with 1 tablespoon minced fresh dill and ¼ teaspoon onion powder.

EQUIPMENT: Spider

More often referred to as a mesh skimmer or strainer, this piece of equipment is invaluable when it comes to working with boiling water or hot oil. Compared with a slotted spoon, which generally retrieves only a few pieces of food at a time, this not so itsy-bitsy spider has a wide basket made of open webbed (hence the name) mesh that can cradle food and lets excess water or oil drain away quickly.

7 QUICK AND EASY DIPS

WHAT COULD BE MORE HANDY THAN A quick, last-minute dip? Yet those made from dried soup mix are often overly salty and dreadfully stale. Luckily, there are lots of other ideas for flavoring dips that are just as fast and taste worlds better. With our Creamy Dip Base, you can whip up any number of fresh-flavored dips by stirring in one of our flavor add-ins, depending on your mood, the season, or the confines of your pantry.

CREAMY DIP BASE
Makes about 1½ CUPS

Mix together ¾ cup mayonnaise, ¾ cup sour cream, and 1 tablespoon lemon juice. Stir in a flavor-add in (see our favorites below for inspiration), then season with salt and pepper to taste. Allow the dip to sit for at least 15 minutes to allow the flavors to meld. The prepared dip will keep, covered and refrigerated, for up to 2 days.

FLAVOR ADD-INS

SUN-DRIED TOMATO AND BASIL DIP:
¼ cup finely chopped sun-dried tomatoes and 2 tablespoons minced fresh basil leaves
JALAPENO-LIME DIP:
Lime juice (instead of fresh lemon juice) in the dip base, ¼ cup chopped pickled jalapeños, and 3 thinly sliced scallions
SALSA DIP:
Lime juice (instead of fresh lemon juice) in the dip base, ½ cup drained salsa, and 2 tablespoons minced fresh cilantro leaves
PESTO DIP:
½ cup pesto and ½ head roasted garlic (page 34)
CUCUMBER-CURRY DIP:
1 tablespoon curry powder, ½ cucumber, seeded and minced, and 1 tablespoon minced fresh cilantro leaves
LEMONY FETA DIP:
½ cup crumbled feta cheese, an additional 1 tablespoon lemon juice, and 1 tablespoon chopped fresh mint leaves or dill
SMOKED SALMON AND CHIVE DIP:
4 ounces chopped smoked salmon and 1 tablespoon minced chives

PARTY DIPS

ONE BIG DIFFERENCE BETWEEN COOKBOOKS from the '60s and '70s and cookbooks from today is the dip recipes. The former have lots of creamy party dips based on sour cream and mayonnaise, while newer cookbooks have recipes for more eclectic sorts of dips made with pureed beans, roasted vegetables, and exotic ingredients such as pomegranate molasses and tahini. Yet there is something very satisfying about dipping a crisp carrot stick or salty potato chip into a cool, savory, creamy dip, and, in fact, these old standbys can be just as delicious as their modern competitors. However, the richness of both sour cream and mayonnaise can easily dominate a dip that is seasoned too timidly. These dips need to be seasoned with gusto. That means mostly fresh ingredients—and plenty of them.

After playing around with these dips for quite a while, we found the combination of mayonnaise and sour cream to be the ideal medium for carrying fresh and vibrant flavors. This combination also has the perfect consistency for dipping and scooping. As for the ratio, we found equal portions to be ideal. The mayonnaise adds body and richness, while the sour cream brings a bright freshness to the dip. We also found that "lite" mayonnaise and sour cream fare pretty well in these dips. They tend to taste a bit flatter and result in a dip that is slightly less creamy and silky, but they are certainly worth trying.

Preparing these dips at least one hour ahead of time or even a day in advance allows the flavors to blend. They are also best served cool rather than at room temperature.

Green Goddess Dip
MAKES ABOUT 1¾ CUPS

³/₄	cup sour cream (regular or light)
³/₄	cup mayonnaise (regular or light)
2	medium garlic cloves, chopped
¼	cup fresh parsley leaves
2	teaspoons chopped fresh tarragon leaves
1	tablespoon juice from 1 lemon
2	anchovy fillets

¼   cup minced fresh chives
     Salt and ground black pepper

In a food processor, process the sour cream, mayonnaise, garlic, parsley, tarragon, lemon juice, and anchovy fillets until smooth and creamy, scraping down the sides of the bowl once or twice. Transfer the mixture to a medium bowl; stir in the chives. Season to taste with salt and pepper. Chill until the flavors meld, about 1 hour. (The dip can be covered and refrigerated for up to 2 days.)

Smoky, Spicy Avocado Dip with Cilantro

MAKES ABOUT 2¼ CUPS

See page 64 for illustrations of pitting an avocado.

¾   cup sour cream (regular or light)
¾   cup mayonnaise (regular or light)
1   ripe avocado, halved, pitted, and flesh scooped
     from the skin
1   tablespoon juice from 1 lime
½   cup fresh cilantro leaves
1½   chipotle chiles in adobo sauce, plus 1 teaspoon
     adobo sauce
2   medium scallions, sliced thin
     Salt and ground black pepper

In a food processor, process the sour cream, mayonnaise, avocado, lime juice, cilantro leaves, and chipotle chiles with adobo sauce until smooth and creamy and the cilantro leaves are chopped fine, scraping down the sides of the bowl once or twice. Transfer the mixture to a medium bowl; stir in the scallions. Season to taste with salt and pepper. Chill until the flavors meld, about 1 hour. (The dip can be covered and refrigerated for up to 2 days.)

Clam Dip with Bacon and Scallions

MAKES ABOUT 2 CUPS

4   slices (about 4 ounces) bacon, cut into
     ¼-inch pieces
¾   cup sour cream (regular or light)

¾   cup mayonnaise (regular or light)
1   teaspoon juice from 1 lemon
1   teaspoon Worcestershire sauce
2   (6½-ounce) cans minced clams, drained
2   medium scallions, sliced thin
     Salt and ground black pepper
     Cayenne pepper

1. Fry the bacon in a small skillet over medium heat until crisp, 6 to 8 minutes. Transfer the bacon with a slotted spoon to a paper towel–lined plate and let cool.

2. Whisk together the sour cream, mayonnaise, lemon juice, and Worcestershire sauce in a medium bowl. Stir in the minced clams, scallions, and bacon. Season to taste with salt, pepper, and cayenne. Chill until the flavors meld, about 1 hour. (The dip can be covered and refrigerated for up to 2 days.)

Smoked Salmon Dip with Dill and Horseradish

MAKES ABOUT 2 CUPS

See page 36 for information on smoked salmon.

¾   cup sour cream (regular or light)
¾   cup mayonnaise (regular or light)
3   ounces smoked salmon
2   teaspoons juice from 1 lemon
1   teaspoon prepared horseradish
2   tablespoons minced fresh dill
     Salt and ground black pepper

In a food processor, process the sour cream, mayonnaise, salmon, lemon juice, and horseradish until smooth and creamy, scraping down the sides of the bowl once or twice. Transfer the mixture to a medium bowl; stir in the dill. Season to taste with salt and pepper. Chill until the flavors meld, about 1 hour. (The dip can be covered and refrigerated for up to 2 days.)

8 QUICK AND EASY CREAM CHEESE SPREADS

IN THE SPIRIT OF OUR QUICK AND EASY Dips (page 26), we developed a versatile spread for crackers; it's based on a simple cream cheese mixture to which any number of flavorings can be added.

CREAM CHEESE SPREAD BASE   Makes about 1 cup

Microwave an 8-ounce block of cream cheese on high power until very soft, 20 to 30 seconds, then stir in 2 tablespoons milk along with a flavor add-in (see our ideas below for inspiration). Allow the spread to chill for 1 hour before serving (the milk will help ensure that it remains spreadable, even when cold). The prepared spread will keep, covered and refrigerated, for up to 1 week.

FLAVOR ADD-INS

LEMONY HERB SPREAD:
¼ cup chopped fresh herbs and 1 tablespoon lemon juice
CHEDDAR AND ROASTED RED PEPPER SPREAD:
1½ cups shredded sharp cheddar cheese and ¼ cup chopped roasted red peppers
RED PEPPER JELLY–ALMOND SPREAD:
¼ cup red pepper jelly or mango chutney and 2 tablespoons chopped toasted almonds
PIMENTO SPREAD:
¼ cup chopped pimento-stuffed green olives and 1 tablespoon lemon juice
SUN-DRIED TOMATO–PARMESAN SPREAD:
¼ cup chopped sun-dried tomatoes, ½ cup grated Parmesan cheese, and 1 tablespoon minced fresh oregano leaves
CHIPOTLE-LIME SPREAD:
2 minced chipotle chiles in adobo sauce, 1 tablespoon lime juice, and 2 thinly sliced scallions
SHRIMP SPREAD:
8 ounces minced cooked shrimp, 1 table-spoon Old Bay seasoning, and 1 tablespoon lemon juice
SMOKED SALMON SPREAD:
4 ounces finely chopped smoked salmon, 2 tablespoons minced red onion, 2 tablespoons capers, and 1 tablespoon minced fresh dill

SPINACH DIP

SPINACH DIP—A SIMPLE CONCOCTION OF vegetable soup mix, sour cream, and frozen spinach—often tastes flat, exorbitantly salty, and nowhere near fresh. We wanted a rich, thick, and creamy spinach dip brimming with big, bold flavors, especially of spinach.

To begin, we gathered five varieties of spinach: curly (or crinkly), flat (or smooth), semi-savoy (a hybrid of the two), baby, and, for the sake of comparison, frozen spinach. We then trimmed, washed, chopped, and wilted the fresh spinaches in hot pots (we simply thawed the frozen spinach), made the dips, chilled them to set (cool and thicken), and let tasters dig in. The results were so surprising we had to tally them twice. Frozen spinach was the victor. Tasters liked its "familiar," "intense" flavor and even used the word "fresh" to describe it. The fresh varieties were too "meek," their flavor lost among the other ingredients. After a few more tests to determine consistency, we found that 20 to 30 seconds in the food processor chopped the thawed frozen spinach into small, manageable bits and made the dip smooth and creamy.

Armed with a host of fresh herbs and other pungent ingredients, we began developing the flavor components for the dip sans soup mix. Among the herbs, parsley and dill were by and large the standards, and they worked appealingly well when combined. Onions and shallots were problematic, however, as they required cooking to mellow their astringency and soften their crunch. We weren't cooking the spinach and thought it would be a waste of time and effort to start pulling out pots and pans now. In the end, a combination of raw scallion whites and a single small clove of garlic added the perfect amount of bite and pungency. With a dash of hot pepper sauce for a kick of heat and some salt and pepper, the dip came out of the food processor light, fresh, and full of bold flavors—far better than the soup mix recipe and not much more work.

The only problem remaining was that the dip, which took only about 15 minutes to make, took almost two hours to chill. Wanting to save time, we found the solution was simple. Instead of thawing the spinach completely, we thawed it only partially. Before processing, we microwaved the frozen block for three minutes on low, broke it into icy chunks, and squeezed each to extract a surprising amount of liquid. The chunks were still ice cold, and they thoroughly cooled the dip as they broke down in the processor. Although our hands were slightly numb, the dip was quick to make, thick, creamy, and cool enough for immediate service.

Herbed Spinach Dip

MAKES ABOUT 1½ CUPS

Partial thawing of the spinach produces a cold dip that can be served without further chilling. If you don't own a microwave, the frozen spinach can be thawed at room temperature for 1½ hours, then squeezed of excess liquid. The garlic must be minced or pressed before going into the food processor; otherwise, the dip will contain large chunks of garlic. See pages 22–23 for information about preparing vegetables to accompany this dip.

1	(10-ounce) box frozen chopped spinach
½	cup sour cream
½	cup mayonnaise
3	medium scallions, white parts only, sliced thin
1	tablespoon chopped fresh dill
½	cup packed fresh parsley leaves
1	small garlic clove, minced or pressed through a garlic press (½ teaspoon)
¼	teaspoon hot pepper sauce
½	teaspoon salt
¼	teaspoon ground black pepper
½	medium red bell pepper, cored, seeded, and diced fine

1. Thaw the spinach in a microwave for 3 minutes at 40 percent power. (The edges should be thawed but not warm; the center should be soft enough to be broken into icy chunks.) Squeeze the partially frozen spinach of excess water.

2. In a food processor, process the spinach, sour cream, mayonnaise, scallions, dill, parsley, garlic, hot pepper sauce, salt, and pepper until smooth and creamy, about 30 seconds. Transfer the mixture to a serving bowl and stir in the bell pepper; serve. (The dip can be covered with plastic wrap and refrigerated for up to 2 days.)

EASY, IMPRESSIVE NO-COOK STARTERS

EVERYONE DESERVES TO RELAX AT A party, even the host. Our favorite quick appetizers are a mix of classic crowd-pleasers and simple but distinctive snacks that give the cook time to enjoy the party too.

- Dates Stuffed with Parmesan (page 12)
- Herbed Spinach Dip (at left)
- Hummus (page 31)
- Whipped Goat Cheese with Chives and Lemon (page 11)
- Melon and Proscuitto (page 38)

➤ VARIATIONS

Spinach Dip with Blue Cheese and Bacon

If making this dip in advance, hold off on sprinkling the bacon over it until just before serving.

Cut 3 slices bacon into ¼-inch pieces and fry in a small skillet over medium-high heat until crisp and browned, about 5 minutes; using a slotted spoon, transfer the bacon to a paper towel–lined plate and set aside. Follow the recipe for Herbed Spinach Dip, omitting the dill, hot pepper sauce, salt, and red bell pepper and processing 1½ ounces crumbled blue cheese (about ⅓ cup) along with the spinach. Adjust seasoning with salt; before serving, sprinkle the bacon over the dip.

Spinach Dip with Feta, Lemon, and Oregano

Follow the recipe for Herbed Spinach Dip, omitting the hot pepper sauce, salt, and red bell pepper and processing 2 tablespoons fresh oregano leaves, 2 ounces crumbled feta cheese (about ½ cup), and 1 tablespoon lemon juice and 1 teaspoon grated lemon zest along with the spinach. Adjust seasoning with salt.

Cilantro-Lime Spinach Dip with Chipotle Chiles

This dip is good served with tortilla chips.

Follow the recipe for Herbed Spinach Dip, omitting the hot pepper sauce and red bell pepper and processing ¼ cup packed cilantro leaves, 1 tablespoon seeded and minced chipotle chiles in adobo sauce (about 2 medium chiles), 1 tablespoon lime juice and ½ teaspoon grated lime zest, ½ teaspoon light brown sugar, and ⅛ teaspoon ground cumin along with the spinach.

FREEZING CHIPOTLE CHILES IN ADOBO SAUCE

Chipotles (smoked, dried jalapeño chiles) are among our favorite chiles because they are so flavorful. Chipotles are often packed in adobo sauce (a vinegary tomato sauce flavored with garlic) and canned. Because a little chipotle goes a long way, it can be difficult to use up an entire can once it has been opened. Rather than letting the remaining chiles go bad in the refrigerator, try this trick we also use with tomato paste.

1. Spoon out the chipotles, each with a couple of teaspoons of adobo sauce, onto different areas of a baking sheet lined with parchment or waxed paper. Place the baking sheet in the freezer.

2. Once frozen, the chipotles should be transferred to a zipper-lock plastic bag and stored in the freezer. You can remove them, one at a time, as needed. They will keep indefinitely.

MAKING OLIVE-OIL DIPPING SAUCES

SERVING A CRUSTY LOAF OF BREAD WITH olive oil is probably the simplest last-minute appetizer. The key is to start with very good extra-virgin olive oil. Although good-quality olive oil has great flavor on its own, you can liven it up with one of our additions below. Simply pour the desired amount of oil into a skillet, add one of our flavor combinations, and heat just until warmed through. Remove from the heat and allow to cool to room temperature, 10 to 15 minutes. Serve the flavored oil with slices of crusty bread. (Leftover flavored oil will not keep and should be discarded.)

- Smashed garlic cloves and red pepper flakes
- Minced shallot and grated lemon zest
- Toasted ground fennel seeds and grated orange zest
- Grated Parmesan or Pecorino cheese, cracked black pepper, and coarse sea salt
- Pesto or roasted garlic cloves (page 34) mashed with chopped fresh basil, oregano, or thyme leaves
- Dried porcini mushrooms, rehydrated and chopped, and minced fresh thyme leaves
- Chopped olives and a sprig of rosemary
- Chopped sun-dried tomatoes and balsamic vinegar
- Minced anchovy, chopped garlic, and chopped fresh parsley leaves

HUMMUS

THIS SIMPLE CHICKPEA PUREE, ALTHOUGH relatively new to the American diet, has been eaten since the time of Socrates and Plato—and with good reason. Unfortunately, many of us are more familiar with the packaged tubs of prepared hummus, which are sold in supermarkets across the United States and don't taste very good. We wanted to make a great homemade hummus, similar to versions we'd tasted in Middle Eastern restaurants.

We did some research and found that hummus has multiple interpretations. Across the Middle East and throughout the Mediterranean region, individual families have their own recipes; these vary by texture and flavor. What they have in common is only the combination of chickpeas and tahini (sesame paste). Tasting several hummus interpretations side by side, tasters homed in on a hummus seasoned with lemon and garlic and mixed to a smooth, stiff, diplike texture that was far less oily than that of the other contenders.

We were impressed by the results obtained with canned chickpeas. Typically, the beans are packed in a slippery, water-based liquid, and we found that the hummus tasted cleaner when we rinsed the chickpeas before pureeing them. We also noted that some of the thin skins would come off the beans if they were then quickly towel-dried, ensuring a smoother puree. A 15-ounce can of chickpeas made a good-size batch of hummus.

We tried various amounts of tahini and found that ¼ cup yielded a good balance of flavors. One clove of garlic along with a pinch of cayenne added just the right bite. Three tablespoons of lemon juice contributed just enough brightness.

Last but not least, we needed to address the texture. Extra-virgin olive oil was the obvious choice, but we soon discovered that the amount needed to achieve a smooth yet sturdy consistency was overpowering in flavor. We corrected this by replacing half of the oil with water, which brought all the flavors into line. We also refrigerated the hummus for 30 minutes or so to mellow the flavors. At last, we had realized our goal: hummus that tasted far better than anything one could buy at the store.

Hummus

MAKES ABOUT 2 CUPS

Serve hummus with pita chips (see Easy Homemade Crackers in the box on page 33), fresh pita breads cut into wedges, or crudités (pages 21). Tahini can be found in Middle Eastern markets as well as in the international foods aisle of many supermarkets.

1	(15-ounce) can chickpeas, drained and rinsed
1	medium garlic clove, minced or pressed through a garlic press (1 teaspoon)
¾	teaspoon salt
	Pinch cayenne pepper
3	tablespoons juice from 1 lemon
¼	cup tahini
¼	cup extra-virgin olive oil
¼	cup water

Process all of the ingredients in a food processor until smooth, about 40 seconds. Transfer the hummus to a serving bowl, cover with plastic wrap, and chill until the flavors meld, at least 30 minutes; serve cold. (The hummus can be refrigerated for up to 2 days.)

BABA GHANOUSH

IN MIDDLE EASTERN COUNTRIES, BABA GHAN-oush is served as part of a meze platter—not unlike an antipasto in Italy—which might feature salads, various dips, small pastries, meats, olives, other condiments, and, of course, bread. The driving force behind baba ghanoush is grill-roasted eggplant, sultry and rich. The dip's beguiling creaminess and haunting flavor come from tahini (sesame paste) enhanced with a bit of garlic and brightened with both fresh lemon juice and parsley.

The traditional method for cooking the eggplant for baba ghanoush is to scorch it over a hot, smoky grill. There the purple fruit grows bruised and then blackens, until its inside almost sloshes within its charred carapace. The hot, soft interior is scooped out with a spoon and the ruined exterior is discarded.

While eggplant cooked to the sloshy, soft stage may sound woefully overcooked to some, we realized that undercooked eggplant would taste spongy-green and remain unmoved by seasonings. This finding elicited an important question: Can a decent baba ghanoush be made without a grill? Taking instruction from the hot grill fire, we roasted a few large eggplants in a 500-degree oven. It took about 60 minutes to collapse the fruit and transform the insides to pulp. Though the baba ghanoushes we made with grill-roasted eggplants were substantially superior to those made with the oven-roasted eggplants, the latter were perfectly acceptable.

Eggplant suffers from persistent rumors that it is bitter. Most baba ghanoush recipes call for discarding the seedbed. But the insides of the eggplants we were roasting were veritably paved with seeds. We thought it impractical and wasteful to jettison that amount of produce, so we performed side-by-side tests comparing versions of the dip with and without seeds. We found no tangible grounds for seed dismissal. The dip was not bitter. The seeds stayed.

Our research on this recipe disclosed that one variety of eggplant was sometimes favored over another. That prompted us to make baba ghanoush with standard large globe eggplants, with compact Italian eggplants, and with long, slender Japanese eggplants. Surprisingly, all were good. The globe eggplants resulted in a baba ghanoush that was slightly more moist. The Italian eggplants were drier and contained fewer seeds. The Japanese eggplants were also quite dry. Their very slenderness allowed the smoke of the open flame to permeate the flesh completely, and the resulting dip was meaty and delicious.

The eggplant can be mashed with a fork, but we preferred to use the food processor, which makes it a cinch to incorporate the other ingredients and to pulse the eggplant, leaving the texture slightly coarse.

As for the proportions of said ingredients, tests indicated that less was always more. Minced garlic gathers strength and can become aggressive when added in substantial amounts. Many recipes also called for tahini in amounts that overwhelmed the eggplant. The same can be said for the lemon juice: Too much will dash the smoky richness of the eggplant with astringent tartness.

If you're serving a crowd, the recipe can easily be doubled or tripled. Time does nothing to improve the flavor of baba ghanoush. An hour-long stay in the refrigerator for a light chilling is all that's needed.

Baba Ghanoush

MAKES ABOUT 2 CUPS

Purchase eggplants with shiny, taut, and unbruised skin and an even shape (eggplants with a bulbous shape won't cook evenly). We prefer to serve baba ghanoush only lightly chilled. If yours is cold, let it stand at room temperature for about 20 minutes before serving. Baba ghanoush does not keep well, so make it the same day you plan to serve it. Pita bread, black olives, tomato wedges, and cucumber slices are nice accompaniments.

2	pounds eggplant (about 2 large globe eggplants, 5 medium Italian eggplants, or 8 small Japanese eggplants), each eggplant poked uniformly over its entire surface with a fork to keep it from bursting
I	tablespoon juice from I lemon
I	small garlic clove, minced or pressed through a garlic press (1/2 teaspoon)
2	tablespoons tahini
	Salt and ground black pepper
I	tablespoon extra-virgin olive oil
2	teaspoons chopped fresh parsley leaves

1. Grill the eggplants over a hot fire (you should be able to hold your hand 5 inches above the grill grate for only 2 seconds) until the skins darken and wrinkle on all sides and the eggplants are uniformly soft when pressed with tongs, about 25 minutes for large globe eggplants, 20 minutes for Italian eggplants, and 15 minutes for Japanese eggplants, turning the eggplants every 5 minutes. Transfer the eggplants to a rimmed baking sheet and cool 5 minutes.

2. Set a small colander over a bowl or in the sink. Trim the top and bottom off each eggplant. Slit the eggplants lengthwise. Use a spoon to scoop the hot pulp from the skins and place the pulp in the colander (you should have about 2 cups packed pulp); discard the skins. Let the pulp drain for 3 minutes.

3. Transfer the pulp to a food processor. Add the lemon juice, garlic, tahini, ¼ teaspoon salt, and ¼ teaspoon pepper and process until the mixture has a coarse, choppy texture, about eight 1-second pulses. Adjust the seasonings with salt and pepper

to taste. Transfer to a serving bowl, cover with plastic wrap flush with the surface of the dip, and refrigerate until lightly chilled, 45 to 60 minutes. To serve, use a spoon to make a trough in the center of the dip and spoon the olive oil into it. Sprinkle with the parsley and serve.

➤ VARIATIONS

Baba Ghanoush, Oven Method

Adjust an oven rack to the middle position and heat the oven to 500 degrees. Line a rimmed baking sheet with foil, set the eggplants on the baking sheet, and roast, turning every 15 minutes, until the eggplants are uniformly soft when pressed with tongs, about 60 minutes for large globe eggplants, 50 minutes for Italian eggplants, and 40 minutes for Japanese eggplants. Cool the eggplants on the baking sheet for 5 minutes, then proceed with the master recipe from step 2.

Baba Ghanoush with Sautéed Onion

Sautéed onion gives the baba ghanoush a sweet, rich flavor.

Heat 1 tablespoon extra-virgin olive oil in a small skillet over low heat until shimmering. Add 1 small onion, chopped fine, and cook, stirring occasionally, until the edges are golden brown, about 10 minutes. Follow the recipe for Baba Ghanoush, stirring the onion into the dip after processing.

Israeli-Style Baba Ghanoush

Replacing the tahini with mayonnaise makes this baba ghanoush pleasantly light and brings out the smoky flavor of charcoal-grilled eggplant.

Follow the recipe for Baba Ghanoush, substituting an equal amount of mayonnaise for the tahini.

QUICK HOMEMADE CRACKERS

WHETHER YOU'VE RUN OUT OF CRACKERS and don't have time to get to the store or you want to serve up something a little more special, here are several ideas for making crackers and chips from ingredients that may already be lurking in your kitchen. Spare pita bread, lavash, tortillas, and even day-old bagels can be transformed into crackers that would put the most renowned cracker manufacturer to shame. Although these addictively crunchy snacks are ripe for dipping, they can also be jazzed up with a range of herb and spice variations, a few of which are listed below.

EASY HOMEMADE CRACKERS

Cut pita bread, lavash, or flour tortillas into bite-size wedges or slice bagels thinly into rounds. Arrange on a large baking sheet. Brush the crackers lightly with olive oil (don't use too much or they'll taste greasy), or use one of the flavoring ideas below, and sprinkle with salt and pepper. Bake in a 350-degree oven, flipping the crackers over halfway through baking, until they are golden and fully toasted, about 12 minutes. Allow to cool before serving. These crackers are best served the same day they are prepared.

CHEESY CRACKERS

After lightly brushing the crackers with oil, sprinkle the tops liberally with grated Parmesan cheese and bake.

GARLIC-HERB CRACKERS

Prior to brushing the crackers with oil, heat the oil in a skillet and add a few smashed garlic cloves. Stir for 30 seconds and remove from the heat. Stir in chopped fresh thyme, basil, or oregano. Just before baking, brush the crackers with the oil, leaving behind the garlic cloves.

SPICED CRACKERS

Prior to brushing the crackers with oil, heat the oil in the skillet and add one of the following: smoked paprika, curry powder, or a combination of ground cinnamon, sugar, and chili powder. Stir until fragrant, about 30 seconds, and remove from the heat. Just before baking, brush the crackers with the spiced oil.

BOOSTING FLAVOR WITH ROASTED GARLIC

ROASTED GARLIC IS THE SECRET WEAPON OF GREAT 11TH-HOUR COOKS AND LAST-minute party throwers everywhere. It's easy to prepare (practically mindless) and it keeps, covered, in the refrigerator for several days. In addition to slathering roasted garlic on crusty bread, you can use just a bit of its sweet, roasted flavor and smooth buttery texture to liven up anything that tastes the least bit bland, from dips and spreads to soups and side dishes. You can double this recipe; just make sure to wrap each garlic head separately in foil.

Roasted Garlic

MAKES 1 HEAD

- 1   medium head garlic, outer skin removed but head left intact
- 1   teaspoon extra virgin-olive oil

1. Adjust an oven rack to the lower-middle position and heat the oven to 425 degrees.

2. Following illustration 1 below, slice off the top ½ inch from the head of garlic to expose the cloves. Place the garlic on a piece of aluminum foil measuring at least 10 by 10 inches. Pour the oil over the garlic and then wrap the garlic securely in the foil following illustration 2 below. Place the wrapped garlic on a baking sheet.

3. Roast the garlic until the cloves are soft and the top is golden, 35 to 45 minutes. (You can open the foil packet to check the progress of the garlic, but seal it back up if the garlic is not done.) Remove the sealed foil packet from the oven and let cool for 10 minutes. Unwrap the garlic and cool further. When the cloves are cool enough to handle, squeeze the roasted garlic from the skins, following illustration 3 below.

ULTIMATE GARLIC SPREAD:
Mix with butter and slather onto a split crusty loaf of bread.

"GROWN-UP" MACARONI AND CHEESE:
Stir into your favorite macaroni and cheese.

GARLICKY MARINARA:
Stir into your favorite jarred marinara sauce.

GARLICKY MAYONNAISE:
Mix with mayonnaise and use as a sandwich spread, a dip for crudités, or a dip for steamed shrimp.

ROASTING GARLIC

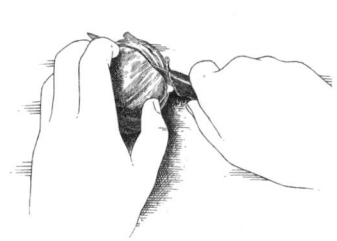 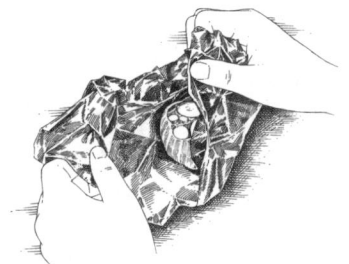 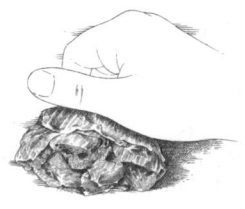

1. Cut ½ inch from the tip end of the head of garlic so that the clove interiors are exposed.

2. Place the garlic, cut-side up, in the center of a 10-inch square of aluminum foil. Drizzle with the oil.

3. After the garlic has roasted, open the foil package and cool. With your hand or the flat edge of a chef's knife, squeeze the garlic from the skins, starting from the root end and working up.

ROASTED RED PEPPER SPREAD

MUHAMMARA, MADE FROM ROASTED RED peppers, walnuts, and pomegranate molasses, is a popular spread made throughout the eastern Mediterranean. We wanted to develop a quicker version, based on pantry staples, without losing the sweet, smoky, savory flavors that make this spread so popular.

The first hurdle was the roasted peppers. Although roasting red peppers is fairly easy, we found that good-quality jarred peppers could be used (see below for more information). The trick is to rinse them of their brine before using them. Our next challenge was to find a replacement for the pomegranate molasses, which is difficult to locate in typical American supermarkets. Seeking its thick, syrupy texture and sweet/sour flavor, we tested a variety of pantry ingredients before coming up with a substitute. In the end, we found that a combination of lemon juice, honey, and mild molasses worked well. Seasoned with cayenne, ground cumin, and salt, the spread required only a small amount of olive oil to help loosen its

consistency and toasted walnuts to enrich it.

At this point, our dip tasted good, but it was still missing something. Taking a look at Paula Wolfert's recipe for muhammara, we quickly realized what it was—crumbled wheat crackers. We added a generic brand of plain wheat crackers from the supermarket and found they contributed both flavor and substance to the mix, turning our roasted red pepper spread into a fair replication of authentic muhammara. Last, we noted that the flavors needed time to meld—at least 30 minutes—before serving.

Roasted Red Pepper Spread
MAKES ABOUT 2 CUPS

Serve this dip with pita chips (see Easy Homemade Crackers in the box on page 33), fresh pitas cut into wedges, or baguette slices. See the information at left on our tasting of jarred roasted red peppers.

1	cup walnuts, toasted in a medium skillet over medium heat until fragrant, about 4 minutes, and cooled
12	ounces jarred roasted red peppers, drained, rinsed, and patted dry with paper towels
1/8	teaspoon cayenne pepper
1/4	cup coarsely ground plain wheat crackers
3	tablespoons juice from 1 lemon
1	tablespoon mild molasses
1	teaspoon honey
1/2	teaspoon ground cumin
3/4	teaspoon salt
2	tablespoons extra-virgin olive oil

Process the toasted walnuts with the remaining ingredients in a food processor until smooth, about ten 1-second pulses. Transfer the mixture to a serving bowl, cover with plastic wrap, and chill until the flavors meld, at least 30 minutes; serve cold. (The spread can be refrigerated for up to 2 days.)

INGREDIENTS:
Jarred Roasted Red Peppers

Jarred peppers are convenient, but are all brands created equal? To find out, we collected six brands from local supermarkets. The top two brands, Divina and Greek Gourmet, were preferred for their "soft and tender texture" (the Divina) and "refreshing," "piquant," "smoky" flavor (the Greek Gourmet) The other brands were marked down for their lack of "roasty flavor" and for the unpleasantly overpowering flavor of the brines These peppers tasted as if they'd been "buried under brine and acid" or were thought to have a "sweet and acidic aftertaste." The conclusion? Tasters preferred peppers with a full, smoky, roasted flavor, a brine that was spicy but not too sweet, and a tender texture.

THE BEST JARRED ROASTED RED PEPPERS
Divina peppers (left) were the top choice of tasters. Greek Gourmet peppers (right) came in a close second.

SMOKED SALMON MOUSSE

POTENT, SALTY-SWEET SMOKED SALMON IS perfect for an appetizer mousse. Its strong, perfumed flavor stands up to the creamy base that often overwhelms less flavorful ingredients. On the other hand, because that flavor is so pervasive, smoked salmon mousse often turns out tasting one-dimensional and unbalanced.

To start, we found that smoked salmon is now sold everywhere in vacuum-sealed packages. Most packages we found held 4 ounces, so we decided to base our recipe on this amount. Turning our attention to the base of the mousse, we tried a variety of ingredients, including cream cheese, sour cream, crème fraîche, yogurt, and mayonnaise. Tossing the yogurt aside as tasting awful

---

6 THINGS TO DO WITH SMOKED SALMON

PRIZED FOR ITS BRINY, SMOKED FLAVOR AND DELICATE TEXTURE, SMOKED SALMON is one of the most accessible delicacies on the market. Yet with so many varieties to choose from, buying smoked salmon can often be confusing.

The two most widely available varieties are called nova (as in Nova Scotia) and lox. Nova has a mild smokiness and is lightly salted, while lox is very salty but has little (if any) smoke flavor. Other varieties, typically found in specialty stores, are Scottish, Irish, and Norwegian salmon (sometimes lumped together as "Euro"). These varieties have a little more punch in terms of smoke and brine.

When possible, purchase smoked salmon from specialty stores that hand-slice their product to order—it is generally of a higher quality than presliced salmon, albeit more expensive. We have found, however, that warehouse clubs (such as BJ's and Costco) sell presliced smoked salmon from Scotland and Norway that is of good quality at a reasonable price. If purchasing presliced packaged smoked salmon, look for firm, well-marbled flesh and steer clear of any with "nitrates" or "nitrites" in the ingredient list. When serving smoked salmon, be sure to cut out the dark brown triangle found at the bottom of each slice. And because of its lush, rich flavor, it's best to serve smoked salmon simply. Here are our favorite serving ideas.

SMOKED SALMON AND WHIPPED GOAT CHEESE SPREAD
Microwave 4 ounces cream cheese on high power until very soft, 20 to 30 seconds, then stir in 4 ounces goat cheese and 2 tablespoons milk. Fold in 4 ounces chopped smoked salmon, 2 tablespoons lemon juice, and cracked black pepper to taste. Chill for 30 minutes to allow flavors to meld before serving with crackers or slices of bread.

SIMPLE SMOKED SALMON PLATE
Arrange thin slices of smoked salmon on a large plate. Add a squeeze of fresh lemon juice, and sprinkle with minced red onion or shallots, finely chopped Hard-Cooked Eggs (page 44), minced fresh dill, and some rinsed capers. Serve with crackers or a thinly sliced baguette.

SMOKED SALMON CANAPÉ
Spread a thin layer of whipped sweet butter onto dense, dark bread such as pumpernickel or rye and top with a generous slice of smoked salmon and a sprig of dill.

SMOKED SALMON RELISH
Combine 4 ounces coarsely chopped smoked salmon, 2 tablespoons chopped capers, 2 tablespoons minced fresh parsley leaves or dill, and 3 tablespoons extra-virgin olive oil; season with pepper to taste. Serve with toast points or Crostini Toasts (see page 47).

SMOKED SALMON–WRAPPED VEGETABLES
Wrap a thin slice of smoked salmon around a spear of blanched asparagus, a baton of cucumber or fennel, or a thin, crisp breadstick smeared with goat cheese, Boursin, or sweet butter. Arrange on a large platter and serve immediately.

SMOKED SALMON POTATO SKINS
Top your favorite potato skins with Boursin cheese and fresh parsley. Sprinkle chopped smoked salmon over the skins just before serving.

with smoked salmon, we thought mayonnaise tasted like a sandwich spread with an unattractive, oily mouthfeel. Sour cream and crème fraîche both tasted fantastic, but they produced textures that were far too loose and diplike. Cream cheese produced a good, spreadable texture but tasted more like a bagel topping than a mousse. By mixing crème fraîche or sour cream with the cream cheese, however, we were able to get just the flavor and texture we were looking for. When rounded out with shallot, lemon juice, and black pepper, the mousse required no additional salt because of the naturally salty character of the smoked salmon.

Up to this point, we had been chopping the salmon by hand and using a rubber spatula to mix it with the other ingredients in a large bowl. Wondering if we could streamline the technique, we were surprised when mousse prepared in a food processor not only tasted as good as the hand-mixed version but also had a better texture. However, neither the shallot nor the crème fraîche processed in the same amount of time as the salmon. Because the shallot didn't break down into small enough pieces, we had to mince it first. As for the crème fraîche, we noted that it turned loose and watery when processed for too long and found it best to pulse it into the mixture at the end.

Smoked Salmon Mousse

MAKES ABOUT 1/4 CUPS

Our favorite way to use this spread is as a canapé topping on squares of black bread. If you have more time, pipe the mousse onto endive leaves. Crème fraîche gives the mousse a slightly creamier, subtler flavor than sour cream does, but sour cream works admirably, too. To soften the cream cheese, cut it into chunks and leave it at room temperature for several minutes while you mince the shallot and measure the other ingredients.

4	ounces sliced smoked salmon
1	large shallot, minced (1/4 cup)
2	ounces cream cheese, softened
2	teaspoons juice from 1 lemon
1/4	cup crème fraîche or sour cream
	Ground black pepper

1. Place the salmon and shallot in a food processor and process, scraping down the sides of the bowl as necessary, until the mixture is finely chopped, about 10 seconds. Add the cream cheese and lemon juice and process until the mixture forms a ball, scraping down the sides of the bowl as necessary. Add the crème fraîche and pulse just to incorporate, about 5 seconds.

2. Scrape the mousse into a serving bowl and season with pepper to taste; serve. (The mousse can be refrigerated in an airtight container for up to 2 days.)

➤ VARIATION

Smoked Trout Mousse

Follow the recipe for Smoked Salmon Mousse, replacing the salmon with 8 ounces smoked trout fillets (about 2 fillets), skinned and pin bones removed, and flaked. Substitute lime juice for the lemon juice and increase the crème fraîche to 1/3 cup. Add 2 tablespoons well-drained prepared horseradish along with the crème fraîche.

MELON AND PROSCIUTTO

THE PAIRING OF JUICY, SWEET MELON and salty, toothsome prosciutto is classic—the quintessentially elegant hors d'oeuvre from Italy. Prosciutto refers to a ham that has been salted and air-dried in the Italian fashion. Unlike many other hams produced elsewhere, prosciutto is not smoked, and it is usually not cooked (because it is cured). As an antipasto, it is served in paper-thin slices. Although prosciutto can be served on its own, the addition of melon (or figs) is customary and delicious. While prosciutto is now produced in various parts of the world and can be quite good, the best comes from two regions of Italy: Parma and San Daniele. Italian prosciutto has been available in the United States for more than a decade, and our tasters found it to be the best choice for this combination.

There are no secrets to assembling this hors d'oeuvre, but there is one caveat: Each ingredient must be prime quality. The prosciutto should be supple and perfumed, and the melon must be sweet and ripe. It is best not to let the melon and prosciutto stand for too long, or the salt from the meat will draw moisture out of the melon, turning the fruit wet and the meat soggy.

Melon and Prosciutto

MAKES 16 PIECES, SERVING 6 TO 8

Cantaloupe is the classic choice, but any ripe melon, including honeydew, can be used in this pairing.

1	medium, ripe cantaloupe
½	pound thinly sliced imported prosciutto

1. Peel the melon and discard the rind. Cut the melon in half and scoop out the seeds with a spoon; discard the seeds. Cut each half into eight ½-inch-wide crescents.

2. If the prosciutto slices are long (over 6 inches in length), wrap one piece of prosciutto around the middle of each melon slice. If the prosciutto slices are short (under 6 inches in length), wrap two around the middle of each melon slice. Arrange on a platter and serve immediately.

➤ VARIATION

Asparagus Wrapped with Prosciutto

MAKES ABOUT 20 PIECES, SERVING 4 TO 6

Let the asparagus spears cool slightly before wrapping them in the prosciutto, but don't let the asparagus cool completely. Part of the charm of this dish comes from the contrasting temperatures (and textures). Make sure you have the same number of asparagus spears (no thicker than your pinkie) and pieces of prosciutto once it has been cut. You need about 20 of each.

1	pound thin asparagus spears, tough ends snapped off (see the illustration on page 165)
1	teaspoon extra-virgin olive oil
	Salt and ground black pepper
1	teaspoon balsamic vinegar
3	tablespoons grated Parmesan cheese
3	ounces thinly sliced imported prosciutto, cut crosswise into 3-inch-long pieces

1. Adjust an oven rack to the highest position and heat the broiler. Toss the asparagus with the oil on a rimmed baking sheet. Sprinkle with salt and pepper to taste. Broil, shaking the pan halfway through to turn the asparagus, until lightly browned, about 5 minutes.

2. Sprinkle the asparagus with the vinegar and Parmesan cheese. Cool slightly. Wrap a piece of prosciutto around the bottom half of each asparagus spear, making sure to leave the tip of the asparagus exposed. Arrange the asparagus on a platter and serve immediately.

CLASSIC SHRIMP COCKTAIL

NOTHING IS MORE BASIC THAN SHRIMP cocktail: "boiled" shrimp served cold with "cocktail" sauce, typically a blend of bottled ketchup or chili sauce spiked with horseradish. Can something so simple and good be improved upon? We thought so and set out to do just that.

If you start with good shrimp and follow a typical shrimp cocktail recipe—that is, simmer the shrimp in salted water until pink—the shrimp will have decent but rarely intense flavor. The easiest way to intensify the flavor of shrimp is to cook them in their shells. But, as we found out, this method has its drawbacks. First of all, it's far easier to peel shrimp when they are raw than when they have been cooked in liquid. More important, however, the full flavor of the shells is not extracted during the relatively short time required for the shrimp to cook through. It takes a good 20 minutes for the shells to impart their flavor to the cooking water, and this is far too long to keep shrimp in a pot.

It's better, then, to make shrimp stock, a simple enough process that takes only 20 minutes using just the shrimp shells. Simply place the shells in a pot with water to cover, then simmer them for 20 minutes.

Next, we thought, it would be best to see what other ingredients would complement the flavor of the shrimp without overpowering it. Our first attempt was to use beer and a spicy commercial seasoning, but this was a near disaster; the shrimp for shrimp cocktail should not taste like a New Orleans crab boil.

After trying about 20 different combinations, involving wine, vinegar, lemon juice, and a near-ludicrous number of herbs and spices, we settled on the mixture given in our recipe. It contains about 25 percent white wine, a dash of lemon juice, and a more-or-less traditional combination of herbs. Variations are certainly possible, but we caution against adding more wine or lemon juice; both were good up to a point, but after that their pungency became overwhelming.

Although we were pleased at this point with the quality of the shrimp's flavor, we thought it could be still more intense. We decided to try to keep the shrimp in contact with the flavorings for a longer period of time. We tried several methods to achieve this, including starting the shrimp in cold water with the seasonings and using a longer cooking time at a lower temperature. But shrimp cook so quickly—this is part of their appeal, of course—that these methods served only to toughen the meat. What worked best, we found, was to bring the cooking liquid to a boil, turn off the heat, and add the shrimp. Depending on their size, we could leave them in the liquid for up to 10 minutes, during which time they would cook through without toughening, all the while taking on near-perfect flavor.

Improving traditional cocktail sauce proved to be a tricky business. We wanted to make a better sauce, but we still wanted it to be recognizable as cocktail sauce. Starting with fresh or canned tomatoes, we discovered, just didn't work. The result was often terrific (some might say preferable), but it was not cocktail sauce. It was as if we had decided to make a better version of liver and onions by substituting foie gras for the calves liver. Undoubtedly, it would be "better," but it would no longer be liver and onions.

We decided to buy bottled ketchup or chili sauce and season it ourselves. First we had to determine which made the better base, ketchup or chili sauce. The answer to this question was surprising but straightforward: ketchup. Bottled chili sauce is little more than vinegary ketchup

PEELING SHRIMP

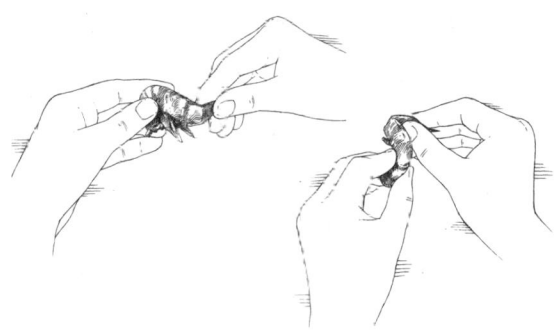

1. Hold the tail end of the shrimp with one hand and the opposite end of the shrimp with the other, then bend the shrimp back and forth and side to side to split the shell.

2. Lift off the tail portion of the shell, then slide your thumb under the legs of the remaining portion and lift it off as well.

DEVEINING SHRIMP

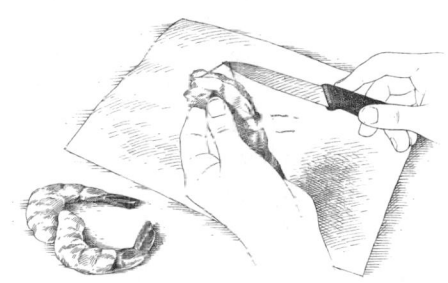

1. With a paring knife, make a shallow slit along the back of each shrimp. With the tip of the blade, lift up and loosen the vein.

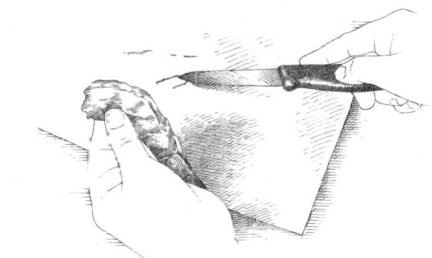

2. Because the vein is quite sticky, we like to touch the knife blade to a paper towel on the counter. The vein will stick to the towel, and you can devein the next shrimp with a clean knife.

with a host of seasonings added. In addition, chili sauce can be four to eight times as expensive as ketchup.

Our preference in cocktail sauce has always been to emphasize the horseradish. But ketchup and horseradish, we knew, were not enough. Cocktail sauce benefits from a variety of heat sources, none of which should overpower the other, and the sum of which should allow the flavor of the shrimp to come through. We liked the addition of chili powder. We also liked a bit of bite from cayenne. Black pepper plays a favorable role as well (as does salt, even though ketchup is already salty). Finally, after trying a variety of vinegars, we went back to lemon juice, the gentlest and most fragrant acidic seasoning.

Now that we had our classic cocktail sauce, we set our sights on developing a more exotically flavored cocktail sauce for our shrimp. One member of our test kitchen staff recalled having enjoyed a spicy-sweet dipping sauce served with shrimp while vacationing in the Caribbean. Making a sauce with lime juice, hot chiles, and brown sugar, we noted this combination had sweet and spicy components similar to those of the classic ketchup-horseradish mixture, yet it was livelier. After a little retooling, we found an equal ratio of sugar to lime juice was necessary to balance the spicy nature of the hot chile. Supplemented with garlic, ginger, and scallions, this sauce was a welcome (and potent) change from classic tomato-based cocktail sauce.

Herb-Poached Shrimp

SERVES 4

Shrimp are sold by size as well as by the number needed to make a pound, usually given in a range (a pound of jumbo shrimp, for example, recommended in this recipe, usually consists of 16 to 20 shrimp and is referred to as 16/20 count). Choosing shrimp by the numerical rating is more accurate than choosing by size label—one store's large might be another's extra-large. When using larger or smaller shrimp, increase or decrease the cooking time by 1 to 2 minutes. For jumbo shrimp, deveining is essential.

I	pound jumbo shrimp (16 to 20 per pound), peeled, deveined, and rinsed, shells reserved
I	teaspoon salt
I	cup dry white wine
4	whole black peppercorns
5	coriander seeds
½	bay leaf
5	sprigs fresh parsley
I	sprig fresh tarragon
I	teaspoon juice from I lemon

1. Bring the reserved shells, 3 cups water, and the salt to a boil in a medium saucepan over medium-high heat; reduce the heat to low, cover, and simmer until fragrant, about 20 minutes. Strain the stock through a sieve, pressing on the shells to extract all the liquid, into a bowl.

2. Bring the stock and remaining ingredients except the shrimp to a boil in a 3- or 4-quart saucepan over high heat; boil 2 minutes. Turn off the heat and stir in the shrimp; cover and let stand until the shrimp are firm and pink, 8 to 10 minutes. Drain the shrimp, reserving the stock for another use. Plunge the shrimp into ice water to stop the cooking, then drain again. Serve the shrimp chilled with cocktail sauce (recipes follow).

Classic Cocktail Sauce

MAKES ABOUT I CUP,
ENOUGH FOR I POUND JUMBO SHRIMP

For maximum flavor, use horseradish from a newly bought jar and mild chili powder.

I	cup ketchup
2½	teaspoons prepared horseradish
¼	teaspoon salt
¼	teaspoon ground black pepper
I	teaspoon ancho or other mild chili powder
	Pinch cayenne pepper
I	tablespoon juice from I lemon

Stir all of the ingredients together in a small serving bowl; adjust the seasonings as necessary.

Spicy Caribbean-Style Cocktail Sauce

MAKES ABOUT ½ CUP,

ENOUGH FOR 1 POUND JUMBO SHRIMP

This cocktail sauce is a sweet and spicy alternative to our classic version. Because this sauce is potent, less is needed to accompany the same amount of shrimp.

1	medium garlic clove, minced to a paste with ⅛ teaspoon salt (see the illustrations on page 11)
1½	tablespoons minced fresh ginger
2	medium scallions, white and green parts, minced
1	large jalapeño chile, cored, seeded, and minced
¼	cup juice from 2–3 limes
¼	cup packed light brown sugar

Mix the garlic paste, ginger, scallions, chile, lime juice, and brown sugar together in a small serving bowl; adjust the seasonings as necessary.

CRAB CAKES

LIKE GOOD SHRIMP COCKTAIL, GOOD CRAB cakes are one of the first seafood starters to disappear at a party, but that's only if they're really good. Too often crab cakes turn out to be greasy, pasty balls light on the crab and heavy on the breading.

Great crab cakes begin with top-quality crabmeat. We tested all the various options, and the differences are stark. Canned crabmeat is horrible; like canned chicken, it bears little resemblance to the fresh product. Fresh pasteurized crabmeat is watery and bland. Frozen crabmeat is stringy and wet. There is no substitute for fresh blue crabmeat, preferably "jumbo lump," which indicates the largest pieces and highest grade. This variety costs a couple of dollars a pound more than other types of fresh crab meat, but, because a 1-pound container is enough to make crab cakes for four, in our opinion, it's money well spent.

Fresh lump blue crab is available year-round but tends to be most expensive from December to March. The meat should never be rinsed, but it does need to be picked over to remove any shells or cartilage the processors may have missed.

Once we figured out what type of crab to use, our next task was to find the right binder. None of the usual suspects worked. Crushed saltines were a pain to smash into small-enough crumbs, potato chips added too much richness, and fresh bread crumbs blended into the crabmeat a little too well. We finally settled on fine dry bread crumbs. They have no overwhelming flavor and are easy to mix in. The trickiest part is knowing when to stop; crab cakes need just enough binder to hold them together but not so much that the filler overwhelms the seafood. We started out with ¾ cup crumbs but ended up reducing it down to just 2 tablespoons for our final recipe. Cooks who economize by padding out their pricey seafood with bread crumbs will end up with dough balls, not crab cakes.

The other ingredients we adopted are equally basic. Good, sturdy commercial mayonnaise (we like Hellmann's) keeps the crabmeat moist (a homemade blend can be too liquidy), and a whole egg, unbeaten, makes the crab, crumbs, and seasonings meld together both before and during cooking.

Classic recipes call for spiking crab cakes with everything from Tabasco to Worcestershire sauce, and those are both fine. But we've decided the best blend of tradition and trendiness is Old Bay seasoning combined with freshly ground white pepper and a tablespoon or more of chopped fresh herbs.

Just as essential as careful seasoning is careful mixing. We found a rubber spatula works best, and it should be used to fold the ingredients together, not stir them. This is important because you want to end up with a chunky consistency. Those lumps aren't cheap.

We were pleased with our basic recipe on most fronts, but we still had trouble keeping the cakes together as they cooked. Our last breakthrough came when we tried chilling the shaped cakes before cooking. As little as half an hour in the refrigerator made an ocean of difference. The cold firmed up the cakes so that they fried into perfect plump rounds without falling apart. We found that formed cakes can be kept, refrigerated and tightly wrapped, for up to 24 hours.

We also tried different cooking methods. After baking, deep-frying, and broiling, we settled on pan-frying in a nonstick skillet over medium-high heat. This method is fast and also gives the cook complete control over how brown and how crisp the cakes get. We first tried frying in butter, but it burned as it saturated the crab cakes. Cut with vegetable oil, it was still too heavy and made a mess of the pan. The ideal medium turned out to be plain old vegetable oil. It can be heated without burning and smoking, it creates a crisp crust, and it never gets in the way of the crab flavor.

Cocktail Crab Cakes

MAKES 24 SMALL CAKES

The amount of bread crumbs you add will depend on the juiciness of the crabmeat. Start with just 2 tablespoons. If the cakes won't hold together once you have added the egg, add more bread crumbs, 1 tablespoon at a time.

CRAB CAKES

I	pound jumbo lump crabmeat, picked over to remove cartilage and shell
4	scallions, green parts only, minced
I	tablespoon chopped fresh parsley leaves
I½	teaspoons Old Bay seasoning
2–4	tablespoons fine dry bread crumbs
¼	cup mayonnaise
	Salt and ground white pepper
I	large egg
½	cup unbleached all-purpose flour
6	tablespoons vegetable oil

CREAMY DIPPING SAUCE

¼	cup mayonnaise
¼	cup sour cream
2	teaspoons minced chipotle chiles in adobo sauce
I	small garlic clove, minced or pressed through a garlic press (about I teaspoon)
2	teaspoons minced fresh cilantro leaves
I	teaspoon juice from I lime

1. FOR THE CRAB CAKES: Gently mix the crabmeat, scallions, parsley, Old Bay, 2 tablespoons of the bread crumbs, and mayonnaise in a medium bowl, being careful not to break up the crab lumps. Season with salt and white pepper to taste. Carefully fold in the egg with a rubber spatula until the mixture just clings together. Add more crumbs if necessary.

2. Line a rimmed baking sheet with parchment paper. Using a generous tablespoon, form the mixture into 24 cakes, each 1½ inches in diameter and ½ inch thick. Place each finished cake on the baking sheet. Cover with plastic wrap and chill at least 30 minutes. (The cakes can be refrigerated for up to 24 hours.)

3. FOR THE DIPPING SAUCE: While the cakes are chilling, combine all the ingredients in a small bowl. Cover and refrigerate to blend flavors, at least 30 minutes and up to 2 days.

4. TO FINISH THE CRAB CAKES: Adjust an oven rack to the middle position and heat the oven to 200 degrees. Line a baking sheet with a double thickness of paper towels. Put the flour in a pie dish. Lightly dredge half of the crab cakes, knocking off the excess.

5. Meanwhile, heat 3 tablespoons of the oil in a large, preferably nonstick skillet over medium-high heat until hot but not smoking. Gently place the floured crab cakes in the skillet; pan fry until the outside is crisp and brown, 1 to 2 minutes. (Flour the remaining cakes while the first batch is browning.) Using a spatula, turn the cakes. Pan fry until the second side is crisp and brown, 1 to 2 minutes. Transfer the finished cakes to a baking sheet lined with paper towels and place the sheet in the oven.

6. Pour off the fat from the hot skillet and wipe clean with paper towels. Return the skillet to the heat, add the remaining 3 tablespoons oil, and heat 1 minute. Add the remaining cakes and pan-fry as above. Serve hot with the dipping sauce.

DEVILED EGGS

DEVILED EGGS SEEM TO BE MAKING A bit of a comeback of late, and with good reason. They are easy to make and tasty, always a crowd-pleaser, and can be quickly put together with ingredients already on hand. When we set out to develop this recipe, we had in mind the deviled eggs of our childhoods: perfectly cooked nests of egg whites cradling a creamy filling, balanced with the flavor of mayonnaise and a hint of spiciness, but no dominant egg overtones.

Great deviled eggs begin with perfectly cooked hard-cooked eggs. We have always considered hard-cooking an egg to be a crapshoot. There's no way to watch the proteins cook under the brittle shell of an uncracked egg, and you certainly can't poke it with an instant-read thermometer, as you can so many other foods. Often the eggs are over-cooked, with rubbery whites and chalky yolks. Of course, undercooked eggs without fully set yolks are even more problematic.

There are two general methods for hard cooking eggs—starting them in cold water and bringing them to a simmer, and lowering them into already simmering water. The first method is not terribly precise. When do you start the clock—when the eggs go into the water, or when the water starts to boil? Also, what temperature is right for simmering? Everyone knows what boiling water looks like (and at sea level the temperature is always 212 degrees), but simmering water can be 180, 190, or even 200 degrees. We never developed a reliable timing mechanism with this technique.

Lowering eggs into simmering water is not easy either, because the eggs are likely to crack. Some sources suggest poking a thumbtack through the large end of the egg where the air hole typically sits, but we had inconsistent results with this "trick." Again, the issue of defining "simmering water" proved problematic.

Not satisfied with either method, we tried a third method—starting the eggs in cold water, bringing the water to a boil, and then turning off the heat. The pan is covered and the eggs are set aside to cook by residual heat for 10 minutes. There's no need to define "simmer" with this method. As long as you can recognize when water is at a boil and can time 10 minutes, you are guaranteed hard-cooked eggs with bright, creamy yolks and tender whites.

FILLING DEVILED EGGS

A pastry bag fitted with a star tip makes the most attractive deviled eggs. If you don't own a pastry bag, spoon the yolk mixture into a small zipper-lock plastic bag. Snip a small piece from one bottom corner of the bag and then gently squeeze the filling through the hole into the egg halves.

PEELING HARD-COOKED EGGS

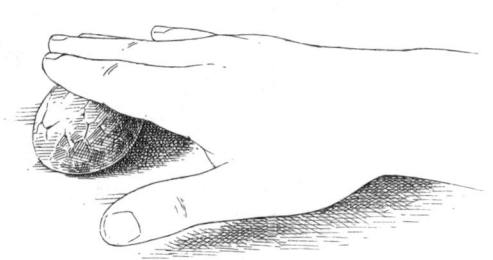

1. Tap the egg against the counter surface, then roll it gently back and forth a few times on the counter to crack the shell all over.

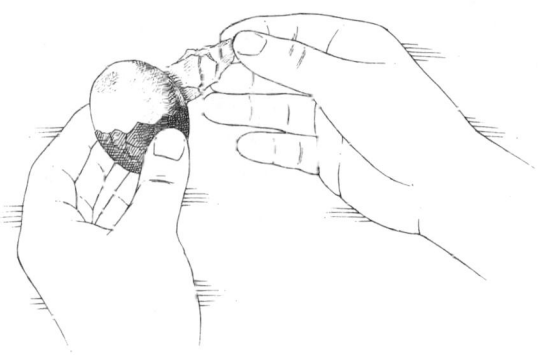

2. Begin peeling from the air-pocket end (the wider end) of the egg. The shell should come off in spiral strips attached to a thin membrane.

With our eggs perfectly cooked, we moved on to testing the main ingredient in most deviled egg recipes—mayonnaise. We sampled deviled eggs made with our favorite commercial mayonnaise (Hellmann's), Miracle Whip salad dressing, butter (several recipes called for butter in addition to or instead of mayonnaise), and homemade mayonnaise. The filling made partially or wholly with butter was dry and bland, and the homemade mayonnaise just wasn't worth the trouble. When it came to salad dressing versus commercial mayonnaise, the results were mixed. Talking over the fine points after the tasting, we discovered that tasters had chosen the eggs made with the ingredient they had had when they were growing up—the one they still associated with deviled eggs. But the majority went with mayonnaise.

To be "deviled," the eggs needed some spiciness. Since mustard was the prevalent source of spicy flavor in most recipes, we made that our next test. We tried French's mustard (the hot dog mustard); dry, or powdered, mustard; Dijon mustard; whole-grain mustard; and brown (Gulden's) mustard. The winner was whole-grain mustard.

Next, we turned to vinegar, another ingredient common to many recipes for deviled eggs. After testing six, we chose cider vinegar. In this case, 1½ teaspoons was just right; add more and that's all you'll taste.

Having made the "big" decisions, we moved on to the accent flavors. We tested sour cream, curry, Worcestershire sauce, and cayenne pepper. Sour cream dulled the impact of the accompanying ingredients, and even the smallest amount of curry dominated all the other flavors, so we left both out of our final recipe. Worcestershire sauce added a touch of savory pungency. Cayenne pepper is a good substitute if you like a bit of heat.

While testing the easiest manner in which to fill the egg whites, we found that stuffing them as close to serving time as possible was key to a fresh, bright flavor. If last-minute preparation is not possible, cook the eggs up to one day ahead and store the whites in an airtight container and the filling in a sealed zipper-lock plastic bag.

Hard-Cooked Eggs
MAKES 6

You can double or triple this recipe as long as you use a pot large enough to hold the eggs in a single layer, covered by 1 inch of water.

   6   large eggs

1. Place the eggs in a medium saucepan, cover with 1 inch water, and bring to a boil over high heat. Remove the pan from the heat, cover, and let sit for 10 minutes. Meanwhile, fill a medium bowl with 1 quart water and 1 tray of ice cubes (or the equivalent).

2. Transfer the eggs to the ice-water bath with a slotted spoon and let sit 5 minutes. Follow the illustrations on page 43 to peel the eggs.

Classic Deviled Eggs
MAKES 1 DOZEN FILLED EGG HALVES

During testing, we found it usual for a couple of the egg whites to rip at least slightly, so you may want to cook an extra hard-cooked egg for a little insurance. If you have a pastry bag, you can use it to fill the eggs with a large open-star tip or a large plain tip. If not, see the illustration on page 43 to improvise with a zipper-lock plastic bag.

1	recipe Hard-Cooked Eggs (above)
³/₄	teaspoon whole-grain mustard
3	tablespoons mayonnaise
1½	teaspoons cider vinegar (or vinegar of your choice)
¼	teaspoon Worcestershire sauce
	Salt and ground black pepper

1. Slice each cooked, peeled egg in half lengthwise with a paring knife. Remove the yolks to a small bowl. Arrange the whites on a serving platter. Mash the yolks with a fork until no large lumps remain. Add the mustard, mayonnaise, vinegar, Worcestershire, and salt and pepper to taste; mix with a rubber spatula, mashing the mixture against the sides of the bowl until smooth.

2. Fit a pastry bag with a large open-star tip. Fill the bag with the yolk mixture, twisting the top of the pastry bag to help push the mixture toward the tip of the bag. Pipe the yolk mixture into the egg white halves, mounding the filling about ½ inch above the flat surface of the whites. Serve immediately.

➤ VARIATIONS

Deviled Eggs with Anchovy and Basil

Rinse, dry, and finely chop 8 anchovy fillets. Mince 4 teaspoons fresh basil leaves. Follow the recipe for Classic Deviled Eggs, mixing the anchovy fillets and 2 teaspoons of the minced basil into the mashed yolks along with the mustard, mayonnaise, vinegar, Worcestershire, and salt and pepper. Continue with the recipe, sprinkling the filled eggs with the remaining 2 teaspoons basil.

Deviled Eggs with Tuna, Capers, and Chives

Drain and finely chop 2 ounces canned tuna (you should have about ½ cup). Rinse and drain 1 tablespoon capers; chop 1 tablespoon fresh chives. Follow the recipe for Classic Deviled Eggs, mixing the tuna, capers, and 2 teaspoons of the chives into the mashed yolks along with the mustard, mayonnaise, vinegar, and salt and pepper. Omit the Worcestershire. Continue with the recipe, sprinkling the filled eggs with the remaining 1 teaspoon chives.

CROSTINI

SMALL TOASTS, CALLED CROSTINI IN ITALIAN, are the vehicle for a variety of spreads. The crostini, which are also commonly served with soup or wedges of cheese, are crusty, rustic pieces of toast lightly flavored with garlic and olive oil. For our spreads, we wanted to make the classics: a white bean puree, chicken liver spread, and olivada.

We started with the crostini itself. Making crostini is easy. Most Italian cookbooks offer similar directions, wherein the bread is toasted then rubbed lightly with a clove of raw garlic. The crisp texture of the toast acts like sandpaper against the garlic,

releasing flavorful, perfumed oils. The dry, garlic-infused toast is then allowed to soak up a bit of olive oil, turning an otherwise ordinary piece of bread into a tasty morsel. We found that the toasting technique is the most important part of this process. We discovered it is best to toast the bread for about 10 minutes in a 400-degree oven. Although this may seem like a slow way to make toast, it dries the interior of the bread so that the crostini are crunchy throughout.

Using canned beans for our white bean puree, we immediately noticed that white navy beans did not work as well as cannellini. Navy beans are small, and their higher ratio of bean skin to creamy interior resulted in a starchy, lumpy spread that was difficult to fix. The larger cannellini beans, on the other hand, produced a silky, creamy puree that tasters liked Flavored simply with a little lemon juice, a clove of garlic, and parsley, the puree was tasty—but too thick. We tried adjusting the texture of the final puree with extra-virgin olive oil. However, the amount of olive oil required to achieve a spreadable texture made the olive flavor overwhelming. Cannellini beans are fairly mild and easily overpowered by the fruity, slightly bitter characteristics of olive oil. To keep the flavors balanced, we wound up using a mixture of half oil and half water to attain the proper texture.

Last, tasters liked the puree left a bit chunky, but the ingredients did need to be processed to blend and meld. We decided to leave one-third of the beans aside until the puree was nearly done, pulsing the reserved beans in only at the end.

For our chicken liver spread we found it necessary to buy the freshest chicken livers we could find and to trim them well. Old, untrimmed livers produced a spread that was overbearingly metallic-tasting, with stringy, fibrous bits. Although most recipes we researched employed similar cooking techniques, we found a few small tricks that made all the difference between good and bad liver puree. First, most recipes cook the livers through until they are no longer pink in the middle (about 15 to 20 minutes). We found, however, that they actually cook much faster (in about six minutes) and produce a better spread when left with a rosy interior. When liver is overcooked, the texture turns chalky and mealy and the delicate nuances of flavor are lost. But when cooked quickly, the liver retains its soft, creamy texture and a clean, mellow flavor that blends easily with other ingredients.

To round out the flavor of the liver mixture, tasters liked the customary additions of white wine, sage, onion, and capers, but not olive oil, anchovy, tomato paste, or parsley. The olive oil and anchovy, for lack of better words, tasted too oily and fishy. The tomato paste turned the pâté sweet, and the parsley added nothing but specks of color.

The remaining problem was that we needed a technique that would cook all the spread ingredients properly, yet accommodate the livers' small cooking window. We started by sautéing the aromatics, then added the livers for a quick sear. We then added the wine and allowed the livers to finish cooking at a gentle simmer as the wine reduced to a light syrup. Transferring the mixture straight from the sauté pan to a food processor fitted with a steel blade, we quickly pulsed it to the correct texture. The resulting spread tasted clean and balanced, with an authentically rustic texture that melts in the mouth.

QUICK AND EASY CROSTINI TOPPINGS

DON'T STOP WITH THE CROSTINI RECIPES ON PAGES 47–48. YOU CAN PUT PRACTICALLY anything from your refrigerator or pantry (within reason) onto crostini for quick and easy hors d'oeuvres. Here are some of our favorite ideas.

FRESH MOZZARELLA AND PESTO
Top crostini with diced fresh mozzarella tossed with pesto, salt, and ground black pepper.

GOAT CHEESE AND TOMATOES
Spread crostini with a thin layer of soft goat cheese and top with seeded, diced tomatoes seasoned with salt, ground black pepper, and minced fresh herbs.

HUMMUS WITH ROASTED RED PEPPER AND LEMON
Spread crostini with hummus and top with roughly chopped roasted red pepper, minced fresh parsley leaves, and a squeeze of lemon juice.

ARTICHOKE, PARMESAN, AND BALSAMIC VINEGAR
Top crostini with roughly chopped canned artichoke hearts tossed with olive oil, balsamic vinegar, and chopped fresh basil leaves. Sprinkle a bit of shaved Parmesan over each crostini.

MINI TUNA MELTS
Spread crostini with tuna salad, top with cheese, and run quickly under the broiler.

MEDITERRANEAN TUNA SALAD
Top crostini with drained oil-packed tuna mixed with capers, fresh parsley leaves, extra-virgin olive oil, and lemon juice.

RICOTTA AND PINE NUTS
Spread crostini with whole-milk ricotta cheese and sprinkle with pine nuts (or walnuts) and minced fresh parsley leaves. Drizzle with extra-virgin olive oil and sprinkle with salt and pepper. Run under the broiler until heated through.

CANNELLINI BEANS WITH LEMON AND GARLIC
Top crostini with rinsed canned cannellini beans slightly mashed and mixed with lemon juice, minced garlic, minced shallot, chopped fresh parsley leaves, salt, and red pepper flakes.

SALAMI AND PROVOLONE SALAD
Top crostini with a combination of thinly sliced strips of salami and cubed provolone seasoned with extra-virgin olive oil, cracked black pepper, and minced fresh basil leaves. Serve as is, or run under the broiler to melt the cheese and serve hot.

Olivada is a paste-like mixture similar to pesto, with black olives taking the place of the basil. Olivada is rich and potent, so it is best used sparingly. Tiny crostini are the perfect way to enjoy these flavors. As with pesto, we find that the food processor is the best tool for preparing this puree. Rich, meaty kalamata olives are the most common choice, and we found they work perfectly in this recipe. Although you could use any high-quality black olive in brine, the kalamata has a high meat-to-pit ratio, and the pit is fairly easy to remove—two factors that make it the most logical choice for this recipe.

Most recipes include capers and anchovies in the puree, and our tasters liked both additions. Olive oil helps bring the ingredients together, but we preferred a slightly rough texture and found it best to use oil sparingly. Too much oil will make the puree perfectly smooth. Herbs are another component of most recipes, and we liked the fresh anise flavor of basil coupled with woodsy rosemary. That said, tasters felt that thyme or oregano could easily replace the rosemary and that parsley could stand in for the basil, with slightly different but still delicious results.

Crostini Toasts

MAKES ABOUT 20 TOASTS

You want small slices for crostini, so try to find a loaf with a diameter of 2½ to 3 inches.

| | large baguette or thin Italian loaf, cut on the bias into ½-inch-thick slices (about 20 slices)
| | large garlic clove, peeled
| | Salt and ground black pepper

Adjust an oven rack to the middle position and heat the oven to 400 degrees. Arrange the bread slices in a single layer on a baking sheet and bake until the bread is dry and crisp, 8 to 10 minutes, turning over the slices halfway through baking. While still hot, rub each slice of bread with the raw garlic clove and season with salt and pepper to taste. (Crostini are best straight from the oven, but they can be set aside on a plate for several hours.)

Crostini with White Bean Puree

MAKES ABOUT 20 CROSTINI

In a tasting of several brands of canned cannellini beans, our favorite brand was Progresso. This crostini topping is the leanest of the three and calls for a drizzle of extra-virgin olive oil to add a bit of richness.

| | (15-ounce) can cannellini beans, drained, rinsed, and patted dry
| 4 | tablespoons extra-virgin olive oil
| 2 | tablespoons water
| | tablespoon juice from I lemon
| | medium garlic clove, crushed
| | tablespoon packed fresh parsley leaves
| | recipe Crostini Toasts (this page)

Process two-thirds of the beans with 2 tablespoons of the oil, the water, lemon juice, garlic, and parsley in a food processor until smooth, about 10 seconds. Scrape down the sides of the workbowl, add the remaining beans, and pulse to incorporate them, but do not make the puree perfectly smooth—about five 1-second pulses. To serve, spread the dip onto the bread slices and drizzle the remaining 2 tablespoons oil over the crostini.

Crostini with Chicken Liver Spread

MAKES ABOUT 20 CROSTINI

We think it's best to spread the warm liver mixture on the toasts and serve immediately, but the warm (or room-temperature) spread can be served in a bowl alongside the garlic-rubbed toasts so that guests can help themselves. The spread will keep in the refrigerator for up to 1 day.

| 8 | tablespoons (I stick) unsalted butter
| | small onion, minced
| 8 | small fresh sage leaves, chopped
| | Salt
| | pound chicken livers, rinsed and patted dry, fat and connective tissue removed
| ½ | cup dry white wine
| 2 | tablespoons capers, rinsed

Ground black pepper

1 **recipe Crostini Toasts (page 47)**

1. Heat the butter in a large skillet over medium-high heat until the foaming subsides, about 2 minutes. Add the onion, sage, and ¼ teaspoon salt and cook until the onion softens, about 5 minutes. Add the chicken livers and toss, cooking briefly, about 1 minute. Add the wine and simmer until the liquid is slightly syrupy and the livers have a rosy interior, 4 to 5 minutes.

2. Transfer the pan contents to a food processor and process until coarsely chopped, about seven 1-second pulses. Transfer the liver spread to a clean bowl, stir in the capers, and adjust the seasonings with salt and pepper to taste. Spread about 1 tablespoon warm liver mixture on each piece of toast and serve immediately.

Crostini with Olivada
MAKES ABOUT 20 CROSTINI

A puree of black olives, called olivada in Italy and tapenade in southern France, often appears spread on little toasts as an antipasto. The paste is similar to pesto, but black olives take the place of the basil. Olivada is rich and potent, so it is best used sparingly. Tiny crostini are the perfect way to enjoy these flavors. If you have any leftover olivada, toss it with linguine or spaghetti, the same way you might use pesto.

1½ **cups pitted kalamata olives**

3 **tablespoons extra-virgin olive oil**

1 **tablespoon capers, rinsed**

4 **anchovy fillets**

2 **tablespoons shredded fresh basil leaves**

2 **teaspoons fresh rosemary**

1 **recipe Crostini Toasts (page 47)**

1. Place the olives, oil, capers, anchovies, basil, and rosemary in a food processor. Process, scraping down the sides of the bowl, until the mixture is finely minced and forms a chunky paste, about 1 minute. Transfer the olivada to a small bowl. (The paste can be refrigerated for 1 or 2 days or longer if covered with a film of oil.)

2. When ready to serve, spread about 2 teaspoons olivada over each piece of toast and serve immediately.

BRUSCHETTA

AUTHENTIC ITALIAN GARLIC BREAD, CALLED bruschetta, is never soggy or soft. Slices of country bread are first toasted, then rubbed with raw garlic, brushed with extra-virgin olive oil (never butter), and topped with various ingredients. These combinations can be as simple as salt and pepper or fresh herbs. Ripe tomatoes, sautéed peppers, and pureed white beans make more substantial offerings.

We found that narrow loaves of Italian bread are not suitable for bruschetta. Crusty country loaves that yield larger slices are preferable. Oblong loaves that measure about 5 inches across are best, but round loaves will work, too. As for the actual thickness of each bruschetta, slices cut about 1 inch thick provide enough heft to support weighty toppings and provide good chew.

Toasting the bread, which can be done over a grill fire or under the broiler, makes little jagged edges in the crumb of the bread that hook tiny bits of garlic when the raw clove is rubbed over the surface. One piece of toast is enough for a single serving, and a few slices make a light lunch.

Toasted Bread for Bruschetta
MAKES 8 TO 10 SLICES

Toast the bread as close as possible to the time you plan to assemble the bruschetta. If you prefer, grill the bread.

1 **loaf country bread (about 12 by 5 inches), cut crosswise into 1-inch-thick slices, ends discarded**

3 **tablespoons olive oil, preferably extra-virgin**

1 **large garlic clove, peeled and halved**

Adjust an oven rack to about 4 inches from the heating element and heat the broiler; broil the bread slices until golden brown on both sides. Brush both sides of each slice with the oil and rub with the garlic clove.

Bruschetta with Sautéed Sweet Peppers

SERVES 8

3	tablespoons plus 1 teaspoon extra-virgin olive oil
4	large red bell peppers, cored, seeded, and cut into 3 by $1/4$-inch strips
2	medium onions, halved and thinly sliced
$3/4$	teaspoon salt
3	medium garlic cloves, minced or pressed through a garlic press (about 1 tablespoon)
$1/4$	teaspoon red pepper flakes
1	(14.5-ounce) can diced tomatoes, drained, $1/4$ cup juice reserved
$1^1/2$	teaspoons chopped fresh thyme leaves
4	teaspoons sherry vinegar
1	recipe Toasted Bread for Bruschetta (facing page)
2	ounces Parmesan cheese, shaved with a vegetable peeler (see the illustration on page 109)

1. Heat the 3 tablespoons of the oil, the bell peppers, onions, and ½ teaspoon of the salt in a large skillet over medium-high heat; cook, stirring occasionally, until the vegetables are softened and browned around the edges, 10 to 12 minutes. Reduce the heat to medium, push the vegetables to the side of the skillet, making a clearing in the center, and add the remaining 1 teaspoon oil, the garlic, and red pepper flakes to the clearing; cook, mashing the garlic with a wooden spoon, until fragrant, about 30 seconds, then stir into the vegetables. Reduce the heat to low and stir in the tomatoes, reserved juice, and thyme. Partially cover and cook, stirring occasionally, until the moisture has evaporated, 15 to 18 minutes. Off the heat, stir in the vinegar and remaining ¼ teaspoon salt.

2. Divide the pepper mixture evenly among the toasted bread slices, top with the shaved Parmesan, and serve.

Bruschetta with Tomatoes and Basil

SERVES 8

This is the classic bruschetta, although you can substitute other herbs. If using more boldly flavored herbs, such as thyme or oregano, decrease the amount called for below.

4	medium ripe tomatoes, cored, seeded, and cut into $1/2$-inch dice
$1/3$	cup shredded fresh basil leaves
	Salt and ground black pepper
1	recipe Toasted Bread for Bruschetta (facing page)

1. Mix the tomatoes, basil, and salt and pepper to taste in a medium bowl. Set aside.

2. Use a slotted spoon to divide the mixture evenly among the toasted bread slices. Serve immediately.

Bruschetta with Arugula, Red Onion, and Rosemary–White Bean Spread

SERVES 8

In a recent tasting, we preferred Progresso cannellini beans—by far—to the other brands sampled.

1	(19-ounce) can cannellini beans, drained and rinsed
3	tablespoons extra-virgin olive oil
2	tablespoons water
1	tablespoon juice from 1 lemon
1	small garlic clove, crushed
$3/4$	teaspoon salt
$1/4$	teaspoon ground black pepper
$1/4$	teaspoon chopped fresh rosemary
1	tablespoon balsamic vinegar
1	recipe Toasted Bread for Bruschetta (facing page)
$1/4$	medium red onion, sliced thin (about $1/4$ cup)
1	small bunch arugula, washed, dried, and cut into $1/2$-inch strips (about 3 cups)

1. In a food processor, process two-thirds of the beans, 2 tablespoons of the oil, the water, lemon juice, garlic, ½ teaspoon of the salt, and ⅛ teaspoon of the pepper until smooth, about 10 seconds. Add the remaining beans and the rosemary; pulse until incorporated but not smooth, about five 1-second pulses.

2. Whisk the remaining 1 tablespoon oil, the vinegar, the remaining ¼ teaspoon salt, and the remaining ⅛ teaspoon pepper together in a medium bowl; add the onion and toss.

3. Divide the bean spread evenly among the toasted bread slices. Add the arugula to the onions and toss until coated. Top each bread slice with a portion of the arugula mixture. Serve immediately.

Bruschetta with Summer Squash, Bacon, and Blue Cheese
SERVES 8

The topped bruschetta goes back under the broiler for a couple of minutes before being served.

4	medium summer squash and/or zucchini, halved lengthwise, seeded, and cut into matchstick-size pieces
2	tablespoons extra-virgin olive oil
1	tablespoon red wine vinegar
½	teaspoon salt
¼	teaspoon ground black pepper
4	ounces (about 4 slices) bacon, minced and fried in small skillet over medium-high heat until crisp, about 8 minutes, then drained on paper towels
4	ounces blue cheese, crumbled (about 1 cup)
¼	cup fresh basil leaves, chopped
1	recipe Toasted Bread for Bruschetta

1. Combine the squash, oil, vinegar, salt, and pepper in a medium bowl; let stand 5 minutes, then toss in the bacon, cheese, and basil. Stir to combine.

2. Divide the mixture evenly among the toasted bread slices; broil the bruschetta until the cheese begins to melt, about 1½ minutes. Serve immediately.

MINI STEAK SANDWICHES WITH ARUGULA AND HORSERADISH

THE COMBINATION OF ROAST BEEF AND horseradish sauce is a classic often found on the hors d'oeuvre table. Wanting to find a fast way to get this pair to the party, we focused on a few key issues. First, we tried simply serving toothpicked slices of beef alongside a horseradish dip, but we found the presentation was just a bit off. The skewered pieces of beef released some of their juices on the platter and wound up sitting in an unappetizing pool of liquid. The toothpicks were also a bit awkward, as the beef often slid off them into the dip. Moving on to the idea of little sandwiches, we found it easy to slice a baguette into small rounds, toast the slices, and fill two with both the horseradish dressing and the beef. These little morsels held up on the platter for some time, looking almost as good as they did when freshly made. ·

Having settled on sandwiches, we turned our attention more specifically to the beef. We tried using sliced roast beef from the deli, but the results were disappointing. Although fast, the deli-sliced beef was much too dry and often came in shaggy, ragged pieces. Roasting a large piece of meat ourselves was out of the question, so we began to search for small, quick-cooking steaks that could be seared on the stovetop, then sliced. Flank steak turned out to be the answer. With a thin profile that cooks in less than 10 minutes, we found that a 1½-pound flank steak yielded the perfect balance of economy and ease and offered a full, meaty flavor and handsome appearance when sliced.

After making a few sandwiches, we discovered a couple of tricks to cooking a flank steak on top of the stove. We noted the importance of using a heavy-bottomed pan that has been preheated for several minutes. The meat simply doesn't brown properly in pans that aren't sturdy enough or hot enough. Although many steaks have enough fat to pan-sear with little or no oil, we discovered that lean flank steak requires a tablespoon of vegetable oil in the pan. Once the steak is well browned on both sides, it is imperative to let the meat rest before slicing it; when cut too soon, the steak loses most of its natural juice and turns out dry. To make the sandwiches easy to eat, we found it important to slice the meat thinly across the grain. When sliced either thickly or with the grain, the beef was unpleasantly tough and chewy.

As for the horseradish sauce, we tried making it with sour cream, crème fraîche, and mayonnaise. In the end, we liked a simple mixture of mayonnaise, prepared horseradish, and a pinch of black pepper on the sandwiches. Rounded out with a small, spicy sprig of arugula and a sliver of fresh red onion, these quick sandwiches look as good as they taste and leave you with plenty of time to enjoy the party.

Mini Steak Sandwiches with Arugula and Horseradish

MAKES ABOUT 40 PIECES,

SERVING 10 TO 12

This appetizer is a bit fancier than the other recipes in this chapter and is appropriate for a larger and more formal gathering. Slicing the bread crosswise rather than on the bias (as in Crostini Toasts on page 47) will yield more slices. If you can't find baby arugula (it is sold in packages or loose in many markets), simply tear regular arugula leaves into bite-size pieces.

I	large baguette, cut crosswise into ½-inch-thick slices (about 40 slices)
I	tablespoon vegetable oil
1½	pounds flank steak, trimmed of excess fat and patted dry with paper towels Salt and ground black pepper
¾	cup mayonnaise
3	tablespoons prepared horseradish
3	cups packed baby arugula
I	small red onion, halved and sliced thin

1. Adjust an oven rack to the middle position and heat the oven to 400 degrees. Arrange the bread slices in a single layer on a large baking sheet. Bake, turning over the slices halfway through baking, until the bread is dry and crisp, about 10 minutes. Remove the baking sheet from the oven and cool for about 5 minutes.

2. Meanwhile, heat the oil in a heavy-bottomed 12-inch skillet over medium-high heat until it begins to smoke. Season the steak liberally with salt and pepper and lay it in the pan. Cook, not moving the steak until it is well browned, 4 to 5 minutes. Turn over the steak with tongs and reduce the heat to medium. Continue to cook until the second side is browned, about 5 minutes. Transfer the steak to a plate and let rest for 10 minutes. Slice the steak crosswise on the bias into ⅛-inch-thick slices. Halve the longer slices into roughly 3-inch lengths (you should have about 40 slices).

3. Mix together the mayonnaise, horseradish, and a pinch of pepper in a small bowl.

4. To assemble the sandwiches, spread 1 teaspoon horseradish mayonnaise on a piece of bread and curl a piece of steak on top. Place a piece of arugula and a sliver of onion within the curl of beef and serve.

PIZZA

WHEN CUT INTO SMALL WEDGES, SIMPLE, lightly topped pizzas make a relatively easy hors d'oeuvres. Pizza with tomato sauce, cheese, pepperoni, and the like are simply too unwieldy (and messy) to serve at a cocktail party.

While pizza dough is nothing more than bread dough with oil added for softness and suppleness, we found in our testing that minor changes in the ingredient list can yield dramatically different results. Our goal in testing was threefold. The recipe had to be easy to put together; the dough had to be easy to shape and stretch thin; and the crust needed to bake up crisp and chewy, not tough and leathery.

After initial tests, it was clear that bread flour was delivering the best texture. Bread flour makes pizza crust that is chewy and crisp. All-purpose flour can be used in a pinch, but the resulting crust is less crisp.

The second key to perfect crust is water. We found that using more water makes the dough softer and more elastic. Soft dough stretches more easily than a stiffer, harder dough with less water. We prefer to jump-start the yeast in a little warm

PUTTING STORE-BOUGHT PIZZA DOUGH TO WORK

PREPARED PIZZA DOUGH IS NOT JUST FOR MAKING PIZZA. ALTHOUGH FRESH, HOMEMADE dough always tastes best, many local pizzerias sell their dough for just a dollar per pound. Pick up a stash and toss the dough in your freezer (provided that the dough hasn't been previously frozen), and you'll be able to quickly turn out such treats as last-minute breadsticks, rolls, focaccia, pretzels, and more. All of the following recipes use a 1-pound ball of pizza dough and are baked in a 400-degree oven. In lieu of store-bought pizza dough, you can use our homemade pizza dough on page 53. Just remember to use half a recipe, as the yield makes double what you need here.

Soft Breadsticks

Roll out the dough ½ inch thick and cut into 1-inch-wide strips. Arrange the breadsticks on a well-oiled baking sheet. Brush with 2 tablespoons extra-virgin olive oil and sprinkle with ½ cup grated Parmesan cheese, ½ teaspoon kosher salt, and 1 teaspoon ground black pepper. Bake until golden brown, about 15 minutes. Cool on a wire rack; serve warm.

Thin, Extra-Crunchy Breadsticks

Roll out the dough as thinly as possible and cut into ¼-inch-wide strips. Arrange the breadsticks on a well-oiled baking sheet. Brush with 2 tablespoons extra-virgin olive oil, ½ cup grated Parmesan cheese, ½ teaspoon kosher salt, and 1 teaspoon ground black pepper. Bake until dark golden and crisp, about 10 minutes. Cool 5 minutes on a wire rack; serve warm.

Dinner Rolls

Cut the dough into 8 even pieces and roll each into a ball. Arrange the rolls on a well-oiled baking sheet. Brush the top of each roll lightly with extra-virgin olive oil, sprinkle with ½ teaspoon salt and ½ teaspoon ground black pepper, and bake until golden brown, about 20 minutes. Cool 5 minutes on a wire rack; serve warm.

Stromboli

Roll the dough into a 12 by 10-inch rectangle. Place 2 to 3 ounces each of deli-cut salami, pepperoni, and prosciutto over the dough, leaving a 1-inch border on all sides. Top with ½ cup roasted red bell peppers (page 10), ½ cup caramelized onions (page 58), 1 cup shredded mozzarella, and ½ cup grated Parmesan. Starting from a long side, roll the dough into a long cylinder, being sure to seal the ends well to prevent leaking. Transfer the stromboli to a well-oiled baking sheet. Brush the dough with extra-virgin olive oil, sprinkle liberally with salt and pepper, and bake until well browned, about 45 minutes. Cool 5 minutes on a wire rack. Transfer to a cutting board, slice, and serve.

Pretzels

Roll out the dough into eight 15-inch ropes, about ½ inch in diameter. Twist into the classic hot pretzel shape and arrange on a parchment-lined baking sheet. Brush the pretzels with 3 tablespoons melted unsalted butter and sprinkle with coarse sea salt (or poppy, sesame, or caraway seeds). Bake until golden brown, 10 to 15 minutes. Cool 5 minutes and serve warm.

Focaccia

Press the dough into a well-oiled 13 by 9-inch baking pan or a 10-inch pie dish and dimple the surface with your fingers. Brush the dough liberally with extra-virgin olive oil and sprinkle with ¼ cup chopped olives, ½ teaspoon minced fresh rosemary, ½ teaspoon kosher salt, and ½ teaspoon cracked black pepper. Bake until golden brown, about 30 minutes. Cool 5 minutes on a wire rack; serve warm.

DIMPLING FOCACCIA DOUGH

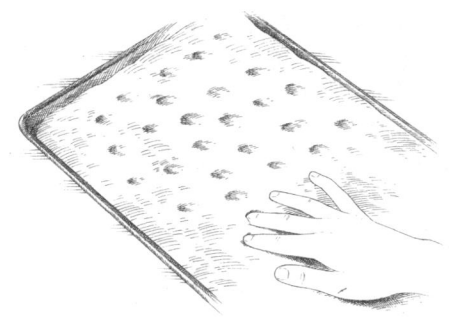

After the dough has been pressed into an oiled pan, wet two fingers and use them to make indentations at regular intervals.

water for five minutes. We then add more water, at room temperature, along with oil.

For combining the dry ingredients (flour and salt) with the wet ingredients, the food processor is our first choice. The liquid is evenly incorporated into the dry ingredients, and the blade kneads the dough in just 30 seconds. Of course, the dough can be kneaded by hand or with a standing mixer. If you make the dough by hand, resist the temptation to add a lot of flour as you knead.

We use plastic wrap to cover the oiled bowl that holds the rising dough. We found that the tight seal offered by plastic wrap keeps the dough moist and protects it from drafts better than the standard damp cloth. We reserve the damp cloth for use when the dough has been divided into balls and is waiting to be stretched.

To stretch dough to its maximum diameter, let it rest once or twice during the shaping process. Once you feel some resistance, cover the dough with a damp cloth and wait five minutes before going at it again. Fingertips and hands generally do a better job of stretching dough than a rolling pin, which presses air out of the risen dough and makes it tough. This low-tech method is also superior to flipping dough in the air and other frivolous techniques that may work in a pizza parlor but can lead to disaster at home. For illustrations of shaping pizza dough, see page 54.

Even if you're baking just one medium pizza, make a full dough recipe. After the dough has risen and been divided, place the extra pieces in separate airtight containers and freeze them for up to 1 month. Defrost and stretch the dough when desired.

Pizza Dough

MAKES ENOUGH FOR 3 MEDIUM PIZZAS

We find that the food processor is the best tool for making pizza dough. However, only a food processor with a capacity of at least 11 cups can handle this much dough. You can also knead this dough by hand or in a standing mixer. Unbleached all-purpose flour can be used in a pinch, but the resulting crust will be less crisp. If you want to make pizza dough in the morning and let it rise on the counter all day, decrease the yeast to ½ teaspoon and let

the covered dough rise at cool room temperature (about 68 degrees) until doubled in size, about 8 hours.

½	cup warm water (about 110 degrees)
1	envelope (about 2¼ teaspoons) instant yeast
1¼	cups water, at room temperature
2	tablespoons extra-virgin olive oil
4	cups (22 ounces) bread flour, plus more for dusting the work surface and hands
1½	teaspoons salt
	Olive oil or nonstick cooking spray for oiling the bowl

1. Measure the warm water into a 2-cup liquid measuring cup. Sprinkle in the yeast and let stand until the yeast dissolves and swells, about 5 minutes. Add the room-temperature water and oil and stir to combine.

2. Process the flour and salt in a large food processor, pulsing to combine. Continue pulsing while pouring the liquid ingredients (holding back a few tablespoons) through the feed tube. If the dough does not readily form into a ball, add the remaining liquid and continue to pulse until a ball forms. Process until the dough is smooth and elastic, about 30 seconds longer.

3. The dough will be a bit tacky, so use a rubber spatula to turn it out onto a lightly floured work surface. Knead by hand for a few strokes to form a smooth, round ball. Put the dough in a deep oiled bowl and cover with plastic wrap. Let rise until doubled in size, 1 to 2 hours. Press the dough to deflate; it is now ready to use in the following recipes.

Pizza Bianca with Garlic and Rosemary

MAKES 3 MEDIUM PIZZAS, SERVING 6

Pizza bianca translates as "white pizza," referring to the fact that there are no tomatoes—just garlic, oil, rosemary, and salt—in this recipe. See the illustrations on page 54 for tips on shaping and topping pizza dough. Serve this simple and light starter with a bowl of marinated olives.

1	recipe Pizza Dough (this page)
¼	cup extra-virgin olive oil, plus more for brushing the stretched dough

6   medium garlic cloves, minced or pressed
    through a garlic press
4   teaspoons minced fresh rosemary
    Salt and ground black pepper
    Semolina or cornmeal for dusting the pizza peel

1. Prepare the dough as directed in the Pizza Dough recipe. Place a pizza stone on a rack in the lower third of the oven. Heat the oven to 500 degrees for at least 30 minutes. Turn the dough out onto a lightly floured work surface. Use a chef's knife or dough scraper to divide the dough into three pieces. Form each piece of dough into a smooth, round ball and cover it with a damp cloth. Let the dough relax for at least 10 minutes but no more than 30 minutes.

2. While preparing the dough, combine the oil, garlic, rosemary, and salt and pepper to taste in a small bowl. Set the herb oil aside.

3. Working with one piece of dough at a time and keeping the others covered, shape the dough as directed in the illustrations below, then transfer it to a pizza peel that has been lightly dusted with semolina.

SHAPING AND TOPPING PIZZA DOUGH

1. Working with one ball of dough at a time and keeping the rest covered with a damp cloth, flatten the dough ball into a disk using the palms of your hands.

2. Starting at the center of the disk and working outward, use your fingertips to press the dough until it is about ½ inch thick.

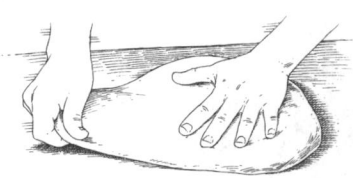

3. Holding the center in place, stretch the dough outward. Rotate the dough a quarter turn and stretch again. Repeat until the dough reaches a diameter of 12 inches.

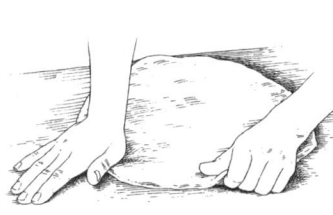

4. Use your palm to press down and flatten the thick edge of the dough.

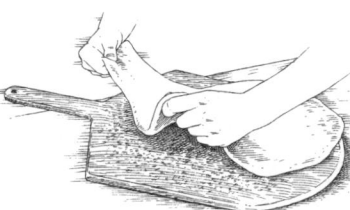

5. Carefully lift the dough round and transfer it to a peel dusted with semolina or cornmeal.

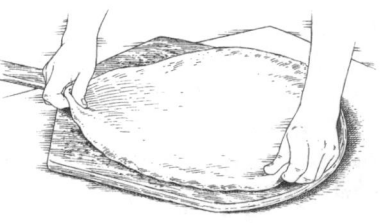

6. If the dough loses its round shape, adjust it on the peel to return it to the original shape.

7. Brush the entire dough round with a little olive oil. Add the toppings. To make it easier to hold pizza slices when eating, leave a ½-inch border of dough uncovered.

8. Use a quick jerking action to slide the topped dough off the peel and onto the hot tiles or stone. Make sure that the pizza lands far enough back so that the front edge does not hang off the tiles or stone.

4. Lightly brush the dough round with plain olive oil. Prick the dough all over with a fork to prevent ballooning in the oven.

5. Slide the dough onto the heated stone. Bake until the crust begins to brown in spots, 6 to 10 minutes. Brush the crust with a third of the herb oil and continue baking until the garlic is fragrant, 1 to 2 minutes. Remove the pizza from the oven, cut into wedges, and serve immediately. Repeat steps 3, 4, and 5 with the remaining two pieces of dough and the remaining herb oil.

➤ VARIATION

Lemon–Sea Salt Pizza

Follow the recipe for Pizza Bianca with Garlic and Rosemary through step 3. Brush the dough round with plain olive oil as directed in step 4. Arrange 1 small lemon, sliced paper-thin, over the dough round, leaving a ½-inch border uncovered. Sprinkle with coarse sea salt to taste. (Do not prick the dough.) Bake and brush with the herb oil as directed in step 5.

PISSALADIÈRE

PISSALADIÈRE IS PROVENÇAL STREET FOOD, a fragrant, pizzalike tart prized for its contrast of salty black olives and anchovies against a backdrop of sweet caramelized onions and thyme. Supporting this rough and rustic flavor combination is a wheaty crust with a texture that is part chewy pizza and part crisp cracker. Commonly eaten as an appetizer or even a light supper alongside a salad, this classic French favorite is still something of a foreigner to most Americans.

The ingredients, however, are simple enough. The crust is basically pizza dough, and the toppings are caramelized onions, herbs, anchovies, and olives. The key is to balance all of these strong flavors so that they work together. We knew we could figure out how to make a great version of this French classic.

To come up with our version of pissaladière, we had to start with a series of "get acquainted" tests to fully comprehend the range of possibilities. Most recipes produced a crust in the style of

a pizza, others called for savory pie dough fit into a fluted tart pan, and we even found a few that used squares of store-bought puff pastry. All of them called for caramelized onions, black olives, thyme, and anchovies, but additional sources of flavor, such as Parmesan, sun-dried tomatoes, basil, and oregano, were not uncommon. As for the basic flavor ingredients, almost all of the caramelized onions were underdone, while the bullish flavor of anchovies overran the olives and thyme. Anchovies, we thought, should not rule but rather act as a counterpoint to the sweet onions, briny olives, and fragrant thyme.

As for the crust, the test kitchen quickly eliminated puff pastry and pie dough. Unfortunately, the more authentic pizzalike crusts weren't very good, either. Textures were too short (think shortbread) and crackery or overly soft and doughy. Tasters thought that good pissaladière should have a dual-textured crust: crisp on the outside (like a cracker) and chewy on the inside.

Although pizza crust isn't exactly right for pissaladière, we whipped up three versions to see if any could be used as a jumping-off point. The thin crust wasn't sturdy enough and the deep-dish crust was too doughy, but the traditional crust was the right thickness (about half an inch) and had the right flavor. Knowing that we wanted it to be chewier, with a more crackerlike exterior, we took a closer look at each of its four major ingredients—bread flour, oil, water, and yeast—to see where we could make adjustments.

We replaced various amounts of bread flour with all-purpose flour but made zero headway. Bread flour has more protein than all-purpose,

RISING THE DOUGH

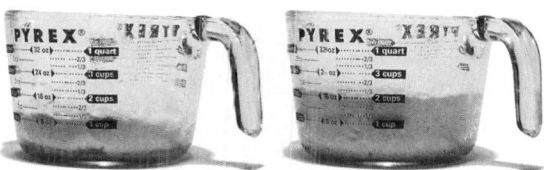

A quart-size liquid measuring cup is good for more than just measuring liquid. We let the pissaladière dough rise in a measuring cup covered with plastic wrap. The lines on the measuring cup make it easy to tell when the dough has doubled in size.

and that translates into a more substantial chew. Testing amounts of olive oil ranging from none at all up to 6 tablespoons, we again found that the original recipe (which called for 1 tablespoon) produced the best balance of crisp to tender without causing the dough to be brittle (a problem when the amount of oil dropped below 1 tablespoon) or greasy (a problem when the amount of oil exceeded 1 tablespoon).

Next on the list of ingredients to tinker with was water. The original recipe called for ¾ cup of water to 2 cups of flour. Less water made the crust drier (no surprise) and tougher. More water made the dough chewier, but we soon learned that there was such a thing as too chewy. When we increased the water to 1¼ cups, the crust baked up with huge holes and was as chewy as bubble gum. The crust made with 1 cup of water proved to be a happy medium—chewier than the original pizza crust but not over the top.

When we varied the amount of yeast, the flavor changed (as did the rising time), but not the texture. Less yeast and an overnight rise—a common flavor-enhancing technique—did produce a crust with a slightly more complex flavor, but it was awfully hard to detect once it came up against the onions, olives, and anchovies. One teaspoon of yeast pumped the dough through the first rise in a convenient 75 minutes (give or take 15 minutes, depending on the humidity and the kitchen temperature), during which there was ample time to prepare and caramelize the onions.

Doughs made in a standing mixer, a food processor, and by hand showed substantial differences and, surprisingly, tasters preferred the method most professional bakers would scoff at. Doughs made by hand and in the mixer were tough and snappy after being baked, requiring a full set of well-rooted molars. To achieve the best texture, this dough apparently would accept only minimal handling. We knew that bread dough could be kneaded in a food processor in a two-step process. Step 1 is to whiz the ingredients for a mere 15 seconds until they come together; step 2 is to wait for two minutes and then knead the dough in the food processor for an additional 30 seconds. It turned out that the secret to perfect pissaladière dough was to complete step 1 and simply ignore step 2! This crust was a winner, unanimously favored for its crackerlike exterior

SHAPING PISSALADIÈRE

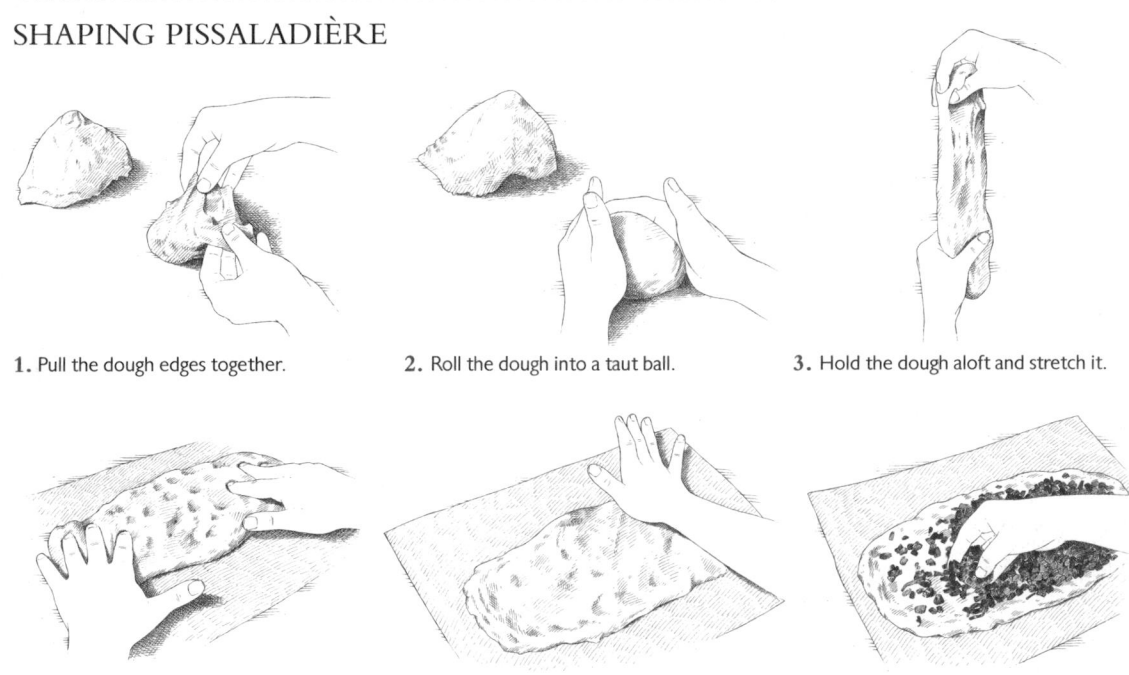

1. Pull the dough edges together.

2. Roll the dough into a taut ball.

3. Hold the dough aloft and stretch it.

4. Dimple the dough with your fingers.

5. Push the dough into an oval.

6. Add the toppings.

and decently chewy crumb. (We eventually figured out how to make the dough by hand and in a standing mixer, but the process for both was more time-consuming and difficult, and the timing and results were never as consistent.) The best part of the food processor technique is that it's foolproof. You know that the dough has been processed properly when it comes together in a ball. Nothing could be simpler.

Dough pressed onto a rimmed baking sheet didn't brown nearly as well as a free-form oval baked directly on a preheated baking stone at 500 degrees. Pressing the dough out on parchment paper made for an easy transfer to the oven. Tasters also preferred the rustic texture of dough that was pressed out by hand as opposed to the uniform consistency of dough flattened by a rolling pin.

A key problem with this recipe was the stickiness of the dough. We had been using plenty of flour when shaping the dough, until, on a whim, we tried oil instead. Good idea. Not only was it a snap to shape the dough on the parchment, but the extra oil pressed into the bottom of the crust made it even crispier. Brushing the dough with yet more olive oil before adding the toppings further ensured a crackerlike exterior, officially turning this crust from pizza to pissaladière.

Most recipes for caramelized onions subscribe to one of two methods—low and slow or fast and furious—yet neither works. Low (heat) and slow dries out the onions before they have a chance to darken, while fast and furious (high heat) leaves the onions crunchy and burnt tasting. Taking a cue from our caramelized onion recipe (page 58), we used a combination of high and low heat, starting the onions on high to release their juices and soften them, then turning the heat to medium-low to let the juices caramelize.

A nonstick skillet works best for caramelizing onions. The low sides of a skillet (as opposed to the high sides of a Dutch oven) allow the steam to evaporate rather than interfere with browning, while the nonstick surface ensures that the caramelization sticks to the onions, not the pan. Once the onions were cooked, though, we had problems sprinkling them over the pizza, as they tended to clump. The solution? We stirred in just a bit of water once we removed the onions from the heat.

Whereas most recipes call for whole black olives, we found that they rolled around and occasionally fell off the crust. In addition, the intense heat of the oven dried them to a leathery texture. A better method was to chop the olives coarsely and layer them underneath the onions, which protect the olives from overcooking. This same trick also worked with the leaves of fresh thyme.

It's traditional to arrange anchovies across the top of a pissaladière in a crosshatch pattern. This was too much anchovy for the test kitchen staff, so we focused on how to incorporate their strong flavor without offending anyone. As with the olives, we found it best to chop and spread them underneath the onions. Just four anchovies per tart was perfect, and rinsing them first made sure they weren't too salty or fishy. (Still, several fish lovers missed the crosshatching, so we included it as an option.) The only untraditional flavors that passed our relatively strict code of authenticity were fennel seeds and freshly minced parsley, and both are optional.

~

Pissaladière

MAKES 2 TARTS, SERVING 8 TO 10

If your food processor includes a plastic dough blade attachment, use it; its short blades and dull edges make kneading easier on the motor. If not, the regular metal blade works almost as well. For best flavor, use high-quality, oil-packed anchovies; in a recent tasting, Ortiz was our favorite brand. The dough in this recipe rises for 1 to 1½ hours. If a longer or overnight rise is more convenient, make the dough with ½ teaspoon of instant yeast and let it rise in the refrigerator for 16 to 24 hours. The caramelized onions can also be made a day ahead and refrigerated.

DOUGH

- 2 cups (11 ounces) bread flour, plus more for dusting the work surface
- 1 teaspoon instant yeast
- 1 teaspoon salt
- 1 tablespoon olive oil, plus more for brushing the dough and greasing hands
- 1 cup warm water (about 110 degrees)

CARAMELIZED ONIONS

2	tablespoons olive oil
2	pounds yellow onions, sliced 1/4 inch thick
1/2	teaspoon salt
I	teaspoon brown sugar
I	tablespoon water

OLIVES, ANCHOVIES, AND GARNISHES

Olive oil

1/2	teaspoon ground black pepper
1/2	cup niçoise olives, pitted and chopped coarse
8	anchovy fillets, rinsed, patted dry, and chopped coarse (about 2 tablespoons), plus 12 fillets, rinsed and patted dry for garnish (optional)
2	teaspoons minced fresh thyme leaves
I	teaspoon fennel seeds (optional)
I	tablespoon minced fresh parsley (optional)

1. FOR THE DOUGH: In a food processor fitted with the plastic dough blade (see note), pulse the flour, yeast, and salt to combine, about five 1-second pulses. With the machine running, slowly add the oil, then the water, through the feed tube; continue to process until the dough forms a ball, about 15 seconds. Generously dust the work surface with flour. Using floured hands, transfer the dough to the work surface and knead lightly, shaping the dough into a ball. Lightly oil a 1-quart measuring cup or small bowl, place the dough in the measuring cup (see the photo on page 55), cover tightly with plastic wrap, and set aside in a draftfree spot until doubled in volume, 1 to 1½ hours.

2. FOR THE CARAMELIZED ONIONS: While the dough is rising, heat the oil in a large nonstick skillet over high heat until shimmering but not smoking. Stir in the onions, salt, and brown sugar and cook, stirring frequently, until the moisture released by the onions has evaporated and the onions begin to brown, about 10 minutes. Reduce the heat to medium-low and cook, stirring frequently, until the onions have softened and are medium golden brown, about 20 minutes longer. Off the heat, stir in the water; transfer to a bowl and set aside. Adjust the oven rack to the lowest position, set a baking stone on the rack, and heat the oven to 500 degrees.

3. TO SHAPE, TOP, AND BAKE THE DOUGH: When the dough has doubled, remove it from the measuring cup and divide into two equal pieces using a dough scraper. Working with one piece at a time, form each piece into a rough ball by gently pulling the edges of the dough together and pinching to seal (see illustration 1 on page 56). With floured hands, turn the dough ball seam-side down. Cupping the dough with both hands, gently push the dough in a circular motion to form a taut ball (illustration 2). Repeat with the second piece. Brush each piece lightly with oil, cover with plastic wrap, and let rest 10 minutes. Meanwhile, cut two 20-inch lengths of parchment paper and set aside.

4. Coat your fingers and the palms of your hands generously with oil. Using a dough scraper, loosen one piece of dough from the work surface. With well-oiled hands, hold the dough aloft and gently stretch it to a 12-inch length (illustration 3). Place the dough on a parchment sheet and gently dimple the surface of the dough with your fingertips (illustration 4). Using oiled palms, push and flatten the dough into a 14 by 8-inch oval (illustration 5). Brush the dough with oil and sprinkle with ¼ teaspoon of the pepper. Leaving a ½-inch border around the edge, sprinkle ¼ cup of the olives, 1 tablespoon of the chopped anchovies, and 1 teaspoon of the thyme evenly over the dough, then evenly scatter with half of the onions (illustration 6). Arrange 6 whole anchovy fillets, if using, on the tart and sprinkle with half of the fennel seeds, if using. Slip the parchment with the tart onto a pizza peel (or inverted rimless baking sheet), then slide it onto the hot baking stone. Bake until deep golden brown, 13 to 15 minutes. While the first tart bakes, shape and top the second tart.

5. Remove the first tart from the oven with a peel or pull the parchment onto a baking sheet. Transfer the tart to a cutting board and slide the parchment out from under the tart. Cool 5 minutes then sprinkle with 1½ teaspoons of the parsley, if using. Cut the tart into 8 pieces; serve immediately. While the first tart cools, bake the second tart.

NACHOS

NACHOS ARE A SIMPLE CULINARY PLEASURE many of us crave: crisp, warm tortilla chips mingling with melted cheese under a colorful banner of spicy salsa, luxurious guacamole, and a dollop of sour cream. Yet as elementary and popular as nachos are, finding a good plate of them can be hard. The worst examples appear at the snack counters of airports and large discount marts, where trays of chips that taste like cardboard are squirted with a few pumps of unnaturally fluid "cheese," doused with watery jarred salsa, and (if you're lucky) served with a miniscule portion of ready-made guacamole. But it doesn't have to be this way.

After sampling some local nacho fare and trying out a few recipes, we homed in on some key issues. First, the chips must be crisp and hot, not lukewarm, soggy, or charred. Second, there must be no shortage of cheese; a chip without cheese is just not a nacho. Third, there is no such thing as minimalist nachos. Good nachos require not only a hearty helping of cheese but also ample amounts of garnishes, such as salsa, guacamole, sour cream, jalapeños, and scallions. Finally, although it may seem blindingly obvious, we noted that fresh, good-quality ingredients make good nachos, while processed ingredients make airport nachos. With these insights in mind, we were ready to create a good plate of nachos, and tasters were already jockeying for position at the counter.

Finding that 8 ounces of chips made enough nachos for four to six people and fit easily onto a 13 by 9-inch baking dish, we made batches with increasing cups of shredded cheese until tasters called uncle. Four cups was just right; lesser amounts left some chips neglected, and more nearly drowned the chips. To ensure an even distribution, it was necessary to toss the cheese with the chips before cooking. But the act of tossing, we quickly discovered, was brutal on the delicate chips, and some of the cheese was lost to the bottom of the baking dish. Instead, we tried building the nachos in layers—two layers of chips topped with cheese—which ensured even distribution. Not surprisingly, these first few batches tasted far better than any nachos we had eaten elsewhere.

The simple pairing of good-quality chips with a generous amount of evenly distributed cheese had already made a huge difference.

Next we held a cheese tasting. Although most recipes call for cheddar or Monterey Jack, we wondered how tasters would react to other types of cheese, such as American, Havarti, Gouda, Muenster, or any of the jalapeño-studded varieties, such as pepper cheddar, pepper Jack, and pepper Havarti. Cheddar turned out to be the test kitchen's overall favorite, with a potent and legitimate flavor, although Gouda was surprisingly good and garnered second place. To our great surprise, Monterey Jack was disappointingly bland and tasteless, while American and the peppered varieties of cheddar, Monterey Jack, and Havarti all tasted commercial and overprocessed. The other oddball contestants, Muenster and regular Havarti had decent if unremarkable flavors but were quick to turn rubbery as they cooled. We tried using preshredded cheddar to save time but found the flavor dull and the texture dry. We got much better results by shredding a block of cheese in a food processor fitted with the shredding disk, which was easy enough and took little time. A greased box grater (see the illustration on page 61) is another good way to accomplish this task quickly and easily.

We had been baking the nachos in a 350-degree oven for 20 minutes to melt the cheese and heat the chips through but wanted to experiment with speedier methods. The broiler caused the top layer of chips to burn before the inner layers of cheese had time to melt. Hot ovens set between 425 and 450 degrees produced chips with charred edges, but a 400-degree oven managed to both melt the cheese and warm the chips through to a lightly toasted crisp in merely 10 minutes. Not only was this a time saver, but the nachos tasted more fresh and less dried out than those baked for a longer period of time in a cooler oven.

Chips and cheese may be the nacho plate's workhorses, but without salsa, guacamole, and sour cream, nachos look naked. When and where they are placed on the chips and cheese are crucial to success. As for when, they must be added after the chips emerge from the oven to provide contrast in temperature, texture, and flavor. As for where, while many recipes tell the cook to spread each topping evenly over each chip. This instruction is both silly and time-consuming. We found that it's easier to simply dump a few scoops of sour cream, salsa, and guacamole on a small portion of the chips, off to the side, so that most of the chips remain unencumbered and easy to pick up.

Tasters liked the spicy addition of thinly sliced jalapeños, preferring them fresh rather than canned. They tasted best when sprinkled into the layers along with the cheese, which, when melted, helped the peppers adhere to the chips. Fresh sliced scallions and wedges of lime—both added when the nachos emerged from the oven—were also welcome additions. The issue of spicy, ground beef and refried beans—common additions to a nacho plate—provoked some controversy in the

INGREDIENTS: Tortilla Chips

Most tortilla chips are made from just three basic ingredients—corn, oil, and salt—and processed in a similar fashion, yet our tasters found a wide range of textures and flavors in the 10 brands we sampled. How, we wondered, could such simple ingredients and a consistent manufacturing process yield such different results?

To understand what gave the chips we tasted such different flavors and textures, we began by examining the manufacturing process and the primary ingredient, corn. Tortilla chips begin with masa, or corn dough. Masa can be made from a number of different corn products, including corn flour, which has the texture of fine sand; stone-ground corn flour, which has a rougher, grittier texture; and stone-ground corn (made from softened whole corn kernels), which is very rough, like pebbly sand. Water is added to the corn product and the dough is mixed, cut into triangles, baked, cooled, and then fried. Cooled once more, the chips are then salted and bagged.

Many manufacturers tout chips made from stone-ground masa, saying they have more texture, are stronger, and absorb less oil. However, we found that tasters preferred the finer and more fragile chips made with corn flour, like second-place Miguel's, described as "delicate," or third-place Newman's Own, called "crisp." (Frito-Lay, which manufactures our top-rated Doritos chips, would not comment on the ingredients in its masa, but given the delicate texture of Doritos, it seems likely that corn flour is used here, too.) In contrast, two of the roughest, heartiest stone-ground chips, Nana's Cocina and Kettle Foods, ended up at the bottom of the scorecard. Their textures were described as "stale" and like "cardboard," respectively. In addition, the Nana's Cocina chips were described as "slick" and "oily," despite the fact that they are made from stone-ground whole corn kernels. Although both Miguel's and Newman's chips are made from fine flours, we found that neither was greasy. It's worth noting that all of the chips we sampled contain similar amounts of fat, from 5.5 to 7 grams per 1-ounce serving.

We then turned our focus to the flavor of the masa itself. We thought there might be a continental divide between those who preferred white or yellow corn tortilla chips, but we found that we liked both types. Our first-, third-, and fourth-place chips are all yellow corn varieties, while our second-, fifth-, and sixth-place picks are made with white corn. In general, we found white corn chips to be more subtly corn flavored, whereas yellow corn chips tasted "toasty" and "nutty."

Salt also has a big impact on flavor. More salt makes a tastier chip. Among the top five brands, four have sodium levels between 110 and 120 milligrams per ounce. The sodium level in the five lowest-ranked brands ranges from 40 to 90 milligrams per ounce.

Finally we turned our focus to the oil. Miguel's pairs canola oil with its white corn masa chips, giving them what tasters described as a "toasted," "authentic" flavor. Why, then, were the Cape Cod chips, also made with white corn masa and canola oil, deemed "bland" and "unremarkable"? The answer lies in the packaging. Miguel's tortilla chips—as well as the other top-rated chips, Doritos and Newman's Own—are packaged in a "metalized" bag, meaning that the bag's surface has been lined with a very thin film of aluminum. This metal lining helps to ward off oxidation of the oil by blocking light and also creates a moisture barrier to help the chips stay crunchy.

In the end, the results of our tasting were unexpected. Doritos won over smaller, boutique brands like Nana's Cocina and Kettle Foods. Although many boutique brands make a big deal about the organically raised, stone-ground corn they use, it seems that the secret to a great tortilla chip isn't all that complicated. Just use fine corn flour (not coarse stone-ground), add plenty of salt, and then pack the chips in a foil-lined bag to keep the oil from oxidizing.

test kitchen. The result? We decided to use these ingredients in variations, as they quickly transform nachos into an indulgent, artery-clogging meal.

Cheesy Nachos with Guacamole and Salsa

SERVES 4 TO 6

See our tasting of tortilla chips (facing page) to see which brands we recommend.

8	ounces tortilla chips
16	ounces cheddar cheese, shredded (about 5^1/$_3$ cups)
2	large jalapeño chiles, stemmed and sliced thin (about ^{1}/$_4$ cup)
2	scallions, sliced thin
	Guacamole (page 64)
^{1}/$_2$	cup (4 ounces) sour cream
	Fresh Tomato Salsa (page 63)
1	lime, cut into 6 wedges

Adjust an oven rack to the middle position and heat the oven to 400 degrees. Spread half of the chips in an even layer in a 13 by 9-inch baking dish; sprinkle evenly with half of the cheese and half of the jalapeño slices. Repeat with the remaining chips, cheese, and jalapeños. Bake until the cheese is melted, 7 to 10 minutes. Remove the nachos from the oven and sprinkle with the scallions. Along the edge of the baking dish, drop scoops of guacamole, sour cream, and salsa. Serve immediately, passing the lime wedges separately.

➤ VARIATIONS

Cheesy Nachos with Refried Beans
Follow the recipe for Cheesy Nachos with Guacamole and Salsa, dropping ¾ cup (about 6 ounces) refried beans in small spoonfuls on each chip layer before sprinkling with the cheese.

Cheesy Nachos with Spicy Beef
A quickly made ground beef mixture turns nachos into a meal.

2	teaspoons corn or vegetable oil
1	small onion, chopped fine

1	large garlic clove, minced or pressed through a garlic press (about 1^1/$_2$ teaspoons)
1	tablespoon chili powder
^{1}/$_4$	teaspoon dried oregano
^{1}/$_2$	teaspoon ground cumin
^{1}/$_2$	teaspoon ground coriander
^{1}/$_4$	teaspoon cayenne
^{1}/$_8$	teaspoon salt
^{1}/$_2$	pound 90 percent lean (or leaner) ground beef

1. Heat the oil in a medium skillet over medium heat until shimmering but not smoking. Add the onion and cook, stirring occasionally, until softened, about 4 minutes. Add the garlic, spices, and salt; cook, stirring constantly, until fragrant and combined with the onion, about 1 minute. Add the ground beef and cook, breaking up the meat with a wooden spoon and scraping the pan bottom to prevent scorching, until the

SHREDDING SOFT CHEESES

Soft cheeses such as cheddar, Monterey Jack, and mozzarella can stick to a box grater and cause a real mess. Here's how to keep the holes on the grater from becoming clogged.

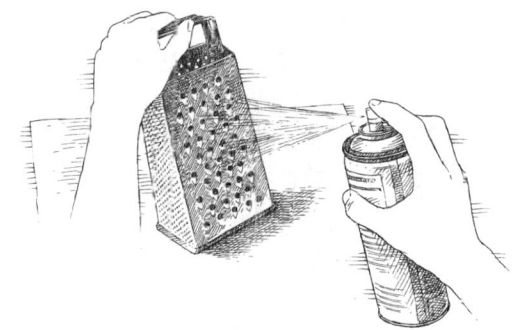

1. Use nonstick cooking spray to lightly coat the side of the box grater with large holes.

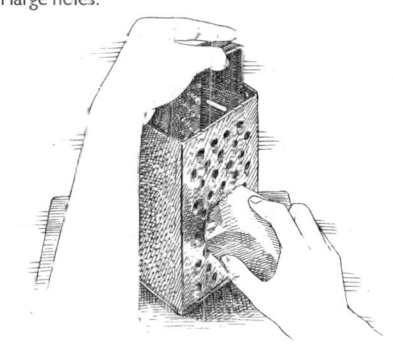

2. Shred the cheese as usual. The cooking spray will keep the cheese from sticking to the grater.

beef is no longer pink, about 5 minutes.

2. Follow the recipe for Cheesy Nachos with Guacamole and Salsa, sprinkling half of the beef mixture on each chip layer before sprinkling with cheese.

FRESH TOMATO SALSA

BACKYARD, FARM-STAND, AND SUPERMARKET summertime tomatoes alike should be sweet, juicy, and ready for top billing in a fresh tomato salsa. But even in the midst of tomato season, some can be less than stellar. Complicating matters, salsa's popularity has opened the door to versions employing extravagant (smoked paprika) and extraneous (canned tomato juice) ingredients, relegating fresh tomatoes to a minor role. One such recipe had us fishing around—literally—in water for miniscule pieces of tomato, while another used four different chiles but only one measly tomato. We wanted a fresh, chunky Mexican-style salsa, or salsa cruda, that would emphasize the tomatoes; the other traditional flavors—lime, garlic, onion, chile, and cilantro—would have supporting roles. We also wanted to get the texture just right for scooping up and balancing on a tortilla chip.

Simply combining salsa ingredients in one bowl for mixing and serving turned out to be a bad idea. The tomatoes exuded so much juice that the other ingredients were submerged in liquid within minutes. The first step, then, was to solve the problem of watery salsa. Peeling and seeding are often-employed techniques for removing excess moisture from tomatoes. Peeling, however, removed the structure that kept the diced pieces intact, resulting in a salsa that was too mushy. Seeding diminished the tomatoes' flavor, and tasters did not mind the presence of seeds. So much for peeling and seeding.

We recalled that here in the test kitchen we often salt tomatoes to concentrate flavor and exude liquid. This technique was promising, but because much more surface area was exposed when the tomatoes were diced, the salt penetrated too deeply and broke them down too much. We were left with mealy, mushy tomatoes, and the salsa was just as watery as before. Dicing the tomatoes larger to expose less surface area was out of the question; the tomato pieces would be too large to balance on a tortilla chip. Taking round slices of tomatoes, salting them, and then dicing them after they had drained was just too much work.

Frustrated, we diced a few tomatoes whole (skin, seeds, and all), threw them into a colander, and walked away. Thirty minutes later, to our surprise, a few tablespoons of liquid had drained out; after a few shakes of the colander, the tomatoes were chunky and relatively dry. We found that in fewer than 30 minutes, not enough liquid drained out, whereas more time didn't produce enough additional juice to justify the wait. Overall, we found that really ripe tomatoes exude more juice than less ripe supermarket tomatoes. This simple technique, with minimal tomato prep, had accomplished a major feat: It put all tomatoes, regardless of origin, ripeness, or juiciness, on a level—and dry—playing field.

CUTTING TOMATOES FOR SALSA

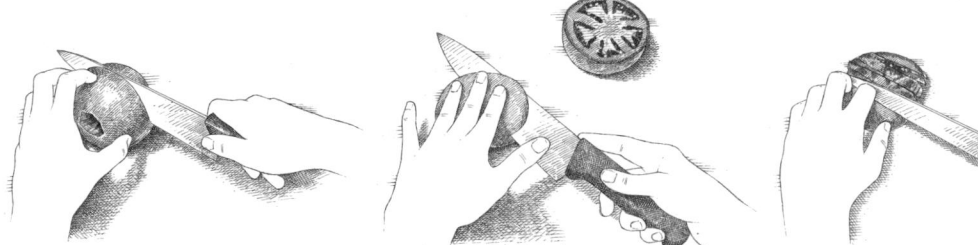

1. Cut each cored tomato in half through the equator.

2. Cut each half into ⅜-inch-thick slices.

3. Stack two slices, cut them into ⅜-inch strips, and then cut them into ⅜-inch dice.

With the main technique established, we fixed the spotlight on the supporting ingredients. Red onions were preferred over white, yellow, and sweet onions for color and flavor. Jalapeño chiles were chosen over serrano, habanero, and poblano chiles because of their wide availability, slight vegetal flavor, and moderate heat. Lime juice tasted more authentic (and better) than red wine vinegar, rice vinegar, or lemon juice. Olive oil, while included at the beginning of the recipe testing process, was rejected later on when tasters found it dulled the other flavors.

We also investigated the best way to combine the ingredients and rejected all but the simplest technique. Marinating the tomatoes, onion, garlic, and chile in lime juice resulted in dull, washed-out flavors and involved extra bowls and work. We tried letting the drained tomatoes, onion, chile, garlic, and cilantro sit for a bit before adding the lime juice, sugar, and salt. Now the flavors of the chile and onion stole the show. It was much more efficient to chop the chile, onion, garlic, and cilantro and layer each ingredient on top of the tomatoes while they drained in the colander. Once the tomatoes were finished draining, the chile, onion, garlic, cilantro, and tomatoes needed just a few stirs before being immediately finished with the lime juice, sugar, and salt, and then served.

Fresh Tomato Salsa

MAKES ABOUT 3 CUPS

Heat varies from jalapeño to jalapeño, and because much of the heat resides in the ribs, or pale-colored, interior flesh, we suggest mincing the ribs (along with the seeds) separately from the dark green, exterior flesh, then adding the minced ribs and seeds to taste. The amount of sugar and lime juice to use depends on the ripeness of the tomatoes. The salsa can be made 2 to 3 hours in advance, but hold off adding the salt, lime juice, and sugar until just before serving. The salsa is perfect for tortilla chips, but it's also a nice accompaniment to grilled steaks, chicken, and fish.

1½	pounds firm, ripe tomatoes, cored and cut into ³⁄₈-inch dice (about 3 cups)
1	large jalapeño chile, seeded (ribs and seeds reserved and minced; see note), exterior flesh minced (about 2 tablespoons)
½	cup minced red onion
1	small garlic clove, minced or pressed through a garlic press (about ½ teaspoon)
¼	cup chopped fresh cilantro leaves
½	teaspoon salt
	Pinch ground black pepper
2–6	teaspoons juice from 1 to 2 limes
	Sugar to taste (up to 1 teaspoon)

1. Set a large colander in a large bowl. Place the tomatoes in the colander and let them drain for 30 minutes. As the tomatoes drain, layer the jalapeño, onion, garlic, and cilantro on top. Shake the colander to drain off the excess tomato juice. Discard the juice; wipe out the bowl.

2. Transfer the contents of the colander to the now-empty bowl. Add the salt, pepper, and 2 teaspoons of the lime juice; toss to combine. Taste and add the minced jalapeño ribs and seeds, sugar, and additional lime juice to taste.

QUICK CHIPS—IN THE MICROWAVE

WHEN WE HEARD THAT YOU COULD MAKE tortilla chips in the microwave, we were skeptical, to say the least. With nothing to lose, we tossed a couple wedges of corn tortilla in the microwave and were surprised at what came out: fresh-tasting chips! Although you wouldn't want to do this for a party, it is a good trick to know when you want a spur-of-the-moment snack or a crispy accompaniment to a bowl of soup or salad.

HOMEMADE TORTILLA CHIPS
Cut 3 corn tortillas into 6 wedges each and spray with vegetable oil spray. Arrange them in a single layer on a paper towel–lined plate and sprinkle generously with salt. Microwave on high for 2 minutes. Carefully flip the chips over and spray again with the vegetable spray. Continue to cook on high until the chips are browned and crisp, 2 to 4 minutes longer.

Guacamole

GUACAMOLE HAS TRAVELED A LONG ROAD. Once a simple Mexican avocado relish, it has become one of America's favorite party dips. Unfortunately, the journey has not necessarily been kind to this dish. The guacamole we are served in restaurants, and even in the homes of friends, often sacrifices the singular, extraordinary character of the avocado—the culinary equivalent of velvet—by adding too many other flavorings. Even worse, the texture of the dip is usually reduced to an utterly smooth, listless puree.

We wanted our guacamole to be different. First, it should highlight the dense, buttery texture and loamy, nutty flavor of the avocado. Any additions should provide bright counterpoints to the avocado without overwhelming it. Just as important, the consistency of the dip should be chunky rather than perfectly smooth.

Good guacamole starts with good (that is, ripe) avocados. Assuming you have ripe avocados, how should you handle and mix them with the other ingredients? Most guacamole recipes direct you to mash all the avocados, and some recipes go so far as to puree them in a blender or food processor. After making dozens of batches, we came to believe that neither pureeing nor simple mashing was the way to go. Properly ripened avocados break down very easily when stirred, and we were aiming for a chunky texture. To get it, we ended up mashing only one of the three avocados in our recipe lightly with a fork and mixing it with most of the other ingredients, then dicing the remaining two avocados into substantial ½-inch cubes and mixing them into the base using a very light hand. The mixing action breaks down the cubes somewhat, making for a chunky, cohesive dip.

Other problems we encountered in most recipes were an overabundance of onion and a dearth of acidic seasoning. After extensive testing with various amounts of onion, tasters found that 2 tablespoons of finely minced or grated onion gave the guacamole a nice spike without an overwhelming onion flavor. We also tried various amounts of fresh lemon and lime juice. The acid was absolutely necessary, not only for flavor but also to help preserve the mixture's green color. Tasters preferred 2 tablespoons of lime juice in our three-avocado guacamole.

❧

Chunky Guacamole

MAKES 2½ TO 3 CUPS

Like our Fresh Tomato Salsa (page 63), our guacamole makes an excellent dip for tortilla chips and Mexican-style dishes. To minimize the risk of discoloration, prepare the minced ingredients first so that they are ready to mix with the avocados as soon as they are cut. Ripe avocados

PITTING AN AVOCADO

Digging out the pit of an avocado with a spoon can mar the soft flesh and is generally a messy proposition. This method avoids that problem.

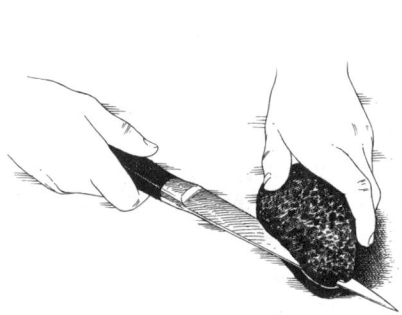

1. Start by slicing around the pit and through both ends with a chef's knife. With your hands, twist the avocado to separate the two halves.

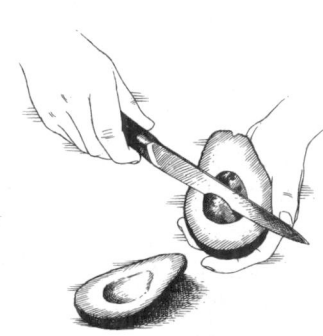

2. Stick the blade of the chef's knife sharply into the pit. Lift the knife, twisting the blade to loosen and remove the pit.

3. Don't pull the pit off the knife with your hands. Instead, use a large wooden spoon to pry the pit off the knife safely.

are essential here. If you like, garnish the guacamole with diced tomatoes and chopped cilantro just before serving. See the illustrations on the facing page and below to pit and dice the avocados.

3	medium, ripe avocados, preferably pebbly-skinned Hass
2	tablespoons minced onion
1	medium garlic clove, minced or pressed through a garlic press (about 1 teaspoon)
1	small jalapeño chile, stemmed, seeded, and minced
¼	cup minced fresh cilantro leaves
	Salt
½	teaspoon ground cumin (optional)
2	tablespoons juice from 1 lime

1. Halve one of the avocados, remove the pit, and scoop the flesh into a medium bowl. Mash the flesh lightly with the onion, garlic, chile, cilantro, ¼ teaspoon salt, and cumin (if using) with the tines of a fork until just combined.

2. Halve, pit, and cube the remaining 2 avocados. Add the cubes to the bowl with the mashed avocado mixture.

3. Sprinkle the lime juice over the diced avocado and mix the entire contents of the bowl lightly with a fork until combined but still chunky. Adjust the seasonings with salt, if necessary, and serve. (Guacamole can be covered with plastic wrap, pressed directly onto the surface of the mixture, and refrigerated for up to 1 day. Return the guacamole to room temperature, removing the plastic wrap at the last moment, before serving.)

➤ VARIATION

Guacamole with Bacon, Scallions, and Tomato

Follow the recipe for Chunky Guacamole, substituting 3 large scallions, sliced thin (about ⅓ cup), for the onion and adding 6 slices bacon, cooked, drained, and crumbled, with 1 teaspoon rendered fat and ½ medium tomato, seeded and diced small.

DICING AN AVOCADO

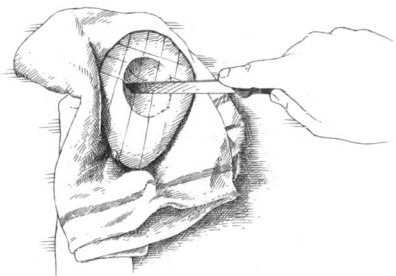

1. Use a dish towel to hold the avocado steady. Make ½-inch crosshatch incisions in the flesh of each avocado half with a dinner knife, cutting down to but not through the skin.

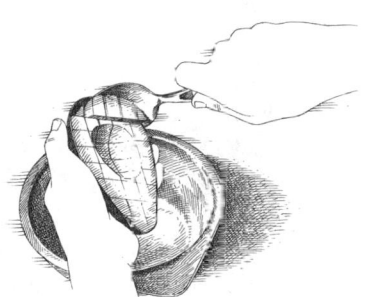

2. Separate the diced flesh from the skin using a spoon inserted between the skin and the flesh and gently scoop out the avocado cubes.

QUESADILLAS

QUESADILLAS ARE NOT HARD TO PREPARE. Yet all too often they taste terrible, with bland, unmelted cheese sandwiched between flabby, floury tortillas. Quesadillas may appear to be effortless, but we realized they need thoughtful attention.

Noting that flour tortillas come in a variety of sizes, we preferred those with an 8-inch diameter because they easily fit into a 10-inch pan. As for cheese, we tried a few varieties; although many tasted good, we found that Monterey Jack melted well and had an easygoing flavor that paired well with other quesadilla-friendly ingredients. We tried using preshredded cheese but were unimpressed with its artificial flavor and gummy texture. Take a couple of minutes to shred the cheese yourself.

For a quick appetizer, we liked potent flavors, such as roasted red peppers, cilantro, and red onion, along with the spicy, smoky flavor of chipotle chiles in adobo sauce. We tried putting avocado inside the quesadilla, but tasters disliked its texture when warm; served on the side, however, it provided a smooth, cool, contrast to the hot, crisp tortilla that tasters really liked. To help prevent the filling from leaking out of the sides, we found it necessary to leave a 1-inch border of plain tortilla.

Cooking quesadillas is fairly straightforward, but after making a few batches we discovered a few little tricks. Although both regular and nonstick pans work, we liked the absolutely effortless release guaranteed by using nonstick. The nonstick pan also allowed us to use less oil, resulting in less greasy quesadillas. Wanting to use the smallest amount of oil possible, we found it easy to just brush the outside of the tortillas with oil rather than adding it to the pan. A hot pan is absolutely necessary to a well-toasted crust, but if the pan is too hot, the tortillas will burn in spots. Medium heat, we found, toasted both sides of the quesadillas and melted the cheese without either burning the tortillas or requiring an oven finish.

Last, we discovered that placing a small weight on the quesadilla as it cooked ensured a crisp, even crust. Using an empty saucepan with a diameter of roughly 8 inches, we found the weight flattened the nooks and crannies of the tortilla against the hot pan without forcing the filling out of the sides. The result was a crisp, toasty quesadilla with melted cheese throughout and a flavor that left tasters wanting more than just one slice.

Spicy Roasted Red Pepper Quesadillas

MAKES 16 SLICES, SERVING 4 TO 6

The avocado salsa takes just 5 minutes to prepare and adds a pleasing contrast of flavors and textures to the quesadillas. However, if you are pressed for time, the salsa can be omitted; the quesadillas are tasty enough to serve as is. See page 35 for information about buying jarred roasted red peppers. Soft taco-size tortillas work best in this recipe.

QUICK AVOCADO SALSA

1   medium avocado, pitted, peeled, and cut into ½-inch dice (see the illustrations on pages 64–65)

1   tablespoon juice from 1 lime
     Salt and ground black pepper

QUESADILLAS

8   ounces jarred roasted red peppers, minced (about 1 cup)
1   small chipotle chile in adobo sauce, minced
½   small clove garlic, minced
2   tablespoons minced fresh cilantro leaves
     Salt and ground black pepper
4   (8-inch) soft flour tortillas
3   thin slices red onion, rings separated
4   ounces Monterey Jack cheese, shredded (about 1⅓ cups)
2   tablespoons vegetable oil

1. FOR THE SALSA: Gently toss the avocado with the lime juice and season to taste with salt and pepper in a small bowl; set aside.

2. FOR THE QUESADILLAS: Combine the roasted red peppers, chipotle, garlic, and cilantro in a small bowl and season to taste with salt and pepper. Spread half of the mixture evenly over 1 tortilla, leaving a 1-inch border bare. Arrange half of the onion slices over the pepper mixture and sprinkle with half of the cheese, again leaving a 1-inch border. Place a second tortilla over the cheese and press slightly to position. Repeat with the remaining ingredients to make a second quesadilla.

3. Set a 10-inch nonstick skillet over medium heat for 2 minutes. Brush 1 side of 1 quesadilla with 1½ teaspoons of the oil and place the quesadilla, greased-side down, in the heated pan. Place a clean saucepan on the quesadilla as a weight and cook until the bottom of the quesadilla is golden brown and crisp, 3 to 4 minutes. Remove the weight and brush the top with 1½ teaspoons oil. Using a wide metal spatula, flip the quesadilla over in the pan and replace the weight. Cook until the second side is golden brown and crisp, about 3 minutes more.

4. Transfer the quesadilla to a cutting board to cool slightly; return the skillet to medium heat. Cook the second quesadilla. Cut each quesadilla into 8 wedges and serve warm with the avocado salsa.

STUFFED MUSHROOMS

MORE THAN A RELIC OF THE 1970S COCKTAIL party set, stuffed mushrooms make a welcome hors d'oeuvre, especially during the cold winter months. Although small enough to eat in one bite, stuffed mushrooms are meant to be potently flavored with the earthy, robust flavors of the forest. The trick is to tease this flavor out of the mushrooms found at the local grocery store. Sure, a great wild mushroom will taste woodsy when stuffed, but what about the common white button mushroom?

We began by trying a few recipes and immediately noted two main issues: the lack of any true mushroom flavor and the mushy, wet texture of the fillings. As the stuffed mushrooms cooked in the oven, they released their moisture, becoming watery and turning the filling wet. We realized that the mushrooms had to be cooked before they were stuffed and knew that roasting was the answer. The dry heat would allow the released moisture to evaporate while the roasting would intensify the mushroom flavor. By roasting the mushroom caps upside down, we were able to drain much of their natural moisture before flipping them over and roasting the other side.

Although this technique produced better flavor, the mushrooms still tasted too bland. In an effort to introduce flavor to the mushrooms as they cooked, we tossed them with olive oil, garlic, lemon juice, salt, and pepper before roasting. This last-minute boost worked wonders, and the mushroom caps emerged from their roast dry, full of flavor, and ready for the stuffing.

Wanting to pack the stuffing with even more mushroom flavor, we thought it would be great to use the mushroom stems as the main ingredient, but after several trials we noted that they were simply too bland and watery, even with a quick marinade and a roast. Instead, we used dried porcini mushrooms and quickly found the potent mushroom flavor we were looking for. Pancetta (Italian-style bacon), Parmesan, and fresh parsley rounded out the stuffing in terms of flavor, yet we were still having trouble with its texture, having gone from wet and mushy to dry and crumbly. To correct this, we used bread soaked in milk, a combination often used in meatballs to help hold the mixture together

without making it sodden or greasy.

Once stuffed and topped with a pinch of grated Parmesan, the mushrooms took only 10 minutes to heat through. They emerged from the oven with the unmistakable, earthy aroma of mushrooms cooked to perfection.

Stuffed Mushrooms

MAKES 24 MUSHROOMS, SERVING 8

Roasting the mushrooms drives off excess moisture and concentrates their flavor. The roasted mushrooms are then stuffed and quickly heated through. We found that mushroom caps that measure between 1½ and 2 inches in diameter (before roasting) are ideal for this recipe. See the illustrations on page 316 for tips on rehydrating dried porcini mushrooms.

ROASTED MUSHROOMS

24	medium mushroom caps
¼	cup extra-virgin olive oil
3	large garlic cloves, minced or pressed through a garlic press (about 2 tablespoons)
½	teaspoon juice from 1 lemon
¼	teaspoon salt
	Pinch ground black pepper

STUFFING

¾	ounce dried porcini mushrooms
2	slices high-quality white sandwich bread
2	tablespoons milk
3	ounces pancetta, minced
2	large garlic cloves, minced or pressed through a garlic press (about 1½ tablespoons)
¼	cup plus 2 tablespoons grated Parmesan cheese
1	tablespoon minced fresh parsley leaves
	Salt and ground black pepper

1. FOR THE MUSHROOMS: Adjust an oven rack to the middle position and heat the oven to 450 degrees. Toss the mushrooms with the oil, garlic, lemon juice, salt, and pepper in a medium bowl. Place the mushrooms, gill-side down, on a large rimmed baking sheet and roast until the brown juices are released, about 20 minutes. Turn the caps over and roast until the liquid has evaporated completely and the

mushrooms are brown all over, about 10 minutes. Remove the baking sheet from the oven and turn the mushrooms gill-side down to drain any excess moisture. (Do not turn off the oven.)

2. FOR THE STUFFING: Meanwhile, mix the dried porcini mushrooms with ½ cup hot tap water in a small microwave-safe bowl. Cover with plastic wrap, cut several steam vents in the plastic wrap with a paring knife, and microwave on high power for 30 seconds. Let stand until the mushrooms soften, about 5 minutes. Lift the mushrooms from the liquid with a fork and mince. Pour the liquid through a small strainer lined with a single sheet of paper towel and placed over a measuring cup.

3. Process the sandwich bread in a food processor fitted with a metal blade until the bread has a coarse texture resembling Grape-Nuts cereal, about eight 1-second pulses. Transfer the crumbs to a small bowl and toss with the milk.

4. Cook the pancetta in a small nonstick pan over medium heat until lightly browned, about 5 minutes. Add the minced porcini and cook for 1 minute. Add the porcini soaking liquid and simmer until the liquid evaporates, about 2 minutes. Add the garlic and sauté until aromatic, about 30 seconds. Remove the pan from the heat and scrape the mixture into a medium bowl. Add the soaked bread crumbs, ¼ cup of the Parmesan, the parsley, and salt and pepper to taste.

5. TO STUFF THE MUSHROOMS: Flip the cooked mushroom caps gill-side up and stuff each with about 1 teaspoon of the stuffing. Top each mushroom with a pinch of the remaining 2 tablespoons cheese. Bake at 450 degrees until the cheese has melted and is browning in spots and the stuffing is heated through, about 10 minutes. Serve immediately.

BUFFALO WINGS

FIRST CONCEIVED OF AT THE ANCHOR bar in Buffalo, N.Y., in the 1960s, Buffalo wings are now found throughout the country at any bar or Super Bowl party worth its salt. The odd combination of chicken wings slathered with hot sauce and dunked in blue cheese dressing may seem like a drunken concoction best forgotten the next morning, but it is actually a harmonious union. The sauce's bright heat is tamed by the soothing, creamy dip.

For Buffalo wings, the raw chicken wing itself is almost always cut in two segments, and the relatively meatless wingtip is removed. The wings come packaged whole or cut into pieces affectionately referred to as drumettes. We found that precut wings were often poorly cut and unevenly sized, so we chose to buy whole wings and butcher them ourselves, which was easy and economical. With kitchen shears or a sharp chef's knife, the wing is halved at the main joint and the skinny tip of the wing is lopped off and discarded (or saved for stock).

While the wings were easy to butcher, cooking them proved a little trickier because of their high fat content. At the Anchor Bar, Buffalo wings are deep-fried, which renders the fat and leaves the skin crisp and golden. But deep-frying can be a daunting project in a home kitchen, with hot fat splattering about, coating the stovetop and stinging uncovered arms. We found that if we used a deep Dutch oven and kept the oil at a constant 360 degrees, splattering oil was kept to a (much safer) minimum and cleanup was easy.

We tossed the wings with salt, pepper, and cayenne and then fried them for about 12 minutes, or until golden. While these wings were juicy and crisp, most tasters wanted an even crispier exterior. We did not want to resort to a batter, so we tried dredging the wings, testing one batch dredged in flour and another in cornstarch. The cornstarch provided a thin and brittle coating, not unlike tempura, that was the tasters' favorite. We found that thoroughly drying the chicken with paper towels prior to tossing it with the cornstarch and seasonings ensured crisp skin and no gumminess.

Now we were ready to tackle the sauce. Most recipes we found agreed that authentic Buffalo wing sauce, as made at the Anchor Bar, is nothing but Frank's Louisiana Hot Sauce and butter or margarine, blended in a 2-to-1 ratio. Most recipes also suggest intensifying the sauce's heat with a bit of Tabasco or other hot pepper sauce because, on its own, Frank's is not quite spicy enough. While we liked this simple sauce, most tasters wanted something a little more dynamic. We included brown sugar to round out the flavors. A little cider vinegar balanced out the sugar and added a pleasing sharpness.

CUTTING UP CHICKEN WINGS

1. With a chef's knife, cut into the skin between the larger sections of the wing until you hit the joint.

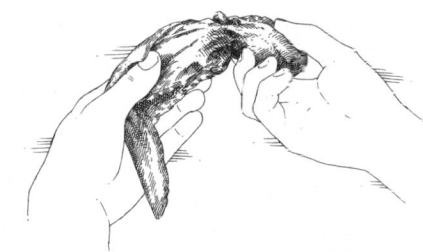

2. Bend back the two sections to pop and break the joint

3. Cut through the skin and flesh to completely separate the two meaty portions.

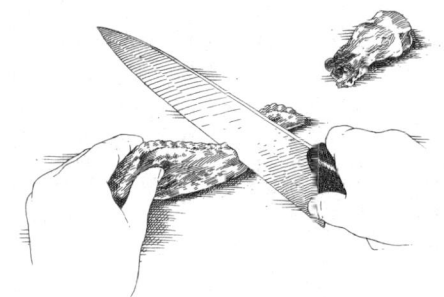

4. Hack off the wingtip and discard (or save for making stock).

Creamy blue cheese dressing and carrot and celery sticks are the classic accompaniments to Buffalo wings. For our dressing, we picked a mild blue cheese and combined it with buttermilk and sour cream for tang and richness and with mayonnaise for body. A little white wine vinegar brightened the flavors, a pinch of sugar added just the right touch of sweetness, and garlic powder, which we normally shy away from, added a subtle background note rather than the assertive bite that comes with fresh garlic.

Our final Buffalo wings buck tradition just a bit. But they do so only in the service of delivering a close-to-foolproof and tasty recipe for a crowd-pleasing favorite.

Buffalo Wings
SERVES 6 TO 8

Frank's Louisiana Hot Sauce is not terribly spicy. We like to combine it with a more potent hot sauce, such as Tabasco, to bring up the heat. You will need to double the ingredients in the blue cheese dressing recipe.

SAUCE
4	tablespoons (½ stick) unsalted butter
½	cup Frank's Louisiana Hot Sauce
2	tablespoons hot pepper sauce, plus more to taste
1	tablespoon dark brown sugar
2	teaspoons cider vinegar

WINGS
1–2	quarts peanut oil for frying
1	teaspoon cayenne pepper
1	teaspoon ground black pepper
1	teaspoon salt
3	tablespoons cornstarch
18	chicken wings (about 3 pounds), wingtips removed and the remaining wings separated into 2 parts at the joint (see the illustrations at left)

VEGETABLES AND DRESSING
4	medium celery ribs, cut into thin sticks
2	medium carrots, peeled and cut into thin sticks
1½	cups Blue Cheese Dressing (page 91)

1. FOR THE SAUCE: Melt the butter in a small saucepan over low heat. Whisk in the hot sauces, brown sugar, and vinegar until combined. Remove from the heat and set aside.

2. FOR THE WINGS: Heat the oven to 200 degrees. Line a baking sheet with paper towels. Heat 2½ inches of the peanut oil in a large Dutch oven over medium-high heat to 360 degrees. While the oil heats, mix the cayenne, black pepper, salt, and cornstarch together in a small bowl. Dry the chicken with paper towels and place the pieces in a large mixing bowl. Sprinkle the spice mixture over the wings and toss with a rubber spatula until evenly coated. Fry half of the chicken wings until golden and crisp, 10 to 12 minutes. With a slotted spoon, transfer the fried chicken wings to the baking sheet. Keep the first batch of chicken warm in the oven while frying the remaining wings.

3. TO SERVE: Pour the sauce mixture into a large bowl, add the chicken wings, and toss until the wings are uniformly coated. Serve immediately with the celery and carrot sticks and the blue cheese dressing on the side.

BREADED CHICKEN FINGERS

FEW KIDS (WHETHER YOUNG OR OLD) DON'T like the crunchy simplicity of chicken fingers—tender, boneless lengths of chicken pan-fried with a cloak of mildly flavored crumbs. They are easily served with a variety of dipping sauces, as shown on pub menus everywhere. Yet, as with most things so simple, they are best made well or not at all. Wanting to avoid rubbery chicken and a bland coating that falls off the chicken, we set out to find the best, yet simplest, way to make chicken fingers.

Cutting boneless, skinless chicken breasts into finger-length pieces was incredibly simple and required little skill. We did note, however, that chicken breasts can range drastically in size. We found it easiest to cut uniformly sized fingers from breasts weighing 5 to 6 ounces each. Cutting the chicken diagonally into ¾-inch-wide strips, we found it unnecessary to pound them. Also, the chicken tenderloins attached to the back of each breast make perfect fingers after the white tendon is removed.

What really makes or breaks a good chicken finger is the coating. Ideally, it should taste mild and comforting and have a solid crunch. It should not be dull or greasy. To get the coating to adhere to the chicken, we found it necessary to use a bound breading, or panade, whereby the chicken is dipped in flour, dragged through a lightly whisked egg, and then coated with bread crumbs. We found that the type of bread crumbs used can make a big difference. Making our own out of sliced bread tasted great but required too much time and effort for a midweek meal. Packaged bread crumbs from the store were disappointing, offering only a stale, mass-market flavor that pleased no one. Japanese panko crumbs (commonly found in the ethnic aisle of the supermarket) offered a mild wheaty flavor and shatteringly crisp texture that not only won the test kitchen over but also required no work beyond the opening of a bag.

We tried to omit the flouring step noted above but found that without it, the coating merely peeled off. The flour ensured that the surface of the chicken was absolutely dry before being dipped into the egg, which guaranteed a coating with staying power. We also learned that mixing a little oil into the egg wash helped to keep the breading from getting too heavy and produced a deeper, golden brown color during frying. Last, we noted the importance of pressing the crumbs into the chicken for an absolutely even distribution. As for seasoning, we found it easiest to add salt and pepper to the egg wash.

Using a heavy-bottomed 12-inch skillet, we were able to fry all the fingers in only two batches. Although this makes for a fairly crowded pan, usually a no-no when frying, we found that the small chicken fingers did not suffer a bit. Rather, they cooked through quickly and browned evenly. Pitting vegetable oil against olive oil, we preferred the light, unobtrusive flavor of the vegetable oil to the potent and slightly bitter flavor of olive oil.

We found it unnecessary to use fresh oil for the second round of frying. After cooking the first batch over medium-high heat, we simply reduced the heat to medium for the second batch to prevent burning.

Breaded Chicken Fingers

MAKES 25 TO 30 PIECES

Look for panko (extra-crunchy Japanese bread crumbs) in the ethnic food aisle at your supermarket. The fingers can be held in a 200-degree oven for up to 20 minutes before serving. Serve with any of the dipping sauces on page 72.

I	pound boneless, skinless chicken breasts, patted dry, trimmed, and sliced crosswise ½ inch thick
I	cup unbleached all-purpose flour
3	cups panko (Japanese-style bread crumbs)
2	large eggs
I	tablespoon plus I cup vegetable oil
	Salt and ground black pepper
I	lemon, cut into wedges, or one of the dipping sauces on page 72

1. Adjust an oven rack to the middle position and heat the oven to 200 degrees. Thoroughly dry the breasts with paper towels. Spread the flour and panko in two separate shallow dishes. Lightly beat the eggs, 1 tablespoon of the oil, 1 teaspoon salt, and ½ teaspoon pepper in a third shallow dish. Working with several pieces of chicken at a time, drop the chicken into the flour and shake the pan to coat them. Shake the excess flour from each piece; then, using tongs, dip the chicken into the egg mixture, turning to coat well and allowing the excess to drip off. Drop the chicken into the panko and press the crumbs lightly onto the chicken. Shake off excess crumbs and place the breaded chicken on a wire rack set over a rimmed baking sheet. Repeat with the remaining chicken.

2. Heat the remaining 1 cup oil in a heavy-bottomed 12-inch skillet over medium-high heat until it reaches 350 degrees—the oil will shimmer but should not smoke—3 to 4 minutes. Place half of the chicken gently in the skillet and cook until golden brown and crisp on the first side, about 2 minutes. Using tongs, flip the chicken; continue to cook until the second side is deep golden brown and crisp and the chicken is no longer pink in the center, about 2 minutes longer. Transfer the chicken to a clean rimmed baking sheet lined with paper towels and place it in the warm oven. Return the skillet to medium heat and repeat with the remaining chicken. Serve immediately with the lemon wedges or one of the dipping sauces.

➤ VARIATIONS

Sesame Chicken Fingers

Follow the recipe for Breaded Chicken Fingers, tossing 3 tablespoons sesame seeds with the panko. Serve with the Sweet and Sour Duck Sauce (page 72).

Curried Chicken Fingers with Chutney

Follow the recipe for Breaded Chicken Fingers, tossing 1½ tablespoons curry powder and a pinch of cayenne with the panko. Serve with Quick Apricot Chutney (page 72).

TRIMMING CHICKEN BREASTS

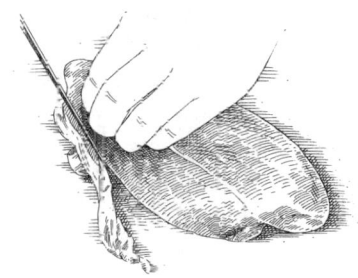

1. Lay each breast tenderloin-side down and smooth the top with your fingers. Any fat will slide to the periphery, where it can be trimmed with a knife.

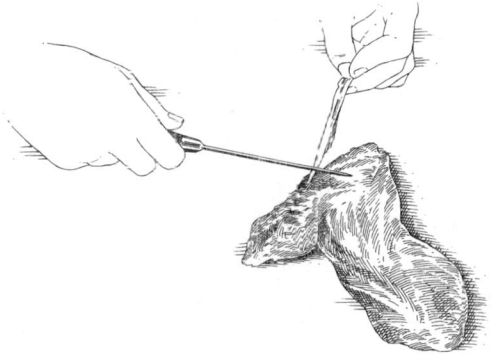

2. To remove the tough, white tendon, turn the breasts tenderloin-side up and peel back the thick half of the tenderloin so that it lies top-down on the work surface. Use the point of a paring knife to cut around the top of the tenderloin to expose the tendon, then scrape the tendon free with the knife.

FOUR DIPPING SAUCES FOR BREADED CHICKEN FINGERS

THE SAUCES AND CHUTNEY CAN BE COVERED AND REFRIGERATED FOR UP TO I WEEK.

Honey-Mustard Sauce

MAKES ABOUT I CUP

6 tablespoons honey
1/2 cup Dijon mustard

Mix the honey and mustard in a small bowl until smooth.

Quick Apricot Chutney

MAKES ABOUT I CUP

I large shallot, chopped coarse
I medium jalapeño chile, stemmed and chopped coarse
8 ounces dried apricots (about 1 1/4 cups)
2 whole cloves
I (1-inch) piece fresh ginger, cut crosswise into 4 coins
1/3 cup cider vinegar
1/4 cup packed light or dark brown sugar
Salt and ground black pepper
1/2 cup water

Process the shallot and jalapeño in a food processor until finely chopped, about ten 1-second pulses. Add the apricots and process until finely chopped, about twenty-five 1-second pulses, scraping down the sides of the workbowl with a rubber spatula as necessary. Transfer the mixture to a small saucepan and add the cloves, ginger, vinegar, brown sugar, 1/4 teaspoon salt, and water. Bring to a simmer over medium-high heat, reduce the heat to low, and cook, stirring occasionally, until the mixture is stiff and the liquid is evaporated, about 15 minutes. Remove and discard the cloves and ginger; adjust the seasonings with salt and pepper to taste. Cool the chutney to room temperature before serving.

Sweet-and-Tangy Barbecue Sauce

MAKES ABOUT I 1/4 CUPS

I cup ketchup
2 tablespoons finely grated onion
2 tablespoons Worcestershire sauce
2 tablespoons Dijon mustard
3 tablespoons molasses
2 tablespoons maple syrup
3 tablespoons cider vinegar
I teaspoon chili powder
1/4 teaspoon cayenne

Combine all the ingredients in a small saucepan and simmer over medium heat, stirring often, until the sauce is thick and glossy, about 30 minutes. Cool the sauce to room temperature before serving.

Spicy Sweet-and-Sour Duck Sauce

MAKES ABOUT I CUP

I cup rice wine vinegar
I cup apricot jam or preserves
I (1-inch) piece fresh ginger, cut into 4 coins
4 teaspoons light brown sugar
1/8 teaspoon red pepper flakes
Salt and ground black pepper

Combine all the ingredients in a medium saucepan and bring to a boil over medium heat. Reduce the heat to medium-low and simmer for 20 minutes, until slightly thickened. Strain the mixture through a fine-mesh sieve into a bowl, pressing on the solids to extract as much liquid as possible. Season with salt and pepper to taste and cool the sauce to room temperature before serving.

HOMEMADE SPRING ROLLS

SOUTHEAST ASIAN SPRING ROLLS (NOT THE deep-fried Chinese variety) are made with translucent rice paper wrappers that have been softened in water and then filled with cool rice vermicelli, raw vegetables, and fragrant herbs. A popular menu item, they offer a textural symphony (soft wrapper, toothsome noodles, and crunchy vegetables) as well as stark but appealing contrasts in flavor (mint, basil, cilantro, chiles, peanuts, and fish sauce). But spring rolls can be disappointing, as lesser establishments use gummy noodles, iceberg lettuce, soggy wrappers, shriveled herbs, and saccharine "peanut" sauces that taste not a whit like peanuts. Given that they require only a short list of fresh ingredients and no cooking other than boiling noodles, it occurred to us that a home cook could easily produce a four-star spring roll worthy of the best Asian restaurant.

We began our investigation with the wrapper. Wrappers come out of the package hard and inedible and so must be soaked in water before use. It quickly became apparent that timing was crucial. When soaked too long (more than 30 seconds), the wrappers simply disintegrated; when soaked for just two or three seconds, they remained stiff. We found the ideal soak time to be 10 seconds.

Even after just 10 seconds of soaking, however, the wrappers were so delicate that they fell apart if simply placed on a kitchen counter for rolling. The trick, we discovered, is to use a damp kitchen towel, which supports the wrappers without sticking to them. We also found it best to make the rolls one at a time and to cover them with a second damp towel once finished to keep the wrappers moist and pliable.

With the wrappers taken care of, we turned to the filling, starting with the noodles. Thin vermicelli-style rice noodles are cooked just like American or Italian pasta. However, we did note that the thickness ranges from brand to brand, which affects cooking time. It's best to taste the noodles every minute or so during cooking until they are tender. A rinse under cold water is then needed to stop the cooking and keep these starchy noodles from congealing into an inseparable mass.

As for the vegetables, we tried jícama, a root vegetable, which had a nice crunch but was too sweet, and daikon, an Asian radish, which was good but hard to find. These two possibilities were out. Two more possibilities were carrot and cucumber. Carrot contributed a pleasantly sweet flavor and nice texture when grated. We tried grating cucumber as well but ended up with watery, soggy rolls. When sliced into substantial planks, however, the cucumber added significant crunch without dampening the wrappers. We also liked its cool, subtle flavor.

For the herbs, fragrant cilantro and Thai basil (we found that mint can be used as a substitute for the latter) sparkle when used in tandem, and their frilly leaves are a visual bonus. We ran into trouble, though, when we inadvertently got a few whole large basil leaves in a single bite. The solution was twofold: Tear large leaves into pieces before using and sprinkle them over the inner section of the rice paper before rolling (rather than piling them up, as most recipes suggest).

SLICING THE CUCUMBER

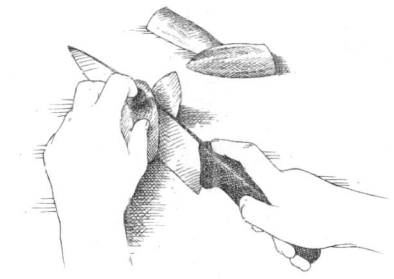

1. Cut the peeled cucumber in half crosswise. Cut ¼-inch planks from the outermost part of each cucumber half, leaving the seeds behind.

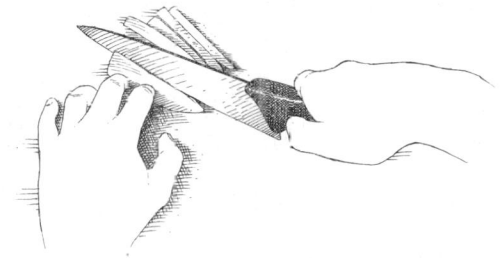

2. Cut each plank into five ⅛-inch strips. You should have about 40 strips of cucumber.

Despite our liberal dose of herbs, the rolls remained bland. We went back to our library of cookbooks and discovered spring roll recipes that included an acidic marinade for the vegetables and noodles that adds both flavor and moisture. The liquid ingredients for the marinade included a few typical Southeast Asian flavorings: lime juice, rice vinegar, and fish sauce (a pungent liquid made from fermented fish). We settled on a simple mixture based on fish sauce and lime juice. A teaspoon of sugar and some chopped fresh chiles balanced the acidity and gave the rolls a sweet-hot punch, while chopped peanuts added substance.

As for serving, we found that a leaf of lettuce makes a fresh-tasting, bright-colored wrap for the finished spring roll. We chose a gently sweet and spicy peanut sauce for dipping (see page 77).

Now we finally had flavorful spring rolls that could be made easily and quickly at home. They are so good, in fact, that we won't be ordering them off a menu anytime soon.

Southeast Asian–Style Spring Rolls

MAKES 8 SPRING ROLLS

If you can't find Thai basil, do not substitute regular basil; its flavor is too gentle to stand up to the other, more assertive flavors in the filling. Mint makes a better substitute. If you are unable to obtain fish sauce, substitute an equal amount of rice vinegar plus ¼ teaspoon salt. Spring rolls are best eaten immediately, but they can be held for up to 4 hours in the refrigerator, covered with a clean, damp kitchen towel.

1	teaspoon sugar
1½	tablespoons fish sauce
2½	tablespoons juice from 1 to 2 limes
1	teaspoon salt
3	ounces rice vermicelli
1	large carrot, peeled and grated on the large holes of a box grater (about ½ cup)
⅓	cup coarsely chopped roasted unsalted peanuts
1	medium jalapeño or 2 Thai chiles, cored, seeded, and minced, or ½ teaspoon red pepper flakes
1	large cucumber, peeled and cut according to the illustrations on page 73
4	large leaves red leaf or Boston lettuce, halved lengthwise
8	(8-inch) round rice paper wrappers
½	cup loosely packed fresh Thai basil leaves or mint leaves, small leaves left whole, medium and large leaves torn into ½-inch pieces
½	cup loosely packed fresh cilantro leaves Spicy Peanut Dipping Sauce (page 77)

1. Combine the sugar, fish sauce, and lime juice in a small bowl; set aside.

2. Bring 2 quarts water to boil in a medium saucepan. Stir in the salt and rice vermicelli. Cook until the noodles are tender but not mushy, 3 to 4 minutes. Drain the noodles and rinse under cold running water until cool. Drain again and transfer to a medium bowl; toss 2 tablespoons of the fish sauce mixture with the noodles and set aside.

3. Combine the carrot, peanuts, and jalapeño in a small bowl. Add 1 tablespoon fish sauce mixture;

ASSEMBLING THE SPRING ROLLS

  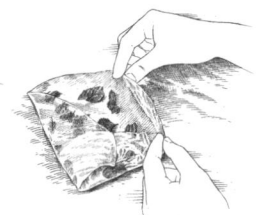 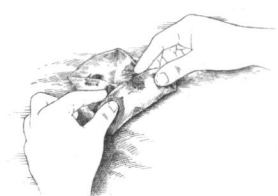

1. Place the herbs and cucumber on the wrapper, followed by the carrot mixture and noodles.

2. Fold up the bottom 2-inch border of the wrapper over the filling.

3. Fold the left, then the right edge of the wrapper over the filling.

4. Roll the filling to the top edge of the wrapper to form a tight cylinder.

toss to combine. Toss the cucumber in the remaining 1 tablespoon fish sauce mixture.

4. Place the lettuce on a platter. Spread a clean, damp kitchen towel on a work surface. Fill a 9-inch pie plate with 1 inch of room-temperature water. Working one at a time, immerse each wrapper in the water until just pliable, about 10 seconds; place the softened wrapper on the towel. Scatter 6 Thai basil leaves and 6 cilantro leaves over the wrapper. Arrange 5 cucumber sticks horizontally on the wrapper (see illustration 1 on the facing page); top with 1 tablespoon of the carrot mixture, then arrange about 2½ tablespoons of the noodles on top of the carrot mixture. Wrap the spring roll according to illustrations 2 through 4; set it on 1 lettuce piece on the platter. Cover the platter with a second damp kitchen towel; repeat with the remaining wrappers and filling. Serve with the dipping sauce, wrapping a piece of lettuce around the exterior of each roll.

➤ VARIATION

Southeast Asian–Style Spring Rolls with Shrimp

Peel and remove the tails from 8 ounces medium (40 to 50 per pound) shrimp. Follow the recipe for Southeast Asian–Style Spring Rolls, adding the shrimp to the boiling water along with the salt in step 2; cook until the shrimp are opaque, about 3 minutes. Using a slotted spoon, transfer the shrimp to a small bowl; use the same water to cook the rice vermicelli, as directed in step 2. When cool enough to handle, coarsely chop the shrimp. When assembling the spring rolls, place about 2 tablespoons of the chopped shrimp on top of the noodles.

BEEF SATAY

SLENDER SLICES OF MARINATED BEEF WOVEN onto bamboo skewers and thrown briefly on the grill are a traditional Indonesian favorite known as satay or sate. The meat has a sweet yet salty flavor, and the skewers make a perfect appetizer, served alongside a spicy peanut sauce. When done correctly, the tender meat is easily pulled apart

SLICING FLANK STEAK THINLY FOR SATAYS

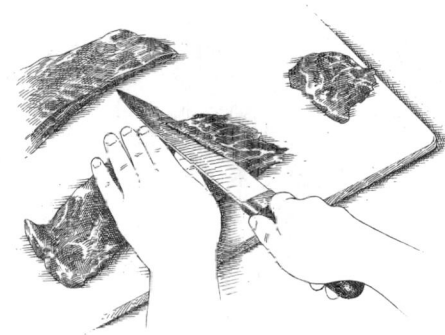

Using a chef's knife, slice the partially frozen flank steak crosswise into ¼-inch-thick slices. You will be cutting against the grain of the meat.

into small bites right off the skewer. All too often, however, the beef is tough and sliced so thickly that it doesn't pull apart, leaving the diner with an ungainly mouthful of meat. The peanut sauce can be graceless, with a gluelike consistency and muddy peanut flavor. Finding the right cut of beef and slicing it correctly would be key for a tender satay, as would finding just the right balance of ingredients for the spicy-sweet marinade and the accompanying peanut sauce.

Starting with the beef, we surveyed the local butcher counter for possibilities. Skipping over expensive cuts such as top loin, rib eye, and tenderloin, we focused on the cheaper cuts more appropriate for marinating and skewering—sirloin, sirloin flap, round, skirt, flank, and blade steaks. Bringing these cheaper cuts back to the test kitchen, we immediately noted that slicing the raw beef into thin strips was a difficult task. To make it easier, we found it best to firm the meat in the freezer for about 30 minutes. Sliced, skewered, and cooked, these various cheaper cuts of meat produced substantially different textures. Steaks from the round were the worst, with a tough, dry texture, followed closely by chewy sirloin and stringy sirloin flap (a cut from the bottom sirloin). The blade steaks tasted great and were fairly tender, but their small size made it difficult to slice them into long, elegant strips. Both the skirt and flank steak were easy to slice and tasted best. Because skirt steak can be difficult to find and is a bit more expensive, flank steak was the best option.

We found the key to tenderness hinged on slicing the meat perpendicular to its large, obvious grain (see the illustration on page 75). Using a small, 2-pound flank steak, we could make about 30 skewers, enough for 12 to 18 people as an appetizer. Although satay is classically grilled, we found the broiler to be a simpler and more party-friendly cooking method. Thin wooden skewers worked better than metal skewers, which tend to be thicker and tore up the small pieces of meat. It was necessary, however, to wrap the ends of the skewers (the part not covered with meat) in foil to keep them from burning or catching fire. Cooked roughly 6 inches from the broiler element, these thinly sliced pieces of meat were done in only six to seven minutes.

Having found a tender cut of meat, we focused next on adding flavor with the marinade. Researching a variety of traditional Indonesian recipes, we noted that most were based on a combination of fish sauce and oil. Using vegetable oil, we tested various amounts of fish sauce, but tasters simply did not like its fermented fish flavor in combination with the beef. Soy sauce, though not traditional, made for a good replacement, lending its salty, fermented flavor without any fishiness. We then tried adding other flavors,

such as coconut milk, lime juice, Tabasco, Asian chili sauce, sugar, and an array of fresh herbs. Coconut milk dulled the beef's natural flavor, while the tart, acidic flavor of lime juice tasted out of place. Asian chili sauce added a pleasant, spicy heat without the sour, vinegary flavor that Tabasco contributed. The sweet, molasses flavor of brown sugar added a welcome balance to the hot chili sauce and salty soy, while enhancing the beef's ability to brown under the broiler. Scallions, garlic and cilantro rounded out all of these flavors nicely. Marinating the beef for more than one hour turned the texture of the thin sliced beef mushy, while less time didn't give the meat long enough to pick up the marinade flavors. One hour was perfect.

Last, we focused on the peanut sauce. Using creamy peanut butter, we tried spicing it up with a variety of flavorings. In the end, the same ingredients used in the marinade also tasted good in the peanut sauce—soy sauce, Asian chili sauce, dark brown sugar, garlic, cilantro, and scallions. This time, however, lime juice added a welcome burst of tart acidity. We then stumbled on the obvious way to keep the sauce from being too thick or pasty: Thin it with hot water. Pairing perfectly with the flavor of the marinated beef, the peanut sauce turns these subtly sweet-and-spicy skewers into an authentic satay.

COVERING THE SKEWERS WITH FOIL

To keep the handle portion of the wooden skewers from burning, cover the ends with foil, leaving just the meat exposed to the heat of the broiler.

Beef Satay with Spicy Peanut Dipping Sauce

MAKES 25 TO 30 LARGE SKEWERS OR ABOUT 50 SMALL SKEWERS, SERVING 12 TO 18

Thirty 6-inch wooden skewers, or fifty 4-inch skewers, are required for this recipe. If you cannot find Asian chili sauce, substitute 1 tablespoon of ketchup mixed with ½ teaspoon of Tabasco. If you would like to halve this recipe, buy a 1-pound flank steak and cut the remaining ingredients in half.

2	pounds flank steak
4	tablespoons soy sauce
4	tablespoons vegetable oil
1	tablespoon Asian chili sauce
¼	cup packed dark brown sugar

¼ cup minced fresh cilantro leaves

2 medium garlic cloves, minced or pressed through a garlic press (about 2 teaspoons)

4 scallions, sliced thin

1 recipe Spicy Peanut Dipping Sauce (recipe follows)

1. Cut the flank steak in half lengthwise and freeze for 30 minutes.

2. Combine the soy sauce, oil, chili sauce, brown sugar, cilantro, garlic, and scallions in a large bowl. Following the illustrations on page 75, slice the meat crosswise (against the grain) into ¼-inch-thick strips. Add the meat to the marinade and refrigerate for 1 hour only. Do not over-marinate.

3. Adjust an oven rack 6 inches from the broiler element and heat the broiler. Line the bottom of a broiler pan with foil and top with the slotted broiler pan top. Thread the skewers through each piece of meat several times (use two pieces of meat for large skewers and one piece for small skewers). Place the skewers on a rimmed baking sheet and, following the illustration on the facing page, cover the skewer ends with foil (the skewers can also be packed together more tightly than shown). Broil, flipping over the skewers halfway through, until the meat is browned, about 7 minutes. Serve immediately with the peanut sauce.

➤ VARIATION
Chicken Satay

Follow the recipe for Beef Satay, substituting 2 pounds boneless, skinless chicken breasts, chilled in the freezer for 30 minutes, for the flank steak. Cut the chicken on the diagonal into ¼-inch-thick strips about 3 inches long, and marinate for only 30 minutes. Do not over-marinate. Continue to skewer and broil as directed in the beef recipe.

Spicy Peanut Dipping Sauce
MAKES ABOUT 1½ CUPS

This sauce can be made a day in advance and refrigerated. Bring the sauce to room temperature before serving.

½ cup creamy peanut butter

¼ cup hot water

1 tablespoon soy sauce

2 tablespoons juice from 1 to 2 limes

1 tablespoon Asian chili sauce

1 tablespoon dark brown sugar

1 medium garlic clove, minced or pressed through a garlic press (about 1 teaspoon)

1 tablespoon chopped fresh cilantro leaves

2 scallions, sliced thin

Whisk the peanut butter and hot water together in a medium bowl, then whisk in the remaining ingredients. Transfer to a small serving bowl.

BROILED SHRIMP SKEWERS

WHEN WE THINK OF SEAFOOD SKEWERS, we think of plump, briny shrimp carefully threaded onto a bamboo skewer, their flavor singing the praises of the sea. Unfortunately, the real thing often involves shriveled, vulcanized shrimp barely hanging on to a carbonized, splinter-ridden stick. And don't even get us started on dipping sauces: insipid, oily, and just plain boring. After seeing all the sad examples of skewered shrimp floating around at cocktail parties, we were determined to examine the process and see what was going wrong. After all, when done right, skewered appetizers are the epitome of party chic. Packed with flavor, you can eat half a dozen without feeling full, getting your hands messy, or even putting your beverage down. For all these reasons, we were determined to reinvigorate the skewered shrimp.

Because we were looking to make enough shrimp skewers to feed a crowd, we needed a cooking method that could produce a lot of food in a little time. Grilling was an option, but the problems of hot spots, charred skewers, and sprints out to the backyard while your guests are arriving nixed that idea. Broiling was a better option—it allowed us to prepare upward of 30 skewers at a time, keeping our guests satisfied and our sanity intact. After settling on our cooking method, we moved on to the shrimp. Tasters preferred extra-large shrimp (21 to

25 per pound) because they have great flavor and require very little (if any) prep.

Because we wanted a user-friendly appetizer, we decided to peel and devein our shrimp prior to threading them on the skewers. Two pounds of raw shrimp made 20 to 25 skewers (with two shrimp on each), enough for 10 to 12 people. Because these hors d'oeuvres would be eaten out of hand, tasters preferred bamboo to metal skewers; the bamboo skewers are disposable and easier to handle out of the oven. The only downside to bamboo skewers is that they run the risk of smoldering, or even catching fire, under the broiler. To combat this issue, we lined up all the shrimp on the same side of the roasting pan and protected the exposed bamboo with a strip of aluminum foil. Arranged about 6 inches below the broiler element, the shrimp cooked through in five to six minutes and the skewers remained unfazed.

Now that we had our shrimp skewered, we needed to pump up their flavor. By tossing them with salt, pepper, and a little oil, we figured that the broiler would impart a beautiful brown color to our shrimp. But by the time the shrimp did turn brown, we no longer had shrimp skewers, we had shrimp jerky. Something had to give. We tried sprinkling sugar on the shrimp, but even the sugar wouldn't promote browning or crisp the shrimp's exterior. Next we tried marinating the shrimp for about 30 minutes in a variety of herbs and spices, hoping that this would encourage caramelization. Instead, the marinating process just seemed to draw out liquid from the shrimp, making them soggy and unappetizing.

Getting a bit frustrated, we used a wet rub—a paste made from oil, herbs, and spices—to flavor the shrimp. Finally, we were on the right track. The wet rub was flavorful, and more oil in the rub insured that the shrimp cooked evenly. Still, the pasty consistency of the rub turned off some of our tasters. We gradually reduced the amount of rub, finally settling on 2 teaspoons of vegetable oil combined with minced parsley, scallions, and garlic. We coated the shrimp with the herb rub just before skewering, ensuring that the shrimp's texture and the herbal flavor would be at their height. With a sprinkling of salt and fresh ground pepper,

only one thing was missing—a dipping sauce.

Any dipping sauce worth its salt complements and enhances its partner. Because the shrimp skewers would be eaten out of hand, we needed a thick sauce that wouldn't run down our arms or drip on our shirts. Tasters really liked the viscosity and richness of a mayonnaise-based dip, and everyone agreed that it matched well with the broiled shrimp. Keeping things simple, we used store-bought mayonnaise doctored with flavors that paired easily with shrimp. We added lemon juice and lemon zest for acidity, garlic for a heady bite, and cayenne pepper for a bit of a kick. Finally, we had found what we were looking for. The briny, crisp-tender shrimp were perfectly balanced by the slightly tart, slightly spicy mayonnaise. With broiled, herbed shrimp and a downright delicious dip, you just can't go wrong.

Shrimp Skewers

MAKES 20 TO 25 SKEWERS

Choose shrimp that are extra-large (21 to 25 per pound) for this recipe, as they're easier to skewer.

2	tablespoons minced fresh parsley leaves
2	scallions, minced
I	medium garlic clove, minced or pressed through a garlic press (about I teaspoon)
2	teaspoons vegetable oil
¼	teaspoon salt
⅛	teaspoon ground black pepper
2	pounds extra-large shrimp (21 to 25 per pound), peeled and deveined (see the illustrations on page 39)
I	recipe Lemon-Cayenne Mayonnaise (recipe follows)

1. Adjust an oven rack 6 inches from the broiler element and heat the broiler. Line a broiler-pan bottom with foil and top with a slotted broiler-pan top.

2. Toss the parsley, scallions, garlic, oil, salt, and pepper together in a large bowl. Add the shrimp, and gently toss to coat. Following the illustration on the facing page, thread 2 shrimp onto each skewer, place on the broiler-pan top,

and cover the skewer ends with foil.

3. Broil the shrimp for about 6 minutes, flipping them over halfway through cooking, until they are pink and the herbs are toasted. Serve immediately with the Lemon-Cayenne Mayonnaise.

➤ VARIATION
Scallop Skewers
Use large sea scallops in this variation. Be sure to remove the tendon, which if left on will be unpleasantly chewy. See the illustration for removing the tendon on page 80.

Follow the recipe for Shrimp Skewers, substituting 2 pounds sea scallops for the shrimp.

Lemon-Cayenne Mayonnaise

MAKES ABOUT 1 CUP

The mayonnaise will keep, covered, in the refrigerator, for up to 1 week.

1	cup mayonnaise
1	medium garlic clove, minced or pressed through a garlic press (about 1 teaspoon)
3	tablespoons juice and 1 teaspoon grated zest from 1 lemon
1/8	teaspoon cayenne pepper or hot pepper sauce
1/8	teaspoon salt
1/4	teaspoon ground black pepper

Whisk all of the ingredients together in a small bowl, and refrigerate for at least 30 minutes.

SKEWERING SHRIMP

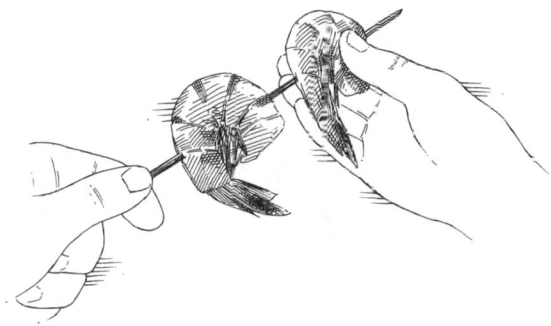

Thread the skewer through both the tail and main body of each shrimp to keep it from spinning around on the skewer. Wrap the ends of the skewers with foil.

BACON-WRAPPED SHRIMP

BACON-WRAPPED SHRIMP ARE ONE OF those cocktail party stand-by's that rarely make an appearance in today's trendy food magazines. And that's a shame, because it's such a simple dish—dare we say, elegant—and, most of all, downright tasty. The smoky flavor of the bacon is a rich complement to the briny flavor of the shellfish. Too often, though, this dish is marred by soggy, chewy bacon and rubbery, overcooked shrimp. We set out to find a never-fail recipe for this cocktail party classic.

As with most seafood dishes, the key is not to skimp on the quality of your seafood. And size matters, too. You don't want shrimp so small that the bacon acts as a blanket and completely overwhelms the flavor of the shrimp. We like extra-large shrimp for this dish. (Our variation substitutes scallops for the shrimp, and the rule on size applies here as well—buy large sea scallops, not tiny bay scallops.)

As for the bacon, we found that a whole slice was too much for one shrimp. Not only was the smoky flavor overwhelming, but it also turned the appetizer unappetizingly greasy. We found that cutting the bacon slices into smaller strips worked much better.

Now we were on to broiling the shrimp. The results were frustrating. The shrimp seemed to finish cooking before the bacon had time to brown and crisp. Time and again we couldn't get these two ingredients to finish cooking simultaneously. Because the bacon takes longer to cook than the shrimp, we would have to parcook it. The question was, how?

We turned to the microwave. Hauling out a skillet seemed like an unnecessary and messy proposition. We simply placed the bacon pieces over four layers of paper towels on a microwave-safe plate, then covered them with two more layers of paper towels. We wanted to cook the bacon just enough so that it was still pliable enough to wrap around the shrimp. After a few tries, we found that one to two minutes on high worked well. From there, it was a cinch to wrap the bacon around the shrimp and pop the whole ensemble under the broiler. We found it was important to tuck the bacon ends under the shrimp so that the bacon would not curl back. One final, finishing touch was minced fresh chives, sprinkled on just before serving.

Broiled Bacon-Wrapped Shrimp

MAKES 21 TO 25 PIECES

4	slices bacon
1/4	teaspoon salt
1/8	teaspoon ground black pepper
	Pinch cayenne pepper
1	pound extra-large (21 to 25 per pound) shrimp, peeled and deveined (see the illustrations on page 39)
2	tablespoon minced fresh chives

1. Adjust an oven rack 6 inches from the broiler element and heat the broiler. Line a broiler-pan bottom with foil and top with the slotted broiler-pan top.

2. Slice each piece of bacon lengthwise into two, long thin strips, then cut each strip into three short pieces (you should have a total of 24 bacon pieces). Spread the bacon pieces out over 4 layers of paper towels on a microwave-safe plate, then cover with 2 more layers of paper towels. Microwave on high until the bacon fat begins to melt but the bacon is still pliable, 1 to 2 minutes.

3. Meanwhile, place the shrimp in a medium bowl. Sprinkle the salt, pepper, and cayenne over the shrimp and toss to coat.

4. Wrap a piece of the microwaved bacon around the center of each shrimp, and place on the broiler-pan top, pinning the bacon ends underneath the shrimp. Broil until the shrimp are pink and the edges of the bacon are brown, spinning around the broiler pan halfway through cooking, 3 to 4 minutes. Skewer the shrimp and bacon with toothpicks, transfer to a serving platter, and sprinkle with the chives. Serve immediately.

➤ VARIATION
Broiled Bacon-Wrapped Sea Scallops
When buying scallops, be sure to buy large sea scallops rather than the small bay scallops. Also make sure to remove and discard the side muscle attached to each scallop before using. (See the illustration below.)

Follow the recipe for Broiled Bacon-Wrapped Shrimp, substituting 24 large sea scallops (about 1 pound) for the shrimp.

REMOVING TENDONS FROM SCALLOPS

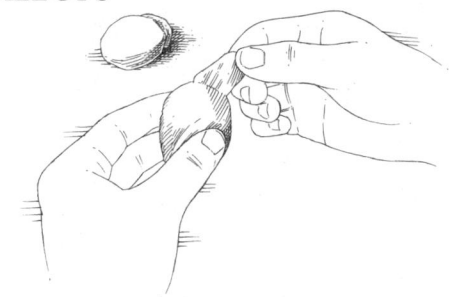

The small, rough-textured, crescent-shaped muscle that attaches the scallop to the shell toughens when cooked. Use your fingers to peel the tendon away from the side of each scallop before cooking.

2

SALADS

IS THERE A RIGHT WAY TO PREPARE A SALAD? We think so. After having eaten our share of soggy salads swimming in dressing or salads with unwashed leaves so gritty we needed a toothpick, we decided to take a look at this seemingly simple course. After all, preparing a salad needn't be difficult.

Most salads require no cooking at all, and, unlike other dishes, salads allow for a fair amount of improvisation. Supermarkets offer a wide variety of salad greens these days—a far cry from the shrink-wrapped globes of iceberg lettuce that once dominated the supermarket greens aisle. Salad greens like watercress can be substituted for arugula, which in turn can be substituted for dandelion greens or mizuna. Making salad can be creative, but some broad guidelines should be followed to achieve optimal results.

SHOP CAREFULLY

Most greens have a short shelf life, so it's especially important to buy greens that look healthy at the market. Greens with stems and roots will stay fresher longer and should be purchased when possible. Also look for any rot among bunches of greens as you shop. Decay can spread quickly, and it's best to avoid greens on which this process has already begun. If once you get the greens home you notice a few slimy leaves, pick them out immediately rather than waiting until you make a salad. If you wait, the rot may well spread throughout the bunch.

KEEP GREENS CRISP

Because they are mostly water, greens should be stored in the crisper drawer of the refrigerator, where the humidity is the highest. But while moist air will help prolong their freshness, excessive amounts of water won't. Therefore, don't wash lettuces until you are ready to use them, and drain off any standing water in bags of greens before refrigerating them.

WASH AND DRY THOROUGHLY

Because they grow in such close proximity to the ground, salad greens are often quite sandy. For information about cleaning salad greens, see page 85.

DON'T TEAR UNTIL READY TO EAT

While you can wash and dry whole leaves in advance, do not tear them until you are ready to dress the salad. Tearing the leaves leads to oxidation and browning in delicate greens. And don't take a knife to salad greens. The more violently they are cut, the quicker they will brown. Gentle tearing of large leaves by hand is best.

DRESS GREENS LIGHTLY

Nothing is worse than a limp, soggy salad with too much dressing. Dressed greens should just glisten, not shine. For our recommended ratios of salad greens to dressings, see pages 83 and 91.

SERVE IMMEDIATELY

Once a salad is dressed, the clock is ticking. Waiting even 15 minutes to eat the salad may cause some loss in freshness and crispness. The longer salad greens sit under a coating of dressing, the less appetizing they become, as the salt in the dressing draws moisture out of the greens and causes them to become limp.

We also offer salads made with vegetables, legumes, pasta, or grains that can serve as a side dish or light meal. Vegetable salads can be divided into two categories based on the dressing. Creamy salads dressed with mayonnaise, buttermilk, or yogurt, such as coleslaw, potato salad, and cucumber-yogurt salad, are perfect accompaniments to warm-weather meals because they can be refrigerated. A second type of vegetable salad is dressed with vinaigrette, such as bean salad and carrot salad. These dishes are generally best served at room temperature, when flavors are brightest. Also, unlike creamy mayonnaise-based salads, many vegetable salads that have been dressed with a vinaigrette should be served immediately. This is especially true of salads made with green vegetables, which will lose their bright color and become soggy rather quickly.

As for main course salads, you want to use enough protein to make the salad seem substantial without overwhelming the greens. Somewhere between 3 and 6 ounces of protein per person is best. When choosing greens for these salads, it's better not to use tender, soft lettuces. The greens must have enough crunch and flavor to stand up to the cooked protein, the vegetables, and the tangy dressings used in these salads. See our glossary on page 90 for more information on choosing heartier greens.

VINAIGRETTES

AFTER MAKING HUNDREDS OF VINAIGRETTES and tasting them straight and on salads, we've come to a few conclusions. First, a ratio of 4 parts oil to 1 part vinegar generally works best. A lower ratio of oil is preferred when the acidic component of the dressing is unusually mild (rice vinegar or lemon juice) or when the dressing is heavily flavored by another ingredient that needs a good kick (such as tomatoes). Second, because of its richer flavor, extra-virgin is the olive oil of choice for most vinaigrettes, the exception being dressings that have strong Asian flavors. Third, the most efficient way to combine vinaigrette ingredients is to shake them together in a jar with a sealed lid; no extra dishes or utensils need to be dirtied, the dressing can be quickly recombined with just a shake, and leftover dressing can be stored right in the jar. Most simple vinaigrettes have a lifespan of about a week in the refrigerator; those with added fresh ingredients such as raspberries or orange juice last about three days. Before being used, a refrigerated dressing should be brought to room temperature for 15 to 20 minutes and then shaken vigorously. Last, we find that ½ cup of dressing is ample to coat 2 quarts of loosely packed greens, which would serve about six people as a side salad. Our vinaigrette recipes make enough for two salads.

White Wine Vinaigrette
MAKES 1 CUP

See page 103 for our tasting of extra-virgin olive oil.

- ³/₄ cup extra-virgin olive oil
- 3 tablespoons white wine vinegar
- 2 teaspoons minced shallot or red onion

SCIENCE: Emulsion and Vinaigrette

Vinaigrette is a relatively thin emulsion made of oil, vinegar, and seasonings. Mayonnaise is a thick, creamy emulsion (see page 88 for information on the science of mayonnaise). An emulsion is a mixture of two things that don't ordinarily mix, such as oil and water, or oil and vinegar. The only way to mix them is to stir or whisk so strenuously that the two ingredients break down into tiny droplets. Many of these droplets will continue to find each other and re-coalesce into pure fluid. (This is what happens when the emulsion breaks.) Eventually, one of the fluids (usually the less plentiful one) will break into droplets so tiny that they remain separated, suspended in the other fluid, at least temporarily.

The liquid in droplet form makes up what is called the dispersed phase of the emulsion because the droplets are dispersed throughout; the liquid that surrounds the droplets makes up what is called the continuous phase. Because the continuous phase forms the surface of the emulsion, that's what the mouth and tongue feel and taste first. In a vinaigrette, the oil makes up the continuous phase and is tasted first, coating your tongue and thereby cushioning the impact of the acid.

- 1 medium garlic clove, minced or pressed through a garlic press (about 1 teaspoon)
- 1½ teaspoons minced fresh tarragon leaves or dill
- 2 teaspoons Dijon mustard (optional)
- ½ teaspoon salt
- ¼ teaspoon ground black pepper

Combine all of the dressing ingredients in a jar, seal the lid, and shake vigorously until emulsified, about 20 seconds. The vinaigrette can be refrigerated in the tightly sealed jar for up to 1 week.

Red Wine Vinaigrette
MAKES 1 CUP

See page 137 for our tasting of red wine vinegar.

- ³/₄ cup extra-virgin olive oil
- 3 tablespoons red wine vinegar
- 2 teaspoons minced shallot or red onion
- 1 medium garlic clove, minced or pressed through a garlic press (about 1 teaspoon)
- 1½ teaspoons minced fresh thyme leaves

2   teaspoons Dijon mustard (optional)
1/2   teaspoon salt
1/4   teaspoon ground black pepper

Combine all of the dressing ingredients in a jar, seal the lid, and shake vigorously until emulsified, about 20 seconds. The vinaigrette can be refrigerated in the tightly sealed jar for up to 1 week.

Balsamic Vinaigrette

MAKES 1 CUP

See page 110 for our tasting of balsamic vinegar.

3/4   cup extra-virgin olive oil
3   tablespoons balsamic vinegar
2   teaspoons minced shallot or red onion
1   small garlic clove, minced or pressed through a garlic press (about 1/2 teaspoon)
2   teaspoons Dijon mustard
1 1/2 teaspoons minced fresh oregano leaves
1/2   teaspoon salt
1/4   teaspoon ground black pepper

Combine all of the dressing ingredients in a jar, seal the lid, and shake vigorously until emulsified, about 20 seconds. The vinaigrette can be refrigerated in the tightly sealed jar for up to 1 week.

Raspberry Vinaigrette

MAKES 1 CUP

Raspberry vinegar can be found with other vinegars in well-stocked supermarkets or gourmet shops.

3/4   cup extra-virgin olive oil
3   tablespoons raspberry vinegar
1   tablespoon minced shallot or red onion
2   teaspoons minced fresh tarragon leaves
1/2   teaspoon salt
1/4   teaspoon sugar
1/4   teaspoon ground black pepper

Combine all of the dressing ingredients in a jar, seal the lid, and shake vigorously until emulsified, about 20 seconds. The vinaigrette can be refrigerated in the tightly sealed jar for up to 1 week.

Lemon-Shallot Vinaigrette

MAKES ABOUT 1 CUP

Grated parmesan lends richness to this dressing, but the cheese can be omitted for a lighter version.

3/4   cup extra-virgin olive oil
3   tablespoons juice from 1 lemon
1   medium garlic clove, minced or pressed through a garlic press (about 1 teaspoon)
1   large shallot, minced (about 4 tablespoons)
1 1/2 teaspoons minced fresh thyme leaves
2   teaspoons Dijon mustard
1/4   teaspoon salt
1/8   teaspoon ground black pepper
1/3   cup grated Parmesan cheese (optional)

Combine all of the dressing ingredients in a jar, seal the lid, and shake vigorously until emulsified, about 20 seconds. The vinaigrette can be refrigerated in the tightly sealed jar for up for 3 days.

JUICING LEMONS

Everyone seems to have a trick for juicing lemons. We find that this one extracts the most juice possible from lemons as well as limes.

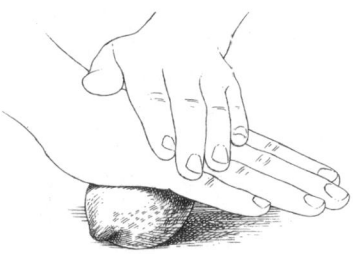

1. Roll the lemon on a hard surface, pressing down firmly with the palm of your hand to break the membranes inside the fruit.

2. Cut the lemon in half. Use a wooden reamer (preferably one with sharp ridges and a pointed tip) to extract the juice into a bowl. To catch the seeds and pulp, place a mesh strainer over the bowl.

Salad 101

CLEANING GREENS

Nothing ruins a salad faster than gritty leaves, so the first step in making any salad is cleaning the greens. (Unwashed greens should be carefully stowed away in the crisper with the rubber band or twist tie removed, as the constriction encourages rotting.) Our favorite way to wash small amounts of greens is in the bowl of a salad spinner; larger amounts require a sink. Make sure there is ample room to swish the leaves about and rid them of sand and dirt. The dirt will sink to the bottom. Exceptionally dirty greens (spinach and arugula often fall into this category) may take at least two changes of water. Do not run water directly from the faucet onto the greens as the force of the water can bruise them. When you are satisfied that the leaves are grit-free, lift them out of the water, leaving the dirt behind, and spin them dry in a salad spinner. Greens must be quite dry; otherwise, the vinaigrette will slide off and taste diluted. Here are some guidelines for washing and drying greens:

 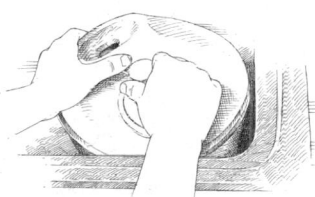

1. Using your hands, gently move the greens about under water to loosen grit, which should fall to the bottom of the salad spinner bowl. Lift the greens out of the water rather than pouring the water out of the bowl with the greens still inside.

2. If you own a crank-style salad spinner, place it in the corner of your sink. This increases your leverage by pushing the spinner into the floor and walls of the sink, thereby stabilizing it.

3. Line the salad spinner with paper towels, then layer in the greens, covering each layer with additional towels. In this manner, the greens will keep for at least 2 days.

4. To store greens for up to a week, loosely roll the greens in paper towels and then place the rolled greens inside a large zipper-lock bag and place in the refrigerator.

THE BEST SALAD SPINNERS

After testing eight salad spinners, we ended up with a two-way tie between spinners made by Zyliss and Oxo Good Grips. They both excelled at drying greens, though they had minor trade-offs: The Zyliss finished the task nominally faster, but the Oxo had a more ergonomic handle and a nonskid bottom, a big bonus. The design enhancements lifted the Oxo's price to $26, $5 more than the Zyliss.

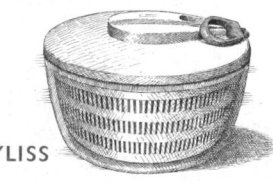 

ZYLISS   OXO

DRESSING AND TOSSING GREENS

We found that an ideal salad bowl is wide-mouthed and relatively shallow, so that the greens become evenly coated with vinaigrette quickly. A wide bowl also facilitates gentle handling of the greens. The bowl should be roughly 50 percent larger than the amount of greens to make sure there is adequate room for tossing. Whatever utensils you choose to toss the salad—wooden spoons, hands (our favorite method), or tongs—a light touch is crucial. A roughly tossed salad will wilt much faster than a lightly tossed salad. Here's how we dress and toss greens:

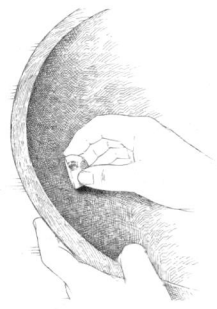 

1. Add mild garlic flavor. Peel and cut a clove of garlic. With the cut-side down, rub the interior of your salad bowl.

2. Measure the greens: Loosely pack the greens into a large measuring cup, figuring on 2 cups per serving.

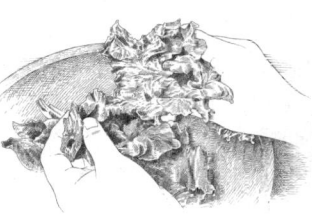 

3. Tear the greens: If the greens are too large, tear them gently into manageable pieces with your hands just before serving the salad. If torn ahead of time, they will discolor and wilt.

4. Shake the dressing: Just before adding the dressing, give it a quick shake to make sure that it is fully combined and that the solid ingredients, such as shallots, are evenly dispersed.

 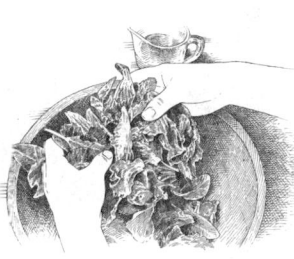

5. Drizzle the dressing: To prevent overdressed greens, add the dressing in small increments as you toss the salad.

6. Toss the salad: Coat the greens by gently "fluffing" them, adding more vinaigrette only when you are certain the greens need it.

Orange-Sesame Vinaigrette

MAKES ABOUT 1 CUP

This vinaigrette tastes best when made with a mildly flavored oil, such as vegetable. Any orange juice will work in this recipe, but we find fresh squeezed is worth the extra effort. The bright flavor of the orange juice will mellow quickly, so it is best to use this vinaigrette within 3 days. Dried ground ginger cannot be substituted for fresh.

1/2	cup vegetable oil
6	tablespoons orange juice
1	tablespoon red wine vinegar
2	teaspoons honey
4	scallions, sliced thin
1	teaspoon grated fresh ginger
4	teaspoons sesame seeds, toasted in a small dry skillet over medium heat until fragrant, about 4 minutes
1/2	teaspoon salt

Combine all of the dressing ingredients in a jar, seal the lid, and shake vigorously until emulsified, about 20 seconds. The vinaigrette can be refrigerated in the tightly sealed jar for up to 3 days.

Tomato-Basil Vinaigrette

MAKES ABOUT 2 CUPS

Depending on the ripeness of the tomatoes, the flavor of this dressing will dissipate sometime within 3 days.

3/4	cup extra-virgin olive oil
1/4	cup red wine vinegar
2	ripe tomatoes, cored, seeded, and minced
4	scallions, sliced thin
1	medium garlic clove, minced or pressed through a garlic press (about 1 teaspoon)
2	tablespoons minced fresh basil leaves
1	teaspoon salt
1	teaspoon ground black pepper

Combine all of the dressing ingredients in a jar, seal the lid, and shake vigorously until emulsified, about 20 seconds. The vinaigrette can be refrigerated in the tightly sealed jar for up to 3 days.

Honey-Dijon Vinaigrette

MAKES 1 1/4 CUPS

This sweet-and-sour dressing is thicker than our other vinaigrettes, but it should be poured in the same amounts, using 1/2 cup to coat 2 quarts of greens.

3/4	cup vegetable oil
3	tablespoons cider vinegar
2	tablespoons Dijon mustard
2	tablespoons honey
1	tablespoon poppy seeds (optional)
1/2	teaspoon salt
1/2	teaspoon ground black pepper

Combine all of the dressing ingredients in a jar, seal the lid, and shake vigorously until emulsified, about 20 seconds. The vinaigrette can be refrigerated in the tightly sealed jar for up to 1 week.

MINCING SHALLOTS

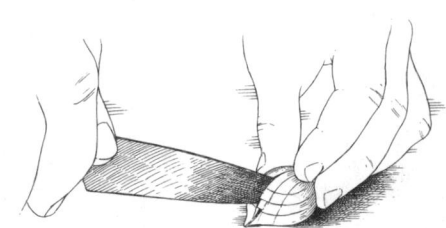

1. Place the peeled bulb flat-side down and make several slices parallel to the work surface, almost to (but not through) the root end. Then make a number of very closely spaced parallel cuts through the top of the shallot down to the work surface.

2. Finish the mincing by making very thin slices perpendicular to the lengthwise cuts.

Catalina Dressing

MAKES ABOUT 1 1/2 CUPS

This sweet and tangy dressing must be prepared at least 1 hour before serving to allow the flavors to develop completely.

2/3	cup vegetable oil
1/4	cup ketchup
1/4	cup sugar
1/4	cup white wine vinegar
1	tablespoon grated onion
1/4	teaspoon salt
1/2	teaspoon Worcestershire sauce
2–3	dashes hot pepper sauce

Combine all of the dressing ingredients in a jar, seal the lid, and shake vigorously until emulsified, about 20 seconds. The dressing can be refrigerated in the tightly sealed jar for up to 1 week.

CHOOSING VINEGAR AND OIL

ALL VINEGARS ARE NOT CREATED EQUAL. Some, like red and white wine vinegars, have a searingly high acidity of 5 to 7 percent. Lemon juice, in comparison, is milder, about 4 percent. And depending on age and quality, balsamic vinegars can have a wide range of acidity (the cheap stuff being nothing more than caramel-colored red wine vinegar). We adjust the ratio of oil to vinegar to suit the vinegar's strength; the oil mellows the acidity. Extra-virgin olive oil is our top choice for salads because it tastes good with all greens and vinegars. See the results of our tasting of extra-virgin olive oils on page 103, of red wine vinegars on page 137, and of balsamic vinegars on page 110.

FRUIT JUICE VINAIGRETTES

ALTHOUGH VINAIGRETTES ARE TRADITIONally made of oil and vinegar, we came across an interesting variation in our research—reduced fruit juice dressings, which are touted as a low-fat alternative to vinaigrettes. Fruit juices are simmered and reduced to a thick syrup before being mixed with the other ingredients, thus enabling the dressing to cling to the lettuce without using much oil. What excited us about these dressings was not the lack of fat but the potential for flavor. Oil tends to dilute fruit flavors; by replacing most of the oil in a vinaigrette with thick and syrupy reduced fruit juice, we were able retain the rich fruit flavor. Testing a few approaches, we found that nearly any fruit juice will work. In addition to the standard vinaigrette ingredients of herbs, shallots, and vinegar, a small dash of good extra-virgin olive oil is still necessary for well-rounded flavor.

Orange-Lime Dressing

MAKES 1 CUP

Any type of orange juice will work here, from fresh squeezed to reconstituted frozen concentrate.

2	cups orange juice
3	tablespoons juice from 2 to 3 limes
2	tablespoons extra-virgin olive oil
1	tablespoon honey
1	tablespoon minced shallot
1/2	teaspoon salt
1/2	teaspoon ground black pepper

1. Bring the orange juice to a boil in a small saucepan over medium-high heat. Reduce the heat to medium and simmer briskly until the juice is thick, syrupy, and measures 2/3 cup, 25 to 35 minutes. Transfer the orange juice syrup to a small bowl and refrigerate until cool, about 15 minutes. (The syrup can be refrigerated in a covered container for up to 2 days.)

2. Transfer the cooled orange juice to a jar and add the lime juice, olive oil, honey, shallot, salt, and pepper. Seal the lid and shake the mixture

vigorously until emulsified, about 20 seconds. The dressing can be refrigerated in the tightly sealed jar for up to 4 days.

➤ VARIATIONS

Pomegranate and Honey Dressing

Follow the recipe for Orange-Lime Dressing, substituting 2 cups pomegranate juice for the orange juice and 3 tablespoons red wine vinegar for the lime juice.

Ruby Red Grapefruit and Sesame Dressing

Follow the recipe for Orange-Lime Dressing, substituting 2 cups ruby red grapefruit juice for the orange juice and 3 tablespoons rice vinegar for the lime juice; add 1 tablespoon minced fresh cilantro leaves and 1 teaspoon toasted sesame seeds.

Apple Cider–Sage Dressing

Follow the recipe for Orange-Lime Dressing, substituting 2 cups apple cider for the orange juice and 3 tablespoons cider vinegar for the lime juice; add ½ teaspoon minced fresh sage leaves.

Pear-Rosemary Dressing

Follow the recipe for Orange-Lime Dressing, substituting 2 cups pear juice for the orange juice and 3 tablespoons lemon juice for the lime juice; add ¼ teaspoon minced fresh rosemary.

Cranberry-Balsamic Dressing

Follow the recipe for Orange-Lime Dressing, substituting 2 cups cranberry juice for the orange juice and 3 tablespoons balsamic vinegar for the lime juice; add 1 small garlic clove, minced, and 1 teaspoon minced fresh thyme leaves.

MAYONNAISE

MAYONNAISE IS USED TO DRESS VEGETABLE salads—especially potato salad and coleslaw. It acts as a creamy binder and adds richness to any salad. The science of mayonnaise is fairly complex and unusual. Whisking transforms three liquids—vegetable oil, lemon juice, and egg yolk—into a thick, creamy sauce known as an emulsion. In mayonnaise, the egg yolk and lemon juice are the continuous phase of the emulsion and the oil is the dispersed phase—that is, it's broken into tiny droplets; this is why mayonnaise, which is about 95 percent oil, doesn't taste greasy.

Mayonnaise works because an egg yolk is such a good emulsifier and stabilizer. But sometimes mayonnaise can "break," as the ingredients revert back to their original liquid form. To keep mayonnaise from breaking, it is first necessary to whisk the egg yolk and lemon juice thoroughly (the egg yolk itself contains liquid and fats that must be emulsified). It is equally important to add the oil slowly to the egg yolk, as a mere 2 tablespoons of yolk and lemon juice must be "stretched" around ¾ cup of oil.

We like the flavor of corn oil in our basic mayonnaise. It produces a dressing that is rich and eggy with good body. Canola oil makes a slightly lighter, more lemony mayo. We find that extra-virgin olive oil can be harsh and bitter, especially if used alone in mayonnaise. While pure olive oil produces a mellower mayonnaise, it costs more than corn or canola oil and does not deliver better results.

Although homemade mayonnaise is a delicious addition to salads, many cooks prefer the convenience and safety of commercial brands made without raw eggs. See our tasting of commercial brands of mayonnaise on page 89.

Mayonnaise

MAKES ABOUT ¾ CUP

Each time you add oil, make sure to whisk until it is thoroughly incorporated. It's fine to stop for a rest or to measure the next addition of oil. If the mayonnaise appears grainy or beaded after the last addition of oil, continue to whisk until smooth.

I	large egg yolk
¼	teaspoon salt
¼	teaspoon Dijon mustard
I½	teaspoons juice from I lemon
I	teaspoon white wine vinegar
¾	cup corn oil

1. Whisk the egg yolk vigorously in a medium bowl for 15 seconds. Add all of the remaining ingredients except for the oil and whisk until the yolk thickens and the color brightens, about 30 seconds.

2. Add ¼ cup of the oil in a slow, steady stream, continuing to whisk vigorously until the oil is incorporated completely and the mixture thickens, about 1 minute. Add another ¼ cup oil in the same manner, whisking until incorporated completely, about 30 seconds more. Add the remaining ¼ cup oil all at once and whisk until incorporated completely, about 30 seconds more. Serve. (The mayonnaise can be refrigerated in an airtight container for several days.)

➤ VARIATIONS
Lemon Mayonnaise
Follow the recipe for Mayonnaise, adding 1½ teaspoons grated lemon zest along with the lemon juice.

Dijon Mayonnaise
Follow the recipe for Mayonnaise, whisking an additional 2 tablespoons Dijon mustard into the finished mayonnaise.

Tarragon Mayonnaise
Follow the recipe for Mayonnaise, stirring 1 tablespoon minced fresh tarragon leaves into the finished mayonnaise.

Food Processor Mayonnaise
MAKES ABOUT 1½ CUPS
Use 1 whole large egg and double the quantities of the other ingredients in the recipe for Mayonnaise. Pulse all of the ingredients except the oil in a food processor three or four times to combine. With the machine running, add the oil through the feed tube in a thin, steady stream until incorporated completely.

INGREDIENTS: Mayonnaise

Although we love homemade mayonnaise on occasion, we realize that it's not always convenient to whip up a batch, so we set up a tasting of seven nationally available brands of commercially prepared mayonnaise along with Kraft Miracle Whip. Even though the U.S. Food and Drug Administration does not recognize Miracle Whip as a real mayonnaise, we included it in our tasting because of its resounding popularity. Why is Miracle Whip considered a salad dressing and not a mayonnaise? The FDA defines mayonnaise as an emulsified semisolid food that is at least 65 percent vegetable oil by weight, is at least 2.5 percent acidifying ingredient (vinegar and/or lemon juice) by weight, and contains whole eggs or egg yolks. Miracle Whip, which is also sweeter than regular mayo, weighs in with only 40 percent soybean oil. (Water makes up the difference.)

A good mayonnaise will have a clear egg flavor and a touch of acidity to offset the significant amount of fat from the oil. Our tasters liked Hellmann's Real Mayonnaise for having that balance, and Kraft Real Mayonnaise was thought to be "flavorful but not overpowering." Which one should you buy? We recommend Hellmann's, but the difference between the two contenders is not overwhelming.

Finally, is it possible for a light mayo to be as flavorful as the full-fat original? We put five brands to the test: Kraft Light Mayonnaise, Hellmann's Light Mayonnaise, Miracle Whip Light Salad Dressing, Spectrum Light Canola Mayonnaise, and Nayonaise (a soy-based sandwich spread), all with a fat content of 3 to 5 grams per serving. To see if our tasters could tell the difference, we also threw the winner of the full-fat tasting into the mix (Hellmann's Real Mayonnaise, 11 grams of fat per serving).

The results? Last place went to Nayonaise. Tasters were unanimous in thinking it bore no resemblance to mayonnaise. Miracle Whip and Spectrum didn't fare much better. Tasters thought Kraft was too sweet. Hellmann's Light came in second place, very nearly beating out the winner, Hellmann's Real Mayonnaise. Although the light version had a pastier texture than regular Hellmann's, the bright, balanced flavors were similar.

THE BEST COMMERCIAL MAYONNAISE

Hellmann's (left), which is known as Best Foods west of the Rockies, took top honors in our tasting. Among the five brands of reduced-fat mayonnaise tested, Hellmann's Light (right) was the clear winner and rated nearly as well as its full-fat cousin.

INGREDIENTS: Salad Greens

The following glossary starts with the four main varieties of lettuce and then covers the most commonly available specialty greens (called mesclun or mesclun mix when sold in combination). When substituting one green for another, try to choose greens with a similar intensity. For example, peppery arugula could be used as a substitute for watercress or dandelion greens, but not for red leaf lettuce, at least not without significantly altering the flavor of the salad.

Main Varieties of Lettuce

BUTTERHEAD LETTUCES Boston and Bibb are among the most common varieties of these very mild-tasting lettuces. A head of butterhead lettuce has a nice round shape and loose outer leaves. The color of the leaves is light to medium green (except, of course, in red-tinged varieties), and the leaves are extremely tender.

ICEBERG LETTUCE Iceberg is the best-known variety of crisphead lettuce. Its shape is perfectly round, and the leaves are tightly packed. A high water content makes iceberg especially crisp and crunchy but also robs it of flavor.

LOOSELEAF LETTUCES Red leaf, green leaf, red oak-leaf, and lolla rossa are the most common varieties. These lettuces grow in a loose rosette shape, not a tight head. The ruffled leaves are perhaps the most versatile because their texture is soft yet still crunchy and their flavor is mild but not bland.

ROMAINE LETTUCE The leaves on this lettuce are long and broad at the top. The color shades from dark green in the outer leaves (which are often tough and should be discarded) to pale green in the thick, crisp heart. Also called Cos lettuce, this variety has more crunch than either butterhead or looseleaf lettuces and a more pronounced earthy flavor. Romaine lettuce is essential in Caesar salad, where the greens must stand up to a thick, creamy dressing.

Specialty Greens

ARUGULA Also called rocket, these tender, dark green leaves can be faintly peppery or downright spicy. Larger, older leaves tend to be hotter than small, young leaves, but the flavor is variable, so taste arugula before adding it to a salad. Try to buy arugula in bunches with the stems and roots still attached—they help keep the leaves fresh. Arugula bruises and discolors quite easily. If possible, keep stemmed leaves whole. Very large leaves can be torn just before they are needed.

BELGIAN ENDIVE With its characteristic bitter chicory flavor, endive is generally used sparingly in salads. Endive is crisp and crunchy, not tender and leafy. The yellow leaf tips are usually mild in flavor, while the white, thick leaf bases are more bitter. Endive is the one salad green we routinely cut rather than tear. Remove whole leaves from the head and then slice them crosswise into bite-size pieces.

CHICORY Also known as curly endive, chicory has curly, jagged leaves that form a loose head. The leaves are bright green, and their flavor is usually fairly bitter. The outer leaves can be tough, especially at the base. Inner leaves are generally more tender.

DANDELION GREENS Dandelion greens are tender and pleasantly bitter. The leaves are long and have ragged edges. The flavor is similar to that of arugula or watercress, both of which can be used interchangeably with dandelion greens. Tougher, older leaves that are more than several inches long should be cooked, not eaten raw.

ESCAROLE The smooth, broad leaves of escarole are bunched together in a loose head. With its long ribs and softly ruffled leaves, it looks a bit like leaf lettuce. As a member of the chicory family, escarole can have an intense flavor, although not nearly as strong as that of endive or chicory.

MIZUNA This Japanese spider mustard has long, thin, dark green leaves with deeply cut, jagged edges. Sturdier than arugula, watercress, or dandelion greens, it can nonetheless be used interchangeably with these slightly milder greens in salads when a strong peppery punch is desired. Note that larger, older leaves are better cooked, so choose small "baby" mizuna for salads.

RADICCHIO This most familiar chicory was almost unknown in this country two decades ago. The tight heads of purple leaves streaked with prominent white ribs are now a supermarket staple. Radicchio has a decent punch but is not nearly as bitter as other chicories, especially Belgian endive.

SPINACH Of all the cooking greens, spinach is the most versatile in salads because it can be used in its miniature or full-grown form. Flat-leaf spinach is better than curly spinach in salads because the stems are usually less fibrous and the spade-shaped leaves are thinner, more tender, and sweeter. Curly spinach is often dry and chewy, while flat-leaf, sold in bundles rather than in cellophane bags, is usually tender and moist, more like lettuce than a cooking green.

TATSOI This Asian green has thin white stalks and round, dark green leaves. A member of the cruciferous family of vegetables that includes broccoli and cabbage, tatsoi tastes like a mild Chinese cabbage, especially bok choy. However, the texture of these miniature leaves is always delicate.

WATERCRESS With its small leaves and long stalks, watercress is easy to spot. It requires some patience in the kitchen because the stalks are really quite tough and must be removed one at a time. Like arugula, watercress usually has a mildly spicy flavor.

CREAMY SALAD DRESSINGS

AFTER MANY TRIALS, WE DISCOVERED THAT the key to a well-rounded, creamy dressing—one that didn't taste dull, fatty, or overly tangy—is to use a trio of dairy ingredients: buttermilk, sour cream, and mayonnaise. Whenever we tried to eliminate any one of them for the sake of convenience, tasters complained of a seriously compromised flavor, except for those that were aggressively flavored, such as Creamy Garlic Dressing and Thousand Island Dressing. We realize that buttermilk isn't often on hand in some households, so we tried substituting either cream or milk. Neither tasted as good as buttermilk; however, milk was an acceptable substitute though it produced a lighter, milder dressing (cream made the dressing heavy and dull). We also noted that lowfat mayonnaise and nonfat sour cream produced less flavorful but acceptable results. Nonfat mayonnaise, however, turned the dressings unbearably sweet and should be avoided. Last, we noted that ½ cup creamy dressing coats 2 quarts of loosely packed greens, which would serve about six people as a side salad. The exception to this is the thicker Blue Cheese Dressing, which uses 1¼ cups per 2 quarts greens.

Blue Cheese Dressing

MAKES 2½ CUPS

Use a generous 1¼ cups of this thick and creamy dressing to coat 2 to 3 quarts of salad, and be sure to use sturdy greens such as romaine, green leaf, or iceberg lettuce, which remain crisp under the weight of the dressing. We also like to pair this recipe with the Buffalo Wings on page 69.

6	ounces blue cheese, crumbled (about 1½ cups)
1	medium garlic clove, minced or pressed through a garlic press (about 1 teaspoon)
½	cup plus 2 tablespoons buttermilk
½	cup plus 2 tablespoons sour cream
6	tablespoons mayonnaise
2	tablespoons white wine vinegar
½	teaspoon sugar
½	teaspoon salt
½	teaspoon ground black pepper

1. Using a fork, mash the blue cheese, garlic, and buttermilk together in a small bowl until the mixture resembles cottage cheese with small curds.

2. Stir in the sour cream, mayonnaise, vinegar, sugar, salt, and pepper until combined. The dressing can be refrigerated in an airtight container for up to 4 days.

Creamy Garlic Dressing

MAKES 1½ CUPS

Substitute mayonnaise for the sour cream, if you have none on hand. This creamy, assertive dressing is delicious tossed with bitter greens. And because this dressing is made with tangy sour cream, we prefer the less fruity flavor of regular olive oil instead of extra-virgin.

¾	cup olive oil
6	tablespoons sour cream
1	tablespoon white wine vinegar
3	tablespoons juice from 1 lemon
4	teaspoons Dijon mustard
3	medium garlic cloves, minced or pressed through a garlic press (about 1 tablespoon)
½	teaspoon salt
½	teaspoon ground black pepper

Combine all of the dressing ingredients in a jar, seal the lid, and shake vigorously until emulsified, about 20 seconds. The dressing can be refrigerated in the tightly sealed jar for up to 4 days.

Ranch Dressing

MAKES 1½ CUPS

This salad dressing also makes a good dip for crudités.

½	cup buttermilk
½	cup mayonnaise
6	tablespoons sour cream
1	tablespoon minced shallot or red onion
1	tablespoon minced fresh parsley leaves
1	tablespoon minced fresh cilantro leaves or dill
1	medium garlic clove, minced or pressed through a garlic press (about 1 teaspoon)
1	teaspoon juice from 1 lemon
	Pinch sugar

¹/₂	teaspoon salt
¹/₄	teaspoon ground black pepper

Stir all of the ingredients together until smooth. The dressing can be refrigerated in a tightly sealed container for up to 4 days.

Thousand Island Dressing

MAKES 1 ¹/₂ CUPS

Do not be tempted to use sweet relish in place of the chopped sweet pickles—the resulting flavor will be muddy and overpowering.

1	cup mayonnaise
¹/₄	cup chili sauce
¹/₂	cup minced sweet pickles
4	green olives with pimentos, minced
1	medium garlic clove, minced or pressed through a garlic press (about 1 teaspoon)
2	tablespoons minced fresh parsley leaves
2	teaspoons juice from 1 lemon
¹/₂	teaspoon salt
¹/₄	teaspoon ground black pepper
1	tablespoon water

Stir all of the ingredients together until smooth. The dressing can be refrigerated in an airtight container for up to 4 days.

Green Goddess Dressing

MAKES 1 ¹/₂ CUPS

This dressing is named for the beautiful pale green hue and vibrant herbaceous flavor that can be achieved only by pureeing a trio of tender-leafed fresh herbs. The parsley and chives are essential, but, if you prefer, you can substitute basil or dill for the tarragon.

¹/₂	cup mayonnaise
¹/₂	cup buttermilk
6	tablespoons sour cream
1	medium garlic clove, minced or pressed through a garlic press (about 1 teaspoon)
¹/₂	cup minced fresh parsley leaves
¹/₄	cup minced fresh chives
3	tablespoons minced fresh tarragon leaves

1	tablespoon juice from 1 lemon
¹/₂	teaspoon salt
¹/₂	teaspoon ground black pepper

14 WAYS TO GUSSY UP GREEN SALADS

IT'S EASY TO FALL INTO A SALAD RUT. Tomatoes and cucumber (yawn!) are obvious additions to any leafy salad. But if you open the fridge or pantry, you probably have the makings of a more exciting—yet still simple—salad. Break out of the salad doldrums with these easy, interesting additions to any green salad.

- Crumbled bacon, halved cherry tomatoes, and diced avocado
- Thinly sliced prosciutto, halved red grapes, and toasted pine nuts
- Diced salami, diced provolone, and minced sun-dried tomatoes
- Flaked canned tuna, diced hard-boiled egg, and sliced scallions
- Shredded carrots, raisins, and sunflower seeds
- Canned black beans, thawed frozen corn, and chopped, jarred roasted red peppers
- Canned chickpeas or white beans, crumbled feta cheese, and fresh mint leaves
- Canned artichoke hearts, kalamata olives, and grated Asiago cheese
- Sliced, roasted (or canned) beets, toasted walnuts, and crumbled goat cheese
- Diced jícama, sectioned oranges, and toasted pumpkin seeds
- Sliced green apple, diced cheddar cheese, and dried cranberries or cherries
- Sliced pear, shaved fennel, and shaved Parmesan cheese
- Sectioned ruby red grapefruit, crumbled feta cheese, and torn mint or basil leaves
- Fresh raspberries, crumbled goat cheese, and toasted sliced almonds

Process all of the ingredients together in a blender or food processor until smooth, about 20 seconds. The dressing can be refrigerated in an airtight container for up to 4 days.

CROUTONS

HOMEMADE CROUTONS TASTE FAR SUPERIOR to any you can purchase at the supermarket, and they are an easy way to add flavor and texture to a boring salad. We found that nearly any type of bread will make a good crouton, from stale pieces of baguette to the end slices of a sandwich loaf. After tasting croutons side by side, we determined that good croutons follow these basic rules: (1) the bread is cut into uniformly sized pieces (about ½-inch cubes), (2) the bread is tossed with olive oil that has been laced with garlic, spices, or herbs, and (3) they are baked in a 350-degree oven until golden. We made croutons with melted butter, vegetable oil, olive oil, and extra-virgin olive oil and generally preferred the flavor and storability of croutons made with regular olive oil. Each of the following recipes makes enough for at least two salads; any leftovers will keep in an airtight container or zipper-lock bag for about one week.

Garlic Croutons

MAKES 4 CUPS

Toss croutons into salad or into soup for some welcome crunch.

- 3 tablespoons olive oil
- 2 medium garlic cloves, minced or pressed through a garlic press (about 2 teaspoons)
- ¼ teaspoon salt
- 4 cups (½-inch) bread cubes

Adjust an oven rack to the center position and heat the oven to 350 degrees. Whisk the oil, garlic, and salt together in a large bowl. Add the bread and toss until thoroughly coated. Spread the bread on a baking sheet and bake until golden brown, 15 to 20 minutes. Allow croutons to cool to room temperature before serving.

➤ VARIATIONS

Chili-Garlic Croutons

Follow the recipe for Garlic Croutons, whisking 1 teaspoon chili powder, ¼ teaspoon ground black pepper, and ⅛ teaspoon cayenne into the oil with the garlic and salt.

Warm-Spiced Croutons

Follow the recipe for Garlic Croutons, omitting the garlic and whisking ½ teaspoon ground cumin, ½ teaspoon ground coriander, ¼ teaspoon paprika, and ⅛ teaspoon cayenne into the oil with the salt.

Herb and Garlic Croutons

Follow the recipe for Garlic Croutons, whisking 2 teaspoons minced fresh (or ½ teaspoon dried) rosemary, 2 teaspoons minced fresh (or ½ teaspoon dried) thyme leaves, sage leaves, or dill, and ¼ teaspoon ground black pepper, into the oil with the garlic and salt.

Parmesan-Garlic Croutons

Follow the recipe for Garlic Croutons, increasing the amount of oil to 6 tablespoons and tossing 2 ounces grated Parmesan cheese (about 1 cup) with the oil and bread before baking.

INSALATA MISTA

USED AS A PALATE CLEANSER AND DIGESTIVE aid, an insalata mista (Italian green salad) is usually spicy and robust, containing several varieties of greens dressed with a small amount of simple vinaigrette. To re-create this type of salad at home, we found it easiest to group lettuce types into three groups: mild, spicy, and bitter. Because of its even balance of mild greens and spicy and bitter greens, the salad is refreshingly vigorous without being overly harsh.

Unlike the bottles of "Italian" dressing sold at the supermarket, an authentic dressing for an insalata mista should be simple and fresh. Most recipes contain only extra-virgin olive oil, red wine vinegar, and salt, but we liked the sweet, complex addition of balsamic vinegar as well. By using a 4:1 ratio of oil to vinegar, we were able to make a dressing with good balance and flavor.

Insalata Mista

SERVES 4 TO 6

Any number of vegetables can be used to garnish the salad, depending on what is in season. Carrot, cucumber, and red onion are always available, adding nice color and contrasting texture to the greens.

1½	teaspoons red wine vinegar
1½	teaspoons balsamic vinegar
⅛	teaspoon salt
4	tablespoons extra-virgin olive oil
4	cups mild greens (Boston, Bibb, green leaf, red oak leaf, or baby romaine), washed and dried and torn into bite-size pieces
2	cups spicy greens (arugula or watercress), washed, dried, and stemmed
2	cups bitter greens (radicchio or endive) washed and dried and torn into bite-size pieces
1	medium carrot, peeled and shredded on the large holes of a box grater
½	cucumber (cut whole cucumber in half lengthwise), peeled, seeded (see illustration 1 on page 113), and cut into ⅛-inch slices
¼	medium red onion, sliced very thin

1. Whisk the vinegars and salt together in a small bowl. Whisk in the oil until the mixture is smooth.

2. Place the greens, carrot, cucumber, and red onion in a large bowl. Drizzle with the dressing and toss gently. Serve immediately.

GREEK SALAD

MOST PIZZA-PARLOR VERSIONS OF GREEK salad consist of iceberg lettuce, chunks of green pepper, and a few pale wedges of tomato, sparsely dotted with cubes of feta and garnished with one forlorn olive of questionable domain. The accompanying dressing is loaded with musty dried herbs. We set out to make this pizzeria staple worthy of the dinner table.

We started by testing different vinaigrette recipes, with ingredients ranging from cider vinegar and lemon juice to yogurt and mustard. Tasters thought that the yogurt-based dressing overwhelmed the salad and that the mustard and cider vinegar versions were just "wrong." Lemon juice was harsh and distilled white vinegar was dull, but a dressing that combined lemon juice and red wine vinegar had the balanced flavor we were looking for. There was no place for dried herbs in this salad. Fresh herbs typically used in Greek cuisine include dill, oregano, parsley, mint, and basil. Tasters loved the idea of mint and parsley, but they lost their zip when mixed with the vinaigrette. Oregano's bold flavor stood up well to the vinegar and lemon juice and was the clear favorite. Pure olive oil and extra-virgin olive oil worked equally well, and the addition of a small amount of garlic gave the dressing the final kick it needed.

The next ingredients up for scrutiny were the vegetables. Although lettuce is not commonly found in traditional Greek salad, it is a main ingredient in the American version. The iceberg lettuce had to go. Romaine, which has the body and crunch of iceberg but also more color and flavor, was the natural choice. Tomatoes were also essential, and only the ripest ones would do. Green bell pepper got a unanimous thumbs down. Everyone preferred the sweeter red variety, which was improved even further by being roasted. In the interest of saving time, we also tried jarred roasted red peppers, which tasters liked even better. The jarred peppers are packaged in a vinegary brine and have more depth of flavor than freshly roasted peppers.

Onion was next. When the pungency of the raw onion sent some tasters running for breath mints, someone suggested soaking the onion in water to eliminate its caustic bite. We took that idea one step further: Why not marinate the onion in the vinaigrette? On a whim, we included some cucumber as well. The results were striking. The cucumber, which had been watery and bland just minutes before, was bright and flavorful, and the onion had lost its unpleasant potency.

Now the vinaigrette recipe was finalized and the vegetables selected, but something was still missing. We returned to the mint and parsley that had been eliminated from the vinaigrette. Instead, we simply mixed them with the vegetables, tossed this mixture together with the onion and cucumber marinating in the vinaigrette, generously sprinkled the salad with feta and kalamata olives, and offered it all to tasters. It was a hit. This was a Greek salad worthy of being served on china—not in an aluminum takeout container.

Greek Salad

SERVES 6 TO 8

Marinating the onion and cucumber in the vinaigrette tones down the onion's harshness and flavors the cucumber. For efficiency, prepare the other salad ingredients while the onion and cucumber marinate. Use a salad spinner to dry the lettuce thoroughly after washing; any water left clinging to the leaves will dilute the dressing.

VINAIGRETTE

3	tablespoons red wine vinegar
1½	teaspoons juice from 1 lemon
2	teaspoons minced fresh oregano leaves
½	teaspoon salt
⅛	teaspoon ground black pepper
1	medium garlic clove, minced or pressed through a garlic press (about 1 teaspoon)
6	tablespoons olive oil

SALAD

½	medium red onion, sliced thin
1	medium cucumber, peeled, halved lengthwise, seeded (see illustration 1 on page 113), and cut into ⅛-inch-thick slices
2	romaine hearts, washed, dried thoroughly, and torn into 1½-inch pieces
2	medium ripe tomatoes, cored, seeded, and cut into 12 wedges
¼	cup loosely packed torn fresh parsley leaves
¼	cup loosely packed torn fresh mint leaves
6	ounces jarred roasted red peppers, cut into 2 by ½-inch strips (about 1 cup)
20	large kalamata olives, each olive pitted and quartered lengthwise
5	ounces feta cheese, crumbled (1¼ cups)

1. FOR THE VINAIGRETTE: Whisk all of the ingredients together in a large bowl until combined.

2. FOR THE SALAD: Add the onion and cucumber to the vinaigrette and toss; let stand to blend the flavors, about 20 minutes. Add the romaine, tomatoes, peppers, parsley, and mint to the bowl with the onion and cucumber; toss to coat with the dressing.

3. Transfer the salad to a wide, shallow serving bowl or platter; sprinkle the olives and feta over the salad. Serve immediately.

VARIATION
Country-Style Greek Salad
This salad, made without lettuce, is served throughout Greece, where it is known as country or peasant salad. It is excellent with garden-ripe summer tomatoes.

Follow the recipe for Greek Salad, reducing the red wine vinegar to 1½ tablespoons and the lemon juice to 1 teaspoon. Omit the romaine and use 2 medium cucumbers, peeled, halved lengthwise, seeded, and cut into ⅛-inch-thick slices (about 4 cups), and 6 medium tomatoes (about 2 pounds), each tomato cored, seeded, and cut into 12 wedges.

WILTED SPINACH SALADS

MANY COOKS CONSIDER WILTED SPINACH salad—in which a warm, fragrant dressing gently wilts fresh spinach leaves—to be a restaurant indulgence. While these elegant salads are surprisingly easy to make at home, there are potential problems. After sampling several recipes in the test kitchen, tasters concurred that these salads can disappoint in two major ways: with greasy, dull-tasting dressings and with spinach reduced to mush in puddles of dressing as deep as a fish pond.

The first hurdle—having to wash, dry, and trim mature curly spinach—was easily overcome. Kitchen tests determined that prewashed, bagged baby spinach works well in this salad, as it is both more tender and sweet than the mature variety.

Next, we wanted to identify the best type of oil to use in these salads. Though dressings made with pure olive oil were fine—use it if that's what you have on hand—the flavor nuances of extra-virgin oil gave the dressings more depth and dimension.

When it came to the acidic component, tasters favored fresh lemon juice for its bright, tangy flavor. We discovered that dressings in which the lemon juice was added early and heated through lacked brightness. The punch was restored when we swirled in the lemon juice after the oil and other ingredients had been heated.

We also tested the ratio of oil to acid. The ratio we use for most vinaigrettes, 4 parts oil to 1 part acid, produced greasy dressings. Mindful that we didn't want too much oil overpowering the tender spinach, we scaled back the ratio to 3 parts oil to 1 part acid. A little extra acid made the dressings sharp and fresh tasting.

Several of us in the test kitchen had in the past encountered wilted salads swimming in dressing, which gave the greens a decidedly drowned, slimy texture. After tasting salads tossed with various quantities of dressing, our tasters settled on just ¼ cup of dressing for 6 cups of greens. The ¼ cup coated the greens generously yet allowed them to retain enough structural integrity to leave these wilted salads with a slight but satisfying crunch. Serve these salads without delay to enjoy the best of their singular texture.

Wilted Spinach Salad with Goat Cheese, Olives, and Lemon Vinaigrette

SERVES 4

If you prefer, use feta in place of the goat cheese.

5	ounces baby spinach (about 6 cups loosely packed), washed and dried
3	tablespoons extra-virgin olive oil
1	medium shallot, minced (about 3 tablespoons)
1	medium garlic clove, minced or pressed through a garlic press (about 1 teaspoon)
1	teaspoon minced fresh oregano leaves
¼	teaspoon salt
⅛	teaspoon ground black pepper
⅛	teaspoon sugar
1	tablespoon juice from 1 lemon
2	ounces goat cheese, cut into small chunks
6	black olives, sliced thin

Place the spinach in a large bowl. Cook the oil, shallot, garlic, oregano, salt, pepper, and sugar in a small skillet over medium heat until the shallot is slightly softened, 2 to 3 minutes. Add the lemon juice and swirl to incorporate. Pour the warm dressing over the spinach, add the cheese and olives, and toss gently with tongs to wilt. Serve immediately.

➤ VARIATIONS

Wilted Spinach Salad with Oranges, Radishes, and Citrus Vinaigrette

See the illustrations on page 117 for tips on segmenting the oranges.

Follow the recipe for Wilted Spinach Salad with Goat Cheese, Olives, and Lemon Vinaigrette, substituting ¼ teaspoon grated orange zest for the oregano. After pouring the warm dressing over the spinach, replace the cheese and olives with 2 medium seedless oranges, divided into segments, and ⅓ cup grated radishes (about 4 medium).

Wilted Spinach Salad with Bacon Dressing

We prefer thick-cut bacon for the dressing, finding that it offers more presence and textural interest than thin-cut. (Slab bacon can also be used, but it fries up chewy, not crisp.) The easiest way to achieve substantial, uniform pieces (and avoid tiny Baco-style bacon bits) is to cut the strips before frying them rather than crumbling them afterward. This salad comes together quickly, so have the ingredients ready before you begin cooking. When adding the vinegar mixture to the skillet, step back from the stovetop—the aroma is quite potent.

6	ounces baby spinach (about 7 cups loosely packed), washed and dried
3	tablespoons cider vinegar
½	teaspoon sugar
¼	teaspoon ground black pepper
	Pinch salt
10	ounces (about 8 slices) thick-cut bacon, cut into ½-inch pieces
½	medium red onion, chopped

1   small garlic clove, minced or pressed through a
     garlic press (about ¹/₂ teaspoon)

3   Hard-Cooked Eggs (page 44), peeled and
     quartered lengthwise

1. Place the spinach in a large bowl. Stir the vinegar, sugar, pepper, and salt together in a small bowl until the sugar dissolves; set aside.

2. Fry the bacon in a medium skillet over medium-high heat, stirring occasionally, until crisp, about 10 minutes. Using a slotted spoon, transfer the bacon to a paper towel–lined plate. Pour the bacon fat into a heatproof bowl, then return 3 tablespoons bacon fat to the skillet. Add the onion to the skillet and cook over medium heat, stirring frequently, until slightly softened, about 3 minutes. Stir in the garlic and cook until fragrant, about 15 seconds. Add the vinegar mixture, then remove the skillet from the heat. Working quickly, scrape the bottom of the skillet with a wooden spoon to loosen the browned bits. Pour the hot dressing over the spinach, add the bacon, and toss gently with tongs until the spinach is slightly wilted. Divide the salad among individual plates, arrange the egg quarters over each, and serve immediately.

BLUE CHEESE SALADS

LIKE A WELL-SPOKEN DINNER GUEST, BLUE cheese is intense, complex, and sophisticated. But pair the life of the party with a dull companion (tender lettuce leaves) and the dinner magic all but disappears. Yet the reward of a properly executed blue cheese salad—a rich, interesting appetizer—makes the proposition worth investigating.

Blue cheese runs the gamut from mild to potent and creamy to crumbly. To see if all types were appropriate for salad, we assembled a half-dozen recipes, each made with a different supermarket blue cheese. Salty, crumbly Danish blue and middle-of-the-road generic cheeses simply labeled "blue" (sold crumbled and in wedge form) were compared with cheeses with stronger flavors or creamier textures—Gorgonzola (sweet and smooth), Stilton (salty and nutty), and Roquefort (tangy and sweet). While all of the cheeses were perfectly acceptable, our tasting panel favored the pungent, somewhat spicy Roquefort. Regardless of variety, blue cheese should be refrigerated wrapped in either plastic wrap or cheese paper (change the wrapping each time you use some cheese) and served at room temperature.

The trick to including blue cheese in a salad, we found, is to have a free hand when introducing a wide range of other flavors and textures; strong cheese really shines when tasted with sweet, tart, bitter, and crunchy ingredients. A good shot of vinegar lent necessary tartness to the dressing, and a spoonful of honey performed double duty, both tempering the acidity of the vinegar and highlighting the saltiness of the cheese. As for the greens, tasters particularly liked bitter radicchio and peppery arugula mixed with milder lettuces. Sweetness and crimson tones come from dried fruit (cherries), fresh fruit (apple), or beets. Good teeth-sinking texture comes by way of crunchy chopped toasted nuts, fresh celery slices, or a flurry of fried shallots. With balanced, flavorful salad recipes at the ready, guess who's coming to dinner?

Salad with Fennel, Dried Cherries, Walnuts, and Roquefort

SERVES 6

This salad and those that follow call for Roquefort, a type of blue cheese that is rich and creamy, with an assertive but not overpowering blue cheese flavor. If you prefer to use a very mild and mellow blue cheese, we recommend Danish blue; if you prefer a sharp and piquant one, try Stilton.

2   teaspoons honey

3   tablespoons red wine vinegar

¹/₂ cup dried sweetened cherries or cranberries

3   tablespoons extra-virgin olive oil
     Salt and ground black pepper

1   small fennel bulb (about 12 ounces), trimmed
     of stalks, cored, and sliced very thin (see the
     illustrations on page 118); fronds chopped
     coarse

1 small head red or green leaf lettuce, washed, dried, and torn into bite-size pieces (about 7 cups loosely packed)

1 small head radicchio, quartered, cored, and cut crosswise into $\frac{1}{8}$-inch-wide strips (about 3 cups loosely packed)

$\frac{1}{2}$ cup chopped walnuts, toasted in a medium dry skillet over medium heat until fragrant, about 4 minutes

6 ounces Roquefort, crumbled (about 1$\frac{1}{2}$ cups)

1. Whisk the honey and vinegar in a medium microwave-safe bowl; stir in the cherries. Cover with plastic wrap, cut several steam vents in the plastic, and microwave on high until the cherries are plump, about 1 minute. Whisk in the oil, $\frac{1}{4}$ teaspoon salt, and $\frac{1}{8}$ teaspoon pepper; while the mixture is still warm, add the sliced fennel (reserving the fronds) and toss to combine. Let cool to room temperature.

2. Toss the lettuce, radicchio, fennel fronds, and dried cherry/fennel mixture in a large bowl; adjust seasonings with salt and pepper. Divide the salad among individual plates; top each with a portion of nuts, Roquefort, and any dried cherries remaining in the bowl. Serve immediately.

Salad with Roquefort, Avocado, Tomatoes, and Bacon
SERVES 6

5 slices bacon (about 5 ounces), cut crosswise into $\frac{1}{2}$-inch strips

3 tablespoons red wine vinegar

3 tablespoons extra-virgin olive oil
Salt and ground black pepper

$\frac{1}{2}$ pint cherry tomatoes, halved

1 ripe Hass avocado, cut into $\frac{1}{4}$-inch dice (see the illustrations on page 65)

1 small bunch arugula, washed, dried, stemmed, and torn into bite-size pieces (about 3 cups loosely packed)

1 medium head butterhead lettuce, washed, dried, and torn into bite-size pieces (about 6 cups loosely packed)

3 medium scallions, green parts only, sliced thin

6 ounces Roquefort, crumbled (about 1$\frac{1}{2}$ cups)

1. Fry the bacon in a small skillet over medium heat until browned and crisp, about 8 minutes; transfer with a slotted spoon to a paper towel–lined plate and set aside.

2. Whisk the vinegar, oil, $\frac{1}{4}$ teaspoon salt, and $\frac{1}{8}$ teaspoon pepper in a small bowl until combined.

3. In a medium bowl, toss the tomatoes and avocado with 1 tablespoon of the vinaigrette; set aside 5 minutes.

4. Toss the arugula, lettuce, and remaining vinaigrette in a large bowl; adjust seasonings with salt and pepper. Divide the greens among individual plates; top each with a portion of tomato-avocado mixture, then sprinkle with a portion of bacon, scallions, and Roquefort. Serve immediately.

Salad with Roasted Beets, Fried Shallots, and Roquefort
SERVES 6
Use paper towels to rub the skins from the cooked and cooled beets.

3 small or 2 medium beets (about 12 ounces), washed and trimmed of root tips and stems

6 tablespoons extra-virgin olive oil

2 tablespoons sherry vinegar

2 teaspoons honey
Salt and ground black pepper

3 medium shallots, sliced thin and separated into thin rings

2 tablespoons unbleached all-purpose flour

1 large bunch arugula, washed, dried, stemmed, and torn into bite-size pieces (about 6 cups loosely packed)

1 medium head butterhead lettuce, washed, dried, and torn into bite-size pieces (about 6 cups loosely packed)

6 ounces Roquefort, crumbled (about 1$\frac{1}{2}$ cups)

1. Adjust an oven rack to the lower-middle position; heat the oven to 400 degrees. Wrap each beet in foil and bake until a paring knife can be inserted and removed with little resistance, 50 to 60 minutes. Unwrap the beets; when cool enough to handle, peel and cut the beets into $\frac{1}{4}$-inch-thick wedges and place in a medium bowl.

2. Whisk 3 tablespoons of the oil, the vinegar, honey, ¼ teaspoon salt, and ⅛ teaspoon pepper in a small bowl until combined. Add 1 tablespoon of the vinaigrette to the beets, season the beets to taste with salt and pepper, and toss to combine.

3. While the beets are roasting, toss the shallots with ¼ teaspoon salt, ⅛ teaspoon pepper, and the flour in a medium bowl. Heat the remaining 5 tablespoons oil in a 12-inch nonstick skillet over medium-high heat until smoking; add the shallots and cook, stirring frequently, until golden and crisp, about 5 minutes. Using a slotted spoon, transfer the shallots to a plate lined with a triple layer of paper towels.

4. Toss the arugula, lettuce, and remaining vinaigrette in a large bowl; adjust seasonings with salt and pepper. Divide greens among individual plates; top each with a portion of beets, fried shallots, and Roquefort. Serve immediately.

Salad with Apple, Celery, Hazelnuts, and Roquefort
SERVES 6

Blanched slivered almonds can be substituted for hazelnuts.

I	tablespoon honey
3	tablespoons cider vinegar
3	tablespoons extra-virgin olive oil
¼	teaspoon salt
⅛	teaspoon ground black pepper
I	sweet red apple, such as Braeburn or Fuji, cored and sliced very thin (about 2 cups)
2	medium celery ribs, sliced very thin on the bias (about 1¼ cups)
I	medium head red or green leaf lettuce, washed, dried, and torn into bite-size pieces (about 9 cups)
¼	cup loosely packed torn fresh parsley leaves
½	cup hazelnuts, toasted in a medium dry skillet over medium heat until fragrant, about 4 minutes, then skinned and chopped fine
6	ounces Roquefort, crumbled (about 1½ cups)

CORING APPLES

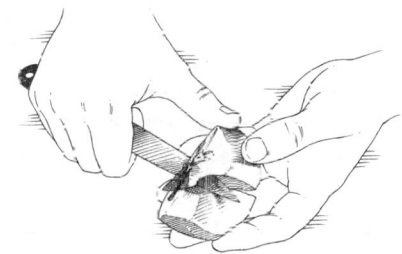

1. Remove the peel (we prefer a paring knife, but you may use a vegetable peeler), then quarter the apple through the stem end. The core can now be removed from each quarter. However, the direction you cut is very important. We find that when we start at the stem end, the quarters often break.

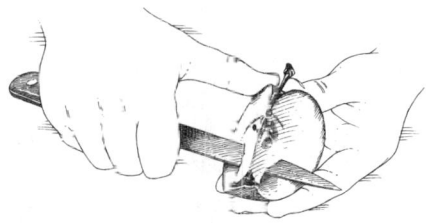

2. Instead, start removing the core at the blossom end. The cored quarter can now be sliced as needed.

1. Whisk the honey, vinegar, oil, salt, and pepper in a small bowl until combined. In a medium bowl, toss the apple and celery with 2 tablespoons of the vinaigrette; let stand 5 minutes.

2. Toss the lettuce, parsley, and remaining vinaigrette in a large bowl; adjust seasonings with salt and pepper. Divide the greens among individual plates; top each with a portion of the apple-celery mixture, nuts, and Roquefort. Serve immediately.

Arugula and Escarole Salad with Roquefort, Figs, and Warm Port Dressing
SERVES 6

⅓	cup port
½	teaspoon sugar
4	ounces dried figs (6 large or 12 small), stems removed
2	tablespoons balsamic vinegar

2 medium shallots, minced, or ¼ cup minced red onion

¼ teaspoon salt

¼ teaspoon ground black pepper

¼ cup extra-virgin olive oil

2 small bunches arugula, washed, dried, stemmed, and torn into bite-size pieces (about 6 cups loosely packed)

I medium head escarole, washed, dried, and torn into bite-size pieces (about 6 cups loosely packed)

4 ounces Roquefort, crumbled (about I cup)

1. Bring the port, sugar, and figs to a boil in a medium saucepan over high heat. Cover the pan, reduce the heat to low, and simmer until the figs are very soft but not mushy, about 15 minutes. Reserving the liquid in the pan, remove the figs with a slotted spoon and, when cool enough to handle, quarter and set them aside.

2. Whisk the vinegar, shallots, salt, and pepper into the port; gradually whisk in the oil. Return the figs to the dressing and reheat over medium heat, stirring occasionally, until warm but not steaming.

3. Toss the greens with the warm dressing to coat in a large mixing bowl. Divide the dressed greens among individual plates and sprinkle each with a portion of Roquefort. Serve immediately.

BAKED GOAT CHEESE SALADS

WARM GOAT CHEESE SALAD HAS BEEN A FIX-ture on restaurant menus for years, featuring artisanal cheeses, organic baby field greens, barrel-aged vinegars, and imported oils. Marketing being what it is, the jargon is often more intriguing than the execution: tepid, crumb-dusted cheese on overdressed designer greens at a price that defies reason. When we've tried to prepare this salad at home, the results have been equally disappointing, albeit less expensive. We usually end up with flavorless warm cheese melted onto the greens. What we wanted was quite different: creamy cheese rounds infused with flavor and surrounded

SLICING GOAT CHEESE

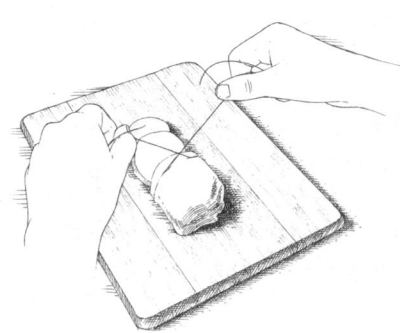

A knife quickly becomes covered with goat cheese, making it difficult to cut clean, neat slices. A piece of dental floss makes much neater cuts. Just slide an 18-inch length of floss under the log of goat cheese, cross the ends of the floss above the cheese, and pull the floss through the cheese to make slices at ⅓-inch intervals.

by crisp, golden breading, all cradled in lightly dressed greens.

Coating and heating the cheese is clearly the major challenge of this recipe. Techniques uncovered in the recipes we researched included pan-frying, broiling, and baking. We began by coating portions of goat cheese in herbs (thyme and chives), then dipping the goat cheese rounds in beaten egg (with a little Dijon mustard added for bite), and finally fresh bread crumbs (the most common option for coating).

We first tried pan-frying the rounds of cheese (the most common option in cookbook recipes and the classic restaurant technique). Although the bread crumbs crisped up nicely after a short stay in the hot oil, there was also a problem: The interior of the cheese rounds began to melt while the first side was browning, which made turning the disks a nightmare. Nevertheless, we continued to pursue this method, chilling the rounds in the refrigerator for 30 minutes before they hit the oil, which we hoped would prevent the centers from overheating before the crust had crisped, but this, too, failed. One recipe suggested broiling the goat cheese rounds, but the rounds simply melted under the intense heat of the broiler.

It was time to try baking. Baking the cheese at temperatures ranging from 300 to 400 degrees for four to seven minutes resulted in pallid, soggy crusts across the board, with varying degrees of unpleasant melting. Curious whether higher temperatures would yield the crust we were searching for, we turned the oven up to 475 degrees and ended up with goat cheese fondue.

Logic (or stubbornness) had persuaded us that higher temperatures had the potential to produce a crisp crust, but reality had shown that we needed a more durable breading. Then we hit upon the idea of using Melba toasts—perhaps these extremely dry (and extremely hard) crackers would work. We pulverized them, dunked the cheese in beaten egg, and then coated the rounds in the sandy crumbs. Appearing to fuse with the egg, the Melba crumbs formed a cohesive, shell-like barrier in the oven. Finally, our crust was crisp, although there still was some oozing of the cheese.

Theorizing that if the oven were blistering hot and the cheese arctic cold we would get a crisp crust and no oozing cheese, we placed our goat cheese rounds in the freezer for 30 minutes rather than the refrigerator. Baking our "frozen" cheese at 475 degrees for seven minutes, we struck gold. Although a few kitchen naysayers found the Melba crust a bit dry, a quick brush of olive oil onto the exterior of the breaded and chilled rounds solved this problem.

It was time to add the baked goat cheese rounds to a salad. Most tasters preferred a mix of heartier greens, such as arugula and frisée, and all tasters preferred a classic vinaigrette, as this dressing echoed and complemented the flavors of the goat cheese rounds. Given the fat in the cheese,

we found that it's important to dress the greens lightly. Hundreds of goat cheese rounds later, we had developed an easy if unorthodox recipe that could give any bistro a run for its money.

Herbed Baked Goat Cheese
MAKES 12 ROUNDS (FOR SIX SALADS)
The baked goat cheese should be served warm. Prepare the salad while the cheese is in the freezer, then toss the greens and vinaigrette while the cheese cools a bit after baking.

3	ounces white Melba toasts
1	teaspoon ground black pepper
3	large eggs
2	tablespoons Dijon mustard
1	tablespoon chopped fresh thyme leaves
1	tablespoon chopped fresh chives
12	ounces firm goat cheese
	Extra-virgin olive oil

1. In a food processor, process the Melba toasts to fine, even crumbs, about 1½ minutes; transfer the crumbs to a medium bowl (you should have 2 cups of crumbs). Stir in the pepper. Whisk the eggs and mustard in another medium bowl until combined. Combine the thyme and chives in a small bowl.

2. Using dental floss or kitchen twine, divide the cheese into 12 equal pieces (see the illustration on page 100). Roll each piece of cheese into a ball; roll each ball in the combined fresh herbs to coat lightly. Transfer 6 pieces to the egg mixture, turn each piece to coat; transfer to the Melba crumbs and turn each piece to coat, pressing the crumbs into the cheese. Flatten each ball gently with your fingertips into a disk about 1½ inches wide and 1 inch thick and set on a baking sheet. Repeat with the remaining 6 pieces of cheese. Transfer the baking sheet to the freezer and chill the rounds until firm, about 30 minutes. (The cheese rounds can be wrapped tightly in plastic wrap and frozen for up to 1 week.) Adjust an oven rack to the uppermost position; heat the oven to 475 degrees.

3. Remove the cheese from the freezer and brush the tops and sides evenly with olive oil. Bake until the crumbs are golden brown and the cheese is slightly soft, 7 to 9 minutes (or 9 to

GETTING THE CHEESE RIGHT

PAN-FRIED   BAKED AT 350°   BAKED AT 475°

Pan-fried goat cheese develops a crisp crust, but it's very tricky to turn the rounds over without crushing the melting interior and causing the cheese to ooze out. Goat cheese coated with bread crumbs and baked in a 350-degree oven is soggy and pale. Goat cheese coated with ground Melba toasts, partially frozen, and baked at 475 degrees is crisp, it doesn't ooze, and it maintains its shape. It has all the benefits of pan-frying with none of the disadvantages.

12 minutes if the cheese was completely frozen). Using a thin metal spatula, transfer the cheese to a paper towel–lined plate and cool 3 minutes before serving with the salad.

Salad with Herbed Baked Goat Cheese, Apples, Walnuts, and Dried Cherries
SERVES 6

1	cup dried cherries
2	medium Granny Smith apples
2	tablespoons cider vinegar
1	tablespoon Dijon mustard
1	teaspoon finely minced shallot
1/4	teaspoon salt
1/4	teaspoon sugar
6	tablespoons extra-virgin olive oil
	Ground black pepper
18	ounces mixed hearty greens (about 14 cups loosely packed), washed and dried
1/2	cup walnuts, chopped coarse and toasted in a medium dry skillet over medium heat until fragrant, about 4 minutes
1	recipe Herbed Baked Goat Cheese

1. Plump the cherries in ½ cup hot water in a small bowl, about 10 minutes; drain. Quarter and core the apples and cut into ⅛-inch-thick slices.

2. Combine the vinegar, mustard, shallot, salt, and sugar in a small bowl. Whisking constantly, drizzle in the oil; season to taste with pepper. Place the greens in a large bowl, drizzle the vinaigrette over them, and toss to coat. Divide the greens among individual plates; divide the cherries, apples, and walnuts among the plates, and place 2 rounds of goat cheese on each salad. Serve immediately.

Salad with Herbed Baked Goat Cheese and Vinaigrette
SERVES 6

2	tablespoons red wine vinegar
1	tablespoon Dijon mustard
1	teaspoon finely minced shallot
1/4	teaspoon salt
6	tablespoons extra-virgin olive oil
	Ground black pepper
18	ounces mixed hearty greens (about 14 cups loosely packed), washed and dried
1	recipe Herbed Baked Goat Cheese

1. Combine the vinegar, mustard, shallot, and salt in a small bowl. Whisking constantly, drizzle in the olive oil; season with pepper to taste. Set aside.

2. Place the greens in a large bowl, drizzle the vinaigrette over them, and toss to coat. Divide the greens among individual plates; place 2 rounds of goat cheese on each salad. Serve immediately.

FANCY FIRST-COURSE SALADS

ALTHOUGH THERE ARE MANY SALADS IN this book that could be termed "fancy first course," these are our favorites. They are a little more work than your typical mixed green salad, so it's best to enjoy them on their own as a first course—you don't want any other dishes trying to steal the limelight. Think of them as an easy way to give a celebratory meal an upscale touch.

- Arugula and Escarole Salad with Roquefort, Figs, and Warm Port Dressing (page 99)
- Wilted Spinach Salad with Bacon Dressing (page 96)
- Wilted Spinach Salad with Oranges, Radishes, and Citrus Vinaigrette (page 96)
- Salad with Herbed Baked Goat Cheese, Apples, Walnuts, and Dried Cherries (this page)
- Romaine and Roasted Pear Salad with Fennel and Lemon-Mint Vinaigrette (page 105)
- Sweet-and-Sour Cabbage Salad with Apple and Fennel (page 123)

INGREDIENTS: Supermarket Extra-Virgin Olive Oils

When you purchase an artisanal oil in a high-end shop, certain informational perks are expected (and paid for). These typically include written explanations of the character and nuances of the particular oil as well as the assistance of knowledgeable staff. But in a supermarket, it's just you and a price tag (usually $8 to $10 per liter). How do you know which supermarket extra-virgin olive oil best suits your needs? To provide some guidance, we decided to hold a blind tasting of the nine best-selling extra-virgin olive oils typically available in American supermarkets.

The label extra-virgin denotes the highest quality of olive oil, with the most delicate and prized flavor. (The three other grades are virgin, pure, and olive pomace. Pure oil, often labeled simply olive oil, is the most commonly available.) To be tagged as extra-virgin, an oil must meet three basic criteria. First, it must contain less than 1 percent oleic free fatty acids per 100 grams of oil. Second, the oil must not have been treated with any solvents or heat. (Heat is used to reduce strong acidity in some nonvirgin olive oils to make them palatable. This is where the term cold-pressed comes into play meaning that the olives are pressed into a paste using mechanical wheels or hammers and are then kneaded to separate the oil from the fruit.) Third, it must pass taste and aroma standards as defined by groups such as the International Olive Oil Council (IOOC), a Madrid-based intergovernmental olive oil regulatory committee that sets the bar for its member countries.

Tasting extra-virgin olive oil is much like tasting wine. The flavors of these oils range from citrusy to herbal, musty to floral with every possibility in between. And what one taster finds particularly attractive—a slight briny flavor, for example—another might find unappealing. Also like wine, the flavor of a particular brand of olive oil can change from year to year, depending on the quality of the harvest and the olives' place of origin.

We chose to taste extra-virgin olive oil in its most pure and unadulterated state: raw. Tasters were given the option of sampling the oil from a spoon or on neutral-flavored French bread and were asked to eat a slice of green apple—for its acidity—to cleanse the palate between oils. The olive oils were evaluated for color, clarity, viscosity, bouquet, depth of flavor, and lingering of flavor.

Whereas in a typical tasting we are able to identify a clear winner and loser, in this case we could not. In fact, the panel seemed to quickly divide itself into those who liked a gutsy olive oil with bold flavor and those who preferred a milder, more mellow approach. Nonetheless, in both camps one oil clearly had more of a following than any other—the all-Italian-olive Da Vinci brand. Praised for its rounded and buttery flavor, it was the only olive oil we tasted that seemed to garner across-the-board approval with olive oil experts and in-house staff alike. Tasters in the mild and delicate camp gave high scores to Pompeian and Whole Foods oils. Among tasters who preferred full-bodied, bold oils, Colavita and Filippo Berio also earned high marks.

THE BEST ALL-PURPOSE OLIVE OIL
Da Vinci Extra-Virgin Olive Oil was the favorite in our tasting of leading supermarket brands. It was described as "very ripe," "buttery," and "complex."

THE BEST MILD OIL
Pompeian Extra-Virgin Olive Oil was the favorite among tasters who preferred a milder, more delicate oil. It was described as "clean," "round," and "sunny."

THE BEST FULL-BODIED OIL
Colavita Extra-Virgin Olive Oil was the favorite among tasters who preferred a bolder, more full-bodied oil. It was described as "heavy," "complex," and "briny."

ROASTED PEAR SALADS

PEARS ARE THE PERFECT WINTER FRUIT—AND an ideal ingredient for a winter salad. Even hard and unfragrant specimens have the capacity to become juicy and butterscotch-brown after a brief spell in a blazing oven. Add them to bitter greens with some sharp cheese, and you have an impressive salad to either dress up a buffet table or serve as a side dish with a light meal.

Our parameters for a simple roasted pear salad were elementary: The roasted pears should be crisp yet tender, sweet but not syrupy, and caramel-colored on both sides. But which type of pear would beget the best roasting results? After roasting one batch each of Anjou, Bartlett, and Bosc (chosen for their availability during the winter), we were torn between Anjou (delicate pear flavor with a grainy texture and good bite) and Bartlett (soft texture with a floral pear essence); the big loser was Bosc (mealy, dry, and flat tasting).

Determining that either Bartlett or Anjou could be used, we turned to the question of slicing. Too thin a slice and the pear wouldn't hold up to the roasting process, but if cut too thickly, the pear would be awkward to bite into, especially in a salad. We found our solution with a thickness of about ⅓ inch, or roughly five slices per half.

Next we tossed the thinly sliced, raw pears with various brews of fats, oils, wines, and broths and roasted them for 20 minutes at 425 degrees. Butter bestowed the highest glories on the pears, but their flavor and color were still slack. We

upped the oven temperature to 500 degrees, decreased the roasting time by five minutes, and turned the pears two-thirds of the way through roasting (at halfway through, the pears hadn't browned enough on the first side). To help draw out their untapped sweetness, we sprinkled some sugar onto the butter-coated pears prior to roasting. Not only were these roasted pears sweet and juicy, but, with the help of sugar to accelerate the caramelization process, they positively glistened.

❧

Roasted Pears

The pears can be roasted up to 3 hours before serving, but keep them at room temperature; refrigeration adversely affects their texture. See below for illustrations of coring the pears.

4	firm Anjou or Bartlett pears (about 2 pounds)
1	tablespoon unsalted butter, melted
2	tablespoons sugar

1. Adjust an oven rack to the lower-middle position, place a baking sheet or broiler pan bottom on the rack, and heat the oven to 500 degrees.

2. Peel and halve each pear lengthwise. With a melon baller, remove the core (see the illustrations below). Set each half cut-side down and slice lengthwise into fifths.

3. Toss the pears with the butter; add the sugar and toss again to combine. Spread the pears in a single layer on the preheated baking sheet, making sure each

CORING PEARS

Pears are best halved, from stem to blossom end, and then cored. We like to use a melon baller for the task.

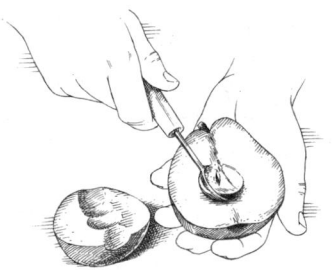  

1. Use a melon baller to cut around the central core with a circular motion.

2. Draw the melon baller from the central core to the top of the pear, removing the interior portion of the stem as you go.

3. Use the melon baller to remove the blossom end as well.

slice lies flat. Roast until browned on the bottom, about 10 minutes. Flip each slice and roast until tender and deep golden brown, about 5 minutes longer. Let the pears cool while preparing the salad.

Pear and Beet Salad with Watercress and Blue Cheese

SERVES 4 TO 6

This salad is great served with warm pears. Roast the pears immediately after the beets and toss them into the salad while still warm.

3	small or 2 medium beets (about 12 ounces)
1½	tablespoons extra-virgin olive oil
1	teaspoon red wine vinegar
½	teaspoon salt
	Ground black pepper
4	ounces blue cheese, crumbled (about 1 cup)
2	medium bunches watercress, washed, dried, and stemmed (about 6 cups loosely packed)
1	recipe Roasted Pears

1. Adjust an oven rack to the lower-middle position; heat the oven to 350 degrees. Wrap each beet in foil and roast until a fork can be inserted and removed with little resistance, 1 to 1½ hours; unwrap the beets. When cool enough to handle, peel and cut the beets lengthwise into quarters; cut each quarter in half into wedges.

2. Whisk together the oil, vinegar, salt, and pepper to taste in a small bowl.

3. Combine the beets, blue cheese, and watercress in a large serving bowl. Add the pears and vinaigrette; toss gently to combine. Serve immediately.

Romaine and Roasted Pear Salad with Fennel and Lemon-Mint Vinaigrette

SERVES 4 TO 6

1½	tablespoons extra-virgin olive oil
1	tablespoon minced fresh mint leaves
1	teaspoon grated zest and 1½ tablespoons juice from 1 lemon
½	teaspoon salt

	Ground black pepper
1	head romaine lettuce, washed, dried, and torn into bite-size pieces (about 8 cups loosely packed)
1	small fennel bulb (about 12 ounces), trimmed of stalks, cored, and sliced very thin (see the illustrations on page 118)
1	recipe Roasted Pears

1. Whisk together the oil, mint, lemon zest and juice, salt, and pepper to taste in a small bowl.

2. Combine the romaine and fennel in a large serving bowl. Add the vinaigrette and toss gently to combine; scatter the pears on top. Serve immediately.

Arugula and Roasted Pear Salad with Walnuts and Parmesan Cheese

SERVES 4 TO 6

Hazelnuts can be substituted for the walnuts in this salad.

VINAIGRETTE

1½	tablespoons extra-virgin olive oil
2	teaspoons white wine vinegar
½	teaspoon salt
	Ground black pepper

SALAD

2	small bunches arugula, washed, dried, stemmed, and torn into bite-size pieces (about 6 cups loosely packed)
4	ounces Parmesan cheese, shaved with a vegetable peeler (see the illustration on page 109)
1	recipe Roasted Pears
1	cup walnuts, chopped coarse and toasted in a small dry skillet over medium heat until fragrant, about 4 minutes

1. Whisk the oil, vinegar, salt, and pepper to taste together in a small bowl.

2. Combine the arugula and cheese in a large serving bowl. Add the vinaigrette and pears and toss gently to combine; sprinkle with the chopped walnuts. Serve immediately.

ORANGE SALADS

WITH THEIR SWEET JUICE, ORANGES CAN turn a simple salad into something special. Unfortunately, they often sink to the bottom of the bowl. And when you try to remix the salad, the greens bruise and the oranges fall apart. In addition, their abundant juice dilutes the dressing.

We started our testing by trying to determine the best way to cut the oranges so that they would retain their shape. The winning method turned out to be cutting the oranges pole to pole, removing the center pith, cutting each half in thirds (pole to pole), and then finishing with ¼-inch slices cut crosswise.

For the dressing, our first thought was to make a quick vinaigrette, using the juice from the oranges along with the standard ingredients of mustard, oil, salt, and pepper, but the result was too sweet. More acidity was needed, and the addition of lime juice, rather than lemon juice, did the trick. But when we tasted the dressing on the salad, we found it had became diluted. What to do? Make a bold vinaigrette using only lime juice—no orange juice, as the oranges would release some juice into the dressing no matter what. We did find, though, that letting the cut oranges sit in a fine-mesh strainer while we prepared the other ingredients relieved them of excess juice.

For the salad ingredients, we found that small amounts of greens (or no greens at all) worked best, keeping the oranges in the forefront. As for the oranges falling to the bottom of the bowl while the salad is tossed, our advice is, don't try to fight gravity. Toss the salad as little as possible and then plate individual portions, evenly distributing the oranges and other weightier ingredients that remain at the bottom of the bowl.

Orange, Avocado, and Watercress Salad
SERVES 4

Be sure to use a Hass avocado, which has a dark green pebbly skin.

1½	cups prepared oranges (see the illustrations below) from 3 medium oranges
1	teaspoon grated fresh ginger
¼	teaspoon Dijon mustard
1	tablespoon juice from 1 lime
	Pinch cayenne
1	tablespoon finely chopped fresh mint leaves
	Salt
3	tablespoons vegetable oil
¼	small red onion, sliced very thin
1	medium Hass avocado, ripe but firm
1	small bunch watercress, washed, dried, stemmed, and cut into 2-inch pieces (about 2½ cups loosely packed)

1. Place the orange pieces in a nonreactive mesh strainer set over a bowl; let stand to drain excess juice. Meanwhile, whisk the ginger, mustard, lime juice, cayenne, mint, and ⅛ teaspoon salt in a large bowl until combined. Whisking constantly, gradually add the oil. Toss the onion in the dressing and set aside.

2. Halve and pit the avocado; cut each half lengthwise to form quarters. Using a paring knife,

CUTTING ORANGES

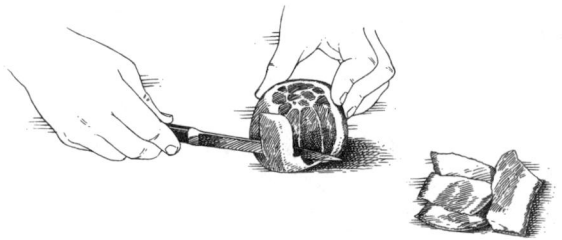

1. Cut a thin slice from the top and bottom of the orange, stand it on end, and slice away the rind and white pith.

2. Cut the orange in half from end to end, remove the stringy pith, cut each half into three wedges, and cut crosswise into ¼-inch pieces.

slice the flesh of each quarter (do not cut through the skin) lengthwise into fifths. Using a soup spoon, carefully scoop the flesh out of the skin and fan the slices from each quarter onto the perimeter of individual plates; season the avocado lightly with salt.

3. Add the oranges to the bowl with the onions; toss to coat. Add the watercress and toss gently. Lift out the watercress and divide among individual plates, mounding it in the center; place a portion of the orange pieces and onions on top of the watercress. Drizzle any dressing in the bowl over the avocado. Serve immediately.

Orange-Jícama Salad with Sweet-and-Spicy Peppers
SERVES 4

If you're not a fan of cilantro, substitute an equal amount of parsley.

1½	cups prepared oranges (see the illustrations on the facing page) from 3 medium oranges
3	tablespoons juice from 2 to 3 limes
¼	teaspoon Dijon mustard
½	teaspoon ground cumin, toasted in a small dry skillet until fragrant, about 30 seconds Salt
4	tablespoons vegetable oil
1	medium jícama (about 1 pound), peeled and cut into 2-inch-long matchsticks
1	medium red bell pepper, cored, seeded, and cut into ⅛-inch-wide strips
2	medium jalapeño chiles, cored, seeded, and quartered lengthwise, then cut crosswise into ⅛-inch-thick slices
½	cup loosely packed fresh cilantro leaves, chopped coarse
3	medium scallions, green parts sliced thin on the bias

1. Place the orange pieces in a nonreactive mesh strainer set over a bowl; let stand to drain excess juice. Meanwhile, whisk the lime juice, mustard, cumin, and ¼ teaspoon salt in a large bowl until combined. Whisking constantly, gradually add the oil.

2. Toss the jícama and red bell pepper with ⅛ teaspoon salt in a medium bowl until combined.

Add the jícama mixture, oranges, jalapeños, cilantro, and scallions to the bowl with the dressing and toss well to combine. Divide among individual plates, drizzle with any dressing in the bowl, and serve immediately.

Orange and Radish Salad with Arugula
SERVES 4

1½	cups prepared oranges (see the illustrations on the facing page) from 3 medium oranges
5	teaspoons juice from 1 to 2 limes
¼	teaspoon Dijon mustard
½	teaspoon ground coriander, toasted in a small dry skillet until fragrant, about 30 seconds
⅛	teaspoon salt Ground black pepper
3	tablespoons vegetable oil
5	radishes, quartered lengthwise and cut crosswise into ⅓-inch-thick slices (about 1⅓ cups)
1	medium bunch baby arugula (about 4 cups loosely packed)

REFRESHING WINTER SALADS

THE FRESH CRUNCH OF SALAD IS synonymous with summer, but it's in the winter when tired palates really need a wake-up call. Try these citrusy salads the next time you think you'll never be able to eat another spoonful of soup or serving of stew.

- Orange-Jícama Salad with Sweet-and-Spicy Peppers (this page)
- Fennel, Orange, and Olive Salad (page 119)
- Orange and Radish Salad with Arugula (this page)
- Fennel and Tangerine Salad (page 119)
- Orange, Avocado, and Watercress Salad (facing page)

1. Place the orange pieces in a nonreactive mesh strainer set over a bowl; let stand to drain excess juice. Meanwhile, whisk the lime juice, mustard, coriander, salt, and pepper to taste in a large bowl until combined. Whisking constantly, gradually add the oil.

2. Add the oranges, radishes, and arugula to the bowl and toss gently to combine. Divide the arugula among individual plates, place a portion of oranges and radishes over the arugula on each plate, and drizzle with any dressing in the bowl; serve immediately.

TOMATO SALADS

TOMATOES ARE THE BASIS FOR COUNTLESS summer salads. A bonus of summer tomato salads is that the mildly acidic juices from the tomatoes themselves provide a delicious base for a dressing, so little additional acid is needed. To make this work, you need to extract a little of the juice from the tomatoes before you make the salad. This is easily done. Simply cutting the tomatoes into wedges and letting them sit for 15 minutes allows them to exude their juices. Salting the cut tomatoes helps this process and seasons the tomatoes and their juices at the same time.

Some cooks recommend peeling the tomatoes, but we find the skin on local vine-ripened tomatoes to be thin and unobtrusive. If home-grown or locally grown tomatoes are unavailable, substitute halved cherry tomatoes.

Tomato Salad with Canned Tuna, Capers, and Black Olives

SERVES 6

Oil-packed tuna is more consistent with the Mediterranean flavors, but you can use water-packed tuna if you prefer. See page 154 for information about buying oil-packed tuna.

4–5	medium ripe tomatoes
1/2	teaspoon salt
3	tablespoons extra-virgin olive oil
1	tablespoon juice from 1 lemon
3	tablespoons capers, chopped
12	large black olives, such as kalamata or another brine-cured variety, pitted and chopped
1/4	cup finely chopped red onion
2	tablespoons chopped fresh parsley leaves
	Ground black pepper
1	(6-ounce) can tuna, drained

1. Core and halve the tomatoes lengthwise, then cut each half into 4 or 5 wedges. Toss the wedges with the salt in a large bowl; let rest until a small pool of liquid accumulates, 15 to 20 minutes.

2. Meanwhile, whisk the oil, lemon juice, capers, olives, onion, parsley, and pepper to taste

8 GREAT SUMMER SALADS

WHETHER YOU GET YOUR FRUITS AND vegetables from your own overflowing garden or a stand at the farmers market, we offer a variety of ways to enjoy summer's bounty. Salads always make an excellent side dish or main course, but they're even better when it's too hot to cook.

- Tomato Salad with Canned Tuna, Capers, and Black Olives (this page)
- Tomato Salad with Arugula and Shaved Parmesan (facing page)
- Tomato Salad with Feta and Cumin-Yogurt Dressing (facing page)
- Tomato, Mozzarella, and Basil Salad (Insalata Caprese) (page 111)
- Israeli Tomato and Cucumber Salad (page 110)
- Peach and Raspberry Salad with Toasted Almonds (page 157)
- Strawberry and Nectarine Salad with Orange and Basil (page 156)
- Honeydew, Mango, and Blueberry Salad with Crystallized Ginger (page 157)

SHAVING PARMESAN

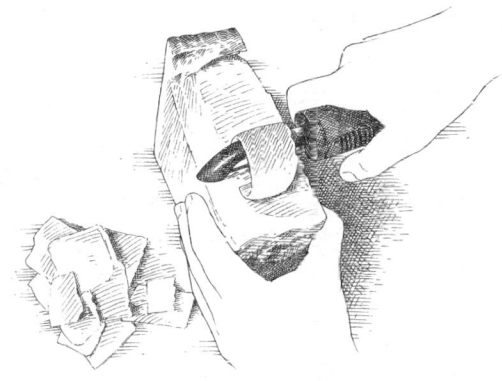

Thin shavings of Parmesan can be used to garnish salads as well as vegetable dishes. Simply run a sharp vegetable peeler along the length of a piece of cheese to remove paper-thin curls.

in a small bowl. Pour the mixture over the tomatoes and their accumulated liquid; toss to coat. Set aside to blend flavors, about 5 minutes.

3. Crumble the tuna over the tomatoes; toss to combine. Adjust the seasonings and serve immediately.

Tomato Salad with Arugula and Shaved Parmesan

SERVES 6

Use a vegetable peeler to remove thin shavings from the chunk of cheese. (See the illustration above.)

4–5	medium ripe tomatoes
¹/₂	teaspoon salt
2	tablespoons extra-virgin olive oil
1	tablespoon balsamic vinegar
1	small garlic clove, minced or pressed through a garlic press (about ¹/₂ teaspoon) Ground black pepper
1	small bunch arugula, washed, dried, stemmed, and chopped coarse (about 1 cup loosely packed)
24	shavings Parmesan cheese

1. Core and halve the tomatoes lengthwise, then cut each half into 4 or 5 wedges. Toss the wedges

with the salt in a large bowl; let rest until a small pool of liquid accumulates, 15 to 20 minutes.

2. Meanwhile, whisk the oil, vinegar, garlic, and pepper to taste in a small bowl. Pour the mixture over the tomatoes and their accumulated liquid; toss to coat. Set aside to blend flavors, about 5 minutes.

3. Add the arugula and Parmesan; toss to combine. Adjust the seasonings and serve immediately.

Tomato Salad with Feta and Cumin-Yogurt Dressing

SERVES 6

Draining the yogurt in a fine sieve gives it a creamier, denser texture, which is better suited to use in a dressing.

4–5	large ripe tomatoes
¹/₂	teaspoon salt
¹/₄	cup plain yogurt, drained in a fine sieve about 30 minutes (discard liquid)
1	tablespoon extra-virgin olive oil
1	tablespoon juice from 1 lemon
1	small garlic clove, minced or pressed through a garlic press (about ¹/₂ teaspoon)
1	teaspoon ground cumin
3	small scallions, white and green parts, sliced thin
1	tablespoon chopped fresh oregano leaves Ground black pepper
1	small chunk feta cheese (about 3 ounces)

1. Core and halve the tomatoes, then cut each half into 4 or 5 wedges. Toss the wedges with the salt in a large bowl; let rest until a small pool of liquid accumulates, 15 to 20 minutes.

2. Meanwhile, whisk the drained yogurt, oil, lemon juice, garlic, cumin, scallions, oregano, and pepper to taste in a small bowl. Pour the mixture over the tomatoes and accumulated liquid; toss to coat. Set aside to blend flavors, about 5 minutes.

3. Crumble the feta over the tomatoes; toss to combine. Adjust seasonings and serve immediately.

Israeli Tomato and Cucumber Salad

SERVES 6

Thin-skinned English cucumbers, with or without the peel, work well in this salad.

2	medium cucumbers
	Salt
4–5	large ripe tomatoes
3	tablespoons extra-virgin olive oil
3	tablespoons juice from 1 lemon
¼	cup finely chopped red onion
¼	cup chopped fresh mint leaves
	Ground black pepper

1. Peel the cucumbers, halve lengthwise, and remove seeds (see illustration 1 on page 113); cut halves in half lengthwise, then cut crosswise into ¼-inch-thick pieces (see illustration 2). Toss cucumbers with 2 teaspoons salt in a colander and place a gallon-size plastic bag filled with water on top of the cucumbers to weigh them down and force out the liquid (see illustration 3). Let drain for at least 1 hour and up to 3 hours; discard liquid.

INGREDIENTS: Balsamic Vinegar

There are balsamic vinegars you can buy for $2.50 and ones that nudge the $300 mark. The more expensive vinegars bear the title *tradizionale* or *extra-vecchio tradizionale* (traditional or extra-old traditional). According to Italian law, these traditional vinegars must come from the northern Italian provinces of Modena or Reggio Emilia and be created and aged in the time-honored fashion.

For hundreds of years, traditional balsamic vinegar has been made from Trebbiano grapes grown in the Modena or Reggio Emilia regions of northern Italy. The grapes are crushed and slowly cooked into must over an open flame. The must begins mellowing in a large wooden barrel, where it ferments and turns to vinegar. The vinegar is then passed through a series of barrels made from a variety of woods. To be considered worthy of the *tradizionale* title, the vinegar must be moved from barrel to barrel for a minimum of 12 years. An extra-vecchio vinegar must be aged for at least 25 years.

Because of its complex flavor and high production cost, traditional balsamic vinegar is used by those in the know as a condiment rather than an ingredient. The longer the vinegar ages, the thicker and more intense it becomes, maturing from a thin liquid into a spoon-coating, syrupy one—perfect for topping strawberries or cantaloupe. This is the aristocrat of balsamic vinegars.

The more common varieties, those with a price tag under $30, are categorized as commercial or industrial balsamic vinegars. These vinegars are the kind with which most Americans are familiar and are often used to complete a vinaigrette or flavor a sauce. Commercial balsamic vinegar may or may not be aged and may or may not contain artificial caramel color or flavor.

We wondered how bad—or good—inexpensive commercial balsamic vinegars would be when compared in a blind tasting. To level the playing field—and ease the burden on our budget—we limited the tasting to balsamic vinegars that cost $15 and under. We included samples of the many production styles, including some aged in the traditional fashion, some with added caramel color and flavor, and some made from a blend of aged red wine vinegar and grape must.

We found that a higher price tag did not correlate with a better vinegar. In addition, age seemed to play a less important role than we had expected. Across the board, tasters found balsamic vinegars containing caramel or artificial color or flavor "sour" and "uninteresting." The top brands from our tasting contain no artificial colors or flavors whatsoever. Our findings led us to believe that must is paramount to making a full-flavored balsamic vinegar. As the must ages, it becomes thick and sweet, contributing a character almost like sherry or port. Producers who substitute artificial color and flavor for must end up with a shallow product.

So how can consumers figure out what type of balsamic vinegar to buy? The easy answer is to check the label. If it discloses that artificial ingredients or sweetener have been added, don't buy it.

THE BEST INEXPENSIVE BALSAMIC VINEGARS

Among the dozen vinegars tested, we preferred 365 Every Day Value (left), Masserie di Sant'Eramo (middle), and Fiorucci Riserva (right).

2. Core and halve the tomatoes, then cut each half into 4 or 5 wedges. Toss the wedges with ½ teaspoon salt in a large bowl; let rest until a small pool of liquid accumulates, 15 to 20 minutes.

3. Meanwhile, whisk the oil, lemon juice, red onion, mint, and pepper to taste in a small bowl. Pour the mixture over the tomatoes and accumulated liquid and toss to coat. Let rest to blend flavors, about 5 minutes.

4. Add the drained cucumber pieces; toss to combine. Adjust seasonings and serve immediately.

Tomato, Mozzarella, and Basil Salad (Insalata Caprese)

SERVES 4 TO 6

Served as an appetizer, light lunch, or snack, this salad is best eaten with a crust of bread to help sop up the tasty tomato-flavored dressing that pools in the bottom of the platter. It is not necessary to salt the tomatoes for this salad. For best presentation, discard the first and last slice from each tomato.

4	medium, very ripe tomatoes, cored and cut into ¼-inch-thick slices
16	ounces fresh mozzarella, cut into ¼-inch-thick slices
2	tablespoons roughly chopped fresh basil leaves
¼	teaspoon kosher salt or sea salt
⅛	teaspoon ground black pepper
¼	cup extra-virgin olive oil

Layer the tomatoes and mozzarella alternately and in concentric circles on a medium platter. Sprinkle the tomatoes and cheese with the basil, salt, and pepper. Drizzle the oil over the platter and allow the flavors to meld for 5 to 10 minutes. Serve immediately.

CUCUMBER SALADS

MORE OFTEN THAN NOT, BY THE TIME YOU eat a cucumber salad, the cucumbers have gone soft and watery, losing their appealing texture and diluting the dressing to near tastelessness. This made the primary goal of our testing simple: Maximize the crunch.

The standard recommendation for ridding watery vegetables such as cucumbers, zucchini, and eggplant of unwanted moisture is to salt them. The salt creates a higher concentration of ions (tiny, charged particles) at the surface of the vegetable than exists deep within its cells. To equalize the concentration levels, the water within the cells is drawn out through permeable cell walls. In the case of cucumbers, this leaves them wilted, yet very crunchy. Of course, some culinary questions remain: How much salt should be used? Should the cucumber slices be weighted, or pressed, to squeeze out the liquid? How long should they drain?

To find out if pressing salted cucumbers really squeezes out more liquid, we trimmed and seeded six cucumbers to a weight of 8 ounces each, sliced them on the bias, and tossed each batch with 1 teaspoon of salt in its own colander set over a bowl. Three batches had zipper-lock freezer bags filled with water placed on top; no additional weight was added to the other three. Then we left them all to drain, measuring the liquid each had released after 30 minutes and after one, two, three, and 12 hours. At each time point, the weighted cucumbers had released about 1 tablespoon more liquid than the unweighted cucumbers; 3 versus 2 tablespoons after 30 minutes, 4 versus 3 after one hour, and so on. Interestingly, the weighted cukes gave off no more liquid after 12 hours than they had after three hours (7 tablespoons at both points). So weighting the cucumbers is worthwhile, but forget about draining the cucumbers overnight; it's not necessary.

At the one-hour mark, we could not detect an appreciable difference in flavor or texture between weighted and unweighted cukes. But we wanted to see how they would perform in salads with different types of dressings. We mixed one batch each of the weighted and unweighted cucumbers with three types of sauces—creamy, oil-based, and water-based—and allowed each to sit at room temperature for one hour. This is where the true value of better-drained cucumbers became obvious; every single taster preferred the salads made with pressed cucumbers for their superior crunch and less diluted dressings.

As for the amount of salt, some cooks recommend simply using the quantity with which you would normally season the cucumber, while others say you should use more, up to 2 tablespoons per cucumber, and then rinse off the excess before further use. We tried a few cucumbers prepared exactly as those described above except with 2 tablespoons of salt. The cucumbers tossed with 2 tablespoons of salt did give up about 1 tablespoon more liquid within the first hour than those tossed with 1 teaspoon had, but they also required rinsing and blotting dry with paper towels. And despite this extra hassle, they still tasted much too salty in the salads. We decided to forgo the extra salt.

SALADS TO FEED A CROWD

ALL OF THESE SALADS DOUBLE EASILY, serving up to 16, and are fairly sturdy, so a bumpy ride in the back seat of the car (or in your lap on the subway) won't bruise any tender leaves.

- Tabbouleh (page 144)
- Rice Salad with Cherry Tomatoes, Parmesan, Peas, and Prosciutto (page 141)
- Pasta Salad with Arugula and Sun-Dried Tomato Vinaigrette (page 136)
- Sesame Noodle Salad with Shredded Chicken (page 138)
- Macaroni Salad (page 134)
- Three-Bean Salad (page 124)
- Chopped Salad (page 147)
- American Potato Salad (page 129)
- Sesame-Lemon Cucumber Salad (facing page)
- Grape and Strawberry Salad with Champagne (page 157)
- Multi-Colored Plum Salad with Orange and Thyme (page 157)
- Pineapple-Kiwi Salad with Brown Sugar and Lime (page 156)

Yogurt-Mint Cucumber Salad
SERVES 4

Known as raita, this creamy salad is traditionally served as a cooling contrast to curry dishes.

3	medium cucumbers, peeled, seeded, sliced, salted, and drained, as shown on the facing page
	Salt
1	cup plain low-fat yogurt
2	tablespoons extra-virgin olive oil
1/4	cup minced fresh mint leaves
1	medium garlic clove, minced or pressed through a garlic press (about 1 teaspoon)
	Ground black pepper

Let the salted cucumbers drain, weighted, in the colander for at least 1 hour and up to 3 hours. Whisk the yogurt, oil, mint, garlic, and salt and pepper to taste in a medium bowl. Add the drained cucumbers; toss to coat. Serve chilled, adjusting seasonings if necessary.

Creamy Dill Cucumber Salad
SERVES 4

Salting and draining the onion along with the cucumbers in this recipe removes the sharp sting of raw onion.

3	medium cucumbers, peeled, seeded, sliced, salted, and drained, as shown on the facing page
1/2	medium red onion, sliced very thin, salted and drained with the cucumbers
	Salt
1	cup sour cream
3	tablespoons cider vinegar
1	teaspoon sugar
1/4	cup minced fresh dill
	Ground black pepper

Let the salted cucumbers and onion drain, weighted, in the colander for at least 1 hour and up to 3 hours. Whisk the sour cream, vinegar, sugar, dill, and salt and pepper to taste in a medium bowl. Add the drained cucumbers and onion; toss to coat. Serve chilled, adjusting seasonings if necessary.

Sesame-Lemon Cucumber Salad

SERVES 4

Mild rice vinegar works well in this Asian-inspired dressing.

3	medium cucumbers, peeled, seeded, sliced, salted, and drained, as shown below
1	tablespoon salt
1/4	cup rice vinegar
1	tablespoon juice from 1 lemon
2	tablespoons toasted sesame oil
2	teaspoons sugar
1/8	teaspoon dried red pepper flakes plus more to taste
1	tablespoon sesame seeds, toasted in a small dry skillet over medium heat until fragrant, about 4 minutes

Let the salted cucumbers drain, weighted, in the colander for at least 1 hour and up to 3 hours. Whisk all of the ingredients except the cucumbers in a medium bowl. Add the drained cucumbers; toss to coat. Serve chilled or at room temperature.

Sweet-and-Tart Cucumber Salad

SERVES 4

Based on a common Thai relish served with saté, this salad is also great with grilled salmon or grilled chicken breasts.

3	medium cucumbers, peeled, seeded, sliced, salted, and drained, as shown below
1/2	medium red onion, sliced very thin, salted and drained with the cucumbers
1	tablespoon salt
2/3	cup water
1/2	cup rice vinegar
2 1/2	tablespoons sugar
2	small jalapeño chiles (or more to taste), cored, seeded, and minced

1. Let the salted cucumbers and onion drain, weighted, in the colander for at least 1 hour and up to 3 hours.

2. Bring the water and vinegar to a boil in a small nonreactive saucepan over medium heat. Stir in the sugar to dissolve; reduce the heat and simmer 15 minutes. Cool to room temperature.

3. Meanwhile, mix the drained cucumbers, onion, and jalapeños in a medium bowl. Pour the dressing over the cucumber mixture; toss to coat. Serve chilled.

SALTING CUCUMBERS

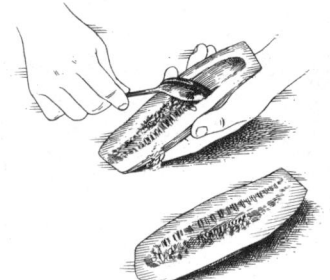

1. Peel each cucumber and halve lengthwise. Use a small spoon to remove the seeds and surrounding liquid from each cucumber half.

2. Place the cucumber halves flat-side down on a work surface and slice them on the diagonal into 1/4-inch-thick pieces.

3. Toss the cucumbers and salt (1 teaspoon for each cucumber) in a colander set in a bowl. Place a gallon-size zipper-lock plastic bag filled with water on top of the cucumbers to weigh them down and force out the liquid. Drain for at least 1 hour and up to 3 hours.

Cucumber Salad with Greek Dressing

SERVES 4

This juicy salad makes an excellent accompaniment to grilled fish or chicken.

3   medium cucumbers, peeled, seeded, sliced, salted, and drained, as shown on page 113
1   tablespoon salt
2   tablespoons red wine vinegar
2   teaspoons minced fresh oregano leaves
1   tablespoon minced fresh mint leaves
1   medium garlic clove, minced or pressed through a garlic press (about 1 teaspoon)
6   tablespoons extra-virgin olive oil
2   ounces feta cheese, crumbled (about ½ cup)

1. Let the salted cucumbers drain, weighted, in the colander for at least 1 hour and up to 3 hours.

2. Whisk the vinegar, oregano, mint, garlic, and oil together in a medium bowl. Add the drained cucumbers and toss to coat. Sprinkle with the feta and serve immediately.

Cucumber Salad with Spicy Soy Dressing

SERVES 4

Red chili paste can be found in the Asian food section of most large grocery stores. If it is unavailable, ½ teaspoon red pepper flakes can be used instead. Make sure you are using toasted sesame oil; it will be golden in color and have a distinct, nutty aroma.

3   medium cucumbers, peeled, seeded, sliced, salted, and drained, as shown on page 113

INGREDIENTS: Chili Paste

Sometimes labeled chili sauce, chili paste is a spicy seasoning made with crushed chile peppers, vinegar, and usually garlic. The texture is thick and smooth and the color is bright red. Brands vary from mild to incendiary, so taste before using and adjust the amount as needed. Opened jars can be refrigerated for many months.

1   tablespoon salt
1   tablespoon soy sauce
3   tablespoons rice vinegar
1   teaspoon chili paste
1   medium garlic clove, minced or pressed through a garlic press (about 1 teaspoon)
1   tablespoon sugar
3   tablespoons toasted sesame oil
1   tablespoon sesame seeds, toasted in a small dry skillet over medium heat until fragrant, about 4 minutes

1. Let the salted cucumbers drain, weighted, in the colander for at least 1 hour and up to 3 hours.

2. Whisk the soy sauce, rice vinegar, chili paste, garlic, sugar, sesame oil, and sesame seeds together in a medium bowl. Add the drained cucumbers and toss to coat. Serve chilled or at room temperature.

ASPARAGUS SALADS

LONG, GRACEFUL ASPARAGUS SPEARS CAN BE an excellent addition to a leafy green salad. But the beauty of these salads is often only skin-deep. Either bland or overseasoned, mushy or nearly raw, this first-course tease can prove to be an unsatisfying encounter. Tired of this ongoing disappointment, we wanted some recipes for asparagus salad that combined good taste with good looks: the asparagus perfectly cooked and seasoned, other fresh and flavorful ingredients added in a way that let the flavors unify, and the salad overall both attractive and easy to assemble.

We knew that boiling or steaming asparagus would introduce water that would dilute (or at the very least, not enhance) its flavor. Grilling or broiling would concentrate the flavor, but these were unwanted added steps. We soon found that quickly sautéing and caramelizing the asparagus over high heat was the easiest way to concentrate flavor. Best of all, this skillet method was ideal for adding other ingredients right to the pan, where the flavors could meld.

The vinaigrette was all about balance. Adding the bold flavors of shallots, garlic, jalapeños, fresh herbs, or even tart cornichons and salty capers to the oil and vinegar made for zesty dressings that contrasted nicely with the mellow asparagus. To offset the leanness of the lettuce and the vegetables and to counter the sharpness of the dressing, we added a small amount of nuts, beans, cheese, or hard-cooked eggs, making the salads more substantial as well as flavorful.

Asparagus, Red Pepper, and Spinach Salad with Goat Cheese
SERVES 4 TO 6

Substitute feta for the goat cheese, if you like.

6   tablespoons extra-virgin olive oil
I   small red bell pepper, cored, seeded, and cut into 1/4-inch strips
I   pound asparagus, tough ends snapped off (see the illustration on page 165) and cut on the diagonal into 1-inch pieces
    Salt and ground black pepper
I   medium shallot, sliced thin
I   tablespoon plus 1 teaspoon sherry vinegar
I   medium garlic clove, minced or pressed through garlic press (about 1 teaspoon)
6   ounces baby spinach (about 8 cups loosely packed)
4   ounces goat cheese, cut into small chunks

1. Heat 2 tablespoons of the oil in a 12-inch nonstick skillet over high heat until it begins to smoke. Add the red pepper and cook until lightly browned, about 2 minutes, stirring only once, after 1 minute. Add the asparagus, 1/4 teaspoon salt, and 1/8 teaspoon pepper and cook until the asparagus is browned and almost tender, about 2 minutes, stirring only once, after 1 minute. Stir in the shallot and cook until softened and the asparagus is crisp-tender, about 1 minute, stirring occasionally. Transfer the vegetables to a large plate and cool for 5 minutes.

2. Meanwhile, whisk the remaining 4 tablespoons oil, the vinegar, garlic, 1/4 teaspoon salt, and 1/8 teaspoon pepper in a medium bowl until combined. In a large bowl, toss the spinach with 2 tablespoons of the dressing and divide among individual plates. Toss the asparagus mixture with the remaining dressing and place a portion over the spinach. Divide the goat cheese among the salads and serve immediately.

Asparagus and Mesclun Salad with Capers, Cornichons, and Hard-Cooked Eggs
SERVES 4 TO 5

Mesclun is a mixture of such specialty greens as arugula, Belgian endive, and radicchio, to name a few. To read more about specialty greens, see page 90.

5   tablespoons extra-virgin olive oil
I   pound asparagus, tough ends snapped off (see the illustration on page 165) and cut on the diagonal into 1-inch pieces
    Salt and ground black pepper
2   tablespoons white wine vinegar
I   small shallot, minced (about 2 tablespoons)
2   tablespoons minced cornichons
I   teaspoon minced capers
2   teaspoons chopped fresh tarragon leaves
6   ounces mesclun mix
3   large Hard-Cooked Eggs (page 44), chopped medium

1. Heat 1 tablespoon of the oil in a 12-inch nonstick skillet over high heat until it begins to smoke. Add the asparagus, 1/4 teaspoon salt, and 1/4 teaspoon pepper and cook until browned and crisp-tender, about 4 minutes, stirring once every minute. Transfer the asparagus to a large plate and cool for 5 minutes.

2. Meanwhile, whisk the remaining 4 tablespoons oil, the vinegar, shallot, cornichons, capers, tarragon, and 1/4 teaspoon pepper together in a medium bowl until combined. In a large bowl, toss the mesclun with 2 tablespoons of the dressing and divide among individual plates. Toss the asparagus with the remaining dressing and place a portion over the mesclun. Divide the chopped eggs among the salads and serve immediately.

Asparagus, Watercress, and Carrot Salad with Thai Flavors
SERVES 4 TO 6

The asparagus in this salad tastes best chilled. To do so, place the plate of just-cooked asparagus in the freezer.

2 tablespoons juice from 1 to 2 limes
2 tablespoons fish sauce
2 tablespoons water
2 teaspoons sugar
1 small garlic clove, minced or pressed through a garlic press (about ½ teaspoon)
1 small jalapeño chile, cored, seeded, and minced
2 medium carrots, peeled and cut into matchsticks
1 tablespoon peanut or vegetable oil
1 pound asparagus, tough ends snapped off (see the illustration on page 165) and cut on the diagonal into 1-inch pieces
1 large bunch watercress, washed, dried, and stemmed (about 4 cups loosely packed)
¼ cup chopped fresh mint leaves
⅓ cup chopped unsalted roasted peanuts, toasted in a small dry skillet over medium heat until fragrant, about 4 minutes

1. Whisk the lime juice, fish sauce, water, sugar, garlic, and jalapeño together in a medium bowl until the sugar dissolves. Reserve 1 tablespoon of the dressing in a large bowl; toss the carrots with the remaining dressing and set aside.

2. Heat the oil in a 12-inch nonstick skillet over high heat until it begins to smoke. Add the asparagus and cook until browned and crisp-tender, about 4 minutes, stirring once every minute. Transfer the asparagus to a large plate and place in the freezer for 5 minutes.

3. Toss the watercress with the reserved 1 tablespoon dressing and divide among individual plates. Toss the asparagus and mint with the carrot mixture and place a portion over the watercress. Sprinkle the salads with the peanuts and serve immediately.

Moroccan-Style Carrot Salad

WHEN CARROT SALADS WERE MENTIONED IN the test kitchen, there was a collective groan. Everybody seemed to remember a tired carrot and raisin salad from childhood—an overly sweet mix of shredded carrots and chewy raisins bound by a little too much mayonnaise. But not long ago, one of us had a carrot salad in a local Moroccan restaurant. The shredded carrots were the same, but this time they were tossed with slices of oranges and flavored with cumin, coriander, and cinnamon—all spices characteristic of Moroccan cooking. This was not your mother's carrot salad.

In our research, we found a wide range of North African carrot salads. The ingredients and procedures for the salads were all similar. Most recipes called for grated carrots tossed with olive oil, lemon juice, and Moroccan spices. Many recipes specified additional flavors, such as olives, toasted almonds, orange flower water, and, yes, even raisins. In the spirit of simple, quick cooking, however, we decide to stick to the basics.

Our first question was how to cut the carrots. Some recipes called for the carrots to be pared into thin ribbons with a vegetable peeler. While this made a pretty salad, the vinaigrette had nothing to cling to, so the carrots were rather bland. Remembering the positive aspects of mom's carrot salad and figuring we shouldn't mess with a good thing, we turned to grating. We tried several methods of grating the carrots with a box grater and with a food processor. We found the large holes on the box grater worked the best. The food processor grated the carrots too finely; the resulting salad didn't have enough body or texture and was watery. The carrot pieces from the box grater were a little larger.

Considering that we were going to add oranges to the salad, we decided to build a vinaigrette around orange juice. The orange juice didn't provide enough acidity, however, resulting in a salad that was too sweet. A squeeze of lemon juice did the trick. As for the oil, extra-virgin olive oil worked best. A touch of honey added a pleasing floral note.

Moving to the spices in the vinaigrette, we initially tried ½ teaspoon each coriander, cumin, and cinnamon. This was entirely too overpowering; none of the spices dominated, and the total amount gave the salad a grainy mouthfeel. So we tried reducing the amount of spices and making one spice the dominant flavor. Tasters felt that

SEGMENTING AN ORANGE

1. Start by slicing a ½-inch-thick piece off the top and bottom of the orange.

2. With the fruit resting flat against the work surface, use a very sharp paring knife to slice off the rind, including all of the bitter white pith. Try to follow the contours of the fruit as closely as possible.

3. Working over a bowl to catch the juices, slip the blade between a membrane and one section of fruit and slice to the center, separating one side of the section.

4. Turn the blade of the knife so that it is facing out and is lined up along the membrane on the opposite side of the section. Slice the blade from the center out along the membrane to free the section completely. Continue until all of the sections are removed.

cinnamon and coriander were too sweet to serve as dominant flavors, failing to provide enough contrast. Cumin, on the other hand, worked perfectly in the starring role. The musty aroma and slight nuttiness of the cumin complemented the sweetness of the carrots. With a hint of cinnamon (the coriander seemed redundant and was dropped) and a little heat provided by cayenne pepper, we finally had our dressing. Now all we had to do was to dress the carrots—or so we thought.

Several minutes after we dressed the salad, a pool of juice—water being expelled by the carrots—developed in the bowl. We explored several ways of getting rid of this liquid. We tried salting the carrots as we would cucumbers to rid them of unwanted juices, but this process required at least half an hour. We also tried squeezing the carrots in a towel after we grated them, but this resulted in a loss of flavor. We then turned to the idea of letting the carrots sit in a strainer for several minutes after being dressed. While this certainly got rid of the extra water, it also got rid of flavor. We finally settled on increasing the amount of spices in the vinaigrette; the carrots thus received an initial overdose of spices that would stand up to the inevitable excess of liquid. By straining some of the liquid from the salad, we reached a proper level of seasoning.

Moroccan-Style Carrot Salad

SERVES 6

Make sure to segment the oranges over a small bowl to catch their juices. You should have several tablespoons of juice in the bowl by the time you are done segmenting both oranges. The flavor combinations in this slawlike salad make it a natural to serve with couscous or North African stews. It also works well with firm white fish, such as halibut.

I	pound carrots, peeled and grated on the large holes of a box grater
2	medium seedless oranges, peeled and segmented (see the illustrations at left)
I	teaspoon honey
I	tablespoon juice from I lemon
4	tablespoons extra-virgin olive oil
¾	teaspoon ground cumin
½	teaspoon salt
¼	teaspoon cayenne pepper
⅛	teaspoon ground cinnamon
3	tablespoons chopped fresh cilantro leaves

1. Place the grated carrots and orange segments in a large bowl. Set aside.

2. Whisk the honey, lemon juice, oil, cumin, salt, cayenne, and cinnamon together with the reserved orange juice in a small bowl.

3. Pour the dressing over the carrots, add the cilantro, and toss to coat. Let stand until liquid starts to pool in the bottom of the bowl, about 3 minutes.

Place the salad in a fine-mesh strainer and let it sit undisturbed for 2 minutes. Remove the salad from the strainer and serve immediately.

FENNEL SALADS

FENNEL HAS A DELICATE, SWEET, LIGHT anise flavor and a delicious crunch that is similar to celery, only without the strings. This vegetable makes a distinctive salad when paired with complementary flavors, of which we found orange (and tangerine) to be popular among recipes we researched.

We decided to model our first salad after a Sicilian-style salad of fennel, orange, and olive. Although we found many recipes for this simple combination, we noted a few tricks in the preparation of both the fennel and the orange. We liked the fennel best when it was sliced as thin as possible. A very sharp knife makes quick work of this task. Second, we noted the importance of cutting the orange into bite-size pieces; the trick is to avoid letting the orange segments fall apart as the salad is tossed. We achieved this by trimming the outer rind and bitter white pith from the orange

with a sharp knife, then breaking the orange down into quarters. We trimmed the inner pith and seeds from inside each quarter, then cut crosswise through each quarter (across the segments). By cutting crosswise, the segment borders and connective tissue helped keep the orange from breaking down further as it was tossed in the salad.

To finish the salad off, we added a small amount of potent black olives, some fresh mint, good extra-virgin olive oil, salt, and black pepper. Because this dish is so simple, the quality of

---

PREPARING FENNEL

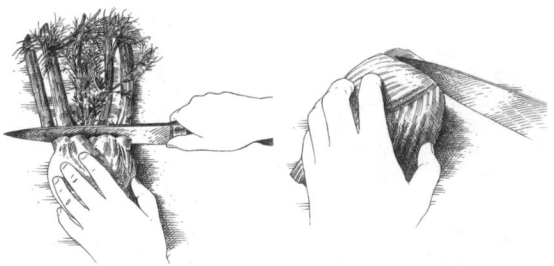

1. Cut off the stems and feathery fronds. (The fronds can be minced and used for a garnish.)

2. Trim a very thin slice from the base and remove any tough or blemished outer layers from the bulb.

3. Cut the bulb in half through the base. Use a small, sharp knife to remove the pyramid-shaped core.

4. Lay the cored fennel on a work surface and, with the knife parallel to the cutting board, cut the fennel in half crosswise. With the knife perpendicular to the cutting board, cut the fennel pieces lengthwise into ½-inch-thick strips.

NOT YOUR AVERAGE SLAWS

THINK SLAWS ARE LIMITED TO THE TYPICAL creamy or sweet-and-sour versions? Or that they always need to be made with cabbage? Think again. Here are our favorite slaws and slaw-like salads:

- Confetti Cabbage Salad with Spicy Peanut Dressing (page 123)
- Cabbage and Red Pepper Salad with Lime-Cumin Vinaigrette (page 123)
- Curried Coleslaw with Apples and Raisins (page 121)
- Fennel and Tangerine Salad (facing page)
- Moroccan-Style Carrot Salad (page 117)

each ingredient, from the fennel to the salt, must be the best.

In our second fennel salad, we chose to work with similar flavors, but we opted to leave out the black olives and employ a French-style vinaigrette for an equally satisfying and refreshing salad. Both can be served as first courses or side salads and are particularly nice served with grilled fish, chicken, or pork.

Fennel, Orange, and Olive Salad
SERVES 4 TO 6

Blood oranges, with their red skin and reddish-orange flesh, are traditional in this dish; use them if you can find them.

2 medium fennel bulbs (about 2 pounds), trimmed of stalks, cored, and sliced thin (see the illustrations on the facing page)
3 large oranges, peeled, quartered, and cut into 1/4-inch pieces (see the illustrations on page 106)
1/2 cup mild black olives, such as gaeta or niçose, pitted and slivered
1/4 cup roughly chopped fresh mint leaves
1/4 cup extra-virgin olive oil
2 tablespoons juice from 1 lemon
Salt and ground black pepper

Toss the fennel, oranges, olives, and mint in a large bowl. Whisk the oil, lemon juice, salt, and pepper together in a small bowl. Toss the dressing with the fennel mixture and adjust seasonings. Serve. (The salad can be refrigerated in an airtight container for 2 days.)

Fennel and Tangerine Salad
SERVES 4 TO 6

Make sure to reserve the juice from the tangerines as you segment them.

2 medium fennel bulbs (about 2 pounds), trimmed of stalks, cored, and sliced thin (see the illustrations on the facing page)

2 tangerines or small oranges, peeled and segmented (see the illustrations on page 117), segments halved crosswise and seeded
1/4 cup chopped fresh parsley leaves
1/4 cup extra-virgin olive oil
2 tablespoons juice from 1 lemon
2 tablespoons whole-grain mustard
1 medium garlic clove, minced or pressed through a garlic press (about 1 teaspoon)
Salt and ground black pepper

Toss the fennel, tangerines, and parsley in a large bowl. Whisk the oil, lemon juice, mustard, and garlic together in a small bowl. Toss the dressing with the fennel mixture and season with salt and pepper to taste. Serve. (The salad can be refrigerated in an airtight container for 2 days.)

COLESLAW

DESPITE ITS SIMPLICITY, COLESLAW HAS always bothered us for two reasons: the pool of watery dressing that appears at the bottom of the bowl after a few hours, and the salad's sharp flavor, no matter what kind or quantity of vinegar is used. Our slaw always seemed to taste better when we tried it again the next day, but by then the dressing was the consistency of skim milk.

While most recipes instruct the cook to toss the shredded cabbage with the dressing immediately, a few add an extra step. Either the shredded (or merely quartered) cabbage is soaked in ice water for crisping and refreshing, or it is salted, drained, and allowed to wilt.

Cabbage soaked in ice water was crisp, plump, and fresh. If looks were all that mattered, this cabbage would have scored high next to the limp, salted cabbage in the neighboring colander. But its good looks were deceiving. Even though we drained the cabbage and dried it thoroughly, the dressing didn't adhere. Furthermore, within minutes, the cabbage shreds started to lose their recently acquired water, creating a large puddle of water that was diluting the creamy dressing. The stiff cabbage shreds were strawlike, making them difficult to fork and even more difficult to get into the mouth without leaving a creamy trail.

Quite unlike the ice-water cabbage, the salted shreds lost most of their liquid while sitting in the salt; this left them wilted but pickle-crisp. Because the cabbage had already lost most of its liquid, little was left to be drawn out by the salt in the dressing. We had found the solution to the

SHREDDING CABBAGE

1. Cut a whole head of cabbage into quarters. Cut away the hard piece of the core attached to each quarter.

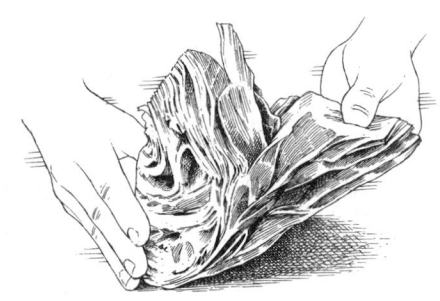

2. Separate the cored cabbage quarters into stacks of leaves that flatten when pressed lightly.

3. Use a chef's knife to cut each stack of cabbage diagonally into long, thin pieces. Alternatively, roll the stacked leaves crosswise to fit them into the feed tube of a food processor fitted with the shredding disk.

problem of watery dressing. In addition, we found that this cabbage, having less water in it, took on more of the dressing's flavors and that, unlike the stiff shreds of ice-water cabbage, this limp cabbage was also easier to eat.

We did discover that the salting process leaves the cabbage a bit too salty, but a quick rinse washes away the excess salt. After the cabbage has been rinsed, just pat it dry with paper towels and refrigerate until you are ready to combine it with the dressing. If the coleslaw is to be eaten immediately, rinse it quickly in ice water rather than tap water, then pat it dry. Coleslaw, at least the creamy style, should be served cold.

Having figured out how to keep the cabbage from watering down the dressing, we were ready to tackle the problem of acidity in the dressing. We found a few creamy coleslaw recipes in which the cabbage was tossed with sour cream only or with a combination of mayonnaise and sour cream—no vinegar. Although we were looking for ways to tone down the tang, a mix of sour cream and mayonnaise proved too mild for our taste. Other recipes called for lemon juice rather than vinegar. Although the lemon juice gave the coleslaw a pleasantly tart flavor, it lacked the depth that vinegar could offer. We decided to give low-acidity rice vinegar a try. We drizzled a bit of rice vinegar over the mayonnaise-tossed cabbage and found its mild acidity to be just right.

Although there are several styles of coleslaw, the two that follow are classics—one mild and creamy, the other sweet and sour. Adjust either recipe to your taste. If sour cream is a must for you in creamy slaw, then substitute it for some or all of the mayonnaise. Also, try adding green pepper, celery, red onions, or apples. Caraway seeds, fresh dill, radishes, or nuts are also good additions.

Creamy Coleslaw
SERVES 4

If you like caraway or celery seed in your coleslaw, you can add ¼ teaspoon of either with the mayonnaise and vinegar. You can shred, salt, rinse, and pat the cabbage dry a day ahead, but dress it close to serving time.

½ medium head (1 pound) red or green cabbage, shredded (see the illustrations on the facing page)
1 large carrot, peeled and grated
1 teaspoon salt
½ cup mayonnaise
¼ cup minced onion
2 tablespoons rice vinegar
   Ground black pepper

1. Toss the cabbage and carrot with the salt in a colander or large mesh strainer set over a medium bowl. Let stand until the cabbage wilts, at least 1 hour and up to 4 hours.

2. Dump the wilted cabbage and carrot into the bowl and rinse thoroughly in cold water (use ice water if serving slaw immediately). Pour the vegetables back into the colander, pressing, but not squeezing, to drain. Pat dry with paper towels. (The vegetables can be stored in a zipper-lock bag and refrigerated overnight.)

3. Pour the cabbage and carrot back into the bowl. Add the mayonnaise, onion, and vinegar; toss to coat. Season with pepper to taste. Cover and refrigerate until ready to serve.

Sweet-and-Sour Coleslaw
SERVES 4

Because rice vinegar tends to mellow, you may want to use cider vinegar if making the slaw a day ahead. The presence of the sugar in this recipe keeps you from having to rinse off salt from the cabbage, as is ordinarily the case.

½ medium head (1 pound) red or green cabbage, shredded (see the illustrations on the facing page)
1 large carrot, peeled and grated
½ cup sugar
1 teaspoon salt
¼ teaspoon celery seed
6 tablespoons vegetable oil
¼ cup rice wine vinegar
   Ground black pepper

1. Toss the cabbage and carrot with the sugar, salt, and celery seed in a colander or large mesh strainer set over a medium bowl. Let stand until the

cabbage wilts, at least 1 hour and up to 4 hours.

2. Pour the draining liquid from the bowl; rinse and dry the bowl. Transfer the wilted cabbage and carrot to the bowl.

3. Add the oil and vinegar; toss to coat. Season with pepper to taste. Cover and refrigerate until ready to serve. (The slaw can be refrigerated for up to 2 days.)

➤ VARIATION
Curried Coleslaw with Apples and Raisins
SERVES 6

With the addition of apple and raisins, this variation makes 2 additional servings

Follow the recipe for Sweet-and-Sour Coleslaw, adding 1 teaspoon curry powder, 1 medium apple, peeled and cut into small dice, and ¼ cup raisins (optional) with the oil and vinegar.

BUTTERMILK COLESLAW

THERE IS ONE THING ABOUT COLESLAW WITH buttermilk dressing that can be bothersome: the tangy flavor of buttermilk often turns harsh and one-dimensional. We wanted a buttermilk slaw that was creamy and piquant.

While many recipes simply call for buttermilk seasoned with a few spices and herbs, we found that the flavor of the buttermilk itself needed to be tempered. By adding a couple of tablespoons each of mayonnaise and sour cream, we were able to round out its tart, dairy flavor without losing its distinctive bite. The mayonnaise and sour cream also added body to the dressing, helping it cling to the cabbage.

After trying a variety of flavorings and vegetables, we found that carrot, shallot, and parsley seasoned with mustard, cider vinegar, and a pinch of sugar turned the buttermilk-cabbage mixture into a fresh and authentic-tasting coleslaw that doesn't weep.

Buttermilk Coleslaw
SERVES 4

Serve this tangy slaw with grilled foods, sandwiches, or burgers.

½	medium head (1 pound) red or green cabbage, shredded (see the illustrations on page 120)
	Salt
1	medium carrot, peeled and shredded
½	cup buttermilk
2	tablespoons mayonnaise
2	tablespoons sour cream
1	small shallot, minced (about 2 tablespoons)
2	tablespoons minced fresh parsley leaves
½	teaspoon cider vinegar
½	teaspoon sugar
¼	teaspoon Dijon mustard
⅛	teaspoon ground black pepper

1. Toss the shredded cabbage and 1 teaspoon salt in a colander or large mesh strainer set over a medium bowl. Let stand until the cabbage wilts, at least 1 hour or up to 4 hours. Rinse the cabbage under cold running water (or in a large bowl of ice water if serving immediately). Press, but do not squeeze, to drain; pat dry with paper towels. Place the wilted cabbage and the carrot in the bowl.

2. Whisk together the buttermilk, mayonnaise, sour cream, shallot, parsley, vinegar, sugar, mustard, ¼ teaspoon salt, and the pepper in a small bowl. Pour the buttermilk dressing over the wilted cabbage and carrot and refrigerate until ready to serve. (The coleslaw can be refrigerated for up to 3 days.)

➤ VARIATIONS

Buttermilk Coleslaw with Scallion and Cilantro

Follow the recipe for Buttermilk Coleslaw, substituting 1 tablespoon minced cilantro leaves for the parsley, 1 teaspoon lime juice for the cider vinegar, omitting the mustard, and adding 2 scallions, sliced thin.

Buttermilk Coleslaw with Lemon and Herbs

Follow the recipe for Buttermilk Coleslaw, substituting 1 teaspoon lemon juice for the cider vinegar and adding 1 teaspoon minced fresh thyme leaves and 1 tablespoon minced chives to the dressing.

CABBAGE SALADS

CABBAGE MAKES A GREAT SALAD—NOT JUST as coleslaw or a picnic side dish but a crunchy, flavorful, dress-up kind of salad. Cabbage's natural spicy-sweetness and crunchy texture work well with many strong and unconventional flavor combinations. Dressings with spicy chiles, sweeteners, tangy acids, and strong herbal or spice flavors highlight the natural flavors in cabbage without overpowering them. Also, unlike lettuce salads, cabbage salads can be made well in advance, and leftovers don't have to go to waste—they make a great addition to a sandwich or lunchbox.

One problem with cabbage salads is their tendency to become watery and bland when dressed and allowed to sit. This occurs because the cells of the cabbage are full of water that leaches out into the salad, diluting its consistency and flavor. Salting the cabbage and setting it over a colander allows a good bit of this liquid to be drawn out. Salads made with this salted and drained cabbage do not become overly watery, and the flavors of the dressing remain undiluted (see the photos below). Because salting does soften cabbage a bit, these salads won't have the intense crispness of some coleslaws, but their pickle-crisp texture is ideal for forking and eating. Red and green cabbage work equally well, either singly or in combination, in these salads.

THE EFFECTS OF SALTING

Unsalted cabbage is too crunchy and leaches moisture, which makes the salad watery (left). Salted cabbage has already shed its moisture and makes a salad that is tender but not watery (right).

Sweet-and-Sour Cabbage Salad with Apple and Fennel

SERVES 6

See the illustrations on page 118 for preparing the fennel.

1/2	medium head (1 pound) red or green cabbage, shredded (see the illustrations on page 120)
	Salt
1/2	small red onion, chopped fine
2	tablespoons rice vinegar
2	tablespoons extra-virgin olive oil
1	tablespoon honey
2	teaspoons minced fresh tarragon leaves
1	teaspoon Dijon mustard
1	large Granny Smith apple, peeled, cored, and cut into 1/4-inch dice
1	medium fennel bulb (about 1 pound), trimmed of stalks, cored, and sliced thin
	Ground black pepper

1. Toss the shredded cabbage and 1 teaspoon salt in a colander or large-mesh strainer set over a medium bowl. Let stand until the cabbage wilts, at least 1 hour or up to 4 hours. Rinse the cabbage under cold running water (or in a large bowl of ice water if serving immediately). Press, but do not squeeze, to drain; pat dry with paper towels. (The cabbage can be stored in a zipper-lock plastic bag and refrigerated overnight.)

2. Stir together the onion, vinegar, oil, honey, tarragon, and mustard and in a medium bowl. Immediately toss the cabbage, apple, and fennel in the dressing. Season to taste with salt and pepper. Cover and refrigerate until ready to serve. (The salad is best the day it is made but will keep for several days.)

Cabbage and Red Pepper Salad with Lime-Cumin Vinaigrette

SERVES 6

Serve this Southwestern-flavored slaw with grilled meat, poultry, or fish.

1/2	medium head (1 pound) red or green cabbage, shredded (see the illustrations on page 120)
	Salt
1	teaspoon grated zest and 2 tablespoons juice from 1 or 2 limes
2	tablespoons extra-virgin olive oil
1	tablespoon rice or sherry vinegar
1	tablespoon honey
1	teaspoon ground cumin
	Pinch cayenne pepper
1	medium red bell pepper, cored, seeded, and cut into thin strips

1. Toss the shredded cabbage and 1 teaspoon salt in a colander or large mesh strainer set over a medium bowl. Let stand until the cabbage wilts, at least 1 hour or up to 4 hours. Rinse the cabbage under cold running water (or in a large bowl of ice water if serving immediately). Press, but do not squeeze, to drain; pat dry with paper towels. (The cabbage can be stored in a zipper-lock plastic bag and refrigerated overnight.)

2. Stir together the lime zest and juice, oil, vinegar, honey, cumin, and cayenne in a medium bowl. Toss the cabbage and red pepper in the dressing. Season to taste with salt. Cover and refrigerate until ready to serve. (The salad is best the day it is made but will keep for several days.)

Confetti Cabbage Salad with Spicy Peanut Dressing

SERVES 6

Grate the carrot on the large holes of a box grater or with the cabbage on the shredding disk of a food processor.

1/2	medium head (1 pound) red or green cabbage, shredded (see the illustrations on page 120)
1	large carrot, peeled and grated
	Salt
2	tablespoons smooth peanut butter
2	tablespoons peanut oil
2	tablespoons rice vinegar
1	tablespoon soy sauce
1	teaspoon honey
2	medium garlic cloves, minced or pressed through a garlic press (about 2 teaspoons)
1	(1 1/2-inch) piece fresh ginger, peeled
1/2	jalapeño chile, cored and seeded

4   medium radishes, halved lengthwise and
    sliced thin
4   medium scallions, sliced thin

1. Toss the shredded cabbage, carrot, and 1 teaspoon salt in a colander or large mesh strainer set over a medium bowl. Let stand until the cabbage and carrot wilt, at least 1 hour or up to 4 hours. Rinse the cabbage and carrot under cold running water (or in a large bowl of ice water if serving immediately). Press, but do not squeeze, to drain; pat dry with paper towels. (The cabbage and carrot can be stored in a zipper-lock plastic bag and refrigerated overnight.)

2. Place the peanut butter, oil, vinegar, soy sauce, honey, garlic, ginger, and jalapeño in a food processor. Process until a smooth dressing is formed. Toss the cabbage and carrot, radishes, scallions, and dressing together in a medium bowl. Season to taste with salt. Cover and refrigerate until ready to serve. (The salad is best the day it is made but will keep for several days.)

BEAN SALADS

IF YOUR MOTHER MADE THREE-BEAN SALAD, it probably featured a sweet, vinegary dressing mixed with canned green, yellow, and kidney beans and a bite of red onion. This salad was good but never great. We wondered if this classic American recipe could be improved with fresh ingredients and techniques.

Our goal was a fresh taste (something other than canned beans came to mind) and a light, sweet, and tangy dressing that united the subtle flavors of the beans without overpowering them. To that end, our testing divided itself into three categories: improving the flavor and the texture of the beans; determining the right mix of vinegar and oil for the marinade; and addressing the question of sweetness, which was handled differently in almost every recipe we looked at. (Although we did find a few recipes that did not include a sweetener, sugar in one form or another seemed to differentiate three-bean salad from a simple oil-and-vinegar vegetable salad.)

We decided to first test boiling, blanching, and steaming the green and yellow beans. Not surprisingly, the less time the beans were cooked, the better they stood up in the dressing. Our 10- and 20-minute boiled beans were soft and flavorless, but those blanched for one and two minutes each weren't cooked enough. We eventually settled on boiling the beans for five minutes. This was long enough to remove their waxy exterior and thereby allow the marinade to penetrate, but not long enough to break down their cell structure and make them mushy. After draining the beans, we plunged them into cold water to stop the cooking process. Steamed beans held up fairly well, but they didn't have the crunch of the boiled and shocked beans.

Next we moved on to the kidney beans. None of the recipes recommended cooking dried beans—they all called for canned. Just to be sure, we cooked up two batches of dried beans, then marinated them overnight. Not only were the canned beans a lot easier to use, but they tasted just as good.

With the beans ready for dressing, we moved on to the marinade. After testing eight oil varieties and seven types of vinegar, we found that we preferred canola oil for its mild flavor and red wine vinegar for its tang.

We were ready to test types of sugar. We also wanted to test an idea we had run across in several recipes—cooking the sugar, vinegar, and oil together. We quickly realized that this step dramatically improved the flavor of the dressing. We tried cooking vinegar mixed with brown sugar, with honey, and with white sugar over medium heat. The white sugar version won hands down: The cooking process created a syrup with its own unique flavor—sweet and tangy at the same time. It turns out that both heat and the type of sugar used make all the difference between a so-so marinade and a tasty one.

Three-Bean Salad

SERVES 8 TO 10

This recipe is the all-American classic. Prepare this salad at least 1 day before you plan on serving it: The beans taste better after marinating in the dressing.

1 cup red wine vinegar
³/₄ cup sugar
¹/₂ cup canola oil
2 medium garlic cloves, minced or pressed through a garlic press (about 2 teaspoons)
Salt and ground black pepper
8 ounces green beans, cut into 1-inch pieces
8 ounces yellow wax beans, cut into 1-inch pieces
1 (15.5-ounce) can red kidney beans, drained and rinsed
¹/₂ medium red onion, chopped medium
¹/₄ cup minced fresh parsley leaves

1. Heat the vinegar, sugar, oil, garlic, 1 teaspoon salt, and pepper to taste in a small nonreactive saucepan over medium heat, stirring occasionally, until the sugar dissolves, about 5 minutes. Transfer to a large nonreactive bowl and cool to room temperature.

2. Bring 3 quarts water to a boil in a large saucepan over high heat. Add 1 tablespoon salt and the green and yellow beans and cook until the beans are crisp-tender, about 5 minutes. Meanwhile, fill a medium bowl with ice water. When the beans are done, drain and immediately plunge them into the ice water to stop the cooking process; let sit until chilled, about 2 minutes. Drain well.

3. Add the green and yellow beans, kidney beans, onion, and parsley to the vinegar mixture and toss well to coat. Cover and refrigerate overnight to let the flavors meld. Let stand at room temperature 30 minutes before serving. (The salad can be covered and refrigerated for up to 4 days.)

➤ VARIATION

Three-Bean Salad with Cumin, Cilantro, and Oranges

This variation gives the salad a Southwestern spin.

¹/₄ cup juice from 3 limes
³/₄ cup red wine vinegar
³/₄ cup sugar
¹/₂ cup canola oil
2 medium garlic cloves, minced or pressed through a garlic press (about 2 teaspoons)
1 teaspoon ground cumin

Salt and ground black pepper
8 ounces green beans, cut into 1-inch pieces
8 ounces yellow wax beans, cut into 1-inch pieces
1 (15.5-ounce) can red kidney beans, drained and rinsed
2 medium oranges, peeled and segmented (see the illustrations on page 117)
¹/₂ medium red onion, chopped medium
¹/₄ cup minced fresh cilantro leaves

1. Heat the lime juice, vinegar, sugar, oil, garlic, cumin, 1 teaspoon salt, and pepper to taste in a small nonreactive saucepan over medium heat, stirring occasionally, until the sugar dissolves, about 5 minutes. Transfer to a large nonreactive bowl and cool to room temperature.

2. Bring 3 quarts water to a boil in a large saucepan over high heat. Add 1 tablespoon salt and the green and yellow beans and cook until the beans are crisp-tender, about 3 minutes. Meanwhile, fill a medium bowl with ice water. When the beans are done, drain and immediately plunge them into the ice water to stop the cooking process; let sit until chilled, about 2 minutes. Drain well.

3. Add the green and yellow beans, kidney beans, oranges, onion, and cilantro to the vinegar mixture and toss well to coat. Cover and refrigerate overnight to let the flavors meld. Let stand at room temperature 30 minutes before serving. (The salad can be covered and refrigerated for up to 4 days.)

Green and White Bean Salad with Pancetta

White cannellini beans stand in for kidney beans in this Italian-style bean salad. Serve this salad warm with grilled meat.

Salt
8 ounces green beans, cut into 1-inch pieces
¹/₂ head radicchio, torn into ¹/₂-inch pieces (about 1 cup)
3 tablespoons olive oil
2 ounces thinly sliced pancetta, cut into ¹/₈-inch pieces

½   white onion, chopped fine

1   (15-ounce) can cannellini beans, drained and rinsed

2   tablespoons red wine vinegar
     Ground black pepper

1. Bring 2½ quarts water to a boil in a large saucepan over high heat. Add 1 teaspoon salt and the green beans, return to a boil, and cook until the beans are bright green and crisp-tender, about 3 minutes. Meanwhile, fill a medium bowl with ice water. Drain the beans in a colander and immediately transfer them to the ice water. When the beans no longer feel warm to the touch, drain them well in the colander again. Place the beans in a large bowl with the radicchio and set the bowl aside.

2. Heat the oil and pancetta in a large skillet over medium heat. Cook until the pancetta has rendered its fat and become slightly crisp, about 6 minutes. Add the onion and cook, stirring occasionally, until slightly softened, about 3 minutes. Add the cannellini beans and cook, stirring occasionally, until heated through, about 3 minutes. Remove the pan from the heat and swirl in the vinegar.

3. Pour the white bean mixture over the green beans and radicchio and toss to combine. Adjust the seasonings with salt and pepper to taste. Serve immediately.

Tuna and White Bean Salad

THIS QUICK TUSCAN SALAD IS A STANDARD in Florence, where hearty portions of round, white beans and good canned tuna are lightly dressed with vinegar and olive oil. Wanting to duplicate this classic dish in the test kitchen, we focused on finding an easy recipe that wouldn't sacrifice flavor.

Although beans always taste better when cooked slowly for several hours, we found this was simply too much time to invest for such a simple salad. We were pleasantly surprised at the quality of canned cannellini beans, finding they needed only a good rinse after coming out of the can. Moving on to the tuna, we found that tuna packed in olive

oil was far superior to any packed in spring water. With a luxurious texture and an honest flavor, good olive oil–packed tuna made all the difference in this salad. We found that one 15-ounce can of cannellini beans and two 4-ounce cans of tuna resulted in a good ration of beans to fish.

Red onion and fresh parsley were the only flavoring garnishes needed to finish the salad. Dressed with good extra-virgin olive oil, red wine vinegar, and a little lemon, this salad is among the most basic and delicious lunches that can be made in less than five minutes. But because it is so simple, all of the ingredients—even the salt—must be absolutely fresh and of high quality.

Tuna and White Bean Salad
SERVES 4

See page 154 for information about buying tuna packed in olive oil.

2   (4-ounce) cans tuna packed in olive oil, drained

1   (15-ounce) can cannellini beans, drained and rinsed

2   tablespoons minced red onion

1   tablespoon minced fresh parsley leaves

½   teaspoon kosher salt or sea salt

⅛   teaspoon ground black pepper

3   tablespoons extra-virgin olive oil

2   teaspoons red wine vinegar

½   lemon, cut into 4 wedges

Gently mix all of the ingredients except the lemon wedges together in a medium bowl and allow the flavors to meld for 5 minutes. Serve with the lemon wedges.

Lentil Salad

COMMON ON FRENCH BISTRO MENUS, LENTIL salad is a tasty, toothsome dish whose popularity in the home kitchen is long overdue. We began our research with the main ingredient: the lentil, a legume, of which there are several varieties. Not surprisingly, lentils du Puy (French green

The fact that nothing seemed to penetrate the potatoes got us wondering: Does the potato skin act as a barrier? We performed an experiment by cooking two batches of unpeeled potatoes, the first in heavily salted water and the second in unsalted water. We rinsed them quickly under cold running water and tasted. Sure enough, both batches of potatoes tasted exactly the same. We tried boiling peeled potatoes, but they were waterlogged compared with their unpeeled counterparts.

SCIENCE: Keeping Potato Salad Safe

Mayonnaise has gotten a bad reputation, being blamed for spoiled potato salads and upset stomachs after many summer picnics and barbecues. You may think that switching from a mayonnaise-based dressing to a vinaigrette will protect your potato salad (and your family) from food poisoning. Think again.

The main ingredients in mayonnaise are raw eggs, vegetable oil, and an acid (usually vinegar or lemon juice). The eggs used in commercially made mayonnaise have been pasteurized to kill salmonella and other bacteria. The acid is another safeguard; because bacteria do not fare well in acidic environments, the lemon juice or vinegar inhibits bacteria growth. Mayonnaise, even when homemade, is rarely the problem. It's the potatoes that are more likely to go bad.

The bacteria usually responsible for spoiled potato salad are Bacillus cereus and Staphylococcus aureus (commonly known as staph). Both are found in soil and dust, and they thrive on starchy foods like rice, pasta, and potatoes. If they find their way to your potato salad via unwashed vegetables, an unwashed cutting board, or contaminated hands, they can wreak havoc on your digestive system.

Most food-borne bacteria grow well at temperatures between 40 and 140 degrees Fahrenheit. This is known as the temperature danger zone, and if contaminated food remains in this zone for too long, the bacteria can produce enough toxins to make you sick. The U.S. Food and Drug Administration recommends refrigerating food within two hours of its preparation, or one hour if the room temperature is above 90 degrees.

Even with our German Potato Salad (page 132), which contains ½ cup of vinegar, we think it's best to play it safe and follow the FDA's guidelines. Don't leave any potato salad out for more than two hours, and promptly refrigerate any leftovers in a covered container.

We found the paper-thin skin of the boiled red potato not unpleasant to taste and certainly pleasant to look at in what is often a monochromatic salad. Although this saved the peeling step, we found the skin tended to rip when the potato was cut. Because the skin was particularly susceptible to ripping when the potatoes were very hot, we solved the problem in two ways. First, we cut the potatoes with a serrated knife, which minimized ripping, and second, we let them cool before cutting them.

Now, it was on to our last step. To find out if the now-cool potatoes would have the capacity to absorb seasoning, we made two salads, letting one cool completely before dressing with vinegar, salt and pepper, and mayonnaise and letting the other cool just until warm and preseasoning it with vinegar and salt and pepper well before adding the mayonnaise. (We found the potatoes could still be cut cleanly as long as they were warm but not hot.) The results were clear. The salad made with potatoes seasoned when still warm was zesty and delicious. The other salad was bland in comparison.

American Potato Salad with Hard-Cooked Eggs and Sweet Pickles

SERVES 4 TO 6

Use sweet pickles, not relish, for the best results.

2	pounds red potatoes (about 6 medium or 18 small), scrubbed
¼	cup red wine vinegar
	Salt and ground black pepper
3	Hard-Cooked Eggs (page 44), peeled and cut into ½-inch dice
1	medium celery rib, minced (about ½ cup)
2	tablespoons minced red onion
¼	cup sweet pickles, minced
½	cup mayonnaise
2	teaspoons Dijon mustard
2	tablespoons minced fresh parsley leaves

1. Cover the potatoes with 1 inch water in a stockpot or Dutch oven. Bring to a simmer over medium-high heat. Reduce the heat to medium

and simmer, stirring once or twice to ensure even cooking, until the potatoes are tender (a thin-bladed paring knife or metal cake tester can be slipped into and out of the center of the potatoes with no resistance), 25 to 30 minutes for medium potatoes or 15 to 20 minutes for small potatoes.

2. Drain; cool the potatoes slightly and peel if you like. Cut the potatoes into ¾-inch cubes (use a serrated knife if they have skins) while still warm, rinsing the knife occasionally in warm water to remove the starch.

3. Place the warm potato cubes in a large bowl. Add the vinegar, ½ teaspoon salt, and ¼ teaspoon pepper and toss gently. Cover the bowl with plastic wrap and refrigerate until cool, about 20 minutes.

4. When the potatoes are cool, toss with the remaining ingredients and season with salt and pepper to taste. Serve immediately or cover and refrigerate for up to 1 day.

FRENCH POTATO SALAD

HAVING LITTLE IN COMMON WITH ITS American counterpart, French potato salad is served warm or at room temperature and is composed of sliced potatoes glistening with olive oil, white wine vinegar, and plenty of fresh herbs. We knew we wanted to go the traditional route and use red potatoes for our salad. Cut into slices, the red potatoes don't crumble and are therefore more aesthetically pleasing for a composed salad. We expected quick success with this seemingly simple recipe—how hard could it be to boil a few potatoes and toss them in vinaigrette? We sliced the potatoes, dressed them while they were still warm (warm potatoes are more absorbent than cool ones), and served them up. Our confidence plummeted as taster after taster remarked on how dull and bland our salad was.

We shifted our focus toward the vinaigrette ingredients—all traditional components of French potato salad: olive oil, white wine vinegar, herbs, mustard, minced onion, chicken stock, and white wine. We decided to experiment with each component until we found a surefire way to pump up the flavor. The first improvement came by using slightly more vinegar than is called for in the test kitchen's standard formula for vinaigrette, 4 parts oil to 1 part vinegar. These bland potatoes could handle extra acid. We loved the sharp flavor notes added by champagne vinegar but found that white wine vinegar worked well, too. As for the olive oil, extra-virgin or pure olive oil made an equally good base for the dressing; tasters found little distinction between the two (the former being more flavorful than the latter), presumably because of the other potent ingredients in the vinaigrette. However, expensive fruity olive oils were rejected for their overpowering nature.

We liked the extra moisture and layer of complexity that chicken stock (or broth) and wine added (salads made strictly with oil and vinegar were a tad dry), but it seemed wasteful to uncork a bottle or open a can to use only a few tablespoons. We found a solution to this problem and a revelation when we consulted Julia Child's *The Way to Cook* (Knopf, 1989). She suggests adding some of the potato cooking water to the vinaigrette, a quick and frugal solution that also added plenty of potato flavor and a nice touch of saltiness. Two teaspoons of Dijon mustard and a sprinkle of ground black pepper perked things up, while the gentle assertiveness of minced shallot and a partially blanched garlic clove (raw garlic was too harsh) added even more depth. As for the fresh herbs, we made salads with all manner of them, including chives, dill, basil, parsley, tarragon, and chervil. But an inherently French fines herbes mixture seemed appropriate in theory and was heavenly in reality. Chives, parsley, tarragon, and chervil make up this classic quartet, with its anise undertones.

The last but not least fine point: How to toss the cooked, warm potatoes with the vinaigrette without damaging the slices? The solution was simple. We carefully laid the potatoes in a single layer on a rimmed baking sheet, then poured the vinaigrette over them. Spreading out the potatoes in this way also allowed them to cool off a bit, preventing residual cooking and potential mushiness. While we let the vinaigrette soak into the potatoes, we had just enough time to chop the herbs and shallot before sprinkling them on the finished salad.

French Potato Salad

SERVES 4 TO 6

If fresh chervil isn't available, substitute an additional ½ tablespoon of minced parsley and an additional ½ teaspoon of minced tarragon. For best flavor, serve the salad warm, but to make ahead, follow the recipe through step 2, cover with plastic wrap, and refrigerate. Before serving, bring the salad to room temperature, then add the shallot and herbs.

2	pounds (about 6 medium or 18 small) red potatoes, scrubbed and cut into ¼-inch-thick slices
2	tablespoons salt
1	medium garlic clove, peeled and threaded on a skewer
1½	tablespoons champagne vinegar or white wine vinegar
2	teaspoons Dijon mustard
¼	cup olive oil
½	teaspoon ground black pepper
1	small shallot, minced (about 2 tablespoons)
1	tablespoon minced fresh chervil leaves
1	tablespoon minced fresh parsley leaves
1	tablespoon minced fresh chives
1	teaspoon minced fresh tarragon leaves

1. Place the potatoes, 6 cups cold water, and the salt in a large saucepan. Bring to a boil over high heat, then reduce the heat to medium. Lower the skewered garlic into the simmering water and partially blanch, about 45 seconds. Immediately run the garlic under cold tap water to stop the cooking process; remove the garlic from the skewer and set aside. Simmer the potatoes, uncovered, until tender but still firm (a thin-bladed paring knife can be slipped into and out of the center of a potato slice with no resistance), about 5 minutes. Drain the potatoes, reserving ¼ cup cooking water. Arrange the hot potatoes close together in a single layer on a rimmed baking sheet.

2. Press the garlic through a garlic press or mince by hand. Whisk the garlic, reserved potato cooking water, vinegar, mustard, oil, and pepper together in a small bowl until combined. Drizzle the dressing evenly over the warm potato slices; let stand 10 minutes.

3. Meanwhile, toss the shallot and herbs gently together in a small bowl. Transfer the potatoes to a large serving bowl. Add the shallot-herb mixture and mix lightly with a rubber spatula to combine. Serve immediately.

➤ VARIATIONS

French Potato Salad with Arugula, Roquefort, and Walnuts

Follow the recipe for French Potato Salad, omitting the herbs and tossing the dressed potatoes with ½ cup walnuts, toasted and chopped coarse, 4 ounces Roquefort cheese, crumbled, and 1 small bunch arugula, washed, dried, stemmed, and torn into bite-size pieces (about 3 cups), along with the minced shallot in step 3.

French Potato Salad with Radishes, Cornichons, and Capers

Follow the recipe for French Potato Salad, omitting the herbs and substituting 2 tablespoons minced red onion for the shallot. Toss the dressed potatoes with 2 medium red radishes, thinly sliced (about ⅓ cup), ¼ cup capers, rinsed and drained, and ¼ cup cornichons, thinly sliced, along with the red onion in step 3.

French Potato Salad with Hard Salami and Gruyère

Follow the recipe for French Potato Salad, omitting the herbs and substituting 2 teaspoons whole-grain mustard for the Dijon mustard and 2 tablespoons minced red onion for the shallot. Toss the dressed potatoes with 3 ounces hard salami, cut into ¼-inch matchsticks, 2 ounces Gruyère, very thinly sliced or shaved with a vegetable peeler, and 1 tablespoon minced fresh thyme leaves along with the red onion in step 3.

GERMAN POTATO SALAD

SERVED HOT OR WARM, PUNGENTLY TANGY from its vinegar dressing, and chock-full of bacon flavor, German potato salad should be a welcome change from the cold comfort of American-style potato salad. But a recent tasting of German potato salad recipes brought about quite different results. These were the comments, across the board: tasteless, broken-down potatoes; unbalanced, flavorless vinaigrettes; and greasy. It was time to take this recipe into the 21st century.

Starting with the potatoes, we chose low-starch red. We decided to cut the potatoes before boiling, thus dramatically reducing their cooking time. Using heavily salted water ensured that the potatoes were also well seasoned.

The beauty of the dressing for this potato salad is the foundation of rendered bacon fat (vegetable and olive oils were tested and flatly rejected). However, we knew that we wanted to eschew the usual overly greasy vinaigrette. We fried up pounds of bacon, increasing the amount of bacon fat (and crumbled bacon pieces) until tasters were satisfied. Half a pound of bacon was the right amount for 2 pounds of potatoes, with plenty of bacon to bite into. It also produced a hefty ⅓ cup of bacon fat for the dressing. Tasty? Yes. Light? No way. This heavy dressing was just what we were trying to avoid. Part of the solution to the greasiness problem was to spoon off some excess bacon fat; 2 pounds of potatoes required a dressing with just ¼ cup. Any more and the salad was just too fatty.

Choosing the right vinegar to balance the bacon fat was also key. Along with cider vinegar (the usual choice in most recipes), we tested white wine, red wine, distilled white, and rice vinegars. Surprisingly, tasters preferred the distilled white vinegar, which is often the last choice in the test kitchen owing to its bland flavor. But in this case, that was exactly what we needed—clean acidity without much personality of its own to mask the flavor of the bacon. One cup of vinegar made the right quantity of dressing (the hot potatoes soaked up an amazing amount), but now tasters' palates were assaulted with a harsh, unbalanced dressing. We diluted the acidity with some of the potato cooking water, a trick we picked up when researching our French Potato Salad (page 131).

Sautéed onion was a must (raw onion was too harsh), and after trying red, white, and yellow, we found that you really can't go wrong with any of them. Mustard appears in some German potato salad recipes, but certainly not all. After starting out with salads made with no mustard, tasters were receptive to its addition. We first tried Dijon (both smooth and cracked varieties), but tasters weren't crazy about the wine flavor that it added. Brown mustard was neither here nor there. Whole-grain German-style mustard (of course) proved the best bet. Dotted with flecks of whole mustard seeds, the salad now had both the right flavor and a rustic appearance. A half teaspoon of sugar offset the tartness of the vinegar and mustard, and some chopped parsley added freshness.

Mixing the dressing and potatoes in a big serving bowl is typically how the salad is combined. We found, though, that the potatoes lost most of their heat that way. Instead, we dumped the potatoes right into the skillet where the vinaigrette was waiting, giving them a quick toss right in the hot pan before piling the whole thing into a serving dish. Nice and warm, tangy and full of flavor, this was German potato salad at its very best.

German Potato Salad

SERVES 4 TO 6

Unlike a nonstick skillet, a traditional skillet will allow the bacon to form caramelized bits on the pan bottom. This will result in a richer-tasting dressing and a more flavorful salad.

2	pounds red potatoes (about 6 medium or 18 small), scrubbed and halved if small or quartered if medium
	Salt
8	ounces (about 8 slices) bacon, cut crosswise into ½-inch pieces
1	medium onion, chopped fine
½	teaspoon sugar
½	cup distilled white vinegar
1	tablespoon whole-grain German-style mustard

¼ teaspoon ground black pepper

¼ cup loosely packed chopped fresh parsley leaves

1. Place the potatoes, 1 tablespoon salt, and water to cover in a large saucepan or Dutch oven; bring to a boil over high heat, then reduce the heat to medium and simmer until the potatoes are tender (a thin-bladed paring knife can be slipped into and out of the potatoes with little resistance), about 10 minutes. Reserve ½ cup potato cooking water, then drain the potatoes; return the potatoes to the pot and cover to keep warm.

2. While the potatoes are cooking, fry the bacon in a large skillet over medium heat, stirring occasionally, until browned and crisp, about 5 minutes. With a slotted spoon, transfer the bacon to a paper towel–lined plate; pour off all but ¼ cup bacon grease. Add the onion to the skillet and cook, stirring occasionally, over medium heat until softened and beginning to brown, about 4 minutes. Stir in the sugar until dissolved, about 30 seconds. Add the vinegar and reserved potato cooking water; bring to a simmer and cook until the mixture is reduced to about 1 cup, about 3 minutes. Off the heat, whisk in the mustard and pepper. Add the potatoes, parsley, and bacon to the skillet and toss to combine; adjust the seasonings with salt to taste. Transfer to a bowl and serve immediately, while still warm.

Macaroni Salad

MACARONI SALAD IS AN AMERICAN DELI staple. For many people, it's hard to imagine a picnic or summer barbecue without this salad of tender elbow noodles and creamy dressing. Although relatively easy to make, it is also easy to make badly. Few dishes are less appetizing than a bowl of underseasoned, overcooked noodles accompanied by flavorless, limp celery, killer-sweet pickle relish, and an excess of mayonnaise. Good macaroni salad, however, is dreamy when made with perfectly cooked, well-seasoned noodles and crisp vegetables dressed lightly in mayonnaise.

To start, we focused on the noodles. We tried cooking them al dente, and although we prefer a slightly resistant texture in hot noodles, we found them overly toothsome and stiff when cold. Thoroughly cooked noodles, which offered no resistance when eaten hot, took on a pleasantly yielding and bouncy texture when cool and were also able to maintain their shape without becoming mushy. Noodles that were overcooked even just slightly tasted mushy and slimy and tore into pieces when tossed with the other ingredients. We also found that adding more salt than usual to the cooking water made for a more evenly seasoned salad. While the noodles will taste a little salty on their own, they will be perfectly seasoned when mixed with the other ingredients and served cold. We found that 2 tablespoons of table salt to 4 quarts of water was just right to season 1 pound of macaroni.

Another trick we picked up was how to turn the hot noodles into a cold salad quickly. When the hot noodles were allowed to cool on their own, they clumped together into a starchy mass and began to overcook from their own residual heat. Going against all we have learned about how to cook

NEW TWISTS ON OLD FAVORITES

WHILE THERE ARE TIMES WHEN ONLY classic potato, three-bean, or macaroni salad will do, sometimes we want to spice things up a little. Here are some variations to keep dinner interesting.

- Macaroni Salad with Chipotles and Cilantro (page 134)
- Macaroni Salad with Curried Apples (page 134)
- Chopped Salad with Fennel, Green Apple, and Radishes (page 148)
- Three-Bean Salad with Cumin, Cilantro, and Oranges (page 125)
- French Potato Salad with Arugula, Roquefort, and Walnuts (page 131)
- French Potato Salad with Hard Salami and Gruyere (page 131)

pasta, we rinsed the hot noodles under cold water, which both stopped them from cooking any further and washed away some of the extra starch. (When serving pasta hot with sauce, this starch is a good thing, because it helps the sauce cling to the pasta.) We then spread out the noodles on paper towels to help drain off this extra water (see the illustrations below). If we skipped this step, water was caught in the curves of the macaroni and turned the dressing watery.

We found the noodles were best mixed with the classic assortment of fresh vegetables and seasonings: celery, red onion, hard-cooked egg, and sweet pickles. Fresh parsley added a clean, herbal flavor and a little mustard provided some kick. Wary of burying this fresh-tasting mixture with too much mayonnaise, we started off using only ½ cup per pound of noodles but found that they readily soaked up mayonnaise until we hit 1 cup. Although many recipes call for vinegar, we preferred the light, fresh acidity of lemon juice. The salad tastes best when allowed to cool for at least one hour in the refrigerator. The seasonings mellow substantially, so use a liberal hand with salt and pepper.

DRYING MACARONI

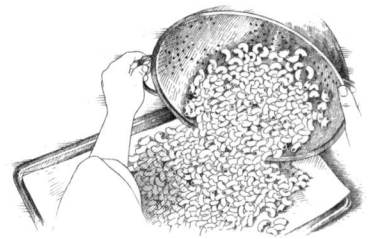

1. Shake the macaroni dry in the colander and spread it in an even layer on a rimmed baking sheet lined with paper towels. Let the macaroni dry for 3 minutes.

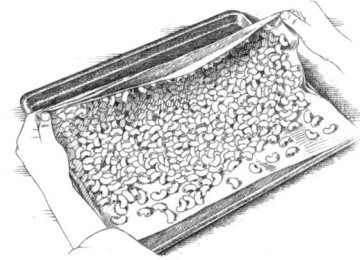

2. Roll the macaroni in paper towels to blot any remaining moisture, then transfer to a large bowl.

Macaroni Salad

SERVES 8 TO 10

Make sure to drain the cooked and rinsed macaroni thoroughly. See the illustrations at left.

	Salt
1	**pound elbow macaroni**
1	**medium celery rib, minced**
¼	**small red onion, minced**
3	**Hard-Cooked Eggs (page 44), peeled and diced small**
¼	**cup minced sweet pickles**
¼	**cup minced fresh parsley leaves**
¼	**cup juice from 2 lemons**
1	**cup mayonnaise**
2	**teaspoons Dijon mustard**
	Ground black pepper

1. Bring 4 quarts water to a boil in a large pot and add 2 tablespoons salt. Stir in the macaroni and cook until thoroughly done, 10 to 12 minutes. Drain the macaroni into a colander and rinse with cold water until cool. Shake the macaroni dry in the colander and then spread it in an even layer on a rimmed baking sheet lined with paper towels. Let the macaroni dry for 3 minutes.

2. Roll the macaroni in paper towels to blot any remaining moisture and transfer the drained macaroni to a large bowl. Toss with the remaining ingredients and season liberally with salt and pepper to taste. Refrigerate the macaroni salad for at least 1 hour or up to 1 day.

➤ VARIATIONS

Macaroni Salad with Curried Apples

Follow the recipe for Macaroni Salad, replacing the hard-cooked eggs, sweet pickles, parsley, and mustard with 1 medium Granny Smith apple, cored and cut into ¼-inch dice (about 1½ cups), and ¼ cup minced fresh basil leaves. Mix 1 tablespoon curry powder into the mayonnaise and proceed as directed.

Macaroni Salad with Chipotles and Cilantro

Toast 1½ cups frozen corn kernels and 2 medium unpeeled garlic cloves in a nonstick skillet set over high heat until the corn turns spotty brown, about 5 minutes; peel and mince the garlic. Follow the recipe for Macaroni Salad, replacing the hard-cooked eggs, sweet pickles, parsley, and mustard with the corn and garlic, 3 scallions, minced (about ¼ cup), and 1 cup cherry tomatoes, quartered. Mix 1 tablespoon minced chipotle chiles in adobo sauce into the mayonnaise and proceed as directed.

Pasta Salad

BECAUSE PASTA SALADS MAKE THE MOST SENSE as a side dish for a summer meal, we've always found it odd that many recipes are heavy and creamy. A good pasta salad should be light and refreshing, with a fair amount of vegetables. (We find little bits of salami a greasy and distressing addition to deli pasta salads.) The dressing should help convey flavors and keep the pasta moist, not weigh it down. Vinaigrette, not mayonnaise, is the obvious choice.

Almost every deli in America sells a pasta salad dressed with vinaigrette. Often made with fusilli (tricolor fusilli in trendier markets), this salad invariably looks unappetizing. The pasta is so mushy you can see it falling apart through the glass deli case. And the vegetables are tired and sad. The broccoli has faded to drab olive green and the shredded carrots that most markets add have wilted. And as for the flavor—these unattractive salads usually look better than they taste.

The problem with most of these pasta salads is that the acid causes the pasta to soften and dulls the color and flavor of many vegetables, especially green ones. But leave out the lemon juice or vinegar and the salad tastes flat. We wanted to develop a light, vinaigrette-dressed vegetable pasta salad that looked good and tasted even better.

We started by making salads with four very simple vinaigrettes. Each contained a different acidic liquid, along with olive oil, salt, and pepper. Each was used to dress a simple pasta salad with blanched and cooled broccoli. The salad made with white wine vinegar looked fine but tasted too acidic. The salad made with lemon juice was clearly the best. It had a nice bright flavor but was neither puckery

nor sour. After half an hour, we noticed that the broccoli in the three salads with vinegar was turning olive green and starting to fall apart. But even after several hours, the broccoli in the salad with lemon juice was green and crunchy.

With lemon juice now our choice of acid, we focused on the sequence of assembling the dish. Would hot vegetables absorb more dressing and taste better? Should we run the vegetables under cold water after cooking to set their color? Neither idea panned out. We found that green vegetables like broccoli are most susceptible to the effects of acid when they are hot. Letting them cool to room temperature helped stem any color loss, but unfortunately you can t speed up the process by running them under cold water. No matter how well we drained them, the vegetables tasted waterlogged after being rinsed in cold water. The best method is to let the vegetables rest in the colander for at least 20 minutes, or until barely warm to the touch, before tossing them with the pasta and dressing.

At this point, we had a master recipe that we liked pretty well, but it needed some other flavors. An herb—we chose basil, but almost anything will work—perked things up. Olives (or sun-dried tomatoes) made everything more lively by adding some acidity and saltiness to a dish that was otherwise a bit bland. And for our variation with Arugula and Sun-Dried Tomatoes, we preferred the more robust flavor of a red wine vinaigrette to a dressing made with lemon juice.

Pasta Salad with Broccoli and Olives

SERVES 6 TO 8

If you prefer, increase the red pepper flakes or replace them with a few grindings of black pepper.

    Salt

2   pounds broccoli (about 2 small heads), florets cut into bite-size pieces (about 7 cups)

¼   cup juice and ½ teaspoon grated zest from 2 lemons

1   medium garlic clove, minced or pressed through a garlic press (about 1 teaspoon)

½   teaspoon red pepper flakes

½   cup extra-virgin olive oil

1   pound short, bite-size pasta, such as fusilli, farfalle, or orecchiette

20   large black olives, such as kalamata or another brine-cured variety, pitted and chopped

15   large fresh basil leaves, shredded

1. Bring 4 quarts water to a boil in a large pot over high heat. Bring several quarts water to boil in a large saucepan. Add salt to taste and broccoli to the saucepan and cook until crisp-tender, about 2 minutes. Drain and cool to room temperature.

2. Meanwhile, whisk the lemon juice and zest, garlic, ¾ teaspoon salt, and the red pepper flakes in a large bowl; whisk in the oil in a slow, steady stream until smooth.

3. Add pasta and 1 tablespoon salt to the boiling water. Cook until the pasta is al dente and drain. Whisk the dressing again to blend; add the hot pasta, cooled broccoli, olives, and basil; toss to mix thoroughly. Cool to room temperature, adjust seasonings, and serve. (The pasta salad can be covered with plastic wrap and refrigerated for 1 day; return to room temperature before serving.)

Pasta Salad with Eggplant, Tomatoes, and Basil

SERVES 6 TO 8

The eggplants can be broiled until golden brown if you prefer not to grill them.

2   medium eggplants (about 1 pound total), cut into ½-inch-thick rounds

½   cup extra-virgin olive oil, plus extra for brushing on the eggplant
     Salt and ground black pepper

¼   cup juice and ½ teaspoon grated zest from 2 lemons

1   medium garlic clove, minced or pressed through a garlic press (about 1 teaspoon)

½   teaspoon red pepper flakes

1   pound short, bite-size pasta, such as fusilli, farfalle, or orecchiette

2   large ripe tomatoes, cored, seeded, and cut into ½-inch dice

15   large fresh basil leaves, shredded

1. Light the grill. Bring 4 quarts water to a boil in a large pot over high heat.

2. Lightly brush the eggplant with oil and sprinkle with salt and pepper to taste. Grill, turning once, until marked with dark stripes, about 10 minutes. Cool and cut into bite-size pieces.

3. Meanwhile, whisk the lemon juice and zest, garlic, ¾ teaspoon salt, and the red pepper flakes in a large bowl; whisk in the oil in a slow, steady stream until smooth.

4. Add the pasta and 1 tablespoon salt to the boiling water. Cook until the pasta is al dente and drain. Whisk dressing again to blend; add hot pasta, cooled eggplant, tomatoes, and basil; toss to mix thoroughly. Cool to room temperature, adjust seasonings, and serve. (The pasta salad can be covered with plastic wrap and refrigerated for 1 day; return to room temperature before serving.)

Pasta Salad with Arugula and Sun-Dried Tomato Vinaigrette

SERVES 6 TO 8

   Salt

1   pound fusilli

1   tablespoon extra-virgin olive oil

1   (8-ounce) jar sun-dried tomatoes packed in olive oil

2   tablespoons red wine vinegar

1   large garlic clove, minced to a paste (about 1½ teaspoons)

¼   teaspoon salt

⅛   teaspoon ground black pepper

1   medium bunch arugula, washed, dried, stemmed, and torn into bite-size pieces (about 4 cups loosely packed)

½   cup green olives, pitted and sliced

6   ounces fresh mozzarella cheese, cut into ½-inch cubes

1. Bring 4 quarts water to a boil in a large pot over high heat. Add 1 tablespoon salt and the pasta to the boiling water. Cook until al dente. Drain, rinsing the pasta well with cold water. Drain the cold pasta well, transfer it to a large mixing bowl, and toss it with the olive oil. Set aside.

2. Drain the tomatoes, reserving the oil. (You should have ⅓ cup reserved oil. If necessary, make up the difference with extra-virgin olive oil.) Coarsely chop the tomatoes. Whisk the reserved oil from the tomatoes with the vinegar, garlic, salt, and pepper in a small bowl.

3. Add the arugula, olives, mozzarella, and chopped tomatoes to the bowl with the pasta. Pour the tomato vinaigrette over the pasta, toss gently, and serve immediately.

INGREDIENTS: Red Wine Vinegar

The source of that notable edge you taste when sampling any red wine vinegar is acetic acid, the chief flavor component in all vinegar and the byproduct of the bacterium Acetobacter aceti, which feeds on the alcohol in wine. The process of converting red wine to vinegar once took months, if not years, but now, with the help of an acetator (a machine that speeds the metabolism of the bacteria), red wine vinegar can be made in less than 24 hours.

Does this faster, cheaper method—the one used to make most supermarket brands—produce inferior red wine vinegar? Or is this a case in which modern technology trumps Old World craftsmanship, which is still employed by makers of the more expensive red wine vinegars? To find out, we included in our tasting vinegars made using the fast process (acetator) and the slow process (often called the Orleans method, after the city in France where it was developed).

We first tasted 10 nationally available supermarket brands in two ways: by dipping sugar cubes in each brand and sucking out the vinegar (to cut down on palate fatigue) and by making a simple vinaigrette with each and tasting it on iceberg lettuce. We then pitted the winners of the supermarket tasting against four high-end red wine vinegars.

Although no single grape variety is thought to make the best red wine vinegar, we were curious to find out if our tasters were unwittingly fond of vinegars made from the same grape. We sent the vinegars to a food lab for an anthocyanin pigment profile, a test that can detect the 10 common pigments found in red grapes. Although the lab was unable to distinguish specific grape varieties (Cabernet, Merlot, Pinot Noir, Zinfandel, and the like), it did provide us with an interesting piece of information: Some of the vinegars weren't made with wine grapes (known as Vitus vinifera), but with less expensive Concord-type grapes, the kind used to make Welch's grape juice.

Did the vinegars made with grape juice fair poorly, as might be expected? Far from it. The taste-test results were both shocking and unambiguous: Concord-type grapes not only do just fine when it comes to making vinegar, they may be a key element in the success of the top-rated brands in our tasting. Spectrum our overall winner, is made from a mix of wine grapes and Concord

grapes. Pompeian, which came in second among the supermarket brands, is made entirely of Concord-type grapes.

What else might contribute to the flavor of these vinegars? One possibility we thought, was the way in which the acetic acid is developed. Manufacturers that mass-produce vinegar generally prefer not to use the Orleans method because it's slow and expensive. Spectrum red wine vinegar is produced with the Orleans method, but Pompeian is made in an acetator in less than 24 hours.

What, then, can explain why Spectrum and Pompeian won the supermarket tasting and beat the other gourmet vinegars? Oddly enough, for a food that defines sourness, the answer seems to lie in its sweetness. It turns out that Americans like their vinegar sweet (think balsamic vinegar).

The production of Spectrum is outsourced to a small manufacturer in Modena, Italy, that makes generous use of the Trebbiano grape, the same grape used to make balsamic vinegar. The Trebbiano, which is a white wine grape, gives Spectrum the sweetness our tasters admired. Pompeian vinegar is finished with a touch of sherry vinegar, added to give the red vinegar a more fruity, well-rounded flavor. Also significant to our results may be that both Spectrum and Pompeian start with wines containing Concord grapes, which are sweet enough to be a common choice when making jams and jellies.

When pitted against gourmet vinegars, Spectrum and Pompeian still came out on top. Which red wine vinegar should you buy? The answer comes faster than it takes an acetator to convert red wine to vinegar: Skip the specialty shop and head to the supermarket.

THE BEST RED WINE VINEGARS

Spectrum and Pompeian vinegars are available in supermarkets and bested gourmet brands costing eight times as much.

SESAME NOODLE SALAD WITH SHREDDED CHICKEN

GOOD SESAME NOODLE SALADS CAN BE addictive: They may appear to be just a humble bowl of cold noodles, but don't be fooled—just one bite and you're hooked on these toothsome noodles with shreds of tender chicken, all tossed with a fresh sesame sauce. Once you get the craving, good versions of the dish are hard to find. The cold noodles have a habit of turning gummy, the chicken often dries out, and the sauce is notorious for turning bland and pasty. We wanted a recipe that could not only quell a serious craving but do it in less time than it would take to grab a bus to Chinatown.

Though immediately drawn to the softer texture and milder flavor of fresh Asian-style noodles, we conceded that dried spaghetti could serve as a second-string substitute. The trouble with both types of noodles, however, was that after being cooked and chilled, they gelled into a rubbery skein. After trying a number of ways to avoid this problem, we found it necessary to rinse the noodles under cold tap water directly after cooking. This not only cooled the hot noodles immediately but washed away much of their sticky starch. To further forestall any clumping, we tossed the rinsed noodles with a little toasted sesame oil; this kept them slack and separated for hours.

Boneless, skinless chicken breasts are quick to cook and easy to shred; the real question is how to cook them. Cooking the chicken under the broiler became our method of choice.

To be authentic, the sesame sauce should be made with an Asian sesame paste (not to be confused with Middle Eastern tahini), but most recipes substitute peanut butter because it's easier to find. Somewhat surprisingly, tasters preferred chunky peanut butter over smooth, describing its flavor as fresh and more peanutty. We had been making the sauce in a blender and realized that the chunky bits of peanuts were being freshly ground into the sauce, resulting in the cleaner, stronger flavor. We found the flavors of both garlic and fresh ginger

necessary, along with soy sauce, rice vinegar, hot pepper sauce, and brown sugar. We then stumbled on the obvious way to keep the sauce from being too thick or pasty: Thin it with water.

Although the sauce was good, tasters still complained that there was not enough sesame flavor. We tried adding toasted sesame seeds. Blended into the sauce along with the peanut butter, the seeds added the final kick of authentic sesame flavor we were all hankering for.

Sesame Noodle Salad with Shredded Chicken

SERVES 4 TO 6

In our experience, chicken takes longer to cook in a gas broiler than in an electric one, which is why the cooking times in the recipe range widely. Although our preference is for fresh Chinese egg noodles, we found that dried spaghetti works well, too. Because dried pasta swells so much more than fresh pasta during cooking, use 12 ounces of dried spaghetti, not 1 pound.

¼	cup sesame seeds, toasted in medium dry skillet over medium heat until fragrant, about 4 minutes
¼	cup chunky peanut butter
2	medium garlic cloves, minced or pressed through a garlic press (about 2 teaspoons)
I	tablespoon minced fresh ginger
5	tablespoons soy sauce
2	tablespoons rice vinegar
I	teaspoon hot pepper sauce
2	tablespoons light brown sugar
	Hot water
I	tablespoon salt
I	pound fresh Asian-style noodles or 12 ounces dried spaghetti
2	tablespoons toasted sesame oil
3	boneless, skinless chicken breast halves (1½ pounds), trimmed of excess fat
4	scallions, sliced thin on the diagonal
I	medium carrot, peeled and grated on the large holes of a box grater (about ⅔ cup)

1. Reserve 1 tablespoon of the sesame seeds in a small bowl. In a blender or food processor, process the remaining 3 tablespoons sesame seeds, the peanut butter, garlic, ginger, soy sauce, vinegar, hot pepper sauce, and brown sugar until smooth, about 30 seconds. With the machine running, add hot water 1 tablespoon at a time until the sauce has the consistency of heavy cream, about 5 tablespoons; set the mixture aside (it can be left in the blender jar or food processor workbowl).

2. Bring 6 quarts water to a boil in a stockpot. Add the salt and noodles to the boiling water; boil the noodles until tender, about 4 minutes for fresh and 10 minutes for dried. Drain, then rinse the noodles under cold running water until cool to the touch; drain again. In a large bowl, toss the noodles with the sesame oil until evenly coated. Set aside.

3. Meanwhile, adjust an oven rack to 6 inches from the broiler element; heat the broiler. Spray the broiler pan top with vegetable cooking spray; place the chicken breasts on top and broil until lightly browned, 4 to 8 minutes. Using tongs, flip the chicken over and continue to broil until the thickest part is no longer pink when cut into and registers about 160 degrees on an instant-read thermometer, 6 to 8 minutes. Transfer to a cutting board and let rest 5 minutes. Using two forks, shred the chicken into bite-size pieces. Add the shredded chicken, scallions, carrot, and sauce to the prepared noodles; toss to combine. Divide among individual bowls, sprinkle each bowl with some of the reserved sesame seeds, and serve.

➤ VARIATION

Sesame Noodle Salad with Sweet Peppers and Cucumbers

Core, seed, and cut into ¼-inch slices 1 medium red bell pepper; peel, halve lengthwise, seed, and cut crosswise into ⅛-inch slices 1 medium cucumber. Follow the recipe for Sesame Noodle Salad with Shredded Chicken, omitting the chicken, adding the bell pepper and cucumber to the noodles along with the sauce, and sprinkling each bowl with a portion of 1 tablespoon chopped fresh cilantro leaves along with the sesame seeds.

RICE SALAD

RICE MAKES A LIGHT, BRIGHT SALAD WHEN dressed properly and studded with vegetables and herbs. The concept of making rice salad seems quite simple, yet it presents two basic problems. For starters, this understated grain does not hold up to assertive flavors the way pasta can. It is readily bogged down by a vinaigrette that would be well suited to a green salad. Even more troubling than the delicate dance of flavors is the texture of the rice. Long-grain rice normally just isn't good cold: it tends to turn hard, clumpy, and slightly crunchy. Short-grain rice holds up better as it cooks, but it has a sticky heaviness that we didn't want in a rice salad. We needed to isolate a cooking method for long-grain rice that would preserve its fresh-from-the-pan characteristics once cooked.

We began with our favorite technique for cooking rice pilaf. This made for a nice pilaf dish, but its buttery flavor was ill suited to a rice salad; what's more, as the rice cooled, it lost its appealing fluffiness. We then began to test every method of cooking rice imaginable. While many methods cooked up great rice, inevitably the quality deteriorated upon cooling.

We finally realized that the source of these failures was also the source of its initial fluffiness after cooking: amylose, one of the two primary starches contained in rice. When long-grain rice cools, the long amylose molecules form rigid crystals that squeeze out liquid and turn the rice rock-hard. Technically speaking, this process is called retrogradation. We realized that if we were going to come up with a palatable rice salad, we would need to apply some kind of sorcery to the starch.

In a last-ditch effort, we tried cooking the long-grain rice with the "abundant water" technique, whereby rice is boiled in a large volume of water, just like pasta, until it is toothsome and cooked through but has not yet begun to fray. At this point, the water is simply strained out. The drawback of this technique is that it tends to turn out rice that tastes waterlogged, but the light texture and separate grains held up so well after cooling that we did not dare to disregard it.

Instead, we added a couple of steps to the process to cope with the waterlogging problem.

Taking a cue from the pilaf recipe, we toasted the rice before boiling to tease out its nutty essence. Actually, its aroma might be better likened to popcorn. We did this, however, without the oil, as we found that oil made the rice heavy and greasy in salad form. (A bonus is that all that's needed to clean the pan is a swipe with a dry towel.)

After the rice was boiled, we spread it across a baking sheet to cool. This creates a great deal of surface area, which allows the excess moisture to evaporate. Spreading the rice to cool also prevents it from clumping, as it would if left to rest in a bowl. In addition, because the rice cools to room temperature in about 10 minutes, the salad can be assembled quickly.

Rice salads are not meant to be doused in oil and vinegar—just a small amount does the trick. This also permits you to use a dark-colored vinegar, such as balsamic, without discoloring the rice.

Rice salad is particularly suited to flavors that are politely understated, not especially bold or loud. It is a side dish that should taste light, not at all filling, yet every forkful should have character. Rice salads pair particularly well with grilled fish or chicken and are best served at room temperature. Toss the rice with the dressing about 20 minutes before serving so that the subtle flavors

have time to develop. If you dress it too far ahead, the rice absorbs the flavor and mutes it. The rice in this salad does stand up to refrigeration. Simply let it rest at room temperature for 30 minutes before serving.

Boiled Rice for Rice Salad
MAKES ABOUT 6 CUPS COOKED RICE

Taste the rice as it nears the end of its cooking time; it should be cooked through and toothsome but not crunchy. Be careful not to overcook the rice or the grains will blow out and fray.

1½ cups long-grain rice
1½ teaspoons salt

1. Bring 4 quarts water to a boil in a large stockpot. Meanwhile, heat a medium skillet over medium heat until hot, about 3 minutes. Add the rice and toast, stirring frequently, until faintly fragrant and some grains turn opaque, about 5 minutes.

2. Add the salt to the boiling water and stir in the toasted rice. Return to a boil and cook, uncovered, until the rice is tender but not soft, 8 to 10 minutes. Meanwhile, line a rimmed baking sheet with foil or parchment paper. Drain the rice in a large fine-mesh strainer or colander and then spread it on the prepared baking sheet. Let the rice cool while you prepare the salad ingredients in the following recipes.

HANDLING THE RICE

1. Start by toasting the rice in a hot skillet until it is faintly fragrant and some grains turn opaque, about 5 minutes. Toasting adds flavor and helps to keep the rice from becoming waterlogged.

2. When the rice has been cooked, cool it on a baking sheet to help evaporate excess moisture quickly.

Rice Salad with Oranges, Olives, and Almonds
SERVES 6 TO 8

This salad is inspired by southern Italian flavors. It is especially good with grilled fish.

2 tablespoons olive oil
1 small garlic clove, minced or pressed through a garlic press (about ½ teaspoon)
¼ teaspoon grated zest and 1 tablespoon juice from 1 orange
2 teaspoons red wine vinegar
1 teaspoon salt

½   teaspoon ground black pepper

I   recipe Boiled Rice for Rice Salad

⅓   cup coarsely chopped pitted green olives

2   medium oranges, peeled and segmented (see the illustrations on page 117)

⅓   cup slivered almonds, toasted in a small dry skillet over medium heat until fragrant and golden, about 2 minutes

2   teaspoons minced fresh oregano leaves

Stir together the oil, garlic, orange zest and juice, vinegar, salt, and pepper in a small bowl. Combine the rice, olives, oranges, almonds, and oregano in a large bowl. Drizzle the dressing over the rice and toss thoroughly to combine. Let stand 20 minutes to blend flavors and serve.

Rice Salad with Cherry Tomatoes, Parmesan, Peas, and Prosciutto

SERVES 6 TO 8

Cherry tomatoes are less juicy and a better choice than regular tomatoes for rice salad.

2   tablespoons extra-virgin olive oil

I   tablespoon balsamic vinegar

I   small garlic clove, minced or pressed through a garlic press (about ½ teaspoon)

I   teaspoon salt

½   teaspoon ground black pepper

I   recipe Boiled Rice for Rice Salad

½   cup frozen peas, thawed

6   ounces cherry tomatoes, quartered (about I cup)

I   ounce thinly sliced prosciutto, chopped fine (about ¼ cup)

¼   cup grated Parmesan cheese

¼   cup shredded fresh basil leaves

Stir together the oil, vinegar, garlic, salt, and pepper in a small bowl. Combine the rice, peas, tomatoes, prosciutto, Parmesan, and basil in a large bowl. Drizzle the dressing over the rice and toss thoroughly to combine. Let stand 20 minutes to blend flavors and serve.

BREAD SALAD

TO THE ITALIANS, BREAD IS HOLY; IT IS almost unthinkable to throw it away. It is not surprising, then, that there are so many uses for bread throughout Italy. One of the most delightful and perhaps surprising dishes that evolved in this part of the world is what amounts to a stale bread salad.

Such thrifty salads are superb dishes because they allow flavorful and fresh tomatoes to be fully experienced, along with fragrant mint, parsley, and fresh cilantro. Another crucial ingredient is high-quality extra-virgin olive oil. Because the dry bread so readily absorbs moisture, much of the flavor of the dish is derived from the dressing.

Last but not least, fundamental to the success of these salads is the quality of the bread. Sliced white bread or airy supermarket bread that is highly refined and becomes rock-hard within a few days simply won't do. Ideally, the bread used in bread salads should not contain sugar or sweeteners of any kind, which would conflict with the savory nature of the other ingredients, nor should it include such ingredients as raisins or nuts. What the bread should have is a sturdy texture and a good wheaty flavor.

Depending on how stale the bread is, it may need to be dampened with a little water. The extent of dampening is determined by the dryness

SCIENCE: The Starch Story

Learning how rice cooks helps explain why this unorthodox method of boiling rice works best for rice salad. Starch granules, which are the primary component of rice, tend not to absorb water. As you heat rice in water, however, the energy from the rapidly moving water molecules begins to loosen the bonds between the starch molecules so that water can seep in. This in turn causes the starch molecules to swell, softening the rice but also making it more sticky, or "starchy." If you use the abundant water method for cooking long-grain rice, some of this starch leaches into the water, which is ultimately drained off. The result is a pot of long-grain rice with less concentrated starch. This is what allows the grains to cook up so remarkably light and separate and to maintain that consistency as they cool to room temperature.

of the bread; if the bread is made too damp, it will collapse into a soggy mess when the dressing is added. Therefore, it's best to assemble the salad, see how much the bread softens, and then adjust the texture by sprinkling lightly with water.

Because the bread becomes soggy fairly quickly, none of these salads should be made much in advance of serving (see individual recipes for suggested preparation ahead of time). The best approach is to assemble all of the salad ingredients, then combine them just before serving.

Bread Salad with Tomatoes, Herbs, and Red Onions

SERVES 4 TO 6

Use coarse peasant bread or any sturdy Italian-style bread in this classic Italian recipe.

1	pound day-old coarse peasant bread or sturdy Italian-style bread, crusts removed, cut or torn into 1-inch cubes (about 6 cups)
$1/2$	cup extra-virgin olive oil
3	tablespoons red wine vinegar
2	large ripe tomatoes, cored, seeded, and cut into medium dice
$1/2$	red onion, sliced very thin
2	tablespoons torn fresh basil or mint leaves
2	teaspoons whole fresh oregano leaves
1	tablespoon minced fresh parsley leaves
$1/2$	teaspoon salt
$1/4$	teaspoon ground black pepper

Place the bread cubes in a shallow bowl. Mix the oil, vinegar, tomatoes, onion, and half of the herbs in a medium bowl. Let stand to allow the flavors to develop, about 10 minutes, then add to the bread, along with the remaining herbs, and toss well. Season with the salt and pepper to taste. If the bread still seems dry, sprinkle with 1 or 2 tablespoons water to rehydrate it a bit. Serve. (If the bread used is quite sturdy, the salad can be covered and set aside up to 2 hours.)

Bread Salad with Roasted Peppers and Olives

SERVES 4 TO 6

Sourdough or a sturdy peasant bread is needed for this salad. Airy, unsubstantial bread will become soggy quickly.

1	pound sturdy Italian bread, crusts removed, cut or torn into 1-inch cubes (about 6 cups)
2	medium bell peppers, 1 red and 1 yellow, roasted (see page 10), cored, seeded, and cut into $1/2$-inch strips
$1/2$	cup extra-virgin olive oil
$1/4$	cup cider vinegar
1	small red or white onion, quartered and sliced thin
1	medium scallion, sliced thin, including 2 inches of green part
3	tablespoons pitted and sliced green olives
1	tablespoon minced fresh oregano leaves
$1/2$	teaspoon salt
$1/4$	teaspoon ground black pepper

1. Mix the bread cubes and pepper strips in a large bowl; set aside.

2. Mix the oil, vinegar, onion, scallion, olives, oregano, salt, and pepper in a medium bowl; let stand to allow the flavors to develop, about 10 minutes. Add the dressing to the bread and peppers; toss to combine. If the bread still seems dry, sprinkle with 1 or 2 tablespoons water to rehydrate it a bit. Serve. (If the bread used is quite sturdy, the salad can be covered and set aside up to 2 hours.)

PITA BREAD SALAD

TRADITIONALLY, FATTOUSH CONSISTS OF small bites of pita bread mixed with cucumbers and tomatoes and dressed with lemon juice and a fruity olive oil. But after making several of these traditional Middle Eastern salads, we noticed a few minor flaws. While the salads we tested were tasty, they lacked body and texture.

Wanting to create a more substantial salad—one that could be eaten as a light entrée—we decided that cheese would be a key ingredient. Feta cheese naturally came to mind, as it is one of the more popular cheeses consumed in countries in the eastern Mediterranean. Feta's bright, fresh flavor would also meld well in the salad without making it too heavy.

Continuing our ingredient search, we wanted to select items that would lend crispness to the salad without adding excess moisture. Romaine lettuce was perfect. It added crunch without making the other ingredients soggy, and it contributed body as well. We wanted to avoid tomatoes, but tasters missed their sweetness, so we tried several varieties with less moisture than traditional vine-ripened tomatoes. We found that halved cherry tomatoes contributed deep tomato flavor with less liquid. Some briny kalamata olives and thinly sliced red onion rounded out our ingredient list.

To finish our pita bread salad, we needed a dressing. We knew we wanted to stay with the traditional trio of olive oil, lemon, and mint, but we found that our normal ratio of 4 parts oil to 1 part acid resulted in a boring salad, short on brightness. So we played with the ratio until settling on 2 parts oil to 1 part acid. While this seemed extreme, it gave the salad a tartness that tasters preferred.

PITTING OLIVES

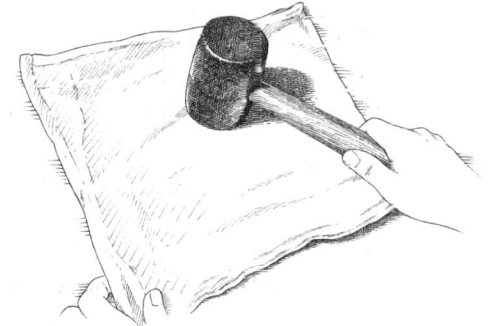

Removing the pits by hand from olives is not an easy job. We found the following method to be the most expedient. Cover a cutting board with a clean kitchen towel and spread the olives on top, spacing them about 1 inch apart. Place a second clean towel over the olives. Using a mallet, pound the olives firmly for 10 to 15 seconds, being careful not to split the pits. Remove the top towel and, using your fingers, press the pit out of each olive.

Finally, we added chopped mint. The only problem with the mint was that with one bite you might get intense mint flavor, and with the next you might not get any. For some reason, the mint was not evenly distributed throughout the chunky salad. To solve this problem, we threw all of the dressing ingredients in a blender and processed them until the mint was finely minced. The salad made with this dressing was just right; the mint flavor was evenly distributed and complemented the other ingredients without overpowering them.

Pita Bread Salad with Olives, Feta, and Mint

SERVES 6

Let the onions sit in the dressing for 5 minutes to remove some of their sting.

4	(8-inch) pita breads, torn into ¹/₂-inch pieces
¹/₄	cup packed fresh mint leaves, torn into small pieces
¹/₄	cup juice from 2 lemons
¹/₂	cup extra-virgin olive oil
¹/₂	small red onion, sliced thin
1	small head romaine lettuce, cut or torn into 1-inch pieces (about 6 cups loosely packed)
20	cherry tomatoes, halved
¹/₂	cup kalamata olives, pitted and sliced
6	ounces feta cheese, crumbled (about 1¹/₂ cups)

1. Adjust an oven rack to the middle position and heat the oven to 375 degrees. Place the bread on a rimmed baking sheet and bake until crisp but not brown, 7 to 10 minutes. Remove the bread from the oven and cool to room temperature.

2. Meanwhile, process the mint, lemon juice, and oil in a blender until the mint is finely chopped, using a rubber spatula to scrape the sides of the blender as necessary, about twenty 1-second pulses. Combine the dressing and onion in a large bowl, toss to coat, and let stand for 5 minutes.

3. Add the pita, romaine, tomatoes, and olives to the bowl with the onion and toss to coat. Arrange the salad on a large serving platter or individual plates, sprinkle with the feta, and serve immediately.

TABBOULEH

PERHAPS THE BEST-KNOWN ARAB DISH IN THE United States is tabbouleh. However, the tabbouleh typically served here is very different from the original. In its Middle Eastern home, this dish is basically a parsley salad with bulgur rather than a bulgur salad with parsley—what is frequently found here.

In addition to finely minced parsley, a perfect tabbouleh includes morsels of bulgur—crushed, parboiled wheat—tossed in a penetrating, minty lemon dressing with bits of ripe tomato. While these principal ingredients remain the same, a variety of preparation techniques exist, each Arab cook being convinced that his or her method produces the finest version.

We tried processing the bulgur in the five most commonly used ways. First we rinsed the grain, combined it with the minced tomato, and set it aside to absorb the tomato juices. With this method, the bulgur remained unacceptably crunchy. Next we marinated the bulgur in a lemon juice and olive oil dressing. This approach produced bulgur that was tasty but still crunchy. The third method, soaking the grain in water until fluffy and then squeezing out the excess moisture, produced an acceptable but somewhat bland-flavored wheat. Next we soaked the wheat in water for about five minutes, then drained the liquid and replaced it with the lemon–olive oil dressing. We discovered that the wheat's texture was good and the flavor much improved.

But the all-out winner came as a surprise. We first rinsed the bulgur, then mixed it with fresh lemon juice. We then set the mixture aside to allow the juice to be absorbed. When treated in this way, bulgur acquires a fresh and intense flavor even better than our last method.

Once the remaining ingredients—parsley, finely chopped scallions, fresh mint, and tomatoes—and the dressing were added to the wheat, we found it best to let the mixture sit for an hour or so to blend the flavors; after five or six hours, though, the scallions became too strong and overpowered the other flavors.

The final question to answer concerned the proportion of parsley to bulgur. Although some Lebanese restaurateurs favor a 9:1 ratio of parsley to bulgur, we found that the wholesome goodness of the wheat was lost. We recommend a more balanced proportion of 5 parts parsley to 3 or 4 parts wheat.

Tabbouleh

SERVES 4 TO 6

Middle Eastern cooks frequently serve this salad with crisp inner leaves of romaine lettuce, using them as spoons to scoop the salad from the serving dish. Fine-grain bulgur is best in this recipe, but medium-grain will work; avoid coarse-grain bulgur, which must be cooked.

1/2	cup fine-grain bulgur wheat, rinsed under running water and drained
1/3	cup juice from 2 lemons
1/3	cup extra-virgin olive oil
	Salt
1/8	teaspoon Middle Eastern red pepper or cayenne pepper (optional)
2	cups minced fresh parsley leaves
2	medium ripe tomatoes, halved, cored, seeded, and cut into very small dice
4	medium scallions, green and white parts, minced
2	tablespoons minced fresh mint leaves

1. Mix the bulgur with 1/4 cup of the lemon juice in a medium bowl; set aside until the grains are tender and fluffy, 20 to 40 minutes, depending on the age and type of the bulgur.

2. Mix the remaining lemon juice, the olive oil, salt to taste, and red pepper (if using) together in a small bowl. In a large bowl, combine the bulgur, parsley, tomatoes, scallions, and mint; add the dressing and toss to combine. Cover and refrigerate to let the flavors blend, 1 to 2 hours. Serve.

CHICKEN CAESAR SALAD

SINCE ITS DEBUT IN THE 1920S, CAESAR SALAD has suffered at the hands of chefs and home cooks alike. The Caesar was conceived as a salad of whole lettuce leaves, cloaked with a rich dressing made from such unlikely partners as egg, Worcestershire sauce, lemon juice, garlic, and Parmesan cheese and garnished with garlic croutons. Over time, however, this salad has been subjected to such oddball additions as chickpeas, palm hearts, and barbecued ribs.

We wanted to bring Caesar salad back to its roots. We were struck, however, by the not inconsiderable effort required to make the salad. Given this investment of time and effort, we decided to make our Caesar heartier by adding one untraditional (but now familiar) ingredient: sliced chicken breast. We wanted the chicken to add heft to the salad without disturbing the underlying magic of the dressing.

Most Caesar salad dressings have at least one of two common problems. The first is texture, which should be thick and smooth, not thin or gluey. The second is lack of balance among the dressing's key flavors—lemon, Worcestershire, and garlic (and often anchovies)—which are frequently so out of whack that they assault your palate with a biting surplus of garlic or lip-sucking profusion of lemon.

We took on texture first. The classic thickening agent in this olive oil–based dressing is egg, which is either added raw or simmered in the shell very briefly in a process called coddling. The recipes we dug up in our research also included dressings that relied on mayonnaise and sour cream for thickening, but tasters summarily rejected both, finding that the former seemed better suited to a sandwich topping and the latter to a party dip. In side-by-side tests of raw and coddled eggs, tasters preferred the noticeably smoother consistency of the coddled-egg dressing. The brief exposure to heat caused the yolk to thicken slightly, thereby giving the dressing a creamier texture. Many tasters wanted the dressing to be thicker still, so we decided to discard the egg white, which

contributed extra liquid, and to double the number of yolks to two. Keep in mind, however, that such a brief exposure to heat does not render the egg as safe as if it were cooked fully; you are still essentially consuming raw egg, which may be of concern to some diners.

A series of tests led us to a well-balanced dressing. Based on an oil quantity of ⅓ cup and our 2 coddled yolks, tasters favored just under 2 tablespoons of lemon juice and a modest teaspoon each of Worcestershire sauce and garlic. The last touch was anchovy, which tasters felt gave the dressing a welcome flavor dimension.

As for the lettuce, romaine is the standard choice. Our tasters stuck to it for its pleasantly sweet flavor and crunchy texture.

The chicken added to Caesar salad in restaurants is often dry and leathery. For our Caesar, we wanted chicken that was moist, well seasoned, and quick and easy to prepare.

Skinless, boneless breasts were the overwhelming choice of tasters, who felt that dark meat tasted out of place. With an eye toward speed and ease, we tested three cooking methods: grilling, sautéing, and broiling. Grilling was too much work for a simple salad. Sautéing was eliminated because it required an extra step (flouring the chicken) and produced (believe it or not) chicken that was too flavorful for this purpose. Broiling, on the other hand, gave us what we wanted—a quick, simple cooking method and chicken that would blend right into the landscape of an already full-flavored salad.

We tried making croutons from various types of white bread and determined that any type made without sweetener tasted fine. Buy a baguette or country white loaf instead of sliced sandwich bread, as the latter usually contains added sugar.

We tested three different methods of making croutons, including toasting, sautéing, and baking the bread cubes, and we tried each method with and without oil and garlic. We quickly learned that infusing olive oil with garlic flavor—rather than using minced garlic—was a key step. Whereas the minced garlic became burnt and bitter in the oven, allowing raw garlic to steep in olive oil for 20 minutes produced a pleasantly garlicky flavor. In the end, we simply tossed raw bread cubes with the seasoned oil and baked them until crisp and golden.

Chicken Caesar Salad

SERVES 4 TO 6

Turn this main-dish salad into a first course by omitting the chicken and reducing the total amount of dressing used to ⅔ cup. Both the croutons and the dressing can be made 1 day in advance of serving.

GARLIC CROUTONS

- 3 tablespoons extra-virgin olive oil
- 2 large garlic cloves, minced or pressed through a garlic press (about 1 tablespoon)
- ¼ teaspoon salt
- 3 cups ¾-inch bread cubes from 1 baguette or country loaf

BROILED CHICKEN BREASTS

- 4 boneless, skinless chicken breast halves (about 6 ounces each), trimmed of excess fat
  Salt and ground black pepper

CAESAR DRESSING

- 2 large eggs
- 1 tablespoon plus 2 teaspoons juice from 1 lemon
- 1 teaspoon Worcestershire sauce
  Salt
  Ground black pepper
- 1 medium garlic clove, minced or pressed through a garlic press (about 1 teaspoon)
- 4 anchovy fillets, minced to a paste (about 1½ teaspoons)
- ⅓ cup extra-virgin olive oil

SALAD

- 2 medium heads romaine lettuce (large outer leaves removed) or 2 large romaine hearts, washed, dried, and torn into 1½-inch pieces (about 10 cups loosely packed)
- ⅓ cup grated Parmesan cheese

1. FOR THE CROUTONS: Adjust an oven rack to the middle position and heat the oven to 350 degrees. Mix the oil, garlic, and salt in a small bowl; let stand 20 minutes to infuse the flavors. Add the bread cubes and toss to coat. Spread the bread cubes in an even layer on a rimmed baking sheet; bake, stirring occasionally, until golden, 15 to 20 minutes. Cool on the baking sheet to room temperature. (The croutons can be covered and stored at room temperature for up to 24 hours.)

2. FOR THE CHICKEN: Season the chicken with salt and pepper. Adjust an oven rack to 6 inches from the broiler element; heat the broiler. Spray the broiler pan top with vegetable cooking spray; place the chicken breasts on top and broil until lightly browned, 4 to 8 minutes. Using tongs, flip the chicken over and continue to broil until the thickest part is no longer pink when cut into and registers about 160 degrees on an instant-read thermometer, 6 to 8 minutes. Transfer the chicken to a plate and set aside.

3. FOR THE DRESSING: Bring 2 inches water to a boil in a small saucepan over high heat. Lower the eggs into the water and cook 45 seconds; remove with a slotted spoon. When cool enough to handle, crack the eggs open; reserve the yolks in a small bowl and discard the whites. Add the lemon juice, Worcestershire, ¼ teaspoon salt, ⅛ teaspoon pepper, the garlic, and anchovies; whisk until smooth. Whisking constantly, add the oil in a slow, steady stream. Adjust the seasonings with salt and pepper to taste. (The dressing can be refrigerated in an airtight container for up to 1 day; shake well before using.)

4. TO FINISH THE SALAD: In a large bowl, toss the lettuce, Parmesan, and about two-thirds of the dressing to coat; divide evenly among individual plates. Remove the tenderloins from the chicken breasts; place in the bowl used to dress the lettuce along with the remaining dressing. Cut the chicken breasts crosswise into ½-inch slices, add to the bowl, and toss to coat. Divide the dressed chicken evenly among the plates, arranging the slices on the lettuce. Sprinkle each plate with a portion of the croutons and serve immediately.

CHOPPED SALAD

THIS CLASSIC LADIES' LUNCH DISH, designed to be easy to eat using only a fork while balancing the plate atop your knees, had its heyday during the 1950s. All the components of the salad are chopped into bite-size pieces and lightly dressed with oil and vinegar.

There's still much to love about this recipe. When correctly made, this salad combines lettuces and vegetables in a pleasing fashion and offers a range of textures, colors, and flavors. While many recipes for chopped salad call for numerous and lavish vegetable garnishes, we found that simpler, more modern salads made with only a few fresh vegetables—cucumber, bell pepper, and radish, as well as tomato—and mild greens tasted best. Although these salads may be simple, we found that a couple of key points distinguish mediocre versions from truly stellar ones.

First, we found that the vegetables should be cut into pieces of similar size. Small pieces (cherry tomatoes cut in half, cucumber and bell pepper cut into ¼-inch dice) are just right. Although this entails slightly more work and attention than rough chopping, the results are worth the extra effort. As for the greens, we found that romaine, Boston, green leaf, and red leaf lettuces were easy to cut into forkable bites and paired well with the vegetables. Tasters did not like spicy greens in this salad. Better to let the tomatoes, cucumbers, and other additions contribute contrasting flavors; our tasters liked mild greens in the background. Finally, it's imperative to use a light hand with the dressing. Too many recipes douse the lettuces and vegetables in dressing, and the resulting salad is limp and heavy.

As for the dressing, we found that a light lemon vinaigrette with some fresh herbs set off the fresh vegetables and lettuces best. Heavier dressings made with sour cream or mayonnaise literally swamped the small pieces of vegetable, while more potent vinaigrettes, made with balsamic or red wine vinegar, were overpowering. We also noted that a little sugar in the vinaigrette helped to boost the flavors of the vegetables, making the overall salad much more lively.

When serving the chopped salad, we preferred to use the lettuce as a base for the chopped vegetables. Wanting all of the components to be properly dressed, we used half of the vinaigrette to dress the greens and the other half to dress the collective garnishes. This two-step dressing process ensures that everything is properly coated and also allows the salad to be plated in the most attractive fashion.

Chopped Salad

SERVES 4 TO 6

This basic recipe can be altered depending on the vegetables you have on hand. See the variations for some ideas.

LEMON-HERB VINAIGRETTE

¼	cup olive oil
1	tablespoon juice from 1 lemon
2	teaspoons Dijon mustard
1	teaspoon minced shallot
1	teaspoon minced fresh parsley leaves
1	teaspoon minced fresh chives
1	teaspoon minced fresh thyme leaves
¼	teaspoon salt
⅛	teaspoon ground black pepper
⅛	teaspoon sugar

SALAD

8	cups mild salad greens (such as romaine, Boston, Bibb, green leaf, or red leaf), cut into 1-inch pieces
½	pint cherry tomatoes, halved
1	small cucumber, peeled, halved lengthwise, seeded (see illustration 1 on page 113), and cut into ¼-inch dice
1	small yellow bell pepper, cored, seeded, and cut into ¼-inch dice
5	medium radishes, stems trimmed, cut in half lengthwise, then sliced thin

1. FOR THE DRESSING: Whisk all of the ingredients together in a small bowl and set aside.

2. FOR THE SALAD: Toss the salad greens with half of the dressing in a medium bowl. Mix the tomatoes, cucumber, bell pepper, and radishes

together in another medium bowl and toss with the remaining dressing.

3. Arrange the salad greens on a serving platter or on individual plates. Spoon the chopped vegetables over the greens and serve immediately.

➤ VARIATIONS

Chopped Salad with Fennel, Green Apple, and Radishes

Follow the recipe for Chopped Salad, omitting the mustard and thyme from the dressing. For the salad, replace the tomatoes, cucumber, and bell pepper with 2 medium Granny Smith apples, peeled, cored, and cut into ¼-inch dice, and 1 small fennel bulb, trimmed of stalks, cored, and cut into ¼-inch dice. (See the illustrations on page 118 for tips on handling fennel.)

Chopped Salad with Avocado, Jícama, and Cucumber

Follow the recipe for Chopped Salad, replacing the lemon juice in the dressing with lime juice, omitting the mustard, and replacing the parsley, chives, and thyme with 1 tablespoon minced fresh cilantro leaves. For the salad, replace the tomatoes, bell pepper, and radishes with ½ medium jícama, peeled and cut into ¼-inch dice, and 1 medium avocado, peeled, pitted, and cut into ¼-inch dice.

WALDORF SALAD

WALDORF SALAD WAS CREATED BY OSCAR Tschirky, maître d'hôtel at the Waldorf-Astoria Hotel in New York. Although the original salad (which dates back to 1896) contained only tart apples and crisp celery bound with a little mayonnaise, walnuts and raisins were added to the mix in subsequent years. In recent decades, recipe writers have tried to "update" the Waldorf by adding everything from oranges and marshmallows to Cajun spices and whipped cream. After making several of these concoctions, we were unanimous in preferring this crisp, clean salad with only walnuts and raisins added to the apples and celery.

Because this simple salad calls for only a few ingredients, each must be fresh and thoughtfully prepared. To start, we found that both the apples and the celery tasted better when they were peeled. The outer layer of the celery was both stringy and bitter, while the skin on the apples tasted tough and tannic. Granny Smiths are traditional in this salad, and we liked the crispness and tartness they brought to this dish. Tasters also preferred salads with an equal proportion of celery and apples. Instead of mincing the celery into tiny bits, as if it were a garnish, we sliced it into substantially sized, attractive half-moon shapes, which made the salad taste more balanced.

Toasting the walnuts is also essential. With so few ingredients, the walnuts add much more punch when toasted in a dry skillet until fragrant. Tossing the apples, celery, walnuts, and raisins with mayonnaise yielded a rather one-dimensional, flat-tasting salad. We found that seasoning the salad ingredients with salt, pepper, and lemon juice before adding the mayonnaise made everything taste brighter. The only liberty we took in updating this recipe was to add a little tarragon, which brought a pleasant herbal, anise flavor to this simple salad.

➤

Waldorf Salad
SERVES 4

This salad can be served in place of coleslaw as a side dish to sandwiches and grilled foods.

¼	cup walnuts, toasted in a small dry skillet over medium heat until fragrant, about 4 minutes, cooled, and chopped
2	medium Granny Smith apples, peeled, cored, and cut into ½-inch dice (about 2½ cups)
4	medium celery ribs, peeled and cut crosswise into ¼-inch pieces ⅓ cup raisins
1	tablespoon juice from 1 lemon
1	teaspoon minced fresh tarragon leaves
¼	teaspoon salt
	Pinch ground black pepper
⅓	cup mayonnaise

Toss the walnuts, apples, celery, and raisins together in a medium bowl. Season with the lemon juice, tarragon, salt, and pepper and toss again. Stir in the mayonnaise and serve immediately.

CHEF'S SALAD

MOST CHEF'S SALAD RECIPES READ LIKE loose guidelines for cleaning out the fridge: Toss whatever greens you have lying around with some aging cold cuts and serve with a sigh. The resulting piles of oily ham, characterless Swiss cheese, and bland iceberg lettuce should not be eaten but taken as an object lesson, demonstrating that recipes, even for simple salads, need structure and discipline.

After all, a hearty green salad topped with boiled eggs, tomatoes, cold meats, and cheese is a more than presentable potluck offering or even dinner for a warm summer night. Unfortunately, the versions we sampled in the test kitchen were far from classic in either taste or technique. Their ingredient lists were haphazard and vague, resulting in bland, muddled flavors, while the procedures were often fussy, time-consuming, and ultimately self-defeating. Why spend an hour julienning ingredients into stringy, unwieldy shapes? Why arrange them in an exacting pattern only to toss the salad into a jumbled mess, with the meat and cheese drowning in a pool of dressing at the bottom of the bowl?

As the foundation, the greens would have to stand up to the strong flavors of the meat and cheese—and support their physical weight as well. Bland iceberg lettuce failed the first test, while tender field greens such as mesclun flunked the second. Other common mild greens, including romaine, Bibb, Boston, and red- and green-leaf lettuces, all held their shape under the weight of the other ingredients, but tasters preferred them mixed with the stronger flavors of spicy greens such as watercress or arugula. A 3:1 ratio of mild to spicy greens worked best.

Personal tastes varied when it came to types of meat and cheese, but tasters agreed on one thing: Thin, stringy strips were unappealing, especially when covered with oily dressing. We readily solved the thin-slice problem by ordering ¼-inch-thick slices at the deli counter. These were easy to stack and cut into 2-inch-long matchsticks, a convenient size for spearing with a fork.

Many recipes suggested creamy Russian or ranch-style dressings, but tasters opposed them. Combined with the meat and cheese, these dressings made the salad far too rich. Vinaigrettes, on the other hand, could not hold their own against the other ingredients, even when livened up with shallot, garlic, and fresh herbs. Tasters declared salad after salad to be bland and oily. Our classic vinaigrette recipe calls for a 4:1 ratio of oil to vinegar, but we decided to balance the meat and cheese with a leaner, more acidic dressing. We reduced the ratio of oil to vinegar first to 3:1, then to 2:1, before tasters were satisfied.

From the way tasters scowled at piles of meat and cheese at the bottom of the salad bowl, we knew a traditional toss was out. The heavier ingredients fell right to the bottom. We discovered that it wasn't necessary to dress the meat and cheese. Other components—greens, radishes, cucumbers, tomatoes, and hard-cooked eggs—could be tossed individually or placed on the salad and then drizzled with vinaigrette. When placed in a wide serving bowl, with the meat and cheese piled on top, the salad could be served family-style but still accommodate individual (even vegetarian) preferences. Diners could serve themselves greens and vegetables from around the sides of the salad, then take whatever meat and cheese they desired from the center.

Chef's Salad

SERVES 8

At the deli counter, be sure to have the meats and cheeses sliced ¼ inch thick.

VINAIGRETTE

6	tablespoons extra-virgin olive oil
3	tablespoons red wine vinegar
2	teaspoons minced shallot
1	small garlic clove, minced or pressed through a garlic press (about ½ teaspoon)
1	teaspoon minced fresh thyme leaves
¼	teaspoon salt
⅛	teaspoon ground black pepper

SALAD

1   medium cucumber, peeled, halved lengthwise, seeded (see illustration 1 on page 113), and sliced crosswise ¼ inch thick

2   medium heads leaf lettuce, washed, dried, and torn into bite-size pieces (about 3 quarts loosely packed)

4   ounces arugula, washed, dried, stemmed, and torn into bite-size pieces (about 4 cups loosely packed)

6   ounces radishes, trimmed, halved, and sliced thin
     Salt and ground black pepper

1   pint cherry tomatoes, halved, or quartered if large

3   large Hard-Cooked Eggs (page 44), each cut into 4 wedges

8   ounces deli ham, sliced ¼ inch thick and cut into 2-inch-long matchsticks

8   ounces deli turkey, sliced ¼ inch thick and cut into 2-inch-long matchsticks

8   ounces sharp cheddar cheese, sliced ¼ inch thick and cut into 2-inch-long matchsticks

1½   cups Garlic Croutons (page 93)

1. FOR THE VINAIGRETTE: Whisk the ingredients in a medium bowl until combined. Add the cucumber and toss; let stand 20 minutes.

2. FOR THE SALAD: Toss the lettuce, arugula, and radishes in a large, wide serving bowl. Add the

---

INGREDIENTS: Deli Turkey and Ham

Supermarkets offer a baffling assortment of packaged meats, but do any of them hold a candle to sliced-to-order deli meats? We began this tasting with a dozen widely available presliced ham and turkey products, most costing about $2 for a 6-ounce package. All were categorically rejected by tasters. Things improved at the deli counter.

Deli Turkey: At the deli counter, we purchased six national brands of sliced-to-order turkey breast. Tasters liked Sara Lee's Oven Roasted Turkey Breast ($6.50 per pound), describing it as "moist," "meaty," and "honest," but the house brand produced by Stop & Shop ($6.50 per pound), a local supermarket chain, ranked just as highly. Also included in the lineup was an in-store roasted turkey breast ($10 per pound) purchased from a gourmet market, which—to our surprise—tasters rejected as bland and incredibly dry. Why did "real" turkey perform so poorly? Processed turkey breast is injected with water, salt, and seasonings. Because turkey breast meat is naturally dry, some extra moisture is desirable—even necessary—to produce a palatable product.

Deli Ham: The processing of deli ham is more involved than that of processing deli turkey, making the choices more confusing. "Boiled" hams are forced into a mold before being cooked, and the gaps are filled in with an emulsified puree of water, fat, and pork trimmings. These hams, easily identifiable by their rectangular shape and pale pink exterior, are generally cheaper than baked or smoked hams, but tasters disliked their wet, plastic texture. Baked or smoked hams are generally injected with salt, water, and phosphates but retain the texture of a real ham. At the deli counter, these hams sport an impressive variety of labels, including baked, smoked, Virginia, maple, Black Forest, and honey. What the names really indicate, however, is merely the particular flavoring blend that has been injected into the ham. We tasted seven hams in this category and uncovered a wide variety of flavors—some sweet, some smoky, some spicy—but most of the samples were quite good. Baked ham costs a bit more than boiled ham, but the money is well spent.

BEYOND HORRIBLE
Tasters utterly rejected presliced ham.

PRETTY BAD
A square boiled ham from the deli counter was not much better.

PRETTY GOOD
A baked Virginia ham from the deli counter was the best choice by far.

PERFECTLY SLICED DELI MEAT

Deli meat should be cut thick enough to prevent clumping in the bowl but trim enough to be easily incorporated into the salad. At the deli counter, ask for ham and turkey sliced ¼ inch thick. At home, cut the deli meats into matchstick pieces that measure ¼ inch thick and 2 inches long.

cucumbers and all but 1 tablespoon of the dressing and toss to combine. Season to taste with salt and pepper. Toss the tomatoes in the dressing remaining in the bowl; arrange the tomatoes around the perimeter of the greens. Arrange the egg wedges in a ring inside the tomatoes and drizzle with any dressing left in the bowl. Arrange the ham, turkey, and cheese over the center of the greens; sprinkle with the croutons and serve immediately.

CLASSIC COBB SALAD

CREATED IN THE 1920S AT THE FAMOUS Hollywood hangout the Brown Derby, a classic cobb salad depends on a large supporting cast for flavor and texture—cool, crunchy greens (both mild and spicy), tender chicken, buttery avocado, juicy tomato, crisp smoky bacon, and tangy blue cheese—to produce a vibrant salad that is substantial enough to satisfy the hankerings for a main course yet still be light and fresh-tasting.

Cobb salad's classic vinaigrette dressing is both the tie that binds the dish together and its biggest problem. Unifying the disparate elements of this salad is a lot to ask of any dressing. This notion was confirmed when we tested a half-dozen recipes and, in each case, the vinaigrette didn't pass its screen test. More often than not, the flavors were dull and muted, with the salad components either drowned in inch-deep puddles of liquid or sitting high and unhappily dry. We wanted a dressing that both stood up to and integrated cobb's multitude of flavors and textures and a method of applying it that would season every ingredient lightly yet thoroughly.

Most of the dressing recipes we consulted called for a quartet of flavorings—garlic, lemon juice, Worcestershire sauce, and mustard—in addition to the basic red wine vinegar, olive oil, salt, and pepper. In an attempt to streamline the formula, we systematically eliminated each of the first four items, but tasters protested. Each one contributed a necessary dimension to the dressing. In fact, we ended up adding a tiny amount of sugar to help soften the double punch of the two acids—lemon juice and vinegar—and to balance the piquancy of the savory ingredients.

The recipes disagreed, however, over the particulars of those four ingredients. Recipes called for mustard in various forms, although dry was the most common choice. In side-by-side tastings of dry, spicy brown (like Gulden's), and Dijon mustards, we preferred the Dijon for its winey complexity. In addition, it is more of a staple ingredient in home kitchens than mustard powder.

Another common addition that we ultimately rejected was water, which made the dressing, well, watery. The third point of contention was oil. All of the recipes specified olive oil (we liked extra-virgin best), but a number of them cut it with plain vegetable oil. Rather like the water, the vegetable oil diluted the dressing's flavor, so we passed on it. The last big question was about blue cheese, which is a standard component of the salad. Some recipes included it in the dressing, others simply added it to the salad itself. Our tasters agreed that the cheese, when incorporated in the dressing, hogged the spotlight in what should be an ensemble performance.

For the greens, we tasted four common mild salad greens—iceberg, Boston, Bibb, and romaine lettuce—and voted unanimously in favor of the romaine for its combination of flavor and crunch. That hearty crunch provided a nice backdrop for the copious toppings, so we used it in greater proportion than the spicy greens. The tasting of spicy salad greens—chicory, curly endive, arugula, and watercress—was less cut-and-dried. Each had its supporters, but watercress won out because it is the traditional choice.

Cooking the chicken with a minimum of fuss was another concern. For sheer ease, broiling won out over grilling, sautéing, and braising.

We also made slight adjustments to several other ingredients. First, we switched from pale, tasteless supermarket beefsteak tomatoes to cherry tomatoes (the small, sweet, widely available grape tomatoes were our favorites), which taste better at any time but the few last weeks of summer when local tomatoes are in season. The bacon and chives, both classic cobb salad additions, remained untouched, but we doubled the quantity of another key ingredient, avocado, from one to two, because otherwise there wasn't enough to go around.

The typical blueprint for cobb salad is to lay down a bed of lettuce, arrange the chicken, tomatoes, eggs, and avocado in rows on top, sprinkle the whole arrangement with crumbled bacon, blue cheese, and chives, and toss it together at the table. It was the last step that lost us, as the individual character of each element was compromised when they were flung about in the bowl into one indistinguishable tangle. We tried drizzling the dressing over the composed salad, but that method failed to season the separate elements evenly. Tasters encountered dry spots with no dressing right next to other spots drowning in puddles of the stuff. The best method by far was to dress each ingredient independently, before arranging it on the platter. To do this without dirtying every bowl in the kitchen, we used the same one over and over, dressing and plating each ingredient as we went. This guaranteed that each morsel of each ingredient would be correctly seasoned. By dint of their delicate structures, only the eggs and avocados were exempted from this routine. Instead, we drizzled a bit of dressing evenly over them.

Classic Cobb Salad

SERVES 8

You'll need a large platter or wide, shallow pasta bowl to accommodate this substantial salad. Avocado discolors quickly, so prepare it at the last possible minute, just before assembling the salad. Though watercress is traditional in cobb salad, *feel free to substitute an equal amount of* arugula, chicory, curly endive, or a mixture thereof. Use more blue cheese if your taste dictates.

VINAIGRETTE

1	teaspoon Dijon mustard
1	medium garlic clove, minced or pressed through a garlic press (about 1 teaspoon)
1/4	teaspoon sugar
1/2	teaspoon salt
1/8	teaspoon ground black pepper
1	teaspoon Worcestershire sauce
2	teaspoons juice from 1 lemon
2	tablespoons red wine vinegar
1/2	cup extra-virgin olive oil

SALAD

3	boneless, skinless chicken breast halves (about 6 ounces each), trimmed of excess fat
	Salt and ground black pepper
1	large head romaine lettuce, washed, dried, and torn into bite-size pieces (about 8 cups loosely packed)
1	medium bunch watercress, washed, dried, and stemmed (about 4 cups loosely packed)
1	pint cherry tomatoes, preferably grape tomatoes, halved
3	Hard-Cooked Eggs (page 44), peeled and cut into 1/2-inch cubes
2	medium, ripe Hass avocados, pitted and cut into 1/2-inch cubes (see the illustrations on pages 64 and 65)
8	slices bacon (about 8 ounces), cut crosswise into 1/4-inch pieces, fried in a medium skillet over medium heat until crisp, about 7 minutes, and drained on a plate lined with paper towels
2	ounces blue cheese, crumbled (about 1/2 cup)
3	tablespoons minced fresh chives

1. FOR THE VINAIGRETTE: Whisk all the ingredients together in a medium bowl until well combined (alternatively, shake vigorously in a tightly sealed jar); set aside. (The dressing can be refrigerated in an airtight container for 1 day; bring to room temperature and shake well before using.)

2. FOR THE SALAD: Meanwhile, season the chicken with salt and pepper. Adjust an oven rack to 6 inches from the broiler element; heat the broiler. Spray the broiler pan top with vegetable cooking spray; place the chicken breasts on top and broil until lightly browned, 4 to 8 minutes. Using tongs, flip the chicken over and continue to broil until the thickest part is no longer pink when cut into and registers about 160 degrees on an instant-read thermometer, 6 to 8 minutes. When cool enough to handle, cut the chicken into ½-inch cubes and set aside.

3. TO FINISH THE SALAD: Toss the romaine and watercress with 5 tablespoons of the vinaigrette in a large bowl until coated; arrange on a very large, flat serving platter. Place the chicken in the now-empty bowl, add ¼ cup vinaigrette, and toss to coat; arrange in a row along one edge of the greens. Place the tomatoes in the now-empty bowl, add 1 tablespoon vinaigrette, and toss gently to combine; arrange on the opposite edge of the greens. Arrange the reserved eggs and avocados in separate rows near the center of the greens and drizzle with the remaining vinaigrette. Sprinkle the bacon, cheese, and chives evenly over the salad and serve immediately.

SALADE NIÇOISE

ALONG THE FRENCH RIVIERA, SALADE niçoise, the composed salad from the city of Nice, is renowned. Unfortunately for many Americans, the salade niçoise most of us encounter in this country is forgettable—bland and lifeless—little more than a bed of lettuce on which lazily strewn piles of overcooked, underseasoned green beans and potatoes, unripened tomatoes, rubbery eggs, and soggy tuna drown in a sea of dull dressing.

The components of salade niçoise seldom vary from the aforementioned lettuce, beans, potatoes, eggs, tomatoes, and tuna. These are joined by slivered red onion and piquant Mediterranean garnishes—always olives and sometimes capers and anchovies—as well as the occasional sweet bell pepper, cucumber, and artichoke heart and perhaps a few whole herb leaves. After trying a few salades niçoise in the test kitchen, we dismissed those platters crowded with an unwieldy collection of ingredients and focused on three basic elements that we considered key (beyond the quality of the produce itself): the dressing, the manner in which the salad components are dressed and assembled, and the tuna, which is what makes this salad so special.

Clearly, the dressing plays a crucial role in flavoring the salad, so we investigated it thoroughly. The importance of extra-virgin olive oil cannot be overstated here, and the fruitier the better. Our tasters preferred the tang of lemon juice over vinegar as the acidic element in the dressing and shallots over garlic to add a mild bite. A little mustard was also welcome in the vinaigrette for the depth of flavor it contributed, and, as another flavor boost, we replaced the standard parsley with the flavorful trio of fresh thyme, basil, and oregano.

Just as important as the ingredients in the dressing, we learned, was the way in which we applied the dressing to the salad. Though we were rooting for the simplest approach—pouring the dressing carefully over the ingredients after they had been placed on the platter—this method won no fans. Because this salad is not tossed, the dressing was never perfectly distributed, so some bites were seasoned while others were not. At this point, we took a cue from some classic French recipes in which each ingredient is dressed individually before being added to the platter. Dressing the components separately paid off, guaranteeing that every bite of each ingredient was fully and evenly seasoned. The downside of this method was the parade of bowls it occasioned—seven in all. After several experiments with the process, however, we decreased the number of bowls by three, and everyone here in the test kitchen agreed that they would happily wash four bowls to achieve such a harmonious salad.

Many authorities consider tuna a defining element of salade niçoise, so we tested several types. Tasters were enthusiastic about grilled fresh tuna, but not everyone would fire up the grill for this dish, so we did not pursue that option for our recipe. By way of canned tuna, we sampled it packed in olive oil (see "Tuna Packed in Olive Oil," below), vegetable oil, and water. Without exception, tasters preferred the tuna packed in olive oil for its rich flavor and meaty, silky texture. We were surprised, though, that the second choice was tuna packed in a pouch, which tasted clean and allowed the flavors of the dressing to come through loud and clear. Tuna packed in vegetable oil, with its faded, faintly rancid flavor, was nobody's favorite.

INGREDIENTS:
Tuna Packed in Olive Oil

Given our preference for tuna packed in olive oil for salade niçoise, we wondered if all brands are created equal. The six we found in grocery stores fell into three categories: light (made from bluefin, yellowfin, or skipjack tuna or a mixture thereof), white (made from albacore tuna), and imported "white tuna" (made from bonito tuna).

Our panel of tasters did not care for light tuna. The representative brands, Cento Solid Pack Light Tuna and Pastene Fancy Light Tuna, were thought to have "potent" and "metallic" flavors, with a "bitter finish," as well as "chewed" and "unpleasant" textures. Surprisingly, our albacore contender, Dave's Albacore Fillets, came in dead last. "It's like eating nothing" was the comment that summed up all others.

The three best-tasting tunas were made by Ortiz, a small Spanish company. Ortiz cans primarily northern bonito white tuna fished off the coast of Spain, a tuna not used by American packers. Europeans consider this tuna to be of the highest quality because of its extremely white meat, tender texture, and full, clean flavor. The superior flavor is attributed to the migratory nature of the bonito tuna, a high-energy fish. High energy is equated with a high oil content, which in turn is equated with flavor—and lots of it.

THE BEST TUNA PACKED IN OLIVE OIL

ORTIZ BONITO DEL NORTE

The "flaky," "tender," and "pleasant" texture of this "intense and delicious" tuna was perfect for salade niçoise.

We tested various ratios of the salad components and found them to be a matter of taste, provided they were in relative balance and were plentiful enough to afford every diner with a generous taste of each. What mattered more was the precise nature of the ingredients. For instance, butterhead lettuces, such as Boston and Bibb, were more tender than romaine, red leaf, or green leaf. And Red Bliss potatoes had better integrity and texture when boiled than russets.

As we found in the end, this salad, when prepared with the right ingredients and some attention to detail, would give even a native of Nice a moment of pause.

Salade Niçoise
SERVES 6

Prepare all of the vegetables before you begin cooking the potatoes and this salad will come together very easily. The classic garnish of tiny, briny, piquant niçoise olives is a hallmark of salade niçoise. If they're not available, substitute another small, black, brined olive (do not use canned olives). Anchovies are another classic garnish, but they met with mixed reviews from our tasters, so they are optional. If you cannot find tuna packed in olive oil, substitute tuna in a pouch, not tuna packed in vegetable oil (see the results of our tuna tasting at left). Compose the salad on your largest, widest, flattest serving platter. Do not blanket the bed of lettuce with the other ingredients; leave some space between the mounds of potatoes, tomatoes and onions, and beans so that leaves of lettuce peek through.

VINAIGRETTE
- ¹/₂ cup juice from 2 or 3 lemons
- ³/₄ cup extra-virgin olive oil
- 1 medium shallot, minced (about 3 tablespoons)
- 1 tablespoon minced fresh thyme leaves
- 2 tablespoons minced fresh basil leaves
- 2 teaspoons minced fresh oregano leaves
- 1 teaspoon Dijon mustard
  Salt and ground black pepper

SALAD
- 1¹/₄ pounds red potatoes (about 10 small), each potato scrubbed and quartered

Salt
2 tablespoons dry vermouth
Ground black pepper
2 small heads Boston or Bibb lettuce, leaves washed, dried, and torn into bite-size pieces (about 8 cups loosely packed)
2 (6-ounce) cans (or three 4-ounce cans) tuna packed in olive oil, drained
3 small ripe tomatoes, each cored and cut into eight wedges
1 small red onion, sliced very thin
8 ounces green beans, stem ends trimmed and each bean halved crosswise
4 Hard-Cooked Eggs (page 44), peeled and quartered lengthwise
¼ cup niçoise olives
10–12 anchovy fillets (optional)
2 tablespoons capers, rinsed (optional)

1. FOR THE VINAIGRETTE: Whisk the lemon juice, oil, shallot, thyme, basil, oregano, and mustard together in a medium bowl; season with salt and pepper to taste and set aside.

2. FOR THE SALAD: Bring the potatoes and 4 quarts cold water to a boil in a large Dutch oven or stockpot over high heat. Add 1 tablespoon salt and cook until the potatoes are tender when poked with a paring knife, 5 to 8 minutes. With a slotted spoon, gently transfer the potatoes to a medium bowl (do not discard the cooking water). Toss the warm potatoes with the vermouth and salt and pepper to taste; let stand 1 minute. Toss with ¼ cup of the vinaigrette; set aside.

3. While the potatoes cook, toss the lettuce with ¼ cup vinaigrette in a large bowl until coated. Arrange a bed of lettuce on a very large, flat serving platter. Place the tuna in the now-empty bowl and break up with a fork. Add ½ cup vinaigrette and stir to combine; mound the tuna in the center of the lettuce. Toss the tomatoes, red onion, 3 tablespoons vinaigrette, and salt and pepper to taste in the now-empty bowl; arrange the tomato-onion mixture in a mound at the edge of the lettuce bed. Arrange the reserved potatoes in a separate mound at the edge of the lettuce bed.

4. Fill a large bowl with ice water. Return the water used to cook the potatoes to a boil; add 1 tablespoon salt and the green beans. Cook until tender but crisp, 3 to 5 minutes. Drain the beans, transfer to the ice water, and let stand until just cool, about 30 seconds; dry the beans well on a triple layer of paper towels. Toss the beans, 3 tablespoons vinaigrette, and salt and pepper to taste in the now-empty bowl; arrange in a separate mound at the edge of the lettuce bed.

5. Arrange the eggs, olives, and anchovies (if using) in separate mounds at the edge of the lettuce bed. Drizzle the eggs with the remaining 2 tablespoons vinaigrette, sprinkle the entire salad with the capers (if using), and serve immediately.

FRUIT SALADS

READY-MADE FRUIT SALADS HAVE BECOME a produce department staple. Simple? Sure. But are they often watery, tasteless, and boring? Absolutely. We wanted a knockout fruit salad—one bursting with so much flavor that it could serve as a refreshing dessert at a summer barbecue—or hold its own against baked goods at brunch.

The problem with many fruit salads is that they're not much more than a hodgepodge of moderately ripe, cut-up fruit. If the salad is really going to sparkle, the fruit needs to be top-notch and the flavors thoughtfully put together. This is not a place to "use up" what you have on hand. When shopping, let the ripeness of the fruit guide you as to what should go in the salad—and what shouldn't. And don't be seduced by pretty-looking fruit that you know is out of season, such as strawberries or raspberries in February.

Next, limit the variety of fruits in your salad to just two or three. Not only does this make it easier when shopping, but the salad will look more interesting and taste far better. The distinct flavors of each fruit will be allowed to shine through. When choosing fruit combinations, think of how their different flavors will meld. Pair very sweet or acidic fruits, such as pineapple, with mild flavors, such as kiwi, and so on.

To heighten the fruits' natural flavors, add a pinch of salt, sugar, and a little fruit juice (lime juice works well, as do other fruit juices and even liqueurs). You can also make your fruit salad more lively by adding toasted nuts, dried fruit, and/or herbs. These and other fruit salad add-in ideas are listed on page 158. Finally, allow fruit salads to sit for at least 15 minutes before serving to allow the flavors to meld.

Summer Fruit Salad

To dress up the fruit salad further, see our ideas for fruit salad add-ins on page 157.

1	medium cantaloupe, peeled, seeded and cut into bite-size pieces (about 2 cups)
2	cups blueberries, picked over
2	cups strawberries, hulled and quartered
1	tablespoon sugar
1	tablespoon juice from 1 lime
	Pinch salt

Toss the fruit gently with the sugar, lime juice, and salt; allow to sit for 15 minutes before serving.

➤ VARIATIONS

Pineapple-Kiwi Salad with Brown Sugar and Lime

Follow the recipe for Summer Fruit Salad, substituting 2 parts sliced pineapple and 1 part sliced kiwi for the fruit and brown sugar for the white, and adding 1 teaspoon grated lime zest. Just before serving, add 1½ teaspoons minced fresh mint leaves.

Strawberry and Nectarine Salad with Orange and Basil

Follow the recipe for Summer Fruit Salad, substituting equal parts quartered strawberries and sliced nectarines for the fruit and orange juice for the lime juice. Just before serving, add 1½ teaspoons minced fresh basil leaves.

HULLING STRAWBERRIES

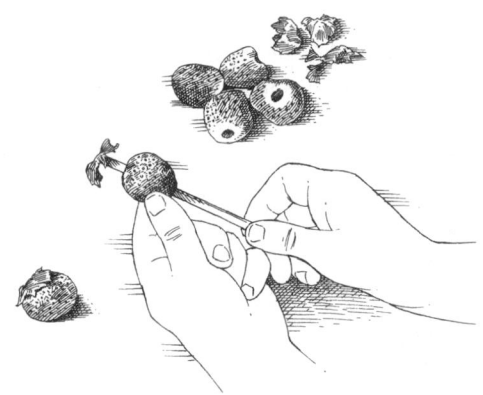

Early-season strawberries can have tough, white cores that are best removed. If you don't own a strawberry huller (and almost no one does), you can improvise with a plastic drinking straw. Push the straw through the bottom of the berry and up through the leafy stem end. The straw will remove the core as well as the leafy top.

PEELING KIWI

A vegetable peeler can crush soft kiwi flesh if you attempt to remove the hairy skin with this tool. We like this method, which won't bruise the fruit.

1. Trim the ends of the fruit and insert a small spoon between the skin and the flesh, with the bowl of the spoon facing the flesh. Push the spoon down and carefully move it around the fruit, separating the flesh from the skin.

2. Gently remove the spoon and pull the loosened skin away from the flesh.

Honeydew, Mango, and Blueberry Salad with Crystallized Ginger

Follow the recipe for Summer Fruit Salad, substituting equal parts sliced honeydew, mango, and blueberries for the fruit, and adding 2 tablespoons minced crystallized ginger.

Multicolored Plum Salad with Orange and Thyme

Follow the recipe for Summer Fruit Salad, substituting several types and colors of sliced plums for the fruit and orange juice for the lime juice. Just before serving, add ½ teaspoon whole fresh thyme leaves.

Peach and Raspberry Salad with Toasted Almonds

Follow the recipe for Summer Fruit Salad, substituting 4 cups sliced peaches and 2 cups raspberries for the fruit. Toss the peaches with the sugar, lime juice, and salt. Just before serving, gently fold in the raspberries and sprinkle with a few tablespoons toasted, slivered almonds.

Papaya and Mango Salad with Tequila and Lime

Follow the recipe for Summer Fruit Salad, substituting equal amounts of sliced papaya and mango for the fruit, and adding 1 teaspoon grated lime zest and 2 tablespoons tequila.

Grape and Strawberry Salad with Champagne

Follow the recipe for Summer Fruit Salad, substituting equal amounts of red grapes and quartered strawberries for the fruit and champagne for the lime juice, and adding 1 teaspoon grated orange zest.

ADDING INTEREST TO FRUIT SALAD

NO ONE WILL MISTAKE YOUR FRUIT salad for cafeteria fare if you take us up on a few of these add-in ideas. Choose just two or three and use a light hand—you want to enhance the fruit flavor, not overwhelm it.

- Brown sugar or crunchy turbinado sugar instead of white sugar
- A little lime, lemon, or orange zest
- Finely chopped crystallized ginger or candied citrus peels
- Fruit juices, such as orange, grapefruit, cranberry
- A touch of rum, champagne, schnapps, or other liqueur
- A dash of high-quality balsamic vinegar
- A little caramel sauce or maple syrup
- Vanilla, almond, or peppermint extract
- A little cinnamon
- Minced fresh herbs, such as mint, basil, or thyme
- Chopped dried fruits, such as apricots or cranberries
- Toasted or candied nuts, such as almonds or pecans (sprinkled on just before serving)
- Granola (sprinkled on just before serving)
- Toasted coconut, sweetened or not (sprinkled on just before serving)

PREPARING PINEAPPLE

A pineapple can seem daunting to peel and core. We find that the following method is reliable and easy.

1. Start by trimming the ends of the pineapple so it will sit flat on a work surface. Cut the pineapple through the ends into four quarters.

2. Place each quarter, cut-side up, on a work surface and slide a knife between the skin and the flesh to remove the skin.

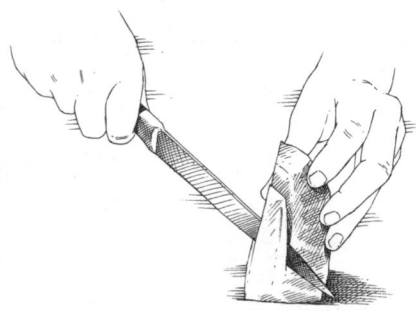

3. Stand each peeled quarter on end and slice off the portion of the tough, light-colored core attached to the inside of the piece. The peeled and cored pineapple can be sliced as desired.

PEELING MANGOES

Because of their odd shape and slippery texture, mangoes are notoriously difficult to peel. Here's how we handle this task. This method ensures long, attractive strips of fruit.

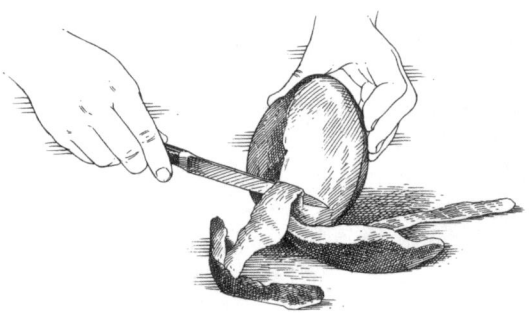

1. Remove a thin slice from one end of the mango so that it sits flat on a work surface. Hold the mango cut-side down and remove the skin with a sharp paring knife in thin strips, working from top to bottom.

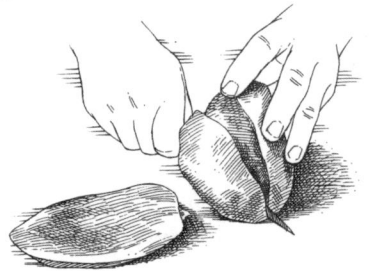

2. Cut down along the side of the flat pit to remove the flesh from one side of the mango. Do the same on the other side of the pit.

3. Trim around the pit to remove any remaining flesh. The mango flesh can now be chopped or sliced as desired.

3

VEGETABLE SIDES AND CASSERCLES

PREPARING VEGETABLE SIDE DISHES SHOULD be quick and easy because no one wants to labor over the vegetables when there is a main course to tend to. Even so, vegetables seem to cause problems for many cooks. Perhaps it is because there are so many ways to cook almost every vegetable or because making vegetable side dishes that let the essence of the vegetable shine through is not as easy as it seems. Far too many cooks overcook their vegetables and then make matters worse by disguising them by covering them with too much cheese or too many bread crumbs.

In this chapter we've examined dozens of vegetables—from artichokes to zucchini—and considered all the relevant cooking methods. The recipes showcase our preferred techniques and offer up plenty of variations so you'll never be stuck in a rut again when it comes to vegetable side dishes, whether they are for Tuesday night's dinner or your Thanksgiving meal.

ARTICHOKES

ARTICHOKES ARE COMMONLY MARKETED IN three sizes: small (2 to 5 ounces each), medium (6 to 11 ounces each), and large (12 ounces or more each). Surprisingly, different-size artichokes bud simultaneously on the same plant; the artichokes that grow on the plant's center stalk are the largest, and those that grow at the juncture between the plant's leaves and the stem are the smallest. After preparing, cooking, and eating all three sizes, we found that we preferred the small and medium artichokes to the large, which can be tough and fibrous.

When selecting fresh artichokes at the market, follow these rules of thumb. The artichokes should be tight and compact, like a flower blossom (which is what they are), and an unblemished bright green. They should "squeak" when you rub the leaves together—evidence that the artichoke still retains much of its moisture. If you tug at a leaf, it should cleanly snap off. If it bends, it's old. Also be on the watch for leaves that look dried out and feathery about the edges, a sure sign of an over-the-hill artichoke.

There are two basic approaches to artichokes: leave them whole (with minimal trimming before cooking) and let your dinner guests eat them leaf-by-leaf at the table, or trim them to the heart before cooking (removing all inedible portions) and let your guests reap the benefit of your labor. Medium artichokes can be left whole or trimmed to the heart. Because of their size, small artichokes are best trimmed to the heart.

Whether you are working with small or medium artichokes, leaving them whole or trimming them to the heart, artichokes will turn brown almost as soon as they are cut. It is crucial to submerge them in acidulated water, which neutralizes the enzymes responsible for oxidation. We tried a variety of acids to prevent oxidation, including white wine vinegar, cider vinegar, and lemon juice, and were most pleased with lemon juice because of its bright

INGREDIENTS: Artichokes
What's Edible and What's Not

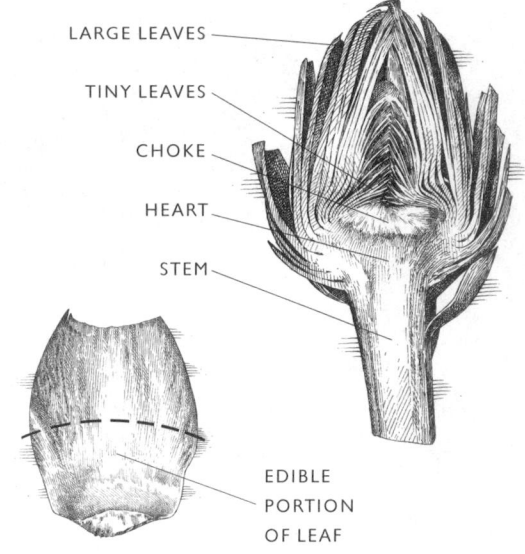

LARGE LEAVES

TINY LEAVES

CHOKE

HEART

STEM

EDIBLE
PORTION
OF LEAF

Much of an artichoke is inedible. The entire exterior (including several layers of leaves) as well as the fuzzy choke and the tiny inner leaves in the center cannot be eaten. Only the heart and the bottom portions of the inner leaves become meaty and tender when cooked. The cooked heart can be eaten with a knife and fork. The edible portion at the bottom of the leaves is best scraped off with your teeth.

yet neutral flavor. Simply add the juice of one lemon per quart of water. Drop each artichoke into the bowl of acidulated water right after you've cleaned it.

Medium artichokes are our favorite for serving whole because they are easy to prepare and each artichoke conveniently serves one person. After experimenting with a variety of methods for cooking whole artichokes, including boiling, steaming, and microwaving, we concluded that steaming is the best choice. Steamed artichokes had the deepest, most pronounced flavor. We discovered that artichokes steam nicely when set on top of thick-sliced onion rings (see the illustration below), which keep them from becoming waterlogged. If you do not have onions on hand, a steaming rack also works. After steaming, allow the artichokes to cool down for at least 15 minutes before serving. It is easy to burn your fingers on them as the dense artichokes retain a lot of heat. Steamed artichokes can also be chilled and eaten cool if you prefer.

In the test kitchen, we find that small artichokes are best roasted, in part because there's no choke to remove. Roasting concentrates the delicate artichoke flavor and lightly crisps the exterior. This cooking method also intensifies the nuttiness of artichokes. The inedible outer portions must be trimmed, but otherwise small artichokes can be roasted as is. To promote browning (and prevent the edges from burning) we found it best to coat the trimmed baby artichokes with olive oil. A 400-degree oven promotes maximum browning but does not run the risk of charring, which can happen at higher temperatures.

Steamed Artichokes

SERVES 4

Artichokes steam nicely when set on top of thickly sliced onion rings, which keep the artichokes from becoming waterlogged. If you don't have onions on hand, a steaming rack works as well.

1	lemon, cut in half
4	medium artichokes (8 to 10 ounces each)
2	medium onions

1. Squeeze the lemon juice into a large bowl filled with one quart of cold water. Drop the spent lemon halves into the water.

2. Prepare the artichokes according to illustrations 1 through 3 below. Drop the trimmed artichokes into the acidulated water. Cut two

PREPARING ARTICHOKES FOR STEAMING

Medium artichokes (each weighing 8 to 10 ounces) are the best choice for steaming.

  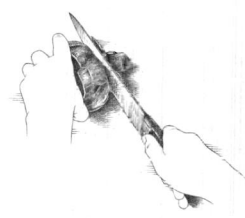 

1. Removing the pin-sharp thorns from the tips of the leaves makes for easier handling and a more attractive presentation. Grasp the artichoke by the stem and hold it horizontal to the work surface. Use kitchen shears to trim the tips off the leaves row by row, skipping the top two rows.

2. Rest the artichoke on a cutting board. Holding the stem in one hand, cut off the top quarter (the top two rows) of the artichoke with a sharp chef's knife.

3. With the sharp thorns and leaf tips removed the stem can now be cut flush with the base of the bulb. Drop the trimmed artichoke into a bowl of acidulated water.

4. Set each trimmed artichoke on a thick onion ring.

1½-inch-thick slices from the middle of each onion; using your fingers, pop out the outer three or four rings from the rest of each slice. Space the onion rings evenly across the bottom of a large pot or Dutch oven and set one trimmed artichoke on top of each ring (see illustration 4 on page 161).

3. Fill a large pot with water to ½ inch below the top of the onion rings. Bring the water to a boil over medium-high heat. Cover and cook until the outer leaves release easily when pulled, about 30 minutes. Check the pot periodically to make sure the water has not boiled away.

4. With tongs, carefully remove the artichokes from the pot and cool for at least 15 minutes before serving. Steamed artichokes can also be chilled and eaten cool. Serve with one of the following vinaigrettes.

Mustard–Tarragon Vinaigrette
MAKES ABOUT ½ CUP

Although the vinaigrettes can be made ahead, the herbs should be added just before serving to preserve their fresh flavor.

6	tablespoons extra-virgin olive oil
I	tablespoon red wine vinegar
I	tablespoon Dijon mustard
I	tablespoon minced fresh tarragon leaves
I	medium garlic clove, minced or pressed through a garlic press (about I teaspoon)
	Salt and ground black pepper

Whisk all of the ingredients, including salt and pepper to taste, together in a medium bowl until thoroughly blended. Serve with steamed artichokes.

Lemon–Mint Vinaigrette
MAKES ABOUT ½ CUP

Basil can be substituted for the mint.

6	tablespoons extra-virgin olive oil
I	teaspoon grated zest and 2 tablespoons juice from I lemon
I	tablespoon minced fresh mint leaves
I	medium shallot, minced

| ½ | teaspoon honey |
| | Salt and ground black pepper |

Whisk all of the ingredients, including salt and pepper to taste, together in a medium bowl until thoroughly blended. Serve with steamed artichokes.

Roasted Baby Artichokes
SERVES 4

Plan on about four small (or baby) artichokes per serving.

I	lemon, cut in half
16	small artichokes (2 to 4 ounces each)
2	tablespoons extra-virgin olive oil
	Salt and ground black pepper

1. Adjust the oven racks to the upper-middle and lower-middle positions and heat the oven to 400 degrees.

2. Squeeze the lemon juice into a large bowl

PREPARING ARTICHOKES FOR ROASTING

Small artichokes (each weighing 2 to 4 ounces) are the best choice for roasting.

1. After cutting off the top quarter of the artichoke, snap off the fibrous outer leaves until you reach the yellow leaves.

2. With a paring knife, trim the dark green exterior from the base of the artichoke as well as the exterior of the stem. Trim a thin slice from the end of the stem and cut the artichoke in half, slicing from tip to stem. Drop the trimmed artichoke into a bowl of acidulated water.

filled with cold water. Drop the spent lemon halves into the water.

3. Cut off the top quarter of each artichoke and snap off the fibrous outer leaves until you reach the inner leaves (see illustration 1 on the facing page). With a paring knife, trim the dark green exterior from the base of the artichoke as well as the exterior of the stem. Trim a thin slice from the end of the stem, then cut the artichoke in half, slicing from tip to stem (see illustration 2 on the facing page). Drop the trimmed artichoke into the bowl of acidulated water until ready to cook.

4. Drain the artichokes and toss them in a large bowl with the olive oil. Place the oiled artichokes cut-side down on 2 rimmed baking sheets. Season the artichokes lightly with salt and pepper to taste. Roast for 15 minutes. Using tongs, turn the artichokes. Reverse the position of the baking sheets, from top to bottom and front to back. Roast until the artichokes can be pierced easily with a skewer, about 10 minutes longer. Season with additional salt and pepper to taste, if desired, and serve.

➤ VARIATION

Roasted Baby Artichokes with Roasted Garlic Aïoli

Aïoli is France's renowned garlicky mayonnaise.

1	lemon, cut in half
16	small artichokes (2 to 4 ounces each)
1	head garlic, cloves separated, skins left on
1	cup extra-virgin olive oil
	Salt and ground black pepper
1	large egg yolk
½	teaspoon dry mustard
	Pinch cayenne pepper

1. Adjust the oven racks to the upper-middle and lower-middle positions and heat the oven to 400 degrees.

2. Reserve 1½ teaspoons juice from the lemon and set aside for the aïoli. Squeeze the rest of the lemon juice into a large bowl filled with one quart of cold water. Drop the spent lemon halves into the water.

EQUIPMENT: Paring Knives

A paring knife is useful for coring tomatoes, slivering garlic, and trimming artichokes. But which paring knife is best? Prices range from a modest $5 plus change to a grand $50, which invites the obvious question for a home cook: Is the most expensive knife really 10 times better than the cheapest model? To find out, we put seven all-purpose paring knives through a series of kitchen tests, including peeling and slicing shallots, peeling and slicing apples and turnips, coring tomatoes, peeling and mincing fresh ginger, and slicing lemons and limes.

The way the knives were made (by forging or stamping) wasn't much of a factor in our ratings of paring knives. By definition, a paring knife is used for light tasks where weight and balance are not terribly important (it doesn't take huge effort to peel an apple). The way the handle felt in testers' hands was much more important. Most testers preferred medium-size, ergonomically designed plastic handles. Slim wooden handles were harder to grasp.

Testers also preferred paring knives with flexible blades, which make it easier to work in tight spots. Peeling turnips or sectioning oranges is much easier with a flexible blade than a stiff one. Stiffer blades are slightly better at mincing and slicing, but

these are secondary tasks for paring knives. Among the knives tested, expensive forged knives from Wüsthof and Henckels performed well, as did an inexpensive stamped knife made by Forschner.

THE BEST PARING KNIVES

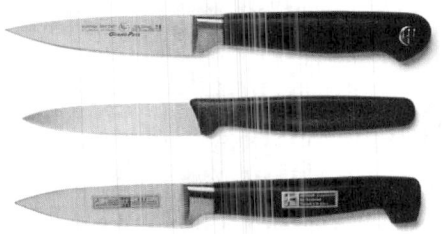

The Wüsthof-Trident Grand Prix (top) is extremely agile and was the clear favorite of our testers. The Forschner (Victorinox) Fibrox (center) is quite light, and the blade is very flexible. The Henckels Four Star (bottom) has an especially comfortable handle, but the blade is a bit less flexible and somewhat less sharp than the blades on our other top picks. Note that the Forschner knife costs just $6, while you should expect to spend about $20 for the Henckels and about $28 for the Wüsthof.

3. Cut off the top quarter and snap off the fibrous outer leaves of each artichoke until you reach the inner leaves (see illustration 1 on page 162). With a paring knife, trim the dark green exterior from the base of the artichoke as well as the exterior of the stem. Trim a thin slice from the end of the stem, then cut the artichoke in half, slicing from tip to stem (see illustration 2 on page 162). Drop the trimmed artichoke into the bowl of acidulated water until ready to cook.

4. Drizzle the garlic cloves with 1 tablespoon of the oil and wrap the oiled cloves in aluminum foil. Drain the artichokes and toss them in a large bowl with 3 tablespoons oil; toss to coat. Place the foil-wrapped garlic and the oiled artichokes, cut-side down, on 2 rimmed baking sheets. Season the artichokes lightly with salt and pepper to taste. Roast for 15 minutes. Using tongs, turn the artichokes. Reverse the position of the baking sheets, from top to bottom and front to back. Roast until the artichokes can be pierced easily with a skewer and the garlic cloves are soft, about 10 minutes longer.

5. When the garlic is cool enough to handle, squeeze the cloves from the skins into a small nonreactive bowl and press or mince the cloves finely. Add the egg yolk, dry mustard, cayenne, and reserved lemon juice and whisk together thoroughly. Add the remaining ¾ cup oil in a thin, steady stream while whisking constantly until a thick emulsion forms. Season with salt and pepper to taste and serve with the roasted artichokes.

ASPARAGUS

ASPARAGUS PRESENTS ONE MAIN PREPARATION issue—should the spears be peeled, or is it better to discard the tough, fibrous ends entirely? In our tests, we found that peeled asparagus has a silkier texture, but we preferred the contrast between the crisp peel and tender inner flesh. Peeling also requires a lot of work. We prefer to simply snap off the tough ends and proceed with cooking.

Asparagus can be cooked in numerous ways. We first investigated moist-heat cooking methods—namely, boiling and steaming—both of which yielded similar results. Although some sources suggest boiling asparagus, we found that steaming is equally appealing (and easy) and leaves the tips just a bit crisper. Simply arrange the trimmed spears in a steamer basket above boiling water and cook until the asparagus is tender but not mushy, a process that will take four to five minutes. Steamed asparagus is pretty bland. At the very least, we found that it should be drizzled with good olive oil and sprinkled with salt and pepper. More flavorful dressings are another good option.

A second option for asparagus is stir-frying. Many recipes for stir-fried asparagus begin by steaming or blanching the spears. The asparagus is then quickly stir-fried with the sauce ingredients. There are two problems with this scenario. First, two cooking methods mean two dirty pots. Second, the flavor of the asparagus is diluted during the first cooking step and then the asparagus doesn't spend enough time with the sauce ingredients to absorb much of their character.

We wanted to solve these problems and knew that skipping the precooking part of the recipe would be necessary. But would this work? The answer is yes, as long as you follow a few rules. First, try to use thinner asparagus that can cook through strictly by stir-frying. If thicker spears are what you have on hand, cut them in half lengthwise so they will cook more quickly.

The second key to success is heat, and plenty of it. Asparagus, even thin spears, will be crunchy if stir-fried for just a minute or two. We found that medium spears cut into 1½-inch lengths need five minutes over intense heat to soften properly. All this heat ensures that the asparagus browns, which improves its flavor. Also, use a skillet large enough to hold the asparagus in a single layer. We also discovered that adding a fairly liquidy sauce (which will reduce quickly to a syrup) helps finish the cooking process.

Two other cooking options, neither of which most cooks consider, are grilling and broiling. The intense dry heat concentrates the flavor of the asparagus, and the exterior caramelization makes the spears especially sweet. The result is asparagus with a heightened and, we think, delicious flavor.

The two primary questions related to broiling concerned the thickness of the stalks and the distance they should be kept from the heat source as they cook. In our tests with thicker asparagus, anywhere from ¾ to 1 inch in diameter, the peels began to char before the interior of the spears became fully tender. When we used thinner spears (no thicker than ⅝ inch), the interior was tender by the time the exterior was browned.

We then focused on how far to keep the spears from the heating element. At 3 inches, the asparagus charred a bit. At 5 inches, the asparagus took a little too long to cook, and it failed to caramelize properly. The middle ground, 4 inches, proved perfect for cooking speed, control, and browning.

As with broiling, we found that thicker spears will char before they become tender on the grill. Stick with spears ⅝ inch in diameter (or smaller) and the asparagus will be tender by the time the exterior is lightly charred. Grilled and broiled asparagus should be lightly oiled before cooking—use extra-virgin olive oil for the most flavor. After cooking, grilled and broiled asparagus can be tossed or drizzled with a vinaigrette for even more flavor.

Steamed Asparagus

SERVES 4

To steam asparagus, you will need a collapsible steamer basket that fits into the pot. Make sure the asparagus is above the water level and keep the pot covered. If you are using asparagus with thicker stalks, add a few minutes to the cooking time. You can flavor steamed asparagus with a drizzle of extra-virgin olive oil and salt and pepper, but the recipes that follow use more flavorful vinaigrettes for better results. If the asparagus is not going to be served right away, plunge it in ice water to stop the cooking process. The cooled and drained asparagus can be covered and refrigerated overnight.

> 1½ pounds asparagus, preferably with thin stalks about ½ inch in diameter, tough ends snapped off (see the illustration at right)
> Extra-virgin olive oil
> Salt and ground black pepper

1. Place a steamer basket in a large pot or Dutch oven. Add enough water so that the water barely reaches the bottom of the steamer basket. Turn the heat to high and bring the water to a boil. Add the asparagus, cover, and reduce the heat to medium-high. Steam until the asparagus bends slightly when picked up and the stalks yield slightly when squeezed, 4 to 5 minutes.

2. Using tongs, transfer the asparagus to a platter. Drizzle with olive oil and sprinkle with salt and pepper to taste. Serve immediately.

➤ VARIATIONS

Steamed Asparagus with Lime-Ginger Vinaigrette
Parsley can be substituted for the cilantro.

> 2 tablespoons juice and 1 teaspoon grated zest from 1 or 2 limes
> 1 tablespoon chopped fresh cilantro leaves
> 1½ teaspoons minced fresh ginger
> ½ teaspoon sugar
> 6 tablespoons canola or vegetable oil
> Salt and ground black pepper
> 1 recipe Steamed Asparagus (without the olive oil, salt, and pepper)

1. Whisk the lime juice, lime zest, cilantro, ginger, and sugar together in a medium bowl. Whisk in the oil until thoroughly combined. Season with salt and pepper to taste.

TRIMMING TOUGH ENDS FROM ASPARAGUS

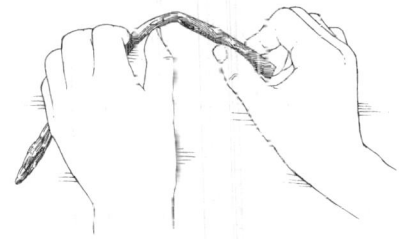

In our tests, we found that the tough, woody part of the stem will break off in just the right place if you hold the spear the right way. With one hand, hold the asparagus about halfway down the stalk; with the thumb and index fingers of the other hand, hold the spear about an inch up from the bottom. Bend the stalk until it snaps.

2. Arrange the steamed asparagus on a platter and drizzle with the dressing. Serve warm or at room temperature.

Steamed Asparagus with Ginger-Hoisin Vinaigrette

Hoisin sauce is a sweet and spicy condiment used in Chinese cooking. Look for it in Asian markets and the Asian aisle of most well-stocked supermarkets. Rice vinegar is typically shelved along with the other vinegar varieties.

2½	tablespoons rice vinegar
1½	tablespoons hoisin sauce
2½	teaspoons soy sauce
1½	teaspoons minced fresh ginger
1½	tablespoons canola oil
1½	teaspoons toasted sesame oil
1	recipe Steamed Asparagus (without the olive oil, salt, and pepper)

1. Whisk the vinegar, hoisin sauce, soy sauce, and ginger together in a medium bowl. Whisk in the oils until thoroughly combined.

2. Arrange the steamed asparagus on a platter and drizzle with the dressing. Serve warm or at room temperature.

Steamed Asparagus with Roasted Red Pepper Vinaigrette

The roasted red peppers are packed in a vinegary brine that lends a bright flavor to the vinaigrette. See page 35 for more information about buying jarred peppers.

¼	cup jarred roasted red peppers
1	tablespoon red wine vinegar
2	medium garlic cloves, minced or pressed through a garlic press (about 2 teaspoons)
6	tablespoons extra-virgin olive oil
1	tablespoon minced fresh parsley leaves
	Salt and ground black pepper
1	recipe Steamed Asparagus (without the olive oil, salt, and pepper)

1. Combine the peppers, vinegar, garlic, and olive oil in a food processor. Pulse until thoroughly combined, about 10 seconds. Scrape the

dressing into a small bowl. Stir in the parsley and season with salt and pepper to taste.

2. Arrange the steamed asparagus on a platter and drizzle with the dressing. Serve warm or at room temperature.

Stir-Fried Asparagus
SERVES 4

Thicker stalks should be halved lengthwise, then cut into 1½-inch pieces to ensure that the centers cook through. The flavors of chicken broth and garlic are basic; the variations are more intriguing.

½	cup low-sodium chicken broth
½	teaspoon salt
¼	teaspoon ground black pepper
2½	tablespoons peanut oil
1½	pounds asparagus, tough ends snapped off (see the illustration on page 165) and cut on the bias into 1½-inch pieces
3	medium garlic cloves, minced or pressed through a garlic press (about 1 tablespoon)

1. Mix the chicken broth, salt, and pepper together in a small bowl.

2. Heat 2 tablespoons of the oil in a large, nonstick heavy-bottomed skillet over high heat until almost smoking. Add the asparagus and cook, stirring frequently, until well browned, about 5 minutes.

3. Clear a space in the center of the pan, add the garlic, and drizzle with the remaining ½ tablespoon oil. Cook until fragrant, about 30 seconds, then mix with the asparagus. Add the chicken broth mixture and toss to coat the asparagus. Cook until the sauce is syrupy, about 30 seconds. Serve immediately.

Stir-Fried Asparagus with Black Bean Sauce

Chinese fermented black beans are available in Asian food shops. They should be moist and soft to the touch. Don't buy beans that are dried out or shriveled. Quality fermented beans should not taste overly salty.

3	tablespoons dry sherry
2	tablespoons low-sodium chicken broth
1	tablespoon soy sauce
1	tablespoon toasted sesame oil
1	tablespoon chopped fermented black beans
1	teaspoon sugar
¼	teaspoon ground black pepper
2½	tablespoons peanut oil
1½	pounds asparagus, tough ends snapped off (see the illustration on page 165) and cut on the bias into 1½-inch pieces
3	medium garlic cloves, minced or pressed through a garlic press (about 1 tablespoon)
1½	teaspoons minced fresh ginger
2	medium scallions, white and green parts, sliced thin on the bias

1. Mix the sherry, chicken broth, soy sauce, sesame oil, black beans, sugar, and pepper together in a small bowl.

2. Heat 2 tablespoons of the peanut oil in a large, nonstick heavy-bottomed skillet over high heat until almost smoking. Add the asparagus and cook, stirring frequently, until well browned, about 5 minutes.

3. Clear a space in the center of the pan, add the garlic and ginger, and drizzle with the remaining ½ tablespoon peanut oil. Cook until fragrant, about 30 seconds, then mix with the asparagus. Add the black bean mixture and toss to coat the asparagus. Cook until the sauce is syrupy, about

30 seconds. Sprinkle with the scallions and serve immediately.

Stir-Fried Asparagus with Soy Sauce, Maple Syrup, and Scallions

Here is an imaginative way to use maple syrup in an Asian sauce to achieve the always-sought-after balance of sweet and salty flavors.

1½	tablespoons soy sauce
1½	tablespoons maple syrup
1	tablespoon dry sherry
2½	tablespoons peanut oil
1½	pounds asparagus, tough ends snapped off (see the illustration on page 165) and cut on the bias into 1½-inch pieces
3	medium garlic cloves, minced or pressed through a garlic press (about 1 tablespoon)
2	medium scallions, white and green parts, sliced thin on the bias

1. Mix the soy sauce, maple syrup, and sherry together in a small bowl.

2. Heat 2 tablespoons of the oil in a large, nonstick heavy-bottomed skillet over high heat until almost smoking. Add the asparagus and cook, stirring frequently, until well browned, about 5 minutes.

CUTTING ASPARAGUS ON THE BIAS

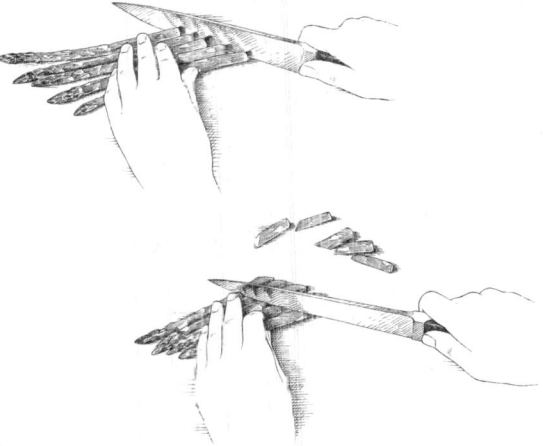

To cut the asparagus quickly and evenly, arrange the stalks in staggered groups of five on a cutting board and then cut them into 1-inch pieces on the bias.

3. Clear a space in the center of the pan, add the garlic, and drizzle with the remaining ½ tablespoon oil. Cook until fragrant, about 30 seconds, then mix with the asparagus. Add the soy sauce mixture and toss to coat the asparagus. Cook until the sauce is syrupy, about 30 seconds. Sprinkle with the scallions and serve immediately.

Broiled Asparagus

SERVES 4 TO 6

Choose asparagus no thicker than ⅜ inch for this recipe.

2	pounds thin asparagus, tough ends snapped off (see the illustration on page 165)
1	tablespoon extra-virgin olive oil
	Salt and ground black pepper

Adjust an oven rack to the uppermost position (about 4 inches from the heating element) and heat the broiler. Toss the asparagus with the oil and salt and pepper to taste, then arrange the stalks in a single layer on a heavy rimmed baking sheet. Broil, shaking the pan halfway through to turn the spears, until the asparagus is tender and lightly browned, 8 to 10 minutes. Cool the asparagus for 5 minutes and arrange it on a platter.

➤ VARIATIONS

Broiled Asparagus with Balsamic Glaze and Parmesan Shards

The balsamic glaze can be made ahead; it will keep in the refrigerator, covered, for up to a week.

¾	cup balsamic vinegar
1	recipe Broiled Asparagus
¼	cup extra-virgin olive oil
¼	cup shaved Parmesan cheese (see the illustration on page 109)

Bring the vinegar to a boil in an 8-inch skillet over medium-high heat. Reduce the heat to medium and simmer slowly until the vinegar is syrupy and reduced to ¼ cup, 15 to 20 minutes. Arrange the asparagus on a platter. Drizzle the balsamic glaze and olive oil over the asparagus. Scatter the cheese shavings on top and serve immediately.

GREAT SIDES FOR ROAST CHICKEN

SIMPLE AND SATISFYING, IT'S NO wonder that roast chicken appears on tables so often. To keep things interesting, it helps to have a wide variety of side dishes to choose from, whether it's for a weeknight supper or Saturday night dinner with friends.

- Broiled Asparagus with Balsamic Glaze and Parmesan Shards (this page)
- Roasted Baby Carrots with Rosemary, Thyme, and Shallots (page 188)
- Buttered Edamame with Shallots and Basil (page 203)
- Garlic-Lemon Skillet Green Beans with Toasted Bread Crumbs (page 213)
- Sugar Snap Peas with Pine Nuts and Garlic (page 225)
- Sugar Snap Peas with Sesame Seeds (page 225)
- Boiled Potatoes with Butter and Chives (page 264)
- Boiled Potatoes with Lemon, Parsley, and Olive Oil (page 265)
- Mashed Potatoes with Garlic (page 267)
- Roasted Potatoes with Garlic and Rosemary (page 277)
- Roasted Potatoes with Lemon-Chive Butter (page 277)
- Rice Pilaf with Currants and Pine Nuts (page 307)
- Brown Rice with Parmesan, Lemon, and Herbs (page 311)
- Toasted Orzo Pilaf with Peas and Parmesan (page 313)
- Bulgur and Mushroom Pilaf (page 316)

Broiled Asparagus with Soy-Ginger Vinaigrette

Putting the garlic through a press ensures a very fine mince. If you don't own a press, mince the garlic to a paste with a knife (see the illustration on page 11).

2	medium scallions, white and green parts, minced
I	tablespoon minced fresh ginger
I	medium garlic clove, minced or pressed through a garlic press (about I teaspoon)
3	tablespoons toasted sesame oil
3	tablespoons soy sauce
1/4	cup juice from 2 or 3 limes
I	tablespoon honey
I	recipe Broiled Asparagus

Whisk the scallions, ginger, garlic, sesame oil, soy sauce, lime juice, and honey together in a small bowl. Arrange the asparagus on a platter. Drizzle the vinaigrette over the asparagus and serve immediately.

Grilled Asparagus
SERVES 4

Thick stalks will burn on the surface before they cook through. Purchase asparagus no thicker than ⅜ inch.

1½	pounds asparagus, tough ends snapped off (see the illustration on page 165)
I	tablespoon extra-virgin olive oil
	Salt and ground black pepper

1. Toss the asparagus with the oil in a medium bowl or on a heavy rimmed baking sheet.

2. Grill the asparagus over a medium-low fire (you should be able to hold your hand 5 inches above the cooking grate for 7 seconds), turning once, until tender and streaked with light grill marks, 5 to 7 minutes. Transfer the asparagus to a platter. Season with salt and pepper to taste. Serve hot, warm, or at room temperature.

➤ VARIATIONS

Grilled Asparagus with Grilled Lemon Vinaigrette

Grilling the lemon not only mellows its flavors but also helps to release its juices.

I	lemon, cut in half crosswise
6	tablespoons extra-virgin olive oil
I	medium shallot, minced
1/2	teaspoon minced fresh thyme leaves
	Salt and ground black pepper
I	recipe Grilled Asparagus

1. Place the lemon halves on the grill cut-side down and grill until tender and streaked with light grill marks, about 3 minutes. When the lemon is cool enough to handle, squeeze and strain the juice into a medium nonreactive bowl; you should have about 2 tablespoons. Whisk in the olive oil, shallot, and thyme. Season with salt and pepper to taste.

TAKING THE TEMPERATURE OF A GRILL FIRE

Use the chart below to determine the intensity of a grill fire. The terms hot, medium-hot, medium, and medium-low are used throughout this book. When using a gas grill, ignore dial readings such as medium or medium-low in favor of actual measurements of the temperature, as described here.

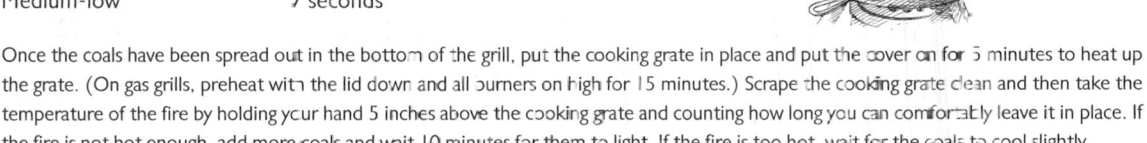

INTENSITY OF FIRE	TIME YOU CAN HOLD YOUR HAND 5 INCHES ABOVE GRATE
Hot	2 seconds
Medium-hot	3 to 4 seconds
Medium	5 to 6 seconds
Medium-low	7 seconds

Once the coals have been spread out in the bottom of the grill, put the cooking grate in place and put the cover on for 5 minutes to heat up the grate. (On gas grills, preheat with the lid down and all burners on high for 15 minutes.) Scrape the cooking grate clean and then take the temperature of the fire by holding your hand 5 inches above the cooking grate and counting how long you can comfortably leave it in place. If the fire is not hot enough, add more coals and wait 10 minutes for them to light. If the fire is too hot, wait for the coals to cool slightly.

2. Arrange the asparagus on a platter and drizzle with the dressing. Serve immediately.

Grilled Asparagus with Orange–Sesame Vinaigrette

Tahini, a paste made from ground sesame seeds, is used in Middle Eastern cooking. If tahini is unavailable, increase the sesame seeds to 3 tablespoons and the sesame oil to 1 teaspoon; instead of whisking the ingredients together, pulse them in a food processor for 10 seconds.

1 tablespoon sesame seeds, toasted in a small dry skillet over medium heat until fragrant, about 4 minutes

1 teaspoon tahini

1 teaspoon grated zest and 1 tablespoon juice from 1 orange

1 tablespoon rice vinegar

1 teaspoon soy sauce

1/2 teaspoon minced fresh ginger

1/2 teaspoon toasted sesame oil

GRILLING VEGETABLES AT A GLANCE

Use this chart as a guide to grilling the following vegetables. Lightly toss the vegetables or brush them on both sides with olive oil, preferably extra-virgin, before grilling. Unless otherwise specified, vegetables should be cooked over a medium fire.

VEGETABLE	PREPARATION	GRILLING DIRECTIONS
Asparagus	Snap off tough ends.	Grill over a medium-low fire, turning once, until tender and streaked with light grill marks, 5 to 7 minutes.
Corn	Remove all but the last layer of husk.	Grill, turning every 1 to 2 minutes, until the husk chars and begins to peel away at the tip, exposing some kernels, 8 to 10 minutes.
Eggplant	Remove the ends. Cut into ¾-inch-thick rounds or ¾-inch-thick strips.	Grill, turning once, until the flesh is darkly colored, 8 to 10 minutes.
Endive	Cut in half lengthwise through the stem end.	Grill, flat-side down, until streaked with dark grill marks, 6 to 8 minutes.
Fennel	Remove the stalks and fronds. Slice vertically through the base into ½-inch-thick pieces.	Grill, turning once, until streaked with dark grill marks and quite soft, 10 to 15 minutes.
Mushrooms, cremini and white	Clean with a damp towel and trim a thin slice from the bottom of each stem.	Grill on a vegetable grid, turning several times, until golden brown, 6 to 7 minutes.
Mushrooms, portobello	Clean with a damp towel and remove the stems.	Grill, with the gill-like underside facing up, until the cap is streaked with grill marks, 8 to 10 minutes.
Onions	Peel and cut into ½-inch-thick slices.	Grill, turning occasionally, until lightly charred, 5 to 6 minutes.
Peppers	Core, seed, and cut into large wedges.	Grill, turning once, until streaked with dark grill marks, 9 to 10 minutes.
Tomatoes, cherry	Remove stems.	Grill on a vegetable grid, turning several times, until streaked with dark grill marks, about 3 minutes.
Tomatoes, plum	Cut in half lengthwise and seed.	Grill, turning once, until streaked with dark grill marks, about 8 minutes.
Zucchini and Summer Squash	Remove the ends. Slice lengthwise into ½-inch-thick strips.	Grill, turning once, until streaked with dark grill marks, 8 to 10 minutes.

6 tablespoons extra-virgin olive oil
Salt and ground black pepper
1 recipe Grilled Asparagus

1. Combine the toasted sesame seeds, tahini, orange zest and juice, rice vinegar, soy sauce, ginger, and oils in a medium bowl and whisk thoroughly to combine. Season with salt and pepper to taste.

2. Arrange the asparagus on a platter and drizzle with the dressing. Serve immediately.

BEETS

THE BEETS MOST OF US REMEMBER FROM childhood are the canned version or the pickled kind (the ones in the giant jars nestled among pink pickled eggs). Freshly cooked beets are altogether different, with sweet, earthy flavors and a firm, juicy texture.

To find the best way of cooking fresh beets, we tried three methods: boiling, steaming, and roasting. Boiled beets were diluted in flavor. Looking at the pink water, it was clear that some of that flavor had escaped into the cooking water. Steaming proved to be a slightly better method, but the flavors weren't as concentrated as we would have liked. Roasting was the next option. We tried wrapping the beets in foil as well as leaving them unwrapped. The unwrapped beets dried out and

REMOVING BEET STAINS

When cut, beets can stain everything they touch, including hands and cutting boards. To help remove these stains, sprinkle the stained area with salt, rinse, and then scrub with soap. The salt crystals help lift the beet juices away.

became leathery, but the wrapped beets were juicy and tender and had the concentrated sweetness we were looking for. The wrapped beets had another significant advantage: The roasting pan remained stain-free.

Roasted beets can be peeled after cooking (the skins can be rubbed off with a paper towels), which further reduces the mess. We found that an oven temperature of 400 degrees delivered good results. Medium beets were done in 45 minutes to an hour. Smaller beets will take less time. We don't recommend roasting very large beets because they can be woody.

Roasted Beets
SERVES 4

To keep your hands from turning a shocking shade of pink, use a paper towel when skinning the beets. Cradle the roasted beet in a paper towel, pinch the skin between your thumb and forefinger, and peel it off. If the beets do stain your hands or the cutting board, see the tips at left to remove the stains. You can simply toss the roasted beets with olive oil, as we suggest below, or flavor them with a vinaigrette or flavored butter. See the recipe variations that follow.

4 medium beets (about 1 pound without greens)
2 tablespoons extra-virgin olive oil
Salt and ground black pepper

1. Adjust an oven rack to the middle position and heat the oven to 400 degrees. Trim all but about 1 inch of the stems from the beets. Wash the beets well and remove any dangling roots. Wrap the beets in aluminum foil and place the wrapped beets in a shallow roasting pan or on a rimmed baking sheet. Roast until a skewer inserted in a beet comes out easily, 45 minutes to 1 hour.

2. Remove the beets from the oven and carefully open the foil packet (make sure to keep your hands and face away from the steam). When the beets are cool enough to handle, carefully peel the skins from the beets. Slice the beets ¼ inch thick and place in a medium bowl. Add the olive oil and salt and pepper to taste and toss together gently. Serve warm or at room temperature.

➤ VARIATIONS

Roasted Beets with Dill–Walnut Vinaigrette

Dill and beets are a combination frequently found in Russian cuisine. Because dill quickly loses its fresh flavor when heated, it's best suited for cold preparations such as vinaigrettes and dips.

1	tablespoon red wine vinegar
2	teaspoons juice from 1 lemon
1	medium shallot, minced
1½	tablespoons minced fresh dill
6	tablespoons extra-virgin olive oil
	Salt and ground black pepper
1	recipe Roasted Beets (without the olive oil, salt, and pepper)
½	cup chopped walnuts, toasted in a medium dry skillet over medium heat until fragrant, about 4 minutes

Whisk the vinegar, lemon juice, shallot, dill, and oil together in a small bowl until thoroughly combined. Add salt and pepper to taste. Toss the dressing, sliced beets, and walnuts together in a medium bowl. Serve immediately.

Roasted Beets with Ginger Butter and Chives

To cut the ginger into matchsticks, first slice it into ⅛-inch-thick rounds. Stack the rounds on top of each other and cut them into thin sticks.

4	tablespoons (½ stick) unsalted butter
1	(1-inch) piece fresh ginger, peeled and cut into matchsticks (see note)
1	tablespoon minced fresh chives
1	recipe Roasted Beets (without the olive oil, salt, and pepper)
	Salt and ground black pepper

Melt the butter in a small skillet over medium heat. When the foaming subsides, add the ginger and cook until fragrant and crisp, 3 to 4 minutes. Add the chives. Toss the butter mixture, sliced beets, and salt and pepper to taste together in a medium bowl. Serve immediately.

BROCCOLI

BROCCOLI REQUIRES A MOIST-HEAT COOKING method to keep the florets tender and to cook the stalks. We tested boiling, blanching then sautéing, and steaming. Boiled broccoli is soggy-tasting and mushy, even when cooked for just two minutes. The florets absorb too much water. We found the same thing happened when we blanched the broccoli for a minute and then finished cooking it in a hot skillet.

Delicate florets are best cooked above the water in a steamer basket. We found that the stalk can be cooked along with the florets as long as it has been peeled and cut into small chunks. Broccoli will be fully cooked after about five minutes of steaming. At this point, it can be tossed with a flavorful dressing. A warning: Cook broccoli just two or three minutes too long and chemical changes cause this vegetable to lose color and texture. (See "Why Broccoli Turns Olive Green" on page 178 for more information.) Steaming also works best to prepare broccoli for a traditional stir-fry; the broccoli is removed from the steamer a little early and then finishes cooking in the stir-fry.

PREPARING BROCCOLI

1. Place the head of broccoli upside down on a cutting board and, using a large knife, trim off the florets very close to their heads. Cut the florets into 1-inch pieces.

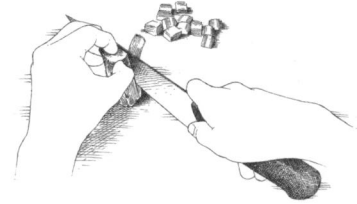

2. The stalks can also be trimmed and cooked. Stand each stalk up on the cutting board and square it off with a large knife. This will remove the outer ⅛ inch from the stalk, which is quite tough. Now cut the stalk in half lengthwise and into 1-inch pieces.

Another option is to sauté the broccoli for several minutes in hot oil, add some liquid ingredients (chicken broth is ideal), cover, and let the steam from the liquid finish cooking the broccoli. The advantage to the sauté-then-steam method is that all the cooking takes place in a single pot. In contrast, traditional stir-frying requires two pots—one to steam the broccoli and one to stir-fry it.

ASIAN-STYLE SIDE DISHES

IF YOU'RE LOOKING TO LEND AN Asian flair to a simple main course like grilled salmon, roast chicken or pork, or a pan-seared steak, try these dishes.

- Steamed Asparagus with Ginger-Hoisin Vinaigrette (page 166)
- Broiled Asparagus with Soy-Ginger Vinaigrette (page 169)
- Stir-Fried Asparagus with Black Bean Sauce (page 167)
- Stir-Fried Asparagus with Soy Sauce, Maple Syrup, and Scallions (page 167)
- Steamed Broccoli with Sesame Vinaigrette (this page)
- Stir-Fried Broccoli with Hot-and-Sour Sauce (page 176)
- Stir-Fried Broccoli with Spicy Black Bean Sauce (page 175)
- Grilled Corn with Soy-Honey Glaze (page 198)
- Edamame with Ginger, Garlic, and Sesame (page 203)
- Sweet-Spicy Edamame with Cilantro and Peanuts (page 203)
- Spicy Green Beans with Sesame Seeds (page 211)
- Sugar Snap Peas with Sesame Seeds (page 225)
- Sugar Snap Peas with Asian Dressing (page 226)
- Braised Winter Squash with Asian Flavors (page 236)

Steamed Broccoli
SERVES 4 TO 6

Cutting the florets and peeled stalks into equal-size pieces ensures that they will all cook at the same rate. The sweet flavor of the steamed broccoli pairs well with bold, bright flavors. Serve it with best-quality olive oil or your favorite vinaigrette, or try one of the vinaigrette recipes that follow. For maximum absorption, toss steamed broccoli with the oil or dressing when hot. The broccoli can be served immediately or cooled to room temperature.

1½	pounds broccoli (about 1 medium bunch), prepared according to the illustrations on the facing page (about 8 cups)
2	tablespoons extra-virgin olive oil
	Salt and ground black pepper

Fit a wide saucepan with a steamer basket. Add water, keeping the water level below the basket. Cover and bring the water to a boil over high heat. Add the broccoli to the basket. Cover and steam until the broccoli is just tender, 4½ to 5 minutes. Transfer the broccoli to a serving bowl and toss with the oil and salt and pepper to taste. Serve hot or at room temperature.

➤ VARIATIONS

Steamed Broccoli with Sesame Vinaigrette

Sesame seeds can be found in any supermarket but are usually much less expensive where they are sold in volume—often at Asian grocery stores or natural foods stores.

¼	cup sesame seeds toasted in a medium dry skillet over medium heat until fragrant, about 4 minutes
1	tablespoon soy sauce
1½	tablespoons rice vinegar
1	tablespoon sugar
1	teaspoon toasted sesame oil
6	tablespoons vegetable or canola oil
1	recipe Steamed Broccoli (without the olive oil, salt, and pepper)

Process the sesame seeds, soy sauce, vinegar, sugar, and oils in a food processor until the sesame seeds are ground and the vinaigrette is well blended, about 15 seconds. Toss the dressing with the broccoli in a serving bowl. Serve hot or at room temperature.

Steamed Broccoli with Balsamic-Basil Vinaigrette

Use a good-quality balsamic vinegar for the vinaigrette.

2   tablespoons balsamic vinegar
6   tablespoons extra-virgin olive oil
I   tablespoon minced fresh basil leaves
I   medium garlic clove, minced or pressed through a garlic press (about I teaspoon)
I   small shallot, minced
    Salt and ground black pepper
I   recipe Steamed Broccoli (without the olive oil, salt, and pepper)

Mix the vinegar, oil, basil, garlic, shallot, and salt and pepper to taste together in a medium bowl until well blended. Toss the dressing with the steamed broccoli in a serving bowl. Serve hot or at room temperature.

Steamed Broccoli with Spanish Green Herb Sauce

Make sure to scrape down the sides of the food processor's workbowl to incorporate all the ingredients into the sauce.

1/2   cup loosely packed fresh parsley leaves
1/2   cup loosely packed fresh cilantro leaves
2   medium garlic cloves, peeled
3   tablespoons extra-virgin olive oil
I   tablespoon juice from I lemon
1/2   teaspoon salt
I   recipe Steamed Broccoli (without the olive oil, salt, and pepper)

Process the parsley, cilantro, garlic, oil, lemon juice, and salt in the workbowl of a food processor until smooth. Toss the herb sauce with the steamed broccoli in a serving bowl. Serve hot or at room temperature.

Stir-Fried Broccoli

SERVES 4 TO 6

We tried stir-frying broccoli without precooking it and found that the florets started to fall apart long before the stems were tender. While blanching and then stir-frying helped the broccoli to cook more evenly, the florets became soggy. We found that partially cooking the broccoli in a steamer basket and then adding it to a stir-fry pan was the solution. This technique is best used when you want to sauce broccoli rather than dress it with vinaigrette.

1/2   cup low-sodium chicken broth
1/2   teaspoon salt
    Ground black pepper
1 1/2   tablespoons plus I teaspoon peanut oil
I   recipe Steamed Broccoli (page 173), cooked for just 2 1/2 minutes and then removed from the steamer
3   medium garlic cloves, minced or pressed through a garlic press (about I tablespoon)

1. Mix the broth, salt, and pepper to taste together in a small bowl.

2. Heat 1½ tablespoons oil in a large nonstick skillet over high heat until shimmering. Add the partially steamed broccoli and cook, stirring every 30 seconds, until fully cooked and heated through, about 2½ minutes.

3. Clear the center of the pan and add the remaining 1 teaspoon oil and the garlic. Mash the garlic with the back of a spatula. Cook 10 seconds, then mix the garlic with the broccoli. Add the

INGREDIENTS: Peanut Oil

You may think all peanut oils are the same. Think again. Highly refined oils, such as Planters, are basically tasteless. They are indistinguishable from safflower, corn, or vegetable oils. In contrast, unrefined peanut oils (also labeled roasted or cold-pressed peanut oil) have a rich nut fragrance straight from the bottle. When heated, these oils smell like freshly roasted peanuts.

In the test kitchen, we find that unrefined or roasted peanut oil is a real plus in simple stir-fries. Like good olive oil, good peanut oil makes many dishes taste better. Three brands that we particularly like are Loriva, Hollywood, and Spectrum.

STIR-FRY BASICS

To stir-fry properly, you need plenty of intense heat. The pan must be hot enough to caramelize sugars, deepen flavors, and evaporate unnecessary juices. All this must happen in minutes. The problem for most American cooks is that the Chinese wok and the American stovetop are a lousy match that generates moderate heat at best.

Woks are conical because in China they traditionally rest in cylindrical pits containing the fire. Food is cut into small pieces to shorten cooking times, thus conserving fuel. Only one vessel is required for many different cooking methods, including sautéing (stir-frying), steaming, boiling, and deep-frying.

Unfortunately, what is practical in China makes no sense in America. A wok was not designed for stovetop cooking, where heat comes only from the bottom. On an American stove, the bottom of the wok gets hot but the sides are only warm. A horizontal heat source requires a horizontal pan. Therefore, for stir-frying at home, we recommend a large skillet, 12 to 14 inches in diameter, with a nonstick coating (see page 176 for details of our testing of nonstick skillets). If you insist on using a wok for stir-frying, choose a flat-bottomed model. It won't have as much flat surface area as a skillet, but it will work better on an American stove than a conventional round-bottomed wok

Our favorite oil for stir-frying is peanut oil (see the facing page), although vegetable oil or canola oil will work. Make sure that the oil is properly heated before adding any food—the oil should almost be smoking before the vegetables are added to the pan.

Many stir-fry recipes add the aromatics (scallions, garlic, and ginger) too early, causing them to burn. In our tests, we found it best to add the aromatics after cooking the vegetables. When the vegetables are done, we push them to the sides of the pan, add a little oil and the aromatics to the center of the pan (see the illustration on page 177), and cook the aromatics briefly until they are fragrant but not colored, 15 to 30 seconds. To keep the aromatics from burning and becoming harsh tasting, we then stir them into the vegetables. At this point, the sauce is usually added to the pan and cooked just until it thickens and coats the vegetables.

---

chicken broth mixture and cook until the sauce is syrupy, about 30 seconds. Serve immediately.

➤ VARIATIONS

Stir-Fried Broccoli with Spicy Black Bean Sauce

Black bean sauce is a salty mixture made from small fermented black soybeans and garlic. It can be found in the Asian food section of most large grocery stores.

1/2	cup low-sodium chicken broth
2	tablespoons black bean sauce
1	tablespoon dry sherry
1	teaspoon toasted sesame oil
1 1/2	tablespoons peanut oil
1	recipe Steamed Broccoli (page 173), cooked for just 2 1/2 minutes and then removed from the steamer
1	teaspoon red pepper flakes
1	tablespoon sesame seeds, toasted in a small dry skillet over medium heat until fragrant, about 4 minutes

1. Mix the broth, black bean sauce, sherry, and sesame oil together in a small bowl.

2. Add the peanut oil to the empty skillet and raise the heat to high. When the oil is shimmering, add the partially steamed broccoli and pepper flakes and cook, stirring every 30 seconds, until fully cooked and heated through, about 2 1/2 minutes. Add the broth mixture and cook until the sauce is syrupy, about 1 minute. Sprinkle with the toasted sesame seeds and serve immediately.

Stir-Fried Broccoli with Hot-and-Sour Sauce

Adjust the heat in this dish as desired by increasing or decreasing the amount of chile.

- 3 tablespoons cider vinegar
- 1 tablespoon low-sodium chicken broth
- 1 tablespoon soy sauce
- 2 teaspoons sugar
- 1½ tablespoons plus 1 teaspoon peanut oil
- 1 recipe Steamed Broccoli (page 173), cooked for just 2½ minutes and then removed from the steamer
- 2 teaspoons minced fresh ginger
- 1 small jalapeño chile, stemmed, seeded, and minced

EQUIPMENT: Inexpensive Nonstick Skillets

Our favorite choice for stir-frying is a large nonstick pan. Although you could spend $100 or more on this pan, most cooks would rather buy a cheaper pan. This makes sense to us, especially when buying nonstick pans, where the increased browning afforded by heavier and more expensive pans is not an issue. To find the best pan for the job, we rounded up eight inexpensive nonstick skillets, all purchased at hardware or discount stores for no more than $50 a piece.

Every pan in our group received a good score in release ability and cleaning tests, the raisons d'être for nonstick. We tested both traits in a purposefully abusive manner by burning oatmeal into the pans over high heat for 45 minutes. That kind of treatment would trash a traditional pan, but the scorched cereal slid out of our nonstick pans with no fuss, and the pans practically wiped clean.

Most manufacturers recommend using plastic, rubber, coated, or wooden utensils to avoid scratching the nonstick coating (and all caution against using any sharp utensil such as a knife, fork, or beater). Makers of only three of our pans, the Farberware, Innova, and Bialetti, sanction the use of metal utensils.

In their new, off-the-shelf condition, all of our pans turned in a reasonable-to-good performance when cooking the foods best suited to nonstick cooking: eggs and fish. In fact, every pan but the Revere produced evenly cooked omelets and released them with ease. The omelet made in the Farberware pan was especially impressive. The Farberware also did a particularly nice job searing salmon fillets to an even, crusty, medium brown. (Salmon is much higher in fat than skinless chicken cutlets and therefore browns more easily, even in a nonstick pan.) Overall, however, our tests indicate that any of these pans could easily handle such light-duty tasks as cooking eggs. Low cost does not mean a big trade-off here.

Sauté speed is also an important measure of a pan's performance. We tested this by sautéing 1½ cups of hand-chopped onions over medium heat for 10 minutes in the hope of ending up with pale gold onions that bore no trace of burning. And you know what? For the most part, we did. The Wearever, T-Fal, Innova, and Revere pans, which were all on the light side in terms of weight, turned out the darkest onions, but they were still well within an acceptable color range. Onions sautéed in the Farberware, Meyer, Calphalon, and Bialetti were a shade lighter, indicating a slightly slower sauté speed; the Farberware onions, however, took top honors based on the evenness of the coloring.

Of course, construction quality is a concern with any piece of cookware, but especially with inexpensive models. Will the thing hold up, or will you have to replace it in six months? Based on our experience, you may well sacrifice a measure of construction quality with a budget pan. Pans with handles that were welded or riveted on to the pan body, including the Farberware, Innova, Meyer, and Calphalon, all felt solid and permanent. But the heat-resistant plastic (called phenolic) handles on the T-Fal, Revere, Bialetti, and Wearever pans were not riveted in place, and all three of them came loose during testing. That does not bode well for their future.

THE BEST INEXPENSIVE NONSTICK SKILLET

The Farberware Millennium 18/10 Stainless Steel 12-Inch Nonstick Skillet costs around $30 and delivered superior results in our tests. It was heavier than the other inexpensive pans we tested and had the most solid construction, which contributed greatly to its success.

KEEPING BURNT GARLIC OUT OF STIR-FRIES

Many recipes add the garlic as well as the ginger and scallions at the beginning of the stir-frying process. This is a recipe for burnt garlic. We prefer to stir-fry the vegetables until they are crisp-tender, clear the center of the pan, and then add the garlic and other aromatics to the clearing. We usually add a little oil to the pan to help the aromatics cook. Once the aromatics are fragrant, they should be stirred back into the vegetables and the sauce should be added to keep them from burning.

1. Mix the vinegar, chicken broth, soy sauce, and sugar together in a small bowl.

2. Heat 1½ tablespoons oil in a large nonstick skillet over high heat until shimmering. Add the partially steamed broccoli and cook, stirring every 30 seconds, until fully cooked and heated through, about 2½ minutes.

3. Clear the center of the pan and add the remaining 1 teaspoon oil, the ginger, and the chile. Mash the ginger and chile with the back of a spatula. Cook 10 seconds, then mix the ginger and chile with the broccoli. Add the vinegar mixture and cook until the sauce is syrupy, about 30 seconds. Serve immediately.

Sautéed Broccoli

SERVES 4 TO 6

Adding broth to the sautéing broccoli and steaming it lightly eliminates the need to steam the broccoli beforehand. This cooking method is well suited to Italian flavors.

2 tablespoons olive oil
1½ pounds broccoli (about 1 medium bunch), prepared according to the illustrations on page 172 (about 8 cups)
½ cup low-sodium chicken broth
Salt and ground black pepper

Heat the oil in a large nonstick skillet over medium-high heat until shimmering. Add the broccoli and cook, stirring frequently, until it turns bright green, 2 to 3 minutes. Increase the heat to high and add the broth. Cover and cook until the broccoli begins to become tender, about 2 minutes. Uncover and cook, stirring frequently, until the liquid has evaporated and the broccoli is tender, 3 to 4 minutes longer. Season with salt and pepper to taste and serve immediately.

➤ VARIATION

Sautéed Broccoli with Garlic, Pine Nuts, and Parmesan
The rich flavors in this recipe work well with pizzas and chicken dishes.

2½ tablespoons olive oil
¼ cup pine nuts
1½ pounds broccoli (about 1 medium bunch), prepared according to the illustrations on page 172 (about 8 cups)
4 medium garlic cloves, sliced thin
¼ cup low-sodium chicken broth
¼ cup dry white wine
¼ cup grated Parmesan cheese
2 tablespoons thinly sliced fresh basil leaves
Salt and ground black pepper

1. Heat 2 tablespoons of the oil in a large nonstick skillet over medium-high heat until shimmering. Add the pine nuts and cook, stirring often, until golden, about 2 minutes.

2. Add the broccoli and cook, stirring frequently, until it turns bright green, 2 to 3 minutes. Clear a space in the center of the pan and add the remaining ½ tablespoon oil and the garlic. Cook until the garlic is fragrant, about 30 seconds. Increase the heat to high and add the broth and wine. Stir, cover, and cook until the broccoli begins to become tender, about 2 minutes. Uncover and cook, stirring frequently, until the liquid has evaporated and the broccoli is tender, 3 to 4 minutes longer. Sprinkle with the cheese and basil and season with salt and pepper to taste. Serve immediately.

Broccoli and Cheese Casserole

IT'S OUR STRONG BELIEF IN THE TEST KITCHEN that smothering broccoli with cheese sauce is more than just a sneaky way to get kids to eat their vegetables. Adults love it, too. Shamefully, and all too often, this classic dish comes to the table with overcooked and washed-out-looking broccoli swimming in a gloppy, greasy, broken cheese sauce. We wanted to create an attractive broccoli and cheese casserole with character and dimension—one you could serve to company and that would entice even the pickiest eaters. Our challenge, then, was to construct a casserole with bright green broccoli—tender, not mushy—an elegant cheese sauce, and a golden bread-crumb topping.

In our initial tests, we tried a variety of methods to cook the broccoli. Sautéing the broccoli before assembling the casserole brought out the strong sulfur compounds found in this member of the cabbage family: This batch had a faint but distinct odor of rotten eggs. And the final product was unevenly colored, exhibiting alternating splotches of olive drab and bright emerald green. Thinking we could save some time and effort, we tried throwing the broccoli into the casserole raw. The results were abysmal: By the time the broccoli was tender, it was army green, the sauce was curdled and broken, and the bread crumbs were overly browned.

The tests confirmed what we already knew to be true—namely, that broccoli requires a moist-heat cooking method to keep the florets tender and to make sure the tough stalks cook through. Ordinarily, our test-kitchen recommendation is to steam broccoli, as it tends to absorb too much moisture when boiled. For this casserole, however, we didn't mind the extra moisture and thought boiling would be quick and easy. In addition, partially cooking, or blanching, the broccoli in salted boiling water would ensure that the broccoli would be fully seasoned to its core, not unlike pasta boiled in salted water. Most important, we favored blanching as a fast way to set that fresh green color. The test kitchen's food scientist explained that as broccoli cooks, some of the air between its cells expands and bubbles off, bringing the cell walls closer together. As the cell walls become closer, the amount of chlorophyll per square inch is concentrated, making the vegetable appear to be a brighter green. The success of this technique, however, is contingent on cooking time. If broccoli is overcooked, the bright green chlorophyll converts to pheophytin, turning the broccoli an ugly olive drab.

With the broccoli cooked, we could now focus on the cheese sauce. Recipes we found included a variety of styles, though most of them were implausibly rich. Yolks and cream seemed too heavy; this was a vegetable dish, after all. We looked to some classic French recipes for inspiration and saw flour-thickened, milk-based sauces (béchamels) ladled over a variety of blanched vegetables (proving that the idea of camouflaging vegetables for finicky eaters is nothing new). The lighter consistency and flavor of the béchamel better allowed the taste of the vegetables to come through. What's more, this flour-bound sauce didn't separate into a curdled mess while in the oven, as some of the richer sauces had.

But the béchamel alone didn't give this dish

SCIENCE:
Why Broccoli Turns Olive Green

We've found that broccoli has an internal clock that starts ticking once the broccoli has steamed for seven minutes. At this point, chemical changes begin to occur that cause an initial undesirable loss of color and texture. This loss intensifies as cooking continues. By nine minutes, the broccoli has become discolored and mushy and it begins to take on a sulfurous flavor.

This deterioration is due to two factors: heat and acid. As broccoli is heated during cooking, chlorophyll begins to break down, resulting in a change of color and texture. In addition, all vegetables contain acids that leach out during cooking and create an acidic environment, further contributing to the breakdown of the chlorophyll. None of this is an issue as long as the steaming time does not exceed seven minutes. We find that broccoli has the best texture, color, and flavor after steaming for just five minutes, which also happens to provide the cook with a decent cushion before this chemical reaction begins.

enough punch, so we added sharp cheddar cheese—the customary accompaniment to broccoli—to our working béchamel. Now closer to a Mornay sauce, our sauce tasted good, but it seemed somewhat heavy and cloying to most of the tasters. Cutting the milk with a portion of chicken broth lightened the sauce and gave it a rounder, more savory edge that tasters enjoyed.

But the sauce still required some help. Sharp cheddar imparted a grainy texture to the otherwise supple sauce. We experimented with other styles of cheddar and found that cutting the sharp cheese with mild-tasting, creamy colby cheese yielded the best-textured sauce. For a little nuance, we added a pinch of cayenne pepper, minced garlic, and dried mustard, flavorings we borrowed from our favorite macaroni and cheese sauce. Also borrowed from our macaroni and cheese was the crispy golden topping, made with a simple combination of white sandwich bread and butter. Far from its French roots, perhaps, this casserole with its creamy "Mornay" sauce is good enough to attract even the pickiest eater.

Broccoli and Cheese Casserole
SERVES 6 TO 8

If you cannot find colby cheese, longhorn will work just as well.

TOPPING
2 slices white sandwich bread, torn into quarters
1 tablespoon unsalted butter, melted

FILLING
Salt
2 pounds broccoli (about 1 large bunch), florets trimmed to 1-inch pieces, stalks peeled and chopped medium (see the illustrations on page 172)
3 tablespoons unsalted butter
1 medium garlic clove, minced or pressed through a garlic press (about 1 teaspoon)
1/2 teaspoon dry mustard
Pinch cayenne pepper
3 tablespoons unbleached all-purpose flour
1 1/2 cups whole milk

1 cup low-sodium chicken broth
8 ounces colby cheese, shredded (about 2 2/3 cups)
4 ounces sharp cheddar cheese, shredded (about 1 1/3 cups)
Ground black pepper

1. FOR THE TOPPING: Process the bread and butter in a food processor until coarsely ground, about six 1-second pulses; set aside.

2. FOR THE FILLING: Adjust an oven rack to the middle position and heat the oven to 400 degrees. Bring 4 quarts water to a boil in a large pot. Add 1 tablespoon salt and the broccoli to the boiling water; cover and cook until bright green and crisp-tender, about 3 minutes. Drain the broccoli and leave it in the colander; set aside.

3. Meanwhile, melt the butter in a medium saucepan over medium heat. Stir in the garlic, mustard, and cayenne; cook until fragrant, about 30 seconds. Add the flour and cook, stirring constantly, until the flour turns golden, about 1 minute. Slowly whisk in the milk and broth; bring to a simmer and cook, whisking often, until large bubbles erupt at the surface and the mixture is slightly thickened, about 5 minutes. Off the heat, whisk in the colby and cheddar. Season to taste with salt and pepper.

4. TO ASSEMBLE AND BAKE: Spread the broccoli in a 13 by 9-inch baking dish (or shallow casserole dish of similar size). Whisk the cheese sauce again briefly and pour over the broccoli. Sprinkle with the bread-crumb topping. Bake until golden brown and bubbling around the edges, about 15 minutes. Cool for 5 minutes before serving.

➤ VARIATION

Broccoli and Cheese Casserole with Roasted Red Peppers

Follow the recipe for Broccoli and Cheese Casserole, adding a 13-ounce jar of roasted red peppers, drained, rinsed, patted dry, and chopped medium, to the seasoned sauce in step 3.

Broccoli Rabe

A PERFECT PLATE OF BROCCOLI RABE SHOULD be intensely flavored but not intensely bitter. You want to taste the other ingredients and flavors in the dish. So we set our sights on developing a dependable, quick method of cooking that would deliver less bitterness and a rounder, more balanced flavor.

Parcooking any bitter greens helps to rid them of some bitter flavor. We found that steaming produced little change in the broccoli rabe—it was still very intense. When blanched in a small amount of salted boiling water (1 quart of water for about 1 pound of broccoli rabe), the rabe was much better. But the bitterness was still overwhelming, so we increased the boiling salted water to 3 quarts. Sure enough, the broccoli rabe was delicious; it was complex, mustardy, and peppery as well as just slightly bitter, and the garlic and olive oil added later complemented rather than competed with its flavor. Depending on personal taste, you can reduce the amount of blanching water for stronger flavor or, to really tone down the bitterness, increase the amount of water.

During testing, we found that the lower 2 inches

PREPARING BROCCOLI RABE

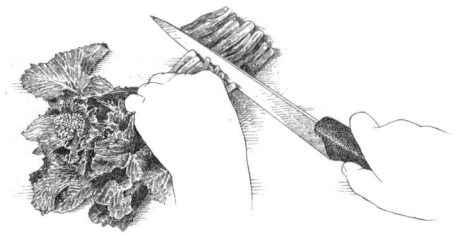

1. The thick stalk ends on broccoli rabe should be trimmed and discarded. Use a sharp knife to cut off the thickest part (usually the bottom 2 inches) of each stalk.

2. Cut the remaining stalks and florets into bite-size pieces, about 1 inch long.

or so of the stems were woody and tough while the upper portions of the stems were tender enough to include in the recipes. When we used only the upper portions, there was no need to go through the laborious task of peeling the stems. Cutting the upper portion of the stems into pieces about an inch long made them easier to eat and allowed them to cook in the same amount of time as the florets and the leaves.

Once the broccoli rabe has been blanched, it should be shocked in cold water to stop the cooking process and then dried well. It can be dressed with a vinaigrette or quickly sautéed with flavorful ingredients.

Blanched Broccoli Rabe

SERVES 4

A salad spinner makes easy work of drying the cooled, blanched broccoli rabe. See page 85 for tips on buying a salad spinner.

| 1 | bunch broccoli rabe (about 14 ounces), bottom 2 inches of stems trimmed and discarded, remainder cut into 1-inch pieces (see the illustrations at left) |
| 2 | teaspoons salt |

1. Bring 3 quarts water to a boil in a large saucepan. Stir in the broccoli rabe and salt and cook until wilted and tender, 2 to 3 minutes. Drain the broccoli rabe and set aside.

2. Cool the empty saucepan by rinsing it under cold running water. Fill the cooled saucepan with cold water and submerge the broccoli rabe to stop the cooking process. Drain again; squeeze well to dry and proceed with one of the following variations.

➤ VARIATIONS

Broccoli Rabe with Balsamic Vinaigrette

This sweet vinaigrette complements the bitter, mustardy flavors of broccoli rabe.

2	tablespoons balsamic vinegar
1	tablespoon maple syrup
1	medium shallot, minced

1/4 teaspoon dry mustard
6 tablespoons extra-virgin olive oil
Salt and ground black pepper
I recipe Blanched Broccoli Rabe

Whisk the vinegar, maple syrup, shallot, mustard, and oil together in a medium bowl until well blended. Season with salt and pepper to taste. Add the broccoli rabe and toss to combine. Serve at room temperature.

Broccoli Rabe with Red Bell Pepper, Olives, and Feta

Sweet red bell peppers and briny olives complement peppery broccoli rabe in both color and flavor.

3 tablespoons extra-virgin olive oil
I medium red bell pepper, cored, seeded, and diced
I recipe Blanched Broccoli Rabe
10 kalamata olives, pitted and chopped coarse
I teaspoon minced fresh oregano leaves
Salt and ground black pepper
I ounce feta cheese, crumbled (about 1/4 cup)

Heat the oil in a large skillet over medium-high heat until shimmering. Add the red bell pepper and cook until barely tender, about 3 minutes. Add the broccoli rabe, olives, and oregano, and cook, stirring to coat with oil, until the broccoli rabe is heated through, about 1 minute. Season with salt and pepper to taste, sprinkle with the feta, and serve immediately.

Broccoli Rabe with Asian Flavors

Although we think of broccoli rabe mainly in terms of Italian cooking, its strong flavor works well with Asian flavorings, too. See the illustration on page 189 for tips on grating ginger.

I tablespoon soy sauce
1 1/2 teaspoons rice vinegar
I teaspoon toasted sesame oil
I teaspoon sugar
2 tablespoons peanut oil

3 medium garlic cloves, minced or pressed through a garlic press (about I tablespoon)
1/2 teaspoon grated fresh ginger
1/4 teaspoon red pepper flakes
I recipe Blanched Broccoli Rabe
Salt

1. Mix the soy sauce, vinegar, sesame oil, and sugar together in a small bowl.

2. Heat the peanut oil, garlic, ginger, and red pepper flakes in a large skillet over medium heat until the garlic starts to sizzle, about 15 seconds. Increase the heat to medium-high and add the broccoli rabe and the soy sauce mixture. Cook, stirring to coat the broccoli rabe with the other ingredients, until heated through, about 1 minute. Season with salt to taste and serve immediately.

BRUSSELS SPROUTS

THE TASTE OF BRUSSELS SPROUTS IS OFTEN maligned simply because the sprouts are not prepared properly. True, they can be bitter and soggy if overcooked, but they can also be crisp, tender, and nutty flavored when handled appropriately. To find the best and simplest way to prepare Brussels sprouts, we chose to investigate boiling, steaming, microwaving, and braising. The result we were looking for was a tender, not-too-bitter, attractively green-colored Brussels sprout that could be prepared with little fuss.

We began our testing with boiling and steaming, the two most popular methods of cooking vegetables. Boiling, we decided, took too much time. It can take up to 20 minutes to bring a pot of water to a boil, and we learned that it then took the sprouts eight to 10 more minutes to cook till just tender. Thirty minutes seemed like a long time to wait for Brussels sprouts that weren't particularly good anyway. Boiling produced only a waterlogged, bitter sprout colored a drab olive green.

Steaming was next. Certainly, steaming is a great way to cook vegetables—fewer nutrients are washed away in the water, the vegetables keep their vibrant colors, and, because less boiled water is used, the cooking time is dramatically reduced. We were convinced that this would be the ideal cooking method for these "little cabbages." However, after several trials, we found that steamed Brussels sprouts also had quite a bitter taste, even when we were very careful not to overcook them.

If steaming wasn't the answer, what would produce the tender, nutty-tasting sprouts we desired?

Braising, which refers to cooking food with a small amount of liquid in a tightly covered pan, was the next cooking method we tried. As we thought about it, we realized that microwaved Brussels sprouts actually are braised—rapidly. Perhaps cooking them on the stovetop would produce equally satisfying results. We braised 1 pound of sprouts on top of the stove, using only ½ cup of water, cooking them until they were just tender enough to be pierced easily by the tip of a knife, about eight to 10 minutes. This method met all of the criteria we had established for the perfectly cooked Brussels sprout, producing a tender, nutty-flavored, bright green vegetable.

Because braising in water was so successful, we decided to try braising in other liquids as well. We tried cooking the sprouts in unsalted butter but found that it was difficult to regulate the heat with the lid on and keep the butter from burning. They ended up tasting fine, but they took longer to cook than the water-braised sprouts and required too much attention. Adding broth to the butter helped reduce the attention needed and produced a very green vegetable, but the taste was merely acceptable. Braising in chicken stock produced a sprout that didn't taste much different from those braised in water.

Overall, the tastiest Brussels sprouts we cooked came from braising them in whipping cream, a classic French technique for cooking vegetables. Lightly seasoned with salt, pepper, and nutmeg, the finished sprouts absorbed most of the cream, creating a slightly sweet, nutty flavor that was in no way bitter. Because the results were so tasty, we almost hesitate to offer any additional ideas for preparing Brussels sprouts. Alas, cooking this healthy vegetable in cream on a regular basis simply goes against the goal of a healthy lifestyle. Save this method for the holidays, when you can throw caution to the wind. For everyday cooking, you can

SCIENCE: Does "X" Mark the Spot?

What about that age-old idea of cutting a small "X" in the stem end of each Brussels sprout before cooking? The idea behind this technique is to produce faster, more even cooking throughout by allowing the water or steam to penetrate the thicker stem end. If you have ever practiced this technique, you know that it is time-consuming to cut that little "X," especially if the sprouts are small; and, because they're round, they tend to roll away from the knife. Was this extra step really necessary?

We carved an "X" into the bottom of half of each batch of Brussels sprouts we tested—whether boiled, steamed, microwaved, or braised. While monitoring cooking times, we tested one sprout with an "X" and one without. Interestingly, we found that the sprouts with an "X" cut in the stem end did, indeed, seem to be more evenly cooked when tested early in the cooking, before the sprout was completely tender. By the time the sprout top was cooked through, however, it was impossible to tell the difference in the tenderness or cooking evenness between the marked and unmarked sprouts.

Further tests showed that the same result held true for other vegetables commonly carved with an "X" for even cooking: broccoli stems and pearl onions. Pearl onions cooked at exactly the same rate whether they had been marked or not, while carved broccoli stalks cooked slightly faster up to the three-minute point, after which they showed no difference at all.

So the notorious "X" appears to be a tenet of kitchen wisdom based on myth. Cutting an "X" into the stem end of a Brussels sprout, broccoli stalk, or pearl onion has no effect on producing evenly cooked, tender vegetables.

still produce wonderful sprouts by braising them in water. The braised sprouts should be drained and then seasoned—either simply with just butter or olive oil and salt and pepper or in slightly more complex sauces (several recipes follow).

The best Brussels sprouts are available in late fall through early winter, peaking in late November. They are often associated with the holidays because of their short season. When buying Brussels sprouts, choose those with small, tight heads, no more than 1½ inches in diameter, for the best flavor. The sprouts should also be bright green; yellow or brown-tipped leaves usually indicate that they are older. Once purchased, keep the sprouts in a vented container in the refrigerator for no longer than four to five days.

Braised Brussels Sprouts

SERVES 4

Serve these tender Brussels sprouts seasoned simply with ground black pepper and either butter or extra-virgin olive oil. Or, use braised Brussels sprouts in one of the following variations.

I	pound small Brussels sprouts (no greater than 1½ inches in diameter), stem ends trimmed with a knife and discolored leaves removed by hand
½	teaspoon salt

Bring the sprouts, ½ cup water, and salt to a boil in a 2-quart saucepan over medium-high heat. Cover and simmer (shaking the pan once or twice to redistribute the sprouts) until a knife tip inserted into the center of a sprout meets no resistance, 8 to 10 minutes. Drain well and season (with ground black pepper and either olive oil or butter), or use in one of the following recipes.

➤ VARIATIONS
Glazed Brussels Sprouts with Chestnuts
If chestnuts are unavailable, substitute ½ cup toasted chopped hazelnuts.

3	tablespoons unsalted butter
I	tablespoon sugar
I	(16-ounce) can peeled chestnuts in water, drained (about 1½ cups)
I	recipe Braised Brussels Sprouts
	Salt and ground black pepper

1. Heat 2 tablespoons of the butter and the sugar in a medium skillet over medium-high heat until the butter melts and the sugar dissolves. Stir in the chestnuts. Reduce the heat to low and cook, stirring occasionally, until the chestnuts are glazed, about 3 minutes.

2. Add the remaining 1 tablespoon butter and the sprouts and cook, stirring occasionally, to heat through, about 1 minute. Season with salt and pepper to taste. Serve immediately.

Brussels Sprouts with Cider and Bacon
Stay away from maple-flavored bacon; it will give this dish an unpleasant flavor. To keep the bacon crisp, add the cooked bacon to the Brussels sprouts immediately before serving.

3	ounces (about 3 slices) bacon, cut into ½-inch pieces
2	medium garlic cloves, minced or pressed through a garlic press (about 2 teaspoons)
½	teaspoon minced fresh thyme leaves
¾	cup apple cider or juice
⅛	teaspoon ground black pepper
I	recipe Braised Brussels Sprouts

1. Cook the bacon in a large skillet over medium-high heat until crisp, about 5 minutes. Transfer the bacon to a paper towel–lined plate; set aside.

2. Add the garlic and thyme to the rendered bacon fat in the skillet (there should be 2 to 3 tablespoons of fat) and cook until fragrant, about 1 minute. Add the cider and pepper and cook until the liquid is reduced by half, about 4 minutes. Add the sprouts and cook until heated through, about 1 minute longer. Sprinkle with the reserved bacon and serve immediately.

Brussels Sprouts Braised in Cream

This rich dish is perfect for holidays. Don't drain the sprouts after braising—the cream reduces to form a thick sauce.

1	pound small Brussels sprouts (no greater than 1½ inches in diameter), stem ends trimmed with a knife and discolored leaves removed by hand
1	cup heavy cream
½	teaspoon salt
	Pinch grated nutmeg
	Ground black pepper

Bring the sprouts, cream, and salt to a boil in a 2-quart saucepan over medium-high heat. Cover and simmer (shaking the pan once or twice to redistribute the sprouts) until a knife tip inserted into the center of a sprout meets no resistance, 10 to 12 minutes. Season with nutmeg and pepper to taste and serve immediately.

CABBAGE

COOKED PROPERLY, CABBAGE IS PLIANT AND mildly sweet. When overcooked, it turns mushy and has an unpleasant aroma. We set out to find the best way to cook this surprisingly fickle vegetable, reasoning that quick cooking would minimize the negative side effects.

Focusing on green cabbage, we chose to shred it for the quickest cooking and also to provide the greatest surface area for flavoring. We began with the fastest possible method: blanching. Plunging cabbage into boiling water for exactly one minute produced the desired crisp-tender texture and pleasant, mild flavor, but this technique also left the cabbage waterlogged.

Steaming turned out to be a better solution to the problem of water uptake, but cooking times varied too much: four to six minutes with an electric steamer appliance; two to four minutes on the stovetop in a basket insert; less time for tender specimens, more time for fibrous heads. With steaming, there is a thin line between perfectly cooked cabbage and the wan, flavorless, mealy kind.

We were not optimistic about the remaining options. Past experience had taught us that cabbage sautés terribly, and a quick test proved that nothing had changed. Sautéed cabbage scorched before it could soften. In addition, the cooking fat remained resolutely on the surface and contributed nothing to flavor other than an oily taste.

Then we recalled our recipe testing with Brussels sprouts—also a member of the cabbage family—in particular, the traditional French technique of braising in cream. We tried it, and seven minutes later we had found our ideal. For the first time, we could taste a subtle mix of flavors, complemented by a slight residual crunch. The cream also provided the perfect vehicle for both sweet and savory flavor variations. The only problem—as with the Brussels sprouts—was the use of the decidedly decadent cream in an everyday recipe.

But we found that other liquids—including white wine, chicken broth, apple juice, and tomato juice—worked just as well, particularly when a small amount of fat or oil was added to the equation. In each case, the cabbage cooked in liquid alone tasted characterless, while the addition of fat—butter, bacon fat, or vegetable oil—provided more depth of flavor as well as improved texture.

Contrary to the common advice to buy a tight, heavy head of cabbage, we had better success with smaller, looser heads that were covered with thin outer leaves.

Braised Cabbage with Parsley and Thyme

SERVES 4

This dish is delicate and simple. For additional richness, increase the amount of butter.

1	tablespoon unsalted butter
¼	cup low-sodium chicken broth
½	medium head (1 pound) green cabbage, shredded (see the illustrations on page 120)
¼	teaspoon minced fresh thyme leaves
1	tablespoon minced fresh parsley leaves
	Salt and ground black pepper

Melt the butter in a large skillet over medium-high heat. Add the broth, and then the cabbage and thyme. Bring to a simmer, cover, and cook, stirring occasionally, until the cabbage is wilted but still bright green, 7 to 9 minutes. Sprinkle with the parsley and season with salt and pepper to taste. Serve immediately.

> VARIATIONS

Cabbage and Apples Braised in Cider

Because Granny Smith apples maintain their shape during cooking, they are the best choice for this recipe. Do not substitute McIntosh apples, as they will turn to mush.

2	tablespoons unsalted butter
I	Granny Smith apple, peeled, cored, and cut into ½-inch dice
½	cup apple cider or juice
I	teaspoon minced fresh thyme leaves
I	teaspoon caraway seeds
½	medium head (I pound) green cabbage, shredded (see the illustrations on page 120) Salt and ground black pepper

Melt the butter in a large skillet over medium-high heat. When the foaming subsides, add the apple and cook until it just begins to brown, about 5 minutes. Add the cider, thyme, and caraway seeds and simmer until the cider is slightly reduced, about 3 minutes. Add the cabbage, stir to combine, cover, and simmer until the cabbage is wilted but still bright green, 7 to 9 minutes. Season with salt and pepper to taste. Serve immediately.

Cream-Braised Cabbage with Lemon and Shallots

The French have been cooking cabbage in cream for ages.

¼	cup heavy cream
I	teaspoon juice from I lemon
I	small shallot, minced
½	medium head (I pound) green cabbage, shredded (see the illustrations on page 120) Salt and ground black pepper

Heat the cream, lemon juice, and shallot in a large skillet over medium-high heat. Add the cabbage, stir to combine, cover, and simmer until the cabbage is wilted but still bright green, 7 to 9 minutes. Season with salt and pepper to taste. Serve immediately.

GLAZED CARROTS

GLAZING IS PROBABLY THE MOST POPULAR way to prepare carrots. However, glazed carrots are often saccharine and ill-suited as a side dish on a dinner plate. These defamed vegetables, adrift in a sea of syrup, often lie limp and soggy from overcooking or retain a raw, fibrous resistance from undercooking. Most recipes for glazed carrots are hopelessly dated. These recipes never deliver what we hope for in glazed carrots: fully tender, well-seasoned carrots with a glossy, clingy, yet modest glaze.

We began with how to prepare the carrots for cooking. Matchsticks were out from the get-go—we were looking for simplicity, not to improve our knife skills. We peeled regular bagged carrots and cut them on the bias into handsome oblong shapes. Once cooked, these comely carrots earned much praise for their good flavor.

Most recipes suggest that the carrots need to be steamed, parboiled, or blanched prior to glazing, resulting in a battery of dirtied utensils. Instead, we put the carrots with a bit of liquid in a skillet (non-stick, for the sake of easy cleanup), along with some salt and sugar for flavor, covered the skillet, and simmered. Mission accomplished: The carrots were cooked through without much ado. Chicken broth as a cooking liquid lent the carrots savory backbone and a full, round flavor, whereas water left them hollow and wine turned them sour and astringent. We tried swapping the sugar for more compelling sweeteners but found brown sugar too muddy-flavored, maple syrup too assertive, and honey too floral (but good for a variation, we noted). We stood by clear, pure, easy-to-measure granulated sugar.

We moved on to finessing the glaze. After the carrots simmered for a few minutes, when just on the verge of tender (they would see more heat during glazing, so we simmered them shy of done), we lifted the lid from the skillet, stepped up the heat, and let the liquid reduce down. (If the liquid is not reduced, it is thin and watery.) Finally, we added butter (cut into small pieces for quick melting) and a bit more sugar to encourage glaze formation and to favorably increase sweetness. All of this resulted in a light, clingy glaze that with a few more minutes of high-heat cooking took on a pale amber hue and a light caramel flavor. A sprinkle of fresh lemon juice gave the dish sparkle, and a twist or two of freshly ground black pepper provided depth. We were surprised, as were our tasters, that glazed carrots could be this good and this easy.

Glazed Carrots

SERVES 4

Glazed carrots are a good accompaniment to roasts of any kind—beef, pork, lamb, or poultry. A nonstick skillet is easier to clean, but this recipe can be prepared in any large skillet with a cover.

1	pound carrots (about 6 medium), peeled and sliced 1/4 inch thick on the bias (see the illustration on the facing page)
1/2	teaspoon salt
3	tablespoons sugar
1/2	cup low-sodium chicken broth
1	tablespoon unsalted butter, cut into 4 pieces
2	teaspoons juice from 1 lemon
	Ground black pepper

1. Bring the carrots, salt, 1 tablespoon of the sugar, and the broth to a boil in a large nonstick skillet, covered, over medium-high heat. Reduce the heat to medium and simmer, stirring occasionally, until the carrots are almost tender when poked with the tip of a paring knife, about 5 minutes. Uncover, increase the heat to high, and simmer rapidly, stirring occasionally, until the liquid is reduced to about 2 tablespoons, 1 to 2 minutes.

2. Add the butter and the remaining 2 tablespoons sugar to the skillet. Toss the carrots to coat and cook, stirring frequently, until the carrots are completely tender and the glaze is light gold, about 3 minutes. Off the heat, add the lemon juice and

toss to coat. Transfer the carrots to a serving dish, scraping the glaze from the pan into the dish. Season with pepper to taste. Serve immediately.

➤ VARIATIONS

Glazed Carrots with Bacon and Pecans

Granulated sugar works best in our traditional glazed carrots, but in this variation light brown sugar was the best choice. Its rich caramel flavor goes well with the bacon and pecans.

3	ounces (about 3 slices) bacon, cut into 1/2-inch pieces
1/3	cup chopped pecans
1	pound carrots (about 6 medium), peeled and sliced 1/4 inch thick on the bias (see the illustration on the facing page)
1/2	teaspoon salt
3	tablespoons light brown sugar
1/2	cup low-sodium chicken broth
1/2	teaspoon minced fresh thyme leaves
1	tablespoon unsalted butter, cut into 4 pieces
2	teaspoons juice from 1 lemon
	Ground black pepper

1. Cook the bacon in a large nonstick skillet over medium-high heat until crisp. Transfer the bacon to a paper towel–lined plate to drain.

2. Remove all but 1 tablespoon of the bacon drippings from the pan. Add the pecans and cook until fragrant and lightly browned, about 4 minutes. Transfer to the plate with the bacon.

3. Add the carrots, salt, 1 tablespoon of the brown sugar, the broth, and thyme to the skillet. Bring to a boil, covered, over medium-high heat. Reduce the heat to medium and simmer, stirring occasionally, until the carrots are almost tender when poked with the tip of a paring knife, about 5 minutes. Uncover, increase the heat to high, and simmer rapidly, stirring occasionally, until the liquid is reduced to about 2 tablespoons, 1 to 2 minutes.

4. Add the butter and the remaining 2 tablespoons brown sugar to the skillet. Toss the carrots to coat and cook, stirring frequently, until the carrots are completely tender, about 3 minutes. Off the heat, add the lemon juice and toss to coat.

Transfer the carrots to a serving dish, scraping the glaze from the pan into the dish. Season with pepper to taste and serve immediately.

Glazed Carrots with Orange and Cranberries

Dried cherries can be used in place of the cranberries if you prefer.

1	pound carrots (about 6 medium), peeled and sliced 1/4 inch thick on the bias (see the illustration below)
1/4	cup dried cranberries
1/2	teaspoon salt
2	tablespoons sugar
1/4	cup low-sodium chicken broth
1/2	teaspoon grated zest and 1/4 cup juice from 1 orange
1	tablespoon unsalted butter, cut into 4 pieces Ground black pepper

1. Bring the carrots, cranberries, salt, 1 tablespoon of the sugar, the broth, and orange zest and juice to a boil in a large nonstick skillet, covered, over medium-high heat. Reduce the heat to medium and simmer, stirring occasionally, until the carrots are almost tender when poked with the tip of a paring knife, about 5 minutes. Uncover, increase the heat to high, and simmer rapidly, stirring occasionally, until the liquid is reduced to about 2 tablespoons, 1 to 2 minutes.

SLICING CARROTS ON THE BIAS

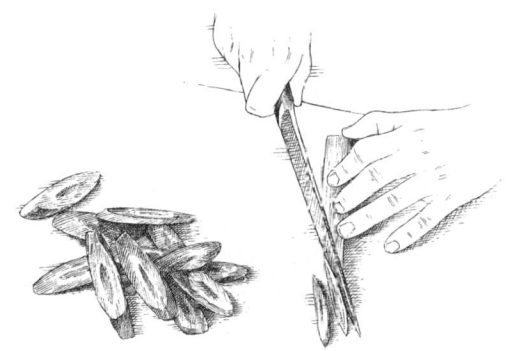

Cut the carrots on the bias into rounds about 1/4 inch thick and 2 inches long.

2. Add the butter and the remaining 1 tablespoon sugar to the skillet. Toss the carrots to coat and cook, stirring frequently, until they are completely tender, about 3 minutes. Transfer the carrots to a serving dish, scraping the glaze from the pan into the dish. Season with pepper to taste and serve immediately.

ROASTED CARROTS

THE SUBLIME NATURE OF ROASTED CARROTS lies in their rustic charm. Simple, sweet, and pure, their perfectly caramelized outer layer gently gives way to a smooth, tender interior—unless they are undercooked and have a crisp, bitter center or, on the opposite end of the spectrum, are subjected to such intense heat that they become wan, limp, and utterly unpalatable. Our ideal roasted carrot recipe, we decided, would be one that would let us throw a couple of ingredients together, toss the carrots into the oven, and let them roast until they were done—a tasty, simple, and effortless side dish.

We chose baby carrots for this recipe because they needed no peeling, trimming, or chopping. They were effortless and easy, just what we had in mind. Our first batches turned out sweet and tender. Still, without a little help from a fatty cohort, we knew that the glossy, bronzed carrots we envisioned would not be possible. So we tossed batches of carrots with vegetable oil, olive oil, extra-virgin olive oil, butter, and clarified butter and roasted them. We were surprised to discover that our favorite was plain olive oil; it neither masked the carrots' sweetness, as did extra-virgin olive and vegetable oils, nor changed their texture, as did butter.

We next examined roasting methods, times, and temperatures. We tried covering a broiler pan with foil to help keep the carrots moist and hasten the roasting, but when we pulled these carrots out from their sealed bed, they had become reminiscent of cafeteria carrots: slightly bitter, pale, and soggy. Carrots covered for only part of the roasting time fared little better. The best batch was the most straightforward: roasted at 475 degrees, uncovered, for 20 minutes, until the carrots were brown and caramel-colored.

We proceeded to roast carrots in different sorts of pans to see which would give us the best color and the easiest cleanup. After pitting broiler pan bottoms against rimmed baking sheets and roasting pans against Pyrex dishes and nonstick aluminum pans, we found the broiler pan bottom to be the best for browning the carrots without burning them.

During these tests, we came to wonder just what a baby carrot is. Bagged baby carrots are made by taking long, thin carrots (usually carrot varieties grown for their high sugar and beta-carotene content, which makes them sweet and bright in color) and forcing them through a machine that peels the carrots and cuts them down to their ubiquitous baby size.

Real baby carrots are varieties of carrots that are miniature in size when mature; contrary to popular belief, they are not carrots of the standard length that are picked early. Unfortunately, real baby carrots are available only through specialty produce purveyors that sell to restaurants and other professional kitchens. If you are lucky enough to spy true, greens-still-attached, tapered carrots in your grocery store or farmers market, buy them and roast according to our recipe. They're best in the cooler months; baby carrots harvested in the warmer spring and summer months tend to be less sweet.

Roasted Carrots
SERVES 8

Inspect your bag of baby carrots carefully for pockets of water. Carrots taken from the top of the supermarket's carrot pile are often waterlogged. This not only makes carrots mealy but dashes any hopes of caramelization in the oven.

2	pounds baby carrots (two 16-ounce bags)
2	tablespoons olive oil
½	teaspoon salt

Adjust an oven rack to the middle position and heat the oven to 475 degrees. Toss the carrots, oil, and salt in the broiler pan bottom. Spread the carrots in a single layer and roast for 12 minutes.

Shake the pan to toss the carrots. Continue roasting, shaking the pan twice more, until the carrots are browned and tender, about 8 minutes longer. Serve immediately.

➤ VARIATIONS

Roasted Baby Carrots with Rosemary, Thyme, and Shallots

Follow the recipe for Roasted Carrots, tossing 1 tablespoon minced fresh rosemary, 2 teaspoons minced fresh thyme leaves, and 2 shallots, sliced, with the carrots, oil, and salt.

Roasted Baby Carrots with Sage and Walnuts

Toast the walnuts in a small dry skillet over medium heat until fragrant, about 4 minutes, then cool and chop.

Follow the recipe for Roasted Carrots, tossing 1 tablespoon minced fresh sage leaves with the carrots, oil, and salt. Just before serving, sprinkle the roasted carrots with ⅓ cup chopped toasted walnuts.

Roasted Maple Carrots with Browned Butter

Follow the recipe for Roasted Carrots, decreasing the oil to 1½ teaspoons. After the carrots have roasted for 10 minutes, heat 1 tablespoon unsalted butter in a small saucepan over medium heat, swirling the pan occasionally, until deep gold, about 1 minute. Off the heat, stir in 1 tablespoon maple syrup. Drizzle the maple-butter mixture over the carrots after 12 minutes of roasting. Shake the pan to coat and continue roasting as directed.

Roasted Carrots with Ginger-Orange Glaze

Follow the recipe for Roasted Carrots. After the carrots have roasted for 10 minutes, bring 1 heaping tablespoon orange marmalade, 1 tablespoon water, and ½ teaspoon grated fresh ginger to a simmer in a small saucepan over medium-high heat. Drizzle the marmalade mixture over the carrots after 12 minutes of roasting. Shake the pan to coat and continue roasting as directed.

GRATING GINGER

Most cooks who use fresh ginger have scraped their fingers on the grater when the piece of ginger gets down to a tiny nub. Instead of cutting a small chunk of ginger off a larger piece and then grating it, try this method. Peel a small section of the large piece of ginger. Grate the peeled portion, using the rest of the ginger as a handle to keep fingers safely away from the grater.

GLAZED WINTER ROOT VEGETABLES

ASK MOST PEOPLE HOW TO PREPARE TURNIPS, celery root, and parsnips and you can expect some blank stares. This wan trio of root vegetables might not be as popular as some of its more colorful cousins—carrots, radishes, and beets, for instance—but that doesn't mean these vegetables couldn't hold their own as a side dish if prepared properly. Perhaps the secret was to find a way to enhance, rather than mask, their naturally bitter, earthy, and sweet flavors.

Our goal was to produce root vegetables with a nicely browned exterior and a tender, creamy interior, coated with a lightly sweetened glaze. For the vegetables to cook evenly, the first step was to cut them into large pieces of equal size. For round vegetables such as celery root and turnips, ¾-inch cubes made the most sense; ½-inch cubes were reminiscent of hash, and 1-inch cubes took too long to cook through. Long roots such as carrots and parsnips were best sliced ½ inch thick on the bias: easy and attractive.

Roasting tended to dry out most root vegetables, leaving the exterior tough and leathery, with little glaze. Boiling, even briefly, washed away flavor. The most promising results were achieved using a large nonstick skillet and a basic method of steaming the vegetables and reducing the remaining liquid.

To avoid a drab appearance and to provide a deep, virtually roasted flavor, we found that these vegetables needed to be browned first in melted butter over moderately high heat. It was important to leave the vegetables alone for the first few minutes of cooking, as constant stirring hindered caramelization. To get the vegetables to a tender-but-not-mushy state, we then had to simmer them, covered, in a combination of broth, seasonings, and a small amount of sweetener. Once the vegetables were tender, creating a glaze out of the remaining liquid was easy. All we had to do was remove the lid, increase the heat to high, and allow the sugar and broth to quickly reduce down to a slightly sticky, caramelized coating, stirring constantly to prevent burning.

With a simple technique that worked across the board and a few complementary ingredients, the most maligned of root vegetables finally got the respect they deserve.

Glazed Parsnips and Celery
SERVES 4

When selecting parsnips, try to choose those with tops no larger than 1 inch in diameter. If they are larger, the fibrous core should be removed.

1½	tablespoons unsalted butter
1	pound parsnips, peeled, tapered ends sliced ½ inch thick on the bias and large upper portions halved lengthwise, then cut ½ inch thick on the bias
3	large celery ribs, strings removed with a vegetable peeler, sliced ½ inch thick on the bias
½	cup low-sodium chicken or vegetable broth
1	tablespoon sugar
½	teaspoon salt
⅛	teaspoon ground black pepper

1. Heat the butter in a large nonstick skillet over medium-high heat; when the foaming subsides, swirl to coat the skillet. Add the parsnips in an even layer; cook without stirring over medium-high heat until browned, 2 to 3 minutes. Stir in the celery and cook, stirring occasionally, until well browned, about 2 minutes longer. Add

the broth, sugar, salt, and pepper; cover the skillet, reduce the heat to medium-low, and simmer until the vegetables are tender, about 6 minutes.

2. Uncover, increase the heat to high, and cook, stirring frequently, until the liquid in the skillet reduces to a glaze, about 1 minute. Transfer to a serving dish; serve immediately.

Glazed Celery Root with Onion, Grapes, and Pistachios

SERVES 4

Sliced almonds can be substituted for the pistachios.

2	tablespoons chopped roasted unsalted pistachios
1½	tablespoons unsalted butter
½	medium red onion, cut into ¼-inch wedges
1	medium celery root (1 to 1¼ pounds), trimmed, peeled, and cut into ¾-inch cubes
½	cup low-sodium chicken or vegetable broth
1½	tablespoons sugar
2	teaspoons red wine vinegar
½	teaspoon salt
⅛	teaspoon ground black pepper
1	cup seedless red grapes, halved lengthwise

1. Toast the pistachios in a large, nonstick skillet over medium heat, stirring frequently, until lightly browned, about 4 minutes. Transfer to a small bowl; set aside.

2. Heat the butter in the now-empty skillet over medium-high heat; when the foaming subsides, swirl to coat the skillet. Add the onion and celery root in an even layer; cook without stirring until browned, about 3 minutes. Stir and continue to cook, stirring occasionally, until all sides are browned, about 3 minutes longer. Add the broth, sugar, vinegar, salt, and pepper; cover the skillet, reduce the heat to medium-low, and simmer until the vegetables are just tender, about 10 minutes.

3. Uncover, increase the heat to high, add the grapes, and cook, stirring frequently, until the liquid in the skillet reduces to a glaze, about 1 minute. Transfer to a serving dish and sprinkle with the pistachios; serve immediately.

Lemon-Thyme Glazed Turnips and Carrots

SERVES 4

When selecting turnips, choose the smallest available (about the size of plums), as they tend to be less fibrous and less bitter than their larger counterparts. Do not substitute yellow turnips for the white turnips called for in this recipe.

1½	tablespoons unsalted butter
1	pound white turnips, peeled and cut into ¾-inch cubes
3	medium carrots (about 9 ounces), peeled, tapered ends sliced ½ inch thick on the bias and large upper portions halved lengthwise, then cut ½ inch thick on the bias
⅔	cup low-sodium chicken or vegetable broth
1½	tablespoons brown sugar
½	teaspoon salt
⅛	teaspoon ground black pepper
1	teaspoon fresh thyme leaves
1	teaspoon grated zest and 1 teaspoon juice from 1 lemon

1. Heat the butter in a large nonstick skillet over medium-high heat; when the foaming subsides, swirl to coat the skillet. Add the turnips and carrots in an even layer; cook without stirring until browned, about 4 minutes. Stir and continue to cook, stirring occasionally, until well browned on all sides, about 4 minutes longer. Add the broth, brown sugar, salt, pepper, thyme, and lemon zest; cover the skillet, reduce the heat to medium-low, and simmer until the vegetables are just tender, about 8 minutes.

2. Uncover, increase the heat to high, and cook, stirring frequently, until the liquid in the skillet reduces to a glaze, about 1 minute. Stir in the lemon juice, transfer to a serving dish, and serve immediately.

CAULIFLOWER

MANY OF US IN THE TEST KITCHEN GREW UP eating soggy, overcooked cauliflower cloaked in a thick layer of congealing neon-yellow cheese. Some of us ate the cheesy sauce, but no one remembers liking (or eating) the cauliflower. With time (and experience), we have learned that cauliflower doesn't have to be prepared this way. When properly cooked and imaginatively flavored, cauliflower can be nutty, slightly sweet, and absolutely delicious.

We started our testing by trying to develop a quick stovetop method for cooking cauliflower. During our first round at the stove, we made an important observation: Cauliflower is very porous. This can work to its advantage or disadvantage, depending on what the cauliflower absorbs during cooking. We identified two basic cooking methods that went hand in hand with this observation. In the first method, the cauliflower is fully cooked (boiled or steamed), then flavored with a light vinaigrette or with a brief sauté in simply seasoned butter or oil. In this scenario, keeping the water out is key. In the second method, the cauliflower is flavored as it cooks, which means that you want to get the liquid in. Our new goal was to test the variables for both methods and devise two master recipes with plenty of creative variations.

We first worked on perfecting the "cook first, flavor later" technique and began by comparing boiling and steaming. The boiled cauliflower tasted watery; no matter how long we boiled it, from underdone to overcooked, the first flavor to reach our taste buds was the cooking water. Steaming the cauliflower for seven to eight minutes, on the other hand, produced evenly cooked florets with a clean, sweet flavor. To verify our strong impression that steamed cauliflower was less watery than the boiled version, we compared the raw and cooked weights of cauliflower cooked by each method. With steaming, there was no weight increase. With boiling, the cauliflower gained approximately 10 percent of its original weight.

Next we moved to the "flavor while cooking" approach. The basic technique was braising, or cooking with a small amount of liquid in a covered container. We hoped that the cooking liquid—our foe in the previous method—would now become our friend. But we were curious as to the best way to accomplish this. Should the cauliflower simply be braised with no previous cooking? Or should it be sautéed first, then finished by braising? Or what about partially cooking via the steaming method and then braising?

After testing these three methods, we immediately realized the benefits of sautéing the cauliflower first, then adding some flavorings and liquids and braising the vegetable until tender. Braising the dense vegetable with no precooking simply took too long. Not only did we have to stand over the stove to make sure it did not overcook, but this method also created some of the same problems of liquid absorption that we had come across when boiling. When we partially cooked the cauliflower by steaming it and then braising it, the taste was lackluster and flat.

PREPARING CAULIFLOWER

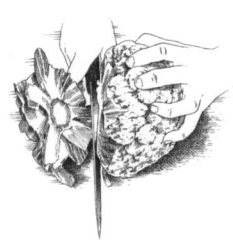

1. Start by pulling off the outer leaves and trimming off the stem near the base of the head.

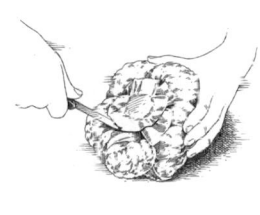

2. Turn the cauliflower upside down so that the stem is facing up. Using a sharp knife cut around the core to remove it.

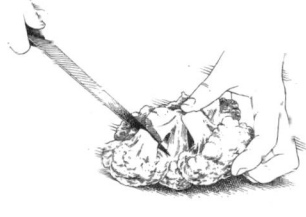

3. Using the tip of a chef's knife, separate the florets from the inner stem.

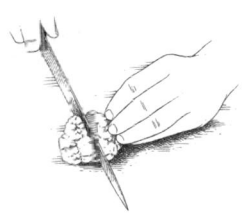

4. Cut the florets in half, or in quarters, if necessary, so that individual pieces are about 1 inch square.

191

Sautéing it for seven minutes on medium-high heat and then braising it, however, intensified the cauliflower's naturally mild flavors. Not only did the cauliflower absorb the flavors from the braising liquid, but the browned cauliflower also tasted wonderfully smoky and earthy.

Cooking cauliflower too long can release unpleasant sulfur-containing compounds that break down when exposed to heat. To avoid this problem, we found it best to cut the cauliflower into 1-inch pieces that will cook uniformly and quickly. We also liked the fact that the cut surface of the florets lay flat in the sauté pan. The cut surfaces browned beautifully, and the sweetness of the florets was pronounced.

We also discovered that the usual way of testing doneness—slipping the tip of a knife in and out of the stem of the cauliflower—was not always accurate. The best way to test for doneness is, quite simply, to sample a piece.

Steamed Cauliflower

SERVES 4

The best complements to the fresh, delicate flavor of steamed cauliflower are mild herbs, nuts, citrus, or simple flavor combinations such as those below. Steamed cauliflower can also be served as is, with just a drizzle of extra-virgin olive oil and a sprinkle of salt.

I   medium head (about 2 pounds) cauliflower, prepared according to the illustrations on page 191

Fit a large saucepan with a steamer basket. Fill the pan with enough water to reach just below the bottom of the basket. Cover and bring the water to a boil over high heat. Add the florets to the basket, reduce the heat to medium, cover, and steam until the cauliflower is tender but firm, about 7 minutes. Remove the cauliflower from the basket and serve, or finish with one of the variations.

VARIATIONS

Steamed Cauliflower with Browned Butter, Walnuts, and Crispy Sage

4   tablespoons (½ stick) unsalted butter
¼   cup walnuts, chopped coarse
I   tablespoon thinly sliced fresh sage leaves
I   recipe Steamed Cauliflower
     Salt and ground black pepper

Heat the butter in a small, heavy-bottomed saucepan over medium heat and cook, swirling frequently, until the butter begins to brown, 3 to 4 minutes. Add the walnuts and cook, stirring constantly, until the nuts become fragrant, about 1 minute longer. Add the sage and cook until crispy, about 30 seconds. Toss the cauliflower gently with the browned butter mixture in a serving bowl. Season with salt and pepper to taste. Serve immediately.

Steamed Cauliflower with Cheddar-Mustard Cream Sauce

Because this sauce does not include flour (therefore eliminating the need for the sauce to boil), it is lighter in texture and quicker to make than most other cheese sauces.

I   cup heavy cream
4   ounces cheddar cheese, shredded
     (about 1⅓ cups)
I   tablespoon whole-grain mustard
     Pinch cayenne pepper
     Salt and ground black pepper
I   recipe Steamed Cauliflower

Place the cream in a small saucepan and bring to a bare simmer over medium heat. When the cream is steaming and just starting to bubble around the edges of the pan, turn off the heat and add the cheese, mustard, and cayenne. Whisk together until smooth. Season with salt and pepper to taste. Toss the cauliflower gently with the cheese sauce in a serving bowl. Adjust the seasonings and serve immediately.

Braised Cauliflower with Garlic and Tomatoes

SERVES 4

We found that you can braise cauliflower in almost any liquid—broth, canned tomatoes, or wine.

2½   tablespoons olive oil
1   medium head (about 2 pounds) cauliflower, prepared according to the illustrations on page 191
3   medium garlic cloves, minced or pressed through a garlic press (about 1 tablespoon)
¼   teaspoon red pepper flakes
1   (14.5-ounce) can diced tomatoes
2   tablespoons minced fresh basil leaves
    Salt

1. Heat 2 tablespoons of the oil in a large skillet over medium-high heat until shimmering. Add the cauliflower and cook, stirring occasionally, until the florets begin to brown, 6 to 7 minutes. Clear a space in the center of the pan and add the remaining ½ tablespoon oil and the garlic and red pepper flakes. Mash and stir the garlic mixture in the center of the pan until it becomes fragrant, about 1 minute. Stir to combine the garlic mixture and cauliflower and cook 1 minute longer.

2. Add the tomatoes, cover, and cook until the cauliflower is tender but still offers some resistance to the tooth when sampled, 4 to 5 minutes. Add the basil and season with salt to taste. Serve immediately.

Braised Cauliflower with Anchovies, Garlic, and White Wine

SERVES 4

Adjust the amount of red pepper flakes to increase the heat of this dish. See the illustrations on page 227 for tips on mincing the anchovies.

2½   tablespoons olive oil
1   medium head (about 2 pounds) cauliflower, prepared according to the illustrations on page 191
2   medium anchovy fillets, minced to a paste
3   medium garlic cloves, minced or pressed through a garlic press (about 1 tablespoon)
½   teaspoon red pepper flakes
⅓   cup dry white wine
⅓   cup low-sodium chicken broth
2   tablespoons minced fresh parsley leaves
    Salt

1. Heat 2 tablespoons of the oil in a large skillet over medium-high heat until shimmering. Add the cauliflower and cook, stirring occasionally, until the florets begin to brown, 6 to 7 minutes. Clear a space in the center of the pan and add the remaining ½ tablespoon oil and the anchovies, garlic, and red pepper flakes. Mash and stir the garlic mixture in the center of the pan until fragrant, about 1 minute. Stir to combine the garlic mixture and cauliflower and cook 1 minute longer.

2. Add the white wine and broth, cover, and cook until the cauliflower is tender but still offers some resistance to the tooth when sampled, 4 to 5 minutes. Add the parsley and season with salt to taste. Serve immediately.

CAULIFLOWER GRATIN

ONCE WE HAD DEVELOPED OUR BROCCOLI and Cheese Casserole (see page 179), we thought that we could simply substitute cauliflower for broccoli for a simple variation. But we were wrong. The cooking times didn't quite match up, and the flavor and texture of the sauce weren't as complementary as we had hoped. With a few alterations, however, we thought it could work.

Blanching worked as well with cauliflower as it did with the broccoli, with one major exception: the denser cauliflower absorbed a good deal of water. Subsequently, when we baked the casserole, a fair amount of water pooled in the bottom of the pan, diluting the sauce. To remedy the situation, we blotted the cauliflower dry on paper towels after blanching and effectively absorbed the excess moisture.

As for the sauce, we much preferred a richer Mornay, prepared exclusively with cream, not the leaner whole milk and broth combination we used in the sauce for the broccoli. The richer flavor better matched the stronger flavor and denser texture of the cauliflower. Because the cream was so much thicker, we found that we had to reduce the amount of flour in the original sauce by two-thirds. Just 1 tablespoon provided all of the thickening power the cream needed.

To match the cauliflower's stronger flavor, we slightly altered the sauce's components. We added minced shallot along with the garlic for a fuller allium flavor, and we substituted minced fresh thyme for the mustard (cauliflower can have a slight mustardy flavor all on its own). And with these simple changes, we were able to develop a few variations—variations on a variation.

Cauliflower Gratin
SERVES 6 TO 8

Gruyère or cheddar can be used in place of the Parmesan. See the illustrations on page 191 for information about cutting up cauliflower.

TOPPING

| 2 | slices white sandwich bread, torn into quarters |
| I | tablespoon unsalted butter, melted |

FILLING

Salt
I	large head (about 3 pounds) cauliflower, trimmed and cut into 3/4-inch florets
2	tablespoons unsalted butter
I	medium shallot, minced
I	medium garlic clove, minced or pressed through a garlic press (about I teaspoon)
I	tablespoon unbleached all-purpose flour
I1/2	cups heavy cream
	Pinch ground nutmeg
	Pinch cayenne pepper
1/8	teaspoon ground black pepper
I	teaspoon minced fresh thyme leaves
2	ounces Parmesan cheese, grated fine (about I cup)

1. FOR THE TOPPING: Process the bread and butter in a food processor until coarsely ground, about six 1-second pulses; set aside.

2. FOR THE FILLING: Adjust an oven rack to the middle position and heat the oven to 450 degrees. Bring 4 quarts water to a boil in a large pot and add 1 tablespoon salt. Add the cauliflower and cook until tender on the outside but slightly crunchy inside, about 3 minutes. Drain the cauliflower in a colander and rinse with cold water to cool. Place the blanched cauliflower on a rimmed baking sheet lined with paper towels.

3. Melt the butter in a large skillet over medium heat. Add the shallot and cook, stirring frequently, until softened, about 2 minutes. Add the garlic and cook until fragrant, about 30 seconds. Stir in the flour until well combined, about 1 minute. Whisk in the cream and bring to a boil. Stir in the nutmeg, cayenne, 1/4 teaspoon salt, the pepper, thyme, and 2/3 cup of the Parmesan until well combined, about 1 minute. Remove the pan from the heat.

4. TO ASSEMBLE AND BAKE: Arrange the cauliflower in a 13 by 9-inch baking dish (or shallow casserole dish of similar size). Pour the cream mixture over the cauliflower and mix gently to coat the cauliflower evenly. Sprinkle with the remaining 1/3 cup Parmesan. Sprinkle the bread-crumb topping evenly over the cheese. Bake until the top is golden brown and the sauce is bubbling around the edges, about 10 minutes. Serve immediately.

CLEANING LEEKS

1. Hold the leek under running water and shuffle the cut layers like a deck of cards.

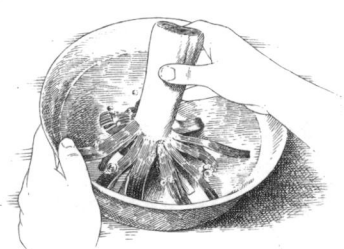

2. Slosh the cut end of the leek up and down in fresh, still water. Repeat as necessary.

Cauliflower Gratin with Leeks and Gruyère

Halve 3 small leeks lengthwise, using the white and light green parts only, and rinse well (see the facing page for information on cleaning leeks); slice crosswise into ¼-inch pieces (you should have about 1 cup). Follow the recipe for Cauliflower Gratin, adding the leeks along with the shallot and substituting 1 cup shredded Gruyère for the Parmesan.

CORN

DESPITE FARM-STAND SIGNS ACROSS THE COUNTRY announcing "butter and sugar" corn for sale, no one really grows old-time butter and sugar corn anymore. Nor does anybody grow most of the other old-fashioned nonhybrid varieties. These bygone varieties of corn have disappeared for a reason. They converted sugar into starch so rapidly once picked that people literally fired up their kettles before going out to gather the corn. Corn has since been crossbred to make for sweeter ears that have a longer hold on their fresh flavor and tender texture.

Basically, there are three hybrid types: normal sugary, sugar enhanced, and supersweet. Each contains dozens of varieties, with fancy names such as Kandy Korn, Double Gem, and Mystique. Normal sugary types, such as Silver Queen, are moderately sweet, with traditional corn flavor. The sugars in this type of corn convert to starch rapidly after being picked. The sugar-enhanced types are more tender and somewhat sweeter, with a slower conversion of sugar to starch. Supersweet corn has heightened sweetness, a crisp texture, and a remarkably slow conversion of sugar to starch after being picked. It is a popular type for growers who supply distant markets and require a product with a longer shelf life. Any corn sold in your supermarket during the off-season is likely a variety of supersweet.

Beyond the above generalizations, it's impossible to tell which kind of corn you have unless you taste it. With that in mind, we developed cooking methods that would work with all three kinds of corn hybrids. Boiling is probably the most all-purpose cooking method. To increase sweetness, we tried adding milk to the water but found it muddied the corn flavor. Salt toughens the corn up a bit and is best added at the table. Sugar can be added to the water to enhance the corn's sweetness, but when we tried this with supersweet corn, it tasted too sweet, almost like dessert.

Boiled Corn
SERVES 8

If you want to serve more corn, bring a second pot of water to a boil at the same time, or cook the corn in batches in just one pot. If you know that you have supersweet corn, omit the sugar.

4	teaspoons sugar (optional)
8	ears fresh corn, husks and silk removed
	Salt and ground black pepper
	Unsalted butter (optional)

Bring 4 quarts water and the sugar, if using, to a boil in a large pot. Add the corn, return to a boil, and cook until tender, 5 to 7 minutes. Drain the corn and season with salt and pepper to taste. Serve immediately, with butter if desired.

Boiled Corn with Lime-Cilantro Butter

6	tablespoons (¾ stick) unsalted butter, softened
½	teaspoons grated zest from 1 lime
1	tablespoon minced fresh cilantro leaves
	Pinch cayenne pepper
1	recipe Boiled Corn (without the salt, pepper, and butter)

Using a fork, beat the butter in a small bowl until light and fluffy. Beat in the lime zest, cilantro, and cayenne until well combined. Serve with the boiled corn.

DRY-TOASTING GARLIC

Toasting garlic cloves in a dry skillet tames their harsh flavor and loosens the skins for easy peeling. The garlic does not become soft and creamy like garlic roasted in the oven.

1. Place the unpeeled garlic cloves in a dry skillet over medium-high heat. Toast, shaking the pan occasionally, until the skins are golden brown, about 5 minutes. Transfer the toasted cloves to a cutting board and cool.

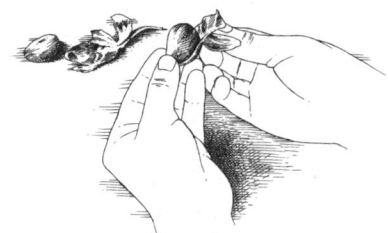

2. When cooled, the once-clingy skins peel off readily. The garlic can now be sliced, chopped, or minced.

Boiled Corn with Toasted Garlic and Herb Butter

Dry-toasting garlic is a good option when you want to mellow the punch of raw garlic but don't want to take the time to roast a whole head of garlic in the oven.

10	medium garlic cloves, skins left on, dry-toasted and then peeled according to the directions above
6	tablespoons (³/₄ stick) unsalted butter, softened
I	tablespoon minced fresh parsley leaves
I	tablespoon minced fresh basil leaves
¹/₈	teaspoon ground black pepper
I	recipe Boiled Corn (without the salt, pepper, and butter)

1. Mince the garlic cloves with a chef's knife or press them through a garlic press.

2. Using a fork, beat the butter in a small bowl until light and fluffy. Beat in the garlic, herbs, and pepper until thoroughly combined. Serve with the boiled corn.

GRILLED CORN

THE IDEAL EAR OF GRILLED CORN RETAINS the juiciness of boiled corn without sacrificing the toasty caramelization and smoke-infused graces of the grill. We started our tests with the bare ear cooked directly over a medium-hot fire. The outcome seemed too good to be true. The lightly caramelized corn was still juicy, with a toasty hit of grilled flavor. In fact, it was too good to be true. The variety of corn we used was fittingly called Fantasy, which is a supersweet variety. When we tried grilling a normal sugary corn variety with the husks off, the outcome was a flavorless, dry, gummy turnoff. The end result was no better with sugar-enhanced corn. The direct heat was just too much for the fleeting flavors and tender texture of the normal sugary and sugar-enhanced corn types.

We went on to test another popular grilling technique: Throw the whole ear on the grill, husk and all, as is. We tried this with all three sweet corn types at various heat levels. Half of the ears of corn were soaked beforehand; the other half were not. In sum, the husk-on method makes for a great-tasting ear of corn, and a particularly crisp, juicy one. But if it were not for the sticky charred husks that must be awkwardly peeled away at the table if you are to serve the corn hot, you would think you were eating boiled corn. The presoaked corn, in particular, just steams in the husks and picks up absolutely no grilled flavor.

Because grilling with the husks off was too aggressive for varieties other than supersweet, and because grilling with the husks on produced results no different from boiling, we turned to a compromise approach. We peeled off the outer layers of the husk but left the final layer that hugs the ear. This layer is much more moist and delicate than the outer layers, so much so that you can practically see the kernels through the husk. This thin husk gave the kernels a jacket heavy enough to prevent dehydration yet light enough to allow a gentle toasting. After the corn had spent about eight minutes over a medium-hot fire (we rolled the corn one-quarter turn every two minutes), we could be certain that it was cooked just right because the husk picked up a dark silhouette of the kernels and began to pull back at the corn's tip.

Grilled Corn

SERVES 8

While grilling husk-on corn delivers great pure corn flavor, it lacks the smokiness of the grill; essentially, each ear is steamed in its protective husk. By leaving only the innermost layer, we were rewarded with perfectly tender corn graced with the grill's flavor. Prepared in this way, the corn does not need basting with oil. See the illustration at bottom right for tips on judging when the corn is ready to come off the grill.

8   ears fresh corn, prepared according to the illustrations at right
Salt and ground black pepper
Unsalted butter (optional)

1. Grill the corn over a medium-hot fire (you should be able to hold your hand 5 inches above the cooking grate for 3 to 4 seconds), turning the ears every 1½ to 2 minutes, until the dark outlines of the kernels show through the husk and the husk is charred and beginning to peel away from the tip to expose some kernels, 8 to 10 minutes.

2. Transfer the corn to a platter. Carefully remove and discard the charred husks and silk. Season the corn with salt and pepper to taste and butter, if desired. Serve immediately.

➤ VARIATIONS

Grilled Corn with Spicy Chili Butter

Sautéing the spices with the butter and garlic brings out their flavor. Because salt does not dissolve readily in butter, it's best to serve the salt on the side.

6   tablespoons (¾ stick) unsalted butter
2   medium garlic cloves, minced or pressed through a garlic press (about 2 teaspoons)
1   teaspoon chili powder
½   teaspoon ground cumin
½   teaspoon paprika
⅛   teaspoon cayenne pepper
1   recipe Grilled Corn (without the salt, pepper, and butter)
1   lime, cut into 8 wedges
Salt

1. Melt the butter in a 10-inch skillet over medium heat. When the foaming subsides, add the garlic, chili powder, cumin, paprika, and cayenne and cook until fragrant, about 1 minute. Turn off the heat and set aside.

2. Using tongs, take each ear of grilled, husked corn and roll it in the spicy butter. Serve immediately, with lime wedges and salt to taste.

PREPARING CORN FOR GRILLING

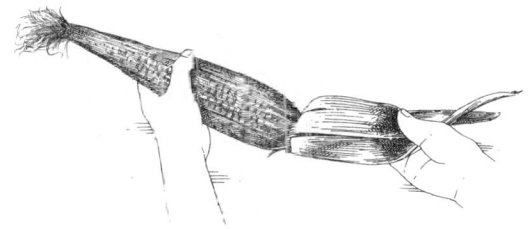

1. Remove all but the innermost layer of the husk. The kernels should be covered by, but visible through, the innermost layer.

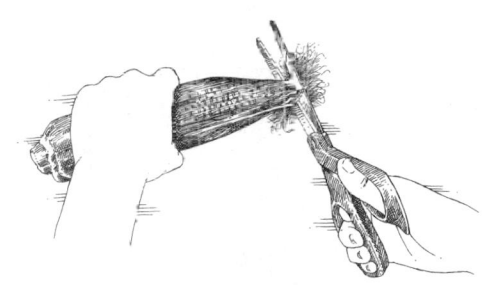

2. Use scissors to snip off the tassel, or long silk ends, at the tip of the ear.

JUDGING WHEN GRILLED CORN IS DONE

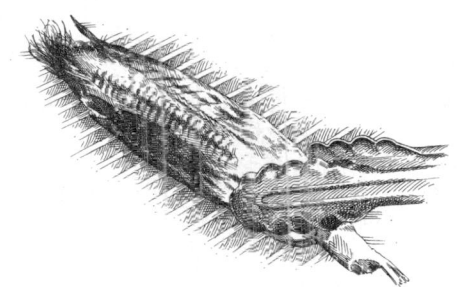

As soon as the husk picks up the dark silhouette of the kernels and begins to pull away from the tip of the ear, the corn is ready to come off the grill.

Grilled Corn with Soy-Honey Glaze

Corn grilled with soy sauce is a familiar sight at summer fairs and festivals in Japan. Returning the glazed ears of corn to the grill caramelizes the sugar in the sauce and gives the corn a deep, smoky flavor.

- ⅓   cup honey
- ⅓   cup soy sauce
- I   recipe Grilled Corn (without the salt, pepper, and butter)

1. Mix the honey and soy sauce together in a 10-inch skillet. Bring to a simmer over medium-high heat. Reduce the heat to medium and simmer until slightly syrupy and reduced to about ½ cup, about 5 minutes. Turn off the heat and set aside.

2. Transfer the corn to a platter. Carefully remove and discard the charred husks and silk. Using tongs, take each ear of grilled, husked corn and roll it in the soy mixture. Return the glazed corn to the grill for an additional 1 to 2 minutes, turning once. Serve immediately.

MEASURING HONEY

Sticky ingredients like honey and molasses take their time flowing out of a measuring cup and require a spoon to scrape out the remainder. Spraying the measuring cup with nonstick cooking spray before filling it will ensure that, when emptied, the liquid will slip right out of the cup.

OUR FAVORITE THANKSGIVING SIDES

WHEN IT COMES TO DECIDING ON OUR Thanksgiving menus, we have as hard a time as the next person in narrowing down our choices, but here are the dishes that most often pop up on our holiday tables, year after year.

- Skillet Green Beans with Orange Essence and Toasted Maple Pecans (page 213)
- Green Bean Casserole (page 215)
- Glazed Brussels Sprouts with Chestnuts (page 183)
- Brussels Sprouts Braised in Cream (page 184)
- Glazed Carrots with Orange and Cranberries (page 187)
- Roasted Baby Carrots with Sage and Walnuts (page 188)
- Sautéed Corn with Bacon and Scallions (page 202)
- Glazed Parsnips and Celery (page 189)
- Faster Acorn Squash with Brown Sugar (page 234)
- Mashed Potatoes (page 267)
- Mashed Sweet Potatoes with Ginger and Brown Sugar (page 299)
- Candied Sweet Potato Casserole with Toasted Marshmallow Topping (page 302)

CREAMED CORN

ALTHOUGH CREAMED CORN IS AVAILABLE AT any time of year out of the can, it doesn't compare with the clean, sweet flavor of late summer corn gently simmered with fresh cream. But if you don't handle the fresh corn and cream correctly, you wind up with that overcooked, just-out-of-the-can flavor you were trying to avoid.

Many recipes start by boiling the corn on the cob, then cutting the kernels off the cob and mixing them with a cream sauce. This technique, however, loses much of the sweet, delicate corn flavor to the cooking water. We quickly rejected this method in favor of recipes that simmer the corn kernels (which are first cut free from the cobs) directly in the cream. This technique releases their sugary, summery flavor into the sauce, which is where you want it to be.

Simply simmering fresh corn kernels in cream, however, wasn't enough. It produced a thin, lumpy mixture that lacked the thickened, spoonable texture we desired. Scraping the pulp out of the spent cobs helped a bit, but we wanted the sauce a bit thicker. Flour and cornstarch just made the sauce gummy and overwhelmed the flavor of the corn. We then tried grating a few of the ears, which broke down some of the kernels into smaller pieces. This did the trick. By grating some of the raw kernels off the cob, we were able to release more of the corn's natural thickener. We found that grating about half of the corn in our recipe thickened the sauce sufficiently.

After making a few batches of this recipe with different types of corn, we realized that the cooking times can differ, depending on the corn's variety and age. While some batches cooked perfectly in only 10 minutes, others needed five minutes longer. We also found that as the corn and cream cook and thicken, the heat needs to be adjusted to keep the mixture at a simmer to prevent the bottom from burning.

As for other ingredients, we tried using half-and-half instead of heavy cream, but tasters missed the luxurious flavor and heft provided by the latter. A little shallot, garlic, and fresh thyme complemented the delicate flavor of the corn, while a pinch of cayenne added a little kick.

Creamed Corn
SERVES 6 TO 8

For the best texture and flavor, we like a combination of grated corn, whole kernels (cut away from the cobs with a knife), and corn milk (scraped from all ears with the back of a knife). See the illustrations on page 200 for tips on cutting the kernels off some ears of corn and grating (milking) the rest of the corn.

5	medium ears fresh corn, husks and silk removed
2	tablespoons unsalted butter
1	medium shallot, minced
1	medium garlic clove, minced or pressed through a garlic press (about 1 teaspoon)
1½	cups heavy cream
½	teaspoon minced fresh thyme leaves
	Pinch cayenne pepper
	Salt and ground black pepper

1. Cut the kernels from 3 ears of corn and transfer them to a medium bowl. Firmly scrape the cobs with the back of a butter knife to collect the pulp and milk in the same bowl. Grate the remaining 2 ears of corn on the coarse side of a box grater set in the bowl with the cut kernels. Firmly scrape these cobs with the back of a butter knife to collect the pulp and milk in the same bowl.

2. Melt the butter in a medium saucepan over medium-high heat. When the foaming subsides, add the shallot and cook until softened but not browned, 1 to 2 minutes. Add the garlic and cook until aromatic, about 30 seconds. Stir in the corn kernels and pulp as well as the cream, thyme, cayenne, ¼ teaspoon salt, and ⅛ teaspoon pepper. Bring the mixture to a simmer and cook, adjusting the heat as necessary and stirring occasionally, until the corn is tender and the mixture has thickened, 10 to 15 minutes. Remove the pan from the heat, adjust the seasonings with salt and pepper to taste, and serve immediately.

➤ VARIATION

Creamed Corn with Bacon and Blue Cheese

Use your favorite kind of blue cheese for this variation. Gorgonzola works as well. Because of the saltiness of the bacon and blue cheese, it may not be necessary to add salt. See the illustrations below for cutting and grating corn kernels.

- 5 medium ears fresh corn, husks and silk removed
- 4 ounces (about 4 slices) bacon, cut into 1/2-inch pieces
- 1 medium shallot, minced
- 1 medium garlic clove, minced or pressed through a garlic press (about 1 teaspoon)

- 1 1/2 cups heavy cream
- 1/2 teaspoon minced fresh thyme leaves
  Pinch cayenne
- 2 ounces blue cheese, crumbled (about 1/2 cup)
  Salt and ground black pepper

1. Cut the kernels from 3 ears of corn and transfer them to a medium bowl. Firmly scrape the cobs with the back of a butter knife to collect the pulp and milk in the same bowl. Grate the remaining 2 ears of corn on the coarse side of a box grater set in the bowl with the cut kernels. Firmly scrape these cobs with the back of a butter knife to collect the pulp and milk in the same bowl.

2. Cook the bacon in a large nonstick skillet over medium-high heat until crisp and brown, about 5 minutes. Transfer the bacon to a paper towel–lined plate to drain; set aside.

3. Remove and discard all but 2 tablespoons rendered bacon fat from the pan. Add the shallot and cook until softened but not browned, 1 to 2 minutes. Add the garlic and cook until aromatic, about 30 seconds. Stir in the corn kernels and pulp as well as the cream, thyme, and cayenne. Bring the mixture to a simmer and cook, adjusting the heat as necessary and stirring occasionally, until the corn is tender and the mixture has thickened, 10 to 15 minutes. Remove the pan from the heat and stir in the cheese. Adjust the seasonings with salt and pepper to taste and serve immediately.

REMOVING KERNELS FROM CORN COBS

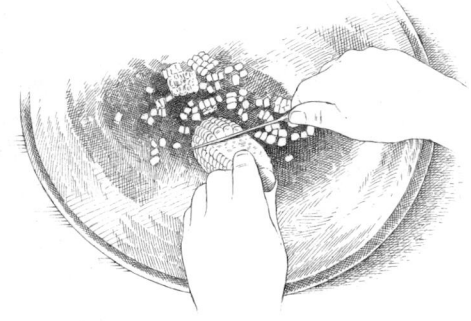

Hold the cob on its end inside a large, wide bowl and use a paring knife to cut off the kernels.

MILKING CORN

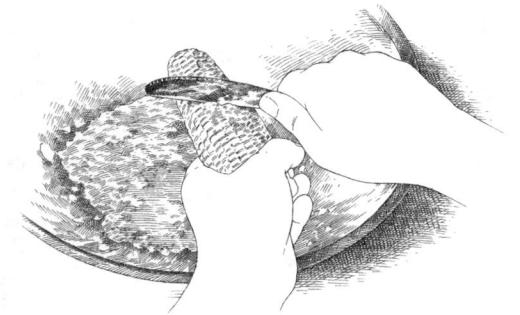

Once you have cut off the kernels, scrape the remaining pulp off the cob and squeeze out the milk by pressing firmly on the cob with the back of a butter knife.

CORN ON THE COB AT THE HEIGHT OF THE summer season is hard to beat, but summer is fleeting. Eating corn doesn't have to be. In addition to our recipes for Sautéed Corn (this page), we've come up with a variety of ideas that will inspire you to stock the freezer with this versatile vegetable.

MEDITERRANEAN CORN SALAD

Combine 3 cups (one 16-ounce bag) thawed frozen corn with 1 cup halved cherry tomatoes, ½ cup pitted kalamata olives, and 1 cup chopped baby spinach. Toss with salt, ground black pepper, 2 tablespoons extra-virgin olive oil, and 1 tablespoon lemon juice.

COOL CORN SALAD

Combine 3 cups (one 16-ounce bag) thawed frozen corn, 1 medium cucumber (peeled, seeded, and diced), and 1 small, thinly sliced red onion. Add 1 tablespoon chopped fresh parsley leaves, 1 teaspoon chopped mint leaves, ½ teaspoon sugar, 3 tablespoons lemon or lime juice, and ½ cup plain yogurt. Stir until combined.

ROASTED CORN AND RED PEPPER SALSA

Pour 2 tablespoons olive oil into a large nonstick skillet set over medium-high heat and sauté 1 minced shallot, 1 minced garlic clove, and 3 cups (one 16-ounce bag) frozen corn until warmed through, about 3 minutes. Stir in 1 cup diced roasted red bell peppers, ¾ teaspoon salt, 3 tablespoons red wine vinegar, and 2 tablespoons minced fresh parsley leaves; remove from the heat and allow to cool to room temperature. This salsa goes perfectly with grilled items, quesadillas, or even tortilla chips.

SAUTÉED CORN

ALTHOUGH ITS CONVENIENCE IS SECOND TO none, we all know that frozen corn lacks the crisp bite and clean flavor of fresh corn on the cob. To put the pop back into frozen corn, we discovered it was best to ignore the cooking instructions on the packaging and sauté the frozen corn in a hot, nonstick skillet. To make up for its lack of flavor, we also added some aromatics, such as shallots and garlic, as well as celery, jalapeño, and fresh herbs. Beyond being sautéed, the thawed corn can also be used in salads, soups, salsas, relishes, or condiments—see our ideas (opposite).

Sautéed Corn with Thyme and Shallot

SERVES 4 TO 6

2	tablespoons unsalted butter
1	shallot, minced
1	medium garlic clove, minced or pressed through a garlic press (about 1 teaspoon)
1	pound frozen corn (do not thaw)
1	teaspoon minced fresh thyme leaves
	Salt and ground black pepper

Melt the butter in a large nonstick skillet over medium-high heat. Add the shallot and garlic

---

SCIENCE: Corn Storage

While the general rule of thumb is to buy and eat corn the same day it has been harvested (as soon as the corn is harvested, the sugars start converting to starches and the corn loses sweetness), most of us have been guilty of trying to break that rule for one reason or another. We tried a variety of methods for overnight storage using Silver Queen corn, one of the more perishable varieties. We found that the worst thing you can do to corn is to leave it sitting out on the counter. Throwing it into the refrigerator without any wrapping is nearly as bad. Storing it in an airtight bag helps, but the hands-down winner entailed wrapping the corn (husks left on) in a wet paper bag and then in a plastic bag (any shopping bag will do). After 24 hours of storage, we found the corn stored this way to be juicy and sweet—not starchy—and fresh-tasting.

and cook until softened, about 2 minutes. Increase the heat to high and add the corn; cook, stirring often, until heated through but still crunchy, about 2 minutes. Stir in the thyme and season with salt and pepper to taste.

➤ VARIATIONS

Sautéed Corn with Cherry Tomatoes and Basil

Follow the recipe for Sautéed Corn with Thyme and Shallot, substituting 2 tablespoons extra-virgin olive oil for the butter. Substitute fresh basil leaves for the thyme and stir in 8 ounces halved cherry tomatoes with the basil.

Sautéed Corn with Fennel, Tomatoes, and Tarragon

Follow the recipe for Sautéed Corn with Thyme and Shallot, adding 1 bulb fennel, halved, cored, and thinly sliced, with the shallot and garlic, and cook until softened, about 5 minutes. Substitute 1 tablespoon minced tarragon leaves for the thyme and stir in 8 ounces halved cherry tomatoes with the tarragon.

Sautéed Southwestern Corn

Follow the recipe for Sautéed Corn with Thyme and Shallot. Before adding the shallot to the melted butter, cook 8 ounces diced chorizo sausage until lightly browned, about 2 minutes. Add 1 finely chopped red bell pepper and 1 minced jalapeño to the pan with the chorizo and shallot and cook until the red pepper just begins to brown, about 5 minutes. Stir in the corn and substitute 2 teaspoons minced cilantro leaves for the thyme.

Sautéed Corn with Bacon and Scallions

Follow the recipe for Sautéed Corn with Thyme and Shallot, omitting the thyme. Fry 6 ounces (about 6 slices) chopped bacon in the skillet until crisp, about 5 minutes. Using a slotted spoon, transfer the bacon to a paper towel–lined plate and pour off all but 2 tablespoons of the bacon fat; substitute the bacon fat for the butter. Sprinkle the corn with 3 thinly sliced scallions and the crisp bacon before serving.

Sautéed Corn Succotash

Follow the recipe for Sautéed Corn with Thyme and Shallot, adding 1 finely chopped red bell pepper to the skillet with the shallot, and cook until the pepper just begins to brown, about 5 minutes. Add 8 ounces frozen lima beans and continue to cook until the beans are softened, about 6 minutes. Stir in 8 ounces frozen corn and cook until heated through, about 2 minutes. Substitute 1 tablespoon minced parsley for the thyme.

EDAMAME

EDAMAME (EH-DAH-MAH-MEH), OR GREEN soybeans, are often served as a simple appetizer in Japanese restaurants. Because they are usually served in their shell (the pods themselves are inedible) as a finger food, the versatility of these protein-rich beans is often overlooked. Possessing a sweet, slightly nutty flavor redolent of fava beans, edamame have always been a test kitchen favorite. So recently, when shelled edamame started showing up in the frozen food section at our local markets, we got to thinking: Why not elevate edamame from snack to side dish? As soon as we started cooking, it was clear that the creamy-crisp edamame were up to the challenge.

The main preparation issue here was the cooking method. For edamame in their shells, our sources suggested either steaming or boiling, but for shelled edamame, we took a different approach. Using only ¼ cup of water, we poached the frozen edamame in a large covered skillet over high heat. After two minutes, we removed the lid from the skillet and allowed the excess liquid to evaporate. From here we added butter, garlic, and shallots to the hot skillet and allowed them to bloom for about 30 seconds. The richness of the butter, combined with the aromatic qualities of the garlic and shallot, gave the dish substance and depth, while a sprinkling of parsley just before serving accentuated the edamame's clean vegetal flavor.

But we had only scratched the surface. Our tasters loved the sturdy texture and especially the full flavor of the edamame, which held its own even when paired with assertive (and sometimes exotic) ingredients, from Parmesan cheese to oyster sauce. The next time you're in the frozen food aisle, pick up some shelled edamame—they make a simple, delicious, and adaptable addition to any meal.

Buttered Edamame with Shallot and Basil

SERVES 4

Beyond turning them into simple side dishes (see the recipes that follow), try adding these crunchy, clean-flavored beans to soups, salads, stir-fries, or fried rice. Don't like lima beans? Use shelled edamame instead in succotash or cold bean salads.

¼	cup water
12	ounces frozen, shelled edamame beans (do not thaw)
	Salt
2	tablespoons unsalted butter
1	medium garlic clove, minced or pressed through a garlic press (about 1 teaspoon)
1	medium shallot, minced
1	tablespoon minced fresh basil leaves
	Ground black pepper

Bring the water to a boil in a large, nonstick skillet over high heat. Add the frozen edamame and a pinch of salt, cover, and cook until the beans have thawed, about 2 minutes. Remove the lid and continue to cook until the water has evaporated and the edamame are heated through, about 2 minutes. Add the butter, garlic, and shallot, and cook until the shallot is soft, about 3 minutes. Off the heat, stir in the basil and season with salt and pepper to taste.

➤ VARIATIONS

Edamame with Garlic, Balsamic, and Parsley Leaves

Follow the recipe for Buttered Edamame with Shallot and Basil, substituting extra-virgin olive oil for the butter and parsley leaves for the basil. Stir in 1 tablespoon balsamic vinegar and 1 teaspoon brown sugar with the parsley. Season with additional oil and vinegar to taste, and serve.

Edamame with Ginger, Garlic, and Sesame

Follow the recipe for Buttered Edamame with Shallot and Basil, substituting vegetable oil for the butter and omitting the basil. Add 1 tablespoon grated ginger with the shallot. Before seasoning with salt and pepper, add 1 tablespoon rice wine vinegar, 2 teaspoons toasted sesame seeds, and ½ teaspoon toasted sesame oil.

Sweet-Spicy Edamame with Cilantro and Peanuts

Follow the recipe for Buttered Edamame with Shallot and Basil, substituting vegetable oil for the butter and cilantro leaves for the basil. Replace the water with a mixture of 2 tablespoons lime juice, 1 tablespoon water, 1 tablespoon white vinegar, 1 tablespoon fish sauce, 1 tablespoon sugar, and ⅛ teaspoon red pepper flakes. After removing the lid, allow the steaming mixture to reduce to a glaze, about 2 minutes, before adding the oil, garlic, and shallot. Before seasoning with salt and pepper, add 2 tablespoons chopped roasted peanuts.

EGGPLANT

EGGPLANT CAN BE PREPARED IN SEVERAL ways, including sautéing, grilling, and stir-frying. The biggest challenge that confronts the cook when preparing eggplant is excess moisture. While the grill will evaporate this liquid and allow the eggplant to brown nicely, this won't happen in a hot pan. The eggplant will steam in its own juices, and the result can be an insipid flavor and mushy texture.

Salting is the classic technique for drawing moisture out of the eggplant before cooking. We experimented with both regular table salt and kosher salt and preferred kosher salt because the crystals are large enough to wipe away after the salt has done its job. Finer table salt crystals dissolved into the eggplant flesh and had to be flushed out with water. Although traditional recipes call for letting the salted eggplant drain in a colander, we had better results when we placed the salted eggplant on a baking sheet lined with paper towels. In a colander, the eggplant juices tended to fall from one piece to another. On the baking sheet lined with paper towels, the juices were absorbed as soon as they were drawn out of the eggplant. The eggplant must then be thoroughly dried, especially if it has been diced for sautéing. We prefer to dice eggplant that will be sautéed to increase the surface area that can brown and absorb flavorings.

When grilling, we prefer thicker slices that won't fall apart on the cooking grate. We found ¾-inch rounds to be just the right size. And because the liquid can fall onto the coals, there's no need to salt eggplant destined for the grill.

Stir-frying is basically the same as sautéing except that the finished dish is saucier. In this case, liquid from the eggplant is not such a problem. The eggplant is browned and then sauced quite generously so its texture will be soft rather than crisp or firm. In addition, stir-fry sauces often contain soy sauce and are quite salty. For all these reasons, we found it best to skip salting eggplant when using it in a stir-fry. However, stir-frying works best with small, firm eggplants (sometimes labeled Asian eggplants in markets). Rather than dicing the eggplant (as we do for sautéing), we had the best results when we cut small eggplants in half lengthwise and then crosswise into ½-inch-thick half-moons.

Sautéed Eggplant

SERVES 4

Very small eggplants (weighing less than 6 ounces each) can be cooked without salting. However, we found that larger eggplants generally have a lot of moisture, which is best removed before sautéing.

I	large eggplant (about I½ pounds), ends trimmed, cut into ³/₄-inch cubes
I	tablespoon kosher salt
2	tablespoons extra-virgin olive oil
	Ground black pepper
I	medium garlic clove, minced or pressed through a garlic press (about I teaspoon)
2	tablespoons minced fresh parsley leaves or finely shredded fresh basil leaves

1. Place the eggplant cubes on a paper towel–lined rimmed baking sheet and sprinkle the cubes with the salt, tossing to coat them evenly. Let the eggplant stand for at least 30 minutes. Using additional paper towels, pat any excess moisture from the eggplant.

2. Heat the oil in a large heavy-bottomed skillet over medium-high heat until shimmering. Add the eggplant cubes and cook until they begin to brown, about 4 minutes. Reduce the heat to medium-low and cook, stirring occasionally, until the eggplant is fully tender and lightly browned, about 10 minutes. Stir in pepper to taste and add the garlic. Cook to blend the flavors, about 2 minutes. Off the heat, stir in the parsley. Serve immediately.

➤ VARIATIONS
Sautéed Eggplant with Cumin and Garlic
Sautéing the spices in the oil makes their flavors bloom.

I	large eggplant (about I½ pounds), ends trimmed, cut into ³/₄-inch cubes
I	tablespoon kosher salt
2	tablespoons vegetable oil
I	teaspoon ground cumin
½	teaspoon chili powder
2	medium garlic cloves, minced or pressed through a garlic press (about 2 teaspoons)
I	teaspoon sugar
I	tablespoon minced fresh parsley leaves

1. Place the eggplant cubes on a paper towel–lined rimmed baking sheet and sprinkle the cubes with the salt, tossing to coat them evenly. Let the eggplant stand for at least 30 minutes. Using additional paper towels, pat any excess moisture from the eggplant.

2. Heat the oil in a large heavy-bottomed skillet over medium-high heat until shimmering. Add the cumin and chili powder and cook until fragrant, about 20 seconds. Add the eggplant cubes and cook until they begin to brown, about 4 minutes. Reduce the heat to medium-low and cook, stirring occasionally, until the eggplant is fully tender and lightly browned, about 10 minutes. Stir in the garlic and sugar. Cook to blend the flavors,

about 2 minutes. Off the heat, stir in the parsley. Serve immediately.

Sautéed Eggplant with Pancetta and Rosemary

Pancetta is unsmoked Italian bacon (for more information, see below). It can be found in the deli section of most large grocery stores. If pancetta is unavailable, bacon can be substituted.

1	large eggplant (about 1½ pounds), ends trimmed, cut into ¾-inch cubes
1	tablespoon kosher salt
3	ounces pancetta, diced fine
1	small onion, halved and sliced thin
½	teaspoon minced fresh rosemary
	Ground black pepper

1. Place the eggplant cubes on a paper towel–lined rimmed baking sheet and sprinkle the cubes with the salt, tossing to coat them evenly. Let the eggplant stand for at least 30 minutes. Using additional paper towels, pat any excess moisture from the eggplant.

2. Cook the pancetta in a large heavy-bottomed skillet over medium-high heat until crisp, about 5 minutes. Use a slotted spoon to transfer the pancetta to a plate. Add the onion and rosemary to the rendered fat in the pan and cook, stirring frequently, until golden, about 4 minutes. Add the eggplant cubes and cook until they begin to brown, about 4 minutes. Reduce the heat to medium-low and cook, stirring occasionally, until the eggplant is fully tender and lightly browned, about 10 minutes. Stir in the pancetta and add pepper to taste. Serve immediately.

INGREDIENTS: Pancetta

Just like bacon, pancetta comes from the belly of the pig, but it has a very different flavor. American bacon is cured with salt, sugar, and spices and then smoked. Pancetta is not smoked, and the cure does not contain sugar—just salt, pepper, and, usually, cloves. As a result, pancetta has a richer, meatier flavor than bacon. Pancetta is rolled tightly, packed in a casing, and then sliced thin or thick, as desired.

Grilled Eggplant
SERVES 4

There's no need to salt eggplant destined for the grill; the intense heat will vaporize excess moisture.

3	tablespoons extra-virgin olive oil
2	medium garlic cloves, minced or pressed through a garlic press (about 2 teaspoons)
2	teaspoons minced fresh thyme or oregano leaves
	Salt and ground black pepper
1	large eggplant (about 1½ pounds), ends trimmed, cut crosswise into ¾-inch-thick rounds

1. Combine the oil, garlic, thyme, and salt and pepper to taste in a small bowl. Place the eggplant on a platter and brush both sides with the oil mixture.

2. Grill the eggplant over a medium-hot fire (you should be able to hold your hand 5 inches above the cooking grate for 3 to 4 seconds), turning once, until both sides are marked with dark stripes, 8 to 10 minutes. Serve hot, warm, or at room temperature.

➤ VARIATIONS

Grilled Eggplant with Basil Oil

Make sure to cook the garlic until it is barely starting to sizzle. The oil will then be just hot enough to slightly wilt the basil when they are processed together.

¼	cup extra-virgin olive oil
1	medium garlic clove, minced or pressed through a garlic press (about 1 teaspoon)
½	cup packed fresh basil leaves
	Salt and ground black pepper
1	recipe Grilled Eggplant

1. Place the oil and garlic in a skillet and turn the heat to medium. Cook until the garlic just starts to sizzle and becomes fragrant, about 2 minutes.

2. Place the basil in a food processor. Very carefully pour the hot oil over the basil. Process until the mixture is fragrant and almost smooth, about

30 seconds. Season with salt and pepper to taste.

3. Transfer the grilled eggplant to a platter and drizzle with the basil oil. Serve immediately.

Grilled Eggplant with Cherry Tomato and Cilantro Vinaigrette

Grape tomatoes can also be used in this recipe. Choose the ripest tomatoes for the best, most flavorful vinaigrette.

1/2	pint cherry tomatoes, each tomato quartered (about 1 cup)
1/4	teaspoon salt
	Pinch cayenne pepper
1	medium shallot, minced
2	tablespoons minced fresh cilantro leaves
2	tablespoons juice from 1 or 2 limes
6	tablespoons olive oil
1	recipe Grilled Eggplant

1. Mix the tomatoes, salt, cayenne, shallot, cilantro, lime juice, and oil together in a medium bowl. Let stand at room temperature until the tomatoes are juicy and seasoned, about 20 minutes.

2. Transfer the grilled eggplant to a platter. Pour the vinaigrette over the eggplant and serve immediately.

Stir-Fried Eggplant

SERVES 4

Small, firm eggplants, sometimes labeled Asian eggplants, work best in this stir-fry.

1/4	cup low-sodium chicken broth
2	tablespoons soy sauce
1 1/2	teaspoons toasted sesame oil
1	tablespoon plus 1 teaspoon peanut oil
2	small eggplants (about 8 ounces each), ends trimmed, cut in half lengthwise, and cut crosswise into 1/2-inch-thick half-moons
1	medium garlic clove, minced or pressed through a garlic press (about 1 teaspoon)
1	teaspoon minced fresh ginger
2	medium scallions, sliced thin

1. Whisk the broth, soy sauce, and sesame oil together in a small bowl.

2. Heat 1 tablespoon of the peanut oil in a large, nonstick heavy-bottomed skillet over high heat until shimmering. Add the eggplant and cook, stirring frequently, until browned, about 3 minutes. Clear a space in the center of the pan and add the remaining 1 teaspoon peanut oil and the garlic and ginger. Cook until fragrant, about 15 seconds. Stir the garlic mixture into the eggplant and add the broth mixture. Cover, reduce the heat to medium, and cook until the sauce has thickened and the eggplant has softened, about 3 minutes. Garnish with the scallions and serve immediately.

OVEN-BAKED RATATOUILLE

A CLASSIC DISH IN SOUTHERN FRANCE, ratatouille is the embodiment of all things summer captured in a humble side dish. Eggplant, squash, tomato, onion, garlic, and herbs are all perfectly cooked, drenched with extra-virgin olive oil, and seasoned with herbs and garlic. The flavors are light and multilayered; each vegetable can be tasted independently, heightened by the presence of the others. But what sounds like an easy dish is actually far from it. Each of the vegetables is cooked separately before combining to maximize its flavor and texture, but this requires multiple pans and a lot of supervision. Ratatouille is derived from *touiller,* the French verb "to stir," pointing—for French speakers at least—to the amount of work involved. We love the flavors of ratatouille, but we don't love the work required to prepare it; side dishes shouldn't require a full battery of pans. We wanted to develop a simpler, less hands-on approach to preparing ratatouille, one in which the vegetables could be blended and cooked in unison.

Intuition led us to believe that roasting would be the best approach. The high heat could concentrate the flavors of the vegetables and evaporate those exuded juices that turn most of the "one-pot" versions of ratatouille we have tried soupy and one-dimensional. The oven-cooked vegetables might not be cooked as perfectly as they are in stovetop recipes, but our hopes were high.

Our intuition proved only partially correct. While the vegetables retained their distinct flavors and discrete shapes at temperatures above 400 degrees, they tended to cook unevenly and burn around the edges. Reducing the temperature 25 degrees at a time, we found the results more consistent with each batch. We found the best compromise between flavor and texture at 375 degrees; the vegetables cooked evenly and retained their shapes. None were too mushy, aside from the tomatoes, but they are supposed to be that way.

With a basic method in hand, we could return to the fundamentals: the specific choice and preparation of the vegetables. Eggplant is usually the 800-pound gorilla of ratatouille, but we weren't having any problems with it in our oven-roasted version. Many recipes salt the eggplant prior to cooking to drain off its excess moisture, but the oven's high heat made this step (thankfully) unnecessary. We simply peeled it and cut it into largish cubes. Within the hour the ratatouille cooked, the eggplant shrank dramatically in size as the moisture evaporated, and its flavor intensified. We tried the three commonly available types of eggplant—globe, Italian, and Japanese—and found that they all tasted similar in the end. We stuck with the widely available globe variety.

Like eggplant, summer squash is often salted before cooking to draw off excess moisture, and, once again, we found this step unnecessary. We preferred the flavor and texture of the squash "as is," unpeeled and cut into fairly large cubes. Summer squash and zucchini are interchangeable here, because their flavors are so similar.

As for the onion, yellow onions tasted fine, but we preferred the sweetness and color of red onions. The onion caramelized in the high heat, even lightly charring in spots to add an occasional (pleasantly) bitter bite to the dish. Minced and chopped onion both disappeared among the mix of vegetables; thinly sliced, the onion added textural and visual contrast.

Fresh tomatoes made little sense in this instance because we knew that, outside of the peak summer months, they would have little flavor and a poor texture. Picked at the height of the season, canned tomatoes are guaranteed to be ripe and sweet. And easy, too—canned diced tomatoes require no preparation outside of draining. At first we thought it would be imperative to thoroughly drain the tomatoes to prevent the ratatouille from becoming soggy, but the resulting dish was too dry and the vegetables burned around the edges. A less thorough draining left enough juice in the tomatoes to moisten the other vegetables and prevent burning.

As for the seasonings, ratatouille is all about the vegetables, and any auxiliary flavorings should be kept to a minimum. A hint of garlic, a spray of herbs, and a shot of acidity are the norm. Minced garlic lent a harsh flavor that was too dominant. Thinly slivered garlic proved a better option because it added a milder, sweeter flavor as it melted into the vegetables. As for herbs, a little went a long way. Thyme, parsley, oregano, marjoram, and basil are all common options, but we chose to let the woodsy flavor of thyme fly solo.

Once the vegetables were roasted, we added a sprinkle of vinegar to brighten the ratatouille's flavors, and the casserole was good to go; a near perfect rendition with a minimum of fuss. To gild the lily, we added a handful of pine nuts, a not uncommon addition in classic recipes. The oily nuts lent just the right richness and a pleasing crunch.

Oven-Baked Ratatouille
SERVES 6 TO 8

This dish can be served either hot or at room temperature. It works not only as a side dish but as a topping for rice or pasta or even a chunky sauce to accompany roasted chicken. If serving at room temperature, you may want to season with additional vinegar and salt to perk up the flavor. This dish tastes best when prepared and served on the same day; however, it can be refrigerated for up to 2 days. Allow the ratatouille to come to room temperature before serving.

1 medium eggplant (about 1 pound), peeled and cut into 3/4-inch cubes
1 medium red onion, halved pole to pole and sliced 1/4 inch thick

2   medium zucchini or summer squash, cut into
    ¹/₂-inch cubes
1   (28-ounce) can diced tomatoes, drained, with
    ¹/₃ cup juice reserved
5   medium garlic cloves, sliced thin
¹/₄ cup extra-virgin olive oil
1   teaspoon fresh thyme leaves
1   teaspoon salt
¹/₈ teaspoon ground black pepper
1¹/₂ tablespoons red wine vinegar
¹/₄ cup pine nuts, toasted in a small dry skillet
    over medium heat until fragrant and golden,
    about 4 minutes

1. Adjust an oven rack to the middle position and heat the oven to 375 degrees. Combine the eggplant, onion, zucchini, tomatoes and reserved juice, garlic, olive oil, thyme, salt, and pepper in a large bowl and mix well. Transfer to a 13 by 9-inch baking dish (or shallow casserole dish of similar size). Roast until the vegetables have softened and browned in spots, about 1 hour, stirring thoroughly halfway through the cooking time.

2. Stir the vinegar into the vegetables and sprinkle the pine nuts over the top. Serve hot or cooled to room temperature.

Green Beans

WHO DOESN'T LIKE GREEN BEANS? ON THEIR own or gussied up with seasonings, green beans are always a crowd pleaser. We favor three basic treatments for cooking them.

For the first method, green beans are boiled or steamed and then sautéed or simply dressed with flavorful ingredients. Sounds simple (and it is), but we still had questions. Is boiling better than steaming? Should the beans be cut (either into pieces or lengthwise) before cooking? Should salt be added to the water? How long should the beans cook? After a number of experiments with boiling and steaming, we came to prefer boiling. Steaming takes twice as long as boiling, and when steaming a pound or more of beans we found it necessary to turn them during cooking because those at the bottom of the pile cooked faster than those at the top. Also, the beans cook more evenly when boiled; steamed beans are often tender on the outside but raw-tasting in the middle. Finally, boiling permits the addition of salt during cooking. This is important because even though the beans need additional salting after they are drained, adding salt during cooking results in more even seasoning, as the beans have time to absorb some of the salt.

As for preparation, we prefer to trim the tops and tails with our fingers but leave the beans whole otherwise. Cutting the beans into shorter lengths exposes the tender flesh to too much heat. Because the skin cooks more slowly than this exposed flesh, the inside of the bean tends to become mushy before the outside has had time to become tender.

Boiling times varied greatly in the sources we consulted. We found in our testing that the freshness and thickness of the beans drastically affects cooking time. Really fresh, thin beans, not much wider than a strand of linguine, may be done in as little as two minutes. Most beans from the supermarket, though, have traveled some distance and are considerably thicker. Because of their age and size, they need five to six minutes to become tender. We don't like mushy green beans, but beans that are too crisp or raw-tasting are likewise unappealing.

After being boiled and promptly drained, the beans can be flavored in two ways. They can be quickly sautéed or "dressed" (drizzled with a flavorful oil or vinaigrette). Beans that will be sautéed can be set aside at room temperature for a few hours. If dressing the beans, do so when they are hot for maximum absorption of flavor. Whether sautéing or dressing beans, use very flavorful ingredients—a drizzle of walnut oil and the addition of toasted walnuts and tarragon, for example, or a quick sauté with onions that have been browned in bacon fat.

The next method we explored is braising. We prefer to braise green beans when we have a lot of pots on the stovetop and are rushing to finish many dishes at once. Braising, or simmering in a small amount of liquid in a covered pan over low heat, requires little attention from the cook. Once the beans, seasonings, and liquid are in the pan, you are free to tend to other matters, returning only to give the beans a quick stir now and then. We found that it takes 20 minutes to braise green

PAIRING GREEN BEAN
SIDE DISHES WITH POPULAR
MAIN COURSES

PAIRING GREEN BEAN SIDE DISHES WITH POPULAR MAIN COURSES

YOU CAN SERVE GREEN BEANS WITH almost any main course. This endlessly adaptable vegetable takes to a wide variety of flavors. Whether you're looking for a subtle side dish to complement the delicate flavor of chicken or fish, or a more assertive partner to stand up to beef or pork, green beans can step up to the plate. Here are the test kitchen's favorite pairings:

BEEF OR LAMB WITH . . .
- Green Beans Braised with Shiitake Mushrooms (page 212)
- Green Beans with Sauteed Shallots and Vermouth (page 210)

PORK WITH . . .
- Green Beans with Quatre-Épices (page 210)
- Spicy Green Beans with Sesame Seeds (page 211)

FISH OR CHICKEN WITH . . .
- Garlic-Lemon Skillet Green Beans with Toasted Bread Crumbs (page 213)
- Braised Green Beans (page 212)

TURKEY OR DUCK WITH . . .
- Skillet Green Beans with Orange Essence and Toasted Maple Pecans (page 213)
- Green Beans with Pickled Red Onions and Toasted Walnuts (page 211)

crisp-tender point, until they are meltingly tender. (And it's no big deal if the beans need to be kept warm on the stove for a few minutes while you finish cooking the rest of your meal.)

Braising is also particularly well suited to supermarket green beans, which tend to be relatively thick and sturdy and can stand up to prolonged cooking. As for braising mediums, we found chicken broth, tomatoes, or a combination of dried mushrooms and soy sauce each provide rich flavor.

The third method we like for cooking green beans is one designed for 11th-hour cooks. We began by steaming the beans in a covered skillet with a little water, then removed the lid partway through cooking to evaporate the water, and built a quick pan sauce around the beans as they finished cooking. The beans, however, steamed in only eight minutes, leaving little time to make a decent sauce after the water had evaporated. Switching the cooking order around, we then tried making the sauce first. Building good flavor and texture by sautéing aromatics and a little flour, we then added to the pan some fresh herbs, the beans, and some chicken broth instead of just plain water. We covered the skillet and cooked the lot until the beans were almost tender. At that point, we removed the lid to thicken the sauce, and this also allowed us to monitor the progress of the green beans.

When made in a nonstick skillet, these beans are easy to dress up with some toasted bread crumbs or glazed nuts. By making the toppings first, you can simply wipe the skillet clean with paper towels and return it to the stovetop.

Blanched Green Beans
SERVES 4

This recipe is extremely simple. If you want, add some chopped toasted nuts, diced tomatoes, or fried bacon and onions to jazz up the beans.

    Salt
1   pound green beans, ends trimmed (see the illustration on page 211)
1   tablespoon extra-virgin olive oil
1   tablespoon minced fresh basil, tarragon, or parsley leaves

beans, give or take a few minutes.

Braising does rob green beans of their brilliant color, but the tradeoff is that the beans pick up lots of flavor during the gentle cooking process. It's difficult, if not impossible, to overcook the beans because they are meant to be cooked well past the

Bring 2½ quarts water to a boil in a large saucepan over high heat. Add 1 teaspoon salt and the green beans and cook until tender, about 5 minutes. Drain the beans well and transfer them to a bowl. Toss with the oil and your herb of choice, season to taste with salt, and serve immediately.

➤ VARIATIONS

Green Beans with Quatre-Épices

Quatre-épices is a classic French blend of four spices used to flavor soups, stews, vegetables, and roasts. There is no set recipe or combination, but it is usually made from any four of the following: ginger, cloves, black or white pepper, nutmeg, cinnamon, and allspice.

	Salt
I	pound green beans, ends trimmed (see the illustration on the facing page)
2	tablespoons unsalted butter
¼	teaspoon ground black pepper
¼	teaspoon ground nutmeg
¼	teaspoon ground ginger
⅛	teaspoon ground cloves
3	tablespoons heavy cream

1. Bring 2½ quarts water to a boil in a large saucepan over high heat. Add 1 teaspoon salt and the green beans and cook until tender, about 5 minutes. Drain the beans well.

2. Melt the butter in a large skillet over medium-high heat. When the foaming subsides, add the spices and cook, stirring frequently, until fragrant, about 30 seconds. Add the cream and beans and cook until heated through, about 1 minute. Season to taste with salt and serve immediately.

Green Beans with Sautéed Shallots and Vermouth

See the information at right about buying vermouth.

	Salt
I	pound green beans, ends trimmed (see the illustration on the facing page)
4	tablespoons (½ stick) unsalted butter
4	large shallots, sliced thin
2	tablespoons dry vermouth
	Ground black pepper

1. Bring 2½ quarts water to a boil in a large saucepan over high heat. Add 1 teaspoon salt and the green beans and cook until tender, about 5 minutes. Drain the beans well.

2. Meanwhile, heat 2 tablespoons of the butter in a large skillet over medium heat. When the foaming subsides, add the shallots and cook, stirring often, until golden brown and just crisp around the edges, about 10 minutes. Add the vermouth and bring to a simmer. Whisk in the remaining 2 tablespoons butter, 1 tablespoon at a time. Add the beans and toss to combine. Season with salt and pepper to taste and serve immediately.

INGREDIENT: Dry Vermouth

Though it's often used in cooking, and even more often in martinis, dry vermouth is a potable that receives very little attention. Imagine our surprise, then, when we did a little research and turned up nearly a dozen different brands. We pared them down to eight and tasted the vermouths straight (chilled) and in simple pan sauces for chicken (containing only shallots, chicken broth, and butter in addition to the vermouth).

First, a quick description of what dry vermouth is. Its base is a white wine, presumably not of particularly high quality, as evidenced by the relatively low prices of most vermouths. The wine is fortified with neutral grape spirits that hike the alcohol level up a few percentage points to 16 to 18 percent, and it is "aromatized," or infused with "botanicals," such as herbs, spices, and fruits. In this country, dry vermouth, also called extra-dry vermouth, is imported from France and Italy (Italian vermouths being the most common here) or is made domestically in California.

Two vermouths found their way into the top three in both tastings: Gallo Extra Dry and Noilly Prat Original French Dry. Gallo is the fruitier of the two and made the favorite pan sauce, which tasters called "balanced," "complex," "smooth," and "round." Noilly Prat is more woodsy and herbaceous and made a pan sauce that tasted fresh and balanced.

Green Beans with Garlic

The green beans served in Chinese restaurants are actually Chinese long beans. They have a flavor similar to that of green beans and can grow up to 3 feet in length. Green beans make a perfectly fine substitute and—unless you live in California—are much more readily available. Because the beans are cooked in the skillet with the seasonings for some time, the blanching time should be reduced.

Salt
1	pound green beans, ends trimmed (see the illustration below)
1	tablespoon vegetable oil
3	medium garlic cloves, minced or pressed through a garlic press (about 1 tablespoon)
1	teaspoon minced fresh ginger
1/4	teaspoon red pepper flakes
1	tablespoon soy sauce

1. Bring 2½ quarts water to a boil in a large saucepan over high heat. Add 1 teaspoon salt and the green beans and cook until crisp-tender, 3 to 4 minutes. Drain the beans well.

2. Heat 2 teaspoons of the oil in a large nonstick skillet over high heat until shimmering. Add the green beans and cook, stirring frequently, until the beans are spotty brown, about 2 minutes. Clear a space in the center of the pan and add the garlic, ginger, and red pepper flakes. Drizzle the remaining teaspoon oil over the aromatics. Cook, stirring frequently, until fragrant, about 15 seconds. Add the soy sauce, mix together, and serve immediately.

TRIMMING ENDS FROM GREEN BEANS

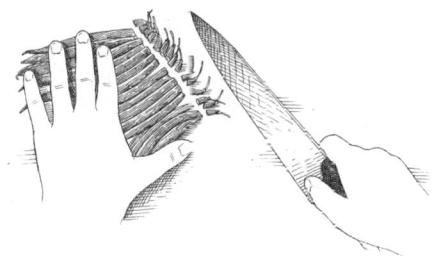

Instead of trimming the end from one green bean at a time, line up the beans on a cutting board and trim all of the ends with just one slice.

Spicy Green Beans with Sesame Seeds

SERVES 4

Avoid buying beans that are very thick—an indication that they were harvested late and will remain tough and chewy after cooking. Also, choose pods that are fairly uniform in size, as their thickness determines the cooking time. If using haricots verts—very thin green beans—reduce the boiling time to just 2 or 3 minutes.

Salt
1	pound green beans, ends trimmed (see the illustration below)
1	teaspoon toasted sesame oil
1½	teaspoons Asian garlic-chili sauce
2	tablespoons minced fresh cilantro leaves
1	tablespoon sesame seeds, toasted in a small dry skillet over medium heat until fragrant, about 4 minutes

Bring 2½ quarts water to a boil in a large saucepan over high heat. Add 1 teaspoon salt and the beans and cook until tender, about 5 minutes. Drain the beans and transfer them to a large serving bowl. Toss with the oil, chili sauce, cilantro, and toasted sesame seeds. Season with salt to taste and serve immediately.

Green Beans with Pickled Red Onions and Toasted Walnuts

SERVES 4

Although the vinegar left over from the quick-pickled onions is not used in this recipe, it is quite flavorful and can be stored in the refrigerator to be used in a vinaigrette or sauce.

1/2	cup red wine vinegar
1	tablespoon sugar
	Salt
1/2	medium red onion, sliced thin
1	pound green beans, ends trimmed (see the illustration at left)
1/2	cup walnuts, toasted in a medium dry skillet over medium heat until fragrant, about 4 minutes
2	teaspoons extra-virgin olive oil

1 tablespoon minced fresh tarragon leaves
Ground black pepper

1. Bring the vinegar, sugar, and ¼ teaspoon salt to a boil over high heat in a small saucepan. Add the onion, return the mixture to a boil, then immediately remove the pan from the heat. Transfer the mixture to a small bowl to cool.

2. Meanwhile, bring 2½ quarts water to a boil in a large saucepan over high heat. Add 1 teaspoon salt and the beans and cook until tender, about 5 minutes. Drain the beans and transfer them to a large serving bowl. Strain the onions from the vinegar, reserving the liquid for another use. Toss the onions with the beans, toasted walnuts, oil, and tarragon. Season with salt and pepper to taste and serve immediately.

Braised Green Beans

SERVES 4

This is a good way to use older, end-of-season green beans.

1 tablespoon extra-virgin olive oil
1 medium shallot, minced
½ teaspoon minced fresh thyme leaves
1 pound green beans, ends trimmed
(see the illustration on page 211)
¾ cup low-sodium chicken broth
Salt and ground black pepper

Heat the oil in a large sauté pan over medium heat until shimmering. Add the shallot and cook until golden, about 5 minutes. Add the thyme, green beans, and broth. Stir, cover, and reduce the heat to low. Simmer, stirring occasionally, until the beans are tender but still offer some resistance to the bite, 15 to 20 minutes. Season to taste with salt and pepper and serve immediately.

➤ VARIATIONS
Green Beans Braised in Tomatoes
This Italian recipe uses a simple tomato sauce flavored with onions and garlic as the braising medium. Add the parsley at the end for extra color; basil can be substituted for the parsley.

2 tablespoons extra-virgin olive oil
1 small onion, diced
2 medium garlic cloves, minced or pressed
through a garlic press (about 2 teaspoons)
1 cup diced canned tomatoes
1 pound green beans, ends trimmed
(see the illustration on page 211)
Salt and ground black pepper
2 tablespoons minced fresh parsley leaves

1. Heat the oil in a large sauté pan over medium heat until shimmering. Add the onion and cook until softened, about 5 minutes. Add the garlic and cook until fragrant, about 1 minute. Add the tomatoes and simmer until the juices thicken slightly, about 5 minutes.

2. Add the green beans, ¼ teaspoon salt, and pepper to taste. Stir, cover, and cook, stirring occasionally, until the beans are tender but offer some resistance to the bite, about 15 to 20 minutes. Stir in the parsley and adjust the seasonings, adding salt and pepper to taste. Serve immediately.

Green Beans Braised with Shiitake Mushrooms
Dried shiitakes have a wonderful earthy, smoky flavor. They are often used in Japanese cooking to flavor soups. You can find them in the Asian food section of most large grocery stores. See page 316 for tips on rehydrating dried mushrooms.

½ ounce dried shiitake mushrooms
(about 6 small or 4 medium)
1 tablespoon soy sauce
1 teaspoon sugar
1 teaspoon vegetable oil
1 teaspoon grated fresh ginger
(see the illustration on page 189)
1 pound green beans, ends trimmed
(see the illustration on page 211)
Salt and ground black pepper

1. Place the shiitakes in a medium bowl. Add 1 cup boiling water, cover the bowl with plastic wrap, and let the shiitakes steep for 5 minutes. Remove the shiitakes from the water (reserving the liquid), let cool, remove and discard the stems,

and dice the shiitake caps. Strain the soaking liquid through a sieve lined with a paper towel. Add the soy sauce and sugar to the shiitake liquid. Set aside.

2. Heat the oil in a large sauté pan over medium-high heat until shimmering. Add the ginger and cook until fragrant, about 30 seconds. Add the green beans, shiitakes, and shiitake liquid. Stir, cover, and reduce the heat to low. Simmer, stirring occasionally, until the beans are tender but still offer some resistance to the bite, 15 to 20 minutes. Season to taste with salt and pepper and serve immediately.

Garlic-Lemon Skillet Green Beans with Toasted Bread Crumbs

SERVES 6

Reduce the amount of garlic if you prefer more subtle flavoring.

2	slices high-quality sandwich bread, each slice torn into quarters
3	tablespoons unsalted butter
	Salt and ground black pepper
2	tablespoons grated Parmesan cheese
6	medium garlic cloves, minced or pressed through a garlic press (about 2 tablespoons)
2	teaspoons unbleached all-purpose flour
1/8	teaspoon red pepper flakes
I	teaspoon minced fresh thyme leaves
1 1/2	pounds green beans, ends trimmed (see illustration on page 211)
I	cup low-sodium chicken broth
I	tablespoon juice from I lemon

1. Process the bread in a food processor to produce even, fine crumbs, about ten 1-second pulses. Heat 1 tablespoon of the butter in a large nonstick skillet over medium-high heat; when melted, add the bread crumbs and cook, stirring frequently, until golden brown, 3 to 5 minutes. Transfer to a medium bowl and stir in ¼ teaspoon salt, ⅛ teaspoon pepper, and the cheese; set aside.

2. Wipe out the skillet. Add the remaining 2 tablespoons butter, the garlic, and ¼ teaspoon

salt; cook over medium heat, stirring constantly, until the garlic is golden, 3 to 5 minutes. Stir in the flour, red pepper flakes, and thyme, then toss in the green beans. Add the chicken broth and increase the heat to medium-high; cover and cook until the beans are partly tender but still crisp at the center, about 4 minutes. Uncover and cook, stirring occasionally, until the beans are tender and the sauce has thickened slightly, about 4 minutes. Off the heat, stir in the lemon juice and adjust the seasonings with salt and pepper to taste. Transfer to a serving dish, sprinkle evenly with the bread crumbs, and serve.

Skillet Green Beans with Orange Essence and Toasted Maple Pecans

SERVES 6

The flavors in this dish work well as part of Thanksgiving dinner.

3/4	cup pecans, chopped coarse
3	tablespoons unsalted butter
2	tablespoons maple syrup
	Salt
2	medium shallots, minced
1/2	teaspoon grated zest and 1/3 cup juice from I orange
	Pinch cayenne pepper
2	teaspoons unbleached all-purpose flour
1 1/2	pounds green beans, ends trimmed (see illustration on page 211)
2/3	cup low-sodium chicken broth
I	teaspoon minced fresh sage leaves
	Ground black pepper

1. Toast the pecans in a large nonstick skillet over medium-high heat, stirring occasionally, until fragrant, about 4 minutes. Off the heat, stir in 1 tablespoon of the butter, the maple syrup, and ⅛ teaspoon salt. Return the skillet to medium heat and cook, stirring constantly, until the nuts are dry and glossy, about 45 seconds; transfer to a plate.

2. Wipe out the skillet. Heat the remaining 2 tablespoons butter in the skillet over medium

heat; when the foaming subsides, add the shallots, orange zest, and cayenne and cook, stirring occasionally, until the shallots are softened, about 2 minutes. Stir in the flour until combined, then toss in the green beans. Add the chicken broth, orange juice, and sage; increase the heat to medium-high, cover, and cook until the beans are partly tender but still crisp at the center, about 4 minutes. Uncover and cook, stirring occasionally, until the beans are tender and the sauce has thickened slightly, about 4 minutes. Off the heat, adjust the seasonings with salt and pepper to taste. Transfer to a serving dish, sprinkle evenly with the pecans, and serve.

GREEN BEAN CASSEROLE

OFTEN REFERRED TO AS THE CLASSIC GREEN Bean Bake, this casserole was developed by Campbell's in 1955 using frozen green beans, canned cream of mushroom soup, and a topping of canned fried onions. The company touted the recipe as "delicious and easy to make, easy to remember, and leaves room for creativity." We thought we would exercise the creativity clause. We started by making the original recipe and then began to experiment.

The frozen beans recommended in the original recipe were certainly easy to use, but they also had a watery taste and a mushy texture. Fresh beans not only offered more flavor, but we were able to cook them to the appropriate doneness and leave a little bit of crunch. We tried sautéing and steaming the green beans but ended up liking the bright green color and seasoned flavor obtained when they were blanched in boiling, salted water. We found that the beans tasted best when blanched in 4 quarts of water heavily seasoned with 2 tablespoons of salt for four to five minutes. We then plunged the beans into ice water (a process called shocking) to stop them from further cooking. Blanching then shocking allowed us maximum control over the cooking process, which meant that the beans were perfectly cooked every time.

Our next concern was the cream-based mushroom sauce. We did not enjoy the thick, pasty texture and lackluster flavor of condensed soup. What we wanted was a smooth, velvety sauce filled with potent mushroom flavor. We began by testing two popular methods for making a cream sauce: reducing the cream to the proper consistency, and thickening the cream with flour and butter (also known as a roux). Sauces made by simply reducing cream were too heavy and took too much time for our holiday-size casserole, while sauces thickened with flour tasted pasty and lacked depth of flavor. By combining the methods—using a little flour and reducing the sauce a bit—we got a smooth, flavorful sauce that was neither too rich nor too floury. After testing half-and-half and whole milk, we found neither up to sharing the title ring with lush heavy cream. We tried adding cheese but found the extra flavor to be both overpowering and unnecessary.

Up until now, we had been using white button mushrooms but were disappointed with their lack of flavor. By replacing half of the button mushrooms with cremini and using some dried porcini, we were able to give the sauce a full, earthy, and complex mushroom flavor. We also tried portobellos and liked their flavor, but we found that their meaty texture required more cooking than button mushrooms, making the portobellos difficult to incorporate into our otherwise streamlined recipe. Onion, garlic, and fresh thyme were great companion flavors for the mushrooms, while chicken broth helped to pull all the flavors in the sauce together. We also tried adding bacon, white wine, Madeira, and shallots to the sauce but found their flavors unwelcome and discordant.

With the green beans and mushroom sauce nailed down, all that was left was the fried onion topping. While deep frying our own onions was out of the question because of the time it takes, we found the canned fried onions simply tasted too commercial to use on their own. By mixing the canned, fried onions with some fresh, seasoned bread crumbs, we were able to remove the "from the can taste" of the traditional topping.

Green Bean Casserole

SERVES 8 TO 10

All the components of this dish can be cooked ahead of time. The assembled casserole needs only 15 minutes in a 375-degree oven to heat through and brown. A gratin dish works nicely for this recipe.

TOPPING

4	slices white sandwich bread, torn into quarters
2	tablespoons unsalted butter, melted
1/4	teaspoon salt
1/8	teaspoon ground black pepper
3	cups canned fried onions (about 6 ounces)

FILLING

Salt

2	pounds green beans, ends trimmed (see the illustration on page 211) and cut on the diagonal into 2-inch pieces
1/2	ounce dried porcini mushrooms
6	tablespoons (3/4 stick) unsalted butter
1	medium onion, minced
3	medium garlic cloves, minced or pressed through a garlic press (about 1 tablespoon)
12	ounces white button mushrooms, wiped clean, stems trimmed, and sliced 1/4 inch thick
12	ounces cremini mushrooms, wiped clean, stems trimmed, and sliced 1/4 inch thick
2	tablespoons minced fresh thyme leaves
1/4	teaspoon ground black pepper
2	tablespoons unbleached all-purpose flour
1	cup low-sodium chicken broth
2	cups heavy cream

1. FOR THE TOPPING: Process the bread, butter, salt, and pepper in a food processor until coarsely ground, about ten 1-second pulses. Transfer to a large bowl and toss with the onions; set aside.

2. FOR THE FILLING: Heat the oven to 375 degrees. Bring 4 quarts water to a boil in a large pot. Add 2 teaspoons salt and the beans. Cook until bright green and crisp-tender, 4 to 5 minutes. Drain the beans and plunge them immediately into a large bowl filled with ice water to stop the cooking process. Remove the beans from the ice water and spread them out on a paper towel–lined baking sheet to drain.

3. Meanwhile, cover the dried porcini with 1/2 cup hot tap water in a small microwave-safe bowl; cover with plastic wrap, cut several steam vents with a paring knife, and microwave on high power for 30 seconds. Let stand until the mushrooms soften, about 5 minutes. Lift the mushrooms from the liquid with a fork and mince using a chef's knife (you should have about 2 tablespoons). Pour the liquid through a paper towel–lined sieve and reserve.

4. Melt the butter in a large nonstick skillet over medium-high heat until the foaming subsides, about 1 minute. Add the onion, garlic, button mushrooms, and cremini mushrooms and cook until the mushrooms release their moisture, about 2 minutes. Add the porcini mushrooms along with their reserved liquid, the thyme, 1 teaspoon salt, and the pepper and cook until the mushrooms are tender and the liquid has reduced to 2 tablespoons, about 5 minutes. Add the flour and cook for about 1 minute. Stir in the broth and reduce the heat to medium. Stir in the cream and simmer gently until the sauce has the consistency of dense soup, about 15 minutes.

5. TO ASSEMBLE AND BAKE: Spread the beans in a 3-quart gratin dish. Pour the mushroom mixture over the beans and mix to coat the beans evenly. Sprinkle with the bread-crumb mixture and bake until the top is golden brown and the sauce is bubbling around the edges, about 15 minutes. Serve immediately.

GREENS

MANY COOKS THINK THEY CAN TREAT ALL leafy greens the same way, even though some are delicate enough for salads while others seem as tough as shoe leather. After cleaning, stemming, and cooking more than 100 pounds of leafy greens, we found that they fell into two categories—tender and mild flavored, and tougher and assertively flavored—each of which should be handled quite differently.

Tender greens include spinach (which is also good in salads; see page 90), beet greens, and Swiss chard, all of which taste of the earth and minerals but are still rather delicate. We tested boiling, steaming, and sautéing these greens. Boiling produced the most brilliantly colored greens, but they were also very mushy and bland. The water cooked out all of their flavor and texture. Steamed greens were less mushy, but clearly these tender greens, with their high moisture content, did not need any added liquid. Damp greens that were tossed in hot oil (which could be flavored with aromatics and spices) wilted in just two to three minutes in a covered pan. Once wilted, we found it best to remove the lid so the liquid in the pan would evaporate. This method has the advantage of flavoring the greens as they cook.

We found that tougher greens, such as kale, mustard, turnip, and collard, don't have enough moisture to be wilted in a hot pan; they scorch before they wilt. Steaming these assertively flavored greens produces a better texture but does nothing to tame their bitter flavor. Oddly, it turned them an unattractive yellowish green. It was clear to everyone in the test kitchen that tough greens benefit from cooking in some water, which will wash away some of their harsh notes.

We tested boiling 2 pounds of greens in an abundant quantity of salted water and what might be called shallow blanching in several cups of salted water. Greens blanched in larger quantities of salted water had a lot going for them. They were tender, brilliantly colored, and less bitter than those cooked by other methods, and the salt rounded out their flavor. But blanching was not ideal. Once boiled, drained, rinsed, and squeezed, the greens had lost much of their individual character and tasted rather pallid. Cooking the greens in lots of water diluted their flavor too much.

So we tried cooking these assertive greens in small quantities of water. We started by cooking leaves from 1 pound of greens in 1 cup of salted water, checking at five and then again at seven minutes. The five-minute leaves had a sharp, raw bite and were starting to acquire that dull look. The seven-minute greens were fully cooked but still tasted bitter. We decided to double the water from 1 to 2 cups. The greens cooked in this quantity of water weren't as grossly bitter as those

cooked in only 1 cup of liquid, but they were still a bit too bold. On the verge of settling for conventional blanching, we gave this shallow-cook method one more shot, by once again doubling the water from 2 cups to a quart and cooking the greens for the full seven minutes. The resulting greens offered the perfect balance we wanted: good color, full flavor without bitterness, and a tender green, ready for a quick, final cooking to unite them with other flavorful ingredients.

When you think about it, it stands to reason that a shallow blanch would work best with assertive

PREPARING LEAFY GREENS

SWISS CHARD, KALE, AND COLLARD AND MUSTARD GREENS
To prepare Swiss chard, kale, and collard and mustard greens, hold each leaf at the base of the stem over a bowl filled with water and use a sharp knife to slash the leafy portion from either side of the thick stem.

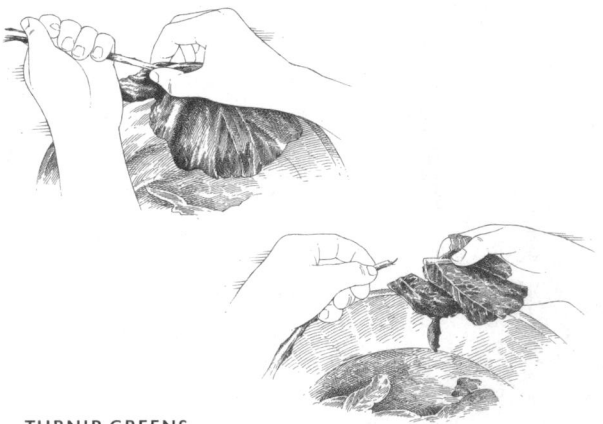

TURNIP GREENS
1. Turnip greens are most easily stemmed by grasping the leaf between your thumb and index finger at the base of the stem and stripping it off by hand.
2. When using this method, however, the very tip of the stem will break off along with the leaves. It is tender enough to cook along with the leaves.

greens. The more water you use when blanching porous vegetables, the more diluted the flavor of the vegetable becomes. That's one reason why steaming is the preferred way to cook so many vegetables—you want as little of the flavor as possible to escape into the cooking liquid. Assertive greens are different. You want to rid them of some of the bitterness, but not all of it. A shallow blanching removes enough bitterness to make these greens palatable but not so much as to rob them of their assertive and often peppery character.

Shallow blanching not only preserves the color and flavor, but it also saves time. We were surprised to learn that a gallon of water takes almost 20 minutes to boil. Two quarts (the amount you need to cook enough greens for four, about 2 pounds) can be brought to a boil in half the time.

We found that while cut leaves cook faster than whole ones, the leaves are much easier to cut once cooked. Tediously stacking 2 pounds of leaves in batches, rolling them up like big cigars, and cutting them into ribbons seemed a waste of time when the same leaves boiled down to just 2 cups seven minutes later. We found it simpler to rough-chop them before blanching. Then, after blanching, it was easy to cut the dramatically shrunken greens as fine as we liked. Once the blanched greens have been cut, they can be quickly cooked with seasonings.

Sautéed Tender Greens

SERVES 4

To stem spinach and beet greens, simply pinch off the leaves where they meet the stems. A thick stalk runs through each Swiss chard leaf, so it must be handled differently; see the illustration on the facing page for instructions. A deep Dutch oven or soup kettle is best for this recipe. The greens should be moist but not soaking when they go into the pot.

3   tablespoons extra-virgin olive oil
2   medium garlic cloves, minced or pressed
    through a garlic press (about 2 teaspoons)
2   pounds damp tender greens, such as spinach,
    beet greens, or Swiss chard, stemmed, washed
    in several changes of cold water, shaken to
    remove excess water and chopped coarse

Salt and ground black pepper
Lemon wedges (optional)

Heat the oil and garlic in a Dutch oven or other deep pot over medium-high heat until the garlic sizzles and turns golden, 1 to 2 minutes. Add the damp greens, cover, and cook, stirring occasionally, until the greens wilt completely, 2 to 3 minutes. Uncover and season with salt and pepper to taste. Raise the heat to high and cook until the liquid evaporates, 2 to 3 minutes. Serve immediately, with lemon wedges if desired.

➤ VARIATIONS

Sautéed Tender Greens with Pine Nuts and Currants

Raisins (either dark or golden) can be used in place of the currants.

3   tablespoons extra-virgin olive oil
1   medium garlic clove, minced or pressed
    through a garlic press (about 1 teaspoon)
¼   cup pine nuts, chopped coarse
2   tablespoons currants
2   pounds damp tender greens, such as spinach,
    beet greens, or Swiss chard, stemmed, washed
    in several changes of cold water, shaken to
    remove excess water, and chopped coarse
    Salt and ground black pepper

Heat the oil, garlic, and pine nuts in a Dutch oven or other deep pot over medium-high heat until the garlic and nuts sizzle and turn golden, 1 to 2 minutes. Add the currants and damp greens, cover, and cook, stirring occasionally, until the greens wilt completely, 2 to 3 minutes. Uncover and season with salt and pepper to taste. Raise the heat to high and cook until the liquid evaporates, 2 to 3 minutes. Serve immediately.

Sautéed Tender Greens with Mustard and Pecans

For best results, use whole-grain mustard. If it is unavailable, regular Dijon mustard can be substituted.

1   tablespoon whole-grain mustard
1   teaspoon light or dark brown sugar
3   tablespoons extra-virgin olive oil
1   medium shallot, minced
2   pounds damp tender greens, such as spinach, beet greens, or Swiss chard, stemmed, washed in several changes of cold water, shaken to remove excess water, and chopped coarse
    Salt and ground black pepper
¼   cup chopped pecans, toasted in a medium dry skillet over medium heat until fragrant, about 4 minutes

1. Mix the mustard, brown sugar, and 2 tablespoons water together in a small bowl. Set aside.

2. Heat the oil and shallot in a Dutch oven or other deep pot over medium-high heat until the shallot sizzles and turns golden, about 2 minutes. Add the damp greens and mustard mixture, cover, and cook, stirring occasionally, until the greens completely wilt, 2 to 3 minutes. Uncover and season with salt and pepper to taste. Raise the heat to high, and cook until the liquid evaporates, 2 to 3 minutes. Garnish with the toasted pecans and serve immediately.

Sautéed Tender Greens with Cumin, Tomatoes, and Cilantro

Indian flavors enliven greens in this simple recipe. See the information at right about seeding plum tomatoes.

3   tablespoons vegetable or canola oil
1   small onion, minced
2   medium garlic cloves, minced or pressed through a garlic press (about 2 teaspoons)
1   medium jalapeño chile, stemmed, seeded, and minced
1½ teaspoons ground cumin
2   large plum tomatoes, cored, seeded, and chopped
2   pounds damp tender greens, such as spinach, beet greens, or Swiss chard, stemmed, washed in several changes of cold water, shaken to remove excess water, and chopped coarse
2   tablespoons minced fresh cilantro leaves
    Salt and ground black pepper
    Lime wedges (optional)

Heat the oil and onion in a Dutch oven or other deep pot over medium-high heat until the onion sizzles and softens, about 2 minutes. Add the garlic, chile, and cumin and cook until fragrant, about 1 minute. Add the tomatoes and cook until they release their juices, about 1 minute. Add the damp greens, cover, and cook, stirring occasionally, until the greens completely wilt, 2 to 3 minutes. Uncover, stir in the cilantro, and season with salt and pepper to taste. Raise the heat to high and cook until the liquid evaporates, 2 to 3 minutes. Serve immediately, with lime wedges if desired.

SEEDING TOMATOES

The seeds are watery and sometimes bitter and are often removed before chopping a tomato. These techniques work for both peeled and unpeeled tomatoes. Because of their different shapes, round and plum (also called Roma) tomatoes are seeded differently.

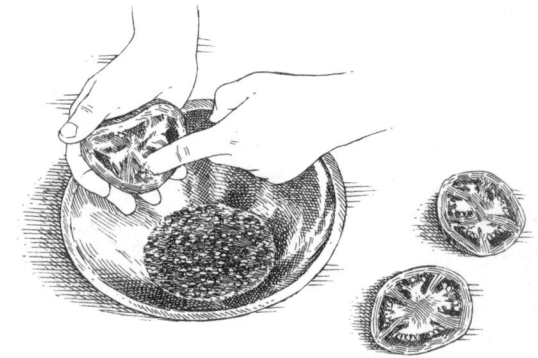

ROUND TOMATOES
Halve the cored tomato along its equator. If the tomato is ripe and juicy, gently give it a squeeze and shake out the seeds and gelatinous material. If not, scoop them out with your finger or a small spoon.

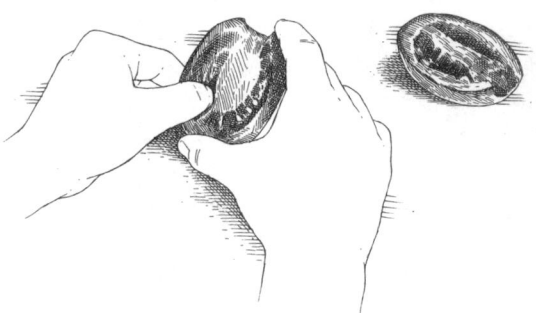

PLUM TOMATOES
Halve the cored tomato lengthwise, cutting through the core end. Break through the inner membrane with your finger and scoop out the seeds and gelatinous material.

Sautéed Tender Greens with Bacon and Red Onion

This dish also makes a great filling for omelets.

- 2 ounces (about 2 slices) bacon, cut crosswise into ½-inch strips
- ½ small red onion, minced
- 1 medium garlic clove, minced or pressed through a garlic press (about 1 teaspoon)
- ½ teaspoon minced fresh thyme leaves
- 2 pounds damp tender greens, such as spinach, beet greens, or Swiss chard, stemmed, washed in several changes of cold water, shaken to remove excess water, and chopped coarse
  Salt and ground black pepper

1. Cook the bacon in a Dutch oven or other deep pot over medium heat until the bacon is crisp, about 5 minutes. Transfer the bacon to a paper towel–lined plate to drain, leaving the bacon drippings in the pot.

2. Raise the heat to medium-high. Add the onion to the drippings and cook, stirring frequently, until golden brown, about 3 minutes. Stir in the garlic and cook until fragrant, about 1 minute longer. Add the thyme and damp greens, cover, and cook, stirring occasionally, until the greens wilt completely, 2 to 3 minutes. Uncover and season with salt and pepper to taste. Raise the heat to high and cook until the liquid evaporates, 2 to 3 minutes. Garnish with the reserved bacon and serve immediately.

Sautéed Tender Greens with Caramelized Onion and Dried Apricots

Adding sugar to the onion speeds its cooking time and balances the sherry vinegar in this recipe.

- 1 tablespoon extra-virgin olive oil
- 1 tablespoon unsalted butter
- 1 large onion, chopped fine
- 1 teaspoon sugar
- 2 medium garlic cloves, minced or pressed through a garlic press (about 2 teaspoons)
- 2 medium anchovy fillets, minced
- ¼ cup chopped dried apricots
- 1 tablespoon sherry vinegar

DRAINING LEAFY GREENS

Many recipes for greens recommend adding them to the cooking pot with a little water from their washing still clinging to their leaves. To keep the damp leaves from turning your work surface into a watery mess, let them drain in an empty dish rack next to the sink.

- 2 pounds damp tender greens, such as spinach, beet greens, or Swiss chard, stemmed, washed in several changes of cold water, shaken to remove excess water, and chopped coarse
  Salt and ground black pepper

Heat the oil and butter in a Dutch oven or other deep pot over medium heat. When the foaming subsides, add the onion and sugar and cook, stirring often, until the onion is soft and golden, about 10 minutes. Add the garlic and anchovies and cook, mashing the anchovies to a paste with a wooden spoon, until fragrant, about 1 minute. Stir in the apricots, vinegar, and damp greens. Raise the heat to medium-high, cover, and cook, stirring occasionally, until the greens completely wilt, 2 to 3 minutes. Uncover and season with salt and pepper to taste. Raise the heat to high and cook until the liquid evaporates, 2 to 3 minutes. Serve immediately.

Blanched Assertive Greens

MAKES ABOUT 2 CUPS

Once the greens have been blanched and drained, they can be used in any of the recipes that follow.

- 1½ teaspoons salt
- 2 pounds assertive greens, such as kale or collard, mustard, or turnip greens, stemmed, washed in several changes of cold water, and chopped coarse

Bring 2 quarts water to a boil in a Dutch oven or large, deep sauté pan. Add the salt and greens and stir until wilted. Cover and cook until the greens are just tender, about 7 minutes. Drain into a colander. Rinse the Dutch oven or pan with cold water to cool, then refill with cold water. Pour the greens into the cold water to stop the cooking process. Gather a handful of greens, lift out of the water, and squeeze dry. Repeat with the remaining greens. Chop each bunch of greens further, if desired, and proceed with one of the following recipes.

➤ VARIATIONS

Assertive Greens with Bacon and Onion

SERVES 4

The strong flavors of bacon and sautéed onion make a good match with assertive greens.

2	ounces (about 2 slices) bacon, cut crosswise into thin strips
	Vegetable oil
1/2	medium onion, chopped fine
2	medium garlic cloves, minced or pressed through a garlic press (about 2 teaspoons)
1	recipe Blanched Assertive Greens
1/4	cup low-sodium chicken broth
2	teaspoons cider vinegar
	Salt

1. Fry the bacon in a large sauté pan over medium heat until crisp, about 5 minutes. Transfer the bacon to a plate lined with paper towels, leaving the drippings in the pan.

2. If necessary, add oil to the bacon drippings in the pan to make 2 tablespoons of fat. Add the onion and cook until softened, about 3 minutes. Add the garlic and cook until fragrant, about 30 seconds. Add the greens and stir to coat them with the fat. Add the broth, cover, and cook until the greens are heated through, about 2 minutes. If any excess liquid remains, remove the lid and continue to simmer until the liquid has thickened slightly, about 1 minute longer. Sprinkle the greens with the vinegar and reserved bacon and season with salt to taste. Serve immediately.

Assertive Greens with Shallots and Cream

SERVES 4

The sweetness of shallots and the richness of cream mellow the bitterness of the greens.

2	tablespoons unsalted butter
2	medium shallots, chopped fine
1	recipe Blanched Assertive Greens
1/4	cup heavy cream
1/2	teaspoon sugar
1/2	teaspoon minced fresh thyme leaves
1/8	teaspoon freshly grated nutmeg
	Salt and ground black pepper

Melt the butter in a large sauté pan over medium heat. When the foaming subsides, add the shallots and cook, stirring frequently, until golden brown, 3 to 4 minutes. Add the greens and stir to coat them with the fat. Stir in the cream, sugar, thyme, and nutmeg. Cover and cook until the greens are heated through, about 2 minutes. If any excess liquid remains, remove the lid and continue to simmer until the cream has thickened slightly,

DRAINING BLANCHED GREENS

Assertive greens should be blanched, drained, and then sautéed with seasonings. After blanching, it's important to squeeze out as much water as possible. Here's an unusual but quick way to accomplish this task.

1. Instead of squeezing the greens by hand, place them in the hopper of a potato ricer.

2. Close the handle and squeeze the water from the greens. Don't squeeze harder than is necessary or you could puree the greens.

about 1 minute longer. Season with salt and pepper to taste and serve immediately.

Assertive Greens with Honey Mustard Sauce

SERVES 4

Serve this dish with German sausages and boiled potatoes for a hearty dinner.

1½	tablespoons Dijon or whole-grain mustard
1	tablespoon honey
¼	cup low-sodium chicken broth
2	tablespoons unsalted butter
1	medium garlic clove, minced or pressed through a garlic press (about 1 teaspoon)
1	recipe Blanched Assertive Greens
	Salt and ground black pepper

1. Mix the mustard, honey, and broth together in a small bowl.

2. Heat the butter in a large sauté pan over medium heat. When the butter melts, add the garlic and cook until the garlic is fragrant and starts to sizzle, about 1 minute. Add the greens and stir to coat them with the fat. Stir in the mustard mixture. Cover and cook until the greens are heated through, about 2 minutes. If any excess liquid remains, remove the lid and continue to simmer until the liquid has thickened slightly, about 1 minute longer. Season with salt and pepper to taste and serve immediately.

OKRA

OKRA HAS A FRESH, SLIGHTLY SWEET FLAVOR, somewhat like a cross between zucchini and green beans. However, the most memorable characteristic of okra may be its texture. The interior of the okra pod contains a substance that becomes gelatinous when it is boiled or braised, which is how many Southern cooks prepare this vegetable.

We wanted to find a way to prepare okra that would make it appeal to all Americans, not just Southerners raised on this summer vegetable. Our okra could not be slimy. As we soon found out,

prolonged cooking exacerbates the problem. The longer okra simmers or stews, the more objectionable it becomes. In addition, moist heat (as supplied in boiling or braising) tends to accelerate the softening. We needed to cook okra with dry heat so that it would remain crisp-tender, like other green vegetables.

We had seen several recipes that called for sautéing. Our first test was a revelation. Sautéing whole pods over medium-high heat not only minimizes the slipperiness but also maintains the okra's fresh flavor and crisp texture. Even test cooks who claimed not to like okra were happily munching on whole pods that had been quickly sautéed in olive oil and flavored with garlic.

As we later discovered, snipping is the other key factor involved in preparing crisp rather than slimy okra. Small pods (no longer than 3 inches) will stay crisp when cooked this way, but larger pods tended to become slimy no matter how we cooked them. The keys to crowd-pleasing okra are simple: Buy small pods and sauté them quickly.

Sautéed Okra

SERVES 4 TO 6

Okra pods that are less than 3 inches in length will be the most tender and the least likely to become slimy when cooked.

2	tablespoons plus 1 teaspoon extra-virgin olive oil
1	pound small okra (no more than 3 inches long), stems removed
1	medium garlic clove, minced or pressed through a garlic press (about 1 teaspoon)
	Salt and ground black pepper

Heat 2 tablespoons of the oil in a large skillet over medium-high heat until shimmering. Add the okra and cook, stirring occasionally, until the okra is bright green, 3 to 4 minutes. Clear a space in the center of the pan and add the remaining 1 teaspoon oil and the garlic. Cook until fragrant, about 15 seconds. Stir the garlic mixture into the okra, season with salt and pepper to taste, and serve immediately.

➤ VARIATION

Sautéed Okra with Quick Tomato Sauce

Tomatoes and okra are a classic combination. This juicy side dish, served with rice or pasta, makes a perfect accompaniment to chicken or fish such as halibut or catfish.

3 tablespoons extra-virgin olive oil
1 pound small okra (no more than 3 inches long), stems removed
Salt and ground black pepper

INGREDIENTS: Canned Tomatoes

Canned whole tomatoes are the closest product to fresh. Whole tomatoes, either plum or round, are steamed to remove their skins and then packed in tomato juice or puree. We prefer tomatoes packed in juice; they generally have a fresher, livelier flavor than tomatoes packed in puree, which has a cooked tomato flavor that imparts a slightly stale, tired taste to the whole can.

Diced tomatoes are simply whole tomatoes that have been roughly chopped during processing and then packed with juice. For pasta sauces, we prefer diced tomatoes because they save time and effort. Why chop canned tomatoes (a messy proposition at best) if you don't have to?

To find the best canned whole tomatoes, we tasted eight brands, both straight from the can and in a simple tomato sauce. Muir Glen (an organic brand available in most supermarkets and natural foods stores) finished at the head of the pack, along with S&W, a West Coast brand, and Redpack (called Redgold on the West Coast).

THE BEST CANNED TOMATOES

The winners of our diced canned tomato tasting are packed in juice, not puree, and are recipe-ready.

MUIR GLEN	S&W	REDPACK
Organic Diced Tomatoes	Ready-Cut Premium, Peeled Tomatoes	Ready-Cut Diced Tomatoes (Redgold on the West Coast)

4 medium garlic cloves, minced or pressed through a garlic press (about 4 teaspoons)
½ teaspoon red pepper flakes
1 (14.5-ounce) can diced tomatoes
1 teaspoon sugar
1 tablespoon minced fresh basil leaves

1. Heat 2 tablespoons of the oil in a large skillet over medium-high heat until shimmering. Add the okra and cook, stirring occasionally, until the okra is bright green, 3 to 4 minutes. Season with salt and pepper to taste and transfer the okra to a bowl.

2. Add the remaining 1 tablespoon oil to the empty pan. Add the garlic and red pepper flakes and cook until fragrant, about 15 seconds. Stir in the tomatoes and sugar, bring to a simmer, and cook until slightly reduced, about 2 minutes. Stir in the okra and cook for 1 minute longer. Stir in the basil and adjust the seasonings, adding salt and pepper to taste. Serve immediately.

PEAS

THERE ARE THREE VARIETIES OF PEAS SOLD in most markets—shell peas, snow peas, and sugar snap peas. We find that fresh shell peas are generally mealy and bland. Frozen peas are usually sweeter and better tasting and are the better option. The key to cooking frozen peas is to ignore the instructions printed on the package. It's far better to sauté them (still frozen) in a large nonstick skillet along with some aromatics and a little sugar.

As for other pea varieties, the flat, light green snow pea has a long history, especially in the Chinese kitchen. The peas are immature and the pod is tender enough to eat. Sugar snap peas are a relatively recent invention that dates back just 20 years. They are a cross between shell peas and snow peas. The sweet, crisp pod is edible and holds small, juicy peas. Good sugar snaps look like compact fresh garden peas in the shell. They are firm and lustrous, with barely discernible bumps along the pods. Expect to find robust fresh peas from late spring through summer.

Sugar snap and snow peas should be cooked quickly so that they retain some crunch and color.

Stir-frying works well with snow peas, which have a fairly sturdy pod, but sugar snap peas are too delicate for such intense heat. The pods become mushy by the time the peas inside have heated through.

We found that microwaving did not cook the sugar snaps evenly. Opening the microwave and stirring helped, but we soon abandoned this method. Steaming yielded tender peas, but they tasted flat. We found that sugar snaps benefit greatly from the addition of some salt as they cook, something that

can be done only if the peas are blanched.

Although blanching yielded sugar snaps with excellent taste and texture, we found that the blanched peas tended to shrivel or pucker a bit as they cooled. We solved this problem by plunging the cooked peas into ice water as soon as they were drained. This also helped to set their bright color and prevent further softening from residual heat. Once blanched and shocked, the peas can be held for up to an hour before seasoning.

ADDING ZING TO STEAMED VEGETABLES

PLAIN STEAMED VEGETABLES CAN BE PRETTY HO-HUM EVEN WHEN SEASONED WITH butter, but stirring in a *compound* butter can elevate your vegetables to star status. Compound butter, which is traditionally served with steak or fish as an alternative to sauce, is easy to prepare and keeps well. Try stirring some into plain white rice or mashed potatoes for a flavor boost.

BASIC COMPOUND BUTTER

Soften 4 tablespoons (½ stick) unsalted butter, then stir in ½ teaspoon salt and flavorings to taste (see our list below for inspiration). The butter can then be rolled into a log. Compound butter can be kept refrigerated for several days or frozen for up to a month. To use, simply slice off the desired amount and continue to store the rest.

COMPOUND BUTTER FLAVORINGS

- Chopped roasted red bell peppers and smoked paprika
- Lemon juice, grated lemon zest, and minced fresh parsley leaves
- Chopped fresh rosemary and grated Parmesan cheese
- Crumbled Roquefort and ground black pepper
- Chopped chipotle chiles in adobo sauce, minced garlic, minced fresh cilantro leaves, and lime juice
- Minced shallot and chopped fresh thyme leaves
- Curry powder, minced shallot, and chopped fresh mint or cilantro leaves
- Minced sage leaves and finely chopped toasted walnuts
- Honey, fresh orange juice, and grated orange zest
- Roasted garlic and minced caramelized onions (page 58)
- Minced sun-dried tomatoes, pesto, or tapenade

ROLLING THE COMPOUND BUTTER

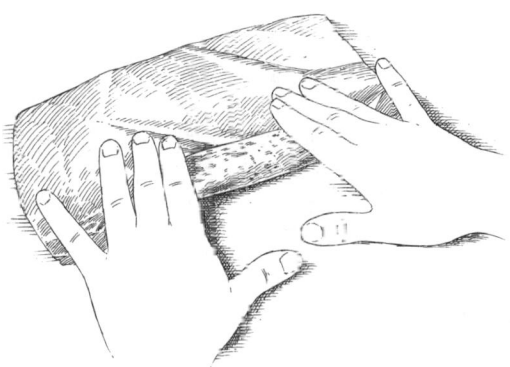

Once the ingredients have been combined, place the butter mixture in the center of a piece of plastic wrap. Fold one edge of the plastic wrap over the butter. Glide your hands back and forth over the butter to shape it into a cylinder. Twist the ends of the plastic wrap shut and refrigerate until firm.

PUTTING FROZEN PEAS TO WORK

WE ALWAYS KEEP A COUPLE OF BAGS of frozen peas in our freezer—and not just for serving as a hot side dish. Their sweet vegetal flavor and vibrant green color make them an ideal ingredient for a variety of dishes. Here are our favorites:

DILLY PEA SALAD

Toss 3 cups (one 16-ounce bag) thawed frozen peas with 1 small, minced red onion, 1 tablespoon chopped fresh dill, 1 tablespoon chopped fresh parsley leaves, 1 tablespoon lemon juice, and 2 tablespoons extra-virgin olive oil. Season to taste with salt and ground black pepper.

HOT-AND-TANGY PEA DIP

In a food processor, puree 2 cups thawed frozen peas, ½ cup mayonnaise, ½ cup sour cream, 3 scallions, 1 tablespoon fresh dill, ½ cup fresh parsley leaves, 1 medium garlic clove, ¼ teaspoon hot pepper sauce (such as Tabasco), ½ teaspoon salt, and ¼ teaspoon ground black pepper until smooth. Transfer to a 1-quart baking dish. Top with ½ cup grated Parmesan cheese and serve cold, or broil for 5 minutes until golden brown and heated through. Serve warm or cold with crackers or toast points.

LEMONY PEA SPREAD

Using a potato masher, mash 3 cups (one 16-ounce bag) thawed frozen peas, flesh from 1 cooked russet potato, 3 tablespoons fresh lemon juice, and ¼ cup extra-virgin olive oil until combined but still lumpy. Season with salt and pepper to taste and serve warm or at room temperature with crusty bread.

PEA PESTO

In a food processor, process 2 cups thawed frozen peas with 1 cup fresh basil leaves, ¼ cup toasted walnuts, ¼ cup grated Parmesan cheese, 2 medium garlic cloves, and ¼ cup extra-virgin olive oil until smooth. Serve as you would any other pesto: spread on crostini, tossed with hot pasta, or stirred into mashed potatoes or plain rice.

Buttered Peas with Thyme

SERVES 4 TO 6

Frozen peas may just be the perfect vegetable. Not only are they inexpensive, but they require no washing, stemming, or chopping, and they cook in a matter of minutes.

- 2 tablespoons unsalted butter
- 1 shallot, minced
- 1 medium garlic clove, minced or pressed through a garlic press (about 1 teaspoon)
- 2 teaspoons sugar
- 1 pound frozen peas (do not thaw)
- 1 teaspoon minced fresh thyme leaves
  Salt and ground black pepper

Melt the butter in a large nonstick skillet over medium-high heat. Add the shallot, garlic, and sugar; cook until softened, about 2 minutes. Stir in the peas; cook, stirring often, until just heated through, about 2 minutes. Off the heat, stir in the thyme and season with salt and pepper to taste.

➤ VARIATIONS

Peas with Feta and Mint

Follow the recipe for Buttered Peas with Thyme, substituting 1 tablespoon minced mint leaves for the thyme. Just before serving, crumble 3 ounces feta cheese (about ¾ cup) over the peas.

Peas with Bacon, Shallot, and Sherry Vinegar

Fry 6 ounces (about 6 slices) chopped bacon in a nonstick skillet until crisp, about 5 minutes. Using a slotted spoon, transfer the bacon to a paper towel–lined plate and pour off all but 2 tablespoons of the bacon fat. Follow the recipe for Buttered Peas with Thyme, substituting the bacon fat for the butter. Off the heat, add 2 teaspoons sherry vinegar and the crisp bacon to the pan along with the thyme.

Peas with Pearl Onions and Lemon

Follow the recipe for Buttered Peas with Thyme, omitting the shallot and garlic. After melting the butter, add 8 ounces frozen pearl onions and ½ cup water to the skillet. Cover the pan and cook, shaking occasionally, until the onions are tender, about 5 minutes. Uncover the pan and simmer until the water has evaporated and the onions have browned, about 5 minutes, then add the frozen peas. Off the heat, add 2 teaspoons lemon juice to the pan along with the thyme.

Peas with Tarragon Cream

Follow the recipe for Buttered Peas with Thyme, substituting 1 tablespoon minced fresh tarragon leaves for the thyme. Before adding the peas to the skillet, pour ½ cup heavy cream into the pan, bring to a simmer, and cook until almost clotted and the mixture measures ⅓ cup. Add the frozen peas and cook until they have heated through and the cream has loosened to form a sauce.

Blanched Sugar Snap Peas
SERVES 4

Have a bowl of ice water ready to shock the drained peas and prevent further softening and shriveling. Snow peas can be used in any of the following recipes, although they are probably best stir-fried (see page 226). To string sugar snap peas, see the illustration on page 226 for stringing snow peas, as the method is identical.

>   Salt
> 1 pound sugar snap peas, stems snapped off and strings removed, if necessary (about 4 cups)
> 1 tablespoon unsalted butter
>   Ground black pepper

1. Bring 6 cups water to a boil in a large saucepan. Add 1 teaspoon salt and the peas and cook until crisp-tender, 1½ to 2 minutes. Drain the peas, shock them in ice water, and drain again. Dry the peas well on a baking sheet lined with paper towels.

2. Melt the butter in a large skillet over medium-high heat. When the foaming subsides, add the peas and cook, stirring frequently, until the peas are heated through, 1 to 2 minutes. Season to taste with salt and pepper and serve immediately.

➤ VARIATIONS

Sugar Snap Peas with Pine Nuts and Garlic

Pine nuts burn very easily. Keep a sharp eye on them in the pan and adjust the heat as necessary.

>   Salt
> 1 pound sugar snap peas (about 4 cups), stems snapped off and strings removed if necessary
> 1 tablespoon extra-virgin olive oil
> ¼ cup pine nuts, chopped coarse
> 1 medium garlic clove, minced or pressed through a garlic press (about 1 teaspoon)
>   Ground black pepper

1. Bring 6 cups water to a boil in a large saucepan. Add 1 teaspoon salt and the peas and cook until crisp-tender, 1½ to 2 minutes. Drain the peas, shock them in ice water, and drain again. Dry the peas well on a baking sheet lined with paper towels.

2. Heat the oil in a large skillet over medium heat until shimmering. Add the pine nuts and cook, stirring frequently, until they are light golden brown, 1 to 2 minutes. Stir in the garlic and cook until fragrant, about 30 seconds. Add the peas and cook, stirring frequently, until the peas are heated through, 1 to 2 minutes. Season to taste with salt and pepper and serve immediately.

Sugar Snap Peas with Sesame Seeds

Sesame oil has a low smoke point and should not be used in high-heat cooking. It is usually used at the end of cooking or as a condiment. There are two different kinds of sesame oil: toasted and plain. Toasted (or Asian) sesame oil is golden in color and has a distinct, nutty aroma. See page 166 for more information about sesame oil.

>   Salt
> 1 pound sugar snap peas (about 4 cups), stems snapped off and strings removed if necessary
> 2 teaspoons vegetable oil
> 2 tablespoons sesame seeds
> 1 teaspoon toasted sesame oil
>   Ground black pepper

1. Bring 6 cups water to a boil in a large sauce-pan. Add 1 teaspoon salt and the peas and cook until crisp-tender, 1½ to 2 minutes. Drain the peas, shock them in ice water, and drain again. Dry the peas well on a baking sheet lined with paper towels.

2. Heat the vegetable oil in a large skillet over medium heat until shimmering. Add the sesame seeds and cook, shaking the pan occasionally, until the seeds are light golden brown and begin to pop, 1 to 2 minutes. Add the sesame oil and peas and cook, stirring frequently, until the peas are heated through, 1 to 2 minutes. Season to taste with salt and pepper and serve immediately.

Sugar Snap Peas with Asian Dressing

To mingle the flavors, you can let the peas and dressing sit for up to 10 minutes—any longer and the peas start to lose their bright green color.

2	tablespoons orange juice
2	tablespoons rice vinegar
1	teaspoon honey
½	teaspoon soy sauce
1	medium scallion, sliced thin
½	teaspoon grated fresh ginger
2	tablespoons peanut oil
1	teaspoon toasted sesame oil
	Salt and ground black pepper
2	teaspoons sesame seeds, toasted in a small dry skillet over medium heat until fragrant, about 4 minutes
1	pound sugar snap peas (about 4 cups), stems snapped off and strings removed if necessary

1. Combine the orange juice, vinegar, honey, soy sauce, scallion, and ginger in a small bowl. Whisk in the oils. Season to taste with salt and pepper. Stir in the sesame seeds. (The dressing can be set aside for several hours.)

2. Bring 6 cups water to a boil in a large sauce-pan. Add 1 teaspoon salt and the peas and cook until crisp-tender, 1½ to 2 minutes. Drain the peas, shock them in ice water, and drain again. Dry the peas well on a baking sheet lined with paper towels.

3. Toss the peas with the dressing, adjust the seasonings with salt and pepper to taste, and serve.

Stir-Fried Snow Peas

SERVES 4

Snow peas are sturdier than sugar snap peas and hold up well when stir-fried.

¼	cup low-sodium chicken broth
¼	teaspoon salt
	Ground black pepper
1	tablespoon plus 1 teaspoon peanut oil
1	pound snow peas (about 4 cups), tips pulled off and strings removed (see the illustration below)
2	medium garlic cloves, minced or pressed through a garlic press (about 2 teaspoons)
½	teaspoon minced fresh ginger

1. Mix the chicken broth, salt, and pepper to taste together in a small bowl.

2. Heat 1 tablespoon of the oil in a large non-stick skillet over high heat until shimmering. Add the snow peas and cook, stirring frequently, until bright green, about 2 minutes. Clear the center of the pan and add the remaining 1 teaspoon oil and the garlic and ginger. Mash the garlic and ginger with the back of a spatula. Cook for 10 seconds, then mix with the snow peas. Off the heat, add the chicken broth mixture (it should immediately reduce down to a glaze). Serve immediately.

STRINGING SNOW PEAS

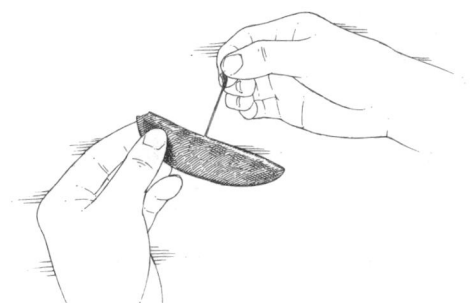

Snap off the tip of the snow pea and at the same time pull down along the flat side of the pod to remove the string.

SAUTÉED CHERRY TOMATOES

MOST COOKS DON'T THINK ABOUT COOKING cherry tomatoes, using them only for salads; when it comes to heating tomatoes, they turn to plum or round beefsteak varieties. But cherry tomatoes can be sautéed in minutes to make a quick side dish. In addition, they generally taste pretty good, even in the dead of winter, which makes them even more appealing.

We wanted to explore the ins and outs of this simple technique. We knew it was important to cook the tomatoes as quickly as possible so they wouldn't fall apart. We found a large skillet (which allows the tomatoes to cook in a single layer) and medium-high heat to be essential.

We also discovered that some batches of cherry tomatoes were bitter. We liked the results when we sprinkled a little sugar over the tomatoes before they went into the pan. The sugar helped with caramelization and balanced the acidity in the tomatoes. Olive oil was tasters' favorite choice for fat, but butter was a close second. Sautéed cherry tomatoes can be seasoned in numerous ways; fresh herbs, however, are a must.

Sautéed Cherry Tomatoes

SERVES 4

If the cherry tomatoes are especially sweet, you may want to reduce or omit the sugar. Serve this juicy side dish with fish, chicken, or beef.

1	tablespoon extra-virgin olive oil
4	cups (2 pints) cherry tomatoes, halved unless very small
2	teaspoons sugar
1	medium garlic clove, minced or pressed through a garlic press (about 1 teaspoon)
2	tablespoons thinly sliced fresh basil leaves
	Salt and ground black pepper

Heat the oil in a large skillet over medium-high heat until shimmering. Mix the tomatoes and sugar in a medium bowl and add them to the hot oil. (Do not mix the tomatoes ahead of time or you will draw out their juices.) Cook for 1 minute, stirring frequently. Stir in the garlic and cook for another 30 seconds. Remove the pan from the heat, add the basil, and season with salt and pepper to taste. Serve immediately.

MINCING ANCHOVIES

Anchovies often stick to the side of a chef's knife, making it hard to cut them into small bits. Here are two better ways to mince them.

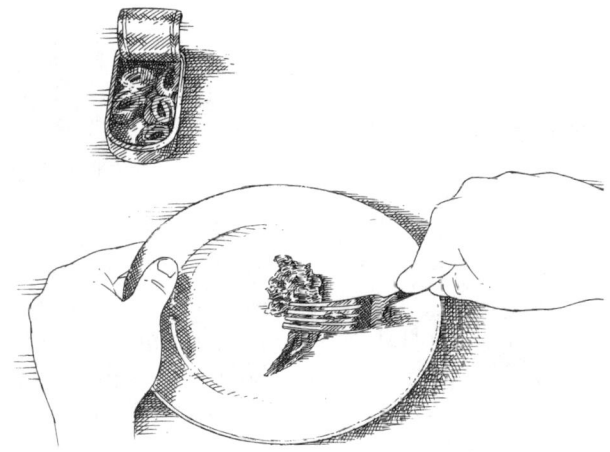

A. Use a dinner fork to mash delicate anchovy fillets into a paste. Mash the fillets on a small plate to catch any oil the anchovies give off.

B. A garlic press will turn anchovies into a fine puree. This method is especially handy when you have already dirtied the press with garlic.

➤ VARIATION
Sautéed Cherry Tomatoes with Capers and Anchovy

These tomatoes work well with any Mediterranean dish and are especially good with mild, white fish, including swordfish and red snapper.

1	tablespoon extra-virgin olive oil
2	medium anchovy fillets, minced
4	cups (2 pints) cherry tomatoes, halved unless very small
2	teaspoons sugar
2	tablespoons capers
2	medium garlic cloves, minced or pressed through a garlic press (about 2 teaspoons)
2	tablespoons minced fresh parsley leaves
	Salt and ground black pepper

Heat the oil and anchovies in a large skillet over medium-high heat until the anchovies begin to sizzle. Mix the tomatoes and sugar in a medium bowl and add them to the hot oil along with the capers. (Do not mix the tomatoes ahead of time or you will draw out their juices.) Cook for 1 minute, stirring frequently. Stir in the garlic and cook for another 30 seconds. Remove the pan from the heat, add the parsley, and season with salt and pepper to taste. Serve immediately.

SLOW-ROASTED TOMATO GRATIN

ROASTING FLAWLESS, VINE-RIPENED TOMA-toes with garlic and olive oil takes them to a new level of perfection; the tomatoes' juices are concentrated by the steady heat and become one with the garlic and herb-scented olive oil. As a relish for grilled or roasted meats or a topping for toasted bread, this dish is hard to beat. It is the distillation of summer in one easy-to-assemble and foolproof dish.

There are only five ingredients in this dish and, for the best results, each must be flawless. In other words, this is not a place to use pale, cardboardlike supermarket tomatoes and cheap oil, as roasting merely magnifies their flaws. The tomatoes must be the best you can find, preferably from your local farmers market—or your garden, if you are so lucky. In the heart of a New England winter, we used "vine-ripened" tomatoes from our gourmet market with some success, but we longed for the beauties of August, still warm from the sun's touch.

The oil should be good quality, extra-virgin olive oil. We tried batches with varying oils and the differences were profound: The best-quality oil was in a league of its own, heady, with a herbaceous, peppery aroma and a taste that elevated the tomatoes beyond what they could attain on their own. (For recommendations about brands of olive oil, see page 103.)

For flavoring the tomatoes, garlic and basil were the only choices, according to our tasters. Oregano, mint, thyme, and rosemary all seemed inappropriate. Slivered garlic fared better than minced, and it looked much more attractive, too. The fine slivers practically melted during the slow bake, reduced to sweet and slightly chewy tidbits.

As this is a rustic dish, hand-torn basil leaves were the logical choice. Because they shrivel to mere shadows of themselves in the oven, we tore the large leaves into pieces and left small leaves whole. Layering the leaves both on top of and underneath the tomatoes guaranteed potent flavor.

For seasoning, a coarse salt, such as kosher or sea salt, was the unanimous choice of tasters for its crunchy texture and intense bursts of salinity. Regular table salt will do in a pinch, of course.

Preparation takes mere moments, but the roasting takes some time. These are neither oven-dried tomatoes—which can take upward of eight hours in a tepid oven—nor classic oven-roasted tomatoes—heat-shriveled to a near candylike sweetness and intensity. Aiming for something in between, we set the baking temperature parameters between 300 and 400 degrees and began testing.

In a 400-degree oven, the garlic browned too quickly and turned acrid, ruining the dish. Erring on the side of caution, we lowered the temperature to 325 degrees and were pleased with the results. Within 1½ hours, the tomatoes were slightly wrinkled and touched with brown; more important, their juices had largely evaporated and been replaced by the olive oil. A lower temperature yielded no better-tasting results and took longer, so we stuck with 325 degrees.

Slow-Roasted Tomato Gratin

SERVES 4 TO 6

For flavor and color contrast, feel free to mix and match varieties of tomatoes. Use whatever tomatoes you can find, as long as they are flawlessly ripe. If you are left with a pool of olive oil in the pan, save it for flavoring a vinaigrette or brushing on bruschetta. Serve these tomatoes with roast chicken or fish. This dish tastes best prepared and served on the same day. It can be served slightly warm or at room temperature.

½	cup extra-virgin olive oil
4	medium garlic cloves, sliced thin
1	cup lightly packed fresh basil leaves, large leaves torn into pieces
2	pounds vine-ripened tomatoes, cored, seeded, and sliced ½ inch thick
1	teaspoon kosher salt

1. Adjust an oven rack to the lower-middle position and heat the oven to 325 degrees. Grease the bottom of a 13 by 9-inch nonreactive glass or ceramic baking dish (or shallow casserole dish of similar size) with 2 tablespoons of the oil. Sprinkle half of the garlic and half of the basil leaves across the bottom of the dish. Lay the tomato slices in the dish, overlapping the edges, if necessary, to fit. Sprinkle with the salt and the remaining garlic, basil, and oil.

2. Roast until the tomatoes are slightly shriveled and their juices have been replaced with oil, about 1½ hours. Cool at least 20 minutes or up to 1 hour before serving. Serve warm or at room temperature.

STUFFED TOMATOES

OUR PAST EXPERIENCES WITH OVEN-BAKED stuffed tomatoes have not exactly been great. Still, when we are presented with one, the thought of its potential juicy tenderness and warmth is too

tempting to pass up. We succumb to the hope that maybe this time the stuffed tomato will live up to its potential, only to be let down by the first bite into sodden mediocrity.

What irks us is that the stuffed tomato's singular components hold forth the promise of perfection. What could be better than a ripe, sun-drenched summer tomato, garden-fresh herbs, garlicky bread crumbs, and a sprightly bite of sharp cheese? When these elements are brought together into one vessel, however, their divinity dissipates. The once buxom tomato becomes mealy and bland, and the flavor of the stuffing is drowned within the waterlogged texture of the bread. Determined to save this traditional dish from the bland and watery depths, we set out to prove that an oven-baked stuffed tomato can taste as good as we've always imagined.

We began testing by following the directions called for in most cookbook recipes: stuff some hollowed-out, raw beefsteak tomatoes with a bread-crumb filling and bake at 375 degrees for 30 minutes. The outcome was a soggy mess. The tomatoes were bland and watery, and the stuffing tasted dull and overly moist. What's more, the tomatoes seemed to lack the structural strength to keep the filling intact. The problem, no doubt, was the water in the tomatoes.

Ridding the tomatoes of excess liquid was our goal. At first we tested oven drying, rationalizing that the slow, low heat would concentrate the tomatoes' sweetness and vaporize the water. The dried tomatoes were laden with rich flavor notes, but they were also shriveled and shrunken, collapsed vessels that were in no condition to hold any stuffing.

We then thought that if we chose a tomato with a naturally lower water content, such as a plum tomato, we might eliminate the water issue altogether. While we did end up with meaty and sweet stuffed tomatoes, they lacked the complexity of flavor that the beefsteaks possessed, and the effort required to stuff the smaller shells—coupled with the fact that we would have to make twice as many if we were substituting for beefsteaks—turned us off the plum variety.

Recalling how salt is used to sweat eggplant,

we thought it might do the same for the tomatoes. We cored and seeded a beefsteak, rubbed salt into its interior, and placed it upside down on a stack of paper towels. Within 30 minutes, our dry paper towels had absorbed a tremendous amount of liquid. In addition, the salt brightened and enhanced the tomato's flavor.

Now that we had solved the moisture problem, we moved on to stuffing, baking times, and temperatures. For the stuffing, we tested store-bought bread crumbs, homemade bread crumbs made from stale French bread, and variations in the ratio of crumbs to cheese to herbs. The fine, store-bought

crumbs were dry and gritty. Their homemade counterpart, on the other hand, absorbed the tomato's juices yet still provided an interesting chew and crunch, especially when paired with garlic, olive oil, and tangy Parmesan cheese.

Our previous oven-roasting experiment negated a low temperature and long baking period, whereas experiments baking the tomatoes at an extremely high temperature (450 degrees) for a short time yielded burnt, crusty stuffing and raw tomatoes. Baked at 375 degrees for 20 minutes, the tomatoes were tender and topped with a lovely golden crust. The result: a sweet-and-savory tomato triumph.

EQUIPMENT: Cheese Graters

In the old days, you grated cheese on the fine teeth of a box grater. Now cheese graters come in several distinct designs. Unfortunately, many of them don't work all that well. With some designs, you need Herculean strength to move the cheese over the teeth with sufficient pressure for grating; with others, you eventually discover that a large portion of the grated cheese has remained jammed in the grater instead of going where it belongs, on your food. Whether you are dusting a plate of pasta or grating a full cup of cheese to use in a recipe, a good grater should be efficient and easy to use.

We rounded up 15 models and set about determining which was the best grater. We found five basic configurations. Four-sided box graters have different-size holes on each side to allow for both fine grating and coarse shredding. Flat graters consist of a flat sheet of metal that is punched through with fine teeth and attached to some type of handle. With rotary graters, you put a small chunk of cheese in a hopper and use a handle to press it down against a crank-operated grating wheel. Porcelain dish graters have raised teeth in the center and a well around the outside edge to collect the grated cheese. We also found a model that uses an electric motor to push and rotate small chunks of cheese against a grating disk.

After grating more than 10 pounds of Parmesan, we concluded that success was due to a combination of sharp grating teeth, a comfortable handle or grip, and good leverage for pressing the cheese onto the grater. Our favorite model was a flat grater based on a small, maneuverable woodworking tool called a rasp. Shaped like a ruler, but with lots and lots of tiny, sharp raised teeth, the Microplane Grater (as it is called) can grate large quantities of cheese smoothly and almost effortlessly.

The black plastic handle, which we found more comfortable than any of the others, also earned high praise. Other flat graters also scored well.

What about traditional box graters? Box graters can deliver good results and can do more than just grate hard cheese. However, if grating hard cheese is the task at hand, a box grater is not our first choice.

We also had good results with rotary graters made from metal, but we did not like flimsy versions made from plastic. A metal arm is rigid enough to do some of the work of pushing the cheese down onto the grating drum. The arms on the plastic models we tested flexed too much against the cheese, thus requiring extra pressure to force the cheese down. Hand strain set in quickly. A rotary grater can also chop nuts finely and grate chocolate.

The two porcelain dish graters we tested were duds; the teeth were quite ineffective. And the electric grater was a loser of monumental proportions. True, the grating effort required was next to nothing, but so were the results. A child could have grated cheese faster and more efficiently.

THE BEST GRATER

The Microplane Grater has very sharp teeth and a solid handle, which together make grating cheese a breeze. This grater also makes quick work of ginger and citrus zest.

Stuffed Tomatoes

SERVES 6

To make homemade bread crumbs, grind any chunk of stale country, Italian, or French bread in the food processor. Use your fingers to gently pull the seeds from the cored tomatoes.

6	large (about 8 ounces each) firm, ripe tomatoes, 1/8 inch sliced off stem end, cored, and seeded
1	teaspoon kosher salt
3/4	cup coarse homemade bread crumbs
3	tablespoons plus 1 teaspoon olive oil
1/3	cup grated Parmesan cheese
1/3	cup chopped fresh basil leaves
2	medium garlic cloves, minced or pressed through a garlic press (about 2 teaspoons) Ground black pepper

1. Sprinkle the inside of each tomato with the salt and place it upside down on several layers of paper towels. Let stand to remove any excess moisture, about 30 minutes.

2. Meanwhile, toss the bread crumbs with 1 tablespoon of the olive oil, the Parmesan, basil, garlic, and pepper to taste in a small bowl; set aside. Adjust an oven rack to the upper-middle position and heat the oven to 375 degrees. Line the bottom of a 13 by 9-inch baking dish with foil.

3. Roll up several sheets of paper towels and pat the inside of each tomato dry. Arrange the tomatoes in a single layer in the baking dish. Brush the cut edges of the tomatoes with 1 teaspoon oil. Mound the stuffing into the tomatoes (about 1/4 cup per tomato) and drizzle with the remaining 2 tablespoons oil. Bake until the tops are golden brown and crisp, about 20 minutes. Serve immediately.

VARIATION

Stuffed Tomatoes with Pecorino Romano, Oregano, and Olives

Pecorino Romano is a hard grating cheese made from sheep's milk. Its pungent flavors complement the briny olives. If you like, substitute finely crumbled feta for the Pecorino.

Follow the recipe for Stuffed Tomatoes, replacing the Parmesan and basil with 1/3 cup grated Pecorino Romano cheese, 2 tablespoons chopped fresh oregano leaves, and 12 briny black olives (such as kalamatas), pitted and chopped.

WINTER SQUASH

THERE ARE MANY WAYS TO COOK WINTER squash, but the ideal method for one kind may not necessarily be the best for another. We quickly discovered this when we set out to find the optimum way to cook the two most common winter squash, acorn and butternut. After only a few tests, we found that they responded very differently. We figured that we should develop several basic cooking methods, then recommend the kinds of squash for each method.

One thing that all winter squash have in common is that, counter to the current fashion for al dente vegetables, they must be cooked until well-done to develop the sweetest flavor and smoothest texture. With this as the only given, we tried cooking various kinds of squash by baking, roasting, steaming, boiling, and even microwaving.

After some experimentation, we found that baking the unpeeled and seeded halves cut-side down produced a slightly better texture than baking them cut-side up. We found it best to cook the squash on a foil-lined baking sheet that had been oiled. The oil promoted browning and reduced the risk of sticking, and the foil made cleanup easy.

Although this method was a success, when we began thinking about serving the squash, we realized that a baked squash half was fine if you could find relatively small squash, but what about those times when the market has only 3-pound butternut squashes? Roasting chunks of peeled squash proved to be a much more successful way to cook such big squash.

We peeled the squash and cut it into 1-inch cubes, then roasted it uncovered at varying oven temperatures. The squash became quite caramelized, with a good chewy texture and a much sweeter and more pronounced flavor. The ideal temperature turned out to be 425 degrees (a bit higher than the 400 degrees at which we like to roast squash halves). At lower temperatures, the squash was no better and took much longer to cook, and at higher temperatures it burned on the outside before it was fully cooked inside. A few sources suggested parboiling the cubed squash in lightly salted water for five to six minutes, until it was about half-cooked, then roasting it. Squash cooked this way was bland, so we discarded this idea.

Because sautéing also caramelizes, we decided to try sautéing diced squash in butter and oil until it became lightly caramelized and tender. This process took about 20 minutes and produced very satisfactory squash, but the flavor was not as deep as that of the roasted squash, and roasting also had the advantage of requiring less attention during cooking. By adding some liquid and seasonings to the

CUTTING BUTTERNUT SQUASH

With its thick skin and odd shape, butternut squash is notoriously difficult to cut, even with the best chef's knife. We prefer to use a cleaver and mallet.

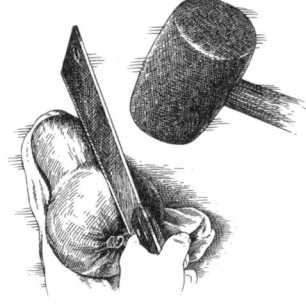

1. Set the squash on a damp kitchen towel to hold it in place. Position the cleaver on the skin of the squash.

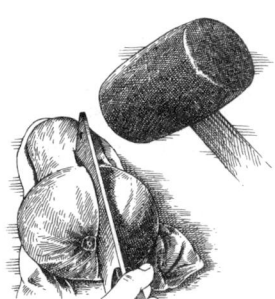

2. Strike the back of the cleaver with a mallet to drive the cleaver deep into the squash. Continue to hit the cleaver with the mallet until the cleaver cuts completely through the squash.

pan, an easy way to add flavor, we turned the sauté into a braise. Braising became our third method for handling squash, along with roasting halves and roasting smaller peeled chunks of squash.

During our research we had come across a recipe on the internet that suggested microwaving winter squash. We have always been somewhat skeptical of the microwave oven because of its finicky nature and its poor powers of flavor enhancement; the only vegetable we have had any real success cooking in the microwave is the potato—and even then we use it just to partially cook the potatoes (see Faster Baked Potatoes on page 273). Nonetheless, we set aside our reservations and proceeded to try the microwave, choosing halved acorn because of its smaller size. Surprisingly, we were pleased with the results. The squash was tender and silky smooth, with nary a trace of dryness or stringiness. The only problem was that the top of the squash hadn't browned and the traditional glaze didn't caramelize, as it does with traditional roasting. We found a quick fix by running the squash, post-microwave, under the broiler for just a few minutes, giving us the flavor of baked acorn squash in a fraction of the time it would take to actually bake it.

Roasted Winter Squash Halves
SERVES 4

This recipe can be made with acorn, buttercup (kabocha), butternut, or delicata squash. The cooking time will vary depending on the kind of squash you use. Start checking for doneness after the first 30 minutes.

2   tablespoons extra-virgin olive oil
1   medium or 2 small winter squash
    (about 2 pounds total), halved lengthwise
    and seeded (see the illustrations at left and on
    the facing page)
    Salt and ground black pepper

1. Adjust an oven rack to the lower-middle position and heat the oven to 400 degrees. Line a rimmed baking sheet with aluminum foil. Brush the oil on the foil and the cut sides of the squash. Place the squash cut-side down on the foil. Roast

until a skewer inserted in the squash meets no resistance, 40 to 50 minutes.

2. Remove the squash from the oven and turn it cut-side up. If necessary, cut large pieces in half. Season the squash with salt and pepper to taste and serve immediately.

➤ VARIATIONS

Roasted Winter Squash Halves with Browned Butter and Sage

The warm flavors of sage and winter squash complement each other beautifully. Serve with roast turkey or chicken.

2   tablespoons extra-virgin olive oil
1   medium or 2 small winter squash (about 2 pounds total), halved lengthwise and seeded (see the illustrations below and on the facing page)
6   tablespoons (¾ stick) unsalted butter
6   medium fresh sage leaves, sliced thin
     Salt and ground black pepper

1. Adjust an oven rack to the lower-middle position and heat the oven to 400 degrees. Line a rimmed baking sheet with aluminum foil. Brush the oil on the foil and the cut sides of the squash. Place the squash cut-side down on the foil. Roast until a skewer inserted in the squash meets no resistance, 40 to 50 minutes.

2. When the squash is almost done, melt the butter in a small skillet over medium heat. Add the sage and cook, swirling the pan occasionally, until the butter is golden brown and the sage is crisp, 4 to 5 minutes. Remove the skillet from the heat.

3. Remove the squash from the oven and turn it cut-side up. If necessary, cut large pieces in half. Season the squash with salt and pepper to taste, drizzle with the sage butter, and serve immediately.

Roasted Winter Squash Halves with Soy and Maple Flavors

While soy sauce and squash might seem to make an unlikely pair, the salty flavor of the soy sauce and the sweetness of the squash enhance each other. This recipe works especially well with buttercup (kabocha) or acorn squash. Given the strong flavors of soy and maple, we find it best to brush the squash with vegetable oil, rather than olive oil, before roasting.

2   tablespoons vegetable oil
1   medium or 2 small winter squash (about 2 pounds total), halved lengthwise and seeded (see the illustrations below and on the facing page)
3   tablespoons maple syrup
2   tablespoons soy sauce
½   teaspoon minced fresh ginger
     Salt and ground black pepper

1. Adjust an oven rack to the lower-middle position and heat the oven to 400 degrees. Line a rimmed baking sheet with aluminum foil. Brush the oil on the foil and the cut sides of the squash. Place the squash cut-side down on the foil. Roast until a skewer inserted in the squash meets no resistance, 40 to 50 minutes. Do not turn off the oven.

2. While the squash is in the oven, mix the maple syrup, soy sauce, and ginger together in a small bowl.

3. Remove the squash from the oven and turn it cut-side up. Brush the cut sides of the squash with the maple-soy mixture and return the squash to the oven. Roast until the cut sides of the squash begin to caramelize, about 5 minutes. Remove the squash from the oven. If necessary, cut large pieces in half. Season the squash with salt and pepper to taste and serve immediately.

REMOVING SQUASH SEEDS

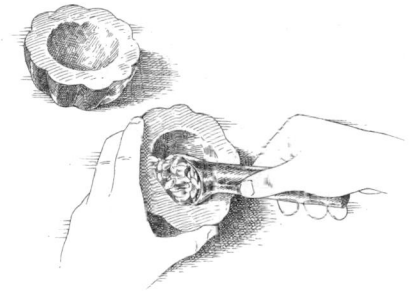

Use an ice cream scoop with a curved bowl to remove all the seeds and strings without damaging the flesh. Because the edge on this kind of scoop is very sharp, it cuts easily, and because the scoop is larger than a spoon, it can remove more seeds in a single swipe.

Roasted Winter Squash

SERVES 4

Peeled and cut squash pieces (usually butternut) are available in the produce section of most grocery stores. It is preferable to peel and cut your own, but if you are short on time, the bagged variety is an acceptable substitute. One whole 2-pound squash yields about 1½ pounds of trimmed pieces. This recipe is best with butternut or buttercup (kabocha) squash. If peeling the squash yourself, use a heavy-duty vegetable peeler that will remove a thick layer of the skin and tough greenish flesh right below the skin. With most squash, it's easiest to cut the squash in half, remove the seeds, and then start peeling.

2   **pounds winter squash, peeled, seeded (see the illustration on page 233), and cut into 1-inch cubes**
1   **medium shallot, minced**
2   **tablespoons extra-virgin olive oil**
2   **teaspoons minced fresh thyme leaves**
    Salt and ground black pepper

Adjust an oven rack to the lower-middle position and heat the oven to 425 degrees. Toss the squash, shallot, oil, thyme, and salt and pepper to taste in a large bowl. Spread the squash pieces on a rimmed baking sheet large enough to hold them without crowding. Roast, shaking the pan every 10 minutes, until the squash is tender and evenly browned, 25 to 35 minutes. Adjust the seasonings, adding salt and pepper to taste. Serve immediately.

➤ VARIATION

Roasted Winter Squash with Parsley, Sage, Rosemary, and Thyme

This isn't just a great song, it's also a delicious combination of herbs. To preserve the parsley's fresh flavor, add it at the end of the recipe. Serve with roast chicken or turkey.

2   **pounds winter squash, peeled, seeded (see the illustration on page 233), and cut into 1-inch cubes**
2   **tablespoons extra-virgin olive oil**
1   **teaspoon minced fresh thyme leaves**
1   **teaspoon minced fresh sage leaves**
½   **teaspoon minced fresh rosemary**
    Salt and ground black pepper
1   **tablespoon minced fresh parsley leaves**

Adjust an oven rack to the lower-middle position and heat the oven to 425 degrees. Toss the squash, oil, thyme, sage, rosemary, and salt and pepper to taste together in a large bowl. Spread the squash pieces on a rimmed baking sheet large enough to hold them without crowding. Roast, shaking the pan every 10 minutes, until the squash is tender and evenly browned, 25 to 35 minutes. Stir in the parsley and adjust the seasonings, adding salt and pepper to taste. Serve immediately.

Faster Acorn Squash with Brown Sugar

SERVES 4

This half-and-half method relies on the microwave oven and broiler and was developed using acorn squash. Squash smaller than 1½ pounds will likely cook a little faster than the recipe indicates, so begin checking for doneness a few minutes early. Likewise, larger squash will take slightly longer to cook. However, keep in mind that the cooking time is largely dependent on the microwave. If microwaving the squash in Pyrex, the manufacturer recommends adding water to the dish (or bowl) prior to cooking. To avoid a steam burn when uncovering the cooked squash, peel back the plastic wrap very carefully, starting from the side that is farthest away from you.

2   **acorn squash (about 1½ pounds each), halved pole to pole and seeded (see the illustrations on pages 235 and 233)**
    Salt
3   **tablespoons unsalted butter**
3   **tablespoons dark brown sugar**

1. Sprinkle the squash halves with salt and place the halves cut-side down in a 13 by 9-inch microwave-safe baking dish or arrange the halves in a large (about 4-quart) microwave-safe bowl so that the cut sides face out. If using Pyrex, add ¼ cup water to the dish or bowl. Cover tightly with plastic wrap, using multiple sheets, if necessary;

with a paring knife, poke about 4 steam vents in the wrap. Microwave on high power until the squash is very tender and offers no resistance when pierced with a paring knife, 15 to 25 minutes. Using potholders, remove the baking dish or bowl from the oven and set on a clean, dry surface (avoid damp or cold surfaces).

2. While the squash is cooking, adjust an oven rack to the uppermost position (about 6 inches from the heating element); heat the broiler. On the stovetop, melt the butter, brown sugar, and ⅛ teaspoon salt in a small saucepan over low heat, whisking occasionally, until combined.

3. When the squash is cooked, carefully pull back the plastic wrap from the side farthest from

you. Using tongs, transfer the cooked squash cut-side up to a rimmed baking sheet. Spoon a portion of the butter-sugar mixture onto each squash half. Broil until brown and caramelized, 5 to 8 minutes, rotating the baking sheet as necessary and removing the squash halves as they are done. Set the squash halves on individual plates and serve immediately.

➤ VARIATION

Faster Acorn Squash with Rosemary–Dried Fig Compote

1. Follow the recipe for Faster Acorn Squash with Brown Sugar, omitting the brown sugar–butter mixture. While the squash is cooking, combine 1 cup orange juice; 4 dried black figs, chopped medium (scant ½ cup); ½ teaspoon minced fresh rosemary; 1 tablespoon dark brown sugar; ¼ teaspoon ground black pepper; and ⅛ teaspoon salt in a small saucepan. Simmer rapidly over medium-high heat, stirring occasionally, until syrupy and the liquid is reduced to about 3 tablespoons, 15 to 20 minutes. Stir in 1 tablespoon butter.

2. Continue with the recipe to fill and broil the squash halves, substituting the fig compote for the brown sugar–butter mixture.

TWO WAYS TO CUT ACORN SQUASH SAFELY

KNIFE AND RUBBER MALLET

1. Set the squash on a damp kitchen towel to hold it in place. Position the knife on the rind.

2. Strike the back of the knife with a rubber mallet to drive it into squash. Continue to hit the knife with the mallet until the knife cuts through the squash.

METAL BENCH SCRAPER AND HAMMER

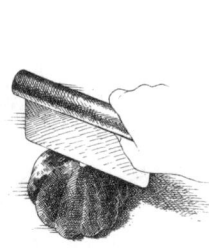 

1. Set the squash on a damp kitchen towel. Position the bench scraper on the rind.

2. Strike the handle of the bench scraper with a hammer to drive the blade into the squash. Continue to hit the bench scraper with the hammer until the blade cuts through the squash.

Braised Winter Squash
SERVES 4

This simple recipe is a great way to cook squash quickly. Braise the squash until it just begins to fall apart and absorb the juicy braising liquid. The recipe is best with butternut, buttercup (kabocha), or delicata squash. Cooking times may differ depending on the type of squash you are using.

- 2 tablespoons unsalted butter
- 1 medium shallot, minced
- 2 pounds winter squash, peeled, seeded (see the illustration on page 233), and cut into 1-inch cubes
- ½ cup low-sodium chicken broth
- 1 teaspoon minced fresh thyme leaves
  Salt and ground black pepper

Heat the butter in a Dutch oven or large saucepan over medium-high heat. When the foaming subsides, add the shallot and cook, stirring occasionally, until golden, about 4 minutes. Add the squash, broth, thyme, and salt and pepper to taste. Stir, cover, reduce the heat to medium, and cook until the squash is very tender, 15 to 20 minutes. Adjust the seasonings, adding salt and pepper to taste. Serve immediately.

EQUIPMENT: Microwave Ovens

Because every cook's microwave oven varies in size, wattage, type, and age, we were concerned about writing a recipe using equipment whose power is difficult to quantify. Would microwaving on "high" power produce consistent results among different machines? We were doubtful.

The amount of microwave energy absorbed by a food is a function of the cooking time, the power (wattage) of the machine, the portion size, and the amount of water in the food to be cooked (the energy produced by the microwave is absorbed primarily by water). Roughly speaking, the more watts, the faster food will cook. Theoretically, a microwave with 1,000 watts of power would cook the same volume of food twice as quickly as a machine with 500 watts.

To gauge real-life differences, we sent armfuls of acorn squash and bags of microwave popcorn (an easy gauge of cooking power) home with colleagues to cook in their microwaves. When they reported back, we found that differences in cooking times correlated roughly—though not reliably—to the power of the microwave used. For example, popcorn took 3 minutes and 45 seconds in the only 700-watt microwave tested, while the same brand of popcorn was ready in just 2 minutes in several 1,100-watt models. The same thing held true for squash, with cooking times running from a low of 15 minutes in several powerful microwaves to a high of 27 minutes in the same weak 700-watt microwave.

What to do, then, when cooking squash in your microwave? Check the label inside the machine (or your owner's manual) to determine its wattage. If your microwave runs on fewer than 900 watts of power, you will likely need to increase the cooking time by a few minutes. If you own a high-wattage machine (more than 1,100 watts), you may need to decrease the cooking time. That said, it always pays to use your senses, not a timer, to judge when food is ready.

➤ VARIATION

Braised Winter Squash with Asian Flavors

Buttercup squash, also called kabocha, is often used in braises and stews in Asian cooking and is the most traditional choice for this dish.

2	tablespoons vegetable oil
I	small onion, diced
2	pounds winter squash, peeled, seeded (see illustrations on page 233), and cut into 1-inch cubes
1/2	cup low-sodium chicken broth
I	tablespoon soy sauce
I	tablespoon mirin (Japanese sweet rice wine)
	Salt and ground black pepper
I	medium scallion, sliced thin

Heat the oil in a Dutch oven or large saucepan over medium-high heat until shimmering. Add the onion and cook, stirring occasionally, until golden, about 4 minutes. Add the squash, broth, soy sauce, mirin, and salt and pepper to taste. Bring to a simmer, cover, and reduce the heat to medium-low. Simmer until the squash is very tender, 15 to 20 minutes. Remove the lid and simmer until the liquid thickens, 2 to 3 minutes. Adjust the seasonings, adding salt and pepper to taste. Sprinkle with the scallion and serve immediately.

ZUCCHINI, SUMMER, AND PATTYPAN SQUASH

GARDENS OVERFLOW WITH ZUCCHINI AND other summer squash every summer, but cooks are often at a loss for ideas for using this bounty. The biggest problem that confronts the cook when preparing zucchini is its wateriness. This vegetable is about 95 percent water and becomes soupy if just thrown into a hot pan. If zucchini cooks in its own juices, it won't brown—and because it is fairly bland, zucchini really benefits from browning. Clearly, some of the water must be removed before sautéing.

The first precautions against wateriness must take place in the supermarket. Size and firmness are the most important factors when purchasing zucchini. After extensive testing, we found that smaller zucchini are more flavorful and less watery. Smaller zucchini also have fewer seeds. Look for zucchini no larger than 8 ounces and preferably just 6 ounces each. Mammoth zucchini may look impressive in the garden (or supermarket), but they will only cause problems in the kitchen. Finally, look for small zucchini with tiny prickly hairs around the stem end; the hairs are a sign of freshness.

Even if you've bought small zucchini, you still need to remove moisture before cooking it. Many sources recommend salting sliced zucchini before cooking it. We tested salting to draw off some water and found that sliced and salted zucchini sheds about 20 percent of its weight after sitting for 30 minutes. One pound of sliced zucchini threw off almost 3 tablespoons of liquid, further confirmation that salting works. We tested longer periods and found that little additional moisture is extracted after 30 minutes.

Given that you don't always have 30 minutes, we wanted to develop quicker methods for cooking zucchini. We tried shredding the zucchini on the large holes of a box grater and then squeezing out excess water by hand. We were able to reduce the weight of shredded zucchini by 25 percent by wrapping it in paper towels and squeezing until dry. Because sliced zucchini has so much less surface area than shredded zucchini, the process works much more efficiently with the latter.

We also tried extracting moisture from shredded zucchini by placing it in batches in a potato ricer fitted with a very fine disk. This method was equally effective at removing moisture but tended to bruise the zucchini. Stick with paper towels.

Another quick-prep option is the grill. The intense heat quickly expels excess moisture, and that moisture drops harmlessly onto the coals rather than sitting in the pan. We found that so much evaporation occurs during grilling that neither salting nor shredding is necessary.

Pattypan squash (also known as custard squash or scallop squash) is characterized by its starburst shape and scalloped edges. While zucchini and other summer squash, such as yellow crookneck, can be prepared and cooked in the same fashion, pattypan squash is meatier and requires some different approaches. It seems a shame to finely chop or slice this squash. We wanted to cut it into larger pieces in order to retain its pretty shape.

We tried steaming and boiling the squash—two common methods touted in many sources as the best way to preserve its flavor and shape—but we had poor results. Even though pattypans are not as watery as zucchini and other summer squash, they don't respond well to moist-heat cooking. Grilling is out because of their odd shape (they can easily fall through the grate onto the coals), and sautéing can be problematic unless they are cut into very small pieces. We had the best results

SHREDDING ZUCCHINI AND SUMMER SQUASH

1. For quick indoor cooking, shred trimmed zucchini or squash on the large holes of a box grater or in a food processor fitted with the shredding disk.

2. Wrap the shredded zucchini or squash in paper towels and squeeze out excess liquid. Proceed immediately with sautéing.

with roasting. Coating the squash pieces with olive oil and roasting them at 425 degrees brought out their natural sweetness.

Shredded Zucchini or Summer Squash

SERVES 4

This recipe is best when you're pressed for time and want to cook zucchini indoors. If you like, replace one of the zucchini with two medium carrots that have been peeled and shredded on the large holes of a box grater—there's no need to squeeze the carrots dry.

   3   tablespoons extra-virgin olive oil
   4   medium zucchini or summer squash (about 1½ pounds), trimmed, shredded, and squeezed dry (see the illustrations on page 237)
   3   medium garlic cloves, minced or pressed through a garlic press (about 1 tablespoon)
   2   tablespoons minced fresh parsley, basil, mint, or tarragon leaves, or chives
      Salt and ground black pepper

Heat the oil in a large nonstick skillet over medium-high heat until shimmering. Add the zucchini and garlic and cook, stirring occasionally, until tender, about 7 minutes. Stir in the parsley and salt and pepper to taste. Serve immediately.

➤ VARIATIONS

Sautéed Shredded Zucchini or Summer Squash with Sweet Corn and Chives
This recipe also works with frozen corn—just defrost the corn and add it during the last minute or two of the cooking time. See the illustrations on page 200 for removing the kernels from fresh corn.

   3   tablespoons unsalted butter
   1   medium shallot, minced
   4   medium zucchini or summer squash (about 1½ pounds), trimmed, shredded, and squeezed dry (see the illustrations on page 237)
   2   medium ears sweet corn, kernels cut away with a knife (about 1¼ cups)
   1   tablespoon minced fresh chives
      Salt and ground black pepper

Heat the butter in a large nonstick skillet over medium-high heat. When the foaming subsides, add the shallot and cook, stirring occasionally, until soft, 2 to 3 minutes. Add the zucchini and corn and cook, stirring occasionally, until tender, about 7 minutes. Stir in the chives and salt and pepper to taste. Serve immediately.

Spicy Sautéed Shredded Zucchini or Summer Squash with Anchovy
Contrary to popular belief, anchovies (when used in moderation) add a deep, salty flavor without any hint of fishiness.

   3   tablespoons extra-virgin olive oil
   3   medium garlic cloves, minced or pressed through a garlic press (about 1 tablespoon)
   2   medium anchovy fillets
  ¼   teaspoon red pepper flakes
   4   medium zucchini or summer squash (about 1½ pounds), trimmed, shredded, and squeezed dry (see the illustrations on page 237)
      Salt and ground black pepper

Heat the oil in a large nonstick skillet over medium-high heat until shimmering. Add the garlic, anchovies, and red pepper flakes and cook, mashing the anchovies into the oil, until fragrant, about 30 seconds. Add the zucchini and cook, stirring occasionally, until tender, about 7 minutes. Add salt and pepper to taste. Serve immediately.

Grilled Zucchini or Summer Squash

SERVES 4

Excess water evaporates over hot coals, so salting the zucchini before cooking is not necessary. If you like, drizzle the zucchini with a little balsamic vinegar just before serving.

   4   medium zucchini or summer squash (about 1½ pounds), trimmed and sliced lengthwise into ½-inch-thick strips (see the illustrations on the facing page)
   2   tablespoons extra-virgin olive oil
      Salt and ground black pepper

1. Lay the zucchini slices on a large baking sheet and brush both sides with the oil. Sprinkle generously with salt and pepper to taste

2. Grill the zucchini over a medium-hot fire (you should be able to hold your hand 5 inches above the cooking grate for 3 to 4 seconds), turning once, until marked with dark stripes, 8 to 10 minutes. Serve hot, warm, or at room temperature.

Sautéed Zucchini or Summer Squash

SERVES 4

If you like browned zucchini, you must salt it before cooking. Salting drives off excess water and helps the zucchini sauté rather than stew in its own juices. Coarse kosher salt does the best job of driving off liquid and can be wiped away without rinsing. Do not add more salt when cooking or the dish will be too salty.

4	medium zucchini or summer squash (about 1½ pounds), trimmed and sliced crosswise into ¼-inch-thick rounds
1	tablespoon kosher salt
3	tablespoons extra-virgin olive oil
1	small onion, minced
1	teaspoon grated zest and 1 tablespoon juice from 1 lemon

1–2 tablespoons minced fresh parsley, basil, mint, or tarragon leaves, or chives
Ground black pepper

1. Place the zucchini slices in a colander and sprinkle with the salt. Set the colander over a bowl until about ½ cup water drains from the zucchini, about 30 minutes. Remove the zucchini from the colander and pat dry with a clean kitchen towel or several paper towels, wiping off any remaining crystals of salt.

2. Heat the oil in a large skillet over medium heat. Add the onion and cook until almost softened, about 3 minutes. Increase the heat to medium-high and add the zucchini and lemon zest. Cook until the zucchini is golden brown, about 10 minutes. Stir in the lemon juice and parsley and season with pepper to taste. Serve immediately.

➤ VARIATION

Sautéed Zucchini or Summer Squash with Olives and Oregano

Follow the recipe for Sautéed Zucchini or Summer Squash, adding ¼ cup chopped kalamata olives with the lemon juice and using 1 teaspoon minced fresh oregano leaves as the herb.

SLICING ZUCCHINI OR SUMMER SQUASH FOR THE GRILL

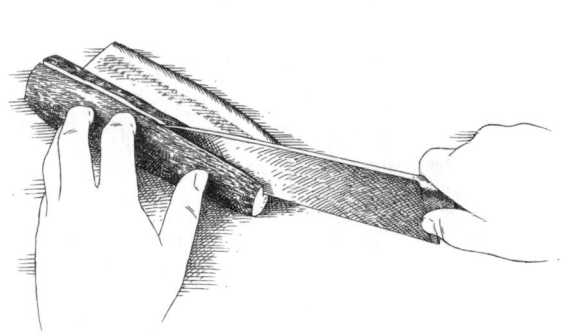

1. Cut a thin slice from each end of the zucchini or summer squash. Slice the trimmed squash lengthwise into ½-inch-thick strips.

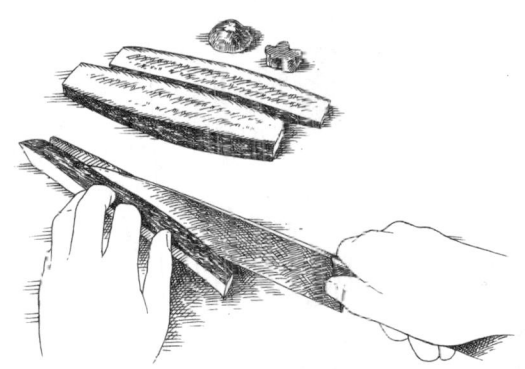

2. For aesthetic reasons, you may want to trim the peel from the outer slices so they match the others. (You can do the same thing with outer eggplant slices.) Besides developing more attractive grill marks, the flesh cooks better when directly exposed to the heat.

STUFFED ZUCCHINI

IN OUR EXPERIENCE, STUFFED ZUCCHINI has either been a healthy but bland attempt at a vegetarian dinner or a thrifty, last-ditch effort to use up some leftovers. Either way, the dish has never garnered any points with us. We prefer the delicate flavor of zucchini in basic preparations, usually sautéed or grilled. But we wondered if we had been premature in giving this stuffed vegetable a bad rap. Realizing that a simple summer recipe would make a handy addition to our repertoire, we set out to create a stuffed zucchini worth making.

We began by testing several recipes. One after another, each turned out to be a disappointment. Simpler recipes stuffed raw zucchini with rice and vegetables and threw it in the oven. Not only did these zucchini take a while to cook through, but the filling on top dried out while the filling on the bottom absorbed the zucchini's moisture and became mushy. Other recipes called for blanching the squash in water or stock before stuffing it, draining the zucchini of flavor and leaving behind a dull, limp shell. Still others filled the squash raw and baked it in tomato juice or a sauce that succeeded only in imparting a tinned tomato flavor. As for the fillings, most recipes used precooked rice, which proceeded to absorb the moisture in the zucchini and take on a toothless texture and monotonous flavor. The reasons for our long-standing bias against this stuffed vegetable were now more obvious than ever. To make a dish worth eating, we would have to figure out how to parcook the zucchini before stuffing it, then find something exciting to stuff it with.

The moisture in the zucchini was clearly the biggest problem. Roasting, with its hot, dry heat, seemed a promising way to lose this moisture while also precooking the squash. We experimented by roasting zucchini whole, roasting it halved, and roasting it halved and seeded. The whole zucchini took too long to cook and steamed itself soggy. Although the halved squash cooked in less time, the seeds still held onto some moisture, leaving behind a soggy shell. The seeded squash, on the other hand, retained the toothsome texture we were looking for and also developed a more concentrated flavor. With the heat of the oven able to hit the flesh of the zucchini directly, more moisture evaporated, intensifying the flavor.

Next we did side-by-side roasting tests. When the zucchini were roasted cut-side up, the moisture that did not evaporate pooled in the hollow space once occupied by the seeds and later seeped into the stuffing, making it watery. When roasted cut-side down, however, the squash dripped moisture onto the hot roasting pan, where it turned to steam. Some of this steam got trapped underneath the overturned squash, speeding up the cooking process. Using a preheated pan further reduced the roasting time while creating a flavorful, golden brown crust along the rim. Salt and pepper brought out flavor, while olive oil prevented sticking. With its lightly browned edges and toothsome texture, the seeded squash, roasted cut-side down on a preheated pan, was by far the best of the class. We could now turn our attention to the filling.

Right off the bat, we set up a few guidelines. We wanted to use ingredients that home cooks would likely have on hand, and we wanted to prepare the filling while the squash roasted. To start, we tried using a simple combination of sautéed vegetables and cheese, but tasters were left wanting something more substantial. We then tested fillings made with rice, couscous, bread cubes, bread crumbs, and roasted potatoes. The rice and couscous, two predictable choices, tasted fine, but the bread cubes and bread crumbs were mushy and wanting in texture. Somewhat unexpectedly, the roasted potatoes stole the show, giving the dish a satisfying oomph that none of the contenders could match. After trying several varieties of potatoes, including russet, Yukon Gold, and red, we found that red potatoes, with their high-moisture and low-starch content, had the best texture when roasted. Best of all, both the squash and the potatoes roasted at about the same speed when placed on preheated pans in a 400-degree oven.

To get the summery flavor mix we were after, we added some fresh tomatoes, a bit of sautéed garlic, and some slightly caramelized onions along with fresh basil. We also found that a little cheese helped to bind the filling. After trying eight different types, tasters voted unanimously for Monterey Jack cheese (it edged out even the Parmesan). The flavor of the Jack cheese was evident without being overpowering, and it melted and browned nicely along the top. Finally, we had a stuffed zucchini worth making; it was even worth serving to company.

Stuffed Zucchini with Tomatoes and Jack Cheese

SERVES 4

Buy firm zucchini with tiny prickly hairs around the stem end; the hairs are a sign of freshness.

4	medium zucchini (about 6 ounces each), washed
	Salt and ground black pepper
1/4	cup olive oil
3	medium red potatoes (about 1 pound), cut into 1/2-inch cubes
1	medium onion, chopped fine
5	large garlic cloves, minced or pressed through a garlic press (about 2 1/2 tablespoons)
3	medium tomatoes (about 1 1/4 pounds), cored, seeded and chopped
1/3	cup chopped fresh basil leaves
6	ounces Monterey Jack cheese, shredded (about 2 cups)

1. Adjust one oven rack to the upper-middle position and a second oven rack to the lowest position, then place a rimmed baking sheet on each rack and heat the oven to 400 degrees.

2. Meanwhile, halve each zucchini lengthwise. With a small spoon, scoop out the seeds and most of the flesh so that the walls of the zucchini are 1/4 inch thick (see the illustration at right). Season the cut sides of the zucchini with salt and pepper, and brush with 2 tablespoons of the olive oil; set the zucchini halves cut-side down on the hot baking sheet on the lower rack. Toss the potatoes with 1 tablespoon olive oil, salt, and pepper in a small bowl and spread them in a single layer on the hot baking sheet on the upper rack. Roast the zucchini until it is slightly softened and the skins are wrinkled, about 10 minutes; roast the potatoes until tender and lightly browned, 10 to

12 minutes. Using tongs, flip the zucchini halves over on the baking sheet and set aside.

3. Meanwhile, heat the remaining 1 tablespoon of olive oil in a large skillet over medium heat until shimmering but not smoking, about 2 minutes. Add the onion and cook, stirring occasionally, until softened and beginning to brown, about 10 minutes. Increase the heat to medium-high; stir in the garlic and cook until fragrant, about 30 seconds. Add the tomatoes and cooked potatoes; cook, stirring occasionally, until heated through, about 3 minutes. Off the heat, stir in the basil, 3/4 cup of the cheese, and salt and pepper to taste.

4. Divide the filling evenly among the squash halves on the baking sheet, spooning about 1/2 cup into each, and pack lightly; sprinkle with the remaining cheese. Return the baking sheet to the oven, this time to the upper rack, and bake until the zucchini are heated through and the cheese is spotty brown, about 6 minutes. Serve immediately.

SEEDING ZUCCHINI

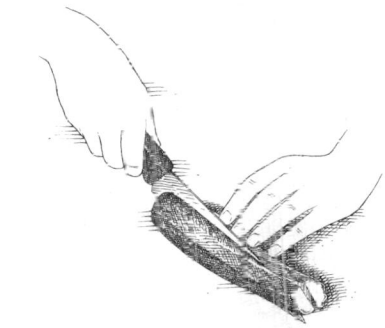

1. After slicing off the stem end, halve each zucchini lengthwise.

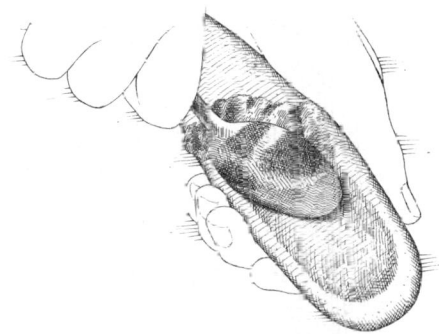

2. With a small spoon, scoop out the seeds and most of the flesh, making the walls of the zucchini 1/4 inch thick.

➤ VARIATION

Stuffed Zucchini with Corn, Black Beans, and Chipotle Chiles

4	medium zucchini (about 6 ounces each), washed
	Salt and ground black pepper
¼	cup olive oil
1	medium red potato (about 5 ounces), cut into ½-inch cubes
1	medium onion, chopped fine
1	cup fresh corn kernels cut from 2 medium ears
5	large garlic cloves, minced or pressed through a garlic press (about 2 tablespoons)
3	medium chipotle chiles in adobo sauce, minced (about 3 tablespoons)
2	medium tomatoes (about 12 ounces), cored, seeded, and chopped
1	(15-ounce) can black beans, drained and rinsed (about 1½ cups)
⅓	cup chopped fresh cilantro leaves
6	ounces Monterey Jack cheese, shredded (about 2 cups)

1. Follow recipe for Stuffed Zucchini with Tomatoes and Jack Cheese through step 2.

2. Heat the remaining tablespoon olive oil in a large skillet over medium heat until shimmering but not smoking, about 2 minutes. Add the onion and cook, stirring occasionally, until softened and beginning to brown, about 10 minutes. Increase the heat to medium–high; stir in the corn and cook until almost tender, about 3 minutes. Add the garlic and chipotle chiles; cook until fragrant, about 30 seconds. Stir in the tomatoes, black beans, and cooked potatoes; cook, stirring occasionally, until heated through, about 3 minutes. Off the heat, stir in the cilantro, ¾ cup of the cheese, and salt and pepper to taste.

3. Continue with the recipe for Stuffed Zucchini with Tomatoes and Jack Cheese from step 4.

Roasted Pattypan Squash

SERVES 4

Choose squash that are 3 inches or smaller in diameter; as the squash gets larger, it loses its buttery flavor.

1½	pounds pattypan squash, stem ends trimmed and halved (or quartered if large)
2	tablespoons extra-virgin olive oil
1	medium garlic clove, minced or pressed through a garlic press (about 1 teaspoon)
	Salt and ground black pepper
1	tablespoon minced fresh parsley leaves or chives

Adjust an oven rack to the lower-middle position and heat the oven to 425 degrees. Toss the squash, oil, garlic, and salt and pepper to taste together in a large bowl. Arrange the squash on a rimmed baking sheet and roast until lightly browned and tender, about 20 minutes. Sprinkle with the parsley and adjust the seasonings, adding salt and pepper to taste. Serve immediately.

➤ VARIATION

Roasted Pattypan Squash with Shallot, Lemon, and Parmesan

Serve this preparation along with fish or pasta. Feel free to use basil, mint, chives, chervil, or tarragon in place of the parsley.

1½	pounds pattypan squash, stem ends trimmed and halved (or quartered if large)
3	tablespoons extra-virgin olive oil
1	medium shallot, minced
	Salt and ground black pepper
1	tablespoon minced fresh parsley leaves
1	teaspoon grated zest and 1 teaspoon juice from 1 lemon
2	teaspoons honey
¼	cup grated Parmesan cheese

1. Adjust an oven rack to the lower-middle position and heat the oven to 425 degrees. Toss the squash, 2 tablespoons of the oil, the shallot, and salt and pepper to taste in a large bowl. Arrange the squash on a rimmed baking sheet (save the bowl for later use) and roast until lightly browned and tender, about 20 minutes.

2. Mix the remaining 1 tablespoon olive oil, the parsley, lemon zest and juice, and honey together in the reserved bowl. Add the roasted squash and toss to combine. Adjust the seasonings, adding salt and pepper to taste. Sprinkle with the cheese and serve immediately.

PROVENÇAL SUMMER SQUASH CASSEROLE

IN PROVENCE, THE ABUNDANCE OF SUMMER vegetables is often dealt with in simple vegetable dishes called tians, or gratins. One of the classic versions includes nothing but summer squash and zucchini. The squashes are thinly sliced, shingled in an alternating pattern, and showered with herbs and broth. Baked until the vegetables are tender and the flavors blend, this dish is both visually pleasing and easy to prepare—just the thing to use up the never-ending surplus of squash that always seems to arise by midsummer.

Provence-grown squash must taste better than our local squash, because the dishes we prepared from authentic recipes were pretty uninspiring. Bland and boring, they failed to capture the clean flavors and crisp texture of the squash in the way we assumed they would. The squash was either dried out and leathery or waterlogged and mushy. It was pretty obvious to us that baking temperature had a major impact on both the flavor and texture of the casserole.

Recipes we had tried differed by more than 100 degrees in cooking temperature—from 350 to 450—and yielded very different results. On the lower end of the scale, the squash shed torrents of liquid and turned mushy; the casserole looked like vegetable soup. At the higher end, the squash slices shriveled up to a dried, leathery consistency, even when doused liberally with broth. We baked casseroles at varying temperatures for different lengths of time until we reached the best compromise of flavor and texture by cooking for about 45 minutes at 400 degrees. The top half of the squash slices withered a bit and intensified in flavor, and the bottom half stayed moist and tender.

At the lowest temperatures, broth had been superfluous because the squash itself exuded so much liquid; at the highest temperatures, it had been essential to keep the squash from drying out completely. We experimented with adding varying amounts of broth at the temperature of 400 degrees and settled on 1 cup. By the time the squash was tender, most of the broth had evaporated, leaving a few spoonfuls, or just enough to dribble over top of the squash after serving. We had initially been using chicken broth, but we found that we much preferred the cleaner, more complementary flavor of vegetable broth. The chicken broth imparted its distinctive flavor to the mild-flavored squash, while the vegetable broth merely reinforced the vegetal qualities of the squash.

We next experimented with spiking the broth with various acids—vinegar, lemon juice, and wine—to brighten the casserole's flavor, and we liked the results. Our top choice was wine because it packed more flavor than either of the other two. Lemon juice and vinegar added sharpness but no depth. A substantial ½ cup of dry, fruity (not oaky) white wine contributed the best flavor (we left out ½ cup of the broth to accommodate the added volume).

We knew we wanted to add aromatic onions to the dish in some fashion. Minced raw onion, tossed in between the layers of squash, lent little but a sharp bite and slightly crunchy texture because the onion barely cooked, sandwiched as it was between the layers. Sautéing the onion first in olive oil proved more successful; its sharpness was tempered and the natural sweetness of the onion intensified the squash's own mild sweetness. We favored red onions over yellow because of their inherent sweetness. We also chose to spread the onion slices in a layer across the bottom of the pan to simplify the assembly process. The bubbling broth percolated up from the bottom, diffusing the onion's flavor through the squash. As an added

ASSEMBLING THE CASSEROLE

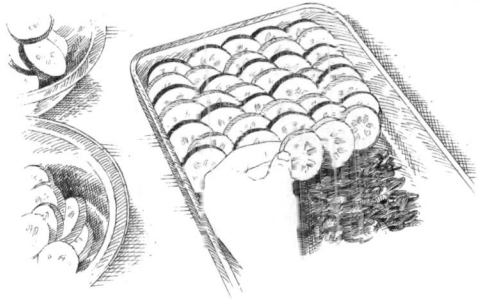

Tightly shingle the slices of squash and zucchini in alternating rows over the top of the onions (the slices will be nearly vertical).

bonus, the onion slices provided some traction for the squash slices, keeping them from sliding on the slippery bottom of the casserole dish during assembly. For a hint of fire, we added a pinch of crushed red pepper flakes along with the onions.

Some of the recipes we tried were heavily laced with garlic, a kick from which we knew our version could benefit. We sprinkled raw, finely minced garlic among the sliced squash, as we had the onion in the first tests, but the flavor proved too assertive—the garlic, like the onion, required cooking first. In our next version, we sautéed the garlic with the onion, which tempered its sharpness and pungency, but the flavor was too localized: The bottom portion of squash had a potent garlicky flavor, but the top had none (mysteriously, the flavor of the onion spread more than that of the garlic). Then it finally occurred to us that we should just add the garlic to the broth and wine we sprinkled over the shingled squash. Evenly dispersed throughout the casserole, the sautéed garlic added just the edge the squash needed. We also decided to add herbs to the broth. Basil, marjoram, oregano, savory, and parsley were all good choices, but woodsy thyme proved to be the favorite among tasters because they felt its flavor paired especially well with the squash and onions.

Provençal Summer Squash Casserole

SERVES 6 TO 8

While we like the flavor and colors of this dish when made with a combination of summer squash and zucchini, it tastes just as good when made only with one or the other. This dish is best served right away, so plan accordingly.

- 3 tablespoons extra-virgin olive oil
- I large red onion, halved and sliced thin
  Pinch red pepper flakes
  Salt

- 4 medium garlic cloves, minced or pressed through a garlic press (about 4 teaspoons)
- ½ cup dry white wine
- ½ cup low-sodium vegetable broth
- I teaspoon minced fresh thyme leaves
  Ground black pepper
- I pound summer squash, sliced ¼ inch thick
- I pound zucchini, sliced ¼ inch thick

1. Adjust an oven rack to the middle position and heat the oven to 400 degrees. Heat 2 tablespoons of the oil in a large skillet over medium-high heat until shimmering. Add the onion, pepper flakes, and ½ teaspoon salt; cook, stirring frequently, until the onion has softened and browned around the edges, about 10 minutes. Spread evenly over the bottom of a 13 by 9-inch baking dish (or shallow casserole dish of similar size); set aside.

2. Add the remaining tablespoon oil and the garlic to the skillet and return to medium heat until fragrant, about 30 seconds. Stir in the wine, broth, and thyme, scraping the bottom of the pan to loosen any browned bits. Season to taste with salt and pepper; remove the skillet from the heat and set aside.

3. Following the illustration on page 243, shingle the slices of squash and zucchini in alternating rows over the onions. Pour the broth mixture evenly over the squash. Bake until the squash has softened and is just beginning to brown, 40 to 45 minutes. Serve hot.

➤ VARIATION

Summer Squash Casserole with Feta, Lemon, and Oregano

Follow the recipe for Provençal Summer Squash Casserole, making the following changes: Substitute 1 teaspoon minced fresh oregano leaves and 1 teaspoon grated lemon zest for the thyme. Sprinkle 2 ounces feta, crumbled (about ½ cup), over the squash before baking.

SOUTHEAST ASIAN-STYLE SPRING ROLLS **PAGE 74**

245

CHEESE TRAY WITH WHIPPED GOAT CHEESE WITH CHIVES AND LEMON **PAGE 11**; MARINATED BLACK AND GREEN OLIVES **PAGE 5**; TOASTED ALMONDS **PAGE 4**; AND CHEESE STRAWS **PAGE 16**

246

CRUDITÉS **PAGE 21**
GREEN GODDESS DIP **PAGE 26**
CLAM DIP WITH BACON AND SCALLIONS **PAGE 27**

BRUSCHETTA WITH SAUTÉED SWEET PEPPERS; BRUSCHETTA WITH ARUGULA, RED ONION, AND ROSEMARY–WHITE BEAN SPREAD; BRUSCHETTA WITH SUMMER SQUASH, BACON, AND BLUE CHEESES **PAGES 49–50**

ORANGE, AVOCADO AND WATERCRESS SALAD **PAGE 106**

CLASSIC COBB SALAD **PAGE 152**

ASPARAGUS, RED PEPPER, AND SPINACH SALAD WITH GOAT CHEESE **PAGE 115**

251

SALADE NIÇOISE **PAGE 154**

SAUTÉED CHERRY TOMATOES WITH CAPERS AND ANCHOVY **PAGE 228**

253

STUFFED ZUCCHINI WITH TOMATOES AND JACK CHEESE **PAGE 241**

SKILLET GREEN BEANS WITH ORANGE ESSENCE AND TOASTED MAPLE PECANS **PAGE 213**

POMMES ANNA **PAGE 294**

MASHED POTATOES WITH GARLIC **PAGE 267**

BOILED POTATOES WITH BUTTER AND CHIVES **PAGE 264**

PARMESAN RISOTTO **PAGE 319**

RISOTTO CAKES **PAGE 321**

4

POTATO SIDES AND CASSEROLES

WHAT'S A HAMBURGER WITHOUT FRENCH fries, meat loaf without mashed potatoes, or eggs without hash browns? Admittedly, there are countless ways to enjoy potatoes, so it comes as no surprise that it was necessary for us to devote an entire chapter to the starchy spud.

The cook has two challenges when preparing any recipe with potatoes. The first is to determine the best cooking method. Is it necessary to prick a potato prior to baking? Does the order in which you add butter and milk to mashed potatoes matter? Secondly, what kind of potato works best in a specific recipe? While other vegetables in most markets vary by size and freshness, in most cases, shoppers will find only one variety of that vegetable—broccoli is broccoli, carrots are carrots. Even when several varieties are available (as in heirloom tomatoes), most can be used interchangeably. Yes, one tomato might look a bit different from or be a bit sweeter than another, but they are closely related. With potatoes, this is not the case.

Dozens of potato varieties are grown in this country, and at any time you may see as many as five or six in your supermarket. Some potatoes are sold by varietal name (such as Yukon Gold), but others are sold by generic name (baking, all-purpose, and so on). To make sense of this confusion, we find it helpful to group potatoes into three major categories, based on the ratio of solids (mostly starch) to water. The categories are high-starch/low-moisture potatoes, medium-starch/medium-moisture potatoes, and low-starch/high-moisture potatoes.

The high-starch/low-moisture category includes baking, russet, and white creamer potatoes. (The formal name for the russet is the russet Burbank potato, named after its developer, Luther Burbank. This type of potato is also known as the Idaho. In all of our recipes, we call them russets.) These potatoes are best suited for baking and mashing but also make the best french fries. The medium-starch/medium-moisture category includes all-purpose, Yukon Gold, Yellow Finn, and purple Peruvian potatoes. These potatoes can be mashed, baked, or roasted, but generally they are not as fluffy as the high-starch potatoes. The low-starch/high-moisture category includes Red Bliss

(we refer to them as red potatoes), red creamer, new, white rose, and fingerling potatoes. These potatoes, which are often called waxy potatoes, are best roasted or boiled and used in salad.

Within each category, you can safely make substitutions, but cross-category substitutions can cause poor results. For instance, if you try to fry red potatoes rather than the recommended russet potatoes, you will get soggy, limp fries.

In addition to categorizing potatoes by starch content, it is useful to divide them into two groups based on how they have been handled after harvesting. Most potatoes are cured in specially lit, well-ventilated rooms after harvesting to toughen their skins and protect their flesh. They are then held in cold storage, often for months. These potatoes are called storage potatoes. Almost all of the potatoes in the supermarket fall into this category. Occasionally, potatoes are harvested before they have developed their full complement of starch. New potatoes are always low in starch and high in moisture, even if they are actually a high-starch variety. Although all new potatoes are small, not all small potatoes are new. You can pick out a true new potato by examining the skin. If the skin feels thin and you can rub it off with your fingers, you are holding a new potato. New potatoes have a lot of moisture, and their flesh is almost juicy when cut. We liken a new potato to the perfect summer tomato—they each have an incomparable flavor that is not to be missed.

Raw potatoes should be stored in a cool, ventilated dark area. Sun promotes the development of solanine, recognizable by the greenish tinge that develops on the skin, which imparts a bitter flavor to the potato. Although solanine can be cut away, it can be toxic and so is best avoided altogether (in other words, throw out potatoes with a greenish tinge). Keep potatoes in a paper bag, not plastic (plastic traps air and will cause the potatoes to sprout). Do not refrigerate raw potatoes—the cold temperature will encourage the starches to turn to sugar and will also darken the flesh.

Sweet potatoes are also included in this chapter. Even though sweet potatoes are not really potatoes, they do share similar preparation techniques. Also like potatoes, sweet potatoes come in different varieties. But, contrary to popular belief, they are not interchangeable with yams. (Yams have a hairy, off-white or brown skin and white, light yellow, or pink flesh. This tuber is usually sold in log-shaped chunks that weigh several pounds each. Unlike sweet potatoes, yams have a bland flavor and ultrastarchy texture.)

Sweet potatoes come in two very distinct types, dry and moist. Endless varieties allow for confusion with sizes and shapes, but the most basic rule is that dry sweet potatoes have white to yellow flesh while moist ones have varying shades of deep orange. Dry sweet potatoes are slightly sweet and, because they have a relatively high starch content, are also somewhat mealy. Moist sweet potatoes have a higher sugar content and are dense, watery, and more easily caramelized.

Most commercially grown sweet potatoes are harvested in the fall. They are then transferred to ventilated curing rooms where, for a period of days, high heat and humidity levels allow cuts and bruises from harvesting to heal. In this controlled environment, starches begin converting to sugar, so that a cured sweet potato is literally sweeter than a freshly harvested one.

Once you get sweet potatoes home, do not wash them until you are ready to use them because this exposes the vulnerable skin and causes them to go bad more quickly. (Neither should regular potatoes be washed until you're ready to cook them.) Refrigeration is also not recommended; it causes the core of the potato to gradually change texture until it resembles a soft, damp cork. The best storage is a dark, well-ventilated spot. Sweet potatoes should not be stored in plastic bags.

As there are multiple varieties of potatoes, there are multiple ways to prepare them. Whether you're looking for a simple potato dish to serve with your favorite meat loaf or burger or something a bit more special to round out a holiday meal, this chapter features recipes for all occasions.

BOILED POTATOES

MOST OFTEN, WE BOIL POTATOES FOR SALAD (see pages 129–133 for potato salad recipes). However, freshly dug baby or new potatoes can be boiled, buttered, and served hot as a side dish. In many ways, this simple preparation is the best way to highlight the flavor of really good potatoes. That said, much can go wrong with this dish. The potatoes can split open and become soggy. The key is to cook the potatoes until they are just tender and then drain and butter them immediately.

From our initial tests, we concluded that having potatoes of varying sizes in the pot was problematic. The small potatoes overcooked and their skins split open while we waited for the larger potatoes to cook through. (The best test for doneness is a paring knife or skewer; it should glide easily through the potato without causing it to fall apart.)

While larger potatoes are fine for salad, we found that the best potatoes for boiling and buttering are small—to be exact, smaller than 2½ inches in diameter. These potatoes cooked more evenly. Larger potatoes tended to get a bit mushy right under the skin by the time the center was cooked through.

From previous tests, we knew that you must boil potatoes with their skins on to prevent them

HANDLING HOT BOILED POTATOES

Potatoes should be boiled whole and unpeeled to keep them from getting soggy. After boiling, however, the potatoes should be cut in half because the fleshy portion is much better at absorbing butter and seasonings than the skin. To halve a hot potato, steady it with a pair of tongs while cutting with a sharp knife.

from becoming watery. However, we found that the flesh on a boiled potato must be exposed at some point so that it can soak up the butter and seasonings. When we tossed drained, whole, skin-on potatoes with butter, the butter just stayed in the bowl—it could not penetrate the skin.

We tried peeling a thin band around the center of each potato before boiling to eliminate the need to cut them after cooking. This test failed. Once the potatoes were cooked, the skin that had been left on started to break away from the flesh, and the flesh, too, began breaking apart.

For the best results, we found it necessary to cut the potatoes in half after boiling. Although a bit tedious, we found that holding the hot potatoes one at a time with a pair of tongs and then slicing them with a knife worked well. Once all of the potatoes were cut in half, we immediately added them to the bowl with the butter. As soon as the potatoes are coated with fat, the seasonings can be added.

Boiled Potatoes with Butter

SERVES 4

The cooking time will vary depending on the size of the potatoes. For potatoes that measure 2 to 2½ inches in diameter (you will need 12 to 17 potatoes to make 2 pounds), plan on 15 to 18 minutes of cooking time. For potatoes that measure 1½ to 2 inches in diameter (you will need 18 to 24 potatoes to make 2 pounds), plan on 12 to 15 minutes of cooking time. For potatoes that measure 1 to 1½ inches in diameter (you will need 25 to 31 potatoes to make 2 pounds), plan on 10 to 12 minutes of cooking time. For potatoes that measure less than 1 inch in diameter (you will need 32 or more potatoes to make 2 pounds), plan on 8 to 10 minutes of cooking time.

3   tablespoons unsalted butter
2   pounds small red or new potatoes, scrubbed
     Salt and ground black pepper

1. Place the butter in a medium serving bowl and set aside to soften while you prepare and cook the potatoes.

2. Place the potatoes and 1 tablespoon salt in a Dutch oven and fill with enough cold water to cover the potatoes by about 1 inch. Bring to a boil over high heat, cover, reduce the heat to medium-low, and simmer, stirring once or twice, until the potatoes are just tender when pierced with a thin-bladed knife or skewer, 8 to 18 minutes, depending on the size of the potatoes (see note). Drain the potatoes.

3. Cut the potatoes in half (see the illustration on page 263). Place the halved potatoes in the bowl with the butter and toss to coat. Season with salt and pepper to taste and toss again. Serve immediately.

➤ VARIATIONS

Boiled Potatoes with Butter and Chives
Follow the recipe for Boiled Potatoes with Butter, adding 3 tablespoons thinly sliced fresh chives along with the salt and pepper in step 3.

FAVORITE SIDES FOR STEAK

WHAT'S STEAK WITHOUT POTATOES? AND because potatoes are so versatile, your choices for choosing sides are seemingly endless. Here are some of the test kitchen's favorite potato sides for steak:

SIMPLE
- Boiled Potatoes with Butter and Chives (this page)
- Boiled Potatoes with Shallot and Sage (facing page)

CRUNCHY
- French Fries (page 282)
- Steak Fries (page 284)

RICH AND CREAMY
- Mashed Potatoes with Garlic (page 267)
- Smashed Potatoes with Bacon and Parsley (page 271)

ELEGANT
- Pommes Anna (page 294)
- Scalloped Potatoes with Mushrooms (page 298)

Boiled Potatoes with Lemon, Parsley, and Olive Oil

Follow the recipe for Boiled Potatoes with Butter, replacing the butter with 3 tablespoons extra-virgin olive oil. Add the minced zest from 1 lemon and 3 tablespoons chopped fresh parsley leaves along with the salt and pepper in step 3.

Boiled Potatoes with Shallot and Sage

Melt 3 tablespoons unsalted butter in a small skillet over medium-high heat. When the foaming subsides, add 1 medium shallot, minced, and cook until golden, 2 to 3 minutes. Add 1 tablespoon minced fresh sage leaves and cook until fragrant, about 1 minute. Scrape this mixture into a medium serving bowl and proceed with the recipe for Boiled Potatoes with Butter from step 2.

MASHED POTATOES

MOST OF US WHO MAKE MASHED POTATOES would never consider consulting a recipe. We customarily make them by adding chunks of butter and spurts of cream until our conscience—or a back-seat cook—tells us to stop. Not surprisingly, we produce batches of mashed potatoes that are consistent only in their mediocrity.

For us, the consummate mashed potatoes are creamy, soft, and supple, yet with enough body to stand up to the sauce or gravy from an accompanying dish. As for flavor, the sweet, earthy, humble potato comes first, then the buttery richness that keeps you coming back for more. In addition, we wanted to develop mashed potato variations spiked with complementary flavors, such as the garlic mashed potatoes we've eaten in restaurants over the years.

We quickly determined that high-starch potatoes, such as russets, are best for mashing. Next we needed to address the simple matter of the best way to cook the potatoes. We started by peeling and cutting some potatoes into chunks to expedite their cooking while cooking others unpeeled and whole. Even when mashed with identical amounts of butter, half-and-half (recommended by a number of trustworthy cookbooks), and salt, the two

batches were very different. The potatoes that had been peeled and cut made mashed potatoes that were thin in taste and texture and devoid of potato flavor. Peeling and cutting before simmering increases the surface area of the potatoes, through which they lose soluble substances such as starch, proteins, and flavor compounds to the cooking water. The greater surface area also enables lots of water molecules to bind with the potatoes' starch molecules. Combine these two effects and you've got bland, thin, watery mashed potatoes. The potatoes cooked whole and peeled after cooking yielded mashed potatoes that were rich, earthy, and sweet.

Next were the matters of butter and dairy. Working with 2 pounds of potatoes, which serve four to six, we stooped so low as to add only 2 tablespoons of butter. The dish ultimately deemed best in flavor by tasters contained 8 tablespoons. It was rich and full and splendid.

When considering dairy, we investigated both the kind and the quantity. Heavy cream made heavy mashed potatoes that were sodden and unpalatably rich, even when we scaled back the amount of butter. On the other hand, mashed potatoes made with whole milk were watery, wimpy, and washed-out. Half-and-half, which we'd used in our original tests, was just what was needed, and 1 cup was just the right amount. The mashed potatoes now had a lovely, light suppleness and a full, rich flavor that edged toward decadent.

The issues attending butter and dairy did not end there. We had heard that the order in which they are added to the potatoes can affect texture. As it turns out, when the butter goes in before the dairy, the result is a silkier, creamier, smoother texture than when the dairy goes in first; by comparison, the dairy-first potatoes were pasty and thick. Also, using melted rather than softened butter made the potatoes even more creamy, smooth, and light.

When the half-and-half is stirred into the potatoes before the butter, the water in it works with the starch in the potatoes to make the mashed potatoes gluey and heavy. When the butter is added before the half-and-half, the fat coats the starch molecules, inhibiting their interaction with the water in the half-and-half added later and thereby yielding silkier, creamier mashed potatoes. The benefit of using melted butter results from its liquid form, which enables it to coat the starch molecules quickly and easily. This buttery coating not only affects the interaction of the starch molecules with the half-and-half, it also affects the starch molecules' interaction with one another. All in all, it makes for smoother, more velvety mashed potatoes. (Melting the butter, as well as warming the half-and-half, also serves to keep the potatoes warm.)

There is more than one way to mash potatoes. In our testing, we had been using either a ricer or a food mill. We preferred the food mill because its large hopper accommodated half of the potatoes at a time. A ricer, which resembles an oversize garlic press, required processing in several batches. Both, however, produced smooth, light, fine-textured mashed potatoes.

A potato masher is the tool of choice for making chunky mashed potatoes, but it cannot produce smooth mashed potatoes on a par with those processed through a food mill or ricer. With a masher, potatoes mashed within an inch of their lives could not achieve anything better than a namby-pamby texture that was neither chunky nor perfectly smooth. Since the sentiment among our tasters was that mashed potatoes should be either smooth or coarse and craggy, a masher is best left to make the latter.

There are two styles of potato masher—one is a disk with large holes in it, the other a curvy wire loop. We found the disk to be more efficient for reducing both mashing time and the number of lumps in the finished product.

KEEPING SIDE DISHES WARM

AS THANKSGIVING DINNER PROVES YEAR after year, getting several side dishes to the table before they've cooled off can test anyone's holiday spirit. Here are our favorite ways to guarantee a festive (and hot) family meal for Thanksgiving or any other multicourse dinner:

USE YOUR SLOW COOKER OR FONDUE POT

Mashed potatoes seem to cool off faster than anything else you can serve. We like this method for keeping mashed potatoes piping hot. Simply transfer the potatoes to a slow cooker set to low; adjust the consistency with hot cream or milk as needed before serving.

Keep sauces and gravy hot by transferring them to a fondue pot set to low. Other creamy dishes you can keep hot using this method include creamed onions, candied sweet potatoes, and macaroni and cheese. A fondue pot works especially well on a buffet.

USE KITCHEN APPLIANCES TO YOUR ADVANTAGE

If your cooktop has an oven located just underneath, the oven's vents are typically located just behind the back burners. You can make use of the hot air coming out of the oven vent to warm up serving dishes and dinner plates by stacking them on top of one of the back burners. Make sure the burner itself is cold and clean and that the stack of plates is stable.

Warmed serving dishes can keep sides warm for an extra 10 to 20 minutes. Briefly heat your empty serving dishes in a warm oven or the rinse/dry cycle of the dishwasher.

EMPLOY A LOW-TECH HEATING METHOD TO KEEP FOODS CRISP

Fried foods cool off quickly. To make matters worse, the crust, or exterior, becomes soft and soggy the longer the food sits. To keep your favorite fried dishes (like french fries) from losing their crunch, place them on a rack set over a baking sheet and transfer to a warm oven. Your food will stay crisp, without drying out, for 15 to 30 minutes.

PUT FOIL AND GROCERY BAGS TO WORK

Cold dinner rolls are a dinner-party travesty. Wrap dinner rolls, biscuits, or other self-contained foods, such as corn on the cob, in several layers of foil and nestle them in paper grocery bags. Your food will stay hot for up to 30 minutes.

Mashed Potatoes

SERVES 4 TO 6

Russet potatoes make slightly fluffier mashed potatoes, but Yukon Golds have an appealing buttery flavor and can be used if you prefer. Mashed potatoes stiffen and become gluey as they cool, so they are best served piping hot. If you must hold mashed potatoes before serving, place them in a heatproof bowl, cover the bowl tightly with plastic wrap, and set the bowl over a pot of simmering water. Be sure to occasionally check the water level in the pan. The potatoes will remain hot and soft-textured for 1 hour. This recipe can be increased by half or doubled as needed. It yields smooth mashed potatoes. If you don't mind (or prefer) lumps, use a potato masher, as directed in the variation.

2	pounds russet potatoes (about 4 medium), scrubbed
8	tablespoons (1 stick) unsalted butter, melted
1	cup half-and-half, warmed
1½	teaspoons salt
	Ground black pepper

1. Place the potatoes in a large saucepan with cold water to cover by about 1 inch. Bring to a boil over high heat, reduce the heat to medium-low, and simmer until the potatoes are just tender when pricked with a thin-bladed knife, 20 to 30 minutes. Drain the potatoes.

2. Set a food mill or ricer over the now-empty but still-warm saucepan. Following the illustrations at right for using a food mill, spear each potato with a dinner fork, then peel back the skin with a paring knife. Working in batches, cut the peeled potatoes into chunks and drop them into the hopper of a food mill or ricer (see the illustrations at right). Process or rice the potatoes into the saucepan.

3. Stir in the melted butter with a wooden spoon until incorporated. Gently whisk in the half-and-half, salt, and pepper to taste. Serve immediately.

➤ VARIATIONS

Mashed Potatoes with Garlic

The garlic can be peeled after toasting, when the skins will slip right off. Just make sure to keep the heat low and to let the garlic stand off the heat until fully softened.

Toast 20–25 small to medium garlic cloves (about ⅔ cup), skins left on, in a small covered skillet over the lowest possible heat, shaking the pan frequently, until the cloves are spotty dark brown and slightly softened, about 22 minutes. Remove the pan from the heat and let stand, covered, until the cloves are fully softened, 15 to 20 minutes. Peel the cloves and, using a paring knife, cut off the woody root ends. Follow the recipe for Mashed Potatoes; in step 2, drop the peeled garlic cloves into the food mill or ricer with the peeled potatoes and continue as directed.

Mashed Potatoes with Scallions and Horseradish

Follow the recipe for Mashed Potatoes through step 2. Stir the butter into the potatoes until just incorporated. Sprinkle the salt and pepper over

MAKING MASHED POTATOES

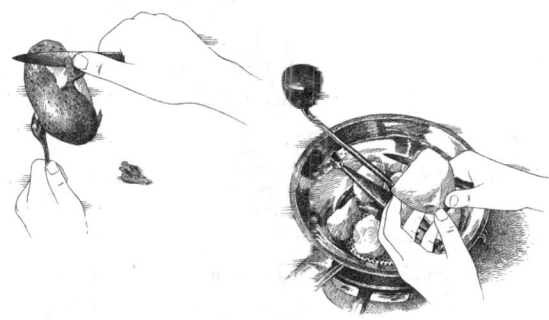

WITH A FOOD MILL

1. Hold the drained potato with a dinner fork and peel off the skin with a paring knife.
2. Cut the peeled potato into rough chunks, and drop the chunks into the food mill.

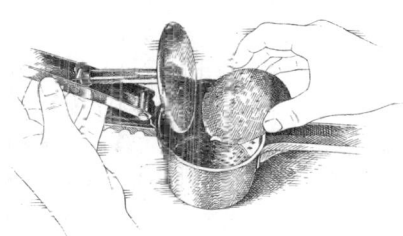

WITH A RICER

Cut each potato in half and place one half cut-side down in the ricer. Press down with the handle of the ricer to force the flesh through the holes. The skin will remain in the hopper. Discard the skin and repeat with the next potato half.

the potatoes. Whisk ¼ cup grated fresh horse-radish and the green parts of 3 scallions, minced, into the warm half-and-half; add the mixture to the mashed potatoes and stir until just combined. Serve immediately.

Mashed Potatoes with Smoked Cheddar and Grainy Mustard

If you can't find smoked cheddar, plain cheddar is good in this dish, too.

Follow the recipe for Mashed Potatoes through step 2. Stir the butter into the potatoes until just incorporated. Sprinkle the salt and pepper over the potatoes; add the warm half-and-half, 2 table-spoons whole-grain mustard, and 3 ounces smoked cheddar cheese, shredded (about 1 cup); stir until just combined. Serve immediately.

Colcannon
SERVES 4 TO 6

Colcannon is a traditional Irish mashed potato dish made with onions and cabbage or kale. Some recipes call for the potatoes and kale to be boiled together, but we found that doing so transferred some of the kale's bitterness to the potatoes.

2½	teaspoons salt
1	pound kale, stemmed, thoroughly washed, and roughly chopped
2	pounds russet potatoes (about 4 medium), scrubbed
9	tablespoons unsalted butter (with 7 tablespoons melted)
1	medium onion, diced

EQUIPMENT: Food Mills

A food mill is no longer a fixture in American kitchens, but it is a terrific tool to have on hand. Think of it as part food processor—because it refines soft foods to a puree—and part sieve—because it separates waste such as peels, seeds, cores, and fiber from the puree. And it accomplishes all of this with the simple turn of a crank, which rotates a gently angled, curved blade. The blade catches the food and forces it down through the holes of a perforated disk at the bottom of the mill. The separation of unwanted material from the puree is the food mill's raison d'être, but another benefit is that it does not aerate the food as it purees, as do food processors and blenders, so you are able to avoid an overly whipped, lightened texture. (In the case of mashed potatoes, a food processor or blender creates a gummy texture.)

Because you can spend as little as $15 and as much as $100 on a food mill (some really huge mills cost as much as $200), we wondered if some were better than others. We gathered five different models and used them to make mashed potatoes and applesauce. Honestly, there was very little difference in the resulting purees—they were all fine, smooth, and free of unwanted material. Thus, we evaluated the mills more on design factors, such as how easy it was to turn the crank, how efficiently the food was processed, and whether the mills offered adjustments in the texture of the puree produced.

The best mills in the group were the beautiful stainless steel Cuisipro, the VEV Vigano, and the white plastic Moulinex. Each one was easy to crank and efficient, and they all came with fine, medium, and coarse disks. The top performer of the three was the Cuisipro, but, at $90, it was also the most expensive. The $15 Moulinex did nearly as well, so it became the pick of the pack for its combination of low price and high performance. The plastic is surely not as strong as the Cuisipro's stainless steel, but for occasional use, it is just fine.

Both the Foley and the Norpro mills were noticeably less efficient; their blades pushed the food around instead of forcing it though the perforated disk. In addition, neither one offered additional disks for different textures. There was just one medium disk, fixed in place.

THE BEST FOOD MILLS

In our test of five food mills, the Cuisipro (left) took top honors. If its $90 price tag seems high for an item that won't see much action in your kitchen, the $15 Moulinex (right) did nearly as well in our tests. The plastic is not as strong as Cuisipro's stainless steel, but for occasional use it works just fine.

1 cup half-and-half, warmed
Ground black pepper

1. Bring 2 quarts water to boil in a large saucepan. Add 1 teaspoon of the salt and the kale, stir, cover, and cook until the greens are just tender, about 6 minutes. Drain the greens and plunge them into a large bowl of cold water to halt the cooking process. Drain the greens again and squeeze them dry. Chop finely and set aside.

2. Meanwhile, place the potatoes in a large saucepan with cold water to cover by about 1 inch. Bring to a boil over high heat, reduce the heat to medium-low, and simmer until the potatoes are just tender when pricked with a thin-bladed knife, 20 to 30 minutes. Drain the potatoes well.

WHAT TO SERVE WITH MEAT LOAF

IT'S NOT DIFFICULT FINDING SIDES that go well with meat loaf, but too often we turn to the same old peas and mashed potatoes. When you're short on ideas, try these dishes:

- Brussels Sprouts Braised in Cream (page 184)
- Glazed Carrots (page 186)
- Steamed Cauliflower with Cheddar-Mustard Cream Sauce (page 192)
- Green Beans Braised with Shiitake Mushrooms (page 212)
- Assertive Greens with Bacon and Onion (page 220)
- Peas with Bacon, Shallot, and Sherry Vinegar (page 224)
- Mashed Potatoes with Smoked Cheddar and Grainy Mustard (facing page)
- Weekday Scalloped Potatoes (page 297)
- Rice Pilaf with Vermicelli (page 307)
- Bulgur and Mushroom Pilaf (page 316)
- Baked Macaroni and Cheese (page 330)
- Savory Noodle Kugel with Caramelized Onions and Cauliflower (page 332)

3. As the potatoes cook, place the 2 tablespoons unmelted butter in a small skillet over medium heat. When the foaming subsides, add the onion and cook, stirring occasionally, until light golden brown, 7 to 10 minutes. Set the onion aside.

4. Set a food mill or ricer over the now-empty but still-warm saucepan. Following the illustrations on page 267 for using a food mill, spear each potato with a dinner fork, then peel back the skin with a paring knife. Working in batches, cut the peeled potatoes into chunks and drop them into the hopper of a food mill or ricer (see the illustrations on page 267). Process or rice the potatoes into the saucepan.

5. Stir in the onions and the 7 tablespoons melted butter with a wooden spoon until incorporated. Gently whisk in the half-and-half, kale, 1½ teaspoons salt, and pepper to taste. Serve immediately.

SMASHED POTATOES

SILKY SMOOTH MASHED POTATOES ARE AT their best when topped with a rich gravy or napped with a highly seasoned pan sauce. Either way, it's a partnership, a question of the whole being greater than the sum of its parts. But there are times when there is no gravy to be had, and that's when smashed potatoes are just the thing. Their bold flavor and rustic, chunky texture give them the brawn to stand on their own, whether served with a grilled steak or a roast chicken.

Unfortunately, most recipes for this dish are plagued by a multitude of variations and refinements. Running the gamut from lean and mean to dangerously close to mashed (no skin, no texture, no oomph), smashed potatoes suffer from an identity crisis. We wanted chunks of potato textured with skins and bound by a rich, creamy puree.

Using the test kitchen's standard add-ins—melted butter and half-and-half—we smashed our way through five different varieties of potato: russet, all-purpose, Yukon Gold, medium-size red, and tiny new potatoes (with red skins).

The russets and all-purpose potatoes had strong potato flavor, but their dry texture caused them to crumble quickly when smashed, and their skins were too thick and tough against the soft, mealy flesh. The texture of the butter-colored Yukon Golds was slightly firmer, but these potatoes were still fluffy enough to break down. The two red varieties fared much better; their compact structure held up well under pressure, maintaining its integrity. The thin skins were pleasantly tender and paired nicely with the chunky potatoes. Clearly, this dish was meant for moist, low-starch potatoes. But because the tiny new potatoes had too high a ratio of skin to flesh, the medium-size red won out.

We cooked the red potatoes both whole and cut into 1-inch chunks. Even though cutting the potatoes reduced the cooking time, the end result was leaden, soggy smashed potatoes with diluted potato flavor. Cooked whole, the potatoes retained their naturally creamy texture, as less potato surface was exposed to the water. We cooked the unpeeled potatoes in plain water and in salted water. The salted water outdid the plain water, penetrating the skins and heightening the potato flavor. Next we added garlic and herbs (fresh rosemary and thyme, dried bay leaves) to the cooking water, but the garlic flavor was just too strong, so we reserved it for a recipe variation. As for the herbs, the bay leaf imparted the most complementary flavor, adding depth.

While a potato masher and fork are good tools for making chunky mashed potatoes, they took the smashed potatoes a little too far, smoothing out the rough, uneven chunks of potato that define this dish. We took a cue from the recipe name, grabbed a plain old wooden spoon, and began smashing each potato with the back of it. If they were cooked just right, they burst apart, splitting the skins when they broke. This was even easier once the potatoes had dried for a few minutes so that their skins were no longer slippery. Then, making the spoon serve double duty, we used it to stir in the remaining ingredients. In fact, this technique was so simple that it even worked with a stiff rubber spatula, a better tool for folding in ingredients.

With the key ingredient and basic technique settled, we turned to the other component that would make these potatoes really stand out: the dairy. Using only butter and half-and-half with the mildly flavored red potatoes resulted in flat-tasting smashed potatoes. To boost the flavor, we tried sour cream, trusted partner of the baked potato. Sour cream alone didn't give the potatoes enough body, so we tried supplementing it with both half-and-half and heavy cream. Both of these additions served only to dull the acidity of the sour cream. A fellow test cook then suggested the rather unconventional cream cheese. Surprisingly, ½ cup of cream cheese—and no sour cream—gave these savory potatoes just the right touch of tang and creaminess. All they needed now was some butter to add richness, and 4 tablespoons was just the right amount for a deeper flavor without greasiness.

Then, as happens often in recipe development, we were confronted with a last-minute surprise. After our sensational smashed potatoes sat in the pot for a few minutes, their luscious texture went from creamy and smooth to dry and unpalatable. The potatoes had quickly absorbed what little moisture the butter and cream cheese had to offer. Not wanting to make the potatoes any richer, we tried a little milk and then chicken broth to moisten the potatoes. Both improved the texture, but they also diluted the potato flavor. Then we thought of a technique the test kitchen favors when making thick pasta sauces: Some of the water used to cook the pasta is reserved, and, if the sauce becomes too thick, the pasta water is added until the desired consistency is achieved. We applied this concept to the thick smashed potatoes, using the potato cooking water (nicely seasoned with salt and bay leaf and thickened with potato starch). We started with ¼ cup and added more as needed until we had a unified and creamy consistency. Just thick enough to be scooped up with a fork, these potatoes were thinner in terms of texture but not flavor.

To finish seasoning the potatoes, we added a little more salt and a dash of ground black pepper. Tasters thought something green and fresh would be nice, so we tried parsley, scallions, and chives.

The parsley was a bit dull and the scallions were too oniony, but the sprinkling of chopped fresh chives brightened the flavor just enough.

Smashed Potatoes

SERVES 4 TO 6

White potatoes can be used instead of red, but their skins lack the pleasing rosy color of red skins. Try to get potatoes of equal size; if that's not possible, test the larger potatoes for doneness. If only larger potatoes are available, increase the cooking time by about 10 minutes. Check for doneness with a paring knife.

2   pounds red potatoes (about 16 small to medium; 2 inches in diameter), scrubbed
     Salt
1   bay leaf
4   tablespoons (½ stick) unsalted butter, melted and warm
½   cup cream cheese (4 ounces), room temperature
     Ground black pepper
3   tablespoons chopped fresh chives (optional)

1. Place the potatoes in a large saucepan and cover with 1 inch cold water; add 1 teaspoon salt and the bay leaf. Bring to a boil over high heat, then reduce the heat to medium-low and simmer gently until a paring knife can be inserted into the potatoes with no resistance, 35 to 45 minutes. Reserve ½ cup cooking water, then drain the potatoes. Return the potatoes to the pot, discard the bay leaf, and allow the potatoes to stand in the pot, uncovered, until the surfaces are dry, about 5 minutes.

2. While the potatoes dry, whisk the melted butter and softened cream cheese in a medium bowl until smooth and fully incorporated. Add ¼ cup of the reserved cooking water, ½ teaspoon pepper, the chives (if using), and ½ teaspoon salt. Using a rubber spatula or the back of a wooden spoon, smash the potatoes just enough to break the skins. Fold in the butter–cream cheese mixture until most of the liquid has been absorbed and chunks of potatoes remain. Add more cooking water 1 tablespoon at a time as needed, until the potatoes are slightly looser than desired (the potatoes will thicken slightly with standing). Adjust the seasonings with salt and pepper; serve immediately.

VARIATIONS
Smashed Potatoes with Bacon and Parsley

Halve 6 slices of bacon lengthwise, then cut them crosswise into ¼-inch pieces. Fry the bacon in a medium skillet over medium heat until crisp and browned, about 8 minutes. Using a slotted spoon, transfer the bacon to a paper towel–lined plate; reserve 1 tablespoon bacon fat. Follow the recipe for Smashed Potatoes, substituting 1 tablespoon bacon fat for an equal amount of butter, substituting 2 tablespoons chopped fresh parsley leaves for the chives, and reducing the salt added to the cream cheese mixture to ¼ teaspoon. Sprinkle individual servings with a portion of the fried bacon.

SCIENCE: Starch in Potatoes

Potatoes are composed mostly of starch and water. The starch is in the form of granules, which in turn are contained in starch cells. The higher the starch content of the potato, the more packed the cells. In high-starch potatoes (russets are a good example), the cells are completely full—they look like plump little beach balls. In medium-starch (Yukon Golds) and low-starch (red) potatoes, the cells look more like underinflated beach balls. The spaces between these less-than-full cells is taken up mostly by water.

In our tests, we found that the starch-packed cells of high-starch potatoes are most likely to maintain their integrity and stay separate when mashed, giving the potatoes a delightfully fluffy texture. In addition, the low water content of these potatoes allows them to absorb milk, cream, and/or butter without becoming wet or gummy. Starch cells in lower-starch potatoes tend to clump when cooked and break more easily, allowing the starch to dissolve into whatever liquid is present. The broken cells and dissolved starch tend to produce sticky, gummy mashed potatoes.

The high moisture content of red potatoes makes them an excellent choice for dishes such as potato salad, however, where you want the potatoes to hold their shape. Because they contain a fair amount of moisture, they don't absorb much water as they boil. In contrast, low-moisture russets suck up water when boiled and fall apart. The resulting potato salad tastes starchy and looks sloppy.

Garlic-Rosemary Smashed Potatoes

Heat the butter in a small skillet over medium heat; when the foaming subsides, add ½ teaspoon chopped fresh rosemary and 1 medium garlic clove, minced or pressed through a garlic press. Cook until just fragrant, about 30 seconds; set the skillet aside. Follow the recipe for Smashed Potatoes, adding 2 medium peeled garlic cloves to the potatoes in the saucepan along with the salt and bay leaf; substitute the butter-garlic mixture for the melted butter, add the whole cooked garlic cloves to the cream cheese along with the butter mixture, and omit the chives.

BAKED POTATOES

IN THE WORLD OF JUNE CLEAVER, POTATOES were baked at 350 degrees because they were put into the oven along with the roast, which cooked at 350 degrees. The world has changed a lot since Wally and Beav sat down to dinner. We wondered if there was a quicker or better route to perfect baked potatoes.

We baked all-purpose potatoes, Yukon Golds, and russets. We tried baking them poked and unpoked, greased and ungreased, with ends dipped in salt, microwaved all the way, microwaved and finished in the oven, baked with gadgets that are supposed to decrease cooking time, and baked at various temperatures. And, against the wishes of all the potato experts we spoke with, we also tried baking them in foil.

After all this experimentation, we discovered that the traditional slow-baking method is best, mainly because of the effect it had on the skin. The skin of a potato baked at 350 degrees for an hour and 15 minutes simply has no peer. Just under the skin, a well-baked potato will develop a substantial brown layer. This is because the dark skin absorbs heat during cooking, and the starch just inside the skin is broken down into sugar and starts to brown. If you love baked potato skin, this is the best method.

Potatoes cooked at 400 and 450 degrees will indeed cook faster—at 450 degrees they may even cook in 45 minutes—but because they cook for a shorter time, the inner browned layer isn't as even or as flavorful as it is with the slower roast method. In addition, the skin isn't quite as thick and chewy. Cooked long enough to develop chewy skin at these higher temperatures, the inner, browned layer becomes thick and unpleasant and somewhat overbrowned.

We also tried starting potatoes at 500 degrees for 10 minutes and then lowering the oven to 350 degrees, but this method also failed to promote even browning. The microwave does a decent job of shortening the overall cooking time and yields decent flesh. What's missing is the delicious browned layer under the skin and the chewy, dry skin that skin lovers covet. We found that cooking the potatoes for half the recommended microwave time and then finishing them in a 450-degree oven produced fluffy, dry flesh, some browning, and pretty good skin. If you're in a hurry, this half-and-half method works best.

As for some of our more unusual tests: Oiling the skin caused the potatoes to cook somewhat more quickly and made the skin crispier—something that some tasters liked but was not what most considered ideal for a basic baked potato (we felt differently when it came to our Twice-Baked Potatoes recipe, on page 275). We found that the expensive metal pokers that you stick into potatoes to decrease cooking time did not seem to have that effect. Another tip that's supposed to shorten the cooking time—cutting off the ends of

SCRUBBING POTATOES

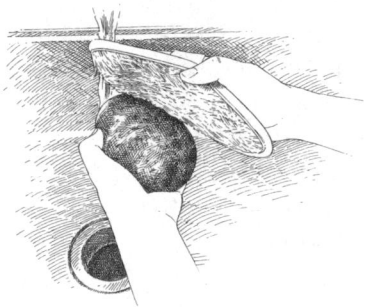

Buy a rough-textured bathing or exfoliating bath glove especially for use in the kitchen. The glove cleans dirt away from potatoes and other root vegetables, but it's relatively gentle and won't scrub away the skin.

the potatoes and dipping them in salt—made for crusty, salty ends but didn't measurably alter baking time. Finally, poking the potato before baking did not noticeably affect the amount of moisture retained after baking. The flesh of a potato that had not been poked was just as dry as one that had. However, it is a good idea to poke a hole or two in any potato you are going to microwave; unpoked potatoes can explode when microwaved.

If slow baking is essential to good skin, the consistency of the flesh also requires some attention. Letting the potato sit awhile after baking without opening it up will steam the potato and cause the flesh to become more dense. For fluffy potatoes, it's best to create a wide opening as soon as the potatoes come out of the oven to let the steam escape.

And what about foil-wrapped potatoes? They are a notion perpetuated by mediocre steakhouses that want to keep potatoes warm indefinitely. Foil

is an insult to potatoes—it holds the steam in, making for limp, damp skin and dense flesh.

Baked Potatoes
SERVES 4

We found neither benefit nor harm in poking the potatoes with the tines of a fork before putting them in the oven. Do use a fork to open the skins as soon as the potatoes come out of the oven.

> 4   **medium russet potatoes**
>   **(7 to 8 ounces each), scrubbed**
>   **Unsalted butter**
>   **Salt**

Adjust an oven rack to the middle position and heat the oven to 350 degrees. Place the potatoes directly on the rack and bake for 1¼ hours. Remove the potatoes from the oven and pierce them with a fork to create a dotted X on the top of each potato (see illustration 1 at left). Press in at the ends of each potato to push the flesh up and out (see illustration 2 at left). Serve immediately with butter and salt.

➤ VARIATION
Faster Baked Potatoes

This half-and-half method (which takes 35 minutes, start to finish) produces far superior results than straight microwaving. By the time you have scrubbed and micro-waved the potatoes, the oven will be preheated. To cook fewer potatoes by this method, plan on 2 minutes total cooking time in the microwave for each potato.

> 4   **medium russet potatoes**
>   **(7 to 8 ounces each), scrubbed**
>   **Unsalted butter**
>   **Salt**

1. Adjust an oven rack to the middle position and heat the oven to 450 degrees.

2. Use a fork to poke a few holes in each potato. Microwave the potatoes on high power for 4 minutes. Turn the potatoes over and microwave them on high power for another 4 minutes.

3. Transfer the potatoes to the hot oven and

OPENING A BAKED POTATO

To ensure that the flesh does not steam and become dense, it's best to open a baked potato as soon as it comes out of the oven. This technique maximizes the amount of steam released and keeps the potato fluffy and light; it also helps to trap and melt the butter.

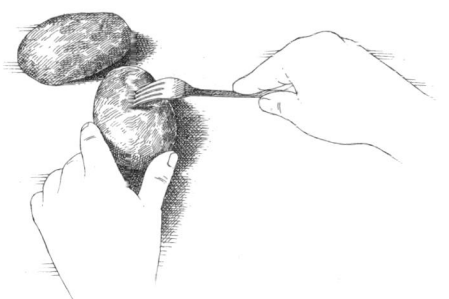

1. Use the tines of a fork to make a dotted X on the top of each potato.

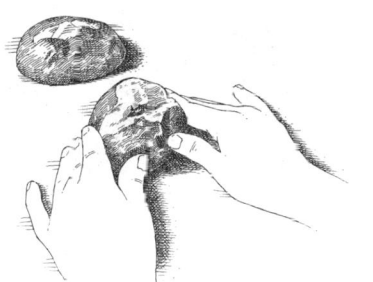

2. Press in at the ends of the potato to push the flesh up and out.

Twice-Baked Potatoes with Indian Spices and Peas

Heat the 2 tablespoons unsalted butter in a medium skillet over medium heat. Add 1 medium onion, chopped fine, and cook until soft, 3 to 4 minutes. Add 1 teaspoon finely grated ginger, 3 medium garlic cloves, minced, 1 teaspoon each ground cumin and ground coriander, and ¼ teaspoon each ground cinnamon, ground turmeric, and ground cloves; cook until fragrant, about 30 seconds more, taking care not to brown the garlic or ginger. Off the heat, stir in 1 cup thawed frozen peas; set aside. Follow the recipe for Twice-Baked Potatoes, omitting the cheese and stirring the spiced peas into the filling mixture in step 2. Proceed as directed.

ROASTED POTATOES

THE PERFECT ROASTED POTATO IS CRISP AND deep golden brown on the outside, with moist, velvety, dense interior flesh. The potato's slightly bitter skin is intact, providing a contrast to the sweet, caramelized flavor that the flesh develops during the roasting process. It is rich but never greasy, and it is accompanied by the heady taste of garlic and herbs.

To start, we roasted several kinds of potatoes. We liked high-starch/low-moisture potatoes (we used russets) the least. They did not brown well, their dry, fluffy texture was more like that of baked potatoes, and their flavor seemed raw. The medium-starch all-purpose potatoes (we used Yukon Golds) produced a beautiful golden crust, but the interior flesh was still rather dry. The best roasting potatoes came from the low-starch/high-moisture category (we used red). These potatoes emerged from the oven with a light, delicate crust and a moist, dense interior that had a more complex, nutty flavor than the others, with hints of bitterness and tang.

After choosing the red potatoes, we began to test oven temperatures. At 425 degrees, the result was an even-colored, golden brown potato with a thin, crisp crust and an interior that was soft and dense, although still slightly dry.

During our research, we came across some recipes that called for parboiling the potatoes before roasting them. Hoping that this approach would produce a texturally superior potato that retained more of its moisture after cooking, we tried boiling the potatoes for seven minutes prior to roasting. This produced a potato closer to our ideal, but preparation required considerable (that is, too much) time owing to the additional step.

We then tried covering the potatoes for a portion of their roasting time. We were especially drawn to this technique because it allowed the potatoes to steam in their own moisture with little extra effort on the part of the cook. The results were perfect. The crisp, deep golden brown crust was perfectly balanced by a creamy, moist interior. These potatoes had a sweet and nutty caramelized flavor, with just a hint of tang from the skin. This simplest of methods produced the very best roasted potatoes.

The next step in the process was figuring out how to add garlic flavor, which makes a good variation on the standard roasted potatoes. If we added minced garlic during the last five minutes of cooking, it burned almost instantly; coating the potatoes with garlic-infused oil failed to produce the strong garlic flavor that we were after; and roasting whole, unpeeled garlic cloves alongside the potatoes and squeezing the pulp out afterward to add to the potatoes was too tedious. The best method turned out to be both simple and flavorful: Mash raw garlic into a paste, place it in a large stainless steel bowl, put the hot roasted potatoes

FLIPPING ROASTED POTATOES

Press the metal spatula against the roasting pan as you slide it under the potatoes to protect the crisp crust. Flip the potatoes so that the other cut sides come into contact with the hot pan.

in the bowl, and toss. This method yields potatoes that have a strong garlic flavor without the raw spiciness of uncooked garlic.

Roasted Potatoes

SERVES 4

To roast more than 2 pounds of potatoes at once, use a second pan rather than crowding the first. If your potatoes are small (as are new potatoes), cut them into halves instead of wedges and turn them cut-side up during the final 10 minutes of roasting.

2   pounds red or other low-starch potatoes
(4 to 6 medium), scrubbed, halved, and cut
into 3/4-inch wedges
3   tablespoons extra-virgin olive oil
Salt and ground black pepper

1. Adjust an oven rack to the middle position and heat the oven to 425 degrees. Toss the potatoes and oil in a medium bowl to coat; season generously with salt and pepper and toss again.

2. Place the potatoes flesh-side down in a single layer in a shallow roasting pan. Cover tightly with aluminum foil and cook for 20 minutes. Remove the foil and roast until the side of the potato touching the pan is crusty and golden brown, about 15 minutes more. Remove the pan from the oven and, with a metal spatula, carefully turn the potatoes. (Press the spatula against the pan as it slides under the potatoes to protect the crusts; see the illustration on the facing page.) Return the pan to the oven and roast until the side of the potato now touching the pan is crusty and golden brown and the skins have raisinlike wrinkles, 5 to 10 minutes more. Transfer the potatoes to a serving dish (again, using a metal spatula and taking care not to rip the crusts) and serve hot or warm.

➤ VARIATIONS
Roasted Potatoes with Garlic and Rosemary

Thyme or oregano can be substituted for the rosemary.

Follow the recipe for Roasted Potatoes. While the potatoes roast, mince 2 medium garlic cloves with 1/8 teaspoon salt with the flat side of a chef's

knife blade until a paste forms. Transfer the garlic paste to a large bowl; set aside. In the last 3 minutes of roasting time, sprinkle 2 tablespoons chopped fresh rosemary evenly over the potatoes. Immediately transfer the finished potatoes to the bowl with the garlic, toss, and serve warm.

Roasted Potatoes with Lemon-Chive Butter

Lemon and chives are a classic combination. Chives should be added at the end of cooking to preserve their delicate flavor.

Follow the recipe for Roasted Potatoes. While the potatoes roast, combine 2 tablespoons unsalted butter, melted, 1 tablespoon minced fresh chives, 1 teaspoon grated lemon zest, and 2 tablespoons lemon juice in a large bowl. Transfer the roasted potatoes to the bowl with the lemon-chive butter, toss, and serve immediately.

Roasted Potatoes with Southwestern Spices

Serve these potatoes with barbecued ribs and grilled corn.

Follow the recipe for Roasted Potatoes. While the potatoes roast, melt 2 tablespoons unsalted butter in a small skillet over medium heat. When the butter starts to sizzle, add 1 teaspoon ground cumin, 1 teaspoon chili powder, 1 teaspoon dry mustard, 1/8 teaspoon cayenne pepper, and 1 medium garlic clove, minced, and cook until fragrant, 30 seconds to 1 minute. Transfer the roasted potatoes to a serving bowl. Pour the spiced butter over the potatoes, toss, and serve immediately.

GREEK-STYLE POTATOES

AS SURE AS YOU'LL FIND A HUGE PICTURE of the Parthenon on the wall at your local Greek diner, you'll also find Greek-style lemon-garlic potatoes on the menu. Often cut in small cubes and either baked in the oven or sautéed on a huge griddle, these popular potatoes are at once tangy with lemon, sharp with garlic, and earthy with oregano. Served alongside every meal from breakfast through dinner, they can accompany an omelet or a simple roast chicken with authority.

Done well, the potatoes are crusty, well browned, and accented by a full (but not overpowering) lemon flavor and plenty of garlic bite. If things go wrong, though, they turn out soggy and sour.

Most of the recipes we found revealed that the standard home-cooking technique for Greek potatoes is to cube raw potatoes, toss them in a baking dish with a mixture of lemon juice, garlic, oregano, and oil, add a little water, and then bake them until the water has evaporated and the potatoes have absorbed the flavors of the seasoning mixture. A number of recipes demanded what seemed to us an unreasonably long baking time of 90 minutes as well as constant monitoring and stirring of the potatoes near the end of cooking. As we discovered when we made the potatoes according to this traditional method, they didn't turn out even close to perfect anyway. The texture was downright soggy, and most tasters felt that the lemon flavor was harsh and acidic. Worse yet was the total absence of the crisp, browned crust we wanted on the potatoes. We decided our first task would be reducing the cooking time.

POTATOES DONE RIGHT

Don't cut the potatoes into haphazardly shaped pieces or crowd the pan (top). For even cooking and proper browning, the potatoes should be sliced evenly and cooked in a single layer (bottom).

More research turned up two possible solutions: oven roasting without the seasonings and stovetop cooking in a skillet. Oven-roasting the potatoes and then adding a lemon-garlic-herb mixture when they emerged from the oven made for a huge improvement. These simple steps cut the cooking time in half, to 45 minutes, while also producing a flavorful, caramelized crust. The results we got from the skillet method were even better. With the intense heat of the hot pan over a medium-high flame, the potatoes developed a gorgeous, flavorful, mahogany brown crust in just 11 minutes. Although perfect on the outside, the potatoes were not completely cooked on the inside. After a number of tests, we found that simply covering the skillet and allowing the browned potatoes to cook for an additional six minutes gave them a tender and velvety interior. Now we had cut the time down from 90 minutes to less than 20, and the results were crisp and flavorful rather than soggy and acidic.

We tested different skillets and found that a heavy-bottomed, 12-inch nonstick model was best suited to the task. The heavy construction translates into even heat distribution, which reduces the risk of burning and maximizes browning. And don't skimp on size: The large diameter provides enough space to arrange the potatoes in a single layer for optimal browning (if cramped, the potatoes will steam rather than brown). However, while the nonstick finish made cleanup a breeze, it is not essential. We successfully cooked the potatoes in a conventional pan (without a nonstick coating), but the pan required a fair amount of elbow grease to clean. In the course of testing, we learned to use only four potatoes, so as not to compromise the browning by crowding the pan, and to make sure the potatoes were evenly sized, so all the pieces would cook at the same rate.

In terms of the cooking medium, we liked the flavor of extra-virgin olive oil, but using it over high heat destroyed its delicate fruitiness. Next we tried pure olive oil and then vegetable oil, and tasters found the flavor differences to be minimal (we chose vegetable oil because it is a pantry staple). Some butter was necessary to boost the flavor of the oil. Finally, because we wanted the flavor of extra-virgin olive oil, we decided to add some to the cooked potatoes along with the seasonings.

We were surprised that few recipes specified the type of potato to use. Surely there would be differences among high-starch/low-moisture potatoes such as russets (commonly used for baking), medium-starch potatoes such as all-purpose or Yukon Gold, and low-starch/high-moisture potatoes such as red, which are often used for roasting and boiling. After testing representatives from the three categories, our tasters consistently favored Yukon Golds for their appealing blend of smooth, velvety texture, rich yellow hue, and buttery flavor. Red potatoes took a close second for their supple, creamy texture. Russets were rejected because the pieces broke apart easily and were mealy. With regard to preparing the Yukon Golds, tasters preferred peeled potatoes cut into wedges ¾ inch thick as opposed to thicker wedges, slices, or cubes.

Lemon, garlic, and oregano give this dish its character. Most of the recipes we consulted called for lemon juice, some as little as 2 tablespoons and others as much as ½ cup. Throughout our tests, tasters agreed that potatoes flavored with lemon juice alone tasted sharp, shallow, and acidic. So we tried adding some grated lemon zest to impart a deeper lemon flavor. Indeed it did; tasters responded well to batches made with a full tablespoon of grated zest per 2 pounds of potatoes, along with a modest 2 tablespoons of juice for brightness and moderate acidity.

Garlic is another key flavoring. At first we thought that raw garlic might have too much bite for the dish, but tasters dismissed our attempts to tame the garlic flavor by toasting the whole cloves or cooking the minced garlic in oil until it was sweet and mellow. Judging the flavor of these batches too "docile" and "wimpy," they agreed that raw garlic was the way to go. One clove, two cloves, and even three cloves were deemed too weak. We were shocked when tasters chose the batch of potatoes with four cloves of minced raw garlic, describing it as "bright, fresh, and gutsy." Last, we replaced the dusty-tasting dried oregano used in so many recipes with fresh, and all the tasters approved.

The only thing left to determine was the optimum amount of time for the potatoes and seasonings to get acquainted. Testing showed that adding the lemon, garlic, and herbs to the pan midway through the potatoes' cooking time (or any earlier) not only diminished their flavor but also increased the risk of burning the garlic. Instead, we mixed the seasonings into the potatoes once they were fully cooked, which provided the strong hits of flavor that our tasters demanded.

Now that these classic potatoes are so quick and easy to make, chances are you can get them on the table at home in less time than it would take you to drive to the nearest diner. Even better, the technique of sautéing potato wedges in a skillet can be used with almost any kind of seasonings—even something you might never see in a diner.

~

Greek-Style Potatoes
SERVES 4

This recipe could really be called Skillet Potatoes because that's the technique employed. Although garlic, lemon, and oregano are traditional Greek flavors, other combinations are possible, as demonstrated in the variations. If your potatoes are larger than the size we recommend, you may have to increase the covered cooking time by up to 4 minutes. While a nonstick pan makes cleanup easier, it is not essential.

I	tablespoon vegetable oil
I	tablespoon unsalted butter
2	pounds Yukon Gold potatoes (about 4 medium), scrubbed, peeled, and cut lengthwise into 8 wedges (see the illustration on page 280)
4	medium garlic cloves, minced or pressed through a garlic press (about I heaping tablespoon)
I	tablespoon extra-virgin olive oil
I	tablespoon grated zest and 2 tablespoons juice from I lemon
2	tablespoons minced fresh oregano leaves
I	teaspoon salt
½	teaspoon ground black pepper
2	tablespoons minced fresh parsley leaves

1. Heat the vegetable oil and butter in a heavy-bottomed 12-inch nonstick skillet over medium-high heat until the butter melts and the foaming subsides, swirling the pan occasionally. Add the potatoes cut-side down in a single layer and cook until golden brown (the pan should sizzle but not smoke), about 6 minutes. Using tongs, turn the potatoes so the second cut side is down. Cook until deep golden brown on the second side, about 5 minutes longer. Reduce the heat to medium-low, cover tightly, and cook until the potatoes are tender when pierced with the tip of a paring knife, about 6 minutes.

2. While the potatoes cook, combine the garlic, olive oil, lemon zest and juice, and oregano in a small bowl. When the potatoes are tender, add the garlic-lemon mixture, salt, and pepper. Stir carefully (so as not to break potato wedges) to distribute. Cook, uncovered, until the seasoning mixture is heated through and fragrant, 1 to 2 minutes. Sprinkle the potatoes with the parsley and stir gently to distribute it. Serve immediately.

➤ VARIATIONS

Greek-Style Potatoes with Olives and Feta

Follow the recipe for Greek-Style Potatoes, adding 3 ounces crumbled feta cheese (about ¾ cup) and 8 kalamata (or other black, brine-cured) olives, pitted and sliced (about ¼ cup), along with the parsley.

CUTTING POTATO WEDGES

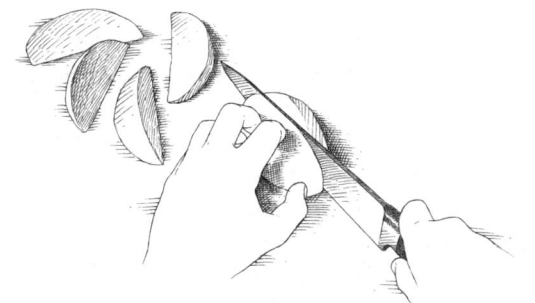

Halve the potato lengthwise and, holding the knife perpendicular to the board, cut each half in half lengthwise to make quarters. Holding the knife at 45 degrees to the board, cut each quarter in half lengthwise, dividing the potato into a total of eight equal-size wedges.

Greek-Style Potatoes with Spinach and Anchovies

If you don't like anchovies, this dish can be made without them.

Follow the recipe for Greek-Style Potatoes, adding 1 teaspoon minced anchovies (about 3 fillets) to the garlic-lemon mixture. Stir the mixture into the potatoes, then add 2½ ounces baby spinach leaves (about 3 cups), and gently stir the mixture again to distribute. Omit the parsley.

Spicy Greek-Style Potatoes

In keeping with the bold flavors of the dish, this variation is very spicy.

Follow the recipe for Greek-Style Potatoes, adding 2 small jalapeño chiles, cut into ¼-inch slices (with seeds and membranes), to the pan just before covering the skillet in step 1.

Greek-Style Garlic-Lemon Potatoes with Sun-Dried Tomatoes and Scallions

Follow the recipe for Greek-Style Potatoes, adding 1 ounce oil-packed sun-dried tomatoes, sliced (about ¼ cup), and 2 medium scallions, sliced (about ¼ cup), to the garlic-lemon mixture.

FRENCH FRIES

THE IDEAL FRENCH FRY HAS A DEFINITE crunch on the outside and is cooked to tender perfection on the inside. It should taste of earthy potato, with just a hint of the oil in which it was cooked. A french fry should definitely not droop—it should be long, but with crisply defined, right-angled edges—and its coloring should be two-toned, golden brown with hints of true brown.

We chose starchy russets for our fries. This potato was ideal, frying up with all the qualities that we were looking for. Because these are starchy potatoes, it is important to rinse the starch off the surface after cutting each potato into fries. To do this, simply put the cut fries in a bowl, place the bowl in the sink, and run cold water into it, swirling with your fingers until the water runs clear. This might seem like an unimportant step, but it makes a real difference.

When we skipped the starch rinse, the fries weren't quite right, and the oil clouded.

At this point, you take the second crucial step: Fill the bowl with clear water, add ice, and refrigerate the potatoes for at least 30 minutes. That way, when the potatoes first enter the hot oil, they are nearly frozen; this allows a slow, thorough cooking of the inner potato pulp. When we tried making fries without this chilling, the outsides started to brown well before the insides were fully cooked.

Our preference is to peel potatoes for french fries. A skin-on fry keeps the potato from forming those little airy blisters that we like. Peeling the potato also allows home cooks to see—and remove, if they want to—any imperfections and greenish coloring.

What is the best cooking medium for french fries? To find out, we experimented with lard, vegetable shortening, canola oil, corn oil, and peanut oil. Tasters agreed that lard made the best-tasting fry. But how could we propose cooking with something most cooks don't have at home? To keep in step with the times, we put the other fats through their paces to see if there was an adequate substitute for the lard. Vegetable-shortening fries rivaled the lard fries, providing an exquisite flavor balance between oil and potato. But many cooks are worried about their health and don't like to use vegetable shortening. We moved on to canola oil but were unhappy with the results: bland, almost watery fries, with little texture.

Our next try, corn oil, was the most forgiving oil in the test kitchen. It rebounded well to temperature fluctuations and the fries tasted great. We felt we were getting close to finding an oil that really worked. Fries cooked in peanut oil had the earthy flavor of the potato—as they did in the corn oil—but it wasn't overbearing. We were now very close, but there was still something missing. The high flavor note, which is supplied by the animal fat in lard, was lacking.

We tried a dollop of strained bacon grease in peanut oil, about 2 generous tablespoons per quart of oil. The meaty flavor came through, but not overwhelmingly so. To be certain of this, we added bacon grease to each of the oils, with these results: canola oil, extra body, but still short on flavor; corn oil, more body, more flavor, nearly perfect; peanut oil, flavor, bite, and body. At last, an equivalent to lard.

Now it was time to get down to the frying, which actually means double-frying. First, we par-fried the potatoes at a relatively low temperature to release their rich and earthy flavor. Then we quick-fried them at a higher temperature until they were nicely browned.

The garden-variety cookbook recipe calls for par-frying at 350 degrees and final frying at 375 to 400 degrees. But we found these temperatures to

CUTTING POTATOES FOR FRYING

REGULAR FRIES

Slice the peeled potatoes lengthwise into ovals about ¼ inch thick. Stack several ovals on top of each other and slice them into ¼-inch-thick lengths.

STEAK FRIES

1. Cut each potato in half lengthwise. Place the potato half flat-side down and cut into thirds lengthwise.

2. Cut each piece of potato in half lengthwise to yield 2 wedges that measure about ¾ inch across on the skin side.

be far too aggressive. We prefer an initial frying at 325 degrees, with the final frying at 350 degrees. Lower temperatures allowed for easier monitoring; with higher temperatures, the fries can get away from the cook.

For the sake of convenience, we also attempted a single, longer frying. Like many cooks before us, we found that with standard french fries (as opposed to the much thinner shoestring fries), we could not both sear the outside and properly cook the inside with a single visit to the hot fat. When we left them in long enough to sear the outside, we wound up with wooden, overcooked fries.

French Fries

SERVES 4

For those who like it, flavoring the oil with a few table-spoons of bacon grease adds a subtle, meaty flavor to the fries. Their texture, however, is not affected if the bacon grease is omitted. See the illustrations on page 281 for tips on cutting the potatoes.

2½	pounds russet potatoes (about 4 large), scrubbed, peeled, and cut into lengths ¼ inch thick
2	quarts peanut oil
¼	cup strained bacon grease (optional)
	Salt and ground black pepper

1. Rinse the cut fries in a large bowl under cold running water until the water turns from milky colored to clear. Cover with at least 1 inch water, then cover with ice. Refrigerate at least 30 minutes and up to 1 day.

2. In a 5-quart pot or Dutch oven fitted with a clip-on candy thermometer, or in a larger electric fryer, heat the oil over medium-low heat to 325 degrees. As the oil heats, add the bacon grease, if using. (The oil will bubble up when you add the fries, so be sure you have at least 3 inches of room at the top of the pot.)

3. Pour off the ice and water, quickly wrap the potatoes in a clean kitchen towel, and pat them thoroughly dry. Increase the heat to medium-high and add the fries, a handful at a time, to the hot oil. Fry, stirring with a Chinese skimmer or large-hole slotted

spoon, until the potatoes are limp and soft and start to turn from white to blond, 6 to 8 minutes. (The oil temperature will drop 50 to 60 degrees during this frying.) Use the skimmer or slotted spoon to transfer the fries to a triple thickness of paper towels to drain; let rest at least 10 minutes. (The fries can stand at room temperature for up to 2 hours or be wrapped in paper towels, sealed in a zipper-lock bag, and frozen for up to 1 month.)

4. When ready to serve the fries, reheat the oil to 350 degrees. Using a paper bag as a funnel, pour the potatoes into the hot oil. Fry the potatoes, stirring fairly constantly, until golden brown and puffed, about 1 minute. Transfer the fries to another triple thickness of paper towels and drain again. Season with salt and pepper to taste. Serve immediately.

➤ VARIATION

Spicy Fries

Combine 1 teaspoon chili powder, 1 teaspoon paprika, ½ teaspoon ground cumin, and ⅛ to ¼ teaspoon cayenne pepper in a small bowl. Follow the recipe for French Fries, using this mixture in place of the black pepper (and with the salt) in step 4.

DISPOSING OF OIL NEATLY

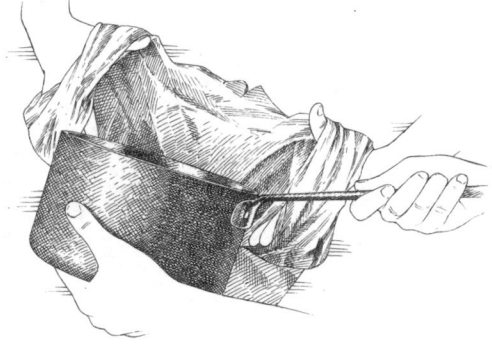

Deep-fried foods, such as french fries, are a real treat, but cleaning up after frying is not. Disposing of the spent oil neatly and safely is a particular challenge. Here's how we do it. First we allow the oil to cool completely. Then we make a quadruple- or quintuple-layered bag using four or five leftover plastic grocery bags. With someone holding the layered bags open over a sink or in an outdoor area, we carefully pour the cooled frying oil from the pot into the innermost bag. We tie the bag handles shut and dispose of the oil in the garbage.

EQUIPMENT: Chef's Knives

A good chef's knife is probably the most useful tool any cook owns. Besides chopping vegetables, it can be used for myriad tasks, including cutting up poultry, mincing herbs, and slicing fruit. So what separates a good knife from an inferior one? To understand the answer to this question, it helps to know something about how knives are constructed.

The first pieces of cutlery were made about 4,000 years ago with the discovery that iron ore could be melted and shaped into tools. The creation of steel, which is 80 percent iron and 20 percent other elements, led to the development of carbon steel knives, which were the standard for 3,000 years. Although this kind of steel takes and holds an edge easily, it also stains and rusts. Something as simple as cutting an acidic tomato or exposing the knife to the salt air of the seacoast can corrode carbon steel.

Today, new alloys have given cooks better options. Stainless steel, made with at least 4 percent chromium and/or nickel, will never rust. Used for many cheap knives, stainless steel is also very difficult to sharpen. The compromise between durable but dull stainless steel and sharp but corrodible carbon steel is a material called high-carbon stainless steel. Used by most knife manufacturers, this blend combines durability and sharpness.

Until recently, all knives were hot drop forged—that is, the steel was heated to 2,000 degrees, dropped into a mold, given four or five shots with a hammer, and then tempered (cooled and heated several times to build strength). This process is labor-intensive (many steps must be done by hand), which explains why many chef's knives cost almost $100.

A second manufacturing process feeds longs sheets of steel through a press that punches out knife after knife, much like a cookie cutter slicing through dough. Called stamped blades, these knives require some hand finishing but are much cheaper to produce because a machine does most of the work.

While experts have long argued that forged knives are better than stamped ones, our testing did not fully support this position. We liked some forged knives and did not like others. Likewise, we liked some stamped knives, but not others. The weight and shape of the handle (it must be comfortable to hold and substantial but not too heavy), the ability of the blade to take an edge, and the shape of the blade (we like a slightly curved blade, which is better suited to the rocking motion often used to mince herbs or garlic than a straight blade) are all key factors in choosing a knife.

When shopping, pick up the knife and see how it feels in your hand. Is it easy to grip? Does the weight seem properly distributed between the handle and blade? In our tests, we liked knives made by Henckels and Wüsthof. An inexpensive knife by Forschner, with a stamped blade, also scored well.

Buying a good knife is only half the challenge. You must keep the edge sharp. To that end, we recommend buying an electric knife sharpener. Steels are best for modest corrections, but all knives will require more substantial sharpening at least several times a year, if not more often, if you cook a lot. Stones are difficult to use because they require that you maintain a perfect 20-degree angle between the stone and the blade. An electric knife sharpener (we like models made by Chef's Choice) takes the guesswork out of sharpening and allows you to keep edges sharp and effective.

THE BEST CHEF'S KNIVES

The Henckels Four Star (left) and Wüsthof-Trident Grand Prix (center) are top choices, but expect to spend about $80 for one of these knives. The Forschner (Victorinox) Fibrox (right) is lighter but still solid and costs just $30.

STEAK FRIES

STEAK FRIES ARE THE RUSTIC COUNTRY cousin to french fries. With their skin left on and their shape determined largely by the shape of the potato, these wedge-shaped fries are easier to prepare and less wasteful than the typical french fry, where much effort is expended to obtain ruler-perfect consistency. Much like good french fries, however, good steak fries should be crisp on the outside and tender on the inside. They should not be oily, dry, mealy, or soggy.

As with regular french fries, we found that starchy russets fried up beautifully. Russets we bought in 5-pound bags, however, came in various sizes and were difficult to cut into uniform wedges. We found russets that are sold loosely are more consistent in size and are easier to cut into same-size wedges for more consistent cooking times. After cooking up fries of various thicknesses, we preferred wedges with an outside edge that measures ¾ inch wide (this works out to one large potato cut into 12 wedges). Any thicker or thinner and the ratio of tender interior to crisp exterior was thrown off.

Many recipes for deep-fried potatoes suggest refrigerating the raw wedges before frying them, and we found this step to be crucial. Cooling the potatoes down before plunging them into the hot oil allows them to cook more slowly and evenly. By soaking the wedges in a bowl of ice water in the refrigerator for at least 30 minutes, we were able to ensure that the inner pulp was fully cooked before the outside turned overly brown.

From previous testing, we found that simply dunking the chilled, raw fries in hot oil and cooking them until done will not produce a good fry. By the time the inside of the fry is cooked and the outside is well browned, the fry itself is wooden and overcooked. We first par-fried them at a relatively low temperature to help them cook through without much browning. We then gave them a brief repose to cool off before refrying them quickly in oil at a higher temperature until nicely browned. In combination with the ice-water bath, this technique worked like a dream. The thick wedges of potato were evenly cooked, with tender middles and crisp, browned exteriors.

Steak Fries

SERVES 4

See the illustrations on page 281 for tips on cutting potatoes for steak fries.

2½   pounds russet potatoes (about 4 large), scrubbed and cut lengthwise into ¾-inch-thick wedges (about 12 wedges per potato)
2   quarts peanut oil
    Salt and ground black pepper

1. Place the cut fries in a large bowl, cover with cold water by at least 1 inch, and then cover with ice cubes. Refrigerate at least 30 minutes or up to 1 day.

2. In a 5-quart pot or Dutch oven fitted with a clip-on candy thermometer, or in a large electric fryer, heat the oil over medium-low heat to 325 degrees. (The oil will bubble up when you add the fries, so be sure you have at least 3 inches of room at the top of the pot.)

3. Pour off the ice and water, quickly wrap the potatoes in a clean kitchen towel, and pat them thoroughly dry. Increase the heat to medium-high and add the fries, one handful at a time, to the hot oil. Fry, stirring with a Chinese skimmer or slotted spoon, until the potatoes are limp and soft and have turned from white to gold, about 10 minutes. (The oil temperature will drop 50 to 60 degrees during this frying.) Use the skimmer or slotted spoon to transfer the fries to a triple thickness of paper towels to drain; let rest at least 10 minutes. (The fries can stand at room temperature for up to 2 hours or be wrapped in paper towels, sealed in a zipper-lock bag, and frozen for up to 1 month.)

4. When ready to serve the fries, reheat the oil to 350 degrees. Using the paper towels as a funnel, pour the potatoes into the hot oil. Discard the paper towels and line a wire rack with another triple thickness of paper towels. Fry the potatoes, stirring fairly constantly, until medium brown and puffed, 8 to 10 minutes. Transfer the fries to the paper towel–lined rack to drain. Season with salt and pepper to taste. Serve immediately.

OVEN FRIES

LOW FAT IS NEVER A GOOD EXCUSE FOR LOUSY food, and oven fries should be no exception. Abysmal flavor and texture just aren't worth the savings in calories, especially when these "lite" fries taste like over-roasted potatoes with thick, leathery crusts and hollow interiors. In other cases, they are limp, whitish, mealy, and bland—a complete failure in all respects. Yet easy and clean oven-cooking—as opposed to deep-frying in a pot of hot, splattering oil—is such an engaging proposition that we decided to enlist temporarily in the low-fat army to see if we could make an oven fry worth eating on its own terms. If it didn't have a golden, crisp crust and a richly creamy interior, we were going back to the deep fryer.

First off, we tested russet, Yukon Gold, and boiling potatoes. Tasting wimpy and sporting spotty crusts, both the Yukon Gold and boiling potatoes couldn't hold a candle to the russets, with their hearty flavor and facility for turning golden brown. Equally obvious were the results of the peeled-versus-unpeeled-potato test. The unpeeled fries were tougher and had the distinct flavor of baked potatoes, whereas the peeled fries—unanimously preferred by tasters—had a clean and more characteristically "french" fry flavor. Tasters also liked the ample size and easy preparation of potatoes cut into wedges, as opposed to the fussy and wasteful option of trimming potatoes down into squared, fast-food-fry wannabes.

Next we baked the fries at 400, 425, 450, 475, and 500 degrees. At lower temperatures, the fries didn't brown sufficiently. The 500-degree oven was a bit too hot and burned the fries at the edges. Baking at 475 degrees was best, but the fries still needed a deeper golden color and a crispier texture. Adjusting the oven rack to the lower-middle position was only moderately helpful, but moving it to the lowest position made for a significant improvement in the fries. The intense heat from the bottom of the oven browned them quickly and evenly, which, in turn, prevented the interiors from overcooking and melding into the crust (thereby becoming the unlikable hollow fry). Lightweight baking sheets can't handle this extreme temperature, so a heavy pan is a must (see "A Weighty Matter," below).

Up until now, we had been simply tossing the potatoes with oil, salt, and pepper before spreading them out on the baking sheet. Turning our attention to the amount of oil, we found that any fewer than 5 tablespoons left some of the fries uncoated and caused them to bake up dry and tough; any more than 5 tablespoons made them disagreeably greasy. Exactly 5 tablespoons, however, ensured that each wedge was evenly coated with oil as it baked. To guarantee even distribution of oil, we found it best to spread 4 tablespoons on the baking sheet and to toss the raw fries with the fifth. Slightly glistening as they emerge from the oven, the fries require a brief drain on paper towel to keep them from tasting oily. Although 5 tablespoons is much less oil than the couple of quarts or more called for when deep-frying potatoes, we felt our oven fries no longer qualified as "low fat," But neither were they pale, soggy, or dry.

A WEIGHTY MATTER

HEAVYWEIGHT PAN: EVEN BROWNING

LIGHTWEIGHT PAN: SPOTTY BROWNING

The heavyweight pan (left) makes all the difference when baking oven fries. A lightweight pan (right) yields fries that are either pale or burnt. A heavy-duty baking sheet is a better conductor of heat and ensures that the fries color evenly and deeply.

Olive oil tasted slightly bitter and out of place, while the mild flavor of vegetable oil and the slight nuttiness of peanut oil (which we prefer to use when deep-frying) both worked well. Although the fries were now sticking to the pan far less than before, we were still plagued by the occasional stuck-on fry until we discovered one last trick. Rather than tossing the potatoes with salt and pepper, we sprinkled the seasonings over the oiled baking sheet. Acting like little ball bearings, the grains of salt and pepper kept the potatoes from sticking to the pan without getting in the way of browning.

Even though we had nailed down the basic method for cooking the fries, they were still beset with crusts that were too thick and interiors that were unappealingly mealy. Wondering what would happen if we steamed the fries before baking them (a technique we'd seen in a few other recipes), we steamed one batch on top of the stove in a steamer basket and another in the oven by covering the baking sheet tightly with foil. This seemingly odd method delivered just the thing we had been after: an oven fry with the creamy, smooth core of an authentic french fry. Steaming on the stovetop had been a counter-clogging, time-consuming affair, but wrapping a baking sheet with foil was easy. The foil trapped the potatoes' natural moisture as they steamed themselves in the oven, and it then came off so that the crusts could crisp for the balance of cooking. Five minutes of steaming was just right, turning the dry, starchy centers of the fries to a soft, creamy consistency without interfering with browning.

Now the only problem remaining was the crust. Steaming, although beneficial for the interior, turned the already thick crust even tougher; this was a far cry from the thin, brittle crust of a good french fry. To solve this problem, we decided to try the techniques of rinsing and soaking, which are often employed when making french fries. Rinsing the raw fries under running water made for a slightly more delicate crust, but soaking them for about an hour in cold tap water was pure magic. Slowly turning the water cloudy as they soaked, the fries emerged from the oven with thin, shatteringly crisp crusts and interiors more

velvety than any oven fry we had tasted (for more information, see "The Power of Soaking" on page 287). But perhaps the biggest surprise came when we tried soaking the fries in water at different temperatures: ice cold, cold from the tap, and hot from the tap. The ice water took hours to become cloudy, the cold tap water took about an hour, and the hot tap water took a convenient 10 minutes, which meant that we could peel, cut, and soak the potatoes in roughly the same time it took to heat up the oven.

Oven Fries

SERVES 3 TO 4

Take care to cut the potatoes into even wedges so that all of the pieces will cook at about the same rate. Although it isn't required, a nonstick baking sheet works particularly well for this recipe. It not only keeps the fries from sticking but, because of its dark color, encourages deep and even browning. Whether you choose a nonstick baking sheet or a regular baking sheet, make sure that it is heavy-duty. The heat of the oven may cause lighter pans to warp.

1½   pounds russet potatoes (about 3 medium), scrubbed and peeled, each potato cut lengthwise into 10 to 12 even wedges

5   tablespoons vegetable or peanut oil
     Salt and ground black pepper

1. Adjust an oven rack to the lowest position; heat the oven to 475 degrees. Place the potatoes in a large bowl and cover with hot tap water; soak 10 minutes. Meanwhile, coat an 18 by 12-inch heavy-duty rimmed baking sheet with 4 tablespoons of the oil and sprinkle evenly with ¾ teaspoon salt and ¼ teaspoon pepper; set aside.

2. Drain the potatoes. Spread the potatoes out on a triple thickness of paper towels and pat them thoroughly dry with additional paper towels. Rinse and wipe out the now-empty bowl; return the potatoes to the bowl and toss with the remaining 1 tablespoon oil. Arrange the potatoes in a single layer on the prepared baking sheet; cover tightly with foil and bake 5 minutes. Remove the foil and continue to bake until the bottoms

of the potatoes are spotty golden brown, 15 to 20 minutes, rotating the baking sheet after 10 minutes. Using a spatula and tongs, scrape to loosen the potatoes from the pan, then flip each wedge, keeping the potatoes in a single layer. Continue baking until the fries are golden and crisp, 5 to 15 minutes longer, rotating the pan as needed if the fries are browning unevenly.

3. Transfer the fries to a second baking sheet lined with paper towels to drain. Season with additional salt and pepper to taste and serve immediately.

➤ VARIATION

Sweet Potato Oven Fries

When buying sweet potatoes for oven fries, try to choose those with a uniform shape. When peeling, shave away odd bumps and curves to make them even more uniform. Because sweet potatoes have more sugar and moisture than russets, the fries will not be as crisp, but they are tasty nonetheless.

Follow the recipe for Oven Fries, substituting 2 sweet potatoes (13 to 15 ounces each) for the russet potatoes. Do not soak the potatoes in water before cooking, and do not cover them with foil during the initial 5 minutes of baking. Bake the fries on the first side until they are spotty golden brown, about 25 minutes. Flip them over and continue to bake until completely golden brown,

---

SCIENCE: The Power of Soaking

Experts agree (just ask McDonald's or our test cooks) that russet potatoes are the best variety for frying—either in a vat of bubbling oil or on a baking sheet in the oven. Unlike other potato varieties, russets produce fries with light, ethereal centers. But they are not perfect.

Russets can produce excessively thick crusts and somewhat dry interiors. The thick crust is caused by the browning of simple sugars in the russet, and the best way to remove some of the surface sugar is to soak the potatoes in water. The water has an added benefit. Potato starches gelatinize completely during cooking. The water introduced during soaking improves the creaminess and smoothness by working its way between the strands of gelatin starch. The final result is a fry that has a good surface crunch married to a smooth interior.

---

15 to 20 minutes longer. Be sure to rotate the baking sheet several times during cooking so that the fries brown evenly, and jockey the position of the fries on the baking sheet as needed. If some fries are done before others, remove them from the pan while letting the others continue to cook. Proceed as directed in the recipe for Oven Fries, and serve immediately.

HASH BROWNS

MANY PEOPLE LIKE HOME FRIES—SAUTÉED chunks of potato that retain their shape and individuality when cooked. Others prefer hash browns, which are thin, crisply sautéed potato cakes made with grated or chopped potatoes, raw or precooked. Unlike other potato cakes (such as the latkes on page 291), hash browns do not contain eggs. The starch from the grated potatoes provides the binder needed to hold the cake together. With just salt and pepper added for seasoning, the focus remains on the potato flavor. Hash browns are probably most closely related to roesti (a Swiss potato pancake), although the latter are thicker and usually served for dinner whereas hash browns are more familiar on the breakfast table.

Even though we assumed that a starchier potato would be best suited for this assignment, we began by testing all the major varieties. After thorough testing, the only type we completely eliminated were the waxy or low-starch varieties, such as red potatoes, which did not stay together or brown well and were also lacking in flavor in this recipe. The all-purpose potatoes sold in plastic bags in the supermarket, which have a medium starch content, worked well enough to be considered an adequate choice. We also liked the buttery color, as well as the taste, of Yukon Golds, another medium-starch potato. However, we found that the high-starch russets yielded the best overall results. They adhered well, browned beautifully, and had the most pronounced potato flavor.

Our next challenge was to decide between raw and precooked potatoes. Precooked potatoes tasted good, but when cut into chunks they did not stay together in a cohesive cake, and when grated they needed to be pressed very hard to form a cake. Unfortunately, this gave them the texture of fried mashed potatoes. Although this is an acceptable alternative if you have leftover cooked potatoes, we preferred using raw, grated potatoes. We also liked the more textured interior, the pronounced potato taste, and the way the raw shreds of potato formed an attractive, deeply browned crust.

Choosing the best method for cutting the potatoes was easy. Grating on the large-hole side of a box grater or with the shredding disk on a food processor yielded hash browns that formed a coherent cake when cooked. Chopped potatoes, even when finely chopped, did not hold together as well. To peel or not to peel the potatoes is a matter of personal preference. The presence of the grated peel altered the taste a bit, but it did not negatively affect the overall cooking method or desired outcome.

After cooking countless batches of hash browns, we found that the pan itself was an important factor. A skillet with sloping sides made it considerably easier to press the potatoes into a flattened shape, invert them, and slide them from the pan. All these tasks were more difficult in a straight-sided frying pan. As for browning, properly seasoned cast-iron pans and uncoated stainless steel pans produced the best exterior, with potatoes that were evenly colored and crusty; however, nonstick pans browned adequately and, obviously, were easier to use and clean.

We found that cooking hash browns with butter provided good color and a very rich flavor. We tested bacon fat (figuring that many cooks might have some in the kitchen at breakfast time) and were disappointed. The color was a bit anemic and the potato flavor was lacking. Vegetable oil could not produce the same rich golden brown color that butter did, and the flavor was again lacking. Butter is clearly the best choice.

Our last test of cooking methods was to try covering the potatoes during cooking. What we found was that the cover trapped steam in the pan, which reduced the crispness of the crust. Since we began with a thin layer of potatoes in the pan anyway, we didn't need steam to help cook them through. Cooking the hash browns without the cover is the way to go.

While testing, we used only salt and pepper for seasonings, planning to experiment with other ingredients at a later time. However, we became so fond of the buttery salt and pepper taste that we decided to keep the seasonings as is for the master recipe. Of course, adding grated onion or chopped scallions and parsley (or other fresh herbs) is an option. The onion or herbs can either be tossed with the grated potatoes before cooking or sprinkled over the potatoes in the pan before they are pressed.

Hash browns can be made into one or more individual servings or one large portion that can be cut into wedges. We also liked using hash

EXTRA-CRISP HASH BROWNS

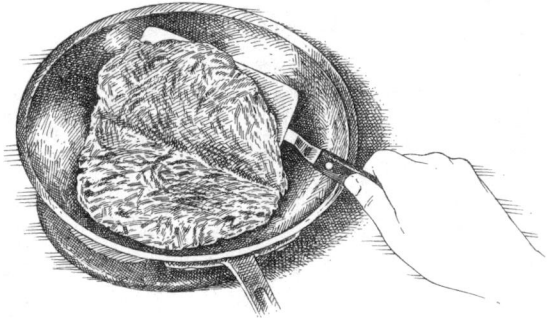

Folding the hash browns ensures that every bite has maximum crunch. Once the potatoes have been browned on both sides, fold the cake over, omelet style, with a spatula. When cut into wedges, each piece will now have four crisp surfaces—two inside and two outside.

DRYING GRATED POTATOES

To release the water from the grated potatoes, place them in a clean kitchen towel. Using two hands twist the towel tightly to squeeze out as much moisture as possible.

browns as a base for toppings or as an omelet-like envelope for fillings. No matter how you choose to present the hash browns, make sure you serve them piping hot.

Hash Browns
SERVES 4

To keep the potatoes from turning brown, grate them just before cooking. This recipe cooks the potatoes in one large cake. For individual servings, simply divide the raw grated potatoes into four equal-sized patties and reduce the cooking time to 5 minutes per side. To vary flavor, add 2 tablespoons grated onion, 1 to 2 tablespoons of an herb of your choice, or roasted garlic to taste to the raw grated potatoes. You can also garnish the cooked hash browns with minced chives or scallion greens just before serving. For extra-crisp hash browns, see the illustration on the facing page. See the same page for tips on squeezing as much moisture as possible from the potatoes.

I	pound russet potatoes (about 2 medium), scrubbed, peeled, rinsed, dried, grated on the large holes of a box grater, and squeezed dry in a kitchen towel (about 1½ cups loosely packed grated potatoes)
¼	teaspoon salt
	Ground black pepper
I	tablespoon unsalted butter

1. Toss the dried grated potatoes with the salt and pepper to taste in a medium bowl.

2. Heat half of the butter in a 10-inch skillet over medium-high heat until it just starts to brown, and then scatter the potatoes evenly over the entire pan bottom. Using a wide spatula, firmly press the potatoes to flatten them. Reduce the heat to medium and continue cooking until the potatoes are dark golden brown and crisp, 7 to 8 minutes.

3. Invert the hash browns, browned-side up, onto a large plate. Add the remaining butter to the pan. Once the butter has melted, slide the hash browns back into the pan to cook the second side. Continue to cook over medium heat until dark golden brown and crisp, 5 to 6 minutes longer.

4. Slide the hash browns onto a plate or cutting board, cut into wedges, and serve immediately.

➤ VARIATION

Spicy Hash Browns with Cheddar and Red Bell Pepper

In this variation, the potatoes themselves are flavored before they go into the pan. If you want your hash browns to be really spicy, just stem the chile and mince it; the heat resides largely in the whitish pith (or membrane or ribs), to which the seeds are attached. For extra-crisp hash browns, see the illustration on the facing page. See the same page for tips on squeezing as much moisture as possible from the potatoes.

2	tablespoons unsalted butter
I	small red bell pepper, cored, seeded, and chopped fine
I	small jalapeño chile, cored, seeded, and minced
I	pound russet potatoes, scrubbed, peeled, rinsed, dried, grated on the large holes of a box grater, and squeezed dry in a kitchen towel (about 1½ cups loosely packed grated potatoes)
2	ounces cheddar cheese, shredded (about ⅔ cup)
I	tablespoon minced fresh parsley leaves
¼	teaspoon salt
	Ground black pepper

1. Heat 1 tablespoon of the butter in a 10-inch skillet over medium-high heat. When the foaming subsides, add the red bell pepper and chile and cook, stirring occasionally, until they soften, about 4 minutes. Transfer the cooked peppers to a medium bowl; set the skillet aside. Add the dried grated potatoes, cheese, parsley, salt, and pepper to taste to the bowl with the peppers and toss to combine.

2. Heat ½ tablespoon of the remaining butter in the empty skillet over medium-high heat until it just starts to brown, then scatter the potatoes evenly over the entire pan bottom. Using a wide spatula, firmly press the potatoes to flatten them. Reduce the heat to medium and continue cooking until the potatoes are dark golden brown and crisp, 7 to 8 minutes.

3. Invert the hash browns, browned-side up, onto a large plate. Add the remaining butter to the pan. Once the butter has melted, slide the hash browns back into the pan to cook the second side.

Continue to cook over medium heat until dark golden brown and crisp, 5 to 6 minutes longer.

4. Slide the hash browns onto a plate or cutting board, cut into wedges, and serve immediately.

LATKES

LATKES ARE THICK, SHREDDED POTATO pancakes that are flavored with onion, bound with eggs and (usually) matzo meal, and pan-fried in vegetable oil. They should be golden and very crisp on the outside and creamy and moist on the inside. To figure out how to make these ideal latkes, we had to find the best potato, the best grating method, and the best frying technique.

We began with the potatoes. We tested russets, which are high in starch; Yukon Golds, which have a medium starch content; and red potatoes, which are low in starch. The russet potato pancakes had a pleasantly pronounced potato flavor and a dry texture. The red potatoes were at the other end of the spectrum: very creamy, almost gluey on the inside. The Yukon Golds were the biggest surprise; the pancakes made with these potatoes were an attractive deep yellow–gold color, tasted somewhat sweet and mild, and were creamy in texture without being either gluey or sticky. Everyone who tried the Yukon Gold latkes judged them superior in taste.

Some experts feel that latkes made with potatoes shredded by hand on a box grater are superior to those made with potatoes shredded in a food processor. We tried both methods and found a negligible difference in texture between the two. We did, however, discover a very useful two-step grating procedure.

For the first step, we put the peeled potatoes through the feed tube of the food processor, using the coarse shredding blade. We then removed about half to two-thirds of the shreds and placed them in a separate mixing bowl. Next, we inserted the metal blade, added chunks of onion to the shreds left in the processor bowl, and processed the mixture in spurts until we had a very coarse puree, each piece being no larger than ⅛ inch. Then we combined the pureed potatoes and onions with the shredded potatoes. This two-step procedure gave us latkes that had some larger shreds that cooked up quite crisp along the outside perimeters, while the center portion remained thicker and chewier, like a traditional pancake. Thus we had met our ideal of crisp on the outside and creamy and moist on the inside.

After we pressed the potatoes in a fine sieve to remove their moisture, we set them aside. We allowed the mixing bowl with the potato water to sit for a minute and then very slowly poured off the potato water that had accumulated. At the bottom of the bowl there was a layer of thick, white potato starch. In our tests, this starch proved so helpful in binding the latkes that we found we didn't need to add flour or matzo meal; but because matzo meal is traditional in latkes, we made it optional in our recipe.

Now we began to test the most crucial part of the whole process: frying. First we tested three different frying mediums: a combination of chicken fat (schmaltz) and vegetable oil; solid vegetable shortening (Crisco); and vegetable oil.

The chicken fat and vegetable oil combination was impractical; chicken fat is just not readily available. We thought solid vegetable shortening might work well, but it was difficult to add more solid shortening to the frying pan to maintain a consistent depth (after cooking a couple of batches of latkes, the frying medium must be replenished). Vegetable oil was easier to work with.

We tried cooking latkes in several depths of oil, from ⅟₁₆ inch to ½ inch, and found that more oil does not necessarily result in oilier pancakes as long as the oil is at the right temperature. It is much easier to regulate the temperature of the oil if you have at least ⅛ inch of oil in the pan, and that was the minimum amount required for thin pancakes. Also, if the oil is deep enough from the start, you don't have to add oil in between batches as frequently. We determined that the optimum amount was ¼ inch.

The temperature of the oil is crucial to frying the perfect latke. Unfortunately, it's very hard to accurately measure the temperature of oil that is only ¼ inch deep. The key is to have the oil really hot, but not smoking, when the latkes go in. The temperature of the oil will fall as more batter is added, but the goal is to restore it to a constant lively bubble throughout the cooking of all the pancakes. When the oil is hot enough to start frying, it begins to shimmer on the surface and appears somewhat wavy. If it is smoking, it's too hot and the heat should be turned down. We tested the oil initially by dropping in about a teaspoon of batter and observing how quickly it cooked. If it browned in less than a minute, the oil was too hot. Two minutes was just about right.

With every batch of latkes we made, we held some in a 200-degree oven and tried a bite every five to 10 minutes. With every bite after the first one, the latkes tasted progressively more old and chewy. We concluded that you cannot hold latkes for more than 10 minutes at the most. They may still be hot, but the taste diminishes and the texture deteriorates so much that after all the trouble you have gone to in preparing them, you might as well have chosen something else to cook.

We did discover, however, that latkes that have been left to cool at room temperature for a few hours and are then reheated in a 375-degree oven for about five minutes are the next best thing to freshly fried.

We also reserved some of the latkes for the freezer. We placed them on a parchment-lined baking sheet and allowed them to freeze for about 15 minutes before placing them in zipper-lock freezer bags. When we were ready to serve the latkes, we reheated them on a baking sheet in the middle of a 375-degree oven for about eight minutes per side. All tasters agreed that there was only a slight difference in quality compared with the freshly fried latkes.

Latkes

MAKES ABOUT FOURTEEN 3-INCH PANCAKES

If you don't have a food processor, you can obtain similar results with a traditional box grater. Simply shred the potatoes on the largest holes of the grater and place half of the shreds in a sieve set over a bowl. Then, using a chef's knife, finely chop the remaining shreds along with all of the onions. Add the mixture to the potatoes in the sieve and proceed with the recipe. Matzo meal is a traditional binder, though we found that the pancake's

texture does not suffer without it. Cooled latkes can be covered loosely with plastic wrap, held at room temperature for 4 hours, transferred to a heated baking sheet, and baked in a 375-degree oven until crisp and hot, about 5 minutes per side. They can also be frozen: Place them on a baking sheet in the freezer and, when frozen, transfer them to zipper-lock bag for storage. Reheat in a 375-degree oven until crisp and hot, about 8 minutes per side.

2	pounds Yukon Gold or russet potatoes (about 4 medium), scrubbed and peeled
1	medium onion, peeled and cut into eighths
1	large egg
4	medium scallions, white and green parts, minced
3	tablespoons minced fresh parsley leaves
2	tablespoons matzo meal (optional)
1½	teaspoons salt
	Ground black pepper
1	cup vegetable oil
	Applesauce and/or sour cream, for serving (optional)

1. Shred the potatoes in a food processor fitted with the coarse shredding blade. Place half of the potatoes in a fine-mesh sieve set over a medium bowl and reserve. Fit the food processor with the steel blade, add the onion, and pulse with the remaining potatoes until all the pieces measure roughly ⅛ inch and are coarsely chopped, five to six 1-second pulses. Mix with the reserved potato shreds in the sieve and press against the sieve to drain as much liquid as possible into the bowl below. (See note if you don't have a food processor.) Let the potato liquid stand until the thick, white starch settles to the bottom, about 1 minute. Pour off the liquid, leaving the starch in the bowl. Beat the egg and then the potato mixture, scallions, parsley, matzo meal (if using), salt, and pepper to taste into the starch.

2. Meanwhile, pour the oil to a depth of ¼ inch into a large skillet (you should have some oil left in the cup). Heat over medium-high until shimmering but not smoking. Working with one portion at a time, place ¼ cup potato mixture, squeezed

of excess liquid and pressed into a ½-inch-thick disk, onto a spatula and lower it into the oil. Press gently with a metal spatula; repeat until 5 latkes are in the pan.

3. Maintaining the heat so that the oil bubbles around the edges of the latkes, fry them until they are golden brown on the bottom and edges, about 3 minutes. Turn with a spatula and continue frying until they are golden brown all over, about 3 minutes more. Drain on a triple thickness of paper towels set on a wire rack over a rimmed baking sheet. Repeat with the remaining potato mixture, returning the oil to temperature between each batch and replacing the oil after every second batch. Season with salt and pepper to taste and serve immediately with applesauce and/or sour cream, if desired.

➤ VARIATION

Potato Pancakes with Pepper Jack Cheese and Cilantro

These untraditional pancakes are great with sour cream, freshly made salsa, and a splash of hot pepper sauce.

Follow the recipe for Latkes, replacing the parsley with an equal amount of minced cilantro leaves, omitting the matzo meal, and adding ½ cup shredded Pepper Jack cheese with the scallions and other ingredients in step 1.

POMMES ANNA

IMAGINE THIN POTATO SLICES LAYERED meticulously in a skillet with nothing but butter, salt, pepper, and more butter, left to cook until the inverted dish reveals a potato cake with a lovely crisp, deep brown, glassine crust belying the soft, creamy potato layers within. This is pommes Anna, the queen of potato cookery.

Legend has it that Anna was a fashionable woman who lived during the reign of Napoleon III. Whoever Anna was, the creator of this dish was, to be sure, a chef with an inordinate amount of time on his hands, as the recipe requires painstaking procedures and the patience of Job. Given the amount of effort required to make just one dish of pommes Anna, it was particularly irritating when, in our preliminary recipe testing, those we

made suffered a 50 percent rate of failure to cleanly release from the pan. It's no surprise, then, that pommes Anna is rarely seen on menus or home dinner tables and that recipes for it are sequestered in only the staunchest of French cookbooks.

We hoped to find a means of simplifying and foolproofing this classic. If we could do away with some of the maddening work and guarantee more than a crapshoot's chance of perfect unmolding, pommes Anna could find her way back onto the culinary map . . . and certainly onto the dining room table.

First we needed a pan for the perilous pommes. Of the four different cooking vessels we employed in tests—a cast-iron skillet, a copper pommes Anna pan, a heavy-bottomed skillet with a stainless steel cooking surface, and a heavy-bottomed nonstick skillet—only the nonstick effortlessly released the potatoes onto the serving platter. As reluctant as we were to make such specific equipment requisite for pommes Anna, a nonstick skillet is essential to the dish's success. After all, once having expended the effort of slicing and arranging the potatoes, it is disheartening to later witness them clinging stubbornly to the pan.

Most, if not all, recipes for pommes Anna begin with clarified butter. To make it, butter is melted, the foamy whey is spooned off the top, and the pure butterfat is poured or spooned off the milky casein at the bottom. Because it lacks solids and proteins, clarified butter has a higher smoke point (and so is more resistant to burning) than whole butter, but it also lacks the full, buttery flavor that those solids and proteins provide. We have always been annoyed by clarified butter because of the time required to make it, the waste involved (typically, about 30 percent of the butter is lost with clarifying), and the loss of flavor. But pommes Anna, which spends a substantial amount of time cooking at moderately high temperatures, is always made with clarified butter. Our big coup, we thought, would be to circumvent this centuries-old "requirement." But sure enough, the surface of the potatoes was dotted with unappealing black flecks. Still, as a few tasters noticed, the whole butter gave the potatoes a richer, fuller flavor that we missed in the versions made with clarified butter. We thought to replace the butter in the bottom of the skillet with oil, then drizzle melted whole butter between potato layers. This worked better than we could have hoped. Our newfangled pommes Anna had a crisp brown crust rivaling that of any made with clarified butter.

Thinly sliced potatoes (russets are traditional but our tasters also liked Yukon Golds) are a defining characteristic of pommes Anna, as is the overlapping arrangement of the slices in concentric circles. In the early stages of our testing, we preferred to slice the potatoes by hand (for no good reason), but as numbers increased, we took to a food processor fitted with a fine slicing disk that could get the job done with effortless speed. If you own and are adept with a mandoline, it offers another quick means of slicing the potatoes.

Slicing wasn't the only obstacle presented by the potatoes. Because they will discolor if peeled, sliced, and then kept waiting to be arranged in the skillet, they must be soaked in water, which in turn means that the slices must be dried before being layered. To avoid this inconvenience, we opted to slice and arrange the potatoes in batches, making sure each group of slices was arranged in the skillet before slicing the next batch. This method prevented discoloration, but it was also awkward and inefficient. Someone suggested tossing the sliced potatoes in the melted butter to prevent them from discoloring. We tried this, and though the butter did not prevent the discoloration, it did slow it down to the extent that all slices could be layered in the skillet before severe discoloration set in. That the butter no longer required drizzling between each layer was a bonus.

Most pommes Anna recipes have the cook start

PREPARING POMMES ANNA

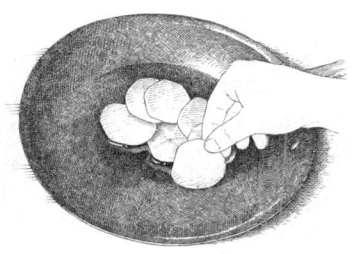

1. Using the nicest slices to form the bottom layer, place one slice in the center of the skillet. Overlap more slices in a circle around the center slice.

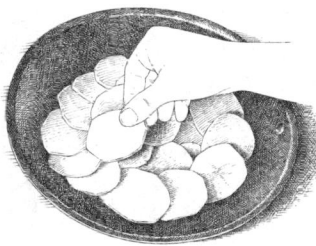

2. Use more slices to form an outer circle of overlapping slices in the bottom of the pan. Continue layering, alternating the direction of the slices in each layer.

3. To drain off excess fat before unmolding, press a cake pan against the potatoes while tilting the skillet. Be sure to use heavy potholders or oven mitts to hold the hot skillet.

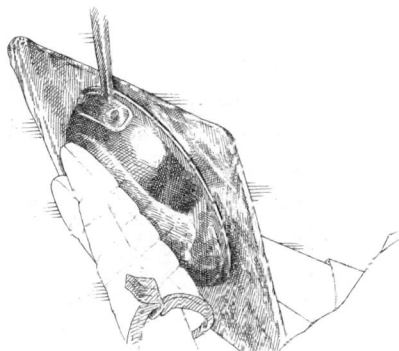

4. To invert, set a prepared baking sheet flat on top of the skillet. Invert the skillet and baking sheet together. Lift the skillet off the potatoes.

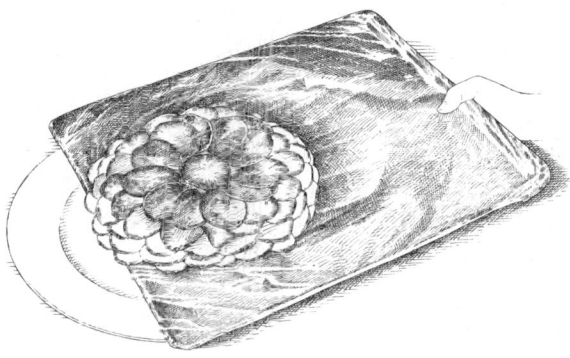

5. Carefully slide the pommes Anna from the baking sheet onto a serving platter.

layering potato slices in the skillet as it heats on the stovetop. It may sound dangerous, but it isn't, really, and it saves much time. After all the slices are in, the skillet is transferred to a hot oven or left on the stovetop to complete cooking. After many tests, we determined that the potatoes—started in a cold skillet—require 30 minutes on the stovetop at medium-low heat (if it takes you longer to get them in the skillet, next time try mashed potatoes), then—after a firm pressing with the bottom of a cake pan to compact the potatoes into a cohesive cake—25 minutes more in a 450-degree oven. The time on the stovetop gets the browning going on the bottom, and the oven time cooks through the potatoes' thickness while completing the bottom browning. Now our recipe required not only a nonstick skillet but a nonstick ovenproof skillet.

SCIENCE: Why Potatoes Turn Brown

As many of us find out the hard way, peeled and sliced potatoes take on a brick-red hue when left to sit out for several minutes before cooking. This was of particular concern in our pommes Anna recipe, because the peeled, sliced potatoes must wait to be layered in the skillet. We consulted spud expert Dr. Alfred Bushway, professor of food science at the University of Maine, to find out what causes potatoes to turn color. He explained that with slicing and peeling, potato cells are broken down and the enzyme polyphenol oxidase is released. Two major substrates, chlorogenic acid and tyrosine, are also released.

The enzyme and substrates combine with oxygen to form a compound called orthoquinone. The orthoquinone quickly polymerizes (a process in which many molecules link up to form a chain of more complex molecules with different physical properties) and creates the brownish-red color that we see in the potatoes.

Tossing the potatoes with butter, as in the pommes Anna recipe, helps limit oxygen exposure and therefore retards discoloration. We had also noted that certain potatoes discolor more rapidly than others. Bushway said that from cultivar to cultivar and over the storage season, potatoes vary in their enzyme and/or substrate concentrations and enzyme activity, so differences in discoloration rates can be expected. In our experience, russet potatoes seem to discolor most rapidly, so if you're a slow hand, opt for Yukon Golds for pommes Anna.

The final step of pommes Anna is, of course, unmolding. If only it could be so easy as inverting a layer cake onto a cooling rack, but with a heavy, hot-handled skillet, the process is awkward and clumsy and can make an experienced cook feel like a bumbling one. Rather than trying to invert the potatoes directly onto a serving platter, where they cannot be unmolded in dead center because of the skillet's protruding handle, we lined the back of a baking sheet (a rimless cookie sheet will do) with lightly greased foil. We inverted the potatoes onto this surface, much as we would invert a cake onto a cooling rack, then slid them onto the serving platter. We found this technique a little less dangerous and much less complicated than going straight from pan to serving dish.

A last word on pommes Anna. Even simplified and streamlined, this recipe requires a good amount of patience, but it is no less a tour de force of culinary art and engineering than the classic rendition.

Pommes Anna

SERVES 6 TO 8

Do not slice the potatoes until you are ready to start assembling. Remember to start timing when you begin arranging the potatoes in the skillet—no matter how quickly you arrange them, they will need 30 minutes on the stovetop to brown properly. Use a mandoline or V-slicer (see page 296 for the results of our testing) or food processor to slice the potatoes; a chef's knife may not get them thin enough. See the illustrations on page 293 for tips on preparing this recipe.

3	pounds russet or Yukon Gold potatoes (about 6 medium), scrubbed, peeled, and sliced $1/16$ to $1/8$ inch thick
5	tablespoons unsalted butter, melted
$1/4$	cup vegetable or peanut oil, plus more for greasing the baking sheet
	Salt and ground black pepper

1. Toss the potato slices with the melted butter in a large bowl until the potatoes are evenly coated. Adjust an oven rack to the lower-middle position and heat the oven to 450 degrees.

2. Pour the oil into a 10-inch heavy-bottomed ovenproof nonstick skillet. Swirl to coat the pan bottom with oil and set the skillet over medium-low heat. Begin timing, and arrange the potato slices in the skillet, using the nicest slices to form the bottom layer. To start, place one slice in the center of the skillet. Overlap more slices in a circle around the center slice, then form another circle of overlapping slices to cover the pan bottom. Sprinkle evenly with a scant ¼ teaspoon salt and ground black pepper to taste. Arrange a second layer of potatoes, working in the opposite direction of the first layer; sprinkle evenly with a scant ¼ teaspoon salt and ground black pepper. Repeat, layering the potatoes in opposite directions and sprinkling with salt and pepper, until no slices remain (broken or uneven slices can be pieced together to form whole slices; the potatoes will mound in the center of the skillet). Continue to cook over medium-low heat until 30 minutes elapse from the time you began arranging the potatoes in the skillet.

3. Using the bottom of a 9-inch cake pan, press the potatoes down firmly to compact them. Cover the skillet and place it in the oven. Bake until the potatoes begin to soften, about 15 minutes. Uncover and continue to bake until the potatoes are tender when a paring knife is inserted in the center and the edge of the potatoes touching the skillet is browned, about 10 minutes longer. Meanwhile, line a rimless cookie sheet or the back of a baking sheet with foil and coat very lightly with oil. Drain off excess fat from the potatoes by pressing the bottom of the cake pan against the potatoes while tilting the skillet. (Be sure to use heavy potholders or oven mitts.)

4. Set the foil-lined cookie sheet on top of the skillet. With your hands protected by oven mitts or potholders, hold the cookie sheet in place with one hand and carefully invert the skillet and cookie sheet together. Lift the skillet off the potatoes. Carefully slide the potatoes from the baking sheet onto a platter. Cut into wedges and serve immediately.

SCALLOPED POTATOES

TRADITIONALLY RESERVED FOR HOLIDAYS and special events, scalloped potatoes are luxuriously waist-defying. Cooked in fantastic amounts of heavy cream, butter, and cheese, their richness is hardly suitable for your average supper (or diet). We wanted a lighter, more convenient recipe, but we also wanted a recipe that would taste good (and not come out of a box).

To begin, we made several standard scalloped potato recipes. We rubbed shallow dishes with garlic, sliced potatoes and laid them in rows, topped them with heavy cream and cheese, and baked them. The ingredient lists were similar in their inclusion of garlic, cream, and sliced russets, but some also called for half-and-half or milk, while others called for butter and flour. All of the recipes were unabashedly rich and took as long as 1½ hours to make from start to finish. Several tasted pasty from the flour (used as a thickener for the sauce), and nearly all were a bit dull from the sheer lack of aromatics beyond garlic. Not only did these stodgy potato dishes need to be lightened up considerably, but they begged for more flavor, as well as a realistic midweek cooking time.

Starting with the potatoes, we cooked russet, all-purpose, and Yukon Gold varieties side by side in basic scalloped fashion. While Yukon Gold and all-purpose potatoes weren't bad, tasters found them a bit waxy. The traditional russets, with their tender bite and earthy flavor, were the unanimous favorite. The russets also formed tighter, more cohesive layers owing to their higher starch content.

Heavy cream is the obvious, diet-crushing ingredient in traditional scalloped potatoes, so we figured it was probably to blame for their usual heft. To relieve some of the heaviness, we tried replacing the heavy cream with a number of less fatty liquids. We tried half-and-half, but the sauce curdled as it bubbled away in the oven. Half-and-half, as it turns out, doesn't have enough fat to keep the dairy proteins from coagulating under high heat. Supplementing some of the heavy cream with whole milk worked well (no curdling), but the potatoes still tasted a bit heavy and dairy-rich for an everyday meal. Next we tried

EQUIPMENT: Mandolines and V-Slicers

What's cheaper than a food processor and faster (if not also sharper) than a chef's knife? A mandoline. This hand-operated slicing machine comes in two basic styles—the classic stainless steel model, supported by legs, and the plastic hand-held model, often called a V-slicer. We put both types of machines—ranging in price from $8.99 to $169—to the test. To determine the winners, we sliced melons, cut carrots into julienne (matchstick pieces), cut potatoes into batonettes (long, skinny french fry pieces), and sliced potatoes into thin rounds. Then we evaluated three aspects of the mandolines: ease of use, including degree of effort, adjustment ease, grip/handle comfort, and safety; quality, including sturdiness and uniformity/cleanliness of slices; and cleanup.

The Progressive Mandoline Multi Slicer ($8.99) and the Target Mandoline Slicer ($9.99) are plastic V-slicers with similar designs. Testers gave these models high marks for safety, handle comfort, and blade sharpness, which helped them whip through melon and potato slices. Interchangeable blade platforms cut respectable batonettes and julienne, though these cuts required more effort on the part of testers.

The two other V-slicers tested were the Börner V-Slicer Plus ($34.95) and the Joyce Chen Asian Mandoline Plus ($49.95). The latter produced flawless melon slices, carrot julienne, and potato batonettes but got low marks for its small, ineffective safety mechanism and tricky blade adjustment. Testers also downgraded the poorly designed and not very sturdy base. The Börner unit sliced melons and carrots with little effort, but the potato slices were inconsistent and required more effort to produce. The Börner's well-designed safety guard, however, kept hands away from blades, and its adjustments were quick and easy to make. In the end, testers preferred the cheaper V-slicers made by Progressive and Target to either of these more expensive options.

We also tested two classic stainless steel mandolines. The deBuyer mandoline from Williams-Sonoma ($169) was controversial. Shorter testers had difficulty gaining leverage to cut consistently; some melon slices were ⅛ inch thicker on one side. However, the safety mechanism, sturdiness, and adjustment mechanism were lauded by taller testers. With some practice, all testers were able to produce perfect slices, julienne, and batonettes with the Bron Coucke mandoline ($99). This machine has fewer parts to clean and switch out than its plastic counterparts and requires less effort to operate once the user becomes familiar with it. Still, the quality comes at an awfully high price.

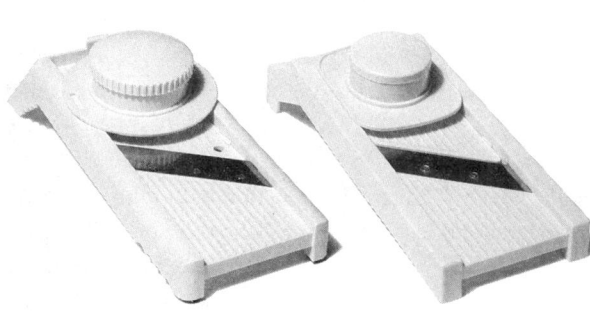

THE BEST V-SLICERS
Plastic mandolines (also called V-slicers) may not be as sturdy as stainless steel versions, but their quality far exceeds the minimal dollar investment. Among the four models tested, we liked the Progressive and Target slicers, which are similar in design.

THE BEST CLASSIC MANDOLINE
Of the two stainless steel mandolines tested, we preferred this model made by Bron Coucke. Note, however, that it costs 10 times more than a good V-slicer.

...eam with chicken
replacing some of the he...tigated some of the
broth. The broth effect...g a variety of broth-
cream's heaviness. A... ned up, it was time to
to-cream ratio... on a 50/50 split.
With the ...ered, the delicate flavor of shal-
tweak its fla... a little sautéed onion
lot was e...dried bay leaves also helped to
and ga...e with an herbaceous flavor that
of fr...vy nor distracting.
...w, we had been using the tiresome
...layering the raw potatoes and sauce
...v dish and baking them in the oven for
...To speed things up, we tried parboiling
...toes in water, then combining them with
...e (thickened with flour to achieve a saucy
...istency in less time), and finishing them in the
...en. Although this did shave nearly 45 minutes
...ff the cooking time, the potatoes had a hollow
flavor, the sauce tasted gummy and flat, and we
spent much of the time we had saved washing
dirty pots.

Next we tried parcooking the sliced potatoes
in the chicken broth and cream in a covered pot
on top of the stove before dumping it all into a
shallow casserole dish and finishing it in the oven.
Here was our solution. This technique gave the
potatoes a head start on the stovetop, where they
released some of their starch into the sauce. This
starch, a natural thickening agent, transformed the
consistency of the cooking liquid into a rightful
sauce, negating the need for flour.

When slowly simmered on the stovetop for 10
minutes, at which time the potatoes were about
halfway cooked, the casserole required only 15
minutes in a 425-degree oven to finish. We
sprinkled a handful of cheddar over the top, and
the potatoes emerged from the oven as a bubbling inferno with a golden crown. Although
ripping-hot potatoes and sauce make for a sloppy
casserole straight out of the oven, a rest of 10 minutes is all that's needed for them to cool off a bit
and cohere.

Weekday Scalloped Potatoes
SERVES 4 TO 6

*The quickest way to slice the potatoes is in a food proces-
sor fitted with an ¼-inch slicing blade. If the potatoes are
too long to fit into the feed tube, halve them crosswise and
put them in the feed tube cut-side down so that they sit on
a flat surface. If the potato slices discolor as they sit, put
them in a bowl and cover with the cream and chicken broth.
A mandoline or V-slicer (see the facing page) is the other
option. Don't try to slice the potatoes with a knife; you won't
get them thin enough. If you like, use Parmesan instead of
cheddar cheese to top the casserole.*

2   tablespoons unsalted butter
1   medium onion, minced
2   medium garlic cloves, minced or pressed
    through a garlic press (about 2 teaspoons)
1   tablespoon chopped fresh thyme leaves
1¼ teaspoons salt
¼   teaspoon ground black pepper
2½ pounds russet potatoes (about 5 medium),
    scrubbed, peeled, and sliced ⅛ inch thick
1   cup low-sodium chicken broth
1   cup heavy cream
2   bay leaves
4   ounces cheddar cheese, shredded (about 1⅓
    cups)

1. Adjust an oven rack to the middle position
and heat the oven to 425 degrees.

2. Melt the butter in a Dutch oven over
medium-high heat. When the foaming subsides, add
the onion and cook, stirring occasionally, until soft
and lightly browned, about 4 minutes. Add the garlic, thyme, salt, and pepper and cook until fragrant,
about 30 seconds. Add the potatoes, broth, cream,
and bay leaves and bring to a simmer. Cover, reduce
the heat to medium-low, and simmer until the potatoes are almost tender (a paring knife can be slid
into and out of a potato slice with some resist...
about 10 minutes. Discard the bay leaves.

3. Transfer the mixture to an 8-inch squ...
ing dish (or any other 1½-quart gratin dish...
evenly with the cheese. Bake until the c...
bling around the edges and the top is g...
about 15 minutes. Cool 10 minutes b...

➤ VARIATIONS

Scalloped Potatoes with Mushrooms

Slice 8 ounces cremini mushrooms ¼ inch thick; trim the stems off 4 ounces fresh shiitake mushrooms and slice the caps ¼ inch thick. Follow the recipe for Weekday Scalloped Potatoes, adding the mushrooms to the butter along with the onion. Cook until the moisture released by the mushrooms has evaporated, about 5 minutes. Proceed as directed.

GREAT SIDES FOR HOLIDAY HAM

BAKED HAM IS A GREAT CENTERPIECE for a holiday meal, whether it be Christmas, New Year's, or Easter. Most recipes for ham require little preparation, allowing the cook to choose interesting sides that might be a little more involved. Here are some of the test kitchen's favorite accompaniments for ham:

- Glazed Brussels Sprouts with Chestnuts (page 183)
- Steamed Cauliflower with Browned Butter, Walnuts, and Crispy Sage (page 192)
- ...eamed Cauliflower with Cheddar-...rd Cream Sauce (page 192)
- ...eans with Quatre-Épices

...Greens with Mustard
...17)

...Shallots and

...297)

297

Scalloped Potato... and Smoked Ched...

Chipotle Chile ...se

Follow the recipe for Wee... adding 1 large chipotle ... minced (about 1½ tablespo... garlic and substituting smoked... the regular cheddar.

...ped Potatoes, ...obo sauce, ...ith the ...e for

Scalloped Potatoes with Fontin... Artichokes

Fontina is a semisoft cow's milk cheese with a m... flavor.

Thoroughly drain 4 ounces jarred or can... artichoke hearts and cut them into ½-inch piece... (You should have about 1 cup.) Follow the recipe for Weekday Scalloped Potatoes, adding the artichokes with the potatoes in step 2. Proceed as directed, replacing the cheddar with an equal amount of shredded fontina cheese.

BAKED SWEET POTATOES

SWEET POTATOES HAVE BEEN SERVED AT holiday meals long enough. They have wonderful flavor, and they're available all year, so why not bake and eat one anytime, just like a potato? We believed we should do just that, so we set out to find the best way to bake sweet potatoes. We were looking for evenly cooked, moist flesh and softened, slightly caramelized skin. In trying to reach this goal, we considered and tested 23 variables.

Oven variables included temperature, rack level, and use of a baking sheet to hold the potatoes as opposed to letting them sit on the oven rack. We found that the best oven temperature was 400 degrees. Lower temperatures took longer with no improvement, while higher temperatures left burnt spots on the bottom of the potatoes. Similarly, the best rack position was the center. Placing the rack either higher or lower caused the potatoes' thin skins to blacken. When we placed the potatoes directly on the rack, sticky juice oozed straight down and burned, so we decided on a baking sheet lined with foil.

We also tested a few quirky baking tips we

came across, such as placing the potatoes on unglazed oven tiles and beds of rock salt, but neither proved productive. We even tried cooking the potatoes halfway in the microwave and then transferring them to the oven, but the skin did not soften and there was no caramelization.

We also did a number of tests to find the best way to deal with the skin, which can be the best part of the potato when cooked properly. Uncoated skin stayed tough and unappealing, but coating it with butter tended to cause burning. Lightly rubbing it with vegetable or olive oil, though, softened the skin just the right amount. We also found that piercing the skin was essential to prevent the infamous exploding potato. But the big payoff in our search for tasty skin was the discovery that you should not turn the potatoes during baking. This method resulted in a perfectly browned bottom skin that was beautifully caramelized.

Baked Sweet Potatoes

SERVES 4

This recipe is for the moist, orange-fleshed varieties of sweet potato that generally show up in supermarkets. If you have white-fleshed sweet potatoes, increase the baking time by 10 minutes and use plenty of butter to moisten their drier flesh. You can cook up to 6 potatoes at once without altering the cooking time. Buying potatoes of the same size is a good idea because they will cook in the same amount of time. As with regular baked potatoes, we find it best to open the baked sweet potatoes as wide as possible so that steam can quickly escape; this ensures that the flesh is fluffy rather than dense.

4   small sweet potatoes (about 2 pounds), scrubbed and lightly pricked with a fork
2   tablespoons vegetable or olive oil
     Salt and ground black pepper
     Unsalted butter

1. Adjust an oven rack to the center position and heat the oven to 400 degrees. Rub the potatoes with the oil, then arrange them on a foil-lined baking sheet as far apart from each other as possible.

2. Bake until a knife tip slips easily into the center of a potato, 40 to 50 minutes. Remove the potatoes from the oven and pierce them with a fork to create a dotted X on the top of each potato (see illustration 1 on page 273). Press in at the ends of each sweet potato to push the flesh up and out (see illustration 2 on page 273). Season with salt and pepper to taste. Dot with butter to taste and serve immediately.

MASHED SWEET POTATOES

MASHED SWEET POTATOES ARE A NICE CHANGE from their usual candied guise. Yet even with a simple recipe, mashed sweet potatoes can pose problems. Nailing a fork-friendly puree every time is a form of cooking roulette. Mashed sweet potatoes often turn out thick and gluey or, at the other extreme, sloppy and loose. We also found that most recipes overload the dish with pumpkin pie seasonings that obscure the potato's natural flavor. We wanted a recipe that pushed that deep, earthy sweetness to the fore and that reliably produced a silky puree with enough body to hold its shape on a fork.

To determine the best cooking method, we tested a variety of techniques: baking potatoes unpeeled, boiling them whole and unpeeled, boiling them peeled and diced, steaming them peeled and diced, and microwaving them whole and unpeeled. Adding a little butter and salt to the potatoes after mashing, we found, yielded a huge improvement in texture, flavor, and ease of preparation.

The baked sweet potatoes produced a mash with a deep flavor and bright color, but the potatoes took more than an hour to bake through, and handling them hot from the oven was risky. Boiling whole sweet potatoes in their skins yielded a wet puree with a mild flavor. When we used a fork to monitor the potatoes as they cooked, we made holes that apparently let the flavor seep out and water seep in. Steaming and boiling pieces of peeled potato produced the worst purees, with zero flavor and loose, applesauce-like textures. The microwave, although fast and easy, was also a disappointment. The rate of cooking was difficult to control, and the difference between undercooked and overdone was only about 30 seconds. Over-microwaving the potatoes, even slightly, produced a pasty mouthfeel and an odd plastic flavor. By all accounts, this first round of testing bombed. Yet it did end up pointing us in a promising direction.

We had certainly learned a few facts about cooking sweet potatoes. First, their deep, hearty flavor is surprisingly fleeting and easily washed out. Second, the tough, dense flesh reacts much like winter squash when it's cooked, turning wet and sloppy. We also found it safer to peel the sweet potatoes when raw and cold rather than cooked and hot. Taking all of this into account, we wondered if braising the sweet potatoes might work. If cut into uniform pieces and cooked over low heat in a covered pan, the potatoes might release their own moisture slowly and braise themselves.

Adding a little water to the pan to get the process going, we found the sweet potatoes were tender in about 40 minutes. We then simply removed the lid and mashed them right in the pot. To our delight, they were full of flavor because they had essentially cooked in their own liquid. We tried various pots and heat levels and found that a medium pot (accommodating two or three layers of potatoes) in combination with low heat worked best.

Up to this point, we had been adding only butter to the mash; we wondered what the typical additions of cream, milk, or half-and-half would do. Making four batches side by side, we tasted mashes made with only butter, with butter and milk, with butter and half-and-half, and with butter and heavy cream. Tasters found the butter batch boring, while milk turned the mash bland and watery. The batch made with half-and-half came in second, with heartier flavor and fuller body, but the heavy cream stole the show.

EQUIPMENT: Potato Mashers

The two classic styles of potato masher are the wire-looped masher with a zigzag presser and the disk masher with a perforated round or oval plate. Modern mashers, as it turns out, are simply variations of these two original designs. We tested eight mashers to see which had the most comfortable grip and the most effective means of mashing.

When we wrapped up our mash-fest, we concluded that the wire-looped mashers were second-rate. The space between the loops made it hard to achieve a good, fast mash, and most of the potato pieces escaped between the loops unscathed. One model, the Exeter Double Masher ($9.99), is worth mentioning, however, as it is spring-loaded and uses a double-tiered set of wire loops for mashing. It took some muscle to use this masher, but it was the fastest of all the mashers tested, turning a pot of cooked potatoes into a smooth puree in just 20 strokes.

In general, the disk mashers outperformed the wire-looped models, and the Profi Plus ($15.99) was our favorite. With its small holes, this oval-based masher turned out soft and silky spuds with a reasonable 40 thrusts. Its rounded edges snuggled right into the curves of the saucepan, enhancing its efficacy, and its round handle was easy to grip. The runner-up, the Oxo Smooth Masher ($9.99), has an oval metal base and rectangular perforations. The larger perforations allowed a bit more potato through, so it took 50 mashes to get the job done; still, this squat device with its cushiony handle was easy to use. We did not like the all-plastic Oxo Good Grips Masher—it has an awkward grip and ineffective mash—so shop carefully if buying this brand.

THE BEST POTATO MASHERS

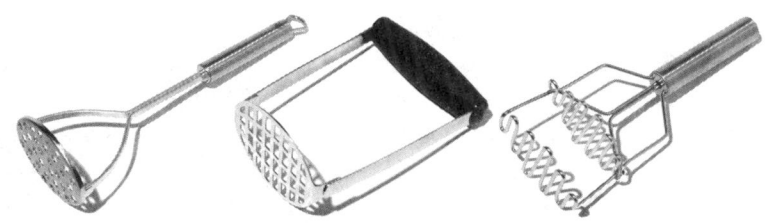

The Profi Plus Masher (left) yielded silky spuds with little effort and was testers' top choice. The Oxo Smooth Masher (center) was comfortable but slower than the winner, making it our runner-up. The spring-loaded Exeter Double Masher (right) was the best of the wire-loop mashers. Although fast, it was a bit awkward to use.

As we had now made this recipe many times, a glaring oversight became obvious. Why didn't we replace the small amount of water used to cook the potatoes with the butter and heavy cream? Curious about how the recipe would react without the water, we were gratified when this stream-lined technique produced the ultimate mash. The puree stood up on a fork, with a luxurious texture that was neither loose nor gluey. And with the water out of the picture, the sweet potato flavor was more intense than ever.

Mashed Sweet Potatoes

SERVES 4

Cutting the sweet potatoes into slices of even thickness is important in getting them to cook at the same rate. The potatoes are best served immediately, but they can be covered tightly with plastic wrap and kept relatively hot for 30 minutes. This recipe can be doubled and prepared in a Dutch oven; the cooking time must be doubled as well.

> 4 tablespoons (½ stick) unsalted butter, cut into 4 pieces
> 2 tablespoons heavy cream
> ½ teaspoon salt
> 1 teaspoon sugar
> 2 pounds sweet potatoes (about 2 large or 3 medium), scrubbed, peeled, quartered lengthwise, and cut crosswise into ¼-inch-thick slices
> Pinch ground black pepper

1. Combine the butter, cream, salt, sugar, and sweet potatoes in a 3- to 4-quart saucepan. Cover and cook over low heat, stirring occasionally, until the potatoes fall apart when poked with a fork, 35 to 45 minutes.

2. Off the heat, mash the sweet potatoes in the saucepan with a potato masher. Stir in the pepper and serve immediately.

➤ VARIATIONS

Mashed Sweet Potatoes with Ginger and Brown Sugar

If you like, garnish these potatoes with chopped crystallized ginger.

Follow the recipe for Mashed Sweet Potatoes, replacing the sugar with 1½ tablespoons light or dark brown sugar and adding 2 teaspoons minced or grated fresh ginger along with the sweet potatoes in step 1.

Mashed Sweet Potatoes with Sesame and Scallions

The tahini gives these potatoes a wonderful, nutty flavor. Toast the sesame seeds in a small dry skillet until fragrant, which should take about 4 minutes.

Follow the recipe for Mashed Sweet Potatoes, adding ½ teaspoon toasted sesame oil along with the sweet potatoes in step 1. Proceed as directed, stirring in 2 tablespoons toasted sesame seeds, 1 tablespoon tahini, and 1 medium scallion, sliced thin, along with the pepper in step 2.

Garlic-Scented Mashed Sweet Potatoes with Coconut Milk and Cilantro

Thai flavors provided the inspiration for this variation.

Follow the recipe for Mashed Sweet Potatoes, substituting ½ cup coconut milk for the butter and cream and adding ¼ teaspoon red pepper flakes and 1 small garlic clove, minced, to the saucepan along with the sweet potatoes. Stir in 1 tablespoon minced fresh cilantro leaves along with the black pepper.

CANDIED SWEET POTATO CASSEROLE

CANDIED SWEET POTATOES ARE A TRADI-tional side dish served alongside a roast ham or Thanksgiving turkey. All too often, how-ever, they turn out watery, overseasoned, and overly sweet, tasting more like a loose, crustless pumpkin pie than a savory side dish. We wanted lightly seasoned and perfectly cooked sweet potatoes soft enough to slice with a fork, yet resilient enough not to fall through the fork tines while being eaten.

To start, we followed the method touted in many cookbooks and boiled peeled pieces of sweet potato before tossing them with a brown sugar–and–butter sauce. Despite the popularity of this method, we found these sweet potatoes to be watery and lacking in flavor. Boiling them washed away vital flavors and added moisture that was difficult to get rid of. Next we tossed raw, peeled pieces of sweet potato with brown sugar and butter and baked them in a covered casserole dish. This method produced a watery sauce as well as unevenly cooked sweet potatoes. As the brown sugar and butter began to melt, the potatoes leached some of their liquid, making a watery cooking solution in which the potatoes began to float. It was difficult to keep these floating sweet potatoes completely submerged, and any unsubmerged parts of the potatoes dried out.

We had better luck once we tried cooking the sweet potatoes on the stovetop. When we cooked the potatoes in a Dutch oven with butter and brown sugar, the flavors of the potatoes and the sauce melded. Moistened with a little water and covered, the sweet potatoes cooked perfectly in about 50 minutes, resulting in the ultimate candied sweet potatoes, with a rich and complex sauce. Although the sauce was still a bit watery when we removed the lid, it was easy to crank up the heat and reduce it quickly to a thicker consistency.

Now that the potatoes were done, we could focus on the topping. Pecans are a natural with sweet potatoes. We decided to leave them whole instead of chopping them, and this made for a nice presentation. Pecans mixed with a beaten egg white, brown sugar, and some cayenne and cumin made for a topping that could hold its own against the robust sweet potatoes. After just 15 minutes in a hot oven, this casserole was cooked through and the flavors had melded.

Candied Sweet Potato Casserole

SERVES 10 TO 12

To make ahead, follow the recipe through step 2. Refrigerate the sweet potato mixture in a large bowl tightly wrapped with plastic wrap for up to 1 day. To bake: Poke several holes in the plastic wrap and microwave on medium-high until hot, 3 to 5 minutes. Continue to assemble and bake the casserole as directed in steps 3 and 4.

SWEET POTATOES

8	tablespoons (1 stick) unsalted butter, cut into 1-inch chunks
5	pounds sweet potatoes (about 8 medium), scrubbed, peeled, and cut into 1-inch cubes
1	cup packed light brown sugar
1½	teaspoons salt
½	teaspoon ground black pepper
½	cup water

TOPPING

1	egg white, lightly beaten
½	cup packed light brown sugar
⅛	teaspoon salt
	Pinch cayenne pepper
	Pinch ground cumin
2	cups pecan halves

1. FOR THE SWEET POTATOES: Melt the butter in a large Dutch oven over medium-high heat. Add the sweet potatoes, brown sugar, salt, pepper, and water; bring to a simmer. Reduce the heat to medium-low, cover, and cook, stirring often, until the sweet potatoes are tender (a paring knife can be slipped into and out of the center of the potatoes with very little resistance), 45 to 60 minutes.

2. When the sweet potatoes are tender, remove the lid and bring the sauce to a rapid simmer over medium-high heat. Continue to simmer until the sauce has reduced to a glaze, 7 to 10 minutes.

3. FOR THE TOPPING: Meanwhile, mix all the ingredients for the topping together in a medium bowl; set aside.

4. Adjust an oven rack to the middle position and heat the oven to 450 degrees. Pour the potato mixture into a 13 by 9-inch baking dish. Spread the topping over the potatoes. Bake until the pecans are toasted and crisp, 10 to 15 minutes. Serve immediately.

➤ VARIATION

Candied Sweet Potato Casserole with Toasted Marshmallow Topping

Follow the recipe for Candied Sweet Potato Casserole, substituting 4 cups mini-marshmallows for the pecan topping. Bake until the marshmallows are crisp and golden, about 5 minutes.

5

RICE, GRAIN, AND BEAN
SIDES AND CASSEROLES

WHAT DOES A STEAMING DISH OF MACARONI and cheese have in common with a bowl of garlicky black beans or a creamy risotto? They're all side dishes that we associate with comfort foods. Many of them are also versatile enough that with a little added protein or served in larger portions, they make a hearty main meal.

And these sides needn't require hours of preparation. After all, who wants to spend a lot of time preparing a side dish when there's the main course to attend to? With a little advance planning, dried beans and whole grains can be soaked the night before and still be part of a weeknight meal. Cooks also have the option of choosing canned beans, quick-cooking grains such as rice and polenta, or pastas such as orzo and couscous for even speedier dishes.

Many of the more simple dishes can easily be transformed into something special. Throughout this chapter, we offer easy tips for jazzing up basic sides. Try stirring a tablespoon or two of pesto into plain white rice or spooning tomato sauce and diced mozzarella over hot polenta. We also offer suggestions for pairing sides with main courses, whether you're looking for something to serve with meat loaf or with grilled fish.

In developing these recipes, we've found myriad tips and techniques that guarantee successful results. Brown rice, for example, is best baked in the oven, not cooked on the stovetop. Baking the rice turns out evenly cooked grains with a pleasant chew. Using a heavy-bottomed pot to slow-cook polenta evenly is essential in unlocking the grain's smooth texture and sweet, corny flavor. Small white navy beans are the best legume for Boston Baked Beans. These beans become creamy yet remain intact during the long simmer this flavorful dish requires.

The recipes in this chapter run the gamut from side-dish workhorses—those that you'll make again and again, such as Basic White Rice and Baked Macaroni and Cheese—to more elegant fare such as Toasted Orzo Pilaf with Peas and Parmesan and Risotto Cakes. While you may be tempted to serve these dishes with abandon, remember that many of them are rich and filling and should complement your main course, not overtake it—so be judicious with portions.

WHITE RICE

FEW FOODS ARE AS SATISFYING AS perfectly cooked rice. But this elemental food can be temperamental—it can resist the cook and become a pot of true grit or dissolve into an unpleasant, gummy mess. Advertisements stress perfect rice, but package instructions are unreliable when you want a tasty bowl of fluffy rice with separate grains. We wanted to find an easy method for making really great long-grain white rice.

We started our tests by following the package directions on four brands of long-grain rice. The technique was a variation on a simmer-covered method, with 1 cup rice to 2 to 2½ cups water. Some of the directions called for salt, some didn't, and there were recipes with and without butter. All the recipes were disappointing—the results mostly insipid, with mushy, frayed grains. There was gritty rice, there was chalky rice, but there was no rice that we liked.

Next we tried a method popular with French and Indian cooks—boiling the rice in a generous quantity of salted water, as if cooking pasta. Cooked this way, all types of rice came to the table evenly done, with individual grains, but they were also waterlogged and bland-tasting.

Then we experimented with baking the rice in casseroles, with 1¾ to 2½ parts water to 1 part rice, some with butter, some salted and others unsalted. Boiling water was poured over the rice, and then the pots were sealed with foil and baked for 25 to 30 minutes. The rice made with less water and with salt was better. This result was somewhat beside the point, however, because baked rice, while slightly creamy, did not have the well-defined grains we wanted.

The perfect method was still eluding us, but we had discerned a pattern: Less water and an even, gentle heat worked better. So we tried a pilaf method, because pilaf recipes generally use less water and produce distinct grains of rice. First we sautéed the rice in 2 teaspoons butter or oil, with the amount of water added varying from 1 to 2 cups. After the water came to a boil, we covered the pan and let the rice simmer for 15 minutes, then removed it from the heat and let it rest a bit prior to serving. With this method, the rice cooked up light and tender but not mushy or clumped, and the sauté added a rich dimension of flavor

No matter the variety of rice, we preferred the ratio of 1 cup rice to 1½ cups water. The grains should be sautéed and stirred until some have become milky white. For a stronger, nuttier flavor, the raw rice can be fried to a toasted golden brown.

We were curious to try the same formula (1 cup rice, 1½ cups water, ½ teaspoon salt) without sautéing. Fluffed with a fork, rice cooked in this manner is almost as fluffy as the pilaf-method rice, with a mild flavor that highlights the subtly floral, "ricey" aromatics. At a small sacrifice of texture, this is the ideal rice for many chicken stews and fish dishes.

There was some flexibility in cooking time, as long as the rice was allowed to rest, covered, after cooking. We got the most consistent results with a cooking time of 15 to 18 minutes from when the pot was sealed to the time the rice was done, with a 15-minute rest on the turned-off burner. (Don't pull the cover off the pot to peek—you want the pot to hold in the heat.) Before serving, fluff the rice with a fork.

White Rice
SERVES 4

This recipe is designed for 1 cup of raw rice in a tight-lidded pot. As you cook more rice, you should reduce the proportion of water. With 2 cups of rice, you can get these results with 2½ to 2¾ cups of water. It is very hard to get a reliable result with less than a cup of rice, however, so we do not advise halving the recipe.

2   teaspoons unsalted butter or vegetable or olive oil
1   cup long-grain white rice (not converted)
1½ cups water
½   teaspoon salt

1. Heat the butter in a 2-quart medium saucepan over medium heat. Add the rice; cook, stirring constantly, for 1 to 3 minutes, depending on the desired amount of nutty flavor. Add the water and salt; bring to a boil, swirling the pot to blend the ingredients.

2. Reduce the heat to low, cover tightly, and cook until the water is absorbed, about 15 minutes.

3. Turn off the heat; let the rice stand on the burner, still covered, to finish cooking, about 15 minutes longer. Fluff with a fork and serve.

RICE PILAF

ACCORDING TO MOST CULINARY SOURCES, rice pilaf is long-grain rice that has been cooked in hot oil or butter before being simmered in hot liquid, typically either water or stock. At its most basic, pilaf is a simple rice dish, made rich and flavorful from the sauté and the addition of an aromatic such as onion or garlic. In Middle Eastern cuisines, the term "pilaf" also refers to a more substantial dish in which the rice is cooked in this manner and then flavored with other ingredients—spices, nuts, dried fruits, and/or chicken or other meat. To avoid confusion, we decided to call the simple master recipe for our dish "pilaf-style" rice, designating the flavored versions as rice pilaf.

The logical first step in this process was to isolate the best type of rice for pilaf. We immediately limited our testing to long-grain rice, as medium- and short-grain rice inherently produce a rather sticky, starchy product and we were looking for fluffy, separate grains.

Plain long-grain white rice worked well in our pilaf, but basmati rice was even better: Each grain was separate, long, and fluffy, and the rice had a fresh, delicate fragrance. That said, we would add that you can use plain long-grain white rice if basmati is not available.

Most sources indicate that the proper ratio of rice to liquid for long-grain white rice is 1 to 2, but many cooks use less water. After testing every possibility, from 1:1 to 1:2, we found that we got the best rice using 1¾ cups of water for every cup of rice. To make this easier to remember, as well as easier to measure, we increased the rice by half to 1½ cups and the liquid to 2½ cups.

With our rice-to-water ratio set, we were ready to test the traditional method, which called for rinsing the rice before cooking it. Most recipes declare this step to be essential to producing rice with distinct, separate grains that are light and fluffy. Rinsing the rice made a substantial difference, particularly with basmati rice. We simply covered 1½ cups of rice with water, gently moved the grains around using our fingers, and drained the water from the rice. We repeated this process four or five times until the rinsing water was clear enough for us to see the grains distinctly. We then drained the rice and cooked it in oil and liquid. The resulting rice was less hard and more tender, and it had a slightly shinier, smoother appearance.

We allowed the rice to steam for 10 minutes after being removed from the heat to ensure that the moisture was distributed throughout. We wondered if a longer or shorter steaming time would make much of a difference in the resulting pilaf. We made a few batches of pilaf, allowing it to steam for 5 minutes, 10 minutes, and 15 minutes. The pilaf that steamed for 5 minutes was heavy and wet. The batch that steamed for 15 minutes was the lightest and least watery. We also decided to try placing a clean kitchen towel between the pan and the lid right after we took the rice off the stove. We found that this produced the best results of all, while reducing the steaming time to only 10 minutes. It seems that the towel (or two layers of paper towels) prevents condensation and absorbs the excess water in the pan during steaming, producing drier, fluffier rice.

From previous kitchen tests, we knew that sautéing the rice was essential for a light, nutty

flavor and tender texture, but we were surprised to see that many Middle Eastern recipes called for as much as a cup of butter per cup of rice. Because we like the extra flavor and richness that butter lends to the rice, we decided to use it but to cut down on the amount. We tried from 1 to 4 tablespoons per 1½ cups rice. Three tablespoons turned out to be optimal. The rice was buttery and rich without being overwhelmingly so, and each grain was shinier and more distinct than when cooked with less fat.

The addition of flavorings, seasonings, and other ingredients is what gives pilaf its distinctive character. We found that dried spices, minced ginger, and onion and garlic are best sautéed briefly in the fat before the raw rice is added to the pan. Saffron and dried herbs are best added to the liquid as it heats up, while fresh herbs and toasted nuts should be added to the pilaf just before serving to maximize freshness, texture (in the case of nuts), and flavor. Dried fruits such as raisins, currants, or figs can be incorporated just before steaming the rice, which gives them enough time to heat through and plump up without becoming soggy.

Basic Pilaf–Style Rice
SERVES 4

If you like, olive oil can be substituted for the butter depending on what you are serving with the pilaf. For the most evenly cooked rice, use a wide-bottomed saucepan with a tight-fitting lid.

1½	cups basmati or plain long-grain rice
2½	cups water
1½	teaspoons salt
	Ground black pepper
3	tablespoons unsalted butter
1	small onion, minced

1. Place the rice in a medium bowl and add enough water to cover the rice by 2 inches; using your hands, gently swish the grains to release excess starch. Carefully pour off the water, leaving the rice in the bowl. Repeat 4 or 5 times, until the water runs almost clear. Using a colander or

STEAMING RICE

After the rice is cooked, cover the pan with a clean kitchen towel, replace the lid, and allow the pan to sit for 10 minutes.

fine-mesh strainer, drain the water from the rice; place the colander over the bowl and set aside.

2. Bring the water to a boil, covered, in a small saucepan over medium-high heat. Add the salt and season with pepper to taste; cover to keep hot. Meanwhile, heat the butter in a large saucepan over medium heat until the foam begins to subside; add the onion and sauté until softened but not browned, about 4 minutes. Add the rice and stir to coat the grains with butter; cook until the edges of the grains begin to turn translucent, about 3 minutes. Stir the hot seasoned water into the rice; return to a boil, then reduce the heat to low, cover, and simmer until all the water is absorbed, 16 to 18 minutes. Off the heat, remove the lid, and place a clean kitchen towel folded in half over the saucepan (see the illustration on the facing page); replace the lid. Let stand 10 minutes; fluff the rice with a fork and serve.

➤ VARIATIONS

Rice Pilaf with Currants and Pine Nuts

When toasting the pine nuts, note that they can go from toasted to burnt and inedible very quickly.

Toast ¼ cup pine nuts in a small dry skillet over medium heat until golden and fragrant, about 5 minutes; set aside. Follow the recipe for Basic Pilaf-Style Rice, adding ½ teaspoon turmeric, ¼ teaspoon ground cinnamon, and 2 medium garlic cloves, minced or pressed through a garlic press, to the sautéed onion; cook until fragrant, about 30 seconds longer. After taking the pilaf off the heat but before covering the saucepan with the kitchen towel, sprinkle ¼ cup currants over the rice in the pan (do not mix in). When fluffing the rice with a fork, toss in the toasted pine nuts and mix in the currants.

Indian-Spiced Rice Pilaf with Dates and Parsley

Follow the recipe for Basic Pilaf-Style Rice, adding 2 medium garlic cloves, minced or pressed through a garlic press, 2 teaspoons grated fresh ginger, ⅛ teaspoon ground cinnamon, and ⅛ teaspoon ground cardamom to the sautéed onion; cook until fragrant, about 30 seconds longer. When the rice is off the heat, before covering the saucepan with the kitchen towel, add ¼ cup chopped dates and 2 tablespoons chopped fresh parsley leaves (do not mix in). Let stand and fluff as directed.

Rice Pilaf with Vermicelli

Break 4 ounces vermicelli into 1-inch pieces (you should have about 1 cup); set aside. Follow the recipe for Basic Pilaf-Style Rice, increasing the water to 3 cups and melting only 1½ tablespoon butter in a saucepan over medium heat; add the vermicelli and cook, stirring occasionally, until browned, about 3 minutes. Remove to a small bowl and set aside. Sauté the onion in the remaining 1½ tablespoons butter in the now-empty saucepan; add 2 medium garlic cloves, minced or pressed through a garlic press, ½ teaspoon ground cumin, ½ teaspoon ground coriander, and a pinch of allspice to the sautéed onion; cook until fragrant, about 30 seconds longer. Add the vermicelli along with the rice; proceed with the recipe as directed.

MEXICAN RICE

IN MEXICO, RICE PILAF, OR SOPA SECA (dry soup), often serves as a separate course, in the manner that Italians serve pasta; on the American table, it makes a unique side dish. Yet for a basic dish with a remarkably short ingredient list, we found it vexing. Variable ingredient quantities and cooking techniques produced disparate results when we put a selection of recipes from respected Mexican cookbook authors to the test. Two of these recipes turned out soupy and greasy. These supersoggy, oily versions were clearly off-track. Other recipes seemed misguided in terms of ingredient amounts. Some had just a hint of garlic, others tasted of tomato and nothing else, and one was overtaken by pungent cilantro.

To our thinking, the perfect version of this dish would exhibit clean, balanced flavors and tender, perfectly cooked rice. It would be rich but not oily, moist but not watery.

The liquid traditionally used in this dish is a mixture of chicken broth and pureed fresh tomatoes (plus a little salt); experiments with a variety of ratios helped us to settle on equal parts of each. With too much tomato puree, the rice tasted like warm gazpacho; with too little, its flavor waned.

Each and every recipe we consulted called for fresh tomatoes, and when we pitted rice made with canned tomatoes against rice made with fresh, the reason for using the latter crystallized for us. Batches made with fresh tomatoes tasted, well, fresh. Those made with canned tomatoes tasted overcooked and too tomatoey; the rice should be scented with tomatoes, not overtaken by them. To capture the one benefit of canned tomatoes—an intense, tomato-red color—we stirred in an untraditional ingredient: tomato paste. It gave the rice an appealing red hue while adding a little flavor to boot.

The usual method for making Mexican rice is to sauté rinsed, long-grain white rice in oil before adding the cooking liquid. Rice that was rinsed indeed produced more distinct, separate grains when compared with unrinsed rice. While some recipes call for only a quick sauté, cooking the rice until it was golden brown proved crucial in providing a mild, toasted flavor and satisfying texture. As for the amount of oil, we experimented with a wide range, from 3 tablespoons to 1¼ cups. When we essentially deep-fried the rice in copious amounts of oil, as more than one recipe suggested, the rice was much too oily; even straining off excess oil from the rice, as directed, didn't help, and it was a messy process. Insubstantial amounts of oil made rice that was dry and lacking richness. One-third of a cup seemed just right—this rice was rich but not greasy.

We had questions about whether to sauté other components of the recipe, such as the aromatics and the tomato pulp. We tried multiple permutations

---

INGREDIENTS: Long-Grain Rice

The beauty of white rice resides in its neutral flavor, which makes it good at carrying other flavors, as it does so well in our Mexican rice. But is all long-grain white rice created equal? We set up a taste test to find out.

We rounded up a converted rice, three standard supermarket options, and an organic white rice available in bulk from a natural foods market. These samples were tasted plain and in our Mexican rice recipe. All five brands rated well in the Mexican rice. Flavor differences were miniscule. With so many potent ingredients in this recipe (tomatoes, chiles, lime juice), these results are not terribly surprising. The most noticeable difference was an unpredictable variance in cooking time. According to the U.S. Rice Producers Association, the age of the rice, its moisture content, and the variety used can affect the rate of water uptake. Inconsistent cooking times are barely noticeable in plain rice, but

they can become more apparent when other ingredients—such as tomatoes and aromatics—are added to the pot. (In the case of our Mexican rice, you'll want to first check doneness after 30 minutes because of the unpredictable cooking time.)

When tasted plain, all of the rices but one were noted for being "clean" and "like rice should be." The exception was Uncle Ben's, a converted rice that failed to meet our standards on all fronts. Converted rice is processed in a way that ensures separate grains, a firm texture, and more pronounced flavor. Those "round," "rubbery" grains and the telltale yellowish tint immediately brought back not-so-fond memories of "dining hall rice." Tasters agreed that some "stickiness" and minor "clumping" make for more natural-looking and better-tasting rice. The recommended brands were universally liked and are listed here alphabetically.

THE BEST LONG-GRAIN RICE

The flavor of Canilla Extra Long (left) was likened to that of jasmine rice, and tasters found Carolina Extra Long Grain Enriched Rice (center) to have a good, clean slate on which to add flavor. Sem-Chi Organically Grown Florida Long Grain Rice (right) was rated the chewiest, with roasted and nutty flavors.

and landed on a compromised technique of sautéing a generous amount of garlic and jalapeños, then mixing in a raw puree of tomato and onion. This technique produced the balanced yet fresh-tasting flavor we were after; it also allowed us to process the onion in the food processor along with the tomatoes rather than having to chop it by hand.

We were having trouble achieving properly cooked rice on the stovetop. The grains inevitably scorched and then turned soupy when we attempted a rescue with extra broth. Prolonged cooking didn't solve the problem; what did was stirring the rice partway through cooking to reincorporate the tomato mixture, which had been settling on top of the pilaf. With this practice in place, every last grain cooked evenly.

While many traditional recipes consider fresh cilantro and minced jalapeño optional, in our book they are mandatory. The raw herbs and pungent chiles complement the richer tones of the cooked tomatoes, garlic, and onions. When a little something still seemed missing from the rice, we thought to offer wedges of lime. A squirt of acidity illuminated the flavor even further.

Mexican Rice

SERVES 6 TO 8

Because the spiciness of jalapeños varies from chile to chile, we try to control the heat by removing the seeds and ribs (the latter being the source of most of the heat) from the chiles that are cooked in the rice. Use an ovensafe pot about 12 inches in diameter so that the rice cooks evenly and in the time indicated. The pot's depth is less important than its diameter; we've successfully used both a straight-sided sauté pan and a Dutch oven. Whichever type of pot you use, it should have a tight-fitting, ovensafe lid. Vegetable broth can be substituted for the chicken broth.

2	medium ripe tomatoes, cored and quartered
1	medium onion, preferably white, peeled, trimmed of the root end and quartered
3	medium jalapeño chiles
2	cups long-grain white rice
1/3	cup canola oil
4	medium garlic cloves, minced or pressed through a garlic press (about 4 teaspoons)
2	cups low-sodium chicken broth
1	tablespoon tomato paste
1 1/2	teaspoons salt
1/2	cup minced fresh cilantro leaves
1	lime, cut into wedges

1. Adjust an oven rack to the middle position and heat the oven to 350 degrees. Process the tomatoes and onion in a food processor until smooth and thoroughly pureed, about 15 seconds, scraping down the bowl if necessary. Transfer the mixture to a liquid measuring cup; you should have 2 cups (if necessary, spoon off any excess so that the volume equals 2 cups). Remove the ribs and seeds from 2 jalapeños and discard; mince the flesh and set aside. Mince the remaining jalapeño, including the ribs and seeds; set aside.

2. Place the rice in a large fine-mesh strainer and rinse it under cold running water until the water runs clear, about 1 1/2 minutes. Shake the rice vigorously in a strainer to remove excess water.

3. Heat the oil in a large, heavy-bottomed, ovensafe straight-sided sauté pan or Dutch oven with a tight-fitting lid over medium-high heat for 1 to 2 minutes. Drop 3 or 4 grains of rice in the oil; if the grains sizzle, the oil is ready. Add the rice and sauté, stirring frequently, until the rice is light golden and translucent, 6 to 8 minutes. Reduce the heat to medium and add the garlic and seeded minced jalapeños; cook, stirring constantly, until fragrant, about 1 1/2 minutes. Stir in the pureed tomatoes and onion, chicken broth, tomato paste, and salt; increase the heat to medium-high and bring to a boil. Cover the pan and transfer it to the oven; bake until the liquid is absorbed and the rice is tender, 30 to 35 minutes, stirring well after 15 minutes.

4. Stir in the cilantro and reserved minced jalapeño with ribs and seeds to taste. Serve immediately, passing the lime wedges separately.

✒ VARIATION

Mexican Rice with Charred Tomatoes, Chiles, and Onion

Because the spiciness of jalapeños varies from chile to chile, we try to control the heat by removing the seeds and ribs (the latter being the source of most of the heat) from those chiles that are cooked into the rice. In this variation, the vegetables are charred in a cast-iron skillet, which gives the finished dish a deeper color and a slightly toasty, smoky flavor. A cast-iron skillet works best—a traditional or a nonstick skillet will be left with burnt spots that are difficult to remove, even with vigorous scrubbing.

2	medium ripe tomatoes, cored
I	medium onion, preferably white, peeled and halved
6	medium garlic cloves, unpeeled
3	medium jalapeño chiles, 2 halved, with seeds and ribs removed, I with seeds and ribs intact, minced
2	cups long-grain white rice
1/3	cup canola oil
2	cups low-sodium chicken broth
I	tablespoon tomato paste
1 1/2	teaspoons salt
1/2	cup minced fresh cilantro leaves
I	lime, cut into wedges

1. Heat a large cast-iron skillet over medium-high heat for about 2 minutes. Add the tomatoes, onion, garlic, and halved chiles; toast the vegetables, using tongs to turn them frequently, until softened and almost completely blackened, about 10 minutes for the tomatoes and 15 to 20 minutes for the other vegetables. When cool enough to handle, trim the root end from the onion and halve each piece. Remove the skins from the garlic and mince the cloves. Mince the jalapeños.

2. Adjust an oven rack to the middle position and heat the oven to 350 degrees. Process the toasted tomato and onion in a food processor until smooth and thoroughly pureed, about 15 seconds, scraping down the bowl if necessary. Transfer the mixture to a liquid measuring cup; you should have 2 cups (if necessary, spoon off any excess so that the volume equals 2 cups).

3. Place the rice in a large fine-mesh strainer and rinse it under cold running water until the water runs clear, about 1½ minutes. Shake the rice vigorously in the strainer to remove the excess water.

4. Heat the oil in a large, heavy-bottomed, ovensafe straight-sided sauté pan or Dutch oven with a tight-fitting lid over medium-high heat for

1 to 2 minutes. Drop 3 or 4 grains of rice in the oil; if the grains sizzle, the oil is ready. Add the rice and sauté, stirring frequently, until the rice is light golden and translucent, 6 to 8 minutes. Stir in the pureed tomato mixture, roasted jalapeños and garlic, chicken broth, tomato paste, and salt; bring to a boil. Cover the pan and transfer it to the oven; bake until the liquid is absorbed and the rice is tender, 30 to 35 minutes, stirring well after 15 minutes.

5. Stir in the cilantro and reserved minced jalapeño with ribs and seeds to taste. Serve immediately, passing the lime wedges separately.

BROWN RICE

BROWN RICE SHOULD BE SLIGHTLY STICKY, with a hint of chew and a nutty flavor. An ideal version should be easy to come by: Just throw rice and water in a pot and set the timer, right? Yet cooks who have attempted to prepare brown rice know it isn't that simple. Most cooks make the mistake (born of impatience) of cranking up the flame in an effort to hurry along the slow-cooking grains (brown rice takes roughly twice as long to cook as white), which inevitably leads to a burnt pot and crunchy rice. Adding plenty of water isn't the remedy, either; excess liquid swells the rice into a gelatinous, wet mass.

We used an expensive, heavy-bottomed pot with a tight-fitting lid (many recipes caution against using inadequate cookware), fiddled with the traditional absorption method (cooking the rice with just enough water), and eventually landed on a workable recipe. Yet when we tested the recipe with less-than-ideal equipment—namely, a flimsy pan with an ill-fitting lid—we were back to burnt, underdone rice. With the very best pot and a top-notch stove, it is possible to cook brown rice properly on top of the stove, but we wanted a surefire method that would work no matter the cook, no matter the equipment.

Although we rarely use the microwave, we thought it might work well in this instance, given that it cooks food indirectly, without a burner. Sadly, it delivered inconsistent results, with one batch turning brittle and another, prepared in a different microwave, too sticky. A rice cooker yielded flawless brown rice on the first try, but many Americans don't own one.

We set out to construct a homemade cooker that would approximate the controlled, indirect heat of a rice cooker. We started with an everyday collapsible vegetable steamer, lined the steamer basket successively with cheesecloth, a coffee filter, and a thin kitchen towel. In each case, it was impossible to stir neatly and consistently during cooking, and the result was irregularly cooked rice. A long-handled fine-mesh strainer used in place of the steamer also failed; the strainer's handle precluded a tight seal between pot rim and lid, and the rice was still raw after two hours.

We then began to consider the merits of cooking the rice in the oven. We'd have more precise temperature control, and we figured that the oven's encircling heat would eliminate the risk of scorching. Our first try yielded extremely promising results: With the pan tightly covered in aluminum foil, the rice steamed to near perfection. Fine-tuning the amount of water, we settled on a ratio similar to that used for our white rice recipe: 2⅓ cups of water to 1½ cups of rice, falling well short of the 2:1 water-to-rice ratio advised by most rice producers and nearly every recipe we consulted. Perhaps that is why so much brown rice turns out sodden and overcooked.

Our next task was to spruce up the recipe by bringing out the nutty flavor of the otherwise plain grains. Adding a small amount (2 teaspoons) of either butter or oil to the cooking liquid added mild flavor while keeping the rice fluffy.

To reduce what was a long baking time of 90 minutes at 350 degrees, we tried starting with boiling water instead of cold tap water and raising the oven temperature to 375 degrees. These steps reduced the baking time to a reasonable one hour. (A hotter oven caused some of the fragile grains to explode.)

Oven-Baked Brown Rice

SERVES 4 TO 6

Base your decision on whether to use oil or butter in the recipe on the dish the rice will accompany; for example, if you are serving a stir-fry, use oil for the rice. To minimize

any loss of water through evaporation, cover the saucepan as the water is heating, and use the water as soon as it reaches a boil. If you own an 8-inch ceramic baking dish with a lid, use it instead of the glass baking dish and foil. To double the recipe, use a 13 by 9-inch baking dish; the baking time need not be increased.

1½	cups long-, medium-, or short-grain brown rice
2⅓	cups water
2	teaspoons unsalted butter or vegetable oil
½	teaspoon salt

1. Adjust an oven rack to the middle position and heat the oven to 375 degrees. Spread the rice in an 8-inch-square glass baking dish.

2. Bring the water and butter to a boil, covered, in a medium saucepan over high heat; once boiling, immediately stir in the salt and pour the water over the rice. Cover the baking dish tightly with a double layer of foil. Bake the rice until tender, about 1 hour.

3. Remove the baking dish from the oven and uncover. Fluff the rice with a fork, then cover the dish with a clean kitchen towel; let the rice stand for 5 minutes. Uncover and let the rice stand 5 minutes longer; serve immediately.

➤ VARIATIONS

Brown Rice with Parmesan, Lemon, and Herbs

2	tablespoons unsalted butter
1	small onion, chopped medium
1½	cups long-, medium-, or short-grain brown rice
2⅓	cups low-sodium chicken broth
⅛	teaspoon salt
⅛	teaspoon ground black pepper
¼	cup minced fresh parsley leaves
¼	cup chopped fresh basil leaves
1	ounce Parmesan cheese, freshly grated (about ½ cup)
1	teaspoon grated zest and ½ teaspoon juice from 1 lemon

1. Heat the butter in a medium nonstick skillet over medium-high heat until foaming; add the

onion and cook, stirring occasionally, until translucent, about 3 minutes.

2. Adjust an oven rack to the middle position; heat the oven to 375 degrees. Spread the rice in an 8-inch-square glass baking dish.

3. Bring the chicken broth to a boil, covered, in a medium saucepan over high heat; once boiling, immediately stir in the salt and pour the broth over the rice. Cover the baking dish tightly with a double layer of foil. Bake the rice until tender, about 1 hour and 10 minutes.

4. Remove the baking dish from the oven, uncover, and fluff the rice with a fork. Stir in the pepper, parsley, basil, Parmesan, lemon zest, and lemon juice. Cover the dish with a clean kitchen towel; let the rice stand for 5 minutes. Uncover and let the rice stand 5 minutes longer; serve immediately.

Curried Brown Rice with Tomatoes and Peas

2	tablespoons unsalted butter
I	small onion, chopped medium
I¹/₂	teaspoons hot curry powder
I	tablespoon minced fresh ginger
I	medium garlic clove, minced or pressed through a garlic press (about I teaspoon)
	Salt
I	(14.5-ounce) can diced tomatoes, drained
I¹/₂	cups long-, medium-, or short-grain brown rice
2¹/₃	cups low-sodium vegetable broth
¹/₂	cup frozen peas, thawed

1. Heat the butter in a medium nonstick skillet over medium-high heat until foaming; add the onion and cook, stirring occasionally, until translucent, about 3 minutes. Add the curry powder, ginger, garlic, and ¼ teaspoon salt; cook until fragrant, about 1 minute. Add the tomatoes and cook until heated through, about 2 minutes; set the skillet aside.

2. Adjust an oven rack to the middle position; heat the oven to 375 degrees. Spread the rice in an 8-inch-square glass baking dish.

3. Bring the vegetable broth to a boil, covered, in a medium saucepan over high heat; once boiling, immediately stir in ⅛ teaspoon salt and pour the broth over the rice. Stir the tomato mixture into the rice and spread the rice-tomato mixture in an even layer. Cover the baking dish tightly with a double layer of foil. Bake the rice until tender, about 1 hour and 10 minutes.

4. Remove the baking dish from the oven, uncover, and stir in the peas. Cover the dish with a clean kitchen towel; let the rice stand for 5 minutes. Uncover and let the rice stand for 5 minutes longer; serve immediately.

TOASTED ORZO PILAF

ORZO, LIKE COUSCOUS, IS A SMALL PASTA that is sometimes treated like a grain and used in pilaf recipes. Shaped like a grain of rice, orzo can be used to produce a pilaf similar in texture to risotto—but requiring a quarter of the work. Cookbooks are packed with ersatz recipes for no-stir risotto that fail to deliver as promised; the secret may be in using rice-shaped pasta over genuine Arborio rice—admittedly inauthentic, but delicious nonetheless.

The basic concept of orzo pilaf varies little from rice pilaf—sauté aromatics, toast the orzo, and simmer in liquid until tender—but cooking pasta, obviously, is different from cooking rice. Our testing thus focused on how long and at what temperature to toast the orzo for optimum flavor and texture and how much liquid was necessary for an al dente texture. For flavor, we decided simple was best and borrowed elements from a basic risotto—butter, shallots, white wine, chicken broth, and Parmesan cheese. In homage to the Venetian dish risi e bisi, or rice and peas, we included peas.

After toasting orzo to shades varying from pale yellow to golden brown, we found that the darker the orzo, the richer the flavor (shy of burning it, of course). Well-browned orzo possessed a full, nutty flavor that tasters favored over that of more lightly toasted orzo. Temperature alone appeared to have little effect on the orzo's flavor; the key, it turned out, was timing. We opted for medium-high heat, which produced golden orzo in about six minutes, though it did require diligent stirring and a watchful eye to prevent scorching.

Rice, predictably, requires about 1½ times its volume in liquid to plump, but we were not sure if this ratio would work for orzo. The pilaf is not drained of excess liquid, so we needed to ascertain the minimum amount of liquid necessary. In our first test, we added 6 cups chicken broth to 1 pound orzo (2½ cups), which resulted in an extraordinarily soupy pilaf. We then tried just 3 cups broth, but the orzo was chalky and undercooked. Four cups came closer to the mark, and an additional ¼ cup proved perfect; the orzo plumped to a tender yet firm consistency, somewhere between that of pasta and rice. We replaced part of the broth with an equal amount of vermouth and tasters liked the result. (White wine also worked well.)

We tried cooking the orzo as we would risotto by adding the liquid a little at a time but found this time-consuming technique unnecessary, as was a low, covered simmer, the standard when making rice pilaf. The easiest way proved the best. Once the broth came to a boil, we reduced the heat to medium-low and left the orzo uncovered and unattended, outside of a few sporadic stirs, until done— a mere 10 minutes. To preserve the color and flavor of the peas, we added them at the last minute, once the orzo was cooked through. The peas needed only about two minutes of ambient heat to warm through, despite directions on the package that suggested cooking them much longer.

Toasted Orzo Pilaf with Peas and Parmesan

SERVES 4 TO 6

Because the pan gets extremely hot while the orzo is toasting, be sure to add the broth off the heat and after the pan has cooled a bit; otherwise, the ensuing steam can be dangerous. For additional flavor, a couple of bay leaves, a few sprigs of thyme, or a small pinch of saffron can be added with the garlic. Just remember to remove the herbs prior to serving. Serve this basic pilaf with almost any dish, including red meat, poultry, and fish.

2	tablespoons unsalted butter
1	medium onion, chopped fine

	Salt
2	medium garlic cloves, minced or pressed through a garlic press (about 2 teaspoons)
1	pound orzo (about 2½ cups)
¾	cup vermouth or dry white wine
3½	cups low-sodium chicken broth
8	ounces frozen peas, thawed
2	ounces grated Parmesan cheese (about 1 cup)
	Pinch ground nutmeg
	Ground black pepper

1. Melt the butter in a large nonstick skillet over medium-high heat. Once the foaming subsides, add the onion and ¾ teaspoon salt and cook, stirring frequently, until the onion has softened and is just beginning to brown, about 4 minutes. Add the garlic and cook until fragrant, about 30 seconds. Stir in the orzo and cook, stirring frequently with a wooden spoon, until most of the grains are lightly browned and golden, 5 to 6 minutes.

2. Slide the skillet off the heat, cool for 30 seconds, then pour in the vermouth and broth, being careful to avoid the steam. Return the skillet to the burner and bring to a boil over medium-high heat. Reduce the heat to medium-low and simmer, stirring occasionally, until all of the liquid has been absorbed and the orzo is tender, 10 to 12 minutes.

3. Stir in the peas, cheese, and nutmeg. Remove the skillet from the heat and allow to sit for 2 minutes to heat the peas through. Adjust the seasonings, adding salt and pepper to taste. Serve immediately.

> VARIATIONS

Toasted Orzo Pilaf with Fennel, Orange, and Olives

1. Trim 1 small fennel bulb of stalks and fronds; trim the bottom ½ inch. Halve the bulb lengthwise and, using a paring knife, remove the core. Slice the bulb lengthwise into ¼-inch-thick strips, then cut the strips crosswise into ¼-inch dice.

2. Follow the recipe for Toasted Orzo Pilaf with Peas and Parmesan, adding the fennel, ¾ teaspoon fennel seeds, and a pinch of red pepper flakes along with the onion; increase the cooking time to about 6 minutes. Add 1 teaspoon grated orange zest along with the garlic and substitute ½ cup coarsely chopped oil-cured olives for the peas.

Toasted Orzo Pilaf with Bacon, Rosemary, and Peas

1. Fry 4 ounces (about 4 slices) of bacon, cut into ¼-inch pieces, in a large nonstick skillet over medium-high heat until brown and crisp, about 5 minutes. Using a slotted spoon, transfer the bacon to a paper towel–lined plate and set aside.

2. Follow the recipe for Toasted Orzo Pilaf with Peas and Parmesan, substituting the fat in the skillet for the butter. Add 1 sprig fresh rosemary with the vermouth and chicken broth and add the reserved bacon with the peas, Parmesan, and nutmeg. Discard the rosemary sprig before serving.

SAFFRON COUSCOUS PILAF

IN NORTH AFRICAN COOKING, THE LINE between sweet and savory dishes is fuzzy. Meats and vegetables are frequently combined with dried fruits, nuts, and warm spices generally reserved for sweets in European-style cooking. So a couscous pilaf with almonds and raisins is far from extraordinary; in fact, it's a staple dish throughout Morocco and Algeria. The pilaf's short list of ingredients and rapid cooking time are appealing. We had little to do to simplify the flavors, but we did find ways to save time.

Couscous is, technically, pasta—the tiny size is deceiving. It is made from semolina flour "rolled" with lightly salted water until the minute balls form; these are then steamed and dried for long-term storage. Traditionally, couscous is cooked in a special pot called a couscoussier, which is essentially a stockpot fitted with a small-holed colander. The couscous sits in the colander and plumps in the steam produced by the pot's contents—stock, soup, or stew. While an ersatz couscoussier can be rigged with a saucepan and colander, a much easier method produces entirely acceptable couscous. Hot water or stock is poured over couscous in a bowl, which is then sealed with plastic wrap. Within minutes—12, to be exact—the couscous is tender and ready to eat.

The drawback to this technique is that the couscous tends to clump into tight balls that must be separated—a labor-intensive chore that inevitably leads to burned fingertips. We found the addition of a little oil or butter to the hydrating liquid helped but didn't completely rectify the situation. Borrowing a technique from rice pilaf, we tried toasting the raw couscous in a little butter before adding the liquid. The resulting couscous was our best batch yet; the grains were discrete and the flavor nutty.

With our couscous plumped and smooth, we were ready to address the pilaf flavorings. As we had already heated a skillet to toast the couscous, it was easy to toast the almonds and sauté aromatics. We favored sliced almonds for both appearance and ease of use; the pale slivers rimmed with brown looked appealing against the couscous and required no preparation beyond the quick toasting. For aromatics, onions sautéed in butter lent the couscous both sweetness and a subtle sharpness.

We initially added the raisins after the onions were cooked, but they failed to fully plump and tasted too mild. We then tried adding them with the onions so that they were heated for several minutes, which markedly improved their flavor and texture.

Saffron gives couscous an alluring golden hue as well as a distinct aroma. Despite its stiff price tag, saffron can be an economical spice, as a little goes a long way. The fine threads are intensely potent, and we found that a small pinch—not even a quarter teaspoon—was ideal. Any more conveyed an unappealingly medicinal flavor.

For liquid, water was the easiest choice, but it made for a bland couscous, even with the onions, raisins, and saffron. We then tried chicken broth, but it was too strong; the chicken flavor overpowered the mild couscous. A combination of chicken broth and water, however, worked fine, giving the couscous body and a pleasant richness. As a final touch, we chose to add a little lemon juice, which sharpened the seasonings and balanced the sweet elements in the pilaf.

Saffron Couscous Pilaf with Raisins and Almonds

SERVES 4 TO 6

If you don't have saffron or dislike its potent flavor, don't skip this dish; substitute a couple of cinnamon sticks for a pleasant flavor and aroma. Add them with the onion so that they are exposed to dry heat, which intensifies their flavor. For the fluffiest texture, use a large fork to fluff the grains; a spoon or spatula can destroy the light texture. The simple flavors of the pilaf pair well with a wide variety of meat, poultry, and vegetable dishes. Specialty markets may carry couscous of varying sizes, but stick to the basic kind. Other sizes require different cooking methods.

4	tablespoons (½ stick) unsalted butter
2	cups couscous
¾	cup sliced almonds
1	small onion, chopped fine
	Pinch saffron threads, crumbled with fingertips
¾	cup raisins
	Salt
1¾	cups low-sodium chicken broth
2	cups water
1½	teaspoons juice from 1 lemon
	Ground black pepper

1. Melt 2 tablespoons of the butter in a large skillet over medium-high heat. When the foaming subsides, add the couscous and cook, stirring frequently with a wooden spoon, until some grains are just beginning to brown, about 3 minutes. Scrape the grains from the skillet into a large bowl and return the pan to medium heat. Add the almonds and cook, stirring frequently, until they are lightly toasted and aromatic, about 1½ minutes. Scrape them into a small bowl.

2. Add the remaining 2 tablespoons butter to the skillet. Once it melts, add the onion, saffron, raisins, and ¾ teaspoon salt and cook, stirring occasionally, until the onion has softened and is beginning to brown, about 5 minutes. Add the broth and the water, increase the heat to medium-high, and bring to a boil.

3. Add the boiling liquid to the bowl with the toasted couscous, cover tightly with plastic wrap, and allow to sit until the couscous is tender, about 12 minutes. Remove the plastic wrap, fluff the grains with a fork, and gently stir in the almonds and lemon juice. Adjust the seasonings with salt and pepper to taste and serve immediately.

BULGUR AND MUSHROOM PILAF

THROUGHOUT THE COUNTRIES OF THE eastern Mediterranean, including Turkey and Greece, bulgur is a staple grain. Produced from whole wheat kernels, it is highly nutritious and packed with an earthy, nutty flavor that is quite distinctive. Bulgur is used in everything from tabbouleh (most famously) to meatballs (called kibbeh) and—our top choice—pilaf. The relatively bland bulgur makes an ideal canvas for any number of assertive flavors. One of our favorites is a pilaf with mushrooms. Our goal was to reinvent this Mediterranean classic as a one-pan, quick-cooking pilaf—ready in minutes with a minimum of effort.

When bulgur is made, the whole wheat kernels are steamed, dried, and crushed into one of three grades—coarse, medium, or fine—each of which requires a different cooking method. Fine-grain bulgur, the variety most often seen in Middle Eastern dishes, must be rehydrated in hot liquid, not unlike couscous. Larger-grain bulgur, which we prefer for pilafs, must be simmered until tender, usually about 15 minutes.

Based on our work developing other pilaf recipes, we already had a cooking method in mind; we would use a large skillet from start to finish. The aromatics and mushrooms would be sautéed, then the bulgur and cooking liquid added and simmered until tender. Testing, then, was a matter of developing the fullest mushroom flavor and discovering how long and at what temperature to simmer the bulgur for the best texture.

To get intense mushroom flavor without resorting to pricey exotics, we frequently combine standard cultivated mushrooms—white button or cremini—with dried shiitake or porcini mushrooms. Relatively inexpensive and packed with flavor, the dried mushrooms impart an intensely earthy flavor and pungent aroma to the most mild-mannered fresh mushrooms. After rehydrating in hot water, the dried mushrooms are ready to cook, and the leftover soaking water can be used as a portion of the cooking liquid. After testing a few combinations, tasters favored the pairing of dried porcini and fresh cremini mushrooms; shiitakes tasted too Asian, and white button mushrooms lacked presence. To boost the mushroom flavor, we added both onion and garlic (pressed for the biggest impact) as well as soy sauce—odd in a Mediterranean dish but welcome nonetheless for its dramatic impact on mushroom flavor. Not identifiable as soy sauce per se once added to the dish, it deepened the mushroom flavor and color.

REHYDRATING DRIED PORCINI MUSHROOMS

We find that the microwave cuts soaking time for dried porcini from 20 minutes at room temperature to just 5 minutes. Place the dried porcini in a small strainer and rinse under cool running water. Transfer the porcini to a microwave-safe bowl, add ½ cup hot tap water, and cover with plastic wrap. Cut several steam vents in the plastic wrap and microwave on high power for 30 seconds. Remove the bowl from the microwave and let stand, covered, until the mushrooms soften, about 5 minutes. Here's how to remove the softened mushrooms from the liquid and leave the sand behind.

1. When soaking dried porcini mushrooms, most of the sand and dirt will fall to the bottom of the bowl. Use a fork to lift the rehydrated mushrooms from the liquid without stirring up the sand. If the mushrooms still feel gritty, rinse them briefly under cool running water.

2. The soaking liquid is quite flavorful and should be reserved. To remove the grit, pour the liquid through a small strainer lined with a coffee filter or a single sheet of paper towel and set over a measuring cup.

For the liquid, we tried both chicken broth and water. Independently, chicken broth was too strong and muddied the dish's flavors, but water made the pilaf too lean-tasting. A combination of the two gave the pilaf body without calling attention to the chicken flavor. Roughly 2 parts broth to 1 part water was just right.

As we explored the best way to cook the bulgur, we tried every approach from a full boil to a quiet simmer. Rapid simmering cooked the bulgur unevenly and gave it an unpleasant chewiness. Very low heat cooked the bulgur more evenly. While some recipes we found called for toasting the bulgur before adding liquid, we found this step unnecessary.

Herbs, however, were necessary to enliven the monotonous palette of browns as well as for flavor. Thyme reinforced the pilaf's earthy edge but lacked visual presence. Parsley brightened both flavor and color, so we chose it over the thyme and opted for a fairly generous amount—¼ cup.

Bulgur and Mushroom Pilaf

SERVES 4 TO 6

Watch for the term "cracked wheat" when purchasing bulgur; while it looks like bulgur, the two are not the same. Cracked wheat is uncooked, whereas bulgur is parcooked, and the two require different cooking methods. We prefer moderately coarse bulgur, which has a texture like that of kosher salt, to finer, sandy bulgur. Cremini mushrooms, also sold as baby bellas, are juvenile portobellos.

Despite its bold flavors, this pilaf is at home with a wide variety of main courses, including roast chicken, pork, and firm-fleshed fish such as halibut, swordfish, and sea bass.

½ ounce dried porcini mushrooms, rinsed

3 tablespoons unsalted butter

I medium onion, chopped fine
  Salt

8 ounces cremini (preferably) or white button mushrooms, wiped clean, stem ends trimmed, then quartered (or cut into 6 pieces if large)

2 medium garlic cloves, minced or pressed through a garlic press (about 2 teaspoons)

- 1½ cups bulgur, preferably medium-grain
- 1¾ cups low-sodium chicken broth
- 1½ teaspoons soy sauce
- ¼ cup chopped fresh parsley leaves
  Ground black pepper

1. Mix the dried porcini mushrooms with ½ cup hot tap water in a small microwave-safe bowl. Cover the bowl with plastic wrap, cut several steam vents with a paring knife, and microwave on high power for 30 seconds. Let stand until the mushrooms soften, about 5 minutes. Lift the mushrooms from the liquid with a fork and mince. Pour the liquid through a small strainer lined with a single layer of paper towel and placed over a measuring cup. Add enough water to the soaking liquid to total 1 cup and set aside.

2. Meanwhile, melt the butter in a large skillet over medium-high heat. When the foaming subsides, add the onion and ¼ teaspoon salt and cook, stirring occasionally, until the onion has softened, 3 to 4 minutes. Add the fresh mushrooms and cook until reduced in volume and beginning to brown, 3 to 4 minutes. Add the garlic and cook until fragrant, about 30 seconds. Stir in the bulgur, broth, soy sauce, and reserved mushroom soaking liquid and bring to a boil. Cover, reduce the heat to low, and simmer until the bulgur is tender, about 15 minutes. Using a fork, stir in the parsley and fluff the bulgur. Adjust the seasonings with salt and pepper to taste. Serve immediately.

RISOTTO

RISOTTO IS A SIMPLE RICE DISH ELEVATED TO ambrosia by the presence of a simple starchy sauce. Encouraged by judicious additions of wine and stock, the starch in the rice is transformed into a velvety, creamy sauce that clings to the toothsome grains.

Obviously, the rice is key to a texturally flawless risotto. We found that medium-grain rice is the best choice for risotto, where we want some starchiness but not too much. But not all medium-grain rice is the same. In our kitchen tests, we found that the risotto technique can be applied to non-Italian medium-grain rice, but the finished texture will pale in comparison to risotto made with Italian rice, which provides the best contrast between supple sauce and firm, toothsome rice. We think Italian rice is a must.

The Italian rice used for risotto comes in two grades: superfino and fino. Varieties include Arborio (the most widely available), Carnaroli, and Vialone Nano. In a side-by-side taste test of Arborio, Carnaroli, and Vialone Nano, tasters were split evenly between the Arborio and Carnaroli; those liking firmer rice grains chose Arborio, and those liking softer, creamier rice chose Carnaroli. Vialone Nano was deemed too soft and had a "pasty" texture, as if the grains lacked a firm center. One source suggested that Vialone Nano is most popular in and around Venice, where a decidedly loose, soupy texture is the desired consistency for risotto.

Luckily, risotto is so popular that most markets carry at least one brand of Italian rice, generally Arborio. Because this rice is so widely available, we call for it in our recipe. If you like a softer, creamier rice and can find Carnaroli, buy it; it can be used in all the risotto recipes that follow.

But having good-quality rice is only half the battle; cooking is the rest. After making countless batches with minute variations, we became certain about a few points. First, slowly cooking the diced onion until it yielded its juices and softened was imperative to the final flavor and texture. The sweetness of properly cooked onion gave this dish depth, and its softness allowed the onion to melt into the risotto by serving time. The next step was sautéing the rice, which prompts its starches to turn translucent—a good visual cue for adding liquid. When we did not cook the rice prior to adding liquid, the risotto was mushy and chalky and the rice grains lacked their distinctive toothsomeness.

Once the rice is toasted, the liquids are added. The wine must be added before the broth so that the boozy flavor has a chance to cook off. Otherwise, we found the alcohol punch was too much. Virtually all risottos are made with a light, dry white wine (although there are some regional specialties made with red wine). Risotto made without wine lacked dimension and tasted bland, so don't skip this ingredient.

The recipes we researched offered a wide range of options for broth, from plain water to veal stock. Water did little for us, and veal stock is rare in all but the best-provisioned professional kitchens. Straight beef broth and chicken broth proved too intense, but diluting chicken broth with an equal amount of water was just right. The chicken broth added richness and depth without taking over. We found that homemade stock was preferable to commercial broth, but the latter still makes a good risotto.

On an interesting note, several prominent cookbook authors suggest using bouillon cubes, but we found the cubes muddied the risotto's clean flavor. We can only assume that the quality of Italian bouillon cubes is superior to what we found on our grocer's shelves.

Although our next discovery runs contrary to conventional wisdom and the instructions in most cookbooks, we found it to be true nonetheless: Constant stirring of the risotto is unnecessary. We added half the broth once the wine had cooked off and allowed the rice to simmer for about 10 minutes, or half the cooking time, with little attention. The rice floated freely, individual grains suspended by the bubbling broth. During this period, we stirred the rice infrequently—about every three minutes—to ensure that it was not sticking to the bottom of the pan. Once all the broth was absorbed by the rice, we added more, a scant half cup at a time. For this period, stirring every minute or so was important; if we did not, the rice stuck to the bottom of the pan.

BEST SIDES FOR SALMON

SALMON IS AMERICA'S MOST POPULAR fish. Unlike delicate sole, salmon is rich and meaty, making it an ideal partner for rich and/or assertively flavored side dishes. Here are some of the test kitchen's favorites:

- Grilled Asparagus with Orange-Sesame Vinaigrette (page 170)
- Roasted Beets with Ginger Butter and Chives (page 172)
- Brussels Sprouts with Cider and Bacon (page 183)
- Green Beans Braised with Shiitake Mushrooms (page 212)
- Garlic-Lemon Skillet Green Beans with Toasted Bread Crumbs (page 213)
- Peas with Tarragon Cream (page 225)
- Slow-Roasted Tomato Gratin (page 229)
- Brown Rice with Parmesan, Lemon, and Herbs (page 311)
- Toasted Orzo with Fennel, Orange, and Olives (page 313)
- Asparagus Risotto with Lemon and Mint (page 319)

INGREDIENTS: Saffron

While many people know that saffron is the most expensive spice in the world, few are aware that it is grown in a variety of locations and that its price and quality can vary considerably. Though the bulk of commercially produced saffron comes from Spain and Iran, it is also harvested on a small scale in India, Greece, France, and, closer to home, in Lancaster County, Pennsylvania. We decided to toss saffron from different places purchased at different prices into a few pots and set up a test. We prepared three batches of Saffron Risotto—the purest way to taste the subtle differences and discern the different shades of orange—and flavored one with Spanish saffron, one with Indian, and one with American.

The finished risotti were similar in hue, though the Indian "Kashmir" saffron threads were darkest prior to cooking. In a blind tasting, we overwhelmingly chose the Pennsylvania-grown saffron over both the Spanish and Indian, judging it the "most potent" and "perfumed" of the three. Surprisingly, no one cared much for the Indian saffron, which is almost twice as costly as the other two and generally regarded as one of the best in the world. Greider's Saffron is exclusively available from the Pennsylvania General store (www.pageneralstore.com).

There is quite a bit of controversy surrounding the doneness of risotto. Some insist it should have a chalky, solid bite, while others feel it should be soft to the core. Tasters expressed individual preferences quite strongly, so you must taste as the rice nears completion and decide for yourself. Generally, we began tasting our rice after about 20 minutes of cooking; you can always cook it longer for a softer texture, but you can never bring back bite.

The remaining ingredient, Parmesan cheese, goes in at the very end to preserve its distinctive flavor and aroma. Grated cheese proved best, as it melted almost instantaneously. The quality of the cheese is paramount, as its taste is so prominent. This is the perfect occasion for buying authentic Parmesan freshly cut from the wheel, with its branded trademark boldly displayed on the rind.

Parmesan Risotto

SERVES 6

This is risotto at its simplest. It can accompany a variety of meals, from grilled or braised cuts to a mélange of roasted vegetables. Parmesan risotto is also appropriate as a first course. Don't fret if you have broth left over once the rice is finished cooking; different brands of rice all cook differently, and we prefer to err on the side of slightly too much broth rather than too little. If you do use all the broth and the rice has not finished cooking, add hot water.

3½	cups low-sodium chicken broth
3	cups water
4	tablespoons (½ stick) unsalted butter
1	medium onion, diced fine
	Salt
2	cups Arborio rice
1	cup dry white wine
2	ounces grated Parmesan cheese (1 cup)
	Ground black pepper

1. Combine the broth and water and bring to a simmer in a medium saucepan over medium-high heat. Reduce the heat to the lowest possible setting to keep the broth warm.

2. Melt the butter in a 4-quart saucepan over medium heat. Once the foaming subsides, add the onion and ½ teaspoon salt and cook, stirring occasionally, until the onion is very soft and translucent, about 9 minutes. Add the rice and cook, stirring frequently, until the edges of the grains are transparent, about 4 minutes. Add the wine and cook, stirring frequently, until the wine is completely absorbed by the rice, about 2 minutes. Add 3 cups of the warm broth and, stirring infrequently (about every 3 minutes), simmer until the liquid is absorbed and the bottom of the pan is dry, 10 to 12 minutes.

3. Add more of the broth, ½ cup at a time, as needed to keep the pan bottom from becoming dry (every 3 to 4 minutes); cook, stirring frequently, until the grains of rice are cooked through but still somewhat firm in the center, 10 to 12 minutes. Stir in the cheese, season with salt and pepper to taste, and serve immediately in warmed shallow bowls.

➤ VARIATIONS

Saffron Risotto

Also known as risotto alla Milanese in honor of the city of Milan, saffron risotto is one of the simplest and best variations on basic risotto. While this risotto is the traditional accompaniment to the classic Italian braised veal dish, osso buco, it is just as good with roast pork, veal, or poultry.

Follow the recipe for Parmesan Risotto. In step 2, just after you add the rice to the pot, crumble ¼ teaspoon saffron threads over the rice. Proceed as directed.

Asparagus Risotto with Lemon and Mint

The flavors in this dish are light, making it a suitable accompaniment to broiled or poached salmon or a simple roast chicken. It is essential to use thin asparagus for this recipe, so that it cooks through by the time the rice is done.

Snap the tough ends off 1 pound thin asparagus (see the illustration on page 165). Cut the spears on the bias into ½-inch lengths. Follow the recipe for Parmesan Risotto through step 2. In step 3, add the broth to the rice and stir as directed. After 5 minutes, stir in the asparagus and continue as directed. When adding the Parmesan to the rice, stir in ½ teaspoon grated lemon zest and 2 tablespoons minced fresh mint leaves. Accompany each serving of risotto with a lemon wedge.

RISOTTO CAKES

REHEATED RISOTTO, WHETHER WARMED ON the stovetop, in the oven, or in the microwave, never has quite the same texture as freshly made. The grains of rice turn mushy, and the velvety sauce, the heart and soul of risotto, becomes downright gluey. The butter can also leach from the rice and make a greasy mess.

Instead of suffering through mediocre leftover risotto or relinquishing it to the garbage, Italians turn it into something entirely new: risotto cakes. Breaded and pan-fried, the cakes become browned and crunchy on the outside and soft and creamy on the inside, especially when stuffed with soft, stringy cheese. There are several variations on this dish, including *arancini* and *suppli al telefono*. Literally "little oranges," arancini take their name from their color, not their flavor—they are tinted orange with a spoonful of tomato paste. Suppli al telefono, or "telephone wires," are a Roman specialty named for the cheese stuffing that, when bitten into, stretches into strings resembling telephone cables.

While both versions are delicious, we wanted a streamlined cake that wouldn't have us frying at the stovetop all day. This would mean increasing the size of the cake, so that one cake, rather than two or three, would serve one person as a side dish. Increasing the size from the traditional small ball to a larger patty or cake was an easy step. However, we needed to keep the size of the cake small enough so that the interior would heat through in the same time that it would take the exterior to brown. When the cakes were too thick, the inside was barely warm by the time the exterior was deeply browned.

Borrowing from suppli al telefono, we stuffed the center of each cake with a soft cheese that would melt, like mozzarella or provolone. We started off using grated cheese but found that bits of cheese worked their way to the exterior and burned in the oil. Diced cheese proved easier to manage and melted just as thoroughly.

We hoped to simply dust the cakes with flour prior to frying, but we found that the cakes absorbed a great quantity of oil and turned sodden. A thicker coating of beaten egg and bread crumbs was substantial enough to shield the rice from the oil and turned quite crisp when fried. Seasoning the bread crumbs with black pepper, cayenne, and minced parsley improved the flavor and appearance of the coating.

For frying the cakes, we had expected to use olive oil, but tasters preferred vegetable oil, which produced a lighter-flavored and less greasy-tasting cake.

SHAPING RISOTTO CAKES

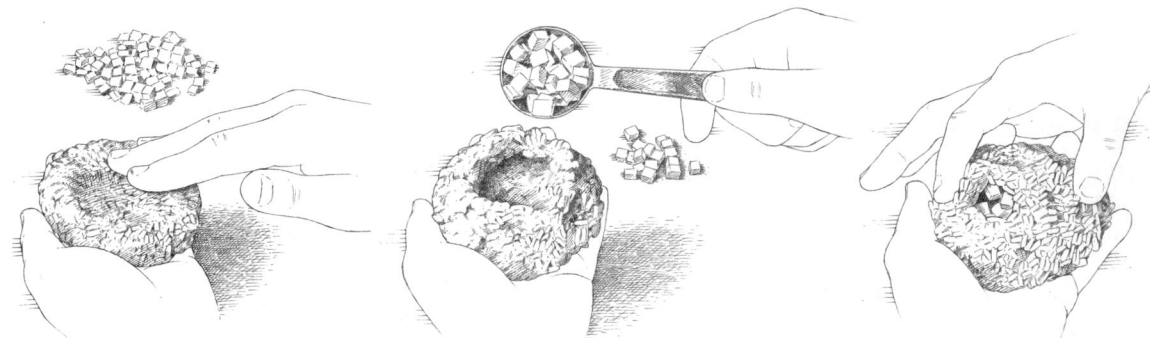

1. Using both hands, shape ½ cup chilled risotto into a uniform disk roughly 3 inches wide and 1 inch thick.

2. With your thumb, make an indentation in the center of the disk and pack it with 1 tablespoon finely diced cheese.

3. Carefully cover the cheese with the risotto mounded around the edges of the indentation. Pat the surface smooth, making sure that no cheese is exposed.

Risotto Cakes

MAKES 2 CAKES (SERVING 2)

Parmesan and saffron risotto are the best bets for this recipe. Spraying the measuring cup with nonstick cooking spray before measuring the risotto facilitates easy removal. To use the minimal amount of oil for frying, choose a pan just large enough to accommodate the risotto cakes without letting them touch. Two cakes can be fried in an 8-inch skillet. Although a spritz of lemon cuts the richness of the cakes and sharpens the flavors, feel free to serve the cakes with tomato sauce, a smear of pesto, or olivada (page 48). Depending on how much leftover risotto you have, the ingredients can be easily multiplied for more servings. Note that four cakes will require a 12-inch skillet and more oil, which should reach halfway up the sides of the cakes as they cook.

½	cup fresh bread crumbs
	Pinch salt
	Pinch ground black pepper
	Small pinch cayenne pepper (optional)
1	teaspoon minced fresh parsley leaves
1	large egg
1	cup leftover risotto, chilled
2	tablespoons finely diced mozzarella, fontina, or provolone cheese
½–⅔	cup vegetable oil for frying
	Lemon wedges

1. Mix the bread crumbs, salt, ground black pepper, cayenne pepper (if using), and parsley together in a small shallow dish. Beat the egg in another small shallow dish. Measure ½ cup chilled risotto, then shape and fill it with 1 tablespoon cheese, as directed in the illustrations on the facing page. Repeat with the remaining risotto and cheese to form a second cake. Dip each cake into the egg, allowing excess to drip back into the bowl. Dip both sides of each cake in the bread crumb mixture, pressing the crumbs with your fingers to form an even, cohesive coat.

2. Pour enough oil into an 8-inch nonstick skillet to reach a depth just under ½ inch. Turn the heat to medium-high and heat until the oil is shimmering but not smoking, about 2 minutes. With a spatula, gently lower each cake into the pan and cook until golden brown, about 3 minutes. Flip the cakes with the spatula and cook until browned on the other side, about 3 minutes. Transfer the cakes to a paper towel–lined plate, blot any excess oil, and serve immediately with lemon wedges.

MUSHROOM RISOTTO

A FAVORITE RISOTTO DISH OF OURS IS ONE packed with earthy, robust flavor courtesy of myriad wild mushrooms—the puffball, hen-of-the-woods, and trompette de la mort—whose fanciful names match their exotic flavor. The trouble is, these exotically flavored wild mushrooms are both elusive and expensive. We wondered if we could approximate (even surpass) that paragon of risottos with supermarket mushrooms and a bit of test kitchen determination.

Most of the mushroom risotto recipes we found were divided into two camps: authentic recipes using wild mushrooms and workaday ones using cultivated mushrooms. But there was a small third group of recipes that relied largely on dried porcini mushrooms for flavor. Sold by the ounce and packing a punch, dried porcini are both robustly flavored and aromatic—just the thing for that earthy edge we craved. We prepared several of these recipes to mixed reviews. Tasters appreciated the porcini flavor but missed the firm texture and visual presence of fresh mushrooms. Some combination of the two, then, looked to be the best tack to take.

As far as fresh mushrooms go, experience has taught us that they are at their best when cooked via the dry, intense heat of a smoking skillet or a fiery oven. Moist cooking, such as simmering in risotto, renders them rubbery and bland. A preliminary test of roasted mushrooms versus sautéed showed little difference, so we opted for the skillet to keep things on the stovetop. We sautéed the three most common supermarket mushrooms—the standard white button, the brown-capped, meaty cremini, and the cremini's larger though similarly flavored sibling, the portobello—and added them to separate batches of the porcini-flavored risotto.

Tasters found the button mushrooms mild and better appreciated the fuller flavor and meatier texture of the cremini and portobellos. Cremini were easier to prepare than portobellos, as the latter's feathery gills must be trimmed before cooking lest they stain the risotto inky black. Tasters favored larger-size pieces over slices, so we opted to quarter the mushrooms. Over medium-high heat and lightly sprinkled with salt, the cremini first shed their liquid, then browned deeply. To preserve their texture and flavor, we didn't add the mushrooms to the risotto until the rice was fully cooked.

The hot skillet and a knob of butter (which tasters preferred to olive oil) did wonders for the mushrooms' flavor, but we wanted more. With onions prepped for the rice, we purloined a portion to sauté with the mushrooms. This step proved successful, as the onions lent both sweetness and piquancy. On a roll, we added a couple of cloves of minced garlic and scored again: These mushrooms were good enough to eat on their own.

The risotto's flavor was emphatically mushroomy but one-dimensional and in need of refinement. We went from ½ cup to a full cup of wine to bring some much-needed acidity to the fore. As for herbs, thyme pairs well with mushrooms, so we added 1 teaspoon minced thyme and then, heeding tasters' demands, minced parsley as well. We kept the Parmesan cheese to 1 cup.

Even with these changes, the risotto still fell short of our expectations, being milder and less dynamic than we wanted. We wondered if we were missing any obvious flavor enhancements, hemmed in by the confines of Italian cooking. Throwing tradition out the window, we turned to a cuisine known for its deft touch with mushrooms: Chinese. A quick thumbing through several Chinese cookbooks inspired us to try replacing the chicken broth with mushroom broth. We combined the dried porcini with the cremini's trimmed stems, bundled herbs, and chicken broth cut with water and simmered the mixture until the mushrooms were tender, about 15 minutes (time enough to prep the other ingredients). We then strained the fungi from the broth and finely minced them before returning them to the rice. The results were promising: The risotto was much

fuller flavored than before, and we had cut preparation time. The cremini's stems appeared to add little besides bulk, so we ended up excluding them for the sake of convenience.

Borrowing again from the Chinese palette, we added soy sauce to the broth. Sweet, salty, and earthy, soy sauce has a galvanizing effect on the flavor of mushrooms that we sensed might pay off in the risotto. The scantest splash rounded out the broth's flavor and gave it indescribable depth. Tasters couldn't detect the soy sauce in the finished risotto, but everyone commented on the dish's fuller, earthier flavor.

Mushroom Risotto

SERVES 6

If cremini mushrooms are not available, button mushrooms make a fine, though somewhat less flavorful, substitute.

2	bay leaves
6	sprigs fresh thyme
4	sprigs fresh parsley
I	ounce dried porcini mushrooms, rinsed in a fine-mesh strainer under running water
3½	cups low-sodium chicken broth
2	teaspoons soy sauce
3¾	cups water
6	tablespoons (¾ stick) unsalted butter
I¼	pounds cremini mushrooms, stems discarded, caps wiped clean, and cut into quarters if small or sixths if larger
2	medium onions, chopped fine (about 2 cups)
	Salt
3	medium garlic cloves, minced or pressed through a garlic press (about I tablespoon)
2	cups Arborio rice
I	cup dry white wine
2	ounces grated Parmesan cheese (I cup)
2	tablespoons finely chopped fresh parsley leaves
	Ground black pepper

1. Tie the bay leaves, thyme sprigs, and parsley sprigs together with kitchen twine. Bring the bundled herbs, porcini mushrooms, broth, soy sauce,

and 3½ cups of the water to a boil in a medium saucepan over a medium-high heat; reduce the heat to medium-low and simmer until the dried mushrooms are softened and fully hydrated, about 15 minutes. Remove and discard the herb bundle and strain the broth through a fine-mesh strainer set over a medium bowl (you should have about 6½ cups strained liquid); return the liquid to the saucepan and keep warm over low heat. Finely mince the porcini and set aside.

2. Adjust an oven rack to the middle position and heat the oven to 200 degrees. Heat 2 tablespoons of the butter in a large nonstick skillet over medium-high heat. When the foaming subsides, add the cremini mushrooms, 1 cup of the onions, and ½ teaspoon salt; cook, stirring occasionally, until the moisture released by the mushrooms evaporates and the mushrooms are well browned, about 7 minutes. Stir in the garlic until fragrant, about 1 minute, then transfer the mushrooms to an ovensafe bowl and keep them warm in the oven. Off the heat, add the remaining ¼ cup water to the now-empty skillet and scrape with a wooden spoon to loosen any browned bits on the pan bottom; pour the liquid from the skillet into the saucepan with the broth.

3. Heat 3 tablespoons butter in a large saucepan over medium heat. When the foaming subsides, add the remaining 1 cup onions and ¼ teaspoon salt; cook, stirring occasionally, until the onions are softened and translucent, about 9 minutes. Add the rice and cook, stirring frequently, until the edges of the grains are transparent, about 4 minutes. Add the wine and cook, stirring frequently, until the rice absorbs the wine, about 2 minutes. Add the minced porcini and 3½ cups of the broth and cook, stirring every 2 to 3 minutes, until the liquid is absorbed, 9 to 11 minutes. Stir in an additional ½ cup broth every 2 to 3 minutes until the rice is cooked through but the grains are still somewhat firm at the center, 10 to 12 minutes (the rice may not require all of the broth). Stir in the remaining 1 tablespoon butter, then stir in the cremini (and any accumulated juices), cheese, and chopped parsley. Adjust the seasonings with salt and pepper to taste; serve immediately.

➤ VARIATION

Mushroom Risotto with Pancetta and Sage

Follow the recipe for Mushroom Risotto through step 2, omitting the thyme from the broth. Cook 2 ounces finely chopped pancetta and 1 tablespoon unsalted butter in a large saucepan over medium heat, stirring frequently, until the pancetta has rendered some fat, about 5 minutes. Add the remaining 1 cup onions, cooking the onions until softened and translucent, about 7 minutes; continue with the recipe, adding and cooking the rice as in step 3 and adding 1 tablespoon minced fresh sage leaves along with the chopped parsley.

BAKED RICE CASSEROLE

BAKED RICE CASSEROLES PROMISE A SOLUtion to the vexing problem of how to serve rice for a crowd. Unlike rice cooked on a stovetop, a rice casserole baked in a serving dish is ready for the table or buffet, and it retains its heat much longer than regular rice, thanks to a protective topping and a creamy sauce. With these advantages come numerous challenges, however, as we discovered when we tested several of the dozens of recipes we found in cookbooks and on the Internet. A dry, pasty texture plagued some recipes; others were overloaded with cheese and other fatty ingredients. Either way, swallowing more than a mouthful was a trial. And the texture of the rice never failed to disappoint; "blown out" grains were commonplace, as were pockets of crunchy, undercooked rice.

The flavor combinations we encountered in these recipes were too numerous to mention, but all the recipes were sorely in need of a fundamental technique for cooking the rice thoroughly and evenly. We set out to develop a basic recipe for a rice casserole with a simple cheese sauce that could be easily varied by adding or substituting any number of ingredients.

We considered our options for cooking the rice. Many recipes call for "cooked rice," which we found unhelpful. The amount of rice needed to fill a casserole dish precluded the use of leftovers, and, in any event, starting with fully cooked rice guaranteed that the grains would overcook in the oven, at least around the edges. Other recipes suggested the compromise of parboiling the rice in salted water, then draining and adding it to a sauce made separately. We objected for two reasons: the extra pot and the wasted opportunity to flavor the rice by cooking it together with aromatics and the sauce.

With this in mind, we began testing recipes in which the rice is cooked in the flour-thickened liquid that becomes the sauce. Our plan was to build the entire dish in a Dutch oven on the stovetop, then pour it into a baking dish, add a bread crumb topping, and finish it in the oven. This would allow us to boost flavor by sautéing aromatics in butter (tasters liked onion and garlic) before adding the flour, liquids, and rice.

The chief question became how long to cook the rice on the stovetop before transferring the mixture to the oven. We tried a variety of cooking times and were surprised to learn that the best results were obtained by cooking the rice for a full 20 minutes before pouring the mixture into the baking dish. Any less and the rice came out of the oven chalky and underdone, especially at the center. And any increase in the oven time only worsened the discrepancy in doneness between edges and center, and it dried out the dish as well. Under normal circumstances, 20 minutes in boiling water would be enough to overcook rice, yet ours was just tender. The reason, we discovered, was the flour. Rice cooks more slowly in a flour-bound sauce because much of the water is trapped by swollen starch granules. The rice grains thus have less water available to absorb. This same principle helped with the problem of uneven doneness. Once in the oven, the rice cooked more slowly and, therefore, more evenly because of the limited quantity of readily available moisture.

Next we tested the type and quantity of liquid to use when cooking the rice. Our options were water, milk, chicken broth, and cream, but tasters found that the latter, in addition to the butter and cheese, made the dish too rich. Even whole milk, in the volume necessary to cook the 3 cups of raw rice needed to fill a casserole dish, made

for a heavy sauce. The casserole made entirely with broth was, not surprisingly, too "chickeny" for what was otherwise a vegetarian dish. Tasters found the right balance of flavor and richness with an even mixture of milk and chicken broth, diluted with a few cups of water.

Even with only ¼ cup of flour to thicken 10 cups of liquid, our casseroles were turning out a little pasty, thanks to all the extra starch released from the rice grains as they cooked. We tried rinsing the rice to remove some of it, but this was only marginally effective. Much better results were obtained by reducing the flour even further, down to a mere 2 tablespoons. With all that liquid, the sauce started out very thin—perfect for cooking rice—then thickened as the rice absorbed water and leached starch.

We had only to adjust the flavors in our basic cheese sauce. Tasters favored sharp cheddar over milder cheeses, as it contrasted with the rich starchiness of the dish; a dash of cayenne pepper was approved for the same reason. The fresh flavors of lemon and parsley contributed a welcome brightness but only when sprinkled on the finished dish; even a relatively short spell in the oven left them washed out and muted.

Baked Rice Casserole

SERVES 8

Stir the sauce frequently for the first few minutes after adding the rice, as this is when the rice is most likely to clump and stick to the bottom of the pan.

TOPPING

4	slices white sandwich bread, torn into quarters
2	tablespoons unsalted butter, melted

RICE

4	tablespoons (½ stick) unsalted butter
1	medium onion, minced
3	medium garlic cloves, minced or pressed through a garlic press (about 1 tablespoon)
2	tablespoons unbleached all-purpose flour
4	cups low-sodium chicken broth
4	cups whole milk
2	cups water

3   cups long-grain white rice
1   teaspoon salt
¼   teaspoon ground black pepper
⅛   teaspoon cayenne pepper
8   ounces sharp cheddar cheese, shredded
    (about 2⅔ cups)
2   tablespoons chopped fresh parsley leaves
1   lemon, cut into wedges

1. FOR THE TOPPING: Process the bread and butter in a food processor until coarsely ground, about six 1-second pulses; set aside.

2. FOR THE RICE: Adjust an oven rack to the middle position and heat the oven to 400 degrees. Melt the butter in a Dutch oven over medium heat. Add the onion and cook until softened and beginning to brown, about 8 minutes. Add the garlic and cook until fragrant, about 30 seconds. Add the flour and cook, stirring constantly, until the flour turns golden, about 1 minute. Slowly whisk in the broth, milk, and water; bring to a simmer, whisking often. Stir in the rice, salt, pepper, and cayenne; return to a simmer. Reduce the heat to medium-low, cover, and cook, stirring often, until the rice has absorbed much of the liquid and is just tender, 20 to 25 minutes. Off the heat, stir in the cheddar.

3. TO ASSEMBLE AND BAKE: Pour the rice mixture into a 13 by 9-inch baking dish (or shallow casserole dish of similar size) and sprinkle with the bread crumb topping. Bake until the topping is browned and the casserole is bubbling, 20 to 25 minutes. Cool for 10 minutes. Sprinkle with the parsley and serve with the lemon wedges.

➤ VARIATIONS

Coconut Cardamom Rice Casserole

Most of a chile's heat resides in the ribs; if you prefer more heat, we suggest mincing the ribs along with the seeds and adding them to the recipe to taste; if you prefer less heat, discard the seeds and ribs.

TOPPING

1   cup roasted, unsalted cashews
4   slices white sandwich bread, torn into quarters
2   tablespoons unsalted butter, melted

RICE

2   tablespoons unsalted butter
1   medium onion, minced
2   jalapeño chiles, seeds and ribs removed and
    set aside (see note), flesh minced
1   tablespoon minced fresh ginger
2   medium garlic cloves, minced or pressed
    through a garlic press (about 2 teaspoons)
1   teaspoon ground cardamom
4   cups low-sodium chicken broth
4   cups unsweetened coconut milk
2   cups water
3   cups jasmine or plain long-grain rice
1   teaspoon salt
¼   teaspoon ground black pepper
2   tablespoons chopped fresh cilantro leaves
1   lime, cut into wedges

1. FOR THE TOPPING: Process the cashews in a food processor until coarsely ground, 5 to 10 seconds. Add the bread and butter and process to a uniformly coarse crumb, about six 1-second pulses; set aside.

2. FOR THE RICE: Adjust an oven rack to the middle position and heat the oven to 400 degrees. Melt the butter in a Dutch oven over medium heat. Add the onion and jalapeños; cook until the vegetables have softened, about 8 minutes. Add the ginger, garlic, and cardamom; cook until fragrant, about 1 minute. Add the broth, coconut milk, and water; bring to a simmer. Add the rice, salt, and pepper; return to a simmer. Turn the heat to medium-low, cover, and cook, stirring often, until the rice has absorbed much of the liquid and is just tender, 20 to 25 minutes.

3. Pour the rice mixture into a 13 by 9-inch baking dish (or shallow casserole dish of similar size) and sprinkle with the bread crumb topping. Bake until the topping is browned and the casserole is bubbling, 20 to 25 minutes. Cool for 10 minutes. Sprinkle with the cilantro and serve with the lime wedges.

POLENTA

NOTHING MORE THAN CORNMEAL MUSH, polenta is made from dried, ground corn cooked in liquid until the starches in the corn hydrate and swell into soft, balloonlike structures. For many purposes, this soft stage is the most delicious way to serve polenta. The stiff polenta you often see in restaurants starts out as a soft mass but is spread into a thin layer on a baking sheet or marble surface, cooled until stiff, sliced, and then sautéed, fried, or grilled until it resembles a crouton. These crisp rectangles are rarely more than a garnish. However, a smooth, piping-hot mound of soft polenta can be a meal. More commonly, soft polenta is used as a filler to stretch out meager servings of small game birds, like quail, or to cut the richness of sausages. Most stews and braised dishes—everything from osso buco to braised rabbit—can be ladled over a bowl of soft polenta.

Although making polenta sounds easy, the traditional Italian method for cooking it is a lot of work. The polenta must be slowly added to boiling salted water and stirred constantly (to prevent scorching) during the entire 30- to 40-minute cooking time. Thirty minutes of such constant stirring can seem like an eternity.

Of course, this assumes that you have avoided the biggest pitfall of all, the seizing problem at the beginning of the cooking process. Cornmeal is a starch, and starch thickens when mixed with water and heated. If this happens too quickly, the cornmeal seizes up into a solid, nearly immovable mass. We tested adding cornmeal to cold water, using more water, using less water, and using different grinds of cornmeal, all to no avail. Yes, we learned how to prevent seizing (add the cornmeal very slowly), but we still needed to stir constantly for at least 30 minutes to prevent scorching.

This testing did, however, reveal some important information. We found that medium-grind cornmeal makes the best polenta. Finely ground cornmeal, such as the Quaker brand sold in many supermarkets, is too powdery and makes gummy polenta. Cornmeal with a texture akin to granulated sugar, not table salt, makes the best polenta. We also discovered that a ratio of 4 parts water to 1 part cornmeal delivers the right consistency. As for salt, 1 teaspoon is the right amount for 1 cup of cornmeal.

At this point in our testing, we started to explore alternative cooking methods. The microwave was a bust, yielding sticky, raw-tasting polenta. The pressure cooker was even worse: The polenta took a long time to cook and then stuck firmly to the pot. We finally got good results when we prepared polenta in a double boiler. The polenta is cooked over simmering water, so it cannot scorch or seize up the way it can when cooked over direct heat. It emerges with a soft, light texture and sweet corn flavor. There is only one drawback, and it is a big one: time.

While a double boiler produced undeniably rich, creamy polenta, the cooking time was

MAKING POLENTA

When the water comes to a boil, add the salt, then pour the polenta from a measuring cup into the water in a very slow stream, stirring all the while in a circular motion with a wooden spoon to prevent clumping.

INGREDIENTS: Instant Polenta

After testing dozens of ways to prepare polenta, we still had one question: What about quick-cooking, or instant, polenta? Quick polenta, like quick grits and instant rice, has been cooked and then dried. All you need to do is reconstitute it with boiling water and let it simmer for a few minutes. We tested several brands (all imported from Italy) and found that instant polenta is a great way to make polenta in a hurry. The flavor is good (although not nearly as good as our basic polenta), and it's done in no more than 10 minutes. On the downside, quick polenta costs at least three times as much as regular cornmeal and doesn't have the smooth texture and full corn flavor of regular polenta.

prohibitively long. Even with the minimum attention that the technique required, 1½ hours of cooking was simply impractical. We wondered whether we could produce similar results via more conventional methods. The double-boiler method proved to us that slow, very gentle heat, not vigilant stirring, was the key to unlocking cornmeal's smooth texture. Could we approximate a double boiler's low heat with a conventional saucepan?

We could. A heavy-bottomed saucepan on the stove's lowest possible setting (or in conjunction with a flame tamer) kept the polenta from cooking too rapidly, allowed for the gradual release of the starches, and permitted the flavor of the cornmeal

EQUIPMENT: Large Saucepans

In the test kitchen (and at home), most of us reach for a 3- to 4-quart saucepan more than any other because its uses go beyond boiling water. This begs an obvious question: Does the brand of pan matter? With prices for these large saucepans ranging from $24.99 for a Revere stainless steel model with thin copper cladding at the base up to $140 for an All-Clad pan with a complete aluminum core and stainless steel interior and exterior cladding, a lot of money is riding on the answer. To let us offer guidance, we tested eight models, all between 3 and 4 quarts in size, from well-known cookware manufacturers.

The tests we performed were based on common cooking tasks and designed to highlight specific characteristics of the pans' performance. Sautéing minced onions illustrated the pace at which the pan heats up and sautés. Cooking white rice provided a good indication of the pan's ability to heat evenly as well as how tightly the lid sealed. Making pastry cream let us know how user-friendly the pan was—was it shaped such that a whisk could reach into the corners without trouble, was it comfortable to pick up, and could we pour liquid from it neatly? These traits can make a real difference when you use a pan day in and day out.

Of the tests we performed, sautéing onions was the most telling. In our view, onions should soften reliably and evenly (and with minimal attention and stirring) when sautéed over medium heat. In this regard, the All-Clad, Calphalon, KitchenAid, and Sitram pans all delivered. The Chantal and Cuisinart pans sautéed slightly faster, necessitating a little more attention from the cook, but still well within acceptable bounds. Only the Revere and Farberware Millennium sautéed so fast that we considered them problematic.

Incidentally, the Revere and Farberware pans that sautéed onions too fast for us were the lightest pans of the bunch, weighing only 1 pound 10 ounces and 2 pounds 6 ounces, respectively. This indicates that they were made from thinner metal, which is one reason they heat up quickly. On the flip side of the weight issue, however, we found that too heavy a pan, such as the 4-pound Calphalon, could be uncomfortable to lift when full.

The ideal was about 3½ pounds; pans near this weight, including the All-Clad, KitchenAid, Chantal, Sitram, and Cuisinart, balanced good heft with easy maneuverability.

While none of the pans failed the rice test outright, there were performance differences. In the Sitram, Revere, and Farberware pans, the rice stuck and dried out at the bottom, if only a little bit. Although this did not greatly affect the texture, the flavor, or the cleanup, we'd still choose a pan for which this was not an issue.

Every pan in the group turned out perfect pastry cream. During this test, we did observe one design element that made it easy to pour liquid from the pan neatly, without dribbles and spills. A rolled lip that flares slightly at the top of the pan helped control the pour. Only two pans in the group did not have a rolled lip: the All-Clad and the Calphalon.

So which pan should you buy? That depends largely on two things: your budget and your attention span. Based on our tests, we'd advise against really inexpensive pans—those that cost less than $50. For between $50 and $100, you can get a competent pan such as the Chantal, Sitram, or Cuisinart. The only caveat is that you may have to watch them carefully; they offer less room for error than our favorite pans, made by All-Clad, Calphalon, and KitchenAid.

THE BEST LARGE SAUCEPAN

The All-Clad (left), Calphalon (center), and KitchenAid (right) saucepans are our favorites, but they are not flawless. The Calphalon ($110) is heavy, both it and the All-Clad pan ($140) lack rolled lips, and the KitchenAid pan ($119) has a relatively short curved handle. However, these three pans provide moderate, steady heat, even when you are distracted.

to develop. Keeping the cover on the pot held in moisture and reduced the risk of scorching the polenta, even when we stirred infrequently rather than constantly. Within 30 minutes, a third of the time it took in the double boiler, we had creamy polenta ready for the table. We did find, however, that with the slightly higher temperature, stirring was a more significant issue. When we left the polenta unattended for more than seven minutes, it tended to stick to the pot bottom and corners, where it remained until washing. Stirring vigorously every five minutes took care of this problem.

DRESSING UP POLENTA

SERVED STRAIGHT OUT OF THE PAN IN ITS soft, creamy state, polenta has a subtle sweet corn flavor that works well with a variety of toppings. In addition to serving polenta with a grating of Parmesan or a slice of creamy cheese such as Gorgonzola, we've found several other ways to enjoy this tasty grain. Try serving it with the following:

- Your favorite tomato sauce and grated Parmesan cheese
- Halved cherry tomatoes warmed in a skillet with olive oil, then mixed with diced fresh mozzarella and minced fresh basil leaves
- Broiled or sautéed asparagus or green beans and crumbled goat cheese
- Crisp bacon or pancetta and balsamic vinegar
- Sautéed radicchio with crumbled blue cheese and toasted walnuts
- Sautéed mushrooms with chopped fresh thyme leaves and grated pecorino cheese
- Sautéed bitter greens with thinly sliced garlic
- Sautéed broccoli or broccoli rabe with crumbled sausage and red pepper flakes
- Roasted chopped fennel or frozen artichokes with chopped olives and orange zest
- Grilled, roasted, or sautéed summer squash with chopped bell peppers seasoned with sherry vinegar

---

Basic Polenta

SERVES 4 TO 6

If you do not have a heavy-bottomed saucepan, you may want to use a flame tamer to manage the heat. A flame tamer can be purchased at most kitchen supply stores, but you can also make one out of aluminum foil (see the illustration on the following page). It's easy to tell whether you need a flame tamer or not. If the polenta bubbles or sputters at all after the first 10 minutes, the heat is too high, and you need a flame tamer. Properly heated polenta will do little more than release wisps of steam. When stirring the polenta, make sure to scrape the sides and bottom of the pan to ensure even cooking. Use this polenta as a base for any stew or braise.

6	cups water
	Salt
1½	cups medium cornmeal, preferably stone-ground
3	tablespoons unsalted butter, cut into large chunks
	Ground black pepper

1. Bring the water to a boil in a heavy-bottomed 4-quart saucepan over medium-high heat. Once boiling, add 1½ teaspoons salt and pour the cornmeal into the water in a very slow stream from a measuring cup, all the while stirring in a circular motion with a wooden spoon (see the illustration on page 326).

2. Reduce the heat to the lowest possible setting and cover. Cook, vigorously stirring the polenta for about 10 seconds every 5 minutes, making sure to scrape clean the bottom and corners of the pot, until the polenta has lost its raw cornmeal taste and become soft and smooth, about 30 minutes. Stir in the butter, season with salt and pepper to taste, and serve immediately.

➤ VARIATIONS

Polenta with Parmesan and Butter
Follow the recipe for Basic Polenta, stirring in 1½ ounces (about ¾ cup) grated Parmesan cheese with the butter. Divide the polenta among individual bowls and top each with a small pat of butter. Sprinkle generously with more grated Parmesan to taste and serve immediately.

Polenta with Gorgonzola

Choose a Gorgonzola dolce or other mild, creamy blue cheese such as Saga blue. Do not use an aged Gorgonzola for this dish. Other aged blue cheeses will also be too salty, crumbly, and pungent.

Follow the recipe for Basic Polenta, dividing the finished polenta among individual bowls. Top each bowl with a 1-ounce slice of Gorgonzola cheese and serve immediately.

EQUIPMENT: Flame Tamer

A flame tamer (or heat diffuser) is a metal disk that can be fitted over an electric or gas burner to reduce the heat transfer. This device is especially useful when trying to keep a pot at the barest simmer. If you don't own a flame tamer (it costs less than $10 and is stocked at most kitchenware stores), you can fashion one from aluminum foil. Take a long sheet of heavy-duty foil and shape it into a 1-inch-thick ring that will fit on your burner. Make sure that the ring is of an even thickness so that a pot will rest flat on it. A foil ring elevates the pot slightly above the flame or electric coil, allowing you to keep a pot of polenta at the merest simmer.

BAKED MACARONI AND CHEESE

BAKED MACARONI AND CHEESE IS THE KING of all casseroles, to which thousands of recipes have tried to pay homage. At its finest, it emerges from the oven with a golden crumb topping, underneath which a creamy cheddar cheese sauce gracefully cloaks tender pasta elbows and fills their curves. More often, however, it is pulled out of the oven with a texture so dense and dried out that it has be cut into squares and served like lasagna. Our goal was clear: Find a way to keep the sauce creamy as it baked, thereby returning this casserole king to glory.

Before diving into the testing, we tried several existing recipes to get the lay of the land. Most recipes used a similar technique: a flour-and-milk-based sauce (aka béchamel) is made, then enriched with the cheese, mixed with the cooked pasta, and baked. A few untraditional recipes used eggs rather than flour to thicken the sauce (making it more like a custard) or replaced the milk with evaporated milk. Although none of these recipes produced the baked mac and cheese of our dreams, we did learn a thing or two. First, casseroles cook very unevenly in the oven—the edges of the casserole are often done long before the center is even warm. Because of this phenomenon, we noted that egg-thickened recipes just don't work. The egg at the edges becomes overcooked and solidified by the time the center is hot. Second, the hot air of the oven will quickly dry out a casserole unless it is either covered with foil or has quite a loose texture to begin with. Therefore it is no surprise that the sauces made with evaporated milk, which is essentially milk with some of the water taken out, baked up to a dry, gloppy mess; using foil to protect these casseroles simply prevented the bread crumb topping from toasting. The most promising recipes from this initial testing used a béchamel, but none of them was perfect. Overall, they tasted bland, dry, and grainy. We clearly had our work cut out for us.

Setting the issue of flavor aside, we began by focusing on the béchamel. Testing how much béchamel we needed for 1 pound of pasta (which fills a 13 by 9-inch casserole dish perfectly), we made three sauces using 3, 4, and 5 cups of milk. Although they produced casseroles that were decreasingly dry, we found that even the sauce made with 5 cups of milk was not enough. Increasing the amount of milk seemed the obvious answer, yet as we added more we noted that the sauce began to turn sticky and taste, well, too milky. As the casserole baked in the oven, the sauce lost some of its moisture but none of the milk fat or flavor. We then tried replacing some of the milk with water or chicken broth. While eliminating some of the milk loosened the sauce up significantly so that it could withstand the evaporation in the oven, the water made the sauce taste somewhat bland. The chicken broth, however, was fantastic. It helped the sauce remain creamy without adding or losing any significant flavor. Testing various amounts of milk and broth to flour (the sauce thickener), we found 3½ cups of milk and one can of chicken broth (about 1¾ cups) to 6 tablespoons of all-purpose flour was perfect.

Up until now, we had been adding a pound of cheddar to the sauce as a baseline; we wondered if either less or more would be better. Testing casseroles with amounts of cheese ranging from 12 to 24 ounces, we found the tasters' penchant for cheese was simply insatiable. At 24 ounces (8 cups), we cried uncle—the casserole tasted sufficiently cheesy. A problem that had been annoying us since the beginning, however, was now impossible to ignore—the grainy texture of the

cooked cheddar. To get around this, many recipes mix cheddar with other types of cheese. We tried replacing some of the cheddar with Gruyère, but its potent flavor—an acquired taste—did not sit well with all of the tasters. Monterey Jack helped to smooth out the sauce, but it also was too bland for a dish in which the cheese was so critical. Gouda, Havarti, and fontina were all given a shot, but none tasted just right. Last, we tried colby and hit the jackpot. Offering a cheddarlike flavor and an unbelievably silky texture when melted, colby was the clearly the answer. Trying various ratios of colby to cheddar, we found that the best balance of flavor and texture was 2 parts colby to 1 part extra-sharp cheddar. Adding a pinch of cayenne, dried mustard, and a single clove of garlic also did wonders to enhance the cheddar flavor.

As for the topping, we immediately canned the idea of using store-bought bread crumbs, finding their flavor stale and lifeless. Rather, we preferred the fresh, somewhat sweet flavor of sliced sandwich bread when ground to crumbs in a food processor. Tossed with a little melted butter, these crumbs brown nicely in a 400-degree oven in about the same time it takes for the sauce and macaroni to bind together.

KID-FRIENDLY SIDES

GETTING KIDS TO EAT SOMETHING AT dinnertime can be a struggle, especially when it comes to vegetables. Nevertheless, we have found success in getting kids to eat more than just a bite of the following dishes:

- Roasted Carrots with Ginger-Orange Glaze (page 188)
- Broccoli and Cheese Casserole (page 179)
- Skillet Green Beans with Orange Essence and Toasted Maple Pecans (page 213)
- Green Bean Casserole (page 215)
- French Fries (page 282) or Oven Fries (page 286)
- Latkes (page 291)
- Scalloped Potatoes (page 297)
- Candied Sweet Potato Casserole with Marshmallow Topping (page 302)
- Baked Rice Casserole (page 324)
- Baked Macaroni and Cheese (this page)

Baked Macaroni and Cheese
SERVES 6 TO 8
Although the classic pasta shape for this dish is elbow macaroni, any small, curvaceous pasta will work.

TOPPING
4   slices white sandwich bread, torn into quarters
2   tablespoons unsalted butter, melted

MACARONI AND CHEESE
Salt
1   pound elbow macaroni
6   tablespoons (¾ stick) unsalted butter
1   medium garlic clove, minced or pressed through a garlic press (about 1 teaspoon)
1   teaspoon dry mustard
¼   teaspoon cayenne pepper
6   tablespoons all-purpose flour
1¾ cups low-sodium chicken broth

3½   cups whole milk
16   ounces colby cheese, shredded
     (about 5⅓ cups)
8   ounces extra-sharp cheddar cheese,
     shredded (about 2⅔ cups)
     Ground black pepper

1. FOR THE TOPPING: Process the bread and butter in a food processor until coarsely ground, about six 1-second pulses; set aside.

2. FOR THE MACARONI AND CHEESE: Adjust an oven rack to the middle position and heat the oven to 400 degrees. Bring 4 quarts of water to a boil in a Dutch oven over high heat. Stir in 1 tablespoon salt and the macaroni; cook, stirring occasionally, until al dente, about 5 minutes. Drain the pasta and leave it in the colander; set aside.

3. Wipe the pot dry. Add the butter and return to medium heat until melted. Add the garlic, mustard, and cayenne; cook until fragrant, about 30 seconds. Add the flour and cook, stirring constantly, until golden, about 1 minute. Slowly whisk in the chicken broth and milk; bring to a simmer and cook, whisking often, until large bubbles form on the surface and the mixture is slightly thickened, 5 to 8 minutes. Off the heat, whisk in the colby and cheddar gradually until completely melted. Season with salt and pepper to taste.

4. Add the drained pasta to the cheese sauce and stir, breaking up any clumps, until well combined. Pour into a 13 by 9-inch baking dish (or a shallow casserole dish of similar size) and sprinkle with the bread crumb topping. Bake until golden brown and bubbling around the edges, 25 to 30 minutes. Remove from the oven and cool for 10 minutes before serving.

SAVORY NOODLE KUGEL

SAVORY NOODLE KUGELS AREN'T REALLY ALL that common. Of the few recipes we found, most feature everyday vegetables in a bland, dry, and forgettable side dish. We knew we needed to go back to the drawing board if we were going to create a kugel with chutzpah. Our desire was for a side dish that would pair as well with juicy roast beef as it would with crisp-skinned chicken. The perfect candidate would have a custardy bottom with a slightly crunchy top and be driven by an intense vegetable flavor.

We wanted to keep the flavors of our kugel simple. After trying several different types of savory kugels, including those built around onions, cabbage, and carrots, tasters preferred the onion version, believing that it would be the most neutral complement to a wide range of main courses. While the onions were only lightly browned in the recipe we had prepared, we knew that the dish would benefit if the onions were more deeply caramelized.

From experience, we knew there are a variety of techniques for caramelizing onions, most of which take a good deal of burner time. Starting with gentle heat, we cooked the onions in vegetable oil over a medium-low flame. This produced well-browned onions but required nearly an hour. Aiming to trim the cooking time, we increased the heat to medium and cut the time by half. Over medium heat, the onions developed a complexity and multilayered flavor that tasters preferred, but the final product made for a messy cleanup, with lots of flavor stuck to the pan as fond, or browned bits. We switched to a nonstick pan, which was not only easier to clean but which helped to concentrate the flavorful juices in the onions rather than leaving them clinging to the pan surface.

One last opportunity for flavor development in caramelizing the onions resided in our choice of fat. We had been using vegetable oil for all of our testing and liked it because it allowed for a clean onion flavor. In one test we used olive oil, which was overpowering, with a bitter edge, and in another we used butter, which also muted the onion flavor, though without a bitter edge. What worked best was a combination of vegetable oil and butter, which released a clean, well-defined onion flavor lightly tempered with the rich taste of butter.

There was no doubt that the caramelized onions increased the flavor intensity of the kugel; however, tasters wanted more flavor dimension. Liking the clean subtle flavors of cauliflower, we thought it would be a good vegetable for rounding out the intense onion flavor. How to incorporate it into the dish became our next challenge.

Wanting to draw out some sweet nuttiness from the cauliflower, we tried to come up with an efficient way of browning it. Our first thought was to cook it along with the onions; this gave us decent results, but the moisture from the cauliflower slowed down the caramelization of the onions. And, in the end, the cauliflower broke down too much, never getting to the nut-brown color we were looking for. However, it did soak up the succulent caramelized onion flavor, which brought out more of the nutty cauliflower flavor—and gave us a new idea.

For our next test, we partially cooked the cauliflower on its own (boiling it in water for about 5 minutes until mostly tender but still crunchy), hoping it would absorb caramelized onion flavor after being mixed into the casserole with the other ingredients and baked. We were right—the cauliflower came out perfectly tender, not mushy, as in our initial tests, and it had picked up some good flavor from the onions.

We were now close to the end of recipe development, but we still had one more problem to solve: Our test kugels came out dry in places, creating a patchy custard bottom. This savory recipe lacked the moist richness of dairy. To make sure that we had an even layer of custard on the bottom, we decided to add extra eggs, which worked. However, after 40 minutes in a hot, dry oven, the noodles above the custard were still drying out.

By adding ½ cup chicken broth to the kugel before baking and covering the casserole with foil, we managed to solve our moisture problems. And to get our golden top, we added small dots of butter to the kugel before baking. In addition, we found it best to remove the foil halfway through the baking to achieve a crunchy top.

Savory Noodle Kugel with Caramelized Onions and Cauliflower

SERVES 8 TO 10

We recommend serving this kugel hot, when the custard, cauliflower, and noodles are soft and steamy (unlike sweet kugel, which can be served either hot or cold).

INGREDIENTS: Egg Noodles

Egg noodles are not the stars of the pasta world. They lack the panache of penne, the sultriness of spaghetti, the rotundity of rotini. Yet in their role as trusty sidekick to dishes like beef stroganoff and chicken paprikash, egg noodles can make or break a meal. Noodles that are mealy, pasty, or fishy have no place in your cupboard.

Classic egg noodles are thick, wide ribbons of pasta that have a slightly higher fat content than other kinds of pasta because of their high percentage (up to 20 percent) of eggs. Their firm, sturdy texture is what makes them so appealing in casseroles or heavy soups and stews.

We chose eight widely available brands, cooked them in salted water, and tasted them plain (tossed in a small amount of canola oil to prevent clumping). We were looking for a clean, slightly buttery flavor and firm yet yielding texture. The top two finished within one point of each other and were clearly superior to the rest. Problems with the rest of the field included excessive thickness, gumminess, off flavors, or no flavor (the only no-yolk brand in the test fell victim to the last problem).

The top choice, Light 'n Fluffy, was praised for its "clean, neutral" flavor and superior texture. Close behind was Black Forest Girl, a German brand found in the international aisle of some supermarkets (or by mail order from www.germandeli.com) and described by fans as "yummy," with a "wheaty" flavor and "firm" texture. Either brand will make an excellent partner to your next stew.

THE BEST EGG NOODLES
Light 'n Fluffy Extra Wide Egg Noodles won fans with their "buttery flavor" and "firm, delicate" texture.

8   tablespoons (1 stick) unsalted butter
2   tablespoons vegetable oil
2   large onions, minced
     Salt and ground black pepper
1   medium head (about 2 pounds) cauliflower,
     cored and cut into ¾-inch florets (about
     6 cups) (see page 191)
1   pound extra-wide egg noodles
6   large eggs, lightly beaten
½   cup low-sodium chicken broth

1. Adjust an oven rack to the middle position and heat the oven to 350 degrees. Grease a 13 by 9-inch baking dish (or shallow casserole dish of similar size) with 1 tablespoon of the butter; set aside.

2. Melt 3 more tablespoons butter with the oil over high heat in a large nonstick skillet. Add the onions and ½ teaspoon salt; cook until the onions begin to soften, about 5 minutes. Reduce the heat to medium and continue to cook, stirring frequently, until they are golden brown and sweet, about 25 minutes longer. Remove from the heat and season with salt and pepper to taste.

3. Meanwhile, bring 4 quarts of water to boil in a large pot (with a perforated pasta insert, if available) over high heat. Add 1 tablespoon salt and the cauliflower; cook until the cauliflower is mostly tender but still slightly crunchy at the core, about 5 minutes. Transfer the cauliflower to a baking sheet lined with paper towels, using a slotted spoon (or by lifting out the pasta insert, if using).

4. Return the water to a boil and add the noodles; cook until almost tender but still firm to the bite, about 6 minutes. Drain the noodles, transfer them to a large bowl, and toss with 2 more tablespoons butter. Allow the noodles to cool to room temperature.

5. Add the onions, cauliflower, and eggs to the cooled noodles; toss to combine. Transfer the mixture to the prepared baking dish. Pour the chicken broth evenly over the noodles and dot with the remaining 2 tablespoons butter. Cover the dish tightly with foil and bake until the kugel is warm, about 20 minutes. Remove the foil and continue to bake until the noodles on the surface are golden and the center is hot, about 20 minutes longer. Cool for 5 minutes before serving.

BLACK BEANS

BLACK BEANS AS MADE IN LATIN AMERICA are more than a side dish. They are also flavorful enough to serve as a main course with rice. Just as important as flavor is texture. The perfect bean is tender without being mushy, with enough bite to make a satisfying chew.

In pursuit of this perfect texture, we discovered that it was important to cook the beans in enough water; too little water and the beans on top cooked more slowly than the beans underneath, and the whole pot took forever to cook. (Twelve cups is a sufficient amount of water to cook one pound of beans.) We did some further testing by comparing beans that had been soaked overnight with a batch of unsoaked beans, as well as with a batch softened by a "quick-soak" method in which the beans were brought to a boil, simmered 2 minutes, and then covered to let stand 1 hour off the heat. The quick-soak method caused a large percentage of the beans to burst during cooking. This reduced the chew we were after, so we nixed that method. Contrary to our expectations, overnight soaking decreased the cooking time by only about half an hour and didn't improve the texture. Because we are rarely organized enough to soak the night before, we no longer soak.

Now that we had discovered how to cook beans with the texture we wanted, it was time to discover the best way to build more layers of flavor without drowning the earthy taste of the beans.

We determined that meat gave the beans a necessary depth of flavor. We tested cooking beans with a ham hock, bacon, ham, and pork loin. We liked all four, and each gave the beans a slightly different flavor. The ham hock provided a smooth background taste, while bacon and ham produced a more assertive flavor. Pork loin was the most subtle.

In many Caribbean recipes, a sofrito is added to the cooked beans for flavor. Chopped vegetables—usually onion, garlic, and green bell pepper—are sautéed in olive oil until soft and then stirred into the beans. This mixture adds another layer of fresh flavor to beans without overwhelming them.

Some recipes suggest pureeing the sofrito with

some of the beans, while others call for mashing some beans with the sofrito. We found that pureeing intensified the flavor of the vegetables enough to almost overwhelm the beans. Simply mashing some beans and the sofrito by hand gets the job done.

We experimented with cumin, the traditional spice for black beans, simmered with the beans or mixed into the sofrito. The flavor of the spice got lost when simmered with the beans; we decided to save the cumin for the sofrito.

Black Beans

SERVES 6

Serve with White Rice (page 305) and garnish with a spoonful of sour cream, minced red onion, and a dash or two of hot pepper sauce.

BEANS

12	cups water
1	pound (about 2½ cups) dried black beans, picked over and rinsed (see the illustration at right)
1	smoked ham hock (about ⅔ pound), rinsed
1	medium green bell pepper, cored, seeded, and quartered
1	medium onion, minced
6	medium garlic cloves, minced or pressed through a garlic press (about 2 tablespoons)
2	bay leaves
1½	teaspoons salt

SOFRITO

2	tablespoons extra-virgin olive oil
1	medium onion, minced
1	small green bell pepper, cored, seeded, and minced
8	medium garlic cloves, minced or pressed through a garlic press (about 3 tablespoons)
2	teaspoons dried oregano
¾	teaspoon salt
1½	teaspoons ground cumin
1	tablespoon juice from 1 lime
½	cup chopped fresh cilantro leaves
	Salt and ground black pepper

1. For the beans: Bring all the bean ingredients to a boil over medium-high heat in a large, heavy-bottomed saucepan or Dutch oven, skimming the surface as the scum rises. Reduce the heat to low and simmer, partially covered, adding more water if the cooking liquid reduces to the level of the beans, until the beans are tender but not splitting (taste several, as they cook unevenly), about 2 hours. Remove the ham hock. When cool enough to handle, remove the ham from the bone, discard the bone and skin, and cut the meat into bite-size pieces; set aside. Remove and discard the bay leaves.

2. For the sofrito: Meanwhile, heat the oil in a large skillet over medium heat; add the onion, bell pepper, garlic, oregano, and salt; sauté until the vegetables soften, 8 to 10 minutes. Add the cumin; sauté until fragrant, about 1 minute longer.

3. To finish the dish: Scoop 1 cup of the beans and 2 cups of the cooking liquid into the pan with the sofrito; mash the beans with a potato masher or fork until smooth. Simmer over medium heat until the liquid is reduced and thickened, about 6 minutes. Return the sofrito mixture with the meat from the ham hock to the bean pot; simmer until the beans are creamy and the liquid thickens to a sauce consistency, 15 to 20 minutes. Add the lime juice; simmer 1 minute longer. Stir in the cilantro, adjust the seasonings with pepper and salt, if necessary, and serve hot over white rice. (The beans can be refrigerated in an airtight container for several

SORTING DRIED BEANS WITH EASE

It is important to rinse and pick over dried beans to remove any stones or debris before cooking. To make this task easier, sort dried beans on a white plate or cutting board. The neutral background makes any unwanted matter easy to spot and discard.

days. To reheat, thin with water, if necessary, and warm over medium-low heat.)

➤ VARIATIONS

Black Beans with Dry Sherry

Follow the recipe for Black Beans, adding 1 teaspoon ground coriander to the sofrito along with the cumin, substituting dry sherry for the lime juice, and omitting the cilantro.

Black Beans with Bacon, Balsamic Vinegar, and Sweet Pepper

Fry 8 ounces (about 8 slices) bacon, cut into ½-inch strips, in a medium skillet over medium heat until crisp and browned, about 5 minutes. Transfer with a slotted spoon to a paper towel–lined plate. Follow the recipe for Black Beans, omitting the ham hock and substituting bacon fat for the olive oil and 1 medium red bell pepper for the green bell pepper in the sofrito. Add the cooked bacon to the beans with the sofrito and substitute 2 teaspoons balsamic vinegar for the lime juice.

REFRIED BEANS

AUTHENTIC REFRIED BEANS ARE LEFTOVER stewed beans cooked in copious quantities of lard until they soften to a smooth paste; they are served garnished with toppings like sharp, crumbly cheese, scallions, bacon, and jalapeño chiles. The texture is sinfully lush and the flavor unbeatably rich and satisfying. Delicious, yes—but healthy? We wanted to revise traditional refried beans to make them both healthier and faster—quick enough to cook a skilletful with time left in the hour to chop garnishes, assemble burritos, or fry eggs to serve with the beans for a platter of huevos rancheros.

The beans were the first hurdle to overcome. Canned beans are undeniably convenient, but in flavor and texture they generally pale compared to dried beans cooked slowly with aromatics. In this case, the canned beans were to be smashed smooth, so texture wasn't an issue. But flavor was paramount, as most refried bean recipes have few ingredients outside of the beans, lard, a little onion, and salt. In preliminary testing, we tried a few traditional recipes with canned beans filling in for dried, and the flavors were boring. Clearly, we needed to boost the dish with additional flavors. First, however, we needed to identify a cooking method that would break down the beans quickly (the traditional recipes took up to an hour) and a fat to replace the lard.

The standard procedure we came across most often involved simply mashing the beans in the pan as they cooked, with a wooden spoon or potato masher. The method was labor-intensive and yielded mediocre results; the chunky mash was punctuated with bits of tough, leathery bean skins. Canned beans apparently have tougher skins than dried beans. It was apparent we needed more force than that generated by a potato masher and an arm—like a food processor or blender. The food processor did a miraculous job. The skins virtually disappeared, and the resulting puree was completely smooth.

With our beans pureed, it was time to fry them. Lard is a tough act to follow; we tried corn, canola, vegetable, and olive oil, and the latter won for its full flavor and rich mouthfeel—mild compared to lard but infinitely healthier. We tried every quantity from a scant tablespoon (unnoticeable) to cup (overkill) for three cans of beans and settled on 5 tablespoons, which is generous but not hedonistic.

The last task was to choose seasonings that would deepen the flavor of the otherwise plain-tasting beans. Onions, which are traditional, added depth and body as well as sweetness. Jalapeño chiles brought a hint of heat and a vegetal edge that tasters liked. Garlic and cumin rounded out the seasonings. We cooked the flavorings in the olive oil and added the bean puree; within 10 minutes, the beans were rich-tasting and smooth.

Refried Beans
SERVES 4 TO 6

If you have a spice grinder, you can enjoy freshly ground whole cumin seeds. The flavor is markedly better than that of store-bought ground cumin. Simply toast the seeds in a dry skillet for a couple of minutes or until fragrant, then grind them until finely processed. If you like your beans on the spicy side, don't bother to seed the chile.

Refried beans can be served with a variety of garnishes, including tortilla chips, salsa, pickled jalapeño chiles (sold in cans in most supermarkets), sliced scallions, shredded Monterey Jack or cheddar cheese, and sour cream.

3	(15-ounce) cans red kidney beans, drained and rinsed
1	cup water
5	tablespoons olive oil
1	medium onion, chopped fine
1	large jalapeño chile, cored, seeded, and minced
	Salt
2	medium garlic cloves, minced or pressed through a garlic press (about 2 teaspoons)
1	teaspoon ground cumin (see note for using ground cumin seeds)
½	cup coarsely chopped fresh cilantro leaves (optional)
	Hot pepper sauce

1. Process the beans and water in a food processor until smooth, scraping down the sides of the workbowl with a rubber spatula as necessary, about 30 seconds; set aside.

2. Heat the oil, onion, chile, and 1 teaspoon salt in a large nonstick skillet over medium-high heat. Cook, stirring occasionally, until the onion softens and just begins to brown, about 5 minutes. Add the garlic and cumin and cook, stirring frequently, until aromatic, about 30 seconds. Stir in the bean mixture until thoroughly combined, then reduce the heat to medium. Cook, stirring occasionally, until the beans have thickened and the flavors have blended, about 10 minutes. Stir in the cilantro, if using, and adjust the seasonings with salt and hot pepper sauce to taste. Serve immediately.

BOSTON BAKED BEANS

HEADY WITH SMOKY PORK AND BITTERSWEET molasses, authentic Boston baked beans are both sweet and savory, a unique combination of the simplest ingredients, unified and refined during a long simmer—a fine example of the whole being greater than the sum of its parts.

A close reading of recipes—and there are thousands out there—made it clear that authentic Boston baked beans are not about fancy seasonings. They are about developing intense flavor by means of the judicious employment of canonical ingredients (beans, pork, molasses, mustard, and sometimes onion) and slow cooking. Tasters quickly rejected recipes with lengthy lists of nontraditional ingredients and short cooking times.

The most important item on the shopping list is, of course, the beans, the classic choice being standard dried white beans in one of three sizes: small white beans, midsize navy or pea beans, or large great northern beans. While the latter two choices were adequate, tasters preferred the small white beans for their dense, creamy texture and their ability to remain firm and intact over the course of a long simmer. (The two larger sizes tended to split.) Consistent with the test kitchen's previous findings, we found that there was no need to soak the beans before cooking, so we gladly skipped that step. We did test canned white beans and were not impressed by their lackluster performance. Within two hours of baking, they turned to mush and lacked the full flavor of the dried beans.

Next came the meat. Some type of cured pork is essential for depth of flavor and lush texture, though its flavor should never dominate. Although traditionalists swear by salt pork, we first tried pork brisket, which is a meatier version of salt pork. Its flavor was enjoyable, but tasters felt the beans lacked richness—the brisket was too lean. Not surprisingly, salt pork scored high with tasters, although some felt the flavor was too mild. Bacon, a more modern choice, was deemed "too smoky and overwhelming" for most, though the heartier pork flavor was appreciated. On a whim, we put both salt pork and bacon into the pot and found the perfect solution. The bacon brought the desired depth to the beans, and the salt pork muted the bacon's hickory tang. Twice as much salt pork as bacon proved the right balance.

In traditional recipes, the salt pork is cast raw into the beans (often as a large piece) and melts into the sauce, but during tests it failed to render completely. Gelatinous chunks of fatty pork bobbing among the beans left even the most carnivorous taster cold. We first diced the pork into smaller bits, but this was only a partial remedy; unmelted fat remained. Next we browned it in the Dutch oven prior to adding the beans, and the results were surprising. This simple step (not recommended in any of the recipes we'd found) made the flavor of the beans significantly fuller and better than anything we had yet tasted. Apparently, the melted fat more readily flavored the cooking liquid, and the browned bits of meat tasted richer.

While yellow onion is a controversial ingredient in classic recipes, we sensed its flavor could be important, and our intuition proved right. Tasters loved the sweetness and full flavor that it gave to the beans, especially once sautéed in the rendered pork fat. Tasters favored a fine dice so that the onion all but disappeared by the time the beans were ready.

Next we tackled the final two ingredients: mustard and molasses. Dried mustard, the standard choice, had worked fine up until now, but we felt home cooks were more likely to have prepared mustard on hand. And it provides a nice perk—vinegar—to cut the beans' sweetness. We tested several varieties, including Dijon, German whole grain, yellow, and brown. They all brought a unique angle to the beans, but brown mustard—Gulden's brown mustard, in particular—was best, imparting a pleasant sharpness without calling attention to itself. Even with the mustard's tang, though, we found it necessary to add vinegar for acidity. Most classic recipes that include cider vinegar add it at the start of the cooking time, but we found the acidity stayed sharper when added to the beans once finished. A scant teaspoon proved enough to cut the sweetness of the molasses and to accent the other flavors.

The molasses, we discovered, would take some finessing, as its brutish flavor and intense sweetness dominated the beans when added carelessly. After tasting batches made with mild, full-flavored (also known as "robust"), and blackstrap varieties, most tasters preferred the subtler tones of the mild variety. We settled on just ½ cup molasses baked with the beans for a balance of moderate sweetness and palate-cleansing bitterness. A tablespoon added after cooking gently reemphasized its character.

All that was left to do now was tweak the cooking time. For testing purposes, we had been cooking the beans at 250 degrees for six to seven hours. While pleased with the results, we were curious to see what other temperatures might accomplish. We knew that to a certain extent, flavor and texture were in opposition. The longer the beans cooked, the better the sauce's flavor, but past a certain crucial moment of equilibrium, time worked against the beans, turning them to mush.

We tested cooking temperatures in increments of 25 degrees between 200 and 350 degrees and met with interesting results. At 200 degrees, the beans took upward of eight hours to cook and were still on the crunchy side. At 350 degrees, the beans percolated vigorously and exploded. Midpoints of 275 and 300 degrees were more successful. The beans were creamy textured and the sauce full flavored. With little difference in the outcome when either temperature was used, we chose 300 degrees, which made the beans cook faster, finishing in just about five hours—less time than we had thought possible.

While pleased with the texture and flavor, we still wanted a thicker sauce—soupy beans were not acceptable. We discovered that it was not simply a matter of reducing the volume of water, however, as this led to unevenly cooked beans. We had been cooking the beans from start to finish covered with

BUYING SALT PORK

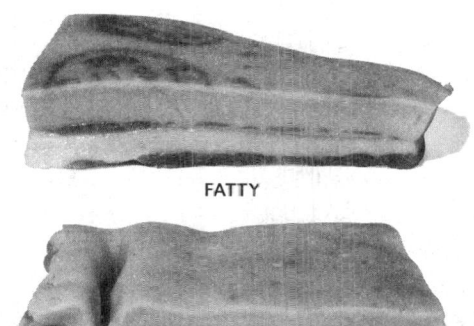

FATTY

LEAN

The salt pork shown at top has a high ratio of fat to meat and is preferable in our baked bean recipe to leaner, meatier salt pork, like the piece shown below.

337

a lid, which had prevented the cooking liquid from reducing effectively. When we removed the lid for the last hour in the oven, we got the results we were seeking—the sauce was reduced to a syrupy, intensified state that perfectly coated the beans.

Boston Baked Beans

SERVES 4 TO 6

If you prefer a stronger molasses flavor, substitute dark or "robust" molasses for the mild. For the richest flavor, look for chunks of salt pork with a high fat-to-meat ratio.

4	ounces salt pork, trimmed of rind and cut into ½-inch cubes
2	ounces (about 2 slices) bacon, chopped fine
1	medium onion, minced
½	cup plus 1 tablespoon mild molasses
1½	tablespoons prepared brown mustard, such as Gulden's
1	pound (about 2½ cups) dried small white beans, rinsed and picked over (see the illustration on page 334)
	Salt
9	cups water
1	teaspoon cider vinegar
	Ground black pepper

Adjust an oven rack to the lower-middle position and heat the oven to 300 degrees. Cook the salt pork and bacon in a large Dutch oven over medium heat, stirring occasionally, until it is lightly browned and most of the fat is rendered, about 7 minutes. Add the onion and cook until softened and beginning to brown, about 8 minutes. Add ½ cup of the molasses, the mustard, beans, 1¼ teaspoons salt, and the water; increase the heat to medium-high and bring to a boil. Cover the pot and set in the oven. Bake until the beans are tender, about 4 hours, stirring once after 2 hours. Remove the lid and continue to bake until the liquid has thickened to a syrupy consistency, 1 to 1½ hours longer. Remove the beans from the oven; stir in the remaining 1 tablespoon molasses and the vinegar. Season to taste with salt and pepper. Serve.

➤ VARIATION

Barbecued Baked Beans

Barbecued baked beans are slow-simmered, oven-cooked beans that are similar to Boston baked beans. Barbecued baked beans are a bit brasher in flavor, however, so they stand up better to the big flavors of grilled and barbecued foods. Black coffee is not such a strange companion to beans. It often appears in chili recipes, "cowboy" cooking, and barbecue sauce recipes. If you do not have time to make freshly brewed coffee, instant will do.

4	ounces (about 4 slices) bacon, chopped fine
1	medium onion, minced
4	medium garlic cloves, minced or pressed through a garlic press (about 4 teaspoons)
1	pound (about 2½ cups) dried small white beans, rinsed and picked over (see the illustration on page 334)
1	cup strong black coffee
¼	cup packed dark brown sugar
1	tablespoon mild molasses
1½	tablespoons prepared brown mustard, such as Gulden's
½	cup plus 1 tablespoon barbecue sauce
½	teaspoon hot pepper sauce
	Salt
8	cups water
	Ground black pepper

Adjust an oven rack to the lower-middle position and heat the oven to 300 degrees. Cook the bacon in a large Dutch oven over medium heat, stirring occasionally, until it is lightly browned and most of the fat is rendered, about 7 minutes. Add the onion and cook until softened and beginning to brown, about 8 minutes. Add the garlic and cook until fragrant, about 30 seconds. Add the beans, coffee, brown sugar, molasses, mustard, ½ cup of the barbecue sauce, the hot sauce, 2 teaspoons salt, and water; increase the heat to medium-high and bring to a boil. Cover the pot and set in the oven. Bake until the beans are tender, about 4 hours, stirring once after 2 hours. Remove the lid and continue to bake until the liquid has thickened to a syrupy consistency, 1 to 1½ hours longer. Remove from the oven and stir in the remaining 1 tablespoon barbecue sauce. Season to taste with salt and pepper.

ITALIAN WHITE BEAN CASSEROLE

CANNELLINI ALL'UCCELLETTO, OR "BEANS cooked like a little bird," is a traditional Tuscan dish as ubiquitous to the region as baked beans are to Boston and cheese steaks are to Philadelphia. So what exactly are "beans cooked like a little bird"? Essentially, they are white beans stewed for hours with tomatoes, garlic, and sage—a common Italian method for preparing small game birds like quail. The flavors blend and sweeten, the beans turn creamy, and the piercing sage flavor mellows to a tame undertone. We liked the concept and flavors of the dish, but not the time required to prepare it. We sought to rework the classic into a faster-to-the-table side dish, complete with a crisp, rustic bread topping. The flavor was classic; the method we developed was anything but.

Traditionally, the dish is prepared with dried cannellini beans, which easily account for much of the long cooking time. While we generally prefer the superior flavor and texture of dried beans, milder-tasting, softer-textured canned beans can be an acceptable substitution when time is tight. The trick, however, is infusing them with flavor without turning them to mush. Canned beans simply cannot withstand extended cooking. (See page 340 for the results of a tasting of canned white beans.)

That said, we knew we had to develop much of the flavor of the dish prior to the beans' introduction. Following the lead of traditional recipes, we prepared a sofrito (a slow-cooked mélange of vegetables) using sautéed onion, carrot, and celery. Cooked slowly over moderate heat, the vegetables shrunk to a fraction of their raw volume and developed a sweet, vegetal flavor base for the beans. Once we added the beans, however, we found the sharp flavor of the celery was too pronounced, so we left it out. We also favored red onion over yellow for the way its sweet flavor intensified the inherent sweetness of the beans.

As for the garlic, northern Italian cooks are much more reserved than southern Italian cooks. In other words, a little goes a long way. When we added minced garlic to the beans, its flavor was deemed too assertive by most tasters, even when we reduced the volume. A milder, subtler hint of garlic seemed more fitting. We borrowed a traditional technique and lightly toasted slivered cloves in the oil before adding the vegetables for the sofrito. Started in the cold oil, the garlic slowly cooked and developed a sweet, nutty flavor and golden color. But it's a fine line between toasted and burnt: any hue darker than light gold and the garlic can taste bitter and acrid. The addition of the vegetables effectively prevented the garlic from browning any further. A pinch of crushed red pepper flakes, toasted with the garlic, added a hint of smoky heat.

Following tradition, we had been adding the tomatoes to the sofrito once it had cooked down, just before adding the beans. Surprisingly, the flavor of canned tomatoes contributed little. Yes, they were fruity and acidic, but most tasters thought they required a good deal of cooking to develop the fullness that this dish required. Breaking with the original concept, we substituted jarred roasted red peppers for the tomatoes. Sweeter, slightly smoky, and richer, they were more densely packed with flavor than the tomatoes and required less cooking.

Without tomatoes and the liquid in which the beans were supposed to cook, the dish needed some liquid to keep things moist. Neutral-tasting chicken broth filled the role well. To replace the tomatoes' acidity, we added a splash of white wine.

As the original dish is typically served with a crusty loaf of hearty bread, we sought a topping that contributed a similar flavor and texture. Finely ground crumbs didn't quite cut it. The bread crumbs were too sandy in texture and "wheaty" in flavor. We wanted more texture and flavor—the crunchy crust and tough pull of a rustic loaf as well as the flavor variation between crumb and crust. We opted to leave the bread in large chunks and toss them in garlic-flavored olive oil (so they would taste like bruschetta) before scattering them over the beans. Dusted with Parmesan, the croutons browned attractively while in the hot oven and had a flavorful distribution of crisp crust and tender, sweet crumb.

Italian White Bean Casserole with Rustic Crouton Crust

SERVES 8 TO 10

If canned cannellini beans prove hard to find, substitute canned navy or great northern beans. Serve this dish alongside roasted chicken or pork.

TOPPING

2	medium garlic cloves, minced or pressed through a garlic press (about 2 teaspoons)
3	tablespoons extra-virgin olive oil
1	ounce Parmesan cheese, grated fine (about 1/2 cup)
1/4	teaspoon black pepper
1	loaf (about 12 ounces) rustic Italian bread, cut into 1-inch chunks (about 6 cups)

BEANS

1/4	cup extra-virgin olive oil
6	medium garlic cloves, sliced thin
1/4	teaspoon red pepper flakes
1	medium red onion, minced
1	medium carrot, peeled and chopped fine
1/2	teaspoon salt
1/2	cup dry white wine
4	(15.5-ounce) cans cannellini beans, drained and rinsed
1	(13-ounce) jar roasted peppers, drained and chopped medium (about 1 1/2 cups)
1/4	cup chopped fresh sage leaves
1	cup low-sodium chicken broth
2	tablespoons minced fresh parsley leaves

1. FOR THE TOPPING: Combine the garlic, oil, Parmesan, and pepper in a large bowl. Add the bread and toss until evenly coated; set aside.

2. FOR THE BEANS: Adjust an oven rack to the middle position and heat the oven to 400 degrees. Heat the oil, garlic, and red pepper flakes in a large skillet or Dutch oven over medium heat. As the oil begins to sizzle, shake the pan back and forth so that the garlic does not stick (stirring with a wooden spoon may cause the garlic to clump). Cook until the garlic turns very pale gold, about 4 minutes. Add the onion, carrot, and salt; cook, stirring occasionally, until softened and beginning to brown, about 10 minutes. Stir in the wine and cook until partially evaporated, about 30 seconds. Stir in the beans, roasted peppers, sage, and broth; bring to a simmer.

3. TO ASSEMBLE AND BAKE: Pour the bean mixture into a 13 by 9-inch baking dish (or shallow casserole dish of similar size). Arrange the bread crumb topping in an even layer over the beans. Bake until the bread has browned and the filling is bubbly, 25 to 30 minutes. Let cool for 10 minutes. Sprinkle with the parsley before serving.

INGREDIENTS: Canned White Beans

While it is hard to beat the full flavor and firm texture of dried beans cooked from scratch, canned beans can be perfectly acceptable in certain applications, including our Italian White Bean Casserole with Rustic Crouton Crust (this page). The dish is so richly flavored that the stronger flavor of the dried beans isn't missed, and the cooking time is short enough that the softer canned beans do not have a chance to overcook and turn mushy.

But are all canned cannellini beans of equal caliber? We looked for multiple brands of nationally distributed cannellini beans to taste against one another and found so few that we decided to include both great northern and navy beans in the tasting as well. From sweet to bland and chalky to mushy, the different brands ran the gamut in quality. Our favorite of the bunch tasted straight from the can were Westbrae Organic great northern beans, which won accolades for their "earthy" flavor and "creamy" texture. In second place, tasters liked Progresso cannellini beans for their "plump shape" and "sweet, slightly salty" flavor. While the "weird" grayish hue of the cannellini beans from Goya was off-putting to many tasters, the beans possessed a solid flavor and scored well enough to come in third.

BEST CANNED WHITE BEANS

WESTBRAE	PROGRESSO	GOYA
ORGANIC GREAT NORTHERN BEANS	CANNELLINI BEANS	CANNELLINI BEANS
"Earthy flavor" and "creamy texture"	"Plump and sweet"	"Weird" gray color but solid flavor

INDEX

A

Acorn squash, 231
  cutting safely, 235
  faster
    with Brown Sugar, 234–35
    with Rosemary–Dried Fig
      Compote, 235
    Roasted Winter Squash Halves,
      232–33
Adobo–Cheddar Cheese Straws, 16
Aïoli, Roasted Garlic, 163–64
Almond(s):
  Mexican-Spiced Peanuts,
    Pumpkin Seeds and, 3
  Quick Toasted, 4, *246*
  Red Pepper Jelly Spread, 28
Ancho–Cinnamon Sugar Straws,
  17
Anchovies:
  mincing, 227
  Pissaladière, 55–58
Appetizers, 1–80
  Almonds, Quick Toasted, 4, *246*
  Asparagus Wrapped with
    Prosciutto, 33
  Beef Satay, 75–77
  Bruschetta, 48–50, *248*
  Cheese Straws, 15–17, *246*
  Cheese Trays, 14–15, *246*
  chicken
    Buffalo Wings, 68–70
    Fingers, Breaded, 70–72
    Satay, 77
  Crab Cakes, Cocktail, 41–42
  Crostini, 45–48
  Crudités, 21–24
  Dates Stuffed with Parmesan,
    12
  Eggs, Deviled, 42–45
  Frico, 13
  goat cheese
    Marinated, 11
    Warm Figs with Honey and,
      12
    Whipped, with Chives and
      Lemon, 11, *246*
    Whipped, with Garlic and
      Mint, 12
  Gougères, 17–21
  holiday, 18
  Melon and Prosciutto, 37–38

Appetizers *(cont.)*
  mushrooms
    Marinated, 7–8
    Stuffed, 67–68
  Nachos, Cheesy, 59–62
  no-cook, 29
  Nuts, Spiced, 2–4
  Olive Oil Dipping Sauce, 30
  Olives, Marinated, 5–6, *246*
  Peppers, Roasted Red Bell, 8–10
  Pissaladière, 55–58
  Pizza, 51–55
  Quesadillas, 65–66
  salads, fancy first-course, 102
  scallop(s)
    Bacon-Wrapped, Broiled, 80
    Skewers, Broiled, 77
  shrimp
    Bacon-Wrapped, Broiled, 79–80
    Cocktail, 38–41
    Skewers, Broiled, 75–77
  Smoked Salmon Mousse, 36–37
  Smoked Trout Mousse, 37
  Spring Rolls, Southeast Asian–
    Style, 73–75, *245*
  Steak Sandwiches, Mini, 50–51
  Straws (puff pastry), 15–17, *246*
  Sweet Potato Chips, 24–25
  see also Dips; Spreads
Apple(s):
  Cabbage and, Braised in Cider, 185
  Cider-Sage Dressing, 88
  coring, 99
  Curried, Macaroni Salad with, 134
  Curried Coleslaw with Raisins
    and, 121
  Green, Chopped Salad with
    Fennel, Radishes and, 148
  Salad with Celery, Hazelnuts,
    Roquefort and, 99
  Salad with Herbed Baked Goat
    Cheese, Walnuts, Dried
    Cherries and, 102
  Sweet-and-Sour Cabbage Salad
    with Fennel and, 123
  Waldorf Salad, 148–49
Apricot Chutney, Quick, 72
Artichoke(s), 160–64
  Baby, Roasted, 162–64
    with Roasted Garlic Aïoli,
      163–64

Artichoke(s) *(cont.)*
  Crostini with Parmesan,
    Balsamic Vinegar
    and, 46
  edible portions of, 160
  Scalloped Potatoes with Fontina
    and, 298
  Steamed, 161–62
    Lemon–Mint Vinaigrette for,
      162
    Mustard–Tarragon Vinaigrette
      for, 162
Arugula, 90
  and Escarole Salad with
    Roquefort, Figs, and Warm
    Port Dressing, 99–100
  Orange and Radish Salad with,
    107–8
  Pasta Salad with, and
    Sun-Dried Tomato
    Vinaigrette, 136–37
  and Roasted Pear Salad with
    Walnuts and Parmesan
    Cheese, 105
  Tomato Salad with Shaved
    Parmesan and, 109
Asian side dishes (list), 173
Asparagus, 164–71
  Broiled, 168–69
    with Balsamic Glaze and
      Parmesan Shards, 168
    with Soy-Ginger Vinaigrette,
      169
  cutting on bias, 167
  Grilled, 169–71
    with Grilled Lemon
      Vinaigrette, 169–70
    with Orange-Sesame
      Vinaigrette, 170–71
  grilling guide for, 170
  preparing for crudités, 22, 24
  Risotto with Lemon and Mint,
    319
  Salad, 114–16
    Mesclun and, with Capers,
      Cornichons, and Hard-
      Cooked Eggs, 115
    Red Pepper, Spinach and, with
      Goat Cheese, 115, *251*
    Watercress, Carrot and, with
      Thai Flavors, 115–16

Asparagus (cont.)
  Steamed, 165–66
    with Ginger-Hoisin Vinaigrette, 166
    with Lime-Ginger Vinaigrette, 165–66
    with Roasted Red Pepper Vinaigrette, 166
  Stir-Fried, 166–68
    with Black Bean Sauce, 167
    with Soy Sauce, Maple Syrup, and Scallions, 167–68
  trimming tough ends from, 165
  Wrapped with Prosciutto, 38
Avocado(s):
  Chopped Salad with Jícama, Cucumber and, 148
  Cobb Salad, Classic, 151–53, 250
  dicing, 65
  Dip with Cilantro, Smoky, Spicy, 27
  guacamole
    with Bacon, Scallions, and Tomato, 65
    Cheesy Nachos with Salsa and, 61
    Chunky, 64–65
  Orange, and Watercress Salad, 106–7, 249
  pitting, 64
  Salad with Roquefort, Tomatoes, Bacon and, 98
  Salsa, Quick, 66

B

Baba Ghanoush, 31–33
  Israeli-Style, 33
  with Sautéed Onion, 33
Bacon:
  Bruschetta with Summer Squash, Blue Cheese and, 50, 248
  Cobb Salad, Classic, 151–53, 250
  Dressing, Wilted Spinach Salad with, 96–97
  Garlic, and Thyme Gougères, 20
  -Wrapped Sea Scallops, Broiled, 80
  -Wrapped Shrimp, Broiled, 79–80
Baked beans:
  Barbecued, 338
  Boston, 336–38
Balsamic vinegar:
  Basil Vinaigrette, 174
  Cranberry Dressing, 88
  tasting of, 110
  Vinaigrette, 84

Barbecued Baked Beans, 338
Barbecue Sauce, Sweet-and-Tangy, 72
Basil:
  Balsamic Vinaigrette, 174
  Oil, 205–6
  Sun-Dried Tomato Dip, 26
  Tomato Vinaigrette, 86
  see also Pesto
Bean(s), 304, 333–40
  baked
    Barbecued, 338
    Boston, 336–38
  dried, sorting, 334
  Refried, 335–36
    Cheesy Nachos with, 61
  Salad, 124–26
    Green and White, with Pancetta, 125–26
    Three-, 124–25
  see also Black bean(s); Green bean(s); White bean(s)
Beef:
  Satay with Spicy Peanut Dipping Sauce, 75–77
  Spicy, Cheesy Nachos with, 61–62
  steak
    favorite sides for, 264
    pairing green bean side dishes with, 209
  Sandwiches with Arugula and Horseradish, Mini, 50–51
Beet(s), 171–72
  and Pear Salad with Watercress and Blue Cheese, 105
  Roasted, 171–72
    with Dill-Walnut Vinaigrette, 172
    with Ginger Butter and Chives, 172
  Roasted, Salad with Fried Shallots, Roquefort and, 98
  stains, removing, 171
Beet greens. See Greens—Sautéed Tender
Belgian endive, 90
Black bean(s):
  with Bacon, Balsamic Vinegar, and Sweet Pepper, 335
  Basic, 333–35
  with Dry Sherry, 335
  Stuffed Zucchini with Corn, Chipotle Chiles and, 242
Black bean sauce (Chinese fermented):
  Spicy, Stir-Fried Broccoli with, 175
  Stir-Fried Asparagus with, 167
Black Pepper and Parmesan Butter, 6

Blanching vegetables, 24
Blueberry(ies):
  Honeydew, and Mango Salad with Crystallized Ginger, 157
  Summer Fruit Salad, 156
Blue cheese:
  Bruschetta with Summer Squash, Bacon and, 50, 248
  Cobb Salad, Classic, 151–53, 250
  Creamed Corn with Bacon and, 200
  Dressing, 91
  Gorgonzola, Polenta with, 329
  Pear and Beet Salad with Watercress and, 105
  Salad, 97–100
  Spinach Dip with Bacon and, 29
  Twice-Baked Potatoes with Thyme and, 275
  Walnut Cheese Straws, 16
  see also Roquefort
Boston Baked Beans, 336–38
Bread:
  for cheese trays, 14
  Bruschetta, 48–50
  Crostini, 45–48
  Croutons, 93, 146
  Focaccia, 52
  Olive Oil Dipping Sauce for, 30
  Pita, Salad with Olives, Feta, and Mint, 142–43
  Pizza, 51–55
  Salad, 141–42
    with Roasted Peppers and Olives, 142
    with Tomatoes, Herbs, and Red Onions, 142
  see also Pizza; Toasts
Breadsticks, 52
Broccoli, 172–79
  and Cheese Casserole, 178–79
    with Roasted Red Peppers, 179
  cooked, olive green color of (science), 178
  Pasta Salad with Olives and, 135–36
  preparing, 172
  for crudités, 22, 24
  Sautéed, 177
    with Garlic, Pine Nuts, and Parmesan, 177
  Steamed, 173–74
    with Balsamic-Basil Vinaigrette, 174
    with Sesame Vinaigrette, 173–74
    with Spanish Green Herb Sauce, 174

Broccoli *(cont.)*
Stir-Fried, 174–77
with Hot-and-Sour Sauce,
176–77
with Spicy Black Bean Sauce,
175
Broccoli rabe, 180–81
with Asian Flavors, 181
with Balsamic Vinaigrette,
180–81
Blanched, 180
preparing, 180
with Red Bell Pepper, Olives, and
Feta, 181
Brown Rice, Oven-Baked,
310–12
Curried, with Tomatoes and Peas,
312
with Parmesan, Lemon, and
Herbs, 311–12
Bruschetta, 48–50
with Arugula, Red Onion, and
Rosemary–White Bean
Spread, 49–50, *248*
with Sautéed Sweet Peppers, 49,
248
with Summer Squash, Bacon, and
Blue Cheese, 50, *248*
Toasted Bread for, 48
with Tomatoes and Basil, 49
Brussels sprouts, 181–84
Braised, 183–84
with Cider and Bacon, 183
in Cream, 184
cutting small "X" in stem end of
(science), 182
Glazed, with Chestnuts, 183
Buffalo Wings, 68–70
Bulgur:
and Mushroom Pilaf, 315–17
Tabbouleh, 144
Buttercup squash (kabocha):
Braised Winter Squash, 235–36
Roasted Winter Squash, 234
Halves, 232–33
Butterhead lettuces, 90
Buttermilk Coleslaw, 121–22
Butternut squash, 231
Braised Winter Squash, 235–36
cutting up, 232
Roasted Winter Squash, 234
Halves, 232–33
Butters, flavored (compound):
Basic, 223
Cajun-Spiced, 6
Chili, Spicy, 197
flavorings for, 223
Garlic and Herb, 6
Toasted, 196

Butters, flavored (compound) *(cont.)*
Ginger, 172
Hot and Sweet, 6
Lime-Cilantro, 195
Parmesan and Black Pepper, 6
popcorn with, 6
rolling, 223
Super-Garlic, 6
Warm Spiced, 6

C
Cabbage, 184–85
braised
Apples and, in Cider, 185
Cream-, with Lemon and
Shallots, 185
with Parsley and Thyme, 184–85
Salad, 122–24
Confetti, with Spicy Peanut
Dressing, 123–24
Red Pepper and, with Lime-
Cumin Vinaigrette, 123
Sweet-and-Sour, with Apple
and Fennel, 123
salting, 122
shredding, 120
see also Coleslaw
Caesar Salad, Chicken, 145–46
Cajun-Spiced Butter, 6
Cannellini beans. *See* White bean(s)
Cantaloupe:
Melon and Prosciutto, 37–38
Summer Fruit Salad, 156
Caprese, Insalata, 111
Caribbean-Style Cocktail Sauce,
Spicy, 41
Carrot(s), 185–88
Asparagus, and Watercress Salad
with Thai Flavors, 115–16
Baby, Roasted, 187–88
with Ginger-Orange Glaze, 188
Maple, with Browned Butter,
188
with Rosemary, Thyme, and
Shallots, 188
with Sage and Walnuts, 188
Glazed, 185–87
with Bacon and Pecans, 186–87
with Orange and Cranberries,
187
Turnips and, Lemon-Thyme,
190
preparing for crudités, 22, 24
Salad, Moroccan-Style, 116–18
slicing on bias, 187
Cashews, Indian-Spiced Pistachios
and, with Currants, 3–4

Casseroles:
baked beans
Barbecued, 338
Boston, 336–38
Broccoli and Cheese, 178–79
Brown Rice, Oven-Baked, 310–12
Cauliflower Gratin, 193–95
Green Bean, 214–15
Macaroni and Cheese, 329–31
Noodle Kugel, Savory, 331–33
Rice, Baked, 323–25
Scalloped Potatoes, 295–98
summer squash
with Feta, Lemon, and Oregano,
244
Provençal, 243–44
Sweet Potato, Candied, 301–2
White Bean, Italian, 339–40
Catalina Dressing, 87
Cauliflower, 191–95
braised
with Anchovies, Garlic, and
White Wine, 193
with Garlic and Tomatoes,
192–93
Gratin, 193–95
with Leeks and Gruyère, 195
preparing, 191
for crudités, 22, 24
Savory Noodle Kugel with
Caramelized Onions and,
331–33
Steamed, 192
with Browned Butter, Walnuts,
and Crispy Sage, 192
with Cheddar-Mustard Cream
Sauce, 192
Celery:
Glazed Parsnips and, 189–90
preparing for crudités, 22
Waldorf Salad, 148–49
Celery Root, Glazed, with Onions,
Grapes, and Pistachios, 190
Cheddar:
Cheese Straws, 16, *246*
Chef's Salad, 149–51
Mustard Cream Sauce, Steamed
Cauliflower with, 192
Nachos, Cheesy, 59–62
Rice Casserole, Baked, 323–25
and Roasted Red Pepper Spread,
23
smoked
Mashed Potatoes with Grainy
Mustard and, 268
Scalloped Potatoes with
Chipotle Chile and, 298
Spicy Hash Browns with Red Bell
Pepper and, 289–90

Cheese, 13
  Broccoli and, Casserole, 178–79
  Crackers, Cheesy, 33
  cream, spreads, 28
  Fontina, Scalloped Potatoes with
    Artichokes and, 298
  Frico, 13
  Gougères, 17–21
  macaroni and
    Baked, 329–31
    "Grown-Up," 34
  mozzarella
    Crostini with Pesto and, 46
    Tomato Salad with Basil and
      (Insalata Caprese), 111
  Nachos, Cheesy, 59–62
  Pepper Jack, Potato Pancakes with
    Cilantro and, 292
  soft, shredding, 61
  storing, 13
  Straws, 15–17, *246*
  Trays, 14–15, *246*
  see also Blue cheese; Cheddar;
    Feta; Goat cheese; Gruyère;
    Monterey Jack; Parmesan;
    Roquefort
Cheese graters, rating of, 230
Chef's knives, rating of, 283
Chef's Salad, 149–51
Chestnuts, Glazed Brussels Sprouts
  with, 183
Chicken:
  breasts, trimming, 71
  Buffalo Wings, 68–70
  Caesar Salad, 145–46
  Cobb Salad, Classic, 151–53, *250*
  Fingers, Breaded, 70–72
    Curried, with Chutney, 71
    dipping sauces for, 72
    Sesame, 71
  Liver Spread, Crostini with, 47–48
  pairing green bean side dishes
    with, 209
  roast, great sides for, 168
  Satay, 77
  Shredded, Sesame Noodle Salad
    with, 138–39
Chickpeas, in Hummus, 30–31
Chicory, 90
Child-friendly sides, 330
Chile(s):
  Ancho–Cinnamon Sugar Straws,
    17
  Jalapeño–Lime Dip, 26
  see also Chipotle chile(s)
Chili:
  Butter, Spicy, 197
  Garlic Croutons, 93
  paste, 114

Chipotle chile(s):
  in adobo sauce, freezing, 30
  Cilantro-Lime Spinach Dip with,
    30
  Lime Spread, 28
  Scalloped Potatoes with Smoked
    Cheddar Cheese and, 298
  Smoky, Spicy Avocado Dip with
    Cilantro, 27
  Stuffed Zucchini with Corn,
    Black Beans and, 242
  Twice-Baked Potatoes with
    Onion and, 275
Chips:
  Sweet Potato, 24–25
  see also Tortilla chips
Chopped Salad, 147–48
  with Avocado, Jícama, and
    Cucumber, 148
  with Fennel, Green Apple, and
    Radishes, 148
Cilantro:
  and Cherry Tomato Vinaigrette, 206
  Lime Butter, 195
Cinnamon Sugar–Ancho Straws, 17
Citrus Vinaigrette, 96
Clam Dip with Bacon and Scallions,
  27, *247*
Cobb Salad, Classic, 151–53, *250*
Cocktail sauces:
  Classic, 40
  Spicy Caribbean-Style, 41
Coconut Cardamom Rice Casserole,
  Baked, 325
Colcannon, 268–69
Coleslaw, 119–22
  Buttermilk, 121–22
    with Green Onion and
      Cilantro, 122
    with Lemon and Herbs, 122
  Creamy, 120–21
  Curried, with Apples and Raisins,
    121
  Sweet-and-Sour, 121
Collard greens:
  preparing, 216
  see also Greens—Blanched
    Assertive
Compound butter. *See* Butters,
  flavored
Corn, 195–202
  Boiled, 195–96
    with Lime-Cilantro Butter, 195
    with Toasted Garlic and Herb
      Butter, 196
  on the cob
    keeping warm, 266
    milking, 200
    removing kernels from, 200

Corn *(cont.)*
  Creamed, 199–200
    with Bacon and Blue Cheese,
      200
  frozen, ideas for, 201
  Grilled, 196–98
    with Soy-Honey Glaze, 198
    with Spicy Chili Butter, 197
  grilling guide for, 170
  Roasted, and Red Pepper Salsa,
    210
  salads
    Cool, 201
    Mediterranean, 201
  Sautéed, 201–2
    with Bacon and Scallions, 202
    with Cherry Tomatoes and
      Basil, 202
    with Fennel, Tomatoes, and
      Tarragon, 202
    Shredded Zucchini or Summer
      Squash with Chives and, 238
    Southwestern, 202
    with Thyme and Shallots,
      201–2
  storing (science), 201
  Stuffed Zucchini with Black
    Beans, Chipotle Chiles and,
    242
Couscous Pilaf with Saffron, Raisins,
  and Almonds, 314–15
Crab Cakes, Cocktail, 41–42
Crackers:
  for cheese trays, 14
  Cheesy, 33
  cream cheese spreads for, 28
  Garlic-Herb, 33
  Homemade, Easy, 33
  Spiced, 33
Cranberry(ies):
  Balsamic Dressing, 88
  Glazed Carrots with Orange and,
    187
Cream cheese spreads, 28
Crostini, 45–48
  with Chicken Liver Spread,
    47–48
  with Olivada, 48
  quick and easy toppings for, 46
  Toasts, 47
  with White Bean Puree, 47
Croutons, 93, 146
Crudités, 21–24
  arranging, 21
  blanching vegetables for, 24
  preparing vegetables for, 22–23
Cucumber(s):
  Chopped Salad, 147–48
    with Avocado and Jícama, 148

Cucumber(s) *(cont.)*
　Curry Dip, 26
　Salad, 111–14
　　Creamy, 112
　　with Greek Dressing, 114
　　Sesame-Lemon, 113
　　with Spicy Soy Dressing, 114
　　Sweet-and-Tart, 113
　　Yogurt Mint, 112
　salting, 111–12, 113
　Sesame Noodle Salad with Sweet
　　Peppers and, 139
　slicing, 73
　and Tomato Salad, Israeli,
　　110–11
Cumin:
　Lime Vinaigrette, 123
　Yogurt Dressing, 109
Curry(ied):
　Apples, Macaroni Salad with,
　　134
　Brown Rice with Tomatoes and
　　Peas, 312
　Chicken Fingers with Chutney,
　　71
　Coleslaw with Apples and Raisins,
　　121
　Cucumber Dip, 26

D
Dandelion greens, 90
Dates Stuffed with Parmesan, 52
Delicata squash:
　Braised Winter Squash,
　　235–36
　Roasted Winter Squash Halves,
　　232–33
Deli meat:
　slicing, 151
　turkey and ham, tasting of, 151
Deviled Eggs, 42–45
Dijon:
　Honey Vinaigrette, 86
　Mayonnaise, 89
Dill:
　Cucumber Salad, Creamy, 112
　Walnut Vinaigrette, 172
Dips:
　Avocado, with Cilantro, Smoky,
　　Spicy, 27
　Baba Ghanoush, 31–33
　Clam, with Bacon and Scallions,
　　27, 247
　Creamy, Base for, 26
　Cucumber-Curry, 26
　Green Goddess, 26–27, 247
　Guacamole, Chunky, 64–65

Dips *(cont.)*
　Hummus, 30–31
　Jalapeño-Lime, 26
　Lemony Feta, 26
　party, 26–27
　Pea, Hot-and-Tangy, 224
　Pesto, 26
　quick and easy, 26
　Salsa, 26
　smoked salmon
　　and Chive, 26
　　with Dill and Horseradish, 27
　Spinach, 28–30
　Sun-Dried Tomato and Basil, 26
　see also Spreads
Dressings, 83–93
　Bacon, 96–97
　Blue Cheese, 91
　Caesar, 145
　Cranberry–Balsamic, 88
　Cumin-Yogurt, 109
　Garlic, Creamy, 91
　Greek, 114
　Green Goddess, 92–93
　Orange-Lime, 87–88
　Peanut, Spicy, 123–24
　Pear-Rosemary, 88
　Pomegranate and Honey, 88
　Port, Warm, 99–100
　Ranch, 91–92
　Ruby Red Grapefruit and Sesame,
　　88
　Soy, Spicy, 114
　Thousand Island, 92
　see also Mayonnaise; Vinaigrettes
Duck Sauce, Spicy Sweet-and-Sour, 72

E
Edamame, 202–3
　Buttered, with Shallots and Basil,
　　203
　with Garlic, Balsamic, and Parsley
　　Leaves, 203
　with Ginger, Garlic, and Sesame,
　　203
　Sweet-Spicy, with Cilantro and
　　Peanuts, 203
Egg noodles, tasting of, 332
Eggplant, 203–6
　Baba Ghanoush, 31–33
　Grilled, 205–6
　　with Basil Oil, 205–6
　　with Cherry Tomato and
　　　Cilantro Vinaigrette, 206
　grilling guide for, 170
　Pasta Salad with Tomatoes, Basil
　　and, 136

Eggplant *(cont.)*
　Ratatouille, Oven-Baked, 206–8
　salting, 203–4
　Sautéed, 204–5
　　with Cumin and Garlic, 204–5
　　with Pancetta and Rosemary, 205
　Stir-Fried, 206
Eggs:
　Deviled, 42–45
　　with Anchovy and Basil, 45
　　Classic, 44–45
　　with Tuna, Capers, and Chives, 45
　Hard-Cooked, 44
　　peeling, 43
Emulsion and vinaigrette (science), 83
Endive:
　grilling guide for, 170
　preparing for crudités, 22
Equipment:
　flame tamers, improvised, 329
　microwave ovens, 236
　ratings of
　　cheese graters, 230
　　chef's knives, 283
　　food mills, 268
　　mandolines and V-slicers, 296
　　nonstick skillets, inexpensive,
　　　175
　　paring knives, 163
　　potato mashers, 300
　　salad spinners, 85
　　saucepans, large, 327
　spiders, 25
　woks, 175
Escarole, 90
　and Arugula Salad with
　　Roquefort, Figs, and Warm
　　Port Dressing, 99–100

F
Fattoush, 42–43
Fennel:
　Chopped Salad with Green Apple,
　　Radishes and, 148
　grilling guide for, 170
　preparing, 118
　　for crudités, 23, 24
　Romaine and Roasted Pear
　　Salad with Lemon-Mint
　　Vinaigrette and, 105
　Salad, 118–19
　　with Dried Cherries, Walnuts,
　　　and Roquefort, 97–98
　　with Oranges and Olives, 118–19
　　with Tangerines, 119
　Sweet-and-Sour Cabbage Salad
　　with Apple and, 123

Feta:
    Dip, Lemony, 26
    Greek Salad, 94–95
    Greek-Style Potatoes with Olives
        and, 280
    Kalamata Olive, and Oregano
        Cheese Straws, 17
    Peas with Mint and, 224
    Pita Bread Salad with Olives,
        Mint and, 143
    Spinach Dip with Bacon and, 29
    Summer Squash Casserole with
        Lemon, Oregano and, 244
    Tomato Salad with
        Cumin-Yogurt
        Dressing and, 109
Fig(s):
    Arugula and Escarole Salad with
        Roquefort, Warm Port
        Dressing and, 99–100
    Dried, Rosemary Compote, 235
    with Goat Cheese and Honey,
        Warm, 12
Fines Herbes Straws, 16
Fish:
    pairing green bean side dishes
        with, 209
    Smoked Trout Mousse, 37
    see also Salmon, smoked; Shellfish;
        Tuna
Five-spice (powder):
    Almonds, 4
    Sweet Potato Chips, 24–25
Flame tamers, improvised, 329
Focaccia, 52
Fontina, Scalloped Potatoes with
        Artichokes and, 298
Food mills:
    making mashed potatoes with,
        267
    rating of, 268
French Potato Salad, 130–31
French Fries, 280–82
    Spicy, 282
Frico, 13
Fried foods:
    keeping crisp, 266
    oil disposal and, 282
Fries:
    French, 280–82
    Oven, 285–87
        Sweet Potato, 287
    Steak, 284
Fruit:
    for cheese trays, 14
    juice vinaigrettes, 87–88
    salads, 155–57
    Adding interest to, 157
    see also specific fruits

G

Garlic:
    Croutons, 93, 146
    Dressing, Creamy, 91
    dry-toasting, 196
    Herb Butter, 6
    mincing to paste, 11
    Roasted, 34
    Roasted, Aïoli, 163–64
    stir-frying and, 177
    Super-, Butter, 6
    Toasted, and Herb Butter, 196
German Potato Salad, 132–33
Ginger:
    Butter, 172
    grating, 189
    Hoisin Vinaigrette, 166
    Lime Vinaigrette, 165
    Orange Glaze, 188
    Soy Vinaigrette, 169
Goat cheese:
    Asparagus, Red Pepper, and
        Spinach Salad with, 115,
        251
    Crostini with Tomatoes and, 46
    Herbed Baked, 101–2
    Herbed Baked, Salad, 100–102
        with Apples, Walnuts, and Dried
            Cherries, 102
        with Vinaigrette, 102
    Marinated, 11
    slicing, 100
    Warm Figs with Honey and, 12
    whipped
        with Chives and Lemon, 11,
            246
        with Garlic and Mint, 12
        and Smoked Salmon Spread,
            36
    Wilted Spinach Salad with
        Olives, Lemon Vinaigrette
        and, 96
Gorgonzola, Polenta with, 329
Gougères, 17–21
    Bacon, Garlic, and Thyme, 20
    Scallion, Parmesan, and Black
        Pepper, 21
Grape(s):
    Glazed Celery Root
        with Onions, Pistachios
        and, 190
    and Strawberry Salad with
        Champagne, 157
Grapefruit, Ruby Red, and Sesame
        Dressing, 88
Graters:
    cheese, rating of, 230
    ginger and, 189
    shredding soft cheeses with, 61

Gratins:
    Cauliflower, 193–95
    Tomato, Slow-Roasted, 228–29
Gravy, keeping warm, 266
Greek:
    Dressing, Cucumber Salad with,
        114
    Potatoes, 277–80
    Salad, 94–95
        Country-Style, 95
Green bean(s), 208–15
    Blanched, 209–10
    Braised, 212
        with Shiitake Mushrooms,
            212–13
        in Tomatoes, 212
    Casserole, 214–15
    with Garlic, 211
    with Pickled Red Onions and
        Toasted Walnuts, 211–12
    preparing for crudités, 22, 24
    with Quatre-Épices, 210
    Salade Niçoise, 153–55, 252
    with Sautéed Shallots and
        Vermouth, 210
    side dishes, pairing with favorite
        main courses, 209
    skillet
        Garlic-Lemon, with Toasted
            Bread Crumbs, 213
        with Orange Essence and
            Toasted Maple Pecans,
            213–14, 255
    Spicy, with Sesame Seeds, 211
    Three-Bean Salad, 124–25
    trimming ends from, 211
    and White Bean Salad with
        Pancetta, 125–26
Green goddess:
    Dip, 26–27, 247
    Dressing, 92–93
Greens, 215–21
    Blanched Assertive, 219–21
        with Bacon and Onion, 220
        draining, 220
        with Honey Mustard Sauce,
            221
        with Shallots and Cream,
            220–21
    leafy
        draining, 219
        preparing, 216
    salad
        buying and storing, 82
        cleaning, 82, 85
        dressing and tossing, 82, 85
        glossary of, 90
        guidelines for, 82
        for main course salads, 83

Greens (cont.)
Sautéed Tender, 217–19
with Bacon and Red Onion,
219
with Caramelized Onions and
Dried Apricots, 219
with Cumin, Tomatoes, and
Cilantro, 218
with Mustard and Pecans,
217–18
with Pine Nuts and Currants,
217
see also specific greens
Grilled:
Asparagus, 169–71
Corn, 196–98
Eggplant, 205–6
Lemon Vinaigrette, 169
Zucchini or Summer Squash,
238–39
Grill fire, taking temperature of, 169
Grilling vegetables (chart), 170
Gruyère:
Cauliflower Gratin with Leeks
and, 195
French Potato Salad with Hard
Salami and, 137
Gougères, 17–20
Guacamole:
with Bacon, Scallions, and Tomato,
65
Cheesy Nachos with Salsa and, 61
Chunky, 64–65

H
Ham:
Chef's Salad, 149–51
deli, tasting of, 150
holiday, sides for, 298
Hash Browns, 287–90
Spicy, with Cheddar and Red Bell
Pepper, 289–90
Herb(s):
Fines Herbes Straws, 16
and Garlic Butter, 6
and Garlic Croutons, 93
Green, Sauce, Spanish, 174
Lemon Vinaigrette, 147
Spread, Lemony, 28
and Toasted Garlic Butter, 196
see also specific herbs
Hoisin-Ginger Vinaigrette, 166
Honey:
Dijon Vinaigrette, 86
measuring, 158
Mustard Sauce, 72
and Pomegranate Dressing, 88

Honeydew, Mango, and Blueberry
Salad with Crystallized
Ginger, 157
Horseradish and Grainy Mustard
Straws, 17
Hummus, 30–31
Crostini with Roasted Red
Pepper, Lemon and, 46

I
Iceberg lettuce, 90
Ingredients:
artichokes, edible portions of, 160
cheese, 13
chili paste, 114
olives, 5
pancetta, 205
peanut oil, 174
polenta, instant, 326
salad greens, glossary of, 90
salt pork, 337
sesame oil, 166
sticky, measuring, 198
tastings of
balsamic vinegar, 110
deli turkey and ham, 150
egg noodles, 332
mayonnaise, commercial, 89
olive oil, supermarket extra-
virgin, 103
popcorn, microwave, 7
red peppers, jarred roasted, 35
red wine vinegar, 137
rice, long-grain, 308
tomatoes, canned, 222
tortilla chips, 60
tuna packed in olive oil, 154
vermouth, dry, 210
white beans, canned, 340
Insalata Caprese, 111
Insalata Mista, 93–94
Israeli:
Baba Ghanoush, 33
Tomato and Cucumber Salad,
110–11
Italian White Bean Casserole, 339–40

J
Jalapeño-Lime Dip, 26
Jicama:
Chopped Salad with Avocado,
Cucumber and, 148
Orange Salad with Sweet-and-
Spicy Peppers, 107
preparing for crudités, 23

K
Kabocha. See Buttercup squash
Kale:
Colcannon, 268–69
preparing, 216
see also Greens—Blanched
Assertive
Kid-friendly sides, 330
Kiwi:
peeling, 156
Pineapple Salad with Brown Sugar
and Lime, 156
Knives:
chef's, rating of, 283
paring, rating of, 163

L
Lamb, pairing green bean side dishes
with, 209
Latkes, 290–92
Leeks:
Cauliflower Gratin with Gruyère
and, 195
cleaning, 194
Lemon(s):
Cayenne Mayonnaise, 79
Grilled, Vinaigrette, 169
Herb Vinaigrette, 147
juicing, 84
Mayonnaise, 89
Mint Vinaigrette, 105, 162
Sea Salt Pizza, 55
Shallot Vinaigrette, 84
Vinaigrette, 96
Lentil Salad, 126–28
with Caraway and Radish,
128
with Walnuts and Scallions,
127–28
Lettuce, varieties of, 90
Lime:
Chipotle Spread, 28
Cilantro Butter, 195
Cumin Vinaigrette, 123
Ginger Vinaigrette, 165
Jalapeño Dip, 26
Orange Dressing, 87–88
Looseleaf lettuces, 90

M
Macaroni:
and cheese
Baked, 329–31
"Grown-Up," 34
drying, 134

Macaroni *(cont.)*
    Salad, 133–35
        with Chipotles and Cilantro,
            134–35
        with Curried Apples, 134
Mandolines, rating of, 296
Mango(es):
    Honeydew, and Blueberry Salad
        with Crystallized Ginger, 157
    and Papaya Salad with Tequila and
        Lime, 157
    peeling, 158
Maple:
    Pecans, Toasted, 213
    Roasted Carrots with Browned
        Butter and, 188
    Roasted Winter Squash Halves
        with Soy and, 233
Marinara, Garlicky, 34
Mayonnaise, 88–89
    Basic, 88–89
    commercial, tasting of, 89
    Dijon, 89
    Food Processor, 89
    Garlicky, 34
    Lemon, 89
    Lemon-Cayenne, 79
    potato salad safety and, 129
    Roasted Garlic Aïoli, 163–64
    Tarragon, 89
Measuring sticky ingredients, 198
Meat loaf, side dishes for, 269
Mediterranean:
    Bulgur and Mushroom Pilaf, 315–17
    Corn Salad, 201
Melon:
    Cantaloupe, in Summer Fruit
        Salad, 156
    Honeydew, Mango, and Blueberry
        Salad with Crystallized
        Ginger, 157
    and Prosciutto, 37–38
Mexican Rice, 307–10
Mexican-Spiced Almonds, Peanuts,
    and Pumpkin Seeds, 3
Microwave (ovens), 236
    popcorn, tasting of, 7
    Tortilla Chips, Homemade, 63
Mizuna, 90
Molasses, measuring, 198
Monterey Jack:
    Spicy Roasted Red Pepper
        Quesadillas, 65–66
    Stuffed Zucchini with Tomatoes
        and, 241, *254*
    Twice-Baked Potatoes with Pesto
        and, 275
Moroccan-Style Carrot Salad,
    116–18

Mousse:
    Smoked Salmon, 36–37
    Smoked Trout, 37
Mozzarella:
    Crostini with Pesto and, 46
    Tomato Salad with Basil and
        (Insalata Caprese), 111
Mushroom(s):
    and Bulgur Pilaf, 315–17
    grilling guide for, 170
    Marinated, 7–8
    porcini, dried, rehydrating, 316
    Risotto, 321–23
        with Pancetta and Sage, 323
    Scalloped Potatoes with, 298
    Shiitake, Green Beans Braised
        with, 212–13
    Stuffed, 67–68
Mustard:
    Dijon
        Honey Vinaigrette, 86
        Mayonnaise, 89
    Grainy, and Horseradish Straws,
        17
    Honey Sauce, 72
    Tarragon Vinaigrette, 162
Mustard greens:
    preparing, 216
    see also Greens—Blanched
        Assertive

N

Nachos, Cheesy, 59–62
    with Guacamole and Salsa,
        61
    with Refried Beans, 61
    with Spicy Beef, 61–62
Nectarine and Strawberry Salad
    with Orange and Basil,
    156
Nonstick skillets, inexpensive,
    rating of, 176
Noodle(s):
    egg, tasting of, 332
    Kugel, Savory, with Caramelized
        Onions and Cauliflower,
        331–33
    Sesame, Salad, 138–39
        with Shredded Chicken,
            138–39
        with Sweet Peppers and
            Cucumbers, 139
    see also Pasta
Nuts:
    for cheese trays, 14
    Spiced, 2–4
    see also specific nuts

O

Oils:
    Basil, 205–6
    choosing, for salads, 87
    disposing neatly of, 282
    olive, supermarket extra-virgin,
        tasting of, 103
    peanut, 174
    sesame, 166
    for stir-fried dishes, 174, 175
Okra, 221–22
    Sautéed, 221–22
        with Quick Tomato Sauce, 222
Olivada, Crostini with, 48
Olive(s), 5
    Black and Green, Marinated, 5–6,
        246
    Fennel, and Orange Salad, 119
    Kalamata, Feta, and Oregano
        Cheese Straws, 17
    Pissaladière, 55–58
    Pita Bread Salad with Feta, Mint
        and, 143
    pitting, 143
Olive oil:
    Dipping Sauce, 30
    supermarket extra-virgin, tasting
        of, 103
Onions:
    Caramelized, Savory Noodle Kugel
        with Cauliflower and, 331–33
    grilling guide for, 170
    Pearl, Peas with Lemon and, 224–25
    Pissaladière, 55–58
Orange(s):
    cutting, 106
    Fennel, and Olive Salad, 119
    Ginger Glaze, 188
    Lime Dressing, 87–88
    Rice Salad with Olives, Almonds
        and, 140–41
    Salad, 106–8
        with Avocado and Watercress,
            106–7, *249*
        Jícama, with Sweet-and-Spicy
            Peppers, 107
        Radish and, with Arugula, 107–8
    segmenting, 117
    Sesame Vinaigrette, 86, 170–71
    Three-Bean Salad with Cumin,
        Cilantro and, 125
Orzo, Toasted, Pilaf, 312–14
    with Bacon, Rosemary, and Peas,
        314
    with Fennel, Orange, and Olives,
        313–14
    with Peas and Parmesan, 313
Oven Fries, 285–87
    Sweet Potato, 287

P

Pancakes, potato:
  Latkes, 290–92
  with Pepper Jack Cheese and
    Cilantro, 292
Pancetta, 205
  Green and White Bean Salad with,
    125–126
  Sautéed Eggplant with Rosemary
    and, 205
Papaya and Mango Salad with
  Tequila and Lime, 157
Paring knives, rating of, 163
Parmesan:
  and Black Pepper Butter, 6
  Crostini with Artichoke, Balsamic
    Vinegar and, 46
  cutting into shards, 12
  Dates Stuffed with, 12
  -Garlic Croutons, 93
  Polenta with Butter and, 328–29
  Risotto, 259, 319
  Scallion, and Black Pepper
    Gougères, 21
  Shaved, Tomato Salad with
    Arugula and, 109
  shaving, 109
Parsnips, Glazed Celery and,
  189–90
Pasta:
  Couscous Pilaf with Saffron,
    Raisins, and Almonds,
    314–15
  Salad, 135–37
    with Arugula and Sun-Dried
      Tomato Vinaigrette, 136–37
    with Broccoli and Olives,
      135–36
    with Eggplant, Tomatoes, and
      Basil, 136
    see also Macaroni; Noodle(s); Orzo
Pattypan squash, 237
  Roasted, 242
Pea(s), 222–26
  with Bacon, Shallots, and Sherry
    Vinegar, 224
  Buttered, with Thyme, 224
  Dip, Hot-and-Tangy, 224
  with Feta and Mint, 224
  frozen, ideas for, 224
  with Pearl Onions and Lemon,
    224–25
  Pesto, 224
  Salad, Dilly, 224
  snow, 222–23
    preparing for crudités, 22, 24
    Stir-Fried, 226
    stringing, 226
  Spread, Lemony, 224

Pea(s) (cont.)
  sugar snap, 222–23
    with Asian Dressing, 226
    Blanched, 225
    with Pine Nuts and Garlic, 225
    preparing for crudités, 22, 24
    with Sesame Seeds, 225–26
Peach and Raspberry Salad with
  Toasted Almonds, 157
Peanut(s):
  Dipping Sauce, Spicy, 77
  Dressing, Spicy, 123–24
  Mexican-Spiced Almonds,
    Pumpkin Seeds and, 3
Peanut oil, 174
Pear(s):
  coring, 104
  Roasted, 104–5
  Roasted, Salad, 104–5
    Arugula and, with Walnuts and
      Parmesan Cheese, 105
    Beet and, with Watercress and
      Blue Cheese, 105
    Romaine and, with Fennel and
      Lemon-Mint Vinaigrette,
      105
  Rosemary Dressing, 88
Pecans:
  Spiced, with Rum Glaze, 2–3
  Toasted Maple, 213
Pepper(s) (bell):
  Chopped Salad, 147–48
  grilling guide for, 170
  preparing for crudités, 23
  red
    Asparagus, and Spinach Salad
      with Goat Cheese, 115, 251
    and Cabbage Salad with Lime-
      Cumin Vinaigrette, 123
    Jelly-Almond Spread, 28
    Roasted, 8–10
    Roasted, and Cheddar Spread,
      28
    roasted, jarred, tasting of, 35
    Roasted, Quesadillas, Spicy,
      65–66
    Roasted, Spread, 35
    Roasted, Vinaigrette, 166
    and Roasted Corn Salsa, 201
    Sautéed, Bruschetta with, 49,
      248
    Sesame Noodle Salad with
      Cucumbers and, 139
    Sweet-and-Spicy, Orange-
      Jícama Salad with, 107
  Roasted, Bread Salad with Olives
    and, 142
Pepper Jack, Potato Pancakes with
  Cilantro and, 292

Pesto:
  Crostini with Mozzarella and,
    46
  Dip, 26
  Pea, 224
  Twice-Baked Potatoes with
    Monterey Jack and, 275
Pilafs:
  Bulgur and Mushroom, 315–17
  Orzo, Toasted, 312–14
  Rice, 305–7
    Mexican, 307–10
  Saffron Couscous, 314–15
Pimiento Spread, 28
Pineapple:
  Kiwi Salad with Brown Sugar and
    Lime, 156
  preparing, 158
Pissaladière, 55–58
Pistachio(s):
  Golden Raisin Straws with
    Cardamom, 17
  Indian-Spiced Cashews and, with
    Currants, 3–4
Pita Bread Salad with Olives, Feta,
  and Mint, 142–43
Pizza, 51–55
  Bianca with Garlic and Rosemary,
    53–55
  Dough (recipe), 53
  dough
    shaping and topping, 54
    store-bought, uses for, 52
  Lemon–Sea Salt, 55
Plum Salad, Multicolored, with
  Orange and Thyme, 157
Polenta, 326–29
  Basic, 328
  dressing up, 328
  with Gorgonzola, 329
  instant, 326
  with Parmesan and Butter,
    328–29
Pomegranate and Honey Dressing,
  88
Pommes Anna, 256, 292–95
Popcorn:
  flavored butters for, 6
  microwave, tasting of, 7
  Perfect Popped, 6
Porcini mushrooms, dried,
  rehydrating, 316
Pork:
  pairing green bean side dishes
    with, 209
  salt, buying, 337
Port Dressing, Warm, 99–100
Portobello mushrooms, grilling
  guide for, 170

Potato(es), 261–98
    Baked, 272–74
        Faster, 273–74
        opening, 273
    Boiled, 263–65
        with Butter, 264
        with Butter and Chives, *258,* 264
        with Lemon, Parsley, and Olive Oil, 265
        with Shallots and Sage, 265
    discoloration of (science), 294
    favorite sides for steak, 264
    French Fries, 280–82
        Spicy, 282
    frying
        cutting potatoes for, 281
        soaking before (science), 287
    grated, drying, 288
    Greek-Style, 277–80
        Garlic-Lemon, with Sun-Dried Tomatoes and Scallions, 280
        with Olives and Feta, 280
        Spicy, 280
        with Spinach and Anchovies, 280
    Hash Browns, 287–90
        Spicy, with Cheddar and Red Bell Pepper, 289–90
    Latkes, 290–92
    Mashed, 265–68
        Colcannon, 268–69
        with Garlic, *257,* 267
        keeping warm, 266
        with Scallions and Horseradish, 267–68
        with Smoked Cheddar and Grainy Mustard, 268
    new, 262
    Oven Fries, 285–87
    Pancakes with Pepper Jack Cheese and Cilantro, 292
    Pommes Anna, *256,* 292–95
    Roasted, 276–77
        with Garlic and Rosemary, 277
        with Lemon-Chive Butter, 277
        with Southwestern Spices, 277
    Salad, 128–33
        American, 128–30
        French, 130–31
        German, 132–33
        safety of (science), 129
    Salade Niçoise, 153–55, *252*
    Scalloped, 295–98
        with Chipotle Chile and Smoked Cheddar Cheese, 298
        with Fontina and Artichokes, 298
        with Mushrooms, 298
        Weekday, 297

Potato(es) *(cont.)*
    scrubbing, 272
    slicing, mandolines and V-slicers for, 296
    Smashed, 269–72
        with Bacon and Parsley, 271
        Garlic-Rosemary, 272
        starch in (science), 271
    Steak Fries, 284
    storing, 262
    Twice-Baked, 274–76
        with Blue Cheese and Thyme, 275
        with Chipotle Chiles and Onion, 275
        with Indian Spices and Peas, 276
        with Monterey Jack and Pesto, 275
    varieties of, 262
    wedges, cutting, 280
    see also Sweet potato(es)
Potato mashers, rating of, 300
Pretzels, 52
Prosciutto:
    Asparagus Wrapped with, 38
    Melon and, 37–38
Provençal Summer Squash Casserole, 243–44
Provolone and Salami Salad, Crostini with, 46
Puff pastry, in Cheese Straws, 15–17
Pumpkin Seeds, Mexican-Spiced Almonds, Peanuts and, 3

Q

Quatre-Épices, Green Beans with, 210
Quesadillas, Spicy Roasted Red Pepper, 65–66

R

Radicchio, 90
Radish(es):
    Chopped Salad with Fennel, Green Apple and, 148
    and Orange Salad with Arugula, 107–8
    preparing for crudités, 23
Raita, 112
Ranch Dressing, 91–92
Raspberry:
    and Peach Salad with Toasted Almonds, 157
    Vinaigrette, 84
Ratatouille, Oven-Baked, 206–8

Ratings. *See* Equipment—ratings of; Ingredients—tastings of
Red Wine Vinaigrette, 83–84
Red wine vinegar, tasting of, 137
Refried Beans, 335–36
    Cheesy Nachos with, 61
Rice, 303–12
    boiling for salad (science), 141
    Brown, Oven-Baked, 310–12
        Curried, with Tomatoes and Peas, 312
        with Parmesan, Lemon, and Herbs, 311–12
    Casserole, Baked, 323–25
        Coconut Cardamom, 325
    long-grain, tasting of, 308
    Mexican, 307–10
        with Charred Tomatoes, Chiles, and Onion, 309–10
    Pilaf, 305–7
        Basic, 306–7
        with Currants and Pine Nuts, 307
        Indian-Spiced, with Dates and Parsley, 307
        with Vermicelli, 307
    Salad, 139–41
        Boiled Rice for, 140
        with Cherry Tomatoes, Parmesan, Peas, and Prosciutto, 141
        with Oranges, Olives, and Almonds, 140–41
    steaming, 306
    White, 304–5
    see also Risotto
Ricers, mashing potatoes with, 267
Ricotta, Crostini with Pine Nuts and, 46
Risotto, 317–19
    Asparagus, with Lemon and Mint, 319
    Cakes, *260,* 320–21
    Mushroom, 321–23
        with Pancetta and Sage, 323
    Parmesan, *259,* 319
    Saffron, 319
Rolls:
    Dinner, 52
    keeping warm, 266
Romaine, 90
    and Roasted Pear Salad with Fennel and Lemon-Mint Vinaigrette, 105
Root vegetables:
    Winter, Glazed, 189–90
    see also specific root vegetables

Roquefort:
  Arugula and Escarole Salad with
    Figs, Warm Port Dressing
    and, 99–100
  French Potato Salad with Arugula,
    Walnuts and, 131
  Salad with Apple, Celery,
    Hazelnuts and, 99
  Salad with Avocado, Tomatoes,
    Bacon and, 98
  Salad with Fennel, Dried Cherries,
    Walnuts and, 97–98
  Salad with Roasted Beets, Fried
    Shallots and, 98
Rosemary:
  Dried Fig Compote, 235
  Pear Dressing, 88

S

Saffron:
  Couscous Pilaf with Raisins and
    Almonds, 314–15
  Risotto, 319
Sage–Apple Cider Dressing, 88
Salade Niçoise, 153–55, 252
Salads, 81–158
  Asparagus, 114–16, 251
  Bean, 124–26
  Blue Cheese, 97–100
  Bread, 141–42
  Cabbage, 122–24
  Carrot, Moroccan-Style, 116–18
  Chef's, 149–51
  Chicken Caesar, 145–46
  Chopped, 147–48
  Cobb, Classic, 151–53, 250
  Coleslaw, 119–22
  Corn, 201
  Croutons for, 93
  Cucumber, 111–14
  Fennel, 118–19
  first-course, 102
  for a crowd, 112
  Fruit, 155–58
  Goat Cheese, Baked, 100–102
  Greek, 94–95
  green, gussying up, 92
  greens for
    buying and storing, 82
    cleaning, 82, 85
    dressing and tossing, 82, 85
    glossary of, 90
    guidelines for, 82
    for main course salads, 83
  Insalata Caprese, 111
  Insalata Mista, 93–94
  Lentil, 126–28

Salads (cont.)
  Macaroni, 133–35
  main course, guidelines for, 82–83
  Niçoise, 153–55, 252
  Orange, 106–8, 249
  Pasta, 135–37
  Pea, Dilly, 224
  Pear, Roasted, 104–5
  Pita Bread, 142–43
  Potato, 128–33
  Rice, 139–41
  Sesame Noodle, 138–39
  Spinach, Wilted, 95–97
  summer, 108
  Tabbouleh, 144
  Tomato, 108–11
  Tuna and White Bean, 126
  Waldorf, 148–49
  winter, 107
  see also Dressings; Vinaigrettes
Salad spinners, rating of, 85
Salami:
  Hard, French Potato Salad with
    Gruyère and, 131
  and Provolone Salad, Crostini
    with, 46
Salmon, smoked:
  and Chive Dip, 26
  Dip with Dill and Horseradish, 27
  ideas for, 36
  Mousse, 36–37
  Spread, 28
Salsa(s):
  Avocado, Quick, 66
  Corn and Red Pepper, Roasted,
    210
  Dip, 26
  Tomato, Fresh, 62–63
Salt pork, buying, 337
Sandwiches, Mini Steak, 50–51
Satays:
  Beef, with Spicy Peanut Dipping
    Sauce, 75–77
  Chicken, 77
Saucepans, large, rating of, 327
Sauces:
  Aïoli, Roasted Garlic, 163–64
  Apricot Chutney, Quick, 72
  Barbecue, Sweet-and-Tangy, 72
  Cheddar-Mustard Cream, 192
  cocktail
    Classic, 40
    Spicy Caribbean-Style, 41
  Duck, Spicy Sweet-and-Sour, 72
  Green Herb, Spanish, 174
  Honey-Mustard, 72
  keeping warm, 266
  Marinara, Garlicky, 34
  Olive Oil Dipping, 30

Sauces (cont.)
  Peanut Dipping, Spicy, 77
  see also Butters, flavored;
    Dips; Dressings;
    Mayonnaise; Salsa(s);
    Spreads; Vinaigrettes
Scallion, Parmesan, and Black Pepper
    Gougères, 21
Scallop(s):
  Bacon-Wrapped, Broiled, 80
  removing tendons from, 80
  Skewers, 77
Science of cooking:
  broccoli cooked, olive green color
    of, 178
  Brussels sprouts, cutting small "X"
    in stem end of, 182
  corn storage, 201
  emulsion and vinaigrette, 83
  potatoes
    discoloration of, 294
    soaking before frying, 287
    starch in, 271
  potato salad safety, 129
  rice, boiling for salad, 141
Sesame:
  Chicken Fingers, 71
  Noodle Salad, 138–39
    with Shredded Chicken,
      138–39
    with Sweet Peppers and
      Cucumbers, 139
  Orange Vinaigrette, 86,
    170–71
  and Ruby Red Grapefruit
    Dressing, 88
  Vinaigrette, 173–74
Sesame oil, 166
Shallot(s):
  Lemon Vinaigrette, 84
  mincing, 86
Shellfish:
  Clam Dip with Bacon and
    Scallions, 27, 247
  Crab Cakes, Cocktail, 41–42
  see also Scallop(s); Shrimp
Shiitake Mushrooms, Green Beans
    Braised with, 212–13
Shrimp:
  Bacon-Wrapped, Broiled,
    79–80
  Cocktail 38–41
  deveining, 39
  Herb-Poached, 40
  peeling, 39
  Skewers, Broiled, 77–79
  Spread, 28
  Spring Rolls with, Southeast
    Asian-Style, 73–75, 245

Skewers:
  satays
    Beef, with Spicy Peanut
      Dipping Sauce, 75–77
    Chicken, 77
    Scallop, 79
    Shrimp, Broiled, 77–79
Skillets, inexpensive nonstick,
    rating of, 176
Slaws:
  favorite, 118
  see also Coleslaw
Snow peas, 222–23
  preparing for crudités, 22, 24
  Stir-Fried, 226
  stringing, 226
Sofrito, 334
Southeast Asian Spring Rolls, 73–75,
    245
Southwestern:
  Sautéed Corn, 202
  Spices, Roasted Potatoes with,
    277
Soy:
  Dressing, Spicy, 114
  Ginger Vinaigrette, 169
Spanish Green Herb Sauce, 174
Spiders, 25
Spinach, 90
  Asparagus, and Red Pepper
    Salad with Goat Cheese,
    115, 251
  Dip, 28–30
    with Blue Cheese and Bacon,
      29
    Cilantro-Lime, with Chipotle
      Chiles, 30
    with Feta, Lemon, and
      Oregano, 29
    Herbed, 28–29
  Wilted, Salad, 95–97
    with Bacon Dressing, 96–97
    with Goat Cheese, Olives, and
      Lemon Vinaigrette, 96
    with Oranges, Radishes, and
      Citrus Vinaigrette, 96
  see also Greens—Sautéed Tender
Spreads:
  cream cheese, 28
  Garlic, Ultimate, 34
  Pea, Lemony, 224
  Roasted Red Pepper, 35
  Smoked Salmon and Whipped
    Goat Cheese, 36
  whipped goat cheese
    with Chives and Lemon, 11,
      246
    with Garlic and Mint, 12
  see also Dips

Spring Rolls, Southeast Asian–Style,
    73–75, 245
  with Shrimp, 75
Squash, summer, 236–39
  Bruschetta with Bacon, Blue
    Cheese and, 50, 248
  casseroles
    with Feta, Lemon, and Oregano,
      244
    Provençal, 243–44
  Grilled, 238–39
  grilling guide for, 170
  Pattypan, Roasted, 242
  preparing for crudités, 23
  Ratatouille, Oven-Baked, 206–8
  Sautéed, 239
    with Olives and Oregano,
      239
  Sautéed Shredded, 238
    Spicy, with Anchovy, 238
    with Sweet Corn and Chives,
      238
  shredding, 237
  slicing for grill, 239
  see also Zucchini
Squash, winter, 231–36
  acorn
    cutting safely, 235
    Faster, with Brown Sugar,
      234–35
    Faster, with Rosemary–Dried
      Fig Compote, 235
  Braised, 235–36
    with Asian Flavors, 236
  butternut, cutting up, 232
  removing seeds from, 233
  Roasted, 234
    Halves, 232–33
    Halves with Browned Butter
      and Sage, 233
    Halves with Soy and Maple,
      233
    with Parsley, Sage, Rosemary,
      and Thyme, 234
Starters. See Appetizers
Steak:
  favorite sides for, 264
  pairing green bean side dishes
    with, 209
  Sandwiches, Mini, with Arugula
    and Horseradish, 50–51
Steak Fries, 284
Sticky ingredients, measuring,
    198
Stir-fried dishes:
  Asparagus, 166–68
  basics for, 175
  Broccoli, 174–77
  Eggplant, 206

Stir-fried dishes (cont.)
  garlic in, 177
  oils for, 174, 175
  Snow Peas, 226
Strawberry(ies):
  and Grape Salad with Champagne,
    157
  hulling, 156
  and Nectarine Salad with Orange
    and Basil, 156
  Summer Fruit Salad, 156
Straws (puff pastry), 15–17, 246
Stromboli, 52
Sugar snap peas, 222–23
  with Asian Dressing, 226
  Blanched, 225
  with Pine Nuts and Garlic, 225
  preparing for crudités, 22, 24
  with Sesame Seeds, 225–26
Summer Fruit Salad, 156–57
Summer salads, 108
Summer squash. See Squash, summer
Sweet-and-sour:
  Cabbage Salad with Apple and
    Fennel, 123
  Coleslaw, 121
  Duck Sauce, Spicy, 72
Sweet potato(es), 262–63, 298–302
  Baked, 298–99
  Candied, Casserole, 301–2
    with Toasted Marshmallow
      Topping, 302
  Chips, 24–25
  Mashed, 299–301
    Garlic-Scented, with
      Coconut Milk and
      Cilantro, 301
    with Ginger and Brown
      Sugar, 301
    with Sesame and Scallions,
      301
  Oven Fries, 287
  varieties of, 263
  yams vs., 263
Swiss chard:
  preparing, 216
  see also Greens—Sautéed Tender

T

Tabbouleh, 144
Tangerine and Fennel Salad,
    119
Tarragon:
  Mayonnaise, 89
  Mustard Vinaigrette, 162
Tastings. See Ingredients—
    tastings of

Tatsoi, 90
Thai Flavors, Asparagus, Watercress, and Carrot Salad with, 115–16
Thanksgiving, favorite sides for, 198
Thousand Island Dressing, 92
Three-Bean Salad, 124–25
   with Cumin, Cilantro, and Oranges, 125
Toasts:
   Bruschetta, 48–50, *248*
   Crostini, 45–48
Tomato(es), 227–31
   Basil Vinaigrette, 86
   Bread Salad with Herbs, Red Onions and, 142
   Bruschetta with Basil and, 49
   canned, tasting of, 222
   Cauliflower Braised with Garlic and, 192–93
   cherry
      and Cilantro Vinaigrette, 206
      grilling guide for, 170
      Sautéed, 227–28
      Sautéed, with Capers and Anchovy, 228, *253*
   Chopped Salad, 147–48
   cutting, for salsa, 62
   Gratin, Slow-Roasted, 228–29
   Green Beans Braised in, 212
   plum, grilling guide for, 170
   Ratatouille, Oven-Baked, 206–8
   Salad, 108–11
      with Arugula and Shaved Parmesan, 109
      with Canned Tuna, Capers and Black Olives, 108–9
      Cucumber and, Israeli, 110–11
      with Feta and Cumin-Yogurt Dressing, 109
      with Mozzarella and Basil (Insalata Caprese), 111
   Salsa, Fresh, 62–63
   Sauce, Quick, Sautéed Okra with, 222
   seeding, 218
   Stuffed, 229–31
      with Pecorino Romano, Oregano, and Olives, 23
   sun-dried
      Caper, and Garlic Straws, 17
      Dip, 26
      Parmesan Spread, 28
      Vinaigrette, 136–37

Tortilla(s):
   chips
      Homemade, 63
      Nachos, Cheesy, 59–62
      tasting of, 60
   Spicy Roasted Red Pepper Quesadillas, 65–66
Trout, Smoked, Mousse, 37
Tuna:
   Canned, Tomato Salad with Capers, Black Olives and, 108–9
   Melts, Mini, 46
   packed in olive oil, tasting of, 154
   Salad, Mediterranean, Crostini with, 46
   Salade Niçoise, 153–55, *252*
   and White Bean Salad, 126
Turkey:
   Chef's Salad, 149–51
   deli, tasting of, 150
   pairing green bean side dishes with, 209
Turnip greens:
   preparing, 216
   see also Greens—Blanched Assertive
Turnips, Lemon-Thyme Glazed Carrots and, 190

V

Vegetable(s), 159–244
   blanching, 24
   Crudités, 21–24
   Smoked Salmon–Wrapped, 36
   steamed, adding zing to, 223
   Winter Root, Glazed, 189–90
   see also specific vegetables
Vermouth, dry, tasting of, 210
Vinaigrettes, 83–87, 105, 149–50, 152, 154–55
   Balsamic, 84
   Basil, 174
   Catalina Dressing, 87
   Cherry Tomato and Cilantro, 206
   choosing vinegar and oil for, 87
   Citrus, 96
   Dill-Walnut, 172
   emulsion and (science), 83
   fruit juice dressings, 87–88
   Ginger-Hoisin, 166
   Greek, 95
   Honey-Dijon, 86

Vinaigrettes *(cont)*
   Lemon, 96
      Grilled, 169
      Herb, 147
      Mint, 105, 162
      Shallot, 84
   lime
      Cumin, 123
      Ginger, 165
   Mustard-Tarragon, 162
   Orange-Sesame, 86, 170–71
   Raspberry, 84
   Red Wine, 83–84
   Roasted Red Pepper, 166
   Sesame, 173–74
   Soy-Ginger, 169
   Sun-Dried Tomato, 136–37
   Tomato-Basil, 86
   White Wine, 83
Vinegars:
   choosing, for salads, 87
   red wine, tasting of, 137
   see also Balsamic
V-slicers, rating of, 296

W

Waldorf Salad, 148–49
Walnut:
   Blue Cheese Straws, 16
   Dill Vinaigrette, 172
Watercress, 90
   Asparagus, and Carrot Salad with Thai Flavors, 115–16
   Orange, and Avocado Salad, 106–7, *249*
White bean(s):
   canned, tasting of, 340
   Casserole with Rustic Crouton Crust, Italian, 339–40
   Crostini with Cannellini Beans, Lemon, and Garlic, 46
   and Green Bean Salad with Pancetta, 125–26
   Puree, Crostini with, 47
   Rosemary Spread, Bruschetta with Arugula, Red Onion and, 49–50, *248*
   and Tuna Salad, 126
White Wine Vinaigrette, 83
Wilted Spinach Salad, 95–97
Winter Root Vegetables, Glazed, 189–90
   see also specific root vegetables
Winter salads, 107
Winter squash. *See* Squash, winter
Woks, 175

Y

Yams, 263
Yogurt-Cumin Dressing, 109

Z

Zucchini, 236–42
  Grilled, 238–39
  grilling guide for, 170
  preparing for crudités, 23

Zucchini *(cont.)*
  Ratatouille, Oven-Baked, 206–8
  salting, 237
  Sautéed, 239
    with Olives and Oregano, 239
  Sautéed Shredded, 238
    Spicy, with Anchovy, 238
    with Sweet Corn and Chives, 238
  seeding, 241
  shredding, 237
  slicing for grill, 239

Zucchini *(cont.)*
  Stuffed, 240–42
    with Corn, Black Beans,
      and Chipotle Chiles,
      242
    with Tomatoes and Jack
      Cheese, 241, *254*
  summer squash casseroles
    with Feta, Lemon, and Oregano,
      244
    Provençal, 243–44

A NOTE ON CONVERSIONS

SOME SAY COOKING IS A SCIENCE AND AN art. We would say that geography has a hand in it, too. Flour milled in the United Kingdom and elsewhere will feel and taste different from flour milled in the United States. So we cannot promise that the loaf of bread you bake in Canada or England will taste the same as a loaf baked in the States, but we can offer guidelines for converting weights and measures. We also recommend that you rely on your instincts when making our recipes. Refer to the visual cues provided. If the bread dough hasn't "come together in a ball," as described, you may need to add more flour—even if the recipe doesn't tell you so. You be the judge. For more information on conversions and

ingredient equivalents, visit our Web site at www.cooksillustrated.com and type "conversion chart" in the search box.

The recipes in this book were developed using standard U.S. measures following U.S. government guidelines. The charts below offer equivalents for U.S., metric, and Imperial (U.K.) measures. All conversions are approximate and have been rounded up or down to the nearest whole number. For example:

1 teaspoon = 4.9292 milliliters, rounded up to 5 milliliters

1 ounce = 28.3495 grams, rounded down to 28 grams

Volume Conversions

U.S.	METRIC
1 teaspoon	5 milliliters
2 teaspoons	10 milliliters
1 tablespoon	15 milliliters
2 tablespoons	30 milliliters
¼ cup	59 milliliters
⅓ cup	79 milliliters
½ cup	118 milliliters
¾ cup	177 milliliters
1 cup	237 milliliters
1¼ cups	296 milliliters
1½ cups	355 milliliters
2 cups	473 milliliters
2½ cups	592 milliliters
3 cups	710 milliliters
4 cups (1 quart)	0.945 liter
1.06 quarts	1 liter
4 quarts (1 gallon)	3.8 liters

Weight Conversions

OUNCES	GRAMS
½	14
¾	21
1	28
1½	43
2	57
2½	71
3	85
3½	99
4	113
4½	128
5	142
6	170
7	198
8	227
9	255
10	283
12	340
16 (1 pound)	454

Conversions for Ingredients Commonly Used in Baking

Baking is an exacting science. Because measuring by weight is far more accurate than measuring by volume, and thus more likely to achieve reliable results, in our recipes we provide ounce measures in addition to cup measures for many ingredients. Refer to the chart below to convert these measures into grams.

INGREDIENT	OUNCES	GRAMS
1 cup all-purpose flour*	5	142
1 cup whole-wheat flour	5½	156
1 cup granulated (white) sugar	7	198
1 cup packed brown sugar (light or dark)	7	198
1 cup confectioners' sugar	4	113
1 cup cocoa powder	3	85
Butter†		
4 tablespoons (½ stick, or ¼ cup)	2	57
8 tablespoons (1 stick, or ½ cup)	4	113
16 tablespoons (2 sticks, or 1 cup)	8	227

*U.S. all-purpose flour, the most frequently used flour in this book, does not contain leaveners, as some European flours do. These leavened flours are called self-rising or self-raising. If you are using self-rising flour, take this into consideration before adding leavening to a recipe.

† In the United States, butter is sold both salted and unsalted. We generally recommend unsalted butter. If you are using salted butter, take this into consideration before adding salt to a recipe.

Oven Temperatures

FAHRENHEIT	CELSIUS	GAS MARK (IMPERIAL)
225	105	¼
250	120	½
275	130	1
300	150	2
325	165	3
350	180	4
375	190	5
400	200	6
425	220	7
450	230	8
475	245	9

Converting Temperatures from an Instant-Read Thermometer

We include doneness temperatures in many of our recipes, such as those for poultry, meat, and bread. We recommend an instant-read thermometer for the job. Refer to the table at left to convert Fahrenheit degrees to Celsius. Or, for temperatures not represented in the chart, use this simple formula:

Subtract 32 degrees from the Fahrenheit reading, then divide the result by 1.8 to find the Celsius reading.

EXAMPLE:
"Roast until the juices run clear when the chicken is cut with a paring knife or the thickest part of the breast registers 160 degrees on an instant-read thermometer." To convert:

$160°\text{ F} - 32 = 128°$
$128° \div 1.8 = 71°\text{ C}$ (rounded down from 71.11)

FDR AND THE AMERICAN CRISIS

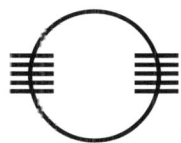

ALSO BY ALBERT MARRIN

Thomas Paine: Crusader for Liberty

A Volcano Beneath the Snow: John Brown's War Against Slavery

Black Gold: The Story of Oil in Our Lives

Flesh and Blood So Cheap: The Triangle Fire and Its Legacy

FDR AND THE AMERICAN CRISIS

ALBERT MARRIN

Alfred A. Knopf · New York

THIS IS A BORZOI BOOK PUBLISHED BY ALFRED A. KNOPF

Text copyright © 2015 by Albert Marrin
Jacket photographs courtesy of U.S. National Archives (top) and the Franklin D. Roosevelt Presidential
Library and Museum (all others)

For image credits, please see page 312.

Visit us on the Web! randomhouseteens.com

Educators and librarians, for a variety of teaching tools, visit us at RHTeachersLibrarians.com

Library of Congress Cataloging-in-Publication Data
Marrin, Albert.
FDR and the American crisis / Albert Marrin.
p. cm.
Includes bibliographical references and index.
ISBN 978-0-385-75359-3 (trade) — ISBN 978-0-385-75360-9 (lib. bdg.) —
ISBN 978-0-385-75361-6 (ebook)
1. Roosevelt, Franklin D. (Franklin Delano), 1882–1945—Juvenile literature. 2. Presidents—United States—
Biography—Juvenile literature. 3. World War, 1939–1945—United States—Juvenile literature. 4. United
States—Politics and government—1933–1945—Juvenile literature. I. Title.
E807.M29 2015
973.917092—dc23
[B]
2013042351

The text of this book is set in 12-point Requiem.

MANUFACTURED IN CHINA
January 2015
10 9 8 7 6 5 4 3 2 1

First Edition

History, by apprizing [people] of the past, will enable them to judge of the future; it will avail them of the experience of other times and other nations; it will qualify them as judges of the actions and designs of men.

—THOMAS JEFFERSON, *Notes on the State of Virginia* (1785)

CONTENTS

Prologue: A Great Bundle of Grief I

   I. A Boy of Many Advantages 8

   II. All the Best People Killed 36

   III. Polio and Politics 61

   IV. Boom to Bust 82

   V. The New Deal 106

   VI. The Supreme Crisis 135

   VII. The War at Home 175

VIII. The Survival War 205

   IX. Roosevelt and Stalin 229

   X. Triumph and Tragedy 250

Notes 285

Some Books on FDR and His Times 309

Image Credits 312

Index 313

A GREAT BUNDLE OF GRIEF

In the darkness with a great bundle of grief
the people march.
In the night, and overhead a shovel of stars for
keeps, the people march:
"Where to? what next?"
—*Carl Sandburg,* The People, Yes *(1936)*

Washington, D.C., March 4, 1933. Inauguration Day. A dull, damp, dismal winter day with thick gray clouds gliding overhead.

Half a million people, standing ten deep in places, lined Pennsylvania Avenue, the capital's main thoroughfare stretching from the White House to Capitol Hill. To gain a better view, some stood on stepladders and soapboxes; a few brave souls climbed into trees, clinging to leafless branches. One hundred thousand others waited on the lawn in front of the U.S. Capitol, their feet squishing in the sodden earth.

Despite the festive decorations, the crowd was as gloomy as the weather.

America was losing faith in itself. "Now is the winter of our discontent the chilliest," an onlooker wrote. "Fear, bordering on panic, loss of faith in everything, our fellowman, our institutions private and government. Worst of all, no faith in ourselves, or the future."[1]

Now in the fourth year of the Great Depression, America was suffering the worst economic crisis in its history. Such misery, and the outrage it stirred, frightened the authorities. There was no telling what desperate people might do; perhaps they might even rise in bloody rebellion, as the Russians had sixteen years earlier. Soldiers with sniper rifles crouched on rooftops overlooking the

Mar. 4, 1933   THE   Price 15 cents

NEW YORKER

peter Arno

A *New Yorker* cover depicting President Hoover and FDR on their way to the inauguration. (March 4, 1933)

door of the White House. A big man in a fur-trimmed coat, striped suit, and tall silk hat sat in the backseat. From the expression on his face, Franklin D. Roosevelt seemed anything but frightened. Born into one of America's oldest families—a man with great personal charm and a "presence" that drew others to him—he radiated self-confidence.

"FDR," as everyone called him, had always believed in his destiny. When he was five years old, his parents brought him to the White House to meet President Grover Cleveland, a family friend. Cleveland patted the child's head and said, "My little man, I am making a strange wish for you. It is that you may never be president of the United States." By that, Cleveland meant the job was so strenuous he would not wish it on anyone he liked. Its physical and emotional demands could wear down the strongest person.[3]

Roosevelt ignored the advice. He thought the presidency the greatest prize this side of paradise. "Wouldn't you be President if you could?" he once asked a guest. "Wouldn't anybody?"[4]

Now president-elect, he waited in the limousine. Moments after it arrived, a butler opened the door, and Herbert Hoover, the outgoing president, took a seat beside him. A sullen, bone-weary

Capitol grounds—just in case. "What are those things that look like little cages?" asked a woman, pointing to a rooftop. "Machine guns," answered a friend, giggling nervously.[2] The guns had shields that resembled cages at a distance.

Meanwhile, a gleaming limousine of the blackest black pulled up to the front

man "tired almost to death," with dark rings under his eyes, Hoover sat silently, his face frozen into a frown. Defeated by the crisis, he wanted only to fish in a quiet stream—and sleep the night through. For private and political reasons, these men despised each other. Hoover refused to speak to him, so a smiling FDR kept waving to the crowd with his silk top hat.[5]

Upon arriving at the Capitol, the limousine stopped under the main stairway leading to the Rotunda, hidden from the crowd's view. Only family members, trusted aides, and his Secret Service detail ever saw Roosevelt get into or out of a car. A victim of polio, he dragged along his withered legs. No president had faced such a physical challenge when he took office. Fearing the public would lose confidence in his leadership, FDR treated his disability as a secret, hiding its full extent from the American people.

Two husky Secret Service men lifted him out of the vehicle. Carefully, they placed him in a wheelchair, of Roosevelt's own design, and rolled him into the Capitol along a ramp built for the inauguration. Once inside, they lifted him out of the wheelchair and stood him up, locking the steel leg braces he wore under his trousers. Each brace weighed ten pounds and extended from his waist to his heel. Holding a cane in one hand, he leaned heavily on the arm of his eldest son, James, with the other. After steadying himself, he swung his legs from the hips and "walked" the thirty-five feet to the platform on the East Portico.

Apart from having to use a cane, FDR seemed to glow with health. Six feet two inches tall and 190 pounds, he was once admired as the "handsomest man in America." Now, at age fifty-one, he had a broad face, light brown hair turning silvery gray, and blue-gray eyes, with a brown mole over his left eyebrow. Years of exercise to regain his health had given him the shoulders of a wrestler, a barrel-like chest, and rock-hard arm muscles. World heavyweight boxing champion Jack Dempsey envied those muscles, saying he wished his were just like them. Roosevelt's large freckled hands gave a bone-crushing handshake.[6]

At precisely 1:08 p.m., FDR put his left hand on the Bible his ancestors had brought from Holland nearly three centuries earlier. The chief justice of the United States, Charles Evans Hughes, then led him through the oath first taken by George Washington Following Hughes "like a bridegroom repeating his marriage vows," as a newspaper reporter stated, he swore to "preserve, protect, and defend the Constitution of the United States" to the best of his ability, "so help me God."[7]

For the first time as president, Roosevelt stood before a bank of microphones to address the nation. No longer smiling, his face stern, he spoke with a cultured accent, the product of years spent with private tutors and in elite schools. Just then, millions of Americans leaned toward their radios. Families had gathered to hear his speech; parents told their children to pay close attention so they could one day tell *their* children about this historic event. They hoped for great things from this man.

Roosevelt began by stating the obvious. The country was in bad shape, and getting worse. However, he saw no reason for despair. "This great Nation," he said, "will endure as it has endured, will revive and will prosper. So, first of all, let me assert my firm belief that the only thing we have to fear is fear itself—nameless, unreasoning, unjustified terror which paralyzes needed efforts to convert retreat into advance."[8]

Nothing to fear but fear itself!

Fine words, though listeners knew they had plenty to fear. What FDR meant was that while Americans stayed frozen in fear, they could not forcefully meet the crisis. His words flew to people's hearts.

FDR delivers his inaugural address at the Capitol. (March 4, 1933)

Courage! Being down does not mean we must stay down, must bow our heads in defeat! Our country had faced other crises in its history and had always overcome them, growing stronger by meeting the challenge. So it would again.

"This Nation asks for action, and action now," the president said firmly. "Our greatest primary task is to put people to work." FDR then asked Americans to unite with him against the Great Depression as they would in wartime. He would lead boldly. Of course, he would obey the law. Yet he would also demand that lawmakers, whatever their political party, support his plans for the sake of the country. If necessary, he would ask Congress for power "as great as the power that would be given to me if we were in fact invaded by a foreign foe."[9]

That night, after the inaugural parade, Roosevelt turned in early. As a valet wheeled him to his bedroom, someone said that if he "licked" the Depression, history would remember him as the greatest president ever—and the worst if he failed. "If I fail," he replied "I shall be the *last* one." Failure, he felt, would bring revolution, followed by the end of American liberty.[10]

Roosevelt went on to capture the nation's imagination as no president since Abraham Lincoln had, or would. In doing so, he became our most controversial twentieth-century president. Millions came to see him as a savior; other millions hated his guts. Had he taken office in a quieter time there might not have been such strong reactions. But we cannot choose the time in which we live. An old Chinese curse says, "May you live in interesting times"—meaning times of trouble and woe, when everything seems about to fall apart. Except for the Civil War in the 1860s, FDR's time was the most "interesting" in our nation's history. Besides the Great Depression America would soon face the Second World War, the most awful conflict in history.

To fight the Depression, Roosevelt began the New Deal—scores of new government programs to revive the economy. A radical step, the New Deal forever changed the relationship between the American people and their government. FDR's actions ignited a national debate about the proper role of the federal government in citizens' lives. That debate still rages. Thanks to FDR, generations of Americans have come to expect more government benefits and protections—to expect, in short, a social "safety net." But nothing is free. And the cost of the safety net has been more rules, more government power, and more taxes.

When Roosevelt took office, tyranny was on the march overseas and democracy was in retreat across the globe. In Asia, a group of generals and admirals led by General Hideki Tōjō controlled Japan; in Europe, a blustering bully named Benito Mussolini ruled Italy. Yet both were amateurs compared to the leaders of the Communists in Soviet Russia and the Nazis in Germany: Joseph Stalin and Adolf Hitler, respectively. They are among the worst—perhaps *the* worst—human beings ever to exist. Because these men lived, millions died. Cruel and cynical, without conscience or regret, each held a human life less valuable than a speck of dust; each caused the deaths of millions through murder and torture, slavery and starvation. Hitler and Stalin loathed each other, but they had the same goal—world domination.

Hitler began the Second World War in 1939 by invading Poland. Overnight, Americans faced life-and-death questions. Should they aid the European democracies, chiefly Great Britain and France? If not, could their country survive in a world dominated by a monster with the most powerful war machine that ever existed? If America must fight, at what cost in blood and treasure? How should America relate to the equally evil

Stalin after Hitler attacked the Soviet Union?

President Roosevelt wrestled with these questions, and many others besides. He had to make hard, even morally doubtful, decisions, raising timeless questions for American democracy.

Given the vast resources of the federal government, including secret information, any president knows, or *should* know, more about world events than any private citizen. Does this knowledge give him special privileges? Should ordinary citizens, even the ignorant and the stupid, have a voice in deciding vital issues like going to war? Must citizens be "guided" for their "own good" by the "wise" and the "informed"? May the president bend the truth to lead the country in a direction he thinks necessary but in which the public is unready or unwilling to go? Can there be such a thing as a "noble" lie? Do the ends justify the means? If so, can the rule of law, the basis of liberty, endure? Must one be a "nice," open person to be a great president? There are no simple answers. However, this much is certain: we need to know about the thirty-second president because we cannot understand our world today without understanding his role in shaping it.

A heartily smiling FDR, clenching his cigarette holder, in an image that has become iconic. (1939)

A BOY OF MANY ADVANTAGES

His father and I always expected a great deal of Franklin. We thought he ought to take prizes, and we were not surprised when he did. After all, he had many advantages that other boys did not have.
—*Sara Roosevelt,* My Boy Franklin *(1933)*

A PRIVILEGED CHILDHOOD

Hyde Park, the Roosevelt estate, is in walking distance of the village of Hyde Park. Located in Dutchess County, on the east bank of the Hudson River, the village lies seventy-five miles north of New York City. On the evening of January 30, 1882, James Roosevelt sat at his desk in the library of his estate overlooking the river. On this bitter cold night, snow lay deep on the ground, and ice floes in the river sparkled in the moonlight like flecks of silver.[1]

At once happy and relieved, James reached for a steel-nibbed pen as he opened his wife Sara's diary. Turning to a fresh page, he wrote, "At quarter to nine my Sallie had a splendid large boy, but

was unconscious when he was born. Baby weighs ten pounds without clothes."[2]

It was a close call, as mother and child nearly died. Sara had gone into labor twenty-four hours earlier, but had trouble giving birth. She was in such agony that the doctor administered chloroform to knock her out. He gave too much. When her baby finally arrived, it was not breathing. Quickly, the doctor grabbed the newborn and began blowing into his mouth, forcing air into his lungs until he began to breathe normally.

A few days later, once they were sure he would live, the grateful parents named their son Franklin Delano Roosevelt. Despite his birth ordeal, baby Franklin had a sweet disposition. Sara wrote that he "crows and laughs all the time" and was "always bright and happy" and "never cries."[3]

Franklin was born into a family whose roots lay deep in American history. In 1644, Claes Martenszen van Rosenvelt and his wife, Jannetje, sailed from Holland bound for New Amsterdam, a tiny Dutch settlement at the southern tip of Manhattan Island. Van Rosenvelt means "of the field of roses" in Dutch, but what the family had to do with roses is a mystery. Anyhow, within twenty years of the couple's arrival, an English army under the Duke of York seized New Amsterdam. Overjoyed at the easy victory, His Grace renamed the colony New York in his own honor.

A portrait of three-year-old FDR. (1885)

Claes was a practical man, more interested in making his fortune than battlefield heroics. Frugal and hardworking, he accumulated land, buildings, and money. Over the years, his sons and grandsons chose brides from equally frugal and hardworking families. In the process, the van Rosenvelt name changed to its English form, Roosevelt.

By the mid-1700s the family had split into two branches. Its Hudson Valley branch settled near Hyde Park; the other made its home in New York City and Oyster Bay, Long Island. Both families gained respect for their wealth, public service, and patriotism. Isaac the Patriot, a Roosevelt ancestor, was among those who ratified the Constitution in 1788. The following year, he led George Washington's horse in the first inaugural parade, held in New York City. In the twentieth century, both branches of the family would give America a president.

Baby Franklin's mother was a Delano. Sara's people counted themselves among the bluest of American blue bloods, their ancestors having come with the Pilgrims in 1620 aboard the *Mayflower*. Fiercely proud of her heritage, Sara boasted, "My son Franklin is a Delano, not a Roosevelt at all!" It was she who insisted on naming him Franklin Delano, after a childless uncle.[4]

Friends said that Delano men had salt water, not blood, in their veins. Over the years, Sara's family had grown wealthy by hunting whales for their fat, which, when melted and burned in lamps, lit the nation's homes. Other Delanos owned merchant ships, trading American manufactured goods for Asian spices, silk, and tea. Warren Delano, Sara's father, went into a less upright, but more profitable, business. He struck it rich selling opium.

In the 1820s, China had much to sell foreigners but bought little from them in return. From the Forbidden City, the imperial palace in Beijing, the emperor declared that China already had everything worth having. Thus, Chinese people must shun the "hairy monkey men" and "foreign devils," as they called whites. British merchants disagreed, bribing Chinese officials to allow entry of opium, a highly addictive drug produced in British-ruled India. Though the emperor banned opium in his realm, in the 1840s British forces defeated China in the first of two conflicts called the Opium Wars. Before long, millions of Chinese became slaves to a drug that enriched foreigners, filling their strongboxes with silver and China with misery.

Warren Delano had no qualms about dealing in "black dirt," as Chinese people called the tarlike opium they smoked in pipes. He wrote his family: "I do not pretend to justify . . . the opium trade [from] a moral . . . point of view, but as a merchant I insist it has been a fair, honorable and legitimate trade." Selling opium, he claimed, was no better or worse than selling wine and whiskey.[5]

The American Civil War made Warren Delano richer than ever. As the conflict raged, he imported huge chests of raw opium, which he sold to the Medical Bureau of the U.S. War Department at a handsome profit. Purified opium relieved the agony of gunshot wounds and amputations, though not without ill effects. A few injections turned wounded men into addicts, creating a drug problem never before seen in America. Opium use was legal in the 1800s. Groceries sold it in syrup form, sweetened with sugar to mask the bitter taste. A few drops of this stuff put crying infants to sleep and stopped diarrhea, a common cause of infant death. Opium also eased women's "monthly complaints." The only problem was that it created yet more addicts.

When Warren finally settled down ashore, he invested his profits in various business ventures. His family lived in a mansion on the west bank of the Hudson, not far upriver from Hyde Park. His children enjoyed the best of everything: private tutors, fine clothes, and long vacations in Europe.

Daughter Sara, his favorite, was a slim, attractive woman. When she married James Roosevelt in 1880, he was a widower with an adult son, also named James but nicknamed "Rosy." At twenty-six, the bride was exactly half her groom's age. James was a soft-spoken, formal man. He sported muttonchops, or extra-thick side-whiskers, favored English-cut clothes, and described himself as a country squire. The term, seldom used today, meant a man who lived in the style of a wealthy English landowner.

James liked to ride horses, sail his yacht, and see that everything ran smoothly on his estate. Rich but not super-rich, he had a steady income from investments in coal companies and real estate. As a director of several railroads, he traveled in his private railroad car. The car was really a spacious hotel suite on wheels, complete with plush carpets, crystal chandeliers, and servants to cater to his every wish.

James and Sara raised their son as if he were a little prince. Franklin's parents came from "old money," their families having made their fortunes long before there was a United States of America. As people who saw themselves as cultured

and refined, they sneered at the "newly rich," immigrants and those of humble origin who might have become wealthy in "shady" ways. This snobbery kept Franklin's parents at a distance even from wealthier Hyde Park neighbors like Mr. and Mrs. Frederick Vanderbilt. James once refused a dinner invitation to the Vanderbilts' elegant fifty-four-room mansion, worth many times his own fifteen-room home. "If we accept," he told Sara, "we shall have to invite these people to our home." And that would "not do."[6]

The Roosevelt house was the center of a 600-acre estate with woods,

〰 FDR, age three, and his dog, Buddy, on a donkey in Hyde Park. (1885)

meadows, gardens, and farmland. The village of Hyde Park seemed to exist solely to serve it and the neighboring estates. Village men worked as butlers, handymen, coachmen, gardeners, blacksmiths, and farmers. Women from select village families served in the same house for generations as cooks, maids, and laundresses. Everyone assumed that a daughter would take over from her mother in the "big house" when she came of age.

Franklin knew his parents were special people. It followed that he, as their son, was also special. Almost from the moment he could walk, he joined James on his daily rounds of the farm, barn, greenhouse, and stables. As they passed, hand in hand, workers stopped what they were doing. Greeting their employer as "Mr. James," they respectfully lifted their caps to him and to "Master Franklin." The little boy saw his father give orders in a calm, matter-of-fact tone, certain that his "people" would obey without question. Raising one's voice in command or in anger showed "bad breeding" and lack of self-control.

By observing his father, young Franklin began to gain the habit of authority that became part of his very being. Though he smiled when asking a servant to do something, his body language commanded respect. That was his due,

something owed him because of the person he was. Studies in child development have found that those raised like Franklin are usually self-confident and optimistic. They believe that anything is possible and that they can succeed at whatever they decide to do. Yes, life had its setbacks; these were a natural part of the human condition. However, FDR, as he signed his earliest letters, would never admit defeat.

Families like his had a strict moral code called *noblesse oblige*. French for "nobility obligates," the term means that high social rank carries duties toward the less fortunate. James, for example, was a member of the local school board and a churchwarden, and he gave generously to charity. "Help the helpless!" he urged his son. "Help the poor, the widow, the orphan; help the sick, the fallen man or woman, for the sake of our common humanity. Help all who are suffering. . . . Work for humanity. Work for your Lord."[7]

Franklin idolized his father, whom he called "Popsy." A good companion, Popsy taught him to swim, fish, sail, shoot a rifle, and ride horses. By the time Franklin was five, he had his own pony, Debby. In winter, as father and son coasted down a slope, icy wind gusts turned their faces fiery red. More than

FDR with his father, James. (1887)

once their sled overturned, sending them rolling in the snow while roaring with laughter. Though a strict disciplinarian, James ignored the old saying "Spare the rod and spoil the child." He never touched his son in anger. On the rare occasion that Franklin acted up, James would calmly ask him why, then explain his error. Once, Sara demanded that he give Franklin a spanking; spankings were the father's responsibility in nineteenth-century households. James took the boy into his library, shut the door, and said, "Consider yourself spanked." But the look in Popsy's eyes had the force of a whack on the backside.[3]

Nevertheless, it was Sara who dominated Franklin's childhood. Because she had nearly died in childbirth, doctors advised her not to have another child. She reacted by focusing all her energy, all her hopes and dreams, on Franklin. "You are my life," she told him time and again. He would always be her darling little boy, her pride and joy, her reason for existing. "What a difference in our lives you have made," she said, "and how I thank God for having given you to me." Everything she did for Franklin was to make him feel loved, safe, wanted, and appreciated. This, in turn, reinforced the sense of worth he gained from observing Popsy on his daily rounds.[9]

Still, the woman Franklin called "Mummy" and "Mama" had the last word on all that concerned him. Mummy knew what was best for her son—always had, always would—and always would say so, even after he became president. A strong-willed woman, Sara tried to control the boy's life down to the tiniest detail. From the moment he awoke in the morning to the moment his head touched the pillow at night, Franklin obeyed Mummy's orders. "He can't help being good," Sara told a houseguest. "He has no brothers and sisters to bother him." Frustrated, he once moaned, "Oh, for freedom!"[10]

Sara kept her son in long curls and short dresses until the age of six. Photographs show him with shoulder-length hair, in dresses and Mary Janes, black patent leather shoes with a strap across the instep. Wearing dresses was common among upper-class boys in the nineteenth century; the dress symbolized the child's dependence on women. A boy usually got his first pair of trousers by the age of five. Franklin was nearly eight before Sara let him wear a sailor suit with trousers, and nearly nine before she allowed him to bathe himself. Until then, she bathed and dressed him herself. "Mama left this morning," a delighted Franklin wrote Popsy, "and I am to take my bath alone!"[11]

Franklin spent little time with children his own age. Mummy would not allow him to play with village boys; they were too rough, too "common," for her son. Occasionally, she invited boys from nearby estates to visit, warning that Franklin would knock his head against the wall if they refused to come. A bossy playmate, he demanded that everyone play the games he chose, and by his rules. When Sara asked why he always gave orders, he replied, "Mummy, if I didn't give the orders, nothing would happen."[12]

Like many youngsters of his social class, Franklin began his schooling at

FDR at age four, wearing the long hair and dress customary of a young upper-class boy at the time. (1886)

home. Sara taught him the basics: reading, writing, and arithmetic. Words enchanted the youngster. He savored them, sounding them out, feeling them roll over his tongue, tasting them. At night, he would sit propped up in bed, reading *Webster's Unabridged Dictionary* (but we don't know how far into it he got). Private tutors, usually refined French, Swiss, and German ladies, taught him foreign languages. French and German were musts for those who traveled widely.

When Franklin learned to read, he began collecting books. He ordered them by mail, paying out of his small allowance. Fearing his mother would object, he hid his purchases—stacks of them—under his bed. Like a human sponge, he soaked up facts: American history, science, exploration. Maps and postage stamps helped him learn geography. When Sara was a child, she saved stamps from letters her father sent from the Far East. The colorful pictures so interested Franklin that he took up her hobby. Franklin mounted his stamps in albums, locating the issuing countries on maps, then reading about them in his books. Stamp collecting became his lifelong hobby and favorite way of relaxing. Over time, he amassed a collection of more than a million stamps, kept in 156 identical albums. When he was president, the Post Office Department sent a sheet of every new stamp to the White House; Roosevelt paid for them himself. Many of these first-issue stamps are worth a fortune to today's collectors.

To escape the summer heat, the Roosevelts went to Campobello, a Canadian island near the northeastern tip of Maine. Before his marriage to Sara, James had built a seaside house on "Campo." In 1883, when Franklin was one, his parents brought him there He took to the sea as readily as his Delano ancestors. The Franklin D. Roosevelt Presidential Library in Hyde Park has photos of the boy, age six, at the helm of James's yacht, the *Half Moon,* in a stiff breeze. When Franklin was fourteen, James gave him the twenty-one-foot *New Moon.* Franklin grew to know the treacherous coastal waters off Campobello like his own bedroom in the dark.

FDR and a friend at the helm of a boat at Campobello Island, off the coast of Canada. (1888)

The sea was in his blood. While visiting Grandfather Warren's house, he discovered the attic. Between the discarded tables and chairs covered with dust thick enough to write his name in, he found old seamen's trunks. These held long-forgotten treasures: handwritten log-books bound in canvas sailcloth. The logs were day-to-day accounts of life aboard whalers and clippers, swift sailing vessels designed for the China trade. They told heart-pounding tales of hunting whales, outrunning Chinese pirates, and surviving raging storms. Fascinated, Franklin began collecting books on naval history and warfare, pictures of ships, and ship models. He dreamed of attending the U.S. Naval Academy at Annapolis, Maryland, and becoming a naval officer. The boy's love of the sea would serve his country well in the wars to come.

Wealthy Americans took their children to Europe to experience a more "uplifting" culture than the one at home. By his fourteenth birthday, Franklin had crossed the Atlantic Ocean eight times. The Roosevelts toured museums, churches, and palaces galore. They stayed in first-class hotels, surrounded by uniformed servants, and ate in the best restaurants. During their travels, Franklin came to love the French people, so warmhearted, and their beautiful country. He spoke French fluently.

Germany was another matter. When he was nine, his parents enrolled Franklin for six weeks in a German school to sharpen his language skills. Besides his academic subjects, Franklin took military map reading and drawing, making detailed pictures of the countryside. As his father aged, he developed a heart ailment; seeking rest and treatment, he took the family to German spas, places noted for their healthful mineral waters. But being surrounded by Germans annoyed Franklin's parents. They made no secret of their contempt for what they saw as crude, rude, "filthy," loud "German swine." Franklin caught their prejudice and always had a low opinion of Germans.[13]

Local newspapers were forever bragging about Germany's military might and its "destiny" to become a world power. Soldiers, their heads encased in spiked helmets, paraded as bands played the national anthem, "Deutschland, Deutschland über Alles" ("Germany, Germany Above All"). Everyone from kindergartners to railroad ticket clerks seemed to wear a uniform and take pride in it. Franklin thought such behavior ridiculous. In a letter to his parents, he wrote in a mock German accent, "Blease expectorate me onze dwenty ninse." Years later, as president, he claimed that his childhood experiences gave him an understanding of Germany deeper than most diplomats'.[14]

SCHOOL DAYS

Sara dreaded having to part from her son for a moment, let alone for months at a time. In 1894, Franklin turned twelve, the age at which the wealthy normally sent their sons to boarding school. Boys went to these elite private schools to prepare for college and learn to speak, dress, and act like gentlemen. Equally important, they mingled with their peers, making friends and contacts that might later help their careers. Finally, in 1896, after a two-year delay, Sara decided to let go of her son just a little. Franklin would attend the Groton School.

Sara Delano Roosevelt with FDR at age eleven. (1893)

Located thirty-five miles north of Boston, the Groton School was known as the "bastion of the elite." The Reverend Endicott Peabody, its founder and headmaster, claimed that he held no *opinions,* for opinions are open to question. Instead, he held *beliefs* that were always true, always just, always beyond question. Like the Roosevelt family, he believed in noblesse oblige. God, Peabody insisted several times a day, had not favored certain people with wealth so they could waste time in idle luxury. The Lord wanted them to help others through public service, defined as clean, honest politics. "If some Groton boys do not enter political life and do something for our land," Peabody would say, "it won't be because they have not been urged."[15]

Peabody also believed in "muscular Christianity." To do God's will, one needed more than good intentions. One needed a sound mind in a sound body. Groton offered the standard nineteenth-century courses: Latin and Greek, ancient history, French and English literature, algebra, geometry, science, and Bible study. However, Peabody said, "I am not sure I like boys who think too much." Those who thought too much, he felt, tended to act very little. Peabody wanted active young men. What really counted at Groton, then, was sports. Sports built "character," a catchall term for courage and duty, confidence and honor. A Grotonian had to take up at least one sport: baseball, football, or rowing.[16]

Franklin never truly fit in at Groton. His schoolmates, all sons of wealth, thought it "rather showy" for the new boy to arrive in a private railroad car. He seemed like a goody-goody, always eager for the teachers' praise, as when he won the prize for punctuality. The best he could do at his chosen sport, baseball, was the second-worst squad. He called it the "BBBBs," for Bum Base Ball Boys.

〰 A portrait of FDR at age eleven in riding clothes. (1893)

Franklin decided that he needed to show some school spirit. To blend in, he deliberately got demerits for petty offenses like whispering in class. However, he avoided the penalties imposed by fellow students. Those disliked by upperclassmen went into the "boot-box," a tiny, pitch-black basement locker in which students kept their mud boots. Better yet, Franklin avoided "pumping." While two upperclassmen held the offender's head, a third poured a pitcher of water down his throat for eight or ten seconds at a time. Today, we call pumping "waterboarding," which most authorities regard as torture. However, nineteenth-century parents seldom objected to it, as it supposedly "made men" out of their boys.[17]

Franklin did well in certain fields. While clumsy on the baseball diamond, he became an excellent manager of the baseball team. His love of words made him a star of the debating society. He also took Peabody's ideal of service to heart, volunteering to care for an aged black woman in town. "I count it among the blessings of my life that it was given to me in my formative years to have the privilege of your guiding hand," Franklin wrote Peabody after he became president. "For all that you have been and are to me I owe a debt of gratitude."[18]

Upon graduating from Groton in June 1900, Franklin entered Harvard College. His family had close ties to the school. Popsy held a degree from Harvard Law School, and a distant cousin, Theodore Roosevelt, was a graduate of Harvard College. Theodore belonged to the New York City–Oyster Bay branch of the family. A man of boundless energy, he had been a New York State legislator, a Dakota rancher, a New York City police commissioner, and an assistant secretary of the navy. With the outbreak of the Spanish-American War in 1898, "Cousin Ted" formed the Rough Riders, a cavalry regiment he led to glory in Cuba. Returning as a war hero, he was elected governor of New York, then ran for vice president on the winning Republican ticket with William McKinley. When President McKinley died from an assassin's bullet in September 1901, he moved into the White House.

Cousin Ted had always liked Franklin. "I'm so fond of the boy I'd be shot for him," he told Sara. Franklin admired his famous cousin, too. Ted became a role model. If something really pleased Franklin, he used the older man's favorite expressions: "bully" and "deelighted." Like Ted, he wore a pince-nez, eyeglasses clipped to the bridge of the nose by a spring.[19]

At Harvard, Franklin majored in history and political science. Yet he showed no interest in gaining a rounded education. When he got bored, which was often, he cut classes. During one lecture, he slipped out a window and climbed down a fire escape while the professor stood at the lectern, head down, eyes glued to his notes. Franklin's average was a "gentleman's C," a grade for students who just managed to squeak by. Not to worry! Grades meant little to men of Franklin's social class, as graduation would usually be followed by a job in a top-notch law firm, bank, or stock brokerage firm. Classmates, however, often

THE HARVARD CRIMSON. SENIOR BOARD

W. DRINKWATER   H. OTIS   W. E. SACHS   A. V. DE ROODE   A. A. BALLANTINE   R. T. HOLT   E. B. KRUMBHAAR
C. W. BLOSSOM   W. R. BOWIE   F. D. ROOSEVELT   P. DANA   H. DE H. HUGHES

FDR as president of the *Harvard Crimson*, posing with its senior board. (1904)

mocked Franklin, calling him "Feather Duster"—a lightweight. His other nicknames were equally demeaning: "Miss Nancy," "Sweetness," "Cunning Little Thing," and "Pretty Face." Cousin Ted's elder daughter, the sharp-tongued Alice, once said, "He was a good little mother's boy whose friends were dull, who belonged to the minor clubs, and who never was at the really gay parties."[20]

The insults hurt, but Franklin brushed them away without showing how he really felt. Instead, he set out to prove himself by trying out for the boxing squad. After taking a beating for two rounds, he threw in the towel and never stepped into a ring again. Unfazed, he joined the staff of the *Crimson,* Harvard's student newspaper, eventually becoming its editor in chief. This was a solid achievement, as the *Crimson* was the nation's foremost college newspaper. Staff members praised his ability to inspire and lead. He had, they said, "a kind of frictionless command." Popsy would have been proud that his son had mastered the very qualities he displayed on his daily rounds at Hyde Park.[21]

James Roosevelt died in 1900, at the age of seventy-two, during Franklin's first year at Harvard. Losing his father was hard in two ways. Not only did Franklin miss the old man, but now his mother, lonely in her big house, focused her attention on him more than ever. To be near him, Sara rented an apartment in Boston, close to the Harvard campus. By now, he had grown into a handsome fellow of eighteen. Women of his own age found him charming, considerate, and amusing. And he found them appealing, too. "Nothing," he once observed, "is more pleasing to the eye than a good-looking lady, nothing more refreshing to the spirit than the company of one, nothing more flattering to the ego than the affection of one." However, Sara saw these young women as rivals for his affections. She always discovered something to criticize in anyone he dated. In Mummy's eyes, nobody was good enough for "my precious Franklin."[22]

Franklin loved his mother very much, as she loved him. He wanted to please her. Yet her attitude put him in a bind. "She was an indulgent mother," a family friend recalled, "but would not let her son call his soul his own." That was no exaggeration. Sara constantly asked personal questions, even read her son's diary without his permission. Franklin, wanting to be his own person, felt he must protect himself from her meddling and prying. The question was how to assert his independence without hurting his mother's feelings.[23]

 Franklin and Sara Roosevelt sailing around Campobello Island. (1904)

Franklin probably realized he could not challenge Sara openly. Starting in childhood, he gradually figured out how to win without conflict. Take the "Sunday headache." If he wanted to skip church, he developed a raging headache. To avoid piano practice, he claimed his hand hurt "just a little." As the boy grew, he found that he had a talent for deception. Depending on the situation, there might be a world of difference between how he *really* felt, which was strictly private, and how he knew he must *appear* to feel. In short, he became an "operator," one who gets what he wants through shrewd, even sneaky, means.[4]

To get his way, Franklin told half-truths, omitting key details, and outright lies. For example, when faced by his mother with a matter he did not wish to discuss or do anything about, he dodged the issue. He became sly and evasive, telling Sara what she wanted to hear while quietly doing as he wished. Mostly, he just turned on the charm. Franklin would become as pleasant as he possibly

could. Without the other person's realizing he was changing the subject, he
laughed, joked, flattered, and talked
about anything but the matter at hand.
Over the years, he became confident in
his ability to charm people into almost
anything. Yet Franklin never confided
in anyone, never revealed his innermost
self. This quality later became part of his
personality as a politician.

LOVE AND MARRIAGE

The most important event during the
Harvard years had nothing to do with
education. In the summer of 1902,
Franklin boarded a train in New York
City bound for Hyde Park. While walking to his seat, he noticed a young woman
sitting by herself. Instantly he recognized his fifth cousin. Born in 1884, she
was christened Anna Eleanor Roosevelt,
but everyone called her Eleanor, and she
seldom used her given first name. Eleanor had recently returned from boarding school in England.

Both branches of the family knew
Eleanor's sad story. Her mother, Anna
Hall Roosevelt, had died of diphtheria
when Eleanor was eight. Two years later,
her father, Elliott, Theodore Roosevelt's
younger brother, died an alcoholic and
a drug addict. An orphan, Eleanor lived

Eleanor Roosevelt at age fourteen in her school portrait. (1898)

with Grandmother Hall until the stern,
sour-faced lady decided to send her to
Allenswood, a famous English school for
upper-class young women.

Although Eleanor's father had ruined his life, he was known as a warm,
affectionate person, lavish with hugs and
kisses. Her mother was not. Among the
great beauties of the day, Anna also had a
cruel streak. Since Eleanor was so plain,
compared to Anna, she called the child
"Granny" in front of strangers. Eleanor
wanted to sink through the floor with
shame.[25]

Franklin and Eleanor had known
each other since childhood. When Eleanor was two, her parents took her on

a day visit to Hyde Park. Poor Eleanor. She stood in the doorway sucking her thumb until, she recalled, gallant Cousin Franklin began "crawling around the nursery . . . bearing me on his back." At a Christmas party when she was fourteen, Franklin asked the wallflower in the plain dress to dance. Afterward, he said, "Cousin Eleanor has a very good mind."[26]

The Harvard man found his cousin unlike any of the young women in his social circle. She was slender and nearly six feet tall, with a shapely figure, golden blond hair, and striking blue eyes. She also had buckteeth, which made her voice high-pitched and shrill. But when she spoke with Franklin, he scarcely noticed her teeth, because she was so smart and mature. Invitations to Harvard football games, college dances, and Campobello quickly followed their meeting on the train. So began their courtship.

It was a courtship typical of upper-class families at the dawn of the twentieth century. The couple obeyed all the rules of polite society. To prevent whispering, they seldom met without a chaperone, an older woman to accompany them in public. Besides, Eleanor said, "the idea that you would permit any man to kiss you before you were engaged to him never even crossed my mind. Ladies of "good breeding" were supposed to faint on proper occasions with very slight provocation. . . . Young ladies received instruction in the art of fainting gracefully. Ladies who fainted were sometimes revived by burning feathers under their noses." Nor would Franklin dream of giving Eleanor a personal gift, such as jewelry. Only "fast" and "forward" women accepted gifts from men they were not engaged to marry.[27]

In the fall of 1903, Franklin proposed. Eleanor accepted, and they agreed to marry after he graduated the following June. Still, Eleanor was torn by doubt. "I shall never be able to hold him," she told a cousin. "He is too attractive." Time would prove her right.

Whenever Eleanor visited Oyster Bay, her uncle fairly burst with joy. Theodore Roosevelt loved his orphaned niece. The moment she came, he would hug her so tightly that she thought the buttons of her dress would pop. An athlete, TR insisted that his children go in for sports, too. Swimming in Long Island Sound was a favorite summer activity. But since Eleanor did not know how to swim, he taught her, as he had his own children. He tossed her off the dock, letting her flail around in deep water until she got the hang of it. Now she

〰 FDR (top row, third from left) with his Harvard class of 1904 in a group shot at Nantasket Beach, Massachusetts. (1904)

was going to marry Cousin Franklin, another favorite of the president's. One day, a letter arrived at Hyde Park from the White House. "Dear Franklin," it said. "We are greatly rejoiced to hear the good news. I am as fond of Eleanor as if she were my daughter; and I like you, and trust you, and believe in you.... Your aff[ectionate] Cousin, Theodore Roosevelt."[28]

Sara Roosevelt did not rejoice. At the ages of twenty-two and nineteen, the couple were too young and immature to marry, she said. Let them wait a few years, and think it over, before taking such a big step. Was this Sara's real concern, or did she want to keep Franklin to herself for a few more years? No historian can answer this question for certain.

We do know that Franklin, gently but firmly, held his ground. "Dearest Mama," he wrote. "I know my own mind, have known it for a long time. . . . Result: I am the happiest man just now in the world; likewise the luckiest—And for you, dear Mummy, you know that nothing can ever change what we have always been & always will be to each other." You, Mummy, will not lose a son, but gain "a daughter to you in every true way." End of debate. Franklin *would* marry Eleanor. And he did, with Sara's grudging blessing.[29]

On March 17, 1905, family and friends gathered in a relative's Manhattan town house for the ceremony. It was St. Patrick's Day, and New York's Irish were having a grand, noisy parade a block away. President Theodore Roosevelt, the parade's guest of honor, took time out to attend the wedding. When Endicott Peabody asked, "Who giveth this woman in marriage?" he answered with a loud

Eleanor Roosevelt in her wedding dress. (1905)

"I do!" The couple then exchanged rings and vows. "Well, Franklin," said TR, moving to kiss the bride, "there's nothing like keeping the name in the family." After the ceremony, the president went into the next room for refreshments, all the guests following him, which left the newlyweds alone with their wedding presents. TR, daughter Alice explained, "always wanted to be the bride at every wedding and the corpse at every funeral."[30]

Though Franklin was now a married man, his mother still doted on him, still tried to control his life. Years later, Eleanor bitterly recalled that her mother-in-law "determined to bend [our] marriage to the way she wanted it to be." At Hyde Park, Eleanor felt like a stranger when servants put two easy chairs near the fireplace. One chair was marked SARA, the other FRANKLIN. Eleanor had no chair of her own.[31]

As a Christmas present, in 1908 Sara built twin town houses at 47–49 East Sixty-Fifth Street in New York City. The redbrick buildings shared a common wall, with connecting doors on three of their six levels. Sara furnished and decorated the couple's house without telling Eleanor or asking her opinion. Worse, Sara would open an unlocked door to enter their home whenever she pleased. "You were never quite sure when [she] would appear, day or night," Eleanor recalled. Such high-handedness made her daughter-in-law burst into tears. When Franklin saw this, he left the room, saying Eleanor was "quite mad."[32]

On May 3, 1906, Eleanor gave birth to a daughter named Anna. For the next decade, she recalled, she was "always getting over a baby or having one." James arrived in 1907; Franklin Jr. in 1909 (he lived only seven months); Elliott in 1910; the second Franklin Jr. in 1914; and John in 1916.[33]

Eleanor had a lot to learn about mothering. "I was certainly not an ideal mother," she admitted years later. "It did not come naturally to me to understand little children or to enjoy them." Some examples of her shortcomings may seem hilarious today, others dreadful. Wanting to be a model modern mother, she read the latest books on the subject, such as Dr. G. Stanley Hall's bestselling *Youth: Its Education, Regimen, and Hygiene* (1906). These books recommended things like toilet training at three months! After reading that young children need fresh air, Eleanor hung a basket made of wood and chicken wire outside the window of their first home, a rented town house. On a frigid winter's day, she placed Anna and James in the basket for their "airing." The children cried so loudly that a neighbor rushed over, angrily threatening to report Eleanor to the Society for the Prevention of Cruelty to Children. Later, to keep three-year-old Anna from touching herself "indecently," she tied her hands above her head to the bedposts at night. This was not unusual at the time; other mothers used tiny handcuffs prescribed by doctors for the same purpose.[34]

"There is something locked up within me," Eleanor wrote. Like her husband, she could not be entirely open with others. The reason almost surely lay in her childhood. As the daughter of a cold and critical mother, she was often cold and critical with her own children. Eleanor seemed distant and detached, unable to unwind around, let alone play with, her children. They all agreed that their mother neglected their emotional needs. Her firstborn, Anna, thought her "very critical, very demanding, and very difficult to be with." Franklin Jr. noted, "She did her duty," but "she didn't enjoy us." Elliott recalled, "None of us children in our growing-up years had turned to her for comfort, guidance, or protection. We saw her principally as an austere, rather distant woman who seldom could communicate with us." His brother James said it best: his mother "did not know how to let her children love her."[35]

Their father was different. Anna spoke for all her siblings when she said, "Father was my childhood hero—not politically or as a world leader—just as a man and *my* father." He seemed to have an instinct for what children needed emotionally, and he gladly satisfied their needs. When they were small, he called them his "chicks." Even as adults, with children of their own, "they called him Pa." And did Pa know how to play! He tickled the chicks, rolled with them on the floor, and carried them piggyback.

Eleanor with her children James, Elliott, and Anna in Hyde Park. (June 27, 1911)

When they felt sad, they cried on his shoulder and, recalled John, "Pa would melt."[36]

Nevertheless, Pa, like his father before him, was no softy. While a serious offense, like Elliott's biting James, brought a spanking with a hairbrush, Franklin preferred words to whacks. Once, James took ten dollars from his father's wallet to buy Anna a birthday gift. In private,

Pa stared at the thief hard and said—nothing. Minutes passed in total silence. If silence could ever seem deafening, it did so then. James squirmed. He broke into a cold sweat. Finally, Pa praised his son for remembering his sister's birthday, but warned that if he stole another cent, he would call the police. James quietly repaid the money out of his allowance. Another time, Pa lectured a friend of James's about some misdeed. Tearfully, the boy said, "I wish my own father would talk to me as you have."[37]

Much as the chicks craved Pa's attention, they realized he was not theirs alone. They must share him with the world outside their home. The world of politics.

POLITICS

Money was no problem for the newlyweds. Each had a trust fund, which together earned $12,000 a year in interest and dividends. As her husband's heir, Sara inherited the Hyde Park estate and James's wealth of about $1.5 million in cash, stocks, and bonds. This was a fortune; $12,000 in 1905 would have the same buying power as $302,000 in 2015; $1.5 million the buying power of $37.7 million.

If Franklin needed extra money, Sara opened her checkbook. She was always generous toward her family, and her son was always ready to let her be so. Sara paid his family's medical bills, school tuitions, and insurance premiums. During Franklin's presidency, she paid for living expenses not covered by the yearly congressional appropriation for White House upkeep. Once, during a discussion of the federal budget, Sara misheard the reference. "Budget? Budget?" she exclaimed. "Franklin knows nothing about the budget. I always make the budget."[38]

Though financially secure, Franklin faced a question we all must answer: What shall I do with my life? He decided to become a lawyer. Lawyers dealt with property rights, leases, deeds, and contracts. A man of his social standing needed to know at least some law, even if he did not make it a career.

Two months before his marriage, Franklin enrolled at Columbia Law School in New York City. From the day his courses began, he knew it was not for him. Bored and restless, he cut classes often, as at Harvard, and failed two courses. As a professor noted, "Franklin Roosevelt... didn't appear to have any aptitude for law, and made no effort to overcome that handicap by hard work." Nevertheless, he learned enough to pass the bar exam without ever graduating.[39]

In the fall of 1907, Franklin became an unpaid clerk in the law firm of Carter, Ledyard & Milburn. The firm, with offices on Wall Street, the nation's financial center, represented tycoons like John D. Rockefeller, head of the Standard Oil Company, and the banker J. P. Morgan. The quality of Franklin's work, however, impressed no one. A partner described it as "utterly worthless."[40]

Lacking his employers' trust Franklin handled only minor cases in the city courts, and described himself as "a full-fledged office boy." Not to worry. One day he told a fellow clerk that he would not grow old in a law office. Politics offered him the chance to be a leader, which appealed to his sense of self-worth and the ideal of noblesse oblige. He would take Cousin Ted's career as his model. Like him, Franklin planned to get elected to the state legislature, become assistant secretary of the navy, and run for governor. "Once you're elected governor of New York," he explained, "if you do well enough in that job, you have a good show to be President."[41]

Franklin's entry into politics came on a silver platter. As his father had been, he was active in Hyde Park community affairs. This caught the attention of Democratic Party leaders, who in 1910 asked him to run for the state senate from Dutchess County. He had the right qualifications. Local people liked Franklin. He was rich—at least his mother was—so he could pay his own campaign expenses. Though Cousin Ted was a Republican and Franklin a Democrat, the leaders expected the Roosevelt name to attract votes. Franklin welcomed the offer but hesitated to accept it. He said he must first ask his mother for permission to run. Taking the twenty-eight-year-old aside, a party leader explained that the others "won't like to hear that you had to speak to your mother." Franklin immediately decided to accept the nomination. "I'll take it," he shot back.[42]

FDR, as everyone now began calling him, eagerly plunged into his first campaign. To reach as many voters as possible, he used the automobile, then a rare thing in American politics. For twenty dollars a day, he hired a Maxwell touring car and a driver. The vehicle, a fiery red beast decked out with American flags, barreled along dirt roads at the dizzying speed of twenty-two miles an hour; the country had few paved roads in 1910. Since the car had no top or windshield, driver and passenger wore coats, called "dusters," to keep their clothes clean and goggles to protect their eyes. Farmers hated motorcars, as they scared horses and cattle. The roar of a passing car, farmers said, so upset chickens that they would lay no eggs for a week. So whenever the Maxwell met a horse-drawn wagon, the driver pulled over and switched off the engine until it was out of sight.[43]

Franklin perfected the skills he had learned in the Groton Debating Society on the campaign trail. Always at ease on the speaker's platform, he could sense the mood of a crowd, shaping his speeches to gain the widest appeal. Often, he gave ten speeches a day—in the open air, without a microphone. The candidate presented himself as a "goo-goo," slang for one pledged to good government. Without making specific promises, he said he stood for honesty, efficiency, and thrift. Better yet, he was his own man; he did not owe anybody any favors.[44]

Voters had heard similar claims before, but seldom from such an appealing candidate. FDR impressed them with his personality. He wooed them. He charmed them. He flashed his smile, showing his gleaming white teeth. His firm handshake suggested sincerity. And he was ever so handsome! Though women would not win the right to vote for another decade, they brought their menfolk to his rallies. A reporter noted how "they came to see as well as hear the handsomest candidate that ever asked

for votes in their district. He might have stepped out of a magazine cover picturing a typical college man of the day, descended from the best honest-to-goodness American stock." Franklin coasted to victory.[45]

In Albany, the state capital, Roosevelt did not get along well with certain lawmakers. Here, it seemed, history was repeating itself. In the 1880s, Cousin Ted's calls for reform had infuriated fellow Republicans, many of whom took bribes for passing laws favorable to big business. Now some fellow Democrats worried about the newcomer from Dutchess County.

FDR in his state senate seat in Albany, New York. (1911)

The worriers belonged to Tammany Hall, the Democratic organization that controlled New York City politics. Tammany men saw public office as their private cash register. Some grew rich from selling jobs—as teachers, police officers, firefighters, court clerks, and tax assessors—to the highest bidder. Others made fortunes from "boodle," slang for bribery and selling contracts to build subways, sewer lines, and parks. FDR had contempt for these corrupt men. Because many were of Irish heritage, he called them "hopelessly stupid" children of "hillbillies" and imitated their brogues. Tammany men thought him a pampered snob, a "silly prig," and a spoiled mama's boy with a swollen head.[46]

Roosevelt got under Timothy "Big Tim" Sullivan's skin. Big Tim was Tammany's boss, or district leader, of the Lower East Side. An outgoing, open-handed man, he held street festivals on holidays, offering entertainment and all the food you could eat. Just for the asking, he helped the poor with money, meals, and clothing. Yet Big Tim also helped gangsters, for a price, and was definitely no Santa Claus. He expected votes in return for his favors—or else. Goo-goos despised Tammany corruption. Big Tim despised goo-goos, and

particularly Harvard men named Roosevelt. "You know these Roosevelts," he snorted. "This fellow [FDR] is still young. Wouldn't it be safer to drown him before he grows up?"[47]

The bosses had reason to resent the newcomer. Until 1913, state legislatures elected U.S. senators. Soon after FDR took office, Tammany Hall backed William F. Sheehan for the Senate. Nicknamed "Blue-Eyed Billy," Sheehan was a crooked politician from Buffalo. In opposing Sheehan's nomination, Roosevelt became the leader of a group of like-minded reformers. They met regularly in a downstairs parlor at Hyde Park to plan strategy. Everyone but Roosevelt puffed cigars—he preferred cigarettes—as the meetings dragged into the early-morning hours. Sara hated the "horrid, blue tobacco smoke," claiming it seeped through the ceiling, "poisoning" the nursery above. Finally, after ten weeks, Tammany withdrew Sheehan's nomination in favor of a candidate both sides could support. FDR was the big winner. His battle against bossism made headlines nationwide, energizing the drive for the direct election of U.S. senators by the people.[48]

Roosevelt was up for reelection in 1912, also a presidential election year. The leading contender for the

Democratic nomination was Woodrow Wilson, a former president of Princeton University and governor of New Jersey. Seeing Wilson as a fellow reformer, FDR became his chief supporter in upstate New York. Wilson welcomed the support of "the handsomest young giant I have ever seen."[49]

Meanwhile, the handsome young giant faced disaster. As his reelection campaign got under way, he came down with typhoid fever. Unable to campaign, he lay in bed for weeks, weak as a lamb. All seemed lost until he remembered an Albany newspaper reporter he had once met.

"ROOSEVELT'S SHADOW"

Louis McHenry Howe, born in 1871, was a scrawny scarecrow of a man whose clothes hung on him like rags. Howe stood five feet four inches in his socks, which had holes in them, and weighed barely a hundred pounds. Frail and high-strung, he suffered from a host of ailments, the worst being asthma. Despite his poor health, he drank gallons of black coffee and constantly smoked Sweet Caporal cigarettes, a brand said to contain dried horse manure, not tobacco, rolled in an ancient death certificate. With each puff, the little fellow coughed

so violently it seemed his lungs would burst; trouble breathing forced him to sleep sitting up. He also had bulging eyes and black scars on his face, the result of a boyhood bicycle accident. Howe described himself as "one of the four ugliest men in the State of New York. . . . Children take one look at me on the street and run from 'the man with the wicked kidnapping eyes.'" Some said he looked "like a troll out of a Catskill cave."[50]

The Roosevelt women despised Howe. Eleanor thought him a vulgar "nuisance." Sara called him "that ugly, dirty little man," half devil and half lunatic. When Howe had a temper tantrum, his face turned scarlet and his body quivered. He cursed, screamed, and threw things. Nevertheless, Franklin hired him to manage his campaign. While he lay bedridden, Howe bombarded voters with "personal" letters bearing FDR's stamped signature, press releases, pamphlets, and advertisements vowing to protect the interests of upstate farmers. FDR easily won reelection, without appearing once in public.[51]

Roosevelt's hiring the "dirty little man" was a stroke of genius. Louis Howe was living proof that we should not judge a person by outward appearances, any more than a book by its cover. He had the keenest political mind of his day.

Though deeply committed to the ideals of fair play and social justice, Howe was also cynical, believing selfishness guided most politicians. Experience as an Albany reporter had made him detest the Big Tim Sullivans and Blue-Eyed Billy Sheehans. These men preyed upon ordinary folks, folks like him, the very ones they had pledged to serve. Though outraged, Howe felt he could not right their wrongs by himself. He was too poor, too sick, and too ugly to run for office. He needed to act through someone else, a reformer able to check the corruption he saw. That person was FDR.

Since Roosevelt, at thirty, was not a seasoned politician, Howe began to teach him. Politics is not a squeaky-clean enterprise, nor a tender one. Howe explained: "You can't adopt politics as a profession and remain honest. If you are going to make your living out of politics, you can't do it honestly." He did not mean that one should be a crook. What he meant is that politics operates by rules different from those that guide ordinary human relations.[52]

Politics is about power. Howe believed that however decent and honest they might be as human beings, politicians are constantly torn between their principles and self-interest. Politicians do what they must to get elected and

FDR clasping hands with his "shadow," Louis McHenry Howe. (April 13, 1932)

reelected. For without gaining power, keeping power, and using power, one cannot get anything done. Wheeling and dealing, horse-trading, and reversing "firm" positions to defeat opponents are the stuff of politics. To win votes, a politician must talk much and say little.

He must offer hope, though he knows he cannot turn hope into reality, or at least not right away. He must charm, smile, flatter, kiss babies, shake hands with anyone who'll shake his, make promises, and show confidence despite worries and doubts. He must stay in touch with a wide range of people, butter them up, praise them, court them, and bully them if need be. He must ask their opinion, even if he thinks them idiots or has already made up his mind. Nor is it always wise, politically, to tell the whole truth. But to deceive voters in what he thinks are their own best interests by lying? Yes, that too. "If you say a thing often enough," Howe insisted, "it has a good chance of becoming a fact."[53]

Fiercely loyal, Howe had an almost religious faith in FDR's destiny. Howe's entire being revolved around him and his career. His reason for existing, Howe said, was to make Franklin Roosevelt president of the United States. To that end, he sacrificed his private life; he became part of the Roosevelt household, visiting his wife and two children on weekends, or whenever he got the chance. Howe became what journalists called "Roosevelt's Shadow" and his "Other I." FDR's ease with words and his charm combined with Howe's savvy to make them a formidable team.[54]

The little fellow wore many hats: companion, adviser, troubleshooter, and fixer. Roosevelt jokingly called him, in mock German, "Dear Ludwig." Howe often began his letters to FDR, half jokingly, with "Beloved and Revered Future President" and signed off as "Your slave and servant." Yet he was no yes-man. Howe told FDR the truth, whether he liked hearing it or not. "You damned fool!" Howe would bark over the telephone. "You can't do that! ... If you do, you're a fool—just a damned idiotic fool!" Nobody but Howe dared call him a fool to his face, let alone shout "I hope to God you drown!" and "Go to hell!" FDR listened because he respected Howe's judgment and integrity.[55]

When Roosevelt returned to Albany after the 1912 election, he knew he had no future in the state legislature. He was a marked man; the Tammany bosses had not forgiven him for making them abandon Billy Sheehan. If they could not drown him in the Hudson, they could, and would, block any measure he put forward. The only way to escape their vengeance was to return to private life or enter national politics.

Woodrow Wilson came to the rescue. Having won the presidential election, he remembered Roosevelt's early support. Wilson owed him a favor. So, on the morning of the inauguration, an official arrived with a message from the president-elect. "How would you like to come to Washington as assistant secretary of the Navy?" In other words, take Cousin Ted's old job.

"How would I like it? How would I like it?" FDR cried, bursting with joy. "I'd like it bully well.... All my life I have been crazy about the Navy." He immediately resigned as state senator and told Eleanor to prepare to move with the chicks to Washington.[56]

ALL THE BEST PEOPLE KILLED

*Why does it all have to be? It isn't possible that it can be for any ultimate good that
all the best people in the world have to be killed.*
—Flora Payne Whitney to her fiancé, Quentin Roosevelt, 1917

ASSISTANT SECRETARY OF THE NAVY

On March 17, 1913, a letter from Theodore Roosevelt reached the Navy Department. As Franklin sat at Ted's old oak desk, he read: "It is interesting that you are in another place which I myself once held. I am sure you will enjoy yourself to the full as Ass't Secty of the Navy and that you will do capital work."[1]

For one who so loved the sea, it was heaven to go to work. Franklin, at thirty-one, was the youngest man ever to hold the naval post. A bundle of energy, he could not sit still, but kept jumping up and walking around his office. His chief, Navy Secretary Josephus Daniels, was a landsman, easily sickened on the rolling deck of a ship. FDR called him "the funniest looking hillbilly I had ever seen." As a former newspaper publisher, Daniels preferred to leave routine naval business to FDR. "Bully" for that! And the devoted Louis Howe, now his personal assistant, handled paperwork in the outer office. Franklin dealt with real ships and real seamen.[2]

Truly a "big shot," Roosevelt rated a seventeen-gun salute when boarding a warship, only four guns fewer than the president. Like Cousin Ted, he could not stop "talking ship." He spent hours discussing complex subjects with the experts: armor plate, engines, developments in aviation. However, he had nothing to do with matters of war and peace; these were up to President Wilson and his cabinet. Instead, the assistant secretary managed dockyards, handled labor relations, and inspected ships. He especially liked to christen new vessels. In March 1914, FDR visited the Brooklyn Navy Yard to hammer the first bolt, of solid silver, into the keel of the battleship *Arizona*. He could not have imagined that Japanese planes would sink this floating fortress at Pearl Harbor during his second term as president.[3]

〰️ FDR in his post as assistant secretary of the navy. (1913)

EUROPE EXPLODES

In July 1914, four months after the silver-bolt ceremony, war broke out in Europe. The conflict that had simmered for forty years now swept the Continent. FDR understood its meaning before most Americans, including his superiors. "These are history-making days," he wrote. "It will be the greatest war in the world's history." Since his life story is part of the larger story of this war, we cannot understand him without understanding it.[4]

Those who experienced the conflict called it various names: Great War, World War, and First World War. Many favored First World War, for never had so many nations fought in nearly every part of the globe or battled in every natural element: on land, on the seas, under the seas, and in the air. Simply put, it was a struggle for power in Europe and colonies in Asia and Africa. At stake were immense overseas empires and markets and vital natural resources such as oil. On one side stood the Central powers: Germany, Austria-Hungary, Bulgaria, and Turkey. Ranged against them were the Allies: France, Russia, Belgium, Italy, Japan, and the British Empire—Great Britain, Canada, Australia, New Zealand, India, and South Africa.

Never had history recorded such a

The front page of the *New York Times* announcing the onset of World War I. (August 8, 1914)

calamity as the First World War. In its opening days, Great Britain rushed to help France. As its army landed, German forces seized much of Belgium and swept into France. In savage fighting, the defenders drove the invaders back, saving Paris, the capital, but leaving the northern part of France in enemy hands. Unable to strike a knockout blow, both sides dug trenches opposite each other. Within weeks, the trench lines stretched 500 miles, from the English Channel to France's border with Switzerland. Between the lines lay no-man's-land. Literally a place without people, it was a moonscape of shell craters, blasted forests, shattered villages, and barbed wire entanglements.

Soldiers described duty in the trenches as living "eye-deep in hell." On a quiet day, with no fighting, they endured raw nature. In summer, they broiled under the blazing sun. In winter, they froze. In all seasons, rain turned their world into mud. Tommy—the British common soldier—sang:

The world wasn't made in a day,
And Eve didn't ride in a bus.
But most of the world's in a sandbag,
And the rest of it's plastered on us.[5]

Nobody sang about constant exposure to wet and damp. Men's feet and legs swelled, cutting off the blood supply. This, in turn, led to gangrene, a painful condition that causes flesh to decay, followed by fatal blood poisoning. With fresh water so scarce in the trenches, soldiers dared not "waste" any on washing. As a result, uniforms became filthy; *men* became filthy. Their heads and bodies crawled with lice. These tiny terrors often carried typhus, a disease causing splitting headaches and high fever, leading to death. The dead lay where they fell or in shallow graves, good eating for rats. Such rats! "Huge rats. So big they would eat a wounded man if he couldn't defend himself," a horrified Canadian wrote.[6]

Most days, however, were not quiet. For the first time, armies used modern weapons, developed since the 1880s, on a massive scale. Their effect stunned Alfred Joubaire, a French lieutenant.

Shortly before dying in action, Joubaire wrote in his diary: "Humanity is mad! It must be mad to do what it is doing. What a massacre! What scenes of horror and bloodshed! Hell cannot be so terrible. Men are mad!"[7]

Soldiers called the trenches the "kingdom of death." One could never relax, never enjoy restful sleep there. Without warning, low-flying enemy aircraft dropped bombs and fired hailstorms of machine-gun bullets. Nothing, however, equaled what British poet Wilfred Owen called "the monstrous anger of the guns." A bombardment with heavy cannons was pure terror. Shells fell where they fell, randomly killing hero and coward. Explosions sent shock waves crashing into stomachs, chests, and heads like hammer blows. The whooshing, whizzing, and shrieking of flying shells seemed to have physical substance, like "a solid ceiling of sound." Men whimpered, "Oh, Christ, make it stop. It must stop because I can't bear it any more." Mommy, *Maman,* and *Mütter,* they wailed, like children having a nightmare.[8]

Thousands cracked under the stress. Physicians dubbed their illness, new to medical science, "shell shock." Victims stared blankly into space, babbling and shaking like leaves in a windstorm. Some recovered after a time, with rest and

Russian troops in the trenches, awaiting a German attack. (1917)

ics unable to form healthy relationships with others.

When soldiers charged enemy trenches across no-man's-land, artillery shells, repeating rifles, and machine guns usually shattered the attackers. Casualties were dreadful. For example, on July 1, 1916, the first day of the Battle of the Somme in France, entrenched Germans killed around 20,000 British soldiers. Another 37,000 were wounded or declared missing. "Missing" meant a man vanished in a red mist, as an explosion blew him into bloody fragments too tiny to identify. The Somme battle lasted nineteen days.[9]

Often sirens in forward observation posts wailed. Gas! In the 1890s, chemists learned that releasing mixtures of certain chemicals into the air turned them into deadly gases. When they did not kill outright, poison gases blinded men, burned their skin, and seared their lungs. Severe cases might linger five weeks—five weeks of continuous, sleepless torment. Victims slowly drowned in fluids produced in their burnt lungs. "Gas cases are terrible," Nurse Millard wrote from a British army hospital. "[Men] cannot breathe lying down or sitting up. They just struggle for breath, but nothing can be done [for them]. . . . Where will it end?"[10]

quiet in rear areas. Others never did recover. A slamming door or an automobile's screeching brakes threw them into a panic. Hearts pounding, they dove for "cover" in the gutter or hid behind garbage cans. Often they became alcohol-

DRIFTING TOWARD WAR

Americans were dumbfounded as the war unfolded in their daily newspapers. Though most favored the Allies, many Americans had no desire to join them. The roots of that restraint ran deep. The Founders believed America did best by minding her own business. In his farewell address, George Washington urged the young country to have friendships with other nations, "but to have with them as little political connection as possible." The fourth president, James Madison, went further, denouncing war as liberty's worst enemy. "War is the parent of armies," he declared. "From these proceed debts and taxes; and armies, and debts, and taxes are the known instruments for bringing the many under the domination of the few." To remain free, we must avoid foreign wars.[11]

The Founders, however, did not want their country to cut herself off from the world. America, they believed, should honor the freedom struggles of others but steer clear of participation in them. The third president, Thomas Jefferson, said she should have "peace, commerce, and honest friendship with all nations, entangling alliances with none." John Quincy Adams, the sixth president, agreed. Though America wished freedom for all, "she does not go abroad in search of monsters to destroy."[12]

When the First World War began, President Wilson urged Americans to be "neutral in thought as well as in action." Like the Founders, whose writings he had studied carefully, he believed neutrality did not mean isolation. America, an industrial giant, had to trade with anyone willing to buy her products.

Wilson's call for neutrality, however, defied reality. Great Britain, the world's leading naval power, had blockaded Germany, sweeping her merchant ships from the seas. The blockade became pitiless as the Royal Navy seized weapons, metals, machinery, chemicals, and medicines—and even food from neutral vessels bound for Germany. Britain seized their food cargoes because these fed civilians, which in effect saved German-grown food for the military. In reply to the British "starvation" blockade, Germany ordered her U-boats (short for "undersea boats"), or submarines, to sink Allied ships. Each month, the stealthy hunters sent scores of vessels to the bottom of the Atlantic.

Congress, seeing trouble ahead, passed a law that barred American ships from carrying war materials to *any* fighting nation, but it excluded food destined for civilian use. All the belligerents need do was order their munitions, pay for them, and carry them away in their own ships. Germans, however, regarded the law as a farce. With their own merchant ships blockaded in port, America became the Allies' chief foreign supplier. Also, in the name of "free trade," New York banks lent the Allies billions of dollars to pay for their munitions. American loans and Allied purchases, in turn, supported jobs for American workers.

Critics warned that Germany could not view America as neutral because she was supplying only one side in the conflict. Equally important, they faulted Wilson for insisting that Americans had a perfect right to sail aboard Allied ships, even munitions ships, and be immune from U-boat attack. In fact, neither international law nor common sense recognized such a right. By insisting on it, the president gave the Allies a gift. Wilson, in effect, allowed them to use American citizens as shields, or "guardian angels," to protect their ships from attack.[13]

Trouble came soon enough. In May 1915, the British liner *Lusitania* sailed from New York. Before she left port, the German embassy placed ads in leading American newspapers. These warned passengers that she was sailing into a war zone—the waters around the British Isles—and might well be sunk. To make matters worse, the ship carried a secret cargo: tons of American-made munitions. On May 7, the German *U-20* torpedoed the *Lusitania* in the Irish Sea. Of her 1,965 passengers and crew, 1,201 drowned, including 128 Americans.

Germans celebrated. To them, U-boat crews were not cowardly killers but heroes out to break the starvation

NOTICE!

TRAVELLERS intending to embark on the Atlantic voyage are reminded that a state of war exists between Germany and her allies and Great Britian and her allies; that the zone of war includes the waters adjacent to the British Isles; that, in accordance with formal notice given by the Imperial German Government, vessels flying the flag of Great Britian, or of any of her allies, are liable to destruction in those waters and that travellers sailing in the war zone on ships of Great Britian or her allies do so at their own risk.

IMPERIAL GERMAN EMBASSY,
WASHINGTON, D. C., APRIL 22, 1915.

One of the ads placed in the *New York Times* by the Imperial German embassy warning passengers about their route. (May 1, 1915)

blockade. Many Americans, however, saw the sinking as a crime against humanity, an act of "brazen piracy" demanding revenge.

President Wilson refused to rush into war. He had been born in Virginia in 1856, and his most vivid childhood memories were of the Civil War and its horrors. Now America must try to avoid war while defending her rights. "There is such a thing as a man being too proud to fight," he said after the *Lusitania* disaster. "There is such a thing as a nation being so right that it does not need to convince others by force that it is right." Rather than fight, the United States threatened to break relations with Germany, a clear warning of worse to come if the country continued its reckless ways.[14]

In Berlin, the government decided it did not need another enemy just then. It backed down. U-boat captains got orders not to sink passenger ships, Allied or neutral, without warning. They must surface and allow the crew and passengers to board lifeboats before opening fire. Though the order saved lives, it did not solve the basic problem. American factories continued to fill Allied munitions orders. Profits soared. Payrolls increased.

The German military vowed to cut the flow of war supplies at the source.

As a result, agents carried out some 200 acts of sabotage—this while Germany was still at peace with America. One team of agents placed bombs disguised as lumps of coal on outbound munitions ships; another spread anthrax, a horse disease that can be deadly to humans, by injecting thousands of horses bound for Allied forces with the bacteria, which were smuggled into the country by German diplomats.

The worst act of sabotage was at Black Tom, a mile-long strip of land jutting into New York Harbor from Jersey City. Located close to Liberty Island, home of the Statue of Liberty, Black Tom was the main loading terminal for British munitions ships. Toward midnight on July 30, 1916, a guard noticed fires in freight cars holding a thousand tons of explosives. The resulting blast broke countless windows in Lower Manhattan, near the future site of the World Trade Center. Seven people died. Chunks of hot metal riddled the Statue of Liberty; to this day, her torch is closed to visitors because of structural weaknesses. The names of the saboteurs remain unknown. After the war, the German government had to pay $50 million in damages, an admission of guilt.[15]

Theodore Roosevelt demanded war over Black Tom; when President Wilson held back, he called him a whining "sissy" with the spine of a "chocolate éclair." Cousin Franklin favored war, too. Since childhood, he had viewed Germany as a bully seeking world domination. Yet Wilson and his cabinet still rejected war. "These dear good people," an irate FDR wrote his wife, "have as much conception of what a general European war means as [four-year-old] Elliott has of the higher mathematics."[16]

Roosevelt wanted America to prepare for the inevitable clash. As part of the preparations, he urged drafting every adult, male and female, into the war effort. Some would fight in the trenches, some work in factories, and some produce food. Whenever Wilson spoke of peace, FDR accused him, but never to his face, of preaching "a lot of soft mush about everlasting peace." More than once, he stormed into Secretary Daniels's office, crying, "We've got to get into this war [and] force peace at Berlin." From the outset, then, FDR wanted America not only to fight but to dictate harsh peace terms to a humiliated enemy. Nor, apparently, did he object to the starvation blockade.[17]

Despite the *Lusitania* and Black Tom, a majority of Americans still opposed war. In November 1916, voters elected Wilson to a second term on the basis of the slogan "He Kept Us Out of War." So he had—for just a little longer.

By then, German leaders had decided to go all out for victory in two ways. First, they sent a coded radio message asking the Mexican government for an alliance. Should the United States declare war on Germany, they promised to help Mexico conquer Texas, New Mexico, and Arizona, lost during the Mexican-American War of 1846. British agents intercepted the message, decoded it, and gave it to the American ambassador in London. When printed in the newspapers, it enraged the American public, as the British intended it should.

Second, the German high command planned an all-out offensive. To choke off Allied supplies, in January 1917 it declared "unrestricted submarine warfare." This meant that U-boats would sink without warning any vessel, Allied or neutral, found in the waters around the British Isles. If those aboard drowned, so be it! Early in March, just days after Wilson's inauguration, U-boats sank three American ships, causing serious loss of life.

With his peace policy a failure, on April 2 Wilson asked a joint session of Congress to declare war on Germany, receiving its approval two days later. Yet, out of respect for the Founders, America did not join the Allies, but became an "associated power." Her forces would fight only under their own officers, carrying out plans made in cooperation with the Allied high command in Paris.

Franklin and Eleanor Roosevelt sat in the audience as the president spoke. She "listened breathlessly," returning home "half-dazed" because great changes were coming. Her husband wasted no time in readying the U.S. Navy for action.[18]

A WORLD SAFE FOR DEMOCRACY

Woodrow Wilson, like Groton's Endicott Peabody, held strong beliefs—yet unlike this educator and headmaster, Wilson acted smug and self-righteous. Some described him as cold and aloof, with a handshake "like a dead fish." A know-it-all, this former college professor lectured seasoned politicians as if they were his students. Wilson could convince himself that whatever he wished was right, just, pure, moral, and, yes, godly. In his war message, he portrayed a European struggle for power and empire as a holy war commanded by God: Germany's rulers, he declared, were the "natural foe of liberty." In this struggle between good and evil, "America is privileged to spend her blood." She was not fighting for gain but "for the ultimate

peace of the world and for the liberation of its people"—in effect, "a war to end all war." "The world must be made safe for democracy," Wilson famously said.[19]

Americans have never gone to war eagerly or, once involved, been unanimous in their support. In 1917, a vocal minority in Congress denounced "Mr. Wilson's War" in biting terms. They charged the president with being arrogant and preachy, spouting fine phrases to disguise an obscene reality. His war message! What hogwash!

The natural foe of liberty? Critics accused Wilson of using this emotional phrase to excuse the British blockade. That blockade was inhuman, declared Senator Robert M. La Follette, Republican of Wisconsin, a respected reformer.

President Woodrow Wilson asking Congress to declare war on Germany, bringing the United States into World War I. (April 2, 1917)

America had joined Britain "in starving to death the old men and women, the children, the sick and the maimed of Germany." If the president felt that the country must fight, he should at least have asked the people to vote for war, as they were "the ones called upon to rot in the trenches."[20]

Privileged to spend her blood? Senator George W. Norris, Republican of Nebraska, called that brave phrase, coming from one who had no sons, a cover for the greed of bankers and munitions makers. America was entering "the greatest holocaust that the world has ever known . . . upon the command of gold. We are going to run the risk of sacrificing millions of our countrymen's lives in order that other countrymen may coin their lifeblood into money." Echoing James Madison, Norris noted that "unborn millions will bend their backs in toil in order to pay for the terrible step we are about to take."[21]

A war to make the world safe for democracy? Not at all! Congressman Ernest Lundeen, Farmer Laborite of Minnesota, noted that America had joined monarchs who oppressed the peoples they ruled. The British Empire held Ireland, India, Egypt, and much of Africa in its iron grip. The Russian Empire, dubbed the "prison of peoples," ruled dozens of small nationalities such as the Chechens. France, a republic, kept the people of Indochina (today's Vietnam) in virtual slavery on rice and rubber plantations. Even when rice crops were poor and people starved, French plantation owners exported rice to the profitable European market.[22]

Many ordinary Americans opposed the war for similar reasons. College students, professors, and members of labor unions staged protests. Marching mothers expressed opposition in a song, "I Didn't Raise My Boy to Be a Soldier."

I didn't raise my boy to be a soldier,
I brought him up to be my pride and joy,
Who dares to put a musket on his shoulder,
To shoot some other mother's darling boy? . . .
It's time to put the gun away,
There'd be no war today,
If mothers all would say,
I didn't raise my boy to be a soldier.[23]

CIVIL LIBERTIES IN WARTIME

Woodrow Wilson compared a nation at war to a chain with millions of individual links. Just as a chain is no stronger than its weakest link, a nation's wartime strength depends on unity. Questioning a war's purpose, morality, and conduct weakens the will to win. In wartime, then, unity is as important as raising armies and building weapons. For that reason, during every major war, the federal government has tried to build support through propaganda while also limiting the rights of those deemed "unpatriotic." During the Civil War, for example, Abraham Lincoln closed newspapers opposed to his policies and jailed editors.

A wise proverb says: "Truth is the first casualty of war." In wartime, each side tries to show itself in the best light. One way is to accuse the other of atrocities. Sometimes, the charges are true. During the invasion of Belgium, for example, civilian snipers fired on German troops. When they did, the soldiers took hostages. If locals refused to name the snipers, soldiers shot the hostages and, in certain cases, burned the town. Often, however, atrocity charges are cooked up to incite hatred and frighten civilians into sacrificing for the war effort.

Within days of the declaration of war, Wilson created America's first official propaganda agency. The Committee on Public Information used the mass media of the day—newspapers, magazines, movies, posters, sound recordings—to mobilize the nation mentally. Atrocity stories abounded, as when the committee cited British reports of Germans crucifying Allied prisoners. Charges made by "eyewitnesses" had Germans tossing Belgian babies into the air and catching them on bayonets. German pilots supposedly dropped exploding toys and poisoned candy into French schoolyards. Propagandists even accused Germans of collecting bodies from the battlefield to grind into fertilizer. Germans made similar charges against the Allies.[24]

The First Amendment to the Constitution guarantees freedom of speech. However, at President Wilson's urging, Congress passed the Espionage and Sedition Acts. These made it a crime to use "disloyal, profane, or abusive language" about the president, the government, or the military. Violators faced fines of $10,000 and twenty years in federal prison.

This attack on free speech inspired a civil liberties nightmare. "Disloyalty," defined as questioning the morality of the war, had no place in America. Wilson said. He insisted that the disloyal "had sacrificed their right to civil liberties." Thus, in this time of need, the Constitution no longer protected them. Accordingly, schools fired teachers who refused to take loyalty oaths, colleges banned study of the German language, and libraries burned books by German authors. Orchestras refused to perform works by German and Austrian composers. Sauerkraut was renamed "liberty cabbage," and frankfurters "liberty sausage."[25]

Self-appointed "guardians of liberty" formed groups with names like Knights of Liberty, Liberty League, and American Rights League. The American Protective League had 250,000 members nationwide. Acting as an unofficial secret police force, these busybodies made illegal searches and "citizen" arrests. Children had the Anti–Yellow Dog League, their own group for rooting out "disloyalty." On the word of his five-year-old daughter, a California man received a five-year prison term for criticizing the president in his own home.[26]

Franklin Roosevelt's letters and speeches suggest that he cared little about civil liberties during the war to make the world "safe for democracy." What did concern him was his role in the conflict. To do his patriotic duty, and to further his political career, Cousin Ted urged him to resign from the Navy Department and get into the fighting at once. Ted's four sons had already enlisted, becoming decorated war heroes. Quentin, the youngest, a fighter pilot, died in combat over the German trenches. Their sister Ethel became an operating-room nurse in a French field hospital. President Wilson, however, thought FDR more valuable at home than in uniform. "Tell the young man to stay where he is," he ordered Secretary Daniels. Ted's wife and children never forgave FDR for "shirking" combat, and never voted for him, either.[27]

FDR'S WAR

The young secretary directed construction of training camps, placed contracts for supplies, and kept naval dockyards humming. Though he did not fight, he influenced the way others did.

Roosevelt believed that "the submarine has come to stay" and the navy had to learn to counter its menace. For that reason, he had built 400 wooden speedboats, a "splinter fleet," designed to patrol coastal waters and call in destroyers to attack the German U-boats when they surfaced. Submarines had to come to the surface and run for several hours each day to recharge the giant batteries that powered them underwater. Destroyers could then easily dispatch the fragile craft with cannon fire, and if a U-boat dove under, destroyers' listening devices could detect the engine and propeller sounds. Depth charges—bombs set to explode at various depths—did the rest. The crew of a depth-charged submarine had almost no chance of survival.[28]

A World War I German U-boat propaganda poster reading "U-boats are out!" (1917)

Roosevelt's most ambitious project was aimed at preventing U-boats from leaving their bases in northern Germany. To keep them from reaching the Atlantic shipping lanes, he wanted to place a barrage, or chain of mines, across the North Sea from Scotland to Norway, a distance of 250 miles. Royal Navy experts scoffed at the idea, saying it would require 400,000 mines.

One day, Roosevelt met a man named Ralph C. Browne. An electrical engineer, Browne had invented a "sub-merged gun" that did not shoot bullets. Instead, it consisted of an iron globe packed with 300 pounds of TNT and an electric battery. Dangling on a chain beneath a floating buoy, each globe bristled with copper wires connected to the battery. A submarine need only brush against a wire to trigger an explosion. British and American admirals approved the invention, and mine laying began in July 1918.

Admiral William Sims, the U.S. Navy commander in Europe, called FDR's project "one of the wonders of the war." Mine laying was an engineering marvel. Working around the clock, crews put 71,093 of these deadly globes in place within three months. In the deepest waters, U-boats easily dove under them to reach the Atlantic. Yet the mines sank four U-boats by the time the war ended in November. Had the war continued, they probably would have destroyed many more.[29]

Meanwhile, the pace of the land war quickened. A revolution in Russia had forced it to sue for peace, freeing vast numbers of German troops for the Western Front. Outnumbered at key points, Allied soldiers died by the thousands each day. A French surgeon captured his army's mood. After an exhausting seventy-two-hour shift in a field hospital, Dr. Le Brun took a short break. As he left the operating tent, he growled, "*La gloire, la gloire! Bah! C'est de la merde!*" (Glory, glory! . . . It's all shit!) Entire French divisions mutinied, until loyal troops shot "cowards" and drove their comrades into the trenches at gunpoint. Ordered to counterattack, Tommies chanted "baaa, baaa, baaa," like sheep going to slaughter.[30]

The help that the Allies so desperately needed came in the nick of time. At the peak, 250,000 American troops landed in France each month, for a total of 2.3 million. Having yet to taste trench warfare, the rookies were in high spirits. Their favorite song swept the Allied armies. "Over There" by George M. Cohan, a writer of Broadway musicals, was lively and upbeat. It went in part:

> *Johnnie, get your gun, get your gun,*
> * get your gun,*
> *Take it on the run, on the run, on the run,*
> *Hear them calling you and me,*
> *Ev'ry son of liberty.*
> *Hurry right away, no delay, go today,*
> *Make your daddy glad to have had such a lad,*
> *Tell your sweetheart not to pine,*
> *To be proud her boy's in line.*
>
> *Over there, over there*
> *Send the word, send the word over there*

> *That the Yanks are coming,*
> * the Yanks are coming,*
> *The drums rum-tumming ev'rywhere*
> *So prepare, say a pray'r*
> *Send the word, send the word to beware*
> *We'll be over, we're coming over,*
> *And we won't come back till it's over*
> * over there!*

In July 1918, as mine laying began, Roosevelt went "over there" to inspect American naval bases. It was the only time he experienced war firsthand, and it was the peak of his navy career. The visit revealed a man who had much growing up to do.

Roosevelt's visit was a glorified tourist outing; he called it "sightseeing." Though ordinary French people had to tighten their belts in wartime, nothing was too good for the favored few. As a VIP, the assistant secretary traveled in style. He and his staff rode in two luxurious limousines driven by French soldiers. In Paris, the French government put them up in "wonderful rooms" (FDR's words) at the stylish Hôtel de Crillon. The honored guest took in the show at the glamorous Folies-Bergère nightclub. He enjoyed, all expenses paid, the best food and the best wines in the best restaurant, the Café de Paris.[31]

On August 4, the tourists visited

FDR at Fort Douaumont in France.
(August 6, 1918)

Next day, Roosevelt visited Verdun, where over 900,000 French and German men had been killed or wounded. "For a few moments it didn't look like a battlefield," he wrote. "When you look at the ground immediately about you, you realize that the earth has been churned by shells, and churned again. You see no complete shell holes, for one runs into another, and trench systems, and forts, and roads have been swallowed up in a brown chaos." In his excitement, FDR left behind a briefcase filled with secret papers; a French soldier found it by the roadside and turned it in. Looking back at his adventure, FDR wrote: "It would be wonderful to be a war president." Time and maturity would change his mind.[33]

THE BETRAYAL

Meanwhile, Eleanor was doing her "bit" for the war effort. She wanted to be "useful," to help others. In Washington, while servants looked after the children, she worked three days a week in a canteen for troops heading overseas. "I loved it," she recalled "I simply ate it up." Two days a week, she visited military hospitals and the shell-shocked. This Eleanor did not love; she never forgot the sights of "some chained to their

the front. According to historian Frank Freidel, Roosevelt "was fascinated rather than repelled" by the awful sights. At Belleau Wood, recently captured by the marines, he saw the debris of battle. Bloodstained clothing, rusted bayonets, broken rifles, and other war junk littered the ground. Briefly, the tourists came under German artillery fire, and marines let FDR fire a cannon in reply. Back in Paris, he had "a splendid dinner" of roast beef and truffles, which no marine ever saw in his rations.[32]

beds, others unable to stop shouting of the horrors they had seen."[34]

Franklin's return from France was a near-death experience. His ship, the transport *Leviathan,* bounced and rolled in high seas. Sailors leaned over the rails to vomit, but not he. The real danger was from influenza, or flu, an epidemic that had broken out in Europe and America. The disease struck every fall, as it still does, killing thousands. However, in 1918 a new strain of the virus killed over 100 million people worldwide. Men died aboard the *Leviathan* every day, and the survivors buried them at sea. Roosevelt fell ill, too. When the ship docked at New York, he had a temperature of 104 degrees and double pneumonia.

Eleanor and Sara rushed down from Hyde Park to care for the patient. While he lay helpless, his wife began to unpack his suitcase. Suddenly she stopped, dazed by what she had found. Buried amid his clothes lay a packet of love letters from another woman. Nobody living today knows what they said because she destroyed them. Then Eleanor also destroyed every letter Franklin sent to her during their courtship. Somehow, she also learned that he and the woman had spent a night in a Virginia hotel registered as husband and wife. The bottom dropped out of Eleanor's world. "All my

confidence is gone," she wrote in her diary.[35]

The other woman was Lucy Mercer, Eleanor's former secretary. Born into a Maryland family that had lost its fortune, the twenty-six-year-old was pretty and easygoing, with a keen sense of humor. As a cousin said, "Every man who ever knew her fell in love with her." Franklin was no exception. Lucy was so different from his wife, and the Roosevelt children adored her. Unlike their mother, Elliott recalled, "she was gay, smiling, and relaxed. She had the same brand of charm as Father, and . . . there was a hint of fire in her warm dark eyes."[36]

≈ A portrait of Lucy Mercer. (1913)

Eleanor offered Franklin his "freedom"—a divorce. Though he could have taken the offer and asked Lucy to marry him, he did not, because his mother and Louis Howe gave him a bitter dose of reality. In the early 1900s, "divorce" was a dirty word. Respectable people thought it "scandalous," reserved for "cads" and "loose" women. Divorced people became outcasts. One never mentioned their names in "polite company." They were cut off by friends and relatives, and nobody "received" them in their homes or spoke to them on the street. They were, as the term went, "socially dead."

If Franklin left Eleanor, disgracing the Roosevelt family name, Sara vowed to cut him off without a penny. Franklin relied on Mummy, as he could not make ends meet on his own. Louis Howe reminded him that a divorced politician had no future. President Wilson would fire him instantly. Worse, he might as well kiss his presidential hopes goodbye, since voters would not trust a man who had cheated on his wife. Franklin saw the light. For the sake of his children and career, he promised never to see Lucy again—a promise he would break.

Franklin's betrayal left Eleanor with a lifelong wound, always open, always raw, always painful. "Eleanor could be hard," said Marion Dickerman, a close friend. "I know she tried to forgive, but hers was not a forgiving nature, really. Eleanor never forgot a hurt, never." After the affair, their son James recalled, "father and mother had an armed truce that endured to the day he died." When he became president, she let him kiss her cheek in public so photographers could snap pictures of the "devoted" couple. In 1920, Lucy Mercer married Winthrop Rutherfurd, a wealthy widower twice her age with six children [37]

STRUGGLE FOR THE LEAGUE OF NATIONS

By the fall of 1918, time had run out for Germany. Allied forces, reinforced by fresh American troops, attacked along the entire front line. As the German army retreated, the Allied blockade tightened. Signs of imminent collapse appeared. Civilians' clothing grew tattered. For want of shoe leather, people wore wooden clogs or went barefoot. The sick lacked medicine. Soap vanished from store shelves. Everything had a stale, musty smell. Fertilizer shortages reduced crop yields, causing widespread hunger. In Berlin, skinny children with bloated bellies fought over garbage pails. Mothers had no milk to nurse their babies, tiny bags of bones who died in droves. With no wood available for coffins, parents buried them in cardboard boxes. An American study noted, "The death rate among old people is huge, as it is with small children. . . . [Everywhere people just] drop in the streets, faint from hunger." Some three-quarters of a million German civilians died of malnutrition in the last year of the war.[38]

Sensing defeat, the German government decided to ask for an armistice—a cease-fire—based on President Wilson's peace program. This program, called the Fourteen Points, supported the right of all people to choose their government, the return of all occupied territory in Europe, and the freedom of the seas. The most important point came last: the call for the League of Nations. Wilson wanted a world organization that could in effect abolish war by forcing nations to negotiate their disputes and punish aggressors. The league would do this by cutting off trade and, if necessary, by using military force. Both sides agreed to the armistice, which took effect on November 11, 1918.

FDR sailed on New Year's Day 1919 to close American naval bases in France. Eleanor came along for company and to keep an eye on him. Her distrust ran deep, and her mood was bitter. Photos show her face drawn and gaunt, her jaws clenched into a scowl. While they were at sea, a wireless message announced the death of her beloved uncle, Theodore Roosevelt.

During his free time, FDR attended the Paris Peace Conference. He did not give his opinion of the sessions, at least not for the record. Yet he must have known that British and French leaders mocked the president as a naive fool. "God Almighty gave mankind Ten Commandments," snorted French premier Georges Clemenceau. "Now comes Wilson with his Fourteen Points."[39]

Germany soon learned that the Fourteen Points meant nothing to the victors. The war had cost them millions of lives, untold misery, and mountains of treasure. For that reason, the treaty signed at the Palace of Versailles, outside Paris, required Germany to take sole blame for the war and repay its entire cost to the Allies. She also had to reduce her military to the size of a national police force, without heavy weapons, and give one-third of her territory to neighboring Poland and Czechoslovakia. The surrender of her Asian and African colonies would give Britain and France over a million square miles of land with nearly 14 million people. Under another treaty, Germany's partner, Turkey, lost her Middle

East territories. Palestine, Jordan, and Iraq went to Britain; France took Syria and Lebanon.

At first, outraged German delegates threatened to reject the treaty as harsh and unfair. In reply, the Allies promised to tighten the blockade further. To show they meant business, the Allies refused to let the German fishing fleet put to sea. Faced with mass starvation, on June 28, 1919, Berlin ordered its delegates to sign at once. Marshal Ferdinand Foch, supreme commander of all Allied armies in France, witnessed the ceremony. As the Germans signed, a grim-faced Foch grumbled, "This is not peace; it is an armistice of twenty years." The old soldier knew the German people would never honor the Treaty of Versailles, to them a scrap of paper with no moral authority. Germany would regain its power and take back all it lost in a second world war. A wounded veteran, temporarily blinded by poison gas, agreed. We will meet Corporal Adolf Hitler again.[40]

Before leaving Washington for the conference, President Wilson met with his aides. "Tell me what's right," he said, "and I'll fight for it." Nevertheless, he gave in to everything Allied leaders wanted. Why? Wilson did not see the main issue at Versailles as money, territory, or even the fate of millions handed

Woodrow Wilson and his wife riding in the backseat of a carriage to his second presidential inauguration. (March 5, 1917)

over to foreign rule. It was world peace. For him, the League of Nations was humanity's best hope for the future. Since its covenant (charter) was part of the treaty, he backed the treaty to gain the league.[41]

Franklin and Eleanor sailed aboard the *George Washington,* the liner that took President Wilson home. One night, he opened his heart to Franklin. His voice quivering with emotion, Wilson said

America must join the league. If not, he warned, "it will break the heart of the world, for she is the only nation that . . . all trust." Wilson was wrong; all nations did not trust America. Nor could he prove that God had commanded the United States to "show the way to the nations of the world how they shall walk in the path of liberty." Nevertheless, he planted an idea in FDR's mind that would bear fruit in his plans for the United Nations.[42]

Under our Constitution, only the Senate can ratify (approve) treaties. However, Senate critics balked when Wilson presented the Treaty of Versailles. Henry Cabot Lodge, the powerful chair of the Foreign Relations Committee, favored united action to halt aggression. Yet the Massachusetts Republican drew the line at one article of the covenant. This obliged the League of Nations members to defend other members' territory, including Britain's and France's colonies, by force. If Wilson dropped that article, Lodge promised to get the treaty passed. When Wilson refused, the Senate rejected the treaty and with it the league, which came into being without the United States. By then, however, Americans had lost interest in foreign crusades.

RED TERROR, RED SCARE

The end of the war did not bring peace to America. Almost from the moment the guns fell silent, fear of communism replaced fear of Germany.

Communism (or Marxism) was the brainchild of Karl Marx, a nineteenth-century German economist who wanted to better the lives of working people. According to Marx, "capitalists," those whose wealth enabled them to command others, controlled governments. To win their rights, he said, workers, led by Communists, must overthrow these governments by force. Communists would then seize all private wealth: land, banks, buildings, businesses, stocks, bonds, railroads, factories, mines, docks, and ships. These would be used not for private gain but for the benefit of all who worked for wages. Marx believed the result would be a utopia, a society where perfect justice and harmony existed, free of poverty and war.

In March 1917, two weeks before Congress declared war on Germany, war-weary Russians overthrew Czar (Emperor) Nicholas II. In November, Communists, also called Bolsheviks (Russian for "majority"), overthrew the reform government that had replaced the monarchy. Soon afterward, they changed the country's name to the Union of Soviet Socialist Republics (USSR), or Soviet Union.

Vladimir Ilyich Lenin, the Bolshevik leader and fervent revolutionary, was a fussy little man with a pointy red beard and shiny bald head. He believed ordinary people were incapable of self-government. Rather than allow free elections, he wanted Communists to rule in the people's best interests. To his mind, Communists' good intentions and superior wisdom released them from the moral restraints on ordinary people. Thus, they could use any and all means, even extreme violence, to achieve their goal of a perfect society. As the slogan went, "We will drive mankind to happiness by force."[43]

Once in power, Lenin and his aides, men like Joseph Stalin, banned all other political parties. Private property became "social property" as Lenin tore the Russian economy from private hands. The Communists declared themselves liberators of the workers. Claiming to know best, they abolished independent trade unions, replacing them with unions run by the party, and demanded longer work hours than before the revolution. Eventually, people began to resist—with words, strikes, and weapons.

Lenin confronted this resistance by unleashing the Red Terror. He defined

A portrait of Vladimir Ilyich Lenin. (1920)

it as "unrestrained power based on force and not on law." The Communist leader did not believe the role of law was to protect citizens' rights, as it is in a democracy. Instead, he saw the law as a tool of the Communist Party of the Soviet Union, and the courts as servants of the state. Both existed to enforce "political correctness," a term Lenin seems to have invented. Anything that advanced a party goal was politically correct in his eyes and therefore "just." Thus, under the Red Terror, individuals suffered not only for what they did but also for who they were. Political correctness labeled broad sections of the population "class enemies," foes of the working class. Mass arrests and mass executions removed those Lenin deemed "harmful insects": nobles, landowners, businessmen, priests, and prosperous peasants. For him, it was necessary to torment and kill millions, sacrificing the living to create utopia for unborn generations.[44]

Seizing power was just the first step. Lenin hoped to use the USSR as a base from which, he said, to "conquer the whole world" by igniting "world revolution" and "world Civil War." To that end, he created the Communist International—Comintern for short. Headquartered in Moscow and controlled and funded by the Soviet government, the Comintern organized Communist political parties across the globe. These were not normal political parties, bound by the laws of their country. Instead, they were agents of a conspiracy, directed from a foreign capital, to seize power.[45]

Benjamin Gitlow, twice Communist Party USA (CPUSA) candidate for vice president (in 1924 and 1928), described his comrades' mentality. After losing faith in communism, Gitlow wrote: "Soviet Russia was our fatherland, its Red Army our army, its red flag our flag. Patriots of Soviet Russia, we would not hesitate to commit any act of violence or

treason against the country in which we lived, if ordered to do so by the Party." Historians have shown that the vast majority of CPUSA members were not traitors but sincere people who wanted social justice. They were, however, not in the party's inner circle, which used their idealism to serve Moscow's ends. Those in control aided Soviet intelligence, checking out likely spies, providing hideouts, supplying false passports, and recruiting couriers to carry messages from spies to their Soviet controllers. The Soviet government financed their activities with smuggled gold and diamonds. Party leaders also borrowed money at sky-high interest rates from New York gangsters.[46]

The American economy had boomed in wartime. However, after the armistice, the government suddenly canceled billions of dollars in contracts for war materials. Three million jobs vanished almost overnight. Returning veterans wandered the streets in their uniforms, searching in vain for work.

Meanwhile, millions who still had jobs went on strike to protest wage cuts. More than 3,000 strikes rocked the nation in 1919, often resulting in violence between strikers and the police. While the CPUSA welcomed strikes, there is no proof that the infant party led any.

Nevertheless, employers found it useful to blame Communists. Headlines in business-friendly newspapers declared OUR AMERICAN WAY OF LIFE IN DANGER! RED TERROR FEARED and REDS THREATEN BLOOD IN THE STREETS.[47]

Terrorism fed the hysteria. On April 29, 1919, a package arrived at the Atlanta, Georgia, home of former senator Thomas W. Hardwick. When his housekeeper cut the string, a bomb exploded, blowing her hands off. Next day, a postal clerk in New York City found sixteen packages addressed to oil tycoon John D. Rockefeller, banker J. P. Morgan, and other business leaders. Each contained a bomb.

The most spectacular bombing shocked the Roosevelt family. In Washington, D.C., at 11:15 p.m. on June 2, Franklin and Eleanor returned home from a dinner party. Just as Franklin turned his key in the lock, a bomb exploded nearby, collapsing a neighboring house belonging to Attorney General A. Mitchell Palmer, the nation's chief law enforcement officer. Apparently, the bomb went off too soon, blowing the man who carried it to bits. For the next hour, bombs went off in other cities: Philadelphia, Cleveland, Pittsburgh, Boston, and New York. Clearly, there was a plot to spread fear by attacks in different places at once.

Pieces of the Washington bomber's body fell onto rooftops, hung from trees, and lay in the gutter. "We could not take a step without seeing or feeling the grinding of a piece of flesh," noted a police report. "The house across the street was plastered with the pieces."[48]

That house, at 2132 R Street NW, was the Roosevelts'. Some of the children had gone to Hyde Park; only twelve-year-old

"COME UNTO ME, YE OPPREST!"

〰 A political cartoon warning that the USSR's practices are working their way into American life. (July 5, 1919)

James had stayed behind to study for his Groton entrance exam. With his ears ringing from the blast, Franklin bounded up the stairs to his son's second-floor bedroom. He found James standing at a broken window in his pajamas, mesmerized, staring at the Palmers' house. James recalled that his father "grabbed me in an embrace that almost cracked my ribs." His mother arrived seconds later. She coolly asked, "What are you doing out of bed at this hour, James?" Next morning, after breakfast, the boy returned with a piece of collarbone wrapped in a napkin. Franklin turned pale and gave the "souvenir" to the police. Eleanor wrote Sara: "James glories in every new bone found."[49]

Though the bombers' names may never be known, printed leaflets scattered at the scene pointed to anarchists, people believing that all forms of government are evil. The blasts occurred just when Americans were primed to believe that Communists were responsible for the country's ills. Caught up in the hysteria of the Red Scare, respected newspapers like the *New York Times* demanded a crackdown on all "undesirables."

Having survived the blast, the attorney general attacked what he called the "disease of evil thinking." On Palmer's orders, federal agents rounded up more than 6,000 foreigners living in the United States. Of these, hundreds were deported, without trial, to their native lands or to the USSR. "America," *Harper's Magazine* protested, "is no longer a free country. . . . Everywhere, on every hand, free speech is choked off in one direction or another."[50]

Franklin Roosevelt encouraged the crackdown. No doubt the Red Terror and the Red Scare frightened him, as well as others of his background and upbringing. He had seen the face of terrorism from his front door. A son of wealth, he knew what enemies of what he called "the sacred cause of Americanism" had in store for people like him. So he gave his blessing to those who roused the nation "to the great task of ridding this land of . . . anti-Americans."[51]

The Red Scare slowly burned itself out. By 1920, the economy had recovered. For FDR, the war years had been an important time. In his public life, he learned that he had a talent for getting things done and that he had a conservative side, which dreaded sudden, violent change; in his private life, he learned he had an unsatisfying marriage. Before long, he would face the supreme test of body and spirit.

POLIO AND POLITICS

[Polio] proved a blessing in disguise, for it gave [Franklin] the strength and courage
he had not had before. He had to think out the fundamentals of living and learn the
greatest of all lessons—infinite patience and never-ending persistence.
—Eleanor Roosevelt, This I Remember (1949)

A FALSE START

If anyone had asked Franklin Roosevelt to describe himself in a word, it is a safe bet that he would have said "politician." Politics was his chosen profession, the presidency his life's goal. Though it was important, he saw his navy job as a stepping-stone, a way of showing his readiness for the challenges of national office. It was also a means of networking, of meeting people who might later help advance his career. After nearly six years, however, the job had become routine, boring. He needed a change.

FDR's chance came in 1919. At their convention in San Francisco in July, the Democrats met to choose a candi-

date to succeed Woodrow Wilson. The president had suffered a stroke while campaigning for the League of Nations. Though partially paralyzed, and barely able to speak, he refused to resign. Instead, he lived like a hermit in a darkened room in the White House while his wife, Edith, and aides ran the government. Whenever Wilson had to sign official papers, the First Lady guided his hand. The press and the public were told that the president was exhausted by years of devoted service, but otherwise fit. FDR knew better. During a visit, he found Wilson in a wheelchair, his paralyzed left arm covered with a shawl, unable to speak above a whisper.

The Democrats nominated Governor James M. Cox of Ohio, a millionaire who had made a fortune from newspapers and in other ways he chose not to discuss. A super-patriot during the war, Cox had banned the teaching of the German language in Ohio schools. As a midwesterner, he wanted to "balance" the ticket with a vice-presidential running mate from a large eastern state.

As a New Yorker who had served in a high post during the war, Roosevelt was Cox's logical choice. He also selected Franklin because of his appeal to women, recently granted the vote in national elections by the Nineteenth Amendment to the Constitution. An admiring reporter described the thirty-seven-year-old as having "the figure of an idealized college football player . . . always with a smile ready to share. . . . He speaks with a strong clear voice . . . with [a] vote-winning quality."[1]

Franklin jumped at the chance to follow again in Cousin Ted's footsteps. After resigning from the Navy Department, he began campaigning. With energy and good humor, he traveled thousands of miles by train, giving up to twenty speeches a day. Both parties made the League of Nations a major issue. Taking his lead from Wilson, Roosevelt described America as part of a world community. "The lives of civilized men," he told audiences, "[are] so interwoven with the lives of other men in

FDR campaigning with Governor James M. Cox in Dayton, Ohio. (August 7, 1920)

other countries as to make it impossible to be in this world and not of it."[2]

Warren G. Harding, the Republican nominee, used a surefire slogan. Americans, he said, demanded a "return to normalcy." That meant a return to life as they imagined it before the war—a happy, carefree time. The very words "League of Nations" grated on people's nerves. Harding and his running mate, Massachusetts governor Calvin Coolidge, attacked their opponents as "starry-eyed" idealists living in a dreamworld. Roosevelt could almost taste audiences' scorn for the man who had kept them out of war in 1916, only to take them into war in 1917. Millions now saw the war as just another of Europe's age-old bloodbaths. They wanted an end to Wilson and "Wilsonism." A Republican campaign song put it this way:

> We'll throw out Wilson and his crew,
> They really don't know what to do.[3]

Harding won in a landslide, with 61 percent of the popular vote (16,152,200 to 9,147,353) and the electoral votes from thirty-seven of the forty-eight states. FDR's candidacy had not kept the Republicans from carrying every New York county, including his own Dutchess County and Hyde Park.

Yet, for him, defeat was no setback. The vice-presidential race had given him experience in a national campaign and valuable contacts among party leaders. When the time came, with the help of Louis Howe's savvy, Roosevelt would seek his party's presidential nomination. Nobody thought, in 1920, that his plans would take a sharp detour.

THE ORDEAL BEGINS

After the election, Roosevelt returned to private life. He became a partner in Emmet, Marvin & Roosevelt, a Wall Street law firm he helped found. He also ran the New York office of the Fidelity and Deposit Company, a firm that insured executives who handled large sums of money. Neither job took much effort; assistants did the routine work, leaving him ample time to plan his political future. Meanwhile, Louis Howe kept him in the public eye by arranging interviews with reporters and visits to places where he could make a good impression. In his role as president of the Greater New York Boy Scouts Council, FDR visited a summer camp at Bear Mountain, New York, late in July 1921. That visit changed his life.

Afterward, Roosevelt joined his family at Campobello for the summer.

On August 10, he took the three older chicks—Anna, James, and Elliott—sailing in the *Vireo,* his twenty-four-foot sloop. The weather was glorious. After sailing an hour, they noticed a brush fire on a tiny island. Landing, they beat out the flames with evergreen boughs. "Late in the afternoon," he recalled, "we brought it under control. . . . Our eyes were bleary with smoke; we were begrimed, smarting with spark burns, exhausted."[4]

Hoping a swim would perk them up, Roosevelt led a two-mile jog to a freshwater lake. After that, they dove into the icy waters of Herring Cove. Back home, the children changed into dry clothes. Their father sat on the porch in his wet bathing suit, catching up on the newspapers. "I sat reading for a while, too tired even to dress," he wrote. "I'd never felt quite that way before." A chill ran through his body. His leg muscles ached, and he felt feverish. Too tired to eat supper, he went straight to bed.[5]

Next morning, his left leg gave way as he tried to get out of bed. Soon it would not move at all, nor would his right leg. Louis Howe, vacationing with the family, called a local doctor, who diagnosed a severe cold. No need to worry, he said, the legs would get better on their own.

They didn't. Over the next two days,

FDR's condition worsened. Sharp pains radiated through his legs and back, then stabbed into his shoulders, arms, and hands. His temperature rose to 102. His skin became ultra-sensitive. Like a soldier with poison gas burns, he could not bear anything on his skin, however light; the gentlest breeze brought searing pain. He became delirious. Eleanor recalled, "One night he was out of his head."[6]

By August 13, Roosevelt lay paralyzed from the waist down. Another doctor, called in from Bar Harbor, Maine, diagnosed a blood clot on the spinal cord. Why he thought so without X-rays is a mystery. Nonetheless, he prescribed frequent massages, which Eleanor and Louis Howe gave. Having his sensitive legs massaged hurt terribly, and probably made the paralysis worse.

In this crisis, Eleanor's basic decency overcame her anger at the Lucy Mercer affair. She became Franklin's angel of mercy. Several times a day, she gave him enemas to empty his bowels and inserted a glass catheter to drain urine from his bladder. She bathed her husband, brushed his teeth, fed him, shaved him, and combed his hair. She slept on a couch in his room, should he need help at night. Finally, the family sent for Robert Lovett, a prominent Boston physician. One look told Lovett that FDR had poliomyelitis, commonly known as infantile paralysis—"polio" for short.[7]

POLIO

"Poliomyelitis" is Greek for swelling (*itis*) of the gray (*polios*) matter (*myelon*) in the spinal cord. Polio is mainly a childhood disease, but it can also infect adults. For centuries, nobody knew its cause, how it spread, or how to prevent it. Scientists now know that it is a virus, a microscopic organism, that attacks the nerve cells of the brain and spinal cord, causing paralysis. Should it attack the nerves that control breathing, the victim can suffocate. Poliovirus enters the body through the mouth in water or food contaminated by infected feces. FDR had probably become infected during his visit to the Boy Scout camp.

The 1700s saw scattered polio outbreaks in Western Europe. America had small, localized outbreaks in colonial days and in the years following the War for Independence. Vermont had the first full-fledged epidemic in 1894; the disease struck 133 people, killing 18. In the summer of 1916, while Europeans butchered each other in the trenches, America had an epidemic unlike any ever recorded. New York City was hit hardest. There were 8,900 cases and

2,400 deaths—or about one infected child in four. Nationwide, there were 27,000 cases and 6,000 deaths. After 1916, polio became "the summer plague." It returned like clockwork during the warm months, though outbreaks varied by location and in severity from year to year. Scientists are still unsure why the virus strikes in this season.[8]

Without knowing its cause, people blamed polio on various things, from poor immigrants to dirt in doctors' beards. Flies, known carriers of bacteria that cause illnesses like food poisoning, became suspects. According to one slogan,

A watched child is a safe child.
Swat the fly![9]

Since dogs and cats carried rabies, a disease that affects the central nervous system, it seemed logical that they carried polio, too. New York authorities put a bounty on stray cats (but not dogs, for some unknown reason). Club-wielding gangs hunted their feline prey through streets, alleys, and vacant lots. On July 26, 1916, a *New York Times* headline read 72,000 CATS KILLED IN PARALYSIS FEAR. Later, some neighborhoods had more rats and mice than usual.

The city's health department ordered

polio victims quarantined in their homes for up to eight weeks. By law, their families had to display an orange quarantine placard in their front window or on their apartment door. No one could enter or leave; grocers had to leave food outside. Wealthier families hired nurses to care for victims at home. The poor wound up in hospital charity wards. Frantic parents turned to prayers like "The Bonds of Motherhood":

> *"Lord, bless my little child,"—*
> *The one boon from Heaven sought*
> *"O Thou, with mercy mild,*
> *Keep this dread spectre from our door"*
> *Is the one prayer of rich and poor.*[10]

During that frightful summer of 1916, FDR was as worried as any parent. From Washington, he wrote Eleanor to

ANTERIOR POLIOMYELITIS!
INFANTILE PARALYSIS

"Act of Assembly approved May 14, 1909, provides that anyone violating the provisions of this Act, upon conviction thereof may be sentenced to pay a fine of not less than $10.00 or more than $100.00, to be paid to the use of said county, or to be imprisoned in the county jail for a period of not less than ten days or more than thirty days, or both, at the discretion of the court."
BY ORDER OF THE BOARD OF HEALTH.

Health Officer.

Address.

〰 This cardboard sign was required by the government to be placed in the windows of residences where patients were quarantined due to poliomyelitis. (1915)

swat every fly in the house at Campobello. At the end of the vacation season, he telegraphed the captain of the USS *Dolphin:* bypass polio-ridden New York City. The destroyer must take Eleanor and the chicks directly to the Hyde Park dock on the Hudson River. Few citizens had a warship for their private use.

THE ROAD BACK

Roosevelt knew that his illness was also an ordeal for the children. Though most of his early symptoms had cleared up by late August, the strong, vibrant father they had known was paralyzed from the waist down. Would he live? What would become of them?

To reassure them, he put on a brave show when attendants carried him by stretcher aboard a boat to the mainland. "Father left the house," James recalled, "with his favorite fedora on his head, a cigarette in his lips, and his Scottie of that time, Duffy, cradled in his arms. His chin was out like a bulldozer blade and he managed a big, flashy smile and a wisecrack—that was for the benefit of us kids. I said, 'So long, Father,' and bit my lip until it hurt." FDR would not see Campobello for twelve years, returning in 1933 as president of the United States.[11]

His battle with disability began in September 1921 at Presbyterian Hospital in New York and lasted the rest of his life. Just as Roosevelt had modeled his career on Cousin Ted's, he found inspiration in the former president's own struggle for health. A weak, scrawny child with asthma, Ted, through sheer grit and vigorous exercise, had made himself into a he-man, admired the world over for his strength and courage.

Doctors said Franklin's only hope of getting out of bed was to strengthen his arm and shoulder muscles. So he spent hours pulling himself up by a strap hung over the bed. After a month in the hospital, he went to Hyde Park. Weather permitting, he exercised on parallel bars set up on the lawn. Again and again, he told Margaret Suckley, a favorite cousin, "I'm not going to be conquered by a childish disease." Indoors, he crawled on the floor of the library, his legs trailing behind, grasping a book in his teeth. After a while, he crawled up and down the stairs, though the house had an elevator. He crawled to regain mobility and to practice escaping fire. He had witnessed a tragedy when he was two. An alcohol lamp exploded, burning his aunt Laura Delano to death. Should a fire break out, he told young Elliott, "I might be able to save myself by crawling."[12]

In March 1922, seven months after he contracted polio, doctors fitted Roosevelt with leg braces. Made of steel and leather, each brace weighed ten pounds and reached from his hip to the sole of his foot. He learned to rise from a chair by lifting one leg with both hands and locking its brace at the knee, repeating the action with the other leg. His legs now rigid, he pushed himself up from the chair with his arms and began to "walk." With a crutch under each arm, he inched ahead by swiveling the right leg from the hip, then the left. He set himself a goal: "walk" to the end of his Hyde Park driveway, a distance of 300 feet. "I must get down the driveway today—all the way down the driveway." Anna heard her father mutter to himself. Exercise gave him immense upper-body strength, but he never got to the end of the driveway.[13]

Though visitors might pity Roosevelt, he would have none of it. He wanted respect, not pity. Proud and defiant, he never used his disability to gain sympathy. "Now, I don't want any sob stuff," he would insist. To prove his strength, he arm-wrestled his sons. Pa's grip made them howl.[14]

Meanwhile, his mother looked to the future. Sara had always tried to interfere in her son's life. Now that he had survived polio, she wanted to keep him beside her always. She may have had selfish motives; Eleanor thought she viewed his disability as a way of controlling him completely. Yet she had another motive—one born of love and fear.

Throughout history, the disabled have had to bear the twin burden of their affliction and others' ignorance. People with disabilities were considered cursed by God or the gods. In ancient Greece, for example, the Spartans, fierce warriors, left "imperfect" infants to die on mountaintops and threw the disabled off cliffs. During the Middle Ages and into modern times, many Europeans believed the disabled had the "evil eye," a magical power to harm others merely by staring at them. Sometimes, disabled people were hanged or burned alive as witches.

Such attitudes persisted into the 1920s and beyond. American society held prejudices against the disabled. A leading child care book, *The Care of Invalid and Crippled Children in School* (1911), defined disability as "a failure in the moral training of a cripple"—that is, the disability was the outward sign of a moral or personality defect. R. C. Elmslie, the book's author, further condemned the disabled as "detestable in character, a menace and a burden to the community."[15]

So as not to "offend" the community, Elmslie and others advised, families should lock their "cripples" away at home. Some communities went further, barring them from public schools and forbidding them to use public transportation. In New York City, health officials might force disabled poor people into bleak, prison-like asylums. These places had sinister names like House of St. Giles the Cripple, Home for Incurables, and New York Society for the Relief of the Ruptured and Crippled. Inmates had little chance of entering the mainstream of society. Women learned sewing, and men basketry and caning— hardly skills leading to prosperity. That one with a disability could succeed in the rough-and-tumble of politics was unthinkable.[16]

Hoping to spare Franklin humiliation, Sara wanted him to retire to Hyde Park. There, with him safe from prying eyes and wagging tongues, she would protect her darling boy while he lived out his years reading, collecting stamps, and dabbling in small-business ventures.

Eleanor rebelled. Just as polio had withered FDR's legs, she feared isolation would wither his spirit. She also knew that in fighting for him, she was fighting for herself. Giving in to Sara, she later told a friend, would have been tragic. "She dominated me for years," Eleanor said. However, Franklin's illness made her "stand on my own two feet in regard to my husband's life, my own life, and my children's training." Yielding to Sara would have made her "a completely colorless echo of my husband and my mother-in-law and torn between them. I might have stayed a weak character forever if I had not found that cut."[17]

Would Eleanor have had the courage to stand up to Sara without Louis Howe's support? It is an important question, but we cannot answer it. However, when Sara described her plan, Howe stared her down. "I expect [Franklin] to be President," he said calmly, almost whispering. "Anyway, he is going to have his chance."[18]

Like her mother-in-law, Eleanor had always thought of Howe as that ugly, dirty little man Franklin hired as a political aide. But her view of him had already begun to change during the 1920 presidential race. In what felt like an eternity aboard the campaign train, he would engage Eleanor in discussions of the day's events and issues. Through these talks she discovered a sensitive, witty person who, incidentally, was a political genius. They became friends. No longer was it Mrs. Roosevelt and Mr. Howe, but Eleanor and Louis.

FDR's polio cemented their friendship. By 1922, Eleanor was on the verge of a nervous breakdown. One day, while reading, she "went to pieces" (her term). Suddenly she burst into tears. She cried for hours until, it seemed, she had run dry. Howe came to the rescue. He held her in his arms, stroked her hair, and caressed her with soothing words. With Louis, she felt safe. She became playful, a quality her children never saw. The two would debate who looked ugliest in photographs. Eleanor once said of Louis, "He probably cared for me as a person . . . more than anyone else has."[19]

Together, they devised a scheme. Eleanor would be Franklin's stand-in, appearing for him and keeping his name before the public until he could return to politics. Howe would teach her about government and politics. Though the niece of a president, she was almost totally ignorant of the American system of government. For example, during their honeymoon in Europe, Eleanor could not explain to their English hosts the difference between the federal and state governments. Howe also tutored her in public speaking. At first, she giggled nervously and wandered off the subject. "Have something to say, then say it and sit down," Howe ordered. Finally, he taught her to write magazine articles and to speed-read, the art of zipping through a newspaper in a half hour without missing a key fact or idea.[20]

As Eleanor gained confidence, she lost her shyness. She became independent in ways she had never dreamed of. She joined women's political groups like the League of Women Voters, the Women's Trade Union League, and the Women's Division of the New York State Democratic Committee. She made scores of female friends, including Lorena Hickok, a cigar-smoking 200-pound newspaper reporter. "Hick" became her best friend and lived in the White House during FDR's first term. Encouraged by Hick, Eleanor learned to drive a car—badly. She once hit a tree, wrecking the vehicle, bruising her face, and knocking out several front teeth.

Eleanor's new interests often took her away for weeks at a time. Her son James recalled that "the more she did, the more she wanted to do. She felt herself filled with a passion for politics through which she saw the chance to right wrongs, to be of use."[21]

If Franklin's disability gave Eleanor the opportunity to develop as a person, it influenced his outlook on life, too. Louis Howe saw the change happen before his very eyes. "You see," Howe told an aide, "[FDR] had a thousand interests. He did about every damn thing under the sun a man could think of doing. Then suddenly there he was flat on his back, with nothing to do but think. . . . He thought of others who were ill and afflicted and in want. He dwelt on many things which had not bothered him much before. Lying there, he grew bigger by the day." A decade later, Harry Hopkins, his chief White House aide, told reporters, "The guy *never* knows when he is licked." In short, battling disability helped "the guy" grow up.[22]

Eleanor Roosevelt (fifth from right) with members of the Women's Trade Union League in New York City. (1958)

HAPPY WARRIORS

In 1922, barely a year after being stricken with polio, Roosevelt returned to his law firm and the Fidelity and Deposit Company. During his abundant spare time, and with Louis Howe's help, he kept in touch with Democratic Party leaders by mail and telephone.

Among these was Alfred E. Smith. A school dropout at fourteen, "Al," as everyone called him, was raised in a tenement on New York's Lower East Side. With his outgoing, backslapping manner and mile-a-minute way of talking, he made friends easily. And his natural talent for politics caught the eye of Tammany Hall bosses. With their support, Al rose through the Democratic Party ranks to become the majority leader of the New York State Assembly. Unlike the bosses, however, he was honest and had real sympathy for the poor—"my people." Following the 1911 Triangle Shirtwaist fire, where 146 garment workers died, he led a commission to investigate working conditions statewide. Its findings led to dozens of laws to improve safety in the workplace. In 1918, he won election to the first of his four terms as governor.

Smith decided to seek the 1924 Democratic presidential nomination. To better his chances, he asked Roosevelt to chair his nomination campaign. It was a figurehead post, with no power, since the governor's advisers made the impor-

tant decisions. The advisers wanted the man from Hyde Park because of his contacts and national reputation.

FDR welcomed the chance to get back into politics. With Louis Howe working in the background, Franklin formed committees and wrote letters to possible supporters. One letter went to Babe Ruth, the greatest baseball player of the day. The "Sultan of Swat" answered, "Sure, I'm for Al Smith.... Maybe you know I wasn't fed with a gold spoon when I was a kid. No poor boy can go any too high in the world for me."[23]

As chair of the Smith campaign, Roosevelt would place his name in nomination at the Democratic convention.

From left to right, lieutenant governor of New York George Lunn, FDR (with crutches), John W. Davis, and Al Smith on the porch of the Roosevelt home in Hyde Park. (August 7, 1924)

While politicians wondered if he could do it, FDR aimed to show that his disability had not affected his mind. On June 26, as New York sizzled in a heat wave, 12,000 delegates jammed Madison Square Garden. A circus had just left, and the lingering smell of animal manure mixed with that of human sweat and tobacco smoke.

The huge arena fell silent as Roosevelt shuffled toward the speaker's platform. The only sounds were a rapid, repeated metallic *click-click-click*. Eleanor sat in the gallery, knitting furiously to calm her nerves.[24]

While steadying himself with a crutch under his left arm, FDR grasped the arm of sixteen-year-old James. "As we walked—struggled, really—down the aisle to the rear of the platform, he leaned heavily on my arm so hard it hurt," James wrote fifty years later. "It was hot, but the heat in that building did not alone account for the perspiration that beaded on his brow. His hands were wet. His breathing was labored. Leaning on me with one arm, working a crutch with the other, his legs locked stiffly in their braces, he went on his awkward way."[25]

At last they reached the platform. Roosevelt released his grip on James's arm and took a second crutch, which had been put there earlier. Louis Howe barked, "Spunky damn Dutchman."[26]

FDR made his way to the podium alone, floodlights blazing hot in his face. When he reached it, he tossed his crutches aside, grasped the podium with both hands, and grinned from ear to ear. *See, I did it!* he seemed to shout. That smile broke the tension. Cheers and applause filled the arena. "I never in my life was so proud of my father as I was at that moment," James recalled.[27]

At first, the speech seemed like the usual politician's prittle-prattle. FDR called for Democratic unity and recited the governor's achievements. Then he practically sang the punch line. His voice rising, he called Al Smith "the Happy Warrior of the political battlefield." The effect was magical. Cheers rocked the arena. Whistles blew. Sirens wailed. A band struck up Smith's theme song, "The Sidewalks of New York."

East Side, West Side, all around the town
The tots sang "ring-around-rosie," "London
*   Bridge is falling down"*
Boys and girls together, me and Mamie
*   O'Rourke*
Tripped the light fantastic on the sidewalks of
*   New York*

Though Roosevelt had spoken for

Smith, delegates viewed him as the real Happy Warrior. One day, the party would turn to him, many predicted. Even so, he could not gain the nomination for Smith; it went to John W. Davis, a prominent Wall Street lawyer and former ambassador to Great Britain. Davis lost the election to Calvin Coolidge in another Republican landslide.

WARM SPRINGS

Despite his personal triumph at the convention, FDR was hesitant about a full return to politics. He still sought to regain use of his legs, and full-time politics would interfere with that effort.

A few weeks earlier, he had received a letter from George Foster Peabody. The millionaire banker mentioned a polio victim whose legs had improved after bathing at a resort Peabody owned in Georgia. Located sixty-two miles southwest of Atlanta, Warm Springs, population 550, had a decrepit hotel with a few run-down cottages. The resort's sole attraction was a swimming pool fed by springs with a constant temperature of eighty-eight degrees. Originating miles beneath the earth's surface, the mineral waters kept bathers afloat, making them feel almost weightless.

In October 1924, Roosevelt arrived at Warm Springs with Eleanor and Marguerite "Missy" LeHand, his private secretary. It was love at first dip. "I walk around in water four feet deep without braces or crutches almost as well as if I had nothing the matter with my legs," he wrote. He stayed six weeks, returning for ever-longer periods.[28]

Warm Springs became Roosevelt's home away from home. He built a cottage and lived there with his secretary, sharing the bathroom between their bedrooms. Though sixteen years younger than Roosevelt, Missy spent more time with him than anyone else, including Louis Howe. To her, he was always "FD," not "Mr. Roosevelt" or even "Mr. President." Unlike serious, high-minded Eleanor, Missy was easygoing,

〰 FDR with Missy LeHand (far left) and two friends in Florida. (1924)

frequently smiling and joking. Sensitive to FD's every mood, she seemed to know what he needed before he did. He could relax with Missy, enjoying small talk and parlor games like Ma and Pa Cheesy. Observers thought Missy loved him, and she probably did, though there is no evidence of an affair.[29]

Eleanor did not seem to mind Franklin's living so close to a vivacious young woman who sometimes sat on his lap; she had her own life to lead now. Besides, she despised rural Georgia. The nagging heat, the Southern drawl, the crude bigotry toward black people made her cringe. Locals responded in kind. "We didn't like her one bit," a Warm Springs resident recalled.[30]

The presence of a nationally known figure drew other "polios," as sufferers called themselves, to the resort. Serving them became FDR's most practical and personal expression of noblesse oblige, the ideal drummed into him in childhood. He felt it a God-given duty to help fellow polios help themselves to regain dignity and to lead as normal a life as possible.

He started an informal poolside clinic. Already he had read nearly everything available on polio. He became a self-taught expert on muscles, their functions and connections to nerves and

≋ FDR enjoying a swim in Warm Springs, Georgia. (1930)

bones. Their Latin names fascinated him; he loved their sounds and to roll the words, like "gluteus maximus," off his tongue. Aided by charts drawn by Missy, he explained how various muscle groups worked and how to strengthen them by exercise, which he often led in person. Sharing the wisdom gained from his own ordeal, he urged polios to have faith in life. He was dubbed "Old Doc Roosevelt." Never lose your zest for living, he urged, because while there is life, there is hope. As self-appointed social director, he helped polios rebuild their self-image by making friends, dating, falling in love.

Old Doc Roosevelt gained as much as he gave. Through the polios, he learned to relate to ordinary folks not as a boss giving orders, however politely, but as a fellow human being. FDR had a car fitted with the gas and brake pedals on the steering wheel. Now that he could control a vehicle by hand, he took long drives into the Georgia countryside. He drove fast, often wildly, shouting "Hiya, neighbor!" to everyone he passed. "He had sense enough to talk to a man who didn't have any education," an old-timer recalled. "He was easy to talk to. He could talk about anything."[31]

In 1926, Roosevelt bought the Warm Springs resort for $201,668, more than two-thirds of his personal wealth. His wife, always prudent, worried about where the money to educate their children would come from. No problem "Ma will always see the children through," he said. He could count on Sara's generosity to help with his family's expenses.[32]

Soon after buying Warm Springs, Roosevelt formed the Warm Springs Foundation, later renamed the National Foundation for Infantile Paralysis. A nonprofit organization it raised money to turn Warm Springs into a modern polio treatment center. During his second term as president, FDR launched

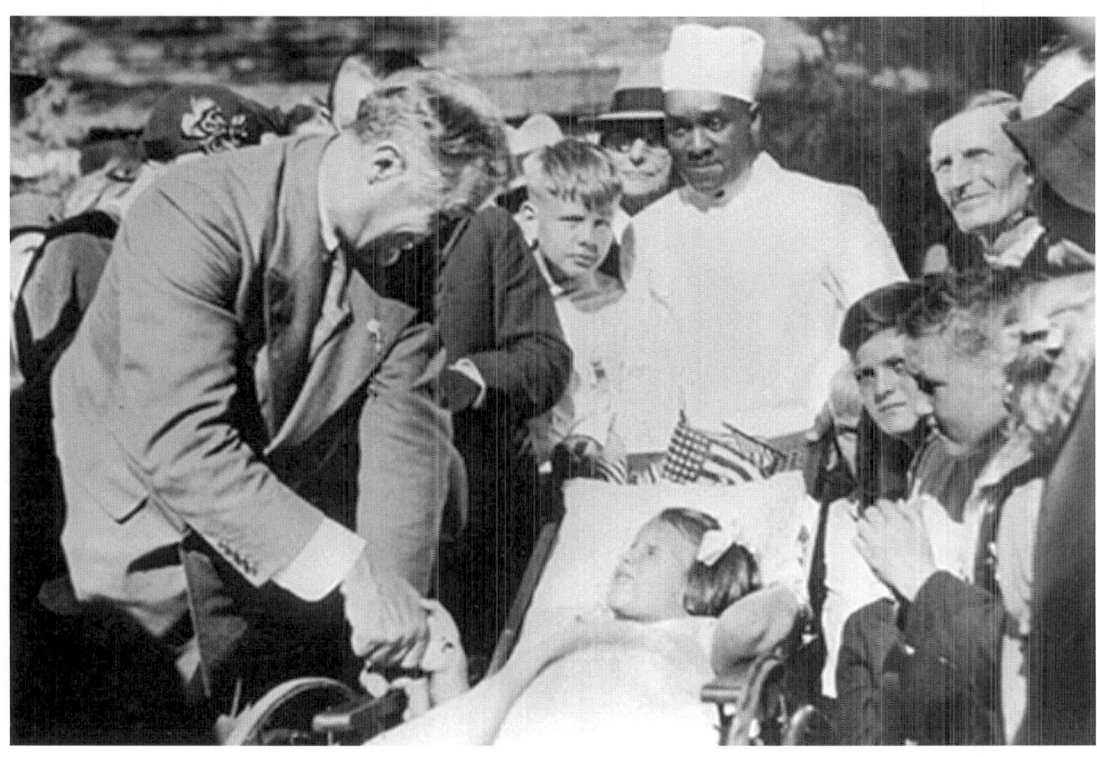

FDR greeting a child patient at Warm Springs. (1930)

the March of Dimes campaign to fund polio research. The name referred to the dimes sent to the White House for the annual fund-raising drive. America's worst polio epidemics struck between 1952 and 1954, with over 100,000 victims. In 1955, on the tenth anniversary of Roosevelt's death, Dr. Jonas Salk announced that March of Dimes aid had enabled him to develop a vaccine to prevent polio. With polio defeated in the United States, in 1958 it became an organization that turned its attention to preventing birth defects. In 1979, it changed its name to National Foundation–March of Dimes.

GOVERNOR

Early in 1928, Al Smith again sought the Democratic presidential nomination. To win the general election, he knew he must carry the big industrial states, particularly New York. This meant having a strong candidate—FDR—run for governor in his place and carry New York.

Roosevelt refused, saying he wanted to spend more time at Warm Springs. Pleading by party leaders had no effect, until a call came from Albany. Smith gave him an offer he dared not refuse. A wealthy Democrat would pay $50,000 toward the upkeep of Warm Springs. If, despite that, he did not help the party, he could say goodbye to his political career.

Smith's offer and warning forced FDR to admit a hard truth. Admirers would later say that he "conquered" polio. He did not. Warm Springs was no miracle place. After four years there, he suddenly realized he would never walk on his own; poliovirus had damaged his legs too badly for that. While he would keep returning there for rest and exercise, politics became the focus of his life, his only passion. He accepted Smith's offer.

In June, Roosevelt nominated Smith at the Democratic convention in Houston, Texas. This son of the Empire State was a man of the highest integrity and strongest character, said FDR. "Victory is his habit—the Happy Warrior—Alfred E. Smith." Though Roosevelt won the convention's heart as before, Smith won its head. This time it gave him the nomination.

Republicans promptly and falsely attacked Smith for sacrificing a "poor cripple" (their term) to his selfish ambitions. Obviously, said supporters of their candidate, Herbert Hoover, Roosevelt was not up to such a strenuous job. Smith shot back: "A governor does not have to be an acrobat. We do not elect him for his ability to do a double back-flip or a handspring. The work of the Governorship is brainwork. Ninety-nine percent of it is accomplished at a desk."[33]

It was not so simple. FDR believed that voters would not think him capable unless he appeared fit. To overcome popular prejudice, Louis Howe laid down a strict rule: Admit you have a disability, but never reveal its full extent.

Howe's rule held throughout the rest of FDR's career. His public appearances became carefully staged events. Of the 35,000 photographs in the Roosevelt Presidential Library, only two show him in a wheelchair. Nor are there any newsreels of him being carried or falling when he lost his balance. He fell in public at least three times, but the press kept mum.[34]

To hide his braces, Roosevelt had their lower part painted black and wore black socks. When meeting people, he turned on the charm full blast, smiling, laughing, cracking jokes, and talking constantly to divert attention from his legs. In taking stairs, he stiffened his arms so aides could lift him by the elbows. From a distance, it looked like he was climbing the stairs in the midst of a group. Whenever possible, he came to a gathering before the other guests arrived. When they entered the room, they found him sitting not in a wheelchair but on a chair behind a table. Afterward, he left last.

Roosevelt campaigned actively, speaking more often, in more places, than any previous candidate for governor. On the campaign trail, he rode in the backseat of an open car fitted with a special iron bar. Upon reaching his destination, he followed the same routine. As the vehicle came to a stop, FDR locked his braces, grabbed the bar, pulled himself to a standing position, and spoke to the crowd. To tease doubters, he'd ask, "Not bad for a sick man?"[35]

The 1928 election marked a low in presidential politics. Al Smith had two problems. First, he was a New Yorker in a country where rural and small-town voters still decided the outcome of elections. Al's pin-striped suit, raspberry-colored shirt, brown derby hat, and cigar clenched between his teeth branded him a "city slicker." To many, Gotham was the sewer of humanity, of immigrant "refuse" and "harlots and sinners," where "Satan's seat is." Al's "Noo Yawkese" accent grated on Southern and Western ears. When he spoke on the "raddio," he said he wanted to "woik" to make a "betta" life for every "poissun" in America. Each

〰 A rare photo of FDR in his wheelchair, in Hyde Park, New York, with a caretaker's granddaughter, Ruthie Bie, and the family dog, Fala, in his lap. (1941)

rally began with "The Sidewalks of New York." As Al sang along, it sounded, an observer noted, like "the bullfrogs had met their master."[36]

Al's second problem was his religion. He was a devout Roman Catholic in a Protestant-majority country, and many feared he would obey Pope Pius XI rather than the Constitution. A whispering campaign spread rumors as vile as any wartime atrocity story. President Smith would declare Protestant marriages illegal! To better give him orders, the pope was coming to America! Opponents circulated doctored photos of the Holland Tunnel linking New York and New Jersey, then under construction. The tunnel, bigots said, was really a "secret passage" to bring His Holiness from Rome to New York, a 4,300-mile trip![37]

Anti-Catholic speakers crisscrossed the country, spewing their poison in parks, on the steps of country courthouses, and in churches. The Ku Klux Klan, an organization of violent racists dedicated to "Americanism," accused Catholics of helping black people "pollute white blood." Catholics had, supposedly with the aid of the devil, invented "a powder" to bleach the skin of black men so they could have sex with white women! In private, the Hoover campaign encouraged anti-Catholic attitudes.[38]

Religious bigotry infuriated Roosevelt. Attack Smith's ideas—that is logical! Attack his record—that is fair! But attacking him on his religion is just crazy. Attackers, said FDR, "ought not to be put in jail, but ought to be put on the first ship and sent away from the United States." Nevertheless, attackers grew bolder, targeting Katie Smith, the candidate's wife. She was, some said, a gross drunkard, an Irish washerwoman in a silk dress. "Can you imagine Mrs. Smith in the White House?" opponents sneered.[39]

The season of hatred ended on Election Day. Herbert Hoover trounced Al Smith in the popular vote (21,392,190 to 15,016,443) and the electoral vote (444 to 87). States that had voted Democrat for decades voted Republican. Worse, Smith lost the Empire State. However, the man from Hyde Park squeaked to victory, beating his Republican opponent, Albert Ottinger, by 26,010 votes out of the 4,234,322 cast.

On January 1, 1929, Franklin Roosevelt, age forty-six, took the oath of office on his family's Dutch Bible. The ceremony took place in the State Assembly chamber, the same room in which Cousin Ted had been sworn in

FDR reading the family's Dutch Bible in Hyde Park. (February 27, 1933)

as governor thirty years earlier. It was a joyful occasion, as much a personal as a political triumph. Not only had Franklin come to terms with his disability, but he had proved to his mother that he need not spend his life in seclusion. Sara agreed. "Now Franklin has grown up and is the Governor!" she said proudly.[40]

Franklin's victory allowed Eleanor to become more useful than ever. At the time they moved into the Executive Mansion, American buildings were not accessible to people with disabilities. Buildings often lacked elevators, not to mention wheelchair ramps. Unable to make inspections in person, the gover-

nor needed another set of eyes, ears, and legs.

Eleanor fit the bill perfectly. Before she toured a state hospital, for example, Franklin gave her pointers. Do not announce your visit in advance; the staff will quickly tidy up and show you what they wish you to see. Don't be shy; ask lots of pointed questions. Look everywhere. Poke into pots to make sure they contain the food listed on the day's menu. Notice patients' facial expressions, sure guides to their satisfaction or unhappiness. Whenever Eleanor returned from an inspection tour, he questioned her in minute detail. Before long, she wrote, she "had become a fairly expert reporter on state institutions."[41]

During his first two-year term, Governor Roosevelt was as keen a reformer as Al Smith had been. He got the State Assembly to lower farmers' taxes, protect state forests, improve prison conditions, and pass pension laws to aid the elderly. After reelection in 1930—he won by 725,000 votes this time—New York became the first state to pass a law requiring unemployment insurance, a much-needed benefit. For by then, the era of prosperity known as the Roaring Twenties had given way to the Great Depression, an economic collapse that shook the nation to its core. This disaster would catapult the governor into the White House. To understand why, we must take a closer look at FDR's America.

FDR seated with Al Smith. Note the braces on FDR's legs. (1930)

BOOM TO BUST

With the end of the winter . . . a fresh picture of life in America began to form before my eyes.
The uncertainties of 1919 were over—there seemed no doubt about what was going to happen—America
was going on the greatest, gaudiest spree in history and there was going to be plenty to tell about it.
The whole golden boom was in the air.
—F. Scott Fitzgerald, The Crack-Up *(1937)*

THE GOLDEN BOOM

In June 1928, Herbert Hoover, fifty-three, won his party's nomination for president. It was, the former secretary of commerce told cheering Republicans, a good time to be alive. "We in America today are nearer to the final triumph over poverty than ever before in the history of any land. . . . We shall soon . . . be in sight of the day when poverty will be banished from this nation."[1]

Hoover's optimism seemed justified. Once the economy revived after the Red Scare, the nation's mood soared. As he spoke, many felt America had entered a golden age of prosperity. Few imag-ined the disaster lurking just around the corner.

Prosperity grew out of new methods pioneered by American business. More than anyone, Henry Ford, a mechanical genius who began life as a Michigan farm boy, gets the credit. In 1912, Ford toured a Chicago meatpacking plant. That tour changed everything for the already suc-cessful automaker. Until then, a motor vehicle was a high-priced luxury, thanks to the time and skills needed to build it. A team of expert mechanics took four-teen hours to build an entire auto from the ground up. When they finished, and only then, they started work on the next.

In Chicago, Ford saw machines moving cattle carcasses on hooks suspended from overhead conveyor belts. As a belt carrying the animal slowly passed each worker, a single task was accomplished: the blood drained, the body gutted, or various cuts of meat separated. Eventually, neat packages emerged with labels showing the type and weight of their contents. Ford made the mental leap from meatpacking to automaking. "Nothing is particularly hard, if you divide it into small jobs," he explained. The result was the assembly line, with unskilled workers doing jobs once done by skilled mechanics.[2]

Ford's teams built a vehicle from thousands of separate parts. They began with the frame, merely an empty metal shell stamped out by a machine. Each worker did one small task on the car part as it was slowly conveyed by his station on a moving belt. "The man who places a part doesn't fasten it," Ford wrote. "The man who puts in a bolt does not put on the nut; the man who puts on the nut does not tighten it."[3]

Though he paid five dollars a day, the highest wage in American industry, working for Henry Ford was no picnic. A demanding employer, he considered wasted seconds lost dollars. Assembly-

⌇⌇ An assembly line at the Ford Motor Company. (May 7, 1923)

line workers felt like slaves to machines. Not only did they have to serve their machine, but they had to fight the boredom of countless repeated motions. Ford forbade workers to sit or relax on the job. You spoke when the supervisor was not looking and without moving your lips in the "Ford whisper," and you wore a frozen expression called "Fordization of the face." You were hardly human, a worker recalled. "Where you used to be a man, now you are far less than the cheapest tool."[4]

Nevertheless, mass production gave spectacular results. In 1925, Ford's plant in Dearborn, Michigan, turned out a car every ten seconds. Assembly-line methods allowed him to lower the price of the Model T, nicknamed the "Tin Lizzie," from $1,200 in 1909 to $295 in 1928. Thanks to Ford and fellow automakers, between 1919 and 1929 the number of motor vehicles in the United States rose from 6.7 million to 27 million—that is, one for every five Americans. What had been a luxury for the wealthy few became a necessity for the many. "We'd rather do without clothes than give up the car," said the wife of a factory worker.[5]

Other industries copied Ford's methods. For example, dressmakers and tailors had always made clothing one item at a time. By the early 1900s, mechanical knives could cut many layers of cloth into a garment's various parts: legs, sleeves, collars, and so on. Workers then assembled these using electric sewing machines. By the First World War, manufacturers produced all types of low-cost, stylish ready-to-wear clothes in standard sizes. Similarly, mass-produced vacuum cleaners, irons, toasters, and washers eased what women called the "domestic slavery" of housework. In 1900, meal preparation, laundry, and housecleaning took fifty-eight hours a week; by 1925, they took forty-four hours a week.[6]

Still, the auto was the powerhouse of the economy. By the 1920s, the industry employed a quarter of the nation's workforce. Not that all worked on assembly lines; most did not. Instead, they supplied the assembly lines with parts made in small, specialized plants. Automaking also spurred growth in the steel, nickel, lead, copper, glass, leather, paint, rubber, and electrical industries. Inexpensive gasoline (21–30 cents a gallon) became available, thanks to giant oil fields discovered in Texas and Oklahoma. Since motor vehicles need fuel and repairs, gas stations and repair shops sprang up to meet the demand.

The face of America changed. Planners redesigned cities, paving and widening streets to handle motor traffic. In the countryside, dirt roads gave way to paved highways. Though only several hundred miles of highway were built each year, the road ahead was clear: twentieth-century America would be bound together by concrete ribbons, just as it had been by the transcontinental railroads in the nineteenth century. Accidents spurred the insurance industry, too. In the 1920s, auto accidents killed more than 25,000 and injured 600,000 Americans each year. New York City alone had over a thousand traffic deaths a year.[7]

Americans called the postwar era the "Roaring Twenties." Change was in the air, with millions adopting new attitudes and lifestyles. As never before, the auto freed the young from adult supervision. The freedom it offered prompted a judge to brand it a "house of prostitution on wheels," as the number of babies born out of wedlock skyrocketed.[8]

Jazz became the rage during the Roaring Twenties. Invented by New Orleans blacks in the 1890s, jazz combines African rhythms with European harmonies and encourages improvisation. Youngsters thrilled to jazz, as their grandchildren would to rock and roll. "Hot" dances like the Charleston, shimmy, bunny hug, and skunk waltz were wildly popular. New "crazes" constantly swept

the nation. Couples danced in marathons until all but one collapsed from exhaustion, the winners receiving a cash prize. Young men sat atop flagpoles just to set a record; a fellow claimed to have spent 210 hours, in freezing weather, on one. Others swallowed live goldfish and jammed into telephone booths to see how many would fit.

But no one captured the era's vitality better than the "flapper," a term that probably came from young women wearing their galoshes unbuckled so they flapped as they walked. The flapper

Representative T. S. McMillan of Charleston, South Carolina, admiring the footwork of flappers Ruth Bennett and Sylvia Clavins doing the Charleston atop a railing, with the U.S. Capitol in the background. (1920–1930)

ranged in age from her mid-teens to mid-twenties. Unlike traditional women, who avoided makeup, which was favored by "loose" actresses, she used lots of it. "She is frankly," author Bruce Bliven observed, "heavily made up, not to imitate nature, but for an altogether artificial effect—poisonously scarlet lips [and] richly ringed eyes." No tight corsets, petticoats, or dresses reaching from chin to ankle for her! She wore a sleeveless dress "cut low where it might be high, and . . . just an inch below her knees. . . . The idea is that when she walks . . . you shall now and then observe the knee." She smoked

Detroit police inspecting equipment found in a clandestine underground brewery. (1920–1933)

cigarettes, drove cars fast, and favored illegal taverns called "speakeasies."[9]

Prohibition created the speakeasy. Next to the abolition of slavery, Prohibition—the banning of alcoholic drinks—was *the* moral crusade of the nineteenth century. Drunkenness often led to work accidents, broken homes, and crime. Though reformers condemned alcohol, they made little progress until the First World War. To save grain for bread and reduce accidents in war plants, in 1917 Congress passed the Eighteenth Amendment to the Constitution. This prohibited the manufacture, transport, and sale of wine, liquor, and beer. After the states ratified the amendment in 1919, Congress passed the Volstead Act to enforce it.

Prohibition shows how banning an "evil" can lead to other, unexpected evils. Americans simply refused to do without their occasional drink just because reformers said they should. Ongoing demand led to "bootlegging," the illegal making, transporting, and selling of alcoholic drinks. Speakeasies opened in basements, garages, and private clubs. By 1929, America had over 219,000 speakeasies; New York City alone had 32,000. To enter, you "spoke easy"—whispered a password. Inside, patrons listened to jazz, danced, and drank so much "booze" that speakeasy slang entered everyday speech. We still say a drunken person is "high," "lit," "loaded," "plastered," "pie-eyed," and "soused." One who refused to give a friend a drink was a "drip" or a "wimp."[10]

The "best" people broke the law. George Cassiday, dubbed 'the unofficial bootlegger to Congress," sold whiskey in the House Office Building. While Eleanor and Sara Roosevelt were definitely "dry" (opposed to strong drink), Franklin was definitely "wet." FDR loved his evening cocktails, which he mixed himself. As governor, he allowed a bodyguard to take his sons to speakeasies. When he moved into the Executive Mansion in Albany, the outgoing governor, Al Smith, sprinkled his luggage with champagne for good luck. At Warm Springs, FDR sipped the local "moonshine" from Mason jars.[11]

As bootlegging became profitable, competition grew. Criminal gangs forced speakeasies to buy liquor only from them and killed competitors. A few gangsters became underworld royalty. Chicago's Al "Scarface" Capone employed a thousand gunmen and had a yearly income of $60 million—nearly $820 million in 2014 dollars. Asked if he was a bootlegger, Capone bragged, "Sure, and some of our best judges use my stuff." To re-

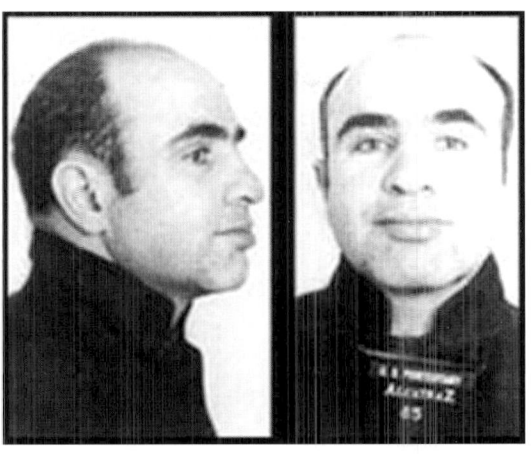

Al Capone's "mug shots" from Alcatraz prison. (1934)

duce violence and increase profits, top gangsters created what we now call "organized crime." At secret meetings, they assigned territories, set prices, and gave "contracts" to "triggermen" to enforce their rules. As money from illegal alcohol poured in, they invested profits in gambling and narcotics.[12]

So it went. Prosperity. Automobiles. Jazz. Flappers. Prohibition. Booze. Organized crime. "Let the good times roll" was a motto of the era. Then, like Humpty Dumpy on his wall, the U.S. economy had its great fall. On October 29, 1929, the Roaring Twenties crashed to an end.

THE CRASH

America has a capitalist economy. Individual citizens or groups of citizens can own land, factories, and businesses, keeping for themselves any profits earned after paying taxes. It is also called a "free market" economy, because people compete with one another, freely buying, selling, and trading within the limits of the law.

Money is the lifeblood of capitalism. To buy equipment, expand production, and develop new products, businesses need money, which they can get in various ways. One way is for a firm to set aside a portion of its profits for future development. Since most firms seldom have enough ready cash, however, they must raise it elsewhere.

Often they borrow what they need from a bank. If we imagine the capitalist economy as a human body, banks are the heart that pumps the blood—money—that nourishes the economy and keeps it healthy. When you deposit money into an account, the bank pays you interest, a fee for using your money. Should a firm need money, it applies to the bank for a loan. If bank officials think the firm is a good credit risk, they will give it a loan at a higher rate of interest than paid to depositors like you. Normally, since not all depositors want all their money back at once, bankers lend most of what is deposited to earn money for their bank, keeping only a relatively small cash supply in reserve to cover daily withdrawals. By pumping revenue into new invest-

ments and expanding businesses, banks help create wealth that can lead to new business opportunities and new jobs. This process, in turn, generates more savings for banks to use for more loans. Thus, without a healthy banking system, a capitalist economy could not prosper. It would, in effect, suffer a "heart attack" and possibly even death.

Businesses (and governments) can also raise money by selling bonds. A bond is a certificate, or written promise issued by a firm, to repay with interest the money the firm "borrowed" from the buyer of the bond. Besides its dollar value, printed on its face, each certificate provides coupons showing the interest amount due on a given date. On the due date, the bondholder could present the appropriate coupon to a bank, which would pay the interest, less a service charge. Then the bank would send the coupon to the "borrowing" firm for collection. (Today, bonds are issued and registered in the owner's name and payment is made electronically to his or her bank account.) Should an owner wish to get his or her money back before the bond's due date, he or she can offer it for sale at a reduced price. Various private companies buy and sell bonds for their customers.

Finally, rather than borrow, a firm may

decide to issue stock certificates. Each certificate represents a share, or portion, of a company and entitles its holder—really a part owner—to a portion of its profits, called dividends. Investors buy and sell stocks in a central place, called a stock exchange. Prices rise or fall depending on a firm's sales and profits, investor confidence, and demand for the stock. Located on Wall Street near the southern tip of Manhattan Island, the New York Stock Exchange is the world's leading stock market. The trouble began there.

After 1920, stock prices rose along with the profits earned by businesses adopting assembly-line methods. At first, most investors were buying for the dividends companies paid. Yet, as profits soared, a kind of insanity took hold. Greedy for "easy money," investors began to speculate. Expecting the price of a stock to rise, they bought it not for future income but for quick resale at a profit. Most bought "on margin"—that is, "buying" by giving a small down payment but borrowing the rest from their broker (stock dealer) or a bank. Suppose John Simpleman wanted a $100 share of the Silly Putty Company. Simpleman would pay $10 of his own money and borrow the remaining $90. Later, he might sell the share for $300. Thus, a $10 investment returned $195.50 ($300

less the $90 loan, $4.50 interest on the loan, and the original $10 down payment), a profit of almost 2,000 percent!

Mr. Simpleman bet that stock prices would keep rising—and they did. The sky was the limit! "When I left my house," an investor recalled, "I checked with my broker. By the time I reached my office, I had made sixty-five points.... Everything you bought just seemed to have no ceiling." Wherever you went, you met people who boasted about their winnings. Even shoeshine boys bought $50,000 worth of stock with $500 down, making fortunes. Yet stock prices have natural limits. This is because, in the end, the value of a stock depends on company earnings. Clearly, it makes no sense to pay hundreds of dollars for a share that pays a dividend of a dollar a year—or zero.[13]

The "smart money" grew uneasy. Joseph P. Kennedy, the father of a future president, was shocked when a Wall Street shoeshine boy gave him a tip on a "hot" oil stock. Such advice from a none-too-sophisticated person made him realize greed and stupidity would surely lead to disaster. "Only a fool holds out for the top dollar," Kennedy said. He sold all his stocks, took his winnings, and got out of the market. So did Herbert Hoover and other savvy investors.[14]

Most investors, however, did not know when to quit. They kept on gambling. By the spring of 1929, as Governor Roosevelt settled into his job, stocks began to "seesaw" violently. Prices rose one day, plunged and recovered the next day, then plunged again. In October, the New York Stock Exchange had its "black" days. Historians still disagree on exactly what set off the wave of panic selling. What is clear is that on October 24, "Black Thursday," prices fell sharply, then recovered some of their losses. On October 29, "Black Tuesday," the market collapsed. Next morning, the show business newspaper *Variety* declared: WALL STREET LAYS AN EGG. By November, stocks lost $30 billion ($420 billion in 2014 dollars) in value.

What happened on the stock exchange floor was more like a fire in a crowded theater than the closing of a bad Broadway show. Everyone tried to escape at once. Wild-eyed speculators bombarded brokers with sell orders. "Sell! Sell! Sell!" they cried. "Get me out at any price!" Overwhelmed brokers grew hysterical. An observer said that they "hollered and screamed, they clawed at one another's collars. It was like a bunch of crazy men. Every once in a while . . . you'd see some poor devil collapse and fall on the floor."[15]

Remember John Simpleman? While the price of Silly Putty Company shares kept rising, he was in gamblers' heaven. But when its price fell, a telephone call came from his broker: "I need more margin, more cash, to cover your loan." If he failed to cough up the cash, the bank took his stock, then went after him for the rest of the loan, plus interest. Thousands of investors got such calls each day. As investors tried to dump stocks to rescue part of their investment, prices fell further and faster. Many stocks found no buyers at all. Within minutes, people with millions in paper winnings lost everything. Some could not take the stress; they died of heart attacks. Others, facing poverty, committed suicide. Hotel clerks in the Wall Street area asked if guests wanted a room for sleeping or jumping.

By late November, the American economy was sliding into a depression, defined as an extended period of sluggish business activity and rising unemployment. Its coming so soon after the Wall Street "crash" suggests that one caused the other. It did not. Two million people owned stocks. Their losses, while personally tragic, could not bring down the world's largest economy. Instead, the crash shook people's confidence, allowing other forces—wages, agricul-

A crowd of people gathers outside the New York Stock Exchange following the market crash. (1929)

ture, and the banks—to ignite the Great Depression.

THE WAGE SQUEEZE

The prosperity of the Roaring Twenties hid serious flaws. Simply put, it is not enough for vast amounts of goods to pour from assembly lines. Consumers must demand these goods *and* have the money to pay for them. Yet increases in wages, though real, failed to keep pace with soaring output. American workers did not earn enough to buy all they produced. As a result, prices fell when unsold goods collected on store shelves, in warehouses, and in auto showrooms.

To spur sales, companies offered easy credit. Consumers could buy with a small down payment, paying off the balance, with interest, over months or years. "Buy now, pay later" was new to Americans. Companies borrowed to improve their operations, increasing profits. Traditionally, however, consumers avoided debt. Only "wastrels," worthless good-for-nothings, fell into debt. Responsible people bought only what they could pay for in cash, or they did without. Now they borrowed to buy things ads told them were glamorous, healthful, and essential to happiness. For a time, easy credit drove up prices. But they could not stay up, because wages still lagged.

By the late 1920s, many debtors could no longer make payments, so lenders took back their purchases. A vicious cycle began. Gradually, orders for new goods slowed. Unable to sell all they produced, factory owners closed assembly lines. Unemployment rose, further reducing workers' spending ability. After the Wall Street crash, investors who still had money feared risking it in new ventures. In this way, the downturn fed on itself.

DOWN ON THE FARM

Meanwhile, Mother Nature turned against farmers, particularly on the Great Plains, the vast grassland reaching from Canada into Texas. For generations, farmers had plowed under the native grasses to make way for wheat and other crops. They scarcely realized (or cared) that for millions of years, these tough, deep-rooted grasses had held down the soil. Beginning in 1930, a decade-long drought turned the soil to dust.

Strong winds blew the dust away, creating the Dust Bowl. Immense clouds of dust, fine as talcum powder, hid the sun at noontime, burying farms and suffocating livestock. Known as "black blizzards," these clouds were awesome and terrifying. A farmer wrote:

By mid-morning, a gale was blowing, cold and black. By noon it was blacker than night, because one can see through night and this was an opaque black. It was a wall of dirt one's eyes could not penetrate, but it could penetrate the eyes and ears and nose. It could penetrate the lungs until one coughed up black. If a person was outside, he tied a handkerchief around his face, but he still coughed up black. When the wind died and the sun shone forth again, it was on a different world. There were no fields, only sand drifting into mounds and eddies that swirled in what was now but an autumn breeze.[16]

Those caught outside during a black blizzard often lost their way and were choked to death by the dust.

In rickety Tin Lizzies, a million people left the Great Plains states. Now refugees in their own country, they fled Texas, Oklahoma, Kansas, Arkansas, Colorado, and New Mexico. Called "Okies," because so many came from Oklahoma, they headed for California, seeking work as migrant fruit and vegetable pickers.

Yet the Dust Bowl was just the tip of the farm problem. During the First World War, the Allies depended upon imported food. Rising prices encouraged American farmers to borrow from banks for tractors, harvesters, fertilizer, and more land. Food production soared, as did profits. Still, nothing lasts forever. When the war ended, European agriculture recovered, leaving American farmers with a home market unable to use all they grew. Food prices tumbled. Farmers boosted production further, hoping to make up for lower prices by selling more. Soon it cost more to grow a crop or raise

〰 A dust storm approaching Spearman, Texas. (April 14, 1935)

〰 A farmer and his sons walking in the face of a dust storm in Cimarron County, Oklahoma. (April 1936)

livestock than the product was worth at market value. When farmers were unable to repay their loans, banks took over their farms. More than anything else, the nation's banks turned a crisis into a catastrophe.

THE BANKING COLLAPSE

"Our entire banking system does credit to a collection of imbeciles," wrote William Gibbs McAdoo, a former secretary of the Treasury. It certainly seemed that way. Though vital to the American economy, banking was its weakest link. Traditionally, the federal government followed a hands-off policy; it did not inspect bank records, regulate loans, or insure deposits. During the Roaring Twenties, banking became another word for high-stakes gambling with other people's money. Bankers did much as they pleased. Eager for quick profits, they made risky loans without keeping sufficient cash reserves to cover losses.[17]

The economic downturn stunned the banks. First, rural banks failed when farmers—nearly all their customers—could not repay their loans. Second, loans to stock speculators threatened urban banks, which also "played the market" on their own. Often, top bank officials gave themselves low-interest or no-interest loans to gamble in stocks. After Wall Street laid its egg, these bad investments wrecked their banks.

Bank failures were as contagious as poliovirus. With the country already jittery over the slowing economy, any failure set off rumors about other banks. Their depositors panicked, rushing to withdraw their money. Since banks never kept enough cash to cover all deposits at once, even healthy ones had to close. Each "run," in turn, triggered runs on other banks, with the same result. People who acted quickly enough to get their money out hid it under mattresses or buried it in their gardens for safety. One father taped hundred-dollar bills to his son's chest!

The worst run was in New York. On December 10, 1930, a false rumor that the Bank of the United States was about to go under swept the city. Depositors, mainly Jewish and Italian immigrants, had trusted the bank because its name suggested a branch of the United States Treasury, a false impression bank officials did not bother to correct. Now, in the pouring rain, a jittery crowd surrounded its main office near Wall Street. When tellers ran out of cash, a heartwrenching wail rose from the crowd. It was America's largest bank failure up to that time. If such a huge bank, with

450,000 depositors, could fail, then nobody's money was safe anywhere. Bank runs multiplied. About 700 banks failed in a "normal" year. From 1931 to 1932, some 5,100 banks closed their doors.[18]

Bank failures drove the already ailing economy off the cliff. Overnight, millions of families lost their life savings. Their money, like billions in unrepaid loans and company accounts, simply vanished. The amount of money in circulation fell by fully one-third. Credit evaporated. Investment came to a standstill. Companies closed their doors or cut production to the bone. Prices tumbled. Unemployment skyrocketed. The elderly became destitute, for pensions hardly existed at this time. Workers saved for retirement; if not, they worked until they died. By destroying old people's savings, failed banks literally took their lives.

Bank failures also sent shock waves across the Atlantic. When the First World War ended, American bankers lent European banks, businesses, and governments billions to aid their recovery. Now troubled U.S. banks called in their loans. As they did, cash-starved European economies collapsed. By 1931, the Great Depression had struck in full force, engulfing the entire developed world.

One of the most iconic images from the Great Depression, captured by famed photographer Dorothea Lange. The original caption reads: "Destitute pea pickers in California. Mother of seven children. Age thirty-two." (February 1936)

A WORLD OF WOE

It is difficult for twenty-first-century Americans to conceive of what life was like during the Great Depression. Recent economic downturns, though severe, cannot compare with it.

Soviet tyrant Joseph Stalin used to

say, "One death is a tragedy; a million deaths is a statistic." Stalin meant that we can relate to another person's suffering, empathizing with their pain. However, a calamity involving millions is too vast for the mind to grasp, merely a number in which human faces get lost. Countless individual tragedies formed the tapestry of misery that was the Great Depression. Let us try to give the tragedies faces.

The numbers speak for themselves. Between 1929 and 1933, national income—the combined earnings of all citizens—fell by over half, from $87 billion to $40 billion. On the day Franklin Roosevelt took the oath of office as president, 24.9 percent (up from 3.2 percent in 1929) of the workforce, men and women, was jobless. Thus, out of a population of 120 million, 12.5 million had no income whatsoever. That figure, though, left out the farmers barely surviving by working every day from dawn to dusk and the factory workers scraping by on two days of work a week.[19]

Observers likened long-term unemployment to "unraveling." It felt as if one's life was coming apart a bit more each day. Joblessness put severe stress on families. To begin with, they had to cut purchases to the bare necessities. This brought harsh choices, for their savings—if they had any, and if their bank was still open—could only stretch so far. "We did not dare to use even a little soap, when it will pay for an extra egg [and] a few more carrots for our children," a man wrote. Yet, without soap, families grew dirtier and more prone to disease—this in a country where health insurance barely existed.[20]

Inevitably, the unemployed had to seek help. That was a big step, for reaching out meant swallowing one's pride. Americans still believed in "rugged individualism," the idea that you must stand on your own feet. Anything less showed a "moral defect" akin to a physical disability such as polio.

At first, the unemployed tried to borrow from better-off relatives, but relatives had to be careful; there was no telling when they might lose their jobs. In small towns and big-city neighborhoods, residents bought most of what they needed from local shops. Merchants knew them. The grocer, butcher, druggist, or gas station owner gladly put a purchase on the "tab" until payday. Now there were no more paydays. Merchants could no longer take risks because they also had bills to pay. Extending credit might ruin their business and impoverish their families.

Hunger stalked the land. While there was no mass starvation, millions had to scrounge for food. That could be degrading and disgusting. "We saw a crowd of some fifty men fighting over a barrel of garbage which had been set outside the back door of a restaurant. American citizens fighting for scraps of food like animals!" a Chicago reporter wrote. An elderly woman removed her eyeglasses so as not to see the maggots crawling over the trash she ate. In the Pennsylvania coalfields, unemployed miners' families ate weeds and roots.[21]

The lucky ones got a bowl of stew, a slice of bread, and a mug of black coffee from a church or charity like the Salvation Army. In New York, in wintertime, breadlines stretched around Times Square and for blocks along the Great White Way, the Broadway theater district. The hungry waited silently for hours, their clothes stuffed with newspapers for warmth, "old before their time, shoulders broken by responsibility, faces that look into a black abyss," drained of any interest in life. Every day, a physician noted, "people were flopping on the streets from hunger"—as they had in Germany in 1918. New York hospitals reported ninety-five deaths from "simple starvation" in 1931.[22]

Nor did hunger spare the youngest. "Have you ever heard a hungry child cry?" asked New York social worker Lillian Wald. "Have you seen the uncontrollable trembling of parents who have gone half starved for weeks so that the children may have food?" When a teacher tried to send a little girl home because she was weak from hunger, she said, "I can't. It's my sister's turn to eat." Undernourished children were listless and inattentive; often they fell asleep at their desks. In 1932, in New York, school officials counted 20,000 malnourished children. Teachers dipped into their own meager salaries to buy food for needy students. But teachers, too, lost their jobs. As tax revenues plummeted, budget cutters targeted the public schools.

A breadline outside St. Peter's Mission in New York City. (1932)

In Alabama, five out of six schools closed for lack of funds. New York City laid off 11,000 teachers from 1932 to 1933.[23]

Should jobless couples have babies? Many thought not. A father of two exclaimed, "Worker's got no right to have kids anymore." He thought it immoral to condemn children to a life of hunger and rags. A New York doctor noted that "boys and girls saw the economic agony and frustration of their elders and they figured—girls more frequently than boys—that it would be sheer madness to marry."[24]

Single mothers might abandon infants. A note pinned to the diaper of a two-month-old left on a car parked on Broadway read: "His name is Billie. I have tried to keep him but I can't keep myself. I am a young widow almost starving." Another mother left her infant on the doorstep of an animal shelter. "You put animals out of their misery. Why not my baby?" the note asked.[25]

Young or old, married or single, people worried about keeping a roof over their heads. "We haven't paid 4 months rent," an anxious twelve-year-old Chicago boy told a social worker. "Everyday the landlord rings the door bell, we don't open the door for him. We are afraid they will put us out. . . . We haven't paid the gas bill, and the electric

bill, haven't paid [the] grocery bill for 3 months."[26]

Tenants who failed to pay rent, and homeowners who missed mortgage payments, faced eviction. Rain or shine, movers put them into the street. Pedestrians in most American cities became used to passing furniture, household goods, and people lying on the sidewalk. "Why, Daddy," a girl said, "there are people lying on the newspapers. And children." Daddy said nothing, but when she looked up, he was crying.[27]

While most families eventually crowded in with relatives, others became homeless. People that had never known want, with babies and small children, gathered in makeshift encampments, some tiny, others the size of city blocks. In these communities of grief, they pitched tents and built scrap-wood huts lacking electricity, heat, light, water, sanitation—and hope. In 1932, author Matthew Josephson visited one on East Tenth Street, at the foot of the East River in New York. He saw

a hundred or so dwellings, each the size of a dog house or chicken coop, often constructed with much ingenuity out of wooden boxes, metal cans, strips of cardboard or old tar paper. Human beings lived on the margin of civilization by foraging for garbage, junk, and waste lumber. I found some splitting or sawing wood with dull tools to make fires; others were picking through heaps of rubbish they had gathered . . . or cooking over open fires on battered stoves. . . . They were of all sorts, young and old, some of them rough-looking and suspicious of strangers. They lived in fear of forcibly being removed by the authorities, though the neighborhood people in many cases helped them and the police tolerated them for the time being [23]

Some homeless "hit the road," hitchhiking or riding in railroad boxcars. Americans knew them by various names. "Hoboes" were ordinary folks forced to travel to find work; "tramps" traveled but would not work. Whatever you called them, they lived dangerously. While running to "hop a freight"—leap onto a moving freight train—one might trip and fall under the wheels. Then there were the "bulls" and "dicks," brawny railroad police, quick with their clubs and shotguns.

Seeing no future at home, an estimated 250,000 people under twenty-one, including thousands of teenage

≋ Two boys "hopping a freight." (1925–1935)

girls, roamed America in 1932. They took odd jobs, begged for food scraps, and slept in camps called "hobo jungles" along the tracks. Henry Ford famously, and foolishly, said of hobo life, "Why, it's the best education in the world for those boys, that traveling around! They get more experience in a few months than they would in years at school." We may wonder if the auto tycoon wanted this "best education" for his own sons.[29]

The Great Depression often hit adult men hardest. Searching for a job was a difficult job itself. To save precious pennies, rather than take public transportation, a man walked to where he thought an employer might be hiring. But walking long distances wore out shoes, and a hole in the sole raised blisters, which would be followed by an infection if untreated. Journalist Martha Gellhorn captured the mood of the long-term unemployed: "I find them all in the same shape—fear, fear driving them into a state of semi-collapse; cracking nerves, and an overpowering terror of the future."[30]

Tenant farmers, now homeless, walk from county to county in Oklahoma. (1936)

A young Oklahoma mother, age eighteen, stranded in a tent city in Imperial Valley, California. (March 1937)

Fear tore down one's self-image. Since colonial times, the husband "wore the pants" in the family, because he "brought home the bacon"—put food on the table. American men grew up believing that hard work, thrift, and honesty would bring a decent living, if not a fortune. Work, to them, was not only for earning dollars. It was the basis of their self-esteem.

Every day, like a strong acid, joblessness ate away at one's humanity. Men often felt that losing a job was their own fault, not the result of forces beyond their control. Unemployment, they felt, proved their worthlessness. "I haven't had a job in more than two years," one said, echoing many others. "Sometimes I feel like a murderer. What's wrong with me, that I can't protect my children?" A Texas schoolteacher explained: "If I can't make a living, I'm just no good, I guess." Self-hatred bred higher rates of mental illness, suicide, and alcoholism among the unemployed than among those with jobs.[31]

JIM CROW

Most African Americans lived in poor conditions, even in boom times. Though the Civil War ended slavery seventy years before the Great Depression, black people endured hardships not for what they did but because of who they were. Segregation, or forced separation from the rest of society, was endemic in the Southern states. Each state had its "Jim Crow" laws, covering many aspects of daily life. Jim Crow said black children must attend all-black schools. Public facilities had FOR WHITES ONLY and COLORED signs at toilets and water fountains. Trains had a "Jim Crow car" reserved for blacks. Blacks sat in the "colored balcony" of movie theaters, so high up that patrons joked about nosebleeds. Buses had black-only sections in the rear, but black riders had to give their seats to whites if asked. Jobs had colors, too. "Negro jobs" were heavy, hot, dirty, and low-paid. These included garbage collectors, street cleaners, ditch diggers, railroad porters, and track workers. Women often became laundresses, cleaners, and servants in white homes.

Racism justified Jim Crow. Racists hold that while people may share the same language and customs, they belong to separate breeds, or races. These, supposedly, are naturally unequal and arranged in a sort of pyramid, with the "superior" race on top. Thus, racists insisted, blacks were "inferior" to whites in their intelligence, morals, and abilities.

Jim Crow rested less on theory than on lynching, the mob killing, usually by hanging, of an accused person without a lawful trial. White mobs, often led by masked Ku Klux Klan thugs, lynched blacks for "getting out of line," which included charges of raping white women, trying to register to vote, "disputing with a white man," testifying in court against a white, and simply being "uppity," or outspoken. Like the Red Terror in the USSR, lynching aimed to terrorize people into submission. Between 1882 and 1944, mobs lynched 3,417 blacks, chiefly in the Southern states. Most were hanged; others were burned alive or hacked to pieces. To attract a white audience, newspaper advertisements announced the time and place of a lynch murder. Families came as if to an outing, the children also witnessing the grisly event. Afterward, shops sold postcards showing the victim's body, and the post office delivered them. Until 1952, not a year passed without a lynching somewhere in the country.[32]

"The Negro was born in depression," a black man told an interviewer. "It only became official when it hit the white man." Normally, blacks were hired last and fired first. However, the Great Depression intensified racial prejudice. "No jobs for niggers until every white man has a job," whites cried. Employers often yielded to these demands, firing black workers. At other times, the Ku Klux Klan ordered blacks to quit their jobs—or else. In 1933, snipers in Mississippi killed seven black railroad workers and wounded seven others to create vacancies for whites. That year, too, African American joblessness reached 50 percent, still the all-time high.[33]

HOOVER'S FAILURE

President Herbert Hoover seemed the ideal person to deal with the crisis. He was born poor, and after working his way through college, pinching pennies or going without, he spent twenty years as a mining engineer on projects around the world. Upon retiring as a millionaire, he entered public service during the First World War. Woodrow Wilson admired his organizing skills and put him in charge of feeding Europe's hungry, especially in the USSR, where crop failures created a massive famine. In that role, he saved at least 9 million people from certain death, more than any individual in history. That achievement earned Hoover the nickname the "Great Humanitarian."[34]

When the Great Depression struck, the federal government barely played a role in citizens' daily lives. It was not supposed to. The Founders feared big government. For generations, leaders believed that federal interference would only make things worse. America had suffered serious depressions in 1837, 1873, and 1893, when Franklin Roosevelt was eleven years old. Each time, Washington did nothing. Depressions were supposedly "natural" in a capitalist economy. Like hurricanes and earthquakes, they must "run their course" until the economy recovered on its own, usually within three years. Thus, the United States was the only industrial nation without a social safety net: retirement pensions, aid for those injured on the job, and unemployment benefits.

Critics branded Hoover a "do-nothing" president who let Americans suffer due to his commitment to old-fashioned ideas. It is untrue. The Great Humanitarian did not have it in him to let people suffer needlessly. Just the opposite. Hoover was the first president to use federal power to fight a depression. That immense effort made his daily life a blur of activity. To save time, he installed a telephone in the Oval Office, the first president to do so. Hoover worked himself and his staff to exhaustion. "I often thought," an aide recalled, "that the only difference between the executive offices and an insane asylum was that we went home at night."[35]

Hoover called business leaders to the White House, urging them to sacrifice profits to save jobs. They should not, he said, cut wages, reduce hours, or fire workers unless absolutely necessary. In that way, workers could retain their self-respect, feed their families, and continue buying goods. To help the unemployed, the president increased federal spending on public works: roads, bridges, tunnels, dams, schools, sewage systems, canals, and hospitals. These included famous projects like the San Francisco–Oakland Bay Bridge and the Los Angeles Aqueduct. Work began on Hoover Dam, on the Colorado River, for flood control and hydroelectric power and to irrigate crops in California and Arizona. Hoover also set up the Reconstruction Finance Corporation to make loans to troubled banks, insurance companies, and railroads. The loans would keep them operating, providing opportunities for investing and creating jobs. To pay for his programs, he persuaded Congress to double income taxes.

However, Hoover drew the line at so-called "handouts," direct federal aid to the jobless. The president insisted that only private citizens, businesses, charities, and churches should aid the needy. Like earlier presidents, he believed federal relief would make people soft, losing their drive to get ahead. "Direct relief to individuals from the Federal government," he warned, "would bring an inevitable train of corruption and waste such as our nation had never witnessed." Nevertheless, millions could not understand why government should aid big corporations but not the unemployed.[36]

WHERE TO?

Everything Hoover tried failed. As the Great Depression deepened, the country's mood turned ugly. Each day, newspaper stories told of rising class hatred. Letters poured into the White House, condemning the American system of

〰 A migrant worker on a California highway. (1935)

government. "In the Public Schools," one said, "our little children stand and salute and recite a 'rig ma role' in which is mentioned 'Justice to all' what a lie, what a naked lie." The writer's punctuation was poor, but his outrage was razor-sharp.[37]

Justice! If it meant anything in America, the unjust would get what they deserved. "Banksters" (bankers) were worse than gangsters. Oklahoma-born Woody Guthrie was a well-known folksinger and "people's troubadour" who gave voice to popular feeling. In "The Ballad of Pretty Boy Floyd," he turned a bank robber into a modern-day Robin Hood.

Yes, as through this world I've wandered
I've seen lots of funny men;
Some will rob you with a six-gun,
And some with a fountain pen.

Pretty Boy Floyd and his kind—John Dillinger, "Baby Face" Nelson, Bonnie Parker and Clyde Barrow—were vicious bandits who died in shoot-outs with lawmen. Though Americans condemned stealing, many believed well-spoken men in nice suits, with soft hands and fine manners, had stolen their livelihoods.[38]

Voices of rebellion rose in farm country. "By God I won't stand for it," cried an Oklahoma rancher. "I've played the game according to the rules. . . . I saved my money. . . . I didn't booze [or] gamble . . . and still I'm cleaned out and by God, I won't stand for it. . . . What we've got to do is have this here revolution."[39]

Rebellion might take the form of "penny auctions." When a bank auctioned a seized farm, grim men in faded denim overalls came with shotguns and pitchforks. As the auctioneer called for bids, a man offered, say, a nickel for a tractor or two cents for a horse. Nobody dared bid higher. Afterward, buyers returned the farm to its original owner. In the cities, hungry people crying "Starve or fight!" broke shopwindows and grabbed anything they could before the police came. Bands of ragged children stormed grocery stores.

The still-wealthy hired armed guards to protect themselves and their property. On March 7, 1932, company police at a Ford plant killed four and wounded fifty others demanding work to feed their families. Forty thousand mourners attended their funeral. The bodies lay beneath a red Communist banner with the words FORD GAVE BULLETS FOR BREAD. Later, California senator Hiram Johnson told colleagues, "The time may come when fat old men like you and me will be lined up against a stone wall."[40]

Where would it end? Revolution? Red Terror? Soviet-style tyranny? As Americans faced the dark unknown, Governor Roosevelt made his move.

THE NEW DEAL

Divine justice weighs the sins of the cold-blooded and the sins of the warm-hearted on different scales.
Better the occasional faults of a Government that lives in the spirit of charity than the consistent
omissions of a Government frozen in the ice of its own indifference.
—Franklin D. Roosevelt, 1936

NOMINATION

The Wall Street crash surprised New York's governor, as it did most other politicians. At first, he dismissed Black Tuesday as "the recent little flurry downtown," nothing to worry about. When the little flurry became the blizzard of the Great Depression, FDR realized the country was in deep crisis. But he also saw the crisis as an opportunity. Since 1932 was a presidential election year, he would toss his hat into the ring.[1]

Roosevelt asked Raymond Moley, a political science professor he knew at Columbia University, to gather a select group of experts to inform him on various issues. Moley recruited several young lawyers and economists. Nicknamed the "Brain Trust," they often met at Hyde Park to discuss the situation.

These meetings reveal a lot about how the future president learned. Though he was a Harvard graduate and an attorney, there were wide gaps in FDR's knowledge. Never a reader of serious books, he preferred detective novels, histories of the navy, and newspapers. His information came mostly from listening. "Every pore in his body was an ear," a journalist observed. An avid brain-picker, he would pose a problem, then sit back while the professors chewed it over. "You tell me what you think, and what you think I ought to do," he told them.

"You leave the politics to me. That's a dirty business."[2]

In late June, the Democratic National Convention was held in Chicago. While FDR stayed in Albany, Louis Howe ran his nominating campaign. Sweltering heat and asthma made him miserable. Howe lay on the floor of his hotel room surrounded by whirring electric fans, smoking Sweet Caporals and coughing violently. "We thought the little boss was going to die," an aide said. "Hell," said another, "Louis Howe has come this far, half alive, and you know damned well he isn't going to die until he sees Franklin Roosevelt nominated for President."[3]

This was what Howe had waited for since their meeting twenty years earlier. "What's your price?" he whispered to delegates as they knelt beside him, their ears near his lips. By "price," he meant not money but backing for their own election bids and government jobs for their supporters. Eventually, he made a deal with a leading contender, John Nance Garner of Texas, Speaker of the House of Representatives. "Cactus Jack" would support Roosevelt in return for the vice-presidential nomination. On July 1, 1932, FDR won the nomination on the fourth ballot.[4]

According to custom, the nominee waited at home to receive official no-

tice from party leaders. Not FDR. He decided to fly to Chicago to give his acceptance speech immediately. This was a calculated move, since it would signal his intention to act boldly. Flying would also show that, despite his disability, he was fit to hold the nation's highest office. Today, air travel is as routine as brushing your teeth. In 1932, it was so risky that passenger planes never flew at night or in rainy weather.

On the morning of July 2, the governor left Albany in a chartered plane with his wife, two of their sons, Missy Le-Hand, and a few aides. Nine hours and two refueling stops later, they landed in Chicago. At this time, only one politician regularly took to the sky. Adolf Hitler flew to several cities a day for speeches. His slogan: "Hitler Over Germany! Tomorrow the World!"

✺ Adolf Hitler in his personal airplane at an airport in Bremen, Germany. (1932)

Roosevelt went straight from the airport to Chicago Stadium. In these trying times, he told the convention, Democrats must "break foolish traditions" and create "a workable program of reconstruction." Ending his speech with a promise, he said, "I pledge you, I pledge myself, to a new deal for the American people." The phrase stuck. History knows FDR's recovery program as the New Deal.[5]

THE GREAT DEBATE

The year 1932 would see a landmark election. Herbert Hoover, again the Republican candidate, agreed with Roosevelt that the contest was a great debate,

FDR shaking hands with a farmer en route to Warm Springs, Georgia. (October 23, 1932)

a clash of ideas unlike any since the Civil War. The question: What is the proper role and size of the federal government? The outcome would set the nation's course for the rest of the twentieth century.

Distrust of big government was an American tradition, old as the Republic itself. Basically, the Founders aimed to protect citizens from their government. "If men were angels, no government would be necessary," wrote James Madison, a key figure in drafting the Constitution. But men are not angels. History taught that humans seek power for selfish reasons, not for the good of society. To avoid tyranny by the few, the Founders devised a system of "checks and balances." The Constitution separates the federal government into three branches—Congress, president, Supreme Court—each meant to keep the others from growing too powerful. It also limits the government's role to defending the nation, regulating trade between the states, keeping public order, and making "public improvements" such as roads, canals, bridges, and dams.[6]

Hoover saw danger in all that New Deal talk. Though he admitted that Roosevelt meant well, he warned that "so-called new deals" would "break down our form of government [and] crack the timbers of our Constitution." Of course, Hoover said, government should aid the needy "in times of great emergency," as he had done, but only in a very limited way and for the shortest time possible.

Hoover further explained that reliance on government promoted "special interests," dividing the nation into rival groups. Special interests attract career politicians, those who live to win and hold office. Given the chance, he predicted, they would turn increased dependency on government to their advantage. By making "raids on the Treasury," selfish politicians would use taxpayer money to buy votes, in effect bribing voters with their own dollars. Ultimately, America would become a tyranny. "You cannot," Hoover declared, "extend the mastery of government over the daily life of a people without somewhere making it master of the people's souls and thoughts."[7]

Roosevelt saw things differently. He extended the ideal of noblesse oblige—that the privileged have duties toward the less fortunate—to the government. FDR championed what historian Irving Bernstein called "a caring society." This means Americans have duties toward one another, and government is their tool for turning duties into action. The candidate declared that in a democracy, government "is not the master but the creature of the people." Elected by the people, it has a duty to care for those of its citizens made needy through no fault of their own. Government must be big and powerful enough to provide food, clothing, and shelter until they get back on their feet. Aid is not charity, FDR argued, but "a matter of social duty" based on our shared humanity.[8]

LANDSLIDE

The candidates crisscrossed the country by train. The Democrat traveled aboard the "Roosevelt Special" at a steady thirty miles an hour, since going faster caused rocking and discomfort. At each stop, a band struck up "Happy Days Are Here Again," a snappy show tune used as his theme song. FDR locked his braces and, grasping his son James's arm, spoke to the crowd. Turning on the charm full blast, he projected calm, strength, optimism, and, yes, joy. To draw attention away from his legs, he joked about "my little boy, Jimmy," now a strapping giant. The crowds roared with laughter. Then he scolded Hoover as both a "do-nothing" and "the greatest spender in history." Crying "Stop the deficits!" he vowed to "throw out the spenders" and balance the budget.[9]

〰 FDR, with his son James, waving to a crowd from the back of the "Roosevelt Special." (1932)

their shacks "Hoover hotels." Families slept under "Hoover blankets," newspapers. The hungry waited on "Hoover breadlines" with "Hoover flags," pockets turned inside out. They lined their worn-out shoes with "Hoover leather," cardboard strips. Wherever he appeared, crowds shook their fists, thumbed their noses, and chanted, "Hang Hoover!" The newly poor sang,

We'd like to thank you, Herbert Hoover,
For really showing us the way.
You dirty rat, you Bureaucrat,
You made us what we are today.[10]

First World War veterans blasted any hopes Hoover had of reelection. After the war, Congress had voted a bonus, due in 1945, for ex-servicemen. In the spring of 1932, jobless veterans and their families, over 25,000 strong, came to Washington to ask Congress to pay the bonus early. In a takeoff on George M. Cohan's "Over There," they sang,

Yet FDR's main appeal was that he was not Herbert Hoover. By 1932, Hoover himself had become the issue. Voters looked for someone to blame for their troubles, and he was the ideal target. For this reason, his name became a curse word. People called the economic collapse "the Hoover Depression." Homeless encampments were "Hoovervilles,"

Pay the bonus,
Pay the bonus,
Pay the bonus everywhere, everywhere,
For the Yanks are starving,
The Yanks are starving,
The Yanks are starving everywhere.[11]

Veterans stage a Bonus March in Washington, D.C. (April 8, 1932)

Calling themselves the "Bonus Army," veterans descended on Washington with their families. There they set up a sprawling Hooverville beside the Anacostia River, across from the capital, while some occupied empty federal buildings on Pennsylvania Avenue. When Congress rejected their plea on July 28, Hoover ordered the buildings cleared. In the riot that followed, police shot two veterans to death. Next Hoover sent war hero General Douglas MacArthur to evict the veterans with 550 troops and five tanks. After clearing the buildings with rifle butts and tear gas, he had the troops burn the shantytown. A baby died, most likely from inhaling the caustic gas.

"This ain't going to stop here," shouted a veteran, tears streaming down his face. An American president's use of American troops against American war veterans waving American flags disgusted the nation. The incident made FDR despise Hoover. "There is nothing inside the man but jelly," he barked. "Why didn't Hoover offer the men coffee and sandwiches, instead of turning . . . Doug MacArthur loose?" Ever the practical politician, he added, "This will elect me."[12]

It did. Roosevelt won in a landslide. He took 22.8 million votes, or 57 percent of the total, to Hoover's 15.7 million votes and carried forty-two of the forty-eight states. Democrats also won large majorities in the Senate and House of Representatives.

After Hoover conceded defeat, the president-elect went to his New York town house. The thrill of victory had already worn off. Now came the letdown as he realized, *truly* realized, what lay ahead. Despite his show of confidence, inwardly he was troubled.

That night, James helped his father into bed. After getting him settled, James kissed him good night, as the chicks did even as adults.

FDR looked up from his pillow and said, "You know, Jimmy, all my life I have been afraid of only one thing—fire. Tonight, I think I'm afraid of something else."

"Afraid of what, Pa?"

"I'm just afraid that I may not have the strength to do this job."

When James turned out the light, Pa said, "After you leave me tonight, Jimmy,

I'm going to pray. I am going to pray that God will help me, that He will give me the strength and the guidance to do this job and do it right. I hope you will pray for me, too, Jimmy."[13]

It was only a passing fear, and Roosevelt mastered it long before taking the oath of office.

THE HUNDRED DAYS

In the four months between his election and inauguration on March 4, 1933, the economy went into free fall. Dozens of banks closed every day as rumors triggered runs. By the time Roosevelt took the oath of office, every governor had ordered his state's banks closed to stop runs. FDR took his cue from them. On March 5, he declared a "bank holiday," a polite term for officially closing the nation's 19,000 banks. Next he called a special session of Congress, which lasted from March 9 to June 16. During this time—known as the Hundred Days, or the First New Deal—he focused on the so-called three R's: relief, recovery, and reform. Relief from suffering. Recovery of the economy. Reform to avert future depressions.

FDR shaped the modern presidency during the Hundred Days. He became both the nation's chief law enforcer and lawmaker. The man in the White House presented, and Congress passed, fifteen major laws drafted by the Brain Trust. His actions set the pattern. As President John F. Kennedy would say, "Ever since Roosevelt's day, all the laws have pretty much been written downtown"—that is, in the White House.[14]

Congress did not quibble over details. As measures came up for discussion, panicky lawmakers shouted, "Vote! Vote!" America was going under, and there was no time for debating, or even reading, a proposed law. "The whole country is with him," said humorist Will Rogers. "If [FDR] burned down the Capitol, we would cheer and say, 'well we at least got a fire started anyhow.'"[15]

The Emergency Banking Act took effect on March 9. Designed to check the economy's downward slide, it gave FDR authority to send Treasury inspectors into banks. Any bank they declared "sound," with enough good investments and cash to cover withdrawals, could reopen immediately. The Treasury would help weaker banks recover, with generous loans if needed, or close them for good. Cash grew scarce during the four-day holiday. No matter. Merchants gave credit or took anything of value in exchange for their goods. A New York store sold dresses for pickled herring!

On March 12, the president broadcast his first "Fireside Chat." Roosevelt had a marvelous radio voice, clear, warm, and comforting. Years later, President Ronald Reagan remembered how "when he came on, it was *the* biggest radio audience ever." The Republican added, "This was one of his great strengths . . . his ability to communicate." It seemed as if FDR spoke to each listener personally. One could almost feel him physically in the room.[16]

As 60 million Americans listened, FDR became teacher in chief. Calling the radio audience "my friends," he explained what he had done, why, and what to expect. "I can assure you," he concluded, "it is safer to keep your money in

≋ FDR conducting one of many Fireside Chats. (April 28, 1935)

a reopened bank than under a mattress." It worked. Next day, millions opened new bank accounts. Within a week, 13,500 banks reopened.[17]

Laws to reform the financial system quickly followed. At Roosevelt's request, Congress passed the Banking Act, which forbade banks to invest depositors' money in the stock market and created the Federal Deposit Insurance Corporation (FDIC). This agency insured savings accounts up to $5,000 ($250,000 in 2012), preventing future bank runs. To check stock market abuses, another law created the Securities and Exchange Commission (SEC).

These reforms, while necessary, could not bring recovery. Other than vowing to cut government spending, Roosevelt did not have a detailed recovery program. Instead, he had a way of tackling problems. "Take a method and try it," he said. "If it fails, admit it frankly and try another. But above all, try something." Experiments might lead to costly errors, but they also made sense—because nobody knew exactly how to revive the economy. FDR even borrowed ideas from Hoover, but without giving him credit.[18]

At first, Roosevelt tried to balance the budget. At his request, Congress passed the Economy Act, which slashed the pay of federal workers; the president dramatized this by sending part of his first paycheck to the Treasury. For one whose mother paid his bills whenever he ran short, this was no sacrifice. Moreover, the act cut benefits for veterans, repealing all laws "granting medical or hospital treatment" to them and their families. For good measure, it halved the pensions of disabled veterans, from forty to twenty dollars a month. Finally, the White House urged states to cut teachers' salaries, as they were "too high."[19]

Roosevelt soon found that cutting only made things worse. It was a simple fact that workers who made less had less to spend, thus driving prices down further and destroying more jobs. So, while the cuts stayed in place, FDR changed course. He began pouring money into the economy, spending and borrowing far more than Hoover.

His calmness and willingness to change amazed aides. Brain Truster Raymond Moley compared Roosevelt to a fairy prince "who didn't know how to shudder. . . . His courage was absolute." The source of that courage was no mystery—to FDR. It came from battling polio. "If you spent two years in bed trying to wiggle your big toe," he explained, "after that anything would seem easy."[20]

ALPHABET SOUP

During the Hundred Days, the president asked Congress to create scores of agencies to spur relief and recovery. They were best known by their initials, and Americans called them "alphabet soup," after a popular kind of canned soup.

These agencies made public service honorable, even romantic. Hundreds of lawyers, economists, planners, and educators flocked to Washington "The climate was exciting," economist Joe Marcus recalled. "You were part of a society that was on the move. You were involved in something that could make a difference."[21]

FDR's cabinet embodied the can-do spirit. Frances Perkins became secretary of labor, the first woman to hold a cabinet post. A veteran New York social reformer, Perkins had led the investigation into the Triangle Shirtwaist Company fire. Henry Morgenthau Jr., a top-notch lawyer and insurance company executive, served as secretary of the Treasury. Harold L. Ickes, of Chicago, former head of the Chicago chapter of the National Association for the Advancement of Colored People (NAACP), became secretary of the interior. Inspired by FDR, reform-minded young people ran for Congress, among them a tall Texan

named Lyndon B. Johnson, later thirty-sixth president of the United States.

The first alphabet soup agency targeted single jobless men (but not women). To keep them out of trouble, Congress created the Civilian Conservation Corps (CCC). Growing up at Hyde Park, Roosevelt came to love the land, especially the trees. A secretary called him "an ardent tree lover," who wanted to preserve as much of America's natural heritage as possible. For that reason, between 1933 and 1942, the CCC recruited 2.5 million men between the ages of eighteen and twenty-five. Recruits lived in army-style camps, under the discipline of army officers commanded by General MacArthur. Besides

Secretary of Labor Frances Perkins shortly before addressing the Conference of Industry and Labor in Washington, D.C. (December 11, 1936)

room, meals, and clothing, they earned thirty dollars a month, from which they had to send twenty-five home. In return, they planted trees in forests depleted by loggers, fought forest fires, built recreation facilities, and cleaned beaches. Many used their off-duty time to earn high school equivalency diplomas.[22]

Since the CCC helped only a tiny fraction of the needy, Congress created

---

A POCKETFUL OF ALPHABET SOUP AGENCIES

(Their names give a good idea of their aim.)

Agricultural Adjustment Administration (AAA)
Civilian Conservation Corps (CCC)
Civil Works Administration (CWA)
Farm Credit Administration (FCA)
Farm Security Administration (FSA)
Federal Art Project (FAP)
Federal Deposit Insurance Corporation (FDIC)
Federal Emergency Relief Administration (FERA)
Federal Farm Board (FFB)
Federal Housing Administration (FHA)
Federal Music Project (FMP)
Federal Theatre Project (FTP)
Federal Writers' Project (FWP)
Home Owners' Loan Corporation (HOLC)
National Labor Relations Board (NLRB)
National Recovery Administration (NRA)
National Youth Administration (NYA)
Public Works Administration (PWA)
Rural Electrification Administration (REA)
Tennessee Valley Authority (TVA)
United States Housing Authority (USHA)
Works Progress Administration (WPA)

---

the Federal Emergency Relief Administration (FERA). Led by Harry Hopkins, a New York social worker, FERA sent the states $500 million to aid families in distress. The agency set up school lunch programs to ensure that children got at least one square meal a day. Children also benefited from health clinics set up in rural areas, which seldom had a full-time doctor, let alone a hospital.

Critics said the money spent on FERA would not reduce unemployment "in the long run." Hopkins bristled. "People don't eat in the long run—they eat every day." For good measure, a few days after creating FERA in February, Congress repealed Prohibition by passing the Twenty-First Amendment to the Constitution. While waiting for the states to ratify the amendment, Congress ended the ban on beer and wine.[23]

The CCC and FERA helped many get by. However, plans that looked good on paper often had unexpected results. For example, aid to farmers was a mixed bag. Their problem, we recall, was low prices due to overproduction. It followed that producing less would create scarcity, driving prices up. Thus, Congress passed the Agricultural Adjustment Act, which allowed government agents to pay farmers to plant crops on only part of their land. During the first year, farmers

~~ Children enjoy a meal from the school lunch program. (1936)

plowed under millions of acres of wheat and corn. Dairy farmers spilled "excess" milk into ditches. Livestock raisers killed 6 million piglets and 200,000 sows. While some pigs were turned into soap or fertilizer, most ended up burned, buried, or dumped into rivers.

Yet the rise in farmers' incomes came at the expense of others just as hard up as they. An irate Southern woman asked an Agricultural Adjustment Administration (AAA) official, "Why do you dump all these little pigs into the Mississippi, when there are thousands of people in the country starving?" She thought it immoral that those least able to afford food should have to pay more because of the government. Nor did the Agricultural Adjustment Act benefit farmers equally. Big landlords gained, since they had plenty of land to take out of production. In doing so, they evicted 3 million of rural America's poorest: tenants, who rented their land for cash, and sharecroppers, who gave part of their crops as rent.[24]

The Hundred Days also saw the birth of the Tennessee Valley Authority (TVA). Covering an area of 600,000 square miles in seven states, the valley of the Tennessee River had always been a backward region. Lacking electricity, their farms ravaged by floods, the people there suffered from malaria, tuberculosis, and malnutrition. Eventually, the TVA built twenty-one dams and power plants to control flooding and generate electricity. For those who had never had electricity, it was magical. "The women went around turning the switches on and off," an inspector wrote. "The light and wonder in their eyes were brighter than that from the lamps." Still, the TVA had its downsides. Nearly 16,000 valley people had to leave their homes to make way for the various projects. Landowners got government checks for their property.

〰 The Tennessee Valley Authority's Norris Dam converts the force of falling water into electric power. (January 1937)

Tenants and sharecroppers got nothing. They joined the ranks of the homeless.[25]

To aid industry, Congress created the National Recovery Administration (NRA). This agency aimed at promoting recovery through a partnership of business, labor, and government. Together, they would draw up "codes of fair competition" to regulate all aspects of an industry, from output to quality, and set minimum prices to ensure profits. Finally, codes would set working conditions: wages, hours, discipline, and safety.

There were 557 NRA codes. These covered industries as varied as making steel, silk flowers, lightning rods, hair tonic, undergarments, macaroni, and dog food. Plays and musical comedies had codes, too, as did chorus-line dancers. Yet most codes did little for recovery. Drawn up by lawyers from each industry's largest firms, they harmed smaller firms, which were unable to make a profit by obeying all their rules.

Pity anyone who charged less! For example, a court found Jacob Maged of Jersey City, New Jersey, guilty of asking thirty-five cents to press a suit, not the forty cents set by the NRA's dry-cleaning code. Maged paid a fine and went to jail for three months. While industries agreed to improve workplace safety, most employers ignored their pledges. As with the AAA, the codes often rewarded the few at the expense of the many. By setting minimum prices, they made those struggling to make ends meet pay more. Clearly, the NRA was not, as an official said, a "Holy Thing, the Greatest Social Advance Since the Days of Jesus Christ."[26]

RAW DEAL

The First New Deal treated African Americans as second-class citizens. In reporting on a civil rights conference, black leaders captured their community's mood. "The New Deal was criticized, denounced, and condemned. Nothing good was found in it." Many blamed the president personally, branding him a racist. Yet it was not that simple.[27]

White supremacy was as much a part of Roosevelt's upbringing as noblesse oblige or public service. In his childhood and youth, derogatory views of black people were all but universal in white America. Part of the reason for this was the legacy of slavery. Though the Thirteenth Amendment to the Constitution, adopted in 1865, formally abolished slavery, the attitudes and ideas that had sustained it continued. In the post–Civil War era, blacks formed the bulk of America's underclass, largely uneducated and doing low-paid, menial work. Education, even in the North, supported notions of black "inferiority." I remember how, in elementary school in the early 1940s, our teacher explained why nature had suited blacks for bondage: having dark skin supposedly made it easy to do hard physical labor, like raising cotton under the blazing sun. Similarly, in the movies, an actor with the screen name Stepin Fetchit personified popular attitudes among whites. Fetchit, an African American, came across as a creature of racist mythology, the caricature of a bowing, scraping, head-scratching, eye-rolling nitwit.

It is hardly surprising, then, that racial slurs should have easily fallen from Franklin's lips. He used the foul insult "nigger" for anyone, including whites, who did manual labor. At Groton, white mail sorters were known as "mail niggers," and package deliverers as "express niggers." As assistant secretary of the navy, FDR wrote, "I worked like niggers all day." Polio, too, had its "color line." When, for example, the Reverend J. S. Brookens applied to send his nine-year-old son to Warm Springs, he learned that "Negroes were never admitted to that institution." Its owner always labeled his Georgia property tax return "White Taxpayer."[28]

Eleanor was different. As a young married woman, she had looked down on black people, calling her house servants "my darkies" and small black children "pickaninnies," but in time, she overcame her prejudice. She joined the NAACP and proudly posed for photos with black friends. This, according to an FBI report, made many Southerners uneasy, and they regarded her as "the most dangerous individual in the United States today." Her husband, however, seems never to have outgrown the language of prejudice. As president, FDR, the word "nigger" still in his vocabulary, discussed the "nigger vote" and joked about colored "pussons," though never in public. His language shocked an eminent attorney. Thurgood Marshall, later the first African American Supreme Court justice, once visited Attorney General Francis Biddle; as chief counsel for the NAACP, Marshall came to him to describe the case of a black man accused of murder in Virginia. Biddle wanted the president's opinion on the case. Dialing the president, he motioned Marshall to pick up an extension phone. Marshall heard an angry Roosevelt say, "I warned you not to call me again about any of Eleanor's niggers. Call me one more time and you are fired." We would love to know how Marshall felt about Roosevelt after this, but he never said, at least for the record.[29]

If the definition of a racist, however, is one who believes in the natural inferiority or inborn evil of another group, FDR was no racist. Instead, he believed all Americans had the right to go as far as ambition and talent could take them. Yet he was also a professional politician. He felt that to win and hold power, he must be careful about the causes he supported. His wife understood this perfectly. "Franklin," Eleanor wrote, "frequently refrained from supporting causes in which he believed, because of

political realities." While he was not actively opposed to African American equality, political reality, as he understood it, kept him from sticking out his neck for a cause he believed in.[30]

FDR's idea of political reality clashed with his ideas about lynching. In private, the president called it by its true name: "a vile form of collective murder," a violation of everything America stands for. However, when a bill came before Congress to make lynching a federal crime, he refused to endorse it. This, he claimed, was because the likes of Senator Theo-

A flag announcing a lynching is flown from the window of the NAACP headquarters on Fifth Avenue in New York City, meant to raise awareness of the mistreatment of blacks throughout the United States. (1936)

dore Bilbo, Democrat of Mississippi, held the New Deal hostage. Fanatical racists like Bilbo controlled key committees in Congress. If FDR favored the bill, he felt, they would take revenge on the New Deal. "I did not choose the tools with which I must work. But I've got to get legislation passed by Congress to save America," he told NAACP executive secretary Walter White. "If I come out for the anti-lynching bill now, [bigots] will block every bill I ask Congress to pass to keep America from collapsing. I just can't take the risk." Nor would he ever.[31]

Blacks rejected FDR's stand as callous and gutless. Thurgood Marshall was bitter. "We couldn't get a damned thing through Congress," the NAACP lawyer said. "You can't name one bill passed in the Roosevelt administration for Negroes. Nothing. We couldn't even get the anti-lynching bill through." Roy Wilkins, editor of the NAACP magazine the *Crisis,* agreed, denouncing the president's "expedient cowardice." More, Wilkins added, the president's measures "to keep America from collapsing" often directly harmed blacks. FDR kept quiet when the CCC and TVA put them in segregated work camps. The AAA's paying landlords not to plant crops meant turning out black laborers and tenant farmers. From 1933 to 1934 alone, AAA policies drove over 100,000 African Americans from the land. NRA codes allowed Southern employers to pay blacks less than the federal minimum wage. Northern employers fired blacks rather than pay them the same as whites. Labor unions banned African Americans, too. No wonder they said NRA stood for "Negroes Robbed Again," "Negro Run Around," "Negro Removal Act," "Negroes Rarely Allowed"—and "No Roosevelt Again."[32]

THE FIRST FAMILY

As the First New Deal got under way, the First Family moved into the White House. By 1933, the once-elegant mansion had become seedy, its carpets musty and threadbare, its furniture dull and scratched. The First Lady found the kitchen unsanitary and the refrigerator "bad smelling." There were rats. Sometimes you met them in the hallways or heard them rummaging in the walls. Not that any of this bothered Eleanor. The night Franklin won the presidency, she sat in a corner, weeping. "Now I will have no identity. I'll only be the wife of the president."[33]

Eleanor soon found that being "only" the president's wife allowed her to make

Eleanor Roosevelt meets with the press in Los Angeles, California. (June 6, 1933)

her life count as never before. The White House became her base, not her home. During breaks from her travels, she stopped by for a few days or weeks. She seemed always busy. Visitors saw her padding down a hallway barefoot, in a bright yellow bathing suit. A friend found her standing on her head, "straight as a column, feet up in the air," doing a yoga exercise. She did not spend much time with her husband. The servants sensed an invisible barrier between the first couple. "Even if Eleanor was home," a butler recalled, "she did not see her husband for stretches at a time, except for 'Good Morning' as they passed in the hall."[34]

Eleanor was so earnest about her "causes" that whenever she stayed in the White House, she bombarded the president with long, detailed memos. Overwhelmed, he put an "Eleanor box" near his bed and declared a three-memo-a-night limit. Sometimes, she got carried away. "She could pester the hell out of him," daughter Anna recalled. *Read this! See so-and-so! Franklin, you must!* His patience exhausted, FDR replied, "Oh, Eleanor, shut up!" Another time, Anna saw her mother hold out a thick folder. "And sure enough, he blew his top. He took every single speck of that whole pile of papers, threw it across the desk at me and said, 'Sis, you handle this tomorrow morning.'" Shocked, Anna "almost went through the floor." Her mother left the room, murmuring, "I'm sorry."[35]

The First Lady believed her husband resented women who saw themselves as his equal. "I don't think," she remarked, "that Franklin likes women who think they are as good as he is." Her daughter agreed. "Pa," Anna wrote, "seems to take for granted that all females should be quite content to 'keep the home fires burning,' and that their efforts outside of this are merely rather amusing and to be aided by a patronizing male world only as a last resort to keep some individually troublesome female momentarily appeased." Anna added that her mother "goes along very strongly with me in our feeling that the OM [Old Man] is a stinker in his treatment of the female members of his family." The word "stinker" also applied to his treatment of certain other women. "If Father became friendly with a princess or a secretary," Anna noted, "he'd reach out and give a pat to her fanny and laugh like hell." Today, this would be considered sexual harassment.[36]

FDR's every waking moment reminded him of his disability. A family friend recalled that he was "totally immobile, like a doll." Life would have been impossible without others to help at every turn. Someone always had to be with him or near him, within the sound of his voice. If not, he was stranded, as when he sat in a chair for hours because his valet did not hear the bell summoning him.[37]

Waking by 8:30 a.m., Roosevelt smoked the first of his forty daily Camel cigarettes. As he puffed, he rang for breakfast—usually coffee, toast, ham, and eggs—eaten in bed while he read the morning papers. The valet then helped him sit on, and get off, the toilet. To dress him, the valet stretched him out on the bed and removed his pajamas. That done, he fastened FDR's leg braces and then put on every stitch of clothing, from his shirt and tie to his socks and shoes. The whole process took up to forty-five minutes.

When the president was ready, a Secret Service man wheeled him to the Oval Study, two doors away from his bedroom on the second floor of the East Wing of the White House. (FDR used the Oval Office, a very formal room in the West Wing, chiefly for ceremonial occasions such as signing bills, receiving important visitors, and holding press conferences.) The study was his favorite White House room. This was where he felt most comfortable working and relaxing with his stamp collection Here, too, he unwound in the evening, inviting guests for poker, small talk—no politics allowed—and drinks. For his guests, FDR enjoyed mixing what he called "yummy" cocktails. The room reflected the president's interests. Ship pictures hung on the walls. Trinkets cluttered the desk: porcelain animals, mechanical toys, clocks, tiny flags, and model ships. From time to time, the deskbound man distracted himself by glancing at the trinkets and fondling them. Staff members nicknamed him the "Dynamo," a good name, because he radiated energy. "I *never* get tired!" FDR boasted. Even so, he couldn't forget that he needed others to meet his most basic needs. Curtis Roosevelt, Anna's son, remembered a valet bringing a bottle to Grandpa's desk for him to urinate into.[38]

Roosevelt greeted visitors with a smile and a handshake. Depending on how well he knew the person, he might take a few moments to share gossip. "I love it! I love it!" he laughed at a spicy story. His laugh was "as joyous, hearty, rolling, thunderous laughter as ever was heard on this sorrowful globe," said author Fulton Oursler. However, FDR was also a master of the brush-off. If he did not wish to discuss something, he "ate time." He would keep talking, not letting the visitor get a word in, until the time allotted for the meeting passed. Or he would say "I see, I see" as the visitor spoke. Many thought he agreed with them, but he meant only that he was listening. To speed some visitors out the door, he let Fala, his Scottish terrier, lick his luncheon plate or wet the rug.[39]

Twice a week, Roosevelt met the press. No president has ever been so available to reporters as he; in total, he held 998 press conferences, an all-time record. On a normal conference day, 180 to 200 reporters (whites only) assembled outside the Oval Study. "All right," FDR told an aide, "bring in the wolves." Upon entering, they found him seated at his desk, smiling broadly, an ivory cigarette holder clamped between his teeth. They gathered around, pencils and notebooks poised, attentive to his every word. He was their bread and butter, because their jobs depended on what FDR provided for their articles. In return, the president used their articles, as he used the Fireside Chats, to educate the public about his policies.[40]

Roosevelt came across as charming and relaxed. Everything went smoothly if reporters obeyed the rules—his rules. No recording equipment, if you please. No wheelchair photos, either. If a reporter snapped such a picture, a Secret Service man hustled him out the door and seized his camera, exposing the film. He would never attend another press conference.

A reporter could ask any question, but Roosevelt did not have to answer. He might brush it aside with "The weather is very hot" or by pretending not to hear it. If asked for the source of a fact, he might say it came from "friends." Reporter Merriman Smith called these "imaginary playmates," for he doubted if they existed outside the president's mind. Should a reporter keep probing, FDR might say in mock politeness, "No cross-examination, please!" Should he continue, FDR got nasty. "Go to a good psychologist," he snapped at one reporter. Others he told to "put on a dunce cap and stand in the corner." That shut them up, while warning the others to hold their tongues. No president could get away with this in our age of live television.[41]

Despite appearances, FDR was never really open with anyone. A mystery man, always secretive, he kept part of himself locked away. This trait, we recall, developed in childhood as protection from his bossy mother. Even after he grew up, Sara ordered him around. She would butt into his conversations and eavesdrop on important phone calls at Hyde Park. "Mama, will you *please* get off the line," the president of the United States once said. "I can hear you breathing. Come on, now."[42]

Roosevelt's secretiveness affected his presidency. He trusted nobody, refusing to share his thoughts and feelings. Interior Secretary Harold Ickes reported a conversation:

Ickes: You are a wonderful person, but you are one of the most difficult men to work with that I have ever seen.

FDR: Because I get too hard at times?

Ickes: No, [because] you won't talk frankly even with people who are loyal to you and of whose loyalty you are fully convinced.[43]

Secretary of the Interior Harold Ickes. (1938)

Roosevelt did not dispute Ickes's remarks. The "Juggler," he called himself. "Never let your left hand know what your right is doing," he told Treasury Secretary Henry Morgenthau. Sometimes, the president gave the same task to more than one person without telling them he had done so. Perhaps he did this to get different opinions, which he could then evaluate on his own. On the other hand, newsman John Gunther believed that "he was tricky for fun."[44]

FDR puzzled those closest to him. Daughter Anna said, "He doesn't know any man and no man knows him. Even his own family doesn't know anything about him." Her brother James agreed. "Of what was inside him, of what really drove him, Father talked with no one." Their mother realized she had never shared his life fully and never would. Eleanor told James, "He had no real confidantes. . . . I don't think I was his confidante, either. . . . He lived his own life exactly as he wanted it." Sadly, while FDR had a great many acquaintances, "he was really incapable of a personal friendship with anyone," Missy LeHand thought. He always protected himself, always defended his inner core from others.[45]

The presidency reinforced these traits. Her husband became, Eleanor noted, a *completely political person.*" We may say that the office eventually absorbed the man. FDR thought of himself, and of his political needs, first. Ruthlessly, he used people but had scant loyalty to them. "The President," Eleanor said, "uses those who suit his purposes. He makes up his own mind and discards people when they no longer fulfill a purpose." Another time, she noted with sorrow, "I was one of those who served his purpose." Despite years of dedicated service, top officials like Harry Hopkins and Postmaster General James Farley never got a thank-you for anything they did. Louis Howe did not say if Roosevelt thanked him or confided in him.[46]

Though those in Roosevelt's inner circle admired his political skills, they grew to dislike him personally. Brain Truster Raymond Moley took offense at his habit of "telling, not asking," as if people must accept his decisions without question, otherwise they were guilty of "corruption or stupidity." Henry Morgenthau noted that, when riled, the president became "very excited, very dictatorial, and very disagreeable." During cabinet meetings, he enjoyed nailing members with sarcastic remarks. He once gave Morgenthau such a dressing-down that Harold Ickes, who disliked the Treasury secretary, took pity. Ickes said he "looked and acted like a spanked child." Ambassador W. Averell Harriman noted that FDR "always enjoyed other people's discomfort. I think it is fair to say that it never bothered him very much when other people were unhappy." This showed up in his crude nicknames for top aides. Harry Hopkins was "Harry the Hop," Morgenthau was "Henry the Morgue," and Ickes was "Donald Duck." To them, of course, he was always "Mr. President."[47]

Many of those who watched FDR closely for any length of time left unflattering descriptions. He seemed vain and petty. For example, Judge Samuel Rosenman, his favorite speechwriter, thought that "he liked flattery . . . and he seemed frequently to be jealous of compliments paid to others." Dwight D Eisenhower, a general and later president, thought the commander in chief "almost an egoist in his belief in his own wisdom."[48]

To others, Roosevelt seemed false and insincere. His bright smile was phony, coming "from the teeth out," according to William Allen White, a leading journalist. As to his charm, Henry Wallace, his third-term vice president, thought he "turned this on automatically." Wallace added that the key to FDR's character was "the desire to be the dominating figure, to demonstrate on all occasions his superiority."[49]

The president's warmth also struck insiders as fake. Ickes noted, "He is as cold as ice inside." Harry S. Truman, the vice president when FDR died in 1945, thought him a superb leader but an awful human being. Using nearly the exact words as Ickes, Truman said, "Inside he was the coldest man I ever met. He didn't care about you or me or anyone else in the world on a personal level, as far as I could see." Even worse: "He lies." Historian Arthur Schlesinger Jr., an expert on the New Deal and a Roo-

sevelt admirer, thought him "glittering, impersonal, impenetrable, superficially warm, basically cold." Nevertheless, he brought far-reaching changes in American life.[50]

THE SECOND NEW DEAL

While millions benefited from alphabet soup programs, the economy had not recovered. Thus, as his first term neared its end, Roosevelt decided America needed a stronger dose of the three R's. Because 1936 was a presidential election year, he launched the Second New Deal.

FDR asked Congress to pass three key measures. The first created the Works Progress Administration (WPA). A more ambitious program than the Civilian Conservation Corps or Federal Emergency Relief Administration, the WPA paid over 3 million people to work on thousands of projects. They built or improved 572,000 miles of roads, 67,000 miles of city streets, 40,000 buildings, 78,000 bridges, 8,000 parks, 2,500 hospitals, 5,900 schools, 13,000 playgrounds, and 353 airports. The National Youth Administration (NYA), a WPA branch, aided high school and college students, paying them for part-time work in libraries and as research assistants.

≈ A dance performance in New York produced by the WPA Federal Theatre Project. (1935)

≈ A WPA bookmobile attracts readers. (Date unknown)

WPA cultural programs funded projects for artists, writers, and performers. "Hell! They've got to eat just like other people," said WPA chief Harry Hopkins. Painters decorated walls of post offices, schools, and federal buildings with murals. Field units collected folk songs and Native American music and crafts. A WPA agency, the Federal Theatre Project (FTP), staged plays, poetry readings, puppet shows, and circuses. The Federal Music Project (FMP) gave live performances free of charge. Other WPA programs sent bookmobiles into rural districts that had no public libraries or where the libraries had closed for lack of funds. These activities exposed millions to the fine arts for the first time. When the WPA ended during the Second World War, it had pumped $11 billion into the economy.

Another measure, the National Labor Relations Act of 1935, became "Labor's Bill of Rights." It was sponsored by New York senator Robert F. Wagner, and under it the federal government recognized labor unions for the first time. This law guaranteed workers' right to organize unions, join them, and have them bargain with employers over wages, hours, and safety. Workers voted for the union they wished to represent them. Once chosen, the union could declare a "closed shop"—that is, prevent anyone from working unless they joined the union and paid dues. A federal agency, the National Labor Relations Board (NLRB), enforced the law, as it still does.

Roosevelt, however, opposed unions for federal employees. Unlike workers in private industry, where a union can strike to gain its demands, federal employees serve all Americans, whose welfare depends on government operations running smoothly. Striking would mean paralyzing the government they had sworn to support, an "unthinkable and intolerable" action, according to the president.[51]

The Second New Deal's most important measure, however, was the Social Security Act. Drafted by Secretary of Labor Frances Perkins, this was the crown jewel of the caring society. FDR said it aimed at full protection: "Cradle to the grave—from the cradle to the grave [everyone] ought to be in a social insurance system." Social Security protected the most vulnerable. It provided pensions for the elderly, aid to needy children and the disabled, and unemployment benefits for the jobless. Roosevelt did not want the program to become a political football, perhaps killed years later by Congress. Rather than finance it with federal funds, he used a payroll tax matched by employer

contributions, thus giving everyone a stake in the system. "With these taxes in there," he insisted, "no damn politician can scrap my Social Security program." Yet Social Security had serious flaws. Originally, it excluded whole categories of workers: farmers, day laborers, housecleaners, cooks, and laundresses.[52]

The Second New Deal harmed but also helped African Americans. Its support for the closed shop permitted "lily-white" unions to bar blacks from the workplace. Social Security did not cover household workers, most of whom were black women. Yet, by 1935, Roosevelt began to help blacks—if he could do it without paying a political price.

Quietly, FDR formed a "black Cabinet" of civil rights leaders to advise him on "Negro" issues. Chief among these was the president of Bethune-Cookman College in Florida, Mary McLeod Bethune, a woman much admired by the First Lady. Roosevelt even appointed the first black federal judge, William Hastie. African Americans appreciated these small victories over Jim Crow, particularly the WPA, which Roosevelt ordered to pay blacks the same as whites. Some sang,

Oh, I'm for you, Mr. President,
I'm for you all the way.

You can take away the alphabet
But don't take away this WPA.[53]

Nevertheless, lynching continued, prompting the bitter remark that America remained "the land of the tree and the home of the grave."

VICTORY AND DEFEAT

The 1936 election season began sadly. Though Roosevelt expected to win his party's nomination easily, Louis Howe would not be able to help. The faithful "gnome" died in April. Though his life was ebbing away, Howe still thought of his chief. "Franklin," he gasped, "is on his own now." With Howe's death, Harry Hopkins became the president's closest adviser on domestic and foreign affairs.[54]

Roosevelt's opponents attacked him from every angle. The political left, particularly Communists, railed against this "puppet of big-money" who was more interested in saving capitalism than serving economic justice. Some Democrats, among them the Happy Warrior, Al Smith, charged him with wasting money on "boondoggles," worthless make-work programs. Kansas governor Alfred M. "Alf" Landon, the Republican candidate, accused him of favoring "big government" at the expense of individual lib-

erty. The letters *FDR*, he said, stood for "Franklin Deficit Roosevelt."[55]

Landon was gentle compared to Republican extremists. The very sound of Roosevelt's name made them hysterical. With red faces and bulging neck veins, they damned him as a "traitor to his class." One fellow bellowed so loudly into a microphone that he nearly swallowed it. An exclusive Connecticut country club forbade the mention of FDR's name to prevent heart attacks among its elderly members. A whispering campaign spread tales of the drooling "simpleton," a "hopeless drug addict" who spent his days cutting out paper dolls. "This vile Communist," "this little Lenin," wished to "sovietize America" with a new Red Terror. He was so despised that "a couple of well-placed bullets would be the best thing for the country." A few Republicans idiotically said they would rather vote for Adolf Hitler than the Democrat.[56]

Roosevelt struck back by pitting haves against have-nots. A son of inherited wealth, he had never thought highly of the businessmen he met. In private, he called them "generally stupid." On the campaign trail, he hammered Republicans as tools of "economic royalists" and "privileged princes," sellouts to "entrenched greed" and "special interests" hoping to end poverty "by starvation."

FDR claimed to wear their hatred as a badge of honor. "They are unanimous in their hate for me—and I welcome their hatred." As for Alf Landon, what a poor imitation of the Kansas state flower! Like the sunflower, he "was yellow, had a black heart, was useful only as parrot food, and always died before November."[57]

Landon died politically long before November. FDR's popularity scared as victims of the Depression rallied to him. "It takes a hungry man to appreciate Roosevelt," a Washington cabdriver said, speaking for millions. Many thought him straight from heaven. "You are the next 'Moses' that God has sent to lead the country to the promised land,' wrote a Louisiana farmer's wife. A Detroit Sunday-school teacher had to settle an argument between two pupils. "Auntie," asked Frankie, "was it Moses or President Roosevelt who led the children of Israel through the Red Sea? Freddie said it was Moses, but I said it was President Roosevelt."[58]

Martha Gellhorn reported from an impoverished South Carolina mill town: "The President stands between them and despair, and all the violence which desperation can produce. . . . Every house I visited—mill worker or unemployed— had a picture of the President. . . . He was at once God and their intimate friend;

he knows them all by name, knows their little town and mill, their little lives and problems. And though everything else fails, he is there, and will not let them down." Some devout Christians hung his picture on the wall next to Jesus Christ's. In a poll of New York City public schools, God ranked a distant second to FDR in popularity. In short, millions sensed that the man in the White House *cared*. He was okay, a good guy. Sure, he made mistakes, but he was on their side.[59]

Election Day saw an epic Roosevelt landslide: 27.7 million to 16.6 million votes. He carried every state but Maine and Vermont. Moreover, Democrats took both houses of Congress by majorities of four to one, raising doubts that the Republican Party could survive. Yet this stunning victory set the stage for

Public health nursing is made available in rural areas through Child Welfare Services. (Date unknown)

the worst blunder of FDR's peacetime presidency.

The problem was the Supreme Court. As early as 1929, FDR decided it was too conservative, too fearful of federal power. Suspicion turned to certainty in May 1935. In unanimous rulings, the justices declared the NRA and AAA unconstitutional because Congress had wrongly given the president its lawmaking powers. As Justice Louis D. Brandeis, among the court's most eminent members, told a White House aide, "This is the end of centralization, and I want you to go back and tell the president that we're not going to let this government centralize everything. It's come to an end."[60]

The Supreme Court is not supposed to follow election results. It must remain neutral to decide legal issues, interpret laws, and define the meaning of the Constitution. That is why, under Article III of the Constitution, justices, nominated by the president and confirmed by the Senate, serve life terms unless they resign, retire, or lose their seats for a serious crime. The Constitution says nothing about how many justices the court can have. Six times before in the nation's history, Congress changed the number, increasing or decreasing it. In 1869, Congress set the number at nine, as it is today.

Roosevelt's stunning victory at the polls went to his head, making him arrogant. Soon afterward, he asked Congress to pass a law allowing the president to add a new justice for every one who refused to retire after the age of seventy. This would allow FDR to appoint six new justices immediately. In a Fireside Chat, he made it seem as if the kindly gentleman in the White House wished only to ease the burden of these "aged and infirm judges," men no longer up to the job. Americans, of course, could trust him never to abuse his presidential powers![61]

FDR may have believed what he said, but countless others did not. Polls showed that 50 percent of Americans thought he was acting for purely political reasons. People began calling the "reorganization" a "court-packing" scheme—a brazen power grab. As a comic song put it:

> It's deliberate, it's deceptive,
> It's deplorable, it's delirious . . .
> It's de-bunk, it's de-lousy.

Citizens' groups, the press, and members of Congress reminded him that the Founders had built the separation of powers into the Constitution. No branch of government could override or dictate to the others.[62]

Democrats and Republicans buried their political hatchets to bury FDR's plan. During a reading of it in the Senate, Vice President John Nance Garner showed his displeasure by holding his nose and giving it a thumbs-down. In rejecting the proposal, the Senate Judiciary Committee came down hard:

> We recommend the rejection of the bill as a needless, futile and utterly dangerous abandonment of constitutional principle. . . . It is a proposal without precedent or justification. It would subjugate the courts to the will of Congress and the President, and thereby destroy the independence of the judiciary, the only certain shield of individual rights. . . . It points the way to the evasion of the Constitution and . . . violates every sacred tradition of American democracy. . . . Its ultimate operation would be to make this government one of men rather than one of law, . . . [making] the Constitution what the executive or legislative branches say it is.

Eventually, Roosevelt packed the court the old-fashioned way. Deaths and retirements allowed him to appoint eight justices.[63]

Still, his troubles were far from over. By early 1937, the economy was showing signs of recovery. FDR mistakenly took this as a signal to trim New Deal spending. At his urging, Congress made deep budget cuts. More, to reduce federal borrowing, it raised taxes on businesses and the wealthy. The effect was like a doctor's telling a patient to do vigorous exercise before fully recovering from a serious illness.

Budget cuts bled relief and recovery programs. State and local governments began to reduce salaries and hours and to fire employees. Higher income taxes led companies to hunker down rather than hire more workers; so did the National Labor Relations Act, which drove up labor costs. Social Security payroll taxes cut into workers' purchasing power further. Before long, the economy slipped into a depression within the Great Depression. Factory output plunged. Unemployment skyrocketed. As a result, Republicans made big gains in the congressional election of 1938. Joining with conservative Democrats, they killed plans for further federal programs. The New Deal was fast running out of steam.

What, then, did it achieve? A lot. Under FDR's leadership, the federal government put in place a series of crucial and long-overdue reforms. Picking up where Hoover had left off, FDR expanded the size and scope of the federal government, taking responsibility for the nation's economic well-being. The New Deal built needed public works, many still in use today. It saved lives through food and public health programs. Its work projects restored dignity and hope to millions. Labor gained the legal right to organize and bargain collectively with bosses. With Social Security, the elderly, children, and the unemployed became entitled to public support. Bank and stock market reforms protected savings and investments. Through these programs, and many others, Roosevelt began weaving the social safety net we now take for granted as "entitlements." Above all, he sustained democracy, avoiding the chaos born of economic collapse and despair.

That said, the New Deal failed to achieve its main goal: recovery. Historians disagree why. Some say the government did not spend enough to jolt the economy back into prosperity. Others say it spent too much to gain too little. Henry Morgenthau thought so, because he could see no end to the crisis. In March 1939, the frustrated Treasury secretary wrote in his diary: "We are spending more than we have ever spent and it does not work. . . . We have just as much unemployment as when we started [in 1933]. . . . And an enormous debt to boot! . . . . I can't see any daylight." It would take a second world war to end the Great Depression.[64]

A Social Security poster featuring a mother and child. (Date unknown)

THE SUPREME CRISIS

It must be said that had [President Roosevelt] not resolved to give aid to Britain in the supreme crisis through which we have passed, a hideous fate might have overwhelmed mankind and made its whole future for centuries sink into shame and ruin.
—Winston Churchill, 1945

THE DEVIL'S TWINS

Woodrow Wilson called the First World War the "war to end all war" and to "make the world safe for democracy." It did neither. The slaughter in the trenches, followed by a harsh peace treaty, planted the seeds of another and far more terrible conflict.

The Second World War sprang from a unique kind of dictatorship that emerged in Europe in the 1920s and 1930s. Dictators were nothing new in history. Until the twentieth century, however, they used force much as gangsters did: for their own material gain and survival. While controlling a government, they interfered in people's lives just enough to exploit them and crush opposition. Totalitarian dictators were different.

As the word suggests, totalitarianism is about total control of a nation by a leader and a political party. Through the party, the leader seeks not merely to command the government but to make every aspect of private life fit his ideology. An ideology is a body of ideas held as perfect, true, and good—in effect, a program of "social engineering" to reshape human nature and dominate the world. Thus, totalitarianism aims to steal more than material things. It aims to control everything that makes us human. Under it, individuals can have nothing of their own. No soul, no will, no privacy, no mind, no ideas, no thoughts, no desires, no doubts, no religion, no life.

Vladimir Lenin laid the foundations of Soviet totalitarianism. We recall that he, like Karl Marx, the founder of communism, wanted to create a utopia by seizing all private property and using it for the workers' benefit. In theory, the workers owned everything, because they produced it. In return for their labor and obedience, the Communist Party promised food, clothing, housing, education, recreation, and medical care. The reality, however, was quite different. Since they meant well, Lenin said, followers were entitled to do anything to achieve their goals. As the magazine *Red Sword* insisted, "To us, everything is permitted, for we are the first to raise the sword not to oppress races and reduce them to slavery, but to liberate humanity from its shackles."[1]

Soviet totalitarianism was firmly in place when Joseph Stalin took power after Lenin's death in 1924. Born in 1879, Joseph Djughashvili was the son of a drunken cobbler who beat him and his mother savagely. Leaving home in his teens, he changed his last name to Stalin—"man of steel"—after joining the Communist Party, which was then a small, secret organization hunted by the police.

Stalin was five feet four inches tall and not handsome, so different from Franklin Roosevelt. "He had a round, tubby figure and walked clumsily, like a small bear," an American diplomat noted. The tyrant had a pale complexion, short black hair flecked with gray, a shaggy mustache, and a withered left arm, the result of a childhood infection. His teeth were rotten, because he feared dentists, and his breath stank. Deep pits left over from smallpox dotted his cheeks. When he met people, his eyes darted to and fro, studying their every movement and expression. Zoya Zarubina, a government

Joseph Stalin, the leader of Russia from 1924 to 1953. (1942)

worker, noted, "His eyes were . . . golden yellowish. . . . But once, all of a sudden, you get eyeball to eyeball it is scary in the sense that he just pierces through you." It felt as if he were boring into your soul, reading your every thought.[2]

Though expelled from the seminary where his mother sent him to study for the priesthood, Stalin was a highly intelligent man; Harry Hopkins called him "an intelligent machine." He never forgot a face, fact, or conversation. Self-educated, he loved serious books, as FDR did not. Stalin had a private library of more than 20,000 volumes and read as much as 500 pages a day. His interests ranged from history and politics to economics, literature, philosophy, the arts and sciences. A careful reader, he underlined key sentences and ideas, writing comments in the margins and detailed summaries on separate slips of paper. Stalin, too, "read" people by the books they read. "If you want to know the people around you," he'd say "find out what they read." Following his own advice, he made a beeline for the bookshelves whenever he visited someone's house.[3]

In the USSR, people rarely saw him in person or heard his voice over the radio. Yet wherever they turned, his image followed them from the giant post-ers that covered city buildings. There was no escaping him. A woman wrote in her diary: "Stalin here, Stalin there, Stalin, Stalin everywhere. You can't go out to the kitchen, or sit on the toilet, or eat without Stalin following you. . . . He creeps into your guts and your very soul . . . gets into bed with you under the blanket, haunts your memories and your dreams."[4]

Stalin's official title, general secretary of the Communist Party, seemed too humble. Here are a few of the grand titles he preferred:

Great Leader

Great Helmsman

Great Master of Daring Revolutionary
  Decisions

Greatest Genius of All Times and
  Peoples

Greatest Military Leader of All
  Times and Peoples

Genius of Mankind

Leader of Progressive Humanity

Leader and Teacher of the Workers
  of the World

Leading Light of Science

Transformer of Nature

Father, Leader, Friend, and Teacher

Father of the Peoples

Driver of the Locomotive of History

Best Friend of All Children

He was praised as God Almighty, Creator and Lord of the World: "O Great Stalin, O Leader of the Peoples, Thou who didst give birth to man, Thou who didst make fertile the earth." Before starting the day's lessons, schoolchildren chanted, "Thank you, Comrade Stalin, for our happy childhoods." In these and other ways, he sought to control people's thoughts, instilling in them automatic obedience.[5]

Meeting the Genius of Mankind was a never-to-be-forgotten experience. A born actor, Stalin came across as modest, polite, and reasonable. On more than one occasion, senior German diplomats reported, "He could charm anyone." But this was a mask, and behind it the demon lurked. A Red Army general, author of a classic biography of Stalin, said it best: "It was impossible to find and touch in him any chords of human feeling. . . . He despised pity, sympathy, mercy. . . . Even worse, Stalin found no place for moral values in politics, either."[6]

Those closest to Stalin knew the real man. Once, his wife, Nadya, burst out, "You're a torturer, that's what you are! You torture your own son, you torture your wife, you've tortured the whole people till they can take no more." His son Yakov, made miserable by his verbal abuse, shot himself but lived. "Ha! You missed!" Stalin snarled. Nadya did not miss; she put a bullet into her heart rather than endure life with him. Though Stalin pampered their daughter, Svetlana, as a child, she saw behind the mask, too. As she grew up, he became harsh, even brutal, toward her, slapping her face and taunting her as ugly. In her twenties, during a New Year's party, he grabbed her hair with his fist and dragged her onto the dance floor. Shortly before her death at age eighty-five, Svetlana denounced her father as "a moral and spiritual monster." She never forgave his cruelty. "He broke my life," she said. "He broke my life."[7]

Stalin trusted no one, "not even myself." His favorite sayings reveal a hard, cynical person. Asked if he knew the meaning of gratitude, Stalin replied, "Oh, yes, I know; I know very well: it is a sickness suffered by dogs." The truth was whatever he said, and freedom of the press was meaningless because "paper has no shame; it will take anything printed on it." He had an iron rule: Never forget, never forgive, always get even. Disagreement signaled disloyalty. Criticism was an insult. When in doubt, Stalin had one solution: "Death solves all problems—no man, no problem." The Great Leader enjoyed setting traps for "enemies" and watching them squirm. A patient man, he planned his moves long, often years, in advance, like a diabolical chess master. "The sweetest thing in life," he noted, "is to mark a victim, prepare the blow carefully, strike hard, and then go to bed and sleep peacefully." It was said that "every killing is a treat" for Stalin.[8]

In the early 1930s, as the First New Deal began, Stalin abolished private ownership of land. To eat, peasants must now surrender their farms and work on large state-owned farms under Communist managers. Rather than abandon their age-old way of life, based on hard work and religious devotion, millions resisted. Stalin crushed them. He sent the NKVD (secret police), Red Army units, and "activists" from the cities to seize food supplies, crops, and livestock, leaving peasants only grass, weeds, and tree bark to eat. When resisters fled to the forests, the Red Army used poison gas to kill them. Stalin had no regrets. Later, he told Winston Churchill, the British prime minister, he had "dealt with" 10 million peasants, as "it was absolutely necessary" to modernize Soviet agriculture. Most had starved to death. Others survived by cannibalism, killing and eating even their own children.[9]

Stalin's Great Terror mirrored Lenin's Red Terror, only on an immensely deadlier scale. The "Boss," an aide said, "treated everyone politically"—that is, Stalin judged people in terms of his political needs. In the late 1930s, he ordered the NKVD to "purge," or cleanse, the USSR of "bad elements." These bloodhounds were everywhere. The NKVD had offices not only in every city and town but in all army camps, railroad stations, hotels, universities, and factories. Anyone who doubted the Great Helmsman, or who he thought *might* oppose him, along with his or her family, relatives, friends, neighbors, and co-workers, became "enemies of the people."[10]

Each night, the NKVD arrested hundreds and took them to secret prisons in "black crows," black vans with blackened windows. There, torturers made them confess to "crimes," implicating yet others. "Beat, beat and, once again, beat!" Stalin shouted at NKVD thugs. Many victims, however, did not undergo the formality of torture and confession; upon arrest, they got a bullet in the head and an unmarked grave. Still not satisfied, Stalin purged the NKVD itself, the Communist Party, and the armed forces, murdering 43,000 officers, including top generals and admirals. Stalin even had some of his late wife's relatives shot, because, he said, "they knew too much."

From 1937 to 1939 alone, he signed more than 400 death lists. On December 12, 1937, a typical day, Stalin approved 3,167 death sentences, and then went to his private movie theater to see *The Merry Fellows,* a comedy. The Best Friend of All Children also ordered boys and girls, starting at age twelve, shot for stealing. If you were hungry and unlucky, you could die for a potato![11]

To test their loyalty, the Driver of the Locomotive of History put his closest aides through humiliating ordeals. One New Year's Eve, for example, he rolled pieces of paper into tubes and put them on the fingers of his private secretary. Then he lit a match. The man squirmed in pain but dared not put them out. Stalin laughed at this little "joke." Another time, during a meeting of his close advisers, he growled at one, "Shut up, imbecile." Others he addressed in words we cannot repeat here. Battle-hardened generals trembled and stammered in his presence.[12]

Russians had a saying, whispered only if they felt safe: "In the Soviet Union, there are only three categories of people—those who were in prison, those who are in prison, and those who will be in prison." Stalin sent millions of political "undesirables" to lingering deaths in prisons or in the Gulag, short for the Russian words for Chief Administration for Corrective Labor Camps. First used by Lenin, the Gulag consisted of hundreds of camps in the wilds of Siberia, Central Asia, and the Arctic.[13]

Under its Great Leader, the USSR became the only major twentieth-century country to have a permanent slave labor system. In the Gulag, the rule was, if you don't work, you don't eat. It was a matter of survival of the fittest, and most inmates, both men and women, fell behind because of the backbreaking work. As a result, they died of hunger and exhaustion while cutting trees, digging canals, and mining coal and gold. Historians believe that around a million Gulag inmates died in an "average" year. Stalin also ordered that, starting at age fifteen, so-called "socially dangerous children" go to the Gulag with their parents. Younger children went to state orphanages, where their names were changed, and they grew up not knowing anything about their families. In all, Stalin caused the deaths of around 20.8 million of his own people in peacetime.

Meanwhile, in 1933, Adolf Hitler took power in Germany. He was born in Austria in 1889 to a civil servant and his wife. Five feet nine inches tall, Hitler looked, some said, like a waiter in a cheap restaurant with his pasty complexion, mousy hair, and toothbrush-like mustache. His eyes, like Stalin's, were his most striking physical feature. Brilliant blue in color, they had a magnetic, almost hypnotic, effect. Foreign diplomats and journalists who met him noted that they "seem at times to spurt fire" and were "the eyes of a fanatic." There was no evading their power. American newsman Louis Lochner heard Germans constantly saying, "Once you look into Hitler's eyes, you are his devoted follower forever." If he locked eyes with you, it took every ounce of will to turn away.[14]

In his youth, Hitler dreamed of becoming a great artist but lacked the talent. After years of drifting, doing odd jobs and living in flophouses, he enlisted in the German army at the start of the First World War. Rising to the rank of corporal, he was wounded during trench fighting in France and Belgium; twice he won medals for bravery. With Germany's defeat in 1919, as Franklin Roosevelt closed naval bases in France, Hitler left the army. Soon afterward, he joined the tiny German Workers' Party, which shared his determination to scrap the Treaty of Versailles.

Almost immediately, Hitler learned something terrible and yet amazing about himself. He had a gift for public speaking. The ex-soldier would begin a

~~~ Adolf Hitler poses with a group of SS members soon after his appointment as chancellor of Germany. (February 1, 1933)

speech slowly, sensing his listeners' mood by their facial expressions and body language. Suddenly he'd whip himself into a frenzy. His face flushed, his eyes bulging, he spat hatred for Germany's enemies. Violent words—"fight," "smash," "crush," "destroy," "annihilate"—gushed from his mouth.

Hitler's raw emotion ignited the audience as if a diabolical magician had seized their minds. People got carried away, cheering, trembling, sobbing, screaming, shrieking, howling, moaning, and swooning. "They reminded me," wrote the American journalist William L. Shirer, "of the crazed expression I once saw in the back country of Louisiana on the faces of some Holy Rollers who were about to hit the trail. They looked up at him as if he were a Messiah, their faces transformed into something positively inhuman." However, like Stalin, Hitler could come across as likable and sincere, even charming, when he met people face to face. But if things did not go his way, he lost all self-control, flying into a furious, arm-flailing rage.[15]

Millions of Germans were ready to listen to Hitler's ranting. Angry at the loss of the war and humiliated by the Versailles treaty, they were also desperate. Germany had never fully recovered from the economic hardship brought on by the First World War. In the 1930s, as the Great Depression spread to Europe, unemployment skyrocketed. In Germany, the hardest-hit country, hunger and misery were every bit as severe as in America during those years. Dreadful living conditions, and his own talents, enabled Hitler to gain control of the party, renaming it the National Socialist German Workers' Party—Nazi for

short. In March 1933, as FDR declared a bank holiday, Hitler won a free election, vowing to create the Third Reich, a Nazi empire to last a thousand years.

Once in power, Hitler used his control of the government to install a totalitarian system. Like Stalin, he ruled through force, fear, and brainwashing. His Gestapo (secret state police) could arrest anyone for anything and do anything to him or her without fear of the law, for Hitler was the law in Germany. On his orders, Nazis seized all newspapers, radio stations, and private organizations: social clubs, sports clubs, youth groups, business associations, law and medical societies, schools and universities. Nazi bullyboys called Storm Troopers scoured libraries, making bonfires of "degenerate" books. Authors who did not follow the Nazi line were forbidden to write. For Hitler, as for Stalin, truth was what he said it was. A believer in the "big lie," he felt that if he lied long enough and loud enough, people would eventually believe it, no matter how absurd.

Brainwashing meant portraying Hitler as the nation's savior, heaven-sent to rescue her in a time of need. God, supposedly, had revealed himself to Germany through this failed artist. Whenever Germans met, they had to raise their right arms in the Nazi salute and cry, *"Heil*

Hitler" (Hail Hitler). Schoolchildren gave the Hitler salute anywhere from 50 to 150 times a day. Wherever you turned, you saw the swastika displayed on flags, banners, armbands, posters, lapel pins, buttons, money, and postage stamps. The swastika is a cross with the ends of the arms bent clockwise, at right angles. An ancient good-luck symbol, it was used by Native Americans in clothing decorations and pottery designs. Hitler made the swastika the most feared and hated symbol of the twentieth century.

Hitler was the *Fuehrer* (leader) of the German people. His image, like Stalin's, was everywhere. Nazis often had "Hitler corners" in their homes, flower-decorated shrines with candles burning

A book burning of "un-German" literature in Berlin. (May 11, 1933)

before his photograph and a swastika flag. Signs covered hillsides, declaring,

We believe in Holy Germany
Holy Germany is Hitler!
We believe in Holy Hitler!

Kindergartners sang:

Adolf Hitler is our savior, our hero,
He is the noblest thing in the whole wide
*   world.*
For Hitler we live,
For Hitler we die.
Our Hitler is our Lord,
Who rules a brave new world.

Four members of the Hitler Youth blowing horns draped with Nazi flags, here showing the *sig* rune, which symbolizes victory (*Sieg* in German) and is also the symbol of the SS. (1934)

And he also performed "miracles." Newspapers carried stories of women calling his name in childbirth and their pain vanishing instantly. Even animals praised him. When asked "Who is Adolf Hitler?" a dog barked, in perfect German, "My Fuehrer." This, the reporter noted, was because Hitler loved animals.[16]

Hitler aimed to plant totalitarianism in the minds and hearts of Germany's young. He would make them, he told leaders of Nazi youth organizations, "learn nothing else but to think as Germans and act as Germans" by surrounding them with an all-Nazi environment.

From nursery school through college and the army, they would learn to see the world through his eyes, and his alone. By the time he finished with them, Hitler boasted, "they will not be free again for the rest of their lives." They would glorify war, as he did. Thus, the League of German Girls learned it was their duty, married or not, to give the Fuehrer a child, a future soldier or bearer of future soldiers. The Hitler Youth, the Nazi boys' organization, taught members how to die before they learned how to live. While doing military exercises, they chanted, "We were born to die for

Germany." And they did, in vast numbers, having spent most of their conscious lives undergoing brainwashing. In the closing days of the Second World War, Allied soldiers considered fanatical fourteen-years-olds nicknamed "Werewolves" more dangerous than regular Nazi soldiers, since they fought so recklessly. Some seriously wounded Werewolves preferred to die staring at wallet-size photographs of Hitler rather than accept medical treatment from "racially inferior" doctors.[17]

Darkness and monstrosities filled the Fuehrer's mental world. A racist since his teenage years, Hitler believed a "master race," embodied by "pure-blooded" German or Aryan "supermen," should rule the world through mass murder. He regarded others' lives as his property to preserve or destroy as he saw fit. "If I can send the flower of the German nation into the hell of war without the smallest pity," he told a follower, "then I surely have the right to remove millions of an inferior race that breeds like vermin!"[18]

Above all, Hitler despised Jews. Violent anti-Semitism—hatred of Jews— dates from the Middle Ages, when Christian mobs massacred Jews throughout Europe, claiming their ancestors killed Jesus Christ. In modern times, religious hatred gave way to racism. Rather than see Jewish people as a religious community, Hitler thought them a separate race, human only in outward appearance. "The Jew is the anti-man, the creature of another god. He must have come from another root of the human race," declared the Fuehrer. "He is a creature outside nature and alien to nature."[19]

Believing Jews the cause of all evil, Hitler always referred to them in degrading terms such as "the Jewish virus," "the Jewish cancer," and "Jewish parasites." The Fuehrer blamed Jews for everything wrong in the world, from disease and war to the Great Depression and communism. Jews, he insisted, aimed at destroying the Aryan race by violating it sexually—"poisoning" its blood through intermarriage or "mating." Like racism itself, these charges were myth and superstition stirred in a cauldron of ignorance and hatred. Jews are no more a race than Christians or Muslims, Americans or baseball fans. No matter. Hitler believed what he preached—that is what counted. And he acted on his beliefs when he got the chance. He launched a war to dominate the world *and* annihilate the Jews.

A mass assembly of German troops at a Nuremberg rally. (November 9, 1935)

PARTNERS IN CRIME

We remember that the Great Depression affected all capitalist countries. But Hitler wanted war, so, unlike Roosevelt, he did not create alphabet soup agencies. Instead, he revived Germany's economy by rebuilding its military. In violation of the Treaty of Versailles, factories produced advanced types of aircraft, ships, tanks, artillery, and munitions. Young men went into the armed forces, ending unemployment. Within five years of taking power, Hitler commanded the world's most modern war machine.

For his plans to succeed, the Fuehrer decided, he must conquer the Soviet Union, for two reasons. First, he said, Germany's expanding population required *Lebensraum,* or "living space," in the east, lands at that point inhabited by "subhumans," people of "inferior blood." Second, Germany lacked the vast amounts of raw materials—oil, minerals, and metals—needed "for waging war against continents," his term for seeking world domination. Moreover, the Allied "hunger blockade" during the First World War was an experience no German could forget. Nor could Hitler. Since the USSR had abundant fertile soil and raw materials, seizing these would make Germany self-sufficient in wartime.

Poland was the gateway to the USSR. To position himself to open that gate, Hitler in 1938 seized Austria and Czechoslovakia through threats of war. Poland's turn came the next year. Now, however, he expected a war to break out. Great Britain and France had defense treaties with Poland. If he attacked and they honored the treaties, he must divide Germany's forces, as in the First World War. Thus, to avoid a dangerous two-front war, Hitler turned to Stalin, whose country he secretly aimed to destroy.

Though Stalin despised Nazism, he decided to help his fellow totalitarian. By doing so, he hoped to gain eastern Poland, securing the USSR's western border with Germany. He also had a broader, more sinister aim. Like Lenin, Stalin thought only another world war would enable communism to spread across the globe. If Germany and the democracies fought, he meant to sit on the sidelines. "The worse the fight between them, the better for us," he told his henchmen. "Our advantage lies in their fight being without a quick victory for one side or the other." After they exhausted themselves on the battlefield, and their starving citizens rebelled, he would send the Red Army to overrun Western Europe.[20]

Through Hitler, Stalin ignited the

Second World War. On August 23, 1939, as the smiling tyrant looked on, Soviet and Nazi diplomats signed a treaty pledging to stay neutral if the other country fought a third one. The Fuehrer was jubilant. When the telephone call came from Moscow, he hammered his fists on his office wall, shouting, "Now I have the world in my pocket!" Winston Churchill compared the Nazi-Soviet Pact to "shaking hands with murder."[21]

The murdering began at dawn on September 1 as Nazi armies invaded Poland. "Have no pity," Hitler ordered his generals. "Mercilessly send to death men, women, and children of Polish descent or language." Later that day, he secretly ordered the murder of some 200,000 incurably ill German hospital patients. He also planned to do away with tens of thousands of crippled German veterans of the First World War—and later the Second World War. One crime, war, was to cover another—the mass murder of Germans deemed "useless eaters" and "lives unworthy of life."[22]

Though Britain and France declared war on Germany, they were unable, geographically or militarily, to fight in Eastern Europe. There, Hitler had all the advantages. The First World War had taught him to avoid trench warfare. Instead, he decided that victory depended on fast-paced battles of constant movement. Thus, his generals devised a style of fighting called *Blitzkrieg* (lightning war), combining attacks by aircraft, tanks, and infantry units. Caught by surprise, Polish forces saw their resistance crumble after a few days.

Stalin delivered the fatal blow. On September 17, he sent the Red Army to stab Poland in the back. Next day, the *New York Times* observed: "Germany having killed the prey, Soviet Russia will seize that part of the carcass that Germany cannot use. It will play the noble role of hyena to the German lion." At-

Soviet foreign minister Vyacheslav Molotov signs the Nazi-Soviet Non-Aggression Pact as Stalin smiles in the background. (August 23, 1939)

tacked front and rear, outnumbered and outgunned, Poland gave up on September 20. After the formal surrender, the lion and the hyena held a joint victory parade. Nazi and Soviet generals saluted and grinned, shook hands and drank champagne toasts to each other. Stalin seized eastern Poland, about a third of the country; Hitler took the rest. Meanwhile, tens of thousands of Polish civilians, soldiers, and airmen escaped to neighboring countries. Over the next few months, they made their way to France, where they formed new units to carry on the fight against Hitler. Polish officials fled to England, setting up a government-in-exile.

With the Fuehrer's blessing, Stalin seized the small countries along the Baltic Sea: Estonia, Latvia, and Lithuania. However, he and Hitler most wanted to destroy the Polish nation, not merely conquer it. To crush resistance, they sought to terrorize the people, creating a climate of anxiety and fear. They began by "decapitating" Poland: eliminating its leaders. This basically was anyone with an education and initiative. In the nightmare time that followed, NKVD and Gestapo officers met to draw up and share lists of likely victims. Whole categories of people were condemned not for anything they'd done but because

they might influence others. Victims included politicians, government officials, university graduates, schoolteachers, professors, librarians, clergymen, judges, lawyers, doctors, journalists, company managers, trade union leaders, landowners, and members of the nobility.

The conquerors scoured the areas under their control. Altogether, they shot 225,000 Poles within a few weeks, often before horrified bystanders "to set an example." In addition, the Soviets shipped over 1.2 million Poles to the Gulag. To stun and demoralize them, a squad of Red Army or NKVD men would bang on the door in the middle of the night, jarring the household awake. *Quick! Quick! You have twenty minutes to pack your things!* Fathers and sons were forced to kneel, faces to the wall, while the mothers and daughters gathered whatever they could. Trucks took the prisoners to the local railroad station, where guards forced them into cattle cars—often sixty to a car—with no food, windows, or heat. The toilet was a hole in the floor. To relieve themselves, people had to squat over the hole in full view of everyone.

Wiesława Saternus was twelve at the time of her family's deportation. She recalled: "Then they locked the wagons. It was very noisy. I remember that noise, like the knocking on the door at night. I will never forget it.... We knew then that we had been locked in and were in slavery." The journey might take from a week to two months, depending on the destination and weather; in Siberia, in winter, snowdrifts might block the tracks for days. Many died along the way. Occasionally, NKVD men went from car to car, shouting, "Are there any frozen children?" No wonder that survivors called the USSR "that hell" and prayed for the devil to "take Stalin away."[23]

Meanwhile, Stalin became the Nazis' eager helper. Calling the USSR Germany's "new partner" and Hitler her "great Fuehrer," he promised that, should his ally face defeat, "the Soviet people will come to Germany's aid" with a huge army. For good measure, he blamed the democracies for starting the war, a blatant lie. "It is not Germany who has attacked England and France," he announced, "but England and France who have attacked Germany." Stalin also fed the Nazi war machine. To evade the British naval blockade, he bought rubber in Asia, sending it to Germany on the Trans-Siberian Railway. His railways also delivered 3 million tons of Soviet goods vital to the Nazi war machine: oil, meat, grain, cotton, copper, and chemicals used to make explosives.[24]

BRITAIN ALONE

After Britain declared war, her army moved into northern France to block a German advance through Belgium. Similarly, Hitler shifted the bulk of his forces to the German-French-Belgian border after crushing Poland. Throughout the winter of 1939–1940, the armies prepared for battle when the weather improved.

Come spring, Hitler unleashed a devastating blitzkrieg. April 1940 saw Nazi forces quickly overrun Denmark and Norway. In May, they seized Belgium and Holland. France was next. In the First World War, she fought fiercely for four years. Now resistance fell away in two weeks.

Stalin helped defeat France. He had the head of the French Communist Party broadcast from Moscow, urging French troops to surrender. Communist-led labor unions disabled arms factories; railway unions refused to move supplies to the front. The civilized world stood aghast as beautiful Paris, the City of Light, lay at the Nazis' feet. When Hitler's troops marched in, Stalin sent congratulations on "the brilliant success of the German Army." Elsewhere, German tank columns trapped the remaining Allied units on the beach near Dunkirk, a French seaport on the English Channel.

From May 26 to June 4, British warships and civilian boats rescued 338,000 British, French, Belgian, and Polish troops. They left with just the clothes on their backs. On the beach lay all their heavy equipment: tanks, trucks, artillery, and communications gear. "Never has a great nation been so naked before her foes," said Prime Minister Winston Churchill.[25]

This time Stalin helped Hitler by repairing Nazi vessels in Soviet shipyards. He even let Hitler build a submarine base on the Arctic Ocean. Within days of the Dunkirk rescue, the Fuehrer sent his *Luftwaffe* (air force) against England. Advanced Soviet weather reports enabled Luftwaffe planners to mount raids when conditions were best. Hitler hoped to terrorize the English, paving the way for his invasion fleet. During the Battle of Britain that followed bombs rained on airfields, dockyards, and cities for weeks on end.

Through the magic of radio, people across the Atlantic experienced the bombings in real time. In 1940, Edward R. Murrow led a team of American

An aircraft spotter on the roof of a building in London, with St. Paul's Cathedral in the background. (Date unknown)

newscasters based in London. As Nazi bombers droned overhead, Murrow stood on a rooftop with his microphone. He made Americans feel, and not just hear, what the English were going through. Sirens wailing. Antiaircraft guns blazing. Bombs exploding. Streets lit by the glow of burning buildings. The courage of "little people," the "unsung heroes," "those black-faced men with bloodshot eyes fighting fires, the girls who cradle the steering wheel of a heavy ambulance in their arms, the policeman who stands guard over that unexploded bomb." Despite all, he reported, "not once have I heard man, woman, or child suggest that Britain should throw in her

hand." When the air raids began, polls showed that only 16 percent of Americans favored aiding Britain. Within weeks, the number rose to 52 percent, largely because of Murrow's broadcasts.[26]

Another struggle, the Battle of the Atlantic, raged out of sight of land. During the First World War, U-boats had to take a roundabout route to the Atlantic. Now, with France's surrender, the Nazis built bases along the coast, giving them direct access to the Atlantic sea-lanes. Hitler's "gray wolves" were bigger, faster, and better armed than those of the previous war.

Two-thirds of Britain's food and 95 percent of her oil came from North and South America. Cargo ships sailed in convoys of up to 160 that were escorted by destroyers equipped with sonar, a recent invention to detect U-boats with sound waves. Once the submarines were located, these sleek vessels raced in with depth charges.

Unfortunately, Britain lacked sufficient destroyers to protect convoys properly. Aircraft, too, had limitations. As in the First World War, submarines had to run on the surface to recharge their electric batteries, exposing themselves to attack. However, land-based planes could not carry enough fuel to patrol the "Black Pit," a 600-mile-wide

CBS news correspondent Edward R. Murrow at his typewriter in wartime London. (1939–1945)

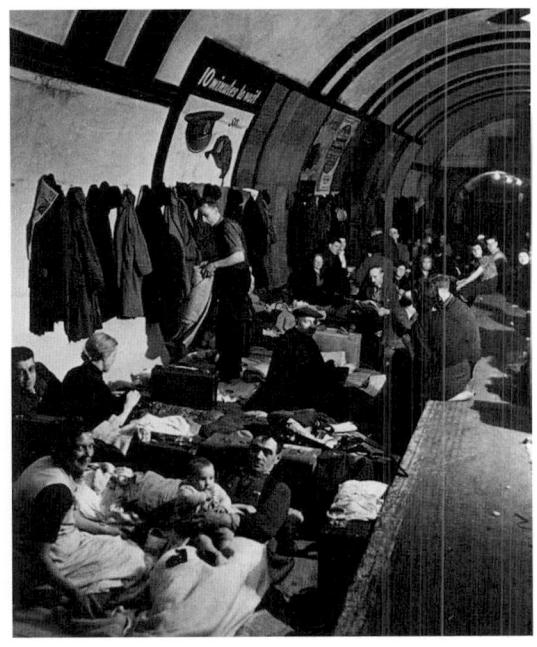

An underground tube station converted into an air-raid shelter in London's West End. (Date unknown)

area of the Atlantic southeast of Greenland. Since this was the most trafficked part of the Atlantic, groups of submarines called "wolf packs" hunted there. In the first fifteen months of the war, they sank 1,281 ships, or a quarter of Britain's entire merchant marine. With them torpedoing ships faster than shipyards could build new ones, it seemed only a matter of time before Hitler starved Britain into surrender.

NEUTRALITY

Americans were too busy with their own problems to worry about Europe. Be-

sides, the First World War had soured them on foreign wars. Nearly 120,000 Yanks had died, and thousands more had returned blind, crippled, or so disfigured they wore face masks in public. Critics claimed that America had fought merely to enrich "merchants of death," greedy bankers and arms makers. Ordinary folks were disgusted with Europe. It was "a goddamn madhouse," said novelist John Dos Passos. "To hell with Europe!" Though Americans would fight if attacked, they vowed to stay out of future European bloodbaths. So, in 1935, Congress passed the Neutrality Act; other acts followed in 1936 and 1937. These banned lending money or selling weapons to any nation at war, including victims of aggression.[27]

Nevertheless, there was Adolf Hitler. Even before the war, Franklin Roosevelt, to his credit, understood the Nazi leader better than almost anyone else in the democracies. While listening to his speeches crackling over the radio, which he translated for aides, FDR realized this man was not right in the head. Hitler's effect on audiences revolted him. "He shrieks, his histrionics and the effect on the huge audience—They did not applaud—they made noises like animals," FDR wrote a cousin. Privately, he described Hitler as "this wild man," "a nut," "pure, unadulterated evil," and "that sonofabitch." "Hitler," declared FDR, "is the most devastating and all-pervading conqueror and destroyer in the last thousand years. We believe there is no geographic limit whatsoever to his infamous plans."[28]

Roosevelt was right, though he did not have Hitler's own words to prove it. We do. Years earlier, in 1928, he had dictated a secret book, which was discovered and published three decades later under the title *Hitler's Second Book*. In it, the future Fuehrer admitted that he would not—*could* not—stop himself. Given the chance, he would carry aggression across the globe. "Wherever our success ends," he insisted, "that will always be the starting point of a new battle." Thus, for the sake of humanity, the man in the White House felt he dared not let this "madman" succeed.[29]

Early in 1940, with Nazi armies massing along the French border, Roosevelt asked Congress to revise the Neutrality Acts. Members agreed. While American ships could not deliver war supplies to a fighting nation, such nations could buy these through "cash-and-carry"—that is, a nation could pay cash for its purchases and carry them away in its own ships, as in the First World War. Even so, FDR had to be careful. Congress and the public would not tolerate anything that might drag America into war. So he cleverly described cash-and-carry as an economic program aimed at creating jobs.

Everything changed in the spring. In the days after Dunkirk, orders flew from the Oval Study. Roosevelt demanded that Britain's losses be replaced, but the military protested, saying it had no weapons to spare. Driven by the White House, the army turned up "surplus" First World War–era rifles (500,000), machine guns (80,000), cannons (900), and ammunition (130 million rounds). Roosevelt went further, with secret programs to aid the island nation. He allowed RAF pilots and British Tank Corps soldiers to train at American bases. East Coast shipyards quietly repaired vessels damaged in clashes with wolf packs.

These measures did not go far enough for Britain's prime minister, Winston Churchill. Eight years older than FDR, Churchill had been born in a palace, the son of an English lord and an American mother. Bald with puffy red cheeks, a sagging belly, and weak, puny muscles, he was a plain-looking man who ate rich food, smoked big cigars, and drank as much whiskey as he pleased, which was a lot. Among his many interests, he painted landscapes, gardened, and wrote

 Winston Churchill, the prime minister of England during World War II. (March 1943)

bestselling history books. Of this bundle of nervous energy, an aide observed: "When he isn't fast asleep he's a volcano." Having served for a time in the trenches during the First World War, Churchill was tough-minded and ruthless. He would do anything to save Britain from that "bloodthirsty guttersnipe" Hitler.[30]

The guttersnipe nevertheless had the upper hand. Churchill knew there was no way Britain could survive, let alone defeat Hitler, by herself. On the morning of May 19, 1940, four days before the Dunkirk evacuation began, his son Randolph came by while he was shaving. Randolph, downhearted, feared the worst. Suddenly his father brightened, as if a brilliant idea had popped into his mind. While drying his face, Churchill said with deep feeling. "I shall drag the United States in."[31]

THE SECRET WAR

In June, an RAF plane landed in Virginia. It carried William S. Stephenson, a former fighter pilot and champion boxer who had made millions in various business ventures, including an early version of the fax machine. Code-named Intrepid, he embodied the word's meaning: courageous and dauntless.

Stephenson was the prime minister's personal representative to the president. During a White House meeting, he presented Churchill's letter of introduction and explained his mission. What he planned was so daring, and so illegal, he needed presidential approval. Intrepid intended to wage "secret warfare" on, and from, American soil—*neutral* American soil. First, he would locate and kill Nazi agents operating in North and South America. Second, he would train agents for special operations in Nazi-held Europe. Finally, he would convince Americans to enter the war.

Roosevelt was enthusiastic. "I'm your most valuable secret agent," he said. He also told J. Edgar Hoover, director of the Federal Bureau of Investigation, that he wanted "the closest marriage possible between the FBI and British Intelligence." Hoover agreed, suggesting a bland, say-nothing cover name for Stephenson's operation: British Security Coordination (BSC).[32]

Stephenson set up headquarters in Rockefeller Center on Fifth Avenue in New York City, opposite St. Patrick's Cathedral. The Rockefeller family rented BSC two floors of prime Manhattan real estate for a penny a year. Insiders called BSC a "full size secret police." Its activities often violated American law, but Intrepid operated with White House consent. As his *Secret History of British Intelligence in the Americas* shows, the White House "winked at" BSC activities. In 1999, historian David Stafford noted that evidence recently released in Britain proves FDR knew about and "gladly played along with British 'dirty tricks.'" Had the press learned of this in 1940, the resulting scandal might well have led to Roosevelt's impeachment. But that was a risk he felt he must take. The stakes were too high to do otherwise.[33]

Eventually, Stephenson had about 3,000 agents, members of Britain's regular secret services, plus Canadian and American recruits. To teach agents the "black arts," skills needed to work behind enemy lines, he built a secret base.

Known as Camp X, it lay on the Canadian shore of Lake Ontario, opposite Rochester, New York. There, members of the underworld joined veteran British and Canadian police officers to give courses in burglary, safecracking, document forging, and assassination by gun, knife, and bomb. In effect, Stephenson created a University of Dirty Tricks.

In America, Intrepid's men guarded Britain-bound supplies. Thanks to their vigilance, there was no repeat of the Black Tom explosion; German agents never damaged or delayed an arms shipment in an American port. Nor did Stephenson blink at violence. He told Americans what to expect if they joined BSC. "For security reasons," he advised recruit Ernest Cuneo, "I can't tell you what sort of job it would be. All I can say is that if you join us . . . you mustn't be afraid of murder." He meant it. Once, a BSC "disposal squad" shot a British sailor caught selling information to a German spy. Another time, a taxi sped away after "accidentally" running over Captain Ulrich von der Osten, of German naval intelligence, in New York's Times Square. Texas oilman William Rhodes Davis suffered a fatal "heart attack"; he had been smuggling Mexican oil to Germany. At BSC's request, the FBI asked local police not to investigate Davis's death.[34]

Finally, Stephenson set out to influence American public opinion. The idea was to show how helping Britain helped America and to brand opponents as unpatriotic. Intrepid funded newspapers, set up aid-to-Britain committees, and even used a Boston radio station to get the British message across. Walter Winchell and Drew Pearson, prominent journalists, interpreted the news in Britain's favor, as did *New York Times* columnists. BSC put out fake public opinion polls to discredit Roosevelt's critics. It also issued pamphlets instructing American friends how to harass critics. They could, for example, call late at night and hang up or drop dead rats into water tanks and sand into automobile gas tanks.[35]

THE THIRD TERM

Nineteen forty was a presidential election year. Should Roosevelt run again? George Washington had served two terms, creating a tradition. FDR hesitated about breaking that tradition. Besides, he was tired—very tired. One day, he lost control. "I am chained to this chair from morning till night," he shouted at Senator George Norris. "You sit in your office too, but if something goes wrong or you get irritated or tired, you can get up and walk around, or you can go into another room. But I can't. I am tied down to this chair day after day, week after week, and month after month. And I can't stand it any longer. I can't go on with it."[36]

Nevertheless, there was Hitler, victorious and menacing. What to do? Vanity played a role in Roosevelt's decision; he felt only he could lead the nation through the deepening crisis. Also, the ideal of duty bred into him in childhood influenced his decision. In accepting the Democratic nomination, he said, "My conscience will not let me turn my back on a call to service."[37]

The Republican candidate, Indiana businessman Wendell L. Willkie, feared that a third term for Roosevelt might bring "the destruction of our democracy." Where would it end? Would a popular president get elected and reelected, for life? While Willkie knew nothing of Intrepid and BSC, he warned that aiding Britain would drag America into the war. Willkie's supporters hammered away on the war issue. A Republican radio commercial bluntly told voters, "When your boy is dying on some battlefield . . . crying out, 'Mother! Mother!' . . . blame YOURSELF, because you sent Franklin D. Roosevelt back to the White House!"[38]

As the campaign heated up, FDR took political risks he would not have dared in normal times. Britain's situation had become desperate. When Churchill asked for help in protecting the Atlantic convoys, he agreed. On September 3, FDR gave fifty First World War–era destroyers in return for leases on bases in Canada and the British West Indies. Churchill would call the destroyer deal "a decidedly unneutral act by the United States." So it was. The president's action raised British morale, signaling that he was with them.[39]

Another signal came on September 16. To meet the Nazi threat, America had to rebuild her armed forces. Yet that involved something Roosevelt knew voters would dislike. At his urging, however, Congress enacted the first peacetime draft in the nation's history. Called "selective service," the draft began on October 29, a week before Election Day. To reassure the country, FDR addressed the draft issue in a speech. "I will say it again and again and again: Your boys are not going to be sent into any foreign wars. They are going into training to form a

〰 Secretary of the Navy Frank Knox, blindfolded, drawing a number during the first peacetime draft lottery for compulsory military service. Behind him, from left to right, are FDR, Major Edward S. Shattuck, and Lt. Colonel Charles R. Morris. (October 29, 1940)

force so strong that...it will keep the threat of war from our shores."[40]

His gamble over the destroyers and the draft paid off. Voters still trusted Roosevelt's leadership. He defeated Willkie by almost 5 million votes, carrying thirty-eight of the forty-eight states. Hitler took the result badly. FDR, he raged, "is more responsible for keeping up Britain's resistance...than any other factor in the war except Winston Churchill." The very sound of FDR's name drove him into a frenzy. The Nazi press became hysterical, too, calling him a "butcher," a "cannibal in a white collar," and a "depraved Jewish scoundrel."[41]

ARSENAL OF DEMOCRACY

After his reelection, Roosevelt boarded a navy cruiser for a Caribbean vacation. While he was sunbathing on deck, a seaplane arrived with a letter from Churchill. Cash-and-carry, the prime minister said, had outlived its usefulness. Britain would soon run out of cash to pay for American war supplies and could not borrow what she needed because of the Neutrality Acts. FDR must exert every effort to help; otherwise Britain might well be forced to surrender to Hitler's terms.

The president decided to ask Congress for a law allowing him to sell, give, lend, or lease equipment to any nation fighting the Nazis. FDR called the program "Lend-Lease." In a Fireside Chat on December 29, 1940, he showed a keen understanding of the danger Hitler posed to humanity. Experience, he said, taught that "no nation can appease the Nazis. No man can tame a tiger into a kitten by stroking it.... We know now that a nation can have peace with the Nazis only at the price of total surrender." Britain, he continued, did not want American troops, nor would he send them if she did. She wanted only the weapons to defend herself, and thus also America. If the island nation

American-built 155 mm howitzers, shipped to England as Lend-Lease, reach an ordnance depot on their way to action. (1941)

went down, so would we. America had no choice. "We must become the great arsenal of democracy." A few days later (January 6, 1941), he told Congress that America was duty-bound to defend the Four Freedoms—freedom of speech, freedom of religion, freedom from want, freedom from fear—"everywhere in the world." Congress passed the Lend-Lease Act on March 7, 1941.[42]

A tiny minority, dubbed the "lunatic fringe," opposed Lend-Lease because they wanted a Nazi victory. Consisting largely of recent German immigrants, the German-American Bund (league) received $5 million from Hitler's intelligence services for its activities. Bund members wore Nazi uniforms at their rallies, spouted anti-Semitic slogans, and howled, "Stop Roosevelt's war machine!" Some Ku Klux Klan racists joined Bund rallies, as did a group called the Friends of Hitler. Father Charles Coughlin, a Roman Catholic priest famous for his radio sermons, blamed the war on the Jews, calling Roosevelt a "warmonger [and] hireling of the Jews."[43]

Loyal to his Nazi partner, Stalin ordered the CPUSA to oppose the draft and Lend-Lease. Its speakers denounced these "outrages" at every turn. Crowds chanted, "Let's skip the next war." Marchers carried signs reading NO WAR FOR THE USA BUT A HOUSE AND A LOT FOR EVERYONE. Moscow-funded newspapers, notably New York's *Daily Worker,* unleashed a barrage of abuse at Roosevelt. This was the same newspaper that called the Hitler-Stalin Pact a "master stroke" for peace, and the Red Army "liberators" of Poland.[44]

Folksingers lent their voices to Stalin, too. American folk music, which began in colonial days, dealt with ordinary people's daily lives, their sorrows and longings for love, happiness, and God. In the 1930s, however, the CPUSA, on orders from Moscow, asked musicians to write "folk" songs with political messages. Their goal, said the *Daily Worker,* was to "sing them so loudly that all the warmakers . . . will hear . . . and tremble."[45]

The Almanac Singers, a group founded by Woody Guthrie and Pete Seeger, set the tone. While Guthrie was "sympathetic" to the CPUSA, Seeger later admitted he had joined the party. On their album *Songs for John Doe,* the Almanacs taunted FDR as a liar and hypocrite:

> *Oh, Franklin Roosevelt told the people how*
> *   he felt*
> *We damn near believed what he said*
> *He said, "I hate war, and so does Eleanor*
> *But we won't be safe 'till everybody's dead."*

And the song "Plow Under" likened the draft to the slaughter of pigs during the New Deal, when millions had been killed to raise pork prices. Now FDR wanted to slaughter American boys like pigs:

Plow the fourth one under
Plow under, plow under
Plow under
Every fourth American boy.

The First Lady heard these songs and thought them "in poor taste." When her husband asked, "Can we forbid this?" Eleanor reminded him that the Constitution guarantees free speech.[46]

Meanwhile, the CPUSA tried to disrupt Lend-Lease aid to Britain. Communist-led unions held work stoppages, as they had in France in 1940. Union bosses would take a genuine grievance, such as low wages, and use it to create a crisis. Most strikers were loyal Americans and had no idea they were being used to serve Stalin's purposes. Nevertheless, a seventy-six-day strike crippled the Allis-Chalmers plant in Milwaukee, Wisconsin, a major supplier of equipment for destroyers. In Cleveland, Ohio, the Die Casters Union shut down the Aluminum Company of America plant, a maker of airplane parts.

The state of California, which accounted for half the nation's aircraft production, saw a wave of strikes. The Vultee Aircraft plant in Downey and the North American Aviation plant in Inglewood shut down for weeks. So serious were the closings that FDR ordered the army to intervene. Soldiers took over the manufacturing plants and protected anyone willing to return to work.[47]

Non-Communists questioned Lend-Lease on patriotic grounds A mass organization, the 800,000-strong America First Committee, attracted politicians, educators, and other concerned citizens. These included Herbert Hoover, Henry Ford, and aviator Charles Lindbergh, the first to fly solo across the Atlantic. Younger members included John F. Kennedy and Gore Vidal, later a famous author.

Members of America First argued that it made no sense to "lend" Britain supplies sure to wind up on the ocean floor. Eventually, the U.S. Navy would have to escort the convoys. That, in turn, would lead to clashes with the wolf packs and, finally, to war. Worse yet, they feared another war would change America for the worse, and forever. To wage it, the White House would have to control the economy—and keep control after victory. "Armament economics" would forge an alliance between government, the military, and industry. America would go on a permanent war footing. Fearing foreign "enemies," it would seek overseas bases from which to strike them.[48]

Roosevelt did not take such criticism lightly. In his view, Hitler was the great present danger. Anything that confused or divided Americans tended to benefit the Nazis, he felt. Lend-Lease supporters agreed, dubbing members of America First "isolationists," a label that has stuck until today. The term implies they were not serious people worried about FDR's policies, but fools wishing to isolate America from the outside world. Interior Secretary Harold Ickes dubbed them "Nazi fellow travelers." Others called them part of the "Nazi underground in America." We cannot be sure if the president actually believed these charges. The fact remains that he had the FBI investigate America First, and Herbert Hoover, to uncover Nazi connections. None were found. Roosevelt also told newspaper and magazine editors that certain writers "should be barred hereafter" from their columns for criticizing his foreign policy. Meanwhile, Hitler unleashed his most destructive blitzkrieg.[49]

RUSSIA'S TURN

Her own war industries and Lend-Lease enabled Britain to survive—barely. While the Battle of the Atlantic raged, the RAF denied Hitler air superiority, forcing him to shelve his invasion plans. Now he prepared to violate his own rule against a two-front war. Despite Stalin's aid, the Fuehrer always meant to destroy the USSR. He could not get it out of his mind: "I just can't help it," he told aides time and again. The thought of the Communist country gnawed at him. "Everything that I undertake is directed against Russia."[50]

Hitler gathered a gigantic invasion

English members of the Auxiliary Territorial Service, the women's branch of the British army during World War II, move armfuls of American rifles just arrived from the United States under Lend-Lease. (Date unknown)

force in eastern Poland: over 3 million ground troops, 3,400 tanks, and 2,000 aircraft. So large a force was impossible to hide. Local people saw the camps, tank parks, and airfields and told others about them. Rumors spread throughout Poland. In turn, Stalin's agents reported what they heard to Moscow. Richard Sorge, a spy in the German embassy in Tokyo, reported the date of the attack. Stalin cursed Sorge, calling him "a little shit." In all, Stalin received and ignored eighty-seven warnings. Angrily, he ordered intelligence officers shot for daring to suggest that Hitler would double-cross him.[51]

For six decades, historians wondered why the ever-suspicious Stalin should have trusted Hitler, a notorious liar. Recently, researchers found two letters in Stalin's personal files that suggest the reason. In them, the Fuehrer swore, "on my honor as a chief of state," that he had no intention of attacking the USSR. Those armies massing in Poland were there, he said, to keep them out of range of RAF bombers until he ordered Britain invaded. Should Nazi forces attack, Stalin must not strike back, because some of his hotheaded generals would be acting without orders, hoping to provoke war. When the invasion began on June 22, 1941, Stalin waited four hours before allowing Soviet troops to return fire.[52]

Stalin regretted the end of Soviet-Nazi "friendship" (his term). His daughter, Svetlana, remembered his habit of repeating, even after the war, "Together with the Germans we would have been invincible." Winston Churchill, however, was thrilled. Upon learning of the invasion, he said that if Hitler invaded hell, he would say something nice about the devil.[53]

Churchill had no illusions about Stalin. Soviet totalitarianism was as evil as Nazi Germany's. What counted was that Britain no longer stood alone. Now she had a partner, though not a friend, in her war for survival. FDR agreed. He realized that if the USSR went down, Hitler would use its resources to attack liberty everywhere, and ultimately the United States. Besides, the harder the Red Army fought, the costlier it would be for Germany. So, to keep the USSR in the fight, on June 24 he approved the first billion of a total of $11 billion in Lend-Lease aid for it

Moscow decided that nothing must interfere with the flow of American aid. Thus, fresh orders reached CPUSA headquarters in New York. Stop calling Roosevelt a warmonger! He is a champion of peace and friend of workers the world over—at least for now! Declare defense plant strikes "treason"! Brand strikers guilty of endangering "the unity of the American people," "sabotaging the war effort," and guaranteeing the triumph of Nazism! Let black people end their "divisive" calls for civil rights and equal opportunity![54]

The Almanac Singers changed their tune. *Songs for John Doe* vanished from record shops as if by magic, replaced by a new album, *Dear Mr. President*. Overnight, the group sang of a startling discovery: Stalin's former partner was a demon after all. Also, since FDR was commander in chief, patriots must obey his orders. Pete Seeger sang,

> *Now, I hate Hitler, and I can tell you why*
> *He's caused lots of good folks to suffer and die*
> *He's got a way of shovin' folks around . . .*
> *Give him a dose of his own medicine . . .*
>   *lead poisoning.*

> *Dear Mister President,*
> *You're commander-in-chief of our armed*
>   *forces*
> *The ships, the planes, the tanks, the horses*
> *And I guess you know best just where I can*
>   *fight. . . .*
> *So if need be I want you to give me a gun*
> *So we can hurry up and get the job done![55]*

UNDECLARED WAR AT SEA

For Roosevelt, the summer of 1941 was a turning point. Though Britain still held out, the Nazis continued grinding up Stalin's forces. War Department analysts gave the USSR at most six weeks before collapsing. This news made FDR decide that he and Churchill must discuss the crisis in person.

On August 9, 1941, the new battleship *Prince of Wales,* pride of the Royal Navy, sailed into Placentia Bay, Newfoundland, off the east coast of Canada. There, American warships rode at anchor around the cruiser *Augusta.* For three days, the president and prime minister met aboard each other's flagships, in a series of gatherings called the Atlantic Conference. Afterward, they declared their support for human rights. In a joint press release called the Atlan-

Winston Churchill and FDR at the Atlantic Conference, with Franklin D. Roosevelt Jr. (left) and Elliott Roosevelt (far right). (August 9, 1941)

tic Charter, they pledged to defend freedom of the seas, the right of all peoples to choose their government, and "the final destruction of Nazi tyranny." Eventually, thirty nations, including the USSR, pledged to uphold this "new charter for Humanity."[56]

When Roosevelt returned to Washington, reporters asked if the meeting had brought America closer to war. "I should say no," he replied firmly. It was not true.[57]

The American and British public only learned the full story of the meeting in 1972, with the release of Churchill's secret War Cabinet papers. These reveal that he begged Roosevelt to declare war on Germany. FDR said he could not—under the Constitution, only Congress may declare war. Besides, polls showed that, while Americans favored aid to Britain, the vast majority opposed going to war for any reason other than a direct attack.

Back in London, Churchill held a top-secret meeting of his War Cabinet. The prime minister explained FDR's position:

If he [Roosevelt] were to put the issue of peace and war to Congress, they would debate it for months. The President had said

he would wage war but not declare it, and that he would become more and more provocative. If the Germans did not like it, they could attack American forces. . . . Everything was to be done to force an incident. . . . The President . . . made it clear that he would look for an incident to justify opening hostilities.[58]

Wage war but not declare it.

Become more and more provocative.

Force an incident.

Most likely, Roosevelt decided on war before meeting with Churchill. War seemed the lesser evil. Without American intervention, it looked as if Hitler would win. The president could not allow that to happen, but he also felt he could not ask America to intervene, not with public opinion dead set against fighting. There seemed only one thing to do. FDR would say he wanted peace—and keep saying it. Meanwhile he would provoke Hitler into striking the first blow. Only then could he take "defensive" action, sure of public support.

This raises grave questions. Can a president trust the American people if he is honest with them about his policy? May he deceive them for reasons he believes vital to their safety? Roosevelt thought so. For him, the crisis was so dire that it outweighed even the law—in this case the Neutrality Acts. In the run-up to the Atlantic Conference, Harry Hopkins visited London to brief Churchill. During the visit, he said FDR "was convinced that if England lost, America, too, would be encircled and beaten. . . . [So] *he would not scruple to interpret existing laws for the furtherance of his aim*" of saving Britain and destroying Hitler.[59]

After America entered the war, Roosevelt spoke with his son James. Perhaps this was the only time he shared his deepest thoughts with anyone. James began by saying how troubled he was by his father's "dishonesty" (James's word) in dealing with the public. FDR replied,

> Jimmy, I knew we were going to war. I was sure there was no way out of it. . . . But I couldn't come out and say a war was coming, because the people would have panicked and turned from me. I had to educate the people to the inevitable, gradually, step by step. . . . If I don't say I hate war, then people are going to think I don't hate war. If I say we're going to get into this war, people will think I want us in it. If I don't say I won't send our sons to fight on foreign battlefields, then people will think I

want to send them. I do hate war. I don't want to send our men to war. I tried to say these things in such a way as to say we won't go to war until we have to go to war. . . . Jimmy, I would have loved to have said that as president I was in a position to know what was happening in the world much more than was the public or even members of Congress, and that I can see we are going to have to go to war sooner or later. . . . But I couldn't say that because the public and congressmen didn't want to hear it and so wouldn't have believed it and would have turned on me.[60]

The president put a chip on America's shoulder and dared the Fuehrer to knock it off. He began by ordering navy destroyers to escort British convoys as far as Iceland, the Black Pit's closest point to land. On September 4, the *U-652,* Lieutenant Georg-Werner Fraatz commanding, fired two torpedoes at the USS *Greer,* narrowly missing her. On September 11, FDR gave a Fireside Chat. He was grim, not only due to the attack but because Sara Roosevelt had died on September 7, two weeks before her eighty-seventh birthday. Back at Hyde Park, he wept when he found a box of his baby clothes she'd kept as mementos. Eleanor was dry-eyed. "I kept being appalled at myself because I couldn't feel any grief, and that seemed terrible after thirty-six years of fairly close association," she wrote.[61]

FDR was not weeping as he addressed the nation. He was angry, and his voice had a sharp edge. The *Greer,* he said, was flying the Stars and Stripes on a peaceful mission to deliver mail to American troops stationed in Iceland One of Hitler's "rattlesnakes of the Atlantic" had attacked her without cause or warning! "We have sought no shooting war with Hitler. We do not seek it now," he said. However, in future, if German warships entered waters essential to U.S. security, "they do so at their own peril," as the navy had orders to "shoot on sight."[62]

Roosevelt knew, but did not tell, the whole story of the attack. The *Greer* had been on a mail run. But she had also been tracking a submerged U-boat with sonar, radioing its position to a British bomber flying nearby. The plane dropped four depth charges, which exploded harmlessly, then left to refuel in Iceland. Though Lieutenant Fraatz tried to slip away, the *Greer* continued to track his boat. Not knowing that the depth charges came from an airplane, Fraatz thought a destroyer had dropped them.

A convoy escort in the Atlantic Ocean. (1942)

Since the *Greer* was the only destroyer around, he fired torpedoes, assuming she was British. The *Greer* replied by dropping her own depth charges, before breaking off the engagement.[63]

U-boat commanders reacted violently to Roosevelt's shoot-on-sight order. On October 17, while the USS *Kearny* escorted a convoy near Iceland, a torpedo slammed into the destroyer's side, killing eleven sailors. "We have wished to avoid shooting," FDR told his radio audience. "America has been attacked. The USS *Kearny* is not just a Navy ship. She belongs to every man, woman, and child in this Nation." The nation must now do her part "to end the curse of Hitlerism." Again, he told only part of the story. The *Kearny* had been helping British destroyers battle a wolf pack before the torpedo struck.[64]

On October 31, a U-boat sank the destroyer *Reuben James* while on convoy duty. She broke in two. Of her 160-man crew, 115 died. Americans were outraged. Woody Guthrie asked in song,

Tell me what were their names?
Tell me what were their names?
Did you have a friend
On the good Reuben James?

While the public still did not demand war, this tragedy allowed FDR to gut the Neutrality Acts. At his request, Congress voted to allow American merchantmen to carry war materials directly to British and Soviet ports. It also allowed them to mount deck guns to fire on surfaced U-boats.[65]

Hitler held back. With fighting raging in the USSR, he did not want war with America—just yet. After the *Reuben James,* he ordered U-boat commanders not to tangle with the U.S. Navy. If attacked, they must escape as best they could, returning fire only in self-defense. Just then, another blow fell. It came not in the icy Atlantic but in the warm waters of the Pacific.

THE PACIFIC BOILS OVER

Over 60 million Japanese inhabited four mountainous islands. Though Japan had some coal and iron ore, she lacked the raw materials essential to modern industry: oil, rubber, tin, copper. Many resented that Westerners—British, French, Dutch, Americans—had seized colonies in Asia. These included India, Burma (now Myanmar), Malaya (Malaysia), the Dutch East Indies (Indonesia), Indochina (Vietnam and Laos), and the Philippines. Japan's other Asian neighbors—industrially less advanced, yet rich in natural resources—were tempting targets. By the 1890s, Japan had scrimped and saved enough to modernize her armed forces. In 1895, they occupied Formosa (now Taiwan), an island off the coast of China. In 1910, Japan easily took over Korea.

Japan fought on the Allied side during the First World War. Afterward, as a reward, she gained control of several Pacific islands held by Germany. By the 1920s, her generals and admirals had become so powerful that they established a dictatorship. While the emperor was worshiped as a living god, the military controlled Japan's affairs. Society became militarized. Boys learned to fight and girls to nurse the wounded. Men had to wear clothes modeled on military uniforms. Assassins killed anyone who protested, including high officials appointed by the emperor. In 1931, Japanese forces swept northward from Korea into Manchuria, a mineral-rich Chinese province. When the League of Nations condemned the invasion, Japan quit the group. The league did nothing.

In 1937, Japanese forces invaded China herself, acting with incredible cruelty. After taking the city of Nanjing, troops went on a rampage, murdering 300,000 civilians within a few days. Later, during the infamous "Three Alls" campaign—"Kill All, Burn All, Loot All"—they massacred over a million Chinese. Officers even held contests to see how many Chinese they could behead with their swords in a given time. As if that were not enough, the army used some 200,000 Chinese and Koreans as "comfort women," a polite term for sex slaves. A secret outfit, Unit 731, experimented with poison gas on captives, including babies. When studying the effects of bacterial infections, its doctors dissected living victims without anesthetics.[66]

China was a massive country with a population six times that of Japan's. Fighting it was like punching an immense feather pillow; though pushed in, it absorbed the blows. As the war dragged on, Japan's resources became stretched to the limit. Food, fuel, cloth, and leather were rationed. Travelers' reports told of workers tanning rat skins to make leather substitutes and recycling burnt matchsticks.[67]

Tokyo's warlords decided that easier pickings lay to the south of China. The Dutch East Indies had oil, British Malaya had rubber and tin, French Indochina had rice. After Hitler defeated France, the Japanese forced France's colonial authorities in August 1940 to let them occupy ports and airfields in northern Indochina. In July 1941, the Japanese army seized the entire country. The cities of Hanoi in the north and Saigon in the south became major military bases.

Roosevelt feared Japan might conquer all Southeast Asia. To signal the administration's disapproval, the State Department froze Japanese assets in the United States, preventing her from buying American goods. Worse yet, the president banned shipments of industrial machinery, iron, and oil to Japan. Since America supplied about 85 percent of her oil, the ban threatened Japan with economic and military collapse.

If FDR thought Japan would back down, he was mistaken. A Japanese proverb says, "A cornered rat will bite a cat." Tokyo's warlords felt cornered.

While they still had fuel reserves, they decided on a fateful gamble. They would follow two courses of action at once. First, they would try to make a deal allowing Japan to keep her conquests if she made no others. Meanwhile, they prepared for war—just in case. If diplomacy failed, they would destroy the Pacific Fleet based at Pearl Harbor. They had no intention of invading the American mainland. Instead, while America tended her wounds, they meant to complete their conquests. They thought that by the time America recovered, perhaps in five years, their defenses would be too strong to overcome.

Not that they thought America would put up much of a fight. Like Hitler, the warlords believed her a weak and cowardly nation. Japanese soldiers were taught that "money-making is the one aim in life [of Americans]. The men make money to live luxuriously and over-educate their wives and daughters who are allowed to talk too much.... [While] outwardly civilized [America] is inwardly corrupt and decadent" and could never match Japan's fighting spirit.[68]

Negotiations in Washington broke down over American demands that Japan withdraw from China. So, on the morning of Sunday, December 7, 1941,

six aircraft carriers turned into the wind north of Pearl Harbor. In less than an hour, their planes sank or damaged eighteen American warships, including eight battleships. One bomb penetrated the battleship *Arizona,* still carrying the silver bolt Franklin Roosevelt had hammered into her keel twenty-seven years earlier. The *Arizona* exploded and sank, taking 1,200 crewmen with her. They remain entombed in the ship's hull to this very day. Raiders also destroyed 180 aircraft, mostly on the ground. In all, 2,403 American servicemen died at Pearl Harbor.

News of the attack stunned the president. "No!" he gasped, then fell silent for several minutes. Navy experts had broken the Japanese diplomatic code, so he had expected an attack. But where? Neither FDR nor his advisers thought the Japanese would strike Pearl Harbor, the very heart of our sea power in the Pacific. The Dutch East Indies and the Philippines, where America had important bases, seemed the most likely targets.[69]

That night, Ed Murrow, on leave from London, had a dinner invitation to the White House. Please wait, an aide told him; the president is busy, but will see you later. Around midnight, Murrow stepped into the Oval Study. Roosevelt had recovered his composure. "Never have I seen one so calm and so steady," Murrow recalled. FDR invited him to share a quickie meal of sandwiches and beer. As they ate, he asked about conditions in London. Soon the conversation turned to Pearl Harbor. FDR began to recite the day's losses, ships sunk, men killed. When he came to the airplanes destroyed, he pounded his fist on the table. "On the ground, by God, on the ground!" he roared.[70]

Almost from the day of the attack, critics claimed Roosevelt knew the Japanese had targeted Pearl Harbor but did nothing to prevent it. Supposedly, he sought a "back door" to war with Germany by provoking an attack by Japan, Hitler's principal ally.

Battleships USS *West Virginia* and USS *Tennessee*, both severely damaged, and USS *Arizona*, sinking, after being hit in the attack on Pearl Harbor. (December 7, 1941)

There are no documents or witnesses to prove this charge. To believe Roosevelt guilty, one must also believe that the commander in chief deliberately sacrificed American lives and ships. If so, his closest advisers must have known *something* about the plan, since he would have needed their cooperation in carrying it out. But, all reports agree, they were as shocked by the attack as he. Then there is the personal factor. FDR loved the navy; he often spoke of it as "us" and the army as "they." To sacrifice the fleet, he would have needed the murderous mentality of a Stalin or Hitler. Nothing we know about him suggests he was like that.[71]

Next day, December 8, the president addressed a joint session of Congress. With controlled anger, he gripped the podium and said, "Yesterday, December 7, 1941—a day that will live in infamy—the United States was suddenly and deliberately attacked by naval and air forces of the Empire of Japan.... With confidence in our armed forces—with the unbounding determination of our people—we will gain the inevitable triumph—so help us God." Congress declared war on Japan without a debate. Immediately the cry "Remember Pearl Harbor!" went up from coast to coast.

Japan's attack left Hitler in a strong position. Americans demanded all-out war with Japan, not Nazi Germany. Germany and Japan had a treaty pledging to help each other if attacked by a third power, but Japan attacked America first. So Hitler was not obliged to declare war for Japan's sake, a fact Roosevelt well knew.

FDR's December 9 Fireside Chat is often overlooked. Yet it is just as important as his "Day of Infamy" speech. The president spoke of "powerful and resourceful gangsters" banding together "to make war on the whole human race." He accused the most vile gangster, Adolf Hitler, of promising Japan control of the entire Pacific as a reward for attacking America. "We know also that Germany and Japan are conducting their military and naval operations in accordance with a joint plan." How "we" knew this remains a mystery. Perhaps FDR got some faulty intelligence, which has still not come to light. Moreover, though Hitler would have welcomed an attack on British possessions in Asia, German documents captured after the war show that the Fuehrer promised Japan nothing. Just as he did not want to provoke America in the Atlantic, for the same reason he did not want war with her over events in the Pacific. Pearl Harbor surprised him, too; the Japanese had not told him about

DRAFT No. 1   December 7, 1941.

PROPOSED MESSAGE TO THE CONGRESS

Yesterday, December 7, 1941, a date which will live in ~~world history~~ *infamy* ——

the United States of America was ~~simultaneously~~ *suddenly* and deliberately attacked

by naval and air forces of the Empire of Japan. ~~without warning~~

The United States was at the moment at peace with that nation and ~~was~~

~~continuing the~~ *still in* conversation with its Government and its Emperor looking

toward the maintenance of peace in the Pacific. Indeed, one hour after

Japanese air squadrons had commenced bombing in *Oahu* ~~Hawaii and the Philippines~~

the Japanese Ambassador to the United States and his colleague delivered

to the Secretary of State a formal reply to a ~~former~~ *recent American* message. ~~from the~~

~~Secretary.~~ *While* This reply ~~contained a statement~~ *stated* that diplomatic negotiations *it seemed useless to*

~~must be considered at an end, it~~ *it* contained no threat ~~and no~~ *or* hint of ~~an~~ *war or*

armed attack.

It will be recorded that the distance ~~of Hawaii~~ of

Hawaii, from Japan makes it obvious that the attack *was* deliberately

planned many days *or even weeks* ago. During the intervening time the Japanese Govern-

ment has deliberately sought to deceive the United States by false

statements and expressions of hope for continued peace.

A first draft of the renowned "Day of Infamy" speech, with FDR's own edits. (December 7, 1941)

their plans. When the news came, he refused to believe the early reports. Aides
recalled that a "stunned" look came over
the Fuehrer's face. Germany and Japan
did not have a joint military plan, and
never would.[72]

Yet the fact remains that on December 11, the Nazi leader responded to
Roosevelt's Fireside Chat with a ranting, hate-filled tirade lasting an hour
and a half. In it, he blamed "this man
alone" for causing the war by his provo-
cations in the Atlantic and personal insults. Hitler ended with a declaration of
war on America; his ally Italian dictator
Benito Mussolini followed suit. Later,
in a calmer moment, Hitler admitted
that he'd acted hastily and that war with
America "was a tragedy and illogical." So
it was—for Nazi Germany.[73]

FDR signing the declaration of war against
Japan at the White House. Note the black armband
he wears as a symbol of mourning for his mother's
recent death. (December 8, 1941)

THE WAR AT HOME

We are now in this war. We are all in it—all the way. Every single man, woman and child is a partner in the most tremendous undertaking of our American history. We must share together the bad news and the good news, the defeats and the victories—the changing fortunes of war.
—*Franklin D. Roosevelt, December 9, 1941*

NATIONAL SECURITY

In the same December 9, 1941, Fireside Chat in which Roosevelt called Hitler a gangster, he also called for national unity and sacrifice. If Americans pulled together, they could overcome any obstacle. To win the war, they must do three things. First, secure the homeland from attack. Second, harness its resources to make the tools of war. Finally, hurl these against the enemy with devastating force.

Security began with the White House. The president holds a unique position. He is not only the head of the military but the living symbol of the nation. In terms of morale, of fighting spirit, his as-

sassination would be worse than almost any military setback.

Like Abraham Lincoln, FDR believed what will be, will be, no matter what we may do. "If anyone wants to kill me, there is no possible way to prevent him," he said. But that was not quite true. He had already survived an assassination attempt. On February 15, 1933, while returning from a brief vacation before the inauguration, he visited Bayfront Park in Miami, Florida. He had just addressed the crowd from the backseat of an open car when a deranged bricklayer named Giuseppe Zangara fired five pistol shots at close range. As Zangara took aim, a woman bystander slammed her handbag into his arm. The bullets missed the president-elect but hit Chicago mayor Anton Cermak, wounding him fatally.

With America at war, the Secret Service tightened presidential security. Before Pearl Harbor, anyone could picnic on the White House lawn in daytime. There were no guard posts at any of the four entrances, nor bag checks or metal detectors. Now guards let only those with official passes, including cabinet members, through the gates. To conceal the building at night, the Secret Service ordered blackout curtains hung over windows and skylights painted black. Since the mansion had no bomb shelter, construction crews dug a 761-foot-long tunnel to an immense steel-and-concrete vault in the basement of the Treasury. The improvised bomb shelter had a bed, a desk, and chairs and was stocked with provisions for the president and his staff. For a test, the Secret Service timed how long it took to push an agent sitting in a wheelchair to safety. The wheelchair was equipped with a gas mask—just in case.

Whenever the president left the White House, he went in a bulletproof vehicle. At first, he used Al Capone's car; the notorious gangster was in prison for tax evasion. "I hope," FDR joked, "Mr. Capone won't mind." Later, the Ford Motor Company built an armored lim-ousine for him. For long-distance travel within the United States, he went by special train, code-named POTUS (an acronym for President of the United States). It had communications gear, radio operators, a dining car, and rooms for guests and the Secret Service detail. Roosevelt's car came last. Named the *Ferdinand Magellan* after the great Portuguese explorer, this rolling fortress had steel plates thick enough to withstand a direct hit by a cannon shell.[1]

During the Second World War, as ever, Americans disagreed on how far a president may go in the name of national security. Some feared that unless checked by Congress and the courts, Roosevelt might use the crisis as an excuse for crushing liberty. Others, however, saw no greater danger than the war itself, as defeat meant the certain end of liberty. Some legal experts thought so. For example, Wayne Morse, dean of the University of Oregon School of Law and later a distinguished senator, held that security came first. "The war power," Morse wrote, "implies the right to do *anything* that may seem necessary to carry out the war successfully, *even to the extent of performing otherwise unconstitutional acts.*" Translation: The president may, for good cause, break the law in wartime.[2]

Roosevelt agreed with Morse and

told him so. Moreover, cabinet members knew his rule: "What must be done to defend the country must be done." Attorney General Francis Biddle claimed FDR "thought that rights should yield to the necessities of war. Rights came after victory, not before." According to Robert H. Jackson, whom Roosevelt appointed to the Supreme Court, he thought in terms not of legal and illegal but of right and wrong. For FDR, worthy ends were more important than the means of achieving them. Since the president wished only well for America, "he found difficulty in thinking there could be legal limitations on them."[3]

Regarding security, Roosevelt was both petty and ruthless. He once demanded to know if FBI director J. Edgar Hoover had "cleaned out" waiters who were not citizens from Washington hotels, as they might eavesdrop on officials' conversations. More serious yet, he allowed the FBI to engage in illegal activities. Hoover's men carried out "black-bag jobs," burglaries of the homes of known or suspected enemy sympathizers. Agents also opened mail in New York and Washington post offices. Along with Intrepid's agents, they routinely read telegrams sent to and from neutral European countries: Switzerland, Sweden, Spain, and Portugal.[4]

A portrait of J. Edgar Hoover, the FBI director during World War II. (April 5, 1940)

Though sworn to uphold the law, the president ignored a Supreme Court ruling against telephone wiretaps as "destructive of personal liberty." On his orders, Hoover's agents installed 6,769 illegal wiretaps and 1,306 listening devices, some in rooms in the nation's leading hotels. "Hell," said John Roosevelt, "my father just about invented bugging. [He] had them spread all over, and thought nothing of it."[5]

The First Lady, whose zeal for reform raised FBI suspicions, was also a target. Years before Pearl Harbor, the agency began to gather material on her. After a worker at the Chicago hotel in which she was staying tipped her off, Eleanor complained to her husband. He ordered Hoover to stop spying on his wife. Hoover said he would but did not. The surveillance continued; at nearly 3,900 pages, her file is among the FBI's largest. When Eleanor learned the FBI was investigating her social secretary, Edith Helm, she wrote Hoover, protesting that his tactics "smack too much of the Gestapo methods" used by Hitler's secret police.[6]

FDR showed no mercy toward captured enemy agents. On June 12, 1942,

U-boats landed two four-man teams on beaches in Florida and New York. Their mission: destroy key bridges, tunnels, power plants, and factories. In addition, they were to set off bombs in department stores, movie theaters, and railroad stations, slaughtering civilians and sowing panic. Fortunately, George Dasch, leader of the New York team, had second thoughts. Dasch went to FBI headquarters in Washington, asking to see Hoover in person. Agents thought him crazy, until he plunked down $84,000 in crisp new bills, which German military intelligence had given him for expenses. Within days, the FBI arrested both teams.

Department of Justice lawyers argued that the would-be terrorists had been arrested before they did any harm. Therefore, a civilian court should try them for entering the country illegally, a crime punishable by two years in prison. FDR called this approach "splitting hairs," a legal technicality, dangerous in the life-and-death struggle with Nazism. He wanted the prisoners dead, and their deaths given the widest publicity. He suspected (correctly) that their masters in Berlin aimed at more than destroying property and spreading panic. They aimed to convince Americans that their government could not protect them—

Guarded by an army lieutenant, two of eight men on trial as alleged Nazi spies sit in the courtroom in the Department of Justice building in Washington, D.C.; from left to right: Herbert H. Haupt, Lieutenant Meakin, and George Dasch. (1942)

this while U-boats prowled American waters and shore defenses were weak.[7]

To reassure the country, and discourage future terrorist missions, Roosevelt decided to set an example by holding the trial in a military court. Should civilian courts try to interfere, he would ignore them. "I want one thing understood, Francis," he warned Attorney General Biddle. "I won't give them up. . . . I won't hand them over to any United States marshal armed with a writ of habeas corpus. Understand?" Biddle understood. A secret trial before a military court composed of seven generals tried the intruders as soldiers captured out of uniform. According to the laws of war, they were spies, and thus not entitled to treatment as soldiers taken on the battlefield. Finding them guilty, the court sentenced six to death. Dasch and another man who had helped the prosecution received thirty-year prison terms.[8]

On August 8, the condemned went to the electric chair in the District of Columbia jail. Newspapers and radio reports made a great to-do over the executions. Yet FDR had sent Nazi intelligence a "message" in the form of six burnt bodies. Thinking American defenses stronger than they actually were, Germany sent no more terrorists.[9]

ISSEI, NISEI, AND OTHERS

Sometimes Roosevelt went overboard, as when security concerns involved him in the most sweeping violation of human rights since slavery. The internment—confinement during wartime—of Japanese Americans will forever be a blot on his name.

Immigrants from Japan began arriving in the 1880s. Frugal and hardworking, most earned their living as small-scale farmers, artisans, and shopkeepers. Because they often undercut white competitors, racial resentments grew so strong that federal law barred Japanese and Chinese immigrants from citizenship. However, also by law, anyone born on American soil is automatically a citizen. So, while the first Japanese arrivals, called Issei, were not citizens, their children, called Nisei, were. By 1941, more than 126,000 people of Japanese heritage lived in the United States, chiefly in California.

In the wake of Pearl Harbor, panic swept the West Coast. It was spread by word of mouth and by the press, which printed the most absurd rumors as fact. *Time* magazine, for example, told readers how to distinguish the Chinese (allies) from the Japanese (enemies). Chinese people are "more placid, kindly, open; the Japanese more positive, dogmatic, arrogant.... Japanese walk stiffly erect... Chinese more relaxed... sometimes shuffle." Comic books depicted the Japanese as "murderous little ape-men," squinting beasts with thick eyeglasses and buckteeth.[10]

Rumors spread like wildfire. The "Japs" were coming, aided by the disloyal Issei and Nisei! A Japanese submarine had surfaced off Santa Barbara, California, and fired cannon shells into an oil refinery! During the so-called Battle of Los Angeles, raiders from Japanese aircraft carriers ran into a hail of anti-aircraft fire over the city! Nisei workers also lit a gigantic "fire arrow" in a field, pointing toward Seattle, Washington! Still others ignited trees at night on a cliff near Santa Cruz, California, as a beacon for enemy warships! And Japanese farmers "will send their peas and potatoes and squash full of arsenic to the markets."[11]

Despite these dire reports, nothing happened. Puzzled, J. Edgar Hoover ordered West Coast agents to investigate. Before long, they reported that Japanese Americans were entirely loyal. "I thought the Army was getting a little bit hysterical," the tough-minded FBI director wrote the president. A follow-up investigation by a State Department official, Curtis B. Munson, confirmed the

FBI findings. According to Munson, people of Japanese descent "are pathetically eager to show their loyalty."[12]

Oddly enough, the absence of trouble caused further alarm. General John DeWitt, chief of West Coast defenses, thought he knew why. Issei and Nisei, said he, were lying low until they could launch a crippling attack. While they had adopted American ways and spoke perfect English, by nature they were "an enemy race." For "a Jap's a Jap.... It makes no difference whether he is an American citizen or not," the general declared. "I don't want any of them." Nor did many others, including Earl Warren, California's attorney general and a future Supreme Court justice. An outcry arose for the government to move "the dirty Japs" from coastal areas to "safe" places inland.[13]

FDR's defenders later claimed he "gave in" to pressure to intern them in camps, implying that the man who had so fiercely battled polio was weak-willed. The written record tells a more complicated story. It goes back to his 1923 *Asia* magazine article, "Shall We Trust Japan?" and to a 1925 article in the *Macon (Georgia) Daily Telegraph*. These reveal a bias against Japanese people nearly two decades before Pearl Harbor. There, FDR declared that Japanese immigrants could never be true Americans because they were "not capable of assimilation into the American population." As people of "Oriental blood," they remained Japanese wherever they happened to live. For that reason, FDR supported discrimination against them to preserve what he termed white "racial purity."[14]

As Japanese armies rampaged across Asia, Roosevelt said aggressiveness was "in the blood" of their leaders After Pearl Harbor, he believed, or claimed to believe, the most outlandish charges. For example, he told the cabinet that "friends of his" had found "numerous secret Japanese air bases" in the "lower California" (Baja) region of Mexico. Nobody else reported seeing them. Perhaps those friends were the ones a reporter had called his "imaginary playmates." Anyhow, the bases never existed. Had they, he would have been obliged to demand that Mexico remove them or to send American bombers to do it. In conversations the FBI secretly taped at his request in the Oval Office, Roosevelt spoke crudely of "the Japs" and "any damn Jap." In public statements, he condemned the brutality of "the Nazis and the Japs."[15]

On February 19, 1942, the president signed Executive Order 9066. Not even Woodrow Wilson, no champion of civil

The *San Francisco Examiner* announcing the implementation of Executive Order 9066. (February 1942)

liberties in wartime, had put his name to such a shameful document. It showed that in Roosevelt's eyes, all American citizens were *not equal*, *not* entitled to the rights safeguarded by the Constitution. His order violated a principle basic to the very meaning of America. Under our system, you are judged by what you *do*, not by who you *are*. Race, religion, color, and social group must play no role in a court's decision. In the case of the Japanese Americans, none were charged with a crime or had their day in court, and surely not the children.

With a stroke of his pen, Roosevelt set the stage for the uprooting of entire communities. Often families had forty-eight hours to prepare for the move. They either sold possessions and property at knockdown prices or left them behind for looters and squatters to take. FDR also wanted Hawaii's 140,000 Japanese Americans interned, but the military objected. Skilled workers of whatever race were needed to repair the damage at Pearl Harbor.

People close to Roosevelt criticized his internment order. Though Secretary of War Henry Stimson approved of it as necessary, he thought it would "make a tremendous hole in our constitutional system." The First Lady strongly objected, too. "These people were not convicted of any crime," Eleanor noted. The government must "adhere strictly to the American rule that a man is innocent until he is proved guilty." When she questioned her husband's decision, he gave her an icy look and said she should not raise the subject again.[16]

The army sent 110,000 Japanese Americans, mostly citizens, to "relocation centers" in California, Arizona, Utah, Colorado, Wyoming, Idaho, and Arkansas. Forty years later, Grace Nakamura recalled the hectic scene, the noise, confusion, and fear, of her family's departure:

On May 16, 1942 at 9:30 a.m. we departed . . . for an unknown destination. To this day I can remember the plight of the elderly, some on stretchers, orphans herded on the train by caretakers, and especially a young couple with four preschool children. The mother had two frightened toddlers hanging on to her coat. In her arms, she carried two crying babies. The father had diapers and other baby paraphernalia strapped to his back. In his hands he struggled with a duffel bag and suitcase. The shades were drawn on the train for our entire trip. Military police patrolled the aisles.

Japanese Americans who were forced to evacuate wait in Los Angeles for a train that will take them to Owens Valley, some 250 miles north. (April 1942)

At least FDR called the centers by their correct name: "concentration camps." In ten remote camps, inmates lived in flimsy wooden barracks, each with several one-room apartments, one per family, no matter the size. Barbed wire fences with watchtowers, searchlights, and armed guards surrounded each camp.[17]

Inmates formed lasting friendships and taught their children as best they could. Adults worked at jobs for which the government paid eight to sixteen dollars a month; an army private got twenty-four dollars a month. Yet this

WESTERN DEFENSE COMMAND AND FOURTH ARMY
WARTIME CIVIL CONTROL ADMINISTRATION
Presidio of San Francisco, California
April 1, 1942

INSTRUCTIONS TO ALL PERSONS OF JAPANESE ANCESTRY

Living in the Following Area:

An evacuation order posted on a street corner in San Francisco. (April 1942)

hardly made up for treating innocents as criminals.

In 1943, despite their bitterness, Nisei men began volunteering for the army; the navy and marines would not have them as yet. Enlisting was, Nisei believed, the only way to prove their loyalty. By the war's end, 33,000 had enlisted. Nisei made valiant, dedicated soldiers. No Nisei ever deserted; desertion was "dishonorable" and would "shame" one's family. The all-Nisei 442nd Regimental Combat Team fought in Europe, becoming the most decorated outfit in American history. Other Nisei served as translators and intelligence officers in the Pacific campaigns. This took extraordinary courage, as they knew that capture by Japanese forces meant death by torture.

While history textbooks discuss Executive Order 9066 and its effects, none that I have seen mention a related issue. During the Second World War, our government arranged mass kidnapping from Latin America to the United States. It did so with the president's full knowledge and approval.[18]

Like the United States, Latin American countries attracted immigrants seeking a better life. Starting in the 1890s, Germans, Italians, and Japanese flocked to Central and South America. As in the

United States, too, newcomers tended to gather in certain areas, forming communities that spoke the language and kept the customs of the old country. In time, many became citizens. Many others, however, remained "aliens," foreigners living legally in a country but owing allegiance to their homeland.

With war clouds gathering over Europe and Asia, Roosevelt worried about Latin America. Not only did it have oil and other essential raw materials, but the Panama Canal allowed the navy to shift forces readily between the Atlantic and Pacific oceans. Without the canal, warships would have to sail around South America or Africa, adding thousands of miles to a voyage. If war came, enemy agents and sympathizers would threaten the waterway and perhaps overthrow friendly governments. War would also put American travelers, tourists, businesspeople, and civilians living abroad under enemy control.

After Hitler invaded Poland in 1939, J. Edgar Hoover sent teams of agents to Latin America. Working with U.S. embassies and host governments, FBI men compiled "black lists" of German, Italian, and Japanese aliens. Soon after Pearl Harbor, the State Department pressured host governments to round up "enemy aliens" for deportation to the United States. Twelve governments agreed, but Argentina, Brazil, Chile, and Mexico refused.[19]

Latin American governments hustled 6,600 people, including children, aboard ships bound for the United States, where immigration officials seized their passports upon landing. This meant they entered "illegally," allowing Washington to intern them during the war, and deport them afterward, without the formality of a trial. As with the Issei and Nisei, they lived in guarded camps, the largest located outside Crystal City, Texas.

Without charging internees with any crime, the authorities held them, said a State Department memo, "for bargaining purposes." Eventually, Tokyo traded about a thousand Japanese Latin Americans for American civilians. The Nazis traded 2,000 German internees for Americans they held. President Roosevelt saw seizing foreigners as a necessary, if harsh, way of saving American civilians from a harsher fate. In Asia, for example, British and Dutch civilians suffered terribly in Japanese prison camps. Nevertheless, FDR's policy had no basis in American or international law. It was, for lack of a gentler word, kidnapping.[20]

BUILDING THE WAR MACHINE

Hitler mocked American military power. "What is America," he sneered, "but millionaires, beauty queens, stupid records and Hollywood?" Though it had economic power, he thought it too silly, too selfish, and too soft to mobilize for war.[21]

The Great Depression had nearly crippled the American military. In 1933, within days of telling the people they had nothing to fear but fear itself, the new president slashed the defense budget further than Hoover had. Although FDR loved the navy, he drastically limited construction of new fighting ships. The army, however, suffered worse, as he cut its already meager budget by 51 percent. With 140,000 men it was eighteenth in size among the world's armies, behind that of tiny Holland.

The army's chief of staff, General Douglas MacArthur, protested that these cuts made him scrap key training programs. During one meeting, he warned the president that his policy courted disaster. Lives were at stake. "When we lost the next war," he said, "and an American boy, lying in the mud with an enemy bayonet through his belly . . . spat out his last curse, I wanted the name not to be MacArthur, but Roosevelt." FDR's face turned ashen, and he roared, "You must not talk that way to the President!" The general apologized. The president accepted his apology, but MacArthur was more upset than he showed. Upon leaving, he recalled, "I just vomited on the steps of the White House."[22]

Everything changed when Hitler began his march of conquest. On October 13, 1939, six weeks after Poland's fall, Roosevelt made perhaps the most fateful decision in modern history. That morning, Alexander Sachs sat in the Oval Study. Sachs, an economist, had known FDR for years. He also knew friends of Albert Einstein, the leading scientist of the age and a German Jew driven from his homeland by the Nazis.

Einstein had written the president about new developments in his field. German researchers had recently made important strides in nuclear physics. Their work suggested the possibility of purifying a rare silvery-white metal, uranium 235, to build a superbomb—an atomic bomb. Having such a weapon would make it easy for Hitler to fulfill his dreams of world conquest. How to get the letter to Roosevelt? Einstein could not simply drop it into a mailbox and hope for the best. Instead, he gave it to a scientist who knew Sachs.

At first, Roosevelt seemed impatient. It was going to be a busy day. He

〰️ Albert Einstein during a lecture in Vienna, more than a decade before he would escape to the United States. (1921)

had other appointments. Sachs, however, stuck to his agenda. Finally, FDR let him read Einstein's letter aloud. One sentence fairly leaped from the page. Purified uranium 235 might lead to the building of "extremely powerful bombs." Worse, "a single bomb of this type, carried by boat and exploded in a port, might very well destroy the whole port together with some of the surrounding territory." *That* got the president's attention.[23]

"Alex, what you are after is to see that the Nazis don't blow us up."

"Precisely."

Instantly Roosevelt summoned General Edwin "Pa" Watson, his military aide.

"Pa," he said, holding up Einstein's letter, "this requires action."[24]

So began the Manhattan Project, a say-nothing name for the largest scientific effort up till that time. Working in secret, project directors scoured universities for scientific talent: physicists, mathematicians, chemists, engineers, machine designers, explosives experts, and planners. These worked in three secret installations at Oak Ridge, Tennessee; Los Alamos, New Mexico; and Hanford, Washington.

Meanwhile, Roosevelt had to supply America's growing forces and, before long, those of her allies. This called for a complete about-face. Never mind that he had bashed leaders of big business as "economic royalists." FDR buried his verbal hatchet, reaching out to business for the sake of the country.

On May 30, 1940, as British troops waded out to rescue ships at Dunkirk, a tall, lean man with gray hair and rough hands visited the White House. Born in Denmark, William "Big Bill" Knudsen had come to America as a child. No stranger to hard work, he was a living legend in the auto industry. A loyal Republican, he had worked himself up from the shop floor to the front office to become Henry Ford's chief technical adviser. Knudsen, a mass-production wizard, designed Ford's plants and assembly lines. Later, he did the same for Ford's chief competitor, General Motors, becoming its president.

America must rearm, and fast, Roosevelt said. Could Knudsen lead the effort to convert private industry to war production? The president could offer only the token salary of a dollar a year. Knudsen said he could, and would, help put industry on a war footing. He welcomed the opportunity to serve. "This country has been good to me," he said, "and I want to pay it back."[25]

Big Bill had a simple formula for success. Running a modern war seemed not all that different from running a modern factory. "If we get into war, the winning of it will be purely a question of material and production. If we know how to get out twice as much material as anyone else—know how to get it . . . and use it— we are going to come out on top—and win."[26]

Knudsen knew almost every leader of American industry, and he would call upon their patriotism, expertise, *and* desire for profits. Washington must do its part, too. Let the military tell indus-

Stop this monster that stops at nothing... PRODUCE to the limit! This is YOUR War!

A propaganda poster created by the Office of War Information, a U.S. government agency, encouraging Americans to increase production to defeat Germany and Japan. (1941–1945)

try what it needs, how many "pieces" it needs, and by when it needs them. Forget alphabet-soup-like agencies! Rearming would be too complicated for centralized control. Washington must stay out of the production process as much as possible. Instead, it must see that industry got the raw materials it needed, in the right quantities, and on time. Thanks to Roosevelt's appeal and Knudsen's organizing skills, when Japan struck Pearl Harbor eighteen months later, America's war machine was already humming.

Conversion to war production was a complex, costly process. To ease the change, Washington gave generous tax breaks to key industries. In turn, Americans responded with an astonishing outburst of creativity. Across the country, architects redesigned factories while engineers retooled machinery to suit wartime needs. Civilian automobile production came to a halt. Instead, auto plants made military vehicles: tanks, trucks, and jeeps. Makers of pleasure boats switched to landing craft. Adding machine companies made automatic pistols, and sewing machine companies machine guns.

We still marvel at some changes. For example, makers of musical instruments fashioned precision parts for airplane engines. Manufacturers of baby cribs turned out cots and sleeping bags. A merry-go-round manufacturer made rotating antiaircraft gun mounts. A pinball machine maker produced armor-piercing shells. Makers of ladies' compacts switched to artillery shell fuses and tiny radio parts. Lace companies went in for camouflage netting.

In describing his new role, Roosevelt said that "Dr. New Deal" had become "Dr. Win-the-War." Dr. New Deal had failed to end the Great Depression. Now, as war drew near, the downturn became a sharp, steady upturn. Defense spending soared. By July 1940, with the Luftwaffe bombing London, Congress was spending $165 million a month on defense. By July 1941, with Nazi tanks stabbing into the USSR, spending rose to $500 million a month. By December 1941, as Japanese planes bore down on Pearl Harbor, spending reached $2 billion a month, and kept climbing.[27]

Business boomed. Unemployment, which stood at 17 percent on the "Day of Infamy," vanished like a bad dream. When men came home from work, families gathered around to open the first pay envelope. A miner took his wife and children to a Pittsburgh clothing store. "Fit us out with new clothes," he said, bursting with pride. None of them had put on a new shirt or pair of shoes in ten years.[28]

The inner wounds inflicted by the Great Depression—hopelessness, doubt, and loss of self-respect—healed. "Going to work in the navy yard," a worker recalled, "I felt like something had come down from heaven. . . . It made a different man out of me. . . . After all the years of the Depression, the war completely turned my life around." Prosperous-again farmers put new words to a children's song:

The farmer's in the dough.
The farmer's in the dough.
Hi-ho, the merry-o,
The farmer's in the dough.[29]

There was plenty of "dough" to go around. The war industries became magnets, drawing people to them. Brand-new towns sprang up around factories, naval bases, and training camps. Old towns and cities expanded, taking on fresh life. As never before, even during the expansion westward in the 1800s, America became a nation on the move. Seeking opportunity, as many as 20 million people—or one in nine—left home. They traveled by car, bus, and train, individually and in family groups. Upon arrival, the hardest part was putting a roof over one's head. All wartime boomtowns had housing shortages, so newcomers were glad to find any room, motel, or house. Finding a job was easiest.

The scene that greeted a newcomer to Mobile, Alabama, on the Gulf of Mexico, was like any in hundreds of places. One reported seeing

a milling crowd; soldiers, sailors, stout women with bundled up babies, lanky backwoodsmen with hats tipped over their brows and a cheek full of chewing tobacco, hatless young men in light colored sports shirts open at the neck, countrymen with creased red necks and well-washed overalls, cigarsmoking men in business suits . . . girls in bright dresses with carefully curled hair piled upon their heads and high-heeled shoes and bloodred fingernails, withered nutbrown old people with glasses, carrying ruptured suitcases, broadshouldered men in oilstained khaki with shiny brown helmets on their heads, negroes in flappy jackets and little felt hats with turned-up brims, teenage boys in jockey caps, here and there a fluttered negro woman dragging behind her a string of white-eyed children.[30]

HOME FRONT

"Home front" is a term coined in Europe during the First World War. When nations fought in centuries past, most civilians escaped the horrors unless they lived in a battle zone. In the new warfare, every person and resource had a role to play in the national effort. Thus, the home front became as important as the battlefront. Without home front support, the bravest fighters were doomed.

War industries drained raw materials from the civilian economy. This meant factories could not meet demands for consumer goods. As a result, "nonessential" metal products vanished from store shelves. A partial list includes buttons, baby carriages, vacuum cleaners, electric irons, ovens, toasters, refrigerators, pots, pans, bicycles, typewriters, bobby pins, safety pins, clothes hangers, flyswatters, window screens, and most toys. Washington also banned production of rubber products for civilian use: tires, rubber bands, gloves, galoshes, shower caps, tennis balls, and golf balls. Copper pennies vanished. Everything from ships to planes required copper wire. The Manhattan Project used so much copper that

directors asked for a substitute: tons of gold bars. New pennies, dull, ugly things, had a steel core with a zinc coating.

Despite the halt in production of many civilian items, certain raw materials remained scarce. To get these, Washington began two programs. The first was a massive conservation campaign. Radio broadcasters and schoolteachers, posters and newspapers, hammered home the message: "Wear it out, use it up, make it do, or do without."

The second program involved collecting and recycling essential materials. As a slogan put it, "Hit Hitler with Junk." For example, the lumber saved by recycling newspapers and magazines went into shipping crates for weapons. Schools and churches recruited millions of young "paper troopers" to collect millions of tons of scrap paper. Schoolchildren also attended weekly "fat parades," ceremonies in which they turned in containers of kitchen fats saved by their mothers. Fats yielded glycerin, used in making explosives. Other drives collected used tinfoil, chewing gum wrappers, batteries, and toothpaste tubes. The humblest bits of metal became weapons. For example, 30,000 used razor blades had enough steel to make 50 heavy machine guns; 30 discarded lipstick tubes had brass for 50 rifle cartridges.

Youngsters in Roanoke, Virginia, line up to turn in fat and grease to be recycled for glycerin. (October 1942)

Through rationing, planners aimed at giving everyone a fair share of scarce goods. Rationing took many forms, touching nearly every aspect of daily life. While Americans loved their cars, wartime driving followed this rule: "Petroleum products are the blood of battles that bring victory." To buy more than five gallons of gasoline a week, a driver employed in war work needed an official "priority." Even with a priority, you could not drive above the national speed limit of forty-five miles an hour, because higher speeds burned more fuel. Gasoline rationing all but ended pleasure driving. It also encouraged car pools and reduced highway deaths dramatically. Meanwhile, tires became precious as diamonds. To buy a new tire, or get a worn tire recapped, you needed a certificate from a government agency. Many drivers simply gave up and left their cars parked until the war was over.

Gasoline and tires were not the only items rationed. Americans needed ration coupons to buy meat, fish, bread, and butter. Coffee became a luxury. Housewives waited in long lines to buy a few ounces of sugar; alcohol obtained from sugar was an ingredient in smokeless gunpowder. People planted "victory gardens" in their backyards and open spaces, including Boston Common in

Left: A member of the Washington, D.C., Boys' Club wheels in a load of old sneakers to add to the nation's scrap-rubber collection. (June 1942)

Below: Plowing the Boston Common victory garden. (April 11, 1944)

the center of the city, growing their own food so crops from farms could go to troops. To get enough leather for military footwear, civilians could only buy two pairs of shoes a year. To save cloth for uniforms, men's suits, called "victory suits," had no lapels, vests, patch pockets, or cuffs. Women made do without girdles, garters, and dresses that went more than three inches below the knee. Ladies' silk and nylon stockings were things "to die for," the fabric going into parachutes. On the rare occasions that stores got a shipment of stockings, women rushed the counters as if their lives depended on it.

Many Americans resented enforced sacrifice. They should not have. Though no war is good, they had a more comfortable war than anyone else. In England, for example, onions were so scarce they became prizes in raffles. People got two ounces of butter a week. They were lucky to see one egg every two weeks; some gave eggs as Christmas gifts. Englishmen could buy a new suit every two years; Americans could buy all they wanted, though without cuffs or lapels. Englishwomen learned to do without personal items: undies, garter belts, stockings, and toiletries. If you were lucky, you could buy a tiny bar of foul-smelling brown soap every two weeks. Too many

Americans, FDR believed, whined like pampered children. Exasperated, he told Harold Ickes, "It really would be a good thing for us if a few German bombs could be dropped over here." *That* would wake people up.[31]

WOMEN'S WORK

A total of 16.3 million men served in America's armed forces during the war, including FDR's sons, who volunteered for combat duty. With so many men in uniform, industry had to find replacement workers. Desperate, it sought out people commonly labeled "abnormal" and "unemployable." For the first time in our history, such people took an important role in society. For example, "little people"—dwarfs—became airplane inspectors, slipping inside wings and other tight places. The deaf became riveters and drill operators, noisy jobs the hearing often found unbearable. The blind worked by "feel," sorting the sweepings of aircraft plants to salvage steel rivets. Mentally ill people found work, too. One lady, a fine machinist, thought she was the queen of England. Convicts, too, joined the war effort. "We are prisoners, true—but we are AMERICAN prisoners," said men in a Georgia penitentiary. Prisoners nationwide made tents, gun

Installing control wires on a ship. (Date unknown)

parts, cartridge clips, and antisubmarine nets. Inmates at a federal prison on Puget Sound, Washington, built navy patrol boats.[32]

Women were the nation's largest reserve of labor. This was nothing new. During the First World War, many European and American women took jobs in factories. Others became telegraphers and telephone operators, until then exclusively male occupations. As members of all-women units, they served as nurses, drove staff cars, coded and decoded messages, and did routine office work.

The Second World War demanded women's service on an unheard-of scale. On the Allied side, Britain drafted 125,000 women into the armed forces; another 400,000 volunteered. Army women became radio operators and code clerks, loaded bombs into planes, and staffed radar stations. All-women antiaircraft crews shot down Nazi bombers. Elsewhere, Soviet women were in the thick of the fighting. About 40 percent of the Red Army's frontline doctors and all its frontline nurses were women. Over a million Soviet women served as military police, tank commanders, artillery gunners, and snipers. Officers decided that graduates of the Central Women's School for Sniper Training were better shots than men because they tended to be calmer and more patient. The champion female sniper Lyudmila Pavlichenko killed 309 Nazi "supermen." Luftwaffe pilots dreaded the "Night Witches," a women's fighter squadron that flew at night.[33]

While American women did not fight, 350,000 joined the Women's Army Corps (WAC) and other military outfits, serving at home and behind the lines overseas. Though not allowed to fly combat missions, Women Airforce Service Pilots (WASP) ferried bombers from factories to American and British airfields. Some joined the elite Office of

Strategic Services (OSS), a dirty-tricks outfit modeled on Intrepid's British Security Coordination. Parachuted into Nazi-occupied Europe, they organized local resistance groups, led raids, and radioed information to OSS headquarters in London.

Best of all, American women were the backbone of the war industries. At first, male co-workers objected to them. "Women's place is in the home," they griped. Besides, "the ladies" were "not mechanical." Supposedly, they lacked the "natural ability" and "temperament" for precise tasks on delicate machinery. Objectors were right in one respect: certain jobs were impossible to do without a long training period. But the nation had no time to spare. Big Bill Knudsen had the answer. As with an auto assembly line, weapons could be mass-produced by breaking each task into its smallest parts.

Women who had never worked outside the home, or who had worked in lower-paying industrial jobs like making clothing, flocked to the war industries. "Rosie the Riveter" became their symbol. Featured in a propaganda poster, the fictional Rosie was a picture of health and determination. Flexing her muscles, she exclaimed, "We Can Do It!" As Redd Evans and John Jacob Loeb's song "Rosie the Riveter" put it:

Rosie the Riveter, flexing her biceps, became an icon for American women wanting to fight the war on the home front. (1942)

All the day long,
Whether rain or shine,
She's a part of the assembly line.
She's making history,
Working for victory,
Rosie the Riveter.

Like the woman in the poster, real-life Rosies wore thick-soled work shoes, a brightly colored bandanna, a denim shirt, and pants. Pants were more comfortable and safer around machinery than dresses—and they saved cloth.

Nearly 500,000 women went into the aircraft industry. Another 225,000 worked in shipyards. Fifteen million more mined coal, made steel, poured concrete, became lumberjacks, and did countless other war-related jobs. Gradually, they won the respect of male coworkers. Supervisors thought women a good influence in the workplace, as no man wanted his output to lag behind a woman's.

As with Soviet snipers, women tended to be calmer and more careful than men. Munitions work demanded these qualities, and courage, too. Women were 67 percent of the workforce at the Huntsville and Redstone Arsenals in Alabama. Each day, these busy plants turned out tons of high-explosive and incendiary bombs, artillery shells, and hand grenades. A wrong move around this dangerous stuff would have blown everything sky-high. War work taught women an important lesson: "You can do anything you want to do. You can be anybody you want to. And you can go anywhere you want to."[34]

Assembly-line methods also reshaped the two main war industries employing women. A division of the Ford Motor Company converted to making B-24 "Liberator" bombers. Its factory at Willow Run, west of Detroit, had a mile-long assembly line. As with making a car, work crews at "the Run" did hundreds of small, repetitive tasks. A visitor found the process awesome: "[It was] impossible in words to convey the feel and smell and tension of Willow Run under full headway.... The roar of the machinery, the special din of the riveting gun absolutely deafening nearby, the throbbing crash of the giant metal presses ... the far-reaching line of half-born sky ships growing wings under swarms of workers, the restless cranes swooping overhead." A Liberator rolled off Ford's assembly line every sixty-three minutes. Had Hitler seen the Run, workers boasted, he would have slit his throat. Better yet, at the height of production in March 1944, American factories turned out one plane every 295 seconds.[35]

Henry J. Kaiser used assembly-line methods to build cargo ships. An engineer by profession, Kaiser had built highways in California and played a key role in constructing Hoover Dam in Nevada. At his shipyards, Kaiser mass-produced "Liberty ships." Teams worked on several at once. As one team finished its task and moved on to the next vessel, a crane hoisted another numbered, factory-made section into place. Waiting teams, usually including women, then connected the sections to each other and to the hull. Meanwhile, yet more teams strung electrical wire, installed plumbing, and did the thousands of other things needed to launch a ship. Kaiser cut construction time from 355 to 41 days. Other shipbuilders copied Kaiser's methods, with the same results. Their efforts were essential to winning the Battle of the Atlantic.[36]

AFRICAN AMERICANS

Before Pearl Harbor, FDR told embattled Europeans, "We Americans are vitally concerned in the defense of your freedom." But he said nothing about defending the freedoms of millions of fellow citizens.[37]

The Second World War touched minorities, particularly African Americans, in many ways. At first, they barely shared in the economic recovery. Jim Crow still rode tall in the saddle. Job ads linked defense work to skin color. A typical ad went: "Wanted—white mechanics, tool and die makers, sheet metal workers." If a firm hired blacks, it was for "3-H" jobs—hot, hard, heavy. A North Ameri-

〰️ A view up one of the assembly lines at Ford's Willow Run plant, where B-24 Liberator bombers are being made. (February 1943)

can Aviation executive bluntly stated company policy: "The Negro will be considered only as janitors and in other similar capacities. Regardless of their training as aircraft workers, we will not employ them." Many "lily-white" unions belonged to the American Federation of Labor (AFL). Even if a firm wished to hire blacks, union rules kept them from entering the closed shop. Whites often walked off the job, willing to lose pay rather than work beside newly hired blacks. After all, they could get another job quickly in the war economy.[38]

Appeals for equal opportunity were ignored. As he had during the Great Depression, the president feared antagonizing racists. Apparently, FDR believed, the less said about Jim Crow, the better. With war drawing near, rearmament must go ahead with as little fuss as possible.

A tall black man with the rich baritone voice of an opera singer decided to make a fuss. A. Philip Randolph led the Brotherhood of Sleeping Car Porters, the only black union in the AFL. A man of iron principle, he spoke out against injustice wherever he found it. During the First World War, he earned a nickname: "The most dangerous Negro in America." Officials thought him dan-

A. Philip Randolph, leader of the Brotherhood of Sleeping Car Porters and a crusader for the empowerment of black Americans. (November 1942)

gerous because he opposed America's crusade to make the world safe for democracy while ignoring the plight of her black citizens.[39]

Randolph never called for violence, let alone revolution. Yet life had taught him that power speaks louder than fine words. "Only power," Randolph declared, "can effect the enforcement and adoption of a given policy, however meritorious it may be."[40]

In June 1941, six months before Pearl Harbor, Randolph sounded his call to action. "Be not dismayed in these terrible times," he told blacks. "You possess power, great power. The Negro stake in national defense is big. It consists of jobs, thousands of jobs. It consists of new industrial opportunities and hope. This is worth fighting for."[41]

How to fight? Randolph demanded that Roosevelt issue an executive order banning Jim Crow in the war industries. Should the president refuse, the National March on Washington Committee he'd formed would help change his mind. Randolph's idea caught on, energizing the African American community. Black churches and civic groups collected money to rent buses. Schoolchildren saved their allowances to pay for advertising. For the first time, thousands of blacks planned to act as one,

challenging Jim Crow in the nation's capital. FDR had preached the Four Freedoms. Now let him live up to them!

Roosevelt wanted to stop the march before it began. On June 18, as Hitler's armies made last-minute preparations for invading the USSR, "the most dangerous Negro in America" entered the Oval Study.

As usual, when he wanted to avoid an issue, FDR turned on the charm. "Hello, Phil. Which class were you in at Harvard?" he asked, smiling broadly. "Phil" did not smile. "I have never been to Harvard," Randolph replied. He had only graduated from an all-black high

What Are Our Immediate Goals?

1. To mobilize five million Negroes into one militant mass for pressure.

2. To assemble in Chicago the last week in May, 1943, for the celebration of

"WE ARE AMERICANS - TOO" WEEK

And to ponder the question of Non-Violent Civil Disobedience and Non-Cooperation, and a Mass March On Washington.

WHY SHOULD WE MARCH?

15.000 Negroes Assembled at St. Louis, Missouri
20.000 Negroes Assembled at Chicago, Illinois
23.500 Negroes Assembled at New York City
Millions of Negro Americans all Over This Great
Land Claim the Right to be Free!

FREE FROM WANT!
FREE FROM FEAR!
FREE FROM JIM CROW!

"Winning Democracy for the Negro is Winning the War for Democracy!" — A. Philip Randolph

A flyer rallying participants for a march on Washington for equality in the war industries. (1941)

school in Florida. The president then tried to change the subject by telling old political stories. The black leader would have none of it. FDR must issue an executive order ending discrimination in the defense industries. Period![42]

Roosevelt replied that no president could appear to give in to pressure. Let Randolph call off the march, then "we'll talk again." Talk is cheap, Randolph knew, and FDR was never at a loss for words. He would keep talking, keep smiling, keep delaying until blacks lost interest in marching. Randolph held his ground.[43]

How many would march? One hundred thousand, Randolph said, locking eyes with the man behind the desk. Roosevelt gave in, not because he wanted to but because he had to. A huge civil rights march, he declared, "would make the country look bad in wartime," tarnishing its image as a bastion of freedom.[44]

In return for Randolph's canceling the march, FDR issued Executive Order 8802. The order banned racial discrimination in the war industries and created the Fair Employment Practices Committee (FEPC) to handle complaints. As one African American newspaper noted, Randolph had proved that united action—power—for a just cause brought results. For it could "persuade, embarrass, compel and shame our government and our nation . . . into a more enlightened attitude toward a tenth of its people." It is no accident that Martin Luther King Jr. said he "idolized" Randolph, considering him the greatest living black man.[45]

Randolph set an example of nonviolent protest. In 1942, police in Tennessee savagely beat Bayard Rustin, a follower of Randolph's, for refusing to ride in the back of a bus. That same year, James Farmer, of the Congress of Racial Equality (CORE), led a sit-in at a Detroit restaurant, demanding it serve blacks. In Washington, students from all-black, all-female Howard University picketed segregated restaurants. Their signs read, OUR BOYS, OUR BROTHERS ARE FIGHTING FOR YOU. WHY CAN'T WE EAT HERE?[46]

Nevertheless, progress came slowly. The FEPC could only examine complaints, not force companies and unions to change their ways. Nor did Executive Order 8802 mention the armed forces. In 1941, the air corps and marines barred blacks entirely. The navy admitted them, but only as mess hall "boys." The army put them into segregated units under white officers. Barred from combat, black soldiers did various kinds of physical labor, such as hauling supplies. On the battlefield, some drove ambulances and carried stretchers.

Black soldiers faced prejudice at every turn. Since many training camps were located in the South, Jim Crow rules applied. Barracks, showers, mess halls, and toilets were strictly segregated. Black nurses could only tend to black soldiers; the navy had only four black nurses. In 1940, Charles Drew, an African American doctor, invented the method of preserving blood plasma still used today. The Red Cross and War Department knew blood transfusions saved lives and did not affect future generations. Yet, to satisfy those who claimed interracial transfusions would "mongrelize the nation," they segregated blood plasma into "colored" and "white."[47]

Outside camp, black soldiers met Jim Crow around every corner. German prisoners got more respect than they. Prisoners of war (POWs) and their guards ate at lunch counters with WHITES ONLY signs. Lunch counter segregation caused deep hurt and resentment. Poet Witter Bynner wrote,

On a train in Texas, German prisoners eat
With white American soldiers, seat by seat,
While black American soldiers sit apart—
The white men eating meat, the black men heart.[48]

Discrimination outraged the First Lady. While visiting an all-black army camp in Australia, she stepped into the canteen for a snack. Private Calvin Johnson was sitting at the counter, eating an ice cream cone. Eleanor went behind the counter and shook hands with each soldier in turn. When she came to Johnson, she looked into his eyes and said, "May I have some of that ice cream?" Everyone was shocked; blacks and whites did not share ice cream cones. "Very gently Mrs. Roosevelt took the cone out of my hand, took a big bite, and handed it back to me. 'You see,' she said, and smiled real wide, 'that didn't hurt a bit, did it?'" Her message: We are the same, and never think otherwise.[49]

However, her husband's hands-off policy raised questions. "What are we fighting for?" many blacks asked. "Why die for democracy for some foreign country when we don't even have it here?" A few sang, only half joking,

My country's tired of me
I'm going to Germany
Where I belong.[50]

Most, however, realized that Hitler must not be allowed to win. The Fuehrer embodied all the poisons of racism. Victory for him would go beyond Jim

Crow at its worst, promising to bring back slavery and, quite possibly, extermination. Therefore, the call went out for a "Double-V." The letter *V* was a powerful wartime symbol. Immediately after Pearl Harbor, V FOR VICTORY posters appeared everywhere. I remember how we third graders tapped the letter *V* in Morse code on our desks. Double-V stood for "Double Victory"—victory over foreign enemies and homegrown racism. "By fighting for our rights now," A. Philip Randolph declared, "American Negroes are helping make America a moral and spiritual arsenal of democracy."[51]

Racism threatened unity on the home front and, as a result, victory. When the war began, most blacks still lived in the rural South. However, the lure of jobs, decent wages, and escape from Jim Crow drew 1.6 million northward and westward. But as the black population rose in cities, friction with whites grew. During the long, hot summer of 1943, tensions erupted—242 race riots rocked the cities. Detroit and Harlem, a nearly all-black section of New York City, saw the worst riots. These left scores dead, hundreds injured, and millions of dollars' worth of property destroyed.

FDR sent troops to restore order in Detroit. Beyond that, he held true to form. Ever cautious, he reacted to the riots as he had to the proposed anti-lynching law. When civil rights leaders asked him to mount an educational campaign against racism, he issued bland statements expressing "regret" over the violence. Civil rights lawyer and activist Pauli Murray spoke for many in the biting poem "Mr. Roosevelt Regrets." In it, she asked a victim, a "black boy," what he got when bigots knocked him down, kicked out his teeth, and cracked his skull with a club.

> *What'd you get when you cried out to the Top*
> *Man?*
> *When you called out to the man next to God,*
> *so you thought,*
> *And you asked him to speak out and save you?*
> *What'd the Top Man say, black boy?*
> *"Mr. Roosevelt regrets. . . ."*[52]

Despite the turmoil, America began, very slowly, to change for the better. The 1943 riots were a wake-up call. The country simply could not afford such mayhem in wartime. To restore peace, communities acted on their own to form interracial committees to resolve local issues. For example, Detroit police officers had to attend classes dealing with social problems. Chicago added sections on black history to grade school textbooks.

Just as necessity is the mother of invention, she may also become the mother of justice. With the military demanding ever more production, ever more job opportunities opened to blacks. Of the million-plus blacks who found work in war industries, the vast majority—600,000—were women. Although they often faced prejudice, daily contact with whites gradually changed attitudes.

The experiences of Sybil Lewis were typical of this process. Sybil grew up in poverty in Oklahoma. Segregation was a way of life in her small town. When the war industries got going, Sybil headed for Lockheed Corporation in Burbank, California. "The war and defense work gave black people opportunities to work in jobs they never had before," she recalled. Sybil worked as a riveter beside a white farm girl from Arkansas. "Although we had our differences, we both learned to work together and talk together. We learned that despite our hostilities and resentments we could open up to each other and get along.... She learned that Negroes were people, too, and I saw her as a person also, and we both gained from it."[53]

Of necessity, the armed forces began to change, too. In 1943, a presidential order required them to accept blacks. White air corps officers, who had claimed "blacks were not smart enough to fly," trained pilots at the segregated Tuskegee Institute in Alabama. Fast learners, two all-black units, the 99th Pursuit Squadron and the 332nd Fighter Group, chalked up distinguished combat records. Nicknamed the "Little Friends," they escorted their "Big Friends," the heavy bombers, on missions over Germany. Bomber squadrons remained all-white. Yet their crews asked commanders to assign a black fighter squadron to "ride shotgun" for them. The blacks, they said, were reliable and lucky—and they never lost a bomber to German fighters.

The navy assigned black sailors to work details, handling supplies and am-

Twenty-year-old Annie Tabor, a highly skilled lathe operator, manufacturing parts for aircraft engines. (October 1942)

African American aviators in flight suits at the Tuskegee Army Air Field. (1941–1945)

munition. During enemy raids, however, whites found that black machine gunners shot straight as any. The marine corps recruited 20,000 blacks for segregated combat and construction units.

A million blacks served in the army, chiefly as service troops in segregated outfits. As part of the "Red Ball Express," they drove the miles-long columns of supply trucks needed as it advanced after the invasion of France in 1944. During heavy fighting, commanders attached black outfits to white units. One commander, General George S. Patton, gave the 761st Tank Battalion a pep talk. "I don't care what color you are as long as you go up there and kill those [blankety-blank Nazis]!" Patton growled. "Everyone has their eyes on you and is expecting great things from you. Most of all, your race is looking forward to you. Don't let them down and, damn you, don't let me down!" The 761st let nobody down. It captured thirty towns in France, Belgium, and Germany. However, segregation in the armed forces outlived Roosevelt and the Second World War. President Harry S. Truman banned it in 1948.[54]

We have gotten ahead of our story. To win on the battlefield, America had first to win the battles of production. This she did—magnificently. Thanks to FDR's leadership, she truly became the arsenal of democracy.

The numbers are mind-boggling. From July 1940 to August 1945, American assembly lines and shipyards produced two-thirds of all the equipment used by the Allies in the Second World War. This included 286,000 warplanes, 88,410 tanks and self-propelled guns, 2.6 million trucks, 141 aircraft carriers, 8 battleships, 807 cruisers and destroyers, 208 submarines, 50 million tons of merchant shipping, 257,000 artillery pieces, 2.6 million machine guns, and 41 *billion* rounds of ammunition. In 1944 alone, America built as many weapons as Germany, Japan, and Italy combined.[55]

Joseph Stalin knew what these numbers meant. After the war, the Soviet tyrant said the Nazis lost because Hitler "could not understand that war is won in the factories."[56]

THE SURVIVAL WAR

So I am looking for a word . . . I want a name for the war. . . . My own thought is that perhaps there is one word that we could use for this war, the word "survival." The Survival War. That is what it comes pretty close to being—the survival of our civilization, the survival of democracy.
—*Franklin D. Roosevelt, April 14, 1942*

ARCADIA

December 22, 1941. Anacostia Flats Naval Air Station. Night. The darkened plane eased to a stop beside Al Capone's former limousine. As attendants rolled the stairway into place, its door opened and chubby, rosy-cheeked Winston Churchill appeared with a cigar clenched between his teeth. Franklin Roosevelt stood below, leaning on the arm of a naval aide. Moments later, they shook hands, got into the limousine, and sped off toward the White House.

Churchill had come at a grim time. In the two weeks since Pearl Harbor, the war news seemed to worsen by the hour. In Europe, Hitler's tank divisions neared the outskirts of Moscow. In the Middle East, General Erwin Rommel, the famed "Desert Fox," landed with his Afrika Korps (Africa Corps) in Italian-ruled Libya. Once ashore, Rommel drove east toward Egypt and the Suez Canal, Britain's lifeline to India and Burma, the core of its empire in the Far East.

In Asia, Japanese forces had already seized, or soon would seize, the Philippines, Wake Island, Guam, Malaya, Hong Kong, Thailand, and the Dutch East Indies. In the Indian Ocean, Japanese carrier planes easily sank the mighty *Prince of Wales* and her escort, the cruiser *Repulse*. With each victory announcement, jubilant crowds gathered outside the Imperial Palace in Tokyo to shout *banzai* to Emperor Hirohito—"May you live ten thousand years!" Children stuck tiny Rising Sun flags into maps to mark each triumph. In all, Japan would add a million square miles of territory, 150 million people, and priceless natural resources to her empire.

Now, three days before Christmas, Churchill led his top military men to a conference in Washington. Code-named for a region in ancient Greece famed for its peace and quiet, the Arcadia Conference was the first time the leaders of the democracies met as war-

A portrait of Japanese emperor Hirohito. (1935)

time allies. Together with the USSR, they formed what the prime minister called the "Grand Alliance."

Churchill stayed at the White House. He proved a difficult guest, with habits the Roosevelt women found hard to take. The Englishman filled the mansion with cigar smoke and used snuff, powdered tobacco, lavishly. "The sneezes which follow the latter," Anna wrote her brother John, "practically rock the foundations of the house and he then blows his nose about three times like a fog horn." His night-owl ways kept FDR up till three in the morning, smoking and talking about war. Eleanor thought Churchill glorified war, treating it as a game. "They looked," she said, "like two little boys playing soldier. They seemed to be having a wonderful time, too wonderful in fact. It made me a little sad somehow."[1]

What bothered her most was Churchill's love of strong drink, the very thing that had killed her father and spoiled her childhood. Churchill could not get along without regular doses of alcohol. On his first morning in the White House, he took butler Alonzo Fields aside. "Now, Fields," said he, "we had a lovely dinner last night but I have a few orders for you. . . . I must have a tumbler of sherry in my room before breakfast [as a waker-upper], a couple of glasses of scotch and soda before lunch, and French champagne and 90-year-old brandy before I go to sleep at night." Despite all that alcohol, he seemed clearheaded and alert.[2]

Churchill had a quick wit, too, as Roosevelt found to his surprise. One day, the prime minister wrapped himself in an enormous towel after he got out of the bathtub. Walking into his bedroom, he began dictating a memo to his male secretary. As he paced back and forth, the towel fell to the floor, leaving him all pink and naked. No matter; he kept pacing and dictating amid clouds of cigar smoke. Suddenly the door opened and an aide wheeled FDR into the room. Startled, the president apologized for not knocking. Churchill grinned and said, "You see, Mr. President, I have nothing to conceal from you." He meant it. Later, he revealed that British intelligence had been reading State Department messages since the First World War.[3]

The result of Arcadia, the public learned, was a grandly worded Declaration of the United Nations. Roosevelt coined the term "United Nations" for those countries united against the Nazis. The name only later applied to an organization, also FDR's idea, to keep the peace after the war. Eventually, representatives of twenty-six nations signed the declaration. In doing so, they promised to fight until "complete victory" for the principles of the Atlantic Charter. They would fight to defend "life, liberty, independence and religious freedom" and "to preserve human rights and justice in their own lands as well as in other lands." Not all who signed were sincere, least of all Joseph Stalin. Nor would Roosevelt and Churchill keep their promises, as time would tell.[4]

The important doings at Arcadia went on behind closed doors. At these meetings, the leaders worked out their overall plan for fighting the Second World War. It was really *two* wars—against Germany and Italy in Europe and the Japanese in Asia. How to fight them at once? Should the democracies divide their efforts equally? Or should they concentrate on one enemy? If so, which one? These questions had already occurred to Hitler. A week before Churchill arrived in Washington, the Nazi leader wondered aloud: "Is there any possibility that the U.S.A. and Britain will abandon East Asia for a time in order to crush Germany and Italy first?" Yes, there was.[5]

Japan was dangerous; Pearl Harbor had proved that. Her "sneak attack" enraged Americans, who wanted all-out war in the Pacific, treating Europe as a sideshow. However, Roosevelt and Churchill decided there was no chance of Japan's dominating the world. Tokyo's warlords, vicious as they were, seemed content to seize the resource-rich lands of Asia. Germany was different. Hitler aimed at world domination, and he had the most powerful war machine ever built. So the two leaders decided to fight Japan with the smallest forces they could safely spare, while throwing their main strength against Germany. After victory in Europe, they would settle with the Japanese, hopefully with the aid of the USSR.

Waging war on a global basis required a large-scale organization. That, in turn, meant breaking with tradition. The British and American militaries had their own high commands: the Imperial General Staff and the Joint Chiefs of Staff, respectively. Each staff chief headed an armed service—army, navy, or air force. Their experts planned operations, assigned missions to the services, and made sure they worked together.

Roosevelt and Churchill knew this setup could not work in a global war. Each country's acting on its own would be like two horses pulling a wagon in different directions. Instead, the leaders wanted unity of command under the Combined Chiefs of Staff (CCS). The CCS would advise the civilian leaders, the president and prime minister, who set broad goals, like defeating Germany before Japan. The CCS would then draw up plans for various military operations, deciding when, how, and with what forces to carry them out. Depending on the situation, an American might take charge, giving orders to British forces, and vice versa. Based in Washington, the CCS eventually had hundreds of specialized committees and planning groups. By 1945, nearly 10,000 British officers had crowded into the capital and the Pentagon, the new headquarters of the U.S. military in Arlington, Virginia.[6]

The Combined Chiefs of Staff in Quebec almost two years after the Arcadia Conference. (August 23, 1943)

GLIMMERINGS OF HOPE

Though Arcadia set out a war strategy, nothing changed immediately. Nearly all the news for the first half of 1942 continued to be bad for the democracies. The Japanese, however, had less to cheer about than they first thought. While Allied strategy called for defeating Hitler first, America scored her earliest victories against the Empire of the Rising Sun.

Their seeds lay in Pearl Harbor. The Pacific Fleet had not died there—far from it. Despite the damage, Pearl Harbor was still a working naval base, its dockyards, warehouses, and repair shops intact. Its fuel depots, holding 5 million barrels of oil and gasoline, had received not a scratch. Apart from the battleships, most vessels were undamaged or easily repaired. Even the battleships were luckier than it seemed at first glance. The harbor's waters are shallow, easily allowing salvage operations. In time, five battleships rose from the mud to take their revenge. Best of all, the base's three aircraft carriers—*Saratoga, Enterprise,* and *Lexington*—had been at sea when the attack came. In 1942, they were worth their weight in gold.

Before Pearl Harbor, navies had fought the same way for centuries. Lines of ships stood at a distance, hurling at each other tons of solid iron cannonballs and, later, explosive shells. The side that lost the fewest of its largest, or "capital," ships won the battle. In the 1920s, however, America, Britain, and Japan pioneered in flying planes off ships and recovering them when they returned from a mission. Though no one knew it then, the aircraft carrier would change sea warfare. For without air cover, the mightiest warship was helpless against dive-bombers and torpedo planes. Aircraft carriers allowed fighter planes to fly and refuel in the middle of the ocean. Now the battleships existed not to sink the enemy fleet but to protect the floating air bases. "Get the flattops" became *the* rule of the Pacific war.

The first good news to reach the White House came from America's flattops. On April 18, the *Hornet,* fresh from California, and the *Enterprise* entered Japanese home waters. All aboard knew the significance of that date. It was the 167th anniversary of Paul's Revere's ride to warn that the British meant to seize patriot guns stored at Concord, Massachusetts.

The *Enterprise,* under Admiral William F. "Bull" Halsey, was there to protect her sister ship with fighter planes. The *Hornet* had no fighters. Instead, she carried sixteen army B-25 twin-engine bombers. With the warm support of the president, their commander, Colonel James H. Doolittle, had trained his men to do the "impossible": launch land-based bombers from the rolling deck of a carrier. Doolittle's mission was to bomb military targets in Tokyo and three other cities. Afterward, the raiders would land on Chinese airfields. Nobody, least of all FDR, expected the raid to do serious damage. Instead, it would raise American morale while telling the enemy to expect a long war.

Caught by surprise, the Japanese failed to shoot down a single B-25. The trouble began afterward. Fuel ran low as the bombers headed across the Sea of Japan. Three went down off the China coast; the rest crash-landed in China, where villagers led their crews to safety in the interior. Upon learning that civilians had helped "Yankee air pirates," vengeful Japanese forces ravaged eastern China. A Chinese official wrote FDR: "These Japanese troops slaughtered every man, woman and child in those areas—let me repeat—slaughtered every man, woman and child in those areas." Not only did troops shoot and bayonet civilians, they sprayed cholera, typhoid, and bubonic plague germs. This made Japan the only country to use biological weapons in the Second World War. No fewer than 250,000 Chinese died in reprisal for the Doolittle raid.[7]

Less than a month later, American carriers had their first victory against enemy ships. On May 6, a Japanese invasion force steamed into the Coral Sea, bound for New Guinea, a large, jungle-covered island north of Australia. Navy cryptographers (code experts) had broken Japan's naval codes and could read every message the force sent or received. The Americans sprang a trap, and while each side lost a carrier in the Battle of the Coral Sea, the Japanese turned back.

On June 4, a huge Japanese force made for Midway Island, northwest of Pearl Harbor. Again, cryptographers learned of the enemy's plan. Over two days, dive-bombers sank four of the six carriers that had launched the Pearl Harbor attack, sending almost all aboard to the bottom—because no Japanese warship carried rafts or life belts, as it was considered "shameful" and "cowardly" for the defeated to survive. The Americans lost one carrier, the *Yorktown*. With the disaster at Midway, Japan's winning streak snapped. "After Midway," recalled Japan's navy minister, Admiral Mitsumasa Yonai, "I was certain there was no chance of success." He was right, though it would take three years of bitter fighting and two atomic bombs to force Japan's surrender.[8]

America began to retake key islands, a job that fell to navy "task forces." By definition, a task force had a specific task, such as seizing an island. To do that, it had hundreds of ships, spread over hundreds of square miles of Pacific Ocean. By 1943, West Coast shipyards were turning out bigger, faster, deadlier aircraft carriers. These rode at the center of the task force, screened from enemy aircraft by battleships, cruisers, destroyers, and their own fighter planes. "Fleet trains" of oil tankers, ammunition ships, and general goods vessels kept the fighting ships supplied, so they could stay at sea for months without having to return to port. Each task force had its own assault force of marines or army troops. The idea was not to take every Japanese-held island, a lengthy, costly, and unnecessary process.

The USS *Yorktown* is hit by a torpedo amid heavy antiaircraft fire during the Battle of Midway. (June 4, 1942)

Instead, task forces would take an island, then "leapfrog"—bypass—other, nearby enemy strongholds. Cut off from supplies, and attacked constantly by carrier planes, their garrisons would starve or die of tropical diseases.

Nothing showed America's industrial might better than these leapfrogging operations. The Japanese fought bravely, often to the last man, killing many Americans. Yet Big Bill Knudsen and his colleagues had given the troops every material advantage. As the saying went, "Never send a man where you can send a bomb, a shell, or a bullet." Planners calculated it cost $40,000 to kill each Japanese soldier. War is never cheap.[9]

Yet this was just the tip of the iceberg. For every four tons of supplies sent to American fighting men in the Pacific, Japan sent only two pounds to her own troops. When landing on an enemy-held island, every marine and soldier could count on forty-five pounds of supplies supporting him each day, including a ration of exactly twenty-two and a half sheets of toilet paper. Almost from the moment assault troops gained a foothold, navy construction units, called Seabees, built airfields so fighters could give them close support. "Why was it that it took the Americans only a few days to build an airbase and the Japanese more

than a month?" Emperor Hirohito asked his naval chief of staff. Admiral Osami Nagano could only say, "I am very sorry." He did not say that the Seabees had masses of bulldozers, tractors, and steam shovels, while the Japanese had mostly hand shovels and muscles.[10]

CASABLANCA

Americans carried nearly the entire burden of the war against Japan in the Pacific. Meanwhile, in North Africa, they joined the British to prepare for the liberation of Western Europe.

German general Erwin Rommel, also known as the Desert Fox. (1942)

General Rommel had lived up to his nickname. In a series of ferocious tank battles, the Desert Fox raced toward the Suez Canal in Egypt. Winston Churchill admired the German's ability and fighting spirit. "We have," said the prime minister, "a very daring and skillful opponent against us, and may I say across the havoc of war, a great general."[11]

Yet Rommel met his match in a general Churchill put in charge of British forces in the Middle East. Bernard Law Montgomery, a much-decorated and much-wounded veteran of the First World War, met the Afrika Korps at a remote desert outpost called El Alamein. Recently, his Eighth Army had received massive Lend-Lease shipments of Sherman tanks, Ford trucks, artillery, aircraft guns, ammunition, and fuel. "Monty" used these well. On October 23, 1942, he unleashed his own version of blitzkrieg. British artillery pounded the enemy for six hours nonstop. When the big guns fell silent, tanks and infantry advanced under an umbrella of dive-bombers and low-flying fighters. Monty's victory was a turning point. "Before Alamein we never had a victory," Churchill wrote. "After Alamein we never had a defeat."[12]

Months before the battle, the Combined Chiefs of Staff had begun to lay plans to destroy the Afrika Korps. Now,

British soldiers advance through dust and smoke in the Battle of El Alamein. (October 24, 1942)

as Rommel fell back to Libya, the plans were set in motion. Three invasion forces—two from England, and one from Norfolk, Virginia—sailed for North Africa. General Dwight Eisenhower, a brilliant organizer with a gift for getting people to work together, was in overall command. Luckily, few U-boats prowled the South Atlantic that fall, as most were busy attacking convoys far to the north. So, on November 8, Allied troops landed at Casablanca in Morocco and at Algiers and Oran in Algeria. As they splashed ashore, the telephone rang in the White

House. The big man's hand shook as he raised the receiver to his ear. "Thank God. Thank God," Roosevelt said, much relieved. "We have landed in North Africa. Casualties are below expectations. We are striking back."[13]

Caught between Eisenhower's and Montgomery's forces, Rommel fought with his usual skill, but it was no use. Desperately short of supplies, especially fuel for his tanks, the Desert Fox knew the end was near. Though he would escape across the Mediterranean Sea with the remnants of the Afrika Korps, he left behind 350,000 German and Italian dead and prisoners. Nearly all the captives went to camps in the Southern states—and got more respect than African American soldiers.

FDR observes the troops at Camp Anfa during his trip to the Casablanca Conference. (January 18, 1943)

With victory near in North Africa, Roosevelt and Churchill had to discuss their next moves in person. From January 14 to 24, 1943, they met at Casablanca. For FDR, the meetings set two precedents. He became the first president to leave America in wartime and to fly to a foreign destination. Though presidents now use Air Force One, a luxurious flying hotel and command center, Roosevelt had no official plane. Aides warned that the long flight would worsen a sinus condition that had troubled him since his teens. The president scoffed at their concern; he was "sick and tired of people telling him it was dangerous to ride in airplanes." The presidential party flew in the four-engine *Sacred Cow*, a transport specially equipped with an elevator to lift the president aboard. After a refueling stop in Brazil, it headed across the South Atlantic to Africa, a flight lasting eighteen hours.[14]

Roosevelt, Churchill, and the Combined Chiefs of Staff met several times a day. Between meetings, the military brass relaxed on the beach, sunbathing, swimming, and building sand castles. Escorted by General Eisenhower, the president inspected American troops. When a surprised soldier cried, "Gosh—it's the old man himself," FDR burst out laughing. He also held his hat over his heart out of respect and gratitude for the soldiers' service.[15]

The meetings were all business. Allied leaders planned to crush Germany in the jaws of a gigantic vise. The Soviet jaw would close from the east. The Anglo-American jaw would close from the west in two stages. From bases in North Africa, their armies would cross the Mediterranean Sea to Europe. First, they would seize the island of Sicily at the tip of the Italian "boot," then invade Italy itself. Later, the largest seaborne invasion force in history would sail from England. Dubbed Operation Overlord, it would start with American, British, and Canadian forces crossing the English Channel to Normandy in northern France. After liberating France, they would drive east, into the heart of Germany.

Roosevelt also demanded "unconditional surrender." This meant the Allies would not agree to anything less than total victory. There would be no armistice to sign, as in the First World War, only a surrender document. If the enemy—Germany, Italy, and Japan—refused to surrender, they faced annihilation. Then, as now, critics questioned the wisdom of this demand. It would, supposedly, force the other side to fight to the last ditch, prolonging the war needlessly.

FDR saw things differently. He had thought the idea through carefully, discussing it with Churchill, who agreed with his reasoning. Unconditional surrender would prevent Germany from claiming she had lost not on the battlefield but at the peace table. After the First World War, Hitler had used the anger stirred by the Treaty of Versailles to win votes and, finally, absolute power. It was clear that the Fuehrer would rather die than surrender, even if that meant dragging his country down in flames. "Negotiation with Hitler was impossible," Churchill later wrote. "He was a maniac with supreme power to play his hand to the end, which he did; and so did we."[16]

On their last night in Casablanca, Roosevelt and Churchill toasted each

❧ FDR with Winston Churchill at the Casablanca Conference. (January 18, 1943)

other with champagne. Since the president was leaving before dawn, he insisted the prime minister stay in bed. "Now, Winston," he said, "don't you get up in the morning to see me off. I'll be wheeled into your room to kiss you goodbye." As promised, FDR came before dawn. But no kisses. Instead, Churchill leaped out of bed, dressed quickly, and rode with him to the airport. As the *Sacred Cow* took off, Churchill told aides, "If anything happens to that man, I couldn't stand it. He is the greatest man I've ever known."[17]

VICTORY IN THE ATLANTIC

To launch Overlord, the democracies first had to build up their forces in Great Britain, an enormously difficult and dangerous task. American armies had to assemble in camps across the island nation, along with mountains of supplies for the invasion. But none of this could happen without first securing the North Atlantic shipping lanes. More, the Allies needed to cripple Germany's war industries and transportation network. At Casablanca, the civilian and military leaders discussed both problems in detail.

As Hitler tried to cut Britain's supply line at its source—the United States—the Battle of the Atlantic escalated. In January 1942, just days after Pearl Harbor, he ordered Operation Drumbeat to begin. "Drumbeat" was code for sending U-boats to the East Coast of the United States. Wolf packs with code names like Leopard, Panther, and Puma began hunting close to shore. Crewmen sang about this "happy time," when they felt invincible.

> *High over the waves or deep under the sea*
> *We sail as fast as a storm wind.*
> *And like the shark sharing blood*
> *We seek the enemy brood.*
> *Nothing can stop us, we defy the elements*
> *Forward to duty, U-boat soldier.*[18]

It was truly their happy time. The U.S. Navy was not prepared to deal with submarines in its own front yard. Overconfident, its chiefs had ignored basic precautions, as the British had at such terrible cost in lives and ships. Instead of ordering ships to form convoys in coastal waters, navy brass let them sail individually, without radio silence, destroyer escorts, or air cover. So U-boats picked them off individually. In the first three months of Drumbeat, they sank 216 vessels, 8 outside New York Harbor in just twelve hours.

Nobody seems to have thought about turning off the lights as a safety measure. Seaside resorts from Atlantic City, New Jersey, to Miami, Florida, and the Gulf of Mexico kept their lights burning brightly at night. Resort owners said colorful neon lights created a festive mood, attracting vacationers and dollars. They also attracted U-boats like moths to flames. A bold skipper even raised his periscope in New York Harbor, near the Statue of Liberty. "It's absolutely unbelievable," he said as he peered at the glittering city. Why, he joked, he could make out tourists on the observation deck of the Empire State Building![19]

Ships' crews saw death written in bright lights. Silhouetted against the illuminated shoreline, outbound vessels fell easy prey to waiting U-boats. A sailor pulled from the water off New Jersey told reporters he had lost twenty shipmates because "it was lit up like daylight all along the beach. The submarine was right there, waiting for the first boat to come along." In one night, U-123 skipper Reinhard Hardegen sank three merchantmen and blew a hole in a fourth. Taken together, this represented a material loss to the Allies

⌁ U.S. servicemen sleep aboard ship as they journey to one of the fighting fronts. (June 29, 1943)

of 42 tanks, 24 armored cars, 96 heavy guns, 5,210 tons of ammunition, and 2,000 tons of food and general supplies.[20]

Tanker crews faced the greatest danger. When fully loaded, a tanker moved slowly and rode low in the water—a perfect target for a submarine. Seaman Frank Trubisz told how it was aboard the *Esso Baton Rouge.* "It was like a shooting gallery. You were in a constant state of tension," he recalled. "You couldn't get enough guys to go on tankers. One guy told me, 'Hell, I'm gonna go join the army, it's safer. Picture yourself sitting out there on about 140,000 barrels of high-octane gas. That's something to think about!'" Years later, Trubisz still could not get over the experience of being torpedoed. "I'm one of the lucky ones. I mean, nerves. Some of the other guys are worse off than I am, especially those that got burnt. But I still get nightmares."[21]

Beaches became gooey with oil from torpedoed tankers. Charred bodies and splintered lifeboats washed ashore at high tide. Off Virginia Beach, Virginia, bathers watched, horror-stricken, as two ships exploded in broad daylight. One night, off Jacksonville, Florida, a U-boat surfaced to sink a tanker with its deck cannon. With flames lighting the sky, guests rushed from hotels and restaurants to see the spectacle. "All the vacationers had seen an impressive special performance at Roosevelt's expense," the U-boat's skipper wrote in his logbook. "A burning tanker, artillery fire, the silhouette of a U-boat—how often had all of that been seen in America?"[22]

No wonder U-boat men felt invincible. After sinking nine ships, one off Cape Hatteras, North Carolina, Captain Jochen Mohr, of the *U-124,* sent an unencoded radio signal for all to read:

> *The new-moon night is black as ink.*
> *Off Hatteras the tankers sink.*
> *While sadly Roosevelt counts the score—*
> *Some fifty thousand tons—by MOHR.*[23]

Roosevelt vowed to stop Mohr and his kind. Like Abraham Lincoln during the Civil War, he followed events closely. In the White House Map Room, built specially for him, officers constantly updated wall maps showing the fighting fronts worldwide. However, flashy uniforms, shiny medals, and colored ribbons did not impress the former assistant secretary of the navy. He had been around military men long enough to know they were just men, not gods. Usually, he left details to the experts, preferring to focus on the military "big picture" and diplomacy. Yet, should their advice clash with his ideas, he did not hesitate to overrule them. The Battle of the Atlantic showed FDR at his best.

So it was that navy brass, on White House orders, imposed a coastal blackout from Maine to Florida and the Gulf of Mexico. Drivers had to turn off their headlights near the ocean at night or face a year in jail and a $5,000 fine. No vessel could sail along the coast without joining a convoy. Coast Guard patrols doubled, and doubled again. With most destroyers assigned to large Britain-bound convoys, Roosevelt ordered an updated version of his First World War splinter fleet of sleek wooden patrol boats. Two thousand prime oak trees even came from his estate at Hyde Park. Nicknamed "Donald Duck's Navy," the vessels built from Roosevelt's trees spotted German submarines running on the surface recharging their batteries.

Though America's coastal waters became safer, the Battle of the Atlantic still raged. The problem was that the widest part of the Black Pit in mid-ocean was beyond the range of land-based aircraft. Unless a way was found to put "eyes in the sky," keeping it under constant observation, the buildup for Overlord could not go forward.

There was only one plane able to cover the Black Pit. The navy had 112 VLRs—Very Long Range B-24 Liberator bombers. With their extra-large fuel tanks, these planes could patrol for many hours, day or night. Equipped with radar, a radio-wave device for tracking objects on a screen, a VLR might spot a submarine on the surface up to ten miles away. The VLR then radioed for destroyers or attacked on its own with bombs, cannons, and machine guns. At night, the pilot switched on Leigh Lights, a British invention, to illuminate a patch of ocean the size of several football fields.

However, the admirals had reserved these planes for the Pacific. After Casablanca, Roosevelt intervened again, personally ordering sixty VLRs to patrol the Black Pit. He also favored a new type of aircraft carrier. Henry J. Kaiser wanted to build a class of small "escort carriers," or "baby flattops," that could carry up to twenty planes, a third the capacity of full-size "fleet" carriers. This, Kaiser believed, would enable convoys to bring their own air cover along, rather than rely on land-based planes. When the navy turned him down, Kaiser went to the White House. FDR loved the idea. According to one historian, "The escort carrier was forced upon the Navy by the President." Before long, Kaiser's shipyards were building one baby flattop a week.[24]

Prodded by FDR, the navy formed "hunter-killer" groups of destroyers, VLRs, and escort carriers. A secret weapon known only to the highest-ranking civilian and military leaders aided them in countless ways. Code-named Ultra, it was Poland's most precious gift to the democracies. The Germans had invented a machine, called "Enigma," for making "unbreakable" codes. In the late 1930s, Polish intelligence learned of Enigma and began to unlock its secrets. Days before Poland's surrender, agents escaped to France, then to England, with their models and drawings of Enigma. The British then built exact copies of the machine, which allowed them to read most German radio messages, often before Nazi receivers decoded them. Not only did the British, who shared Ultra with the Americans (but not the Soviets), know many Nazi plans in advance, but they could track the movements of the wolf packs and route the convoys away from the lurking U-boats. Next to the atomic bomb, Ultra was the most closely guarded Allied secret of the Second World War.

Before long, the hunters became the hunted, their "happy time" ending in explosions and screams. Even those U-boat crews who survived an attack were left unfit for duty. "We crash-dived seven times and shook off twenty-eight attacks by bombs and depth charges," a skipper wrote in his log. "By sunrise, we were stunned, deaf, and exhausted." Within a month, May 1943, fifty-six U-boats were destroyed, nearly a third of the total at sea. Hitler ordered the rest back to their bases in France. When they returned to action later that year, the hunter-killer groups tore them to shreds. The Battle of the Atlantic was over.[25]

It had been history's longest sea battle, fought round the clock, in all seasons

〰 A scout plane from the aircraft carrier USS *Ranger* returns from a patrol flight of the area through which a convoy is passing. (1940–1946)

and weather. Germany lost a staggering 696 of her 830 U-boats. Of the 40,900 men who served aboard them, 25,870 never returned, a 63 percent death rate, the highest of any fighting service of any country in the war. Still, victory cost the Allies dearly. Out of some 2,000 convoys that sailed from America and Canada, German submarines sank 2,779 cargo ships and tankers and 148 warships. Over 85,000 seamen, mostly British, lost their lives. But none died in vain. After May 1943, over 1.5 million American soldiers arrived safely in England. U-boats sank not one troopship.[26]

THE AIR WAR

At Casablanca, the leaders also focused on the air war, the second part of the buildup for Overlord. When the conference ended, the Combined Chiefs of Staff issued a secret order called the Casablanca Directive. It instructed the American and British air staffs to plan the Combined Bomber Offensive, which was aimed at destroying Germany's war-making ability. The full weight of Allied airpower would fall on her industry and transportation network and on her civilian population, too. In other words, the Allies planned to make ordinary Germans so miserable that they would lose the will to resist and would perhaps even rebel against Hitler.

The Allies did not start the bombing of civilians; their enemies did. Beginning in 1937, Japanese planes pummeled undefended Chinese cities to spread panic. A famous photo shows a crying baby surrounded by wreckage, the only living soul in a Shanghai railroad station. Around the same time, during his conquest of Ethiopia in East Africa, Benito Mussolini bombed defenseless villages of mud-and-straw huts. The dictator's son Vittorio, a pilot, compared the fiery explosions to luscious red blossoms opening.

The Nazis proudly began what they themselves called the "terror bombing" of cities. For openers, they deliberately targeted Polish civilians. Pilots swooped in low, machine-gunning women and girls picking potatoes in the fields. They bombed churches and hospitals, even shot at toddlers fleeing burning nursery schools. Warsaw, the Polish capital, "had become a gigantic bonfire," the glow of flames reflecting blood-red off the clouds. "What had become of the beautiful city I had known?" a German officer wondered. But his Fuehrer was delighted. "Take a good look around

A young Polish boy amid the ruins of Warsaw. (September 1939)

Warsaw," he told newspaper reporters after its surrender. "That is how I can deal with any European city." And he did. Later, the Luftwaffe bombed the sprawling Dutch seaport of Rotterdam and pounded London and other English cities. Just before the Casablanca Conference, German airmen killed over 40,000 Soviet civilians in the city of Stalingrad.[27]

What the enemy started, the Allies would finish, only on what was then an unimaginably larger scale. In war, as in life, we must make moral choices. For this reason, Allied actions raise questions about the morality of bombing cities. Can a worthy end—defeating a monstrous tyranny like Hitler's—ever justify killing civilians wholesale? Did bombing cities put Allied leaders on the same moral level as their enemies? Would future generations say, as critics said of the Puritans' wars against the Massachusetts Indians in the 1600s, "that we were wolves with the minds of men?" Thoughtful people still ponder the morality of the Allies' air war. However, many (perhaps most) of those who lived through the terror bombing of Warsaw and the Battle of Britain believed the German people deserved what they got. Had it not been for them, the argument went, Hitler would not have come to power in the first place.[23]

Winston Churchill had no qualms about bombing enemy civilians. In 1920, during an uprising in British-controlled Iraq, Churchill, as minister of aviation, wished to drop poison gas on rebels. "I am strongly in favor of using poisoned gas against uncivilized tribes," he wrote in a secret memo. "It is not necessary to use the most deadly gases . . . [just those able to] spread a lively terror and yet leave no serious permanent effects on most of those affected." This was nonsense. A "mild" poison gas could easily kill the infirm, the elderly, and young children. Anyhow, the military had yet to devise a method of spreading poison gas by airplane.[29]

Later, as prime minister, Churchill returned to his idea of "lively terror."

The prime minister vowed to defeat Hitler at *any* cost. In this struggle for survival, he thought, the end justified the means. And so moral boundaries vanished. "There are no sacrifices we will not make, no lengths of violence to which we will not go, to destroy Nazi tyranny," Churchill told British lawmakers. For that reason, he ordered the RAF to launch "an absolutely devastating, exterminating attack by heavy bombers from this country upon the Nazi homeland."[30]

It followed that German civilian morale was a proper target. By the summer of 1944, Churchill went even further, returning to the subject of poison gas. He asked his air chiefs "to think very seriously" about drenching "cities in Germany with poison gas" so that "most of the population would be requiring constant medical attention." The chiefs wisely rejected his idea. Hitler, they feared, would retaliate by moving British and American war prisoners into likely target areas.[31]

FDR said different things to different people at different times about bombing civilians. At first, he called it murder, pure and simple. When the Japanese bombed Chinese cities in 1937, he called their actions "ruthless" and "barbarous." The maiming and death "of thousands of defenseless men, women and children has sickened the hearts of every civilized man and woman, and has profoundly shocked the conscience of humanity," he added. Congress agreed, formally declaring city bombing a "crime against humanity." America's initial policy, then, was to use airpower strictly against military targets: troops, fortifications, naval bases, factories, bridges, and railroads.[32]

Events persuaded the president to change his mind. When Churchill sent bombers to German cities, they flew at night because it was safer. Darkness, however, prevented aiming at individual targets. So the RAF took to "area bombing," striking densely populated areas to "de-house" workers and exhaust them from lack of sleep. Even before Pearl Harbor, Roosevelt became convinced that Churchill was on the right track. Hitler had so brainwashed the German people that it seemed only relentless bombing could undermine their loyalty to him. In August 1941, Harry Hopkins described FDR as "a believer in bombing as the only means of gaining victory." The president told Secretary of the Treasury Henry Morgenthau that "the only way to break German morale" was to bomb every small town to show ordinary folks what war meant. FDR felt that all Germans, not just Nazis, would

have to pay for what their Fuehrer had begun.[33]

At Casablanca, Churchill proposed a simple formula: "Bomb the devils around the clock." The British would come by night, the Americans by day. After the defeat of the U-boats, the Americans began a massive bomber buildup in southern England. Airfields, hangars, barracks, control towers, warehouses, repair shops, and fuel depots seemed to spring from the earth. Ships delivered so many bombs to the U.S. Eighth Air Force that ground crews had to store them under camouflage nets in rows, one atop the other, for miles along country roads. By then, too, Allied assembly lines had hit full stride, mass-producing heavy bombers. Besides the B-24 Liberator, the Americans had the B-17 Flying Fortress; Britain had the Lancaster and Halifax. These four-engine planes were simply big trucks with wings, able to haul tons of bombs long distances. Bombs like the RAF's Grand Slam weighed 22,000 pounds. Blockbusters came in two sizes: 4,000 and 2,000 pounds. Demolition bombs, the most commonly used, weighed 500 pounds. Bombers also carried containers holding hundreds of 4-pound incendiaries. When the containers sprang open, it literally rained firebombs.

A B-24 Liberator releases its bombs on the rail yards at Mühldorf, Germany. (March 19, 1945)

The Combined Bomber Offensive opened with a devastating blow. Hamburg, Germany's second-largest city behind Berlin, lies on the Elbe River a little way inland from the North Sea and was a major center of Germany's home front. Its shipyards built U-boats while hundreds of factories turned out a host of other goods for Hitler's war machine. Between July 24 and August 3, 1943, the RAF and Eighth Air Force unleashed Operation Gomorrah. The name was well chosen, for the Bible tells how God, in his wrath, deluged the sinful city of Gomorrah with fire.

While the Americans bombed Hamburg's docks, shipyards, and factories by day, at night the British area-bombed its residential districts, where the workers lived. The RAF deliberately ignited history's first man-made "firestorm." Incendiary bombs started so many fires at once that firefighters could not cope with them all. Scattered fires joined to

〰 A British bomber over Hamburg during Operation Gomorrah. (1943)

form an all-consuming blaze. As superheated air shot skyward, it created a vacuum at ground level, sucking in cool air from surrounding areas. The oxygen-rich air made the fire hotter, spawning winds of up to 170 miles an hour. The result was horrors no human being should have to endure. A German civil defense report said it all:

> Before half an hour had passed, the districts upon which the weight of the attack fell ... were transformed into a lake of fire covering an area of twenty-two square kilometers. The effect of this was to heat the air to a temperature which at times was estimated to approach [1,472 degrees Fahrenheit]. A vast suction was in this way created so that the air stormed through the streets with immense force, bearing upon it sparks, timber and roof beams and thus spreading the fire still further and further till it became a typhoon such as had never before been witnessed, and against which all human resistance was powerless. Trees three feet thick were broken off or uprooted, human beings were thrown to the ground or flung alive into the flames by winds which exceeded 150 miles an hour. The panic-stricken citizens knew not where to turn. Flames drove them from the shelters, but high-explosive bombs sent them scurrying back again. Once inside, they were suffocated by carbon-monoxide poisoning and their bodies reduced to ashes as though they had been placed in a crematorium, which was indeed what each shelter proved to be.[34]

The firestorm leveled eight square miles of Hamburg, an area one-fourth the size of Manhattan Island. No fewer than 45,000 civilians died; a million others became homeless. Many vanished without a trace, burned to dust. Others shriveled where they fell, overcome by heat and smoke, forcing workmen to pry them up with shovels for burial "The smallest children," a survivor wrote, "lay like fried eels on the pavement." Hitler never visited Hamburg or any other bombed city to see what he had brought upon the German people.[35]

Joseph Goebbels, Hitler's propaganda minister, called Hamburg "a catastrophe" that "simply staggers the imagination." President Roosevelt called it "an impressive demonstration" of airpower. When the Fellowship of Reconciliation, a Christian peace group, condemned city bombing, FDR "delivered a stinging rebuke." Though "disturbed and horrified" by the "destruction of life," he believed the only way to save yet more lives was to blast and burn Germany into submission as quickly as possible. The First Lady agreed. Protests against city bombing, she insisted, were "sentimental nonsense."[36]

The Hamburg firestorm sent a shudder into every corner of Hitler's domain. If this vast city, with its strong defenses, could suffer such a blow, no place and no person were safe. Stunned, the chief

〰️ Damage to residential buildings in Hamburg after the Allied bombings. (1943–1945)

of Luftwaffe fighter command noted, "A wave of terror radiated from the suffering city and spread throughout Germany," even to the most remote village.[37]

City by city, the Allied air forces would lay waste to the Nazi homeland. After Hamburg, they bombed more than 120 major cities and industrial centers. Sometimes, a thousand bombers took part in a raid. The Luftwaffe fought back fiercely and skillfully. When bomber formations appeared, antiaircraft shells and fighters rose to meet them. Air battles ranged over hundreds of square miles at speeds of over a hundred miles an hour. Machine gunners aboard bombers joined their "little friends," the long-range fighters, to meet the defenders. Nevertheless, for Germany, the tide of war had turned in the sky, as it had at sea.

But at what a price! The air war claimed the lives of 140,000 American and British flyers and 21,000 bombers. Yet the Combined Bomber Offensive was critical to the Allied effort. It paralyzed Germany's war industries, particularly oil refining and gasoline production. It brought her transportation system to a near standstill and destroyed the Luftwaffe as a fighting force. Though air raids killed 635,000 German civilians, the survivors learned to endure what they could not prevent. Yet daily life became harder and harder. Clearing damage after a thousand-bomber raid was like cleaning up after a massive earthquake—every day and night. Tense and fearful, groggy from lack of sleep, people described the bombing as "the hardest thing for civilians during the war." It convinced millions that Nazi Germany was doomed.[38]

They were right, as events in the Soviet Union would prove.

ROOSEVELT AND STALIN

It is unlikely that history holds a stranger, more improbable, and withal [more important] relationship than that between President Roosevelt and Marshal Stalin in World War II. It was more a courtship than a relationship in the ordinary sense; a courtship initiated by the President and regarded warily by the Marshal throughout, almost as though he could scarcely credit what was before his eyes.
—Robert Nisbet, Roosevelt and Stalin: The Failed Courtship (1989)

STALIN'S WAR

No day passed at Casablanca without Roosevelt and Churchill thinking of the man who wasn't there. As they well knew, Joseph Stalin would play a decisive role in shaping the course of the war and the world after it. Also, they knew the English saying: "He who sups with the devil should have a long spoon." In other words, if you must deal with bad people, you should never get too close to them. Next to fighting the war, dealing with Adolf Hitler's former partner was the greatest challenge they faced.

During the early days of the Nazi invasion in June 1941, the USSR seemed

hopeless. Observers compared the Red Army's retreat to a human tidal wave, hundreds of miles wide, flowing eastward away from the front. The sight of Soviet planes parked in neat rows on airfields amazed Luftwaffe pilots; they destroyed 1,200 on the first day alone and over 6,500 by mid-July. Dive-bombers hammered Soviet tank formations, turning them into twisted junk. Fast-moving Nazi tank columns encircled entire divisions.

At first, Stalin panicked, locking himself in a room and shouting about "betrayal." Yet he quickly recovered, declaring himself Marshal of the Soviet

Union and Generalissimo, supreme commander on land, at sea, and in the air. As the Red Army retreated, he sent the ferocious NKVD (secret police) into action. After seizing the Baltic countries, we recall, Stalin had ordered the arrest and execution of anyone who might oppose Soviet rule. Nevertheless, many were still in jail, awaiting their fate. Echoing his master, NKVD chief Lavrenti Beria declared, "When you stop murdering people by the millions, they start to get notions." So, rather than have prisoners "get notions" about aiding the Nazis, the NKVD shot them. In some jails, Germans found the floors covered with a layer of dried blood several inches thick.[1]

At first, the survivors, including many Soviet citizens, saw the Nazis as liberators. They preferred the demon they did not know as yet, in Berlin, to the demon they knew all too well, in Moscow. Oppressed people prayed for the Nazis to arrive quickly. When they did, cheering crowds gave them flowers, bread, and salt, traditional welcoming gifts. In some areas, men joined the invaders; about a million put on Nazi uniforms. When news of the invasion reached the Gulag, slave laborers whispered, "They are coming!" Even in Moscow, one heard excited cries of "Down with Soviet power! Long live good old Hitler!" Surely, he would deliver them from their Communist tormentors![2]

Stalin clamped down—hard. "In the Red Army it takes more courage to retreat than advance," he said by way of warning. He meant it. When, for example, a general asked for permission to withdraw to avoid being trapped, Stalin asked if his division had spades. Of course it had spades; every division did. What should be done with them? His men, Stalin growled, "should take their spades and dig their own graves." Let them die fighting, or he would hand them over to the NKVD.[3]

Stalin turned his terror machine on those who surrendered. In August,

~ Lavrenti Beria with Joseph Stalin's daughter, Svetlana, while Stalin reads in the background. (Date unknown)

Order No. 270 decreed that Soviet soldiers must kill themselves when faced with capture, branding captives "traitors to the Motherland." The families of these traitors might wind up in the Gulag or, at the very least, have their food rations cut and children expelled from school. That went for the tyrant's own family, too. When his son Yakov was captured, Stalin sent his daughter-in-law, Yulia, to prison. Stalin refused to exchange Yakov for a captured Nazi general; he died in a prison camp. Those who escaped and made it back to Soviet lines faced immediate execution: 158,000 escapees were shot during the war. The "lucky" ones were allowed to live a little longer. Formed into units without camouflage uniforms, they were sent forward to draw enemy fire. Others cleared minefields with their bodies. When the British offered a Red Army general land mine detectors, he refused because "in the Soviet Union we use people."[4]

Without meaning to, Hitler did Stalin a huge favor. While millions of Soviet citizens had initially welcomed the Nazis, the invaders soon showed their true colors. Shortly before the invasion, Hitler, sure of victory, gave an assignment to Heinrich Himmler, chief of the black-uniformed SS (elite guard). Himmler's experts were to draw up the General Plan for the East, the blueprint for empire in Eastern Europe and the USSR. The result was the most wicked document ever written.

The General Plan for the East totally disregarded humane values and morality. To exploit their conquests, the plan called for the Nazis to seize all farmland and turn it over to German settlers. All food grown and harvested would go to feed Germany's armed forces and civilian population. As for the Soviet people, they fell under another part of the plan, called the Hunger Plan. The Nazis would level every Soviet city Except for a few million people destined for slavery, the document defined the rest as "superfluous eaters"—useless mouths to feed. Accordingly, *"many tens of millions of people* in this area will become redundant [unneeded] and will either die or have to emigrate to Siberia. Any attempt to save the population . . . from death by starvation would undermine Germany's power to resist the blockade. This must be clearly and absolutely understood."[5]

Hunger planners expected between 30 million and 50 million civilians to starve or die of hunger-related diseases within a year after the collapse of the USSR. As for those who fled to Siberia, most would surely die of hunger, cold, and exposure. The plan had already gone into effect with Soviet war prisoners. POW camps were usually barren fields, without shelter, surrounded by barbed wire and armed guards. Of some 5.7 million captives, 3.5 million died from cold, disease, abuse, and starvation. To relieve their hunger, some prisoners resorted to cannibalism. No nation in history has ever lost so many men after their capture.

The Soviet people found themselves caught between two barbarous tyrannies. Evil as it was, most came to see Stalin's as the lesser evil. Though many despised him and the Communists, they would fight doggedly to defend their homeland, "Mother Russia," rather than those who ruled it. Hitler gave them no choice. Nazi rule meant certain death or slavery—that is, "death through work." So it would be a total war, a war of extermination, but not the one Hitler imagined when he began it. A popular poem, "A Soldier's Oath," set the tone:

> *The tears of women and children are boiling*
> *in my heart*
> *Hitler the murderer and his hordes shall pay*
> *for these tears with their wolfish blood*
> *For the avenger's hatred knows no mercy.*[6]

As the spring of 1941 turned to summer, and summer to fall, Soviet resistance

A Russian poster reading "To the west!" inspiring Russians to defend their homeland to their western border. (1943)

stiffened. Stalin ordered a "scorched earth" campaign. People obeyed, taking away or burning anything the Nazis might eat, wear, or use. Autumn found the invaders moving across a barren land. All around, flaming wheat fields lit the night sky. In thousands of villages, only charred rubble greeted them, the inhabitants having fled to Soviet-held territory or to guerrilla bands in the forests. Organized and supplied by the

Red Army, these operated behind enemy lines, ambushing patrols, attacking supply columns, and overrunning outposts. Guerrillas seldom took prisoners.

November found Hitler's tanks bearing down on Moscow. By then, they had driven more than 600 miles into the USSR, conquering a combined area the size of Britain, Spain, Italy, and France. Then it happened. Heavy rains turned dirt roads to sticky, clinging mud that fouled engines and sucked the boots off soldiers' feet. Temperatures dropped. Snow began to fall—and fall. Winter had arrived early, the worst in decades. Red Army men said they had many generals, but none as brutal as "General Winter."

The arrogant Nazis had not prepared for a winter campaign. Now they paid the price. In subzero temperatures, tank and airplane engines froze. Artillery and machine guns broke down. Soldiers, still in summer uniforms, slogged through snowdrifts, wrapped in any rags they could find. Each day, surgeons hacked off frostbitten fingers and toes. Worse yet, Japan gave Stalin a gift of 2 million fresh Soviet troops fully equipped for winter fighting. A Soviet spy reported that Japan was preparing to attack America in the Pacific. Until then, Stalin had stationed a large army in Siberia to keep tabs on Japanese forces in Manchuria. There had

already been border clashes, and Stalin feared a full-scale invasion if he moved the Siberians westward. The spy's report solved his problem. The focus of the Japanese would be elsewhere. Immediately troops boarded trains heading west along the Trans-Siberian Railway. On December 6, as Japanese aircraft carriers neared Pearl Harbor, the Siberians halted Hitler's advance on Moscow.

"OUR GREAT SOVIET ALLY"

Americans watched the Nazi-Soviet war with mixed feelings. Pro-Nazis wished Hitler success. Communists gave Stalin their blessing. The vast majority, however, saw little to choose from. "The principal difference between Mr. Hitler and Mr. Stalin," the saying went, "is the size of their respective mustaches." Dubbed "the twin princes of darkness," they were seen as equally evil. "Stalin is as bloody-handed as Hitler," said Senator Bennett Champ Clark. "I don't think we should help either." It would be good if Hitler destroyed the Soviet demon; best if the devil's twins destroyed each other.[7]

Roosevelt could not just wish for good things to happen. Presidents must make choices all the time, often with incomplete information—that is what leadership means. One thing FDR never doubted: the evil of the Soviet system. Early in 1940, he told a gathering of the American Youth Congress, a Communist-leaning group, that "the Soviet Union, as everybody knows who has courage to face the known facts, is run by a dictatorship as absolute as any dictatorship in the world." At those words, the audience heartily booed the president.[8]

Yet FDR also knew that the realities of war create strange alliances. Like it or not, the democracies needed the USSR to defeat Hitler. There was no arguing with arithmetic. FDR had made a cold calculation. "The Russians," he wrote Churchill, "are killing more Germans and destroying more equipment than you and I put together." In fact, from June 1941 to April 1945, Hitler kept less than 10 percent of his troops in the west. The rest fought in the USSR, where they suffered 93 percent of all German military casualties—4.2 million killed, wounded, and missing. In the process, the Red Army lost some 8 million soldiers. Put another way, by spilling so much German blood, and so much of their own besides, Stalin's armies spared the Americans and British untold losses.[9]

Roosevelt wanted the Soviets to continue killing Nazis. However, he worried that Stalin might try to make a deal with his former partner in crime. He was right. In 2004, historians discovered a set of documents in Soviet-era files. These show that in February 1942, Stalin sent V. N. Merkulov, deputy chief of the NKVD, to meet secretly with Karl Wolff, an SS general and aide of Hitler's. The main document bears Stalin's signature. In it, he offers "to begin military actions with German forces against England and the USA." Stalin also promised to blame the Jews "represented by England and the USA [for] instigating the war." After victory, Stalin proposed that the USSR and Germany join forces to create what he called "a new world order." Hitler, still confident of victory, rejected the offer.[10]

Roosevelt wanted Stalin's help not only in winning the war but also in securing the peace. Though Stalin was a ruthless tyrant, the president felt he could make him a partner for peace. It was all a matter of the right person approaching him with the right attitude. And FDR thought himself that person.

Since his childhood at Hyde Park, Roosevelt had had unlimited faith in his ability to connect with others. Even opponents found him hard to resist when he turned on the charm and flashed that brilliant smile of his. He had spent his adult life managing men, and Stalin, he imagined, could not be much different from other people. To win the grand prize—peace lasting generations—he decided to appeal to Stalin's human side. As he put it, the Soviet leader was "get-atable," and he, FDR, "can personally handle Stalin" better than any diplomat. This certainty came from one who had yet to meet Stalin, who had never been to the USSR or read a book about it. Stalin's early religious schooling, the president told Labor Secretary Frances Perkins, had "entered his nature," so he would behave "the way in which a Christian gentleman should behave." FDR failed to explain how he knew this. Nevertheless, he felt sure he could win over Stalin, gaining his trust and friendship, his cooperation and gratitude.[11]

George F. Kennan was more realistic. A high-ranking diplomat in the U.S. embassy in Moscow, Kennan was a leading expert on the USSR. He had studied Russian history and politics closely and spoke Russian fluently. To his mind, the president's view of Stalin was "puerile"—childish—wishful thinking "unworthy of a statesman of FDR's stature."[12]

Stalin might have been a creature from outer space, so different was he from anyone Roosevelt had ever dealt with. Kennan believed the president

George F. Kennan, an American diplomat in Moscow and expert on the USSR. (1947)

lacked the life experiences and imagination to relate to the likes of the Soviet leader. "I don't think FDR was capable of conceiving of a man of such profound iniquity, coupled with enormous ... cleverness as Stalin." When Stalin met foreigners, Kennan noted, he tried to give a good impression. However, should anything annoy him, "the yellow eyes lit up and you suddenly realized what sort of an animal you had by the tail."[13]

Charm Stalin? Kennan thought FDR could as easily charm a hungry wolf. Stalin had not taken over the largest nation on earth by being truthful, loyal, and kind. As a man who had betrayed and tortured, enslaved and murdered, millions of his own people, he lacked normal human feelings. Gratitude? Stalin, we recall, defined that as "a sickness suffered by dogs." Friendship? Stalin, described by Kennan as "a man of absolutely diseased suspiciousness," viewed any overture of friendliness as a trick to throw him off guard and then betray him, as he had betrayed others.[14]

Kennan's boss, William C. Bullitt, agreed. As America's first ambassador to the USSR, Bullitt knew everyone worth knowing there. He and Stalin were on kissing terms, a common Russian greeting. Once, Bullitt recalled, "Stalin took my head in his two hands and gave me a large kiss! I swallowed my astonish-

FDR and William C. Bullitt, the first U.S. ambassador to Russia. (1933)

ment, and when he turned up his face for a return kiss, I delivered it." But Bullitt was too shrewd to be taken in by a kiss. He knew that Stalin, like Hitler, had one aim. The ambassador wrote: "Hitler's aim was to spread the power of the Nazis to the ends of the earth. Stalin's aim was to spread the power of the communists to the ends of the earth. Stalin, like Hitler, will not stop. He can only *be* stopped."[15]

Early in the war, Roosevelt and Bullitt met for three hours in the White House. It made sense, Bullitt said, to help anyone, however nasty, in a war for survival. Give Stalin what he needs to fight Hitler, but don't fool yourself about him and what he stands for. Aiding the USSR was simply a matter of grim necessity, and nothing more. In return for Lend-Lease aid, Stalin should be made to give ironclad guarantees to abandon all claims to Poland and the Baltic countries after the Nazi defeat.

FDR gave a revealing reply. "Bill, I don't dispute your facts; they are accurate. I don't dispute the logic of your reasoning. I just have a hunch that Stalin is not that kind of man. . . . I think that if I give him everything I possibly can, and ask nothing of him in return, noblesse oblige, he . . . will work with me for a world of democracy and peace. . . . I am going to play my hunch." Seldom has a president so misread a foreign leader or disproved the soundness of his own hunches.[16]

To play his hunch, Roosevelt needed the American people's support. That, in turn, required changing attitudes toward the USSR. So the White House inspired (but did not control) a propaganda campaign to convince the public that Stalin was a morally worthy ally. One critic called it an effort to "prettify Stalin, whose homicide record is even longer than Hitler's." Likewise, in Britain, the government and media went all out to show the Soviets in a favorable light. George Orwell, among the finest writers of his generation, bitterly protested "this nation-wide conspiracy to flatter our ally," this "fog of lies and misinformation."[17]

In what critics dubbed "Operation Whitewash," the American media glorified Stalin and the Soviet system. Forgotten, as if by a sudden attack of amnesia, were his reign of terror, his Gulag, and his alliance with Hitler. *Time* magazine named him its 1943 "Man of the Year." Hundreds of articles "humanized" Stalin, portraying him as "Uncle Joe," a jovial, pipe-smoking gentleman. A leader

Time touting Stalin as "Man of the Year." (January 4, 1943)

of the Daughters of the American Revolution gushed, "Stalin is a university graduate and a man of great studies. He is a man who, when he sees a great mistake, admits it and corrects it." She had no idea that Stalin corrected "mistakes" by shooting their makers.[18]

The media developed a teenager's crush on the Red Army. Many took its heroic resistance to the Nazis as proof of its love for Stalin and the blessings of communism. The New York *Daily News* compared the "gallant and mighty Red

Army" to the patriots George Washington led at Valley Forge. Radio commercials sold the USSR like soda pop. One ad set new words to the Pepsi-Cola jingle:

Soviet Union hits the spot
Twelve million soldiers that's a lot
Timoshenko and Stalin too
Soviet Union is Red, White and Blue.

President Roosevelt agreed. He publicly welcomed the USSR to "the common cause of all free men." Yet Stalin knew better. The tyrant told a visitor that the common people fought for their homeland, "not for us," meaning him and the Communist Party.[19]

Life, the nation's leading picture magazine, took first prize for silliness. Its editors devoted the entire March 29, 1943, issue to "Soviet-American Cooperation." The Soviets, it declared with smug ignorance, were "one hell of a people" who "look like Americans, dress like Americans, and think like Americans." The NKVD was "a national police similar to the FBI" whose job was "tracking down traitors." As for the Gulag, *Life* never mentioned it. It did say, however, that Stalin and his henchmen were trustworthy: "We can afford to take their word for it."[20]

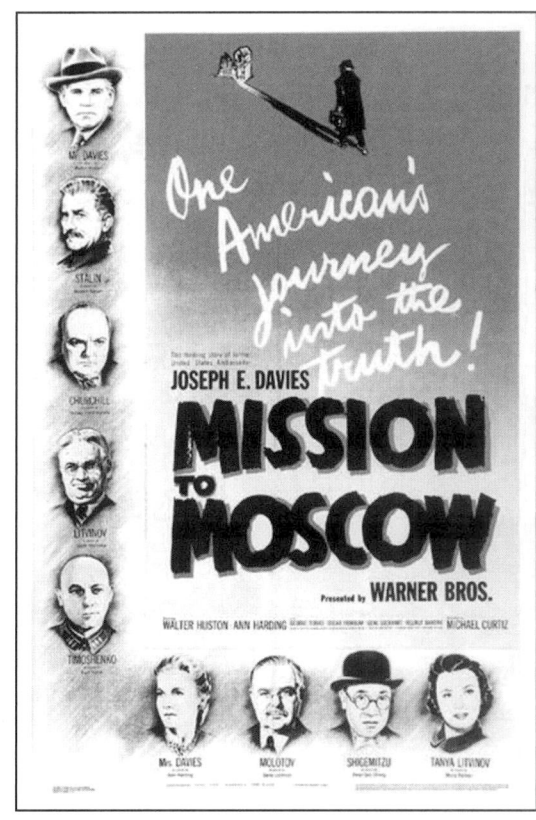

The movie poster for *Mission to Moscow,* which praised Stalin's leadership. (1943)

The White House asked Hollywood to make pro-Soviet movies. If paper has no shame, as Stalin claimed, neither does film—both take anything imprinted on them. Thus, Hollywood studios turned out dozens of salute-to-our-great-ally films. Productions like *Song of Russia, Three Russian Girls, The Boy from Stalingrad, The North Star,* and *Days of Glory* focused on the heroism and idealism of ordinary Soviet people and their unwavering loyalty to Moscow. These films were pure propaganda disguised as entertainment, as close to Soviet reality as portrayals of the Land of Oz, Middle-earth, and cloud-cuckoo-land.[21]

The president took a personal interest in the 1943 Warner Bros. release of *Mission to Moscow,* based on a book of the same title that Roosevelt had encouraged Joseph E. Davies to write. Davies, a former ambassador to Moscow, was a gullible man, easily duped. He famously praised Stalin for his "kindness and gentle simplicity." The Soviet leader was so warm and cuddly, Davies wrote, that "a child would like to sit in his lap." Advertised as "one American's journey into the truth," *Mission to Moscow* showed how the Soviet people loved Stalin and lived happily under the "protection" of his NKVD. When FDR saw the film at a private White House showing, he adored it. Viewing it in Moscow, Stalin praised it warmly. Robert Buckner, its producer, hated it bitterly—and himself for making it. Buckner called the film "an expedient lie for political purposes, glossily covering important facts with full or partial knowledge of their false presentation."[22]

Nevertheless, media propaganda worked. Polls showed that most Americans had come to trust their Soviet ally. More, they believed that Soviet leaders were "democratic," having abandoned their aim of world revolution. Only 7 percent of Americans distrusted Soviet intentions. The president felt encouraged.[23]

THE ROAD TO TEHRAN

By 1943, the tide had turned on every fighting front. After killing 140,000 Germans and capturing 91,000 others at Stalingrad in January, the Red Army destroyed 2,500 tanks at Kursk in August, the largest tank battle in history. Things went badly for Nazi captives. The NKVD shot many upon surrender; it marched the rest to Siberia, where most died of hunger, exhaustion, and exposure along the way or in prison camps.

〰 A wounded German prisoner of war taken at the Battle of Stalingrad. (1943)

Of those taken at Stalingrad, only 5,000 saw their homes again, and not until 1955. After Kursk, Soviet offensives steadily pushed the invaders back. Meanwhile, America and Britain, having defeated the U-boats and begun the air assault on Germany, invaded Sicily and then Italy proper from bases in North Africa. Benito Mussolini fell from power, and Italy switched sides, joining the Allies.

In the Pacific, the U.S. Navy waged unrestricted submarine warfare, for which FDR had denounced Germany in the First World War. During the next two years, submarines based at Pearl Harbor went all out to sink any vessel flying the Rising Sun flag. Gradually, they cut the lifeline bringing raw materials from the conquered lands Japan's civilians and military depended upon. By February, marines and army troops secured Guadalcanal in the Solomon Islands and began island-hopping northward, toward the Philippines. In the Central Pacific, marines took the Gilbert Islands, the first step on the road to Japan itself. Each island became a launchpad for seizing others, gradually bringing heavy bombers within range of Japan's crowded cities.

The "Big Three"—Roosevelt, Churchill, and Stalin—had important matters to decide, which they could only do in person. Because of his disability, FDR wanted the meeting held close to home, perhaps in Alaska. Stalin refused, claiming he had to stay near the front. A lie; he never visited a combat zone. Instead, he suggested they meet in Tehran, Iran, jointly occupied by Soviet and British forces to secure its oil fields. Roosevelt protested. He would have to travel 6,000 miles, while Stalin traveled only 600 miles from Soviet territory. He asked Stalin not to let him down, ending with a plea: "I am begging you." Stalin held his ground. FDR gave in. The Big Three would meet in Tehran from November 28 to December 2, 1943.[24]

MURDER IN THE FOREST

The conference might easily have been wrecked before it began. For in April 1943, Radio Berlin announced that German troops had uncovered mass graves in the Katyn Forest near the Soviet city of Smolensk.

When Poland surrendered in 1939, over 250,000 of its soldiers became Soviet prisoners. Of these, the NKVD placed 21,857 officers, the cream of Poland's military, in three prison camps. None ever returned. Though the Germans uncovered the graves of some at Katyn, the others' remains have never been found; Russia still has many unopened Stalin-era mass grave sites in Siberia. The Katyn site held the bodies of 4,143 officers, including generals, packed in layers like sardines in a tin can.

Though it was a top-secret operation, three Poles who had escaped from a Soviet prisoner-of-war camp saw some of the killings from their hiding place. Upon leading victims into the forest, a witness said, "two [NKVD men] seized their hands and held them in back and one of the [NKVD men] lifted [the victim's] chin up, took him by the head, opened his mouth and shoved a handful of sawdust into his mouth." Unable to scream, their hands often bound with rope or barbed wire, most died of a bullet in the back of the head.[25]

Germany accused the USSR of the atrocity, and vice versa. For once, the Nazis told the truth. Their reason, however, had nothing to do with justice; they hoped Katyn would drive a wedge between the Soviets and their Western allies. Letters and diaries later found on the corpses ended with dates in April 1940—that is, while the Red Army still held Smolensk. Finally in 1992, Russian president Boris Yeltsin released

One of the mass graves discovered at Katyn Forest. (1943)

the original execution order, signed by Stalin and his top aides, to shoot "hardened and uncompromising enemies of Soviet authority." Translation: Stalin feared that these officers, if ever set free, would lead resistance to Soviet rule. So Stalin "solved" the problem in his usual manner—by murder. After the shootings, NKVD squads rounded up the victims' families, deporting them to the Gulag in railroad boxcars. The killers were proud of their work. In NKVD slang, Katyn was *mokraya rabota*—a "wet job"—because it shed so much blood. Stalin rewarded the NKVD men who did the job with medals and promotions.[26]

Even without Stalin's signed order, the Western leaders soon learned the truth about Katyn. Neither Churchill nor Roosevelt seemed surprised. Both had known about the existence of the Gulag, if not all the grisly details, for years; they were also well aware of the Great Terror, the mass murder purges of the 1930s. Now, through contacts in the Polish resistance, British diplomat Sir Owen O'Malley found clear evidence of Soviet guilt. O'Malley told Churchill that the evidence posed a grave moral problem for the democracies. For the sake of human decency, they must speak out. "We now stand in danger of . . . falling under St. Paul's curse on those who

can see cruelty and burn not [with righteous anger]." Yet the prime minister swore the diplomat to silence, then sent his report to the White House. FDR may or may not have read it; there is no record of his having discussed it with anyone.[27]

Nevertheless, the president did order John F. Carter, head of a special intelligence team, to investigate the massacre. Roosevelt told Carter the Soviets were probably guilty, but said he "didn't want to believe it." However, if he must believe it, he said, he would "pretend not to"; in other words, he would lie. When Carter confirmed O'Malley's findings, Roosevelt turned to George H. Earle, a navy commander and former governor of Pennsylvania. Earle confirmed Soviet guilt, too. But FDR was "absolutely convinced" of their innocence, or so he told Earle. When Earle asked for permission to release his findings anyhow, FDR sent a written order: "I specifically forbid you to publish any information or opinion [about Katyn]." For good measure, he sent Earle to a remote Pacific outpost for the rest of the war.[28]

The leaders of the democracies deliberately hid their knowledge of Soviet guilt for a major war crime. "We should, none of us, ever speak a word about it," Churchill told his War Cabinet. Moreover, he pressured the London-based Polish press not to write about Katyn. In America, FDR spared no effort to keep the truth under wraps. Knowledge of Katyn might easily have undone propaganda about "our great Soviet Ally," turning American opinion against the alliance. For that reason, the Office of War Information, the official government propaganda agency, even threatened to cancel the licenses of Polish-language radio stations in Detroit and Buffalo if their newscasters dared mention the massacre. Ultimately, the nation learned everything. In September 2012, the U.S. National Archives released a thousand pages of once-secret documents proving the White House's cover-up.[29]

Roosevelt and Churchill knew what they were doing. The Polish officers were dead. That was a tragedy, but nothing could bring them back. Both men believed that creating an uproar would harm, perhaps even wreck, the Grand Alliance, so vital to the defeat of Hitler. Countless lives were at stake, too, since the Red Army prevented the transfer of Nazi combat units to the west, sparing American and British soldiers. Therefore, the leaders felt obliged to stifle the truth while pretending to believe Soviet lies. However, what O'Malley told Churchill also applied to Roosevelt: "We

have used the good name of England to cover up a massacre."[30]

Herein lies a lesson. In any war, however just the cause and noble the aim, nobody emerges with clean hands or, if they are honest, with a clear conscience. To fight an evil enemy, leaders may feel it necessary to adopt, however reluctantly, some of his methods. Such is the tragedy of war. History is also a tattletale. Unless destroyed, documents eventually come to light, and then there is always a price to pay. Today, more than seventy years after the murders in the forest, Polish people rightly feel betrayed by those who spoke so movingly about the Four Freedoms and the ideals expressed in the Atlantic Charter. Katyn, however, would not be the Poles' only reason for feeling betrayed, nor their most serious one.

MEETING AT TEHRAN

Roosevelt left for Tehran bent upon a full-scale charm offensive. He was, Frances Perkins recalled, "prepared to like Stalin and determined to make himself liked" by the tyrant. Upon arriving, as a gesture of goodwill, he accepted Stalin's invitation to stay in a villa in the Soviet embassy compound; Churchill stayed at the British embassy nearby.[31]

On Roosevelt's first night in Tehran,

 Joseph Stalin, FDR, and Winston Churchill pose at the Tehran Conference. (November 29, 1943)

"a frightening figure with his slit, bear eyes."[33]

Meanwhile, Stalin took no chances. The NKVD kept tabs on Roosevelt and his staff while in Tehran. Three thousand NKVD officers handled security, far outnumbering the president's Secret Service team. Several dozen NKVD men, all over six feet tall, attended their master's guests as servants. Dressed in spotless white coats, they had odd bulges at their hips. A careless move revealed a holstered pistol. During a banquet, Americans saw one of their "servants" now decked out in the uniform of an NKVD general.

Stalin welcomed him. "I am glad to see you," said the president as they shook hands. "I have tried for a long time to bring this about." The Soviet leader was on his best behavior, and FDR found him "altogether impressive." He told his son Elliott that he was "sure we'll hit it off" and that there was "nothing devious" about Stalin![32]

Others were not so sure. General George C. Marshall knew Stalin's history and despised him for it. "He was a rough SOB," said the chairman of the Joint Chiefs of Staff, "who made his way by murder and everything else, and should be talked to that way." Sarah Churchill, the prime minister's daughter, cringed when she first saw Stalin. She found him

Yet Stalin had gone further. In 2003, a study by the Central Intelligence Agency (CIA) concluded that at Tehran, Roosevelt "was bugged like no other American president in history." Stalin had ordered microphones planted in FDR's living quarters. Sergo Beria, the man in charge, was the son of NKVD chief Lavrenti Beria. Each morning, the younger Beria, who spoke English fluently, brought Stalin a word-for-word translation of the president's conversations. Stalin wanted to know not only what FDR said but also the tone of his voice. However, the president may have outfoxed his host. Secret Service men had already found bugs in

the Moscow embassy. Perhaps he suspected the NKVD was listening in Tehran, too, and said what he wanted Stalin to hear. Perhaps it was just good luck that he gave away nothing important. We will probably never know for sure. However, according to young Beria, during his conversations FDR always spoke highly of Stalin.[34]

But hard as he tried, Roosevelt found Stalin not "getatable." His charm offensive fell flat. Recalling their early meetings, he told Frances Perkins, "I made absolutely no progress. I couldn't get any personal connection with Stalin." At the conference table, the man from Moscow sat quietly, took in everything, and doodled wolf heads on a pad with a red pencil. However, FDR noticed that Stalin liked to needle Churchill. Perhaps, he asked the prime minister, Britain wanted a "soft peace" with the Nazis? Churchill, who had led the fight against Hitler while Stalin helped him, held his temper. He just sat there, grasping his cigar with clenched jaws, his face flushed[35]

Roosevelt took his cue from Stalin. Before one meeting, he told Churchill not to take offense at what he was about to do. He began by whispering aloud to Stalin: "Winston is cranky this morning; he got off the wrong side of the bed." Then he teased Churchill about his Britishness, his cigars, and his personal habits. Slowly, Stalin's eyes brightened and a smile creased the corners of his mouth. Finally, he broke into a hearty laugh. After that, as FDR would later tell Frances Perkins, "the ice was broken and we talked like men and brothers."[36]

Seen another way, the president mocked Churchill, who admired him, to get a laugh from a mass murderer who distrusted everybody. George Kennan was appalled at such behavior. Poking fun at the prime minister, he believed, was "one of the saddest manifestations of the almost childish failure on FDR's part to understand the personality of Stalin." Yet there was more to come.[37]

Between meetings, the Big Three socialized. Events hosted by Stalin were not what they seemed. The Soviet leader had always used social gatherings to learn others' thoughts by getting them to lower their guard. He would loosen their tongues with strong drink, tell jokes, and say outrageous things. Meanwhile, he watched their reactions, sizing them up. Not looking him in the eye when speaking was dangerous, for it made him think a person had something to hide. Thus, any social event might end in disaster. From time to time, Soviet bigwigs returned home after an all-night drinking party with Stalin to find NKVD men waiting at their front door.

One evening, a smiling Stalin declared that 50,000 German officers should be "rounded up and shot after the war." No charges! No lawyers! No trials! Just shoot them!

Churchill was flabbergasted. "The British Parliament and public will never tolerate mass executions," he growled.

"Fifty thousand must be shot," Stalin insisted.

Churchill could listen no more. "I would rather be taken into the garden here and now and be shot myself than sully my own and my country's honor by such infamy."

With that, he stormed out of the room. Moments later, he felt a tap on his shoulder. Stalin. He was only joking, he said. Churchill followed him back to the banquet room.[38]

Then Stalin asked what Roosevelt thought. How many should be shot? The president urged compromise. "Shall we say forty-nine thousand five hundred?" FDR laughed. Stalin laughed. Churchill frowned.[39]

Why? Not because Churchill shrank from bloodshed. He did not. The reason almost certainly lay in the Katyn Forest. The Big Three knew the truth behind the massacre. Yet, as if by an unspoken agreement, nobody mentioned it for the sake of the Grand Alliance. Knowing how Stalin operated, it seems likely that his proposal to shoot German officers was a test to see how far he could go. Churchill may have sensed that his and Roosevelt's silence about Katyn told Stalin he could get away with anything. As Churchill later put it, "Stalin is an unnatural man." No wickedness was beyond him.[40]

During the formal meetings, Roosevelt and Churchill promised to open the long-awaited Second Front. Operation Overlord would begin in May or June 1944, with General Eisenhower commanding the armies landing in France. To draw away German forces, Stalin promised to start a powerful offensive a few days before the invasion got under way. He also promised to declare war on Japan soon after victory in Europe.

Stalin expected a reward for his efforts. A big reward. His armies would soon drive the Nazis out of the USSR and enter Eastern Europe. The Soviet leader made it clear that he intended to claim everything Hitler had given him in 1939, meaning that Poland would lose nearly half her prewar territory and a third of her population. To make up for this loss, Stalin wanted to shift the Polish border hundreds of miles to the west, giving eastern Germany to Poland in exchange. Around 12 million Germans would have to leave homes their ancestors had lived in for centuries. Everything would be lost, except the clothes they wore and the few possessions they might cram into a suitcase. Forced into what remained of Germany, they would survive as best they could. Today, we call this "ethnic cleansing."

Though Roosevelt agreed to Stalin's demand, he felt he could not say so publicly. It was all a matter of presidential politics. FDR had already decided to run for a fourth term. Privately, he told Stalin there were 6 million to 7 million Americans of Polish heritage. As a "practical man," he "would not wish to lose their vote" by revealing his position on Poland's future borders. Let Stalin and Churchill work out the details, but keep them secret until after his reelection. Whatever happened, FDR added, he had no intention of fighting the USSR. Stalin said he understood. The boundaries he and Churchill worked out exist to this day.[41]

Historians have viewed Roosevelt's decision harshly. While the Atlantic Charter said all peoples should choose their form of government, FDR did not think that right absolute. Poland's fate carried little weight with him, compared to the realities and risks of fighting a world war. According to Robert A. Divine, an expert on American foreign affairs, "The President had little genuine concern for Poland; it was the unity of the Big Three that he wished to preserve." Only their unity could achieve victory, and peace afterward, FDR believed.[42]

Roosevelt thus put his vision of peace with Stalin's help ahead of the welfare of Eastern Europe. He told W. Averell Harriman, his last ambassador to Moscow, that he "didn't care whether the countries bordering Russia went Communist or not." For the greater good, these must learn to live under Soviet rule, however harsh. In a generation or so, he hoped, the Soviets might "become less barbarian." As he told Archbishop (later Cardinal) Francis Spellman of New York, "The European people will simply have to endure the Russian domination, in the hope that in ten or twenty years they will be able to live well with the Russians." Eastern Europeans, particularly Poles, still blame FDR for writing off their countries to satisfy Stalin. Even if he could not have prevented a Soviet takeover, they say, he had a moral duty to protest strongly.[43]

The president returned from Tehran in high spirits. On Christmas Eve, he gave a Fireside Chat about the conference. He could not praise Stalin enough: "I believe he is truly representative of the heart and soul of Russia; and I be-

FDR addresses a joint session of Congress shortly after the Tehran Conference. (January 7, 1944)

lieve that we are going to get along very well with him and the Russian people—very well indeed." When a reporter asked what type of person Stalin was, he replied, "I would call him something like me . . . a realist," one who sees things as they really are.[44]

FDR might not have spoken so highly about the Soviet leader had he known Stalin's feelings about him and Churchill. Thieves! That's what they were—greedy capitalist thieves! Churchill, he sneered, was the kind of man who would pick your pocket for a kopek, a small copper coin. Not Roosevelt. He was fussier: "He dips in his hand only for bigger coins."[45]

No amount of presidential charm and friendliness would win Stalin's trust, nor could they ever. The tyrant lived by an inflexible rule: "One can never be too suspicious." As George Kennan well knew, Stalin saw any display of goodwill as the exact opposite, a pretend friend's trick to deceive him—as he deceived others. Stalin also had contempt for Roosevelt's disability, perhaps because he thought it showed weakness of character. But he was too good an actor to say it to FDR's face. Once, when the conference broke for lunch, everyone got up to leave. An aide wheeled the president out of the room. As they left, Stalin's interpreter heard him say sarcastically, "Some will walk and some will ride." When the interpreter asked if he should translate the remark, Stalin snapped, "Nyet." No.[46]

TRIUMPH AND TRAGEDY

The courage of life is often . . . a magnificent mixture of triumph and tragedy.
A man does what he must—in spite of personal consequences, in spite of obstacles and
dangers and pressures—and that is the basis of all human morality.
—*John F. Kennedy,* Profiles in Courage *(1956)*

"I FEEL LIKE HELL"

Shortly after returning from Tehran, Roosevelt reached a turning point in his life. Those who saw him regularly, his aides and daughter, Anna, now living in the White House as an unpaid special assistant, noticed the changes immediately. Awakening tired from a full night's sleep, FDR complained of constant fatigue and splitting headaches. Dark rings appeared under his eyes. He was pale and short of breath, and his lips and the skin under his fingernails had a blue tinge. Anna also noticed that his hands trembled when he lit a cigarette, and he dozed off while dictating letters. Food tasted like straw. He lost his appe-

tite and grew thinner, seeming to shrink inside his clothes. Asked how he felt, he answered "rotten," like "boiled owl," or simply "like hell."[1]

Anna insisted that he get a checkup at Bethesda Naval Hospital. Howard Bruenn, a cardiologist (heart specialist), did a complete physical examination. Appalled, he found the president's condition "God-awful." Even the medical terms he used were chilling: "malignant hypertension" and "acute congestive heart failure." Malignant hypertension is the most serious form of high blood pressure. It's called the "silent killer," and a person may have it for years without showing symptoms. Eventually, it can cause an artery in the brain to burst—Dr. Bruenn said "pop"—producing a fatal hemorrhage. Not only was FDR's blood pressure dangerously high, but the blue tinges pointed to his heart's inability to pump enough oxygen-rich blood to his vital organs. This, in turn, could result in a fatal heart attack or a stroke caused by a blockage of an artery in the brain.[2]

Since science had yet to find drugs to treat these ailments, Dr. Bruenn could only put his patient on a low-salt, low-fat diet, also a common procedure nowadays. Roosevelt must rest often and avoid stress. From forty Camel cigarettes a day, he must cut down to six. However, even with the best of care, he could die at any time. Most likely, the doctor thought, the end would come in less than a year. We may never know what he told FDR about his condition. All the president's medical records were kept in the hospital's vault, and only the cardiologist and Admiral Ross McIntire, FDR's personal physician, had access to them. Somehow, they went missing right after the president's death. Nobody has ever explained how or why this could have happened or what became of them. One thing is certain: they did not walk away on their own.

PERSONAL MATTERS

We do know that Roosevelt was painfully lonely toward the end of his life. On weekends, he was often alone in the White House, except for the servants. The First Lady was no comfort at all. Eleanor bore a deep, though invisible, wound. Opened by the Lucy Mercer affair, it was still, twenty-five years later, raw as the day she learned of her husband's infidelity. "I have the memory of an elephant," she would say. "I can forgive, but I cannot forget."[3]

Around 1943, Franklin asked if they might again live as husband and wife. Eleanor refused. Dr. Bruenn noticed that she gave him no attention, let alone warmth and affection. When he held out his arms, son James recalled, "she refused flatly to enter his embrace." Later, when Anna mentioned his health problems, Eleanor said she was not "interested in psychology"—as if these were only in his mind.[4]

Unwilling to give up her independence, Eleanor was happiest away from the White House. Under the code name Rover, she traveled constantly. Her longest trip, 23,000 miles aboard an army transport plane dubbed *Our Eleanor*, took her to the South Pacific. She visited Australia, New Guinea, and Guadalcanal; the last two islands still had pockets of

Japanese resistance in the jungle. "Gosh, there's Eleanor," men cried when she appeared as if out of thin air.[5]

Dressed in a brown Red Cross uniform, the First Lady inspected military hospitals, going into every ward, stopping at every bed, and speaking to every patient. These men's wounds were not "psychological." Seeing them unlocked her, revealing a tender side few ever saw. Admiral William F. Halsey was amazed. "She walked for miles, and saw patients who were grievously and gruesomely wounded. But I marveled most at their expressions as she leaned over them." For them, it was as if their mother, wife, or sweetheart had come across the world just to comfort them.[6]

In his loneliness, Roosevelt turned to Lucy Mercer, now the Widow Rutherfurd with grown children. Despite his promise to Eleanor, he had never completely broken ties with her. He sent a limousine for Lucy so she could watch his first inauguration from a discreet distance. Now and then, they exchanged letters. On visits to Warm Springs, he might take side trips to meet her at financier Bernard Baruch's estate in South Carolina. Under the name "Mrs. Johnson," she stayed in the White House while Eleanor was away. Lucy would massage his legs. Franklin relaxed, laughed, and talked about how it had been when they were young. Lucy, visibly happy, listened intently, taking in his every word. Anna arranged the meetings, but kept them secret from her mother, not wanting to hurt her feelings. Lucy, Anna recalled, was "a wonderful listener, an intelligent listener in that she knew the right questions, while mother would get in there and say 'I think you are wrong, Franklin.'"[7]

Eleanor Roosevelt at a naval hospital at Pearl Harbor, Honolulu, Hawaii. (September 21, 1943)

THE FOURTH TERM

At Tehran, Roosevelt had told Stalin before anyone else that he would run for a fourth term. Dr. Bruenn's findings, however, raised questions. Should one in failing health take on the challenge of an election campaign? And if he did, and won, could he carry out the strenuous duties of office?

Ever the politician, Roosevelt felt he had no choice. Fearing a Republican comeback, Democratic leaders urged him to run. Only he, they said, could hold Congress for their party. As a patriot, he also felt he alone could finish the war and secure a lasting peace. It was his duty to serve, whatever might happen to him. "If the people command me to continue in this office, I have as little right to withdraw as a soldier has to leave his post in the line."[8]

His health, however, continued to decline. Alonzo Fields, the White House butler, dreaded going to work each day. The man he so admired seemed to wither before his eyes. "You could see him just fade away," Fields recalled. "He would come to the table sometimes and he would be bright and cheerful, but [then] he would sag and he'd sort of droop and drop his head, or he would drop his jaw." Roosevelt began to have fainting spells, falling off his chair. Secret Service agent

Milton Lipson recalled, "You'd have to come in and there was the president of the United States helpless on the floor, and you [had to] gently pick him up, say nothing about it, put him back on the chair and that was it. But your heart would break."[9]

Hoping to regain his strength, Roosevelt spent a month (from April 9 to May 6, 1944) at Bernard Baruch's estate. Shielded from reporters by the Secret Service, he was only a part-time president. On a good day, he awoke at noon, worked two hours, took a long nap, and then worked another two hours. Most days, however, he spent just an hour or two on public business. Usually, he slept more than sixteen hours a day. "Sleep and sleep . . . and let the world go hang," he replied when asked what he wished for most.[10]

FDR returned to Washington in time to celebrate a string of Allied victories. On June 5, American troops captured Rome, the Italian capital. Before dawn the next day, Operation Overlord got under way. By sundown, 150,000 Allied troops had landed in Normandy. In New York, Teletype machines came alive in newsrooms, clattering, FLASH. INVASION HAS BEGUN. The sound of pealing church bells rolled across America. Railroad engines and factories blew whistles.

〜 American soldiers
plunge down the ramp
of a Coast Guard–
manned landing barge
and onto the beach at
Normandy on D-Day.
(June 6, 1944)

Air-raid sirens wailed. Yet, amid the excitement ran a current of anxiety.

That night, the president found the strength to lead the nation in prayer. As they had done so often, millions gathered around their radios to hear his comforting voice:

In this poignant hour, I ask you to join with me in prayer:

Almighty God: Our sons, pride of our Nation, this day have set upon a mighty endeavor, a struggle to preserve our Republic, our religion, and our civilization, and to set free a suffering humanity.

Lead them straight and true; give strength to their arms, stoutness to their hearts, steadfastness in their faith.

They will need Thy blessings. Their road will be long and hard. For the enemy is strong.... And, O Lord, give us Faith. Give us Faith in Thee; Faith in our sons; Faith in each other; Faith in our united crusade.... Amen.[11]

Early in July, the Democrats nominated Roosevelt and Missouri senator Harry S. Truman as his running mate. The Republicans chose New York governor Thomas E. Dewey. Young and dynamic, Dewey was a "gangbuster," famous for jailing kingpins of organized crime. The Republican made his opponent's health a campaign issue, describing FDR as "old and tired," a polite way of saying "unfit for office."[12]

To counter the charge, Roosevelt had to show himself fit and able, though he was anything but. Acting "presidential," he left (on July 17, 1944), for Pearl Harbor aboard the cruiser *Baltimore* to discuss strategy with his Pacific commanders. Before sailing, and unbeknownst to the public, he had stabbing chest pains unlike any before. Fortunately, he recovered after about an hour. When he arrived, General MacArthur was stunned to see "just a shell of the man I had known." As for the meeting, the general thought it "purely political," a stunt to deceive voters. It accomplished little that the Joint Chiefs of Staff could not have done in Washington.[13]

Before leaving Hawaii, Roosevelt made an unannounced visit to a military hospital. An aide wheeled him through the amputee wards, without reporters or Secret Service men tagging along.

From left to right, General MacArthur, FDR, Admiral Nimitz, and Admiral Leahy in Waikiki, Hawaii. (July 28, 1944)

No hiding his disability now! He rolled down the aisles slowly, visible to everyone. Again he was "Old Doc Roosevelt," as he had been at Warm Springs before many of them were born. He knew how they felt, because he had felt that way himself. They were depressed, and why not? *But look at me,* he said wordlessly, *we are not that different. Where there is life, there is hope. Really!* He had heard about one exceptionally brave man who had amputated his own legs with a bayonet during combat to stay alive. FDR came over to his bed and said, "I understand you are something of a surgeon. I'm not a bad orthopedist myself."[14]

Back home, he took a leaf from Winston Churchill's book. The prime minister liked to say that in wartime, truth is so precious it needs a "bodyguard of lies." By that, Churchill meant one must spread lies to deceive the enemy. During the 1944 election, Roosevelt devised his own bodyguard of lies.

His first line of defense was Admiral McIntire, an ear, nose, and throat specialist. The admiral swore Dr. Bruenn, whom he outranked, to secrecy at all costs. Asked by reporters about Roosevelt's health, McIntire insisted, "The president's health is perfectly okay." Democratic Party officials joined the bodyguard, too. "The president is very vigorous, the picture of health," they announced straight-faced. When rumors of his failing health spread through several major hospitals, J. Edgar Hoover sent FBI agents to find the culprits and warn them to keep quiet. Though the rumors stopped, FDR's health continued to decline. When Joseph P. Kennedy, the former ambassador to Britain and father of a future president, visited the White House in late October, he found the president looking "very badly." Kennedy noted, "His face was as gray as his hair. He is thin, he has an unhealthy color. His hands shake violently when he tries to take a drink of water."[15]

In November, Roosevelt coasted to victory on Election Day. Polish American votes helped; after he promised to demand the Allies treat their homeland justly at the end of the war, their leaders heartily endorsed him. On January 2, 1945, FDR took the oath of office for the fourth time. Standing on the South Portico of the White House in the bitter cold, without a hat or an overcoat, he spoke for less than five minutes to a small crowd gathered in the slush.

Even that speech, the shortest inaugural in American history, took its toll. Vice President Truman noticed the pain lines etched into FDR's face. Secretary of State Edward Stettinius noted that he "seemed to tremble all over. It was not just his hands that shook but his whole body as well." His appearance upset Edith Wilson. "I feel terrible," the former First Lady told Frances Perkins. "He looks exactly as my husband looked when he went into his decline." Perkins made her promise not to tell anyone about her fears, for she understood that "he has a great and terrible job to do, and he's got to do it even if it kills him."[16]

Roosevelt must have known how gravely ill he was, if not how little time he had left. Yet he chose to keep his condition secret from the American people. They had a right to know, since his health affected how he did his job. For months, they had no full-time president. At the same time, the Holocaust raged.

HOLOCAUST

"Holocaust" comes from the Greek *holokauston,* meaning "a sacrifice that is completely burned." Since the Second World War, it has referred to Hitler's effort to annihilate Europe's Jews. Churchill called the Holocaust "probably the greatest and most horrible crime ever committed in the whole history of the world." For many, Roosevelt's reaction to it is the most troubling aspect of his presidency.[17]

We remember that anti-Semitism, hatred of Jews, lay at the center of Hitler's mental world. It was no accident, then, that his coming to power began a horrific time for Germany's 525,000 Jews. For starters, in April 1933, a month after FDR's first term began, Hitler's henchmen organized boycotts and vandalism against Jewish-owned businesses. The pace of oppression picked up in 1935 with a series of laws on race and citizenship aimed at humiliating, denigrating, and separating Jews from German society. These laws stripped Jews of their citizenship, meaning they were in the country illegally. Sexual relations, let alone marriage, between Jews and people of "Aryan blood" were forbidden; violators faced fines and jail. Eventually, some 2,000 laws, decrees, orders, rulings, and regulations limited what Jews could and could not do.

Jews lost their civil rights and property. Signs reading JEWS KEEP OUT, JEWS NOT WANTED, and JEWS AND DOGS NOT ALLOWED appeared in every German city, town, and village. Jews were barred from public transportation, restaurants, theaters, museums, libraries, movie houses, swimming pools, and parks. Nor could they buy or own an ever-growing list of things, including cars, motorcycles, bicycles, pets, flowers, fruit, coffee, typewriters, radios, cameras, woolen blankets, newspapers, and books. Public schools taught that "the Devil is the father of the Jew" and expelled Jewish pupils. Nazi thugs chased Jewish students and professors off university campuses. The government seized Jewish-owned bank accounts, real estate, businesses, and insurance policies. Ousted from the professions—law, medicine, dentistry, engineering, science, and teaching—Jews had to sell whatever they had in exchange for basic necessities.

On the night of November 9, 1938, mobs ransacked the remaining Jewish businesses and burned most synagogues, Jewish houses of worship. As grinning policemen stood by, storm troopers invaded Jewish homes, trashing them and throwing out anything that fit through a window: furniture, bedding, even pianos. And people, too. In Berlin, an

〰️ Germans pass by the broken shop window of a Jewish-owned business that was destroyed during Kristallnacht. (November 10, 1938)

American diplomat reported that Nazis tossed a little boy from a second-story window into the howling mob below. "His leg broken, the boy tried to crawl on hands and knees through the forest of kicking black boots until my friend plunged in and rescued him." This night of terror became known as Kristallnacht, German for "Crystal Night," also often called the "Night of Broken Glass." Later, Jews were ordered to sew a six-pointed star created with black lines—a Star of David—on yellow cloth with the word *Jude* in the center on their outer garments.[18]

But Hitler was not satisfied. He wanted a "Final Solution" to the "Jewish problem." Today, we call his policy genocide, from the Greek *genos* (race) and Latin *cída* (killer). Hitler had always been clear about his murderous objective. As early as 1922, the future Fuehrer shrieked at journalist Josef Hell: "Once I am really in power, my first and foremost task will be the annihilation of the Jews." For starters, he said, he would set up gallows across Germany, where the Jews "will remain hanging until they stink." On January 30, 1939, eight months before attacking Poland, Hitler announced that war would bring "the annihilation of the Jewish race in Europe." Eventually, he meant to kill every Jew on earth, including those in America. He promised, "We will exterminate this Jewish democracy and Jewish blood will mix with the dollars."[19]

The Holocaust began in Poland. Following their victory in 1939, the Nazis forced Jews into urban ghettos, sections of cities enclosed by high brick walls topped with barbed wire and broken bottles cemented into place. Driven from their homes, Jews had to live in overcrowded conditions, often a big family in a tiny room. The Warsaw Ghetto, the largest, held over 400,000 people in a two-square-mile area, a little

Heinrich Himmler (in front, with glasses) inspects a prisoner-of-war camp in Russia. (1940–1941)

bigger than New York's Central Park. Ghettos became testing grounds for the Hunger Plan. For days at a time, Nazi guards forbade food to enter. Then they allowed a little to trickle in for a day or so before cutting it off again. Starvation and its related diseases killed hundreds of ghetto dwellers each day. Pedestrians got used to walking around bodies sprawled in the streets. Starving orphans with bloated bellies died in droves. People driven insane by hunger stood against walls with outstretched hands, babbling and pleading for a crust of bread or a moldy potato.

In July 1941, soon after Germany invaded the Soviet Union, Hitler secretly ordered SS chief Heinrich Himmler, like him a fanatical racist, to begin full-scale murder operations. He did not put the order in writing but gave it to Himmler verbally, thus distancing himself from blame. By the end of the war, Himmler had organized the murder of between 5.5 million and 6 million Jews and around 500,000 Roma, or Gypsies, also considered a "racial menace."

However, murdering millions quickly and disposing of their bodies are not easy tasks. At first, Himmler relied on SS units called Einsatzgruppen, Special Action Groups. As the German army cut deeper into the USSR, these units followed closely behind. Appearing suddenly in a village, they rounded up the Jews, marched them to out-of-the-way spots (usually in forests), shot them, and buried their bodies in mass graves. Sometimes, a unit killed thousands in a single *Aktion* (action). The largest began on September 29, 1941, at Babi Yar, a ravine outside the city of Kiev. Teams shot 33,771 men, women, and children in thirty-six hours. Though SS commanders gave orders to conceal the murders, killers often snapped photos and wrote home about their activities. As one told his family, "Wherever there is a German soldier, the Jews are no more." Another simply said, "The Jew was not acknowledged by us to be a human being."[20]

Shooting proved too slow and messy to suit Himmler. The SS chief had a delicate stomach and got sick during a "demonstration" execution; he never watched another. Besides, shooting was too personal, because shooters saw the effects of their bullets up close. SS men wrote home, telling how "infants flew in great arcs through the air, and we shot them to pieces in flight, before their bodies fell into the pit." Spattered with blood and brains, hundreds of the shooters cracked under the strain, becoming alcoholics and drug addicts. One Special Action Group commander, an SS general, suffered a nervous breakdown. Sent to rest in a hospital, he spent the nights screaming as gory images appeared whenever he closed his eyes. "Don't you know what's happening in Russia?" he shouted at doctors. "The entire Jewish people is being exterminated there."[21]

Some killers, overcome by guilt and disgust, volunteered for regular front-line units, seeking a soldier's death in combat. Those who remained, the vast majority, saw the murder of innocents as a duty to their Fuehrer and the Aryan race. Racial brainwashing had dehumanized Jews in their eyes, erasing any humane inclinations they may have had.

Himmler wanted to speed up the killing while reducing stress on the killers. For that reason, he had several concentration camps set up in Poland: Treblinka, Belzec, Sobibor, Majdanek, and Chelmno. Auschwitz, the largest, was located in the southern part of the country.

From the moment Hitler took power, he had built concentration camps for Germans. While many inmates died as a result of SS brutality, these camps were really prisons to hold "enemies of the state." However, the camps in Poland had just one purpose. Designed solely as murder factories, they drew victims from across Nazi-occupied Europe. Death camps operated according to a sick version of Henry Ford's methods. Hitler admired Ford, who was also a notorious anti-Semite. In the 1920s, Hitler kept a life-size portrait of Ford next to his desk in Nazi Party headquarters

Instead of making cars, however, death camps mass-produced corpses. The idea was to break the killing process into several distinct stages: arrival, processing, killing, and disposal. When a trainload of Jews arrived, SS doctors selected victims for ghastly "medical" experiments or to be worked to death as slaves, a process called "extermination through work." The rest, the overwhelming majority, were slated for immediate death by Zyklon B. Originally used to rid warehouses of insects,

≈≈ Newly arrived Jews undergo a selection on the ramp at Auschwitz. (May 1, 1944)

Jewish women and children who have been selected for death at Auschwitz walk unknowingly toward the gas chambers. (May 1, 1944)

Zyklon B came as bluish crystals that turned into cyanide gas when exposed to air. Depending on the temperature and humidity on any given day, the gas usually killed within ten to twenty-five minutes. Working round the clock, Germans could murder as many as 2,000 people in a single gas chamber each day.

A report to Himmler detailed assembly-line murder in the sterile prose of an engineering textbook:

The Jews arrive in special trains (freight cars) toward evening and are driven on special tracks to areas of the camp specifically set aside for this purpose. There the Jews are unloaded and examined for their fitness to work.... The unfit go to cellars in a large house which are entered from outside. They go down five or six steps into a fairly long, well-constructed and well-ventilated cellar area, which is lined with benches to the left and right. It is brightly lit, and the benches are numbered. The prisoners are told that they are to be cleansed and disinfected for their new assignments. They must therefore completely undress to be bathed.... Everything proceeds in a perfectly orderly fashion. Then they pass through a small corridor and enter a large cellar room which resembles a shower bath. In this room are three large pillars, into which [Zyklon B] can be lowered from outside the cellar room. When three- to four-hundred people have been herded into this room, the doors are shut, and containers filled with [Zyklon B] are dropped down into the pillars. As soon as the containers touch the base of the pillars, they release [gases] that put the people to sleep.... A few minutes later, the door opens on the other side, where the elevator is located.

The hair of the corpses is cut off, and their [gold-filled] teeth are extracted. . . . Then the corpses are loaded into elevators and brought up to the first floor, where ten large crematoria are located. . . . The job itself is performed by Jewish prisoners, who never step outside this camp again.[22]

Slaves collected victims' possessions for further use. Adult and baby clothes, shoes, socks, underwear, spectacles, and even toys were sent to Germany for distribution to the needy, chiefly sufferers from Allied air raids. The hair of victims was used to stuff mattresses and woven into warm socks for U-boat crews; some received looted watches as prizes for a successful cruise. At Auschwitz, daily "output" reached 12,000 victims. In all, some 1.5 million people died in this hellish place, now preserved as a museum and monument to the victims of Nazi genocide.

Though a few Jews escaped from the camps, joined guerrilla bands in the forests, and fought back, nothing they did could slow, let alone stop, the murder machine. They needed Allied help, and of that they got precious little.

FDR AND THE HOLOCAUST

How President Roosevelt dealt with the Holocaust is important, as it reflects on his image as a humanitarian. Critics have said he was, at best, a heartless man who allowed mass murder to happen; at worst, he was an anti-Semite who wanted Jews killed. Defenders have said he wished to help Jews but had his hands tied by American public opinion and the demands of waging global war. The facts are complicated. There were no easy answers back then, nor are there any today.

FDR grew up in an anti-Semitic environment—this we know for sure. In his youth, upper-class people, as a rule, disliked Jews and resented their presence in America. This was not because they saw Jews as "race enemies" deserving extermination; instead Jews were considered outsiders who held different religious beliefs from the Protestant majority. Poor immigrants who worked hard and rose in the world alarmed families that had controlled the nation's economic and political life for generations.

Like black people, Jews faced discrimination, though little violence. Elite private schools such as Groton barred Jews. During Franklin's years at Harvard, and until the late 1920s, its social, athletic, and cultural organizations excluded Jews. Similarly, American universities had fewer than a hundred Jews on their liberal arts and sciences faculties. Well into the 1940s, top schools—Harvard, Princeton, Yale, Brown, Columbia, and the University of Pennsylvania, among others—had quotas on the number of Jewish freshmen admitted each year. Employment ads often said that only Christians need apply. Leading banks, businesses, and law firms refused to hire Jews. Nor could Jews, however rich, buy homes in neighborhoods where the "best" people lived or vacation at the resorts they favored. FDR never protested such discrimination, if he ever thought about it, probably because he considered it normal.[23]

Franklin's family shared the prejudices of their time and social class. His mother, Sara, thought Jews "common" and "horrid." His young wife held them in contempt. Eleanor used phrases like "very Jew" and "loathsome little Jew" to describe offensive things and people. Jews, she huffed, were "very unlike ourselves." In 1915, after a party given by Bernard Baruch, she wrote Sara: "The Jew party [was] appalling. . . . I never wish to hear money, jewels or sables mentioned again." She also found Harvard Law School professor and later Supreme Court justice Felix Frankfurter "an interesting little man, but very Jew."

Franklin told jokes about immigrant Jews on New York's Lower East Side.[24]

However, as the couple matured, they rejected anti-Semitism as bigoted and ignorant. Eleanor became especially sensitive to the Jews' plight. In a way, she believed, we are all Jews, united by our humanity. Ultimately, anti-Semitism was a form of suicide. "It looks to me," she said, "as though the future of the Jews [is] tied up . . . with the future of all the world, [and] if they perish, we perish sooner or later." Those who knew Franklin said he did not have an anti-Semitic bone in his body. He placed Jews in top-level posts, which inspired opponents to brand the New Deal the "Jew Deal." Accused of being Jewish himself, he snapped, "I wish I was."[25]

Until the war began, Hitler allowed Jews to leave Germany, but with little more than the clothes on their backs; he would kill them later, at his convenience. However, refugees need a place to go. While Britain admitted several thousand German Jews, most countries barred them. Since 1924, federal quotas based on age, ethnicity, and country of origin had set limits on the number of immigrants admitted to America each year. These quotas favored northern Europeans, chiefly Protestants. Roosevelt did what he thought he safely could—

that is, without raising a political storm. Between 1933 and 1940, about 105,000 German and Austrian Jews came to America—more than to any other country. As it turned out, Hitler's loss was our country's gain. Jewish refugees were usually city-bred people with high levels of education. Among them were 900 lawyers, 2,000 physicians, 1,500 writers, 1,500 musicians, and 3,000 professors. The scientists included physicists who would soon play key roles in developing the atomic bomb: Eugene Wigner, John von Neumann, Hans Bethe, and Victor Weisskopf. Albert Einstein came in 1934.[26]

Sadly, Roosevelt was no more willing to take risks for Jews than for blacks terrorized by lynching. As Eleanor explained, political considerations often made her husband back away from causes he believed in. Anti-Semitism was rampant in Depression-era America, as workers resented immigrants competing for scarce jobs. Members of Congress like John E. Rankin were brazen bigots, blaming the crisis on "a little group of our international Jewish brethren." In one poll, 72 percent of Americans opposed allowing Jewish refugees into the country. With war drawing near, in 1939 New York senator Robert F. Wagner and Massachusetts representative Edith

N. Rogers introduced a bill to admit 20,000 Jewish children above the German quota on an emergency basis. After polls showed 66 percent of Americans opposed even such an expression of decency, the bill died without a vote in either house of Congress. In effect, this lack of action condemned the children to death. As for FDR, he was unwilling to defy public opinion and risk a voter backlash. Ever the politician, he said, "It is a terrible thing to look over your shoulder when you are trying to lead— and find no one there." So, rather than educate Americans on the plight of refugees, as he had about the Hitler peril, he evaded the issue in public.[27]

In June 1939, the *St. Louis* steamed along the Florida coast with 936 Jews fleeing Germany. Denied entry to Cuba as promised, they cabled the White House from the ship, pleading for sanctuary in the United States. FDR did not reply. Instead, he had the State Department work quietly to see that none went back to Germany against their will. When the *St. Louis* returned to Europe, most passengers found refuge in England. Of those who went to France and Holland, some later died in Auschwitz.

Several Jews owed their lives to the First Lady. Through some hocus-pocus with paperwork, she managed to get eighty-three refugees from the ship *Quanza* into the country. Eleanor's failure to persuade her husband to admit more troubled her always. It was, her son James said, "her deepest regret at the end of her life." On the other hand, in the 1930s, few non-Germans thought Hitler actually meant what he said about exterminating the Jews. Even to suggest such a crime seemed over the top, like the atrocity propaganda of the last war.[28]

When war came again, the president left the refugee issue for the State Department to handle. Jews in countries allied to Germany but not yet under direct Nazi control—Hungary, Romania, Bulgaria—scrambled for American entry permits. However, Breckinridge Long, chief of the department's passport division, despised Jews. Admitting any, Long insisted, would also admit Nazi spies disguised as refugees. Long instructed his division to tie up passport applications in red tape. Other department officials refused to forward information received from various sources on the death camps to Jewish organizations in America.

No matter. By mid-1942, the Allies knew the broad outlines, if not all the details, of the Holocaust. The machinery of death was never the total secret Hitler hoped for; survivors of mass shootings and escapees from trains bound for the death camps told their stories to fellow Jews and Poles. These stories, in turn, passed from mouth to mouth, until they reached the West. In March 1943, a huge rally in New York's Madison Square Garden denounced the murders.

President Roosevelt got an in-person report from Poland. Twenty-nine-year-old Jan Karski, a devout Catholic, was a courier between the Polish Home Army, or underground, and the Polish government-in-exile in London. He would sneak into Poland, gather intelligence from a network of contacts, and follow secret routes back to London—dangerous work that once landed him in a Nazi prison. He was tortured for days before Polish agents freed him in a daring raid.

In the summer of 1942, Karski met with two members of the Jewish underground. At great risk, they had left the Warsaw Ghetto through a tunnel dug in the cellar of a house near the wall. They calculated that in what they called "Hitler's war against the Polish Jews," the Germans had already murdered over 1.8 million fellow Jews. Clearly, unless the Allies acted soon, and decisively, every Jew was doomed. They wanted

Karski to see for himself, and then report to the Allied leaders, particularly the American president.

In late August, a Jewish contact gave Karski some ragged clothes and an armband with a Star of David and led him through the tunnel. The horrific things Karski saw when he emerged burned themselves into his soul, making him a lifelong crusader for human rights. In May 2012, President Barack Obama awarded the Medal of Freedom, America's highest civilian award, posthumously to Karski.

The Germans had recently rounded up tens of thousands of Warsaw Ghetto Jews for the gas chambers. Those left behind (for the time being) seemed hardly human. Karski recalled:

Jan Karski lectures at the United States Holocaust Memorial Museum in Washington, D.C., many decades after the end of World War II. (1994)

These were still living people, if you could call them such. For apart from their skin, eyes, and voice there was nothing human left in these palpitating figures. Everywhere there was hunger, misery, the atrocious stench of decomposing bodies, the pitiful moans of dying children, the desperate cries and gasps of a people struggling for life against impossible odds. . . . As we picked our way across the mud and rubble, the shadows of what had once been men or women flitted by us in pursuit of someone or something, their eyes blazing with some insane hunger or greed. . . . Everything there seemed polluted by death, filth, and decay. I was careful to avoid touching a wall or a human being.[29]

Karski felt he needed to see more—a death camp. Soon after he'd visited the Warsaw Ghetto, a Jewish guide turned him over to a member of the Polish underground. The Pole had bribed an

Estonian guard working under German command to take the day off and lend him his uniform. Another Estonian guard, also for a price, led him past a checkpoint to a field enclosed by barbed wire. Karski was dazed, scarcely able to believe his eyes. The field seemed like a corner of hell vomited onto the earth's surface. It was a temporary holding area for Warsaw Jews destined for the Belzec gas chambers. There, thousands of people, many stark naked, suffered for days in the open, without food or water. "The Jewish mass vibrated, trembled, and

Two inmates suffering from starvation at the Amphing concentration camp in Germany. This photo was taken after the camp was liberated by Allied troops. (May 4, 1945)

moved to and fro as if united in a single, insane, rhythmic trance," Karski wrote later. "They waved their hands, shouted, quarreled, cursed and spat at each other. Hunger, thirst, fear, and exhaustion had driven them all insane."[30]

Back in London, British officials said they could do little, if anything, to aid the Jews; they had their hands full fighting the war. With the blessings of his own government, Karski went to Washington.

On July 28, 1943, he entered the Oval Study. William Bullitt had arranged the visit so Karski could relate his experiences to the president in person. Karski found FDR "amazingly well-informed about Poland . . . and [he] asked me to verify stories told about the German practices against the Jews." Karski did, naming Auschwitz as "the most horrible concentration camp" of the lot. "More than 1,800,000 Jews have been murdered in my country," he told FDR, echoing his Warsaw contacts. The president listened, seemingly wrapped up in his report. Yet, when the Pole said goodbye, he felt disappointed. For Roosevelt was, as he delicately put it, "rather noncommittal." Translation: The president sympathized with the plight of the Jews and Poland but gave no promises, refusing to be pinned down.[31]

However, Treasury Secretary Henry Morgenthau wanted to do just that: pin his boss down. Morgenthau, the cabinet's only Jew, had received reports from secret contacts in Switzerland. Ever loyal to Roosevelt, he kept these to himself, until one day he exclaimed, "I cannot take any more!" In January 1944, he sent the White House his "Report on the Acquiescence of This Government in the Murder of the Jews." The report accused Breckinridge Long and his aides of "willful attempts to prevent action from being taken to rescue Jews from Hitler." Morgenthau also noted that if the State Department's policy became public in a presidential election year, a "nasty scandal" would result. Prodded into action, Roosevelt created the War Refugee Board (WRB), a government agency to rescue victims of Nazi oppression.[32]

Established on January 22, 1944, the WRB received few taxpayer dollars, its funds coming almost entirely from private Jewish organizations. Within weeks, it sent agents to Nazi-allied countries. The WRB's most successful agent was Swedish diplomat Raoul Wallenberg. Though Sweden was neutral in the war, its heart was in the right place. With his government's blessing, Wallenberg went to Hungary to set up a rescue network. Warned of the danger, the thirty-one-

A statue of Raoul Wallenberg in Tel Aviv, Israel. This is one of many statues around the world honoring his heroism. (2007)

year-old said simply: "Every day costs human lives. I'm going to get ready to leave immediately."[33]

After unexpected delays, Wallenberg finally arrived in July 1944, just as Nazi troops took over Hungary. Acting on orders from Adolf Eichmann, Himmler's extermination "expert," they sent four trains a day to Auschwitz. Before long, they had deported all Hungarian Jews except those in Budapest, the nation's capital. Meanwhile, Wallenberg worked feverishly, recruiting several hundred helpers. Using bribes and forged exit permits printed in the Swedish embassy, they saved 120,000

Jews. Wallenberg also had help from a Roman Catholic priest. Father Angelo Roncalli (the future Pope John XXIII) provided certificates saying their holders were Christians. But Wallenberg could not save himself. When Stalin's troops captured Budapest in January 1945, the NKVD arrested the hero as an American spy and, later, murdered him.[34]

In the meantime, Roosevelt had to consider the Auschwitz murder factory. In the summer of 1944, the World Jewish Congress and other Jewish organizations asked the War Department to bomb the gas chambers and rail lines serving the camp. The nearest strike force, B-24 Liberators based in Italy, had already flown over Auschwitz to bomb oil refineries only five miles away.

When Assistant Secretary of War John J. McCloy raised the issue at a White House meeting, he recalled, the president became "irate." Bombing would kill hundreds of prisoners, FDR said, handing the Nazis a propaganda victory. The president was not alone in rejecting such a raid. After the war, survivors were appalled at the idea of bombing. One exclaimed, "Bomb Auschwitz! I would never have survived—if the bombs did not kill us, the Nazis would have shot us down like dogs if we tried to escape." Other survivors, however, favored bombing. Being marked for death anyhow, they felt they had nothing to lose if Auschwitz were attacked.[35]

On a deeper level, Roosevelt probably did not see how bombing a murder factory could do any good. Nazi work crews usually repaired damaged rail lines within hours; that is why bombers had to return to the same target repeatedly. Even if bombing destroyed every mile of track serving Auschwitz, Hitler had other camps beyond the range of Liberators. As for gas chambers, it was easy to replace them. All the killers had to do was cement the outer walls of a building to make it airtight and install ducts for the Zyklon B crystals.

Most Holocaust scholars think no pleas for mercy, or threats of punishment, could have influenced Hitler and his Nazi fanatics. Racism had poisoned their minds. The reality was that they had decided an entire people had no right to exist. So they would go on killing while they had the means to do it—in fact, until the very last hours of the war. Only swift, total defeat could stop them.

Thus, Roosevelt faced the brutal arithmetic of life and death. As Raoul Wallenberg said, "Every day costs human lives." Similarly, every day that shortened the war saved human lives. This suggests that the president believed the Allies' only real chance of saving Jews was by focusing every resource on destroying Nazism quickly. But nagging questions remain. How many more might have lived had FDR admitted more refugees before the war, as the First Lady wished? Even if bombing could not halt the gassing, might it have been worthwhile as a gesture of moral solidarity with the victims?[36]

Whatever answers we may give, the failure to bomb Auschwitz echoes down to the present. Citing its example, in 2012 high officials of the State of Israel warned, "Never again will we not be masters of the fate of our very survival." In short, if threatened with another Holocaust, they vowed to rely on their own armed forces, not the promises or goodwill of others.[37]

YALTA

By early 1945, the Nazis were fighting on their own soil. While General Eisenhower's armies invaded Germany from the west, Allied bomber fleets pounded it as never before. Its cities became moonscapes of deep craters with shells of burnt-out buildings. Hundreds of miles of streets were impassable, blocked by mounds of rubble and twisted steel. When British troops took Cologne on the Rhine River, some said, "The great city looks like a corpse and smells like one, too." Nuremberg, site of gigantic prewar Nazi rallies, became a sea of rubble. "Nuremberg is a city of the dead," wrote an American journalist. High-explosive and incendiary bombs deluged Berlin, demolishing entire neighborhoods in a night. Driven underground, millions of Berliners called dank, dark cellars home. At the all-clear siren, they emerged trembling and bleary-eyed, to scrounge for anything edible or useful.[33]

Roosevelt had far worse in store for Germany. For five years, scientists had been working on the atomic bomb. FDR meant to use it. General Leslie Groves, chief of the military side of the project, recalled the president telling him that "he wished for us to be prepared to drop the bomb on Germany, if we had the first bombs before the end of the war in Europe." Only Germany's collapse spared her the calamity that overtook Japan.[39]

In the east, Stalin's forces rolled ahead, unstoppable. By January 1945, the Red Army had overrun much of Eastern Europe, liberated Auschwitz, and crossed into Germany. As Soviet tank columns drove to within fifty miles of Berlin, FDR left Washington for another Big Three meeting, to last from February 4 to 11.

〰 Winston Churchill, FDR, and Joseph Stalin at the Yalta Conference. (February 1945)

Traveling by warship, then aboard the *Sacred Cow,* he reached Yalta, a Soviet vacation resort on the Black Sea. Given his failing health, he had not wanted to venture so far from home—over 7,000 miles, with stopovers in Africa—but Stalin insisted. Again, the tyrant said that "military matters" kept him from going any further. At Yalta, as at Tehran, he had his guests' rooms bugged. There were six-legged bugs, too. The Americans stayed at the Livadia Palace, recently retaken from the Nazis. They had left it so filthy that delousing teams had to work overtime to get the pests under control. Still, guests complained of being "eaten up by bedbugs at night."[40]

The change in Roosevelt since Tehran shocked everyone. To Churchill, he "seemed placid and frail. I felt that he had a slender contact with life." The president's hands shook, his face was drawn, and his eyes had a glassy, faraway look. Lord Moran, Churchill's personal doctor, saw him with a physician's trained eyes. He noted in his diary that FDR "had gone all to bits physically" and "appears a very sick man. He has all the symptoms of hardening of the arteries of the brain in an advanced stage, so that I give him only a few months to live." FDR was so ill and so tired that he stayed in bed for much of the day, saving his strength for the formal meetings. Photographs showed a sick man, but the White House staff concealed most of them. Only the kindest appeared in newspapers.[41]

Those who watched Roosevelt at the conference table differed on his mental condition. British diplomat Sir Alexander Cadogan, for example, thought that "most of the time he hardly knew what it was about." Roosevelt's interpreter Charles Bohlen, an expert on Soviet affairs and a future ambassador to Moscow, thought "our leader was ill at Yalta . . . but he was effective." Both men were right. It all depended on when they saw the president in action. Humans are living beings, not mechanical robots. Even the very ill have good days and bad days. At meetings, the president's mind was usually, but not always, sharp.[42]

Roosevelt still believed Stalin was "getatable." For that reason, he met with the tyrant privately to avoid giving the impression that the democracies were ganging up on him. Churchill was angry, but realized that Britain had become the junior partner in the Grand Alliance.

"I'm more bloodthirsty than a year ago," Roosevelt said, urging Stalin to repeat his demand to shoot 50,000 German officers. For his part, Stalin came across as cool, confident, and firm. During a luncheon, for example, Anna Roosevelt noticed a "most sinister gent" sitting across the table. Short and dumpy, he was bald, with dark, beady eyes and thick glasses. When FDR asked his name, Stalin replied with a sneer. "Ah, that's our Himmler," NKVD chief Lavrenti Beria. It was a startling admission, for Stalin had linked his own bloody deeds with the Nazi mass murderer. Beria said nothing. He smiled broadly, revealing his yellowed teeth.[43]

Roosevelt aimed to get Stalin's help in defeating Japan, as promised at Tehran. This was important because scientists had not tested the atomic bomb yet and did not know if it would work. Mean-while, a new long-range bomber, the B-29 Superfortress, struck Japanese cities from recently captured island bases. "Bomb and burn 'em till they quit," declared the man in charge, General Curtis LeMay. And so they did. The March 9, 1945, raid on Tokyo killed around 100,000 people and left another million homeless. But the Japanese military preferred national annihilation to surrender. "We will fight," they said, "until we eat stones." In some island battles, they unleashed the *kamikaze,* or "divine wind"—suicide pilots who crashed their planes into American ships In Washington, the War Department estimated up to a million American casualties in an invasion of Japan.[44]

A Soviet attack would shorten the war, sparing American lives. Stalin agreed to declare war on Japan within three months of Germany's surrender. In return, and without asking the Chinese government, Roosevelt said he had no objections to Soviet forces occupying parts of Manchuria. Stalin also agreed to support the president's plans for the United Nations. The UN was of prime importance to Roosevelt, who felt that America's failure to join the League of Nations had reduced its chances for success and contributed to the coming of the Second World War.

The interior of a B-29 Superfortress, showing the rear pressurized cabin, equipped with four bunks to give crew members a chance for rest on a long mission. (June 1944)

Next the conference turned to the fate of postwar Germany. Churchill and Stalin agreed with Roosevelt's insistence on harsh, punishing treatment. The German people, FDR felt, must be made to realize they had lost the war and would never become a military power again. They had only themselves to blame for supporting Hitler. While FDR did not want civilians to starve, he did not want to treat them like other Europeans, either. The Allies would feed them enough to keep them going—the barest ration of hard bread and thin soup. Moreover, they would carve Germany into zones of occupation and try Nazi leaders for war crimes. Not a word was said about the Katyn massacre, a Soviet war crime.[45]

Eastern Europe was the last major item on the agenda. At Tehran, Stalin could only demand the lands Hitler had ceded to him. Now the Red Army occupied them all, or soon would. As promised at Tehran, the Big Three agreed to redraw the map. While the Soviets kept eastern Poland, an area the size of Missouri, Poland would get a large slice of eastern Germany in exchange. Ignoring the inevitable human tragedies, Roosevelt said the Germans "deserved" to be expelled and Churchill promised "a clean sweep." Within two years, 12 million Germans were driven from their homes. Of these, perhaps a million died of hunger and cold, exhaustion and brutality. Finally, at FDR's urging, the leaders issued the Declaration of Liberated Europe. Modeled on the Atlantic Charter, it pledged democracy, representative government, and free elections in the lands liberated from the Nazis.[46]

Roosevelt and Churchill were blamed for selling out Eastern Europe to Stalin. In England, when exiled Poles heard the news from Yalta on the radio, many wept from rage and disgust. General Władysław Anders, commander of Polish forces serving with the British army, called the agreement a "mockery of the Atlantic Charter." Before taking off on a bombing raid, a Polish airman said, "If the Germans get me now, I won't even know what I am dying for. For Poland? For Britain? Or for Russia?" In the Gulag, when news of Yalta filtered in, slave laborers cursed the leaders of the democracies for their "shortsightedness and stupidity."[47]

Roosevelt did not see it that way. Like it or not, the Red Army occupied Eastern Europe, and only another war could drive it out. However, in 1945, few sane Americans or British could imagine fighting the USSR. Equally important, FDR needed Stalin's help against Japan and in creating the United Nations. By yielding Eastern Europe to the Soviet tyrant, he thought he had gotten the best deal possible, given the situation.

On March 1, Roosevelt reported to a joint session of Congress. When he appeared, a loud gasp rose from the audience. Never before, a reporter noted, had the president "uncloaked his infirmity so openly, so frankly, before so many people." At last, Americans realized how ill their president was. Pale and trembling, he read the speech from his wheelchair,

often losing his place on the page and slurring his words. Vice President Truman thought it "the most poorly delivered speech he ever made." Still, FDR said that he'd returned from Yalta in high spirits and "with a firm belief that we have made a good start on the road to peace." When he finished, Congress gave a thunderous round of applause. It seemed as if members sensed he would never appear before them again.[48]

Roosevelt had been too optimistic about the road to peace. In getting Stalin to sign the Declaration of Liberated Europe, he'd hoped to pin "Uncle Joe" down in writing. Unfortunately, this was another example of paper taking whatever is written on it. Paper promises meant nothing to Stalin unless they suited his purposes. He had no intention of abiding by any written pledge limiting his freedom of action, not when he commanded a victorious army 12 million strong. When an aide worried that he had signed away too much at Yalta, Stalin replied, "Never mind. We'll do it our own way later."[49]

What "our own way" meant became clear in the spring of 1945. Disturbing reports began to reach Washington from Eastern Europe. These told of wholesale arrests of those likely to challenge Soviet rule. "Our Himmler's" NKVD

FDR addresses Congress after the Crimean Conference. (March 1, 1945)

worked overtime, sending most victims to the Gulag and the rest to the grave. Poland's "liberators" executed heroes of the resistance, who had fought the Nazis tooth and nail, by firing squad. Reports also told of Soviet abuse of thousands of American and British soldiers found in Nazi prisoner-of-war camps. Many said they would have starved if not for the decency of ordinary Poles, themselves hungry. Late into 1946, nearly a year after Germany's surrender, Polish patriots waged a losing battle against the Red Army, the NKVD, and Stalin's Polish Communist stooges.

On March 21, Ambassador W. Averell

Harriman sent a warning to the White House from Moscow. We face a "20th century barbarian invasion," it said. "We must clearly recognize that the Soviet program is the establishment of totalitarianism, ending personal liberty and democracy as we know and respect it."[50]

Roosevelt was stunned. Finally, he realized that Stalin was not "getatable," that he was no partner for peace. "Averell is right," he cried, pounding his wheelchair with his hands. "We can't do business with Stalin. He has broken every one of his promises to me at Yalta."[51]

FDR did not know that Stalin was already thinking about the next war. Around the time Stalin left Moscow for Yalta, he had meetings with a high-ranking foreign Communist official. At one meeting, the tyrant suddenly stood up and declared, "The war shall soon be over. We shall recover in fifteen or twenty years, and then we'll have another go at it." Stalin said much the same to his inner circle. "During all the sittings of his government," Sergo Beria recalled, "he said that the Third World War would take place, and that this war would take place during his life."[52]

So George Kennan and the other Soviet experts had been right all along. Stalin despised the democracies, their liberties, and their capitalist economies.

He had never asked them to be allies. The Grand Alliance had been forced upon him by Hitler's betrayal. He had not given up on Lenin's dream of world domination, and nothing short of the democracies' surrender would satisfy him. We should be glad neither that nor a third world war happened. Instead, despite Stalin's death in 1953, humanity endured a half century of the "Cold War," a dangerous rivalry between groups of Communist nations led by the USSR and non-Communist nations led by the United States. The rivalry was "cold" because it did not escalate into a "hot" war, an armed conflict with atomic bombs.

Two of three or four thousand inmates at Lager Nordhausen, a Gestapo concentration camp. These two men were liberated from the camp by Allied soldiers. (April 14, 1945)

DEATH OF A PRESIDENT

Toward the end of March 1945, a very tired president returned to Warm Springs. All he wanted to do now was "sleep & sleep & sleep" at the place he loved so much.[53]

In Germany, on April 12, while FDR slept, Generals Eisenhower and Patton toured the Ohrdruf concentration camp. American troops had liberated this little corner of hell the day before. Though it was not a murder factory like Auschwitz, the SS had stopped trying to keep its inmates alive in the closing weeks of the war. Before fleeing, guards shot many of them out of spite, just hours before liberation.

No strangers to violent death, the American generals could scarcely believe their eyes—or their noses. Corpses with bulging eyes, little more than bones covered with paper-thin flesh, lay scattered on the ground or heaped in piles. Patton, a hard-bitten soldier nicknamed "Old Blood and Guts," cringed. Unable to take it anymore, he ran behind a building and vomited until he had nothing left to throw up. A few hours later, Patton's troops liberated Buchenwald, a major concentration camp nearby.

There, too, the dead and dying lay everywhere. One of the liberators saw this as more than a Jewish tragedy. Leon Bass, a black sergeant, saw it as Jim Crow writ large. "So, you see what I mean?" Bass said years later. "Segregation, racism, can lead to the ultimate, to what I saw at Buchenwald."[54]

That afternoon, Roosevelt sat at a table in the living room of his cottage, reviewing the speech he expected to give at the opening session of the United Nations in San Francisco. Three of his favorite people kept him company. Laura Delano and Margaret Suckley, elderly cousins, sat on a sofa, chatting and crocheting. Lucy Mercer Rutherfurd sat on a chair in front of him, watching Elizabeth Shoumatoff at her easel. Lucy had hired the artist to paint his portrait as a gift for her daughter, Barbara.

A few minutes before one o'clock, the president raised his left hand to his forehead. "I have a terrific pain in the back of my head," he said. Those were FDR's last words. He slumped forward, unconscious. As Dr. Bruenn feared, a blood vessel had burst in his brain, causing a massive hemorrhage. Though he clung to life, his mouth open, gasping rather than breathing, there was no hope. At 3:35 p.m., the president died on the eighty-third day of his fourth term. He was sixty-three years old. Lucy, not wanting to cause a scandal, hastily packed her bags and drove away.[55]

It was nearly midnight when the First Lady arrived. Eleanor sat down on the sofa and asked what had happened. Cousin Laura told her. The woman Franklin had sworn never to see again had been with him at the end, and also at other times. Daughter Anna had arranged their White House meetings.

Though devastated by this second betrayal, Eleanor reflected on their marriage after the funeral. She had regrets. Deep regrets. "I should have tried much *harder* to help him through this awful war," she told her son Elliott. "Oh, I was pigheaded! Unbending during all those years since the first war. Always so insistent on doing what *I* wanted to do.... If I had only found the *courage* to talk to Franklin as I wanted to do, I could have said, 'Let us bury this whole [Lucy Mercer] matter and begin again together.' ... I contributed to his loneliness. I should have shared his burdens."[56]

Meanwhile, at 5:48 p.m., the White House made the official announcement. In New York, anguished cries rose from the crowds in Times Square: "Roosevelt is dead. Roosevelt is dead." Shopkeepers put radios in their doorways, turning them on full blast. Though a boy of nine,

Franklin and Eleanor Roosevelt with their thirteen grandchildren in Washington, D.C., in one of the last photographs taken of FDR. (January 20, 1945)

I remember people walking the streets dazed, unable to believe their ears. By 1945, we had grown used to FDR, and most took comfort in his leadership. Millions thought it natural, like the changing seasons, that he should be president. And now he was gone. "What will we do?" people asked. A lanky Texas congressman stood in the Rotunda of the Capitol, speaking for those millions. "He was just like a Daddy to me always; he always talked to me just that way," said Lyndon B. Johnson. "God! God! How he could take it for us all."[57]

The news spread overseas. Winston Churchill would later write, "I felt as if I had been struck a physical blow." Joseph Stalin held Ambassador Harriman's hand, saying not a word. Stalin suspected Roosevelt had died not of natural causes but of poison, which he had often used to get rid of troublesome people.[58]

Despite the blockade and fire raids, Radio Tokyo played soft music "in honor of the passing of the great man." In Berlin, a telephone rang in the steel-and-concrete bunker hidden beneath the city. "My Fuehrer!" propaganda chief Joseph Goebbels bawled. "I congratulate you! Roosevelt is dead! It is written in the stars that the second half of April will be the turning point for us. This is Friday the thirteenth of April. It is the turning point!" Hitler was thrilled. The death "of the greatest war criminal of all times," he announced, meant victory for Germany.[59]

That morning of April 13, Roosevelt's funeral train left Warm Springs with his coffin. As it headed north, countryfolk lined the tracks waiting for it to pass, many on their knees in prayer.

Next morning, April 14, the train pulled into Union Station in Washington, D.C. From there, six white horses drew the caisson bearing the coffin to the White House. Crowds along Pennsylvania Avenue stood silent and tearful.

〰️ A grieving Chief Petty Officer Graham Jackson plays "Goin' Home" on the accordion as FDR's funeral procession passes by in Warm Springs, Georgia. (April 14, 1945)

Now and then, a mourner called out a goodbye. "Oh, he's gone. He's gone forever. I loved him so. He's never coming back," a black woman cried. After the funeral service in the East Room, where Abraham Lincoln's body had lain in state almost eighty years earlier to the day, the honor guard put the body aboard another train. On Sunday, April 15, Franklin Delano Roosevelt was buried in his mother's rose garden, where he had played as a child.[60]

Night had fallen by the time his widow returned to New York City. Eleanor was alone, carrying a small suitcase. As she walked toward the apartment she rented on Washington Square, reporters saw her. "What next for you, Mrs. Roosevelt?" they asked. The former First Lady shook her head. "The story is over now," she murmured. But it was not over. In time, she would become the guiding spirit behind the United Nations Commission on Human Rights and, as President Truman said, the "First Lady of the World." She died on November 7, 1962, and is buried alongside her husband.[61]

On the day Roosevelt died, his top aides briefed his successor. President Truman had much to learn in a short time. For reasons Roosevelt never explained, he had not prepared his vice president to take over if need be, keeping him ignorant of the most urgent matters. Truman knew nothing about FDR's private talks with Churchill and Stalin, military plans, or even the atomic bomb project—a lack he could not forgive. Now Truman must make decisions involving the lives of millions.

Hitler decided one matter by himself. By April 30, he admitted that nothing could save Nazi Germany. Hysterical, he ran around his foul-smelling cavern, shrieking to echoes of Soviet shells bursting overhead. He married Eva Braun, his longtime mistress, and the couple went into his private apartment. The bride sat on the couch and took poison. Her groom sat beside her, put a pistol to his head, and pulled the trigger. On May 7, the German High Command surrendered unconditionally.

On July 16, scientists successfully tested an atomic bomb in the New Mexico desert. An amazed scientist recalled that the ball of fire rising into the sky was "brighter than a thousand suns." We still live under its shadow.

Since Japan's military rulers refused to give up, Truman ordered the bomb used. He never doubted that it was the right thing to do, or that FDR would have done the same. Nor did he think

FDR observing a globe given to him by the United States Army. (December 1942)

that using this weapon of mass destruction was a choice between good and evil. It was a choice between two evils. Truman chose what he thought the lesser evil: killing enemy civilians to spare American lives and many more Japanese who would have died during an invasion. Having made his decision, Truman said, he never lost five minutes' sleep over it.[62]

On August 6, an atomic bomb equal in power to 20,000 tons of high explosives leveled the naval base city of Hiroshima, killing an estimated 80,000 people outright. As a survivor put it, Hiroshima "just didn't exist" anymore. Three days later, a second atomic bomb destroyed Nagasaki, a shipbuilding center, killing another 39,000 people. In years to come, thousands more would die of radiation poisoning. On September 2, Japanese leaders signed the Instrument of Surrender aboard the battleship *Missouri,* anchored in Tokyo Bay. General MacArthur signed the document on behalf of the United States.[63]

Late in 1941, during the war's darkest time, Winston Churchill met Edward R. Murrow on a London street. "One day, the world and history will recognize and acknowledge what it owes to your President," the prime minister told the broadcaster, his eyes glistening with tears.[64]

Churchill was right. Nevertheless, Franklin Roosevelt's is not a simple story. Those who have praised him as a saintly miracle worker are as wrong as those who bitterly cursed him as a monster. FDR was a complicated person, and nobody, not even his wife of forty years, ever really figured him out. Flawed in many ways, he was not always truthful or loyal or fair. Ever the shrewd "operator," he used people, casting them aside when he no longer needed them. He refused to support worthy causes, such as a federal anti-lynching law, for political reasons. He deceived voters about his health, especially in the last year of his life. Convinced of his own virtue and wisdom, he thought too highly of his personal charm and powers of persuasion. He misjudged the murderous Stalin.

Despite everything, Roosevelt is among our great presidents. Though his New Deal failed to end the nation's worst economic crisis, it convinced millions that government had a vital role in protecting basic human dignity. FDR also judged Hitler correctly. By doing so, he helped his countrymen to rethink their relationship with the world, to think globally. Roosevelt saw there was no returning to the days of the Founders, when Americans had no need to "go abroad in search of monsters to destroy." Like it or not, there were now monsters who would gladly destroy them. This insight moved him to prepare the nation to wage the most terrible war in history. If not for him, our world today would be a far different—and a far worse—place than we dare to imagine. By realizing that great power carries great responsibilities, FDR did more than anyone else to save democracy in its hour of supreme peril. Above all, the thirty-second president showed that our liberty is tied to that of others, and Americans must lead in freedom's fight.

A World War II veteran happy to be "home alive in '45," and a small boy look out over San Francisco Bay (September 1945)

NOTES

PROLOGUE: A GREAT BUNDLE OF GRIEF

1. Fred I. Greenstein, ed., *Leadership in the Modern Presidency* (Cambridge, MA: Harvard University Press, 1988), 12.

2. Nathan Miller, *New World Coming: The 1920s and the Making of Modern America* (New York: Scribner's, 2003), 387.

3. Ted Morgan, *FDR: A Biography* (New York: Simon & Schuster, 1985), 43.

4. Doris Kearns Goodwin, *No Ordinary Time: Franklin and Eleanor Roosevelt; The Home Front in World War II* (New York: Simon & Schuster. 1994), 606.

5. Adam Cohen, *Nothing to Fear: FDR's Inner Circle and the Hundred Days That Created Modern America* (New York: Penguin Press, 2009), 35.

6. Nathan Miller, *FDR: An Intimate History* (Garden City, NY: Doubleday, 1983), 192.

7. "500,000 in Streets Cheer Roosevelt," *New York Times,* March 5, 1933.

8. Franklin Delano Roosevelt, *Great Speeches,* ed. John Grafton (Mineola, NY: Dover Publications, 1999), 28–33.

9. Ibid.

10. Gene Smith, *The Shattered Dream: Herbert Hoover and the Great Depression* (New York: William Morrow, 1970), 242; William Manchester, *The Glory and the Dream: A Narrative History of America, 1932–1972* (Boston: Little, Brown, 1974), 95.

I. A BOY OF MANY ADVANTAGES

1. Springwood is the official name of the estate. but the Roosevelt family never used it preferring the name Hyde Park instead.

2. Jan Pottker, *Sara and Eleanor: The Story of Sara Delano Roosevelt and Her Daughter-in-Law, Eleanor Roosevelt* (New York: St. Martin's Press, 2004). 59.

3. Jonathan Alter, *The Defining Moment: FDR's First Hundred Days and the Triumph of Hope* (New York Simon & Schuster, 2006). 16–17.

4. John Gunther, *Roosevelt in Retrospect: A Profile in History* (New York: Harper & Brothers, 1950), 157; Geoffrey C. Ward, *Before the Trumpet: Young Franklin Roosevelt, 1882–1905* (New York Harper & Row, 1985), 112.

5. Pottker, *Sara and Eleanor,* 15.

6. Miller, *FDR,* 17.

7. Joseph E. Persico, *Franklin and Lucy: President Roosevelt, Mrs. Rutherfurd, and the Other Remarkable Women in His Life* (New York: Random House, 2008), 20.

8. Miller, *FDR,* 16.

9. Pottker, *Sara and Eleanor,* 295; Morgan, *FDR,* 60.

10. Persico, *Franklin and Lucy,* 18; Goodwin, *No Ordinary Time,* 76.

11. Ward, *Before the Trumpet,* 125; James Roosevelt and Sidney Shalett, *Affectionately, F.D.R.: A Son's Story of a Lonely Man* (New York: Harcourt, Brace, 1959), 28–29.

12. Peter Collier, *The Roosevelts: An American Saga* (New York: Simon & Schuster, 1994), 103; Miller, *FDR,* 20.

13. Morgan, *FDR,* 43–44, 49, 176.

14. Robert N. Rosen, *Saving the Jews: Franklin D. Roosevelt and the Holocaust* (New York: Thunder's Mouth Press, 2006), 13–14.

15. Frank Freidel, *Franklin D. Roosevelt: A Rendezvous with Destiny* (Boston: Little, Brown, 1990), 8.

16. Geoffrey C. Ward, *A First-Class Temperament: The Emergence of Franklin Roosevelt* (New York: Harper & Row, 1989), 180.

17. James Roosevelt, ed., *F.D.R.: His Personal Letters, Early Years* (New York: Duell, Sloan and Pearce, 1947), 37.

18. Miller, *FDR,* 26.

19. Morgan, *FDR,* 61.

20. Alter, *Defining Moment,* 24–25; Ward, *First-Class Temperament,* 551; Joseph Lash, *Eleanor and Franklin: The Story of Their Relationship, Based on Eleanor Roosevelt's Private Papers* (New York: W. W. Norton, 1971), 103.

21. Frank Freidel, *Franklin D. Roosevelt: The Apprenticeship* (Boston: Little, Brown, 1952), 11.

22. James Roosevelt, *My Parents: A Different View* (Chicago: Playboy Press, 1976), 17; Pottker, *Sara and Eleanor,* 110.

23. Ward, *Before the Trumpet,* 245.

24. Freidel, *Franklin D. Roosevelt: The Apprenticeship,* 24; Curtis Roosevelt, *Too Close to the Sun: Growing Up in the Shadow of My Grandparents, Franklin and Eleanor* (New York: Public Affairs, 2008), 43.

25. Lash, *Eleanor and Franklin,* 28.

26. Nathan Miller, *The Roosevelt Chronicles* (Garden City, NY: Doubleday, 1979), 231; Lash, *Eleanor and Franklin,* 101.

27. Elliott Roosevelt and James Brough, *An Untold Story: The Roosevelts of Hyde Park* (New York: G. P. Putnam's Sons, 1973), 24.

28. Lash, *Eleanor and Franklin,* 138.

29. James Roosevelt, ed., *F.D.R.: His Personal Letters, 1905–1928* (New York: Duell, Sloan and Pearce, 1948), 516.

30. Ward, *Before the Trumpet,* 340; Persico, *Franklin and Lucy,* 64.

31. Lash, *Eleanor and Franklin,* 198; Doris Kearns Goodwin, *Booknotes,* January 1, 1995.

32. Miller, *Roosevelt Chronicles*, 271; Pottker, *Sara and Eleanor*, 141.

33. Miller, *FDR*, 57.

34. Lash, *Eleanor and Franklin*, 198; Roosevelt and Shalett, *Affectionately, F.D.R.*, 35; Ward, *First-Class Temperament*, 109; Morgan, *FDR*, 103; Mary Cable, *The Little Darlings: A History of Child Rearing in America* (New York: Scribner's, 1975), 117.

35. Roosevelt, *Too Close to the Sun*, 23; Bernard Asbell, ed., *Mother and Daughter: The Letters of Eleanor and Anna Roosevelt* (New York: Fromm, 1983), 9; Lash, *Eleanor and Franklin*, 241; Elliott Roosevelt and James Brough, *A Rendezvous with Destiny: The Roosevelts of the White House* (New York: G. P. Putnam's Sons, 1975), 247; Roosevelt, *My Parents*, 59.

36. Ward, *First-Class Temperament*, 54; Roosevelt and Shalett, *Affectionately, F.D.R.*, 16.

37. Roosevelt and Shalett, *Affectionately, F.D.R.*, 86–87, 98.

38. Pottker, *Sara and Eleanor*, 277.

39. Ward, *First-Class Temperament*, 62.

40. Burton Folsom Jr., *New Deal or Raw Deal? How FDR's Economic Legacy Has Damaged America* (New York: Threshold Books, 2008), 20.

41. Michael Beschloss, *Kennedy and Roosevelt: The Uneasy Alliance* (New York: W. W. Norton, 1980), 36.

42. Morgan, *FDR*, 112.

43. Ibid., 114–15.

44. Freidel, *Franklin D. Roosevelt: A Rendezvous with Destiny*, 18.

45. Ward, *First-Class Temperament*, 117.

46. Alter, *Defining Moment*, 34.

47. Miller, *Roosevelt Chronicles*, 274.

48. Roosevelt and Shalett, *Affectionately, F.D.R.*, 16.

49. Miller, *FDR*, 82.

50. Earle Looker, *The American Way: Franklin Roosevelt in Action* (New York: John Day, 1933), 166; Blanche Wiesen Cook, *Eleanor Roosevelt, 1884–1933* (New York: Viking, 1992), 199.

51. Pottker, *Sara and Eleanor*, 157; Roosevelt and Brough, *Untold Story*, 172; Ward, *First-Class Temperament*, 196.

52. Lela Stiles, *The Man Behind Roosevelt: The Story of Louis McHenry Howe* (New York: World Publishing, 1954), 233.

53. Alter, *Defining Moment*, 36.

54. Stiles, *Man Behind Roosevelt*, 220.

55. Ward, *First-Class Temperament*, 230; Roosevelt and Shalett, *Affectionately, F.D.R.*, 226; H. W. Brands, *Traitor to His Class: The Privileged Life and Radical Presidency of Franklin Delano Roosevelt* (New York: Doubleday, 2008), 311.

56. James N. Rosenau, ed., *The Roosevelt Treasury* (Garden City, NY: Doubleday, 1951), 46

II. ALL THE BEST PEOPLE KILLED

1.   Ward, *First-Class Temperament,* 200.

2.   Ibid., 217.

3.   "Lay Keel of Navy's New Dreadnought," *New York Times,* March 17, 1914.

4.   Miller, *Roosevelt Chronicles,* 284.

5.   John Ellis, *Eye-Deep in Hell: Trench Warfare in World War I* (New York: Pantheon Books, 1976), 43.

6.   Ibid., 54.

7.   Ibid., 5.

8.   Wilfred Owen, "Anthem for a Doomed Youth"; Denis Winter, *Death's Men: Soldiers of the Great War* (New York: Viking Penguin, 1978), 118.

9.   Martin Gilbert, *The First World War: A Complete History* (New York: Henry Holt, 1994), 541.

10. Winter, *Death's Men,* 123.

11. "Washington's Farewell Address, 1796," http://avalon.law.yale.edu/18th_century/washing.asp; *Letters and Other Writings of James Madison* (Philadelphia: J. B. Lippincott, 1876), 4:491.

12. "First Inaugural Address," March 4, 1801, in *Thomas Jefferson: Writings* (New York: Library of America, 1983), 494; "John Quincy Adams on U.S. Foreign Policy," http://www.fff.prg/cpmment/AdamsPolicy .asp.

13. Thomas Parrish, *The Submarine: A History* (New York: Viking, 2004), 101.

14. Diana Preston, *Lusitania: An Epic Tragedy* (New York: Walker, 2002), 333.

15. Black Tom took its name from a legend about a black man who once lived there named Tom. Jules Witcover's *Sabotage at Black Tom: Imperial Germany's Secret in America, 1914–1917* (Chapel Hill, NC: Algonquin Books, 1989) tells the whole story of the explosion and its aftermath.

16. Joseph E. Persico, *Roosevelt's Secret War: FDR and World War II Espionage* (New York: Random House, 2001), 89.

17. Lash, *Eleanor and Franklin,* 202, 204, 206; Morgan, *FDR,* 163.

18. Ward, *First-Class Temperament,* 342–43.

19. "Woodrow Wilson: War Message," http://mtholyoke.edu/acad/intrel/ww18.htm.

20. "Speech by Robert M. LaFollette," https://www.mtholyoke.edu/acad/intrel/doc19.htm.

21. "Speech by George W. Norris," https://www.mtholyoke.edu/acad/intrel/doc19.htm.

22. Scott Nearing, "The Great Madness," www.bigeye.com.madness.htm.

23. "I Didn't Raise My Boy to Be a Soldier," http://staff.isma.edu/socsci/jvictory/antiwar_04/I_didn .htm.

24. "Of Fraud and Force Fast Woven: Domestic Propaganda During the First World War," www .firstworldwar.com/features/propaganda.htm.

25. Geoffrey R. Stone, *Perilous Times: Free Speech in Wartime, from the Sedition Act of 1798 to the War on Terrorism* (New York: W. W. Norton, 2004), 37, 172–73.

26. Thomas Fleming, *The Illusion of Victory: America in World War I* (New York: Basic Books, 2003), 90.

27. Ward, *First-Class Temperament,* 346.

28. Parrish, *Submarine,* 166.

29. Brands, *Traitor to His Class,* 108–14

30. Fleming, *Illusion of Victory,* 210–11.

31. Roosevelt, *F.D.R.: His Personal Letters, 1905–1928,* 421; Ward, *First-Class Temperament,* 396, 398.

32. Freidel, *Franklin D. Roosevelt: The Apprenticeship,* 358–61.

33. Ward, *First-Class Temperament,* 401–2; Fleming, *Illusion of Victory,* 254.

34. Meirion and Susie Harries, *The Last Days of Innocence: America at War, 1917–1918* (New York: Random House, 1997), 453.

35. Roosevelt, *My Parents,* 101; Persico, *Franklin and Lucy,* 131.

36. Persico, *Franklin and Lucy,* 93; Goodwin, *No Ordinary Time,* 375.

37. Pottker, *Sara and Eleanor,* 185; Roosevelt, *My Parents,* 98–102.

38. Fleming, *Illusion of Victory,* 194–95; Lizzie Collingham, *The Taste of War: World War II and the Battle for Food* (New York: Penguin Press, 2012), 25.

39. Page Smith, *America Enters the World: A People's History of the Progressive Era and World War I* (New York: McGraw-Hill, 1985), 642.

40. Ruth Henig, *Versailles and After, 1919–1933* (London: Routledge, 1995), 52.

41. Thomas A. Bailey, *Woodrow Wilson and the Lost Peace* (New York: Macmillan. 1947), 110.

42. Robert Dallek, *Franklin Roosevelt and American Foreign Policy, 1932–1945* (New York: Oxford University Press, 1979), 11; Lynne Olson and Stanley Cloud, *A Question of Honor: The Kosciuszko Squadron, Heroes of World War II* (New York: Knopf, 2003), 144.

43. Richard Pipes, *Russia Under the Bolshevik Regime* (New York: Knopf, 1993), 512.

44. Dmitri Volkogonov, *Lenin: A New Biography* (New York: Free Press, 1994), 236; Pipes, *Russia,* 401–2; Paul Johnson, *Modern Times: The World from the Twenties to the Eighties* (New York: Harper & Row, 1982), 69–70.

45. Richard Pipes, *Communism: A History* (New York: Modern Library, 2001), 49; Paul Kengor *Dupes: How America's Adversaries Have Manipulated Progressives for a Century* (Wilmington, DE: ISI Books, 2010), 18–19.

46. Benjamin Gitlow, *I Confess: The Truth About American Communism* (New York: E. P. Dutton, 1940), 217–18; John Earl Haynes and Harvey Klehr, *In Denial: Historians, Communism, and Espionage* (San Francisco: Encounter Books, 2003), 82, 219. During the 1930s, new members of the CPUSA recited a pledge to "defend the Soviet Union" and to bring about "the triumph of Soviet power in the United States." Haynes and Klehr, 196.

47. Robert K. Murray, *Red Scare: A Study of National Hysteria, 1919–1920* (New York: McGraw-Hill, 1964), 82–104.

48. Paul Avrich, *Sacco and Vanzetti: The Anarchist Background* (Princeton, NJ: Princeton University Press, 1991), 153–54.

49. Roosevelt and Shalett, *Affectionately, F.D.R.*, 59–61.

50. Cook, *Eleanor Roosevelt,* 241; Frederick Lewis Allen, *Only Yesterday: An Informal History of the Nineteen-Twenties* (New York: Harper & Brothers, 1931), 61–62.

51. Cook, *Eleanor Roosevelt,* 281.

III. POLIO AND POLITICS

1. Folsom, *New Deal,* 27.

2. Freidel, *Franklin D. Roosevelt: A Rendezvous with Destiny,* 39.

3. Francis Russell, *The Shadow of Blooming Grove: Warren G. Harding and His Times* (New York: McGraw-Hill, 1968), 400.

4. Hugh Gregory Gallagher, *FDR's Splendid Deception* (Arlington, VA: Vamdaere Press, 1999), 2.

5. Ibid., 2.

6. Ibid., 10–11, 14.

7. Persico, *Franklin and Lucy,* 149.

8. Naomi Rogers, *Dirt and Disease: Polio Before FDR* (New Brunswick, NJ: Rutgers University Press, 1992), 10–11; Jeffrey Kluger, "Conquering Polio," *Smithsonian,* April 2005, 84.

9. Rogers, *Dirt and Disease,* 57.

10. Gallagher, *FDR's Splendid Deception,* 29; Rogers, *Dirt and Disease,* 30.

11. Roosevelt and Shalett, *Affectionately, F.D.R.,* 144.

12. Geoffrey C. Ward, ed., *Closest Companion: The Unknown Story of the Intimate Friendship Between Franklin Roosevelt and Margaret Suckley* (Boston: Houghton Mifflin, 1995), xvii; Roosevelt and Brough, *Untold Story,* 174.

13. Gallagher, *FDR's Splendid Deception,* 26.

14. Miller, *Roosevelt Chronicles,* 305.

15. Gallagher, *FDR's Splendid Deception,* 30.

16. Ibid., 29, 59.

17. Lash, *Eleanor and Franklin,* 276.

18. Roosevelt and Brough, *Untold Story,* 126.

19. Miller, *Roosevelt Chronicles,* 268; Ward, *First-Class Temperament,* 627–28; Lash, *Eleanor and Franklin,* 341; Roosevelt, *My Parents,* 110.

20. Cook, *Eleanor Roosevelt,* 174; Roosevelt, *Untold Story,* 184.

21. Roosevelt, *My Parents,* 80.

22. Stiles, *Man Behind Roosevelt,* 83; Gunther, *Roosevelt in Retrospect,* 241.

23. Morgan, *FDR,* 269.

24. Gallagher, *FDR's Splendid Deception,* 61.

25. Roosevelt, *My Parents,* 92–93.

26. Robert S. Slayton, *Empire Statesman: The Rise and Redemption of Al Smith* (New York Free Press, 2001) 210.

27. Roosevelt, *My Parents,* 92–93.

28. Roosevelt, *Untold Story,* 224.

29. Persico, *Franklin and Lucy,* 160.

30. Goodwin, *No Ordinary Time,* 116.

31. Alter, *Defining Moment,* 67; Ward, *First-Class Temperament,* 765.

32. Gallagher, *FDR's Splendid Deception,* 43.

33. Morgan, *FDR,* 291.

34. Rogers, *Dirt and Disease,* 232n19.

35. Slayton, *Empire Statesman,* 356–57.

36. Oscar Handlin, *Al Smith and His America* (Boston: Little, Brown, 1958), 132–33; Slayton, *Empire Statesman,* 166.

37. Slayton, *Empire Statesman,* 310.

38. Tony Gould, *A Summer Plague: Polio and Its Survivors* (New Haven, CT: Yale University Press, 1995) 251.

39. Slayton, *Empire Statesman,* 314–15.

40. Gunther, *Roosevelt in Retrospect,* 165.

41. Lash, *Eleanor and Franklin,* 331.

IV. BOOM TO BUST

1. Brands, *Traitor to His Class,* 221.

2. Henry Ford, *My Life and Work* (Garden City, NY: Doubleday, Page, 1922), 81.

3. Miller, *New World Coming,* 181.

4. Robert S. McElvaine, *The Great Depression America, 1929–1941* (New York: Random House, 1984), 291–92.

5. Robert S. Lynd and Helen Merrell Lynd, *Middletown: A Study in Modern American Culture* (New York: Harcourt, Brace, 1929), 254–57.

6. Bradford DeLong, "Slouching Towards Utopia," http://econ161.berkeley.edu/TCEH/Slouch_roaring13.html.

7. Geoffrey Perrett, *America in the Twenties: A History* (New York: Simon & Schuster, 1982), 251.

8. Allen, *Only Yesterday,* 100.

9. Bruce Bliven, "Flapper Jane," *New Republic,* September 9, 1925, http://faculty.pittstate/edu/~knichols/flapperjane.html.

10. Andrew Sinclair, *Prohibition: The Era of Excess* (Boston: Little, Brown, 1962), 230, 236–37; Miller, *New World Coming,* 258.

11. Paul Dickson and Thomas B. Allen, *The Bonus Army: An American Epic* (New York: Walker, 2004), 20, 33; Miller, *FDR,* 171; Ward, *First-Class Temperament,* 679; Roosevelt and Brough, *Untold Story,* 245, 280.

12. "Al Capone," http://www.alcaponebio.com/al_capone_quotes.htm.

13. Studs Terkel, *Hard Times: An Oral History of the Great Depression* (New York: Pantheon, 1970), 65, 68.

14. Lindley H. Clark Jr., "After the Fall," *Wall Street Journal,* October 26, 1979.

15. "The Wall Street Crash," www.eyewitnesstohistory.com/pfsnpmech5.htm.

16. T. H. Watkins, *The Great Depression: America in the 1930s* (Boston: Back Bay Books, 1993), 191.

17. Adam Cohen, *Nothing to Fear: FDR'S Inner Circle and the Hundred Days That Created Modern America* (New York: Penguin Press, 2009), 51.

18. "False Rumor Leads to Trouble at Bank," *New York Times,* December 11, 1930; Amity Shlaes, *The Forgotten Man: A New History of the Great Depression* (New York: HarperCollins, 2007), 246.

19. Shlaes, *Forgotten Man,* 246; David M. Kennedy, *Freedom from Fear: The American People in Depression and War, 1929–1945* (New York: Oxford University Press, 1999), 163.

20. McElvaine, *Great Depression,* 172.

21. Manchester, *Glory and the Dream,* 47; Watkins, *Great Depression,* 56; William E. Leuchtenburg, *The Perils of Prosperity, 1914–1932* (Chicago: University of Chicago Press, 1958), 254.

22. Louis Adamic, *My America, 1928–1938* (New York: Harper & Brothers, 1938), 29; Irving Bernstein, *A Caring Society: The New Deal, the Worker, and the Great Depression* (Boston: Houghton Mifflin, 1985), 19; Milton Meltzer, *Brother, Can You Spare a Dime? The Great Depression, 1929–1933* (New York: Knopf, 1969), 29; Edward Robb Ellis, *A Nation in Torment: The Great American Depression, 1929–1939* (New York: Kodansha International, 1995), 242.

23. Caroline Bird, *The Invisible Scar* (New York: David McKay, 1965), 29, 30, 34; Kennedy, *Freedom from Fear,* 86; Meltzer, *Brother,* 46.

24. Meltzer, *Brother,* 29; Adamic, *My America,* 293.

25. Smith, *Shattered Dream,* 222.

26. McElvaine, *Great Depression,* 176.

27. Smith, *Shattered Dream,* 80.

28. Meltzer, *Brother,* 87–88.

29. Manchester, *Glory and the Dream,* 23.

30. Bernstein, *Caring Society,* 23.

31. Smith, *Shattered Dream,* 81; Ellis, *Nation in Torment,* 253.

32. Philip Dray, *At the Hands of Persons Unknown: The Lynching of Black America* (New York: Random House, 2002), viii.

33. Terkel, *Hard Times,* 82; Bernstein, *Caring Society,* 293.

34. Richard Pipes, *A Concise History of the Russian Revolution* (New York: Knopf, 1995), 360.

35. Eugene Lyons, *Herbert Hoover: A Biography* (Garden City, NY: Doubleday, 1964), 260.

36. Ellis, *Nation in Torment*, 119.

37. McElvaine, *Great Depression*, 82.

38. Woody Guthrie, "The Ballad of Pretty Boy Floyd," https://www.youtube/com/watch?v= AVUEgycfb5s.

39. Page Smith, *Redeeming the Time: A People's History of the 1920s and the New Deal* (New York: McGraw-Hill, 1986), 290.

40. McElvaine, *Great Depression*, 92–93; Smith, *Shattered Dream*, 146.

V. THE NEW DEAL

1. Roosevelt and Brough, *Untold Story*, 292.

2. Alter, *Defining Moment*, 238; Cohen, *Nothing to Fear*, 61.

3. Stiles, *Man Behind Roosevelt*, 177.

4. Manchester, *Glory and the Dream*, 56.

5. "Roosevelt's Nomination Address," July 2, 1932, www.newdeal.feri.org/speeches/1932b/htm

6. *The Federalist*, 1788, Number 51.

7. "Herbert Hoover Address Accepting the Republican Presidential Nomination," August 11, 1932, www.americanhistory.about.com/library/docs/blhooverspeech1932.htm; Herbert Hoover, "Address at Madison Square Garden in New York City," October 31, 1932, http://presidency.ucsb.edu/ws/index .php?pid=23317.

8. Bernstein, *Caring Society*, 23; "Message to the New York State Legislature," August 28, 1931, in Roosevelt, *Great Speeches*, 10.

9. Roosevelt and Shalett, *Affectionately, F.D.R.*, 230; Lyons, *Herbert Hoover*, 295; John T. Flynn, *The Roosevelt Myth* (New York: Devin-Adair, 1948), 36–37.

10. Manchester, *Glory and the Dream*, 26; Michael E. Parrish, *Anxious Decades: America in Prosperity and Depression, 1920–1941* (New York: W. W. Norton, 1992), 240.

11. Smith, *Shattered Dream*, 145.

12. Manchester, *Glory and the Dream*, 19–20; Dickson and Allen, *Bonus Army*, 177, 184–85.

13. Roosevelt, *My Parents*, 142.

14. Patrick J. Maney, *The Roosevelt Presence: A Biography of Franklin D. Roosevelt* (New York: Twayne Publishers, 1992), 198.

15. Morgan, *FDR*, 376; Miller, *FDR*, 310; Shlaes, *Forgotten Man*, 150.

16. Murray N. Rothbard, "The Roosevelt Myth." http://www.lewrockwell.com/rothbard/rothbard58 .html.

17. "Address of the President Delivered by Radio from the White House, March 12, 1933," www.mhrcc /org/fdr/chat1/html.

18. Richard Thayer Goldberg, *The Making of Franklin D. Roosevelt: Triumph Over Disability* (Cambridge, MA: Abt Books, 1981), 132.

19. Economy Act, March 20, 1933, Sec. 17; Paul Johnson, *A History of the American People* (London: Weidenfeld & Nicolson, 1997), 255; Alter, *Defining Moment,* 275–76.

20. Raymond Moley, *After Seven Years* (New York: Harper & Brothers, 1939), 191–92; Alter, *Defining Moment,* 327.

21. Terkel, *Hard Times,* 266.

22. Cohen, *Nothing to Fear,* 209.

23. Watkins, *Great Depression,* 124.

24. Lash, *Eleanor and Franklin,* 383.

25. George Brown Tindall and David Emory Shi, *America: A Narrative History* (New York: W. W. Norton, 1999), 1250. The Tennessee River winds through Kentucky, Virginia, North Carolina, Georgia, Alabama, and Mississippi, as well as Tennessee.

26. Folsom, *New Deal,* 45.

27. Harvard Sitkoff, *A New Deal for Blacks: The Emergence of Civil Rights as a National Issue* (New York: Oxford University Press, 1978), 58.

28. Ward, *Before the Trumpet,* 190; Ward, *First-Class Temperament,* 205; Goldberg, *Making,* 146; Morgan, *FDR,* 277; David Pilgrim, "The Coon Caricature," http://www.ferris.edu/jimcrow/coon/. Pilgrim surveys the history of white attitudes toward blacks in cartoons and the movies.

29. Lynne Olson, *Freedom's Daughters: The Unsung Heroines of the Civil Rights Movement from 1830 to 1970* (New York: Scribner's, 2001), 56–57; Morgan, *FDR,* 53, 509; Persico, *Franklin and Lucy,* 134; Kati Marton, *Hidden Power: Presidential Marriages That Shaped Our Recent History* (New York: Pantheon Books, 2001), 74.

30. Eleanor Roosevelt, *This I Remember* (New York: Harper & Brothers, 1949), 161.

31. Watkins, *Great Depression,* 224; Walter White, *A Man Called White: The Autobiography of Walter White* (New York: Viking, 1948), 169–70.

32. Juan Williams, *Thurgood Marshall: American Revolutionary* (New York: Times Books, 1998), 82; Kenneth O'Reilly, "The Roosevelt Administration and Black America: Federal Surveillance Policy and Civil Rights During the New Deal and World War II Years," *Phylon* 48, no. 1 (1987): 12–25; Joe William Trotter Jr., *From a Raw Deal to a New Deal? African Americans, 1929–1945* (New York: Oxford University Press, 1995), 31–36; Gerald D. Nash, *The Crucial Decade: The Great Depression and World War II, 1929–1945* (New York: St. Martin's Press, 1990), 88; Sitkoff, *A New Deal for Blacks,* 50–55; Jim Powell, "Why Did FDR's New Deal Harm Blacks," www.cato.org/dailys/12-03-03-2.html.

33. Alter, *Defining Moment,* 134, 223; David McCullough, *Truman* (New York: Simon & Schuster, 1992), 373.

34. Persico, *Franklin and Lucy,* 218, 219; Stella K. Hershan, *A Woman of Quality* (New York: Crown Publishers, 1970), 57.

35. Eleanor Roosevelt, *This Is My Story* (New York: Harper & Brothers, 1937), 172.

36. Marton, *Hidden Power,* 67, 68.

37.   Alter, *Defining Moment*, 53; Gallagher, *FDR's Splendid Deception*, 115.

38.   Manchester, *Glory and the Dream*, 98; Gunther, *Roosevelt in Retrospect*, 63; Persico, *Franklin and Lucy*, 234.

39.   Alter, *Defining Moment*, 239; Gallagher, *FDR's Splendid Deception*, 134; John Morton Blum, *The Progressive Presidents: Theodore Roosevelt, Woodrow Wilson, Franklin D. Roosevelt, Lyndon B. Johnson* (New York: W. W. Norton, 1980), 135.

40.   Rosenau, *Roosevelt Treasury*, 286.

41.   Flynn, *Roosevelt Myth*, 178; Rosenau, *Roosevelt Treasury*, 147; Gunther, *Roosevelt in Retrospect*, 136; Thomas A. Bailey and Paul B. Ryan, *Hitler vs. Roosevelt: The Undeclared Naval War* (New York: Free Press, 1979), 209.

42.   Goodwin, *No Ordinary Time*, 273.

43.   Persico, *Roosevelt's Secret War*, 96.

44.   Ward, *Before the Trumpet*, 8–9; Persico, *Roosevelt's Secret War*, 96.

45.   Robert H. Ferrell, *The Dying President: Franklin D. Roosevelt, 1944–1945* (Columbia: University of Missouri Press, 1998), 143; Roosevelt and Shalett, *Affectionately, F.D.R.*, 315; Goodwin, *No Ordinary Time*, 306.

46.   Goodwin, *No Ordinary Time*, 202, 204, 306 (italics added); Gallagher, *FDR's Splendid Deception*, 122; Terkel, *Hard Times*, 265; Ferrell, *Dying President*, 101.

47.   Michael Hiltzik, *The New Deal: A Modern History* (New York: Free Press, 2011), 384; W. Averell Harriman and Elie Abel, *Special Envoy to Churchill and Stalin, 1941–1946* (New York: Random House, 1975), 191; Persico, *Franklin and Lucy*, 218; Alter, *Defining Moment*, 242.

48.   Jon Meacham, *Franklin and Winston: An Intimate Portrait of an Epic Partnership* (New York: Random House, 2003), 327; Ferrell, *Dying President*, 145.

49.   Collier, *Roosevelts*, 347; Thomas Fleming, *The War Within World War II: Franklin Delano Roosevelt and the Struggle for Supremacy* (Oxford: Perseus Press, 2001), 55; Olson and Cloud, *Question of Honor*, 245.

50.   Goodwin, *No Ordinary Time*, 245; Fleming, *War*, 219, 560–61; McCullough, *Truman*, 328; Arthur M. Schlesinger Jr., "The Supreme Partnership," *Atlantic Monthly*, October 1984.

51.   "FDR to Luther C. Steward, July 1937," http://sweetness-light.com/archive/even-fdr-opposed-public-sector-unions.

52.   Brands, *Traitor to His Class*, 413; Alter, *Defining Moment*, 315.

53.   Kennedy, *Freedom from Fear*, 378; Morgan, *FDR*, 437.

54.   Roosevelt and Brough, *Untold Story*, 318.

55.   George Wolfskill and John A. Hudson, *All but the People: Franklin D. Roosevelt and His Critics, 1933–39* (New York: Macmillan, 1969), 17.

56.   Goodwin, *No Ordinary Time*, 34; Wolfskill and Hudson, *All but the People*, 6–16; Johnson, *History*, 636–37; Manchester, *Glory and the Dream*, 127; Johnson, *Modern Times*, 258; Bird, *Invisible Scar*, 219.

57.   Larry Schweikart and Michael Allen, *A Patriot's History of the United States: From Columbus's Great Discovery to the War on Terror* (New York: Sentinel, 2004), 561; Franklin D. Roosevelt, "State of the Union Address, January 3, 1936," http://www.infoplease.com/t/hist/state-of-the-union/147.html; "Speech at Madison Square Garden, October 21, 1936," http://millercenter.org/president/speeches

/detail/3307; Arthur M. Schlesinger, *The Age of Roosevelt: The Politics of Upheaval* (Boston: Houghton Mifflin, 1960), 503; Miller, *FDR,* 383–84; Manchester, *Glory and the Dream,* 169; Morgan, *FDR,* 440.

58.   Rosen, *Saving the Jews,* 67; Lawrence W. Levine and Cornelia R. Levine, *The People and the President: America's Conversation with FDR* (Boston: Beacon Press, 2002), 181, 245.

59.   Bernstein, *Caring Society,* 206–7; Manchester, *Glory and the Dream,* 99.

60.   Burt Solomon, *FDR v. Constitution: The Court-Packing Fight and the Triumph of Democracy* (New York: Walker, 2009), 73.

61.   "Fireside Chat on Reorganization of the Judiciary, February 9, 1937," www.mhric.org/fdr/chat9.html.

62.   Solomon, *FDR v. Constitution,* 177.

63.   Moley, *After Seven Years,* 361.

64.   Folsom, *New Deal,* 143–44; Hiltzik, *New Deal,* 414.

VI. THE SUPREME CRISIS

1.   Stéphane Courtois, ed., *The Black Book of Communism: Crimes, Terror, Repression* (Cambridge, MA: Harvard University Press, 1999), 102.

2.   Charles E. Bohlen, *Witness to History, 1929–1969* (New York: W. W. Norton, 1973), 131; Laurence Rees, *World War II Behind Closed Doors: Stalin, the Nazis and the West* (New York: Pantheon Books, 2008), 268.

3.   Brands, *Traitor to His Class,* 601; Simon Sebag Montefiore, *Stalin: The Court of the Red Tsar* (New York: Knopf, 2004), 97; Nadezhda Mandelstam, *Hope Against Hope: A Memoir* (New York: Atheneum, 1970), 13.

4.   Edvard Radzinsky, *Stalin* (New York: Doubleday, 1996), 540.

5.   Anton Antonov-Ovseyenko, *The Time of Stalin: Portrait of a Tyranny* (New York: Harper Colophon Books, 1980), 229–30; Mikhail Heller and Alexandr M. Nekrich, *Utopia in Power: The History of the Soviet Union from 1917 to the Present* (New York: Summit Books, 1986), 245, 505, 507.

6.   Robert C. Tucker, *Stalin in Power: The Revolution from Above, 1928–1941* (New York: W. W. Norton, 1990), 597; Volkogonov, *Stalin,* 155.

7.   Edvard Radzinsky, *Stalin: The First In-Depth Biography Based on Explosive New Documents from Russia's Secret Archives* (New York: Doubleday, 1996), 286; Volkogonov, *Stalin,* 149; Montefiore, *Stalin,* 87; "Stalin's Daughter, Whose Escape Was Obscurity," *New York Times,* November 28, 2011; Nikita Khruschev, *Khruschev Remembers* (Boston; Little, Brown, 1970), 290.

8.   Nikolai Tolstoy, *Stalin's Secret War* (New York: Holt, Rinehart and Winston, 1981), 24, 26; Kennedy, *Freedom from Fear,* 3; Montefiore, *Stalin,* 230.

9.   Winston S. Churchill, *The Second World War: The Hinge of Fate* (Boston: Houghton Mifflin, 1950), 498.

10.   Montefiore, *Stalin,* 151.

11.   Tolstoy, *Stalin's Secret War,* 26; Johnson, *Modern Times,* 302; Pipes, *Communism,* 66.

12.   Tolstoy, *Stalin's Secret War,* 22; Sergo Beria, *Beria, My Father: Inside Stalin's Kremlin* (London: Duckworth, 1999), 141.

13. Olson and Cloud, *Question of Honor,* 211.

14. Andrew Nagorski, *Hitlerland: American Eyewitnesses to the Nazi Rise to Power* (New York: Simon & Schuster, 2012), 21, 112, 179.

15. Ibid., 173.

16. Walter Langer, *The Mind of Adolf Hitler: The Secret Wartime Report* (New York: Basic Books, 1972), 62; John Toland, *Adolf Hitler* (Garden City, NY: Doubleday, 1976), 528: Richard Grunberger, *The 12-Year Reich: A Social History of Nazi Germany, 1933–1945* (New York: Holt, Rinehart and Winston, 1971), 86.

17. Michael Burleigh and Wolfgang Wippermann, *The Racial State: Germany 1933–1945* (Cambridge: Cambridge University Press, 1991), 206–7 (italics added): Grunberger, *12-Year Reich,* 282.

18. Hermann Rauschning, *The Voice of Destruction* (New York: G. P. Putnam's Sons, 1940), 137–38.

19. Ibid., 241–42.

20. Donald Rayfield, *Stalin and His Hangmen* (New York: Random House, 2004), 265.

21. Anthony Read and David Fisher, *The Deadly Embrace: Hitler, Stalin, and the Nazi-Soviet Pact, 1939–1941* (New York: W. W. Norton, 1988), 223; Fleming, *War,* 307.

22. Alexander B. Rossino, *Hitler Strikes Poland: Blitzkrieg, Ideology, and Atrocity* (Lawrence: University Press of Kansas, 2003), 9–10; Gerhard L. Weinberg, *Visions of Victory: The Hopes of Eight World War II Leaders* (Cambridge: Cambridge University Press, 2005), 17.

23. Rees, *World War II,* 49; Read and Fisher, *Deadly Embrace,* 469; Olson and Cloud, *Question of Honor,* 213; Irena Grudzinska-Gross and Jan Tomasz eds., *War Through Children's Eyes: The Soviet Occupation of Poland and the Deportations, 1939–1941* (Stanford CA: Hoover Institution Press, 1981), 61, 81, 137.

24. Rees, *World War II,* 9, 31; Robert Nisbet, *Roosevelt and Stalin: The Failed Courtship* (Washington, DC: Regnery Gateway, 1988), 19; Read and Fisher, *Deadly Embrace,* 430–31.

25. Johnson, *Modern Times,* 362; Tolstoy, *Stalin's Secret War,* 113–15, 187; William L. Shirer, *The Collapse of the Third Republic: An Inquiry into the Fall of France in 1940* (New York: Simon & Schuster, 1969), 484; Olson and Cloud, *Question of Honor,* 91

26. Lynne Olson, *Citizens of London: The Americans Who Stood with Britain in Its Darkest, Finest Hour* (New York: Random House, 2010), 46–47; Olson and Cloud, *Question of Honor,* 161; John Lukacs, *June 1941 Hitler and Stalin* (New Haven, CT: Yale University Press, 2006), 62.

27. Justus D. Doenecke, "American Isolationism, 1939–1941," *Journal of Libertarian Studies* 6, no. 3 (Summer/Fall 1982): 201–16; Rosen, *Saving the Jews,* 45.

28. Ward, *Closest Companion,* 124; Freidel, *Franklin D. Roosevelt: A Rendezvous with Destiny,* 113; Richard Overy, *The Dictators: Hitler's Germany and Stalin's Russia* (New York: W. W. Norton, 2004), 23 Smith, *Redeeming the Time,* 652; William Stevenson, *A Man Called Intrepid: The Secret War* (New York: Harcourt Brace Jovanovich, 1976), 173.

29. Gerhard L. Weinberg, ed., *Hitler's Second Book: The Unpublished Sequel to 'Mein Kampf'* (New York: Enigma Books, 2003), 45.

30. Russell D. Buhite, *Decisions at Yalta: An Appraisal of Summit Diplomacy* (Wilmington, DE: Scholarly Resources, 1986), 16; Edward R. Murrow, *In Search of Light: The Broadcasts of Edward R. Murrow, 1938–1961* (New York: Knopf, 1967), 47.

31. Martin Gilbert, *Churchill and America* (New York: Free Press, 2005), 186.

32. Robert Goldston, *Sinister Touches: The Secret War Against Hitler* (New York: Dial Press, 1982), 67;
     H. Montgomery Hyde, *The Quiet Canadian: The Secret Service Story of Sir William Stephenson* (London:
     Hamish Hamilton, 1962), 26, 52.

33. Lukacs, *June 1941*, 140; Thomas E. Mahl, *Desperate Deception: British Covert Operations in the United States,
     1939–44* (Washington, DC: Brassey's, 1998), 11; David Stafford, *Roosevelt and Churchill: Men of Secrets*
     (Boston: Little, Brown, 1999), 78.

34. William Boyd, "The Secret Persuaders," *Guardian,* August 18, 2006, http:
     //www.guardian/co/uk/uk/2006/aug/19/military.secondworldwar/print; Stevenson, *Man Called
     Intrepid,* 176; Hyde, *Quiet Canadian,* 64–65; Dale Harrington, *Mystery Man: William Rhodes Davis, Nazi
     Agent of Influence* (Dulles, VA: Brassey's, 1999), 189–97.

35. Boyd, "Secret Persuaders."

36. Goodwin, *No Ordinary Time,* 107.

37. Miller, *FDR,* 453.

38. Freidel, *Franklin D. Roosevelt: A Rendezvous with Destiny,* 355–56.

39. Ibid., 352.

40. FDR Speech, October 10, 1940, www.commandposts.com/ . . . /from-the-president-your-boys-are-
     not-g . . .

41. Miller, *FDR,* 457; William L. Shirer, *The Rise and Fall of the Third Reich: A History of Nazi Germany* (New
     York: Simon & Schuster, 1960), 560–61; Mark Bernstein and Alex Lubertozzi, *World War II on the
     Air: Edward R. Murrow and the Broadcasts That Riveted a Nation* (Naperville, IL: Sourcebooks, 2003), 114.

42. Roosevelt, *Great Speeches,* 82–91, 92–100.

43. Sheldon Marcus, *Father Coughlin: The Tumultuous Life of the Priest of the Little Flower* (Boston: Little,
     Brown, 1973), 209.

44. Ronald Radosh and Allis Radosh, *Red Star Over Hollywood: The Film Colony's Romance with the Left* (San
     Francisco: Encounter Books, 2005), 78–79; Irving Howe and Lewis Coser, *The American Communist
     Party: A Critical History* (New York: Frederick A. Praeger, 1962), 387–88.

45. R. Serge Denisoff, " 'Take It Easy, but Take It': The Almanac Singers," *Journal of American Folklore* 83
     (January–March 1970): 23.

46. Alec Wilkinson, *The Protest Singer: An Intimate Portrait of Pete Seeger* (New York: Knopf, 2009), 116;
     "Songs for John Doe," www.geocites.com/Nashville/3448/doe.html; Denisoff, " 'Take It Easy,' " 25;
     Will Kaufman, *Woody Guthrie, American Radical* (Urbana: University of Illinois Press, 2011), 60–69.

47. Kennedy, *Freedom from Fear,* 638–39; Louis Stark, "Tares in the Wheat," *Survey Graphic: Magazine
     of Social Interpretation,* November 1941, 1–11; Eugene Lyons, *The Red Decade* (New Rochelle, NY:
     Arlington House, 1970), 394–95.

48. Doenecke, "American Isolationism," 201; Murray N. Rothbard, "The Foreign Policy of the Old
     Right," *Journal of Libertarian Studies* 2, no. 1, 90–91.

49. Rothbard, "Foreign Policy," 87–88; Doenecke, "American Isolationism," 212–13; Richard W. Steele,
     "Franklin D. Roosevelt and His Foreign Policy Critics," *Political Science Quarterly* 94, no. 1 (Spring
     1979): 23; Ronald Radosh, *Prophets of the Right: Profiles of Conservative Critics of American Globalism* (New
     York: Simon & Schuster, 1975), 204–5.

50. Allen Paul, *Katyn: The Untold Story of Stalin's Polish Massacre* (New York: Scribner's, 1991), 161; Johnson, *Modern Times,* 361.

51. Lukacs, *June 1941,* 74; Overy, *Dictators,* 93.

52. David E. Murphy, *What Stalin Knew: The Enigma of Barbarossa* (New Haven, CT: Yale University Press, 2005), 257–58; Volkogonov, *Stalin,* 399–400; Montefiore, *Stalin,* 343.

53. Svetlana Alliluyeva, *Only One Year* (New York: Harper & Row, 1969), 392; Winston S. Churchill, *The Second World War: The Grand Alliance* (Boston: Houghton Mifflin, 1951), 370.

54. Howe and Coser, *American Communist Party,* 415.

55. *"Dear Mr. President,"* www.geocites.com/Nashville/3448/prez.html; Denisoff, " 'Take It Easy,' " 27.

56. Persico, *Roosevelt's Secret War,* 123.

57. Brands, *Traitor to His Class,* 609.

58. "War-Entry Plans Laid to Roosevelt," *New York Times,* January 2, 1972. Churchill later repeated the story to a South African diplomat: "He [Roosevelt] went on to say to me, 'I shall never declare war; I shall make war. If I were to ask Congress to declare war they might argue about it for three months.' " Kimball, "Franklin D. Roosevelt and World War II," *Presidential Studies Quarterly,* March 2004, note 37.

59. Gilbert, *Churchill and America,* 214 (italics added).

60. Roosevelt, *My Parents,* 160–61.

61. Goodwin, *No Ordinary Time,* 274.

62. "On Maintaining Freedom of the Seas," September 11, 1941, http://docs.fdrlibrary.marist.edu/091141.html.

63. Persico, *Roosevelt's Secret War,* 124–25.

64. "President Franklin Delano Roosevelt Address, October 27, 1941," http://www.usmm.org/fdr/kearny.html.

65. Michael Gannon, *Operation Drumbeat: The Dramatic True Story of Germany's First U-Boat Attacks Along the American Coast in World War II* (New York: HarperPerennial, 1991), 92.

66. Max Hastings, *Retribution: The Battle for Japan, 1944–45* (New York: Knopf, 2008), 209; Iris Chang, *The Rape of Nanking: The Forgotten Holocaust of World War II* (New York: Basic Books, 1997), 83–87, 99–104; Dick Wilson, *When Tigers Fight: The Story of the Sino-Japanese War, 1937–1945* (New York: Viking, 1982), 66–85; Sheldon H. Harris, *Factories of Death: Japanese Biological Warfare 1932–45 and the American Cover-Up* (London: Routledge, 1994) 33–82.

67. Johnson, *Modern Times,* 318.

68. Hastings, *Retribution,* 35.

69. Persico, *Franklin and Lucy,* 267.

70. Joseph E. Persico, *Edward R. Murrow: An American Original* (New York: McGraw-Hill, 1988), 194.

71. Forrest C. Pogue, *George C. Marshall: Ordeal and Hope, 1939–1942* (New York: Viking, 1965), 22.

72. "Broadcast from the Oval Room of the White House, December 9, 1941," www.mhric.org/fdr/chat19.html; Hastings, *Retribution,* 4; Toland, *Adolf Hitler,* 694.

73. H. L. Trefousse, "Germany and Pearl Harbor," *Far Eastern Quarterly* (November 1951): 46, 47; Shirer, *Rise,* 897–98; Robert G. L. Waite, *The Psychopathic God: Adolf Hitler* (New York: Basic Books, 1977), 407.

VII. THE WAR AT HOME

1. David Brinkley, *Washington Goes to War* (New York: Knopf, 1988), 88–89; Ferrell, *Dying President,* 18.

2. Freidel, *Franklin D. Roosevelt: A Rendezvous with Destiny,* 437 (italics added).

3. Francis Biddle, *In Brief Authority* (Garden City, NY: Doubleday, 1962), 226; Robert H. Jackson, *That Man: An Insider's Portrait of Franklin D. Roosevelt* (New York: Oxford University Press, 2003), 74.

4. Tim Weiner, *Enemies: A History of the FBI* (New York: Random House, 2012), 109–10.

5. Weiner, *Enemies,* 84, 88; Burton Folsom Jr. and Anita Folsom, *FDR Goes to War: How Expanded Executive Power, Spiraling National Debt, and Restricted Civil Liberties Shaped Wartime America* (New York: Threshold Books, 2011), 212.

6. Weiner, *Enemies,* 106. Eleanor Roosevelt's FBI file is available online at vault.fbi.gov /Eleanor%Roosevelt and on the CD-ROM *Eleanor Roosevelt FBI Files* (BACM Research, 2008).

7. Biddle, *In Brief Authority,* 330–31.

8. Ibid., 331. Judges issue writs of habeas corpus (from the Latin for "produce the body") to bring jailed persons before a court to decide if the authorities are holding them lawfully.

9. The story of the failed mission is told in two books: Pierce O'Donnell, *In Time of War: Hitler's Terrorist Attack on America* (New York: New Press, 2005), and Michael Dobbs, *Saboteurs: The Nazi Raid on America* (New York: Random House, 2004).

10. John Morton Blum, *V Was for Victory: Politics and American Culture During World War II* (New York: Harcourt Brace Jovanovich, 1976), 46–47.

11. Ibid., 158.

12. Folsom and Folsom, *FDR Goes to War,* 228; "Japanese American Internment," www.asianamericans .com/JapaneseAmericanInternment.html.

13. Blum, *V Was for Victory,* 159.

14. Greg Robinson, *By Order of the President: FDR and the Internment of Japanese Americans* (Cambridge, MA: Harvard University Press, 2001), 37–43, 242.

15. Robinson, *Order,* 115, 120; R. J. C. Butow, "The FDR Tapes: Secret Recordings Made in the Oval Office of the President in the Autumn of 1940," *American Heritage,* February–March 1982, 12; "President Roosevelt's Statement Condemning War Crimes," March 24, 1944, www.historyplace .com/worldwar2/holocaust/h-roos-statement.htm.

16. Stone, *Perilous Times,* 294; Goodwin, *No Ordinary Time,* 321, 323.

17. Emmy E. Werner, *Through the Eyes of Children: Children Witness World War II* (Boulder, CO: Westview Press, 2000), 81. In 1998, President Ronald Reagan signed the Civil Liberties Restoration Act, an official apology for Executive Order 9066 and the misery it caused. The act also provided a tax-free payment of $20,000 to each person who had been forced to leave home.

18. Thomas Connell, *America's Japanese Hostages: The World War II Plans for a Japanese Latin America* (Westport, CT: Greenwood Publishing Group, 2002), 5.

19. Bolivia, Colombia, Costa Rica, the Dominican Republic, Ecuador, El Salvador, Guatemala, Haiti, Honduras, Nicaragua, Panama, and Peru agreed to the roundups and deportations.

20. This subject is treated best in Max Paul Friedman, *Nazis and Good Neighbors: The United States Campaign Against the Germans of Latin America in World War II* (New York: Cambridge University Press, 2003).

21. Arthur Herman, *Freedom's Forge: How American Business Produced Victory in World War II* (New York: Random House, 2012), 13.

22. Douglas MacArthur, *Reminiscences* (New York: McGraw-Hill, 1964), 101.

23. Kenneth S. Davis, *Experience of War: The United States in World War II* (Garden City, NY: Doubleday, 1965), 17–18.

24. Dan Kurzman, *Day of the Bomb* (London: Weidenfeld and Nicolson, 1986), 30–31.

25. Herman, *Freedom's Forge,* 67.

26. Ibid., 83.

27. Geoffrey Perrett, *Days of Sadness, Years of Triumph: The American People, 1939–1945* (New York: Coward, McCann & Geoghegan, 1973), 257.

28. Herman, *Freedom's Forge,* 88–89.

29. Kennedy, *Freedom from Fear,* 644; Perrett, *Days,* 407.

30. Richard R. Lingeman, *Don't You Know There's a War On? The American Home Front, 1941–1945* (New York: G. P. Putnam's Sons, 1970), 66, 74.

31. Olson, *Citizens of London,* 231.

32. Lee Kennett, *For the Duration: The United States Goes to War, Pearl Harbor–1942* (New York: Scribner's, 1985), 195–96; Perrett, *Days,* 255, 259, 336–37; Biddle, *In Brief Authority,* 281–82.

33. Chris Bellamy, *Absolute War: Soviet Russia in the Second World War* (New York: Vintage Books, 2007), 486–89.

34. Kaylene Hughes, "Women at War: Redstone's WWII Female 'Production Soldiers,'" www.library.csi.cuny/edu/dept/history/lavender/redstone.html; Goodwin, *No Ordinary Time,* 613.

35. Kennedy, *Freedom from Fear,* 653; Morgan, *FDR,* 667.

36. Herman, *Freedom's Forge,* 283.

37. Blum, *V Was for Victory,* 183.

38. Richard Polenberg, *War and Society: The United States, 1941–1945* (Philadelphia: J. B. Lippincott, 1972), 114.

39. Trotter, *Raw Deal,* 68.

40. Goodwin, *No Ordinary Time,* 247.

41. Ibid., 248.

42. Ronald Takaki, *Double Victory: A Multicultural History of America in World War II* (Boston: Little, Brown, 2000), 41.

43.   Morgan, *FDR,* 594.

44.   Brinkley, *Washington Goes to War,* 83.

45.   Kennedy, *Freedom from Fear,* 768; Stephen B. Oates, *Let the Trumpet Sound: The Life of Martin Luther King, Jr.* (New York: New American Library, 1982), 116.

46.   Brinkley, *Washington Goes to War,* 250–51.

47.   Ibid., 247.

48.   Trotter, *Raw Deal,* 97.

49.   Hershan, *Woman of Quality,* 162–64.

50.   Takaki, *Double Victory,* 24; Perrett, *Days,* 312.

51.   A. Philip Randolph, "The March on Washington Committee," www.teachers.sduhsd.k12.ca.us /mmontgomery/us_history/greatdepression/march/htm.

52.   Glenda Elizabeth Gilmore, *Defying Dixie: The Radical Roots of Civil Rights, 1919–1950* (New York: W. W. Norton, 2008), 373–74.

53.   Mark Jonathan Harris et al., *The Home Front: America During World War II* (New York: G. P. Putnam's Sons, 1984), 251–52.

54.   Carlo D'Este, *Patton: A Genius for War* (New York: HarperCollins, 1995), 726.

55.   Herman, *Freedom's Forge,* 334–35.

56.   Johnson, *Modern Times,* 401.

VIII. THE SURVIVAL WAR

1.   Goodwin, *No Ordinary Time,* 310–11, 438–39.

2.   Stanley Weintraub, *Pearl Harbor Christmas: The World at War, December 1941* (New York: Da Capo Press, 2011), 51.

3.   Ibid., 111–12; Hastings, *Retribution,* 398.

4.   "Declaration of the United Nations," www.ibiblio.org/pha/policy/1942/420101a.html.

5.   Weintraub, *Pearl Harbor Christmas,* 58.

6.   Stafford, *Roosevelt and Churchill,* 128.

7.   James Bradley, *Flyboys: A True Story of Courage* (Boston: Little, Brown, 2003), 112–13.

8.   Richard Overy, *Why the Allies Won* (New York: W. W. Norton, 1995), 43.

9.   Michael C. C. Adams, *The Best War Ever: America and World War II* (Baltimore: Johns Hopkins University Press, 1994), 67.

10.   Hastings, *Retribution,* 53; Johnson, *Modern Times,* 401.

11.   Norman Polmar and Thomas B. Allen, *World War II: America at War* (New York: Random House, 1991), 590.

12. Churchill, *The Second World War: The Hinge of Fate,* 603.

13. Goodwin, *No Ordinary Time,* 388.

14. Brands, *Traitor to His Class,* 696.

15. Goodwin, *No Ordinary Time,* 405.

16. Gilbert, *Churchill and America,* 269.

17. D'Este, *Patton,* 484.

18. "Torpedo Away!," http://uboat.net/special/songs/.

19. Tom Parrish, *The Submarine* (New York: Viking, 2004), 252; Hughes and Costello, *Battle of the Atlantic* (New York: Dial, 1977), 195.

20. Parrish, *Submarine,* 254, 255.

21. Andrew Williams, *The Battle of the Atlantic: Hitler's Gray Wolves of the Sea and the Allies' Desperate Struggle to Defeat Them* (New York: Basic Books, 2003), 179, 184.

22. Gannon, *Operation Drumbeat,* 363.

23. Parrish, *Submarine,* 257.

24. Scot MacDonald, "Emergence of the Escort Carriers," *Naval Aviation News,* December 1962, 50.

25. Richard Hough, *The Longest Battle: The War at Sea, 1939–1945* (New York: William Morrow 1986), 272.

26. Gary Sheffield, "The Battle of the Atlantic," www.bbc.co.uk/history/war/wwtwo/battle_atlantic_print.html; Parrish, *Submarine,* 295.

27. Olson and Cloud, *Question of Honor,* 55, 68; Andrew Roberts, *The Storm of War: A New History of the Second World War* (New York: Harper, 2011), 27.

28. C. P. Snow, *Science and Government: The Godkin Lectures at Harvard University* (London: Oxford University Press, 1961), 48.

29. "Winston Churchill's Secret Poison Gas Memo," http://globalresearch.ca/articles/CHU407A.html

30. A. C. Grayling, *Among the Dead Cities: The History and Moral Legacy of WWII Bombing of Civilians in Germany and Japan* (New York: Walker, 2006), 188; Bradley, *Flyboys,* 257.

31. "Winston Churchill's Secret Poison Gas Memo."

32. Bradley, *Flyboys,* 64.

33. Overy, *Why the Allies Won,* 109.

34. Keith Lowe, *Inferno: The Fiery Destruction of Hamburg, 1943* (New York: Scribner's, 2007), 184; John Terraine, *A Time of Courage: The Royal Air Force in the European War, 1939–1945* (New York: Macmillan, 1985), 546.

35. Richard Rhodes, *The Making of the Atomic Bomb* (New York: Simon & Schuster, 1986), 474.

36. Max Hastings, *Bomber Command* (New York: Dial Press, 1979), 208; Fleming, *War,* 276; Grayling, *Among the Dead Cities,* 203.

37. Lowe, *Inferno,* 221–22.

38. Overy, *Why the Allies Won,* 133.

IX. ROOSEVELT AND STALIN

1. Robert Dallek, *The Lost Peace: Leadership in a Time of Horror and Hope, 1945–1953* (New York: HarperCollins, 2010), 54; Tolstoy, *Stalin's Secret War,* 246.

2. Overy, *Russia's War,* 161–62; Tolstoy, *Stalin's Secret War,* 237; Rodric Braithwaite, *Moscow 1941: A City and Its People at War* (New York: Knopf, 2006), 228.

3. Robert Service, *Stalin: A Biography* (Cambridge, MA: Harvard University Press, 2005), 454.

4. Nikolai Tolstoy, *The Secret Betrayal* (New York: Scribner's, 1977), 397; Overy, *Russia's War,* 200; Tolstoy, *Stalin's Secret War,* 282.

5. Timothy Snyder, *Bloodlands: Europe Between Hitler and Stalin* (New York: Basic Books, 2010), 163. The text of the General Plan for the East is in the records of the postwar trial of Nazi war criminals. "Nazi Conspiracy and Aggression," Volume I, http://www.nizkor.org.ftp.cgi/imt/nca/nca-01/nca-01-13-spoliation-03 (italics added).

6. Overy, *Russia's War,* 157.

7. William C. Bullitt, "How We Won the War and Lost the Peace," *Life,* August 30, 1948, 88; Goodwin, *No Ordinary Time,* 255.

8. Roosevelt and Brough, *Rendezvous with Destiny,* 250–51.

9. Francis L. Lowenheim, *Roosevelt and Churchill: Their Secret Wartime Correspondence* (New York: E. P. Dutton, 1975), 202.

10. Jochen von Lang, *Top Nazi: SS General Karl Wolff, the Man Between Hitler and Himmler* (New York: Enigma Books, 2005), 366–71.

11. Robert E. Sherwood, *Roosevelt and Hopkins: An Intimate History* (New York: Harper & Brothers, 1948), 799; Churchill, *The Second World War: The Hinge of Fate,* 201; Olson, *Citizens of London,* 303.

12. George F. Kennan, *Russia and the West Under Lenin and Stalin* (Boston: Little, Brown, 1961), 355.

13. "Interview with Professor George F. Kennan," www.cnn.com/SPECIALS/cold.war/episodes/01/interviews/kennan/index.html.

14. Ibid.

15. Will Brownell and Richard N. Billings, *So Close to Greatness: A Biography of William C. Bullitt* (New York: Macmillan, 1987), 144; John Lewis Gaddis, *The United States and the Origins of the Cold War* (New York: Columbia University Press, 1972), 54.

16. Bullitt, "How We Won," 95.

17. Gordon Thomas, *The Secret Wars: One Hundred Years of British Intelligence Inside MI5 and MI6* (New York: St. Martin's Press, 2009), 160.

18. Howe and Coser, *American Communist Party,* 433–34.

19. Paul Willen, "Who 'Collaborated' with Russia?" *Antioch Review* (Autumn 1954): 259–83; Nisbet, *Roosevelt and Stalin,* 19; Lingeman, *Don't You Know,* 222; Tolstoy, *Stalin's Secret War,* 257. Marshal Semyon Timoshenko was a leading Red Army commander.

20. *Life,* March 29, 1943, 20–49.

21. Melvin Small, "Buffoons and Brave Hearts: Hollywood Portrays the Russians, 1949–1944," *California Historical Quarterly* (Winter 1973): 333.

22. Joseph E. Davies, *Mission to Moscow* (New York: Simon & Schuster, 1941), 356–57; Todd Bennett, "Culture, Power, and *Mission to Moscow*: Film and Soviet-American Relations During World War II," *Journal of American History* (September 2001): 499.

23. Willen, "Who 'Collaborated' with Russia?," 260.

24. Gary Kern, "How 'Uncle Joe' Bugged FDR," Central Intelligence Agency, *Studies in Intelligence* (2003): 19–31.

25. "US Congress Hearings in 1951/52 on Katyn Wood War Crime," kanada.net/war/us_congress_doc.html.

26. Rayfield, *Stalin and His Hangmen*, 375.

27. Tim Tzouliadis, *The Forsaken: An American Tragedy in Stalin's Russia* (New York: Penguin Press, 2008), 239.

28. Fleming, *War*, 303; Paul, *Katyn*, 314, 315.

29. Tolstoy, *Stalin's Secret War*, 179; Paul, *Katyn*, 227, 313–14; Olson and Cloud, *Question of Honor*, 169; Jabusz K. Zawodny, "The Katyn Massacre: Morals in American Foreign Policy," http://www.pacwashmetrodiv.org/projects/katyn.zawodny.htm; Randy Herschaft, "AP Exclusive: Memos Show US Hushed Up Soviet Crime," September 10, 2012, http://www.google.com/hostednews/ap/article/AleqM5gelpYyGgcvS92ulKrle-RVkp9Cig.

30. Olson and Cloud, *Question of Honor*, 169.

31. Frances Perkins, *The Roosevelt I Knew* (New York: Viking, 1946), 83.

32. Bohlen, *Witness to History*, 139; Eliott Roosevelt and James Brough, *As He Saw It* (New York: Duell, Sloan and Pearce, 1946), 76, 183.

33. Keith Eubank, *Summit at Teheran* (New York: William Morrow, 1985), 311; Meacham, *Franklin and Winston*, 263.

34. Kern, "How 'Uncle Joe' Bugged FDR"; Beria, *Beria, My Father*, 93.

35. Perkins, *Roosevelt I Knew*, 83; Bohlen, *Witness to History*, 145; Meacham, *Franklin and Winston*, 259.

36. Perkins, *Roosevelt I Knew*, 84, 85.

37. Olson and Cloud, *Question of Honor*, 193.

38. Winston Churchill, *The Second World War: Closing the Ring* (Boston: Houghton Mifflin, 1951), 373–74.

39. Roosevelt and Brough, *As He Saw It*, 189.

40. Harriman and Abel, *Special Envoy*, 226.

41. Tzouliadis, *Forsaken*, 240; Bohlen, *Witness to History*, 151.

42. Robert A. Divine, "Roosevelt the Pragmatist," *Discovery: Research and Scholarship at the University of Texas at Austin*, 1997, www.utexas.edu/opa/pubs/discovery/disc1997v14n2/disc-roosevelt.html.

43. Olson, *Citizens of London*, 305; Geoffrey Warner, "From Teheran to Yalta: Reflections on FDR's Foreign Policy," *International Affairs* (July 1967): 533.

44. "Address by the President Broadcast from Hyde Park, New York, December 24, 1943," http://www.mhric.org/fdr/chat27.html; Dallek, *Lost Peace*, 49.

45. Milovan Djilas, *Conversations with Stalin* (New York: Harcourt, Brace & World, 1962), 73.

46. Beria, *Beria, My Father*, 147; Tzouliadis, *Forsaken*, 241.

X. TRIUMPH AND TRAGEDY

1.   Steven Lomazow and Eric Fettmann, *FDR'S Deadly Secret* (New York: PublicAffairs, 2009), 97; Ferrell, *Dying President,* 30.

2.   Ferrell, *Dying President,* 37.

3.   Goodwin, *No Ordinary Time,* 377.

4.   Ferrell, *Dying President,* 32; Roosevelt, *My Parents,* 101; Goodwin, *No Ordinary Time,* 492.

5.   Roosevelt, *This I Remember,* 307.

6.   Lash, *Eleanor and Franklin,* 685, 688.

7.   Michael Dobbs, *Six Months in 1945: FDR, Stalin, Churchill, and Truman—from World War to Cold War* (New York: Knopf, 2012), 153.

8.   Manchester, *Glory and the Dream,* 388.

9.   Lomazow and Fettmann, *FDR'S Deadly Secret,* 152, 153.

10. Ibid., 108–9.

11. "Franklin Roosevelt's D-Day Prayer, June 6, 1944," www.fdrlibrary.marist.edu/odddayp.html.

12. Perrett, *Days,* 292.

13. Roosevelt, *My Parents,* 278; Freidel, *Franklin D. Roosevelt: A Rendezvous with Destiny,* 540–41.

14. Gallagher, *FDR's Splendid Deception,* 172–73.

15. Fleming, *War,* 444–45; Ferrell, *Dying President,* 87; David Nasaw, *The Patriarch: The Remarkable Life and Turbulent Times of Joseph P. Kennedy* (New York: Penguin Press, 2012).

16. Lomazow and Fettmann, *FDR'S Deadly Secret,* 158–59; Olson and Cloud, *Question of Honor,* 165.

17. Michael Makovsky, *Churchill's Promised Land: Zionism and Statecraft* (New Haven, CT: Yale University Press, 2007), 179.

18. Nagorski, *Hitlerland,* 244.

19. Gerald Fleming, *Hitler and the Final Solution* (Berkeley: University of California Press, 1984), 17; Norman H. Baynes, ed., *The Speeches of Adolf Hitler* (London: Oxford University Press, 1942), 1:740; Persico, *Roosevelt's Secret War,* 216.

20. Daniel Jonah Goldhagen, *Hitler's Willing Executioners: Ordinary Germans and the Holocaust* (New York: Knopf, 1996), 280, 404.

21. Snyder, *Bloodlands,* 205; Heinz Höhne, *The Order of the Death's Head: The Story of Hitler's S.S.* (New York: Coward-McCann, 1969), 363. The SS general was Erich von dem Bach-Zelewski. See Robert E. Conot, *Justice at Nuremberg* (New York: Carroll & Graf Publishers, 1983), 275.

22. Fleming, *Hitler,* 142–43.

23. Morgan, *FDR,* 22–23; Blanche Wiesen Cook, *Eleanor Roosevelt, 1933–1938* (New York: Viking, 1999), 317; Ward, *First-Class Temperament,* 251n43; Rosen, *Saving the Jews,* 9, 10; Collier and Horowitz, *Roosevelts,* 191; Lash, *Eleanor and Franklin,* 214.

24. Leonard Dinnerstein, *Anti-Semitism in America* (New York: Oxford University Press, 1994), 85–86, 88.

25.   Theodore S. Hamerow, *Why We Watched: Europe, America, and the Holocaust* (New York: W. W. Norton, 2008), 221–22; Roosevelt, *My Parents,* 241–42.

26.   Petra Moser et al., "German-Jewish Émigrés and U.S. Intervention," extranet.isnie.org/upload /isnie2011/moser_veona_waldinger.pdf.

27.   Rosen, *Savings the Jews,* 63, 163; Kennedy, *Freedom from Fear,* 406.

28.   Goodwin, *No Ordinary Time,* 174 176.

29.   Jan Karski, *Story of a Secret State* (Boston: Houghton Mifflin, 1944), 330, 334.

30.   Ibid., 345.

31.   Ibid., 387–88; E. Thomas Wood and Stanislaw M. Jankowski, *Karski: How One Man Tried to Stop the Holocaust* (New York: John Wiley & Sons, 1994), 196, 198–99; Rafael Medoff, "Holocaust Witness Jan Karski's Confrontation with FDR." www.jspace.com.articles/holocaust-witness-jan-karski . . . fdr/14736.

32.   Rosen, *Saving the Jews,* 346; Michael Beschloss, *The Conquerors: Roosevelt, Truman and the Destruction of Hitler's Germany, 1941–1945* (New York: Simon & Schuster, 2002), 43; Rosen. *Savings the Jews,* 345–47.

33.   Alex Kershaw, *The Envoy: The Epic Rescue of the Last Jews in Europe in the Desperate Closing Months of World War II* (New York: Da Capo Press, 2010), 55.

34.   Arthur D. Morse, *While Six Million Died. A Chronicle of American Apathy* (New York: Random House, 1968), 356–66.

35.   Beschloss, *Conquerors,* 66; William J. vanden Heuvel, "In Praise of FDR," George Mason University History News Network, www.hnn.us/articles/4268.html.

36.   Michael J. Newfield and Michael Berenbaum. eds., *The Bombing of Auschwitz: Should the Allies Have Attempted It?* (New York: St. Martin's Press, 2000), 24–26.

37.   David Remnick, "Letter from Tel Aviv: The Vegetarian," *New Yorker,* September 3, 2012, 26.

38.   William I. Hitchcock, *The Bitter Road to Freedom: A New History of the Liberation of Europe* (New York: Free Press, 2008), 183, 192.

39.   Frederick Taylor, *Dresden: Tuesday, February 13, 1945* (New York: Perennial, 2005), 454–55.

40.   Lord Moran, *Churchill Taken from the Diaries of Lord Moran: The Struggle for Survival, 1940–1965* (Boston: Houghton Mifflin, 1966), 237.

41.   Winston S. Churchill, *The Second World War. Triumph and Tragedy* (Boston: Houghton Mifflin, 1951), 397; Moran, *Churchill,* 239, 242.

42.   Lomazow and Fettmann, *FDR's Deadly Secret,* 162; Susan Butler, ed., *My Dear Dear Mr. Stalin: The Complete Correspondence Between Franklin D. Roosevelt and Joseph V. Stalin* (New Haven, CT: Yale University Press, 2005), x.

43.   Bohlen, *Witness to History,* 173; Montefiore, *Stalin,* 483; Dobbs, *Six Months in 1945,* 71; Beria, *Beria. My Father,* 337n32.

44.   Hastings, *Retribution,* 296, 305; Rhodes. *Atomic Bomb,* 597.

45.   Hitchcock, *Bitter Road to Freedom,* 171.

46.   Snyder, *Bloodlands,* 315.

47. Rees, *World War II,* 349; Olson and Cloud, *Question of Honor,* 272–73; Alexandr I. Solzhenitsyn, *The Gulag Archipelago, 1918–1956* (New York: Harper & Row, 1973), 259n12.

48. Dobbs, *Six Months in 1945,* 105; Beschloss, *Conquerors,* 190; "Report to Congress by President Franklin D. Roosevelt, March 1, 1945," http//history.sandiego.edu/gen/text/ww2/yaltareport.html.

49. Eric Alterman, *When Presidents Lie: A History of Official Deception and Its Consequences* (New York: Viking, 2004), 35.

50. Herbert Feis, *Churchill, Roosevelt, Stalin: The War They Waged and the Peace They Sought* (Princeton, NJ: Princeton University Press, 1967), 597.

51. Nisbet, *Roosevelt and Stalin,* 81.

52. Djilas, *Conversations with Stalin,* 114–15; www.cnn.com/SPECIALS/cold.war.episodes/01/interviews .beria.

53. Ferrell, *Dying President,* 111.

54. "I Saw the Walking Dead," http://historymatters.gmu.edu.search.php?function=print&id=142.

55. Persico, *Franklin and Lucy,* 339.

56. Elliott Roosevelt and James Brough, *Mother R.: Eleanor Roosevelt's Untold Story* (New York: G. P. Putnam & Sons, 1977), 37–38.

57. Louis L. Snyder and Richard B. Morris, eds., *A Treasury of Great Reporting* (New York: Simon & Schuster, 1949), 673, 674; Robert A. Caro, *The Years of Lyndon Johnson: The Path to Power* (New York: Knopf, 1982), 766.

58. Bernard Asbell, *When FDR Died* (New York: Holt, Rinehart and Winston, 1961), 95.

59. Ibid., 94; John Toland, *The Last 100 Days* (New York: Random House, 1966), 337; Overy, *Why the Allies Won,* 280.

60. Lingeman, *Don't You Know,* 352.

61. Joseph Lash, *Eleanor: Years Alone* (New York: W. W. Norton, 1972), 15.

62. Thomas Fleming, "Eight Days with Harry Truman," *American Heritage Magazine,* July–August 1992, http://www.americanheritage.com/print/57623?page=show.

63. Andrew Roberts, *The Storm of War: A New History of the Second World War* (New York: Harper, 2011), 575, 577; Rhodes, *Atomic Bomb,* 728.

64. Murrow, *In Search of Light,* 95.

SOME BOOKS ON FDR AND HIS TIMES

Adams, Michael C. C. *The Best War Ever: America and World War II.* Baltimore: Johns Hopkins University Press, 1994.

Alter, Jonathan. *The Defining Moment: FDR's First Hundred Days and the Triumph of Hope.* New York: Simon & Schuster, 2006.

Asbell, Bernard, ed. *Mother and Daughter: The Letters of Eleanor and Anna Roosevelt.* New York: Fromm, 1988.

Bailey, Thomas A., and Paul B. Ryan. *Hitler vs. Roosevelt: The Undeclared Naval War.* New York: Free Press, 1979.

Barber, Lucy G. *Marching on Washington: The Forging of an American Political Tradition.* Berkeley: University of California Press, 2002.

Bierman, John. *Righteous Gentile: The Story of Raoul Wallenberg, Missing Hero of the Holocaust.* New York: Penguin, 1996.

Blum, John Morton. *V Was for Victory: Politics and American Culture During World War II.* New York: Harcourt Brace Jovanovich, 1976.

Burns, James MacGregor. *Roosevelt: The Lion and the Fox.* New York: Harcourt, Brace & World, 1956.

————. *Roosevelt: The Soldier of Freedom.* New York: Harcourt Brace Jovanovich, 1970.

Cohen, Adam. *Nothing to Fear: FDR's Inner Circle and the Hundred Days That Created Modern America.* New York: Penguin Press, 2009.

Conquest, Robert. *Stalin, Breaker of Nations.* New York: Viking, 1991.

Dobbs, Michael. *Saboteurs: The Nazi Raid on America.* New York: Alfred A. Knopf, 2004.

Ellis, Edward Robb. *A Nation in Torment: The Great American Depression, 1929–1939.* New York: Kodansha International, 1995.

Eubank, Keith. *Summit at Teheran.* New York: William Morrow, 1985.

Ferrell, Robert H. *The Dying President: Franklin D. Roosevelt, 1944–1945.* Columbia: University of Missouri Press, 1998.

Finan, Christopher M. *Alfred E. Smith: The Happy Warrior.* New York: Hill & Wang, 2002.

Freidel, Frank. *Franklin D. Roosevelt: A Rendezvous with Destiny.* Boston: Little, Brown, 1990.

————. *Franklin D. Roosevelt: The Apprenticeship.* Boston: Little, Brown, 1952.

Friedman, Max Paul. *Nazis and Good Neighbors: The United States Campaign Against the Germans of Latin America in World War II.* New York: Cambridge University Press, 2003.

Gallagher, Hugh Gregory. *FDR's Splendid Deception.* Arlington, VA: Vandamere Press, 1999.

Gannon, Michael. *Operation Drumbeat: The Dramatic True Story of Germany's First U-Boat Attacks Along the American Coast in World War II.* New York: HarperPerennial, 1991.

Gilbert, Martin. *Auschwitz and the Allies.* New York: Holt, Rinehart and Winston, 1981.

Goldberg, Richard Thayer. *The Making of Franklin D. Roosevelt: Triumph Over Disability.* Cambridge, MA: Abt Books, 1981.

Goodwin, Doris Kearns. *No Ordinary Time: Franklin and Eleanor Roosevelt; The Home Front in World War II.* New York: Simon & Schuster, 1994.

Gould, Tony. *A Summer Plague: Polio and Its Survivors.* New Haven, CT: Yale University Press, 1995.

Hastings, Max. *Armageddon: The Battle for Germany, 1944–45.* London: Macmillan, 2004.

———. *Winston's War: Churchill, 1940–1945.* New York: Vintage Books, 2009.

Herman, Arthur. *Freedom's Forge: How American Business Produced Victory in World War II.* New York: Random House, 2012.

Hyde, H. Montgomery. *The Quiet Canadian: The Secret Service Story of Sir William Stephenson.* London: Hamish Hamilton, 1962.

Kennedy, David M. *Freedom from Fear: The American People in Depression and War, 1929–1945.* New York: Oxford University Press, 1999.

Lash, Joseph. *Eleanor and Franklin: The Story of Their Relationship, Based on Eleanor Roosevelt's Private Papers.* New York: W. W. Norton, 1971.

Lingeman, Richard R. *Don't You Know There's a War On? The American Home Front, 1941–1945.* New York: G. P. Putnam's Sons, 1970.

McElvaine, Robert S. *The Great Depression: America, 1929–1941.* New York: Random House, 1984.

Meacham, Jon. *Franklin and Winston: An Intimate Portrait of an Epic Partnership.* New York: Random House, 2003.

Miller, Nathan. *New World Coming: The 1920s and the Making of Modern America.* New York: Scribner's, 2003.

Morgan, Ted. *FDR: A Biography.* New York: Simon & Schuster, 1985.

Murray, Robert K. *Red Scare: A Study of National Hysteria, 1919–1920.* New York: McGraw-Hill, 1964.

Newfield, Michael J., and Michael Berenbaum, eds. *The Bombing of Auschwitz: Should the Allies Have Attempted It?* New York: St. Martin's Press, 2000.

Olson, Lynne. *Citizens of London: The Americans Who Stood with Britain in Its Darkest, Finest Hour.* New York: Random House, 2010.

Overy, Richard. *The Dictators: Hitler's Germany and Stalin's Russia.* New York: W. W. Norton, 2004.

Paul, Allen. *Katyn: The Untold Story of Stalin's Polish Massacre.* New York: Scribner's, 1991.

Perkins, Frances. *The Roosevelt I Knew.* New York: Viking, 1946.

Perlmutter, Amos. *FDR and Stalin: A Not So Grand Alliance, 1943–1945.* Columbia: University of Missouri Press, 1993.

Perrett, Geoffrey. *America in the Twenties: A History.* New York: Simon & Schuster, 1982.

———. *Days of Sadness, Years of Triumph: The American People, 1939–1945.* New York: Coward, McCann & Geoghegan, 1973.

Persico, Joseph E. *Franklin and Lucy: President Roosevelt, Mrs. Rutherfurd, and the Other Remarkable Women in His Life.* New York: Random House 2008.

Pottker, Jan. *Sara and Eleanor: The Story of Sara Delano Roosevelt and Her Daughter-in-Law, Eleanor Roosevelt.* New York: St. Martin's Press, 2004.

Quarles, Benjamin. *A. Philip Randolph. Labor Leader at Large.* Chicago University of Illinois Press, 1986.

Rhodes, Richard. *The Making of the Atomic Bomb.* New York: Simon & Schuster, 1986.

Robinson, Greg. *By Order of the President: FDR and the Internment of Japanese Americans.* Cambridge, MA: Harvard University Press, 2001

Rogers, Naomi. *Dirt and Disease: Polio Before FDR.* New Brunswick, NJ: Rutgers University Press, 1992.

Roosevelt, Eleanor. *This I Remember.* New York: Harper & Brothers, 1949.

———. *This Is My Story.* New York: Harper & Brothers, 1937.

Roosevelt, Elliott, and James Brough. *As He Saw It.* New York: Duell, Sloan and Pearce, 1946.

———. *Mother R.: Eleanor Roosevelt's Untold Story.* New York: G. P. Putnam's Sons, 1977.

———. *A Rendezvous with Destiny: The Roosevelts of the White House.* New York: G. P. Putnam's Sons, 1975.

Roosevelt, James. *My Parents: A Differing View.* Chicago: Playboy Press, 1976.

Small, Melvin. "Buffoons and Brave Hearts: Hollywood Portrays the Russians, 1949–1944." *California Historical Quarterly* (Winter 1973): 326–37.

Smith, Gene. *The Shattered Dream: Herbert Hoover and the Great Depression.* New York: William Morrow, 1970.

Snyder, Timothy. *Bloodlands: Europe Between Hitler and Stalin.* New York: Basic Books, 2010.

Takaki, Ronald. *Double Victory: A Multicultural History of America in World War II.* Boston Little, Brown, 2000.

Terkel, Studs. *Hard Times: An Oral History of the Great Depression.* New York: Pantheon, 1970.

Ward, Geoffrey C. *Before the Trumpet: Young Franklin Roosevelt, 1882–1905.* New York: Harper & Row, 1985.

———. *A First-Class Temperament: The Emergence of Franklin Roosevelt.* New York: Harper & Row, 1989.

Weintraub, Stanley. *Pearl Harbor Christmas: The World at War, December 1941.* New York: Da Capo Press, 2011.

Welch, Steven R. "'Annihilation of Superfluous Eaters': Nazi Plans for and Uses of Famine in Eastern Europe." www.yale.edu/gsp/publications/Annihila.doc.

IMAGE CREDITS

Ed Clark—Time & Life Pictures/Getty Images
280

Federal Bureau of Prisons
87

Franklin D. Roosevelt Presidential Library and Museum
9, 11, 13, 14, 15, 17, 18, 19, 21, 22, 25, 27, 30, 33, 51, 62, 70, 71, 73, 74, 75, 78, 80, 81, 93 (top), 93 (bottom), 95, 97, 100, 101, 104, 108, 110, 113, 117, 118, 122, 128 (top), 128 (bottom), 131, 134, 153, 159, 162, 164, 171, 174, 181, 183, 190, 191 (top), 191 (bottom), 193, 196, 214, 215, 217, 244, 248, 252, 254, 255, 272, 276, 277, 279, 282, 283

German Federal Archives
143, 212, 239

Imperial War Museums
155

Library of Congress
4, 7, 37, 45, 55, 83, 85, 91, 99, 111, 115, 120, 125, 136, 144, 152, 158, 167, 177, 178, 182, 197, 198, 202, 203, 206, 220, 235, 236, 245, 268

National Archives
24, 86, 146, 148, 151, 173, 211, 259

National Archives and Records Administration, College Park, Maryland, Bildarchiv Abraham Pisarek
258

National Geographic Magazine
40

The New York Times
38, 42

The New Yorker
2

PD-US
49, 52, 57, 59, 66, 186, 187, 194, 208, 213, 222, 226, 227, 230, 232, 241, 269

Time Magazine
237

United States Air Force
225, 274

United States Holocaust Memorial Museum
141

United States Holocaust Memorial Museum, courtesy of Donald Chumley
107

Warner Bros.
238

E. Thomas Wood
267

Yad Vashem
261, 262

INDEX

Note: *Italic* page numbers refer to illustrations.

Adams, John Quincy, 41
African Americans; *see also* segregation
    FDR and, 119–121, 129, 197–199, 265, 282
    New Deal and, 118–121, 129
    Second World War and, 196–204, *198, 202 203*
Agricultural Adjustment Act, 116–117
Agricultural Adjustment Administration
    (AAA), 117, 118, 121, 132
Allies
    First World War and, 37, 41–42, 43, 44, 47,
      49–50, 53, 55, 93, 147, 168
    Second World War and, 150–151, 193, 204,
      207, 209, 215, 221–228, 243, 245, 266–267,
      270–271, 274
Almanac Singers, 160–161, 164
America First Committee, 161, 162
American Federation of Labor (AFL), 197
American Protective League, 48
American Rights League, 48
American Youth Congress, 234
Anders, Władysław, 275
anti-Semitism, 145, 160, 257–258, 261,
    263–265, 266
Anti–Yellow Dog League, 48
Arcadia Conference, 205–208, 209
assembly-line methods, 83–84, *83, 89,* 92,
    195–196, *196*
Atlantic Charter, 164–165, 207, 243, 248,
    274–275
Atlantic Conference, 164–165, *164*
Augusta, 164
Auschwitz concentration camp, 261, *261, 262,*
    263, 265, 268, 269–271, 277
Auxiliary Territorial Service, *162*

B-17 Flying Fortresses, 224
B-24 Liberators, 224, *225,* 270
B-29 Superfortresses, 273, *274*
Banking Act, 114
banking system, 88, 90, 94–95, 104–105, 112,
    113–114, 134

Bank of the United States, 94–95
Barrow, Clyde, 105
Baruch, Bernard, 252, 253, 264
Bass, Leon, 278
Bear Mountain, New York, 63
Bennett, Ruth, *85*
Beria, Lavrenti, 230, *230,* 244, 273
Beria, Sergo, 244, 245, 276
Bernstein, Irving, 109
Bethe, Hans, 265
Bethune, Mary McLeod, 129
Biddle, Francis, 120, 177, 179
Bie, Ruthie, *78*
Bilbo, Theodore, 120–121
Black Tom, New York Harbor, 43, 44 156
Bliven, Bruce, 86
Bohlen, Charles, 272
Bolsheviks, 56–57
bonds, 88
Bonus March, 111, *111*
bootlegging, 86–87, *86*
Brandeis, Louis D., 132
Braun, Eva, 281
breadlines, 97, *97*
British Security Coordination (BSC), 156–157
Brookens, J. S., 119
Brotherhood of Sleeping Car Porters, 197
Browne, Ralph C., 49
Bruenn, Howard, 250–251, 253, 256, 278
Buckner, Robert, 239
Bullitt, William C., 236, *236,* 268
Bynner, Witter, 200

Cadogan, Alexander, 272
Capone, Al "Scarface," 87, *87,* 176, 205
Carter, John F., 242
Cassiday, George, 87
Central Intelligence Agency (CIA), 244
Central Women's School for Sniper Training,
    193
Cermak, Anton, 176
Child Welfare Services, *131*
China, 169, 170, 210, 223, 273
Churchill, Randolph, 155

Churchill, Sarah, 244
Churchill, Winston
    air war and, 223, 224
    Arcadia Conference and, 205–208
    Atlantic Conference and, 164, *164*
    Casablanca Conference and, 214–216, *215,*
        224, 229
    on Dunkirk, 151
    on FDR, 135, 282
    FDR and, 158, 165, 166, 205, 206–207, 214,
        215–216, *215,* 234, 255–256, 281
    on FDR's death, 279
    First World War and, 155
    on Hitler, 155, 163
    Hitler on, 159
    on Holocaust, 257
    Murrow and, 282
    on Nazi-Soviet Non-Aggression Pact, 148
    as prime minister, 154–155, *155*
    Rommel and, 213
    Stalin and, 139, 242–244, 249
    Tehran Conference and, 240, 243–249, *244*
    War Cabinet of, 165, 242–243
    Yalta Conference and, 272–275, *272*
Civilian Conservation Corps (CCC), 115–116,
    121, 127
Civil War, 10, 43, 47
Clark, Bennett Champ, 233
Clavins, Sylvia, *85*
Clemenceau, Georges, 54
Cleveland, Grover, 2
Cohan, George M., 50, 110
Cold War, 277
Columbia Law School, 28
Combined Bomber Offensive, 221, 225, 228
Combined Chiefs of Staff (CCS), 208, *208,* 221
Comintern, 58
Committee on Public Information, 47
communism
    philosophy of, 56–57, 136, 147
    red scare and, 58–60, 82
    Red Terror and, 57–58, 60, 102
Communist Party USA (CPUSA), 58, 160, 161,
    163
Congress of Racial Equality (CORE), 199
conservation campaigns, 190
Coolidge, Calvin, 63, 73
Coughlin, Charles, 160
Cox, James M., 62, *62*
credit, 92, 95, 96, 113
Crisis, 121

Cuneo, Ernest, 156

Daily Worker, 160
Daniels, Josephus, 36, 44, 48
Dasch, George, 178–179, *178*
Davies, Joseph E., 239
Davis, John W., *71,* 73
Davis, William Rhodes, 156
Declaration of Liberated Europe, 274, 275
Declaration of the United Nations, 207
Delano, Laura, 67, 278
Delano, Warren, 10–11, 15–16
democracy
    debates on, 109
    FDR's legacy and, 283
    First World War and, 45, 46, 48, 135
    tyranny threatening, 6
Dempsey, Jack, 3
Depression, *see* Great Depression
Dewey, Thomas E., 255
DeWitt, John, 180
Dickerman, Marion, 53
Dillinger, John, 105
Divine, Robert A., 248
Doolittle, James H., 210
Dos Passos, John, 153
Double-V, 201
Drew, Charles, 200
Dust Bowl, 92–94, *93*
Dutch East Indies, 170

Earle, George H., 242
economy; *see also* Great Depression
    banking collapse, 94–95, 112
    capitalism and, 87–89, 103, 130
    crash of 1929, 89–91, *91,* 92, 106
    New Deal and, 128
    prosperity of 1920s, 82–87, 91, 94
    recovery of, 133, 134
    Second World War and, 188–190, 196,
        197–198
    wages and, 91–92
Economy Act, 114
Eichmann, Adolf, 269
Eighteenth Amendment, 86
Einsatzgruppen (Special Action Groups), 260
Einstein, Albert, 185–186, *186,* 265
Eisenhower, Dwight D., 127, 213, 214, 247, 271,
    277

Elmslie, R. C., 68
Emergency Banking Act, 113
Enterprise, 209
Espionage and Sedition Acts, 47
Esso Baton Rouge, 218
Evans, Redd, 194
Executive Order 8802, 199
Executive Order 9066, 181, 183

Fair Employment Practices Committee
    (FEPC), 199
Fala (family dog), *78,* 124
Farley, James, 126
Farmer, James, 199
farmers and farming
    Dust Bowl and, 92–94, *93*
    First World War and, 93
    Great Depression and, 96
    New Deal and, 116–117, 161
    tenant farmers, *100,* 117, 118, 121
Federal Bureau of Investigation (FBI), 155–156,
    162, 177–178, 180, 181, 184, 238, 256
Federal Deposit Insurance Corporation
    (FDIC), 114
Federal Emergency Relief Administration
    (FERA), 116, 127
federal government
    banking system and, 94
    debate on role of, 108–109, 134
    Great Depression and, 103
    New Deal and, 5–6, 108–109, 283
    reforms in, 134
Federal Music Project (FMP), 128
Federal Theatre Project (FTP), 128, *128*
Fellowship of Reconciliation, 227
Fidelity and Deposit Company, 63, 71
Fields, Alonzo, 206–207, 253
films, on Soviet Union, 238–239, *238*
Fireside Chats
    on banking system, 113–114
    FDR's policies and, 124
    on Hitler as gangster, 172, 175
    Hitler's response to, 174
    Lend-Lease and, 159–160
    photograph of, *113*
    on Supreme Court, 132
    on Tehran Conference, 248–249
    USS *Greer* attack and, 166–167
First Amendment, 47
First World War

Allies and, 37, 41–42, 43, 44, 47, 49–50, 53, 55,
    93, 147, 168
American involvement in, 37, 41–43, 153
Battle of the Somme, 40
civil liberties during, 46–48, 181
FDR's role in, 37, 44, 48–51, 60, 219
fighting conditions of, 38–39
Hitler in, 55, 141, 148, 215
home front and, 189
New York Times announcement of, *38*
shell shock and, 39–40, 51–52
trenches of, 38, 39, 40, *40,* 46, 50, 51, 135, 148
veterans of, 110–111, *111*
Wilson and, 37, 41, 42, 43–48, *45,* 54, 135, 181
Wilson's Fourteen Points and, 54
Fitzgerald, F. Scott, 82
flappers, 85–86, *85*
Floyd, Pretty Boy, 104–105
Foch, Ferdinand, 55
Ford, Henry, 82–84, 100, 161, 187, 261
Ford Motor Company, *83,* 105, 176, 195
Fraatz, Georg-Werner, 166, 167
France
    FDR's childhood experiences in, 16
    First World War and, 37, 38, 49–51, 54–55,
        150
    Second World War and, 148, 150, 151, 169, 215
Frankfurter, Felix, 264
Freidel, Frank, 51
Friends of Hitler, 160

Garner, John Nance, 107, 133
Gellhorn, Martha, 100, 131
General Motors, 187
German-American Bund, 160
Germany; *see also* Hitler, Adolf
    Amphing concentration camp, 268
    Arcadia Conference and, 208
    blitzkrieg and, 148, 150, 162
    book burning in, 142, *143*
    Buchenwald concentration camp, 277–278
    Casablanca Conference and, 215
    concentration camps, 261
    FDR's childhood experiences in, 16, 44
    First World War and, 37, 38, 41–44, 45, 46,
        47–48, 53–55, 56, 142, 147
    General Plan for the East, 231
    Great Depression in, 142, 147
    Hamburg bombing, 225–228, *226, 227*
    Holocaust in, 257–263

Hunger Plan, 231–232, 259
    Japan and, 172, 174
    Kristallnacht, 258, *258*
    Lager Nordhausen concentration camp, *277*
    mass assembly of German troops at
        Nuremberg rally, *146*
    Ohrdruf concentration camp, 277
    Soviet Union and, 147–150
    totalitarianism of, 163
Gestapo, 142, 149
Gitlow, Benjamin, 58
Goebbels, Joseph, 227, 279–280
Great Britain; *see also* Churchill, Winston
    First World War and, 37, 38, 41, 43, 44, 45, 46,
        47, 49, 54–55
    Jews and, 264, 268
    Opium Wars and, 10
    Second World War and, 148, 150–153, *151, 153,*
        159–162, 192, 193, 212–221
Great Depression
    anti-Semitism during, 265
    conditions of, 95–101
    economic crisis of, 1–2, 81, 106
    effect on American military, 185
    in Europe, 142
    FDR's inauguration address of 1933 and, 4–5
    Hoover and, 102–104
    hunger and, 96–98, 131
    Lange's photographs of, *95*
    racial prejudice and, 102
    unemployment and, 90, 95, 96, 97, 98,
        100–101, 102, 103, 104–105, 133, 134, 188
Greater New York Boy Scouts Council, 63
Groton School, 17–19, 30, 60, 119, 263
Groves, Leslie, 271
Gunther, John, 125
Guthrie, Woody, 104–105, 160, 168
Gypsies, 260

Hall, G. Stanley, 26
Halsey, William F. "Bull," 209, 252
"Happy Days Are Here Again," 109
Hardegen, Reinhard, 217
Harding, Warren G., 63
Hardwick, Thomas W., 59
Harper's Magazine, 60
Harriman, W. Averell, 126, 248, 276, 279
Harvard College, 19–21, 23, 263–264
Harvard Crimson, 19, 20
Hastie, William, 129

Haupt, Herbert H., *178*
health clinics, 116
Hell, Josef, 258
Helm, Edith, 178
Hickok, Lorena, 70
highways, 84–85
Himmler, Heinrich, 231, 259–263, *259,* 269
Hirohito, 206, *206,* 212
Hiroshima, Japan, 282
Hitler, Adolf
    Allies' strategy and, 207, 209, 223, 224, 225,
        227, 243, 245, 274
    on American military power, 185
    anti-Semitism of, 145, 257–258, 264, 265, 266
    attack on Soviet Union, 6, 162–164, 168, 205,
        229, 231–233, 234, 259–260
    Churchill on, 155, 163
    factory production and, 204
    on FDR, 159, 174
    FDR on, 153–154, 157, 159, 162, 165, 166, 167,
        172, 175, 283
    on FDR's death, 279–280
    First World War and, 55, 141, 148, 215
    France and, 169
    Gestapo methods of, 178
    Great Britain's supply line and, 216
    Holocaust and, 257–263, 266, 269, 270
    invasion of Poland, 6, 147, 148–49, 184,
        221–222, 258
    Japan as ally of, 171
    as leader of Nazi Germany, 6, 140–145
    military buildup of, 147
    murderous mentality of, 172
    in personal airplane, 107, *107*
    personal appearance of, 140–141
    personality of, 142
    public speaking of, 141–142, 153
    racism of, 145, 200–201
    with SS members, *141*
    Stalin compared to, 141, 142, 143, 233, 236, 237
    Stalin's alliance with, 147–150, 151, 160,
        162–163, 229, 234, 237, 247, 274, 277
    suicide of, 281
    Third Reich and, 142
    totalitarianism and, 142, 144, 147
    U-boats and, 152, 168, 220
    view of United States, 170
    world domination as goal of, 208
Hitler Youth, 144–145, *144*
hoboes, 99–100
Holocaust, 256, 257–271, 277–278

homelessness, 98–100, *100,* 110
Hoover, Herbert
    American First Committee and, 161, 162
    budget cuts of, 185
    election of 1928, 76, 79, 82
    election of 1932, 108–112
    FDR's borrowing ideas of, 114
    federal government's role and, 108, 109, 134
    Great Depression and, 102–104
    inauguration of 1933, 2–3, *2*
    stock market investments of, 89
Hoover, J. Edgar, 155–156, 177–178, *177,* 180,
    184, 256
Hoovervilles, 110, 111
Hopkins, Harry, 70, 116, 126, 128, 130, 137, 166,
    224
hopping a freight, 99, *99*
Hornet, 209–210
Howard University, 199
Howe, Louis McHenry
    death of, 130
    with FDR, *33*
    as FDR's personal assistant, 36, 73
    FDR's polio and, 64, 69, 77
    FDR's political career and, 32–34, 53, 63, 69,
        71, 72, 107, 126
    Eleanor Roosevelt's relationship with, 69–70
Hughes, Charles Evans, 3
Hundred Days, 112–118
Hyde Park, 8, 11–12, 28, 31, 106

Ickes, Harold, 115, 125, *125,* 126, 127, 162, 192
individualism, 96
Indochina, 169
influenza, 52
Israel, 271

Jackson, Graham, *280*
Jackson, Robert H., 177
Japan
    atomic bomb and, 271, 273, 281–282
    First World War and, 168
    Germany and, 172, 174
    Second World War and, 168–172, 174,
        205–208, 209, 210–212, 233, 240, 247, 273,
        275
    surrender of, 282
Japanese Americans, internment of, 179–184,
    181, 182, 183

jazz, 85
Jefferson, Thomas, 41
Jews, *see also* anti-Semitism
    Coughlin on, 160
    discrimination against, 263–264
    Hitler's anti-Semitism, 145, 257–258, 264,
        265, 266
    Holocaust and, 256, 257–271, 277–278
    Stalin and, 234
Jim Crow laws, 101–102, 197, 198, 200; *see also*
    segregation
Johnson, Calvin, 200
Johnson, Hiram, 105
Johnson, Lyndon B., 115, 279
John XXIII, 270
Josephson, Matthew, 98–99
Joubaire, Alfred, 39

Kaiser, Henry J., 195–196, 219–220
Karski, Jan, 266–268, *267*
Kennan, George F., 235–236, *235,* 246, 249, 276
Kennedy, John F., 113, 161, 250
Kennedy, Joseph P., 89, 256
King, Martin Luther, Jr., 199
Knights of Liberty, 48
Knox, Frank, *158*
Knudsen, William "Big Bill," 186–187, 194, 212
Korea, 168, 169
Ku Klux Klan, 79, 102, 160

labor unions, 128–129, 134, 161, 164, 197, 199
La Follette, Robert M., 45–46
Landon, Alfred M. "Alf," 130, 131
Lange, Dorothea, photographs of Great
        Depression, *95*
League of German Girls, 144
League of Nations, 54, 55–56, 61, 62, 63, 165,
    273
League of Women Voters, 70
Leahy, William D., 255
LeHand, Marguerite "Missy," 73–74, *73,* 107, 126
LeMay, Curtis, 273
Lend-Lease, 159–162, *159, 162, 163,* 236
Lenin, Vladimir Ilyich, 57–58, *57,* 136, 139, 140,
    147, 277
Leviathan, 52
Lewis, Sybil, 202
Lexington, 209
Liberty League, 48

Life magazine, 238
Lincoln, Abraham, 5, 47, 175, 218, 281
Lindbergh, Charles, 161
Lipson, Milton, 253
Lochner, Louis, 141
Lodge, Henry Cabot, 56
Loeb, John Jacob, 194
Long, Breckinridge, 266, 269
Lovett, Robert, 64–65
Lundeen, Ernest, 46
Lunn, George, *71*
Lusitania, 42, 43, 44
lynching, 102, 120–121, *120,* 130, 265, 282

MacArthur, Douglas, 111, 112, 115, 185, 255, *255,*
    282
Madison, James, 41, 46, 108
Maged, Jacob, 118
Manchuria, 169, 233, 273
Manhattan Project, 186, 190
March of Dimes campaign, 76
Marcus, Joe, 115
Marshall, George C., 244
Marshall, Thurgood, 120, 121
Marx, Karl, 56, 136
mass production, 84, 187, 194, 212
McAdoo, William Gibbs, 94
McCloy, John J., 270
McIntire, Ross, 251, 256
McKinley, William, 19
McMillan, T. S., *85*
Meakin, *178*
Mercer Rutherfurd, Lucy, 52–53, *52,* 64, 251,
    252, 278
Merkulov, V. N., 234
Mexican-American War of 1846, 44
migrant workers, 93, *104*
Mission to Moscow poster, *238, 239*
Mohr, Jochen, 218
Moley, Raymond, 106, 114, 126
Molotov, Vyacheslav, *148*
Montgomery, Bernard Law, 213, 214
Moran, Charles McMoran Wilson, Lord, 272
Morgan, J. P., 29, 59
Morgenthau, Henry, Jr., 115, 125, 126, 134, 224,
    269
Morris, Charles R., *158*
Morse, Wayne, 176–177
Munson, Curtis B., 180
Murray, Pauli, 201

Murrow, Edward R., 151–152, *152,* 170–171, 282
Mussolini, Benito, 6, 174, 221, 240
Mussolini, Vittorio, 221

Nagano, Osami, 212
Nagasaki, Japan, 282
Nakamura, Grace, 182
National Association for the Advancement of
    Colored People (NAACP), 119, *120,* 121
National Foundation for Infant Paralysis, 75
National Foundation–March of Dimes, 76
National Labor Relations Act, 128, 133
National Labor Relations Board (NLRB), 129
National March on Washington Committee,
    198–199, *198*
National Recovery Administration (NRA), 118,
    121, 132
National Youth Administration (NYA), 127
Nazis, *see* Germany; Hitler, Adolf
Nazi-Soviet Non-Aggression Pact, 148, *148*
Nelson, "Baby Face," 105
Neutrality Acts, 153, 154, 159, 166, 168
New Deal
    African Americans and, 118–121, 129
    alphabet soup agencies of, 115–118, *116*
    budget cuts and, 133–134
    failures of, 134, 161
    Hundred Days, 112–118
    role of federal government in, 5–6, 108–109,
        283
    Second New Deal, 127–130
New Yorker, cover on inauguration of 1933, *2*
New York State Democratic Committee,
    Women's Division, 70
New York Stock Exchange, 89, 90, *91*
New York Times
    First World War announcement, *38*
    German embassy warnings in, 42, *42*
    red scare and, 60
    Second World War and, 157
Nicholas II, 56
Nimitz, Chester W., *255*
Nineteenth Amendment, 62
Nisbet, Robert, 229
NKVD
    American media on, 238
    in Eastern Europe, 275–276
    Hitler and, 234
    in Poland, 149–150, 240–242
    Soviet rule and, 139, 230, 239

Tehran Conference and, 244–246
Wallenberg and, 270
noblesse oblige, 12, 17, 29, 74, 109, 119, 236–237
Norris, George W., 46, 157
Norris Dam, *118*

Obama, Barack, 267
Office of Strategic Services (OSS), 193–194
Office of War Information, *187,* 243
O'Malley, Owen, 242, 243
Opium Wars, 10
organized crime, 87
Orwell, George, 237
Ottinger, Albert, 79
Oursler, Fulton, 124
Owen, Wilfred, 39

Palmer, A. Mitchell, 59, 60
Paris Peace Conference, 54–55
Parker, Bonnie, 105
Patton, George S., 203, 277
Pavlichenko, Lyudmila, 193
Peabody, Endicott, 17–18, 25, 45
Peabody, George Foster, 73
Pearl Harbor attack
    Arcadia Conference and, 207–208
    battleships sinking following, *171*
    deportation of enemy aliens to United States
        following, 184
    FDR and, 170–172, 179, 181
    home front war production and, 187, 188
    salvage operations after, 209
Pearson, Drew, 157
Perkins, Frances, 115, *115,* 129, 235, 243, 245, 246,
    256
Philippines, 170, 240
Pius XI, 79
Poland
    concentration camps in, 261–262, *261, 262,*
        263, 265, 268, 269–271, 277
    Hitler's invasion of, 6, 147, 148–49, 184,
        221–222, 258
    Holocaust in, 258–259, 261, 266, 267, 268
    mass graves in Katyn Forest, 240–43, *241,* 247,
        274
    Stalin's invasion of, 148–150, 240
    Stalin's proposal for borders of, 247, 248,
        274–275
    Ultra and, 220

Warsaw bombing, 221–222, *222,* 223
Warsaw Ghetto, 258–259, 266, 267
poliomyelitis
    African Americans and, 119
    FDR's polio, 3, 61, 63–65, 67–69, 77, 114,
        123–124, 180, 249
    outbreaks of, 65–66
    quarantine sign for, 66, *66*
political correctness, 57–58
Prince of Weles (battleship), 164, 205
prisoners of war (POWs), 200, 232, 239, *239,*
    240–243, *241,* 276
Prohibition, 86, *86,* 116
public service
    FDR and, 17, 18, 119, 157, 253
    New Deal and, 115

Quanza, 266

race riots, 201
racism, 102, 119–120, 145, 160, 179–181, 197,
    200–201; *see also* African Americans;
    Holocaust; segregation
Randolph, A. Philip, 197–199, *197,* 201
Rankin, John E., 265
rationing, 191–192
Reagan, Ronald, 113
Reconstruction Finance Corporation, 104
recycling programs, 190–191, *190,* 191
Red Army
    Eastern Europe occupied by, 274, 275–276
    Great Terror and, 139
    Hitler's attack on Soviet Union, 163, 229,
        230, 231, 232–233, 234
    liberation of Auschwitz and, 271
    media on, 237–238
    in Poland, 148, 149, 160, 241, 276
    Stalin's use of, 147
    women in, 193
red scare, communism and, 58–60, 82
Red Terror, 57–58, 60, 102
relief, recovery, and reform, 112–114
Repulse, 205
Reuben James, 168
Revere, Paul, 209
Rockefeller, John D., 29, 59
Rogers, Edith N., 265
Rogers, Will, 113
Roma, 260

Rommel, Erwin, 205, *212*, 213, 214
Roosevelt, Alice, 20, 25
Roosevelt, Anna (daughter)
  birth of, 26
  on Churchill, 206
  photograph with mother, *27*
  relationship with father, 27, 64, 67, 122–123,
    125–126, 250, 251, 252, 278
  relationship with mother, 27, 122, 123, 252
  at Yalta Conference, 273
Roosevelt, Anna Hall, 22
Roosevelt, Curtis (grandson), 124
Roosevelt, Eleanor (wife)
  African Americans and, 119, 120, 129, 200
  on air war, 227
  alcoholic beverages and, 87, 206
  childhood of, 22–23
  with children James, Elliott, and Anna, *27*
  on Churchill, 206
  death of, 281
  family background of, 22
  FBI surveillance of, 177–178
  FDR as assistant secretary of the navy and, 35
  FDR as New York governor and, 80–81
  FDR's correspondence with, 44
  FDR's death and, 278, 281
  FDR's early relationship with, 22–23
  FDR's polio and, 61, 64, 68–70, 72
  as First Lady, 121–123, 161, 177–178
  First World War and, 45, 51–52, 54, 55
  with grandchildren, *279*
  on Howe, 32
  on Japanese American internment, 182
  on Jews, 264, 265–268, 271
  marriage of, 25–26, 52–53, 60, 64–65, 74,
    122, 126, 251, 278, 282
  meeting press in Los Angeles, *122*
  as mother, 26–27, 69
  at Pearl Harbor naval hospital, *252*
  polio outbreaks and, 66
  political career of, 69–70
  portrait at age fourteen, *22*
  portrait in wedding dress, *25*
  presidential election of 1932, 107
  red scare and, 59, 60
  relationship with Sara Roosevelt, 25–26, 60,
    68, 69–70, 167, 264
  relationship with Theodore Roosevelt, 22,
    23–24, 25, 54
  travel of, 251–252
  Warm Springs and, 73, 74

  in White House, 121–123
  with Women's Trade Union League members,
    70
Roosevelt, Elliott (Eleanor Roosevelt's father),
    22–23
Roosevelt, Elliott (son)
  Atlantic Conference, *164*
  birth of, 26
  FDR on Stalin and, 244
  on Lucy Mercer, 52
  photograph with mother, *27*
  relationship with father, 64, 67
  relationship with mother, 27, 278
Roosevelt, Ethel, 48
Roosevelt, Franklin, Jr. (son; 1909), 26
Roosevelt, Franklin, Jr. (son; 1914), 26, 27, *164*
Roosevelt, Franklin Delano
  addressing Congress after Crimean
    Conference, *276*
  African Americans and, 119–121, 129,
    197–199, 265, 282
  at age four, *14*
  air war and, 223–224, 227
  alcoholic beverages and, 87, 123
  assassination attempt on, 175–176
  as assistant secretary of the navy, 35, 36–37, *37*,
    48–51, 54, 61
  Atlantic Conference, 164, *164*
  atomic bomb and, 185–186, 271, 273
  birth of, 8–9
  "Brain Trust" of, 106–107, 113, 114, 126
  Bullitt and, *236*
  Casablanca Conference and, 214–216, *214*,
    229
  childhood of, *2*, 11–16
  Churchill and, 158, 165, 166, 205, 206–207,
    214, 215–216, *215*, 234, 255–256, 281
  Churchill on, 135, 282
  with cigarette holder, *7*, 124
  with James M. Cox, *62*
  "Day of Infamy" speech, 172, *173*, 188
  death of, 278–281
  deception and lies of, 21–22, 127, 165–166,
    242, 256, 282
  with dog, Buddy, on a donkey, *11*
  education of, 4, 14, 16, 17–22, 23, 28, 30
  election of 1928 for New York governor,
    76–77, 79–80
  election of 1930 for New York governor, 81
  family background of, 9–11
  with father, James, *13*

as father, 27–28, 66, 87, 112
Fireside Chats, 113–114, *113*, 124, 132,
    159–160, 166–167, 172, 174, 175, 248–249
at Fort Douaumont in France, *51*
with grandchildren, *279*
with Harvard class of 1904 at Nantasket
    Beach, *24*
with *Harvard Crimson* senior board, *19*
Hawaii meeting, 255, *255*
health of, 3, 32, 52, 250–251, 253, 255, 256,
    272–273, 275, 282
at helm of boat at Campobello Island, *15*
on Hitler, 153–154
Holocaust and, 257, 263–271
with Howe, *33*
inauguration of 1933, 1–4, *2, 4*, 112, 252
Japanese American internment and, 179–184
law career of, 28–29, 63, 70–71
legacy of, 283
with Lunn, Davis, and Smith, *71*
marriage of, 25–26, 52–53, 60, 64–65, 74,
    122, 126, 251, 278, 282
with mother, Sara, *17*
with mother, Sara, sailing around Campobello
    Island, *21*
national security and, 175–179
as New York governor, 90, 105, 106
on North Africa, 214
observing globe, *282*
peacetime draft lottery, 158–159, *158*
Pearl Harbor attack and, 170–172, 179, 181
polio of, 3, 61, 63–65, 67–69, 77, 114,
    123–124, 180, 249
polio treatments of, 66–70, 73–76, *74*
political career of, 29–33, 34, 61, 62–63, 73,
    76–77, 79–81, 265
portrait as three-year-old, *9*
portrait at age eleven in riding clothes, *18*
as president, 96, 112–114, 123–127
presidential election of 1932, 105–109, *108,
    110*, 111–112
presidential election of 1936, 127, 130–134
presidential election of 1940, 157–159
presidential election of 1944, 247, 253–256
press conferences of, 124–125
public appearances of, 77
reading family's Dutch Bible in Hyde Park, *80*
role in shaping modern world, 6–7
Eleanor Roosevelt's early relationship with,
    22–23
secretiveness of, 125–126, 256

self-confidence of, 2, 12
signing declaration of war against Japan, *174*
with Al Smith, *81*
Stalin and, 234–239, 242, 248–249, 253, 273,
    275, 276, 283
Stalin compared to, 137
stamp collecting of, 15, 123
in state senate seat, 30
on Survival War, 205
Tehran Conference and, 240, 243–249, *244,
    245, 248*, 253, 273
in Warm Springs, *74, 75*
in wheelchair, 77, *78*, 124, 255, 275, 276
White House Map Room and, 218–219
Yalta Conference and, 271–275, *272, 275*
Roosevelt, Isaac the Patriot, 9
Roosevelt, James (father)
    death of, 20
    education of, 19
    FDR's birth and, 8
    FDR's childhood and, 12–13, 14, 27
    health of, 16
    inheritance left by, 28
    marriage of, 11
    photograph with FDR, *13*
    yacht of, 15
Roosevelt, James (son)
    birth of, 26
    FDR's polio and, 3, 66, 72, 109
    on parents' relationship, 53, 251
    photograph with mother, *27*
    relationship with father, 27–28, 60, 64, 66,
        72, 109, *110*, 112, 126, 166
    relationship with mother, 27, 70
Roosevelt, James "Rosy" (half brother), 11
Roosevelt, John (son), 26, 27, 177, 206
Roosevelt, Quentin, 36, 48
Roosevelt, Sara Delano (mother)
    alcoholic beverages and, 87
    death of, 166–167
    family background of, 10–11
    FDR's childhood and, 8–9, 13–14
    FDR's education and, 14, 16, 17
    FDR's polio and, 67–69
    FDR's relationship with, 20–21, 25–26, 28,
        29, 31, 52, 53, 75, 80, 114, 125
    on Howe, 32
    on Jews, 264
    marriage of, 11
    photograph with FDR at age eleven, *17*
    photograph with FDR sailing around

Campobello Island, *21*
Theodore Roosevelt and, 19
Eleanor Roosevelt's relationship with, 25–26, 60, 68, 69–70, 167, 264
stamp collecting of, 15
Roosevelt, Theodore
death of, 54
education of, 19
FDR's relationship with, 19, 29, 35, 36, 48, 62
First World War and, 43–44, 48
health of, 67
political career of, 19, 29, 30, 79–80
Eleanor Roosevelt's relationship with, 22, 23–24, 25, 54
Rosenman, Samuel, 127
Rosie the Riveter, 194, *194*
Rustin, Bayard, 199
Ruth, Babe, 71
Rutherfurd, Winthrop, 53

Sachs, Alexander, 185–186
St. Louis, 265
Salk, Jonas, 76
Salvation Army, 97
Sandburg, Carl, 1
Saratoga, 209
Saternus, Wiesława, 149–150
Schlesinger, Arthur, Jr., 127
school lunch programs, 116, *117*
Second World War
African Americans and, 196–204, *198, 202, 203*
air war and, 221–228, *225, 226, 227,* 271
Arcadia Conference, 205–208, 209
atomic bomb and, 185–186, 211, 220, 265, 271, 273, 281
Battle of Britain, 151, 223
Battle of Midway, 210, *211*
Battle of Stalingrad, 239–240, *239*
Battle of the Atlantic, 152, 162, 196, 216, 219, 220–221
Battle of the Coral Sea, 210
building American military, 185–189, 204, 212
Casablanca Conference, 214–215, *214,* 221–222, 224, 229
convoy escort in Atlantic Ocean, *167*
D-Day, 253–254, *254*
dictators and, 135, 168
Hitler's invasion in Poland and, 6, 147, 148–149, 184, 221–222, 258

Holocaust and, 256, 257–271, 277–278
home front and, 189–196, *190*
internment of Japanese Americans, 179–184, *181, 182, 183*
Japan and, 168–172, 174, 205–208, 209, 210–212, 233, 240, 247, 273, 275
mass kidnapping from Latin America, 183–184
national security and, 175–179
North Africa and, 212–216
Operation Drumbeat, 216–218
Operation Gomorrah, 225–226, *226*
Operation Overlord, 215, 216, 219, 221, 247, 253
peacetime draft lottery, 158–159, *158,* 160
secret war, 155–157
servicemen sleeping aboard ship, *217*
Tehran Conference, 240, 243–249, *244, 245,* 272
veteran of, *283*
Yalta Conference, 271–275, *272*
Secret Service men
FDR's health and, 253
FDR's polio and, 3, 123, 124
Second World War security and, 176, 244–245
Securities and Exchange Commission (SEC), 114
Seeger, Pete, 160, 164
segregation, 101–102, 121, 199–200, 202, 203–204, 278
sharecroppers, 117, 118
Shattuck, Edward S., *158*
Sheehan, William F., 31, 33, 34
Shirer, William L., 142
Shoumatoff, Elizabeth, 278
Sims, William, 49
slavery, legacy of, 119
Smith, Alfred E., 71–73, *71,* 76–77, 79, 81, *81,* 87, 130
Smith, Katie, 79
Smith, Merriman, 124
Social Security Act, 129, 133, 134, *134*
Sorge, Richard, 163
Soviet Union; *see also* Red Army; Stalin, Joseph
dictatorship of, 234
famine in, 103
formation of, 56–57
Germany and, 147–150
Gulags of, 140, 149–150, 230–231, 237, 238, 242, 275, 276

Hitler's attack of, 6, 162–164, 168, 205, 229, 231–233, 234, 259–260
Japan and, 273
mass graves in Katyn Forest, 240–243, *241*, 247, 274
Poland and, 148–149, 240
political cartoon warning of practices of, *59*
red scare and, 58–59
Red Terror and, 57–58, 60, 102
slave labor system in, 140
totalitarianism of, 136, 163
women in Red Army, 193, 195
Spanish-American War, 19
speakeasies, 86–87
special interests, 109
Spellman, Francis, 248
Stafford, David, 156
Stalin, Joseph
  Atlantic Charter and, 207
  with Lavrenti Beria, *230*
  death of, 277
  on factory production, 204
  FDR and, 234–239, 242, 248–249, 253, 273, 275, 276, 281, 283
  on FDR's death, 279
  Great Terror, 139–140, 230–231 237, 242
  Hitler compared to, 141, 142, 143, 233, 236, 237
  Hitler's alliance with, 147–150, 151, 160, 162–163, 229, 234, 237, 247, 274, 277
  Japan and, 233, 273, 275
  as leader of Soviet Russia, 6, 136–140
  Lend-Lease opposition, 160, 161
  Lenin and, 57
  murderous mentality of, 172, 236, 237, 242, 246, 283
  Nazi-Soviet Non-Aggression Pact and, 148, *148*
  personality of, 138, 142
  physical appearance of, 136–137
  policies of, 139, 140, 142
  portrait of, *136*
  scorched earth campaign, 232
  Tehran Conference and, 240, 243–249, *244, 245*, 253, 272, 273, 274
  as *Time* "Man of the Year," 237, *237*
  titles of, 137–138
  on tragedy, 95–96
  Wallenberg's capture and, 270
  Yalta Conference and, 271–275, *272, 276*
Stalin, Nadya, 138

Stalin, Svetlana, 138, 163, *230*
Stalin, Yakov, 138, 231
Stalin, Yulia, 231
Statue of Liberty, 43
Stephenson, William S., 155–157
Stettinius, Edward, 256
Stimson, Henry, 182
stock market, 89, 94, 114, 134
Storm Troopers, 142
Suckley, Margaret, 67, 278
Sullivan, Timothy "Big Tim," 31 33
Supreme Court, 132–133, 177
Sweden, 269–270

Tabor, Annie, *202*
Tammany Hall, New York City, 31, 34, 71
Tehran Conference, 240, 243–249, *244, 245*, 253. 272, 273, 274
tenant farmers, *100*, 117, 118, 121
Tennessee Valley Authority (TVA), 117–118, *118*, 121
tent cities, *101*
Thirteenth Amendment, 119
Time magazine, 179
Tōjō, Hideki, 6
totalitarianism, 135–136, 142, 144
Trans-Siberian Railway, 150, 233
Treaty of Versailles, 54–55, 56, 135, 141, 142, 147, 215
Triangle Shirtwaist Company fire, 71, 115
Trubisz, Frank, 218
Truman, Harry S., 127, 204, 255 256, 275, 281–282
Tuskegee Army Air Field, *203*
Tuskegee Institute, 202
Twenty-First Amendment, 116

U-boats
  First World War and, 41, 42–43, 44, 48–49, 152
  Second World War and, 152–153, 167, 168, 178, 179, 216–217, 218, 220, 221, 224, 225 240
unemployment
  Civilian Conservation Corps and 115–116
  Great Depression and, 90, 95, 96, 97, 98, 100–101, 102, 103, 104–105, 133, 134, 188
United Nations, 56, 207, 273, 275, 278
United Nations Commission on Human

Rights, 281
United States; *see also* Second World War; *specific presidents*
   First World War and, 37, 41–48, 153
   Jewish immigration and, 264–265
United States Constitution, 108, 132–133, 161, 165; *see also specific amendments*
United States Holocaust Memorial Museum, 267
USS *Arizona,* 37, 170, *171*
USS *Greer,* 166, 167
USS *Kearny,* 167–168
USS *Ranger,* 220
USS *Tennessee,* 171
USS *West Virginia,* 171
USS *Yorktown,* 210, *211*
utopias, 56, 136

Vanderbilt, Mr. and Mrs. Frederick, 11
van Rosenfelt, Claes Martenszen, 9
van Rosenfelt, Jannetje, 9
victory gardens, 191–192, *191*
Vidal, Gore, 161
Vireo, 64
Volstead Act, 86
von der Osten, Ulrich, 156
von Neumann, John, 265

Wagner, Robert F., 128, 265
Wald, Lillian, 97
Wallace, Henry, 127
Wallenberg, Raoul, 269–270, *269, 270*
Warm Springs, Georgia, 73–76, *74, 75,* 87, 119, 252, 277, 280, *280*
Warm Springs Foundation, 75
War Refugee Board (WRB), 269
Warren, Earl, 180
Washington, George, 3, 9, 41, 157, 238
Watson, Edwin "Pa," 186
Weisskopf, Victor, 265
White, Walter, 121

White, William Allen, 127
White House
   Roosevelt family in, 121–127
   Second World War security and, 176
white supremacy, 119
Whitney, Flora Payne, 36
Wigner, Eugene, 265
Wilkins, Roy, 121
Willkie, Wendell L., 157, 159
Wilson, Edith, *55,* 61, 256
Wilson, Woodrow
   election of 1912, 32
   election of 1916, 44
   FDR's relationship with, 34–35, 62
   First World War and, 37, 41, 42, 43–48, *45,* 54, 135, 181
   Hoover and, 103
   League of Nations and, 54, 55–56, 61, 63
   photograph of second presidential inauguration, *55*
   stroke of, 61
Winchell, Walter, 157
Wolff, Karl, 234
women, in Second World War, 192–196, 202, *202*
Women Airforce Service Pilots (WASP), 193
Women's Army Corps (WAC), 193
Women's Trade Union League, 70, *70*
Works Progress Administration (WPA), 127–130, *128*
World Jewish Congress, 270
writs of habeas corpus, 179

Yalta Conference, 271–275, *272, 276*
Yeltsin, Boris, 241–242
Yonai, Mitsumasa, 210

Zangara, Giuseppe, 175–176
Zarubina, Zoya, 136–137
Zyklon B, 261–262, 270